Indicating words in *italics*
Indicadores semánticos en *cursiva*

Headwords in blue
Lemas en azul

Information on Spanish conjugations
Información sobre las conjugaciones verbales

Latin American Spanish
Español latinoamericano

Grammatical information
Información gramatical

British variants
Variantes del inglés británico

Examples and phrases in ***bold italics***
Ejemplos y frases en ***negrita y cursiva***

Register labels
Marcas de registro

Spanish compounds
Compuestos españoles

mañoso *adj* **1** *(habilidoso)* skillful, *Br* skilful **2** *desp (astuto)* crafty **3** *L.Am. animal* stubborn

mapa *m* map; ***desaparecer del ~*** F disappear off the face of the earth ◇**mapa de carreteras** road map; **mapa mudo** skeleton map, outline map; **mapa del tiempo** weather map

mapache *m* raccoon

mapamundi *m* map of the world

maqueta *f* **1** *de edificio, barco* model **2** TIP dummy

maquetista *m/f* TIP compositor, page make-up artist

maquiavélico *adj tb fig* Machiavellian

maquillador *m*, **~a** *f* make-up artist

maquillaje *m* make-up

maquillar ⟨1a⟩ *v/t* make up; **maquillarse** *v/r* put on one's make-up

máquina *f* **1** machine **2** FERR locomotive; ***a toda ~*** at top speed **3** *C.Am., Carib* car **4**: ***pasar algo a ~*** type sth ◇**máquina de afeitar** (electric) shaver; **máquina de coser** sewing machine; **máquina de escribir** portable typewriter; **máquina expendedora de bebidas / billetes / tabaco** drinks / ticket / cigarette machine; **máquina fotográfica, máquina de fotos** camera; **máquina herramienta** machine tool; **máquina recreativa** arcade game; **máquina de vapor** steam locomotive, *Br* steam engine

maquinaciones *fpl* scheming *sg*

maquinador **I** *adj* scheming **II** *m*, **~a** *f* schemer

maquinal *adj fig* mechanical

maquinar ⟨1a⟩ *v/t* plot

maquinaria *f* machinery

◇**maquinilla de afeitar** *f* razor

◇**maquinilla eléctrica** *f* electric razor

maquinista *m/f* FERR engineer, *Br* train driver

mar *m* (*also f*) GEOG sea; ***los ~es del Sur*** the South Seas; ***alta ~*** high seas *pl*; ***sudaba a ~es*** *fig* F the sweat was pouring off him F; ***llover a ~es*** *fig* F pour, bucket down F; ***la ~ de bien*** *(muy bien)* really well; ***hacerse a la ~*** put to sea ◇**mar Bermejo** Gulf of California; **mar Caribe** Caribbean Sea; **mar de fondo** ground swell; **mar interior** inland sea; **mar Muerto** Dead Sea; **mar Negro**

◆ get up to *v/t mischief* hacer; ***what have those two been getting up to?*** qué han estado haciendo esos dos?; ***what are you getting up to these days?*** qué haces ahora?
'get•a•way *from robbery* fuga *f*, huida *f*; **'get•a•way car** coche *m* utilizado en la fuga; **'get-to•geth•er** reunión *f*; **'get-up** F indumentaria *f*
gey•ser ['gaɪzər] GEOL géiser *m*
ghast•ly ['gæstlɪ] *adj* terrible
gher•kin ['gɜːrkɪn] pepinillo *m*
ghet•to ['getoʊ] ***(pl -o(e)s)*** gueto *m*
ghost [goʊst] fantasma *m*
ghost•ly ['goʊstlɪ] *adj* fantasmal
'ghost sto•ry historia *f* de fantasmas; **'ghost town** ciudad *f* fantasma; **'ghost train** tren *m* fantasma; **'ghost writ•er** negro(-a) *m(f)*
ghoul [guːl] macabro(-a) *m(f)*, morboso(-a) *m(f)*
ghoul•ish ['guːlɪʃ] *adj* macabro, morboso
gi•ant ['dʒaɪənt] **I** *n* gigante *m* **II** *adj* gigantesco, gigante
'gi•ant kil•lers *npl* matagigantes ***m inv***
gib•ber ['dʒɪbər] *v/i* farfullar
gib•ber•ish ['dʒɪbərɪʃ] F memeces *fpl* F, majaderías *fpl* F; ***talk ~*** decir memeces
gib•bon ['gɪbən] gibón *m*
gibe [dʒaɪb] pulla *f*
gib•lets ['dʒɪblɪts] *npl* menudillos *mpl*
gid•di•ness ['gɪdɪnɪs] mareo *m*
gid•dy ['gɪdɪ] *adj* mareado; ***feel ~*** estar mareado; ***become ~*** marearse
gift [gɪft] regalo *m*; ***have a ~ for sth*** tener un don para algo
'gift cer•ti•fi•cate vale *m* de regalo
gift•ed ['gɪftɪd] *adj* con talento
'gift shop tienda *f* de artículos de regalo; **'gift to•ken** vale *m* de regalo; **'gift-wrap I** *n* papel *m* de regalo **II** *v/t* ***(pret & pp -ped)*** envolver para regalo
gig [gɪg] F concierto *m*, actuación *f*
gi•ga•byte ['gɪgəbaɪt] COMPUT gigabyte *m*
gi•gan•tic [dʒaɪ'gæntɪk] *adj* gigantesco
gig•gle ['gɪgl] **I** *v/i* soltar risitas **II** *n* risita *f*; ***get the ~s*** tener un ataque de risa
gig•gly ['gɪglɪ] *adj* que suelta risitas
gild [gɪld] *v/t* dorar
gill [gɪl] *of fish* branquia *f*
gilt [gɪlt] dorado *m*; ***~s*** FIN valores *mpl* del Estado

Título de página
Running head

Phrasal Verbs presentados como lemas
Phrasal verbs entered as headwords

Compuestos ingleses
English compounds

Transcripción fonética
International phonetic alphabet

Plurales irregulares
Irregular plurals

Información gramatical
Grammatical information

' identifica la sílaba acentuada
Stress shown in headwords

Formas de los verbos
Verb forms

Indicación de división
Hyphenation points

Dominio de uso
Subject area labels

Langenscheidt
Compact Dictionaries

Langenscheidt Compact Spanish Dictionary

Spanish – English
English – Spanish

Edited by the
Langenscheidt Editorial Staff

Langenscheidt

New York · Berlin · Munich · Vienna · Zurich

Compiled by LEXUS
with
Beatriz Membrado Dolz
José A. Gálvez · Jane Goldie
Tim Gutteridge · Jane Horwood
Roy Russell · Peter Terrell

on the basis of Langenscheidt's
Pocket Spanish Dictionary
revised by
José A. Gálvez · Roy Russell
Jane Goldie · Peter Terrell
Monica Tamariz-Martel Mirêlis · Rafael Alarcón Gaeta
Andrew Wilkes · Stephanie Parker
Mike Gonzalez

This dictionary is also available in a larger type size in the Langenscheidt Standard Dictionary Series.

2. 3. 4. 5. 08 07 06 05

Printed in Germany

Preface

This is a new dictionary of English and Spanish, a tool with well over 90,000 headwords, compounds and phrases for those who work with the English and Spanish languages at beginner's or intermediate level.

The dictionary offers a broad coverage of everyday language and includes vocabulary from areas such as computers, business and sport. American English is used as the standard, with rich coverage of British English too. Spanish is both European Spanish and Latin American, with an extensive range of country labels to identify the language of the Latin American continent.

Ease and speed of reference are facilitated by the clearly set out blue headwords and compounds. The use of paragraphed grammatical and sense categories avoids the occurrence of unwieldly or over-dense blocks of text. And within these categories there is a wealth of indicating words to guide you, the dictionary user, to whatever particular sense or usage you may be wanting to translate.

In this dictionary you'll also find the grammatical information that you need to be able to construct correct sentences in a foreign language. There are irregular verb forms, in both English and Spanish, irregular English plural forms, guidance on Spanish feminine endings and on prepositional usage with verbs.

And where a translation equivalent in English or Spanish requires a full context of usage in order to be meaningfully demonstrated, concise and idiomatic example phrases are given to show how the two languages correspond in specific contexts.

This dictionary will, we think, become a valuable part of your language toolkit.

Prólogo

Éste es nuestro nuevo diccionario de inglés y español, una obra con más de 90.000 palabras, compuestos y locuciones, destinado a todos aquellos usuarios que trabajan con la lengua inglesa y española a nivel principiante o intermedio.

El diccionario cubre ampliamente el lenguaje cotidiano e incluye vocabulario especializado de áreas como la informática, los negocios y el deporte. Se ha tomado como lengua de referencia el inglés americano, aunque el inglés británico también está ricamente representado. En cuanto al español, incluye la variedad europea y la latinoamericana, y se utiliza un amplio abanico de marcas para identificar el país o países de procedencia de las palabras latinoamericanas.

Para facilitar y agilizar la consulta, las palabras y compuestos del diccionario aparecen en color azul. El uso de categorías gramaticales y de significado dispuestas en párrafos independientes evita que se formen farragosos bloques de texto, difíciles de manejar. Además, dentro de estas categorías abundan indicadores que ayudan a encontrar fácilmente las distintas acepciones y el uso de cualquier palabra que se quiera traducir.

En este diccionario encontrará la información gramatical necesaria para poder construir frases correctas en un idioma extranjero. También se señalan las formas verbales irregulares, tanto inglesas como españolas, las formas plurales irregulares en inglés, y se dan orientaciones sobre las terminaciones femeninas en español y el régimen preposicional de los verbos.

Cuando un vocablo español o inglés requiere ser bien contextualizado para que la traducción sea correcta, el diccionario ofrece valiosos y concisos ejemplos de construcciones idiomáticas que permiten establecer la equivalencia de los dos idiomas en contextos específicos.

Creemos que este diccionario puede ser una de las herramientas más útiles a su alcance para el aprendizaje del idioma.

Contents

Índice

How to use the dictionary

To get the most out of your dictionary you should understand how and where to find the information you need. Whether you are yourself writing text in a foreign language or wanting to understand text that has been written in a foreign language, the following pages should help.

1. How and where do I find a word?

1.1 Spanish and English headwords. The word list for each language is arranged in alphabetical order and also gives irregular forms of verbs and nouns in their correct alphabetical order.

Sometimes you might want to look up terms made up of two separate words, for example **shooting star**, or hyphenated words, for example **absent-minded**. These words are treated as though they were a single word and their alphabetical ordering reflects this.

There are two exceptions to this strict alphabetical ordering. One is made for English phrasal verbs - words like **go off**, **go out**, **go up**. These are positioned in a block directly after their main verb (in this case **go**), rather than being split up and placed apart in strict alphabetical order. The other is for Spanish compounds. These are identified with a ◇ and grouped in a block directly after the entry for the first word of the compound.

Spanish words beginning with **ch** and **ll** are positioned in their alphabetical position in letters C and L. Words beginning with **ñ** are listed after N.

1.2 Spanish feminine headwords are shown as follows:

abogado *m*, **-a** *f* lawyer
embajador *m*, **~a** *f* ambassador
danzarín *m*, **-ina** *f* dancer
pibe *m*, **-a** *f Rpl* F kid F
aprendiz *m*, **~a** *f* apprentice, trainee

The feminine forms of these headwords are: **abogada**, **fumadora**, **bailarina**, **piba** and **aprendiza**.

When a Spanish headword has a feminine form which translates differently from the masculine form, the feminine is entered as a separate headword in alphabetical order:

empresaria *f* businesswoman; **empresario** *m* businessman

1.3 Running heads

If you are looking for a Spanish or English word you can use the **running heads** printed in bold in the top corner of each page. The running head on the left tells you the *first* headword on the left-hand page and the one on the right tells you the *last* headword on the right-hand page.

2. How do I split a word?

The bold dots in English headwords show you where you can split a word at the end of a line but you should avoid having just one letter before or after the hyphen as in **a•mend** or **thirst•y**. In such cases it is better to take the entire word over to the next line.

2.1 If a word is split at the end of a line in the dictionary, a hyphen is used to indicate this split. So that you can tell which hyphens are really part of the way a word is written, we use the following system:

> **despampanante** *adj* F striking, eye-
> -catching

The repeated hyphen before '-catching' means that the word is written 'eye-catching'.
But in:

> **rebrote** *m* BOT new shoot; *fig* new out-
> break

the hyphen is a 'dictionary' hyphen only. The word is written 'outbreak'.

3. Swung dashes and long dashes

3.1 A swung dash (~) replaces the entire headword when the headword is repeated within an entry:

> **face** [feɪs] **I** *n* **1** cara *f*; ***~ to ~*** cara a cara …

Here ***~ to ~*** means ***face to face***.

> **rencor** *m* resentment; ***guardar ~ a alguien*** bear s.o. a grudge

Here ***guardar ~ a alguien*** means ***guardar rencor a alguien***.

3.2 When a headword changes form in an entry, for example if it is put in the past tense or in the plural, then the past tense or plural ending is added to the swung dash - but only if the rest of the word doesn't change:

> **flame** [fleɪm] **1** llama *f*; ***go up in ~s*** ser pasto de las llamas …
> **parch** [pɑːrʧ] *v/t* secar; ***be ~ed*** F *of person* estar muerto de sed F

But:

> **sur•vive** [sər'vaɪv] **I** *v/i* sobrevivir; ***how are you? – I'm surviving*** ¿cómo estás? - voy tirando
> **saltón** *adj*: ***ojos saltones*** bulging eyes

3.3 Double headwords are replaced by a single swung dash:

> **Pan•a•ma Ca'nal**: ***the ~*** el Canal de Panamá

one-track 'mind *hum*: ***have a ~*** ser un obseso

3.4 In the Spanish-English part of the dictionary, when a headword is repeated in a phrase or compound with an altered form, a long dash is used:

escaso *adj* … ***-as posibilidades de*** not much chance of, little chance of

Here ***-as posibilidades*** means ***escasas posibilidades***

4. What do the different numbers mean?

Roman numbers are used to identify different grammatical categories:

sil•hou•ette [sɪlu:'et] **I** *n* silueta *f* **II** *v/t*: ***be ~d against*** perfilarse *or* recortarse sobre

recluso I *adj* reclusive; ***población -a*** prison population **II** *m*, **-a** *f* prisoner

Arabic numbers are used to identify distinct senses or uses of a word:

let•ter ['letər] **1** *of alphabet* letra *f* **2** *in mail* carta *f*

enviado *m*, **-a** *f* **1** POL envoy **2** *de periódico* reporter, correspondent

5. What do the different typefaces mean?

5.1 All Spanish and English headwords and the Roman and Arabic numbers appear in **bold**:

neoyorquino I *adj* New York *atr* **II** *m*, **-a** *f* New Yorker

◆ **go into** *v/t* **1** *room, building* entrar en **2** *profession* meterse en **3** (*discuss*) entrar en

5.2 *Italics* are used for:

a) abbreviated grammatical labels: *adj*, *adv*, *v/i*, *v/t* etc

b) gender labels: *m*, *f*, *mpl* etc

c) all the indicating words which are the signposts pointing to the correct translation for your needs:

sport•y ['spɔ:rtɪ] *adj person* deportista; *clothes* deportivo

◆ **work out I** *v/t problem, puzzle* resolver; *solution* encontrar, hallar **II** *v/i* **1** *at gym* hacer ejercicios **2** *of relationship etc* funcionar, ir bien

completo *adj* complete; *autobús*, *teatro* full

5.3 All phrases (examples and idioms) are given in ***secondary bold italics***:

sym•pa•thet•ic [sɪmpə'θetɪk] *adj* (*showing pity*) compasivo; (*understanding*) comprensivo; ***be ~ toward a person / an idea*** simpatizar con una persona / idea

salsa 1 *f* GASTR sauce; ***en su ~*** *fig* in one's element **2** *baile* salsa

5.4 The normal typeface is used for the translations.

5.5 If a translation is given in italics, and not in the normal typeface, this means that the translation is more of an *explanation* in the other language and that an explanation has to be given because there just is no real equivalent:

> **'walk-up** *apartamento en un edificio sin ascensor*
> **adobera** *f Méx type of mature cheese*

6. What do the various symbols and abbreviations tell you?

6.1 A solid blue diamond is used to indicate a phrasal verb:

> ◆ **call off** *v/t* (*cancel*) cancelar; *strike* desconvocar

6.2 A white diamond ◇ is used to indicate a Spanish compound:

> ◇**imagen de archivo** library photograph; ***imágenes de archivo*** archive footage *sg*
> ◇**imagen pública** public image

Where more than two Spanish compounds occur consecutively, they are put in a block and only the first is given the ◇.

6.3 The abbreviation F tells you that the word or phrase is used colloquially rather than in formal contexts. The abbreviation V warns you that a word or phrase is vulgar or taboo. Words or phrases labeled P are slang. Be careful how you use these words.

These abbreviations, F, V and P, are used both for headwords and phrases (placed after) and for the translations of headwords and phrases (placed after). If there is no such label given, then the word or phrase is neutral.

6.4 A colon before an English or Spanish word or phrase means that usage is restricted to this specific example (at least as far as this dictionary's translation is concerned):

> **catch-22** [kætʃtwentɪ'tu:]: ***it's a ~ situation*** es como la pescadilla que se muerde la cola
> **co-au•thor** ['koʊɒ:θər] … **II** *v/t*: ***~ a book*** escribir un libro conjuntamente
> **decantarse** *v/r*: ***~ por*** opt for

7. Does the dictionary deal with grammar too?

7.1 All English headwords are given a part of speech label:

> **tooth•less** ['tu:θlɪs] *adj* desdentado
> **top•ple** ['tɑ:pl] **I** *v/i* derrumbarse **II** *v/t government* derrocar

But if a headword can only be used as a noun (in ordinary English) then no part of speech is given, since none is needed and the Spanish gender label makes it clear that this is a noun:

> **'tooth•paste** pasta *f* de dientes, dentífrico *m*

7.2 Spanish headwords have part of speech labels. Spanish gender markers are given:

barbacoa *f* barbecue – feminine noun
bocazas *m/f inv* F loudmouth F – masculine or feminine noun with no distinct plural form
budista *m/f & adj* Buddhist – masculine or feminine noun or adjective

7.3 If an English translation of a Spanish adjective can only be used in front of a noun, and not after it, this is marked with *atr*:

bursátil *adj* stock market *atr*
campestre *adj* rural, country *atr*

7.4 If an English translation of a Spanish adjective can only be used after a noun, and not in front of it, this is marked with *pred*:

adormilado *adj* asleep *pred*

7.5 If the Spanish, unlike the English, doesn't change form if used in the plural, this is marked with *inv*:

cortacircuitos *m inv* circuit breaker
microondas *m inv* microwave

7.6 If the English, in spite of appearances, is not a plural form, this is marked with *nsg*:

nu•cle•ar 'phys•ics *nsg* física *f* nuclear
mea•sles ['mi:zlz] *nsg* sarampión *m*

English translations are given a *pl* or *sg* label (for plural or singular) in cases where this does not match the Spanish:

... ***acciones*** *pl* stock *sg*, *Br* shares
entarimado *m* **1** (*suelo*) floorboards *pl* ...

7.7 Cross-references are given to the tables of Spanish conjugations at the back of this dictionary:

gemir ⟨3l⟩ *v/i* moan, groan
esconder ⟨2a⟩ *v/t* hide, conceal

7.8 Grammatical information is provided on the prepositions you'll need in order to create complete sentences:

'switch•o•ver *to new system* cambio *m* (***to*** a)
sneer [sni:r] **I** *n* mueca *f* desdeñosa **II** *vi* burlarse (***at*** de)
escindirse *v/r* **1** (*fragmentarse*) split (***en*** into) **2** (*segregarse*) break away (***de*** from)
enviciarse *v/r* get addicted (***con*** to), get hooked (***con*** on)

Cómo utilizar el diccionario

Para sacar el máximo partido al diccionario es necesario saber dónde y cómo buscar la información. En las próximas páginas encontrará información que le ayudará tanto si está escribiendo en el idioma extranjero como si quiere entender algo escrito en ese mismo idioma.

1. ¿Dónde encuentro las palabras?

1.1 Lemas españoles e ingleses. La lista de lemas de cada idioma está ordenada alfabéticamente. Contiene las formas irregulares de verbos y nombres, ordenadas también alfabéticamente.

Habrá ocasiones en las que busque términos formados por dos palabras, por ejemplo **shooting star**, o palabras compuestas como **absent-minded**. Estas palabras reciben el mismo tratamiento que las palabras sencillas y aparecen por tanto en orden alfabético.

Hay dos excepciones a esta ordenación alfabética estricta. Una de ellas son los *phrasal verbs* ingleses, palabras como **go off**, **go out**, **go up**, que aparecen en un bloque, inmediatamente después del verbo principal (en este caso **go**), en vez de estar desperdigadas en su correspondiente posición alfabética.

La otra excepción la constituyen los compuestos españoles, que aparecen identificados con un ◇ y están agrupados en un bloque, inmediatamente después del lema de la primera palabra del compuesto.

Las palabras españolas que empiezan con **ch** y **ll** están colocadas en orden alfabético dentro de las letras C y L. Las palabras que empiezan con **ñ** aparecen después de N.

1.2 Las formas femeninas del español aparecen así:

abogado *m*, **-a** *f* lawyer
embajador *m*, **~a** *f* ambassador
danzarín *m*, **-ina** *f* dancer
pibe *m*, **-a** *f Rpl* F kid F
aprendiz *m*, **~a** *f* apprentice, trainee

Cuando un lema español tiene una forma femenina cuya traducción es diferente a la de la masculina, la forma femenina aparece presentada como un lema aparte, en orden alfabético:

empresaria *f* businesswoman; **empresario** *m* businessman

1.3 Título de página

Los **títulos de página** le permiten encontrar palabras españolas e inglesas. Éstos aparecen en negrita en la esquina superior de cada página. En el título de la izquierda aparece la *primera* palabra de la página izquierda mientras que en el de la derecha aparece la *última* palabra de la página derecha.

1.4 ¿Cómo se escribe una palabra?

Con este diccionario también podrá comprobar cómo se escriben correctamente las palabras. Las variantes del inglés británico aparecen marcadas con *Br.*

2. ¿Cómo se parte una palabra?

La partición de palabras inglesas es muy difícil para los hablantes de español. En este diccionario no tiene más que buscar los círculos negros que aparecen entre las sílabas. Estos círculos muestran dónde se puede partir una palabra al final de una línea, aunque es mejor evitar dejar una sola letra colgada como en **a•mend** o **thirst•y**. En esos casos es mejor pasar toda la palabra a la línea siguiente.

2.1 Si una palabra queda partida al final de una línea del diccionario, se utiliza un guión. Para que estos guiones se puedan distinguir de los que forman parte de la propia palabra, utilizamos el siguiente sistema:

> **despampanante** *adj* F striking, eye-
> -catching

El guión repetido antes del lema '-catching' indica que la palabra se escribe 'eye-catching'.

Sin embargo, en:

> **rebrote** *m* BOT new shoot; *fig* new out-
> break

el guión que aparece es un guión propio del diccionario. La palabra se escribe 'outbreak'.

3. Tildes y rayas

3.1 Una tilde (~) reemplaza al lema cuando éste aparece dentro de una entrada:

> **face** [feɪs] **I** *n* **1** cara *f*; ***~ to ~*** cara a cara …

En este caso ***~ to ~*** quiere decir ***face to face***.

> **rencor** *m* resentment; ***guardar ~ a alguien*** bear s.o. a grudge

Aquí ***guardar ~ a alguien*** quiere decir ***guardar rencor a alguien***.

3.2 En los casos en los que el lema cambia de forma en la entrada, por ejemplo si aparecen pasados o plurales, se le añade al lema la terminación del pasado o del plural, pero sólo si el resto de la palabra no cambia:

> **flame** [fleɪm] **1** llama *f*; ***go up in ~s*** ser pasto de las llamas …
> **parch** [pɑːrʧ] *v/t* secar; ***be ~ed*** F *of person* estar muerto de sed F

En cambio:

sur•vive [sər'vaɪv] **I** *v/i* sobrevivir; ***how are you? – I'm surviving*** ¿cómo estás? - voy tirando …
saltón *adj*: ***ojos saltones*** bulging eyes

3.3 A los lemas compuestos los sustituye una única tilde:

Pan•a•ma Ca'nal: ***the ~*** el Canal de Panamá
one-track 'mind *hum*: ***have a ~*** ser un obseso

3.4 En la parte Español-Inglés del diccionario se utiliza una raya para reemplazar el lema cuando éste aparece repetido en una frase:

escaso *adj* ... ***-as posibilidades de*** not much chance of, little chance of

Aquí ***-as posibilidades*** quiere decir ***escasas posibilidades***.

4. ¿Qué significan los distintos números?

Los números romanos se utilizan para identificar categorías gramaticales diferentes:

sil•hou•ette [sɪluː'et] **I** *n* silueta *f* **II** *v/t*: ***be ~d against*** perfilarse *or* recortarse sobre
recluso I *adj* reclusive; ***población -a*** prison population **II** *m*, **-a** *f* prisoner

Los números arábigos se utilizan para mostrar distintas acepciones o usos de una palabra:

let•ter ['letər] **1** *of alphabet* letra *f* **2** *in mail* carta *f*
enviado *m*, **-a** *f* **1** POL envoy **2** *de periódico* reporter, correspondent

5. ¿Qué significan los diferentes tipos de letra?

5.1 Todos los lemas españoles e ingleses, así como los números romanos y arábigos aparecen en **negrita**:

neoyorquino I *adj* New York *atr* **II** *m*, **-a** *f* New Yorker
◆ **go into** *v/t* **1** *room, building* entrar en **2** *profession* meterse en **3** (*discuss*) entrar en

5.2 *La cursiva* se utiliza para:

a) las abreviaturas de categorías gramaticales: *adj*, *adv*, *v/i*, *v/t*, etc.

b) marcas de género: *m*, *f*, *mpl*, etc.

c) todas las palabras que se utilizan para indicar cuál es la traducción correcta para cada contexto:

sport•y ['spɔːrtɪ] *adj person* deportista; *clothes* deportivo
◆ **work out I** *v/t problem, puzzle* resolver; *solution* encontrar, hallar **II** *v/i* **1** *at gym* hacer ejercicios **2** *of relationship etc* funcionar, ir bien
completo *adj* complete; *autobús, teatro* full
grano *m* **1** *de café* bean; *de cereales* grain … **2** *en la piel* pimple, spot

5.3 Todas las frases (ejemplos y expresiones idiomáticas) aparecen en ***negrita y cursiva***:

sym•pa•thet•ic [sɪmpə'θetɪk] *adj* (*showing pity*) compasivo; (*understanding*) comprensivo; ***be ~ toward a person / an idea*** simpatizar con una persona / idea
salsa *f* **1** GASTR sauce; ***en su ~*** *fig* in one's element **2** *baile* salsa

5.4 El tipo de letra normal se utiliza para las traducciones.

5.5 Si una traducción aparece en cursiva y no en el tipo de letra normal, quiere decir que esta traducción es más una *explicación* en el otro idioma, explicación necesaria porque no hay un equivalente natural:

'walk-up *apartamento en un edificio sin ascensor*
adobera *f Méx type of mature cheese*

6. Acento

La marca de acento tónico ' aparece delante de la sílaba sobre la que recae el principal acento en las palabras inglesas:

mo•tif [moʊ'tiːf] motivo *m*
rec•ord[1] ['rekɔːrd] *n* **1** MUS disco *m* **2** SP *etc* récord *m* …
re•cord[2] [rɪ'kɔːrd] *v/t electronically* grabar; *in writing* anotar

El acento aparece en la transcripción fonética o, si ésta no aparece, en el mismo lema o palabra compuesta:

'rec•ord hold•er plusmarquista *m/f*

7. ¿Qué indican los diferentes símbolos y abreviaturas?

7.1 Un rombo azul identifica un *phrasal verb* (verbo con partícula):

◆ **call off** *v/t* (*cancel*) cancelar; *strike* desconvocar

7.2 Un rombo blanco ◇ se utiliza para identificar un compuesto español:

◇**imagen de archivo** library photograph; ***imágenes de archivo*** archive footage *sg*
◇**imagen pública** public image

Cuando aparecen seguidos más de dos compuestos españoles, éstos se colocan en un bloque y sólo el primero está identificado con el ◇.

7.3 La abreviatura F indica que la palabra o frase se utiliza más en contextos coloquiales que formales. La abreviatura V alerta sobre una palabra vulgar o tabú. Tenga cuidado al utilizar estas palabras. Las palabras con la abreviatura P son de argot.

Las abreviaturas F, V y P aparecen tanto con lemas y ejemplos (colocadas detrás) como con sus traducciones (colocadas detrás). Cuando no aparece ninguna abreviatura la palabra o frase es neutra.

7.4 Los dos puntos delante de una frase o ejemplo en inglés o español indican que el uso se restringe al ejemplo que aparece en el texto (por lo menos en lo que respecta a la traducción ofrecida en este diccionario):

catch-22 [kætʃtwentɪ'tuː]: ***it's a ~ situation*** es como la pescadilla que se muerde la cola
co•au•thor ['koʊɒːθər] … **II** *v/t*: ***~ a book*** escribir un libro conjuntamente
decantarse ⟨1a⟩ *v/r*: ***~ por*** opt for

8. ¿Este diccionario contiene también información gramatical?

8.1 Todos los lemas ingleses llevan una marca de categoría gramatical:

tooth•less ['tuːθlɪs] *adj* desdentado
top•ple ['tɑːpl] **I** *v/i* derrumbarse **II** *v/t government* derrocar

Pero si un lema sólo se puede utilizar como nombre (en inglés corriente), no aparece ninguna marca de categoría gramatical porque no hace falta y, además, la marca de género de la palabra española deja bien claro que se trata de un nombre.

'tooth•paste pasta *f* de dientes, dentífrico *m*

8.2 Todas los lemas españoles llevan abreviatura de categoría gramatical y, si corresponden, marcas de género:

barbacoa *f* barbecue
bocazas *m/f inv* F loudmouth F
budista *m/f & adj* Buddhist

8.3 Si la traducción al inglés de un adjetivo español sólo se puede utilizar delante de un nombre, y nunca detrás, se identifica con la marca *atr*:

bursátil *adj* stock market *atr*
campestre *adj* rural, country *atr*

8.4 Si la traducción al inglés de un adjetivo español sólo se puede utilizar detrás de un nombre, y nunca delante, se identifica con la marca *pred*:

adormilado *adj* asleep *pred*

8.5 Si la forma del plural del español es invariable, al contrario que la del inglés, se identifica con la marca *inv*:

cortacircuitos *m inv* circuit breaker
microondas *m inv* microwave

8.6 Cuando, a pesar de su apariencia, el inglés no es una forma plural, se identifica con *nsg*:

nu•cle•ar 'phys•ics *nsg* física *f* nuclear
mea•sles ['miːzlz] *nsg* sarampión *m*

Las traducciones inglesas reciben una marca *pl* o *sg* (para plural o singular) en los casos en los que no se corresponden con el español:

... ***acciones*** *pl* stock *sg*, *Br* shares
entarimado *m* **1** (*suelo*) floorboards *pl* ...

8.7 Los plurales ingleses irregulares aparecen identificados:

the•sis ['θiːsɪs] (*pl* ***theses*** ['θiːsiːz]) tesis *f inv*
thief [θiːf] (*pl* ***thieves*** [θiːvz]) ladrón(-ona) *m(f)*
trout [traʊt] (*pl* ***trout***) trucha *f*

8.8 Si el plural de un nombre inglés que acaba en **-o** se forma simplemente añadiendo una **-s**, no se identifica con ninguna marca. En cambio, si el plural de un nombre inglés que acaba en **-s** se forma añadiendo **-es**, o bien añadiendo indistintamente **-es** o **-s**, esto aparece indicado:

car•go ['kɑːrgoʊ] (*pl* ***-o(e)s***) cargamento *m*
to•ma•to [tə'meɪtoʊ] (*pl* ***-oes***) tomate *m*, *Mex* jitomate *m*

8.9 Las formas irregulares y semi-irregulares de los verbos aparecen identificadas:

sim•pli•fy ['sɪmplɪfaɪ] *v/t* (*pret & pp* ***-ied***) simplificar
sing [sɪŋ] *v/t & v/i* (*pret* ***sang***, *pp* ***sung***) cantar
la•bel ['leɪbl] **I** *n* etiqueta *f* ... **II** *v/t* (*pret & pp* ***-ed***, *Br* ***-led***) *bags* etiquetar

8.10 Se incluyen remisiones a las conjugaciones verbales españolas que se encuentran al final del diccionario:

gemir ⟨3l⟩ *v/i* moan, groan
esconder ⟨2a⟩ *v/t* hide, conceal

8.11 Se ofrece información gramatical sobre las preposiciones necesarias para formar frases:

'switch•o•ver *to new system* cambio *m* (***to*** a)
sneer [sniːr] **I** *n* mueca *f* desdeñosa **II** *v/i* burlarse (***at*** de)
escindirse *v/r* **1** (*fragmentarse*) split (***en*** into) **2** (*segregarse*) break away (***de*** from)
enviciarse *v/r* get addicted (***con*** to), get hooked (***con*** on)

The pronunciation of Spanish

Stress

1. If a word ends in a vowel, or in *n* or *s*, the penultimate syllable is stressed: **espada**, **biblioteca**, **hablan**, **telefonean**, **edificios**.

2. If a word ends in a consonant other than *n* or *s*, the last syllable is stressed: **dificultad**, **hablar**, **laurel**, **niñez**.

3. If a word is to be stressed in any way contrary to rules 1 and 2, an acute accent is written over the stressed vowel: **rubí**, **máquina**, **crímenes**, **carácter**, **continúa**, **autobús**.

4. **Diphthongs and syllable division.** Of the 5 vowels *a*, *e*, *o* are considered "strong" and *i* and *u* "weak":

a) A combination of weak + strong forms a diphthong, the stress falling on the stronger element: **reina**, **baile**, **cosmonauta**, **tiene**, **bueno**.

b) A combination of weak + weak forms a diphthong, the stress falling on the second element: **viuda**, **ruido**.

c) Two strong vowels together remain two distinct syllables, the stress falling according to rules 1 and 2: **ma/estro**, **atra/er**.

d) Any word having a vowel combination not stressed according to these rules has an accent: **traído**, **oído**, **baúl**, **río**.

Sounds

Since the pronunciation of Spanish is (unlike English) adequately represented by the spelling of words, Spanish headwords have not been given a phonetic transcription. The sounds of Spanish are described below.

The pronunciation described is primarily that of a Spaniard. But the main features of Latin American pronunciation are also covered.

Vowels

a As in English *father*: **paz**, **pata**.

e Like *e* in English *they* (but without the following sound of *y*): **grande**, **pelo**. A shorter sound when followed by a consonant in the same syllable, like *e* in English *get*: **España**, **renta**.

i Like *i* in English *machine*, though somewhat shorter: **pila**, **rubí**.

o As in English *November*, *token*: **solo**, **esposa**. A shorter sound when followed by a consonant in the same syllable, like *au* in English *fault* or the *a* in *fall*: **costra**, **bomba**.

u Like *oo* in English *food*: **pura**, **luna**. Silent after **q** and in **gue**, **gui**, unless marked with a dieresis (**antigüedad**, **argüir**).

y when occurring as a vowel (in the conjunction **y** or at the end of a word), is pronounced like *i*.

Diphthongs

ai like *i* in English *right*: **baile**, **vaina**.

ei like *ey* in English *they*: **reina**, **peine**.

oi like *oy* in English *boy*: **boina**, **oigo**.

au like *ou* in English *bout*: **causa**, **audacia**.

eu like the vowel sounds in English *may-you*, without the sound of the *y*: **deuda**, **reuma**.

Semiconsonants

i, y like *y* in English *yes*: **yerno**, **tiene**; in some cases in *L.Am.* this *y* is pronounced like the *s* in English *measure*: **mayo**, **yo**.

u like *w* in English *water*: **huevo**, **agua**.

Consonants

b, v These two letters represent the same value in Spanish. There are two distinct pronunciations:

1. At the start of a word and after *m* and *n* the sound is like English *b*: **batalla**, **ventaja**; **tromba**, **invierno**.
2. In all other positions the sound is what is technically a "bilabial fricative". This sound does not exist in English. Go to say a *b* but do not quite bring your lips together: **estaba**, **cueva**, **de Vigo**.

c
1. *c* before *a*, *o*, *u* or a consonant is like English *k*: **café**, **cobre**.
2. *c* before *e*, *i* is like English *th* in *thin*: **cédula**, **cinco**. In *L.Am.* this is pronounced like an English *s* in *chase*.

ch like English *ch* in *church*: **mucho**, **chocho**.

d Three distinct pronunciations:

1. At the start of a word and after *l* and *n*, the sound is like English *d*: **doy**, **aldea**, **conde**.
2. Between vowels and after consonants other than *l* and *n* the sound is relaxed and approaches English *th* in *this*: **codo**, **guardar**; in parts of Spain it is further relaxed and even disappears, particularly in the **-ado** ending.
3. In final position, this type 2 is further relaxed or omitted altogether: **usted**, **Madrid**.

f like English *f*: **fuero**, **flor**.

g Three distinct pronunciations:

1. Before *e* and *i* it is the same as the Spanish j (below): **coger**, **general**.
2. At the start of a word and after *n*, the sound is that of English *g* in *get*: **granada**, **rango**.
3. In other positions the sound is like 2 above, but much softer, the *g* almost disappearing: **agua**, **guerra**. N.B. In the group **gue**, **gui** the **u** is silent (**guerra**, **guindar**) unless marked with a dieresis (**antigüedad**, **argüir**). In the group **gua** all letters are sounded.

h	always silent: **honor**, **búho**.
j	A strong guttural sound not found in English, but like the *ch* in Scots *loch*, German *Achtung*: **jota**, **ejercer**.
k	like English *k*: **kilogramo**, **ketchup**.
l	like English *l*: **león**, **pala**.
ll	approximating to English *lli* in *million*: **millón**, **calle**. In *L.Am.* like the *s* in English *measure*.
m	like English *m*: **mano**, **como**.
n	like English *n*: **nono**, **pan**; except before **v**, when the group is pronounced like *mb*: **enviar**, **invadir**.
ñ	approximating to English *ni* in *onion*: **paño**, **ñoño**.
p	like English *p*: **Pepe**, **copa**.
q	like English *k*; always in combination with **u**, which is silent: **que**, **quiosco**.
r	a single trill stronger than any *r* in English, but like Scots *r*: **caro**, **querer**. Somewhat relaxed in final position. Pronounced like **rr** at the start of a word and after **l**, **n**, **s**: **rata**.
rr	strongly trilled: **carro**, **hierro**.
s	like *s* in English *chase*: **rosa**, **soso**. But before **b**, **d**, hard **g**, **l**, **m** and **n** it is like English *s* in *rose*: **desde**, **mismo**, **asno**. Before "impure **s**" in loanwords, an extra *e*-sound is inserted in pronunciation: **e-sprint**, **e-stand**.
t	like English *t*: **patata**, **tope**.
v	see *b*.
w	found in a few recent loan-words only and pronounced pretty much as the English *w*, but sometimes with a very slight *g* sound before it: **whisky**, **windsurf**. In one exceptional case it is pronounced like an English *v* or like Spanish **b** and **v**: **wáter**.
x	like English *gs* in *big sock*: **máximo**, **examen**. Before a consonant like English *s* in *chase*: **extraño**, **mixto**.
z	like English *th* in *thin*: **zote**, **zumbar**. In *L.Am.* like English *s* in *chase*.

The Spanish Alphabet

a [ah]	f ['ef-feh]	l ['eleh]	p [peh]	u [oo]
b [beh]	g [Heh]	ll ['el-yeh]	q [koo]	v ['ooveh]
c [theh]	h ['acheh]	m ['emeh]	r ['ereh]	w ['oovehdoh-bleh]
ch [cheh]	i [ee]	n ['eneh]	rr ['erreh]	x ['ekees]
d [deh]	j ['Hota]	ñ ['en-yeh]	s ['eseh]	y [eegree-'eh-ga]
e [eh]	k [ka]	o [oh]	t [teh]	z ['theh-ta]

H *is pronounced as in the Scottish way of saying loch*

Written Spanish

I. Capitalization

The rules for capitalization in Spanish largely correspond to those for the English language. In contrast to English, however, adjectives derived from proper nouns are not capitalized (*americano* American, *español* Spanish).

II. Word division

Spanish words are divided according to the following rules:

1. If there is a **single consonant** between two vowels, the division is made between the first vowel and the consonant (*di-ne-ro*, *Gra-na-da*).
2. **Two consecutive consonants** may be divided (*miér-co-les*, *dis-cur-so*). If the second consonant is an *l* or *r*, however, the division comes before the two consonants (*re-gla*, *nie-bla*; *po-bre*, *ca-bra*). This also goes for ch, ll and rr (*te-cho*, *ca-lle*, *pe-rro*).
3. In the case of **three consecutive consonants** (usually including an *l* or *r*), the division comes after the first consonant (*ejem-plo*, *siem-pre*). If the second consonant is an *s*, however, the division comes after the *s* (*cons-tan-te*, *ins-ti-tu-to*).
4. In the case of **four consecutive consonants** (the second of these is usually an *s*), the division is made between the second and third consonants (*ins-tru-men-to*).
5. **Diphthongs** and **triphthongs** may not be divided (*bien*, *buey*). Vowels which are part of different syllables, however, may be divided (*frí-o*, *acre-e-dor*).
6. **Compounds**, including those formed with prefixes, can also be divided morphologically (*nos-otros*, *des-ali-ño*, *dis-cul-pa*).

III. Punctuation

In Spanish a comma is often placed after an adverbial phrase introducing a sentence (*sin embargo, todos los esfuerzos fueron inútiles* however, all efforts were in vain). A subsidiary clause beginning a sentence is also followed by a comma (*si tengo tiempo, lo haré* if I have time, I'll do it, **but**: *lo haré si tengo tiempo* I'll do it if I have time).

Questions and exclamations are introduced by an inverted question mark and exclamation point respectively, which immediately precedes the question or exclamation (*Perdone, ¿está en casa el señor Pérez?* Excuse me, is Mr. Pérez at home?; *¡Que lástima!* What a shame!).

La pronunciación del inglés

A. Vocales y diptongos

[ɑː] sonido largo parecido al de *a* en *raro*: *far* [fɑːr], *father* ['fɑːðər].

[ʌ] *a* abierta, breve y oscura, que se pronuncia en la parte anterior de la boca sin redondear los labios: *butter* ['bʌtər], *come* [kʌm], *color* ['kʌlər], *blood* [blʌd], *flourish* ['flʌrɪʃ].

[æ] sonido breve, bastante abierto y distinto, algo parecido al de *a* en *parra*: *fat* [fæt], *ran* [ræn], *after* ['æftər].

[ɒː] vocal larga, bastante cerrada, entre *a* y *o*; más cercana a la *a* que a la *o*: *fall* [fɒːl], *fault* [fɒːlt], *inaudible* [ɪn'ɒːdəbl].

[e] sonido breve, medio abierto, parecido al de *e* en *perro*: *bed* [bed], *less* [les], *hairy* ['herɪ].

[aɪ] sonido parecido al de *ai* en *estáis*, *baile*: *I* [aɪ], *lie* [laɪ], *dry* [draɪ].

[aʊ] sonido parecido al de *au* en *causa*, *sauce*: *house* [haʊs], *now* [naʊ].

[eɪ] *e* medio abierta, pero más cerrada que la *e* de *hablé*; suena como si la siguiese una [ɪ] débil, sobre todo en sílaba acentuada: *date* [deɪt], *play* [pleɪ], *obey* [oʊ'beɪ].

[ə] 'vocal neutra', siempre átona; parecida al sonido de la *a* final de *cada*: *about* [ə'baʊt], *butter* ['bʌtər], *connect* [kə'nekt].

[iː] sonido largo, parecido al de *i* en *misa*, *vino*: *scene* [siːn], *sea* [siː], *feet* [fiːt], *ceiling* ['siːlɪŋ].

[ɪ] sonido breve, abierto, parecido al de *i* en *silba*, *tirria*, pero más abierto: *big* [bɪg], *city* ['sɪtɪ].

[oʊ] *o* larga, más bien cerrada, sin redondear los labios ni levantar la lengua: *note* [noʊt], *boat* [boʊt], *below* [bɪ'loʊ].

[ɔː] vocal larga, bastante cerrada; es algo parecida a la *o* de *por*: *abnormal* [æb'nɔːrml], *before* [bɪ'fɔːr].

[ɔɪ] diptongo cuyo primer elemento es una *o* abierta, seguido de una *i* abierta pero débil; parecido al sonido de *oy* en *doy*: *voice* [vɔɪs], *boy* [bɔɪ], *annoy* [ə'nɔɪ].

[ɜː] forma larga de la 'vocal neutra' [ə], algo parecida al sonido de *eu* en la palabra francesa *leur*: *word* [wɜːrd], *girl* [gɜːrl].

[uː] sonido largo, parecido al de *u* en *cuna*, *duda*: *fool* [fuːl], *shoe* [ʃuː], *you* [juː], *rule* [ruːl].

[ʊ] *u* pura pero muy rápida, más cerrada que la *u* de *burra*: *put* [pʊt], *look* [lʊk].

B. Consonantes

[b] como la *b* de *cambiar*: *bay* [beɪ], *brave* [breɪv].

[d] como la *d* de *andar*: *did* [dɪd], *ladder* ['lædər].

[f] como la *f* de *filo*: *face* [feɪs], *baffle* ['bæfl].

[g] como la *g* de *golpe*: *go* [goʊ], *haggle* ['hægl].

[h] se pronuncia con aspiración fuerte, sin la aspereza gutural de la *j* en *Gijón*: *who* [huː], *ahead* [ə'hed].

[j] como la *y* de *cuyo*: *you* [juː], *million* ['mɪljən].

[k] como la *c* de *casa*: *cat* [kæt], *kill* [kɪl].

[l] como la *l* de *loco*: *love* [lʌv], *goal* [goʊl].

[m] como la *m* de *madre*: *mouth* [maʊθ], *come* [kʌm].

[n] como la *n* de *nada*: *not* [nɑːt], *banner* ['bænər].

[p] como la *p* de *padre*: *pot* [pɑːt], *top* [tɑːp].

[r] Cuando se pronuncia, es un sonido muy débil, más bien semivocal, que no tiene nada de la vibración fuerte que caracteriza la *r* española; se articula elevando la punta de la lengua hacia el paladar duro: *rose* [roʊz], *pride* [praɪd], *there* [ðer]. (v. también 'Diferencias entre la pronunciación del inglés americano y la del inglés británico').

[s] como la *s* de *casa*: *sit* [sɪt], *scent* [sent].

[t] como la *t* de *pata*: *take* [teɪk], *patter* ['pætər].

[v] inexistente en español; a diferencia de *b*, *v* en español, se pronuncia juntando el labio inferior con los dientes superiores: *vein* [veɪn], *velvet* ['velvɪt].

[w] como la *u* de *huevo*: *water* ['wɒːtər], *will* [wɪl].

[z] como la *s* de *mismo*: *zeal* [ziːl], *hers* [hɜːrz].

[ʒ] inexistente en español; como la *j* en la palabra francesa *jour*: *measure* ['meʒər], *leisure* ['liːʒər]. Aparece a menudo en el grupo [dʒ], que se pronuncia como el grupo *dj* de la palabra francesa *adjacent*: *edge* [edʒ], *gem* [dʒem].

[ʃ] inexistente en español; como *ch* en la palabra francesa *chose*: *shake* [ʃeɪk], *washing* ['wɑːʃɪŋ]. Aparece a menudo en el grupo [ʧ], que se pronuncia como la *ch* en *mucho*: *match* [mæʧ], *natural* ['næʧrəl].

[θ] como la *z* de *zapato* en castellano: *thin* [θɪn], *path* [pæθ].

[ð] forma sonorizada del anterior, algo como la *d* de *todo*: *there* [ðer], *breathe* [briːð].

[ŋ] como la *n* de *banco*: *singer* ['sɪŋər], *tinker* ['tɪŋkər].

El alfabeto inglés

a [eɪ]	e [iː]	i [aɪ]	m [em]	q [kjuː]	u [juː]	y [waɪ]
b [biː]	f [ef]	j [dʒeɪ]	n [en]	r [ɑːr]	v [viː]	z [ziː],
c [siː]	g [dʒiː]	k [keɪ]	o [oʊ]	s [es]	w ['dʌbljuː]	*Br* [zed]
d [diː]	h [eɪʧ]	l [el]	p [piː]	t [tiː]	x [eks]	

Diferencias entre la pronunciación del inglés americano y la del inglés británico

Entre la pronunciación del inglés en Gran Bretaña (British English, BE) y la del inglés en Estados Unidos (American English, AE) existen múltiples diferencias que es imposible tratar aquí en forma adecuada. Señalamos únicamente las diferencias más notables:

1. Las palabras que tienen dos sílabas o más después del acento principal ['] llevan en AE un acento secundario que no tienen en BE, p.ej. ***dictionary*** [AE ''dɪkʃə'nerɪ = BE 'dɪkʃənrɪ], ***secretary*** [AE ''sekrə'terɪ = BE 'sekrətrɪ].

2. La **r** en posición final después de una vocal o entre vocal y consonante es normalmente muda en BE, pero se pronuncia claramente en AE, p.ej. ***car*** [AE kɑːr = BE kɑː], ***care*** [AE ker = BE keə], ***border*** [AE 'bɔːrdər = BE 'bɔːdə].

3. Una de las peculiaridades más notables del AE es la **nasalización** de las vocales antes y después de las consonantes nasales [m, n, ŋ].

4. La **o** [BE ɒ] suele pronunciarse en AE casi como una **a** oscura [AE ɑː], p.ej. ***dollar*** [AE 'dɑːlər = BE 'dɒlə], ***college*** [AE 'kɑːlɪdʒ = BE 'kɒlɪdʒ], ***lot*** [AE lɑːt = BE lɒt], ***problem*** [AE 'prɑːbləm = BE 'prɒbləm].

5. La **a** [BE ɑː] se pronuncia en AE como [æ] en palabras del tipo ***pass*** [AE pæs = BE pɑːs], ***answer*** [AE 'ænsər = BE 'ɑːnsə], ***dance*** [AE dæns = BE dɑːns], ***laugh*** [AE læf = BE lɑːf].

6. La **u** [BE juː] en sílaba acentuada se pronuncia en AE como [uː], p.ej. ***Tuesday*** [AE 'tuːzdeɪ = BE 'tjuːzdeɪ], ***student*** [AE 'stuːdnt = BE 'stjuːdnt], pero no en ***music*** [AE, BE = 'mjuːzɪk], ***fuel*** [AE, BE = 'fjʊəl].

7. La sílaba final **-ile** (BE generalmente [-aɪl]) se pronuncia a menudo en AE como [-əl] o bien [-ɪl], p.ej. ***missile*** [AE 'mɪs(ə)l, 'mɪsɪl = BE 'mɪsaɪl].

8. Hay otras palabras que se pronuncian de distinto modo en BE y AE, p.ej. ***lever*** [AE 'levər = BE 'liːvə], ***lieutenant*** [AE lʊ'tenənt = BE lef'tenənt], ***tomato*** [AE tə'meɪtoʊ = BE tə'mɑːtəʊ], ***clerk*** [AE klɜːrk = BE klɑːk], ***vase*** [AE veɪz = BE vɑːz], leisure [AE 'liːʒər = BE 'leʒə].

Diferencias entre la ortografía del inglés americano y la del inglés británico

Existen ciertas diferencias entre el inglés escrito de Gran Bretaña (British English, BE) y el inglés escrito de Estados Unidos (American English, AE).

Son las principales:

1. La **u** que se escribe en BE en las palabras que terminan en **-our** (p.ej. col*our*) se suprime en AE: col*or*, hum*or*, hon*or*able.

2. Muchas palabras que en BE terminan en **-re** (p.ej. cent*re*) se escriben en AE **-er**, p.ej. cent*er*, met*er*, theat*er* (pero no massacre).

3. En muchos casos, las palabras que en BE tienen **ll** en posición media en sílabas no acentuadas se escriben en AE con una **l**, p.ej. counci*l*or, quarre*l*ed, trave*l*ed. Sin embargo, hay palabras que en BE se escriben con una **l** que en AE se escriben con **ll**, p.ej. enro*ll*(s), ski*ll*ful, insta*ll*ment.

4. En ciertos casos, las palabras que en BE terminan en **-ence** se escriben en AE con **-ense**, p.ej. def*ense*, off*ense*.

5. Ciertas vocales finales, que no tienen valor en la pronunciación, se escriben en BE (p.ej. catalog*ue*) pero no en AE: catalog, dialog, prolog, program.

6. Se ha extendido más en AE que en BE la costumbre de escribir **e** en lugar de **ae** y **oe**, p.ej. an(a)*e*mia, an(a)*e*sthetic.

7. Algunas consonantes que en BE se escriben dobles pueden en AE escribirse sencillas, p.ej. kidna(p)*p*ed, worshi(p)*p*ed.

8. En AE se suprime a veces la **u** del grupo **ou** que tiene BE, p.ej. m*o*(*u*)ld, sm*o*(*u*)lder, y se escribe en AE pl*ow* en lugar del BE pl*ough*.

9. En AE suele suprimirse la **e** muda en las palabras como judg(*e*)ment, acknowledg(*e*)ment.

10. Hay otras palabras que se escriben de distinto modo en BE y AE, p.ej. BE cosy = AE *cozy*, BE moustache = AE *mustache*, BE sceptical = AE *skeptical*, BE grey = AE *gray*.

English pronunciation

Vowels

[ɑː] *father* ['fɑːðər]
[æ] *man* [mæn]
[e] *get* [get]
[ə] *about* [ə'baʊt]
[ɜː] *absurd* [əb'sɜːrd]
[ɪ] *stick* [stɪk]
[iː] *need* [niːd]
[ɒː] *in-laws* ['ɪnlɒːz]
[ɔː] *more* [mɔːr]
[ʌ] *mother* ['mʌðər]
[ʊ] *book* [bʊk]
[uː] *fruit* [fruːt]

Diphthongs

[aɪ] *time* [taɪm]
[aʊ] *cloud* [klaʊd]
[eɪ] *name* [neɪm]
[ɔɪ] *point* [pɔɪnt]
[oʊ] *oath* [oʊθ]

Consonants

[b] *bag* [bæg]
[d] *dear* [dɪr]
[f] *fall* [fɒːl]
[g] *give* [gɪv]
[h] *hole* [hoʊl]
[j] *yes* [jes]
[k] *come* [kʌm]
[l] *land* [lænd]
[m] *mean* [miːn]
[n] *night* [naɪt]
[p] *pot* [pɑːt]
[r] *right* [raɪt]
[s] *sun* [sʌn]
[t] *take* [teɪk]
[v] *vain* [veɪn]
[w] *wait* [weɪt]
[z] *rose* [roʊz]
[ŋ] *bring* [brɪŋ]
[ʃ] *she* [ʃiː]
[ʧ] *chair* [ʧer]
[dʒ] *join* [dʒɔɪn]
[ʒ] *leisure* ['liːʒər]
[θ] *think* [θɪŋk]
[ð] *the* [ðə]
['] means that the following syllable is stressed: *ability* [ə'bɪlətɪ]

Vocabulario Español-Inglés
Spanish-English Dictionary

A

a *prp* **1** *dirección* to; ***al este de*** to the east of; ***~ casa*** home; ***ir ~ la cama / al cine*** go to bed / to the movies; ***¡~ trabajar!*** get to work!; ***vamos ~ Buenos Aires*** we're going to Buenos Aires; ***voy ~ casa de Marta*** I'm going to Marta's (house)
2 *situación* at; ***~ la mesa*** at the table; ***al lado de*** next to; ***~ la derecha*** on the right; ***al sol*** in the sun; ***~ treinta kilómetros de Cuzco*** thirty kilometers from Cuzco; ***está ~ cinco kilómetros*** it's five kilometers away
3 *tiempo*: ***¿~ qué hora llegas?*** what time do you arrive?; ***~ las tres*** at three o'clock; ***de once ~ doce*** from eleven (o'clock) to twelve; ***estamos ~ quince de febrero*** it's February fifteenth; ***~ los treinta años*** at the age of thirty; ***~ la llegada del tren*** when the train arrives
4 *modo*: ***~ la española*** the Spanish way; ***~ mano*** by hand; ***~ pie*** on foot; ***~ 50 kilómetros por hora*** at fifty kilometers an hour
5 *precio*: ***¿~ cómo*** *o* ***cuánto está?*** how much is it?; ***están ~ dos pesos el kilo*** they are two pesos a kilo
6 *objeto indirecto*: ***dáselo ~ tu hermano*** give it to your brother
7 *objeto directo*: ***vi ~ mi padre*** I saw my father
8 *en perífrasis verbal*: ***empezar ~*** begin to; ***jugar ~ las cartas*** play cards; ***decidirse ~ hacer algo*** decide to do sth; ***voy ~ comprarlo*** I'm going to buy it; ***~ decir verdad*** to tell the truth
9 *para introducir pregunta*: ***¿~ que no lo sabes?*** I bet you don't know; ***~ ver*** OK, right; ***~ ver lo que pasa ahora*** let's see what happens now

(a) *abr* (= ***alias***) aka (= also known as)

AA.EE. *abr* (= ***Asuntos Exteriores***) foreign affairs

abacería *f* grocery store, *Br* grocer's

abacero *m*, **-a** *f* grocer

abacial *adj*: ***iglesia ~*** abbey (church)

ábaco *m* abacus

abad *m* abbot

abadejo *m pez* pollack

abadía *f* abbey

abajeño *m*, **-a** *f L.Am.* lowlander

abajo I *adv* **1** *situación* below, underneath; *en edificio* downstairs; ***ponlo ahí ~*** put it down there; ***el ~ firmante*** the undersigned; ***el cajón de ~*** *siguiente* the drawer underneath *o* below; *último* the bottom drawer
2 *dirección* down; *en edificio* downstairs; ***cuesta ~*** downhill; ***empuja hacia ~*** push down; ***ir para ~*** *fig* drop, go down
3 *con cantidades*: ***de diez para ~*** ten or under, ten or below
II *prp*: ***~ de*** *L.Am.* under
III *int*: ***¡~ los traidores!*** down with the traitors!

abalanzarse ⟨1f⟩ *v/r* rush *o* surge forward; ***~ sobre algo / alguien*** leap *o* pounce on sth / s.o.

abalaustrado *adj*: ***columna -a*** ARQUI baluster

abalear ⟨1a⟩ *v/t S.Am.* shoot

abaleo *m Andes, C.Am., Ven* shootout

abalón *m* ZO abalone

abalorio *m* bead

abanderado I *m*, **-a** *f* standard-bearer **II** *part* ☞ ***abanderar***

abanderar ⟨1a⟩ *v/t* register

abandonado I *adj* abandoned **II** *part* ☞ ***abandonar***

abandonar ⟨1a⟩ **I** *v/t* **1** *lugar* leave; *a alguien* abandon; *a esposa, hijos* desert; *objeto* abandon, dump **2** *idea* give up, abandon; *actividad* give up, drop **II** *v/i* DEP pull out; **abandonarse** *v/r* let o.s. go; ***~ a*** abandon o.s. to

abandono *m* **1** abandonment; ***~ del do-***

micilio conyugal desertion; ***~ de la energía nuclear*** abandonment of nuclear power **2** DEP *de carrera* retirement **3**: ***en un estado de ~*** in a state of neglect

abanicar ⟨1g⟩ *v/t* fan; **abanicarse** *v/r* fan o.s.

abanico *m* **1** fan **2** *fig* range

◇ **abanico eléctrico** *Méx* electric fan

abaratar ⟨1a⟩ *v/t* reduce *o* lower the price of; *precio* reduce, lower; **abaratarse** *v/r* become cheaper; *de precio* drop, go down

abarca *f* sandal

abarcable *adj pormenores, historia, vista* which can be taken in; ***la historia del país no es ~ en una hora*** the history of the country cannot be dealt with *o* covered in one hour

abarcar ⟨1g⟩ *v/t* **1** *territorio* cover; *fig* comprise, cover **2** *L.Am.* (*acaparar*) hoard, stockpile **3**: ***~ con la vista*** take in

abarrotado I *adj* packed **II** *part* ☞ ***abarrotar***

abarrotar ⟨1a⟩ *v/t* **1** *lugar* pack **2** *L.Am.* COM buy up, stockpile; **abarrotarse** *v/r L.Am. del mercado* become glutted

abarrotería *f Méx, C.Am.* grocery store, *Br* grocer's

abarrotero *m*, **-a** *f Méx, C.Am.* storekeeper, *Br* shopkeeper

abarrotes *mpl L.Am.* (*mercancías*) groceries; (***tienda de***) ***~s*** grocery store, *Br* grocer's

abastecer ⟨2d⟩ *v/t* supply (***de*** with); **abastecerse** *v/r* stock up (***de*** on *o* with)

abastecimiento *m* supply

abasto *m*: ***no dan ~*** (***con***) they can't cope (with)

abatí *m* **1** *Rpl* corn, *Br* maize **2** *Parag*: *fermented maize drink*

abatible *adj* collapsible, folding *atr*

abatido I *adj* depressed **II** *part* ☞ ***abatir***

abatimiento *m* depression

abatir ⟨3a⟩ *v/t* **1** *edificio* knock *o* pull down; *árbol* cut down, fell; AVIA shoot *o* bring down **2** *fig* kill; (*deprimir*) depress; **abatirse** *v/r*: ***~ sobre*** swoop down on

abdicación *f* abdication

abdicar ⟨1g⟩ *v/t* abdicate; ***~ en alguien*** abdicate in favor *o Br* favour of s.o.

abdomen *m* abdomen

abdominal *adj* abdominal

abdominales *mpl* sit-ups *pl*

abecé *m fig* ABCs *pl*, *Br* ABC, basics *pl*

abecedario *m* alphabet

abedul *m* birch

abeja *f* ZO bee

◇ **abeja obrera** worker bee

◇ **abeja reina** queen bee

abejarrón *m* bumblebee

abejaruco *m* bee eater

abejón *m* drone

abejorro *m* bumblebee

aberración *f* aberration

aberrante *adj* aberrant

abertura *f* opening

abeto *m* fir (tree)

◇ **abeto blanco** silver fir

◇ **abeto rojo** spruce

abiertamente *adv* openly

abierto I *part* ☞ ***abrir*** **II** *adj tb persona* open; ***está ~ a nuevas ideas*** *fig* he's open to new ideas

abigarrado *adj* multicolored, *Br* multicoloured

abisal *adj* deep-sea *atr*; ***fauna ~*** creatures of the deep

abismal *adj diferencias* deep, huge

abismarse ⟨1a⟩ *v/r fig*: ***~ en*** become engrossed in

abismo *m* abyss; *fig* gulf; ***estar al borde del ~*** be staring into the abyss

abjurar ⟨1a⟩ **I** *v/t* foreswear, renounce **II** *v/i*: ***~ de*** foreswear, renounce

ablación *f* MED removal

ablandamiento *m tb fig* softening

ablandar ⟨1a⟩ *v/t* **1** *tb fig* soften **2** *CSur, Cuba* AUTO run in; **ablandarse** *v/r* soften, get softer; *fig* relent

ablución *f* REL ablution, cleansing

abnegación *f* self-denial

abnegado *adj* selfless

abobado *adj* dim-witted

abocado I *adj* doomed; ***~ al fracaso*** doomed to failure, destined to fail **II** *part* ☞ ***abocar***

abocar ⟨1g⟩ *v/i* **1**: ***~ en un puerto*** enter port **2**: ***~ a una calle*** lead to a street; **abocarse** *v/r* **1** head (***hacia*** for) **2** *CSur*: ***~ a algo*** face up to sth; ***verse abocado a algo*** be faced with sth

abochornado I *adj* embarrassed **II** *part* ☞ ***abochornar***

abochornante *adj* embarrassing

abochornar ⟨1a⟩ *v/t* embarrass; **abochornarse** *v/r* feel embarrassed
abofetear ⟨1a⟩ *v/t* slap
abogacía *f* law
abogado *m*, **-a** *f* lawyer, *Br* solicitor; *en tribunal superior* attorney, *Br* barrister; ***no le faltaron ~s*** *fig* there were plenty of people who defended him
◇ **abogado del Estado** attorney general
◇ **abogado de oficio** court-appointed lawyer
abogar ⟨1h⟩ *v/i*: ***~ por alguien*** defend s.o., plead for s.o.; ***~ por algo*** advocate sth
abolengo *m* ancestry; ***de rancio ~*** of noble ancestry
abolición *f* abolition
abolir ⟨3a⟩ *v/t* abolish
abolladura *f* dent
abollar ⟨1a⟩ *v/t* dent
abombado I *adj S.Am.* **1** (*tonto*) dopey **2** *comida* rotten, bad **II** *part* ☞ ***abombar***
abombar ⟨1a⟩ *v/t*: ***~ algo*** make sth sag, warp sth; **abombarse** *v/r* **1** sag, warp **2** *S.Am. de comida* go off, go bad
abominable *adj* abominable
abominación *f* abomination
abominar ⟨1a⟩ **I** *v/t* detest, loathe **II** *v/i*: ***~ de*** detest, loathe
abonable *adj* COM payable
abonado I *adj* **1**: ***campo*** *o* ***terreno ~*** *fig* fertile ground **2**: ***estar ~ a*** TEA have a season ticket for **II** *m*, **-a** *f a revista* subscriber; *a teléfono, gas, electricidad* customer; *a ópera, teatro* season-ticket holder
abonar ⟨1a⟩ *v/t* **1** COM pay; ***~ en cuenta a alguien*** credit s.o.'s account with **2** *Méx* pay on account **3** AGR fertilize; ***~ el terreno*** *fig* sow the seeds; **abonarse** *v/r*: ***~ a*** *espectáculo* buy a season ticket for; *revista* take out a subscription to
abono *m* **1** COM payment; ***pagar en ~s*** *Méx* pay in installments *o Br* instalments **2** AGR fertilizer **3** *para espectáculo, transporte* season ticket
◇ **abono mensual** monthly season ticket; **abono orgánico** organic fertilizer; **abono químico** chemical fertilizer; **abono semanal** weekly season ticket
abordable *adj fig* approachable
abordaje *m* MAR boarding
abordar ⟨1a⟩ *v/t* **1** MAR board **2** *tema, asunto* broach, raise **3** *problema* tackle, deal with **4** *a una persona* approach
aborigen I *adj* native *atr*, indigenous **II** *m/f* native
aborrascado *adj tiempo* stormy
aborrascarse ⟨1g⟩ *v/r* become stormy
aborrecer ⟨2d⟩ *v/t* loathe, detest
aborrecible *adj* detestable
aborrecido *adj* detested, loathed
aborrecimiento *m* loathing
aborregarse ⟨1h⟩ *v/r* lose one's individuality
abortar ⟨1a⟩ **I** *v/i* MED *espontáneamente* miscarry; *de forma provocada* have an abortion **II** *v/t plan* foil
abortista *m/f* abortionist
abortivo *adj* abortion *atr*; ***píldora -a*** abortion pill; ***clínica -a*** abortion clinic
aborto *m espontáneo* miscarriage; *provocado* abortion; *fig* F freak F; ***tener un ~*** have a miscarriage
abota(r)garse ⟨1h⟩ *v/r fig* become bloated
abota(r)gado *adj por gordura* bloated, swollen; *por hinchazón* swollen
abotonar ⟨1a⟩ *v/t* button up
abovedado *adj* ARQUI vaulted, arched
abra *f L.Am.* clearing
abrasador *adj* scorching, burning
abrasar ⟨1a⟩ **I** *v/t* burn **II** *v/i* **1** *del sol* be scorching **2** *de bebida, comida* be boiling hot; **abrasarse** *v/r*: ***~ de calor*** F be sweltering; ***~ de pasión*** *lit* be aflame with passion *lit*
abrasión *f* abrasion
abrasivo *m* TÉC abrasive; ***~ líquido*** abrasive fluid
abrazadera *f* TÉC (hose) clamp
abrazar ⟨1f⟩ *v/t* hug, embrace; *fig* embrace; **abrazarse** *v/r* hug (each other), embrace (each other)
abrazo *m* hug, embrace; ***dar un ~ a alguien*** hug s.o., embrace s.o.; ***un ~*** *en carta* best wishes; *más íntimo* love
abrebotellas *m inv* bottle opener
abrecartas *m inv* letter opener
abrelatas *m inv* can opener, *Br tb* tin opener
abrevadero *m* watering hole
abrevar ⟨1a⟩ *v/t* water
abreviación *f* shortening

abreviadamente *adv* in brief
abreviar ⟨1b⟩ *v/t* shorten; *palabra tb* abbreviate; *texto tb* abridge
abreviatura *f* abbreviation
abridor *m* bottle opener
abrigado I *adj* sheltered **II** *part* ☞ ***abrigar***
abrigar ⟨1h⟩ *v/t* **1** wrap up **2** *esperanzas* hold out; *duda* entertain; **abrigarse** *v/r* **1** wrap up warmly **2**: ***~ del frío*** (take) shelter from the cold
abrigo *m* **1** coat; ***~ de entretiempo*** light coat **2** (*protección*) shelter; ***ropa de ~*** warm clothes; ***al ~ de*** in the shelter of **3**: ***de ~*** F real; ***un proyecto de ~*** a huge project
◇ **abrigo de pieles** fur coat
abril *m* April; ***de quince ~es*** 15 fifteen years old
abrillantado *adj Rpl* (*esarchado*) glacé
abrillantador *m* polish
abrillantar ⟨1a⟩ *v/t* polish
abrir ⟨3a; abierto⟩ **I** *v/t* **1** open; *nuevos mercados* open (up); ***~ los ojos*** open one's eyes; ***~ al tráfico*** open to traffic; ***~ camino*** *fig* pave the way; ***le abrió el apetito*** it gave him an appetite **2** *túnel* dig **3** *grifo* turn on
II *v/i de persona* open up; *de ventana, puerta* open (***a*** onto); ***a medio ~*** half-open; ***en un ~ y cerrar de ojos*** in the twinkling of an eye
abrirse *v/r* open; ***~ la cabeza*** split one's head open; ***~ paso*** get through; ***~ paso entre*** make one's way through; ***~ a algo*** *fig* open up to sth
abrochador *m*, ***~a*** *f Rpl* stapler
abrochar ⟨1a⟩ *v/t* **1** do up; *cinturón de seguridad* fasten **2** *Rpl* (*grapar*) staple; **abrocharse** *v/r* do up; *de cinturón de seguridad* fasten; ***tendremos que abrocharnos el cinturón*** *fig* we'll have to tighten our belts
abrogación *f* repeal
abrogar ⟨1h⟩ *v/t* repeal
abroncar ⟨1g⟩ *v/t* F tell off
abrumador *adj* overwhelming
abrumar ⟨1a⟩ *v/t* overwhelm (***con*** *o* ***de*** with); ***abrumado de*** *o* ***con trabajo*** snowed under with work; **abrumarse** *v/r* be overwhelmed
abrupto *adj* **1** *terreno* rough; *pendiente* steep **2** *tono, respuesta* abrupt; *cambio* sudden
absceso *m* MED abscess
absenta *f* absinthe
absentismo *m* absenteeism
◇ **absentismo escolar** truancy
absentista I *adj* absentee *atr* **II** *m/f* absentee
ábside *m* ARQUI apse
absolución *f* **1** JUR acquittal; ***el juez anunció la ~ por falta de pruebas*** the judge acquitted the accused for lack of evidence **2** REL absolution; ***dar la ~ a alguien*** give s.o. absolution
absolutamente *adv* absolutely; ***no entendió ~ nada*** he didn't understand a thing, he understood absolutely nothing
absolutismo *m* absolutism
absoluto *adj* absolute; ***en ~*** not at all; ***nada en ~*** absolutely nothing; ***la casa no ha cambiado nada en ~*** the house hasn't changed at all, the house hasn't changed in the slightest; ***se negó en ~*** he refused outright
absolutorio *adj*: ***sentencia -a*** JUR not-guilty verdict
absolver ⟨2h; absuelto⟩ *v/t* **1** JUR acquit **2** REL absolve
absorbente *adj* absorbent; ***ser muy ~*** *papel de cocina* be highly absorbent; *libro* be engrossing; *persona* demand a great deal of attention
absorber ⟨2a⟩ *v/t* **1** absorb **2** (*consumir*) take (up) **3** (*cautivar*) absorb **4** COM take over; **absorberse** *v/r* become absorbed (***en*** in)
absorción *f* **1** absorption **2** COM takeover
absorto I *adj* absorbed (***en*** in), engrossed (***en*** in); ***~ en sus pensamientos*** absorbed *o* engrossed in his thoughts **II** *part* ☞ ***absorber***
abstemio I *adj* teetotal **II** *m*, **-a** *f* teetotaler, *Br* teetotaller
abstención *f* abstention
abstencionismo *m* abstentionism
abstenerse ⟨2l⟩ *v/r* **1** refrain (***de*** from) **2** POL abstain; ***~ de votar*** abstain (from voting)
abstinencia *f* abstinence; ***síndrome de ~*** MED withdrawal symptoms *pl*
abstracción *f* abstraction; ***hacer ~ de*** leave aside, exclude
abstracto *adj* abstract
abstraer ⟨2p⟩ *v/t* abstract; **abstraerse**

v/r shut o.s. off (**de** from)
abstraído *adj* preoccupied; **~ en algo** engrossed in sth
abstruso *adj* abstruse
absuelto *part* ☞ **absolver**
absurdo I *adj* absurd **II** *m* **1** absurdity; ***es un ~ que*** it's absurd that **2:** ***teatro del ~*** theater *o Br* theatre of the absurd
abubilla *f* ZO hoopoe
abuchear ⟨1a⟩ *v/t* boo
abucheo *m* booing, boos *pl*; **~s** booing, boos *pl*
abuela *f* **1** grandmother; ***¡cuéntaselo a tu ~!*** F tell me another one F, *Br* pull the other one! F; ***no tener ~, no necesitar ~*** F be good at blowing one's own trumpet **2** F *persona mayor* old lady
abuelo *m* **1** grandfather **2** F *persona mayor* old man **3:** **~s** grandparents
abulia *f* apathy, lack of energy
abúlico *adj* apathetic, lacking in energy
abultado *adj* **1** bulging **2** *derrota* heavy
abultar ⟨1a⟩ **I** *v/t* **1** swell **2** (*aumentar*) increase **II** *v/i* be bulky; ***no abulta casi nada*** it takes up almost no room at all
abundamiento *m* **1** abundance **2:** ***a mayor ~*** moreover
abundancia *f* abundance; ***había comida en ~*** there was plenty of food; ***nadar en la ~*** be rich
abundante *adj* plentiful, abundant
abundantemente *adv* **1** abundantly; ***estar ~ plagado de faltas de ortografía*** be absolutely riddled with spelling mistakes; ***una zona ~ habitada por liebres*** an area with an abundance of hares *o* an abundant population of hares **2** *llover* heavily
abundar ⟨1a⟩ *v/i* be plentiful *o* abundant; **~ en** abound in
abundoso *adj C. Am., Méx* abundant, plentiful
aburguesado *adj desp* bourgeois
aburguesarse ⟨1a⟩ *v/r desp* become bourgeois *o* middle class
aburrido *adj que aburre* boring; *que se aburre* bored; **~ de algo** bored *o* fed up F with sth
aburrimiento *m* boredom
aburrir ⟨3a⟩ *v/t* bore; **aburrirse** *v/r* get bored **~ de algo** get bored *o* fed up F with sth; ***~ como una ostra*** F get bored stiff F
abusado *adj Méx* **1** smart, clever **2:** ***¡~!*** look out!
abusador *adj L.Am.* bullying
abusar ⟨1a⟩ *v/i*: **~ de** *poder, confianza* abuse; *persona* take advantage of; ***~ sexualmente de alguien*** sexually abuse s.o.; ***~ del alcohol*** drink too much
abusivo *adj* **1** JUR unfair **2** *precio* exorbitant
abuso *m* abuse; ***estos precios son un ~*** these prices are outrageous *o* an outrage
◇ **abuso de autoridad** abuse of one's authority; **abuso de confianza** breach of trust; **abuso sexual** sexual abuse; **abusos deshonestos** indecent assault
abusón *m*, **-ona** *f* F bully
abyecto *adj* despicable
a.C. *abr* (= ***antes de Cristo***) BC (= before Christ)
a/c *abr* (= ***a cuenta***) on account
acá *adv* **1** here; ***~ y allá*** here and there; ***de ~ para allá*** from here to there; ***¡ven ~!*** come here! **2:** ***de entonces para ~*** since then
acabado I *adj persona* finished; ***producto ~*** finished product **II** *m* TÉC finish
acabar ⟨1a⟩ **I** *v/t* **1** finish **2:** ***acabé haciéndolo yo*** I ended up doing it myself **II** *v/i* **1** *de persona* finish; *de función, acontecimiento* finish, end; ***~ con*** put an end to; *caramelos* finish off; *persona* destroy; ***~ en*** end in; ***~ en punta*** end in a point; ***~ bien / mal*** end well / badly; ***va a ~ mal*** F this is going to end badly; *persona* he'll come to no good *o* to a bad end; ***acabó por comprender*** in the end he understood; ***no acabo de comprender*** I still don't understand; ***~ con sus huesos en*** end up in; ***es cosa de nunca ~*** it's never-ending; ***¡acabáramos!*** now I get it!; ***¡acaba ya!*** hurry up and finish!; ***la cosa no acaba aquí*** and that's not all, and there's worse
2: ***~ de hacer algo*** have just done sth; ***acabo de escribirlo*** I've just written it
acabarse *v/r de actividad* finish, end; *de pan, dinero* run out; ***se nos ha acabado el azúcar*** we've run out of sugar; ***¡se acabó!*** that's it!, that's that!
acabóse *m* F: ***¡es el ~!*** it's the limit!
acacia *f* acacia
◇ **acacia blanca, acacia falsa** locust tree, false acacia

academia *f* academy
◇ **academia de idiomas** language school
◇ **academia militar** military academy
académico I *adj* academic **II** *m*, **-a** *f* academician, *member of an academy*
acaecer ⟨2d⟩ *v/i* occur
acalenturarse ⟨1a⟩ *v/r L.Am.* (*afiebrarse*) get a temperature *o* fever
acallar ⟨1a⟩ *v/t tb fig* silence
acalorado *adj fig* heated; ***estar*** **~** be agitated
acaloramiento *m fig* heat, passion; *de persona* agitation
acalorar ⟨1a⟩ *v/t fig* inflame; **acalorarse** *v/r* **1** (*enfadarse*) get agitated **2** (*sofocarse*) get embarrassed
acampada *f* camp; ***ir de*** **~** go camping
acampanado *adj* bell-shaped; ***falda -a*** flared skirt
acampar ⟨1a⟩ *v/i* camp
acanalado *adj* **1** grooved, corrugated **2** ARQUI fluted
acanaladura *f* ARQUI flute; *diseño* fluting
acantilado *m* cliff
acanto *m* BOT acanthus
acantonamiento *m* MIL quarters *pl*
acantonar ⟨1a⟩ *v/t* MIL quarter
acaparador *adj* greedy
acaparar ⟨1a⟩ *v/t* **1** hoard, stockpile **2** *tiempo* take up **3** *interés* capture **4** F (*monopolizar*) monopolize, hog F
acápite *m L.Am.* **1** section **2** (*párrafo*) paragraph
acaramelado *adj fig* F lovey-dovey F
acaramelarse ⟨1a⟩ *v/r* whisper sweet nothings to each other, bill and coo
acariciar ⟨1b⟩ *v/t* **1** caress; *perro* stroke **2**: **~ *una idea*** *fig* contemplate an idea
ácaro *m* mite
acarrear ⟨1a⟩ *v/t* **1** carry **2** *fig* give rise to, cause
acarreo *m* transportation
acartonado *adj piel, persona* wizened
acartonarse ⟨1a⟩ *v/r de piel* become wizened
acaso *adv* by any chance, perhaps; ***por si*** **~** just in case; ***si*** **~** maybe; ***¿~ crees que ...?*** do you really think that ...?
acatamiento *m* compliance (***de*** with)
acatar ⟨1a⟩ *v/t* comply with, obey
acatarrado *adj*: ***estar*** **~** have a cold
acatarrarse ⟨1a⟩ *v/r* catch a cold
acaudalado *adj* wealthy, well-off
acaudillar ⟨1a⟩ *v/t* lead
acceder ⟨2a⟩ *v/i* **1** (*ceder*) agree (***a*** to), *fml* accede (***a*** to); **~ *a un ruego*** agree to a request; **~ *a los deseos de alguien*** bow to s.o.'s wishes **2**: **~ *a*** *lugar* gain access to, access; *cargo* accede to
accesibilidad *f* accessibility
accesible *adj* accessible
accésit *m* second prize
acceso *m* **1** *a un lugar* access; ***de difícil*** **~** inaccessible, difficult to get to **2** INFOR access; **~ *a Internet*** Internet access **3** *de fiebre* attack, bout; *de tos* fit; **~ *de rabia*** fit of anger
accesorio I *adj* incidental **II** *m* accessory
accidentado I *adj* **1** *terreno, camino* uneven, rough **2** *viaje* eventful **3**: ***personas -as*** people who have had an accident; ***el vehículo*** **~** the vehicle involved in the accident **II** *m*, **-a** *f* casualty
accidental *adj* **1** (*no esencial*) incidental **2** (*casual*) chance
accidentalidad *f*: ***nivel de*** **~** *de tráfico* accident rate
accidentarse ⟨1a⟩ *v/r* have an accident, be involved in an accident
accidente *m* **1** accident; ***sufrir un*** **~** have an accident, be involved in an accident **2** (*casualidad*) chance **3** GEOG feature
◇ **accidente aéreo** plane crash; **accidente en cadena** multiple vehicle pile-up; **accidente de circulación** road (traffic) accident; **accidente laboral** accident in the workplace; **accidente de trabajo** accident in the workplace; **accidente de tráfico** road (traffic) accident
acción *f* **1** action; ***entrar en*** **~** come into action; ***poner en*** **~** put into action **2** COM share; ***acciones*** *pl* stock *sg*, *Br* shares
◇ **acción civil** JUR civil action; **acción popular** JUR class action; **acciones nominativas** registered stock; **acciones al portador** bearer stock; **acciones preferentes** preference stock
accionamiento *m* TÉC activation
accionar ⟨1a⟩ *v/t* activate
accionariado *m* stockholders *pl*, shareholders *pl*
accionarial *adj* stock *atr*, *Br* share *atr*
accionista *m/f* stockholder, share-

holder
◇ **accionista mayoritario** majority stockholder *o* shareholder
◇ **accionista principal** main stockholder *o* shareholder
acebo *m* BOT holly
acebuche *m* BOT wild olive (tree)
acechar ⟨1a⟩ *v/t* lie in wait for
acecho *m*: ***al ~*** lying in wait
acedera *f* BOT sorrel
◇ **acedera menor** ☞ ***acederilla***
acederilla *f* BOT sheep sorrel
acéfalo *adj* headless
aceite *m* oil; ***echar ~ al fuego*** add fuel to the fire
◇ **aceite de girasol** sunflower oil; **aceite de hígado de bacalao** cod-liver oil; **aceite de linaza** linseed oil; **aceite lubricante** lubricating oil; **aceite de oliva** olive oil; **aceite de oliva virgen** virgin olive oil; **aceite vegetal** vegetable oil
aceitera *f* **1** TÉC oilcan **2** GASTR cruet
aceitero *adj* oil *atr*; ***molino ~*** oil mill
aceitoso *adj* oily
aceituna *f* olive
aceitunado *adj* olive *atr*
aceitunero *m*, **-a** *f* **1** olive seller **2** *peón* olive picker
aceleración *f* acceleration
acelerado I *adj* **1** nervous, het-up **2**: ***curso ~*** intensive course **II** *part* ☞ ***acelerar***
acelerador *m* gas pedal, accelerator; ***pisar el ~ a fondo*** step on the gas, *Br* put one's foot down
acelerar ⟨1a⟩ **I** *v/t motor* rev up; *fig* speed up; ***aceleró el coche*** she accelerated; ***~ el paso*** walk faster **II** *v/i* accelerate; **acelerarse** *v/r L.Am.* (*enojarse*) lose one's cool
acelerón *m*: ***dar un ~*** step on the gas, *Br* put one's foot down; ***dio semejante ~ con el coche que ...*** he accelerated so hard that ...
acelgas *fpl* BOT Swiss chard *sg*
acémila *f* mule
acendrado *adj* pure
acendrar ⟨1a⟩ *v/t fig* purify
acento *m* **1** *en ortografía*, *pronunciación* accent; ***hablar sin ~*** speak without an accent **2** *énfasis* stress, emphasis; ***poner el ~ en*** *fig* stress, emphasize
acentuación *f* accentuation
acentuado *adj* pronounced, distinct
acentuar ⟨1e⟩ *v/t* stress; *fig* accentuate, emphasize; **acentuarse** *v/r* become more pronounced
acepción *f* sense, meaning
aceptable *adj* acceptable
aceptación *f* **1** acceptance; ***encontrar buena ~*** *de plan* receive a warm welcome, be welcomed; *de producto*, *novela* be successful (***entre*** with) **2** *éxito* success
aceptar ⟨1a⟩ *v/t* accept
acequia *f* irrigation ditch
acera *f* sidewalk, *Br* pavement; ***ser de la otra ~, ser de la ~ de enfrente*** F be gay
acerbo *adj* **1** *sabor* sour, sharp **2** *comentario* sharp, acerbic
acerca *adv*: ***~ de*** about
acercamiento *m tb fig* approach
acercar ⟨1g⟩ *v/t* **1** bring closer **2**: ***~ a alguien a un lugar*** give s.o. a ride *o* lift somewhere **3** (*pasar*): ***acércame el pan*** pass me the bread
acercarse *v/r* **1** approach; *de fecha* draw near; ***se acercó a mí*** she came up to me *o* approached me; ***no te acerques a la pared*** don't get close to the wall; ***¡acércate!*** come closer! **2** *ir* go; ***me acercaré a tu casa*** I'll drop by **3** *de grupos*, *países* develop closer ties
acería *f* steel mill
acerico *m* **1** cushion **2** *costura* pin cushion
acero *m* steel; ***tener nervios de ~*** have nerves of steel
◇ **acero dulce** mild steel
◇ **acero inoxidable** stainless steel
acérrimo *adj* staunch
acertado I *adj* **1** *comentario* apt **2** *elección* good, wise; ***estar ~*** F be right; ***estar muy ~*** F be dead right F **II** *part* ☞ ***acertar***
acertante *m/f de apuesta* winner
acertar ⟨1k⟩ **I** *v/t respuesta* get right; *al hacer una conjetura* guess; ***~ el blanco, ~ en la diana*** *fig* hit the nail on the head **II** *v/i* **1** be right; ***~ con algo*** get sth right **2**: ***no acierto a hacerlo*** I don't seem to be able to do it
acertijo *m* riddle, puzzle
acervo *m fig* heritage
◇ **acervo cultural** cultural heritage
acetato *m* acetate
acético *adj* acetic

acetileno *m* acetylene
acetilsalicílico *adj*: ***ácido ~*** aspirin
acetona *f* acetone
achacar ⟨1g⟩ *v/t* attribute (***a*** to); ***~ la culpa a alguien*** blame s.o., put the blame on s.o.
achacoso *adj* ailing
achampanado, achampañado *adj* sparkling
achantarse ⟨1a⟩ *v/r* F keep quiet, keep one's mouth shut F
achaparrado *adj persona* squat
achaque *m* ailment; ***~s de la edad*** ailments typical of old age
achatado *adj* flattened
achatar ⟨1a⟩ *v/t* flatten; **achatarse** *v/r* be flattened
achicar ⟨1g⟩ *v/t* **1** make smaller **2** MAR bail out; **achicarse** *v/r* get smaller; *fig* feel intimidated
achicharrar ⟨1a⟩ *v/t* burn; **achicharrarse** *v/r fig* F roast F
achicoria *f* BOT chicory
achinado *adj L.Am.* oriental-looking
achinero *m C.Am. vendedor* peddler
achique *m* MAR bailing; ***bomba de ~*** bilge pump
achiquitarse ⟨1a⟩ *v/r L.Am.* become frightened *o* scared
¡achís! *onomatopeya* atchoo!
achisparse ⟨1a⟩ *v/r* F get tipsy
acholar ⟨1a⟩ *v/t S.Am.* embarrass
achuchado *adj* F tough
achuchar ⟨1a⟩ *v/t fig* F pester, nag
achuchón *m* F **1** squeeze, hug **2** (*empujón*) push **3**: ***le dio un ~*** *desmayo* she felt faint
achurar ⟨1a⟩ *v/t Arg animal* gut; *persona* knife, kill
achuras *fpl S.Am.* variety meat *sg*, *Br* offal *sg*
aciago *adj* fateful; ***día ~*** fateful day
acíbar *m* BOT aloes *pl*
acicalarse ⟨1a⟩ *v/r* get dressed up
acicate *m fig* incentive, stimulus
acicatear ⟨1a⟩ *v/t* spur on
acidez *f* acidity
◇ **acidez de estómago** heartburn
acidificar ⟨1g⟩ *v/t* acidify
ácido I *adj* **1** *sabor* sour, sharp **2** *comentario* caustic, acid **II** *m* acid
◇ **ácido acético** acetic acid; **ácido ascórbico** ascorbic acid; **ácido butírico** butyric acid; **ácido carbónico** carbonic acid; **ácido clorhídrico** hydrochloric acid; **ácido fólico** folic acid; **ácido fórmico** formic acid; **ácido graso** fatty acid; **ácido láctico** lactic acid; **ácido sulfhídrico** hydrogen sulfide; **ácido sulfúrico** sulfuric *o Br* sulphuric acid; **ácido úrico** uric acid
acídulo *adj* acidic
acierto *m* **1** (*idea*) good idea; ***fue un ~*** it was a wise decision *o* good move **2** (*respuesta*) correct answer **3** (*habilidad*) skill
aclamación *f* acclaim
aclamado I *adj* acclaimed **II** *part* ☞ ***aclamar***
aclamar ⟨1a⟩ *v/t* acclaim
aclaración *f* clarification
aclarar ⟨1a⟩ **I** *v/t* **1** *duda, problema* clarify, clear up **2** *ropa, vajilla* rinse **II** *v/i* **1** *de día* break, dawn **2** *de tiempo* clear up; **aclararse** *v/r* **1**: ***~ la voz*** clear one's throat **2**: ***no me aclaro*** F I can't decide, I can't make my mind up; (*no entiendo*) I don't understand; *por cansancio, ruido etc* I can't think straight
aclimatación *f* acclimatization
aclimatar ⟨1a⟩ *v/t* acclimatize; **aclimatarse** *v/r* acclimatize, become acclimatized
acné *m* acne
acobardar ⟨1a⟩ *v/t* intimidate; **acobardarse** *v/r* get frightened, lose one's nerve
acodado I *adj* elbow *atr*, offset **II** *part* ☞ ***acodar***
acodar ⟨1a⟩ *v/t* **1** bend **2** AGR layer; **acodarse** *v/r* lean (one's elbows) (***en*** on)
acodo *m* AGR layer
acogedor *adj* welcoming; *lugar* cozy, *Br* cosy
acoger ⟨2c⟩ *v/t* **1** receive; ***~ con satisfacción*** welcome **2** *en casa* take in, put up; **acogerse** *v/r*: ***~ a algo*** have recourse to sth
acogida *f* **1** reception; ***una calurosa ~*** a warm reception; ***tener buena ~*** get a good reception, be well received **2**: ***centro de ~*** reception center *o Br* centre; ***casa de ~*** (***para mujeres maltratadas***) women's shelter
acogotar ⟨1a⟩ *v/t* F **1** intimidate **2** (*matar*): ***~ a alguien*** break s.o.'s neck
acojonado *adj*: ***está ~*** V he's scared

shitless V
acojonante *adj* V terrifying F
acojonar ⟨1a⟩ V *v/t* **1** (*asustar*) scare the shit out of V **2** (*asombrar*) knock out F, blow away P; **acojonarse** *v/r* be scared shitless V
acolchado *Rpl* **I** *adj* quilted **II** *m* bedspread
acolchar ⟨1a⟩ *v/t* quilt, pad
acolchonar ⟨1a⟩ *v/t Rpl* quilt
acólito *m tb fig* acolyte
acomedido *L.Am.* **I** *adj* obliging, helpful **II** *part* ☞ ***acomedirse***
acomedirse ⟨3l⟩ *v/r Méx* offer to help
acometer ⟨2a⟩ **I** *v/t* **1** attack **2** *tarea, proyecto* undertake, tackle **II** *v/i* attack; **~ *contra algo*** attack sth
acometida *f* **1** attack **2** TÉC supply
acometimiento *m* **1** undertaking **2** (*ataque*) attack
acometividad *f* commitment
acomodable *adj* adaptable
acomodación *f* **1** accommodation **2** (*acuerdo*) agreement, accommodation
acomodadizo *adj* accommodating, adaptable
acomodado **I** *adj* well-off **II** *part* ☞ ***acomodar***
acomodador *m*, **~a** *f* usher; *mujer* usherette
acomodamiento *m* agreement
acomodar ⟨1a⟩ *v/t* **1** (*adaptar*) adapt **2** *a alguien* accommodate; **acomodarse** *v/r* **1** make o.s. comfortable **2** (*adaptarse*) adapt (***a*** to)
acomodaticio *adj* accommodating; *desp* weak
acomodo *m* lodgings *pl*
acompañamiento *m* accompaniment
acompañante *m/f* **1** companion **2** MÚS accompanist
acompañar ⟨1a⟩ *v/t* **1** (*ir con*) go with, accompany **2** (*permanecer con*): **~ *a alguien*** keep s.o. company **3** MÚS accompany **4** GASTR accompany, go with
acompaño *m C.Am.* (*reunión*) meeting
acompasado *adj* regular, rythmic
acompasar ⟨1a⟩ *v/t* keep in time
acomplejado **I** *adj*: ***un niño* ~** a child with a complex **II** *part* ☞ ***acomplejar***
acomplejar ⟨1a⟩ *v/t*: **~ *a alguien*** give s.o. a complex; ***estar acomplejado*** have a complex; **acomplejarse** *v/r* get a complex
acondicionado *adj*: ***aire* ~** air conditioning
acondicionador *m* conditioner
acondicionamiento *m* equipping, fitting-out
◇ **acondicionamiento de aire** air conditioning
acondicionar ⟨1a⟩ *v/t* **1** *un lugar* equip, fit out **2** *pelo* condition
aconfesional *adj* non-confessional
acongojar ⟨1a⟩ *v/t lit* grieve *lit*, distress
acónito *m* BOT aconite
aconsejable *adj* advisable
aconsejado *adj*: ***mal* ~** badly advised
aconsejar ⟨1a⟩ *v/t* advise
acontecer ⟨2d⟩ *v/i* take place, occur
acontecimiento *m* event
acopiar ⟨1b⟩ *v/t* gather, stockpile
acopio *m* stockpile; ***hacer* ~ *de*** gather, stockpile; ***hacer* ~ *de valor*** pluck up courage
acoplado *m Rpl* trailer
acoplamiento *m* TÉC, EL connection
acoplar ⟨1a⟩ *v/t piezas* fit together; **acoplarse** *v/r* **1** *de persona* fit in (***a*** with) **2** *de nave espacial* dock (***a*** with); *de piezas* fit together
acoquinar ⟨1a⟩ *v/t* intimidate; **acoquinarse** *v/r* feel intimidated
acorazado **I** *adj* armored, *Br* armoured; ***división -a*** armored division **II** *m* MAR battleship
acorazar ⟨1f⟩ *v/t* armor-plate, *Br* armour-plate; **acorazarse** *v/r fig* protect o.s. (***contra*** against)
acorazonado *adj* heart-shaped
acordado **I** *adj* agreed **II** *part* ☞ ***acordar***
acordar ⟨1m⟩ *v/t* agree; ***lo acordado*** what was agreed; **acordarse** *v/r* remember; ***¿te acuerdas de él?*** do you remember him?; ***si mal no me acuerdo*** if I remember right
acorde **I** *adj*: **~ *con*** in keeping with; ***estar* ~ *con*** *con alguien* be in agreement with; *de reglamento, principios, creencias etc* be in keeping with **II** *m* MÚS chord
acordeón *m* **1** accordion **2** *Méx* F *en examen* cheat sheet, *Br* crib
acordeonista *m/f* accordionist
acordonamiento *m* cordoning off
acordonar ⟨1a⟩ *v/t* cordon off
acorralar ⟨1a⟩ *v/t tb fig* corner
acortar ⟨1a⟩ **I** *v/t* shorten **II** *v/i* take a

short cut; **acortarse** *v/r* get shorter
acosar ⟨1a⟩ *v/t* hound, pursue; ***me acosaron a preguntas*** they bombarded me with questions
acosijar ⟨1a⟩ *v/t Méx* badger, pester
acoso *m fig* hounding, harassment
◇ **acoso sexual** sexual harassment
acostar ⟨1m⟩ *v/t* put to bed; ***estar acostado*** be in bed; **acostarse** *v/r* **1** go to bed; (*tumbarse*) lie down; ***~ con las gallinas*** go to bed very early **2**: ***~ con alguien*** go to bed with s.o., sleep with s.o.
acostumbrado *adj* **1** (*habitual*) usual **2**: ***estar ~ a algo*** be used to sth
acostumbrar ⟨1a⟩ **I** *v/t* get used (***a*** to) **II** *v/i*: ***acostumbraba a venir a este café todas las mañanas*** he used to come to this café every morning; **acostumbrarse** *v/r* get used (***a*** to); ***se acostumbró a levantarse temprano*** he got used to getting up early
acotación *f* **1** *en texto* note, annotation **2** *de terreno* fencing-off
acotamiento *m* **1** fencing-off **2** *Méx* AUTO hard shoulder
acotar ⟨1a⟩ *v/t* **1** *terreno* fence off **2** *texto* annotate
ácrata I *adj* anarchist *atr* **II** *m/f* anarchist
acre I *adj* **1** *olor* acrid **2** *crítica* biting **II** *m* acre
acrecentamiento *m* increase, growth
acrecentar ⟨1k⟩ *v/t* increase; **acrecentarse** *v/r* increase, grow
acreditación *f documento* credentials *pl*
acreditado I *adj* well-known, reputable **II** *part* ☞ ***acreditar***
acreditar ⟨1a⟩ *v/t* **1** *diplomático, etc* accredit (***como*** as) **2** (*avalar*) prove; ***un documento que lo acredita como el propietario*** a document that proves his ownership **3** FIN: ***~ en cuenta*** credit an account; **acreditarse** *v/r* gain a good reputation, achieve fame
acreditativo *adj* supporting; ***documento ~*** supporting document
acreedor I *adj fig* worthy (***de*** of), deserving (***de*** of) **II** *m*, ***~a*** *f* **1** creditor; ***junta de ~es*** creditors' meeting **2**: ***hacerse ~ de la confianza de alguien*** gain s.o.'s confidence
acreencia *f L.Am.* credit
acribillar ⟨1a⟩ *v/t*: ***~ a alguien a balazos*** riddle s.o. with bullets; ***me acribillaron a preguntas*** they bombarded me with questions
acrílico *m/adj* acrylic
acrimonia *f fig* bitterness, acrimony
acristalamiento *f* glazing
acristalar ⟨1a⟩ *v/t* glaze
acrítico *adj* uncritical, non-critical
acritud *f* harshness
acrobacia *f* acrobatics *pl*
acróbata *m/f* acrobat
acrobático *adj* acrobatic; ***vuelo ~*** stunt flight
acrofobia *f* fear of heights
acrónimo *m* acronym
acta(s) *f(pl)* **1** minutes *pl*; ***~ de una sesión*** minutes of a meeting; ***hacer constar algo en ~*** include sth in the minutes, minute sth; ***levantar ~*** take the minutes **2**: ***~s*** *pl* JUR proceedings
◇ **acta judicial** record of proceedings
◇ **acta notarial** notarial deed
actitud *f* **1** (*disposición*) attitude **2** (*posición*) position
activación *f* **1** *de economía* boosting, stimulation **2** *de bomba*, activation, setting off; *de sistema de seguridad tb* triggering
activar ⟨1a⟩ *v/t* **1** (*estimular*) stimulate **2** *bomba* activate, set off; *sistema de seguridad tb* trigger
actividad *f* activity; ***~ comercial*** trade
activista *m/f* POL activist
activo I *adj* **1** active; ***en ~*** on active service **2** LING: ***voz -a*** active voice **II** *m* COM assets *pl*
acto *m* **1** TEA act **2** (*ceremonia*) ceremony **3** (*acción*): ***~ violento*** act of violence; ***en ~ de servicio*** on active service; ***hacer ~ de presencia*** put in an appearance **4**: ***~ seguido*** immediately afterward(s); ***en el ~*** instantly, there and then
◇ **acto de clausura** closing ceremony; **acto inaugural** opening ceremony; **acto oficial** official ceremony; **acto reflejo** reflex action; **acto sexual** sexual intercourse, sex act
actor *m* actor
◇ **actor de cine** movie *o* film actor
◇ **actor de reparto, actor secundario** supporting actor
actriz *f* actress, actor
actuación *f* **1** TEA performance **2** (*inter-*

vención) intervention **3**: ***actuaciones*** *pl* JUR proceedings
actual *adj* **1** present, current **2**: ***un tema muy ~*** a very topical issue
actualidad *f* **1** current situation; ***en la ~*** at present, presently; (*hoy en día*) nowadays **2**: ***de gran ~*** very topical **3**: ***~es*** *pl* current affairs
actualización *f* updating
actualizar ⟨1f⟩ *v/t* bring up to date, update
actualmente *adv* at the moment
actuar ⟨1e⟩ *v/i* **1** (*obrar*, *ejercer*), TEA act; ***~ de*** act as **2** MED work, act
actuario *m* JUR clerk of the court
◇ **actuario de seguros** actuary
acuarela *f* watercolor, *Br* watercolour
acuarelista *m/f* watercolorist, *Br* watercolourist
acuariano *L.Am* **I** *adj* Aquarian; ***ser ~*** be (an) Aquarius, be (an) Aquarian **II** *m*, **-a** *f* Aquarian
acuario *m* aquarium
Acuario ASTR **I** *adj* Aquarian; ***soy ~*** I'm (an) Aquarian, I'm (an) Aquarius **II** *m/f inv* Aquarius
acuartelamiento *m* **1** quartering **2** *lugar* barracks *pl*
acuartelar ⟨1a⟩ *v/t* quarter; *en casas particulares* billet
acuático *adj* aquatic, water *atr*; ***deporte ~*** water sport
acuchillar ⟨1a⟩ *v/t* stab
acuciante *adj* pressing, urgent
acuciar ⟨1b⟩ *v/t* pester, hassle
acuclillarse ⟨1a⟩ *v/r* squat, crouch down
acudir ⟨3a⟩ *v/i* come; ***~ a alguien*** turn to s.o.; ***~ al médico*** go to the doctor; ***~ a las urnas*** go to the polls; ***~ al trabajo*** go to work
acueducto *m* aqueduct
acuerdo *m* **1** agreement; ***~ comercial*** trade agreement; ***estar de ~ con*** agree with, be in agreement with; ***llegar a un ~***, ***ponerse de ~*** come to *o* reach an agreement (***con*** with); ***tomar un ~*** reach an agreement; ***de común ~*** by mutual agreement; ***¡de ~!*** all right!, OK! **2**: ***de ~ con algo*** in accordance with sth
◇ **Acuerdo General sobre Aranceles y Comercio** General Agreement on Tariffs and Trade (GATT)
◇ **acuerdo marco** enabling agreement
acuicultura *f* aquaculture
acuífero *m* aquifer
acullá elsewhere; ***acá y ~*** here and there
acumulación *f* accumulation
acumulador *m* EL accumulator, storage battery
acumular ⟨1a⟩ *v/t* accumulate; **acumularse** *v/r* accumulate
acunar ⟨1a⟩ *v/t* rock
acuñación *f* minting
acuñar ⟨1a⟩ *v/t* **1** *monedas* mint **2** *término*, *expresión* coin
acuoso *adj* watery
acupuntor *m*, **~a** *f* acupuncturist
acupuntura *f* acupuncture
acupunturista *m/f* acupuncturist
acurrucarse ⟨1g⟩ *v/r* curl up
acusación *f* accusation
◇ **acusación particular, acusación privada** private prosecution
acusado **I** *adj fig* marked, pronounced **II** *m*, **-a** *f* accused, defendant
acusador *m* **1** accuser **2** JUR prosecuting attorney
◇ **acusador privado** *person bringing a private law suit*
acusar ⟨1a⟩ *v/t* **1** accuse (***de*** of) **2** JUR charge (***de*** with) **3** (*manifestar*) show **4**: ***~ recibo de*** acknowledge receipt of
acusativo *m* GRAM accusative
acusatorio *adj* accusing
acuse *m*: ***~ de recibo*** acknowledgement of receipt
acusetas *m/f inv S.Am.* F tattletale F, *Br* tell-tale F
acusica *m/f* F tattletale F, *Br* tell-tale F
acusón *m* tattletale F, *Br* tell-tale F
acústica *f* acoustics *pl*
acústico acoustic
adagio *m* MÚS adagio
adalid *m fig* champion (***of*** de)
Adán *m* **1** ANAT: ***bocado*** *o* ***nuez de ~*** Adam's apple **2**: ***ir hecho un ~*** look a mess
adaptabilidad *f* adaptability
adaptable *adj* adaptable
adaptación *f* adaptation
◇ **adaptación cinematográfica** movie *o* screen version
◇ **adaptación escénica** stage version
adaptado *adj* adapted (***a*** for)
adaptador *m* adaptor
adaptar ⟨1a⟩ *v/t* adapt; **adaptarse** *v/r*

adapt (***a*** to)
adarme *m*: (***ni***) ***un ~ de*** *de compasión, verdad* an ounce of; *de comida, pintura* a little bit of; ***no hizo*** (***ni***) ***un ~ de frío*** it wasn't the slightest bit cold
adecentar ⟨1a⟩ *v/t* straighten up, tidy up; **adecentarse** *v/r* F clean o.s. up, tidy o.s. up
adecuación *f* suitability, appropriateness; ***... gracias a la ~ de los servicios a las necesidades de la clientela ...*** because services have been adapted to customer requirements
adecuado *adj* suitable, appropriate
adecuar ⟨1d⟩ *v/t* adapt (***a*** to); **adecuarse** *v/r* fit in (***a*** with)
adefesio *m fig* F **1** monstrosity, hideous thing **2** *persona* freak F; ***estar hecho un ~*** look a sight
adelantado I *adj* **1** advanced; ***estar muy ~*** be very well advanced **2**: ***ir ~*** *de reloj* be fast **3**: ***por ~*** in advance; ***pagar por ~*** pay in advance **II** *part* ☞ ***adelantar***
adelantamiento *m* AUTO passing maneuver, *Br* overtaking manoeuvre
adelantar ⟨1a⟩ **I** *v/t* **1** (*mover*) move forward; *reloj* put forward **2** AUTO pass, *Br* overtake **3** *dinero* advance **4** (*conseguir*) achieve, gain **II** *v/i* **1** *de reloj* be fast **2** (*avanzar*) make progress **3** AUTO pass, *Br* overtake; **adelantarse** *v/r* **1** (*mover*) move forward; (*ir delante*) go on ahead; ***se me adelantó*** she beat me to it, she got there first **2** *de estación, cosecha* come early **3** *de reloj* gain
adelante I *adv* **1** *en espacio* forward; ***un paso ~*** *tb fig* a step forward; ***llevar*** *o* ***sacar ~*** *familia* bring up; ***salir ~*** *fig de persona* succeed; *de proyecto* go ahead; ***seguir ~*** carry on, keep going; ***¡~!*** come in! **2** *en tiempo*: ***más ~*** later on; ***de ahora*** *o* ***aquí en ~*** from now on **II** *prp*: ***~ de*** *L.Am.* in front of
adelanto *m tb* COM advance; ***~s*** advances
adelfa *f* BOT oleander
adelgazamiento *m* slimming; ***cura de ~*** controlled weight loss; ***dieta de ~*** (weight-loss) diet
adelgazante *adj* weight-reducing, slimming *atr*
adelgazar ⟨1f⟩ **I** *v/t* lose **II** *v/i* lose weight
ademán *m* **1** gesture; ***en ~ de*** in a gesture of; ***hacer ~ de*** make as if to **2**: ***ademanes*** *pl* manners *pl*
además I *adv* as well, besides **II** *prp*: ***~ de*** as well as
ADENA *f abr Esp* (= ***Asociación para la Defensa de la Naturaleza***) *wildlife and habitat conservancy organization*
adenoma *m* MED adenoma
adentrarse ⟨1a⟩ *v/r tb fig* go deep (***en*** into); *en tema* go into (in depth)
adentro I *adv* **1** inside; ***¡~!*** get inside!; ***mar ~*** out to sea; ***tierra ~*** inland **2** *L.Am.* ***~ de*** inside **II** *mpl*: ***para sus ~s*** to o.s.; ***decir para sus ~s*** say to o.s.
adepto *m* follower; *fig* supporter
aderezar ⟨1f⟩ *v/t con especias* season; *ensalada* dress; *fig* liven up; **aderezarse** *v/r* F dress up
aderezo *m* GASTR *con especias* seasoning; *para ensalada* dressing
adeudar ⟨1a⟩ *v/t* owe; ***~ en cuenta*** debit an account; **adeudarse** *v/r* get into debt
adeudo *m* **1** debit **2** *Méx* (*deuda*) debt ◇ **adeudo en cuenta** debit from an account
adherencia *f* MED adhesion ◇ **adherencia al suelo** AUTO roadholding
adherente *adj* adhesive
adherir ⟨3i⟩ *v/t* stick; **adherirse** *v/r* **1** *a superficie* stick (***a*** to), adhere (***a*** to) *fml* **2**: ***~ a una organización*** become a member of *o* join an organization **3**: ***~ a una idea*** support an idea
adhesión *f* FÍS adhesion
adhesivo I *adj* adhesive **II** *m* adhesive
adicción *f* addiction; ***~ a las drogas*** drug addiction
adición *f* **1** MAT addition **2** *Rpl en restaurante* check, *Br* bill
adicional *adj* additional
adicionar ⟨1a⟩ *v/t* MAT add, add up
adictivo *adj* addictive
adicto I *adj* **1** addicted (***a*** to); ***ser ~ al trabajo*** be a workaholic **2**: ***ser ~ al régimen*** be a supporter of the regime, support the regime **II** *m*, **-a** *f* addict
adiestramiento *m* training
adiestrar ⟨1a⟩ *v/t* train; **adiestrarse** *v/r*: ***~*** (***en***) train (in)
adinerado *adj* wealthy
adiós I *int* **1** goodbye, bye; *al cruzarse* hi, hello **2**: ***¡~!*** F *sorpresa* good heavens!;

disgusto oh no!, oh god! **II** *m* goodbye; ***decir ~ (a)*** say goodbye (to)
adiposo *adj* adipose; ***tejido ~*** adipose tissue
aditamento *m* accessory
aditivo *m* additive
adivinación *f* **1** guessing **2** *de adivino* prediction
adivinanza *f* riddle
adivinar ⟨1a⟩ *v/t* **1** guess **2** *de adivino* foretell
adivino *m*, **-a** *f* fortune teller
adjetivo *m* adjective
adjudicación *f* awarding; ***~ de una obra*** award of a contract
adjudicar ⟨1g⟩ *v/t* award; **adjudicarse** *v/r* win
adjudicatorio *m*, **-a** *f* successful bidder *o* tenderer
adjuntar ⟨1a⟩ *v/t* enclose
adjunto I *adj* deputy *atr*; ***profesor ~*** assistant teacher; *en universidad* associate professor, *Br* lecturer **II** *m*, **-a** *f* assistant **III** *adv*: ***~ le remitimos ...*** please find enclosed ...
adlátere *m* crony
adminículo *m* accessory
administración *f* **1** management, administration; *de empresa* management **2** (*gobierno*) administration, government
◇ **administración de bienes** asset management; **administración de fincas** property management; **administración de justicia** justice system; **administración de lotería** lottery outlet; **administración municipal** local council; **administración pública** government, administration
administrador *m*, **~a** *f* administrator; *de empresa* manager
administrar ⟨1a⟩ *v/t* **1** *medicamento, sacramentos* administer, give **2** *empresa* run, manage; *bienes* manage
administrativo I *adj* administrative **II** *m*, **-a** *f* administrative assistant
admirable *adj* admirable
admiración *f* **1** admiration **2** TIP: ***signo de ~*** exclamation mark
admirado I *adj*: ***quedarse ~*** be amazed **II** *part* ☞ ***admirar***
admirador *m*, **~a** *f* admirer
admirar ⟨1a⟩ *v/t* admire; **admirarse** *v/r* be amazed (***de*** at *o* by)
admisible *adj* admissible, acceptable
admisión *f* admission; ***derecho de ~*** right of admission
admitir ⟨3a⟩ *v/t* **1** (*aceptar*) accept; ***~ en pago*** accept as payment **2** (*reconocer*) admit **3** (*permitir*): ***el poema admite varias interpretaciones*** the poem can be interpreted in different ways, the poem admits of various interpretations *fml*; ***no admite duda*** there's no doubt about it
admonición *f* reprimand
ADN *m abr* (= ***ácido desoxirribonucleico***) DNA (= deoxyribonucleic acid)
adobar ⟨1a⟩ *v/t* GASTR marinate
adobe *m* adobe
adobera *f Méx type of mature cheese*
adobo *m* GASTR marinade
adoctrinar ⟨1a⟩ *v/t* indoctrinate
adolecer ⟨2d⟩ *v/i* suffer (***de*** from)
adolescencia *f* adolescence, teens *pl*
adolescente I *adj* teenage *atr*, adolescent *atr* **II** *m/f* teenager, adolescent
adonde *adv* where
adónde *interr* where; ***¿~ vas?*** where are you going?
adondequiera *adv* wherever
adopción *f* adoption
adoptar ⟨1a⟩ *v/t* adopt
adoptivo *adj padres* adoptive; ***hijo ~*** adopted child; ***patria -a*** adopted country
adoquín *m* paving stone
adoquinado *m* paving
adoquinar ⟨1a⟩ *v/t* pave
adorable *adj* adorable
adoración *f* adoration, worship
adorador *m* **1** admirer **2** REL worshipper
adorar ⟨1a⟩ *v/t* **1** adore **2** REL worship
adormecedor *adj* soporific
adormecer ⟨2d⟩ *v/t* make sleepy; **adormecerse** *v/r* doze off
adormecido *adj* **1** asleep *pred* **2** *extremidades* numb
adormecimiento *m* **1** sleepiness **2** *de extremidades* numbness
adormidera *f* BOT poppy
adormilado *adj* asleep *pred*
adormilarse ⟨1a⟩ *v/r* doze off
adornar ⟨1a⟩ *v/t* decorate; **adornarse** *v/r* dress up
adorno *m* ornament; *de Navidad* decoration

adosar ⟨1a⟩ *v/t*: **~ *algo a algo*** put sth (up) against sth
adquirir ⟨3i⟩ *v/t* **1** acquire **2** (*comprar*) buy, purchase *fml*
adquisición *f* acquisition; ***hacer una buena ~*** make a good purchase; ***gastos de ~*** acquisition costs; ***~ de clientes*** client acquisition
adquisidor *m*, **~a** *f* buyer, purchaser *fml*
adquisitivo *adj*: ***poder ~*** purchasing power
adrede *adv* on purpose, deliberately
adrenalina *f* adrenaline; ***descarga de ~*** adrenaline rush
Adriático *m* Adriatic; ***mar ~*** Adriatic Sea
adscribir ⟨3a; adscrito⟩ *v/t* assign; **adscribirse** *v/r* POL join
aduana *f* customs; ***derechos de ~*** customs duty *sg*; ***exento de ~*** duty-free
aduanero **I** *adj* customs *atr* **II** *m*, **-a** *f* customs officer
aducir ⟨3o⟩ *v/t* **1** *razones*, *argumentos* give, put forward **2** (*alegar*) claim
adueñarse ⟨1a⟩ *v/r*: **~ *de*** take possession of
adulación *f* flattery
adulador *adj* flattering *atr*, sycophantic
adular ⟨1a⟩ *v/t* flatter
adulón **I** *adj S.Am.* fawning **II** *m*, **-ona** *f* flatterer
adulteración *f* adulteration
adulterador *adj* adulterating
adulterar ⟨1a⟩ *v/t* adulterate; **adulterarse** *v/r* become adulterated
adulterino *adj* adulterous
adulterio *m* adultery; ***cometer ~*** commit adultery
adúltero **I** *adj* adulterous **II** *m*, **-a** *f* adulterer; *mujer* adulteress
adultez *f* adulthood
adulto **I** *adj persona* adult *atr*; *opinión*, *comportamiento* adult; ***edad -a*** adulthood **II** *m*, **-a** *f* adult
adusto *adj* **1** *paisaje* harsh **2** *persona* stern, severe **3** *L.Am.* (*inflexible*) stubborn
advenedizo **I** *adj* upstart, parvenu *atr* **II** *m*, **-a** *f* upstart, parvenu
advenimiento *m* advent
adventicio *adj* adventitious
adventista **I** *adj* Adventist *atr* **II** *m/f* Adventist
adverbio *m* adverb
adversario *m*, **-a** *f* adversary, opponent
adversidad *f* adversity, hard times *pl*
adverso *adj* adverse; ***suerte -a*** bad luck
advertencia *f* warning
advertido *part* ☞ ***advertir***
advertir ⟨3i⟩ *v/t* **1** warn (***de*** about, of); ***quedas*** *o* ***estás advertido*** you have been warned **2** (*notar*) notice
adviento *m* REL Advent
advierto *vb* ☞ ***advertir***
adyacente *adj* adjacent
AENA *f abr* (= ***Aeropuertos Españoles y Navegación Aérea***) *Spanish civil aviation organization*
AENOR *f abr* (= ***Asociación Española de Normalización y Certificación***) *Spanish standardization association*
aéreo *adj* **1** air *atr*; ***compañía -a*** airline; ***navegación -a*** flying, flight **2** *vista*, *fotografía* aerial *atr*
aerobic, aeróbic *m* aerobics *sg*
aeróbica *f L.Am.* aerobics *sg*
aerobús *m* airbus
aeroclub *m* flying club
aerodeslizador *m* hovercraft
aerodinámico *adj* aerodynamic
aeródromo *m* airfield, aerodrome
aeroespacial *adj* aerospace *atr*
aerofagia *f* MED wind, aerophagia *fml*
aerofaro *m* AVIA beacon, runway marker
aerograma *m* air mail letter, air letter
aerolínea *f* airline
aeromodelismo *m* model airplane making
aeromodelo *m* model aircraft
aeromozo *m*, **-a** *f L.Am.* flight attendant
aeronáutica *f* aeronautics *sg*
aeronáutico *adj* aeronautical; ***industria -a*** aviation industry
aeronaval *adj* MIL, MAR air and sea *atr*; ***fuerzas ~es*** naval and air forces
aeronave *f* airplane, *Br* aeroplane
aeroplano *m* airplane, *Br* aeroplane
aeroportuario *adj* airport *atr*
aeropuerto *m* airport
aerosilla *f Arg, Chi* chair lift
aerosol *m* aerosol
aerostático *adj* aerostatic
aeróstato, aerostato *m* balloon
aerotaxi *m* air taxi
aerotransportado *adj*: ***tropas -as*** airborne troops

aerovía *f* air route
afabilidad *f* affability, pleasantness
afable *adj* affable, pleasant
afamado *adj* famous
afán *m* **1** (*esfuerzo*) effort **2** (*deseo*) eagerness; ~ ***de aprender*** eagerness to learn; ~ ***de saber*** hunger *o* thirst for knowledge; ~ ***de poder*** hunger for power; ***sin*** ~ ***de lucro*** *organización* not-for-profit, non-profit; ***con*** ~ enthusiastically
afanador *m*, **~a** *f Méx* cleaner
afanar ⟨1a⟩ **I** *v/i C.Am.* (*ganar dinero*) make money **II** *v/t* **1** *C.Am. dinero* make **2** *Rpl* F (*robar*) swipe F, *Br tb* pinch F; **afanarse** *v/r* F make a real effort
afanoso *adj* painstaking, industrious
afasia *f* aphasia
afear ⟨1a⟩ *v/t*: ~ ***algo / a alguien*** make sth / s.o. look ugly
afección *f* MED complaint, condition
afectación *f* affectation
afectado I *adj* **1** (*afligido*) upset (***por*** by) **2** (*amanerado*) affected **II** *m*, **-a** *f*: ***es un*** ~ he is so affected
afectar ⟨1a⟩ *v/t* **1** (*producir efecto en*) affect **2** (*conmover*) upset, affect **3** (*fingir*) feign
afectividad *f* affectivity
afectivo *adj* emotional
afecto I *adj*: ~ ***a algo*** keen on sth; POL sympathetic to sth **II** *m* affection; ***tener*** ~ ***a alguien*** be fond of s.o.
afectuosidad *f* affection
afectuoso *adj* affectionate
afeitada *f* shave
afeitado *m* shave
afeitadora *f* electric razor
afeitar ⟨1a⟩ *v/t* shave; *barba* shave off; **afeitarse** *v/r* shave, have a shave
afelpado *adj* velvety
afeminado I *adj* effeminate **II** *m*: ***es un*** ~ he is very effeminate
afeminar ⟨1a⟩ *v/t* soften, feminize; ~ ***sus cualidades varoniles*** get in touch with one's feminine side
aferrado *part* ☞ ***aferrar***
aferramiento *m* clinging (***a*** to)
aferrar ⟨1k⟩ *v/i* cling to; ***aferrado a*** clinging to; **aferrarse** *v/r fig* cling (***a*** to)
Afganistán *m* Afghanistan
afgano I *adj* Afghan **II** *m*, **-a** Afghan
afianzamiento *m* strengthening
afianzar ⟨1f⟩ *v/t fig* strengthen; **afianzarse** *v/r* become stronger
afiche *m L.Am.* poster
afición *f* **1** love (***por*** of); ***tener*** ~ ***por algo*** like sth; ***tomar*** ~ ***a algo*** take a liking to sth **2** *pasatiempo* pastime, hobby; ***por*** ~ as a hobby **3**: ***la*** ~ DEP the fans *pl*
aficionado I *adj*: ***ser*** ~ ***a*** be interested in, *Br tb* be keen on **II** *m*, **-a** *f* **1** enthusiast; ~ ***a la música*** music enthusiast *o* buff; ~ ***al deporte*** sports fan **2** *no profesional* amateur; ***un partido de*** **~*s*** an amateur game
aficionar ⟨1a⟩ *v/t* get interested (***a*** in); **aficionarse** *v/r* become interested (***a*** in)
afiebrarse ⟨1a⟩ *v/r L.Am.* develop a fever
afilado I *adj* sharp **II** *m* sharpening
afilador *m* sharpener; *Chi* pencil sharpener
afiladora *f* **1** sharpener **2** *L.Am.* (*piedra*) whetstone
afilalápices *m inv* pencil sharpener
afilar ⟨1a⟩ *v/t* **1** sharpen **2** *L.Am.* F (*halagar*) flatter, butter up F **3** *S.Am* (*seducir*) seduce; **afilarse** *v/r S.Am.* F (*prepararse*) get ready
afiliación *f* affiliation (***a*** to), becoming a member (***a*** of)
afiliado *m*, **-a** *f* member; ~ ***a un sindicato*** member of a union, union member
afiliar ⟨1b⟩ *v/t* enroll (***a*** in); **afiliarse** *v/r* become a member, join; ~ ***a un partido*** become a member of a party, join a party
afín *adj* related, common
afinación *f* MÚS tuning
afinador *m*, **~a** *f* MÚS (piano) tuner
afinar ⟨1a⟩ **I** *v/t* **1** MÚS tune; *fig* fine-tune **2** *punta* sharpen **II** *v/i* play in tune; **afinarse** *v/r* become thinner
afincarse ⟨1g⟩ *v/r* settle
afinidad *f* affinity
afirmación *f* **1** statement **2** *declaración positiva* affirmation
afirmar ⟨1a⟩ *v/t* state, declare; ~ ***con la cabeza*** nod; **afirmarse** *v/r*: ~ ***en algo*** repeat sth
afirmativa *f* affirmative answer
afirmativo *adj* affirmative; ***en caso*** ~ if so, if that turns out to be the case
aflicción *f* grief, sorrow
aflictivo *adj* very sad

afligido *adj* upset
afligir ⟨3c⟩ *v/t* **1** afflict **2** (*apenar*) upset **3** *L.Am. F* (*golpear*) beat up; **afligirse** *v/r* get upset
aflojamiento *m* loosening
aflojar ⟨1a⟩ **I** *v/t* **1** *nudo, tornillo* loosen **2** F *dinero* hand over **3**: ***~ el paso*** slow down **II** *v/i de tormenta* abate; *de viento, fiebre* drop; **aflojarse** *v/r* come *o* work loose
afloramiento *m* appearance, coming to the surface
aflorar ⟨1a⟩ *v/t* surface, come to the surface
afluencia *f fig* influx, flow; ***horas de ~*** peak times
afluente I *adj* **1** *calle* adjoining; *río* tributary *atr* **2** *persona* vociferous **II** *m* tributary
afluir ⟨3g⟩ *v/i* flock, flow
afonía *f* loss of voice, aphonia *fml*
afónico *adj*: ***está ~*** he has lost his voice
aforado *adj which holds a royal charter*
aforismo *m* aphorism
aforo *m* capacity; ***el teatro tiene un ~ de mil personas*** the theater has a capacity of *o* holds a thousand people
afortunadamente *adv* fortunately, luckily
afortunado *adj* fortunate, lucky
afrancesado *adj* Frenchified
afrancesarse ⟨1a⟩ *v/r* become Frenchified
afrecho *m Arg* bran
afrenta *f* insult, affront
afrentar ⟨1a⟩ *v/t* insult, affront
África *f* Africa
◇ **África del Sur** South Africa
africano I *adj* African **II** *m*, **-a** *f* African
afroantillano, afrocaribeño *adj* Afro-Caribbean
afrodisíaco *m* aphrodisiac
afrontar ⟨1a⟩ *v/t* face (up to); *desafío* face; ***~ un peligro*** face up to a danger
afrutado *adj* fruity
afta *f* MED sore, ulceration
aftoso *adj*: ***fiebre -a*** foot-and-mouth disease
afuera I *adv* outside; ***de ~*** from the outside; ***¡~!*** get out! **II** *prp*: ***~ de*** *L.Am.* outside
afueras *fpl* outskirts *pl*
agachadiza *f* ZO snipe
agachar ⟨1a⟩ *v/i* duck; **agacharse** *v/r* **1** bend down **2** (*acuclillarse*) crouch down **3** *L.Am.* (*rendirse*) give in
agalla *f* **1** ZO gill **2**: ***tener ~s*** F have guts F
ágape *m* banquet
agarrada *f* F run-in F, fight
agarradera *f L.Am.* handle
agarrado *adj* **1** F mean, stingy F **2**: ***bailar ~*** dance close together
agarrador *m* oven mitt
agarrar ⟨1a⟩ **I** *v/t* **1** (*asir*) grab **2** (*atrapar, pescar*), *resfriado* catch **3** *L.Am.* (*tomar*) take **4** *L.Am. velocidad* gather, pick up **5** *L.Am.* ***~ una calle*** go up *o* along a street **II** *v/i* **1** (*asirse*) hold on **2** *de planta* take root **3** *L.Am. por un lugar* go; ***agarró y se fue*** he upped and went; **agarrarse** *v/r* **1** (*asirse*) hold on **2** *L.Am. a golpes* get into a fight
agarrón *m* **1** *Rpl* (*pleito*) fight, argument **2** *L.Am.* (*tirón*) pull, tug
agarrotar ⟨1a⟩ *v/t* make stiff; **agarrotarse** *v/r* **1** *de músculo* stiffen up **2** TÉC seize up
agasajado *adj* acclaimed
agasajar ⟨1a⟩ *v/t* fête
agasajo *m*: ***en ~ de*** in honor *o Br* honour of
ágata *f* MIN agate
agave *f* agave
agavilladora *f* AGR reaper
agazaparse ⟨1a⟩ *v/r* **1** crouch (down) **2** (*ocultarse*) hide
agencia *f* agency
◇ **agencia de colocación** recruitment agency; **agencia inmobiliaria** real estate office, *Br* estate agency; **agencia de marketing** marketing agency; **agencia matrimonial** marriage bureau; **agencia de noticias** news agency; **agencia de prensa** press agency; **agencia de publicidad** advertising agency; **agencia de transportes** freight company; **Agencia Tributaria** *Esp* IRS office, tax office; **agencia de viajes** travel agency
agenciar ⟨1b⟩ *v/t* F wangle F, get hold of; **agenciarse** *v/r* F wangle F, get hold of; ***agenciárselas para ...*** F manage to ...
agenda *f* **1** (*diario*) diary **2** (*programa*) schedule; ***tener una ~ muy apretada*** have a very busy schedule **3** *de mitin* agenda

agente I *m* agent **II** *m/f* agent ◇ **agente de aduanas** customs officer; **agente de cambio y bolsa** stockbroker; **agente comercial** sales representative, sales rep; **agente forestal** (forest) ranger; **agente patógeno** MED pathogen; **agente de policía** police officer; **agente de la propiedad inmobiliaria** realtor, *Br* estate agent; **agente de publicidad** advertising agent; **agente secreto** secret agent; **agente de seguridad** security man; **agente de seguros** insurance agent; **agente de tráfico** traffic officer; **agente de transportes** freight forwarder, shipping agent; **agentes sociales** POL social partners

agigantado *adj* gigantic; ***a pasos ~s*** by leaps and bounds

ágil *adj* agile

agilidad *f* agility

agilizar ⟨1f⟩ *v/t* speed up; **agilizarse** *v/r* be speeded up; ***si no se agiliza lo del visado…*** if the visa doesn't come through quickly …

agio *m* COM speculation

agiotaje *m* speculation

agiotista *m/f* speculator

agitación *f* POL unrest

agitado *adj* **1** *mar* rough, choppy **2** *día* hectic

agitador *m*, **~a** *f* agitator

agitanado *adj* gypsy-like

agitar ⟨1a⟩ *v/t* **1** shake; *fig* stir up **2** *brazos, pañuelo* wave; **agitarse** *v/r* become agitated *o* worked up

aglomeración *f de gente* crowd ◇ **aglomeración urbana** built-up area

aglomerado *m* particle board ◇ **aglomerado de madera** chipboard

aglomerar ⟨1a⟩ *v/t* pile up; **aglomerarse** *v/r* crowd together

aglutinante I *adj* agglutinating *atr* **II** *m* agglutinating agent

aglutinar ⟨1a⟩ *v/t fig* bring together

agobiado *adj fig* stressed out; ***~ de trabajo*** snowed under with work

agobiante *adj* **1** *trabajo* exhausting **2** *calor* stifling

agobiar ⟨1b⟩ *v/t* **1** *de calor* stifle **2** *de problemas* get on top of, overwhelm; ***~ de trabajo*** overload with work; **agobiarse** *v/r* F get stressed out

agobio *m*: ***es un ~*** it's unbearable, it's a nightmare F

agolparse ⟨1a⟩ *v/r* crowd together

agonía *f* agony; ***la espera fue una ~*** the wait was unbearable

agónico *adj* dying

agonizante *adj* dying

agonizar ⟨1f⟩ *v/i* **1** *de persona* be dying **2** *de régimen* be crumbling, be in its death throes

agorafobia *f* MED agoraphobia

agorero I *adj* ominous; ***ave -a*** bird of ill omen **II** *m*, **-a** *f* prophet of doom

agosto *m* August; ***hacer su ~*** F make a fortune *o* F a killing

agotado *adj* **1** (*cansado*) exhausted, worn out **2** (*terminado*) exhausted **3** (*vendido*) sold out; ***-as las localidades*** TEA sold out

agotador *adj* exhausting

agotamiento *m* exhaustion

agotar ⟨1a⟩ *v/t* **1** (*cansar*) wear out, exhaust **2** (*terminar*) use up, exhaust; **agotarse** *v/r* **1** (*cansarse*) get worn out, exhaust o.s. **2** (*terminarse*) run out, become exhausted **3** (*venderse*) sell out; ***la primera edición se ha agotado*** the first edition has sold out

agracejo *m* BOT West Indian box

agraciado *adj* **1** *persona* attractive **2**: ***salir ~*** be a winner; ***número ~*** winning number

agraciar ⟨1b⟩ *v/t* suit

agradable *adj* pleasant, nice; ***~ a la vista*** good-looking

agradar ⟨1a⟩ *v/i fml*: ***me agrada la idea*** I like the idea; ***nos ~ía mucho que …*** we would be delighted *o* very pleased if …

agradecer ⟨2d⟩ *v/t*: ***~ algo a alguien*** thank s.o. for sth; ***te lo agradezco*** I appreciate it; ***se agradece*** *como respuesta* I really appreciate it

agradecido *adj* grateful, appreciative; ***le estaría muy ~ si*** (*+subj*) I would be very grateful if

agradecimiento *m* gratitude, appreciation

agrado *m*: ***ser del ~ de alguien*** be to s.o.'s liking; ***recibió la invitación con ~*** he was delighted to receive the invitation

agrandamiento *m* enlargement

agrandar ⟨1a⟩ *v/t* make bigger, enlarge; **agrandarse** *v/r* get bigger

agrario *adj* land *atr*, agrarian; *política* agricultural; ***reforma -a*** agrarian reform
agravación *f* MED worsening
agravante I *adj* JUR aggravating *atr*; ***circunstancia ~*** aggravating circumstance **II** *f* aggravating factor *o* circumstance
agravar ⟨1a⟩ *v/t* make worse, aggravate; **agravarse** *v/r* get worse, deteriorate
agraviar ⟨1b⟩ *v/t* offend, affront
agravio *m* offense, *Br* offence
agredir ⟨3a⟩ *v/t* attack, assault
agregado *m*, **-a** *f* **1** *en universidad* senior lecturer; *en colegio* senior teacher **2** POL attaché
◇ **agregado cultural** cultural attaché
agregar ⟨1h⟩ *v/t* add; **agregarse** *v/r*: ***~ a algo*** join sth
agresión *f* aggression; ***una ~*** an assault, an attack
◇ **agresión sexual** sexual assault
agresividad *f* aggression, aggressiveness
agresivo *adj* aggressive
agresor *m*, **~a** *f* aggressor; ***no pudo identificar a su ~*** she could not identify her attacker
◇ **agresor sexual** sex attacker
agreste *adj terreno* rough; *paisaje* wild
agriar ⟨1b *o* 1c⟩ *v/t fig* sour, turn sour; **agriarse** *v/r* **1** *de vino* go sour **2** *de carácter* become bitter
agrícola *adj* agricultural, farming *atr*
agricultor *m*, **~a** *f* farmer
agricultura *f* agriculture
agridulce *adj* bittersweet
agriera *f L.Am.* heartburn
agrietado *adj jarrón de barro, pared* cracked; *labios, manos* chapped
agrietarse ⟨1a⟩ *v/r* crack; *de manos, labios* chap
agrimensor *m*, **~a** *f* surveyor
agrimensura *f* surveying
agringarse ⟨1h⟩ *v/r L.Am.* become Americanized
agrio *adj* **1** *fruta* sour **2** *disputa, carácter* bitter
agrios *mpl* BOT citrus fruit *sg*
agriparse ⟨1a⟩ *v/r Méx* catch the flu
agro *m* field
agronomía *f* agronomy
agrónomo *adj*: ***ingeniero ~*** agronomist
agropecuario *adj* farming *atr*, agricultural
agroturismo *m* agrotourism, rural tourism
agrupación *f* group, association
agrupar ⟨1a⟩ *v/t* group, put into groups; **agruparse** *v/r* form a group, gather
agua *f* **1** water; ***claro como el ~*** obvious, as plain as day; ***como ~ de mayo*** a godsend; ***te ha estado esperando como ~ de mayo*** he's been longing to see you; ***es ~ pasada*** it's water under the bridge; ***está con el ~ al cuello*** *fig con problemas* he's up to his neck in problems F; *con deudas* he's up to his neck in debt F; ***ha corrido mucha ~*** a lot of water has flowed under the bridge since then; ***estar como ~ para el chocolate*** *Méx* F be fuming, be hopping mad F; ***hacer ~*** MAR take in water, have a leak; ***pasado por ~*** *huevo* soft-boiled; (*muy lluvioso*) very wet; ***llevar ~ al mar*** be a waste of time, *Br tb* carry coals to Newcastle; ***se me hace la boca ~*** it makes my mouth water
2: ***~s*** *pl* waters; ***~s abajo*** dowstream; ***~s arriba*** upstream; ***hacer ~s mayores*** defecate, move one's bowels; ***hacer ~s menores*** urinate, pass water; ***las ~s vuelven a su cauce*** *fig* things are getting back to normal; ***estar entre dos ~s*** *para satisfacer a otros* be caught in the middle; ***rompió ~s*** her waters broke; ***tomar las ~s*** take the waters
◇ **agua bendita** holy water; **agua de la canilla** *Rpl* branch water, *Br* tap water; **agua de Colonia** eau de cologne; **agua corriente** running water; **agua destilada** distilled water; **agua dulce** fresh water; **agua fuerte** nitric acid; **agua del grifo** branch water, *Br* tap water; **agua de la llave** *L.Am.* branch water, *Br* tap water; **agua de mar** seawater; **agua mineral** mineral water; **agua oxigenada** (hydrogen) peroxide; **agua potable** drinking water; **agua salada** salt water; **agua de Seltz** soda water, seltzer (water); **aguas bravas** rough waters, white water *sg*; **aguas freáticas** water table *sg*; **aguas jurisdiccionales** territorial waters; **aguas residuales** effluent *sg*, sewage *sg*; **aguas subterráneas** underground water *sg*; **aguas termales** thermal waters
aguacate *m* BOT avocado

aguacero *m* downpour
aguachento *adj CSur* watery
aguachirle *f* F dishwater F
aguacil *m Rpl* dragonfly
aguada *f* **1** MAR water supply **2** PINT wash drawing
aguado *adj* **1** watered-down, weak **2** *C.Am., Méx, Ven* F boring
aguafiestas *m/f inv* partypooper, killjoy
aguafuerte *m* PINT etching
aguaitar ⟨1a⟩ *v/t S.Am.* spy on
aguamala *f S.Am.* jellyfish
aguamanil *m* **1** pitcher, *Br* jug **2** *lavamanos* wash basin; *palangana* wash bowl
aguamarina *f* MIN aquamarine
aguamiel *f* **1** *L.Am. water and honey* **2** *Méx* (*jugo de maguey*) agave sap
aguanieve *f* sleet
aguantable *adj* bearable
aguantar ⟨1a⟩ **I** *v/t* **1** *un peso* bear, support **2** *respiración* hold **3** (*soportar*) put up with; ***no lo puedo ~*** I can't stand *o* bear it **II** *v/i*: ***no aguanto más*** I can't take (it) any more, I can't bear it any longer; **aguantarse** *v/r* **1** (*contenerse*) keep quiet **2** (*conformarse*): ***me tuve que aguantar*** I had to put up with it
aguante *m* **1** patience; ***tener mucho ~*** be very patient, have a lot of patience **2** *física* stamina, endurance
aguar ⟨1a⟩ *v/t* spoil; ***~ la fiesta*** spoil the fun
aguardar ⟨1a⟩ **I** *v/t* wait for, await *fml* **II** *v/i* wait
aguardiente *m fruit-based alcoholic spirit*
aguarrás *m* turpentine, turps F
aguatero *m*, **-a** *f S.Am.* water-seller
aguatinta *f* PINT aquatint
aguaturma *f* BOT Jerusalem artichoke
aguaviva *f Rpl* jellyfish
agudeza *f* **1** *de voz, sonido* high pitch **2** MED intensity **3** (*perspicacia*) sharpness
◇ **agudeza visual** sharp-sightedness
agudizar ⟨1f⟩ *v/t* **1** *sentido* sharpen **2**: ***~ un problema*** make a problem worse; **agudizarse** *v/r* **1** MED get worse **2** *de sentido* become sharper
agudo *adj* **1** acute **2** (*afilado*) sharp **3** *sonido* high-pitched **4** (*perspicaz*) sharp **5** LING: ***acento ~*** acute accent
agüero *m* omen; ***ser de mal ~*** be a bad omen; ***pájaro de mal ~*** prophet of doom
aguerrido *adj* brave, valiant
aguijada *f* goad
aguijón *m* ZO sting; *fig* spur
aguijonear ⟨1a⟩ *v/t* ZO goad; *fig* drive
águila *f* **1** eagle; ***ser un ~*** *fig* be very sharp **2** *Méx*: ***¿~ o sol?*** heads or tails?
◇ **águila bicéfala** two-headed eagle; **águila caudal** golden eagle; **águila imperial** imperial eagle; **aguila pescadora** fish eagle, *Br* osprey; **aguila ratonera** buzzard; **águila real** golden eagle
aguileño *adj*: ***nariz -a*** aquiline nose
aguilucho *m* eaglet
aguinaldo *m* **1** *Esp* tip *given at Christmas* **2** *L.Am. month's salary paid as a bonus at Christmas*
agüita *f L.Am.* F **1** (*agua*) water **2** (*infusión*) infusion
aguja *f* **1** needle; ***buscar una ~ en un pajar*** *fig* look for a needle in a haystack **2** *de reloj* hand **3** FERR switch, *Br* point **4** GASTR rib roast
◇ **aguja de coser** (sewing) needle; **aguja de hacer media, aguja de hacer punto** knitting needle; **aguja de zurcir** darning needle
agujerear ⟨1a⟩ *v/t* make holes in; *billete* punch; **agujerearse** *v/r* develop holes
agujeta *f Méx* shoelace
agujero *m* hole
◇ **agujero en la capa de ozono** hole in the ozone layer
◇ **agujero negro** AST black hole
agujetas *fpl* stiffness *sg*; ***tener ~*** be stiff
agutí *m* agouti
aguzanieves *f* ZO pied wagtail
aguzar ⟨1f⟩ *v/t* sharpen; ***~ el ingenio*** sharpen one's wits; ***~ el oído*** prick up one's ears
ah *interj* ah!
ahí *adv* there; ***~ mismo*** right there; ***está por ~*** it's (somewhere) over there; *dando direcciones* it's that way; ***irse por ~*** go out; ***por ~ voy*** that's what I'm getting at; ***~ me las den todas*** F I couldn't *o* could care less, *Br* I couldn't care less; ***¡~ va!*** F there you go! F; ***de ~ que*** that is why
ahijado *m*, **-a** *f* **1** *en bautizo* godchild **2** (*adoptado*) adopted child
ahijar ⟨1a⟩ *v/t* adopt

ahínco *m* effort; ***trabajar con ~*** work hard; ***poner ~ en*** put a lot of effort into
ahíto *adj* sated
ahogado I *adj* **1** *en agua* drowned; ***~ en lágrimas*** in floods of tears **2** (*asfixiado*) suffocated **II** *m*, **-a** *f* drowned person, victim of drowning
ahogar ⟨1h⟩ *v/t* **1** *en agua* drown **2** (*asfixiar*) suffocate; *protestas* stifle **3** AUTO flood; **ahogarse** *v/r* **1** *en agua* drown; ***~ en un vaso de agua*** *fig* F get in a state over nothing, make a mountain out of a molehill **2** *con comida* choke **3** (*asfixiarse*) suffocate **4** AUTO flood
ahogo *m* breathlessness
ahondar ⟨1a⟩ **I** *v/i*: ***~ en algo*** go into sth in depth **II** *v/t* make … deeper; **ahondarse** *v/r* go deeper (***en*** into)
ahora *adv* **1** (*pronto*) in a moment; ***¡hasta ~!*** see you soon! **2** (*en este momento*) now; ***~ mismo*** right now; ***por ~*** for the present, for the time being; ***desde ~***, ***de ~ en adelante*** from now on; ***~ que*** now that; ***es ~ o nunca*** it's now or never **3**: ***~ bien*** however; ***y ¿~ qué?, esperas que …*** and then you expect …
ahorcado *m*, **-a** *f* hanged person; ***jugar al ~*** play hangman
ahorcar ⟨1g⟩ *v/t* hang; **ahorcarse** *v/r* hang o.s.
ahorita *adv* **1** *L.Am.* (*en este momento*) (right) now **2** *Méx*, *C.Am.* (*pronto*) in a moment **3** *Méx*, *C.Am.* (*hace poco*) just now
ahorrador I *adj* thrifty **II** *m*, **~a** *f* saver, investor; ***pequeño ~*** small saver, small investor
ahorrar ⟨1a⟩ **I** *v/t* save; ***~ algo a alguien*** save s.o. (from) sth; ***no ~ sacrificios*** make all sorts of sacrifices **II** *v/i* save (up); **ahorrarse** *v/r dinero* save; *fig* spare o.s., save o.s.
ahorrativo *adj* thrifty
ahorro *m* **1** saving; ***~ energético***, ***~ de energía*** energy saving **2**: ***~s*** *pl* savings *pl*; ***caja de ~s*** savings bank
ahuecar ⟨1g⟩ *v/t* **1** hollow out **2** *pelo* give volume to **3**: ***~ la voz*** deepen one's voice **4**: ***~ el ala*** F beat it F; **ahuecarse** *v/r* F get bigheaded, get a swollen head
ahulado *m C.Am.*, *Méx* oilskin
ahumado *adj* **1** smoked **2**: ***cristal ~*** tinted glass
ahumar ⟨1a⟩ *v/t* smoke; **ahumarse** *v/r* get blackened by smoke
ahuyentar ⟨1a⟩ *v/t* scare off *o* away; **ahuyentarse** *v/r L.Am.* run away
AI *abr* (= ***Amnistía Internacional***) AI (= Amnesty International)
airado *adj* angry
airbag *m* AUTO airbag
◇ **airbag lateral** side airbag
airbus *m* AVIA airbus
aire *m* **1** air; ***al ~ libre*** in the open air; ***traer ~ fresco a algo*** bring a breath of fresh air to sth; ***estar en el ~*** *fig* F be up in the air F; ***dejar en el ~*** *fig* leave … up in the air; ***vivir del ~*** F live on thin air; ***a mi ~*** in my own way **2** MÚS tune **3** (*viento*): ***hace mucho ~*** it is very windy; ***corre mucho ~*** it is very windy; ***cambiar de ~s*** have a change of scene **4**: ***darse ~s*** F give o.s. airs, put on airs and graces
◇ **aire acondicionado** air-conditioning; **aire comprimido** compressed air; **aire enrarecido** stuffy atmosphere; **aire popular** MÚS traditional tune; **aire viciado** stuffy atmosphere
airear ⟨1a⟩ *v/t tb fig* air; **airearse** *v/r* get some air
airoso *adj*: ***salir ~ de algo*** do well in sth
aislacionismo *m* POL isolationism
aislado *adj* isolated
aislador *m* insulator
aislamiento *m* TÉC, EL insulation; *fig* isolation
◇ **aislamiento acústico** soundproofing
◇ **aislamiento térmico** thermal insulation
aislante I *adj* insulating *atr*, insulation *atr* **II** *m* insulator
aislar ⟨1a⟩ *v/t* **1** isolate **2** EL insulate; **aislarse** *v/r* cut o.s. off
ajá *int* aha
ajado *adj* **1** *flores* withered **2** (*desgastado*) worn
ajar ⟨1a⟩ *v/t* **1** *flores* wither **2** (*desgastar*) wear; **ajarse** *v/r* **1** *de flores* wither **2** (*desgastarse*) wear
ajardinado *adj* landscaped; ***zona -a*** area with parks and gardens
ajardinar ⟨1a⟩ *v/t* landscape
a.J.C. *abr* (= ***antes de Jesucristo***) BC (= before Christ)

ajedrea *f* BOT savory
ajedrecista *m/f* chess player
ajedrez *m* chess
ajedrezado *adj* checked
ajenjo *m* **1** BOT wormwood **2** *bebida* absinthe
ajeno *adj* **1** *propiedad, problemas etc* someone else's; ***me era totalmente ~*** it was completely alien to me; ***lo ~*** *fig* other people's property **2**: ***por razones -as a nuestra voluntad*** for reasons beyond our control **3**: ***estar ~ a*** be unaware of, be oblivious to
ajete *m* BOT garlic shoot
ajetrearse ⟨1a⟩ *v/r* F get het up F
ajetreo *m* bustle
ají *m S.Am.* chili, *Br* chilli
ajiaceite *m* GASTR garlic dressing; *mayonesa* garlic mayonnaise, aïoli
ajiaco *m Col*: *spicy potato stew*
ajilimoje, ajilimójili *m* **1** GASTR spicy garlic sauce **2**: ***~s*** *pl fig* F trimmings F
ajillo *m*: ***al ~*** with garlic
ajo *m* BOT garlic; ***estar*** *o* ***andar en el ~*** F be in the know F
ajoaceite *m* GASTR garlic dressing; *mayonesa* garlic mayonnaise, aïoli
ajoarriero *m* GASTR *Basque dish containing salt cod, garlic, and eggs*
ajonjolí *m* BOT sesame
ajuar *m de novia* trousseau
ajuntarse ⟨1a⟩ *v/r* start living together
ajustable *adj* adjustable
ajustado I *adj* tight **II** *part* ☞ ***ajustar***
ajustador *m Cu* bra
ajustar ⟨1a⟩ **I** *v/t* **1** *máquina etc* adjust; *tornillo* tighten **2** *precio* set; ***~(le) las cuentas a alguien*** *fig* have a settling of accounts with s.o., settle accounts with s.o. **II** *v/i* fit; **ajustarse** *v/r* **1** *el cinturón* tighten **2**: ***~ a algo*** *fig* keep within sth; ***~ a la ley*** comply with the law, keep within the law
ajuste *m* adjustment; ***~ de cuentas*** settling of scores
ajusticiamiento *m* execution
ajusticiar ⟨1b⟩ *v/t* execute
al *prp* ***a*** *y art* ***el***; ***~ entrar*** on coming in, when we / they *etc* came in
ala *f* **1** wing; ***cortar las ~s a alguien*** clip s.o.'s wings; ***dar ~s a alguien*** encourage s.o. **2** MIL flank; DEP wing; *en baloncesto* forward **3** *Esp*: ***está tocado del ~*** he's mad, he's not right in the head F
◇ **ala delta** hang glider; **ala pivot** *en baloncesto* power forward; **ala del sombrero** hat brim
Alá *m* Allah
alabanza *f* acclaim
alabar ⟨1a⟩ *v/t* praise, acclaim
alabastro *m* alabaster
alacena *f* larder
alacrán *m* ZO scorpion
alacridad *f lit* alacrity
alado *adj* winged
alambicado *adj* **1** (*inteligente*) sharp, ingenious **2** (*complicado*) complicated, complex
alambique *m* still
alambrada *f* wire fence
alambrar ⟨1a⟩ *v/t* fence
alambre *m* wire
◇ **alambre de espino, alambre de púas** barbed wire
alameda *f* **1** boulevard **2** *de álamos* poplar grove
álamo *m* BOT poplar
◇ **álamo blanco** white poplar
◇ **álamo temblón** aspen
alarde *m* show, display; ***hacer ~ de*** make a show of
alardear ⟨1a⟩ *v/i* show off (**de** about)
alargado *adj cuello, nariz* long and thin; *habitación, mesa* long and narrow
alargador *m* TÉC extension cord, *Br* extension lead
alargamiento *m* lengthening, extension
alargar ⟨1h⟩ *v/t* **1** lengthen; *prenda* let down **2** *en tiempo* prolong **3** *mano, brazo* stretch out; **alargarse** *v/r de sombra, día* get longer, lengthen
alargue *m Rpl* extension cord, *Br* extension lead
alarido *m* shriek; ***dar ~s*** shriek
alarma *f* (*mecanismo, miedo*) alarm; ***dar la voz*** *o* ***el grito de ~*** raise the alarm; ***falsa ~*** false alarm; ***dispositivo de ~*** alarm; ***hacer saltar la ~*** set off *o* trigger the alarm; ***señal de ~*** alarm (signal)
◇ **alarma social** public disquiet; ***para evitar la ~*** so as not to alarm people
alarmante *adj* alarming
alarmar ⟨1a⟩ *v/t* alarm; **alarmarse** *v/r* become alarmed
alarmismo *m* alarmism
alarmista *m/f* alarmist

alazán *m* sorrel
alba *f* dawn; ***al rayar el ~*** at first light; ***levantarse con el ~*** get up at the crack of dawn
albacea *m/f* executor
albahaca *f* BOT basil
Albania *f* Albania
albañil *m* bricklayer
albano I *adj* Albanian **II** *m*, **-a** *f* Albanian
albanés *f* **I** *adj* Albanian **II** *m*, **-esa** *f* Albanian **III** *m idioma* Albanian
albarán *m* delivery note
albarda *f* packsaddle
albardear ⟨1a⟩ *v/t C.Am.* F bug F, pester
albardilla *f* light saddle
albaricoque *m* BOT apricot
albaricoquero *m* apricot tree
albatros *m inv* ZO albatross
albedrío *m*: ***libre ~*** free will; ***a su ~*** of his own free will
alberca *f* **1** reservoir **2** *Méx* (swimming) pool
albergar ⟨1h⟩ *v/t* **1** (*hospedar*) put up **2** (*contener*) house **3** *esperanzas* hold out **4** INFOR host; **albergarse** *v/r* to lodge
albergue *m* hostel; *benéfico* refuge, shelter; ***dar ~ a alguien*** take s.o. in
◇ **albergue de carreteras** motel
◇ **albergue juvenil** youth hostel
albino *m*, **-a** *f* albino
albis: ***me quedé en ~*** I didn't understand a thing; *estupefacto* I was speechless; *en blanco* my mind was a complete blank
albo *adj lit* white
albóndiga *f* meatball
albor *m lit* dawn, daybreak; ***~es*** *fig* dawn *sg*; ***en los ~es de la vida*** in one's youth
alborada *f* dawn
alborear ⟨1a⟩ *v/i*: ***alboreaba*** day was breaking
albornoz *m* (bath)robe
alborotado I *adj* **1** rowdy **2** (*imprudente*) reckless **II** *part* → ***alborotar***
alborotador I *adj* rowdy, noisy **II** *m*, **~a** *f* rioter
alborotar ⟨1a⟩ **I** *v/t* **1** stir up **2** (*desordenar*) disturb **II** *v/i* make a racket; **alborotarse** *v/r* **1** get excited **2** (*inquietarse*) get worked up
alboroto *m* commotion
alborozado *adj* delighted, overjoyed
alborozar ⟨1f⟩ *v/t* fill with joy; **alborozarse** *v/r* be overjoyed, rejoice
alborozo *m* rejoicing
albricias *fpl* congratulations; ***¡~!*** hooray!
albufera *f* lagoon
álbum *m* album
◇ **álbum de fotos** photo album
◇ **álbum de sellos** stamp album
albúmina *f* albumin
albuminoso *adj* albuminous
albur *m* **1** fate, chance **2** ZO dace
albura *f lit* whiteness
alcachofa *f* **1** BOT artichoke **2** *de ducha* shower head **3** F mike
alcahuete *m*, **-a** *f* **1** go-between **2** *Rpl* (*chivato*) snitch F, tattletale F, telltale F; *entre delincuentes* stool pigeon, *Br tb* grass F
alcahuetear ⟨1a⟩ *v/i* act as a go-between
alcaide *m* **1** warden, *Br* governor **2** HIST keeper
alcaldable *m* mayoral hopeful, *potential future mayor*
alcaldada *f* abuse of authority
alcalde *m*, **-esa** *f* mayor
◇ **alcalde de barrio** district mayor
alcaldía *f* mayor's office, city hall, *Br* town hall
álcali *m* alkali
alcalino *adj* alkaline
alcaloide *m* alkaloid
alcance *m* **1** reach; ***al ~ de la mano*** within reach; ***poner algo al ~ de alguien*** put sth within s.o.'s reach; ***dar ~ a alguien*** catch up with s.o.; ***al ~ de la vista*** visible, in view; ***¿está al ~ de tu bolsillo?*** can you afford it? **2** *de arma etc* range; ***de largo ~*** long-range **3** *de medida* scope **4** *de tragedia* extent, scale **5** *fig*: ***un hombre de mucho ~*** a talented *o* gifted man; ***de pocos ~s*** F untalented
alcancía *f L.Am.* piggy bank
alcanfor *m* camphor
alcantarilla *f* **1** sewer **2** (*sumidero*) drain
alcantarillado *m* **1** sewer system **2** *de sumideros* drainage system
alcanzar ⟨1f⟩ **I** *v/t a alguien* catch up with; *lugar* reach, get to; *en nivel* reach; *objetivo* achieve; *cantidad* amount to; ***~ la cifra de*** amount to, stand at **II** *v/i* **1** *en altura* reach **2** *en cantidad* be enough; ***el***

dinero no alcanza I / we *etc* can't afford it **3**: **~ *a oír / ver*** manage to hear / see
alcaparra *f* BOT caper
alcatraz *f* ZO gannet
alcaucil *f Rpl* artichoke
alcaudón *m* ZO shrike
alcayata *f* hook
alcazaba *f* citadel, castle
alcázar *m* fortress
alce *m* ZO elk
alcista *adj en bolsa* rising, bull *atr*; ***tendencia ~*** upward trend
alcoba *f S.Am.* bedroom
alcohol *m* **1** alcohol; ***prueba / test de ~*** breath test; ***la policía le sometió a la prueba de ~*** the police breathalyzed him; ***bajo la influencia*** *o* ***los efectos del ~*** under the influence of alcohol **2** MED rubbing alcohol, *Br* surgical spirit
◇ **alcohol etílico** ethyl alcohol; **alcohol metílico** methyl alcohol; **alcohol de quemar** denatured alcohol, *Br* methylated spirits *sg*
alcoholemia *f* blood alcohol level; ***prueba de ~*** drunkometer test, *Br* Breathalyser® test
alcohólico I *adj* alcoholic **II** *m*, **-a** *f* alcoholic
alcoholímetro *m* Breathalyzer®, *Br* Breathalyser®; ***soplar en el ~*** F blow into the bag
alcoholismo *m* alcoholism
alcoholizado *adj*: ***persona -a*** drunk, alcoholic; ***estar ~*** be a drunk *o* an alcoholic
alcoholizarse ⟨1f⟩ *v/r* become an alcoholic
alcornoque *m* BOT cork oak; ***pedazo de ~*** F blockhead F
alcotán *m* ZO hobby
alcurnia *f* ancestry; ***de noble ~*** of noble birth *o* ancestry
aldaba *f* doorknocker
aldabón *m* doorknocker
aldea *f* (small) village
◇ **aldea global** global village
aldeanismo *m desp* parochialism
aldeano I *adj* village *atr* **II** *m*, **-a** *f* villager
aldehído *m* QUÍM aldehyde
¡ale! ☞ ***hala***
aleación *f* alloy
alear ⟨1a⟩ *v/t* alloy
aleatorio *adj* random
aleccionador *adj* instructive
aleccionamiento *m* **1** instruction **2** (*reprimenda*) lecture
aleccionar ⟨1a⟩ *v/t* **1** instruct **2** (*regañar*) lecture
aledaño *adj* bordering, neighboring, *Br* neighbouring
aledaños *mpl* surrounding area *sg*; *de ciudad* outskirts
alegación *f* JUR declaration, statement
alegador *adj L.Am.* argumentative
alegar ⟨1h⟩ **I** *v/t motivo, razón* cite; **~ *que*** claim *o* allege that **II** *v/i L.Am.* **1** (*discutir*) argue **2** (*quejarse*) complain, gripe F
alegato *m* JUR *fig* speech; *Andes* argument
alegoría *f* allegory
alegórico *adj* allegorical
alegrar ⟨1a⟩ *v/t* **1** make happy **2** (*animar*) cheer up; **alegrarse** *v/r* **1** cheer up; ***¡alegra esa cara!*** cheer up! **2** F *bebiendo* get tipsy **3**: ***me alegro*** I am pleased; ***me alegro de que hayas venido*** I'm pleased you could make it; **~ *por alguien*** be pleased *o* happy for s.o. (***de*** about)
alegre *adj* **1** (*contento*) happy; *por naturaleza* happy, cheerful **2** F (*bebido*) tipsy
alegría *f* happiness; ***me has dado una gran ~*** you've made me very happy
◇ **alegría de vivir** joie de vivre, ebullience
alegrón *m* thrill; ***llevarse un ~*** be thrilled
alejado *adj* remote, far away
alejamiento *m* removal, separation; *fig* distancing
alejar ⟨1a⟩ *v/t* **1** move away **2** *pensamiento* banish; ***debes tratar de ~ de ti esa idea absurda*** you must try to get that absurd idea out of your head; **alejarse** *v/r* move away (***de*** from); *de situación, ámbito* get away (***de*** from); ***¡no te alejes mucho!*** don't go too far away!
alelado *adj*: ***estar ~*** be in a daze
alelar ⟨1a⟩ *v/t* stupefy
aleluya *m & interj* hallelujah
alemán I *adj* German **II** *m*, **-ana** *f persona* German **III** *m idioma* German
Alemania *f* Germany

alentado *adj L.Am.* encouraged
alentador *adj* encouraging
alentar ⟨1k⟩ *v/t* **1** (*animar*) encourage **2** *esperanzas* cherish; **alentarse** *v/r L.Am.* get better
aleonado *adj*: ***melena -a*** mane
alerce *m* BOT larch
alergénico **I** *adj* allergenic **II** *m* allergen
alergia *f* allergy
alérgico *adj* allergic (***a*** to)
alergólogo *m*, **-a** *f* MED allergist
alero *m* **1** *de tejado* eave; ***estar en el ~*** *fig* F be up in the air **2** *en baloncesto* forward
alerón *m* **1** AVIA aileron **2** AUTO spoiler
alerta **I** *adv*: ***estar ~*** be on the alert; ***estar ojo ~*** keep an eye out; ***¡~!*** watch out!, be careful! **II** *f* alert; ***dar la ~*** raise the alarm; ***poner en ~*** alert; ***en estado de ~*** on alert, in a state of alert
◇ **alerta roja** red alert
◇ **alerta por vibración** TELEC vibration mode
alertar ⟨1a⟩ *v/t* alert (***de*** to)
aleta *f* **1** ZO fin **2** *de buzo* flipper **3** *de la nariz* wing
aletargar ⟨1h⟩ *v/t* make feel lethargic; **aletargarse** *v/r* feel lethargic
aletear ⟨1a⟩ *v/i* flap one's wings
alevín *m* **1** ZO young fish **2** *fig* beginner; DEP junior
alevosía *f* treachery; ***con ~*** treacherously
alevoso *adj* treacherous
alfa *f* alpha
alfabético *adj* alphabetical; ***por orden ~*** in alphabetical order
alfabetización *f* teaching of basic literacy
alfabetizar ⟨1f⟩ *v/t* **1** *lista etc* put into alphabetical order **2**: ***~ a alguien*** teach s.o. to read and write
alfabeto *m* alphabet
alfajor *m almond sweet, traditionally associated with Christmas*
alfalfa *f* BOT alfalfa
alfanumérico *adj* alphanumeric
alfar *m*, **alfarería** *f* pottery
alfarero *m*, **-a** *f* potter
alféizar *m* sill, windowsill
alfeñique *m* F wimp F
alférez *m* second lieutenant
◇ **alférez de fragata** ensign
◇ **alférez de navío** second lieutenant
alfil *m* bishop
alfiler *m* pin; ***no cabe un ~*** *fig* F there's no room for anything else; ***prendido con ~*** *fig* held together with spit
◇ **alfiler de corbata** tiepin
◇ **alfiler de gancho** *Arg* safety pin
alfiletero *m* **1** (*cojín*) pincushion **2** (*estuche*) needlecase
alfombra *f* carpet; *más pequeña* rug
◇ **alfombra persa** Persian carpet *o* rug
alfombrado *m L.Am.* carpeting, carpets *pl*
alfombrar ⟨1a⟩ *v/t* carpet
alfombrilla *f* **1** mat **2** MED *illness similar to measles*
◇ **alfombrilla de baño** bathmat
◇ **alfombrilla de ratón** INFOR mouse pad, mouse mat
alfóncigo, alfónsigo *m* BOT pistachio
alforfón *m* BOT buckwheat
alforja *f* saddlebag
alga *f* BOT alga; *marina* seaweed
algalia *f* civet
algarabía *f fig* rejoicing, jubilation
algarada *f* HIST incursion; *fig* brawl, commotion
algarroba *f* BOT carob, carob bean
algarrobo *m* BOT carob, carob tree
álgebra *f* algebra
algebraico *adj* algebraic
álgido *adj fig* decisive; ***punto ~*** climax, high point
algo **I** *pron* **1** *en frases afirmativas* something; ***~ es ~*** it's something, it's better than nothing; ***o ~ así*** or something like that; ***unas 5.000 personas o ~ así*** 5,000 or so people, 5,000 people more or less; ***por ~ será*** there must be a reason **2** *en frases interrogativas o condicionales* anything **II** *adv* rather, somewhat
algodón *m* cotton; ***criado entre algodones*** F mollycoddled, pampered
◇ **algodón hidrófilo** absorbent cotton, *Br* cotton wool
◇ **algodón en rama** raw cotton
algodonero **I** *adj* cotton *atr* **II** *m*, **-a** *f* cotton farmer
algorítmico *adj* algorithmic
algoritmo *m* algorithm
alguacil *m*, **~esa** *f* bailiff
alguacilillo *m* TAUR (bullfight) official
alguien *pron* **1** *en frases afirmativas* somebody, someone; ***en su empresa***

es ~ he's a somebody in his company **2** *en frases interrogativas o condicionales* anybody, anyone
algún *adj* **1** *en frases afirmativas* some; ***~ día*** some day **2** *en frases interrogativas o condicionales* any
alguno I *adj* **1** *en frases afirmativas* some; ***~ que otro de sus libros*** a few of his books; ***~ que otro jueves*** occasionally on a Thursday; ***fumo ~ que otro cigarrillo de vez en cuando*** I smoke the odd cigarette, I have a cigarette from time to time; ***de modo ~*** in the slightest, at all; ***de -a manera*** somehow; ***en -a parte*** somewhere **2** *en frases negativas, interrogativas o condicionales* any; ***no la influyó de modo ~*** it didn't influence her in any way; ***si -a vez ...*** if at any time ... **II** *pron*: *persona* someone, somebody; ***~s opinan que*** some people think that; ***~ se podrá usar*** *objeto* we'll be able to use some of them; ***si ~ de vosotros / aquéllos ...*** if one of you / them ...
alhaja *f* piece of jewelry *o Br* jewellery; *fig* gem; ***~s*** jewelry *sg*; ***¡buena ~!*** F he's / she's a real so-and-so! F
alhelí *m* BOT wallflower
alheña *f* BOT henna
alhucema *f* BOT lavender
aliado I *adj* allied **II** *m*, **-a** *f* ally
alianza *f* **1** POL alliance **2** *anillo* wedding band, wedding ring
aliar ⟨1c⟩ *v/t conocimientos* pool, combine; ***~ fuerzas*** join forces; **aliarse** *v/r* form an alliance (***con*** with)
alias I *m inv* alias **II** *adv* alias
alicaído *adj* F down *pred*
alicatado *m* tiling, tiles *pl*
alicatar ⟨1a⟩ *v/t* tile
alicates *mpl* **1** pliers **2** *L.Am.* (*cortaúñas*) nail clippers
aliciente *m* **1** (*estímulo*) incentive **2** (*atractivo*) attraction
alienación *f* JUR alienation
◇ **alienación mental** insanity
alienado I *adj* alienated **II** *part* ☞ ***alienar***
alienar ⟨1a⟩ *v/t* alienate
alienígena I *adj* alien **II** *m/f* alien
aliento *m* **1** breath; ***mal ~*** bad breath; ***cobrar ~*** catch one's breath, get one's breath back; ***perder el ~*** be out of breath, be breathless; ***cortar el ~ a alguien*** take s.o.'s breath away; ***sin ~*** breathless, out of breath; ***que quita el ~*** breathtaking; ***hasta el último ~*** to his / her dying day **2** *fig* encouragement
aligátor *m* ZO alligator
aligerar ⟨1a⟩ *v/t* **1** *carga* lighten **2**: ***~ el paso*** quicken one's pace; **aligerarse** *v/r*: ***~ de ropa*** take off some of one's clothes, shed a layer or two
aligustre *m* BOT privet
alijo *m* MAR consignment
alimaña *f* pest; ***~s*** *pl* vermin *pl*
alimentación *f* **1** (*dieta*) diet **2** *acción* feeding; ***~ de papel*** INFOR paper feed **3** EL power supply
alimentador *m* TÉC feed, feeder
alimentar ⟨1a⟩ **I** *v/t tb* TÉC, *fig* feed; EL power **II** *v/i* be nourishing; **alimentarse** *v/r* feed o.s.; ***~ de algo*** *de persona, animal* live on sth; *de máquina* run on sth
alimentario, alimenticio *adj* food *atr*; ***industria -a*** food industry; ***producto ~*** foodstuff
alimento *m* **1** (*comida*) food **2**: ***tiene poco ~*** it has little nutritional value
◇ **alimentos básicos** basic foods; **alimentos congelados** frozen foods; **alimentos dietéticos (de régimen)** slimming aids; **alimentos infantiles** baby foods
alimón *m*: ***al ~*** in chorus
alineación *f* DEP line-up
alinear ⟨1a⟩ *v/t* **1** line up, align **2** DEP select **3**: ***países no alineados*** POL non-aligned countries; **alinearse** *v/r* **1** (*ponerse en fila*) line up **2** POL align o.s. (***con*** with)
aliñar ⟨1a⟩ *v/t* dress; **aliñarse** *v/r* get dressed up
aliño *m* dressing
alioli *m* GASTR garlic mayonnaise, aïoli
alirón *m* DEP: ***cantar o entonar el ~*** sing a victory song
alisar ⟨1a⟩ *v/t* smooth
aliscafo *m Rpl* hydrofoil
alisios *mpl* trade winds
aliso *m* BOT alder
alistamiento *m* MIL enlistment
alistar ⟨1a⟩ MIL *v/t* draft; **alistarse** *v/r* **1** enlist **2** *L.Am.* (*prepararse*) get ready
aliteración *f* alliteration
aliviar ⟨1b⟩ *v/t* alleviate, relieve; **aliviarse** *v/r de dolor* ease (off); ***¡que se alivie!*** get well soon!

alivio *m* **1** relief **2**: ***de ~*** F horrendous; ***me he dado un golpe de ~*** I gave myself a helluva knock F
aljibe *m* cistern, tank
allá *adv* **1** *de lugar* (over) there; ***~ abajo*** down there; ***~ arriba*** up there; ***más ~*** further on; ***más ~ de*** beyond; ***muy ~*** a long way off; ***el más ~*** the hereafter; ***¡~ voy!*** here I come! **2** *de tiempo*: ***~ por los años veinte*** back in the twenties **3** F: ***~ él / ella*** that's up to him / her; ***~ se las arregle*** that's his problem
allanamiento *m*: ***~ de morada*** JUR breaking and entering
allanar ⟨1a⟩ *v/t* **1** (*alisar*) smooth **2** (*aplanar*) level (out) **3** *obstáculos* overcome
allegado I *adj* close **II** *m*, **-a** *f* relation, relative
allende *prep* beyond, on the other side of
allí *adv* there; ***por ~*** over there; *dando direcciones* that way; ***¡~ está!*** there it is! ***~ mismo*** right there; ***de ~*** from there; ***hasta ~*** that far
alma *f* soul; ***se me cayó el ~ a los pies*** F my heart sank; ***llegar al ~*** *conmover* move deeply; *herir* hurt deeply; ***lo siento en el ~*** I am truly sorry; ***¡~ mía!*** my love!; ***arrancarle a uno el ~***, ***destrozar*** *o* ***partir el ~ a uno*** break s.o.'s heart; ***como ~ que lleva el diablo*** like a bat out of hell; ***con el ~ en un hilo*** worried sick; ***con toda el ~*** with all one's heart; ***me duele en el ~*** it hurts me deeply; ***romperle a uno el ~*** F beat the living daylights out of s.o. F; ***no se ve un ~*** there isn't a soul to be seen
◇ **alma de cántaro** kind soul; **alma de Dios** kind-hearted person; **alma en pena** lost soul
almacén *m* **1** warehouse **2** (*tienda*) store, *Br* shop; ***grandes almacenes*** *pl* department store *sg* **3** *Andes*, *Rpl* grocery store, *Br* grocer's
almacenaje *m* storage; ***derechos de ~*** storage charges
almacenamiento *m* storage
◇ **almacenamiento de datos** data storage
almacenar ⟨1a⟩ *v/t tb* INFOR store; ***~ en disquete*** save to disk
almacenero *m*, **-a** *f* storekeeper, shopkeeper
almacenista *m/f* wholesaler
almagre *m* MIN red ocher *o Br* ochre
almanaque *m* almanac
almazara *f* olive press
almeja *f* ZO clam
almenas *fpl* battlements
almendra *f* almond
◇ **almendra amarga** bitter almond
◇ **almendra garrapiñada** caramel-coated almond
almendrado I *adj* almond-shaped **II** *m almond candy*
almendro *m* almond tree
almendruco *m unripe almond*
almíbar *m* syrup; ***en ~*** in syrup
almibarado *adj fig* syrupy
almibarar ⟨1a⟩ *v/t fruta* preserve in syrup
almidón *m* starch
almidonado *adj fig* stuffy, starchy
almidonar ⟨1a⟩ *v/t* starch
alminar *m* minaret
almirantazgo *m* admiralty
almirante *m* admiral
almirez *m* mortar
almizcle *m* ZO musk
almizclero *m* ZO musk deer
almohada *f* pillow; ***consultarlo con la ~*** sleep on it
almohadilla *f* **1** small cushion **2** TÉC pad **3** *en béisbol* bag
almohadillado *adj codera*, *hombrera* padded
almohadón *m* large cushion
almoneda *f* auction
almorranas *fpl* piles
almorta *f* BOT vetch
almorzada *f Méx* lunch
almorzar ⟨1f & 1m⟩ **I** *v/i al mediodía* have lunch; *a media mañana* have a mid-morning snack **II** *v/t*: ***~ algo*** *al mediodía* have sth for lunch; *a media mañana* have sth as a mid-morning snack; ***vengo almorzado*** I've already eaten
almuerzo *m al mediodía* lunch; *a media mañana* mid-morning snack
◇ **almuerzo de trabajo** working lunch
¿alo? *L.Am. por teléfono* hello?
alocado I *adj* crazy **II** *m*, **-a** *f* crazy fool
alocución *f* speech, address
aloe, áloe *m* BOT aloe
alojamiento *m* accommodations *pl*, *Br* accommodation
alojar ⟨1a⟩ *v/t* accommodate; **alojarse** *v/r* **1** stay (**en** in) **2** (*colocarse*) lodge

(**en** in); ***la bala se alojó en el pulmón*** the bullet lodged in the lung
alojo *m L.Am.* ☞ ***alojamiento***
alondra *f* ZO lark
alopatía *f* MED allopathy
alopecia *f* MED alopecia
alpaca *f animal, lana* alpaca
alpargata *f Esp* espadrille
alpargatería *f Esp shop where espadrilles are sold*
alpinismo *m* mountaineering, climbing
alpinista *m/f* mountaineer, climber
alpino *adj* Alpine
alpiste *m* **1** birdseed **2**: ***le gusta mucho el ~*** F he likes a drink, he's very fond of the bottle F
alquería *f* farm
alquilar ⟨1a⟩ *v/t de usuario* rent; *de dueño* rent out; **alquilarse** *v/r* **1** *de casa* be for rent; ***se alquila*** for rent, *Br tb* to let **2** *de persona* hire o.s. out
alquiler *m* **1** *acción*: *de coche etc* rental; *de casa* renting; ***de ~*** rental *atr*, *Br tb* hire *atr* **2** *dinero* rental, *Br tb* rent
◇ **alquiler de bicicletas** bicycle rental, *Br tb* bicycle hire
◇ **alquiler de coches** car rental, *Br tb* car hire
alquimia *f* alchemy
alquimista *m* alchemist
alquitrán *m* tar
alquitranado *m* tarring
alquitranar ⟨1a⟩ *v/t* tar
alrededor **I** *adv* around; ***a mí ~*** around me **II** *prp*: ***~ de*** around
alrededores *mpl* surrounding area *sg*
alta *f* **1** MED discharge; ***dar de ~ a alguien***, ***dar el ~ a alguien*** discharge s.o.; ***recibir el ~*** be allowed to go back to work **2**: ***darse de ~*** *en organismo* register
◇ **alta médica** discharge
altamente *adv* highly
altanería *f* arrogance
altanero *adj* arrogant
altar *m* altar; ***llevar al ~*** marry, lead to the altar; ***elevar a los ~es*** canonize
◇ **altar mayor** high altar
altavoz *m* loudspeaker
alterable *adj* changeable, volatile
alteración *f* alteration
alterado *adj* **1** *persona* upset **2** (*modificado*): ***~ genéticamente*** genetically altered *o* modified
alterar ⟨1a⟩ *v/t* **1** (*cambiar*) alter **2** *a alguien* upset **3**: ***~ el orden público*** cause a breach of the peace; **alterarse** *v/r* **1** (*cambiarse*) change, alter **2** get upset (***por*** because of)
altercado *m* argument, altercation *fml*
altercar ⟨1g⟩ *v/i* argue
alternador *m* EL alternator
alternancia *f* alternation
alternar ⟨1a⟩ **I** *v/t* alternate; ***~ el trabajo con el descanso*** alternate work and relaxation **II** *v/i* **1** *de persona* mix **2**: ***~ con*** alternate with; **alternarse** *v/r* alternate, take turns
alternativa *f* **1** alternative **2** TAUR: ***dar la ~ a alguien*** confirm s.o. as a fully-fledged bullfighter; ***tomar la ~*** become a fully-fledged bullfighter
alternativamente *adv* alternately, turn and turn about; ***~ rojo y verde*** now red, now green
alternativo *adj* alternative
alterne *m* F hospitality *in hostess bars*; ***bar de ~*** hostess bar; ***chica de ~*** hostess
alterno *adj* **1** alternate; ***en días ~s*** on alternate days **2** EL: ***corriente -a*** alternating current
Alteza *f título* Highness
◇ **Alteza Real** Royal Highness
altibajos *mpl* ups and downs
altillo *m* **1** (*desván*) attic **2** *en armario* top (part) of the closet
altímetro *m* altimeter
altiplanicie *f*, **altiplano** *m* high plateau; ***El Altiplano*** the Bolivian plateau, the Bolivian Altiplano
altísimo *adj* **1** very high **2** REL: ***el Altísimo*** the Almighty
altisonante *adj* high-flown
altitud *f* altitude; ***~ sobre el nivel del mar*** height above sea level
altivez *f* pride, haughtiness
altivo *adj* proud, haughty
alto[1] **I** *adj persona* tall; *precio, número, montaña* high; ***en -a mar*** on the high seas; ***el ~ Salado*** the upper (reaches of the) Salado; ***los pisos ~s*** the top floors; ***en voz -a*** out loud; ***a -as horas de la noche*** in the small hours; ***clase -a*** high class; ***-a calidad*** high quality **II** *adv volar, saltar* high; ***hablar ~*** speak loudly; ***pasar por ~*** overlook; ***poner más ~*** TV, RAD turn up; ***por todo lo ~*** F lavishly; ***en ~*** on high ground, high

up; ***llegar ~*** go far
III *m* **1** (*altura*) height; ***dos metros de ~*** two meters high **2** *Chi* pile **3**: ***los altos de Golán*** GEOG the Golan Heights
◇ **alta sociedad** high society; **altas presiones** high pressure *sg*; **alto horno** blast furnace

alto[2] *m* **1** halt; ***¡~!*** halt!; ***dar el ~ a alguien*** order s.o. to stop; ***¡~ ahí!*** stop right there! **2** (*pausa*) pause; ***hacer un ~*** stop
◇ **alto el fuego** ceasefire

altoparlante *m L.Am.* loudspeaker

altorrelieve *m* high relief

altozano *m* hillock

altramuz *m planta* lupin; *semilla* lupin seed

altruismo *m* altruism

altruista I *adj* altruistic **II** *m/f* altruist

altura *f* **1** height; ***de diez metros de ~*** 10 meters in height, 10 meters high; ***a la ~ de*** on a par with; ***estar a la ~ de algo*** be up to sth; ***a estas ~s*** by this time, by now **2** MÚS pitch **3** AVIA altitude; ***tomar ~*** gain altitude **4** GEOG latitude
◇ **altura de vuelo** cruising altitude

alubia *f* BOT kidney bean

alucinación *f* hallucination

alucinado *adj* F blown away P, *Br tb* gobsmacked F

alucinante *adj* F incredible

alucinar ⟨1a⟩ **I** *v/i* hallucinate **II** *v/t* F amaze

alucine *m*: ***de ~*** F amazing

alucinógeno *m* hallucinogen

alud *m* avalanche

aludido: ***darse por ~*** take it personally; ***no darse por ~*** take no notice

aludir ⟨3a⟩ *v/i*: ***~ a algo*** allude to sth

alumbrado I *adj* lit **II** *m* lighting
◇ **alumbrado público** street lighting

alumbramiento *m* birth

alumbrar ⟨1a⟩ **I** *v/t* (*dar luz a*) light (up) **II** *v/i* give off light

alúmina *f* QUÍM aluminum oxide, *Br* aluminium oxide

aluminio *m* aluminum, *Br* aluminium; ***papel de ~*** aluminum foil

alumnado *m* students *pl*, student body

alumno *m*, **-a** *f* student

alunizaje *m* moon landing

alunizar ⟨1f⟩ *v/i* land on the moon

alusión *f* allusion (***a*** to); ***hacer ~ a*** refer to, allude to; ***en ~ a*** with reference to

alusivo *adj*: ***~ a*** regarding

aluvión *m* **1** flood *tb fig* **2** GEOL alluvium

alvéolo, alveolo *m* ANAT, TÉC alveolus

alverja *f* ☞ ***arveja***

alza *f* rise; ***~ de precios*** price rise; ***en ~*** *en bolsa* rising; ***jugar al ~*** *en bolsa* gamble on a bull market; ***revisar al ~*** *precios* revise upward

alzacuellos *m inv* clerical collar, dog collar F

alzada *f* JUR appeal

alzado I *adj* **1** (*elevado*) high, raised **2** (*rebelde*) rebel *atr* **3** (*soberbio*) arrogant **4** *L.Am.* ***un animal ~*** an animal that has escaped into the wild **5**: ***precio ~*** fixed building cost **II** *m*, **-a** *f L.Am.* insurgent **III** *m* **1** ARQUI elevation **2** TIP pagination

alzamiento *m* MIL, POL uprising
◇ **alzamiento de bienes** JUR concealment of assets

alzapaño *m* tieback

alzar ⟨1f⟩ *v/t barrera, brazo* lift, raise; *precios* raise; ***~ velas*** hoist the sails; ***~ la vista*** raise one's eyes, look up; ***~ el vuelo*** take off; **alzarse** *v/r* rise; *en armas* rise up; ***~ con el triunfo*** win; ***~ con el dinero*** run off with the money

alzo *m C.Am.* theft

a.m. *abr* (= ***ante meridiem***) a.m. (= ante meridiem)

ama *f* (*dueña*) owner
◇ **ama de casa** housewife, homemaker; **ama de cría, ama de leche** *L.Am.* wetnurse; **ama de llaves** housekeeper

amabilidad *f* kindness; ***tener la ~ de hacer algo*** be kind enough to do sth

amable *adj* kind (***con*** to); ***¿sería tan ~ de ayudarme?*** would you be so kind as to help me?; ***muy ~, es Vd muy ~*** it's very good *o* kind of you

amado *m*, **-a** *f* love, sweetheart

amaestrado *adj* trained

amaestrar ⟨1a⟩ *v/t* train

amagar ⟨1h⟩ **I** *v/t* **1**: ***la tarde amaga lluvia*** it looks like rain this afternoon **2** *enfermedad* show symptoms of **3**: ***~ una sonrisa*** try to smile **II** *v/i* **1** fake **2** DEP dummy

amago *m* **1** threat **2**: ***hizo ~ de levantarse*** she made as if to get up **3** DEP dummy

◇ **amago de infarto** minor heart attack
amainar ⟨1a⟩ *v/i de lluvia, viento* ease up, slacken off
amalgama *f* amalgam, mixture
amalgamar ⟨1a⟩ *v/t fig* combine; **amalgamarse** *v/r* amalgamate
amamantar ⟨1a⟩ *v/t bebé* breastfeed; *cría* feed
amancebamiento *m* living together
amancebarse ⟨1a⟩ *v/r* move in together
amanecer ⟨2d⟩ **I** *v/i* **1** get light **2** *de persona* wake up **II** *m* dawn; ***al ~*** at dawn, at daybreak; **amanecerse** *v/r Andes, Carib, Méx* stay up all night
amanerado *adj* affected
amaneramiento *m* affectation
amanerarse ⟨1a⟩ *v/r* become affected
amanita *f* BOT amanita
amansar ⟨1a⟩ *v/t* break in, tame; **amansarse** *v/r* become tame, become quieter
amante I *adj* loving; ***es ~ de la buena vida*** he's fond of good living; ***ser ~ de los animales*** be an animal lover **II** *m/f en una relación* lover; ***los ~s de la naturaleza*** nature lovers
amanuense *m/f* scribe
amañar ⟨1a⟩ *v/t* F rig F; *partido* fix F; **amañarse** *v/r* manage
amaño *m* cunning trick
amapola *f* BOT poppy
amar ⟨1a⟩ *v/t* love; ***hacerse ~*** be lovable
amarrado *adj Méx* F mean, stingy F
amaraje *m* AVIA landing *on water*
amarar ⟨1a⟩ *v/i* AVIA land *on water*
amargado *adj fig* bitter, embittered
amargamente *adv fig* bitterly
amargar ⟨1h⟩ *v/t* **1** *día, ocasión* spoil **2**: ***~ a alguien*** make s.o. bitter; **amargarse** *v/r* **1** get bitter **2**: ***~ la vida*** get upset
amargo *adj tb fig* bitter
amargor *m* bitterness
amargura *f tb fig* bitterness
amariconado *adj* P *fig* effeminate, camp
amarilis *f* BOT amaryllis
amarillear ⟨1a⟩ *v/t* go yellow, turn yellow
amarillento *adj* yellowish
amarillez *f* yellowness
amarillismo *m* muckraking journalism
amarillo *m/adj* yellow
amarizaje *m* splashdown
amarizar ⟨1f⟩ *v/i* splash down
amarra *f* MAR mooring rope; ***soltar** o **largar las ~s*** cast off her moorings; ***tener buenas ~s*** *fig* have contacts; ***cortar** o **romper las ~s*** *fig* strike out on one's own; ***cortar las ~s del hogar familiar*** leave home
amarradero *m* MAR bollard
amarraje *m* MAR wharfage
amarrar ⟨1a⟩ *v/t* (*atar*) tie
amarre *m* MAR mooring, berth
amasar ⟨1a⟩ *v/t* **1** *pan* knead **2** *fortuna* amass
amasijo *m* jumble
amateur I *adj* amateur *atr* **II** *m/f* amateur
amatista *f* amethyst
amatorio *adj* love *atr*, love-making *atr*
amazacotado *adj* sticky, stodgy
amazona *f* horsewoman
Amazonas: ***el ~*** the Amazon
amazónico *adj* GEOG Amazonian
ambages *mpl*: ***decirlo sin ~*** say it straight out, come straight out with it
ámbar I *adj* amber; *luz* yellow, *Br* amber **II** *m* amber; ***el semáforo está en ~*** the lights are yellow, *Br* the lights are at amber
ambición *f* ambition; ***sin ambiciones*** unambitious
ambicionar ⟨1a⟩ *v/t* aspire to
ambicioso *adj* ambitious
ambidextro, ambidiestro *adj* ambidextrous
ambientación *f de película, obra de teatro* setting
ambientado *part* ☞ ***ambientar***
ambientador *m* air freshener
ambiental *adj* environmental
ambientar ⟨1a⟩ *v/t película, novela* set; ***estar ambientado en*** be set in; **ambientarse** *v/r* be set
ambiente I *adj*: ***medio ~*** environment; ***temperatura ~*** room temperature **II** *m* **1** (*entorno*) environment **2** (*situación*) atmosphere; ***crear ~*** create an atmosphere **3** *Andes, Rpl* (*habitación*) room
◇ **ambiente laboral, ambiente de trabajo** work environment
ambigú *m* buffet
ambigüedad *f* ambiguity
ambiguo *adj* ambiguous
ámbito *m* **1** area **2** (*límite*) scope

ambivalencia *f* ambivalence
ambivalente *adj* ambivalent
ambo *m Arg* two-piece suit
ambos, ambas I *adj* both **II** *pron* both (of us / you / them)
ambrosía *f* MYTH ambrosia
ambulancia *f* ambulance
ambulante I *adj* traveling, *Br* travelling; ***venta ~*** peddling, hawking; ***vendedor ~*** hawker, street seller **II** *m/f L.Am. vendedor* hawker, street seller
ambulatorio I *adj* MED out-patient *atr* **II** *m* out-patient clinic
ameba *f* ameba, *Br* amoeba
amebiano *adj* amebic, *Br* amoebic
amedrentar ⟨1a⟩ *v/t* terrify; **amedrentarse** *v/r* be terrified, feel terrified
amén I *m* amen; ***en un decir ~*** in a flash; ***decir a todo ~*** agree to everything **II** *prp*: ***~ de*** as well as
amenaza *f* threat
◇ **amenaza de bomba** bomb scare
amenazador *adj* threatening
amenazante *adj* threatening
amenazar ⟨1f⟩ **I** *v/t* threaten (***con***, ***de*** with); ***~ a alguien de muerte*** threaten to kill s.o.; ***~ ruina*** threaten to collapse, be on the verge of collapse; ***amenaza tempestad*** there's a storm brewing **II** *v/i*: ***~ con*** threaten to
amenidad *f* interest, enjoyment
amenizar ⟨1f⟩ *v/t*: ***~ algo*** make sth more entertaining *o* enjoyable
ameno *adj* enjoyable
amento *m* BOT catkin
América *f* America; ***hacer las ~s*** make a fortune
◇ **América Central** Central America; **América Latina** Latin America; **América del Norte** North America; **América del Sur** South America
americana *f* **1** American woman **2** *prenda* jacket
americanismo *m* Americanism
americanizar ⟨1f⟩ *v/t* Americanize
americano *m/adj* American
amerindio I *adj* Amerindian **II** *m*, **-a** *f* Amerindian
ameritar ⟨1a⟩ *v/t L.Am.* deserve, merit
amerizaje *m de avión* landing *on water*; *de nave espacial* splashdown
amerizar ⟨1f⟩ *v/i de avión* land *on water*; *de nave espacial* splash down
ametralladora *f* machine gun
ametrallar ⟨1a⟩ *v/t* machine-gun, fire at … with a machine gun
amianto *m* MIN asbestos
amiba *f* ☞ ***ameba***
amigable *adj* friendly
amígdala *f* ANAT tonsil
◇ **amígdala faríngea** adenoids *pl*, pharyngeal tonsil *fml*
amigdalitis *f* MED tonsillitis *sg*
amigo I *adj* friendly; ***ser ~ de algo*** be fond of sth; ***no soy ~ de esquiar*** I'm not a big skier, I'm not fond of skiing; ***ser ~ de lo ajeno*** be light-fingered F **II** *m*, **-a** *f* friend; ***hacerse ~s*** make friends; ***somos muy ~s*** we're very close, we're very good friends; ***~ de la naturaleza*** nature lover
amigote *m* F buddy F, pal F
amiguete *m* F crony F
amiguismo *m* nepotism, cronyism F
amilanar ⟨1a⟩ *v/t* daunt; **amilanarse** *v/r* be daunted
amina *f* QUÍM amine
aminoácido *m* QUÍM amino acid
aminorar ⟨1a⟩ *v/t* reduce; ***~ la marcha*** slow down
amistad *f* **1** friendship; ***hacer*** *o* ***trabar ~ con alguien*** strike up a friendship with s.o.; ***hacer las ~es*** make it up **2**: ***~es*** *pl* friends
amistosamente *adv* amicably
amistoso I *adj* friendly; ***partido ~*** DEP friendly (game) **II** *m* DEP friendly
amnesia *f* amnesia
amniocentesis *f* MED amniocentesis
amniótico *adj*: ***bolsa -a*** amniotic sac; ***líquido ~*** amniotic fluid
amnistía *f* amnesty
◇ **Amnistía Internacional** Amnesty International
amnistiar ⟨1c⟩ *v/t* grant an amnesty to, amnesty
amo *m* **1** (*dueño*) owner **2** HIST master; ***ser el ~ del cotarro*** be the leader of the pack
amoblado *S.Am.* **I** *adj* furnished **II** *m* furniture
amoblar ⟨1a⟩ *v/t S.Am.* furnish
amodorramiento *m* drowsiness
amodorrarse ⟨1a⟩ *v/r* feel sleepy
amolar ⟨1a⟩ *v/t*: ***~ a alguien*** F get on s.o.'s nerves, *Br* get up s.o.'s nose F; *de muelas, artritis etc* bother s.o., give s.o. trouble; ***¡no amueles!*** F you're jok-

ing!, you're kidding (me)! F; **amolarse** *v/r* grin and bear it
amoldar ⟨1a⟩ *v/t* adapt (***a*** to); **amoldarse** *v/r* adapt (***a*** to)
amonestación *f* **1** warning; DEP *tb* caution **2**: ***amonestaciones*** *pl* REL banns
amonestar ⟨1a⟩ *v/t* **1** *reñir* reprimand **2** DEP caution
amoniacal *adj* ammoniac(al)
amoníaco, amoniaco *m* ammonia
amonio *m* ammonium
amontillado *m* amontillado
amontonamiento *m* stack, pile; *de gente* crowd
amontonar ⟨1a⟩ *v/t* pile up; **amontonarse** *v/r de objetos, problemas* pile up; *de gente* crowd together
amor *m* **1** love; ***~ mío*** my love, darling; ***~ al prójimo*** love for one's fellow man; ***por ~ a alguien*** for the love of s.o.; ***por ~ al arte*** *fig* just for the fun of it; ***por ~ de Dios*** for God's sake; ***hacer el ~ a alguien*** *uso antiguo* court *o* woo s.o.
2 (*acto sexual*): ***hacer el ~*** make love; ***hacer el ~ con alguien*** make love to *o* with s.o.
3: ***de*** *o* ***con mil ~es*** with the greatest of pleasure
4: ***al ~ de la lumbre*** around the fire
◇ **amor brujo** true love
◇ **amor propio** self-respect
amoral *adj* amoral
amoratado *adj* bruised; ***~ de frío*** blue with cold
amordazar ⟨1f⟩ *v/t* gag; *animal, prensa* muzzle
amorfo *adj* shapeless
amorío *m* affair
amoroso *adj* amorous
amortajar ⟨1a⟩ *v/t* shroud
amortiguador *m* AUTO shock absorber
amortiguar ⟨1i⟩ *v/t impacto* cushion; *sonido* muffle
amortizable *adj* redeemable
amortización *f* repayment, redemption
amortizar ⟨1f⟩ *v/t* **1** pay off **2** COM *bienes* charge off, *Br* write off
amotinado I *adj* rebel *atr*, insurgent *atr* **II** *m*, **-a** *f* rebel, insurgent
amotinamiento *m* mutiny, uprising
amotinar ⟨1a⟩ *v/t* incite to rebellion *o* mutiny; **amotinarse** *v/r* rebel, mutiny
amp. *abr* (= ***amperios***) amp (= amperes)
amparar ⟨1a⟩ *v/t* protect; (*ayudar*) help; **ampararse** *v/r* seek shelter (***de*** from); ***~ en algo*** seek protection in sth
amparo *m* protection; (*cobijo*) shelter; ***al ~ de*** under the protection of
amperímetro *m* EL ammeter
amperio *m* EL ampere, amp
ampliable *adj contrato de trabajo, alquiler* renewable; ***es ~*** it can be extended
ampliación *f* **1** increase; *de negocio* expansion; *de plazo, edificio* extension **2** FOT enlargement, blow-up
◇ **ampliación de capital** COM increase in capital
ampliadora *f* FOT enlarger
ampliamente *adv* widely
ampliar ⟨1c⟩ *v/t* **1** *plantilla* increase; *negocio* expand; *plazo, edificio* extend; ***~ estudios*** continue one's education; ***~ sus horizontes*** broaden one's horizons **2** FOT enlarge, blow up; **ampliarse** *v/r* broaden
amplificación *f* amplification
amplificador *m* amplifier
amplificar ⟨1g⟩ *v/t* amplify
amplio *adj casa* spacious; *gama, margen* wide; *falda* full
amplitud *f* **1** breadth; ***~ de miras*** broadmindedness; ***~ de surtido*** COM range, choice **2** FÍS amplitude
ampolla *f* **1** MED blister; ***levantar ~s*** *fig* get people's backs up **2** (*botellita*) vial, ampoule, *Br* phial
ampollarse ⟨1a⟩ *v/r* blister
ampolleta *f Arg, Chi* light bulb
ampulosidad *f* pomposity, pompousness
ampuloso *adj* pompous
amputación *f* amputation
amputar ⟨1a⟩ *v/t brazo, pierna* amputate
amueblar ⟨1a⟩ *v/t* furnish
amuermar ⟨1a⟩ F *v/t* bore; **amuermarse** *v/r* be bored
amuleto *m* charm
amurallar ⟨1a⟩ *v/t* wall, build a wall around
anabaptista *m/f* REL Anabaptist
anabolizante *m* anabolic steroid
anacarado *adj* mother-of-pearl *atr*
anacardo *m* BOT cashew
anaconda *f* ZO anaconda
anacoreta *m/f* hermit

anacrónico *adj* anachronistic
anacronismo *m* anacronism
ánade *m* ZO duck
◇ **ánade real** mallard
◇ **ánade silbón** wigeon
anadón *m* duckling
anaerobio I *adj* anaerobic **II** *m* anaerobe
anagrama *m* anagram
anal *adj* anal
anales *mpl* annals
analfabetismo *m* illiteracy
analfabeto I *adj* illiterate **II** *m*, **-a** *f* illiterate
analgesia *f* MED analgesia
analgésico I *adj* painkilling, analgesic **II** *m* painkiller, analgesic
análisis *m inv* analysis
◇ **análisis de mercado** market research; **análisis de sangre** blood test; **análisis de sistemas** INFOR systems analysis
analista *m/f* analyst
◇ **analista programador** INFOR programmer-analyst
analítico *adj* analytic
analizar ⟨1f⟩ *v/t* analyze
analogía *f* analogy
analógico *adj* analog, *Br* analogue
análogo *adj* analogous
ananá(s) *m S.Am.* BOT pineapple
anaquel *m* shelf
anaranjado *adj* orangish
anarco *m/f* F anarchist
anarquía *f* anarchy
anárquico *adj* anarchic
anarquismo *m* anarchism
anarquista I *adj* anarchist *atr* **II** *m/f* anarchist
anatema *m* anathema
anatematizar ⟨1f⟩ *v/t* anathematize, condemn
anatomía *f* anatomy
anatómico *adj* anatomical; ***asiento ~*** AUTO ergonomically designed seat
anca *f* haunch
◇ **ancas de rana** GASTR frogs' legs
ancestral *adj* ancestral
ancestro *m* ancestor
ancho I *adj* **1** wide, broad **2** (*cómodo, tranquilo*): ***a sus -as*** at ease, relaxed; ***quedarse tan ~*** F carry on as if nothing had happened **3** (*orgulloso*): ***ponerse muy ~*** be very proud **4**: ***venir ~ a*** be too much for; ***le viene ~ el cargo*** the job is too much for her **II** *m* width; ***dos metros de ~*** two meters wide
◇ **ancho de banda** bandwidth
◇ **ancho de vía** FERR gauge
anchoa *f* anchovy
anchura *f* width, breadth
anciana *f* old woman
ancianidad *f* old age
anciano I *adj* old **II** *m* old man
ancla *f* MAR anchor; ***echar ~s*** drop anchor; ***levar ~s*** weigh anchor
anclado *adj*: ***estar ~*** MAR be at anchor; *fig* be rooted (***en*** in)
anclaje *m* **1** TÉC anchoring, fixing **2** MAR anchorage
anclar ⟨1a⟩ **I** *v/i* MAR anchor **II** *v/t* **1** TÉC anchor, fix **2** MAR anchor
áncora *f* anchor
andadas *fpl*: ***volver a las ~*** F fall back into one's old ways
andaderas *fpl* baby harness *sg*, reins *pl*
andador I *adj*: ***una persona ~a*** (*que anda mucho*) a person who walks a lot; (*que le gusta andar*) a person who is fond of walking **II** *m para bebé* baby walker; *para anciano* walker, Zimmer®
andadura *f* journey
andamiaje *m* (*conjunto de andamios*) scaffolding
andamio *m* scaffolding
◇ **andamio colgante** cradle
andante I *adj*: ***caballero ~*** knight errant **II** *m* MÚS andante
andanzas *fpl* adventures
andar ⟨1q⟩ **I** *v/i* **1** (*caminar*) walk; ***andando*** on foot; ***¡andando!*** come on!, move it! F
2 (*funcionar*) work
3: ***~ alegre / triste*** be happy / sad; ***~ bien / mal*** do well / badly; ***~ bien / mal de algo*** have a lot of / be short of sth; ***~ con cuidado*** be careful; ***~ con alguien*** mix with s.o., hang out with s.o. F; ***~ en algo*** (*buscar*) rummage in sth; ***~ en el cajón*** rummage around in the drawer; ***~ en*** *o* ***por los 30 años*** be around 30; ***~ tras algo*** be after sth F; ***~ haciendo algo*** be doing sth; ***~ a golpes, ~ a palos*** be always fighting; ***~ a una*** work together; ***¡anda!*** *sorpresa* wow!; *incredulidad* come on!
II *v/t* walk
III *m*: ***~es*** gait, walk

andarse *v/r*: **~ *con bromas*** kid around F; ***todo se andará*** F all will become clear
andariego *adj* fond of walking
andarín *adj* fond of walking
andarivel *m Rpl* DEP lane
andarríos *m* ZO sandpiper
andas *fpl*: ***llevar en ~*** carry on one's shoulders
andén *m* **1** platform **2** *L.Am.* sidewalk, *Br* pavement
Andes *mpl* Andes
andinismo *m L.Am.* mountaineering, climbing
andinista *m/f L.Am.* mountaineer, climber
andino *adj* Andean
Andorra *f* Andorra
andrajoso *adj* ragged
andrógino BIO **I** *adj* androgynous **II** *m*, **-a** *f* hermaphrodite
andurriales *mpl*: ***por estos ~*** F around here, in this neck of the woods F
anea *f* BOT cattail
anécdota *f* anecdote
anecdótico *adj* anecdotal
anegar ⟨1h⟩ *v/t* flood; **anegarse** *v/r de campo, terreno* be flooded; ***~ en llanto*** dissolve into tears
anejo I *adj* attached **II** *m* annex, *Br* annexe
anélidos *mpl* ZO annelids
anemia *f* MED anemia, *Br* anaemia
anémico *adj* anemic, *Br* anaemic
anemómetro *m* anemometer, wind gauge
anemona, anémona *f* BOT anemone
◇ **anemona de mar** ZO sea anemone
anestesia *f* MED anesthesia, *Br* anaesthesia
◇ **anestesia general** general anesthetic *o Br* anaesthetic
◇ **anestesia local** local anesthetic *o Br* anaesthetic
anestesiado *adj* anesthetized, *Br* anaesthetized, under F
anestesiar ⟨1b⟩ *v/t* anesthetize, *Br* anaesthetize
anestésico *m* anesthetic, *Br* anaesthetic
anestesista *m/f* anesthesiologist, *Br* anaesthetist
aneurisma *m* MED aneurism, aneurysm
anexar ⟨1a⟩ *v/t territorio* annex; *comentario* append
anexión *f* POL annexation
anexionar ⟨1a⟩ *v/t* POL annex
anexo I *adj* attached **II** *m edificio* annex, *Br* annexe
anfeta F, **anfetamina** *f* MED amphetamine, speed F
anfibio I *adj* amphibious; ***vehículo ~*** amphibious vehicle **II** *m* amphibian
anfiteatro *m* amphitheater, *Br* amphitheatre; *de teatro* dress circle
anfitrión *m* host
anfitriona *f* hostess
ánfora *f* **1** *L.Am.* POL ballot box **2** HIST amphora
anfractuoso *adj* rough, uneven
ángel *m* angel; ***tener ~*** (*tener gracia*) be witty; (*tener encanto*) have charm
◇ **ángel custodio** guardian angel; **ángel exterminador** *en Biblia* angel of death; **ángel de la guarda** guardian angel
angélica *f* BOT angelica
angelical *adj* angelic
angélico *adj* REL angelic
angelino I *adj* of / from Los Angeles, Los Angeles *atr* **II** *m*, **-a** *f* Angelino
angelito *m* little angel
angelote *m* angel
ángelus *m* angelus
angina *f* MED: **~*s*** *pl* sore throat *sg*, strep throat *sg*
◇ **angina de pecho** angina
angioma *m* MED angioma
anglicanismo *m* Anglicanism
anglicano I *adj* Anglican **II** *m*, **-a** *f* Anglican
anglicismo *m* Anglicism
angloamericano *adj* Anglo-American
anglófono *adj* English-speaking
angloparlante *adj* English-speaking
anglosajón I *adj* Anglo-Saxon **II** *m*, **-ona** *f* Anglo-Saxon
angoleño I *adj* Angolan **II** *m*, **-a** *f* Angolan
angora *f* angora; ***gato / conejo de Angora*** Angora cat / rabbit
angosto *adj* narrow
angostura *f* angostura
anguila *f* ZO eel
angula *f* ZO, GASTR elver
angular I *adj* angular; ***piedra ~*** cornerstone **II** *m* **1** TÉC angle iron **2** FOT: ***gran ~*** wide-angle lens *sg*

ángulo *m* MAT, *fig* angle
◇ **ángulo agudo** acute angle; **ángulo complementario** complementary angle; **ángulo obtuso** obtuse angle; **ángulo recto** right angle
anguloso *adj* angular
angustia *f* anguish
angustiado *adj* distraught
angustiante *adj* distressing
angustiar ⟨1b⟩ *v/t* distress; **angustiarse** *v/r* agonize (***por*** over)
angustioso *adj* agonizing
anhelante *adj* longing (***de*** for)
anhelar ⟨1a⟩ *v/t* long for
anhelo *m* longing, desire (***de*** for)
anheloso *adj* ☞ ***anhelante***
anhídrido *m* QUÍM anhydride
◇ **anhídrido carbónico** carbon dioxide
◇ **anhídrido sulfuroso** sulfur *o Br* sulphur dioxide
anidación *f* **1** nesting **2** MED implanting
anidar ⟨1a⟩ *v/i* nest; **anidarse** *v/r* MED implant
anilina *f* QUÍM aniline
anilla *f* **1** ring; ***cuaderno de ~s*** ring binder **2**: ***~s*** *pl* DEP rings
anillar ⟨1a⟩ *v/t* ring
anillo *m* ring; ***te viene como ~ al dedo*** F it suits you perfectly; ***no se te caerán los ~s*** it won't kill you
◇ **anillo de boda** wedding ring *o* band
ánima *f* **1** REL soul; ***~ en pena*** *fig* soul in torment **2** TÉC bore
◇ **ánima bendita, ánima del purgatorio** soul in purgatory
animación *f* **1** liveliness; ***hay mucha ~*** it's very lively **2** *en películas* animation
animado *adj* lively
animador *m* TV host
◇ **animador turístico** events organizer
animadora *f* **1** TV hostess **2** DEP cheerleader
animadversión *f* antagonism, hostility
animal I *adj* **1** animal *atr*; ***reino ~*** animal kingdom **2** *fig* stupid **II** *m tb fig* animal
◇ **animal de carga** beast of burden; **animal de compañía** pet; **animal de costumbres** *fig* creature of habit; **animal doméstico** *mascota* pet; *de granja* domestic animal; **animal experimental, animal de experimentación** laboratory animal; **animal de presa** predator
animalada *f*: ***decir / hacer una ~*** F say / do something nasty
animar ⟨1a⟩ *v/t* **1** cheer up **2** (*alentar*) encourage; **animarse** *v/r* cheer up; ***¿te animas?*** do you feel like it?, are you interested?
anímico *adj* mental; ***estado ~*** state of mind
ánimo *m* **1** spirit; ***tener ~s de*** *o* ***para*** feel up to **2** (*coraje*) encouragement; ***dar*** *o* ***infundir ~ a alguien*** give s.o. encouragement; ***¡~!*** cheer up! **3** (*mente*): ***presencia de ~*** presence of mind; ***estado de ~*** state of mind **4** (*intención*): ***con ~ de*** with the intention of
animosidad *f* animosity
animoso *adj* spirited
aniñado *adj* childlike
anión *m* anion
aniquilación *f*, **aniquilamiento** *m* annihilation
aniquilar ⟨1a⟩ *v/t* annihilate
anís *m* **1** BOT aniseed **2** *bebida* anisette
◇ **anís estrellado** star anis
anisado I *adj* aniseed-flavored, *Br* aniseed-flavoured **II** *m* anisette
anisete *m* anisette
aniversario *m* anniversary; ***~ de muerte*** anniversary of s.o.'s death; ***el quinto ~ de muerte del abuelo*** the fifth anniversary of grandfather's death
◇ **aniversario de boda** wedding anniversary
ano *m* ANAT anus
◇ **ano artificial, ano contra natura** colostomy
anoche *adv* last night; ***antes de ~*** the night before last
anochecer I ⟨2d⟩ *v/i* get dark; ***anocheció*** night fell, it got dark **II** *m* dusk; ***al ~*** at dusk, at nightfall
anodino *adj* anodyne; *fig* bland
ánodo *m* EL anode
anomalía *f* anomaly
anómalo *adj* anomalous
anonadar ⟨1a⟩ *v/t*: ***~ a alguien*** take s.o. aback
anonimato *m* anonymity; ***guardar*** *o* ***mantener el ~*** remain anonymous; ***salir del ~*** reveal one's identity; (*sobresalir*) emerge from obscurity
anónimo I *adj* anonymous **II** *m* poison pen letter
anorak *m* anorak

anorexia *f* MED anorexia
anoréxico *adj* anorexic
anormal *adj* abnormal
anormalidad *f* abnormality
anotación *f* note
anotado *adj* annotated
anotador *m*, **~a** *f* DEP scorer
anotar ⟨1a⟩ *v/t* note down; **anotarse** *v/r tanto*, *victoria* notch *o* rack up
anovulatorio *m* MED anovulant
anquilosarse ⟨1a⟩ *v/r* **1** get stiff, stiffen up **2** *fig*: *de planes*, *creación de empleo* grind to a halt
ánsar *m* ZO goose
ansia *f* **1** yearning; **~ de saber** thirst for knowledge; **~ de poder** desire *o* yearning for power **2** (*inquietud*) anxiety, anxiousness **3**: **~s** *pl* nausea *sg*
ansiar ⟨1b⟩ *v/t* yearn for, long for
ansiedad *f* anxiety
ansioso *adj* **1** anxious **2**: **está ~ por verlos** he's longing to see them; **~ de placer** anxious *o* eager to please
anta *f* *L.Am.* ZO tapir
antagónico *adj* conflicting
antagonismo *m* antagonism
antagonista *m/f* antagonist
antaño *adv* long ago
antártico *adj paisaje*, *fauna* Antarctic
Antártico *m* Antarctic
Antártida *f* Antarctica
anteanoche *adv* the night before last
anteayer *adv* the day before yesterday
antebrazo *m* forearm
antecámara *f* anteroom
antecedente I *adj* previous; **~ a** prior to **II** *m* **1** precedent; **sin ~s** unprecedented **2**: **poner a alguien en ~s** put s.o. in the picture, bring s.o. up to speed; **estar en ~s** be up to speed **3** JUR: **sin ~s** without precedent; **tener ~s** have a criminal record
◇ **antecedentes penales** previous convictions; **sin ~** without a criminal record
anteceder ⟨2a⟩ *v/t* precede, come before
antecesor *m*, **~a** *f* **1** predecessor **2** *familia* ancestor
antedatar ⟨1a⟩ *v/t* backdate
antedicho *adj* aforesaid, aforementioned
antediluviano *adj* prehistoric *hum*
antefechar ⟨1a⟩ *v/t* backdate
ante I *m* **1** suede **2** ZO moose **3** *Méx* (*postre*) *egg and coconut dessert* **II** *prp posición* before; *dificultad* faced with; **~ todo** above all
antelación *f*: **con ~** in advance; **con la debida ~** with plenty of notice; **con la mayor ~ posible** in plenty of time
antemano: **de ~** beforehand
antena *f* **1** TV, RAD antenna, *Br* aerial; **estar en ~** be on the air **2** ZO antenna
◇ **antena colectiva** communal antenna, *Br* communal aerial
◇ **antena parabólica** satellite dish
antenista *m/f* antenna *o Br* aerial installer
anteojeras *fpl inv* blinders, *Br* blinkers
antojitos *mpl Méx* snacks, appetizers
anteojos *mpl inv* **1** binoculars **2** *L.Am.* (*gafas*) glasses, eyeglasses
antepasado *m*, **-a** *f* ancestor; **~s** ancestors, forefathers
antepecho *m* **1** *de ventana* sill **2** (*barandilla*) parapet
antepenúltimo *adj* third last
anteponer ⟨2r⟩ *v/t*: **~ algo a algo** put sth before sth
anteproyecto *m* draft
anterior *adj* previous, former
anterioridad *f*: **con ~** before, previously; **con ~ a** before
anteriormente *adv* **1** previously, before; **sus amigos habían acudido ~ a la casa** his friends had gone to the house earlier *o* beforehand **2**: **~ a** prior to
antes I *adv* before; **cuanto ~**, **lo ~ posible** as soon as possible; **poco ~** shortly before; **~ que nada** first of all; **~ bien** on the contrary; **de ~** old **II** *prp*: **~ de** before; **~ de hora**, **~ de tiempo** early, ahead of time; **~ de llegar el tren** before the train arrived **III** *conj*: **~ de que** *subj* before
antesala *f* lobby; **hacer ~** hang around
antiabortista *m/f* right-to-lifer, anti-abortionist
antiadherente *adj* non-stick
antiaéreo I *adj* anti-aircraft *atr* **II** *m* anti-aircraft gun
antialérgico *adj* anti-allergy *atr*
antiarrugas *adj* antiwrinkle *atr*
antiautoritario *adj* antiauthoritarian
antibala(s) *adj* bulletproof; **cristal ~** bulletproof glass
antibelicista *adj* anti-war *atr*

antibiótico *m* antibiotic
antibloqueo *adj*: ***sistema ~ de frenos*** AUTO ABS
antichoque(s) *adj* shock-resistant
anticiclón *m* anticyclone
anticiclónico *adj* anticyclonic
anticipación *f* anticipation; ***con ~*** in advance
anticipadamente *adv pagar* in advance; *presentarse, reunirse* ahead of time
anticipado *adj pago* advance *atr*; *elecciones* early; ***por ~*** in advance
anticipar ⟨1a⟩ *v/t* **1** *sueldo* advance **2** *fecha, viaje* move up, *Br* bring forward **3** *información, noticias* give a preview of; **anticiparse** *v/r* **1** *de suceso* come early **2**: ***~ a alguien*** get there ahead of s.o.
anticipo *m* advance
anticlericalismo *m* anticlericalism
anticoncepción *f* contraception
anticonceptivo I *adj* contraceptive *atr* **II** *m* contraceptive
anticongelante *m* antifreeze
anticonstitucional *adj* unconstitutional
anticontaminante *adj* non-polluting, which does not harm the environment; *energía* clean
anticorrosivo *m/adj* anticorrosive
anticristo *m* Antichrist
anticuado *adj* antiquated
anticuario *m* antique dealer
anticuarse ⟨1d⟩ *v/r* become old-fashioned
anticuerpo *m* BIO antibody
antideportivo *adj* unsporting, unsportsmanlike
antidepresivo *m* antidepressant
antideslizante *adj* non-slip
antideslumbrante *adj* anti-glare
antidetonante AUTO **I** *adj* anti-knock *atr* **II** *m* anti-knock agent
antidisturbios *adj*: ***policía ~*** riot police
antidopaje, antidoping *adj*: ***control*** *o* ***prueba ~*** dope test, drugs test; ***dar positivo en el test ~*** fail the drugs test
antídoto *m* MED antidote; *fig* cure
antidroga *adj* drug *atr*; *campaña, proyecto* anti-drug
antieconómico *adj* uneconomic
antiespasmódico *adj* MED antispasmodic
antiestético *adj* unattractive, unesthetic, *Br* unaesthetic
antifascista *m/f & adj* anti-Fascist
antifaz *m* mask
antígeno *m* BIO antigen
antigripal *adj* influenza *atr*, flu *atr*
antigualla *f* F piece of old junk F; ***~s*** *pl* old junk F *sg*
antiguamente *adv* in the past
antigubernamental *adj* antigovernment
antigüedad *f* **1** age **2** *en el trabajo* length of service, seniority **3**: ***~es*** *pl* antiques
antiguo *adj* old; *del pasado remoto* ancient; ***su ~ novio*** her old *o* former boyfriend; ***a la -a*** in the old-fashioned way; ***edad -a*** ancient times *pl*
antihéroe *m* antihero
antihigiénico *adj* unhygienic
antiincendios *adj*: ***sistema ~*** fire detection and alarm system
antiinflacionista *adj* anti-inflation *atr*
antiinflamatorio *adj* MED anti-inflammatory
antillano *adj* West Indian
Antillas *fpl* West Indies; ***Grandes / Pequeñas Antillas*** Greater / Lesser Antilles
antílope *m* ZO antelope
antimateria *f* antimatter
antimilitarista *adj* antimilitarist
antimísil *m* antimissile
antimonio *m* QUÍM antimony
antinatural *adj* unnatural
antinuclear *adj* anti-nuclear *atr*
antioxidante *m/adj* antioxidant
antiparasitario I *adj*: ***producto ~*** antiparasitic product **II** *m* antiparasitic
antiparras *fpl* F specs F
antipatía *f* antipathy, dislike
antipático *adj* disagreeable, unpleasant
antipirético *m* MED antipyretic
antípodas *mpl* antipodes
antiquísimo *adj* incredibly ancient *o* old
antirreglamentario *adj* DEP *posición* offside; ***una jugada -a*** a foul
antirrobo *m* AUTO antitheft device
antisemita *m/f* anti-Semite
antisemítico *adj* anti-Semitic
antisemitismo *m* anti-Semitism
antiséptico *m/adj* antiseptic
antisida *adj* Aids *atr*; ***vacuna ~*** Aids vaccine
antisísmico *adj* earthquake-proof

antisocial *adj* antisocial
antitabaco *adj*: ***campaña ~*** anti-smoking campaign
antitérmico *m* MED antifebrile
antiterrorista *adj brigada* antiterrorist; ***la lucha ~*** the fight against terrorism
antítesis *f inv* antithesis
antivirus *adj*: ***programa ~*** INFOR virus program
antojadizo *adj*: ***ser ~*** want everything one sees
antojarse ⟨1a⟩ *v/r* **1** (*apetecer*): ***se le antojó salir*** he felt like going out **2** (*parecer*): ***se me antoja que …*** it seems to me that …; ***se me antoja que va a llover*** it looks like rain to me
antojo *m* whim; *de embarazada* craving; ***a mi ~*** as I please
antología *f* anthology; ***de ~*** *fig* F fantastic, incredible F
antónimo *m* antonym
antonomasia *f*: ***por ~*** par excellence
antorcha *f* torch
antracita *f* MIN anthracite
ántrax *m* MED anthrax
antro *m* F dive F, dump F
antropofagia *f* cannibalism
antropófago *m*, **-a** *f* cannibal
antropología *f* anthropology
antropólogo *m*, **-a** *f* anthropologist
antropomorfo *adj* anthropomorphic
anual *adj* annual
anualidad *f* annual payment
anualmente *adv* yearly
anuario *m* yearbook
anubarrado *adj* cloudy, overcast
anudar ⟨1a⟩ *v/t* knot; *corbata* knot, tie; ***anudado a mano*** *alfombra*, *moqueta* hand-knotted; **anudarse** *v/r fig*: ***se le anudaba la garganta*** he got a lump in his throat; *de miedo* he found it difficult to swallow
anulación *f* cancellation; *de matrimonio* annulment
anular[1] ⟨1a⟩ *v/t* cancel; *matrimonio* annul; *gol* disallow; *ley repeal*
anular[2] *adj* ring-shaped; ***dedo ~*** ring finger
anunciación *f* **1** announcement **2** REL: ***Anunciación*** Annunciation
anunciante *m/f* COM advertiser
anunciar ⟨1b⟩ *v/t* **1** announce **2** COM advertise; **anunciarse** *v/r* **1** take out a newspaper advertisement, advertise **2** *en forma de comunicado* be announced
anuncio *m* **1** announcement **2** (*presagio*) sign **3** COM advertisement; ***sección de ~s*** advertisement section; ***~ luminoso*** illuminated sign
◊ **anuncios clasificados** classified advertisements *o* ads, *Br* small ads F
◊ **anuncios por palabras** classified advertisements *o* ads, *Br* small ads F
anverso *m* obverse
anzuelo *m* (fish) hook; ***echar el ~*** cast; ***morder*** *o* ***tragar el ~*** *fig* F take the bait
añada *f* year
añadido I *adj* added **II** *m* extra piece
añadidura *f*: ***por ~*** in addition
añadir ⟨3a⟩ *v/t* add
añejo *adj* mature
añicos *mpl*: ***hacer ~*** F smash to smithereens; ***estar hecho ~*** *fig* be shattered
añil *m* indigo
año *m* **1** year; ***~ tras ~*** year after year; ***el ~ que viene*** next year; ***el ~ pasado*** last year; ***los ~s veinte*** the twenties; ***¡por muchos ~s!*** long may it last!; ***ser del ~ de la nanita*** *o* ***de la pera*** F be as old as the hills
2 *de edad*: ***cumplir diez ~s*** be ten (years old), turn ten; ***¿cuándo cumples ~s?*** when's your birthday?; ***¿cuántos ~s tienes?*** how old are you?; ***a los diez ~s*** at the age of ten; ***a mis ~s*** at my age; ***entrado*** *o* ***metido en ~s*** elderly; ***quitarse ~s*** claim to be younger than one is; ***por ti no pasan los ~s*** you don't seem to age at all
◊ **año bisiesto** leap year; **año civil** calendar year; **año eclesiástico** ecclesiastic year; **año fiscal** fiscal year, *Br* tax year; **año litúrgico** ecclesiastic year; **año luz** light year; ***estar a años luz*** be light years ahead; **año nuevo** New Year; ***día de Año Nuevo*** New Year's Day; **año sabático** sabbatical
añoranza *f* yearning, longing (**de** for)
añorar ⟨1a⟩ *v/t* miss
añublo *m* AGR rust
aorta *f* ANAT aorta
aovar ⟨1a⟩ *v/i* lay eggs
apabullante *adj* overwhelming
apabullar ⟨1a⟩ *v/t* overwhelm
apacentar ⟨1k⟩ *v/t* graze
apache *m/f* & *adj* Apache
apacible *adj* mild-mannered

apaciguador *adj* pacifying
apaciguar ⟨1i⟩ *v/t* pacify, calm down; **apaciguarse** *v/r* calm down
apadrinar ⟨1a⟩ *v/t* **1** be godparent to **2**: **~ *a la novia*** give the bride away **3** *político* support, back **4** *artista etc* sponsor
apagado *adj* **1** *fuego* out; *luz* off **2** *persona* dull **3** *color* subdued
apagador *m* **1** snuffer **2** *Méx* EL switch
apagar ⟨1h⟩ *v/t televisor, luz* turn off; *fuego* put out; *vela* snuff, put out; ***apaga y vámonos*** we may as well call it a day; **apagarse** *v/r de luz* go off; *de fuego* go out
apagón *m* blackout
apaisado *adj* landscape *atr*
apalabrar ⟨1a⟩ *v/t* agree (verbally); **apalabrarse** *v/r* reach an agreement
apalancar ⟨1g⟩ *v/t* lever; **apalancarse** *v/r* F settle
apaleamiento *m* beating
apalear ⟨1a⟩ *v/t* beat; ***ha sido apaleada por la vida*** she's had a hard life
apañado **I** *adj* F resourceful **II** *part* ☞ ***apañar***
apañar ⟨1a⟩ *v/t* **1** tidy up **2** *aparato* repair **3** *resultado* rig F, fix F **4**: ***estamos apañados*** F we've had it F; **apañarse** *v/r* manage; ***apañárselas*** manage, get by
apaño *m fig* F makeshift repair
aparador *m* **1** sideboard **2** *Méx* (*escaparate*) store window, *Br* shop window
aparato *m* **1** piece of equipment; *doméstico* appliance; ***al ~*** TELEC speaking **2** BIO, ANAT system **3** *de partido político* machine
◇ **aparato administrativo** state machinery; **aparato circulatorio** ANAT circulatory system; **aparato digestivo** digestive system; **aparato respiratorio** respiratory system; **aparato locomotor** ANAT skeletomuscular system
aparatosidad *f* **1** *de vestido, collar* fanciness **2** *de caída* spectacular nature **3** *de vendaje, armazón* bulkiness
aparatoso *adj* **1** *vestido, collar* fancy **2** *caída* spectacular **3** *vendaje, armazón* bulky
aparcacoches *m inv* valet
aparcamiento *m* parking lot, *Br* car park
◇ **aparcamiento subterráneo** underground parking garage, *Br* underground car park
aparcar ⟨1g⟩ **I** *v/t* **1** park; ***~ en batería*** angle park; ***~ en línea*** parallel park; ***~ en doble fila*** double park **2** *tema, proyecto* shelve **II** *v/i* park
aparcería *f* AGR sharecropping
aparcero *m*, **-a** *f* AGR sharecropper
apareamiento *m* ZO mating
aparear ⟨1a⟩ ZO *v/t* mate; **aparearse** *v/r* mate
aparecer ⟨2d⟩ *v/i* appear; **aparecerse** *v/r* turn up
aparecido *m* ghost
aparejado *part* ☞ ***aparejar***
aparejador *m*, **~a** *f architectural technician*, *Br* quantity surveyor
aparejar ⟨1a⟩ *v/t* **1** prepare **2** *caballo* saddle **3** MAR rig **4**: ***traer*** *o* ***llevar aparejado*** entail, bring with it
aparejo *m* **1** preparation **2** MAR rigging **3**: **~s** *pl* tack *sg*
◇ **aparejos de pesca** fishing gear *sg*
aparentar ⟨1a⟩ *v/t* **1** pretend; ***~ hacer algo*** pretend to do sth **2**: ***no aparenta la edad que tiene*** she doesn't look her age
aparente *adj* **1** (*evidente*) apparent **2** *L.Am.* (*fingido*) feigned
aparentemente *adv* apparently
aparición *f* **1** appearance; ***hacer su ~*** make one's appearance **2** (*fantasma*) apparition
apariencia *f* appearance; ***en ~*** outwardly; ***las ~s engañan*** appearances can be deceptive; ***salvar las ~s*** keep up appearances; ***según todas las ~s*** judging by appearances
apart(h)otel *m* apartment hotel
apartadero *m* FERR siding
apartado **I** *adj* isolated **II** *m* section
◇ **apartado de correos** P.O. Box
apartamento *m Esp* apartment, *Br* flat
apartamiento *m* **1** separation **2** *L.Am.* (*apartamento*) apartment, *Br* flat
apartar ⟨1a⟩ *v/t* **1** separate; *para después* set *o* put aside; *de un sitio* move away (**de** from) **2**: ***~ a alguien de hacer algo*** dissuade s.o. from doing sth; **apartarse** *v/r* move aside (**de** from); ***~ del camino*** leave the main road; ***~ del tema*** stray from the subject; ***no se aparta de mi lado*** he won't move from my side, F he sticks like glue; ***¡apártate!*** move!
aparte **I** *adv* **1** to one side; ***llevar a al-***

guien ~ take s.o. aside *o* to one side **2** (*por separado*) separately **3**: ***~ de*** aside from, *Br* apart from; ***~ de guapa, es rica*** she's not only pretty, she's rich too, she's rich as well as pretty; ***~ de que*** apart from the fact that
II *m* **1** TEA aside **2** TIP new line; ***punto y ~*** new paragraph

apasionado I *adj* passionate **II** *m/f* enthusiast

apasionamiento *m* passion

apasionante *adj* fascinating

apasionar ⟨1a⟩ *v/t* fascinate; **apasionarse** *v/r* develop a passion (***por*** for)

apatía *f* apathy

apático *adj* apathetic

apátrida *adj* stateless

apdo. *abr* (= ***apartado (de correos)***) P.O. Box (= Post Office Box)

apeadero *m* FERR halt

apear ⟨1a⟩ *v/t* **1** get … off **2**: ***~ a alguien del cargo*** remove s.o. from their position; **apearse** *v/r* get off, alight *fml*; ***~ de algo*** get off sth, alight from sth *fml*

apechar *vb* ☞ ***apechugar***

apechugar ⟨1h⟩ *v/i*: ***~ con algo*** cope with sth

apedrear ⟨1a⟩ *v/t* throw stones at; *matar* stone (to death)

apegado *adj*: ***~ a alguien / algo*** be attached to s.o. / sth

apego *m* attachment

apelable *adj* JUR appealable

apelación *f* JUR, DEP appeal; ***interponer ~*** appeal

apelar ⟨1a⟩ *v/t tb* JUR appeal (***a*** to)

apelativo *m* form of address; ***~ cariñoso*** pet name

apellidarse ⟨1a⟩ *v/r*: ***¿cómo se apellida?*** what's your / his / her surname?; ***se apellida Ocaña*** his / her surname is Ocaña

apellido *m* surname
◇ **apellido de soltera** maiden name

apelmazado *adj lana* matted; *arroz* stodgy

apelmazarse ⟨1f⟩ *v/r de lana* get matted; *de arroz* stick together

apelotonarse ⟨1a⟩ *v/r* crowd together

apenado *adj* **1** sad **2** *L.Am.* (*avergonzado*) ashamed **3** *L.Am.* (*incómodo*) embarrassed **4** *L.Am.* (*tímido*) shy

apenar ⟨1a⟩ *v/t* sadden; **apenarse** *v/r* **1** be upset *o* distressed **2** *L.Am.* (*avergonzarse*) be ashamed **3** *L.Am.* (*sentirse incómodo*) be embarrassed **4** *L.Am.* (*ser tímido*) be shy

apenas I *adv* hardly, scarcely; ***falta ~ una hora*** there's barely an hour left; ***la película ha comenzado hace ~ unos minutos*** the movie started just a few minutes ago, the movie has only just started; ***~ nada*** hardly anything **II** *conj* as soon as

apéndice *m* appendix
◇ **apéndice cecal, apéndice vermiforme** vermiform appendix

apendicitis *f* MED appendicitis

apercibimiento *m* warning

apercibir ⟨3a⟩ *v/t* warn (***de*** of); **apercibirse** *v/r*: ***~ de algo*** notice sth

apergaminado *adj fig* wrinkled

aperitivo *m* **1** *comida* appetizer **2** *bebida* aperitif

apero *m* **1** *utensilio* implement **2** *L.Am.* (*arneses*) harness
◇ **aperos de labranza** farming implements

apertura *f* **1** opening **2** FOT aperture **3** POL opening up

apesadumbrado *adj* heavy-hearted

apesadumbrar ⟨1a⟩ *v/t* sadden; **apesadumbrarse** *v/r* be saddened

apestado *part* ☞ ***apestar***

apestar ⟨1a⟩ **I** *v/t* stink out F **II** *v/i* reek, stink (***a*** of); ***huele que apesta*** it stinks

apestoso *adj* smelly

apetecer ⟨2d⟩ **I** *v/i*: ***me apetece ir a dar un paseo*** I feel like going for a walk; ***¿qué te apetece?*** what do you feel like? **II** *v/t*: ***me apetece una cerveza*** I feel like a beer

apetecible *adj* appetizing

apetito *m* appetite; ***falta de ~*** lack of appetite

apetitoso *adj* appetizing

API *m/f abr* (= ***agente de la propiedad inmobiliaria***) realtor, real estate agent, *Br* estate agent

apiadarse ⟨1a⟩ *v/r* take pity (***de*** on)

ápice *m*: ***ni un ~*** *fig* not an ounce; ***no ceder ni un ~*** *fig* not give an inch; ***no falta un ~*** not a thing is *o* absolutely nothing is missing

apícola *adj* beekeeping *atr*

apicultor *m*, ***~a*** *f* beekeeper

apicultura *f* beekeeping

apilar ⟨1a⟩ *v/t* pile up; **apilarse** *v/r* pile up
apiñado *adj* packed, squashed
apiñar ⟨1a⟩ *v/t* pack, squash; **apiñarse** *v/r* crowd together, squash together
apio *m* BOT celery
apiolar ⟨1a⟩ *v/t* F bump off F
apisonadora *f* steamroller
apisonar ⟨1a⟩ *v/t* roll
aplacar ⟨1g⟩ *v/t* **1** *hambre* satisfy; *sed* quench **2** *a alguien* calm down, placate *fml*; **aplacarse** *v/r* calm down, die down
aplanado *part* ☞ **aplanar**
aplanadora *f L.Am.* steamroller
aplanar ⟨1a⟩ *v/t* **1** level, flatten **2** *C.Am., Pe*: **~ las calles** hang around the streets; **aplanarse** *v/r fig* (*descorazonarse*) lose heart
aplastante *adj* overwhelming; *calor* suffocating; ***una mayoría ~*** an overwhelming majority
aplastar ⟨1a⟩ *v/t tb fig* crush
aplaudida *f L.Am.* applause
aplaudir ⟨3a⟩ **I** *v/i* applaud, clap **II** *v/t tb fig* applaud
aplauso *m* round of applause
aplazable *adj* which can be postponed
aplazamiento *m de visita, viaje* postponement
◇ **aplazamiento de pago** deferred terms *pl*
aplazar ⟨1f⟩ *v/t* **1** *visita, viaje* put off, postpone **2** *Arg* fail
aplicable *adj* applicable
aplicación *f* application
aplicado *adj* hard-working
aplicar ⟨1g⟩ *v/t* apply; *sanciones* impose; **aplicarse** *v/r* apply o.s.
aplique *m* wall light
aplomado *adj* self-assured, composed
aplomo *m* composure, aplomb
apnea *f* MED apnea, *Br tb* apnoea; ***~ del sueño*** sleep apnea
apocado *adj* timid
Apocalipsis *f* Apocalypse
apocalíptico *adj* apocalyptic
apocar ⟨1g⟩ *v/t* daunt; **apocarse** *v/r* be intimidated, be daunted
apócrifo *adj* apocryphal
apodado *part* ☞ **apodar**
apodar ⟨1a⟩ *v/t* nickname, call; **apodarse** *v/r* be nicknamed *o* called
apoderado *m*, **-a** *f* COM agent
apoderamiento *m* authorization
apoderar ⟨1a⟩ *v/t* authorize; **apoderarse** *v/r* take possession *o* control (***de*** of); ***se apoderó de todo el dinero*** he took all the money
apodo *m* nickname
apogeo *m fig* height, peak; ***estar en su ~*** be at its height
apolillado *adj* moth-eaten
apolillarse ⟨1a⟩ *v/r* get moth-eaten
apolíneo *adj fig* handsome
apolítico *adj* apolitical
apolo *m fig* Greek god
apologético *adj* apologetic
apología *f* defense, *Br* defence
apologista *m/f* apologist
apoltronarse ⟨1a⟩ *v/r en asiento* settle down; *en trabajo, rutina* get into a rut
apoplejía *f* MED apoplexy; ***ataque de ~*** stroke; ***~ cerebral*** stroke
apoquinar ⟨1a⟩ *v/t & v/i* F cough up F
aporrear ⟨1a⟩ *v/t* pound on
aportación *f* **1** contribution **2** COM investment
aportar ⟨1a⟩ *v/t* contribute; ***~ pruebas*** JUR provide evidence; ***~ al matrimonio*** JUR bring to the marriage
aposentar ⟨1a⟩ *v/t* settle; **aposentarse** *v/r* settle in
aposento *m* room, chamber
aposición *f* GRAM apposition
apósito *m* dressing
aposta *adv* on purpose, deliberately
apostante *m person who places a bet*, *Br* punter
apostar ⟨1m⟩ **I** *v/t* bet (***por*** on); ***~ doble contra sencillo*** bet double or quits; ***¿qué apostamos?*** do you want to bet? **II** *v/i* **1** bet **2**: ***~ por algo*** opt for sth; ***~ fuerte por*** be firmly in favor of; **apostarse** *v/r* MIL position o.s.
apostasía *f* apostasy
apóstata *m/f* apostate
a posteriori *adj & adv* a posteriori
apostilla *f* comment, note
apostillar ⟨1a⟩ *v/t* add
apóstol *m* **1** apostle **2** *fig*: *de la paz, la solidaridad etc* advocate
apostolado *m* ministry
apostólico *adj* apostolic
apóstrofe, apóstrofo *m* apostrophe
apoteósico *adj* spectacular
apoteosis *f fig* climax, apotheosis *fml*
apoyabrazos *m inv* armrest

apoyacabezas *m inv* headrest
apoyar ⟨1a⟩ *v/t* **1** lean (***en*** against), rest (***en*** against) **2** (*respaldar, confirmar*) support; **apoyarse** *v/r* **1** lean (***en*** on; ***contra*** against) **2** *en persona* rely (***en*** on) **3**: ***¿en qué te apoyas para decir eso?*** what are you basing that comment on?
apoyatura *f* MÚS appoggiatura
apoyo *m fig* support; ***en ~ de*** in support of
apreciable *adj* **1** (*visible*) appreciable, noticeable **2** (*considerable*) considerable, substantial
apreciación *f* appreciation
apreciado *adj* valued
apreciar ⟨1b⟩ *v/t* **1** appreciate **2** (*sentir afecto por*) be fond of, think highly of; **apreciarse** *v/r* FIN appreciate
apreciativo *adj* appreciative
aprecio *m* respect; ***tener un gran ~ por alguien*** have a great deal of respect for s.o.
aprehender ⟨2a⟩ *v/t* apprehend, capture
aprehensión *f* capture, seizure
apremiante *adj* pressing, urgent
apremiar ⟨1b⟩ **I** *v/t* pressure, put pressure on **II** *v/i*: ***el tiempo apremia*** time is pressing
apremio *m* pressure, harassment; ***~ de tiempo*** pressure of time
aprender ⟨2a⟩ *v/t* learn; ***~ a leer / conducir*** learn to read / drive; ***~ de la experiencia*** learn from experience; **aprenderse** *v/r* learn; ***se aprendió la lección*** he learned his lesson; ***~ algo de memoria*** learn sth (off) by heart
aprendiz *m*, **~a** *f* apprentice, trainee; ***estar de ~*** be a trainee
aprendizaje *m* **1** apprenticeship; ***puesto o plaza de ~*** apprenticeship **2**: ***capacidad de ~*** ability to learn
aprensión *f* **1** (*miedo*) apprehension **2** (*asco*) squeamishness; ***me da ~ hacerlo*** I don't like the thought of doing it
aprensivo *adj* apprehensive
apresamiento *m* **1** MAR seizure **2** *de ladrón, animal* capture
apresar ⟨1a⟩ *v/t* **1** *nave* seize **2** *ladrón, animal* catch, capture
aprestarse ⟨1a⟩ *v/r*: ***~ a*** get ready to
apresurado *adj* quick, rushed
apresuramiento *m* hurry, haste
apresurar ⟨1a⟩ *v/t* hurry; **apresurarse** *v/r* hurry up; ***~ a hacer algo*** hurry *o* rush to do sth
apretado *adj* **1** tight **2**: ***iban muy ~s en el coche*** they were very cramped *o* squashed in the car
apretar ⟨1k⟩ **I** *v/t* **1** *botón* press; ***apretó contra el pecho la fotografía / el niño*** she held the photograph / the child close, she pressed the photograph / the child to her breast; ***~ los puños*** clench one's fists; ***~ los dientes*** grit one's teeth
2 (*pellizcar, pinzar*) squeeze
3 *tuerca* tighten
4: ***~ el paso*** quicken one's pace
II *v/i* **1** *de ropa, zapato* be too tight **2**: ***~ a correr*** start to run, start running
apretarse *v/r* **1** squeeze *o* squash together **2**: ***~ el cinturón*** *fig* tighten one's belt
apretón *m* squeeze
◇ **apretón de manos** handshake
apretujar ⟨1a⟩ *v/t* F squeeze, squash; **apretujarse** *v/r* F squash *o* squeeze together
apretujón *m* F hug
apretura *f* crush
aprieto *m* predicament; ***poner a alguien en un ~*** put *o* place s.o. in a predicament
a priori *adj & adv* a priori
aprisa *adv* quickly
aprisco *m* fold, pen
aprisionar ⟨1a⟩ *v/t fig* trap
aprobación *f* approval; *de ley* passing
aprobado I *adj* passed **II** *m* EDU pass
aprobar ⟨1m⟩ *v/t* **1** approve; *comportamiento, idea* approve of; *ley* pass **2** *examen* pass
aprobatorio *adj* approving *atr*
aprontar ⟨1a⟩ *Rpl v/t* get ready; **aprontarse** *v/r* get ready
apropiación *f* appropriation
◇ **apropiación indebida** JUR misappropriation
apropiado *adj* appropriate, suitable
apropiarse ⟨1b⟩ *v/r*: ***~ de algo*** take sth
aprovechable *adj* usable
aprovechado I *adj desp* opportunistic **II** *m*, **-a** *f desp* opportunist
aprovechamiento *m* exploitation, use; ***~ de residuos*** waste recycling
aprovechar ⟨1a⟩ **I** *v/t* **1** take advantage

of **2** *tiempo, espacio* make good use of; ***quiero ~ la ocasión para ...*** I would like to take this opportunity to ... **II** *v/i* **1** take the opportunity (***para*** to) **2**: ***¡que aproveche!*** enjoy your meal!; **aprovecharse** *v/r* take advantage (***de*** of)

aprovisionamiento *m* provisioning, supply

aprovisionar ⟨1a⟩ *v/t* provision, supply; **aprovisionarse** *v/r* stock up (***de*** on)

aproximación *f* **1** approximation **2** (*acercamiento*) approach **3** *en lotería* consolation prize (*won by those with numbers immediately before and after the winning number*)

aproximadamente *adv* approximately

aproximado *adj* approximate

aproximar ⟨1a⟩ *v/t* bring closer; **aproximarse** *v/r* approach; ***~ a la verdad*** get close to the truth; ***~ a los setenta*** be approaching seventy; ***se aproxima el invierno*** winter is coming

aproximativo *adj* approximate, rough

aptitud *f* aptitude (***para*** for), flair (***para*** for)

apto *adj* **1** suitable (***para*** for); ***~ para menores*** *película* suitable for underage children; ***~ para todos los públicos*** G (general audiences), *Br* universal **2** *para servicio militar* fit **3** EDU pass

apuesta *f* bet

apuesto *adj* handsome

apunado *adj Andes* suffering from altitude sickness

apunamiento *m Andes* altitude sickness

apunarse ⟨1a⟩ *v/r Andes* get altitude sickness

apuntado *part* ☞ **apuntar**

apuntador *m*, **~a** *f* TEA prompter

apuntalar ⟨1a⟩ *v/t edificio* shore up; *fig* prop up

apuntar ⟨1a⟩ **I** *v/t* **1** (*escribir*) note down, make a note of **2** TEA prompt **3** *en curso, para viaje etc* put one's name down (***en, a*** on; ***para*** for) **4**: ***~ con el dedo*** point at *o* to
II *v/i* **1** *con arma* aim; ***~ alto*** *fig* aim high, have big ambitions **2**: ***apunta el día*** *lit* day is breaking
apuntarse *v/r* **1** put one's name down (***en, a*** on; ***para*** for); ***~ a la victoria*** take all the credit; ***¡me apunto!*** count me in! **2**: ***~ un tanto*** score a point

apunte *m* note; **~s** *pl* EDU notes; ***tomar ~s*** take notes

apuñalar ⟨1a⟩ *v/t* stab

apurado *adj* **1** *L.Am.* (*con prisa*) in a hurry; ***ir ~ de tiempo*** be pressed for time, be short of time **2** (*pobre*) short (of cash); ***ir ~ de dinero*** be short of cash, be strapped for cash; ***estoy ~*** F I'm struggling

apurar ⟨1a⟩ **I** *v/t* **1** *vaso* finish off **2** *a alguien* pressure, put pressure on **II** *v/i Chi*: ***no me apura*** I'm not in a hurry for it; **apurarse** *v/r* **1** worry; ***¡no te apures!*** don't worry! **2** *L.Am.* (*darse prisa*) hurry (up); ***¡no te apures!*** there's no rush

apuro *m* **1** predicament, tight spot F; ***sacar a alguien de un ~*** F get s.o. out of trouble *o* a jam F; ***en caso de ~*** in case of trouble **2** (*estrechez, necesidad*): ***pasar ~s*** suffer hardship **3** (*compromiso*): ***poner a alguien en un ~*** put s.o. in an awkward situation **4** (*vergüenza*) embarrassment; ***me da ~*** I'm embarrassed **3** *L.Am.* (*prisa*) rush

aquaplaning *m* hydroplaning, *Br* aquaplaning

aquejado *adj*: ***estar ~ de*** be suffering from

aquejar ⟨1a⟩ *v/t* afflict; ***le aqueja una rara enfermedad*** he suffers from *o* is afflicted with a rare disease

aquél, aquélla, aquéllos, aquéllas *pron singular* that (one); *plural* those (ones)

aquel, aquella, aquellos, aquellas *det singular* that; *plural* those

aquelarre *m* witches' sabbath

aquello *pron* that

aquí *adv* **1** *en el espacio* here; ***desde ~*** from here; ***por ~*** here; ***¡ven ~!*** come here!; ***ir de ~ para allá*** go backwards and forwards; *ociosamente* wander around; ***he ~*** this / that is **2** *en el tiempo* now; ***de ~ en adelante*** from now on; ***de ~ que ocurra*** by the time it happens; ***de ~ a ocho días*** within the next week, by next week

aquiescente *adj* acquiescent

aquietarse ⟨1a⟩ *v/r* calm down

ara *f* **1** altar **2**: ***en ~s de*** in the interests of

árabe I *m/f* & *adj* Arab **II** *m idioma* Ara-

bic
arabesco I *adj* Arabic **II** *m* arabesque
Arabia Saudí *f* Saudi Arabia
arábico, arábigo *adj* Arabic
arabista *m/f* Arabist
arable *adj* arable; ***suelo ~*** arable land
arácnidos *mpl* ZO arachnids
arado *m* plow, *Br* plough
arador *m* ZO mite
arancel *m* tariff
arancelario *adj* tariff *atr*; ***barreras -as*** tariff barriers
arándano *m* blueberry
arandela *f* washer
araña *f* **1** ZO spider **2** *lámpara* chandelier
◇ **araña de mar** ZO spider crab
arañar ⟨1a⟩ *v/t* scratch; **arañarse** *v/r* scratch (***con*** on); ***se arañó los brazos con las ramas*** he scratched his arms on the branches
arañazo *m* scratch
arar ⟨1a⟩ *v/t* plow, *Br* plough
arbitraje *m* **1** arbitration **2** DEP refereeing
arbitral *adj* arbitration *atr*
arbitrar ⟨1a⟩ *v/t* **1** *en conflicto* arbitrate **2** *en fútbol, boxeo* referee; *en tenis, béisbol* umpire
arbitrariedad *f* arbitrariness
arbitrario *adj* arbitrary
árbitro *m* **1** *en fútbol, boxeo* referee; *en tenis, béisbol* umpire **2** *en conflicto* arbitrator
◇ **árbitro asistente** DEP assistant referee
árbol *m* **1** tree **2** TÉC shaft
◇ **árbol caducifolio** deciduous tree; **árbol de la ciencia** tree of knowledge; **árbol de hoja caduca** deciduous tree; **árbol de levas** camshaft; **árbol de Navidad** Christmas tree; **árbol genealógico** family tree
arbolado I *adj* wooded **II** *m* woodland
arboladura *f* MAR spars *pl*
arbolar ⟨1a⟩ *v/t* MAR mast, fit the mast on
arboleda *f* grove
arbóreo *adj* **1** tree *atr*, arboreal **2** *zona* wooded
arboricultor *m*, **~a** *f* forest worker
arboricultura *f* forestry
arbotante *m* ARQUI flying buttress
arbusto *m* shrub, bush
arca *f* chest
◇ **arca de la alianza** REL Ark of the Covenant
◇ **arca de Noé** Noah's Ark
arcada *f* MED: ***me provocó ~s*** it made me retch *o* heave F
arcaico *adj* archaic
arcaísmo *m* archaism
arcángel *m* archangel
arce *m* BOT maple
arcén *m* shoulder, *Br* hard shoulder
archiconocido *adj* extremely well known
archidiócesis *f inv* archdiocese
archifamoso *adj* super famous
archipiélago *m* archipelago
archisabido *adj* very well known
archivador *m* file cabinet, *Br* filing cabinet
archivar ⟨1a⟩ *v/t* **1** *papeles, documentos* file **2** *asunto* shelve
archivero *m*, **-a** *f* archivist
archivo *m* **1** archive **2** INFOR file
arcilla *f* clay
arcilloso *adj* clayey
arcipreste *m* archpriest
arco *m* **1** ARQUI arch **2** MÚS bow **3** *para tirar flechas* bow **4** *L.Am.* DEP goal
◇ **arco iris** rainbow; **arco de medio punto** round arch; **arco ojival** gothic arch; **arco triunfal** triumphal arch; **arco voltaico** electrical arc
arcón *m* chest
arder ⟨2a⟩ *v/i* **1** burn; **~ *de*** *o* ***en*** be burning with **2** *estar muy caliente* be exceedingly hot; ***la reunión está que arde*** F the meeting is about to erupt F
ardid *m* trick, ruse
ardiente *adj* **1** *persona, amor* passionate; *defensor* ardent **2** *bebida* scalding
ardilla *f* ZO squirrel
ardor *m* *entusiasmo* fervor, *Br* fervour; ***en el ~ de la batalla*** *o* ***disputa*** in the heat of battle
◇ **ardor de estómago** heartburn
ardoroso *adj* ardent, passionate
arduo *adj* arduous
área *f* area; ***~ de influencia*** area of influence
◇ **área de castigo** DEP penalty area; **área de descanso** rest area, *Br* lay-by; **área de embarque** AVIA departure lounge; **área grande** *en fútbol* eighteen-yard box; **área metropolitana**

metropolitan area; **área de no fumar** no-smoking area; **área operativa** *de policía* area, *Br* F patch; **área de penalty** DEP penalty area; **área pequeña** *en fútbol* six-yard box; **área de servicio** service area
arena *f* **1** sand **2** TAUR, *de gladiadores* arena
◇ **arenas movedizas** quicksand *sg*
arenal *m* sandy area
arenga *f* morale-boosting speech; (*sermón*) harangue
arengar ⟨1h⟩ *v/i* harangue
arenilla *f* **1** grit, sand **2**: **~s** *pl* MED gravel *sg*
arenisca *f* MIN sandstone
arenoso *adj* sandy
arenque *m* herring
◇ **arenque ahumado** kipper
aréola *f*, **areola** *f* ANAT, MED areola
arepa *f C.Am., Ven cornmeal roll*
arete *m L.Am. joya* earring
argamasa *f* mortar
Argel *m* Algiers
Argelia *f* Algeria
argelino I *adj* Algerian **II** *m*, **-a** *f* Algerian
argénteo *adj* silver *atr*
argentífero *adj* silver-bearing
Argentina *f* Argentina
argentino I *adj* Argentinian **II** *m*, **-a** *f* Argentinian
argolla *f L.Am.* ring
argón *m* QUÍM argon
argot *m* slang
argucia *f* clever argument
argüir ⟨3g⟩ *v/t & v/i* argue
argumentación *f* argumentation
argumentar ⟨1a⟩ *v/t* argue
argumento *m* **1** *razón* argument **2** *de libro, película etc* plot
aria *f* aria
ariano *L.Am.* **I** *adj* Arian; ***ser ~*** be (an) Aries, be (an) Arian **II** *m*, **-a** *f* Aries, Arian
aridez *f* aridity, dryness
árido *adj* arid, dry; *fig* dry
Aries ASTR **I** *adj* Arian; ***soy ~*** I'm (an) Arian, I'm (an) Aries **II** *m/f inv* Aries
ariete *m* **1** HIST battering ram **2** DEP striker
arisco *adj* unfriendly
arista *f* **1** MAT edge **2** BOT beard
aristocracia *f* aristocracy
aristócrata *m/f* aristocrat
aristocrático *adj* aristocratic
aritmética *f* arithmetic
arma *f* weapon; ***alzarse en ~s*** rise up in arms; ***tomar las ~s*** take up arms; ***llamar a las ~*** call to arms; ***pasar por las ~s*** shoot; ***presentar ~*** present arms; ***de ~s tomar*** *fig* F formidable
◇ **arma blanca** knife; **armas de destrucción masiva** weapons of mass destruction, WMDs; **arma de doble filo, arma de dos filos** *fig* two-edged sword; **arma de fuego** firearm; **arma punzante** sharp weapon; **armas nucleares** nuclear weapons
armada *f* **1** navy **2** HIST: ***la Armada*** the (Spanish) Armada
armadillo *m* ZO armadillo
armado *adj* armed
armador *m*, **~a** *f* MAR shipowner
armadura *f* **1** armor, *Br* armour **2** TÉC framework
armamentista, armamentístico *adj* armaments *atr*, arms *atr*
armamento *m* armaments *pl*
armar ⟨1a⟩ *v/t* **1** MIL arm **2** TÉC assemble, put together **3**: ***~ un escándalo*** F kick up a fuss F, make a scene F; ***~la*** cause trouble; **armarse** *v/r* **1** arm o.s. **2**: ***~ de valor*** pluck up courage; ***~ de paciencia*** be patient **3**: ***la que se va a armar*** F all hell will break loose F, the shit will really hit the fan P
armario *m* closet, wardrobe; *de cocina* cabinet, *Br* cupboard
◇ **armario de luna** closet *o Br* wardrobe with mirrors
◇ **armario ropero** closet, *Br* wardrobe
armatoste *m* F huge thing
armazón *f* skeleton, framework; *Rpl* (*de gafas*) frame
armería *f* gunstore
armero *m* gunsmith
armiño *m* **1** ZO stoat **2** *piel* ermine
armisticio *m* armistice
armonía *f* harmony
armónica *f* harmonica, mouth organ
armónico I *adj* harmonic **II** *m* MÚS harmonic
armonio *m* MÚS harmonium
armonioso *adj* harmonious
armonizar ⟨1f⟩ **I** *v/t* harmonize; *diferencias* reconcile **II** *v/i* **1** *de color, estilo* blend (**con** with) **2** *de persona* get on

(**con** with)
arnés *m* **1** harness **2** *para niños* leading strings *pl*, *Br* leading reins *pl* **3**: ***arneses*** *pl* tack *sg*
árnica *f* BOT arnica
aro *m* **1** hoop; ***entrar*** *o* ***pasar por el ~*** *fig* F bite the bullet, knuckle under; ***hacer pasar a alguien por el ~*** make s.o. knuckle under *o* toe the line **2** *L.Am.* (*pendiente*) earring
aroma *m* aroma; *de flor* scent
aromaterapia *f* aromatherapy
aromático *adj* aromatic
aromatizar ⟨1f⟩ *v/t* perfume
arpa *f* harp
arpegiar ⟨1a⟩ *v/i* MÚS play an arpeggio
arpegio *m* MÚS arpeggio
arpía *f* harpy
arpista *m/f* harpist
arpón *m* harpoon
arponear ⟨1a⟩ *v/t* harpoon
arponero *m* harpooner
arqueado *adj* curved; ***tener las piernas -as*** be bowlegged
arquear ⟨1a⟩ *v/t* *espalda* arch; *cejas* raise; ***~ el lomo de*** *gato* arch its back; **arquearse** *v/r de balda* bend, sag; ***se le está arqueando la espalda*** he's becoming stooped *o* hunched
arqueo *m* **1** MAR capacity **2** COM: ***~ (de caja)*** cashing up
arqueología *f* archeology, *Br tb* archaeology
arqueológico *adj* archeological, *Br tb* archaeological
arqueólogo *m*, **-a** *f* archeologist, *Br tb* archaeologist
arquería *f* ARQUI arcade
arquero *m* **1** archer **2** *L.Am. en fútbol* goalkeeper
arqueta *f* small chest
arquetipo *m* archetype
arquitecto *m*, **-a** *f* architect
arquitectónico *adj* architectural
arquitectura *f* architecture
arquitrabe *m* ARQUI architrave
arrabal *m* poor outlying area
arrabalero *adj* of / from a poor outlying area
arraigado *adj* entrenched
arraigar ⟨1h⟩ *v/i* take root; **arraigarse** *v/r de persona* settle (**en** in); *de costumbre, idea* take root
arraigo *m*: ***tener ~*** be deep-rooted
arramblar ⟨1a⟩ *v/t* (*destruir*) destroy
arrancada *f*: ***pegar una ~, salir en una ~*** pull away quickly
arrancado *part* ☞ ***arrancar***
arrancar ⟨1g⟩ **I** *v/t* **1** *planta, página* pull out **2** *vehículo* start (up) **3** (*quitar*) snatch; ***le ~on el bolso*** they snatched her purse **II** *v/i* **1** *de vehículo, máquina* start (up) **2** INFOR boot (up) **3**: ***~ a hacer algo*** start to do sth, start doing sth **4** *Chi* (*huir*) run away; **arrancarse** *v/r* **1** *Chi* run away **2**: ***~ por sevillanas*** start dancing a *sevillana*
arranque *m* **1** AUTO starter (motor); ***no hay ningún problema con el ~*** there's no problem starting it **2** INFOR start (-up), boot **3** (*energía*) drive **4** (*ataque*) fit
◇ **arranque en frío** INFOR cold start *o* boot
arras *fpl* **1** *en una boda* coins (*given by the bridegroom to the bride*) **2** (*depósito*) deposit
arrasar ⟨1a⟩ **I** *v/t* devastate **II** *v/i* F be a big hit
arrastrado **I** *adj* wretched, miserable **II** *part* ☞ ***arrastrar***
arrastrar ⟨1a⟩ **I** *v/t* **1** *por el suelo*, INFOR drag (**por** along) **2** (*llevarse*) carry away **II** *v/i* **1** *por el suelo* trail on the ground **2** *en juegos de cartas* draw trumps; **arrastrarse** *v/r* crawl; *fig* (*humillarse*) grovel, crawl (***delante de*** to)
arrastre *m*: ***estar para el ~*** *fig* F be fit to drop F
arrayán *m* BOT myrtle
arre *int* gee up!
arreada *f Rpl* round-up
arrear ⟨1a⟩ **I** *v/t* **1**: ***~ una bofetada a alguien*** thump s.o. F, hit s.o. **2** *el ganado* drive **II** *v/i*: ***¡arrea!*** F get on with it!
arrebatado *part* ☞ ***arrebatar***
arrebatador *adj* breathtaking, dazzling
arrebatamiento *m* anger
arrebatar ⟨1a⟩ *v/t* snatch (***a*** from); ***el ladrón le arrebató el bolso*** the thief snatched her purse
arrebato *m* fit; ***~ de cólera*** fit of rage
arrebujarse ⟨1a⟩ *v/r* F wrap o.s. up; *en cama* snuggle up
arrechucho *m* F **1** (*ataque*) fit **2**: ***me dio un ~*** *indisposición* I felt strange
arreciar ⟨1b⟩ *v/i de tormenta* get worse; *de viento* get stronger

arrecife *m* reef
◇ **arrecife de coral** coral reef
arredrar ⟨1a⟩ *v/t* intimidate; **arredrarse** *v/r* be intimidated (***ante*** by)
arreglado I *adj* **1** *casa, escritorio etc* neat **2** (*bien vestido*) well-groomed **3**: ***si empieza a llover estamos ~s*** *irón* if it starts to rain, that'll be just dandy **II** *part* ☞ ***arreglar***
arreglar ⟨1a⟩ *v/t* **1** (*reparar*) fix, repair **2** (*ordenar*) tidy (up) **3** (*solucionar*) sort out; ***~ cuentas*** settle up; *fig* settle scores **4** MÚS arrange **5**: ***¡ya te arreglaré yo!*** *amenaza* I'll show you!, I'll soon settle your hash! F
arreglarse *v/r* **1** get (o.s.) ready **2** *de problema* get sorted out; ***¡todo se arreglará!*** everything will work out **3**: ***el tiempo se arregla*** it's clearing up **4** (*apañarse*) manage; ***arreglárselas*** manage; ***¡arréglate como puedas!*** you'll just have to manage!, you'll just have to sort something out!; ***~ con algo*** get by with sth, make do with sth
arreglista *m/f* MÚS arranger
arreglo *m* **1** (*reparación*) repair **2** (*solución*) solution; ***esto no tiene ~*** there's nothing to be done; ***no tienes ~*** you're the limit, you're impossible **3** (*acuerdo*) arrangement, agreement **4** MÚS arrangement **5**: ***con ~ a*** in accordance with **6** F *amoroso* affair
◇ **arreglo de cuentas** settling of scores
arrejuntarse ⟨1a⟩ *v/r* F shack up (together) F
arrellanarse ⟨1a⟩ *v/r* settle
arremangarse ⟨1h⟩ *v/r* roll up one's sleeves
arremeter ⟨2a⟩ *v/i*: ***~ contra*** charge (at); *fig* (*criticar*) attack
arremetida *f* MIL charge
arremolinarse ⟨1a⟩ *v/r* mill around
arrendajo *m* ZO (blue) jay
arrendamiento *m* renting; ***dar en ~*** rent (out); ***tomar en ~*** rent
arrendar ⟨1k⟩ *v/t* *L.Am.* **1** (*dar en alquiler*) rent (out), let; ***se arrienda*** for rent **2** (*tomar en alquiler*) rent
arrendatario *m*, **-a** *f* tenant
arreo *m* **1** *Rpl* driving, herding **2** *Rpl* (*manada*) herd **3**: ***~s*** *pl* tack *sg*
arrepentido *part* ☞ ***arrepentirse***
arrepentimiento *m* **1** repentance **2** (*cambio de opinión*) change of heart
arrepentirse ⟨3i⟩ *v/r* **1** be sorry; ***~ de algo*** regret sth; ***estar arrepentido de algo*** regret sth, be sorry for sth **2** (*cambiar de opinión*) change one's mind, have a change of heart
arrestado I *adj* arrested, under arrest **II** *part* ☞ ***arrestar***
arrestar ⟨1a⟩ *v/t* arrest
arresto *m* **1** arrest; ***orden de ~*** arrest warrant **2**: ***~s*** *pl* spirit *sg*, daring *sg*
◇ **arresto domiciliario** house arrest
arriar ⟨1c⟩ *v/t* lower, strike; ***~ velas*** lower *o* strike the sails
arriba I *adv* **1** *situación* up; ***ponlo ahí ~*** put it up there; ***el cajón de ~*** *siguiente* the next drawer up, the drawer above; *último* the top drawer; ***más ~*** higher (up), further up; ***~ del todo*** right at the top; ***las plantas de ~*** the top floors; ***los de ~*** the ones on top; ***~ mencionado*** above-mentioned; ***véase ~*** see above; ***de*** *o* ***desde ~*** from above; ***~ de*** above; (*encima de*) on top of; ***volver lo de ~ abajo*** turn everything upside down
2 *en edificio* upstairs; ***vete ~*** go upstairs
3 *dirección* up; ***sigan hacia ~*** keep going up; ***me miró de ~ abajo*** *fig* she looked me up and down
4 *con cantidades*: ***de diez para ~*** ten or above; ***de cincuenta (años) para ~*** over 50, 50 and over
II *prp*: ***~ de*** *L.Am.* on, on top of
III *interj*: ***¡~!*** long live …!
arribada *f*, **arribaje** *m* MAR arrival
arribar ⟨1a⟩ *v/i* MAR arrive, put in
arribeño *m*, **-a** *f* *L.Am.* uplander, highlander
arribismo *m* social climbing
arribista *m/f* social climber, arriviste
arriesgado *adj* risky
arriesgar ⟨1h⟩ *v/t* risk; **arriesgarse** *v/r* take a risk; ***~ a hacer algo*** risk doing sth
arrimar ⟨1a⟩ *v/t* move closer; ***~ el hombro*** F pull one's weight; **arrimarse** *v/r* move closer (***a*** to); ***~ al sol que más calienta*** swim with the tide
arrinconar ⟨1a⟩ *v/t* **1** (*acorralar*) corner **2** *libros etc* put away **3** *persona* cold-shoulder
arritmia *f* MED arrhythmia
arroba *f* INFOR at sign, @; ***josé ~…*** josé

at …
arrocero I *adj* rice-growing *atr* II *m*, **-a** *f* rice grower
arrodillarse ⟨1a⟩ *v/r* kneel (down)
arrogancia *f* arrogance
arrogante *adj* arrogant
arrogarse ⟨1h⟩ *v/r* assume
arrojadizo *adj*: ***arma -a*** throwing weapon
arrojado I *adj* brave, daring II *part* ☞ ***arrojar***
arrojar ⟨1a⟩ *v/t* **1** (*lanzar*) throw **2** *resultado* produce **3** (*vomitar*) throw up; **arrojarse** *v/r* throw o.s; ***~ por la ventana*** throw o.s. out of the window
arrojo *m* bravery, daring
arrolladito *m Rpl*: ***~ de primavera*** spring roll
arrollador *adj* overwhelming
arrollar ⟨1a⟩ *v/t* **1** AUTO run over **2** *fig* crush, overwhelm
arropar ⟨1a⟩ *v/t* wrap up; *fig* protect; ***arropado por*** protected by; **arroparse** *v/r* cover o.s. up, wrap up
arrope *m Rpl*, *Chi*, *Pe* fruit syrup
arroyo *m* stream; ***sacar a alguien del ~*** *fig* pull s.o. out of the gutter
arroz *m* rice
◇ **arroz integral** brown rice; **arroz largo** long-grain rice; **arroz con leche** rice pudding
arrozal *m* ricefield, paddy
arruga *f* wrinkle
arrugado *adj* wrinkled
arrugar ⟨1h⟩ *v/t* wrinkle; ***~ el ceño*** *o* ***la frente*** frown; **arrugarse** *v/r de piel*, *ropa* get wrinkled
arruinado *adj* ruined, broke F
arruinar ⟨1a⟩ *v/t* ruin; **arruinarse** *v/r* be ruined
arrullar ⟨1a⟩ I *v/t* (*adormecar*) to lull to sleep II *v/i de paloma* coo
arrullo *m* **1** *de paloma* cooing **2** *para niño* lullaby
arrumaco *m* F: ***~s*** kissing and cuddling; ***hacer ~s*** bill and coo
arrumbar ⟨1a⟩ I *v/t* put away II *v/i* MAR: ***~ hacia el norte*** steer a course north
arsenal *m* arsenal
arsénico *m* arsenic
art *abr* (= ***artículo***) art. (= article)
arte *m* (*pl f*) **1** art; ***bellas ~s*** *pl* fine art *sg*; ***el séptimo ~*** cinema, the movies *pl*; (***como***) ***por ~ de magia*** as if by magic; ***no tener ~ ni parte*** have absolutely no say **2** (*argucia*): ***malas ~s*** *pl* guile *sg*
◇ **arte dramático** dramatic art; **artes de pesca** fishing tackle *sg*; **artes plásticas** plastic arts
artefacto *m* (*dispositivo*) device
artemisa *f* BOT artemisia
arteria *f* artery
arterial *adj* arterial; ***tensión ~*** blood pressure
arterio(e)sclerosis *f* arteriosclerosis
artero *adj* artful, cunning
artesa *f* trough
artesana *f* craftswoman
artesanado *m* craftspeople *pl*
artesanal *adj* craft *atr*
artesanía *f* (handi)crafts *pl*
artesano *m* craftsman
artesiano *adj*: ***pozo ~*** artesian well
artesonado I *adj* coffered II *m* coffering
ártico *adj paisaje*, *fauna* Arctic
Ártico *m zona*, *océano* Arctic
articulación *f* **1** ANAT, TÉC joint **2** *de sonidos* articulation
articulado I *adj* **1** *lenguaje* articulated **2** TÉC: ***tren ~*** articulated train II *mpl*: ***~s*** ZO articulate animals
articular I *adj* ANAT of the joint II ⟨1a⟩ *v/t* **1** TÉC articulate **2** *palabras* articulate, say
articulista *m/f* columnist
artículo *m* **1** *de periódico*, GRAM, JUR article **2** COM product, item; ***~s de escritorio*** stationery *sg*
◇ **artículo de consumo** consumer item; **artículo de fe** article of faith; **artículo de fondo** editorial; **artículo de lujo** luxury item; **artículo de primera necesidad** essential (item); **artículos de marca** brand goods
artífice *m/f* author
artificial *adj* artificial
artificio *m* **1** trick **2** (*artefacto*) device
artificioso *adj* **1** sly **2** (*falto de naturalidad*) affected, contrived
artillería *f* artillery
◇ **artillería antiaérea** antiaircraft guns *pl*; **artillería ligera** light artillery; **artillería pesada** heavy artillery
artillero *m* artillery gunner
artilugio *m aparato* gadget
artimaña *f* trick
artista *m/f* artist; ***~ de circo*** circus performer

artístico *adj* artistic
artritis *f* MED arthritis
artrópodos *mpl* ZO arthropods
artroscopia *f* MED arthroscopy
artrosis *f* MED rheumatoid arthritis
arveja *f Rpl, Chi, Pe* BOT pea
arzobispado *m* archbishopric
arzobispal *adj* archbishop's, archiepiscopal
arzobispo *m* archbishop
as *m tb fig* ace; ***~ del volante*** ace driver
asa *f* handle
asadera *f CSur* roasting dish
asadero *m* griddle; *fig* F oven F
asado I *adj* roast *atr* **II** *m* **1** roast **2** *Rpl* (*barbacoa*) barbecue
asador *m* rotisserie
asadura *f* offal
asaetear ⟨1a⟩ *v/t*: ***~ a*** *o* ***con preguntas*** bombard with questions
asalariado *m*, **-a** *f* **1** wage earner **2** *de empresa* employee
asaltante *m/f* assailant
asaltar ⟨1a⟩ *v/t* **1** *persona* attack; *banco* rob **2** *fig*: ***le asaltó una duda*** he was suddenly struck by doubt
asalto *m* **1** *a persona* attack (***a*** on); *robo* robbery, raid; ***tomar por ~*** take by storm **2** *en boxeo* round
asamblea *f* **1** *reunión* meeting **2** *ente* assembly
◇ **asamblea general** general meeting; **asamblea general anual** COM stockholders' meeting, *Br* annual general meeting; **asamblea plenaria** plenary session; **asamblea de trabajadores** employees' meeting, *Br* works meeting
asambleísta *m/f* assembly member
asar ⟨1a⟩ *v/t* roast; ***~ a la parrilla*** broil, *Br* grill; **asarse** *v/r fig* F be roasting F
asaz *adv lit* extremely
asbesto *m* MIN asbestos
ascendencia *f* ancestry
ascendente I *adj* rising, upward **II** *m* ASTR ascendant
ascender ⟨2g⟩ **I** *v/t a empleado* promote **II** *v/i* **1** *de precios, temperatura etc* rise **2** *de montañero* climb **3** DEP, *en trabajo* be promoted (***a*** to)
ascendiente *m/f* ancestor
ascensión *f* ascent
◇ **ascensión al trono** ascent to the throne
Ascensión *f* REL Ascension
ascenso *m* **1** *de temperatura, precios* rise (***de*** in) **2** *de montaña* ascent **3** DEP, *en trabajo* promotion
ascensor *m* elevator, *Br* lift
ascensorista *m/f* elevator operator, *Br* lift operator
asceta *m/f* ascetic
ascético *adj* ascetic
ascetismo *m* asceticism
asco *m* disgust; ***me da ~*** I find it disgusting; ***¡qué ~!*** how revolting *o* disgusting!; ***estar hecho un ~*** be a real mess; ***morirse de ~*** be bored to death; ***no hacer ~s a*** not turn one's nose up at
ascua *f* ember; ***estar en*** *o* ***sobre ~s*** be on tenterhooks; ***tener a alguien sobre ~s*** keep s.o. in suspense *o* on tenterhooks; ***arrimar el ~ a su sardina*** *fig* work things to one's own advantage
aseado *adj* clean
asear ⟨1a⟩ *v/t* clean; **asearse** *v/r* wash up, *Br* have a wash
asechanza *f* trap
asediar ⟨1b⟩ *v/t tb fig* besiege
asedio *m* **1** MIL siege, blockade **2** *a alguien* hounding
asegurado I *adj* insured **II** *m*, **-a** *f* insured
asegurador I *adj* insurance *atr* **II** *m* insurer
aseguradora *f* **1** insurance company **2** *persona* insurer
asegurar ⟨1a⟩ *v/t* **1** (*afianzar*) secure **2** (*prometer*) assure; ***te lo aseguro*** I assure you **3** (*garantizar*) guarantee **4** COM insure; ***~ algo contra incendios*** insure sth against fire, take out fire insurance on sth; **asegurarse** *v/r* make sure
asemejarse ⟨1a⟩ *v/r*: ***~ a*** look like
asentaderas *fpl* F behind, rear end F
asentado *adj* **1** located, situated **2** (*establecido*) settled
asentamiento *m* settlement
asentar ⟨1k⟩ *v/t* **1** *refugiados* place, settle **2** *objeto* place; **asentarse** *v/r* settle
asentimiento *m* approval, agreement
asentir ⟨3i⟩ *v/i* **1** agree (***a*** to), consent (***a*** to) **2** *con la cabeza* nod
aseo *m* **1** cleanliness **2** (*baño*) restroom, *Br* toilet
◇ **aseo personal** personal hygiene
asepsia *f* asepsis
aséptico *adj* aseptic

asequible *adj* **1** *precio* affordable **2** *obra* accessible
aserción *f* assertion
aserradero *m* sawmill
aserrar ⟨1k⟩ *v/t* saw
aserrín *m L.Am.* sawdust
asesinar ⟨1a⟩ *v/t* murder; POL assassinate
asesinato *m* murder; POL assassination
asesino *m*, **-a** *f* murderer; POL assassin
◇ **asesino en serie** serial killer
◇ **asesino a sueldo** hired killer, hitman
asesor I *adj* advisory **II** *m*, **~a** *f* consultant, advisor, *Br* adviser
◇ **asesor financiero** financial advisor *o Br* adviser; **asesor fiscal** tax advisor *o Br* adviser; **asesor de imagen** public relations consultant, image consultant; **asesor jurídico** legal advisor *o Br* adviser
asesoramiento *m* advice; ***~ de empresas*** management consultancy
asesorar ⟨1a⟩ *v/t* advise; **asesorarse**: ***~ con alguien*** consult s.o.
asesoría *f* consultancy
asestar ⟨1a⟩ *v/t golpe* deal (***a*** to); ***me asestó una puñalada*** he stabbed me
asexual *adj* asexual
asfaltado I *adj* asphalted **II** *m* asphalting
asfaltadora *f* asphalting machine
asfaltar ⟨1a⟩ *v/t* asphalt
asfalto *m* asphalt
asfixia *f* asphyxiation, suffocation
asfixiante *adj* asphyxiating, suffocating
asfixiar ⟨1b⟩ *v/t* asphyxiate, suffocate; **asfixiarse** *v/r* asphyxiate, suffocate
así I *adv* **1** (*de este modo*) like this; ***~ de grande*** this big; ***~ o asá*** this way or that (way)
2 (*de ese modo*) like that; ***una cosa ~*** a thing like that, something like that; ***soy ~ (yo)*** that's how I am; ***una casa ~*** a house like that; ***~ es*** that's right; ***~ no más*** *S.Am.* just like that; ***~ como ~*** just like that; ***~ ~*** so-so
II *conj*: ***~ como*** *al igual que* while, whereas; ***~ y todo*** even so; ***~ pues*** so; ***~ que*** so; ***~ (es) que*** so that's how, so that's why; ***¿~ que no vienes?*** so you're not coming?; ***tanto es ~, que*** ... and (as a result) ...; ***... tanto es ~, que varias estaciones han cerrado*** ... and (as a result) a number of stations are closed
Asia *f* Asia
◇ **Asia Menor** Asia Minor
asiático I *adj* Asian **II** *m*, **-a** *f* Asian
asidero *m* handle
asiduidad *f* frequency; ***con ~*** *con frecuencia* regularly
asiduo *adj* regular; ***cliente ~*** regular customer
asiento *m* **1** seat; ***tomar ~*** take a seat **2** COM entry
◇ **asiento del acompañante** front passenger seat; **asiento abatible** folding seat; **asiento catapulta** AVIA ejector seat; **asiento del conductor** driver's seat; **asiento delantero** front seat; **asiento eyectable** AVIA ejector seat; **asiento de pasillo** aisle seat; **asiento trasero** back seat; **asiento de ventanilla** window seat
asignación *f* **1** *acción* allocation **2** *dinero* allowance
asignar ⟨1a⟩ *v/t* allocate; *persona, papel* assign
asignatura *f* EDU subject
◇ **asignatura facultativa** elective *o* optional subject; **asignatura obligatoria** compulsory *o* required subject; **asignatura optativa** elective *o* optional subject; **asignatura pendiente** EDU failed subject; *asunto* unfinished business, unresolved matter
asilado *m*, **-a** *f* POL asylum seeker
asilarse ⟨1a⟩ *v/r* POL seek asylum
asilo *m* **1** home, institution **2** POL asylum; ***derecho de ~*** right to asylum; ***solicitante de ~*** asylum seeker
◇ **asilo de ancianos** retirement home, old people's home
asilvestrarse ⟨1a⟩ *v/r* go wild
asimetría *f* assymetry
asimétrico *adj* asymmetrical
asimilable *adj* which can be assimilated, assimilable
asimilación *f* assimilation
asimilar ⟨1a⟩ *v/t* assimilate; **asimilarse** *v/r*: ***~ a*** resemble
asimismo *adv* **1** (*también*) also **2** (*igualmente*) in the same way, likewise
asintomático *adj* MED asymptomatic
asir ⟨3a; asgo, ases⟩ *v/t* grab (hold of); **asirse** *v/r*: ***~ de*** grab onto, grab hold of
asistemático *adj* unsystematic
asistencia *f* **1** (*ayuda*) assistance; ***~ a***

(los) ancianos home help (for the elderly) **2** *a lugar* attendance (**a** at); **récord de ~** attendance record; **~ a las urnas** voter turnout **3** DEP assist
◇ **asistencia en carretera** AUTO roadside assistance; **asistencia a domicilio** home help; **asistencia jurídica** legal aid; **asistencia médica** medical care; **asistencia social** social work; **asistencia técnica** technical support
asistenta *f* cleaner, cleaning woman
asistente *m/f* **1** (*ayudante*) assistant **2**: **los ~s** *pl* those present
◇ **asistente social** social worker
asistir ⟨3a⟩ **I** *v/t* help, assist **II** *v/i* be present; **~ a una boda** go to a wedding; **~ a clase** attend class, go to class
asma *m o f* asthma
asmático *adj* asthmatic
asno *m* **1** ZO donkey **2** *persona* idiot
asociación *f* association; **~ de ideas** association of ideas
◇ **asociación de consumidores** consumer association; **asociación empresarial** employers' association; **asociación de padres de alumnos** parent-teacher association, PTA; **asociación profesional** professional association; **asociación de vecinos** residents' association
asociado *m*, **-a** *f* member
asocial *adj* antisocial
asociar ⟨1b⟩ *v/t* associate; **~ a alguien con algo** associate s.o. with sth; **asociarse** *v/r* **1** team up (**con** with), go into partnership (**con** with) **2**: **~ a** *grupo, club* become a member of, join
asolador *adj* devastating
asolar ⟨1m⟩ *v/t* devastate
asoleada *f*: **pegarse una ~** *Bol, Pe* sunbathe
asolearse ⟨1a⟩ *v/r L.Am.* sunbathe
asomar ⟨1a⟩ **I** *v/t* put *o* stick out **II** *v/i* show; **asomarse** *v/r* lean out; **~ a** *o* **por la ventana** lean out of the window
asombrado *adj* amazed
asombrar ⟨1a⟩ *v/t* amaze, astonish; **asombrarse** *v/r* be amazed *o* astonished
asombro *m* amazement, astonishment; **no salía de su ~** he couldn't get over his amazement *o* astonishment
asombroso *adj* amazing, astonishing
asomo *m*: **ni por ~** no way
asonante *adj rima* assonant
asorocharse ⟨1a⟩ *v/r Pe, Bol* get altitude sickness
aspa *f de molino* sail; *de ventilador* blade
aspavientos *mpl* waving *sg*, flapping *sg*; **hacer muchos ~** wave *o* flap one's arms wildly
aspecto *m* **1** *de persona, cosa* look, appearance; **tener buen ~** look good; **tener ~ de ser / estar** seem (to be); **tenía ~ de ser una persona simpática** he seemed (to be) *o* he looked a nice guy **2** (*faceta*) aspect
aspereza *f* roughness, unevenness; **limar ~s** knock the rough edges off
áspero *adj* **1** *superficie* rough **2** *sonido* harsh **3** *persona* abrupt
aspersión *f* **1** AGR sprinkler system **2** REL sprinkling with holy water
aspersor *m* sprinkler
◇ **aspersor para césped** lawn sprinkler
◇ **aspersor circular** rotary sprinkler
áspid *m* ZO asp
aspiración *f* **1** TÉC draft, aspiration **2** GRAM aspiration
aspiraciones *fpl* aspirations
aspirado **I** *adj*: **sonido ~** GRAM aspirated sound **II** *part* ☞ **aspirar**
aspirador *m*, **~a** *f* vacuum cleaner; **pasar la ~** vacuum
aspirante **I** *adj* aspiring **II** *m/f a cargo* candidate (**a** for); *a título* contender (**a** for)
aspirar ⟨1a⟩ **I** *v/t* **1** suck up **2** *al respirar* inhale, breathe in **II** *v/i*: **~ a** aspire to
aspirina *f* aspirin
asqueado *adj* disgusted
asquear ⟨1a⟩ *v/t* disgust
asquerosidad *f* **1** filthiness **2**: **es una ~** it is disgusting
asqueroso **I** *adj* **1** (*sucio*) filthy **2** (*repugnante*) revolting, disgusting **II** *m*, **-a** *f* creep
asta *f* **1** flagpole, flagstaff; **a media ~** at half-staff, *Br* at half-mast **2** (*pitón*) horn; **dejar a alguien en las ~s del toro** drop s.o. right in it F
astenia *f* asthenia
aster *m* BOT aster
asterisco *m* asterisk
astigmatismo *m* astigmatism
astilla *f* **1** splinter **2**: **~s** *pl para fuego*

kindling *sg*; ***hacer ~s algo*** *fig* smash sth to pieces **3**: ***~s*** *pl fig* F bribe *sg*, kickback F *sg*
astillar ⟨1a⟩ *v/t* splinter; **astillarse** *v/r* splinter
astillero *m* shipyard
astracán *m* astrakhan
astrágalo *m* ANAT astragalus, anklebone
astral *adj* astral
astringente *m/adj* astringent
astro *m* AST, *fig* star; ***~ de la pantalla*** movie star, film star
◇ **astro rey** sun
astrofísica *f* astrophysics *sg*
astrofísico *m*, **-a** *f* astrophysicist
astrología *f* astrology
astrólogo *m*, **-a** *f* astrologer
astronauta *m/f* astronaut
astronáutica *f* space travel, astronautics *sg fml*
astronave *f* spaceship
astronomía *f* astronomy
astronómico *adj* astronomical
astrónomo *m*, **-a** *f* astronomer
astucia *f* shrewdness, astuteness
Asturias: ***el Príncipe de ~*** *title conferred on the king of Spain's eldest son*
astuto *adj* shrewd, astute
asueto *m* time off; ***día de ~*** day off, rest day
asumir ⟨3a⟩ *v/t* **1** assume **2** (*aceptar*) accept, come to terms with
asunceno I *adj* of / from Asunción, Asunción *atr* **II** *m*, **-a** *f* native of Asunción
Asunción *f* **1** REL Assumption **2** GEOG Asunción
asunción *f* assumption; ***bajo la ~ de que*** on the assumption that
asunto *m* **1** matter; ***mal ~*** that's bad (news); ***no es ~ tuyo*** it's none of your business **2** F (*relación*) affair
◇ **asunto de Estado** matter of State
◇ **asuntos exteriores** foreign affairs
asustadizo *adj* easily frightened
asustar ⟨1a⟩ *v/t* frighten, scare; **asustarse** *v/r* be frightened *o* scared
atacante *m/f* **1** attacker, assailant **2** DEP forward
atacar ⟨1g⟩ **I** *v/t* **1** attack; ***le atacó un fuerte lumbago*** he had a severe attack of lumbago; ***me atacaron ganas de ...*** I was seized *o* gripped by a desire to ... **2** *fig*: *tarta* attack, tackle; *tema* address, tackle **II** *v/i* attack
atadijo *m* bundle
atado *m Arg* packet
atadura *f* tie
atajar ⟨1a⟩ **I** *v/t* **1** check the spread of, contain **2** *L.Am. pelota* catch **II** *v/i* take a short cut
atajo *m* short cut
atalaya I *f* watchtower **II** *m/f* sentinel
atañer ⟨2f⟩ *v/t* concern; ***eso no me atañe*** that's no concern of mine, that doesn't concern me
ataque *m* **1** (*agresión*), DEP attack **2** (*acceso*) fit; ***le dio un ~ de risa*** she burst out laughing
◇ **ataque cardíaco, ataque al corazón** MED heart attack
atar ⟨1a⟩ *v/t* **1** tie (up); ***~ a alguien de pies y manos*** tie s.o.'s hands and feet, truss s.o. up; ***loco de ~*** mad as a hatter **2** *fig* tie down; ***los niños atan mucho*** kids really tie you down; ***~ corto a alguien*** *fig* keep s.o. on a tight leash; **atarse** *v/r fig* tie o.s. down
atardecer I ⟨2d⟩ *v/i* get dark **II** *m* dusk; ***al ~*** at sunset
atareado *adj* busy
atarearse ⟨1a⟩ *v/r* busy o.s.
atascar ⟨1g⟩ *v/t* block; **atascarse** *v/r* **1** *de mecanismo* jam, stick; *de cañería* get blocked; ***se ha atascado el tubo*** the pipe's blocked **2** *al hablar* dry up
atasco *m* AUTO traffic jam; ***~ de papel*** *de impresora* paper jam
ataúd *m* coffin, casket
ataviar ⟨1c⟩ *v/t* dress s.o. up; **ataviarse** *v/r* dress up
ate *m Méx* quince jelly
ateísmo *m* atheism
atemorizar ⟨1f⟩ *v/t* frighten; **atemorizarse** *v/r* be frightened (***de*** of)
atemperar ⟨1a⟩ *v/t* temper
atenazar ⟨1f⟩ *v/t* grip
atención *f* **1** attention; ***¡~!*** your attention, please!; ***falta de ~*** lack of attention, inattentiveness; ***prestar ~*** pay attention (***a*** to); ***llamar la ~ a alguien*** *reñir* tell s.o. off; *por ser llamativo* attract s.o.'s attention; ***llamar la ~ de alguien sobre algo*** call s.o.'s attention to sth; ***dar un toque de ~ a alguien*** pull s.o. up
2 (*cortesía*) courtesy; ***atenciones*** *pl* at-

tentiveness *sg*; ***nos han tratato con mil atenciones*** they were extremely attentive
3: ***a la ~ de*** *carta* for the attention of; ***en ~ a*** *fml* with regard to
◇ **atención a domicilio, atención domiciliaria** home help
◇ **atención médica** medical attention
atender ⟨2g⟩ **I** *v/t* **1** *a enfermo* look after **2** *en tienda* attend to, serve **II** *v/i* **1** pay attention (***a*** to) **2**: ***que atiende por el nombre de …*** whose name is …; who answers to the name of …
ateneo *m Esp* atheneum, *Br* athenaeum
atenerse ⟨2l⟩ *v/r*: ***~ a*** *normas* abide by; *consecuencias* face, accept; ***me atengo a lo dicho*** I'm sticking to what I said; ***saber a qué ~*** know where one stands
atentado *m* attack (***contra, a*** on)
◇ **atentado con bomba** bomb attack
◇ **atentado terrorista** terrorist attack
atentamente *adv* **1** attentively **2** *en carta* sincerely, Yours truly, *Br* Yours sincerely
atentar ⟨1k⟩ *v/i*: ***~ contra*** *vida* make an attempt on; *moral etc* be contrary to
atento *adj* attentive; ***estar ~ a algo*** pay attention to sth
atenuación *f* lessening
atenuante *adj* JUR extenuating; ***circunstancia ~*** extenuating circumstance
atenuar ⟨1e⟩ *v/t* lessen, reduce; **atenuarse** *v/r* **1** *de violencia, dolor* lessen, die down **2**: ***se atenuan los castigos por …*** the penalties for … are being made less severe; ***se han atenuado las medidas de seguridad*** security has been scaled down
ateo I *adj* atheistic **II** *m*, **-a** *f* atheist
aterciopelado *adj tb fig* velvety
aterido *adj*: **~ (*de frío*)** frozen
atero(e)sclerosis *f* MED arteriosclerosis
aterrador *adj* frightening, terrifying
aterrar[1] ⟨1a⟩ *v/t persona* frighten, terrify
aterrar[2] ⟨1k⟩ *v/t con tierra* fill with earth
aterrizaje *m* AVIA landing
◇ **aterrizaje de emergencia, aterrizaje forzoso** emergency landing
aterrizar ⟨1f⟩ *v/i* land
aterrorizado *adj* terrified, petrified
aterrorizar ⟨1f⟩ *v/t* **1** terrify, petrify **2** (*amenazar*) terrorize; **aterrorizarse** *v/r* be terrified *o* petrified
atesorar ⟨1a⟩ *v/t* amass
atestado *adj* overcrowded
atestiguar ⟨1i⟩ *v/t* JUR testify; *fig* bear witness to
atiborrar ⟨1a⟩ *v/t* cram; **atiborrarse** *v/r* F stuff o.s. F (***de*** with)
ático *m piso* top floor; *apartamento* top floor apartment *o Br* flat; (*desván*) attic
atinado *part* ☞ ***atinar***
atinar ⟨1a⟩ *v/i* **1** manage (***a*** to) **2**: ***no atinó con la respuesta correcta*** she couldn't come up with the right answer; ***~ en el blanco*** hit the bull's eye
atiparse ⟨1a⟩ *v/r* eat one's fill
atípico *adj* atypical
atirantar ⟨1a⟩ *v/t* tighten; **atirantarse** *v/r de situación* become more tense
atisbar ⟨1a⟩ *v/t* see, make out
atisbo *m* sign
atizador *m* poker
atizar ⟨1f⟩ *v/t* **1** *fuego* poke **2** *pasiones* stir up **3**: ***le atizó un golpe*** she hit him **4**: ***¡atiza!*** wow!; **atizarse** *v/r bebida, comida* put away; ***~ un trago*** F knock back a drink F; ***se atizó un trago de coñac*** he took a gulp of brandy; ***me he atizado tres horas de gimnasio*** I put in a solid three hours at the gym
Atlántico *m*/*adj* Atlantic
atlas *m inv* atlas
atleta *m*/*f* athlete
atlético *adj* athletic
atletismo *m* athletics *sg*
atmo. *abr* (= ***atentísimo***): ***su ~*** Yours truly
atmósfera *f* atmosphere
atmosférico *adj* atmospheric; ***presión -a*** atmospheric pressure
atn *abr* (= ***atención***) attn (= for the attention of)
atoar ⟨1a⟩ *v/t* MAR *barco* tow
atole *m Méx flavored hot drink made with maize flour*
atolladero *m fig*: ***sacar a alguien del ~*** F get s.o. out of a jam *o* a tight spot; ***estar en un ~*** F be in a jam *o* a tight spot
atollarse ⟨1a⟩ *v/r* get stuck
atolón *m* atoll
atolondrado *adj* scatterbrained
atolondramiento *m* bewilderment
atolondrar ⟨1a⟩ *v/t* **1** *de golpe, noticia*

stun, daze **2** (*confundir*) bewilder, confuse; **atolondrarse** *v/r* **1** be stunned, be dazed **2** (*confundirse*) be bewildered, be confused

atómico *adj* atomic

atomización *f* **1** spraying **2** TÉC atomization

atomizador *m* spray

atomizar ⟨1f⟩ *v/t* **1** spray **2** TÉC atomize

átomo *m* atom; ***ni un ~ de*** *fig* not an iota of

atonal *adj* MÚS atonal

atonía *f* MED, *fig* sluggishness

atónito *adj* astonished, amazed; ***me dejas ~*** you astonish *o* amaze me

átono *adj* GRAM unstressed

atontado *adj* dazed, stunned

atontamiento *m* dazed state

atontar ⟨1a⟩ *v/t* **1** make groggy *o* dopey; (*volver tonto*) turn into a zombie **2** *de golpe* stun, daze; **atontarse** *v/r* go into a daze

atontolinar ⟨1a⟩ *v/t* F ☞ ***atontar***

atorar ⟨1a⟩ *L.Am. v/t cañería etc* block (up); **atorarse** *v/r* **1** choke **2** *de cañería etc* get blocked (up)

atormentar ⟨1a⟩ *v/t* torment; **atormentarse** *v/r* torment o.s.

atornillador *m CSur* screwdriver

atornillar ⟨1a⟩ *v/t* screw on

atorrante *m Rpl, Chi* F **1** bum F, *Br* tramp **2** (*holgazán*) bum F, *Br* layabout F

atosigar ⟨1h⟩ *v/t* pester

atrabancado *adj Méx* clumsy

atracadero *m* MAR mooring

atracador *m*, **~a** *f* robber

atracar ⟨1g⟩ **I** *v/t* **1** *banco, tienda* hold up; *a alguien* mug **2** *Chi* F make out with F, neck with *Br* F **II** *v/i* MAR dock; **atracarse** *v/r* stuff o.s. (***de*** with), pig out (***de*** on) F

atracción *f* **1** attraction; ***fuerza de ~*** force of attraction **2**: ***parque de atracciones*** amusement park

atraco *m de banco, tienda* robbery; *de persona* mugging

◇ **atraco a mano armada** armed robbery

atracón *m*: ***darse un ~ de*** stuff o.s. with F; ***hoy me he dado un ~ de trabajar*** F I've done more than enough work for the day

atractivo **I** *adj* attractive **II** *m* appeal, attraction

atraer ⟨2p⟩ *v/t* attract; ***~ todas las miradas*** be the center *o Br* centre of attention; **atraerse** *v/r* **1** be attracted (to each other) **2** *simpatía etc* draw, attract; ***~ el odio de la gente*** be greatly disliked

atragantarse ⟨1a⟩ *v/r* choke (***con*** on); ***se le ha atragantado*** *fig* she can't stand *o* stomach him

atrajo *vb* ☞ ***atraer***

atrancar ⟨1g⟩ *v/t puerta* barricade; **atrancarse** *v/r fig* get stuck

atrapada *f en béisbol* catch

atrapar ⟨1a⟩ *v/t* catch, trap

atraque *m* MAR mooring

atrás **I** *adv* **1** *para indicar posición* at the back, behind; ***sentarse ~*** sit at the back; *en coche* sit in back, *Br* sit at the back; ***de*** *o* ***por ~*** behind, in back of; ***quedarse ~*** get left behind; ***dejar ~*** leave behind; ***años ~*** years ago *o* back

2 *para indicar movimiento* back; ***hacia ~*** back, backwards; ***echar ~ el asiento*** push one's seat back; ***¡~!*** get back!; ***venir de ~*** come from behind; *fig* go back a long way; ***mi amistad con Carlos viene de ~*** *fig* Carlos and I go back a long way; ***venir por ~*** come from behind; ***volverse*** *o* ***echarse ~*** *fig* F back out

II *prp*: ***~ de*** *L.Am.* behind

atrasado *adj* **1** *en estudios, pago* behind (***en*** in *o* with) **2** *reloj* slow; ***ir ~*** be slow **3** *pueblo* backward

atrasar ⟨1a⟩ **I** *v/t reloj* put back; *fecha* postpone, put back **II** *v/i de reloj* lose time; **atrasarse** *v/r* fall behind

atraso *m* **1** backwardness **2** COM: ***~s*** *pl* arrears

atravesado *adj*: ***~ en algo*** stuck across sth; ***tener a alguien ~*** *fig* F not be able to stand s.o.

atravesar ⟨1k⟩ *v/t* **1** cross; ***~ el lago nadando*** swim across the lake **2** (*perforar*) go through, pierce **3** *crisis* go through; **atravesarse** *v/r* **1** (*cruzar*) cross **2** (*atascarse*) get stuck **3**: ***se me ha atravesado la física*** I can't stand physics

atrayente *adj* appealing

atreverse ⟨2a⟩ *v/r* **1** dare; ***~ a hacer algo*** dare (to) do sth; ***¿cómo te atreves?***

how dare you? **2**: **~ a algo** take sth on; **~ con alguien** take s.o. on
atrevido *adj* **1** (*insolente*) sassy F, *Br* cheeky F **2** (*valiente*) brave, daring
atrevimiento *m* nerve
atrez(z)o *m* TEA props *pl*
atribución *f* attribution
atribuible *adj*: **ser ~ a algo** be attributable to sth
atribuir ⟨3g⟩ *v/t* attribute (**a** to); **atribuirse** *v/r* claim
atributo *m* attribute
atril *m* lectern
atrincherarse ⟨1a⟩ *v/r* MIL dig o.s. in, entrench o.s.; **se atrincheró en su postura** *fig* he dug his heels in
atrio *m* atrium
atrocidad *f* **1** atrocity **2** (*disparate*): **decir / hacer ~es** say / do stupid things **3**: **una ~ de película / libro** F an atrocious movie / book
atrofia *f* atrophy, degeneration
atrofiado *adj* atrophied
atrofiarse ⟨1b⟩ *v/r* atrophy
atronador *adj* deafening
atropellado *adj* in a rush
atropellamiento *m* running over
atropellar ⟨1a⟩ *v/t* knock down; **le atropelló un coche** he was knocked down by a car; **atropellarse** *v/r* rush
atropello *m* **1** running over **2** *escándalo* outrage
atroz *adj* **1** appalling, atrocious **2**: **un éxito ~** a smash hit
ATS *m/f abr* (= **ayudante técnico sanitario**) registered nurse
atte. *abr* (= **atentamente**) sincerely (yours), *Br* Yours sincerely
atuendo *m* outfit
atufar ⟨1a⟩ F **I** *v/t* stink out F **II** *v/i* (*apestar*) stink to high heaven F
atún *m* tuna (fish)
atunero *m* tuna boat
aturdido *adj* dazed, in a daze
aturdimiento *m* bewilderment
aturdir ⟨3a⟩ *v/t* **1** *de golpe*, *noticia* stun, daze **2** (*confundir*) bewilder, confuse; **aturdirse** *v/r* **1** be stunned, be dazed **2** (*confundirse*) be bewildered, be confused
aturullar ⟨1a⟩ *v/t* confuse; **aturullarse** *v/r* get confused
atusar ⟨1a⟩ *v/t* smooth (down); **atusarse** *v/r* smooth (down)
audacia *f* audacity
audaz *adj* daring, bold, audacious
audible *adj* audible
audición *f* **1** hearing **2** *Rpl* RAD program, *Br* programme **3** TEA audition **4** JUR hearing
audiencia *f* **1** audience; **~ pontificia** audience with the Pope **2** TV: **índice de ~** ratings *pl* **3** JUR court
audífono I *m para sordos* hearing aid **II ~s** *mpl L.Am.* (*cascos*) headphones
audímetro, audiómetro *m* MED, TÉC audiometer
audiovisual *adj* audiovisual; **medios ~es** audiovisual equipment *sg*, audiovisual aids
auditar ⟨1a⟩ *v/t* audit
auditivo *adj* auditory; *problema* hearing *atr*; **conducto ~** auditory canal
auditor *m*, **~a** *f* auditor
auditoría *f* audit
auditorio *m* (*público*) audience; *sala* auditorium
auge *m* peak; **estar en ~** *aumento* be enjoying a boom
augurar ⟨1a⟩ *v/t de persona* predict, foretell; *de indicio* augur
augurio *m* omen, sign; **un buen / mal ~** a good / bad omen
augusto *adj* august
aula *f* classroom; *en universidad* lecture hall, *Br* lecture theatre
◇ **aula magna** main lecture hall
aulaga *f* BOT gorse
aullar ⟨1a⟩ *v/i* howl
aullido *m* howl
aumentable *adj* which may be increased; **la dosis es ~** the dose may be increased
aumentar ⟨1a⟩ **I** *v/t* increase; *precio* increase, raise, put up **II** *v/i de precio*, *temperatura* rise, increase, go up
aumentativo *m* GRAM augmentative
aumento *m de precios*, *temperaturas etc* rise (**de** in), increase (**de** in); **~ salarial** *o* **de sueldo** raise, *Br* (pay) rise; **ir en ~** be increasing
aún *adv* **1** *en oraciones no negativas* still **2** *en oraciones negativas* yet; **~ no** not yet **3** *en comparaciones* even
aun *adv* even; **~ así** even so; **~ cuando** even if, even when; **ni ~** not even
aunar ⟨1a⟩ *v/t* combine; **~ esfuerzos** join forces; **si aunamos ideas** if we

put our heads together
aunque *conj* **1** although, even though **2** + *subj* even if
aúpa *int* F **1** up you get! **2**: ***de ~*** tremendous; *comida* enormous, *Br* F slap-up *atr*; ***una borrachera / un follón de ~*** one hell of a hangover / a fight F
au pair *m/f* au pair
aupar ⟨1a⟩ *v/t* lift up; **auparse** *v/r* stand on something; ***~ encima de una silla*** stand on a chair
aura *f* **1** aura **2** *L.Am.* ZO turkey buzzard
áureo *adj lit* golden
aureola *f* halo
aurícula *f* ANAT auricle
auricular *m* **1** *de teléfono* receiver; ***descolgar el ~*** take the phone off the hook **2**: ***~es*** *pl* headphones, earphones
aurífero *adj* gold-bearing
aurora *f* dawn
◇ **aurora austral** southern lights *pl*; **aurora boreal** northern lights *pl*; **aurora polar** polar lights *pl*
auscultación *f* MED auscultation
auscultar ⟨1a⟩ *v/t*: ***~ a alguien*** listen to s.o.'s chest
ausencia *f* **1** *de persona* absence; ***en ~ de*** in the absence of; ***brillaba por su ~*** he was conspicuous by his absence **2** *no existencia* lack (***de*** of)
ausentarse ⟨1a⟩ *v/r* leave, go away
ausente *adj* absent; ***últimamente está siempre ~*** *fig* his mind has been elsewhere lately
auspiciar ⟨1b⟩ *v/t* sponsor
auspicio *m* sponsorship; ***bajo los ~s de*** under the auspices of
austeridad *f* austerity; ***programa de ~*** POL austerity program
austero *adj* austere
austral *adj* southern
Australia *f* Australia
australiano I *adj* Australian **II** *m*, **-a** *f* Australian
Austria *f* Austria
austríaco, austriaco I *adj* Austrian **II** *m* **-a** *f* Austrian
austriano I *adj* Austrian **II** *m*, **-a** *f* Austrian
autarquía *f* self-sufficiency
autárquico *adj* self-sufficient
autenticar ⟨1g⟩ *v/t* authenticate
autenticidad *f* authenticity
auténtico *adj* authentic
autentificar ⟨1g⟩ *v/t* authenticate
autillo *m* ZO tawny owl
autismo *m* autism
autista I *adj* autistic **II** *m/f* autistic person
autito *m CSur* bumper car
auto[1] *m* **1** JUR order; ***dictar ~ de detención*** issue an arrest warrant **2**: ***~s*** *pl* JUR proceedings; ***consta en ~s*** it is a matter of record **3**: ***lugar de ~s*** crime scene **4** *L.Am.* AUTO car
◇ **auto de choque** *L.Am.* AUTO bumper car; **auto de fe** HIST auto-da-fé; **auto de procesamiento** JUR committal proceedings *pl*; **auto sacramental** TEA mystery play
auto[2] *pref* self
autoabastecerse ⟨2d⟩ *v/r* be self-sufficient (***de*** in)
autoabastecimiento *m* self-sufficiency
autoadhesivo *adj* self-adhesive
autoafirmación *f* self-affirmation
autoayuda *f* self-help
autobanco *m* ATM, cash machine
autobiografía *f* autobiography
autobiográfico *adj* autobiographical
autobombo *m* F self-glorification
autobronceador *m* artificial tanning lotion
autobús *m* bus
◇ **autobús escolar** school bus; **autobús interurbano** (long-distance) bus, *Br tb* coach; **autobús de línea** (long-distance) bus, *Br tb* coach
autocar *m Esp* bus, *Br tb* coach
autocaravana *f* camper van
autocine *m* drive-in (movie theater)
autoclave *m o f* autoclave
autocompadecerse ⟨2d⟩ *v/r* feel sorry for o.s.
autocomplacencia *f* smugness
autoconfianza *f* self-confidence
autocontrol *m* self-control
autocrítica *f* self-criticism
autocross *m* autocross
autóctono I *adj* indigenous, native **II** *m* indigenous person, native
autodefensa *f* self-defense, *Br* self-defence
autodenominarse ⟨1a⟩ call o.s., refer to o.s. as
autodeterminación *f* self-determination
autodidacta I *adj* self-taught **II** *m/f* self-taught person

autodisciplina *f* self-discipline
autodisparador *m* FOT automatic shutter release
autodominio *m* self-control
autódromo *m* racetrack
autoedición *f* desktop publishing, DTP
autoescuela *f* driving school; ***profesor de ~*** driving school instructor
autoestima *f* self-esteem
autoestop *m* hitchhiking
autoestopista *m/f* hitchhiker
autofinanciación *f* self-financing
autofinanciarse ⟨1b⟩ *v/r* finance o.s.
autofoco *m* FOT autofocus
autoformato *m* INFOR automatic formatting
autógeno *adj* autogenous; ***soldadura -a*** welding
autogestión *f* self-management
autogobierno *m* POL self-government
autogol *m* own goal
autógrafo *m* autograph
autómata *m* automaton, automatic system
automático **I** *adj* automatic **II** *m L.Am.* AUTO automatic
automatización *f* automation
automatizar ⟨1f⟩ *v/t* automate
automedicación *f* self-medication
automoción *f* self-propulsion
automotor **I** *adj* self-propelled **II** *m* motor vehicle
automóvil *m* car, automobile
automovilismo *m* driving
automovilista *m/f* motorist
automovilístico *adj* automobile *atr*
automutilación *f* self-mutilation
autonomía *f* **1** autonomy **2** *en España* autonomous region
autonómico *adj* autonomous; ***elecciones -as*** *Esp* elections in the autonomous regions
autónomo **I** *adj* autonomous; *trabajador* self-employed **II** *m*, **-a** *f* self-employed person
autopista *f* freeway, *Br* motorway
◇ **autopista de la comunicación** INFOR information (super)highway; **autopista de cuota** *Méx* turnpike, *Br* toll motorway; **autopista de la información** INFOR information (super)highway; **autopista de peaje** turnpike, *Br* toll motorway
autopropulsión *f* TÉC self-propulsion
autopsia *f* post mortem, autopsy
autor *m*, **~a** *f* author; *de crimen* perpetrator; ***los ~es del atentado*** those who carried out the attack; *con bomba* the bombers
◇ **autor material** JUR actual perpetrator
◇ **autor teatral** playwright
autoría *f de un acto* responsibility; *de un libro* authorship
autoridad *f* authority; ***hacer valer toda su ~*** *fig* assert one's authority, bring the full weight of one's authority to bear
autoritario *adj* authoritarian
autoritarismo *m* authoritarianism
autorización *f* authority
autorizado *adj* authorized; ***~ a firmar*** authorized to sign; ***no ~*** unauthorized
autorizar ⟨1f⟩ *v/t* authorize
autorradio *m* car radio
autorretrato *m* self-portrait
autoservicio *m* **1** supermarket **2** *restaurante* self-service restaurant
autostop *m* hitchhiking; ***hacer ~*** hitch (-hike)
autostopista *m/f* hitchhiker
autosuficiencia *f* self-sufficiency; *desp* smugness
autosuficiente *adj* self-sufficient; *desp* smug
autosugestión *f* autosuggestion
autovía *f* divided highway, *Br* dual carriageway
auxiliar **I** *adj* **1** auxiliary; ***verbo ~*** auxiliary verb **2** *profesor* assistant *atr* **II** *m/f* assistant **III** *f Rpl* AUTO spare wheel **IV** ⟨1b⟩ *v/t* help
◇ **auxiliar administrativo** administrative assistant; **auxiliar de clínica** nurses' aide, *Br* nursing auxiliary; **auxiliar de geriatría** geriatric nurse; **auxiliar de vuelo** stewardess, flight attendant
auxilio *m* help; ***primeros ~s*** *pl* first aid *sg*
◇ **auxilio en carretera** AUTO breakdown assistance
Avda *abr* (= ***Avenida***) Ave (= Avenue)
aval *m* guarantee
◇ **aval bancario** bank guarantee
avalancha *f* avalanche; ***~ de coches*** stream of cars
avalar ⟨1a⟩ *v/t* guarantee; *fig* back
avalista *m/f* guarantor

avalúo *m L.Am.* valuation
avance *m* **1** advance; **~ de papel** *en impresora* paper advance **2** *en cine* trailer
◇ **avance informativo** newsflash
◇ **avance de programas** (program) preview
avanzada *f* MIL scouting party
avanzadilla *f* MIL scouting party; *fig* vanguard
avanzado *adj* advanced
avanzar ⟨1f⟩ **I** *v/t* **1** move forward, advance; **~ un pie** take a step forward **2** *dinero* advance **II** *v/i* **1** advance, move forward; MIL advance (**hacia** on) **2** *en trabajo* make progress
avaricia *f* greed, avarice
avaricioso *adj* greedy, avaricious
avaro I *adj* miserly; **ser ~ de algo** be sparing with sth; **es muy ~ de su vida personal** he gives very little away about his private life **II** *m*, **-a** *f* miser
avasallador *adj* domineering
avasallar ⟨1a⟩ *v/t* subjugate; **no dejes que te avasallen** *fig* don't let them push you around
avatares *mpl* changes
ave *f* **1** bird **2** *S.Am.* (*pollo*) chicken
◇ **ave migratoria** migratory bird; **ave del paraíso** bird of paradise; **ave de paso** migratory bird; **ave de presa, ave de rapiña** bird of prey; **aves de corral** poultry
AVE *m abr* (= **alta velocidad española**) high speed train
avechucho *m* **1** *desp* ugly bird **2** *fig* ugly customer
avecinarse ⟨1a⟩ *v/r* approach
avefría *f* ZO lapwing
avejentado *adj* aged
avejentar ⟨1a⟩ *v/t* age; **avejentarse** *v/r* age
avellana *f* BOT hazelnut
avellano *m* BOT hazel
avemaría *f* REL Hail Mary
avena *f* oats *pl*
avenamiento *m* draining
avenar ⟨1a⟩ *v/t terreno* drain
avenida *f* avenue
avenido *adj*: **bien ~** well-matched; **mal ~** badly-matched
avenirse ⟨3s⟩ *v/r* agree (**a** to)
aventajado *adj* outstanding
aventajar ⟨1a⟩ *v/t* be ahead of
aventar ⟨1k⟩ *L.Am v/t* **1** throw **2** (*empujar*) push; **aventarse** *v/r* **1** F throw o.s. **2**: **~ a hacer algo** dare to do sth
aventón *m Andes, C.Am., Méx* F: **dar ~ a alguien** give s.o. a ride *o* lift
aventura *f* **1** adventure **2** (*riesgo*) venture **3** *amorosa* affair
aventurado *adj* risky, hazardous
aventurar ⟨1a⟩ *v/t* **1** risk **2** *opinión* venture; **aventurarse** *v/r* venture; **~ a hacer algo** dare (to) do sth
aventurero I *adj* adventurous; **espíritu ~** sense *o* spirit of adventure **II** *m*, **-a** *f* adventurer
avergonzado *adj* **1** embarrassed **2** *de algo reprensible* ashamed
avergonzar ⟨1n & 1f⟩ *v/t* **1** (*aborchornar*) embarrass **2**: **le avergüenza** *de algo reprensible* she's ashamed of it; **avergonzarse** *v/r* be ashamed (**de** of)
avería *f* **1** TÉC fault **2** AUTO breakdown
averiado *adj* broken down
averiarse ⟨1c⟩ *v/r* break down
averiguar ⟨1i⟩ **I** *v/t* find out **II** *v/i C.Am., Méx* (*discutir*) argue
aversión *f* aversion
avestruz *m* ZO ostrich; **del ~** *política, táctica* head-in-the-sand *atr*
avetoro *m* ZO bittern
aviación *f* **1** aviation; **campo de ~** airfield **2** MIL air force
◇ **aviación deportiva** flying (*as a hobby*), leisure flying
aviador *m*, **~a** *f* pilot, aviator
avícola *adj* poultry *atr*; **granja ~** poultry farm
avicultor *m*, **~a** *f* poultry farmer
avicultura *f* poultry farming
avidez *f* eagerness
ávido *adj* eager (**de** for), avid (**de** for)
avifauna *f* birds *pl*
avinagrado *adj* vinegary
avinagrar ⟨1a⟩ *v/t* turn vinegary; *fig* make bitter; **avinagrarse** *v/r de vino* turn vinegary; *fig* become bitter *o* sour
avío *m* useful item; **~s de coser** *pl* sewing kit *sg*
avión *m* airplane, plane; **por ~** *mandar una carta* (by) airmail; **ir en ~** fly
◇ **avión de carga** cargo airplane; **avión chárter** chartered airplane; **avión a chorro** jet (plane); **avión cisterna** tanker aircraft; **avión de combate** fighter (plane); **avión comercial** commercial airplane; **avión de hélice**

propeller aircraft; **avión nodriza** tanker aircraft; **avión a reacción** jet (plane); **avión de reconocimiento** reconnaissance airplane; **avión supersónico** supersonic airplane
avionazo *m Méx* airplane crash, plane crash
avioneta *f* light plane, light aircraft
avisador *m* **1** warning light; *sonoro* alarm **2** *L.Am.* (*anunciante*) advertiser
avisar ⟨1a⟩ *v/t* **1** (*notificar*) tell, inform; *de peligro* warn, inform; ***sin ~*** without warning **2** (*llamar*) call, send for
aviso *m* **1** (*comunicación*) notice; ***hasta nuevo ~*** until further notice; ***sin previo ~*** without any notice *o* warning; ***último ~*** AVIA final call; ***~ de llamada por vibración*** TELEC vibration mode **2** (*advertencia*) warning; ***estar sobre ~*** have been warned; ***poner a alguien sobre ~*** give s.o. a warning, warn s.o. **3** *L.Am.* (*anuncio*) advertisement
◇ **aviso de recibo** *de correos* acknowledgement of receipt
avispa *f* ZO wasp
avispado *adj* bright, sharp
avisparse ⟨1a⟩ *v/r* wake up, become more alert; ***se ha avispado mucho*** he's a lot more on the ball F
avispero *m* wasps' nest; ***meterse en un ~*** *fig* get o.s. into trouble
avispón *m* ZO hornet
avistar ⟨1a⟩ *v/t* sight, spot
avitaminosis *f* MED vitamin deficiency
avituallamiento *m*: ***nos hicimos con un ~ de vino*** we stocked up on wine
avivar ⟨1a⟩ *v/t* **1** *fuego* revive **2** *interés* arouse **3**: ***~ el paso*** speed up; **avivarse** *v/r* **1** *de fuego* flare up **2** *de persona* get one's act together
avizor *adj*: ***estar ojo ~*** be alert
avutarda *f* ZO bustard
axial *adj* axial
axil *adj* axial
axila *f* armpit
axioma *m* axiom
axiomático *adj* axiomatic
ay *interj de dolor* ow!, ouch!; *de susto* oh!; ***¡~ de mí!*** *lit* woe is me! *lit*
ayer *adv* yesterday; ***~ por la mañana*** yesterday morning; ***de ~*** yesterday's; ***parece que fue ~*** it seems like yesterday
ayuda I *f* help, assistance; ***~ financiera*** financial help *o* aid *o* assistance; ***con la ~ de*** with the help of; ***prestar ~*** help; ***pedir ~ a alguien*** ask s.o. for help; ***venir en ~ de*** come to the aid *o* help of **II** *m* aide
◇ **ayuda de cámara** valet
◇ **ayuda al desarrollo** development aid *o* assistance
ayudante *m/f* assistant
◇ **ayudante técnico sanitario** registered nurse
ayudar ⟨1a⟩ *v/t* help; ***¿le ayudo?*** can I help?, would you like some help?; ***le ayudó a ponerse el abrigo*** he helped her put on her coat
ayudarse *v/r* help o.s.; ***~ con las manos para hacer algo*** use one's hands to do sth; ***se ayudó con las manos para levantarse del sofá*** he levered himself up off the sofa
ayunar ⟨1a⟩ *v/i* fast
ayunas: ***estoy en ~*** I haven't eaten anything; ***quedarse en ~*** *fig* be left completely in the dark
ayuno *m* fast
ayuntamiento *m* city council, town council; *edificio* city hall, town hall
◇ **ayuntamiento carnal** carnal knowledge
azabache *m* MIN jet
azada *f* hoe
azadón *m* mattock
azafata *f* flight attendant
◇ **azafata de congresos** hostess
azafato *m* flight attendant
◇ **azafato de congresos** steward
azafrán *m* BOT saffron
azahar *m* BOT orange *o* lemon blossom
azalea *f* BOT azalea
azar *m* fate, chance; ***al ~*** at random; ***por ~*** by chance
azarar *vb* ☞ ***azorar***
azaroso *adj* **1** risky, daring **2**: ***una vida -a*** an eventful life
Azerbaiján, Azerbaiyán *m* Azerbaijan
ázimo *adj* unleavened
azogue *m* mercury
azor *m* ZO hawk
azorar ⟨1a⟩ *v/t* embarrass; **azorarse** *v/r* be embarrassed
azotador *m Méx* caterpillar
azotaina *f* F spanking
azotar ⟨1a⟩ *v/t* **1** *con látigo* whip, flog; *con mano* smack **2** *de enfermedad, hambre* grip **3** *Méx puerta* slam

azote *m* **1** *con látigo* lash; *con mano* smack; ***dar un ~ a alguien*** smack s.o. **2** *fig* scourge
azotea *f* flat roof; ***estar mal de la ~*** *fig* F be crazy
azteca *m/f & adj* Aztec
azúcar *m* (*also f*) sugar
◇ **azúcar cande, azúcar candi** candy cane; **azúcar de caña** cane sugar; **azúcar de cortadillo** sugar lumps *pl o* cubes *pl*; **azúcar glas** confectioners' sugar, *Br* icing sugar; **azúcar impalpable** *Rpl* confectioners' sugar, *Br* icing sugar; **azúcar lustre** superfine sugar, *Br* castor sugar; **azúcar moreno** brown sugar; **azúcar en terrones** sugar lumps *pl o* cubes *pl*
azucarado *adj* sweetened, *fig* sugary
azucarar ⟨1a⟩ *v/t* add sugar to, sugar
azucarera *f* sugar bowl
azucarero I *adj* sugar *atr* **II** *m* sugar bowl
azucarillo *m* sugar cube, lump of sugar
azucena *f* BOT Madonna lily
azufre *m* sulfur, *Br* sulphur
azul I *adj* blue **II** *m* blue
◇ **azul celeste** sky-blue; **azul claro** light blue; **azul marino** navy(-blue); **azul turquesa** turquoise
azulado *adj* bluish
azulejo *m* **1** tile **2** BOT cornflower **3** ZO bee-eater
azulete *m* bluing
azulino *adj* bluish
azulón *adj* dark-bluish
azuzar ⟨1f⟩ *v/t*: ***~ los perros a alguien*** set the dogs on s.o.; *fig* egg s.o. on

B

B.A. *abr* (= ***Buenos Aires***) Buenos Aires
baba *f* drool, dribble; ***se le caía la ~*** F he was drooling F (***con*** over); ***tener mala ~*** be mean
babear ⟨1a⟩ *v/i* dribble
babel *m* (*also f*) chaos
babero *m* bib
babi *m* smock, overall
Babia *f*: ***estar en ~*** be miles away
bable *m dialect of Asturias*
babor *m* MAR port
babosa *f* ZO slug
babosada *f L.Am.* F stupid thing to do / say
baboso *L.Am.* F **I** *adj* stupid **II** *m*, **-a** *f* idiot
babucha *f* slipper
babuino *m* ZO baboon
baca *f* AUTO roof rack
bacaladilla *f pescado* blue whiting
bacalao *m* cod; ***cortar el ~*** F call the shots F
◇ **bacalao seco** salt cod
bacán *m Arg* F big shot F
bacanal *f* **1** MYTH bacchanal **2** *fig* orgy
bacante *f* MYTH bacchante
bacar(r)á *m juego de naipes* baccarat
bache *m* **1** *en carretera* pothole **2** *fig* rough patch
bachicha I *m/f Rpl, Chi desp* wop *desp* **II** *f Méx* cigarette stub
bachiller *m/f* high school graduate
bachillerato *m Esp high school leaver's certificate*; ***estudiar el ~*** be in high school, *Br* be at secondary school
bacía *f* shaving bowl
bacilar *adj* bacillary
bacilo *m* bacillus
bacín *m* chamber pot
backup *m* INFOR backup
Baco *m* MYTH Bacchus
bacón *m* bacon
bacteria *f* bacteria
bacteriano *adj* bacterial
bactericida I *adj* bactericidal, antibacterial **II** *m* bactericide
bacteriología *f* bacteriology
bacteriológico *adj* bacteriological
bacteriólogo *m*, **-a** *f* bacteriologist
báculo *m* staff; *fig* support
badajo *m* clapper
badana *f* F: ***zurrar a alguien la ~*** give s.o. a good hiding
badén *m* dip
badil *m*, **badila** *f* fire shovel
bádminton *m* badminton
badulaque *m/f* F idiot F, fool
bafle *m* loudspeaker
bagaje *m fig* heritage

B

bagatela *f* trinket
baguette *f* baguette, French stick
¡bah! *int* bah
bahía *f* bay
bailable *adj*: ***música ~*** dance music
bailador I *adj*: ***ser muy ~*** love dancing **II** *m*, **~a** *f* dancer
bailaor *m*, **~a** *f* flamenco dancer
bailar 〈1a〉 **I** *v/i* **1** dance; ***~ al son que le tocan*** toe the line; ***~ con la más fea*** draw the short straw **2** *de zapato* be loose **II** *v/t* dance; ***se lo bailó*** *Méx* F he swiped it F; ***~le a alguien el agua*** suck up to s.o.; ***¡que me quiten lo bailado!*** nobody can take away the good times I've had
bailarín I *adj*: ***es muy ~*** he loves dancing **II** *m*, **-ina** *f* dancer
baile *m* **1** dance **2** *fiesta formal* ball
◇ **baile de disfraces** costume ball, fancy dress ball; **baile de máscaras** masked ball; **baile de salón** ballroom dancing; **baile de San Vito** St. Vitus's dance
bailón I *adj* F: ***ser muy ~*** love dancing **II** *m*, **-ona** *f* F big dancer F
bailongo *m* F dance
bailotear 〈1a〉 *v/i* dance
bailoteo *m* dancing
baja *f* **1** *descenso* fall, drop; ***jugar a la ~*** FIN gamble on a bear market **2** *persona* casualty; ***~s*** *pl* MIL casualties **3** (*dimisión, cese*): ***causar ~*** resign, leave; ***dar de ~*** dismiss; ***darse de ~*** resign, leave (***por*** because of); ***estar de ~*** (***por enfermedad***) be off sick, be on sick leave
◇ **Baja California** Baja, Lower California; **baja por enfermedad** sick leave; ***darse de ~*** resign for health reasons; **baja por maternidad** maternity leave
bajá *m* pasha
bajada *f* fall, drop
◇ **bajada de tipos** drop in interest rates
bajamar *f* low tide
bajante *m* drainpipe, downspout, *Br* downpipe
bajar 〈1a〉 **I** *v/t* **1** *voz, precio* lower; ***~ la mirada*** lower one's eyes *o* gaze, look down; ***~ algo de arriba*** get sth down **2** *TV, radio* turn down **3** *escalera* go down **4** INFOR download **II** *v/i* **1** go down **2** *de intereses* fall, drop; **bajarse** *v/r* **1** get down **2** *de automóvil* get out (***de*** of); *de tren, autobús* get off (***de*** sth) **3**: ***~ los pantalones*** drop one's pants *o Br* trousers
bajel *m lit* ship
bajeza *f* **1** (*calidad*) baseness **2** (*acto*) despicable thing to do
bajinis: ***por lo ~*** F under one's breath
bajío *m L.Am.* lowland
bajista I *adj*: ***tendencia ~*** downward trend **II** *m/f* **1** FIN bear **2** MÚS bass player, bassist
bajo I *adj* **1** low; ***~ en sal*** low in salt **2** *persona* short **II** *m* **1** MÚS bass **2** *piso* first floor, *Br* ground floor; *de edificio* first floor apartment, *Br* ground floor flat **3** *de vestido, pantalón* hem **4**: ***por lo ~*** at least **III** *adv* **1** *cantar, hablar* quietly, softly **2** *volar* low **IV** *prp* under; ***tres grados ~ cero*** three degrees below zero; ***~ juramento*** *o* ***palabra*** on *o* under oath
◇ **bajo continuo** MÚS continuo
bajón *m* sharp decline; ***dar un ~*** decline sharply, slump; ***tener un ~*** *de salud* take a turn for the worse
bajorrelieve *m* bas-relief
bakalao *m* MÚS F techno
bala *f* bullet; ***como una ~*** like lightning; ***ni a ~*** *L.Am.* F no way F
◇ **bala de fogueo** blank
balacear 〈1a〉 *v/t L.Am.* shoot
balaceo *m L.Am.*, **balacera** *f L.Am.* shooting
balada *f* ballad
baladí *adj* trivial
baladronada *f* boast
baladronear 〈1a〉 *v/i* boast, brag
balance *m* COM balance; ***hacer ~*** do the books; ***hacer el ~*** *fig*: *de situación* take stock
balancear 〈1a〉 *v/t caderas* swing, sway; **balancearse** *v/r* **1** swing, sway **2** MAR rock
balanceo *m* **1** swinging, swaying **2** MAR rocking
balancín *m* **1** TÉC rocker **2** (*mecedora*) rocking chair
bálano *m* ANAT glans penis
balanza *f* scales *pl*; ***~ para cartas*** letter scales *pl*; ***inclinar la ~*** *fig* tip the balance *o* scales
◇ **balanza comercial** balance of trade; **balanza de pagos** balance of pay-

B

ments; **balanza de precisión** precision scales *pl*
balar ⟨1a⟩ *v/i de oveja, cabra* bleat
balasto *m* ballast
balaustrada *f* balustrade
balaustre *m* spindle
balazo *m* shot
balboa *m* FIN balboa
balbucear ⟨1a⟩ **I** *v/i* **1** stammer **2** *de niño* babble **II** *v/t* stammer
balbuceo *m* stammer
balbucir ⟨3f; *defective*⟩ *v/t & v/i* ☞ ***balbucear***
Balcanes *mpl* Balkans
balcánico *adj* Balkan
balcón *m* balcony
◇ **balcón corrido** ☞ ***balconada***
balconada *f* continuous balcony
balda *f* shelf
baldado *adj fig* F bushed F
baldaquín *m* canopy
balde I *m* bucket **II** *adv*: ***de ~*** for nothing; ***en ~*** in vain
baldear ⟨1a⟩ *v/t* MAR wash down, sluice
baldío I *adj terreno* uncultivated; *fig* useless **II** *m* uncultivated land
baldón *m* dishonor, *Br* dishonour
baldosa *f* floor tile
baldosín *m* tile
baldragas *m* F wimp F
balear[1] **I** *adj* Balearic; ***las islas Baleares*** the Balearic Islands **II** *m/f* native of the Balearic Islands
balear[2] ⟨1a⟩ *v/t L.Am.* shoot
Baleares *fpl* Balearics
baleárico *adj* Balearic
baleo *m L.Am.* shooting
balido *m* bleat
balín *m* pellet
balística *f* ballistics *sg*
balístico *adj* ballistic
baliza *f* **1** MAR buoy **2** AVIA runway light
balizamiento *m* AVIA runway lights *pl*; ***~ luminoso*** *en carretera* warning lights *pl*
balizar ⟨1f⟩ *v/t carretera* mark with warning lights
ballena *f* ZO whale
ballenato *m* ZO whale calf
ballenero I *adj* whaling *atr*; ***barco ~*** whaler **II** *m persona, barco* whaler
ballesta *f* **1** crossbow **2** TÉC spring
ballestero *m* crossbowman
ballet *m* ballet
balneario *m* spa
balneoterapia *f* balneotherapy
balompédico *adj* soccer *atr*, *Br tb* football *atr*
balompié *m* soccer, *Br tb* football
balón *m* ball; ***echar balones fuera*** avoid the issue; ***recibir un ~ de oxígeno*** *fig* get a boost
◇ **balón muerto** *en baloncesto* dead ball
balonazo *m* DEP: ***recibir un ~*** get hit by the ball
baloncestista *m/f* basketball player
baloncestístico *adj* basketball *atr*
baloncesto *m* basketball
balonmano *m* handball
balonvolea *m* volleyball
balotaje *m L.Am.* POL ballot(t)ing
balsa *f* raft; ***como una ~ de aceite*** *fig* like a mill pond
balsámico *adj* soothing
bálsamo *m* balsam
balsera *f* **1** ferrywoman **2** *inmigrante* illegal Cuban immigrant
balsero *m* **1** ferryman **2** *inmigrante* illegal Cuban immigrant
báltico I *adj* Baltic; ***el mar Báltico*** the Baltic Sea **II** *m*: ***el Báltico*** the Baltic
baluarte *m* **1** MIL stronghold **2** *persona* pillar, stalwart
balumba *f* **1** *L.Am.* F heap, pile **2** *(ruido)* noise, racket F
bambolearse ⟨1a⟩ *v/r* **1** *de persona* sway **2** *(oscilar)* swing, rock
bamboleo *m* **1** *de persona* swaying **2** *(oscilación)* swinging, rocking
bambolla *f L.Am.* F fuss
bambú *m* BOT bamboo
banal *adj* banal
banalidad *f* banality
banana *f L.Am.* banana
bananero I *adj* banana *atr* **II** *m* banana tree
banano *m* banana tree
banasta *f* basket
banasto *m* round-bottomed basket
banca *f* **1** *actividad* banking; *conjunto de bancos* banks *pl* **3** *en juego* bank; ***saltar la ~*** break the bank **4** *Méx* DEP *(asiento)* bench
◇ **banca electrónica** electronic banking
bancal *m* **1** *en pendiente* terrace **2** *divi-*

sión de terreno plot

bancario *adj* bank *atr*

bancarrota *f* bankruptcy; ***estar en ~*** be bankrupt; ***hacer ~*** go bankrupt

banco *m* **1** COM bank **2** *para sentarse* bench

◇ **banco de arena** sand bank; **banco de carpintero** carpenter's bench; **banco en casa** home banking; **Banco Central Europeo** Central European Bank; **banco de crédito** credit bank; **banco de datos** data bank; **banco emisor** issuing bank; **Banco Europeo de Inversiones** European Investment Bank; **Banco Europeo de Reconstrucción y Desarrollo** European Bank for Reconstruction and Development; **banco de genes** gene bank; **banco de hielo** ice floe; **Banco Mundial** World Bank; **banco de niebla** bank of fog, fog bank; **banco de órganos** organ bank; **banco de peces** shoal of fish; **banco de pruebas** test bed; **banco de sangre** blood bank; **banco de semen** sperm bank; **banco de trabajo** workbench

banda *f* **1** MÚS (*grupo*) band **2** *de delincuentes* gang **3** (*cinta*) sash **4** *en fútbol* touchline **5** *de billar* cushion **6**: ***cerrarse en ~*** F stand firm, dig one's heels in F

◇ **banda de frecuencia** frequency band; **banda magnética** INFOR magnetic strip *o* stripe; **banda de rodadura** *de ruedas* tread; **banda sonora** soundtrack; **banda terrorista** terrorist group

bandada *f de pájaros* flock; ***a ~s*** *fig* in hordes

bandazo *m*: ***dar ~s*** *de coche* swerve

bandeja *f* **1** tray; ***servir en ~*** hand on a plate; ***pasar la ~*** pass the plate around **2** *en balconcesto* lay-up

bandera *f* flag; **(*lleno*) *hasta la ~*** packed (out); ***bajar la ~*** *de taxi* start the meter running; ***de ~*** F great F, fantastic F; ***jurar la ~*** swear allegiance to the flag

banderilla *f* **1** TAUR banderilla (*dart stuck into bull's neck during bullfight*) **2** GASTR *tapa on a cocktail stick*

banderillear ⟨1a⟩ *v/t* TAUR stick the *banderilla* in

banderillero *m* TAUR banderillero (*person who wields the banderillas*)

banderín *m* pennant; *en fútbol* flag

◇ **banderín de córner** *en fútbol* (corner) flag

bandido *m*, **-a** *f* bandit

bando *m* **1** (*aviso*) edict **2** *en disputa* side

bandolera *f* **1** MIL bandoleer; ***en ~*** across one's chest **2** *mujer* bandit

bandolerismo *m* banditry

bandolero *m* bandit

bandoneón *m Rpl* MÚS *large accordion*

bandurria *f* MÚS mandolin

banjo *m* MÚS banjo

banquero *m*, **-a** *f* banker

banqueta *f* **1** (*taburete*) stool **2** AUTO: ***~ trasera*** back seat **3** *L.Am.* (*acera*) sidewalk, *Br* pavement

banquete *m* banquet

◇ **banquete de bodas** wedding reception

banquetear ⟨1a⟩ *v/i* feast

banquillo *m* **1** JUR dock **2** DEP bench; ***estar en el ~*** DEP be on the bench

◇ **banquillo de los acusados** dock

◇ **banquillo de suplentes** DEP bench

banquina *f Rpl* AUTO shoulder, *Br* hard shoulder

banquisa *f* ice field

bañadera *f Rpl* (*baño*) bath

bañador *m* swimsuit

bañar ⟨1a⟩ *v/t* **1** *de sol, mar* bathe **2** *a un niño, un enfermo* bathe, *Br* bath; ***bañado en lágrimas*** bathed in tears **3** GASTR coat (***con*** with, ***en*** in); **bañarse** *v/r* **1** have a bath **2** *en el mar* go for a swim

bañera *f* (bath)tub, bath

◇ **bañera de hidromasaje** whirlpool, Jacuzzi®

bañero *m*, **-a** *f Rpl* lifeguard

bañista *m/f* swimmer

baño *m* **1** *en la bañera* bath; ***celebraron su victoria con un ~ de masas*** *o* ***de multitudes*** *fig* a huge crowd celebrated their victory **2** *en el mar* swim **3** *esp L.Am.* bathroom; (*ducha*) shower **4** TÉC plating **5**: ***~s*** *pl* spa *sg*

◇ **baño de asiento** hip bath; **baño de azúcar** sugar coating; **baño fijador** FOT fixing bath; **baño María** bain-marie; **baño de sangre** blood bath; **baño de sol** sunbathing session; **baño termal** (thermal) baths *pl*; **baño de vapor** steam bath; **baños de sol** sunbathing *sg*; **baños termales** thermal baths,

thermal spa *sg*
baobab *m* BOT baobab, monkey bread tree
baptista *m/f* REL Baptist
baptisterio *m* baptistry
baqueta *f* **1** MIL ramrod; ***correr ~s*** run the gauntlet **2** MÚS drumstick
baqueteado *adj fig* experienced
baquetear ⟨1a⟩ *v/t fig*: **~ *a alguien*** give s.o. a hard time
baquiano *L.Am.* **I** *adj* expert *atr* **II** *m*, **-a** *f* guide
báquico *adj* drunken; MYTH Bacchanalian
bar *m* bar
◇ **bar de copas** nightclub
barahúnda *f* commotion
baraja *f* deck of cards; ***jugar con dos ~s*** *fig* not play straight; ***se rompe la ~*** *fig* the whole deal's off
barajar ⟨1a⟩ **I** *v/t* **1** *naipes* shuffle **2** *fig* consider **II** *v/i* quarrel
baranda *f en billar* cushion
barandilla *f* handrail, banister
barata *f* **1** *Méx* (*engaño*) bargain counter **2** *Méx* (*saldo*) sale **3** *Chi* (*cucaracha*) cockroach
baratear ⟨1a⟩ *v/t* sell off
baratero *m*, **-a** *f Chi tendero* junk-shop owner
baratija *f* trinket
baratillo *m* **1** *tienda* cut-price store **2** (*mercadillo*) street market
barato *adj* cheap
baratura *f* cheapness
baraúnda *f* ☞ ***barahúnda***
barba *f tb* BOT beard; ***dejarse (la) ~*** grow a beard; ***en las ~s de alguien*** under s.o.'s nose; ***subirse a las ~s de alguien*** get fresh with s.o. F, *Br* be cheeky to s.o. F; ***por ~*** F a head, per person
◇ **barba de chivo, barba en punta** goatee (beard)
barbacana *f* MIL barbican
barbacoa *f* barbecue
barbado **I** *adj fml* bearded **II** *m* BOT rooted cutting
Barbados *m* Barbados
barbaridad *f* **1** barbarity **2** (*disparate*): ***decir ~es*** say outrageous things; ***¡qué ~!*** what a thing to say / do! **3**: ***una ~ de*** F a load of F, loads of F; ***costar una ~*** cost a fortune
barbarie *f* barbarism
barbarismo *m* **1** GRAM (*extranjerismo*) loan word **2** (*incorrección*) barbarism
bárbaro **I** *adj* F tremendous, awesome F; ***¡qué ~!*** amazing!, wicked! F; ***lo pasamos ~*** F we had a whale of a time **II** *m*, **-a** *f* F punk F
barbechar ⟨1a⟩ *v/t* AGR plow, *Br* plough
barbecho *m* AGR fallow land; ***estar de ~*** be lying fallow
barbería *f* barber's shop
barbero *m* barber
barbilampiño *adj* beardless
barbilla *f* chin
barbitúrico *m* barbiturate
barbo *m pescado* barbel
barbotar ⟨1a⟩, **barbotear** ⟨1a⟩ *v/t & v/i* mutter
barbudo *adj* bearded
barca *f* boat; ***dar un paseo en ~*** go on a boat trip
◇ **barca de pesca** fishing boat
barcada *f* boatload
barcaza *f* MAR barge
barcelonés *adj* of / from Barcelona, Barcelona *atr*
barco *m* boat; *más grande* ship; ***estar en el mismo ~*** *fig* be in the same boat
◇ **barco ballenero** whaler; **barco de escolta** escort ship; **barco pesquero** fishing boat; **barco salvador** *L.Am.* lifeboat; **barco de vela** sailing ship
barda *f Méx* wall
bardana *f* BOT burdock
bardo *m* bard
baremo *m* (*tabla*) scale; *fig* scale of values
bargueño *m* bureau (*furniture*)
bario *m* QUÍM barium
barítono *m* MÚS baritone
barlovento *m* MAR windward
barman *m* bartender, barman
barniz *m para madera* varnish
barnizado *m* varnishing
barnizar ⟨1f⟩ *v/t* varnish
barómetro *m* barometer
barón *m* baron
baronesa *f* baroness
barquero *m* boatman
barquillo *m* **1** (*galleta crujiente*) wafer **2** *Méx, C.Am.* ice-cream cone
barra *f* **1** *de metal*, *en bar* bar; ***en la ~*** at the bar; ***no te fíes de ellos, que no se paran en ~s*** *fig* don't trust them, they'll

B

stop at nothing **2** *de cortinas* rod **3** MÚS bar; ***doble ~*** double bar
◇ **barra adhesiva** glue stick; **barra americana** hostess bar; **barra de comandos** INFOR command bar; **barra desodorante** deodorant stick; **barra de equilibrio** DEP beam; **barra diagonal** INFOR slash; **barra diagonal inversa** INFOR backslash; **barra espaciadora** space-bar; **barra fija** DEP horizontal bar; **barra de herramientas** INFOR tool bar; **barra invertida** backslash; **barra de labios** lipstick; **barra libre** free bar; **barra de menús** INFOR menu bar; **barra de pan** baguette; **barra de protección lateral** AUTO side protection bar, side impact bar; **barras asimétricas** DEP asymmetric bars; **barras paralelas** DEP parallel bars
barrabasada *f* F mean trick
barraca *f* **1** (*chabola*) shack **2** *de tiro* stand; *de feria* stall **3** *L.Am.* (*depósito*) shed **4**: **~s** *pl L.Am.* shanty town *sg*
barracón *f* MIL barrack room
barracuda *m* barracuda
barranco *m* ravine
barredera I *f* street sweeper **II** *adj*: ***red ~*** trawl net
barredora *f* ☞ ***barredera***
barredura *f* sweeping; **~s** *pl* sweepings
barrena *f* **1** gimlet **2** AVIA: ***entrar en ~*** go into a spin
barrenar ⟨1a⟩ *v/t* drill
barrendero *m*, **-a** *f* street sweeper
barreno *m* drill hole
barreño *m* washing up bowl
barrer ⟨2a⟩ *v/t* sweep; ***~ hacia dentro*** *o* ***para casa*** look after number one; ***~ algo bajo la alfombra*** *fig* sweep sth under the carpet
barrera *f* **1** barrier; ***sin ~s*** (***arquitectónicas***) readily accessible (to the disabled), with easy disabled access; ***~s comerciales*** *pl* trade barriers **2** DEP jump; *de carreras* hurdle; *en fútbol* wall
◇ **barrera del sonido** sound barrier
◇ **barreras aduaneras, barreras arancelarias** tariff barriers
barretina *f traditional Catalan cap*
barriada *f C.Am.* (*barrio marginal*) slum, shanty town
barrial *m L.Am.* bog
barrica *f* barrel
barricada *f* barricade
barrida *f L.Am.* **1** sweep **2** (*redada*) police raid
barrido *m* sweep; ***servir lo mismo para un ~ que para un fregado*** F be able to turn one's hand to anything
barriga *f* belly; ***echar ~*** *fig* F get a belly *o* paunch; ***rascarse la ~*** *fig* F sit on one's butt F
barrigudo F **I** *adj* pot-bellied, paunchy **II** *m*, **-a** *f*: ***es un ~*** he has a pot belly, he has a paunch
barril *m* barrel
barrilero *m*, **-a** *f* cooper
barrilete *m* **1** cask **2** *Arg* (*cometa*) kite
barrio *m* neighborhood, *Br* neighbourhood, area; ***irse al otro ~*** *fig* F kick the bucket P
◇ **barrio de chabolas** *Esp* shanty town; **barrio chino** red-light district; **barrio obrero** working-class area; **barrio residencial** residential area; **barrios bajos** poor areas
barriobajero I 1 *adj* slum *atr* **2** *desp* common **II** *m*, **-a** *f* **1** slum dweller **2** *desp* common person
barritar ⟨1a⟩ *v/i de elefante* trumpet
barrizal *m* mire
barro *m* mud
barroco *m/adj tb fig* baroque
barroquismo *m* **1** ARQUI, PINT Baroque **2** *fig*: *de diseño, lenguaje* extravagance
barroso *adj* muddy
barrote *m* bar; ***entre ~s*** *fig* F behind bars
barruntar ⟨1a⟩ *v/t* suspect
barrunto *m* suspicion, feeling
bartola: ***tumbarse a la ~*** F take it easy
bártulos *mpl* F things, gear *sg* F; ***liar los ~*** pack one's bags
barullero I *adj* careless **II** *m*, **-a** *f* shoddy worker
barullo *m* uproar, racket
basa *f* ARQUI base
basal *adj* basal
basalto *m* MIN basalt
basamento *m* ARQUI pedestal
basar ⟨1a⟩ *v/t* base (**en** on); **basarse** *v/r* be based (**en** on)
basca *f* crowd, gang
báscula *f* scales *pl*
bascular ⟨1a⟩ *v/i* swing
base I *f* **1** QUÍM, MAT, MIL, DEP base **2**: **~s** *pl de concurso etc* conditions **3**: ***una***

dieta a ~ de frutas a diet based on fruit, a fruit-based diet; ***consiguió comprarse una casa a ~ de ahorrar*** he managed to buy a house by (dint of) saving; ***nos divertimos a ~ de bien*** we had a really *o* F a real good time **II** *m/f en baloncesto* guard
◇ **base aérea** MIL air base; **base por bolas** *en béisbol* base on balls, walk; **base de datos** INFOR database; **base imponible** tax base; **base de maquillaje** foundation (cream); **base naval** MIL naval base; **base robada** *en béisbol* stolen base
básicamente *adv* basically
básico *adj* basic
basílica *f* basilica
basilisco *m* MYTH basilisk; ***estar hecho un ~*** *fig* F be furious
basket *m* basketball
básquet *m L.Am.* basketball
basquetbol, básquetbol *m L.Am.* basketball
basquetbolista *m/f L.Am.* basketball player
basta *f* basting stitch, *Br* tacking stitch
bastante I *adj* **1** enough **2** *número o cantidad considerable* plenty of; ***quedan ~s plazas*** there are plenty of seats left **II** *adv con adjetivos* quite, fairly; ***bebe ~*** she drinks quite a lot
bastar ⟨1a⟩ *v/i* be enough; ***basta con uno*** one is enough; ***¡basta!*** that's enough!; ***basta y sobra*** I've / you've etc got more than enough; **bastarse** *v/r*: ***~ solo para hacer algo*** be perfectly able to do sth on one's own
bastardilla *f* italics *pl*
bastardo I *adj* bastard *atr* **II** *m* bastard
bastedad, basteza *f* roughness, coarseness
bastidor *m* **1** (*armazón*) frame **2** TEA wing; ***entre ~es*** *tb fig* behind the scenes
bastión *m* bastion
basto I *adj* rough, coarse **II** *mpl*: ***~s*** (*en naipes*) *suit in Spanish deck of cards*; ***pintar ~s*** *de situación* get rough
bastón *m* **1** (*vara*) stick; ***empuñar el ~*** *fig* take charge *o* command **2** ANAT rod
◇ **bastón de esquí** ski pole *o* stick
bastonazo *m* blow with a stick
bastoncillo *m* ANAT (retinal) rod
◇ **bastoncillo de algodón** Q-Tip®, *Br* cotton bud
basura *f tb fig* trash, *Br* rubbish; ***cubo de la ~*** garbage *o* trash can, *Br* rubbish bin
◇ **basura doméstica** domestic waste
◇ **basura orgánica** organic waste
basural *m L.Am.* dump, *Br tb* tip
basurero *m* garbage collector, *Br* dustman
bat *m Méx* DEP bat
bata *f* **1** *de estar por casa* robe, *Br* dressing gown **2** MED (white) coat **3** TÉC lab coat
◇ **bata de cola** *dress with a train, as worn by flamenco dancer*
batacazo *m* F bang; ***darse*** *o* ***pegarse un ~*** give o.s. a bang, bang o.s.; *fig* fail
batahola *f* F racket, din
batalla *f* battle; ***de ~*** *ropa* everyday
◇ **batalla campal** *fig* pitched battle
batallar ⟨1a⟩ *v/i* battle
batallita *f* F story, anecdote
batallón *m* battalion
batán *m* TÉC fulling machine
batata *f* BOT sweet potato
batazo *m en béisbol* hit
◇ **batazo de línea** *en béisbol* line drive; **batazo de sacrificio** *en béisbol* sacrifice hit
bate *m* DEP bat
◇ **bate de béisbol** baseball bat
batea *f* **1** (*bandeja*) tray **2** MAR flat-bottomed boat
bateador *m*, **~a** *f* batter
◇ **bateador corredor** *en béisbol* hitter runner
◇ **bateador designado** *en béisbol* designated hitter
batear ⟨1a⟩ **I** *v/t* hit **II** *v/i* bat
bateo *m* DEP batting
batería I *f* **1** MIL, EL, AUTO *en béisbol* battery; ***aparcar en ~*** AUTO angle park **2** MÚS drums *pl*, drum kit **II** *m/f* MÚS drummer
◇ **batería de cocina** set of pans
baterista *m/f* MÚS *L.Am.* drummer
batiborrillo *m*, **batiburrillo** *m* F jumble
batida *f* **1** *de caza* beating **2** *de policía* search
batido I *adj camino* well-trodden **II** *m* GASTR milkshake
batidor I *m* GASTR *manual* whisk; *eléctrico* hand mixer **II** *m*, **~a** *f* **1** *de caza* beater **2** MIL scout

batidora *f* mixer
batiente *m* jamb
batín *m* robe, *Br* dressing gown
batir ⟨3a⟩ *v/t* **1** *huevos* beat; *nata* whip **2** *récord* break **3** *territorio* comb **4** *monedas* mint; **batirse** *v/r* beat a retreat; **~ en duelo** fight a duel
batiscafo *m* bathyscaph(e)
Batuecas: ***estar en las ~*** F be in a world of one's own
baturro **I** *adj* **1** Aragonese **2** *fig* dumb **II** *m*, **-a** *f* Aragonese
batuta *f* MÚS baton; ***bajo la ~ de*** MÚS under the baton of; ***llevar la ~*** *fig* F be the boss F, rule the roost F
baúl *m* **1** *mueble* chest, trunk; ***salir del ~ de los recuerdos*** *fig* F come flooding back; ***henchir*** *o* ***llenar el ~*** *fig* P fill one's belly F, stuff one's face F **2** *L.Am.* AUTO trunk, *Br* boot
bauprés *m* MAR bowsprit
bautismal *adj* baptismal
bautismo *m* baptism, christening; ***partida de ~*** certificate of baptism
◇ **bautismo de fuego** baptism of fire
bautizar ⟨1f⟩ *v/t* baptize, christen; *barco* name; *vino* F water down
bautizo *m* baptism, christening
bauxita *f* MIN bauxite
baya *f* berry
bayeta *f* cloth
bayo **I** *adj horse* cream-colored, *Br* cream-coloured **II** *m*, **-a** *f* cream-colored *o* *Br* cream-coloured horse
bayoneta *f* bayonet
bayunco *adj C.Am.* P dumb F, stupid
baza *f* **1** *en naipes* trick; *fig* trump card; ***jugar sus ~s*** *fig* play one's cards right **2**: ***meter ~*** F interfere; ***no dejar a alguien meter ~*** F not let s.o. get a word in edgewise
bazar *m* **1** *tienda* hardware and fancy goods store **2** *mercado* bazaar
bazo *m* ANAT spleen
bazofia *f fig* F load of trash F
bazoka *f*, **bazuca** *f* MIL bazooka
BCE *m abr* (= ***Banco Central Europeo***) CEB (= Central European Bank)
be *f* letter 'b'
beatería *f desp* exaggerated piety
beatificación *f* REL beatification
beatificar ⟨1g⟩ *v/t* REL beatify
beatífico *adj* REL beatific
beatitud *f* REL beatitude
beato **I** *adj* pious; *desp* over-pious **II** *m*, **-a** *f* pious person; *desp* Holy Joe F
bebé *m* baby
bebedero *m para pájaros* water bowl
bebedizo **I** *adj* drinkable **II** *m* magic potion; *del amor* love potion
bebedor *m*, **~a** *f* **1** *de café, té* drinker **2** *de alcohol* (heavy) drinker
bebé-probeta *m* test-tube baby
beber ⟨2a⟩ **I** *v/i* drink; ***~ a o por*** drink to; ***~ en exceso*** drink too much, drink to excess; ***~ en un vaso*** drink from a glass; ***~ de la botella*** drink straight from the bottle **II** *v/t* drink; ***~ los vientos por alguien*** *fig* be crazy about s.o.; ***~ las palabras de alguien*** *fig* hang on *o* drink in s.o.'s every word; **beberse** *v/r* drink up
bebestible, bebible *adj* drinkable
bebida *f* drink
◇ **bebida energética** energy drink
◇ **bebida refrescante** soft drink
bebido **I** *pp* ☞ ***beber*** **II** *adj* drunk
bebistrajo *m* F vile concoction
beca *f* **1** *de organización* scholarship **2** *del estado* grant
becada *f* ZO woodcock
becado *m*, **-a** *f* **1** *de organización* scholarship holder **2** *del estado* grant holder
becar ⟨1g⟩ *v/t* **1** *de organización* award a scholarship to **2** *del estado* award a grant to
becario *m*, **-a** *f* ☞ ***becado***
becerrada *f bullfight featuring young bulls*
becerrillo *m* calfskin
becerro *m*, **-a** *f* calf
◇ **becerro de oro** golden calf
béchamel *f* GASTR béchamel (sauce)
becuadro *m* MÚS natural sign
bedel *m* porter
beduino **I** *adj* Bedouin **II** *m*, **-a** *f* Bedouin
befa *f* mockery; ***hacer ~ de*** mock, make fun of
befar ⟨1a⟩ *v/t* mock, make fun of; **befarse de** *v/r* mock, make fun of
befo *adj* thick-lipped
begonia *f* BOT begonia
BEI *m abr* (= ***Banco Europeo de Inversiones***) EIB (= European Investment Bank)
beicon *m* bacon
beige *adj* beige

Beijing *m* Beijing
beisbol *m Cu, Méx* baseball
béisbol *m* baseball
beisbolero *m*, **-a** *f L.Am.* baseball player
beisbolista *m/f L.Am.* baseball player
Belcebú *m* Beelzebub
beldad *f lit* beauty
belén *m* crèche, *Br tb* nativity scene
beleño *m* BOT henbane
belfo I *adj* thick-lipped **II** *m de animal* lip
belga *m/f & adj* Belgian
Bélgica *f* Belgium
Belice *m* Belize
beliceño I *adj* Belizean **II** *m*, **-a** *f* Belizean
belicismo *m* warmongering
belicista I *adj* warmongering **II** *m/f* warmonger
bélico *adj* war *atr*
belicosidad *f* bellicosity, aggressiveness
belicoso *adj* **1** warlike, bellicose **2** *fig persona* belligerent
beligerancia *f* belligerence
beligerante *adj nación, pueblo etc* belligerent
bellaco I *adj* rascally, roguish **II** *m*, **-a** *f* rascal, rogue
belladona *f* BOT deadly nightshade, belladonna
bellaquería *f* rascally trick
belleza *f* beauty
bellísimo *adj* extremely beautiful; ***una -a persona*** a lovely person
bello *adj* beautiful
bellota *f* BOT acorn
bemba *f L.Am.* thick lips *pl*
bemol *m* MÚS flat; ***mi ~*** E flat; ***tener ~es*** *fig* F be tricky F
benceno *m* QUÍM benzene
bencina *f* **1** QUÍM benzine **2** *Pe, Bol* (*gasolina*) gas, *Br* petrol
bendecir ⟨3p⟩ *v/t* bless; ***~ la mesa*** say grace
bendición *f* blessing; ***con la ~ de*** F with the blessing of; ***ser una ~*** (***de Dios / del cielo***) *fig* be a godsend
◇ **bendición de la mesa** grace
◇ **bendiciones nupciales** wedding ceremony *sg*
bendigo *vb* ☞ ***bendecir***
bendijo *vb* ☞ ***bendecir***
bendito I *adj* blessed **II** *m*, **-a** *f* simple soul; ***dormir como un ~*** sleep like a baby, sleep the sleep of the just
benedictino I *adj* Benedictine **II** *m*, **-a** *f* Benedictine
benefactor *adj* charitable
beneficencia *f* charity
beneficiar ⟨1b⟩ *v/t* **1** benefit; ***~ a alguien*** benefit s.o. **2** *Rpl ganado* slaughter; **beneficiarse** *v/r* benefit (***de, con*** from)
beneficiario I *adj*: ***la persona -a de*** the recipient of; ***la parte -a*** the beneficiary / beneficiaries **II** *m*, **-a** *f* beneficiary
beneficio *m* **1** (*ventaja*) benefit; ***en ~ de*** in aid of **2** COM profit **2** *Rpl para ganado* slaughterhouse **3** *C.Am.* coffee-processing plant
beneficioso *adj* beneficial
benéfico *adj* charity *atr*; ***función -a*** charity function *o* event; ***para fines ~s*** for charity
Benemérita *f Esp*: ***la ~*** the Civil Guard
benemérito *adj* distinguished
beneplácito *m* approval; ***dar su ~*** give one's approval
benevolencia *f* benevolence
benevolente *adj* ☞ ***benévolo***
benévolo *adj* **1** (*bondadoso*) benevolent, kind **2** (*indulgente*) lenient
bengala *f* flare
bengalí I *adj* Bengali **II** *m/f* Bengali **III** *m idioma* Bengali
benigno *adj* **1** MED benign **2** *clima* mild **3** *persona* benevolent
benito *m*, **-a** *f* Benedictine
benjamín *m* youngest son
benjamina *f* youngest daughter
beodez *f fml* drunkenness
beodo *fml* **I** *adj* drunk, inebriated *fml* **II** *m*, **-a** *f* drunkard, drunk
berberecho *m* ZO cockle
berbiquí *m* brace
BERD *m abr* (= ***Banco Europeo de Reconstrucción y Desarrollo***) EBRD (= European Bank for Reconstruction and Development)
beréber, bereber *m/f* Berber
berenjena *f* BOT eggplant, *Br* aubergine
berenjenal *m*: ***meterse en un ~*** *fig* F get o.s. into a jam F
bergamota *f* BOT bergamot
bergante *m* scoundrel
bergantín *m* MAR brigantine, brig

B

berilio *m* QUÍM beryllium
berilo *m* MIN beryl
Berlín *m* Berlin
berlina *f* AUTO four-door sedan, *Br* four-door saloon
berlinés **I** *adj* of / from Berlin, Berlin *atr* **II** *m*, **-esa** *f* Berliner
berma *f Andes* (hard) shoulder
bermejo *adj* reddish; ***Mar Bermejo*** Gulf of California
bermellón *m* vermilion, *Br* vermillion
bermudas *mpl*, *fpl* Bermuda shorts
berrear ⟨1a⟩ *v/i* **1** *de animal, persona* bellow **2** *de niño* bawl, yell
berrido *m* **1** *de animal, persona* bellow **2** *de niño* yell
berrinche *m* F tantrum; ***agarrar un ~*** F throw a tantrum
berro *m* BOT watercress
berrueco *m* granite rock *o* crag
berza *f* BOT cabbage
berzas, berzotas *m/f inv* F dope F
besamel *f* GASTR béchamel (sauce)
besar ⟨1a⟩ *v/t* kiss; ***~ el suelo*** *fig* F fall flat on one's face; ***lo suyo fue llegar y ~ el santo, quedó primero en su primera carrera*** he was incredibly lucky and won his first race; **besarse** *v/r* kiss
besito *m* little kiss
beso *m* kiss; ***comerse a alguien a ~s*** smother s.o. in kisses
◇ **beso de tornillo** French kiss
bestia **I** *f* beast; ***trabajar como una ~*** work like a dog **II** *m/f* **1** (*zopenco*) F brute; *antipático* swine F; *mujer* bitch; ***ser un ~*** be a brute **2**: ***conducir a lo ~*** F drive like a madman
◇ **bestia de carga** *tb fig* beast of burden
◇ **bestia negra** bête noire
bestial *adj* F tremendous F
bestialidad *f* act of cruelty
bestiario *m* bestiary
best-seller *m* best-seller
besugo *m* **1** ZO bream; ***ojos de ~*** bulging eyes **2** *fig* F idiot; ***no seas ~*** F don't be stupid
besuquear ⟨1a⟩ *v/t* F smother with kisses
besuqueo *m* F necking, *Br* F snogging
betabel *m Méx* red beet, *Br* beetroot
betabloqueador *m* MED beta-blocker
betarraga *f Andes* red beet, *Br* beetroot
betún *m* shoe polish
BEX *m abr* (= ***Banco Exterior de España***) *Overseas Bank of Spain*
bianual *adj* biannual, twice-yearly
biatleta *m/f* biathlete
biatlón *m* biathlon
biberón *m* baby's bottle
Biblia *f* Bible
bíblico *adj* biblical
bibliobús *m* bookmobile, *Br* mobile library
bibliófilo *m*, **-a** *f* bibliophile
bibliografía *f* bibliography
bibliográfico *adj* bibliographic
biblioteca *f* **1** library **2** *mueble* bookcase
◇ **biblioteca de consulta (directa), biblioteca presencial** reference library
bibliotecario *m*, **-a** *f* librarian
biblioteconomía *f* librarianship, library science
bicameralismo *m* POL two-chamber system
bicampeón *m*, **-ona** *f* DEP two-times champion
bicarbonato *m*: **~ (*de sodio*)** bicarbonate of soda, bicarb F
bicéfalo *adj* two-headed
bicentenario *m* bicentennial, *Br* bicentenary
bíceps *mpl* biceps *sg*
bicha *f* F snake
bicharraco *m*, **-a** *f fig* F nasty piece of work
bicherío *m L.Am.* bugs *pl*, *Br tb* creepy-crawlies *pl*
bichero *m* MAR boat hook
bicho *m* **1** (*insecto*) bug, *Br tb* creepy-crawly; ***¿qué ~ te ha picado?*** what's eating you?; ***no hay ~ viviente*** F there isn't a living soul **2** (*animal*) creature; **(*mal*) ~** *fig* F nasty piece of work; ***~ raro*** weirdo F
bici *f* F bike
bicicleta *f* bicycle; ***ir*** *o* ***montar en ~*** go cycling
◇ **bicicleta de carreras** racing bicycle; **bicicleta de ejercicio, bicicleta estática** exercise bicycle; **bicicleta de montaña** mountain bike; **bicicleta plegable** folding bicycle
bicicross *m* cyclocross
bicoca *f* F bargain
bicolor *adj* two-colored, *Br* two-col-

oured

BID *m abr* (= ***Banco Interamericano de Desarollo***) IADB (= Inter-American Development Bank)

bidé *m* bidet

bidón *m* drum

biela *f* TÉC connecting rod

Bielorrusia *f* Belarus

bielorruso I *adj* Belarussian **II** *m*, **-a** *f* Belarussian

bien I *m* good; ***por tu ~*** for your own good; ***~es*** *pl* goods, property *sg*; ***hombre de ~*** good man; ***estar por encima del ~ y del mal*** be above the law **II** *adj*: ***¡está ~!*** it's OK!, it's alright!; ***estoy ~*** I'm fine, I'm OK; ***¿estás ~ aquí?*** are you comfortable here?; ***la gente ~*** well-to-do people **III** *adv* **1** well; (*muy*) very; ***¡~ hecho!*** well done!; ***~ está lo que ~ acaba*** all's well that ends well **2** (*correctamente*) well, properly **3** *en locuciones*: ***más ~*** rather; ***tener a ~ hacer algo*** see fit to do sth; ***hicieron ~ en reservar los billetes con tanta antelación*** they did the right thing booking the tickets so far ahead; ***haces ~ en llevarte el paraguas*** it's a good idea to take your umbrella; ***estar (a) ~ con alguien*** be on good terms with s.o. **IV** *conj*: ***o ~ … o …*** either … or …; ***si ~***, ***~ que*** although; ***no ~*** as soon as **V** *int*: ***¡ya está ~!*** that's it!, that's enough!; ***pues ~*** well
◇ **bienes de capital** capital goods; **bienes de consumo** consumer goods, consumer durables; **bienes de equipo** capital goods; **bienes immuebles** real estate *sg*; **bienes muebles** moveable items, personal property *sg*

bienal I *adj* biennial **II** *f* biennial event

bienaventurado *adj* REL blessed

bienaventuranza *f* REL eternal life; ***las Bienaventuranzas*** the Beatitudes

bienestar *m* well-being

bienhablado *adj* well-spoken

bienhechor I *adj* beneficent **II** *m*, **~a** *f* benefactor

bienintencionado *adj* well-meant

bienio *m* period of two years

bienquerencia *f* **1** affection **2** (*buena voluntad*) good will

bienquisto *adj fml* well-liked

bienvenida *f* welcome; ***dar la ~ a alguien*** welcome s.o.

bienvenido *adj* welcome

bienvivir ⟨3a⟩ *v/i* live comfortably

bies *m en costura* bias; ***al ~*** on the cross

bifásico *adj* EL two-phase

bife *m Rpl* steak

bifocal *adj* bifocal

biftec *m* steak

bifurcación *f de camino, río etc* fork; *de línea férrea* junction

bifurcado *adj* forked

bifurcarse ⟨1g⟩ *v/r de camino, río etc* fork

bigamia *f* bigamy

bígamo I *adj* bigamous **II** *m*, **-a** *f* bigamist

bigardo *m* F bruiser F, beefy type

bígaro *m* ZO winkle

bigote *m* mustache, *Br* moustache; ***tener ~s*** have a mustache; ***~s*** *pl de gato etc* whiskers; ***de ~s*** F fantastic, amazing

bigotudo *adj* with a big mustache *o Br* moustache

bikini *m* bikini

bilateral *adj* bilateral

bilbaíno I *adj* of / from Bilbao **II** *m*, **-a** *f* native of Bilbao

bilet *m Méx* lipstick

biliar *adj* ANAT bile *atr*

bilingüe *adj* bilingual

bilingüismo *m* bilingualism

bilioso *adj tb fig* bilious

bilis *f* **1** bile **2** *fig* spleen; ***tragar ~*** put up with it, grin and bear it

billar *m* billiards *sg*; ***jugar al ~*** play billiards
◇ **billar americano** pool

billete *m* ticket
◇ **billete abierto** open ticket; **billete de autobús** bus ticket; **billete de avión** plane ticket; **billete de banco** bill, *Br* banknote; **billete de ida** one-way ticket, *Br* single (ticket); **billete de ida y vuelta** round-trip ticket, *Br* return (ticket); **billete infantil** child's ticket; **billete de lotería** lottery ticket; **billete premiado** *lotería* winning ticket; **billete sencillo** one-way ticket, *Br* single (ticket)

billetera *f L.Am.*, **billetero** *m* billfold, *Br* wallet

billón *m* trillion

bimensual *adj* twice-monthly, *Br tb* fortnightly

B

bimestral *adj* bimonthly, two-monthly
bimotor I *adj* twin-engined **II** *m* twin-engined plane
binar ⟨1a⟩ *v/t* dig over
binario *adj* binary
bingo *m* **1** *juego* bingo **2** *lugar* bingo hall
binocular *adj* binocular
binóculo *m* pince-nez
binóculos *mpl L.Am.* binoculars, pair of binoculars *sg*
binomio *m* MAT binomial
bioactivo *adj* bioactive
biodegradable *adj* biodegradable
biodinámico *adj* biodynamic
biodiversidad *f* biodiversity
biofísica *f* biophysics *sg*
biogás *m* biogas
biogenético *adj* biogenetic
biografía *f* biography
biográfico *adj* biographical
biógrafo *m*, **-a** *f* biographer
biología *f* biology
biológico *adj* biological; AGR organic
biólogo *m*, **-a** *f* biologist
biomasa *f* biomass
biombo *m* folding screen
biopsia *f* MED biopsy
bioquímica *f* biochemistry
bioquímico I *adj* biochemical **II** *m*, **-a** *f* biochemist
biorritmo *m* biorhythm
biosfera *f* biosphere
biotecnología *f* biotechnology
biotopo *m* biotope
bipartidismo *m* POL two-party system
bipartidista *adj* POL two-party
bípedo I *adj* bipedal, biped **II** *m* biped
biplano *m* AVIA biplane
biplaza *m/adj* two-seater *atr*
bipolar *adj* bipolar
biquini *m* bikini
BIRD *m abr* (= ***Banco Internacional de Reconstrucción y Desarrollo***) IBRD (= International Bank for Reconstruction and Development)
birlar ⟨1a⟩ *v/t* F lift F, swipe F
birlibirloque *m* F: ***por arte de ~*** as if by magic
Birmania *f* Burma
birmano I *adj* Burmese **II** *m*, **-a** *f* Burmese **III** *m idioma* Burmese
birome *m Rpl* ballpoint (pen)
birra *f* F beer
birreta *f de cardenal* biretta
birrete *m de catedrático* mortarboard
birria *f* F piece of junk F; ***va hecha una ~*** F she looks a real mess F
bis *m* encore; ***9 ~*** 9A
bisabuela *f* great-grandmother
bisabuelo *m* great-grandfather
bisagra *f* hinge
bisbisar, bisbisear ⟨1a⟩ *v/t* whisper
biscocho *m* ☞ ***bizcocho***
biscote *m* rusk
bisecar ⟨1g⟩ *v/t* bisect
bisección *f* MAT bisection
bisector *adj* MAT bisecting
bisel *m* bevel
biselado *adj* beveled, *Br* bevelled
biselar ⟨1a⟩ *v/t* bevel
bisemanal *adj* twice-weekly
bisexual *m/f* & *adj* bisexual
bisiesto *adj*: ***año ~*** leap year
bisílabo *adj* with two syllables, two-syllable
bismuto *m* QUÍM bismuth
bisnieta *f* great-granddaughter
bisnieto *m* great-grandson
bisojo *adj* cross-eyed
bisonte *m* ZO bison
bisoñé *m* hairpiece, toupee
bisoño I *adj* **1** *en un oficio* inexperienced, green F **2** MIL inexperienced, raw **II** *m*, **-a** *f* **1** F (*novato*) greenhorn F **2** MIL rookie F
bisté, bistec *m* steak
bisturí *m* MED scalpel
bisutería *f* costume jewelry *o Br* jewellery
bit *m* INFOR bit
bitácora *f* MAR binnacle; ***cuaderno de ~*** logbook
bíter *m aperitivo* bitters *pl*
bituminoso *adj* bituminous
Bizancio *m* Byzantium
bizantino *adj fig* pointless
bizarría *f lit* valor, *Br* valour, bravery
bizarro *adj lit* valiant, brave
bizcar ⟨1g⟩ *v/i* squint, be cross-eyed
bizco *adj* cross-eyed
bizcocho *m* sponge (cake)
biznieta *f* great-granddaughter
biznieto *m* great-grandson
bizquear ⟨1a⟩ *v/i* F squint, be cross--eyed
bizquera *f* F squint
blanca *f* **1** *persona* white **2** MÚS half note, *Br* minim **3**: ***estar sin ~*** *fig* F

be broke F
Blancanieves *f* Snow White
blanco I *adj* **1** white; ***no distinguir lo ~ de lo negro*** not know what's what; ***ponerse*** *o* ***quedarse ~*** go white **2** (*sin escrito*) blank; ***en ~*** COM blank; ***me quedé en ~, me quedé con la mente en ~*** my mind went blank; ***pasar la noche en ~*** have a sleepless night **3**: ***arma -a*** knife
II *m* **1** *persona* white **2** (*diana*), *fig* target; ***dar en el ~*** hit the nail on the head; ***errar el ~*** miss the target; ***hacer ~*** hit the target; ***ser el ~ de todas las miradas*** be the center *o Br* centre of attention
◇ **blanco de España** whiting; **blanco de plomo** white lead; **blanco y negro** GASTR *iced coffee with cream*
blancor *m*, **blancura** *f* whiteness
blancuzco *adj* whitish
blandengue F *desp* **I** *adj* soft F **II** *m/f* softy F
blandir ⟨3a⟩ *v/t arma* brandish
blando I *adj* soft **II** *m*, **-a** *f*: ***ser un ~*** be too soft
blanducho *adj desp* soft
blandura *f* softness
blanquear ⟨1a⟩ **I** *v/t* **1** whiten; *pared* whitewash; *ropa* bleach **2** *dinero* launder **3** GASTR blanch **II** *v/i* go white
blanquecino *adj* off-white
blanqueo *m de pared* whitewashing; *con lejía* bleaching
◇ **blanqueo de dinero** money laundering
blanquillo I *adj* whitish **II** *m Méx* egg
blanquinegro *adj* black-and-white
blasfemar ⟨1a⟩ *v/i* **1** (*maldecir*) curse, swear **2** REL blaspheme
blasfemia *f* REL blasphemy
blasfemo I *adj* blasphemous **II** *m*, **-a** *f* blasphemer
blasón *m* coat of arms
blasonar ⟨1a⟩ **I** *v/t* emblazon **II** *v/i*: ***~ de*** *lit* boast about
blazer *m* blazer
bledo *m* F: ***me importa un ~*** I don't give a damn F
blenorragia *f* MED gonorrhea, *Br tb* gonorrhoea
blindado *adj* **I 1** *vehículo* armored, *Br* armoured **2** *puerta* reinforced **3** EL shielded **II** *m* armored *o Br* armoured vehicle
blindaje *m* **1** *de vehículo* armor *o Br* armour plating **2** EL shield
blindar ⟨1a⟩ *v/t* **1** *vehículo* armor-plate, *Br* armour-plate **2** EL shield
blíster *m* (*envase*) blister pack, bubble pack
bloc *m* pad
◇ **bloc de cartas** writing pad
◇ **bloc de notas** notepad
blocao *m* MIL blockhouse
blocar ⟨1g⟩ *v/t* DEP *balón* stop; *jugador* bodycheck
blof *m L.Am.* bluff
blofear ⟨1a⟩ *v/i L.Am.* bluff
blondo *adj lit* flaxen *lit*
bloomer *m Cu* panties *pl*
bloque *m* **1** *de piedra* block **2** POL bloc; ***en ~*** en masse
◇ **bloque de apartamentos** apartment building, *Br* block of flats
bloquear ⟨1a⟩ *v/t* **1** block **2** DEP obstruct; *en baloncesto* screen **3** (*atascar*) jam **4** MIL blockade **5** COM freeze
bloqueo *m* **1** MIL blockade **2** *en baloncesto* screen
bluf(f) *m L.Am.* bluff
blusa *f* blouse
blusón *m* loose blouse *o* shirt
BM *m abr* (= ***Banco Mundial***) World Bank
B.o *abr* (= ***visto bueno***) approved, OK
boa *f* ZO boa constrictor
boato *m* ostentation
bob *m* DEP bob
bobada *f* piece of nonsense
bobalicón *m*, **-ona** *f* F dope F, *Br tb* twit F
bobear ⟨1a⟩ *v/i* fool around, act the fool
bobería *f*: ***hacer / decir una ~*** do / say something silly
bóbilis: ***de ~ ~*** F (*sin esfuerzo*) just like that F; (*gratis*) for nothing
bobina *f* **1** *de hilo* bobbin **2** FOT reel, spool **3** EL coil
bobinado *m* EL winding
bobinar ⟨1a⟩ *v/t* wind
bobo I *adj* silly, foolish **II** *m*, **-a** *f* fool; ***pájaro ~*** penguin
bobsleigh *m* bob(sled), *Br* bob(sleigh)
boca *f* **1** mouth; ***~ a ~*** mouth to mouth; ***hacer el ~ a ~ a alguien*** MED give s.o. mouth-to-mouth resuscitation; ***~ abajo*** upside down; *persona, cartas, libro* face

B

down; **~ arriba** right way up; *persona*, *cartas*, *libro* face up; **dejar con la ~ abierta** leave open-mouthed; **quedarse con la ~ abierta** be dumbfounded, be open-mouthed with astonishment; **se me hace la ~ agua** my mouth is watering; **abrir** *o* **hacer ~** whet one's appetite; **a pedir de ~** perfectly; **andar** *o* **ir** *o* **correr de ~ en ~** circulate, go around; **callar la ~** shut up; **estar en ~ de todos** be on everybody's lips; **hablar por ~ de ganso** *o* **de otro** F parrot someone else's views; **no decir esta ~ es mía** not say a word; **meterse en la ~ del lobo** put one's head in the lion's mouth; **taparle la ~ a alguien** *fig* keep s.o. quiet, F shut s.o. up; **con la ~ chica** without much conviction; **partirle la ~ a alguien** P smash s.o.'s face in F; **poner algo en ~ de alguien** attribute sth to s.o.; **quitarle a alguien la palabra de la ~** take the words right out of s.o.'s mouth; **llenarse la ~** (**hablando**) **de** *fig* talk of nothing but; **quitarse algo de la ~** *fig* go *o* do without sth, deny o.s. sth
2 ZO crab claw
◇ **boca de incendios** fireplug, *Br* fire hydrant; **boca de metro** subway entrance; **boca de riego** fireplug, *Br* fire hydrant; **boca de subte** *CSur* subway entrance; **Bocas del Amazonas** Amazon estuary

bocacalle *f* side street
bocadillería *f* sandwich shop
bocadillo *m* sandwich
bocado *m* **1** mouthful, bite; **no probar ~** not have a bite to eat, not eat a thing **2** *para caballos* bit
◇ **bocado de Adán** ANAT Adam's apple
bocajarro *m*: **a ~** at point-blank range; *fig decir* point-blank, straight out
bocallave *f* keyhole
bocamanga *f* cuff
bocamina *f* MIN pithead
bocana *f* river mouth
bocanada *f* **1** mouthful **2** *de viento* gust
bocata *m* F ☞ **bocadillo**
bocazas *m/f inv* F loudmouth F
bocera *f* mustache, *Br* moustache (*left by food or drink*)
boceras *m/f inv* loudmouth
boceto *m* sketch
bocha *f* bowl; **~s** *pl juego* bowls *sg*
bochar ⟨1a⟩ *v/t* **1** *Rpl* F *en examen* fail, flunk F **2** *Méx* (*rechazar*) cold-shoulder, rebuff
boche *m Ven*, *Chi* brawl, fight
bochinche *m Méx* uproar
bochorno *m* **1** sultry weather **2** *fig* embarrassment
bochornoso *adj* **1** *tiempo* sultry **2** *fig* embarrassing
bocina *f* MAR, AUTO horn; **tocar la ~** blow *o* toot one's horn
bocinazo *m* MAR, AUTO toot
bocio *m* MED goiter, *Br* goitre
boda *f* wedding
◇ **bodas de oro** golden wedding *sg*; **bodas de diamante** diamond wedding *sg*; **bodas de plata** silver wedding *sg*
bodega *f* **1** wine cellar **2** MAR, AVIA: **~** (**de carga**) hold **3** *L.Am.* bar **4** *C.Am.*, *Pe*, *Bol* grocery store, *Br* grocer's
bodegón *m* PINT still life
bodeguero *m*, **-a** *f C.Am.*, *Pe*, *Ven* storekeeper, *Br* shopkeeper
bodrio *m fig* piece of garbage
body *m prenda* body
BOE *m abr* (= **Boletín Oficial del Estado**) Official Gazette of Spain
bofe *m* ZO lights *pl*; **echar los ~s** work one's butt off F, *Br* slog one's guts out F
bofetada *f* slap
bofetear ⟨1a⟩ *v/t L.Am.* slap
bofetón *m* hard slap (in the face)
bofia *f* F cops *pl* F
boga *f*: **estar en ~** *fig* be in fashion
bogador *m*, **~a** *f* rower
bogar ⟨1h⟩ *v/i* row
bogavante *m* ZO lobster
Bogotá *m* Bogota
bogotano I *adj* of / from Bogota, Bogota *atr* **II** *m*, **-a** *f* native of Bogota
bohemio I *adj* bohemian **II** *m*, **-a** *f* bohemian
bohío *m Cu*, *Ven* hut
boicot *m* boycott
boicotear ⟨1a⟩ *v/t* boycott
boicoteo *m* boycotting
boiler *m Méx* boiler
boina *f* beret
boj *m* BOT box
bojote *m L.Am. fig* bundle
bol *m* bowl
bola *f* **1** ball; **no dar pie con ~** get every-

thing wrong; ***dejar que ruede la ~*** *fig* let things take their course **2** TÉC ball bearing **3** *de helado* scoop **4** F (*mentira*) fib F **5**: ***~s*** *pl* P balls P, nuts P; ***en ~s*** F stark naked
◇ **bola de billar** billiard ball; **bola buena** *en béisbol* fair ball; **bola con curva** *en béisbol* curve ball; **bola de fuego** fireball; **bola mala** *en béisbol* foul ball; **bola muerta** *en béisbol* dead ball; **bola del mundo** globe; **bola de nieve** snowball; **bola rápida** *en béisbol* fast ball

bolada *f* **1** *L.Am.* (*tiro*) throw **2** (*suerte*) piece of luck

bolado *m* **1** *S.Am.* deal **2** *L.Am.* F (*mentira*) fib F

bolchevique *m/f* & *adj* Bolshevik

bolchevismo *m* Bolshevism

boleada *f Arg* hunt

boleador *m*, **~a** *f Méx* (*limpiabotas*) bootblack

boleadoras *fpl L.Am. para cazar* bolas

bolear ⟨1a⟩ **I** *v/i L.Am.* DEP have a knockabout **II** *v/t* **1** *L.Am.* DEP bowl **2** *Rpl con boleadoras* bring down **3** *Méx zapatos* shine; **bolearse** *v/r* **1** *Rpl* fall **2** (*apenarse*) get embarrassed

bolera *f* bowling alley

bolero I *m* MÚS bolero **II** *m*, **-a** *f Méx* F bootblack

boleta *f* **1** *L.Am. de tren, cine* ticket **2** *L.Am.* (*pase*) pass, permit **3** *L.Am.* (*voto*) ballot paper; ***dar (la) ~ a alguien*** F break with s.o.

boletería *f L.Am.* **1** *en estación* ticket office **2** *en cine, teatro* box office

boletero *m*, **-a** *f L.Am.* **1** *en estación* ticket clerk **2** *en cine, teatro* box office employee

boletín *m* bulletin, report
◇ **boletín de evaluación** report card;- **boletín informativo** news bulletin; **boletín meteorológico** weather report; **boletín oficial** official bulletin; **boletín de pedido** order form

boleto *m L.Am.* ticket
◇ **boleto de autobús** *L.Am.* bus ticket
◇ **boleto de ida y vuelta** *L.Am.*, **boleto redondo** *Méx* round-trip ticket, *Br* return

boli *m* ballpoint (pen)

boliche *m* **1** AUTO jack **2** (*bolera*) bowling alley **3** *CSur* (*tienda*) grocery store, *Br* grocer's **4** *CSur* (*bar*) bar **5** *L.Am. juego* cup and ball game

bólido *m* **1** racing car **2** AST meteor; ***como un ~*** *fig* F like greased lightning

bolígrafo *m* ballpoint pen

bolillo *m* **1** *para labores* bobbin; ***encaje de ~s*** (handmade) lace **2** *Méx* bread roll

bolina *f* MAR bowline; ***ir** o **navegar de ~*** sail close to the wind

bolita *f CSur* (*canica*) marble

bolívar *m* bolivar (*currency unit of Venezuela*)

Bolivia *f* Bolivia

boliviano I *adj* Bolivian **II** *m*, **-a** *f* Bolivian

bollería *f* bakery

bollo *m* **1** *de repostería* bun **2** (*abolladura*) bump

bolo *m* **1** *para el juego* pin **2** *C.Am., Méx regalo* christening present

bolos *mpl* **1** bowling *sg*, *Br* tenpin bowling *sg*; ***jugar a los ~*** go bowling, *Br* play tenpin bowls **2** TEA: ***hacer ~*** tour

bolsa *f* **1** bag **2** COM stock exchange; ***salida a ~*** flotation **3** *L.Am.* (*bolsillo*) pocket **4** *C.Am., Méx de mujeres* purse, pocketbook, *Br* handbag **5** (*dinero*): ***aflojar la ~*** F fork out F **6** ANAT: ***~s bajo los ojos*** bags under the eyes
◇ **bolsa de agua caliente** hot-water bottle; **bolsa de aseo** toilet kit, *Br* sponge bag; **bolsa de la basura** garbage bag, *Br* bin bag; **bolsa de la compra** shopping bag; **bolsa de deporte** sport bag; **bolsa de estudios** (study) grant; **bolsa isotérmica** cool bag; **bolsa nevera** cool bag; **bolsa de trabajo** employment exchange; **bolsa de valores** stock exchange; **bolsa de viaje** travel bag

bolsero *m*, **-a** *f Méx* F scrounger

bolsillo *m* pocket; ***de ~*** pocket *atr*; ***meterse a alguien en el ~*** F win s.o. over; ***rascarse el ~*** F fork out F; ***llenarse los ~s*** *fig* make a fortune; ***los tuvo a todos en el ~ en seguida*** he soon had them all eating out of his hand; ***el Boca Juniors tiene la liga en el ~*** the league is in the bag for Boca Juniors
◇ **bolsillo trasero** back pocket

bolsín *m* COM small stock exchange

bolsista *m/f* stockbroker

bolso *m* purse, *Br* handbag
◇ **bolso de bandolera** shoulder bag

B

bolsón *m Arg, Pe* travel bag
bomba *f* **1** (*explosivo*) bomb; ***caer como una ~*** *fig* F come as a bombshell **2** TÉC pump **3** *S.Am.* gas station, *Br* petrol station **4** *Esp*: ***pasarlo ~*** F have a great time
◇ **bomba de aire** pump; **bomba aspiradora** suction pump; **bomba atómica** atomic bomb; **bomba de calor** heat pump; **bomba de cobalto** MED cobalt bomb; **bomba fétida** stink bomb; **bomba de fragmentación** fragmentation bomb; **bomba de gasolina** gas pump, *Br* petrol pump; **bomba de hidrógeno** hydrogen bomb; **bomba de humo** smoke bomb; **bomba incendiaria** incendiary bomb; **bomba de inyección** injection pump; **bomba lacrimógena** tear gas canister; **bomba de mano** hand grenade; **bomba de neutrones, bomba neutrónica** neutron bomb; **bomba de presión** pressure pump; **bomba de relojería** time bomb; **bomba de vacío** vacuum pump
bombacha *f Arg* panties *pl*, *Br tb* knickers *pl*
bombacho *m*: ***~s*** *pl*, ***pantalón ~*** baggy pants *pl*
bombardear ⟨1a⟩ *v/t desde el aire* bomb; *con artillería* bombard
bombardeo *m desde el aire* bombing; *con artillería* bombardment
bombardero *m* bomber
bombástico *adj* bombastic
bombazo *m* **1** explosion **2** *fig* F bombshell
bombear ⟨1a⟩ *v/t* **1** *líquido* pump **2** *balón* lob
bombeo *m de líquido* pumping
bombero *m*, **-a** *f* firefighter; ***~s*** *pl* fire department *sg*, *Br* fire brigade *sg*; ***llamar a los ~s*** call the fire department
bombilla *f* **1** light bulb; ***se me encendió la ~*** *fig* I had a brainstorm *o Br* brainwave **2** *Rpl metal drinking tube for maté* **3** *en baloncesto* key
bombillo *m C.Am., Pe, Bol* light bulb
bombín *m* derby, *Br* bowler hat
bombita *f Arg* light bulb
bombo *m* **1** MÚS bass drum; *persona* bass drummer; ***dar ~ a algo*** F hype sth up F; ***darse ~*** F blow one's own trumpet F; ***a ~ y platillo*** F with a great song and dance F, with a lot of hoo-ha F; ***tengo la cabeza como un ~*** *fig* my head is splitting **2** TÉC drum **3** *fig* F *de embarazada* bump
bombón *m* **1** *dulce* chocolate **2** *fig* F *persona* babe F
◇ **bombón helado** ice-cream bomb
bombona *f de oxígeno, líquido etc* cylinder
◇ **bombona de gas** gas cylinder
bombonera *f* candy box, *Br* sweet box
bombonería *f* candy store, *Br* sweet shop
bonachón *adj* good-natured
bonaerense **I** *adj* of / from Buenos Aires, Buenos Aires *atr* **II** *m/f* native of Buenos Aires
bonanza *f fig* boom, bonanza
bondad *f* goodness, kindness; ***tenga la ~ de*** please be so kind as to
bondadoso *adj* caring
bonete *m* **1** *sombrero* mortarboard **2** ZO reticulum
bongo *m L.Am.* bongo
boniato *m* BOT sweet potato
bonificación *f* **1** (*gratificación*) bonus **2** (*descuento*) discount
bonificar ⟨1g⟩ *v/t* **1** (*gratificar*) give a bonus to **2** (*descontar*) give a discount of
bonísimo *adj sup* (*bueno*) very good
bonito **I** *adj* pretty **II** *m* ZO tuna **III** *adv L.Am.* well
bono *m* **1** (*vale*) voucher **2** COM bond
◇ **bono del Tesoro** Treasury bond
bonsái *m* bonsai
boñiga *f* dung
bookmark *m* INFOR bookmark
boom *m* boom
boqueada *f por sorpresa, dolor etc* gasp; ***dar la última ~*** breathe one's last
boquear ⟨1a⟩ **I** *v/i* **1** *por sorpresa, dolor etc* gasp **2** *fig* be at death's door **II** *v/t palabra* utter
boquera *f* cold sore
boquerón *m* ZO anchovy
boquete *m* hole
boquiabierto *adj fig* F speechless; ***quedarse ~*** be speechless
boquilla *f* **1** MÚS mouthpiece **2** TÉC *de manguera* nozzle **3**: ***lo dice de ~*** he doesn't mean a word of it; ***promete mucho de ~ pero luego no hace nada*** he's all talk and no action
boquirroto *adj* garrulous

borbollar ⟨1a⟩ *v/i* bubble
borbollón *m* ☞ ***borbotón***
Borbones *mpl*: ***los ~*** the Bourbons
borborigmo(s) *m(pl)* rumbling *sg*
borbotar ⟨1a⟩ *v/i* bubble
borbotón *m*: ***salir a borbotones*** *de agua* gush out; ***hablaba a borbotones*** *fig* it all came out in a rush
borceguí *m* ankle boot
borda *f* MAR gunwale; ***echar*** *o* ***tirar por la ~*** throw overboard
bordado I *adj* embroidered; ***~ a mano*** hand-embroidered **II** *m* embroidery
bordador *m*, **~a** *f* embroiderer
bordar ⟨1a⟩ *v/t* embroider; ***~ algo*** *fig* do sth brilliantly
borde[1] *adj* F *persona* rude, uncouth
borde[2] *m* edge; ***al ~ de*** *fig* on the verge *o* brink of
bordear ⟨1a⟩ *v/t* (*rodear*) border
bordillo *m* curb, *Br* kerb
bordo *m*: ***a ~*** MAR, AVIA on board; ***ir*** *o* ***subir a ~*** go on board
bordó *m Rpl* burgundy
bordón *m* **1** (*bastón*) staff **2** MÚS bass string
boreal *adj* northern
borgoña *m* Burgundy (wine)
bórico *adj* QUÍM boric; ***ácido ~*** boric acid
borla *f en cojín, cortina etc* tassel
borne *m* TÉC, EL terminal
boro *m* QUÍM boron
borona *f* corn, *Br* maize
borrachera *f* drunkenness; ***agarrar una ~*** get drunk; ***~ de poder*** excitement that power brings
borrachería *f Méx*, *Rpl* ☞ ***borrachera***
borrachín *m*, **-ina** *f* F boozer F
borracho I *adj* drunk; ***~ de poder*** drunk with power **II** *m*, **-a** *f* drunk
borrador *m* **1** *para pizarra* eraser **2** *de texto* draft **3** (*boceto*) sketch
borraja *f* BOT borage
borrajear ⟨1a⟩ *v/t* & *v/i* scribble
borrar ⟨1a⟩ *v/t* **1** erase **2** INFOR delete **3** *pizarra* clean **4** *recuerdo* blot out **5** *huellas* wipe off; **borrarse** *v/r* **1** *de imagen, rótulo* fade **2** *de club* resign
borrasca *f* area of low pressure
borrascoso *adj* **1** *tiempo* stormy; *viento* squally **2** *fig*: *vida* tempestuous
borrego *m* **1** ZO lamb **2** *fig persona* sheep; ***~s*** *pl* fluffy white clouds
borreguillo *m* sheepskin
borricada *f fig* F stupid thing, dumb thing F
borrico[1] *m* TÉC ☞ ***borriqueta***
borrico[2] *m*, **-a** *f* **1** ZO donkey **2** *fig* F (*torpe*) dummy F
borriqueta *f*, **borriquete** *m* TÉC sawhorse
borrón *m* **1** (*tachón*) blot; ***hacer ~ y cuenta nueva*** *fig* wipe the slate clean; ***¡~ y cuenta nueva!*** let's wipe the slate clean! **2** *mancha* smudge
borronear ⟨1a⟩ *v/t* scribble on
borroso *adj escritura, perfil, foto* blurred, fuzzy
boscaje *m* thicket
boscoso *adj* wooded
Bósforo *m* Bosphorus
Bosnia *f* Bosnia
Bosnia-Herzegovina *f* Bosnia-Herzegovina
bosnio I *adj* Bosnian **II** *m*, **-a** *f* Bosnian
bosque *m* wood; *grande* forest
bosquejar ⟨1a⟩ *v/t* **1** *dibujo* sketch **2** *fig concepto, plan* outline
bosquejo *m* **1** *de dibujo* sketch **2** *fig de concepto, plan* outline
bosta *f de caballo* dropping, roadapple F; *de vaca* cowpat
bostezar ⟨1f⟩ *v/i* yawn
bostezo *m* yawn
bota *de vino* wineskin
bota *f* boot; ***ponerse las ~s*** *fig* F coin it F, rake it in F; (*comer mucho*) make a pig of o.s. F; ***morir con las ~s puestas*** *fig* die with one's boots on; ***colgar las ~s*** DEP hang up one's boots
◇ **bota campera** cowboy boot; **bota de caña alta** knee-high boot; **bota de esquiar** ski boot; **bota de fútbol** football boot; **bota de media caña** calf-length boot; **bota de montar** riding boot
botado *L.Am.* F **I** *adj* (*barato*) dirt cheap F **II** *m*, **-a** *f* abandoned child
botador *m* MAR punt pole
botadura *f* MAR launching
botalón *m* MAR boom
botana *f Méx* snack
botánica *f* botany
botánico I *adj* botanical **II** *m*, **-a** *f* botanist
botar ⟨1a⟩ **I** *v/t* **1** MAR launch **2** *pelota* bounce; ***está que bota*** F he's seething **3** *L.Am.* (*echar*) throw **4** *L.Am.* (*dese-*

B

char) throw out **5** *L.Am.* (*despedir*) fire **II** *v/i de pelota* bounce
botavara *f* MAR boom
bote *m* **1** (*barco*) boat **2** *de pelota* bounce; ***pegar un ~*** *de persona* jump; ***a ~ pronto*** off the top of one's head; ***darse el ~*** *Esp* F take off **3** *L.Am.* (*lata*) can, *Br tb* tin **4** (*tarro*) jar; ***tener a alguien en el ~*** F have s.o. in one's pocket F; ***chupar del ~*** *fig* F line one's pockets F; ***de ~ en ~*** packed out **5** *para propinas* kitty **6** *Méx* F (*cárcel*) slammer P
◇ **bote de la basura** *Méx* trash can, *Br* rubbish bin; **bote neumático** rubber dinghy; **bote salvavidas** lifeboat
botella *f* **1** bottle; ***verde ~*** *color* bottle-green; ***~ de vino*** *con viño* bottle of wine; *envase* wine bottle **2** *en baloncesto* key
◇ **botella no retornable** non-returnable bottle
◇ **botella retornable** returnable bottle
botellero *m* wine rack
botellín *m* small bottle (*esp of beer*)
botepronto *m* DEP drop kick; ***a ~*** off the top of one's head
botica *f* pharmacy, *Br* chemist's (shop)
boticario *m*, **-a** *f* pharmacist, *Br tb* chemist
botija *f* earthenware pitcher
botijo *m container with a spout for drinking water*
botín *m* **1** *de dinero, provisiones etc* loot **2** *calzado* ankle boot
botiquín *m* **1** *armario* medicine chest **2** *estuche* first-aid kit
botón *m* **1** *en prenda*, TÉC button; ***dar al ~*** press the button **2** BOT bud
◇ **botón de muestra** *fig* example; **botón de oro** BOT buttercup; **botón de presión** F snap fastener, *Br* press stud
botonadura *f* buttons *pl*
botones *m inv en hotel* bellhop, bellboy
botulismo *m* MED botulism
boutique *f* boutique
bóveda *f* ARQUI vault
◇ **bóveda celeste** firmament, vault of heaven
◇ **bóveda craneal** ANAT cranial cavity
bovino I *adj* bovine **II** *mpl*: ***~s*** cattle *pl*
box *m* **1** DEP pit **2** *Méx* (*boxeo*) boxing
boxeador *m*, **~a** *f* boxer
boxear ⟨1a⟩ *v/i* box
boxeo *m* boxing
bóxer *m* boxer (dog)
boya *f* **1** MAR buoy **2** *de caña* float
boyada *f* drove of oxen
boyante *adj fig* buoyant
boyera *f*, **boyeriza** *f* cattle shed
boyero *m* drover
bozal *m para perro* muzzle
bozo *m* fuzz (*on a boy's face*)
BPI *m abr* (= ***Banco de Pagos Internacionales***) BIS (= Bank for International Settlements)
bracear ⟨1a⟩ *v/i* wave one's arms around, flail one's arms
bracero *m*, **-a** *f* agricultural laborer, *Br* farm labourer
bracete *m*: ***de ~*** F arm in arm
bracista *m/f* breaststroke swimmer
braga-pañal *m* pull-up diaper, *Br* pull-up nappy
bragas *fpl* panties, *Br tb* knickers; ***estar / quedarse en ~s*** *fig* not have a cent *o Br* penny / be left without a cent *o Br* penny
bragazas *m inv* F henpecked husband
braguero *m* MED truss
bragueta *f* fly
braguetazo *m* P: ***dar un*** *o* ***el ~*** marry for money
brahmán *m* Brahmin
braille *m* braille
brama *f* bream
bramante *m* twine
bramar ⟨1a⟩ *v/i* **1** *de animal* bellow, roar **2** *del viento* howl; *del mar* roar
bramido *m* roar, bellow
brandy *m* brandy
branquia *f* ZO gill
branquial *adj* ZO branchial, gill *atr*
braquial *adj* brachial
brasa *f* ember; ***a la ~*** GASTR char-broiled, *Br* char-grilled
brasero *m* **1** *de carbón* brazier **2** *eléctrico* electric heater
brasier *m C.Am., Méx* bra
Brasil *m* Brazil
brasileño I *adj* Brazilian **II** *m*, **-a** *f* Brazilian
brasilero *L.Am.* **I** *adj* Brazilian **II** *m*, **-a** *f* Brazilian
bravata *f* **1** (*fanfarronada*) boast **2** (*amenaza*) threat
braveza *f* **1** *de animal* ferocity **2** *de persona* bravery **3** *de mar* wildness
bravío *adj* **1** *animal* fierce **2** *persona*

brave **3** *mar* wild
bravo I *adj* **1** *animal* fierce **2** *mar* rough, choppy **3** *persona* brave **4** *L.Am.* (*furioso*) angry **5**: ***a*** *o* ***por las -as*** forcibly, by force **II** *int* well done!; *en concierto etc* bravo!
bravucón I *adj* boastful **II** *m*, **-ona** *f* boaster, braggart
bravuconada *f* boast
bravura *f* **1** *de animal* ferocity **2** *de persona* bravery
braza *f* **1** *en natación* breaststroke **2** MAR fathom
brazada *f* **1** *en natación* stroke **2** *cantidad* armful
brazado *m* armful
brazal *m distintivo* armband
brazalete *m* **1** (*pulsera*) bracelet **2** (*banda*) armband
brazo *m* **1** arm; **(cogidos)** ***del ~*** arm in arm; ***con los ~s abiertos*** with open arms; ***dar su ~ a torcer*** give in; ***no dar su ~ a torcer*** hold out, not give in; ***luchar a ~ partido*** fight tooth and nail; ***cruzarse de ~s, quedarse con los ~s cruzados*** sit back and do nothing; ***echarse en los ~s de alguien*** *fig* put o.s. in s.o.'s hands; ***ser el ~ derecho de alguien***; be s.o.'s right-hand man / woman **2** TÉC: ***de tres ~s*** *lámpara* three-arm *atr* **3**: ***~s*** *pl* (*trabajadores*) hands *pl*
◇ **brazo armado** *fig* armed wing; **brazo de gitano** GASTR jelly roll, *Br* Swiss roll; **brazo de mar** inlet; ***estar hecho un ~*** F be smartly dressed
brea *f* tar, pitch
brear ⟨1a⟩ *v/t* F: ***~ a alguien a preguntas*** bombard s.o. with questions; ***~ a alguien a palos*** give s.o. a hiding
brebaje *m desp* concoction
brecha *f* **1** *en pared, valla etc* breach; ***abrir ~*** break through; ***seguir en la ~*** F hang on in there F; ***estar siempre en la ~*** be always in the thick of things **2** *fig* F gap **3** MED gash
brécol *m* broccoli
brega *f* **1** (*lucha*) struggle **2** (*trabajo*) hard work; ***andar a la ~*** work hard, toil
bregar ⟨1h⟩ *v/i* **1** (*luchar*) struggle **2** (*trabajar*) work hard
breque *m C.Am.* brake
bresca *f* honeycomb
Bretaña *f* Brittany
brete *m fig* F: ***poner a alguien en un ~*** put s.o. on the spot; ***estar en un ~*** be in a jam F
bretel *m CSur* strap
breva *f* BOT early fig; ***no caerá esa ~*** *fig* F no such luck!
breve *adj* brief, short; ***en ~*** shortly; ***ser ~*** be brief
brevedad *f* briefness, shortness; ***a la mayor ~ posible*** as soon as possible
brevemente *adv* briefly
breviario *m* breviary
brezal *m* heathland
brezo *m* BOT heather
bribón I *adj* rascally **II** *m*, **-ona** *f* rascal
bribonada *f* trick
bricolador *m*, **~a** *f* do-it-yourself enthusiast, DIY enthusiast
bricolaje *m* do-it-yourself, DIY
brida *f* **1** *de caballo* bridle; ***a toda ~*** at top speed **2** TÉC clamp
bridge *m* bridge
brigada I *f* **1** MIL brigade **2** *en policía* squad **II** *m* MIL warrant officer
brillante I *adj* **1** (*luminoso*) bright **2** *fig* brilliant **II** *m* diamond
brillantez *f* **1** (*luminosidad*) brightness, brilliance **2** *fig* brilliance
brillantina *f* brilliantine
brillar ⟨1a⟩ *v/i fig* shine
brillo *m de ojos, madera* shine; *de estrella, luz* brightness; ***dar*** *o* ***sacar ~ a algo*** polish sth
brincar ⟨1g⟩ *v/i* jump up and down
brinco *m* F leap, bound; ***dar ~s*** jump up and down; ***dar*** *o* ***pegar un ~*** *fig* jump, start
brindar ⟨1a⟩ **I** *v/t* **1** *oportunidad, ayuda* offer **2** TAUR dedicate (***a*** to) **II** *v/i* drink a toast (***por*** to); **brindarse** *v/r* offer, volunteer
brindis *m inv* toast; ***hacer un ~*** drink a toast (***por*** to)
brío *m fig* F verve, spirit
brioche *m* brioche
brioso *adj* F spirited, lively
brisa *f* MAR breeze
brisca *f Esp*: *popular card game*
brisera *f L.Am.* windshield, *Br* windscreen
británico I *adj* British **II** *m*, **-a** *f* Briton, Brit F
brizna *f* **1** *de hierba* blade **2**: ***una ~ de*** *pan, tela* a tiny bit of; *verdad* a grain

of; *esperanza* a gleam *o* ray of; *viento* a breath of
broca *f* TÉC (drill) bit
brocado *m* brocade
brocal *m de pozo* parapet
brocha *f* brush
◇ **brocha de afeitar** shaving brush
brochazo *m* brush stroke
broche *m* **1** (*prendedor*) brooch **2** (*cierre*) fastener **3** *L.Am.* (*pinza*) clothes pin
◇ **broche de oro** *fig* perfect end (***de*** to)
brocheta *f* skewer
brócoli *m* broccoli
broma *f* joke; ***en ~*** as a joke; ***entre ~s y veras*** half joking; ***~s aparte*** joking apart; ***gastar ~s*** play jokes; ***estaba de ~*** he was joking; ***tomar algo a ~*** take sth as a joke; ***no estoy para ~s*** I'm not in the mood for jokes
◇ **broma de mal gusto** joke in bad taste
◇ **broma pesada** bad joke
bromatología *f* food science, nutrition
bromatólogo *m*, **-a** *f* nutritionist
bromear ⟨1a⟩ *v/i* joke
bromista **I** *adj*: ***es muy ~*** he loves a joke **II** *m/f* joker
bromo *m* QUÍM bromine
bromuro *m* QUÍM bromide
bronca *f* **1** F telling off F; ***echar la ~ a alguien*** F give s.o. a telling off, tell s.o. off **2** *Méx* P fight; ***armar una ~*** get into a fight **3**: ***armar ~*** (*hacer ruido*) cause a rumpus; ***se armó ~ tras anunciarse la subida de los impuestos*** there was an outcry *o* a rumpus when the tax increase was announced
broncazo *m* F: ***un ~*** a real telling-off
bronce *m* bronze; ***edad del ~*** Bronze Age
bronceado **I** *adj* tanned **II** *m* suntan; ***centro de ~*** solarium
bronceador *m* suntan lotion
broncearse ⟨1a⟩ *v/r* get a tan
bronco *adj voz* harsh, gruff
bronconeumonía *f* MED bronchopneumonia
broncoscopia *f* MED bronchoscope
bronquedad *f* harshness, gruffness
bronquial *adj* bronchial
bronquios *mpl* bronchial tubes, bronchi
bronquitis *f* MED bronchitis
broquel *m tb fig* shield
broqueta *f* skewer
brotar ⟨1a⟩ *v/i* **1** BOT sprout, bud **2** *fig de sospecha*, *chispa* appear, arise; *de epidemia* break out
brote *m* **1** BOT shoot **2** MED, *fig* outbreak
◇ **brotes de bambú** bamboo shoots
◇ **brotes de soja** beansprouts
broza *f* **1** dead leaves *pl* **2** *en artículo* padding
bruces: ***de ~*** face down; ***caer de ~*** F fall flat on one's face; ***darse de ~ con alguien*** bump into s.o.
bruja *f* **1** witch; ***caza de ~s*** *tb fig* witch hunt **2** *Méx*: ***andar*** *o* ***estar ~*** F be broke F
brujería *f* witchcraft
brujo **I** *adj* bewitching **II** *m* wizard
brújula *f* compass; ***perder la ~*** *fig* lose one's bearings
bruma *f* mist
brumoso *adj* misty
bruñido *m* burnishing, polishing
bruñir ⟨3h⟩ *v/t* **1** burnish, polish **2** *C.Am.* F (*molestar*) annoy
brusco *adj* **1** *cambio* abrupt, sudden **2** *respuesta*, *persona* brusque, curt
Bruselas *f* Brussels
brusquedad *f* **1** *de cambio* sharpness, abruptness **2** *de respuesta*, *persona* brusqueness, curtness; ***con ~*** curtly, brusquely
brut *adj* dry
brutal *adj* **1** *procedimiento*, *lenguaje* brutal **2** P *fiesta* incredible F, terrific
brutalidad *f* brutality
brutalizar ⟨1f⟩ *v/t* harden, brutalize
bruto **I** *adj* **1** brutish; ***a lo ~*** using brute force **2** (*inculto*) ignorant **3** (*torpe*) clumsy **4** COM gross; ***peso ~*** gross weight **5** *diamante* uncut; ***en ~*** *petróleo* crude; **II** *m*, **-a** *f* brute; (*idiota*) idiot
bu *m* F boogeyman, bogeyman
buba *f*, **bubón** *m* MED bubo
bucal *adj* oral
buceador *m*, **~a** *f* diver
bucear ⟨1a⟩ *v/i* **1** dive **2** *fig* (*investigar*) delve (***en*** into)
buceo *m* diving
◇ **buceo deportivo** diving
buche *m* **1** *de ave* crop; ***guardar algo en el ~*** *fig* F keep sth under one's hat F **2** *de persona* F belly F

bucle *m* **1** (*rizo*) curl **2** INFOR loop
bucólica *f* pastoral poem
bucólico *adj* bucolic
Buda *m* Buddha
budín *m* pudding
budismo *m* Buddhism
budista *m/f & adj* Buddhist
buen *adj* ☞ ***bueno***
buenamente *adv* **1** (*fácilmente*) easily **2** (*voluntariamente*) willingly
buenaventura *f* fortune; ***decir la ~ a alguien*** tell s.o.'s fortune
buenazo I *adj* kind-hearted **II** *m*, **-a** *f*: ***ser un ~*** F be a softy F
buenísimo *sup* very good
bueno I *adj* **1** good; ***-a voluntad*** goodwill; ***lo ~ es que …*** the best thing about it is that …; ***estar de -as*** be in a good mood; ***ponerse ~*** get well; ***dar algo por ~*** approve sth; ***ahora viene lo ~*** *irón* here comes the good bit; ***¡ésta sí que es -a!*** *irón* F that's a good one!; ***¡estaría ~!*** *irón* F oh, terrific!; ***lo ~, si breve, dos veces ~*** brevity is the soul of wit
2 (*bondadoso*) kind; ***ser -a gente*** be nice
3 (*sabroso*) nice
4: ***por las -as*** willingly; ***por las -as o por las malas*** whether we / they / etc like it or not; ***de -as a primeras*** without warning; ***a la -a de Dios*** any which way, *Br* any old how
II *int*: ***¡~!*** well!; ***¿~?*** *Méx* hello; ***¡-as!*** hello!; ***~s días***, *Rpl* ***~ día*** good morning; ***-as noches*** good evening; ***-as tardes*** good evening
Buenos Aires *m* Buenos Aires
buey *m* ZO ox
búfalo *m* ZO buffalo
bufanda *f* **1** scarf **2** *fig* F (*gratificación*) perk F
bufar ⟨1a⟩ *v/i* **1** *de gato* spit; *de caballo, toro* snort **2**: ***está que bufa*** *fig* F he's seething
bufé *m* buffet
búfer *m* INFOR buffer
bufete *m* lawyer's office; ***abrir ~*** start up a law practice, F put up one's shingle
buffet *m* GASTR buffet
◇ **buffet de desayuno** breakfast buffet
◇ **buffet frío** cold buffet
bufido *m* **1** *de gato* spit; *de caballo, toro* snort **2** *fig*: *por enfado* snort
bufo *adj* comic; ***ópera -a*** comic opera
bufón *m* buffoon, fool
bufonada *f* silly joke
buganvilla *f* BOT bougainvillea
bugle *m* MÚS bugle
buhardilla *f* attic, *Br tb* loft
búho *m* ZO owl
buhonero *m* peddler, *Br* pedlar
buitre *m* ZO vulture
◇ **buitre negro** black buzzard
bujía *f* AUTO spark plug
bula *f* REL bull; ***tiene ~*** *fig* F he's got pull F *o* connections
bulbo *m* BOT bulb
bulboso *adj* bulbous
buldog *m* ZO bulldog
bulevar *m* boulevard
Bulgaria *f* Bulgaria
búlgaro I *adj* Bulgarian **II** *m*, **-a** *f* Bulgarian **III** *m idioma* Bulgarian
bulimia *f* MED bulimia
bulla *f* din, racket; ***meter*** *o* ***armar ~*** make a din *o* racket
bullabesa *f* GASTR fish soup, bouillabaisse
bullanguero F **I** *adj* rowdy **II** *m*, **-a** *f* troublemaker
bulldog *m* ☞ ***buldog***
bullicio *m* **1** (*ruido*) hubbub, din **2** (*actividad*) bustle
bullicioso *adj* bustling
bullir ⟨3h⟩ *v/i fig* **1** *de sangre* boil **2** *de lugar* swarm, teem (***de*** with)
bulo *m* F rumor, *Br* rumour
bulto *m* **1** (*paquete*) package; ***escurrir el ~*** F duck out F **2** MED lump **3** *en superficie* bulge **4** (*silueta*) (vague) shape **5** (*pieza de equipaje*) piece of baggage; ***~s*** *pl* baggage *sg*, *Br tb* luggage *sg*; ***~s de mano*** hand baggage *sg*, *Br tb* hand luggage *sg* **6** (*volumen*): ***hacer ~*** swell the numbers; ***de ~*** *error* glaring; ***a ~*** roughly, at a guess
bumerán *m* boomerang
búnker *m* MIL bunker
buñuelo *m Esp* fritter
◇ **buñuelo de viento** GASTR *cream donut*
buqué *m* bouquet (*of wine*)
buque *m* ship
◇ **buque almirante** flagship; **buque de carga** freighter; **buque cisterna** tanker; **buque escuela** training ship;

B

buque frigorífico refrigerated vessel, reefer F; **buque de guerra** warship; **buque insignia** flagship; **buque mercante** merchant ship; **buque nodriza (de aviones)** mother ship; **buque de pasajeros** passenger ship; **buque portacontenedores** container ship; **buque de vapor** steamship
burbuja *f* bubble
burbujear ⟨1a⟩ *v/i* **1** (*bullir*) bubble **2** *de champán* fizz
burdel *m* brothel
Burdeos *m* Bordeaux
burdo *adj* rough
bureta *f* buret, *Br* burette
burgalés *adj* of / from Burgos
burgo *m* **1** fortified town **2** (*pueblo*) village
burgués I *adj* middle-class, bourgeois **II** *m*, **-esa** *f* middle-class person, member of the bourgeoisie
burguesía *f* middle class, bourgeoisie; ***alta / pequeña ~*** upper / lower middle class
buril *m* burin, graver
burilar ⟨1a⟩ *v/t* engrave
burla *f* **1** (*mofa*) joke; ***hacer ~ de alguien*** F make fun of s.o. **2** (*engaño*) trick
burladero *m* TAUR *barrier behind which a bullfighter can hide*
burlador *m* Don Juan
burlar ⟨1a⟩ **I** *v/t* **1** *riesgo, dificultad* get round **2** (*engañar*) trick, take in **II** *v/i* mock; **burlarse** *v/r* make fun (**de** of)
burlesco *adj* **1** *tono* joking **2** *gesto* rude
burlete *m L.Am.* draft excluder, *Br* draught excluder
burlón I *adj* mocking **II** *m*, **-ona** *f* mocker
buró *m* bureau
burocracia *f* bureaucracy
burócrata *m/f* bureaucrat
burocrático *adj* bureaucratic
burocratizar ⟨1f⟩ *v/t* bureaucratize
burrada *f fig* F piece of nonsense; ***hay una ~*** F there's loads F; ***costar una ~*** F cost a packet F
burro *m*, **-a** *f* **1** ZO donkey; ***caer** o **bajarse** o **apearse del ~*** F back down; ***no ver tres en un ~*** be as blind as a bat **2** F *persona* idiot **3** *Méx* (*tabla de planchar*) ironing board
bursátil *adj* stock market *atr*
bus *m* **1** (*autobús*) bus **2** INFOR bus
busca I *f* search; ***en ~ de*** in search of; ***encontrarse en ~ y captura*** have a warrant out for one's arrest **II** *m* F pager
◇ **busca de tesoros** treasure hunt
buscador I *m*, **~a** *f* searcher **II** *m* INFOR search engine
buscapersonas *m inv* pager
buscapiés *m inv type of firecracker, Br* jumping jack
buscapleitos *m/f inv* F troublemaker
buscar ⟨1a⟩ *v/t* search for, look for; ***ir / venir a ~*** fetch; ***se la estaba buscando*** he was asking for trouble *o* for it
buscón *m* rogue
buscona *f* prostitute
busilis *m* F snag, problem; ***ahí está el ~*** F that's the problem
búsqueda *f* search; ***~ en el texto*** INFOR search *o* find in the text
◇ **búsqueda automática** TV, RAD automatic channel search
bustier *m* bustier
busto *m* bust
butaca *f* **1** (*sillón*) armchair **2** TEA seat
butano *m* butane
butén: ***de ~*** F terrific, fantastic F
butifarra *f type of sausage*
butrón *m hole made by robbers in order to break into a building*
buzo *m* **1** *persona* diver **2** *CSur prenda* tracksuit **3** *Urug* (*jersey*) sweater
buzón *m* mailbox, *Br* postbox
◇ **buzón electrónico** INFOR mailbox
◇ **buzón de voz** TELEC voicemail
buzoneo *m* direct mailing
bypass *m* bypass
byte *m* INFOR byte

C

C *abr* **1** (= ***centígrado***) C (= centigrade) **2** (= ***compañía***) Co. (= company) **3** c (= ***calle***) St. (= street) **4** (= ***capítulo***) ch. (= chapter)

cabal *adj*: ***no estar en sus ~es*** not be in one's right mind; ***un hombre ~*** a man of integrity

cábala *f fig* intrigue; ***hacer ~s*** speculate

cabalgadura *f* mount

cabalgar ⟨1h⟩ *v/i* ride

cabalgata *f* procession

caballa *f* ZO mackerel

caballada *f Rpl*: ***decir / hacer una ~*** say / do sth stupid

caballar *adj* horse *atr*; ***cría ~*** horse breeding

caballeresco *adj* chivalrous

caballerete *m desp* youth

caballería *f* **1** MIL cavalry **2** (*caballo*) horse

caballeriza *f* stable

caballerizo *m*, **-a** *f* groom

caballero I *adj* gentlemanly, chivalrous **II** *m* **1** *hombre educado* gentleman; *hombre* gentleman, man; (***servicio de***) ***~s*** *pl* men's room *sg*, *Br* gents *sg*; *en tienda de ropa* menswear *sg* **2** HIST knight; ***armar a alguien ~*** HIST knight s.o. **3** *trato* sir

◇ **caballero blanco** COM white knight

caballerosidad *f* chivalry

caballeroso *adj* gentlemanly, chivalrous

caballete *m* **1** PINT easel **2** TÉC trestle

caballista I *m* horseman **II** *f* horsewoman

◇ **caballito del diablo** ZO dragonfly

◇ **caballito de mar** ZO seahorse

caballitos *mpl* carousel *sg*, merry-go--round *sg*

caballo *m* **1** horse; ***a ~*** on horseback; ***montar** o **andar** Rpl **a ~*** ride (a horse); ***me gusta montar a ~*** I like riding; ***ir a ~*** go on horseback; ***a ~ entre*** halfway between; ***a mata ~*** at breakneck speed; ***a ~ regalado no le mires el diente*** don't look a gift horse in the mouth **2** *en ajedrez* knight

◇ **caballo con arcos** *en gimnasia* (pommel) horse; **caballo balancín** rocking horse; **caballo de carreras** racehorse; **caballo de montar** saddle horse; **caballo de saltos** *en gimnasia* vaulting horse; **caballo de Troya** MYTH Trojan horse; **caballo de vapor** horsepower

cabaña *f* **1** cabin **2** *Méx en fútbol* goal

cabaret *m* cabaret

cabaretero I *adj* cabaret *atr* **II** *m*, **-a** *f* cabaret artist

cabeceada *f L.Am.* **1** nod **2** *en fútbol* header

cabecear ⟨1a⟩ **I** *v/i* nod **II** *v/t el balón* head

cabeceo *m* nod

cabecera *f* **1** *de mesa*, *cama* head **2** *de periódico* masthead **3** *de texto* top **4** INFOR header

cabecero *m de cama* headboard

cabecilla *m/f* ringleader

cabellera *f* **1** hair; ***le cortaron la ~*** they cut his hair; ***con la ~ a lo Sid Vicious*** with a Sid Vicious hairstyle **2** *de cometa* tail

cabello *m* hair

◇ **cabello de ángel** GASTR *confectionery made from pumpkin*

cabelludo *adj* hairy

caber ⟨2m⟩ *v/i* **1** fit; ***ya no me cabe el vestido*** the dress doesn't fit me anymore

2 *en un sitio*: ***caben tres litros*** it holds three liters *o Br* litres; ***cabemos todos*** there's room for all of us; ***aquí no cabe nadie más*** there's no room here for anyone else; ***no me cabe en la cabeza*** I just don't understand, I just can't get my head around it; ***no ~ en sí de alegría** o **de gozo*** be beside o.s. with joy **3** (*ser posible*): ***no cabe duda*** *fig* there's no doubt; ***cabe preguntarse si*** I wonder if; ***no cabe / cabe esperar que …*** there's no hope that… / it is to be hoped that …; ***si cabe*** if that's possible

cabestrillo *m* MED sling; ***tener el brazo en ~*** have one's arm in a sling

cabestro *m* halter

cabeza I *f* **1** ANAT head; ***de ~*** *caerse*, *ti-*

C

rarse etc headlong; ***estar mal** o **no estar bien de la ~*** F not be right in the head F; ***írsele la ~*** feel giddy *o* dizzy; ***con la ~ alta*** with one's head held high; ***subírsele a alguien a la ~*** *fig* go to s.o.'s head; ***llevarse las manos a la ~*** *fig* throw one's hands up (in the air); ***andar** o **ir de ~*** be snowed under; ***sentar la ~*** settle down; ***levantar ~*** (*recuperarse*) pick up; ***no levantar ~*** *fig* be knocked sideways; ***tras la derrota, el equipo no consiguió levantar ~*** the team was knocked sideways by the defeat

2 (*razón*): ***perder la ~*** *fig* lose one's head; ***llevar** o **traer a alguien de ~*** drive s.o. crazy;

3 (*memoria*): ***tener mala ~*** have a bad memory

4 (*pensamiento*): ***pasarle a alguien por la ~*** occur to s.o.; ***se me viene a la ~ …*** it occurs to me …; ***meterse algo en la ~*** get sth into one's head; ***quitarse algo de la ~*** get sth out of one's head; ***calentarle la ~ a alguien*** *fig* fill s.o.'s head with ideas; ***calentarse la ~*** get worked up; ***mantener la ~ fría*** keep a cool head; ***romperse la ~*** *fig* rack one's brains

5 (*persona*): ***por ~*** per head, per person

6: ***el equipo a la ~** o **en ~*** the team at the top; ***estar a la ~*** be out in front, be the leader

II *m/f de familia, grupo* head

◇ **cabeza de ajo** head of garlic; **cabeza cuadrada** F bigot; **cabeza de familia** head of the family; **cabeza de ganado** head of cattle; **cabeza lectora** INFOR read head; **cabeza de lista** POL *candidate heading an electoral list*; **cabeza loca** fool, *Br tb* thickhead F; **cabeza nuclear** nuclear warhead; **cabeza de partido** major town, county town; **cabeza de puente** MIL bridgehead; **cabeza rapada** skinhead; **cabeza de turco** scapegoat

cabezada *f* **1**: ***echar una ~*** have a nap **2** (*golpe*) bang on the head

cabezal *m* TÉC head

cabezazo *m* **1** *con la cabeza* head butt; *en la cabeza* bang on the head; ***darse un ~*** hit one's head **2** *en fútbol* header; ***~ en plancha*** diving header

cabezo *m* **1** hillock **2** *de montaña* peak

cabezón I *adj*: ***mi hermana es muy cabezona*** my sister has a very large head; *fig* my sister is very pigheaded **II** *m* large head **III** *m*, **-ona** *f*: ***es un ~*** he's so pigheaded

cabezonada *f* pigheaded thing to do

cabezonería *f* pigheadedness; *acto* pigheaded thing to do

cabezota I *adj* pigheaded **II** *m/f* pigheaded person

cabezudo I *adj*: ***es ~*** he has a very large head **II** *m large-headed carnival figure*

cabida *f* capacity; ***dar ~ a*** hold; ***tener ~ en*** have room in

cabildo *m* POL council

cabina *f* cabin

◇ **cabina del piloto** AVIA cockpit

◇ **cabina telefónica** phone booth

cabizbajo *adj* dejected, downhearted

cable *m* **1** EL cable; ***se le cruzaron los ~s*** F he got mixed up **2** MAR line, rope; ***echar un ~ a alguien*** give s.o. a hand

◇ **cable de fibra óptica** fiber-optic cable, *Br* fibre-optic cable

◇ **cable de remolque** tow rope

cableado *m* wiring

cablear ⟨1a⟩ *v/t* wire up

cablegrafiar ⟨1c⟩ *v/t* cable

cabo *m* **1** end; ***al ~ de*** after; ***de ~ a rabo*** F from start to finish; ***estar al ~ de la calle*** know the score F, be clued up F; ***llevar a ~*** carry out **2** GEOG cape **3** MAR rope; ***quedan muchos ~s sueltos*** *fig* there are still a lot of loose ends; ***atar ~s*** F put two and two together F **4** MIL corporal

◇ **Cabo de Buena Esperanza** Cape of Good Hope

◇ **Cabo de Hornos** Cape Horn

cabra *f* ZO goat; ***estar como una ~*** F be nuts F; ***la ~ siempre tira al monte*** a leopard never changes its spots

◇ **cabra montesa** *Esp* mountain goat, Spanish ibex

cabracho *m* ZO scorpion fish

cabreado *adj*: ***estar ~*** F be annoyed *o* furious

cabrear ⟨1a⟩ *v/t* P bug F; **cabrearse** *v/r* P get mad F

cabreo *m* P: ***tener un ~*** be in a foul mood

cabrerizo *m*, **-a** *f*, **cabrero** *m*, **-a** *f* goatherd

cabrestante *m* **1** TÉC winch **2** MAR

capstan
cabria *f* hoist
cabrillas *fpl* MAR whitecaps, white horses
cabrillear ⟨1a⟩ *v/i* MAR form whitecaps *o* white horses
cabrío *adj* goat *atr*; ***macho ~*** billy goat
cabrio *m* rafter
cabriola *f*: ***hacer ~s*** *de niño* jump around
cabritas *fpl Chi* popcorn *sg*
cabritilla *f* kid(skin)
cabrito *m* kid
cabro *m Chi* boy; ***~ chico*** *Chi* baby
cabrón *m* V bastard P, son of a bitch P
cabronada *f* P dirty trick
cabruno *adj* goat *atr*
caca *f* F **1** poop F, *Br* pooh F; ***hacer ~*** F poop F, *Br* do a pooh F **2** *cosa mala* piece of trash F
cacahuate *m Méx* peanut
cacahuete *m* peanut
cacalote *m C.Am., Cuba, Méx* crow
cacao *m* **1** cocoa; ***no valer un ~*** *L.Am. fig* F not be worth a bean F **2** *de labios* lip salve
cacaotal *m* cocoa plantation
cacarear ⟨1a⟩ **I** *v/i de gallo* crow; *de gallina* cluck **II** *v/t* F crow about F, boast about
cacareo *m de gallo* crowing; *de gallina* clucking; *fig* F crowing F, boasting
cacatúa *f* ZO cockatoo
cacería *f* hunt
cacerola *f* pan
cacha *f*: ***estar metido hasta las ~s en algo*** F be up to one's neck in sth F
cachalote *m* ZO sperm whale
cachar ⟨1a⟩ *v/t* **1** *L.Am.* (*engañar*) trick **2** *L.Am.* (*sorprender*) catch out **3**: ***¿me cachas?*** *Chi* get it?
cacharrería *f* kitchenware store
cacharro *m* **1** pot; ***lavar los ~s*** *Méx, C.Am.* wash the dishes **2** *Méx, C.Am.* (*trasto*) piece of junk **3** *Méx, C.Am. coche* junkheap
cachas *adj*: ***estar ~*** F be a real hunk F
cachaza *f* F: ***la gente de hoy tiene mucha ~*** people today are very laidback F
cachazudo *adj* F laidback F
caché *m* cachet
cachear ⟨1a⟩ *v/t* frisk
cachemira *f* cashmere
cacheo *m* frisking
cácher *m/f en béisbol* catcher
cachería *f L.Am.* small business
cachet *m* cachet
cachetada *f* slap
cachete *m* cheek
cachetear ⟨1a⟩ *v/t L.Am.* slap
cachetudo *adj* chubby-cheeked
cachilo *m Rpl* F old jalopy F, *Br tb* old banger F
cachimba *f* pipe
cachimbo *m L.Am.* pipe
cachipolla *f* ZO mayfly
cachiporra *f* billy club, *Br* truncheon
cachivache *m* thing; ***~s*** *pl* (*cosas*) things, stuff *sg* F; (*basura*) junk *sg*
cacho *m* **1** F bit **2** *Rpl* (*cuerno*) horn **3** *Ven, Col* F (*marijuana*) joint F **4**: ***jugar al ~*** *Bol, Pe* play dice **5**: ***ponerle ~s a alguien*** cheat on s.o. **6** *Rpl de bananas* bunch
cachondearse ⟨1a⟩ *v/r* F make fun (**de** of)
cachondeo *m*: ***estar de ~*** F be joking; ***tomar a ~*** F take as a joke; ***¡vaya ~!*** F what a laugh! F
cachondo *adj* F **1** (*caliente*) horny F; ***poner ~ a alguien*** F make s.o. horny F **2** (*gracioso*) funny
cachorro *m* ZO pup
cachucha *f Andes, C.Am., Méx* cap
cacillo *m* (small) saucepan
cacique *m* **1** chief **2** POL *local political boss* **3** *fig* F tyrant
caciquismo *m system of rule by a local political boss*
cacle *m Méx* shoe
caco *m* F thief
cacofonía *f* cacophony
cacto, cactus *m inv* BOT cactus
cacumen *m* F brains *pl* F; ***qué poco ~ tienes*** you don't have any brains
cada *adj* **1** *considerado por separado* each; *con énfasis en la totalidad* every; ***~ cosa en su sitio*** everything in its place; ***~ uno, ~ cual*** each one; ***~ vez*** every time, each time; ***~ tres días*** every three days; ***uno de ~ tres*** one out of every three; ***uno de ~*** one of each **2**: ***~ vez más*** more and more, increasingly
cadalso *m* scaffold
cadáver *m* (dead) body, corpse
cadavérico *adj* cadaverous
cadena *f* **1** chain; ***~ humana*** human chain; ***~ de tiendas*** chain of stores; ***~***

hotelera hotel chain **2** *de perro* leash, *Br tb* lead **3** TV channel **4**: ***~s*** *pl* AUTO snow chains
◇ **cadena alimentaria** BIO food chain; **cadena de montaje** assembly line; **cadena de montañas** mountain range; **cadena perpetua** life sentence; **cadena de producción** TÉC production line; **cadena de música, cadena de sonido** hi-fi, sound system
cadencia *f* MÚS rhythm, cadence
cadencioso *adj* rhythmic
cadeneta *f de decoración* chain stitch
cadera *f* hip
cadete *m* **1** MIL cadet **2** *Rpl, Chi* office junior, errand boy
cadí *m* caddy
cadmio *m* QUÍM cadmium
caducado *adj documento* out of date, expired; *alimento* past its sell-by date / use-by date; ***está ~*** *de tarjeta* it is out of date
caducar ⟨1g⟩ *v/i* expire
caducidad *f*: ***fecha de ~*** expiration date, *Br* expiry date; *de alimentos, medicinas* use-by date
caducifolio *adj* BOT deciduous
caduco *adj* **1** BOT deciduous **2** *persona* senile **3** *belleza* faded
caer ⟨2o⟩ **I** *v/i* **1** fall; ***~ sobre*** fall on; ***dejar ~ algo*** drop sth; ***~ enfermo*** fall ill; ***~ en lunes*** fall on a Monday; ***al ~ la noche*** at sunset *o* nightfall; ***caiga quien caiga*** no matter whose head has to roll; ***~ muy bajo*** *fig* stoop very low; ***dejarse ~*** F flop down
2: ***me cae bien / mal*** *fig* I like / don't like him
3 *de un lugar*: ***cae cerca*** it's not far; ***¿por dónde cae este pueblo?*** whereabouts is this village?
4: ***estar al ~*** be about to arrive; ***¡ahora caigo!*** *fig* now I get it!
caerse *v/r* fall (down); ***~ de risa*** fall about laughing; ***~ de sueño*** be ready to drop; ***~ de viejo*** be falling apart with age; ***este coche se cae de viejo*** the car is so old it's falling apart; ***no tener dónde ~ muerto*** not have a penny to one's name
café *m* **1** coffee **2** (*bar*) café
◇ **café cantante** *café with live entertainment*; **café descafeinado** decaffeinated coffee, decaf F; **café exprés** espresso; **café instantáneo** instant coffee; **café irlandés** Irish coffee; **café con leche** white coffee; **café solo** black coffee; **café soluble** instant coffee; **café torrefacto, café tostado** high-roast coffee
cafeína *f* caffeine
cafetal *m* coffee plantation
cafetalero *m*, **-a** *f L.Am.* coffee grower
cafetera *f* coffee maker *o* pot; *para servir* coffee pot
◇ **cafetera automática** coffee machine
◇ **cafetera exprés** espresso coffee pot
cafetería *f* coffee shop
cafetero **I** *adj* coffee *atr*; ***ser muy ~*** F be very fond of coffee, be a big coffee drinker **II** *m*, **-a** *f* coffee grower
cafeto *m* coffee bush
cafre *m/f & adj* savage
caftán *m* caftan
cafúa *f Rpl* F (*cárcel*) slammer P
cagada *f* P *tb fig* shit V, crap P
cagado **I** *adj* P scared shitless V; ***estar ~ de miedo*** P be scared shitless V **II** *m*, **-a** *f* P coward
cagalera *f* P: ***tener una ~*** have the runs F
cagar ⟨1h⟩ V **I** *v/i* have a shit V **II** *v/t*: ***~la*** screw up P, *Br tb* cock up F; ***¡ya la hemos cagado!*** F now we've really screwed up! F; **cagarse** *v/r* shit o.s. V; ***~ de miedo*** shit o.s. V; ***me cago en diez*** *o* ***en tu tía*** P shit! V
cagarruta *f* dropping, pellet
cagón F **I** *adj*: ***es muy ~*** *bebé* he's always pooping in his diaper F, *Br* he's always poohing in his nappy F **II** *m*, **-ona** *f* wimp F
caguama *f Méx* (*tortuga*) turtle
cagueta *m/f* F chicken F
caída *f* fall; ***a la ~ del sol*** at sunset; ***a la ~ de la tarde*** at sunset; ***~ del gobierno*** fall of the government; ***~ del pelo*** hair loss
◇ **caída libre** free fall
caído **I** *adj* **1** fallen; ***~ de ánimo*** downhearted, dispirited **2** *hombros* sagging **II** *mpl*: ***los ~s*** MIL the fallen, the (war) dead
caigo *vb* ☞ ***caer***
caimán *m* **1** ZO alligator **2** *Méx, C.Am. útil* monkey wrench
Caín *m* Cain; ***pasar las de ~*** *fig* go

through hell F
Cairo: ***El ~*** Cairo
cairota *adj* of / from Cairo, Cairo *atr*
caja *f* **1** box; ***la ~ tonta*** F the idiot box F, *Br* the goggle-box F; ***echar a alguien con ~s destempladas*** F send s.o. packing **2** *de reloj, ordenador* case, casing **3** COM cash desk; *en supermercado* checkout; ***hacer ~*** COM cash up **4**: ***entrar en ~*** MIL enlist, *Br* join up
◇ **caja de ahorros** savings bank; **caja de cambios** gearbox; **caja de cambios automática** AUTO automatic gearbox; **caja de cartón** cardboard box; **caja de caudales** safe, strongbox; **caja de cerillas** matchbox; **caja de colores** box of crayons; **caja de la escalera** stairwell; **caja fuerte** safe, strongbox; **caja de herramientas** tool box; **caja de música** music box; **caja negra** AVIA black box; **caja nido** nesting box; **caja de pinturas** paint box; **caja postal** post office savings bank; **caja de reclutamiento** MIL recruiting office; **caja registradora** cash register; **caja de resonancia** sound box; **caja de seguridad** safe-deposit box; **caja torácica** rib cage; **caja de zapatos** shoe box
cajero *m*, **-a** *f* cashier; *de banco* teller
◇ **cajero automático** ATM, *Br tb* cash point
cajeta *f Méx* caramel spread
cajetilla *f* pack, packet
cajilla *f Rpl de tabaco* packet
cajista *m/f* compositor, typesetter
cajita *f* (small) box
cajón *m* **1** drawer **2** *L.Am.* casket, coffin **3**: ***ser de ~*** F be obvious **4** *Méx* AUTO parking space
◇ **cajón del bateador** *en béisbol* batter's box; **cajón del receptor** *en béisbol* catcher's box; **cajón de sastre** F hodgepodge F, *Br* hotchpotch F
cajuela *f Méx* AUTO trunk, *Br* boot
cajuelita *f C.Am., Méx* glove compartment
cal *f* lime; ***una de ~ y otra de arena*** F mixed fortunes; ***cerrar algo a ~ y canto*** *fig* shut sth tight
◇ **cal viva** quicklime
cala *f* cove
calabacín *m* BOT zucchini, *Br* courgette
calabacita *f Méx* zucchini, *Br* courgette
calabaza *f* pumpkin; ***dar ~s a alguien*** F *en examen* fail s.o., flunk s.o. F; *en relación* give s.o. the brush off F
calabobos *m* F drizzle
calabozo *m* cell
calada *f* puff, drag F
caladero *m* fishing ground
calado I *adj* soaked; ***~ hasta los huesos*** soaked to the skin **II** *m* **1** MAR draft, *Br* draught; ***de gran ~*** *fig* important, significant **2** AUTO stall
calamar *m* ZO squid
calambre *m* **1** EL shock **2** MED cramp
calambur *m* play on words
calamidad *f* calamity
calamina *f* MIN calamine
calamita *f* MIN lodestone
calamitoso *adj* catastrophic
cálamo *m* BOT stem
calandria *f* **1** ZO lark **2** *Méx (carroza)* carriage
calaña *f desp* sort, type; ***de mala ~*** *gente* nasty; ***son de la misma ~*** they're as bad as each other
calar ⟨1a⟩ **I** *v/t* **1** *(mojar)* soak; *techo, tela* soak through **2** *persona, conjura* see through **II** *v/i* **1** *de zapato* leak **2** *de ideas, costumbres* take root; ***~ hondo en*** make a big impression on; **calarse** *v/r* **1** *de motor* stall **2**: ***~ hasta los huesos*** get soaked to the skin
calato *adj Chi, Pe* naked
calavera I *f* skull **II** *m fig* F rake, libertine
calcáneo *m* ANAT heel bone
calcañar *m* heel
calcar ⟨1g⟩ *v/t* trace
calcáreo *adj* limy
calce *m* wedge
calceta *f*: ***hacer ~*** knit
calcetín *m* sock
calcificación *f* MED calcification
calcificarse ⟨1g⟩ *v/r* calcify
calcinación *f* calcination
calcinado *adj* burned, burnt
calcinar ⟨1a⟩ *v/t* burn; **calcinarse** *v/r* be reduced to ashes
calcio *m* calcium
calco *m* tracing; *fig* copy
calcomanía *f* decal, *Br* transfer
calculable *adj* calculable
calculador *adj fig* calculating
calculadora *f* calculator
◇ **calculadora de bolsillo** pocket calculator
calcular ⟨1a⟩ *v/t tb fig* calculate

C

cálculo *m* **1** calculation **2** MED stone ◇ **cálculo biliar** MED gallstone; **cálculo de costes** estimate of costs; **cálculo diferencial** differential calculus; **cálculo integral** integral calculus; **cálculo mental** mental arithmetic; **cálculo de probabilidades** calculation of probabilities; **cálculo renal** MED kidney stone
caldas *fpl* hot springs
caldear ⟨1a⟩ *v/t* **1** warm up **2** *ánimos* inflame; **caldearse** *v/r* heat up, warm up
caldera *f* **1** boiler **2** *Rpl*, *Chi* kettle ◇ **caldera de vapor** steam boiler
calderero *m* boilermaker
caldereta *f* GASTR *de carne* lamb stew; *de pescado* fish stew
calderilla *f* small change
caldero *m* (small) boiler
calderón *m* MÚS *tb signo* pause
caldillo *m Méx* GASTR stock
caldo *m* GASTR stock; ***hacer el ~ gordo a alguien*** F make things easy for s.o.; ***poner a ~ alguien*** F tell s.o. off ◇ **caldo de carne** meat stock; **caldo de cultivo** *fig* breeding ground; **caldo de verduras** vegetable stock
caldoso *adj* watery
calé I *adj* gypsy *atr* **II** *m/f* gypsy
calefacción *f* heating ◇ **calefacción central** central heating ◇ **calefacción individual** individually controlled central heating
calefactor I *m* heater **II** *m*, **~a** *f* heating engineer
calefón *m Rpl* (water) heater
caleidoscopio *m* ☞ ***calidoscopio***
calendario *m* **1** calendar **2** (*programa*) schedule ◇ **calendario escolar** school year; **calendario de pared** wall calendar; **calendario de taco** tear-off calendar
caléndula *f* BOT marigold
calentador *m* heater; ***~ de agua*** water heater
calentamiento *m* **1** heating **2** DEP warm-up ◇ **calentamiento global** global warming
calentar ⟨1k⟩ **I** *v/t* **1** heat (up) **2**: ***~ a alguien*** *fig* provoke s.o.; P *sexualmente* get s.o. hot F **II** *v/i* DEP warm up; **calentarse** *v/r* warm up, have a warm-up; *fig*: *de discusión*, *disputa* become heated
calentito *adj* F *noticia* hot F
calentón *m* F: ***darse un ~*** feel horny F
calentura *f* fever; ***estar con ~*** have a temperature
calenturiento *adj* feverish
calenturón *m* fever
calera *f* quarry
calero *adj* lime *atr*
calesita *f Rpl* merry-go-round
caleta *f* cove
caletre *m* F gumption F
calibración *f* calibration
calibrador *m* TÉC gauge
calibrar ⟨1a⟩ *v/t* gauge, calibrate; *fig* gauge, weigh up
calibre *m tb fig* caliber, *Br* calibre
calidad *f* **1** quality; ***de primera ~*** top-quality *atr*; ***de ~ inferior***, ***de baja ~*** poor-quality *atr*; ***de ~ superior*** superior-quality *atr*, high-quality *atr* **2**: ***en ~ de médico*** as a doctor ◇ **calidad de vida** quality of life
cálido *adj tb fig* warm
calidoscopio *m* kaleidoscope
calientapiernas *m inv* legwarmers *pl*
calientapiés *m inv* foot warmer
calientaplatos *m inv* plate warmer
caliente *adj* **1** hot; ***en ~*** in the heat of the moment **2** F (*cachondo*) horny F
calificable *adj* gradable
calificación *f* **1** description **2** EDU grade, *Br* mark
calificado *adj* qualified; *trabajador* skilled
calificar ⟨1g⟩ *v/t* **1** describe, label (***de*** as) **2** EDU grade, *Br* mark; **calificarse** *v/r*: ***con esa actitud se califica él solo*** *fig* that attitude sums him up
calificativo I *adj* qualifying **II** *m* description
California *f* California
caligrafía *f* calligraphy
caligráfico *adj* handwriting *atr*
calígrafo *m* calligrapher; (***perito***) **~** handwriting expert
calima, calina *f* haze
calimocho *m* red wine and cola
cáliz *m* BOT calyx
caliza *f* limestone
calizo *adj* limy
callada *f*: ***dar la ~ por respuesta*** not reply, remain silent; ***de ~*** secretly
callado *adj* quiet
callampas *fpl Chi* shanty town *sg*

callar ⟨1a⟩ **I** *v/i* (*dejar de hablar*) go quiet; (*guardar silencio*) be quiet, keep quiet; ***¡calla!*** be quiet!, shut up! **II** *v/t* silence; **callarse** *v/r* (*dejar de hablar*) go quiet; (*guardar silencio*) be quiet, keep quiet; ***~ algo*** keep sth quiet
calle *f* **1** street; ***echar a alguien a la ~*** *fig* throw s.o out on the street; ***quedarse en la ~*** *fig* fall on hard times; ***llevarse a alguien de ~*** have s.o. chasing after one; ***traer*** *o* ***llevar a alguien por la ~ de la amargura*** make s.o.'s life a misery; ***hacer la ~*** F *de prostituta* turn tricks F, *Br* walk the streets **2** DEP lane
◇ **calle comercial** shopping street; **calle de dirección única** one-way street; **calle lateral** side street; **calle mayor** main street, *Br* high street; **calle peatonal** pedestrian street; **calle principal** main street, *Br* high street
calleja *f* narrow street, side street
callejear ⟨1a⟩ *v/i* stroll (around the streets)
callejero I *adj* street *atr* **II** *m* street directory
callejón *m* alley
◇ **callejón sin salida** blind alley; *fig* dead end
callejuela *f* narrow street, side street
callicida *m* corn remover
callista *m/f* podiatrist, *Br* chiropodist
callo *m* **1** callus; ***dar el ~*** *fig* F slog away F **2** *fig* F ugly man / woman; ***ser un ~*** be plug ugly F, be as ugly as sin **3**: ***~s*** *pl* GASTR tripe *sg*
callosidad *f* callus
calloso *adj* callused, rough
calma *f* calm; ***¡~!*** calm down!; ***tómatelo con ~*** take it easy; ***la ~ que precede a la tormenta*** the calm before the storm
◇ **calma chicha** dead calm
calmante I *adj* soothing **II** *m* MED sedative
calmar ⟨1a⟩ *v/t* **1** calm (down) **2** *sed* quench; **calmarse** *v/r* calm down
calmoso *adj* calm; *desp* slow
caló *m* **1** *language spoken by Spanish gypsies* **2** *Méx* criminal slang
calor *m* **1** heat; ***hace mucho ~*** it's very hot; ***tengo ~*** I'm hot **2** *fig* warmth; ***entrar en ~*** get warm **3**: ***al ~ de*** *fig*: *ayuda económica, contactos* thanks to
caloría *f* calorie; ***comida baja / rica en ~s*** low- / high-calorie food
calorífero *adj* heat-producing
calorífico *adj* calorific
calostro *m* BIO colostrum
calumnia *f oral* slander; *por escrito* libel
calumniador I *adj oral* slanderous; *por escrito* libelous, *Br* libellous **II** *m*, **~a** *f oral* slanderer; *por escrito* libeler, *Br* libeller
calumniar ⟨1b⟩ *v/t oralmente* slander; *por escrito* libel
calumnioso *adj oral* slanderous; *por escrito* libelous, *Br* libellous
caluroso *adj* hot; *fig* warm; ***una acogida -a*** a warm welcome
calva *f* bald patch
calvario *m fig* torment
calvero *m* clearing
calvicie *f* baldness
calvo I *adj* **1** bald; ***estar ~*** be bald; ***ni tanto ni tan ~*** *fig* F there's no need to go to extremes **2** *región* bare, barren **II** *m* bald man
calza *f* **1** wedge **2**: ***~s*** *fpl* HIST hose *pl*
calzada *f* road (surface), pavement; ***salirse de la ~*** go off the road
calzado I *adj* with shoes on; ***iba ~ de botas*** he had boots on, he was wearing boots **II** *m* footwear
calzador *m* shoe horn; ***entrar con ~*** F squeeze in
calzar ⟨1f⟩ *v/t* **1** *zapato, bota etc* put on; ***¿qué número calza?*** what size (shoe) do you take? **2** *mueble, rueda* wedge; **calzarse** *v/r zapato, bota etc* put on
calzo *m* chock
calzón *m* **1** DEP shorts *pl* **2** *L.Am. de hombre* shorts *pl*, *Br* (under)pants *pl*; *L.Am. de mujer* panties *pl*, *Br tb* knickers *pl* **3**: ***calzones*** *pl L.Am.* shorts, *Br* (under)pants
calzonazos *m inv* F *marido* henpecked husband
calzoncillos *mpl* shorts, *Br* (under-) pants
cama *f* bed; ***hacer la ~*** make the bed; ***irse a la ~*** go to bed; ***estar en ~*** be in bed; ***guardar ~*** be confined to bed
◇ **cama de agua** water bed; **cama camera** three-quarter bed; **cama de campaña** cot, *Br* camp bed; **cama con dosel** four-poster bed; **cama elástica** trampoline; **cama individual** single bed; **cama de matrimonio** double bed; **cama nido** truckle bed, trundle

bed; **cama plegable** folding bed; **cama turca** divan (bed)
camachuelo *m* ZO: **~ *común*** common bullfinch
camada *f* ZO litter; *fig desp* gang; ***ser de la misma ~*** be as bad as each other
camafeo *m* cameo
camaleón *m* chameleon
camaleónico *adj* chameleon-like
camama *f* F lie
camandulero *m*, **-a** *f* hypocrite
cámara I *f* **1** FOT, TV camera; ***chupar ~*** F TV hog the limelight F; ***a ~ lenta*** in slow motion **2** (*sala*) chamber; ***de ~*** MÚS chamber *atr* **II** *m/f* cameraman; *mujer* camerawoman
◇ **cámara acorazada** strong room; **cámara de aire** AUTO inner tube; **cámara alta** POL upper house, upper chamber; **cámara baja** POL lower house, lower chamber; **cámara de comercio e industria** chamber of commerce and industry; **cámara de diputados** chamber of deputies (*Spanish lower house*); **cámara fotográfica** camera; **cámara frigorífica** cold room; **cámara de gas** gas chamber; **cámara oscura** camera obscura; **cámara de televisión** television camera; **cámara de video**, *Esp* **cámara de vídeo** video camera
camarada *m/f* **1** comrade **2** *de trabajo* colleague, co-worker
camaradería *f* camaraderie, comradeship
camarera *f* waitress
camarero *m* waiter
camarilla *f* POL inner circle; *fig* clique
camarín *m* **1** dressing room **2** REL chapel
camarógrafo *m*, **-a** *f L.Am.* camera operator
camarón *m L.Am.* ZO shrimp, *Br* prawn
camarote *m* MAR cabin
camarotero *m L.Am.* steward
camastro *m* uncomfortable old bed
cambalache *m Arg* F second-hand store
cambalachear ⟨1a⟩ *v/t* F swap F
cambiable *adj* changeable
cambiador *m* money changer
◇ **cambiador de calor** heat exchanger
cambiante *adj* changing; *tiempo* changeable
cambiar ⟨1b⟩ **I** *v/t* change (***por*** for); *compra* exchange (***por*** for) **II** *v/i* change; ***~ de lugar*** change places; ***~ de marcha*** AUTO shift gear, *Br* change gear; ***~ de domicilio*** move house; ***~ de tren*** change trains; ***~ de coche*** get a new car; ***~ de opinión*** *o* ***parecer*** change one's mind; **cambiarse** *v/r* change; ***~ de ropa*** change (one's clothes)
cambiario *adj* COM exchange *atr*
cambiazo *m* F switch; ***dar el ~*** (***a alguien***) F pull a switch (on s.o.) F
cambio *m* **1** change; ***~ de domicilio*** change of address; ***~ de aires*** change of scene; ***~ de turno*** change of shift; ***~ de aceite*** AUTO oil change; ***¡~!*** *al hablar por radio* over!
2 COM exchange rate; ***el ~ del día*** the day's (exchange) rate; ***libre ~*** COM free trade
3 (*suelto*): ***¿tiene ~?*** do you have change?
4: ***no se admiten ~s*** goods will not be exchanged
5 *en locuciones*: ***a ~ de*** in exchange for; ***en ~*** on the other hand
◇ **cambio automático (de marchas)** automatic transmission; **cambio climático** climate change; **cambio de marchas** AUTO gear shift, *Br* gear change; **cambio de sentido** U-turn; *señal de tráfico* exit here to join opposite highway; **cambio del tiempo** change in the weather
cambista *m/f* money changer
cambriano, cámbrico *adj* GEOL Cambrian
camelar ⟨1a⟩ *v/t* F sweet-talk F; ***~ a alguien para que haga algo*** F sweet-talk s.o. into doing sth F
camelia *f* BOT camellia
camella *f* (female) camel
camello I *m* ZO camel **II** *m/f* F (*vendedor de drogas*) pusher F, dealer
camellón *m Méx* median strip, *Br* central reservation
camelo *m* F con F; (*broma*) joke; ***dar el ~ a alguien*** F pull s.o.'s leg F
camerino *m* TEA dressing room
camilla *f* **1** stretcher **2**: ***mesa ~*** *small round table*
camillero *m*, **-a** *f* stretcher bearer

caminante *m/f* traveler, *Br* traveller
caminar ⟨1a⟩ **I** *v/i* **1** walk; *fig* move; ***caminando*** on foot **2** *L.Am.* (*funcionar*) work **II** *v/t* walk
caminata *f* long walk
caminero *adj*: ***peón ~*** road mender, *Br* navvy
camino *m* **1** (*senda*) path; ***no es*** (***todo***) ***un ~ de rosas*** it isn't all a bed of roses **2** INFOR path
3 (*ruta*) way; ***a medio ~*** halfway; ***de ~ a*** on the way to; ***por el ~*** on the way; ***~ de*** on the way to; ***abrirse ~*** *fig* make one's way; ***estar en ~*** be on the way; ***ponerse en ~*** set out; ***abrirse ~*** *en la vida* get on; ***ir por buen / mal ~*** *fig* be on the right / wrong track; ***abrir ~ hacia algo*** *fig* pave the way for sth; ***quedarse a medio*** *o* ***mitad de ~*** *fig* leave sth half finished
◇ **camino forestal** forest track; **camino de herradura** bridle path; **camino rural** country road; **camino vecinal** minor road
camión *m* **1** truck, *Br tb* lorry **2** *Méx* bus
◇ **camión de la basura** garbage truck; **camión cisterna** tanker; **camión frigorífico** refrigerated truck; **camión de mudanzas** moving van, *Br* removal van; **camión pesado** heavy truck, *Br* heavy goods vehicle
camionero *m*, **-a** *f* **1** truck driver, *Br tb* lorry driver **2** *Méx* bus driver
camioneta *f* van; ***~ (de reparto)*** delivery van
camisa *f* shirt; ***dejar a alguien sin ~*** *fig* F leave s.o. without a cent; ***meterse en ~ de once varas*** F stick one's nose in (s.o. else's business) F; ***no le llegaba la ~ al cuerpo*** he was petrified; ***cambiar de ~*** *fig* POL switch allegiance
◇ **camisa de fuerza** straitjacket
camisería *f* men's outfitters
camisero I *adj*: ***blusa -a*** woman's shirt; ***vestido ~*** shirt dress **II** *m*, **-a** *f* shirtmaker
camiseta *f* **1** T-shirt **2** DEP jersey, *Br* shirt
camisola *f* sport shirt
camisón *m* nightdress
camomila *f* BOT camomile
camorra *f* F fight; ***armar ~*** F cause trouble; ***buscar ~*** F look for a fight *o* for trouble
camorrista *m/f* F troublemaker
camote *m Andes*, *C.Am.*, *Méx* sweet potato
campal *adj*: ***batalla ~*** pitched battle
campamento *m* camp
campana *f* **1** bell; ***doblar las ~s*** toll the bells; ***echar las ~s al vuelo*** *fig* get excited, get carried away; ***dar una vuelta de ~*** AUTO flip over **2** *de chimenea* hood
◇ **campana de buzo** diving bell
◇ **campana extractora** extractor hood
campanada *f* chime; ***dar la ~*** cause a stir; ***la noticia fue una ~*** F the news came as a bombshell
campanario *m* bell tower; ***política de ~*** local politics, *Br* parish-pump politics
campanazo *m L.Am.* warning
campaneo *m* pealing
campanero *m*, **-a** *f* bell ringer
campaniforme *adj* bell-shaped
campanil *m* bell tower
campanilla *f* **1** small bell; ***de muchas ~s*** high-class **2** ANAT uvula **3** BOT bell flower, campanula
campante *adj*: ***tan ~*** F as calm as anything F
campanudo *adj* **1** *voz* resonant **2** *persona* pompous
campánula *f* BOT campanula
campaña *f* campaign; ***~ antitabaco*** anti-smoking campaign
◇ **campaña electoral** election campaign
◇ **campaña publicitaria** advertising campaign
campar ⟨1a⟩ *v/i* **1** *fig* stand out **2**: ***~ por sus respetos*** do as one likes; ***~ a sus anchas*** do as one pleases
campear ⟨1a⟩ *v/i* stand out
campechanía *f* down-to-earth nature
campechano *adj* down-to-earth
campeón *m*, **-ona** *f* champion
campeonato *m* championship; ***de ~*** F terrific F
◇ **campeonato mundial, campeonato del mundo** world championship
campera *f* **1** *L.Am.* jacket **2**: ***~s*** *pl botas* cowboy boots
campero *adj* country *atr*, rural
campesinado *m* peasantry, peasants *pl*
campesino I *adj* peasant *atr* **II** *m*, **-a** *f* peasant
campestre *adj* rural, country *atr*

camping *m* campground, *Br tb* campsite; ***ir de ~*** go camping
campiña *f* countryside
campista *m/f* camper
campo *m* **1** field
2: ***el ~*** (*área rural*) the country; ***en el ~*** in the country(side); ***ir al ~*** go to the country; ***a ~ abierto*** *o* ***raso*** in (the) open country; ***a ~ traviesa***, ***~ a través*** cross-country
3 DEP field, *Br tb* pitch; (*estadio*) stadium, *Br tb* ground
4: ***en el ~ de la técnica*** in the technical field; ***dejar el ~ libre*** leave the field free (***a*** for), make way (***a*** for); ***tener ~ libre para hacer algo*** have a free hand to do sth
◇ **campo de acción** scope; ***la empresa está ampliando su ~*** the firm is expanding (the scope of) its operations; **campo de acogida** reception camp; **campo de aplicación** scope; **campo atrás** *en baloncesto* backcourt violation; **campo de aviación** airfield; **campo de batalla** battlefield; **campo de concentración** concentration camp; **campo de deportes** sports field; **campo para entradas** INFOR entry field; **campo de exterminio** death camp; **campo de golf** golf course; **campo magnético** magnetic field; **campo de opción** INFOR optional field; **campo de refugiados** refugee camp; **campo de tiro** firing range; **campo visual** field of vision
camposanto *m* cemetery
campus *m inv*: ***~ universitario*** university campus
camuflaje *m* camouflage
camuflar ⟨1a⟩ *v/t* camouflage
can *m lit*, *hum* dog
cana *f* **1** (*pelo gris*) gray *o Br* grey hair; (*pelo blanco*) white hair; ***echar una ~ al aire*** F let one's hair down F; ***peinar ~s*** be getting on, be getting old **2** *Cu*, *Rpl* F (*cárcel*) can F **3** *Rpl* F (*policía*): ***la ~*** the cops F *pl*
Canadá *m* Canada
canadiense *m/f & adj* Canadian
canal *m* **1** channel **2** TRANSP canal **3**: ***abrir en ~*** cut open (from top to bottom)
canalete *m* paddle
canalización *f* **1** *de río* canalization **2** *de ideas* channeling, *Br* channelling
canalizar ⟨1f⟩ *v/t* **1** channel **2** *río* canalize
canalla **I** *m/f* swine F, rat F **II** *f* riff-raff
canallada *f* rotten trick
canallesco *adj* rotten, mean
canalón *m* gutter
canana *f* cartridge belt
canapé *m* **1** (*sofá*) couch **2** *para cama* base **3** GASTR canapé
Canarias *fpl* Canaries; ***Islas ~*** Canary Islands
canario **I** *adj* Canary *atr* **II** *m* ZO canary
canasta *f* **1** basket **2** *juego* canasta
◇ **canasta de dos puntos** *en baloncesto* two-pointer
◇ **canasta de tres puntos** *en baloncesto* three-pointer
canastero *m*, **-a** *f* basket maker; *vendedor* basket seller
canastilla *f*, **canastillo** *m* (small) basket
canasto *m* basket
cáncamo *m* TÉC eyebolt
cancel *m* inner door
cancela *f* (wrought-iron) gate
cancelación *f* **1** cancellation; *de billetes* punching **2** *de deuda*, *cuenta* settlement, payment
cancelar ⟨1a⟩ *v/t* **1** *tb* INFOR cancel **2** *deuda*, *cuenta* settle, pay
cáncer *m* MED, *fig* cancer
◇ **cáncer de mama** breast cancer
◇ **cáncer hepático** liver cancer
Cáncer ASTR **I** *adj* Cancerian; ***soy ~*** I'm (a) Cancer, I'm (a) Cancerian **II** *m/f inv* Cancer
cancerbero *m* **1** DEP goalkeeper **2**: ***el Cancerbero*** MYTH Cerberus
canceriano *L.Am.* ASTR **I** *adj* Cancerian; ***soy ~*** I'm (a) Cancer, I'm (a) Cancerian **II** *m*, **-a** *f* Cancerian, Cancer
cancerígeno *adj* carcinogenic
cancerología *f* MED oncology
cancerólogo *m*, **-a** *f* cancer specialist, oncologist
canceroso *adj* cancerous
cancha *f* **1** DEP court; *L.Am. de fútbol* field, *Br tb* pitch; ***~ de tenis*** tennis court **2** *Rpl*: ***¡~!*** gangway!; ***abrir*** *o* ***hacer ~*** make room
canchear ⟨1a⟩ *v/i L.Am.* climb
canciller *m* **1** Chancellor **2** *S.Am. de asuntos exteriores* Secretary of State, *Br* Foreign Minister

cancillería *f* **1** *de gobierno* chancellorship **2** *de embajada* chancellery
canción *f* song; ***esa*** *o* ***eso es otra ~*** *fig* F that's another story F; ***siempre la misma ~*** F the same old story F
◇ **canción de cuna** lullaby; **canción popular** folk song; **canción de protesta** protest song
cancionero *m* song book
candado *m* padlock
candeal *adj*: ***trigo ~*** durum wheat
candela *f L.Am.* fire; ***¿me das ~?*** do you have a light?; ***dar*** *o* ***arrear ~ a alguien*** beat s.o. up
candelabro *m* candelabra
Candelaria *f* REL Candlemas
candelero *m* candlestick; ***estar en el ~*** *de persona* be in the limelight
candente *adj* **1** red-hot **2** *tema* topical
candidato *m*, **-a** *f* candidate
candidatura *f* candidacy; ***presentar su ~ para*** apply for
candidez *f* naivety
cándido *adj* naïve
candil *m* oil lamp
candileja *f* **1** small oil lamp **2**: **~*s*** *pl* TEA footlights
candor *m* innocence; (*franqueza*) candor, *Br* candour
candoroso *adj* innocent; (*franco*) candid
canear ⟨1a⟩ *v/i* go gray *o Br* grey
canela *f* cinnamon; ***ser ~ fina*** *fig* F be very fine, be wonderful
◇ **canela en rama** stick cinnamon
canelo I *adj* cinnamon *atr*; ***color -a*** cinnamon-colored, *Br* cinnamon-coloured **II** *m* cinnamon tree; ***hacer el ~*** F make a fool of o.s.
canelón *m de tejado* gutter
canelones *mpl* GASTR cannelloni *sg*
canesú *m* bodice
cangilón *m* scoop, bucket
cangreja *f* MAR gaff sail
cangrejo *m* ZO crab
◇ **cangrejo de mar** crab
◇ **cangrejo de río** crawfish, *Br* crayfish
canguelo *m* F: ***tener ~*** be scared stiff F; ***entrarle a alguien el ~*** get jittery F
canguro I *m* ZO kangaroo **II** *m/f* F babysitter
caníbal I *adj* cannibal *atr* **II** *m/f* cannibal
canibalismo *m* cannibalism
canica *f* marble
caniche *m* poodle
canícula *f* dog days *pl*
canijo *adj* F puny
canilla *f L.Am.* faucet, *Br* tap
canillita *m/f CSur* newspaper vendor
canino I *adj* dog *atr*, canine; ***diente ~*** canine (tooth); ***tener un hambre -a*** be ravenous **II** *m* canine (tooth)
canje *m* exchange
canjeable *adj* exchangeable (***por*** for)
canjear ⟨1a⟩ *v/t* exchange (***por*** for)
cano *adj* (*pelo*: *blanco*) white; (*gris*) gray, *Br* grey
canoa *f* canoe
canódromo *m* dog track
canon *m* MÚS, REL canon; ***como mandan los cánones*** *fig* in accordance with the rules
canónico *adj* canonical; ***derecho ~*** canon law
canónigo *m* canon
canonización *f* canonization
canonizar ⟨1f⟩ *v/t* canonize
canoro *adj* tuneful; ***aves -as*** songbirds
canoso *adj* (*gris*: *pelo*) gray, *Br* grey; *persona* gray-haired, *Br* grey-haired; (*blanco*: *pelo*) white; *persona* white-haired
canotier *m* straw hat, boater
cansado *adj* tired; ***vista -a*** farsightedness, *Br* longsightedness
cansancio *m* tiredness
cansar ⟨1a⟩ *v/t* **1** tire **2** (*aburrir*) bore; **cansarse** *v/r* **1** get tired; ***~ de algo*** get tired of sth **2** (*aburrirse*) get bored
cansino *adj* weary
cantable *adj* singable
Cantabria *f* Cantabria
cantábrico *m/adj*: ***el*** (***mar***) ***Cantábrico*** the Bay of Biscay
cantada *f* F *en fútbol* (goalkeeping) error
cantado *adj*: ***estaba ~*** F it was a foregone conclusion
cantamañanas *m/f inv* F: ***ser un ~*** be all talk
cantante *m/f* singer
cantaor *m*, **~a** *f* flamenco singer
cantar ⟨1a⟩ **I** *v/i* **1** sing **2** P *de delincuente* squeal P **II** *v/t* sing **III** *m*: ***ése es otro ~*** *fig* F that's a different story
cántara *f* pitcher
cantárida *f* ZO Spanish fly
cantarín *adj* **1** *persona* fond of singing **2**

voz singsong
cántaro *m* pitcher; ***llover a ~s*** F pour (down); ***alma de ~*** F simple soul
cantata *f* cantata
cantautor *m*, **~a** *f* singer-songwriter
cante *m*: ***dar el ~*** *fig* F make an exhibition of o.s.
◇ **cante flamenco, cante hondo, cante jondo** flamenco singing
cantegril *m Urug* shanty town
cantera *f* **1** quarry; *fig* source **2** DEP youth squad
cantero *m* **1** quarryman **2** *S.Am.* (*parterre*) flowerbed
cántico *m* canticle
cantidad I *f* quantity, amount; ***había ~ de*** there was (*pl* were) a lot of; ***en ~*** in large amounts; ***tenemos seda en ~*** we have lots of *o* plenty of silk **II** *adv*: ***es ~ de barato*** it's really cheap; ***nos divertimos ~*** we had a really great time
cantil *m* **1** coastal shelf **2** (*acantilado*) cliff
cantilena *f* ☞ ***cantinela***
cantimplora *f* water bottle
cantina *f* canteen
cantinela *f fig* F: ***la misma ~*** the same old story
canto[1] *m* **1** singing **2** *de pájaro* song
◇ **canto coral** choral singing
◇ **canto del gallo** cockcrow
canto[2] *m* **1** edge; ***de ~*** on its side (*pl* on their sides); ***por el ~ de un duro*** *fig* F by the skin of one's teeth F **2** (*roca*) stone; ***darse con un ~ en los dientes*** count o.s. lucky
◇ **canto rodado** boulder
cantón *m* **1** POL canton **2** MIL cantonment
cantonera *f* corner piece
cantor I *adj* singing; ***niño ~*** choirboy; ***pájaro ~*** songbird **II** *m*, **~a** *f* singer
canturrear ⟨1a⟩ *v/t* sing softly
canutas: ***las pasé ~*** F it was really tough F
canutillo *m*: ***paño de ~*** needlecord
canuto *m* **1** tube **2** F *de marihuana* joint F
caña *f* **1** BOT reed **2** *L.Am.* straw **3** (*tallo*) stalk **4** *bambú* cane; ***muebles de ~*** cane furniture **5** *Esp cerveza* small glass of beer **6**: ***dar*** *o* ***meter ~ a alguien*** F pull s.o.'s leg, *Br tb* wind s.o. up F; ***¡dale ~!*** F get off your butt! F; *no tengas compasión* give him hell! F; *animando* go for it!, come on! **7** *L.Am. type of rum*
◇ **caña de azúcar** sugar cane
◇ **caña de pescar** fishing rod
cañada *f* **1** ravine **2** *L.Am.* (*arroyo*) stream
cañadilla *f* ZO whelk
cáñamo *m* **1** hemp **2** *L.Am.* marijuana plant
cañamón *m* hemp seed
cañaveral *m* **1** reedbed **2** *L.Am.* sugarcane plantation
cañazo *m L.Am.* cane liquor
cañería *f* pipe; ***~ de agua*** water pipe
cañero I *adj L.Am.* sugar-cane *atr* **II** *m*, **-a** *f* plantation worker
cañí I *adj* gypsy *atr* **II** *m/f* gypsy
cañizal *m*, **cañizar** *m* reedbed
cañizo *m* wattle
caño *m* **1** pipe **2** *de fuente* spout
◇ **caño de escape** *Rpl* AUTO exhaust (pipe)
cañón I *adj* F great, fantastic F; ***lo pasamos ~*** we had a great time **II** *m* **1** HIST cannon **2** *antiaéreo, antitanque etc* gun **3** *de fusil* barrel **4** GEOG canyon
◇ **cañón de agua** water cannon
cañonazo *m* **1** gunshot **2**: ***lanzar un ~*** *en fútbol* hit a powerful shot, fire off a tremendous kick
cañonear ⟨1a⟩ *v/t* shell, bombard
cañoneo *m* shelling, bombardment
cañonera *f* gunboat
cañonero I *adj*: ***lancha -a*** gunboat **II** *m* gunboat
caoba I *adj* mahogany *atr* **II** *f* mahogany
caolín *m* MIN china clay, kaolin
caos *m* chaos; ***~ circulatorio*** traffic chaos
caótico *adj* chaotic
cap *abr* (= ***capítulo***) ch. (= chapter)
CAP *m abr* (= ***Centro de Atención Primaria***) Primary Care Center *o Br* Centre
capa *f* **1** layer; ***~ de nieve*** layer of snow; ***~ social*** social stratum
2 *prenda* cloak; ***andar*** *o* ***ir de ~ caída*** F *de persona* be down F; *de negocio* not be doing well, be on the skids F; ***defender algo a ~ y espada*** fight tooth and nail for something; ***hacer de su ~ un sayo*** do as one likes; ***bajo la ~ de hacer algo*** on the pretext of doing sth

3 TAUR cape
◇ **capa de ozono** ozone layer
◇ **capa de pintura** coat of paint
capacho *m* basket
capacidad *f* **1** capacity; ***medida de ~*** cubic measure **2** (*aptitud*) competence
◇ **capacidad de almacenamiento** INFOR storage capacity; **capacidad de carga** freight capacity; **capacidad competitiva** competitiveness; ***un sector con una alta ~*** a highly competitive industry; **capacidad jurídica** legal authority; ***el magistrado no tiene ~ alguna para actuar en ese caso*** the case is outside the judge's jurisdiction, the judge has no jurisdiction over the case; **capacidad de memoria** INFOR memory capacity; **capacidad organizativa** organizational ability
capacitación *f* training; ***curso de ~*** training course
capacitado *adj* trained, qualified
capacitar ⟨1a⟩ *v/t* train, prepare; ***~ a alguien para hacer algo*** qualify s.o. to do sth; **capacitarse** *v/r* train, qualify
capadura *f* castration
capar ⟨1a⟩ *v/t* castrate
caparazón *m* ZO shell
capataz *m* foreman
capataza *f* forewoman
capaz *adj* able (***de*** to); ***ser ~ de*** be capable of; ***ser ~ de todo*** be capable of anything
capazo *m* basket
capcioso *adj*: ***pregunta -a*** trick question
capea *f* TAUR *bullfight featuring young bulls*
capear ⟨1a⟩ *v/t* **1** *temporal* weather **2** TAUR make passes at with one's cape
capacete *m Méx* bonnet
capellán *m* chaplain
capellanía *f* chaplaincy
capelo *m* cardinal's hat
Caperucita *f*: ***~ Roja*** Little Red Riding Hood
caperuza *f* **1** *tb* TÉC hood **2** *de bolígrafo* top
capicúa *adj*: ***número ~*** reversible number
capilar I *adj* capillary *atr*; *loción* hair *atr* **II** *m* capillary; ***vaso ~*** ANAT capillary
capilla *f* chapel; ***estar en ~*** be on tenterhooks
◇ **capilla ardiente** chapel of rest
capirotada *f Méx*: *type of French toast with honey, cheese, raisins etc*
capirotazo *m* F flick
capirote *m* F hood; ***ser tonto de ~*** F be dumb F, be a complete idiot
capitación *f* HIST capitation, poll tax
capital I *adj importancia* prime; ***pena ~*** capital punishment **II** *f de país* capital **III** *m* COM capital
◇ **capital circulante** circulating capital; **capital de explotación** working capital; **capital fijo, capital inmovilizado** fixed capital; **capital de inversión** investment capital; **capital líquido** liquid assets *pl*; **capital (de) riesgo** venture capital; **capital social** share capital
capitalidad *f* capital city status
capitalino I *adj* of / from the capital city, capital *atr* **II** *m*, **-a** *f* native of the capital city
capitalismo *m* capitalism
capitalista I *adj* capitalist *atr* **II** *m/f* capitalist
capitalización *f* capitalization
capitalizar ⟨1f⟩ *v/t* capitalize; *fig* capitalize on
capitán *m*, **-ana** *f* captain
◇ **capitán de fragata** lieutenant commander; **capitán general** *Esp* field marshal; **capitán de navío** captain, sea captain
capitanear ⟨1a⟩ *v/t* captain
capitanía *f* **1** captaincy **2** *edificio* headquarters *sg o pl*
capitel *m* ARQUI capital
Capitolio *m* Capitol
capitoste *m* F bigwig F
capitulación *f* **1** capitulation, surrender **2** (*pacto*) agreement; ***capitulaciones matrimoniales*** marriage settlement *sg*
capitular ⟨1a⟩ **I** *v/i* surrender, capitulate **II** *adj* REL: ***sala ~*** chapterhouse
capítulo *m* chapter; ***ser ~ aparte*** F be a separate issue; ***llamar a alguien a ~*** call s.o. to account
capo *m*, **-a** *f* **1** *de mafia* capo, don **2** *CSur* star
capó *m* AUTO hood, *Br* bonnet
capón *m* **I** *adj* castrated **II** *Rpl* mutton
caporal *m* foreman
capot *m* ☞ ***capó***
capota *f* AUTO top, *Br* hood
capotar ⟨1a⟩ *v/i* AUTO, AVIA overturn

C

capote *m* cloak; MIL greatcoat; ***decir algo para su ~*** say sth to o.s.; ***echar un ~ a alguien*** *fig* F give s.o. a hand F
capotear ⟨1a⟩ *v/t* TAUR make passes at with one's cape
capotera *f L.Am.* coat stand
capricho *m* **1** whim; ***a ~*** at the drop of a hat; *sin orden aparente* willy-nilly, at random **2** MÚS capriccio
caprichoso *adj* capricious
capricorniano *L.Am.* ASTR **I** *adj* ***soy ~*** I'm (a) Capricorn **II** *m*, **-a** *f* Capricornian, Capricorn
Capricornio ASTR **I** *adj* Capricornian; ***soy ~*** I'm (a) Capricorn, I'm (a) Capricornian **II** *m/f inv* Capricorn
cápsula *f* capsule
◇ **cápsula espacial** space capsule
capsular *adj* capsular
captación *f* **1** (*percepción*) understanding **2** RAD reception **3** *de aguas* channeling, *Br* channelling **4** *de clientes* gaining, acquiring; ***la ~ de clientes*** expansion of the customer base
captar ⟨1a⟩ *v/t* **1** understand **2** RAD pick up **3** *aguas* channel **4** *clientes* acquire, win **5** *negocio* take **6** FOT, *datos* capture
captor *m*, **~a** *f de personas, animales* captor
captura *f* capture; *en pesca* catch; ***tasa de ~s*** fishing quota
capturar ⟨1a⟩ *v/t* capture; *peces* catch
capturista *m/f Méx* keyboarder
capucha *f* hood
capuchina *f* BOT nasturtium
capuchino *m* **1** GASTR cappuccino **2** REL Capuchin
capuchón *m de bolígrafo* top; *de ropa* hood
capullo *m* **1** ZO cocoon **2** BOT bud **3** P *persona* jerk F, *Br* dickhead P
caqui I *adj* khaki **II** *m* **1** BOT persimmon **2** (*tela*) khaki
cara *f* **1** face; ***a ~ descubierta*** not wearing a mask; ***~ a algo*** facing sth; ***~ a ~*** face to face; ***en el ~ a ~*** face to face; ***de ~ a*** facing; *fig* with regard to; ***de ~ al exterior*** on the surface, outwardly; ***hacer ~ a*** face up to; ***dar la ~*** face the consequences; ***sacar la ~ por alguien*** stick one's neck out for s.o.; ***plantar ~ a*** stand up to; ***echar algo en ~ a alguien*** remind s.o. of sth; ***decir algo en*** *o* ***a la ~ de alguien*** say sth to s.o.'s face; ***lo hizo por su ~ bonita*** *o* ***por su linda ~*** *fig* he did it just because he felt like it; ***cruzar la ~ a alguien*** slap s.o. in the face, slap s.o.'s face; ***romper*** *o* ***partir la ~ a alguien*** P smash s.o.'s face in; ***¡nos veremos las ~s!*** you haven't heard the last of this!; ***tenían el viento / el sol de ~*** they had the wind in their faces / the sun in their eyes; ***todo le sale de ~*** everything goes right for him
2 (*expresión*) look; ***tiene ~ de pocos amigos*** he doesn't look very friendly; ***tiene ~ de preocupación / alegría*** he looks worried / happy; ***~ larga*** long face; ***tener buena / mala ~*** *de comida* look good / bad; *de persona* look well / sick; ***poner buena ~ a mal tiempo*** look on the bright side
3 *fig* nerve; ***tener ~ dura*** have a nerve
4: ***la otra ~ de la moneda*** *fig* the other side of the coin
◇ **cara o cruz** heads or tails
carabina *f* carbine; *fig* F chaperone
carabinero *m* **1** GASTR (large) shrimp, *Br* prawn **2** (*agente de aduana*) border guard
cárabo *m* ZO tawny owl
Caracas *m* Caracas
caracol *m* **1** snail **2**: ***¡~es!*** wow! F; *enfado* damn! F
caracola *f* ZO conch
caracolear ⟨1a⟩ *v/i de caballo* prance
carácter *m* **1** character **2** INFOR,TIP character; ***caracteres de imprenta*** block letters **3** (*naturaleza*) nature
característica *f* **1** characteristic **2** *L.Am.* TELEC area code
característico *adj* characteristic (***de*** of)
caracterización *f* characterization; TEA portrayal
caracterizar ⟨1f⟩ *v/t* characterize; TEA play (the part of); **caracterizarse** *v/r* be characterized (***por*** by)
caradura *m/f* F guy / woman with a nerve, *Br* cheeky devil F
carajillo *m coffee with a shot of liquor*
carajo *m*: ***irse al ~*** F go down the tubes F; ***¡~!*** F damn! F
¡caramba! *int* wow! F; *enfado* damn! F
carámbano *m* icicle
carambola *f billar* carom, *Br* cannon; ***por*** *o* ***de ~*** F by sheer chance
caramelizar ⟨1f⟩ *v/t* coat in caramel

caramelo *m* **1** *dulce* candy, *Br* sweet **2** (*azúcar derretido*) caramel
◇ **caramelo de palo** lollipop
caramillo *m* MÚS flageolet
carantoña *f* caress; ***hacer ~s a alguien*** caress s.o.
carapacho *m* ZO shell
caraqueño I *adj* of / from Caracas, Caracas *atr* **II** *m*, **-a** *f* native of Caracas
carátula *f* **1** *de disco* jacket, *Br tb* sleeve **2** *L.Am. de reloj* face
caravana *f* **1** (*remolque*) trailer, *Br* caravan **2** *de tráfico* traffic jam, *Br* queue of traffic **3** *Méx* (*reverencia*) bow **4** *Urug* (*pendiente*) earring
caravaning *m touring with car and trailer*, *Br* caravanning
caray *int* F wow! F; *enfado* damn! F
carbohidrato *m* carbohydrate
carbón *m* coal
◇ **carbón de leña** charcoal; **carbón mineral, carbón de piedra** coal; **carbón vegetal** charcoal
carbonato *m* carbonate
carboncillo *m* charcoal; ***dibujo al ~*** charcoal drawing
carbonera *f* **1** coal cellar **2** MAR collier
carbonería *f* coalyard
carbonero I *adj* coal *atr* **II** *m* **1** ZO coal tit **2** (*vendedor*) coal merchant
carbonífero I *adj* carboniferous **II** *m* GEOL Carboniferous period
carbonilla *f* coal dust
carbonizar ⟨1f⟩ *v/t* **1** char **2** QUÍM carbonize; **carbonizarse** *v/r* be reduced to ashes
carbono *m* QUÍM carbon
carbunco *m* MED anthrax
carburador *m* AUTO carburet(t)or
carburante *m* fuel
carburo *m* carbide
carca *m/f & adj* F reactionary
carcacha *f Méx* F old jalopy F, *Br tb* old banger F
carcaj *m* quiver
carcajada *f* laugh, guffaw; ***reír a ~s*** roar with laughter; ***estallar en ~s*** burst out laughing; ***soltar una ~*** burst out laughing
carcajear ⟨1a⟩ *v/i* roar with laughter; **carcajearse** *v/r* have a good laugh (***de*** at)
carcamal *m/f* F old crock F
carcasa *f* TÉC casing
cárcava *f* gully
cárcel *f* prison
carcelero I *adj* prison *atr* **II** *m*, **-a** *f* guard, *Br* warder
carcinógeno *adj* ☞ ***cancerígeno***
carcinoma *f* MED carcinoma
carcoma *f* ZO woodworm
carcomer ⟨2a⟩ *v/t* eat away; *fig*: *de envidia* eat away at, consume; **carcomerse** *v/r* be eaten away; ***~ de*** *fig* be consumed with
carcomido *adj* worm-eaten; ***~ de envidia*** *fig* eaten up with envy
carda *f* TÉC carding; *máquina* carding machine
cardamomo *m* BOT cardamom
cardán *m* TÉC universal joint
cardar ⟨1a⟩ *v/t lana* card; *pelo* backcomb
cardenal *m* **1** REL cardinal **2** (*hematoma*) bruise
cardenillo *m* verdigris
cárdeno *adj* purple
cardiaco, cardíaco I *adj* cardiac **II** *m*, **-a** *f* heart patient
cárdigan *m* cardigan
cardinal *adj* cardinal; ***número ~*** cardinal number; ***puntos ~es*** points of the compass, cardinal points; ***virtudes ~es*** cardinal virtues
cardiocirujano *m*, **-a** *f* heart surgeon
cardiograma *m* MED cardiogram
cardiología *f* cardiology
cardiólogo *m*, **-a** *f* cardiologist
cardiópata I *adj*: ***ser ~*** have heart trouble **II** *m/f* heart patient
cardiopatía *f* heart disease
cardiovascular *adj* cardiovascular
cardo *m* BOT thistle
cardumen *m* shoal
carear ⟨1a⟩ *v/t* bring face to face
carecer ⟨2d⟩ *v/i*: ***~ de algo*** lack sth; ***~ de interés*** not be interesting, be lacking in interest
carena *f* MAR careening
carenar ⟨1a⟩ *v/i* MAR careen
carencia *f* lack (***de*** of)
carencial *adj dieta* deficient; ***enfermedad ~*** wasting disease
carente *adj*: ***~ de*** lacking in
careo *m* confrontation
carestía *f* high cost
◇ **carestía de la vida** high cost of living

C

careta *f* mask; ***quitar la ~ a alguien*** *fig* unmask s.o.
◇ **careta antigás** gas mask

carey *m* ZO turtle

carga *f* **1** load; *de buque* cargo **2** MIL, EL charge **3**: ***volver a la ~*** return to the attack **4** (*responsabilidad*) burden; ***llevar la ~*** take responsibility; ***ser una ~ para alguien*** be a burden to s.o.
◇ **carga explosiva** explosive charge; **carga fiscal, carga impositiva** tax burden; **carga de profundidad** MIL depth charge; **cargas sociales** social security contributions; **carga útil** payload

cargadero *m* loading bay

cargado *adj* **1** loaded (***de*** with) **2**: ***~ de años*** bowed with old age; ***~ de espaldas*** *o* ***hombros*** bowed **3** *aire* stuffy **4** *ambiente* tense **5** *café* strong

cargador I *m* **1** *de arma* magazine **2** EL (battery) charger **II** *m*, **~a** *f* loader; **~** (***de muelle***) MAR longshoreman, *Br* docker

cargadores *mpl Col* suspenders, *Br* braces

cargamento *m* load

cargante *adj* F annoying

cargar ⟨1h⟩ **I** *v/t* **1** *arma, camión* load **2** *batería, acusado* charge **3** COM charge (***en*** to); ***~ algo en cuenta a alguien*** charge sth to s.o.'s account **4** *L.Am.* (*traer*) carry **5**: ***esto me carga*** *L.Am.* I can't stand this
II *v/i* **1** (*apoyarse*) rest (***sobre*** on) **2** (*fastidiar*) be annoying **3**: ***~ con algo*** carry sth; ***~ con la culpa*** *fig* shoulder the blame; ***tuvo que ~ con toda la familia durante las vacaciones*** I had the whole family to contend with during the vacation **4**: ***~ contra alguien*** MIL, DEP charge (at) s.o.
cargarse *v/r* **1** *con peso, responsabilidad* weigh o.s. down **2** F (*matar*) bump off F **3** F (*romper*) wreck F **4** INFOR load

cargazón *f* heaviness

cargo *m* **1** position; ***alto ~*** high-ranking position; *persona* high-ranking official; ***~ ministerial*** ministerial post
2 JUR charge
3: ***a ~ de la madre*** in the mother's care; ***tener algo a su ~***, ***estar a ~ de algo*** be in charge of sth; ***está a ~ de Gómez*** Gómez is in charge of it; ***hacerse ~ de algo*** take charge of sth; ***tomar a su ~*** take charge of
4 COM: ***con ~ a nosotros*** on our account
5: ***me da ~ de conciencia*** it makes me feel guilty

carguero *m* MAR cargo ship, freighter

cariacontecido *adj* crestfallen

cariado *adj* decayed

cariarse ⟨1b⟩ *v/r* decay

cariátide *f* ARQUI caryatid

caribe *adj* Carib

Caribe *m* Caribbean

caribeño *adj* Caribbean

caricato *m fig* comedian, impressionist

caricatura *f* **1** caricature **2** *Méx* (*dibujos animados*) cartoon

caricaturista *m/f* caricaturist

caricaturizar ⟨1f⟩ *v/t* caricature

caricia *f* caress; ***hacer ~s a*** caress, stroke

caridad *f* charity

caries *f* MED caries *sg*

carilla *f de papel* side

cariño *m* **1** affection, fondness; ***con ~*** with love; ***tener ~ a alguien*** be fond of s.o.; ***tomar ~ a*** become fond of **2**: ***hacer ~ a alguien*** *L.Am.* (*acariciar*) caress s.o.; (*abrazar*) hug s.o. **3**: ***¡~!*** darling! **4** *Rpl*: ***~s*** (*en carta*) love

cariñoso *adj* affectionate

carioca *adj* of / from Rio de Janeiro, Rio de Janeiro *atr*

carisma *m* charisma

carismático *adj* charismatic

caritativo *adj* charitable

cariz *m* look; ***tomar mal ~*** start to look bad

carlinga *f* AVIA cockpit

carmelita REL **I** *adj* Carmelite **II** *m/f* Carmelite

carmen *m*: (***orden del***) ***Carmen*** Carmelite order

carmesí *m/adj* crimson

carmín *m de labios* lipstick

carnada *f* bait

carnal I *adj* **1** carnal; ***acto ~*** sex, sex act **2** *primo* first; *sobrino, tío*: *related by blood, as opposed to marriage*; ***mi sobrino ~*** my brother's / sister's boy; ***mi tío ~*** my mother's / father's brother **II** *m Méx* F (*amigo*) chum F, pal F

carnaval *m* carnival

carnavalesco *adj* carnival *atr*

carnaza *f* bait

carne *f* **1** meat; ***echar** o **poner toda la ~ en el asador*** pull out all the stops; ***ni ~ ni pescado*** *fig* neither fish, flesh, nor fowl **2** *de persona* flesh; ***de ~ y hueso*** flesh and blood; ***de color ~*** flesh-colored, *Br* flesh-coloured; ***tenía la rodilla en ~ viva*** his knee was raw; ***sufrir algo en sus propias ~s*** *fig* go through sth o.s.; ***echar ~s*** put on weight

◇ **carne adobada** marinaded meat; **carne ahumada** smoked meat; **carne de ave** poultry; **carne de cañón** *fig* cannon fodder; **carne de cerdo** pork; **carne congelada** frozen meat; **carne en conserva** canned meat, *Br* tinned meat; **carne de gallina** *fig* goose bumps *pl*, *Br* goose pimples *pl*; **carne de lata** canned meat, *Br* tinned meat; **carne de membrillo** quince jelly; **carne molida** *L.Am.* ground meat, *Br* mince; **carne picada** ground meat, *Br* mince; **carne de vacuno** beef

carné *m* ☞ ***carnet***

carnear ⟨1a⟩ *v/t L.Am.* slaughter

carnero *m* ram

carnet *m* card

◇ **carnet de conducir** driver's license, *Br* driving licence; **carnet de identidad** identity card; **carnet de socio** membership card

carnicería *f* butcher's; *fig* carnage

carnicero I *m*, **-a** *f* butcher **II** *adj animal* carnivorous

cárnico *adj* meat *atr*; ***industria -a*** meat industry

carnívoro I *adj* carnivorous **II** *m* carnivore

carnoso *adj* fleshy

caro *adj* expensive, dear; ***costar ~*** *fig* cost dear

carota *m/f* F guy / woman with a nerve, *Br* cheeky devil F; ***es un ~*** he's got a nerve

caroteno *m* QUÍM carotene

carótida *f* ANAT carotid (artery)

carotina *f* QUÍM carotene

carozo *m Chi*, *Rpl* pit

carpa *f* **1** *de circo* big top **2** ZO carp **3** *L.Am. para acampar* tent **4** *L.Am. de mercado* stall

carpanta *f* F: ***tener ~*** be starving F

carpeta *f* **1** file; ***~ portadocumentos*** briefcase **2** INFOR folder **3** *Cu en hotel* reception

◇ **carpeta de anillas** ring binder

carpetazo: ***dar ~ a algo*** F shelve sth

carpintería *f* **1** carpentry **2** *de obra* joinery

carpintero I *adj* ZO: ***pájaro ~*** woodpecker **II** *m*, **-a** *f* **1** carpenter **2** *de obra* joiner

carpir ⟨3a⟩ *v/t L.Am.* hoe

carpo *m* ANAT carpus

carraca *f* **1** rattle **2** *persona* wreck **3** ZO common roller

carraspear ⟨1a⟩ *v/i* clear one's throat

carraspeo *m*: ***los ~s del público la distrajeron*** the sound of people in the audience clearing their throats distracted her

carraspera *f* hoarseness

carrasposo *adj voz* rough, gravelly

carrera *f* **1** race; ***a las ~s*** at top speed; *con prisas* in a rush; ***hacer la ~*** F *de prostituta* turn tricks F, *Br* be on the game F **2** EDU degree course; ***dar ~ a alguien*** put s.o. through college, *Br* put s.o. through university **3** *profesional* career; ***hacer ~*** pursue a career; ***militar de ~*** professional soldier **4** *en béisbol* run **5** *Méx en el pelo* part, *Br* parting

◇ **carrera de armamento** arms race; **carrera de caballos** horse race; **carrera de coches** motor race; **carrera completa** *en béisbol* home run; **carrera de fondo** long-distance race; **carrera del émbolo** AUTO piston stroke; **carrera de medio fondo** middle-distance race; **carreras de caballos** horse racing *sg*, races; **carreras de coches** motor racing *sg*

carrerilla *f*: ***tomar ~*** take a run up; ***decir algo de ~*** reel sth off

carreta *f* cart

carretada *f* cartload; ***a ~s*** F by the cartload F

carrete *m* FOT (roll of) film

◇ **carrete de hilo** reel of thread

carretear ⟨1a⟩ *v/t L.Am. avión* taxi

carretera *f* highway, (main) road

◇ **carretera de circunvalación** beltway, *Br* ring road

carretero I *m*: ***fumar como un ~*** *fig* F smoke like a chimney F; ***jurar** o **blasfemar como un ~*** swear like a trooper **II** *adj* road *atr*; road-traffic *atr*

carretilla *f* wheelbarrow

◇ **carretilla elevadora, carretilla de horquilla** forklift (truck)
carretón *m* small cart
carricoche *m* **1** covered wagon **2** AUTO F old jalopy F, *Br tb* old banger F
carril *m* lane
◇ **carril-bici** cycle lane; **carril-bus** bus lane; **carril de adelantamiento** fast lane, passing lane
carrillo *m* cheek; ***comer a dos ~s*** F stuff o.s. F
carrilludo *adj* chubby-cheeked
carrito *m* cart, *Br* trolley
◇ **carrito de bebé** buggy, *Br* pushchair; **carrito de la compra** shopping cart, *Br* shopping trolley; **carrito para equipajes** baggage cart, *Br* luggage trolley; **carrito de servicio, carrito de té** hostess cart, *Br* tea trolley
carrizal *m* reedbed
carrizo *m* reed
carro *m* **1** cart; ***subirse al ~*** *fig* jump on the bandwagon; ***¡para el ~!*** F hold your horses! F; ***poner el ~ delante de los bueyes*** *fig* put the cart before the horse; ***untar el ~ a alguien*** F grease s.o.'s palm F **2**: ***el Carro*** AST the Charioteer **3** *L.Am.* (*coche*) car **4** *L.Am.* (*taxi*) taxi, cab **5** *Méx* FERR car
◇ **carro de combate** tank; **carro comedor** *Méx* FERR dining car; **carro de compra** shopping cart, *Br* supermarket trolley; **carro-patrulla** *L.Am.* F patrol car
carrocería *f* AUTO bodywork
carrocero *m*, **-a** *f* bodybuilder, *Br* coachbuilder
carromato *m* covered wagon
carroña *f* carrion
carroñero *adj* **1** ZO carrion *atr* **2** *persona* scavenging
carroza I *adj* old **II** *f* carriage **III** *m/f* F old fog(e)y F
carruaje *m* carriage
carrusel *m* merry-go-round, carousel
carta *f* **1** letter
2 GASTR menu; ***a la ~*** à la carte
3 (*naipe*) playing card; ***jugar a las ~s*** play cards; ***jugar a ~s vistas*** play straight; ***jugarse todo a una ~*** risk everything on one throw; ***tomar ~s en el asunto*** intervene in the matter; ***poner las ~s boca arriba*** *fig* put one's cards on the table; ***honrado a ~ cabal*** utterly honest; ***no saber a qué ~ quedarse*** not know what to do; ***echar las ~s a alguien*** tell s.o.'s fortune
4 (*mapa*) chart
◇ **carta abierta** open letter; **carta de agradecimiento** thank-you letter; **carta de ajuste** TV test card; **carta blanca** *fig* free hand, carte blanche; ***dar ~ a alguien*** give s.o. carte blanche *o* a free hand; **carta-bomba** letter bomb; **carta certificada** registered letter; **carta comercial** business letter; **carta de crédito** letter of credit; **carta de despido** dismissal letter; **Carta Magna** POL Magna Carta; **carta de naturaleza** naturalization papers *pl*; ***tomar ~*** be naturalized; **carta pastoral** pastoral letter; **carta de pésame** letter of condolence; **carta de portes** bill of lading; **carta de presentación** letter of introduction; **carta de recomendación** letter of recommendation; **carta registrada** registered letter; **carta de solicitud** application letter; **carta de vinos** wine list; **carta urgente** special-delivery letter; **carta verde** green card; **cartas al director** letters to the editor
cartabón *m* set square
cartapacio *m* folder
cartearse ⟨1a⟩ *v/r* write to each other
cártel *m* cartel
cartel *m* **1** poster; ***estar en ~*** *de película, espectáculo* be on **2**: ***de ~*** famous; ***tener buen ~*** be well known
◇ **cartel publicitario** advertising poster
cartelera *f* **1** billboard **2** *de periódico* listings *pl*, entertainments section
◇ **cartelera cinematográfica** billboard
cartelero *m*, **-a** *f* billposter, billsticker
cartelista *m/f* poster designer
carteo *m* correspondence
cárter *m* **1** TÉC housing **2**: ***~(de aceite)*** AUTO crankcase, sump
cartera *f* **1** wallet **2** *L.Am.* purse, *Br* handbag **3** (*maletín*) briefcase; *de colegio* knapsack, *Br* satchel **4** COM, POL portfolio **5** *mujer* mailwoman, *Br* postwoman
◇ **cartera de clientes** client portfolio; **cartera de pedidos** order book; **cartera de valores** *de banco* securities portfolio

cartería *f* sorting office
carterista *m/f* pickpocket
cartero *m* mailman, *Br* postman
cartilaginoso *adj* ANAT cartilaginous
cartílago *m* cartilage
cartilla *f* **1** reader; ***leerle a alguien la ~*** F give s.o. a telling off **2** *Méx* identity card
◇ **cartilla de ahorros** savings book
◇ **cartilla sanitaria** health card
cartografía *f* cartography
cartografiar ⟨1a⟩ *v/t* chart
cartógrafo *m*, **-a** *f* cartographer
cartomancia *f* fortune-telling (*using cards*)
cartomántico *m*, **-a** *f* fortune-teller
cartón *m* **1** cardboard **2** *de tabaco* carton **3** *Méx* DEP scoreboard
◇ **cartón ondulado** corrugated cardboard
◇ **cartón piedra** pap(i)er-mâché
cartoné *m*: ***en ~*** hardback
cartuchera *f* **1** cartridge belt **2**: ***~s*** *pl* F flabby hips
cartucho *m* **1** *de arma* cartridge; ***quemar el último ~*** *fig* make a last-ditch attempt
◇ **cartucho sin bala** blank (cartridge)
◇ **cartucho de tinta** ink cartridge
cartuja *f* monastery
cartulina *f* sheet of card
◇ **cartulina roja** DEP red card
casa *f* **1** house; ***como una ~*** F huge F; ***comenzar la ~ por el tejado*** *fig* put the cart before the horse; ***echar*** *o* ***tirar la ~ por la ventana*** spare no expense; ***se me cayó la ~ encima*** *fig* the bottom fell out of my world
2 DEP: ***jugar en ~*** play at home; ***jugar fuera de ~*** play away, play on the road
3 (*hogar*) home; ***en ~*** at home; ***estás en tu ~*** make yourself at home; ***de andar por ~*** *ropa* for (wearing) around the house; *fig*: *arreglo* makeshift; ***llevar la ~*** run the home; ***ser muy de su ~*** be a real home-lover; ***todo queda en ~*** everything stays in the family
◇ **casa adosada** *house sharing one or more walls with other houses*; **casa de campo** country house; **casa de citas** brothel; **casa cuna** children's home; **casa de empeño** pawnshop; **casa de huéspedes** rooming house, *Br* boarding house; **casa de locos** madhouse; **casa matriz** head office; **casa mortuoria** funeral home; **casa pareada** semi-detached house; **casa de pisos** apartment house, *Br* block of flats; **casa prefabricada** prefab; **casa pública** brothel; **casa de putas** brothel; **casa real** royal household; **casa rodante** *Rpl* trailer, mobile home; **casa de socorro** first aid post; **casa de vecindad** tenement
casaca *f* cassock
casación *f* JUR cassation, annulment
casadero *adj* marriageable
casado *adj* married; ***recién ~*** newly-wed
casamentero *m*, **-a** *f* matchmaker
casamiento *m* marriage
casar ⟨1a⟩ **I** *v/i fig* match (up); ***~ con*** go with **II** *v/t* **1** *de sacerdote* marry; *de padres* marry off **2** JUR *sentencia* quash; **casarse** *v/r* get married; ***~ con alguien*** marry s.o.; ***no ~ con nadie*** *fig* refuse to compromise
cascabel *m* small bell; ***poner el ~ al gato*** bell the cat
cascada *f* waterfall; *fig* flood, avalanche
cascado *adj* **1** *voz* hoarse **2** F *persona* worn out
cascajo *m fig* F: ***estar hecho un ~*** be a wreck F
cascanueces *m inv* nutcracker
cascar ⟨1g⟩ **I** *v/t* **1** crack; *algo quebradizo* break **2** *fig* F whack F **3**: ***~la*** peg out F **II** *v/i* F chat; **cascarse** *v/r* crack, chip
cáscara *f de huevo* shell; *de naranja, limón* peel
cascarón *m* shell; ***salir del ~*** hatch (out)
◇ **cascarón de nuez** MAR, *fig* cockleshell
cascarrabias *m/f inv* F grouch F
casco *m* **1** helmet **2** *de barco* hull **3** (*botella vacía*) empty (bottle) **4** *edificio* shell **5** *de caballo* hoof **6** *de vasija* fragment **7**: ***~s*** *pl* (*auriculares*) headphones **8**: ***ligero de ~s*** reckless; ***calentarse*** *o* ***romperse los ~s*** *fig* agonize (***por*** over)
◇ **casco antiguo** old quarter; **casco retornable** returnable bottle; **casco urbano** urban area; **cascos azules** MIL blue berets, UN peace-keeping troops
cascote *m* piece of rubble
caseína *f* QUÍM casein

casera *f* landlady
caserío *m* country house
casero I *adj* home-made; ***comida -a*** home cooking **II** *m* landlord
caserón *m* big old barn
caseta *f* **1** hut; *de feria* stall; ***~ de baño*** beach hut; ***~ de(l) perro*** doghouse, kennel **2** (*vestuario*) locker room, *Br tb* changing room
casete I *f* cassette **II** *m* cassette player
casetón *m* ARQUI caisson
casi *adv* almost, nearly; *en frases negativas* hardly
casilla *f* **1** *en formulario* box; *en tablero* square; ***sacar a alguien de sus ~s*** drive s.o. crazy **2** *de correspondencia* pigeon hole **3** *S.Am.* post office box, P.O. Box
casillero *m mueble* pigeonholes *pl*
casino *m* casino
caso *m* **1** case; ***en ese ~*** in that case; ***en tal ~*** in such a case; ***en ~ contrario*** otherwise, if not; ***en ~ de que***, ***~ de*** in the event that, in case of; ***en todo ~*** in any case, in any event; ***en el peor de los ~s*** if the worst comes to the worst; ***en el mejor de los ~s*** at best; ***en último ~*** as a last resort; ***en ningún ~*** never, under no circumstances; ***dado o llegado el ~*** if it comes to it; ***dado el ~ que*** in the event that; ***si se da el ~*** if the situation arises; ***el ~ es que ...*** the thing is that ...; ***no venir al ~*** be irrelevant; ***¡vamos al ~!*** let's get to the point; ***en su ~*** in his / her case; ***ponerse en el ~ de alguien*** put o.s. in s.o.'s shoes
2: ***~ aislado*** isolated case; ***~ perdido*** *fig* hopeless case; ***ser un ~*** F be a real case F
3 (*atención*): ***hacer ~*** take notice; ***hacer ~ de algo*** pay attention to sth; ***hacer ~ a alguien*** pay attention to s.o.; ***¡no le hagas ~!*** take no notice of him!
casorio *m desp* wedding
caspa *f* dandruff
caspiroleta *f S.Am.* eggnog
¡cáspita! *int* F goodness me!
casquería *f butcher's shop specializing in offal*
casquete *m* skullcap
◇ **casquete polar** polar icecap
casquijo *m* gravel
casquillo *m* **1** *de cartucho* case **2** EL socket, bulb holder **3** *L.Am. de caballo* horseshoe
casquivano *adj* F flighty
cassette *m* (*also f*) cassette
◇ **cassette de video**, *Esp* **cassette de vídeo** video cassette
◇ **cassette virgen** blank cassette
casta *f* caste; ***de ~*** thoroughbred
castaña *f* chestnut; ***~ asada*** roasted chestnut; ***sacar las ~s del fuego a alguien*** *fig* F pull s.o.'s chestnuts out of the fire F; ***a toda ~*** F hell for leather F; ***¡toma ~!*** F how about that! F
◇ **castaña de Indias** horse chestnut
castañazo *m* F thump, bump
castañero *m*, **-a** *f* roast chestnut seller
castañeta *f de dedos* snap
castañetear ⟨1a⟩ **I** *v/i de dientes* chatter **II** *v/t*: ***~ los dedos*** snap one's fingers
castaño I *adj color* chestnut, brown **II** *m* **1** chestnut (tree) **2** *color* chestnut, brown; ***ya pasa de ~ oscuro*** F it's gone too far, it's beyond a joke
◇ **castaño de Indias** horse chestnut (tree)
castañuela *f* castanet; ***estar como unas ~s*** F be over the moon F
castellano I *adj* Castilian **II** *m* (Castilian) Spanish **III** *m*, **-a** *f* Castilian
castellanohablante *adj* Spanish-speaking
casticidad *f*, **casticismo** *m* purity
castidad *f* chastity
castigar ⟨1h⟩ *v/t* punish
castigo *m* punishment
◇ **castigo físico** corporal punishment
Castilla *f* Castile
◇ **Castilla la Nueva** HIST New Castile
◇ **Castilla la Vieja** HIST Old Castile
castillo *m* castle; ***hacer ~s en el aire*** *fig* build castles in the air
◇ **castillo de arena** sandcastle; **castillo de fuegos artificiales** firework display; **castillo de naipes** house of cards; **castillo de popa** MAR afterdeck; **castillo de proa** MAR forecastle, fo'c'sle
casting *m* TEA, *cine* casting
castizo *adj* pure
casto *adj* chaste
castor *m* ZO beaver
castración *f* castration
castrar ⟨1a⟩ *v/t* castrate; *fig* emasculate
castrense *adj* army *atr*; ***capellán ~*** army chaplain
casual *adj* chance *atr*

casualidad *f* chance, coincidence; ***por** o **de ~*** by chance; ***da la ~ que*** it just so happens that
casualmente *adv* by chance
cata *f* tasting
◇ **cata de vinos** wine tasting
cataclismo *m* cataclysm, catastrophe
catacumbas *fpl* catacombs
catador *m*, **~a** *f* taster
catadura *f* tasting; ***de mala ~*** nasty-looking
catafalco *m* catafalque
catafaro, catafoto *m* AUTO cat's eye, reflector
catalán I *adj* Catalan **II** *m*, **-ana** *f* Catalan **III** *m idioma* Catalan
catalejo *m* telescope
catalepsia *f* MED catalepsy
cataléptico *adj* MED cateleptic
catalizador *m* **1** catalyst **2** AUTO catalytic converter
catalizar ⟨1f⟩ *v/t* catalyze
catalogación *f* cataloging, *Br* cataloguing
catalogar ⟨1h⟩ *v/t* catalog, *Br* catalogue; *fig* class
catálogo *m* catalog, *Br* catalogue
Cataluña *f* Catalonia
catamarán *m* MAR catamaran
cataplasma *f* **1** MED poultice **2** *fig: persona* bore
cataplines *mpl* P nuts P
¡cataplum! *int* crash!
catapulta *f* slingshot, *Br* catapult
catapultar ⟨1a⟩ *v/t* catapult
catar ⟨1a⟩ *v/t* taste
catarata *f* **1** GEOG waterfall **2** MED cataract
catarral *adj* catarrhal, catarrh *atr*
catarro *m* **1** cold **2** *inflamación* catarrh
catarsis *f* catharsis
catastral *adj* land registry *atr*
catastro *m* land registry
catástrofe *f* catastrophe
◇ **catástrofe ambiental** environmental disaster; **catástrofe ecológica** ecological disaster; **catástrofe natural** natural disaster
catastrófico *adj* catastrophic
catastrofismo *m* doom and gloom
catastrofista I *adj* catastrophist **II** *m/f* prophet of doom
catavinos *m/f inv* wine taster
catchup *m* ketchup
cate *m* EDU F fail, flunk F
catear ⟨1a⟩ *v/t* F fail, flunk F
catecismo *m* catechism
catecúmeno *m*, **-a** *f* catechumen
cátedra *f* EDU chair; ***sentar** o **poner ~*** pontificate, sound off
catedral *f* cathedral; ***una mentira como una ~*** F a whopping great lie F
catedrático *m*, **-a** *f en universidad* professor; *en colegio* head of department
categoría *f* category; *social* class; (*estatus*) standing; *fig: de local, restaurante* class; DEP division; ***de ~*** first-rate, top-class; ***de segunda ~*** second rate, second class; ***actor de primera ~*** first-rate actor
categórico *adj* categorical
categorizar ⟨1f⟩ *v/t* classify, categorize
catenaria *f* EL overhead power cable
catequesis *f* catechism
catequista *m/f* catechist
catequizar ⟨1f⟩ *v/t* catechize
caterva *f* load
catéter *m* MED catheter
cateterizar ⟨1f⟩ *v/t* MED catheterize
cateto I *m* MAT leg **II** *m*, **-a** *f* P hick F, yokel F
cátodo *m* cathode
catolicismo *m* (Roman) Catholicism
católico I *adj* (Roman) Catholic; ***no estar muy ~*** *fig* F be under the weather F **II** *m*, **-a** *f* (Roman) Catholic
catorce *adj* fourteen
catre *m* bed
caucásico *adj* Caucasian
Cáucaso *m*: ***el ~*** the Caucasus
cauce *m* riverbed; *fig* channel; ***volver a su ~*** *fig* get back to normal
caucho *m* **1** rubber **2** *L.Am.* (*neumático*) tire, *Br* tyre
caución *f* guarantee, security
cauda *f L.Am. de cometa* tail
caudal *m de río* volume of flow; *fig* wealth
caudaloso *adj río* with a great volume of flow
caudillaje, caudillismo *m* rule, leadership
caudillo *m* leader
causa *f* **1** cause; ***ha***
make common cau
fig lost cause **2** (*n*
de because of; ***por***
3 JUR lawsuit

◇ **causa civil** lawsuit
◇ **causa penal** criminal proceedings *pl*
causal *adj* causal
causalidad *f* causality
causante **I** *adj* causal **II** *m* cause
causar ⟨1a⟩ *v/t daño* cause; *placer* provide, give
causticidad *f tb fig* causticity
cáustico *adj tb fig* caustic
cautela *f* caution; ***con ~*** cautiously
cautelar *adj* precautionary; ***medida ~*** precautionary measure, precaution
cautelarmente *adv* as a precaution
cauteloso *adj* cautious
cauterizar ⟨1f⟩ *v/t* cauterize
cautivador *adj* captivating
cautivar ⟨1a⟩ *v/t fig* captivate
cautiverio *m*, **cautividad** *f* captivity
cautivo **I** *adj* captive **II** *m*, **-a** *f* captive; ***es ~ a la droga*** he's a drug addict
cauto *adj* cautious
cava **I** *m* cava (*sparkling wine*) **II** *f* (wine) cellar
cavar ⟨1a⟩ *v/t* dig
caverna *f* cavern
cavernícola **I** *adj* cave-dwelling **II** *m* caveman **III** *f* cavewoman
caviar *m* caviar
cavidad *f* cavity
◇ **cavidad abdominal** abdominal cavity
◇ **cavidad torácica** thoracic cavity
cavilaciones *fpl* deliberation *sg*
cavilar ⟨1a⟩ *v/t* meditate on
caviloso *adj* suspicious
cayado *m* AGR crook
cayo *m* cay, key
cayó *vb* ☞ ***caer***
caza **I** *f* hunt; *actividad* hunting; ***andar a la ~ de algo / alguien*** be after sth / s.o.; ***dar ~ a*** give chase to **II** *m* AVIA fighter
◇ **caza mayor** big game
◇ **caza menor** small game
cazabombardero *m* fighter-bomber
cazacerebros *m/f inv* headhunter
cazador *m* hunter
◇ **cazador furtivo** poacher
cazadora *f* **1** hunter **2** *prenda* jacket
cazadotes *m inv* fortune-hunter
cazaminas *m inv* MAR minesweeper
zar ⟨1f⟩ **I** *v/t* **1** *animal* hunt; *fig: infor- ión* track down **2** (*pillar, captar*) ***~ un buen trabajo*** get o.s. a good job **II** *v/i* hunt; ***ir a ~*** go hunting
cazarrecompensas *m/f inv* bounty hunter
cazasubmarinos *m inv* MIL submarine chaser
cazatalentos *m/f inv* talent scout
cazatesoros *m/f inv* treasure hunter
cazatorpedero *m* MIL torpedo patrol boat
cazo *m* saucepan
cazoleta *f* small saucepan
cazón *m* ZO dogfish
cazuela *f* pan; *de barro, vidrio* casserole
cazurro *adj* **1** stubborn **2** (*basto*) coarse **3** (*lento de entender*) dense F, *Br tb* thick F
c.c. *abr* (= ***centímetro cúbico***) c.c. (= cubic centimeter)
c/c *abr* (= ***cuenta corriente***) C/A (= checking account)
CC.AA. *fpl abr* (= ***Comunidades Autónomas***) Autonomous Regions
CC.OO. *fpl abr* (= ***Comisiones Obreras***) *Spanish labor union*
CD *m* (= ***disco compacto***) **1** CD (= compact disc) **2** *reproductor* CD-player
CD-ROM *m* CD-Rom
CE *f abr* **1** (= ***Comisión Europea***) European Commission **2** (= ***Comunidad Europea***) HIST EC (= European Community)
ce *f letra* C; ***~ por be*** F in minute detail; ***por ~ o por be*** somehow or other
cebada *f* barley
cebador *m Rpl* AUTO choke
cebar ⟨1a⟩ *v/t* **1** fatten **2** *anzuelo* bait **3** TÉC prime **4** *L.Am. mate* prepare; **cebarse** *v/r* **1** feed (**en** on) **2**: ***~ con alguien*** vent one's fury on s.o.
cebo *m* bait
cebolla *f* onion
cebolleta *f*, **cebollino** *m planta* scallion, *Br* spring onion; ***¡vete a escardar ~s!*** F scram! F, get lost! F
cebón **I** *adj* fat
cebra *f* zebra; ***paso de ~*** crosswalk, *Br* zebra crossing
Ceca *f*: ***ir de la ~ a la Meca*** rush around
cecear ⟨1a⟩ *v/i* **1** *en acento regional* pronounce Spanish "s" as "th" **2** *como defecto* lisp
ceceo *m* **1** *en acento regional* pronunciation of Spanish "s" as "th" **2** *como defecto* lisp

cecina *f* cured meat
cedazo *m* sieve
cedente *m/f* JUR assignor
ceder ⟨2a⟩ **I** *v/t* give up; (*traspasar*) transfer, cede; **~ *el paso*** AUTO yield, *Br* give way **II** *v/i* **1** give way, yield **2** *de viento*, *lluvia* ease off
cederrón *m* CD-Rom
cedro *m* BOT cedar
cédula *f L.Am.* identity document
◇ **cédula hipotecaria** mortgage title; **cédula de identidad** *L.Am.* identity document; **cédula personal** *Esp* identity document
cefalea *f* MED migraine
cefalópodos *mpl* ZO cephalopods
cefalorraquideo *adj*: ***líquido ~*** ANAT cerebrospinal fluid
céfiro *m* zephyr
cegador *adj* blinding
cegar ⟨1h & 1k⟩ **I** *v/t* **1** blind **2** *tubería* block **II** *v/i* go blind; **cegarse** *v/r* **1** *fig* become blinded **2** (*obstruirse*) get blocked
cegato *adj* F *fig* nearsighted, shortsighted
ceguedad, ceguera *f tb fig* blindness
◇ **ceguedad nocturna** MED night blindness
ceja *f* eyebrow; ***arquear las ~s*** raise one's eyebrows; ***lo tiene entre ~ y ~*** F she can't stand him F; ***estar hasta las ~s de alguien*** have had it up to here with s.o. F; ***estar entrampado hasta las ~s*** be up to one's eyes in debt; ***quemarse las ~s*** F burn the midnight oil
cejar ⟨1a⟩ *v/i fml* give up; ***no ~ en*** not let up in
cejijunto *adj*: ***es ~*** his eyebrows meet in the middle
cejilla *f* MÚS bridge
cejudo *adj* with bushy eyebrows
celada *f* ambush; *fig* trap
celador *m*, **~a** *f* **1** *de hospital* orderly **2** *de cárcel* guard **3** *de museo* attendant
celar ⟨1a⟩ *v/t* **1** watch over **2** (*ocultar*) conceal
celda *f* cell
◇ **celda de castigo** punishment cell
celdilla *f* cell
celebérrimo *adj* very famous, celebrated
celebración *f* celebration
celebrante *m* REL celebrant
celebrar ⟨1a⟩ *v/t* **1** *misa* celebrate; *reunión*, *acto oficial* hold; *fiesta* have, hold **2**: ***lo celebro mucho*** I'm extremely pleased
célebre *adj* famous
celebridad *f* **1** fame **2** (*persona*) celebrity
celentéreos *mpl* ZO coelenterates
celeridad *f* speed
celeste *adj* light blue, sky blue; ***azul ~*** sky blue
celestial *adj* celestial; *fig* heavenly
celestina *f* matchmaker
celibato *m* celibacy
célibe *m/f* & *adj* celibate
cellisca *f* sleet
celo *m* **1** zeal **2** (*cinta adhesiva*) Scotch® tape, *Br* Sellotape® **3**: **~s** *pl* jealousy *sg*; ***tener ~s de*** be jealous of; ***dar ~s a alguien*** make s.o. jealous **4**: ***en ~*** ZO in heat
celofán *m* cellophane
celosía *f* lattice
celoso *adj* jealous (***de*** of)
celtibérico *adj* Celtiberian
célula *f* cell
◇ **célula fotoeléctrica** photoelectric cell
◇ **célula solar** solar cell
celular I *adj* cellular **II** *m L.Am.* cellular *o* cell phone, *Br* mobile (phone)
celulitis *f* cellulite
celuloide *m* celluloid
celulosa *f* cellulose
cementar ⟨1a⟩ *v/t* **1** TÉC case-harden **2** *L.Am. suelo* cement
cementerio *m* cemetery
◇ **cementerio de coches** wrecker's yard, *Br* scrapyard
◇ **cementerio nuclear** nuclear waste dump
cemento *m* **1** cement **2** *L.Am.* (*pegamento*) glue
◇ **cemento armado** reinforced concrete
cena *f* dinner; *más tarde* supper; ***la Última Cena*** the Last Supper
cenáculo *m fig* circle, group
cenador *m* arbor, *Br* arb
cenagal *m* **1** bog **2** *fig* m
cenagoso *adj* boggy
cenar ⟨1a⟩ **I** *v/t*: ***~ algo*** ha
ner **II** *v/i* have dinner

C

C

cenceño *adj* very thin
cencerro *m* cowbell; ***estar como un ~*** F be as nutty as a fruit cake F
cenefa *f* border
cenicero *m* ashtray
Cenicienta *f* Cinderella
ceniciento *adj* ash-gray, *Br* ash-grey
cenit *m* AST zenith; *fig* peak
cenital *adj* zenithal
ceniza *f* ash; **~s** ashes; ***reducir a ~s*** reduce to ashes
cenizo I *adj* ash-gray, *Br* ash-grey; ***de color ~*** gray, *Br* grey **II** *m* **1** F jinx **2** BOT goosefoot
cenobio *m* monastery
cenozoico *m* Cenozoic
censar ⟨1a⟩ *v/t* take a census of
censo *m* census
◇ **censo electoral** voting register, electoral roll
censor *m*, **~a** *f* censor
◇ **censor jurado de cuentas** certified public accountant, *Br* chartered accountant
censual *adj* census *atr*
censura *f* censorship
censurable *adj* reprehensible
censurar ⟨1a⟩ *v/t* **1** censor **2** *tratamiento* condemn
cent *abr* (= ***céntimo***) cent
centauro *m* MYTH centaur
centavo *m* cent
centella *f* **1** spark **2** (*rayo*) flash of lightning
centelleante *adj* sparkling; *estrella* twinkling
centellear ⟨1a⟩ *v/i* sparkle; *de estrella* twinkle
centelleo *m* sparkle; *de estrella* twinkle
centena *f* hundred; ***una ~ de ...*** about a hundred ...
centenar *m* hundred; ***un ~ de*** a hundred; ***regalos a ~es*** hundreds of gifts
centenario I *adj* hundred-year-old *atr* **II** *m* centennial, *Br* centenary
centeno *m* BOT rye
centesimal *adj* MAT centesimal
centésimo I *adj* hundredth **II** *m*, **-a** *f* hundredth
centígrado *adj* centigrade; ***dos grados ~s*** two degrees centigrade
centigramo *m* centigram
centilitro *m* centiliter, *Br* centilitre
centímetro *m* centimeter, *Br* centimetre
◇ **centímetro cuadrado** square centimeter *o Br* centimetre
◇ **centímetro cúbico** cubic centimeter *o Br* centimetre
céntimo *m* cent; ***estar sin un ~*** not have a red cent F, *Br* be flat broke F
◇ **céntimo de euro** euro cent
centinela *m/f* **1** MIL sentry **2** *de banda criminal* lookout
centolla *f*, **centollo** *m* ZO spider crab
centrado *adj* stable, well-balanced
central I *adj* central; (*principal*) main, central **II** *f* head office **III** *m/f en fútbol* central defender, center-back, *Br* centre-back
◇ **central atómica** atomic power station; **central de correos** main post office; **central eléctrica** power station; **central eólica** wind generated power station; **central hidroeléctrica** hydroelectric power station; **central maremotriz** tidal power station; **central nuclear** nuclear power station; **central telefónica** telephone exchange; **central térmica** coal-fired / oil-fired power station
centralismo *m* POL centralism
centralita *f* TELEC switchboard
centralizar ⟨1f⟩ *v/t* centralize
centrar ⟨1a⟩ *v/t* **1** center, *Br* centre; DEP *tb* cross **2** *esfuerzos* focus (***en*** on); ***~ la atención*** focus, center, *Br* centre (***en*** on); **centrarse** *v/r* concentrate (***en*** on)
céntrico *adj* central
centrifugación *f*, **centrifugado** *m* spin
centrifugadora *f* **1** centrifuge **2** *para ropa* spin-dryer
centrifugar ⟨1h⟩ *v/t* spin
centrífugo *adj* centrifugal; ***fuerza -a*** centrifugal force
centrípeto *adj* centripetal; ***fuerza -a*** centripetal force
centrista I *adj* POL center *atr*, *Br* centre *atr*, of the center *o Br* centre **II** *m/f* POL centrist
centro *m* **1** center, *Br* centre **2** DEP cross **3** *Méx* (*traje*) suit (and shirt and tie)
◇ **centro de atención** *fig* center *o Br* centre of attention; **centro de atención primaria** primary care center *o Br* centre; **centro de cálculo** computer center *o Br* centre; **centro comercial** (shopping) mall, *Br tb* shopping centre;

centro de día day center *o Br* centre, daycare center *o Br* centre; **centro de estética** beauty parlor *o Br* parlour, beauty salon; **centro de gravedad** center *o Br* centre of gravity; **centro hospitalario** health *o* medical center *o Br* centre; **centro de investigación** research center *o Br* centre; **centro de mesa** centerpiece, *Br* centrepiece; **centro sanitario** health *o* medical center *o Br* centre; **centro urbano** *en señal* town center *o Br* centre

centroafricano *adj*: ***República Centroafricana*** Central African Republic

Centroamérica *f* Central America

centroamericano *adj* Central American

centrocampista *m/f* DEP midfield player, midfielder

Centroeuropa Central Europe

centroeuropeo *adj* Central European

centuplicar ⟨1g⟩ *v/t* multiply by a hundred

céntuplo I *adj* centuple, hundredfold **II** *m* centuple

centuria *f* century

ceñido *adj* tight

ceñidor *m* sash

ceñir ⟨3h & 3l⟩ *v/t fig*: ***las fábricas ciñen la ciudad*** the plants surround the city; ***la ciñó con los brazos*** he wrapped his arms around her; **ceñirse** *v/r*: ***~ a algo*** *fig* stick to sth

ceño *m* forehead; ***fruncir el ~*** frown

ceñudo *adj* frowning

CEOE *f abr* (= ***Confederación Española de Organizaciones Empresariales***) *Confederation of Spanish Industry and Trade*

cepa *f de vid* stock; ***peruano de pura ~*** Peruvian through and through

cepellón *m* AGR root ball

cepilladora *f* plane

cepillar ⟨1a⟩ *v/t* brush; **cepillarse** *v/r* **1** brush **2** F (*comerse*) polish off F **3** F (*matar*) kill, knock off F

cepillo *m* brush; ***con el pelo cortado a ~*** with a crew cut

◇ **cepillo de dientes** toothbrush; **cepillo para limosnas** poor box; **cepillo de uñas** nailbrush

cepo *m* **1** trap; ***caer en el ~*** fall into the trap **2** AUTO Denver boot F, (wheel) clamp

ceporro *m*, **-a** *f* **1** *fig* idiot **2**: ***dormir como un ~*** sleep like a log

cera *f* **1** wax; ***museo de ~*** waxworks *sg*, wax museum; ***no hay más ~ que la que arde*** F that's it, that's all there is to it; ***ser*** (***como***) ***una ~*** *fig* be very quiet and pleasant **2** *de los oídos* (ear) wax **3** *para pisos* wax (floor) polish **4** *Méx* (*vela*) candle

◇ **cera depilatoria** hair-removing wax, depilatory wax

cerámica *f* ceramics *sg*

cerámico *adj* ceramic

ceramista *m/f* potter

cerbatana *f* blowpipe

cerca[1] *f* fence

cerca[2] *adv* **1** near, close; ***de ~*** close up; ***seguir de ~*** follow closely; ***vivo muy ~, me coge muy ~*** I live very close by; ***~ de*** near, close to **2** (*casi*) nearly

cercado *m* fence

cercanías *fpl* **1** surrounding area *sg*, vicinity *sg* **2** (*suburbios*) outskirts, suburbs; ***tren de ~*** suburban train

cercano *adj* nearby; ***~ a*** close to, near to

cercar ⟨1g⟩ *v/t* **1** surround **2** *con valla* fence in

cercenar ⟨1a⟩ *v/t* **1** cut off **2** *libertades, derechos* curtail

cerceta *f* ZO teal

cerciorarse ⟨1a⟩ *v/r* make sure (***de*** of)

cerco *m* **1** *de mancha* ring **2**: ***poner ~ a*** lay siege to **3** *de puerta* frame **4** *L.Am.* fence **5** AST ring

cerda *f* **1** *animal* sow; *fig* F *persona* pig F **2** *de brocha* bristle

cerdada *f fig* dirty trick

Cerdeña *f* Sardinia

cerdo *m* hog, *Br* pig; *fig* F *persona* pig F

cerdoso *adj* bristly

cereal I *adj* cereal *atr* **II** *m* cereal; ***~es*** *pl* (breakfast) cereal *sg*

cerebelo *m* ANAT cerebellum

cerebral *adj* cerebral

cerebro *m* ANAT brain; *fig*: *persona* brains *sg*

ceremonia *f* ceremony; ***sin ~s*** without ceremony

ceremonial *m/adj* ceremonial

ceremonioso *adj* ceremonious

céreo *adj* waxen

cereza *f* **1** cherry **2** *L.Am.* (*grano*) bean

cerezo *m* cherry (tree)

cerilla *f* match

C

cerillo *m C.Am., Méx* match
cerner ⟨2g⟩ *v/t* sieve, sift; **cernerse** *v/r*: **~ sobre** *fig* hang over
cernícalo *m* ZO kestrel; *fig* F lout
cero *m* **1** zero; ***bajo / sobre ~*** below / above zero; ***empezar desde ~*** *fig* start from scratch; ***quedarse a ~*** *fig* be left with nothing; ***ser un ~ a la izquierda*** F be a nonentity; ***pelado al ~*** with one's head shaven **2** EDU zero, *Br tb* nought **3** DEP zero, *Br* nil; *en tenis* love; ***vencer por tres a ~*** win three-zero
◇ **cero absoluto** absolute zero
cerquillo *m L.Am.* bangs *pl*, *Br* fringe
cerquita *adv* F close by
cerrado *adj* **1** closed; ***oler a ~*** smell stuffy **2** *persona* narrow-minded **3** (*tímido*) introverted **4** *cielo* overcast **5** *acento* broad **6**: ***curva -a*** tight curve
cerradura *f* lock; ***ojo de la ~*** keyhole
◇ **cerradura de dirección** AUTO steering lock
◇ **cerradura de seguridad** safety lock
cerrajería *f* locksmith's
cerrajero *m*, **-a** *f* locksmith
cerramiento *m* **1** *de acuerdo* closure **2** *de terreno, finca* enclosure
cerrar ⟨1k⟩ **I** *v/t* **1** close; *para siempre* close down; ***~ con llave*** lock; ***~ de golpe*** slam; ***~ al tráfico*** close to traffic **2** *tubería* block **3** *grifo* turn off **4** *terreno, finca* enclose; *frontera* close **5** *acuerdo* close
II *v/i* close; *para siempre* close down; ***la puerta no cierra bien*** the door doesn't shut properly; ***al ~ el día*** at the end of the day
cerrarse *v/r* **1** close; ***~ de golpe*** slam shut **2** *de cielo* cloud over **3** *de persona* shut o.s. off (***a*** from)
cerrazón *f fig* narrow-mindedness
cerrero *adj L.Am. persona* rough
cerril *adj animal* wild; (*terco*) stubborn, pig-headed F; (*torpe*) F dense F
cerro *m* hill; ***irse por los ~s de Úbeda*** *fig* stray from the point
cerrojazo *m*: ***dar el ~ a algo*** bring sth to a (sudden) close
cerrojo *m* bolt; ***echar el ~*** bolt the door
certamen *m* competition
certero *adj* accurate
certeza *f* certainty; ***saber algo con ~*** know sth for sure
certidumbre *f* certainty
certificación *f* certification
certificado **I** *adj carta* registered **II** *m* certificate
◇ **certificado de aptitud** certificate of attainment; **certificado de defunción** death certificate; **certificado de estudios** high school diploma, *Br* school leaving certificate; **certificado de origen** certificate of origin; **certificado médico** medical certificate
certificar ⟨1g⟩ *v/t* **1** certify **2** *carta* register
cerumen *m* earwax
cerval *adj*: ***miedo ~*** terrible fear
cervato *m* fawn
cervecería *f* bar
cervecero **I** *adj* ***empresa -a*** brewery **II** *m*, **-a** *f* brewer
cerveza *f* beer; ***fábrica de ~*** brewery
◇ **cerveza de barril** draft, *Br* draught (beer); **cerveza negra** stout; **cerveza de presión** draft, *Br* draught (beer); **cerveza rubia** lager
cervical *adj* **1** neck; ***vértebras ~es*** cervical vertebrae **2** (*del útero*) cervical
cérvidos *mpl* ZO cervids *fml*, deer *pl*
cerviz *f* nape of the neck; ***doblar la ~*** give in, submit
cesación *f* cessation; ***~ de pagos*** *Rpl* suspension of payments
cesante *Chi* **I** *adj* unemployed, jobless; ***dejar ~ a alguien*** let s.o. go **II** *m/f* unemployed person
cesantía *f Chi* unemployment
cesar ⟨1a⟩ **I** *v/i* **1** stop; ***no ~ de hacer algo*** keep on doing sth; ***sin ~*** non-stop **2**: ***~ en sus funciones*** resign **II** *v/t* dismiss
cesárea *f* MED Cesarean *o Br* Caesarean (section)
cese *m* cessation; ***~ de las hostilidades*** MIL ceasefire, cessation of hostilities; ***liquidación por ~ de negocio*** closing up sale, *Br* closing down sale
◇ **cese el fuego** *L.Am.* ceasefire
cesio *m* QUÍM cesium, *Br* caesium
cesión *f* transfer; ***~ al portero*** DEP back-pass
cesionario *m*, **-a** *f* grantee, assignee
cesionista *m/f* grantor, assignor
césped *m* lawn; ***prohibido pisar el ~*** keep off the grass
cesta *f* basket
◇ **cesta de la compra** shopping basket
cestería *f* **1** basketwork **2** (*tienda*) bas-

ketwork store
cestero *m*, **-a** *f* basket maker
cesto *m* large basket; *en baloncesto* basket
cesura *f* caesura
ceta *f* letter 'z'
cetáceos *mpl* ZO cetaceans
cetona *f* QUÍM ketone
cetrería *f* falconry
cetrero *m*, **-a** *f* falconer
cetrino *adj* sallow
cetro *m*: ***empuñar el ~*** ascend to the throne
C.F. *abr* (= ***club de fútbol***) FC (= football club)
cfc *m abr* (= ***clorofluorocarbono***) CFC (= chlorofluorocarbon)
cg. *abr* (= ***centigramo***) centigram
CGPJ *abr* (= ***Consejo General del Poder Judicial***) *Spanish Judiciary Council*
CGT *f abr* (= ***Confederación General del Trabajo***) *Spanish labor union*
ch *abr* (= ***cheque***) check, *Br* cheque
chabacanería *f* vulgarity, tackiness F
chabacano *adj* vulgar, tacky F
chabola *f* shack; ***barrio de ~s*** shanty town
chabolismo *m* shanty towns *pl*
chacal *m* ZO jackal
chacarero *m*, **-a** *f Rpl*, *Chi* smallholder, farmer
chacha *f* **1** F girl, kid F **2** (*criada*) maid
cháchara *f* chatter
chácharas *fpl L.Am.* junk *sg*, bits and pieces
chacharear ⟨1a⟩ *v/i* F chatter
chacharero *m*, **-a** *f* chatterbox
chachi *adj* F great F; ***pasarlo ~*** have a great time F
chacho *m* F boy, kid F
chacinería *f* pork butcher's
chacinero *m*, **-a** *f* sausage producer, pork butcher
chacolí *m light*, *sharp wine*
chacota *f* F joke; ***hacer ~ de*** make fun of; ***tomarse algo a ~*** treat sth as a joke
chacotear ⟨1a⟩ *v/i* have fun
chacotero *adj*: ***es ~*** he likes a joke
chacra *f L.Am.* AGR smallholding
Chad *m* Chad
chafar ⟨1a⟩ *v/t* **1** squash; *cosa erguida* flatten **2** F *planes etc* ruin
chaflán *m* corner
chabacano *m Méx* apricot
chaira *f* steel
chal *m* shawl
chalado *adj* F crazy F (***por*** about)
chaladura *f* F crazy idea F
chalán *m*, **-ana** *f* horse dealer
chalaneo *m* wheeling and dealing
chalanería *f* trick, con F
chalarse ⟨1a⟩ *v/r* F go crazy F (***por*** about)
chalé *m* ☞ ***chalet***
chaleco *m de traje* vest, *Br* waistcoat; *de sport* gilet, bodywarmer
◇ **chaleco antibalas** bulletproof vest
◇ **chaleco salvavidas** life preserver, life jacket
chalet *m* chalet
◇ **chalet adosado** *house sharing one or more walls with other houses*
◇ **chalet pareado** semi-detached house
chalina *f* cravat
chalote *m* BOT shallot
chalupa *f* **1** MAR small boat **2** *Méx* stuffed tortilla
chamaca *f C.Am.*, *Méx* girl
chamaco *m C.Am.*, *Méx* boy
chamán *m* shaman
chamarilería *f* junk shop
chamarilero *m*, **-a** *f* secondhand dealer
chamarra *f Méx* (*saco*) (short) jacket
chamba *f* **1** *Méx* F job **2**: ***de ~*** F by sheer luck
chambelán *m* HIST chamberlain
chambergo *m* broad-brimmed hat
chambón *m*, **-ona** *f Méx* F klutz F, clumsy idiot F
champán, **champaña** *m* champagne
champiñón *m* BOT mushroom
champión *m Urug* sneaker, *Br* trainer
champú *m* shampoo; ***~ colorante*** tint shampoo
chamullar ⟨1a⟩ **I** *v/i* P jabber F **II** *v/t idioma* P have a smattering of F
chamuscar ⟨1g⟩ *v/t* **1** scorch; *pelo* singe **2** *Méx* (*vender*) sell cheap
chamusquina *f*: ***oler a ~*** F smell fishy F
chance **I** *m L.Am.* chance; ***dame ~*** let me have a go **II** *conj Méx* perhaps, maybe
chancear ⟨1a⟩ *v/i* joke, make wisecracks; **chancearse** *v/r*: ***~ de alguien*** make fun of s.o.
chanchería *f L.Am.* pork butcher's

C

chancero *adj*: ***es ~*** he likes a joke
chanchita *f CSur* piggy bank
chancho *m* **1** *L.Am.* hog, *Br* pig **2** *carne* pork
chanchullero *m*, **-a** *f* F crook F
chanchullo *m* F trick, scam F; ***hacer un ~*** do a dodgy deal F, do some shady business
chancla *f* **1** thong, *Br* flip-flop **2** *Méx*, *C.Am.* (*zapato*) slipper
chancleta *f* **1** thong, *Br* flip-flop **2** *S.Am.* F baby girl
chancletear ⟨1a⟩ *v/i* wear thongs; ***ir chancleteando*** walk around in thongs
chanclo *m* clog
chancro *m* MED chancre
chándal *m* sweats *pl*, *Br* tracksuit
chanfaina *f* GASTR *lamb casserole*
changa *f Rpl* odd job
changarse ⟨1o⟩ *v/r* F break, bust F
chango *Méx* **I** *adj* sharp, smart **II** *m*, **-a** *f* monkey
chanquetes *mpl* GASTR whitebait *sg*
chantaje *m* blackmail; ***hacer ~ a alguien*** blackmail s.o.
chantajear ⟨1a⟩ *v/t* blackmail
chantajista *m/f* blackmailer
chanza *f* wisecrack
chao *int* bye
chapa *f* **1** (*tapón*) cap **2** (*plancha*) sheet (of metal) **3** *de madera* veneer **4** (*insignia*) badge **5** AUTO bodywork **6** *Rpl* AUTO license plate, *Br* number plate **7** *Méx* (*cerradura*) lock
chapado *adj* plated; *con madera* veneered; ***~ en oro*** gold-plated; ***~ a la antigua*** old-fashioned
chapalear ☞ ***chapotear***
chapar ⟨1a⟩ *v/t* **1** plate **2** *con madera* veneer **3** *Arg*, *Pe* catch
chaparro I *adj Méx* small **II** *m* BOT kermes oak
chaparrón *m* downpour; *fig* F *de insultos* barrage; ***aguantar el ~*** F weather the storm
chapear ⟨1a⟩ *v/t* **1** plate **2** *con madera* veneer
chapero *m* F male prostitute, rent boy F
chapín *C.Am.*, *Méx* **I** *adj* Guatemalan **II** *m*, **-ina** *f* Guatemalan
chapista *m* body shop worker, *Br* panel beater
chapistería *f* AUTO body shop
chapitel *m* ARQUI **1** spire **2** *de columna* capital
¡chapó! *int* well done!, bravo!
chapopote *m Méx* tar
chapotear ⟨1a⟩ *v/i* splash
chapucear ⟨1a⟩ *v/t* botch
chapucería *f* botched job
chapucero I *adj* shoddy, slapdash **II** *m*, **-a** *f* shoddy worker
chapulín *m C.Am.*, *Méx* **1** grasshopper **2** (*niño*) kid F
chapurr(e)ar ⟨1a⟩ *v/t*: ***~ el francés*** speak poor French
chapuza *f* **1** (*trabajo mal hecho*) shoddy piece of work **2** (*trabajo menor*) odd job; ***hacer ~s*** do odd jobs
chapuzar ⟨1f⟩ *v/t* duck; **chapuzarse** *v/r* dive in
chapuzón *m* dip; ***darse un ~*** go for a dip
chaqué *m* morning coat
chaqueta *f* jacket; ***cambiar de ~*** F POL change sides
◇ **chaqueta de punto** cardigan
chaquetear ⟨1a⟩ *v/i* POL switch allegiance
chaquetero *m*, **-a** *f* F turncoat
chaquetilla *f* bolero
chaquetón *m* three-quarter length coat
charada *f* charade
charanga *f* brass band
charango *m Pe*, *Bol* five-string guitar
charca *f* pond
charco *m* puddle; ***pasar*** *o* ***cruzar el ~*** cross the Atlantic, cross the pond F
charcutería *f* delicatessen
charcutero *m*, **-a** *f* **1** pork butcher **2** *propietario* deli owner
charla *f* **1** chat **2** *organizada* talk
charlar ⟨1a⟩ *v/i* chat
charlatán I *adj* talkative **II** *m*, **-ana** *f* chatterbox
charlatanería *f* talkativeness
charlestón *m* charleston
charlotada *f* farce
charnela *f* hinge
charol *m* patent leather; ***zapatos de ~*** patent leather shoes
charola *f C.Am.*, *Méx* tray
charqui *m L.Am.* beef jerky
charrán *m* rascal
charranada *f* dirty trick
charrar ⟨1a⟩ *v/i* F chat
charretera *f* MIL epaulette
charro I *adj desp* garish, gaudy **II** *m Méx*

C

(Mexican) cowboy
chárter *adj* charter *atr*
¡chas! *int* smack!
chascar ⟨1g⟩ ☞ ***chasquear***
chascarrillo *m* funny story
chasco *m* joke; ***llevarse un ~*** be disappointed
chasis *m inv* AUTO chassis
chasquear ⟨1a⟩ *v/t* **1** click; ***~ la lengua*** click one's tongue, make a clicking noise with one's tongue **2** *látigo* crack
chasquido *m* **1** click; *de lengua* click, clicking noise **2** *de látigo* crack
chasquilla *f Chi* bangs *pl*, *Br* fringe
chat *m* INFOR chatroom
chata *f* **1** bedpan **2** *Rpl* truck, *Br tb* lorry
chatarra *f* scrap
chatarrería *f* scrap metal business
chatarrero *m*, **-a** *f* scrap merchant
chatear ⟨1a⟩ *v/i* INFOR chat
chato I *adj* **1** *nariz* snub **2** *L.Am. nivel* low **II** *m* wine glass
chau *int Rpl* bye
chaucha *f Rpl* French bean
chaval *m* F kid F, boy
chavala *f* F kid F, girl
chavalo *m C.Am.* F kid F, boy
chavea *m* F kid F, boy
chaveta *f* TÉC (cotter) pin; ***estar ~*** F be crazy F, be nuts F; ***perder la ~*** F go off one's rocker F
chavo *m*, **-a** *f Méx* F **1** (*chico*) kid F **2** *novio etc* partner
che *int Rpl* hey!, look!
checar ⟨1g⟩ *v/t Méx* check
Chechenia *f* Chechnya
checheno I *adj* Chechen **II** *m*, **-a** *f* Chechen
checo I *adj* Czech **II** *m idioma* Czech **III** *m*, **-a** *f* Czech
chef *m* chef
cheli *m* Madrid slang
chelista *m/f* cellist
chelo *m* MÚS cello
chepa I *f* F hump; ***subírsele a la ~*** get too familiar **II** *m/f* (*persona jorobada*) humpback, hunchback
cheposo I *adj* humped **II** *m*, **-a** *f* humpback, hunchback
cheque *m* check, *Br* cheque; ***cobrar un ~*** cash a check
◇ **cheque abierto** open check *o Br* cheque; **cheque en blanco** blank check *o Br* cheque; *fig* carte blanche; **cheque cruzado** check for deposit only, *Br* crossed cheque; **cheque sin fondos** bad check *o Br* cheque; **cheque al portador** check *o Br* cheque made payable to bearer; **cheque-regalo** gift certificate, *Br* gift token, *Br* gift voucher; **cheque de viaje** traveler's check, *Br* traveller's cheque
chequear ⟨1a⟩ *v/t* **1** check **2** *C.Am. equipaje* check in
chequeo *m* MED check-up; ***~ oncológico*** cancer check-up
chequera *f* checkbook, *Br* chequebook
cherna *f*, **cherne** *m pez* stone bass
chévere *adj L.Am.* F cool F
chic *m* chic
chica *f* girl
chicarrón *m* F big strapping fellow
chicha *f L.Am.* corn liquor; ***no ser ni ~ ni limonada*** F be neither one thing nor the other
chícharo *m Méx* pea
chicharra *f* **1** ZO cicada **2** *Méx* (*timbre*) buzzer
chicharro *m* ☞ ***jurel***
chicharrones *mpl* cracklings, *Br* pork scratchings
chiche I *adj C.Am.* F (*fácil*) easy **II** *m* **1** *S.Am.* (*juguete*) toy **2** (*adorno*) trinket
chichera *f C.Am.* F slammer F, jail
chichería *f L.Am. bar selling corn liquor*
chichi *f Méx* F breast, boob F
chichón *m* bump
chicle *m* chewing gum
chico I *adj* small, little; ***dejar ~ a alguien*** *fig* F put s.o. to shame F **II** *m* boy; ***peinado a lo ~*** with short hair, with a boyish haircut
chicota *f* great big girl
chicote *m* **1** great big boy **2** *L.Am.* (*látigo*) whip
chifa *m Pe* **1** Chinese restaurant **2** (*comida china*) Chinese food
chifla *f Méx* whistling
chiflado *adj* F crazy F (***por*** about), nuts F (***por*** about) **II** *m*, **-a** *f* nutcase F, basketcase F
chifladura *f* **1** whistling **2** F (*locura*) craziness F **3** F (*idea*) crazy idea F
chiflar ⟨1a⟩ **I** *v/t* boo **II** *v/i* whistle; **chiflarse** *v/r* F be crazy F (***por*** about)
chifón *m tejido* chiffon
chiísmo *m* REL Shiite religion

C

chiíta I *adj* Shiite **II** *m/f* Shiite
Chile *m* Chile
chile *m* chilli (pepper)
chilena *f en fútbol* scissors kick, overhead kick
chileno I *adj* Chilean **II** *m*, **-a** *f* Chilean
chilindrón *m* GASTR: ***al ~*** cooked in a tomato and pepper sauce
chillar ⟨1a⟩ *v/i* scream, shriek; *de cerdo* squeal
chillería *f* screaming, shrieking
chillido *m* scream, shriek; *de cerdo* squeal
chillón I *adj* **1** *voz* shrill **2** *color* loud **II** *m*, **-ona** *f* loudmouth
chilmol(e) *m C.Am., Méx* GASTR tomato and chilli sauce
chilote *m C.Am.* baby corn
chimenea *f* **1** chimney **2** *de salón* fireplace
chimichurri *m Rpl* hot sauce
chimpancé *m* ZO chimpanzee
China *f* China
china[1] *f* **1** Chinese woman **2** *Rpl* (*criada*) waitress **3** *Rpl* (*niñera*) nursemaid
china[2] *f piedra* small stone; ***me ha tocado la ~*** *fig* I've drawn the short straw
chinchar ⟨1a⟩ *v/t* F pester; **chincharse** *v/r* put up with it; ***¡que se chinche!*** tough!
chinche *f* **1** ZO bedbug **2** *L.Am.* (*chincheta*) thumbtack, *Br* drawing pin
chincheta *f* thumbtack, *Br* drawing pin
chinchilla *f* chinchilla
¡chinchín! *int* bottoms up!, chinchin!
chinchorrero *adj* annoying, irritating
chinchorro *m* hammock
chinchoso *adj* F annoying, irritating
chinear ⟨1a⟩ *v/t C.Am. niños* look after
chinela *f* slipper
chinesco *adj* Chinese
chingar ⟨1h⟩ *v/t Méx* V screw V, fuck V; ***¡chinga tu madre!*** screw you! V, fuck you! V; ***no chingues*** don't screw me around V; **chingarse** *v/r* put up with it
chino I *adj* **1** Chinese **2** *Méx* (*rizado*) curly **II** *m* **1** Chinese man; ***trabajo de ~s*** F hard work **2** *idioma* Chinese; ***me suena a ~*** F it's all Chinese *o* double Dutch to me F **3** *L.Am. desp* half-breed *desp* **4** *Méx* (*rulo*) curler
chip *m* INFOR chip
chipirón *m* baby squid
Chipre *f* Cyprus
chipriota *m/f & adj* Cypriot
chiquero *m* TAUR bull pen
chiquilla *f* girl, kid F
chiquillada *f* childish trick
chiquillería *f* kids *pl* F
chiquillo *m* boy, kid F
chiquito *adj* little; ***no andarse con -as*** F not beat about the bush
chiribita *f* spark; ***los ojos me hacen ~s*** I'm seeing spots before my eyes; ***está que echa ~s*** F he's fuming
chirigota *f* joke
chirimbolo *m* F doodad F, *Br* doodah F
chirimoya *f* BOT custard apple
chiringuito *m* beach bar
chiripa *f*: ***de ~*** F by sheer luck
chirivía *f* BOT parsnip
chirla *f* baby clam
chirona *f*: ***en ~*** F in the can F, inside F; ***meter a alguien en ~*** put s.o. in the can F *o* inside F
chirriar ⟨1c⟩ *v/i* squeak
chirrido *m* squeak
¡chis! *int* ssh!, hush!
chisgarabís *m/f inv* F waste of space F
chisme *m* F **1** bit of gossip; ***~s*** *pl* (*cotilleos*) gossip *sg* **2** *objeto* doodad F, *Br* doodah F
chismear ⟨1a⟩ *v/i* gossip
chismografía *f* F gossip
chismorrear ⟨1a⟩ *v/i* F gossip
chismorreo *m* F gossip
chismoso I *adj* gossipy **II** *m*, **-a** *f* F gossip
chispa I *adj*: ***estar ~*** F be tipsy F **II** *f* **1** spark; ***echar ~s*** be fuming F **2** *fig* F wit **3** (*cantidad pequeña*) spot; ***ni ~*** not one iota; ***una ~ de ...*** a touch of ...; ***eres una ~ revolucionario*** you're a bit of a revolutionary
chispazo *m* spark
chispeante *adj* **1** sparking; *fig* sparkling **2** *lluvia* spitting
chispear ⟨1a⟩ *v/i* **1** spark; *fig* sparkle **2** *de lluvia* spit
chisporrotear ⟨1a⟩ *v/i* **1** *de leña* crackle **2** *de aceite* spit
¡chist! *int* ssh!
chistar ⟨1a⟩ *v/i*: ***sin ~*** without saying a word
chiste *m* joke; ***tener ~*** *L.Am.* F be funny
chistera *f* top hat
chistorra *f* spicy sausage
chistoso *adj* funny
chita *f*: ***a la ~ callando*** F on the quiet

¡chitón! *int* ssh!, hush!
chiva *f* **1** *L.Am.* goat; ***estar como una ~*** F be nuts F **2** *C.Am., Col* bus
chivarse ⟨1a⟩ *v/r* F rat F (***a*** to); ***~ de alguien*** rat on s.o. F
chivatazo *m* F tip-off F; ***dar el ~ a alguien*** F tip s.o. off F, rat to s.o. F
chivato *m*, **-a** *f* F stool pigeon F
chivo *m* **1** ZO kid **2** *C.Am., Méx* wages *pl*
◇ **chivo expiatorio** scapegoat
chocante *adj* **1** (*sorprendente*) startling **2** *que ofende* shocking **3** (*extraño*) odd **4** *L.Am.* (*antipático*) unpleasant
chocar ⟨1g⟩ **I** *v/t*: ***¡choca esos cinco!*** give me five!, put it there! **II** *v/i* **1** crash (***con, contra*** into), collide (***con*** with); ***~ frontalmente*** crash head on; ***~ con un problema*** come up against a problem **2**: ***~le a alguien*** (*sorprender*) surprise s.o.; (*ofender*) shock s.o **3**: ***me choca ese hombre*** that guy disgusts me
chocarrería *f* coarseness
chocarrero *adj* coarse
chocha *f* ZO woodcock
chochear ⟨1a⟩ *v/i* F be senile
chochera *f*, **chochez** *f* F senility
chochín *m* ZO wren
chocho I *adj* F senile; ***estar ~ con*** dote on **II** *m* P beaver P, cunt V
choclo *m Rpl* corn, *Br* corn on the cob
choco *m* ZO cuttlefish
chocolate *m* **1** chocolate **2** F (*hachís*) hashish, hash F
chocolatería *f* chocolate factory
chocolatero I *adj* **1** chocolate *atr* **2** *persona* fond of chocolate **II** *m*, **-a** *f* chocolate maker
chocolatina *f* chocolate bar
chofer *L.Am.*, **chófer** *m* driver
chollo *m* F bargain
cholo *m L.Am.* half-caste *desp*
chomba *f* sweater, *Br tb* jumper; *Arg* polo shirt
chompa *f S.Am.* sweater, *Br tb* jumper
chongo *m Méx* (*moño*) bun
chop *m L.Am.* large beer
chopera *f* poplar grove
chopo *m* BOT poplar
choque *m* **1** collision, crash **2** DEP, MIL clash **3** MED shock
◇ **choque en cadena** pile-up; **choque frontal** head-on collision; **choque múltiple** pile-up
chorar ⟨1a⟩ *v/t* P rip off F
chorbo *m* P guy F
choricear ⟨1a⟩, **chorizar** ⟨1f⟩ *v/t* P swipe F
chorizo I *m* **1** chorizo (*spicy cured sausage*) **2** *Rpl* (*filete*) rump steak **II** *m*, **-a** *f* F thief
chorlito *m* plover; ***cabeza de ~*** F featherbrain F
chorra I *f* luck **II** *m/f* idiot
chorrada *f* F piece of junk; ***decir ~s*** F talk garbage, *Br* talk rubbish
chorrear ⟨1a⟩ *v/i* **1** gush out, stream out **2** (*gotear*) drip
chorreo *m* gushing
chorrera *f de líquido* stream; *de gas* jet
chorro *m* **1** *líquido* jet, stream; *fig* stream; ***sangraba / sudaba a ~s*** he was bleeding / sweating heavily; ***como los ~s del oro*** F clean as a new pin; ***un ~ de*** *Méx* F loads of F **2** *C.Am.* faucet, *Br* tap
◇ **chorro de voz** strong voice
chota *f* ZO kid; ***estar como una ~*** *fig* F be nuts F
chotearse ⟨1a⟩ *v/r* F: ***~ de*** make fun of
choteo *m* F joking
choto *m* ZO *de vaca* calf; *de cabra* kid
chova *f* ZO chough
chovinismo *m* chauvinism
chovinista I *adj* chauvinist(ic) **II** *m/f* chauvinist
choza *f* hut
christmas *m* Christmas card
chubasco *m* shower
chubasquero *m* raincoat
chuchería *f* **1** knick-knack **2** (*golosina*) candy, *Br* sweet
chucho I *adj C.Am.* mean **II** *m* F **1** (*perro*) mutt F, mongrel **2** *Chi* (*cárcel*) can F, *Br* nick F
chucrut *m* GASTR sauerkraut
chueco *adj L.Am.* (*torcido*) twisted
chufa *f* BOT tiger nut
chufla *f* joke; ***estar de ~*** be joking
chulada *f*: ***¡qué ~ de …!*** what a lovely …!
chulapo *m* ☞ ***chulo***
chulearse ⟨1a⟩ *v/r* brag; ***~ de que*** brag that
chulería *f* bragging
chuleta *f* GASTR chop
chulo F **I** *adj* **1** fantastic F, great F **2** *Méx* (*guapo*) attractive **3** (*presuntuoso*)

cocky F; ***ponerse ~*** get cocky **II** *m* pimp
chumbera *f* prickly pear
chumbo *adj*: ***higo ~*** prickly pear
chumpipe *m C.Am.* turkey
chunga *f* F joke; ***tomar algo a ~*** treat sth as a joke
chungo *adj* F **1** terrible, crap V **2** *persona* mean F, nasty
chungón *m*, **-ona** *f* joker
chunguearse ⟨1a⟩ *v/r* F: ***~ de*** make fun of
chupa *f* **1** jacket; ***poner a alguien como ~ de dómine*** lay into s.o. F, *Br* tear s.o. off a strip F **2** *L.Am.* (*ebriedad*) drunkenness
chupada *f* **1** suck; ***dar una ~ a*** suck **2** *de cigarrillo* puff
chupado *adj* **1** F (*delgado*) skinny F **2** F (*fácil*) dead easy F **3** *L.Am.* F (*borracho*) drunk
chupaflor *m L.Am.* hummingbird
chupar ⟨1a⟩ **I** *v/t* **1** suck **2** (*absorber*) soak up; ***~ rueda*** *en ciclismo* tuck in, follow **II** *v/i*: ***~ del bote*** F line one's pockets; **chuparse** *v/r*: ***~ algo*** suck sth; *fig* F put up with sth; ***~ los dedos*** F lick one's fingers; ***estar para ~ los dedos*** *de comida* be delicious, be finger-licking good F
chuparrueda(s) *m/f* (*inv*) hanger-on
chupasangre *m fig* F bloodsucker
chupatintas *m inv* F pencil pusher, pen pusher
chupete *m* **1** *de bebé* pacifier, *Br* dummy **2** (*sorbete*) Popsicle®, *Br* ice lolly
chupetear ⟨1a⟩ *v/t* lick, suck
chupetín *m Rpl* Popsicle®, *Br* ice lolly
chupi *adj* F great F, fantastic F
chupito *m* F shot
chupón I *m* **1** BOT sucker **2** *L.Am. de bebé* pacifier, *Br* dummy **II** *m*, **-ona** *f* sponger F
chupóptero *m*, **-a** *f* F sponger F
churrasco *m Rpl* steak
churre *m* F grease
churrería *f* fritter stall
churrete *m* F mark, stain
churro *m* **1** fritter **2** (*chapuza*) botched job
churruscarse ⟨1g⟩ *v/r* crisp
churumbel *m* F kid F
chusco I *adj* funny **II** *m* piece of bread
chusma *f desp* rabble *desp*
chutar ⟨1a⟩ *v/i* **1** DEP shoot **2**: ***esto va que chuta*** F this is working out fine; ***y vas que chutas*** F and that's your lot! F; **chutarse** *v/r* F *con drogas* shoot up F
chute *m* F fix F
chuzo *m* **1** *Chi* F *persona* dead loss F **2**: ***caer ~s de punta*** F pelt down F
Cía. *abr* (= ***compañía***) Co. (= company)
cianuro *m* cyanide
◇ **cianuro de potasio** potassium cyanide
ciática *f* MED sciatica
ciático *adj* sciatic; ***nervio ~*** sciatic nerve
cibercafé *m* Internet café, cyber café
ciberespacio *m* cyberspace
cibernauta *m/f* Internet surfer
cibernética *f* cybernetics *sg*
cibernético *adj* cybernetic
cicatear ⟨1a⟩ *v/i* be stingy
cicatería *f* stinginess
cicatero I *adj* stingy **II** *m*, **-a** *f* miser, tightwad F
cicatriz *f* scar
cicatrización *f* healing, formation of scar tissue
cicatrizar ⟨1f⟩ *v/i* & *v/t* heal; **cicatrizarse** *v/r* heal
cicerone *m/f* guide
ciclamen *m* BOT cyclamen
cíclico *adj* cyclical
ciclismo *m* cycling
ciclista I *adj* cycling *atr*; ***carrera ~*** cycle race **II** *m/f* cyclist
ciclo *m* **1** cycle **2** *de cine* season; *de conferencias* series *sg*
ciclocross *m* DEP cyclo-cross
ciclomotor *m* moped
ciclón *m* cyclone
ciclópeo *adj fig* gigantic
ciclotrón *m* cyclotron
cicloturismo *m* bicycle touring
cicloturista *m/f* touring cyclist
ciclovía *f L.Am.* cycle lane
cicuta *f* BOT hemlock
cidra *f* BOT citron
ciega *f* blind woman
ciego I *adj* **1** blind; ***quedar(se) ~*** go blind; ***~ de ira*** blind with rage; ***a -as*** blindly **2** ANAT: ***intestino ~*** cecum, *Br* caecum **II** *m* **1** blind man; ***¡eso lo ve un ~!*** even a blind man can see that! **2** ANAT cecum, *Br* caecum
cielito *m Rpl folk dance*
cielo *m* **1** sky; ***minería a ~ abierto*** MIN

strip mining, *Br* opencast mining; ***poner a alguien por los ~s*** F praise s.o. to the skies; ***llovido del ~*** out of the blue; ***remover ~ y tierra*** F move heaven and earth **2** REL heaven; ***estar en el séptimo ~*** *fig* be in seventh heaven; ***ver el ~ abierto*** F see one's chance; ***ser un ~*** F be an angel F; ***¡~s!*** good heavens!

◇ **cielo raso** ceiling

ciempiés *m inv* ZO centipede

cien *adj* a *o* one hundred; ***poner a alguien a ~*** F irritate s.o., get on s.o.'s nerves; ***~ por ~*** *fig* F a hundred per cent, totally

ciénaga *f* marsh

ciencia *f* **1** science; ***a ~ cierta*** for certain, for sure; ***ser un pozo de ~*** F be a fount of knowledge **2**: ***~s*** *pl* EDU science *sg*; ***~s (naturales)*** natural sciences

◇ **ciencia ficción** science fiction; **ciencias de la comunicación** communication sciences; **ciencias económicas** economics *sg*

cieno *m* silt

científico I *adj* scientific **II** *m*, **-a** *f* scientist

cientista *m/f L.Am.* scientist

ciento *pron* **1** a *o* one hundred; ***~s de*** hundreds of; ***~ y la madre*** F the world and his wife F **2**: ***el cinco por ~*** five percent; ***cien por ~*** one hundred per cent, totally

cierne(s): ***en ~*** *fig* potential, in the making; ***estar en ~*** be in its infancy

cierre *m* **1** *de prenda, maleta etc* fastener **2** *de negocio*: *permanente* closure; *a diario* closing; ***~ de la Bolsa*** close of the stock exchange; ***al ~ de la edición*** at the time of going to press

◇ **cierre centralizado** AUTO central locking; **cierre de las emisiones** TV close, closedown; **cierre metálico** metal shutter; **cierre patronal** lockout; **cierre relámpago** *L.Am.* zipper, *Br* zip

ciertamente *adv* certainly

cierto *adj* **1** (*seguro*) certain **2** (*verdadero*): ***es ~*** it's true; ***lo ~ es que ...*** the fact is that ...; ***estar en lo ~*** be right **3**: ***hasta ~ punto*** up to a point; ***un ~ encanto*** a certain charm; ***~ día*** one day **4**: ***por ~*** incidentally

cierva *f* ZO doe

ciervo *m* ZO buck

◇ **ciervo volante** stag beetle

cierzo *m* north wind

c.i.f. *abr* (= ***costo, seguro y flete***) cif (= cost, insurance, freight)

cifra *f* **1** figure **2**: ***en ~*** in code

◇ **cifra de negocios, cifra de ventas** sales figures *pl*, turnover

cifrado *adj* coded

cifrar ⟨1a⟩ *v/t* write in code; ***~ su esperanza en*** pin one's hopes on; **cifrarse** *v/r*: ***~ en*** come to, amount to

cigala *f* ZO crawfish, *Br* crayfish

cigarra *f* ZO cicada

cigarrera *f* cigar / cigarette box, cigar / cigarette case

cigarrería *f L.Am. shop selling cigarettes etc*

cigarrillo *m* cigarette

cigarro *m* **1** cigar **2** *L.Am.* (*cigarillo*) cigarette

cigüeña *f* ZO stork

cigüeñal *m* AUTO crankshaft

cigüeñuela *f* ZO black-winged stilt

cilantro *m* BOT coriander

cilicio *m* hair shirt

cilindrada *f* AUTO cubic capacity

cilíndrico *adj* cylindrical

cilindro *m* cylinder

cilio *m* BIO cilium

cima *f* summit; *fig* peak; ***dar ~ a*** complete successfully

cimarrón I *adj* **1** *L.Am. animal* wild **2** *L.Am. esclavo* runaway **3** *Arg*: ***mate ~*** unsweetened maté **II** *L.Am. m*, **-ona** *f* **1** wild animal **2** *esclavo* runaway slave

címbalo *m* MÚS cymbal

cimborio *m* ARQUI dome

cimbr(e)ar ⟨1a⟩ *v/t* swing; **cimbr(e)arse** *v/r* sway

cimbreante *adj* swaying

cimentación *f* **1** foundation laying **2** (*cimientos*) foundations *pl*

cimentar ⟨1k⟩ *v/t* lay the foundations of; *fig* base (***en*** on)

cimero *adj* highest; *fig* finest

cimientos *mpl* foundations

cimitarra *f* scimitar

cinabrio *m* cinnabar

cinc *m* zinc

cincel *m* chisel

cincelado *m* **1** *de metal* engraving **2** *de piedra* chiseling, *Br* chiselling

cincelar ⟨1a⟩ *v/t* **1** *metal* engrave **2** *pie-*

dra chisel
cincha *f* girth, cinch
cinchar ⟨1a⟩ *v/t* girth, do up the girth of
cincho *m* **1** belt **2** (*aro*) hoop
cinco I *adj* five **II** *m* five; ***no tener ni ~*** F not have a red cent F
cincuenta *adj* fifty
cincuentena *f* fifty; ***una ~ de ...*** about fifty ...
cincuentenario *m* fiftieth anniversary
cincuentón I *adj* in one's fifties **II** *m*, **-ona** *f* person in his / her fifties
cine *m* **1** movies *pl*, cinema; ***llevar al ~*** make into a movie; ***de ~*** *fig* F magnificent **2** *edificio* movie theater, *Br* cinema
◇ **cine de barrio** local movie theater, *Br* local cinema; **cine club** film club *o* society; **cine de estreno** *movie house showing new releases*; **cine mudo** silent movies *pl*; **cine sonoro** talkies *pl*
cineasta *m/f* film-maker
cinéfilo *m*, **-a** *f* movie buff
cinegética *f* (art of) hunting
cinegético *adj* hunting *atr*
cinemateca *f* movie library, *Br* film library
cinematografía *f* cinematography
cinematográfico *adj* movie *atr*
cinematógrafo *m* projector
cinerario *adj*: ***urna -a*** funerary urn
cinética *f* kinetics *sg*
cinético *adj* kinetic
cíngaro I *adj* gypsy **II** *m*, **-a** *f* gypsy
cínico I *adj* cynical **II** *m*, **-a** *f* cynic
cinismo *m* cynicism
cinta *f* **1** ribbon **2** *de música, vídeo* tape **3** BOT spider plant
◇ **cinta adhesiva** adhesive tape; **cinta aislante** electrical tape, friction tape, *Br* insulating tape; **cinta de audio** audio tape; **cinta correctora** correction ribbon; **cinta magnética** magnetic tape; **cinta métrica** tape measure; **cinta transportadora** conveyor belt; **cinta de video**, *Esp* **cinta de vídeo** video tape
cinto *m* belt
cintura *f* waist; ***meter a alguien en ~*** *fig* F take s.o. in hand
cinturón *m* **1** belt; ***apretarse el ~*** *fig* tighten one's belt **2** AUTO: ***llevar el ~ (abrochado)*** have one's seatbelt on
◇ **cinturón de castidad** HIST chastity belt; **cinturón con pretensor** AUTO inertia-reel seatbelt; **cinturón de ronda** beltway, *Br* ring road; **cinturón de seguridad** AUTO seatbelt; **cinturón de tres puntos (de anclaje)** AUTO three-point seatbelt
cíper *m Méx* zipper, *Br* zip
ciprés *m* BOT cypress
circense *adj* circus *atr*
circo *m* circus
circón *m* MIN zircon
circuito *m* circuit; ***corto ~*** EL short circuit
◇ **circuito cerrado** EL closed circuit
circulación *f* **1** movement; ***libre ~*** POL freedom of movement **2** FIN, MED circulation; ***poner en ~*** put into circulation; ***retirar de la ~*** withdraw from circulation ***fuera de ~*** out of circulation **3** AUTO traffic
◇ **circulación sanguínea** circulation (of the blood)
circular I *adj* circular **II** *f* circular **III** ⟨1a⟩ *v/i* **1** circulate **2** AUTO drive, travel **3** *de persona* move (along); ***¡circulen!*** move along!
circulatorio *adj* MED circulatory; ***trastornos ~s*** circulation problems
círculo *m* **1** MAT circle **2**: ***en ~s artísticos*** in artistic circles
◇ **Círculo Polar Antártico** Antarctic Circle; **Círculo Polar Ártico** Arctic Circle; **círculo vicioso** vicious circle
circuncidar ⟨1a⟩ *v/t* circumcise
circuncisión *f* circumcision
circunciso *adj* circumcised
circundante *adj* surrounding
circundar ⟨1a⟩ *v/t* surround
circunferencia *f* circumference
circunloquio *m* circumlocution
circunnavegación *f* circumnavigation
circunnavegar ⟨1h⟩ *v/t* circumnavigate
circunscribir ⟨3a⟩ *v/t* limit (***a*** to)
circunscripción *f* POL electoral district, *Br* constituency
circunscrito I *part* ☞ ***circunscribir*** **II** *adj* limited (***a*** to)
circunspección *f* circumspection, caution
circunspecto *adj* circumspect, cautious
circunstancia *f* **1** circumstance; ***dadas la ~s*** in view of the circumstances; ***en estas ~s*** in these circumstances **2**: ***de ~s*** (*provisional*) temporary

circunstanciado *adj* detailed
circunstancial *adj* circumstantial
circunstante I *adj* present **II** *mpl*: ***los ~s*** those present
circunvalación *f*: (***carretera de***) ~ beltway, *Br* ring road
circunvalar ⟨1a⟩ *v/t* go around
circunvolución *f* circumvolution
cirio *m* candle; ***armar*** *o* ***montar un*** ~ F kick up a fuss F
cirro *m* cirrus
cirrosis *f* MED cirrhosis
◇ **cirrosis hepática** cirrhosis of the liver
ciruela *f* plum
◇ **ciruela claudia** greengage
◇ **ciruela pasa** prune
ciruelo *m* plum tree
cirugía *f* surgery
◇ **cirugía estética** cosmetic surgery
◇ **cirugía plástica** plastic surgery
cirujano *m*, **-a** *f* surgeon
ciscar ⟨1g⟩ *v/t* soil, dirty; **ciscarse** *v/r* F do a poop F, *Br* do a pooh F
cisco *m*: ***hacer*** ~ smash; ***armar*** ~ kick up a fuss
Cisjordania *f* the West Bank
cisma *m* REL schism; *fig* split
cisne *m* ZO swan; ***canto del*** ~ swansong; ***jersey de cuello*** ~ turtleneck (sweater)
Císter *m* Cistercian order
cisterciense *adj* Cistercian
cisterna *f de WC* cistern
cístico *adj* ANAT: ***conducto*** ~ bile duct
cistitis *f* MED cystitis
cisura *f* crack
cita *f* **1** appointment; ~ ***previa*** prior appointment, previous engagement; ***concertar una*** ~ arrange an appointment; ***darse*** ~ arrange to meet **2** *de texto* quote, quotation
citación *f* JUR summons *sg*, subpoena
citadino *L.Am.* **I** *adj* city *atr*, urban **II** *m*, **-a** *f* city dweller, person from the city
citar ⟨1a⟩ *v/t* **1** *a reunión* arrange to meet **2** *a juicio* summon **3** (*mencionar*) mention **4** *de texto* quote; **citarse** *v/r* arrange to meet
cítara *f* MÚS zither
citología *f* Pap test, *Br* smear test
cítrico I *adj* citric; ***ácido*** ~ citric acid **II** *m* citrus fruit; ***~s*** *pl* citrus fruit *sg*
citricultura *f* citrus fruit growing
ciudad *f* town; *más grande* city
◇ **Ciudad del Cabo** Cape Town; **Ciudad Condal**: ***la*** ~ Barcelona; **ciudad dormitorio** bedroom community, *Br* dormitory town; **ciudad-estado** city state; **Ciudad Eterna**: ***la*** ~ the Eternal City; **Ciudad de Guatemala** Guatemala City; **ciudad jardín** garden city; **Ciudad de México** Mexico City; **ciudad universitaria** university campus; **Ciudad del Vaticano** Vatican City
ciudadanía *f* citizenship
ciudadano I *adj* civic; ***seguridad -a*** public safety **II** *m*, **-a** *f* citizen; ***el ~ de a pie*** the man in the street
ciudadela *f* citadel
civeta *f* ZO civet
cívico *adj* civic; ***deber*** ~ civic duty, public duty
civil I *adj* civil; ***casarse por lo*** ~ have a civil wedding **II** *m/f* civilian **III** *m* civil guard
civilidad *f* civility
civilista *m/f* JUR civil lawyer
civilización *f* civilization
civilizado *adj* civilized
civilizar ⟨1f⟩ *v/t* civilize; **civilizarse** *v/r* become civilized
civismo *m* civility
cizalla *f* metal shears *pl*
cizaña *f*: ***sembrar*** *o* ***meter*** ~ cause trouble
cizañero *m*, **-a** *f* F troublemaker
cl. *abr* (= ***centilitro***) cl. (= centiliter)
clamar ⟨1a⟩ *v/i*: ~ ***por algo*** clamor for sth, *Br* clamour for sth, cry out for sth; ~ ***al cielo*** *fig* be an outrage
clamor *m* roar; *fig* clamor, *Br* clamour
clamoroso *adj* clamorous; *ovación* rapturous; *éxito*, *fracaso* resounding
clan *m* clan
clandestinidad *f* POL clandestine nature
clandestino *adj* POL clandestine, underground; ***movimiento*** ~ underground movement
claque *f* TEA claque
claqué *m* tap dancing; ***bailar*** ~ tap-dance
claqueta *f* clapperboard
clara *f* **1** *de huevo* white **2** *bebida* shandy-gaff, *Br* shandy
claraboya *f* skylight
claramente *adv* clearly
clarear ⟨1a⟩ *v/i del cielo* get light; ***al ~ el***

C

día at daybreak
clarete *m* claret
claridad *f* light; *fig* clarity
clarificación *f* explanation, clarification
clarificar ⟨1g⟩ *v/t* clarify
clarín *m* bugle
clarinazo *m* bugle call
clarinete *m* clarinet
clarinetista *m/f* clarinetist
clarividencia *f* clairvoyance
clarividente I *adj* clairvoyant **II** *m/f* clairvoyant
claro I *adj* **1** *tb fig* clear; ***poner en ~*** make clear; ***dejar ~*** make plain; ***quedar ~*** be clear; ***tener algo ~*** be sure *o* clear about sth; ***pasar la noche en ~*** lie awake all night, not sleep a wink; ***a las -as*** clearly **2** *color* light **3** (*luminoso*) bright **4** *salsa* thin
II *adv*: ***hablar ~*** speak plainly; ***¡~!*** of course!; ***~ está*** of course
III *m* **1** METEO clear spell **2** *en bosque* clearing
◇ **claro de luna** moonlight
claroscuro *m* chiaroscuro
clase *f* **1** EDU class; ***dar ~(s)*** teach **2** (*variedad*) kind, sort **3** *social* class; ***la ~ obrera*** the working class **4**: ***tener ~*** have class; ***una mujer con ~*** a classy woman
◇ **clase media** middle class; **clase particular** private lesson; **clase turista** AVIA tourist class; **clases altas** upper classes; **clases bajas** lower classes; **clases pasivas** *people in receipt of state pensions*
clasemediero *adj Méx* middle-class
clasicismo *m* classicism
clásico I *adj* classical **II** *m* classic
clasificable *adj* classifiable
clasificación *f* **1** DEP *en competición* qualification **2** *de liga* league table **3**: ***hacer la ~ de los documentos*** sort the documents out
clasificado *m L.Am.* classified ad
clasificador *m* file cabinet, *Br* filing cabinet
clasificadora *f* sorter
clasificar ⟨1g⟩ *v/t* classify; **clasificarse** *v/r* DEP qualify; ***~ tercero*** come in *o* place third
clasismo *m* classism
clasista *adj* classist; ***sociedad ~*** class-conscious society
claudia *f* BOT greengage
claudicación *f* capitulation
claudicar ⟨1g⟩ *v/i* give in, capitulate
claustro *m* **1** ARQUI cloister **2** *de profesores* staff
claustrofobia *f* claustrophobia
cláusula *f* clause
◇ **cláusula penal** penalty clause
clausura *f* **1** *de acto* closing ceremony **2** *de bar, local* closure **3** REL cloister
clausurar ⟨1a⟩ *v/t* **1** *acto oficial* close **2** *por orden oficial* close down
clavadista *m/f Méx* diver
clavado I *adj*: ***ser ~ a alguien*** be the spitting image of s.o. F; ***dejar a alguien ~*** *fig* F dumbfound s.o. **II** *m Méx* (*salto*) dive
clavar ⟨1a⟩ *v/t* **1** stick (***en*** into) **2** *clavos, estaca* drive (***en*** into); *uñas* sink (***en*** into) **3**: ***~ los ojos en alguien*** fix one's eyes on s.o. **4**: ***~ a alguien por algo*** F overcharge s.o. for sth; **clavarse** *v/r*: ***~ un cuchillo en la mano*** stick a knife into one's hand
clave I *f* **1** *de problema* key **2** (*código*) code; ***en ~*** in code **II** *adj importante* key; ***figura ~*** key figure; ***puesto ~*** key post **III** *m* MÚS harpsichord
◇ **clave de fa** bass clef
◇ **clave de sol** treble clef
clavecín *m* harpsichord
clavecinista *m/f* harpsichord player
clavel *m* BOT carnation
clavellina *f* BOT pink
clavetear ⟨1a⟩ *v/t* adorn with studs, stud
clavicémbalo *m* harpsichord
clavicordio *m* clavichord
clavícula *f* ANAT collarbone
clavija *f* EL pin; ***apretarle a alguien las ~s*** put the screws on s.o. F
clavo *m* **1** *de metal* nail; ***dar en el ~*** hit the nail on the head; ***como un ~*** on the dot; ***está tan desesperado que se agarraría a un ~ ardiendo*** he's so desperate he'd do anything; ***remachar el ~*** make matters worse **2** GASTR clove **3** *CSur* F *persona* dead loss F
claxon *m* AUTO horn; ***tocar el ~*** sound one's horn
clemátide *f* BOT clematis
clemencia *f* clemency, mercy
clemente *adj lit* clement, merciful
clementina *f* BOT clementine

cleptómano I *adj* kleptomaniac **II** *m*, **-a** *f* kleptomaniac
clerical *adj* clerical
clericalismo *m* clericalism
clérigo *m* priest, clergyman
◇ **clérigo secular** lay preacher
clero *m* clergy
clic *m* INFOR click; ***hacer ~ en*** click on; ***doble ~*** double click; ***hacer doble ~*** double click
clicar ⟨1g⟩ *v/i* click
cliché *m* **1** TIP plate **2** (*tópico*) cliché
clienta *f* ☞ ***cliente***
cliente *m/f de tienda* customer; *de empresa* client
◇ **cliente fijo, cliente habitual** regular (customer)
clientela *f* clientele, customers *pl*
clima *m* climate
◇ **clima continental** continental climate
climaterio *m* MED climacteric *fml*, menopause
climático *adj* climatic
climatización *f* air conditioning
climatizado *adj* air-conditioned
climatizador *m* air conditioner
climatizar ⟨1f⟩ *v/t* air-condition
climatología *f* climatology
clímax *m fig* climax
clínic *m en baloncesto* clinic
clínica *f* clinic
◇ **clínica abortiva** abortion clinic; **clínica dental** dental clinic; **clínica ginecológica** gynecological clinic; **clínica veterinaria** veterinary clinic
clínico *adj* clinical
clip *m* **1** *para papeles* paperclip **2** *para el pelo* bobby pin, *Br* hairgrip
clisé *m* **1** TIP plate **2** (*tópico*) cliché
clítoris *m* ANAT clitoris
cloaca *f tb fig* sewer
clon *m* BIO clone
clonación *f* BIO cloning
clonar ⟨1a⟩ *v/t* clone
clónico *adj* BIO clonal, clone *atr*
cloquear ⟨1a⟩ *v/i* cluck
clorar ⟨1a⟩ *v/t* chlorinate
cloro *m* **1** QUÍM chlorine **2** *Méx* (*lejía*) bleach
clorofila *f* chlorophyll
clorofluorocarbono *m* chlorofluorocarbon
cloroformizar ⟨1f⟩ *v/t* chloroform
cloroformo *m* QUÍM chloroform
cloruro *m* QUÍM chloride
◇ **cloruro sódico, cloruro de sodio** sodium chloride
clóset *m L.Am.* closet, *Br* wardrobe
club *m* club
◇ **club deportivo** sports club; **club náutico** yacht club; **club nocturno** nightclub
clueca *f* broody hen
cm *abr* (= ***centímetro***) cm (= centimeter)
CNI *m abr* (= ***Centro Nacional de Inteligencia***) Spanish Intelligence Service
CNT *f abr* (= ***Confederación Nacional de Trabajo***) *Spanish labor union*
coacción *f* coercion
coaccionar ⟨1a⟩ *v/t* coerce
coactivo *adj* coercive
coadyuvante *adj*: ***factor ~*** contributing factor
coadyuvar ⟨1a⟩ *v/i* contribute (***a*** to)
coagulación *f* coagulation; *de sangre* clotting
coagular ⟨1a⟩ *v/t* coagulate; *sangre* clot; **coagularse** *v/r* coagulate; *de sangre* clot
coágulo *m* clot
coala *m* ZO koala
coalición *f* coalition
coaligarse ⟨1h⟩ *v/r tb* POL work together, join forces
coartada *f* JUR alibi
coartar ⟨1a⟩ *v/t* restrict
coautor *m*, **~a** *f* co-author
coba *f*: ***dar ~ a alguien*** F soft-soap s.o. F
cobalto *m* cobalt
cobarde I *adj* cowardly **II** *m/f* coward
cobardía *f* cowardice
cobaya *m/f* guinea pig
cobertera *f* lid
cobertizo *m* shed
cobertor *m* (*manta*) blanket
cobertura *f* **1** *de seguro* cover **2** TV *etc* coverage **3**: ***~ de chocolate*** covering of chocolate, chocolate coating
cobija *f L.Am.* blanket
cobijar ⟨1a⟩ *v/t* **1** give shelter to **2** (*acoger*) take in; **cobijarse** *v/r* take shelter
cobijo *m* shelter, refuge
cobista *m/f* F con artist F
cobra *f* ZO cobra
cobrable *adj dinero* recoverable
cobrador *m*, **~a** *f a domicilio* collector

C

C

cobranza *f* collection
cobrar ⟨1a⟩ **I** *v/t* **1** charge **2** *subsidio, pensión* receive; *deuda* collect; *cheque* cash **3** *salud, fuerzas* recover **4** *importancia* acquire **II** *v/i* **1** be paid, get paid **2**: ***vas a ~*** F (*recibir un palo*) you're going to get it! F; **cobrarse** *v/r* **1**: ***cóbrese por favor*** can I pay, please? **2**: ***el huracán se cobró diez víctimas mortales*** the hurricane claimed ten lives
cobre *m* copper
cobrizo *adj* copper-colored, *Br* copper-coloured
cobro *m* **1** charging; ***llamar a ~ revertido*** call collect, *Br tb* reverse the charges **2** *de subsidio* receipt; *de deuda* collection; *de cheque* cashing
coca *f* **1** BOT coca **2** F *droga* coke F **3**: ***de ~*** *Méx* free
cocacho *m S.Am.* F whack on the head F
cocada *f L.Am.* coconut cookie
cocaína *f* cocaine
cocainómano I *adj* addicted to cocaine **II** *m*, **-a** *f* cocaine addict
cocción *f* cooking; *en agua* boiling; *al horno* baking
cóccix *m* ANAT coccyx
cocear ⟨1a⟩ *v/i* kick
cocer ⟨2b & 2h⟩ **I** *v/t* cook; *en agua* boil; *al horno* bake **II** *v/i* cook; *en agua* boil; ***a medio ~*** half done, half cooked; ***sin ~*** uncooked; **cocerse** *v/r* cook; *en agua* boil; *al horno* bake; *fig* F *de persona* be roasting F
coces ☞ ***coz***
cochambre *m/f* F **1** filth **2** (*basura*) trash, *Br* rubbish
cochambroso *adj* F filthy
coche *m* **1** car **2** *Méx* (*taxi*) cab, taxi **3** FERR car, *Br* carriage
◇ **coche de alquiler** rental car, *Br* hire car; **coche bomba** car bomb; **coche de caballos** horse-drawn carriage; **coche cama** sleeping car; **coche de carreras** racing car; **coche celular** patrol wagon, *Br* police van; **coche de choque** bumper car, *Br tb* dodgem; **coche deportivo** sports car; **coche comedor** *L.Am.* dining car; **coche de época** vintage car; **coche fúnebre** hearse; **coche de línea** (long-distance) bus; **coche de ocasión** used car, second-hand car; **coche oficial** official car; **coche patrulla** police car, patrol car; **coche restaurante** restaurant car; **coche usado** used car, second-hand car
cochecito *m*: ***~ de niño*** stroller, *Br* pushchair
cochera *f* **1** garage **2** *de trenes* locomotive shed
cochero I *adj*: ***puerta -a*** carriage entrance **II** *m* coachman
cochifrito *m* GASTR *dish made with goat and lamb*
cochina *f* sow; F *persona* pig F
cochinada *f* F filth
cochinilla *f* ZO woodlouse
◇ **cochinilla de (la) humedad** woodlouse
cochinillo *m* suckling pig, sucking pig
cochino I *adj* **1** *fig* filthy, dirty **2** (*asqueroso*) disgusting **II** *m* hog, *Br* pig; F *persona* pig F
cochiquera *f tb fig* pigpen, *Br* pig sty
cocido I *adj* boiled **II** *m* stew
cociente *m* quotient
◇ **cociente intelectual** intelligence quotient, IQ
cocina *f* **1** *habitación* kitchen **2** *aparato* stove, cooker **3** *actividad* cooking **4**: ***la ~ francesa*** French cuisine
◇ **cocina eléctrica** electric stove *o* cooker
◇ **cocina de gas** gas stove *o* cooker
cocinar ⟨1a⟩ **I** *v/t* **1** cook **2** *fig* F plot **II** *v/i* cook
cocinero *m*, **-a** *f* cook
cocinilla *f* camp stove, *Br* camping stove
coclearia *f* scurvy grass
coco *m* **1** BOT coconut **2** *monstruo* bogeyman F **3**: ***comer el ~ a alguien*** F softsoap s.o.; *más fuerte* brainwash s.o.; ***comerse el ~*** F worry; ***estar hasta el ~*** F be fed up
cococha *f* GASTR cheek *of cod, hake etc*
cocodrilo *m* crocodile; ***lágrimas de ~*** *fig* crocodile tears
cocoliche *m Arg* pidgin Spanish
cocorota *f* F head, nut F
cocotazo *m L.Am.* F whack on the head F
cocotero *m* coconut palm
cóctel *m* cocktail
◇ **cóctel de gambas** shrimp cocktail, *Br* prawn cocktail

◇ **cóctel Molotov** Molotov cocktail
coctelera *f* cocktail shaker
coctelería *f* cocktail bar
cód *abr* (= ***código***) code
coda *f* MÚS coda
codazo *m*: ***dar a alguien un ~*** elbow s.o.
codear ⟨1a⟩ *v/t & v/i* nudge; *con fuerza* elbow; **codearse** *v/r*: ***~ con alguien*** rub shoulders with s.o.
codeína *f* codeine
codera *f* elbow patch
codeso *m* BOT laburnum
códice *m* HIST codex
codicia *f* greed
codiciable *adj* desirable
codiciar ⟨1b⟩ *v/t* covet
codicilo *m* codicil
codicioso *adj* greedy, covetous
codificación *f* codification, encoding
codificado *adj* TV encrypted
codificar ⟨1g⟩ *v/t* **1** JUR codify **2** (*cifrar*) encode; TV encrypt
código *m* code
◇ **código de barras** COM barcode; **código de la circulación** drivers' manual, *Br* highway code; **código civil** civil code; **código de honor** code of honor *o Br* honour; **código penal** penal code; **código postal** zip code, *Br* postcode
codillo *m* **1** ZO elbow **2** TÉC elbow (joint) **3** GASTR knuckle
codo *m* ANAT elbow; ***~ con ~*** *fig* F side by side; ***hablar por los ~s*** F talk nineteen to the dozen F; ***romperse los ~s*** F bust a gut F
◇ **codo de tenista** MED tennis elbow
codorniz *f* ZO quail
coeducación *f* coeducation
coeficiente *m* coefficient
coerción *f* coercion
coercitivo *adj* coercive
coetáneo I *adj* contemporary **II** *m*, **-a** *f* contemporary
coexistencia *f* coexistence
coexistente *adj* coexistent
coexistir ⟨3a⟩ *v/i* coexist (***con*** with)
cofia *f* cap
cofrade *m* member of a ***cofradía***
cofradía *f* **1** fraternity **2** (*gremio*) guild
cofre *m* **1** *de tesoro* chest **2** *para alhajas* jewelry box, *Br* jewellery box
cofundador *m*, **~a** *f* co-founder
cogedor *m* dustpan
coger ⟨2c⟩ **I** *v/t* **1** (*asir*) take (hold of); *del suelo* pick up **2** *L.Am.* V screw V **3** *ladrón*, *enfermedad* catch **4** TRANSP catch, take; ***~ el tren / bus*** catch the train / bus **5** (*entender*) get **6** *emisora de radio* pick up **II** *v/i* **1** *en un espacio* fit **2** *L.Am.* V screw V **3** *de una planta* take, take root **4**: ***~ por la primera a la derecha*** take the first right
cogerse *v/r* hold on (tight); ***~ de algo*** hold on to sth
cogestión *f* joint management
cogida *f* TAUR goring
cognición *f* cognition
cognitivo *adj* cognitive
cogollo *m de lechuga*, *fig* heart
cogorza *f*: ***agarrar una ~*** F get plastered F
cogotazo *m* rabbit punch
cogote *m* F nape of the neck; ***estar hasta el ~ de algo*** F have had it up to here with sth
cogulla *f* cowl
cohabitación *f* cohabitation, living together
cohabitar ⟨1a⟩ *v/i* live together, cohabit
cohechar ⟨1a⟩ *v/t* bribe
cohecho *m* JUR bribery
coheredero *m*, **-a** *f* joint heir
coherencia *f* coherence
coherente *adj* coherent; ***ser ~ con*** be consistent with
cohesión *f* cohesion
cohesionar ⟨1a⟩ *v/t* unite
cohete *m* rocket
cohibición *f* inhibition
cohibido *adj* inhibited
cohibir ⟨3a⟩ *v/t* inhibit; **cohibirse** *v/r* feel shy
cohombro *m* BOT cucumber
◇ **cohombro de mar** ZO sea cucumber
cohonestar ⟨1a⟩ *v/t* cover up
COI *abr* (= ***Comité Olímpico Internacional***) IOC (= International Olympic Committee)
coima *f L.Am.* bribe
coimear ⟨1a⟩ *v/t L.Am.* bribe
coincidencia *f* coincidence
coincidente *adj* coincident
coincidir ⟨3a⟩ *v/i* coincide
coito *m* intercourse
cojear ⟨1a⟩ *v/i* **1** *de persona* limp, hobble **2** *de mesa*, *silla* wobble
cojera *f* limp

C

cojín *m* cushion
cojinete *m* TÉC bearing
◇ **cojinete de bolas** ball bearing
cojo *adj* **1** *persona* lame; ***es ~*** he walks with a limp; ***andar a la pata -a*** hop **2** *mesa, silla* wobbly
cojón *m* V ball V; ***tener cojones*** P have balls V, have guts F; ***estar hasta los cojones*** V be pissed off V; ***¡cojones!*** V fuck! V, shit! P
cojonudo *adj* P awesome F, brilliant
col *f* cabbage; ***entre ~ y ~, lechuga*** variety is the spice of life
◇ **col blanca** white cabbage
◇ **col de Bruselas** Brussels sprout
col. *abr* (= ***columna***) col. (= column)
cola[1] *f* (*pegamento*) glue
cola[2] *f* **1** AVIA, *de animal* tail; ***traer ~*** have repercussions; ***estar a la ~*** be in last place **2** *de gente* line, *Br* queue; ***hacer ~*** stand in line, *Br* queue (up) **3** *L.Am.* F *de persona* butt F, *Br* bum F
◇ **cola de caballo** **1** ponytail **2** BOT horsetail
cola[3] *f* BOT cola, kola; ***nuez de ~*** cola nut, kola nut
colaboración *f* collaboration
colaboracionista *m/f* POL collaborator, collaborationist
colaborador *m*, **~a** *f* collaborator; *en periódico* contributor
colaborar ⟨1a⟩ *v/i* collaborate
colación *f*: ***traer o sacar a ~*** bring up
colada *f*: ***hacer la ~*** do the laundry *o* washing
coladero *m* ☞ ***colador***
colado *adj*: ***estar ~ por alguien*** F be nuts about s.o. F
colador *m* colander; *para té etc* strainer
coladura *f* **1** straining **2** (*error*) blunder
colágeno *m* BIO collagen
colapsar ⟨1a⟩ **I** *v/t* paralyze; ***~ el tráfico*** bring traffic to a standstill **II** *v/i L.Am.* collapse; **colapsarse** *v/r* **1** grind to a halt **2** *de edificio* collapse
colapso *m* collapse; ***provocar un ~ en la ciudad*** bring the city to a standstill
colar ⟨1m⟩ **I** *v/t* **1** *líquido* strain **2** *billete falso* pass; ***~ algo por la aduana*** F smuggle sth through customs **II** *v/i fig* F: ***no cuela*** I'm not buying it F; **colarse** *v/r* F **1** *en un lugar* get in **2** *en una fiesta* gatecrash; *en una cola* cut in line, *Br* push in **3**: ***~ por alguien*** F fall for s.o.
colcha *f L.Am.* bedspread
colchón *m* mattress; *fig* buffer
◇ **colchón de muelles** spring mattress
◇ **colchón neumático** air mattress, *Br* air bed
colchoneta *f* **1** DEP mat **2** *hinchable* air mattress, *Br* air bed
cole *m* F school
colear ⟨1a⟩ *fig* **I** *v/i*: ***todavía colea la polémica*** the controversy is still dragging on **II** *v/t toro* pull the tail of
colección *f* collection
coleccionable *adj* collectable
coleccionar ⟨1a⟩ *v/t* collect
coleccionista *m/f* collector
colecta *f* collection
colectar ⟨1a⟩ *v/t dinero* collect
colectivero *m*, **-a** *f Arg* bus driver
colectividad *f* community
colectivizar ⟨1f⟩ *v/t* collectivize
colectivo **I** *adj* collective **II** *m* **1** *L.Am.* bus **2** *Méx, C.Am.* taxi **3** *para regalo* collection, *Br tb* whip-round
colector *m* **1** TÉC manifold **2** EL collector
◇ **colector solar** solar panel
colega *m/f* **1** *de trabajo* colleague **2** F pal F
colegiado **I** *adj* belonging to a professional body **II** *m*, **-a** *f* **1** schoolchild **2** DEP referee **3** *member of a professional body*
colegial **I** *adj* school *atr* **II** *m* student, *Br tb* schoolboy
colegiala *f* student, *Br tb* schoolgirl
colegiarse ⟨1b⟩ *v/r* join a professional body
colegio *m* school
◇ **colegio electoral** electoral college; *lugar* polling place; **colegio de médicos** *professional medical body*; **colegio mayor** dormitory, dorm F, *Br* hall of residence; **colegio profesional** professional institute
colegir ⟨3l & 3c⟩ *v/t* deduce (***de, por*** from)
colegui *m/f* F buddy F, pal F
coleóptero *m* ZO coleopteran
cólera **I** *f* anger; ***montar en ~*** get in a rage **II** *m* MED cholera
colérico *adj* angry
colesterol *m* cholesterol
coleta *f* **1** ponytail; ***~s*** *pl de pelo*

bunches **2**: ***cortarse la ~*** *de torero* retire
coletazo *m* swish of the tail
coletilla *f* tag
coleto *m*: ***decir para su ~*** *fig* say to o.s.; ***echarse al ~*** F *comida, bebida* put away; *libro* get through
colgado *adj* **1**: ***dejar ~ a alguien*** F let s.o. down; ***estar*** *o* ***quedarse ~*** be (left) on one's own **2**: ***estar ~ por alguien*** F be nuts about s.o. F
colgador *m L.Am.* hanger
colgaduras *fpl* hangings
colgajo *m* **1** *de tela* shred **2** *de frutas*: *bunch of fruit hung up to dry*
colgante I *adj* hanging **II** *m* pendant
colgar ⟨1h & 1m⟩ **I** *v/t* **1** hang **2** TELEC put down **3**: ***~ los estudios*** give up one's studies **II** *v/i* **1** hang (***de*** from) **2** TELEC hang up; ***¡no cuelgue!*** hold the line!; **colgarse** *v/r* **1** hang o.s. **2**: ***~ de algo*** hang from sth; ***~ de alguien*** hang onto s.o. **3** INFOR F freeze **4** *a telecomedia, pasatiempo etc* get hooked
colibrí *m* ZO hummingbird
cólico *m* MED colic
◇ **cólico gástrico** gastric colic; **cólico hepático** hepatic colic; **cólico nefrítico** renal colic
coliflor *f* cauliflower
coligarse ⟨1h⟩ *v/r* ☞ ***coaligarse***
colilla *f* cigarette butt *o Br tb* end
colín *m* GASTR bread stick
colina *f* hill
colinabo *m* kohlrabi
colindante *adj* adjoining
colindar ⟨1a⟩ *v/i* be adjacent (***con*** to)
colirio *m* MED eyedrops *pl*
coliseo *m* HIST colosseum, coliseum
colisión *f* collision; *fig* clash
◇ **colisión en cadena** multiple vehicle pile-up; **colisión frontal** head-on collision; **colisión múltiple** multiple vehicle pile-up
colisionar ⟨1a⟩ *v/i* collide (***con*** with); ***~ frontalmente*** collide head-on
colista *m* DEP bottom team in the league
colitis *f* MED colitis
collado *m* hill
collage *m* collage
collar *m* **1** necklace **2** *para animal* collar
collarín *m* MED surgical collar
colleras *fpl Chi* cuff links
colmado I *adj* overflowing (***de*** with); ***una cucharada -a*** a heaped spoonful **II** *m* grocery store, *Br* grocer's (shop)
colmar ⟨1a⟩ *v/t deseos, ambición etc* fulfill, *Br* fulfil; ***~ un vaso*** fill a glass to the brim; ***~ a alguien de elogios*** heap praise on s.o.
colmena *f* beehive
colmenar *m* apiary
colmenero *m*, **-a** *f* beekeeper
colmillo *m* ANAT eye tooth; *de perro* fang; *de elefante* tusk; *de rinoceronte* horn; ***escupir por el ~*** F brag; ***enseñar los ~s*** F show one's teeth
colmo *m*: ***¡es el ~!*** this is the last straw!; ***para ~*** to cap it all; ***para ~ de desgracias*** *o* ***de males*** to make matters worse
colocación *f* **1** positioning, placing **2** (*trabajo*) position
colocar ⟨1g⟩ *v/t* put, place; ***~ a alguien en un trabajo*** get s.o. a job; **colocarse** *v/r* **1** *de persona* position o.s.; ***se colocó a mi lado*** he stood next to me; ***se colocaron en primer lugar*** they moved into first place **2** F get plastered F; *con droga* get stoned F
colocón *m* F bender F; *con droga* high F
colofón *m fig* culmination; ***como ~*** to finish
coloide *m* QUÍM colloid
Colombia *f* Colombia
colombiano I *adj* Colombian **II** *m*, **-a** *f* Colombian
colombicultor *m*, **~a** *f* pigeon breeder
colombicultura *f* pigeon breeding
colombino *adj* of Columbus, Columbian
colombofilia *f* pigeon keeping
colombófilo *m*, **-a** *f* pigeon enthusiast, *Br* pigeon fancier
Colón Columbus
colón *m* FIN colon
colon *m* ANAT colon
colonia *f* **1** colony; ***la ~ venezolana en Washington*** the Venezuelan community in Washington **2** *perfume* cologne **3** *Méx* (*barrio*) district
◇ **colonia de verano** summer camp
colonial *adj* colonial; ***estilo ~*** colonial style
colonialismo *m* colonialism
colonialista *m/f* colonialist
colonización *f* colonization
colonizador *m*, **~a** *f* colonizer
colonizar ⟨1f⟩ *v/t* colonize

colono *m*, **-a** *f* **1** colonist **2** AGR tenant farmer
coloquial *adj* colloquial
coloquio *m* talk
color *m* color, *Br* colour; ***de ~*** black, colored, *Br* coloured; ***sacarle a alguien los ~es*** embarrass s.o., make s.o. blush; ***salirle a alguien los ~*** flush, blush; ***se puso de mil ~es*** he turned bright red; ***subido de ~*** risqué; ***mudar*** *o* ***cambiar de ~*** *fig* change color, go pale
◇ **color café** coffee-colored, *Br* coffee-coloured; *L.Am.* brown; **color complementario** complementary color *o Br* colour; **color local** local color, *Br* local colour
coloración *f* coloration
colorado *adj* red; ***ponerse ~*** blush
colorante *m* coloring, *Br* colouring
colorar ⟨1a⟩ *v/t* color, *Br* colour
coloratura *f* MÚS coloratura
colorear ⟨1a⟩ *v/t* color, *Br* colour; ***libro para ~*** coloring book, *Br* colouring book
colorete *m* blusher
colorido *m* colors *pl*, *Br* colours *pl*
colorín *m* **1** ZO goldfinch **2** (*color*) bright color *o Br* colour
colorterapia *f* color therapy, *Br* colour therapy
colosal *adj* colossal
coloso *m* colossus
columbrar ⟨1a⟩ *v/t* (*ver*) make out, glimpse; *fig* perceive
columna *f* column
◇ **columna de dirección** AUTO steering column
◇ **columna vertebral** ANAT spinal column
columnata *f* colonnade
columnista *m/f* columnist
columpiar ⟨1b⟩ *v/t* push; **columpiarse** *v/r* swing
columpio *m* swing
colutorio *m* MED mouthwash
colza *f* BOT rape
coma **I** *f* GRAM comma **II** *m* MED coma
comadre *f L.Am.* godmother
comadrear ⟨1a⟩ *v/i* F gossip
comadreja *f* **1** ZO weasel **2** *Arg* opossum
comadreo *m* gossip
comadrona *f* midwife
comandancia *f* **1** *distrito* command **2** (*cuartel*) command headquarters *sg o pl* **3** *Méx* police station
comandante *m* **1** MIL commander **2** *rango* major **3** AVIA captain **4** *Méx de policía* captain, *Br* superintendent
◇ **comandante en jefe** commander-in-chief
comandar ⟨1a⟩ *v/t* command
comanditario *adj* COM: ***socio ~*** silent partner, *Br* sleeping partner
comando *m* **1** commando **2** INFOR command
comarca *f* area
comarcal *adj* local
comarcano *adj* neighboring, *Br* neighbouring
comba *f* jump rope, *Br* skipping rope; ***jugar*** *o* ***saltar a la ~*** jump rope, *Br* skip; ***no perder ~*** not miss a trick
combar ⟨1a⟩ *v/t* bend; **combarse** *v/r* bend
combate *m* **1** *acción* combat; MIL engagement **2** DEP fight; ***fuera de ~*** out of action
combatiente *m* combatant
combatir ⟨3a⟩ *v/t* & *v/i* fight
combatividad *f* fighting spirit
combativo *adj* combative
combi *m Méx* minibus
combinación *f* **1** combination; ***~ numérica*** combination of numbers **2** *prenda* slip **3**: ***hacer ~*** TRANSP change
combinada *f* DEP combined (event)
combinado *m* **1** cocktail **2** GASTR ☞ ***plato***
combinar ⟨1a⟩ *v/t* combine; **combinarse** *v/r* get together
combinatorio *adj* combinatorial
combo *adj* bent
combustibilidad *f* combustibility
combustible **I** *adj* combustible **II** *m* fuel
◇ **combustible fósil** fossil fuel
combustión *f* combustion
comecocos *m/f inv* F con artist F
comedero *m* trough
comedia *f* **1** comedy; ***hacer ~*** *fig* put on an act **2** *L.Am.* (*telenovela*) soap
◇ **comedia de capa y espada** cloak-and-dagger drama (*seventeenth-century Spanish dramatic genre*); **comedia de costumbres** comedy of manners; **comedia de enredo** comedy of intrigue; **comedia musical** musical
comedianta *f* actress

comediante *m* actor
comedido *adj* moderate
comedimiento *m* moderation
comediógrafo *m*, **-a** *f* playwright
comedirse ⟨3l⟩ *v/r* show restraint (***en*** in)
comedón *m* MED blackhead
comedor **I** *adj*: ***es muy ~*** he's a big eater **II** *m* dining room
◇ **comedor universitario** refectory
comején *m* termite
comendador *m* HIST commander
comensal *m/f* diner
comentador *m*, **~a** *f* commentator
comentar ⟨1a⟩ *v/t* **1** *libro* comment on **2** (*mencionar*) comment, remark
comentario *m* **1** comment; ***¡sin ~s!*** no comment! **2**: **~s** *pl* gossip *sg*
◇ **comentario de texto** textual analysis
comentarista *m/f* commentator
comenzar ⟨1f & 1k⟩ *v/t* begin
comer ⟨2a⟩ **I** *v/t* eat; *a mediodía* have for lunch
II *v/i* eat; *a mediodía* have lunch; ***dar de ~ a alguien*** feed s.o.; ***no tienen qué ~*** they haven't a thing to eat; ***sin ~lo ni beberlo*** F all of a sudden
comerse *v/r* **1** *tb fig* eat up; ***~ de envidia*** be consumed with envy; ***está para comértela*** F she's really tasty F **2** *de color* fade **3**: ***se comió una palabra*** she missed out a word
comerciable *adj* marketable, saleable
comercial **I** *adj* commercial; *de negocios* business *atr*; ***el déficit ~*** the trade deficit **II** *m/f* representative **III** *m L.Am.* (*anuncio*) commercial
comercialización *f* marketing; *desp* commercialization
comercializar ⟨1f⟩ *v/t* market, sell; *desp* commercialize
comerciante *m/f* trader
◇ **comerciante al por mayor** wholesaler
◇ **comerciante al por menor** retailer
comerciar ⟨1b⟩ *v/i* trade (***con*** with; ***en*** in), do business (***con*** with)
comercio *m* **1** *actividad* trade; *fig* dealings *pl*; ***libre ~*** free trade **2** *local* store, shop
◇ **comercio al detalle** retail trade; **comercio electrónico** INFOR e-commerce; **comercio exterior** foreign trade; **comercio interior** domestic trade; **comercio al por mayor** wholesale trade; **comercio al por menor** retail trade; **comercio de ultramar** overseas trade
comestible **I** *adj* eatable, edible **II** *m* foodstuff; **~s** *pl* food *sg*
cometa **I** *m* comet **II** *f* kite
cometer ⟨2a⟩ *v/t* commit; *error* make
cometido *m* task
comezón *f* itch; ***sentir ~ por hacer algo*** F be itching to do sth F
comible *adj* F eatable
cómic *m* comic
comicastra *f* ham actress
comicastro *m* ham actor
comicidad *f* humor, *Br* humour, comic nature
comicios *mpl* elections *pl*
cómico **I** *adj* comical **II** *m*, **-a** *f* comedian
comida *f* **1** (*comestibles*) food **2** *ocasión* meal
◇ **comida basura** junk food; **comida de negocios** business lunch; **comida rápida** fast food; **comida de trabajo** working lunch
comidilla *f*: ***ser la ~ de*** be the talk of
comido **I** *part* ☞ ***comer*** **II** *adj*: ***estoy ~*** I've already eaten; ***llegó ~*** he had eaten before he arrived
comienzo *m* beginning; ***al ~***, ***en un ~*** at first, in the beginning; ***desde el*** *o* ***un ~*** from the start; ***a ~s de junio*** at the beginning of June
comillas *fpl* quotation marks, *Br* inverted commas; ***poner entre ~*** put in quotation marks *o Br* in inverted commas
comilón **I** *adj* greedy **II** *m*, **-ona** *f* big eater
comilona *f* F feast, blowout F
comino *m* BOT cumin; ***me importa un ~*** F I don't give a damn F; ***no vale un ~*** F it isn't worth anything
comisaría *f* precinct (house), *Br* police station
comisariado *m* POL commission
comisario *m* **1** commissioner; ***~ europeo*** European Commissioner **2** *de policía* captain, *Br* superintendent
comisión *f* **1** committee; *de gobierno* commission; ***~ parlamentaria*** parliamentary committee **2** (*recompensa*) commission; ***trabajar a ~*** work on com-

mission
◇ **Comisión Europea** European Commission
comisionado *m*, **-a** *f* commissioner
comisionar ⟨1a⟩ *v/t* commission
comisionista *m/f* commission agent
comiso *m* confiscation
comistrajo *m desp* terrible meal
comisura *f* ANAT: **~ *de los labios*** corner of the mouth
comité *m* committee
◇ **comité de empresa** *committee of workers that discusses industrial relations*, *Br* works council
comitiva *f* retinue
◇ **comitiva fúnebre** cortège, funeral procession
como **I** *adv* **1** as; **~ *amigo*** as a friend **2** (*aproximadamente*): ***había ~ cincuenta*** there were about fifty; ***hace ~ una hora*** about an hour ago **3**: ***así ~*** as well as **II** *conj* **1** if; **~ *si*** as if; **~ *si fuera tonto*** as if he were *o* was an idiot; **~ *no bebas vas a enfermar*** if you don't drink you'll get sick **2** *expresando causa* as, since; **~ *no llegó, me fui solo*** as *o* since she didn't arrive, I went by myself **3**: ***me gusta ~ habla*** I like the way he talks; **~ *quiera*** any way you want
cómo *adv* **1** how; ***¿cómo estás?*** how are you?; ***¿a ~?*** how much?; ***¿~ dice?*** what did you say?; ***no voy a ir - ¿~ que no?*** I'm not going - what do you mean, you're not going? **2** *en exclamaciones*: ***¡~ me gusta!*** I really like it; ***¡~ no!*** *L.Am.* of course!
cómoda *f* chest of drawers
comodidad *f* **1** comfort **2**: ***~es*** *pl* home comforts
comodín *m* **1** *en naipes* joker **2** INFOR wild card **3** *palabra* stand-in word
cómodo *adj* comfortable; ***¡póngase ~!*** make yourself at home, make yourself comfortable
comodón *adj* F **1** comfort-loving **2** (*perezoso*) idle
comodoro *m* MAR commodore
comoquiera *adv*: **~ *que*** however, in whatever way
comp. *abr* (= ***compárese***) cf (= confer)
compacidad *f* compactness
compactar ⟨1a⟩ *v/t* compact, compress
compacto *adj* compact
compadecer ⟨2d⟩ *v/t* feel sorry for; **compadecerse** *v/r* feel sorry (***de*** for)
compadre *m L.Am.* F buddy F
compadrear ⟨1a⟩ *v/i Arg* F brag
compadreo *m desp* nepotism, *Br* old--boy network
compadrito *m Arg* F show-off
compaginable *adj* compatible
compaginación *f* **1** combination **2** TIP makeup
compaginar ⟨1a⟩ *v/t* **1** *fig* combine (***con*** with) **2** TIP make up; **compaginarse** *v/r* tally (***con*** with)
compañerismo *m* comradeship
compañero *m*, **-a** *f* companion; *en una relación, un juego* partner
◇ **compañero de clase** classmate; **compañero de fatigas** fellow sufferer; **compañero de trabajo** coworker, colleague; **compañero de viaje** traveling companion, *Br* travelling companion
compañía *f* company; ***en ~ de*** with, in the company of; ***hacer ~ a alguien*** keep s.o. company; ***malas ~s*** *pl* bad company *sg*
◇ **compañía aérea** airline; **compañía chárter** charter airline; **compañía matriz** COM parent company; **compañía de navegación, compañía naviera** shipping line; **compañía de seguros** insurance company
comparable *adj* comparable
comparación *f* comparison; ***en ~ con*** in comparison with; ***no tiene (ni punto de) ~ con*** there's no comparison with
comparado *adj*: **~ *con*** compared with
comparar ⟨1a⟩ *v/t* compare (***con*** with, to)
comparativo **I** *adj* comparative **II** *m* GRAM comparative
comparecencia *f* JUR appearance
comparecer ⟨2d⟩ *v/i* appear
comparsa **I** *f* TEA: ***la ~*** the extras *pl* **II** *m/f* TEA extra; *fig* rank outsider
comparsería *f* TEA extras *pl*
compartimentar ⟨1a⟩ *v/t* compartmentalize
compartimento *m* FERR car, *Br* compartment
compartir ⟨3a⟩ *v/t* share (***con*** with)
compás *m* **1** MAT compass **2** MÚS rhythm; ***al ~*** to the beat; ***llevar el ~*** MÚS keep time; ***perder el ~*** lose the beat
◇ **compás de espera** MÚS bar rest; *fig*

temporary interruption; ***estar en un ~*** be on hold
compasión *f* compassion; ***sin ~*** without compassion
compasivo *adj* compassionate
compatibilidad *f* compatibility
compatibilizar ⟨1f⟩ *v/t* **1** reconcile; ***~ el negocio con el placer*** combine business with pleasure **2** INFOR make compatible
compatible *adj* INFOR compatible
compatriota *m/f* compatriot
compeler ⟨2a⟩ *v/t* compel
compendiar ⟨1b⟩ *v/t* summarize
compendio *m* summary
compendioso *adj* summarized
compenetración *f* understanding
compenetrado *adj*: ***están muy ~s*** they are very much in tune with each other
compenetrarse ⟨1a⟩ *v/r*: ***~ con alguien*** reach a good understanding with s.o.
compensación *f* compensation
compensador *adj* compensatory
compensar ⟨1a⟩ **I** *v/t* compensate (***por*** for) **II** *v/i fig* be worthwhile
competencia *f* **1** (*habilidad*) competence **2** *entre rivales* competition; ***hacer la ~ a alguien / algo*** compete with s.o. / sth **3** (*incumbencia*) area of responsibility, competency; ***eso no es de mi ~*** that's not my department **4** *L.Am.* DEP competition
◇ **competencia desleal** unfair competition
competente *adj* competent
competer ⟨2a⟩ *v/i*: ***~ a*** be the responsibility of
competición *f* DEP competition
competidor I *adj* rival **II** *m*, **~a** *f* competitor
competir ⟨3l⟩ *v/i* compete (***con*** with)
competitividad *f* competitiveness
competitivo *adj* competitive
compilación *f* compilation
compilador *m* INFOR compiler
compilar ⟨1a⟩ *v/t* compile
compincharse ⟨1a⟩ *v/r* F work together
compinche *m/f* F buddy F; *desp* crony F
compinchería *f*: ***hay ~ entre ellos*** they are planning *o* plotting something together
compite *vb* ☞ ***competir***
compito *vb* ☞ ***competir***
complacencia *f* **1** (*placer*) pleasure **2** (*tolerancia*) indulgence
complacer ⟨2x⟩ *v/t* please; **complacerse** *v/r* take pleasure (***en*** in)
complacido *adj* pleased
complaciente *adj* obliging, helpful
complejidad *f* complexity
complejo I *adj* complex **II** *m* PSI, *industrial etc* complex
◇ **complejo de Edipo** Oedipus complex; **complejo de inferioridad** inferiority complex; **complejo industrial** industrial complex; **complejo turístico** tourist resort
complementar ⟨1a⟩ *v/t* complement
complementario *adj* complementary
complemento *m* **1** complement **2** GRAM complement, object
◇ **complemento circunstancial** GRAM adverbial complement
◇ **complementos de moda** fashion accessories
completamente *adv* completely, totally
completar ⟨1a⟩ *v/t* complete
completo *adj* complete; *autobús, teatro* full; ***por ~*** completely; ***al ~*** whole, entire
complexión *f* constitution
complicación *f* complication
complicado *adj* complicated
complicar ⟨1g⟩ *v/t* **1** complicate **2**: ***~ a alguien en algo*** involve s.o. in sth; **complicarse** *v/r* get complicated; ***~ la vida*** make life *o* things difficult for o.s.
cómplice *m/f* accomplice
complicidad *f* complicity
complot *m* plot
complotar ⟨1a⟩ *v/i L.Am.* plot
componedor *m*, **~a** *f* mediator; ***amigable ~*** JUR arbitrator
componenda *f* shady deal
componente *m* component; ***~s de automóviles*** vehicle parts *o* components
componer ⟨2r⟩ *v/t* **1** make up, comprise **2** *sinfonía, poema etc* compose **3** *algo roto* fix, mend; **componerse** *v/r* **1** be made up (***de*** of) **2** *L.Am.* MED get better **3**: ***componérselas*** manage
comportamiento *m* behavior, *Br* behaviour
comportar ⟨1a⟩ *v/t* involve, entail; **comportarse** *v/r* behave
composición *f* composition

C

compositor *m*, **~a** *f* composer
compost *m* compost
compostura *f fig* composure
compota *f* compote
compotera *f* serving dish (for dessert)
compra *f* **1** *acción* purchase; ***hacer la ~***, ***ir a la ~*** do the shopping; ***ir de ~s*** go shopping **2** (*cosa comprada*) purchase, buy
◇ **compra a plazos** installment plan, *Br* hire purchase
comprador *m*, **~a** *f* buyer, purchaser
comprar ⟨1a⟩ *v/t* buy, purchase
compraventa *f* buying and selling; ***contrato de ~*** bill *o* deed of sale
comprender ⟨2a⟩ *v/t* **1** understand; ***hacerse ~*** make o.s. understood; ***~ mal*** misunderstand **2** (*abarcar*) include
comprensible *adj* understandable
comprensión *f* **1** understanding **2** *de texto*, *auditiva* comprehension
comprensivo *adj* understanding
compresa (higiénica) *f* sanitary napkin, *Br* sanitary towel
compresible *adj* compressible
compresión *f tb* INFOR compression
compresor *m* compressor
comprimido *m* MED pill
comprimir ⟨3a⟩ *v/t* compress; *fig* summarize
comprobable *adj* verifiable
comprobación *f* check
comprobador *m* TÉC tester
comprobante *m* **1** proof **2** (*recibo*) receipt
comprobar ⟨1m⟩ *v/t* **1** check **2** (*darse cuenta de*) realize
comprometer ⟨2a⟩ *v/t* **1** compromise **2** (*obligar*) commit; **comprometerse** *v/r* **1** promise (***a*** to) **2** *a una causa* commit o.s. **3** *de novios* get engaged
comprometido *adj* **1** committed **2**: ***estar ~ en algo*** be implicated in sth **3**: ***estar ~*** *de novios* be engaged
compromisario *m*, **-a** *f* delegate
compromiso *m* **1** commitment **2** (*obligación*) obligation; ***sin ~*** COM without commitment; ***soltero y sin ~*** F footloose and fancy-free **3** (*acuerdo*) agreement **4** (*apuro*) awkward situation **5**: ***~ (matrimonial)*** engagement
compuerta *f* sluice gate
compuesto **I** *adj* composed; ***estar ~ de*** be composed of **II** *m* compound
compulsa *f* **1** certification **2** (*copia*) certified copy
compulsar ⟨1a⟩ *v/t* certify
compulsión *f* PSI compulsion
compulsivo *adj* PSI compulsive
compunción *f* remorse, compunction
compungido *adj* remorseful
compungir ⟨3c⟩ *v/t* make sorry *o* sad; **compungirse** *v/r* feel sorry *o* sad
computable *adj*: ***ser ~ para algo*** count toward sth
computación *f L.Am.* **1** calculation **2** INFOR computer science
computador *m*, **computadora** *f L.Am.* computer
◇ **computadora de a bordo** AUTO on-board computer; **computadora de escritorio** desktop (computer); **computadora de mano** palmtop; **computadora personal** personal computer; **computadora portátil** laptop
computar ⟨1a⟩ *v/t* count; (*calcular*) calculate
computarizar ⟨1f⟩ *v/t* computerize
cómputo *m* **1** count **2** (*cálculo*) calculation
comulgante *m/f* REL communicant
comulgar ⟨1h⟩ *v/i* REL take communion; ***~ con alguien*** (***en algo***) *fig* F think the same way as s.o. (on sth); ***~ con ruedas de molino*** F swallow anything
común **I** *adj* common; ***poco ~*** unusual, rare; ***por lo ~*** generally; ***en ~*** in common; ***tener algo en ~*** have sth in common **II** *m*: ***el ~ de las gentes*** the common man
comuna *f* **1** commune **2** *L.Am.* (*población*) town
comunal *adj* **1** communal **2**: ***elecciones ~es*** *pl L.Am.* municipal elections
comunicación *f* **1** communication **2** TRANSP link; TELEC connection, link; ***comunicaciones*** *pl* communications **3**: ***estar en ~ con alguien*** be in touch with s.o.
comunicado **I** *adj* connected; ***el lugar está bien ~*** the place has good transport links **II** *m* POL press release, communiqué
comunicante *m/f* informant
comunicar ⟨1g⟩ **I** *v/t* **1** TRANSP connect, link **2**: ***~ algo a alguien*** inform s.o. of sth **II** *v/i* **1** communicate **2** TELEC be

busy, *Br tb* be engaged; ***está comunicando*** it's busy, *Br* it's engaged; **comunicarse** *v/r* communicate
comunicativo *adj* communicative
comunicología *f* communication(s) theory
comunidad *f* community; ***~ sucesoria o hereditaria*** heirs *pl*
◇ **comunidad autónoma** autonomous region
comunión *f* **1** REL communion; ***hacer la primera ~*** make one's first communion **2**: ***~ de ideología*** common ideology
comunismo *m* Communism
comunista *m/f & adj* Communist
comunitario *adj* POL EU *atr*, Community *atr*
comúnmente *adv* commonly
con *prp* **1** with; ***voy ~ ellos*** I'm going with them; ***pan ~ mantequilla*** bread and butter; ***estar ~ alguien*** *tb fig* be with s.o. **2**: ***~ todo eso*** in spite of all that; ***~ tal de que*** provided that, as long as; ***~ hacer eso*** by doing that; ***para ~ alguien*** to s.o., toward s.o.; ***~ este calor*** in this heat; ***¡~ lo que he hecho por él!*** after all I've done for him! **3**: ***ser amable ~ alguien*** be kind to s.o.
conato *m*: ***~ de violencia*** minor outbreak of violence; ***~ de incendio*** small fire
concatenación *f* linking
concatenar ⟨1a⟩ *v/t* link together; **concatenarse** *v/r fig* come together, coincide
concavidad *f* concavity
cóncavo *adj* concave
concebible *adj* conceivable
concebir ⟨3l⟩ *v/t* conceive
conceder ⟨2a⟩ *v/t* concede; *entrevista, permiso* give; *premio* award; *importancia* attach
concejal *m*, **~a** *f* councilor, *Br* councillor
concejalía *f* council seat *o* post
concejo *m* council
concentración *f* concentration; *de personas* gathering
◇ **concentración de masas** mass gathering
concentrado **I** *m* concentrate **II** *adj*: ***estar ~ en algo*** be concentrating on sth
concentrar ⟨1a⟩ *v/t* concentrate; **concentrarse** *v/r* **1** concentrate (***en*** on) **2** *de gente* gather
concéntrico *adj* concentric
concepción *f* BIO, *fig* conception; ***la Inmaculada Concepción*** REL the Immaculate Conception
concepto *m* **1** concept **2** (*opinión*): ***tener un alto ~ de alguien*** think highly of s.o. **3** (*condición*): ***bajo ningún ~*** on no account; ***bajo todos los ~s*** in every way, in every respect **4**: ***en ~ de algo*** COM (in payment) for sth
conceptual *adj* conceptual
conceptuar ⟨1e⟩ *v/t* regard; ***~ a alguien de*** regard s.o. as
concerniente *adj*: ***~ a*** concerning, regarding; ***en lo ~ a*** with regard to
concernir ⟨3i⟩ *v/i* concern; ***en lo que concierne a X*** as far as X is concerned
concertación *f* POL agreement
concertar ⟨1k⟩ **I** *v/t* **1** *cita* arrange **2** *precio* agree **3** *esfuerzos* coordinate **II** *v/i* agree; **concertarse** *v/r* work together
concertino *m/f* MÚS concertmaster, *Br* leader (of the orchestra)
concertista *m/f* MÚS soloist
concesión *f* **1** concession; ***hacer concesiones*** make concessions **2** COM dealership
concesionario *m*, **-a** *f* dealer
concha *f* ZO shell; ***meterse en su ~*** *fig* withdraw into one's shell
conchabar ⟨1a⟩ *v/t L.Am. trabajador* hire; **conchabarse** *v/r* F plot
conciencia *f* conscience; ***a ~*** conscientiously; ***con plena ~ de*** fully conscious of; ***en ~*** in all conscience; ***tener la ~ tranquila*** have a clear conscience; ***tener buena / mala ~*** have a clear / guilty conscience; ***tener o tomar ~ de algo*** be / become aware of sth
concienciación *f* consciousness-raising
concienciar ⟨1b⟩ *v/t*: ***~ a alguien de algo*** make s.o. aware of sth; **concienciarse** *v/r* realize (***de*** sth)
concientizar ⟨1f⟩ *L.Am.* ☞ ***concienciar***
concienzudo *adj* conscientious
concierto *m* MÚS concert; *fig* agreement; ***sin orden ni ~*** without rhyme or reason
conciliable *adj* reconcilable
conciliábulo *m* secret meeting

C

conciliación *f* JUR conciliation, reconciliation
conciliador *adj* conciliatory
conciliar ⟨1b⟩ *v/t* **1** reconcile **2**: *~ el sueño* get to sleep
concilio *m* council
concisión *f* conciseness
conciso *adj* concise
concitar ⟨1a⟩ *v/t* arouse, incite; **concitarse** *v/r* gain
conciudadano *m*, **-a** *f* fellow citizen
cónclave *m* **1** REL conclave **2** (*reunión*) meeting, *hum* conclave
concluir ⟨3g⟩ *v/t & v/i* conclude
conclusión *f* conclusion; *en ~* in short; *llegar a la ~ de que …* come to the conclusion that …
concluso *part* ☞ *concluir*
concluyente *adj* conclusive
concomerse ⟨2a⟩ *v/r fig*: *se concome de envidia* he is consumed with *o* eaten up with envy
concomitante *adj* concomitant
concordancia *f* agreement
concordar ⟨1m⟩ **I** *v/t* reconcile **II** *v/i* agree (*con* with)
concordato *m* concordat
concorde *adj*: *estar ~s* agree, be in agreement
concordia *f* harmony, concord
concreción *f* **1** precision **2** GEOL concretion **3** MED stone
concretamente *adv* specifically, precisely
concretar ⟨1a⟩ *v/t* **1** specify **2** (*hacer concreto*) realize; **concretarse** *v/r* **1** materialize; *de esperanzas* be fulfilled **2**: *~ a* limit o.s. to
concretizar ⟨1f⟩ *v/t* fix, set
concreto **I** *adj* **1** specific; *en ~* specifically; *nada en ~* nothing specific **2** (*no abstracto*) concrete **II** *m L.Am.* concrete
concubina *f* concubine
conculcar ⟨1g⟩ *v/t derecho etc* infringe
concupiscencia *f* lust
concupiscente *adj* lustful
concurrencia *f* **1** audience **2** *de circunstancias* combination
concurrente **I** *adj* concurrent **II** *m/f*: *los ~s* the audience
concurrido *adj* crowded
concurrir ⟨3a⟩ *v/i*: *~ a* attend
concursante *m/f* competitor
concursar ⟨1a⟩ *v/i* compete
concurso *m* **1** competition **2** COM tender; *sacar a ~* put out to tender
◇ **concurso de acreedores** JUR creditors' meeting
◇ **concurso-oposición** competitive exam
condado *m* county
condal *adj* ☞ *ciudad*
conde *m* count
condecoración *f* decoration
condecorar ⟨1a⟩ *v/t* decorate
condena *f* **1** JUR sentence **2** (*desaprobación*) condemnation
condenable *adj* reprehensible
condenación *f* REL damnation
condenado **I** *adj* **1** destined, doomed (*a* to) **2** JUR convicted; *~ a muerte* condemned to death **3** REL damned **4** (*maldito*) F damn F **II** *m*, **-a** *f* **1** prisoner **2** REL one of the damned; *los ~s* the damned *pl*; *como un ~ fig* F like a maniac *o* lunatic F
condenar ⟨1a⟩ *v/t* **1** JUR sentence (*a* to) **2** (*desaprobar*) condemn; **condenarse** *v/r* REL be damned
condenatorio *adj* condemnatory
condensación *f* condensation
condensado *adj* condensed
condensador *m* condenser
condensar ⟨1a⟩ *v/t* **1** condense **2** *libro* abridge; **condensarse** *v/r* condense
condesa *f* countess
condescendencia *f* condescension
condescender ⟨2g⟩ *v/i* condescend (*a* to); *~ en hacer algo* agree to do sth
condescendiente *adj actitud* accommodating; *desp* condescending
condición *f* **1** condition; *a ~ de que* on condition that; *~ previa* precondition; *sin condiciones* with no conditions attached **2** (*situación, estado*): *estar en condiciones de* be in a position to; *~ física* physical condition; *estar en buenas / malas condiciones* be in good / bad condition; *estar en condiciones* be fit
condicional **I** *adj* conditional **II** *m* GRAM conditional
condicionante **I** *adj* determining **II** *m* determinant, determining factor
condicionar ⟨1a⟩ *v/t*: *~ algo en* make sth conditional on
condimentar ⟨1a⟩ *v/t* flavor, *Br* flavour

condimento *m* seasoning
condiscípulo *m*, **-a** *f en universidad* fellow student; *en colegio* fellow student, *Br* fellow pupil
condolencia *f*: ***una carta de ~*** a letter of condolence; ***expresar sus ~s*** express one's condolences
condolerse ⟨2h⟩ *v/r* sympathize (***de*** with)
condominio *m* **1** JUR joint ownership **2** *L.Am.* apartment building, *Br* block of flats
condón *m* condom
condonación *f* writing off, cancellation
condonar ⟨1a⟩ *v/t* condone
cóndor *m* ZO condor
conducción *f* **1** AUTO driving **2** *de calor, electricidad* conduction **3** (*tuberías*) piping; (*cables*) cables *pl*, cabling
conducir ⟨3o⟩ **I** *v/t* **1** *vehículo* drive **2** (*dirigir*) lead (***a*** to); ***esto no conduce a nada*** this is getting us nowhere **3** EL, TÉC conduct **4** *programa de TV, radio* host **5** MÚS conduct **II** *v/i* **1** drive **2** *de camino* lead (***a*** to); **conducirse** *v/r* conduct o.s. *fml*, behave (o.s.)
conducta *f* conduct, behavior, *Br* behaviour
conductibilidad *f* FÍS conductivity
conducto *m* pipe; *fig* channel; ***por ~ de*** through
◇ **conducto biliar** bile duct
conductor I *adj* **1** guiding **2** FÍS conductive **II** *m*, **~a** *f* driver **III** *m* FÍS conductor
◇ **conductor de orquesta** *L.Am.* conductor
condujo *vb* ☞ ***conducir***
conectador *m* EL connector
conectar ⟨1a⟩ **I** *v/t* **1** connect, link **2** EL connect; ***~ a tierra*** ground, *Br* earth **II** *v/i* connect; **conectarse** *v/r* INFOR connect (to the Internet), go on line (to the Internet)
conejera *f* burrow
conejillo *m*: ***~ de Indias*** *tb fig* guinea pig
conejo *m* rabbit
conexión *f tb* EL connection; ***~ a Internet*** Internet connection; ***~ telefónica*** INFOR dial-up connection
◇ **conexión a la red** EL mains connection
conexo *adj* connected
confabulación *f* plot, conspiracy
confabularse ⟨1a⟩ *v/r* plot, conspire
confección *f* **1** *de aparatos* making **2** *de vestidos* dressmaking; *de trajes* tailoring
confeccionar ⟨1a⟩ *v/t* **1** *aparatos* make **2** *plan* devise
confeccionista *m/f* clothes manufacturer
confederación *f* confederation
confederarse ⟨1a⟩ *v/r* form a confederation, confederate
conferencia *f* **1** lecture **2** (*reunión*) conference **3** TELEC long-distance call
◇ **conferencia de cobro revertido** TELEC collect call, *Br tb* reverse-charge call
◇ **conferencia de prensa** press conference
conferenciante *m/f* lecturer
conferenciar ⟨1b⟩ *v/i* hold talks
conferencista *m/f L.Am.* lecturer
conferir ⟨3i⟩ *v/t* award
confesar ⟨1k⟩ **I** *v/t* REL confess; *delito* confess to, admit **II** *v/i* JUR confess; **confesarse** *v/r* confess; (*declararse*) admit to being
confesión *f* confession
confesional *adj* denominational
confes(i)onario *m* confessional
confeso *adj* self-confessed
confesor *m* REL confessor
confeti *m* confetti
confiabilidad *f L.Am. esp* TÉC reliability
confiable *adj L.Am.* reliable
confiado *adj* trusting
confianza *f* **1** confidence; ***~ en sí mismo*** self-confidence **2** (*amistad*): ***de ~*** *persona* trustworthy; ***amigo de ~*** good friend; ***en ~*** in confidence **3**: ***tomarse demasiadas ~s*** take liberties
confiar ⟨1c⟩ **I** *v/t* **1** *secreto* confide (***a*** to) **2**: ***~ algo a alguien*** entrust s.o. with sth, entrust sth to s.o. **II** *v/i* **1** trust (***en*** in) **2** (*estar seguro*) be confident (***en*** of); **confiarse** *v/r*: ***~ a alguien*** confide in s.o.
confidencia *f* confidence
confidencial *adj* confidential
confidencialidad *f* confidentiality
confidente I *m* **1** (*soplón*) informer **2** (*amigo*) confidant **II** *f* **1** (*soplón*) informer **2** (*amiga*) confidante
configuración *f* **1** configuration **2** IN-

FOR set-up, configuration
configurar ⟨1a⟩ *v/t* **1** shape **2** INFOR set up, configure; **configurarse** *v/r* form
confín *m lit*: ***los confines de la tierra*** the ends of the earth; ***los confines del horizonte*** the horizon
confinamiento *m* confinement
confinar ⟨1a⟩ **I** *v/t* confine **II** *v/i* border (***con*** on); **confinarse** *v/r* shut o.s. away
confirmación *f* confirmation
confirmar ⟨1a⟩ *v/t* confirm; **confirmarse** *v/r* be confirmed
confirmatorio *adj* confirmatory
confiscación *f* confiscation
confiscar ⟨1g⟩ *v/t* confiscate
confitar ⟨1a⟩ *v/t* crystallize
confite *m* dragée
confitería *f* confectioner's
confitero *m*, **-a** *f* confectioner
confitura *f* preserve
conflagración *f* **1** conflagration **2** (*guerra*) war
◇ **conflagración mundial** world war
conflictividad *f* controversial nature
conflictivo *adj* **1** *época*, *zona* troubled **2** *persona* troublemaking
conflicto *m* conflict
confluencia *f de ríos* confluence; *de calles* intersection, *Br* junction
confluente *adj* confluent
confluir ⟨3g⟩ *v/i* meet, converge
conformación *f* shape
conformar ⟨1a⟩ **I** *v/t* **1** (*constituir*) make up **2** (*dar forma a*) shape **II** *v/i* agree (***con*** with); **conformarse** *v/r* make do (***con*** with)
conforme I *adj* **1** satisfied (***con*** with) **2**: ***¡~!*** agreed!; ***estar ~ con*** agree with **3**: ***ser ~ a*** comply with **II** *prp*: ***~ a*** in accordance with **III** *conj* as
conformidad *f* **1** (*acuerdo*) agreement; ***de*** *o* ***en ~ con*** in accordance with **2** (*consentimiento*) consent
conformismo *m* conformity
conformista I *adj* conformist **II** *m/f* conformist
confort *m* comfort
confortabilidad *f* comfort
confortable *adj* comfortable
confortante *adj* comforting
confortar ⟨1a⟩ *v/t*: ***~ a alguien*** comfort s.o.
confraternidad *f* fraternity
confraternizar ⟨1f⟩ *v/i* fraternize
confrontación *f* confrontation
confrontar ⟨1a⟩ *v/t* **1** compare **2** *a personas* bring face to face **3** *peligro, desafío* face up to; **confrontarse** *v/r*: ***~ con*** face up to
confundido *adj* confused
confundir ⟨3a⟩ *v/t* **1** confuse **2** (*equivocar*) mistake (***con*** for); **confundirse** *v/r* **1** make a mistake; ***~ de calle*** get the wrong street **2** *fig* mingle with; ***~ entre la gente*** disappear into the crowd
confusión *f* confusion
confuso *adj* confused
congelación *f* **1** freezing; ***~ de precios / de salarios*** price / wage freeze **2** MED frostbite
congelado *adj* frozen; ***alimentos ~s*** frozen food *sg*
congelador *m* freezer
congelar ⟨1a⟩ *v/t* freeze; **congelarse** *v/r* freeze
congénere *m/f*: ***este chico y sus ~s*** this boy and others like him
congeniar ⟨1b⟩ *v/i* get on well (***con*** with)
congénito *adj* congenital
congestión *f* MED congestion
◇ **congestión del tráfico** traffic congestion
congestionar ⟨1a⟩ *v/t* congest; **congestionarse** *v/r* MED become congested
conglomerado *m* GEOL conglomerate
conglomerarse ⟨1a⟩ *v/r* conglomerate
Congo *m* Congo
congoja *f* anguish
congoleño, congolés I *adj* Congolese **II** *m*, **-a** *f*, **-esa** *f* Congolese
congraciarse ⟨1b⟩ *v/r* ingratiate o.s. (***con*** with)
congratulaciones *fpl* congratulations
congratular ⟨1a⟩ *v/t* congratulate; **congratularse** *v/r*: ***~ de*** *o* ***por algo*** congratulate o.s. on sth
congregación *f* REL congregation
congregar ⟨1h⟩ *v/t* bring together; **congregarse** *v/r* congregate, assemble
congresal *m/f L.Am.*, **congresista** *m/f* conference *o* convention delegate, conventioneer
congreso *m* **1** conference, convention **2**: ***Congreso*** *en EE.UU.* Congress
◇ **Congreso de los diputados** *lower house of Spanish parliament*

C

congrio *m* ZO conger eel
congruencia *f* **1** consistency **2** MAT congruence
congruente *adj* **1** consistent **2** MAT congruent
cónico *adj* conical; ***sección -a*** conic section
conífera *f* BOT conifer
conjetura *f* conjecture
conjeturar ⟨1a⟩ *v/t* conjecture
conjugación *f* **1** GRAM conjugation **2** *fig* combination
conjugar ⟨1h⟩ *v/t* **1** GRAM conjugate **2** *fig* combine
conjunción *f* GRAM conjunction
conjuntado *adj* coordinated, matching
conjuntamente *adv* jointly
conjuntar ⟨1a⟩ *v/t* coordinate
conjuntiva *f* ANAT conjunctiva
conjuntivitis *f* MED conjunctivitis
conjuntivo *adj* **1** GRAM conjunctive **2** ANAT connective
conjunto I *adj* joint **II** *m* **1** *de personas, objetos* collection; ***en ~*** as a whole **2** *de prendas* outfit **3** MAT set
conjura *f*, **conjuración** *f* plot, conspiracy
conjurado *m*, **-a** *f* plotter, conspirator
conjurar ⟨1a⟩ **I** *v/i* plot, conspire **II** *v/t* **1** *espíritu* exorcise **2** *peligro* ward off; **conjurarse** *v/r* plot, conspire
conjuro *m* spell
conllevar ⟨1a⟩ *v/t* entail
conmemoración *f* commemoration; ***en ~ de algo*** to commemorate sth, in commemoration of sth
conmemorar ⟨1a⟩ *v/t* commemorate
conmemorativo *adj* commemorative
conmigo *pron* with me
conminar ⟨1a⟩ *v/t*: ***~ a alguien a hacer algo*** order s.o. to do sth
conminatorio *adj* threatening
conmiseración *f* commiseration
conmoción *f* **1** shock **2** (*agitación*) upheaval
◇ **conmoción cerebral** concussion
conmocionar ⟨1a⟩ *v/t* shock
conmovedor *adj* moving
conmover ⟨2h⟩ *v/t* move; **conmoverse** *v/r* be moved
conmutación *f* **1** JUR commutation **2** EL, INFOR switching
conmutador *m* **1** EL switch **2** *L.Am.* TELEC switchboard
conmutar ⟨1a⟩ *v/t* **1** exchange **2** JUR commute **3** EL switch
connatural *adj* innate; ***ser ~ a alguien*** be inherent in s.o.
connivencia *f* JUR connivance, collusion; ***en ~ con*** in collusion with
connotación *f* connotation
connotar ⟨1a⟩ *v/t* connote, have connotations of
cono *m tb* GASTR cone
conocedor I *adj*: ***ser ~ de*** know about **II** *m*, **~a** *f* expert (***de*** on)
conocer ⟨2d⟩ **I** *v/t* **1** know; ***dar a ~*** make known; ***darse a ~*** reveal one's identity; *de artista* become famous **2** *por primera vez* meet **3** *tristeza, amor etc* experience, know **4** (*reconocer*) recognize **II** *v/i*: ***~ de*** know about
conocerse *v/r* **1** know each other **2** *por primera vez* meet each other **3** *a sí mismo* know o.s. **4**: ***se conoce que*** it seems that
conocido I *adj* well-known **II** *m*, **-a** *f* acquaintance
conocimiento *m* **1** knowledge; ***con ~ de causa*** *hacer algo* fully aware of the consequences; ***poner alguien en ~ de algo*** inform s.o. of sth; ***para su ~*** for your information; **~s** *pl* (*nociones*) knowledge *sg* **2** MED consciousness; ***perder el ~*** lose consciousness; ***sin ~*** unconscious; ***recobrar el ~*** regain consciousness
◇ **conocimientos generales** general knowledge *sg*
conque *conj* so
conquista *f* conquest
conquistador I *adj* conquering **II** *m*, **~a** *f* conqueror **III** *m* HIST conquistador
conquistar ⟨1a⟩ *v/t* conquer; *persona* win over
consabido *adj* usual
consagración *f* REL consecration
consagrado *adj* REL consecrated; *fig* acclaimed
consagrar ⟨1a⟩ *v/t* **1** REL consecrate **2** (*hacer famoso*) make famous **3** *vida* devote; **consagrarse** *v/r* **1** devote o.s. (***a*** to) **2** *como escritor etc* establish o.s.
consanguíneo *adj*: ***pariente ~*** blood relation
consanguinidad *f* blood relationship
consciencia *f* ☞ ***conciencia***
consciente *adj* **1** MED conscious **2**: ***~ de***

aware of, conscious of; ***ser ~ de algo*** be aware *o* conscious of sth

C

conscripción *f* MIL draft, *Br* conscription

conscripto *m* draftee, *Br* conscript

consecución *f* achievement, attainment

consecuencia *f* consequence; ***a ~ de*** as a result of; ***en ~*** consequently; ***pagar las ~s*** take *o* pay the consequences

consecuente *adj* consistent

consecuentemente *adv* consequently

consecutivo *adj* **1** consecutive; ***tres años ~s*** three years in a row **2** GRAM consecutive

conseguido *adj* successful

conseguir ⟨3l & 3d⟩ *v/t* **1** get; *objetivo* achieve **2**: ***~ hacer algo*** manage to do sth

consejería *f Esp* ministry, department; *de ayuntamiento* department

consejero *m*, **-a** *f* **1** adviser **2** COM, *de ayuntamiento* director **3** *Esp* minister ◇ **consejero matrimonial** marriage guidance counselor, *Br* marriage guidance counsellor

consejo *m* **1** piece of advice; ***~s*** *pl* advice *sg* **2**: ***el Consejo de Seguridad de la ONU*** the UN Security Council ◇ **consejo de administración** board of directors; **consejo de guerra** court-martial; **consejo de ministros** *grupo* cabinet; *reunión* cabinet meeting

consenso *m* consensus; ***llegar a un ~*** reach a consensus

consensuar ⟨1d⟩ *v/t* reach a consensus on

consentido *adj* spoiled, spoilt

consentimiento *m* consent

consentir ⟨3i⟩ **I** *v/t* **1** allow **2** *a niño* indulge **II** *v/i*: ***~ en algo*** agree to sth

conserje *m/f* superintendent, super F, *Br* caretaker

conserjería *f* superintendent's *o* super's F office, *Br* caretaker's office

conserva *f*: ***en ~*** canned, *Br* tinned; ***~s*** *pl* canned *o Br* tinned food *sg*

conservación *f* **1** *de alimentos* preservation **2** *de edificios, especies* conservation

conservacionista *m/f* conservationist

conservado *adj*: ***bien ~*** *persona* well preserved

conservador **I** *adj* conservative **II** *m*, **~a** *f* **1** *de museo* curator **2** POL conservative

conservadurismo *m* conservatism

conservante *m* preservative

conservar ⟨1a⟩ *v/t* **1** conserve **2** *alimento* preserve; **conservarse** *v/r* **1** *de costumbres, edificio etc* survive, remain **2** *de fruta* keep

conservatorio *m* conservatory

conservero **I** *adj* canning *atr*; ***industria -a*** canning industry **II** *m*, **-a** *f* canner

considerable *adj* considerable

consideración *f* **1** consideration; ***en ~ a*** out of consideration for; ***tener*** *o* ***tomar en ~*** take into consideration; ***falta de ~*** lack of consideration **2**: ***de ~*** *herida* serious

considerado *adj* considerate

considerar ⟨1a⟩ *v/t* consider; **considerarse** *v/r* consider o.s.

consigna *f* **1** order **2** *de equipaje* baggage checkroom, *Br* left luggage ◇ **consigna automática** baggage lockers *pl*, *Br* left-luggage lockers *pl*

consignación *f* COM consignment

consignar ⟨1a⟩ *v/t* consign

consignatario *m*, **-a** *f* consignee

consigo *pron* (*con el, con ella*) with him / her; (*con ellos, con ellas*) with them; (*con usted, con ustedes*) with you; (*con uno*) with you, with one *fml*

consiguiente *adj* consequent; ***por ~*** and so, therefore

consistencia *f* consistency

consistente *adj* **1** consistent **2** (*sólido*) solid

consistir ⟨3a⟩ *v/i* consist (***en*** of)

consistorial *adj* council; ***casa ~*** town hall

consocio *m*, **-a** *f* fellow member

consola *f* INFOR console ◇ **consola de mezclas** mixing panel *o* console

consolación *f* consolation

consolador **I** *adj* consoling **II** *m* dildo

consolar ⟨1m⟩ *v/t* console; **consolarse** *v/r* take comfort

consolidación *f* consolidation

consolidar ⟨1a⟩ *v/t* consolidate; **consolidarse** *v/r* strengthen

consomé *m* GASTR consommé

consonancia *f*: ***en ~ con*** in keeping with

consonante **I** *adj*: ***~ con*** in keeping with

II *f* consonant
consorcio *m* consortium
consorte *m/f* spouse
conspicuo *adj* eminent
conspiración *f* conspiracy
conspirador *m*, **~a** *f* conspirator
conspirar ⟨1a⟩ *v/i* conspire
constancia *f* **1** constancy **2**: ***dejar ~ de*** leave a record of; ***tengo ~ de que*** I have evidence *o* proof that
constante I *adj* constant **II** *f* MAT constant
◇ **constantes vitales** MED vital signs
constantemente *adv* constantly
constar ⟨1a⟩ *v/i* **1** be recorded; ***hacer ~*** put on record; ***para que conste*** for the record **2**: ***~ de*** consist of **3**: ***me consta que*** I know for a fact that
constatación *f* verification
constatar ⟨1a⟩ *v/t* verify
constelación *f* AST constellation
consternación *f* consternation, dismay
consternado *adj* dismayed
consternar ⟨1a⟩ *v/t* dismay
constipado I *adj*: ***estar ~*** have a cold **II** *m* cold
constiparse ⟨1a⟩ *v/r* get a cold
constitución *f* constitution
constitucional *adj* constitutional
constituir ⟨3g⟩ *v/t* **1** constitute, make up **2** *empresa, organismo* set up; **constituirse** *v/r* **1** (*reunirse*) meet **2**: ***~ en algo*** (*convertirse*) become sth
constitutivo *adj* constituent
constituyente *adj* POL constituent
constreñir ⟨3h & 3l⟩ *v/t* **1** constrain, oblige **2** (*limitar*) restrict; **constreñirse** *v/r* restrict o.s.
constricción *f* constriction
construcción *f* **1** *actividad, sector* construction; ***~ naval*** shipbuilding **2** (*edificio*) building
◇ **construcción de la frase** sentence construction
constructivo *adj* constructive
constructor *m*, **~a** *f* builder
construir ⟨3g⟩ *v/t* build, construct
consuegra *f mother of one's son- / daughter-in-law*
consuegro *m father of one's son- / daughter-in-law*
consuelo *m* consolation
consuetudinario *adj* **1** habitual, customary **2**: ***derecho ~*** common law
cónsul *m/f* consul
◇ **cónsul general** consul general
◇ **cónsul honorario** honorary consul
consulado *m* consulate
consular *adj* consular
consulta *f* **1** consultation **2** MED *local* office, *Br* surgery; ***pasar ~*** have office hours, *Br* have a surgery
consultar ⟨1a⟩ *v/t* consult; ***~ algo en el diccionario*** look sth up in the dictionary
consultivo *adj* consultative
consultor I *adj*: ***empresa -a*** consulting firm, consultancy **II** *m*, **~a** *f* consultant
consultoría *f* consultancy
consultorio *m* MED office, *Br* surgery
consumación *f* **1** JUR commission **2** *de matrimonio* consummation
consumado *adj* consummate
consumar ⟨1a⟩ *v/t* **1** complete, finish **2** *crimen* carry out **3** *matrimonio* consummate
consumición *f* **1** consumption **2**: ***pago yo la ~*** *en bar* I'll pay, I'll get the drinks
consumido *adj* drawn, haggard
consumidor *m*, **~a** *f* COM consumer
consumir ⟨3a⟩ *v/t & v/i* consume; ***~ preferentemente antes de …*** COM best before …; **consumirse** *v/r* **1** *por enfermedad* waste away **2** *por envidia* be consumed
consumismo *m* consumerism
consumista *adj* consumer *atr*
consumo *m* consumption; ***de bajo ~*** economical; ***artículo de gran ~*** high-volume item
consunción *f* MED consumption
consustancial *adj* REL consubstantial
contabilidad *f* accountancy; ***llevar la ~*** do the accounts
◇ **contabilidad por partida doble** double-entry bookkeeping
◇ **contabilidad por partida simple** single-entry bookkeeping
contabilizar ⟨1f⟩ *v/t* enter
contable I *adj* countable **II** *m/f* accountant
contactar ⟨1a⟩ *v/i*: ***~ con alguien*** contact s.o.
contacto *m* **1** *tb* EL contact **2** AUTO ignition **3**: ***ponerse en ~*** get in touch (***con*** with)
contado I *m*: ***al ~*** in cash **II** *adj*: ***~s*** few; ***-as veces*** seldom

contador I *m* meter **II** *m*, **~a** *f L.Am.* accountant
◇ **contador público** *L.Am.* certified public accountant, *Br* chartered accountant
contaduría *f L.Am.* accountancy
contagiar ⟨1b⟩ *v/t*: ***~ la gripe a alguien*** give s.o. the flu; ***nos contagió su entusiasmo*** he infected us with his enthusiasm; **contagiarse** *v/r* become infected
contagio *m* contagion
contagioso *adj* contagious
contaminación *f de agua etc* contamination; *de río, medio ambiente* pollution; ***residuos de baja ~*** low-level waste
◇ **contaminación acústica** noise pollution; **contaminación ambiental** environmental pollution; **contaminación atmosférica** air pollution; **contaminación radiactiva** radioactive contamination
contaminante I *adj* polluting; ***no ~*** non-polluting, non-contaminating **II** *m* pollutant
contaminar ⟨1a⟩ *v/t agua etc* contaminate; *río, medio ambiente* pollute; *fig* corrupt; **contaminarse** *v/r* become contaminated
contante *adj*: ***pagar en dinero ~ y sonante*** pay hard cash
contar ⟨1m⟩ **I** *v/t* **1** count **2** (*narrar*) tell; ***¡a quién se lo vas a ~!, ¡me lo vas a ~ a mí!*** you're telling me!; ***¿qué (me) cuentas?*** what's new? **II** *v/i* **1** count **2**: ***~ con*** count on
contemplación *f*: ***sin contemplaciones*** without ceremony
contemplar ⟨1a⟩ *v/t* **1** (*mirar*) look at, contemplate **2** *posibilidad* consider
contemplativo *adj* contemplative
contemporáneo I *adj* contemporary **II** *m*, **-a** *f* contemporary
contemporizador *adj* accommodating
contemporizar ⟨1f⟩ *v/i*: ***~ con alguien*** come to an arrangement with s.o., compromise with s.o.
contención *f* containment
contencioso *adj* JUR contentious; ***asunto ~*** JUR subject of litigation
contender ⟨2g⟩ *v/i* **1** fight, struggle **2** DEP compete
contendiente *m/f* contender
contenedor *m* TRANSP container
◇ **contenedor de basura** dumpster, *Br* skip
◇ **contenedor de vidrio** bottle bank
contener ⟨2l⟩ *v/t* **1** contain **2** *respiración* hold; *muchedumbre* hold back; **contenerse** *v/r* control o.s.
contenido *m* content
contentadizo *adj* easy to please
contentamiento *m* contentment
contentar ⟨1a⟩ *v/t* please; **contentarse** *v/r* be satisfied (***con*** with)
contento I *adj* **1** (*satisfecho*) pleased **2** (*feliz*) happy; ***y tan ~s*** F and that is / was no problem F **II** *m* joy
conteo *m* count
contertulio *m*, **-a** *f fellow member of a tertulia*
contestable *adj* debatable
contestación *f* answer; ***en ~ a su carta*** in reply to your letter
contestador *m*: ***~ automático*** TELEC answer machine
contestar ⟨1a⟩ **I** *v/t* answer, reply to **II** *v/i* **1** reply (***a*** to), answer (***a*** sth) **2** *de forma insolente* answer back
contestatario I *adj* anti-establishment **II** *m*, **-a** *f* rebel
contestón *adj* F argumentative, lippy F
contexto *m* context; ***fuera de ~*** out of context; ***sacar de ~*** take out of context
contextura *f de persona* build
contienda *f* **1** conflict **2** DEP contest
contigo *pron* with you
contigüidad *f* proximity
contiguo *adj* adjoining, adjacent
continencia *f* continence
continental *adj* continental
continente[1] *m* continent
continente[2] *adj* continent
contingencia *f* contingency
contingente I *adj* contingent **II** *m* **1** contingent **2** COM quota
continuación *f* continuation; ***a ~*** (*ahora*) now; (*después*) then
continuar ⟨1e⟩ **I** *v/t* continue **II** *v/i* continue; ***continuará*** to be continued; ***~ haciendo algo*** continue *o* carry on doing sth; ***continuó nevando*** it kept on snowing
continuidad *f* continuity; ***sin solución de ~*** uninterrupted
continuo *adj* **1** (*sin parar*) continuous; ***de ~*** constantly **2** (*frecuente*) continual

contonearse ⟨1a⟩ *v/r* wiggle one's hips
contoneo *m* swinging of the hips
contorno *m* **1** outline **2** GEOG contour **3**: **~s** *pl* (*cercanías*) surrounding area *sg*
contorsión *f* contortion
contorsionarse ⟨1a⟩ *v/r* contort o.s.
contorsionista *m/f* contortionist
contra I *prp* against; ***en ~ de*** against; ***en ~*** against **II** *f fig*: ***llevar*** *o* ***hacer la ~ a alguien*** contradict s.o.
contraatacar ⟨1g⟩ *v/i* counterattack
contraataque *m* counterattack; *en baloncesto tb* fast break
contrabajista *m/f* MÚS double bass player
contrabajo *m* double bass
contrabandista *m/f* smuggler
contrabando *m* contraband, smuggled goods *pl*; *acción* smuggling; ***hacer ~*** smuggle; ***pasar algo de ~*** smuggle sth in
contracarro(s) *adj* MIL anti-tank *atr*
contracción *f tb* GRAM contraction
contracepción *f* contraception
contraceptivo *m/adj* contraceptive
contrachapado I *adj*: ***madera -a*** plywood **II** *m* plywood
contracorriente *f* crosscurrent; ***ir a ~*** *fig* swim against the tide
contráctil *adj* contractile
contractual *adj* contractual
contractura *f* MED contraction, spasm
contracultura *f* counterculture
contradecir ⟨3p⟩ *v/t* contradict
contradicción *f* contradiction; ***estar en ~ con algo*** contradict sth, be a contradiction of sth
contradictorio *adj* contradictory
contraer ⟨2p; *part* ***contraído***⟩ *v/t* **1** contract **2** *músculo* tighten **3**: ***~ matrimonio*** marry; **contraerse** *v/r* contract
contraespionaje *m* counterespionage
contrafuerte *m* ARQUI buttress
contrahacer ⟨2s; *part* ***contrahecho***⟩ *v/t* copy
contrahecho I *part* ☞ ***contrahacer*** **II** *adj* deformed
contraindicación *f* MED contraindication
contraindicado *adj* MED contraindicated
contralto MÚS **I** *m* countertenor **II** *f* contralto
contraluz *f*: ***a ~*** against the light
contramaestre *m* MAR boatswain
contramanifestación *f* counterdemonstration
contramano *adv*: ***a ~*** the wrong way, in the wrong direction
contramedida *f* countermeasure
contraofensiva *f* MIL counter-attack, counter-offensive
contraoferta *f* counteroffer
contraorden *f* countermand
contrapartida *f* COM balancing entry; ***como ~*** *fig* in contrast
contrapelo: ***a ~*** *fig* the wrong way
contrapesar ⟨1a⟩ *v/t* counterbalance
contrapeso *m* counterweight
contrapie *adv*: ***a ~*** *fig* off guard
contraponer ⟨2r; *part* ***contrapuesto***⟩ *v/t* compare (***a*** to); **contraponerse** *v/r* contrast (***a*** with)
contraportada *f de libro* half-title
contraposición *f*: ***en ~ a*** in comparison to
contraprestación *f* consideration
contraproducente *adj* counterproductive
contraprogramación *f* TV competitive programming
contraproposición *f* counterproposal
contrapuerta *f portón* storm door
contrapuesto *part* ☞ ***contraponer***
contrapunto *m* MÚS *fig* counterpoint
contrariado *adj* upset
contrariamente *adv*: ***~ a*** contrary to
contrariar ⟨1c⟩ *v/t* **1** (*obstaculizar*) oppose **2** (*enfadar*) annoy
contrariedad *f* **1** setback **2** (*disgusto*) annoyance
contrario I *adj* **1** contrary; *sentido* opposite; ***al ~, por el ~*** on the contrary; ***todo lo ~*** just the opposite; ***de lo ~*** otherwise; ***ser ~ a algo*** be opposed to sth; ***llevar la -a a alguien*** contradict s.o. **2** *equipo* opposing **II** *m*, **-a** *f* adversary, opponent
contrarreloj *f* DEP time trial
contrarrestar ⟨1a⟩ *v/t* counteract
contrarrevolución *f* counterrevolution
contrasentido *m* contradiction
contraseña *f tb* INFOR password
contrastar ⟨1a⟩ *v/t & v/i* contrast (***con*** with)
contraste *m* **1** contrast; ***en ~ con*** in contrast to **2**: (***sustancia / medio de***) **~** MED contrast substance / medium
contrata *f* contract

C

contratación *f* **1** *de trabajadores* hiring, recruitment **2**: **~ *bursátil*** trading
contratar ⟨1a⟩ *v/t trabajadores* hire, take on; *servicios* contract
contratenor *m* MÚS countertenor
contratiempo *m* setback, hitch
contratista *m/f* contractor; **~ *de obras*** main contractor
contrato *m* contract
◇ **contrato de alquiler** rental contract; **contrato indefinido** permanent contract; **contrato laboral** (work) contract; **contrato de obra** contract of employment, job contract; **contrato temporal** temporary contract
contravalor *m* exchange value
contravención *f* contravention
contraveneno *m* antidote
contravenir ⟨3s⟩ **I** *v/t* contravene **II** *v/i*: **~ *a*** contravene
contraventana *f* shutter
contrayentes *mpl*: ***los* ~** the bride and groom
contribución *f* **1** contribution **2** (*impuesto*) tax
◇ **contribuciones sociales** social security contributions
contribuir ⟨3g⟩ *v/t* contribute (***a*** to)
contribuyente *m/f* taxpayer
contrición *f* contrition
contrincante *m/f* opponent
contrito *adj* contrite
control *m* **1** control; ***perder el* ~** lose control; ***tenerlo todo bajo* ~** have everything under control **2** (*inspección*) check
◇ **control de calidad** quality control; **control de divisas** exchange controls *pl*; **control fronterizo** border checkpoint; **control de pasaportes** passport control; **control remoto** remote control; **control de tráfico aéreo** air traffic control
controlable *adj* controllable
controlador *m*, **~a** *f*: **~ *aéreo*** air traffic controller
controlar ⟨1a⟩ *v/t* **1** control **2** (*vigilar*) check; **controlarse** *v/r* control o.s.
controversia *f* controversy
controvertible *adj* debatable
controvertido *adj* controversial
controvertir ⟨3i⟩ *v/i & v/t* debate
contumacia *f* obstinacy
contumaz *adj* obstinate
contundencia *f* forcefulness; ***con* ~** forcefully
contundente *adj arma* blunt; *fig*: *derrota* overwhelming
conturbación *f* dismay
conturbar ⟨1a⟩ *v/t* upset, perturb; **conturbarse** *v/r* get upset, become perturbed
contusión *f* MED bruise
contusionar ⟨1a⟩ *v/t* bruise
contuso *adj* bruised; ***herida -a*** bruise
convalecencia *f* convalescence
convalecer ⟨2d⟩ *v/i* convalesce; **~ *de*** recover from
convaleciente *m/f* convalescent
convalidación *f* validation
convalidar ⟨1a⟩ *v/t* validate
convecino *m*, **-a** *f* neighbor, *Br* neighbour
convencer ⟨2b⟩ *v/t* convince; **convencerse** *v/r* become convinced
convencimiento *m* conviction
convención *f* convention
convencional *adj* conventional
conveniencia *f* **1** *de hacer algo* advisability **2**: ***hacer algo por* ~** to do sth in one's own interest; ***matrimonio de* ~** marriage of convenience
conveniente *adj* **1** convenient **2** (*útil*) useful **3** (*aconsejable*) advisable
convenio *m* agreement
◇ **convenio colectivo** collective agreement
convenir ⟨3s⟩ **I** *v/t* agree; ***a* ~** to be agreed **II** *v/i* **1** be advisable **2**: ***no te conviene*** it's not in your interest; **~ *a alguien hacer algo*** be in s.o.'s interests to do sth **3**: **~ *en*** agree on
conventillo *m CSur* tenement
convento *m de monjes* monastery; *de monjas* convent
convergencia *f* convergence
convergente *adj* convergent
converger ⟨2c⟩ *v/i*, **convergir** ⟨3c⟩ *v/i* converge (***en*** on)
conversa *f L.Am.* chat
conversación *f* conversation; **~ *telefónica*** telephone conversation
conversador I *adj* good at making conversation **II** *m*, **~a** *f* conversationalist
conversar ⟨1a⟩ *v/i* make conversation
conversión *f* conversion
converso *m*, **-a** *f* REL convert
conversor *m* ☞ ***convertidor***

convertibilidad *f* convertibility
convertible I *adj* COM convertible **II** *m L.Am.* convertible
convertidor *m* TÉC converter
convertir ⟨3i⟩ *v/t* convert; **convertirse** *v/r* **1**: **~ *en algo*** turn into sth **2** REL be converted
convexidad *f* convexity
convexo *adj* convex
convicción *f* conviction
convicto *adj* JUR convicted
convidado *m*, **-a** *f* guest
convidar ⟨1a⟩ *v/t* invite (***a*** to)
convincente *adj* convincing
convite *m* banquet
convivencia *f* living together
convivir ⟨3a⟩ *v/i* live together
convocar ⟨1g⟩ *v/t a personas* summon; *oposiciones* organize; *huelga* call; **~ *elecciones*** call elections
convocatoria *f de oposiciones* announcement; *de huelga* call; **~ *electoral*** calling of elections
convoy *m* convoy
convulsión *f* convulsion; *fig* upheaval
convulsionar ⟨1a⟩ *v/t* throw into confusion
convulsivo *adj* convulsive
convulso *adj* convulsed
conyugal *adj* conjugal
cónyuge *m/f* spouse; **~*s*** *pl* married couple *sg*
coña *f*: **1**: ***decir algo de*** **~** F say sth as a joke; ***¡ni de*** **~*!*** F no way! F **2**: ***darle la*** **~ *a alguien*** F bug s.o. F
coñac *m* (*pl* **~*s***) brandy, cognac
coñazo *m* V pain in the butt P, drag F; ***dar el*** **~**V be a pain in the butt P
coño *m* V cunt V; **¡~!** V shit! V, fuck! V; ***¡qué*** **~ *…!*** V fuck! V; ***en el quinto*** **~** V out in the frigging boonies P
cooperación *f* cooperation
cooperador *adj* cooperative, helpful
cooperar ⟨1a⟩ *v/i* cooperate
cooperativa *f* cooperative
cooperativista *m/f* member of a cooperative
cooperativo *adj* cooperative
coordenada *f* MAT coordinate
coordinación *f* coordination
coordinador I *adj* coordinating **II** *m*, **~a** *f* coordinator, organizer
coordinar ⟨1a⟩ *v/t* coordinate
copa *f* **1** *de vino etc* glass; ***tomar una*** **~** have a drink; ***ir de*** **~*s*** go out for a drink; ***beber unas*** **~*s de más*** F have one too many F; ***levantar la*** **~** raise one's glass **2** DEP cup **3**: **~*s*** *pl* (*en naipes*) *suit in Spanish deck of cards*
◇ **copa balón** balloon glass, brandy glass; **copa de helado** bowl of ice cream; **Copa del Mundo** World Cup; **copa de la UEFA** UEFA cup
copar ⟨1a⟩ *v/t* **1** MIL take **2**: **~ *el mercado*** corner the market
coparticipación *f* participation
copartícipe *m/f* collaborator
copear ⟨1a⟩ *v/i* F go out drinking
Copenhague *m* Copenhagen
copeo *m* F: ***ir de*** **~** go out drinking
copete *m* **1** *de ave* tuft; ***de alto*** **~** F *dama* aristocratic; *fiesta*, *restaurante* grand, ritzy F **2** *de persona* quiff
copia *f* copy
◇ **copia pirata** pirate copy
◇ **copia de seguridad** INFOR back-up (copy)
copiadora *f* (photo)copier
copiar ⟨1b⟩ *v/t* copy
copiloto *m/f* copilot
copioso *adj* copious
copla *f* **1** verse **2** (*canción*) popular song
copo *m* flake
◇ **copos de avena** rolled oats; **copos de maíz** cornflakes; **copos de nieve** snowflakes
copra *f* copra
coproducción *f* co-production
coproductor *m*, **~a** *f* co-producer
copropiedad *f* co-ownership, joint ownership
copropietario *m*, **-a** *f* co-owner, joint owner
cópula *f* **1** BIO copulation **2** GRAM copula
copulación *f* copulation
copular ⟨1a⟩ *v/i* copulate
copulativo *adj* GRAM copulative
coque *m* coke
coquetear ⟨1a⟩ *v/i* flirt
coqueteo *m* flirting
coquetería *f* flirtatiousness
coqueto *adj* **1** flirtatious **2** *lugar* pretty **3** (*presumido*): ***ser muy*** **~** be very concerned about one's appearance
coraje *m* courage; ***me da*** **~** *fig* F it makes me mad F
corajudo *adj L.Am.* brave

C

coral[1] *m* ZO coral
coral[2] MÚS **I** *adj* choral **II** *f* choir
Corán *m* Koran
coraza *f* **1** cuirasse; *fig* shield **2** ZO shell
corazón *m* **1** heart; ***a ~ abierto*** MED *operación* open-heart *atr*; ***ser todo ~*** be all heart; ***te digo, con el ~ en la mano, que ...*** I can say, hand on heart, that ...; ***de todo ~*** with all one's heart; ***de buen ~*** good-hearted; ***tener un ~ de oro*** have a heart of gold; ***con el ~ encogido*** upset; ***se me encoge el ~*** I get upset; ***se me parte*** *o* ***rompe el ~*** my heart breaks; ***no tener ~*** be heartless; ***¡(mí) ~!, ¡~ (mío)!*** (my) darling!, sweetheart!
2 *de fruta* core
corazonada *f* hunch
corbata *f* tie
◇ **corbata de moño** *Méx* bow tie
corbatero *m* tie rack
corbatín *m* bow tie
corbeta *f* MAR corvette
Córcega *f* Corsica
corcel *m* *lit* steed
corchea *f* MÚS eighth note, *Br* quaver
corchero *adj* cork *atr*
corcheta *f* eye (*of hook and eye*)
corchete *m* **1** hook and eye **2**: ***~s*** *pl* TIP brackets, *Br* square brackets **3** *Chi* (*grapa*) staple
corchetera *f* *Chi* stapler
corcho *m* cork
¡córcholis! *int* F wow! F
corcova *f* hump(back), hunchback
corcovado *adj* humpbacked, hunchbacked
cordada *f* roped team
cordaje *m* MAR rigging
cordel *m* string
cordero *m*, **-a** *f* lamb; (***carne de***) **~** lamb; (***piel de***) **~** sheepskin
◇ **Cordero de Dios** Lamb of God
cordial I *adj* cordial **II** *m* cordial, tonic
cordialidad *f* cordiality
cordialmente *adv* cordially
cordillera *f* mountain range; ***la Cordillera de los Andes*** the Andes
córdoba *m* FIN cordoba
cordobés I *adj* Cordovan **II** *m*, **-esa** *f* Cordovan
cordón *m* **1** cord; *de zapato* shoelace **2** *Cu, Rpl*: *de la acera* curb, *Br* kerb
◇ **cordón policial** police cordon; **cordón sanitario** cordon sanitaire; **cordón umbilical** ANAT umbilical cord
cordura *f* **1** sanity **2** (*prudencia*) good sense
Corea *f* Korea
◇ **Corea del Norte** North Korea
◇ **Corea del Sur** South Korea
coreano I *adj* Korean **II** *m*, **-a** *f* Korean **III** *m idioma* Korean
corear ⟨1a⟩ *v/t palabras* chorus; *canto* sing together; *consigna* chant
coreografía *f* choreography
coreografiar ⟨1c⟩ *v/t* choreograph
coreográfico *adj* choreographic
coreógrafo *m*, **-a** *f* choreographer
coriandro *m* BOT coriander
corindón *m* MIN corundum
corintio I *adj* Corinthian **II** *m*, **-a** *f* Corinthian
corista I *m/f* chorister **II** *f* TEA chorus girl
cormorán *m* ZO cormorant
cornada *f* TAUR goring
cornamenta *f de toro* horns *pl*; *de ciervo* antlers *pl*
cornamusa *f* MÚS **1** (*gaita*) bagpipes *pl* **2** (*trompeta*) horn
córnea *f* cornea
cornear ⟨1a⟩ *v/t* gore
corneja *f* ZO crow
◇ **corneja negra** carrion crow, hooded crow
córneo *adj* horny, hornlike
córner *m en fútbol* corner (kick)
corneta I *f* MIL bugle **II** *m/f* bugler
cornetín I *m* cornet **II** *m/f* cornet player
cornezuelo *m* BOT ergot
cornisa *f* ARQUI cornice
corno *m* MÚS horn
◇ **corno inglés** English horn, *Br* cor anglais
cornucopia *f* cornucopia, horn of plenty
cornudo I *adj* horned **II** *m* cuckold
coro *m* MÚS choir; *de espectáculo, pieza musical* chorus; ***a ~*** together, in chorus; ***hacer ~ con alguien*** back s.o. up
corola *f* BOT corolla
corolario *m* corollary
corona *f* crown
◇ **corona de flores** garland
◇ **corona fúnebre** wreath
coronación *f* coronation
coronar ⟨1a⟩ *v/t* crown; ***coronado por***

el éxito crowned with success
coronario *adj* MED coronary
coronel *m* MIL colonel
coronilla *f* ANAT crown; ***estoy hasta la ~*** F I've had it up to here F
corotos *mpl L.Am.* bits and pieces
corpachón *m* hefty frame
corpiño *m* **1** bodice **2** *Arg* (*sujetador*) bra
corporación *f* corporation
corporal *adj placer, estética* physical; *fluido* body *atr*
corporativo *adj* corporate
corpóreo *adj* corporeal
corpulencia *f* burliness
corpulento *adj* solidly built, burly
Corpus (Christi) *m* Corpus Christi
corpus *m inv* corpus
corpúsculo *m* corpuscle
corral *m* **1** farmyard **2** *cercado* corral
correa *f de perro* leash, *Br* lead; *de reloj* strap; (*cinturón*) belt; ***tener mucha ~*** *fig* be long-suffering
◇ **correa de transmisión** TÉC drive belt
◇ **correa del ventilador** AUTO fan belt
corrección *f* **1** *de error, test etc* correction **2** *en el trato* correctness
correccional I *adj* corrective **II** *m* reformatory
corre-corre *m en béisbol* rundown
correctivo I *adj* corrective **II** *m* punishment
correcto *adj* **1** correct; ***políticamente ~*** politically correct **2** (*educado*) polite
corrector I *adj* correcting *atr* **II** *m*, **~a** *f* TIP: **~ (*de pruebas*)** proofreader
corredera *f* TÉC slide; ***puerta ~*** sliding door
corredizo *adj* sliding
corredor I *adj* ZO flightless **II** *m*, **~a** *f* **1** DEP runner **2** COM agent **III** *m* ARQUI corridor
◇ **corredor aéreo** air corridor; **corredor de apuestas** bookmaker, bookie F; **corredor de bolsa** stockbroker; **corredor de fincas** real estate broker, *Br* estate agent; **corredor de fondo** long-distance runner; **corredor de medio fondo** middle-distance runner
correduría *f* brokerage
corregible *adj* correctable
corregidor *m* HIST chief magistrate
corregir ⟨3c & 3l⟩ *v/t* correct; **corregirse** *v/r* correct o.s.
correlación *f* correlation
correlativo *adj* correlative
correligionario *m*, **-a** *f*: ***sus ~s republicanos*** his fellow republicans
corremundos *m/f inv* F globetrotter F
correntada *f L.Am.* current
correntoso *adj L.Am.* fast-flowing
correo *m* **1** mail, *Br tb* post; ***por ~*** by mail; ***por ~ aparte*** *o* ***separado*** under separate cover; ***echar al ~*** mail, *Br tb* post **2**: **~*s*** *pl* post office *sg*
◇ **correo aéreo** airmail; **correo electrónico** e-mail; ***enviar algo por ~*** e-mail sth, send sth by e-mail; **correo de voz** INFOR voicemail
correoso *adj* leathery, tough
correr ⟨2a⟩ **I** *v/i* **1** run; ***a todo ~*** at top speed **2** (*apresurarse*) rush **3** *de tiempo* pass **4** *de agua* run, flow **5** *fig*: ***~ con los gastos*** pay the expenses; ***~ con algo*** meet the cost of sth; ***~ a cargo de alguien*** be s.o.'s responsibility, be down to s.o. F
II *v/t* **1** run **2** *cortinas* draw; *mueble* slide, move **3**: ***~ la misma suerte*** suffer the same fate
correrse *v/r* **1** move; *de tinta* run **2** P *en orgasmo* come F
correría *f* **1** MIL raid **2**: **~*s*** *pl* adventures
correspondencia *f* **1** correspondence **2** TRANSP connection (***con*** with)
corresponder ⟨2a⟩ *v/i* **1**: ***~ a alguien*** *de bienes* be for s.o., be due to s.o.; *de responsabilidad* be up to s.o.; *de asunto* concern s.o.; *a un favor* repay s.o. (***con*** with) **2**: ***actuar como corresponde*** do the right thing; **corresponderse** *v/r*: ***~ con algo*** match sth, tally with sth
correspondiente *adj* corresponding
corresponsable *adj* jointly responsible
corresponsal *m/f* correspondent
◇ **corresponsal de guerra** war correspondent
corresponsalía *f* post of correspondent
corretaje *m* brokerage
corretear ⟨1a⟩ *v/i* run around
correveidile *m/f* F snitch F, *Br* telltale
corrida *f* run; ***decir algo de ~*** *fig* rattle sth off
◇ **corrida de toros** bullfight
corrido *adj*: ***decir algo de ~*** *fig* say sth parrot-fashion
corriente I *adj* **1** (*actual*) current **2** (*co-*

C

mún) ordinary; **~ *y moliente*** F run-of--the-mill **3**: ***estar al ~*** be up to date; ***poner alguien al ~ de algo*** bring s.o. up to date on sth **II** *f* EL, *de agua* current; ***~ de aire*** draft, *Br* draught; ***ir*** *o* ***nadar contra la ~*** *fig* swim against the tide; ***llevar*** *o* ***seguir a alguien la ~*** play along with s.o.; ***dejarse llevar por la ~*** *fig* go with the flow
◇ **corriente alterna** alternating current; **corriente continua** direct current; **Corriente del Golfo** Gulf Stream
corrientemente *adv* normally, commonly
corrillo *m* small group
corrimiento *m*: ***~ de tierras*** landslide
corro *m* ring; ***hacer ~*** gather round; ***hacer ~ aparte*** form a separate group
corroboración *f* corroboration
corroborar ⟨1a⟩ *v/t* corroborate
corroer ⟨2a⟩ *v/t* corrode; *fig* eat up; **corroerse** *v/r* corrode
corromper ⟨2a⟩ *v/t* corrupt; **corromperse** *v/r* become corrupted
corrompido *adj* ☞ ***corrupto***
corrosión *f* corrosion
corrosivo *adj* corrosive; *fig* caustic
corrupción *f* decay; *fig* corruption
◇ **corrupción de menores** corruption of minors
corruptela *f* corruption
corruptibilidad *f* corruptibility
corruptible *adj* corruptible
corrupto *adj* corrupt
corruptor I *adj* corruptive **II** *m*, **~a** *f* corrupter
corsario *m* HIST corsair, privateer
corsé *m* corset
corsetería *f* lingerie store
cortaalambres *m inv* wire cutters *pl*
cortabordes *m inv* edger
cortacésped *m* lawnmower
cortacircuitos *m inv* circuit breaker
cortacristales *m inv* glasscutter
cortada *f L.Am.* cut
cortado I *adj* **1** cut **2** *calle* closed **3** *leche* curdled **4** *persona* shy; ***quedarse ~*** be embarrassed **II** *m* coffee with a dash of milk
cortador *m*, **~a** *f de prendas de vestir, zapatos* cutter
cortadura *f* cut
cortafrío *m* cold chisel
cortafuego *m* firebreak; *muro* fire wall
cortante *adj* **1** *filo* sharp **2** *viento* cutting
cortapapeles *m inv* letter opener, *Br tb* paper knife
cortapisa *f* restriction; ***poner ~s a*** *fig* put obstacles in the way of, obstruct
cortaplumas *m inv* penknife
cortar ⟨1a⟩ **I** *v/t* **1** cut; *electricidad* cut off **2** *calle* close **3**: ***~ la respiración*** *fig* take one's breath away **II** *v/i* cut; ***~ con alguien*** split up with s.o.; **cortarse** *v/r* **1** cut o.s.; ***~ el pelo*** have one's hair cut **2**: ***la línea se ha cortado*** TELEC the line has gone dead **3** *fig* F get embarrassed
cortaúñas *m inv* nail clippers *pl*
cortavidrios *m inv* glasscutter
cortavientos *m inv* windbreak
corte[1] *m* **1** *con cuchillo* cut **2**: ***me da ~*** F I'm embarrassed **3**: ***hacerle un ~ de mangas a alguien*** F give s.o. the finger F
◇ **corte de luz** power outage, power cut; **corte de pelo** haircut; **corte publicitario** TV commercial break; **corte de tráfico** F road closure
corte[2] *f* **1** *real* court; ***hacer la ~ a alguien*** woo s.o. **2** *L.Am.* JUR (law) court **3**: ***las Cortes*** *Spanish parliament*
cortedad *f* shortness; ***~ de miras*** short-sightedness
cortejar ⟨1a⟩ *v/t* court
cortejo *m* entourage
◇ **cortejo fúnebre** cortège, funeral procession
cortés *adj* courteous
cortesana *f* courtesan
cortesano I *adj* court *atr* **II** *m* courtier
cortesía *f* courtesy; ***tener la ~ de hacer algo*** be kind enough to do sth; ***por ~ de ...*** by courtesy of ...
corteza *f de árbol* bark; *de pan* crust; *de queso* rind
◇ **corteza cerebral** ANAT cerebral cortex
◇ **corteza terrestre** earth's crust
cortijo *m* farmhouse
cortina *f* curtain
◇ **cortina de baño** shower curtain
◇ **cortina de niebla** blanket of fog
cortisona *f* cortisone
corto *adj* short; ***ir de ~*** be wearing a short dress; ***~ de vista*** nearsighted; ***de -a edad*** young; ***ni ~ ni perezoso*** as bold as brass; ***quedarse ~*** fall short;

(*calcular mal*) underestimate; ***a la -a o a la larga*** sooner or later
cortocircuito *m* EL short circuit
corva *f* back of the knee
corvejón *m de caballo* hock
corvina *f* meager, *Br* meagre
corvo *adj* curved
corzo *m*, -a *f* ZO roe deer
cosa *f* thing; ***¿sabes una ~?*** do you know something?; ***alguna ~*** something; ***ser ~ fina*** be really something F, be something else F; ***son ~s que pasan*** these things happen; ***son ~s de la vida*** that's life; ***entre otras ~s*** among other things; ***como si tal ~*** as if nothing had happened; ***decir a alguien cuatro ~s*** give s.o. a piece of one's mind; ***eso es otra ~*** that's another matter; ***¿qué pasa? – poca ~*** what's new? – nothing much; ***~ de*** about; ***hace ~ de un año*** about a year ago; ***le dijo que había ganado la lotería como quien no quiere la ~*** he told her that he had won the lottery as though it happened to him every day; ***este pintor no es gran ~*** he's not much of a painter; ***no hay tal ~*** there's no such thing; ***¡qué ~!*** that's odd *o* strange!; ***lo que son las ~s*** well, well!, imagine that!; ***~ rara*** oddly enough, strangely enough; ***son ~s de Juan*** that's typical of Juan, that's Juan all over
coscorrón *m* bump on the head
cosecha *f* **1** harvest; *fig* tally, score **2**: ***de ~ propia*** one's own; ***no ser de su ~*** *fig* F not be one's own work
cosechadora *f* combine (harvester)
cosechar ⟨1a⟩ *v/t* harvest; *fig* gain, win
cosedor *m*, **~a** *f* machinist
coseno *m* MAT cosine
coser ⟨2a⟩ *v/t* sew; ***ser ~ y cantar*** F be dead easy F; ***~ a tiros*** riddle with bullets
cosido *m* sewing; ***~ a mano*** hand sewing
cosmética *f* cosmetics (industry)
cosmético *m/adj* cosmetic
cósmico *adj* cosmic
cosmología *f* cosmology
cosmonauta *m/f* cosmonaut
cosmopolita *m/f & adj* cosmopolitan
cosmopolitismo *m* cosmopolitanism
cosmos *m* cosmos
cosmovisión *f L.Am.* world view
coso *m* enclosure; TAUR bullring
cosquillas *fpl*: ***hacer ~ a alguien*** tickle s.o.; ***tener ~*** be ticklish; ***buscarle las ~ a alguien*** annoy s.o.
cosquillear ⟨1a⟩ *v/t* tickle
cosquilleo *m* tickle
cosquilloso *adj* ticklish; *fig* touchy
costa[1] *f*: ***a ~ de*** at the expense of; ***a toda ~*** at all costs
costa[2] *f* GEOG coast
◇ **Costa Azul** Côte d'Azur
costado *m* side; ***por los cuatro ~s*** *fig* throughout, through and through
costal *m* sack, bag
costar ⟨1m⟩ **I** *v/t* **1** *en dinero* cost; ***¿cuánto cuesta?*** how much does it cost? **2** *trabajo, esfuerzo etc* take **II** *v/i* **1** *en dinero* cost; ***cueste lo que cueste*** at all costs; ***~ caro*** *fig* cost dear **2**: ***me costó*** it was hard work
Costa Rica *f* Costa Rica
costarricense *m/f & adj* Costa Rican
coste *m* ☞ ***costo***
costear[1] ⟨1a⟩ *v/t* pay for
costear[2] ⟨1a⟩ *v/i* MAR sail along the coast
costeño, costero *adj* coastal
costilla *f* **1** ANAT rib; ***medirle a alguien las ~s*** beat s.o. **2** GASTR sparerib
costillar *m* GASTR ribs *pl*; *de cordero* rack
costo *m* cost; ***abaratar ~s*** cut costs
◇ **costo de la vida** cost of living *sg*; **costos fijos** fixed costs; **costos procesales** JUR court costs
costoso *adj* costly; *fig* difficult
costra *f* MED scab
costumbre *f* **1** *de país* custom **2** *de una persona* habit; ***mala ~*** bad habit; ***persona de ~s*** creature of habit; ***tengo la ~ de madrugar*** I usually get up early; ***de ~*** usual; ***como de ~*** as usual
costumbrismo *m literary genre focusing on social customs*
costura *f* **1** sewing; ***alta ~*** haute couture **2**: ***sin ~*** seamless
costurar ⟨1a⟩ *v/t*, **costurear** ⟨1a⟩ *v/t L.Am.* sew
costurera *f* seamstress
costurero *m* sewing box
cota *f* height above sea level; ***~ de nieve*** snow level
cotangente *f* MAT cotangent
cotarro *m*: ***manejar el ~*** F be the boss F;

C

animar el **~** F liven things up
cotejar ⟨1a⟩ *v/t* compare
cotejo *m* comparison
cotidianidad *f* daily life
cotidiano *adj* daily; ***vida -a*** daily life
cotiledón *m* BOT cotyledon
cotilla *m/f* F gossip
cotillear ⟨1a⟩ *v/i* F gossip
cotizable *adj* FIN listed; **~ *en bolsa*** quoted on the Stock Market
cotización *f* **1** (*precio*) price; **~ *bursátil*** stock price, share price; (*valor*) value; ***la ~ del actor subió después de obtener el Óscar*** the actor became more sought-after after winning the Oscar **2** (*cuota*) contribution
cotizado *adj* COM quoted; *fig* sought-after
cotizante *m/f* contributor
cotizar ⟨1f⟩ **I** *v/i* **1** *de trabajador* pay social security, *Br* pay National Insurance **2** *de acciones, bonos* be listed (***a*** at); **~ *en bolsa*** be listed on the stock exchange **II** *v/t* **1** (*pagar*) pay **2** *acciones, bonos* quote; **cotizarse** *v/r* COM be quoted (***a*** at); *fig* be valued (***a*** at)
coto[1] *m*: **~ *de caza*** hunting reserve; ***poner ~ a algo*** *fig* put a stop to sth
coto[2] *m S.Am.*, MED goiter, *Br* goitre
cotonete *m Méx* Q-Tip®, *Br* cotton bud
cotorra *f* ZO parrot; F *persona* motormouth F
cotorrear ⟨1a⟩ *v/i* F chatter
cotorreo *m* F chatter
coturno *m* sandal; ***de alto ~*** *fig* upscale, *Br* upmarket
covacha *f* small cave; *casa* hovel
coxal *adj*: ***hueso ~*** coccyx
coxis *m* ANAT coccyx
coyote *m* ZO coyote
coyuntura *f* **1** situation **2** ANAT joint
coyuntural *adj* interim, temporary
coz *f* kick; ***dar coces*** kick
C.P. *abr* (= ***código postal***) zip code, *Br* post code
crac *m* **1** (*crujido*) snap, crack **2** COM crash
crack *m* DEP star, ace
craneal *adj* ANAT cranial
cráneo *m* ANAT skull, cranium
craso *adj ignorancia* crass; *error, engaño* terrible
cráter *m* crater
crayón *m L.Am.* crayon
creación *f* creation
◇ **creación de empleo** job creation
creador I *adj* creative **II** *m*, **~a** *f* creator
crear ⟨1a⟩ *v/t* create; *empresa* set up
creatividad *f* creativity
creativo *adj* creative
crecer ⟨2d⟩ *v/i* grow; **crecerse** *v/r* rise to the challenge *o* occasion
creces *fpl*: ***con ~*** *superar* by a comfortable margin; *pagar* with interest
crecida *f* rise in river level; (*inundación*) flooding
crecido *adj persona* big; *número* large; *pelo* long
creciente I *adj cantidad* growing; *luna* waxing **II** *f*: **~ (*lunar*)** crescent (of the moon)
crecimiento *m* growth; **~ *demográfico*** population growth
◇ **crecimiento cero** zero growth
credencial I *f* document **II** *adj*: ***cartas ~es*** credentials
credibilidad *f* credibility
crediticio *adj* credit *atr*
crédito *m* **1** COM credit; ***a ~*** on credit; **~ *bancario*** (bank) credit **2**: ***no dar ~ a sus oídos / ojos*** F not believe one's ears / eyes; ***dar ~ a algo*** believe sth; ***digno de ~*** reliable, trustworthy
credo *m* REL, *fig* creed
credulidad *f* credulity
crédulo *adj* credulous
creencia *f* belief
creer ⟨2e⟩ **I** *v/i* believe (***en*** in); **~ *en Dios*** believe in God
II *v/t* think; (*dar por cierto*) believe; ***hacer ~ algo a alguien*** make s.o. think *o* believe sth; ***no creo que esté aquí*** I don't think he's here; ***eso no te lo crees ni tú*** F you must be nuts! F; ***¡quién iba a creerlo!*** who would have believed it!; ***¡ya lo creo!*** F you bet! F
creerse *v/r*: **~ *que ...*** believe that ...; ***se cree muy lista*** she thinks she's very clever; ***¡qué te has creído!*** you must be joking!
creíble *adj* credible
creído I *part* → **creer II** *adj* conceited
crema I *adj*: ***color ~*** cream(-colored, *Br* -coloured) **II** *f* GASTR cream
◇ **crema solar** suntan lotion
cremación *f* cremation
cremallera I *f* **1** zipper, *Br* zip **2** TÉC rack **II** *m* cog railway, *Br* rack railway

crematístico *adj* financial
crematorio I *adj*: ***horno ~*** crematory oven **II** *m* crematory, *Br* crematorium
cremoso *adj* creamy
crep *m* → ***crepé***
crepe *f* GASTR crêpe, pancake
crepé *m tela* crêpe
crepitación *f* crackling
crepitar ⟨1a⟩ *v/i* crackle
crepuscular *adj* twilight *atr*
crepúsculo *m tb fig* twilight
crespo *adj* curly
crespón *m* **1** *tela* crêpe **2** *en bandera* black armband
cresta *f* crest; ***estar en la ~ de la ola*** *fig* be riding high, be on the crest of a wave
Creta *f* Crete
creta *f* GEOL chalk
cretáceo GEOL **I** *adj* cretaceous **II** *m* Cretaceous (period)
cretense *m/f & adj* Cretan
cretino I *adj* **1** MED cretinous **2** F cretinous F, moronic F **II** *m*, **-a** *f* **1** MED cretin **2** F cretin F, moron F
cretona *f* cretonne
creyente REL **I** *adj*: ***ser ~*** believe in God **II** *m/f* believer
creyó *vb* → ***creer***
cría *f* **1** *acción* breeding **2** *de zorro, león* cub; *de perro* puppy; *de gato* kitten; *de oveja* lamb; ***sus ~s*** her young
criada *f* maid
criadero *m* **1** *de animales* breeder's, breeding establishment; *de ratas* breeding ground **2** *de plantas* nursery
criadilla *f* GASTR testicle
◇ **criadilla de tierra** BOT truffle
criado I *part* → ***criar*** **II** *adj* raised, brought up; ***bien ~*** well-bred; ***mal ~*** bad-mannered **III** *m*, **-a** *f* servant
criador *m* breeder
crianza *f* **1** *de niños* upbringing **2** *de animales* breeding
criar ⟨1c⟩ *v/t* **1** *niños* raise, bring up **2** *animales* breed; **criarse** *v/r* grow up
criatura *f* **1** creature **2** F (*niño*) baby, child
criba *f* sieve
cribado *m* sieving, sifting
cribar ⟨1a⟩ *v/t* sift, sieve; *fig* select
cric *m* TÉC jack
crimen *m* crime; ***~ sexual*** sex crime
criminal *m/f & adj* criminal
◇ **criminal de guerra** war criminal
criminalidad *f* crime; ***~ informática*** computer crime
criminalista *m/f* criminal lawyer
criminología *f* criminology
crin *f* mane; ***~es*** *pl* mane *sg*
crío *m*, **-a** *f* F kid F
criollo I *adj* Creole **II** *m*, **-a** *f* Creole **III** *f idioma* Creole
cripta *f* crypt
críptico *adj* cryptic
criptografía *f* cryptography
criptograma *m* cryptogram
críquet *m* cricket
crisálida *f* ZO chrysalis
crisantemo *m* BOT chrysanthemum
crisis *f inv* crisis
◇ **crisis nerviosa** attack of hysteria
crisma I *f* F head, nut F; ***romper la ~ a alguien*** F smash s.o's face in F **II** *m* Christmas card
crismas *m inv* Christmas card
crisol *m* **1** crucible **2** *fig* melting pot
crispación *f* irritation
crispado *adj* irritated
crispar ⟨1a⟩ *v/t* irritate; ***~le a alguien los nervios*** get on s.o.'s nerves; **crisparse** *v/r* get irritated
cristal *m* **1** crystal **2** (*vidrio*) glass **3** (*lente*) lens **4** *de ventana* pane
◇ **cristal líquido** liquid crystal
◇ **cristal de roca** MIN rock crystal
cristalera *f* **1** *puerta* glass door **2** (*ventana*) window **3** (*armario*) display cabinet
cristalería *f* **1** *fábrica* glassworks *sg* **2** *objetos* glassware
cristalero *m*, **-a** *f* glazier
cristalino *adj* crystal-clear
cristalizar ⟨1f⟩ *v/i* **1** FÍS, MIN crystallize **2** *de idea, proyecto* jell, gel
cristianar ⟨1a⟩ *v/t* christen, baptize
cristiandad *f* Christendom
cristianismo *m* Christianity
cristianizar ⟨1f⟩ *v/t* convert to Christianity
cristiano I *adj* Christian **II** *m*, **-a** *f* Christian **III** *m*: ***hablar en ~*** use everyday language, talk plain English
Cristo Christ; ***todo ~*** F everyone; ***donde ~ dio las tres voces*** F in the middle of nowhere F
cristo *m* crucifix
criterio *m* **1** criterion **2** (*juicio*) judg(e)ment

crítica *f* criticism; ***muchas ~s*** a lot of criticism
criticable *adj* reprehensible
criticar ⟨1g⟩ *v/t* criticize
crítico **I** *adj* critical **II** *m*, **-a** *f* critic
criticón F **I** *adj* nit-picking **II** *m*, **-ona** *f* nit-picker
Croacia *f* Croatia
croar ⟨1a⟩ *v/i* croak
croata **I** *adj* Croatian **II** *m/f* Croat
crocante **I** *adj* *Rpl* crunchy **II** *m* nougat
croché *m*, **crochet** *m* crochet
crol *m* crawl; ***nadar a ~*** do the crawl
cromar ⟨1a⟩ *v/t* chromium-plate
cromático *adj* chromatic
crómico *adj* chrome *atr*; ***ácido ~*** chromic acid
cromo *m* **1** QUÍM chromium, chrome **2** (*estampa*) picture card, trading card
cromosoma *m* BIO chromosome
crónica *f* chronicle; *en periódico* report
crónico *adj* MED chronic
cronista *m/f* reporter
cronoescalada *f* mountain time trial
cronología *f* chronology
cronológico *adj* chronological
cronometrador *m*, **~a** *f* DEP timekeeper
cronometrar ⟨1a⟩ *v/t* DEP time
cronómetro *m* stopwatch
cróquet *m* croquet
croqueta *f* GASTR croquette
croquis *m inv* sketch
cross *m* DEP cross-country (running); *con motocicletas* motocross
crótalo *m* ZO rattlesnake
crotorar ⟨1a⟩ *v/i* clatter its bill / their bills
cruasán *m* croissant
cruce *m* **1** *de especies* cross **2** *de carreteras* crossroads *sg* **3**: ***~ en las líneas*** TELEC crossed line **4** DEP crossfield pass, cross
cruceiro *m* FIN cruzeiro
crucero *m* **1** cruise **2** MIL cruiser **3** ARQUI transept
cruceta *f* crosspiece
crucial *adj* crucial
crucíferas *fpl* BOT Cruciferae
crucificar ⟨1g⟩ *v/t* crucify
crucifijo *m* crucifix
crucifixión *f* crucifixion
crucigrama *m* crossword
crucis *m* REL Stations *pl* of the Cross, Way of the Cross; ***pasar por un ~*** *fig* go through hell
cruda *f Méx* F hangover
crudeza *f de clima* harshness; *de enfrentamiento* severity; *de lenguaje, imágenes* crudeness, coarseness; *de descripción* harshness; ***con toda ~*** in all its gory detail
crudo **I** *adj alimento* raw; *fig* harsh; ***voy a tenerlo ~ para aprobar*** F I'm going to have a hard job passing the exam, passing the exam isn't going to be easy **II** *m* crude (oil)
cruel *adj* cruel
crueldad *f* cruelty
cruento *adj* bloody
crujido *m de tarima* creak; *al arder* crackle; *de grava* crunch
crujiente *adj* GASTR crunchy
crujir ⟨3a⟩ *v/i de tarima* creak; *al arder* crackle; *de grava* crunch
crup *m* MED croup
crupier *m/f* croupier
crustáceos *mpl* ZO crustaceans
cruz *f* cross; ***cargar con su ~*** *fig* have one's cross to bear; ***con los brazos en ~*** with one's arms outstretched; ***hacerse cruces*** F be astonished (***de cómo*** that)
◇ **cruz gamada** swastika
◇ **Cruz Roja** Red Cross
cruza *f L.Am.* cross
cruzada *f* HIST, *fig* crusade
cruzado **I** *adj* **1** *piernas, cheque* crossed **2** *chaqueta* double-breasted **3**: ***había un tronco ~ en el camino*** there was a tree trunk lying across the road **II** *m* HIST, *fig* crusader
cruzamiento *m* BIO crossing
cruzar ⟨1f⟩ *v/t* cross; **cruzarse** *v/r* **1** pass one another; ***~ con alguien*** pass s.o. **2**: ***~ de brazos*** cross one's arms
c.s.f. *abr* (= ***costo***, ***seguro***, ***flete***) cif (= cost, insurance, freight)
cta *abr* (= ***cuenta***) A/C (= account)
cuaderna *f* MAR rib
cuaderno *m* notebook; EDU exercise book
◇ **cuaderno de bitácora** log, logbook
cuadra *f* **1** stable **2** *L.Am.* (*manzana*) block
cuadrado **I** *adj* square; ***cabeza -a*** F bigot **II** *m* square; ***al ~*** MAT squared; ***elevar al ~*** MAT square

cuadragésimo *m* fortieth
cuadrangular I *adj* quadrangular **II** *m L.Am. en béisbol* home run
cuadrante *m* MAT quadrant
cuadrar ⟨1a⟩ **I** *v/t* MAT square **II** *v/i* tally (***con*** with); **cuadrarse** *v/r* MIL stand to attention
cuadratura *f*: ***la ~ del círculo*** squaring the circle
cuadrícula *f* grid
cuadriculado *adj* **1** *persona* rigid, unbending **2**: ***papel ~*** graph *o* squared paper
cuadricular ⟨1a⟩ *v/t* draw a grid on
cuadrilátero *m/adj* quadrilateral
cuadrilla *f* squad, team
cuadro *m* **1** painting; (*grabado*) picture **2** (*tabla*) table **3** DEP team; POL, MIL staff, cadre; ***~ de actores*** TEA cast **4**: ***de*** *o* ***a ~s*** checked; ***estar*** *o* ***quedarse a ~s*** be short of staff
◇ **cuadro clínico** MED condition, manifestations *pl*; **cuadro de diálogo** INFOR dialog *o Br* dialogue box; **cuadro de distribución** EL switchboard; **cuadro de instrumentos, cuadro de mandos** AUTO dashboard; **cuadro sinóptico** tree diagram
cuadrúpedo *m* quadruped
cuádruple *m/adj* quadruple
cuadruplicar ⟨1g⟩ *v/t* quadruple
cuadruplo ☞ ***cuádruple***
cuajada *f* GASTR curd
cuajado *adj* **1** *leche* curdled **2** (*lleno*): ***~ de algo*** crammed with sth
cuajaleche *m* BOT bedstraw
cuajar ⟨1a⟩ **I** *v/i* **1** *de leche* curdle; *de nieve* settle; *fig*: *de idea, proyecto etc* come together, jell, gel **2** F (*llenar*) cover **II** *v/t leche* curdle; **cuajarse** *v/r de leche* curdle; *de nieve* settle
cuajo *m*: ***de ~*** by the roots
cual I *pron rel*: ***el ~, la ~*** *etc cosa* which; *persona* who; ***por lo ~*** (and) so; ***tiene dos coches, a cuál más caro*** he has two cars, both (of them) equally expensive **II** *adv* like; ***dejó la habitación tal ~ la encontró*** she left the room just as she found it
cuál *interr* which (one); ***~ más, ~ menos*** to a certain extent, to a greater or lesser extent; ***¿~ de vosotros ...?*** which one of you ...?
cualidad *f* quality
cualificación *f* qualification
cualificado *adj*: (***altamente***) ***~*** (highly) qualified
cualificar ⟨1g⟩ *v/t* qualify
cualitativo *adj* qualitative
cualquier *adj* any; ***~ día*** any day; ***~ cosa*** anything; ***de ~ modo*** *o* ***forma*** anyway; ***en ~ caso*** in any case
cualquiera *pron* **1** *persona* anyone, anybody; ***un ~*** a nobody; ***¡~ lo comprende!*** nobody can understand it!; ***¡así ~!*** anyone can do it like that!; ***~ diría ...*** you *o* anyone would think ... **2** *cosa* any (one); ***~ que sea*** *o* ***fuera*** whichever it is *o* was
cuán *adv* how
cuando I *conj* when; *condicional* if; ***~ quieras*** whenever you want **II** *adv* when; ***de ~ en ~*** from time to time; ***~ menos*** at least; ***~ más, ~ mucho*** at (the) most
cuándo *interr* when
cuantía *f* amount, quantity; *fig* importance
cuántico *adj* FÍS quantum *atr*; ***mecánica -a*** quantum mechanics *sg*; ***teoría -a*** quantum theory
cuantificar ⟨1g⟩ *v/t* quantify
cuantioso *adj* substantial
cuantitativo *adj* quantitative
cuanto[1] **I** *adj*: ***~ dinero quieras*** as much money as you want; ***unos ~s chavales*** a few boys
II *pron* all, everything; ***se llevó ~ podía*** she took all *o* everything she could; ***le dio ~ necesitaba*** he gave her everything she needed; ***unas -as*** a few; ***todo ~*** everything
III *adv*: ***~ antes, mejor*** the sooner the better; ***en ~*** as soon as; ***en ~ a*** as for; ***~ más*** the more; ***~ más, mejor*** the more the better; ***~ más ... más ...*** the more ..., the more ...; ***por ~*** inasmuch as; ***todos ~s*** all those who
cuanto[2] *m* FÍS quantum; ***teoría de los ~s*** quantum theory
cuánto I *interr adj* how much; *pl* how many; ***¿~ café?*** how much coffee?; ***¿~s huevos?*** how many eggs?; ***¿~ tiempo?*** how long?
II *pron* how much; *pl* how many; ***¿~ necesita Vd.?*** how much do you need?; ***¿~s ha dicho?*** how many did you say?; ***¿a ~ están?*** how much are they?;

¿a ~s estamos? what's the date today?
III *exclamaciones*: ***¡cuánta gente había!*** there were so many people!; ***¡~ me alegro!*** I'm so pleased!; ***¡~ lo siento!*** I can't tell you how sorry I am!
cuáquero *m*, **-a** *f* Quaker
cuarenta *adj* forty; ***cantar las ~ a alguien*** *fig* F give s.o. a piece of one's mind
cuarentena *f* quarantine; ***una ~*** a quarantine period
cuarentón I *adj* in one's forties **II** *m*, **-ona** *f* person in his / her forties, forty-something F
Cuaresma *f* Lent
cuaresmal *adj* Lent *atr*
cuarta *f* MÚS fourth
cuartear ⟨1a⟩ *v/t* cut up, quarter; **cuartearse** *v/r* crack
cuartel *m* **1** barracks *pl* **2**: ***lucha sin ~*** fight to the death; ***no dar ~*** give no quarter, show no mercy
◇ **cuartel general** headquarters *sg o pl*
cuartelazo *m L.Am.* military uprising
cuartelero *adj* barracks *atr*
cuarterón *m*, **-ona** *f L.Am.* quadroon
cuarteto *m* MÚS quartet; ***~ de cuerda*** string quarter
cuartilla *f* sheet of paper
cuarto I *adj* fourth **II** *m* **1** (*habitación*) room **2** (*parte*), DEP quarter; ***~ de hora*** quarter of an hour; ***~ de kilo*** quarter of a kilo; ***las diez y ~*** (a) quarter after *o Br* past ten; ***las tres menos ~*** a quarter to three, quarter of three; ***de tres al ~*** F third-rate; ***tres ~s*** *prenda* three-quarter length **3**: ***~s*** *pl* P dough *sg* F, *Br tb* dosh *sg* F; ***estar sin un ~*** be broke F
◇ **cuarto de baño** bathroom; **cuarto creciente** *de luna* first quarter; **cuarto de estar** living room; **cuartos de final** DEP quarter finals; **cuarto menguante** *de luna* last quarter
cuartucho *m desp* horrible little room
cuarzo *m* quartz
cuate *m Méx* **1** (*gemelo*) twin **2** F (*tío*) guy F
cuaternario GEOL **I** *adj* quaternary **II** *m* Quaternary
cuatrero *m* rustler
cuatrienal *adj* quadrennial, four-year *atr*; ***plan ~*** four-year plan
cuatrillizos *mpl* quad(ruplet)s
cuatrimestral *adj* four-monthly
cuatrimotor *m* AVIA four-engined plane
cuatripartito *adj* POL four-party *atr*
cuatro *adj* four; ***~ gotas*** F a few drops
cuatrocientos *adj* four hundred
Cuba *f* Cuba
cuba *f*: ***estar como una ~*** F be plastered F
cubalibre *m* rum and coke, cubalibre
cubano I *adj* Cuban **II** *m*, **-a** *f* Cuban
cubata *m* F ☞ ***cubalibre***
cubero *m* cooper; ***a ojo de buen ~*** roughly
cubertería *f* (set of) flatware, *Br* cutlery
cubeta *f* **1** *rectangular* tray **2** (*cubo*) bucket **3** (*cubitera*) ice tray
cubicaje *m* AUTO cubic capacity
cubicar ⟨1g⟩ *v/t* MAT cube
cúbico *adj* MAT cubic
cubículo *m* cubicle
cubierta *f* **1** MAR deck **2** AUTO tire, *Br* tyre **3** ARQUI roof
cubierto I *part* ☞ ***cubrir*** **II** *adj* covered (***de*** with, in) **III** *m* **1** piece of flatware, *Br* piece of cutlery; ***~s*** *pl* flatware *sg*, *Br* cutlery *sg* **2** *en la mesa* place setting **3**: ***ponerse a ~*** take cover (***de*** from)
cubil *m* den
cubilete *m* cup (*for dice*)
cubismo *m* cubism
cubista *m/f & adj* cubist
cubitera *f* **1** *bandeja* ice tray **2** (*cubo*) ice bucket
cúbito *m* ANAT ulna
cubito *m*: ***~ (de hielo)*** ice cube
◇ **cubito de caldo** bouillon cube, *Br* stock cube
cubo *m* **1** *figura* cube **2** *recipiente* bucket
◇ **cubo de la basura** *dentro* garbage can, *Br* rubbish bin; *fuera* garbage can, *Br* dustbin; **cubo de hielo** ice cube; **cubo de pedal** pedal bin
cubrecama *f* bedspread
cubreobjetos *m inv* slide cover
cubrir ⟨3a⟩ *v/t* cover (***de*** with); **cubrirse** *v/r* cover o.s.
cucamonas *fpl* F: ***hacerle ~ a alguien*** get around s.o., sweet-talk s.o.
cucaña *f* greasy pole
cucaracha *f* ZO cockroach
cuchara *f* **1** spoon; ***meter su ~*** *L.Am.* F stick one's oar in F **2** *L.Am.* (*paleta*) trowel

cucharada *f* spoonful
cucharadita *f* teaspoonful
cucharilla *f* teaspoon
cucharón *m* ladle
cuchichear ⟨1a⟩ *v/i* whisper
cuchicheo *m* whispering
cuchilla *f* razor blade
cuchillada *f* stab; *herida* stab wound
cuchillo *m* knife; ***~ de monte*** hunting knife; ***pasar a ~*** put to the sword
cuchipanda *f* F *comida* blow-out P, *Br tb* slap-up meal
cuchitril *m desp* hovel
cuchufleta *f* F joke
cuclillas: ***en ~*** squatting
cuclillo *m* ZO cuckoo
cuco I *m* ZO cuckoo; ***reloj de ~*** cuckoo clock **II** *adj* (*astuto*) sharp, crafty
cucurucho *m* **1** *de papel etc* cone **2** *sombrero* pointed hat
cuece *vb* ☞ ***cocer***
cuelgo *vb* ☞ ***colgar***
cuelgue *m* F high F
cuello *m* **1** ANAT neck; ***estar metido hasta el ~ en algo*** be up to one's neck in sth **2** *de camisa etc* collar; ***~ postizo*** detachable collar **3** *de botella* neck
◇ **cuello uterino** ANAT cervix, neck of the uterus
cuelo *vb* ☞ ***colar***
cuenca *f* **1** GEOG basin; ***~ hidrográfica*** (river) basin **2**: ***~ hullera** o **minera*** coalfield **3** *del ojo* socket
cuenco *m* bowl; ***el ~ de la mano*** the hollow of one's hand
cuenta *f* **1** (*cálculo*) sum; ***echar ~s de algo*** work sth out; ***perder la ~*** lose count
2 *de restaurante* check, *Br* bill; ***pasar la ~ a alguien*** send s.o. the bill; ***no me gusta pedirle favores porque siempre te pasa la ~*** *fig* I don't like asking him for favors because he always wants something in return; ***tener una ~ pendiente con alguien*** F have unfinished business with s.o.
3 COM account; ***a ~*** on account; ***póngamelo en la ~*** put it on the slate
4 (*justificación*): ***dar ~ de*** give an account of; ***pedir ~s a alguien*** ask s.o. for an explanation
5 (*responsabilidad*): ***corre por mi / su ~*** I'll / he'll pay for it; ***por su propia ~*** off one's own bat; ***trabajar por ~ ajena / propia*** be employed / self-employed
6: ***más de la ~*** too much; ***caer en la ~*** realize; ***darse ~ de algo*** realize sth; ***tener** o **tomar en ~*** take into account; ***en resumidas ~s*** in short; ***dar buena ~ de*** finish off, polish off F; ***a fin de ~s*** after all
◇ **cuenta de ahorros** savings account, *Br* deposit account; **cuenta atrás** countdown; **cuenta bancaria** bank account; **cuenta bloqueada** frozen account; **cuenta corriente** checking account, *Br* current account; **cuenta de gastos** expense account; **cuenta de pérdidas y ganancias** profit and loss account
cuentagotas *m inv* dropper; ***a** o **con ~*** *fig* F in dribs and drabs
cuentakilómetros *m inv* odometer, *Br* mileometer
cuentapropista *m/f L.Am.* self-employed person
cuentarrevoluciones *m inv* tachometer, *Br* rev counter
cuentista *m/f tb* F (*mentiroso*) storyteller
cuento *m* **1** (short) story; ***~ de nunca acabar*** *fig* never-ending story; ***ir con el ~ a alguien*** tell s.o. tales **2** (*pretexto*) excuse; ***tener mucho ~*** put it on F; ***vivir del ~*** F live off other people **3**: ***venir a ~*** be relevant; ***eso no viene a ~*** that's irrelevant; ***traer a ~*** bring up
◇ **cuento chino** F tall story F; **cuento de hadas** fairy tale; **cuento de viejas** old wives' tale
cuerda *f* **1** rope; ***~ de trepar*** climbing rope; ***~ para tender la ropa*** clothes line; ***poner a alguien contra las ~s*** get s.o. on the ropes; ***bajo ~*** on the side **2** *de guitarra, violín* string; ***ser de la misma ~*** be two of a kind
3 *mecanismo*: ***dar ~ al reloj*** wind the clock up; ***dar ~ a algo*** *fig* F string sth out F; ***dar ~ a alguien*** encourage s.o.; ***cuando cuenta historias, mi abuelo tiene ~ para rato*** when he's telling stories, my grandfather can talk for hours
◇ **cuerda floja** tightrope; ***andar** o **bailar en la ~*** *fig* F be walking a tightrope; **cuerda de tripa** MÚS gut string; **cuerdas vocales** *pl* ANAT vocal chords

C

C

cuerdo *adj* **1** sane **2** (*sensato*) sensible
cuerna *f* horns *pl*; *de ciervo* antlers *pl*
cuerno *m* horn; *de caracol* feeler; ***irse al ~*** F fall through, be wrecked; ***¡un ~!*** F you must be joking!; ***¡vete al ~!*** F go to hell! F; ***romperse los ~s*** F break one's back F, slog one's guts out F; ***poner los ~s a alguien*** F be unfaithful to s.o.
◇ **cuerno de la abundancia** horn of plenty, cornucopia
cuero *m* **1** leather **2** *Rpl* (*fuete*) whip **3**: ***en ~s*** F naked; ***dejar a alguien en ~s*** *fig* leave s.o. broke F, leave s.o. penniless
◇ **cuero cabelludo** scalp
cuerpo *m* **1** body; ***~ a ~*** hand-to-hand; ***retrato de ~ entero / de medio ~*** full-length / half-length portrait; ***a ~ de rey*** like a king; ***en ~ y alma*** body and soul; ***aún estaba de ~ presente*** he had not yet been buried; ***me lo pide el ~*** I feel like it; ***hacer del ~*** *euph* do one's business **2** *de policía* force; ***~ (de ejército)*** corps **3**: ***tomar ~*** take shape
◇ **cuerpo de baile** corps de ballet *sg*; **cuerpo de bomberos** fire department, *Br* fire brigade; **cuerpo celeste** heavenly body; **cuerpo del delito** JUR corpus delicti; **cuerpo diplomático** diplomatic corps *sg*; **cuerpo docente** teachers *pl*, teaching staff *sg o pl*; **cuerpo extraño** MED foreign body
cuervo *m* ZO raven, crow
cuesta *f* slope; ***~ abajo*** downhill; ***~ arriba*** uphill; ***se me hace ~ arriba levantarme a las 7 todos los días*** I find it very hard to get up at 7am every day; ***a ~s*** on one's back
cuestación *f* collection for charity
cuestión *f* **1** question **2** (*asunto*) matter, question; ***en ~ de dinero*** as far as money is concerned; ***no es ~ de dinero*** it's not a question of money; ***en ~*** in question; ***la ~ es que*** the thing is
cuestionable *adj* questionable
cuestionar ⟨1a⟩ *v/t* question
cuestionario *m* questionnaire
cuete *adj Méx* F (*borracho*) blitzed F, plastered F
cueva *f* cave; ***~ de ladrones*** den of thieves
cuévano *m* large, deep basket
cuezo *m*: ***meter el ~*** (*meter la pata*) put one's foot in it; (*ser indiscreto*) poke one's nose in
cuidado *m* care; ***¡~!*** look out!; ***andar con ~*** tread carefully; ***tener ~*** be careful; ***me tiene sin ~*** I couldn't *o* could care less, *Br* I couldn't care less; ***es un niño de ~*** you really have to watch that boy; ***¡pierda Vd. ~!*** don't worry!
cuidador *m* **1** *de niños* childminder; *de ancianos* carer **2** *de animales* keeper
cuidadora *f* **1** *de niños* childminder; *de ancianos* carer **2** *de animales* keeper **3** *Méx* nursemaid
cuidadoso *adj* careful
cuidar ⟨1a⟩ **I** *v/t* look after, take care of **II** *v/i*: ***~ de*** look after, take care of; **cuidarse** *v/r* **1** look after o.s., take care of o.s. **2**: ***~ de hacer algo*** take care to do sth
cuita *f* trouble, worry
cuitado *adj* troubled, worried
culantro *m* cilantro, coriander
culata *f* butt
culatazo *m* kick, recoil
culebra *f* ZO snake
culebrear ⟨1a⟩ *v/i de persona, animal* wriggle; *de carretera, río* wind
culebrilla *f* MED F shingles *sg*
culebrón *m* TV soap
culera *f* seat
culinario *adj* cooking *atr*, culinary
culminación *f* culmination
culminante *adj*: ***punto ~*** peak, climax
culminar ⟨1a⟩ **I** *v/i* culminate (***en*** in); *fig* reach a peak *o* climax **II** *v/t* finish
culo *m* V ass V, *Br* arse V; F butt F, *Br* bum F; ***caer(se) de ~*** fall on one's ass; ***lamer el ~ a alguien*** V brown-nose s.o. F; ***ir de ~*** *fig* F do badly; ***ser ~ de mal asiento*** *fig* F be restless, have ants in one's pants F; ***en el ~ del mundo*** *fig* in the boondocks F, in the middle of nowhere
culpa *f* fault; ***echar la ~ de algo a alguien*** blame s.o. for sth; ***ser por ~ de alguien*** be s.o.'s fault; ***tener la ~*** be to blame (***de*** for); ***sentimiento de ~*** feeling of guilt
culpabilidad *f* guilt
culpabilizar ⟨1f⟩ *v/t* blame
culpable I *adj* guilty; ***declarar ~ a alguien*** find s.o. guilty; ***ser ~ de algo*** be guilty of sth **II** *m/f* culprit
culpar ⟨1a⟩ *v/t*: ***~ a alguien de algo*** blame s.o. for sth

cultismo *m* learned word / expression
cultivable *adj* cultivable
cultivador *m* grower
cultivadora *f* **1** *máquina* cultivator **2** *mujer* grower
cultivar ⟨1a⟩ *v/t* AGR grow; *tierra* farm; *fig* cultivate
cultivo *m* **1** AGR crop **2** AGR *acto* growing, cultivation **3** BIO culture
◇ **cultivo extensivo** AGR extensive farming
culto I *adj* educated **II** *m* worship; ***rendir ~ a*** worship; ***~ a*** *o* ***de la personalidad*** personality cult
cultura *f* culture
◇ **cultura general** general knowledge
cultural *adj* cultural; ***un nivel ~ muy pobre*** a very poor standard of education
culturismo *m* bodybuilding
culturista *m/f* bodybuilder
culturizar ⟨1f⟩ *v/t* enlighten, educate; **culturizarse** *v/r* get o.s. an education
cumbre *f tb* POL summit; ***~ de la economía mundial*** world economic summit
cumpleaños *m inv* birthday
cumplido I *part* ☞ ***cumplir*** **II** *adj* **1** (*cortés*) polite **2**: ***tener 50 años ~s*** be 50 years old **III** *m* compliment; ***no andarse con ~s*** not stand on ceremony; ***por ~*** out of politeness
cumplidor *adj* reliable
cumplimentar ⟨1k⟩ *v/t trámite* carry out
cumplimiento *m de promesa* fulfillment, *Br* fulfilment; *de ley* compliance (***de*** with), observance (***de*** of),
cumplir ⟨3a⟩ **I** *v/t* **1** *orden* carry out; *promesa* fulfill, *Br* fulfil **2** *condena* serve **3**: ***~ diez años*** reach the age of ten, turn ten **II** *v/i* **1**: ***~ con algo*** carry sth out; ***~ con su deber*** do one's duty **2**: ***te invita sólo por ~*** he's only inviting you out of politeness; **cumplirse** *v/r de plazo* expire
cúmulo *m* (*montón*) pile, heap
cuna *f cama* crib, *Br* cot; *con balancín*, *fig* cradle
cundir ⟨3a⟩ *v/i* **1** *de noticia* spread **2** (*dar mucho de sí*) go a long way; ***me cunde el trabajo*** I get a lot of work done; ***nadie la conocía cuando llegó, pero con lo que cunde ...*** nobody knew her when she got here, but the way she's going …
cuneiforme *adj* cuneiform
cuneta *f* ditch; ***dejar a alguien en la ~*** *fig* F leave s.o. way behind
cunicultor *m*, **~a** *f* rabbit breeder
cunicultura *f* rabbit breeding
cuña *f* wedge
◇ **cuña anticiclónica** ridge of high pressure
◇ **cuña publicitaria** commercial break
cuñada *f* sister-in-law
cuñado *m* brother-in-law
cuño *m* stamp; ***de nuevo ~*** brand new
cuota *f* **1** share **2** *de club*, *asociación* fee; ***~ de abono*** TELEC line rental **3** *L.Am.* (*plazo*) installment, *Br* instalment
◇ **cuota empresarial** employer's contribution; **cuota de mercado** COM market share; **cuota patronal** employer's contribution
cupé *m* AUTO coupe, *Br* coupé
cuplé *m type of light cabaret song*
cupletista *m/f singer of* ***cuplés***
cupo[1] *m* quota
cupo[2] *vb* ☞ ***caber***
cupón *m* coupon
cúprico *adj* cupric, copper *atr*
cuprífero *adj* copper-bearing, cupriferous
cúpula *f* **1** dome, cupola **2** *esp* POL leadership; ***~ directiva*** board of directors
cura I *m* priest **II** *f* **1** cure; ***tener ~*** be curable **2** (*tratamiento*) treatment **3** *Méx*, *C.Am.* hangover
◇ **cura de reposo** rest cure
◇ **cura de urgencia** emergency treatment
curable *adj* curable
curación *f* **1** (*recuperación*) recovery **2** (*tratamiento*) treatment
curado *adj* **1** *Méx*, *C.Am.* drunk **2**: ***~ de espanto*** *fig* unshockable
curador *m*, **~a** *f* JUR guardian
curaduría *f* JUR guardianship
curanderismo *m* folk medicine
curandero *m*, **-a** *f* faith healer
curar ⟨1a⟩ **I** *v/t* **1** *tb* GASTR cure **2** (*tratar*) treat; *herida* dress **3** *pieles* tan **II** *v/i* MED recover (***de*** from); **curarse** *v/r* **1** MED recover; ***~ en salud*** F play safe **2** *Méx*, *C.Am.* get drunk
curativo *adj* curative; ***poder ~*** healing power
curato *m* parish
curda *f*: ***agarrarse una ~*** F get plastered F

curdo I *adj* Kurdish **II** *m*, **-a** *f* Kurd
curia *f* JUR legal profession
curiosamente *adv* strangely, oddly
curiosear ⟨1a⟩ **I** *v/t* **1** (*fisgonear*) pry into **2** (*mirar*) look around **II** *v/i* (*mirar*) look around
curiosidad *f* curiosity
curioso I *adj* **1** *persona* curious **2** (*raro*) curious, odd, strange **II** *m*, **-a** *f* onlooker
curita *f L.Am.* Band-Aid®, *Br* Elastoplast®
currante *m/f* F worker
currar ⟨1a⟩ *v/i* F work
curre *m* F work
currelar P ☞ ***currar***
currículo *m* curriculum
currículum vitae *m* résumé, *Br* CV, *Br* curriculum vitae
curro *m* P work
curry *m* GASTR curry
cursar ⟨1a⟩ *v/t* **1** *carrera* take **2** *orden, fax* send; *instancia* deal with
cursi F **I** *adj persona* affected **II** *m/f*: ***es un ~*** he is so affected
cursilería *f* affectation
cursillo *m* short course
cursiva *f* italics *pl*
cursivo *adj* italic
curso *m* **1** course; ***en el ~ de*** in the course of **2** COM: ***moneda de ~ legal*** legal tender **3** EDU: ***pasar de ~*** move up a grade; ***perder el ~*** miss the school year; ***repetir ~*** repeat a grade
◇ **curso acelerado** crash course; **curso por correspondencia** correspondence course; **curso a distancia** correspondence course; **curso escolar** academic year; **curso intensivo** crash course, intensive course
cursor *m* INFOR cursor
curtido I *adj* weather-beaten **II** *m* tanning; ***~s*** *pl* tanned hides
curtidor *m* tanner
curtiduría *f* tannery
curtiente *m* tanning agent
curtir ⟨3a⟩ *v/t* tan; *fig* harden; **curtirse** *v/r* become tanned
curul *m Méx* POL seat
curva *f* curve
curvar ⟨1a⟩ *v/t* bend; **curvarse** *v/r* bend; *de estante* sag
curvatura *f* curvature
curvilíneo *adj* curvilinear, curved
curvo *adj* curved
cuscurro *m* end, tip
cuscús *m* GASTR couscous
cúspide *f de montaña* summit; *de fama etc* height
custodia *f* JUR custody; ***bajo la ~ de alguien*** in s.o.'s custody
custodiar ⟨1b⟩ *v/t* guard
custodio *m*, **-a** *f* custodian
cususa *f C.Am.* corn liquor
cutáneo *adj* skin *atr*
cúter *m* MAR cutter
cutis *m* skin
cutre *adj* F shabby, dingy
cutrez *f* F shabbiness, dinginess
cuyo, -a *adj* whose
CV[1] *m abr* (= ***caballo(s) de vapor***) HP (= horsepower)
CV[2] *m* resumé, *Br* CV

D

D. *abr* (= ***Don***) Mr.
Da. *abr* (= ***Doña***) Mrs
dabute(n), dabuti *adj* F great F, fantastic F
dactilar *adj* finger *atr*
dactilografía *f* typing
dadá, dadaísmo *m* Dada, Dadaism
dádiva *f* gift
dadivosidad *f* generosity
dadivoso *adj* generous
dado[1] *m* dice; ***jugar a los ~s*** play dice
dado[2] **I** *part* ☞ ***dar*** **II** *adj* given; ***ser ~ a algo*** be given to sth **III** *conj*: ***~ que*** since, given that **IV** *prp* given
dador *m*, ***~a*** *f* COM drawer
daga *f* dagger
dalia *f* BOT dahlia
dallar ⟨1a⟩ *v/t hierba* scythe
dálmata *m perro* Dalmatian
daltónico *adj* color-blind, *Br* colour-blind
daltonismo *m* color-blindness, *Br* colour-blindness
dama *f* **1** lady; ***primera ~*** First Lady **2**:

(**juego de**) **~s** checkers *sg*, *Br* draughts *sg*
◇ **dama de compañía** (lady's) companion
◇ **dama de honor** bridesmaid
damajuana *f* demijohn
Damasco *m* Damascus
damasco *m* **1** damask **2** *L.Am. fruta* apricot; *árbol* apricot tree
damasquinado *m* damascene
damero *m* checkerboard, *Br* draughtboard
damisela *f* damsel
damnificado I *adj* affected **II** *m*, **-a** *f* victim
damnificar ⟨1g⟩ *v/t persona* harm; *cosa* damage
dandi *m* dandy
danés I *adj* Danish **II** *m*, **-esa** *f* Dane **III** *m idioma* Danish
danta *f L.Am.* ZO tapir
dantesco *adj fig* nightmarish
Danubio *m* Danube
danza *f* dance; ***estar en ~*** *fig* be on the go; ***meter a alguien en la ~*** F involve s.o.
◇ **danza macabra** danse macabre, dance of death
◇ **danza del vientre** belly dance
danzar ⟨1f⟩ *v/i* dance
danzarín *m*, **-ina** *f* dancer
dañado *adj* damaged
dañar ⟨1a⟩ *v/t* harm; *cosa* damage; **dañarse** *v/r de persona* harm o.s.; *de objeto* get damaged
dañino *adj* harmful; *fig* malicious
daño *m* **1** harm; *a un objeto* damage; ***hacer ~ a*** hurt; ***hacerse ~*** hurt o.s. **2**: ***~s*** *pl* damage *sg*; ***~s ecológicos*** *o* ***ambientales*** environmental damage, damage to the environment **3** *L.Am* F evil eye
◇ **daños materiales** damage *sg* to property; **daños personales** personal injury *sg*; **daños y perjuicios** damages
dañoso *adj* harmful
dar ⟨1r; *part* **dado**⟩ **I** *v/t* **1** give; *fiesta* give, have; ***~ un salto / una patada*** jump / kick, give a jump / kick; ***~ miedo a*** frighten; ***el jamón me dio sed*** the ham made me thirsty; ***~ de comer / beber a alguien*** give s.o. something to eat / drink
2 *fruta* bear; *luz* give off; *beneficio* yield
3 *película* show, screen
4: ***el reloj dio las tres*** the clock struck three
5: ***¡dale*** (***que dale***)***!*** F don't keep on! F; ***y siguió dale que te pego*** F and he kept on and on
II *v/i* **1** give; *de cartas en juego* deal; ***dame*** give it to me, give me it
2: ***~ a*** *de ventana* look onto
3: ***~ con algo / alguien*** come across sth / s.o., find sth / s.o.; ***no di con el nombre*** I couldn't think of the name
4: ***~ de sí*** *de material* stretch, give; ***~ para*** be enough for; ***no da para más*** it's past its best
5: ***le dio por insultar a su madre*** F she started insulting her mother
6: ***¡qué más da!*** what does it matter!; ***da igual*** it doesn't matter
7: ***~ contra*** *o* ***en algo*** hit sth; ***el sol le daba en la cara*** he had the sun in his eyes, the sun was in his eyes
8: ***~ por muerto a alguien*** give s.o. up for dead
9: ***~ que hablar*** give people something to talk about; ***da que pensar*** it makes you think, it gives you something to think about
darse *v/r* **1** *de situación* arise **2**: ***~ a algo*** take to sth **3**: ***esto se me da bien*** I'm good at this **4**: ***dárselas de algo*** make o.s. out to be sth, claim to be sth **5**: ***a mí no me las das*** F you don't fool me
dardo *m* dart
dársena *f* dock
datación *f* dating
datar ⟨1a⟩ **I** *v/i*: ***~ de*** date from **II** *v/t* date
dátil *m* BOT date
datilera *f* date palm; ***palmera ~*** date palm
dativo *m* GRAM dative
dato *m* piece of information; ***~s*** *pl* information *sg*, data *sg*
◇ **datos personales** personal details
D.C. *abr* (= ***después de Cristo***) AD (= Anno Domini)
dcho., dcha. *abr* (= ***derecho***, ***derecha***) r (= right)
de *prp* **1** *origen* from; ***~ Nueva York*** from New York; ***~ … a*** from … to
2 *posesión* of; ***el coche ~ mi amigo*** my friend's car
3 *material* (made) of; ***un anillo ~ oro*** a gold ring
4 *contenido* of; ***un vaso ~ agua*** a glass

of water
5 *cualidad*: ***una mujer ~ 20 años*** a 20 year old woman
6 *causa* with; ***temblaba ~ miedo*** she was shaking with fear
7 *hora*: ***~ noche*** at night, by night; ***~ día*** by day
8 *en calidad de* as; ***trabajar ~ albañil*** work as a bricklayer; ***~ niño*** as a child
9 *agente* by; ***~ Goya*** by Goya
10 *condición* if; ***~ haberlo sabido*** if I'd known
11 *en aposición*: ***la ciudad ~ Lima*** the city of Lima

dé *vb* ☞ ***dar***
d. de J.C. *abr* (= ***después de Jesucristo***) AD (= Anno Domini)
deambular ⟨1a⟩ *v/i* wander around
deán *m* REL dean
debacle *f* debacle
debajo I *adv* underneath **II** *prp*: **(*por*) *~ de*** under; ***un grado por ~ de lo normal*** one degree below normal
debate *m* debate, discussion
debatir ⟨3a⟩ **I** *v/t* debate, discuss **II** *v/i* struggle; **debatirse** *v/r*: ***~ entre la vida y la muerte*** fight for one's life
debe *m* COM debit
deber I *m* **1** duty **2**: ***~es*** *pl* homework *sg* **II** ⟨2a⟩ *v/t* owe; ***~ a alguien 500 pesos*** owe s.o. 500 pesos
III ⟨2a⟩ *v/i* **1** *en presente* must, have to; ***debo llegar a la hora*** I must be on time, I have to be on time; ***no debo llegar tarde*** I mustn't be late
2 *en pretérito* should have; ***debería haberme callado*** I should have kept quiet
3 *en futuro* will have to; ***deberán terminar imediatamente*** they must finish *o* they will have to finish immediately
4 *en condicional* should; ***¿qué debería hacer?*** what should I do?; ***no deberías hacer eso*** you shouldn't do that; ***debería ser lo suficientemente largo*** that should be long enough
5 *como suposición*: ***debe de hacer frío*** it must be cold; ***debe de tener quince años*** he must be about 15; ***debe de hacer poco que viven aquí*** they can't have lived here for long; ***ya deben de haber llegado*** they must *o* should have arrived by now
deberse *v/r*: ***~ a*** be due to, be caused by
debidamente *adv* properly, correctly
debido I *part* ☞ ***deber* II** *adj* **1** due; ***como es ~*** properly; ***a su ~ tiempo*** in due course **2** *en locuciones*: ***~ a*** due to, owing to, on account of; ***ser ~ a*** be due to
débil *adj* weak
debilidad *f* weakness
debilitación *f*, **debilitamiento** *m* debilitation, weakening
debilitar ⟨1a⟩ *v/t* weaken; **debilitarse** *v/r* weaken, become weaker; *de salud* deteriorate
debitar ⟨1a⟩ *v/t* COM debit
débito *m* COM debit
◇ **débito bancario** *L.Am.* direct billing, *Br* direct debit
debut *m* debut
debutante *m/f* beginner
debutar ⟨1a⟩ *v/i* make one's debut
década *f* decade
decadencia *f* decadence; *de imperio* decline
decadente *adj* decadent
decaer ⟨2o; *part* ***decaído***⟩ *v/i tb fig* decline; *de rendimiento* fall off, decline; *de salud* deteriorate
decaído I *part* ☞ ***decaer* II** *adj fig* depressed, down F
decaimiento *m* decline; *de salud* deterioration; ***sufre un ~*** she feels run down
decálogo *m* REL decalogue
decanato *m* deanship
decano *m*, **-a** *f* dean
decantar ⟨1a⟩ *v/t* decant; **decantarse** *v/r*: ***~ por*** opt for
decapitar ⟨1a⟩ *v/t* behead, decapitate
decatleta *m/f* DEP decathlete
decatlón *m* DEP decathlon
deceleración *f* deceleration
decelerar ⟨1a⟩ *v/i* decelerate
decena *f* ten; ***una ~ de*** about ten
decenal *adj* ten-yearly
decencia *f* decency
decenio *m* decade
decente *adj* decent
decepción *f* disappointment
decepcionado *adj* disappointed
decepcionante *adj* disappointing
decepcionar ⟨1a⟩ *v/t* disappoint
deceso *m* death
dechado *m fig* model
decibel *m L.Am.* decibel
decibelio *m* decibel

decidido I *part* ☞ ***decidir*** **II** *adj* decisive; ***estar ~*** be determined (***a*** to)
decidir ⟨3a⟩ **I** *v/t* decide **II** *v/i* decide, make up one's mind; **decidirse** *v/r* make up one's mind, decide
decigramo *m* decigram
decilitro *m* deciliter, *Br* decilitre
décima *f* **1** tenth **2**: ***tener ~s*** MED have a slight fever, *Br* have a slight temperature
decimal I *adj* decimal; ***número ~*** decimal number; ***sistema ~*** decimal system **II** *m* decimal
decímetro *m* decimeter, *Br* decimetre
décimo I *adj* tenth **II** *m de lotería*: *share of a lottery ticket*
decimonónico *adj fig* old-fashioned
decir ⟨3p; *part* ***dicho***⟩ **I** *v/t* **1** say; (*contar*) tell; ***~ misa*** say mass; ***~ que sí*** say yes; ***~ que no*** say no; ***se dice que …*** they say that …, it's said that …; ***diga lo que diga*** whatever he says; ***¿qué quieres que te diga?*** what do you expect me to say?; ***~ entre*** *o* ***para sí*** say to o.s.
2 *con infinitivo*: ***querer ~*** mean; ***es ~*** in other words; ***dar que ~*** set people talking; ***ni que ~ tiene*** (***que***) it goes without saying (that); ***por así ~lo*** so to speak; ***ya es ~*** that's saying something; ***que ya es ~*** which is really something; ***es mucho ~*** that's saying a lot
3 *con participio*: ***¡quién hubiera dicho que María se iba casar!*** who would have thought that Maria would get married!; ***dicho y hecho*** no sooner said than done; ***mejor dicho*** or rather; ***dicho sea de paso*** incidentally; ***está dicho***, ***lo dicho*** as I have already said
4: ***no es rico***, ***que digamos*** let's say he's not rich; ***¡no me digas!*** you're kidding!; ***¡dímelo a mí!*** tell me about it!, you're telling me!; ***como quien dice*** so to speak; ***y que lo digas*** you bet; ***¿y qué me dices de …?*** so what do you think of …?; ***usted dirá*** how can I help you?; ***ya decía yo que iba a acabar mal*** I knew it would end badly; ***¡quién lo diría!*** who would believe it!; ***¡cualquiera diría que tiene setenta años!*** who would have thought he was seventy!, you wouldn't think *o* believe he was seventy!
II *v/i*: ***¡diga!***, ***¡dígame!*** *Esp* TELEC hello **III** *m* saying; ***es un ~*** it's just a figure of speech
decisión *f* **1** decision; ***tomar una ~*** make *o* take a decision **2** *fig* decisiveness
decisivo *adj* critical, decisive
declamación *f* declamation
declamar ⟨1a⟩ *v/i* declaim
declamatorio *adj* declamatory
declaración *f* **1** declaration; *a la prensa*, *la policía* statement; ***hacer una ~*** make a statement; ***tomar ~ a alguien*** take a statement from s.o. **2** JUR: ***prestar ~*** testify, give evidence
◇ **declaración de aduana** customs declaration; **declaración de impuestos** tax return; **declaración jurada** sworn statement, affidavit; **declaración de quiebra** declaration of bankruptcy; **declaración de la renta** tax return; **declaración testimonial** witness statement
declarado I *part* ☞ ***declarar*** **II** *adj* self-confessed
declarante *m/f* JUR deponent
declarar ⟨1a⟩ **I** *v/t* **1** state **2** *bienes* declare **3**: ***~ culpable a alguien*** find s.o. guilty **II** *v/i* JUR give evidence; **declararse** *v/r* **1** declare o.s.; ***~ inocente*** JUR plead not guilty, plead innocent; ***~ a alguien*** declare one's love for s.o. **2** *de incendio* break out
declinación *f* **1** GRAM declension **2** *fig* decline
declinar ⟨1a⟩ *v/t & v/i* decline
declive *m fig* decline; ***en ~*** in decline; ***ir en ~*** decline
decocción *f* decoction
decodificación *f* ☞ ***descodificación***
decodificador *m* ☞ ***descodificador***
decodificar ⟨1g⟩ *v/t* ☞ ***descodificar***
decolaje *m L.Am.* takeoff
decolar ⟨1a⟩ *v/i L.Am.* take off
decolorante *m* bleaching agent
decolorar ⟨1a⟩ *v/t* bleach; **decolorarse** *v/r* bleach one's hair
decomisar ⟨1a⟩ *v/t* confiscate
decomiso *m* confiscation
decompresión *f* decompression
decomprimir ⟨3a⟩ *v/t* decompress
decoración *f* decoration
decorado *m* TEA set
decorador *m*, **~a** *f*. **~** (***de interiores***) interior decorator; TEA set designer
decorar ⟨1a⟩ *v/t* decorate
decorativo *adj* decorative

D

decoro *m* decorum; ***guardar el ~*** maintain decorum
decoroso *adj* decorous
decrecer ⟨2d⟩ *v/i* decrease, diminish
decreciente *adj* decreasing, diminishing
decremento *m* decrease
decrépito *adj* decrepit
decrepitud *f* decrepitude
decretar ⟨1a⟩ *v/t* order, decree; ***~ sanciones económicas*** impose economic sanctions
decreto *m* decree
decreto-ley *m* government decree
decúbito *m* position; ***~ prono / supino*** prone / supine position
décuplo *adj* tenfold
decurso *m* course; ***en el ~ de los años*** over the years
dedal *m* thimble
dedalera *f* BOT foxglove
dédalo *m* labyrinth
dedicación *f* dedication
dedicar ⟨1g⟩ *v/t* dedicate; *esfuerzo* devote; **dedicarse** *v/r* **1** devote o.s. (***a*** to) **2**: ***¿a qué se dedica?*** what do you do (for a living)?
dedicatoria *f* dedication
dedillo *m*: ***conocer algo al ~*** F know sth like the back of one's hand; ***saber algo al ~*** F know sth off by heart
dedo *m* finger; ***a dos ~s*** inches away; ***se pueden contar con los ~s de la mano*** they can be counted on the fingers of one hand; ***a ~ viajar*** hitchhike; ***no tiene dos ~s de frente*** F he doesn't have much commonsense; ***no mover (ni) un ~*** *fig* F not lift a finger F; ***pillarse los ~s*** *fig* F get one's fingers burned
◇ **dedo anular** ring finger; **dedo del corazón** middle finger; **dedo gordo** thumb; **dedo índice** forefinger, index finger; **dedo del pie** toe; **dedo meñique** little finger; **dedo pulgar** thumb
deducción *f* deduction
deducible *adj* **1** *conclusión* deducible **2** COM deductible
deducir ⟨3o⟩ *v/t* **1** deduce **2** COM deduct
defecación *f* defecation
defecar ⟨1g⟩ *v/i* defecate
defección *f* defection
defectivo *adj* defective
defecto *m* **1** defect; *moral* fault **2** INFOR default **3**: ***en ~ de*** for lack of, for want of; ***en su ~*** failing that
◇ **defecto de fabricación** manufacturing defect
defectuoso *adj* defective, faulty
defender ⟨2g⟩ **I** *v/t* **1** defend (***de*** against) **2** *en fútbol* mark **II** *v/i en fútbol* mark; **defenderse** *v/r* **1** defend o.s. (***de*** against); ***~ del frío*** ward off the cold **2** *fig* F manage, get by; ***me voy defendiendo*** I'm managing *o* coping
defendible *adj* defensible
defenestración *f fig* ousting
defenestrar ⟨1a⟩ *v/t fig* oust
defensa I *f* **1** JUR, DEP defense, *Br* defence; ***legítima ~*** self-defense, *Br* self-defence; ***salir en ~ de alguien*** come to s.o.'s defense **2** *L.Am.* AUTO fender, *Br* mudguard **3**: ***~s*** *pl* MED defenses, *Br* defences
II *m/f* DEP defender
◇ **defensa antiaérea** MIL anti-aircraft defenses *pl o Br* defences *pl*; **defensa central** *en fútbol* central defender, center-back, *Br tb* centre-back; **defensa al hombre** DEP man-to-man defense *o Br* defence; **defensa personal** self-defense, *Br* self-defence; **defensa en zona** *en baloncesto* zone defense *o Br* defence
defensiva *f* defensive; ***estar / ponerse a la ~*** be / go on the defensive; ***¡no hace falta que te pongas tan a la ~!*** stop being so defensive!; ***jugar a la ~*** DEP play defensively, play a defensive game
defensivo *adj* defensive
defensor *m*, **~a** *f* **1** defender, champion; ***~ de la naturaleza*** environmentalist **2** JUR defense lawyer, *Br* defending counsel
◇ **defensor de oficio** JUR court-appointed lawyer
◇ **defensor del pueblo** *en España* ombudsman
deferencia *f* deference; ***por ~ a*** in deference to
deferente *adj* deferential
defeño *m*, **-a** *f Méx* inhabitant of Mexico City, person from Mexico City
deficiencia *f* deficiency; ***con ~ auditiva*** with a hearing problem
◇ **deficiencia mental** mental handicap
deficiente I *adj* **1** *dieta* deficient **2** (*insatisfactorio*) inadequate **II** *m/f* mentally

handicapped person
◇ **deficiente visual** visually impaired person; ***los~s visuales*** the visually impaired
déficit *m* deficit
deficitario *adj* loss-making
definible *adj* definable
definición *f* definition; ***de alta~*** TV high definition
definido *adj* GRAM definite
definir ⟨3a⟩ *v/t* define; **definirse** *v/r* come down (***por*** in favor of)
definitivo *adj conclusión* definitive; *respuesta* definite; ***en -a*** all in all
deflación *f* COM deflation
deflacionario *adj* deflationary
deflagrar ⟨1a⟩ *v/i* QUÍM deflagrate *fml*, burst into flames
defoliación *f* defoliation
defoliar ⟨1b⟩ *v/i* defoliate
deforestación *f* deforestation
deforestar ⟨1a⟩ *v/t* deforest
deformación *f* deformation
deformar ⟨1a⟩ *v/t* **1** *forma, sonido* distort **2** MED deform
deforme *adj* **1** MED deformed **2** *zapatos* out of shape, misshapen
deformidad *f* deformity
defraudación *f* fraud
defraudador *m*, **~a** *f* fraudster
◇ **defraudador fiscal** tax evader
defraudar ⟨1a⟩ *v/t* **1** *expectativas* disappoint **2** (*estafar*) defraud; ***~ a Hacienda*** evade taxes
defunción *f* death, demise *fml*; ***certificado de ~*** death certificate
degeneración *f* degeneration
degenerado **I** *adj* degenerate **II** *m*, **-a** *f* degenerate
degenerar ⟨1a⟩ *v/i* degenerate (***en*** into)
deglución *f* swallowing
deglutir ⟨3a⟩ *v/t* swallow
degollar ⟨1n⟩ *v/t* cut the throat of; *fig* F murder F
degollina *f* slaughter
degradación *f* **1** degradation **2** MIL demotion
degradante *adj* degrading
degradar ⟨1a⟩ *v/t* **1** degrade **2** MIL demote **3** PINT gradate; **degradarse** *v/r* demean o.s.
degüello *m* (*degollina*) slaughter
degustación *f* tasting
◇ **degustación de vino** wine tasting
degustar ⟨1a⟩ *v/t* taste
dehesa *f* meadow
deidad *f* deity
deificar ⟨1g⟩ *v/t* deify
dejación *f* JUR abandonment; *de derechos* relinquishment
dejadez *f* **1** slovenliness **2** (*negligencia*) neglect
dejado **I** *part* ☞ ***dejar*** **II** *adj* slovenly
dejar ⟨1a⟩ **I** *v/t* **1** leave; *estudios* give up, quit F; ***~ mucho que desear*** leave a lot to be desired; ***~ algo para mañana*** leave sth until tomorrow; ***dejémoslo aquí*** let's leave it here; ***¡déjalo!*** *persona* leave him alone!; *asunto* drop it!
2 (*permitir*) let, allow; ***déjale marcharse*** let him go; ***~ que algo ocurra*** let sth happen, allow sth to happen
3 (*prestar*) lend
4 *beneficios* yield
5: ***déjame en la esquina*** drop me at the corner; ***~ caer algo*** drop sth
II *v/i* **1** (*parar*): ***~ de hacer algo*** stop doing sth; ***~ de fumar*** give up smoking, stop *o* quit smoking; ***no deja de fastidiarme*** he keeps (on) annoying me; ***no puedo ~ de pensar en ellos*** I can't stop thinking about them **2**: ***no dejes de visitarnos*** be sure to visit us
dejarse *v/r* **1** let o.s. go; ***~ llevar*** let o.s. be carried along **2**: ***déjate de lloros / de quejas*** stop crying / complaining **3**: ***ya se deja sentir el invierno*** it's getting a bit wintry; ***¡qué poco te dejas ver!*** we hardly ever see you!
deje, dejo *m* **1** *acento* slight accent **2** *gusto* aftertaste
del *prp* ***de*** *y art* ***el***
delación *f* denunciation
delantal *m* apron
delante *adv* **1** in front; ***lo tengo~*** I have it in front of me; ***el asiento de ~*** the front seat; ***se abrocha por ~*** it does up at the front; ***tener algo por~*** have sth ahead of *o* in front of one **2** (*más avanzado*) ahead; ***por ~*** ahead; ***¡pase usted~!*** you first!, after you! **3** (*enfrente*) opposite **4**: ***~ de*** in front of
delantera *f* DEP forward line; ***llevar la~*** be ahead, lead; ***tomar la ~ a alguien*** take the lead from s.o.
delantero **I** *adj* front *atr* **II** *m*, **-a** *f* DEP forward **III** *m de prenda* front
◇ **delantero centro** DEP center for-

ward, *Br* centre forward
delatar ⟨1a⟩ *v/t*: **~ *a alguien*** inform on s.o.; *fig* give s.o. away; **delatarse** *v/r* give o.s. away
delator *m*, **~a** *f* informer
delco *m* AUTO distributor
dele *m* deletion mark, delete
delectación *f* delectation
delegación *f* **1** delegation **2** *oficina* local office
◇ **delegación de Hacienda** tax office
◇ **delegación de policía** *Méx* police station, station house
delegado *m*, **-a** *f* delegate; COM representative
delegar ⟨1h⟩ *v/t* delegate
deleitable *adj* delightful
deleitar ⟨1a⟩ *v/t* delight; **deleitarse** *v/r* take delight (***con***, ***en*** in)
deleite *m* delight
deleitoso *adj* delightful
deletéreo *adj* deleterious
deletrear ⟨1a⟩ *v/t* spell
deleznable *adj* contemptible
delfín *m* ZO dolphin
delgadez *f de cuerpo* slimness; (*esbeltez*) thinness
delgado *adj* slim; *lámina*, *placa* thin
delgaducho *adj* F skinny F
deliberación *f* deliberation
deliberado *adj* deliberate
deliberar ⟨1a⟩ **I** *v/i* deliberate (***sobre*** on) **II** *v/t* discuss
delicadeza *f* **1** *de movimientos* gentleness **2** *de acabado*, *tallado* delicacy **3** (*tacto*) tact; ***tener la ~ de hacer algo*** be kind enough to do sth
delicado *adj* delicate
delicia *f* delight; ***hacer las ~s de alguien*** delight s.o.
delicioso *adj* delightful; *comida* delicious
delictivo *adj* criminal; ***acto*** *o* ***hecho ~*** criminal act
delimitar ⟨1a⟩ *v/t* delimit
delincuencia *f* crime
◇ **delincuencia informática** computer crime
◇ **delincuencia juvenil** juvenile delinquency
delincuente *m/f* criminal
◇ **delincuente habitual** habitual criminal, repeat offender; **delincuente juvenil** juvenile delinquent; **delincuente sexual** sex offender
delineador *m* eyeliner
◇ **delineador de labios** lip pencil
delineante *m/f* draftsman, *Br* draughtsman; *mujer* draftswoman, *Br* draughtswoman
delinear ⟨1a⟩ *v/t* draft; *fig* draw up
delinquir ⟨3e⟩ *v/i* offend
delirante *adj* delirious; *fig*: *idea* crazy
delirar ⟨1a⟩ *v/i* be delirious; ***¡tú deliras!*** *fig* you must be crazy!
delirio *m* MED delirium; ***con ~*** *fig* deliriously; ***tener ~ por el fútbol*** *fig* be mad about soccer
◇ **delirios de grandeza** delusions of grandeur
delito *m* offense, *Br* offence
◇ **delito ecológico** ecological crime, eco-crime; **delito fiscal** tax offense, *Br* tax offence; **delito informático** computer crime; **delito de sangre** violent crime; **delito sexual** sex crime
delta *m* GEOG delta
demacrado *adj* haggard
demacrarse ⟨1a⟩ *v/r* waste away
demagogia *f* demagogy
demagógico *adj* demagogic
demagogo *m*, **-a** *f* demagogue
demanda *f* **1** demand (***de*** for); ***en ~ de*** (asking) for **2** COM demand; ***tener mucha ~*** be very popular; ***tiene poca ~*** there's not much demand for it, it's not very popular **3** JUR lawsuit, claim; ***presentar*** *o* ***interponer una ~ contra alguien*** take legal action against s.o.
◇ **demanda civil** JUR civil (law)suit; **demanda de divorcio** JUR divorce suit; **demanda de empleo** demand for work
demandado *m*, **-a** *f* JUR defendant
demandante *m/f* JUR plaintiff
◇ **demandante de trabajo** job seeker
demandar ⟨1a⟩ *v/t* JUR sue
demarcación *f* demarcation
demarcar ⟨1g⟩ *v/t* demarcate
demás **I** *adj* remaining **II** *pron*: ***lo ~*** the rest; ***los ~*** the rest, the others **III** *adv*: ***por lo ~*** apart from that; ***y ~*** and so on; ***por ~*** extremely
demasía *f* excess; ***en ~*** too much
demasiado **I** *adj* too much; *antes de pl* too many; ***-a gente*** too many people; ***hace ~ calor*** it's too hot **II** *adv antes de adj*, *adv* too; *con verbo* too much;

¡esto es ~! *fig* this is too much!
demencia *f* MED dementia; *fig* madness
◇ **demencia senil** MED senile dementia
demencial *adj fig* crazy, mad
demente I *adj* demented, crazy **II** *m/f* mad person
democracia *f* democracy
demócrata I *adj* democratic **II** *m/f* democrat
democrático *adj* democratic
democratizar ⟨1f⟩ *v/t* democratize
democristiano I *adj* Christian Democrat *atr* **II** *m*, **-a** *f* Christian Democrat
demografía *f* demographics *sg*
demográfico *adj* demographic
demoledor *adj* demolition *atr*; *fig* devastating
demoler ⟨2h⟩ *v/t* demolish
demolición *f* demolition
demoniaco, demoníaco *adj* demonic
demonio *m* demon; ***¡~s!*** F hell! F, damn! F; ***a ~s*** F *oler, saber* terrible, hellish F; ***al ~ con …*** F to hell with … F; ***como un ~*** F like a madman F; ***tener el ~ en el cuerpo*** be a handful
demora *f* delay; ***sin ~*** without delay
demorar ⟨1a⟩ **I** *v/i* **1** stay on **2** *L.Am.* (*tardar*) be late; ***no demores*** don't be long **II** *v/t* delay; **demorarse** *v/r* **1** be delayed **2**: ***¿cuánto se demora de Concepción a Santiago?*** how long does it take to get from Concepción to Santiago?
demorón *adj L.Am.* F: ***es ~*** he's always late
demoscópico *adj*: ***instituto ~*** opinion poll institute
demostrable *adj* demonstrable
demostración *f* **1** proof **2** *de método* demonstration **3** *de fuerza, sentimiento* show
demostrar ⟨1m⟩ *v/t* **1** prove **2** (*enseñar*) demonstrate **3** (*mostrar*) show
demostrativo *adj* demonstrative
demudar ⟨1a⟩ *v/t* change, alter; *fig*: *expresión de la cara* distort, contort; **demudarse** *v/r* change, alter
denegación *f* refusal
denegar ⟨1h & 1k⟩ *v/t* refuse
dengue *m* **1** *afectación* fussiness; ***no le hace ~s a nada*** he never makes a fuss about anything **2** MED dengue
denigración *f* denigration
denigrante *adj* **1** *trato* degrading **2** *artículo* denigrating
denigrar ⟨1a⟩ *v/t* **1** degrade **2** (*criticar*) denigrate
denodado *adj* tireless
denominación *f* name
◇ **denominación de origen** *guarantee of provenance and quality of a wine or other product*
denominador *m*: ***~ común*** *fig* common denominator
denominar ⟨1a⟩ *v/t* designate; **denominarse** *v/r* be called
denostar ⟨1m⟩ *v/t* insult
denotación *f* indication
denotar ⟨1a⟩ *v/t* indicate, denote
densidad *f* density
◇ **densidad de población** population density
densificar ⟨1g⟩ *v/t* make denser
densitometría *f*: ***~ ósea*** MED bone-mass measurement
denso *adj bosque* dense; *fig* weighty
dentado *adj* serrated; ***rueda -a*** cogwheel
dentadura *f*: ***~ postiza*** false teeth *pl*, dentures *pl*
dental *adj* dental
dentellada *f* **1** bite; ***rompió la cuerda a ~s*** he bit through the rope **2** *herida* teeth mark
dentera *f*: ***darle ~ a alguien*** set s.o.'s teeth on edge
dentición *f* **1** teething; ***estar con la ~*** be teething **2** (*dientes*) teeth *pl*
dentífrico I *adj*: ***pasta -a*** toothpaste **II** *m* toothpaste
dentista *m/f* dentist
dentro I *adv* inside; ***por ~*** inside; *fig* inside; ***de ~*** from inside **II** *prp*: ***~ de*** *en espacio* in, inside; *en tiempo* in, within
denuedo *m* valor, *Br* valour; ***con ~*** valiantly
denuesto *m* insult
denuncia *f* report; ***poner una ~*** make a formal complaint
denunciante *m/f person who reports a crime*
denunciar ⟨1b⟩ *v/t* report; *fig* condemn, denounce
deontología *f* professional ethics *pl*
deontológico *adj*: ***código ~*** code of ethics
deparar ⟨1a⟩ *v/t alegrías* bring; ***¿qué***

nos deparará el futuro? what does the future have in store *o* hold for us?

departamento *m* **1** department **2** *L.Am.* (*apartamento*) apartment, *Br* flat

◇ **departamento de comercio exterior** foreign trade department; **departamento de contabilidad** accounts *sg* (department); **departamento de ventas** sales *sg* (department)

departir ⟨3a⟩ *v/i* talk, converse *fml*

depauperación *f* impoverishment

depauperar ⟨1a⟩ *v/t* impoverish; **depauperarse** *v/r* become impoverished

dependencia *f* **1** dependence, dependency (***de*** on) **2** COM department

depender ⟨2a⟩ *v/i* **1** depend (***de*** on); ***eso depende*** that all depends **2**: ***~ de alguien*** *en una jerarquía* report to s.o.

dependiente **I** *adj* dependent **II** *m*, **-a** *f* sales clerk, *Br* shop assistant

depilación *f* hair removal; *con cera* waxing; *con pinzas* plucking

depilar ⟨1a⟩ *v/t con cera* wax; *con pinzas* pluck

depilatorio **I** *adj* hair-removing, depilatory; ***crema -a*** hair-removing cream, depilatory **II** *m* hair remover, depilatory

deplorable *adj* deplorable

deplorar ⟨1a⟩ *v/t* deplore

deponer ⟨2r; *part* ***depuesto***⟩ **I** *v/t* **1** *ministro, presidente* dismiss; *rey* depose **2** *armas* lay down **II** *v/i* JUR give evidence, testify

deportación *f* deportation

deportar ⟨1a⟩ *v/t* deport

deporte *m* sport; ***hacer ~*** play sports; ***~ en pista cubierta*** indoor sport

◇ **deporte de alta competición** high-level sport; **deporte de alto riesgo** high-risk sport; **deporte de aventura** adventure activity; **deporte blanco** winter sport; **deporte de invierno** winter sport; **deporte náutico** water sports *pl*; **deporte rey**: ***el ~*** the beautiful game

deportista **I** *adj* sporting **II** *m* sportsman **III** *f* sportswoman

◇ **deportista náutico** sailor

deportividad *f* sportsmanship

deportivo *adj* sports *atr*; *actitud* sporting

deposición *f* deposition

depositante *m/f* COM depositor

depositar ⟨1a⟩ *v/t tb fig* put, place; *dinero* deposit (***en*** in); **depositarse** *v/r* settle

depositario *m*, **-a** *f* COM depositor

depósito *m* **1** COM deposit; ***tomar algo en ~*** take sth as a deposit **2** (*almacén*) store **3** *de agua*, AUTO tank

◇ **depósito de cadáveres** morgue, *Br* mortuary

depravación *f* depravity

depravado *adj* depraved

depravar ⟨1a⟩ *v/t* deprave

depre F **I** *adj* depressed, down F **II** *f* depression

deprecación *f* supplication, entreaty

deprecar ⟨1g⟩ *v/t* beg, entreat

depreciación *f* depreciation

depreciar ⟨1b⟩ *v/t* lower the value of; **depreciarse** *v/r* depreciate, lose value

depredación *f* depredation

depredador **I** *adj* predatory **II** *m*, **~a** *f* ZO predator

depredar ⟨1a⟩ *v/t* ZO prey on

depresión *f* MED depression

◇ **depresión atmosférica** low pressure area, low, depression

depresivo *adj* depressive

deprimente *adj* depressing

deprimido *adj* depressed

deprimir ⟨3a⟩ *v/t* depress; **deprimirse** *v/r* get depressed

deprisa *adv* fast, quickly; ***~ y corriendo*** in a rush

depuesto *part* ☞ ***deponer***

depuración *f* **1** purification **2** POL purge

depuradora *f* purifier; ***planta ~ de aguas residuales*** sewage treatment plant

depurar ⟨1a⟩ *v/t* **1** purify **2** POL purge

derbi *m* derby

derecha *f tb* POL right; ***de ~s*** POL right-wing, of the right; ***la ~*** the right(-hand); ***a la ~*** *posición* on the right; *dirección* to the right; ***a ~s*** right

derechazo *m en boxeo* right

derechista POL **I** *adj* right-wing **II** *m/f* right-winger

derecho **I** *adj* **1** *lado* right **2** (*recto*) straight **3** *C.Am. fig* straight, honest **II** *adv* straight; ***siga ~*** carry straight on; ***tenerse ~*** stand up / sit up straight; ***poner ~ algo*** straighten sth; *vertical* right sth, set sth upright; ***vamos ~ a casa***

we're going straight home
III *m* **1** (*privilegio*) right; ***con ~ a*** with a right to; ***dar ~ a alguien a algo*** entitle s.o. to sth; ***la tarjeta da ~ a entrar gratuitamente*** the card entitles you to free entry; ***tener ~ a*** have a right to, be entitled to; ***tener el ~ de*** have the right to, be entitled to; ***estar en su ~*** be within one's rights; ***no hay ~*** it's not fair, it's not right; ***miembro de pleno ~*** full member **2** JUR law; ***estudiar ~*** study law **3**: ***del ~*** *vestido, jersey* on the right side
IV *mpl*: ***~s*** fees; ***~s de almacenaje*** storage charges
◇ **derecho administrativo** administrative law; **derecho de asilo** right to asylum; **derecho civil** civil law; **derecho exclusivo de venta** exclusive sales rights *pl*; **derecho internacional** international law; **derecho del más fuerte** law of the jungle; **derecho mercantil** commercial law; **derecho penal** criminal law; **derecho procesal** law of procedure; **derecho de voto** right to vote; **derechos de aduana** customs duties; **derechos de autor** royalties; **derechos cívicos** civil rights; **derechos humanos** human rights; **derechos de inscripción** registration fee *sg*

derechura *f* **1** straightness; ***en ~*** straight away **2** *C.Am., Pe* luck

deriva *f*: ***ir a la ~*** MAR, *fig* drift

derivación *f* derivation

derivado *m* QUÍM, GRAM derivative

derivar ⟨1a⟩ *v/i* **1** derive (***de*** from) **2** *de barco* drift; **derivarse** *v/r* be derived (***de*** from)

dermatitis *f* MED dermatitis

dermatología *f* dermatology

dermatólogo *m*, **-a** *f* dermatologist

dérmico *adj* skin *atr*

dermis *f* ANAT dermis

dermofarmacia *f* cosmetology, cosmetic science

derogación *f* repeal

derogar ⟨1h⟩ *v/t* repeal

derrama *f* apportionment

derramamiento *m* spilling
◇ **derramamiento de sangre** bloodshed

derramar ⟨1a⟩ *v/t* **1** spill; *luz, sangre, lágrimas* shed; *fig* waste **2** (*esparcir*) scatter; **derramarse** *v/r* **1** spill **2** *de gente* scatter

derrame *m* MED: ***~ cerebral*** stroke

derrapar ⟨1a⟩ *v/i* AUTO skid

derredor *m*: ***en*** *o* ***al ~*** around

derrengado *adj* exhausted

derrengar ⟨1h⟩ *v/t*: ***~ a alguien*** break s.o.'s back; *fig* exhaust s.o., wear s.o. out; **derrengarse** *v/r fig* collapse

derretimiento *m* melting

derretir ⟨3l⟩ *v/t* melt; **derretirse** *v/r* melt; *fig* be besotted (***por*** with); ***~ por alguien*** be crazy about s.o. F

derribar ⟨1a⟩ *v/t* **1** *edificio, persona* knock down **2** *avión* shoot down **3** POL bring down

derribo *m* **1** *de edificio* demolition **2** *de persona* knocking down **3** *de avión* shooting down **4** POL overthrow

derrocamiento *m* POL overthrow

derrocar ⟨1g⟩ *v/t* POL overthrow

derrochador **I** *adj* wasteful **II** *m*, **~a** *f* spendthrift

derrochar ⟨1a⟩ *v/t* **1** *dinero* waste **2** *salud, felicidad* exude, be bursting with

derroche *m* waste

derrota *f* defeat; ***~ electoral*** election defeat; ***sufrir una ~*** be defeated, suffer a defeat

derrotado *adj fig* **1** (*cansado*) exhausted **2** (*deprimido*) depressed

derrotar ⟨1a⟩ *v/t* MIL defeat; DEP beat, defeat; *fig*: *salud* ruin

derrotero *m* MAR, *fig* course; ***ir por otros ~s*** *fig* change tack

derrotismo *m* defeatism

derrotista *m/f* defeatist

derruir ⟨3g⟩ *v/t edificio* demolish

derrumbamiento *m accidental* collapse; *intencionado* demolition

derrumbar ⟨1a⟩ *v/t* knock down; **derrumbarse** *v/r* **1** collapse, fall down **2** *de persona* go to pieces

derrumbe *m* ☞ ***derrumbamiento***

derviche *m* dervish

desabastecer ⟨2d⟩ *v/t*: ***~ a alguien de algo*** stop s.o.'s supply of sth

desabastecimiento *m* shortage

desabollar ⟨1a⟩ *v/t* take the dents out of

desaborido **I** *adj* bland, insipid **II** *m*, **-a** *f* bore

desabotonar ⟨1a⟩ *v/t* unbutton; **desabotonarse** *v/r* unbutton

desabrido *adj* **1** (*soso*) bland, insipid **2** *persona* surly **3** *tiempo* unpleasant

D

desabrigado *adj*: ***salir ~*** go out without warm enough clothes on
desabrigarse ⟨1h⟩ *v/r* take off one's coat; ***no te desabrigues*** keep your coat on
desabrimiento *m* tastelessness, blandness
desabrochar ⟨1a⟩ *v/t* undo, unfasten; ***~ el cinturón*** AVIA unfasten one's safety belt
desacatar ⟨1a⟩ *v/t orden* disobey; *ley, regla* break
desacato *m* JUR contempt
desaceleración *f* deceleration
desacelerar ⟨1a⟩ *v/t & v/i* slow down
desacertado *adj* misguided
desacertar ⟨1k⟩ *v/i* be wrong
desacierto *m* mistake
desacomplejarse ⟨1a⟩ *v/r* get rid of one's complexes
desaconsejable *adj* inadvisable
desaconsejado *adj*: ***esta ~ el consumo de bebidas alcohólicas durante el embarazo*** drinking during pregnancy is not advised, it is not advisable to drink during pregnancy
desaconsejar ⟨1a⟩ *v/t* advise against
desacoplar ⟨1a⟩ *v/t* uncouple
desacostumbrado *adj*: ***estar ~ a algo*** be unaccustomed to sth, be unused to sth
desacostumbrar ⟨1a⟩ *v/t*: ***~ a alguien de algo*** get s.o. out of the habit of sth; **desacostumbrarse** *v/r*: ***~ a algo*** get out of the habit of sth
desacreditado *adj* discredited
desacreditar ⟨1a⟩ *v/t* discredit
desactivación *f* deactivation
desactivar ⟨1a⟩ *v/t bomba etc* deactivate
desacuerdo *m* disagreement; ***estar en ~ con*** disagree with
desafecto **I** *adj* hostile (***a*** to) **II** *m* disaffection
desafiador, desafiante *adj* defiant
desafiar ⟨1c⟩ *v/t* challenge; *peligro* defy
desafinado *adj* MÚS out of tune
desafinar ⟨1a⟩ *v/i* MÚS be out of tune; *fig* speak out of turn
desafío *m* challenge; *al peligro* defiance
desaforado *adj* **1** *ambición* boundless **2** *grito* ear-splitting
desafortunadamente *adv* unfortunately
desafortunado *adj* unfortunate, unlucky
desafuero *m* outrage
desagradable *adj* unpleasant, disagreeable
desagradar ⟨1a⟩ *v/i*: ***me desagrada tener que ...*** I dislike having to ...; ***les desagradó lo que hizo*** they were unhappy with what he did; ***no me desagradaría ...*** I wouldn't mind ...
desagradecido *adj* ungrateful; ***una tarea -a*** a thankless task
desagradecimiento *m* ingratitude
desagrado *m* displeasure
desagraviar ⟨1b⟩ *v/t*: ***~ a alguien*** (***por algo***) make amends to s.o. (for sth)
desagravio *m* apology
desaguadero *m* drain
desaguar ⟨1i⟩ **I** *v/t* drain **II** *v/i* **1** *de agua* drain away **2** *de río* flow, drain (***en*** into)
desagüe *m* **1** *orificio* drain; (*cañería*) drainpipe **2** *acción* drainage
desaguisado *m* crime
desahogado *adj* spacious
desahogar ⟨1h⟩ *v/t sentimiento* vent; **desahogarse** *v/r fig* F let off steam F, get it out of one's system F
desahogo *m* comfort; ***con ~*** comfortably
desahuciar ⟨1b⟩ *v/t* **1**: ***~ a alguien*** declare s.o. terminally ill **2** *inquilino* evict
desahucio *m* JUR eviction; ***demanda de ~*** eviction order
desairar ⟨1a⟩ *v/t* snub
desaire *m* snub; ***hacer un ~ a alguien*** snub s.o.
desajustar ⟨1a⟩ *v/t* **1** *tornillo, pieza* loosen **2** *mecanismo, instrumento* affect, throw out of balance; **desajustarse** *v/r* TÉC work loose
desajuste *m* **1** disruption **2** COM imbalance **3**: ***existe un ~ en el engranaje*** the gears are not adjusted correctly
desalación *f* **1** *de agua* desalination **2** GASTR soaking (*to remove salt*)
desaladora *f* desalination plant
desalar ⟨1a⟩ *v/t* **1** *agua* desalinate **2** GASTR soak (*to remove salt*)
desalentador *adj* disheartening
desalentar ⟨1k⟩ *v/t* discourage; **desalentarse** *v/r* become disheartened *o* discouraged
desaliento *m* discouragement
desalinización *f* desalination

desalinizador *adj*: ***planta ~a*** desalination plant
desalinizar ⟨1f⟩ *v/t* desalinate
desaliñado *adj* slovenly
desaliño *m* slovenliness
desalmado I *adj* heartless **II** *m*, **-a** *f*: ***es un ~*** he is heartless
desalojar ⟨1a⟩ **I** *v/t* **1** *ante peligro* evacuate **2** (*desahuciar*) evict **3** (*vaciar*) vacate **II** *v/i* move out
desalojo *m* **1** *ante peligro* evacuation **2** *de inquilinos* eviction **3** *de ocupantes* removal
desamor *m* coldness, lack of affection
desamparado *adj* defenseless, *Br* defenceless
desamparar ⟨1a⟩ *v/t*: ***~ a alguien*** abandon s.o., leave s.o. defenseless *o Br* defenceless
desamparo *m* neglect
desamueblado *adj* unfurnished
desandar ⟨1q⟩ *v/t*: ***~ el camino*** retrace one's steps; ***~ lo andado*** *fig* go back to square one
desangelado *adj lugar* soulless; *persona* dull, charmless
desangrar ⟨1a⟩ *v/t* bleed; **desangrarse** *v/r* bleed to death
desanimado *adj* discouraged, disheartened
desanimar ⟨1a⟩ *v/t* discourage, dishearten; **desanimarse** *v/r* become discouraged *o* disheartened
desánimo *m* discouragement
desanudar ⟨1a⟩ *v/t* untie, undo
desapacible *adj* nasty, unpleasant
desaparecer ⟨2d⟩ **I** *v/i* disappear, vanish **II** *v/t L.Am.* disappear F, make disappear
desaparecido I *adj* missing **II** *m*, **-a** *f* **1**: ***el ~*** the deceased **2** *L.Am.* ***un ~*** one of the disappeared
desaparición *f* disappearance
desapasionado *adj* dispassionate
desapegarse ⟨1h⟩ *v/r fig* lose touch, become distanced
desapego *m* indifference; (*distancia*) distance, coolness
desapercibido *adj* unnoticed; ***pasar ~*** go unnoticed; ***pillar ~ a alguien*** catch s.o. unawares
desaplicación *f* laziness, lack of application
desaplicado *adj* lazy
desapoderar ⟨1a⟩ *v/t*: ***~ a alguien de algo*** strip s.o. of sth
desaprensión *f* unscrupulousness
desaprensivo *adj* unscrupulous
desaprobación *f* disapproval
desaprobar ⟨1m⟩ *v/t* disapprove of
desaprovechado *adj oportunidad, talento* wasted
desaprovechamiento *m* waste
desaprovechar ⟨1a⟩ *v/t oportunidad* waste
desarbolar ⟨1a⟩ *v/t* MAR dismast
desarmado *adj* unarmed
desarmador *m Méx*, *tb* F *bebida* screwdriver
desarmante *adj fig* disarming
desarmar ⟨1a⟩ *v/t* **1** MIL disarm **2** TÉC take to pieces, dismantle
desarme *m* MIL disarmament
desarraigar ⟨1h⟩ *v/t tb fig* uproot
desarraigo *m fig* rootlessness
desarreglado *adj* **1** *habitación, aspecto* untidy **2** *vida* disorganized, chaotic
desarreglar ⟨1a⟩ *v/t* **1** *habitación* make untidy **2** *horario* disrupt
desarreglo *m* **1** *hormonal* disorder **2** *de horarios* disruption
desarrollar ⟨1a⟩ *v/t* **1** develop **2** *tema* explain **3** *trabajo* carry out; **desarrollarse** *v/r* **1** develop, evolve **2** (*ocurrir*) take place
desarrollo *m* development
desarrugar ⟨1h⟩ *v/t ropa* remove the creases from
desarticular ⟨1a⟩ *v/t* **1** *banda criminal* break up **2** MED dislocate
desaseado *adj* F scruffy, untidy
desaseo *m* scruffiness, untidiness
desasirse ⟨3a⟩ *v/r*: ***~ de*** get free of, free o.s. from
desasnar ⟨1a⟩ *v/t* F enlighten, educate
desasosegar ⟨1h & 1k⟩ *v/t* make uneasy; **desasosegarse** *v/r* become uneasy *o* restless
desasosiego *m* disquiet, unease
desastrado *adj* untidy
desastre *m tb fig* disaster; ***ser un ~*** *fig* F be a disaster F
◇ **desastre ecológico** environmental disaster
◇ **desastre natural** natural disaster
desastroso *adj* disastrous
desatar ⟨1a⟩ *v/t* untie; *fig* unleash; **desatarse** *v/r* **1** *de animal, persona* get

free **2** *de cordón* come undone; *fig* be unleashed, break out; ***~ en insultos*** let fly a string of insults
desatascar ⟨1g⟩ *v/t* unblock
desatención *f* lack of attention, inattention
desatender ⟨2g⟩ *v/t* **1** *amigos, profesión etc* neglect **2** (*ignorar*) ignore
desatento *adj* **1** (*desconsiderado*) discourteous **2** (*distraído*) inattentive
desatinado *adj* foolish
desatinar ⟨1a⟩ *v/i* (*actuando*) act foolishly; (*hablando*) talk nonsense
desatino *m* mistake
desatornillador *m esp L.Am.* screwdriver
desatornillar ⟨1a⟩ *v/t* unscrew
desatrancar ⟨1g⟩ *v/t cañería* unblock
desautorizado *adj* unauthorized
desautorizar ⟨1f⟩ *v/t* **1** (*prohibir*) refuse permission for **2** (*desacreditar*) discredit
desavenencia *f* disagreement
desavenir ⟨3s⟩ *v/t* make trouble between; **desavenirse** *v/r* fall out (***con*** with)
desaventajado *adj* unfavorable, *Br* unfavourable
desayunar ⟨1a⟩ **I** *v/i* have breakfast **II** *v/t*: ***~ algo*** have sth for breakfast; **desayunarse** *v/r* **1** have breakfast; ***~ con algo*** have sth for breakfast **2**: ***~ de algo*** hear about sth
desayuno *m* breakfast
desazón *f* (*ansiedad*) uneasiness, anxiety
desazonado *adj* worried, anxious
desazonar ⟨1a⟩ *v/t* worry, make anxious
desbancar ⟨1g⟩ *v/t fig* displace, take the place of; *a un alto cargo* oust
desbandada *f*: ***a la ~*** in all directions; ***salir en ~*** scatter
desbandarse ⟨1a⟩ *v/r* disband; *de grupo de personas* scatter
desbarajuste *m* mess
desbaratar ⟨1a⟩ *v/t* **1** *planes* ruin, spoil; *organización* disrupt **2** *dinero* squander; **desbaratarse** *v/r* be spoiled
desbarrancar ⟨1g⟩ *L.Am. v/t* push over the edge of a cliff; **desbarrancarse** *v/r* go over the edge of a cliff
desbarrar ⟨1a⟩ *v/i* talk nonsense
desbastar ⟨1a⟩ *v/t* smooth down
desbloquear ⟨1a⟩ *v/t* **1** *carretera* clear; *mecanismo* free up, unjam; *tubería etc* clear, unblock; *proceso de paz* break the logjam in **2** *cuenta bancaria* unfreeze
desbloqueo *m* **1** *de carretera* clearing; *de mecanismo* freeing up, unjamming; *de tubería etc* clearing, unblocking; ***hasta el ~ del proceso de paz*** until such time as the logjam in the peace process has been broken **2** *de cuenta bancaria* unfreezing
desbocado *adj* **1** *caballo* runaway **2** (*malhablado*) foulmouthed
desbocarse ⟨1g⟩ *v/r de caballo* bolt
desbordamiento *m* overflow
desbordante *adj energía, entusiasmo etc* boundless; ***~ de*** bursting with, overflowing with
desbordar ⟨1a⟩ **I** *v/t* **1** *de río* overflow, burst **2** *de multitud* break through **3** *de acontecimiento* overwhelm; *fig* exceed **II** *v/i* overflow; **desbordarse** *v/r de río* burst its banks, overflow; *fig* get out of control
desbrozar ⟨1f⟩ *v/t* clear
descabalgar ⟨1h⟩ *v/i* dismount
descabellado *adj*: ***idea -a*** F hare-brained idea F
descabellar ⟨1a⟩ *v/t* TAUR *kill with a knife-thrust in the neck*
descabello *m knife thrust to the neck*
descabezado *adj persona* beheaded; *organización* leaderless; *fig* crazy
descabezar ⟨1f⟩ *v/t* **1** *persona* behead, decapitate; *cosa* take the top off; *organización* remove the leader of **2**: ***~ un sueño*** F have forty winks
descacharrante *adj* F hilarious
descafeinado *adj* decaffeinated; *fig* watered-down
descalabrar ⟨1a⟩ *v/t*: ***~ a alguien*** split s.o.'s head open
descalabro *m* calamity, disaster
descalcificación *f* calcium deficiency
descalcificador *m* water softener
descalcificar ⟨1g⟩ *v/t* **1** *water* soften **2** MED decalcify
descalificación *f* disqualification
descalificar ⟨1g⟩ *v/t* disqualify
descalzar ⟨1f⟩ *v/t*: ***~ a alguien*** take s.o.'s shoes off; **descalzarse** *v/r* take one's shoes off
descalzo *adj* barefoot

descamar ⟨1a⟩ *v/t pescado* scale; **descamarse** *v/r de piel* flake off
descambiar ⟨1a⟩ *v/t* F *artículo* exchange, swap
descaminado *adj fig* misguided; ***andar o ir ~*** be on the wrong track
descamisado *adj* shirtless; *fig* ragged
descampado *m* open ground
descansado *adj trabajo* light, undemanding
descansar ⟨1a⟩ **I** *v/i* rest, have a rest; ***¡que descanses!*** sleep well **II** *v/t* **1** rest (***sobre*** on) **2**: ***¡descansen armas!*** MIL order arms!
descansillo *m* landing
descanso *m* **1** rest; ***sin ~*** without a break; ***tomarse un ~*** take a break, have a rest **2** DEP half-time; TEA interval **3** *L.Am.* (*descansillo*) landing
descapitalización *f* decapitalization
descapotable *m* AUTO convertible
descarado *adj* rude, impertinent
descararse ⟨1a⟩ *v/r* be rude *o* impertinent
descarga *f* **1** EL, MIL discharge **2** *de mercancías* unloading **3** INFOR downloading
◇ **descarga eléctrica** electric shock
descargadero *m* wharf
descargar ⟨1h⟩ **I** *v/t* **1** *arma*, EL discharge; *fig*: *ira etc* take out (***en***, ***sobre*** on) **2** *mercancías* unload **3** *de responsabilidad*, *culpa* clear (***de*** of) **4** INFOR download **II** *v/i de tormenta etc* hit; **descargarse** *v/r de pila* go flat
descargo *m* defense, *Br* defence; ***decir algo en ~ de alguien*** say sth in s.o.'s defense
descargue *m* unloading
descarnado *adj* **1** *persona* emaciated **2** *relato* stark
descaro *m* nerve
descarriado *adj*: ***ir ~*** go astray
descarriar ⟨1c⟩ *v/t* misdirect; **descarriarse** *v/r* lose one's way
descarrilamiento *m* FERR derailment
descarrilar ⟨1a⟩ *v/t* derail
descartable *adj L.Am.* disposable
descartar ⟨1a⟩ *v/t* rule out; **descartarse** *v/r en naipes* discard
descascarar ⟨1a⟩ *v/t fruta* peel; *nuez* shell
descascarillar ⟨1a⟩ *v/t* chip
descastado *adj* cold, uncaring
descendencia *f* descendants *pl*
descendente *adj* downward; *escala* descending
descender ⟨2g⟩ **I** *v/i* **1** *para indicar alejamiento* go down, descend; *para indicar acercamiento* come down, descend; *fig* go down, decrease, diminish **2**: ***~ de*** *de civilización* descend from **II** *v/t escalera* go down; *para indicar acercamiento* come down
descendiente *m/f* descendant
descendimiento *m* descent
descenso *m* **1** *de precio etc* drop; *de montaña*, AVIA descent; ***la prueba de ~*** *en esquí* the downhill (race *o* competition) **2** DEP relegation
descentralización *f* decentralization
descentralizar ⟨1f⟩ *v/t* decentralize
descentrar ⟨1a⟩ *v/t fig* shake; **descentrarse** *v/r fig* lose one's concentration
descerebrado *adj* mindless
descerrajar ⟨1a⟩ *v/t* **1** *tiro* fire **2** *puerta* force
descifrar ⟨1a⟩ *v/t* decipher; *fig* work out
desclasificar ⟨1g⟩ *v/t* declassify
desclavar ⟨1a⟩ *v/t clavo*, *chincheta* take out, remove
descocado *adj* daring
descodificación *f* decoding
descodificador *m* decoder
descodificar ⟨1g⟩ *v/t* decode
descolgar ⟨1h & 1m⟩ *v/t* **1** take down **2** TELEC pick up; **descolgarse** *v/r* **1** *por una cuerda* lower o.s. **2** *de grupo* break away **3** *de póster*, *cortina* come down **4** *L.Am.* ***~ con algo*** come out with sth; ***te descuelgas con que no quieres*** F out of the blue you say you don't want to **5** *L.Am.* ***~ por un sitio*** F turn up somewhere unexpectedly
descollante *adj* outstanding
descollar ⟨1m⟩ *v/i* stand out (***sobre*** among)
descolonización *f* decolonization
descolonizar ⟨1f⟩ *v/t* decolonize
descolorar ⟨1a⟩ *v/t* bleach; **descolorarse** *v/r* fade
descolorido *adj* faded; *fig* colorless, *Br* colourless
descombrar ⟨1a⟩ *v/t* clear (up)
descomedido *adj* **1** immoderate **2** (*descortés*) rude
descomedirse ⟨3l⟩ *v/r* be rude (***con*** to)
descompaginar ⟨1a⟩ *v/t plan* upset

descompasado *adj*: ***están ~s*** MÚS they're not keeping time
descompensar ⟨1a⟩ *v/t* unbalance
descomponer ⟨2r; *part* ***descompuesto***⟩ *v/t* **1** (*dividir*) break down **2** *L.Am.* (*romper*) break **3** (*pudrir*) cause to decompose **4** *plan* upset; **descomponerse** *v/r* **1** (*pudrirse*) decompose, rot **2** TÉC break down **3** *Rpl* (*emocionarse*) break down (in tears) **4**: ***se le descompuso la cara*** he turned pale
descomposición *f* **1** breaking down **2** (*putrefacción*) decomposition; ***en avanzado estado de ~*** in an advanced state of decay *o* decomposition **3** (*diarrea*) diarrhea, *Br* diarrhoea
descompostura *f L.Am.* (*avería*) breakdown, fault
descompuesto I *part* ☞ ***descomponer*** **II** *adj* **1** *alimento* rotten; *cadáver* decomposed **2** *persona* upset **3** *L.Am.* tipsy **4** *L.Am. máquina* broken down
descomunal *adj* huge, enormous
desconcentrarse ⟨1a⟩ *v/r* lose one's concentration
desconcertado *adj* disconcerted
desconcertar ⟨1k⟩ *v/t a persona* disconcert; **desconcertarse** *v/r* be disconcerted, be taken aback
desconchado *m place where the paint is peeling*; *en porcelana* chip
desconcharse ⟨1a⟩ *v/r de porcelana* chip; ***se había desconchado la pared*** the paint had peeled off the wall
desconchón *m* ☞ ***desconchado***
desconcierto *m* uncertainty
desconectar ⟨1a⟩ **I** *v/t* EL disconnect **II** *v/i fig* switch off; **desconectarse** *v/r fig* lose touch (***de*** with)
desconexión *f* disconnection
desconfiado *adj* mistrustful, suspicious
desconfianza *f* mistrust, suspicion
desconfiar ⟨1c⟩ *v/i* be mistrustful (***de*** of), be suspicious (***de*** of)
descongelación *f* **1** *de comida* thawing, defrosting **2** *de precios* unfreezing
descongelar ⟨1a⟩ *v/t* **1** *comida* thaw, defrost; *refrigerador* defrost **2** *precios* unfreeze; **descongelarse** *v/r* defrost, thaw
descongestión *f* decongestion
descongestionar ⟨1a⟩ *v/t* **1** MED clear **2**: ***~ el tráfico*** relieve traffic congestion
desconocer ⟨2d⟩ *v/t* not know
desconocido I *adj* unknown **II** *m*, **-a** *f* stranger
desconocimiento *m* ignorance
desconsideración *f* lack of consideration
desconsiderado *adj* inconsiderate
desconsolado *adj* inconsolable
desconsolador *adj* distressing
desconsolar ⟨1m⟩ *v/t* distress
desconsuelo *m* grief
descontado I *part* ☞ ***descontar*** **II** *adj*: ***dar por ~*** take for granted; ***por ~*** certainly
descontaminación *f* decontamination
descontaminar ⟨1a⟩ *v/t* decontaminate
descontar ⟨1m⟩ *v/t* COM deduct, take off; *fig* exclude
descontentadizo *adj* hard to please
descontentar ⟨1a⟩ *v/t* displease
descontento I *adj* dissatisfied **II** *m* dissatisfaction
descontrol *m* chaos
descontrolado *adj* out of control
descontrolarse ⟨1a⟩ *v/r* get out of control; (*enojarse*) lose control
desconvocar ⟨1g⟩ *v/t* call off
descoordinación *f* lack of coordination
descorazonamiento *m* discouragement
descorazonar ⟨1a⟩ *v/t* discourage; **descorazonarse** *v/r* get discouraged
descorchador *m Rpl* corkscrew
descorchar ⟨1a⟩ *v/t botella* uncork
descorrer ⟨2a⟩ *v/t cortina, pestillo* draw (back)
descortés *adj* impolite, rude
descortesía *f* discourtesy, impoliteness
descortezar ⟨1f⟩ *v/t* strip the bark from
descoser ⟨2a⟩ *v/t costura* unpick; **descoserse** *v/r de costura, dobladillo etc* come unstitched; *de prenda* come apart at the seams
descosido I *adj fig* disjointed **II** *m*, **-a** *f*: ***como un ~*** F like mad F; ***hablar como un ~*** F talk non-stop
descoyuntamiento *m* dislocation
descoyuntar ⟨1a⟩ *v/t* dislocate
descrédito *m* discredit; ***caer en ~*** be discredited
descreído I *adj* skeptical, *Br* sceptical **II** *m*, **-a** *f* skeptic, *Br* sceptic
descreimiento *m* skepticism, *Br* scepticism

descremado *adj* skimmed
descremar ⟨1a⟩ *v/t leche* skim
describir ⟨3a; *part* ***descrito***⟩ *v/t* describe
descripción *f* description
descriptivo *adj* descriptive
descriptor *m* INFOR descriptor
descrito *part* ☞ ***describir***
descuajaringarse ⟨1h⟩ *v/r* F fall apart, fall to bits; **~ (*de risa*)** split one's sides (with laughter)
descuartizar ⟨1f⟩ *v/t* quarter
descubierta *f* MIL reconnaissance
descubierto I *part* ☞ ***descubrir*** **II** *adj* **1** uncovered; *persona* bare-headed; ***al ~*** in the open; ***dormir al ~*** sleep outdoors *o* out in the open; ***poner al ~*** *fig* expose; ***quedar al ~*** *fig* be exposed; ***dejar algo al ~*** leave sth uncovered *o* exposed **2** *cielos* clear **3** *piscina* open-air **III** *m* COM overdraft; ***en ~*** *cuenta* overdrawn
descubridor *m*, **~a** *f* discoverer
descubrimiento *m* **1** *de territorio, cura etc* discovery **2** (*revelación*) revelation
descubrir ⟨3a; *part* ***descubierto***⟩ *v/t* **1** *territorio, cura etc* discover **2** (*averiguar*) discover, find out **3** *poner de manifiesto* uncover, reveal; *estatua* unveil; **descubrirse** *v/r* take one's hat off; *fig* give o.s. away
descuento *m* **1** discount **2** DEP stoppage time
descuerar ⟨1a⟩ *v/t L.Am.* skin; ***~ a alguien*** *fig* tear s.o. to pieces
descuidado *adj* careless
descuidar ⟨1a⟩ **I** *v/t* neglect **II** *v/i*: ***¡descuida!*** don't worry!; **descuidarse** *v/r* **1** get careless **2** *en cuanto al aseo* let o.s. go **3** (*despistarse*) let one's concentration lapse
descuidero *m*, **-a** *f* sneak thief
descuido *m* **1** carelessness; ***en un ~*** *L.Am.* in a moment of carelessness; ***por ~*** through carelessness **2** (*error*) mistake **3** (*omisión*) oversight
desde *prp* **1** *en el tiempo* since; ***~ 1993*** since 1993; ***~ que*** since; ***~ hace tres días*** for three days; ***~ hace mucho / poco*** for a long / short time; ***~ mañana*** from tomorrow; ***~ ya*** *Rpl* right away **2** *en el espacio* from; ***~ arriba / abajo*** from above / below; ***te veo ~ aquí*** I can see you from here **3** *en escala* from; ***~ … hasta …*** from … to … **4**: ***~ luego*** of course
desdecir ⟨3p; *part* ***desdicho***⟩ *v/i*: ***la decoración desdice de un lugar tan formal*** the decor is not in keeping with such formal surroundings; ***la corbata desdice de la camisa*** the tie does not go with the shirt; **desdecirse** *v/r*: ***~ de algo*** withdraw *o* retract sth
desdén *m* disdain, contempt
desdentado *adj* toothless
desdeñable *adj* contemptible; ***nada ~*** far from insignificant
desdeñar ⟨1a⟩ *v/t* scorn
desdeñoso *adj* disdainful, contemptuous
desdibujado *adj* blurred
desdibujar ⟨1a⟩ *v/t* blur; **desdibujarse** *v/r* become blurred
desdicha *f* **1** (*desgracia*) misfortune **2** (*infelicidad*) unhappiness
desdichado I *adj* **1** unhappy **2** (*sin suerte*) unlucky **II** *m*, **-a** *f* poor soul
desdicho *part* ☞ ***desdecir***
desdoblamiento *m* **1** unfolding **2** (*división*) splitting; ***~ de la personalidad*** PSI split personality
desdoblar ⟨1a⟩ *v/t* **1** unfold **2** (*dividir*) split; **desdoblarse** *v/r* split in two, divide
desdorar ⟨1a⟩ *v/t fig* tarnish
desdoro *m* dishonor, *Br* dishonour
desdramatizar ⟨1f⟩ *v/t* take the drama out of; *situación* play down
deseable *adj* desirable
deseado *adj* desired; ***niño ~*** wanted child; ***no ~*** unwanted
desear ⟨1a⟩ *v/t* **1** wish for; *suerte etc* wish **2**: ***¿qué desea?*** what would you like?; ***¿desea algo más?*** would you like anything else?
desecación *f de comestibles* drying; *de terreno* drainage
desecar ⟨1g⟩ *v/t comestibles* dry; *terreno* drain; **desecarse** *v/r* dry up, dry out
desechable *adj* disposable
desechar ⟨1a⟩ *v/t* **1** (*tirar*) throw away **2** (*rechazar*) reject
desechos *mpl* waste *sg*
◇ **desechos espaciales** space garbage *sg*; **desechos nucleares** nuclear waste *sg*; **desechos reciclables** recyclable waste *sg*; **desechos tóxicos** toxic waste *sg*
desembalaje *m* unpacking

D

desembalar ⟨1a⟩ *v/t* unpack
desembarazar ⟨1f⟩ *v/t* clear; **desembarazarse** *v/r*: **~ *de*** get rid of
desembarazo *m* ease
desembarcadero *m* MAR landing stage
desembarcar ⟨1g⟩ **I** *v/i* disembark **II** *v/t personas* land; *mercancías* unload
desembarco *m*, **desembarque** *m de personas* disembarkation; *de mercancías* landing
desembarrancar ⟨1g⟩ *v/t & v/i* refloat
desembocadura *f de calle* end; *de río* mouth
desembocar ⟨1g⟩ *v/i* **1** *de río* flow (***en*** into); *de calle* come out (***en*** into) **2** *de situación* end (***en*** in)
desembolsar ⟨1a⟩ *v/t* pay out
desembolso *m* expenditure, outlay
desembozar ⟨1f⟩ *v/t* unmask
desembragar ⟨1h⟩ **I** *v/t embrague* release **II** *v/i* release the clutch, declutch
desembrague *m* declutching
desembrollar ⟨1a⟩ *v/t* untangle; *fig* sort out
desembuchar ⟨1a⟩ *v/i fig* F spill the beans F, come out with it F; ***¡desembucha!*** F out with it! F
desemejante *adj* dissimilar
desemejanza *f* dissimilarity, difference
desempacar ⟨1g⟩ *v/t* unpack
desempacho *m* ease
desempapelar ⟨1a⟩ *v/t pared* strip (the wallpaper from)
desempaquetar ⟨1a⟩ *v/t* unwrap
desempatar ⟨1a⟩ *v/i* DEP, POL decide the winner
desempate *m*: ***fue necesaria una votación de ~*** POL a vote was necessary to decide the winner; (***partido de***) **~** DEP decider, deciding game
desempeñar ⟨1a⟩ *v/t* **1** *deber*, *tarea* carry out **2** *cargo* hold **3** *papel* play **4** *cosa empeñada* redeem
desempeño *m* **1** *de tarea*, *deber* execution, performance **2** *de papel* performance **3** *de cosa empeñada* redemption
desempleado **I** *adj* unemployed **II** *m*, **-a** *f* unemployed person; ***los ~s*** *pl* the unemployed
desempleo *m* unemployment; **~ *de larga duración*** long-term unemployment
desempolvar ⟨1a⟩ *v/t* **1** dust **2** *fig* dust off; *conocimientos teóricos* brush up
desenamorarse ⟨1a⟩ *v/r* fall out of love
desencadenamiento *m* setting off, triggering
desencadenante **I** *adj*: ***factor ~*** trigger **II** *m fig* trigger
desencadenar ⟨1a⟩ *v/t fig* set off, trigger; **desencadenarse** *v/r fig* be triggered
desencajar ⟨1a⟩ *v/t* **1** *mecanismo*, *puerta* remove **2** *mandíbula* dislocate; **desencajarse** *v/r* **1** *de pieza* come out **2**: ***se le ha desencajado la mandíbula*** he has dislocated his jaw
desencallar ⟨1a⟩ *v/t* MAR refloat
desencaminar ⟨1a⟩ *v/t* misdirect; **desencaminarse** *v/r* take the wrong road
desencantado *adj fig* disillusioned, disenchanted (***con*** with)
desencantar ⟨1a⟩ *v/t fig* disillusion, disenchant
desencanto *m fig* disillusionment, disenchantment
desenchufar ⟨1a⟩ *v/t* EL unplug
desencolarse ⟨1a⟩ *v/r* come unstuck *o* unglued
desencriptar ⟨1a⟩ *v/t* INFOR decrypt, decode
desencuentro *m fig* mix-up
desenfadado *adj* **1** self-assured **2** *programa* light, undemanding
desenfadarse ⟨1a⟩ *v/r* calm down
desenfado *m* ease
desenfocado *adj* FOT out of focus
desenfocar ⟨1g⟩ *v/t* FOT: **~ *algo*** get sth out of focus
desenfrenado *adj* frenzied, hectic
desenfrenarse ⟨1a⟩ *v/r de persona* lose control
desenfreno *m* frenzy
desenfundar ⟨1a⟩ *v/t arma* take out, draw
desenganchar ⟨1a⟩ *v/t caballo* unhitch; *carro* uncouple; **desengancharse** *v/r* **1** get loose **2** *fig* F kick the habit F
desengañar ⟨1a⟩ *v/t* disillusion; **desengañarse** *v/r* **1** become disillusioned (***de*** with) **2** (*dejar de engañarse*) stop kidding o.s.
desengaño *m* disappointment
desengrasar ⟨1a⟩ *v/t* clean the grease off
desenlace *m* outcome, ending
desenlazar ⟨1f⟩ *v/t* untie; **desenla-**

zarse *v/r de obra de teatro* end
desenmarañar ⟨1a⟩ *v/t* untangle
desenmascarar ⟨1a⟩ *v/t fig* unmask, expose
desenredar ⟨1a⟩ *v/t* **1** untangle **2** *situación confusa* straighten out, sort out; **desenredarse** *v/r* extricate o.s.
desenredo *m* disentanglement
desenrollar ⟨1a⟩ *v/t rollo de tela, papel etc* unroll; *cable* unwind
desenroscar ⟨1g⟩ *v/t* unscrew
desensillar ⟨1a⟩ *v/t caballo* unsaddle
desentenderse ⟨2g⟩ *v/r* not want to know (***de*** about)
desentendido *adj*: ***hacerse el ~*** F pretend not to notice
desenterramiento *m* disinterment
desenterrar ⟨1k⟩ *v/t* disinter, dig up; *fig*: *viejo amor, odios* resurrect; *escándalo* dig up
desentonar ⟨1a⟩ *v/i* MÚS go off key; ***~ con*** *fig* clash with; ***decir algo que desentona*** say something out of place
desentrañar ⟨1a⟩ *v/t fig* unravel
desentrenado *adj* out of condition
desentrenamiento, desentreno *m* lack of training
desentumecerse ⟨2d⟩ *v/r* loosen up; ***~ las piernas*** stretch one's legs
desenvainar ⟨1a⟩ *v/t espada* draw, unsheathe
desenvoltura *f* ease
desenvolver ⟨2h; *part* ***desenvuelto***⟩ *v/t* unwrap; **desenvolverse** *v/r fig* cope
desenvuelto **I** *part* ☞ ***desenvolver*** **II** *adj* self-confident
deseo *m* wish
deseoso *adj*: ***~ de hacer algo*** eager to do sth
desequilibrado **I** *adj* unbalanced **II** *m*, **-a** *f*: ***ser un ~ mental*** be mentally unbalanced
desequilibrar ⟨1a⟩ *v/t* unbalance; ***~ a alguien*** throw s.o. off balance; **desequilibrarse** *v/r* lose one's balance
desequilibrio *m* imbalance; ***~ Norte-Sur*** North-South divide
◇ **desequilibrio mental** mental instability
deserción *f* desertion
desertar ⟨1a⟩ *v/i* **1** MIL desert **2** POL defect
desértico *adj* desert *atr*
desertización *f* desertification
desertizar ⟨1f⟩ *v/t* desertify; **desertizarse** *v/r* become desertified, turn into a desert
desertor *m*, **~a** *f* **1** MIL deserter **2** POL defector
desescombrar ⟨1a⟩ *v/t* clear (up), remove the rubble from
desescombro *m* clearing (up), removal of rubble
desesperación *f* **1** despair **2**: ***ser una ~*** *tener que hacer cola, esperar etc* be infuriating
desesperado *adj* in despair; ***a la -a*** out of desperation
desesperante *adj* infuriating, exasperating
desesperanzador *adj* gloomy
desesperanzar ⟨1f⟩ *v/t* make lose hope; **desesperanzarse** *v/r* give up hope, lose hope
desesperar ⟨1a⟩ **I** *v/t* infuriate, exasperate **II** *v/i* give up hope (***de*** of), despair (***de*** of); **desesperarse** *v/r* get exasperated
desespero *m* desperation
desestabilizar ⟨1f⟩ *v/t* POL destabilize
desestatización *f L.Am.* privatization
desestatizar ⟨1f⟩ *v/t L.Am.* privatize
desestimar ⟨1a⟩ *v/t queja, petición* reject
desfachatez *f* impertinence
desfalcar ⟨1g⟩ *v/t dinero* embezzle
desfalco *m* embezzlement
desfallecer ⟨2d⟩ *v/i* faint; ***sus fuerzas desfallecieron*** *fig* he lost heart
desfallecimiento *m* **1** (*debilidad*) weakness **2** (*desmayo*) fainting fit
desfasado *adj fig* old-fashioned
desfasarse ⟨1a⟩ *v/r* become old-fashioned
desfase *m fig* gap
desfavorable *adj* unfavorable, *Br* unfavourable
desfavorecer ⟨2d⟩ *v/t* **1** (*no ser favorable a*) not favor, *Br* not favour, be disadvantageous to **2** *de ropa etc* not suit
desfiguración *f* disfigurement
desfigurar ⟨1a⟩ *v/t* disfigure
desfiladero *m* ravine
desfilar ⟨1a⟩ *v/i* parade
desfile *m* parade
◇ **desfile de modas, desfile de modelos** fashion show
desfloración *f* defloration

D

desflorar ⟨1a⟩ *v/t* deflower
desfogarse ⟨1h⟩ *v/r fig* vent one's emotions
desfoliación *f* ☞ ***defoliación***
desfondar ⟨1a⟩ *v/t* **1** *recipiente* knock the bottom out of **2** MAR stave in; **desfondarse** *v/r* **1**: ***se desfondó la bolsa*** the bottom fell out of the bag **2** *fig*: *en competición* run out of steam
desforestación *f* deforestation
desgajar ⟨1a⟩ *v/t rama* break off; **desgajarse** *v/r de rama* break off
desgalichado *adj* F slovenly
desgana *f* loss of appetite; ***con ~*** *fig* reluctantly, half-heartedly
desganado *adj*: ***estar ~*** not have an appetite
desganarse ⟨1a⟩ *v/r* lose one's appetite
desgano *m L.Am.* ☞ ***desgana***
desgañitarse ⟨1a⟩ *v/r* F yell one's head off F
desgarbado *adj* F ungainly
desgarrado *adj* heart-rending
desgarrador *adj* heart-rending
desgarrar ⟨1a⟩ *v/t* tear up; *fig*: *corazón* break; **desgarrarse** *v/r* tear, rip; ***se me desgarra el corazón*** it breaks my heart
desgarro *m* MED tear
desgarrón *m* rip, tear
desgastado *adj* worn out
desgastar ⟨1a⟩ *v/t* **1** *zapatos* wear out **2** *defensas* wear down; **desgastarse** *v/r fig* wear o.s. out
desgaste *m* wear (and tear); ***guerra de ~*** war of attrition
desglosar ⟨1a⟩ *v/t coste* break down, itemize
desglose *m* breakdown, itemization
desgobernar ⟨1k⟩ *v/t* misgovern
desgobierno *m* misrule, misgovernment
desgracia *f* **1** misfortune; ***por ~*** unfortunately **2** *suceso* accident; ***las ~s nunca vienen solas*** when it rains, it pours **3** (*vergüenza*) disgrace; ***caer en ~*** fall from favor *o Br* favour *o* grace
◇ **desgracias personales** casualties
desgraciadamente *adv* unfortunately
desgraciado **I** *adj* **1** unfortunate **2** (*miserable*) wretched **II** *m*, **-a** *f* **1** (*infeliz*) wretch **2** (*sinvergüenza*) swine F
desgraciar ⟨1b⟩ *v/t* injure, hurt; **desgraciarse** *v/r de máquina* break down; *de persona* do o.s. an injury
desgranar ⟨1a⟩ *v/t guisantes* shell
desgrapadora *f* staple remover
desgravable *adj* tax-deductible
desgravación *f* deduction
◇ **desgravación fiscal** tax relief
desgravar ⟨1a⟩ **I** *v/t* deduct **II** *v/i* be tax-deductible
desgreñado *adj* disheveled, *Br* dishevelled
desgreñar ⟨1a⟩ *v/t* dishevel
desguace *m* MAR, AUTO scrapping; ***estar para el ~*** be ready for the scrapheap
desguazar ⟨1f⟩ *v/t* scrap
deshabitado *adj* uninhabited
deshabitar ⟨1a⟩ *v/t* desert
deshabituar ⟨1e⟩ *v/t*: ***~ a alguien de la televisión / las drogas etc*** get s.o. out of the habit of watching TV / taking drugs *etc*; **deshabituarse** *v/r* break the habit; ***~ de fumar*** break the smoking habit
deshacer ⟨2s; *part* ***deshecho***⟩ *v/t* **1** undo; *costura* unpick **2** *maleta* unpack; *cama* strip **3** *pastilla* crush **4** *nieve*, *mantequilla* melt **5** *tratado* break; *planes* wreck, ruin; ***eso los obligó a ~ todos sus planes*** this forced them to cancel their plans
deshacerse *v/r* **1** *de nudo de corbata*, *lazo etc* come undone **2** *de hielo* melt; *fig* go to pieces **3**: ***~ de*** get rid of **4**: ***~ en elogios*** be full of praise; ***~ en insultos*** let fly a series of insults **5**: ***~ por alguien*** F bend over backward for s.o.
desharrapado *adj* ragged
deshecho **I** *part* ☞ ***deshacer*** **II** *adj* F **1** *anímicamente* devastated F **2** *de cansancio* beat F, exhausted
deshelar ⟨1k⟩ *v/t* thaw; **deshelarse** *v/r* thaw, melt
desherbar ⟨1k⟩ *v/t* weed
desheredar ⟨1a⟩ *v/t* disinherit
deshice *vb* ☞ ***deshacer***
deshidratación *f* dehydration
deshidratar ⟨1a⟩ *v/t* dehydrate; **deshidratarse** *v/r* become dehydrated
deshielo *m* thaw
deshilachar ⟨1a⟩ *v/t* fray; **deshilacharse** *v/r* fray
deshilar ⟨1a⟩ *v/t* unpick; **deshilarse** *v/r* fray
deshilvanado *adj fig* disjointed

deshinchado *adj* deflated
deshinchar ⟨1a⟩ *v/t globo* deflate, let down; **deshincharse** *v/r* deflate, go down; *fig* lose heart
deshojar ⟨1a⟩ *v/t* **1** *planta* pull the leaves off; *flor* pull the petals off **2** *libro* tear the pages out of; **deshojarse** *v/r de árbol* lose its leaves; *de flor* lose its petals
deshollinador *m*, **~a** *f* chimney sweep
deshollinar ⟨1a⟩ *v/t chimenea* sweep
deshonestidad *f* dishonesty
deshonesto *adj* dishonest
deshonor *m* dishonor, *Br* dishonour
deshonra *f* dishonor, *Br* dishonour
deshonrar ⟨1a⟩ *v/t* dishonor, *Br* dishonour
deshonroso *adj* dishonorable, *Br* dishonourable
deshora *f*: ***a ~(s)*** at the wrong time
deshuesar ⟨1a⟩ *v/t fruta* stone; *carne* bone
deshumanizar ⟨1f⟩ *v/t* dehumanize
deshumidificación *f* dehumidification
deshumidificador *m* dehumidifier
deshumidificar ⟨1g⟩ *v/t* dehumidify
desidia *f* apathy, lethargy
desidioso *adj* apathetic, lethargic
desierto I *adj* **1** *lugar* empty, deserted; ***isla -a*** desert island **2**: ***el premio fue declarado ~*** the prize was not awarded **II** *m* desert; ***predicar*** *o* ***clamar en el ~*** cry in the wilderness
Desierto Atacama *m* Atacama Desert
designación *f* appointment, naming; *de lugar* selection; *de candidato* designation
designar ⟨1a⟩ *v/t* appoint, name; *lugar* select; *candidato* designate
designio *m* plan
desigual *adj* **1** *reparto* unequal **2** *terreno* uneven, irregular
desigualdad *f* inequality
desilusión *f* disappointment; ***llevarse una ~*** be disappointed
desilusionado *adj* disappointed
desilusionar ⟨1a⟩ *v/t* **1** disappoint **2** (*quitar la ilusión a*) disillusion; **desilusionarse** *v/r* **1** be disappointed **2** (*perder la ilusión*) become disillusioned
desinencia *f* GRAM ending
desinfección *f* disinfection
desinfectante *m/adj* disinfectant
desinfectar ⟨1a⟩ *v/t* disinfect
desinflado *adj* deflated
desinflar ⟨1a⟩ *v/t globo, neumático* let the air out of, deflate; **desinflarse** *v/r* **1** *de neumático* deflate **2** *fig* lose heart
desinformación *f* disinformation
desinformar ⟨1a⟩ *v/t* misinform
desinhibición *f* lack of inhibition
desinhibido *adj* uninhibited
desinhibir ⟨3a⟩ *v/t*: ***~ alguien*** get rid of s.o.'s inhibitions; **desinhibirse** *v/r* lose one's inhibitions
desinsectación *f* fumigation
desinstalar ⟨1a⟩ *v/t* INFOR uninstall
desintegración *f tb* FÍS disintegration
desintegrar ⟨1a⟩ *v/t* **1** FÍS cause to disintegrate, disintegrate **2** *grupo de gente* break up; **desintegrarse** *v/r* **1** FÍS disintegrate **2** *de grupo de gente* break up
desinterés *m* **1** lack of interest **2** (*generosidad*) unselfishness, disinterestedness
desinteresado *adj* unselfish, disinterested
desinteresarse ⟨1a⟩ *v/r* lose interest
desintoxicación *f* detoxification; ***hacer una cura de ~*** go into detox F, have treatment for drug / alcohol abuse
desintoxicar ⟨1g⟩ *v/t* detoxify; **desintoxicarse** *v/r* undergo treatment for drug / alcohol abuse, go into detox F
desistir ⟨3a⟩ *v/i* give up; ***tuvo que ~ de hacerlo*** she had to stop doing it; ***hacer ~ a alguien de algo*** make s.o. stop sth
deslavazado *adj tela* limp; *fig* disjointed
deslave *m L.Am.* landslide
desleal *adj* disloyal
deslealtad *f* disloyalty
deslegalizar ⟨1f⟩ *v/t*: ***~ algo*** make sth illegal
deslegitimar ⟨1a⟩ *v/t* (*minar*) undermine
desleír ⟨3m⟩ *v/t* dissolve; **desleírse** *v/r* dissolve
deslenguado I *adj* foul-mouthed **II** *m*, **-a** *f* foul-mouthed person
desliar ⟨1c⟩ *v/t* untie, undo; **desliarse** *v/r* come undone
desligar ⟨1h⟩ *v/t* separate (***de*** from); *fig*: *persona* cut off (***de*** from); **desligarse** *v/r fig* cut o.s. off (***de*** from)
deslindar ⟨1a⟩ *v/t* mark the boundaries of; *fig* define
deslinde *m* demarcation; *fig* definition

D

desliz *m fig* F slip-up F
deslizadero *m* **1** slide **2** *lugar* slippery place
deslizamiento *m* slip
◇ **deslizamiento de tierras** landslip, landslide
deslizante *adj* slippery; ***puerta*** ~ sliding door
deslizar ⟨1f⟩ **I** *v/t* **1** slide, run (***por*** along); ~ ***algo por debajo de la puerta*** slip sth under the door **2** *idea, frase* slip in **II** *v/i* slide; **deslizarse** *v/r* **1** slide; ~ ***sobre el hielo*** slide over the ice **2**: ***se me ha deslizado un error*** I've slipped up
deslomarse ⟨1a⟩ *v/r fig* kill o.s.
deslucido *adj* **1** *metal, espejo* tarnished **2** *colores* dull, drab
deslucir ⟨3f⟩ *v/t* tarnish; *fig* spoil; **deslucirse** *v/r* **1** *de colores* fade **2** *de persona* be discredited
deslumbrador *adj* dazzling
deslumbramiento *m* dazzle, glare
deslumbrante *adj* dazzling
deslumbrar ⟨1a⟩ *v/t fig* dazzle; **deslumbrarse** *v/r fig* be dazzled
deslustrado *adj* unpolished
deslustrar ⟨1a⟩ *v/t*: ~ ***algo*** take the shine off sth
desmadejado *adj persona* tired, weak
desmadrado *adj* F unruly
desmadrarse ⟨1a⟩ *v/r* F run wild
desmadre *m* F chaos
desmán *m* outrage
desmanchar ⟨1a⟩ *v/t L.Am.* remove stains from
desmandado *adj* unruly, disobedient
desmandarse ⟨1a⟩ *v/r de animal* break loose
desmano: ***a*** ~ out of the way
desmantelamiento *m* dismantling
desmantelar ⟨1a⟩ *v/t* **1** *fortificación, organización* dismantle **2** *barco* demast
desmaña *f* clumsiness
desmañado *adj* clumsy
desmaquillador I *adj*: ***crema*** ~***a*** make-up remover; ***leche*** ~***a*** cleansing milk; ***discos*** ~***es*** make-up removal pads **II** *m* make-up remover
desmaquillante *m* make-up remover
desmaquillar ⟨1a⟩ *v/t* remove make-up from; **desmaquillarse** *v/r* remove one's make-up
desmarcarse ⟨1g⟩ *v/r* **1** DEP lose one's marker, shake off one's marker **2**: ~ ***de*** distance o.s. from
desmayado *adj* **1** *persona* unconscious **2** *voz* weak; *color* pale
desmayar ⟨1a⟩ *v/i* lose heart; **desmayarse** *v/r* faint
desmayo *m* fainting fit; ***sin*** ~ without flagging
desmedido *adj* excessive
desmejorar ⟨1a⟩ **I** *v/t* spoil **II** *v/i* MED get worse, go downhill; ***ha desmejorado mucho con la edad*** he's lost a lot of his good looks as he's got older; **desmejorarse** *v/r* MED get worse, go downhill
desmelenar ⟨1a⟩ *v/t*: ~ ***a alguien*** muss s.o.'s hair; **desmelenarse** *v/r fig* F **1** let one's hair down F **2** (*enfurecerse*) hit the roof F
desmembración *f*, **desmembramiento** *m* dismemberment
desmembrar ⟨1k⟩ *v/t* dismember; **desmembrarse** *v/r* break up, fall apart
desmemoriado *adj* forgetful
desmentido *m* denial
desmentir ⟨3i⟩ *v/t* **1** *acusación* deny **2** *a alguien* contradict
desmenuzar ⟨1f⟩ *v/t* crumble up; *fig* break down; **desmenuzarse** *v/r* crumble
desmerecedor *adj* undeserving
desmerecer ⟨2d⟩ **I** *v/t* not do justice to **II** *v/i* **1** be unworthy (***con*** of) **2**: ~ ***de*** not stand comparison with; ***no*** ~ ***de*** be in no way inferior to
desmesura *f* lack of moderation
desmesurado *adj* excessive
desmigajar ⟨1a⟩ *v/t*, **desmigar** ⟨1h⟩ *v/t* crumble; **desmigajarse** *v/r* crumble
desmilitarización *f* demilitarization
desmilitarizar ⟨1f⟩ *v/t* demilitarize
desmirriado *adj* F skinny F, scrawny F
desmitificar ⟨1g⟩ *v/t* demystify, demythologize
desmochar ⟨1a⟩ *v/t* pollard
desmoche *m* pollarding
desmontable *adj* easily dismantled
desmontaje *m* dismantling
desmontar ⟨1a⟩ **I** *v/t* **1** dismantle, take apart; *tienda de campaña* take down **2** *terreno* level **II** *v/i* dismount; **desmontarse** *v/r*: ~ ***del caballo*** dismount, get off one's horse
desmonte *m* leveling, *Br* levelling

desmoralización *f* demoralization
desmoralizado *adj* demoralized
desmoralizador, desmoralizante *adj* demoralizing
desmoralizar ⟨1f⟩ *v/t* demoralize
desmoronamiento *m tb fig* collapse
desmoronar ⟨1a⟩ *v/t* bring down, cause the collapse of; **desmoronarse** *v/r tb fig* collapse
desmotivar ⟨1a⟩ *v/t* demotivate, discourage
desmovilizar ⟨1f⟩ *v/t* MIL demobilize
desnacionalizar ⟨1f⟩ *v/t* denationalize, privatize
desnatado *adj* skim, skimmed
desnatar ⟨1a⟩ *v/t leche* skim
desnaturalizado *adj* QUÍM denatured
desnaturalizar ⟨1f⟩ *v/t* QUÍM denature; **desnaturalizarse** *v/r* give up one's nationality
desnivel *m* **1** *del terreno* unevenness **2** *entre personas* disparity
desnivelar ⟨1a⟩ *v/t* upset the balance of; **desnivelarse** *v/r fig* become one-sided, become unbalanced
desnucar ⟨1g⟩ *v/t*: **~ a alguien** break s.o.'s neck; **desnucarse** *v/r* break one's neck
desnuclearizado *adj* nuclear-free
desnudar ⟨1a⟩ *v/t* **1** undress **2** *fig*: *en el juego* fleece; **desnudarse** *v/r* **1** undress **2** *fig* bare one's soul
desnudez *f* nudity; *fig* nakedness
desnudo **I** *adj* **1** *persona* naked **2** (*sin decoración*) bare **II** *m* **1** PINT nude **2**: **al ~** *realidad* harsh; *verdad* unvarnished, plain and simple; ***poner al ~*** lay bare
desnutrición *f* undernourishment
desnutrido *adj* undernourished
desobedecer ⟨2d⟩ *v/t* disobey
desobediencia *f* disobedience
desobediente *adj* disobedient
desobstruir ⟨3g⟩ *v/t poros* unblock, unclog
desocupación *f L.Am.* unemployment
desocupado **I** *adj* **1** *apartamento* vacant, empty **2** *L.Am. sin trabajo* unemployed **II** *m*, **-a** *f* unemployed person; ***los ~s*** the unemployed *pl*
desocupar ⟨1a⟩ *v/t* vacate; **desocuparse** *v/r de casa, piso* fall vacant; ***espera a que se desocupe el baño*** wait until the bathroom's free
desodorante **I** *adj* deodorant; ***barra ~*** deodorant stick **II** *m* deodorant ◇ **desodorante de bola** roll-on deodorant
desoído *part* ☞ ***desoír***
desoír ⟨3q; *part* ***desoído***⟩ *v/t* ignore, turn a deaf ear to
desolación *f* desolation
desolado *adj* **1** *lugar* desolate **2** *fig* grief-stricken, devastated
desolador *adj* devastating
desolar ⟨1m⟩ *v/t tb fig* devastate
desollar ⟨1m⟩ *v/t* skin; ***¡te voy a ~ vivo!*** I'll skin you alive!; ***~ a alguien / algo vivo*** *fig* F *de crítica* pull s.o. / sth to pieces *o* shreds
desorbitado *adj* **1** *precio, cantidad etc* astronomical **2**: ***con ojos ~s*** pop-eyed
desorbitar ⟨1a⟩ *v/t fig* exaggerate; **desorbitarse** *v/r de precios* sky-rocket, go sky-high
desorden *m* **1** disorder; *de habitación* untidiness **2**: ***desórdenes*** *pl* disturbances
desordenado *adj* untidy, messy F; *fig* disorganized
desordenar ⟨1a⟩ *v/t* make untidy *o* messy; **desordenarse** *v/r* get untidy *o* messy
desorganización *f* lack of organization
desorganizado *adj* disorganized
desorganizar ⟨1f⟩ *v/t* disrupt; **desorganizarse** *v/r* become disorganized
desorientación *f* disorientation; *fig* confusion
desorientador *adj* disorienting
desorientar ⟨1a⟩ *v/t* disorient; (*confundir*) confuse; **desorientarse** *v/r* get disoriented, lose one's bearings; *fig* get confused
desovar ⟨1a⟩ *v/i de peces, anfibios* spawn; *de insectos* lay eggs
desove *m de peces, anfibios* spawning; *de insectos* egg laying
desoxidar ⟨1a⟩ *v/t* deoxidize
despabilado *adj fig* bright
despabilar ⟨1a⟩ **I** *v/t* wake up **II** *v/i* wake up; ***¡despabila!*** *fig* get your act together!; **despabilarse** *v/r fig* get one's act together
despachar ⟨1a⟩ **I** *v/t* **1** *a persona, cliente* attend to **2** *problema* sort out **3** (*vender*) sell **4** (*enviar*) send (off), dispatch **5** *L.Am.* (*facturar*) check in **II** *v/i* meet (**con** with); **despacharse** *v/r* **1** F polish

off F **2**: ***~ a su gusto*** speak one's mind
despacho *m* **1** office **2** *diplomático, a periódico* dispatch
◇ **despacho de aduana** customs clearance
◇ **despacho de billetes** ticket office
despachurrar ⟨1a⟩ *v/t* F crush
despacio *adv* **1** slowly; ***¡~!*** slow down! **2** *L.Am.* (*en voz baja*) in a low voice
despacioso *adj* slow
despacito *adv* F slowly
despampanante *adj* F striking, eye--catching
despanzurrar ⟨1a⟩ *v/t* F rip apart
desparejado, desparejo *adj calcetín* odd
desparpajo *m* self-confidence; ***con mucho ~*** with great self-confidence, very self-confidently
desparramado *adj* scattered
desparramar ⟨1a⟩ *v/t* **1** scatter; *líquido* spill **2** *dinero* squander; **desparramarse** *v/r* spill; *fig* scatter
despatarrado *adj* sprawled out, spread out
despatarrarse ⟨1a⟩ *v/r* F sprawl
despavorido *adj* terrified
despechado *adj* offended; (*enfadado*) angry
despecho *m* spite; ***a ~ de*** in spite of
despechugado *adj* F *hombre* bare--chested; *mujer* topless
despectivo *adj* contemptuous; GRAM pejorative
despedazar ⟨1f⟩ *v/t* tear apart; *fig*: *honra* destroy; **despedazarse** *v/r* smash
despedida *f* **1** farewell; ***carta de ~*** goodbye letter; ***función de ~*** farewell performance **2** *en carta* close
◇ **despedida de soltera** wedding shower, *Br* hen party
◇ **despedida de soltero** stag party
despedir ⟨3l⟩ *v/t* **1** see off **2** *empleado* dismiss **3** *perfume* give off **4** *de jinete* throw; ***salir despedido del coche*** be thrown out of the car; **despedirse** *v/r* say goodbye (***de*** to); ***~ a la francesa*** F leave without saying goodbye; ***~ de algo*** *fig* kiss sth goodbye
despegado *adj fig* distant
despegar ⟨1h⟩ **I** *v/t* remove, peel off **II** *v/i* AVIA, *fig* take off; **despegarse** *v/r* **1** come unstuck (***de*** from), come off (***de*** sth) **2** *de persona* distance o.s. (***de*** from)
despego *m* ☞ ***desapego***
despegue *m* AVIA, *fig* take-off
despeinado *adj* disheveled, *Br* dishevelled; ***está -a*** her hair's a mess
despeinar ⟨1a⟩ *v/t*: ***~ a alguien*** muss s.o.'s hair; **despeinarse** *v/r* mess one's hair up
despejado *adj cielo, cabeza* clear
despejar ⟨1a⟩ *v/t* **1** *calle, sala etc* clear **2** *persona* wake up **3** DEP *pelota* clear; **despejarse** *v/r* **1** *de cielo* clear up; ***~ la cabeza*** clear one's head **2** *fig* wake o.s. up
despeje *m* DEP clearance
despellejar ⟨1a⟩ *v/t* skin; ***~ a alguien*** *fig* tear s.o. to pieces
despelotarse ⟨1a⟩ *v/r* **1** (*desnudarse*) strip off **2** *de risa* split one's sides
despenalización *f* decriminalization
despenalizar ⟨1f⟩ *v/t* decriminalize
despensa *f* larder
despeñadero *m* cliff, precipice
despeñar ⟨1a⟩ *v/t*: ***~ a alguien*** throw s.o. off a cliff; **despeñarse** *v/r* throw o.s. off a cliff
despepitar ⟨1a⟩ *v/t* remove the pips from; **despepitarse** *v/r* **1** yell **2**: ***~ por algo / hacer algo*** F long for sth / to do sth
desperdiciar ⟨1b⟩ *v/t oportunidad* waste
desperdicio *m* waste; ***~s*** *pl* waste *sg*; ***no tener ~*** be worthwhile
◇ **desperdicios biológicos** biological waste *sg*
◇ **desperdicios industriales** industrial waste *sg*
desperdigar ⟨1h⟩ *v/t* scatter; **desperdigarse** *v/r* be scattered
desperezarse ⟨1f⟩ *v/r* stretch
desperfecto *m* **1** (*defecto*) flaw **2** (*daño*) damage
despertador *m* alarm (clock)
despertar ⟨1k⟩ **I** *v/t* **1** wake, waken **2** *apetito* whet; *sospecha* arouse; *recuerdo* reawaken, trigger **II** *v/i* wake up; **despertarse** *v/r* wake (up) **IV** *m* awakening
despiadado *adj* ruthless
despido *m* **1** dismissal **2** (*indemnización*) severance pay
◇ **despido colectivo, despido masivo** mass dismissal
despiece *m* carving up

despierto *adj* **1** awake; ***soñar ~*** daydream **2** *fig* bright
despiezar ⟨1f⟩ *v/t* **1** *máquina* take apart **2** *animal* cut up
despilfarrador **I** *adj* wasteful **II** *m*, **~a** *f* spendthrift
despilfarrar ⟨1a⟩ *v/t* squander, waste
despilfarro *m* waste
despintar ⟨1a⟩ *v/t* take the paint off, remove the paint from; **despintarse** *v/r*: ***la pared se estaba despintando*** the paint was coming off the wall
despiojar ⟨1a⟩ *v/t* delouse
despistado **I** *adj* scatterbrained **II** *m*, **-a** *f* scatterbrain
despistar ⟨1a⟩ *v/t* **1**: ***~ alguien*** *en persecución* lose s.o., shake s.o. off; *en investigación* throw s.o. off the scent **2** (*confundir*) confuse; **despistarse** *v/r* get distracted
despiste *m* distraction; ***tener un ~*** become distracted
desplantar ⟨1a⟩ *v/t planta* uproot
desplante *m*: ***dar*** *o* ***hacer un ~ a alguien*** *fig* be rude to s.o.
desplazado **I** *adj fig* out of place **II** *m*, **-a** *f* displaced person
desplazamiento *m* **1** trip **2** (*movimiento*) movement
desplazar ⟨1f⟩ *v/t* **1** move **2** (*suplantar*) take over from; **desplazarse** *v/r* **1** (*moverse*) move **2** travel
desplegable *adj* folding
desplegar ⟨1h & 1k⟩ *v/t* **1** unfold, open out **2** MIL deploy; **desplegarse** *v/r* **1** unfold, open out **2** MIL deploy
despliegue *m* **1** MIL deployment **2** *fig*: ***con gran ~ de*** *astucia*, *riqueza* with a great show of
desplomarse ⟨1a⟩ *v/r* collapse
desplome *m* collapse
desplumar ⟨1a⟩ *v/t* **1** *ave* pluck **2** *fig* fleece
despoblación *f* depopulation
despoblado **I** *adj* uninhabited, deserted **II** *m* deserted place
despoblar ⟨1m⟩ *v/t* depopulate; **despoblarse** *v/r* become depopulated *o* deserted
despojar ⟨1a⟩ *v/t* strip (***de*** of); **despojarse** *v/r*: ***~ de*** *prenda* take off
despojos *mpl* **1** (*restos*) left-overs **2** (*desperdicios*) waste *sg*; *fig* spoils **3** *de animal* variety meat *sg*, *Br* offal *sg*
◇ **despojos mortales** *pl* mortal remains
desportillar ⟨1a⟩ *v/t plato* chip
desposados *mpl*: ***los ~*** the bride and groom
desposar ⟨1a⟩ *v/t* marry; **desposarse** *v/r* **1** (*casarse*) get married **2** (*prometerse*) get engaged
desposeer ⟨2e⟩ *v/t de títulos*, *medalla* strip (***de*** of); **desposeerse** *v/r* relinquish
desposeídos *mpl*: ***los ~*** the dispossessed
desposorios *mpl* **1** *ceremonia* marriage *sg* **2** (*compromiso*) betrothal *sg*
déspota *m/f* despot
despótico *adj* despotic
despotismo *m* despotism
despotricar ⟨1g⟩ *v/i* F rant and rave F (***contra*** about)
despreciable *adj* **1** *comportamiento* contemptible, despicable **2** *cantidad*, *coste etc* neglible; ***nada ~*** *cantidad* large, not inconsiderable
despreciar ⟨1b⟩ *v/t* **1** look down on, despise **2** *propuesta* reject
despreciativo *adj* contemptuous
desprecio *m* **1** (*desdén*) contempt **2** *acto* slight **3** (*indiferencia*) disregard
desprender ⟨2a⟩ *v/t* **1** detach, separate **2** *olor* give off; **desprenderse** *v/r* **1** come off **2**: ***~ de*** *fig*: *posesión* part with **3**: ***de este estudio se desprende que*** what emerges from the study is that
desprendido *adj* generous
desprendimiento *m* detachment
◇ **desprendimiento de retina** MED detached retina
◇ **desprendimiento de tierras** landslide
despreocupación *f* indifference
despreocupado *adj* **1** (*descuidado*) careless **2** (*sin preocupaciones*) carefree
despreocuparse ⟨1a⟩ *v/r* not worry (***de*** about)
desprestigiar ⟨1b⟩ *v/t* discredit; **desprestigiarse** *v/r* be discredited
desprestigio *m* loss of prestige
despresurización *f* AVIA depressurization
desprevenido *adj* unprepared; ***pillar*** *o* *L.Am.* ***agarrar ~*** catch unawares
desproporción *f* disproportion
desproporcionado *adj* disproportion-

ate
despropósito *m* stupid thing
desprotección *f* vulnerability
desprotegido *adj* unprotected
desproveer ⟨*2a*⟩ **v/t**: ***~ a alguien de algo*** deprive s.o. of sth
desprovisto *adj*: ***~ de*** lacking in
después *adv* **1** (*más tarde*) afterward, later **2** *seguido en orden* next; ***yo voy ~*** I'm next; ***~ de que se vaya*** after he's gone **3** *en el espacio* after; ***~ de*** after; ***~ de la parada*** after the bus stop **4** *en locuciones*: ***~ de todo*** after all
despuntar ⟨1a⟩ **I** *v/t* blunt **II** *v/i* **1** *de planta* sprout **2** *de día* dawn; ***al ~ el día*** at daybreak **3** *de persona* excel (***en*** in); **despuntarse** *v/r* be blunted
desquiciado *adj fig* crazed, unhinged
desquiciamiento *m fig* chaos (***de*** in)
desquiciar ⟨1b⟩ *v/t* **1** *fig* drive crazy **2** *puerta* take off its hinges; **desquiciarse** *v/r fig* lose one's mind
desquitar ⟨1a⟩ *v/t* compensate (***de*** for); **desquitarse** *v/r* get one's own back (***de*** for)
desquite *m* compensation; ***tomarse el ~*** F get one's own back
desratización *f* rat catching
desregulación *f* deregulation
desrielar ⟨1a⟩ *v/t Chi* derail
desrizar ⟨1f⟩ *v/t cabello* straighten; **desrizarse** *v/r de cabello* go all straight
destacable *adj* noteworthy, notable
destacado *adj* outstanding
destacamento *m* **1** MIL detachment **2** *de policía* (rural) police station
destacar ⟨1g⟩ **I** *v/i* stand out **II** *v/t* emphasize; **destacarse** *v/r* stand out (***por*** because of); (*ser excelente*) be outstanding (***por*** because of)
destajero *m*, **-a** *f*, **destajista** *m/f* pieceworker
destajo *m*: ***trabajar a ~*** do piecework
destapar ⟨1a⟩ *v/t* open, take the lid off; *fig* uncover; **destaparse** *v/r* take one's coat off; *en cama* kick off the bedcovers; *fig* strip (off)
destape *m* nudity
destaponar ⟨1a⟩ *v/t* unblock
destartalado *adj vehículo*, *casa* dilapidated
destellar ⟨1a⟩ *v/i de estrella* twinkle; *de faros* gleam
destello *m de estrella* twinkling; *de faros* gleam; *fig* brief period, moment
destemplado *adj* out of tune
destemplanza *f* tunelessness
destemplar ⟨1a⟩ *v/t* **1** MÚS put out of tune **2** *persona* upset; **destemplarse** *v/r fig* become unwell
destemple *m* ☞ ***destemplanza***
desteñir ⟨3h & 3l⟩ *v/t* discolor, *Br* discolour, fade; **desteñirse** *v/r* fade
desternillante *adj* F hilarious
desternillarse ⟨1a⟩ *v/r*: ***~ (de risa)*** F kill o.s. laughing F
desterrar ⟨1k⟩ *v/t* exile
destetar ⟨1a⟩ *v/t niño*, *cría* wean
destete *m* weaning
destiempo *m*: ***a ~*** at the wrong moment
destierro *m* exile
destilación *f* distillation
destilador *m* still
destilar ⟨1a⟩ *v/t* distill; *fig* exude
destilería *f* distillery
destinado *adj* **1**: ***~ en*** MIL stationed in **2**: ***~ a*** *dinero*, *comida*, *ayuda* intended for, meant for; *programa*, *producto* aimed at, targeted at **3**: ***estar ~ a hacer algo*** be destined to do sth
destinar ⟨1a⟩ *v/t* **1** *fondos* allocate (***para*** for) **2** *a persona* post (***a*** to)
destinatario *m*, **-a** *f* addressee
destino *m* **1** fate, destiny **2** *de viaje etc* destination; ***el tren con ~ a*** the train for **3** *en el ejército etc* posting
destitución *f* dismissal
destituir ⟨3g⟩ *v/t* dismiss; ***~ del cargo*** remove from one's post
destornillado *adj* F crazy F, screwy F
destornillador *m* screwdriver
destornillar ⟨1a⟩ *v/t* unscrew
destreza *f* skill
destripar ⟨1a⟩ *v/t* **1** *animal* gut **2** *cosa* tear open
destronamiento *m* dethronement, overthrow
destronar ⟨1a⟩ *v/t* depose
destrozar ⟨1f⟩ *v/t* **1** destroy **2** *emocionalmente* shatter, devastate; **destrozarse** *v/r* be destroyed
destrozos *mpl* damage *sg*
destrucción *f* destruction
destructivo *adj* destructive
destructor **I** *adj* destructive; ***máquina ~a de documentos*** document shredder **II** *m barco* destroyer
destruir ⟨3g⟩ *v/t* **1** destroy **2** (*estropear*)

ruin, wreck
desunido *adj* divided
desunión *f* lack of unity
desunir ⟨3a⟩ *v/t* divide
desusado *adj* obsolete
desusarse ⟨1a⟩ *v/r* become obsolete
desuso *m* disuse; ***caer en ~*** fall into disuse
desvaído *adj* **1** *color, pintura* faded **2** *fig* dull
desvalido *adj* helpless
desvalijador *m*, **~a** *f* burglar
desvalijar ⟨1a⟩ *v/t persona* rob; *apartamento* burglarize, burgle
desvalimiento *m* robbery
desvalorización *f* devaluation
desvalorizar ⟨1f⟩ *v/t* devalue
desván *m* attic
desvanecer ⟨2d⟩ *v/t sospechas, temores* dispel; **desvanecerse** *v/r* **1** *de niebla* disperse; ***~ en el aire*** vanish into thin air **2** MED faint
desvanecimiento *m* MED fainting fit
desvariar ⟨1c⟩ *v/i* **1** (*decir disparates*) rave **2** MED be delirious
desvarío *m* **1** delirium **2**: ***~s*** *pl* ravings
desvelado *adj* wide awake
desvelar ⟨1a⟩ *v/t* **1** keep awake **2** *secreto* reveal; **desvelarse** *v/r* **1** stay awake **2** *fig* do one's best (***por*** for)
desvelo *m* **1** sleeplessness **2**: ***~s*** *pl* efforts
desvencijado *adj* rickety
desvencijarse ⟨1a⟩ *v/r* fall to pieces
desventaja *f* disadvantage
desventajoso *adj* disadvantageous
desventura *f* misfortune
desventurado I *adj* unfortunate **II** *m*, **-a** *f* unfortunate
desvergonzado *adj* shameless
desvergüenza *f* shamelessness
desvestir ⟨3l⟩ *v/t* undress; **desvestirse** *v/r* get undressed, undress
desviación *f* detour, *Br tb* diversion
desviacionista *m/f* & *adj* POL deviationist
desviar ⟨1c⟩ *v/t* **1** *golpe* deflect, parry; *pelota* deflect; *tráfico* divert; *río* divert, alter the course of; ***~ la conversación*** change the subject; ***~ la mirada*** look away **2**: ***~ a alguien del buen camino*** lead s.o. astray; **desviarse** *v/r* **1** (*girar*) turn off **2** (*bifurcarse*) branch off **3** (*apartarse*) stray (***de*** from)
desvincular ⟨1a⟩ *v/t* dissociate (***de*** from); **desvincularse** *v/r* dissociate o.s. (***de*** from)
desvío *m* detour, *Br tb* diversion
desvirgar ⟨1h⟩ *v/t* deflower
desvirtuar ⟨1e⟩ *v/t* detract from; *fig* (*distorsionar*) distort; **desvirtuarse** *v/r* deteriorate
desvivirse ⟨3a⟩ *v/r*: ***~ por alguien*** *fig* F live for s.o., be devoted to s.o.
detallado *adj* detailed
detallar ⟨1a⟩ *v/t* **1** explain in detail, give details of **2** COM itemize
detalle *m* **1** detail; ***en ~*** in detail; ***con todo lujo de ~s*** in great detail; ***entrar en ~s*** go into details **2** *fig* thoughtful gesture **3**: ***al ~*** COM retail
detallista *m/f* COM retailer
detección *f* detection
◇ **detección precoz** MED early detection
detectable *adj* detectable
detectar ⟨1a⟩ *v/t* detect
detective *m/f* detective
◇ **detective privado** private detective
detector *m* detector
◇ **detector de humos** smoke detector; **detector de mentiras** lie detector; **detector de metales** metal detector; **detector de minas** mine detector; **detector de movimientos** motion detector
detención *f* detention, arrest; ***orden de ~*** arrest warrant
◇ **detención ilegal** unlawful arrest
◇ **detención preventiva** (police) custody
detener ⟨2l⟩ *v/t* **1** stop **2** *de policía* arrest, detain; **detenerse** *v/r* stop
detenidamente *adv* at length, thoroughly; ***leer algo ~*** read something through carefully
detenido I *adj* **1** *coche* held up, delayed **2** (*minucioso*) detailed **3**: ***llevar ~*** *delincuente* detain **II** *m*, **-a** *f* person under arrest
detenimiento *m*: ***con ~*** thoroughly
detentar ⟨1a⟩ *v/t* hold
detergente I *adj* detergent **II** *m* detergent
deteriorado *adj* damaged
deteriorar ⟨1a⟩ *v/t* damage; **deteriorarse** *v/r* deteriorate
deterioro *m* deterioration
determinación *f* **1** (*intrepidez*) determi-

nation **2** (*decisión*) decision
determinado *adj* certain
determinante I *adj* decisive **II** *f* MAT determinant
determinar ⟨1a⟩ *v/t* **1** (*establecer*) determine **2**: ***eso me determinó a llamarlo*** that made me decide to call him; **determinarse** *v/r* decide (***a*** to)
detestable *adj* terrible
detestar ⟨1a⟩ *v/t* detest
detonación *f* detonation
detonador *m* detonator
detonante I *adj* explosive **II** *m* explosive; *fig* trigger
detonar ⟨1a⟩ **I** *v/i* detonate, go off **II** *v/t* detonate, set off
detracción *f* disparagement
detractor I *adj* critical **II** *m*, **~a** *f* detractor, critic
detrás *adv* behind; ***el que está ~*** the one behind; ***por*** *o* ***de ~*** at the back; *fig* behind your / his etc back; ***sentarse ~*** sit at the back; *en coche* sit in back, *Br* sit at the back; ***~ de*** behind; ***uno ~ de otro*** one after the other; ***estar ~ de algo*** *fig* be behind sth; ***ir / andar ~ de algo*** be after sth; ***venir por ~*** come from behind
detrimento *m*: ***en ~ de*** to the detriment of; ***ir en ~ de algo*** be at the expense of sth
detrito, detritus *m* detritus
detuvo *vb* ☞ ***detener***
deuda *f* debt; ***cargado de ~s*** deep in debt; ***libre de ~s*** free of debts; ***estar en ~ con alguien*** *fig* be in s.o.'s debt, be indebted to s.o.
◇ **deuda externa** foreign debt
◇ **deuda pública** national debt
deudo *m*, **-a** *f* relative
deudor I *adj* debtor *atr* **II** *m*, **~a** *f* debtor
devaluación *f* devaluation
devaluar ⟨1e⟩ *v/t* devalue
devanadera *f* spool
devanar ⟨1a⟩ *v/t* wind; **devanarse** *v/r*: ***~ los sesos*** F rack one's brains F
devaneo *m* **1** (*lío amoroso*) affair **2**: ***dejarse de ~s*** stop wasting one's time
devastación *f* devastation
devastar ⟨1a⟩ *v/t* devastate
devengar ⟨1h⟩ *v/t* yield, pay
devengo *m* fee
devenir ⟨3s⟩ *v/i*: ***~ en*** become
devoción *f tb fig* devotion; ***hacer algo con ~*** do sth devoutly
devocionario *m* prayer book
devolución *f* return; *de dinero* refund
devolver ⟨2h; *part* ***devuelto***⟩ *v/t* **1** give back, return; ***devuélvase al remitente*** return to sender **2**: ***~ el cambio*** give change **3** *fig*: *visita, saludo* return **4** F (*vomitar*) throw up F; **devolverse** *v/r L.Am.* go back, return
devorador *adj hambre* ravenous; *fig* all-consuming
devorar ⟨1a⟩ *v/t* devour; ***~ a alguien con los ojos*** devour s.o. with one's eyes; ***el fuego devoró el bosque*** the forest was consumed by the fire; ***le devora la envidia*** he is consumed with jealousy
devoto I *adj* devout **II** *m*, **-a** *f* devotee (***de*** of)
devuelto *part* ☞ ***devolver***
deyección *f* (*tb* ***deyecciones***) **1** MED bowel movement, motion **2** GEOL ejecta *pl*, volcanic ash and lava
D.F. *abr Méx* (= ***Distrito Federal***) Mexico City
dg. *abr* (= ***decigramo***) decigram
DGT *f abr* (= ***Dirección General de Tráfico***) *Spanish Road Transport Department*
di *vb* ☞ ***dar***
día *m* **1** (*veinticuatro horas*) day; ***¿qué ~ es hoy?***, ***¿a qué ~ estamos?*** what day is it today?; ***al ~ siguiente*** the following *o* next day, the day after; ***el otro ~*** the other day; ***un ~ sí y otro no*** every other day; ***un ~ sí y otro también*** every day, day in day out; ***~ por medio*** every other day; ***~ tras ~*** day after day; ***de un ~ a*** *o* ***para otro*** from one day to the next; ***de ~ en ~*** from day to day; ***todo el santo ~*** all day long; ***todos los ~s*** every day; ***de hoy en ocho ~s*** a week from today *o* from now; ***a los pocos ~s*** a few days later; ***mañana será otro ~*** tomorrow's another day
2 *actualidad*: ***al ~*** up to date; ***poner al ~*** update, bring up to date
3: ***de ~*** by day, during the day; ***ya es de ~*** it's light already; ***se hizo de ~*** dawn *o* day broke; ***~ y noche*** night and day; ***¡buenos ~s!*** good morning!
4: ***hace mal ~*** *tiempo* it's a nasty day
5: ***algún ~***, ***un ~*** some day, one day; ***un ~ de estos*** one of these days; ***un ~ es un ~*** this is a special occasion; ***el ~ me-***

nos pensado when you least expect it; ***el ~ de mañana*** in the future, one day; ***el ~ a ~*** the day-to-day routine; ***hoy en ~*** nowadays; ***en su ~*** in due course; ***tiene sus ~s contados*** his / her / its days are numbered; ***¡hasta otro ~!*** see you around!; ***del ~*** *pan* fresh
◇ **día de clase** school day; **día feriado** *L.Am.* (public) holiday; **día de fiesta** holiday; **día de los fieles difuntos** All Souls' Day; **día festivo** holiday; **día hábil** work day; **día laborable** work day; **día de la madre** Mother's Day; **día de los Muertos** *L.Am.* All Souls' Day; **día de puertas abiertas** open house, *Br* open day; **día del santo** saint's day; **día útil** workday
diabetes *f* diabetes *sg*
diabético **I** *adj* diabetic **II** *m*, **-a** *f* diabetic
diabla, diablesa *f* F she-devil
diablillo *m* F little devil F, little horror F
diablo *m* devil; ***un pobre ~*** *fig* a poor devil; ***el ~ anda suelto*** F it's a terrible mess; ***tener el ~ en el cuerpo*** be a handful; ***mandar a alguien al ~*** F tell s.o. to go to hell F; ***¡vete al ~!*** F go to hell! F; ***¡al ~ con …!*** F to hell with …! F; ***quema como un*** *o* ***el ~*** F it's really hot; ***de mil ~s, de*** **(*todos*)** ***los ~s*** F terrible; ***¿qué ~s pasa aquí?*** F what the hell is going on here? F
diablura *f* prank, lark
diabólico *adj* diabolical
diácono *m* deacon
diadema *f* tiara; *para el pelo* Alice band, hairband
diafanidad *f* clarity
diáfano *adj* clear
diafragma *m* diaphragm
diagnosis *f* diagnosis
diagnosticar ⟨1g⟩ *v/t* diagnose
diagnóstico **I** *adj* diagnostic **II** *m* diagnosis
◇ **diagnóstico precoz** early diagnosis
diagonal **I** *adj* diagonal **II** *f* diagonal (line); ***en ~*** diagonally
diagrama *m* diagram
◇ **diagrama de barras** bar chart
◇ **diagrama de flujo** flow chart
dial *m* TELEC, RAD dial
dialectal *adj* dialect *atr*
dialéctica *f* dialectics *pl*
dialéctico *adj* dialectical
dialecto *m* dialect
diálisis *f* MED dialysis
dialogar ⟨1h⟩ *v/i* **1** talk (***sobre*** about), discuss (***sobre*** sth) **2** (*negociar*) hold talks (***con*** with)
diálogo *m* dialog, *Br* dialogue; ***es un ~ de sordos*** it's a dialog of the deaf
diamante *m tb en béisbol* diamond; **~ (*en*) *bruto*** *tb fig* rough diamond
diamantino *adj* diamond-like
diametral *adj* diametrical
diametralmente *adv*: ***~ opuesto*** diametrically opposed
diámetro *m* diameter
diana *f* **1** MIL reveille **2** *para jugar a los dardos* dartboard **3** (*blanco*) target; (*centro de blanco*) bull's eye; ***dar en la ~*** hit the bull's eye; *fig* hit the nail on the head
diantre *int* F hell! F
diapasón *m* tuning fork; ***~ normal*** tuning fork
diapositiva *f* FOT slide, transparency
diariero *m*, **-a** *f* *Arg* newspaper vendor
diario **I** *adj* **1** daily **2**: ***a ~, de ~*** every day, daily **II** *m* **1** diary **2** (*periódico*) daily newspaper, daily
diarrea *f* MED diarrhea, *Br* diarrhoea
diatriba *f* diatribe
dibujante **I** *m* draftsman, *Br* draughtsman **II** *f* draftswoman, *Br* draughtswoman **III** *m/f de viñetas* cartoonist
dibujar ⟨1a⟩ *v/t* draw; *fig* describe; **dibujarse** *v/r fig* appear
dibujo *m arte* drawing; *ilustración* drawing, sketch; *estampado* pattern; ***con ~(s)*** with illustrations
◇ **dibujo lineal** technical drawing; **dibujo técnico** technical drawing; **dibujos animados** cartoons; ***película de ~*** animation
dic.[e] *abr* (= ***diciembre***) Dec. (= December)
dicción *f* diction
diccionario *m* dictionary
dice *vb* ☞ ***decir***
díceres *mpl L.Am.* sayings
dicha *f* **1** (*felicidad*) happiness **2** (*suerte*) good luck
dicharachero **I** *adj* **1** chatty **2** (*gracioso*) witty **II** *m*, **-a** *f* witty conversationalist
dicho **I** *part* ☞ ***decir*** **II** *adj* said **III** *m* saying; ***del ~ al hecho hay gran trecho*** easier said than done
dichoso *adj* **1** happy **2** F (*maldito*)

damn F
diciembre *m* December
diciendo *vb* ☞ **decir**
dictado *m* dictation; ***al ~ de*** dictated by
dictador *m*, **~a** *f* dictator
dictadura *f* dictatorship
dictáfono *m* dictaphone
dictamen *m* **1** (*informe*) report; ***emitir un ~*** publish a report **2** (*opinión*) opinion
◇ **dictamen facultativo, dictamen médico** medical report
dictaminar ⟨1a⟩ **I** *v/t* state **II** *v/i*: ***~ sobre algo*** report on sth
dictar ⟨1a⟩ *v/t* **1** *lección, texto* dictate **2** *ley* announce; ***~ sentencia*** JUR pass sentence **3** *L.Am. clase, conferencia* give
dictatorial *adj* dictatorial
didáctica *f* didactics *sg*
didáctico *adj* educational; ***material ~*** teaching aids *pl*; ***método ~*** teaching method
diecinueve *adj* nineteen
dieciocho *adj* eighteen
dieciséis *adj* sixteen
diecisiete *adj* seventeen
diente *m* tooth; ***echar los ~s*** teethe; ***daba ~ con ~*** his teeth were chattering; ***enseñar los ~s*** bare one's teeth; *fig* show one's teeth; ***armado hasta los ~s*** armed to the teeth; ***hablar entre ~s*** mutter under one's breath; ***tener buen ~*** have a hearty appetite; ***poner los ~s largos a alguien*** make s.o. jealous
◇ **diente de ajo** clove of garlic; **diente de leche** milk tooth; **diente de león** BOT dandelion
diéresis *f* GRAM dieresis *sg*, *Br* diaeresis *sg*
diesel *m* diesel
diestra *f* right hand
diestro I *adj*: ***a ~ y siniestro***, *L.Am.* ***a -a y siniestra*** *fig* F left and right **II** *m* TAUR bullfighter
dieta *f* **1** diet; ***estar a ~*** be on a diet; ***poner a alguien a ~*** put s.o. on a diet **2**: ***~s*** *pl* travel expenses
dietario *m* ledger, account book
dietética *f* dietetics *sg*; ***tienda de ~*** health food store
dietético *adj* dietary
dietista *m/f* dietician, dietitian
diez *adj* ten
diezmar ⟨1a⟩ *v/t* decimate
difamación *f* defamation; *de palabra* slander; *por escrito* libel
difamador I *adj* defamatory; *de palabra* slanderous; *por escrito* libelous, *Br* libellous **II** *m*, **~a** *f de palabra* slanderer; *por escrito* libeler, *Br* libeller
difamar ⟨1a⟩ *v/t* defame; *de palabra* slander; *por escrito* libel
difamatorio *adj* defamatory; *de palabra* slanderous *por escrito* libelous, *Br* libellous
diferencia *f* **1** difference; ***hay una ~ como del día a la noche*** it's like the difference between night and day; ***a ~ de*** unlike; ***con ~*** *fig* by a long way **2**: ***~s*** *pl* (*desacuerdo*) differences
diferenciable *adj* distinguishable
diferencial I *adj* **1** distinguishing **2** MAT differential **II** *m* AUTO differential **III** *f* MAT differential
diferenciar ⟨1b⟩ *v/t* differentiate; **diferenciarse** *v/r* differ (***de*** from); ***no se diferencian en nada*** there's no difference at all between them
diferente *adj* different
diferido *adj* TV: ***en ~*** prerecorded
diferir ⟨3i⟩ **I** *v/t* postpone **II** *v/i* differ (***de*** from)
difícil *adj* **1** difficult; ***ponerlo ~ a alguien*** make it difficult for s.o.; ***~ de decir*** hard *o* difficult to say **2** (*poco probable*): ***es ~ que venga*** he's unlikely to come, it's unlikely that he'll come
difícilmente *adv* with difficulty
dificultad *f* difficulty; ***sin ~*** easily; ***con ~es*** with difficulty; ***poner ~es*** make it difficult
dificultar ⟨1a⟩ *v/t* hinder
dificultoso *adj* difficult, awkward
difracción *f* FÍS diffraction
difteria *f* MED diphtheria
difuminar ⟨1a⟩ *v/t* PINT, *fig* blur; **difuminarse** *v/r* fade
difundir ⟨3a⟩ *v/t* **1** spread **2** *programa* broadcast; **difundirse** *v/r* spread
difunto I *adj* late **II** *m*, **-a** *f* deceased
difusión *f* spread(ing)
difuso *adj* **1** *idea, conocimientos* vague, sketchy **2** *luz* diffuse
digerible *adj* digestible
digerir ⟨3i⟩ *v/t* **1** digest; ***no puedo ~ a Juan*** I can't stomach Juan **2** *ofensa*,

desgracia accept; *noticia* take in, absorb
digestibilidad *f* digestibility
digestible *adj* digestible
digestión *f* digestion
digestivo *adj* digestive; ***aparato ~*** digestive system
digitador *m*, **~a** *f L.Am.* keyboarder
digital I *adj* digital **II** *f* BOT foxglove
digitalizar ⟨1f⟩ *v/t* INFOR digitalize
digitar ⟨1a⟩ *v/t L.Am* key
dígito *m* digit
dignarse ⟨1a⟩ *v/r* deign (***a*** to)
dignatario *m*, **-a** *f* dignitary
dignidad *f* **1** dignity **2** (*cargo*) position
dignificar ⟨1g⟩ *v/t* dignify
digno *adj* **1** worthy; ***~ de mención*** worth mentioning; ***~ de confianza*** trustworthy **2** *trabajo* decent, respectable
digo *vb* ☞ ***decir***
digresión *f* digression
dije *vb* ☞ ***decir***
dijo *vb* ☞ ***decir***
dilación *f*: ***sin ~*** without delay; ***sin más dilaciones*** without further delay
dilapidación *f* waste, squandering
dilapidar ⟨1a⟩ *v/t* waste, squander
dilatación *f* dilation
dilatado *adj* dilated
dilatar ⟨1a⟩ **I** *v/t* **1** *pupilas* dilate **2** (*prolongar*) prolong **3** (*aplazar*) postpone **II** *v/i Méx* (*tardar*) be late; ***no me dilato*** I won't be long
dilatorio *adj*: ***táctica -a*** delaying tactics *pl*
dilema *m* dilemma
diletante *m/f* dilettante
diligencia *f* **1** (*prontitud*) diligence **2** *vehículo* stagecoach **3**: ***~s*** *pl* JUR procedures, formalities **4**: ***hacer ~s*** do some business
diligente *adj* diligent
dilucidación *f* clarification
dilucidar ⟨1a⟩ *v/t* clarify
dilución *f* dilution
diluir ⟨3g⟩ *v/t* dilute; *fig* water down; **diluirse** *v/r fig* be watered down
diluviar ⟨1b⟩ *v/i* pour down
diluvio *m* downpour; *fig* deluge
diluyente *m* solvent
dimanar ⟨1a⟩ *v/i*: ***~ de*** *de situación*, *dificultades* arise from
dimensión *f* **1** dimension; *fig*: *de catástrofe* size, scale **2**: ***dimensiones*** *pl* measurements, dimensions; ***de grandes dimensiones*** large
dimes y diretes *mpl* F **1** gossip *sg*, tittle-tattle *sg* **2**: ***andar en ~ con alguien*** squabble with s.o.
diminutivo *m/adj* diminutive
diminuto *adj* tiny, diminutive
dimisión *f* resignation; ***presentar su ~*** hand in one's resignation
dimisionario *adj* outgoing
dimitir ⟨3a⟩ *v/i* resign
dimos *vb* ☞ ***dar***
Dinamarca *f* Denmark
dinámica *f* dynamics *sg*
◇ **dinámica de grupo** group dynamics *pl*
dinámico *adj fig* dynamic
dinamismo *m* dynamism
dinamita *f* dynamite
dinamitar ⟨1a⟩ *v/t* dynamite
dinamizar ⟨1f⟩ *v/t* invigorate
dínamo, dinamo *f o L.Am. m* dynamo
dinastía *f* dynasty
dinástico *adj* dynastic
dineral *m* F fortune
dinero *m* money; ***andar*** *o* ***estar mal de ~*** be short of money *o* cash; ***el ~ no hace la felicidad*** money doesn't bring happiness
◇ **dinero en efectivo** cash; **dinero fácil** easy money; **dinero en metálico** cash; **dinero negro** undeclared money; **dinero de plástico** plastic money; **dinero suelto** loose change
dinosaurio *m* dinosaur
dintel *m* lintel
diñar ⟨1a⟩ *v/t*: ***~la*** P kick the bucket F
dio *vb* ☞ ***dar***
diócesis *f* diocese
diodo *m* diode
dionisíaco, dionisiaco *adj* MYTH Dionysian
Dios *m* God; ***¡~ mío!*** my God!; ***¡por ~!*** for God's sake!; ***~ mediante*** God willing; ***si ~ quiere*** God willing; ***¡~ nos libre!*** God forbid!; ***¡válgame ~!*** good God!; ***¡vaya por ~!*** oh dear!; ***sabe ~ lo que dijo*** God knows what he said; ***hazlo como ~ manda*** do it properly; ***a la buena de ~*** any old how; ***costar ~ y ayuda*** be very difficult; ***vivir como ~*** F live like a king; ***armar la de ~*** F raise hell F
dios *m tb fig* god

diosa *f* goddess
dióxido *m* dioxide
◇ **dióxido de azufre** sulfur dioxide, *Br* sulphur dioxide
◇ **dióxido de carbono** carbon dioxide
dioxina *f* QUÍM dioxin
diploma *m* diploma
diplomacia *f* diplomacy
diplomado **I** *adj* qualified **II** *m*, **-a** *f* person with a diploma
diplomar ⟨1a⟩ *v/t*: ~ ***a alguien*** give s.o. a diploma; **diplomarse** *v/r* receive one's diploma, graduate
diplomático **I** *adj* diplomatic **II** *m*, **-a** *f* diplomat
diplomatura *f* diploma
dipsomanía *f* MED dipsomania
dipsómano **I** *adj* dipsomaniac **II** *m*, **-a** *f* dipsomaniac
díptico *m* PINT diptych
diptongo *m* GRAM diphthong
diputación *f* deputation
◇ **diputación provincial** *Esp* provincial authority *o* council
diputado *m*, **-a** *f* representative, *Br* Member of Parliament
diputar ⟨1a⟩ *v/t* depute, delegate
dique *m* dike, *Br* dyke
◇ **dique de contención** dam; **dique flotante** floating dock; **dique seco** dry dock
dirá *vb* ☞ ***decir***
diré *vb* ☞ ***decir***
dirección *f* **1** (*sentido*) direction; ***en aquella*** ~ that way, in that direction; ~ ***obligatoria*** one way only
2 COM management; POL leadership
3 *de coche* steering
4 TEA, *de película* direction; ***bajo la*** ~ ***de*** under the direction of, directed by
5 *en carta* address
6 (*rumbo*): ***con*** ~ ***a Lima*** for Lima; ***en*** ~ ***a*** heading for; ***en*** ~ ***sur*** heading south
7: ***direcciones*** *pl* (*instrucciones*) guidelines
◇ **dirección asistida** AUTO power steering
◇ **dirección de correo electrónico** e-mail address
directa *f* AUTO top (gear)
directiva *f de empresa* board of directors; POL executive committee
directivo **I** *adj* governing; COM managing **II** *m*, **-a** *f* COM manager; ***alto*** ~ top executive
directo **I** *adj* **1** direct; ***tren*** ~ direct train, *Br tb* through train **2**: ***en*** ~ TV, RAD live **3**: ***ir*** ~ ***al asunto*** get straight to the point **II** *m en boxeo* jab
director **I** *adj* leading **II** *m*, ~**a** *f* **1** *de empresa* manager **2** EDU principal, *Br* head (teacher) **3** TEA, *de película* director
◇ **director espiritual** spiritual director; **director de orquesta** conductor; **director de recursos humanos** director of human resources; **director técnico** *en fútbol* director of football; **director de ventas** sales manager
directorio *m tb* INFOR directory
directriz *f* guideline
dirigente **I** *adj* ruling **II** *m/f* leader
dirigible **I** *adj* steerable **II** *m* dirigible
dirigir ⟨3c⟩ *v/t* **1** TEA, *película* direct; MÚS conduct **2** COM manage, run **3**: ~ ***una carta a*** address a letter to; ~ ***una pregunta a*** direct a question to **4** (*conducir*) lead; **dirigirse** *v/r* make, head (***a***, ***hacia*** for)
dirimir ⟨3a⟩ *v/t disputa* settle
discapacidad *f* disability
discapacitado **I** *adj* disabled **II** *m*, **-a** *f* disabled person
discar ⟨1g⟩ *v/t L.Am.* TELEC dial
discernimiento *m* discernment
discernir ⟨3i⟩ *v/t* distinguish, discern
disciplina *f* discipline
◇ **disciplina de voto** POL party discipline
disciplinado *adj* disciplined
disciplinar ⟨1a⟩ *v/t* discipline
disciplinario *adj* disciplinary
discípulo *m*, **-a** *f* REL, *fig* disciple
disco *m* **1** disk, *Br* disc **2** DEP discus **3** MÚS record; ***cambiar de*** ~ *fig* F change the record **4** (*discoteca*) disco
◇ **disco de algodón** cotton pad; **disco compacto** compact disc; **disco duro** INFOR hard disk; **disco magnético** INFOR magnetic disk; **disco rígido** *L.Am.* INFOR hard disk
discóbolo *m* HIST discus thrower
discografía *f* records *pl*
discográfica *f* record label *o* company
discográfico *adj* record *atr*; ***industria -a*** recording industry
díscolo *adj* unruly
disconforme *adj*: ***estar*** ~ disagree (***de***

with)
discontinuo *adj* discontinuous; ***línea -a*** AUTO broken line
discordancia *f* discord
discordante *adj* discordant
discordar ⟨1m⟩ *v/i* **1** clash (***de*** with) **2** MÚS be out of tune
discorde *adj* **1** clashing **2** MÚS discordant
discordia *f* **1** discord **2** (*colección de discos*) record collection
discreción *f* **1** (*sensatez*) discretion **2**: ***a ~ de*** at the discretion of **3**: ***a ~*** *disparar* at will
discrecional *adj* **1** *potestad* discretionary **2**: ***parada ~*** flag stop, *Br* request stop; ***servicio ~*** *autobús* private service
discrepancia *f* **1** discrepancy **2** (*desacuerdo*) disagreement
discrepante *adj* dissenting
discrepar ⟨1a⟩ *v/i* disagree
discreto *adj* discreet
discriminación *f* discrimination
discriminante *adj* discriminatory
discriminar ⟨1a⟩ *v/t* **1** discriminate against **2** (*diferenciar*) differentiate
discriminatorio *adj* discriminatory
disculpa *f* apology; ***pedir ~s a alguien*** apologize to s.o. (***por*** for)
disculpable *adj* excusable
disculpar ⟨1a⟩ *v/t* excuse; **disculparse** *v/r* apologize
discurrir ⟨3a⟩ *v/i* **1** *de tiempo* pass; *de acontecimiento* pass off **2** *de río* run **3** (*reflexionar*) reflect (***sobre*** on)
discursivo *adj* discursive
discurso *m* **1** speech **2** *de tiempo* passage, passing
◇ **discurso electoral** election speech
◇ **discurso inaugural** inaugural address
discusión *f* **1** discussion **2** (*disputa*) argument
discutible *adj* debatable
discutido I *part* ☞ ***discutir*** **II** *adj* controversial
discutir ⟨3a⟩ **I** *v/t* discuss **II** *v/i* argue (***sobre*** about)
disecación *f* **1** *de animal* stuffing **2** *de planta* drying
disecar ⟨1g⟩ *v/t* **1** *animal* stuff **2** *planta* dry
disección *f* dissection
diseccionar ⟨1a⟩ *v/t* dissect
diseminación *f* scattering; *fig* spreading
diseminar ⟨1a⟩ *v/t* scatter; *fig* spread; **diseminarse** *v/r situación* be scattered; *acción* scatter
disensión *f* disagreement; ***disensiones*** disagreements, dissension
disentería *f* MED dysentery
◇ **disentería amebiana** amebic *o Br* amoebic dysentery
disentimiento *m* disagreement, dissent
disentir ⟨3i⟩ *v/i* disagree (***de*** with), dissent (***de*** from); ***disiento de tu opinión*** I disagree with you
diseñador *m*, **~a** *f* designer
◇ **diseñador publicitario** commercial artist
diseñar ⟨1a⟩ *v/t* design
diseño *m* design
◇ **diseño gráfico** graphic design; **diseño industrial** industrial design; **diseño publicitario** commercial art
disertación *f* dissertation
disertar ⟨1a⟩ *v/i*: ***~ sobre algo*** lecture about sth, speak on sth
disfraz *m para ocultar* disguise; *para fiestas* costume, *Br* fancy dress
disfrazar ⟨1f⟩ *v/t para ocultar* disguise (***de*** as); *para divertir* dress up (***de*** as); **disfrazarse** *v/r para ocultarse* disguise o.s. (***de*** as); *para divertirse* dress up (***de*** as)
disfrutar ⟨1a⟩ **I** *v/t* enjoy **II** *v/i* **1** have fun, enjoy o.s. **2**: ***~ de buena salud*** be in *o* enjoy good health
disfrute *m* enjoyment
disfunción *f* MED dysfunction
disgregación *f* disintegration, breaking up
disgregar ⟨1h⟩ *v/t* break up; **disgregarse** *v/r* disintegrate
disgustado *adj* upset (***con*** with); ***estar ~ con alguien*** be upset with s.o.
disgustar ⟨1a⟩ *v/t* upset; **disgustarse** *v/r* get upset; ***~ con alguien*** get upset with s.o.
disgusto *m* **1** (*pesar*): ***me causó un gran ~*** I was very upset; ***llevarse un ~*** get upset **2** (*enfado*): ***tener un ~*** have an argument; ***tener un ~ con alguien*** have an argument with s.o., fall out with s.o **3** (*accidente*): ***tener un ~*** have an accident **4**: ***a ~*** unwillingly; ***sentirse a ~*** feel uncomfortable, feel ill at ease

disidencia *f* dissidence
disidente I *adj* dissident **II** *m/f* dissident
disimulación *f* dissimulation
disimulado *adj* furtive, sly
disimular ⟨1a⟩ **I** *v/t* disguise **II** *v/i* pretend
disimulo *m*: ***con ~*** unobtrusively
disipación *f* dissipation
disipado *adj* dissipated
disipador I *adj* spendthrift **II** *m*, **~a** *f* spendthrift
disipar ⟨1a⟩ *v/t* **1** *duda* dispel **2** *dinero* fritter away, squander; **disiparse** *v/r* **1** *de niebla* clear **2** *de duda* vanish
diskette *m* diskette, floppy (disk)
dislate *m* piece of nonsense
dislexia *f* dyslexia
disléxico I *adj* dyslexic **II** *m*, **-a** *f* dyslexic
dislocación *f* MED dislocation; *fig* distortion
dislocar ⟨1g⟩ *v/t* dislocate; *fig* distort; **dislocarse** *v/r* be dislocated
disminución *f* decrease
disminuido I *adj* handicapped **II** *m*, **-a** *f* handicapped person
◇ **disminuido físico** physically handicapped person
disminuir ⟨3g⟩ **I** *v/t gastos, costos* reduce, cut; *velocidad* reduce **II** *v/i* decrease, diminish
disociación *f* dissociation
disociar ⟨1b⟩ *v/t* dissociate; **disociarse** *v/r fig*: ***~ de alguien / algo*** dissociate o.s. from s.o. / sth
disoluble *adj* soluble
disolución *f* dissolution
disoluto *adj* dissolute
disolvente *m* solvent
disolver ⟨1h; *part* ***disuelto***⟩ *v/t* **1** dissolve **2** *manifestación* break up; **disolverse** *v/r* **1** dissolve **2** *de manifestación* break up
disonancia *f* dissonance
disonar ⟨1m⟩ *v/i* be out of tune
dispar *adj* different
disparada *f L.Am.* ***a la ~*** in a rush
disparadero *m de arma* trigger; ***poner a alguien en el ~*** *fig* F drive s.o. to distraction
disparado *adj*: ***salir ~*** rush off; *de un edificio etc* rush out
disparador *m* FOT shutter release
disparar ⟨1a⟩ **I** *v/t* **1** *tiro, arma* fire **2** *foto* take **3** *precios* send (rocketing F) up **3** *en fútbol* shoot **II** *v/i* **1** shoot, fire; ***~ al aire*** fire in the air **2** *en fútbol* shoot;
dispararse *v/r* **1** *de arma, alarma* go off **2** *de precios* rise dramatically, rocket F
disparatado *adj fig* F absurd, crazy F
disparatar ⟨1a⟩ *v/i* talk nonsense
disparate *m* F **1** piece of nonsense; ***es un ~ hacer eso*** it's crazy to do that; ***¡qué ~!*** what a stupid thing to say / do! **2**: ***costar un ~*** cost an arm and a leg F
disparidad *f* disparity
disparo *m* **1** *con pistola* shot; ***~ al aire*** shot in the air **2** *en fútbol* shot
dispendio *m* waste
dispendioso *adj* expensive, costly
dispensa *f* **1** *por defecto físico* exemption **2** REL dispensation
dispensable *adj* dispensable
dispensador *m recipiente* dispenser
◇ **dispensador de jabón** soap dispenser
dispensar ⟨1a⟩ *v/t* **1** dispense; *recibimiento* give; *ayuda* give, afford *fml* **2** (*eximir*) excuse (***de*** from)
dispensario *m* MED clinic
dispepsia *f* MED dyspepsia
dispersar ⟨1a⟩ *v/t* disperse; **dispersarse** *v/r* disperse
dispersión *f* dispersion
disperso *adj* scattered
display *m* INFOR display
displicencia *f* disdain
displicente *adj* disdainful
disponer ⟨2r; *part* ***dispuesto***⟩ **I** *v/t* **1** (*arreglar*) arrange **2** (*preparar*) prepare **3** (*ordenar*) stipulate **II** *v/i*: ***~ de algo*** have sth at one's disposal; **disponerse** *v/r*: ***~ a hacer algo*** get ready to do sth
disponibilidad *f* **1** COM availability **2**: ***~es*** *pl* (financial) resources
disponible *adj* available
disposición *f* **1** disposition; ***estar en ~ de hacer algo*** be prepared *o* willing to do sth **2**: ***~ para*** aptitude for **3**: ***estar a ~ de alguien*** be at s.o.'s disposal; ***poner algo a ~ de alguien*** put sth at s.o.'s disposal; ***pasar a ~ judicial*** come before the courts **4** *de objetos* arrangement
◇ **disposición de ánimo** state of mind
◇ **disposición legal** legal requirement
dispositivo *m* device
dispuesto I *part* ☞ ***disponer*** **II** *adj para*

expresar preparación ready (***a*** to); *para expresar voluntad* willing, disposed (***a hacer algo*** to do sth)
disputa *f* dispute; ***sin ~*** undoubtedly
disputable *adj* debatable, disputable
disputar ⟨1a⟩ **I** *v/t* **1** dispute; *premio* compete for **2** *partido* play **II** *v/i* argue (***sobre*** about); **disputarse** *v/r* compete for
disquera *f L.Am.* record company
disquería *f L.Am.* record store
disquete *m* INFOR diskette, floppy (disk)
◇ **disquete de arranque** INFOR boot disk
◇ **disquete de seguridad** INFOR back-up disk
disquetera *f* disk drive
distancia *f tb fig* distance; ***a ~*** at a distance; ***acortar ~s*** *tb fig* bridge the gap, catch up; ***guardar*** (***las***) ***~s*** *fig* keep one's distance
◇ **distancia de frenado** AUTO braking distance; **distancia focal** focal length *o* distance; **distancia de seguridad** AUTO safe distance
distanciamiento *m afectivo*, *de posturas* distancing
distanciar ⟨1b⟩ *v/t* space out; **distanciarse** *v/r* distance o.s. (***de*** from)
distante *adj tb fig* distant
distar ⟨1a⟩ *v/i* be far (***de*** from); ***~ mucho de*** be very far from
distender ⟨2g⟩ *v/t* **1** MED strain **2** *fig*: *relaciones*, *ambiente* ease
distendido *adj ambiente* relaxed
distensible *adj* MED distensible, distendible
distensión *f* **1** MED strain **2** *fig*: *de relaciones*, *ambiente* easing **3** POL détente
distinción *f* distinction; ***sin ~*** without distinction; ***hacer una ~ entre*** make a distinction between; ***a ~ de*** unlike
distingo *m* subtle distinction
distinguible *adj* distinguishable
distinguido *adj* distinguished
distinguir ⟨3d⟩ *v/t* **1** distinguish (***de*** from) **2** (*divisar*) make out; ***~ algo lejano*** make out sth in the distance **3** *con un premio* honor, *Br* honour; **distinguirse** *v/r* distinguish o.s.
distintivo I *adj* distinctive **II** *m* emblem; MIL insignia
distinto *adj* **1** different; ***ser ~ de*** be different from **2**: ***~s*** (*varios*) several
distorsión *f* **1** distortion **2** MED sprain
distorsionar ⟨1a⟩ *v/t* **1** *verdad* distort **2** MED sprain
distracción *f* **1** distraction **2** (*descuido*) absent-mindedness; ***por ~*** out of absent-mindedness **3** (*diversión*) entertainment **4** (*pasatiempo*) pastime
distraer ⟨2p; *part* **distraído**⟩ *v/t* **1** distract **2**: ***la radio la distrae*** she enjoys listening to the radio; **distraerse** *v/r* **1** get distracted **2** (*disfrutar*) enjoy o.s.
distraído I *part* ☞ ***distraer*** **II** *adj* absent-minded; *temporalmente* distracted
distribución *f* TÉC, COM distribution
distribuidor *m* COM, EL, *de película* distributor
◇ **distribuidor automático** vending machine
distribuidora *f* distributor
distribuir ⟨3g⟩ *v/t* **1** distribute; *beneficio* share out **2**: ***~ en grupos*** divide into groups; **distribuirse** *v/r* be distributed
distributivo *adj* distributive
distrito *m* district
◇ **distrito electoral** (legislative) district, *Br* constituency
◇ **distrito postal** zip code, *Br* post code
disturbio *m* disturbance
disuadir ⟨3a⟩ *v/t* dissuade; POL deter; ***~ a alguien de hacer algo*** dissuade s.o. from doing sth
disuasión *f* dissuasion
disuasivo, disuasorio *adj* disuasive; POL deterrent *atr*
disuelto *part* ☞ ***disolver***
disyuntiva *f* dilemma
disyuntivo *adj* GRAM disjunctive
DIU *m abr* (= ***dispositivo intrauterino***) coil, IUD (= intra-uterine device)
diurético *adj* diuretic
diurno *adj* day *atr*; *servicio de trenes etc* daytime *atr*; ***luz -a*** daylight
diva *f* diva, prima donna
divagación *f* digression
divagar ⟨1h⟩ *v/i* digress
diván *m* couch
divergencia *f* divergence
divergente *adj* divergent
divergir ⟨3c⟩ *v/i* diverge
diversidad *f* diversity
diversificar ⟨1g⟩ *v/t* diversify; **diversificarse** *v/r* diversify

diversión *f* **1** fun **2** (*pasatiempo*) pastime; ***aquí no hay muchas diversiones*** there's not much to do around here
diverso *adj* diverse; **~s** several, various
divertido *adj* **1** funny **2** (*entretenido*) entertaining
divertimiento *m* fun
divertir ⟨3i⟩ *v/t* entertain; **divertirse** *v/r* have fun, enjoy o.s.; ***¡que te diviertas!*** have fun!, enjoy yourself!
dividendo *m* dividend
dividir ⟨3a⟩ *v/t* divide; **dividirse** *v/r* divide
divinamente *adv fig* wonderfully
divinidad *f* divinity
divinizar ⟨1f⟩ *v/t* deify
divino *adj tb fig* divine
divisa *f* currency; **~s** *pl* foreign currency *sg*
divisar ⟨1a⟩ *v/t* make out, see
divisibilidad *f* divisibility
divisible *adj* divisible
división *f* **1** MAT, MIL, DEP division **2**: ***hubo ~ de opiniones*** there were differences of opinion
◇ **división acorazada** MIL armored *o Br* armoured division
divisor *m* MAT divisor
divisoria *f*: ***~ de aguas*** watershed
divisorio *adj* dividing; ***línea -a*** dividing line
divo *m* star
divorciado **I** *adj* divorced **II** *m*, **-a** *f* divorcee
divorciar ⟨1b⟩ *v/t* divorce; **divorciarse** *v/r* get divorced
divorcio *m* divorce
divulgación *f* spread
divulgar ⟨1h⟩ *v/t* spread; **divulgarse** *v/r* spread
divulgativo *adj* informative
dizque *adv Méx* F apparently, supposedly
d.J.C. *abr* (= ***después de Jesucristo***) A.D. (= Anno Domini)
dl. *abr* (= ***decilitro***) deciliter, *Br* decilitre
dm. *abr* (= ***decímetro***) decimeter, *Br* decimetre
Dn. *abr* (= ***Don***) *title of respect used before a man's first name*
DNI *m abr* (= ***documento nacional de identidad***) identity card, ID
D.O. *abr* (= ***denominación de origen***) guarantee of origin
do *m*: ***~ sostenido*** C sharp
dobladillo *m* hem
doblado *adj película* dubbed
doblador *m*, **~a** *f de película* dubber
dobladura *f* dubbing
doblaje *m de película* dubbing; ***actor / actriz de ~*** dubber
doblar ⟨1a⟩ **I** *v/t* **1** fold; *pierna, brazo* bend **2** *cantidad* double; ***me dobla la edad*** he's twice my age **3** *película* dub **4** MAR round; *en una carrera* pass, *Br* overtake; ***~ la esquina*** go round *o* turn the corner **II** *v/i* **1** turn; ***~ a la derecha*** turn right **2** *de campana* toll; ***~ a muerto*** sound the death knell; **doblarse** *v/r* bend; *fig* give in
doble **I** *adj* double; *nacionalidad* dual **II** *m* **1**: ***el ~*** twice as much (***de*** as); ***el ~ de gente*** twice as many people, double the number of people; ***me ofrecieron el ~ que la otra gente*** they offered me double what the others did **2**: **~s** *pl en tenis* doubles; *en baloncesto* double dribble; ***un partido de ~s*** a doubles (match); ***hacer ~s*** *en baloncesto* double dribble **3** *en béisbol* double **III** *m/f en película* double
◇ **doble barbilla** double chin; **doble clic** double click; ***hacer ~ en*** double-click on; **doble falta** double fault; **doble jugada** *en béisbol* double play
doblegar ⟨1h⟩ *v/t fig*: *voluntad* break; *orgullo* humble; **doblegarse** *v/r fig* yield
doblete *m*: ***hacer ~*** TEA double up, play two roles; DEP do the double
doblez **I** *m* fold **II** *f fig* deceit
doce *adj* twelve
docena *f* dozen; ***a ~s*** by the dozen
docencia *f* teaching
docente **I** *adj* teaching *atr*; ***cuerpo ~*** teaching staff; ***centro ~*** school **II** *m/f* teacher
dócil *adj* docile
docilidad *f* docility
docto *adj* learned
doctor *m*, **~a** *f* doctor
◇ **doctor honoris causa** honorary doctor
◇ **doctor de la Iglesia** Doctor of the Church
doctorado *m* doctorate
doctoral *adj* **1** doctoral **2** *desp* pompous

doctorando *m*, **-a** *f* PhD student
doctorarse ⟨1a⟩ *v/r* receive one's doctorate *o* PhD
doctrina *f* doctrine
doctrinario I *adj* doctrinaire **II** *m*, **-a** *f* doctrinarian
documentación *f* **1** documentation **2** *de persona* papers
documentado *adj persona* with papers
documental *m/adj* documentary
documentalista *m/f* documentary maker
documentar ⟨1a⟩ *v/t* document; **documentarse** *v/r* do research
documento *m* document
◇ **documento adjunto** INFOR attachment
◇ **documento nacional de identidad** national identity card
dodecafonía *f*, **dodecafonismo** *m* twelve-tone system
dogal *m para ahorcar* noose
dogaut *m Méx* DEP dugout
dogma *m* dogma
dogmático I *adj* dogmatic **II** *m*, **-a** *f* dogmatist
dogo *m* ZO mastiff
dólar *m* dollar
dolencia *f* ailment
doler ⟨2h⟩ *v/t tb fig* hurt; ***me duele el brazo*** my arm hurts; ***le duele la tripa*** he has a stomach-ache; ***me duele la garganta*** I have a sore throat, my throat hurts; ***le dolió que le mintieran*** *fig* she was hurt that they had lied to her; ***ahí le duele*** *fig* that's his problem **dolerse** *v/r* **1**: **~ *de*** (*sentir tristeza por*) regret; (*estar disgustado por*) be upset about **2**: ***se duele de la rodilla*** his knee hurts
dolido *adj fig* hurt
doliente *adj* **1** sick, *Br* ill **2** (*apenado*) bereaved
dolmen *m* dolmen
dolo *m* JUR fraud
dolor *m tb fig* pain; ***dar ~es de cabeza a alguien*** *fig* cause s.o. problems
◇ **dolor de cabeza** headache; **dolor de estómago** stomach-ache; **dolor de muelas** toothache; **dolores de parto** labor pains, *Br* labour pains
dolorido *adj* sore, aching; *fig* hurt
dolorosa *f* F check, *Br* bill
doloroso *adj tb fig* painful
doloso *adj* JUR fraudulent
doma *f* taming; *de caballo* breaking in
domador *m* **~a** *f* tamer
◇ **domador de caballos** horse-breaker
domar ⟨1a⟩ *v/t tb fig* tame; *caballo* break in
domesticable *adj* which can be domesticated
domesticar ⟨1g⟩ *v/t* domesticate
doméstico I *adj* domestic, household *atr* **II** *m*, **-a** *f* servant
domiciliación *f de sueldo* credit transfer; *de pagos* direct billing, *Br* direct debit
domiciliado *adj* resident (***en*** in)
domiciliar ⟨1b⟩ *v/t pago* pay by direct billing, *Br* pay by direct debit; ***tengo la nómina domiciliada*** my salary is paid directly into my bank account
domiciliario *adj* home *atr*; ***arresto ~*** house arrest
domicilio *m* address; ***sin ~ fijo*** of no fixed abode; ***repartir a ~*** do home deliveries; ***una victoria a ~*** DEP away win
◇ **domicilio social** COM registered address
dominación *f* domination
dominador *adj* dominant
dominancia *f* BIO dominance
dominante *adj* dominant; *desp* domineering
dominar ⟨1a⟩ **I** *v/t* **1** *persona*, *mercado* dominate **2** *idioma* have a good command of **II** *v/i* dominate; **dominarse** *v/r* control o.s.
domingas *fpl* P tits P, boobs P
domingo *m* Sunday
◇ **domingo de Ramos** Palm Sunday
◇ **domingo de Resurrección** Easter Sunday
dominguero I *adj* Sunday *atr* **II** *m*, **-a** *f* F weekender, *Br tb* Sunday tripper
dominical *adj* Sunday *atr*; ***suplemento ~*** Sunday supplement
dominicano GEOG **I** *adj* Dominican **II** *m*, **-a** *f* Dominican
dominico *m monje* Dominican
dominio *m* **1** control; ***~ de sí mismo*** self-control **2** *fig*: *de idioma* command **3** INFOR domain **4**: ***ser del ~ público*** be in the public domain
dominó *m* dominoes *pl*

domótica *f* home automation
don[1] *m* gift; **~ de gentes** way with people; **~ de lenguas** gift for languages
don[2] *m* Mr.; **~ Enrique** Mr. Sanchez *English uses the surname while Spanish uses the first name*
dona *f Méx* donut, *Br* doughnut
donación *f* donation
◇ **donación de órganos** organ donation
◇ **donación de sangre** blood donation
donaire *m al hablar* wit; *al moverse* grace
donante *m/f* donor
◇ **donante de sangre** blood donor
donar ⟨1a⟩ *v/t sangre, órgano, dinero* donate
donatario *m*, **-a** *f* recipient (*of a donation*)
donativo *m* donation
doncel *m* **1** youth **2** HIST squire
doncella *f* maid
donde I *adv* where **II** *prp esp L.Am.* **fui ~ el médico** I went to the doctor's
dónde *interr* where; **¿de ~ eres?** where are you from?; **¿hacia ~ vas?** where are you going?; **¿en ~?** where?
dondequiera *adv* wherever
dondiego *m*: **~ (de noche)** BOT marvel of Peru
donjuán *m fig* womanizer, Don Juan
donoso *adj al hablar* witty; *al moverse* graceful
donostiarra *adj* of / from San Sebastián, San Sebastián *atr*
doña *f* Mrs; **~ Estela** Mrs Sanchez *English uses the surname while Spanish uses the first name*
dopaje, doping *m* doping
dopar ⟨1a⟩ *v/t* dope; **doparse** *v/r* take drugs
doquier(a) *adv*: **por ~** *lit* everywhere
dorada *f* ZO gilthead
dorado I *adj* gold; *montura* gilt **II** *m* gilt
dorar ⟨1a⟩ *v/t* **1** TÉC gild **2** GASTR brown
dórico *adj* ARQUI Doric
dorífora *f* ZO potato beetle
dormido *adj* asleep; **quedarse ~** fall asleep
dormilón *m*, **-ona** *f* F sleepyhead F
dormir ⟨3k⟩ **I** *v/i* sleep; (*estar dormido*) be asleep **II** *v/t* **1** put to sleep; **dejar ~ algo** *fig* let sth lie **2**: **~ a alguien** MED give s.o. a general anesthetic; **dormirse** *v/r* **1** go to sleep; (*quedarse dormido*) fall asleep; **no podía dormirme** I couldn't get to sleep; **se me durmió la pierna** my leg has gone to sleep **2** (*no despertarse*) oversleep
dormitar ⟨1a⟩ *v/i* doze
dormitorio *m* bedroom
dorsal I *adj* dorsal **II** *m* DEP number
dorso *m* back; **al ~** on the back; **~ de la mano** back of the hand
dos *adj* **1** two; **de ~ en ~** in twos, two by two; **los ~** both; **conozco a los ~ hermanos** I know both (of the) brothers; **anda con ojo con los ~** watch out for both of *o* the pair of them; **~ contra uno** *en baloncesto* double team **2**: **cada ~ por tres** all the time, continually; **en un ~ por tres** in a flash
doscientos *adj* two hundred
dosel *m* canopy; **cama con ~** four-poster bed
dosificación *f* dosage
dosificador *m* dispenser
◇ **dosificador de jabón** soap dispenser
dosificar ⟨1g⟩ *v/t* cut down on
dosis *f inv* dose; **una buena ~ de** a good deal of
◇ **dosis de choque** MED large dose
◇ **dosis letal** lethal dose
dotación *f* **1**: **la ~ del premio es de 10 millones de dólares** the total amount of prize money is 10 million dollars; **una ayuda con una ~ de 10 millones de dólares** aid totaling 10 million dollars **2**: **la ~ de doctores es …** the number of doctors is…
dotado *adj* **1** gifted; **~ para las lenguas** with a gift for languages **2**: **~ de algo** equipped with sth
dotar ⟨1a⟩ *v/t*: **~ de** equip with; *fondos* provide with; *cualidades* endow with; **la organización fue dotada con el premio a …** the organization was awarded the prize for …
dote *f* **1** *a novia* dowry **2**: **tener ~s para algo** have a gift for sth
doy *vb* ☞ **dar**
dpto. *abr* (= **departamento**) dept (= department)
Dr. *abr* (= **doctor**) Dr (= doctor)
Dra. *abr* (= **doctora**) Dr (= doctor)

draconiano *adj* draconian; ***medidas -as*** draconian measures
draga *f máquina* dredge; *barco* dredger
dragado *m* dredging
dragaminas *m inv* minesweeper
dragar ⟨1h⟩ *v/t* dredge
drago *m* BOT dragon tree
dragón *m* **1** MYTH dragon **2** MIL dragoon
drama *m* drama; ***hacer un ~ de algo*** *fig* make a drama out of sth, make a big deal out of sth
dramático *adj* dramatic; ***arte ~*** dramatic art
dramatismo *m* dramatic quality, drama
dramatizar ⟨1f⟩ *v/t* dramatize
dramaturgia *f* drama
dramaturgo *m*, **-a** *f* playwright, dramatist
dramón *m desp* melodrama
drástico *adj* drastic
drenaje *m* drainage
drenar ⟨1a⟩ *v/t* drain
driblar ⟨1a⟩ DEP **I** *v/i* dribble **II** *v/t* dribble past
dribling *m* dribbling, dribble
dril *m* drill
droga *f* drug
◇ **droga blanda** soft drug; **droga de diseño** designer drug; **droga dura** hard drug
drogadicción *f* drug addiction
drogadicto I *adj*: ***una mujer -a*** a woman addicted to drugs **II** *m*, **-a** *f* drug addict
drogarse ⟨1h⟩ *v/r* take drugs, do drugs F
drogata *m/f* F junkie F
drogodependencia *f* drug dependency
drogodependiente I *adj* drug-dependent **II** *m/f* drug addict
droguería *f* hardware store (*selling cleaning and household products*)
droguero *m*, **-a** *f*, **droguista** *m/f owner of a **droguería***
dromedario *m* ZO dromedary
d.to *abr* (= ***descuento***) discount
dubitativo *adj* doubtful
ducado *m* dukedom
ducal *adj* ducal
ducha *f* shower; ***ser una ~ de agua fría*** *fig* come as a shock
duchar ⟨1a⟩ *v/t*: ***~ a alguien*** give s.o. a shower; (*mojar*) soak s.o.; **ducharse** *v/r* have a shower, shower
ducho *adj* knowledgeable
dúctil *adj* ductile
ductilidad *f* ductility
duda *f* doubt; ***sin ~*** without doubt; ***poner en ~*** call into question; ***estar fuera de*** (***toda***) ***~*** be beyond (any) doubt; ***no cabe la menor ~*** there is absolutely no doubt; ***salir de ~s*** get things clear; ***todavía tengo mis ~s*** I still have (my) doubts, I'm still dubious
dudar ⟨1a⟩ **I** *v/t* doubt; ***¡no lo dudes!*** of course!, no problem! **II** *v/i* **1** hesitate (***en*** to); ***no ~ en hacer algo*** not hesitate to do sth **2**: ***~ de alguien*** not trust s.o.
dudoso *adj* **1** (*incierto*) doubtful, dubious **2** (*indeciso*) hesitant
duela *f* **1** stave **2** *Méx parquet* parquet
duele *vb* ☞ ***doler***
duelista *m* duelist, *Br* duellist
duelo *m* **1** grief **2** (*combate*) duel; ***batirse en ~*** fight a duel
duende *m* **1** imp **2** *cualidad* magic; ***tener ~*** have a magical quality
dueño *m*, **-a** *f* **1** COM owner; *de perro* owner, master **2**: ***eres muy ~ de hacer lo que quieras*** you are free to do as you wish, you are your own master; ***hacerse ~ de la situación*** take command *o* control of the situation; ***no ser ~ de sí mismo*** be out of control; ***no ser ~ de sus actos*** not be responsible for one's actions
duermo *vb* ☞ ***dormir***
dueto *m* MÚS duet
dulce I *adj* sweet; *fig*: *carácter* gentle **II** *m* candy, *Br* sweet; ***~s*** sweet things
dulcería *f* candy store, *Br* sweetshop
dulcificar ⟨1g⟩ *v/t* GASTR sweeten; *fig* soften
dulzaina *f* MÚS *oboe-like instrument*
dulzón *adj* sickly sweet
dulzor *m*, **dulzura** *f tb fig* sweetness
dumping *m* dumping
duna *f* dune
duo *m* MÚS duo
duodécimo *adj* twelfth
duodeno *m* ANAT duodenum
dúplex *m* duplex (apartment)
duplicación *f* duplication
duplicado I *adj* duplicate; ***por ~*** in duplicate **II** *m* duplicate
duplicar ⟨1g⟩ *v/t* duplicate
duplicidad *f fig* duplicity
duplo *m*: ***el ~ de tres es seis*** two times

three is six, twice three is six
duque *m* **1** duke; ***los ~s de*** the Duke and Duchess of **2** ZO: ***gran ~*** eagle owl
duquesa *f* duchess
durabilidad *f* durability
durable *adj* durable
duración *f* duration; ***de larga ~*** long-life *atr*
duradero *adj* lasting; *ropa, calzado* hard-wearing
durante *prp indicando duración* during; *indicando período* for; ***~ seis meses*** for six months
durar ⟨1a⟩ *v/i* last
duraznero *m L.Am.* BOT peach (tree)
durazno *m L.Am.* BOT peach
Durex® *m Méx* Scotch tape®, *Br* Sellotape®
dureza *f* **1** *de material* hardness; *de carne* toughness **2** *de clima, fig* harshness
durmiente I *adj* sleeping **II** *m/f* sleeper; ***la Bella Durmiente*** Sleeping Beauty **III** *m* FERR tie, *Br* sleeper
duro I *adj* **1** *material* hard; *carne* tough **2** *clima, fig* harsh **3**: ***~ de oído*** F hard of hearing; ***~ de corazón*** hard-hearted; ***ser ~ de pelar*** be a tough nut to crack **II** *adv* hard **III** *m* five peseta coin
DVD *m abr* (= ***disco de vídeo digital***) DVD (= digital versatile *o* video disc)

E

e *conj* (*instead of* ***y*** *before words starting with* ***i*** *or* ***hi***) and
E *abr* (= ***este***) E (= East, Eastern)
¡ea! *int* come on!
EAU *abr* (= ***Emiratos Arabes Unidos***) UAE *pl* (= United Arab Emirates)
ebanista *m/f* cabinetmaker
ebanistería *f* cabinetmaking
ébano *m* ebony
ebriedad *f* drunkenness; *fig* delirium; ***en estado de ~*** in a state of intoxication
ebrio *adj* drunk; ***~ de*** *éxito, felicidad* drunk with; ***~ de amor*** blinded by love; ***~ de ira*** blind with rage
ebullición *f*: ***punto de ~*** boiling point
ebúrneo *adj* ivory *atr*
eccema *m* eczema
echado I *part* ☞ ***echar*** **II** *adj* **1** lying down **2**: ***~ para (a)delante*** F self-reliant
echadora *f*: ***~ de cartas*** fortune-teller
echar ⟨1a⟩ **I** *v/t* **1** (*lanzar*) throw; *de un lugar* throw out; ***lo han echado del trabajo*** he's been fired; ***~ abajo*** pull down, destroy **2** *humo* give off **3** (*poner*) put **4** *carta* mail, *Br tb* post **5**: ***~ la culpa a alguien*** blame s.o., put the blame on s.o.; ***me echó 40 años*** he thought I was 40
II *v/i*: ***~ a*** start to, begin to; ***~ a correr*** start *o* begin to run, start running
echarse *v/r* **1** (*tirarse*) throw o.s.; ***~ al agua*** jump into the water; ***~ al suelo*** throw o.s. to the ground; ***échate a un lado*** move to one side; ***~ sobre algo*** throw o.s. on sth; ***~ detrás de alguien*** go after s.o. **2** (*tumbarse*) lie down **3** (*ponerse*) put on **4**: ***~ a llorar / reír*** start *o* begin to cry / laugh, start crying / laughing **5**: ***echárselas de algo*** make out that one is sth, make o.s. out to be sth **6** F *novia, coche etc* get
echarpe *m* scarf
eclesiástico I *adj* ecclesiastical, church *atr* **II** *m* clergyman
eclipsar ⟨1a⟩ *v/t* eclipse; **eclipsarse** *v/r* **1** *de persona* disappear, vanish **2**: ***la luna se eclipsará a las diez*** there will be a lunar eclipse at ten o'clock
eclipse *m* eclipse
◇ **eclipse de luna** lunar eclipse, eclipse of the moon
◇ **eclipse de sol** solar eclipse, eclipse of the sun
eclosión *f* **1** ZO hatching **2** *fig* sudden emergence *o* appearance
eclosionar ⟨1a⟩ *v/i* **1** ZO hatch **2** *fig* appear, emerge
eco *m* echo; ***hacerse ~ de algo*** echo sth; ***tener ~*** *fig* make an impact
ecografía *f* (ultrasound) scan
ecología *f* ecology
ecológico *adj* ecological; *alimentos* organic
ecologismo *m* environmentalism, conservationism

ecologista *m/f* ecologist, environmentalist
ecólogo *m*, **-a** *f* ecologist
economato *m* co-operative (store)
economía *f* **1** economy; ***hacer ~s*** economize, make economies **2** *ciencia* economics *sg*
◇ **economía doméstica** home economics *sg*; **economía informal** *L.Am.* black economy; **economía de mercado** market economy; **economía planificada** planned economy; **economía política** political economy; **economía sumergida** black economy
económico *adj* **1** economic **2** (*barato*) economical
economista *m/f* economist
economizar ⟨1f⟩ *v/t* economize on, save; ***~ esfuerzos*** save one's energy; ***no debemos ~ esfuerzos*** we must spare no effort
ecosistema *m* ecosystem
ecotest *m* ecotest
ecotienda *f* ecostore, *Br tb* ecoshop
ecoturismo *m* ecotourism
ectoplasma *m* ectoplasm
ecuación *f* equation
Ecuador *m* Ecuador
ecuador *m* equator; ***paso del ~*** *fig* crossing the line
ecualizador *m* TÉC equalizer
ecuánime *adj* **1** (*sereno*) even-tempered **2** (*imparcial*) impartial
ecuanimidad *f* even temper, equanimity; (*imparcialidad*) impartiality
ecuatorial *adj* equatorial
ecuatoriano I *adj* Ecuadorean **II** *m*, **-a** *f* Ecuadorean
ecuestre *adj* equestrian; ***estatua ~*** equestrian statue
ecuménico *adj* ecumenical
ecumenismo *m* REL ecumenicalism
eczema *m* eczema
ed. *abr* (= **edición**) ed (= edition)
edad *f* **1** age; ***a la ~ de*** at the age of; ***a mi ~*** at my age; ***¿qué ~ tienes?*** how old are you?; ***de corta ~*** *niño* young; ***en ~ escolar*** school-age, of school age; ***en ~ penal*** old enough to be sent to prison; ***de mediana ~*** middle-aged; ***la tercera ~*** the over 60s; ***una señora de ~*** an elderly lady; ***estar en la ~ del pavo*** be at that awkward age **2** (*época*): ***la Edad Media*** the Middle Ages *pl*; ***la ~ dorada*** *o* ***de oro*** *fig* the golden age
◇ **edad de jubilación** retirement age; **edad moderna** modern era; **edad de piedra** Stone Age
edecán *m* MIL aide-de-camp
edema *m* MED edema, *Br tb* oedema
edén *m* Eden; *fig* paradise
edición *f* edition
◇ **edición de bolsillo** pocket edition
◇ **edición pirata** pirate edition
edicto *m* edict
edificable *adj* available for development; ***zona ~*** development area
edificación *f* construction, building
edificante *adj* edifying
edificar ⟨1g⟩ *v/t* construct, build
edificio *m* building
◇ **edificio de pisos, edificio de viviendas** apartment building, *Br* block of flats
edil *m* councilor, *Br* councillor, councilman
edila *f* councilor, *Br* councillor, councilwoman
Edimburgo *m* Edinburgh
Edipo Oedipus; ***complejo de ~*** Oedipus complex
editar ⟨1a⟩ *v/t* **1** edit **2** (*publicar*) publish
editor I *m*, **~a** *f* editor **II** *m* INFOR editor
editorial I *adj* publishing *atr* **II** *m* editorial, leading article **III** *f* publishing company *o* house, publisher
editorialista *m/f* editorialist, *Br* leader writer
edredón *m* eiderdown; *utilizado sin sábanas* duvet, *Br tb* continental quilt
educación *f* **1** (*crianza*) upbringing **2** (*modales*) manners *pl*; ***con mucha ~*** *persona* extremely polite; *pedir* extremely politely; ***no tener ~*** have no manners
◇ **educación de adultos** adult education; **educación cívica** civics *sg*; **educación especial** special-needs education; **educación física** physical education, PE; **educación preescolar** preschool education; **educación primaria** elementary education, *Br* primary education; **educación secundaria** secondary education; **educación sexual** sex education; **educación viaria** traffic safety classes *pl*
educado I *adj* polite, well-mannered;

bien ~ polite, well-mannered; **mal ~** rude, ill-mannered **II** *part* ☞ **educar**
educador *m*, **~a** *f* teacher, educator
educar ⟨1g⟩ *v/t* **1** educate **2** (*criar*) bring up **3** *voz* train
educativo *adj* educational; ***política -a*** education(al) policy; ***sistema ~*** education(al) system
edulcorante *m* sweetener
edulcorar ⟨1a⟩ *v/t* sweeten
EE. UU. *abr* (= ***Estados Unidos***) US(A) (= United States (of America))
EEB *f abr* (= ***encefalopatía espongiforme bovina***) BSE (= bovine spongiform encephalopathy)
efebo *m* youth
efectismo *m* theatricality
efectista *adj* theatrical, dramatic
efectivamente *adv* indeed
efectividad *f* effectiveness; ***tener ~*** be effective
efectivo I *adj* **1** effective **2** COM: ***hacer ~*** cash **II** *m* COM: ***en ~*** (in) cash
efecto *m* **1** effect; ***surtir ~*** take effect, work; ***~ a largo plazo*** long-term effect; ***aplicarse con ~ retroactivo*** be applied retroactively; ***la subida con ~ retroactivo de las pensiones*** the retroactive increase in pensions; ***llevar a ~*** carry out; ***dejar sin ~*** negate, undo **2**: ***hacer buen / mal ~*** give *o* create a good / bad impression **3**: ***al ~*** for the purpose; ***en ~*** indeed
◇ **efecto invernadero** greenhouse effect; **efectos especiales** *en película* special effects; **efectos personales** personal effects *o* belongings; **efectos secundarios** side effects
efectuar ⟨1e⟩ *v/t* carry out; **efectuarse** *v/r*: ***la inauguración se efectuará …*** the inauguration will take place …
efeméride *f* anniversary
efervescencia *f* effervescence
efervescente *adj* **1** effervescent; ***tableta ~*** effervescent tablet **2** *bebida* carbonated, sparkling
eficacia *f* efficiency
eficaz *adj* **1** (*efectivo*) effective **2** (*eficiente*) efficient
eficiencia *f* efficiency
eficiente *adj* efficient
efigie *f* effigy
efímera *f* ZO mayfly
efímero *adj* ephemeral, short-lived
eflorescente *adj* efflorescent
efluvio *m* smell, scent
efusión *f* effusiveness; ***con ~*** effusively
efusivo *adj* effusive
Egeo *m/adj*: ***el (mar) ~*** the Aegean (Sea)
égida *f*: ***bajo la ~ de*** under the aegis of
egipcio I *adj* Egyptian **II** *m*, **-a** *f* Egyptian
Egipto *m* Egypt
ego *m* ego
egocéntrico *adj* egocentric, self-centered, *Br* self-centred
egoísmo *m* selfishness, egoism
egoísta I *adj* selfish, egoistic **II** *m/f* egoist
egregio *adj* distinguished, eminent
egresado *m*, **-a** *f L.Am.* graduate
egresar ⟨1a⟩ *v/i L.Am. de universidad* graduate; *de colegio* graduate from high school, *Br* leave school
egreso *m* **1** *L.Am.* graduation **2** *Méx* (*retirada*) withdrawal
eh *int para llamar atención* hey!; ***¿~?*** eh?
eje *m* **1** axis; ***partir a alguien por el ~*** *fig* mess up s.o.'s plans **2** TÉC shaft; AUTO *de ruedas* axle; *fig* linchpin
ejecución *f* **1** (*realización*) implementation, carrying out, execution; ***poner en ~*** execute, carry out **2** *de condenado* execution **3** INFOR running, execution **4** MÚS performance
◇ **ejecución forzosa** JUR enforced execution *o* implementation
ejecutante *m/f* MÚS performer
ejecutar ⟨1a⟩ *v/t* **1** (*realizar*) carry out, implement, execute **2** *condenado* execute **3** INFOR run, execute **4** MÚS play, perform
ejecutiva *f* executive
ejecutivo I *adj* executive; ***el poder ~*** POL the executive **II** *m* **1** executive; ***alto ~*** top executive **2**: ***el Ejecutivo*** the government
ejecutor *m* executor
ejecutora *f* executor, executrix
ejecutorio *adj* executory
ejemplar I *adj alumno*, *padre etc* model *atr*, exemplary **II** *m* **1** *de libro* copy; *de revista tb* issue **2** *animal*, *planta* specimen
◇ **ejemplar gratuito** *de publicación* free copy
ejemplaridad *f* exemplary nature; ***la ~ de su comportamiento*** his exemplary behavior

ejemplarizar ⟨1f⟩ *v/t* set a good example to
ejemplificar ⟨1g⟩ *v/t* exemplify
ejemplo *m* example; ***dar buen ~*** set a good example; ***por ~*** for example; ***poner por ~*** quote as an example; ***tomar ~ de alguien*** follow s.o.'s example; ***predicar con el ~*** practice what one preaches
ejercer ⟨2b⟩ **I** *v/t* **1** *cargo* practice, *Br* practise **2** *influencia* exert **II** *v/i de profesional* practice, *Br* practise; ***ejerce de médico*** he's a practicing doctor
ejercicio *m* **1** exercise; ***hacer ~*** exercise **2** COM fiscal year, *Br* financial year **3** MIL: ***en ~(s)*** on maneuvers, *Br* on manoeuvres
◇ **ejercicios espirituales** REL retreat *sg*
ejercitado *adj* experienced (***en*** in)
ejercitar ⟨1a⟩ *v/t músculo, derecho* exercise; **ejercitarse** *v/r* train; ***~ en*** practice, *Br* practise
ejército *m* army
◇ **ejército de(l) aire** air force
◇ **ejército profesional** professional army
ejido *m Méx traditional communal farming unit*
ejote *m L.Am.* green bean
el I *art* the **II** *pron*: ***~ de ...*** that of ...; ***~ de Juan*** Juan's; ***~ más grande*** the biggest (one); ***~ que está ...*** the one that is ...
él *pron sujeto* he; *cosa* it; *complemento* him; *cosa* it; ***de ~*** his; ***esto es para ~*** this is for him
elaboración *f* production, making; *de metal etc* working; *de plan* drawing up
elaborar ⟨1a⟩ *v/t* produce, make; *metal etc* work; *plan* devise, draw up
elasticidad *f* elasticity
elástico I *adj* elastic **II** *m* **1** elastic **2** (*goma*) elastic band, *Br* rubber band
eléboro *m* BOT hellebore
elección *f* choice
eleccionario *adj L.Am.* election *atr*, electoral
elecciones *fpl* election *sg*, elections
◇ **elecciones generales** general election *sg*; **elecciones legislativas** parliamentary elections; **elecciones municipales** municipal elections; **elecciones presidenciales** presidential election *sg*
electivo *adj* elective
electo *adj* elect
elector *m*, **~a** *f* voter
electorado *m* electorate
electoral *adj* election *atr*, electoral
electricidad *f* electricity
electricista *m/f* electrician
eléctrico *adj luz, motor* electric; *aparato* electrical
electrificación *f* electrification
electrificar ⟨1g⟩ *v/t* electrify
electrizar ⟨1f⟩ *v/t tb fig* electrify
electrocardiograma *m* electrocardiogram
electrochoque *m* electroshock therapy
electrocución *f* electrocution
electrocutar ⟨1a⟩ *v/t* electrocute; **electrocutarse** *v/r* be electrocuted, electrocute o.s
electrodinámica *f* electrodynamics *sg*
electrodo *m* electrode
electrodoméstico *m* electrical appliance
electroencefalograma *m* electroencephalogram
electroimán *m* electromagnet
electrólisis *f* electrolysis
electrón *m* electron
electrónica *f* electronics *sg*
◇ **electrónica de consumo** consumer electronics *sg o pl*
electrónico *adj* electronic
electrotecnia *f* electrical engineering
electrotécnico *adj* electrical; ***el equipo ~*** the electricians *pl*
electroterapia *f* MED electrotherapy
elefante *m* ZO elephant; ***como un ~ en una cacharrería*** like a bull in a china shop
◇ **elefante marino** elephant seal, sea elephant
elegancia *f* elegance, stylishness
elegante *adj* elegant, stylish
elegantoso *adj L.Am.* F stylish, classy F
elegía *f* elegy
elegible *adj* eligible
elegir ⟨3c & 3l⟩ *v/t* choose; *por votación* elect
elemental *adj* **1** (*esencial*) fundamental, essential **2** (*básico*) elementary, basic
elemento *m* element; ***estar en su ~*** *fig* be in one's element
elenco *m* TEA cast

elepé *m* LP, album
elevación *f* GEOG elevation
elevado *adj* high; *fig* elevated
elevador *m* **1** hoist **2** *L.Am.* elevator, *Br* lift
elevadorista *m/f L.Am.* elevator operator, *Br* lift operator
elevalunas *m inv* AUTO: ***~ eléctrico*** electric window
elevar ⟨1a⟩ *v/t* **1** raise **2** MAT: ***~ al cuadrado*** raise to the power of four; **elevarse** *v/r* **1** rise **2** *de monumento* stand **3**: ***~ a*** *de cantidad, número etc* stand at, have reached
elfo *m* MYTH elf
eliminación *f* **1** elimination **2** *de desperdicios* disposal **3** INFOR deletion
◇ **eliminación de desechos, eliminación de residuos** waste disposal
eliminado *adj* DEP out *pred*
eliminar ⟨1a⟩ *v/t* **1** eliminate **2** *desperdicios* dispose of **3** INFOR delete
eliminatoria *f* DEP qualifying round, heat
eliminatorio *adj* DEP qualifying *atr*
elipse *f* ellipse
elíptico *adj* elliptical
élite *f* elite
elitista *adj* elitist
elixir *m* elixir
◇ **elixir bucal** mouthwash
ella *pron sujeto* she; *cosa* it; *complemento* her; *cosa* it; ***de ~*** her; ***es de ~*** it's hers; ***con / para ~*** with / for her
ellas *pron sujeto* they; *complemento* them; ***de ~*** their; ***es de ~*** it's theirs
ello *pron* it; ***por ~*** for this reason; ***¿has reparado la televisión? – estoy en ~*** have you mended the television? – I'm working on it *o* I'm doing it
ellos *pron sujeto* they; *complemento* them; ***de ~*** their; ***es de ~*** it's theirs
elocuencia *f* eloquence
elocuente *adj* eloquent
elogiable *adj* praiseworthy
elogiar ⟨1b⟩ *v/t* praise
elogio *m* praise
elogioso *adj* full of praise, highly complimentary
elote *m L.Am.* **1** corncob **2** *granos* corn, *Br* sweetcorn
El Salvador *m* El Salvador
elucidar ⟨1a⟩ *v/t* elucidate
elucubrar ⟨1a⟩ *v/t* muse on, ponder
eludir ⟨3a⟩ *v/t* evade, avoid
e-mail *m* e-mail; ***mandar un ~ a alguien*** e-mail s.o., send s.o. an e-mail
emanación *f* emanation *fml*, emission
emanar ⟨1a⟩ **I** *v/i fml* emanate (***de*** from) *fml*; *fig* stem (***de*** from), derive (***de*** from) **II** *v/t* exude, emit
emancipación *f* emancipation
emancipar ⟨1a⟩ *v/t* **I** emancipate; **emanciparse** *v/r* become emancipated
emascular ⟨1a⟩ *v/t* castrate
embadurnar ⟨1a⟩ *v/t* smear (***de*** with)
embajada *f* embassy
embajador *m*, **~a** *f* ambassador
embalador *m*, **~a** *f* packer
embalaje *m* packing
embalar ⟨1a⟩ *v/t* pack; **embalarse** *v/r* **1** *de persona* get excited **2**: ***el coche se embaló*** the car went faster and faster; ***no te embales*** don't go so fast
embaldosado *m* **1** *suelo* tiled floor **2** *acto* tiling
embaldosar ⟨1a⟩ *v/t* tile
embalsamar ⟨1a⟩ *v/t* embalm
embalsar ⟨1a⟩ *v/t* dam up
embalse *m* reservoir
embarazada **I** *adj* pregnant **II** *f* pregnant woman
embarazar ⟨1f⟩ *v/t* **1** (*preñar*) get pregnant **2** (*obstaculizar*) hinder, hamper; **embarazarse** *v/r* get embarrassed
embarazo *m* pregnancy; ***interrupción del ~*** termination, abortion
embarazoso *adj* awkward, embarrassing
embarcación *f* vessel, craft
embarcadero *m* wharf
embarcar ⟨1g⟩ **I** *v/t* **1** *pasajeros* board, embark; *mercancías* load **2** *fig* involve (***en*** in) **II** *v/i* board, embark; **embarcarse** *v/r en barco* board, embark; *en avión* board; ***~ en*** *fig* embark on
embargar ⟨1h⟩ *v/t* **1** JUR seize **2** *fig* overwhelm, overcome
embargo *m* **1** embargo **2** JUR seizure **3**: ***sin ~*** however
embarque *m* **1** AVIA boarding; ***puerta de ~*** gate; ***zona de ~*** departure area **2** *de mercancías* loading
embarrancar ⟨1g⟩ *v/i* MAR run aground; **embarrancarse** *v/r* MAR run aground
embarrarse ⟨1a⟩ *v/r* get covered in mud
embarullar ⟨1a⟩ *v/t* confuse, mix up

embarullarse ⟨1a⟩ *v/r* get mixed up
embate *m del mar, del viento* beating, battering; *de las olas* pounding, battering
embaucador I *adj* deceitful **II** *m*, **~a** *f* trickster
embaucar ⟨1g⟩ *v/t* trick, deceive
embeber ⟨2a⟩ *v/t* soak up, absorb; **embeberse** *v/r* get absorbed *o* engrossed (***en*** in)
embelesar ⟨1a⟩ *v/t* captivate; **embelesarse** *v/r* be captivated
embeleso *m* captivation
embellecer ⟨2d⟩ *v/t* make more beautiful, beautify; **embellecerse** *v/r* grow more beautiful
embellecimiento *m* beautification
embestida *f* charge
embestir ⟨3l⟩ **I** *v/t* charge **II** *v/i* charge (***contra*** at)
embetunar ⟨1a⟩ *v/t zapatos* polish
emblandecerse ⟨2d⟩ *v/r* go soft
emblema *m* emblem
emblemático *adj* emblematic
embobar ⟨1a⟩ *v/t* fascinate
embobarse ⟨1a⟩ *v/r* be fascinated
embocadura *f* MÚS mouthpiece
embolarse ⟨1a⟩ *v/r C.Am., Méx* F get plastered F
embole *m Rpl* F bore
embolia *f* MED embolism
◇ **embolia pulmonar** MED pulmonary embolism
émbolo *m* TÉC piston
embolsar ⟨1a⟩ *v/t* pocket; **embolsarse** *v/r* pocket
emboquillado I *adj* tipped **II** *m* filter tip
emborrachar ⟨1a⟩ *v/t* make drunk, get drunk; **emborracharse** *v/r* get drunk
emborronar ⟨1a⟩ *v/t* blot, smudge
emboscada *f* ambush
emboscar ⟨1g⟩ *v/t* ambush; **emboscarse** *v/r* lie in ambush
embotelladora *f* bottling plant
embotellamiento *m* **1** traffic jam **2** *de bebidas* bottling
embotellar ⟨1a⟩ *v/t* bottle
embozar ⟨1f⟩ *v/t* **1** (*obstruir*) block **2** *cara* cover
embozo *m de sábana* turndown; ***sin ~*** openly
embragar ⟨1h⟩ AUTO **I** *v/t* engage **II** *v/i* engage the clutch
embrague *m* AUTO clutch
embravecer ⟨2d⟩ *v/t* enrage, infuriate; **embravecerse** *v/r* **1** *de mar* get rough **2** *de persona* become enraged *o* infuriated
embriagador *adj* intoxicating, heady
embriagar ⟨1h⟩ *v/t fig* intoxicate; **embriagarse** *v/r* become intoxicated
embriaguez *f* intoxication; ***en estado de ~*** *fig* delirious (with joy)
embridar ⟨1a⟩ *v/t caballo* put a bridle on, bridle
embrión *m* embryo; ***en ~*** in an embryonic state, in embryo
embrionario *adj* embryonic; ***en estado ~*** *fig* in embryo
embrollar ⟨1a⟩ *v/t* muddle, mix up; **embrollarse** *v/r* **1** get complicated; ***la situación se embrolla cada vez más*** the situation is getting more and more complicated **2** *de hilos* get tangled up
embrollo *m* tangle; *fig* mess, muddle
embromar ⟨1a⟩ *v/t Rpl* F (*molestar*) annoy
embrujar ⟨1a⟩ *v/t tb fig* bewitch
embrujo *m tb fig* enchantment
embrutecer ⟨2d⟩ *v/t* brutalize; **embrutecerse** *v/r* become brutalized
embrutecimiento *m* brutalization
embuchado *m* GASTR *type of dry sausage*
embuchar ⟨1a⟩ *v/t salchicha* stuff; *fig* wolf down
embudo *m* funnel
embuste *m* lie
embustero I *adj* deceitful **II** *m*, **-a** *f* liar
embutido *m* GASTR *type of dry sausage*
embutir ⟨3a⟩ *v/t salchicha, cojín, colchón* stuff; *fig* wolf down; **embutirse** *v/r*: ***~ en*** *una prenda* squeeze o.s. into
emergencia *f* emergency; ***estado de ~*** state of emergency
emergente *adj* emergent, emerging; ***país ~*** emergent nation
emerger ⟨2c⟩ *v/i* emerge
emérito *adj* emeritus
emético *m* MED emetic
emigración *f* emigration
emigrante *m* emigrant
emigrar ⟨1a⟩ *v/i* **1** emigrate **2** ZO migrate
eminencia *f* **1** *cualidad* eminence **2** *persona* eminent figure; ***Su / Vuestra Eminencia*** REL His / Your Eminence
◇ **eminencia gris** *fig* éminence grise

eminente *adj* eminent
emir *m* emir
emirato *m* emirate
emisario *m*, **-a** *f* emissary
emisión *f* **1** emission; ***emisiones contaminantes*** emissions of pollutants; ***de baja ~ contaminante*** low-emission **2** COM issue **3** RAD, TV broadcast
emisor I *adj* **1** *banco* issuing *atr* **2** *centro* broadcasting *atr* **3**: ***una fuente ~a de luz / calor*** a light- / heat-emitting source **II** *m* transmitter
emisora *f* radio station
◇ **emisora pirata** pirate radio station
emitir ⟨3a⟩ *v/t* **1** *calor, sonido* give out, emit **2** *moneda* issue **3** *opinión* express, give; *veredicto* deliver **4** RAD, TV broadcast **5** *voto* cast
emoción *f* emotion; ***¡qué ~!*** how exciting!
emocionado *adj* excited
emocional *adj* emotional
emocionante *adj* **1** (*excitante*) exciting **2** (*conmovedor*) moving
emocionar ⟨1a⟩ *v/t* **1** excite **2** (*conmover*) move; **emocionarse** *v/r* **1** get excited **2** (*conmoverse*) be moved
emoliente *adj* emollient
emolumentos *mpl* emoluments
emoticón *m* INFOR emoticon
emotivo *adj* **1** emotional **2** (*conmovedor*) moving
empacar ⟨1g⟩ *v/t & v/i L.Am.* pack; **empacarse** *v/r L.Am.* **1** (*ponerse tozudo*) dig one's heels in **2** *tragar* devour
empachar ⟨1a⟩ *v/t*: ***el chocolate me empacha*** chcolate gives me an upset stomach, chocolate upsets my stomach; **empacharse** *v/r* F **1** get an upset stomach (***de*** from) **2**: ***~ de*** *fig* overdose on
empacho *m* F **1** upset stomach; *fig* bellyful F **2**: ***sin ~*** unashamedly; ***no tener ~ en hacer algo*** not be ashamed to do sth
empadronamiento *m* registration
empadronar ⟨1a⟩ *v/t* register; **empadronarse** *v/r* register
empalagar ⟨1h⟩ *v/t*: ***el chocolate me empalaga*** I find chocolate too cloying *o* sickly sweet; ***me empalaga*** *fig* I find it too much
empalago *m* sickliness; *fig* sickly sweetness, cloyingness
empalagoso *adj* sickly; *fig* sickly sweet, cloying
empalizada *f* palisade
empalmar ⟨1a⟩ **I** *v/t* connect, join **II** *v/i* **1** connect (***con*** with), join up (***con*** with) **2** *de idea, conversación* run *o* follow on (***con*** from)
empalme *m* **1** TÉC connection **2** *de carreteras* intersection, *Br* junction
empanada *f* pie
empanadilla *f* turnover, *Br tb* pasty
empanar ⟨1a⟩ *v/t* coat in breadcrumbs
empantanar ⟨1a⟩ *v/t* **1** flood **2** *fig* bring to a halt; **empantanarse** *v/r* **1** become swamped *o* waterlogged **2** *fig* get bogged down
empañado *adj* misty
empañar ⟨1a⟩ *v/t* **1** steam up, mist up **2** *fig* tarnish, sully; **empañarse** *v/r de vidrio* steam up, mist up
empapado *adj* soaked, dripping wet
empapar ⟨1a⟩ *v/t* soak; (*absorber*) soak up; **empaparse** *v/r* **1** get soaked *o* drenched **2**: ***~ de algo*** immerse o.s. in sth
empapelado *m* papering, wallpaper hanging
empapelador *m*, **~a** *f* wallpaper hanger
empapelar ⟨1a⟩ *v/t* wallpaper
empaque *m* **1** presence **2** (*seriedad*) solemnity
empaquetado *m* packing
empaquetador *m*, **~a** *f* packer
empaquetar ⟨1a⟩ *v/t* pack
emparedado *m* sandwich
emparedar ⟨1a⟩ *v/t* wall up
emparejar ⟨1a⟩ *v/t personas* pair off; *calcetines* match up; **emparejarse** *v/r* **1** (*formar parejas*) pair up (***con*** with) **2** (*igualarse*) catch up (***con*** with)
emparentado *adj* related; ***estar bien ~*** be well connected
emparentar ⟨1k⟩ *v/i*: ***~ con alguien*** become related to s.o. by marriage
empastador *m*, **~a** *f L.Am.* bookbinder
empastar ⟨1a⟩ *v/t* **1** *muela* fill **2** *libro* bind
empaste *m* filling
empatar ⟨1a⟩ *v/i* tie, *Br* draw; (*igualar*) tie the game, *Br* equalize; ***~ a cero*** tie zero-zero, *Br* draw nil-nil
empate *m* tie, *Br* draw; ***gol del ~*** *en fútbol* equalizer; ***~ a cero*** goalless tie *o Br* draw
empecinado *adj* stubborn; ***estar ~ en***

(*hacer*) *algo* be set on (doing) sth
empecinarse ⟨1a⟩ *v/r* get an idea into one's head; ~ ***en algo*** insist on sth
empedernido *adj*: ***fumador*** ~ inveterate smoker; ***solterón*** ~ confirmed bachelor
empedrado *m* paving
empedrar ⟨1k⟩ *v/t* pave
empeine *m* instep
empellón *m* shove; ***entró a empellones*** he shoved his way in
empelotarse ⟨1a⟩ *v/r L.Am.* P take one's clothes off, strip off
empeñado *adj* **1** (*endeudado*) in debt **2**: ***estar*** ~ ***en hacer algo*** be determined to do sth
empeñar ⟨1a⟩ *v/t* pawn; **empeñarse** *v/r* **1** (*endeudarse*) get into debt **2** (*esforzarse*) strive (***en*** to), make an effort (***en*** to) **3**: ~ ***en hacer*** *obstinarse* insist on doing, be determined to do
empeñero *Méx* **I** *adj* determined **II** *m*, **-a** *f* determined person
empeño *m* **1** (*obstinación*) determination; ***con*** ~ insistently **2** (*esfuerzo*) effort **3** *Méx* pawn shop
empeñoso *adj L.Am.* hard-working
empeoramiento *m* deterioration, worsening
empeorar ⟨1a⟩ **I** *v/t* make worse **II** *v/i* deteriorate, get worse; **empeorarse** *v/r* deteriorate, get worse
empequeñecer ⟨2d⟩ *v/t fig* diminish; **empequeñecerse** *v/r fig* feel small *o* insignificant
emperador *m* **1** emperor **2** *pez* swordfish
emperatriz *f* empress
emperejilarse, emperifollarse ⟨1a⟩ *v/r* F doll o.s. up F, *Br* tart o.s. up
empero *adv lit* however, nevertheless
emperramiento *m* F stubbornness
emperrarse ⟨1a⟩ *v/r* F: ~ ***en hacer algo*** have one's heart set on doing sth; ~ ***con algo*** set one's heart on sth
empezar ⟨1f & 1k⟩ **I** *v/t* start, begin **II** *v/i* **1** start, begin; ~ ***a hacer algo*** start to do sth, start doing sth; ~ ***por hacer algo*** start *o* begin by doing sth; ~ ***por alguien*** start with s.o.; ***para*** ~ to begin with; ***ya empezamos*** F here we go again
empiezo *m S.Am.* start, beginning
empinado *adj* steep
empinar ⟨1a⟩ *v/t* raise; ~ ***el codo*** F raise one's elbow F; **empinarse** *v/r* stand on tiptoe
empiparse ⟨1a⟩ *v/r* F down F, knock back F
empírico *adj* empirical
empitonar ⟨1a⟩ *v/t* TAUR gore
emplaste *m* mess
emplasto *m* MED poultice; *fig* soggy mess
emplazamiento *m* **1** site, location **2** JUR subpoena, summons *sg*
emplazar ⟨1f⟩ *v/t* locate, situate
empleada *f* (female) employee
◇ **empleada del hogar** maid
empleado **I** *adj* **1**: ***le está bien*** ~ it serves him right **2**: ***dar algo por bien*** ~ consider sth well worthwhile; ***doy el dinero / tiempo por bien*** ~ I consider it money / time well spent **II** *m*, **-a** *f* employee; ~ ***a tiempo parcial*** part-time employee
empleador *m*, ~**a** *f* employer
emplear ⟨1a⟩ *v/t* **1** (*usar*) use **2** *persona* employ; **emplearse** *v/r* **1** spend one's time (***en hacer algo*** doing sth) **2**: ~ ***como*** be employed as, have a job as
empleo *m* **1** employment; ***crear*** ~ create employment *o* jobs; ***plan de*** ~ employment plan; ***pleno*** ~ full employment **2** (*puesto*) job **3** (*uso*) use; ***modo de*** ~ instructions for use *pl*, directions *pl*
emplomar ⟨1a⟩ *v/t S.Am.* fill
empobrecer ⟨2d⟩ **I** *v/t* impoverish, make poor **II** *v/i* become impoverished, become poor; **empobrecerse** *v/r* become impoverished, become poor
empobrecimiento *m* impoverishment
empollar ⟨1a⟩ **I** *v/i* F cram F, *Br* swot F **II** *v/t* **1** ZO sit on, incubate **2** F (*estudiar*) cram F, *Br* swot up on F
empollón *m*, **-ona** *f* F grind F, *Br* swot F
empolvar ⟨1a⟩ *v/t* powder; **empolvarse** *v/r* get dusty
emponzoñamiento *m* poisoning
emponzoñar ⟨1a⟩ *v/t* poison
emporio *m L.Am. almacén* department store
emporrarse ⟨1a⟩ *v/r* F get high F
empotrado *adj* built-in, fitted
empotrar ⟨1a⟩ *v/t* build (***en*** into); **empotrarse** *v/r* crash (***contra*** into)
emprendedor *adj* enterprising; ***espíritu*** ~ entrepreneurship; ***con espíritu*** ~ *per-*

sona entrepreneurial
emprender ⟨2a⟩ *v/t* **1** embark on, undertake **2**: ***~la con alguien*** F take it out on s.o.; ***~la a golpes con alguien*** exchange blows with s.o.; ***~la a tiros con alguien*** start shooting at s.o.
emprendimiento *m CSur* initiative
empreñar *vb* ☞ ***preñar***
empresa *f* **1** company; ***gran ~*** large company; ***pequeña ~*** small business; ***mediana ~*** medium-sized business **2** *fig* venture, undertaking
◇ **empresa fantasma** dummy corporation, front; **empresa de seguridad y vigilancia** security firm; **empresa de servicios públicos** public utility (company); **empresa de trabajo temporal** temping agency
empresaria *f* businesswoman
empresariado *m* employers *pl*
empresarial *adj* business *atr*; ***ciencias ~es*** business studies *sg*
empresario *m* businessman
empréstito *m* loan
empujar ⟨1a⟩ *v/t* push; *fig* urge on, spur on
empuje *m* push; *fig* drive
empujón *m* push, shove; ***salían a empujones*** F they were pushing and shoving their way out; ***dar un ~ a algo*** *fig* give sth a push
empuñadura *f de espada* hilt; *de daga, paraguas* handle
empuñar ⟨1a⟩ *v/t* grasp
emú *m* ZO emu
emulación *f* emulation
emular ⟨1a⟩ *v/t* emulate
emulsión *f* emulsion
emulsionar ⟨1a⟩ *v/t* emulsify
en *prp* **1** (*dentro de*) in; ***~ un mes*** in a month; ***~ junio*** in June; ***~ casa*** at home; ***~ el cielo*** in heaven **2** (*sobre*) on; ***~ la mesa*** on the table; ***~ la calle*** on the street, *Br tb* in the street **3** *con medios de transporte*: ***~ coche / tren*** by car / train **4**: ***~ inglés*** in English; ***póngamelo ~ la cuenta*** put it on my account; ***aumentar ~ un 10 %*** grow (by) 10%, increase (by) 10%
enagua(s) *f(pl)* petticoat *sg*
enajenable *adj* transferable
enajenación *f* JUR transfer
◇ **enajenación mental** insanity
enajenado *adj* insane, out of one's mind
enajenar ⟨1a⟩ *v/t* **1** JUR transfer **2** (*trastornar*) drive insane **3**: ***~ algo*** dispose of sth; **enajenarse** *v/r* go crazy, lose one's mind
enaltecer ⟨2d⟩ *v/t* **1** ennoble **2** (*alabar*) extol, praise
enamoradizo *adj*: ***es muy ~*** he falls in love very easily, he falls in love at the drop of a hat
enamorado *adj* in love (***de*** with)
enamoramiento *m* falling in love
enamorar ⟨1a⟩ *v/t*: ***lo enamoró*** she captivated him; **enamorarse** *v/r* fall in love (***de*** with)
enanismo *m* MED dwarfism
enano I *adj* **1** tiny **2** *perro, árbol* miniature, dwarf *atr* **II** *m* dwarf; ***trabajar como un ~*** *fig* F work like a dog F
enarbolar ⟨1a⟩ *v/t* hoist, raise
enarcar ⟨1g⟩ *v/t*: ***~ las cejas*** raise one's eyebrows; **enarcarse** *v/r por edad* become hunched
enardecer ⟨2d⟩ *v/t fig* **1** *discusión* inflame; *lucha* intensify **2** *persona* excite, arouse; **enardecerse** *v/r* **1** *de discusión* become heated; *de lucha* intensify **2** *de persona* get excited, get aroused
encabezado *m* **1** INFOR header **2** *Méx* headline
encabezamiento *m* heading
encabezar ⟨1f⟩ *v/t* head; *movimiento, revolución* lead
encabritarse ⟨1a⟩ *v/r* **1** *de caballo* rear up **2** *de persona* F get mad F, blow one's stack F
encabronar ⟨1a⟩ *v/t*: ***~ a alguien*** V make s.o. angry, piss s.o. off P; **encabronarse** *v/r* V get fucking angry V, get fucking pissed off V
encadenamiento *m* chaining
encadenar ⟨1a⟩ *v/t* chain (up); *fig* link *o* put together; **encadenarse** *v/r* chain o.s. (***a*** to)
encajar ⟨1a⟩ **I** *v/t* **1** *piezas* fit **2** *golpe* take; *gol* concede **II** *v/i* fit (***en*** in; ***con*** with); **encajarse** *v/r* **1** (*ponerse*) put on **2** (*atascarse*) get stuck
encaje *m* lace
encajonar ⟨1a⟩ *v/t fig* shut in
encalado *m* whitewashing
encalar ⟨1a⟩ *v/t* whitewash
encallar ⟨1a⟩ *v/i* **1** MAR run aground **2** *fig* grind to a halt

encallecerse ⟨2d⟩ *v/r*: ***se me han encallecido las manos*** I've got calluses on my hands
encallecido *adj* callused
encamar ⟨1a⟩ *v/t* confine to bed
encaminar ⟨1a⟩ *v/t* direct; **encaminarse** *v/r* set off (***a*** for), head (***a*** for); *fig* be aimed *o* directed (***a*** at)
encanar *vt Cu, Rpl* F put in the slammer F
encandilar ⟨1a⟩ *v/t* dazzle
encanecer ⟨2d⟩ *v/i* go gray, *Br* go grey; **encanecerse** *v/r* go gray *o Br* grey
encantado *adj* **1** (*contento*) delighted; ***~ de algo / de hacer algo*** delighted with *o* at sth / to do sth; ***¡~ (de conocerle)!*** nice to meet you **2** *castillo* enchanted
encantador I *adj* charming **II** *m*, **~a** *f* magician; ***~ de serpientes*** snake charmer
encantamiento *m* enchantment
encantar ⟨1a⟩ *v/t*: ***me / le encanta*** I love / he loves it; ***me encanta el chocolate*** I love chocolate
encanto *m* **1** (*atractivo*) charm **2** (*hechizo*): ***como por ~*** as if by magic **3**: ***eres un ~*** you're an angel; ***¡~!*** love of my life!
encañonar ⟨1a⟩ *v/t* **1** point one's gun at **2** *agua* pipe
encapotarse ⟨1a⟩ *v/r del cielo* cloud over, become cloudy
encapricharse ⟨1a⟩ *v/r* fall in love (***de*** with)
encapuchada *f* hooded woman
encapuchado I *adj* hooded **II** *m* hooded man
encaramarse ⟨1a⟩ *v/r* climb
encarar ⟨1a⟩ *v/t* **1** approach **2** *desgracia etc* face up to; **encararse** *v/r*: ***~ con alguien*** confront s.o.
encarcelamiento *m* imprisonment
encarcelar ⟨1a⟩ *v/t* put in prison, imprison
encarecer ⟨2d⟩ **I** *v/t* put up the price of, make more expensive **II** *v/i* become more expensive; *de precios* increase, rise; **encarecerse** *v/r* become more expensive; *de precios* increase, rise
encarecidamente *adv*: ***le ruego ~ que ...*** I beg *o* urge you to ...
encarecimiento *m* **1** *de precios* increase, rise **2** (*alabanza*) (exaggerated) praise **3** (*empeño*) insistence
encargado I *adj* in charge (***de*** of), responsible (***de*** for) **II** *m*, **-a** *f* **1** person in charge **2** *de negocio* manager ◇ **encargado de negocios** chargé d'affaires
encargar ⟨1h⟩ *v/t* (*pedir*) order; ***le encargué que me trajera ...*** I asked him to bring me ...; **encargarse** *v/r* (*tener responsabilidad*) be in charge; (*asumir reponsabilidad*) take charge; ***yo me encargo de la comida*** I'll take care of *o* see to the food
encargo *m* **1** job, errand; ***¿te puedo hacer un ~?*** can I ask you to do something for me? **2** COM order; ***hecho por ~*** made to order **3**: ***por ~ de*** at the request of
encariñarse ⟨1a⟩ *v/r*: ***~ con alguien / algo*** grow fond of s.o / sth, become attached to s.o. / sth
encarnación *f* **1** REL incarnation **2** *fig* embodiment
encarnado *adj* **1** red; ***ponerse ~*** blush **2**: ***uña -a*** ingrowing nail
encarnar ⟨1a⟩ **I** *v/t* **1** *cualidad etc* embody **2** TEA play **II** *v/i de herida* heal up; **encarnarse** *v/r* **1** REL become incarnate **2** *de uña* become ingrown
encarnizado *adj* bitter, fierce
encarnizar ⟨1f⟩ *v/t* make cruel; **encarnizarse** *v/r* show no mercy (***con*** to)
encarrilar ⟨1a⟩ *v/t fig* direct, guide; **encarrilarse** *v/r* get on the right track
encasillar ⟨1a⟩ *v/t* **1** class, classify **2** (*estereotipar*) pigeonhole
encasquetar ⟨1a⟩ *v/t* **1** *gorro etc* pull down **2**: ***me lo encasquetó*** F he landed me with it F
encasquillarse ⟨1a⟩ *v/r de arma* jam
encausar ⟨1a⟩ *v/t* prosecute
encauzar ⟨1f⟩ *v/t tb fig* channel
encefálico *adj* brain *atr*, encephalic *fml*
encéfalo *m* brain
encefalopatía *f*: ***~ espongiforme bovina*** bovine spongiform encephalopathy, BSE
encendedor *m* lighter
encender ⟨2g⟩ *v/t* **1** *fuego* light; *luz, televisión* switch on, turn on **2** *fig* inflame, arouse, stir up; **encenderse** *v/r* **1** *de luz, televisión* come on **2** *fig*: ***se le encendió la cara*** her face went bright red; ***se le encendió la sangre*** his blood boiled; ***~ de rabia*** be furious, be incandescent with rage *lit*

encendido **I** *adj* **1** *luz, televisión* (switched) on; *fuego* lit **2** *cara* red **II** *m* AUTO ignition
encerado *m* blackboard
enceradora *f* polishing machine, polisher
encerar ⟨1a⟩ *v/t* polish, wax
encerrar ⟨1k⟩ *v/t* **1** lock up, shut up **2** (*contener*) contain; **encerrarse** *v/r* shut o.s. up

E

encerrona *f tb fig* trap
encestador *m*, **~a** *f en baloncesto* scorer
encestar ⟨1a⟩ *v/t & v/i en baloncesto* score
enceste *m en baloncesto* basket
encharcado *adj* flooded, waterlogged
encharcar ⟨1g⟩ *v/t* flood, waterlog; **encharcarse** *v/r* get flooded, get waterlogged
enchicharse ⟨1a⟩ *v/r* **1** *L.Am.* (*emborracharse*) get drunk **2** *Rpl* (*enojarse*) get angry, get mad F
enchilada *f Méx* GASTR enchilada (*tortilla with a meat or cheese filling*)
enchilarse ⟨1a⟩ *v/r C.Am.* get angry
enchiloso *adj C.Am., Méx* hot
enchironar ⟨1a⟩ *v/t* P put inside F, *Br* bang up F
enchufado *m*: ***es un ~*** F he has connections, he has friends in high places
enchufar ⟨1a⟩ *v/t* EL plug in
enchufe *m* **1** EL *macho* plug; *hembra* socket **2**: ***tener ~*** *fig* F have pull F, have connections
enchufismo *m* string-pulling
enchufista *m/f* F person with friends in high places
encía *f* gum
enciclopedia *f* encyclopedia, *Br tb* encyclopaedia; ***ser una ~ viviente*** *fig* be a walking encyclopedia
enciclopédico *adj* encyclopedic, *Br tb* encyclopaedic
encierro *m* **1** *protesta* sit-in **2** *de toros* bull running
encima *adv* **1** on top; **~ *de*** on top of, on; ***por ~ de*** over, above; ***por ~ de todo*** above all; ***estar por ~ de*** be above; ***echarse ~ de alguien*** *fig* pounce on s.o.; ***estar ~ de alguien*** *fig*: *para que haga algo* keep on top of s.o.; *hacerle caso* be all over s.o.; ***la noche se nos echó ~*** night overtook us
2: ***hacer algo muy por ~*** do sth very quickly; ***leí el artículo por ~*** I skimmed (through) the article
3: ***no lo llevo ~*** I haven't got it on me; ***ponerse algo ~*** put sth on
4 (*cercano*): ***el final del curso ya está ~*** we're nearly at the end of the course already
5 (*además*): ***lo ayudo, y ~ se queja*** I help him and then he goes and complains
encimera *f* **1** *sábana* top sheet **2** *Esp mostrador* worktop
encina *f* BOT holm oak
encinar *m* (holm) oak wood
encinta *adj* pregnant
enclaustrarse ⟨1a⟩ *v/r fig* shut o.s. away
enclave *m* enclave
enclavijar ⟨1a⟩ *v/t* peg
enclenque **I** *adj* sickly, weak **II** *m/f* weakling
encofrado *m* formwork, *Br* shuttering
encofrar ⟨1a⟩ *v/t* put formwork around, *Br* put shuttering around
encoger ⟨2c⟩ **I** *v/t* **1** shrink; *las piernas* tuck in **2** *fig* intimidate **II** *v/i de material* shrink; **encogerse** *v/r* **1** *de material* shrink; **~ *de hombros*** shrug (one's shoulders) **2** *fig*: *de persona* be intimidated, cower
encogido *adj fig* shy
encogimiento *m* **1** *de material* shrinkage; **~ *de hombros*** shrug **2** *de persona* shyness
encolado **I** *adj L.Am.* sticky **II** *m* gluing, sticking
encolar ⟨1a⟩ *v/t* glue, stick
encolerizar ⟨1f⟩ *v/t* anger, make angry; **encolerizarse** *v/r* get angry
encomendar ⟨1k⟩ *v/t* entrust (***a*** to); **~ *algo a alguien*** entrust sth to s.o., entrust s.o. with sth; **encomendarse** *v/r* commend o.s. (***a*** to)
encomiable *adj* commendable
encomiar ⟨1b⟩ *v/t* praise
encomienda *f L.Am.* **1** (*paquete*) parcel **2** HIST *grant of land and labor by colonial authorities after the Conquest*
encomio *m* praise
enconado *adj* fierce, heated
enconar ⟨1a⟩ *v/t lucha* intensify; *discusión* inflame; **enconarse** *v/r de discusión, persona* get heated; *de lucha* intensify

encono *m* rancor, *Br* rancour
encontradizo *adj*: ***hacerse el ~*** engineer a meeting
encontrado *adj* opposing
encontrar ⟨1m⟩ *v/t* find; **encontrarse** *v/r* **1** (*reunirse*) meet; ***~ con alguien*** meet s.o., run into s.o. **2** (*estar*) be; ***me encuentro bien*** I'm fine, I feel fine
encontronazo *m* smash, crash
encopetado *adj* grand, *Br tb* posh F
encorajinarse ⟨1a⟩ *v/r* get angry
encorbatado *adj* wearing a tie
encorsetar ⟨1a⟩ *v/t* confine, restrict
encorvado *adj persona*, *espalda* stooped
encorvadura *f*, **encorvamiento** *m* curve, curvature
encorvar ⟨1a⟩ *v/t* **1** hunch **2** *estantería* (cause to) buckle
encrespado *adj* **1** *pelo* curly **2** *mar* rough, choppy **3** *debate*, *ambiente* heated; *ánimos* inflamed, aroused
encrespar ⟨1a⟩ *v/t* **1** *pelo* curl **2** *mar* make rough *o* choppy **3** *fig ánimos* arouse, inflame; ***su intervención encrespó el debate / el ambiente*** her intervention made the debate / the atmosphere even more heated; **encresparse** *v/r* **1** *del mar* turn choppy **2** *fig de ánimos* become aroused *o* inflamed; *del pelo* curl; *de debate*, *ambiente* become more heated
encriptado *m* INFOR encrypted
encriptar ⟨1a⟩ *v/t* encrypt
encrucijada *f* crossroads *sg*; *fig* dilemma; ***estar en una ~*** be in a dilemma; *al tomar una decisión* be at a crossroads
encuadernación *f* **1** binding; ***~ en piel*** leather binding; ***~ en tela*** cloth binding **2** *acto* bookbinding
encuadernador I *m*, **~a** *f* bookbinder **II** *f* binder, binding machine
encuadernar ⟨1a⟩ *v/t* bind
encuadrar ⟨1a⟩ *v/t* **1** *en marco* frame **2** *en grupo* include, place
encuadre *m* **1** framing **2** FOT setting, background
encuartelar ⟨1a⟩ *v/t L.Am.* billet
encubierto *part* ☞ ***encubrir***
encubridor *m*, **~a** *f* accessory after the fact
encubrimiento *m de delincuente* harboring, *Br* harbouring; *de delito* concealment
encubrir ⟨3a; *part* ***encubierto***⟩ *v/t delincuente* harbor, *Br* harbour; *delito* cover up, conceal
encuentro *m* **1** meeting, encounter; ***salir*** *o* ***ir al ~ de alguien*** meet s.o., greet s.o. **2** DEP game
encuerado *adj L.Am.* naked
encuerar ⟨1a⟩ *L.Am. v/t* undress; **encuerarse** *v/r* get undressed, undress
encuesta *f* **1** survey **2** (*sondeo*) (opinion) poll
◇ **encuesta demoscópica, encuesta de opinión** opinion poll
encuestado *m*, **-a** *f*. ***el 75% de los ~s*** 75% of those surveyed *o* polled
encuestador *m*, **~a** *f* pollster
encuestar ⟨1a⟩ *v/t* poll
encumbrado *adj* **1** *árbol*, *edificio* lofty, tall **2** *persona* distinguished, important
encumbramiento *m* elevation
encumbrar ⟨1a⟩ *v/t* **1** elevate, raise **2** (*alabar*) praise, extol; **encumbrarse** *v/r fig* rise to the top
encurtidos *mpl* pickles
ende *adv*: ***por ~*** therefore, consequently
endeble *adj* weak, feeble
endemia *f* MED endemic disease
endémico *adj* endemic
endemoniado *adj* **1** possessed **2** *fig* F terrible, awful
enderezar ⟨1f⟩ *v/t* straighten out; **enderezarse** *v/r* straighten up, stand up straight; *fig* straighten o.s. out, sort o.s out
ENDESA *f abr Esp* (= ***Empresa Nacional de Electricidad, Sociedad Anónima***) *Spanish power company*
endeudado *adj* in debt
endeudamiento *m* indebtedness
endeudarse ⟨1a⟩ *v/r* get (o.s.) into debt
endiablado *adj fig* **1** (*malo*) terrible, awful **2** (*difícil*) tough
endibia *f* BOT endive
endilgar ⟨1h⟩ *v/t* **1**: ***me lo endilgó a mí*** F he landed me with it F **2**: ***~ un sermón a alguien*** F lecture s.o., give s.o. a lecture
endiñar ⟨1a⟩ *v/t* F: ***~ algo a alguien*** foist sth on s.o.
endiosamiento *m fig* arrogance
endiosar ⟨1a⟩ *v/t* deify; *fig* treat like a god; **endiosarse** *v/r* become arrogant
endocardio *m* ANAT endocardium
endocrino *adj* endocrine

endocrinología *f* endocrinology
endomingado *adj* in one's Sunday best
endomingarse ⟨1h⟩ *v/r* put on one's Sunday best
endosable *adj* COM endorsable
endosante *m/f* COM endorser
endosar ⟨1a⟩ *v/t* COM endorse; ***me lo endosó a mí*** F she landed me with it F
endosatario *m*, **-a** *f* COM endorsee
endoscopia *f* MED endoscopy
endoscopio *m* endoscope
endoso *m* COM endorsement
endrina *f* BOT sloe
endrino *m* BOT blackthorn
endrogarse ⟨1h⟩ *v/r Méx*, *C.Am.* get into debt
endulzar ⟨1f⟩ *v/t* **1** sweeten **2** (*suavizar*) soften
endurecer ⟨2d⟩ *v/t* harden; *fig* toughen up; **endurecerse** *v/r* harden, become harder; *fig* become harder, toughen up
endurecimiento *m* hardening; *fig* toughening up
ene. *abr* (= ***enero***) Jan. (= January)
enea *f* BOT bulrush
enebrina *f* BOT juniper berry
enebro *m* BOT juniper
eneldo *m* BOT dill
enema *m* MED enema
enemigo I *adj* enemy *atr* **II** *m*, **-a** *f* enemy; ***ser ~ de*** *fig* be opposed to, be against
enemistad *f* enmity
enemistarse ⟨1a⟩ *v/r* fall out
energético *adj* **1** *crisis* energy *atr* **2** *alimento* energy-giving; *bebida* energy *atr*
energía *f* energy; ***sin ~*** *golpe* weak, feeble; *persona* listless, lacking in energy; *hacer algo* listlessly; ***con ~*** *hacer algo* energetically; *chutar* hard; ***abrir la puerta con ~*** fling open the door
◇ **energía alternativa** alternative (form of) energy; **energía eólica** wind power; **energía nuclear** nuclear power *o* energy; **energía renovable** renewable form of energy; **energía solar** solar power *o* energy; **energía térmica** thermal power *o* energy
enérgico *adj* energetic; *fig* forceful, strong
energúmeno *m* lunatic; ***ponerse hecho un ~*** go crazy F, blow a fuse F; ***como un ~*** *fig* like a madman, like one possessed
enero *m* January
enervante *adj fml* **1** (*debilitador*) debilitating, enervating *fml* **2** (*irritante*) irritating
enervar ⟨1a⟩ *v/t fml* **1** (*debilitar*) weaken, enervate *fml* **2** (*irritar*) irritate, get on the nerves of; **enervarse** *v/r* get irritated
enésimo *adj* nth; ***por -a vez*** for the umpteenth time
enfadadizo *adj* irritable
enfadado *adj* **1** annoyed (***con*** with) **2** (*encolerizado*) angry (***con*** with)
enfadar ⟨1a⟩ *v/t* **1** (*molestar*) annoy **2** (*encolerizar*) make angry, anger; **enfadarse** *v/r* **1** (*molestarse*) get annoyed (***con*** with) **2** (*encolerizarse*) get angry (***con*** with)
enfado *m* **1** (*molestia*) annoyance **2** (*cólera*) anger
enfadoso *adj* annoying
enfangar ⟨1h⟩ *v/t* get muddy, cover with mud; **enfangarse** *v/r* **1** get muddy **2:** ***~ en*** *fig* get (o.s.) mixed up in
énfasis *m* emphasis; ***poner ~ en*** emphasize, stress
enfático *adj* emphatic
enfatizar ⟨1f⟩ *v/t* emphasize
enfermar ⟨1a⟩ **I** *v/t* drive crazy **II** *v/i* get sick, *Br tb* get ill; **enfermarse** *v/r Rpl* F have one's period
enfermedad *f* illness, disease
◇ **enfermedad infecciosa** infectious disease; **enfermedad mental** mental illness; **enfermedad profesional** occupational disease *o* illness; **enfermedad del sueño** sleep disorder; **enfermedad tropical** tropical disease *o* illness; **enfermedad de las vacas locas** mad cow disease
enfermería *f* **1** *sala* infirmary, sickbay **2** *carrera* nursing
enfermero *m*, **-a** *f* nurse
◇ **enfermero jefe** head nurse, *Br* senior nursing officer
enfermizo *adj* unhealthy
enfermo I *adj* sick, ill; ***gravemente ~*** seriously ill; ***ponerse ~*** get sick, *Br* fall ill **II** *m*, **-a** *f* sick person; ***~ mental*** mentally ill person
◇ **enfermo terminal** terminally ill patient, terminal patient
enfermoso *adj L.Am.* sickly, unhealthy
enfervorizar ⟨1f⟩ *v/t* rouse; **enfervori-**

zarse *v/r* go wild
enfiestarse ⟨1a⟩ *v/r L.Am.* party F, live it up F
enfilar ⟨1a⟩ *v/t* **1** *camino* take **2** *perlas* thread, string
enfisema *m* MED emphysema
◇ **enfisema pulmonar** pulmonary emphysema
enflaquecer ⟨2d⟩ **I** *v/t* cause to lose weight **II** *v/i* lose weight
enflaquecimiento *m* weight loss
enfocar ⟨1g⟩ *v/t* **1** *cámara* focus; *imagen* get in focus **2** *fig*: *asunto* look at, consider
enfoque *m fig* approach
enfrentamiento *m* clash, confrontation; **~ *verbal*** heated argument
enfrentar ⟨1a⟩ *v/t* confront, face up to; **enfrentarse** *v/r* **1** DEP meet **2**: **~ *con alguien*** confront s.o. **3**: **~ *a algo*** face (up to) sth
enfrente *adv* opposite; **~ *del colegio*** opposite the school, across (the street) from the school; ***la casa de* ~** the house opposite, the house across the way; ***tiene a todos los miembros del comité* ~** *fig* all the committee members are against him *o* oppose him
enfriamiento *m* **1** chill **2** *acto* chilling; *fig* cooling
enfriar ⟨1c⟩ *v/t vino* chill; *algo caliente* cool (down); *fig* cool; **enfriarse** *v/r* **1** (*perder calor*) cool down; (*perder demasiado calor*) get cold, go cold; *fig* cool, cool off **2** MED catch a cold, catch a chill
enfundar ⟨1a⟩ *v/t espada* sheathe; *paraguas* put the cover on; ***enfundó su pistola*** he put his pistol (back) in its holster
enfurecer ⟨2d⟩ *v/t* infuriate, make furious; **enfurecerse** *v/r* get furious, get into a rage
enfurecido *adj* furious, enraged
enfurruñado *adj* F sulky
enfurruñarse ⟨1a⟩ *v/r* F go into a huff F
engalanar ⟨1a⟩ *v/t* decorate, deck; **engalanarse** *v/r* dress (o.s.) up
enganchar ⟨1a⟩ *v/t* **1** hook **2** *caballo* harness **3** F *novia*, *trabajo* land F; **engancharse** *v/r* **1** get caught (***en*** on) **2** MIL sign up, enlist **3**: **~ *a la droga*** F get hooked on drugs F
enganche *m* **1** hooking (up) **2** *de caballo* harnessing **3** *mecanismo* catch **4** FERR coupling
engañabobos *m inv* F **1** *persona* swindler, conman F **2** *cosa* swindle, con F
engañadizo *adj* gullible
engañar ⟨1a⟩ *v/t* **1** deceive, cheat; **~ *el hambre*** take the edge off one's appetite; ***te han engañado*** you've been had F **2** (*ser infiel a*) cheat on, be unfaithful to; **engañarse** *v/r* **1** (*mentirse*) deceive o.s., kid o.s. F **2** (*equivocarse*) be wrong
engañifa *f* F swindle, con F
engaño *m* **1** (*mentira*) deception, deceit **2** (*ardid*) trick; ***llamarse a* ~** claim to have been cheated
engañoso *adj persona*, *palabras* deceitful; *apariencias* deceptive
engarce *m* **1** setting, mount **2** *acción* setting, mounting
engarzar ⟨1f⟩ *v/t joya* set, mount
engastar ⟨1a⟩ *v/t joya* set, mount
engaste *m* **1** setting, mount **2** *acción* setting, mounting
engatusar ⟨1a⟩ *v/t* F sweet-talk F
engendrar ⟨1a⟩ *v/t* father; *fig* breed, engender
engendro *m* **1** (*persona fea*) freak, monster **2** *fig* eyesore; ***esa estatua es un* ~** that statue is a monstrosity
englobado *m L.Am. en béisbol* fly ball
englobar ⟨1a⟩ *v/t* include, embrace *fml*
engolado *adj* pompous
engomar ⟨1a⟩ *v/t* glue, put glue on
engordar ⟨1a⟩ **I** *v/t* put on, gain **II** *v/i* **1** *de persona* put on weight, gain weight **2** *de comida* be fattening
engorde *m* fattening (up); ***ganado de* ~** feeder cattle
engorrar ⟨1a⟩ *v/t Méx*, *Carib* annoy
engorro *m* F nuisance, hassle F
engorroso *adj* tricky
engrampadora *f Rpl* stapler
engrampar ⟨1a⟩ *v/t Rpl* staple
engranaje *m* TÉC gears *pl*; *fig* machinery
engranar ⟨1a⟩ *v/i* mesh, engage
engrandecer ⟨2d⟩ *v/t* **1** enlarge **2** (*ensalzar*) praise, extol; **engrandecerse** *v/r* grow in stature
engrandecimiento *m* **1** enlargement **2** (*ensalzamiento*) praise
engrapadora *f L.Am.* stapler
engrapar ⟨1a⟩ *v/t L.Am.* staple

engrasar ⟨1a⟩ *v/t* **1** grease, lubricate **2** *manchar* get grease on, make greasy; **engrasarse** *v/r* get greasy
engrase *m* greasing, lubrication
engreído *adj* conceited
engreimento *m* conceit
engreírse ⟨3m⟩ *v/r* become conceited
engripado *adj Rpl*: ***estar ~*** have the flu
engriparse ⟨1a⟩ *v/r Rpl* get the flu
engrosar ⟨1m⟩ **I** *v/t* swell, increase **II** *v/i* put on weight, gain weight
engrudo *m* (flour and water) paste
engullir ⟨3h⟩ *v/t* bolt (down)
enharinar ⟨1a⟩ *v/t* dip in flour, flour
enhebrar ⟨1a⟩ *v/t* thread, string
enhiesto *adj lit* **1** *persona* erect, upright **2** *torre, árbol* lofty
enhorabuena *f* congratulations *pl*; ***dar la ~ a*** congratulate (***por*** on); ***estar de ~*** have good reason to celebrate
enigma *m* enigma
enigmático *adj* enigmatic
enjabonar ⟨1a⟩ *v/t* soap
enjaezar ⟨1f⟩ *v/t caballo* harness
enjambre *m tb fig* swarm
enjaulado *adj* caged; *fig* jailed, locked up
enjaular ⟨1a⟩ *v/t* cage, put in a cage; *fig* jail, lock up
enjoyado *adj* bejeweled, *Br* bejewelled
enjuagar ⟨1h⟩ *v/t* rinse; **enjuagarse** *v/r* rinse the soap off
enjuague *m* **1** *acto* rinsing **2** *líquido* mouthwash
enjugar ⟨1h⟩ *v/t* **1** *deuda etc* wipe out **2** *líquido* mop up; *lágrimas* wipe away
enjuiciamiento *m* **1** indictment; ***ley de ~ civil / criminal*** code of civil / criminal procedure **2** *fig* judg(e)ment
enjuiciar ⟨1b⟩ *v/t* **1** JUR institute proceedings against **2** *fig* judge
enjundia *f fig* substance
enjuto *adj* lean, thin
enlace *m* link, connection
◇ **enlace ferroviario** rail link
◇ **enlace matrimonial** marriage
enlatar ⟨1a⟩ *v/t* can, *Br tb* tin; ***música enlatada*** canned *o* piped music, Muzak®
enlazar ⟨1f⟩ **I** *v/t* **1** link (up), connect **2** *L.Am. con cuerda* rope, lasso **II** *v/i de carretera* link up (***con*** with); AVIA, FERR connect (***con*** with); **enlazarse** *v/r* link up (***con*** with)
enlentecer ⟨2d⟩ *v/t* slow down; **enlentecerse** *v/r* slow down
enlodar ⟨1a⟩ *v/t*, **enlodazar** ⟨1f⟩ *v/t* cover in mud
enloquecer ⟨2d⟩ **I** *v/t* drive crazy *o* mad **II** *v/i* go crazy *o* mad; ***me enloquece el chocolate*** I'm mad about chocolate
enloquecimiento *m* madness
enlosado *m* flagstones *pl*
enlosar ⟨1a⟩ *v/t* pave (*with flagstones*)
enlozado *adj L.Am.* enameled, *Br* enamelled
enlucido *m* plaster
enlucir ⟨3f⟩ *v/t* plaster
enlutado *adj* (dressed) in mourning
enlutar ⟨1a⟩ *v/t* plunge into mourning; **enlutarse** *v/r* go into mourning
enmadrado *adj*: ***niño ~*** Mama's boy, *Br* Mummy's boy
enmadrarse ⟨1a⟩ *v/r* be tied to one's mother's apron strings
enmarañar ⟨1a⟩ *v/t* **1** *pelo* tangle **2** *asunto* complicate, muddle; **enmarañarse** *v/r* **1** *de pelo* get tangled **2**: ***~ en algo*** get entangled *o* embroiled in sth
enmarcación *f* framing
enmarcar ⟨1g⟩ *v/t* frame; **enmarcarse** *v/r*: ***~ en algo*** *o* ***dentro de algo*** *fig* be in line with sth, be in keeping with sth
enmascaramiento *m de la verdad* concealment
enmascarar ⟨1a⟩ *v/t* hide, disguise
enmendar ⟨1k⟩ *v/t* **1** *asunto* rectify, put right **2** JUR, POL amend **3**: ***~le la plana a alguien*** find fault with what s.o. has done; **enmendarse** *v/r* mend one's ways
enmicado *m L.Am.* laminating
enmicar ⟨1g⟩ *v/t L.Am.* laminate
enmienda *f* POL amendment
enmohecer ⟨2d⟩ *v/t*: ***~ algo*** turn sth moldy *o Br* mouldy; *metal* rust sth; **enmohecerse** *v/r* go moldy *o Br* mouldy; *de metal* rust
enmoquetado *adj* carpeted, with wall-to-wall carpeting
enmoquetar ⟨1a⟩ *v/t* carpet
enmudecer ⟨2d⟩ **I** *v/t* silence **II** *v/i* fall silent
ennegrecer ⟨2d⟩ *v/t* blacken; **ennegrecerse** *v/r* turn black, go black
ennoblecer ⟨2d⟩ *v/t* ennoble

enojadizo *adj* irritable
enojado *adj L.Am.* angry
enojar ⟨1a⟩ *v/t* **1** (*molestar*) annoy **2** *L.Am.* (*encolerizar*) make angry; **enojarse** *v/r L.Am.* **1** (*molestarse*) get annoyed **2** (*encolerizarse*) get angry
enojo *m L.Am.* anger; ***con ~*** angrily
enojón *adj L.Am.* irritable, touchy
enojoso *adj* **1** (*delicado*) awkward **2** (*aburrido*) tedious, tiresome
enología *f* enology, *Br tb* oenology
enorgullecer ⟨2d⟩ *v/t* make proud, fill with pride; **enorgullecerse** *v/r* be proud (***de*** of)
enorme *adj* enormous, huge
enormidad *f* **1** (*barbaridad*) enormity **2** *cantidad* enormous *o* huge amount **3**: ***eso que dijo es una ~*** what an appalling thing for him to say
enquistarse ⟨1a⟩ *v/r* **1** MED form a cyst **2** *fig*: *de economía* stagnate
enraizado *adj fig* deep-rooted
enraizar ⟨1f⟩ *v/i* take root
enrarecer ⟨2d⟩ *v/t* **1** *aire* rarefy **2** *relaciones* strain; **enrarecerse** *v/r* **1** *de aire* become rarefied **2** *de relaciones* become strained
enrarecido *adj* **1** *aire* rarefied **2** *relaciones* strained
enredadera *f* BOT creeper, climbing plant
enredador *m*, **~a** *f* troublemaker
enredar ⟨1a⟩ **I** *v/t* **1** tangle, get tangled **2** *fig* complicate, make complicated **II** *v/i* make trouble; **enredarse** *v/r* **1** get tangled **2** *fig* get complicated **3**: ***~ en algo*** get mixed up *o* involved in sth; ***~ con alguien*** get involved with s.o.
enredo *m* **1** tangle **2** (*confusión*) mess, confusion **3** (*intriga*) intrigue **4** *amoroso* affair
enrejar ⟨1a⟩ *v/t ventana* put bars on
enrevesado *adj* complicated, involved
enriquecer ⟨2d⟩ *v/t* make rich; *fig* enrich; **enriquecerse** *v/r* get rich; *fig* be enriched
enriquecimiento *m* enrichment
enrocar ⟨1g⟩ *v/t & v/i en ajedrez* castle; **enrocarse** *v/r* castle
enrojecer ⟨2d⟩ **I** *v/t* turn red **II** *v/i* blush, go red; **enrojecerse** *v/r de persona* blush, go red; *de cosa* turn red
enrolar ⟨1a⟩ *v/t* MIL enlist; **enrolarse** *v/r*: ***~ en*** *partido* join; *el ejército, la marina* enlist in, join
enrollar ⟨1a⟩ *v/t* **1** roll up; *cable* coil; *hilo* wind **2**: ***me enrolla*** F I like it, I think it's great F; **enrollarse** *v/r* F **1** *hablar* go on and on F; ***¡no te enrolles!*** get to the point! **2**: ***se enrolló mucho con nosotros*** (*se portó bien*) he was great to us F **3**: ***~ con alguien*** *fig* F neck with s.o.
enronquecer ⟨2d⟩ **I** *v/t* make hoarse **II** *v/i* go hoarse
enroque *m en ajedrez* castling
enroscar ⟨1g⟩ *v/t* **1** *tornillo* screw in **2** *cable, cuerda* coil; **enroscarse** *v/r* coil up
enrostrar ⟨1a⟩ *v/t L.Am.* ***~ algo a alguien*** reproach s.o. for sth
ensaimada *f* GASTR *pastry in the form of a spiral*
ensalada *f* GASTR salad
ensaladera *f* salad bowl
ensaladilla *f*: ***~ rusa*** GASTR Russian salad
ensalmo *m*: ***como por ~*** as if by magic
ensalzamiento *m* extolling, praising
ensalzar ⟨1f⟩ *v/t* extol, praise
ensamblador *m* INFOR assembler
ensambladura *f*, **ensamblaje** *m* TÉC assembly
ensamblar ⟨1a⟩ *v/t* assemble
ensanchamiento *m de calle, avenida* broadening; *de falda, pantalón* letting out
ensanchar ⟨1a⟩ *v/t* widen; *prenda* let out; **ensancharse** *v/r* widen, get wider; *de prenda* stretch
ensanche *m* **1** *de carretera* widening **2** *de ciudad* new suburb
ensangrentado *adj* bloodstained
ensangrentar ⟨1k⟩ *v/t* stain with blood, cover with blood
ensañamiento *m* mercilessness, cruelty
ensañarse ⟨1a⟩ *v/r* show no mercy (***con*** to)
ensartar ⟨1a⟩ *v/t* **1** *en hilo* string **2** *aguja* thread **3** *con espada* run through **4** *L.Am.* (*engañar*) trick, trap; **ensartarse** *v/r L.Am. en discusión* get involved, get caught up
ensayar ⟨1a⟩ *v/t* **1** test, try (out) **2** TEA rehearse
ensayista *m/f* essayist
ensayo *m* **1** test **2** TEA rehearsal **3** *escri-*

to essay
◇ **ensayo general** TEA dress rehearsal
enseguida *adv* immediately, right away
ensenada *f* inlet, cove
enseña *f* emblem
enseñanza *f* **1** teaching; ***dedicarse a la ~*** take up teaching, become a teacher **2**: ***sacar una ~ de algo*** learn a lesson from sth
◇ **enseñanza a distancia** distance learning; **enseñanza media** secondary education; **enseñanza primaria** elementary education, *Br* primary education; **enseñanza secundaria** secondary education; **enseñanza superior** higher education; **enseñanza universitaria** university education
enseñar ⟨1a⟩ *v/t* **1** (*dar clases*) teach; ***~ a leer a alguien*** teach s.o. to read **2** (*mostrar*) show
enseñorearse ⟨1a⟩ *v/r*: ***~ de algo*** take possession of sth
enseres *mpl de persona* tools and equipment; *de casa* fixtures and fittings; *de oficina* furniture and equipment *sg*
ensillar ⟨1a⟩ *v/t* saddle
ensimismado *adj* deep in thought
ensimismarse ⟨1a⟩ *v/r* **1** become lost in thought **2** *L.Am.* get conceited *o* big-headed F
ensombrecer ⟨2d⟩ *v/t* cast a shadow over
ensoñar ⟨1a⟩ *v/i* dream
ensordecedor *adj* deafening
ensordecer ⟨2d⟩ **I** *v/t* deafen **II** *v/i* go deaf
ensortijado *adj* in ringlets
ensortijar ⟨1a⟩ *v/t* curl; **ensortijarse** *v/r* form ringlets
ensuciar ⟨1b⟩ *v/t* (get) dirty; *fig* sully, tarnish; **ensuciarse** *v/r* get dirty; *fig* get one's hands dirty
ensueño *m*: ***de ~*** *fig* fairy-tale *atr*, dream *atr*
entablado *m* floorboards *pl*
entablar ⟨1a⟩ **I** *v/t* strike up, start **II** *v/i* DEP tie, *Br* draw
entablillar ⟨1a⟩ *v/t* splint, put in a splint
entallado *adj* tailored, fitted
entallar ⟨1a⟩ *v/t* tailor
entarimado *m* **1** (*suelo*) floorboards *pl* **2** (*plataforma*) stage, platform
entarimar ⟨1a⟩ *v/t* put floorboards on, floor
ente *m* **1** (*ser*) being, entity **2** F (*persona rara*) oddball F **3** (*organización*) body
entejar ⟨1a⟩ *v/t L.Am.* tile
entendederas *fpl*: ***tener malas ~*** F be dumb F, be thick F
entender ⟨2g⟩ **I** *v/t* **1** understand; ***~ mal algo*** misunderstand sth; ***hacerse ~*** make o.s. understood; ***ya me entiendes*** do you catch my drift?, do you know what I mean?; ***dar a ~ a alguien*** give s.o. to understand **2** (*creer*): ***entendemos que sería mejor …*** we believe it would be better …
II *v/i* **1** understand; ***si entiendo bien*** if I understand correctly **2**: ***~ de algo*** know about sth **3**: ***~ en*** JUR hear
III *m*: ***a mi ~*** in my opinion, to my mind
entenderse *v/r* **1** communicate; ***a ver si nos entendemos*** let's get this straight; ***para entendernos***, ***para que me entiendas*** not to put too fine a point on it **2**: ***yo me entiendo*** I know what I'm doing **3**: ***~ con alguien*** get along with s.o., get on with s.o.
entendido **I** *adj* understood; ***¿~?*** do you understand?, understood?; ***tengo ~ que*** I gather *o* understand that **II** *m*, **-a** *f* expert, authority (***en*** on)
entendimiento *m* **1** understanding **2** (*inteligencia*) mind
enterado *adj* **1** knowledgeable, well-informed; ***estar ~ de*** know about, have heard about **2**: ***darse por ~*** get the message, take the hint
enteramente *adv* entirely, wholly
enterar ⟨1a⟩ *v/t* **1** inform, notify (***de*** of) **2** *Méx* (*pagar*) pay; **enterarse** *v/r* **1** find out, hear (***de*** about) **2**: ***¡para que te enteres!*** F so there! F; ***¡se va a enterar!*** F he's in for it! F
entereza *f* fortitude
entérico *adj* enteric
enteritis *f* MED enteritis
enterito *m Rpl* coveralls *pl*, *Br* overalls *pl*
enternecer ⟨2d⟩ *v/t* move, touch; **enternecerse** *v/r* be moved, be touched
entero **I** *adj* **1** (*completo*) whole, entire; ***por ~*** completely, entirely; ***10 años / días ~s*** 10 whole years / days **2** (*no roto*) intact, undamaged **II** *m* **1** (*punto*) point **2** *Rpl* (*mono*) coveralls *pl*, *Br* overalls *pl*

enteropostal *m* aerogram, *Br tb* aerogramme
enterrador *m*, **~a** *f* gravedigger
enterramiento *m* burial
enterrar ⟨1k⟩ *v/t* bury; ***~ a todos*** *fig* outlive everybody; **enterrarse** *v/r*: ***~ en vida*** *fig* turn one's back on everything, drop out F
entibiar ⟨1b⟩ *v/t tb fig* cool down; **entibiarse** *v/r tb fig* cool down
entidad *f* entity, body
◇ **entidad bancaria** bank, banking institution
entierro *m* **1** burial **2** (*funeral*) funeral
entlo. *abr* (= ***entresuelo***) mezzanine
entoldado *m de tienda* awning; *para fiesta* tent, *Br* marquee
entoldar ⟨1a⟩ *v/t* cover with an awning
entomología *f* entomology
entomólogo *m*, **-a** *f* entomologist
entonación *f* intonation
entonado *adj* in tune
entonar ⟨1a⟩ **I** *v/t* **1** intone, sing **2** *fig* F perk up **II** *v/i* sing in tune; **entonarse** *v/r con bebida* get tipsy
entonces *adv* then; ***desde ~*** since, since then; ***por ~***, ***en aquel ~*** in those days, at that time; ***hasta ~*** until then; ***¡pues ~…!*** then…!; ***¿y ~ qué?*** and then what?; *expresando irritación* so?, so what!
entontecer ⟨2d⟩ *v/t*: ***la televisión entontece a los niños*** television addles kids' brains, TV dumbs kids down; **entontecerse** *v/r* get stupid
entorchado *m* **1** MÚS string **2** MIL braid
entornar ⟨1a⟩ *v/t puerta* leave ajar; *ojos* half close
entorno *m tb* INFOR environment
entorpecer ⟨2d⟩ *v/t* **1** hold up, hinder; *paso* obstruct **2** *entendimiento* dull; **entorpecerse** *v/r* slow down
entrada *f* **1** *acción* entry; ***se prohibe la ~*** no entry; ***hacer su ~*** make one's entrance
2 *lugar* entrance; ***~ a la autopista*** on ramp, *Br* slip road
3 *localidad* ticket
4 *pago* deposit, downpayment
5 (*comienzo*): ***~ del año*** start *o* beginning of the year; ***de ~*** from the outset, from the start
6 *de comida* starter
7: ***~s*** *pl en frente* receding hairline *sg*
8 *Cu, Méx en béisbol* inning
9 *en fútbol* tackle; ***hacer una ~ a alguien*** tackle s.o., make a tackle on s.o.
◇ **entrada de artistas** TEA stage door; **entrada en escena** entrance, appearance on stage; **entrada libre** free admission; **entrada en plancha** *en fútbol* sliding tackle; **entrada en vigor** coming into effect
entramado *m* ARQUI framework; *fig* network
entrampar ⟨1a⟩ *v/t* **1** burden with debts **2** *animal* trap; **entramparse** *v/r* get into debt
entrante I *adj semana, mes* next, coming **II** *m* GASTR starter
entrañable *adj amistad* close, deep; *amigo* close, dear; *recuerdo* fond
entrañar ⟨1a⟩ *v/t* entail, involve
entrañas *fpl* entrails; ***no tener ~*** be cruel *o* hard-hearted
entrar ⟨1a⟩ **I** *v/i* **1** *para indicar acercamiento* come in, enter; ***¡entre!*** come in!; ***yo en eso no entro ni salgo*** that has nothing to do with me, I have nothing to do with that
2 *para indicar alejamiento* go in, enter
3 *caber* fit; ***el pantalón no me entra*** these pants don't fit me; ***la llave no entra*** the key doesn't fit; ***no me entra en la cabeza*** I can't understand it
4: ***¿cuántos plátanos entran en un kilo?*** how many bananas are there in a kilo?
5: ***me entró frío / sueño*** I got cold / sleepy, I began to feel cold / sleepy; ***me entró miedo*** I got scared, I began to feel scared
6: ***~ en*** go into; ***~ en los 40 años*** turn 40
7 (*gustar*): ***este tipo no me entra*** I don't like the look of the guy, I don't like the guy's face
8 (*empezar*): ***~ (a trabajar) a las ocho*** start (work) at eight o'clock
II *v/t* **1** *para indicar acercamiento* bring in **2** *para indicar alejamiento* take in **3** INFOR enter **4** *en fútbol* tackle
entre *prp* **1** *dos cosas, personas* between; ***~ las dos y las tres*** between two and three
2 *más de dos* among(st), between; ***~ nosotros*** among *o* between us; ***repartir algo ~ tres*** split sth three ways
3 *expresando cooperación* between; ***lo pagamos ~ todos*** we paid for it among

o between us; ***lo hicieron ~ tres*** they did it between the three of them; ***la relación ~ ellos*** the relationship between them; ***te cuento ~ mis amigos*** I regard you as a friend
4 MAT: ***ocho ~ cuatro son dos*** eight divided by four is two, four into eight is two

entreabierto **I** *part* ☞ **entreabrir** **II** *adj* half-open; *puerta* ajar

E

entreabrir ⟨3a; *part* **entreabierto**⟩ *v/t* half-open

entreacto *m* TEA interval

entrecano *adj pelo* graying, *Br* greying

entrecejo *m*: ***fruncir el ~*** frown

entrecerrar ⟨1a⟩ *v/t ojos* narrow; *puerta* leave ajar

entrechocar ⟨1g⟩ *v/t espadas* clash; *vasos* clink

entrecomillar ⟨1a⟩ *v/t* put in quotation marks

entrecortado *adj respiración* difficult, labored; *habla* halting; ***con la voz -a por lágrimas*** in a voice choked with tears

entrecortarse ⟨1a⟩ *v/r*: ***su voz se entrecortaba*** his voice faltered, he spoke falteringly

entrecot *m* GASTR entrecote

entrecubierta *f* MAR between-decks

entredicho *m*: ***poner en ~*** call into question, question; ***estar en ~*** be in question *o* doubt

entredós *m* decorative trim

entrega *f* **1** handing over; ***~ de premios*** prize-giving, presentation; ***hacer ~ de algo a alguien*** present s.o. with sth **2** *de mercancías* delivery; ***~ a domicilio*** (home) delivery **3** (*dedicación*) dedication, devotion

◇ **entrega de equipajes** baggage reclaim

◇ **entrega contra reembolso** collect on delivery, *Br* cash on delivery, COD

entregar ⟨1h⟩ *v/t* **1** give, hand over **2** *trabajo, deberes* hand in **3** *mercancías* deliver **4** *premio* present; **entregarse** *v/r* **1** give o.s. up **2**: ***~ a*** *fig* devote o.s. to, dedicate o.s. to

entrelazar ⟨1f⟩ *v/t* interweave, intertwine; **entrelazarse** *v/r* interweave, intertwine; ***sus manos se entrelazaron*** their fingers intertwined

entremedias *adv* **1** (*en medio*) in between **2** (*entretanto*) meanwhile, in the meantime

entremeses *mpl* GASTR appetizers, hors d'oeuvres

entremeter ⟨2a⟩ *v/t* insert; **entremeterse** *v/r* ☞ **entrometerse**

entremetido ☞ **entrometido**

entremezclar ⟨1a⟩ *v/t* intermingle, mix; **entremezclarse** *v/r* intermingle, mix

entrenador *m*, **~a** *f* coach

entrenamiento *m* coaching

entrenar ⟨1a⟩ *v/t* train, coach; **entrenarse** *v/r* train

entreoír ⟨3q⟩ *v/t* half-hear

entrepaño *m* **1** shelf **2** ARQUI pier

entrepierna *f* **1** ANAT crotch **2** *medida* inside leg

entresacar ⟨1g⟩ *v/t* extract, select

entresijos *mpl fig* details, complexities; ***tener muchos ~*** be extremely complex

entresuelo *m* **1** mezzanine **2** TEA dress circle

entretanto *adv* meanwhile, in the meantime

entretecho *m Arg, Chi* attic

entretejer ⟨2a⟩ *v/t* interweave

entretener ⟨2l⟩ **I** *v/t* **1** (*divertir*) entertain, amuse **2** (*retrasar*) keep, detain **3** (*distraer*) distract **II** *v/i* be entertaining; **entretenerse** *v/r* **1** (*divertirse*) amuse o.s. (***en hacer algo*** doing sth; ***con algo*** with sth) **2** (*distraerse*) keep o.s. busy **3** (*retrasarse*) linger (***en*** over)

entretenido *adj* **1** (*divertido*) entertaining, enjoyable **2**: ***estar ~*** *ocupado* be busy

entretenimiento *m* entertainment, amusement

entretiempo *m* **1**: ***de ~*** *ropa* mid-season **2** *CSur* DEP half-time

entrever ⟨2v; *part* **entrevisto**⟩ *v/t* make out, see

entreverar ⟨1a⟩ *v/t* intersperse

entrevero *m* **1** *S.Am.* (*lío*) mix-up, mess **2** *Chi* (*discusión*) argument

entrevía *f* gage, *Br* gauge

entrevista *f* interview

◇ **entrevista de trabajo** job interview

entrevistador *m*, **~a** *f* interviewer

entrevistar ⟨1a⟩ *v/t* interview; **entrevistarse** *v/r*: ***~ con alguien*** meet (with) s.o.

entrevisto *part* ☞ **entrever**

entristecer ⟨2d⟩ *v/t* sadden; **entriste-**

cerse *v/r* grow sad
entrometerse ⟨2a; *part* **entrometido**⟩ *v/r* meddle (**en** in)
entrometido I *part* ☞ **entrometerse II** *adj* meddling *atr*, interfering **III** *m* meddler, busybody
entromparse ⟨1a⟩ *v/r* F get sloshed F, tie one on F
entroncar ⟨1g⟩ *v/t* establish a relationship between
entronización *f* enthronement
entronizar ⟨1f⟩ *v/t* **1** enthrone **2** *fig* install
entronque *m* **1** (*parentesco*) relationship **2** FERR junction
entubar ⟨1a⟩ *v/t* MED intubate
entuerto *m* F wrong, injustice; ***deshacer un ~*** right a wrong
entumecer ⟨2d⟩ *v/t* numb; **entumecerse** *v/r* go numb, get stiff
entumecido *adj* numb
entumecimiento *m* numbness
enturbiar ⟨1b⟩ *v/t tb fig* cloud
entusiasmado *adj* excited, delirious
entusiasmar ⟨1a⟩ *v/t* excite, make enthusiastic; **entusiasmarse** *v/r* get excited, get enthusiastic (***con*** about)
entusiasmo *m* enthusiasm
entusiasta I *adj* enthusiastic **II** *m/f* enthusiast
entusiástico *adj* enthusiastic
enumeración *f* list, enumeration
enumerar ⟨1a⟩ *v/t* list, enumerate
enunciación *f*, **enunciado** *m* **1** GRAM statement **2** MAT formulation
enunciar ⟨1b⟩ *v/t* state
enuresis *f* MED enuresis
envainar ⟨1a⟩ *v/t espada* sheathe
envalentonar ⟨1a⟩ *v/t* make bolder *o* more daring; **envalentonarse** *v/r* **1** become bolder *o* more daring **2** (*insolentarse*) become defiant
envanecer ⟨2d⟩ *v/t* make conceited *o* vain; **envanecerse** *v/r* become conceited *o* vain
envanecimiento *m* conceit, vanity
envarado *adj* haughty
envararse ⟨1a⟩ *v/r* stiffen
envasador I *m*, **~a** *f* packer **II** *f*: ***~a de latas / conservas*** canning company, cannery
envasar ⟨1a⟩ *v/t en botella* bottle; *en lata* can; *en paquete* pack
envase *m* **1** container; ***~ de cartón*** carton; ***~ ahorro*** economy pack **2** *botella* (empty) bottle; ***~ no retornable*** nonreturnable bottle; ***~ retornable*** returnable bottle **3** *lata* can, *Br tb* tin **4** *caja* box
envejecer ⟨2d⟩ **I** *v/t* age, make look older **II** *v/i* age, grow old; **envejecerse** *v/r* age, grow old
envejecido *adj* old-looking; (*viejo*) aged
envejecimiento *m* ag(e)ing
envenenamiento *m* poisoning
envenenar ⟨1a⟩ *v/t tb fig* poison
envergadura *f* AVIA wingspan; MAR breadth; *fig* magnitude, importance; ***de gran*** *o* ***mucha ~*** *fig* of great importance
envés *m de hoja* underside; *de tela* wrong side
enviado *m*, **-a** *f* **1** POL envoy **2** *de periódico* reporter, correspondent
◇ **enviado especial 1** POL special envoy **2** *de periódico* special correspondent
enviar ⟨1c⟩ *v/t* send
enviciar ⟨1b⟩ *v/t*: ***~ a alguien con la droga*** get s.o. addicted to drugs; **enviciarse** *v/r* get addicted (***con*** to), get hooked (***con*** on)
envidia *f* envy, jealousy; ***me da ~*** I'm envious *o* jealous; ***tener ~ a alguien de algo*** envy s.o. sth
envidiable *adj* enviable
envidiar ⟨1b⟩ *v/t* envy; ***~ a alguien por algo*** envy s.o. sth; ***no tiene nada que ~le*** you have no reason to be envious of her; ***los Rioja no tienen nada que ~les*** Riojas can easily stand comparison with them
envidioso *adj* envious, jealous
envilecer ⟨2d⟩ *v/t* degrade, debase; **envilecerse** *v/r* degrade o.s., debase o.s.
envilecimiento *m* degradation, debasement
envío *m* shipment; *mercancías* shipment, consignment; ***gastos de ~*** shipping charges; ***~ rehusado*** delivery not accepted
◇ **envío contra reembolso** collect on delivery, *Br* cash on delivery, COD
envite *m* **1** *en naipes* stake **2**: ***al primer ~*** right from the start
enviudar ⟨1a⟩ *v/i* be widowed
envoltorio *m* wrapper

envoltura *f* cover, covering; *de regalo* wrapping; *de caramelo* wrapper
envolvente *adj* pervasive
envolver 〈2h; *part* ***envuelto***〉 *v/t* **1** wrap (up) **2** (*rodear*) surround, envelop **3** (*involucrar*) involve; ***~ a alguien en algo*** involve s.o. in sth; **envolverse** *v/r* **1** wrap o.s. up **2**: ***~ en*** *fig* become involved in
envuelto *part* ☞ ***envolver***
enyesado *m* plastering
enyesar 〈1a〉 *v/t* **1** *pared* plaster **2** MED put in plaster
enzarzarse 〈1f〉 *v/r* get involved (***en*** in)
enzima *f o m* BIO enzyme
eñe *f* letter 'ñ'
eoceno *m* GEOL Eocene
eólico *adj* wind *atr*
EPA *f abr* (= ***Encuesta de Población Activa***) labor *o Br* labour force survey, manpower report
E.P.D. *abr* (= ***en paz descanse***) RIP (= requiescat in pace, rest in peace)
épica *f* epic poetry
épico *adj* epic
epicúreo I *adj* epicurean **II** *m*, **-a** *f* epicure
epidemia *f* epidemic
epidémico *adj* epidemic
epidermis *f* epidermis
epidural *f/adj* MED epidural
Epifanía *f* Epiphany
epiglotis *f inv* ANAT epiglottis
epígrafe *m* epigraph
epigrama *m* epigram
epilepsia *f* MED epilepsy
epiléptico I *adj* epileptic **II** *m*, **-a** *f* epileptic
epílogo *m* epilogue
episcopado *m* **1** *cargo* bishopric, episcopate **2** (*tiempo conjunto de obispos*) episcopate
episcopal *adj* episcopal; ***sede ~*** bishopric
episódico *adj* episodic
episodio *m* episode
epístola *f* epistle
epistolar *adj* epistolary
epistolario *m* collected letters *pl*
epitafio *m* epitaph
epitelio *m* ANAT epithelium
epíteto *m* epithet
época *f* **1** time, period; ***en aquella ~*** at that time; ***hacer ~*** be epoch-making **2** *parte del año* time of year **3** GEOL epoch
epopeya *f* epic, epic poem
equidad *f* fairness
equidistante *adj* equidistant
equidistar 〈1a〉 *v/i*: ***~ de*** be equidistant from
equilátero *adj* MAT equilateral
equilibrado *adj* well-balanced
equilibrar 〈1a〉 *v/t* balance; **equilibrarse** *v/r de balanza, barco* be balanced; *de efecto* be balanced out
equilibrio *m* **1** balance; ***falta de ~*** imbalance; ***mantener / perder el ~*** keep / lose one's balance ***~ ecológico*** ecological balance **2** FÍS equilibrium
equilibrista *m/f* acrobat; *con cuerda* tightrope walker
equino I *adj* equine **II** *m* horse
equinoccio *m* equinox
equipaje *m* baggage
◇ **equipaje de mano** hand baggage
equipamiento *m* AUTO: ***~ de serie*** standard features *pl*; ***~ base*** entry-level equipment
equipar 〈1a〉 *v/t* equip (***con*** with)
equiparable *adj* comparable (***a***, ***con*** with)
equiparar 〈1a〉 *v/t* put on a level (***a***, ***con*** with); ***~ algo con algo*** *fig* compare *o* liken sth to sth
equipo *m* **1** DEP team **2**: ***~ investigador*** investigating team **3** *accesorios* equipment; ***~ de esquiar*** skiing equipment; ***caerse con todo el ~*** *fig* F fall flat
◇ **equipo de alta fidelidad** hi-fi (system); **equipo local** local team; **equipo de música** sound system; **equipo de sonido** sound system; **equipo visitante** visiting team
equis *f* **1** letter 'x' **2**: ***el señor ~*** Mr. So-and-so; ***estar a ~ dólares*** cost so many dollars
equitación *f* riding; ***escuela de ~*** riding school
equitativo *adj* fair, equitable
equivalencia *f* equivalence
equivalente *m/adj* equivalent
equivaler 〈2q〉 *v/i* be equivalent (***a*** to)
equivocación *f* mistake; ***por ~*** by mistake
equivocado *adj* wrong; ***estar ~*** be wrong, be mistaken
equivocar 〈1g〉 *v/t*: ***~ a alguien*** make

s.o. make a mistake; **equivocarse** *v/r* make a mistake; ***te has equivocado*** you are wrong *o* mistaken; ***~ de número*** TELEC get the wrong number; ***~ de camino*** take the wrong road; ***si no me equivoco*** if I'm not mistaken
equívoco I *adj* ambiguous, equivocal **II** *m* **1** misunderstanding **2** (*error*) mistake
era *f* era
erario *m* treasury; ***el ~ público*** the treasury, the public purse
erección *f* erection
erecto *adj* erect
eremita *m/f* hermit
eres *vb* ☞ ***ser***
ergonomía *f* ergonomics *sg*
ergonómico *adj* ergonomic
erguido *adj cuerpo, cabeza* erect; *espalda* straight
erguir ⟨3n⟩ *v/t* **1** raise, lift **2** (*poner derecho*) straighten; **erguirse** *v/r* **1** *de persona* stand up, rise **2** *de edificio* rise
erial *m* uncultivated land
erigir ⟨3c⟩ *v/t* **1** erect **2** *persona* set up (***en*** as); **erigirse** *v/r*: ***~ en*** set o.s. up as
erisipela *f* MED erysipelas *sg*
eritema *m* MED erythema
erizado *adj* bristling (***de*** with)
erizarse ⟨1f⟩ *v/r de pelo* stand on end
erizo *m* ZO hedgehog
◇ **erizo de mar** ZO sea urchin
ermita *f* chapel
ermitaño I *m* ZO hermit crab **II** *m*, **-a** *f* hermit
erogación *f Méx, S.Am.* expenditure, outlay
erogar ⟨1h⟩ *v/t Méx, S.Am.* spend
erógeno *adj* erogenous
erosión *f* erosion
erosionar ⟨1a⟩ *v/t* GEOL erode; **erosionarse** *v/r* **1** GEOL erode, be eroded **2** *fig*: *de confianza, apoyo* crumble; *de relación* deteriorate
erótica *f* eroticism
erótico *adj* erotic
erotismo *m* eroticism
erradicación *f* eradication
erradicar ⟨1g⟩ *v/t* eradicate, wipe out
errado *adj* **1** *respuesta, decisión* wrong; ***estar ~*** *persona* be wrong *o* mistaken **2** DEP: ***un disparo ~*** a mishit
errante *adj* wandering
errar ⟨1l⟩ **I** *v/t* miss; ***~ el tiro / golpe*** miss; ***~ el cálculo*** miscalculate, make a mistake in one's figures **II** *v/i* miss; ***~ es humano*** to err is human
errata *f* mistake, error; *de imprenta* misprint
errático *adj* erratic
erre *f*: ***~ que ~*** F doggedly, stubbornly
erróneamente *adv* wrongly
erróneo *adj* wrong, erroneous *fml*
error *m* mistake, error; ***por ~*** by mistake; ***caer en un ~*** make a mistake; ***estar en un ~*** be wrong *o* mistaken
◇ **error de cálculo** error of judg(e)ment; **error humano** human error; **error judicial** miscarriage of justice; **error médico** medical error; **error de sistema** INFOR system error; **error tipográfico** misprint, typo; **error de transmisión** INFOR transmission error
eructar ⟨1a⟩ *v/i* belch, burp
eructo *m* belch, burp
erudición *f* learning, erudition
erudito I *adj* learned, erudite **II** *m*, **-a** *f* scholar
erupción *f* **1** GEOL eruption; ***entrar en ~*** erupt; ***estar en ~*** be erupting **2** MED: ***~ (cutánea)*** rash
es *vb* ☞ ***ser***
esa *det* ☞ ***ese***
ésa *det* ☞ ***ése***
esbeltez *f* slimness, slenderness
esbelto *adj* slim, slender
esbirro *m* henchman
esbozar ⟨1f⟩ *v/t* sketch; *idea, proyecto etc* outline
esbozo *m* sketch; *de idea, proyecto etc* outline
escabechar ⟨1a⟩ *v/t* **1** GASTR marinade (in ***escabeche***) **2** *fig* (*suspender a*) fail
escabeche *m type of marinade*
escabechina *f* **1** bloodbath, massacre; ***hacer una ~ en la cocina*** F leave the kitchen looking as if a bomb had hit it F **2**: ***hacer una ~*** *fig* F *de profesor* pass very few people
escabel *m* footstool
escabrosidad *f* **1** *de terreno* roughness **2** *de problema* trickiness **3** *de relato* indecency
escabroso *adj* **1** *terreno* rough **2** *problema* tricky **3** *relato* indecent
escabullirse ⟨3h⟩ *v/r* escape, slip away
escachar, escacharrar ⟨1a⟩ F *v/t* bust F; **escacharse** *v/r* bust F, break down

escafandra *f* **1** diving suit **2** AST space suit
escala *f* **1** *tb* MÚS scale; ***a ~*** to scale, life-sized; ***a ~ mundial*** on a world scale; ***en** o **a gran ~*** large-scale *atr*, on a large scale **2** AVIA stopover; ***hacer ~ en*** stop over in
◇ **escala de cuerda** rope ladder
◇ **escala de valores** scale of values
escalada *f* **1** DEP climb, ascent **2**: ***~ de los precios*** increase in prices, escalation of prices
◇ **escalada libre** DEP free climbing
escalador *m*, **~a** *f* climber
escalafón *m fig* ladder
escalar ⟨1a⟩ **I** *v/t* climb, scale; ***~ un alto puesto*** rise to a high position **II** *v/i* climb
escaldado *adj* scalded; *fig* ***salió ~ del proyecto*** he got his fingers burned in the project
escaldar ⟨1a⟩ *v/t* **1** GASTR blanch **2** *manos* scald; **escaldarse** *v/r* scald o.s.
escaleno *adj* scalene
escalera *f* stairs *pl*, staircase
◇ **escalera de caracol** spiral staircase; **escalera de emergencia** fire escape; **escalera extensible** extension ladder; **escalera de incendios** fire escape; **escalera de mano** ladder; **escalera mecánica** escalator
escalerilla *f de avión* steps *pl*; *en barco* gangway
escalfar ⟨1a⟩ *v/t* poach
escalinata *f* (flight of) steps *pl*, staircase
escalofriante *adj* horrifying
escalofrío *m* shiver
escalón *m* step; *de escalera de mano* rung
escalonado *adj* **1** *proceso* gradual, cumulative **2** *corte de pelo* layered
escalonar ⟨1a⟩ *v/t* **1** *en tiempo* stagger **2** *terreno* terrace
escalonia, escaloña *f* BOT escallonia
escalopa *f L.Am.*, **escalope** *m* escalope
escalpelo *m* scalpel
escama *f* **1** ZO scale **2** *de jabón, piel* flake
escamar ⟨1a⟩ *v/t* **1** scale, remove the scales from **2** *fig* make suspicious; **escamarse** *v/r* become suspicious
escamoso *adj* **1** ZO scaly **2** *piel* flaky
escamotear ⟨1a⟩ *v/t* **1** (*ocultar*) hide, conceal **2** (*negar*) withhold
escamoteo *m* **1** (*ocultación*) concealment **2** (*negación*) withholding
escampada *f* (*claro*) clear spell
escampar ⟨1a⟩ *v/i* clear up, stop raining
escanciador *m* wine waiter
escanciar ⟨1b⟩ *v/t fml* pour
escandalizar ⟨1f⟩ *v/t* shock, scandalize; **escandalizarse** *v/r* be shocked
escandallo *m* **1** MAR lead **2** COM pricing
escándalo *m* **1** (*asunto vergonzoso*) scandal **2** (*jaleo*) racket, ruckus; ***armar un ~*** make a scene
escandaloso *adj* **1** (*vergonzoso*) scandalous, shocking **2** (*ruidoso*) noisy, rowdy
Escandinavia *f* Scandinavia
escandinavo I *adj* Scandinavian **II** *m*, **-a** *f* Scandinavian
escanear ⟨1a⟩ *v/t* scan
escáner *m* scanner
◇ **escáner en color** color *o Br* colour scanner
escaño *m* POL seat
escapada *f* escape
escapar ⟨1a⟩ *v/t* **1** escape (***de*** from) **2**: ***dejar ~*** *oportunidad* pass up, let slip; *suspiro* let out, give; **escaparse** *v/r* **1** (*huir*) escape (***de*** from); *de casa* run away (***de*** from); ***~ de*** *situación* get out of **2** (*dejar pasar*): ***se me ha escapado el tren*** I missed the train **3**: ***no se te escapa nada*** nothing gets past you *o* escapes you
escaparate *m* store window, *Br tb* shop window
escaparatismo *m* window-dressing
escaparatista *m/f* window dresser
escapatoria *f*: ***no tener ~*** have no way out
escape *m* **1** *de gas* leak **2** AUTO exhaust **3**: ***salir a ~*** rush out
escapista *m/f* escape artist, escapologist
escápula *f* ANAT shoulder blade, scapula *fml*
escapular *adj* ANAT scapular
escapulario *m* REL scapular
escaque *m* square
escara *f* MED crust
escarabajo *m* ZO beetle
◇ **escarabajo de la patata** Colorado beetle, potato beetle

escaramujo *m flor* wild rose; *fruto* (rose) hip
escaramuza *f* skirmish
escarapela *f* rosette
escarbadientes *m inv* toothpick
escarbar ⟨1a⟩ **I** *v/i tb fig* dig around (**en** in) **II** *v/t* dig around in
escarceo *m* **1** white caps *pl*, white horses *pl* **2**: **~s** *pl* (*incursiones*) forays (**en**, **con** into), dabbling *sg* (**en**, **con** in) ◇ **escarceos amorosos** romantic *o* amorous adventures
escarcha *f* frost
escarchar ⟨1a⟩ *v/t* GASTR crystallize
escarda *f* AGR **1** hoeing **2** (*azada*) hoe
escardar ⟨1a⟩ *v/t* hoe
escarlata *adj inv & m* scarlet
escarlatina *f* MED scarlet fever
escarmentar ⟨1k⟩ **I** *v/t* teach a lesson to **II** *v/i* learn one's lesson; **~ en cabeza ajena** learn from other people's mistakes
escarmiento *m* lesson; **le sirvió de ~** it taught him a lesson
escarnecer ⟨2d⟩ *v/t* ridicule, deride
escarnio *m* ridicule, derision
escarola *f* endive, escarole
escarpa *f* escarpment
escarpado *adj* sheer, steep
escarpadura *f* escarpment
escarpia *f* hook
escarpín *m zapato* pump, *Br* court shoe
escasamente *adv* barely, hardly
escasear ⟨1a⟩ **I** *v/i* be scarce, be in short supply **II** *v/t* use sparingly, be sparing with
escasez *f* shortage, scarcity
escaso *adj* **1** *recursos* limited; **-as posibilidades de** not much chance of, little chance of **2**: **andar ~ de algo** *falto* be short of sth **3** (*justo*): **falta un mes ~** it's barely a month away; **un kilo ~** a scant kilo, barely a kilo
escatimar ⟨1a⟩ *v/t* be mean with, be very sparing with; **no ~ esfuerzos** be unstinting in one's efforts, spare no effort
escayola *f* (plaster) cast
escayolar ⟨1a⟩ *v/t* put in a (plaster) cast; **llevar el pie escayolado** have one's foot in a cast, *Br* have one's foot in plaster
escayolista *m/f* plasterer
escena *f* **1** scene; **hacer una ~** *fig* make a scene; **desaparecer de la ~** *fig* vanish from the scene; **robarle a alguien la ~** steal the show from s.o. **2** *escenario* stage; **entrar en ~**, **salir a ~** come on stage; **poner en ~** stage; **llevar a la ~** *obra de teatro* direct; (*adaptar*) adapt for the stage
escenario *m* stage; *fig* scene
escénico *adj* stage *atr*
escenificación *f* staging
escenificar ⟨1g⟩ *v/t* stage
escenografía *f* **1** *arte* set design **2** (*decorados*) scenery
escenógrafo *m*, **-a** *f* set designer
escepticismo *m* skepticism, *Br* scepticism
escéptico **I** *adj* skeptical, *Br* sceptical **II** *m*, **-a** *f* skeptic, *Br* sceptic
escindible *adj* separable, splittable
escindir ⟨3a⟩ *v/t* split; **escindirse** *v/r* **1** (*fragmentarse*) split (**en** into) **2** (*segregarse*) break away (**de** from)
escisión *f* **1** (*fragmentación*) split **2** (*segregación*) break
esclarecer ⟨2d⟩ **I** *v/t* **1** throw *o* shed light on **2** *misterio* clear up **II** *v/i* dawn
esclarecido *adj* illustrious
esclarecimiento *m* **1** clarification **2** *de misterio* solving
esclava *f* **1** (female) slave **2** (*pulsera*) bangle
esclavina *f* short cape
esclavitud *f* slavery
esclavizar ⟨1f⟩ *v/t* enslave; *fig* tie down
esclavo **I** *adj tb fig* slave *atr* **II** *m* slave
esclerosis *f* MED: **~ múltiple** multiple sclerosis; **~ arterial** arteriosclerosis
esclusa *f* lock
escoba *f* broom
escobajo *m* BOT stem
escobazo *m*: **dar un ~ a algo** give sth a sweep; **echar a alguien a ~s** *o* **a ~ limpio** F kick s.o. out F
escobén *m* MAR hawse (hole)
escobilla *f* **1** small brush **2** AUTO wiper blade
escobón *m* long-handled broom
escocer ⟨2b & 2h⟩ *v/i* **1** sting, smart **2** *fig*: **todavía le escuece la derrota** he's still smarting from the defeat; **escocerse** *v/r* **1** chafe **2** *fig* be irritated *o* irked
escocés **I** *adj* Scottish; **falda escocesa** kilt; **tela escocesa** tartan **II** *m* Scot,

E

Scotsman
escocesa *f* Scot, Scotswoman
Escocia *f* Scotland
escofina *f* rasp, file
escoger ⟨2c⟩ *v/t* choose, select
escogido *adj* select
escolanía *f* boys' choir
escolar I *adj* school *atr* **II** *m/f* student
escolaridad *f* schooling, education; ***libro de ~*** school record
escolarización *f* education, schooling
◇ **escolarización obligatoria** compulsory education
escolarizar ⟨1f⟩ *v/t* educate, provide schooling for
escolástica *f* scholasticism
escolástico *adj* scholarly
escoleta *f Méx* rehearsal
escoliosis *f* MED scoliosis
escollera *f* breakwater
escollo *m* **1** MAR reef **2** (*obstáculo*) hurdle, obstacle
escolta I *f* escort **II** *m/f* **1** *motorista* outrider **2** (*guardaespaldas*) bodyguard **3** *en baloncesto* shooting guard
escoltar ⟨1a⟩ *v/t* escort
escombrera *f* dump
escombros *mpl* rubble *sg*
esconder ⟨2a⟩ *v/t* hide, conceal; **esconderse** *v/r* hide
escondidas *fpl* **1** *S.Am.* hide-and-seek *sg* **2**: ***a ~*** in secret, secretly; ***a ~ de alguien*** behind s.o.'s back
escondite *m* **1** *lugar* hiding place **2** *juego* hide-and-seek
escondrijo *m* hiding place
escopeta *f* shotgun
◇ **escopeta de aire comprimido** air gun, air rifle
◇ **escopeta de caza** shotgun
escopetado *adj*: ***salir ~*** F shoot *o* dash off F
escopetazo *m* gunshot
escopetero *m* hunter
escoplo *m* chisel
escora *f* MAR load line
escorar ⟨1a⟩ **I** *v/t* shore up **II** *v/i* MAR list, heel over
escorbuto *m* scurvy
escoria *f* slag; *desp* dregs *pl*
Escorpio *m/f inv* ASTR Scorpio
escorpión *m* ZO scorpion
escorrentía *f* torrent
escorzo *m* PINT foreshortening
escota *f* MAR sheet
escotado *adj* low-cut
escotar ⟨1a⟩ *v/t* **1** *prenda* cut low in the front **2** *precio* cut
escote *m* **1** neckline; *de mujer* cleavage **2**: ***~ en pico*** V-neck **3**: ***pagar a ~*** share the expenses, go Dutch F
escotilla *f* MAR hatch
escotillón *m* **1** MAR hatch **2** TEA trapdoor
escozor *m* **1** burning sensation, stinging **2** *fig* bitterness
escriba *m* scribe
escribanía *f* **1** set of writing materials **2** *mueble* writing desk, escritoire **3** *L.Am.* (*notaría*) notary's office
escribano I *m* HIST scribe **II** *m*, **-a** *f* *L.Am.* notary
escribiente *m/f* clerk
escribir ⟨3a; *part* ***escrito***⟩ **I** *v/t* **1** write; ***~ a mano*** hand-write, write by hand; ***~ a máquina*** type **2** (*deletrear*) spell **II** *v/i* write; **escribirse** *v/r* **1** write to each other, correspond **2**: ***¿cómo se escribe?*** how do you spell it?
escrito I *part* ☞ ***escribir*** **II** *adj* **1** written; ***por ~*** in writing; ***~ a mano*** handwritten **2**: ***estaba ~*** it was inevitable **III** *m* **1** document **2**: ***~s*** *pl* writings
escritor *m*, **~a** *f* writer, author
escritorio *m* **1** desk; ***artículos de ~*** stationery; ***juego de ~*** desk set **2** INFOR desktop **3** *L.Am.* (*oficina*) office
escritura *f* **1** writing **2** JUR deed **3**: ***Sagradas Escrituras*** Holy Scripture *sg*
◇ **escritura pública** JUR public deed
escriturar ⟨1a⟩ *v/t* register
escroto *m* ANAT scrotum
escrúpulo *m* scruple; ***sin ~s*** unscrupulous
escrupulosidad *f* (*cuidado*) meticulousness
escrupuloso *adj* **1** (*cuidadoso*) meticulous **2** (*honrado*) scrupulous **3** (*aprensivo*) fastidious
escrutador I *adj mirada* penetrating **II** *m*, **~a** *f* scrutineer, *Br* returning officer
escrutar ⟨1a⟩ *v/t* **1** scrutinize **2** *votos* count
escrutinio *m* **1** *de votos* count **2** (*inspección*) scrutiny
escuadra *f* **1** MAT set square; *de carpintero* square **2** MIL squad; MAR squadron **3** DEP: ***el balón entró por la ~***

the ball went in the top corner
escuadrilla *f* MAR, AVIA squadron
escuadrón *m* squadron
escualidez *f* skinniness
escuálido *adj* skinny, emaciated
escualo *m* ZO dogfish
escucha *f*: ***estar a la ~*** be listening out
◇ **escuchas telefónicas** wire-tapping *sg*, *Br tb* phone-tapping *sg*
escuchar ⟨1a⟩ **I** *v/t* **1** listen to **2** *L.Am.* (*oír*) hear **II** *v/i* listen; **escucharse** *v/r* like the sound of one's own voice
escuchimizado *adj* F puny F, scrawny F
escudar ⟨1a⟩ *v/t* shield; **escudarse** *v/r fig* hide (***en*** behind)
escudería *f* stable
escudero *m* HIST squire
escudilla *f* bowl
escudo *m* **1** *arma* shield **2** *insignia* badge **3** *moneda* escudo
◇ **escudo de armas** coat of arms
escudriñar ⟨1a⟩ *v/t* **1** (*mirar de lejos*) scan **2** (*examinar*) scrutinize
escuela *f* school; ***hacer*** *o* ***crear ~*** *fig* create a trend; ***de la vieja ~*** *fig* of the old school
◇ **escuela de arte dramático** drama school; **escuela de Bellas Artes** art school; **escuela de comercio** business school; **escuela de educación especial** special-needs school; **escuela de hostelería** hotel school; **escuela de idiomas** language school; **escuela primaria** elementary school, *Br* primary school; **escuela técnica superior** *Esp* technical college; **escuela universitaria** *Esp junior college*, *Br university college teaching three-year diploma courses*
escuelero I *adj L.Am.* school *atr* **II** *m*, **-a** *f* **1** *L.Am.* (*maestro*) teacher **2** *Pe*, *Bol* (*alumno*) student
escueto *adj* succinct, concise
escuincle *m/f Méx*, *C.Am.* kid
esculpir ⟨3a⟩ *v/t* sculpt
escultismo *m* scouting, scout movement
escultor *m*, **~a** *f* sculptor
escultura *f* sculpture
escultural *adj* **1** sculptural **2** *persona*, *cuerpo* statuesque
escupidera *f* **1** spitoon **2** *L.Am.* chamber pot
escupir ⟨3a⟩ **I** *v/i* spit; ***~ a alguien a*** *o* ***en la cara*** spit in s.o.'s face **II** *v/t* spit out; ***~ fuego*** spew out flames
escupitajo *m* F gob of spit F
escurreplatos *m inv* plate rack
escurrevasos *m inv* drainer
escurridizo *adj* slippery; *fig* evasive
escurrido I *part* ☞ ***escurrir*** **II** *adj* skinny; ***~ de caderas*** with narrow hips, narrow-hipped
escurridor *m* **1** (*colador*) colander **2** (*escurreplatos*) plate rack
escurrir ⟨3a⟩ **I** *v/t* **1** *ropa* wring out **2** *platos*, *verduras* drain **II** *v/i* **1** *de platos* drain **2** *de ropa* drip-dry; **escurrirse** *v/r* **1** *de líquido* drain away **2** (*deslizarse*) slip; (*escaparse*) slip away
escusado *m* bathroom
esdrújula *f word with the stress on the third syllable from the end* (*e.g. teléfono*)
esdrújulo *adj* stressed on the third last syllable
ese *f* letter 's'; ***ir haciendo ~s*** zigzag
ese, esa, esos, esas *det singular* that; *plural* those; ***eso mismo*** exactly that; ***aun con eso*** even then
ése, ésa, ésos, ésas *pron singular* that (one); *plural* those (ones); ***le ofrecí dinero pero ni por ésas*** I offered him money but even that wasn't enough; ***no soy de ésos que*** I'm not one of those who
esencia *f* essence; ***en ~*** essentially, in essence
esencial *adj* essential; ***lo ~ es que*** the main *o* essential thing is that
esencialmente *adv* essentially, in essence
esfera *f* sphere; ***~ de actividad*** *fig* field *o* sphere (of activity); ***las altas ~s*** *fig: de la sociedad* the upper echelons
esférico I *adj* spherical **II** *m* DEP F ball
esfinge *f* sphinx
esfínter *m* ANAT sphincter
esforzar ⟨1f & 1m⟩ *v/t* strain; **esforzarse** *v/r* make an effort, try hard
esfuerzo *m* effort; ***hacer un ~*** make an effort; ***sin ~*** effortlessly
esfumar ⟨1a⟩ *v/t* PINT blur; **esfumarse** *v/r* F *tb fig* disappear
esfumino *m* PINT stump
esgrafiado *m* PINT sgraffito
esgrima *f* fencing

esgrimidor *m*, **~a** *f* fencer
esgrimir ⟨3a⟩ *v/t* **1** *arma* wield **2** *fig: argumento* put forward, use
esguín *m* ZO young salmon
esguince *m* sprain
eslabón *m* link; ***el ~ perdido*** the missing link
eslabonar ⟨1a⟩ *v/t* link (together)
eslalon *m* ☞ ***slalom***
eslavo **I** *adj* Slavic, Slav *atr* **II** *m*, **-a** *f* Slav
eslogan *m* slogan
eslora *f* length
eslovaco **I** *adj* Slovakian, Slovak **II** *m*, **-a** *f* Slovak **III** *m idioma* Slovak
Eslovaquia *f* Slovakia
Eslovenia *f* Slovenia
esloveno **I** *adj* Slovene, Slovenian **II** *m*, **-a** *f* Slovene, Slovenian **III** *m idioma* Slovene
esmachar ⟨1a⟩ *v/t & v/i en baloncesto* dunk, slam dunk
esmaltado *m* enamel
esmaltar ⟨1a⟩ *v/t* enamel; ***~ las uñas*** put nail polish on
esmalte *m* enamel; ***~ (dental)*** (tooth) enamel
◇ **esmalte de uñas** nail polish, *Br tb* nail varnish
esmerado *adj* meticulous
esmeralda *f* emerald
esmerarse ⟨1a⟩ *v/r* take great care (***en*** over)
esmeril *m* emery
esmerilado **I** *adj*: ***cristal ~*** frosted glass **II** *m* grinding
esmerilar ⟨1a⟩ *v/t* grind
esmero *m* care; ***con ~*** carefully
esmirriado *adj* F skinny, scrawny F
esmoquin *m* tuxedo, *Br* dinner jacket
esnifar ⟨1a⟩ *v/t* F *pegamento* sniff F; *cocaína* snort F
esnob **I** *adj* snobbish **II** *m/f* snob
esnobismo *m* snobbishness
ESO *f abr Esp* (= ***educación secundaria obligatoria***) compulsory secondary education
eso *pron* **1** that; ***en ~*** just then, just at that moment; ***~ mismo***, ***~ es*** that's it, that's the way; ***por ~*** that's why; ***¿y ~?*** why's that?; ***~ sí*** yes of course **2** *en locuciones*: ***y ~ que le dije que no se lo contara*** and after I told him not to tell her; ***a ~ de las dos*** at around two
esófago *m* ANAT esophagus, *Br tb* oesophagus
esotérico *adj* esoteric
esoterismo *m* occult
espabilado *adj* **1** (*listo*) bright, smart **2** (*vivo*) sharp, on the ball F
espabilar ⟨1a⟩ **I** *v/t* **1** (*quitar el sueño*) wake up, revive **2**: ***lo ha espabilado*** (*lo ha avivado*) she's got him to wise up F **II** *v/i* **1** (*darse prisa*) hurry up, get a move on **2** (*avivarse*) wise up **3** *del sueño* wake up; **espabilarse** *v/r* **1** *del sueño* wake o.s. up **2** (*darse prisa*) hurry up, get a move on **3** (*avivarse*) wise up F
espaciador *m* space bar
espacial *adj* **1** *cohete*, *viaje* space *atr* **2** FÍS, MAT spatial
espaciar ⟨1a⟩ *v/t* **1** *en el espacio* space out **2**: ***ha empezado a ~ las visitas a sus hijos*** his visits to his children have started to become less frequent; **espaciarse** *v/r* become more (and more) infrequent
espacio *m* **1** space; ***~ en blanco*** (blank) space; ***~ de tiempo*** space of time; ***no tengo suficiente ~*** I don't have enough space *o* room; ***en el ~ de tres meses*** in the space of three months; ***por ~ de una hora*** for a full hour **2** TV program, *Br* programme
◇ **espacio aéreo** airspace; **espacio informativo** TV news program *o Br* programme; **espacio vital** living space; **espacios verdes** green spaces
espaciosidad *f* spaciousness, roominess
espacioso *adj* spacious, roomy
espada **I** *f* **1** sword; ***estar entre la ~ y la pared*** be between a rock and a hard place **2**: ***~s*** *pl* (*en naipes*) *suit in Spanish deck of cards* **II** *m* TAUR matador
◇ **espada de Damocles** *fig* sword of Damocles
espadachín *m* skilled swordsman
espadaña *f* BOT bulrush
espaguetis *mpl* spaghetti *sg*
espalda *f* back; ***ancho de ~s*** broad-shouldered; ***de ~s a*** with one's back to; ***caerse de ~s*** fall flat on one's back; ***nadar a ~*** swim backstroke; ***por la ~*** from behind; ***a ~s de alguien*** behind s.o.'s back; ***no me des la ~*** don't sit with your back to me; ***tener cubiertas las***

~s *fig* keep one' s back covered; ***cubrirse las ~s*** cover one's back; ***volver la ~ a alguien*** *fig* turn one's back on s.o.; ***echarse algo sobre las ~s*** *fig* take on sth, shoulder sth; ***tiene muchos años sobre las ~s y sabe cómo ...*** he has many years of experience behind him and knows how to ...; ***echarse algo a la(s) ~(s)*** *fig* stop worrying about sth, forget sth
espaldarazo *m* **1** slap on the back **2** (*reconocimiento*) recognition; ***dar el ~ a alguien*** *fig* give s.o. support
espalderas *fpl* wall bars
espaldilla *f* ANAT, ZO shoulder blade; ***~ de cordero*** shoulder of lamb
espantadizo *adj* nervous, easily frightened
espantajo *m* scarecrow; *fig* sight
espantapájaros *m inv* scarecrow
espantasuegras *m inv Méx* party blower
espantar ⟨1a⟩ *v/t* **1** (*asustar*) frighten, scare **2** (*ahuyentar*) frighten away, shoo away **3** F (*horrorizar*) horrify, appall; **espantarse** *v/r* **1** get frightened, get scared **2** F (*horrorizarse*) be horrified, be appalled
espanto *m* **1** (*susto*) fright **2** *L.Am.* (*fantasma*) ghost **3**: ***nos llenó de ~*** *desagrado* we were horrified; ***¡qué ~!*** how awful!; ***de ~*** terrible; ***estar curado de ~(s)*** F have seen it all before
espantoso *adj* **1** horrific, appalling **2** *para enfatizar* terrible, dreadful; ***hace un calor ~*** it's terribly *o* incredibly hot
España *f* Spain
español **I** *adj* Spanish **II** *m idioma* Spanish **III** *m*, **~a** *f* Spaniard; ***los ~es*** the Spanish
españolada *f old-fashioned Spanish movie*
españolismo *m* **1** (*afición*) love of Spain **2** *cualidad* Spanishness
esparadrapo *m* Band-Aid®, *Br* plaster
esparceta *f* BOT sainfoin
esparcimiento *m* (*ocio*) recreation
esparcir ⟨3b⟩ *v/t papeles* scatter; *rumor* spread; **esparcirse** *v/r de papeles* be scattered; *de rumor* spread
espárrago *m* BOT asparagus; ***¡vete a freír ~s!*** F get lost! F
◇ **espárrago triguero** wild asparagus
Esparta *f* HIST Sparta
espartano *adj* spartan
esparto *m* BOT esparto grass
espasmo *m* spasm
espasmódico *adj* spasmodic
espatarrarse *vb* ☞ ***despatarrarse***
espato *m* MIN spar
espátula *f en cocina* spatula; *en pintura* palette knife
especia *f* spice
especial *adj* **1** special; ***en ~*** especially; ***nada en ~*** nothing special **2** (*difícil*) fussy
especialidad *f* specialty, *Br* speciality
especialista *m/f* **1** specialist, expert **2** *en cine* stuntman; *mujer* stuntwoman
especialización *f* specialization
especializarse ⟨1f⟩ *v/r* specialize (**en** in)
especialmente *adv* specially
especie *f* **1** BIO species **2** (*tipo*) kind, sort; ***una ~ de*** a kind *o* sort of **3**: ***en ~*** in kind
especiero *m* spice rack
especificación *f* specification
especificar ⟨1g⟩ *v/t* specify
específico *adj* specific
espécimen *m* specimen
espectacular *adj* spectacular
espectacularidad *f* spectacular nature
espectáculo *m* **1** TEA show; ***dar el ~*** *fig* make a spectacle of o.s. **2** (*escena*) sight; ***dar un triste ~*** be a sorry sight
espectador *m*, **~a** *f* **1** *en cine etc* member of the audience; DEP spectator **2** (*observador*) on-looker, observer
espectral *adj* FÍS spectral; ***análisis ~*** spectrum analysis
espectro *m* **1** FÍS spectrum; ***un amplio ~*** *fig* a wide range, a broad spectrum **2** (*fantasma*) ghost; ***el ~ de la guerra*** the specter *o Br* spectre of war
especulación *f* speculation
especulador *m*, **~a** *f* speculator
especular ⟨1a⟩ *v/i* speculate
especulativo *adj* speculative
espéculo *m* MED speculum
espejismo *m* mirage
espejo *m* mirror; (***limpio***) ***como un ~*** spotless, clean as a whistle; (***liso***) ***como un ~ mar*** like a millpond; *lámina de madera* smooth as silk
◇ **espejo deformante** distorting mirror
◇ **espejo retrovisor** rear-view mirror

espeleología *f* spelunking, *Br* potholing
espeleólogo *m*, **-a** *f* spelunker, *Br* potholer
espeluznante *adj* horrific, horrifying
espeluznar ⟨1a⟩ *v/t* scare, frighten; **espeluznarse** *v/r* get scared *o* frightened
espera *f* wait; ***sala de ~*** waiting room; ***en ~ de*** pending; ***estar a la ~ de*** be waiting for
esperanza *f* hope; ***estar en estado de*** (***buena***) **~** be pregnant, be expecting (a baby)
◇ **esperanza de vida** life expectancy
esperanzador *adj* hopeful, encouraging
esperar ⟨1a⟩ **I** *v/t* **1** (*aguardar*) wait for; ***hacerse ~*** keep people waiting **2** *con esperanza* hope; (***así***) ***lo espero*** I hope so, hopefully; ***espero que no*** I hope not, hopefully not; ***es de ~ que*** it is to be hoped that **3** (*suponer, confiar en*) expect **4**: ***~ un hijo*** be expecting a baby **5**: ***de aquí te espero*** F incredible F
II *v/i* (*aguardar*) wait; ***puedes ~ sentado*** you're in for a long wait
esperma *f* sperm
◇ **esperma de ballena** spermaceti
espermatozoide *m* spermatozoid
espermatozoo *m* BIO spermatozoon, sperm
esperpento *m fig* sight
espesante *m* thickener
espesar ⟨1a⟩ *v/t* thicken; **espesarse** *v/r* thicken, become thick
espeso *adj* thick; *vegetación, niebla* thick, dense
espesor *m* thickness
espesura *f* dense vegetation
espetar ⟨1a⟩ *v/t* **1** run through **2** GASTR put on a spit; *en pincho* skewer **3** *decir* come out with, blurt out
espetón *m* spit; (*pincho*) skewer
espía *m/f* spy
espiar ⟨1c⟩ **I** *v/t* spy on **II** *v/i* spy
espichar ⟨1a⟩ *v/t* P die, kick the bucket F
espiga *f* BOT ear, spike; ***dibujo de ~*** herringbone
espigado *adj fig* tall and slim
espigarse ⟨1h⟩ *v/r* shoot up
espigón *m* MAR breakwater
espina *f de planta* thorn; *de pez* bone; ***dar mala ~ a alguien*** F make s.o. feel uneasy; ***por fin me he sacado la ~*** F at last I have managed to do it
◇ **espina dorsal** spine, backbone
espinacas *fpl* BOT spinach *sg*
espinal *adj* spinal
espinazo *m* spine, backbone; ***doblar el ~*** *fig* (*trabajar mucho*) work o.s. into the ground; (*humillarse*) kowtow (***ante*** to)
espineta *f* MÚS spinet
espingarda *f fig* F beanpole F
espinilla *f* **1** *de la pierna* shin **2** *en la piel* pimple, spot
espinillera *f* shinguard, shinpad
espino *m* BOT hawthorn
◇ **espino albar, espino blanco** BOT whitethorn
espinoso *adj* thorny, prickly; *fig* thorny, knotty
espionaje *m* spying, espionage
◇ **espionaje industrial** industrial espionage
espira *f* spiral; *de concha* whorl
espiración *f* exhalation
espiral **I** *adj* spiral *atr* **II** *f* spiral; ***~ precios-salarios*** wage-price spiral
espirar ⟨1a⟩ *v/t* & *v/i* exhale
espiritismo *m* spiritualism
espiritista *m/f* spiritualist
espiritoso *adj* → ***espirituoso***
espíritu *m* **1** spirit; ***pobre de ~*** timid; ***ser el ~ de la contradicción*** be very contrary, be a contrary old buzzard F **2** REL: ***el Espíritu Santo*** the Holy Ghost, the Holy Spirit
◇ **espíritu aventurero** sense *o* spirit of adventure; **espíritu de equipo** team spirit; **espíritu de vino** spirits *pl* of wine
espiritual *adj* spiritual
espiritualidad *f* spirituality
espirituoso *adj*: ***bebidas -as*** spirits
esplendidez *f* **1** splendor, *Br* splendour, magnificence **2** (*generosidad*) generosity
espléndido *adj* **1** splendid, magnificent **2** (*generoso*) generous
esplendor *m* splendor, *Br* splendour
esplendoroso *adj* splendid, magnificent
esplénico *adj* ANAT splenic
espliego *m* BOT lavender

espolear ⟨1a⟩ *v/t tb fig* spur on
espoleta *f* **1** MIL fuse **2** ZO wishbone
espolón *m* **1** *de ave* spur; *de caballo* fetlock **2** ARQUI buttress **3** MED: **~ (*calcáneo*)** (bone) spur
espolvorear ⟨1a⟩ *v/t* sprinkle
esponja *f* sponge; ***beber como una ~*** F drink like a fish
esponjar ⟨1a⟩ *v/t* make fluffy; **esponjarse** *v/r* **1** *de masa* rise **2** *fig* puff up, swell with pride
esponjoso *adj* **1** *bizcocho* spongy **2** *toalla* soft, fluffy
esponsales *mpl* betrothal *sg*
espónsor *m/f* sponsor
esponsorizar ⟨1f⟩ *v/t* sponsor
espontáneamente *adv* spontaneously
espontaneidad *f* spontaneity
espontáneo *adj* spontaneous
espora *f* BOT spore
esporádico *adj* sporadic
esposa *f* wife; ***~s pl*** handcuffs
esposar ⟨1a⟩ *v/t* handcuff, cuff F
esposo *m* husband
esprint *m* sprint
espuela *f* spur
◇ **espuela de caballero** BOT larkspur
espuerta *f*: ***ganar dinero a ~s*** F make money hand over fist F
espulgar ⟨1h⟩ *v/t* delouse
espuma *f* foam; *de jabón* lather; *de cerveza* froth; ***crecer*** *o* ***subir como la ~*** shoot up
◇ **espuma de afeitar** shaving foam; **espuma de mar** meerschaum; **espuma moldeadora** styling mousse
espumadera *f* slotted spoon, skimmer
espumarajo *m* froth, foam
espumilla *f C.Am.* GASTR meringue
espumillón *m* tinsel
espumoso *adj* **1** frothy, foamy **2** *caldo* sparkling
esqueje *m* cutting
esquela *f aviso* death notice, obituary
esquelético *adj* skeletal
esqueleto *m* **1** ANAT skeleton; ***ser un ~***, ***estar en el ~*** be a walking skeleton; ***mover*** *o* ***menear el ~*** *hum* shake a leg, dance **2**: **~ (*arquitectónico*)** framework **3** *Méx, C.Am., Pe, Bol fig* blank form
esquema *m* **1** (*croquis*) sketch, diagram; ***en ~*** *mostrar* in diagrammatic form; *explicar* briefly **2** (*sinopsis*) outline, summary
esquemático *adj* **1** *dibujo* schematic, diagrammatic **2** *resumen* simplified, outline *atr*
esquí *m* **1** *tabla* ski **2** *deporte* skiing
◇ **esquí acuático** waterskiing; **esquí de fondo** cross-country skiing; **esquí náutico** waterskiing
esquiador *m*, **~a** *f* skier
◇ **esquiador acuático** waterskier
◇ **esquiador de fondo** cross-country skier
esquiar ⟨1a⟩ *v/i* ski
esquila *f* **1** *de ovejas* shearing **2** (*cencerro*) cowbell
esquilador *m*, **~a** *f* (sheep) shearer
esquilar ⟨1a⟩ *v/t* shear
esquilmar ⟨1a⟩ *v/t* **1** *fuente de riqueza* overexploit **2** *a alguien* suck dry
esquina *f* corner
esquinado *adj fig* awkward, difficult
esquinar ⟨1a⟩ *v/t fig* set at odds; **esquinarse** *v/r fig* fall out (***con*** with), quarrel (***con*** with)
esquinazo *m* **1** *Arg, Chi* serenade **2**: ***dar ~ a alguien*** F give s.o. the slip F
esquirla *f* splinter
esquirol *m/f* strikebreaker, scab F
esquisto *m* schist
esquite *m C.Am., Méx* popcorn
esquivar ⟨1a⟩ *v/t* avoid, dodge F
esquivo *adj* **1** (*huraño*) unsociable **2** (*evasivo*) shifty, evasive
esquizofrenia *f* schizophrenia
esquizofrénico **I** *adj* schizophrenic **II** *m*, **-a** *f* schizophrenic
esta *det* this
está *vb* ☞ ***estar***
estabilidad *f* stability; ***~ de precios*** price stability
estabilización *f* stabilization
estabilizador *m* TÉC, MAR stabilizer
estabilizante *m* stabilizer
estabilizar ⟨1f⟩ *v/t* stabilize; **estabilizarse** *v/r* stabilize
estable *adj* stable
establecer ⟨2d⟩ *v/t* **1** establish **2** *negocio* set up; **establecerse** *v/r* **1** *en lugar* settle **2** *en profesión* set up
establecimiento *m* establishment
establo *m* stable
estabulación *f* stabling
estaca *f* stake
estacada *f*: ***dejar a alguien en la ~*** F

leave s.o. in the lurch

estación *f* **1** station **2** *del año* season **3** *L.Am.* (*emisora*) station
◇ **estación de autobuses** bus station; **estación central** main station, central station; **estación climática** season; **estación espacial** space station; **estación de esquí** ski resort; **estación de invierno, estación invernal** winter resort; **estación de las lluvias** rainy season; **estación meteorológica** weather station; **estación de metro** subway station, *Br* underground station; **estación orbital** space station; **estación de servicio** service station; **estación termal** spa; **estación de trabajo** INFOR workstation

estacional *adj* seasonal

estacionamiento *m* AUTO **1** parking; **~ *indebido*** illegal parking; **~ *prohibido*** no parking **2** *L.Am.* parking lot, *Br* car park
◇ **estacionamiento en batería** angle parking
◇ **estacionamiento en línea** parallel parking

estacionar ⟨1a⟩ *v/t* AUTO park; **estacionarse** *v/r* stabilize

estacionario *adj* **1** *estado, situación* stable **2** *vehículo* stationary

estacionómetro *m Méx* parking meter

estada *f L.Am.* stay

estadía *f L.Am.* stay

estadio *m* DEP stadium

estadista **I** *m* statesman **II** *f* stateswoman

estadística *f* **1** *cifra* statistic **2** *ciencia* statistics *sg*

estadístico **I** *adj* statistical **II** *m*, **-a** *f* statistician

estado *m* **1** state **2** MED condition; ***en buen / mal ~*** in good / bad condition **3**: ***el Estado*** the State
◇ **estado de alarma, estado de alerta** state of alert; **estado del bienestar** welfare state; **estado civil** marital status; **estado de la cuenta** bank statement; **estado de derecho** democracy; **estado de emergencia** state of emergency; **estado de excepción** state of emergency; **estado federal, estado federado** federal state; **estado de guerra** state of war; **Estado Mayor** MIL general staff; **estado satélite** satellite state; **estado de salud** state of health; **estado de sitio** state of siege

Estados Unidos (**de América**) the United States (of America)

estadounidense **I** *adj* American, US *atr* **II** *m/f* American

estafa *f* swindle, cheat

estafador *m*, **~a** *f* con artist F, fraudster

estafar ⟨1a⟩ *v/t* swindle, cheat; **~ *algo a alguien*** cheat s.o. out of sth, defraud s.o. of sth

estafeta *f*: **~** (***de correos***) mail office, *Br* sub-post office

estalactita *f* stalactite

estalagmita *f* stalagmite

estallar ⟨1a⟩ *v/i* **1** explode **2** *de guerra* break out; *de escándalo* break; ***estalló en llanto*** she burst into tears

estallido *m* **1** explosion **2** *de guerra* outbreak

estambre *m* BOT stamen

Estambul *m* Istanbul

estamento *m* stratum, class
◇ **estamento social** social class

estampa *f* **1** *de libro* illustration **2** (*aspecto*) appearance; ***de buena ~*** good-looking, handsome; ***ser la viva ~ de alguien*** be the spitting image of s.o. **3** REL prayer card

estampación *f* printing

estampado **I** *adj tejido* patterned **II** *m* **1** *acción* printing **2** *diseño* pattern

estampar ⟨1a⟩ *v/t* **1** *sello* put **2** *tejido* print **3** *pasaporte* stamp **4**: ***le estampó una bofetada en la cara*** F she smacked him one F; **estamparse** *v/r* crash (**en**, **contra** into)

estampida *f* stampede; ***salir de ~*** stampede out

estampido *m* bang

estampilla *f L.Am.* stamp

estampillar ⟨1a⟩ *v/t L.Am.* stamp

estancado *adj agua* stagnant; *fig* at a standstill

estancamiento *m tb fig*, stagnation

estancar ⟨1g⟩ *v/t río* dam up, block; *fig* bring to a standstill; **estancarse** *v/r* stagnate; *fig* come to a standstill

estancia *f* **1** stay **2** *Rpl* farm, ranch

estanciero *m*, **-a** *f Rpl* farmer, rancher

estanco **I** *adj* watertight **II** *m* tobacco store, *Br* tobacconist's (*also selling stamps*)

estándar *m* standard

estandarización *f* standardization
estandarizar ⟨1f⟩ *v/t* standardize
estandarte *m* standard, banner
estanque *m* pond
estanquero *m*, **-a** *f* tobacco store clerk, *Br* tobacconist
estante *m* shelf
estantería *f* shelves *pl*; *para libros* bookcase
estaño *m* tin; ***hoja de ~*** tinfoil
estar ⟨1p⟩ *v/i* **1** *situación temporal* be; ***¿cómo está Vd.?*** how are you?; ***estoy mejor*** I'm (feeling) better; ***estoy bien / mal*** I'm fine / I'm not feeling too great; ***~ de tres meses*** be three months pregnant; ***~ sin dinero*** have no money; ***¡ya estoy!*** I'm ready!
2 *situación espacial*: ***¿está Javier?*** is Javier in?; ***mi padre no está*** my father isn't here; ***¡ahí está!*** there it is!; ***ahora estoy con Vd.*** I'll be with you in just a moment; ***¿dónde estábamos?*** where were we?
3: ***~ haciendo algo*** be doing sth; ***estoy leyendo*** I'm reading
4 (*sentar*): ***te está grande*** it's too big for you; ***el vestido te está bien*** the dress suits you
5: ***~ de*** *ocupación* work as, be; ***está de camarero*** he's working as a waiter
6 (*padecer de*): ***~ del corazón / estómago*** have heart / stomach problems
7 *indicando fechas, precios*: ***estamos a 3 de enero*** it's January 3rd; ***el kilo está a un peso*** they're one peso a kilo
8: ***~ con alguien*** agree with s.o.; (*apoyar*) support s.o.; ***~ a bien / mal con alguien*** be on good / bad terms with s.o.; ***~ en algo*** be working on sth; ***~ para hacer algo*** be about to do sth; ***no ~ para algo*** not be in a mood for sth; ***~ por algo*** be in favor of sth; ***está por hacer*** it hasn't been done yet; ***¡ya está!*** that's it!
estarse *v/r* stay; ***~ quieto*** keep still; ***~ muriendo*** be dying
estárter *m* choke
estatal *adj* state *atr*
estático *adj* static; ***electricidad -a*** static (electricity)
estatización *f L.Am.* nationalization
estatizar *vt L.Am.* nationalize
estatua *f* statue
estatuilla *f* statuette
estatura *f* height; ***de baja ~*** short; ***de mediana ~*** of medium height
estatus *m* status
estatutario *adj* statutory
estatuto *m* **1** statute **2**: ***~s*** *pl* articles of association
este[1] *m* east
este[2], **esta, estos, estas** *det singular* this; *plural* these; ***a todas estas*** in the meanwhile
éste, ésta, éstos, éstas *pron singular* this (one); *plural* these (ones)
estela *f* MAR wake; AVIA, *fig* trail
estelar *adj* star *atr*; ***figura ~*** *fig* star; ***momento ~*** *fig* highlight
estenotipia *f* **1** stenotype **2** *máquina* stenotype machine
estentóreo *adj* stentorian, booming
estepa *f* **1** steppe **2** BOT white-leaded rock rose
estepario *adj* steppe *atr*
éster *m* QUÍM ester
estera *f* mat
estercolero *m* dunghill, dung heap
estéreo I *adj* stereo **II** *m* stereo
estereofonía *f* stereophony
estereofónico *adj* stereophonic
estereotipado *adj* stereotyped
estereotipar ⟨1a⟩ *v/t* stereotype
estereotipo *m* stereotype
estéril *adj* **1** MED sterile **2** *trabajo, esfuerzo etc* futile
esterilidad *f* sterility
esterilización *f* sterilization
esterilizar ⟨1f⟩ *v/t tb persona* sterilize
esterilla *f* mat
esterlina *adj*: ***libra ~*** pound sterling
esternón *m* breastbone, sternum
estero *m Rpl* marsh
estertor *m* death rattle
esteta *m/f* esthete, *Br* aesthete
estética *f* **1** esthetics *sg*, *Br* aesthetics *sg*; ***centro de ~*** beauty parlor *o Br* parlour *o* salon **2** MED cosmetic surgery
esteticista *m/f* beautician
estético *adj* esthetic, *Br* aesthetic
estetoscopio *m* MED stethoscope
estiaje *m* **1** low water level **2** *duración* low water
estiba *f* MAR stowage
estibador *m*, **~a** *f* longshoreman, *Br* docker, *Br* stevedore
estibar ⟨1a⟩ *v/t* MAR stow
estiércol *m* **1** dung **2** (*abono*) manure

estigma *m* BOT, REL, *fig* stigma
estigmatizar ⟨1f⟩ *v/t* stigmatize
estilarse ⟨1a⟩ *v/r* be fashionable
estilete *m* **1** *arma* stiletto **2** HIST stylus
estilista *m/f* stylist; *de modas* designer
estilístico *adj* stylistic
estilizado *adj* stylized; *fig* slender
estilizar ⟨1f⟩ *v/t* stylize
estilo *m* style; ***al ~ de*** in the style of; ***algo por el ~*** something like that; ***son todos por el ~*** they're all the same
◇ **estilo directo** GRAM direct speech; **estilo indirecto** GRAM indirect speech; **estilo libre** DEP *en natación* freestyle
estilográfica *f* fountain pen
estima *f* esteem, respect; ***tener a alguien en mucha*** *o* ***gran ~*** hold s.o. in high regard *o* esteem
estimable *adj* estimable
estimación *f* **1** (*cálculo*) estimate **2** (*estima*) esteem, respect
estimar ⟨1a⟩ *v/t* **1** respect, hold in high regard; ***~ (en) poco*** not think much of **2** (*considerar*): ***estimo conveniente que*** I consider it advisable to **3** (*calcular*): ***~ en*** estimate at; *objeto* value at
estimarse *v/r* **1** (*calcularse*): ***se estima que el 80% de ...*** it is estimated that 80% of ... **2** (*considerarse*): ***si se estima necesario*** if it is thought *o* deemed necessary
estimativo *adj* estimated
estimulante I *adj* stimulating **II** *m* stimulant; ***~ del apetito*** appetite enhancer
estimular ⟨1a⟩ *v/t* **1** stimulate **2** (*animar*) encourage
estímulo *m* **1** stimulus **2** (*incentivo*) incentive
estío *m lit* summertime
estipendio *m* **1** (*sueldo*) salary **2** (*tarifa*) fee
estipulación *f* stipulation
estipular ⟨1a⟩ *v/t* stipulate
estirada *f en fútbol* flying save
estirado I *adj* snooty F, stuck-up F **II** *m* face-lift; ***hacerse un ~*** have a face-lift
estiramiento *m* **1** stretching **2** MED: ***~ (facial)*** face-lift
estirar ⟨1a⟩ *v/t* **1** stretch; *dinero* stretch, make go further; ***~ las piernas*** stretch one's legs; ***~ la pata*** F kick the bucket F **2** (*alisar*) smooth out; **estirarse** *v/r* stretch; *fig* last, go on
estirón *m* **1** (*tirón*) tug **2**: ***dar un ~*** F *de niño* shoot up
estirpe *f* stock
estival *adj* summer *atr*; ***época ~*** summertime
esto *pron* this; ***~ es*** that is to say; ***por ~*** this is why; ***a todo ~*** (*mientras tanto*) meanwhile; (*a propósito*) incidentally; ***en ~*** just then, at that moment; ***hablar de ~ y aquello*** talk of this and that
estocada *f* **1** sword thrust **2** *herida* sword wound **3** TAUR *thrust with the estoque that kills the bull*
Estocolmo *m* Stockholm
estofa *f*: ***de baja ~*** *desp* low-class *desp*
estofado I *adj* stewed **II** *m* stew
estofar ⟨1a⟩ *v/t* stew
estoicismo *m* stoicism
estoico I *adj* stoic(al) **II** *m*, **-a** *f* stoic
estola *f* stole
estomacal *adj* stomach *atr*
estómago *m* stomach; ***estar enfermo del ~*** have stomach problems; ***tener ~*** *fig* have a strong stomach; ***tengo el ~ en los talones*** *fig* F I'm starving, my stomach thinks my throat's cut F
estomatología *f* MED stomatology
Estonia *f* Estonia
estonio I *adj* Estonian **II** *m*, **-a** *f* Estonian **III** *m idioma* Estonian
estopa *f* tow; *tela* burlap
estoque *m* (bullfighter's) sword
estor *m* shade, *Br* blind
estorbar ⟨1a⟩ **I** *v/t* (*dificultar*) hinder; ***nos estorbaba*** he was in our way **II** *v/i* get in the way
estorbo *m* hindrance, nuisance
estornino *m* ZO starling
estornudar ⟨1a⟩ *v/i* sneeze
estornudo *m* sneeze
estos ☞ ***este***[2]
estoy *vb* ☞ ***estar***
estrábico *adj* squinting
estrabismo *m* squint
estrado *m* platform
◇ **estrado de testigos** JUR witness stand, *Br* witness box
estrafalario *adj* F eccentric; *ropa* outlandish
estragón *m* BOT tarragon
estragos *mpl* devastation *sg*; ***causar ~ entre*** wreak havoc among
estrambótico *adj* F eccentric; *ropa* outlandish

estrangulación *f* strangulation
estrangulador **I** *m*, **~a** *f* strangler **II** *m* TÉC: **~** (***de aire***) choke
estrangular ⟨1a⟩ *v/t* strangle; **estrangularse** *v/r* strangle o.s.
estraperlo *m* black market; ***de*** **~** on the black market
Estrasburgo *m* Strasbourg
estratagema *f* stratagem
estratega *m/f* strategist
estrategia *f* strategy
estratégico *adj* strategic
estratificación *f* GEOL stratification
estrato *m fig* stratum; **~ *social*** social stratum
estratosfera *f* stratosphere
estraza *f* **1** rag **2**: ***papel de*** **~** gray paper, *Br* grey paper
estrechamiento *m* narrowing
estrechar ⟨1a⟩ *v/t* **1** *ropa* take in **2** *mano* shake **3**: **~ *entre los brazos*** hug, embrace; **estrecharse** *v/r* narrow, get narrower
estrechez *f* **1** *fig* hardship; ***pasar estrecheces*** suffer hardship **2**: **~ *de miras*** narrow-mindedness
estrecho **I** *adj* **1** narrow; **~ *de miras*** narrow-minded **2** (*apretado*) tight; ***el vestido me queda*** **~** the dress is too tight **3** *amistad* close **4**: ***estar*** *o* ***ir*** **~*s*** be cramped (for space) **II** *m* strait, straits *pl*; ***el Estrecho de Gibraltar*** the Strait(s) of Gibraltar; ***Estrecho de Magallanes*** Magellan Straits
estregar ⟨1h & 1k⟩ *v/t* rub; **estregarse** *v/r* rub
estrella *f tb de cine etc* star; ***tener buena / mala*** **~** be born lucky / unlucky; ***nació con buena*** **~** he was born under a lucky star; ***ver las*** **~*s*** *fig* F see stars F; ***hotel de tres*** **~*s*** three-star hotel
◇ **estrella de cine** movie star, *Br tb* film star; **estrella fugaz** falling star, *Br tb* shooting star; **estrella de mar** ZO starfish; **estrella de Navidad** BOT star-of-Bethlehem; **estrella polar** Pole star
estrellado *adj* **1** (*en forma de estrella*) star-shaped **2** (*que tiene estrellas*) starry; ***cielo*** **~** star-studded sky
estrellar ⟨1a⟩ *v/t* smash; **~ *algo contra algo*** smash sth against sth; ***estrelló el coche contra un muro*** he smashed the car into a wall; **estrellarse** *v/r* crash (***contra*** into)
estrellato *m* stardom
estrellón *m Pe, Bol* crash
estremecedor *adj* terrifying
estremecer ⟨2d⟩ *v/t* shock, shake F; **estremecerse** *v/r* shake, tremble; *de frío* shiver; *de horror* shudder
estremecimiento *m* shaking, trembling; *de frío* shiver; *de horror* shudder
estrenar ⟨1a⟩ *v/t* **1** *ropa* wear for the first time, christen F; *objeto* try out, christen F; ***a*** **~** brand new; ***piso a*** **~** new apartment **2** *obra de teatro, película* premiere; **estrenarse** *v/r* make one's debut
estreno *m* **1** *obra de teatro, película* premiere **2** *de persona* debut **3**: ***estar de*** **~** be wearing new clothes
estreñimiento *m* constipation
estreñir ⟨3h & 3l⟩ *v/t* MED make constipated, constipate
estrépito *m* noise, racket
estrepitoso *adj* noisy
estreptococo *m* MED streptococcus
estreptomicina *f* MED streptomycin
estrés *m* stress
estresado *adj* under stress, stressed out
estresante *adj* stressful
estresar ⟨1a⟩ *v/t*: **~ *a alguien*** cause s.o. stress, subject s.o. to stress
estría *f en piel* stretch mark
estriado *adj* **1** *músculo, fibra* striated **2** *madera, piedra* grooved
estribación *f* spur; ***las estribaciones de los Pirineos*** the foothills of the Pyrenees
estribar ⟨1a⟩ *v/i*: **~ *en*** stem from, lie in
estribillo *m* chorus, refrain; *fig* frequently used word or expression
estribo *m* stirrup; ***perder los*** **~*s*** *fig* fly off the handle F; ***estar con un pie en el*** **~** *fig* be on the point of leaving
estribor *m* MAR starboard
estricnina *f* strychnine
estrictez *f S.Am.* strictness
estricto *adj* strict
estridencia *f* shrillness, stridency
estridente *adj* shrill, strident
estrofa *f* stanza, verse
estrógeno *m* estrogen, *Br tb* oestrogen
estroncio *m* strontium
estropajo *m* scourer
estropajoso *adj* **1** *persona* wiry **2** *boca* dry **3** *camisa* scruffy

estropeado *adj* (*averiado*) broken; ***está muy estropeada*** *fig* she is really showing her age
estropear ⟨1a⟩ *v/t* **1** *aparato* break **2** *plan* ruin, spoil; **estropearse** *v/r* **1** break down **2** *de comida* go off, go bad **3** *de plan* go wrong **4**: ***~ la vista*** ruin one's eyesight
estropicio *m* mess
estroquear ⟨1a⟩ *v/i L.Am. en béisbol* be struck out
estructura *f* structure
estructuración *f* **1** structure **2** *acción* structuring
estructural *adj* structural
estructurar ⟨1a⟩ *v/t* structure, organize; **estructurarse** *v/r*: ***~ en*** *de poema, organismo* consist of, be made up of
estruendo *m* racket, din
estruendoso *adj* thunderous
estrujar ⟨1a⟩ *v/t* **1** F crumple up, scrunch up F **2** *trapo* wring out **3** *persona* squeeze, hold tightly; **estrujarse** *v/r* squeeze (***en*** into)
estuario *m* estuary
estucado *m* stucco, plasterwork
estucar ⟨1g⟩ *v/t* stucco, plaster
estuche *m* case, box; ***~ de violín*** violin case
estuco *m* stuccowork
estudiado *adj fig sonrisa* affected; *gesto* studied
estudiantado *m* students *pl*, student body
estudiante *m/f* student
estudiantil *adj* student *atr*
estudiar ⟨1b⟩ *v/t & v/i* study
estudio *m* **1** *disciplina* study **2** *apartamento* studio, *Br* studio flat **3** *de cine, música* studio **4**: ***~s*** (***universitarios***) *pl* university education *sg*; ***tener ~s*** have a degree; ***una persona sin ~s*** a person with no formal education
◇ **estudio de mercado** market research; *resultado* market survey
estudioso *adj* studious
estufa *f* **1** heater **2** *L.Am.* (*cocina*) stove
◇ **estufa eléctrica** space heater, electric fire
estulticia *f* foolishness, folly
estupa *m* F narcotics cop F, *Br* member of the drug squad
estupefacción *f* amazement, stupefaction
estupefaciente *m* narcotic (drug)
estupefacto *adj* stupefied, speechless
estupendo *adj* fantastic, wonderful
estupidez *f* **1** *cualidad* stupidity **2** *acción* stupid thing
estúpido I *adj* stupid **II** *m*, **-a** *f* idiot
estupor *m* **1** astonishment, amazement **2** MED stupor
esturión *m* ZO sturgeon
estuve *vb* ☞ ***estar***
estuvo *vb* ☞ ***estar***
esvástica *f* swastika
ETA *f abr* (= ***Euskadi Ta Askatasuna***) ETA, *Basque separatist movement*
etano *m* QUÍM ethane
etapa *f* **1** DEP stage, leg **2** stage; ***por ~s*** in stages; ***quemar ~s*** cut corners
etarra *m/f* member of ETA
etc *abr* (= ***etcétera***) etc (= etcetera)
etcétera *m* etcetera, and so on; ***y un largo ~ de ...*** and a long list of ..., and many other ...
éter *m* ether
etéreo *adj* ethereal
eternidad *f* eternity
eternizarse ⟨1f⟩ *v/r fig* drag on; ***se eterniza arreglándose*** she takes forever to get ready
eterno *adj* eternal; ***la película se me hizo -a*** the movie seemed to go on for ever
ética *f* **1** *en filosofía* ethics *sg* **2** *comportamiento* principles *pl*
◇ **ética profesional** professional ethics *pl*
ético *adj* ethical
etílico *adj* ethyl *atr*; ***intoxicación -a*** alcohol poisoning
etimología *f* etymology
etimológico *adj* etymological
etíope *m/f & adj* Ethiopian
Etiopía *f* Ethiopia
etiqueta *f* **1** label; ***~ adhesiva*** sticky label **2** (*protocolo*) etiquette; ***traje de ~*** formal wear; ***ir*** *o* ***vestir de ~*** wear evening dress
etiquetado *m* labeling, *Br* labelling
etiquetar ⟨1a⟩ *v/t tb fig* label
etmoides *m inv* ANAT ethmoid bone
etnia *f* ethnic group
étnico *adj* ethnic
etnología *f* ethnology
etología *f* ethology
ETS *abr* (= ***escuela técnica superior***)

technical university
ETT *abr* (= ***empresa de trabajo temporal***) temp agency
eucalipto *m* BOT eucalyptus
eucaristía *f* Eucharist
eufemismo *m* euphemism
eufemístico *adj* euphemistic
eufonía *f* euphony
euforia *f* euphoria
eufórico *adj* euphoric
eunuco *m* eunuch
Eurasia *f* Eurasia
euro *m* euro
eurocheque *m* Eurocheck, *Br* Eurocheque
eurocomisario *m*, **-a** *f* Commission member
Eurocopa *f* DEP European Cup
Eurocuerpo *m* MIL Euro-army, European army
eurodiputado *m*, **-a** *f* MEP, member of the European Parliament
eurodólar *m* eurodollar
euroescéptico *m*, **-a** *f* euroskeptic, *Br* eurosceptic
euromercado *m* euromarket
Europa *f* Europe
europarlamentario *m*, **-a** *f* Member of the European Parliament, MEP
europeísmo *m* Europeanism
europeísta *m/f* pro-European
europeo I *adj* European **II** *m*, **-a** *f* European
eurotúnel *m* Channel Tunnel
eurozona *f* Eurozone, Euroland
Euskadi *m* Basque Country
eusquera *m/adj* Basque
eutanasia *f* euthanasia
evacuación *f* evacuation
evacuar ⟨1d⟩ *v/t* **1** evacuate **2**: ***~ el vientre*** have a bowel movement
evadir ⟨3a⟩ *v/t* avoid; *impuestos* evade; **evadirse** *v/r tb fig* escape
evaluable *adj* which can be assessed *o* evaluated
evaluación *f* **1** evaluation, assessment **2** (*prueba*) test
evaluar ⟨1e⟩ *v/t* assess, evaluate
evanescente *adj* fleeting, evanescent *fml*
evangélico *adj* evangelical
evangelio *m* gospel
evangelista *m* evangelist
evangelizar ⟨1f⟩ *v/t* evangelize
evaporación *f* evaporation
evaporarse ⟨1a⟩ *v/r* evaporate; *fig* F vanish into thin air
evasión *f tb fig* escape; ***literatura de ~*** escapist literature
◇ **evasión de capitales** flight of capital
◇ **evasión fiscal** tax evasion
evasiva *f* evasive reply
evasivo *adj* evasive
evento *m* event
eventual *adj* **1** possible; ***en el caso ~ de*** in the event of **2** *trabajo* casual, temporary
eventualidad *f* eventuality
eventualmente *adv* **1** possibly **2** *trabajar* on a casual basis
evidencia *f* **1** evidence, proof; ***poner en ~*** demonstrate **2**: ***poner a alguien en ~*** show s.o. up
evidenciar ⟨1b⟩ *v/t* demonstrate; **evidenciarse** *v/r*: ***se evidenciaba su nerviosismo*** his nervousness was evident, he was clearly nervous
evidente *adj* evident, clear
evitable *adj* avoidable
evitar ⟨1a⟩ *v/t* **1** avoid; ***no puedo ~lo*** I can't help it **2** (*impedir*) prevent **3** *molestias* save
evocación *f* evocation
evocar ⟨1g⟩ *v/t* evoke
evolución *f* **1** BIO evolution **2** (*desarrollo*) development
evolucionar ⟨1a⟩ *v/i* **1** BIO evolve **2** (*desarrollar*) develop
evolucionismo *m* BIO evolutionism
evolutivo *adj* evolutionary
ex I *pref* ex-; ***mi ~ marido*** F my former husband, my ex F **II** *m/f* F ex F
exabrupto *m* sharp remark
exacerbar ⟨1a⟩ *v/t* **1** exacerbate, make worse **2** (*irritar*) exasperate; **exacerbarse** *v/r* **1** worsen, become exacerbated *fml* **2** *de deseo, hambre* become more acute
exactamente *adv* exactly; ***más ~*** more precisely; ***¡~!*** exactly!, precisely!
exactitud *f* accuracy; *de medida* accuracy, precision
exacto *adj* **1** *medida* exact, precise; *informe* accurate **2**: ***¡~!*** exactly!, precisely!
exageración *f* exaggeration
exagerado *adj* exaggerated; ***¡eres un ~!***

you always overdo things *o* go too far!; *al contar una anécdota* you do exaggerate!
exagerar ⟨1a⟩ *v/t* exaggerate
exaltación *f* **1** (*alabanza*) exaltation **2** (*entusiasmo*) agitation, excitement
exaltado *adj* excited, worked up
exaltar ⟨1a⟩ *v/t* excite, get worked up; **exaltarse** *v/r* get excited, get worked up (***por*** about)
examen *m* **1** test, exam **2** MED examination **3** (*análisis*) study
◇ **examen de conducir** driving test
◇ **examen de ingreso** entrance exam
examinador *m*, **~a** *f* examiner
examinando *m*, **-a** *f* examinee
examinar ⟨1a⟩ *v/t* examine; **examinarse** *v/r* take an exam
exasperación *f* exasperation
exasperante *adj* exasperating
exasperar ⟨1a⟩ *v/t* exasperate; **exasperarse** *v/r* get exasperated
excarcelación *f* release (from prison)
excarcelar ⟨1a⟩ *v/t* release (from prison)
excavación *f* excavation
excavadora *f* digger
excavar ⟨1a⟩ *v/t* excavate; *túnel* dig
excedencia *f* extended leave of absence
excedentario *adj* surplus
excedente **I** *adj* **1** surplus **2** *empleado* on extended leave of absence **II** *m* surplus
exceder ⟨2a⟩ *v/t* exceed; **excederse** *v/r* go too far, get carried away
excelencia *f* **1** excellence; ***por ~*** par excellence **2**: ***Su Excelencia la señora embajadora*** Her Excellency the Ambassador
excelente *adj* excellent
excelentísimo *adj*: ***el ~ señor presidente …*** the President, President …
excelso *adj* lofty, sublime
excentricidad *f* eccentricity
excéntrico **I** *adj* eccentric **II** *m*, **-a** *f* eccentric
excepción *f* exception; ***a ~ de*** except for; ***sin ~*** without exception; ***de ~*** exceptional; ***como ~*** as an exception, as a one-off
excepcional *adj* exceptional
excepcionalmente *adv* for once
excepto *prp* except
exceptuar ⟨1e⟩ *v/t* except; ***exceptuando*** with the exception of, except for
excesivo *adj* excessive
exceso *m* excess; ***en ~*** *beber, fumar* to excess; *preocuparse* in excess, too much; ***ser amable en ~*** be extremely nice; ***trabajar en ~*** overwork
◇ **exceso de equipaje** excess baggage; **exceso de peso** excess weight; **exceso de velocidad** speeding
excipiente *m* MED excipient
excitable *adj* excitable
excitación *f* excitement, agitation
excitado *adj* **1** excited **2** *sexualmente* aroused
excitante **I** *adj* **1** exciting **2**: ***una bebida ~*** a stimulant **II** *m* stimulant
excitar ⟨1a⟩ *v/t* **1** excite **2** *sentimientos, sexualmente* arouse; **excitarse** *v/r* **1** get excited **2** *sexualmente* get aroused
exclamación *f* exclamation
exclamar ⟨1a⟩ *v/t* exclaim
excluir ⟨3g⟩ *v/t* **1** leave out (***de*** of), exclude (***de*** from) **2** *posibilidad* rule out, exclude
exclusión *f* exclusion; ***con ~ de*** with the exception of, except for
exclusiva *f* **1** *privilegio* exclusive rights *pl* (***de*** to) **2** *reportaje* exclusive
exclusivamente *adv* exclusively
exclusive *adv* exclusively; ***hasta junio ~*** up to but not including June
exclusividad *f* exclusiveness; ***no ser una ~ de*** not be exclusive to
exclusivo *adj* exclusive
Excmo. *abr* ☞ ***Excelentísimo***
excombatiente *m* (war) veteran, vet F, *Br* ex-serviceman
excomulgar ⟨1h⟩ *v/t* REL excommunicate
excomunión *f* excommunication
excoriar ⟨1a⟩ *v/t* chafe
excremento *m* excrement
excretar ⟨1a⟩ *v/t & v/i* excrete
excretor(io) *adj* ANAT excretory
exculpación *f* exoneration
exculpar ⟨1a⟩ *v/t* exonerate; **exculparse** *v/r* apologize
excursión *f* trip, excursion; ***~ a pie*** *por ciudad* walk; *por montañas* hike
excursionista *m/f* excursionist; *por ciudad* walker; *por montañas* hiker
excusa *f* **1** excuse **2**: ***~s*** *pl* apologies
excusable *adj* excusable
excusado **I** *adj* excused; ***~ es decir que***

... it goes without saying that ..., needless to say, ... **II** *m* bathroom
excusar ⟨1a⟩ *v/t* **1** excuse; **~ a alguien de hacer algo** excuse s.o. from doing sth **2**: **excuso decirte ...** I need not remind you ...; **excusarse** *v/r* apologize (**por hacer algo** for doing sth; **por algo** for sth)
execrable *adj* abominable, execrable *fml*
execrar ⟨1a⟩ *v/t* abhor
exégesis *f* exegesis
exención *f* exemption
◇ **exención fiscal** tax exemption
exento *adj* exempt (**de** from); **~ de impuestos** tax-exempt, tax-free
exequias *fpl* funeral *sg*
exfoliación *f* exfoliation
exfoliante *m* face scrub
exfoliar ⟨1b⟩ *v/t* exfoliate; **exfoliarse** *v/r* lose its leaves
exhalación *f*: **salir como una ~** *fig* rush *o* dash out
exhalar ⟨1a⟩ *v/t* **1** *olor* give off **2** *suspiro* heave, let out
exhaustivo *adj* exhaustive
exhausto *adj* exhausted
exhibición *f* **1** display, demonstration **2** *de película* screening, showing
exhibicionista *m/f* exhibitionist
exhibir ⟨3a⟩ *v/t* **1** show, display **2** *película* screen, show; *cuadro* exhibit **3** *Méx* (*pagar*) pay; **exhibirse** *v/r* **1** show o.s., let o.s. be seen **2** *de película* be showing
exhortación *f* exhortation
exhortar ⟨1a⟩ *v/t* exhort (**a** to)
exhumación *f* exhumation
exhumar ⟨1a⟩ *v/t* exhume
exigencia *f* demand
exigente *adj* demanding
exigible *adj* JUR enforceable
exigir ⟨3c⟩ *v/t* **1** demand **2** (*requirir*) call for, demand **3**: **le exigen mucho** they ask a lot of him
exigüidad *f* meagerness, *Br* meagreness
exiguo *adj* meager, *Br* meagre
exilado *L.Am.* ☞ **exiliado**
exiliado I *adj* exiled, in exile *pred* **II** *m*, **-a** *f* exile
exiliar ⟨1a⟩ *v/t* exile; **exiliarse** *v/r* go into exile
exilio *m* exile; **en el ~** in exile
eximente *adj* JUR: **circunstancias ~s** mitigating *o* extenuating circumstances
eximio *adj* distinguished, eminent
eximir ⟨3a⟩ *v/t* exempt (**de** from)
existencia *f* **1** existence **2** (*vida*) life **3**: **~s** *pl* COM supplies, stocks; **hasta que se agoten las ~s** while stocks last
existencial *adj* existential
existencialismo *m* existentialism
existencialista *m/f & adj* existentialist
existente *adj* **1** existing **2** *problema, situación* current, present
existir ⟨3a⟩ *v/i* exist; **existen muchos problemas** there are a lot of problems
exitazo *m* F smash hit
éxito *m* success; **con ~** successfully; **sin ~** without success; **~ (musical)** hit; **tener ~** be successful, be a success
◇ **éxito de taquilla** box office hit
◇ **éxito de ventas** best-seller
exitoso *adj* successful
Exmo. *abr* ☞ **Excelentísimo**
éxodo *m* exodus; **~ rural** rural exodus, flight from the land
exoneración *f de culpa* exoneration; *de obligación* exemption
exonerar ⟨1a⟩ *v/t* **1** *de culpa* exonerate; *de obligación* exempt **2**: **~ del cargo** relieve of duty
exorbitante *adj* exorbitant
exorcismo *m* exorcism
exorcista *m/f* exorcist
exorcizar ⟨1f⟩ *v/t* exorcize
exótico *adj* exotic
exotismo *m* exoticism
expandir ⟨3a⟩ *v/t* expand; **expandirse** *v/r* **1** expand **2** *de noticia* spread
expansión *f* **1** expansion; **en ~** growing, expanding; **estar en ~** be growing *o* expanding; **~ económica** economic growth *o* expansion **2** (*recreo*) recreation
expansionarse ⟨1a⟩ *v/r* **1** *de empresa, país* expand **2** (*relajarse*) relax **3** (*desahogarse*) open one's heart (**con** to)
expansivo *adj* expansive
expatriar ⟨1b⟩ *v/t* expel; **expatriarse** *v/r* **1** (*emigrar*) leave one's country **2** (*exiliarse*) go into exile
expectación *f* sense of anticipation; **causar mucha ~** arouse a great deal of excitement
expectante *adj* expectant
expectativa *f* **1** (*esperanza*) expectation; **responder a las ~s** live up to expecta-

tions **2**: ***estar a la ~ de algo*** be waiting for sth **3**: ***~s*** *pl* (*perspectivas*) prospects
◇ **expectativa de vida** life expectancy
expectoración *f* MED expectoration
expectorante I *adj* expectorant *atr* **II** *m* expectorant
expectorar ⟨1a⟩ *v/t* expectorate, cough up
expedición *f* expedition
expedicionario I *adj* expeditionary **II** *m*, **-a** *f* expedition member
expedidor *m*, **~a** *f* sender
expedientar ⟨1a⟩ *v/t*: ***~ a alguien*** take disciplinary action against s.o.
expediente *m* **1** file, dossier; ***cubrir el ~*** do only what is required **2** (*investigación*) investigation, inquiry; ***abrir un ~ a alguien*** take disciplinary action against s.o.
◇ **expediente académico** student record
◇ **expediente disciplinario** disciplinary proceedings *pl*
expedir ⟨3l⟩ *v/t* **1** *documento* issue **2** *mercancías* send, dispatch
expeditar ⟨1a⟩ *v/t L.Am.* **1** (*apresurar*) hurry **2** (*concluir*) finish, conclude
expeditivo *adj* expeditious
expedito *adj camino* clear
expeler ⟨2a⟩ *v/t* expel
expendedor *adj*: ***máquina ~a*** vending machine
◇ **expendedora de bebidas** drinks machine; **expendedora de billetes** ticket machine; **expendedora de tabaco** cigarette machine
expendeduría *f*: ***~ de tabaco*** *shop selling cigarettes*, *Br* tobacconist's (shop)
expendio *m L.Am.* store, shop
expensas *fpl*: ***a ~ de*** at the expense of
experiencia *f* experience; ***por ~*** from experience; ***sin ~*** inexperienced
experimentación *f* **1** *con drogas, nuevo método etc* experimentation **2** *en laboratorio* experiments *pl*
experimentado *adj* experienced; ***no ~*** inexperienced
experimental *adj* experimental
experimentar ⟨1a⟩ **I** *v/t* try out, experiment with **II** *v/i* experiment (***con*** on)
experimento *m* experiment
experto I *adj* expert; ***~ en hacer algo*** expert *o* very good at doing sth **II** *m*, **-a** *f* expert (***en*** on)
expiación *f* expiation, atonement
expiar ⟨1c⟩ *v/t* expiate, atone for
expiatorio *adj* expiatory
expiración *f* expiry, expiration
expirar ⟨1a⟩ *v/i* expire
explanada *f* open area; *junto al mar* esplanade
explanar ⟨1a⟩ *v/t* **1** *terreno* level **2** *fig* explain, set forth
explayarse ⟨1a⟩ *v/r* **1** speak at length; ***~ sobre algo*** expound on sth **2** (*desahogarse*) unburden o.s. **3** (*distraerse*) relax, unwind
explicable *adj* explainable, explicable
explicación *f* explanation; ***pedir explicaciones a alguien*** ask s.o. for an explanation; ***no tengo que dar explicaciones*** I don't need to explain myself; ***dar explicaciones de*** account for
explicar ⟨1g⟩ *v/t* explain; **explicarse** *v/r* **1** (*comprender*) understand; ***no me lo explico*** I can't understand it, I don't get it F **2** (*hacerse comprender*) express o.s.; ***¿me explico?*** any questions?, do you see what I'm getting at?
explicativo *adj* explanatory
explícito *adj* explicit
exploración *f* exploration
explorador *m*, **~a** *f* **1** explorer **2** MIL scout
explorar ⟨1a⟩ *v/t* explore
exploratorio *adj* exploratory
explosión *f* explosion; ***hacer ~*** go off, explode; ***~ de ira*** outburst of anger
◇ **explosión demográfica** population explosion
explosionar ⟨1a⟩ *v/t & v/i* explode
explosivo *m/adj* explosive
explotable *adj* **1** MIN *terreno*, *mina* workable, exploitable **2** *bosque*, *fig* exploitable
explotación *f* **1** *de mina*, *tierra* exploitation, working **2** *de negocio* running, operation **3** *de trabajador* exploitation
◇ **explotación a cielo abierto** MIN *actividad* open-cast mining; *mina* open-cast mine
explotador *m*, **~a** *f* **1** *de mina* operator **2** *desp* exploiter
explotar ⟨1a⟩ **I** *v/t* **1** *tierra*, *mina* work, exploit **2** *situación* take advantage of, exploit **3** *trabajador* exploit **II** *v/i* go off, explode; *fig* explode, blow a fuse F
expoliación *f* plunder, pillage

expoliar ⟨1b⟩ *v/t* plunder, pillage

expolio *m* plunder, pillage

exponente *m* exponent

exponer ⟨2r; *part* ***expuesto***⟩ *v/t* **1** *idea, teoría* set out, put forward **2** (*revelar*) expose **3** *pintura, escultura* exhibit, show **4** (*arriesgar*) risk; **exponerse** *v/r*: **~ a algo** (*arriesgarse*) lay o.s. open to sth

exportación *f* export

exportador *m*, **~a** *f* exporter

exportar ⟨1a⟩ *v/t* export

exposición *f* exhibition

◇ **exposición itinerante** traveling exhibition, *Br* travelling exhibition

◇ **exposición universal** world fair

exposímetro *m* FOT light meter

expositor *m*, **~a** *f* exhibitor

exprés *m* ☞ ***expreso***

expresamente *adv* specifically, expressly

expresar ⟨1a⟩ *v/t* express; **expresarse** *v/r* express o.s.

expresión *f* expression

expresionismo *m* expressionism

expresionista *m/f* & *adj* expressionist

expresivo *adj* expressive

expreso **I** *adj* express *atr*; ***tren ~*** express (train) **II** *m* **1** *tren* express (train) **2** *café* espresso

exprimidor *m* lemon squeezer; *eléctrico* juicer

exprimir ⟨3a⟩ *v/t* squeeze; (*explotar*) exploit

expropiación *f* expropriation

◇ **expropiación forzosa** compulsory purchase

expropiar ⟨1b⟩ *v/t* expropriate

expuesto **I** *part* ☞ ***exponer*** **II** *adj* **1** exposed **2** (*peligroso*) dangerous

expugnar ⟨1a⟩ *v/t* take by storm

expulsar ⟨1a⟩ *v/t* **1** expel, throw out F **2** DEP expel from the game, *Br* send off

expulsión *f* **1** expulsion **2** DEP expelling from the game, *Br* sending off

expulsor *m* TÉC ejector

expurgar ⟨1h⟩ *v/t* expurgate

expuso *vb* ☞ ***exponer***

exquisitez *f* **1** *cualidad* exquisiteness **2** (*cosa exquisita*) delicacy

exquisito *adj* **1** *comida* delicious **2** (*bello*) exquisite **3** (*refinado*) refined

extasiarse ⟨1c⟩ *v/r* be enraptured, go into raptures

éxtasis *m tb droga* ecstasy

extender ⟨2g⟩ *v/t* **1** *brazos* stretch out; *tela, papel* spread out; ***me extendió la mano*** she held out her hand to me **2** (*untar*) spread **3** (*ampliar*) extend; **extenderse** *v/r* **1** *de campos* stretch **2** *de influencia* extend **3** (*difundirse*) spread **4** (*durar*) last **5** (*explayarse*) go into detail

extendido **I** *part* ☞ ***extender*** **II** *adj* **1** *costumbre* widespread **2** *brazos* outstretched; *mapa* spread out

extensamente *adv* extensively

extensible *adj* extending

extensión *f* **1** *tb* TELEC extension; ***por ~*** by extension **2** *superficie* expanse, area; ***en toda la ~ de la palabra*** in the broadest sense of the word

extensivo *adj* extensive; ***hacer algo ~ a*** extend sth to, apply sth to; ***ser ~ a*** extend to, apply to

extenso *adj* **1** extensive, vast; *informe* lengthy, long **2**: ***por ~*** in full

extensor **I** *adj* extensor **II** *m* DEP chest expander

extenuación *f* exhaustion

extenuante *adj* exhausting

extenuar ⟨1e⟩ *v/t* exhaust, tire out; **extenuarse** *v/r* exhaust o.s., tire o.s. out

exterior **I** *adj* **1** *aspecto* external, outward; *capa* outer; ***la parte ~ del edificio*** the exterior *o* the outside of the building **2** *apartamento* overlooking the street **3** POL foreign; ***deudas ~es*** foreign debt *sg*
II *m* **1** (*fachada*) exterior, outside **2** *aspecto* exterior, outward appearance **3**: ***viajar al ~*** (*al extranjero*) travel abroad **4**: ***~es*** *pl* TV *etc* location shots; ***rodar en ~es*** film on location

◇ **exterior central** *en béisbol* center field

◇ **exterior centro** *en béisbol* center fielder

exteriorizar ⟨1f⟩ *v/t* externalize

exteriormente *adv* outwardly, on the outside, externally

exterminación *f* ☞ ***exterminio***

exterminar ⟨1a⟩ *v/t* exterminate, wipe out

exterminio *m* extermination

externalización *f* **1** PSI externalization **2** COM outsourcing

externalizar ⟨1f⟩ *v/t* **1** PSI externalize **2** COM outsource
externo I *adj* **1** *aspecto* external, outward; *influencia* external, outside; *capa* outer **2** *deuda* foreign **II** *m*, **-a** *f* EDU *student who attends a boarding school but returns home each evening*, *Br* day boy / girl
extinción *f*: ***en peligro de ~*** threatened with extinction, facing extinction
extinguidor *m L.Am.* ~ (***de incendios***) (fire) extinguisher
extinguir ⟨3d⟩ *v/t* **1** BIO, ZO wipe out **2** *fuego* extinguish, put out; **extinguirse** *v/r* **1** BIO, ZO become extinct, die out **2** *de fuego* go out **3** *de plazo* expire
extinto *adj* extinct
extintor *m* fire extinguisher
extirpación *f* **1** MED removal **2** *de vicio* eradication
extirpar ⟨1a⟩ *v/t* **1** MED remove **2** *vicio* eradicate, stamp out
extorsión *f* extortion
extorsionar ⟨1a⟩ *v/t* extort money from
extorsionista *m/f* extortionist
extra I *adj* **1** *excelente* top quality **2** *adicional* extra; ***horas ~*** *pl* overtime *sg*; ***paga ~*** extra month's pay **II** *m/f de cine* extra **III** *m* **1** *gasto* additional expense **2** AUTO extra
extracción *f* **1** extraction; ***~ de sangre*** taking blood **2**: ***de baja ~*** of lowly origins, of humble extraction
extracomunitario *adj* non-EU
extraconyugal *adj* extramarital
extracto *m* **1** extract **2** (*resumen*) summary **3** GASTR, QUÍM extract, essence; ***~ de carne*** beef extract
◇ **extracto de cuenta** bank statement
extractor *m* extractor
◇ **extractor de humos** extractor fan
extradición *f* extradition
extraditar ⟨1a⟩ *v/t* extradite
extraer ⟨2p⟩ *v/t* **1** extract, pull out **2** *conclusión* draw
extraescolar *adj* after-school
extrafino *adj* extra fine
extraíble *adj* removable
extrajudicial *adj* out-of-court
extralimitarse ⟨1a⟩ *v/r* go too far, exceed one's authority
extramarital *adj* extramarital
extramatrimonial *adj* extramarital
extramuros *adv* outside the city, out of town
extranjería *f*: ***ley de ~*** immigration laws *pl*; ***oficina de ~*** INS, Immigration and Naturalization Service
extranjerismo *m* LING loan word
extranjero I *adj* foreign **II** *m*, **-a** *f* foreigner **III** *m*: ***en el ~*** abroad
extranjis: ***de ~*** F on the quiet F, on the sly F
extrañar ⟨1a⟩ *v/t L.Am.* miss; **extrañarse** *v/r* be surprised (***de*** at); ***no me extrañaría*** I wouldn't be surprised; ***no es de ~ que*** it's not surprising that
extrañeza *f* **1** strangeness, oddness **2** (*sorpresa*) surprise, astonishment
extraño I *adj* strange, odd **II** *m*, **-a** *f* stranger
extraoficial *adj* unofficial
extraordinario I *adj* extraordinary; ***horas -as*** overtime *sg* **II** *m* special issue
extraparlamentario *adj* extraparliamentary
extrapolable *adj*: ***esta solución no es ~ a otras partes del mundo*** this solution cannot be exported to other parts of the world
extrapolación *f* extrapolation
extrapolar ⟨1a⟩ *v/t* extrapolate
extrarradio *m* outlying districts *pl*, outskirts *pl*
extrasensorial *adj* extrasensory
extraterrestre *adj* extraterrestial, alien
extravagancia *f* eccentric behavior *o Br* behaviour; ***una de sus ~s*** one of his eccentricities
extravagante I *adj* eccentric **II** *m/f* eccentric
extravertido I *adj* extrovert **II** *m*, **-a** *f* extrovert
extraviado *adj* **1** *lugar* out of the way **2** *perro* lost, stray
extraviar ⟨1c⟩ *v/t* lose, mislay; **extraviarse** *v/r* get lost, lose one's way
extravío *m* loss
extremadamente *adv* extremely
extremado *adj* extreme
extremar ⟨1a⟩ *v/t* maximize; **extremarse** *v/r* take great care (***en*** over)
extremaunción *f* REL extreme unction
extremeño I *adj* Extremaduran **II** *m*, **-a** *f* Extremaduran
extremidad *f* **1** end **2**: ***~es*** *pl* ANAT extremities

extremismo *m* POL extremism
extremista I *adj* extreme **II** *m/f* POL extremist
extremo I *adj* **1** extreme **2** POL: ***la -a derecha / izquierda*** the far right / left **II** *m* **1** extreme; ***ir o pasar de un ~ a otro*** go from one extreme to another; ***los ~s se tocan*** opposites attract; ***en ~*** in the extreme **2** *parte primera o última* end **3** (*punto*) point; ***llegar al ~ de*** reach the point of **III** *m/f*: ***~ derecho / izquierdo*** DEP right / left wing
extrínseco *adj* extrinsic
extrovertido I *adj* extrovert **II** *m*, **-a** *f* extrovert
exuberancia *f* **1** exuberance **2** *de vegetación* lushness
exuberante *adj* **1** exuberant **2** *vegetación* lush
exudación *f* exudation
exudar ⟨1a⟩ *v/t* exude
exultante *adj* elated
exultar ⟨1a⟩ *v/i* exult, rejoice (***de*** with)
exvoto *m* ex-voto, votive offering
eyaculación *f* ejaculation
eyacular ⟨1a⟩ *v/t & v/i* ejaculate
eyección *f* ejection
eyectar ⟨1a⟩ *v/t* eject

F

fa *m* F; ***~ sostenido*** F sharp
fabada *f* GASTR *Asturian stew with pork sausage, bacon and beans*
fábrica *f* **1** plant, factory; ***en ~*** COM *de precio* ex works **2** ARQUI stonework; ***de ~*** stone *atr*
◇ **fábrica de sueños** *fig* dream factory
fabricación *f* manufacturing
◇ **fabricación en serie** mass production
fabricante *m/f* manufacturer, maker
fabricar ⟨1g⟩ *v/t* manufacture, make
fabril *adj* manufacturing *atr*
fábula *f* **1** fable; ***de ~*** F fabulous, terrific **2** (*mentira*) lie
fabulador *m*, **~a** *f fig* person with a vivid imagination; ***es un ~*** he has a vivid imagination, he lets his imagination run away with him
fabular ⟨1a⟩ *v/t* make up, invent
fabulista *m/f* fabulist, writer of fables
fabuloso *adj* fabulous, marvelous, *Br* marvellous
facción *f* **1** POL faction **2**: ***facciones*** *pl* (*rasgos*) features
faccioso I *adj* rebel *atr* **II** *m*, **-a** *f* rebel
faceta *f tb fig* facet
facha I *f* **1** look **2** (*cara*) face **II** *m/f desp* fascist
fachada *f tb fig* façade
facho *m*, **-a** *f L.Am. desp* fascist
facial *adj* facial
fácil I *adj* **1** easy; ***~ de entender*** easy to understand; ***~ de manejar*** easy to use, user-friendly; ***~ de usar*** user-friendly; ***eso se dice ~*** that's easy for you / him etc to say, that's easily said; ***ponerlo ~ a alguien*** make things *o* life easy for s.o.; ***sería lo más ~*** that would be easiest *o* simplest
2: ***mujer ~*** loose woman
3: ***es ~ que*** it's likely that
facilidad *f* ease; ***con ~*** easily; ***~ de manejo / uso*** user-friendliness; ***tener ~ para algo*** have a gift for sth; ***tener ~ de palabra*** have a way with words
◇ **facilidades de pago** credit facilities, credit terms
facilitar ⟨1a⟩ *v/t* **1** facilitate, make easier **2** (*hacer factible*) make possible **3** *medios, dinero etc* provide
fácilmente *adv* easily
facilón *adj* F very easy, dead easy F
facineroso I *adj* criminal **II** *m*, **-a** *f* criminal
facistol *m* lectern
facsímil(e) *m* facsimile
factible *adj* feasible
fáctico *adj* factual
factor *m* factor
◇ **factor de protección** protection factor; **factor Rhesus** rhesus factor; **factor de riesgo** risk factor
factoría *f esp L.Am.* plant, factory
factoring *m* COM factoring
factura *f* COM invoice; *de luz, gas etc* bill; ***seguro que luego te pasa la ~*** I'm sure there'll be a price to pay; ***to-***

dos los excesos de su juventud le están empezando a pasar ~ he's starting to pay the price for all his youthful excesses, all his youthful excesses are starting to take their toll

facturación *f* **1** COM invoicing **2** (*volumen de negocio*) turnover **3** AVIA check-in

facturar ⟨1a⟩ *v/t* **1** COM invoice, bill **2** *volumen de negocio* turn over **3** AVIA check in

facultad *f* **1** EDU, *de la vista* faculty **2** (*autoridad*) authority **3**: **~es** *pl mentales* faculties

facultar ⟨1a⟩ *v/t*: ***~ a alguien para hacer algo*** authorize s.o. to do sth

facultativo I *adj* optional **II** *m*, **-a** *f* doctor, physician

facundo *adj* eloquent

faena *f* **1** task, job; ***~s agrícolas*** farmwork *sg*; ***~s de la casa*** household chores **2** TAUR *series of passes with the cape* **3**: ***hacer una ~ a alguien*** play a dirty trick on s.o. **4** *Chi*, *Rpl de ganado* slaughtering

faenar ⟨1a⟩ **I** *v/t Chi*, *Rpl ganado* slaughter **II** *v/i* fish

fagot MÚS **I** *m instrumento* bassoon **II** *m/f músico* bassoonist

faisán *m* ZO pheasant

faja *f prenda interior* girdle; (*banda*) sash

fajar ⟨1a⟩ **I** *v/t herida* dress; *brazo*, *pierna* bandage; *paquete* tie up **II** *v/i Méx* F (*enrollarse*) neck F; **fajarse** *v/r Méx*, *Ven* F **1** get into a fight **2** (*enrollarse*) neck F

fajín *m* sash

fajo *m de billetes* wad; *de periódicos* bundle

falacia *f* **1** fallacy **2** (*engaño*) fraud

falange *f* **1** ANAT phalange **2** MIL phalanx

falaz *adj* false

falda *f* **1** skirt; ***ser muy aficionado a las ~s*** *fig* be a ladies' man; ***por un asunto de ~s*** *dejar de hablarse* because of some woman or other; ***por un asunto de ~s con una de las empleadas*** because of his affair with one of the employees **2** *de montaña* side

◇ **falda pantalón** divided skirt, culottes *pl*; **falda plisada** pleated skirt; **falda recta** straight skirt; **falda tableada** pleated skirt

faldero *adj*: ***perro ~*** lap dog

faldón *m* tail

falencia *f L.Am.* bankruptcy

falibilidad *f* fallibility

falible *adj* fallible

fálico *adj* phallic; ***símbolo ~*** phallic symbol

falla *f* **1** GEOL fault; ***la ~ de San Andrés*** the San Andreas Fault **2** *de fabricación* flaw **3**: **~s** *pl celebrations held in Valencia to mark the feast day of St Joseph*

fallar ⟨1a⟩ **I** *v/i* **1** fail **2** (*no acertar*) miss **3** *de sistema etc* go wrong **4** JUR find (***en favor de*** for; ***en contra de*** against) **5**: ***~ a alguien*** let s.o. down **II** *v/t* **1** JUR pronounce judg(e)ment in **2** *pregunta* get wrong **3**: ***~ el tiro*** miss

fallecer ⟨2d⟩ *v/i* pass away

fallecido *m*, **-a** *f* deceased

fallecimiento *m* demise, passing

fallero 1 *adj relating to the Fallas* **2** *m*, **-a** *f person taking part in the Fallas*

fallido *adj* **1** *esfuerzo* failed, unsuccessful **2**: ***disparo ~*** DEP miss

fallo *m* **1** mistake; ***~ del sistema*** INFOR system error **2** TÉC fault **3** JUR judg(e)ment

◇ **fallo cardíaco** heart failure

◇ **fallo humano** human error

falo *m* phallus

falocracia *f* male chauvinism

falsamente *adv* falsely

falseador *m*, **~a** *f* ☞ ***falsificador***

falseamiento *m de la verdad*, *los hechos* distortion

falsear ⟨1a⟩ *v/t* falsify

falsedad *f* **1** falseness **2** (*mentira*) lie

falsete *m* MÚS falsetto

falsificación *f de moneda* counterfeiting; *de documentos*, *firma* forgery

falsificador *m*, **~a** *f de moneda* counterfeiter; *de documentos*, *firma* forger

falsificar ⟨1g⟩ *v/t moneda* counterfeit; *documento*, *firma* forge, falsify

falso *adj* **1** false **2** *joyas* fake; *documento*, *firma* forged; *monedas*, *billetes* counterfeit **3**: ***jurar*** *o* ***declarar en ~*** commit perjury **4** *persona* false

falta *f* **1** (*escasez*) lack, want; ***~ de*** lack of, shortage of; ***a*** *o* ***por ~ de*** due to *o* for lack of; ***por ~ de tiempo*** due to *o* for *o* through lack of time; ***por ~ de capital*** for lack of capital

2 (*error*) mistake; ***sin ~s*** perfect

3 (*ausencia*) absence; ***echar en ~ a alguien*** miss s.o.
4 *en tenis* fault; *en fútbol, baloncesto* foul; ***hacer una ~*** *en fútbol* commit a foul, foul; ***hacerle ~ a alguien*** foul s.o.; ***doble ~*** *en tenis* double fault; ***cometer doble ~*** double-fault
5 DEP (*tiro libre*) free kick; ***lanzar una ~*** take a free kick; ***marcar de ~*** score from a free kick; ***pitar ~*** blow one's whistle for a free kick
6: ***hacer ~*** be necessary; ***buena ~ le hace*** it's about time; ***no me hace ~*** I don't need it; ***ni ~ que hace*** he / it won't be missed, he's / it's no great loss
7: ***sin ~*** without fail
◇ **falta antideportiva** *en baloncesto* unsportsmanlike foul; **falta en ataque** *en baloncesto* offensive foul; **falta libre** *en fútbol* free kick; **falta libre directa** *en fútbol* direct free kick; **falta libre indirecta** *en fútbol* indirect free kick; **falta personal** *en baloncesto* personal foul

faltante *m L.Am.* deficit

faltar ⟨1a⟩ *v/i* **1** be missing; ***cuando falten mis padres*** when my parents die **2** (*quedar*): ***falta una hora*** there's an hour to go; ***faltan 10 kilómetros*** there are 10 kilometers to go; ***sólo falta hacer la salsa*** there's only the sauce to do; ***falta poco para las diez*** it's almost *o* nearly ten o'clock; ***falta poco para que empiece la película*** it won't be long before the film starts, the film will be starting soon; ***faltó poco para que me cayera*** I almost *o* nearly fell; ***y por si faltaba algo …*** and as if that wasn't enough …
3: ***~ a*** be absent from; ***~ a clase*** miss class, be absent from class
4: ***~ a alguien*** be disrespectful to s.o.; ***~ a su palabra*** not keep one's word
5: ***¡no faltaba*** *o* ***faltaría más!*** (*por supuesto*) certainly!, of course!; (*de ninguna manera*) certainly not!; ***¡lo que faltaba!*** that's all I / we *etc* needed!

falto *adj*: ***~ de*** lacking in, devoid of; ***~ de recursos*** short of resources

faltón *adj* F nervy F, *Br* cheeky F; ***es muy ~*** he's got real nerve, *Br* he's got the cheek of the devil

faltriquera *f* pouch

falúa *f* MAR tender; *de vela* felucca

fama *f* **1** fame; ***de ~ mundial*** world-famous **2** (*reputación*) reputation; ***tener mala ~*** have a bad reputation

famélico *adj* starving

familia *f* family; ***sentirse como en ~*** feel at home; ***ser de la ~*** be one of the family; ***de buena ~*** from a good family
◇ **familia numerosa** large family

familiar I *adj* **1** family *atr*; ***envase ~*** family-size pack **2** (*conocido*) familiar; ***su cara me es*** *o* ***resulta ~*** his face is familiar **3** LING colloquial **II** *m/f* relation, relative

familiaridad *f* familiarity

familiarizar ⟨1f⟩ *v/t* familiarize (***con*** with); **familiarizarse** *v/r* familiarize o.s. (***con*** with)

famoso I *adj* famous **II** *m*, **-a** *f* celebrity; ***los ~s*** celebrities, famous people *pl*

fan *m/f* fan

fanático I *adj* fanatical **II** *m*, **-a** *f* fanatic

fanatismo *m* fanaticism

fandango *m* fandango

faneca *f type of fish common in the Mediterranean*

fanfarria *f* brass band

fanfarrón I *adj* boastful **II** *m*, **-ona** *f* boaster

fanfarronada *f* boast

fanfarronear ⟨1a⟩ *v/i* boast, brag

fanfarronería *f* boasting, bragging

fango *m tb fig* mud; ***aplicación de ~*** MED mud wrap; ***arrastrar por el ~*** *fig* drag through the mud; ***cubrir de ~*** *fig* cast slurs on, attack; ***su nombre quedó cubierto de ~*** his name was mud F

fangoso *adj* muddy

fantasear ⟨1a⟩ *v/i* fantasize

fantasía *f* **1** fantasy **2** (*imaginación*) imagination **3**: ***joyas de ~*** costume jewelry *o Br* jewellery

fantasioso *adj*: ***es una -a*** she tends to imagine things *o* to fantasize

fantasma I *m* ghost; *fig* specter, *Br* spectre **II** *m/f* F show-off F

fantasmagórico *adj* fantastical, dreamlike

fantasmal *adj* ghostly

fantasmón *adj* F bigheaded F

fantástico *adj* fantastic

fantoche *m* puppet; F sight F

fanzine *m* fanzine

F

faquir *m* fakir
faralá *m*: ***traje de faralaes*** flounced dress (*as worn by flamenco dancers*)
farándula *f* show business; ***el mundo de la ~*** show business, show biz F
faraónico *adj* **1** of the pharaohs, Pharaonic *fml* **2** *fig* massive, enormous
fardar ⟨1a⟩ *v/i*: ***~ de algo*** F boast about sth, show off about sth
fardo *m* bundle
farero *m* lighthouse-keeper
farfullar ⟨1a⟩ *v/t & v/i* gabble, jabber
farfullero *m*, **-a** *f* jabberer
faringe *f* ANAT pharynx
faringitis *f* MED inflammation of the pharynx, pharyngitis
fariña *f S.Am.* manioc flour, cassava
fario *m*: ***mal ~*** F bad luck; ***le persigue el mal ~*** he is plagued by bad luck
farisaico *adj fig* hypocritical
fariseo *m*, **-a** *f fig* hypocrite
farmacéutico I *adj* pharmaceutical; ***industria -a*** pharmaceutical industry, pharmaceuticals **II** *m*, **-a** *f* pharmacist, *Br* chemist
farmacia *f* **1** pharmacy, *Br tb* chemist's **2** *estudios* pharmacy
◇ **farmacia de guardia** 24-hour pharmacy, *Br tb* emergency chemist
fármaco *m* medicine
farmacología *f* pharmacology
farmacólogo *m*, **-a** *f* pharmacologist
faro *m* **1** MAR lighthouse **2** AUTO headlight, headlamp
◇ **faro antiniebla** fog light
◇ **faro halógeno** halogen headlight *o* headlamp
farol *m* **1** lantern **2** (*farola*) streetlight, streetlamp **3** *en juegos de cartas* bluff; ***tirarse un ~*** F (*presumir*) shoot a line F
farola *f* streetlight, streetlamp
faroleo *m* F shooting a line F
farolero *m*, **-a** *f* blowhard F, boaster
farolillo *m* **1** Chinese lantern **2** BOT Canterbury bell **3**: ***ser el ~ rojo*** *fig* F be bottom of the league
farra *f L.Am.* F partying; ***irse de ~*** go out on the town F
fárrago *m* jumble, farrago *fml*
farragoso *adj texto* dense
farrear ⟨1a⟩ *v/i L.Am.* F go out on the town F
farrista *adj L.Am.* hard-drinking
farruco *adj* F cocky F
farsa *f tb fig* farce
farsante *m/f* fraud, fake
FAS *fpl abr* (= ***Fuerzas Armadas***) armed forces
fas: ***por ~ o por nefas*** for some reason or another
fascículo *m* installment, *Br* instalment
fascinación *f* fascination
fascinante *adj* fascinating
fascinar ⟨1a⟩ *v/t* fascinate
fascismo *m* fascism
fascista *m/f & adj* fascist
fase *f* phase
faso *m Rpl* F cigarette, *Br tb* fag F
fastidiado *adj*: ***estoy ~*** F I'm not feeling too great
fastidiar ⟨1b⟩ **I** *v/t* **1** annoy; ***¿no te fastidia?*** F would you believe *o* credit it! **2** F (*estropear*) spoil **II** *v/i*: ***¡no fastidies!*** F you're kidding! F; **fastidiarse** *v/r* **1** grin and bear it; ***si no les gusta que se fastidien*** if they don't like it they can lump it
fastidio *m* annoyance; ***¡qué ~!*** what a nuisance!
fastidioso *adj* annoying
fasto *m* splendor, *Br* splendour
fastuosidad *f* lavishness
fastuoso *adj* lavish
fatal I *adj* **1** fatal **2** (*muy malo*) dreadful, awful **II** *adv* very badly; ***lo he pasado ~*** F I had an awful time
fatalidad *f* misfortune
fatalismo *m* fatalism
fatalista I *adj* fatalistic **II** *m/f* fatalist
fatídico *adj* fateful
fatiga *f* tiredness, fatigue
fatigado *adj* tired
fatigar ⟨1h⟩ *v/t* tire; **fatigarse** *v/r* get tired
fatuo *adj* **1** conceited **2** (*necio*) fatuous
fauces *fpl* ZO jaws
faul *f L.Am.* foul
faulear ⟨1a⟩ *v/t L.Am.* foul
fauna *f* fauna
fauno *m* MYTH faun
favor *m* **1** favor, *Br* favour; ***hacer un ~*** do a favor; ***¿me harías el ~ de echarme esta carta?*** could you do me a favor and mail this letter?, could you (please) mail this letter for me?; ***haz el ~ de callarte*** would you please be quiet!; ***pedir un ~ a alguien*** ask s.o. for a favor **2** *en locuciones*: ***a ~ de*** in

favor *o Br* favour of; ***por ~*** please
favorable *adj* favorable, *Br* favourable
favorecedor *adj* flattering
favorecer ⟨2d⟩ *v/t* **1** favor, *Br* favour **2** *de ropa, color* suit
favorecido *m*, **-a** *f L.Am.* winner
favoritismo *m* favoritism, *Br* favouritism
favorito I *adj* favorite, *Br* favourite **II** *m*, **-a** *f* favorite, *Br* favourite
fax *m* fax; ***enviar un ~ a alguien*** send s.o. a fax, fax s.o.
faxear ⟨1a⟩ *v/t* fax, send by fax
fayuca *f Méx* smuggling
fayuquear ⟨1a⟩ *v/t Méx* smuggle
fayuquero *m*, **-a** *f Méx* dealer in smuggled goods
faz *f* face
F.C. *abr* (= ***Fútbol Club***) FC (= Football Club)
fdo. *abr* (= ***firmado***) signed
fe *f* **1** faith (***en*** in); ***tener ~ en*** believe in, have faith in; ***la ~ mueve montañas*** faith moves mountains **2** (*intención*): ***de buena / mala ~*** in good / bad faith **3**: ***dar ~ de*** testify to; ***dar ~ de que*** vouch for the fact that; JUR testify that ◇ **fe de erratas** errata *pl*
fealdad *f* ugliness
feb. *abr* (= ***febrero***) Feb. (= February)
febrero *m* February
febrícula *f* slight fever, *Br* slight temperature
febril *adj* feverish
fecal *adj* fecal, *Br tb* faecal
fecha *f* date; ***hasta la ~*** to date; ***en estas ~s*** at this time of year; ***sin ~*** undated ◇ **fecha de caducidad** *de medicamento* expiry date; *de alimento* use-by date; **fecha límite de consumo** best before date; **fecha de nacimiento** date of birth
fechador *m Chi, Méx* postmark
fechar ⟨1a⟩ *v/t* date; ***fechado el …*** dated the …
fechoría *f* misdemeanor, *Br* misdemeanour
fécula *f* starch
fecundación *f* fertilization ◇ **fecundación artificial** artificial insemination ◇ **fecundación in vitro** MED in vitro fertilization
fecundar ⟨1a⟩ *v/t* fertilize
fecundidad *f* fertility, fecundity *fml*
fecundizar ⟨1f⟩ *v/t* fertilize
fecundo *adj* fertile, fecund *fml*
FEDER *m abr* (= ***Fondo Europeo de Desarrollo Regional***) ERDF (= European Regional Development Fund)
federación *f* federation
federal *adj* federal
federalismo *m* federalism
federar ⟨1a⟩ *v/t* form into a federation, federate; **federarse** *v/r* form a federation, federate
féferes *mpl L.Am.* junk *sg* F, bits and pieces F
felación *f* fellatio
feldespato *m* MIN feldspar
felicidad *f* **1** happiness **2**: ***¡~es!*** congratulations!
felicitación *f* **1** letter of congratulations **2**: ***¡felicitaciones!*** congratulations!
felicitar ⟨1a⟩ *v/t* congratulate (***por*** on)
feligrés *m*, **-esa** *f* REL parishioner
felino I *adj tb fig* feline **II** *m*, **-a** *f* feline, cat
feliz *adj* happy; ***¡~ Navidad!*** Merry Christmas!; ***¡~ Año Nuevo!*** Happy New Year!
felonía *f* crime, felony
felpa *f* toweling, *Br* towelling
felpudo I *adj abrigo, tejido* plush; *pijama, sábanas* soft, downy **II** *m* doormat
femenil *adj Méx* women's *atr*
femenino I *adj* **1** feminine **2** *moda, equipo* women's *atr* **II** GRAM feminine
femin(e)idad *f* femininity
feminismo *m* feminism
feminista *m/f & adj* feminist
fémur *m* ANAT femur
fenecer ⟨2d⟩ *v/i* pass away
fenecimiento *m* passing, demise *fml*
fenicio I *adj* Phoenician **II** *m*, **-a** *f* Phoenician
fénico *adj*: ***ácido ~*** QUÍM phenol, carbolic acid
fénix *m* MYTH phenix, *Br* phoenix
fenol *m* QUÍM phenol, carbolic acid
fenomenal I *adj* F fantastic F, phenomenal F **II** *adv*: ***lo pasé ~*** F I had a fantastic time F
fenómeno I *m* **1** phenomenon **2** *persona* genius **II** *adj* F fantastic F, great F
fenotipo *m* BIO phenotype
feo I *adj* ugly; *fig* nasty; ***la(s) cosa(s) se pone(n) ~(s)*** *fig* things are looking

F

grim **II** *m*: ***hacer un ~ a alguien*** F snub s.o. **III** *adv Méx oler, saber* bad
féretro *m* casket, coffin
feria *f* **1** COM fair **2** *L.Am.* (*mercado*) market **3** *Méx* (*calderilla*) small change
◇ **feria de muestras** trade fair
feriado I *adj L.Am.* ***día ~*** (public) holiday **II** *m L.Am.* (public) holiday; ***abierto ~s*** open on public holidays
ferial I *adj*: ***recinto ~*** fairground **II** *m* fair
feriante *m/f* exhibitor
fermentación *f* fermentation
fermentar ⟨1a⟩ *v/t* ferment
fermento *m* ferment
ferocidad *f* ferocity
feroz *adj* fierce; (*cruel*) cruel
férreo *adj* **1** *tb fig* iron *atr* **2** *del ferrocarril* rail *atr*
ferretería *f* hardware store, *Br tb* ironmonger's
ferretero *m*, **-a** *f* hardware dealer, *Br tb* ironmonger
ferrocarril *m* **1** railroad, *Br* railway **2** *Urug en examen* cheat sheet, *Br* crib
ferrocarrilero *m L.Am.* railroad *o Br* railway worker
ferroviario I *adj* rail *atr* **II** *m*, **-a** *f* railroad *o Br* railway worker
ferry *m* ferry
fértil *adj* fertile; ***en edad ~*** of child-bearing age
fertilidad *f* fertility
fertilización *f* fertilization
◇ **fertilización in vitro** MED in vitro fertilization, IVF
fertilizante *m* fertilizer
fertilizar ⟨1f⟩ *v/t* fertilize
ferviente *adj fig* fervent
fervor *m* fervor, *Br* fervour
fervoroso *adj* fervent
festejar ⟨1a⟩ *v/t* **1** *persona* wine and dine **2** *L.Am.* celebrate
festejo *m* celebration; ***~s*** *pl* festivities
festín *m* banquet
festival *m* festival; ***~ cinematográfico*** film festival; ***~ de música*** music festival
festividad *f* feast; ***~es*** *pl* festivities
festivo *adj* festive
feta *f Rpl* slice
fetal *adj* fetal
fetén I *adj* F **1** (*auténtico*) real, genuine; ***es ~*** it's the real McCoy *o* the real thing F, it's the genuine article F **2** (*estupendo*) fantastic F, terrific F **II** *f* F truth; ***es la pura ~*** it's the pure and simple truth
fetiche *m* fetish
fetichismo *m* fetishism
fetichista I *adj* fetishistic **II** *m/f* fetishist
fétido *adj* fetid
feto *m* fetus, *Br tb* foetus
feúcho *adj* F homely, plain
feudal *adj* feudal
feudalismo *m* feudalism
feudo *m* **1** *fig* domain **2**: ***jugar en su ~*** DEP play at home
fez *m* fez
FF. AA. *abr* (= ***Fuerzas Armadas***) armed forces
FF. CC. *abr* (= ***ferrocarriles***) railroads, *Br* railways
fiable *adj* trustworthy; *datos, máquina etc* reliable
fiado *adj*: ***al ~*** F on credit
fiador I *m* TÉC safety catch **II** *m*, **~a** *f* JUR guarantor; ***salir ~ de alguien*** act as guarantor for s.o.
fiambre *m* **1** cold cut, *Br* cold meat **2** P (*cadáver*) stiff P
fiambrera *f* lunch pail, *Br* lunch box
fiambrería *f L.Am.* delicatessen
fianza *f* **1** deposit **2** JUR bail; ***bajo ~*** on bail
fiar ⟨1c⟩ **I** *v/i* **1** give credit **2**: ***ser de ~*** be trustworthy **II** *v/t* COM sell on credit; **fiarse** *v/r*: ***~ de alguien*** trust s.o.; ***no me fío*** I don't trust him / them *etc*
fiasco *m* fiasco
fibra *f* **1** *en tejido, alimento* fiber, *Br* fibre **2** *Méx* (*estropajo*) scourer
◇ **fibra de vidrio** fiberglass, *Br* fibreglass; **fibra muscular / nerviosa** ANAT muscle / nerve fiber *o Br* fibre; **fibra óptica** optical fiber *o Br* fibre; **fibra sintética** synthetic *o* man-made fiber *o Br* fibre
fibrilación *f* MED fibrillation
fibroso *adj* fibrous
ficción *f* fiction
ficha *f* **1** file card, index card **2** *en juegos de mesa* counter; *en un casino* chip; *en damas* checker, *Br* draught; *en ajedrez* man, piece **3** TELEC token **4** *L.Am.* ***ser una ~*** F be tough *o* formidable
fichaje *m* DEP signing
fichar ⟨1a⟩ **I** *v/t* **1** DEP *jugador* sign up **2** JUR open a file on; ***la policía le tiene fichado*** he's got a (criminal) record **II**

v/i DEP sign (up) (***por*** for)
fichero *m* **1** file cabinet, *Br* filing cabinet **2** INFOR file
◇ **fichero adjunto** INFOR attachment
ficticio *adj* fictitious
ficus *m* BOT rubber plant
fidedigno *adj* reliable
fideicomisario *m*, **-a** *f* trustee
fideicomiso *m* trust
fidelidad *f* fidelity; ***alta ~*** high fidelity, hi-fi
fideo *m* noodle
fiduciario I *adj* fiduciary; ***circulación -a*** fiduciary currency **II** *m*, **-a** *f* fiduciary, trustee
fiebre *f* fever; ***tiene*** (***mucha***) ***~*** he's got a (high) temperature
◇ **fiebre amarilla** yellow fever; **fiebre del heno** hay fever; **fiebre del oro** gold fever; *fenómeno* gold rush; **fiebre palúdica** malaria
fiel I *adj* faithful; (*leal*) loyal **II** *mpl*: ***los ~es*** REL the faithful *pl*
fieltro *m* felt; (***sombrero de***) ***~*** felt hat
fiera *f* wild animal; ***ponerse hecho una ~*** F go wild
fiero *adj* fierce
fierrero *m*, **-a** *f L.Am.* weightlifter
fierro *m L.Am.* **1** iron **2** *en ganado* brand **3** F (*pistola*) gun
fiesta *f* **1** festival; ***¡felices ~s!*** *de pueblo* enjoy the fiesta!; *en Navidad* Happy Holidays!, Merry Christmas! **2** (*reunión social*) party; ***estar de ~*** be in a party mood; ***no estar para ~s*** be in no mood for jokes; ***¡se acabó la ~!*** the party's over! **3** (*día festivo*) public holiday; ***hacer ~*** have a day off
◇ **fiesta de guardar** REL day of obligation; **fiesta mayor** major festival; **fiesta nacional** public holiday; **fiesta de precepto** REL day of obligation
FIFA *f abr* (= ***Fédération Internationale de Football Association***) FIFA
fifar ⟨1a⟩ *v/t & v/i Rpl* V fuck V, screw V
fifí *m L.Am.* P (*afeminado*) sissy F
figura *f* **1** figure; ***tener buena ~*** have a good figure **2** (*estatuilla*) figurine **2** (*forma*) shape **3** *naipes* face card, *Br* picture card
◇ **figura paterna** father figure
figuración *f* **1** *de cine* extras *pl* **2**: ***son figuraciones tuyas*** it's a figment of your imagination, you're imagining things
figurado *adj* figurative; ***sentido ~*** figurative sense
figurante *m*, **-a** *f en película* extra; TEA walk-on
figurar ⟨1a⟩ **I** *v/i* appear (***en*** in); ***aquí figura como ...*** she appears *o* is down here as ... **II** *v/t* **1** (*simular*) pretend **2** (*representar*) represent; **figurarse** *v/r* imagine; ***¡figúrate!*** just imagine!
figurita *f Rpl* picture card
figurativo *adj* figurative
figurilla *f* figurine
figurín *m* **1** design **2** *persona* fashion plate; ***ir hecho un ~*** look like a fashion plate
fijación *f* **1** *acción* fixing **2** (*obsesión*) fixation
fijado *m* FOT fixing
fijador *m* **1** FOT, PINT fixative, fixer **2** *para el pelo* hairspray
fijapelo *m* hairspray, hair lacquer
fijar ⟨1a⟩ *v/t* **1** *espejo*, *balda* fix; *cartel* stick **2** *fecha*, *objetivo* set **3** *residencia* establish **4** *atención* focus; **fijarse** *v/r* **1** (*establecerse*) settle **2** (*prestar atención*) pay attention (***en*** to); ***~ en algo*** (*darse cuenta*) notice sth; ***¡fíjate!*** look!; ***¡fíjate bien!*** look closely!; *aviso* be careful!, mind now!
fijativo *m* PINT fixative
fijeza *f* **1** (*firmeza*) firmness **2** (*persistencia*) persistence
fijo I *adj* **1** *espejo*, *balda* fixed **2** *trabajo* permanent **3** *fecha* definite **4**: ***idea -a*** idée fixe, obsession **II** *adv*: ***mirar ~*** stare at
fila *f* **1** line, *Br* queue; ***en ~ india*** in single file
2 *de asientos* row; ***de primera / segunda ~*** first- / second-rate; ***en primera ~*** *fig*: *flores*, *fotos*, *medallas* prominently displayed; ***siempre tiene que estar en primera ~*** he always has to be the center *o Br* centre of attention
3: ***~s*** *pl* MIL ranks; ***cerrar ~s*** *fig* close ranks; ***romper ~s*** break ranks; ***llamar a alguien a ~s*** draft s.o., *Br* call s.o. up
filamento *m* **1** thread **2** EL, BOT filament
filamentoso *adj textura* stringy
filantropía *f* philanthropy
filantrópico *adj* philanthropic
filántropo *m*, **-a** *f* philanthropist

filarmónica *f* philharmonic (orchestra)
filarmónico *adj* philharmonic; ***orquesta -a*** philharmonic (orchestra)
filatelia *f* philately, stamp collecting
filatélico I *adj* stamp *atr*, philatelic **II** *m*, **-a** *f* → ***filatelista***
filatelista *m/f* philatelist, stamp collector
fildeador *m*, **~a** *f L.Am. en béisbol* fielder
fildear ⟨1a⟩ *v/t & v/i L.Am en béisbol* field
filete *m* GASTR fillet
filfa *f* fake
filiación *f* **1** *política* affiliation **2** *datos* personal details *pl*
filial I *adj* filial **II** *f* COM subsidiary
filibustero *m* HIST buccaneer
filigrana *f* filigree; ***hacer ~s*** *fig* F do marvels
filípica *f* diatribe
Filipinas *fpl* Philippines
filipino I *adj* Philippine, Filipino **II** *m*, **-a** *f* Filipino **III** *idioma* Philipino, Filipino
filisteo REL, *fig* **I** *adj* Philistine **II** *m*, **-a** *f* Philistine
film(e) *m* movie, film
filmación *f* filming, shooting
filmadora *f* movie camera, *Br* cine camera
filmar ⟨1a⟩ *v/t* film, shoot
filmografía *f* movies *pl*, *Br* films *pl*
filmoteca *f* film library
filo *m* **1** *de mesa* edge **2** *de navaja* cutting edge; ***arma de dos ~s*** *o* ***de doble ~*** double-edged sword; ***estar en el ~ de la navaja*** be on a knife edge; ***sacar ~ a*** sharpen, put an edge on **3**: ***al ~ de las siete*** around 7 o'clock; ***al ~ del mediodía*** twelve o'clock on the dot, on the stroke of twelve
filología *f* philology; ***~ hispánica*** EDU Spanish language and literature; ***~ clásica*** EDU classics *sg*
filológico *adj* philological
filólogo *m*, **-a** *f* philologist
filón *m* vein, seam; *fig* goldmine
filoso *adj L.Am.* sharp
filosofal *adj* philosophical; ***la piedra ~*** the philosopher's stone
filosofar ⟨1a⟩ *v/i* philosophize
filosofía *f* philosophy
filosófico *adj* philosophical
filósofo *m*, **-a** *f* philosopher
filtración *f* **1** filtration, filtering **2** (*gotera*) leak
filtrar ⟨1a⟩ *v/t* **1** *agua* filter **2** *información* leak; **filtrarse** *v/r* filter (***por*** through); *de agua, información* leak
filtro *m* filter; **~** (***mágico***) *lit* love potion, philter *lit*, *Br* philtre *lit*
◇ **filtro solar** sun cream
fin *m* **1** end; ***al*** *o* ***por ~*** finally, at last; ***a ~es de mayo*** at the end of May; ***sin ~*** endless, never-ending; ***dar*** *o* ***poner ~ a*** end, bring to an end; *abuso, disputa* put an end to; ***tocar a su ~*** draw to a close, come to an end
2 (*objetivo*) aim, purpose; ***a ~ o con el ~ de que acabemos a tiempo*** in order to finish on time, to ensure that we finish on time; ***el ~ justifica los medios*** the end justifies the means; ***a ~ de*** in order to
3 *locuciones*: ***al ~ y al cabo*** at the end of the day, after all; ***en ~*** anyway
◇ **fin de semana** weekend; ***el ~*** on the weekend
finado *m*, **-a** *f* deceased
final *f & adj* final
final *m* end; ***al ~*** in the end; ***a ~es de mayo*** at the end of May
◇ **final a cuatro** *en baloncesto* final four
finalidad *f* purpose, aim
finalista I *adj*: ***las dos selecciones ~s*** the two teams that reached the final **II** *m/f* finalist
finalización *f* completion
finalizado *adj* complete
finalizar ⟨1f⟩ *v/t & v/i* end, finish
finalmente *adv* eventually
financiación *f*, **financiamiento** *L.Am. m* funding
financiar ⟨1b⟩ *v/t* finance, fund
financiero I *adj* financial; (***sociedad***) ***-a*** finance company **II** *m*, **-a** *f* financier
financista *m/f L.Am.* financier
finanzas *fpl* finances
finca *f* **1** (*bien inmueble*) property; ***~ rústica / urbana*** rural / urban property **2** *L.Am.* (*granja*) farm
finés I *adj* Finnish **II** *m*, **-esa** Finn **III** *m idioma* Finnish
fineza *f* **1** *cualidad* fineness; ***un jarrón de una ~ excepcional*** an exceptionally fine vase **2** *dicho* compliment
fingido *adj* false

fingimiento *m* pretense, *Br* pretence
fingir ⟨3c⟩ *v/t* feign *fml*; ***fingió no haberlo oído*** he pretended he hadn't heard; ***fingió dormir*** he pretended to be asleep; **fingirse** *v/r*: **~ *enfermo*** pretend to be ill, feign illness *fml*
finiquitar ⟨1a⟩ *v/t* COM settle; *fig*: *guerra*, *crisis*, *relación* put an end to, bring to an end
finiquito *m* COM settlement
finisecular *adj* turn-of-the-century, fin de siècle
finito *adj* finite
finlandés I *adj* Finnish **II** *m*, **-esa** *f* Finn **III** *m idioma* Finnish
Finlandia *f* Finland
fino I *adj* **1** *calidad* fine **2** *libro*, *tela* thin; (*esbelto*) slim **3** *modales*, *gusto* refined **4** *sentido de humor* subtle **II** *m* dry sherry, fino
finolis F **I** *adj* affected, precious **II** *m/f* affected *o* precious person
finta *f en baloncesto tb* feint
fintar ⟨1a⟩ *v/i* feint
finura *f* **1** *de calidad* fineness **2** *de tela* thinness; (*esbeltez*) slimness **3** *de modales*, *gusto* refinement, refined nature **4** *de sentido de humor* subtlety
firma *f* **1** signature; *acto* signing; ***recoger ~s*** collect signatures **2** COM firm
firmamento *m* firmament
firmante *m/f* & *adj* signatory
firmar ⟨1a⟩ *v/t* sign
firme I *adj* **1** firm; (*estable*) steady; (*sólido*) solid; ***en ~*** COM firm **2** MIL: ***¡ ~s!*** attention!; ***poner ~ a alguien*** *fig* F take a firm line with s.o. **II** *m* pavement, *Br* road surface **III** *adv*: ***trabajar ~*** work hard
firmeza *f* firmness
fiscal I *adj* tax *atr*, fiscal; ***sistema ~*** tax system **II** *m/f* district attorney, *Br* public prosecutor
◇ **fiscal general del Estado** *Spanish equivalent of Attorney General o Br Director of Public Prosecutions*
fiscalía *f* **1** *oficio* position of district attorney *o Br* public prosecutor **2** *oficina* district attorney's office, *Br* public prosecutor's office
fiscalidad *f* taxation; (*impuestos*) taxes *pl*, taxation
fiscalización *f* tax audit
fiscalizar ⟨1f⟩ *v/t* audit
fisco *m* Treasury, *Br* Exchequer
fisgar ⟨1h⟩ *v/i* F snoop F; **~ *en algo*** snoop around in sth
fisgón I *adj* nosy **II** *m*, **-ona** *f* snoop
fisgonear ⟨1a⟩ *v/i* F snoop around F (***en*** in)
fisgoneo *m* F snooping F
física *f* physics *sg*
◇ **física cuántica** quantum physics *sg*
◇ **física nuclear** nuclear physics *sg*
físico I *adj* physical **II** *m*, **-a** *f* physicist **III** *m de una persona* physique
fisiología *f* physiology
fisiológico *adj* physiological
fisiólogo *m*, **-a** *f* physiologist
fisión *f* fission
◇ **fisión nuclear** nuclear fission
fisionomía *f* ☞ ***fisonomía***
fisioterapeuta *m/f* physical therapist, *Br* physiotherapist
fisioterapia *f* physical therapy, *Br* physiotherapy
fisonomía *f* features *pl*
fistol *m Méx* tie pin
fístula *f* MED fistula
fisura *f* crack; MED fracture
fitófago *adj* plant-eating, phytophagous *fml*
fitoterapia *f* herbal medicine
FIV *f abr* (= ***fecundación in vitro***) IVF (= in vitro fertilization)
flac(c)idez *f* flabbiness
flác(c)ido *adj* flabby
flaco I *adj* **1** (*delgado*) thin **2** (*débil*): ***punto ~*** weak point; **~ *de memoria*** forgetful **II** *m*, **-a** *f* thin person
flacón *adj L.Am.* skinny
flacuchento *adj L.Am.* F skinny
flagelar ⟨1a⟩ *v/t* flagellate
flagrante *adj* flagrant; ***en ~ delito*** red-handed, in flagrante delicto
flama *f Méx* flame
flamable *adj Méx* flammable
flamante *adj* (*nuevo*) brand-new
flambear ⟨1a⟩ *v/t* GASTR flambé
flamear ⟨1a⟩ **1** *v/i de vela* burn brightly **2** *de bandera* flutter
flamenco I *adj* MÚS flamenco *atr*; ***ponerse ~*** get smart *o* fresh; ***estar muy ~ para su edad*** F be in pretty good shape for one's age **II** *m* **1** MÚS flamenco **2** ZO flamingo
flamígero *adj lit* fiery
flan *m* crème caramel; ***estar hecho un ~***

be shaking like a leaf
flanco *m* flank
flanera *f* ramekin
flanquear ⟨1a⟩ *v/t* flank
flaquear ⟨1a⟩ *v/i de fuerzas* weaken; *de entusiasmo* flag
flaqueza *f fig* weakness
flash *m* FOT flash
flashback, flash-back *m* flashback
flato *m* MED stitch
flatulencia *f* MED flatulence
flauta *f* **1** MÚS flute **2** *Méx* fried taco
◇ **flauta dulce** recorder; **flauta de pan** baguette, French loaf *o* stick; **flauta travesera** (transverse) flute
flautín I *m instrumento* piccolo **II** *m/f músico* piccolo player
flautista *m/f* flautist; ***el ~ de Hamelin*** the Pied Piper of Hamelin
flebitis *f* MED phlebitis
flecha *f* arrow; ***fue al aeropuerto como una ~*** he shot off *o* dashed off to the airport; ***regresó al restaurante como una ~*** he shot back *o* dashed back to the restaurant
flechazo *m fig* love at first sight
fleco *m del pelo* fringe, bangs *pl*
flecos *mpl de vestido, cortinas* fringe *sg*
flema *f tb fig* phlegm
flemático *adj* phlegmatic
flemón *m* MED gumboil
flequillo *m del pelo* fringe, bangs *pl*
fletador *m*, **~a** *f* charterer
fletamiento *m* chartering
fletar ⟨1a⟩ *v/t* **1** *avión* charter **2** (*embarcar*) load
flete *m L.Am.* freight, cost of transport
fletero *adj L.Am.* hire *atr*, charter *atr*
flexibilidad *f* flexibility
flexible I *adj* flexible **II** *m* EL cord, *Br tb* flex
flexión *f* **1** *en gimnasia* push-up, *Br* press-up; *de piernas* squat; ***~ de rodillas*** knee bend **2** *de la voz* inflection
flexionar ⟨1a⟩ *v/t* flex; **flexionarse** *v/r* bend
flexo *m* desk lamp
flexor *m/adj*: (***músculo***) **~** flexor (muscle)
flipado *adj* P **1** (*asombrado*) blown away P, *Br* gobsmacked F **2** (*drogado*) stoned F
flipar ⟨1a⟩ P *v/i* **1**: ***le flipa el cine*** he's mad about the movies F **2** *con sorpresa* flip P: ***yo flipé con …*** … blew my mind F
flirt *m* **1** *relación* fling **2** (*novio*) boyfriend; (*novia*) girlfriend
flirtear ⟨1a⟩ *v/i* flirt (***con*** with)
flirteo *m* flirting
flojear ⟨1a⟩ *v/i* weaken, become *o* get weak
flojedad *f* weakness
flojera *f L.Am.* laziness; ***me da ~*** I can't be bothered
flojo *adj* **1** *lazada* loose; ***me la trae -a*** P I couldn't give a damn F **2** *café, argumento* weak; *vino* without any body **3** COM *actividad* slack **4** *novela etc* weak, poor; *redacción, montaje* slack, sloppy **5** *L.Am.* (*perezoso*) lazy
flor *f* flower; ***de ~es*** *vestido, cortinas, papel* flower-patterned, flowery; ***en ~*** in bloom, in flower; ***echar ~es*** bloom, flower; *fig* flatter; ***la ~ y nata de la sociedad*** the cream of society; ***tengo los nervios a ~ de piel*** I'm *o* my nerves are all on edge
◇ **flor de Pascua** poinsettia
◇ **flores cortadas** cut flowers
flora *f* flora
◇ **flora intestinal** MED intestinal flora
floración *f* flowering
floral *adj* floral
floreado *adj tejido* flowery
florear ⟨1a⟩ **I** *v/t* **1** decorate with flowers **2** *Méx* (*halagar*) flatter, compliment **II** *v/i* flower, bloom
florecer ⟨2d⟩ *v/i* BOT flower, bloom; *de negocio, civilización etc* flourish; **florecerse** *v/r* **1** bloom, flower **2** *de pan, queso* go moldy *o Br* mouldy
floreciente *adj* flourishing
florecimiento *m tb fig* flowering
Florencia *f* Florence
florero *m* vase
floresta *f* grove
florete *m* foil
floricultor *m*, **~a** *f* flower grower
floricultura *f* flower growing
florido *adj* **1** *estilo* florid, flowery **2**: ***lo más ~*** *de la sociedad* the cream
floripondio *m desp* flowery monstrosity
florista *m/f* florist
floristería *f* florist's, flower shop
florituras *fpl* MÚS fioritturas; *fig* embellishments; ***no se andó con ~*** he didn't beat about the bush, he didn't mince

his words; ***se andaba con muchas ~*** there was a lot of humming and hawing
florón *m* ARQUI fleuron
flota *f* fleet
◇ **flota de guerra** fleet; **flota mercante** merchant fleet; **flota pesquera** fishing fleet
flotación *f* flotation; ***línea de ~*** water line
flotador *m* **1** float; *para la cintura* (inflatable) ring; *salvavidas* life preserver **2** *Rpl* (*michelín*) spare tire *o Br* tyre
flotante *adj* floating
flotar ⟨1a⟩ *v/i* float
flote *m* MAR: ***a ~*** afloat; ***mantenerse a ~*** *fig* stay afloat; ***poner*** *o* ***sacar algo a ~*** refloat sth; *fig* get sth back on its feet; ***salir a ~*** *fig* get back on one's feet
flotilla *f* MAR flotilla
fluctuación *f* fluctuation
fluctuante *adj* fluctuating
fluctuar ⟨1e⟩ *v/i* fluctuate
fluidez *f* fluidity
fluido I *adj sustancia* fluid; *tráfico* free-flowing; *lenguaje* fluent **II** *m* fluid
fluir ⟨3g⟩ *v/i* flow
flujo *m* flow; ***~ de información*** flow of information
◇ **flujo de caja** cashflow
flúor *m* fluoride
fluorescencia *f* fluorescence
fluorescente I *adj* fluorescent **II** *m* strip light
fluvial *adj* river *atr*
fly *m en béisbol* fly ball
FM *f abr* (= ***frecuencia modulada***) FM (= frequency modulation)
FMI *m abr* (= ***Fondo Monetario Internacional***) IMF (= International Monetary Fund)
fobia *f* phobia; *fig* loathing; ***les tengo ~ a las comidas familiares / le tengo ~ a ir de compras con ella*** I hate *o* detest family meals / going shopping with her
foca *f* ZO seal
focal *adj* focal
focalizar ⟨1f⟩ *v/t cámara, atención* focus; *fig*: *gasto social, inversiones* concentrate, focus
foco *m* **1** MAT, FÍS focus **2** *de infección* center, *Br* centre, focus; *de incendio* seat **3** *de auto* headlight; *de calle* streetlight; TEA, TV spotlight; *L.Am.* (*bombilla*) lightbulb
fofo *adj* flabby
fogata *f* bonfire
fogón *m* **1** *de cocina* stove **2** TÉC burner **3** *L.Am. fuego* bonfire
fogonazo *m* flash
fogosidad *f* ardor, *Br* ardour
fogoso *adj* fiery, ardent
foguear ⟨1a⟩ *v/t* MIL, *fig* give a baptism of fire; **foguearse** *v/r fig* go through a baptism of fire
folclore *m* folklore
folclórico *adj* folk *atr*
foliación *f* BOT foliation
foliar ⟨1a⟩ *v/t* TIP *libro, cuaderno* paginate, number the pages of; *páginas* number
fólico *adj*: ***ácido ~*** folic acid
folículo *m* ANAT follicle
folio *m* sheet (of paper)
folklore *m* folklore
folklórico *adj* folk *atr*
follaje *m* foliage
follar ⟨1a⟩ *v/t & v/i* V fuck V, screw V
folletín *m* newspaper serial; *desp libro* trashy novel; TV (melodramatic) soap opera
folleto *m* pamphlet
◇ **folleto informativo** information leaflet
follón *m* **1** argument **2** (*lío*) mess **3**: ***armar un ~*** kick up a fuss
follonero *m*, **-a** *f* F troublemaker
fomentar ⟨1a⟩ *v/t solidaridad* foster; COM promote; *rebelión* foment, incite
fomento *m* COM promotion
fonazo *m Méx* F call
fonda *f* **1** (simple) restaurant **2** (*pensión*) boarding house
fondeadero *m* MAR anchorage
fondear ⟨1a⟩ *v/t* MAR anchor; **fondearse** *v/r L.Am.* get rich
fondeo *m* MAR anchoring
fondero *m*, **-a** *f L.Am.* restaurant owner
fondillos *mpl*: ***los ~ de los pantalones*** the seat of the pants
fondista *m/f* DEP long-distance runner
fondo *m* **1** bottom; ***doble ~*** false bottom; ***~ marino*** seabed; ***tocar ~*** *fig* reach bottom; ***los bajos ~s*** the underworld *sg*
2 (*profundidad*) depth; ***hacer una limpieza a ~ de algo*** give sth a thorough clean, clean sth thoroughly; ***emplearse a ~*** *fig* give one's all; ***ir al ~ de algo*** look

F

at sth in depth; ***en el ~*** deep down
3 *de sala*, *cuarto etc* back; *de pasillo* end
4 PINT, FOT background; ***música de ~*** background music
5 *de un museo* etc collection
6 COM fund; ***~s*** *pl* money *sg*, funds; ***a ~ perdido*** non-refundable; ***sin ~s*** *cheque* dud
7 DEP: ***de medio ~*** middle distance *atr*
8 (*disposición*): ***tiene buen ~*** he's got a good heart
◇ **fondo de inversión** investment fund; **Fondo Monetario Internacional** International Monetary Fund; **fondo del ojo** ANAT funduscopy, ophthalmoscopy; **fondo de pensiones** pension fund; **fondos públicos** public funds; **fondos reservados** secret funds

fondón *adj* F broad in the beam F
fonema *m* phoneme
fonética *f* phonetics *sg*
fonético *adj* phonetic
foniatra *m/f* speech therapist
foniatría *f* speech therapy
fono *m L.Am.* F phone
fontanería *f* plumbing
fontanero *m* plumber
footing *m* DEP jogging; ***hacer ~*** go jogging, jog
foque *m* MAR jib
forajido *m*, **-a** *f* outlaw
foral *adj* charter *atr*
foráneo *adj* foreign
forastero I *adj* foreign **II** *m*, **-a** *f* outsider, stranger
forcejear ⟨1a⟩ *v/i* struggle
forcejeo *m* struggle
fórceps *m inv* forceps *pl*
forense I *adj* forensic **II** *m/f* forensic scientist
forestación *f* afforestation
forestal *adj* forest *atr*
forestar ⟨1a⟩ *v/t L.Am.* afforest
forfait *m* **1** COM fixed price; ***viaje a ~*** package tour **2** *para el cibercafé*, *el cine* pass
forja *f* **1** *taller* forge **2** *acción* forging
forjador *m*, **~a** *f de metal* forger
forjar ⟨1a⟩ *v/t metal* forge; **forjarse** *v/r futuro* carve out; ***~ ilusiones*** get one's hopes up
forma *f* **1** form
2 (*apariencia*) shape; ***en ~ de*** in the shape of; ***dar ~ a algo*** shape sth
3 (*manera*) way; ***de ~ que*** in such a way that; ***de todas ~s*** in any case, anyway; ***de alguna ~***, ***en cierta ~*** in a way; ***de cualquier ~*** anyway; ***de ninguna ~*** not in the slightest, F no way; ***no hay ~ de que coma / estudie*** nothing will make him eat / study, it's impossible to get him to eat / study
4: ***~s*** *pl* proprieties; ***guardar las ~s*** keep up appearances
5: ***estar en ~*** be fit; ***mantenerse en ~*** stay in shape
6 *Méx* (*formulario*) form
formación *f* **1** *de palabras*, *asociación* formation **2** (*entrenamiento*) training; ***alumno de ~ profesional*** student doing a vocational course
◇ **formación de adultos** adult education; **formación continuada** in-service training; **formación profesional** vocational training; **formación universitaria** university education

formal *adj* **1** formal **2** *niño* well-behaved **3** (*responsable*) responsible
formalidad *f* formality
formalismo *m* formalism, excessive formality
formalizar ⟨1f⟩ *v/t* formalize; *relación* make official
formar ⟨1a⟩ *v/t* **1** form; *asociación* form, set up **2** (*educar*) educate; **formarse** *v/r* form
formatear ⟨1a⟩ *v/t* INFOR format
formateo *m* INFOR formatting
formativo *adj jornada*, *curso*, *materiales*, *centro* training *atr*
formato *m* format; ***en gran / pequeño ~*** *dibujo*, *mueble* large- / small-format, large- / small-size
◇ **formato de caracteres (de impresión)** INFOR character format; **formato horizontal** INFOR landscape; **formato vertical** INFOR portrait

formidable *adj* huge; (*estupendo*) tremendous
formol *m* QUÍM formalin
fórmula *f* **1** MAT formula **2**: ***por pura ~*** as a matter of form
◇ **fórmula de cortesía** *acción* polite custom; *en documento* polite phrase; *en carta* standard opening; *en la despedida* standard closure
◇ **fórmula magistral** prescription medicine

formulación *f* formulation
formular ⟨1a⟩ *v/t teoría* formulate; *queja* make, lodge
formulario *m* form
fornicación *f* fornication
fornicar ⟨1g⟩ *v/i* fornicate
fornido *adj* well-built
foro *m* forum; ***irse** o **desaparecer por el** ~* slip out, slip away
forofo *m*, **-a** *f* F fan
forrado *adj* **1** *prenda* lined; *libro* covered **2** *fig* F (*rico*) loaded F
forraje *m* fodder
forrajero *adj* fodder *atr*; ***planta -a*** fodder plant
forrar ⟨1a⟩ *v/t prenda* line; *libro*, *silla* cover; **forrarse** *v/r* **1** F make a fortune F **2** *L.Am.* F (*llenarse*) stuff o.s. F, have a good feed
forro *m* **1** *de prenda* lining; *de libro* cover; ***no se le parece ni por el ~*** he looks nothing like him; ***pasarse algo por el ~*** F not give a damn about sth F **2** *Méx* F (*bombón*) good looker F **3** *Rpl* F (*condón*) rubber F
fortachón I *adj* F big and strong, burly **II** *m*, **-ona** *f* burly man; *mujer* woman
fortalecedor *adj* strengthening
fortalecer ⟨2d⟩ *v/t tb fig* strengthen; **fortalecerse** *v/r* strengthen
fortalecimiento *m* strengthening
fortaleza *f* **1** strength of character **2** MIL fortress
fortificación *f* fortification
fortificar ⟨1g⟩ *v/t* MIL fortify
fortín *m* MIL small fort
fortísimo *sup* ☞ ***fuerte***
fortuito *adj* chance *atr*, accidental
fortuna *f* **1** fortune; ***hacer una ~*** make a fortune **2** (*suerte*) luck; ***por ~*** fortunately, luckily; ***probar ~*** try one's luck
forúnculo *m* MED boil
forzado *adj* forced
forzar ⟨1f & 1m⟩ *v/t* **1** force; ***~ la voz*** strain one's voice **2** (*violar*) rape; **forzarse** *v/r* force o.s. (***a hacer algo*** to do sth)
forzosamente *adv* of necessity; ***tienes que pasar ~ por el centro de la ciudad*** you have no option but to go through the city center
forzoso *adj aterrizaje* forced
forzudo *adj* brawny
fosa *f* **1** pit **2** (*tumba*) grave **3** GEOL basin
◇ **fosa común** common grave
◇ **fosas nasales** nostrils
fosfato *m* phosphate
fosforescencia *f* phosphorescence
fosforescente *adj* phosphorescent
fosfórico *adj*: ***ácido ~*** phosphoric acid
fósforo *m* **1** QUÍM phosphorus **2** *L.Am.* (*cerilla*) match
fósil I *adj* fossilized **II** *m* fossil
fosilizarse ⟨1f⟩ *v/r* fossilize, become fossilized
foso *m* **1** ditch; *de castillo*, DEP *en campo* moat; *en béisbol* dugout **2** TEA, MÚS pit
foto *f* photo
◇ **foto fija** still
fotocomposición *f* TIP photocomposition, *Br* filmsetting
fotocopia *f* photocopy
fotocopiadora *f* photocopier
fotocopiar ⟨1a⟩ *v/t* photocopy
fotofobia *f* photophobia
fotogenia *f* photogenic nature; ***gracias a su ~*** because she is so photogenic
fotogénico *adj* photogenic
fotograbado *m* photogravure
fotografía *f* **1** *técnica* photography **2** *imagen* photograph
◇ **fotografía aérea** *técnica* aerial photography; *imagen* aerial photograph; **fotografía en blanco y negro** *técnica* black and white photography; *imagen* black and white photograph; **fotografía en color** *técnica* color *o Br* colour photography; *imagen* color *o Br* colour photograph
fotografiar ⟨1c⟩ *v/t* photograph
fotográfico *adj* photographic
fotógrafo *m*, **-a** *f* photographer
◇ **fotógrafo de prensa** press photographer
fotómetro *m* light meter
fotomontaje *m* photomontage
fotosensible *adj* photosensitive
fotosíntesis *f* BIO photosynthesis
fototeca *f* photo library
foul *m L.Am. en béisbol* foul ball
foyer *m Rpl* foyer
FP *f abr* (= ***formación profesional***) vocational training
frac *m* tail coat
fracasado I *adj* unsuccessful **II** *m*, **-a** *f* loser
fracasar ⟨1a⟩ *v/i* fail

fracaso *m* failure
◇ **fracaso escolar** academic failure
fracción *f* fraction; POL faction
fraccionador *m*, **~a** *f Méx* realtor, *Br* estate agent
fraccionamiento *m* **1** *L.Am.* (housing) project, *Br* (housing) estate **2** (*división*) division
fraccionar ⟨1a⟩ *v/t* **1** break up **2** FIN pay in installments *o Br* instalments; **fraccionarse** *v/r* break up (***en*** into); ***un metro se fracciona en 100 centímetros*** a meter divides into 100 centimeters
fraccionario *adj* fractional
fractura *f* MED fracture; ***tener una ~ craneal*** have a fractured skull
fracturar ⟨1a⟩ *v/t* MED fracture; **fracturarse** *v/r costillas, fémur, pierna* break, fracture; *cráneo* fracture
fragancia *f* fragrance
fraganti: ***in ~*** *adv* F in the act F
fragata *f* MAR frigate
frágil *adj* fragile
fragilidad *f* fragility; *de condición física* frailty
fragmentación *f* fragmentation
fragmentar ⟨1a⟩ *v/t* fragment; **fragmentarse** *v/r* fragment
fragmentario *adj* fragmentary
fragmento *m* fragment; *extracto de novela, poema* excerpt, extract
fragor *m* clamor, *Br* clamour, din
fragoroso *adj* deafening
fragoso *adj terreno* rough, uneven; *montaña* rocky; *bosque* dense
fragua *f* forge
fraguar ⟨1i⟩ **I** *v/t* **1** forge **2** *plan* devise; *complot* hatch **II** *v/i de cemento* set; **fraguarse** *v/r de proyecto, sistema* take shape; *de revuelta, revolución* brew
fraile *m* friar, monk
frambuesa *f* raspberry
frambueso *m* raspberry cane
francachela *f* F binge F
francamente *adv* **1** (*sinceramente*) frankly **2** (*realmente*) really
francés **I** *adj* French **II** *m* **1** Frenchman **2** *idioma* French
francesa *f* Frenchwoman
franchute *m/f & adj desp* F Frog *desp* F
Francia *f* France
franciscano REL **I** *adj* Franciscan **II** *m*, **-a** *f* Franciscan
francmasón *m* freemason
francmasonería *f* freemasonry
franco **I** *adj* **1** (*sincero*) frank **2** (*evidente*) distinct, marked **3** COM free **4** *L.Am.* ***estar ~*** have a day off (work) **II** *m moneda* franc
◇ **franco en almacén** ex warehouse; **franco en fábrica** ex works; **franco de porte** carriage free
francófilo **I** *adj* Francophile **II** *m*, **-a** *f* Francophile
francófobo **I** *adj* Francophobe **II** *m*, **-a** *f* Francophobe
francófono **I** *adj* French-speaking **II** *m*, **-a** French-speaker
francotirador *m*, **~a** *f* sniper
franela *f* **1** flannel **2** *Rpl* (*trapo del polvo*) duster
franja *f* **1** (*orilla*) fringe **2** *de tierra* strip
◇ **franja horaria** TV time slot
franqueable *adj* passable
franquear ⟨1a⟩ *v/t* **1** *carta* pay the postage on; ***sin ~*** unstamped; ***a ~ en destino*** postage paid **2** *camino, obstáculo* clear; **franquearse** *v/r* open up, open one's heart (***con*** to)
franqueo *m* postage; ***sin gastos de ~*** postage paid
franqueza *f* frankness; ***con toda ~, …*** quite frankly, …, to be perfectly frank, …
franquicia *f* **1** (*exención*) exemption **2** COM franchise
◇ **franquicia postal** free postage
franquiciado *m*, **-a** *f* COM franchisee
franquiciador *m*, **~a** *f* COM franchisor
franquismo *m* HIST Francoism
franquista HIST **I** *adj* supporting Franco, pro-Franco **II** *m/f* Franco supporter
frasco *m* bottle
frase *f* phrase; (*oración*) sentence
◇ **frase hecha** set phrase
fraseo *m* MÚS phrasing
fraseología *f* phraseology
fraternal *adj* brotherly
fraternidad *f* brotherhood, fraternity
fraternizar ⟨1f⟩ *v/i* POL fraternize
fratricida *m/f* fratricide
fratricidio *m* fratricide
fraude *m* fraud
◇ **fraude electoral** election *o* electoral fraud
◇ **fraude fiscal** tax evasion, tax fraud
fraudulento *adj* fraudulent

fray *m* REL friar, brother; ***Fray Juan*** Brother Juan
frazada *f L.Am.* blanket
freático *adj*: ***aguas -as*** ground water; ***capa -a*** water table
frecuencia *f* frequency; ***con ~*** frequently
◇ **frecuencia modulada** RAD frequency modulation
frecuentado *adj* popular
frecuentar ⟨1a⟩ *v/t* frequent
frecuente *adj* frequent; (*común*) common
frecuentemente *adv* often, frequently
freezer *m L.Am.* freezer
fregadero *m* sink
fregado I *adj L.Am.* annoying **II** *m* **1** *de platos* washing; *del suelo* mopping; *frotando* scrubbing **2** F (*lío*) mess; ***meterse en un buen ~*** *fig* F get into a fine mess F
fregaplatos *m inv* ☞ ***friegaplatos***
fregar ⟨1h & 1k⟩ *v/t* **1** *platos* wash; *suelo* mop; *frotando* scrub **2** *L.Am.* F (*molestar*) bug F
fregasuelos *m inv* ☞ ***friegasuelos***
fregón I *adj* annoying **II** *m L.Am.* F nuisance, pain in the neck F
fregona *f* **1** mop **2** *L.Am.* F nuisance, pain in the neck F
freidora *f* deep fryer
freidura *f* frying
freír ⟨3m; *part* **frito**⟩ *v/t* **1** fry **2** F (*matar*) waste P
frenada *f esp L.Am.* ***dar una ~*** F slam the brakes on, hit the brakes F
frenado *m* braking
frenar ⟨1a⟩ **I** *v/i* AUTO brake; ***~ en seco*** brake sharply **II** *v/t fig* slow down; *impulsos* check; **frenarse** *v/r fig* control o.s.
frenazo *m*: ***pegar*** *o* ***dar un ~*** F slam the brakes on, hit the brakes F
frenesí *m* frenzy
frenético *adj* frenetic
freno *m* brake; ***poner ~ a algo*** *fig* curb sth, check sth
◇ **freno de disco** disc brake; **freno de mano** parking brake, *Br* handbrake; **freno de tambor** drum brake
frente I *f* forehead; ***con la ~ alta / erguida*** *fig* with (one's) head held high; ***lo lleva escrito en la ~*** *fig* it's written all over him
II *m* **1** MIL, METEO front **2** *en locuciones*: ***de ~*** *colisión* head-on; ***de ~ al grupo*** *L.Am.* facing the group; ***foto de ~*** head and shoulders photograph; ***~ a ~*** *fig* face to face; ***estar al ~ de algo*** head sth, lead sth; ***hacer ~ a*** *situación* face up to; *deudas* meet, be able to pay; ***ponte más al ~*** move further forward, move closer to the front; ***ponerse al ~ de la situación*** *fig* take charge (of the situation)
III *prp*: ***~ a*** opposite; ***estar ~ a*** *crisis* be faced with, be facing
◇ **frente cálido** warm front
◇ **frente frío** cold front
fresa *f* strawberry
fresal *m* strawberry field
fresca *f* **1** cool air; ***la ~*** *de la mañana* the cool of the morning; *de la tarde* the cool of the evening **2**: ***soltar una ~ a alguien*** F get fresh with s.o., *Br* be cheeky to s.o.
frescales *m/f inv*: ***¡eres un ~!*** F you have some nerve! F
fresco I *adj* **1** cool; ***conservar en lugar ~*** keep cool, keep in a cool place **2** *pescado etc* fresh **3** *persona* F fresh F, *Br* cheeky F; ***quedarse tan ~*** F stay calm, F keep one's cool
II *m*, **-a** *f*: ***¡eres un ~!*** F you've got some nerve! F, *Br* you've got a cheek! F
III *m* **1** fresh air; ***tomar el ~*** get some fresh air **2**: ***hace ~*** it's cool; ***me trae al ~*** F I couldn't *o* could care less, *Br* I couldn't care less F **3** *C.Am. bebida* fruit drink
frescor *m* freshness
frescura *f* **1** freshness; (*frío*) coolness **2** *fig* nerve
fresno *m* BOT ash tree
fresón *m* strawberry
fresquería *f L.Am.* soda fountain, store selling soda *o* soft drinks
friable *adj* friable
frialdad *f tb fig* coldness
fricasé *m* fricassee
fricativo I *adj* fricative **II** *f* fricative
fricción *f* TÉC, *fig* friction
friccionar ⟨1a⟩ *v/t* rub
friega *f L.Am.* hassle F, drag F
friegaplatos *inv* **I** *m* dishwasher **II** *m/f* dishwasher
friegasuelos *m inv* **1** floor cleaner **2** *utensilio* floor mop

frigider *m Andes* icebox, fridge
frigidez *f* frigidity
frígido *adj* frigid
frigorífico I *adj* refrigerated **II** *m* fridge
frigorista *m/f* refrigeration engineer
fríjol, frijol *m L.Am.* bean
frío I *adj tb fig* cold; ***quedarse ~*** get cold; *fig* be astonished **II** *m* cold; ***hace ~*** it's cold; ***tener ~*** be cold; ***pillar*** *o Esp tb* ***coger ~*** catch cold
friolento *L.Am.* ☞ ***friolero***
friolera *f irón*: ***gana la ~ de 2 millones al mes*** he earns a cool 2 million a month
friolero *adj*: ***es ~*** he feels the cold
frisar ⟨1a⟩ *v/i*: ***~ en los setenta*** *fig* be getting on for seventy
friso *m* ARQUI frieze
fritada *f*: ***una ~ de cerdo para mí, por favor*** (a piece of) fried pork for me, please
fritanga *f desp* fried food, greasy food
fritar ⟨1a⟩ *v/t L.Am.* fry
frito I *part* ☞ ***freír*** **II** *adj* **1** GASTR fried **2**: ***estar ~*** F be dead to the world F; ***quedarse ~*** F fall asleep, crash F; **3**: ***los vecinos me traen ~*** F I'm sick to death of the people next door F **III** *mpl*: ***~s*** fried food *sg*
fritura *f* ☞ ***fritada***
frivolidad *f* frivolity
frivolizar ⟨1f⟩ *v/t tema* trivialize
frívolo *adj* frivolous
fronda *f* leaves *pl*, foliage; *de helecho* frond
frondosidad *f* leafiness
frondoso *adj* leafy
frontal I *adj* **1** frontal; *ataque etc* head-on **2** (*delantero*) front *atr* **II** *m* **1** ANAT frontal bone **2** *de coche* front end
frontera *f* border; *fig* boundary, dividing line; ***no hay ~s para su ambición*** his ambition knows no bounds
fronterizo *adj* border *atr*
frontis *m inv* façade
frontispicio *m* **1** ARQUI façade **2** *de libro* frontispiece
frontón *m* DEP **1** pelota **2** *cancha* pelota court; *pared* fronton
frotar ⟨1a⟩ *v/t* rub; **frotarse** *v/r* rub; ***~ las manos*** rub one's hands; *fig* rub one's hands with glee
frotis *m* MED Pap test, smear
fructífero *adj* fruitful, productive
fructificar ⟨1a⟩ *v/i* bear fruit
fructosa *f* fructose
fructuoso *adj fig* fruitful
frugal *adj persona* frugal
frugalidad *f* frugality
fruición *f* delight; ***con ~*** with delight, delightedly
frunce *m* gather
fruncimiento *m de material* gathering; ***~ del entrecejo*** *o* ***de ceño*** frown; ***a juzgar por el ~ de boca*** judging by his pursed lips
fruncir ⟨3b⟩ *v/t material* gather; ***~ el ceño*** frown
fruslería *f* knick-knack, trinket
frustración *f* frustration
frustrante *adj* frustrating
frustrar ⟨1a⟩ *v/t persona* frustrate; *plan* thwart; **frustrarse** *v/r* **1** get frustrated **2** *de plan* fail
fruta *f* fruit
◇ **fruta bomba** *Cu* papaya
◇ **fruta del tiempo** seasonal fruit
frutal I *adj* fruit *atr* **II** *m* fruit tree
frutera *f Rpl* fruit bowl
frutería *f* fruit store, *Br* greengrocer's
frutero I *adj* fruit *atr* **II** *m* fruit bowl
frutícola *adj* fruit-growing *atr*
fruticultor *m*, ***~a*** *f* fruit grower
fruticultura *f* fruit growing
frutilla *f S.Am.* strawberry
fruto *m tb fig* fruit; *nuez, almendra etc* nut; ***dar ~(s)*** *tb fig* bear fruit
◇ **frutos del mar** seafood *sg*
◇ **frutos secos** nuts
fu: ***ni ~ ni fa*** F so-so
fuagrás *m* liver pâté
fucsia I *adj inv* fuchsia **II** *m* fuchsia **III** *f* BOT fuchsia
fue *vb* ☞ ***ir, ser***
fuego *m* **1** fire; ***pegar*** *o* ***prender ~ a*** set fire to; ***jugar con ~*** *fig* be playing with fire **2**: ***a ~ lento / vivo*** *cocinar* over a low / high heat *o* flame **3**: ***¿tienes ~?*** *para cigarro* do you have a light? **4**: ***romper*** *o* ***abrir el ~*** MIL open fire; ***estar entre dos ~s*** *fig* be between a rock and a hard place
◇ **fuego cruzado** crossfire; **fuego fatuo** will-o'-the-wisp; **fuego de Santelmo** St Elmo's fire; **fuegos artificiales** fireworks
fuel(-oil) *m* fuel oil
fuelle *m* bellows *pl*; ***perder ~*** *fig* F run

out of steam
fuente *f* **1** fountain; *fig* source **2** *recipiente* dish **3** INFOR font **4** *L.Am. bar* soda fountain
fuera I *vb* ☞ ***ir, ser***
II *adv* outside; (*en otro lugar*) away; (*en otro país*) abroad; ***por ~*** on the outside; ***de ~*** *de otro departamento, cuerpo de policía etc* from outside, outside *atr*; *de otro lugar* strange; *persona* stranger; *de otro país* foreign; *persona* foreigner; ***¡~!*** get out!
III *prp*: ***~ de*** outside; ***¡sal ~ de aquí!*** get out of here!; ***está ~ del país*** he's abroad, he's out of the country; ***~ de eso*** aside from that, apart from that; ***estar ~ de sí*** be beside o.s.
◇ **fuera de juega** DEP offside; ***estar en ~*** be offside
fueraborda *m* outboard motor; *barca* boat with an outboard motor
fuereño *m*, **-a** *f Méx* stranger
fuero *m*: ***en el ~ interno*** deep down
fuerte I *adj* **1** strong **2** *dolor* intense; *lluvia* heavy **3** *aumento* sharp **4** *ruido* loud **5**: ***estoy ~ en idiomas*** I'm good at languages **6** *fig* P incredible F; ***¡qué ~!, ¡esto es muy ~!*** F God, this is awful! F
II *adv* hard; ***hablar ~*** speak loudly; ***jugar ~*** bet heavily
III *m* MIL fort; ***hacerse ~*** dig o.s. in
fuerza *f* **1** strength; ***hacer ~*** try hard, make an effort; ***hacer ~ a alguien*** *fig* put pressure on s.o., pressure s.o.; ***sacar ~s de flaqueza*** make a superhuman effort; ***cobrar ~*** *fig* gather *o* gain strength
2 (*violencia*) force; ***este domingo voy a tener que trabajar a la ~ o por ~*** I have no choice *o* option but to work this Sunday
3 EL power
4: ***la ~ de la costumbre*** force of habit; ***a ~ de …*** by (dint of)
5: ***~ es reconocer que …*** it has to be admitted that …
◇ **fuerza aérea** air force; **fuerza bruta** brute force; **fuerza física** physical strength; **fuerza de gravedad** force of gravity; **fuerza mayor** JUR force majeure; *en seguro* act of God; **fuerza pública** police *pl*, police force; **fuerza de reacción rápida** rapid deployment force; **fuerza de voluntad** willpower; **fuerzas armadas** armed forces; **fuerzas de orden público** police *pl*, police force; **fuerzas de seguridad** security forces
fuese *vb* ☞ ***ir, ser***
fuet *m dried sausage from Catalonia*
fuetazo *m L.Am.* lash
fuete *m L.Am.* whip
fuga *f* **1** escape; ***~ masiva*** mass escape; ***darse a la ~*** flee **2** *de gas, agua* leak
◇ **fuga de capitales** flight of capital
◇ **fuga de cerebros** brain drain
fugacidad *f* fleetingness, fleeting nature
fugarse ⟨1h⟩ *v/r* run away; *de la cárcel* escape
fugaz *adj fig* fleeting
fugitivo I *adj* runaway *atr* **II** *m*, **-a** *f* fugitive
fui *vb* ☞ ***ir, ser***
fuimos *vb* ☞ ***ir, ser***
fula *f Cu* dollar, buck F
fulana *f* **1** so-and-so **2** F (*prostituta*) hooker P, whore P, *Br* tart F
fulano *m* so-and-so
fular *m* scarf
fulero *adj* shoddy, slapdash
fulgor *m* brightness
fulgurante *adj fig* dazzling
fulgurar ⟨1a⟩ *v/i* shine; *de foco, mirada* blaze
fullería *f* **1** (*trampa*) trick; ***hacer ~s*** cheat (***a alguien*** s.o.) **2** (*astucia*) cunning
fullero I *adj* deceitful **II** *m*, **-a** *f* cheat
fulminante I *adj* **1** *enfermedad* sudden **2** *mirada* withering **II** *m* percussion cap
fulminar ⟨1a⟩ *v/t*: ***lo fulminó un rayo*** he was killed by lightning; ***~ a alguien con la mirada*** look daggers at s.o. F
fumadero *m*: ***~ de opio*** opium den
fumador I *adj*: ***las personas ~as*** smokers **II** *m*, **~a** *f* smoker; ***no ~*** non-smoker
fumar ⟨1a⟩ **I** *v/t* smoke **II** *v/i* smoke; ***prohibido ~*** no smoking; ***~ en pipa*** smoke a pipe; **fumarse** *v/r* **1** smoke **2** *dinero* F blow F **3**: ***~ una clase*** F skip a class
fumigación *f* fumigation
fumigar ⟨1h⟩ *v/t* fumigate
fumo *m Rpl* F (*maría*) dope F
funámbulo *m*, **-a** *f* tightrope walker
función *f* **1** purpose, function **2** *en el trabajo* duty **3**: ***en funciones*** acting; ***en-***

trar en funciones take office **4** TEA performance **5**: ***en ~ de*** according to
◇ **función matinal** TEA matinée
funcional *adj* functional
funcionalidad *f* functional nature; *de software* functionality; ***una lavadora de excelente ~*** an extremely functional washing machine
funcionamiento *m* working; ***en*** (***perfecto***) ***estado de ~*** in (perfect) working order
funcionar ⟨1a⟩ *v/i* work; ***no funciona*** out of order
funcionariado *m* government employees *pl*, civil servants *pl*
funcionario *m*, **-a** *f* **1** government employee, civil servant **2** *L.Am.* (*empleado*) employee
funda *f* cover; *de gafas* case; *de almohada* pillowcase; ***~ portadocumentos*** credit card holder
fundación *f* foundation; *acto* foundation, founding
fundacional *adj* founding *atr*
fundador *m*, **~a** *f* founder
fundamental *adj* fundamental
fundamentalismo *m* fundamentalism
fundamentalista **I** *adj* fundamentalist **II** *m/f* fundamentalist
fundamentalmente *adv* essentially
fundamentar ⟨1a⟩ *v/t* base (***en*** on); **fundamentarse** *v/r de teoría*, *argumento*, *éxito* be based (***en*** on)
fundamento *m* **1** foundation; ***carecer de ~*** lack foundation, be groundless **2**: ***~s*** *pl* (*nociones*) fundamentals
fundar ⟨1a⟩ *v/t fig* base (***en*** on); **fundarse** *v/r* be based (***en*** on)
fundición *f* **1** *acción* smelting **2** *fábrica* foundry
fundido **I** *adj hierro*, *acero* molten **II** *m en TV*, *película* fade
◇ **fundido en negro** fade-out, fade (to black)
fundir ⟨3a⟩ *v/t* **1** *hielo* melt **2** *metal* smelt **3** COM merge **4** *en TV*, *película* fade; **fundirse** *v/r* **1** melt **2** *de bombilla* fuse; *de plomos* blow **3** COM merge **4** *L.Am. fig*: *de empresa* go under
fúnebre *adj* funeral *atr*; *fig*: *ambiente* gloomy
funeral **I** *adj* funeral *atr* **II** *m* funeral; (*honras fúnebres*) memorial service
funerala *f*: ***a la ~*** MIL reversed; ***ojo a la ~*** black eye
funeraria *f* funeral parlor, *Br* undertaker's
funerario *adj* funeral *atr*; ***empresa -a*** funeral director
funesto *adj* disastrous
fungir ⟨3c⟩ *v/i Méx*: ***~ como*** act as
funicular *m* funicular; (*teleférico*) cable car
furcia *f* P whore P
furgón *m* van; FERR boxcar, *Br* goods van
◇ **furgón de cola** caboose, *Br* guard's van; ***ser el ~ de algo*** be last in sth
◇ **furgón de equipajes** baggage car, *Br* luggage van
furgoneta *f* van
furia *f* fury; ***ponerse hecho una ~*** get into a fury *o* rage
furibundo *adj* furious
furioso *adj* furious
furor *m*: ***hacer ~*** *fig* be all the rage F
◇ **furor uterino** nymphomania
furtivo *adj* furtive
furúnculo *m* MED boil
fusa *f* MÚS thirty-second note, *Br* demisemiquaver
fuselaje *m* fuselage
fusible *m* EL fuse
fusil *m* rifle
◇ **fusil ametrallador** machine gun; **fusil de asalto** assault rifle; **fusil automático** automatic (rifle); **fusil de repetición** repeater
fusilamiento *m* execution (*by firing squad*)
fusilar ⟨1a⟩ *v/t* **1** shoot **2** *fig* F (*plagiar*) lift F
fusilero *m* HIST fusilier
fusión *f* **1** FÍS fusion **2** COM merger
◇ **fusión nuclear** nuclear fusion
fusionar ⟨1a⟩ *v/t* COM, *equipos*, *partidos políticos* merge; ***~ fuerzas*** join forces; **fusionarse** *v/r* merge
fusta *f* riding crop
fuste *m* **1** ARQUI shaft **2** *fig* importance, significance; ***de ~*** *fig* important, of consequence
fustigar ⟨1h⟩ *v/t* whip
futbito *m* indoor five-a-side soccer, *Br tb* five-a-side football
futbol *m Méx* ☞ ***fútbol***
fútbol *m* soccer, *Br tb* football
◇ **fútbol americano** football, *Br tb*

American football
◇ **fútbol sala** indoor five-a-side soccer *o Br tb* football
futbolín *m* Foosball®, table football
futbolista *m/f* soccer player, *Br tb* footballer, *Br tb* football player
futbolístico *adj* soccer *atr*, *Br tb* football *atr*
fútil *adj* trivial
futilidad *f* triviality
futón *m* futon
futre *m Chi* dandy
futurible *adj* possible
futurismo *m* futurism
futuro I *adj* future *atr* **II** *m* future; ***en el ~*** in (the) future
futurología *f* futurology
futurólogo *m*, **-a** *f* futurologist

G

g. *abr* (= ***gramo(s)***) gr(s) (= gram(s))
gabacho *m*, **-a** *f* F *desp* **1** Frog F, Frenchie F **2** *Méx* (*yanqui*) Yank
gabán *m* overcoat
gabardina *f* **1** *prenda* raincoat **2** *material* gabardine
gabarra *f* MAR barge
gabela *f* tax
gabinete *m* **1** (*despacho*) office; *en una casa* study **2** POL cabinet **3** *L.Am. de médico* office, *Br* surgery
◇ **gabinete de crisis** POL crisis cabinet
◇ **gabinete en la sombra** POL shadow cabinet
Gabón *m* Gabon
gacela *f* ZO gazelle
gaceta *f* gazette
gacetilla *f* short news story
gachas *fpl* porridge *sg*
gachí *f* P chick F, *Br tb* bird F
gacho *adj* **1** turned downward; ***con las orejas -as*** ashamed; ***con la cabeza -a*** hanging one's head **2** *Méx* F (*cutre*) ugly, horrible
gachó *m* P guy F
gachupín *m Méx desp* Spaniard
gacilla *f C.Am.* safety pin
gaditano *adj* of / from Cadiz, Cadiz *atr*
gaélico *adj* Gaelic
gafar ⟨1a⟩ *v/t* F jinx
gafas *fpl* glasses; ***llevar ~*** wear glasses
◇ **gafas de alta graduación** strong glasses; **gafas de buceo** diving goggles; **gafas de lectura** reading glasses; **gafas de sol** sunglasses
gafe I *adj* jinxed **II** *m* jinx **III** *m/f*: ***es un ~*** he's jinxed
gafotas *m/f fig* four-eyes *sg* F
gag *m* gag
gaita *f* MÚS bagpipes *pl*; ***templar ~s*** F tread carefully; ***estar de ~*** be happy
gaitero *m*, **-a** *f* piper
gajes *mpl*: ***~ del oficio*** *irón* occupational hazards
gajo *m* segment
GAL *mpl abr* (= ***Grupos Antiterroristas de Liberación***) anti-ETA death squads
gala[1] *f* gala; ***traje de ~*** formal dress; ***vestirse de ~*** wear formal dress; ***función de ~*** gala event; ***hacer ~ de*** show off; ***tener algo a ~*** pride o.s. on sth
gala[2] *f* (*francesa*) Frenchwoman
galán *m* **1** *actor* leading man **2** F (*hombre guapo*) gorgeous *o* cute guy F
◇ **galán de noche** *mueble* valet
galante *adj* gallant
galanteo *m* wooing
galápago *m* ZO turtle
galardón *m* award
galardonado I *adj* prize-winning, award-winning **II** *m*, **-a** *f* prizewinner, award winner
galardonar ⟨1a⟩ *v/t*: ***fue galardonado con ...*** he was awarded ...
galaxia *f* galaxy
galeno *m* F doctor
galeón *m* HIST galleon
galeote *m* HIST galley slave
galera *f* HIST galley
galerada *f* TIP galley proof
galería *f* gallery; ***para la ~, de cara a la ~*** *fig* for *o* to the gallery
◇ **galería de arte** art gallery
◇ **galería comercial** shopping mall
galerista *m/f* gallery owner
galerna *f* strong north-west wind (*that blows on the north coast of Spain*)
galés I *adj* Welsh **II** *m* **1** Welshman; ***los***

galeses the Welsh **2** *idioma* Welsh
Gales *m*: (***País de***) ~ Wales
galesa *f* Welshwoman
galgo *m*, **-a** *f* greyhound
gálibo *m* **1** gauge, gage **2**: ***luces de ~*** AUTO marker lamps, clearance lamps
galimatías *m* gibberish
gallardía *f* gallantry
gallardo *adj* gallant
gallego I *adj* **1** Galician **2** *Rpl* F Spanish **II** *m*, **-a** *f* **1** Galician **2** *Rpl* F Spaniard **III** *m idioma* Galician
gallera *f L.Am.* cockpit
galleta *f* **1** cookie, *Br* biscuit **2** *Méx* F strength

G

gallina I *f* hen; ***matar la ~ de los huevos de oro*** kill the goose that lays the golden eggs **II** *m/f* F chicken
◇ **gallina ciega** blind man's bluff *o Br* buff
gallinazo *m L.Am.* turkey buzzard
gallinero *m* henhouse
gallo *m* **1** ZO rooster, *Br* cock; ***en menos que canta un ~*** in an instant, in no time at all; ***otro ~ le cantaría si*** it would be different if; ***alzar*** *o* ***levantar el ~*** *fig* get on one's high horse **2**: ***soltó un ~*** F his voice cracked
◇ **gallo de pelea** fighting cock, game cock
galo *m* (*francés*) Frenchman
galón *m* **1** *adorno* braid **2** MIL stripe **3** *medida* gallon
galopada *f* gallop
galopante *adj* galloping
galopar ⟨1a⟩ *v/i* gallop
galope *m* gallop; ***a(l) ~*** at a gallop; ***a ~ tendido*** at full gallop; *fig* in a mad rush
galpón *m* **1** *L.Am.* large shed **2** *Carib* HIST slave quarters *pl*
galvanizar ⟨1f⟩ *v/t* galvanize
galvanoplastia *f* electroplating
gama *f* **1** *de tonalidades* range **2** MÚS scale
gamba *f* ZO, GASTR shrimp, *Br* prawn
gamberrada *f*: ***las ~s de los vecinos*** the neighbors' loutish behavior; ***el accidente ferroviario pudo ser debido a una ~*** the rail crash may be due to (an act of) vandalism
gamberrear ⟨1a⟩ *v/i* behave like a lout
gamberrismo *m* loutishness
gamberro *m*, **-a** *f* lout, troublemaker
gambito *m* gambit
gameto *m* BIO gamete
gamín *m*, **-ina** *f Col* street kid
gamo *m* ZO fallow deer
gamonal *m Pe*, *Bol desp* chief
gamulán *m Rpl* sheepskin coat
gamuza *f* ZO, *piel* chamois
gana *f* **1**: ***no me da la ~*** I don't want to; ***hace lo que le da la ~*** he does what he likes, he does as he pleases; ***... me da ~s de ...*** ... makes me want to ...; ***tener ~s de algo / de hacer algo*** feel like sth / like doing sth; ***quedarse con las ~s*** never get (the chance) to do sth **2** (*voluntad*): ***de mala ~*** unwillingly, grudgingly; ***de buena ~*** willingly
◇ **gana(s) de comer** appetite
ganadería *f* stockbreeding
ganadero I *adj* (*del ganado*) cattle *atr*; (*de la ganadería*) stockbreeding *atr* **II** *m*, **-a** *f* stockbreeder
ganado *m* cattle *pl*
◇ **ganado bovino** cattle *pl*; **ganado cabrío** goats *pl*; **ganado lanar** sheep *pl*; **ganado mayor** *cattle or horses*; **ganado menor** *goats, pigs or sheep*; **ganado ovino** sheep *pl*; **ganado porcino** hogs *pl*, pigs *pl*
ganador I *adj* winning **II** *m*, **~a** *f* winner
ganancia *f* profit
ganancial *adj* profit *atr*; ***bienes ~es*** JUR joint possessions, joint property *sg*; ***sociedad de ~es*** joint ownership *sg* (*on marriage*)
ganar ⟨1a⟩ **I** *v/t* **1** win; ***le gané cincuenta dólares*** I won fifty dollars off him; ***~ a alguien*** beat s.o. **2** *mediante el trabajo* earn
II *v/i* **1** *mediante el trabajo* earn **2** (*vencer*) win; ***~ por dos sets a uno*** win (by) two sets to one **3** (*mejorar*) improve; ***salir ganando con algo*** be better off with sth **4** (*aventajar*): ***le gano en velocidad / inteligencia*** I'm faster / more intelligent than him *o* than he is
ganarse *v/r* **1** earn; ***te has ganado unas vacaciones*** you've earned a vacation; ***~ la vida*** earn one's living **2** *a alguien* win over
ganchillo *m* crochet; ***hacer ~*** crochet
gancho *m* **1** hook **2** *L.Am.*, *Arg fig* F sex-appeal; ***tener ~*** F *de un grupo, una campaña* be popular; *de una persona* have that certain something **3** *L.Am.* ***hacer ~*** (*ayudar*) lend a hand

4 *L.Am.* (*grapa*) staple **5** *L.Am.* (*percha*) coat hanger
ganchudo *adj* hook-shaped; ***nariz -a*** hook nose
gandul I *adj* idle **II** *m*, **~a** *f* lazybones *sg*
gandulear ⟨1a⟩ *v/i* F loaf around F
ganga *f* bargain
ganglio *m* ANAT ganglion
gangoso *adj* nasal
gangrena *f* MED gangrene
gangrenarse ⟨1a⟩ *v/r* become gangrenous
gángster *m* gangster
ganguear ⟨1a⟩ *v/r* speak through one's nose
ganoso *adj*: ***estar ~ de algo / de hacer algo*** be dying for sth / to do sth; ***estar ~ de poder*** be hungry for power
gansada *f* F piece of nonsense; ***decir ~s*** talk nonsense
ganso *m* ZO goose; *macho* gander
ganzúa *f* picklock
gañán *m fig* oaf
gañido *m de perro* yelping; *de pájaro* cawing
gañir ⟨3h⟩ *v/i de perro* yelp; *de pájaro* caw
garabatear ⟨1a⟩ *v/i & v/t* doodle
garabateo *m* scrawl, scribble
garabato *m* doodle
garage *m L.Am.* garage
garagista *m/f L.Am.* garage attendant
garaje *m* garage; ***~ de reparaciones*** repair shop, garage
garajista *m/f* garage attendant
garante *m/f* FIN guarantor; ***salir ~*** stand surety (***de*** for)
garantía *f* guarantee
◇ **garantía por defectos** warranty against defects
garantizador *m* guarantor
garantizar ⟨1f⟩ *v/t* guarantee
garañón *m L.Am.* stallion
garapiña *f Cuba, Méx* pineapple squash
garbanzo *m* BOT chickpea; ***el ~ negro*** *fig* F the black sheep F
garbeo *m* stroll; ***darse un ~*** go for a stroll
garbo *m al moverse* grace
garboso *adj* graceful
garceta *f* ZO egret
gardenia *f* BOT gardenia
garete *m*: ***irse al ~*** *fig* F go to pot F
garfio *m* hook
gargajo *m* piece of phlegm
garganta *f* **1** ANAT throat **2** GEOG gorge
gargantilla *f* choker
gárgaras *fpl*: ***hacer ~*** gargle; ***mandar a alguien a hacer ~*** F tell s.o. to get lost F
gárgola *f* gargoyle
garita *f* sentry box
garito *m* gambling den
garra *f* **1** *de gato* claw; *de ave* talon; ***caer en las ~s de alguien*** *fig* fall into s.o.'s clutches **2**: ***tener ~*** F be compelling
garrafa *f* **1** carafe **2** *Rpl* (*bombona*) cylinder
garrafal *adj error etc* terrible
garrafón *m* demijohn
garrapata *f* ZO tick
garrapiñar ⟨1a⟩ *v/t almendras* coat in caramel
garrocha *f* **1** goad **2** *L.Am.* DEP pole; *deporte* pole-vault; ***salto con ~*** pole-vault
garrochista *m/f L.Am.* pole-vaulter
garronear ⟨1a⟩ *v/t & v/i Rpl* F scrounge F
garronero *m*, **-a** *f Rpl* F scrounger F
garrotazo *m* blow with a club, blow with a stick
garrote *m* **1** *tipo de ejecución* garrotte **2** *palo* club, stick
◇ **garrote vil** *tipo de ejecución* garrotte
gárrulo *adj persona* garrulous; *pájaro* twittering; *corriente* babbling
garúa *f L.Am.* drizzle
garuar ⟨1e⟩ *v/i L.Am.* drizzle
garza *f* ZO heron
◇ **garza real** gray *o Br* grey heron
garzón *m Rpl* (*mesero*) waiter
gas *m* **1** FÍS, QUÍM gas; ***con ~*** sparkling, carbonated; ***sin ~*** still **2**: ***~es*** *pl* MED gas *sg*, wind *sg* **3**: ***a todo ~*** flat out; ***a medio ~*** *fig* at reduced capacity; ***perder ~*** *fig* run out of steam
◇ **gas ciudad** town gas; **gas hilarante** laughing gas; **gas invernadero** greenhouse gas; **gas lacrimógeno** tear gas; **gas mostaza** mustard gas; **gas natural** natural gas; **gas nervioso** nerve gas; **gas noble** rare *o* noble gas; **gas propelente** propellant (gas); **gas tóxico** poison gas
gasa *f* gauze
gasear ⟨1a⟩ *v/t* gas
gaseosa *f* lemonade

G

gaseoso *adj* gaseous
gasfitero *m Pe, Bol* plumber
gasificación *f* QUÍM gasification
gasificar ⟨1g⟩ *v/t* QUÍM gasify
gasoducto *m* gas pipeline
gasoil, gasóleo *m* oil; *para motores* diesel
gasolina *f* gas, gasoline, *Br* petrol
◇ **gasolina con plomo** leaded gasoline, *Br* leaded petrol; **gasolina normal** regular (gasoline), *Br* two-star (petrol); **gasolina sin plomo** unleaded (gasoline *o Br* petrol); **gasolina súper** premium gasoline, *Br* four-star (petrol)
gasolinera *f* gas station, *Br* petrol station
gasolinero *m* gas station attendant, *Br* petrol station attendant
gasómetro *m* gasometer
gastado *adj* worn out
gastador *adj* spendthrift
gastar ⟨1a⟩ *v/t* **1** *dinero* spend; *energía, electricidad etc* use **2** (*llevar*) wear; ***¿qué número gastas?*** what size do you take?, what size are you? **3** (*desperdiciar*) waste **4** (*desgastar*) wear out; **gastarse** *v/r* **1** *dinero* spend **2** *de gasolina, agua* run out; *de pila* run down **3** *de ropa, zapatos* wear out
gasto *m* expense; ***~s*** expenses; ***meterse en ~s*** spend money; ***cubrir ~s*** cover one's costs, break even; ***pagar los ~s*** *de juicio* pay the costs; *de viaje* pay the expenses
◇ **gastos por desplazamiento** travel expenses; **gastos de mantenimiento** maintenance costs; **gastos de producción** production costs; **gastos de viaje** travel expenses
gástrico *adj* gastric; ***jugos ~s*** gastric juices
gastritis *f* gastritis
gastroenteritis *f* gastroenteritis
gastrointestinal *adj* gastrointestinal
gastronomía *f* gastronomy
gastronómico *adj* gastronomic
gastrónomo *m*, **-a** *f* gastronome
gata *f* **1** ZO (female) cat; ***a ~s*** F on all fours; ***andar a ~s*** F crawl **2** *Méx* servant, maid **3** *Chi para vehículo* jack
gatear ⟨1a⟩ *v/i* crawl
gatillero *m Méx* gunman; ***~ a sueldo*** hired gunman, hitman
gatillo *m* trigger; ***apretar el ~*** squeeze *o* pull the trigger
gato *m* **1** ZO cat; ***aquí hay ~ encerrado*** F there's something fishy going on here F; ***cuatro ~s*** a handful of people; ***dar ~ por liebre a alguien*** F con s.o. F; ***llevarse el ~ al agua*** *fig* F pull it off F; ***~ escaldado del agua fría huye*** once bitten, twice shy; ***de noche todos los ~s son pardos*** all cats look gray in the dark; ***lavarse a lo ~*** *fig* have a quick wash, have a cat lick
2 AUTO jack
3 *Méx* (*tres en raya*) tick-tack-toe, *Br* noughts and crosses *sg*
◇ **gato montés** ZO wild cat
gatuno *adj* feline, cat *atr*
gaucho *Rpl* **I** *adj* gaucho *atr* **II** *m* gaucho
gaveta *f* drawer
gavia *f* MAR topsail
gavilán *m* ZO sparrowhawk
gaviota *f* (sea)gull
gay I *adj* gay **II** *m* gay (man)
gayola *f Rpl* F slammer F
gayuba *f* BOT bearberry
gayumbos *mpl* F shorts, *Br* underpants
gazapo *m* **1** ZO young rabbit **2** F (*equivocación*) boo-boo F
gazmoño I *adj* **1** (*recatado*) prudish **2** (*santurrón*) sanctimonious **II** *m*, **-a** *f* **1** (*recatado*) prude **2** (*santurrón*) sanctimonious person
gaznápiro I *adj* dumb **II** *m*, **-a** *f* dimwit, dummy F
gaznate *m* gullet
gazpacho *m* gazpacho (*cold soup made with tomatoes, peppers, garlic etc*)
géiser *m* geyser
gel *m* gel
◇ **gel de baño** bath gel
gelatina *f* **1** gelatin(e) **2** GASTR Jell-O®, *Br* jelly
gelatinoso *adj* gelatinous
gélido *adj* icy
gelificar ⟨1g⟩ *v/t* set; **gelificarse** *v/r* set
gema *f* gem
gemebundo *adj fml* groaning
gemelo I *adj* **1** twin *atr*; ***hermano ~*** twin brother **II** *mpl*: ***~s*** **1** twins **2** *de camisa* cuff links **3** (*prismáticos*) binoculars
gemido *m* moan, groan
Géminis *m/f inv* ASTR Gemini
geminiano *L.Am.* ASTR **I** *adj* Gemini; ***soy ~*** I'm (a) Gemini **II** *m*, **-a** *f* Gemini
gemir ⟨3l⟩ *v/i* moan, groan

gemología *f* gemology
gen *m* gene
genciana *f* BOT gentian
gendarme *m* gendarme
gendarmería *f* gendarmerie
genealogía *f* genealogy
genealógico *adj*: ***árbol ~*** family tree
generación *f* generation
generacional *adj* generation *atr*; ***conflicto ~*** generation gap; ***cambio*** *o* ***relevo ~*** passage from one generation to the next
generador I *adj*: ***ser ~ de algo*** generate sth **II** *m* EL generator
general I *adj* general; ***en ~*** in general; ***por lo ~*** usually, generally **II** *m* general
generalidad *f* **1** (*mayoría*) majority **2** (*vaguedad*) general nature
generalización *f* generalization
generalizador *adj* general; *afirmación* sweeping, general
generalizar ⟨1f⟩ **I** *v/t* spread **II** *v/i* generalize; **generalizarse** *v/r* spread
generalmente *adv* generally
generar ⟨1a⟩ *v/t* generate
generativo *adj* generative
generatriz *f* MAT generatrix
genérico *adj* generic; ***nombre ~*** BIO generic name
género *m* **1** (*tipo*) type **2** PINT, *de literatura* genre; ***pintura de ~*** genre painting **3** GRAM gender **4** COM goods *pl*, merchandise **4** BIO genus; ***el ~ humano*** the human race
◇ **géneros de punto** knitwear *sg*
generosidad *f* generosity
generoso *adj* **1** *persona* generous **2** *vino* full-bodied
génesis *f* genesis
Génesis *m* Genesis
genética *f* genetics *sg*
genéticamente *adv* genetically; ***~ alterado*** *o* ***manipulado*** *o* ***modificado*** genetically altered *o* engineered *o* modified
genético *adj* genetic
genetista *m/f* geneticist
genial *adj* brilliant; F (*estupendo*) fantastic F, great F; ***lo pasamos ~*** F we had a fantastic F *o* a great F time
genialidad *f* brilliance
génico *adj* BIO gene *atr*; ***terapia -a*** gene therapy
geniecillo *m* elf
genio *m* **1** *talento*, *persona* genius **2** (*carácter*) temper; ***tener mal ~*** be bad-tempered; ***estar de buen / mal ~*** be in a good / bad mood
genital *adj* genital; ***órgano ~*** genital organ
genitales *mpl* genitals
genitivo *m* GRAM genitive
genocidio *m* genocide
genoma *m* BIO genome
Génova *f* Genoa
gente *f* **1** people *pl*; ***buena ~*** good *o* respectable people *pl*; ***ser buena ~*** be nice; ***la ~ mayor*** grown-ups *pl*; *ancianos* elderly people *pl*, old people *pl*; ***mi ~*** my family **2** *L.Am.* (*persona*) person
◇ **gente bien** well-off *o* well-to-do people *pl*; **gente de bien** good *o* respectable people *pl*; **gente bonita** *Méx*, **gente guapa** beautiful people *pl*; **gente menuda** children *pl*
gentil *adj* **1** kind, courteous **2** REL Gentile
gentileza *f* kindness; ***por ~ de*** by courtesy of
gentilhombre *m* gentleman
gentilicio *m word used to indicate nationality or regional origin*
gentilmente *adv* kindly
gentío *m* crowd
gentuza *f* rabble
genuflexión *f* genuflection
genuino *adj* genuine, real
GEO *m abr* (= ***Grupo Especial de Operaciones***) SWAT team
geodesia *f* geodesy
geodésico *adj* geodesic
geofísica *f* geophysics *sg*
geografía *f* geography; ***en toda la ~ española*** all over Spain
geográfico *adj* geographical
geógrafo *m*, **-a** *f* geographer
geología *f* geology
geológico *adj* geological
geólogo *m*, **-a** *f* geologist
geometría *f* geometry
geométrico *adj* geometric, geometrical
geopolítica *f* geopolitics *sg*
geotérmico *adj* geothermal
geranio *m* BOT geranium
gerbera *f* BOT gerbera
gerencia *f* **1** management **2** *oficina* manager's office **3** *tiempo* time as manager

gerenciar ⟨1b⟩ *v/t L.Am.* manage
gerente *m/f* manager
geriatra *m/f* geriatrician
geriatría *f* geriatrics *sg*
geriátrico *adj* geriatric; ***centro ~*** old people's home
gerifalte *m* ZO gyrfalcon; F bigwig F
germánico *adj* Germanic
germano I *adj* Germanic **II** *m*, **-a** *f* German
germen *m* germ
◇ **gérmenes de trigo** *pl* wheatgerm *sg*
germinación *f* germination
germinal *adj* germinal; ***célula ~*** germ cell
germinar ⟨1a⟩ *v/i tb fig* germinate
gerontocracia *f* POL gerontocracy
gerontología *f* gerontology
gerontólogo *m*, **-a** *f* gerontologist
gerundense *adj* of / from Gerona, Gerona *atr*
gerundio *m* GRAM gerund
gesta *f* heroic deed; ***cantar de ~*** chanson de geste, epic poem
gestación *f* gestation; ***en avanzado estado de ~*** heavily pregnant; ***en ~*** *fig* in gestation
gestante *f* expectant mother
gestarse ⟨1a⟩ *v/r*: ***se está gestando una rebelión*** a rebellion is brewing; ***se está gestando un nuevo plan*** a new plan is being developed
gesticulación *f* gesticulation
gesticular ⟨1a⟩ *v/i* gesticulate
gestión *f* **1** management; ***mala ~*** mismanagement, poor management **2**: ***gestiones*** *pl* (*trámites*) formalities, procedure *sg*; ***hacer gestiones*** attend to some business
◇ **gestión de empresa, gestión empresarial** business management; **gestión de patrimonios** asset management; **gestión de residuos** waste management; **gestión de sistemas** INFOR systems administration
gestionar ⟨1a⟩ *v/t* **1** *trámites* take care of **2** *negocio* manage
gesto *m* **1** *movimiento* gesture; ***hacer ~s*** gesture, make gestures **2** (*expresión*) expression; ***torcer el ~*** make a face, *Br* pull a face
gestor *m*, **~a** *f Esp person who works in a gestoría*
◇ **gestor de redes** INFOR network administrator
gestoría *f Esp agency offering clients help with official documents*
gestual *adj*: ***lenguaje ~*** sign language
giba *f* hump, hunch
gibar ⟨1a⟩ *v/t* F bug F, pester F; ***¿no te giba?*** F would you believe it!; **gibarse** *v/r* F lump it F
gibón *m* ZO gibbon
giboso *adj* humpbacked, hunchbacked
gibraltareño *adj* Gibraltarian
gigabyte *m* gigabyte
gigante I *adj* giant *atr* **II** *m* giant
gigantesco *adj* gigantic
gigantismo *m* MED gigantism
gigoló *m* gigolo
gilí *adj* F dumb F, silly; ***no seas ~*** don't be so dumb F
gilipollas *m/f inv* P jerk P
gilipollez *f Esp* V bullshit V
gilipuertas *m/f inv* F ☞ ***gilipollas***
gimió *vb* ☞ ***gemir***
gimnasia *f* gymnastics *sg*; ***hacer ~*** do exercises
◇ **gimnasia correctiva** remedial exercises *pl*; **gimnasia preparto** antenatal exercises *pl*; **gimnasia rítmica** rhythmic gymnastics *sg*
gimnasio *m* gym
gimnasta *m/f* gymnast
gimnástico *adj* gymnastic
gimo *vb* ☞ ***gemir***
gimotear ⟨1a⟩ *v/i* whine, whimper
gimoteo *m* whining, whimpering
gincana *f* gymkhana
ginebra *f* gin
Ginebra *f* Geneva
ginebrino *adj* Genevan
ginecología *f* gynecology, *Br tb* gynaecology
ginecológico *adj* gynecological, *Br tb* gynaecological
ginecólogo *m*, **-a** *f* gynecologist, *Br tb* gynaecologist
gingivitis *f* gingivitis
gin-tonic *m* gin and tonic, G and T F
gira *f* tour
girador *m*, **~a** *f* drawer
girar ⟨1a⟩ **I** *v/i* **1** (*dar vueltas*, *torcer*) turn; ***~ a la derecha / izquierda*** turn to the right / left; *de coche*, *persona* turn right / left, take a right / left **2** *alrededor de algo* revolve; ***~ en torno a algo*** *fig* revolve around sth **II** *v/t* COM

transfer
girasol *m* BOT sunflower
giratorio *adj* revolving
giro *m* **1** turn; ***~ a la derecha / izquierda*** right / left turn; POL shift to the right / left **2** GRAM idiom
◇ **giro postal** COM money order
gis *m L.Am.* chalk
gitano **I** *adj* gypsy *atr* **II** *m*, **-a** *f* gypsy
glaciación *f* GEOL glaciation
glacial *adj* icy; ***período o época ~*** Ice Age
glaciar **I** *adj*: ***lago ~*** glacier lake **II** *m* glacier
gladiador *m* HIST gladiator
gladiola *f Méx* BOT gladiolus
gladíolo, gladiolo *m* BOT gladiolus
glamoroso *adj* glamorous
glamour *m* glamor, *Br* glamour
glamuroso *adj* glamorous
glande *m* ANAT glans *sg*
glándula *f* ANAT gland
◇ **glándula lacrimal** tear gland
◇ **glándula pituitaria** pituitary gland
glasé *m* (*tela*) *type of thick silk*
glasear ⟨1a⟩ *v/t* GASTR, *papel* glaze
glauco *adj* glaucous
glaucoma *m* MED glaucoma
glicerina *f* glycerin, glycerine
glicin(i)a *f* BOT wisteria
global *adj* **1** (*de todo el mundo*) global **2** *visión*, *resultado* overall; *cantidad* total
globalidad *f*: ***en su ~*** in its entirety
globalización *f* globalization
globalizar ⟨1f⟩ *v/t* (*internacionalizar*) globalize
globo *m* **1** *aerostático*, *de niño* balloon **2** *terrestre* globe **3** DEP lob
◇ **globo aerostático** hot air balloon; **globo ocular** ANAT eyeball; **globo sonda** observation balloon; **globo terráqueo** globe
globoso *adj* globular
globular *adj* globular
glóbulo *m* globule; ANAT blood cell
gloria *f* **1** (*fama*) glory; ***cubrirse de ~*** cover o.s. in glory **2** (*delicia*) delight; ***saber a ~*** taste wonderful **3**: ***estar en la ~*** F be in seventh heaven F
gloriado *m Pe*, *Bol*, *Ecuad*: *type of punch*
glorieta *f* traffic circle, *Br* roundabout
glorificación *f* glorification
glorificar ⟨1g⟩ *v/t* glorify
glorioso *adj* glorious
glosa *f* gloss
glosar ⟨1a⟩ *v/t* gloss
glosario *m* glossary
glosopeda *f* foot-and-mouth (disease)
glotis *f* ANAT glottis
glotón **I** *adj* greedy, gluttonous **II** *m*, **-ona** *f* glutton
glotonear ⟨1a⟩ *v/i* stuff o.s.
glotonería *f* gluttony
glucemia *f* glycemia, *Br tb* glycaemia
glúcido *m* QUÍM glycide
glucosa *f* glucose
gluten *m* gluten
glúteo *m* gluteus
gnomo *m* gnome
gobernabilidad *f* governability
gobernable *adj* governable
gobernación *f* **1** government **2** *Méx*: ***Gobernación*** Department of the Interior, *Br* Home Office
gobernador **I** *adj* governing *atr* **II** *m*, **~a** *f* governor
gobernanta *f* **1** *de hotel* housekeeper **2** *L.Am.* (*institutriz*) governess
gobernante *m* leader
gobernar ⟨1k⟩ *v/t & v/i* rule, govern
gobierno *m* **1** POL government **2** MAR steering
◇ **gobierno de la casa** housekeeping
◇ **gobierno en la sombra** POL shadow cabinet
gobio *m pez* gudgeon
goce *m* pleasure, enjoyment
godo **I** *adj* Gothic **II** *m*, **-a** *f L.Am. desp* Spaniard
gofre *m* waffle
gogó *f* go-go; (***chica***) **~** go-go dancer
gol *m* DEP goal; ***marcar o meter un ~*** score (a goal); ***meter un ~ a alguien*** *fig* F put one over on s.o. F
◇ **gol del empate** tying goal, *Br* equalizer; **gol de oro** golden goal; **gol en propia meta, gol en propia puerta** own goal
gola *f* ruff
golazo *m* terrific *o* amazing goal
goleada *f* DEP F massacre F, crushing win / defeat
goleador *m*, **~a** *f* DEP (goal) scorer
golear ⟨1a⟩ *v/t* beat, thrash F
golero *m*, **-a** *f Rpl* goalkeeper
goleta *f* MAR schooner
golf *m* DEP golf; ***campo de ~*** golf course

golfa *f* P whore P
golfante *m* F ☞ ***golfo* II**
golfear 〈1a〉 *v/i* **1** loaf around **2** (*meterse en líos*) get up to no good
golfillo *m* (street) urchin
golfista *m/f* golfer
golfito *m L.Am.* mini-golf
golfo I *m* GEOG gulf **II** *m*, **-a** *f* good-for-nothing; *niño* little devil
◇ **Golfo de Arica** Chile-Peru Trench; **Golfo de California** Gulf of California; **Golfo de México** Gulf of Mexico
golondrina *f* ZO swallow; ***una ~ no hace verano*** one swallow doesn't make a summer
golondrino *m* MED *tumor in the armpit*
golosina *f* candy, *Br* sweet
goloso I *adj* sweet-toothed **II** *m*, **-a** *f* person with a sweet tooth
golpazo *m* thump
golpe *m* **1** knock, blow; ***un duro ~*** *fig* a heavy blow; ***no da ~*** F she doesn't do a thing, she doesn't lift a finger **2**: ***de ~*** suddenly; ***de ~ y porrazo*** suddenly
◇ **golpe bajo** *en boxeo* low punch, blow below the belt; ***no invitarla fue un ~*** *fig* not inviting her was a low blow *o* a bit below the belt; **golpe de calor** heatstroke; **golpe de Estado** coup d'état; ***dar un ~*** stage a coup (d'état); **golpe de fortuna** stroke of luck; **golpe franco** DEP free kick; **golpe de gracia** coup de grâce; **golpe de mar** huge wave; **golpe militar** military coup; **golpe de tos** coughing fit; **golpe de suerte** stroke of luck; **golpe de viento** gust of wind; **golpe de vista** glance
golpear 〈1a〉 *v/t cosa* bang, hit; *persona* hit; **golpearse** *v/r*: ***se golpeó la cabeza*** he hit his head
golpismo *m*: ***el ~ es característico de la vida política en el país*** coups (d'état) are a feature of the country's political life; ***fue condenado por ~*** he was convicted of involvement in the coup (d'état)
golpista I *adj*: ***un militar ~*** a participant in a military coup (d'état) **II** *m/f* coup participant, participant in a coup (d'état)
golpiza *f L.Am.* beating
goma *f* **1** (*caucho*) rubber **2** (*pegamento*) glue **3** (*banda elástica*) elastic band, *Br* rubber band **4** F (*preservativo*) condom, rubber P **5** *C.Am.* F hangover **6** BOT gum **7** *Méx en béisbol* home plate **8** *CSur* (*neumático*) tire, *Br* tyre
◇ **goma de borrar** eraser; **goma espuma** foam rubber; **goma de mascar** chewing gum
gomina *f* hair gel
gominola *f* jelly bean
gomorresina *f* gum resin
gónada *f* BIO gonad
góndola *f Chi* bus
gong *m* gong
gonorrea *f* gonorrhea, *Br tb* gonorrhoea
gordezuelo *adj* plump
gordinflón *m*, **-ona** *f* F fatso F
gordo I *adj* **1** fat **2**: ***me cae ~*** F I can't stand him; ***se va a armar la -a*** F all hell will break loose F; ***¡ésta sí que es -a!*** F this is a disaster!; ***no veo ni -a*** F I can't see a damn thing F **II** *m*, **-a** *f* fat person **III** *m premio* jackpot; ***me ha caído*** *o* ***tocado el ~*** I've won the jackpot; *fig* I've hit the jackpot
gorgorito *m* trill, warble
gorgotear 〈1a〉 *v/i* gurgle; *al hervir* bubble
gorigori *m* F wailing; ***armar el ~*** F make a racket F
gorila *m* ZO gorilla
gorjear 〈1a〉 *v/i de pájaro* chirp, warble; *de niño* gurgle
gorjeo *m de pájaro* chirping, warbling; *de niño* gurgling
gorra *f* cap; ***de ~*** F for free F; ***vivir de ~*** scrounge F
◇ **gorra de béisbol** baseball cap
◇ **gorra de plato, gorra visera** peaked cap
gorrinada, gorrinería *f fig* dirty trick
gorrinera *f* pigpen, *Br* pigsty
gorrino *m fig* pig
gorrión *m* ZO sparrow
gorro *m* **1** cap; ***estar hasta el ~ de algo*** F be fed up to the back teeth with sth F **2** *en baloncesto* block
gorrón *m*, **-ona** *f* F scrounger F
gorronear 〈1a〉 *v/t & v/i* F scrounge F
gota I *f* drop; ***ni ~*** F *de cerveza, leche etc* not a drop; *de pan* not a scrap; ***no ver ni ~*** F not see a thing; ***la ~ que colma*** *o* ***hace rebosar el vaso*** the last straw; ***parecerse como dos ~s de agua*** be like two peas in a pod; ***una ~ en el***

mar *fig* a drop in the ocean **II** *m*: ***~ a ~*** MED drip
◇ **gota fría** cold front
gotear ⟨1a⟩ *v/i* drip; *filtrarse* leak
goteo *m* dripping
gotera *f* **1** leak **2** (*mancha*) stain
gotero *m* **1** MED drip **2** *L.Am.* (eye)-dropper
gótico I *adj* Gothic **II** *m* ARQUI Gothic
gouache *m* gouache
gozada *f* F: ***fue una ~*** it was fantastic, it was brilliant
gozar ⟨1f⟩ *v/i* **1** (*disfrutar*) enjoy o.s.; ***~ de*** (*disfrutar de*) enjoy; ***~la*** have a good time **2**: ***~ de*** (*poseer*) have, enjoy
gozne *m* hinge
gozo *m* **1** (*alegría*) joy; ***no caber en sí de ~*** be overjoyed; ***mi ~ en un pozo*** F that's the end of that!, so much for that idea! **2** (*placer*) pleasure
gozoso *adj* happy
grabación *f* recording
grabado *m* engraving
grabador *m* tape recorder
grabadora *f* tape recorder
grabar ⟨1a⟩ *v/t* **1** *en video*, *cinta* record **2** PINT, *fig* engrave; ***el accidente quedó ~ en su memoria*** the accident was engraved *o* etched on her memory; **grabarse** *v/r* be engraved (***en*** on)
gracejo *m* wit
gracia *f* **1** (*humor*): ***tener ~*** be funny; ***me hace ~*** I think it's funny, it makes me laugh; ***no le veo la ~*** I don't think it's funny, I don't see the joke; ***tiene ~ que ...*** it's funny that ...; ***eso no tiene la menor ~*** that isn't the least *o* slightest bit funny; ***¡qué ~!*** *irón* well that's just great!
2: ***dar las ~s a alguien*** thank s.o., say thank you to s.o.; ***~s*** thank you; ***¡muchas ~s!*** thank you very much, thanks very much; ***~s a*** thanks to; ***¡~s a Dios!*** thank God, thank goodness; ***con la entrada tienes derecho a una bebida, y ~s*** F the ticket entitles you to one drink, and that's it
3 (*simpatía*): ***le has caído en ~*** he's taken a liking to you
4: ***en estado de ~*** REL in a state of grace
5 *de movimientos* gracefulness; ***tener ~*** be graceful
grácil *adj* dainty
gracilidad *f* gracefulness
gracioso I *adj* funny; ***¡muy ~!*** *irón* very funny! **II** *m* TEA comic character
gradas *fpl* DEP stands, grandstand *sg*
gradería *f L.Am.* stands *pl*
graderío *m* stands *pl*
grado *m* **1** degree; ***de primer grado*** *quemaduras* first-degree **2**: ***de buen ~*** with good grace, readily; ***de mal ~*** with bad grace, reluctantly
graduable *adj* adjustable
graduación *f* **1** TÉC *etc* adjustment **2** *de alcohol* alcohol content **3** EDU graduation **4** MIL rank; ***de alta ~*** high-ranking
◇ **graduación de gafas** eyeglass prescription
graduado I *adj* **1** *aparato de medida* graduated **2** *lentes*, *gafas* prescription *atr* **3** EDU graduate *atr* **II** *m*, **-a** *f* graduate
◇ **graduado escolar** *Esp* elementary school certificate; *persona* person with an elementary school certificate
gradual *adj* gradual
gradualmente *adv* gradually
graduar ⟨1e⟩ *v/t* **1** TÉC *etc* adjust **2**: ***~ las gafas*** *o* ***la vista*** have one's eyes tested; **graduarse** *v/r* EDU graduate, get one's degree
graffiti *mpl* graffiti
grafía *f* spelling
gráfica *f* graph
gráfico I *adj* graphic; ***artes -as*** graphic arts **II** *m* **1** MAT graph **2** INFOR graphic
grafismo *m* graphic design, graphic art
grafista *m/f* graphic designer, graphic artist
grafito *m* MIN graphite
grafología *f* graphology
grafólogo *m*, **-a** *f* graphologist
gragea *f* tablet, pill
grajo *m* ZO rook
Gral. *abr* (= ***general***) Gen (= general)
grama *f* **1** BOT Bermuda grass **2** *L.Am.* (*césped*) lawn
gramática *f* grammar; ***tener mucha ~ parda*** be worldly-wise
gramatical *adj* grammatical
gramático I *adj* grammatical **II** *m*, **-a** *f* grammarian
gramíneas *fpl* BOT grasses
gramo *m* gram
gramófono *m* phonograph, *Br* gramophone

gran *short form of* ***grande*** *before a noun*
Gran Bretaña *f* Great Britain
grana *f / adj* deep red
granada *f* **1** BOT pomegranate **2** MIL grenade
◇ **granada de carga hueca** MIL dummy grenade
◇ **granada de mano** MIL hand grenade
granadilla *f* **1** BOT passionflower **2** *fruta* passion fruit
granadino I *adj* of / from Granada, Granada *atr* **II** *m*, **-a** *f* native of Granada
granado I *adj* **1** (*destacado*) select; ***lo más ~ de*** *fig* the cream of **2** (*maduro*) mature **II** *m* BOT pomegranate tree
granangular *m* wide-angle lens
granate *adj inv* dark crimson
grancanario *adj* of / from Gran Canaria, Gran Canaria *atr*
grande I *adj* **1** big, large; ***el vestido me está*** *o* ***me viene ~*** the jacket is too big for me; ***el cargo le viene ~*** the job is too much for him **2**: ***a lo ~*** in style; ***pasarlo en ~*** have a great time **II** *m/f* **1** *L.Am.* (*adulto*) grown-up, adult; ***~s y pequeños*** young and old **2** (*mayor*) eldest
◇ **grande de España** (Spanish) nobleman *o* grandee
grandeza *f* greatness
◇ **grandeza de alma** nobility
grandilocuencia *f* grandiloquence
grandilocuente *adj* grandiloquent
grandiosidad *f* grandeur
grandioso *adj* impressive, magnificent
grandullón *m*, **-ona** *f* F big kid F
granel *m*: ***vender a ~*** COM sell in bulk; ***había comida a ~*** F there was loads of food F
granero *m* granary
granítico *adj* granite *atr*
granito[1] *m* MIN granite
granito[2] *m*: ***aportar su ~ de arena*** *fig* do one's bit
granizada *f* hailstorm
granizado *m type of soft drink made with crushed ice*
granizar ⟨1f⟩ *v/i* hail
granizo *m* hail
granja *f* farm
◇ **granja marina** fish farm
granjearse ⟨1a⟩ *v/r* win, earn
granjero *m*, **-a** *f* farmer
grano *m* **1** *de café* bean; *de cereales* grain; ***separar*** *o* ***apartar el ~ de la paja*** separate the wheat from the chaff; ***ir al ~*** get (straight) to the point **2** *en la piel* pimple, spot
◇ **grano de uva** grape
granoso *adj* grainy
granuja *m/f* rascal
granujada *f* dirty trick
granulación *f* granulation
granuloma *m* MED granuloma
grapa *f* staple
grapadora *f* stapler
grapar ⟨1a⟩ *v/t* staple
grasa *f* **1** BIO, GASTR fat; ***bajo en ~*** low in fat, low-fat *atr* **2** *lubricante*, *suciedad* grease **3** *Méx* (*betún*) shoe polish
◇ **grasa animal** animal fat
◇ **grasa vegetal** vegetable fat
grasiento *adj* greasy, oily
graso *adj* greasy; *carne* fatty
gratén *m*: ***al ~*** GASTR au gratin
gratificación *f* **1** *por satisfacción* gratification **2** *a un empleado* bonus
gratificante *adj* gratifying
gratificar ⟨1g⟩ *v/t* reward; *a un empleado* give a bonus to
gratinar ⟨1a⟩ *v/t* GASTR cook au gratin
gratis *adj & adv* free
gratitud *f* gratitude
grato *adj* pleasant
gratuidad *f*: ***~ de la enseñanza / los medicamentos*** free education / medicine
gratuito *adj* free; ***ser ~*** *fig* be gratuitous
grava *f* gravel
gravable *adj* taxable
gravamen *m* tax
gravar ⟨1a⟩ *v/t* tax; ***la casa está gravada con una hipoteca*** the house is mortgaged
grave *adj* **1** serious; *tono* grave, solemn; ***estar ~*** be seriously ill **2** *voz* deep; *nota* low **3** LING *acento* grave
gravedad *f* **1** seriousness, gravity; ***herido de ~*** seriously injured **2** FÍS gravity
gravemente *adv* seriously; ***~ enfermo*** seriously ill
gravidez *f* pregnancy
grávido *adj* pregnant; ***el útero ~*** the uterus during pregnancy
gravilla *f* gravel
gravitación *f* gravitation
gravitar ⟨1a⟩ *v/i* **1** FÍS gravitate; ***~ alre-***

dedor de *fig* center round, *Br* centre around **2** (*recaer*) rest (***sobre*** on)
gravitatorio *adj* gravitational
gravoso *adj* expensive, costly
graznar ⟨1a⟩ *v/i de cuervo* caw; *de pato* quack; *de ganso* honk
graznido *m de cuervo* cawing; *de pato* quacking; *de ganso* honking
greca *f* frieze
Grecia *f* Greece
gregario *adj* gregarious; ***instinto ~*** gregariousness
gregoriano *adj* Gregorian; ***canto ~*** Gregorian chant
grelos *mpl* GASTR turnip greens
gremial *adj* HIST guild *atr*
gremio *m* HIST guild; *fig* F (*oficio manual*) trade; (*profesión*) profession
greña *f* **1**: ***andar a la ~*** F quarrel, argue **2**: ***~s*** messy hair *sg*
greñudo *adj* unkempt, disheveled, *Br* dishevelled
gres *m* (*arcilla*) earthenware; *para artesano* potter's clay
gresca *f* **1** (*pelea*) fight; ***armar ~*** start a fight **2** (*escándalo*) din, uproar
grey *f* flock
Grial *m*: ***el Santo ~*** the Holy Grail
griego I *adj* Greek **II** *m*, **-a** *f* Greek **III** *m idioma* Greek
grieta *f* crack
grifa *f* F dope F
grifería *f* faucets *pl*, *Br* taps *pl*
grifo I *adj Méx* F high **II** *m* **1** faucet, *Br* tap **2** *Pe* (*gasolinera*) gas station, *Br* petrol station
grifón *m* griffon
grillado *adj* F crazy, loopy F
grillarse ⟨1a⟩ *v/r* F go crazy
grillete *m* shackle, fetter
grillo *m* **1** ZO cricket **2**: ***~s*** *pl* shackles, fetters
grima *f* **1** *Esp*: ***me da ~*** *de ruido, material etc* it sets my teeth on edge; *de algo asqueroso* it gives me the creeps F **2** *Pe*: ***en ~*** alone
gringo *m*, **-a** *f L.Am. desp* gringo *desp*, foreigner
gripa *f Méx* flu
gripal *adj* MED flu *atr*, influenza *atr*
griparse ⟨1a⟩ *v/r* TÉC seize (up)
gripe *f* flu, influenza
◇ **gripe intestinal** gastric flu
griposo *adj*: ***estar ~*** have flu
gris I *adj* gray, *Br* grey **II** *m*: ***~ perla*** pearl gray *o Br* grey
grisáceo *adj* grayish, *Br* greyish
grisú *m* firedamp
gritar ⟨1a⟩ *v/t & v/i* shout, yell
griterío *m* shouting
grito *m* cry, shout; ***dar ~s*** shout; ***a ~ pelado*** at the top of one's voice; ***pedir algo a ~s*** F be crying out for sth; ***poner el ~ en el cielo*** hit the roof F; ***el último ~ en teléfonos móviles*** the last word in cell phones
grogui *adj* groggy, dazed
grosella *f* redcurrant
◇ **grosella silvestre** gooseberry
grosería *f* rudeness
grosero I *adj* rude **II** *m*, **-a** *f* rude person
grosor *m* thickness
grotesco *adj* grotesque
grúa *f* **1** crane **2** AUTO wrecker, *Br* breakdown truck
◇ **grúa flotante** floating crane
grueso I *adj* **1** *muro, tela* thick **2** *persona* stout **3**: ***mar -a*** rough sea **II** *m* thickness
grulla *f* ZO crane
grumete *m* cabin boy
grumo *m* lump
grumoso *adj* lumpy
gruñido *m* grunt; *de perro* growl
gruñir ⟨3h⟩ *v/i* **1** (*quejarse*) grumble, moan F **2** *de perro* growl; *de cerdo* grunt
gruñón I *adj* F grumpy **II** *m*, **-ona** *f* F grouch F
grupa *f* hindquarters *pl*; ***volver ~s*** turn back
grupo *m* group; ***en ~s*** in groups
◇ **grupo electrógeno** generator; **grupo parlamentario** POL parliamentary group; **grupo de presión** POL pressure group, special interest group; **grupo sanguíneo** blood group
grupúsculo *m esp* POL splinter group
gruta *f* cave; *artificial* grotto
guacamayo *m ave* macaw
guacamol, guacamole *m* guacamole
guache *m* ☞ ***gouache***
guachimán *m Chi* watchman
guacho *S.Am.* **I** *adj* **1** (*sin casa*) homeless **2** (*huérfano*) orphaned **II** *m*, **-a** *f* **1** *sin casa* homeless person **2** (*huérfano*) orphan
guadaña *f* scythe
guadaño *m Cuba, Méx* small boat

guagua *f* **1** *Carib, Ven, Canaries* bus **2** *Pe, Bol, Chi* (*niño*) baby
guajiro *m*, **-a** *f Cu* peasant
guajolote *m Méx, C.Am.* turkey
guanábana *f* BOT soursop (tree)
guanaco **I** *adj L.Am.* F dumb F, stupid **II** *m* ZO guanaco **III** *m*, **-a** *f persona* idiot
guano *m* guano
guantazo *m* slap
guante *m* glove; ***echar el ~ a alguien*** catch s.o., nab s.o. F; ***arrojar el ~ a alguien*** throw down the gauntlet to s.o.; ***recoger el ~*** take up the challenge; ***sentar como un ~*** F fit like a glove; ***tratar a alguien con ~ de seda*** *fig* handle s.o. with kid gloves
guantera *f* AUTO glove compartment
guaperas *m/f* F good-looker
guapetón *adj* F gorgeous F
guapo **I** *adj* **1** *hombre* handsome, good-looking; *mujer* beautiful **2** *S.Am.* gutsy **II** *m* handsome *o* good-looking man **III** **-a** *f* beautiful woman
guapura *f* good looks *pl*
guaracha *f Carib* street band
guarache ☞ ***huarache***
guaraní *m* FIN guaraní
guarapo *m L.Am. alcoholic drink made from sugar cane and herbs*
guarda *m/f* keeper
◇ **guarda de campo** estate guard; **guarda forestal** forest ranger, warden; **guarda jurado** security guard; **guarda rural** estate guard
guardabarrera *m* FERR grade crossing keeper, *Br* level crossing keeper
guardabarros *m inv* AUTO fender, *Br* mudguard
guardabosque(**s**) *m/f* (*inv*) forest ranger, warden
guardacoches *m/f inv* parking lot attendant, *Br* car park attendant
guardacostas **I** *m inv* coastguard vessel **II** *m/f inv* coastguard
guardaespaldas *m/f inv* bodyguard
guardafango *m L.Am.* AUTO fender, *Br* mudguard
guardagujas FERR **I** *m inv* switchman, *Br* pointsman **II** *f* switchwoman, *Br* pointswoman
guardameta *m/f* DEP goalkeeper
guardapolvo *m* **1** (*bata*) overall **2** (*funda*) dust sheet, dust cover
guardar ⟨1a⟩ *v/t* **1** keep; ***~ silencio*** remain silent, keep silent **2** *poner en un lugar* put (away) **3** *recuerdo* have **4** *apariencias* keep up **5** INFOR save **6**: ***~ cama*** stay in bed; **guardarse** *v/r* **1** keep **2**: ***~ de*** refrain from; ***me guardaré muy mucho*** I'll be very careful
guardarraíl *m* safety barrier
guardarropa *m* **1** *en lugar público* checkroom, *Br* cloakroom **2** (*ropa*) wardrobe; *armario* closet, *Br* wardrobe
guardarropía *f* TEA wardrobe
guardavallas *m/f inv L.Am.* goalkeeper
guardavida *m/f Rpl* lifeguard
guardería *f* nursery
guardia **I** *f* **1** guard; ***bajar la ~*** *fig* lower one's guard; ***poner a alguien en ~*** put s.o. on their guard; ***la vieja ~*** *fig* the old guard **2**: ***de ~*** on duty **II** *m/f* **1** MIL guard **2** (*policía*) police officer
◇ **guardia civil** *Esp* civil guard; **guardia de corps** bodyguard; **guardia de seguridad** security guard; **guardia de tráfico** traffic warden; **guardia urbano** city police officer
guardián **I** *adj*: ***perro ~*** guard dog **II** *m*, **-ana** *f* guard; *fig* guardian
guarecer ⟨2d⟩ *v/t* shelter; **guarecerse** *v/r* shelter (***de*** from), take shelter (***de*** from)
guarida *f* **1** ZO den **2** *de personas* hide-out
guarismo *m* figure
guarnecer ⟨2d⟩ *v/t* **1** adorn (***de*** with) **2** GASTR garnish (***con*** with)
guarnición *f* **1** GASTR accompaniment; ***con ~*** with garnish **2** MIL garrison
guaro *m C.Am.* sugar-cane liquor
guarrada, guarrería *f* F filth; ***es una ~*** it's disgusting
guarrear ⟨1a⟩ *v/i* F make a mess
guarro **I** *adj* F *sucio* filthy **II** *m tb fig* F pig
guarura *m Méx* **1** (*guardaespaldas*) bodyguard **2** (*gamberro*) thug
guasa *f L.Am.* joke; ***de ~*** as a joke
guaso **I** *adj S.Am.* rude **II** *m*, **-a** *f Chi* peasant
guasón **I** *adj*: ***es muy ~*** he treats everything as a joke **II** *m*, **-ona** *f* joker
guata *f L.Am.* F paunch
Guatemala *f* Guatemala
guatemalteco **I** *adj* Guatemalan **II** *m*, **-a** *f* Guatemalan
guateque *m* party

guatón *adj* pot-bellied, big-bellied
guau *int* **1** *por asombro, sorpresa etc* wow **2**: *¡~!, ¡~! de perro* bow-wow!
guay *int Esp* F cool F, neat F
guayaba *f* BOT guava
guayabera *f Méx, C.Am., Carib loose embroidered shirt*
guayabo *m* BOT guava tree
guayaco *m* BOT guaiacum
gubernamental *adj* governmental, government *atr*
gubernativo *adj* government *atr*
guepardo *m* ZO cheetah
güero **I** *adj Méx, C.Am.* fair, light-skinned **II** *m*, **-a** *f Méx, C.Am.* blonde, blond
guerra *f* war; ***dar ~ a alguien*** F give s.o. trouble
◇ **guerra civil** civil war; **guerra fría** cold war; **guerra mundial** world war; **guerra de precios** price war; **guerra relámpago** blitzkrieg; **guerra de sucesión** HIST War of Spanish Succession
guerrear ⟨1a⟩ *v/i* wage war
guerrera *f* military jacket
guerrero **I** *adj* warlike **II** *m* warrior
guerrilla *f* **1** *organización* guerillas *pl* **2** *guerra* guerrilla warfare
guerrillero *m*, **-a** *f* guerilla
gueto *m* ghetto
guevear ☞ ***huevear***
guevón ☞ ***huevón***
güey *adj Méx* F stupid, dumb F
guía **I** *m/f* guide **II** *f libro* guide (book)
◇ **guía de montaña** mountain guide; **guía telefónica, guía de teléfonos** phone book; **guía turístico** tourist guide
guiar ⟨1c⟩ *v/t* guide; **guiarse** *v/r*: ***~ por*** follow
guijarro *m* pebble
guillarse ⟨1a⟩ *v/r* go crazy F
guillotina *f* guillotine; ***ventana de ~*** sash window
guillotinar ⟨1a⟩ *v/t* guillotine
guinche, güinche *m L.Am.* winch, pulley
guinda **I** *adj L.Am.* purple **II** *f fresca* morello cherry; *en dulce* glacé cherry
guindar ⟨1a⟩ *v/t* F lift F, *Br* nick F
guindilla *f* GASTR chil(l)i
guindo *m* BOT cherry tree
guiñapo *m* rag; ***estar hecho un ~*** F be a wreck; ***poner a alguien como un ~*** F tear a strip off s.o.
guiñar ⟨1a⟩ **I** *v/t*: ***le guiñó un ojo*** she winked at him **II** *v/i* wink
guiño *m* wink; ***hacer un ~ a alguien*** wink at s.o.
guiñol *m* puppet show; ***muñeco de ~*** puppet
guión *m* **1** *de película* script **2** GRAM *corto* hyphen; *largo* dash
guionista *m/f* scriptwriter
guiri *m Esp* P (light-skinned) foreigner
guirigay *m* F jargon, gibberish
guirnalda *f* garland
guisa *f*: ***a ~ de*** as, like; ***de esta ~*** thus, in this way; ***de tal ~ (que)*** in such a way (that)
guisado *m* GASTR stew, casserole
guisante *m* pea
guisar ⟨1a⟩ *v/t* GASTR stew, casserole; ***ellos se lo guisan y ellos se lo comen*** *fig* they keep it all in the family
guiso *m* GASTR stew, casserole
güisqui *m* whiskey, *Br* whisky
guita *f* **1** string **2** P dough P, cash
guitarra *f* guitar
guitarrista *m/f* guitarist
gula *f* gluttony
guripa *m* F **1** *soldado* private, grunt P **2** *guardia* cop F
gurú *m* guru
gusanillo *m*: ***me tomé una manzana para matar el ~*** F I had an apple to keep myself going
gusano *m* worm; *de mosca* maggot
◇ **gusano de luz** glowworm
◇ **gusano de seda** silkworm
gustar ⟨1a⟩ *v/i*: ***me gusta viajar***, *fml* ***me gusta de viajar*** I like to travel, I like *o* enjoy traveling; ***¿te gusta el ajo?*** do you like garlic?; ***no me gusta*** I don't like it; ***me gusta Ana*** I like Ana, *Br tb* I fancy Ana F; ***me gustaría ...*** I would like ...; ***cuando guste*** whenever you like; ***¿Vd. gusta?*** would you like some? **II** *v/t* taste
gustativo *adj* taste *atr*
gustazo *m* great pleasure
gustillo *m* (slight) taste; ***tiene un ~ amargo*** it has a slightly bitter taste
gusto *m* **1** (*preferencias, sabor*) taste; ***sobre ~s no hay nada escrito*** there's no accounting for taste; ***de buen ~*** in good taste, tasteful; ***de mal ~*** in bad taste, tasteless; ***tomar el ~ a algo*** get

G

to like sth, acquire a taste for sth
2 (*placer*) pleasure; ***con mucho ~*** with pleasure; ***da ~ hacer negocios con usted*** it's a pleasure doing business with you; ***dar ~ a alguien*** please s.o.; ***tener el ~ de*** have the pleasure of; ***mucho** o **tanto ~*** how do you do
3: ***a ~*** at ease; ***sentirse a ~*** feel comfortable *o* at ease
gustoso *adj* gladly, with pleasure
gutural *adj* guttural
Guyana *f* Guyana
Guyana Francesa *f* French Guyana
guyanés **I** *adj* Guyanese **II** *m*, **-esa** Guyanese
gymkhana *f* gymkhana

H

ha *vb* ☞ ***haber***
haba *f* broad bean; ***en todas partes se cuecen ~s*** it's the same the world over; ***o vienes o te quedas, son ~s contadas*** either you come or you stay, it's as simple as that
Habana: ***La ~*** Havana
habanera *f* habanera
habanero **I** *adj* of / from Havana, Havana *atr*; **II** *m*, **-a** *f* citizen of Havana
habano **I** *adj* of / from Havana, Havana *atr* **II** *m*, **-a** *f* citizen of Havana **III** *m* Havana (cigar)
haber ⟨2k⟩ **I** *v/aux* **1** *en tiempos compuestos* have; ***hemos llegado*** we've arrived; ***lo he oído*** I've heard it; ***¿la ha visto?*** has he seen her? **2** *expresando obligación, deber*: ***he de levantarme pronto*** I have to *o* I've got to get up early **3**: ***de ~lo sabido*** if I'd known; ***has de ver*** *Méx* you have *o* ought to see it; ***habérselas con alguien*** have it out with s.o.; ***años ha*** *lit* years ago
II *v/impers* **1** (*existir*): ***hay*** there is *sg*, there are *pl*; ***hubo un incendio*** there was a fire; ***había mucha gente*** there were a lot of people; ***hoy no hay clase*** there aren't any lessons today, school is closed today; ***ya no hay más*** there's none left; there are none left; ***no hay como …*** there's nothing like …; ***esto es de lo que no hay*** this is the limit!
2 *expresando obligación, deber*: ***hay que hacerlo*** it has to be done; ***no hay de qué*** not at all, don't mention it; ***no hay más que decir*** there's nothing more to be said; ***no hay que pagar para entrar*** you don't have to pay to go in; ***no hay que hablar con la boca llena*** you mustn't *o* shouldn't talk with your mouth full
3: ***¿qué hay?***, *Méx* ***¿qué hubo?*** how's it going?, what's happening?; ***es ingenioso donde los haya*** he's as ingenious as they come
III *m* asset; *pago* fee; ***tiene en su ~ 50.000 pesos*** she's 50,000 pesos in credit; ***~es*** *pl* (*bienes*) assets; (*sueldo*) salary *sg*
habichuela *f* kidney bean
hábil *adj* **1** skilled **2** (*capaz*) capable **3** (*astuto*) clever, smart **4**: ***día ~*** working day
habilidad *f* **1** skill **2** (*capacidad*) ability **3** (*astucia*) cleverness
habilidoso *adj* **1** *con las manos* good with one's hands, handy **2** (*inteligente*) clever, skillful, *Br* skilful
habilitación *f* **1** *de lugar* fitting out **2** (*autorización*) permission
habilitado *m*, **-a** *f* paymaster
habilitar ⟨1a⟩ *v/t* **1** *lugar* fit out **2** *persona* authorize
habitable *adj* habitable, fit for habitation
habitación *f* room; (*dormitorio*) bedroom
◇ **habitación doble** double room; **habitación con dos camas** twin room; **habitación individual** single room
habitacional *adj L.Am.* housing *atr*
habitáculo *m* **1** dwelling **2** AUTO passenger compartment
habitante *m/f* inhabitant
habitar ⟨1a⟩ **I** *v/i* live (***en*** in) **II** *v/t* inhabit, live in
hábitat *m* habitat
hábito *m* **1** (*costumbre*) habit; ***crear ~*** be addictive, be habit-forming **2** REL habit; ***colgar los ~s*** *fig de sacerdote* give

up the priesthood; ***tomar el ~*** REL *de hombre* become a monk, take holy orders; *de mujer* become a nun, take the veil **3** (*práctica*) knack

habitual **I** *adj* usual, regular **II** *m/f* regular

habitualmente *adv* usually

habituar ⟨1e⟩ *v/t*: ***~ a alguien a algo*** get s.o. used to sth; **habituarse** *v/r*: ***~ a algo*** get used to sth

habla *f* **1** speech; ***quedarse sin ~*** *fig* be speechless **2** (*idioma*): ***de ~ española*** Spanish-speaking **3**: ***ponerse al ~ con alguien*** contact s.o., get in touch with s.o. ***¡al ~!*** TELEC speaking

hablada *f L.Am.* piece of gossip; ***~s*** *pl* gossip *sg*

hablado *adj* **1** *lengua* spoken **2**: ***mal ~*** foulmouthed; ***bien ~*** well-spoken

hablador **I** *adj* talkative; *Méx* boastful **II** *m*, **~a** *f* chatterbox

habladurías *fpl* gossip *sg*

hablante *m/f* speaker

hablar ⟨1a⟩ *v/i* **1** speak; ***~ alto / bajo*** speak loudly / softly; ***~ claro*** *fig* say what one means; ***~ por sí solo*** *fig* speak for o.s.
2 (*conversar*) talk; ***~ con alguien*** talk to s.o., talk with s.o.
3: ***~ de*** *de libro etc* be about, deal with
4: ***¡ni ~!*** no way!; ***~ por ~*** talk for the sake of it; ***¡mira quién habla!*** look who's talking!; ***no me hagas ~ más*** I don't want to have to say this again!; ***no se hable más (del asunto)*** I don't want to hear anything more about it; ***por no ~ de ...*** not to mention ...
hablarse *v/r* speak to one another; ***no se hablan*** they're not speaking (to each other)

hablilla *f* rumor, *Br* rumour

habón *m* MED bump (*on the skin*)

hacedero *adj* feasible, practicable

hacedor *m*, **~a** *f* maker

hacendado **I** *adj* land-owning **II** *m*, **-a** *f* land-owner

hacendoso *adj* hardworking

hacer ⟨2s; *part* **hecho**⟩ **I** *v/t* **1** (*realizar*) do; ***¡haz algo!*** do something!; ***~ una pregunta*** ask a question; ***tengo que ~ los deberes*** I have to do my homework; !; ***no hace más que quejarse*** all he does is complain; ***no hay nada que ~*** there's nothing we can do; ***se hace lo que se puede*** one does one's best; ***¡eso no se hace!*** that's just not done!
2 (*elaborar, crear*) make; ***~ la comida*** make *o* cook a meal; ***~ que algo ocurra*** make sth happen
3 (*obligar a*): ***~ que alguien haga algo*** make s.o. do sth; ***le hicieron ir*** they made him go
4 (*cumplir*): ***hoy hago veinte años*** I am twenty today, today is my twentieth birthday
5 (*equivaler a*): ***esta botella hace un litro*** this bottle holds a liter
6: ***¡qué le vamos a ~!*** that's life
II *v/i* **1**: ***haces bien / mal en ir*** you are doing the right / wrong thing by going
2 (*sentar*): ***me hace mal*** it's making me ill
3 (*servir de*): ***esto hará de mesa*** *de objeto* this will do as a table
4 (*fingir*): ***~ como que*** *o* ***como si*** act as if
5 *L.Am.* ***no le hace*** it doesn't matter
6 *L.Am.* (*parecer*): ***se me hace que*** it seems to me that
7 (*apetecer*): ***¿hace?*** F does that sound good?
8: ***~ de malo*** TEA play the villain
III *v/impers*: ***hace calor / frío*** it's hot / cold; ***hace tres días*** three days ago; ***hace mucho (tiempo)*** a long time ago, long ago; ***desde hace un año*** for a year
hacerse *v/r* **1** *traje* make; *casa* build o.s.
2 (*cocinarse*) cook
3 (*convertirse, volverse*) get, become; ***~ viejo*** get old; ***~ de noche*** get dark; ***se hace tarde*** it's getting late; ***¿qué se hizo de aquello?*** what happened with that?
4: ***~ el sordo / el tonto*** pretend to be deaf / stupid
5: ***~ a algo*** get used to sth
6: ***~ con algo*** get hold of sth

hacha *f* **1** ax, *Br* axe; ***enterrar el ~ de guerra*** *fig* bury the hatchet **2**: ***ser un ~ para algo*** F be brilliant at sth

hachazo *m* blow with an ax, *Br* blow with an axe

hache *f* letter 'h'; ***por ~ o por be*** for one reason or another

hachís *m* hashish

hacia *prp* **1** *en el espacio* toward; ***~ adelante*** forward; ***~ abajo*** down; ***~ arriba*** up; ***~ atrás*** back(ward); ***~ aquí*** in this

H

direction, this way **2** *en el tiempo*: ***~ las cuatro*** about four (o'clock)
hacienda *f L.Am.* (*granja*) ranch, estate
Hacienda *f* **1** *ministerio* Treasury Department, *Br* Treasury **2** *oficina* Internal Revenue Service, *Br* Inland Revenue **3**: ***la ~ pública*** public funds *pl*, the public purse
hacinamiento *m* overcrowding
hacinar ⟨1a⟩ *v/t* stack; **hacinarse** *v/r* crowd together
hacker *m/f* INFOR hacker
hada *f* fairy
hado *m lit* fate, destiny
haga *vb* ☞ ***hacer***
hagiografía *f* hagiography
hago *vb* ☞ ***hacer***
Haití *m* Haiti
haitiano **I** *adj* Haitian **II** *m*, **-a** *f* Haitian
¡hala! *int animando* come on!; *sorpresa* wow!
halagador *adj* flattering
halagar ⟨1h⟩ *v/t* flatter
halago *m* flattery
halagüeño *adj* encouraging, promising
halar ⟨1a⟩ *v/t L.Am.* haul, pull
halcón *m* ZO falcon
◇ **halcón peregrino** peregrine falcon
halconero *m*, **-a** *f* falconer
¡hale! ☞ ***hala***
halibut *m* ZO halibut
hálito *m lit* breath
halitosis *f* MED halitosis, bad breath
hall *m* hall
hallar ⟨1a⟩ *v/t* **1** *objeto* find; *muerte, destino* meet **2** (*descubrir*) discover; **hallarse** *v/r* **1** be **2** (*sentirse*) feel
hallazgo *m* find; (*descubrimiento*) discovery
halo *m* AST, *de santo* halo; *fig* aura
halógeno *adj* halogen
halógeno *m* QUÍM halogen
haltera DEP **I** *f* barbell **II** *m/f* ☞ ***halterófilo***
halterofilia *f* DEP weight lifting
halterófilo *m*, **-a** *f* weight lifter
hamaca *f* **1** hammock **2** (*tumbona*) deck chair **3** *L.Am.* (*mecedora*) rocking chair, rocker **4** *Rpl* (*columpio*) swing
hamacar ⟨1g⟩ *v/t L.Am.* swing; **hamacarse** *v/r Rpl* swing
hamaquear ⟨1a⟩ *v/t L.Am.* swing
hambre *f* hunger; ***tener ~*** be hungry; ***tener un ~ canina*** be ravenous; ***pasar ~*** be starving; ***morirse de ~*** *fig* be starving; ***ser un muerto de ~*** be on the bread line; *en relaciones* have no luck with the opposite sex
hambreado *adj L.Am.* starving
hambriento *adj tb fig* hungry (**de** for)
hambrón *adj* greedy
hambruna *f* **1** famine **2** *L.Am.* ravenous hunger
hamburguesa *f* GASTR hamburger
hamburguesería *f* hamburger joint
hampa *f* underworld; ***gente del ~*** criminals *pl*, underworld figures *pl*
hampón *m* criminal, underworld figure
hámster *m* ZO hamster
handicap *m* DEP *tb fig* handicap
hangar *m* hangar
haragán *m*, **-ana** *f* shirker
haraganear ⟨1a⟩ *v/i* laze around, idle
haraganería *f* laziness, idleness
harapiento *adj* ragged
harapo *m* rag
hardware *m* INFOR hardware
haré *vb* ☞ ***hacer***
harina *f* flour; ***eso es ~ de otro costal*** *fig* F that's a different kettle of fish; ***estar metido en ~*** F be in the middle of things
◇ **harina integral** wholemeal flour
◇ **harina de trigo** wheat flour
harinero *adj* flour *atr*
harinoso *adj* floury
harmonía *f* ☞ ***armonía***
harnero *m* sieve
hartar ⟨1a⟩ *v/t*: ***~ a alguien con algo*** tire s.o. with sth; ***~ a alguien de algo*** give s.o. too much of sth; **hartarse** *v/r* **1** get sick (***de*** of) F, get tired (***de*** of) **2** (*llenarse*) stuff o.s. (***de*** with); ***~ de dormir*** sleep for hours on end
hartazgo *m* surfeit, excess; ***nos dimos un ~ de pasteles*** we stuffed ourselves with cake F; ***me di un ~ de ver la televisión*** I watched television until I was sick of it F
harto **I** *adj* **1** fed up F; ***estar ~ de algo*** be sick of sth F, be fed up with sth F **2** (*lleno*) full (up) **3**: ***había ~s pasteles*** there were cakes in abundance **II** *adv* very much; *delante del adjetivo* extremely; ***me gusta ~*** *L.Am.* I like it a lot; ***hace ~ frío*** *L.Am.* it's very cold
hartón **I** *adj L.Am.* greedy **II** *m*: ***darse un ~ de algo*** overdose on sth

H

has *vb* ☞ ***haber***
hasta **I** *prp* until, till; ***~ que*** until; ***llegó ~ Bilbao*** he went as far as Bilbao; ***~ aquí*** up to here; ***~ ahora*** so far; ***¿~ cuándo?*** how long?; ***no se levanta ~ las diez*** he doesn't get up until ten o'clock; ***¡~ luego!*** see you (later); ***¡~ la vista!*** see you (later)
II *adv* even; ***~ un niño podría hacerlo*** even a child could do it
hastial *m* ARQUI gable, gable end
hastiar ⟨1c⟩ *v/t* bore; **hastiarse** *v/r* get tired (***de*** of), get bored (***de*** with)
hastío *m* boredom
hatajo *m* bunch
hato *m L.Am.* bundle
hawaiana *f Rpl* thong, *Br* flip-flop
hay *vb* ☞ ***haber***
Haya: ***La ~*** The Hague
haya **I** *vb* ☞ ***haber*** **II** *f* BOT beech
hayuco *m* beechnut
haz **I** *m* **1** (*manojo*) bundle **2** *de luz* beam **II** *f de tela* right side **III** *vb* ☞ ***hacer***
hazaña *f* achievement
hazmerreír *m* laughing stock
HB *m abr* (= ***Herri Batasuna***) HIST *radical Basque nationalist party*
he **I** *vb* ☞ ***haber*** **II** *adv*: ***~ aquí*** *sg* here is; *pl* here are; ***~ me aquí*** here I am
hebdomadario *m/adj* weekly
hebilla *f* buckle
hebra *f* thread; ***pegar la ~*** F start a conversation, get talking F
hecatombe *f* **1** disaster, catastrophe **2** *muertes* loss of life
heces *fpl* ☞ ***hez***
hechicera *f* sorceress
hechicería *f* sorcery, witchcraft
hechicero **I** *adj* bewitching, captivating **II** *m* **1** (*mago*) sorcerer **2** *de tribu* witch-doctor
hechizado *adj* spellbound
hechizar ⟨1f⟩ *v/t fig* bewitch, captivate
hechizo **I** *m* spell, charm; ***romper el ~*** break the spell **II** *adj Méx* makeshift
hecho **I** *part* ☞ ***hacer***, (*confeccionado*): ***~ a mano*** hand-made; ***un traje ~*** an off-the-peg suit; ***muy ~*** *carne* well-done; ***¡bien ~!*** well done!; ***¡~!***, ***¡eso está ~ !*** done!, it's a deal!; ***a lo ~, pecho*** what's done is done
II *adj* finished; ***un hombre ~ y derecho*** a fully grown man
III *m* **1** (*realidad*) fact; ***de ~*** in fact; ***el ~ es que*** the fact is that **2** (*suceso*) event **3** (*obra*) action, deed; ***un ~ consumado*** a fait accompli
hechura *f de ropa* making
hectárea *f* hectare (*approx 2½ acres*)
hectómetro *m* hectometer, *Br* hectometre
heder ⟨2g⟩ *v/i* stink
hediondo *adj* stinking, foul-smelling
hedonismo *m* hedonism
hedonista **I** *adj* hedonistic **II** *m/f* hedonist
hedor *m* stink, stench
hegemonía *f* hegemony
helada *f* frost
heladera *f Rpl* fridge
heladería *f* ice-cream parlor *o Br* parlour
helado **I** *adj* frozen; *fig* icy; ***quedarse ~*** be stunned **II** *m* ice cream
heladora *f* ice-cream maker
helar ⟨1k⟩ **I** *v/t* freeze **II** *v/i* freeze; ***anoche heló*** there was a frost last night; **helarse** *v/r tb fig* freeze
helecho *m* BOT fern
helero *m* ice pocket
hélice *f* propeller
helicoidal *adj* TÉC helicoidal
helicóptero *m* helicopter
◇ **helicóptero de rescate** rescue helicopter
helio *m* QUÍM helium
heliograbado *m* TIP photoengraving
helipuerto *m* heliport
helvético **I** *adj* Swiss **II** *m*, **-a** *f* Swiss
hematoma *m* bruise
hembra *f* ZO, TÉC female
hembrilla *f* TÉC ring, socket
hemeroteca *f* newspaper library
hemiciclo *m* (semicircular) chamber
hemiplejía *f* MED hemiplegia
hemipléjico **I** *adj* hemiplegic **II** *m*, **-a** *f* hemiplegic
hemisférico *adj* hemispherical
hemisferio *m* hemisphere
hemodiálisis *f* MED (kidney) dialysis
hemofilia *f* MED hemophilia, *Br tb* haemophilia
hemofílico **I** *adj* hemophiliac, *Br tb* haemophiliac **II** *m*, **-a** hemophiliac, *Br tb* haemophiliac
hemoglobina *f* hemoglobin, *Br tb* haemoglobin

hemorragia *f* MED hemorrhage, *Br* haemorrhage, bleeding
◇ **hemorragia nasal** nosebleed
hemorroides *fpl* MED hemorrhoids, *Br* haemorrhoids, piles
henchir ⟨3l & 3h⟩ *v/t* fill, fill up (***de*** with); **henchirse** *v/r* swell (***de*** with)
hender ⟨2g⟩ *v/t* crack; **henderse** *v/r* crack, split
hendidura *f* crack
hendir *vb* ☞ ***hender***
heno *m* hay
hepático *adj* liver *atr*, hepatic
hepatitis *f* MED hepatitis
heptágono *m* heptagon
heptatlón *m* DEP heptathlon
heráldica *f* heraldry
heráldico *adj* heraldic
heraldo *m* herald
herbáceo *adj* herbaceous
herbaje *m* grass
herbario *m* herbarium
herbicida *m* herbicide, weedkiller
herbívoro I *adj* herbivorous II *m*, **-a** *f* herbivore
herbolario *m* health-food store
herborista *m* ☞ ***herbolario***
herboristería *f* herbalist
herboso *adj* grassy
hercio *m* FÍS hertz
hercúleo *adj* Herculean
heredable *adj* that can be inherited, inheritable
heredad *f* estate
heredar ⟨1a⟩ *v/t* **1** inherit (***de*** from) **2** *Méx* (*legar*) leave, bequeath
heredera *f* heiress
heredero *m* heir
◇ **heredero del trono** heir to the throne
hereditario *adj* hereditary
hereje *m/f* heretic
herejía *f* heresy
herencia *f* inheritance
herético *adj* heretical
herida *f* **1** *de arma* wound; (*lesión*) injury; ***sufrir ~s de gravedad*** be seriously wounded; *lesionado* be seriously injured **2** *mujer* wounded woman; *mujer lesionada* injured woman
herido I *adj de arma* wounded; (*lesionado*) injured II *m de arma* wounded man; (*lesionado*) injured man; ***los ~s*** the wounded; (*lesionados*) the injured; ***el atentado dejó cuatro heridos graves y dos leves*** the attack left four people seriously injured and two slightly
herir ⟨3i⟩ *v/t con arma* wound; (*lesionar*) injure; *fig* (*ofender*) hurt
hermafrodita I *adj* hermaphroditic, hermaphrodite *atr* II *m/f* hermaphrodite
hermana *f* sister
hermanado *adj*: ***dos ciudades -as*** twinned cities
hermanamiento *m de ciudades* twinning
hermanar ⟨1a⟩ *v/t* **1** *personas* unite **2** *ciudades* twin; **hermanarse** *v/r* **1** (*combinar*) combine **2** *de ciudades* twin
hermanastra *f* stepsister
hermanastro *m* stepbrother
hermandad *f de hombres* brotherhood, fraternity; *de mujeres* sisterhood
hermano *m* brother; ***~s*** *pl sólo varones* brothers; *varones y mujeres* brothers and sisters, siblings
hermético *adj* **1** *al aire* airtight; *al agua* watertight; ***con cierre ~*** hermetically sealed **2** *fig*: *persona* inscrutable
hermetismo *m* **1** secretiveness **2** *de recipiente*: *al aire* airtightness; *al agua* watertightness
hermetizar ⟨1f⟩ *v/t* seal hermetically
hermosear ⟨1a⟩ *v/t* beautify
hermoso *adj* beautiful
hermosura *f* beauty
hernia *f* MED hernia
◇ **hernia discal** slipped disk, *Br* slipped disc; **hernia estrangulada** strangulated hernia; **hernia inguinal** inguinal hernia; **hernia umbilical** umbilical hernia
herniado *adj* suffering from a hernia
herniarse ⟨1a⟩ *v/r* **1** F get a hernia, rupture o.s. **2** *fig* F bust a gut F
Herodes *m*: Herod; ***ir de ~ a Pilatos*** go from pillar to post
héroe *m* hero
heroicidad *f* **1** *hecho* heroic deed, heroic act **2** *cualidad* heroism
heroico *adj* heroic
heroína *f* **1** *mujer* heroine **2** *droga* heroin
heroinómano I *adj* addicted to heroin II *m*, **-a** *f* heroin addict
heroísmo *m* heroism
herpes *m* MED herpes *sg*
◇ **herpes zoster** herpes zoster, shin-

gles *sg*
herradura *f* **1** horseshoe **2**: ***camino de ~*** bridle path
herraje *m* ironwork, iron fittings *pl*
herramienta *f* tool
herrar ⟨1k⟩ *v/t* **1** *caballo* shoe **2** *ganado* brand
herrería *f* smithy, blacksmith's shop
herrerillo *m* ZO great tit; *con manchas azules* blue tit
herrero *m*, **-a** *f* blacksmith
herrumbrarse ⟨1a⟩ *v/r* rust, get rusty
herrumbre *f* rust
herrumbroso *adj* rusty
hertz(io) *m* FÍS hertz
hervidero *m fig* hotbed; ***un ~ de levantamientos*** a hotbed of rebellion; ***esto es un ~ de gente*** the place is teeming with people
hervido *m S.Am.* stew
hervidor *m* kettle
hervir ⟨3i⟩ **I** *v/i* boil; *fig* swarm, seethe (***de*** with) **II** *v/t* boil
hervor *m*: ***dar un ~ a algo*** boil sth
heterodoxo *adj método* unorthodox
heterogeneidad *f* heterogeneity
heterogéneo *adj* heterogeneous
heterosexual *adj* heterosexual
hexágono *m* hexagon
hez *f* **1** *de la sociedad* scum, dregs *pl* **2**: ***heces*** *pl* feces, *Br* faeces
hibernación *f* hibernation
hibernal *adj* winter *atr*
hibernar ⟨1a⟩ *v/i* hibernate
hibisco *m* BOT hibiscus
hibridar ⟨1a⟩ *v/t* BIO hybridize
híbrido **I** *adj* hybrid *atr* **II** *m* hybrid
hice *vb* ☞ ***hacer***
hicimos *vb* ☞ ***hacer***
hidalgo *m* nobleman
hidratante *adj* moisturizing; ***crema ~*** moisturizing cream
hidratar ⟨1a⟩ *v/t* hydrate; *piel* moisturize
hidrato *m*: ***~ de carbono*** carbohydrate
hidráulica *f* hydraulics *sg*
hidráulico *adj* hydraulic
hídrico *adj* water *atr*
hidroala *m* hydrofoil
hidroavión *m* seaplane
hidrocarburo *m* hydrocarbon
hidrocefalia *f* MED hydrocephalus, water on the brain
hidrocultivo *m* BOT hydroponics *sg*
hidroeléctrico *adj* hydroelectric
hidrofobia *f* MED hydrophobia
hidrofoil *m* hydrofoil
hidrógeno *m* hydrogen
hidrografía *f* hydrography
hidrología *f* hydrology
hidropesía *f* MED dropsy
hidroplano *m avión* seaplane
hidrosfera *f* hydrosphere
hidrosoluble *adj* water-soluble
hidroterapia *f* hydrotherapy
hidróxido *m* QUÍM hydroxide
hiedra *f* BOT ivy
hiel *f* bile
hiela *vb* ☞ ***helar***
hielo *m* ice; ***romper el ~*** *fig* break the ice
◇ **hielo seco** dry ice
◇ **hielos flotantes** pack ice *sg*
hiena *f* ZO hyena
hierático *adj* hieratical; *fig* severe, stern
hierba *f* **1** grass; ***mala ~*** weed; ***mala ~ nunca muere*** only the good die young; ***sentir*** *o* ***ver crecer la ~*** *fig* be very sharp **2** *condimento* herb
◇ **hierba medicinal** medicinal herb
hierbabuena *f* BOT mint
hierbaluisa *f* BOT lemon verbena
hiere *vb* ☞ ***herir***
hierro *m* iron; ***de ~*** iron *atr*; ***salud de ~*** iron constitution; ***quitar ~ a algo*** *fig* downplay sth, play sth down
◇ **hierro colado** cast iron; **hierro forjado** wrought iron; **hierro fundido** cast iron
hierve *vb* ☞ ***hervir***
higa *f*: ***me importe una ~*** F I couldn't *o* could care less, *Br* I couldn't care less
higadillo *m* liver
hígado *m* liver; ***ser un ~*** *C.Am., Méx* F be a pain in the butt F; ***tener ~s*** have guts
higiene *f* hygiene; ***~ bucal / corporal*** oral / personal hygiene
higiénico *adj* hygienic
higienista *m/f* hygienist
◇ **higienista dental** dental hygienist
higienizar ⟨1f⟩ *v/t* clean, sanitize
higo *m* BOT fig; ***de ~s a brevas*** F once in a blue moon F; ***me importa un ~*** F I couldn't care less F
higrómetro *m* hygrometer
higuera *f* BOT fig tree; ***estar en la ~*** *fig* F be miles away F
hija *f* daughter

hijastra *f* stepdaughter
hijastro *m* stepson
hijo *m* **1** son; ***como cada*** *o* ***cualquier*** *o* ***todo ~ de vecino*** like everybody else **2**: ***~s*** children *pl*
◇ **hijo de mamá** F momma's boy F, *Br* mummy's boy F; **hijo de papá** spoilt rich kid; **hijo político** son-in-law; **hijo predilecto** favorite *o Br* favourite son; **hijo de puta** P son of a bitch V, bastard P; **hijo único** only child
híjole *interj Méx* F hell! F
hilacha *f* loose thread
hilachos *mpl Méx* rags
hilada *f* row, line
hilado I *adj* spun **II** *m* **1** *acción* spinning **2** *fibra* thread
hilador *m* spinner
hiladora *f* spinning machine
hilandería *f* **1** *arte* spinning **2** *lugar* spinning mill
hilandero *m*, **-a** *f* spinner
hilar ⟨1a⟩ **I** *v/t* spin **II** *v/i*: ***~ delgado*** *o* ***fino*** *fig* split hairs
hilarante *adj* hilarious
hilaridad *f* hilarity
hilatura *f* **1** *arte* spinning **2** *lugar* spinning mill
hilera *f* row, line
hilo *m* **1** *para coser* thread; ***colgar*** *o* ***pender de un ~*** *fig* hang by a thread; ***mover los ~s*** *fig* pull strings; ***perder el ~*** *fig* lose the thread **2**: ***sin ~s*** TELEC cordless **3**: ***con un ~ de voz*** *fig* in a barely audible voice
◇ **hilo conductor** conductor; *fig* central theme; **hilo de coser** thread; **hilo dental** dental floss; **hilo musical** piped music
hilván *m* **1** basting; *puntada* basting stitch **2** *hilo* basting thread
hilvanar ⟨1a⟩ *v/t* baste; *fig* ***no podía ~ una frase*** he couldn't string half a dozen words together
himen *m* ANAT hymen
himno *m* hymn
◇ **himno nacional** national anthem
hincapié *m*: ***hacer ~*** put special emphasis (***en*** on)
hincar ⟨1g⟩ *v/t* thrust, stick (***en*** into); ***~ el diente*** F sink one's teeth (***en*** into); ***~ el diente a algo*** *fig* F get one's teeth into sth; **hincarse** *v/r*: ***~ de rodillas*** kneel down
hincha I *m/f* fan, supporter **II** *f*: ***tener ~ a alguien*** F have a grudge against s.o.
hinchable *adj* inflatable
hinchada *f* fans *pl*, supporters *pl*
hinchado *adj* swollen
hinchar ⟨1a⟩ *v/t* **1** inflate, blow up **2** *Rpl* annoy; **hincharse** *v/r* **1** MED swell **2** (*mostrarse orgulloso*) swell with pride **3** *fig* stuff o.s (***de*** with)
hinchazón *f* swelling
hinduismo *m* Hinduism
hinojo *m* BOT fennel
hipar ⟨1a⟩ *v/i* hiccup, hiccough
híper *m* F supermarket, *Br tb* hypermarket
hiperactividad *f* hyperactivity
hiperactivo *adj* hyperactive
hipérbola *f* MAT hyperbola
hipérbole *f* hyperbole
hipercrítico *adj* hypercritical
hiperenlace *m* INFOR hyperlink
hiperfunción *f* MED hyperfunction
hipermercado *m* supermarket, *Br tb* hypermarket
hipermétrope *adj* MED far-sighted, *Br* long-sighted
hipermetropía *f* MED far-sightedness, *Br* long-sightedness
hipersensibilidad *f* hypersensitivity
hipersensible *adj* hypersensitive
hipertensión *f* MED high blood pressure, hypertension
hipertenso *adj* hypertensive, with high blood pressure
hipertexto *m* hypertext
hipervínculo *m* INFOR hyperlink
hípica *f* equestrian sports *pl*
hípico *adj* equestrian; ***concurso ~*** show-jumping event; ***carrera -a*** horse race
hipismo *m* horse racing
hipnosis *f* hypnosis
hipnótico *adj* hypnotic
hipnotizador *m*, **~a** *f* hypnotist
hipnotizar ⟨1f⟩ *v/t* hypnotize
hipo *m* hiccups *pl*, hiccoughs *pl*; ***quitar el ~*** F take one's breath away
hipocalórico *adj* low-calorie
hipocampo *m* ZO sea horse
hipocondría *f* MED hypochondria
hipocondríaco I *adj* hypochondriac **II** *m*, **-a** *f* hypochondriac
hipocrático *adj* Hippocratic
hipocresía *f* hypocrisy

H

hipócrita I *adj* hypocritical II *m/f* hypocrite
hipodérmico *adj* MED hypodermic
hipódromo *m* racetrack
hipófisis *f* ANAT pituitary gland
hipopótamo *m* ZO hippopotamus
hipoteca *f* COM mortgage
hipotecar ⟨1g⟩ *v/t* COM mortgage; *fig* compromise
hipotecario *adj* mortgage *atr*
hipotensión *f* MED low blood pressure
hipotenusa *f* MAT hypotenuse
hipotermia *f* MED hypothermia
hipótesis *f* hypothesis
hipotético *adj* hypothetical
hiriente *adj* wounding, hurtful
hirsuto *adj* 1 hairy, *fml* hirsute 2 *fig* surly, brusque
hirviente *adj* boiling
hisopo *m* 1 REL holy water sprinkler, aspergillum 2 BOT hyssop
hispalense *adj* of / from Seville, Seville *atr*
hispánico *adj* Hispanic
hispanidad *f*: ***la ~*** the Spanish-speaking world
hispanista *m/f* Hispanicist
hispanizar ⟨1f⟩ *v/t* Hispanicize
hispano I *adj* 1 (*español*) Spanish 2 (*hispanohablante*) Spanish-speaking 3 *en EE.UU.* Hispanic II *m*, **-a** *f* 1 (*español*) Spaniard 2 (*hispanohablante*) Spanish speaker 3 *en EE.UU.* Hispanic
hispanoamericano I *adj* Latin American, Latino F II *m*, **-a** *f* Latin American, Latino F
hispanohablante *adj* Spanish-speaking
histeria *f* hysteria
histérico I *adj* hysterical II *m*, **-a** *f* hysteric
histerismo *m* hysteria
histología *f* MED histology
historia *f* 1 history; ***pasar a la ~*** go down in history 2 (*cuento*) story; ***una ~ de drogas*** F some drugs business; ***déjate de ~s*** F stop making excuses
◇ **historia clínica** MED medical history
◇ **historia universal** world history
historiador *m*, **~a** *f* historian; ***~ del arte*** art historian
historial *m* record
◇ **historial delictivo** criminal record; **historial médico** medical history; **historial profesional** career history
historiar ⟨1b⟩ *v/t*: ***~ algo*** write the history of sth
histórico *adj* 1 *de la historia* historical 2 (*importante*) historic
historieta *f* 1 anecdote 2 (*viñetas*) comic strip
historiografía *f* historiography
historiógrafo *m*, **-a** *f* historiographer
histriónico *adj* histrionic
hito *m tb fig* milestone; ***marcar (un) ~*** be *o* mark a milestone; ***mirar a alguien de ~ en ~*** stare at s.o.
hizo *vb* ☞ ***hacer***
Hnos. *abr* (= ***hermanos***) Bros (= brothers)
hobby *m* hobby
hocico *m* snout; *de perro* muzzle; *desp de persona* mouth, *Br tb* gob P; ***dar o caer de ~s*** fall flat on one's face
hockey *m* hockey
◇ **hockey sobre hielo** hockey, *Br* ice hockey; **hockey sobre hierba** field hockey, *Br* hockey; **hockey sobre patines** roller hockey
hogar *m fig* home
hogareño *adj* 1 home *atr* 2 *persona* home-loving
hogaza *f type of large loaf*
hoguera *f* bonfire
hoja *f* 1 BOT leaf 2 *de papel* sheet; *de libro* page 3 *de cuchillo* blade
◇ **hoja de afeitar** razor blade; **hoja de cálculo** INFOR spreadsheet; **hoja de lata** ☞ ***hojalata***; **hoja de pedido** order form; **hoja de servicios** work record
hojalata *f* tin
hojalatería *f* 1 tinsmith's workshop 2 *Méx* (*chapistería*) body shop
hojalatero *m* 1 tinsmith 2 *Méx* (*chapista*) panel-beater
hojaldre *m* GASTR puff pastry
hojarasca *f* 1 fallen leaves *pl* 2 *fig* padding
hojear ⟨1a⟩ *v/t* leaf through, flip through
hojuela *f* pancake; ***es miel sobre ~s*** F that's the cherry on the cake
hola *int* hello, hi F; *Rpl* TELEC hello?
Holanda *f* Holland
holandés I *adj* Dutch II *m* Dutchman; ***los holandeses*** the Dutch III *m idioma* Dutch

H

holandesa *f* Dutchwoman
holding *m* holding company
holgado *adj ropa* loose, comfortable; ***estar ~ de tiempo*** have time to spare
holganza *f* idleness
holgar ⟨1h & 1m⟩ *v/i* **1** *fml* be idle **2**: ***huelga decir que …*** needless to say, …, it goes without saying that …
holgazán *m* idler
holgazanear ⟨1a⟩ *v/i* laze around
holgazanería *f* laziness, idleness
holgura *f* **1** (*sin dificultad*) ease **2** *de ropa* looseness **3** TÉC play **4**: ***vivir con ~*** live comfortably
hollar ⟨1m⟩ *v/t fml* set foot on
hollejo *m* skin, peel
hollín *m* soot
holocausto *m* holocaust
holograma *m* hologram
hombrada *f* manly thing to do
hombre *m* **1** man; ***de ~ a ~*** man to man; ***~ hecho a sí mismo*** self-made man; ***pobre ~*** poor man *o* soul; ***¡~ al agua!*** man overboard! **2**: ***el ~*** (*la humanidad*) man, mankind **3**: ***¡claro, ~!*** you bet!, sure thing!; ***¡~, qué alegría!*** that's great!
◇ **hombre de acción** man of action; **hombre-anuncio** sandwich man; **hombre de bien** good man; **hombre de la calle** *fig* man in the street; **hombre de Estado** statesman; **hombre de letras** man of letters; **hombre lobo** werewolf; **hombre medio** Mr. Average, your average Joe F; **hombre de negocios** businessman; **hombre de paja** *fig* puppet; **hombre rana** frogman; **hombre del saco** bogeyman
hombrera *f* shoulder pad; MIL epaulette
hombría *f* manliness
hombro *m* shoulder; ***~ con ~*** shoulder to shoulder; ***encogerse de ~s*** shrug (one's shoulders); ***mirar a alguien por encima del ~*** *fig* look down on s.o.
hombruno *adj mujer* mannish, butch F
homenaje *m* homage; ***rendir ~ a alguien*** pay tribute to s.o.; ***en ~ a alguien*** in honor *o Br* honour of s.o.
homenajeado *m*, **-a** *f* guest of honor *o Br* honour
homenajear ⟨1a⟩ *v/t* honor, *Br* honour, pay homage to
homeópata *m/f* homeopath
homeopatía *f* homeopathy
homeopático *adj* homeopathic
homérico *adj* Homeric
homicida **I** *adj* homicidal; ***el arma ~*** the murder weapon **II** *m/f* murderer
homicidio *m* homicide
homilía *f* REL homily
homo *m* F gay (man)
homofobia *f* homophobia
homogeneizar ⟨1f⟩ *v/t* homogenize
homogéneo *adj* homogenous
homologación *f* approval; *de título, diploma* official recognition
homologar ⟨1h⟩ *v/t* certify
homólogo **I** *adj* equivalent **II** *m*, **-a** *f* counterpart, opposite number
homónimo *m* homonym
homosexual *m/f & adj* homosexual
homosexualidad *f* homosexuality; ***hacer pública la ~ de alguien*** out s.o.
honda *f de cuero* sling(shot); *Rpl* (*tirachinas*) slingshot, *Br* catapult
hondo *adj* deep
hondonada *f* hollow
hondura *f* depth; ***meterse en ~s*** *fig* F get into deep water
Honduras *f* Honduras
hondureño **I** *adj* Honduran **II** *m*, **-a** *f* Honduran
honestidad *f* honesty, decency
honesto *adj* honorable, *Br* honourable, decent
hongo *m* **1** fungus; ***brotar como ~s*** *fig* F mushroom **2** *L.Am.* (*seta*) mushroom
honor *m* **1** honor, *Br* honour; ***en ~ a*** in honor of; ***en ~ a la verdad*** to be honest; ***palabra de ~*** word of honor; ***hacer ~ a*** live up to **2**: ***~es*** *pl* (*pompa*) honors, *Br* honours
honorabilidad *f* honorableness, *Br* honourableness
honorable *adj* honorable, *Br* honourable
honorario *adj* honorary
honorarios *mpl* fees
honorífico *adj* honorary
honra *f* honor, *Br* honour; ***¡a mucha ~!*** I'm honored *o Br* honoured; ***tener algo a mucha ~*** be very proud of sth
◇ **honras fúnebres** funeral rites
honradez *f* honesty
honrado *adj* honest
honrar ⟨1a⟩ *v/t* honor, *Br* honour; ***su humildad le honra*** his humility does

him credit; **honrarse** *v/r*: ***~ de hacer algo*** be honored *o Br* honoured to do sth
honroso *adj* honorable, *Br* honourable
hora *f* **1** hour; ***~ y media*** an hour and a half; ***~s muertas*** hour after hour **2** (*momento indeterminado*): ***a todas ~s*** all the time; ***a última ~*** at the last minute; ***a última ~ de la tarde*** late in the afternoon; ***a altas ~s de la madrugada*** in the (wee) small hours, in the early hours of the morning; ***a primera ~ de la tarde*** first thing in the afternoon; ***¡ya era ~!*** about time too!; ***ya es ~ de que te pongas a estudiar*** it's time you started studying; ***comer entre ~s*** eat between meals; ***le ha llegado*** *o* ***tocado su ~*** his time has come; ***a la ~ de …*** *fig* when it comes to … **3** (*cita*): ***pedir ~*** make an appointment; ***tengo ~ con el dentista*** I have an appointment with the dentist **4** (*momento justo*): ***dar la ~*** *de reloj* strike (the hour); ***poner en ~*** *reloj* set; ***¿tiene ~?*** do you have the time?, have you got the time?; ***¿qué ~ es?*** what time is it?; ***llegó a la ~*** he arrived on time
◇ **hora de cierre** closing time; **hora feliz** happy hour; **hora lectiva** class time; **hora de llegada** arrival time; **hora local** local time; **hora pico** *L.Am.* rush hour; **hora punta** rush hour; **hora de salida** departure time; **horas extraordinarias** overtime *sg*; **horas de máxima audiencia** TV prime time *sg*, peak viewing time *sg*; **horas de oficina** office hours
horadar ⟨1a⟩ *v/t* bore through, drill through
horario I *adj* hourly **II** *m* schedule, *Br* timetable; **(*con*) *~ continuado*** open all day
◇ **horario de apertura, horario de atención al público** hours (of business) *pl*, opening hours *pl*; **horario comercial** business hours *pl*; **horario flexible** flextime, *Br* flexitime; **horario de trabajo** (working) hours *pl*; **horario de trenes** train schedule, *Br* train timetable; **horario de visitas** visiting hours *pl*; **horario de vuelos** AVIA flight times *pl*
horca *f* gallows *pl*
horcajadas *fpl*: ***a ~*** astride
horchata *f drink made from tiger nuts*
horchatería *f bar selling horchata*
horda *f* horde
horizontal *f* / *adj* horizontal
horizonte *m* horizon
horma *f* form, mold, *Br* mould; *de zapatos* last
hormiga *f* ant
◇ **hormiga blanca** white ant, termite
hormigón *m* concrete
◇ **hormigón armado** reinforced concrete
◇ **hormigón pretensado** prestressed concrete
hormigonera *f* cement mixer
hormiguear ⟨1a⟩ *v/i*: ***me hormiguea la pierna*** I have pins and needles in my leg
hormigueo *m* pins and needles *pl*
hormiguero *m* ant hill; ***la sala era un ~ de gente*** the hall was swarming with people
hormona *f* hormone
hormonal *adj* hormonal, hormone *atr*
hornacina *f* niche
hornada *f* batch
hornear ⟨1a⟩ *v/t* bake
hornilla *f* ring
hornillo *m de fogón* burner; *de gas* gas ring; *transportable* camping stove
horno *m* **1** oven; ***recién sacado*** *o* ***salido del ~*** freshly baked; ***no está el ~ para bollos*** F this isn't a good time *o* the right moment **2** *de cerámica* kiln; ***alto ~*** blast furnace
horóscopo *m* horoscope
horqueta *f L.Am. de camino* fork
horquilla *f para pelo* hairpin
horrendo *adj* horrendous
hórreo *m* granary
horrible *adj* horrible, dreadful
horripilante *adj* horrible
horripilar ⟨1a⟩ *v/t* horrify; **horripilarse** *v/r* be horrified
horror *m* **1** horror (***a*** of); ***tener ~ a*** be terrified of; ***me da ~ pensar en …*** I dread to think of …; ***¡qué~!*** how awful! **2**: ***me gusta ~es*** F I like it a lot
horrorizar ⟨1f⟩ *v/t* horrify; **horrorizarse** *v/r* be horrified (***de*** at, by)
horroroso *adj* terrible; (*de mala calidad*) dreadful; (*feo*) hideous
hortaliza *f* vegetable

hortelano *m*, **-a** *f* truck farmer, *Br* market gardener
hortensia *f* BOT hydrangea
hortera I F *adj* tacky F **II** *m/f* F tacky person F
horterada *f* F tacky thing F; ***es una ~*** it's tacky F
hortícola *adj* horticultural, garden *atr*
horticultor *m*, **~a** *f* horticulturist
horticultura *f* horticulture
hortofrutícola *adj* fruit and vegetable *atr*
hortofruticultura *f* fruit and vegetable growing
hosco *adj* sullen
hospedaje *m* accommodations *pl*, *Br* accommodation; ***dar ~ a alguien*** put s.o. up
hospedar ⟨1a⟩ *v/t* give accommodations *o Br* accommodation to; INFOR host; **hospedarse** *v/r* stay (***en*** at)
hospicio *m* **1** *para niños* orphanage **2** HIST *para peregrinos* hospice
hospital *m* hospital
◇ **hospital militar** military hospital
◇ **hospital de sangre** field hospital
hospitalario *adj* **1** *gentes* hospitable **2** MED hospital *atr*
hospitalidad *f* hospitality
hospitalización *f* hospitalization
hospitalizar ⟨1f⟩ *v/t* hospitalize
hosquedad *f* surliness, brusqueness; ***con ~*** sullenly, brusquely
hostal *m* hostel
hostelera *f* landlady
hostelería *f* **1** hotel industry **2** *como curso* hotel management
hostelero I *adj* hotel *atr* **II** *m* landlord
hostia *f* **1** REL host **2** P (*golpe*) sock P, wallop F; ***dar una ~ a alguien*** P slap s.o. in the face F; ***darse una ~*** P bash o.s. F **3**: ***¡~s!*** P Christ! P; ***es la ~*** P it's amazing F; ***a toda ~*** *conducir, moverse* P flat out F, balls out P
hostigamiento *m* harassment
hostigar ⟨1h⟩ *v/t* **1** pester **2** MIL harass **3** *caballo* whip
hostil *adj* hostile
hostilidad *f* hostility; ***romper las ~es*** MIL commence hostilities
hostilizar ⟨1f⟩ *v/t* harass
hotel *m* hotel
hotelero I *adj* hotel *atr*; ***industria -a*** hotel industry *o* trade **II** *m*, **-a** *f* hotelier
hoy *adv* today; ***de ~*** of today; ***por ~*** for today; ***~ mismo*** today, this very day; ***los padres de ~*** today's parents, parents today; ***de ~ en adelante*** from now on; ***~ por ~*** at the present time; ***~ en día*** nowadays; ***de ~ a*** *o* ***para mañana*** from one day to the next; ***¡que es para ~!*** F get a move on!
hoya *f* **1** hole **2** *de tumba* grave **3** GEOG plain **4** *S.Am.* river basin
hoyo *m* **1** hole **2** *de tumba* grave; ***estar con un pie en el ~*** *fig* have one foot in the grave F **3** (*depresión*) hollow **4** *de golf* hole
◇ **hoyo negro** *Méx* black hole
hoyuelo *m* dimple
hoz *f* sickle
huachafo *adj Pe* (*cursi*) affected, pretentious
huarache *m Méx rough sandal*
huayno *m Pe, Bol Andean dance rhythm*
hubo *vb* ☞ ***haber***
hucha *f* money box
hueco I *adj* hollow; (*vacío*) empty; *fig: persona* shallow **II** *m* **1** *en pared, escrito* gap **2** (*agujero*) hole; *de ascensor* shaft
huele *vb* ☞ ***oler***
huelga *f* strike; ***declararse en ~, ir a la ~*** go on strike; ***estar en ~*** be on strike
◇ **huelga de brazos caídos** sit-down strike; **huelga de celo** work-to-rule; **huelga general** general strike; **huelga de hambre** hunger strike
huelguista *m/f* striker
huelguístico *adj* strike *atr*
huella *f* mark; *de animal* track; ***seguir las ~s de alguien*** follow in s.o.'s footsteps
◇ **huellas dactilares** fingerprints
huelo *vb* ☞ ***oler***
huérfano I *adj* orphan *atr*; ***quedarse ~*** be orphaned **II** *m*, **-a** *f* orphan
huero *adj* **1** *fig* empty **2** *L.Am.* blond
huerta *f* truck farm, *Br* market garden
huerto *m* kitchen garden; ***llevar a alguien al ~*** F put one over on s.o. F
huesear ⟨1a⟩ *v/t C.Am.* beg
huesillo *m S.Am.* sun-dried peach
hueso *m* **1** ANAT bone; ***estar en los ~s*** be all skin and bone; ***moler / romper los ~s a alguien*** beat s.o. up; ***dar con sus ~s en la cárcel*** end up in jail **2** *de fruta* pit, stone; *persona* tough guy;

~ duro de roer *fig* F hard nut to crack F **3** *Méx* F cushy number F **4** *Méx* F (*influencia*) influence, pull F
huésped *m/f* guest
huestes *fpl lit* host *sg lit*, army *sg*
huesudo *adj* bony
huevada *f* P stupid thing to say / do
huevas *fpl* roe *sg*
huevear ⟨1a⟩ *v/i Chi* P mess around
huevera *f para servir* eggcup; *para almacenar* egg box
huevería *f* egg store
huevo *m* **1** egg **2** P (*testículo*) ball F; ***estar hasta los ~s*** V be fucking fed up V; ***me importa un ~*** V I don't give a fuck V, I don't give a shit P; ***¡y un ~!*** P no way! F; ***un ~ de*** P a load of F; ***costar un ~*** P cost an arm and a leg F
◇ **huevo duro** hard-boiled egg; **huevo escalfado** poached egg; **huevo estrellado** *Méx* fried egg; **huevo frito** fried egg; **huevo pasado por agua** soft-boiled egg; **huevo tibio** *Méx* soft-boiled egg; **huevos revueltos** scrambled eggs
huevón *m*, **-ona** *f* **1** *Chi* P idiot **2** *L.Am.* F (*flojo*) idler F
huida *f* flight, escape
huidizo *adj persona* elusive
huido *adj* on the run
huipil *m C.Am., Méx type of dress traditionally worn by Native American women*
huir ⟨3g⟩ **I** *v/i* **1** flee, escape (***de*** from) **2**: ***~ de algo*** avoid sth **II** *v/t* avoid
huitlacoche *m C.Am., Méx* corn smut
hulado *m C.Am., Méx* rubberized cloth
hule *m* **1** *para mesa* oilcloth **2** *L.Am.* (*caucho*) rubber
hulla *f* coal
hullero *adj* coal *atr*
humanamente *adv* **1** humanely **2**: ***hacer lo ~ posible*** do everything humanly possible
humanidad *f* **1** humanity **2**: ***~es*** *pl* EDU humanities
humanismo *m* humanism
humanista *m/f* humanist
humanístico *adj* humanistic
humanitario *adj* humanitarian
humanización *f* humanization
humanizar ⟨1f⟩ *v/t* humanize; **humanizarse** *v/r* become more human
humano **I** *adj* human **II** *m* human, human being
humareda *f* cloud of smoke
humear ⟨1a⟩ *v/i* **1** *con humo* smoke **2** *con vapor* steam
humedad *f* **1** humidity; ***~ atmosférica*** *o* ***del aire*** relative humidity **2** *de una casa* damp(ness)
humedal *m* wetland
humedecer ⟨2d⟩ *v/t* dampen; **humedecerse** *v/r* become wet *o* damp; *fig* fill with tears
húmedo *adj* **1** *clima, aire* humid **2** *toalla* damp
húmero *m* ANAT humerus
humidificador *m*: ***~*** (***de aire***) humidifier
humidificar ⟨1g⟩ *v/t* humidify
humildad *f* humility
humilde *adj* **1** humble; (*sin orgullo*) modest **2** *clase social* lowly
humillación *f* humiliation
humillante *adj* humiliating
humillar ⟨1a⟩ *v/t* humiliate; **humillarse** *v/r* humiliate o.s.
humita *f S.Am. meat and corn paste wrapped in leaves*
humo *m* **1** *de fuego* smoke; ***echar ~*** *fig* be furious, be fuming; ***me echa ~ la cabeza*** *fig* F I'm fuming F **2** (*vapor*) steam **3**: ***~s*** *pl* fumes; ***tener muchos ~s*** F be a real bighead F; ***bajarle los ~s a alguien*** F take s.o. down a peg or two; ***se le han subido los ~s*** (***a la cabeza***) he's gotten really high and mighty
humor *m* **1** humor, *Br* humour; ***sentido del ~*** sense of humor *o Br* humour **2** (*estado de ánimo*) mood; ***estar de buen*** / ***mal ~*** be in a good / bad mood; ***estar de ~ para hacer algo*** be in the mood to do sth **3** (*genio*): ***tener un ~ de perros*** F be bad-tempered
humorada *f* joke, witty comment
humorado *adj*: ***bien ~*** good-tempered, good-humored, *Br* good-humoured; ***mal ~*** bad-tempered
humorismo *m* humor, *Br* humour
humorista *m/f* humorist; (*cómico*) comedian
humorístico *adj* humorous
humoso *adj* smoky
humus *m* GASTR hummus
hundido *adj fig*: *persona* devastated
hundimiento *m* sinking
hundir ⟨3a⟩ *v/t* sink; *fig*: *empresa* ruin,

bring down; *persona* devastate; **hundirse** *v/r* sink; *fig*: *de empresa* collapse, go under; *de persona* go to pieces
húngaro I *adj* Hungarian **II** *m*, **-a** *f* Hungarian **III** *m idioma* Hungarian
Hungría *f* Hungary
huracán *m* hurricane
huracanado *adj* hurricane-force, gale-force
huraño *adj* unsociable
hurgar ⟨1h⟩ *v/i* rummage (***en*** in); **hurgarse** *v/r*: ***~ la nariz*** pick one's nose
hurgón *m* poker
hurón *m* ZO ferret
huronear ⟨1a⟩ *v/i fig* pry, snoop
hurtadillas *fpl*: ***a ~*** furtively
hurtar ⟨1a⟩ *v/t* steal; **hurtarse** *v/r*: ***~ a alguien*** hide from s.o.
hurto *m* theft
húsar *m* MIL hussar
husmear ⟨1a⟩ **I** *v/i* **1** (*olfatear*) sniff around **2** F (*cotillear*) sniff *o* nose around F, snoop F (***en*** in) **II** *v/t* sniff
husmeo *m* **1** (*olfateo*) sniffing **2** F (*cotilleo*) sniffing *o* nosing around F, snooping F
huso *m* spindle
◇ **huso horario** time zone
¡huy! *int sorpresa* wow!; *dolor* ouch!
huyo *vb* ☞ ***huir***

I

I, i *f* letter 'i'
ib., ibid. *abr* (= ***ibídem***) ibid (= ibidem)
iba *vb* ☞ ***ir***
ibérico *adj* Iberian; ***la Península Ibérica*** the Iberian Peninsula
ibero, íbero *m*, **-a** *f* Iberian
Iberoamérica *f* Latin America
iberoamericano I *adj* Latin American **II** *m*, **-a** *f* Latin American
IBI *m abr* (= ***impuesto sobre bienes inmuebles***) property tax, *Br* rates *pl*
ibicenco *adj* Ibizan
ibis *m inv* ZO ibis
iceberg *m* iceberg; ***la punta del ~*** *fig* the tip of the iceberg
ICEX *m abr* (= ***Instituto Español de Comercio Exterior***) Spanish Overseas Trade Association
icono *m tb* INFOR icon
ictericia *f* MED jaundice
I+D *abr* (= ***investigación y desarrollo***) R&D (= research and development)
ida *f* outward journey; (***billete de***) ***~ y vuelta*** round trip (ticket), *Br* return (ticket); ***~s y venidas*** comings and goings
idea *f* idea; ***dar*** (***una***) ***~ de algo*** give an idea of sth; ***hacerse a la ~ de que …*** get used to the idea that …; ***no tener ni ~*** not have a clue
ideal *m/adj* ideal
idealismo *m* idealism
idealista I *adj* idealistic **II** *m/f* idealist
idealizar ⟨1f⟩ *v/t* idealize
idear ⟨1a⟩ *v/t* think up, come up with
ideario *m* ideology
ídem *pron* ditto; *fml* idem
idéntico *adj* identical; ***es ~ a su padre*** he's the spitting image of his father
identidad *f* identity
identificable *adj* identifiable
identificación *f* **1** *acto* identification **2** INFOR user ID, user name
identificar ⟨1g⟩ *v/t* identify; **identificarse** *v/r* identify o.s.; ***~ con*** identify with
identikit *m Rpl* identikit
ideología *f* ideology
ideológico *adj* ideological
ideólogo *m*, **-a** *f* ideologist
idílico *adj* idyllic
idilio *m* **1** idyll **2** (*relación amorosa*) romance
idioma *m* language
idiomático *adj* idiomatic
idiosincrasia *f* idiosyncrasy
idiota I *adj* idiotic **II** *m/f* idiot
idiotez *f* stupid thing to say / do; ***es una ~ hacer eso*** that's a stupid thing to do
idiotismo *m* **1** LING idiom **2** MED idiocy
idiotizar ⟨1f⟩ *v/t* turn into an idiot; **idiotizarse** *v/r* turn into an idiot
ido I *part* ☞ ***ir*** **II** *adj* F (*chiflado*) nuts F; ***estar ~*** be miles away F
idólatra I *adj* idolatrous *tb fig* **II** *m/f* idolater; *fig* worshipper

idolatrar ⟨1a⟩ *v/t tb fig* worship
idolatría *f* idolatry
ídolo *m tb fig* idol
idoneidad *f* suitability
idóneo *adj* suitable
IES *m abr* (= ***instituto de educación secundaria***) High School, *Br* Secondary School
iglesia *f* church; ***casarse por la ~*** have a church wedding, get married in church
iglú *m* igloo
ígneo *adj* igneous
ignición *f* **1** combustion **2** AUTO ignition
ignífugo *adj* fireproof, fire-resistant
ignominia *f* ignominy, disgrace
ignominioso *adj* ignominious, disgraceful
ignorancia *f* ignorance
ignorante I *adj* ignorant **II** *m/f* ignoramus
ignorar ⟨1a⟩ *v/t* not know, not be aware of; ***ignoro cómo sucedió*** I don't know how it happened
ignoto *adj* unknown
igual I *adj* **1** (*idéntico*) same (***a***, ***que*** as); ***es ~ a su padre*** he's just like his father; ***al ~ que*** like, the same as **2** (*proporcionado*) equal (***a*** to) **3** (*constante*) constant
II *m/f* equal; ***tratar de ~ a ~*** treat as an equal; ***no tener ~*** have no equal; ***sin ~*** unequaled, *Br* unequalled
III *m* MAT equals sign
IV *adv*: ***~ vengo mañana*** I may come tomorrow; ***me da ~*** I don't mind
igualación *f*: ***buscan la ~ de los derechos*** they are trying to achieve equal rights
igualado *adj* even
igualar ⟨1a⟩ **I** *v/t* **1** *precio*, *marca* equal, match; ***~ algo*** MAT make sth equal (***con***, ***a*** to) **2** (*nivelar*) level off **II** *v/i* DEP tie the game, *Br* equalize; ***~ a cero*** tie *o Br* draw nil-nil; **igualarse** *v/r* match
igualdad *f* equality
◇ **igualdad de derechos** equal rights *pl*
◇ **igualdad de oportunidades** equal opportunities *pl*
igualitario *adj* egalitarian
igualmente *adv* equally
iguana *f* ZO iguana
ijada *f*, **ijar** *m* ANAT *de persona* side; *de animal* side, flank
ilegal *adj* illegal
ilegalidad *f* illegality
ilegalizar ⟨1f⟩ *v/t* make illegal, outlaw
ilegible *adj* illegible
ilegitimar ⟨1a⟩ *v/t* make illegal
ilegitimidad *f* illegitimacy
ilegítimo *adj* **1** (*ilegal*) unlawful **2** *hijo* illegitimate
íleon *m* ANAT ileum
ilerdense *adj* of / from Lerida, Lerida *atr*
ileso *adj* unhurt
iletrado *adj* (*analfabeto*) illiterate; (*inculto*) uneducated
ilícito *adj* illicit
ilimitado *adj* unlimited
Ilmo. *abr* (= ***ilustrísimo***) His / Your Excellency
ilocalizable *adj*: ***está ~*** he cannot be found
ilógico *adj* illogical
iluminación *f* illumination
iluminado I *m*, **-a** *f* REL visionary **II** *part* ☞ ***iluminar***
iluminador *m*, **~a** *f* TEA lighting technician
iluminar ⟨1a⟩ *v/t edificio*, *calle etc* light, illuminate; *monumento* light up, illuminate; *fig* light up
ilusión *f* **1** (*ficción*) illusion **2** (*deseo*, *esperanza*) hope; ***hacerse ilusiones*** get one's hopes up **3** (*entusiasmo*): ***me hace mucha ~*** I'm really looking forward to it
ilusionar ⟨1a⟩ *v/t*: ***~ a alguien*** get s.o.'s hopes up; **ilusionarse** *v/r* **1** get one's hopes up **2** (*entusiasmarse*) get excited (***con*** about)
ilusionismo *m* magic, illusionism
ilusionista *m/f* conjurer, illusionist
iluso I *adj* gullible **II** *m*, **-a** *f* dreamer
ilusorio *adj* illusory
ilustración *f* **1** illustration **2** (*saber*) learning; ***la Ilustración*** HIST the Enlightenment
ilustrado *adj* **1** illustrated **2** (*culto*) learned
ilustrador *m*, **~a** *f* illustrator
ilustrar ⟨1a⟩ *v/t* **1** illustrate **2** (*aclarar*) explain; **ilustrarse** *v/r* learn, acquire knowledge
ilustrativo *adj* illustrative

ilustre *adj* illustrious
imagen *f tb fig* image; ***ser la viva ~ de*** be the spitting image of
◇ **imagen de archivo** library photograph; ***imágenes de archivo*** archive footage *sg*
◇ **imagen pública** public image
imaginable *adj* imaginable
imaginación *f* imagination; ***ni me pasó por la ~*** it never crossed my mind
imaginar ⟨1a⟩ *v/t* imagine; **imaginarse** *v/r* imagine; ***¡ya me lo imagino!*** I can just imagine it!; ***¡imagínate!*** just imagine!
imaginario *adj* imaginary
imaginativo *adj* imaginative
imán *m* magnet
iman(t)ar ⟨1a⟩ *v/t* magnetize
imbatibilidad *f* invincibility
imbatible *adj* unbeatable
imbatido *adj* unbeaten
imbécil I *adj* **1** stupid **2** MED imbecilic **II** *m/f* idiot, imbecile
imbecilidad *f* **1** stupidity; ***¡qué ~ decir eso!*** what a stupid thing to say! **2** MED imbecility
imberbe *adj*: ***un joven ~*** a beardless youth
imborrable *adj* indelible
imbricar ⟨1g⟩ *v/t* overlap; **imbricarse** *v/r* overlap
imbuir ⟨3g⟩ *v/t* imbue (***de*** with)
imitable *adj* imitable
imitación *f* imitation; ***de ~*** imitation *atr*; ***a ~ de*** in imitation of, imitating
imitador *m*, **~a** *f* **1** *de producto, técnica* imitator **2** (*cómico*) impressionist
imitar ⟨1a⟩ *v/t* imitate
impaciencia *f* impatience
impacientar ⟨1a⟩ *v/t* make impatient; **impacientarse** *v/r* lose (one's) patience
impaciente *adj* impatient
impactante *adj imagen, espectáculo* stunning; *belleza* striking
impactar ⟨1a⟩ *v/t* **1** hit **2** (*impresionar*) have an impact on
impacto *m tb fig* impact; ***~ ecológico / medioambiental*** ecological / environmental impact
◇ **impacto de bala** bullet hole
impagable *adj* unpayable
impagado I *adj* unpaid **II** *m* unpaid item, outstanding item
impago *m* non-payment
impala *m* ZO impala
impalpable *adj* impalpable
impar *adj número* odd
imparable *adj* unstoppable
imparcial *adj* impartial
imparcialidad *f* impartiality
impartir ⟨3a⟩ *v/t* impart; *clase, bendición* give
impasibilidad *f* impassivity
impasible *adj* impassive
impavidez *f* **1** (*valor*) fearlessness **2** (*impasibilidad*) impassivity
impávido *adj* **1** (*valiente*) fearless, undaunted **2** (*impasible*) impassive
impecable *adj* impeccable
impedido *adj* disabled
impedimento *m* impediment
impedir ⟨3l⟩ *v/t* prevent; (*estorbar*) impede
impeler ⟨2a⟩ *v/t* **1** (*impulsar*) propel, drive **2** (*incitar*) impel, drive
impenetrable *adj* impenetrable
impenitente *adj* unrepentant
impensable *adj* unthinkable
impensado *adj* unexpected
impepinable *adj* F certain
imperante *adj* ruling; *fig* prevailing
imperar ⟨1a⟩ *v/i* rule; *fig* prevail
imperativo I *adj* **1** GRAM imperative **2** *obligación* pressing **II** *m* imperative *also* GRAM
imperceptible *adj* imperceptible
imperdible *m* safety pin
imperdonable *adj* unpardonable, unforgivable
imperecedero *adj* perpetual, everlasting
imperfección *f* **1** (*defecto*) imperfection, flaw **2** (*cualidad*) imperfection
imperfecto I *adj* imperfect **II** *m* GRAM imperfect
imperial *adj* imperial
imperialismo *m* imperialism
imperialista *m/f & adj* imperialist
impericia *f* lack of skill
imperio *m* empire
imperioso *adj* **1** *necesidad* compelling, pressing **2** *persona* imperious
impermeabilidad *f* impermeability
impermeabilizar ⟨1f⟩ *v/t* waterproof, make waterproof
impermeable I *adj* waterproof **II** *m* raincoat

impersonal *adj* impersonal
impertérrito *adj* unperturbed, unmoved
impertinencia *f* impertinence; ***una ~*** an impertinent remark
impertinente I *adj* impertinent **II** *m/f*: ***¡eres un ~!*** you're so impertinent!
imperturbable *adj* imperturbable
ímpetu *m* impetus
impetuosidad *f* impetuosity, impetuousness
impetuoso *adj* impetuous
impiedad *f* impiety
impío *adj* **1** (*sin piedad*) impious **2** (*sin fe*) godless, heathen
implacable *adj* implacable
implantación *f* **1** *de programa, reforma* implementation; *de democracia* establishment; *de pena de muerte* introduction **2** MED implantation
implantar ⟨1a⟩ *v/t* **1** *programa, reforma* implement; *democracia* establish; *pena de muerte* introduce, bring in **2** MED implant; **implantarse** *v/r* be introduced
implante *m* MED implant
implementación *f* implementation
implementar ⟨1a⟩ *v/t* implement
implemento *m* implement
implicación *f* (*participación*) involvement; *en un delito* implication, involvement
implicar ⟨1g⟩ *v/t* **1** mean, imply; ***eso no implica que …*** that does not mean that … **2** (*involucrar*) involve (***en*** in); *en un delito* implicate (***en*** in); **implicarse** *v/r* get involved
implícito *adj* implicit
implorar ⟨1a⟩ *v/t* beg for
impoluto *adj* (*sin mancha*) unmarked, unstained; (*sin contaminar*) unpolluted, uncontaminated; *fig*: *expediente, trayectoria profesional* impeccable
imponderable *adj* & *m* imponderable
imponente I *adj* **1** impressive, imposing **2** F terrific **II** *m/f* FIN depositor
imponer ⟨2r; *part* ***impuesto***⟩ **I** *v/t* **1** impose; *impuesto* impose, levy **2** *miedo, respeto* inspire **II** *v/i* be imposing *o* impressive; **imponerse** *v/r* **1** (*hacerse respetar*) assert o.s. **2** DEP win **3** (*prevalecer*) prevail **4** (*ser necesario*) be imperative **5**: ***~ una tarea*** set o.s. a task
imponible *adj* taxable; ***base ~*** tax base
impopular *adj* unpopular
impopularidad *f* unpopularity
importación *f* **1** *acción* import, importation **2** *artículo* import
importador I *adj* importing *atr* **II** *m*, **~a** *f* importer
importancia *f* importance; ***dar ~ a*** attach importance to; ***quitar*** *o* ***restar ~ a algo*** make light of sth, play sth down; ***tener ~*** be important; ***no tiene ~*** it's not important, it doesn't matter; ***sin ~*** unimportant; ***darse ~*** give o.s. airs
importante *adj* important
importar[1] ⟨1a⟩ *v/i* **1** matter; ***no importa*** it doesn't matter; ***¿qué importa?*** what does it matter? **2**: ***eso a ti no te importa*** that's none of your business **3**: ***¿le importa …?*** do you mind …?; ***¿te importaría que pase por tu casa?*** would you mind if I dropped by?
importar[2] ⟨1a⟩ *v/t* COM import
importe *m* **1** *de factura, compra* amount **2** (*coste*) cost
importunar ⟨1a⟩ *v/t* bother
importuno *adj* inopportune
imposibilidad *f* impossibility
imposibilitado *adj* **1** disabled **2**: ***~ para hacer algo*** unable to do sth
imposibilitar ⟨1a⟩ *v/t*: ***~ algo*** make sth impossible, prevent sth
imposible *adj* impossible; ***hacer lo ~*** do everything in one's power
imposición *f* **1** imposition **2** (*exigencia*) demand **3** COM deposit
◇ **imposición de manos** laying on of hands
impositivo *adj* tax *atr*; ***tipo ~*** rate of tax
impositor *m*, **~a** *f* depositor
impostergable *adj*: ***es ~*** it can't be put off
impostor *m*, **~a** *f* impostor
impostura *f* deception
impotencia *f* **1** helplessness, impotence **2** MED impotence
impotente *adj* **1** helpless, powerless, impotent **2** MED impotent
impracticable *adj* impracticable
imprecación *f* curse
imprecar ⟨1g⟩ *v/t* curse
imprecisión *f* lack of precision
impreciso *adj* imprecise
impredecible *adj* unpredictable
impregnación *f* **1** saturation (***de*** with) **2** TÉC impregnation (***de*** with)
impregnar ⟨1a⟩ *v/t* **1** *esponja* saturate

I

(*de* with); *fig* pervade **2** TÉC impregnate (*de* with); **impregnarse** *v/r*: ***se impregna de …*** it is filled with …
impremeditado *adj* unpremeditated
imprenta *f* **1** *taller* printer's **2** *arte, técnica* printing **3** *máquina* printing press; ***dar a la ~*** send for printing
imprescindible *adj* essential; *persona* indispensable
impresentable *adj* unpresentable
impresión *f* **1** impression; ***causar ~*** make an impression; ***causar buena ~*** make a good impression **2**: ***la sangre le da ~*** he can't stand the sight of blood **3** *acto* printing; ***~ en color*** color printing, *Br* colour printing **4** (*tirada*) print run
impresionable *adj* impressionable
impresionante *adj* impressive
impresionar ⟨1a⟩ *v/t*: ***~le a alguien*** impress s.o.; (*conmover*) move s.o.; (*alterar*) shock s.o.; **impresionarse** *v/r* be shocked
impresionismo *m* Impressionism
impresionista I *adj* impressionist, impresssionistic **II** *m/f* Impressionist
impreso I *part* ☞ ***imprimir*** **II** *m* **1** form **2**: ***~s*** *pl* printed matter *sg*
impresor *m* printer
impresora *f* INFOR, *mujer* printer
◊ **impresora de chorro de tinta** inkjet (printer); **impresora en color** color printer, *Br* colour printer; **impresora de inyección de tinta** inkjet (printer); **impresora láser** laser (printer); **impresora matricial** dot-matrix printer
imprevisible *adj* unpredictable
imprevisión *f* lack of foresight
imprevisor *adj* shortsighted; ***ser ~*** not plan ahead
imprevisto I *adj* unforeseen, unexpected **II** *m* unexpected event
imprimación *f* PINT primer
imprimar ⟨1a⟩ *v/t* PINT prime
imprimir ⟨3a; *part* ***impreso***⟩ *v/t tb* INFOR print; *fig* transmit
improbabilidad *f* improbability
improbable *adj* unlikely, improbable
ímprobo *adj* massive, enormous
improcedencia *f* inadmissibility
improcedente *adj* improper
improductividad *f* unproductiveness
improductivo *adj* unproductive
impronta *f* mark
impronunciable *adj* unpronounceable
improperio *m* insult
impropiedad *f* inappropriateness
impropio *adj* inappropriate; ***ser ~ de alguien*** be inappropriate for s.o.
improrrogable *adj* non-extendable
improvisación *f* improvisation
improvisado *adj* improvised
improvisar ⟨1a⟩ *v/t* improvise
improviso *adj*: ***de ~*** unexpectedly
imprudencia *f* recklessness, rashness
◊ **imprudencia temeraria** criminal negligence
imprudente *adj* reckless, rash
impudicia *f* shamelessness
impúdico *adj* shameless, immodest
impudor *m* shamelessness, immodesty
impuesto I *part* ☞ ***imponer*** **II** *m* tax
◊ **impuesto sobre bienes inmuebles** *Esp* property tax; **impuesto sobre el patrimonio** wealth tax; **impuesto sobre la renta** income tax; **impuesto sobre sociedades** corporate tax, *Br* corporation tax; **impuesto sobre sucesiones** inheritance tax; **impuesto sobre el valor añadido** *o L.Am.* **agregado** sales tax, *Br* value-added tax
impugnable *adj* challengeable, contestable
impugnación *f* challenge
impugnar ⟨1a⟩ *v/t* challenge, contest
impulsar ⟨1a⟩ *v/t* **1** TÉC propel **2** COM, *fig* boost
impulsivo *adj* impulsive
impulso *m* **1** (*arrebato*) impulse **2** (*empuje*) impetus; COM boost; *fig* urge, impulse; ***tomar ~*** take a run up
impulsor I *adj* driving *atr* **II** *m*, **~a** *f* driving force
impune *adj* unpunished
impunidad *f* impunity
impuntual *adj* unpunctual
impuntualidad *f* unpunctuality
impureza *f* impurity
impuro *adj* impure
imputable *adj* attributable
imputación *f* attribution
imputar ⟨1a⟩ *v/t* **1** attribute **2** COM assign
IMSERSO *m abr* (= ***Instituto de Migraciones y Servicios Sociales***) Spanish Social Services and Immigration Department

inabarcable *adj* which cannot be dealt with
inabordable *adj* unapproachable, inaccessible
inacabable *adj* endless, never-ending
inacabado *adj* unfinished
inaccesibilidad *f* inaccessibility
inaccesible *adj* inaccessible; *persona* distant, inaccessible
inacción *f* inactivity, inaction
inaceptable *adj* unacceptable
inactivar ⟨1a⟩ *v/t* deactivate
inactividad *f* inactivity
inactivo *adj* inactive
inadaptación *f* maladjustment, failure to adapt
inadaptado *adj* maladjusted
inadecuado *adj* inadequate
inadmisibilidad *f* inadmissibility
inadmisible *adj* inadmissible
inadvertencia *f* oversight
inadvertido *adj*: ***pasar ~*** go unnoticed
inagotable *adj* inexhaustible
inaguantable *adj* unbearable
inalámbrico TELEC **I** *adj* cordless **II** *m* cordless (telephone)
inalcanzable *adj* unattainable, unachievable
inalienable *adj* inalienable
inalterable *adj* **1** *color* permanent, fast; ***materiales ~s*** materials that do not deteriorate **2** *principios* immutable **2** *carácter* impassive
inalterado *adj* unchanged, unaltered
inamovible *adj* immovable
inane *adj* pointless
inanición *f* starvation
inanimado *adj* inanimate
inapelable *adj* JUR unappealable; *fig* indisputable
inapetencia *f* lack of appetite
inapetente *adj*: ***está ~*** she has no appetite, she has lost her appetite
inaplazable *adj* impossible to postpone
inaplicable *adj* inapplicable
inapreciable *adj* **1** (*valioso*) priceless **2** (*insignificante*) negligible
inaprensible *adj*: ***ser ~*** be hard to get hold of
inapropiado *adj* inappropriate
inaprovechado *adj* unused, unexploited
inaptitud *f* unsuitability
inapto *adj* unsuitable
inarrugable *adj* crease-resistant
inasequible *adj* **1** *objetivo* unattainable **2** *precio* prohibitive
inasistencia *f* absence; ***~ a clase*** absence from class
inastillable *adj* shatterproof
inatacable *adj* unassailable
inatención *f* lack of attention
inaudible *adj* inaudible
inaudito *adj* unprecedented
inauguración *f* official opening
inaugural *adj* opening, inaugural
inaugurar ⟨1a⟩ *v/t* (officially) open
inca *m/f* & *adj* Inca
incaico *adj* Incan
incalculable *adj* incalculable
incalificable *adj* indescribable
incandescencia *f* incandescence
incandescente *adj* incandescent
incansable *adj* tireless
incapacidad *f* **1** disability **2** (*falta de capacidad*) inability; ***~ mental*** mental incapacity **3** (*ineptitud*) incompetence
◇ **incapacidad laboral** unfitness for work
incapacitación *f* JUR disqualification
incapacitado *adj* disabled, handicapped; ***~ para el trabajo*** unfit for work
incapacitar ⟨1a⟩ *v/t* JUR disqualify
incapaz *adj* incapable (***de*** of)
incautación *f* seizure
incautarse ⟨1a⟩ *v/r*: ***~ de*** seize
incauto *adj* unwary
incendiar ⟨1b⟩ *v/t* set fire to; **incendiarse** *v/r* burn, catch fire
incendiario I *adj* incendiary; *fig* inflammatory **II** *m*, **-a** *f* arsonist
incendio *m* fire
◇ **incendio forestal** forest fire
◇ **incendio provocado** arson attack
incentivación *f* motivation
incentivar ⟨1a⟩ *v/t* motivate
incentivo *m* incentive
incertidumbre *f* uncertainty
incesante *adj* incessant
incesto *m* incest
incestuoso *adj* incestuous
incidencia *f* **1** (*efecto*) effect **2** (*frecuencia*) incidence **3** (*incidente*) incident
incidental *adj* incidental
incidente *m* incident
incidir ⟨3a⟩ **I** *v/i*: ***~ en*** (*afectar*) have an effect on, affect; (*recalcar*) stress; ***~ en***

un error make a mistake **II** *v/t* incise
incienso *m* incense
incierto *m* uncertain
incineración *f de basuras* incineration; *de cadáver* cremation
◇ **incineración de basuras** waste incineration
incinerador *adj* incinerator *atr*; ***planta ~a de basuras*** *o* ***residuos*** waste incineration plant
incinerar ⟨1a⟩ *v/t basuras* incinerate; *cadáver* cremate
incipiente *adj* incipient
incisión *f* incision
incisivo *adj* cutting; *fig* incisive; ***diente ~*** incisor
inciso *m* **1** (*oración*) digression **2** (*comentario*) interruption
incitación *f* incitement (***a*** to)
incitador *m*, **~a** *f* agitator
incitante *adj* provocative
incitar ⟨1a⟩ *v/t* incite
incivil *adj* uncivil
incivilizado *adj* uncivilized
inclasificable *adj* impossible to classify
inclemencia *f del tiempo* inclemency
inclemente *adj* inclement
inclinación *f* **1** inclination; ***tener ~ a hacer algo*** have an inclination to do sth **2** *fig*: *propensión* tendency **3** *de un terreno* slope **4** *muestra de respeto* bow
inclinado *adj* sloping
inclinar ⟨1a⟩ **I** *v/t* **1** tilt; ***~ la cabeza*** nod (one's head) **2**: ***me inclina a creer que ...*** it makes me think that ...; **inclinarse** *v/r* **1** *desde la horizontal* bend (down); *desde la vertical* lean; *de un terreno* slope **2** *en señal de respeto* bow **3**: ***~ a*** *fig* tend to, be inclined to
ínclito *adj* illustrious
incluido *prp* inclusive
incluir ⟨3g⟩ *v/t* include; (*comprender*) comprise
inclusa *f* children's home
inclusión *f* inclusion
inclusive *adv* inclusive
incluso *adv*, *prp & conj* even
incoar ⟨1a⟩ *v/t* JUR *procedimiento*, *proceso* initiate
incobrable *adj deuda* irrecoverable, bad
incógnita *f* unknown factor; MAT unknown (quantity)
incógnito *adj*: ***de ~*** incognito
incoherencia *f* incoherence; ***eso que has dicho es una ~*** what you said makes no sense
incoherente *adj* incoherent
incoloro *adj* colorless, *Br* colourless
incólume *adj* unharmed, unscathed
incombustible *adj* fireproof; *fig* ***ser ~*** go on for ever
incomible *adj* inedible
incomodar ⟨1a⟩ *v/t* **1** inconvenience **2** (*enfadar*) annoy; **incomodarse** *v/r* **1** feel uncomfortable **2** (*enfadarse*) get annoyed (***por*** about, over)
incomodidad *f* **1** uncomfortableness **2** (*fastidio*) inconvenience
incómodo *adj* **1** uncomfortable **2** (*fastidioso*) inconvenient
incomodo *m* inconvenience, trouble
incomparable *adj* incomparable
incomparecencia *f* JUR non-appearance, failure to appear
incompatibilidad *f* incompatibility
incompatible *adj tb* INFOR incompatible
incompetencia *f* incompetence
incompetente *adj* incompetent
incompleto *adj* incomplete
incomprendido *adj* misunderstood
incomprensible *adj* incomprehensible
incomprensión *f* lack of understanding, incomprehension
incomprensivo *adj* unsympathetic
incomunicación *f* **1** lack of communication **2** JUR solitary confinement
incomunicado *adj* **1** isolated, cut off **2** JUR in solitary confinement
incomunicar ⟨1g⟩ *v/t* **1** cut off **2** JUR put in solitary confinement
inconcebible *adj* inconceivable
inconciliable *adj* irreconcilable
inconcluso *adj* unfinished
inconcreción *f* imprecision
inconcreto *adj* imprecise
incondicional **I** *adj* unconditional **II** *m/f* staunch supporter, stalwart
inconexo *adj* unconnected
inconfesable *adj* shameful
inconforme *adj* nonconformist
inconformismo *m* non-conformism
inconformista *m/f* non-conformist
inconfundible *adj* unmistakable
incongruencia *f* incongruity
incongruente *adj* incongruous
inconmensurable *adj* immeasurable

inconmovible *adj* unmoved, implacable
inconquistable *adj* unconquerable
inconsciencia *f* **1** MED unconsciousness **2** (*desconocimiento*) lack of awareness, unawareness **3** (*irreflexión*) thoughtlessness
inconsciente *adj* **I 1** MED unconscious **2** (*ignorante*) unaware **3** (*irreflexivo*) thoughtless **II** *m* PSI: ***el ~*** the unconscious (mind)
inconsecuencia *f* inconsistency
inconsecuente *adj* inconsistent
inconsideración *f* lack of consideration, inconsiderateness
inconsiderado *adj* inconsiderate
inconsistencia *f* flimsiness, weakness
inconsistente *adj* flimsy, weak
inconsolable *adj* inconsolable
inconstancia *f* fickleness
inconstante *adj* fickle
inconstitucional *adj* unconstitutional
inconstitucionalidad *f* unconstitutionality
incontable *adj* uncountable
incontenible *adj* uncontainable, uncontrollable
incontestable *adj* indisputable
incontestado *adj* undisputed
incontinencia *f*: **~ (*urinaria*)** MED incontinence
incontinente *adj* MED incontinent
incontrastable *adj que no se puede discutir* incontrovertible
incontrolable *adj* uncontrollable
incontrolado *adj* uncontrolled
incontrovertible *adj* incontrovertible
inconveniencia *f* **1** inconvenience **2** (*impertinencia*) inappropriate remark
inconveniente I *adj* **1** (*inoportuno*) inconvenient **2** (*impropio*) inappropriate **II** *m* **1** (*desventaja*) drawback, disadvantage **2** (*estorbo*) problem; ***no tengo ~*** I don't mind
incordiar ⟨1b⟩ *v/t* annoy
incordio *m* nuisance
incorporación *f* incorporation
incorporar ⟨1a⟩ *v/t* incorporate; **incorporarse** *v/r* **1** sit up **2 ~ *a*** MIL join
incorpóreo *adj* incorporeal
incorrección *f* **1** error, mistake **2** (*descortesía*) discourtesy
incorrecto *adj* **1** incorrect, wrong **2** (*descortés*) impolite, discourteous

incorregible *adj* incorrigible
incorruptible *adj* incorruptible
incredibilidad *f* incredibility, incredible nature
incredulidad *f* disbelief, incredulity
incrédulo *adj* incredulous
increíble *adj* incredible
incrementar ⟨1a⟩ *v/t* increase; **incrementarse** *v/r* increase
incremento *m* growth
increpación *f* rebuke
increpar ⟨1a⟩ *v/t* **1** (*reprender*) reproach **2** (*insultar*) insult
incriminación *f* incrimination
incriminar ⟨1a⟩ *v/t* incriminate
incruento *adj* bloodless
incrustación *f* incrustation; ***un collar con incrustaciones de marfil*** a necklace inlaid with ivory
incrustar ⟨1a⟩ *v/t* incrust (***de*** with); **incrustarse** *v/r de la suciedad* become ingrained
incubación *f* incubation; ***período de ~*** incubation period
incubadora *f* incubator
incubar ⟨1a⟩ *v/t* incubate; **incubarse** *v/r* incubate
incuestionable *adj* unquestionable
inculcar ⟨1g⟩ *v/t* instill, Br instil (***en*** in)
inculpación *f* accusation
inculpado *m*, **-a** *f*: ***el ~*** the accused
inculpar ⟨1a⟩ *v/t* JUR accuse
inculto *adj* **1** ignorant, uneducated **2** AGR uncultivated
incultura *f* ignorance, lack of education
incumbencia *f* responsibility, duty; ***no es de mi ~*** it's not my responsibility
incumbir ⟨3a⟩ *v/i*: ***~ a alguien*** (***hacer algo***) be s.o.'s responsibility (to do sth)
incumplimiento *m* non-fulfillment (***de*** of), *Br* non-fulfilment (***de*** of), non-compliance (***de*** with); ***~ contractual*** breach of contract
incumplir ⟨3a⟩ *v/t* break
incurable *adj* incurable
incurrir ⟨3a⟩ *v/i* **1**: ***~ en un error*** make a mistake **2**: ***~ en gastos*** incur costs
incursión *f* MIL raid; *fig* foray
indagación *f* investigation
indagar ⟨1h⟩ *v/i* investigate
indebido *adj* unjustified
indecencia *f* indecency; *de película* obscenity
indecente *adj* indecent; *película* ob-

scene
indecible *adj* indescribable, unspeakable
indecisión *f* indecisiveness
indeciso *adj* undecided; *por naturaleza* indecisive
indecoroso *adj* indecorous
indefectible *adj* inevitable, unfailing
indefendible *adj* undefendable; *fig* indefensible
indefensión *f* defenselessness, *Br* defencelessness
indefenso *adj* defenseless, *Br* defenceless
indefinible *adj* indefinable
indefinidamente *adv* indefinitely
indefinido *adj* **1** (*impreciso*) vague **2** (*ilimitado*) indefinite; *contrato* permanent **3** GRAM indefinite
indeformable *adj material* that keeps its shape
indeleble *adj* indelible
indelicadeza *f* indelicacy, indiscretion
indelicado *adj* indelicate
indemne *adj* unhurt, unscathed; ***salir ~*** escape unscathed *o* unharmed
indemnidad *f* indemnity
indemnización *f* compensation
indemnizar ⟨1f⟩ *v/t* compensate (***por*** for)
indemostrable *adj* impossible to demonstrate
independencia *f* independence; ***con ~ de*** independently of
independentismo *m* POL pro-independence movement
independentista I *adj* pro-independence *atr* **II** *m/f* supporter of independence
independiente *adj* independent
independientemente *adv* independently; ***~ de*** regardless of
independizarse ⟨1f⟩ *v/r* become independent
indescifrable *adj* indecipherable
indescriptible *adj* indescribable
indeseable I *adj* undesirable **II** *m/f* undesirable
indeseado *adj* unwanted
indesmallable *adj* run-resist, *Br* ladderproof
indestructible *adj* indestructible
indeterminable *adj* indeterminable
indeterminación *f* indecisiveness
indeterminado *adj* indeterminate; (*indefinido*) indefinite
indexación *f* indexing
indexar ⟨1a⟩ *v/t* index
India: (***la***) **~** India
indiada *f L.Am.* group of Indians
indiano *m Spaniard who has returned from Latin America after making his fortune*
indicación *f* **1** indication; ***por ~ médica*** on medical advice **2** (*señal*) sign **3**: ***indicaciones*** *para llegar* directions; (*instrucciones*) instructions
indicado *adj* **1** (*adecuado*) suitable; ***lo más / menos ~*** the best / worst thing **2**: ***hora -a*** specified time
indicador *m* indicator
◇ **indicador de dirección** AUTO indicator
indicar ⟨1g⟩ *v/t* **1** show, indicate **2** (*señalar*) point out **3** (*sugerir*) suggest
indicativo I *adj* indicative **II** *m* **1** GRAM indicative **2** TELEC code
índice *m* **1** index; ***~ de precios al consumo*** consumer price index, *Br tb* retail price index; ***~ bursátil*** stock market index, *Br* share index; ***~ de desempleo*** unemployment rate **2**: ***dedo ~*** index finger
indicio *m* indication, sign; (*vestigio*) trace
índico *adj* Indian; ***Océano Índico*** Indian Ocean
indiferencia *f* indifference
indiferente *adj* **1** indifferent **2** (*irrelevante*) immaterial
indígena I *adj* indigenous, native *atr* **II** *m/f* native
indigencia *f* destitution
indigente I *adj* destitute **II** *m/f* poor person; ***los ~s*** the poor *pl*
indigerible *adj* indigestible
indigestarse ⟨1a⟩ *v/r de persona* get indigestion; *de comida* cause indigestion
indigestión *f* indigestion
indigesto *adj* indigestible
indignación *f* indignation
indignado *adj* indignant
indignante *adj* infuriating
indignar ⟨1a⟩ *v/t*: ***~ a alguien*** make s.o. indignant; **indignarse** *v/r* become indignant
indignidad *f* unworthiness
indigno *adj* unworthy (***de*** of)

índigo *adj* indigo; ***azul ~*** indigo
indio I *adj* Indian **II** *m*, **-a** *f* Indian; ***hacer el ~*** F clown around F, play the fool F
indirecta *f* insinuation; (*sugerencia*) hint
indirecto *adj* indirect
indisciplina *f* lack of discipline, indiscipline
indisciplinado *adj* undisciplined
indiscreción *f* **1** indiscretion, lack of discretion **2** (*declaración*) indiscreet remark
indiscreto *adj* indiscreet
indiscriminado *adj* indiscriminate
indiscutible *adj* indisputable
indiscutido *adj* undisputed
indisoluble *adj* **1** *sustancia* insoluble **2** *matrimonio*, *amistad* indissoluble
indispensable *adj* indispensable
indisponer ⟨2r; *part* ***indispuesto***⟩ *v/t* **1** (*enfermar*) make unwell, upset **2**: ***~ a alguien con alguien*** (*enemistar*) set s.o. against s.o.; **indisponerse** *v/r* **1** become unwell **2**: ***~ con alguien*** fall out with s.o.
indisposición *f* indisposition
indispuesto *adj* indisposed, unwell
indisputable *adj* undeniable
indistintamente *adv* **1** (*sin claridad*) indistinctly **2** (*sin distinción*) without distinction
indistinto *adj* *forma* indistinct, vague; *noción* vague; *sonido* faint
individual *adj* individual; *cama*, *habitación* single
individualidad *f* individuality
individualismo *m* individualism
individualista I *adj* individualistic **II** *m/f* individualist
individualizar ⟨1f⟩ *v/t* set apart; *para crítica*, *elogio* single out
individuo *m* individual
indivisible *adj* indivisible
indiviso *adj* undivided
indócil *adj* troublesome
indocumentado *adj*: ***un hombre ~*** a man with no identity papers
índole *f* nature; ***de esta ~*** of this nature
indolencia *f* laziness, indolence
indolente *adj* lazy, indolent
indoloro *adj* painless
indomable *adj* *animal* untameable; *persona* indomitable
indómito *adj* indomitable
Indonesia *f* Indonesia
inducción *f* induction
inducido *m* EL armature
inducir ⟨3o⟩ *v/t* **1** (*persuadir*) lead, induce (***a*** to) **2** EL induce
inductivo *adj* EL, *en lógica* inductive
inductor *m* EL inductor
indudable *adj* undoubted
indudablemente *adv* undoubtedly
indulgencia *f* indulgence
indulgente *adj* indulgent
indultar ⟨1a⟩ *v/t* pardon
indulto *m* pardon
indumentaria *f* clothing
industria *f* **1** *actividad*, *sector* industry **2** (*esfuerzo*) industriousness, industry ◇ **industria automovilística** automobile industry; **industria electrónica** electronics industry; **industria ligera** light industry; **industria pesada** heavy industry; **industria de transformación, industria transformadora** processing industry; **industria turística** tourist industry
industrial I *adj* industrial; ***cantidad ~*** F massive amount F **II** *m/f* industrialist
industrialización *f* industrialization
industrializar ⟨1f⟩ *v/t* industrialize; **industrializarse** *v/r* industrialize
industrioso *adj* industrious
INE *m abr* (= ***Instituto Nacional de Estadística***) Spanish National Statistics Office
inédito *adj* **1** unpublished **2** *fig* unprecedented
ineducado *adj* uneducated
inefable *adj* indescribable, ineffable *fml*
inefectivo *adj* ineffective
ineficacia *f* inefficiency; *de un procedimiento* ineffectiveness
ineficaz *adj* inefficient; *procedimiento* ineffective
ineficiencia *f* inefficiency
ineficiente *adj* inefficient
inelegible *adj* ineligible
ineludible *adj* unavoidable
INEM *m abr* (= ***Instituto Nacional de Empleo***) Spanish Employment Office
inenarrable *adj* inexpressible, indescribable
ineptitud *f* ineptitude, incompetence
inepto I *adj* inept, incompetent **II** *m*, **-a** *f* incompetent fool
inequívoco *adj* unequivocal
inercia *f* inertia

inerme *adj* **1** (*sin defensa*) defenseless, *Br* defenceless **2** (*sin armas*) unarmed
inerte *adj fig* lifeless; FÍS inert
inescrutable *adj* inscrutable
inesperado *adj* unexpected
inestabilidad *f* instability
inestable *adj situación, persona* unstable; *tiempo* unsettled
inestimable *adj* invaluable
inevitable *adj* inevitable
inexactitud *f* inaccuracy
inexacto *adj* inaccurate
inexcusable *adj* inexcusable
inexistencia *f* lack
inexistente *adj* non-existent
inexorable *adj* inexorable
inexperiencia *f* lack of experience, inexperience
inexperto *adj* inexperienced
inexplicable *adj* inexplicable
inexplorado *adj* unexplored
inexpresable *adj* inexpressible
inexpresividad *f* lack of expression
inexpresivo *adj* inexpressive, expressionless
inexpugnable *adj* impregnable
inextinguible *adj* **1** *fuego* inextinguishable **2** *sed* unquenchable
inextricable *adj* inextricable
infalibilidad *f* infallibility
infalible *adj* infallible
infalsificable *adj documento etc* impossible to forge *o* fake
infamante *adj* defamatory
infamatorio *adj* defamatory
infame *adj* vile, loathsome; (*terrible*) dreadful, awful
infamia *f* **1** (*deshonra*) disgrace **2** (*acción infame*) dreadful *o* awful thing to do **3** (*dicho infame*) slander, slur
infancia *f* childhood; *fig* infancy
infanta *f* infanta, princess
infante *m* infante, prince
infantería *f* MIL infantry
infanticida *m/f* child killer, *fml* infanticide
infanticidio *m* infanticide
infantil *adj* **1** children's **2** *naturaleza* childlike; *desp* infantile, childish
infarto *m*: ~ (***de miocardio***) heart attack; ***de*** ~ *fig* F heart-stopping, incredible; ***nos dio una alegría de*** ~ we were incredibly happy
infatigable *adj* tireless, indefatigable
infausto *adj* unfortunate, unhappy
infección *f* MED infection; ~ ***viral*** viral infection
infeccioso *adj* infectious
infectar ⟨1a⟩ *v/t* infect; **infectarse** *v/r* become infected
infecto *adj* **1** revolting, disgusting **2** MED infected
infecundidad *f* infertility
infecundo *adj tb fig* infertile
infelicidad *f* unhappiness, misery
infeliz I *adj* **1** unhappy, miserable **2** (*inocente*) naive **II** *m/f* **1** poor devil **2** (*inocente*) naive person
inferior I *adj* inferior (***a*** to); *en el espacio* lower (***a*** than) **II** *m/f* inferior
inferioridad *f* inferiority
inferir ⟨3i⟩ *v/t* **1** infer (***de*** from) **2** *daño* do, cause (***a*** to)
infernal *adj* **1** *ruido, calor* infernal **2** (*muy malo*) diabolical
infértil *adj* infertile
infertilidad *f* infertility
infestación *f* infestation
infestar ⟨1a⟩ *v/t* **1** infest; *fig* corrupt **2** (*invadir*) overrun
infición *f Méx* pollution
inficionar ⟨1a⟩ *v/t* infect; *fig* corrupt
infidelidad *f* infidelity
infiel I *adj* **1** *amante* unfaithful **2** (*inexacto*) inaccurate **II** *m/f* unbeliever
infiernillo *m* portable stove
infierno *m* hell; ***vivir en el quinto*** ~ *fig* F live in the back of beyond F
infiltración *f* infiltration; ***aguas de*** ~ seepage water
infiltrar I ⟨1a⟩ *v/t* infiltrate; **infiltrarse** *v/r*: ~ ***en*** infiltrate; *de agua* seep into
ínfimo *adj* **1** *cantidad* very small **2** *calidad* very poor
infinidad *f*: ~ ***de*** countless
infinitesimal *adj* infinitesimal; ***cálculo*** ~ infinitesimal calculus
infinitivo *m* GRAM infinitive
infinito I *adj* infinite **II** *m* infinity
infinitud *f* infinite nature
inflable *adj* inflatable
inflación *f* COM inflation; ***tasa de*** ~ inflation rate
inflacionista *adj* inflationary
inflador *m Rpl* bicycle pump
inflamable *adj* flammable
inflamación *f* MED inflammation
inflamar ⟨1a⟩ *v/t tb fig* inflame; **infla-**

marse *v/r* MED become inflamed
inflamatorio *adj* MED inflammatory
inflar ⟨1a⟩ *v/t* inflate; **inflarse** *v/r* **1** swell (up) **2** *fig* F get a swollen head F
inflexibilidad *f* inflexibility
inflexible *adj fig* inflexible
inflexión *f* inflection; **~ *de la tendencia*** change in the trend
infligir ⟨3c⟩ *v/t* inflict (***a*** on)
influencia *f* influence; ***tener ~s*** have contacts
influenciable *adj* easily influenced
influenciar ⟨1b⟩ *v/t* influence
influir ⟨3g⟩ *v/i*: **~ *en alguien / algo*** influence s.o. / sth, have an influence on s.o. / sth
influjo *m* influence
influyente *adj* influential
infografía *f* computer graphics *pl*
información *f* **1** information; **~ *genética*** BIO genetic information **2** (*noticias*) news *sg*
informador *m*, **~a** *f* **1** *de noticias* informant **2** (*chivato*) informer
informal *adj* **1** informal **2** *irresponsable* unreliable
informalidad *f* **1** informality **2** (*irresponsabilidad*) unreliability
informante *m/f* informer
informar ⟨1a⟩ *v/t* inform (***de***, ***sobre*** about); **informarse** *v/r* find out (***de***, ***sobre*** about)
informática *f* information technology
informático **I** *adj* computer *atr* **II** *m*, **-a** *f* IT specialist
informativo **I** *adj* **1** informative; ***folleto ~*** (information) leaflet **2** *programa* news *atr* **II** *m* TV, RAD news *sg*
informatización *f* computerization
informatizar ⟨1f⟩ *v/t* computerize
informe **I** *adj* shapeless **II** *m* **1** report **2**: **~*s*** *pl* (*referencias*) references
◇ **informe anual** annual report
◇ **informe médico** medical report
infortunado *adj* unfortunate, unlucky
infortunio *m* misfortune, ill fortune
infracción *f* offense, *Br* offence
infractor **I** *adj* offending *atr* **II** *m*, **~a** *f* offender
infraestructura *f* infrastructure
infrahumano *adj* subhuman
infranqueable *adj barrera*, *río* impassable; *obstáculo*, *diferencia* insurmountable
infrarrojo *adj* infrared
infrautilización *f* under-use
infrautilizado *adj* under-used
infravaloración *f* undervaluation
infravalorar ⟨1a⟩ *v/t* undervalue
infrecuencia *f* infrequency
infrecuente *adj* infrequent
infringir ⟨3c⟩ *v/t* JUR infringe, violate
infructuoso *adj* fruitless
ínfulas *fpl fig*: ***tener*** *o* ***darse ~*** give o.s. airs
infumable *adj* unsmokable; *fig* unbearable
infundado *adj* unfounded, groundless
infundio *m* unfounded rumor, *Br* unfounded rumour
infundir ⟨3a⟩ *v/t* inspire; *terror* instill, *Br* instil; *sospechas* arouse
infusión *f* infusion; *de tila*, *manzanilla* tea
ingeniarse ⟨1b⟩ *v/r*: ***ingeniárselas para*** manage to
ingeniería *f* engineering
◇ **ingeniería genética** genetic engineering
ingeniero *m*, **-a** *f* engineer
◇ **ingeniero aeronaútico** aeronautical engineer; **ingeniero agrónomo** agronomist; **ingeniero de minas** mining engineer; **ingeniero de montes** forestry expert; **ingeniero naval** naval architect; **ingeniero de redes** systems engineer; **ingeniero de sonido** sound engineer; **ingeniero técnico** engineer (*after three-year university course*)
ingenio *m* **1** ingenuity; ***golpe de ~*** flash of inspiration **2** (*aparato*) device
◇ **ingenio azucarero** *L.Am.* sugar refinery
ingeniosidad *f* ingenuity
ingenioso *adj* ingenious
ingente *adj* enormous, huge
ingenuidad *f* naivety
ingenuo **I** *adj* naive **II** *m*, **-a** *f* naive person, sucker F
ingerir ⟨3i⟩ *v/t* consume
ingestión *f* consumption
Inglaterra *f* England
ingle *f* groin
inglés **I** *adj* English **II** *m* **1** Englishman; ***los ingleses*** the English **2** *idioma* English
inglesa *f* Englishwoman
ingobernable *adj* ungovernable

ingratitud *f* ingratitude
ingrato *adj persona* ungrateful; *tarea* thankless
ingravidez *f* weightlessness
ingrávido *adj* weightless
ingrediente *m* ingredient
ingresar ⟨1a⟩ **I** *v/i*: *~ **en*** *en universidad* go to; *en asociación, cuerpo* join; *en hospital* be admitted to **II** *v/t cheque* pay in, deposit
ingreso *m* **1** entry; *en una asociación* joining; ***examen de ~*** entrance exam **2** *en hospital* admission **3** COM deposit **4**: ***~s*** *pl* income *sg*
◇ **ingresos fiscales, ingresos impositivos** tax revenue *sg*
inguinal *adj* ANAT groin *atr*
inhábil *adj* **1** unskillful, *Br* unskilful **2**: ***día ~*** non-working day
inhabilidad *f* lack of skill, ineptitude
inhabilitación *f* JUR disqualification
inhabilitar ⟨1a⟩ *v/t* disqualify (***para*** from)
inhabitable *adj* uninhabitable
inhabitado *adj* uninhabited
inhabitual *adj* unusual
inhalación *f* inhalation
inhalador *m* inhaler
inhalar ⟨1a⟩ *v/t* inhale
inherente *adj* inherent
inhibición *f* **1** inhibition **2** JUR disqualification
inhibir ⟨3a⟩ *v/t* inhibit; **inhibirse** *v/r* keep one's distance (***de*** from)
inhibitorio *adj* disqualifying *atr*
inhospitalario, inhóspito *adj* inhospitable
inhumación *f* interment, burial
inhumanidad *f* inhumanity
inhumano *adj* inhuman; (*cruel*) inhumane
inhumar ⟨1a⟩ *v/t* inter, bury
iniciación *f* initiation
iniciador I *adj*: ***la persona ~a de …*** the person initiating …, the initiator of … **II** *m*, **~a** *f* initiator
inicial *f/adj* initial
inicialista *m/f en béisbol* first base
inicializar ⟨1f⟩ *v/t* INFOR initialize
iniciar ⟨1b⟩ *v/t* initiate; *curso* start, begin; **iniciarse** *v/r* begin, commence; ~ ***en*** be initiated into
iniciativa *f* initiative; ***tomar la ~*** take the initiative
inicio *m* start, beginning; ***estar todavía en los ~s*** be still in the early stages; ***~ en caliente*** INFOR warm start
inicuo *adj* iniquitous, wicked
inidentificable *adj* unidentifiable
inigualable *adj* incomparable; *precio* unbeatable
inigualado *adj* unequaled, *Br* unequalled
inimaginable *adj* unimaginable
inimitable *adj* inimitable
ininflamable *adj* non-flammable
ininteligible *adj* unintelligible
ininterrumpido *adj* uninterrupted
iniquidad *f* iniquity, wickedness
injerencia *f* interference
injerirse ⟨3i⟩ *v/r* interfere (***en*** in)
injertar ⟨1a⟩ *v/t* graft
injerto *m* graft
injuria *f* insult
injuriar ⟨1b⟩ *v/t* insult
injurioso *adj* insulting
injusticia *f* injustice
injustificado *adj* unjustified
injusto *adj* unjust
INM *m abr* (= ***Instituto Nacional de Meteorología***) Spanish Meteorological Service
inmaculado *adj* immaculate
inmadurez *f* immaturity
inmaduro *adj* immature
inmanente *adj* immanent
inmaterial *adj* immaterial
inmediaciones *fpl* immediate area *sg* (***de*** of), vicinity *sg* (***de*** of)
inmediatamente *adv* immediately
inmediato *adj* immediate; ***de ~*** immediately
inmejorable *adj* unbeatable
inmemorial *adj* age-old; ***desde tiempo ~*** from time immemorial
inmensidad *f* immensity
inmenso *adj* immense
inmerecido *adj* undeserved; ***el equipo se llevó una victoria -a*** the team did not deserve to win
inmersión *f* immersion; *de submarino* dive
inmerso *adj fig* immersed (***en*** in)
inmigración *f* immigration
inmigrante *m/f* immigrant
inmigrar ⟨1a⟩ *v/i* immigrate
inmigratorio *adj* immigrant *atr*
inminencia *f* imminence

inminente *adj* imminent
inmiscuirse ⟨3g⟩ *v/r* meddle (***en*** in)
inmisericorde *adj* unmerciful
inmobiliaria *f* realtor's office, *Br* estate agent's
inmobiliario *adj* real estate *atr*, property *atr*; ***agente ~*** realtor, *Br* estate agent
inmoderación *f* lack of moderation
inmoderado *adj* excessive, immoderate
inmodestia *f* immodesty, lack of modesty
inmodesto *adj* immodest
inmolación *f* sacrifice
inmolar ⟨1a⟩ *v/t* sacrifice; **inmolarse** *v/r* sacrifice o.s.
inmoral *adj* immoral
inmoralidad *f* immorality
inmortal *adj* immortal
inmortalidad *f* immortality
inmortalizar ⟨1f⟩ *v/t* immortalize
inmotivado *adj* motiveless
inmóvil *adj persona* motionless; *vehículo* stationary
inmovilidad *f* immobility
inmovilización *f* immobilization
inmovilizador *m* AUTO: ***~ antirrobo*** (anti-theft) immobilizer
inmovilizar ⟨1f⟩ *v/t* immobilize; *fig* paralyze
inmueble **I** *adj* JUR: ***bienes ~s*** immovable assets **II** *m* building
inmundicia *f* filth
inmundo *adj* filthy
inmune *adj* immune
inmunidad *f* MED, POL immunity
inmunitario *adj* immune; ***sistema ~*** immune system
inmunizar ⟨1f⟩ *v/t* immunize
inmunodeficiencia *f* immunodeficiency
inmunología *f* immunology
inmunoterapia *f* immunotherapy
inmutable *adj* unchanging
inmutarse ⟨1a⟩ *v/r*: ***no ~*** not bat an eyelid; ***sin ~*** without batting an eyelid
innato *adj* innate, inborn
innecesario *adj* unnecessary
innegable *adj* undeniable
innoble *adj* ignoble
innovación *f* innovation
innovador **I** *adj* innovative **II** *m*, **~a** *f* innovator
innovar ⟨1m⟩ *v/t*: ***~ algo*** introduce innovations into sth
innumerable *adj* innumerable, countless
inobservancia *f* non-observance
inocencia *f* innocence
inocentada *f* practical joke (*played esp on December 28*)
inocente *adj* innocent
inocuidad *f* harmlessness, innocuousness
inoculación *f* inoculation
inocular ⟨1a⟩ *v/t* inoculate
inocuo *adj* **1** *comentario*, *materia* harmless, innocuous **2** *película* bland
inodoro **I** *adj* odorless, *Br* odourless **II** *m* toilet
inofensivo *adj* inoffensive, harmless
inoficioso *adj L.Am.* (*inútil*) useless
inolvidable *adj* unforgettable
inoperable *adj* MED inoperable
inoperante *adj* ineffective
inopia *f*: ***estar en la ~*** F (*distraído*) be miles away F; (*alejado de la realidad*) be on another planet F
inopinado *adj* unexpected
inoportunidad *f* inconvenience, *fml* inopportuneness
inoportuno *adj* inopportune; (*molesto*) inconvenient
inorgánico *adj* inorganic
inoxidable *adj*: ***acero ~*** stainless steel
input *m* INFOR input
inquebrantable *adj* unshak(e)able, unyielding
inquietante *adj* worrying
inquietar ⟨1a⟩ *v/t* worry; **inquietarse** *v/r* worry, get worried *o* anxious
inquieto *adj* worried, anxious
inquietud *f* **1** worry, anxiety **2** *intelectual* interest
inquilino *m*, **-a** *f* tenant
inquina *f* aversion, dislike; ***tener ~ a alguien*** have sth against s.o., have a grudge against s.o.
inquirir ⟨3i⟩ *v/t* investigate, inquire into
inquisición *f* **1** investigation, inquiry **2**: ***la Inquisición*** HIST the Inquisition
inquisidor **I** *adj* inquiring **II** *m* HIST inquisitor
inquisitivo *adj* inquisitive
inquisitorial *adj* inquisitorial
inri *m*: ***para más ~*** to cap it all, on top of all that
insaciabilidad *f* insatiability

insaciable *adj* insatiable
insalubre *adj* unhealthy
insalubridad *f* unhealthiness
INSALUD *m abr* (= ***Instituto Nacional de la Salud***) Spanish Health Service
insalvable *adj obstáculo* insuperable
insano *adj* unhealthy
insatisfacción *f* dissatisfaction
insatisfactorio *adj* unsatisfactory
insatisfecho *adj* dissatisfied
inscribir ⟨3a; *part* ***inscrito***⟩ *v/t* **1** (*grabar*) inscribe **2** *en lista, registro* register, enter; *en curso*, enroll, *Br* enrol, register; *en concurso* enter; **inscribirse** *v/r en curso* enroll, *Br* enrol, register; *en concurso* enter
inscripción *f* **1** inscription **2** *en lista, registro* registration, entry; *en curso* enrollment, *Br* enrolment, registration; *en concurso* entry
inscrito *part* ☞ ***inscribir***
insecticida *m* insecticide
insectívoro I *adj* insectivorous **II** *m*, **-a** *f* insectivore
insecto *m* insect
inseguridad *f* **1** *de una persona* insecurity **2** *de estructura* unsteadiness **3** (*peligro*) lack of safety, danger; ***está aumentando la ~ ciudadana*** the coutry is becoming increasingly dangerous
inseguro *adj* **1** *persona* insecure **2** *estructura* unsteady **3** (*peligroso*) dangerous, unsafe
inseminación *f* insemination
◇ **inseminación artificial** artificial insemination
inseminar ⟨1a⟩ *v/t* inseminate
insensatez *f* foolishness
insensato *adj* foolish
insensibilidad *f* insensitivity
insensibilizar ⟨1f⟩ *v/t tb fig* desensitize; **insensibilizarse** *v/r* become desensitized
insensible *adj* insensitive (***a*** to)
insensiblemente *adv* imperceptibly
inseparable *adj* inseparable
insepulto *adj* unburied
inserción *f* insertion
insertar ⟨1a⟩ *v/t* insert
inservible *adj* useless
insidia *f* treachery; ***actuar con ~*** act treacherously
insidioso *adj* insidious
insigne *adj* famous
insignia *f* insignia; *bandera, estandarte* standard
insignificancia *f* **1** insignificance **2** *cosa* trifle
insignificante *adj* insignificant
insinceridad *f* insincerity
insincero *adj* insincere
insinuación *f* insinuation
insinuante *adj* suggestive
insinuar ⟨1e⟩ *v/t* insinuate; **insinuarse** *v/r*: **~ *a alguien*** make advances to s.o.
insipidez *f* insipidness
insípido *adj* insipid
insistencia *f* insistence
insistente *adj* insistent
insistir ⟨3a⟩ *v/i* **1** insist; ***~ en hacer algo*** insist on doing sth **2**: ***~ en algo*** stress sth
insobornable *adj* incorruptible, impossible to bribe
insociable *adj* unsociable
insolación *f* MED sunstroke
insolencia *f* insolence
insolentarse ⟨1a⟩ *v/r* become insolent
insolente *adj* insolent
insolidario *adj* unsupportive
insólito *adj* unusual
insoluble *adj* insoluble
insolvencia *f* insolvency
insolvente *adj* insolvent
insomne I *adj* insomniac; ***una noche ~*** a sleepless night **II** *m/f* insomniac
insomnio *m* insomnia
insondable *adj* unfathomable
insonorización *f* soundproofing
insonorizar ⟨1f⟩ *v/t* soundproof
insonoro *adj* soundless, noiseless
insoportable *adj* unbearable, intolerable
insoslayable *adj* inevitable, unavoidable
insospechable *adj* unimaginable
insospechado *adj* unexpected
insostenible *adj* **1** *situación* unsustainable **2** *tesis* untenable
inspección *f* inspection
◇ **inspección fiscal** tax audit
◇ **inspección ocular** visual inspection
inspeccionar ⟨1a⟩ *v/t* inspect
inspector *m*, **~a** *f* inspector
◇ **inspector de Hacienda** tax inspector
inspiración *f* **1** inspiration **2** MED inhalation

inspirar ⟨1a⟩ **I** *v/t* **1** inspire **2** MED inhale **II** *v/i* inhale; **inspirarse** *v/r* draw inspiration, be inspired
instalación *f acto* installation
◇ **instalaciones deportivas** sports facilities
instalador *m* fitter
instalar ⟨1a⟩ *v/t* **1** install, *Br* instal; (*colocar*) put **2** *un negocio* set up; **instalarse** *v/r en un sitio* install o.s., *Br* instal o.s.
instancia *f* **1** JUR petition **2** (*petición por escrito*) application; ***a ~s de*** at the request of **3**: ***en última ~*** as a last resort
instantánea *f* FOT snapshot
instantáneo *adj* immediate, instantaneous
instante *m* moment, instant; ***a cada ~*** every moment; ***al ~*** right away, immediately; ***en un ~*** in a flash
instar ⟨1a⟩ *v/t* urge, press
instauración *f* establishment
instaurar ⟨1a⟩ *v/t* establish
instigación *f* instigation; ***por ~ de*** at the instigation of
instigador *m*, **~a** *f* instigator
instigar ⟨1h⟩ *v/t* incite (***a*** to)
instilar ⟨1a⟩ *v/t* instill, *Br* instil
instintivo *adj* instinctive
instinto *m* instinct
◇ **instinto de conservación** survival instinct
◇ **instinto sexual** sex drive
institución *f* institution
◇ **institución benéfica** charitable organization, charity
institucional *adj* institutional
instituir ⟨3g⟩ *v/t* institute
instituto *m* **1** institute **2** *Esp* high school, *Br* secondary school
◇ **instituto de belleza** beauty salon
◇ **instituto de enseñanza media** *Esp* high school, *Br* secondary school
institutriz *f* governess
instrucción *f* **1** education; (*formación*) training **2** MIL drill **3** INFOR instruction **4** JUR hearing
◇ **instrucciones de uso** instructions, directions (for use)
instructivo *adj* educational
instructor I *adj* JUR: ***juez ~*** examining magistrate **II** *m*, **~a** *f* instructor
instruido *adj* educated
instruir ⟨3g⟩ *v/t* **1** educate; (*formar*) train **2** JUR *pleito* hear; **instruirse** *v/r* broaden one's mind, educate o.s.
instrumentación *f* MÚS scoring, orchestration
instrumental I *adj* instrumental **II** *m* MED instruments *pl*
instrumentalizar ⟨1f⟩ *v/t* exploit
instrumentar ⟨1a⟩ *v/t* MÚS score, orchestrate
instrumentista *m/f* MÚS instrumentalist
instrumento *m* instrument; (*herramienta*) tool, instrument; *fig* tool
◇ **instrumento de cuerda** string instrument; **instrumento didáctico** teaching aid; **instrumento musical** musical instrument; **instrumento de percusión** percussion instrument; **instrumento de viento** wind instrument
insubordinación *f* insubordination
insubordinado *adj* **1** *con un superior* insubordinate **2** (*rebelde*) rebellious
insubordinarse ⟨1a⟩ *v/r* **1** *con un superior* be insubordinate **2** (*rebelarse*) rebel
insuficiencia *f* **1** lack **2** MED failure
◇ **insuficiencia cardiaca** heart failure, *fml* cardiac insufficiency
insuficiente I *adj* insufficient, inadequate **II** *m* EDU *nota* fail
insuflar ⟨1a⟩ *v/t* MED blow; *fig* transmit
insufrible *adj* insufferable
insular *adj* island *atr*
insulina *f* insulin
insulsez *f* blandness, insipidness
insulso *adj* bland, insipid
insultada *f L.Am.* (*insultos*) string of insults
insultante *adj* insulting
insultar ⟨1a⟩ *v/t* insult
insulto *m* insult
insumergible *adj* unsinkable
insumiso I *adj* rebellious **II** *m person who refuses to do military service or an alternative social service*
insuperable *adj* insurmountable
insurgente *m/f & adj* insurgent
insurrección *f* insurrection
insurreccionarse ⟨1a⟩ *v/r* revolt
insurrecto I *adj* rebel *atr*, insurgent *atr* **II** *m*, **-a** *f* rebel, insurrectionist
insustancial *adj* **1** *conferencia* lightweight **2** *estructura* flimsy

I

insustituible *adj* irreplaceable
intachable *adj* faultless
intacto *adj* **1** (*íntegro*) intact **2** (*sin tocar*) untouched
intangible *adj* intangible
integración *f* integration
integral I *adj* **1** complete **2** *alimento* wholewheat, *Br* wholemeal **3** MAT integral; ***cálculo ~*** integral calculus **II** *f* integral
integrante I *adj* integral **II** *m/f* member
integrar ⟨1a⟩ *v/t* integrate; *equipo* make up; **integrarse** *v/r* integrate
integridad *f* **1** entirety; ***el texto en su ~*** the text in full, the text in its entirety **2** (*honradez*) integrity
integrismo *m* fundamentalism
integrista *m/f* fundamentalist
íntegro *adj* whole, entire; ***un hombre ~*** *fig* a man of integrity
intelecto *m* intellect
intelectual *m/f & adj* intellectual
inteligencia *f* intelligence; ***servicio de ~*** POL intelligence service
◇ **inteligencia artificial** artificial intelligence
inteligente *adj* intelligent
inteligible *adj* intelligible
intemperancia *f* **1** (*intolerancia*) intransigence **2** (*falta de moderación*) intemperance
intemperie *f*: ***a la ~*** in the open air
intempestivo *adj* untimely
intemporal *adj* timeless
intemporalidad *f* timelessness
intención *f* intention; ***con buena / mala ~*** with good / bad intentions, in good / bad faith; ***doble*** *o* ***segunda ~*** ulterior motive; ***con / sin ~*** intentionally / unintentionally; ***tener la ~ de*** intend to
intencionado *adj* deliberate
intencional *adj* intentional
intencionalidad *f* intent
intendencia *f* **1** quartermaster corps *sg* **2** *Rpl* city council; *edificio* city hall
intendente *m* **1** MIL quartermaster general **2** *Rpl* (*gobernador*) military governor; (*alcalde*) mayor
intensidad *f* **1** intensity **2** (*fuerza*) strength
intensificación *f* intensification
intensificar ⟨1g⟩ *v/t* intensify; **intensificarse** *v/r* intensify
intensivo *adj* intensive
intenso *adj* **1** intense **2** (*fuerte*) strong
intentar ⟨1a⟩ *v/t* try, attempt
intento *m* **1** attempt, try **2** *Méx* (*intención*) aim
intentona *f*: ***~ (golpista)*** POL attempted putsch, attempted coup
interacción *f* interaction
interactividad *f* interaction
interactivo *adj* interactive
interbancario *adj* inter-bank *atr*
intercalar ⟨1a⟩ *v/t* insert
intercambiable *adj* interchangeable
intercambiador *m* interchange
◇ **intercambiador de calor** heat exchanger
intercambiar ⟨1a⟩ *v/t* exchange, swap
intercambio *m* exchange, swap; ***~ de datos / opiniones*** exchange of information / ideas
interceder ⟨2a⟩ *v/i* intercede (***por*** for)
intercepción, interceptación *f* interception
interceptar ⟨1a⟩ *v/t tb* DEP intercept
interceptor *m* MIL interceptor
intercesión *f* intercession
intercesor *m*, **~a** *f* intercessor
intercomunicador *m* intercom
intercomunicar ⟨1g⟩ *v/t* interconnect; **intercomunicarse** *v/r* interconnect
interconexión *f* interconnection
intercontinental *adj* intercontinental
intercostal *adj* ANAT intercostal
interdependencia *f* interdependence
interdependiente *adj* interdependent
interdicción *f* prohibition
◇ **interdicción civil** JUR prohibition, banning order
interdisciplinar(io) *adj* interdisciplinary
interés *m* **1** interest **2** COM interest; ***sin ~*** interest free **3** *desp* self-interest **4**: ***intereses*** *pl* (*bienes*) interests
◇ **interés compuesto** compound interest
interesado I *adj* interested **II** *m*, **-a** *f* interested party
interesante *adj* interesting; ***hacerse el ~*** draw attention to o.s.
interesar ⟨1a⟩ *v/t* interest; **interesarse** *v/r*: ***~ por*** take an interest in
interestatal *adj* interstate *atr*
interface *m*, **interfaz** *f* INFOR interface
interfecto *m*, **-a** *f* murder victim, de-

ceased
interferencia *f* interference
interferir ⟨3i⟩ **I** *v/t* interfere with **II** *v/i* interfere (***en*** in)
interfono *m* intercom, *Br* entryphone
interglaciar *adj* GEOL interglacial; ***período ~*** interglacial period
intergubernamental *adj* intergovernmental
ínterin *m* interim; ***en el ~*** in the interim
interinidad *f* temporary status
interino I *adj* **1** substitute *atr*, replacement *atr* **2** (*provisional*) provisional, acting; ***médico ~*** covering doctor, *Br* locum **II** *m*, **-a** *f* temporary worker
interior I *adj* **1** interior; *bolsillo* inside *atr* **2** COM, POL domestic **II** *m* **1** interior; ***en su ~*** *fig* inwardly **2** DEP inside-forward, central midfielder **3**: ***~es*** *pl* TV *etc* indoor shots
◇ **interior izquierdo** DEP inside left
◇ **interior derecho** DEP inside right
interioridades *fpl* personal *o* private matters
interiorismo *m* interior design
interiorista *m/f* interior designer, interior decorator
interiorizar ⟨1f⟩ *v/t* internalize
interiormente *adv* inwardly
interjección *f* GRAM interjection
interlínea *f* TIP (inter)line spacing, leading
interlineal *adj* interlinear, between the lines
interlocutor *m*, **~a** *f* speaker; ***mi ~*** the person I was talking to
◇ **interlocutores sociales** social partners
interludio *m tb fig* interlude
intermediario I *adj* intermediary **II** *m* COM intermediary, middle man
intermedio I *adj nivel* intermediate; *tamaño* medium; *calidad* average, medium **II** *m* intermission
interminable *adj* interminable, endless
intermitente I *adj* intermittent **II** *m* AUTO turn signal, *Br* indicator
internacional I *adj* international **II** *m/f* DEP international **III** *f* POL *himno* Internationale
internacionalizar ⟨1f⟩ *v/t* internationalize
internado *m* boarding school
internamiento *m* **1** POL internment **2** MED admission (to hospital)
internar ⟨1a⟩ *v/t* **1** POL intern **2** MED admit (to hospital); **internarse** *v/r*: ***~ en*** go into
internauta *m/f* INFOR Internet user, Net surfer
Internet *f* INFOR Internet; ***navegar por ~*** surf the Net; ***en ~*** on the Net
internista *m/f* MED internist
interno I *adj* internal; POL domestic, internal **II** *m*, **-a** *f* **1** EDU boarder **2** (*preso*) inmate **3** MED intern, *Br* houseman
interpelación *f* POL question
interpelar ⟨1a⟩ *v/t* question
interpersonal *adj* interpersonal
interplanetario *adj* interplanetary
interpolar ⟨1a⟩ *v/t* insert, *fml* interpolate
interponer ⟨2r; *part* ***interpuesto***⟩ *v/t* **1** interpose, place **2** JUR lodge; **interponerse** *v/r* intervene
interposición *f* **1** placing **2** JUR lodging
interpretación *f* **1** interpretation **2** TEA performance (***de*** as)
interpretar ⟨1a⟩ *v/t* **1** interpret **2** TEA play
interpretativo *adj* interpretational
intérprete *m/f* interpreter
interpuesto *part* ☞ ***interponer***
interrelación *f* interrelation
interrelacionar ⟨1a⟩ *v/t* interrelate; **interrelacionarse** *v/r* be interrelated
interrogación *f* interrogation; ***signo de ~*** question mark
interrogador I *adj* questioning **II** *m*, **~a** *f* interrogator
interrogante I *adj* questioning **II** *m* (*also f*) question; *fig* question mark, doubt
interrogar ⟨1h⟩ *v/t* question; *de policía* interrogate, question
interrogativo *adj* interrogative
interrogatorio *m* questioning, interrogation
interrumpir ⟨3a⟩ **I** *v/t* interrupt; *servicio* suspend; *reunión, vacaciones* cut short, curtail **II** *v/i* interrupt
interrupción *f* interruption; *de servicio* suspension; *de reunión, vacaciones* curtailment; ***sin ~*** non-stop
interruptor *m* EL switch
intersección *f* intersection; *de carreteras* intersection, *Br* junction
intersticio *m* gap
interurbano *adj* long-distance

intervalo *m* **1** *tb* MÚS interval; ***a ~s*** at intervals **2** (*espacio*) gap
intervención *f* **1** intervention; *en debate, congreso* participation; *en película, espectáculo* appearance **2** MED operation
intervenir ⟨3s⟩ **I** *v/i* intervene; *en debate, congreso* take part, participate; *en película, espectáculo* appear **II** *v/t* **1** TELEC tap **2** *contrabando* seize **3** MED operate on
interventor *m*, **~a** *f* **1** *de cuentas* auditor **2** (*revisor*) (ticket) inspector **3** *electoral* canvasser, *Br* scrutineer
interviú *f* interview
intestado *adj* intestate
intestinal *adj* intestinal
intestino I *adj* internal **II** *m* intestine; ***~s*** intestines
◇ **intestino delgado** small intestine
◇ **intestino grueso** large intestine
intimar ⟨1a⟩ *v/i* **1** (*hacerse amigos*) become friendly (***con*** with) **2** (*tratar*) mix (***con*** with)
intimidación *f* intimidation
intimidad *f* **1** intimacy **2** (*lo privado*) privacy; ***en la ~*** in private
intimidar ⟨1a⟩ *v/t* intimidate
intimidatorio *adj* intimidating
íntimo *adj* **1** intimate; ***somos ~s amigos*** we're close friends **2** (*privado*) private
intocable *adj* **1** (*sagrado*) sacrosanct **2** *tema* taboo
intolerable *adj* intolerable, unbearable
intolerancia *f* intolerance
intolerante *adj* intolerant
intoxicación *f* poisoning
◇ **intoxicación alimenticia** food poisoning
intoxicar ⟨1g⟩ *v/t* poison
intracomunitario *adj* POL intracommunitary
intraducible *adj* untranslatable
intragable *adj* unacceptable; *persona* unbearable
intramuscular *adj* MED intramuscular
intranquilidad *f* **1** *por preocupación* unease **2** (*nerviosismo*) restlessness
intranquilizar ⟨1f⟩ *v/t* make uneasy
intranquilo *adj* **1** (*preocupado*) uneasy **2** (*nervioso*) restless
intransferible *adj* non-transferable
intransigencia *f* intransigence
intransigente *adj* intransigent
intransitable *adj* impassable
intransitivo *adj* GRAM intransitive
intrascendencia *f* insignificance
intrascendente *adj* insignificant
intratable *adj*: ***es ~*** he is impossible (to deal with)
intravenoso *adj* MED intravenous
intrepidez *f* intrepidness
intrépido *adj* intrepid
intriga *f* intrigue; *de novela* plot
intrigado *adj* intrigued
intrigante I *adj* **1** scheming **2** (*curioso*) intriguing **II** *m/f* schemer
intrigar ⟨1h⟩ **I** *v/t* (*interesar*) intrigue **II** *v/i* plot, scheme
intrincado *adj* intricate
intrincar ⟨1g⟩ *v/t* complicate
intríngulis *m inv* F snag
intrínseco *adj* intrinsic
introducción *f* **1** introduction **2** *acción de meter* insertion **3** INFOR input
introducir ⟨3o⟩ *v/t* **1** introduce **2** (*meter*) insert **3** INFOR input; **introducirse** *v/r*: ***~ en*** get into; ***~ en un mercado*** gain access to *o* break into a market
introductor *adj* introductory
introito *m* **1** prolog, *Br* prologue **2** REL introit
intromisión *f* interference
introspección *f* introspection
introvertido I *adj* introverted **II** *m*, **-a** *f* introvert
intrusión *f* intrusion
intrusismo *m*: ***~ profesional*** *entry into a profession of people without appropriate qualifications*
intruso *m*, **-a** *f* intruder
intubación *f* MED intubation
intubar ⟨1a⟩ *v/t* intubate
intuición *f* intuition
intuir ⟨3g⟩ *v/t* sense
intuitivo *adj* intuitive
inundación *f* flood
inundadizo *adj L.Am.* prone to flooding
inundar ⟨1a⟩ *v/t* flood
inusitado *adj* unusual, uncommon
inusual *adj* unusual
inútil I *adj* **1** useless **2** MIL unfit **II** *m/f*: ***es un ~*** he's useless
inutilidad *f* uselessness
inutilizar ⟨1f⟩ *v/t*: ***~ algo*** render sth useless

inútilmente *adv* uselessly
invadir ⟨3a⟩ *v/t* **1** invade; **~ *el carril contrario*** go onto the wrong side of the road **2** *de un sentimiento* overcome
invalidar ⟨1a⟩ *v/t* invalidate
invalidez *f* disability
◇ **invalidez permanente** permanent disability *o* invalidity
inválido I *adj* **1** *persona* disabled **2** *documento, billete* invalid **II** *m*, **-a** *f* disabled person
◇ **inválido de guerra** disabled veteran, *Br* disabled ex-serviceman
invariabilidad *f* invariability
invariable *adj* invariable
invasión *f* MIL invasion
invasivo *adj* MED invasive
invasor I *adj* invading *atr* **II** *m*, **~a** *f* invader
invectiva *f* invective
invencible *adj* invincible; *miedo* insurmountable
invención *f* invention
invendible *adj* unsaleable, unsellable
inventar ⟨1a⟩ *v/t* invent
inventariar ⟨1b⟩ *v/t* inventory, make an inventory of
inventario *m* inventory
inventiva *f* inventiveness
inventivo *adj* inventive
invento *m* invention
inventor *m*, **~a** *f* inventor
invernada *f Rpl* winter pasture
invernadero *m* greenhouse
invernal *adj* winter *atr*
invernar ⟨1k⟩ *v/i* **1** winter, spend the winter **2** ZO hibernate
inverosímil *adj* unlikely
inverosimilitud *f* unlikeliness
inversión *f* **1** reversal **2** COM investment
inversionista *m/f* COM investor
inverso *adj* opposite; *orden* reverse; ***a la -a*** the other way round
inversor *m*, **~a** *f* investor
invertebrado *m/adj* ZO invertebrate
invertido *adj* inverted, upside down
invertir ⟨3i⟩ *v/t* **1** reverse **2** COM invest (***en*** in) **3** INFOR invert
investidura *f* investiture
investigación *f* **1** *policial* investigation **2** EDU, TÉC research; **~ *genética*** genetic research
◇ **investigación y desarrollo** research and development
investigador I *adj* research *atr*; ***comisión ~a*** committee of inquiry **II** *m*, **~a** *f* researcher
◇ **investigador privado** private investigator
investigar ⟨1h⟩ *v/t* **1** *crimen* investigate **2** EDU, TÉC research
investir ⟨3l⟩ *v/t* **1**: ***ser investido algo*** be sworn in as sth **2**: **~ *a alguien de algo*** confer sth on s.o.
inveterado *adj* deep-rooted, deep-seated
inviabilidad *f* nonviability
inviable *adj* nonviable
invicto *adj* unconquered; *equipo* unbeaten, undefeated
invidencia *f* blindness
invidente I *adj* blind **II** *m/f* blind person
invierno *m* winter
inviolabilidad *f* inviolability
inviolable *adj* inviolable
invisibilidad *f* invisibility
invisible *adj* invisible
invitación *f* invitation
invitado *m*, **-a** *f* guest
invitar ⟨1a⟩ *v/t* **1** invite (***a*** to) **2** (*convidar*) treat (***a*** to)
invocación *f* invocation
invocar ⟨1g⟩ *v/t* invoke
involución *f* regression
involucrar ⟨1a⟩ *v/t* involve (***en*** in)
involuntario *adj* involuntary
involutivo *adj* regressive
invulnerabilidad *f* invulnerability
invulnerable *adj* invulnerable
inyección *f* MED, AUTO injection; ***motor de ~*** fuel-injected engine
inyectable MED **I** *adj* injectable **II** *m* injection
inyectar ⟨1a⟩ *v/t* **1** *tb* TÉC inject **2** *fig*: *valor, fuerza* instill, *Br* instil
inyector *m* AUTO injector
ion *m* ion
ionosfera *f* ionosphere
IPC *m abr* (= ***índice de precios al consumo***) CPI (= consumer price index), *Br* RPI (= retail price index)
ir ⟨3t; *part* ***ido***⟩ **I** *v/i* **1** go (***a*** to); **~ *a pie*** walk, go on foot; **~ *en avión*** fly; **~ *en coche* / *en tren*** go by car / train; **~ *a por algo*** go and fetch sth; ***¡ya voy!*** I'm coming!; ***¿quién va?*** who goes there?
2 (*vestir*): ***iba de amarillo* / *de unifor-***

me she was wearing yellow / a uniform
3: ***van dos a dos*** DEP the score is two all
4 (*tratar*): ***¿de qué va la película?*** what's the movie about?; ***el libro va de vampiros*** the book's about vampires
5 (*agradar*): ***el clima no me va*** the climate doesn't suit me, I don't like the climate; ***ella no me va*** she's not my kind of person; ***no me va ni me viene*** I'm not bothered, I don't care one way or the other
6 (*marchar, evolucionar*) go; ***~ bien / mal*** go well / badly
7 (*abarcar*): ***va de la página 12 a la 16*** it goes from page 12 to page 16
8: ***¡qué va!*** you must be joking!; ***¡vamos!*** come on!; ***¡vaya!*** well!; ***¿ha dicho eso? – ¡vamos!*** he said that? – no way!; ***¡vaya una sorpresa!*** *irón* what a surprise!; ***a eso voy*** I'm just getting to that; ***eso va por ti también*** that goes for you too
II *v/aux* **1** *con referencia al futuro*: ***va a llover*** it's going to rain; ***va para abogado*** he's going to be a lawyer
2 *expresando proceso*: ***ya voy comprendiendo*** I'm beginning to understand; ***~ para viejo*** be getting old; ***ya va anocheciendo*** it's getting dark
3 *con referencia al pasado*: ***ya va para dos años*** it's been almost two years now; ***van tirados 3.000*** 3,000 have been printed
irse *v/r* go (away), leave; ***¡vete!*** go away!; ***¡vámonos!*** let's go
ira *f* anger
iracundia *f* irascibility
iracundo *adj* irascible
Irak *m* Irak
Irán *m* Iran
iraní *m/f & adj* Iranian
Iraq *m* Iraq
iraquí *m/f & adj* Iraqi, Iraki
irascible *adj* irascible
irguiendo *vb* ☞ ***erguir***
iridio *m* QUÍM iridium
iridiscente *adj* iridescent
iris *m inv* ANAT iris
irisar ⟨1a⟩ *v/i* be iridescent
Irlanda *f* Ireland
◇ **Irlanda del Norte** Northern Ireland
irlandés I *adj* Irish **II** *m* Irishman; ***los irlandes*** the Irish **III** *idioma* Irish
irlandesa *f* Irishwoman
ironía *f* irony
irónico *adj* ironic
ironizar ⟨1f⟩ **I** *v/i* speak ironically, be ironic (***sobre*** about) **II** *v/t* ridicule
IRPF *m abr* (= ***impuesto sobre la renta de las personas físicas***) Income Tax
irracional *adj tb* MAT irrational
irracionalidad *f* irrationality
irradiación *f* irradiation
irradiar ⟨1b⟩ *v/t* **1** FÍS, *fig* radiate **2** MED irradiate
irrazonable *adj* unreasonable
irreal *adj* unreal
irrealizable *adj* unattainable; *proyecto* unfeasible
irrebatible *adj* irrefutable
irreconciliable *adj* irreconcilable
irreconocible *adj* unrecognizable
irrecuperable *adj* irretrievable
irrecusable *adj* unchallengeable
irreductible *adj* uncompromising
irreflexivo *adj* rash
irrefrenable *adj* uncontrollable
irrefutable *adj* irrefutable
irregular *adj* **1** irregular **2** *superficie* uneven
irregularidad *f* **1** irregularity **2** *de superficie* unevenness
irrelevante *adj* irrelevant
irreligioso *adj* irreligious
irremediable *adj fig* irremediable
irremisible *adj* irremissible
irrenunciable *adj* inalienable
irreparable *adj* irreparable
irrepetible *adj* unrepeatable
irreprimible *adj* irrepressible
irreprochable *adj* irreproachable
irreproducible *adj* which cannot be reproduced, non-reproducible
irresistible *adj* irresistible
irresoluble *adj* unsolvable, unresolvable
irresolución *f* **1** *de problema* failure to resolve **2** *de persona* indecision, indecisiveness
irresoluto *adj* indecisive
irrespetuoso *adj* disrespectful
irrespirable *adj* unbreathable
irresponsabilidad *f* irresponsibility
irresponsable *adj* irresponsible
irresuelto *adj* ☞ ***irresoluto***
irreverencia *f* irreverence

irreverente *adj* irreverent
irreversible *adj* irreversible
irrevocable *adj* irrevocable
irrigación *f* MED, AGR irrigation
◇ **irrigación sanguínea** blood supply
irrigador *m* MED, AGR irrigator
irrigar ⟨1h⟩ *v/t* MED, AGR irrigate
irrisorio *adj* laughable, derisory; *precio* ridiculously low
irritabilidad *f* irritability
irritable *adj* irritable
irritación *f tb* MED irritation
irritante *adj tb* MED irritating
irritar ⟨1a⟩ *v/t tb* MED irritate; **irritarse** *v/r tb* MED get irritated
irrompible *adj* unbreakable
irrumpir ⟨3a⟩ *v/i* burst in
irrupción *f*: ***hacer ~ en*** burst into
isla *f* island
islam *m* Islam
islámico *adj* Islamic
islamismo *m* Islam
islamizar ⟨1f⟩ *v/t* convert to Islam
isleño I *adj* island *atr* **II** *m*, **-a** *f* islander
isleta *f* islet
islote *m* islet, small island
isobara *f* isobar
isósceles *adj* MAT isosceles
isoterma *f* isotherm
isotérmico, isotermo *adj* isothermal; ***camión ~*** refrigerated truck
isótopo *m* isotope
Israel *m* Israel
israelí *m/f* & *adj* Israeli
istmo *m* isthmus
Italia *f* Italy
italiano I *adj* Italian **II** *m*, **-a** *f* Italian **III** *m idioma* Italian
itálico *adj* TIP italic
iterar ⟨1a⟩ *v/t* repeat
iterativo *adj* recurrent
itinerante *adj* traveling, *Br* travelling, itinerant
itinerario *m* itinerary
ITV *f abr Esp* (= ***inspección técnica de vehículos***) *compulsory annual test of motor vehicles of a certain age*, *Br* MOT
IU *f abr* (= ***Izquierda Unida***) Spanish Communist coalition
IVA *m abr* (= ***impuesto sobre el valor añadido*** *o L.Am.* ***agregado***) sales tax, *Br* VAT (= value-added tax)
izada *f* hoisting, raising
izar ⟨1f⟩ *v/t* hoist, raise
izdo., izda *abr* (= ***izquierdo, izquierda***) l (= left)
izquierda *f tb* POL left; ***por la ~*** on the left
izquierdista POL **I** *adj* left-wing **II** *m/f* left-winger
izquierdo *adj* left

J

ja *int* ha!; ***~, ~!*** ha, ha!
jabalí *m* ZO wild boar
jabalina *f* **1** DEP javelin; ***el lanzamiento de ~*** the javelin **2** ZO wild sow
jabalinista *m/f* DEP javelin thrower
jabato *m* **1** ZO young wild boar **2** *fig* daredevil, tough guy F
jabón *m* soap; ***dar ~ a alguien*** F soft-soap s.o. F
◇ **jabón de afeitar** shaving soap; **jabón de sastre** tailor's chalk, French chalk; **jabón de tocador** toilet soap
jabonar ⟨1a⟩ *v/t* soap
jaboncillo *m* tailor's chalk, French chalk
jabonera *f* soap dish
jabonero I *adj* soap *atr* **II** *m*, **-a** *f* soap maker
jabonoso *adj* soapy
jaca *f* pony
jacal *m Méx* hut
jacarandá *m* BOT jacaranda
jacarandoso *adj* F jaunty, jolly
jacinto *m* hyacinth
jactancia *f* boasting
jactancioso I *adj* boastful **II** *m*, **-a** *f* braggart
jactarse ⟨1a⟩ *v/r* boast (***de*** about), brag (***de*** about)
jaculatoria *f* short prayer
jacuzzi *m* jacuzzi®
jade *m* MIN jade
jadear ⟨1a⟩ *v/i* pant
jadeo *m* panting

jaez *m* **1** kind, sort; ***de ese ~*** *desp* of that sort, like that **2**: ***jaeces*** *pl de caballo* trappings
jaguar *m* ZO jaguar
jaiba *f Méx* **1** crab **2**: ***la ~*** F the cops *pl* F
jalada *f L.Am.* pull
jalar ⟨1a⟩ **I** *v/t* **1** *L.Am.* pull; *con esfuerzo* haul **2** *Méx* (*atraer*) attract; ***¿te jala el arte?*** do you feel drawn to art? **3** *Méx* F (*dar aventón a*) give a ride *o Br* a lift to **4** *Esp* F (*zampar*) wolf down
II *v/i* **1** *L.Am.* pull **2** (*trabajar mucho*) work hard **3** *Méx* F (*tener influencia*) have pull F **4** F: ***~ hacia*** head toward; ***~ para la casa*** clear off home F
jalarse *v/r Méx* **1** (*irse*) go, leave **2** F (*emborracharse*) get plastered F
jalea *f* jelly
◇ **jalea real** royal jelly
jalear ⟨1a⟩ *v/t* cheer on, urge on
jaleo *m* **1** (*ruido*) racket, uproar; ***armar ~*** F kick up a fuss F **2** (*lío*) mess, muddle
jalón *m L.Am.* pull; ***dar un ~ a algo*** pull sth; ***de un ~*** *Méx fig* in one go
jalonar ⟨1a⟩ *v/t fig* mark out
jamaica *f Méx* F fair, street party
Jamaica *f* Jamaica
jamaicano **I** *adj* Jamaican **II** *m*, **-a** *f* Jamaican
jamaiquino *L.Am* **I** *adj* Jamaican **II** *m*, **-a** Jamaican
jamar ⟨1a⟩ *v/t & v/i* scoff
jamás *adv* never; ***~ te olvidaré*** I'll never forget you; ***¿viste ~ algo así?*** did you ever see anything like it?; ***nunca ~*** never ever; ***por siempre ~*** for ever and ever
jamba *f* jamb
jamelgo *m* hack, old nag
jamón *m* ham; ***¡y un ~!*** F (*¡no!*) no way! F; (*¡bromeas!*) come off it! F
◇ **jamón cocido, jamón en dulce** boiled ham; **jamón serrano** cured ham; **jamón de York** boiled ham
jamona *f* F big, busty woman
jangada *f S.Am.* F dirty trick
Japón *m* Japan
japonés **I** *adj* Japanese **II** *m*, **-esa** *f* Japanese **III** *m idioma* Japanese
japuta *f* ZO pomfret
jaque *m* check; ***dar ~ a*** checkmate; ***tener en ~ a alguien*** have s.o. scared, have s.o. sweating F
◇ **jaque mate** checkmate
jaqueca *f* MED migraine
jara *f* BOT rockrose, cistus
jarabe *m* **1** syrup; ***dar a alguien ~ de palo*** *fig* F wallop s.o. **2** *Méx*: *type of folk dance*
jarana *f* F **1** partying F; ***irse de ~*** go out on the town F, go out partying F **2** (*alboroto*) racket
jaranear ⟨1a⟩ *v/i* F go out on the town F, go out partying F
jaranero *adj* F: ***es muy ~*** he's a real party animal F
jarcias *fpl* MAR rigging *sg*
jardín *m* garden; ***jardines*** *pl en béisbol* outfield *sg*
◇ **jardín botánico** botanic(al) gardens *pl*; **jardín central** *L.Am. en béisbol* center field; **jardín exterior** *L.Am. en béisbol* outfield; **jardín de infancia** kindergarten; **jardín de infantes** *Rpl* kindergarten; **jardín zoológico** zoo
jardinear ⟨1a⟩ *v/i Chi* do the gardening
jardinera *f* jardiniere
jardinería *f* gardening
jardinero *m*, **-a** *f* **1** gardener **2** *Cu*, *Méx en béisbol* outfielder **3** *Rpl* (*mono*) dungarees *pl*
jarra *f* pitcher, *Br* jug; ***en ~s*** with hands on hips
jarro *m* pitcher, *Br* jug; ***un ~ de agua fría*** *fig* a real blow, a kick in the stomach
jarrón *m* vase
jaspe *m* MIN jasper
jauja *f*: ***¡esto es ~!*** this is the life!
jaula *f* cage
jauría *f* pack
jazmín *m* BOT jasmine
jazz *m* jazz
jazzero *m*, **-a** *f*, **jazzista** *m/f* jazz musician
jazzman *m* jazz musician, jazzman
J.C. *abr* (= ***Jesucristo***) J.C. (= Jesus Christ)
jean *m*, **jeans** *mpl L.Am.* jeans
jefatura *f* **1** *lugar* headquarters *sg o pl* **2** (*dirección*) leadership
◇ **jefatura del Estado** position of head of State
◇ **jefatura de policía** police headquarters *sg o pl*
jefazo *m* F big boss F
jefe *m*, **-a** *f de departamento*, *organización* head; (*superior*) boss; POL leader; *de tribu* chief **3** *Méx* F: ***mi ~*** my dad F;

mi -a my mom F
◇ **jefe de cocina** (head) chef; **jefe de departamento** head of department; **jefe de estación** station manager; **jefe de estado** head of state; **jefe de gobierno** prime minister; **jefe de partido** party leader; **jefe de sección** section chief; **jefe de ventas** sales manager
jején *m L.Am.* mosquito
jengibre *m* BOT ginger
jeque *m* sheik
jerarca *m* leader
jerarquía *f* hierarchy
jerárquico *adj* hierarchic(al)
jerarquizar ⟨1f⟩ *v/t* organize into a hierarchy
jerez *m* sherry
jerezano *adj* of *o* from Jerez, Jerez *atr*
jerga *f* jargon; (*argot*) slang; ***~ del hampa*** underworld slang
jergón *m* straw mattress, palliasse
jeribeque *m* grimace; ***hacer ~s*** grimace
jerigonza *f* **1** gobbledygook **2** (*jerga*) jargon
jeringa *f* MED syringe
jeringar ⟨1h⟩ F *v/t* bug F; **jeringarse** *v/r*: ***si no le gusta, que se jeringue*** he can like it or lump it F
jeringuilla *f* MED syringe
◇ **jeringuilla desechable, jeringuilla de un solo uso** disposable syringe
jeroglífico *m* **1** hieroglyphic **2** *rompecabezas* puzzle
jersey *m* sweater
Jesucristo *m* Jesus Christ
jesuita *m/adj* Jesuit
jesuítico *adj* Jesuitic, Jesuitical
Jesús *m* Jesus; ***¡~!*** good grief!; *por estornudo* bless you!; ***Compañía de ~*** Society of Jesus
jet I *m* AVIA jet **II** *f o L.Am. m*: ***~*** (***set***) jet set
jeta *f* F **1** face, mug F; ***¡qué ~ tiene!*** F he's got nerve! F, *Br* what a cheek! F **2** *Méx* (*siesta*) nap; ***echar una ~*** have a nap, grab some sleep
ji *int*: ***¡~, ~!*** hee, hee!
jibia *f* ZO cuttlefish
jícara *f Méx* drinking bowl
jícaro *m L.Am.* BOT calabash
jilguero *m* ZO goldfinch
jilote *m C.Am., Méx* young corn
jineta *f* ZO civet
jinete *m* rider; *en carrera* jockey
jinetear ⟨1a⟩ **I** *v/i* ride (on horseback) **II** *v/t L.Am.* break (in)
jinetera *f Cu* F prostitute
jingle *m* TV jingle
jipijapa *f* jipijapa (*strips of palm leaf used for making hats*)
jirafa *f* ZO giraffe
jirón *m* shred, rag
jitomate *m Méx* tomato
JJ.OO. *abr* (= ***Juegos Olímpicos***) Olympic Games
¡jo! *int* F *expresando fastidio* darn! F, damn! F; *expresando sorpresa* wow! F, gee! F; *expresando protesta* oh!; ***~, ~*** *expresando risa* ho, ho!
jockey *m* jockey
jocosidad *f* **1** humor, *Br* humour **2** *dicho, hecho* joke
jocoso *adj* humorous, joking
jocundo *adj lit* jovial
joder ⟨2a⟩ **I** *v/i* V screw V, fuck V **II** *v/t* V **1** (*follar*) screw V, fuck V **2** (*estropear*) screw up V, fuck up V **3** *L.Am.* F (*fastidiar*) annoy, irritate; ***¡~!*** fuck! V; ***¡que se joda!*** V fuck him! V; ***me jode un montón*** V it really pisses me off P; ***¡no me jodas!*** V don't jerk me around! P; ***¡no te jode!*** V would you damn well believe it! F, would you fucking believe it! V
jodido *adj* V *persona, máquina etc* fucked V; *situación* fucked up V
jodienda *f* V fucking pain V
jofaina *f* washbowl, washbasin
jol *m L.Am.* hall
jolgorio *m* F partying F
jolín *int* F wow! F, jeez! F
jolines *int* F darn! F, heck! F
jónico *adj* ARQUI Ionic
jonrón *m L.Am. en béisbol* home run
jornada *f* **1** (working) day; ***media ~*** half-day **2** *distancia* day's journey **3** DEP round of games
◇ **jornada intensiva** *working day with no lunch break in order to finish early*; **jornada laboral** work day; **jornada partida** split shift
jornal *m* day's wage
jornalero *m*, **-a** *f* day laborer, *Br* day labourer
joroba I *f* hump; *fig* pain F, drag F **II** *int* F darn! F, heck! F
jorobado I *adj* **1** hump-backed **2** *fig* F in a bad way F **II** *m*, **-a** *f* humpback,

J

hunchback
jorobar ⟨1a⟩ *v/t* F **1** (*molestar*) bug F **2** *planes* ruin; **jorobarse** *v/r* lump it F
jorongo *m Méx* poncho
jota *f* letter 'j'; ***no saber ni ~*** F not have a clue F; ***no ver ni ~*** F not see a thing F
joven I *adj* young **II** *m/f* young man; *mujer* young woman; ***los jóvenes*** young people *pl*
jovial *adj* cheerful
jovialidad *f* cheerfulness
joya *f* **1** jewel; ***~s*** *pl* jewelry *sg*, *Br* jewellery *sg*; ***~ de la corona*** jewel in the crown **2** *persona* gem
joyería *f* jewelry store, *Br* jeweller's
joyero I *m*, **-a** *f* jeweler, *Br* jeweller **II** *m* jewelry *o Br* jewellery box
juanete *m* MED bunion
jubilación *f* retirement
◇ **jubilación anticipada** early retirement
◇ **jubilación forzosa** compulsory retirement
jubilado I *adj* retired **II** *m*, **-a** *f* retiree, *Br* pensioner
jubilar ⟨1a⟩ *v/t* **1** retire **2** (*desechar*) get rid of; **jubilarse** *v/r* **1** retire **2** *C.Am.* play hooky F, be truant, *Br* play truant
jubileo *m* REL jubilee
júbilo *m* jubilation
jubiloso *adj* jubilant
jubón *m* doublet
judaico *adj* Jewish, Judaic
judaísmo *m* Judaism
judería *f* Jewish quarter
judía *f* BOT bean
◇ **judía verde** green bean, runner bean
judicatura *f* **1** *cargo* judgeship **2** (*jueces*) judiciary
judicial *adj* judicial; ***recurrir a la vía ~*** have recourse to law; ***el asunto se resolverá por la vía ~*** the matter will be settled in court
judío I *adj* Jewish **II** *m*, **-a** *f* Jew
judo *m* DEP judo
judoka *m* judoka
juego *m* **1** game; *acción* play; ***fuera de ~*** DEP offside; ***entrar en ~*** *de jugador* enter the game; *de factor* come into play; ***en ~*** *en baloncesto* alive; ***hacer el ~ a alguien*** play along with s.o., go along with s.o. **2** *por dinero* gambling; ***estar en ~*** *fig* be at stake; ***poner en ~*** put at risk **3** (*conjunto de objetos*) set; ***hacer ~ con*** go with, match
◇ **juego aéreo** *en fútbol* aerial game; **juego de azar** game of chance; **juego de café** coffee set; **juego de cama** set of matching bed linen; **juego electrónico** computer game; **juego de manos** conjuring trick; **juego de mesa** board game; **juego de niños** *fig* child's play; **juego de palabras** play on words, pun; **juego de rol** role-playing game; **juego de sociedad** game; **juegos florales** *poetry contest with a flower as the first prize*; **Juegos Olímpicos** Olympic Games; **juegos parolímpicos** paralympic games, paralympics
juerga *f* F partying F; ***irse de ~*** go out on the town F, go out partying F; ***correrse una ~*** have a ball F
juerguista *m/f* F party animal F
jueves *m inv* Thursday; ***no es cosa del otro ~*** F it's nothing special, it's nothing to write home about F
juez *m/f* judge
◇ **juez de instrucción** examining magistrate; **juez instructor** examining magistrate; **juez de línea** *en fútbol* assistant referee, linesman; *en fútbol americano* line judge; **juez de paz** Justice of the Peace; **juez de silla** *en tenis* umpire
jueza *f* ☞ ***juez***
jugada *f* play, *Br* move; *en ajedrez*, DEP move; ***~ individual*** *o* ***personal*** DEP solo effort; ***hacerle una mala ~ a alguien*** play a dirty trick on s.o.
◇ **jugada a balón parado** set piece; **jugada de cuatro puntos** *en baloncesto* four-point play; **jugada de elección** *en béisbol* fielder's choice
jugador *m*, **~a** *f* player
◇ **jugador internacional** international (player); **jugador de primera base** first baseman; **jugador profesional** professional (player *o* sportsperson); **jugador de segunda base** second baseman; **jugador titular** first-team player
jugar ⟨1o⟩ **I** *v/t* play
II *v/i* **1** play; ***~ al baloncesto*** play basketball; ***~ a la bolsa*** play the stock market; ***~ con fuego*** *fig* play with fire; ***~ limpio / sucio*** play clean / dirty **2** *con dinero* gamble
jugarse *v/r* **1** risk; ***~ la vida*** risk one's life; ***¿qué te juegas?*** what do you want

to bet?; ~ ***el todo por el todo*** *fig* go for broke **2**: ***jugársela a alguien*** F do the dirty on s.o. F

jugarreta *f* F dirty trick F

juglar *m* HIST minstrel, jongleur

jugo *m* juice; *de carne* gravy; ***en su*** ~ GASTR in its own juices; ***sacar*** ~ ***a algo*** get the most out of sth; ***sacar el*** ~ ***a alguien*** bleed s.o. dry

jugoso *adj tb fig* juicy

juguera *f Rpl* juicer, juice extractor

juguete *m* toy

◇ **juguetes bélicos** war toys

juguetear ⟨1a⟩ *v/i* play

juguetería *f* toy store, *Br* toy shop

juguetón *adj* playful

juicio *m* **1** judg(e)ment; ***a mi*** ~ in my opinion **2** JUR trial; ***el*** ~ ***final*** REL the Last Judg(e)ment **3** (*sensatez*) sense **4** (*cordura*) sanity; ***estar en su*** ~ be in one's right mind; ***perder el*** ~ lose one's mind

◇ **juicio oral** JUR trial

juicioso *adj* judicious, sensible

julepe *m C.Am. fig* F fright; ***dar*** (***un***) ~ ***a alguien*** F give s.o. a real fright

juliana *f* GASTR julienne; ***cortar en*** ~ cut into julienne strips

julio *m* **1** July **2** FÍS joule

jumento *m* ZO donkey

juncal *m* BOT reed bed

junco *m* BOT reed

jungla *f* jungle

junio *m* June

júnior *tb* DEP **I** *adj* junior **II** *m/f* junior

junta *f* **1** POL (regional) government **2** *militar* junta **3** COM board **4** (*sesión*) meeting **5** TÉC joint

◇ **junta de accionistas** stockholders' *o* shareholders' meeting; **junta directiva** board of directors; **junta general** general meeting; **junta general anual** annual general meeting

juntamente *adv* together, jointly

juntar ⟨1a⟩ *v/t* **1** put together; *bienes* collect, accumulate **2** *gente* gather together; **juntarse** *v/r* **1** (*reunirse*) meet, assemble **2** *de pareja*: *empezar a salir* start going out; *empezar a vivir juntos* move in together **3**: ~ ***con alguien*** *socialmente* mix with s.o. **4** *de caminos, ríos* meet, join

junto I *adj* together; ***todo*** ~ altogether **II** *prp*: ~ ***a*** next to, near; ~ ***con*** together with

juntura *f* TÉC joint

jupa *f C.Am., Méx fig* F head, nut F

jura *f* **1** (*promesa*) oath **2** *ceremonia* swearing (of an oath)

◇ **jura de bandera** swearing allegiance to the flag

◇ **jura del cargo** swearing-in

jurado I *adj* sworn **II** *m* JUR jury

juramentar ⟨1a⟩ *v/t* swear in, administer the oath to

juramento *m* oath; ***bajo*** ~ under oath; ***tomar*** ~ ***a alguien*** swear s.o. in, administer the oath to s.o.

◇ **juramento falso** perjury

◇ **juramento hipocrático** Hippocratic oath

jurar ⟨1a⟩ **I** *v/i* swear; ~ ***en falso*** commit perjury **II** *v/t* swear; ***te lo juro*** I swear; ~ ***la bandera*** swear allegiance to the flag; ~ ***el cargo*** be sworn in; ***tenérsela jurada a alguien*** have it in for s.o.

jurásico GEOL **I** *adj* Jurassic **II** *m* Jurassic (period)

jurel *m* ZO jurel

jurídico *adj* legal

jurisconsulto *m*, **-a** *f* jurist

jurisdicción *f* jurisdiction

jurisperito *m*, **-a** *f* jurist, legal expert

jurisprudencia *f* jurisprudence

jurista *m/f* jurist

justa *f* HIST joust, tournament; *fig* competition, contest

justamente *adv* **1** fairly **2** (*precisamente*) precisely

justicia *f* **1** justice; ***hacer*** ~ ***a*** do justice to; ***es de*** ~ ***que le devuelvan lo que le pertenenece*** it is only right that they give him back what belongs to him **2**: ***la*** ~ (*la ley*) the law; ***tomarse la*** ~ ***por su mano*** take the law into one's own hands

justiciero *adj*: ***un héroe*** ~ a hero who metes out justice

justificable *adj* justifiable

justificación *f tb* TIP justification

justificado *adj tb* TIP justified

justificante *m* **1** *de pago* receipt; ***hay que presentar un*** ~ ***de compra*** you will have to present proof of purchase **2** *de ausencia, propiedad* certificate

justificar ⟨1g⟩ *v/t* **1** justify; *mala conducta* justify, excuse **2** TIP justify; **justificarse** *v/r* justify o.s.

J

justificativo *adj* justificatory; *documento* explaining the reasons, explanatory
justipreciar ⟨1b⟩ *v/t* value
justiprecio *m* valuation
justo I *adj* **1** just, fair **2** (*exacto*) right, exact; **3**: ***este vestido me está muy ~*** this dress is very tight
II *adv* **1** (*exactamente*): ***~ a tiempo*** just in time; ***~ después*** right after, just after; ***~ en aquel momento*** just at that moment; ***¡~!*** right!, exactly! **2**: ***aprobó muy ~*** he only just passed; ***lo ~*** just enough
III *m*, **-a** *f* just person; ***los ~s*** the just *pl*
juvenil *adj* youthful
juventud *f* youth
juzgado I *part* ☞ ***juzgar*** **II** *m* court
juzgar ⟨1h⟩ *v/t* **1** JUR try **2** (*valorar*) judge; ***~ bien a alguien*** judge s.o. fairly; ***~ mal a alguien*** judge s.o. unfairly, misjudge s.o.; ***~ bien las intenciones de alguien*** think that s.o.'s intentions are honest; ***a ~ por*** to judge by, judging by **3** *considerar* consider, judge; ***~ a alguien capaz de hacer algo*** consider s.o. capable of doing sth

K

kafkiano *adj* Kafkaesque
kantiano *adj* Kantian
karaoke *m* karaoke
kárate *m* DEP karate
karateca *m/f* karate expert
kart *m* DEP kart, *Br* go-kart
karting *m* karting, *Br* go-kart racing
kayak *m* DEP kayak
kéfir *m* kefir
keniano I *adj* Kenyan **II** *m*, **-a** *f* Kenyan
kermés *f* charity fête
keroseno *m* kerosene
ketchup *m* ketchup
kg. *abr* (= ***kilogramo***) kg (= kilogram)
kib(b)utz *m inv* kibbutz
kikos *mpl* toasted corn snack
kilim *m* kilim
kilo *m* **1** kilo **2** *fig* F million
kilobyte *m* INFOR kilobyte
kilocaloría *f* kilocalorie
kilociclo *m* EL kilocycle
kilogramo *m* kilogram, *Br* kilogramme
kilometraje *m number of kilometers covered*, mileage
kilométrico *adj* **1** *distancia* in kilometers, *Br* in kilometres **2** F very long
kilómetro *m* kilometer, *Br* kilometre
◇ **kilómetro cuadrado** square kilometer *o Br* kilometre
◇ **kilómetro cúbico** cubic kilometer *o Br* kilometre
kilotón *m* kiloton
kilovatio *m* kilowatt
◇ **kilovatio hora** kilowatt-hour
kinesiterapia *f* physiotherapy
kiosco *m* kiosk
kit *m* kit
kiwi *m* **1** BOT kiwi (fruit) **2** ZO kiwi
kleenex® *m inv* Kleenex®, tissue
km. *abr* (= ***kilómetro***) km (= kilometer)
km/h *abr* (= ***kilómetros por hora***) kph (= kilometers per hour)
koala *m* ZO koala (bear)
kuwaití I *adj* Kuwaiti **II** *m/f* Kuwaiti
kv. *abr* (= ***kilovatio***) kw (= kilo-watt)

L

la[1] I *art* the **II** *pron complemento directo sg* her; *a usted* you; *algo* it; ***~ que está embarazada*** the one who is pregnant; ***~ más grande*** the biggest (one); ***dame ~ roja*** give me the red one
la[2] *m* MÚS A; ***~ bemol*** A flat
laberíntico *adj fig* labyrinthine
laberinto *m* labyrinth, maze
labia *f*: ***tener mucha ~*** have the gift of the gab
labial *adj* labial
labio *m* lip; ***~ inferior / superior***

upper / lower lip; ***~s*** *de vulva* labia *pl*; ***despegar los ~s*** *fig* not say a word; ***morderse los ~s*** *fig* bite one's lip
◇ **labio leperino** harelip
◇ **labios vulvares** labia *pl*
labor *f* work; (*tarea*) task, job; ***hacer ~es*** do needlework; ***no estar por la ~*** F not be enthusiastic about the idea
◇ **labores agrícolas** AGR farmwork *sg*; **labores de la casa, labores del hogar** housework *sg*; **labores de punto** knitting *sg*
laborable *adj* **1** AGR cultivatable **2**: ***día ~*** workday
laboral *adj* labor *atr*, *Br* labour *atr*
laboralista *m/f* labor *o Br* labour relations lawyer
laborar ⟨1a⟩ **I** *v/t tierra* work **II** *v/i* work, strive
laboratorio *m* laboratory, lab F
laborear ⟨1a⟩ *v/t* MIN, AGR work
laboreo *m* **1** AGR working, cultivation **2** MIN working
laboriosidad *f* **1** *de tarea* laboriousness **2** *de persona* industriousness
laborioso *adj* **1** *tarea* laborious **2** *persona* industrious, hard-working
laborista *adj* **I** *Br* POL Labor, *Br* Labour **II** *m/f* Labor *o Br* Labour party supporter
labrado *m* **1** *de metal* working **2** *de piedra, madera* carving
labrador *m*, **~a** *f* farm worker
labrantío *adj* arable
labranza *f de la tierra* cultivation
labrar ⟨1a⟩ *v/t* **1** *tierra, metal* work **2** *piedra, madera* carve
labriego *m*, **-a** *f* farm worker
laburante *m/f Rpl* F worker
laburar ⟨1a⟩ *v/i Rpl* F work
laburo *m Rpl* F job
laca *f* **1** lacquer **2** *para el cabello* hairspray
◇ **laca de uñas** nail varnish *o* polish
lacar ⟨1g⟩ *v/t* lacquer
lacayo *m fig pej* lackey
lacear ⟨1a⟩ *v/t Rpl* lasso
lacerante *adj* **1** *dolor* shooting **2** *palabras* cutting
lacerar ⟨1a⟩ *v/t* **1** *herir* lacerate **2** *fig* hurt, wound
lacio *adj* limp; *pelo* lank
lacón *m* GASTR ham
lacónico *adj lenguaje, persona* laconic
laconismo *m* laconic manner
lacra *f* **1** scar **2** *L.Am.* (*llaga*) sore **3**: ***la corrupción es una ~ social*** corruption is a blot on society
lacrar ⟨1a⟩ *v/t* seal (*with sealing wax*)
lacre *m* sealing wax
lacrimal *adj* tear *atr*; ***glándula ~*** tear gland
lacrimógeno *adj fig*: ***una novela / película -a*** a tearjerker (of a novel / movie)
lacrimoso *adj* **1** *persona* tearful, lachrymose *fml* **2** *novela, película* tear-jerking
lactancia *f* lactation
lactante **I** *adj madre* nursing; ***un bebé ~*** a baby who is still being breastfed **II** *m/f* child who is still breast-feeding
lácteo *adj*: ***Vía Láctea*** Milky Way; ***productos ~s*** dairy products
láctico *adj* lactic; ***ácido ~*** lactic acid
lactosa *f* lactose
lacustre *adj* lake *atr*
ladeado *adj* tilted
ladear ⟨1a⟩ *v/t* **1** tilt **2** *fig*: ***~ a alguien*** leave s.o. out
ladera *f* slope
ladilla *f* crab louse
ladino **I** *adj* cunning, sly **II** *m C.Am. Indian who has become absorbed into white culture*
lado *m* side; (*lugar*) place; ***al ~*** nearby; ***al ~ de*** beside, next to; ***al otro ~ de*** on the other side of; ***de ~*** sideways; ***por todos ~s*** everywhere; ***ir por otro ~*** go another way; ***mirar a otro ~*** look the other way; ***andar de un ~ para otro*** run around; ***por un ~ ... por otro ~*** on the one hand ... on the other hand; ***dejar a un ~*** leave aside; ***hacerse a un ~*** *tb fig* stand aside; ***dar a alguien de ~*** leave s.o. out; ***estar del ~ de alguien*** be on s.o.'s side; ***ponerse del ~ de alguien*** take s.o.'s side; ***cada uno va por su ~*** everyone goes their own way; ***mirar a alguien de (medio) ~*** look sideways at s.o.; ***por el ~ de mi padre*** on my father's side
ladrar ⟨1a⟩ *v/i* bark
ladrido *m* bark; ***~s*** *pl* barks, barking *sg*
ladrillo *m* brick
ladrón *m* EL F adapter
ladrón *m*, **-ona** *f* thief
ladronzuelo *m*, **-a** *f* petty thief
lagaña *f Rpl* ☞ ***legaña***
lagar *m de vino* wine press; *de aceite* oil

press

lagarta *f fig* F bitch P

lagartija *f* ZO small lizard

lagarto I *m* **1** ZO lizard **2** *Méx caiman* alligator **II** *int*: ***¡~, ~!*** God help us!

lago *m* lake

lágrima *f* tear; ***llorar a ~ viva*** cry one's eyes *o* heart out

lagrimal *m* ANAT tear duct

laguna *f* **1** lagoon **2** *fig* gap

laica *f* laywoman, layperson

laico I *adj* lay **II** *m* layman, layperson

lama *m* **1** REL lama **2** *Méx moho* moss **3** *L.Am. musgo* slime

lameculos *m inv* V asslicker V, brown-nose P, *Br* arselicker V

lamentable *adj* deplorable

lamentablemente *adv* regretfully

lamentaciones *fpl* **1** (*lamentos*) groans, groaning *sg* **2** (*quejas*) complaints, complaining *sg*

lamentar ⟨1a⟩ *v/t* **1** regret, be sorry about; ***lo lamento*** I'm sorry **2** *muerte* mourn; **lamentarse** *v/r* complain (***de*** about)

lamento *m* whimper; *por dolor* groan

lamer ⟨2a⟩ *v/t* lick

lamido *adj fig* sharp

lámina *f* **1** *de metal* sheet **2** (*grabado*) print

laminar ⟨1a⟩ *v/t* laminate

laminero *adj* fond of sweet things; ***ser muy ~*** have a sweet tooth

lámpara *f* lamp

◇ **lámpara de cabecera** bedside lamp *o* light; **lámpara halógena** halogen lamp; **lámpara de mesa** table lamp **lámpara de minero** miner's lamp; **lámpara de pared** wall lamp; **lámpara de pie** floor lamp, *Br tb* standard lamp; **lámpara solar** sun lamp; **lámpara de techo** ceiling light

lamparilla *f* oil lamp

lamparón *m* F grease mark

lampazo *m* BOT burdock

lampiño *adj* (*sin barba*) smooth-faced, beardless; (*sin vello*) smooth, hairless

lampista *m/f* plumber

lamprea *f* ZO lamprey

lana *f* **1** wool; ***pura ~ virgen*** pure new wool **2** *Méx* P (*dinero*) dough F

lanar *adj* wool *atr*; ***ganado ~*** sheep *pl*

lance *m* incident, episode; ***de ~*** second-hand

◇ **lance de honor** duel

lancero *m* HIST lancer

lanceta *f* MED lancet

lancha *f* launch

◇ **lancha fueraborda** outboard; **lancha motora** motor launch; **lancha neumática** inflatable (dinghy); **lancha rápida** speedboat

lanero I *adj* wool *atr* **II** *m*, **-a** *f* wool merchant, wool trader

langosta *f* ZO *insecto* locust; *crustáceo* spiny lobster

langostino *m* ZO king prawn

languidecer ⟨2d⟩ *v/i* languish

lánguido *adj* languid

lanolina *f* lanolin

lanoso, lanudo *adj oveja*, *cabra* wooly, *Br* woolly; *perro* shaggy, long-haired

lanza *f* lance; ***romper una ~ por alguien*** *fig* come to s.o.'s defense *o Br* defence, stick up for s.o.

lanzacohetes *m inv* rocket launcher

lanzadera *f* shuttle

◇ **lanzadera espacial** space shuttle

lanzado I *adj fig* go-ahead; ***es muy ~ con las chicas*** he's not shy with girls **III** *part* ☞ ***lanzar***

lanzador *m*, **~a** *f en béisbol* pitcher

◇ **lanzador de cuchillos** knife thrower; **lanzador de disco** discus thrower; **lanzador de jabalina** javelin thrower; **lanzador de martillo** hammer thrower; **lanzador de peso** shot-putter

lanzagranadas *m inv* grenade launcher

lanzallamas *m inv* flamethrower

lanzamiento *m* **1** DEP throw; *en béisbol tb* pitch **2** MIL, COM launch

◇ **lanzamiento de bala** *L.Am.* shot (put); **lanzamiento de disco** discus; **lanzamiento de dos puntos** *en baloncesto* two-pointer; **lanzamiento de jabalina** javelin; **lanzamiento malo** *en béisbol* wild pitch; **lanzamiento de martillo** hammer; **lanzamiento de peso** shot (put); **lanzamiento de tres puntos** *en baloncesto* three-pointer

lanzamisiles *m inv* missile launcher

lanzar ⟨1f⟩ *v/t* **1** throw; *bomba* drop; *en béisbol* throw, pitch **2** *cohete*, *producto* launch; **lanzarse** *v/r* throw o.s. (***en*** into); (*precipitarse*) pounce (***sobre*** on); ***~ al agua*** dive into the water; ***~ en paracaídas*** parachute; ***~ a hacer algo*** rush into doing sth

lanzaroteño *adj* of / from Lanzarote, Lanzarotean
lanzatorpedos *m inv* torpedo tube, torpedo launcher
lapa *f* ZO limpet; ***pegarse como una ~ a alguien*** *fig* F stick to s.o. like a limpet *o* like glue F; ***bomba ~*** limpet bomb
lapicera *f Rpl, Chi* (ballpoint) pen
◇ **lapicera fuente** *L.Am.* fountain pen
lapicero *m L.Am.* automatic pencil, *Br* propelling pencil
lápida *f* memorial stone
◇ **lápida funeraria** tombstone
lapidación *f* stoning
lapidar ⟨1a⟩ *v/t* stone
lapidario *adj* memorable
lapislázuli *m* MIN lapis lazuli
lápiz *m* pencil
◇ **lápiz de cejas** eyebrow pencil; **lápiz de cera** crayon; **lápiz de color** colored *o Br* coloured pencil; **lápiz fluorescente** highlighter; **lápiz labial, lápiz de labios** lipstick; **lápiz de ojos** eyeliner; **lápiz óptico** light pen
lapón I *adj* Lapp, of / from Lapland **II** *m*, **-ona** *f* Laplander **III** *m idioma* Lapp
Laponia *f* Lapland
lapso *m de tiempo* space, period; (*error*) ☞ ***lapsus***
lapsus *m inv* slip; ***tener un ~*** have a momentary lapse
◇ **lapsus linguae** slip of the tongue
laqueado *m* lacquered
laquear ⟨1a⟩ *v/t* lacquer
lar *m* hearth; ***~es*** *pl* MYTH lares, household gods
larga *f*: ***poner las ~s*** put the headlights on full beam; ***dar ~s a alguien*** F put s.o. off
largamente *adv* at length
largar ⟨1h⟩ *v/t* drive away; *persona* get rid of; ***~ un discurso*** F make a speech; **largarse** *v/r* F clear off *o* out F; ***¡lárgate!*** beat it!, get lost!
largavistas *m inv Rpl* binoculars *pl*
largo I *adj* long; *persona* tall; ***esto va para ~*** this will take some time; ***pasar de ~*** go (straight) past; ***tener setenta años ~s*** be a good seventy years old
II *m* length; ***tener tres metros de ~*** be three meters long; ***poner a alguien de ~*** dress s.o. in a long dress
III *int*: ***¡~ (de aquí)!*** get out of here!; ***¡~!*** F scram! F
IV: ***a la -a*** in the long run; ***~ y tendido*** at great length; ***a lo ~ del día*** throughout the day; ***a lo ~ de muchos años*** over the course of many years; ***a lo ~ de la calle*** along the street
largometraje *m* feature film
larguero *m* DEP crossbar
larguirucho *adj* F lanky, gangling
largura *f* length
laringe *f* larynx
laringitis *f* MED laryngitis
larva *f* ZO larva
las I *art fpl* the **II** *pron complemento directo pl* them; *a ustedes* you; ***llévate ~ que quieras*** take whichever ones you want; ***~ de ...*** those of ...; ***~ de Juan*** Juan's; ***~ que llevan falda*** the ones *o* those that are wearing dresses
lasaña *f* GASTR lasagne
lasca *f* chip, chipping
lascivia *f* lewdness, lasciviousness
lascivo *adj* lewd, lascivious
láser *m inv* laser; ***rayo ~*** laser beam
laserterapia *f* laser therapy
lástima *f* **1** pity, shame; ***es una ~*** it's a pity *o* shame; ***¡qué ~!*** what a pity *o* shame!; ***me da ~ no usarlo*** it's a shame *o* pity not to use it **2**: ***estar hecho una ~*** be in terrible shape
lastimar ⟨1a⟩ *v/t* (*herir*) hurt; **lastimarse** *v/r* hurt o.s.
lastimero *adj* pitiful
lastimoso *adj* pitiful; (*deplorable*) shameful
lastrar ⟨1a⟩ *v/t* MAR ballast; *fig* burden
lastre *m* ballast; *fig* burden; ***soltar ~*** drop ballast
lata *f* **1** can, *Br tb* tin **2** *fig* F nuisance, drag F, pain F; ***dar la ~*** F be a nuisance *o* a drag F *o* a pain F; ***¡qué ~!*** what a nuisance *o* a drag F *o* a pain F !; ***es una ~*** it's a nuisance *o* a drag F *o* a pain F
latazo *m* F pain in the neck F; ***dar el ~*** be a real pain in the neck F
latencia *f* **1** latency **2** *de enfermedad* incubation period
latente *adj* latent
lateral I *adj* side *atr*; ***cuestiones ~es*** side issues **II** *m* DEP back
◇ **lateral derecho** DEP right back
◇ **lateral izquierdo** DEP left back
latería *f L.Am.* tin works *sg*
latero *m*, **-a** *f L.Am.* tinsmith

látex *m* BOT, QUÍM latex
latido *m* beat
◇ **latido cardiaco** heartbeat
latifundio *m* large estate
latifundista *m/f* owner of a large estate
latigazo *m* **1** lash; (*chasquido*) crack **2** F *de whisky* shot F
látigo *m* whip
latiguillo *m* (*muletilla*) filler (word)
latín *m* Latin; ***saber mucho ~*** be really sharp
latinajo *m* F *palabra* Latin word; *frase* Latin phrase; (*latín incorrecto*) dog Latin
latino *adj* Latin
Latinoamérica Latin America
latinoamericano I *adj* Latin American **II** *m*, **-a** *f* Latin American
latir ⟨3a⟩ *v/i* beat
latitud *f* GEOG latitude
lato *adj* broad, wide; ***en sentido ~*** in a broad sense, broadly
latón *m* brass
latoso F **I** *adj* annoying **II** *m*, **-a** *f* pain F, nuisance
latrocinio *m* larceny
laucha *f S.Am.* mouse
laúd *m* MÚS lute
laudable *adj* praiseworthy, laudable
laudatorio *adj* laudatory *fml*
laudo *m* JUR decision
laureado *adj* prize-winning
laurear ⟨1a⟩ *v/t*: ***~ a alguien con algo*** *fml* award sth to s.o.
laurel *m* BOT laurel; ***dormirse en los ~es*** *fig* rest on one's laurels
lava *f* lava
lavable *adj* washable
lavabo *m* washbowl
lavacoches *m/f inv* carwash employee
lavada *f L.Am.* wash
lavadero *m* utility room, laundry room
lavado *m* wash; ***de fácil ~*** easy wash
◇ **lavado de cerebro** *fig* brainwashing; **lavado de estómago, lavado gástrico** stomach pump; ***hacer un ~ a alguien*** MED pump s.o.'s stomach; **lavado en seco** dry cleaning
lavadora *f* washing machine
lavamanos *m inv L.Am.* ☞ ***lavabo***
lavanda *f* BOT lavender
lavandera *f* washerwoman, laundress
lavandería *f* laundry
lavandina *f Arg* bleach
lavándula *f* BOT lavender
lavaplatos *m inv* **1** dishwasher **2** *L.Am.* sink
lavar ⟨1a⟩ **I** *v/t* wash; ***~ los platos*** wash the dishes, *Br* do the washing-up; ***~ la ropa*** do the laundry, *Br tb* do the washing; ***~ en seco*** dry clean **II** *v/i* (*lavar los platos*) do the dishes; *de detergente* clean; **lavarse** *v/r* wash up, *Br* have a wash; ***~ los dientes*** brush one's teeth; ***~ las manos*** wash one's hands; ***yo me lavo las manos*** *fig* I wash my hands of it
lavarropas *m inv L.Am.* washing machine
lavativa *f* MED enema
lavatorio *m Rpl* washbasin
lavavajillas *m inv* **1** *líquido* dish-washing liquid, *Br* washing-up liquid **2** *electrodoméstico* dishwasher
lavotear ⟨1a⟩ F *v/t* wash quickly; **lavotearse** *v/r* wash up quickly, have a quick wash
lavoteo *m* F quick wash F
laxante *m/adj* MED laxative
laxar ⟨1a⟩ *v/t* MED give a laxative to, dose with a laxative
laxativo *m/adj* MED laxative
laxitud *f* laxness, laxity
laxo *adj* **1** relaxed **2** (*poco estricto*) lax
lazada *f* bow
lazarillo *m* guide; ***perro ~*** seeing eye dog, *Br* guide dog
lazo *m* **1** knot **2** *de adorno* bow **3** *para atrapar animales* lasso; ***caer en el ~*** *fig* fall into the trap **4**: ***~s*** *pl* ties
le *pron sg complemento indirecto* (to) him; (*a ella*) (to) her; (*a usted*) (to) you; (*a algo*) (to) it; *complemento directo* him; (*a usted*) you
leal *adj* loyal
lealtad *f* loyalty
leasing *m* leasing
lebrada *f* GASTR hare stew
lebrel *m* coursing dog
lección *f* lesson; ***dar una ~ a alguien*** *fig* teach s.o. a lesson; ***esto le servirá de ~*** that will teach him a lesson
◇ **lección inaugural** initial class *given by an eminent figure*
◇ **lección magistral** master class
lechada *f* **1** *de cal* whitewash **2** *de argamasa* grout **3** *de papel* pulp
lechal I *adj* sucking, suckling **II** *m* suck-

ler, suckling
lechar ⟨1a⟩ *v/t L.Am.* (*ordeñar*) milk
leche *f* milk; ***es la ~*** P (*bueno*) he's / it's the best; (*malo*) he's / it's the pits F; ***estar de mala ~*** P be in a foul mood; ***tener mala ~*** P be out to make trouble; ***tener ~*** *L.Am.* F be lucky
◇ **leche condensada** condensed milk; **leche descremada** skim milk, *Br* skimmed milk; **leche desmaquillante** cleansing cream; **leche desnatada** skim milk, *Br* skimmed milk; **leche entera** whole milk; **leche limpiadora** cleansing cream; **leche en polvo** powdered milk; **leche semidescremada, leche semidesnatada** low-fat milk, *Br tb* semi-skimmed milk
lechecillas *fpl* sweetbreads
lechera *f para guardar* milk churn; *para hervir* milk pan; *para servir* creamer, *Br* milk jug; ***es el cuento*** *o* ***las cuentas de la ~*** *fig* it's pie in the sky F, it's pure fantasy
lechería *f* dairy
lechero I *adj* dairy *atr* **II** *m* milkman
lecho *m tb de río* bed; ***ser un ~ de rosas*** *fig* be a bed of roses
◇ **lecho de muerte** deathbed
lechón *m* suckling pig, sucking pig
lechoso *adj* milky
lechuga *f* lettuce; ***ser más fresco que una ~*** F have a lot of nerve
◇ **lechuga iceberg** iceberg lettuce
lechuguino *m* F dandy
lechuza *f* **1** ZO barn owl **2** *Cuba, Méx* (*prostituta*) hooker F
lecitina *f* BIO lecithin
lectivo *adj*: ***día ~*** school day; ***día no ~*** non-school day; ***hora -a*** class time
lector *m*, **~a** *f* **1** reader **2** EDU language assistant
◇ **lector de CD-ROM** CD ROM player
lectorado *m* assistantship
lectura *f* reading; ***dar ~ a algo*** read sth (out); ***tener varias ~s*** *fig* have several interpretations
leer ⟨2e⟩ *v/t & v/i* read; ***~ en voz alta*** read aloud, read out loud; ***~ música*** read music
lega *f* laywoman, layperson; *en orden religiosa* lay sister
legación *f* legation
legado *m* legacy; *persona* legate
legajo *m* file
legal *adj* **1** legal **2** F *persona* great F, terrific F
legalidad *f* legality
legalización *f* legalization
legalizar ⟨1f⟩ *v/t* legalize
legaña *f*: ***tener ~s en los ojos*** have sleep in one's eyes
legañoso *adj ojos* bleary, sleep-filled
legar ⟨1h⟩ *v/t* leave
legatario *m*, **-a** *f* legatee
legendario *adj* legendary
legibilidad *f* legibility
legible *adj* legible
legión *f* legion
legionario *m* **1** *en Roma* legionary **2** *en la actualidad* legionnaire; ***enfermedad del ~*** MED legionnaire's disease
legionella *f* legionnaire's disease
legislación *f* legislation
legislador I *adj* legislative **II** *m*, **~a** *f* legislator
legislar ⟨1a⟩ *v/i* legislate
legislativo *adj* legislative; ***poder ~*** legislature
legislatura *f cuerpo* legislature; *periodo* term of office
legista *m/f* jurist
legitimación *f* **1** legitimization **2** *de documento* authentication
legitimar ⟨1a⟩ *v/t* **1** justify **2** *documento* authenticate **2** *hijo* legitimize
legitimidad *f* **1** legitimacy **2** (*autenticidad*) authenticity
legítimo *adj* **1** legitimate **2** (*verdadero*) authentic
lego *adj* **1** lay *atr* **2** *fig* ignorant; ***ser ~ en la materia*** know little about the subject **II** *m* layman, layperson; *en orden religiosa* lay brother
legrado *m* MED D & C, dilation and curettage
legrar ⟨1a⟩ *v/t* curette, scrape
legua *f*: ***se ve a la ~*** *fig* F you can see it a mile off F; *hecho* it's blindingly obvious F
leguleyo *m*, **-a** *f desp* shyster F
legumbre *f* BOT pulse, legume
leguminosas *fpl* BOT leguminous plants
leída *f L.Am.* reading
leído *adj libro* widely read; *persona* well-read
lejanía *f* distance; ***en la ~*** in the distance
lejano *adj* distant

lejía *f* bleach
lejos **I** *adv* far, far away; ***Navidad queda ~*** Christmas is a long way off; ***a lo ~*** in the distance; ***sin ir más ~*** to give you an example; ***estar muy ~ de algo*** *fig* be a long way from sth; ***ir demasiado ~*** *fig* go too far, overstep the mark; ***llegar ~*** *fig* go far; ***nada más ~ de mi intención*** nothing was further from my mind **II** *prp*: ***~ de*** far from; ***desde ~*** from afar, from far away
lele *adj C.Am.* stupid
lelo *adj* slow(-witted)
lema *m* **1** slogan **2** LING lemma
lempira *m* FIN lempira
lencería *f* lingerie
lengua *f* tongue; ***darle a la ~*** F chatter; ***~ afilada*** *o* ***de doble filo*** sharp tongue; ***tirar a alguien de la ~*** get information out of s.o.; ***con la ~ fuera*** *fig* with one's tongue hanging out; ***irse de la ~*** let the cat out of the bag; ***morderse la ~*** *fig* bite one's tongue; ***sacar la ~ a alguien*** stick one's tongue out at s.o.; ***lo tengo en la punta de la ~*** it's on the tip of my tongue
◇ **lengua de gato** GASTR langue de chat; **lengua materna** mother tongue; **lengua de signos** sign language; **lengua de tierra** strip of land
lenguado *m* ZO sole
lenguaje *m* language
◇ **lenguaje de programación** INFOR programming language
lenguaraz *adj* (*mal hablado*) foul-mouthed
lengüeta **I** *f* **1** *de zapato* tongue **2** (*pestaña*) tab **3** MÚS: ***~*** (***de caña***) MÚS reed; ***doble ~*** double reed **II** *adj*: ***ser ~*** *S.Am.* be a gossip
lengüetazo *m* big lick
lenidad *f fml* lenience
lenitivo *m* balm
lente *f* lens
◇ **lente de aumento** magnifying glass
◇ **lentes de contacto** contact lenses, contacts
lenteja *f* BOT lentil
lentejuela *f* sequin
lentes *mpl LAm.* glasses
◇ **lentes de sol** *L.Am.* sunglasses
lentillas *fpl* contact lenses
lentisco *m* BOT mastic tree
lentitud *f* slowness
lento *adj* slow; ***a fuego ~*** on a low heat
leña *f* (fire)wood; ***echar ~ al fuego*** *fig* add fuel to the fire
leñador *m* woodcutter
leñazo *m* F wallop; ***darse un ~*** take a wallop
¡leñe! *int* P hey!
leño *m* log
leñoso *adj* woody
Leo *m/f inv* ASTR Leo
león *m* ZO lion; *L.Am.* puma
◇ **león marino** sealion
leona *f* lioness
leonado *adj* tawny
leonera *f* **1** lion's den; *jaula* lion's cage **2** *Rpl, Chi fig* F pigpen F, *Br* pigsty F **3** *L.Am.* F *para prisioneros* bullpen F, *Br communal cell for holding prisoners temporarily*
leonino **I** *adj* **1** leonine **2** *L.Am.* ASTR Leo; ***soy ~*** I'm (a) Leo **II** *m*, **-a** *f L.Am.* ASTR Leo
leopardo *m* ZO leopard
leotardo *m de gimnasta* leotard; ***~s*** *pl* tights, *Br* heavy tights
lépero *adj C.Am., Méx* coarse
lepidópteros *mpl* ZO lepidoptera *pl*
leporino *adj*: ***labio ~*** MED harelip
lepra *f* MED leprosy
leprosería *f* leper colony
leproso **I** *adj* leprous **II** *m*, **-a** *f* leper
lerdo *adj* (*torpe*) slow(-witted)
les *pron pl complemento indirecto* (to) them; (*a ustedes*) (to) you; *complemento directo* them; (*a ustedes*) you
lesbiana *f* lesbian
lesbiano *adj* lesbian
lésbico *adj* lesbian
lesión *f* injury
lesionado *adj* injured
lesionar ⟨1a⟩ *v/t* injure; **lesionarse** *v/r* hurt o.s.
lesivo *adj* harmful
leso *adj*: ***delito de lesa majestad*** lese-majesty, treason
letal *adj* lethal
letanía *f tb desp* litany
letárgico *adj* lethargic
letargo *m* **1** lethargy **2** ZO hibernation
◇ **letargo invernal** ZO hibernation
letón **I** *adj* Latvian **II** *m*, **-ona** *f* Latvian **III** *m idioma* Latvian, Lettish
Letonia *f* Latvia
letra *f* **1** letter; ***escribir en ~s de molde***

print; ***la ~ pequeña*** *o* ***menuda*** *fig* the fine print, *Br* the small print; ***al pie de la ~*** word for word **2** *de canción* lyrics *pl* **3**: **~s** *pl* (*literatura*) literature *sg*; EDU arts **4**: ***tener buena / mala ~*** have good / bad handwriting
◇ **letra de cambio** COM bill of exchange; **letra de imprenta** block capital; **letra mayúscula** capital letter; **letra a la vista** COM sight draft, sight bill
letrado I *adj* learned **II** *m*, **-a** *f* lawyer
letrero *m* sign
letrina *f* latrine
letrista *m/f* MÚS lyricist
leucemia *f* MED leuk(a)emia
leucocito *m* ANAT leucocyte
leva *f* **1** MIL levy **2** TÉC cam **3**: ***la ~ de la flota tendrá lugar cuando*** … the fleet will weigh anchor when …
levadura *f* yeast
◇ **levadura de cerveza** brewer's yeast
◇ **levadura en polvo** baking powder
levantador *m*, **~a** *f*: ***~ de pesas*** DEP weightlifter
levantamiento *m* **1** raising **2** (*rebelión*) rising **3** *de embargo* lifting **4** *de cadáver* removal
◇ **levantamiento de peso, levantamiento de pesas** weightlifting
◇ **levantamiento topográfico** topographical survey
levantar ⟨1a⟩ *v/t* **1** raise; *bulto* lift (up); *del suelo* pick up; ***~ los ojos*** raise one's eyes, look up; ***~ la voz*** raise one's voice (***a*** to); ***¡levanta los ánimos!*** cheer up!; ***~ sospechas*** arouse suspicion; ***~ el vuelo*** *de pájaro* fly away, fly off; *de avión* take off **2** *edificio, estatua* put up, erect **3** *embargo* lift **4** F (*robar*) lift F, *Br tb* pinch F
levantarse *v/r* **1** get up; (*ponerse de pie*) stand up **2** *de un edificio, una montaña* rise **3** *de un telón* go up, rise **4** *en rebelión* rise up
levante *m* east
levar ⟨1a⟩ *v/t*: ***~ anclas*** weigh anchor
leve *adj* slight; *sonrisa* faint
levedad *f* lightness
levita *f* frock coat
levitación *f* levitation
levitar ⟨1a⟩ *v/i* levitate
lexema *m* lexeme
lexicalizar ⟨1f⟩ *v/t* lexicalize
léxico *m* lexicon
ley *f* law; ***es la ~ del más fuerte*** might is right; ***una ~ no escrita*** an unwritten law; ***con todas las de la ~*** fairly and squarely
◇ **ley fundamental** constitutional law; **ley marcial** martial law; **ley seca** Prohibition; **ley de la selva** law of the jungle; **ley del Talión** principle of an eye for an eye; **ley de la ventaja** DEP advantage law; ***aplicar la ~*** play advantage
leyenda *f* legend
leyendo *vb* ☞ ***leer***
leyó *vb* ☞ ***leer***
liana *f* BOT liana, creeper
liar ⟨1c⟩ *v/t* **1** tie (up) **2** *en papel* wrap (up); *cigarillo* roll **3** *persona* confuse;
liarse *v/r de una persona* get confused; ***~ a hacer algo*** get tied up doing sth; ***~ con alguien*** F get involved with s.o.; ***~ a golpes*** start fighting
libanés I *adj* Lebanese **II** *m*, **-esa** *f* Lebanese
Líbano *m* Lebanon
libar ⟨1a⟩ *v/t néctar* suck; *fml*: *licor* sip
libelo *m* libel
libélula *f* ZO dragonfly
liberación *f* release; *de un país* liberation
liberal I *adj* liberal **II** *m/f* liberal
liberalidad *f* generosity
liberalismo *m* liberalism
liberalización *f* liberalization
liberalizar ⟨1f⟩ *v/t* liberalize
liberar ⟨1a⟩ *v/t* (set) free, release; *país* liberate; *energía* release; **liberarse** *v/r*: ***~ de algo*** free o.s. of sth
líbero *m en fútbol* sweeper
libérrimo *adj fml* most free
libertad *f* freedom, liberty; ***dejar a alguien en ~*** release s.o., let s.o. go; ***hablar con toda ~*** speak freely; ***tomarse ~es*** take liberties; ***tomarse la ~ de hacer algo*** take the liberty of doing sth
◇ **libertad bajo fianza** JUR bail
◇ **libertad condicional** JUR probation
libertador I *adj* liberating **II** *m*, **~a** *f* liberator
libertar ⟨1a⟩ *v/t* (set) free, release
libertario I *adj* libertarian **II** *m*, **-a** *f* libertarian
libertinaje *m* licentiousness
libertino I *adj* dissolute, libertine **II** *m* libertine

L

Libia *f* Libya
libidinoso *adj* lustful, libidinous *fml*
líbido *f* libido
libio I *adj* Libyan **II** *m*, **-a** *f* Libyan
libra *f* pound; **~ *esterlina*** pound (sterling)
Libra *m/f inv* ASTR Libra
libraco *m* **1** *desp* (*libro malo*) bad book **2** (*libro grueso*) thick book, brick F
librado I *part* ☞ **librar**, ***salir bien / mal ~ de algo*** come out of sth well / badly **II** *m*, **-a** *f* COM drawee
librador *m*, **~a** *f* COM drawer
librano *L.Am.* ASTR **I** *adj* Libran; ***soy ~*** I'm (a) Libra(n) **II** *m*, **-a** *f* Libra(n)
libranza *f* order to pay
librar ⟨1a⟩ **I** *v/t* free (**de** from); *cheque* draw; *batalla* fight **II** *v/i*: ***libro los lunes*** I have Mondays off; **librarse** *v/r*: **~ *de algo*** get out of sth; ***de buena nos hemos librado*** F that was lucky
libre *adj* free; *tiempo* spare, free; ***eres ~ de*** you're free to; ***trabajar por ~*** be self-employed; **~ *de impuestos*** tax free
librea *f* livery
librecambio *m* free trade
librepensador I *adj* freethinking **II** *m*, **~a** *f* freethinker
librera *f* bookseller
librería *f* bookstore
◇ **librería de lance, librería de viejo** second-hand bookstore
librero *m* bookseller; *L.Am. mueble* bookcase
libreta *f* notebook
◇ **libreta de ahorros** bankbook, passbook
◇ **libreta de cheques** *Rpl* checkbook, *Br* chequebook
libretista *m/f* **1** librettist **2** *L.Am. en cine etc* scriptwriter
libreto *m* **1** libretto **2** *en cine etc* script
libriano *L.Am.* ☞ **librano**
libro *m* book; ***colgar los ~s*** quit studying; ***hablar como un ~*** talk like a book, use highfalutin language
◇ **libro de bolsillo** paperback (book); **libro de cabecera** bedtime book; ***¿cuál es tu ~ ahora mismo?*** what's your bedtime reading at the moment?; **libro de caja** COM cash book; **libro de cocina** cookbook, *Br tb* cookery book; **libro de cuentos** book of short stories; **libro diario** COM day book; **libro electrónico** e-book; **libro de escolaridad** school record; **libro de familia** *booklet recording family births, marriages and deaths*; **libro mayor** COM ledger; **libro de pedidos** order book; **libro de reclamaciones** complaints book; **libro de texto** textbook
licencia *f* **1** permit, license, *Br* licence **2** (*permiso*) permission **3** MIL leave **4**: ***tomarse demasiadas ~s*** take liberties **5** *L.Am.* AUTO license, *Br* licence
◇ **licencia absoluta** MIL absolute discharge; **licencia de armas** gun permit, *Br* gun licence; **licencia de caza** hunting permit; **licencia de conducir, licencia de manejar** *L.Am.* driver's license, *Br* driving licence; **licencia de obras** planning permission; **licencia de pesca** fishing permit; **licencia poética** poetic license *o Br* licence
licenciado I *adj* MIL: ***está ~*** he has completed his military service **II** *m*, **-a** *f* graduate
licenciamiento *m* MIL discharge
licenciar ⟨1b⟩ *v/t* MIL discharge; **licenciarse** *v/r* **1** graduate **2** MIL be discharged
licenciatura *f* EDU degree
licencioso *adj* licentious
liceo *m L.Am.* high school, *Br* secondary school
licitación *f L.Am.* bidding
licitador *m*, **~a** *f L.Am.* bidder
licitar ⟨1a⟩ *v/t L.Am. en subasta* bid for
lícito *adj* **1** legal **2** (*razonable*) fair, reasonable
licitud *f fml* legality
licor *m* liquor, *Br* spirits *pl*
licorera *f* decanter
licorería *f* liquor store, *Br* off-licence
licorista *m/f* liquor store clerk, *Br* off-licence assistant
licuado *m Méx* fruit milkshake
licuadora *f* blender
licuar ⟨1d⟩ *v/t* blend, liquidize
licuefacción *f* liquefaction
lid *f lit* battle
líder I *m/f* leader **II** *adj* leading
liderar ⟨1a⟩ *v/t* lead
liderazgo *m* leadership
lidia *f* bullfighting
lidiar ⟨1b⟩ **I** *v/i fig* do battle, struggle **II** *v/t toro* fight
liebre *f* ZO hare; ***levantar la ~ fig*** let the

cat out of the bag, spill the beans
liendre *f* ZO nit
lienzo *m* canvas
lifting *m* facelift; **~ *facial*** facelift; ***hacerse un ~*** have a facelift
liga *f* **1** POL, DEP league; ***la Liga de los Campeones*** the Champions League **2** *de medias* garter
ligado **I** *adj* connected, linked **II** *m* MÚS slur
ligadura *f* MED ligature; **~*s*** *pl fig* ties
ligamento *m* ANAT ligament; **~ *cruzado*** cruciate ligament
ligar ⟨1h⟩ **I** *v/t* **1** bind **2** (*atar*) tie **3** GASTR blend **II** *v/i*: **~ *con*** F pick up; **ligarse** *v/r* pick up
ligazón *f* connection, link
ligereza *f* **1** lightness **2** (*rapidez*) speed **3** *de movimiento* agility, nimbleness **4** *de carácter* shallowness, superficiality
ligero **I** *adj* **1** light; **~ *de ropa*** scantily clad; ***a la -a*** (*sin pensar*) lightly, casually; ***tomarse algo a la -a*** not take sth seriously **2** (*rápido*) rapid, quick **3** *movimiento* agile, nimble **4** (*leve*) slight **II** *adv* quickly
lignito *m* lignite
ligón *m* F: ***es un ~*** he's a real Don Juan F
ligue *m/f* F *persona* pick-up F; ***estar de ~*** be on the pick-up F, *Br* be on the pull F
liguero **I** *m* garter belt, *Br* suspender belt **II** *adj* DEP: ***partido ~*** league game
lija *f*: ***papel de ~*** sandpaper
lijar ⟨1a⟩ *v/t* sand
lila **I** *adj inv* lilac **II** *f* BOT lilac **III** *m color* lilac **IV** *m/f* F dimwit F
lima *f* **1** file **2** BOT lime **3**: ***comer como una ~*** *fig* F eat like a horse F
◇ **lima de uñas** nail file
limaco *m* ZO ☞ ***limaza***
limadura *f* filing
limar ⟨1a⟩ *v/t* file; *fig* polish
limaza *f* ZO slug
limbo *m* REL limbo; ***estar en el ~*** be miles away
limeño **I** *adj* of / from Lima, Lima *atr* **II** *m*, -*a f* native of Lima
limitación *f* limitation
limitado **I** *adj* limited **II** *part* ☞ ***limitar***
limitar ⟨1a⟩ **I** *v/t* limit; (*restringir*) limit, restrict **II** *v/i*: **~ *con*** border on; **limitarse** *v/r* limit *o* restrict o.s. (***a*** to)
límite **I** *m* **1** limit; ***sin ~s*** limitless **2** (*línea de separación*) boundary **II** *adj*: ***situación ~*** extreme situation; ***caso ~*** borderline case
◇ **límite de velocidad** speed limit
limítrofe *adj* neighboring, *Br* neighbouring; ***país ~*** neighboring country
limo *m* silt; *en el suelo* mud
limón *m* **1** lemon **2** *Méx lima* lime
◇ **limón francés** *Méx* lemon
limonada *f* lemonade
limonero *m* lemon tree
limosna *f*: ***una ~, por favor*** can you spare some change?
limosnear ⟨1a⟩ *v/i* beg
limosnero *L.Am.* **I** *adj* beggar *atr*, begging *atr* **II** *m*, -*a f* beggar
limpiabotas *m/f inv* bootblack
limpiacristales *m inv* window cleaner
limpiada *f L.Am.* clean
limpiador **I** *adj* cleansing **II** *m*, **~*a*** *f* cleaner **III** *m Méx* (*limpiaparabrisas*) windshield wiper, *Br* windscreen wiper
limpiahogar *m* cleaning liquid
limpiamanos *m inv L.Am.* hand towel
limpiamente *adv* cleanly
limpiametales *m inv* metal cleaner
limpiamuebles *m inv* furniture polish
limpiaparabrisas *m inv* AUTO windshield wiper, *Br* windscreen wiper
◇ **limpiaparabrisas trasero** rear windshield wiper, *Br* rear windscreen wiper
limpiar ⟨1b⟩ *v/t* clean; *con un trapo* wipe; *fig* clean up; **~ *a alguien*** F clean s.o. out F; **~ *en seco*** dry-clean; **limpiarse** *v/r* clean o.s.
limpiasuelos *m inv* floor cleaner
limpiavidrios *m inv L.Am.* window cleaner
límpido *adj lit* limpid
limpieza *f estado* cleanliness; *acto* cleaning; ***hacer la ~*** do the cleaning; **~ *en seco*** dry-cleaning
◇ **limpieza de cutis** skin cleansing; **limpieza étnica** ethnic cleansing; **limpieza general** spring cleaning
limpio *adj* **1** clean; ***poner algo en ~*** make a fair copy of sth; ***pasar a ~*** copy out neatly; ***gana $5.000 ~s al mes*** he takes home $5,000 a month; ***quedarse ~*** *S.Am.* F be broke F; ***sacar algo en ~*** *fig* make sense of sth **2** (*ordenado*) neat, tidy **3** *político* honest
limusina *f* limousine

linaje *m* lineage
linaza *f* BOT linseed
lince *m* ZO lynx; ***ojos*** *o* ***vista de ~*** *fig* eyes like a hawk; ***ser un ~*** be very sharp
◇ **lince ibérico** Iberian lynx, Spanish lynx
linchamiento *m* lynching
linchar ⟨1a⟩ *v/t* lynch
lindante *adj* adjacent (***con*** to), bordering (***con*** on)
lindar ⟨1a⟩ *v/i*: ***~ con algo*** adjoin sth; *fig* border on sth
linde *m o f* boundary
lindero I *adj*: ***ser ~ con*** border on **II** *m* boundary
lindeza *f* prettiness, loveliness; ***~s*** *pl irón* insults, offensive remarks
lindo *adj* lovely; ***de lo ~*** a lot, a great deal
línea *f* line; ***mantener la ~*** watch one's figure; ***de primera ~*** *fig* first-rate; ***tecnología de primera ~*** state-of-the art technology; ***perdieron en toda la ~*** they were soundly beaten; ***entre ~s*** *fig* between the lines; ***escribir*** *o* ***poner unas*** *o* ***dos*** *o* ***cuatro ~s a alguien*** drop s.o. a line; ***la ~ se ha cortado*** TELEC the line's gone dead; ***no hay ~*** TELEC the line's dead
◇ **línea aérea** airline; **línea de alta tensión** EL high voltage cable; **línea directa** TELEC direct line; **línea divisoria** dividing line; **línea eléctrica** power cable *o* line; **línea erótica** sex phone line; **línea férrea** railroad, *Br* railway; **línea de flotación** water line; **línea de fondo** *en fútbol* goal line; *en baloncesto* end line; **línea de gol** *en fútbol* goal line; **línea de llegada** DEP finishing line, finish; **línea marítima** shipping line; **línea media** *en fútbol* midfield line, *Br* halfway line; **línea de meta** *en fútbol* goal line; **línea de productos** COM product line; **línea de salida** DEP starting line; **línea de seis veinticinco** *en baloncesto* three-point line; **línea de tiros libres** *en baloncesto* free throw line
lineal *adj* linear
linfa *f* lymph
linfático *adj* lymphatic
linfocito *m* ANAT lymphocyte
lingotazo *m* F *de vodka* shot F
lingote *m* ingot; ***~ de oro*** gold bar
lingual *adj* lingual
lingüista *m/f* linguist
lingüística *f* linguistics *sg*
lingüístico *adj* linguistic
linier *m* DEP assistant referee, linesman
linimento *m* MED liniment
lino *m* linen; BOT flax
linóleo *m* linoleum, lino
linotipia *f* TIP Linotype®
linotipista *m/f* TIP Linotype® operator
linterna *f* **1** flashlight, *Br* torch **2** *Méx* F *ojo* eye
◇ **linterna mágica** magic lantern
lío *m* **1** bundle **2** F (*desorden*) mess; ***~ amoroso*** F affair; ***estar hecho un ~*** be all confused; ***hacerse un ~*** get into a muddle; ***meterse en ~s*** get into trouble **3** F (*jaleo*) fuss; ***armar un ~*** F kick up a fuss F
liofilización *f* freeze-drying
liofilizado *adj* freeze-dried
liofilizar ⟨1f⟩ *v/t* freeze-dry
lioso *adj* confusing
liposucción *f* MED liposuction
lipotimia *f* MED blackout
liquen *m* BOT lichen
liquidación *f* **1** COM *de cuenta, deuda* settlement **2** *de negocio* liquidation
◇ **liquidación de fin de temporada** end of season sale
◇ **liquidación total** clearance sale
liquidador *m*, **~a** *f* liquidator
liquidar ⟨1a⟩ *v/t* **1** *cuenta, deuda* settle **2** COM *negocio* wind up, liquidate **3** *existencias* sell off **4** F (*matar*) liquidate F, bump off F
liquidez *f* COM liquidity
líquido I *adj* **1** liquid **2** COM net **II** *m* liquid
lira *f* **1** lira **2** MÚS lyre
lírica *f* lyric poetry
lírico *adj* lyrical
lirio *m* BOT lily
◇ **lirio de los valles** lily of the valley
lirismo *m* lyricism
lirón *m* ZO dormouse; ***dormir como un ~*** *fig* F sleep like a log
lisa *f* ZO grey mullet
lisboeta *adj* Lisboan
lisiado I *adj* crippled **II** *m*, **-a** *f* cripple
lisiar ⟨1b⟩ *v/t* cripple
liso *adj* **1** smooth **2** *terreno* flat; ***cien metros ~s*** DEP one hundred meter sprint, one hundred meters **3** *pelo* straight **4** (*sin adornos*) plain; ***-a y llanamente***

plainly and simply

lisonja *f* flattery

lisonjear ⟨1a⟩ *v/t* flatter

lisonjero *adj* flattering

lista *f* **1** list; ***pasar ~*** take the roll call, *Br* call the register **2** *en tela* stripe

◇ **lista de boda** wedding list; **lista civil** civil list; **lista de correos** general delivery, *Br* poste restante; **lista de espera** waiting list; ***estar en ~*** be on the waiting list, be waitlisted; **lista de precios** price list

listado I *adj* striped **II** *m* INFOR printout

listar ⟨1a⟩ *v/t* list

listillo F **I** *adj* smart **II** *m*, **-a** *f* smart alec F

listín *m*: **~ (*telefónico*)** phone book

listo *adj* **1** (*inteligente*) clever; ***pasarse de ~*** F try to be too smart F; ***ser más ~ que el hambre*** F be a smart cookie **2** (*preparado*) ready; ***estar ~*** *fig* F be finished

listón *m* **1** *de madera* strip **2** DEP bar; ***poner el ~ muy alto*** *fig* set very high standards

lisura *f Rpl*, *Pe* curse, swearword

litera *f* bunk; *de tren* couchette

literal *adj* literal

literario *adj* literary

literata *f* woman of letters

literato *m* man of letters

literatura *f* literature

litigante *m/f & adj* JUR litigant

litigar ⟨1h⟩ *v/i* JUR go to litigation

litigio *m* lawsuit

litigioso *adj persona* litigious

litio *m* QUÍM lithium

litografía *f* lithography

litoral I *adj* coastal **II** *m* coast

litro *m* liter, *Br* litre

litrona *f* F *liter bottle of beer*

Lituania *f* Lithuania

lituano I *adj* Lithuanian **II** *m*, **-a** *f* Lithuanian **III** *m idioma* Lithuanian

liturgia *f* REL liturgy

litúrgico *adj* liturgical

liviano *adj* **1** light **2** (*de poca importancia*) trivial

lividez *f* paleness, pallor

lívido *adj* pale, pallid

living *m* living room

liza *f* HIST lists *pl*; ***entrar en ~*** *fig* enter the fray

llaga *f* sore; ***poner*** *o* ***meter el dedo en la ~*** *fig* put one's finger on it

llagar ⟨1h⟩ *v/t* cause *o* create a sore on

llama *f* **1** flame **2** ZO llama

◇ **llama piloto** pilot light

llamada *f* **1** call; ***hacer una ~*** make a call; ***~ al orden*** call to order; ***última ~*** AVIA last call **2** *en una puerta* knock; *en timbre* ring

◇ **llamada de auxilio** distress call; **llamada a cobro revertido** collect call; **llamada interurbana** long-distance call; **llamada urbana** local call

llamado I *adj* called, named **II** *m L.Am.* call

llamador *m* (door) knocker

llamamiento *m* call; ***hacer un ~ a algo*** call for sth

◇ **llamamiento a filas** MIL draft, *Br* call-up

◇ **llamamiento al orden** call to order

llamar ⟨1a⟩ **I** *v/t* call; TELEC call, *Br tb* ring **II** *v/i* TELEC call, *Br tb* ring; ***~ a la puerta*** knock at the door; *con timbre* ring the bell; ***llaman (a la puerta)*** there's someone at the door; ***el fútbol no me llama nada*** football doesn't appeal to me in the slightest; **llamarse** *v/r* be called; ***¿cómo te llamas?*** what's your name?

llamarada *f* flare-up

llamativo *adj* eyecatching; *color* loud

llamear ⟨1a⟩ *v/i* blaze

llamón *adj Méx* moaning

llana *f* trowel

llaneza *f en el trato* naturalness; *en el habla* plainness, plain speech

llanito *m*, **-a** *f* F Gibraltarian

llano I *adj* **1** *terreno* level **2** *trato* natural; *persona* unassuming **3** *palabra* stressed on the penultimate syllable **II** *m* flat ground

llanta *f* **1** wheel rim **2** *C.Am.*, *Méx* (*neumático*) tire, *Br* tyre **3** *Méx*: *flotador* rubber ring **3**: **~s** *pl Méx* F spare tire *sg*, *Br* spare tyre *sg*

◇ **llanta de refacción** *Méx* spare tire, *Br* spare tyre

llantén *m* BOT plantain

llanto *m* sobbing

llanura *f* plain

llave *f* **1** key; ***bajo ~*** under lock and key; ***cerrar con ~*** lock; ***echar la ~*** lock the door, lock up **2** *para tuerca* wrench, *Br tb* spanner

◇ **llave de contacto** AUTO ignition

L

key; **llave inglesa** TÉC monkey wrench; **llave maestra** master key; **llave en mano** available for immediate occupancy; **llave de paso** stop cock
llavero *m* key ring
llavín *m* small key
llegada *f* arrival; DEP finish
llegar ⟨1h⟩ *v/i* **1** arrive; ***ha llegado la primavera*** spring is here, spring has arrived; ***está al ~*** he'll arrive momentarily, he's about to arrive
2 (*alcanzar*) reach; ***me llega hasta las rodillas*** it comes down to my knees; ***el agua me llegaba a la cintura*** the water came up to my waist; ***no llego a comprender por qué …*** I don't understand why …; ***la comida no llegó para todos*** there wasn't enough food for everyone; ***¡hasta ahí podíamos ~!*** F that's going too far!, that's a bit much! F; ***~ a saber*** find out; ***~ a ser*** get to be; ***~ a viejo*** live to a ripe old age; ***~ a presidente*** get to be president, become president
llegarse *v/r*: ***llégate al vecino*** F run over to the neighbor's
llenar ⟨1a⟩ **I** *v/t* fill; *impreso* fill out *o* in **II** *v/i* be filling; **llenarse** *v/r* fill up; ***me he llenado*** I have had enough (to eat)
llenazo *m* F full house
lleno I *adj* full (***de*** of); *pared* covered (***de*** with); ***estar ~*** F be full **II** *m* TEA full house; ***hubo un ~ total*** it was a complete sellout **III** *adv*: ***de ~*** fully; ***meterse de ~ en algo*** put all one's energy into sth
llevadero *adj* bearable
llevar ⟨1a⟩ **I** *v/t* **1** take; ***~ a alguien en coche*** drive s.o., take s.o. in the car; ***~ dinero encima*** carry money
2 *ropa*, *gafas* wear
3 *ritmo* keep up
4: ***~ las de perder*** be likely to lose; ***me lleva dos años*** he's two years older than me; ***llevo ocho días aquí*** I've been here a week; ***llevo una hora esperando*** I've been waiting for an hour; ***¿te llevó dos horas hacer eso?*** it took you two hours to do that?
II *v/i* lead (***a*** to)
llevarse *v/r* **1** take **2** *susto*, *sorpresa* get **3**: ***~ bien / mal*** get on well / badly **4**: ***se lleva el color rojo*** red is fashionable
llorar ⟨1a⟩ **I** *v/i* cry, weep; ***~ a moco tendido*** F cry one's eyes out **II** *v/t lágrimas* cry, weep; *muerte* mourn
llorera *f* F: ***le entró una ~*** she burst into tears
llorica *m/f* F crybaby F
lloriquear ⟨1a⟩ *v/i* snivel, whine
lloro *m* weeping, crying
llorón I *adj* F: ***ser ~*** be a crybaby F **II** *m*, **-ona** *f* F crybaby F
lloroso *adj* tearful; *ojos* full of tears
llovedera *f L.Am.*, **llovedero** *m L.Am.* rainy season
llover ⟨2h⟩ *v/i* rain; ***llueve*** it is raining; ***~ sobre mojado*** *fig* F be one thing after another; ***es como quien oye ~*** it's like talking to a wall; ***nunca llueve a gusto de todos*** you can't please everybody
llovizna *f* drizzle
lloviznar ⟨1a⟩ *v/i* drizzle
llueve *vb* ☞ ***llover***
lluvia *f* **1** rain **2** *Rpl* (*ducha*) shower
◇ **lluvia ácida** acid rain
◇ **lluvia de estrellas** meteor shower
lluvioso *adj* rainy
lo I *art sg* the; ***~ bueno*** the good thing; ***no sabes ~ difícil que es*** you don't know how difficult it is **II** *pron sg*: *a él* him; *a usted* you; *algo* it; ***~ sé*** I know **III** *pron rel sg*: ***~ que*** what; ***~ cual*** which
loa *f* praise
loable *adj* praiseworthy, laudable
loar ⟨1a⟩ *v/t* praise
loba *f* she-wolf
lobato, lobezno *m* wolf cub
lobo *m* wolf
◇ **lobo de mar** *fig* sea dog
◇ **lobo marino** seal
lóbrego *adj* gloomy
lóbulo *m* lobe; ***~ de la oreja*** earlobe
loca *f* madwoman
locador *m S.Am.* landlord
local I *adj* local **II** *m* premises *pl*; ***~ comercial*** commercial premises *pl*; ***~ nocturno*** nightspot
localidad *f* **1** town **2** TEA seat
localizable *adj*: ***estar ~*** be easily found
localización *f* **1** location **2** INFOR localization
localizador *m Méx* pager
localizar ⟨1f⟩ *v/t* **1** locate; *incendio* contain, bring under control **2** INFOR localize
locatis *m/f inv* F loony F, nutcase F
loción *f* lotion
◇ **loción capilar** hair lotion; **loción**

corporal body lotion; **loción facial** skin lotion; **loción hidratante** moisturizer, moisturizing lotion

loco I *adj* mad, crazy; ***a lo ~*** F (*sin pensar*) hastily; ***es para volverse ~*** it's enough to drive you mad *o* crazy; ***~ de atar*** *o* ***remate*** completely mad; ***estar ~ de alegría*** be insanely happy; ***estar ~ por alguien*** be mad *o* crazy about s.o.
II *m* **1** madman; ***cada ~ con su tema*** each to his own; ***hacer el ~*** make a fool of o.s. **2** *Rpl* F guy; ***~, ayudame*** help me, pal

locomoción *f* locomotion; ***medio de ~*** means of transportation

locomotor *adj* ANAT locomotory

locomotora *f* locomotive

locomotriz *adj* ANAT locomotory

locro *m S.Am. stew of meat, corn and potatoes*

locuacidad *f* talkativeness, loquacity *fml*

locuaz *adj* talkative, loquacious *fml*

locución *f* phrase

locura *f* madness; ***es una ~*** it's madness; ***de ~*** F crazy

locutor *m*, **~a** *f* RAD, TV presenter

locutorio *m* TELEC phone booth

lodazal *m* quagmire

lodo *m* mud; ***arrastrar por el ~*** *fig* drag through the mud
◇ **lodos de depuración, lodos residuales** sludge

logaritmo *m* logarithm

logia *f* **1** *masónica* lodge **2** ARQUI loggia

lógica *f* logic

lógico *adj* logical

logística *f* logistics *sg*

logístico *adj* logistical

logopeda *m/f* speech therapist

logopedia *f* speech therapy

logotipo *m* logo

logrado *adj* excellent

lograr 〈1a〉 *v/t* achieve; (*obtener*) obtain; ***~ hacer algo*** manage to do sth; ***~ que alguien haga algo*** (manage to) get s.o. to do sth; **lograrse** *v/r* succeed

logrero *m L.Am.* F profiteer

logro *m* achievement

LOGSE *f abr* (= ***Ley de Ordenación General del Sistema Educativo***) Education Act

lola *f Rpl* F tit F

loma *f L.Am.* small hill

lombarda *f* BOT red cabbage

lombriz *f*: ***~ de tierra*** earthworm
◇ **lombriz intestinal** tapeworm

lomo *m* back; GASTR loin; ***a ~s de burro*** on a donkey

lona *f* canvas

loncha *f* slice

lonche *m L.Am.* afternoon snack

lonchería *f L.Am.* diner, luncheonette

londinense I *adj* of / from London, London *atr* **II** *m/f* Londoner

Londres *m* London

loneta *f* canvas, sailcloth

longaniza *f type of dried sausage*

longevidad *f* longevity

longevo *adj* long-lived

longitud *f* **1** longitude **2** (*largo*) length; ***tener dos metros de ~*** be two meters long
◇ **longitud de onda** wavelength

longitudinal *adj* longitudinal

longui(s) *m/f Esp*: ***hacerse el ~*** F play *o* act dumb F

lonja *f* **1** *de pescado* fish market **2** (*loncha*) slice

lontananza *f* **1** *lit* distance; ***en ~*** in the distance **2** *de cuadro* background

loor *m* REL, *lit* praise

loquear 〈1a〉 *v/i L.Am.* horse around

loquera *f L.Am.* F shrink F; *enfermera* psychiatric nurse

loquero *m* **1** *L.Am.* F shrink F; *enfermero* psychiatric nurse **2** (*manicomio*) mental hospital, funny farm F

loro *m* parrot; ***estar al ~*** F (*enterado*) be clued up F, be on the ball F

los *mpl* **I** *art* the **II** *pron complemento directo pl* them; *a ustedes* you; ***llévate ~ que quieras*** take whichever ones you want; ***~ de …*** those of …; ***~ de Juan*** Juan's; ***~ que juegan*** the ones *o* those that are playing

losa *f* flagstone

loseta *f* floor tile

lote *m* **1** *en reparto* share, part **2** *L.Am.* (*solar*) lot **3** P: ***darse el ~*** make out F

lotería *f* lottery; ***le cayó*** *o* ***tocó la ~*** he won the lottery

lotero *m*, **-a** *f* lottery ticket seller

loto I *m* BOT lotus **II** *f* F lottery

loza *f material* china; (*vajilla*) china, crockery; ***de ~*** china *atr*

lozanía *f* **1** *de persona* healthiness **2** *de*

planta lushness
lozano *adj* **1** *persona* healthy-looking **2** *planta* lush
lubina *f* ZO sea bass
lubri(fi)cación *f* lubrication
lubri(fi)cante I *adj* lubricating II *m* lubricant
lubri(fi)car ⟨1g⟩ *v/t* lubricate
lubricidad *f* lewdness
lucerna *f*, **lucernario** *m* skylight
lucero *m* **1** bright star **2** (*Venus*) Venus
◇ **lucero del alba, lucero matutino** morning star
◇ **lucero de la tarde, lucero vespertino** evening star
luces ☞ ***luz***
lucha *f* **1** fight, struggle **2** DEP wrestling **3** *en baloncesto* jump ball
◇ **lucha libre** all-in wrestling
luchador I *adj espíritu* fighting II *m*, **~a** *f* fighter
luchar ⟨1a⟩ *v/i* fight (***por*** for); *fig* fight, struggle (***por*** for)
lucidez *f* lucidity
lúcido *adj* lucid, clear
lucido *adj* splendid, magnificent
luciérnaga *f* ZO glowworm
lucimiento *m* (*brillo*) splendor, *Br* splendour; ***le ofrece oportunidades de ~*** it gives him a chance to shine
lucio *m* ZO pike
lucir ⟨3f⟩ *v/i* **1** shine **2** *L.Am.* (*verse bien*) look good II *v/t ropa, joya* wear; **lucirse** *v/r tb irón* excel o.s., surpass o.s.
lucrarse ⟨1a⟩ *v/r* make a profit (***de*** from)
lucrativo *adj* lucrative
lucro *m* profit; ***afán de ~*** profit-making; ***sin ánimo de ~*** non-profit (making), not-for-profit
luctuoso *adj* sad, sorrowful
lúdico *adj* playful
ludópata *m/f* compulsive gambler
ludopatía *f* compulsive gambling
ludoteca *f* toy library
luego I *adv* **1** (*después*) later; ***¡hasta ~!*** see you (later) **2** *en orden, espacio* then **3** *L.Am.* (*en seguida*) right now; ***~ ~*** *Méx* straight away **4**: ***¡desde ~!*** of course! II *conj* therefore; ***~ que*** *L.Am.* after; ***~ de hacer algo*** after doing sth
lugar *m* place; ***en ~ de*** instead of; ***en primer ~*** in the first place, first(ly); ***fuera de ~*** out of place; ***yo en tu ~*** if I were you, (if I were) in your place; ***ponte en mi ~*** put yourself in my place; ***dar ~ a*** give rise to; ***tener ~*** take place; ***~ de destino*** posting; ***sin ~ a dudas*** without a doubt
◇ **lugar de autos** JUR scene of the crime; **lugar común** cliché, commonplace; **lugar de los hechos** JUR scene of the crime; **lugar de nacimiento** place of birth
lugareño I *adj* local II *m*, **-a** *f* local
lugarteniente *m/f* deputy
lúgubre *adj* gloomy
lujo *m* luxury; ***de ~*** luxurious, luxury *atr*; ***permitirse el ~ de …*** afford to …; ***¡cómo se permite el ~ de decirme lo que tengo que hacer!*** how dare he tell me what to do!
lujoso *adj* luxurious
lujuria *f* lust
lujurioso I *adj* lecherous II *m*, **-a** *f* lecher
lumbago *m* MED lumbago
lumbar *adj* lumbar; ***vértebra ~*** lumbar vertebra
lumbre *f* fire
lumbrera *f* genius
luminaria *f* REL altar lamp
luminiscencia *f* FÍS luminescence
luminosidad *f* luminosity; *de lámpara, habitación* brightness
luminoso *adj* luminous; *lámpara, habitación* bright
luminotecnia *f* lighting
luminotécnico I *adj* lighting *atr* II *m*, **-a** *f* lighting engineer
luna *f* **1** moon; ***a la luz de la ~*** in the moonlight; ***estar en la ~*** F have one's head in the clouds F; ***pedir la ~*** ask for the moon, ask the impossible; ***quedarse a la ~ de Valencia*** F have one's head in the clouds; ***media ~*** *L.Am.* GASTR croissant **2** *de tienda* window; *de vehículo* windshield, *Br* windscreen
◇ **luna llena** full moon; **luna de miel** honeymoon; **luna nueva** new moon
lunar I *adj* lunar II *m en la piel* mole; ***de ~es*** spotted, polka-dot
lunático *adj* lunatic
lunes *m inv* Monday
◇ **lunes de Pascua** Easter Monday
luneta *f*: ***~ térmica*** AUTO heated windshield, *Br* heated windscreen
lunfardo *m Arg*: *slang used in Buenos*

Aires
lúnula *f* ANAT lunule
lupa *f* magnifying glass; ***mirar algo con ~*** *fig* go through sth with a fine-tooth comb
lúpulo *m* BOT hop
luso **I** *adj* Portuguese **II** *m*, **-a** *f* Portuguese
lustrabotas *m/f inv L.Am.* bootblack
lustrador *m*, **~a** *f L.Am.* bootblack
lustrar ⟨1a⟩ *v/t* polish
lustre *m* **1** shine; ***sacar ~ a algo*** polish sth **2** *fig* luster, *Br* lustre; ***dar ~ a*** *fig* give added luster to
lustro *m* period of five years
lustroso *adj* **1** shiny **2** *fig* healthy-looking
luthier *m* luthier, maker of stringed instruments
luto *m* mourning; ***estar de ~ por alguien*** be in mourning for s.o.; ***llevar ~, ir de ~*** wear mourning, be in mourning
◇ **luto nacional, luto oficial** national *o* official mourning
luxación *f* MED dislocation
luxar ⟨1a⟩ *v/t* dislocate
Luxemburgo *m* Luxemb(o)urg
luxemburgués **I** *adj* of / from Luxemb(o)urg, Luxemb(o)urg *atr* **II** *m*, **-guesa** *f* Luxemb(o)urger
luz *f* light; ***a la ~ del día*** in daylight; ***dar la ~*** turn on the light; ***arrojar ~ sobre algo*** *fig* shed light on s.th.; ***ver la ~*** *de publicación* be published, see the light of day; ***dar a ~*** give birth to; ***sacar a la ~*** *fig* bring to light; ***salir a la ~*** *fig* come to light; ***a todas luces*** evidently, clearly; ***de pocas luces*** *fig* F dim F, not very bright
◇ **luces altas** *L.Am.* AUTO full *o* main beam headlights; **luces bajas** *L.Am.* AUTO dipped headlights; **luces de carretera** AUTO full *o* main beam headlights; **luces cortas, luces de cruce** AUTO dipped headlights; **luces de emergencia** emergency lights; **luces largas** AUTO full *o* main beam headlights; **luz antiniebla** AUTO foglamp; **luz diurna** daylight; **luz intermitente** AUTO turn signal, *Br* indicator (light); **luz de marcha atrás** AUTO reversing light; **luz trasera** AUTO rear light; **luz verde** *tb fig* green light

M

m *abr* (= ***metro***) m (= meter); (= ***minuto***) m (= minute)
maca *f fig* flaw
macabro **I** *adj* macabre **II** *m*, **-a** *f* ghoul
macaco **I** *m* ZO macaque **II** *adj L.Am.* ugly
macana *f L.Am.* **1** (*porra*) billyclub, *Br* truncheon **2** F (*mentira*) lie, fib F; ***hizo / dijo una ~*** he did / said something stupid; ***¡qué ~!*** *Rpl* P what a drag!
macanear ⟨1a⟩ *v/t L.Am.* (*aporrear*) beat
macanudo *adj S.Am.* F great F, fantastic F
macarra **I** *m* P pimp **II** *adj* F: ***ser ~*** be a bastard P
macarrones *mpl* macaroni *sg*
macarrónico *adj* F: ***habla un francés ~*** he speaks atrocious French; ***latín ~*** dog Latin
Macedonia *f* Macedonia
◇ **macedonia de frutas** *f* fruit salad
◇ **macedonia de verduras** *f* green salad
macerar ⟨1a⟩ *v/t* GASTR (*golpear*) tenderize (*by beating*); (*poner en líquido*) macerate
maceta *f* **1** *para plantas* flowerpot **2** TÉC *de metal* club hammer; *de madera* mallet **3** *Méx* F head
macetero *m* **1** *para macetas* flowerpot holder **2** *L.Am. para plantas* flowerpot
machacar ⟨1g⟩ **I** *v/t* **1** (*triturar*) crush **2** *fig* (*vencer*) thrash **3** *en baloncesto* dunk **II** *v/i* **1** (*insistir*) go on (***con*** about) **2** *en baloncesto* dunk
machacón *adj* insistent
machaconería *f* insistence
machamartillo: ***a ~*** firmly
machaque *m en baloncesto* dunk
machetazo *m* blow with a machete
machete *m* machete

machihembrado *m* TÉC tongue and groove
machihembrar ⟨1a⟩ *v/t* TÉC tongue-and-groove
machismo *m* male chauvinism, machismo
machista **I** *adj* sexist **II** *m* sexist, male chauvinist
macho **I** *adj* **1** (*de sexo masculino*) male **2** (*varonil*) tough **3** *desp* macho **II** *m* **1** *animal* male **2** *apelativo* F man F, *Br* mate F **3** *L.Am.* (*plátano*) banana
machota *f desp* F butch woman F
machote F **I** *adj* macho **II** *m* tough guy
macilento *adj* haggard, gaunt
macillo *m* hammer
macis *f inv* mace
macizo **I** *adj madera*, *oro* solid; (*grande*) massive; ***estar ~*** F *hombre*, *mujer* be dishy F **II** *m* GEOG massif
◇ **Macizo de Brasil** Brazilian Highlands *pl*; **Macizo de las Guayanas** Guiana Highlands *pl*; **macizo de flores** flower bed
macro *m* INFOR macro
macrobiótico *adj* macrobiotic
macroeconomía *f* macroeconomics *sg*
macroeconómico *adj* macroeconomic
mácula *f* blemish; ***sin ~*** unblemished
macuto *m* backpack
Madagascar *m* Madagascar
madalena *f* cupcake
madeja *f de lana*, *hilo* hank
madera *f* wood; ***tener ~ de*** *fig* have the makings of; ***tocar ~*** knock on wood, *Br* touch wood; ***¡toca ~!*** knock on wood, *Br* touch wood
maderaje, maderamen *m* lumber, timber
maderería *f* timber merchant
maderero **I** *adj* timber *atr* **II** *m*, **-a** *f* timber merchant
madero *m* P *fig* cop P
madrastra *f* step-mother
madraza *f* doting mother
madre **I** *f* mother; ***dar en la ~ a alguien*** *Méx* F hit s.o. where it hurts; ***sacar a alguien de ~*** F insult s.o. (*by saying rude things about his / her mother*); ***salirse de ~*** *de un río* burst its banks; *fig* F get out of hand; ***esa es la ~ del cordero*** that's the trouble, that's the problem; ***de puta ~*** V fucking fantastic V; ***¡~ mía!*** good heavens!; ***¡me vale ~!*** *Méx* V I don't give a fuck! V **II** *adj Méx*, *C.Am.* F great F, fantastic F
◇ **madre alquilada, madre de alquiler** surrogate mother; **madre patria** *L.Am.* Spain, mother country; **madre política** mother-in-law; **madre soltera** single mother
madreperla *f* mother-of-pearl
madreselva *f* BOT honeysuckle
Madrid *m* Madrid
madriguera *f* **1** (*agujero*) burrow **2** (*guarida*) *tb fig* den
madrileño **I** *adj* of / from Madrid, Madrid *atr* **II** *m*, **-a** *f* native of Madrid
madrina *f* godmother
madrugada *f* **1** *por la noche* early morning; ***a las dos de la ~*** at two in the morning; ***de ~*** in the small hours **2** (*amanecer*) dawn
madrugador **I** *adj*: ***ser ~*** be an early riser **II** *m*, **~a** *f* early riser
madrugar ⟨1h⟩ *v/i* **1** *L.Am.* (*quedarse despierto*) stay up till the small hours **2** (*levantarse temprano*) get up early; ***a quien madruga, Dios le ayuda*** the early bird catches the worm; **madrugarse** *v/r L.Am.* ***~ a alguien*** get in ahead of s.o.
maduración *f* **1** *de persona* maturing **2** *de fruta* ripening
madurar ⟨1a⟩ **I** *v/t fig*: *idea* think through **II** *v/i* **1** *de persona* mature **2** *de fruta* ripen
madurez *f* **1** *mental* maturity **2** *edad* middle age **3** *de fruta* ripeness
maduro *adj* **1** *mentalmente* mature **2** *de edad* middle-aged **3** *fruta* ripe
maestra *f* teacher; ***~ de preescolar*** kindergarten teacher
maestre *m* **1** MAR mate **2**: ***gran ~*** Grand Master
maestría *f* **1** mastery; ***con ~*** skillfully, *Br* skilfully **2** *Méx* EDU master's (degree)
maestro **I** *adj* master *atr* **II** *m* **1** EDU teacher; ***~ de preescolar*** kindergarten teacher **2** *en oficio* master **3** MÚS maestro
◇ **maestro de ceremonias** master of ceremonies, emcee F
◇ **maestro de obras** foreman
mafia *f* mafia
mafioso **I** *adj* mafia *atr* **II** *m de la Mafia* mafioso; (*gángster*) gangster
magazine *m* magazine

magdalena *f* cupcake; ***llorar como una ~*** *fig* F cry one's eyes out
magenta *m* MIN magenta
magia *f tb fig* magic
◇ **magia negra** black magic
mágico *adj* **1** *truco, varita* magic **2** *lugar, momento* magical
magisterio *m* teaching profession
magistrado *m*, **-a** *f* judge
magistral *adj* masterly
magistratura *f* magistracy
magma *m* GEOL magma
magnanimidad *f* magnanimity
magnánimo *adj* magnanimous
magnate *m* magnate, tycoon
magnesia *f* magnesia
magnesio *m* QUÍM magnesium
magnético *adj* magnetic
magnetismo *m* magnetism
magnetizar ⟨1f⟩ *v/t* **1** magnetize **2** *fig* (*fascinar*) mesmerize
magneto *m* AUTO magneto
magnetofón, magnetófono *m* tape recorder
magnetoscopio *m* VCR, video (cassette recorder)
magnicidio *m* assassination
magnificar ⟨1g⟩ *v/t fig* praise, extol
magnificencia *f* magnificence
magnífico *adj* wonderful, magnificent
magnitud *f* magnitude; ***de primera ~*** *fig* full-scale, of the first magnitude
magno *adj fig* great
magnolia *f* BOT magnolia
mago I *m* magician; (*brujo*) wizard; *fig* magician, wizard **II** *adj*: ***los Reyes Magos*** the Three Wise Men, the Three Kings
magrear ⟨1a⟩ *v/t* F feel up F
Magreb *m* Maghreb
magrebí *adj* of / from the Maghreb, Maghreb *atr*
magreo *m* F feel-up F
magro *adj* **I** *carne* lean **II** *m* loin
magulladura *f* bruise
magullar ⟨1a⟩ *v/t* bruise
magullón *m L.Am.* bruise
maharajá *m* maharaja
mahometano I *adj* Muslim, Moslem **II** *m*, **-a** *f* Muslim, Moslem
mahonesa *f* mayonnaise
mailing *m* mass mailing, mailshot
maillot *m* DEP jersey
maître *m* maitre d'
maíz *m* corn, *Br* maize
maizal *m* cornfield, *Br* field of maize
majada *f CSur* flock of sheep
majaderear ⟨1a⟩ *L.Am.* F **I** *v/t* bug F **II** *v/i* keep going on F
majadería *f*: ***decir / hacer una ~*** say / do sth stupid
majadero F **I** *adj* idiotic, stupid **II** *m*, **-a** *f* idiot
majar ⟨1a⟩ *v/t* crush
majareta *adj* F nutty F, screwy F
maje *adj Méx* F silly
majestad *f* majesty
majestuosidad *f* majesty
majestuoso *adj* majestic
majeza *f* **1** (*simpatía*) charm, pleasant character **2** (*belleza*) beauty
majo I *adj* F nice; (*bonito*) pretty **II** *m*, **-a** *f*: ***¿qué tal estás, ~?*** how are you (buddy, *Br* mate)?; ***¿qué quieres, maja?*** what can I do for you (honey, *Br* love)?
majorero *adj* of / from Fuerteventura, Fuerteventura *atr*
majuelo *m* BOT hawthorn
mal I *adj* ☞ ***malo***
II *adv* badly; ***~ que bien*** one way or the other; ***¡no está ~!*** it isn't bad!; ***¡menos ~!*** thank goodness!; ***no hay ~ que por bien no venga*** every cloud has a silver lining; ***hacer ~ en hacer algo*** be wrong to do sth; ***ir de ~ en peor*** go from bad to worse; ***estar a ~ con alguien*** be on bad terms with s.o.; ***hablar ~ de alguien*** speak ill of s.o.; ***poner ~ a alguien*** criticize s.o.; ***ponerse a ~ con alguien*** fall out with s.o.; ***tomarse algo a ~*** take sth badly; ***ponerse ~*** get sick
III *m* MED illness; ***el ~ menor*** the lesser of two evils
◇ **mal de altura** altitude sickness; **mal de amores** lovesickness; **mal de mar** seasickness; **mal de ojo** evil eye
malabar *m/adj*: (***juegos***) ***~es*** *pl* juggling *sg*
malabarismo *m* juggling; ***hacer ~s*** juggle; ***hacer ~s con algo*** juggle sth
malabarista *m/f* juggler
malaconsejado *adj* ill-advised
malacostumbrado *adj* (*mimado*) spoiled, pampered; ***está muy ~*** (*tiene malos hábitos*) he has some very bad habits
malacrianza *f L.Am.* rudeness
malagueño *adj* of / from Malaga, Ma-

laga *atr*
malandanza *f* misfortune
malaria *f* MED malaria
Malasia *f* Malaysia
malasio I *adj* Malaysian **II** *m*,**-a** *f* Malaysian
malasombra I *adj* tiresome **II** *m/f* nuisance
malaventura *f* misfortune
malaventurado *adj* unfortunate
malayo I *adj* Malay **II** *m*,**-a** *f* Malay **III** *m idioma* Malay
malbaratar ⟨1a⟩ *v/t* sell at a loss
malcarado *adj* ugly
malcasado *adj* unhappily married
malcomer ⟨2a⟩ *v/i* eat badly
malcontento *adj* discontented
malcriadez *f L.Am.* bad upbringing
malcriado *adj* spoilt
malcrianza *f L.Am.* rudeness
malcriar ⟨1c⟩ *v/t* spoil
maldad *f* evil; ***es una ~ hacer eso*** it's a wicked thing to do
maldecir ⟨3p⟩ **I** *v/i* curse; ***~ de alguien*** speak ill of s.o. **II** *v/t* curse
maldiciente I *adj* slanderous **II** *m/f* slanderer
maldición *f* curse
maldispuesto *adj* ill-disposed
maldito *adj* F damn F; ***¡-a sea!*** (god-) damn it!
maleable *adj* malleable
maleante *m/f & adj* criminal
malear ⟨1a⟩ *v/t* corrupt; **malearse** *v/r* go bad
malecón *m* **1** (*rompeolas*) breakwater **2** *C.Am., Cuba: área* seafront
maledicencia *f* slander
maleducado *adj* rude, bad-mannered
maleducar ⟨1g⟩ *v/t* spoil
maleficio *m* curse
maléfico *adj* evil
malentender ⟨2a⟩ *v/t* misunderstand
malentendido *m* misunderstanding
malestar *m* **1** MED discomfort **2** *entre grupo de personas* malaise **3** *social* unrest
maleta I *f* **1** bag, suitcase; ***hacer la ~*** pack one's bags **2** *L.Am.* AUTO trunk, *Br* boot **II** *m/f* F DEP: ***era un ~*** he was hopeless
maletera *f Andes* trunk, *Br* boot
maletero *m* trunk, *Br* boot
maletilla *m* TAUR would-be bullfighter
maletín *m* briefcase
malevolencia *f* malevolence
malévolo *adj* malevolent
maleza *f* undergrowth
malformación *f* MED malformation
malgache *m/f & adj* Madagascan, Malagasy
malgastar ⟨1a⟩ *v/t* waste
malgenioso *adj Méx* bad-tempered
malhablado *adj* foul-mouthed
malhadado *adj lit* ill-fated
malhechor *m*, **~a** *f* criminal
malherir ⟨3i⟩ *v/t* hurt badly
malhumorado *adj* bad-tempered
malicia *f* **1** (*mala intención*) malice; ***no tener ~*** F be very naive **2** (*astucia*) cunning, slyness
maliciar ⟨1b⟩ *v/t* suspect; **maliciarse** *v/r* suspect
malicioso *adj* **1** (*malintencionado*) malicious **2** (*astuto*) cunning, sly
malignidad *f* **1** (*maldad*) harmfulness **2** MED malignancy
maligno *adj* **1** (*malicioso*) harmful **2** MED malignant
malinchismo *m Méx* treason
malintencionado *adj* malicious
malinterpretar ⟨1a⟩ *v/t* misinterpret
malísimo *adj sup* (*malo*) very bad
malla *f* **1** *de metal, plástico* mesh **2** *Rpl* (*bañador*) swimsuit **3**: **~s** *pl* pantyhose, *Br* tights
◇ **malla metálica** *de armadura* chain mail
Mallorca *f* Majorca
mallorquín I *adj* Majorcan **II** *m*,**-quina** *f* Majorcan **III** *m idioma* Majorcan
malmandado *adj* disobedient
malnacido I *adj* swinish **II** *m*,**-a** *f* swine
malnutrición *f* malnutrition
malnutrido *adj* malnourished
malo I *adj* **1** bad **2** *calidad* poor **3** (*enfermo*) sick, ill; ***ponerse ~*** get sick, fall ill **4**: ***por las buenas o por las -as*** whether he / she *etc* likes it or not; ***estar de -as*** be in a bad mood; ***por las -as*** by force; ***andar a -as con alguien*** be on bad terms with s.o.; ***lo ~ es que*** unfortunately **II** *m hum* bad guy, baddy
malogrado *adj* **1** *muerto* dead before one's time; *plan* failed **2** *Andes* broken-down
malograr ⟨1a⟩ *v/t* **1** *tiempo* waste **2** *tra-*

bajo spoil, ruin; **malograrse** *v/r* **1** fail **2** *de plan* come to nothing **3** *fallecer* die before one's time, die young **4** *S.Am.* (*descomponerse*) break down; (*funcionar mal*) go wrong
maloliente *adj* stinking
malparado *adj*: ***quedar*** *o* ***salir ~ de algo*** come out badly from sth
malparido P ☞ ***malnacido***
malpensado *adj*: ***ser ~*** have a nasty mind
malquerencia *f* dislike
malquerer ⟨2u⟩ *v/t* dislike
malquistarse ⟨1a⟩ *v/r* fall out (***con*** with)
malsano *adj* unhealthy
malsonante *adj* rude
malta *f* malt
Malta *f* Malta
maltear ⟨1a⟩ *v/t* malt
maltés I *adj* Maltese **II** *m*,**-esa** *f* Maltese **III** *m idioma* Maltese
maltosa *f* maltose
maltratamiento *m* ill-treatment, abuse
maltratar ⟨1a⟩ *v/t* ill-treat, mistreat
maltrato *m* ill-treatment, mistreatment
maltrecho *adj cosa* damaged; ***dejar ~*** *persona, salud* weaken, damage; ***quedar ~*** *de persona, salud* be weakened, be damaged
malva I *adj* mauve **II** *f* BOT mallow; ***estar criando ~s*** *fig* F be pushing up daisies; ***ser*** (***como***) ***una ~*** *fig* be as gentle as a lamb
malvado I *adj* evil **II** *m*, **-a** *f* evil man; *mujer* evil woman
malvasía *f uva* malvasia
malvavisco *m* BOT marshmallow
malvender ⟨2a⟩ *v/t*: ***~ algo*** sell sth off cheap
malversación *f*: ***~ de fondos*** embezzlement
malversar ⟨1a⟩ *v/t* embezzle
Malvinas: ***las ~*** the Falklands, the Falkland Islands
malvivir ⟨3a⟩ *v/i* scrape by
mama *f* breast
mamá *f* mom, *Br* mum
◇ **mamá grande** *Méx* F grandma
mamada *f* **1** F *de leche materna* feed **2** *S.Am.* (*embriaguez*) binge **3**: ***decir ~s*** *Méx* F talk garbage F
mamadera *f L.Am.* feeding bottle
mamar ⟨1a⟩ *v/i* suck; ***dar de ~ a*** (breast)-feed; **mamarse** *v/r* F get drunk, get sloshed F
mamario *adj* mammary; ***glándula -a*** mammary gland
mamarrachada *f* F mess
mamarracho *m*,**-a** *f*: ***vas hecho un ~*** F *persona* you look a mess F; ***ser un ~ / una -a*** (*chapuza*) look a mess; (*extravagancia*) look ridiculous
mameluco *m L.Am. para niño* rompers *pl*; *para obrero* coveralls *pl*, *Br* overalls *pl*
mamífero *m* mammal
mamila *f Méx* feeding bottle
mamografía *f* MED mammography
mamón I *adj Méx* P cocky F **II** *m* P bastard P
mamona *f* P bitch P
mamotreto *m* F *libro* hefty tome
mampara *f* screen
mamparo *m* MAR bulkhead
mamporro *m* F punch; ***darse un ~ contra algo*** wallop o.s. against sth
mampostería *f* masonry
mamut *m* ZO mammoth
maná *m fig* manna
manada *f de elefantes, ciervos* herd; *de lobos* pack; *fig*: *de gente* herd
manantial *m* **1** spring **2** *fig* (*origen*) source
manar ⟨1a⟩ *v/i de líquidos, ideas* flow
manatí *m* ZO manatee
manazas *m/f inv*: ***ser un ~*** F be ham-handed F, *Br* be ham-fisted
mancebo *m* youth
mancera *f* AGR plow handle, *Br* plough handle
mancha *f* **1** *de suciedad* (dirty) mark; *de grasa, sangre etc* stain **2** *fig*: *en reputación* blot; ***sin ~s*** spotless
Mancha: ***Canal de la ~*** English Channel; ***la ~*** La Mancha
manchado *adj* stained
manchar ⟨1a⟩ *v/t* get dirty; *de grasa, sangre etc* stain; **mancharse** *v/r* get dirty
manchego I *adj* of / from La Mancha, La Mancha *atr* **II** *m*: (***queso***) ***~*** Manchego cheese
mancilla *f* blemish; ***sin ~*** immaculate, unblemished
mancillar ⟨1a⟩ *v/t fig* sully
manco *adj de mano* one-handed; *de brazo* one-armed; ***no ser*** *o* ***quedarse***

~ *fig* F be pretty useful
mancomunar ⟨1a⟩ *v/t* combine; **mancomunarse** *v/r* join together
mancomunidad *f* association; ***la Mancomunidad Británica*** the (British) Commonwealth
mancornas *fpl Pe, Bol* cufflinks
mancuernas *fpl* **1** *C.Am.* cufflinks **2** DEP weights, dumbbells
mandadero *m Rpl* errand boy
mandado I *m* **1** (*recado*) errand **2** *Méx, C.Am.* ***los ~s*** *pl* the shopping *sg* **II** *m*, **-a** *f* subordinate **II** *Méx* F: ***es muy ~*** he's always taking advantage!; ***¡no sea ~, quieto con las manos!*** you're going too far, keep your hands to yourself!
mandamás *m/f inv* F big shot F
mandamiento *m* **1** (*orden*) order **2** JUR warrant **3** REL commandment; ***los Diez Mandamientos*** the Ten Commandments
mandanga *f*: **~*s*** *pl* garbage *sg* F, *Br* rubbish *sg* F; ***tener ~*** F be very laidback; ***tiene una ~ que no veas*** F he's so amazingly laidback, he's Mr. Cool F
mandar ⟨1a⟩ **I** *v/t* **1** (*ordenar*) order; ***a mí no me manda nadie*** nobody tells me what to do; ***~ hacer algo*** have sth done **2** (*enviar*) send **II** *v/i* **1** be in charge **2**: ***¿mande?*** (*¿cómo?*) what did you say?, excuse me?; *Méx* can I help you?; *Méx* TELEC hallo?
mandarín *m* HIST mandarin
mandarina *f* mandarin (orange)
mandatario *m* leader; ***primer ~*** *Méx* President
mandato *m* **1** (*orden*) order **2** POL mandate
mandíbula *f* ANAT jaw; ***reírse a ~ batiente*** laugh one's head off F
mandil *m* leather apron
mandioca *f* cassava
mando *m* command; ***alto ~*** high command; ***~ a distancia*** TV remote control; ***cuadro de ~s*** AVIA instrument panel; ***tablero de ~s*** AUTO dashboard; ***estar al ~ de*** be in charge of
mandolina *f* MÚS mandolin
mandón I *adj* bossy **II** *m*, **-ona** *f* bossy person
mandrágora *f* BOT mandrake
mandril *m* **1** ZO mandrill **2** TÉC mandrel
manduca *f* F food, grub F
manducar F ⟨1g⟩ **I** *v/t* scoff F **II** *v/i* stuff o.s. F
manecilla *f de reloj* hand
manejabilidad *f* maneuverability, *Br* manoeuvrability
manejable *adj* **1** *objeto* easy to handle **2** *automóvil* maneuverable, *Br* manoeuvrable
manejar ⟨1a⟩ **I** *v/t* **1** handle **2** *máquina* operate **3** *negocio* manage, run **4** *L.Am.* AUTO drive **II** *v/i L.Am.* AUTO drive; **manejarse** *v/r* **1** manage, get by; ***manejárselas*** F manage, get by F **2** (*comportarse*) behave
manejo *m* **1** *de situación* handling **2** *de una máquina* operation; ***de fácil ~*** easy to use **3** *de un negocio* management, running **4**: **~*s*** *pl* scheming *sg*, machinations
manera *f* way; ***esa es su ~ de ser*** that's the way he is; **~*s*** *pl* manners; ***lo hace a su ~*** he does it his way; ***a ~ de*** like; ***un cuadro a la ~ de los cubistas*** a Cubist-style picture; ***no hay ~ de*** it is impossible to; ***de mala ~*** *tratar* badly; *responder* rudely; ***de ~ que*** so (that); ***de ninguna ~*** certainly not; ***en gran ~*** greatly; ***sobre ~*** exceedingly; ***de todas ~s*** anyway, in any case; ***de alguna ~*** somehow; ***de cualquier ~*** anyway, anyhow; ***de la misma ~ que*** in the same way that; ***de otra ~*** if not; ***de tal ~ que*** in such a way that, so that
manga *f* **1** *de camisa* sleeve; ***sin ~s*** sleeveless; ***de ~ corta / larga*** short-sleeved / long-sleeved; ***en ~s de camisa*** in shirtsleeves; ***traer algo en la ~*** F have sth up one's sleeve; ***sacarse algo de la ~*** *fig* make sth up; ***sacarse un as de la ~*** *fig* pull a rabbit out of the hat; ***tener*** *o* ***ser de ~ ancha*** *fig* be (too) lenient **2** TÉC hose
◇ **manga de agua** heavy shower; **manga pastelera** GASTR pastry bag; **manga de riego** hosepipe; **manga de viento** windsock
manganeso *m* manganese
mangante *m/f* P thief
mangar ⟨1h⟩ *v/t* P swipe F, *Br tb* pinch F
manglar *m* BOT mangrove swamp
mangle *m* BOT mangrove
mango *m* **1** *de instrumento, utensilio etc* handle **2** BOT mango **3** *CSur* F (*dinero*) dough F, cash; ***estoy sin un ~*** *CSur* F I'm broke F, I don't have a bean F **4**

M

L.Am. F *tío bueno* good-looking guy F; *tía buena* good-looking girl *o* chick F
mangoneador F **I** *adj* **1** (*mandón*) bossy F **2** (*entrometido*) nosey F **II** *m*, **~a** *f* **1** (*mandón*) bossy person F **2** (*entrometido*) nosey parker F
mangonear ⟨1a⟩ F **I** *v/i* **1** boss people around **2** (*entrometerse*) meddle **II** *v/t*: ***~ a alguien*** boss s.o. around
mangoneo *m* **1** F bossiness F **2** F (*entrometimiento*) nosiness F
mangosta *f* ZO mongoose
manguera *f* hose(pipe)
mangui *m/f* P thief
manguito *m* TÉC sleeve; ***~s*** *pl para nadar* waterwings, armbands
mani *f* P demo F
maní *m S.Am.* peanut
manía *f* **1** (*costumbre*) habit, mania; ***tiene sus -s*** she has her little ways **2** (*antipatía*) dislike; ***tener ~ a alguien*** F have it in for s.o. F **3** (*obsesión*) obsession ◇ **manía persecutoria** persecution complex
maniaco I *adj* maniacal **II** *m*, **-a** *f* maniac ◇ **maniaco sexual** sex maniac
maniacodepresivo *adj* MED manic-depressive
maniatar ⟨1a⟩ *v/t*: ***~ a alguien*** *tb fig* tie s.o.'s hands
maniático I *adj* F fussy **II** *m*, **-a** *f* fusspot; ***es un ~ de la limpieza*** he has an obsession with cleaning, he's a cleaning freak F
manicomio *m* lunatic asylum
manicorto *adj* stingy
manicura *f* manicure; ***hacerse la ~*** have a manicure
manicuro *m*, **-a** *f* manicurist
manido *adj fig* clichéd, done to death F
manierismo *m* Mannerism
manierista I *adj* mannerist **II** *m/f* mannerist
manifestación *f* **1** *de gente* demonstration **2** (*muestra*) show **3** (*declaración*) statement
manifestante *m/f* demonstrator
manifestar ⟨1k⟩ *v/t* **1** (*demostrar*) show **2** (*declarar*) declare, state; **manifestarse** *v/r* **1** (*protestar*) demonstrate **2** (*aparecer*) become apparent
manifiesto I *adj* clear, manifest; ***poner de ~*** make clear **II** *m* manifesto
manigua *f Carib* thicket, bush
manija *f L.Am.* (*asa*) handle, crank
manilla *f* **1** *de reloj* hand **2** *de puerta* handle
manillar *m* handlebars *pl*
maniobra *f* maneuver, *Br* manoeuvre; ***~s*** MIL maneuvers, *Br* manoeuvres; ***hacer ~s*** maneuver, *Br* manoeuvre
maniobrabilidad *f* maneuverability, *Br* manoeuvrability
maniobrable *adj* maneuverable, *Br* manoeuvrable
maniobrar ⟨1a⟩ *v/i* maneuver, *Br* manoeuvre
manipulable *adj* manipulable, manipulatable
manipulación *f* **1** *de información*, *persona* manipulation **2** (*manejo*) handling
manipular ⟨1a⟩ *v/t* **1** *información*, *persona* manipulate **2** (*manejar*) handle
maniquí I *m* dummy **II** *m/f* model
manirroto I *adj* extravagant **II** *m*, **-a** *f* spendthrift
manisero *m*, **-a** *f Carib*, *S.Am.* peanut seller
manitas I *m/f inv* F: ***ser un ~*** be handy **II** *fpl*: ***hacer ~*** make out F, neck F
manito *m Méx* pal, buddy
manivela *f* handle
manjar *m* delicacy
mano I *f* **1** ANAT hand; *de animal* paw; (***dispositivo***) ***~s libres*** TELEC hands-free (kit); ***¡~s arriba!*** hands up!; ***lo hicieron ~ a ~*** they did it between them; ***un ~ a ~*** a contest; ***de ~ en ~*** from hand to hand; ***a cuatro ~s*** MÚS for four hands; ***a ~ derecha / izquierda*** on the right / lefthand side; ***a ~s llenas*** *fig* generously; ***con las ~s vacías*** *fig* empty-handed; ***ser ~ de santo*** work wonders; ***bajo ~*** on the quiet; ***de segunda ~*** second-hand; ***de primera ~*** first-hand; ***ser la ~ derecha de alguien*** *fig* be s.o.'s right hand; ***tener mucha ~ izquierda*** be very skillful *o Br* skilful; ***atar las ~s a alguien*** *fig* tie s.o.'s hands; ***dejado de la ~ de Dios*** *fig* godforsaken; ***echar ~ a*** F grab; ***echar ~ de*** *fig* use, make use of; ***echar una ~ a alguien*** give s.o. a hand; ***estar a ~s*** *L.Am.* F be even, be quits; ***hecho a ~*** handmade; ***llegar*** *o* ***venir a las ~s*** come to blows; ***pedir la ~ de alguien*** ask for s.o.'s hand in marriage; ***poner la***

~ en el fuego *fig* swear to it; **poner ~s a la obra** get down to work; **se le fue la ~ con** *fig* he overdid it with; **tender la ~ a alguien** *fig* hold out a helping hand to s.o.; **tener a ~** have to hand; **tener buena / mala ~ para (hacer) algo** be good / bad at (doing) sth; **con ~ dura** *o* **de hierro** with a firm hand *o* with an iron fist; **estar en buenas ~s** be in good hands; **lo dejo en sus ~s** I'll leave it in your hands; **traerse algo entre ~s** be plotting sth; **alzar** *o* **levantar la ~ contra** *o* **a alguien** raise one's hand to s.o.; **llevarse las ~s a la cabeza** *fig* throw up one's hands (in horror); **andar cogidos de la ~** walk hand in hand; **tomar a alguien de la ~** take s.o. by the hand, take s.o.'s hand; **meter ~ a alguien** F feel s.o. up F, grope s.o. F; **dar la última ~ a algo** finish sth off **II** *m Méx* F pal F, buddy F
◇ **mano de obra** labor, *Br* labour, manpower
◇ **mano de pintura** coat of paint
manojo *m* handful; **~ de llaves** bunch of keys; **~ de nervios** *fig* bundle of nerves
manómetro *m* pressure gauge, manometer
manopla *f* mitten
◇ **manopla de baño** washcloth, *Br* facecloth
manoseado *adj* **1** *libro* well-thumbed **2** *tema* well-worn, hackneyed
manosear ⟨1a⟩ *v/t* **1** *fruta* handle **2** *persona* F grope F
manotada *f* slap
manotazo *m* slap
manotear ⟨1a⟩ *Arg, Méx* **I** *v/t* grab **II** *v/i* wave one's hands around
mansalva *f*: **a ~** *gente* in vast numbers; *bebida, comida* in vast amounts
mansarda *f* attic
mansedumbre *f* **1** *de animal* docility **2** *de persona* mildness
mansión *f* mansion
manso I *adj* **1** *animal* docile **2** *persona* mild **II** *m gentle-natured bull, ram etc that leads the herd, flock etc*
manta *f* **I** blanket; **a ~** F in abundance; **tirar de la ~** *fig* uncover the truth; **liarse la ~ a la cabeza** *fig* F throw caution to the wind **II** *m/f*: **ser un ~** F *fig* be a lazy so-and-so F
◇ **manta eléctrica** electric blanket

manteca *f* **1** (*grasa*) fat **2** *Rpl* butter
◇ **manteca de cacao** cocoa butter
◇ **manteca de cerdo** lard
mantecado *m* GASTR *type of cupcake, traditionally eaten at Christmas*
mantecoso *adj* greasy
mantel *m* tablecloth; **~ individual** table mat
mantelería *f* table linen; **una ~** a set of table linen
mantención *f L.Am.* ☞ **manutención**
mantener ⟨2l⟩ *v/t* **1** (*sujetar*) hold; *techo etc* hold up **2** (*preservar*) keep **3** *conversación, relación* have **4** *económicamente* support **5** (*afirmar*) maintain; **mantenerse** *v/r* **1** (*sujetarse*) be held **2** *económicamente* support o.s. **3** *en forma* keep
mantenimiento *m* **1** *de edificio, paz* maintenance **2** *económico* support **3**: **gimnasia de ~** keep-fit
mantequera *f* churn
mantequería *f* dairy
mantequilla *f* butter
mantequillera *f L.Am.* butter dish
mantilla *f de mujer* mantilla; **estar en ~s** *fig* F be in its infancy
mantillo *m* humus
manto *m* **1** GEOL layer, stratum **2** (*capa*) cloak; **un ~ de nieve** a blanket of snow
mantón *m* shawl
mantuvo *vb* ☞ **mantener**
manual *m/adj* manual
manualidades *fpl* handicrafts
manubrio *m* **1** (*manija*) handle **2** *S.Am.* handlebars *pl*
manufactura *f* manufacture
manufacturar ⟨1a⟩ *v/t* manufacture
manumisión *f* HIST emancipation, manumission *fml*
manumitir ⟨3a⟩ *v/t fml* emancipate, manumit *fml*
manuscrito I *adj* handwritten **II** *m* manuscript
manutención *f* maintenance
manzana *f* **1** BOT apple; **~ asada** GASTR baked apple **2** *de casas* block
◇ **manzana de Adán** ANAT Adam's apple
◇ **manzana de la discordia** *fig* bone of contention
manzanilla *f* camomile tea
manzano *m* apple tree
maña *f* **1** (*habilidad*) skill; **darse** *o* **tener**

~ para be good at **2** *desp* (*astucia*) guile; ***tiene muchas ~s*** *L.Am.* she's got lots of tricks up her sleeve F
mañana I *f* morning; ***por la ~*** in the morning; ***~ por la ~*** tomorrow morning; ***de la ~ a la noche*** from morning until night; ***de la noche a la ~*** *fig* overnight; ***esta ~*** this morning; ***muy de ~*** very early (in the morning)
II *adv* tomorrow; ***pasado ~*** the day after tomorrow; ***~ será otro día*** tomorrow is another day; ***no dejes para ~ lo que puedas hacer hoy*** don't put off till tomorrow what you can do today
mañanero *adj* morning *atr*; ***ser ~*** be an early riser
mañanita *f* shawl
mañero *adj Rpl* (*animal*: *terco*) stubborn; (*nervioso*) skittish, nervous
maño F **I** *m*, **-a** *f* Aragonese **II** *adj* Aragonese
mañoso *adj* **1** (*habilidoso*) skillful, *Br* skilful **2** *desp* (*astuto*) crafty **3** *L.Am. animal* stubborn
mapa *m* map; ***desaparecer del ~*** F disappear off the face of the earth
◇ **mapa de carreteras** road map; **mapa mudo** skeleton map, outline map; **mapa del tiempo** weather map
mapache *m* raccoon
mapamundi *m* map of the world
maqueta *f* **1** *de edificio*, *barco* model **2** TIP dummy
maquetista *m/f* TIP compositor, page make-up artist
maquiavélico *adj tb fig* Machiavellian
maquillador *m*, **~a** *f* make-up artist
maquillaje *m* make-up
maquillar ⟨1a⟩ *v/t* make up; **maquillarse** *v/r* put on one's make-up
máquina *f* **1** machine **2** FERR locomotive; ***a toda ~*** at top speed **3** *C.Am.*, *Carib* car **4**: ***pasar algo a ~*** type sth
◇ **máquina de afeitar** (electric) shaver; **máquina de coser** sewing machine; **máquina de escribir** portable typewriter; **máquina expendedora de bebidas / billetes / tabaco** drinks / ticket / cigarette machine; **máquina fotográfica, máquina de fotos** camera; **máquina herramienta** machine tool; **máquina recreativa** arcade game; **máquina de vapor** steam locomotive, *Br* steam engine
maquinaciones *fpl* scheming *sg*
maquinador I *adj* scheming **II** *m*, **~a** *f* schemer
maquinal *adj fig* mechanical
maquinar ⟨1a⟩ *v/t* plot
maquinaria *f* machinery
◇ **maquinilla de afeitar** *f* razor
◇ **maquinilla eléctrica** *f* electric razor
maquinista *m/f* FERR engineer, *Br* train driver
mar *m* (*also f*) GEOG sea; ***los ~es del Sur*** the South Seas; ***alta ~*** high seas *pl*; ***sudaba a ~es*** *fig* F the sweat was pouring off him F; ***llover a ~es*** *fig* F pour, bucket down F; ***la ~ de bien*** (*muy bien*) really well; ***hacerse a la ~*** put to sea
◇ **mar Bermejo** Gulf of California; **mar Caribe** Caribbean Sea; **mar de fondo** ground swell; **mar interior** inland sea; **mar Muerto** Dead Sea; **mar Negro** Black Sea; **mar del Norte** North Sea; **mar Rojo** Red Sea
marabunta *f* F mob, gang; ***~ turística*** swarm of tourists
maraca *f* MÚS maraca
maracuyá *m* BOT passion fruit
marajá *m* maharaja
maraña *f* **1** *de hilos* tangle **2** (*lío*) jumble
marañero *m*, **-a** *f* troublemaker
marasmo *m fig* stagnation
maratón *m* (*also f*) marathon
maratoniano *adj* marathon *atr*
maravilla *f* **1** (*portento*) marvel, wonder; ***de ~*** marvelously, *Br* marvellously, wonderfully; ***a las mil ~s*** marvelously, wonderfully **2** BOT marigold
maravillar ⟨1a⟩ *v/t* amaze, astonish; **maravillarse** *v/r* be amazed *o* astonished (***de*** at)
maravilloso *adj* marvelous, *Br* marvellous, wonderful
marbellí *adj* of / from Marbella, Marbella *atr*
marca *f* **1** (*señal*) mark **2** MED scar, mark **3** COM brand; ***de ~*** brand-name *atr* **4** DEP score; ***batir** o **superar una ~*** break a record; ***mejor ~ personal*** personal best; ***sus 9,93 segundos son la segunda mejor ~*** his 9.93 seconds is the second best time; ***de ~ mayor*** *fig* tremendous
◇ **marca de calidad** top brand; **marca de fábrica** trademark; **marca de fuego**

en res brand; **marca registrada** registered trademark
marcación *f* MAR bearing
marcado *adj* marked
marcador *m* **1** DEP scoreboard **2** (*rotulador*) marker pen
◇ **marcador fluorescente** highlighter
marcaje *m* DEP marking
marcapasos *m inv* MED pacemaker
marcar ⟨1g⟩ *v/t* **1** mark **2** *número de teléfono* dial **3** *gol* score **4** *res* brand **5** *de termómetro, contador etc* read, register **6** *naipes* mark **7** *fig*: *persona* affect **8** *en fútbol etc* mark; **marcarse** *v/r*: ***~ unos pasos de baile*** have a dance
marcha *f* **1** (*salida*) departure
2 (*velocidad*) speed; ***a toda ~*** at top speed; ***a ~s forzadas*** *fig* flat out
3 (*avance*) progress; ***hacer algo sobre la ~*** do sth as one goes along
4 MIL march
5 DEP walk; ***~ a pie*** *en manifestación* march
6 AUTO gear
7 *de máquina* running; ***estar en ~*** (*estar en funcionamiento*) be working, be running; *de coche* be moving; ***bajarse del tren en ~*** get off the train while it is moving; ***poner en ~*** set in motion; ***ponerse en ~*** get started, get going
8 MÚS march
9 *Esp*: ***tener mucha ~*** F be very lively; ***aquí hay mucha ~*** F this place is cool F; ***ir de ~*** F go out partying F
◇ **marcha atrás** AUTO reverse (gear); ***dar ~*** go into reverse; *fig* backpedal
◇ **marcha fúnebre** MÚS dead march
marchador *m*, **~a** *f* walker
marchamo *m* **1** *en aduana* label **2** *fig* stamp
marchante *m/f L.Am. cliente* regular customer
marchantería *f* merchandise
marchar ⟨1a⟩ *v/i* **1** (*progresar*) go **2** (*funcionar*) work **3** (*caminar*) walk **4** MIL march; **marcharse** *v/r* leave, go
marchitamiento *m* withering
marchitarse ⟨1a⟩ *v/r* wilt
marchito *adj* **1** *flor* withered **2** *juventud, lozanía* faded
marchoso *adj* F lively
marcial *adj* martial; ***artes ~es*** martial arts
marciano *m/adj* Martian
marco *m* **1** *moneda* mark **2** *de cuadro, puerta* frame **3** *fig* framework
marea *f* tide; *fig*: *de gente* sea
◇ **marea alta** high tide; **marea baja** low tide; **marea negra** oil slick; **marea viva** spring tide
mareado *adj*: ***estoy ~*** I feel nauseous, *Br* I feel sick; *sin equilibrio* I feel dizzy
marear ⟨1a⟩ **I** *v/t* **1** make feel nauseous, *Br* make feel sick **2** *fig* (*confundir*) confuse **II** *v/i* navigate; **marearse** *v/r* feel nauseous, *Br* feel sick; ***me mareo*** *en barco, avión etc* I get nauseous; *sin equilibrio* I get dizzy
marejada *f* heavy sea
marejadilla *f* slight swell
maremagno, maremágnum *m* mountain
maremoto *m* tidal wave
marengo *adj*: ***gris ~*** dark gray, *Br* dark grey
mareo *m* **1** *por movimiento del barco* seasickness **2** F (*fastidio*) pain F
marfil *m* ivory; **(*de color*) ~** ivory *atr*
marfileño *adj* ivory *atr*
margarina *f* margarine
margarita *f* **1** BOT daisy; ***estar criando ~s*** F be pushing up daisies F; ***deshojar la ~*** *fig* play 'she loves me, she loves me not'; ***echar ~s a los puercos*** cast pearls before swine **2** TÉC daisy wheel
margen *m tb fig* margin; ***al ~ de eso*** apart from that; ***mantenerse al ~*** keep out
◇ **margen de beneficios** profit margin; **margen comercial** margin; **margen de error** margin of error
margen *f de río* bank
marginación *f* marginalization
marginado **I** *adj* marginalized **II** *m*, **-a** *f* social outcast; ***~s sociales*** social outcasts, people on the fringes of society
marginal *adj* marginal; ***nota ~*** note in the margin
marginar ⟨1a⟩ *v/t* marginalize
maría *f* **1** → ***maruja*** **2** (*marihuana*) grass F, marijuana **3** *asignatura* easy option F
mariachi **I** *m* mariachi band **II** *m/f* mariachi player
mariano *adj* REL Marian
marica *m* F fag P, *Br* poof P
Maricastaña: ***en tiempos de ~*** F in the stone age F
maricón *m* P fag P, *Br* poof P

mariconada *f* P dirty trick F
maridaje *m fig* (good) combination
marido *m* husband
mariguana *f Méx* marijuana
marihuana *f* marijuana
marimacho *m* **1** F (*machota*) butch woman **2** P (*lesbiana*) dyke P
marimandón *m*, **-ona** *f* F domineering person, bossy-boots *sg* F
marimba *f* MÚS marimba
marimorena *f* F row F, fuss F; ***armar la ~*** kick up a row F, kick up a fuss F
marina *f* navy
◇ **marina mercante** merchant marine, *Br* merchant navy
marinada *f* GASTR marinade
marinar ⟨1a⟩ *v/t* GASTR marinade
marinería *f* **1** *profesión* sailing **2** (*conjunto de marineros*) sailors *pl*; (*tripulación*) crew
marinero I *adj* sea *atr* **II** *m* sailor
marino I *adj brisa* sea *atr*; *planta, animal* marine; ***azul ~*** navy blue **II** *m* sailor
marioneta *f tb fig* puppet
marionetista *m/f* puppeteer
mariposa *f* butterfly; **(*estilo*) ~** DEP butterfly; ***a otra cosa, ~*** F let's move on
mariposear ⟨1a⟩ *v/i* flutter around; *fig* flit from one subject / job *etc* to another
mariposón *m* **1** F (*afeminado*) fairy F **2** (*ligón*) flirt
mariquita *f* **I** ladybug, *Br* ladybird **II** F *m* fag P, *Br* poof P
marisabidilla *f* F know-it-all, *Br* know-all
mariscada *f* GASTR seafood platter
mariscal *m* marshal
◇ **mariscal de campo** field marshal
marisco *m*, **mariscos** *mpl L.Am.* seafood *sg*
marisma *f* salt marsh
marisquería *f* seafood *o* shellfish restaurant / bar
marital *adj* marital; ***hacer vida ~*** live as husband and wife
marítimo *adj* maritime
marketing *m* marketing
marmita *f* pot, pan
mármol *m* marble
marmóreo *adj* marble *atr*
marmota *f* ZO marmot; ***dormir como una ~*** F sleep like a log
◇ **marmota de América** groundhog
maroma *f* rope; ***hacer ~s*** *L.Am. tb fig* walk a tightrope
maromo *m* F boyfriend, guy F
marqués *m* marquis
marquesa *f* marchioness
marquesina *f* marquee, *Br* canopy
marquetería *f* marquetry
marrana *f* sow
marranada *f* F dirty trick
marrano I *adj* filthy **II** *m* **1** hog, *Br* pig **2** F *persona* pig F
marrar ⟨1a⟩ *v/t tiro, golpe* miss
marras *adv*: ***el computador de ~*** the darned computer
marrón *m/adj* brown; ***comerse un ~*** F own up; ***meterse en un ~*** F get in a fix F
marroquí *m/f & adj* Moroccan
marroquinería *f* leather goods *pl*
Marruecos *m* Morocco
marrullería *f* dirty trick
marrullero I *adj* underhand(ed) **II** *m* cheat
Marsella *f* Marseilles
marsopa *f* ZO porpoise
marsupiales *mpl* ZO marsupials
marta *f* ZO marten
Marte *m* AST Mars
martes *m inv* Tuesday
martillar ⟨1a⟩ *v/t & vi* hammer
martillazo *m* blow with a hammer, hammer blow
martillear ⟨1a⟩ *v/t & v/i* hammer
martilleo *m* hammering
martillero *m S.Am.* auctioneer
martillo *m* hammer
◇ **martillo neumático** pneumatic drill
martín *m*: ***~ pescador*** ZO kingfisher
martinete *m* **1** ZO heron **2** TÉC pile driver **3** MÚS hammer
martingala *f* F trick
mártir *m/f tb fig* martyr
martirio *m tb fig* martyrdom
martirizar ⟨1f⟩ *v/t tb fig* martyr
maruja *f* F housewife
marzo *m* March
mas *conj* but
más I *adj* more
II *adv* **1** *comp* more; ***~ grande / pequeño*** bigger, larger / smaller; ***~ importante*** more important; ***trabajar ~*** work harder; ***éste me gusta ~*** I like this one better; ***~ que, ~ de lo que*** more than; ***~ de*** more than; ***si quieres algo no tie-***

M

nes ~ que pedirlo if you want anything you only have to ask; ***¿qué ~?*** what else?; ***me gustaría ~ …*** I would prefer …; ***~ lejos*** further; ***el que ~ y el que menos*** some more than others
2 *sup* most; ***el ~ grande / pequeño*** the biggest *o* largest / smallest; ***el ~ importante*** the most important; ***a lo ~*** at most; ***tiene tres coches, a cuál ~ caro*** he has three cars, all (of them) equally expensive; ***¡qué vestido ~ bonito!*** what a pretty dress!; ***lo ~ pronto posible*** as soon as possible
3 MAT plus
III *m* MAT plus (sign); ***tener sus ~ y sus menos*** have its pros and cons
IV *en locuciones*: ***~ o menos*** more or less; ***poco ~ o menos*** roughly; ***comimos a ~ y mejor*** we ate a great deal; ***~ y ~*** more and more; ***ni ~ ni menos*** neither more nor less; ***no ~*** *L.Am.* ☞ ***nomás***; ***por ~ que*** however much; ***sin ~*** without more ado; ***tanto ~ cuanto que*** particularly since; ***~ bien*** rather; ***ir a ~*** be on the up; ***como el que ~*** as *o* like anyone else; ***estar de ~*** be superfluous

masa *f* **1** (*volumen*) mass; ***en ~*** en masse **2** GASTR dough; ***pillar a alguien con las manos en la ~*** F catch s.o. red-handed **3**: ***las ~s*** (*el pueblo*) the masses
◇ **masa de bienes** assets *pl*
◇ **masa quebrada** puff pastry
masacrar ⟨1a⟩ *v/t* massacre
masacre *f* massacre
masaje *m* massage; ***dar un ~ a alguien, dar ~s a alguien*** give s.o. a massage
masajear ⟨1a⟩ *v/t* massage
masajista *m/f hombre* masseur; *mujer* masseuse
mascada *f Méx* scarf
mascar ⟨1g⟩ **I** *v/t* chew **II** *v/i L.Am.* chew tobacco
máscara *f* **1** (*careta*) mask; ***quitarse la ~*** *fig* show one's true colors *o Br* colours **2** *cosmetic* mascara
◇ **máscara antigás** gas mask
mascarada *f* masquerade
mascarilla *f* **1** (*antifaz*) mask **2** *cosmética* face pack
◇ **mascarón de proa** *m* MAR figurehead
mascota *f* **1** *de equipo, olimpiada* mascot **2** *animal doméstico* pet
masculinidad *f* masculinity
masculino **I** *adj* masculine **II** *m* GRAM masculine
mascullar ⟨1a⟩ *v/t* mutter
masificación *f* overcrowding
masificarse ⟨1g⟩ *v/r* get overcrowded
masilla *f* putty
masita *f L.Am. small sweet cake or bun*
masivo *adj* massive
masoca *m/f* F masochist
masón *m* mason
masonería *f* masonry
masónico *adj* masonic
masoquismo *m* masochism
masoquista **I** *adj* masochistic **II** *m/f* masochist
máster *m* master's (degree)
masticación *f* chewing
masticar ⟨1g⟩ *v/t* chew
mástil *m* **1** MAR mast **2** *de tienda, bandera* pole
mastín *m* ZO mastiff
mastitis *f* MED mastitis
mastodonte *m* mastodon; *cosa* whopping great thing F; *fig* giant of a man / woman
mastodóntico *adj* colossal, enormous
mastuerzo *m* BOT cress
masturbación *f* masturbation
masturbarse ⟨1a⟩ *v/r* masturbate
mata *f* bush; ***~ de pelo*** mop of hair
matacaballo *adv* F: ***a ~*** at loggerheads
matachín *m* bully
matadero *m* slaughterhouse
matador **I** *adj* killing *atr* **II** *m* TAUR matador
matagigantes *m inv equipo* giant killers *pl*
matalahúga, matalahúva *f* anis, aniseed
matamoscas *m inv* fly swatter; ***papel ~*** flypaper
matanza *f de animales* slaughter; *de gente* slaughter, massacre
matar ⟨1a⟩ **I** *v/t* **1** *persona, tiempo* kill; ***~ a tiros*** shoot dead, shoot to death; ***~las callando*** F be a wolf in sheep's clothing **2** *ganado* slaughter **3** *hambre* satisfy; *sed* quench, slake
II *v/i* kill; ***no matarás*** thou shalt not kill; ***estar a ~ con alguien*** be at daggers drawn with s.o.
matarse *v/r* **1** (*suicidarse*) kill o.s.; ***~ a***

trabajar work o.s. to death **2** *morir* be killed
matarife *m* slaughterman
matarratas *m inv* rat poison
matasanos *m/f inv* F quack F
matasellar ⟨1a⟩ *v/t* frank, cancel
matasellos *m inv* postmark
matasuegras *m inv* party blower
mate I *adj* matt **II** *m* **1** *en ajedrez* mate **2** *L.Am.* (*infusión*) maté **3** *en baloncesto* dunk
matear ⟨1a⟩ **I** *v/t CSur* checkmate **II** *v/i L.Am.* drink maté
matemáticas *fpl* mathematics *sg*
matemático I *adj* mathematical **II** *m*, **-a** *f* mathematician
materia *f* **1** matter **2** (*material*) material **3** (*tema*) subject; ***entrar en ~*** get on to the subject; ***en ~ de*** as regards
◇ **materia gris** ANAT *tb fig* F grey matter
◇ **materia prima** raw material
material *m/adj* material
◇ **material didáctico** *en enseñanza* teaching materials *pl*
◇ **material escolar** (*artículos de papelería*) school supplies *pl*
materialismo *m* materialism
materialista I *adj* materialistic **II** *m/f* **1** materialist **2** *Méx* building contractor **III** *m Méx* builder's truck
materializar ⟨1f⟩ *v/t*: ***~ algo*** make sth a reality; **materializarse** *v/r* materialize
materialmente *adv* absolutely, completely; ***~ imposible*** absolutely *o* completely impossible
maternal *adj* maternal
maternidad *f* maternity, motherhood; ***casa de ~*** maternity hospital
materno *adj*: ***por parte -a*** on one's mother's side, maternal
matero *m*, **-a** *f L.Am.* maté drinker
matinal *adj* morning *atr*
matiz *m* **1** *de ironía* touch **2** *de color* shade
matizar ⟨1f⟩ *v/t comentarios* qualify
matón *m* **1** *de colegio* bully **2** (*criminal*) thug; ***~ a sueldo*** hired killer
matorral *m* thicket
matraca *f* rattle
matraz *m* flask
matriarcado *m* matriarchy
matricida *m/f* matricide
matricidio *m* matricide
matrícula *f* **1** AUTO license plate, *Br* numberplate **2** EDU enrollment, *Br* enrolment, registration
matriculación *f* AUTO registration
matricular ⟨1a⟩ *v/t* AUTO, EDU register; **matricularse** *v/r* EDU enroll, register
matrimonial *adj* marriage *atr*, marital
matrimonio *m* **1** (*unión conyugal*) marriage; ***pedir a alguien en ~*** ask for s.o.'s hand in marriage **2** *boda* wedding
◇ **matrimonio civil** civil wedding *o* ceremony
◇ **matrimonio religioso** church wedding
matriz *f* **1** MAT, TÉC, GEOL matrix **2** ANAT womb
matrona *f* (*comadrona*) midwife
matute *m* smuggling; ***de ~*** (*de contrabando*) smuggled; *fig* (*de manera clandestina*) clandestinely; ***colar de ~*** smuggle
matutero *m* smuggler
matutino *adj* morning *atr*; ***periódico ~*** morning paper
maula *m/f* annoying person
maullar ⟨1a⟩ *v/i* miaow
maullido *m* miaow
Mauritania *f* Mauritania
mauritano I *adj* Mauritanian **II** *m*, **-a** *f* Mauritanian
mausoleo *m* mausoleum
maxilar ANAT **I** *adj* maxillary **II** *m* jaw (-bone); ***~ superior / inferior*** upper / lower jaw
máxima *f* **1** (*dicho*) maxim **2** *temperatura* maximum
máxime *adv* especially
maximizar ⟨1f⟩ *v/t* maximize
máximo *adj* maximum
máximum *m* maximum
maya *m/f & adj* Mayan
mayar ⟨1a⟩ *v/i* miaow
mayate *m Méx* F *desp* fag F, *Br* poof F
mayestático *adj* majestic
mayo *m* May
mayólica *f* majolica
mayonesa *f* GASTR mayonnaise
mayor I *adj* **1** *comp*: *en tamaño* larger, bigger; *en edad* older; *en importancia* greater; ***~ que*** greater than, larger than; ***ser ~ de edad*** be an adult; ***ser (muy) ~*** be (very) elderly; ***~ que*** older than **2** *sup*: ***el ~*** *en edad* the oldest *o* eldest; *en tamaño* the largest *o* biggest; *en im-*

portancia the greatest; ***los ~es*** the adults; ***la ~ parte*** the majority **3** MÚS *tono, modo* major; ***do ~*** MÚS C major **4** COM: ***al por ~*** wholesale **II** *m* MIL major **III**: ***ir*** *o* ***pasar a ~es*** get serious

mayoral *m* **1** (*capataz*) foreman **2** AGR farm manager

mayordomo *m* butler

mayoreo *m*: ***vender al ~*** *Méx* sell wholesale

mayoría *f* majority; ***~ de votos*** majority of votes; ***alcanzar la ~ de edad*** come of age; ***la ~ de*** the majority of, most (of); ***en la ~ de los casos*** in the majority of cases, in most cases; ***la ~ de las veces*** most of the time

◇ **mayoría absoluta** absolute majority

◇ **mayoría relativa, mayoría simple** simple majority

mayorista I *adj* wholesale **II** *m/f* wholesaler

mayoritariamente *adv* mostly

mayoritario *adj* majority *atr*

mayormente *adv* mainly

mayúscula *f* capital (letter), upper case letter

mayúsculo *adj* capital, uppercase

maza *f* mace

mazacote *m* F stodgy mass F

mazamorra *f S.Am. kind of porridge made from corn*

mazapán *m* marzipan

mazazo *m fig* blow

mazmorra *f* dungeon

mazo *m* mallet

mazorca *f* cob

me *pron pers* **I** *complemento directo* me **II** *complemento indirecto* (to) me; ***~ dio el libro*** he gave me the book, he gave the book to me **III** *reflexivo* myself

meada *f* P pee F; ***echar una ~*** P have a pee F

meadero *m* P john F, *Br* loo F

meandro *m* meander

mear ⟨1a⟩ F *v/i* pee F; **mearse** *v/r* pee o.s. F; ***~ de risa*** wet o.s. laughing F

meato *m* ANAT meatus

meca *f fig* mecca

Meca: ***La ~*** Mecca

¡mecachis! *int* F blast! F

mecánica *f* mechanics *sg*

◇ **mecánica cuántica** quantum mechanics *sg*

◇ **mecánica de precisión** precision engineering

mecánico I *adj* mechanical **II** *m*, **-a** *f* mechanic

◇ **mecánico de automóviles** garage mechanic, auto mechanic

◇ **mecánico dentista** dental technician

mecanismo *m* mechanism

mecanización *f* mechanization

mecanizar ⟨1f⟩ *v/t* mechanize

mecanografía *f* typing

mecanografiar ⟨1c⟩ *v/t* type

mecanógrafo *m*, **-a** *f* typist

mecate *m Méx* string, cord

mecedora *f* rocking chair

mecenas *m inv* patron, sponsor

mecer ⟨2b⟩ *v/t* rock; **mecerse** *v/r* rock

mecha *f* **1** *de vela* wick **2** *de explosivo* fuse **3** *del pelo* highlight; ***hacerse ~s*** have highlights put in **4** *Méx* F fear **5**: ***a toda ~*** like greased lightning; ***aguantar ~*** F put up with it

mechero *m* cigarette lighter

mechón *m de pelo* lock

medalla *f* medal; ***~ de oro / plata / bronce*** gold / silver / bronze medal

medallero *m* medal table

medallista *m/f* medalist, *Br* medallist

medallón *m* medallion

médano *m* dune

media *f* **1** *hasta el muslo* stocking; ***~s*** *pl* pantyhose *pl*, *Br* tights *pl* **2** *L.Am. calcetín* sock **3** MAT mean

◇ **media corta** knee highs *pl*

◇ **media de rejilla** fishnet stocking

mediación *f* mediation

mediado *adj*: ***a ~s de junio*** in mid-June, halfway through June

mediador I *m*, **~a** *f* mediator **II** *adj* mediating

medialuna *f L.Am.* croissant

mediana *f* AUTO median strip, *Br* central reservation

medianería *f* party wall, dividing wall

medianero *adj* party *atr*, dividing

medianía *f persona* mediocrity

mediano *adj* **1** *tamaño, altura* medium, average; ***de -a edad*** middle-aged **2** (*no bueno*) average

medianoche *f* **1** midnight **2** GASTR sweet roll

mediante *prp* by means of; ***Dios ~*** God

willing
mediar ⟨1b⟩ *v/i* **1** (*arbitrar*) mediate **2** (*interceder*) intercede **3** (*intervenir*) intervene **4** *de tiempo* elapse; ***median 4km entre los dos pueblos*** the two towns are 4km apart **5**: ***sin ~ palabra*** without a word
mediateca *f* media library
mediático *adj* media *atr*
mediatizar ⟨1f⟩ *v/t* influence
mediatriz *f* MAT bisector
medicación *f* medication
medicamento *m* medicine, drug
◇ **medicamentos genéricos** generic drugs
medicamentoso *adj* medicinal
medicar ⟨1g⟩ *v/t* administer medication to; **medicarse** *v/r* take medication
medicastro *m* quack
medicina *f* medicine
◇ **medicina convencional** conventional medicine; **medicina deportiva** sports medicine; **medicina forense** forensic medicine; **medicina general** general medicine; **medicina legal** forensic medicine; **medicina de la reproducción** reproductive medicine
medicinal *adj* medicinal
medición *f* (act of) measuring
médico I *adj* medical **II** *m/f* doctor
◇ **médico de cabecera, médico de familia** family physician *o* doctor, *Br* GP, *Br* general practitioner; **médico forense** forensic scientist; **médico de guardia** duty doctor; **médico de urgencia** emergency doctor
medida *f* **1** (*unidad*) measure; *acto* measurement; ***hecho a ~*** made to measure; ***está hecho a ~ de mis necesidades*** it's tailor-made for me; ***tomar las ~s a alguien*** take s.o.'s measurements; ***tomar ~s*** *fig* take measures *o* steps **2** (*grado*) extent; ***en mayor ~*** to a greater extent **3**: ***a ~ que*** as
medidor *m S.Am.* meter
medieval *adj* medieval, *Br tb* mediaeval
medievalista *m/f* medievalist, *Br tb* mediaevalist
medievo *m* Middle Ages *pl*
medio I *adj* **1** half; ***las tres y -a*** half past three, three-thirty; ***a ~ camino*** halfway **2** *tamaño* medium **3** (*de promedio*) average **4** *posición* middle
II *m* **1** (*entorno*) environment **2** *en fútbol* midfielder **3** (*centro*) middle; ***en ~ de*** in the middle of **4** (*manera*) means; ***por ~ de*** by means of; ***~s*** *pl dinero* means, resources
III *adv* half; ***hacer algo a -as*** half do sth; ***ir a -as*** go halves; ***a ~ hacer*** half done; ***de ~ a ~*** completely; ***día por ~*** *L.Am.* every other day; ***quitar de en ~ algo*** F move sth out of the way; ***quitarse de en ~*** get out of the way
◇ **medio ambiente** environment; **medio tiempo** *L.Am.* DEP half-time; **medios de comunicación, medios de información** (mass) media; **medios de masas** mass media; **medios de transporte** means of transportation
medioambiental *adj* environmental
mediocampista *m/f* DEP midfield player, midfielder
mediocre *adj* mediocre
mediocridad *f* mediocrity
mediodía *m* midday; ***a ~*** (*a las doce*) at noon, at twelve o'clock; (*a la hora de comer*) at lunchtime
medioevo *m* Middle Ages *pl*
mediofondista *m/f* DEP middle-distance runner
medir ⟨3l⟩ **I** *v/t* measure; ***~ sus palabras*** *fig* weigh one's words **II** *v/i*: ***mide 2 metros de ancho / largo / alto*** it's 2 meters wide / long / tall; **medirse** *v/r* measure o.s.
meditabundo *adj* pensive
meditación *f* meditation
meditar ⟨1a⟩ **I** *v/t* ponder **II** *v/i* meditate
meditativo *adj* meditative
mediterráneo I *adj* Mediterranean; ***el mar Mediterráneo*** the Mediterranean Sea **II** *m*: ***el Mediterráneo*** the Mediterranean
médium *m/f inv* medium
medrar ⟨1a⟩ *v/i* **1** *de planta, animal* grow **2** *de persona* prosper, flourish
medroso *adj* fearful
médula *f* marrow; ***hasta la ~*** *fig* through and through, to the core
◇ **médula espinal** spinal cord
◇ **médula ósea** bone marrow
medular *adj* bone-marrow *atr*
medusa *f* ZO jellyfish
megabyte *m* megabyte
megaciclo *m* megacycle
megafonía *f* public-address *o* PA system

megáfono *m* bullhorn, *Br* loud-hailer
megalomanía *f* megalomania
megalómano *adj* megalomaniacal
megatón *m* megaton
mejicano I *adj* Mexican **II** *m*, **-a** *f* Mexican
Méjico *m* **1** *país* Mexico **2** (*DF*) Mexico City
mejilla *f* cheek
mejillón *m* ZO mussel
mejor I *adj* **1** *comp* better; ***está ~*** that's better; ***ir a ~*** get better; ***tanto ~*** all the better **2** *sup*: ***el ~*** the best; ***lo ~*** the best thing; ***lo ~ posible*** as well as possible; ***dar lo ~ de sí mismo*** do one's best **II**: ***~ para ti*** good for you; ***a lo ~*** perhaps, maybe
mejora *f* improvement
mejorable *adj* improvable; ***es ~*** it can be improved
mejoramiento *m* improvement
mejorana *f* BOT marjoram
mejorar ⟨1a⟩ **I** *v/t* improve **II** *v/i* improve; **mejorarse** *v/r* get better; ***¡que te mejores!*** get well soon!
mejoría *f* improvement
mejunje *m desp* concoction
melancolía *f* melancholy
melancólico *adj* gloomy, melancholic
melancólico *adj* melancholy
melanina *f* BIO melanin
melanoma *m* MED melanoma
melaza *f* molasses
melena *f* **1** *de persona* long hair **2** *de león* mane
melenudo I *adj* long-haired **II** *m* long-haired boy *o* guy
melifluo *adj fig* sickly sweet; ***~s*** *pl* (*afectación*) affected ways; ***andarse con ~s*** be affected
melindroso *adj* affected
melisa *f* BOT lemon balm
mella *f*: ***hacer ~ en alguien*** have an effect on s.o., affect s.o.
mellado *adj dentadura* gap-toothed
mellar ⟨1a⟩ *v/t* nick, chip
mellizo I *adj* twin *atr* **II** *m*, **-a** *f* twin
melocotón *m* peach
melocotonero *m* peach tree
melodía *f* melody
melódico *adj* melodic
melodioso *adj* melodious
melodrama *m* melodrama
melodramático *adj* melodramatic
melómano *m*, **-a** *f* music lover
melón *m* **1** BOT melon; ***~es*** *pl hum* F boobs F, melons F **2** *fig* F (*bobo*) dummy F
meloncillo *m* ZO mongoose
meloso *adj* F sickly sweet
membrana *f* membrane
membrete *m* heading, letterhead; ***papel con ~*** letterhead, headed paper
membrillo *m* quince; ***dulce de ~*** quince jelly
membrudo *adj* muscular
memela *f Méx* corn tortilla
memez *f* stupid thing
memo F **I** *adj* dumb F **II** *m*, **-a** *f* idiot
memorable *adj* memorable
memorándum *m* memo
memoria *f* **1** *tb* INFOR memory; ***si no me falla la ~*** if my memory serves me well; ***traer a la ~*** remind; ***venir a la ~*** come to mind; ***hacer ~*** remember; ***de ~*** by heart **2** (*informe*) report; ***~s*** *pl* (*biografía*) memoirs
◇ **memoria de trabajo** INFOR working memory
memorial *m* memorial
memorizar ⟨1f⟩ *v/t* memorize
mena *f* MIN ore
menaje *m* household equipment
mención *f*: ***hacer ~ de*** mention
mencionar ⟨1a⟩ *v/t* mention
mendaz *adj fml* mendacious *fml*
mendicante I *adj* begging **II** *m/f* beggar
mendicidad *f* begging
mendigar ⟨1h⟩ *v/t* beg for
mendigo *m*, **-a** *f* beggar
menear ⟨1a⟩ *v/t* **1** (*agitar*) shake **2** *las caderas* sway; ***~ la cola*** wag its tail; ***~ la cabeza*** shake one's head; **menearse** *v/r* **1** (*moverse*) fidget **2** (*apresurarse*) hurry up
meneo *m* F telling-off; ***dar un ~ a alguien*** tell s.o. off, give s.o. a telling-off
menester *m* (*trabajo*) job; ***~es*** *pl* F tools, gear *sg*; ***ser ~*** (*necessario*) be necessary
menesteroso *adj* needy
menestra *f* vegetable stew
mengano *m*, **-a** *f* F so-and-so F
mengua *f* decrease, diminution; ***ir en ~ de*** be to the detriment of
menguado *adj* diminished, reduced
menguante *adj* **1** *cantidad, intensidad* decreasing, diminishing **2** *luna* waning

menguar 〈1i〉 **I** *v/i* **1** *de cantidad, intensidad* decrease, diminish **2** *de la luna* wane **II** *v/t* decrease, diminish
meninge *f* ANAT meninx
meningitis *f* MED meningitis
menisco *m* ANAT cartilage
menopausia *f* MED menopause
menopáusico *adj* menopausal
menor I *adj* **1** *comp* less; *en tamaño* smaller; *en edad* younger; ***ser ~ de edad*** be a minor **2** *sup*: ***el ~*** *en tamaño* the smallest; *en edad* the youngest; ***el número ~*** the lowest number; ***no tengo la ~ idea*** I don't have the slightest idea **3** MÚS *tono, modo* minor; ***mi ~*** E minor **4** COM: ***al por ~*** retail
II *m/f* minor
Menorca *f* Minorca
menorquín I *adj* Minorcan **II** *m*, **-quina** *f* Minorcan
menos I *adj* **1** *en cantidad* less; ***cien dólares de ~*** 100 dollars short, 100 dollars too little; ***hay cinco calcetines de ~*** we are five socks short **2** *en número* fewer **II** *adv* **1** *comp*: *en cantidad* less; ***es ~ guapa que Ana*** she is not as pretty as Ana **2** *sup*: *en cantidad* least; ***al ~, por lo ~*** at least **3** MAT minus; ***tres ~ dos*** three minus two
III *m* MAT minus (sign)
IV: ***a ~ que*** unless; ***todos ~ yo*** everyone but *o* except me; ***echar de ~*** miss; ***tener a alguien en ~*** look down on s.o.; ***eso es lo de ~*** that's the least of it; ***ir a ~*** come down in the world; ***ni mucho ~*** far from it; ***no es para ~*** quite right too; ***son las dos ~ diez*** it's ten of two, *Br* it's ten to two
menoscabar 〈1a〉 *v/t* **1** *autoridad* diminish, reduce **2** (*dañar*) harm
menoscabo *m* **1** (*mengua*) reduction, diminution **2** (*daño*) harm
menospreciable *adj* contemptible
menospreciar 〈1b〉 *v/t* **1** (*subestimar*) underestimate **2** (*desdeñar*) look down on
menosprecio *m* contempt
mensaje *m* message
◇ **mensaje publicitario** commercial
mensajería *f* messenger company, *Br* courier service
mensajero *m*, **-a** *f* **1** *de recados, información* messenger **2** COM messenger, *Br* courier
menso *adj Méx* F dumb F
menstruación *f* menstruation
menstruar 〈1h〉 *v/i* menstruate
mensual *adj* monthly
mensualidad *f* COM monthly installment *o Br* instalment, monthly payment
mensualmente *adv* monthly
mensurable *adj* measurable
menta *f* BOT mint
mental *adj* mental
mentalidad *f* mentality
mentalizar 〈1f〉 *v/t*: ***~ a alguien*** make s.o. aware; **mentalizarse** *v/r* mentally prepare o.s.
mentalmente *adv* mentally
mentar 〈1k〉 *v/t* mention
mente *f* mind; ***no se me va de la ~*** I can't stop thinking about it, I can't get it out of my mind
mentecato I *adj* F dim F **II** *m*, **-a** *f* F fool
mentir 〈3i〉 *v/i* lie
mentira *f* lie; ***¡parece ~!*** that's incredible!
mentirijillas *fpl*: ***de ~*** F in jest, jokingly
mentiroso I *adj*: ***ser muy ~*** tell a lot of lies **II** *m*, **-a** *f* liar
mentís *m inv* denial; ***dar un ~ a algo*** deny sth
mentol *m* menthol
mentón *m* chin; ***doble ~*** double chin
mentor *m* mentor
menú *m tb* INFOR menu
◇ **menú de ayuda** INFOR help menu
◇ **menú desplegable** INFOR drop-down menu
menudear 〈1a〉 **I** *v/t*: ***~ algo*** do sth frequently; ***la guerrilla menudéo los ataques*** the guerrillas attacked frequently **II** *v/i L.Am.* be frequent; (*ocurrir*) happen frequently
menudencia *f* trifle
menudencias *fpl Méx* giblets
menudeo *m L.Am.* COM retail trade
menudillos *mpl* giblets
menudo I *adj* small; ***¡-a suerte!*** *fig* F lucky devil!; ***¡-as vacaciones!*** *irón* F some vacation!; ***¡~ lío!*** what a mess!; ***a ~*** often **II** *m L.Am.* small change; ***~s*** *pl* GASTR giblets
meñique *m/adj*: **(*dedo*) ~** little finger
meollo *m fig* heart
meón *m*, **-ona** *f*: ***ser un ~*** have a weak bladder

mequetrefe F *m* good-for-nothing
meramente *adv* merely
mercachifle *m desp fig* money-grubbing store-keeper
mercadear ⟨1a⟩ **I** *v/t* market **II** *v/i* trade
mercadeo *m* marketing
mercader *m* trader
mercadería *f L.Am.* merchandise
mercadillo *m* street market
mercado *m* market; ***abrir nuevos ~s*** open up new markets
◊ **mercado interior** domestic market; **mercado laboral** job market; **mercado negro** black market; **mercado de valores** stock market
mercadotecnia *f* marketing
mercancía *f* merchandise; ***tren de ~s*** freight train, *Br* goods train
mercante *adj* merchant *atr*; ***buque ~*** merchant ship *o* vessel
mercantil *adj* commercial
merced *f*: ***estar a ~ de alguien*** be at s.o.'s mercy; ***~ a*** thanks to
mercenario *m/adj* mercenary
mercería *f* notions *pl*, *Br* haberdashery
MERCOSUR *m abr* (= ***Mercado Común del Sur***) *Common Market including Argentina, Brazil, Paraguay and Uruguay*
mercurial *adj* mercurial
mercurio *m* mercury
Mercurio *m* MYTH, AST Mercury
merecedor *adj* deserving; ***ser ~ de*** deserve, be worthy of; ***~ de confianza*** trustworthy; ***hacerse ~ de algo*** *fig* earn sth
merecer ⟨2d⟩ *v/t* deserve; ***no merece la pena*** it's not worth it; ***no se lo merece*** he doesn't deserve it; ***en edad de ~*** old enough to have a boyfriend / girlfriend
merecido I *adj* well-deserved; ***bien ~ lo tiene*** it serves him right **II** *m* just deserts *pl*
merendar ⟨1k⟩ **I** *v/t*: ***~ algo*** have sth as an afternoon snack **II** *v/i* have an afternoon snack; **merendarse** *v/r* **1** *fig*: *rival* thrash F **2** *fig*: *tarea* finish off
merendero *m* outdoor café
merengue *m* GASTR meringue
meretriz *f fml* prostitute
meridiano *m/adj* meridian
meridional I *adj* southern **II** *m/f* southerner
merienda *f* afternoon snack
◊ **merienda de negros** bedlam, confusion
merino *adj* merino *atr*; ***lana / oveja -a*** merino wool / sheep
mérito *m* merit; ***hacer ~s*** work hard; ***de ~*** worthy
meritorio I *adj* commendable **II** *m*, **-a** *f* (unpaid) trainee
merluza *f* ZO hake; ***agarrar una ~*** *fig* F get plastered F
merluzo *m*, **-a** *f* F idiot
merma *f* reduction, decrease
mermar ⟨1a⟩ **I** *v/t* reduce **II** *v/i* diminish
mermelada *f* jam
mero I *adj* mere; ***el ~ jefe*** *Méx* F the big boss **II** *m* ZO grouper
merodear ⟨1a⟩ *v/i* loiter
mersa *adj Rpl* F tacky F
mersa *mf Rpl* F tacky person F
mersada *f Rpl* F tacky thing F
mes *m* month; ***en el ~ de mayo*** in the month of May; ***al ~ de haber llegado*** a month after she arrived
mesa *f* **1** *mueble* table; ***poner / quitar*** *o* ***alzar*** *o* ***levantar la ~*** set / clear the table; ***sentarse a la ~*** sit at the table **2** GEOG plateau **3** POL committee
◊ **mesa auxiliar** side table; **mesa de centro** coffee table; **mesa electoral** *people who organize a polling station in an election*; **mesa extensible** extending table; **mesa de negociaciones** negotiating table; **mesa redonda** *fig* round table
mesada *f L.Am.* monthly allowance
mesana *f* MAR *mástil* mizzenmast
mesarse ⟨1a⟩ *v/r barba* pull; ***~ los cabellos*** tear one's hair
mescalina *f* mescaline
mescolanza *f* ☞ ***mezcolanza***
mesera *f L.Am.* waitress
mesero *m L.Am.* waiter
meseta *f* plateau; ***Meseta Mato Grosso*** Plateau of the Mato Grosso
mesías *m inv* messiah
mesilla, mesita *f*: ***~*** (***de noche***) night stand, *Br* bedside table
mesón *m traditional restaurant decorated in rustic style*
mesonera *f* **1** landlady, person who runs a mesón **2** *Ven* waitress
mesonero *m* **1** landlord, person who runs a mesón **2** *m Ven* waiter
mesozoico *m* GEOL Mesozoic

M

mestizo *m* person of mixed race
mesura *f*: ***con ~*** in moderation
mesurado *adj* moderate
mesurar ⟨1a⟩ *v/t* moderate; **mesurarse** *v/r* restrain o.s., control o.s.
meta I *f* **1** *en fútbol* goal; ***marcar en propia ~*** score an own goal **2** *en carrera* finishing line **3** *en béisbol* home **4** *fig* (*objetivo*) goal, objective; ***fijarse una ~*** set o.s. an objective *o* a goal **II** *m/f* goalkeeper
metabólico *adj* metabolic
metabolismo *m* metabolism
◇ **metabolismo basal** basal metabolism
metabolizar ⟨1f⟩ *v/t* metabolize
metacarpo *m* ANAT metacarpus
metadona *f* methadone
metafísica *f* metaphysics *sg*
metáfora *f* metaphor
metafórico *adj* metaphorical
metal *m* **1** metal **2** MÚS heavy metal
◇ **metal no férrico** non-ferrous metal; **metal noble** precious metal; **metal pesado** heavy metal; **metal precioso** precious metal
metálico I *adj* metallic **II** *m*: ***en ~*** (in) cash
metalizado *adj*: ***pintura -a*** AUTO metallic paint
metalurgia *f* metallurgy
metalúrgico I *adj* metallurgical **II** *m*, **-a** *f trabajador del metal* metalworker; *científico* metallurgist
metamorfosear ⟨1a⟩ *v/t* metamorphose; **metamorfosearse** *v/r* metamorphose
metamorfosis *f inv* transformation, metamorphosis
metano *m* methane
metedura *f*: ***~ de pata*** F blunder
metegol *m Arg* table football
meteórico *adj* meteoric
meteorito *m* meteorite
meteoro *m* meteor
meteorología *f* meteorology
meteorológico *adj* weather *atr*, meteorological; ***mapa ~*** weather map; ***parte ~*** weather report; ***pronóstico ~*** weather forecast
meteorólogo *m*, **-a** *f* meteorologist
metepatas *m/f inv* F: ***ser un ~*** be prone to making bloopers F, be always putting one's foot in it F
meter ⟨2a⟩ *v/t* **1** put (***en*** in, into) **2** *gol* score **3** (*involucrar*) involve (***en*** in); ***~ a alguien en un lío*** get s.o. into a mess; ***a todo ~*** at full speed
meterse *v/r*: ***~ en algo*** get into sth; (*involucrarse*) get involved in sth, get mixed up in sth; ***~ donde no le llaman*** stick one's nose in where it doesn't belong; ***no saber dónde ~*** *fig* not know what to do with o.s.; ***~ a hacer algo*** start doing sth, start to do sth; ***~ con alguien*** pick on s.o.; ***~ de administrativo*** get a job in admin; ***se metió a bailar*** he became a dancer; ***¿dónde se ha metido?*** where has he got to?
meterete *m/f Rpl* F busybody F
metiche *m/f Méx* F busybody F
meticulosidad *f* meticulousness
meticuloso *adj* meticulous
metida *f*: ***~ de pata*** *L.Am.* F blooper F, blunder
metido *adj* **1** (*involucrado*) involved; ***estar muy ~ en algo*** be very involved in sth **2** *L.Am.* nosy F **3**: ***~ en años*** elderly; ***~ en carnes*** plump; ***~ en sí*** inward-looking
metódico *adj* methodical
metodista REL **I** *adj* Methodist **II** *m/f* Methodist
método *m* method
metomentodo *m/f* F busybody F
metraje *m de película* length
metralla *f pedazos* shrapnel; HIST grapeshot; ***~ de preguntas*** *fig* F barrage of questions
metralleta *f* sub-machine gun
métrico *adj* metric
metro *m* **1** *medida* meter, *Br* metre **2** *para medir* rule **3** *transporte* subway, *Br* underground
◇ **metro cuadrado** square meter *o Br* metre
◇ **metro cúbico** cubic meter *o Br* metre
metrónomo *m* MÚS metronome
metrópoli(s) *f* (*inv*) metropolis
metropolitano I *adj* metropolitan **II** *m* subway, *Br* underground
mexicano I *adj* Mexican **II** *m*, **-a** Mexican
México *m* **1** *país* Mexico **2** (*DF*) Mexico City
mezcal *m Méx* mescal
mezcla *f* **1** mixture; *de tabaco, café etc*

blend **2** *acto* mixing; *de tabaco, café etc* blending
mezclador *m*, **~a** *f*: **~** (***de sonido***) (sound) mixer
mezclar ⟨1a⟩ *v/t* mix; *tabaco, café etc* blend; **~ *a alguien en algo*** get s.o. mixed up *o* involved in sth; **mezclarse** *v/r* mix; **~ *en algo*** get mixed up *o* involved in sth
mezclilla *f Méx* denim; ***pantalón de ~*** jeans *pl*
mezcolanza *f* F jumble
mezquinar ⟨1a⟩ *v/t L.Am.* skimp on
mezquindad *f* meanness
mezquino *adj* mean
mezquita *f* mosque
mg. *abr* (= ***miligramo***) mg (= milligram)
mi *m* MÚS E; **~ *bemol*** E flat
mi, mis *adj pos* my
mí I *pron* me; ***¿y a ~ qué?*** so what?, what's it to me? **II** *reflexivo* myself
miaja *f* crumb; ***una ~ fig*** F a scrap, a bit
mialgia *f* MED myalgia
mica *f* MIN mica
micción *f fml* micturition
michelín *m* F spare tire, *Br* spare tyre
michino *m* F puss F, pussy F
mico *m* ZO monkey
micología *f* mycology
micosis *f* MED mycosis
micro I *m* **1** F (*micrófono*) mike F **2** (*microbús*) minibus **II** *m o f Chi* bus
microbio *m* microbe
microbús *m* minibus
microchip *m* (micro)chip
microcirugía *f* MED microsurgery
microclima *m* microclimate
microcomputador *m L.Am.* microcomputer
microcomputadora *f L.Am.* microcomputer
micro-espía *m fig* F bug F, listening device
microficha *f* microfiche
microfilm(e) *m* microfilm
microfilmar ⟨1a⟩ *v/t* microfilm
micrófono *m* microphone; **~ *oculto*** bug
microondas *m inv* microwave
microordenador *m* microcomputer
microprocesador *m* microprocessor
microscópico *adj* microscopic; *fig* (*diminuto*) minute, tiny
microscopio *m* microscope
◇ **microscopio electrónico** electron microscope
mide *vb* ☞ ***medir***
mieditis *f*: ***tener ~*** F be scared
miedo *m* fear (***a*** of); ***dar ~*** be frightening; ***~ a volar*** fear of flying; ***me da ~ la oscuridad*** I'm frightened of the dark; ***meter ~ a*** frighten; ***tener ~ de que*** be afraid that; ***por ~ a*** for fear of; ***de ~*** F great F, awesome F
miedoso *adj* timid; ***¡no seas tan ~!*** don't be scared!
miel *f* honey; ***quedarse con la ~ en los labios*** have the gift of the gab; ***ser ~ sobre hojuelas*** be even better
◇ **miel de flores** honey
mielga *f* **1** BOT alfalfa, *Br* lucerne **2** ZO spiny dogfish
miembro *m* **1** (*socio*) member; ***estado / país ~*** member state / country **2** (*extremidad*) limb, member *fml*; **~*s*** *pl* ANAT limbs
◇ **miembro viril** ANAT male organ
mientes *fpl*: ***parar ~ en*** consider, contemplate; ***pasarle por las ~ a alguien*** occur to s.o.
mientras I *conj* while; **~ *que*** whereas **II** *adv*: **~ *tanto*** in the meantime, meanwhile
miércoles *m inv* Wednesday
◇ **miércoles de ceniza** REL Ash Wednesday
mierda I *f* P shit P, crap P; ***una ~ de película*** a crap movie P; ***¡una ~!*** no way! F; ***¡vete a la ~!*** go to hell! F; ***a la ~ con …*** to hell with … F; ***me importa una ~*** I don't give a shit P **II** *m/f* P *persona* shit P, piece of shit P
mies *f* (ripe) grain
miga *f de pan* crumb; **~*s*** *pl* crumbs; ***hacer algo ~s*** smash sth to bits; ***hacer buenas / malas ~s*** *fig* F get on well / badly; ***tiene ~*** F there's more to it than meets the eye
migajas *fpl* **1** *de pan* (bread)crumbs **2** *fig* (*restos*) scraps
migra *f Méx* F: ***la ~*** the INS (*the Immigration and Naturalization Service*)
migración *f* migration
migraña *f* MED migraine
migratorio *adj* migratory
mijo *m* BOT millet
mil I *adj* thousand **II** *m* thousand; ***a ~es*** by the thousands
milagro *m* miracle; ***hacer ~s*** work mir-

acles; ***de ~*** miraculously, by a miracle
milagroso *adj* miraculous
Milán *m* Milan
milano *m* ZO kite
mildiu, mildiú *m* BOT mildew
milenario I *adj* thousand-year-old **II** *m* **1** (*mil años*) millennium **2** *aniversario* thousandth anniversary
milenio *m* millennium
milenrama *f* BOT yarrow
milésimo I *adj* thousandth **II** *f*: ***una -a de segundo*** a thousandth of a second
milhojas *m inv* GASTR millefeuille
mili *f* F military service
milibar *m* millibar
milicia *f* militia
miliciano *m* militiaman
milico *m S.Am. desp* soldier
miligramo *m* milligram
mililitro *m* milliliter, *Br* millilitre
milímetro *m* millimeter, *Br* millimetre
militancia *f* militancy
militante I *adj* (politically) active **II** *m/f* activist
militar I *adj* military **II** *m/f* soldier; ***los ~es*** *pl* the military **III** ⟨1a⟩ *v/i* POL: ***~ en*** be a member of
militarista I *adj* militaristic **II** *m/f* militarist
milla *f* mile
◇ **milla marina, milla náutica** nautical mile
millar *m* thousand; ***~es de*** thousands of
millón *m* million; ***mil millones*** a billion
millonario I *adj* millionaire *atr*; ***un yate ~*** a yacht that cost millions **II** *m*, **-a** *f* millionaire
milpa *f Méx*, *C.Am.* **1** corn, *Br* maize **2** *terreno* cornfield, *Br* field of maize
milpiés *m inv* ZO millipede
mimar ⟨1a⟩ *v/t* spoil, pamper
mimbre *m* BOT willow; ***muebles*** *pl* ***de ~*** wicker furniture *sg*
mimbrera *f* BOT willow
mimetismo *m* mimicry
mimetizar ⟨1f⟩ *v/t* mimic
mímica *f* mime
mímico *adj* mimic *atr*
mimo *m* **1** TEA mime **2** (*caricia*) cuddle; ***con ~*** *tb fig* affectionately
mimosa *f* BOT mimosa
mimoso *adj*: ***es muy ~*** he likes being pampered
mina *f* **1** MIN, MIL mine **2** *Rpl* F (*mujer*) broad F, *Br* bird F
◇ **mina antipersonal** MIL antipersonnel mine
◇ **mina terrestre** landmine
minar ⟨1a⟩ *v/t* **1** (*excavar*) mine **2** *fig* (*dañar*) undermine
minarete *m* minaret
mineral *m/adj* mineral
mineralogía *f* mineralogy
minería *f* mining
minero I *adj* mining **II** *m* miner
mingitorio *m fml* urinal *fml*
miniatura *f* miniature
miniaturista *m/f* miniaturist
minifalda *f* miniskirt
minigolf *m* miniature golf, mini-golf
minimizar ⟨1f⟩ *v/t* minimize
mínimo I *adj* minimum; ***como ~*** at the very least; ***no me interesa lo más ~*** I'm not in the least interested **II** *m* minimum
mínimum *m* minimum
minino *m* F puss F, pussy (cat) F
miniserie *f* TV miniseries *sg*
ministerial *adj* (*de ministro*) ministerial; (*de ministerio*) departmental
ministerio *m* POL department
◇ **Ministerio de Asuntos Exteriores** State Department, *Br* Foreign Office; **Ministerio de Hacienda** Treasury Department, *Br* Treasury; **ministerio fiscal** JUR Attorney General's office; **Ministerio del Interior** Department of the Interior, *Br* Home Office; **Ministerio de Relaciones Exteriores** *L.Am.* State Department, *Br* Foreign Office
ministro *m*, **-a** *f* minister; ***primer ~*** Prime Minister
◇ **ministro del Interior** Secretary of the Interior, *Br* Home Secretary
◇ **ministro sin cartera** minister without portfolio
minoría *f* minority
◇ **minoría de edad** minority
minoridad *f* minority
minorista COM **I** *adj* retail *atr* **II** *m/f* retailer
minoritario *adj* minority *atr*
mintió *vb* ☞ ***mentir***
minucia *f* minor detail
minuciosidad *f* attention to detail
minucioso *adj* meticulous, thorough
minué *m* MÚS minuet

minúscula *f* small letter, lower case letter
minúsculo *adj* **1** (*diminuto*) tiny, minute **2** *letra* small, lower-case
minusvalía *f* disability
minusválido I *adj* disabled **II** *m*, **-a** *f* disabled person; ***los ~s*** the disabled, disabled people
minusvalorar ⟨1a⟩ *v/t* undervalue
minuta *f* GASTR menu; (*cuenta de los honorarios*) bill
minutero *m* minute hand
minuto *m* minute
◇ **minutos de la basura** *en baloncesto* garbage time
mío, mía *pron* mine; ***el ~ / la -a*** mine; ***un amigo ~*** a friend of mine; ***los ~s*** my family; ***no es lo ~*** it isn't my thing
mioma *m* MED myoma
miope I *adj* near-sighted, short-sighted **II** *m/f* near-sighted *o* short-sighted person
miopía *f* near-sightedness, short-sightedness
miosotis *m inv* BOT forget-me-not
MIR *m abr* (= ***médico interno residente***) intern, resident
mira *f*: ***con ~s a*** with a view to; ***estar en el punto de ~ de alguien*** be the focus of s.o.'s attention; ***está en el punto de ~ de los Lakers*** the Lakers have an eye on him
◇ **mira telescópica** telescopic sight
mirada *f* look; ***echar una ~*** take a look (***a*** at); ***ser el centro de todas las ~s*** be the center *o Br* centre of attention
mirado *adj* considerate, thoughtful; ***bien ~*** well thought of, highly regarded; *fig* all things considered
mirador *m* viewpoint
miramiento *m* consideration, thoughtfulness; ***sin ~s*** *tratar a alguien* without consideration; *decir algo* abruptly, without ceremony
mirar ⟨1a⟩ **I** *v/t* **1** look at **2** (*observar*) watch; **3** *fig* (*considerar*) look at, consider; ***no ~ el precio*** not worry about the cost; ***mira bien lo que haces*** think carefully about what you're doing **4** *L.Am.* (*ver*) see; ***¿qué miras desde aquí?*** what can you see from here? **II** *v/i* look; ***~ a / hacia algo*** face sth; ***~ al norte*** *de una ventana etc* face north; ***~ por*** look through; (*cuidar*) look after; ***~ por la ventana*** look out of the window; ***¡mira!*** look!; ***¡mira por dónde!*** would you believe it?; ***mirándolo bien*** thinking about it, now that I *etc* come to think about it
mirarse *v/r* look at o.s.; ***~ en el espejo*** look at o.s. in the mirror; ***si bien se mira*** all things considered
mirilla *f* spyhole
miriñaque *m* crinoline
mirlo *m* ZO blackbird; ***ser un ~ blanco*** *fig* be a rare bird
mirón F **I** *adj* nosy **II** *m*, **-ona** *f* busybody, nosy parker F
mirra *f* BOT myrrh
mirto *m* BOT myrtle
mis *adj pos* my
misa *f* REL mass; ***ayudar a ~*** serve at mass; ***ir a ~*** go to mass; ***no sabe de la ~ la media*** F he doesn't know a thing about it; ***ir a ~*** *fig* F be the last word
◇ **misa de difuntos** requiem mass; **misa de gallo** Christmas Eve midnight mass; **misa mayor** high mass; **misa rezada** low mass
misal *m* missal
misántropo *m*, **-a** *f* misanthropist
miscelánea *f* **1** miscellany **2** *Méx* convenience store, *Br* corner shop
misceláneo *adj* miscellaneous
miserable I *adj* wretched **II** *m/f* **1** (*tacaño*) skinflint **2** (*canalla*) swine
miseria *f* **1** poverty **2** *fig* (*sufrimiento*) misery
misericordia *f* mercy, compassion
misericordioso *adj* merciful, compassionate
mísero *adj* **1** *condición, persona* wretched **2** *sueldo* miserable; ***ni un ~ dólar*** not a miserable dollar
misil *m* missile
◇ **misil de corto alcance** short-range missile; **misil de crucero** cruise missile; **misil de largo alcance** long-range missile; **misil de medio alcance** medium-range missile; **misil tierra-aire** surface-to-air missile, SAM
misión *f* mission
misionero *m*, **-a** *f* missionary
misiva *f* missive
mismamente *adv* **1** *como respuesta* exactly, precisely **2** (*justo*) just; ***ayer ~*** just yesterday
mismo I *adj* same; ***el ~*** the (self)same; ***lo***

~ the same; ***lo ~ que*** the same as; ***yo ~*** I myself; ***da lo ~*** it doesn't matter, it's all the same; ***me da lo ~*** I don't care, it's all the same to me; ***el ~ rey*** the king himself **II** *adv*: ***aquí ~*** right here; ***ahí ~*** right there; ***ahora ~*** right now, this very minute; ***hoy ~*** today, this very day; ***lo ~ llueve que hace sol*** you never know whether it's going to be rainy or sunny

misógino I *adj* misogynistic **II** *m* misogynist

misterio *m* mystery

misterioso *adj* mysterious

mística *f* mysticism

místico I *adj* mystic(al) **II** *m*, **-a** *f* mystic

mistificación *f* mystification

mistificar ⟨1g⟩ *v/t* mystify

mitad *f* half; ***en ~ de*** *calle*, *noche etc* in the middle of; ***a ~ del camino*** halfway; ***a ~ de la película*** halfway through the movie; ***a ~ de precio*** half-price; ***~ y ~*** half and half

mítico *adj* mythical

mitificar ⟨1g⟩ *v/t* mythicize

mitigar ⟨1h⟩ *v/t* **1** *pobreza*, *contaminación etc* mitigate **2** *ansiedad*, *dolor etc* ease; **mitigarse** *v/r* ease

mitin *m* POL meeting

mito *m* myth

mitología *f* mythology

mitológico *adj* mythological

mitón *m* fingerless glove

mitra *f* miter, *Br* mitre

mixto I *adj* **1** *colegio* mixed **2** *comisión* joint **II** *m toasted ham and cheese sandwich*

mixtura *f* mixture, mix

mm. *abr* (= ***milímetro***) mm (= millimeter)

moaré *m* moire

mobiliario *m* furniture

◇ **mobiliario urbano** street furniture

moblaje *m* furniture

moca *m* ☞ ***moka***

mocasín *m* moccasin

mocedad *f* youth

mocetón *m*, **-ona** *f* fine strapping boy / girl

mochales *adj* F nuts F

mochila *f* backpack

mochilero *m*, **-a** *f* backpacker

mocho I *adj* blunt **II** *m* (blunt) end

mochuelo *m* ZO little owl; ***cargar con el ~*** F be landed with the job

moción *f* POL motion

◇ **moción de censura** vote of no confidence

◇ **moción de confianza** vote of confidence

moco *m*: ***tener ~s*** have a runny nose; ***se sacó un ~ de la nariz*** he picked a booger *o Br* bogey out of his nose F; ***no es ~ de pavo*** F it's not to be sniffed at

mocoso I *adj* snotty **II** *m*, **-a** *f* F snotty-nosed kid F

moda *f* fashion; ***~ de diseño*** designer fashion; ***~ femenina / masculina*** men's / women's fashion; ***de ~*** fashionable, in fashion; ***estar de ~*** be in fashion; ***estar pasado de ~*** be out of fashion; ***pasarse de ~*** go out of fashion; ***vestirse a la ~*** wear the latest fashions, dress fashionably

modal *adj* GRAM modal

modales *mpl* manners; ***buenos ~*** good manners

modalidad *f* **1** (*modo*) form **2** DEP discipline

◇ **modalidad de pago** method of payment

modelar ⟨1a⟩ *v/t* model

modélico *adj* model *atr*

modelismo *m* model making

modelo I *m* **1** (*maqueta*) model **2** (*ejemplo*) model, example **II** *m/f persona* model

módem *m* INFOR modem

moderación *f* moderation

moderado I *adj* moderate **II** *m*, **-a** *f* moderate

moderador I *adj* moderating **II** *m*, **~a** *f* TV presenter

moderar ⟨1a⟩ *v/t* **1** *exigencias* moderate; *impulsos* control, restrain **2** *velocidad*, *gastos* reduce **3** *debate* chair; **moderarse** *v/r* control o.s., restrain o.s.

modernidad *f* modernity

modernismo *m* modernism

modernización *f* modernization

modernizar ⟨1f⟩ *v/t* modernize

moderno *adj* modern

modestia *f* modesty; ***~ aparte*** though I say so myself

modesto *adj* modest

módico *adj precio* reasonable

modificación *f* modification

modificar ⟨1g⟩ *v/t* modify; **modificarse** *v/r* change, modify

modismo *m* idiom
modista *m/f* **1** (*costurero*) dressmaker **2** (*diseñador*) fashion designer
modisto *m* fashion designer
modo *m* **1** way; ***a mi ~ de ver*** to my way of thinking; ***dicho de otro ~*** to put it another way; ***de este ~*** like this; ***~ de ser*** personality **2** GRAM mood **3** MÚS mode **4**: ***~s*** *pl* manners; ***de malos ~s*** rudely **5**: ***a ~ de*** as; ***de ~ que*** so that; ***de ningún ~*** not at all; ***de otro ~*** otherwise; ***de tal ~ que*** so much that; ***de todos ~s*** anyway; ***de cualquier ~*** anyway, anyhow; ***en cierto ~*** in a way *o* sense
modorra *f* drowsiness
modorro *adj* drowsy
modulación *f tb* MÚS modulation
modular I ⟨1a⟩ *v/t* modulate **II** *adj* modular
módulo *m* **1** module **2** EDU module, unit
mofa *f* mockery; ***hacer ~ de*** make fun of
mofarse ⟨1a⟩ *v/r*: ***~ de*** make fun of
mofeta *f* ZO skunk
mofle *m Méx* AUTO muffler
mofletes *mpl* chubby cheeks
mofletudo *adj* chubby-cheeked
mogol *adj* ☞ ***mongol***
mogollón *m* F (*discusión*) argument; ***~ de*** loads of F; ***de ~*** for free F, without paying
mogrebí *adj* ☞ ***magrebí***
mohín *m* face; ***hacer un ~*** make a face
mohíno *adj* **1** (*triste*) depressed **2** (*enfadado*) annoyed
moho *m* mold, *Br* mould; ***criar ~*** go moldy; ***no criar ~*** *fig* not let the grass grow beneath one's feet
mohoso *adj* moldy, *Br* mouldy
moisés *m inv* Moses basket
Moisés *m* Moses
mojado I *adj* (*húmedo*) damp, moist; (*empapado*) wet **II** *m*, **-a** *f Méx* F wetback
mojama *f* salted dried tuna
mojar ⟨1a⟩ *v/t* **1** (*humedecer*) dampen, moisten; (*empapar*) wet **2** *galleta* dunk, dip; **mojarse** *v/r* **1** get wet **2** F (*orinarse*) wet o.s. **3** (*tener parte en un asunto*) get involved **4** (*comprometerse*) commit o.s.
mojiganga *f* **1** *fig* farce **2** HIST masquerade
mojigatería *f* prudishness
mojigato I *adj* prudish **II** *m*, **-a** *f* prude
mojón *m tb fig* milestone
moka *m* mocha
molar[1] **I** *adj*: ***diente ~*** molar **II** *m* molar
molar[2] ⟨2h⟩ **I** *v/t*: ***me mola ese tío*** P I like the guy a lot; ***me mola ...*** P *actividad, objeto* I love … F **II** *v/i* P be cool P; ***no ~*** *fig* it's not working out
molcajete *m Méx, C.Am.* (*mortero*) grinding stone
molde *m para metal, cera* mold, *Br* mould; *para bizcocho* (cake) tin; ***romper ~s*** *fig* break the mold
moldeable *adj* malleable
moldeado *m* molding, *Br* moulding
moldear ⟨1a⟩ *v/t* mold, *Br* mould
moldura *f* ARQUI molding, *Br* moulding
mole I *f* mass **II** *m Méx* mole (*spicy sauce made with chilies and tomatoes*)
molécula *f* molecule
molecular *adj* molecular
moledor *adj* grinding
moler ⟨2h⟩ *v/t* **1** grind; ***carne molida*** ground meat, *Br* mince **2** *fruta* mash; ***~ a alguien a palos*** *fig* beat s.o. to a pulp
molestar ⟨1a⟩ *v/t* **1** bother, annoy **2** (*doler*) trouble; ***no ~*** do not disturb; **molestarse** *v/r* **1** get upset **2** (*ofenderse*) take offense, *Br* take offence **3** (*enojarse*) get annoyed; ***~ en hacer algo*** take the trouble to do sth
molestia *f* (*incordio*) nuisance; ***~s*** *pl* MED discomfort *sg*; ***tomarse la ~ de*** go to the trouble of
molesto *adj* **1** (*fastidioso*) annoying **2** (*incómodo*) inconvenient **3** (*embarazoso*) embarrassing
molestoso *adj L.Am.* annoying
molicie *f* **1** *al tacto* softness **2** (*comodidad*) comfort
molido *adj* F bushed F
molienda *f* grinding
molinero I *adj* milling *atr* **II** *m*, **-a** *f* miller
molinete *m* pinwheel
◇ **molinillo de café** *m* coffee grinder *o* mill
molino *m* mill
◇ **molino de viento** windmill
mollar *adj fruta* easy to peel; *almendra* easy to shell; ***carne ~*** lean meat
molleja *f de ave* gizzard; ***~s*** *pl* GASTR sweetbreads

mollera *f* F head; ***cerrado*** *o* ***duro de*** **~** F pigheaded F
molón *adj* P cool P
molturar ⟨1a⟩ *v/t* grind, mill
Molucas *fpl*: (***islas***) **~** Moluccas, Moluccan Islands
molusco *m* ZO mollusk, *Br* mollusc
momentáneo *adj* momentary
momento *m* moment; ***a cada*** **~** all the time; ***al*** **~** at once; ***por el*** **~**, ***de*** **~** for the moment; ***hasta el*** **~** up to now, so far; ***de un*** **~** ***a otro*** from one minute to the next; ***desde un primer*** **~** right from the beginning; ***por*** **~*s*** by the minute; ***no es el*** **~** the time isn't right; ***atravesar un mal*** **~**, ***pasar por un*** **~** ***difícil*** go through a bad patch; ***estar en su mejor*** **~** be at one's peak *o* best
momia *f* mummy
momificar ⟨1g⟩ *v/t* mummify
momio *m* F cushy job F
mona *f* ZO (female) monkey; ***dormir la*** **~** F sleep it off
◇ **mona de Pascua** Easter cake
monacal *adj* monastic
Mónaco *m* Monaco
monada *f*: ***su hija es una*** **~** her daughter is lovely; ***¡qué*** **~*!*** how lovely!
monaguillo *m* REL altar boy
monarca *m* monarch
monarquía *f* monarchy
monárquico I *adj* monarchic; POL monarchist **II** *m/f* monarchist
monasterio *m* monastery
monástico *adj* monastic
monda *f* **1** *de frutos* peel; *de patata etc* peelings *pl* **2** *acción* peeling **3**: ***¡es la*** **~*!*** P it's unbelievable!
mondadientes *m inv* toothpick
mondadura *f* **1** peel; **~*s*** *pl* peelings **2** *acción* peeling
mondar ⟨1a⟩ *v/t* **1** *fruta*, *patata* peel **2** *árbol* prune; **mondarse** *v/r*: **~** ***de risa*** F split one's sides laughing
mondo *adj* **1** (*sin complemento*) plain; **~** ***y lirondo*** *fig* pure and simple **2** *cabeza* bald
mondongo *m* tripe
moneda *f* **1** coin; ***casa de la*** **~** mint; ***ser*** **~** ***corriente*** *fig* be an everyday occurrence; ***pagar a alguien con*** *o* ***en la misma*** **~** *fig* pay s.o. back in their own coin **2** (*divisa*) currency
◇ **moneda extranjera** foreign currency; **moneda falsa** counterfeit currency; **moneda única** single currency
monedero *m* **1** change purse, *Br* purse **2** *L.Am.* TELEC pay phone
◇ **monedero electrónico** electronic purse *o* wallet
monegasco I *adj* Monegasque **II** *m*, **-a** *f* Monegasque
monería *f* ☞ ***monada***
monetario *adj* monetary
mongol *m/f* & *adj* Mongol, Mongolian
Mongolia *f* Mongolia
mongólico *adj*: ***niño*** **~** MED child with Down's syndrome
monicaco *m desp* F silly young kid F
monigote *m* **1** (*muñeco*) rag doll; **~** ***de nieve*** snowman **2** F (*tonto*) F idiot
monises *mpl* F dough *sg* F, *Br* dosh *sg* F
monitor[1] *m* TV, INFOR monitor
monitor[2] *m*, **~a** *f* (*profesor*) instructor
monitorear *vt L.Am.* monitor
monitoreo *m L.Am.* monitoring
monja *f* nun
monje *m* monk
mono I *m* **1** ZO monkey **2** *prenda* coveralls *pl*, *Br* boilersuit **3**: ***ser el último*** **~** be the low man on the totem pole; ***tratar como al último*** **~** treat like dirt **II** *adj* pretty, cute
monoambiente *m Arg* studio apartment, *Br* studio flat
monocolor *adj* self-colored, *Br* self-coloured, monochrome
monóculo *m* monocle
monocultivo *m* AGR monoculture
monogamia *f* monogamy
monógamo *adj* monogamous
monograma *m* monogram
monolingüe *adj* monolingual
monólogo *m* monolog(ue)
monomando *m* TÉC mixing faucet, *Br* mixer tap
monomotor AVIA **I** *adj* single-engine **II** *m* single-engine plane
monoparental *adj*: ***familia*** **~** one-parent family, single-parent family
monopartidismo *m* POL one-party system
monopatín *m* **1** skateboard **2** *Rpl patinete* scooter
monoplano *m* AVIA monoplane
monoplaza *m* single-seater
monopolio *m* monopoly
monopolizar ⟨1f⟩ *v/t tb fig* monopolize

monorraíl *m* monorail
monosílabo *adj* monosyllabic
monoteísmo *m* monotheism
monotonía *f* monotony
monótono *adj* monotonous
monovolumen *m* AUTO minivan, *Br* people carrier, MPV
monóxido *m* monoxide
◇ **monóxido de carbono** carbon monoxide
monseñor *m* REL monsignor
monsergas *fpl*: ***déjate de ~*** F stop going on F
monstruo *m* **1** (*adefesio*) monster **2** (*fenómeno*) phenomenon
monstruosidad *f* eyesore, monstrosity
monstruoso *adj* **1** (*deforme, feo*) monstrous **2** (*escandaloso*) outrageous, monstrous
monta *f*: ***de poca ~*** unimportant
montacargas *m inv* hoist
montada *f L.Am.* mounted police
montado *adj*: ***~ a caballo*** on horseback
montador *m*, **~a** *f* **1** TÉC fitter **2** *de película* editor
montaje *m* **1** TÉC assembly **2** *de película* editing **3** TEA staging; *fig* F con F
◇ **montaje fotográfico** photomontage
montante *m* COM total
montaña *f* mountain; ***hacer una ~ de algo*** *fig* make a mountain out of sth; ***tener ~s de trabajo*** have piles of work
◇ **montaña rusa** rollercoaster
montañero *m*, **-a** *f* mountaineer
montañés I *adj* mountain *atr* **II** *m*, **-esa** *f person who lives in the mountains*
montañismo *m* mountaineering
montañoso *adj* mountainous
montaplatos *m inv* dumb waiter
montar ⟨1a⟩ **I** *v/t* **1** TÉC assemble **2** *tienda* put up **3** *negocio* set up **4** TEA stage **5** *película* edit **6** *caballo* mount; ***~ la guardia*** mount guard
II *v/i*: ***~ en bicicleta*** ride a bicycle; ***~ a caballo*** ride a horse; ***tanto monta*** it makes no difference
montarse *v/r* **1** *en coche, moto etc* get in; *en caballo* get on **2** *un negocio* set up **3** F *jaleo, bronca* kick up F; ***montárselo*** F set things up F
montaraz *adj* **1** *persona* uncouth, boorish **2** *animal* wild
monte *m* mountain; (*bosque*) woodland; ***echarse*** *o* ***tirarse al ~*** *fig* take to the hills
◇ **monte alto** forest; **monte bajo** scrubland; **monte de piedad** pawnshop
montera *f* **1** (*gorra*) cap **2** TAUR bullfighter's hat; ***ponerse el mundo por ~*** F take a risk
montería *f* (art of) hunting
montero *m*, **-a** *f* hunter
montés *adj*: ***cabra montesa*** mountain goat; ***gato ~*** wildcat
montevideano I *adj* Montevidean **II** *m*, **-a** *f* Montevidean
montículo *m* mound
monto *m* COM total
montón *m* pile, heap; ***ser del ~*** *fig* be average, not stand out; ***montones de*** F piles of F, loads of F; ***tiene coches a montones*** she has loads of cars; ***había gente a montones*** there were loads of people; ***me gusta un ~*** F I'm crazy about him / her F
montuoso *adj* mountainous
montura *f de gafas* frame
monumental *adj* monumental
monumento *m* monument; ***ser un ~*** *fig* F be very good-looking
◇ **monumento funerario** memorial
monzón *m* monsoon
moña *f Esp* P: ***cogerse una ~*** get plastered F
moñita *f Urug* bow tie
moñito *m Rpl* bow tie
moño *m con el cabello* bun; ***estar hasta el ~*** F be sick and tired
moquear ⟨1a⟩ *v/i*: ***estar moqueando*** *de persona* have a runny nose; *de nariz* run
moqueta *f* (wall-to-wall) carpet
moquillo *m* ZO distemper
mor *m lit*: ***por ~ de*** because of
mora *f* BOT *de zarza* blackberry; *de morera* mulberry
morada *f* dwelling; ***la última ~*** *lit* one's final resting place
morado *adj* purple; ***pasarlas -as*** F have a rough time; ***ponerse ~ de*** F stuff o.s. with F
morador *m*, **~a** *f* inhabitant
moral[1] **I** *adj* moral **II** *f* **1** (*moralidad*) morals *pl* **2** (*ánimo*) morale; ***estar bajo de ~*** be feeling low; ***levantar la ~*** cheer up
moral[2] *m* BOT mulberry tree
moraleja *f* moral

moralidad *f* morality
moralina *f* moral
moralista *m/f* moralist
moralizar ⟨1f⟩ **I** *v/t* raise the moral tone of **II** *v/i* moralize
morapio *m* F cheap (red) wine, *esp Br* plonk F
morar ⟨1a⟩ *v/i lit* dwell *lit*
moratón *m* bruise
moratoria *f* moratorium
mórbido *adj* **1** (*morboso*) morbid **2** *lit* soft
morbo *m* F perverted kind of pleasure; ***le da ~ ver un accidente*** accidents hold a morbid fascination for him
morbosidad *f* morbidness, morbidity
morboso *adj* perverted
morcilla *f* blood sausage, *Br* black pudding; ***¡que te den ~!*** *fig* F go to hell! F
mordacidad *f* sharpness
mordaz *adj* biting, sharp
mordaza *f para la boca* gag
mordedura *f* bite
morder ⟨2h⟩ *v/t* bite; ***está que muerde*** *fig* F he's / she's furious F
mordida *f Méx* F bribe
mordisco *m* bite
mordisquear ⟨1a⟩ *v/t* nibble
morena *f* ZO moray eel
moreno I *adj* **1** *pelo, piel* dark **2** (*bronceado*) tanned **II** *m* tan, suntan
morera *f* BOT white mulberry tree
morería *f* **1** HIST Moorish lands *pl* **2** *barrio* Moorish quarter
moretón *m L.Am.* bruise
morfar *vt Rpl* F eat
morfe *m Rpl* F grub F
morfema *m* morpheme
morfina *f* morphine
morfinómano I *adj* addicted to morphine **II** *m*, **-a** *f* morphine addict
morfología *f* morphology
morgue *f L.Am.* morgue
moribundo I *adj* dying **II** *m*, **-a** *f* dying man / woman
morigerado *adj* well-behaved
morilla *f* BOT wild artichoke
morir ⟨3k; *part* **muerto**⟩ *v/i* die (**de** of); ***~ de hambre*** die of hunger, starve to death; **morirse** *v/r* die; ***~ de*** *fig* die of; ***~ por*** *fig* be dying for; ***~ de sed*** die of thirst; ***~ de risa*** laugh one's head off, die laughing
morisco I *adj* Moorish **II** *m*, **-a** *f* HIST *Moorish convert to Christianity in post-Reconquest Spain*
mormón *m*, **-ona** *f* Mormon
moro I *adj* **1** North African **2** HIST Moorish **II** *m*, **-a** *f* **1** North African **2** HIST Moor; ***no hay ~s en la costa*** F the coast is clear
morocho *adj S.Am. persona* dark
morondo *adj* **1** *persona* bald **2** *árbol* bare
moronga *f C.Am., Méx* blood sausage, *Br* black pudding
morosidad *f* COM slowness in paying
moroso COM **I** *adj* slow to pay **II** *m*, **-a** *f* slow payer
morral *m* knapsack
morralla *f Méx* small change
morrear ⟨1a⟩ P *v/t* kiss, *Br tb* snog F; **morrearse** *v/r* kiss, *Br tb* snog F
morrena *f* GEOL moraine
morriña *f* homesickness
morro *m* ZO snout; ***~s*** *pl* F mouth *sg*, kisser *sg* F; ***beber a ~*** drink straight from the bottle; ***estar de ~s*** F be annoyed (***con*** with); ***tener mucho ~*** F have a real nerve; ***caer*** *o* ***caerse de ~s*** fall flat on one's face
morrocotudo *adj* F massive
morrón *m Rpl* red pepper
morrongo *m* F pussycat F
morsa *f* ZO walrus
mortaja *f* **1** (*sudario*) shroud **2** *L.Am.* cigarette paper
mortal I *adj* **1** *criatura* mortal **2** *accidente, herida* fatal; *dosis* lethal **II** *m/f* mortal
mortalidad *f* mortality; (***tasa de***) ***~*** mortality rate
◇ **mortalidad infantil** infant mortality rate
mortalmente *adv* fatally
mortandad *f* loss of life
mortecino *adj luz* dim; *color* dull
mortero *m tb* MIL mortar
mortífero *adj* lethal
mortificación *f* mortification
mortificante *adj* mortifying
mortificar ⟨1g⟩ *v/t* torment; **mortificarse** *v/r fig* **1** (*angustiarse*) distress o.s. **2** *Méx* (*apenarse*) be embarrassed *o* ashamed
mortuorio *adj* funeral *atr*; ***casa -a*** funeral home
moruno *adj desp* Moorish
mosaico *m* **1** mosaic **2** *L.Am. baldosa*

tile

mosca *f* fly; **~ *muerta*** F hypocrite; ***estar ~*** F smell a rat F; ***estar con*** *o* ***tener la ~ detrás de la oreja*** F smell a rat F; ***por si las ~s*** F just to be on the safe side; ***¿qué ~ te ha picado?*** what's biting you?; ***soltar*** *o* ***aflojar la ~*** F pay up, cough up F; ***caer*** *o* ***morir como ~s*** *fig* drop like flies; ***estar papando ~s*** F be miles away F; ***no es capaz de matar una ~*** he wouldn't hurt a fly

◇ **mosca azul, mosca de la carne** ZO bluebottle

moscada *adj*: ***nuez ~*** nutmeg

moscarda *f* bluebottle, blowfly

moscardón *m* hornet

moscovita I *adj* Muscovite **II** *m/f* Muscovite

Moscú *m* Moscow

mosqueado F *adj Esp* **1** (*molesto*) riled F **2** (*receloso*) suspicious

mosquear ⟨1a⟩ F *v/t Esp* **1** (*molestar*) rile F **2** F (*hacer sospechar*) make suspicious; **mosquearse** *v/r* **1** (*enfadarse*) get hot under the collar F **2** (*sentir recelo*) smell a rat F

mosquete *m* musket

mosquetero *m* musketeer

mosquetón *m* musket

mosquita *f*: **~ *muerta*** F hypocrite

mosquitero *m* mosquito net

mosquito *m* mosquito

mostacho *m* mustache, *Br* moustache

mostaza *f* mustard

mosto *m* grape juice

mostrador *m en tienda, banco etc* counter; *en bar* bar; *Rpl en cocina* worktop

◇ **mostrador de facturación** check-in desk

mostrar ⟨1m⟩ *v/t* show; **mostrarse** *v/r*: **~ *contento*** seem happy

mostrenco *adj* **1** (*torpe*) dense **2** (*gordo*) fat

mota *f* **1** *de polvo* speck **2** *en diseño* dot

mote *m* **1** (*apodo*) nickname **2** *S.Am.* boiled corn *o Br* maize

motear ⟨1a⟩ *v/t* speckle

motejar ⟨1a⟩ *v/t* nickname; **~ *a alguien de algo*** brand sb sth

motel *m* motel

motero *m*, **-a** *f* F biker

motete *m* MÚS motet

motín *m* **1** (*rebelión*) mutiny **2** *en una cárcel* riot

motivación *f* motivation

motivar ⟨1a⟩ *v/t* motivate

motivo *m* **1** motive, reason; ***por ~s de salud*** for health reasons; ***sin ~*** for no reason at all; ***con ~ de*** because of; ***con ~ de la visita*** on the occasion of the visit **2** MÚS, PINT motif

moto *f* motorcycle, motorbike; ***ir / estar como una ~*** *fig* F be very agitated, *Br tb* be in a flat spin

◇ **moto acuática, moto de agua** jet ski

motocicleta *f* motorcycle

motociclismo *m* motorcycle racing

motociclista *m/f* motorcyclist

motocross *m* motocross

motonáutica *f* motorboat racing

motonave *f* motorboat

motoneta *f L.Am.* scooter

motor I *adj* ANAT motor **II** *m* engine; *eléctrico* motor

◇ **motor de búsqueda** INFOR search engine; **motor de cuatro tiempos** four-stroke engine; **motor de dos tiempos** two-stroke engine; **motor eléctrico** electric motor; **motor de inyección** fuel-injected engine; **motor de explosión** internal combustion engine

motora *f* motorboat

motorismo *m* motorcycling

motorista *m/f* motorcyclist

motosierra *f* chain saw

motovelero *m* sailing boat (*with a back-up engine*)

motriz *adj* motor; ***fuerza ~*** driving force

mouse *m L.Am.* INFOR mouse

movedizo *adj fig* restless

mover ⟨2h⟩ *v/t* **1** move **2** (*agitar*) shake **3** (*impulsar, incitar*) drive; **moverse** *v/r* move; ***¡muévete!*** get a move on! F, hurry up!

movible *adj* movable; *fig precio, opinión* fickle

movida *f* F scene

movido *adj* **1** *foto* blurred **2** *mar* rough **3** *mañana, jornada* busy

móvil I *adj* mobile **II** *m* TELEC cell phone, *Br* mobile (phone)

movilidad *f* mobility

movilización *f* MIL mobilization

movilizar ⟨1f⟩ *v/t* mobilize; **movilizarse** *v/r* mobilize

movimiento *m* **1** movement **2** COM, *fig* activity

moza *f* **1** girl; ***buena ~*** good-looking girl **2** (*camarera*) waitress
mozalbete *m* lad, boy
mozambiqueño *adj* Mozambican
mozárabe **I** *adj* Mozarabic **II** *m/f* Mozarab
mozo **I** *adj*: ***en mis años ~s*** in my youth **II** *m* **1** boy; ***buen ~*** good-looking boy **2** (*camarero*) waiter
mu *m* moo; ***no decir ni ~*** F not tell a soul
muaré *m* ☞ ***moaré***
mucama *f Rpl* maid
mucamo *m Rpl* servant
muchacha *f* girl
muchachada *f Arg* group of youngsters
muchacho *m* boy
muchedumbre *f* crowd
mucho **I** *adj* **1** *singular* a lot of, lots of; *en frases interrogativas y negativas tb* much; ***~ tiempo*** a lot of time; ***no tengo ~ tiempo*** I don't have a lot of time *o* much time; ***tengo ~ frío*** I am very cold; ***es ~ coche para mí*** this car's too much for me
2 *plural* a lot of, lots of; *en frases interrogativas y negativas tb* many; ***~s amigos*** a lot of friends; ***no tengo ~s amigos*** I don't have a lot of friends *o* many friends
II *pron* **1** *singular* a lot; *en frases interrogativas y negativas tb* much; ***no tengo ~*** I don't have much *o* a lot
2 *plural* a lot; *en frases interrogativas y negativas tb* many; ***no tengo ~s*** I don't have many *o* a lot; ***~s creen que ...*** a lot of people *o* many people think that ...
III *adv* **1** a lot; *en frases interrogativas y negativas tb* much; ***¿cuesta ~?*** does it cost a lot *o* much?; ***nos vemos ~*** we see each other often *o* a lot; ***hace ~ que no te veo*** I haven't seen you for a long time; ***¿dura / tarda ~?*** does it last / take long?
2: ***como ~*** at the most; ***10 meses dan para ~*** *o* ***dan ~ de sí*** you can do a lot in 10 months; ***no es ni con ~*** he is far from being ...; ***ni ~ menos*** far from it; ***por ~ que*** however much
mucosa *f* ANAT mucous membrane
mucosidad *f* mucus
mucoso *adj* mucous
muda *f de ropa* change of clothes
mudable *adj viento* changeable; *fig opinión, gustos* fickle
mudanza *f de casa* move
mudar ⟨1a⟩ **I** *v/t* **1** change **2** ZO shed **II** *v/i*: ***~ de*** **1** change **2** ZO shed; **mudarse** *v/r*: ***~ de casa*** move house; ***~ de ropa*** change (one's clothes)
mudéjar *adj* Mudéjar (*permitted to live under Christian rule*)
mudez *f* dumbness, muteness
mudo *adj* **1** *persona* mute **2** *letra* silent
mueble **I** *m* piece of furniture; ***~s*** *pl* furniture *sg*; ***~s de época*** period furniture; ***~s por elementos modulares*** modular furniture **II** *adj* JUR: ***bienes ~s*** movable items, personal property *sg*
◇ **mueble bar** cocktail cabinet
◇ **mueble-cama** foldaway bed, Murphy bed
mueblería *f* furniture store
mueblista *m/f artesano* furniture maker; *comerciante* furniture seller
mueca *f de dolor* grimace; ***hacer ~s*** make faces
muecín *m* REL muezzin
muela *f* tooth; ANAT molar; ***dolor de ~s*** toothache
◇ **muela del juicio** wisdom tooth
muelle *m* **1** TÉC spring **2** MAR wharf
◇ **muelle de carga** loading bay
◇ **muelle de descarga** off-loading bay
muérdago *m* BOT mistletoe
muerde *vb* ☞ ***morder***
muere *vb* ☞ ***morir***
muermo *m fig* F boredom; ***ser un ~*** *fig* be a drag F
muerte *f* death; ***a ~*** to the death; ***odiar a ~*** loathe, detest; ***me dio un susto de ~*** it frightened me to death; ***dar ~ a alguien*** kill s.o.; ***de mala ~*** *fig* F lousy F, awful F
◇ **muerte cerebral** brain death
◇ **muerte súbita** *en tenis* tiebreaker, tiebreak
muerto **I** *part* ☞ ***morir***
II *adj* dead; ***~ de hambre*** starving; *fig, desp* penniless, down and out; ***~ de sueño*** dead-tired; ***más ~ que vivo*** *fig* half-dead; ***no tener dónde caerse ~*** F be as poor as a church mouse F
III *m*, **-a** *f* dead person; ***hacer el ~*** *en el agua* float on one's back; ***cargar(le)*** *o* ***colgar(le) a alguien el ~*** *fig* get s.o. to do the dirty work
muesca *f* notch, groove

muestra *f* **1** *de un producto* sample **2** (*señal*) sign **3** (*prueba*) proof; ***como ~, un botón*** for example **4** (*modelo*) model **5** (*exposición*) show
◇ **muestra gratuita** free sample
muestrario *m* collection of samples
muestreo *m en estadística* sample; *acto* sampling
mueve *vb* ☞ ***mover***
mugido *m* moo
mugir ⟨3c⟩ *v/i* moo
mugre *f* filth
mugriento *adj* filthy
mugrón *m* AGR shoot
mugroso *adj* dirty
muguete *m* BOT lily-of-the-valley
mui *f* P mouth, kisser F; ***irse de la ~*** P talk, sing F
mujer *f* **1** woman **2** (*esposa*) wife
◇ **mujer de faenas, mujer de la limpieza** cleaning woman; **mujer de mala vida** prostitute; **mujer de la vida** prostitute
mujeriego I *m* womanizer **II** *adj*: ***montar a -as*** ride sidesaddle
mujerío *m* F group of women
mujerona *f* big fat woman
mujerzuela *f* F slut
mújol *m* ZO gray *o Br* grey mullet
mula *f* **1** ZO mule **2** *Méx* trash, *Br* rubbish
muladar *m* garbage dump, *Br* rubbish dump
mulato *m*,**-a** *f* person of mixed race, mulatto
mulero *m* mule driver
muleta *f* **1** MED crutch **2** TAUR cape
muletilla *f* favorite expression, *Br* favourite expression
muletón *m* flannelette
mullido *adj* soft
mullir ⟨3h⟩ *v/t* **1** *almohada* plump up **2** *tierra* loosen
mulo *m* ZO mule
multa *f* fine; ***poner una ~ a alguien*** fine s.o.
multar ⟨1a⟩ *v/t* fine
multicine *m* multiscreen
multicolor *adj* multicolored, *Br* multicoloured
multicopiar ⟨1b⟩ *v/t* duplicate
multicopista *f* duplicating machine
multicultural *adj* multicultural
multidisciplinar(io) *adj* multidisciplinary
multiétnico *adj* multiethnic
multifacético *adj* multifaceted
multifamiliar *m L.Am.* apartment house, *Br* block of flats
multifuncional *adj* multifunctional
multilateral *adj* multilateral
multilingüe *adj* multilingual
multimedia *f/adj* multimedia
multimediático *adj* multimedia
multimillonario *m*, **-a** *f* multimillionaire
multinacional I *adj* multinational **II** *f* multinational
multipartidismo *m* POL multiparty system
multipartidista *adj* multiparty *atr*
múltiple *adj* multiple; ***de ~ uso*** re-useable
multiplicación *f* multiplication
multiplicador *m* MAT multiplier
multiplicando *m* MAT multiplicand
multiplicar ⟨1g⟩ *v/t* multiply; **multiplicarse** *v/r* multiply
multiplicidad *f* multiplicity
múltiplo *m* MAT multiple
multipropiedad *f* timeshare
multirracial *adj* multiracial
multitud *f* crowd; ***~ de*** thousands of
multitudinario *adj* mass *atr*
multiuso *adj* multipurpose
mundanal *adj* worldly
mundano *adj* **1** *persona, fiesta* society *atr* **2** REL wordly
mundial I *adj* world *atr* **II** *m*: ***el Mundial*** (***de fútbol***) the World Cup
mundialización *f* globalization
mundialmente *adv* throughout the world
mundillo *m* world, circle
mundo *m* world; ***el Nuevo Mundo*** the New World; ***el Tercer Mundo*** the Third World; ***el otro ~*** the next world; ***nada del otro ~*** nothing out of the ordinary; ***todo el ~*** everybody, everyone; ***medio ~*** just about everybody; ***tiene mucho ~*** he's seen life; ***correr*** *o* ***ver ~*** see the world; ***traer a alguien al ~*** bring s.o. into the world, give birth to s.o.; ***venir al ~*** come into the world, be born; ***desde que el ~ es ~*** since time immemorial; ***por nada del ~*** not for anything in the world; ***se le hundió el ~, se le vino*** *o* ***cayó el ~ encima*** his / her world fell

apart
mundología *f* worldly wisdom
Múnich *m* Munich
munición *f* ammunition
municionar ⟨1a⟩ *v/t*: *~ **a alguien*** supply s.o. with ammunition, supply ammunition to s.o.
municipal *adj* municipal
municipalidad *f*, **municipio** *m* municipality
munificencia *f* generosity, munificence *fml*
muñeca *f* **1** *juguete* doll **2** *de sastre* dummy **3** ANAT wrist
muñeco *m* **1** *juguete* doll **2** *fig* puppet
◇ **muñeco de nieve** snowman
muñequera *f* wristband
muñir ⟨3h⟩ *v/t* F (*amañar*) provide, supply
muñón *m* MED stump
mural I *adj* wall *atr* **II** *m* mural
muralla *f de ciudad* wall
murciélago *m* ZO bat
murga *f* band of street musicians; ***dar la ~ a alguien*** F bug s.o. F
murió *vb* ☞ ***morir***
murmullo *m* murmur
murmuración *f*, **murmuraciones** *fpl* gossip *sg*
murmurador *m*, **~a** *f* F gossip
murmurar ⟨1a⟩ **I** *v/i* **1** *hablar* murmur **2** *criticar* gossip **II** *v/t* murmur
muro *m* wall
murria *f* F gloom, depression
murrio *adj* F gloomy, depressed; ***estar ~*** F be down F
mus *m card game, played with a partner*
musa *f* MYTH *tb fig* muse
musaraña *f* ZO shrew; ***pensar en las ~s*** F daydream
musculación *f* bodybuilding
muscular *adj* muscular
musculatura *f* muscles *pl*
músculo *m* muscle
musculoso *adj* muscular
muselina *f* muslin
museo *m de ciencias*, *historia* museum; *de pintura* art gallery
musgo *m* BOT moss
musgoso *adj* mossy
música *f* **I** music; ***leer ~*** read music; ***poner algo en ~, poner ~ a algo*** set sth to music; ***hacer ~*** make music; ***ir con la ~ a otra parte*** *fig* go somewhere else **II** *adj Méx* F: ***ser ~*** be mean; ***ser ~ para algo*** be useless at sth
◇ **música de cámara** chamber music; **música celestial** *fig* empty words *pl*, hot air F; **música enlatada** piped *o* canned music, Muzak®; **música de fondo** background music; **música instrumental** instrumental music; **música ligera** easy listening, light music; **música rock** rock music
musical *m/adj* musical
musicalidad *f* musicality
music-hall *m* vaudeville, *Br* music hall
músico I *adj* musical **II** *m*, **-a** *f* musician
musicología *f* musicology
musicólogo *m*, **-a** *f* musicologist
musicoterapia *f* music therapy
musiquilla *f desp* (simple) music
musitar ⟨1a⟩ *v/i* mumble
muslo *m* thigh
mustiarse ⟨1b⟩ *v/r de planta* wither
mustio *adj* **1** *planta* withered **2** *fig* (*deprimido*) down F
musulmán I *adj* Muslim **II** *m*, **-ana** *f* Muslim
mutación *f* **1** BIO mutation **2** TEA scene change
mutar ⟨1a⟩ *v/t* BIO mutate; **mutarse** *v/r* mutate
mutilación *f* mutilation
mutilado *m*, **-a** *f* disabled person
◇ **mutilado de guerra** disabled war veteran, *Br* disabled ex-serviceman
mutilar ⟨1a⟩ *v/t* mutilate
mutis *m inv* TEA exit; ***hacer ~*** exit; *fig* keep quiet; ***hacer ~ por el foro*** *fig* make o.s. scarce
mutismo *m* silence
mutualidad *f* benefit society, *Br* friendly society
mutuo *adj* mutual
muy *adv* **1** very; ***~ valorado*** highly valued; ***Muy Señor mío*** Dear Sir **2** (*demasiado*) too

N

N *abr* (= ***norte***) N (North(ern))
naba *f* BOT turnip
nabo *m* **I** *adj Arg* F dumb F **II** *m* turnip
nácar *m* mother-of-pearl
nacarado *adj* pearly
nacatamal *m C.Am., Méx meat, rice and corn in a banana leaf*
nacer ⟨2d⟩ *v/i* **1** be born; *de un huevo* hatch **2** *de una planta* sprout **3** *de un río, del sol* rise **4** (*surgir*) arise (***de*** from)
nacido born; ***mal ~*** wicked; ***haber ~ de pie*** be born lucky; ***no nací ~ ayer*** I wasn't born yesterday
naciente *adj* **1** *país, gobierno* newly formed **2** *sol* rising
nacimiento *m* **1** birth; ***de ~*** *defecto físico etc* congenital, that he / she *etc* is born with; ***es ciego de ~*** he was born blind **2** *de Navidad* crèche, nativity scene
nación *f* nation
nacional *adj* national
nacionalidad *f* nationality; ***doble ~*** dual nationality
nacionalismo *m* nationalism
nacionalista *m/f & adj* nationalist
nacionalización *f* COM nationalization
nacionalizar I ⟨1f⟩ *v/t* **1** COM nationalize **2** *persona* naturalize; **nacionalizarse** *v/r* become naturalized
naco *m Col* purée
nada I *pron* nothing; ***no hay ~*** there isn't anything; ***no es ~*** it's nothing; ***~ más*** nothing else; ***~ menos que*** no less than; ***~ de ~*** nothing at all; ***para ~*** not at all; ***no lo entiendes para ~*** you don't understand at all; ***lo dices como si ~*** you talk about it as if it was nothing; ***más que ~*** more than anything; ***no lo haría por ~ del mundo*** I wouldn't do it if you paid me; ***por menos de ~*** for no reason at all; ***~ más llegar*** as soon as I arrived; ***antes de ~*** first of all; ***¡~ de eso!*** F you can put that idea out of your head; ***¡casi ~!*** peanuts!; ***¡de ~!*** you're welcome, not at all; ***pues ~, …*** well, …
II *adv* not at all; ***no ha llovido ~*** it hasn't rained; ***no estoy ~ contento*** I'm not at all happy
III *f* nothingness
nadador *m*, **~a** *f* swimmer; ***~ de fondo*** long-distance swimmer
nadar ⟨1a⟩ *v/i* swim; ***~ y guardar la ropa*** *fig* have one's cake and eat it; ***~ en dinero*** *fig* be rolling in money
nadería *f* trifle
nadie *pron* nobody, no-one; ***no había ~*** there was nobody there, there wasn't anyone there; ***no hablé con ~*** I didn't speak to anybody, I spoke to no-one; ***un don ~*** F a nonentity, a nobody
nado *m* **1** *L.Am.* swimming **2**: ***atravesar a ~*** swim across
nafta *f Arg* gas(oline), *Br* petrol
naftalina *f* naphthalene
naïf *adj* naive
nailon *m* nylon
naipe *m* (playing) card
nalga *f* buttock; ***~s*** *pl* F butt *sg* F, *Br* backside *sg* F
Namibia *f* Namibia
namibio I *adj* Namibian **II** *m*, **-a** *f* Namibian
nana *f* **1** lullaby **2** *Rpl* F (*abuela*) grandma
napias *fpl* F schnozzle *sg* F, *Br* hooter *sg* F
Nápoles *m* Naples
naranja I *f* orange; ***media ~*** F (*pareja*) other half **II** *adj* orange
naranjada *f* orangeade
naranjado *adj* orange
naranjal *m* orange grove
naranjero *m*, **-a** *f* orange grower
naranjo *m* orange tree
narcisismo *m* narcissism
narcisista *adj* narcissistic
narciso *m* BOT daffodil
narco *m/f* F drug trafficker
narcosis *f* narcosis
narcótico *m/adj* narcotic
narcotizar ⟨1f⟩ *v/t* drug
narcotraficante *m/f* drug trafficker
narcotráfico *m* drug trafficking
nardo *m* BOT nard
narguile *m* hookah, hubble-bubble
narigón, narigudo *adj* big nose, P schnozzle

nariz *f* nose; ***¡narices!*** F nonsense!; ***caerse de narices con*** F bump into; ***estar hasta las narices de algo*** F be sick of sth F, be up to here with sth F; ***se le hincharon las narices*** F he blew his top F; ***hincharle las narices a alguien*** F get on s.o.'s nerves F, *Br tb* get up s.o.'s nose F; ***meter las narices en algo*** F stick one's nose in sth F; ***nos restriegan por las narices su victoria*** they're rubbing our noses in the fact that they won; ***no ve más allá de sus narices*** *fig* he can't see further than the end of his nose; ***quedarse con un palmo de narices*** F have the wind taken out of one's sails F
narizón *m* F big nose, schnozzle P, *Br* conk F
narizotas *m/f inv* F person with a big nose *o* schnozzle P
narración *f* narration
narrador *m*, **~a** *f* narrator
narrar ⟨1a⟩ *v/t*: **~ *algo*** tell the story of sth
narrativa *f* **1** narrative **2** *género literario* fiction
narrativo *adj* narrative
narval *m* ZO narwhal
nasal *adj* nasal
nasofaríngeo *adj* ANAT nose and throat *atr*
nata *f* cream
◇ **nata montada** whipped cream
natación *f* swimming
natación sincronizada synchronized swimming
natal **I** *adj* native; ***ciudad*** **~** city of one's birth, home town; ***casa*** **~** house one was born in, birthplace **II** *m/f Méx* native
natalicio **I** *adj* birthday *atr* **II** *m* birthday
natalidad *f* birthrate; ***control de*** **~** birth control; ***de alta / baja*** **~** with a high / low birthrate
natillas *fpl* custard *sg*
Natividad *f* Nativity
nativo **I** *adj* native (***de*** to) **II** *m*, **-a** *f* native
nato *adj* born; ***un poeta*** **~** a born poet
natural **I** *adj* **1** natural; ***es*** **~** it's only natural **2** MÚS *nota* natural **3**: ***ser*** **~ *de*** come from **II** *m*: ***fruta al*** **~** fruit in its own juice
naturaleza *f* **1** nature **2** (*índole*) kind, type
◇ **naturaleza muerta** PINT still life
naturalidad *f* naturalness; ***con toda*** **~** very naturally, as if it were the most natural thing in the world
naturalismo *m* naturalism
naturalista *m/f* naturalist
naturalizar ⟨1f⟩ *v/t* **I** naturalize; **naturalizarse** *v/r* become naturalized
naturalmente *adv* naturally
naturismo *m* MED naturopathy
naturista **I** *adj* **1** nudist, naturist **2** *medicina* natural; ***médico*** **~** naturopath **II** *m/f* nudist, naturist
naturópata *m/f* naturopath
naturopatía *f* natural medicine, naturopathy
naufragar ⟨1h⟩ *v/i* be shipwrecked; *fig* fail
naufragio *m* shipwreck
náufrago **I** *adj* shipwrecked **II** *m*, **-a** *f* shipwrecked person
nauseabundo *adj* nauseating
náuseas *fpl* nausea *sg*; ***tengo*** **~** I feel nauseous, *Br* I feel sick; ***dar*** **~** *fig* be sickening
náutica *f* navigation
náutico *adj* nautical
navaja *f* knife
◇ **navaja de afeitar** straight razor, *Br* cutthroat razor
navajada *f*, **navajazo** *m* knife wound, slash
navajero *m*: ***le asaltó un*** **~** he was attacked by a man with a knife
naval *adj* naval; ***base*** **~** MIL naval base; ***construcción*** **~** shipbuilding
navarro *adj* of Navarre, from Navarre, Navarre *atr*
nave *f* **1** ship; ***quemar las ~s*** *fig* burn one's boats **2** *de iglesia* nave
◇ **nave espacial** spacecraft
◇ **nave industrial** industrial premises *pl*
navegabilidad *f* navigability
navegable *adj* navigable
navegación *f* navigation
◇ **navegación aérea** air travel; **navegación de altura** celestial navigation; **navegación espacial** space travel; **navegación a vela** sailing
navegador *m* INFOR browser
navegante *m/f* **1** MAR navigator **2**: **~** (***por Internet***) (web) surfer, (net) surfer
navegar ⟨1h⟩ **I** *v/i* **1** *por el mar* sail **2** *por*

el aire, *espacio* fly **3**: **~ *por la red*** *o* ***por Internet*** surf the Net **II** *v/t* sail

Navidad *f* Christmas; **¡*Feliz ~!*** Merry *o* Happy Christmas!

navideño *adj* Christmas *atr*

naviero I *adj* shipping *atr* **II** *m*, **-a** *f* shipowner

navío *m* ship

náyade *f* MYTH naiad, water nymph

nazi *m/f* & *adj* Nazi

nazismo *m* Nazi(i)sm

N.B. *abr* (= ***nótese bien***) NB (= nota bene)

NE *abr* (= ***nordeste***) NE, Northeast

neblina *f* mist

neblinoso *adj* misty

nebulosa *f* AST nebula

nebuloso *adj fig* hazy, nebulous

necedad *f* foolishness

necesariamente *adv* necessarily; ***no ~*** not necessarily

necesario *adj* necessary

neceser *m* toilet kit, *Br* toilet bag; ***~ de viaje*** overnight bag

necesidad *f* **1** need; ***en caso de ~*** if necessary; ***por ~*** out of necessity; ***hacer de la ~ virtud*** make a virtue out of a necessity **2** (*cosa esencial*) necessity; ***de primera ~*** essential **3**: ***hacer sus ~es*** F relieve o.s. **4**: ***pasar ~es*** suffer hardship

necesitado *adj* needy; ***estar ~ de algo*** be in need of sth

necesitar ⟨1a⟩ *v/t* need; ***necesito hablarte*** I need to talk to you

necio I *adj* brainless **II** *m*, **-a** *f* fool, idiot

nécora *f* ZO, GASTR *edible sea crab*

necrología, necrológica *f* obituary

necrológico *adj* necrological

necrópolis *f* HIST necropolis

necrosis *f* MED necrosis

néctar *m* BOT nectar

nectarina *f* BOT nectarine

neerlandés I *adj* Dutch **II** *m* **1** Dutchman **2** *idioma* Dutch

neerlandesa *f* Dutchwoman

nefando, nefasto *adj* harmful

nefritis *f* nephritis

negación *f* **1** negation **2** *de acusación* denial **3** (*prohibición*) refusal **4** GRAM negative

negado *adj* useless F; ***ser ~ para algo*** be useless at sth F

negar ⟨1h & 1k⟩ *v/t* **1** *acusación* deny **2** (*no conceder*) refuse; **negarse** *v/r* refuse (***a*** to)

negativa *f* **1** refusal **2** *de acusación* denial

negativo I *adj* negative; ***dar ~*** *de test* be negative **II** *m* FOT negative

negligencia *f* JUR negligence

negligente *adj* negligent

negociable *adj* negotiable

negociación *f* negotiation; ***negociaciones*** *pl* talks, negotiations ◇ **negociación colectiva** collective bargaining

negociado *m* department

negociador I *adj* negotiating **II** *m*, **~a** *f* negotiator

negociante *m/f* businessman; *mujer* businesswoman; *desp* money-grubber

negociar ⟨1b⟩ *v/t* negotiate

negocio *m* **1** business **2** (*trato*) deal

negra *f* **1** black woman **2** MÚS quarter note, *Br* crotchet **3** *L.Am.* (*querida*) honey, dear **4**: ***tener la ~*** F be out of luck

negrero *m*, **-a** *f fig* slave driver

negrilla, negrita *f* bold

negro I *adj* black; ***estar ~*** F be furious; ***poner ~ a alguien*** F make s.o. furious, make s.o. see red; ***verse ~ para hacer algo*** F have one's work cut out to do sth; ***las he pasado -as*** I've had a rough time **II** *m* **1** black man; ***trabajar como un ~*** F work one's butt off F **2** *L.Am.* (*querido*) honey, dear

negrura *f* blackness

negruzco *adj* blackish

nel *adv Méx* F no, nope F

nena *f* F little girl, kid F

nene *m* F little boy, kid F

nenúfar *m* BOT water lily

neocelandés ☞ ***neozelandés***

neofascismo *m* neofascism

neofascista I *adj* neofascist *atr* **II** *m/f* neofascist

neófito *m* REL, *fig* neophyte

neolítico *m* GEOL Neolithic period

neologismo *m* neologism

neón *m* neon

neonazi I *adj* neonazi *atr* **II** *m/f* neonazi

neonazismo *m* neonazism

neoyorquino I *adj* New York *atr* **II** *m*, **-a** New Yorker

neozelandés I *adj* New Zealand *atr* **II** *m*, **-esa** *f* New Zealander

N

neozoico *m* GEOL Neozoic *o* Cenozoic period
Nepal *m* Nepal
nepalés I *adj* Nepalese **II** *m*, **-esa** *f* Nepalese
nepotismo *m* nepotism
nervadura, nervatura *f* **1** BOT vein structure, veins *pl* **2** ARQUI ribbing
nervio *m* ANAT nerve; ***tener ~s*** be nervous; ***tener ~s de acero*** have nerves of steel; ***crispar los ~s a alguien, poner los ~s de punta a alguien*** get on s.o.'s nerves; ***perder los ~s*** fly off the handle
nerviosismo *m* nervousness
nervioso *adj* nervous; ***ponerse ~*** get nervous; (*agitado*) get agitated; ***poner a alguien ~*** get on s.o.'s nerves
nervudo *adj persona* robust; *mano* sinewy
netiqueta *f* INFOR netiquette
neto *adj* COM net
neumático I *adj* pneumatic **II** *m* AUTO tire, *Br* tyre
◇ **neumático sin cámara** tubeless tire *o Br* tyre
neumonía *f* MED pneumonia
neura *f* F: ***le entró la ~*** she got uptight F
neural *adj* neural
neuralgia *f* neuralgia
neurálgico *adj* neuralgic; ***punto ~*** nerve center *o Br* centre; *fig* key point
neurastenia *f* nervous exhaustion
neuritis *f* MED neuritis
neurocirugía *f* neurosurgery, brain surgery
neurocirujano *m*, **-a** *f* brain surgeon
neurología *f* neurology
neurológico *adj* neurological
neurólogo *m*, **-a** *f* neurologist
neurona *f* neurone
neuropatía *f* neuropathy
neurosis *f inv* neurosis
neurótico *adj* neurotic
neutral *adj* neutral
neutralidad *f* neutrality
neutralismo *m* neutralism
neutralizar ⟨1f⟩ *v/t* neutralize
neutro I *adj* neutral **II** *m L.Am.* AUTO neutral
neutrón *m* neutron
nevada *f* snowfall
nevado *adj* snow-covered; *fig* snow-white
nevar ⟨1k⟩ *v/i* snow
nevasca *f* snowstorm
nevazón *f Arg, Chi* snowstorm
nevera *f* refrigerator, fridge
◇ **nevera portátil** cooler
nevería *f Méx, C.Am.* ice-cream parlor, *Br* ice-cream parlour
nevero *m* snowdrift
nevisca *f* light snowfall
neviscar ⟨1g⟩ *v/i* snow gently
nexo *m* link; GRAM connective
ni *conj* neither; **~ … ~** neither … nor; ***~ siquiera*** not even; ***no di ~ una*** I made a real mess of things; ***~ que*** not even if
nica *adj & m/f L.Am.* F Nicaraguan
Nicaragua *f* Nicaragua
nicaragüense *m/f & adj* Nicaraguan
nicho *m* niche
◇ **nicho ecológico** BIO (ecological) niche
◇ **nicho del mercado** COM market niche
nicotina *f* nicotine; ***bajo en ~*** low in nicotine
nidada *f* clutch
nidificar ⟨1g⟩ *v/i* nest
nido *m* nest
niebla *f* fog
nieta *f* granddaughter
nieto *m* **1** grandson **2**: ***~s pl*** grandchildren
nieve *f* **1** snow; ***~ polvo*** powder snow **2** *Méx* water ice, sorbet
◇ **nieves perpetuas** perpetual *o* permanent snow *sg*
NIF *m abr* (= ***Número de Identificación Fiscal***) Fiscal Identification Number
nihilismo *m* nihilism
nihilista I *adj* nihilistic **II** *m/f* nihilist
nilón *m* nylon
nimbo *m* **1** AST nimbus **2** *de santo* halo
nimiedad *f* triviality
nimio *adj* trivial
ninfa *f* ZO, MYTH nymph
ninguno *adj* no; ***no hay -a razón*** there's no reason why, there isn't any reason why
niña[1] *f* **1** girl **2** *forma de cortesía* young lady
niña[2] *f* ANAT pupil; ***es la ~ de sus ojos*** *fig* he is the apple of her eye; ***guardar algo como la ~ de sus ojos*** take very good care of sth, guard sth with one's life

niñada *f* **1** childishness **2** *acto* childish thing to do
niñato *adj desp* bighead
niñato *m*, **-a** *f* brat
niñera *f* nanny
niñería *f*: ***una ~*** a childish thing
niñero *adj* fond of children
niñez *f* childhood
niño I *adj* young; *desp* childish; ***¡no seas ~!*** don't be childish! **II** *m* **1** boy; ***como ~ con zapatos nuevos*** like a child with a new toy **2** *forma de cortesía* young man **3**: ***~s*** *pl* children
◇ **niño bien** rich kid F; **niño de pecho** infant; **niño probeta** test-tube baby
nipón I *adj* Japanese **II** *m*, **-ona** *f* Japanese
níquel *m* nickel
niquelar ⟨1a⟩ *v/t* nickel-plate
níscalo *m* saffron milk cap
níspero *m* BOT loquat
nitidez *f* **1** clarity **2** FOT sharpness
nítido *adj* **1** clear **2** *imagen* sharp
nitrato *m* nitrate
◇ **nitrato de Chile** saltpeter, *Br* saltpetre
nítrico *adj* nitric; ***ácido ~*** nitric acid
nitrógeno *m* nitrogen
nitroglicerina *f* nitroglycerin
nitroso *adj* nitrous
nivel *m* **1** level; ***a ~ mundial / nacional*** at *o* on a global / national level; ***un incremento del 4% a ~ nacional*** a 4% increase nationwide **2** (*altura*) height
◇ **nivel del aceite** AUTO oil level; **nivel del agua** water level; **nivel de aire** spirit level; **nivel cero** Ground Zero; **nivel freático** water table; **nivel del mar** sea level; **nivel de ruido, nivel sonoro** noise level; **nivel de vida** standard of living
nivelación *f* leveling, *Br* levelling
niveladora *f* TÉC bulldozer
nivelar ⟨1a⟩ *v/t* **1** *terreno*, *superficie* level, grade **2** *diferencias* even out
níveo *adj lit* snowy
nixtamal *m Méx*, *C.Am.* *dough from which corn tortillas are made*
no I *adv* **1** no; ***~ del todo*** not entirely; ***~ ya por el gobierno sino por los habitantes del país*** not for the government but for the people; ***ya ~*** not any more; ***~ más*** *L.Am.* ☞ ***nomás***; ***así ~ más*** *L.Am.* just like that **2** *para negar verbo* not; ***no entiendo*** I don't understand, I do not understand; ***~ mejora nada*** it doesn't improve at all; ***~ te vayas*** don't go **3** (*tan pronto como*): ***~ bien*** as soon as; ***~ bien entramos nos recibió una ovación*** no sooner had we entered than we received an ovation **4**: ***te gusta, ¿~?*** you like it, don't you?; ***te ha llamado, ¿~?*** he called you, didn't he?; ***¿a que ~?*** I bet you don't / can't etc **5** *con adjetivos, sustantivos* non-; ***~ optativo*** non-optional; ***para ~ fumadores*** for non-smokers
II *m* no; POL *tb* nay
n.o *abr* (= ***número***) No. (= number)
NO *abr* (= ***noroeste***) NW, Northwest
nobiliario *adj* noble
noble *m/f & adj* noble
nobleza *f* nobility
noche *f* night; ***¡buenas ~s!*** *saludo* good evening; *despedida* good night; ***de ~, por la ~***, *L.Am.* ***en la ~*** at night; ***hacerse de ~*** get dark; ***muy de ~, muy entrada la ~*** well into the night; ***llegó a casa muy entrada la ~*** he got home very late; ***de la ~ a la mañana*** *fig* overnight
Nochebuena *f* Christmas Eve
nochecita *f L.Am.* evening
nochero *m L.Am.* night watchman
Nochevieja *f* New Year's Eve
noción *f* **1** notion **2**: ***nociones*** *pl* rudiments, basics
nocividad *f* harmfulness
nocivo *adj* harmful
noctámbulo *m*, **-a** *f* sleepwalker
nocturno *adj* **1** night *atr*; ***clase -a*** evening class **2** ZO nocturnal
nódulo *m* nodule
nogal *m* BOT walnut
nómada I *adj* nomadic **II** *m/f* nomad
nomás *adv L.Am.* **1** just, only; ***llévaselo ~*** just take it away; ***siga ~*** just carry on **2** (*tan pronto como*): ***~ lo vio, echó a llorar*** as soon as she saw him she started to cry; ***~ llegue, te avisaré*** as soon as he arrives, I'll let you know
nombrado *adj* famous, renowned
nombramiento *m* appointment
nombrar ⟨1a⟩ *v/t* **1** mention **2** *para un cargo* appoint
nombre *m* **1** name; ***un barco de ~ desconocido*** a boat whose name is not

known, an unknown boat; ***un caballo de ~ Arquero*** a horse by the name of Arquero, a horse called Arquero; ***es abogado sólo de ~*** he is a lawyer in name only; ***de ~ amenazador*** with a threatening sounding name; ***llamar las cosas por su ~*** call a spade a spade; ***no tener ~*** *fig* be inexcusable **2** GRAM noun
◇ **nombre artístico** stage name; **nombre de familia** family name, last name, surname; **nombre de guerra** nom de guerre, pseudonym; **nombre de pila** first name; **nombre propio** proper noun; **nombre de soltera** maiden name

nomenclatura *f* nomenclature

nomeolvides *f inv* BOT forget-me-not

nómina *f* pay slip

nominación *f* nomination

nominal *adj* nominal

nominar ⟨1a⟩ *v/t* nominate

non I *adj* odd **II** *m* odd number

nonagenario I *adj* nonagenarian **II** *m*, **-a** *f* nonagenarian, person in his / her nineties

nonagésimo *adj* ninetieth

nonato *adj* born by Cesarean *o Br* Caesarean section

nono *adj* ninth

nopal *m L.Am.* BOT prickly pear

noquear ⟨1a⟩ *v/t* knock out

nor(d)este I *adj* northeastern **II** *m* northeast

noray *m* MAR (mooring) bollard

norcoreano I *adj* North Korean **II** *m*, **-a** *f* North Korean

nórdico I *adj* **1** (*del norte*) Northern European **2** *esquí* nordic **II** *m*, **-a** *f* Northern European

noria *f de agua* waterwheel; *en feria* Ferris wheel

norirlandés I *adj* of / from Northern Ireland, Northern Ireland *atr* **II** *m*, **-esa** *f* man / woman from Northern Ireland

norma *f* **1** standard **2** (*regla*) rule, regulation

normal *adj* normal

normalidad *f* normality; ***volver a la ~*** return to normal

normalización *f* **1** normalization **2** TÉC standardization

normalizar ⟨1f⟩ *v/t* **1** normalize **2** TÉC standardize; **normalizarse** *v/r* normalize

normalmente *adv* normally

normativa *f* rules *pl*, regulations *pl*

normativo *adj código, sistema etc* regulatory

nornordeste *m* north-northeast

nornoroeste *m* north-northwest

noroccidental *adj* northwestern

noroeste *m* northwest

nororiental *adj* northeastern

norte *m* north; ***al ~ de*** north of; ***perder el ~*** *fig* lose one's way

Norteamérica *f* North America

norteamericano I *adj* North American **II** *m*, **-a** *f* North American

norteño I *adj* northern **II** *m*, **-a** *f* northerner

Noruega *f* Norway

noruego I *adj* Norwegian **II** *m*, **-a** *f* Norwegian

nos I *pron complemento directo* us; *complemento indirecto* (to) us; ***~ dio el dinero*** he gave us the money, he gave the money to us **II** *reflexivo* ourselves

nosotras, nosotros *pron* we; *complemento* us; ***ven con ~*** come with us; ***somos ~*** it's us; ***esto queda entre ~*** this is just between us

nostalgia *f* nostalgia; *por la patria* homesickness

nostálgico *adj* nostalgic; *por la patria* homesick

nota *f* **1** MÚS note; ***~ discordante*** *fig* discordant note; ***dar la ~*** F draw attention to o.s. **2** EDU grade, mark; ***sacar buenas / malas ~s*** get good / bad grades **3** (*anotación*): ***tomar ~s*** take notes; ***tomar ~ de algo*** make a note of sth
◇ **nota adhesiva** Post-it® note; **nota de entrega** delivery note; **nota marginal** note in the margin; **nota a pie de página** footnote

notable I *adj* remarkable, notable **II** *m* **1** EDU *B* **2**: ***~s*** *pl* dignitaries

notación *f* MÚS notation

notar ⟨1a⟩ *v/t* **1** notice; ***hacer ~ algo a alguien*** point sth out to s.o.; ***se nota que*** you can tell that; ***hacerse ~*** draw attention to o.s. **2** (*sentir*) feel

notaría *f* notary's office

notario *m*, **-a** *f* notary

notebook *m* INFOR notebook (computer)

noticia *f* piece of news; *en noticiario* news story, item of news; ***tener ~ de algo*** have news of sth; ***~s*** *pl* news *sg*; ***no tengo ~s de él*** I haven't had any news from him
noticiario, noticierio *m L.Am.* RAD, TV news *sg*
notificación *f* notification
notificar ⟨1g⟩ *v/t* notify
notoriedad *f* clarity, clearness
notoriedad *f* **1** clarity, clearness **2** (*fama*) fame
notorio *adj* **1** (*claro*) clear **2** (*famoso*) famous, well-known
novatada *f* practical joke
novato I *adj* inexperienced **II** *m*, **-a** *f* beginner, rookie F
novecientos *adj* nine hundred
novedad *f* **1** novelty **2** *cosa* new thing; *acontecimiento* new development; ***sin ~*** no change, same as always; ***llegar sin ~*** arrive safely **3** (*noticia*) piece of news
novedoso *adj* novel, new; *invento* innovative
novel *adj* new
novela *f* novel
◇ **novela corta** novella; **novela de costumbres** novel of manners; **novela por entregas** serial; **novela negra** crime novel; **novela policíaca** detective novel; **novela rosa** romantic novel
novelar ⟨1a⟩ *v/t* turn into a novel
novelista *m/f* novelist
novelística *f* novel
novelón *m* long novel
noveno *adj* ninth
noventa *adj* ninety
novia *f* **1** girlfriend **2** (*prometida*) fiancée **3** *el día de la boda* bride
noviar ⟨1b⟩ *v/i L.Am.* F: ***~ con alguien*** go out with s.o.
noviazgo *m* engagement
noviciado *m* novitiate
novicio *m*, **-a** *f* REL novice
noviembre *m* November
novilla *f* ZO heifer
novillada *f bullfight featuring novice bulls*
novillero *m* novice (bullfighter)
novillo *m* ZO young bull; ***hacer ~s*** F play hooky F, play truant
novio *m* **1** boyfriend **2** (*prometido*) fiancé **3** *el día de la boda* bridegroom; ***quedarse compuesta y sin ~*** *tb fig* F be left high and dry F **4**: ***los ~s*** the bride and groom; (*recién casados*) the newly-weds
novísimo *adj* newest, latest
nubarrón *m* storm cloud
nube *f* cloud; ***~ tóxica*** toxic cloud, cloud of poison gas; ***estar en las ~s*** *fig* be miles away, be day-dreaming; ***estar por las ~s*** *fig* F be incredibly expensive; ***poner en las ~s*** *fig* praise to the skies
núbil *adj* nubile
nublado I *adj* cloudy, overcast **II** *m* storm cloud
nublarse ⟨1a⟩ *v/r* cloud over
nubosidad *f* clouds *pl*
nuboso *adj* cloudy
nuca *f* nape of the neck
nuclear *adj* nuclear
núcleo *m* **1** nucleus; **~ (*celular*)** BIO (cell) nucleus **2** *de problema* heart
nudillo *m* knuckle
nudismo *m* nudism
nudista *m/f* nudist; ***playa ~*** nudist beach
nudo *m* **1** *tb* BOT knot; ***se me hace un ~ en la garganta*** F I get a lump in my throat **2**: ***~ ferroviario*** railroad *o Br* railway junction
◇ **nudo corredizo** slipknot; **nudo gordiano** Gordian knot; **nudo marinero** sailor's knot, *Br* reef knot
nudoso *adj madera* knotty
nuera *f* daughter-in-law
nuestro I *adj pos* our **II** *pron* ours; ***es ~*** it's ours
nueva *f lit* piece of news
Nueva York *f* New York
Nueva Zelanda *f* New Zealand
nuevamente *adv* again
nueve *adj* nine
nuevo *adj* **1** new; ***sentirse como ~*** feel like new; ***¿qué hay de ~?*** what's new? **2** (*otro*) another; ***de ~*** again
nuez *f* **1** BOT walnut **2** ANAT Adam's apple
◇ **nuez del Brasil** Brazil nut
◇ **nuez moscada** nutmeg
nueza *f* BOT bryony, bryonia
nulidad *f* nullity; *fig* F dead loss F
nulo *adj* **1** JUR null and void **2** F *persona* hopeless **3** (*inexistente*) non-existent, zero **4** DEP: ***salida -a*** false start
núm. *abr* (= ***número***) No. (= number)

numeración *f* **1** numbering **2** (*números*) numbers *pl*
numerador *m* MAT numerator
numeral I *adj*: ***valor ~*** numerical value; ***sistema ~*** numeric system **II** *m* numeral
numerar ⟨1a⟩ *v/t* number
numerario I *adj socio* full; *empleado, profesor* permanent; *catedrático* tenured **II** *m* cash
numérico *adj* numerical; ***teclado ~*** numeric keypad, number pad
número *m* **1** number; ***un gran ~ de*** a large number of; ***sin ~*** countless; ***ser el ~ uno*** be number one, be the best; ***en ~s redondos*** in round figures; ***en ~s rojos*** *fig* in the red; ***hacer ~s*** F add up the figures, *Br* do one's sums **2** *de publicación* issue **3** *de zapato* size **4**: ***montar un ~*** F make a scene **5**: ***de ~*** *socio* full; *empleado, profesor* permanent; *catedrático* tenured
◇ **número complementario** *en lotería* bonus number; **número entero** whole number; **número de identificación fiscal** ☞ ***NIF***; **número premiado** winning number; **número primo** prime number; **número secreto** PIN (number)
numeroso *adj* numerous
numismática *f* numismatics *sg*
numismático I *adj* numismatic, coin *atr*; ***colección -a*** coin collection **II** *m*, **-a** *f* coin collector, *fml* numismatist
nunca *adv* never; ***~ jamás*** *o* ***más*** never again; ***más que ~*** more than ever
nunciatura *f* REL nunciature
nuncio *m* REL nuncio
nupcial *adj* wedding *atr*
nupcias *fpl* wedding *sg*, nuptials; ***casarse en segundas ~*** remarry, marry for the second time
nutria *f* ZO otter
nutrición *f* nutrition
nutricional *adj* nutritional; ***valor ~*** nutritional value
nutricionista *m/f* nutritionist
nutrido *adj fig* large
nutriente *m* nutrient
nutrir ⟨3a⟩ *v/t* nourish; *fig*: *esperanzas* cherish; **nutrirse** *v/r* receive nourishment; ***~ de algo*** feed on sth
nutritivo *adj* nutritious, nourishing
nylon *m* nylon
ñame *m* BOT yam
ñandú *m* ZO rhea
ñandutí *m Parag*: *type of lace*
ñaña *f L.Am.* shit F, crap F
ñapa *f S.Am.* extra, bonus; ***le di dos de ~*** I threw in an extra two
ñato *adj Rpl* snub-nosed
ñeque *m S.Am.* strength; ***de ~*** F gutsy F; ***tener mucho ~*** F have a lot of guts F
ñoñería, ñoñez *f* feebleness F, wimpish behavior *o Br* behaviour F
ñoño I *adj* feeble F, wimpish F **II** *m*, **-a** *f* drip F, wimp F
ñoqui *m*: ***~s*** *pl* GASTR gnocchi *sg*
ñu *m* ZO gnu

O

o *conj* or; ***~ (bien) ... ~*** either … or; ***~ sea*** in other words
O *abr* (= ***oeste***) W (= West(ern))
oasis *m inv* oasis
obcecación *f* obstinacy
obcecado *adj* **1** (*terco*) obstinate, stubborn **2** (*obsesionado*) obsessed (***con*** with)
obcecar ⟨1g⟩ *v/t* blind; **obcecarse** *v/r* **1** (*insistir*) stubbornly insist (***en que*** that) **2** (*obsesionarse*) become obsessed (***con*** with)
obedecer ⟨2d⟩ **I** *v/t* obey **II** *v/i* **1** obey; ***la profesora no sabe hacerse ~*** the teacher cannot control the class *o* cannot command obedience **2** *de una máquina* respond **3**: ***~ a*** *fig* (*ser causa de*) be due to
obediencia *f* obedience
obediente *adj* obedient
obelisco *m* obelisk
obertura *f* MÚS overture
obesidad *f* obesity
obeso *adj* obese
óbice *m* obstacle; ***esto no es ~ para que acuda a la reunión*** *fml* this doesn't prevent me from going to the meeting
obispal *adj* episcopal

obispo *m* bishop
óbito *m fml* demise *fml*
obituario *m* **1** REL register of deaths **2** *en periódico* obituary
objeción *f* objection
◇ **objeción de conciencia** conscientious objection
objetar ⟨1a⟩ **I** *v/t* object; ***tener algo que ~*** have any objection **II** *v/i* become a conscientious objector
objetivar ⟨1a⟩ *v/t* objectivize
objetividad *f* objectivity
objetivo I *adj* objective **II** *m* **1** objective **2** MIL target **3** FOT lens
objeto *m* **1** object; ***~s de regalo*** *pl* gifts, gift items **2**: ***con ~ de*** with the aim of
objetor *m*, **~a** *f* objector
◇ **objetor de conciencia** conscientious objector
oblea *f* (communion) wafer
oblícuo *adj* oblique, slanted
obligación *f* **1** obligation, duty **2** COM bond
◇ **obligación convertible** convertible bond
obligado *adj* obliged (***a*** to)
obligar ⟨1h⟩ *v/t* **1**: ***~ a alguien*** oblige *o* force s.o. (***a hacer algo*** to do sth) **2** *de una ley* apply to s.o.; **obligarse** *v/r*: ***~ a hacer algo*** force o.s. to do sth, make o.s. do sth
obligatoriedad *f* obligatory nature
obligatorio *adj* obligatory, compulsory
obliterar ⟨1a⟩ *v/t* **1** *fml huellas, recuerdos etc* obliterate, wipe away **2** MED block
oblongo *adj* oblong
obnubilar ⟨1a⟩ *v/t* cloud
oboe *m* MÚS oboe
oboísta *m/f* oboist
obra *f* **1** work; ***~s completas*** complete works **2** (*acción*): ***hacer buenas ~s*** do good deeds; ***por ~ de*** thanks to, as a result of; ***poner por*** *o L.Am.* ***en ~*** set in motion; ***¡manos a la ~!*** let's get to work! **3**: ***de ~*** *muro, chimenea* brick *atr* **4**: ***~s*** *pl de construcción* building work *sg*; *en la vía pública* road works
◇ **obra de arte** work of art; **obra de consulta** reference book; **obra maestra** masterpiece; **obra de referencia** reference work; **obra de teatro** play; **obras públicas** public works
obrador *m* workshop; *de pan* bakery
obraje *m Méx* butcher's
obrar ⟨1a⟩ **I** *v/i* **1** act **2**: ***su carta obra en mi poder*** his / her letter is in my possession **II** *v/t* work
obrero I *adj* working **II** *m*, **-a** *f* worker
◇ **obrero de la construcción** construction worker, hard hat F; **obrero especializado** skilled worker; **obrero portuario** longshoreman, *Br* dock worker
obscenidad *f* obscenity
obsceno *adj* obscene
obscu... ☞ ***oscu...***
obsequiar ⟨1b⟩ *v/t*: ***~ a alguien con algo*** present s.o. with sth
obsequio *m* gift; ***en ~ de alguien*** in honor *o Br* honour of s.o.
obsequioso *adj* attentive
observación *f* **1** observation **2** JUR observance
observador I *adj* observant; ***ser muy ~*** be very observant **II** *m*, **~a** *f* observer
observancia *f* observance
observar ⟨1a⟩ *v/t* **1** *con la mirada* observe **2** (*advertir*) notice, observe **3** (*comentar*) remark, observe
observatorio *m* observatory
◇ **observatorio astronómico** observatory
◇ **observatorio meteorológico** weather station
obsesión *f* obsession
obsesionado *adj* obsessed
obsesionar I ⟨1a⟩ *v/t* obsess; **obsesionarse** *v/r* become obsessed (***con*** with)
obsesivo *adj* obsessive
obseso *adj* obsessed
obsoleto *adj* obsolete
obstaculizar ⟨1f⟩ *v/t* hinder, hamper
obstáculo *m* obstacle; ***carrera de ~s*** obstacle race; ***ponerle ~s a alguien*** make things difficult for s.o.; ***ponerle ~s a algo*** make sth difficult
obstante: ***no ~*** nevertheless, nonetheless
obstetra *m/f* obstetrician
obstetricia *f* obstetrics *sg*
obstinación *f* obstinacy
obstinado *adj* obstinate
obstinarse ⟨1a⟩ *v/r* insist; ***~ en hacer algo*** insist on doing sth
obstrucción *f* obstruction, blockage; ***~ de la justicia*** obstruction of justice

obstruccionismo *m* POL obstructionism
obstruir ⟨3g⟩ *v/t* obstruct, block; **obstruirse** *v/r* get blocked
obtener ⟨2l; *part* **obtuvo**⟩ *v/t* get, obtain *fml*
obtenible *adj* obtainable
obturación *f de tubo, orificio etc* blocking, blockage
obturador *m* shutter
obturar ⟨1a⟩ *v/t* plug
obtuso *adj tb fig* obtuse
obtuvo *vb* ☞ ***obtener***
obús *m* MIL shell
obviar ⟨1c⟩ *v/t* avoid, *fml* obviate
obviedad *f* obviousness
obvio *adj* obvious
oca *f* goose
ocarina *f* MÚS ocarina
ocasión *f* **1** occasion; ***con ~ de*** on the occasion of; ***en ocasiones*** on occasion **2** (*oportunidad*) chance, opportunity; ***la ~ hace al ladrón*** F don't put temptation in a thief's way; ***la ~ la pintan calva*** F strike while the iron is hot F **3** COM: ***de ~*** cut-price, bargain *atr*; *de segunda mano* second-hand, used
ocasional *adj* occasional
ocasionar ⟨1a⟩ *v/t* cause
ocaso *m* **1** *del sol* setting **2** *de imperio, poder* decline
occidental **I** *adj* western **II** *m/f* Westerner
occidente *m* west
occipucio *m* ANAT occiput
occiso *adj* JUR: ***persona -a*** victim
OCDE *f abr* (= ***Organización de Cooperación y Desarrollo Económico***) OECD (= Organization for Economic Cooperation and Development)
Oceanía *f* Oceania
oceánico *adj* oceanic
océano *m* ocean
◇ **Océano Atlántico** Atlantic Ocean; **Océano Glacial Antártico** Antarctic Ocean; **Océano Glacial Ártico** Arctic Ocean; **Océano Indico** Indian Ocean; **Océano Pacífico** Pacific Ocean
oceanografía *f* oceanographic
oceanógrafo *m*, **-a** *f* oceanographer
ocelote *m* ZO ocelot
ochenta *adj* eighty
ocho **I** *adj* eight **II** *m* eight
ochocientos *adj* eight hundred
ocio *m* leisure time, free time; *desp* idleness; ***industria del ~*** leisure industry
ociosear ⟨1a⟩ *v/i S.Am.* laze around
ociosidad *f* idleness
ocioso *adj* idle
oclusivo *adj*: ***consonante -a*** GRAM occlusive
ocre *m/adj* ocher, *Br* ochre
oct. *abr* (= ***octubre***) Oct. (= October)
octagonal *adj* ☞ ***octogonal***
octágono *m* ☞ ***octógono***
octano *m* octane
octava *f* MÚS octave
octavilla *f* leaflet
octavo **I** *adj* eighth **II** *m* **1** eighth **2** DEP: ***~s de final*** *pl* last 16
octeto *m* **1** MÚS octet **2** INFOR byte
octogenario **I** *adj* octogenarian **II** *m*, **-a** *f* octogenarian, person in his / her eighties
octogonal *adj* octagonal
octógono *m* octagon
octubre *m* October
OCU *f abr* (= ***Organización de Consumidores y Usuarios***) Consumers' Association
ocular **I** *adj* eye *atr* **II** *m* eyepiece
oculista *m/f* ophthalmologist
ocultación *f* concealment
ocultar ⟨1a⟩ *v/t* hide, conceal; **ocultarse** *v/r* hide
ocultismo *m* occult
oculto *adj* **1** hidden **2** (*sobrenatural*) occult; ***las ciencias -as*** the occult
ocupación *f* **1** *tb* MIL occupation **2** (*actividad*) activity **3**: ***~ hotelera*** hotel occupancy
ocupacional *adj* occupational; ***terapia ~*** occupational therapy
ocupado *adj* **1** busy **2** *asiento* taken
ocupante **I** *adj* MIL occupying **II** *m/f* occupant; ***~s*** *pl* MIL occupying forces
ocupar ⟨1a⟩ *v/t* **1** *espacio* take up, occupy **2** (*habitar*) live in, occupy **3** *obreros* employ **4** *periodo de tiempo* spend, occupy **5** MIL occupy; **ocuparse** *v/r* **1**: ***~ de*** deal with **2** (*cuidar de*) look after
ocurrencia *f* **1** occurrence **2** (*chiste*) quip, witty remark
ocurrente *adj* witty
ocurrir ⟨3a⟩ **I** *v/i* **1** happen, occur; ***¿qué ocurre?*** what's going on?; ***¿qué te ocurre?*** what's the matter? **II** *v/i Méx* go; **ocurrirse** *v/r*: ***se me ocurrió***

it occurred to me, it struck me
oda *f* ode
odiar ⟨1b⟩ *v/t* hate
odio *m* hatred, hate
odioso *adj* odious, hateful
odisea *f fig* odyssey
odómetro *m* odometer, *Br* mil(e)-ometer
odontología *f* dentistry
odontólogo *m*, **-a** *f* dental surgeon
odorífero *adj* fragrant
OEA *f abr* (= ***Organización de los Estados Americanos***) OAS (= Organization of American States)
oeste *m* west; ***al ~ de*** west of
ofender ⟨2a⟩ *v/t* offend; **ofenderse** *v/r* take offense (***por*** at)
ofensa *f* insult
ofensiva *f* offensive
ofensivo *adj* offensive
ofensor I *adj* offending **II** *m*, **~a** *f* offender
oferta *f* offer; ***~ especial*** special offer; ***tener en ~*** have on offer
◇ **oferta de empleo** job offer
◇ **oferta pública de adquisición** takeover bid
ofertante *m/f* bidder
ofertar ⟨1a⟩ *v/t* COM put on special offer
oficial I *adj* official **II** *m/f* MIL officer
oficialidad *f* MIL officers *pl*
oficialista *adj L.Am.* pro-government
oficializar ⟨1f⟩ *v/t* make official
oficiante *m* REL celebrant
oficiar ⟨1b⟩ **I** *v/i* officiate (**de** at) **II** *v/t* REL conduct, officiate at
oficina *f* office
◇ **oficina de correos** post office; **oficina de empleo** employment office; **oficina de objetos perdidos** lost and found, *Br* lost property; **oficina de turismo** tourist office
oficinesco *adj* office *atr*; *desp* bureaucratic
oficinista *m/f* office worker
oficio *m* **1** *trabajo* trade; ***sin ~ ni beneficio*** F with no trade **2**: ***abogado de ~*** public defender, *Br* duty solicitor **3**: ***Santo Oficio*** HIST Holy Office, Inquisition
◇ **oficio de difuntos** funeral service, office of the dead
◇ **oficio divino** divine office
oficioso *adj* unofficial
ofimática *f* INFOR office automation
ofrecer ⟨2d⟩ *v/t* offer; **ofrecerse** *v/r* **1** volunteer, offer one's services (***de*** as) **2** (*presentarse*) appear **3** *fml*: ***¿qué se le ofrece?*** what can I do for you?
ofrecimiento *m* offer
ofrenda *f* offering
ofrendar ⟨1a⟩ *v/t* offer
oftalmóloga *f* ophthalmology
oftalmología *f* ophthalmology
oftalmólogo *m*, **-a** *f* ophthalmologist
ofuscamiento *m* blinding rage
ofuscar ⟨1g⟩ *v/t tb fig* blind
ogro *m tb fig* ogre
ohmio *m* EL ohm
oída *f*: ***conocer algo de ~s*** have heard of sth
oído *m* **1** *sentido* hearing; ***tener el ~ fino*** have sharp hearing
2 ear; ***dolor de ~*** earache; ***me pitan los ~s*** *por música alta* my ears are ringing; ***de ~*** MÚS by ear; ***¡cómo le debían estar pitando los ~s!*** *fig* his ears must have been burning; ***dar*** *o* ***prestar ~s*** listen; ***hacer ~s sordos*** turn a deaf ear; ***entrarle por un ~ y salirle por el otro*** go in one ear and come out the other; ***llegar a ~s de alguien*** come to s.o.'s attention; ***ser todo ~s*** *fig* be all ears
◇ **oído medio** ANAT middle ear
oigo *vb* ☞ ***oír***
oír ⟨3q⟩ *v/t* **1** *tb* JUR hear **2** (*escuchar*) listen to; ***hacerse ~*** make o.s. heard; ***¡oiga!*** TELEC hello!; ***¡oye!*** listen!, hey! F; ***como quien oye llover*** F he turned a deaf ear
OIT *f abr* (= ***Organización Internacional de Trabajo***) ILO (= International Labor Organization)
ojal *m* buttonhole
ojalá *int*: ***¡~!*** let's hope so; ***¡~ venga!*** I hope he comes; ***¡~ tuvieras razón!*** I only hope you're right
ojeada *f* glance; ***echar una ~ a alguien*** glance at s.o.
ojeador *m* DEP scout
ojear ⟨1a⟩ *v/t* look at, have a look at
ojeras *fpl* bags under the eyes
ojeriza *f* grudge; ***tener ~ a alguien*** have a grudge against s.o.
ojeroso *adj*: ***estar ~*** have bags under one's eyes
ojete I *m* eyelet **II** *m/f Méx* V bastard F, son of a bitch P

ojo *m* ANAT eye; ***abrir los ~s*** open one's eyes; ***abrir los ~s como platos*** open one's eyes really wide; ***con mis propios ~s*** with my own eyes; ***en un abrir y cerrar de ~s*** in an instant; ***¡~!*** F watch out!, mind! F; ***andar con ~*** F keep one's eyes open F; ***a ~*** roughly; ***a ~s vistas*** visibly; ***abrir los ~s a alguien*** *fig* open s.o.'s eyes; ***cerrar los ~s ante algo*** turn a blind eye to sth; ***no tener ~s en la cara*** *fig* be blind; ***costar un ~ de la cara*** F cost an arm and a leg F; ***no pegar ~*** F not sleep a wink F; ***echar el ~ a algo / alguien*** eye sth / s.o. up; ***no quitar ~ de*** not take one's eyes off; ***comer(se) a alguien con los ~s*** *fig* devour s.o. with one's eyes, ogle s.o.; ***se le iban los ~s*** *fig* his / her eyes wandered; ***mirar a algo con otros ~s*** *fig* look at sth differently; ***no ver con buenos ~s*** have a low opinion of, not approve of; ***tener mucho ~ para hacer algo*** be very good at doing sth; ***tener ~ clínico*** have a good eye; ***tener ~ clínico*** *o* ***mucho ~ para descubrir errores*** have a good eye for mistakes, be good at spotting mistakes; ***~ por ~ y diente por diente*** an eye for an eye and a tooth for a tooth; ***~s que no ven, corazón que no siente*** what you don't see won't hurt you
◇ **ojo de buey** MAR porthole; **ojo de la cerradura** keyhole; **ojo del culo** V asshole V, *Br* arsehole V; **ojo de gallo** corn

ojota *f* **1** *C.Am.*, *Méx* sandal **2** *Rpl* thong, *Br* flip-flop

okey *interj L.Am.* ok

okupa *m/f Esp* F squatter

ola *f* wave
◇ **ola de calor** heat wave; **ola de frío** cold spell; **ola de gripe** outbreak of flu

¡olé!, ¡ole! *int* olé!

oleada *f fig* wave, flood

oleaginoso *adj* oleaginous

oleaje *m* swell

óleo *m* oil; ***pintura al ~*** oil painting

oleoducto *m* (oil) pipeline

oleoso *adj* oily

oler ⟨2i⟩ **I** *v/i* **1** smell (***a*** of) **2**: ***me huelo algo*** *fig* there's something fishy going on, I smell a rat **II** *v/t* smell

olfatear ⟨1a⟩ *v/t* sniff

olfato *m* sense of smell; *fig* nose; ***tener ~ para algo*** have a good nose for sth

oligoceno *m* GEOL Oligocene

oligopolio *m* COM oligopoly

olimpíada, olimpiada *f* Olympics *pl*

olímpico *adj* Olympic; ***villa -a*** Olympic village

olisquear ⟨1a⟩ *v/t* sniff

oliva *f* BOT olive

olivar *m* olive grove

olivarero *adj* olive *atr*, olive-producing

olivicultor *m*, **~a** *f* olive grower

olivo *m* olive tree

olla *f* pot
◇ **olla exprés** pressure cooker; **olla de grillos** *fig* F madhouse; **olla podrida** GASTR *type of stew containing different kinds of meat*; **olla a presión** pressure cooker

olmo *m* BOT elm

olor *m* **1** smell; *de flores*, *perfume tb* scent **2**: ***en ~ de santidad*** like a saint; ***fue acogido en ~ de multitud(es)*** he was received by a huge crowd
◇ **olor corporal** body odor, *Br* body odour, BO

oloroso *adj* scented

OLP *f abr* (= ***Organización para la Liberación de Palestina***) PLO (= Palestine Liberation Organization)

olvidadizo *adj* forgetful

olvidar ⟨1a⟩ *v/t* forget; **olvidarse** *v/r*: ***~ de algo*** forget sth; ***se le olvidó*** it slipped his mind, he forgot

olvido *m* **1** oblivion; ***caer en el ~*** fall into oblivion **2** (*omisión*) oversight

ombligo *m* ANAT navel; ***el ~ del mundo*** the center *o Br* centre of the universe; ***mirarse el ~*** *fig* contemplate one's navel; ***encogérsele a alguien el ~*** *fig* F get the wind up F

OMC *f abr* (= ***Organización Mundial de Comercio***) WTO (= World Trade Organization)

omelet, omelette *f L.Am.* omelet, *Br* omelette

ominoso *adj* **1** (*despreciable*) detestable **2** (*de mal agüero*) ominous

omisión *f* omission

omiso *adj*: ***hacer caso ~ de algo*** ignore sth

omitir ⟨3a⟩ *v/t* omit, leave out

ómnibus *m inv Cu*, *Urug* bus

omnímodo *adj fml poder* absolute, all-embracing

omnipotente *adj* omnipotent

omnipresencia *f* omnipresence
omnipresente *adj* omnipresent
omnisciente *adj* omniscient
omnívoro I *adj* omnivorous **II** *m* omnivore
omóplato, omoplato *m* ANAT shoulder blade
OMS *f abr* (= ***Organización Mundial de la Salud***) WHO (= World Health Organization)
OMT *f abr* (= ***Organización Mundial del Turismo***) World Tourism Organization
onanismo *m* onanism
ONCE *f abr* (= ***Organización Nacional de Ciegos de España***) Spanish National Association for the Blind
once I *adj* eleven **II** *m* DEP team
onceavo I *adj* eleventh **II** *m* eleventh
oncología *f* MED oncology
oncólogo *m*, **-a** *f* oncologist
onda *f* **1** wave; ***captar la ~*** F get it F; ***estar en la ~*** F be with it F **2** *Méx*: ***¿qué ~?*** F what's happening? F
◇ **onda corta** short wave; **onda expansiva** shock wave; **onda larga** long wave; **onda media** medium wave; **onda sonora** sound wave
ondear ⟨1a⟩ *v/i de bandera* wave
ondulación *f* undulation
ondulado *adj* wavy; *cartón* corrugated; *terreno* undulating
ondular ⟨1a⟩ **I** *v/i* undulate **II** *v/t pelo* wave
ondulatorio *adj*: ***movimiento ~*** waving motion
oneroso *adj* onerous
ONG *f abr* (= ***Organización no Gubernamental***) NGO (= non-governmental organization)
ónice *m* MIN onyx
onomástica *f* saint's day
onomástico *m L.Am.* **1** saint's day **2** (*cumpleaños*) birthday
onomatopeya *f* onomatopoeia
onomatopéyico *adj* onomatopoeic
ONU *f abr* (= ***Organización de las Naciones Unidas***) UN (= United Nations)
onza *f* ounce
OPA *f abr* (= ***oferta pública de adquisición***) takeover bid; ***lanzar una ~ hostil*** launch a takeover bid
opacar ⟨1g⟩ *v/t L.Am.* darken, cast a shadow over
opacidad *f* opacity
opaco *adj* **1** *cristal* opaque **2** *voz, persona etc* dull
ópalo *m* MIN opal
opción *f* **1** option, choice **2** (*posibilidad*) chance
◇ **opción de compra** COM option to buy
◇ **opción de venta** COM option to sell
opcional *adj* optional
OPEP *f abr* (= ***Organización de Países Exportadores de Petróleo***) OPEC (= Organization of Petroleum Exporting Countries)
ópera *f* MÚS opera
◇ **ópera bufa, ópera cómica** comic opera
◇ **ópera prima** first work
operable *adj* MED operable
operación *f* operation
operador *m*, **~a** *f* TELEC, INFOR operator
◇ **operador turístico** tour operator
operar ⟨1a⟩ **I** *v/t* **1** MED operate on **2** *cambio* bring about **3** *L.Am. manejar* operate **II** *v/i* **1** operate **2** COM do business (***con*** with); **operarse** *v/r* **1** MED have an operation (***de*** on) **2** *de un cambio* occur
operario *m*, **-a** *f* operator, operative
operatividad *f de sistema, máquina etc* operating capacity
operativo I *adj* operational; ***sistema ~*** INFOR operating system **II** *m L.Am.* operation
operatorio *adj* MED operating
opereta *f* MÚS operetta
operístico *adj* operatic, opera *atr*
opiáceo I *adj* opiate **II** *m* opiate
opinar ⟨1a⟩ **I** *v/t* think (***de*** about) **II** *v/i* express an opinion
opinión *f* opinion; ***la ~ pública*** public opinion; ***en mi ~*** in my opinion; ***tener buena / mala ~ de alguien*** think highly / little of s.o.
opio *m* opium
opíparo *adj* sumptuous
oponente *m/f* opponent
oponer ⟨2r; *part* ***opuesto***⟩ *v/t resistencia* put up (***a*** to), offer (***a*** to); *razón, argumento* put forward (***a*** against); **oponerse** *v/r* be opposed (***a*** to); (*manifestar oposición*) object (***a*** to)
oporto *m* port

oportunidad *f* **1** opportunity; **~ de gol** DEP chance to score **2**: **~es** *pl* COM sales
oportunista I *adj* opportunistic **II** *m/f* opportunist
oportuno *adj* **1** timely; *momento* opportune **2** *respuesta, medida* suitable, appropriate
oposición *f* **1** POL opposition **2**: ***oposiciones*** *pl* official entrance exams
opositar ⟨1a⟩ *v/i* take an exam
opositor I *adj* opposition *atr* **II** *m*, **~a** *f* opponent
opresión *f* oppression
opresivo *adj* oppressive
opresor I *adj* oppressive **II** *m*, **~a** *f* oppressor
oprimir ⟨3a⟩ *v/t* **1** *pueblo* oppress **2** *botón* press **3** *de zapatos* be too tight for
oprobio *m* ignominy, shame
optar ⟨1a⟩ *v/i* **1** (*elegir*) opt (***por*** for); ***~ por hacer algo*** opt to do sth **2**: ***~ a*** be in the running for
optativo *adj* optional; *asignatura tb* elective
óptica *f* **1** optician's **2** FÍS optics *sg*; *fig* point of view
óptico I *adj* optical; ***nervio ~*** optic nerve **II** *m*, **-a** *f* optician
optimar ⟨1a⟩ *v/t* optimize
optimismo *m* optimism
optimista I *adj* optimistic **II** *m/f* optimist
optimización *f* optimization
optimizar ⟨1f⟩ *v/t* optimize
óptimo *adj* ideal
optometría *f* optometry
opuesto I *part* ☞ ***oponer*** **II** *adj* **1** *en el espacio* opposite **2** *opinión* contrary
opulencia *f* opulence
opulento *adj* opulent
opuso *vb* ☞ ***oponer***
OPV *f abr* (= ***oferta pública de venta***) Public Offering
oquedad *f* cavity
ora *conj*: **~ … ~ …** now …, now …
oración *f* **1** REL prayer **2** GRAM sentence; ***~ principal / subordinada*** main / subordinate clause
oráculo *m* oracle
orador *m*, **~a** *f* orator
oral *adj* oral; ***prueba de inglés ~*** English oral (exam)
órale *interj Méx* F come on
orangután *m* ZO orang-utan
orar ⟨1a⟩ *v/i* pray (***por*** for)
orate *m/f* F lunatic
oratoria *f* oratory
oratorio *m* MÚS oratorio
orbe *m* AST world
órbita *f* orbit; ***colocar*** *o* ***poner en ~*** put into orbit
orbital *adj* orbital
orbitar ⟨1a⟩ *v/i* orbit; ***~ en torno a*** orbit, orbit around
orca *m* ZO killer whale
órdago *m*: ***de ~*** F terrific F
orden[1] *m* **1** order; ***por ~ alfabético*** in alphabetical order; ***por ~ de altura*** in order of height; ***poner en ~*** tidy up, straighten up; ***sin ~ ni concierto*** without rhyme or reason **2** (*clase*): ***de todo ~*** of all kinds *o* types; ***de primer ~*** top-ranking, leading **3**: ***llamar al ~*** call to order **4** ARQUI order
◇ **orden de bateo** batting order
◇ **orden del día** agenda
orden[2] *f* (*mandamiento*) order; ***por ~ de*** by order of, on the orders of; ***hasta nueva ~*** until further notice; ***¡a la ~!*** yes, sir
◇ **orden de caballería** HIST order of knighthood; **orden de pago** order to pay; **orden de registro** JUR search warrant
ordenación *f* REL ordination
ordenado *adj* tidy
ordenador *m Esp* INFOR computer; ***asistido por ~*** computer-aided
◇ **ordenador de a bordo** *Esp* on-board computer; **ordenador doméstico** *Esp* home computer; **ordenador de escritorio** *Esp* desktop (computer); **ordenador de mano** *Esp* palmtop; **ordenador personal** *Esp* personal computer; **ordenador portátil** *Esp* portable (computer), laptop
ordenamiento *m* set of laws
ordenanza I *f* by-law **II** *m* **1** office junior, gofer F **2** MIL orderly
ordenar ⟨1a⟩ *v/t* **1** *habitación* tidy up **2** *alfabéticamente* arrange; INFOR sort **3** (*mandar*) order **4** *L.Am.* (*pedir*) order; **ordenarse** *v/r* REL be ordained
ordeñadora *f* milking machine
ordeñar ⟨1a⟩ *v/t* milk
ordinal I *adj* ordinal **II** *m* ordinal (number)
ordinariez *f* vulgarity

ordinario *adj* **1** ordinary; ***de ~*** usually, ordinarily **2** *desp* vulgar

orear ⟨1a⟩ *v/t* air; **orearse** *v/r* air

orégano *m* BOT oregano; ***no todo el monte es ~*** F it's not all plain sailing

oreja *f* **1** ear; ***~s despegadas*** protruding ears; ***una sonrisa de ~ a ~*** a smile from ear to ear; ***aguzar las ~s*** *L.Am.* prick one's ears up; ***parar la ~*** pay attention; ***asomar*** *o* ***enseñar*** *o* ***descubrir la ~*** show one's true colors *o Br* colours; ***ver las ~s al lobo*** *fig* F wake up to the danger; ***bajar*** *o* ***agachar las ~s*** *fig* back down; ***calentarle a alguien las ~s*** *fig* tell s.o. off; ***hasta las ~s*** *fig* up to one's eyes *o* ears **2** *Méx* F (*delator*) informer

◇ **oreja de mar** ZO abalone

orejeras *fpl* earmuffs

orejudo *adj* big-eared

orfanato *m* orphanage

orfebre *m/f* goldsmith / silversmith

orfebrería *f* goldsmith / silversmith work

orfelinato *m* orphanage

organdí *m* organdy

orgánico *adj* organic; ***ley ~*** organic law

organigrama *m* flow chart; *de empresa* organization chart, tree diagram

organillo *m* barrel organ

organismo *m* **1** organism **2** POL agency, organization

◇ **organismo modificado genéticamente** genetically modified organism

organista *m/f* organist

organización *f* organization

◇ **Organización de Cooperación y Desarrollo Económico** Organization for Economic Cooperation and Development; **Organización de los Estados Americanos** Organization of American States; **Organización Internacional de Trabajo** International Labor Organization; **Organización para la Liberación de Palestina** Palestine Liberation Organization; **Organización Mundial de Comercio** World Trade Organization; **Organización Mundial de la Salud** World Health Organization; **Organización de las Naciones Unidas** United Nations; **Organización de Países Exportadores de Petróleo** Organization of Petroleum Exporting Countries; **Organización del Tratado del Atlántico Norte** North Atlantic Treaty Organization

organizado *adj* organized

organizador I *adj* organizing **II** *m*, **~a** *f* organizer

◇ **organizador personal** personal organizer

organizar ⟨1f⟩ *v/t* organize; **organizarse** *v/r de persona* organize one's time

organizativo *adj*: ***capacidad -a*** organizational skill

órgano *m* MÚS, ANAT, *fig* organ

◇ **órgano sensorial** sense organ

◇ **órgano sexual** sex organ

organza *f* organdy

orgasmo *m* orgasm

orgía *f* orgy

orgiástico *adj* orgiastic

orgullo *m* pride

orgulloso *adj* proud (***de*** of)

orientable *adj lámpara, antena etc* adjustable

orientación *f* **1** orientation **2** (*ayuda*) guidance **3**: ***sentido de la ~*** sense of direction

◇ **orientación profesional** vocational guidance, *Br tb* careers advice

orientador *m*, **~a** *f* counselor, *Br* counsellor

oriental I *adj* **1** oriental, eastern **2** *S.Am.* Uruguayan **II** *m/f* **1** Oriental **2** *S.Am.* Uruguayan

orientar ⟨1a⟩ *v/t* **1** (*aconsejar*) advise **2**: ***~ algo hacia algo*** turn sth toward sth; **orientarse** *v/r* **1** get one's bearings **2** *de una planta* turn (***hacía*** toward)

oriente *m* **1** east **2**: ***Oriente*** Orient; ***Extremo*** *o* ***Lejano Oriente*** Far East; ***Próximo Oriente*** Near East

◇ **Oriente Medio** Middle East

orificio *m* hole; *en cuerpo* orifice; ***~ de entrada*** *de proyectil* entry wound

origen *m* origin; ***ser de ~ …*** be of … origin *o* extraction; ***tener su ~ en*** have its origin in; ***dar ~ a*** give rise to

original *m/adj* original

originalidad *f* originality

originar ⟨1a⟩ *v/t* give rise to; **originarse** *v/r* originate; *de un incendio* start

originario *adj* **1** (*primero*) original **2** (*nativo*) native (***de*** of)

orilla *f* shore; *de un río* bank; ***~s*** *L.Am. pl de ciudad* outskirts

orillar ⟨1a⟩ *v/t* **1** *dificultades* avoid **2** *tela* edge
orín *m* rust
orina *f* urine
orinal *m* urinal
orinar ⟨1a⟩ *v/i* urinate; **orinarse** *v/r* wet o.s.
orita *adv C.Am., Méx* F right away; **~ *voy*** I'll be right there
oriundo *adj* native (***de*** to); ***ser ~ de*** *de persona* come from, be a native of
orla *f* border
orlar ⟨1a⟩ *v/t* edge
ornamentación *f* ornamentation
ornamental *adj* ornamental
ornamentar ⟨1a⟩ *v/t* adorn
ornamento *m* **1** ornament **2**: ***~s*** *pl* REL vestments
ornar ⟨1a⟩ *v/t* adorn
ornato *m* adornment
ornitología *f* ornithology
ornitólogo *m*, **-a** *f* ornithologist
oro *m* **1** gold; ***de ~*** gold; ***no es ~ todo lo que reluce*** all that glitters is not gold; ***guardar como ~ en paño*** *con mucho cariño* treasure sth; *con mucho cuidado* guard sth with one's life; ***prometer el ~ y el moro*** promise the earth; ***hacerse de ~*** get rich **2**: ***~s*** *en naipes*: *suit in Spanish deck of cards*
◇ **oro blanco** white gold
◇ **oro negro** black gold, oil
orondo *adj* **1** fat **2** *fig* smug
oropel *m fig* glitter
oropéndola *f* ZO golden oriole
orozuz *m* BOT licorice, *Br* liquorice
orquesta *f* orchestra
◇ **orquesta de cámara** chamber orchestra
◇ **orquesta sinfónica** symphony orchestra
orquestación *f* orchestration
orquestal *adj* orchestral
orquestar ⟨1a⟩ *v/t fig* orchestrate
orquídea *f* BOT orchid
ortega *f* ZO sand grouse
ortiga *f* BOT nettle
orto *m* AST rising
ortodoncia *f* MED orthodontics *sg*
ortodoncista *m/f* orthodontist
ortodoxia *f* orthodoxy
ortodoxo *adj* orthodox
ortografía *f* spelling
ortográfico *adj* spelling *atr*; ***falta -a*** spelling mistake
ortopedia *f* orthopedics *sg*, *Br tb* orthopaedics *sg*
ortopédico **I** *adj* orthopedic, *Br tb* orthopaedic **II** *m*, **-a** *f* orthopedist, *Br tb* orthopaedist
ortopedista *m/f* orthopedist, *Br tb* orthopaedist
oruga *f* **1** ZO caterpillar **2** TÉC (caterpillar) track
orujo *m liquor made from the remains of grapes*
orzuelo *m* MED stye
os *pron complemento directo* you; *complemento indirecto* (to) you; *reflexivo* yourselves; **~ *lo devolveré*** I'll give you it back, I'll give it back to you
osa *f* AST: ***Osa Mayor*** Great Bear; ***Osa Menor*** Little Bear
osadía *f* **1** daring **2** (*descaro*) audacity
osado *adj* daring
osamenta *f* bones *pl*
osar ⟨1a⟩ *v/i* dare
oscense *adj* of / from Huesca, Huesca *atr*
oscilación *f* oscillation; *de precios* fluctuation
oscilante *adj* oscillating
oscilar ⟨1a⟩ *v/i* oscillate; *de precios* fluctuate
ósculo *m lit* kiss
oscurecer ⟨2d⟩ **I** *v/t* **1** darken **2** *logro, triunfo* overshadow **II** *v/i* get dark; ***al ~*** when it gets dark; **oscurecerse** *v/r* darken
oscurecimiento *m* darkening
oscuridad *f* darkness
oscuro *adj* **1** dark; ***a -as*** in the dark **2** *fig* obscure
óseo *adj* bone *atr*
osezno *m* cub
osito *m*: **~ *de peluche*** teddy bear
oso *m* bear; ***hacer el ~*** F fool around, monkey around F
◇ **oso hormiguero** anteater; **oso panda** panda; **oso pardo** brown bear; **oso polar** polar bear
ostensible *adj* obvious
ostentación *f* ostentation; ***hacer ~ de*** flaunt
ostentar ⟨1a⟩ *v/t* **1** flaunt **2** *cargo* hold
ostentoso *adj* ostentatious
osteoporosis *f* MED osteoporosis
ostra *f* **1** ZO oyster **2**: ***¡~s!*** F hell! F

ostracismo *m* ostracism
ostrero *m* ZO oyster-catcher
OTAN *f abr* (= ***Organización del Tratado del Atlántico Norte***) NATO (= North Atlantic Treaty Organization)
otárido *m*,**-a** *f* ZO sealion
otear ⟨1a⟩ *v/t horizonte* scan
otero *m* hillock
OTI *f abr* (= ***Organización de Televisiones Iberoamericanas***) *Association of Latin American TV stations*
otitis *f* MED earache
otomano *adj* HIST Ottoman
otoñal *adj* fall *atr*, *Br* autumnal
otoño *m* fall, *Br* autumn
otorgamiento *m* award; *de favor* granting
otorgar ⟨1h⟩ *v/t* award; *favor* grant
otorrino *m*,**-a** *f* F,**otorrinolaringólogo** *m*,**-a** *f* MED ear, nose and throat *o* ENT specialist
otro **I** *adj* **1** (*diferente*) another; **~s** other; ***ser muy ~*** be very different **2** (*adicional*): ***~s dos libros*** another two books **3** *con el*, *la* other
II *pron* **1** (*adicional*) another (one) **2** (*persona distinta*) someone *o* somebody else; ***fue ~, no fui yo*** it wasn't me, it was someone else **3** (*cosa distinta*) another one, a different one; **~s** others; ***entre ~s*** among others **4** *siguiente*: ***¡hasta otra!*** see you soon
III *pron recíproco*: ***amarse el uno al ~*** love one another, love each other
otrora *adv* formerly
ovación *f* ovation
ovacionar ⟨1a⟩ *v/t* cheer, give an ovation to
oval, ovalado *adj* oval
óvalo *m* oval
ovario *m* ANAT ovary
oveja *f* sheep
◇ **oveja negra** *fig* black sheep
ovejuno *adj* sheep *atr*
overol *m Méx* overalls *pl*, *Br* dungarees *pl*
ovetense *adj* of / from Oviedo, Oviedo *atr*
oviducto *m* ANAT oviduct
ovillar ⟨1a⟩ *v/t* roll into a ball;**ovillarse** *v/r* curl up (into a ball)
ovillo *m* ball; ***hacerse un ~*** *fig* curl up (into a ball)
ovino **I** *adj* sheep *atr* **II** *m* sheep; **~s** sheep *pl*
OVNI *m abr* (= ***objeto volante no identificado***) UFO (= unidentified flying object)
ovoide *adj* ovoid
ovulación *f* ovulation
ovular ⟨1a⟩ *v/i* ovulate
óvulo *m* egg
oxálico *adj*: ***ácido ~*** oxalic acid
oxidable *adj* oxidizable
oxidación *f* oxidation
oxidado *adj* rusty
oxidar ⟨1a⟩ *v/t* rust;**oxidarse** *v/r* rust, go rusty
óxido *m* **1** QUÍM oxide **2** (*herrumbre*) rust
oxigenado *adj* oxygenated
oxigenar ⟨1a⟩ *v/t* oxygenate
oxigenarse ⟨1a⟩ *v/r fig* get some fresh air, get some air in one's lungs
oxígeno *m* oxygen
oxiuro *m* ZO pinworm, threadworm
oye *vb* ☞ ***oír***
oyendo *vb* ☞ ***oír***
oyente *m/f* **1** listener **2** EDU auditor, *Br* occasional student
oyó *vb* ☞ ***oír***
ozono *m* ozone; ***capa de ~*** ozone layer; ***agujero en la capa de ~*** hole in the ozone layer

P

pabellón *m* **1** *de exposiciones*, *deportes* pavilion **2** *edificio* block **3** MÚS bell **4** MAR flag
◇ **pabellón de la oreja** ANAT outer ear
pábilo, pabilo *m* wick
pábulo *m*: ***dar ~ a*** *rumores* encourage
PAC *f abr* (= ***Política Agraria Común***) CAP (= Common Agricultural Policy)
pacana *f* BOT pecan
pacato *adj* prudish, prim and proper
pacer ⟨2d⟩ *v/t & v/i* graze

pachanga *f*: ***ir de ~*** *Méx, Carib, C.Am.* go on a spree F
pachanguero *adj Esp*: ***música -a*** party music
pacharán *m drink similar to sloe gin*
pachocha *f L.Am.* slowness
pachorra *f* F slowness
pachucho *adj* MED F poorly
pachulí *m* patchouli
paciencia *f* patience; ***se me acaba la ~*** I'm running out of patience; ***~ y barajar*** *fig* keep trying
paciente *m/f & adj* patient
pacificación *f* pacification
pacificador **I** *adj* peace *atr*, pacifying **II** *m*,**~a** *f* peace-maker
pacificar ⟨1g⟩ *v/t* pacify;**pacificarse** *v/r* calm down
pacífico **I** *adj* peaceful; *persona* peaceable; ***el océano Pacífico*** the Pacific Ocean **II** *m*: ***el Pacífico*** the Pacific
pacifismo *m* pacifism
pacifista **I** *adj* pacifist *atr* **II** *m/f* pacifist
pack *m* COM pack
paco *m*,**-a** *f L.Am.* F (*policía*) cop F
pacotilla *f*: ***de ~*** third-rate, lousy F
pacotillero *m*,**-a** *f L.Am.* street vendor
pactar ⟨1a⟩ **I** *v/t* agree; ***~ un acuerdo*** reach (an) agreement **II** *v/i* reach (an) agreement
pacto *m* agreement, pact; ***~ de no agresión*** non-aggression pact
paddle(-tenis) *m* DEP paddle tennis
padecer ⟨2d⟩ **I** *v/t* suffer **II** *v/i* suffer; ***~ de*** have trouble with; ***~ del estómago / corazón*** have stomach / heart trouble
padecimiento *m* suffering
pádel *m* ☞ ***paddle***
padrastro *m* **1** *familiar* stepfather **2** *en los dedos* hangnail
padrazo *m* indulgent father
padre *m* father; REL ***el Padre Martin*** Father Martin; ***~s*** *pl* parents; ***de ~ y muy señor mío*** terrible; ***¡qué ~!*** *Méx* brilliant!
◇ **padre espiritual** (father) confessor; **padre de familia** father, family man; **padre político** father-in-law; **Padre Santo** Holy Father
padrenuestro *m* Lord's Prayer
padrillo *m Rpl* stallion
padrino *m* **1** *en bautizo* godfather **2** (*en boda*) *man who gives away the bride* **3** *fig*: ***tener buenos ~s*** know the right people
padrón *m register of local inhabitants*
paella *f* paella
paellera *f* paella dish
¡paf! *int* wham!, bang!, kapow!
pág. *abr* (= ***página***) p. (= page)
paga *f* **1** (*jornal*) pay **2** *de niño* allowance, *Br* pocket money
pagadero *adj* payable
pagado *adj* paid; ***~ de sí mismo*** *fig* smug, self-satisfied
pagador *m*,**~a** *f* payer
págalo *m* ZO skua
paganismo *m* paganism
pagano **I** *adj* pagan **II** *m*,**-a** *f* pagan; ***ser el ~*** *fig* pay (***de*** for), be the one who suffers
pagar ⟨1h⟩ **I** *v/t* **1** pay; ***¡me las pagarás!*** you'll pay for this! **2** *compra, gastos, crimen* pay for **3** *favor* repay **II** *v/i* pay; ***~ a escote*** F go Dutch F; ***~ a cuenta*** pay on account; ***~ al contado*** pay in cash
pagaré *m* IOU
pagel *m* ZO pandora, red sea bream
página *f* page
◇ **página web** web page
◇ **páginas amarillas** yellow pages
paginación *f* TIP pagination
paginar ⟨1a⟩ *v/t* TIP paginate
pago *m* **1** COM payment; ***en ~ de*** in payment for *o* of **2** *Rpl* (*quinta*) piece of land; ***por estos ~s*** F in this neck of the woods F
◇ **pago anticipado** payment in advance; **pago al contado** payment in cash; **pago a cuenta** payment on account; **pago en efectivo** payment in cash; **pago por visión** TV pay per view
paila *f L.Am* frypan, *Br* frying pan
país *m* country; ***~ en vías de desarrollo*** developing country; ***~ productor*** producer country; ***~ comunitario*** EU country; ***los Países Bajos*** the Netherlands
paisaje *m* landscape
paisajista *m/f* **1** *pintor* landscape artist **2** *jardinero* landscape gardener
paisajístico *adj* landscape *atr*
paisana *f* compatriot, (fellow) countrywoman
paisano *m* **1** compatriot, (fellow) countryman **2**: ***de ~*** MIL in civilian clothes; *policía* in plain clothes

P

paja *f* straw; ***hacerse una*** *o L.Am.* ***la~*** V jerk off V; ***por un quítame allá esas ~s*** over nothing
pajar *m* hayloft
pájara *f fig desp mujer* cow *desp*, bitch *desp*
pajarera *f* aviary
pajarería *f* pet shop
pajarita *f* **1** *corbata* bow tie **2** *de papel* paper bird
pájaro *m* **1** bird; ***matar dos ~s de un tiro*** kill two birds with one stone; ***más vale ~ en mano que ciento volando*** a bird in the hand is worth two in the bush **2** *fig* (*granuja*) ugly customer F, nasty piece of work F
◇ **pájaro bobo** penguin; **pájaro carpintero** woodpecker; **pájaro mosca** hummingbird
pajarraco *m weird-looking bird*
paje *m* page
pajel *m* ☞ ***pagel***
pajita *f* drinking straw, straw
pajizo *adj* **1** *pelo* straw-colored, *Br* straw-coloured **2** *techo* thatched
pajolero *adj* F damn F
pajoso *adj pelo* strawlike
pajuerano *m*, **-a** *f Rpl desp* hick
Pakistán *m* Pakistan
pakistaní *m/f & adj* Pakistani
pala *f* **1** AGR spade **2** *raqueta* paddle **3** *para servir* slice **4** *para recoger* dustpan
◇ **pala mecánica** mechanical shovel
palabra *f tb fig* word; ***~ por ~*** word for word; ***bajo ~*** on parole; ***en una ~*** in a word; ***en pocas ~s*** briefly; ***tomar la ~*** speak; ***de ~*** *acuerdo* verbal; ***de pocas ~s*** *persona* of few words; ***tomar a alguien la ~*** take s.o. at his / her word; ***dejar a alguien con la ~ en la boca*** *fig* cut s.o. off in mid-sentence; ***buenas ~s*** fine words; ***lo de tener un hijo son ~s mayores*** having a child is a serious business *o* is not something to be undertaken lightly; ***con medias ~s dijo ...*** he hinted that ..., he half said that ...
◇ **palabra compuesta** GRAM compound
◇ **palabra de honor** word of honor, *Br* word of honour
palabrería *f*, **palabrerío** *m* talk, hot air
palabrota *f* swearword
palacete *m* small palace
palaciego *adj* palace *atr*
palacio *m* palace
◇ **palacio de deportes** sport center, *Br* sports centre; **palacio de justicia** law courts; **palacio real** royal palace
paladar *m* **1** palate; ***tener un ~ fino, tener buen ~*** *fig* have a discerning palate **2** *Cu*: *small restaurant in a private house*
paladear ⟨1a⟩ *v/t* savor, *Br* savour
paladín *m* HIST paladin
paladino *adj* patently obvious
palafito *m* HIST stilt house
palanca *f* lever; ***tener ~*** *Méx fig* have pull *o* clout
◇ **palanca de cambios** AUTO gear shift, *Br* gear lever
palangana *f plastic bowl for washing dishes*, *Br* washing-up bowl
palanganear ⟨1a⟩ *v/i S.Am.* show off
palanquear ⟨1a⟩ *v/t L.Am.* pull some strings for
palanqueta *f* crowbar
palatal *adj* palatal
palatino *adj* **1** LING palatal **2** *de palacio* palace *atr*
palco *m* TEA box
◇ **palco de platea** *box level with the stage*
palenque *m L.Am.* cockpit (*in cock fighting*)
palentino *adj* of / from Palencia, Palencia *atr*
paleocristiano *adj* paleochristian
paleolítico *m* Paleolithic (period)
paleontología *f* paleontology
Palestina *f* Palestine
palestino I *adj* Palestinian **II** *m*, **-a** *f* Palestinian
palestra *f* arena; ***salir*** *o* ***saltar a la ~*** *fig* hit the headlines
palet *m* TÉC pallet
paleta *f* **1** PINT palette **2** TÉC trowel **3** *Méx*: *polo* popsicle®, *Br* ice lolly
paletada *f de tierra* trowelful; ***a ~s*** *fig* in huge numbers; ***los refugiados llegaban a las costas a ~s*** the refugees were reaching the coasts in huge numbers
paletilla *f* GASTR shoulder
paleto F **I** *adj* hick *atr* F, provincial **II** *m*, **-a** *f* hick *F*, *Br* yokel F
paliar ⟨1b⟩ *v/t problema, efecto dañoso* alleviate; *dolor* relieve
paliativo *m/adj* palliative

palidecer ⟨2d⟩ *v/i* turn pale; *fig* (*parecer menos importante*) pale
palidez *f* paleness
pálido *adj* pale
palillero *m* toothpick holder
palillo *m* **1** *para dientes* toothpick **2** *para comer* chopstick
palíndromo *m* palindrome
palique *m*: ***estar de ~*** F have a chat
palisandro *m* rosewood
palito *m Rpl* popsicle®, *Br* ice lolly
paliza I *f* **1** (*azotaina*) beating **2** (*derrota*) thrashing F, drubbing F **3** F (*pesadez*) drag F; ***dar la ~ a alguien*** F pester s.o. F **II** *m/f* F drag
palma *f* palm; ***dar ~s*** clap (one's hands); ***batir ~s*** clap one's hands; ***el modelo diésel se lleva la ~ en cuanto a ventas*** when it comes to sales, the diesel model wins hands down; ***en cuanto a casos de sida, África se lleva la ~*** Africa leads the world in Aids cases; ***conocer algo como la ~ de su mano*** *fig* know sth like the back of one's hand
palmada *f* **1** *de ánimo, consuelo* pat **2** (*manotazo*) slap
palmar I ⟨1a⟩ *v/t*: ***~la*** P kick the bucket F **II** *m* palm grove
palmarés *m* DEP list of winners
palmario *adj fml* clear, obvious
palmatoria *f* candlestick
palmear ⟨1a⟩ **I** *v/i* clap **II** *v/t* **1** *hombro* slap **2** *en baloncesto* tip in
palmense *adj* of / from Las Palmas (de Gran Canaria), Las Palmas *atr*
palmeo *m en baloncesto* tip-in
palmera *f* **1** BOT palm tree **2** (*dulce*) *heart-shaped pastry*
palmeral *m* palm grove
palmesano *adj* of / from Palma de Majorca, Palma de Majorca *atr*
palmeta *f* cane
palmita *f Rpl*: *heart-shaped pastry*
palmito *m* **1** BOT palmetto **2** GASTR palm heart **3** *fig* F attractiveness
palmo *m* hand's breadth; ***~ a ~*** inch by inch
palmotear ⟨1a⟩ **I** *v/i* clap **II** *v/t*: ***~ (las espaldas) a alguien*** slap s.o. on the back
palo *m* **1** *de madera etc* stick; ***de tal ~ tal astilla*** a chip off the old block F; ***dar ~s de ciego*** (*no saber cómo actuar*) grope in the dark; (*criticar*) lash out wildly **2** MAR mast; ***que cada ~ aguante su vela*** everybody has to stand up and be counted **3** *de portería* post, upright **4** *fig* blow **5**: ***a medio ~*** *L.Am.* half-drunk; ***a ~ seco*** *whiskey* straight up **6** *L.Am.* ***ser un ~*** be fantastic **7**: ***echarse un ~*** *Méx* V have a screw V
◇ **palo dulce** licorice, *Br* liquorice; **palo de golf** golf club; **palo mayor** MAR mainmast
paloma *f* pigeon; *blanca* dove
◇ **paloma de la paz** dove of peace; **paloma mensajera** carrier pigeon; **paloma torcaz** ZO wood pigeon
palomar *m* pigeon loft
palometa *f* ZO pompano
palomilla *f C.Am., Méx* gang
palomino *m* ZO **1** young pigeon, squab **2** *L.Am*: *caballo* palomino
palomita *f* **1** *Méx* checkmark, *Br* tick **2** *en fútbol* diving save
◇ **palomitas de maíz** popcorn *sg*
palomo *m* ZO (cock) pigeon
palpable *adj fig* palpable
palpación *f* MED palpation
palpar ⟨1a⟩ *v/t con las manos* feel, touch; *fig*: *descontento, miedo* feel
palpitación *f* palpitation
palpitante *adj* **1** *corazón* pounding **2** *cuestión* burning
palpitar ⟨1a⟩ *v/i* **1** *del corazón* pound **2** *Rpl fig* have a hunch F, have a feeling
pálpito *m Rpl* feeling, hunch F; ***me da el ~ que ...*** F I have a feeling *o* hunch F that ...
palta *f S.Am.* BOT avocado
palto *m S.Am.* jacket
palúdico *adj terreno* marshy; *vegetación, fauna* marsh *atr*
paludismo *m* MED malaria
palurdo I *adj* F hick *atr* F, provincial **II** *m*, **-a** *f* F hick F, *Br* yokel F
palustre I *adj de la laguna* lake *atr*; *del pantano* marsh *atr* **II** *m* trowel
pamela *f* picture hat
pampa *f* GEOG pampa, prairie; ***la ~ argentina*** the Argentinian Pampas *pl*; ***a la ~*** *Rpl* in the open
pámpano *m* (vine) tendril
pampeano *adj* pampas *atr*, prairie *atr*
pampero I *adj* ☞ **pampeano II** *m cold wind that blows from the pampas*
pamplinas *fpl* nonsense *sg*; ***¡no me vengas con ~!*** F don't try to soft-soap me! F

P

pamplonés, pamplonica *adj* of / from Pamplona, Pamplona *atr*

pan *m* bread; ***un ~*** a loaf (of bread); ***ser ~ comido*** F be easy as pie F; ***con su ~ se lo coma*** that's his / her problem; ***está más bueno que el ~*** F he's gorgeous F; ***es más bueno que el ~*** he's a good-natured sort; ***llamar al ~, ~ y al vino, vino*** call a spade a spade

◇ **pan de azúcar** sugarloaf; **pan de barra** French bread; **pan de caja** *Méx* sliced bread; **pan francés** *L.Am.* French bread; **pan integral** wholemeal bread **pan lactal** *Arg* sliced bread **pan de molde** sliced bread **pan rallado** breadcrumbs *pl*; **pan tostado** toast

pana *f* corduroy

panacea *f* panacea

panadería *f* baker's shop

panadero *m*,**-a** *f* baker

panal *m* honeycomb

panamá *m* panama hat

Panamá *m* Panama; ***el Canal de ~*** the Panama Canal; ***Ciudad de ~*** Panama city

panameño **I** *adj* Panamanian **II** *m*,**-a** *f* Panamanian

pancarta *f* placard

panceta *f* belly pork

pancho **I** *adj* F: ***quedarse tan ~*** act as if nothing had happened **II** *m Rpl* hot dog

páncreas *m inv* ANAT pancreas

panda[1] *f* ☞ ***pandilla***

panda[2] *m* ZO panda

pandemia *f* MED pandemic

pandereta *f* tambourine

pandero *m* tambourine

pandilla *f de amigos* group; *de delincuentes* gang

panecillo *m* (bread) roll

panecito *m L.Am.* (bread) roll

panegírico **I** *adj* panegyrical **II** *m* panegyric

panel *m tb grupo de personas* panel

◇ **panel solar** solar panel

panela *f L.Am.* brown sugar loaf

panera *f* bread basket

pánfilo *adj* gullible

pangolín *m* ZO pangolin

paniaguada *f* protégée

paniaguado *m* protégé

pánico *m* panic; ***sembrar el ~*** spread panic; ***me entró ~*** I panicked; ***tener ~ a alguien*** be scared stiff of s.o.

panificadora *f* bakery

panizo *m* BOT millet

panocha, panoja *f* ear

panoli **I** *adj* F dopey F **II** *m/f* F nitwit

panoplia *f fig* panoply

panorama *m* panorama

panorámico **I** *adj*: ***vista -a*** panoramic view **II** *f vista* view, panorama; FOT panning shot

panqueque *m L.Am.* pancake

pantagruélico *adj fig* huge

pantaleta *f C.Am., Méx* panties *pl*

pantalla *f* **1** TELEC, INFOR screen, monitor; TV, *de cine* screen; ***la pequeña ~*** *fig* the small screen; ***la gran ~*** *fig* the big screen; ***llevar a la ~*** make a movie *o Br* film of **2** *de lámpara* shade **3** *fig* front, cover

◇ **pantalla chica** *L.Am.* small screen; **pantalla de cristal líquido** liquid crystal screen; **pantalla panorámica** wide screen; **pantalla plana** TV flat screen; **pantalla táctil** INFOR touch screen

pantalón *m*,**pantalones** *mpl* pants *pl*, *Br* trousers *pl*; ***llevar los pantalones*** *fig* F wear the pants *o Br* trousers F

pantanal *m* marshland

pantano *m* **1** (*embalse*) reservoir **2** (*ciénaga*) marsh

pantanoso *adj* marshy

panteísmo *m* pantheism

panteón *m* pantheon

pantera *f* ZO panther

pantimedia *f Méx* pantyhose *pl*, *Br tb* tights *pl*

pantomima *f* pantomime

pantorrilla *f* ANAT calf

pants *mpl Méx* tracksuit *sg*

pantufla *f* slipper

panty *m* pantyhose *pl*, *Br* tights *pl*

panza *f de persona* belly, paunch

panzudo *adj* potbellied, paunchy

pañal *m* diaper, *Br* nappy; ***estar aún en ~es*** *fig*: *persona* be inexperienced, be a novice; *proyecto*, *plan* be in its infancy

pañería *f* dry goods store, drapery

paño *m* cloth; ***conocer el ~*** *fig* F know what's what F, know the score F; ***~s calientes*** *o* ***tibios*** *fig* half measures; ***en ~s menores*** in one's underwear

◇ **paño de cocina** dishtowel

◇ **paño de lágrimas** *fig* shoulder to cry on

pañol *m* MAR store
pañuelo *m* handkerchief; ***el mundo es un ~*** *fig* F it's a small world
◇ **pañuelo de cabeza** (head)scarf
◇ **pañuelo de cuello** scarf
Papa *m* Pope
papa *f L.Am.* potato
papas fritas *fpl L.Am. de sartén* French fries, *Br* chips; *de bolsa* chips, *Br* crisps
papá *m* F pop F, dad F; ***~s*** *L.Am.* parents
◇ **Papá Noel** Santa Claus
papada *f* double chin
papado *m* papacy
papagayo *m* ZO parrot
papal **I** *adj* papal **II** *m L.Am.* potato field
papalote *m Méx* kite
papamoscas *m* **1** ZO flycatcher **2** *fig* F dope F, dimwit F
papamóvil *m* popemobile
papanatas *m/f inv* F dope F, dimwit F
Papanicolau *m L.Am.* Pap smear, *Br* smear test
paparruchadas, paparruchas *fpl* F baloney *sg* F
papaya *f* BOT papaya
papear ⟨1a⟩ F **I** *v/t* eat **II** *v/i* chow down F, eat
papel **1** *m* paper; *trozo* piece of paper; ***ser ~ mojado*** *fig* not be worth the paper it's written on **2** TEA, *fig* role; ***hacer buen / mal ~*** *fig* prove useful / useless; ***perder los ~es*** lose control
◇ **papel de aluminio** aluminum foil, *Br* aluminium foil; **papel de calco** carbon paper; **papel carbón** carbon paper; **papel de cartas** notepaper, writing paper; **papel de cocina** kitchen roll; **papel confort** *Chi* toilet paper; **papel continuo** continuous paper; **papel cuché** coated paper; **papel de embalar** wrapping paper; **papel de envolver** wrapping paper; **papel de fumar** cigarette paper; **papel higiénico** toilet paper *o* tissue; **papel moneda** paper money; **papel mural** *Chi* wallpaper; **papel de música, papel pautado** music paper; **papel (de) pergamino** parchment; **papel pintado** wallpaper; **papel de plata** aluminum foil, kitchen foil; **papel principal, papel de protagonista** leading role; **papel de regalo** giftwrap; **papel reciclado** recycled paper; **papel secundario** supporting role; **papel tapiz** *Méx* coated wallpaper; **papel térmico** thermal paper
papelada *f L.Am.* farce
papeleo *m* paperwork
papelera *f* wastepaper basket
papelería *f* stationer's shop
papelerío *m L.Am.* muddle, mess
papelero **I** *adj* paper *atr* **II** *m Rpl* wastepaper basket
papeleta *f* **1** *de rifa* raffle ticket **2** *fig (engorro)* chore
◇ **papeleta de voto** ballot paper
papelina *f* wrap
paperas *fpl* MED mumps
papilla *f para bebés* baby food; *para enfermos* puree; ***hacer ~ a alguien*** F beat s.o. to a pulp F
papiloma *m* MED papilloma
papiroflexia *f* paper-folding
papista *adj*: ***ser más ~ que el papa*** hold extreme views
papo *m* ZO dewlap
paquete *m* **1** package, parcel **2** *de cigarrillos* packet **3** F *en moto* (pillion) passenger
◇ **paquete accionarial, paquete de acciones** block of shares; **paquete bomba** parcel bomb; **paquete turístico** package tour
paquetería *f* parcels office
paquidermo *m* ZO pachyderm
Paquistán *m* Pakistan
paquistaní *m/f & adj* Pakistani
par **I** *f* par; ***es bella a la ~ que inteligente*** she is beautiful as well as intelligent, she is both beautiful and intelligent; ***a la ~*** COM at par (value); ***sin ~*** unequaled, *Br* unequalled, unparalleled **II** *m* pair; ***un ~ de*** a pair of; ***a ~es*** in pairs, two by two; ***abierto de ~ en ~*** wide open
para *prp* **1** for; ***~ mí*** for me
2 *dirección* toward(s); ***ir ~*** head for; ***va ~ directora*** she's going to end up as manager
3 *tiempo* for; ***listo ~ mañana*** ready for tomorrow; ***~ siempre*** forever; ***diez ~ las ocho*** *L.Am.* ten of eight, ten to eight; ***~ Pascua iremos de vacaciones a Lima*** we're going to Lima for Easter; ***espero que ~ Pascua haya terminado la crisis*** I hope the crisis is over by Easter; ***¿~ cuándo?*** when for?
4 *finalidad*: ***lo hace ~ ayudarte*** he does

P

it (in order) to help you; **~ que** so that; **¿~ qué te marchas?** what are you leaving for?; **~ eso no hace falta** it's not necessary just for that
5 *en comparaciones*: **~ su edad es muy maduro** he's very mature for his age
6: **lo heredó todo ~ morir a los 30** he inherited it all, only to die at 30
parabién *m*, **parabienes** *mpl* congratulations *pl*
parábola *f* **1** MAT parabola **2** REL parable
parabólico **I** *adj* parabolic **II** *f* satellite dish
parabrisas *m inv* AUTO windshield, *Br* windscreen
paracaídas *m inv* parachute; **lanzarse** *o* **saltar en ~** parachute
paracaidismo *m* parachuting
paracaidista *m/f* **1** DEP parachutist **2** MIL paratrooper
parachoques *m inv* AUTO bumper
parada *f* **1** stop **2** DEP save, stop
◇ **parada de autobús** bus stop
◇ **parada de taxis** taxi stand, *Br* taxi rank
paradero *m* **1** whereabouts *sg*; **está en ~ desconocido** his / her whereabouts are unknown **2** *L.Am.* ☞ **parada 1**
paradigma *m* paradigm
paradigmático *adj* paradigmatic
paradisiaco, paradisíaco *adj* heavenly
parado **I** *adj* **1** unemployed **2** *L.Am.* (*de pie*) standing (up) **3**: **quedarse ~** stand still; **dejar ~ a alguien de** *noticia, sorpresa* stun s.o.; **salir bien / mal ~** come off well / badly; **II** *m*, **-a** *f* unemployed person; **los ~s de larga duración** the long-term unemployed
paradoja *f* paradox
paradójico *adj* paradoxical
parador *m Esp* parador (*state-run luxury hotel*)
paraestatal *adj* government agency *atr*
parafarmacia *f* drug store (*not authorized to sell prescription medicines*)
parafernalia *f* F paraphernalia
parafina *f* kerosene, *Br* paraffin
parafrasear ⟨1a⟩ *v/t* paraphrase
paráfrasis *f inv* paraphrase
paragolpes *m inv Rpl* bumper
parágrafo *m L.Am.* paragraph
paraguas *m inv* umbrella
Paraguay *m* Paraguay
paraguaya *f* BOT peach
paraguayo **1** *adj* Paraguayan **2** *m*, **-a** *f* Paraguayan
paragüero *m* umbrella stand
paraíso *m* paradise
◇ **paraíso fiscal** tax haven
paraje *m* place, spot
paralela *f* **1** MAT parallel **2** DEP: **~s** *pl* parallel bars
◇ **paralelas asimétricas** asymmetric bars
paralelismo *m* parallel; **establecer un ~** draw a parallel
paralelo *m/adj* parallel; **no admite ~** there is no parallel *o* comparison
paralelogramo *m* parallelogram
paralímpico *adj* ☞ **parolímpico**
parálisis *f tb fig* paralysis
◇ **parálisis infantil** infantile paralysis
paralítico **I** *adj* paralytic **II** *m*, **-a** *f* person who is paralyzed
paralización *f tb fig* paralysis
paralizar ⟨1f⟩ *v/t* **1** MED paralyze **2** *actividad* bring to a halt **3** *país, economía* paralyze, bring to a standstill; **paralizarse** *v/r por miedo* be paralyzed (**por** by); *fig*: *de actividad* be brought to a halt
parámetro *m* parameter
paramilitar *adj* paramilitary
páramo *m* upland moor
parangón *m*: **sin ~** incomparable
parangonar ⟨1a⟩ *v/t* compare (**con** to, with)
paraninfo *m de universidad* auditorium (*used only on very special occasions*)
paranoia *f* paranoia
paranoico **I** *adj* MED paranoid **II** *m*, **-a** *f* MED person suffering from paranoia
paranormal *adj* paranormal
parapente *m artilugio* hang glider; *actividad* hang gliding
parapentista *m/f* hang glider
parapetarse ⟨1a⟩ *v/r* shelter, hide (**tras** behind)
parapeto *m* parapet
parapléjico **I** *adj* MED paraplegic **II** *m*, **-a** *f* paraplegic
parapsicología *f* parapsychology
parar ⟨1a⟩ **I** *v/t* **1** (*detener*) stop **2** *L.Am.* (*poner de pie*) stand up
II *v/i* **1** stop; **~ de llover** stop raining; **ha estado lloviendo tres horas sin ~** it's

been raining for three hours non-stop **2** *en alojamiento* stay; ***no sé dónde para*** I don't know where he's staying **3**: ***ir a ~*** end up; ***¿cómo va a ~ todo eso?*** where is this all going to end?; ***¿dónde quieres ir a ~?*** what are you getting at?
pararse *v/r* **1** (*detenerse*) stop **2** *L.Am.* (*ponerse de pie*) stand up
pararrayos *m inv* lightning rod, *Br* lightning conductor
parasitario *adj* parasitic
parásito *m* parasite; ***~s*** *pl en radio* interference *sg*, atmospherics
parasol *m* parasol; *en la playa* (beach) umbrella
paratiroides *adj*: ***glándula ~*** ANAT thyroid (gland)
parcela *f* lot, *Br* plot
parcelar ⟨1a⟩ *v/t* divide into lots, *Br* divide into plots
parchar ⟨1a⟩ *v/t* **1** *L.Am. ropa* patch **2** (*arreglar*) repair
parche *m* **1** *para ojo, agujero* patch **2** *fig* (*remedio temporal*) band-aid, patch-up
parchear *vb* ☞ ***parchar***
parchís *m* Parcheesi®
parcial *adj* (*partidario*) bias(s)ed
parco *adj* moderate, frugal; ***es ~ en palabras*** he's a man of few words
pardiez *int* good heavens!
pardillo I *adj* gullible, easily fooled **II** *m* ZO linnet **III** *m*, **-a** *f* F *persona* hick
pardo I *adj* **1** *color* dun **2** *L.Am. desp* half-breed *desp*, *Br tb* half-caste *desp* **II** *m* **1** *color* dun **2** *L.Am. desp* half-breed *desp*, *Br tb* half-caste *desp*
pardusco *adj* dun
parear ⟨1a⟩ *v/t* match up, put into pairs
parecer I *m* opinion, view; ***al ~*** apparently; ***de buen ~*** well-dressed; ***dar su ~*** give one's opinion
II ⟨2d⟩ *v/i* seem, look; ***me parece que*** I think (that), it seems to me that; ***me parece bien*** it seems fine to me; ***¿qué te parece?*** what do you think?; ***si a usted le parece*** if you're agreeable, if it suits you; ***parece que va a llover*** it looks like rain, it looks like it's going to rain
parecerse *v/r* resemble each other; ***~ a alguien*** resemble s.o., be like s.o.; ***ese chico se parece a tu novio*** that guy looks like your boyfriend
parecido I *adj* similar; ***bien ~*** good-looking; ***no mal ~*** not bad-looking **II** *m* similarity; ***tener un gran ~*** look a lot alike
pared *f* wall; ***subirse por las -es*** hit the roof; ***las ~es oyen*** walls have ears; ***hacer la ~*** *en fútbol* play a give and go, *Br* play a one-two; ***poner a alguien contra la ~*** *fig* force s.o. into a corner
◇ **pared maestra** supporting wall
paredón *m* thick wall; *para ejecuciones* wall
pareja *f* **1** (*conjunto de dos*) pair **2** *en una relación* couple; ***hacen buena ~*** they make a good couple **3** *de una persona* partner **4** *de un objeto* other one
parejita *f* F couple; ***pero estaba lleno de ~s*** but the whole place was full of couples
parejo *adj L.Am. suelo* level, even; ***andar*** *o* ***correr*** *o* ***ir ~s*** be neck and neck; ***llegaron ~s*** they arrived at the same time
parental *adj* BIO parental
parentela *f* relatives *pl*, family
parentesco *m* relationship
paréntesis *m inv* **1** parenthesis; ***entre ~*** *fig* by the way **2** *fig* (*pausa*) break
pareo *m* wrap-around skirt
paria *m/f* pariah
parida *f* P stupid thing to say / do
paridad *f* COM parity
parienta *f* F wife, old lady F
pariente *m/f* relative; ***~ cercano*** close relative
parietal *adj*: (***hueso***) ***parietal*** ANAT parietal bone
parihuela(**s**) *f*(*pl*) stretcher *sg*
paripé *m*: ***hacer el ~*** F put on an act F
parir ⟨3a⟩ **I** *v/i* give birth **II** *v/t* give birth to; ***poner a alguien a ~*** *fig* F tear s.o. to pieces F
París *m* Paris
parisiense *m/f & adj* Parisian
parisino I *adj* Parisian **II** *m*, **-a** *f* Parisian
paritario *adj comité* joint
paritorio *m* MED delivery room
parka *f* parka
parking *m* parking lot, *Br* car park
parlamentar ⟨1a⟩ *v/i* talk, hold talks
parlamentario I *adj* parliamentary **II** *m*, **-a** *f* member of parliament
parlamentarismo *m* parliamentarianism
parlamento *m* parliament

◇ **Parlamento Europeo** European Parliament
parlanchín **I** *adj* chatty **II** *m*,**-ina** *f* chatterbox
parlante *m L.Am.* loudspeaker
parlar ⟨1a⟩ **I** *v/i* chatter **II** *v/t* reveal, talk about
parlotear ⟨1a⟩ *v/i* chatter
parmesano *m/adj* Parmesan
parné *m* P dough P, *Br* dosh P
paro *m* **1** unemployment; ***estar en ~*** be unemployed; ***cobrar el ~*** collect unemployment benefits **2** ZO tit(mouse)
◇ **paro cardíaco** MED cardiac arrest; **paro forzoso** lay-off; **paro respiratorio** MED respiratory failure
parodia *f* parody
parodiar ⟨1b⟩ *v/t* parody
parolímpico *adj*: ***juegos -s*** paralympic games, paralympics
parón *m* sudden stop, dead stop
parótida *f* ANAT parotid gland
paroxismo *m* MED, *fig* paroxysm
parpadear ⟨1a⟩ *v/i* **1** *de persona* blink **2** *de luz, llama* flicker
parpadeo *m* **1** *de persona* blinking **2** *de luz, llama* flickering
párpado *m* eye lid
parque *m* **1** *zona verde* park **2** *para bebé* playpen
◇ **parque acuático** aquatic *o* water park; **parque de atracciones** amusement park; **parque de bomberos** fire station; **parque de diversiones** amusement park; **parque eólico** wind farm; **parque infantil** children's playground; **parque móvil** fleet of official vehicles; **parque nacional** national park; **parque natural** nature reserve; **parque tecnológico** technology park; **parque temático** theme park
parqué *m* parquet
◇ **parqué flotante** suspended flooring, floating floor
parqueadero *m*,**-a** *f L.Am.* parking lot, *Br* car park
parquear ⟨1a⟩ *v/t L.Am.* park
parquedad *f* moderation, frugality
parquet *m* parquet
parquímetro *m* parking meter
parra *f* (grape)vine; ***subirse a la ~*** F (*vanagloriarse*) get bigheaded F; (*enfurecerse*) hit the roof F
párrafo *m* paragraph; ***echar un ~*** *fig* F have a chat F
parral *m* **1** (*plantación*) vineyard **2** (*parras*) vine arbor, *Br* vine arbour
parranda *f*: ***andar*** *o* ***irse de ~*** F go out on the town F
parricida *m/f* parricide
parricidio *m* parricide
parrilla *f* broiler, *Br* grill; ***a la ~*** broiled, *Br* grilled
◇ **parrilla de salida** *en carreras* starting grid
parrillada *f* **1** GASTR *dish consisting of various kinds of broiled meat*, *Br* mixed grill; *L.Am.* barbecue **2** *L.Am. baca* roof rack
párroco *m* parish priest
parroquia *f* **1** REL parish **2** COM clientele, customers *pl*
parroquial *adj* parish *atr*, parochial; ***iglesia ~*** parish church
parroquiano *m*,**-a** *f* parishioner
parsimonia *f* calm; ***con ~*** calmly
parte **I** *m* report; ***dar ~ a alguien*** inform s.o.; ***dar ~*** file a report
II *f* **1** *trozo* part; ***en ~*** partly; ***en gran ~*** largely; ***la mayor ~ de*** the majority of, most of; ***formar ~ de*** form part of; ***tomar ~ en*** take part in; ***tener ~ en algo*** play a part in sth; ***la ~ del león*** the lion's share; ***ir por ~s*** do a job in stages *o* bit by bit; ***llevar la mejor / peor ~*** be at an advantage / a disadvantage
2 JUR party; ***~s contratantes*** contracting parties, parties to the contract
3 (*lugar*): ***alguna ~*** somewhere; ***en cualquier ~*** anywhere; ***otra ~*** somewhere else; ***en*** *o* ***por todas ~s*** everywhere; ***en ninguna ~*** nowhere; ***no llevar*** *o* ***conducir a ninguna ~*** *fig* be going nowhere; ***en otra ~*** elsewhere
4: ***de ~ de*** on *o* in behalf of
5: ***por ~ de madre / padre*** on one's mother's / father's side; ***estar de ~ de alguien*** be on s.o.'s side; ***ponerse de ~ de alguien*** take s.o.'s side; ***por una ~ … por otra ~*** on the one hand … on the other (hand)
6: ***por otra ~*** moreover
7: ***desde un tiempo a esta ~*** up to now, up until now
◇ **parte contraria** JUR opposing party, other side; **parte médico** medical report; **parte meteorológico** weather report

P

partera *f* midwife
parterre *m* flowerbed
partición *f de bienes* division; *de país* partition
participación *f* participation
participante *m/f* participant
participar ⟨1a⟩ **I** *v/t una noticia* announce **II** *v/i* take part (***en*** in), participate (***en*** in)
partícipe *adj*: ***hacer ~ de algo a alguien*** (*comunicar*) tell s.o. about sth, inform s.o. of sth; (*compartir*) share sth with s.o.
participio *m* GRAM participle
partícula *f* particle
particular **I** *adj* **1** *clase*, *propiedad* private; *asunto* personal **2** (*específico*) particular; ***caso ~*** particular case; ***en ~*** in particular **3** (*especial*) peculiar **II** *m* **1** (*persona*) individual **2**: ***~es*** *pl* particulars **3**: ***sin otro ~ se despide atentamente*** sincerely yours, *Br* yours faithfully **4**: ***sobre el ~*** on the subject
particularidad *f* peculiarity
particularizar ⟨1f⟩ **I** *v/t* **1** (*detallar*) particularize, go into detail about **2** (*distinguir*) distinguish **II** *v/i*: ***no particularices, la responsabilidad fue de todos*** don't point the finger *o* name names, everyone was responsible;**particularizarse** *v/r* stand out, distinguish o.s. (***por*** by)
particularmente *adv* particularly, especially
partida *f* **1** *en juego* game; ***tenemos la ~ ganada*** *fig* it's in the bag **2** (*remesa*) consignment **3** *documento* certificate
◇ **partida de bautismo** certificate of baptism;**partida de defunción** death certificate; **partida de nacimiento** birth certificate
partidario **I** *adj*: ***ser ~ de*** be in favor of, *Br* be in favour of **II** *m*,**-a** *f* supporter
partidismo *m* partisanship
partidista *adj* party *atr*, partisan
partido *m* **1** POL party **2** DEP game; ***~ en casa*** home game **3**: ***sacar ~ de*** take advantage of; ***tomar ~*** take sides
◇ **partido amistoso** friendly;**partido benéfico** benefit game;**partido centrista** center party, party of the center; **partido de consolación** consolation final; **partido ecologista** POL green party;**partido de homenaje** testimonial;**partido de ida** DEP first leg;**partido judicial** *area under the jurisdiction of a court of first instance*;**partido laborista** Labor *o Br* Labour party;**partido de vuelta** DEP second leg
partir ⟨3a⟩ **I** *v/t* **1** (*dividir, repartir*) split **2** (*romper*) break open, split open **3** (*cortar*) cut **II** *v/i* (*irse*) leave; ***~ de*** *fig* start from; ***a ~ de hoy*** (starting) from today; ***a ~ de ahora*** from now on;**partirse** *v/r* (*romperse*) break; ***~ la cabeza*** split one's head open; ***~ de risa*** F split one's sides laughing F
partisano *m*,**-a** *f* partisan
partitura *f* MÚS score
parto *m* **1** birth; ***sala de ~s*** delivery room; ***estar de ~*** be in labor *o Br* labour **2** *fig*: *de artículo*, *libro* creation
parturienta *f en parto* woman in labor *o Br* labour; *que ya parió* woman who has just given birth
parva *f* AGR heap of grain
parvulario *m* kindergarten
párvulo *m* (young) child
pasa *f* raisin
◇ **pasa de Corinto** currant
◇ **pasa de Esmirna** sultana
pasable *adj* passable
pasada *f* **1** *con trapo* wipe; ***dar una ~ a algo*** (*retocar, repasar*) put the finishing touches to sth, go over sth again **2** *de pintura* coat **3**: ***jugar una mala ~ a alguien*** play a dirty trick on s.o. **4** F: ***¡qué ~!*** that's incredible! F; ***este coche es una ~*** this car is so cool! F, this car is something else! F **5**: ***de ~*** in passing
pasadizo *m* passage
pasado **I** *adj tiempo* last; ***el lunes ~*** last Monday; ***~ de moda*** old-fashioned **II** *m* past
pasador *m* **1** *para el pelo* barrette, *Br* (hair) slide **2** (*pestillo*) bolt **3** GASTR strainer
pasaje *m* **1** (*billete*) ticket **2** MÚS *de texto* passage
pasajero **I** *adj situación* temporary; *relación* brief **II** *m*,**-a** *f* passenger
pasamano(s) *m*(*inv*) handrail
pasamontañas *m inv* balaclava (helmet)
pasante *m/f* trainee
pasaporte *m* passport; ***dar ~ a alguien*** *fig* sack s.o. F, fire s.o. F
pasapurés *m inv* food mill

pasar ⟨1a⟩ **I** *v/t* **1** pass; **~ *la mano por*** run one's hand through
2 *el tiempo* spend; ***para ~ el tiempo*** (in order) to pass the time; ***~lo bien*** have a good time; ***¡que lo pases bien!, ¡a pasarlo bien!*** enjoy yourself!, have fun *o* a good time!
3 *un lugar* pass, go past; *frontera* cross
4 *problemas, dificultades* experience
5 AUTO (*adelantar*) pass, *Br* overtake
6 *una película* show
7 TELEC: ***le paso al Sr. Galvez*** I'll put you through to Mr. Galvez
8: ***~ algo a máquina*** type sth
II *v/i* **1** (*suceder*) happen; ***¿qué ha pasado?*** what's happened?; ***¿qué pasa?*** what's happening?, what's going on?; ***¿qué te pasa?*** what's the matter?; ***pase lo que pase*** whatever happens, come what may; ***ya ha pasado lo peor*** the worst is over; ***en el viaje nos pasó de todo*** F just about everything happened on that trip, it was a very eventful trip
2 *en juegos* pass
3: ***¡pasa!, ¡pase usted!*** come in!; ***pasé a visitarla*** I dropped by to see her; ***~ por*** go by; ***pasa por aquí*** come this way; ***pasé por la tienda*** I stopped off at the shop; ***pasaré por tu casa*** I'll drop by your house
4: ***dejar ~*** *oportunidad* miss
5 F: ***~ de alguien*** not want anything to do with s.o.; ***paso de ir al gimnasio*** I can't be bothered to go to the gym
6: ***~ de los 60 años*** be over 60 (years old); ***~ de moda*** go out of fashion; ***hacerse ~ por*** pass o.s. off as; ***poder ~ sin algo*** be able to get by *o* to manage without sth; ***puede ~*** it's OK, it'll do
pasarse *v/r* **1** *tb fig* go too far **2** *del tiempo* pass, go by **3** *tiempo* spend **4** *de molestia, dolor* go (away); ***~ al enemigo*** go over to the enemy; ***se me pasó*** it slipped my mind, I forgot; ***se le pasó llamar*** he forgot to call
pasarela *f* **1** *de modelos* runway, *Br* catwalk **2** MAR gangway, gangplank
◇ **pasarela telescópica** AVIA jetty
pasatiempo *m* pastime
Pascua *f* Easter; ***~s*** (*Navidad*) Christmas *sg*; ***¡felices ~s!*** Merry Christmas!; ***de ~s a Ramos*** once in a blue moon; ***estar como unas ~s*** F be over the moon F, be ecstatic F; ***hacer la ~ a alguien*** F (*molestar*) bother s.o., bug s.o. F; (*perjudicar*) wreck s.o.'s plans; ***¡y santas ~s!*** F and that's that!
◇ **Pascua florida, Pascua de Resurrección** Easter
pascual *adj* Easter *atr*, paschal
pase *m* **1** *tb* DEP, TAUR pass **2** *en el cine* showing
◇ **pase de modelos** fashion show
paseante *m/f* stroller, walker
pasear ⟨1a⟩ **I** *v/t* **1** *perro* take for a walk, walk **2** (*exhibir*) show off **II** *v/i* walk; **pasearse** *v/r* walk
paseíllo *m* TAUR *parade at the beginning of a bullfight*
paseo *m* walk; ***dar un ~*** go for a walk; ***mandar a alguien a ~*** *fig* F tell s.o. to get lost F
◇ **paseo marítimo** seafront
pasillo *m* **1** *en vivienda, hospital* corridor **2** *en avión, cine* aisle
◇ **pasillo aéreo** air corridor
◇ **pasillo rodante** AVIA moving walkway
pasión *f* passion
pasional *adj* passionate; ***crimen ~*** crime of passion, crime passionel
pasionaria *f* BOT passionflower
pasividad *f* passivity
pasivo I *adj* passive; ***voz -a*** GRAM passive voice **II** *m* **1** COM liabilities *pl* **2** GRAM passive (voice)
pasma *f* P cops *pl* F
pasmado *adj* **1** (*aturdido*) stunned **2** (*quieto*) still
pasmar ⟨1a⟩ *v/t* **1** (*asombrar*) amaze, astonish **2** (*dar frío a*) freeze; **pasmarse** *v/r* **1** be amazed, be astonished **2**: ***~ de frío*** freeze
pasmarote *m* F half-wit
pasmoso *adj* amazing, astonishing
paso[1] *m* **1** step; ***~ a ~*** step by step; ***a cada ~*** at every step; ***a dos ~s de*** *fig* a stone's throw (away) from; ***volver sobre sus ~s*** retrace one's steps; ***dar un mal ~ o un ~ en falso*** make a false move; ***seguir los ~s a alguien*** follow s.o., dog s.o.'s footsteps; ***seguir los ~s de alguien*** follow in s.o.'s footsteps; ***~s*** *pl en baloncesto* traveling *sg*, *Br* travelling *sg*; ***hacer ~s*** *en baloncesto* travel
2 (*manera de andar*) walk

3 (*ritmo*) pace, rate; ***a este ~*** *fig* at this rate; ***al ~ que vamos*** at the rate we're going; ***a ~ ligero*** at the double; ***llevar el ~*** MIL keep in step; ***marcar el ~*** MIL mark time
4 *de agua* flow; *de tráfico* movement; ***cerrar el ~ de la calle*** block off *o* close the street; ***prohibido el ~*** no entry; ***ceda el ~*** yield, *Br* give way; ***observaba el ~ del agua / de la gente*** he watched the water flow past / the world go by
5 (*cruce*) crossing
6 *de tiempo* passing
7 (*huella*) footprint
8 (*camino*): ***de ~*** on the way; ***estar de ~*** be passing through; ***dicho sea de ~*** and incidentally; ***¡~!*** make way!, let me through!; ***abrirse ~*** push one's way through; *fig* carve out a path for o.s.; ***salir al ~ de alguien*** waylay s.o.; ***salir del ~*** get out of a tight spot
◇ **paso elevado** overpass, *Br* flyover; **paso a nivel** grade crossing, *Br* level crossing; **paso de peatones** crosswalk, *Br* pedestrian crossing; **paso subterráneo** underpass, *Br* subway

paso[2] *m* REL *float in Holy Week procession*

pasodoble *m* paso doble

pasota F **I** *adj actitud, comportamiento* couldn't-care-less; ***estás muy ~ últimamente*** you couldn't care less about anything lately **II** *m/f*: ***es un ~*** he couldn't care less about anything

pasta *f* **1** *sustancia* paste **2** GASTR pasta **3** P (*dinero*) dough P, *Br* dosh P; ***una ~ (gansa)*** F a fortune; ***soltar la ~*** P cough up F, hand over the cash; ***de buena ~*** good-natured; ***son de la misma ~*** *fig* they're two of a kind
◇ **pasta de dientes** toothpaste; **pasta quebrada** short pastry; **pastas de té** *type of cookie o Br biscuit*

pastar ⟨1a⟩ *v/i* graze

paste(u)rización *f* pasteurization

paste(u)rizar ⟨1f⟩ *v/t* pasteurize

pastel *m* **1** GASTR cake **2** *pintura, color* pastel **3**: ***descubrirse el ~*** F come to light

pastelería *f* cake shop

pastelero *m*, **-a** *f* pastry cook

pastelista *m/f* PINT pastel painter

pastiche *m* pastiche

pastilla *f* **1** *medicina* tablet **2** *de jabón* bar **3**: ***a toda ~*** F at top speed F, flat out F

pastillero *m* pillbox

pastizal *m* pastureland

pasto *m* (*dehesa*) pasture; ***a todo ~*** F for all one is worth F; ***el edificio fue ~ de las llamas*** the building was engulfed by flames; ***fueron ~ de las murmuraciones*** they were the subject of rumors; ***dar ~ a*** *fig* (*fomentar*) encourage

pastón *m* F fortune; ***gastarse un ~*** spend a fortune

pastor **I** *adj*: ***perro ~*** sheepdog **II** *m* **1** *de ovejas* shepherd **2** REL pastor
◇ **pastor alemán** German shepherd

pastoral *f/adj* pastoral

pastorear ⟨1a⟩ **I** *v/i de ganado* pasture, graze **II** *v/t* (*cuidar, atender*) tend

pastoreo *m* pasturage

pastoril *adj* pastoral

pastoso *adj* **1** *masa* doughy **2** *lengua* furry **3** *voz* rich

pata[1] *m/f Pe* F pal F, buddy F

pata[2] *f* leg; ***a cuatro ~s*** on all fours; ***ir a la ~ coja*** hop; ***meter la ~*** F put one's foot in it F; ***tener mala ~*** F be unlucky; ***~s arriba*** upside down, in a mess; ***a la ~ la llana*** F *comportarse* naturally, in a down-to-earth way
◇ **pata de gallo** houndstooth (check); **pata de palo** wooden leg; **patas de gallo** crow's feet

patada *f* kick; ***dar una ~*** kick; ***dar la ~ a alguien*** *fig* kick s.o. out; ***echar a alguien a ~s*** *fig* kick s.o. out; ***tratar a alguien a ~s*** treat s.o. like dirt

Patagonia *f* Patagonia

patagónico *adj* Patagonian

patalear ⟨1a⟩ *v/i* stamp one's feet; *fig* kick and scream

pataleo *m* stamping; ***derecho al ~*** right to complain

pataleta *f* F tantrum

patán *desp* **I** *adj* loutish **II** *m* lout

patata *f* potato; ***no saber ni ~*** *fig* F know nothing at all
◇ **patata caliente** *fig* F hot potato F
◇ **patatas fritas** *de sartén* French fries, *Br* chips; *de bolsa* chips, *Br* crisps

patatús *m*: ***le dio un ~*** F he had a fit F

paté *m* paté

patear ⟨1a⟩ **I** *v/t* **1** *L.Am. de animal* kick **2** (*recorrer*) go all over, walk all around **II** *v/i L.Am. de animal* kick

patena *f* paten; ***limpio como una ~ fig*** spick-and-span
patentar ⟨1a⟩ *v/t* patent
patente **I** *adj* clear, obvious **II** *f* **1** patent; ***oficina de ~s*** patent office **2** *L.Am.* AUTO license plate, *Br* numberplate
◇ **patente de corso** *fig* free hand, carte blanche
patera *f* small boat
paternal *adj* paternal, fatherly
paternalismo *m* paternalism
paternidad *f* paternity, fatherhood; ***prueba de ~*** paternity test
paterno *adj* paternal
patético *adj* pitiful
patetismo *m* pathos *sg*
patíbulo *m* scaffold
paticojo *m*,**-a** *f* F gimp F, cripple
patidifuso *adj* F staggered F, flabbergasted F
patilla *f de gafas* arm; **~s** *pl barba* sideburns
patín *m* **1** skate **2** *Méx*: ***a ~*** on foot; ***fuimos a ~*** we walked
◇ **patín de ruedas** roller skate;**patín (de ruedas) en línea** rollerblade®, inline skate;**patín a vela** catamaran
pátina *f* patina
patinador *m*,**~a** *f* skater
patinaje *m* skating
◇ **patinaje artístico** figure skating;**patinaje sobre hielo** ice-skating;**patinaje sobre ruedas** roller-skating
patinar ⟨1a⟩ *v/i* **1** skate; ***~ sobre hielo*** (ice)skate; ***~ sobre ruedas*** (roller-) skate **2** AUTO skid **3** *fig* (*equivocarse*) slip up
patinazo *m* **1** AUTO skid; ***dar un ~*** skid **2** *fig* F (*equivocación*) slip-up
patinete *m* scooter
patio *m* courtyard, patio
◇ **patio de butacas** TEA orchestra, *Br* stalls *pl*;**patio de luces** (light) well;**patio de recreo** schoolyard, *Br* playground;**patio trasero** back yard
patita *f*: ***poner a alguien de ~s en la calle*** F kick s.o. out F
patitieso *adj fig* F **1** *por el frío* frozen stiff **2** *por sorpresa* staggered F, flabbergasted F
patituerto *adj* bowlegged
patizambo *adj* knock-kneed
pato *m* ZO duck; ***pagar el ~*** F take the rap F, *Br* carry the can F
patochada *f* piece of nonsense; **~s** *pl* nonsense *sg*
patógeno **I** *adj* pathogenic **II** *m* pathogen
patojo *m C.Am.* squat
patología *f* pathology
patológico *adj* pathological
patólogo *m*,**-a** *f* pathologist
patoso *adj* clumsy
patraña *f* tall story
patria *f* homeland
◇ **patria chica** home town
patriarca *m* patriarch
patriarcado *m* patriarchy
patriarcal *adj* patriarchal
patricio **I** *adj* patrician **II** *m*,**-a** *f* patrician
patrimonial *adj* hereditary
patrimonio *m* heritage
◇ **patrimonio artístico** artistic heritage;**patrimonio cultural** cultural heritage; **patrimonio de la humanidad** world heritage
patrio *adj*: ***amor ~*** love of one's country; ***lengua -a*** native tongue
patriota **I** *adj* patriotic **II** *m/f* patriot
patriotería *f* jingoism, chauvinism
patriotero **I** *adj* jingoistic, chauvinistic **II** *m*,**-a** *f* jingoist, chauvinist
patriótico *adj* patriotic
patriotismo *m* patriotism
patrocinador *m*,**~a** *f* sponsor
patrocinar ⟨1a⟩ *v/t* **1** sponsor **2** *Méx* JUR defend
patrocinio *m* **1** sponsorship **2** *Méx* JUR defense, *Br* defence
patrón *m* **1** (*jefe*) boss; MAR skipper **2** REL patron saint **3** *para costura* pattern **4** (*modelo*) standard; ***cortado por el mismo ~ fig*** cast in the same mold *o Br* mould
◇ **patrón oro** gold standard
patrona *f* **1** (*jefa*) boss **2** REL patron saint
patronaje *m* pattern-making
patronal **I** *adj* **1** employers *atr* **2**: ***fiesta ~*** patron saint's day **II** *m* employers *pl*
patronato *m de fundación benéfica* trustees *pl*; *de organización* board
patronista *m/f* pattern-maker
patrono *m* **1** COM employer **2** REL patron saint
patrulla *f* **1** patrol; ***estar de ~*** be on patrol **2** *Méx* patrol car
patrullar ⟨1a⟩ *v/t* patrol

patrullero I *m barco* patrol boat; *Ecuad, Rpl*: *coche* patrol car II *m,-a f* patrolman; *mujer* patrolwoman
patucos *mpl* bootees
paulatino *adj* gradual
paupérrimo *adj* poverty-stricken, impoverished
pausa *f* **1** *en conversación* pause; *en actividad* break **2** MÚS rest
◇ **pausa publicitaria** commercial break
pausado *adj* slow, deliberate
pauta *f* guideline; ***marcar la ~*** set the guidelines
pautar ⟨1a⟩ *v/t* set down guidelines for
pava *f* **1** *animal* (hen) turkey **2** F (*colilla*) cigarette butt, *Br* dog end F **3**: ***pelar la ~*** F whisper sweet nothings
◇ **pava real** peahen
pavada *f* F silly thing
pavimentar ⟨1a⟩ *v/t* surface
pavimento *m* pavement, *Br* road surface
pavisoso *adj* dull
pavo I *adj L.Am.* stupid II *m* ZO turkey; ***se le subió el ~*** *fig* F she blushed
◇ **pavo real** peacock
pavón *m mariposa* peacock butterfly; *ave* peacock
pavonearse ⟨1a⟩ *v/r* boast (***de*** about)
pavor *m* terror; ***me da ~*** it terrifies me
pavoroso *adj* terrifying
pay *m Méx* pie
payada *f Rpl improvised ballad*
payador *m Rpl* gaucho singer
payasadas *fpl* antics; ***hacer ~*** fool *o* clown around
payasear ⟨1a⟩ *v/i L.Am.* clown around
payaso *m,-a f* clown
payo *m,-a f* non-gypsy, Gorgio
paz *f* peace; ***amante de la ~*** peace-loving; ***dejar en ~*** leave alone; ***hacer las paces*** make it up, make things up; ***quedar en ~*** F be quits; ***¡y en ~!*** F and that's that!
pazguato I *adj* dopey F, dumb F II *m,-a f* dope F, dummy F
PBI *m abr Rpl* (= ***producto bruto interno***) GDP (= Gross Domestic Product)
PBN *m abr L.Am.* (= ***producto bruto nacional***) GNP (= Gross National Product)
PC *m abr* (= ***Partido Comunista***) CP (= Communist Party)
P.D. *abr* (= ***posdata***) PS (= postscript)
pe : ***de ~ a pa*** F from start to finish
peaje *m dinero, lugar* toll
peatón *m* pedestrian
peatonal *adj* pedestrian *atr*
pebete *m,-a f Rpl* F kid F
peca *f* freckle
pecado *m* sin
◇ **pecado capital** deadly sin; ***los siete pecados capitales*** the seven deadly sins;**pecado mortal** mortal sin;**pecado original** original sin
pecador *m,~a f* sinner
pecaminoso *adj* sinful
pecar ⟨1g⟩ *v/i* sin; ***~ de ingenuo / generoso*** be very naive / generous
pécari *m*,**pecarí** *m* ZO peccary
pecera *f* fish tank, aquarium
pecho *m* **1** (*caja torácica*) chest **2** (*mama*) breast; ***dar el ~*** breastfeed; ***de ~s planos*** flat-chested; ***tomar algo a ~*** take sth to heart; ***a ~ descubierto*** *luchar* bare-handed; *hablar* openly, frankly; ***echarse*** *o* ***meterse entre ~ y espalda*** F *comida* put away F; *bebida* knock back F; ***sacar ~*** stick one's chest out; *fig* stick one's neck out; ***partirse el ~*** *fig* knock o.s. out **3** *L.Am.* DEP breaststroke
pechuga *f* **1** GASTR breast **2** *L.Am. fig* (*caradura*) nerve F
pechugona *adj* busty F
peciolo, pecíolo *m* BOT petiole
pécora *f*: ***mala ~*** F bitch F
pecoso *adj* freckled
pectina *f* QUÍM pectin
pectoral *m/adj* ANAT pectoral
peculiar *adj* **1** (*singular*) peculiar, odd **2** (*característico*) typical
peculiaridad *f* (*característica*) peculiarity
pecuniario *adj fml* pecuniary *fml*
pedagogía *f* education
pedagógico *adj* educational
pedagogo *m,-a f* teacher
pedal *m* pedal
◇ **pedal de freno** brake pedal
◇ **pedal del acelerador** gas pedal, accelerator pedal
pedalear ⟨1a⟩ *v/i* pedal
pedaleo *m* pedaling, *Br* pedalling
pedante I *adj* **1** (*perfeccionista*) pedantic **2** (*presuntuoso*) pretentious II *m/f* **1** (*perfeccionista*) pedant **2** (*presuntuoso*)

pretentious individual
pedantería *f* **1** (*perfeccionismo*) pedantry **2** (*presunción*) pretentiousness
pedazo *m* piece, bit; **~ *de bruto*** F blockhead F; ***ser un ~ de pan*** be really nice; ***hacer ~s*** F smash to bits F; ***caerse a ~s*** fall to pieces; ***hecho ~s*** F shattered F
pederasta *m* pederast
pederastia *f* pederasty
pedernal *m* flint
pedestal *m* pedestal; ***poner / tener a alguien en / sobre un ~*** *fig* put / have s.o. on a pedestal
pedestre *adj* pedestrian; ***carrera ~*** footrace
pediatra *m/f* pediatrician, *Br tb* paediatrician
pediatría *f* pediatrics *sg*, *Br tb* paediatrics *sg*
pedicura *f* pedicure
pedicuro *m*, **-a** *f* podiatrist, *Br* chiropodist
pedido *m* order; ***a ~ de*** *L.Am.* at the request of; ***hacer un ~*** place an order
pedigrí *m* pedigree
pedigüeño *m*, **-a** *f* person who is always asking to borrow things, moocher F
pedir ⟨3l⟩ **I** *v/t* **1** ask for; ***~ algo a alguien*** ask s.o. for sth; ***me pidió que no fuera*** he asked me not to go; ***te lo pido*** I beg you **2** (*necesitar*) need **3** *en bar, restaurante* order **II** *v/i* **1** (*mendigar*) beg **2** *en bar, restaurante* order
pedo I *adj* drunk **II** *m* F fart F; ***tirarse*** *o* ***echar un ~*** F fart F; ***agarrarse un ~*** F get plastered F
pedorreta *f* F Bronx cheer F, *Br* raspberry F
pedrada *f* blow with a stone; ***me dio una ~ en la cabeza*** he hit me over the head with a stone
pedregal *m* stony ground
pedregoso *adj* stony
pedrera *f* quarry
pedrería *f* precious stones *pl*
pedrero *m* stonecutter
pedrisco *m* hail
Pedro *m*: ***como ~ por su casa*** *fig* F as if he / she owned the place
pedrusco *m* rough stone
pedúnculo *m* BOT, ANAT peduncle
peerse ⟨2e⟩ *v/r* F fart F
pega *f* F snag F, hitch F; ***poner ~s*** raise objections; ***de ~*** fake, bogus
pegadizo *adj* catchy
pegado *adj* (*adherido*) stuck (***a*** to); ***estar ~ a*** (*cerca de*) be right up against; ***estar ~ a alguien*** *fig* follow s.o. around, be s.o.'s shadow
pegajoso *adj* **1** (*pringoso*) sticky **2** *fig*: *persona* clingy
pegamento *m* glue
pegar ⟨1h⟩ **I** *v/t* **1** (*golpear*) hit **2** (*adherir*) stick, glue **3** *bofetada, susto, resfriado* give; ***~ un grito*** shout, give a shout; ***no me pega la gana*** *Méx* I don't feel like it **II** *v/i* **1** (*golpear*) hit **2** (*adherir*) stick **3** *del sol* beat down **4** (*armonizar*) go (together); **pegarse** *v/r* **1** *resfriado* catch **2** *acento* pick up **3** *susto* give o.s.; ***~ un golpe / un tiro*** hit / shoot o.s. **4**: ***~ a alguien*** *fig* stick to s.o.; ***pegársela a alguien*** F con s.o. F
pegatina *f* sticker
pego *m* F: ***dar el ~*** look the part, look real
pegote *m* F (*cosa fea*) eyesore
peinado I *adj*: ***bien ~*** well-groomed; ***va muy mal ~*** his hair is a mess **II** *m* hairstyle
peinador *m*, **~a** *f L.Am.* hairdresser
peinar ⟨1a⟩ *v/t tb fig* comb; ***~ a alguien*** comb s.o.'s hair; **peinarse** *v/r* comb one's hair
peine *m* comb; ***¡te vas a enterar de lo que vale un ~!*** F you're going to find out what's what!
peineta *f* ornamental comb
p. ej. *abr* (= ***por ejemplo***) e.g. (= exempli gratia, for example)
pékari *m S.Am.* ☞ ***pécari***
Pekín *m* Peking; *China actual* Beijing
pela *f* F peseta
peladero *m L.Am.* vacant lot
peladilla *f* sugared almond
pelado *adj* **1** peeled; *fig* bare; F (*sin dinero*) broke F **2** *Méx* F *grosero* rude
peladura *f acción* peeling; ***~s*** *pl* peelings, peel *sg*
pelagatos *m inv* F nobody
pelaje *m* **1** ZO coat **2** *fig* (*aspecto*) look, appearance
pelambre *m*, **pelambrera** *f* F mop of hair
pelandusca *f* F whore F
pelapapas *m inv L.Am.* potato peeler
pelapatatas *m inv* potato peeler
pelar ⟨1a⟩ *v/t manzana, patata etc* peel;

hace un frío que pela F it's freezing; **pelarse** *v/r* **1** (*cortarse el pelo*) have a haircut **2** *Rpl* F (*chismear*) gossip
pelazón *f C.Am.* backbiting
peldaño *m* step
pelea *f* fight
pelear ⟨1a⟩ *v/i* fight; **pelearse** *v/r* **1** *con fuerza física* fight **2** (*discutir*) argue, fight
pelele *m* puppet
peleón *adj* argumentative; ***vino ~*** F jug wine, *Br* plonk F
peletería *f* furrier's
peli *f* F movie, film
peliagudo *adj* tricky
pelícano *m* ZO pelican
película *f* **1** movie, film; ***de ~*** F awesome F, fantastic F **2** FOT film
◇ **película de acción** action movie; **película en blanco y negro** black-and-white movie; **película muda** silent movie; **película del Oeste** Western; **película sonora** talkie; **película de terror** horror movie
peliculón *m* F fantastic movie
peligrar ⟨1a⟩ *v/i* be at risk; ***hacer ~ algo*** put sth at risk
peligro *m* danger; ***correr ~*** be in danger; ***poner en ~*** endanger, put at risk; ***su vida no corre ~*** his life is not at risk; ***fuera de ~*** out of danger; ***sin ~*** without risk
◇ **peligro de incendio** fire hazard
◇ **peligro de muerte** danger
peligroso *adj* dangerous
pelilargo *adj* long-haired
pelillo *m*: ***¡~s a la mar*** *fig* F let's bury the hatchet
pelín: ***un ~*** F a (little) bit; ***por un ~*** F just
pelirrojo *adj* red-haired, red-headed
pellejo *m de animal* skin, hide; ***salvar el ~*** *fig* F save one's (own) skin F; ***arriesgarse*** *o* ***jugarse el ~*** F risk one's neck F; ***estar en el ~ de alguien*** F be in s.o.'s shoes; ***dejarse el ~ en algo*** *fig* slog one's guts out on sth; ***no caber en su ~*** F be bursting with joy
pellizcar ⟨1g⟩ *v/t* pinch
pellizco *m* pinch; ***un buen ~*** F a tidy sum F
pelma **I** *adj* annoying **II** *m/f* pain F
pelmazo **I** *adj* annoying **II** *m*, **-a** *f* F pain F
pelo *m* **1** *de persona, de perro* hair; ***tiene el ~ muy largo*** he has very long hair; ***por los ~s*** F by a hair's-breadth, by a whisker F; ***por un ~*** just, barely; ***los ~s se me ponen de punta*** *fig* my hair stands on end; ***tirarse de los ~s*** *fig* F tear one's hair out; ***traído por los ~s*** *fig* far-fetched; ***soltarse el ~*** *fig* F let one's hair down F **2** *de animal* fur; ***a ~*** F (*sin preparación*) unprepared; ***montar a ~*** ride bareback; ***tomar el ~ a alguien*** F pull s.o.'s leg F; ***con ~s y señales*** in minute detail; ***hombre de ~ en pecho*** real man; (***ni***) ***un ~*** not at all; ***no cortarse*** (***ni***) ***un ~*** not be shy; ***no tiene un ~ de tonto*** *fig* F there are no flies on him F, he's no fool; ***no tener ~s en la lengua*** *fig* F not mince one's words F
pelón *adj Méx* F tough
pelota **I** *f* **1** ball; ***~s*** F nuts F, balls F; ***en ~s*** P stark naked; ***dejar a alguien en ~s*** F clean s.o. out F; ***hacer la ~ a alguien*** suck up to s.o. F; ***devolver la ~*** *fig* give as good as one gets; ***la ~ está*** *o* ***queda en el tejado*** *fig* the whole thing is up in the air **2** *L.Am.* DEP baseball **II** *m/f* F creep F
◇ **pelota vasca** jai alai, pelota
pelotari *m/f* jai alai player, pelota player
pelotazo *m*: ***rompió el cristal de un ~*** he smashed the window with a ball; ***darle a alguien un ~*** hit s.o. with a ball; ***pegar el ~*** *fig* make a quick buck F
pelotera *f* F row F, argument
pelotero *m*, **-a** *f L.Am.* (base)ball player
pelotilla *f*: ***hacer la ~ a alguien*** suck up to s.o. F
pelotillero F **I** *adj* crawling, toadying **II** *m*, **-a** *f* crawler F, toady
pelotón *m* **1** MIL squad **2** DEP bunch, pack
◇ **pelotón de ejecución** firing squad
peluca *f* wig
peluche *m* soft toy; ***oso de ~*** teddy bear
peludo *adj persona* hairy; *animal* furry
peluquearse ⟨1a⟩ *v/r L.Am.* get one's hair cut
peluquería *f* hairdresser's
peluquería de caballeros barber's, gentlemen's hairdresser's; **peluquería canina** canine hairdresser's; **peluquería de señoras** ladies' hairdresser's
peluquero *m*, **-a** *f* hairdresser
peluquín *m* toupee, hairpiece
pelusa *f* fluff

pelviano, pélvico *adj* ANAT pelvic
pelvis *f inv* ANAT pelvis
pena *f* **1** (*tristeza*) sadness, sorrow; ***da ~*** it's sad
2 (*congoja*) grief, distress
3 (*lástima*) pity; ***es una ~*** it's a shame *o* pity; ***¡qué ~!*** what a shame *o* pity!
4 *L.Am.* (*vergüenza*) embarrassment; ***me da ~*** I'm embarrassed
5 JUR sentence
6: ***no vale*** *o* ***no merece la ~*** it's not worth it; ***a duras ~s*** with great difficulty; ***so ~ de*** on pain of; ***con más ~ que gloria*** ingloriously; ***sin ~ ni gloria*** almost unnoticed
◇ **pena capital** death penalty, capital punishment; **pena máxima** DEP penalty; **pena de muerte** death penalty; **pena privativa de libertad** custodial sentence
penal **I** *adj* penal; ***derecho ~*** criminal law **II** *m* **1** penitentiary, pen F, *Br* prison **2** *L.Am.* (*penalti*) penalty
penalidad *f fig* hardship
penalista *m/f* criminal law specialist
penalización *f* **1** *acción* penalization **2** DEP penalty
penalizar ⟨1f⟩ *v/t* penalize
penalti *m* DEP penalty; ***cometer un ~*** concede a penalty; ***marcar de ~*** score a penalty; ***ganar por ~s*** win on penalties
penalty *m* DEP penalty; ***casarse de ~*** F have to get married
penar ⟨1a⟩ **I** *v/t* punish **II** *v/i* suffer
penca **I** *adj Chi* soft, weak **II** *f L.Am.* (*nopal*) leaf of the prickly pear plant
pendejada *f L.Am.* stupid thing to do
pendejo **I** *m* (*pelea*) fight **II** *m*, **-a** *f L.Am.* F dummy F
pendenciero *m*,**-a** *f* troublemaker
pender ⟨2a⟩ *v/i* hang (***sobre*** over)
pendiente **I** *adj* **1** unresolved, unfinished; ***estar ~*** be pending; ***~ de solución*** awaiting a solution, still to be resolved **2** *cuenta* unpaid **3** (*alerta*): ***estar ~ de*** be waiting for **II** *m* earring **III** *f* slope
pendón **I** *adj* swinging F **II** *m*,**-ona** *f* F swinger F
pendular *adj* pendular; ***movimiento ~*** pendular motion
péndulo *m* pendulum
pene *m* ANAT penis
penetración *f* penetration
penetrante *adj* **1** *mirada* penetrating **2** *sonido* piercing **3** *frío* bitter **4** *herida* deep **5** *análisis* incisive
penetrar ⟨1a⟩ **I** *v/t* penetrate **II** *v/i* **1** (*atravesar*) penetrate **2** (*entrar*) enter **3** *de un líquido* seep in
penicilina *f* penicillin
península *f* peninsula
◇ **Península Ibérica** Iberian Peninsula
◇ **Peninsula del Yucatan** Yucatan Peninsula
peninsular *adj* peninsular
penique *m* penny
penitencia *f* penitence
penitenciaría *f* penitentiary, pen F, *Br* prison
penitenciario *adj* penitentiary *atr*, prison *atr*; ***centro ~*** prison
penitente *m/f* penitent
penosamente *adv* with difficulty
penoso *adj* **1** (*angustiante*) distressing **2** *trabajo* laborious **3** *C.Am., Cu, Méx*: *que causa vergüenza* embarrassing **4** *C.Am., Cu, Méx*: *que siente vergüenza* shy
pensado *adj* thought-out; ***lo tengo bien ~*** I've thought about it carefully
pensador *m*,**~a** *f* thinker
pensamiento *m* **1** (*reflexión*) thought **2** BOT pansy
pensar ⟨1k⟩ **I** *v/t* **1** think about; ***¡ni ~lo!*** don't even think about it! **2** (*opinar*) think **II** *v/i* think (***en*** about); ***¿en qué piensas?*** what are you thinking about?; ***sin ~*** without thinking
pensativo *adj* thoughtful
pensión *f* **1** *hotel* rooming house, *Br* guesthouse; ***media ~*** *bed and breakfast and one main meal*, *Br* half board **2** *dinero* pension
◇ **pensión alimenticia** child support, *Br* maintenance; **pensión completa** American plan, *Br* full board;**pensión de invalidez** disability *o* invalidity pension
pensionista *m/f* pensioner
pentágono *m* pentagon; ***el Pentágono*** the Pentagon
pentagrama *m* MÚS stave
pentatleta *m/f* DEP pentathlete
pentatlón *m* DEP pentathlon
Pentecostés *m* Pentecost
penúltimo *adj* penultimate

penumbra *f* half-light
penumbroso *adj* shadowy
penuria *f* **1** (*pobreza*) poverty; ***sufrir ~s*** suffer hardship **2** *fml*: *de medios, espacio* shortage (***de*** of)
peña *f* **1** *cerro* crag, cliff;(*roca*) rock **2** F *de amigos* group, circle; ***~ quinielística*** *syndicate of people doing the sports lottery*, *Br* pools syndicate (*for soccer*)
peñasco *m* boulder
peñazo *m* F pain (in the neck) F
peñón *m*: ***el Peñon de Gibraltar*** the Rock of Gibraltar
peón *m* **1** *en ajedrez* pawn **2** *trabajador* laborer, *Br* labourer
◇ **peón caminero** road mender, *Br tb* navvy
peonada *f trabajo* day's work; *trabajadores* gang of laborers *o Br* labourers
peonía *f* BOT peony
peor *adj* **1** *comp* worse; ***de mal en ~*** from bad to worse; ***ir a ~*** get worse, deteriorate; ***~ que ~, tanto ~*** it will make matters worse **2** *sup*: ***lo ~*** the worst (thing); ***haber pasado lo ~*** be over the worst
pepa *f L.Am.* (*semilla*) seed; ***soltar la ~*** spill the beans
pepenador *m*, **-a** *f C.Am.*, *Méx* scavenger
pepinillo *m* gherkin
pepino *m* cucumber; ***me importa un ~*** F I don't give a damn F
pepita *f* pip
pepito *m* steak sandwich
pepitoria *f meat stew in sauce which contains egg yolk*
pepsina *f* pepsin
peque *m/f* F kid F
pequeñez *f* smallness
pequeño **I** *adj* small, little; ***de ~*** when I was small *o* little; ***en ~*** in miniature **II** *m*, **-a** *f* little one
◇ **pequeños anuncios** classified advertisements *o* ads, *Br tb* small ads
Pequín *m* Peking; *en la China actual* Beijing
pequinés **I** *adj* of / from Peking, Peking *atr*; *en la China actual* of / from Beijing, Beijing *atr* **II** *m* ZO Pekinese, Peke F
pera *f* pear; ***pedir ~s al olmo*** ask the impossible; ***poner a alguien las ~s al cuarto*** *fig* F give s.o. a piece of one's mind F; ***ser la ~*** *fig* P be the limit
peral *m* pear tree
peralte *m* camber
perca *f pez* perch
percal *m* percale
percance *m* mishap
percatarse ⟨1a⟩ *v/r* notice; ***~ de algo*** notice sth
percebe *m* ZO barnacle
percebista *m/f* barnacle collector
percepción *f* **1** perception **2** COM *acto* receipt
perceptible *adj* perceptible, noticeable
perceptivo *adj* perceptive
perceptor **I** *adj* receiving **II** *m*,**~a** *f* recipient
percha *f* (*colgador*) coat hanger; *gancho* coat hook; ***tener buena ~*** *fig* F have a good figure
perchero *m* coat rack
percibir ⟨3a⟩ *v/t* **1** perceive **2** COM *sueldo* receive
percusión *f* MÚS percussion
percusionista *m/f* MÚS percussionist
percusor *m* hammer
percutáneo *adj* MED percutaneous
percutir ⟨3a⟩ *v/t* MED sound
percutor *m* ☞ ***percusor***
perdedor **I** *adj* losing **II** *m*,**~a** *f* loser; ***ser buen / mal ~*** *en juegos* be a good / bad loser
perder ⟨2g⟩ **I** *v/t* **1** *objeto* lose; ***¡piérdete!*** get lost!; ***no te lo pierdas*** *película, acontecimiento* don't miss it; ***no tener nada que ~*** have nothing to lose **2** *tren, avión etc* miss **3** *el tiempo* waste **II** *v/i* lose; ***echar a ~*** ruin; ***echarse a ~*** *de alimento* go bad; ***llevar*** *o* ***tener las de ~*** be at a disadvantage; ***salir perdiendo*** come off worst
perderse *v/r* get lost; ***no se te ha perdido nada aquí*** *fig* there's nothing here for you
perdición *f* downfall
pérdida *f* **1** loss; ***no tiene ~*** you can't miss it; ***~ de tiempo*** waste of time **2** *en baloncesto* turnover
perdidamente *adv* hopelessly; ***estar ~ enamorado*** be hopelessly in love
perdido *adj* lost; ***ponerse ~*** get filthy; ***estar ~*** F be crazy (***por*** about) F, be madly in love (***por*** with) F; ***loco ~*** absolutely crazy
perdigón *m* pellet

P

perdigonada *f* **1** *tiro* shot **2** *herida* gunshot wound
perdiguero *adj*: ***perro ~*** gundog
perdiz *f* ZO partridge; ***marear la ~*** *fig* waste time; ***~ blanca*** *o* ***nival*** rock ptarmigan
perdón *m* **1** *disculpa* pardon; ***¡~!*** sorry!; ***¿~?*** excuse me?, pardon me?; ***pedir ~*** say sorry, apologize; ***con ~*** pardon my French **2** REL forgiveness
perdonable *adj* forgivable
perdonar ⟨1a⟩ **I** *v/t* **1** forgive; ***~ algo a alguien*** forgive s.o. sth **2** JUR pardon **II** *v/i*: ***¡perdone!*** sorry!; ***perdone, ¿tiene hora?*** excuse me, do you have the time?
perdonavidas *m inv* F tough guy F, thug
perdurable *adj* enduring, lasting
perdurar ⟨1a⟩ *v/i* endure
perecedero *adj* perishable
perecer ⟨2d⟩ *v/i* perish; ***~ ahogado*** drown
peregrinación *f* pilgrimage
peregrinar ⟨1a⟩ *v/i* go on a pilgrimage
peregrino I *adj* **1** *ave* migratory **2** *idea* strange, outlandish **II** *m*, **-a** *f* pilgrim
perejil *m* BOT parsley
perengano *m*, **-a** *f* so-and-so
perenne *adj* BOT perennial
perennifolio *adj* BOT evergreen
perentorio *adj* **1** (*urgente*) urgent, pressing **2** (*apremiante*) peremptory
pereza *f* laziness; ***me da ~*** I can't be bothered
perezoso I *adj* lazy **II** *m* ZO sloth
perfección *f* perfection; ***a la ~*** perfectly, to perfection
perfeccionamiento *m* perfecting; ***~ (profesional)*** (professional) training
perfeccionar ⟨1a⟩ *v/t* perfect
perfeccionista I *adj* perfectionist **II** *m/f* perfectionist
perfectamente *adv* perfectly; ***¡~!*** agreed!, all right!; ***lo vi ~*** I saw it as clear as day; ***te comprendo ~*** I know exactly what you mean
perfecto I *adj* perfect **II** *m* GRAM perfect (tense)
perfidia *f* treachery
pérfido *adj* treacherous
perfil *m* profile; ***de ~*** in profile, from the side; ***dar el ~*** *para un cargo* fit the profile
perfilado *adj rostro, nariz* long and thin; ***estar muy ~*** *proyecto* be at an advanced stage
◇ **perfilador de labios** lip pencil
perfilar ⟨1a⟩ *v/t* **1** *dibujo* outline **2** *proyecto* put the finishing touches to; **perfilarse** *v/r* emerge
perforación *f* **1** (*orificio*) puncture; ***perforaciones*** *pl* perforations **2** *en la calle* hole; ***hacer una ~*** make *o* dig a hole
perforadora *f de papeles* punch
perforar ⟨1a⟩ *v/t* **1** (*agujerear*) pierce **2** *calle* dig up
perfumador *m utensilio* atomizer
perfumar ⟨1a⟩ *v/t* perfume
perfume *m* perfume
perfumería *f* perfume shop
perfumista *m/f* perfumer, perfume-maker
pergamino *m* parchment
pergenio *m*, **-a** *f Rpl* F kid F
pergeñar ⟨1a⟩ *v/t* F throw together
pérgola *f* pergola
pericardio *m* ANAT pericardium
pericia *f* expertise
pericial *adj* expert; ***informe*** *o* ***dictamen ~*** technical report
perico *m* parakeet
pericote *m Chi, Pe* ZO large rat
periferia *f de circunferencia* periphery; *de ciudad* outskirts *pl*
periférico I *adj* peripheral; *barrio* outlying **II** *m* INFOR peripheral
perifollo *m* BOT chervil
perifrástico *adj* periphrastic
perilla *f* **1** goatee; ***me viene de ~*** F that'll be very useful; ***tu visita me viene de ~*** F you've come at just the right time **2** *L.Am. pomo* doorknob
perímetro *m* perimeter
perinatal *adj* MED perinatal
perineo *m* ANAT perineum
periodicidad *f* periodicity; ***se publica con ~ trimestral*** it is published quarterly *o* every three months; ***con ~*** periodically
periódico I *adj* periodic **II** *m* newspaper
periodismo *m* journalism
periodista *m/f* journalist; ***~ deportivo*** sport writer *o* columnist
periodístico *adj* journalistic
período, periodo *m* period
periostio *m* ANAT periosteum
peripecia *f* adventure

periplo *m* tour, (long) journey
periquete *m*: ***en un ~*** F in a second, in no time F
periquito *m* ZO budgerigar
periscopio *m* periscope
peritaje *m* **1** *informe* expert's report, specialist report **2** *trabajo* specialist work
peritar ⟨1a⟩ *v/t* value (***en*** at)
perito I *adj* expert **II** *m*, **-a** *f* **1** (*especialista*) expert **2** COM *en seguros* loss adjuster
peritoneo *m* ANAT peritoneum
peritonitis *f* MED peritonitis
perjudicar ⟨1g⟩ *v/t* harm, damage
perjudicial *adj* harmful, damaging; ***~ para la salud*** harmful to one's health
perjuicio *m* harm, damage; ***sin ~ de*** without affecting
perjurar ⟨1a⟩ *v/i* commit perjury, perjure o.s.
perjurio *m* perjury
perla *f* pearl; ***nos vino de ~s*** F it suited us fine F
◇ **perla cultivada** cultured pearl
permanecer ⟨2d⟩ *v/i* remain, stay
permanencia *f* stay
permanente I *adj* permanent **II** *f o Méx m* (*moldeado*) perm
permeabilidad *f* permeability
permeable *adj* permeable; ***ser ~ al agua / la luz*** let in water / light
permisible *adj* permissible
permisividad *f* permissiveness
permisivo *adj* permissive
permiso *m* **1** (*consentimiento*) permission; ***dar ~*** give permission **2** *documento* permit **3**: ***estar de ~*** be on leave; ***con ~*** excuse me
◇ **permiso de circulación** AUTO car registration document; **permiso de conducir** driver's license, *Br* driving licence; **permiso de residencia** residence permit; **permiso de trabajo** work permit
permitir ⟨3a⟩ *v/t* permit, allow; **permitirse** *v/r* afford; ***~ el lujo de*** permit o.s. the luxury of
permuta *f* exchange
permutable *adj* exchangeable
permutación *f* **1** (*permuta*) exchange **2** MAT permutation
permutar ⟨1a⟩ *v/t* exchange
pernera *f* (pants, *Br* trouser) leg
pernicioso *adj* harmful
pernil *m* **1** *de pantalón* leg **2** GASTR ham
perno *m* bolt
pernoctar ⟨1a⟩ *v/i* spend the night
pero I *conj* but **II** *m* flaw, defect; ***no hay ~s que valgan*** no excuses; ***poner ~s*** raise problems
perogrullada *f* platitude
peronismo *m* Peronism
peronista *m/f & adj* Peronist
perorata *f* F lecture
perpendicular *f/adj* perpendicular
perpetrar ⟨1a⟩ *v/t crimen* perpetrate, commit
perpetuación *f* perpetuation
perpetuar ⟨1e⟩ *v/t* perpetuate; **perpetuarse** *v/r* be perpetuated
perpetuidad *f*: ***a ~*** in perpetuity
perpetuo *adj fig* perpetual
perplejidad *f* perplexity
perplejo *adj* puzzled, perplexed
perra *f* dog; ***el perro y la ~*** the dog and the bitch; ***~s*** *pl* F pesetas
perrada *f fig* F dirty trick
perrera *f* **1** *sitio* dog pound, *Br* dogs' home **2** *furgoneta* dog catcher's van, *Br* dog warden's van
perrería *f* F dirty trick
perrero *m*, **-a** *f* dog catcher, *Br* dog warden
◇ **perrito caliente** *m* GASTR hot dog
perro *m* dog; ***hace un tiempo de ~s*** F the weather is lousy F; ***llevarse como el ~ y el gato*** *fig* fight like cat and dog; ***a otro ~ con ese hueso*** *fig* F tell that to the marines! F, *Br* pull the other one (it's got bells on)! F; ***~ ladrador poco mordedor*** his bark is worse than his bite
◇ **perro callejero** stray; **perro de caza** hound; **perro faldero** lap dog; **perro guardián** guard dog; **perro lazarillo** seeing eye dog, *Br* guide dog; **perro lobo** German shepherd, *Br tb* Alsatian; **perro pastor** sheepdog; **perro perdiguero** gundog; **perro de Terranova** Newfoundland; **perro viejo** *fig* F old hand F
perruno *adj* dog *atr*, canine
persecución *f* **1** (*búsqueda*) pursuit **2** (*acoso*) persecution
perseguidor I *adj* in pursuit **II** *m*, **~a** *f* persecutor
perseguir ⟨3l & 3d⟩ *v/t* **1** *objetivo* pur-

sue **2** *delincuente* look for **3** (*molestar*) pester **4** (*acosar*) persecute
perseverancia *f* perseverance
perseverante *adj* persistent, persevering
perseverar ⟨1a⟩ *v/i* persevere (***en*** with)
persiana *f de tablillas fijas* shade, *Br* blind; *enrollable* shade, *Br* roller blind
pérsico *adj* Persian
persignarse ⟨1a⟩ *v/r* cross o.s.
persistencia *f* persistence
persistente *adj* persistent
persistir ⟨3a⟩ *v/i* persist
persona *f* person; ***quince ~s*** fifteen people; **~ (*humana*)** human being; ***~ mayor*** elderly person ***buena / mala ~*** nice / nasty person; ***en ~*** in person
personaje *m* **1** TEA character **2** *famoso* celebrity
personal I *adj* personal **II** *m* **1** personnel, staff; ***~ docente*** teaching staff **2** *en baloncesto* personal foul
◇ **personal de a bordo** AVIA flight crew
◇ **personal de tierra** AVIA ground crew
personalidad *f* personality
personalizar ⟨1f⟩ **I** *v/t* personalize **II** *v/i* get personal
personarse ⟨1a⟩ *v/r* arrive, turn up
personificación *f* personification, embodiment
personificar ⟨1g⟩ *v/t* personify, embody
perspectiva *f* **1** (*vista, ángulo*) perspective **2** *fig* point of view; ***~s*** *pl* outlook *sg*, prospects; ***tener algo en ~*** have the possibility of sth
perspicacia *f* shrewdness, perspicacity *fml*
perspicaz *adj* shrewd, perspicacious *fml*
persuadir ⟨3a⟩ *v/t* persuade; **persuadirse** *v/r* become convinced
persuasión *f* persuasion
persuasivo *adj* persuasive
pertenecer ⟨2d⟩ *v/i* belong (***a*** to)
perteneciente *adj*: **~ *a*** belonging to
pertenencias *fpl* belongings
pértiga *f* pole; ***salto con ~*** DEP pole vault
pertiguista *m/f* DEP pole-vaulter
pertinaz *adj* **1** (*prolongado*) persistent **2** (*terco*) obstinate
pertinencia *f* relevance, pertinence
pertinente *adj* relevant, pertinent
pertrechar ⟨1a⟩ *v/t* equip, supply (***de*** with); **pertrecharse** *v/r* equip o.s.
pertrechos *mpl* MIL equipment *sg*
perturbación *f* disturbance
◇ **perturbación mental** mental disturbance
perturbado *m*,**-a** *f*: **~ (*mental*)** mentally disturbed person
perturbador *adj* disturbing
perturbar ⟨1a⟩ *v/t* **1** (*producir desorden en*) disturb **2** *reunión* disrupt
Perú *m* Peru
peruano I *adj* Peruvian **II** *m*,**-a** *f* Peruvian
perversidad *f* wickedness, evil
perversión *f* perversion
perverso *adj* wicked, evil
pervertido I *adj* perverted **II** *m*,**-a** *f* pervert
pervertir ⟨3i⟩ *v/t* pervert; **pervertirse** *v/r* become perverted *o* corrupted
pervivencia *f* survival
pervivir ⟨3a⟩ *v/i* survive, remain
pesa *f* **1** *para balanza* weight **2** DEP shot; ***hacer ~s*** do weight-training **3** *C.Am., Carib* butcher's shop
pesabebés *m inv* baby scales *pl*
pesadamente *adv* heavily
pesadez *f fig* drag F
pesadilla *f* nightmare
pesado I *adj* **1** *objeto* heavy **2** *libro, clase etc* tedious, boring **3** *trabajo* tough F, difficult **II** *m*, **-a** *f* bore; ***¡qué ~ es!*** F he's a real pain F
pesadumbre *f* grief, sorrow
pésame *m* condolences *pl*; ***dar el ~*** offer one's condolences
pesar ⟨1a⟩ **I** *v/t* weigh
II *v/i* **1** (*ser muy pesado*) be heavy; ***casi no pesa*** it weighs next to nothing **2** (*influir*) carry weight **3** *fig de responsabilidad* weigh heavily (***sobre*** on); ***me pesa tener que informarle …*** I regret to have to inform you …; ***mal que me / le pese*** like it or not, whether I / you like it or not
III *m* sorrow
IV: ***a ~ de*** in spite of, despite; ***a ~ de ello*** nevertheless; ***a ~ de eso*** in spite of that, despite that; ***a ~ de que*** in spite of *o* despite the fact that, even though; ***a ~ mío*** against my wishes

pesario *m* MED pessary
pesaroso *adj* **1** (*apenado*) sad **2** (*arrepentido*) sorry
PESC *f abr* (= ***Política Exterior y de Seguridad Común***) CFSP (= Common Foreign and Security Policy)
pesca *f* **1** *actividad* fishing **2** (*peces*) fish *pl* **3**: ***y toda la ~*** *fig* F the whole gang
◇ **pesca de altura** deep-sea fishing; **pesca de arrastre** trawling;**pesca de bajura, pesca de costera** coastal fishing; **pesca submarina** underwater fishing
pescadería *f* fish shop
pescadero *m*,**-a** *f* fishmonger
pescadilla *f pez* whiting
pescado *m* GASTR fish
pescador *m* fisherman
◇ **pescador de caña** angler
pescante *m* MAR davit
pescar ⟨1g⟩ **I** *v/t* **1** *un pez, resfriado* catch; *trabajo, marido* land F **2** (*intentar tomar*) fish for **II** *v/i* fish; ***~ con caña*** go angling
pescozón *m* slap on the neck
pescuezo *m* neck
pese : ***~ a*** despite, in spite of; ***~ a ello*** nevertheless; ***~ a que*** in spite of *o* despite the fact that, even though
pesebre *m* **1** (*comedero*) manger **2** (*belén*) crèche
pesero *m* **1** *L.Am.* minibus **2** *Méx* (collective) taxi
peseta *f* peseta
pesetero *adj* F money-grubbing F
pesimismo *m* pessimism
pesimista **I** *adj* pessimistic **II** *m/f* pessimist
pésimo *adj sup* awful, terrible
pesista *m/f L.Am.* weightlifter
peso *m* **1** weight; ***ganar ~*** put on *o* gain weight; ***perder ~*** lose weight; *fig* become less important; ***de ~*** *fig* weighty; ***se cae de*** *o* ***por su propio ~*** it goes without saying; ***se me quitó un ~ de encima*** it took a real load off my mind **2** FIN peso
◇ **peso específico** specific gravity; **peso gallo** *en boxeo* bantamweight; **peso mosca** *en boxeo* flyweight;**peso pesado** *en boxeo, fig* heavyweight; **peso pluma** *en boxeo* featherweight; **peso semipesado** *en boxeo* light-heavyweight
pespuntar ⟨1a⟩ *v/t* ☞ ***pespuntear***
pespunte *m* backstitch
pespuntear ⟨1a⟩ *v/t* backstitch
pesquería *f* fishing industry
pesquero **I** *adj* fishing *atr* **II** *m* fishing boat
pesquisa *f* investigation; ***hacer ~s*** investigate
pestaña *f* eyelash; ***quemarse las ~s*** F burn the midnight oil
pestañear ⟨1a⟩ *v/i* blink; ***sin ~*** *fig* without batting an eyelid
pestañeo *m* blink
peste *f* **1** MED plague **2** F *olor* stink F **3**: ***echar ~s*** F curse and swear
◇ **peste porcina** hog cholera, *Br* swine fever
pesticida *m* pesticide
pestilencia *f* stench
pestilente *adj* foul-smelling
pestillo *m* **1** (*picaporte*) door handle **2** (*cerradura*) bolt
petaca *f* **1** *para tabaco* tobacco pouch **2** *para bebida* hip flask **3** *C.Am.* F *insecto* ladybug, *Br* ladybird
petacas *fpl Méx* F buttocks
pétalo *m* petal
petanca *f type of bowls*
petar ⟨1a⟩ *v/i* P: ***me peta / no me peta ...*** I feel like / don't feel like ...
petardear ⟨1a⟩ *v/i* backfire
petardo **I** *m* firecracker **II** *m*,**-a** *f* F (*plasta*) nerd F; ***ser un ~*** *de persona* be a pain in the neck F
petate *m* **1** (*lío*) kit bag; ***liar el ~*** *fig* F pack one's bags **2** *L.Am.* F *en el suelo* mat
petenera *f type of flamenco song*; ***salir(se) por ~s*** *fig* F go off at a tangent F
petición *f* request; ***a ~ de*** at the request of
petigrís *m* ZO gray squirrel, *Br* grey squirrel
petirrojo *m* ZO robin
petiso *L.Am.* **I** *adj* short, tiny **II** *m*,**-a** *f* shorty F **III** *m* pony
peto *m* bib; ***pantalón de ~*** overalls *pl*, *Br* dungarees *pl*
petrel *m* ZO petrel
pétreo *adj* (*de piedra*) stone *atr*, (*similar a la piedra*) stonelike, stony; *fig* stony
petrificación *f* petrification
petrificado *adj* petrified

P

petrificar ⟨1g⟩ *v/t* petrify (*a fig*); **petrificarse** *v/r* become petrified
petrodólar *m* petrodollar
petróleo *m* oil, petroleum
petrolero I *adj* oil *atr*; ***compañía -a*** oil company; ***flota -a*** fleet of oil tankers **II** *m* MAR oil tanker
petrolífero *adj* oil *atr*
petroquímica *f* petrochemical
petulancia *f* smugness
petulante *adj* smug
petunia *f* BOT petunia
peyorativo *adj* pejorative
pez I *m* ZO fish; ***estar ~ en algo*** F be clueless about sth F; ***estar como ~ en el agua*** be in one's element **II** *f* pitch, tar
◇ **pez espada** swordfish; **pez gordo** F big shot F; **pez volador** flying fish
pezón *m* nipple
pezuña *f* ZO hoof
PHN *m abr* (= ***Plan Hidrológico Nacional***) National Hydrological Plan
piadoso *adj* pious
pianista *m/f* pianist
piano *m* piano
◇ **piano de cola** grand piano
◇ **piano de media cola** baby grand
piar ⟨1c⟩ *v/i* tweet, chirrup
piara *f* herd
PIB *m abr* (= ***producto interior bruto***) GDP (= gross domestic product)
pibe *m*, **-a** *f Rpl* F kid F
pica *f* **1** TAUR goad **2** *palo de la baraja* spade **3**: ***poner una ~ en Flandes*** *fig* pull off a coup
picacho *m* peak
picada *f* **1** *de serpiente* bite; *de abeja* sting **2** *L.Am. para comer* snacks *pl*, nibbles *pl* **3** *Rpl* (*camino*) path
picadero *m escuela* riding school
picadillo *m* GASTR *de lomo*: *marinated ground meat*; ***añada un ~ de cebolla y ajo*** add finely chopped onion and garlic; ***hacer ~ a alguien*** *fig* F beat s.o. up
picado I *adj* **1** *diente* decayed **2** *mar* rough, choppy **3** *carne* ground, *Br* minced; *verdura* minced, *Br* finely chopped **3** *fig* (*resentido*) offended **II** *m L.Am.* dive; ***caer en ~*** *de precios* nosedive, plummet
picador *m* **1** TAUR picador **2** MIN face worker
picadora *f en cocina* meat grinder, *Br* mincer
picadura *f* **1** *de reptil*, *mosquito* bite; *de avispa* sting **2** *tabaco* cut tobacco
picaflor *m L.Am.* **1** ZO hummingbird **2** *fig* womanizer
picajoso *adj* touchy
picante I *adj* **1** *comida* hot, spicy **2** *chiste* risqué **II** *m* hot spice
picapedrero *m* stone cutter
picapleitos *m/f inv* F shyster F, *Br unethical lawyer*
picaporte *m* door handle
picar ⟨1g⟩ **I** *v/t* **1** *de mosquito*, *serpiente* bite; *de avispa* sting; *de ave* peck **2** *carne* grind, *Br* mince; *verdura* mince, *Br* chop finely **3** *piedra* break (up) **4** TAUR jab with a lance **5** (*molestar*) annoy **6** *la curiosidad* pique **7** MÚS pick
II *v/i* **1** *tb fig* take the bait **2** *L.Am. de la comida* be hot *o* spicy **3** (*producir picor*) itch **4** *del sol* burn
picarse *v/r* **1** (*agujerearse*) rust **2** (*cariarse*) decay **3** F (*molestarse*) get mad F
picardía *f* **1** (*astucia*) craftiness, slyness **2** (*travesura*) mischievousness **3** *Méx* (*taco*, *palabrota*) swearing, swearwords *pl*
picaresco *adj* picaresque
pícaro I *adj* **1** *persona* crafty, sly **2** *comentario* mischievous **II** *m* rogue
picarón *m Méx*, *Chi*, *Pe* (*buñuelo*) fritter
picatoste *m* piece of fried bread
picazón *f* itching; *fig* unease, disquiet
picha *f* V prick V
pícher *m/f en béisbol* pitcher
pichi *m* **1** jumper, *Br* pinafore dress **2** DEP top scorer
pichicato *m Pe*, *Bol* P coke P
pichichi *m* leading goalscorer
pichincha *f L.Am.* bargain
pichón *m L.Am.* **1** chick **2** F (*novato*) rookie F
Picio: ***más feo que ~*** F as ugly as sin F
pick up *m L.Am.* pick-up (truck)
picnic *m* (*pl* ***~s***) picnic
pico *m* **1** ZO beak **2** F (*boca*) mouth; ***cerrar el ~*** F shut one's mouth F; ***abrir / no abrir el ~*** open / not open one's mouth; ***ser un ~ de oro*** have the gift of the gab **3** *de montaña* peak **4** *herramienta* pickax, *Br* pickaxe **5**: ***a las tres y ~*** some time after three o'clock; ***mil***

pesetas y ~ just over a thousand pesetas; ***irse de ~s pardos*** F paint the town red F

picor *m* itch

picota *f* **1** BOT bigarreau (*type of sweet cherry*) **2** *fig*: ***poner en la ~*** pillory

picotazo *m* peck

picotear ⟨1a⟩ *v/t* **1** *de pájaro* peck **2** *comer* nibble

pictograma *m* pictogram

pictórico *adj* pictorial

pido *vb* ☞ ***pedir***

pie *m* **1** *de estatua, lámpara* base **2** *de persona* foot; ***a ~*** on foot; ***al ~ de*** at the foot of; ***de ~*** standing; ***estar de ~*** be standing (up); ***ponerse de*** *o* ***en ~*** stand up; ***no tenerse en*** *o* ***de ~*** *fig*: *por cansancio* be ready to drop; ***de ~s a cabeza*** from head to foot; ***no tiene ni ~s ni cabeza*** it doesn't make any sense at all, I can't make head nor tail of it; ***a ~s juntillas*** *creer* blindly; ***levantarse con el ~ izquierdo*** get out of bed on the wrong side; ***con buen / mal ~*** *empezar* get off to a good / bad start; ***con los ~s*** *fig* badly; ***andarse con ~s de plomo*** tread warily; ***estar en ~*** be up, be out of bed; ***estar en ~ de guerra*** be on a war footing; ***buscar tres*** *o* ***cinco ~s al gato*** *fig* make things difficult, complicate things; ***dar ~ para*** *o* ***a*** give rise to, generate; ***echar ~ a tierra*** go ashore; ***estar al ~ del cañón*** *fig* be hard at work; ***hacer ~*** touch bottom; ***no hacer ~*** *en piscina* be out of one's depth; ***no dar ~ con bola*** F get *o* do everything wrong; ***parar los ~s a alguien*** take s.o. down a peg or two F; ***saber de qué ~ cojea alguien*** *fig* know where s.o. is coming from; ***poner ~s en polvorosa*** F take to one's heels F; ***salir por ~s*** hotfoot it F, make o.s. scarce; ***~ de la cama*** foot of the bed; ***~s planos*** flat feet

◇ **pie de atleta** MED athlete's foot; **pie equino** MED clubfoot; **pie de página** TIP foot *o* bottom of the page; **pie de pivote** *en béisbol* pivot foot

piedad *f* **1** (*compasión*) pity **2** (*clemencia*) mercy **3** REL piety

piedra *f tb* MED stone; ***quedarse de ~*** *fig* F be stunned; ***el ejército invasor no dejó ~ sobre ~ de la ciudad*** *fig* the invading army razed the city to the ground *o* did not leave a stone standing in the city; ***tirar ~s a su propio tejado*** *fig* F shoot o.s. in the foot F; ***tirar la ~ y esconder la mano*** do things on the sly; ***poner*** *o* ***colocar la primera ~*** lay the foundation stone; ***pasar por la ~*** V lay F, screw V

◇ **piedra angular** cornerstone; **piedra fundamental** foundation stone; **piedra preciosa** precious stone; **piedra semipreciosa** semiprecious stone; **piedra de toque** touchstone

piel *f* **1** *de persona, fruta* skin; ***~ de naranja*** orange peel; ***dejarse la ~*** sweat blood F **2** *de animal* hide, skin; ***abrigo de ~es*** fur coat; ***la ~ de toro*** *fig* the Iberian Peninsula **3** (*cuero*) leather

◇ **piel roja** redskin

pienso[1] *vb* ☞ ***pensar***

pienso[2] *m* animal feed, fodder

piercing *m* (body) piercing

pierdo *vb* ☞ ***perder***

pierna *f* leg; ***~ ortopédica*** artificial leg; ***dormir a ~ suelta*** sleep like a log; ***salir por ~s*** F hotfoot it F, make o.s. scarce

pieza *f* **1** *de un conjunto*, MÚS piece; *de aparato* part; ***de dos / tres ~s*** two-piece / three-piece **2** TEA play **3** (*habitación*) room **4** F: ***quedarse de una ~*** be amazed

◇ **pieza de recambio** spare (part)

pífano *m* MÚS fife

pifia *f* **1** F (*error*) booboo F **2** *Chi, Pe, Rpl* defect

pifiar ⟨1a⟩ *v/t* F mess up F

pigmentación *f* pigmentation

pigmentar ⟨1a⟩ *v/t* color, *Br* colour

pigmento *m* pigment

pigmeo *m*, **-a** *f* pigmy

pignoración *f* pawning

pignorar ⟨1a⟩ *v/t* pawn

pija *f* V cock V, dick V

pijada *f* F stupid thing

pijama *m* pajamas *pl*, *Br* pyjamas *pl*

pijo I *adj* posh **II** *m* V (*pene*) prick V **III** *m*, **-a** *f* F *persona* rich kid F

pijotero *adj* F nitpicking, niggling

pila *f* **1** EL battery; ***cargar las ~s*** *fig* F recharge one's batteries; ***se le acabaron*** *o* ***agotaron las ~s*** *fig* F he ran out of steam **2** (*montón*) pile **3** (*fregadero*) sink

◇ **pila bautismal** font; **pila botón** EL watch battery; **pila seca** dry battery

P

pilar *m tb fig* pillar
píldora *f* pill; ***la ~ (anticonceptiva)*** the (contraceptive) pill; ***dorar la ~*** *fig* F sweeten the pill
pileta *f* **1** *Rpl* sink **2** (*alberca*) swimming pool
pillaje *m* pillage
pillar 〈1a〉 *v/t* **1** (*tomar*) seize **2** (*atrapar*) catch **3** (*atropellar*) hit **4** *chiste* get **4**: ***me pilla muy cerca*** it's very handy for me; ***me pilla de camino*** it's on my way; ***~ a alguien de sorpresa*** catch s.o. by surprise
pillastre *m* F rogue, scoundrel
pillín *m*,**-ina** *f* F rascal
pillo **I** *adj* mischievous **II** *m*,**-a** *f* rascal
pilluelo *m*,**-a** *f* F scamp, little rascal
pilón *m Méx*: ***me dio dos de ~*** he gave me two extra
pilonga *f*: (***castaña***) **~** dried chestnut
píloro *m* ANAT pylorus
pilosidad *f* hairiness
pilotar 〈1a〉 *v/t* **1** AVIA fly, pilot **2** AUTO drive **3** MAR steer
pilote *m* pile
piloto **I** *m/f* **1** AVIA, MAR pilot **2** AUTO driver **II** *m* EL pilot light
◇ **piloto automático** autopilot, automatic pilot
◇ **piloto de pruebas** AVIA test pilot
piltra *f* F bed; ***estar en la ~*** F be in bed, be in the sack F
piltrafa *f*: ***~s*** rags; ***estar hecho una ~*** *fig* be a total wreck *F*
pimentero *m* BOT pepper plant
pimentón *m* paprika
pimienta *f* pepper
pimiento *m* pepper; ***me importa un ~*** F I couldn't *o* could care less, *Br* I couldn't care less
◇ **pimiento morrón** red pepper
pimplar 〈1a〉 *v/i* F *de alcohol* booze;
pimplarse *v/r* F drink
pimpón *m* ping-pong
PIN *m* PIN
pinacoteca *f* art gallery
pináculo *m* ARQUI, *fig* pinnacle
pinar *m* pine forest
pincel *m* paintbrush; ***ir como un ~*** *fig* F look very sharp, be all dressed up
pincelada *f*: ***dar la(s) última(s) ~(s) a*** *fig* put the finishing touches to
pinchadiscos *m/f inv* F disc jockey, DJ
pinchar 〈1a〉 **I** *v/t* **1** (*agujerear*) prick; ***~le a alguien*** MED give s.o. a shot **2** AUTO puncture **3** TELEC tap **4** F (*molestar*) bug F, needle F
II *v/i* **1** (*agujerear*) prick **2** AUTO get a flat tire, *Br* get a puncture **3**: ***no ~ ni cortar*** F not count for anything;
pincharse *v/r* **1** *con aguja etc* prick o.s. **2** F (*inyectarse*) shoot up P **3**: ***se nos pinchó una rueda*** we got a flat (tire) *o Br* a puncture
pinchazo *m* **1** *herida* prick **2** *dolor* sharp pain **3** AUTO flat (tire), *Br* puncture **4** F (*fracaso*) flop F
pinche[1] *m* cook's assistant
pinche[2] *adj* **1** *Méx* F (*mezquino*) rotten F **2** *C.Am.*, *Méx* (*tacaño*) tight-fisted
pinchito *m* GASTR bar snack, tapa
pincho *m* GASTR bar snack
pineda *f* ☞ ***pinar***
pingajo *m* F rag; ***estar hecho un ~*** F be a mess
pingajoso *adj* shabby
pingo *m*: ***poner a alguien como un ~*** F give s.o. a piece of one's mind
ping-pong *m* ping-pong
pingüe *adj fig beneficios* fat, large
pingüino *m* ZO penguin
pinitos *mpl* first steps
pino *m* BOT pine; ***hacer el ~*** do a handstand; ***vivir en el quinto ~*** F live out in the boondocks F
pinol(e) *m* **1** *C.Am.*, *Méx* cornstarch, *Br* cornflour **2** *L.Am.* roasted corn
pinrel *m* F: ***~es*** *pl* feet
pinta *f* **1** *medida* pint **2** *aspecto* looks *pl*; ***tener buena ~*** *fig* look inviting; ***tener ~ de*** look like
pintada *f* piece of graffiti; ***~s*** *pl* graffiti *pl o sg*
pintado *adj*: ***siempre va muy -a*** F she always slaps on loads of makeup F; ***este regalo me viene que ni ~*** it's just what I wanted (as a gift); ***me está que ni ~*** *de prenda* it's perfect for me
pintalabios *m inv* lipstick
pintamonas *m* **1** F *pintor* dauber F **2** (*don nadie*) nobody
pintar 〈1a〉 *v/t* paint; ***~ algo de rojo*** paint sth red; ***no ~ nada*** *fig* F not count; ***¿qué pintas tu aquí?*** what are you doing here?;**pintarse** *v/r* put on one's makeup
pintarraj(e)ar 〈1a〉 *v/t* F daub
pintarrajo *m* F daub

pintarroja *f* ZO dogfish
pintor *m*,**~a** *f* painter; **~ (*de brocha gorda*)** (house) painter
pintoresco *adj* picturesque
pintura *f* **1** *sustancia* paint **2** *obra* painting; ***no le puedo ver ni en ~*** *fig* F I can't stand the sight of him
◇ **pintura al agua** watercolor, *Br* watercolour
◇ **pintura al dedo** finger paint; *obra* finger painting
pinza *f* **1** clothespin, *Br* clothes peg **2** ZO claw **3** *L.Am.* (*alicates*) pliers *pl*; **~s** tweezers; ***pantalón de ~s*** pleated pants *pl*, *Br* pleated trousers *pl*
pinzón *m* ZO finch
piña *f* *del pino* pine cone; *fruta* pineapple; ***formar una ~ en torno a alguien*** *fig* close ranks around s.o.
piñón *m* **1** BOT pine nut **2** TÉC pinion **3**: ***estar a partir un ~ con alguien*** F be bosom buddies with s.o.
pío[1] *adj* pious
pío[2] *m* tweet, chirrup; ***no decir ni ~*** F not say a word
piojo *m* ZO louse; **~s** *pl* lice *pl*
piojoso *adj* lousy, full of lice
piola *f* *L.Am.* cord, twine
piolet *m* ice ax, *Br* ice axe
piolín *m* *Arg* cord, twine
pionero I *adj* pioneering **II** *m*,**-a** *f* *tb fig* pioneer
pipa *f* **1** *de fumar* pipe; ***pasarlo ~*** F have a great time **2**: **~s** *pl* *semillas* sunflower seeds **3** *Méx camión* tanker
pipeta *f* pipette
pipí *m* F pee F; ***hacer ~*** F pee F
pipiolo *m* *C.Am.*, *Méx* F kid F; **~s** *pl* *C.Am.* F (*dinero*) cash *sg*
pique *m* **1** (*disgusto*) resentment **2** (*rivalidad*) rivalry **3**: ***irse a ~*** MAR sink; *fig* go under, go to the wall; ***echar a ~*** MAR sink; *fig* ruin, wreck **4** *L.Am.* *de pelota* bounce
piqueta *f* **1** *herramienta* pickax, *Br* pickaxe **2** *en cámping* tent peg
piquete *m* **1** POL picket **2** *Méx picadura* bite **3** *Méx punzada* sharp pain
pira *f* pyre
pirado F **I** *adj* crazy F **II** *m*,**-a** *f* madman, madwoman
piragua *f* canoe
piragüismo *m* canoeing
◇ **piragüismo en aguas bravas** DEP white-water canoeing
piragüista *m/f* canoeist
piramidal *adj* pyramidal
pirámide *f* pyramid
◇ **pirámide de edades** age graph
piraña *f* ZO piranha
pirarse ⟨1a⟩ *v/r* F (*marcharse*) clear off F; ***pirárselas*** F clear off F; ***~ por alguien*** F lose one's head over s.o. F
pirata I *adj* pirate *atr* **II** *m/f* pirate
◇ **pirata aéreo** hijacker
◇ **pirata informático** hacker
piratear ⟨1a⟩ *v/t* INFOR pirate
piratería *f* piracy
pirenaico *adj* Pyrenean
Pirineos *mpl* Pyrenees
piripi *adj* F tipsy F
pirita *f* MIN pyrite
piro *m*: ***darse el ~*** P hotfoot it F, make o.s. scarce
pirograbado *m* poker-work
pirómano I *adj* MED pyromaniac **II** *m*,**-a** *f* MED pyromaniac; JUR arsonist
piropear ⟨1a⟩ *v/t* pay a flirtatious compliment to
piropo *m* flirtatious compliment
pirotecnia *f* fireworks *pl*, pyrotechnics *pl*
pirotécnico I *adj* fireworks *atr* **II** *m*,**-a** *f* fireworks expert, pyrotechnist
pirrarse ⟨1a⟩ *v/r*: ***~ por*** F (*chiflar*) be crazy about F; (*desear con vehemencia*) be dead set on, have one's heart set on
pírrico *adj*: ***victoria -a*** pyrrhic victory
pirueta *f* pirouette
piruleta *f*, **pirulí** *m* lollipop
pis *m* F pee F; ***hacer ~*** F have a pee F
pisada *f* **1** (*paso*) footstep; ***seguir las ~s de alguien*** *fig* follow in s.o.'s footsteps **2** *huella* footprint
pisapapeles *m inv* paperweight
pisar ⟨1a⟩ **I** *v/t* **1** step on; ***~ a alguien*** step on s.o.'s foot **2** *uvas* tread **3** *fig* (*maltratar*) walk all over **4** *idea* steal **II** *v/i*: ***~ firme o fuerte*** *fig* make a big impact; ***piso fuerte en latín*** I'm good at *o* strong in Latin
pisciano *L.Am.* **I** *adj* ***ser ~*** be (a) Pisces, be a Piscean **II** *m*,**-a** *f* Pisces, Piscean
piscícola *adj* fish-farming *atr*
piscicultura *f* fish farming
piscifactoría *f* fish farm
piscina *f* swimming pool
◇ **piscina cubierta** indoor pool

Piscis *m/f inv* ASTR Pisces
pisco *m Chi, Pe* grape liquor
piscolabis *m inv* F snack
piso *m* **1** apartment, *Br* flat **2** (*planta*) floor; ***primer ~*** second floor, *Br* first floor; *en edificio con piso principal* third floor, *Br* second floor; ***~ principal*** second floor, *Br* first floor; ***de tres ~s*** *hamburguesa* triple-decker *atr*; *tarta* three-layer *atr*
◇ **piso franco** safe house
pisotear ⟨1a⟩ *v/t* trample
pisotón *m* stamp; ***me dio un ~*** he stamped on my foot
pispajo *m* F little rascal
pispar ⟨1a⟩ *v/t* F steal, filch F
pista *f* **1** *vía* track, trail; ***seguir la ~ a alguien*** be on the trail of s.o. ***estar sobre la buena ~*** be on the right track **2** *de atletismo* track; *de tenis etc* court **3** *de circo* ring **4** (*indicio*) clue; ***dar una ~*** give a clue
◇ **pista de aterrizaje** AVIA runway; **pista de baile** dance floor; **pista cubierta** indoor track; ***atletismo en ~*** indoor athletics *sg o pl*; **pista de despegue** AVIA runway; **pista de esquí** ski slope *o* run; **pista de fondo** cross-country trail; **pista forestal** forest trail; **pista de hielo** ice rink, skating rink; **pista de rodadura** AVIA taxiway; **pista de squash** squash court; **pista de tenis** tennis court
pistache *m Méx* BOT pistachio
pistacho *m* BOT pistachio
pistilo *m* BOT pistil
pisto *m* **1** GASTR *mixture of tomatoes, peppers etc cooked in oil* **2** *C.Am., Méx* F (*dinero*) cash, dough F **3**: ***darse ~*** give o.s. airs
pistola *f* pistol; ***~ pulverizadora*** *para pintar* spray gun
pistolera *f* holster
pistolero *m* gunman
pistoletazo *m* pistol shot
◇ **pistoletazo de salida** DEP starting signal
pistón *m* **1** *de motor* piston **2** MÚS key
pita *f* BOT agave, pita
pitada *f* **1** (*abucheo*) whistle **2** *S.Am. de cigarillo* puff
pitar ⟨1a⟩ **I** *v/i* **1** whistle **2** *con bocina* beep, hoot **3** *L.Am.* (*fumar*) smoke **4** F: ***salir pitando*** dash off F **II** *v/t* **1** (*abuchear*) whistle at; *penalti, falta etc* call, *Br* blow for; ***~ el final*** DEP blow the final whistle **2** *silbato* blow
pitazo *m L.Am.* whistle
pitcher *m/f en béisbol* pitcher
pitear ⟨1a⟩ *v/i L.Am.* blow a whistle
pitido *m* **1** *con silbato* whistle **2** *con bocina* beep, hoot
◇ **pitido final** DEP final whistle
◇ **pitido inicial** DEP whistle to start
pitillera *f* cigarette case
pitillo *m* cigarette; *hecho a mano* roll-up; ***~s*** *pl pantalón* drainpipes
pito *m* **1** (*silbato*) whistle; ***me importa un ~*** F I don't give a hoot F; ***entre ~s y flautas*** F with one thing and another **2** (*bocina*) horn **3** *fig: pene* willie F
pitón *m* ZO python
pitonisa *f* fortune-teller
pitorrearse ⟨1a⟩ *v/r*: ***~ de alguien*** F make fun of s.o.
pitorreo *m* F joke, farce; ***tomar algo a ~*** F take sth lightly, think sth is a joke
pitorro *m* spout
pitote *m* F ruckus F
pituitario *adj* ANAT: ***membrana -a*** pituitary membrane
pívot *m en baloncesto* center, *Br* centre
pivotar ⟨1a⟩ *v/i* pivot
pivote *m* **1** TÉC pivot **2** *en baloncesto* center, *Br* centre
piyama *m L.Am.* pajamas *pl*, *Br* pyjamas *pl*
pizarra *f* **1** *en aula* blackboard **2** *piedra* slate
pizarrón *m L.Am.* blackboard
pizca *f* **1** pinch; ***ni ~ de*** not a bit of; ***una ~*** a little bit **2** *Méx* AGR harvest
pizpireta *adj* flirtatious, coquettish
pizza *f* pizza
placa *f* **1** (*lámina*) sheet; ***~s de hielo*** patches of ice **2** (*plancha*) plate **3** (*letrero*) plaque **4** *Méx* AUTO license plate, *Br* number plate
◇ **placa conmemorativa** commemorative plaque; **placa dental** plaque; **placa madre** INFOR motherboard; **placa de matrícula** AUTO license plate, *Br* number plate
placaje *m en fútbol* tackle
placar ⟨1g⟩ **I** *v/t en fútbol* tackle **II** *m Rpl* closet, *Br* built-in wardrobe
placebo *m* placebo

P

pláceme *m* message of congratulations
placenta *f* MED placenta
placentero *adj* pleasant, agreeable
placentino *adj* of / from Plasencia, Plasencia *atr*
placer ⟨2x⟩ **I** *v/i* please; ***siempre hace lo que le place*** he always does as he pleases **II** *m* pleasure; ***es un ~ para mí*** it is my pleasure
plácet *m* assent
placidez *f* placidness
plácido *adj* placid
¡plaf! *int* crash!, bang!
plafón *m* (*lámpara*) ceiling light
plaga *f* **1** AGR pest **2** MED plague **3** *fig* scourge; (*abundancia*) glut
plagado *adj de hormigas*, *ortigas* infested; (*lleno*) full; ***~ de gente*** swarming with people
plagiar ⟨1b⟩ *v/t* **1** (*copiar*) plagiarize **2** *L.Am.* (*secuestrar*) kidnap
plagio *m* **1** (*copia*) plagiarism **2** *L.Am.* (*secuestro*) kidnap
plaguicida *m* pesticide
plan *m* plan; ***~ de emergencia*** emergency plan; ***lo dije en ~ de broma*** F I said it as a joke; ***tener un ~*** F be playing around, be having an affair; ***esto no es ~*** F this isn't good enough
◇ **plan de estudios** syllabus, program, *Br* programme
plana *f*: ***primera ~*** *de periódico* front page; ***a toda ~*** *de periódico* full-page; ***enmendar la ~ a alguien*** correct s.o., put s.o. right
◇ **plana mayor** MIL staff *pl*; *fig* top brass *pl*
plancha *f* **1** *para planchar* iron; ***no precisa ~*** it doesn't need ironing **2** *en cocina* broiler, *Br* grill; ***a la ~*** broiled, *Br* grilled **3** *de metal* sheet **4** F (*metedura de pata*) goof F **5** TIP plate
planchado I *adj* F shattered F, beat F; ***quedarse ~*** F be shattered *o* beat **II** *m* ironing
planchar ⟨1a⟩ *v/t* **1** *ropa* iron **2** *Méx* F (*dar plantón a*) stand up F **3** *L.Am.* (*lisonjear*) flatter
planchazo *m* F booboo F, foul-up F
plancton *m* BIO plankton
planeación *f Méx* planning
planeador *m* glider
planeadora *f* MAR speedboat
planeamiento *m* planning
planear ⟨1a⟩ **I** *v/t* plan **II** *v/i* AVIA glide
planeo *m* gliding
planeta *m* planet
planetario I *adj* planetary **II** *m* planetarium
planicie *f* plain
planificación *f* planning
◇ **planificación familiar** family planning
planificar ⟨1g⟩ *v/t* plan; **planificarse** *v/r* be planned
planilla *f L.Am. formulario* form
planisferio *m* planisphere; ***~ celeste*** star map
plano I *adj* flat **II** *m* **1** ARQUI plan; *de ciudad* map **2** *en cine* shot **3** MAT plane **4** *fig* (*aspecto*) level **5**: ***primer / segundo ~*** foreground / middle ground; ***pasar / relegar a un segundo ~*** *fig* fade / push into the background; ***estar en el primer ~ de la actualidad*** be in the spotlight *o* limelight; ***de ~*** completely; *negar* categorically; *rechazar* outright
◇ **plano inclinado** inclined plane
planta *f* **1** BOT plant **2** (*piso*) floor; ***edificio de nueva ~*** new building
◇ **planta baja, planta calle** first floor, *Br* ground floor; **planta de interior** houseplant, pot plant; **planta medicinal** medicinal plant; **planta del pie** sole of the foot; **planta de reciclaje** recycling plant
plantación *f* plantation
plantado *adj*: ***dejar a alguien ~*** F stand s.o. up F; ***bien ~*** handsome
plantar ⟨1a⟩ *v/t* **1** *árbol etc* plant **2** *tienda de campaña* put up **3** F: ***~ a alguien*** stand s.o. up F; **plantarse** *v/r* **1** put one's foot down **2** (*aparecer*) show up, turn up
planteamiento *m* **1** *de problema* posing **2** (*perspectiva*) approach
plantear ⟨1a⟩ *v/t* **1** *dificultad*, *problema* pose, create **2** *cuestión* raise
plantel *m* **1** (*equipo*) team **2** *L.Am.* staff
plantilla *f* **1** *para zapato* insole **2** (*personal*) staff; ***reducción de ~*** staff cuts *pl* **3** DEP squad **4** *para cortar*, INFOR template
◇ **plantilla ortopédica** orthopedic insole
plantío *m* patch
plantón *m*: ***dar un ~ a alguien*** F stand

P

s.o. up F; ***tener a alguien de ~*** F leave s.o. waiting, stand s.o. up F
plañir ⟨3h⟩ *v/i* lament, grieve
plaqueta *f* ANAT: **~ (*sanguínea*)** platelet
plasenciano, plasentino *adj* of / from Plasencia, Plasencia *atr*
plasma *m* plasma
plasmar ⟨1a⟩ *v/t* **1** (*modelar*) shape **2** *fig* (*representar*) express;**plasmarse** *v/r* be expressed (***en*** in)
plasta I *m/f* F pain F, drag F **II** *adj*: ***ser ~*** F be a pain *o* drag F
plástica *f* EDU *handicrafts*
plasticidad *f* plasticity
plástico *m/adj* plastic
plastificado *adj* laminated
plastificar ⟨1g⟩ *v/t documento* laminate
plastilina *f* Plasticine®
plata *f* **1** *metal* silver **2** *L.Am.* (*dinero*). money; ***gano mucha ~*** I earn a lot of money **3**: ***hablando en ~*** to put it bluntly
plataforma *f tb* POL platform; ***~ cívica*** *o* ***ciudadana*** civic platform; ***~ negociadora*** negotiating platform
◇ **plataforma continental** GEOL continental shelf
◇ **plataforma petrolífera** oil rig
platal *m L.Am.* fortune
plátano *m* banana
platea *f* TEA orchestra, *Br* stalls *pl*
plateado *adj Méx* wealthy
platense *adj* of / from the River Plate, River Plate *atr*
plática *f Méx* chat, talk
platicar ⟨1g⟩ **I** *v/t L.Am.* tell **II** *v/i Méx* chat, talk
platija *f* plaice
platillo *m*: ***~s*** *pl* MÚS cymbals
◇ **platillo volante** flying saucer
platina *f* **1** *de microscopio* slide **2** *de estéreo* tape deck
platino *m* platinum; ***~s*** *pl* AUTO points
plató *m cine* set; TV studio
plato *m* **1** *recipiente* plate; ***parece no haber roto un ~ en su vida*** she looks as though butter wouldn't melt in her mouth; ***pagar los ~s rotos*** F carry the can F **2** GASTR dish **3** *Méx*: *en béisbol* home plate
◇ **plato combinado** GASTR mixed platter; **plato del día** dish of the day; **plato hondo** soup dish; **plato llano** dinner plate;**plato precocinado, plato preparado** ready meal, precooked meal;**plato principal** main course;**plato sopero** soup dish
platónico *adj* platonic
platudo *adj Chi* rich
plausible *adj* plausible
playa *f* beach
◇ **playa de estacionamiento** *L.Am.* parking lot, *Br* car park
playeras *fpl* canvas shoes
playera *f Méx* T-shirt
playero *adj* beach *atr*; ***vestido ~*** beach dress
playo *adj Rpl* shallow
plaza *f* **1** (*glorieta*) square **2** *en vehículo* seat; ***de dos ~s*** two-seater *atr* **3** *de trabajo* position; (*vacante*) job opening, *Br* vacancy
◇ **plaza de aparcamiento** parking space;**plaza mayor** main square;**plaza de parking** parking space; **plaza de toros** bull ring
plazo *f* **1** *de tiempo* period; ***a corto / largo ~*** in the short / long term; ***en el ~ de tres meses*** within three months **2** (*pago*) installment, *Br* instalment; ***a ~s*** in installments; ***meter su dinero a ~ fijo*** put one's money on fixed-term deposit
◇ **plazo de entrega** *de solicitud* deadline; *de paquete* delivery time
plazoleta, plazuela *f* small square
pleamar *f* high tide
plebe *f*: ***la ~*** HIST the masses; *desp* the rabble, the plebs
plebeyo I *adj* plebeian **II** *m*,**-a** *f* plebeian
plebiscito *m* plebiscite
plegable *adj* collapsible, folding
plegamiento *m* GEOL *proceso* folding; *resultado* fold
plegar ⟨1h & 1k⟩ *v/t* fold (up);**plegarse** *v/r fig* submit (***a*** to)
plegaria *f* prayer
pleistoceno *m* GEOL Pleistocene
pleitesía *f* respect
pleito *m* **1** JUR lawsuit; ***poner un ~ a alguien*** sue s.o. **2** *fig* dispute **3** *Méx* DEP fight
plenamente *adv* fully, completely
plenario I *adj* plenary **II** *m Am reg* plenary session
plenilunio *m* full moon
plenipotenciario I *adj* plenipotentiary **II** *m*,**-a** *f* plenipotentiary

plenitud *f* height, pinnacle; ***en la ~ de su carrera*** at the height of his career; ***estar en la ~ de la vida*** be in the prime of life; ***estar en ~ de facultades mentales*** be in full possession of one's mental faculties

pleno I *adj* full; ***en ~ día*** in broad daylight; ***a ~ sol*** in the sun; ***toda la familia estaba allí en ~*** the family turned out in force, the entire family was there; ***en ~ invierno*** in the depths *o* middle of winter **II** *m* plenary session; ***salón de ~s*** meeting room; ***acertar un ~, hacer ~*** *en quiniela* win the sports lottery *o Br* pools

◇ **pleno empleo** full employment

pletina *f* TÉC platen; **~ (*de cassette*)** tape deck, cassette deck

plétora *f* plethora

pletórico *adj*: ***~ de*** full of, brimming with; ***~ de salud*** bursting with health

pleuresía, pleuritis *f* MED pleurisy

pléyade *f fml* famous group

pliego I *vb* ☞ ***plegar*** **II** *m* **1** (*hoja de papel*) sheet (of paper) **2** (*carta*) sealed letter *o* document

◇ **pliego de cargos** JUR list of charges

◇ **pliego de condiciones** COM specifications *pl*, terms and conditions *pl*

pliegue *m de tela, papel* fold, crease

plin *m* F: ***a mí, ~*** I don't care

plinto *m* plinth

plioceno *m* GEOL Pliocene

plisado *adj* pleated

plisar ⟨1a⟩ *v/t tela* put pleats in

plis-plas *m* F: ***en un ~*** in no time at all

plomería *f Méx* plumbing

plomero *m*, **-a** *f Méx* plumber

plomizo *adj* leaden

plomo *m* **1** *metal* lead; ***sin ~*** AUTO unleaded **2** EL fuse **3** *fig* F (*pelma*) drag F

pluma *f* **1** ZO feather **2** *para escribir* fountain pen; ***escribir algo a vuela ~*** scribble sth down **3** *Méx grifo* faucet, *Br* tap

◇ **pluma atómica** *f Méx* ball-point pen

plumada *f* ☞ ***plumazo***

plumado *adj* feathered

plumaje *m* plumage

plumazo *m*: ***de un ~*** *suprimir* with one stroke of the pen

plúmbeo *adj fml* **1** (*de plomo*) leaden *fml* **2** (*pesado*) heavy

plumero *m* **1** *para limpiar* feather duster **2** *CSur: para maquillaje* powder puff **3**: ***vérsele el ~ a alguien*** *fig* F see what s.o. is up to F

plumier *m* pencil case

plumífero *m* F down jacket

plumón *m* down

plural I *adj* plural **II** *m* GRAM plural

pluralidad *f* plurality

pluralismo *m* POL pluralism

plurianual *adj* lasting several years

pluridisciplinar(io) *adj* multidisciplinary

pluriempleo *m* having more than one job

plurilingüe *adj* multilingual

plurilingüismo *m* multilingualism

pluripartidismo *m* POL multi-party system

plus *m* bonus

◇ **plus de antigüedad** long-service bonus

plusmarca *f* record

plusmarquista *m/f* record holder

plusvalía *f* COM capital gain

plutonio *m* QUÍM plutonium

pluvial *adj* rain *atr*

pluviómetro *m* rain gauge, pluviometer

pluviosidad *f* rainfall

PM *abr* (= ***Policía Militar***) MP (= Military Police)

PNB *m abr* (= ***producto nacional bruto***) GNP (= gross national product)

PNV *m abr* (= ***Partido Nacionalista Vasco***) Basque National Party

p.o. *abr* (= ***por orden***) p.p. (= per procurationem, by proxy)

P.o. *abr* (= ***paseo***) Ave (= avenue)

poblacho *m desp* dump *desp*, dead-and-alive hole *desp*

población *f* **1** *gente* population **2** (*ciudad*) city, town; (*pueblo*) village **3** *Chi* shanty town

◇ **población activa** labor *o Br* labour force

◇ **población callampa** *Chi* shanty town

poblado I *adj* **1** *área* populated; ***~ de*** *fig* full of **2** *barba* bushy **II** *m* (*pueblo*) settlement

poblador *m*, **~a** *f Chi* shanty town dweller

poblar ⟨1m⟩ *v/t* populate (***de*** with); **poblarse** *v/r con personas* be settled (***de*** by); *con animales* be populated (***de***

P

with); *fig* (*colmarse*) cover
pobre I *adj económicamente, en calidad* poor; **~ hombre** poor man; **¡~ de mí!** poor me! **II** *m/f* poor person; **los ~s** the poor
pobretón *adj* (*desdichado*) miserable
pobreza *f* poverty
pocho *adj* **1** *planta* sick **2** *de ánimo* down **3** (*con mala salud*) off-color, *Br* off-colour
pochoclo *m Arg* popcorn
pocilga *f* pigpen, *Br* pigsty
pócima *f* concoction
poción *f* potion
poco I *adj sg* little, not much; *pl* few, not many; **un ~ de** a little; **unos ~s** a few **II** *adv* little; **trabaja ~** he doesn't work much; **ahora se ve muy ~** it's seldom seen now; **estuvo ~ por aquí** he wasn't around much; **~ conocido** little known; **~ a ~** little by little; **dentro de ~** soon, shortly; **hace ~** a short time ago, not long ago; **desde hace ~** (for) a short while; **por ~** nearly, almost; **¡a ~ no lo hacemos!** *Méx* don't tell me we're not doing it; **de a ~ me fui tranquilizando** *Rpl* little by little I calmed down; **por si fuera ~** as if that weren't *o* wasn't enough
III *m*: **un ~** a little, a bit
poda *f* AGR pruning
podadera *f* AGR *cuchillo* pruning knife, billhook; *tijeras* pruning shears *pl*
podar ⟨1a⟩ *v/t* AGR prune
podenco *m* hound
poder ⟨2t⟩ **I** *v/aux* **1** *capacidad* can, be able to; **no pude hablar con ella** I wasn't able to talk to her **2** *permiso* can, be allowed to; **¿puedo ir contigo?** can *o* may I come with you? **3** *posibilidad* may, might; **¡podías habérselo dicho!** you could have *o* you might have told him
II *v/i*: **~ con** (*sobreponerse a*) manage, cope with; **me puede** he can beat me; **es franco a más no ~** F he's as frank as they come F; **comimos a más no ~** F we ate to bursting point F; **no puedo más** I can't take any more, I've had enough; **a ~ ser** if possible; **puede ser** perhaps, maybe; **¡no puede ser!** it can't be!, that can't be right!; **puede que** perhaps, maybe; **puede ser que no lo sepa** maybe *o* perhaps he doesn't know; **¿se puede?** can I come in?, do you mind if I come in?; **no pude menos de insultarle** insulting him was the least I could do
III *m tb* POL power; **en ~ de alguien** in s.o.'s hands; **plenos ~es** *pl* full authority *sg*; **por ~es**, *L.Am.* **por ~** JUR by proxy; **los ~ es públicos** the authorities
◇ **poder adquisitivo** purchasing power
◇ **poder judicial** judiciary
poderío *m* power
poderoso I *adj* powerful **II** *mpl*: **los ~s** the people with power
podiatra *m/f L.Am.* podiatrist, *Br* chiropodist
podio *m* podium
podólogo *m*, **-a** *f* MED podiatrist, *Br* chiropodist
podómetro *m* pedometer
podredumbre *f* rottennness, putrefaction
podrido *adj tb fig* rotten; **~ de dinero** F filthy rich F
podrir ⟨3a⟩ *v/t* ☞ **pudrir**
poema *m* poem
◇ **poema épico** epic poem
◇ **poema sinfónico** MÚS symphonic poem
poemario *m* collection of poems
poesía *f* **1** *género* poetry **2** (*poema*) poem
poeta *m/f* poet
poético *adj* poetic
poetisa *f* poet
póker *m* ☞ **póquer**
polaco I *adj* Polish **II** *m*, **-a** *f* Pole **III** *m idioma* Polish
polar *adj* polar
polaridad *f* polarity
polarizar ⟨1f⟩ *v/t* polarize; **polarizarse** *v/r* polarize, become polarized
polea *f* TÉC pulley
polémica *f* controversy
polémico *adj* controversial
polemista *m/f* polemicist
polemizar ⟨1f⟩ *v/i* argue (**sobre** about)
polen *m* BOT pollen
poleo *m* BOT pennyroyal
polera *f Chi* turtle neck (sweater)
poli *m/f* F cop F; **la ~** F the cops *pl* F
policía I *f* **1** *cuerpo* police **2** *agente* police officer, policewoman **II** *m* police offi-

cer, policeman
◇ **policía montada** mounted police
policíaco, policiaco *adj* detective *atr*
policial *adj* police *atr*
policlínica *f* MED private hospital
policromía *f* polychromy
policromo, polícromo *adj* polychrome
polideportivo *m* sports center, *Br* sports centre
poliedro *m* MAT polyhedron
poliéster *m* polyester
polifacético *adj* versatile, multifaceted
polifásico *adj* EL multiphase
polifonía *f* polyphony
polifónico *adj* polyphonic
poligamia *f* polygamy
polígamo *adj* polygamous
políglota **I** *adj* polyglot *atr* **II** *m/f* polyglot
polígloto, poligloto *adj* polyglot
polígono *m* MAT polygon
◇ **polígono de tiro** shooting range; **polígono industrial** industrial zone, *Br* industrial estate; **polígono residencial** housing development
polilla *f* ZO moth
Polinesia *f* Polynesia
polinesio **I** *adj* Polynesian **II** *m*, **-a** *f* Polynesian
polinización *f* BOT pollination
polinizar ⟨1f⟩ *v/t* BOT pollinate
polinosis *f* MED hay fever
polio *f* MED polio
poliomielitis *f* MED poliomyelitis
pólipo *m* MED, ZO polyp
polisemia *f* polysemy
polista *m/f* DEP polo player
politécnico *adj instituto* polytechnic; ***universidad -a*** technical college
política *f* **1** politics *sg* **2** *orientación* policy; ***~ ambiental*** environmental policy
◇ **política exterior** foreign policy
políticamente *adv*: ***~ correcto*** politically correct, PC
político **I** *adj* political **II** *m*, **-a** *f* politician
politizar ⟨1f⟩ *v/t* politicize
politólogo *m*, **-a** *f* political scientist
polivalente *adj* **1** QUÍM polyvalent **2** *fig*: *objeto* multipurpose; *persona* versatile
póliza *f* policy
◇ **póliza de seguros** insurance policy
polizón *m/f* stowaway
polizonte *m/f* F cop F
polla *f* V prick V, cock V
◇ **polla de agua** ZO moorhen
pollada *f* brood
pollera *f L.Am.* skirt
pollería *f* poulterer's
pollino *m* **1** ZO young donkey **2** F idiot, ass F
pollito *m* chick
pollo *m* ZO, GASTR chicken
◇ **pollo asado** GASTR roast chicken
polluelo *m* ZO chick
polo *m* **1** GEOG, EL pole; ***los ~s opuestos se atraen*** opposites attract **2** *prenda* polo shirt **3** DEP polo
◇ **polo acuático** *L.Am.* waterpolo; **Polo Norte** North Pole; **Polo Sur** South Pole
polola *f Chi* girlfriend
pololear ⟨1a⟩ *v/i Chi* be going steady
pololo *m Chi* boyfriend
Polonia *f* Poland
poltrona *f* easy chair
polución *f* pollution; ***~ atmosférica*** air pollution, atmospheric pollution
polucionar ⟨1a⟩ *v/t* pollute
polvareda *f* dust cloud; ***levantar una ~*** *fig* cause an uproar
polvera *f* powder compact
polvo *m* **1** *del camino*, *de muebles* dust; ***limpiar*** *o* ***quitar el ~*** dust; ***morder el ~*** F bite the dust F; ***hacer morder el ~ a alguien*** F crush s.o., wipe the floor with s.o. F **2** *en química*, *medicina etc* powder **3** F: ***estar hecho ~*** be all in F **4** V: ***echar un ~*** have a screw V; ***nada de ~s durante dos semanas*** no nooky V *o* sex for two weeks
pólvora *f* gunpowder; ***no ha inventado la ~*** he'll never set the world on fire; ***gastar la ~ en salvas*** *fig* waste one's energy
polvoriento *adj* dusty
polvorín *m* **1** *almacén* magazine **2** *fig* powder keg
polvorón *m* GASTR *type of small cake*
◇ **polvos de talco** *mpl* talcum powder *sg*
pomada *f* cream
pomelo *m* BOT grapefruit
pómez *f*: ***piedra ~*** pumice stone
pomo *m* **1** doorknob **2** *Méx frasco* bottle
pompa *f* **1** (*ostentación*) pomp **2** *de jabón* bubble
◇ **pompas fúnebres** *ceremonia* funeral ceremony *sg*; *establecimiento* fun-

P

eral home *sg*, funeral parlor *sg*, *Br* funeral parlour *sg*
pompis *m* F bottom F
pomposo *adj* pompous
pómulo *m* ANAT cheekbone
pon *vb* ☞ ***poner***
ponchadura *f Méx* flat, *Br* puncture
ponchar ⟨1a⟩ *v/t L.Am.* **1** puncture **2** *en béisbol* strike out; **poncharse** *v/r* **1** *Méx* get a flat *o Br* puncture **2** *L.Am. en béisbol* strike out
ponche *m* **1** punch **2** *L.Am. en béisbol* strike
ponchera *f* punch bowl
poncho *m* poncho; ***pisarse el ~*** *S.Am.* be mistaken
ponderación *f* **1** *mesura* deliberation **2** *en estadísticas* weighting
ponderar ⟨1a⟩ *v/t* **1** *fml* (*alabar*) praise, speak highly of **2** (*considerar*) consider, ponder
ponedero *m* nest(ing) box
ponencia *f* **1** (*charla*) presentation **2** EDU paper
ponente *m/f* speaker
poner ⟨2r; *part* ***puesto***⟩ *v/t* **1** put; ***~ en escena*** stage; ***~ en marcha*** set in motion; ***pongamos que*** let's suppose *o* assume that
2 *ropa* put on
3 (*añadir*) put in
4 RAD, TV turn on, switch on
5 *la mesa* set
6 (*escribir*) put down
7 *en periódico, libro etc* say; ***la crítica puso muy bien su última película*** the critics gave his last film very good reviews
8 *negocio* set up
9 *telegrama* send
10 *huevos* lay
11 AUTO *marcha* put the car in, move into
12 *dinero* deposit
13: ***~ a alguien furioso*** make s.o. angry; ***~le a alguien con alguien*** TELEC put s.o. through to s.o.; ***~le una multa a alguien*** fine s.o.
ponerse *v/r* **1** *ropa* put on; ***~ de luto*** dress in mourning; ***~ de verano*** put on summer clothes
2 *en un estado*: ***~ palido*** turn pale; ***~ furioso*** get angry; ***~ enfermo*** become *o* fall ill; ***¡no te pongas así!*** don't get so upset!, don't take it like that!; ***~ bien*** recover, get better; ***~ en marcha*** get started, get going
3: ***ponte en el banco*** go and sit on the bench; ***se puso ahí*** she stood over there; ***dile que se ponga*** TELEC tell her to come to the phone; ***~ a*** start to; ***al ~ el sol*** at sunset
poney *m* ☞ ***poni***
pongo[1] *vb* ☞ ***poner***
pongo[2] *m Pe: indentured Indian laborer*
poni *m* ZO pony
poniente *m* west
pontificado *m* pontificate
pontificar ⟨1g⟩ *v/i* REL, *fig* pontificate
pontífice *m* pontiff; ***sumo ~*** Pope
pontificio *adj* pontifical
pontón *m* pontoon
ponzoñoso *adj* poisonous
pop I *adj* pop; ***música ~*** pop music **II** *m* pop
popa *f* MAR stern
popote *m Méx* straw
populachero *adj desp* vulgar, common
populacho *m desp* rabble, plebs *pl*
popular I *adj* **1** (*afamado*) popular **2** (*del pueblo*) folk *atr* **3** *barrio* lower-class **II** *mpl*: ***los ~es*** *Esp* POL the Popular Party
popularidad *f* popularity
popularizar ⟨1f⟩ *v/t* popularize; **popularizarse** *v/r* become popular
populismo *m* populism
populista *m/f* populist
populoso *adj* populous
popurrí *m* MÚS, *fig* potpourri
póquer *m* poker; ***cara de ~*** poker face
poquito *adj*: ***un ~*** a little, a (little) bit
por *prp* **1** *motivo* for, because of; ***lo hace ~ mí*** he does it for me; ***lo hizo ~ amor*** she did it out of *o* for love; ***luchó ~ sus ideales*** he fought for his ideals; ***~ miedo a ofenderle*** for fear of upsetting her; ***vino ~ verme*** he came to see me
2 *medio* by; ***~ avión*** by air; ***~ correo*** by mail, *Br tb* by post
3 *tiempo*: ***~ un año*** / ***un segundo*** for a year / a second; ***~ la mañana*** in the morning; ***~ Navidad*** around Christmas
4 *movimiento*: ***~ la calle*** down the street; ***~ un tunel*** through a tunnel; ***~ aquí*** this way
5 *posición aproximada* around, about; ***está ~ aquí*** it's around here (some-

where); ***vive ~ el centro de la ciudad*** she lives somewhere around the center of town
6 *cambio*: ***~ cincuenta pesos*** for fifty pesos; ***~ cabeza*** each, a head
7 *otros usos*: ***~ hora*** an *o* per hour; ***dos ~ dos*** two times two; ***¿~ qué?*** why?; ***el motivo ~ el cual*** *o* ***~ el que …*** the reason why …; ***esa factura aún está ~ pagar*** that invoice still has to be paid; ***tomar ~ esposa*** marry; ***~ difícil que sea*** however difficult it might be

porcelana *f* porcelain, china; ***de ~*** porcelain *atr*, china *atr*

porcentaje *m* percentage

porcentual *adj* percentage *atr*

porche *f* porch

porcicultor *m*,**~a** *f* hog *o* pig breeder, hog *o* pig farmer

porcicultura *f* hog *o* pig breeding, hog *o* pig farming

porcino *adj* pig *atr*, porcine *fml*; ***ganado ~*** *sg* hogs *pl*, pigs *pl*

porción *f* portion

pordiosero *m*,**-a** *f* beggar

porfía *f* (*insistencia*) insistence

porfiar ⟨1c⟩ *v/i* insist (***en*** on)

pormenor *m* detail

pormenorizar ⟨1f⟩ *v/t* describe in detail

porno **I** *adj* porn *atr* **II** *m* porn

pornografía *f* pornography

pornográfico *adj* pornographic

poro *m* **1** pore **2** *Chi*, *Méx*: *puerro* leek

porosidad *f* porosity, porousness

poroso *adj* porous

poroto *m Rpl*, *Chi* bean
◇ **porotos verdes** *L.Am.* green beans

porque *conj* because; ***~ sí*** just because

porqué *m* reason

porquería *f* **1** (*suciedad*) filth **2** F *cosa de poca calidad* piece of trash F

porqueriza *f* pigpen, *Br* pigsty

porra *f* **1** *de policía* night stick, *Br* baton **2** (*palo*) club **3**: ***¡vete a la ~!*** F go to hell! F

porrada *f*: ***una ~ de*** F loads of F

porrazo *m*: ***darle un ~ a alguien*** F hit s.o.; ***darse*** *o* ***pegarse un ~*** crash (***contra*** into)

porreta *f*: ***en ~s*** F stark naked, in one's birthday suit F

porrillo : ***a ~*** F by the truckload F; ***gana dinero a ~*** he makes a bundle F, he makes loads of money F

porro *m* F joint F

porrón *m container from which wine is poured straight into the mouth*

portaaviones *m inv* aircraft carrier

portacontenedores *m inv* container ship

portada *f* **1** TIP front page; *de revista* cover **2** ARQUI front

portador *m*,**~a** *f* **1** COM bearer **2** MED: ***~ de gérmenes*** carrier

portaequipajes *m inv* **1** AUTO trunk, *Br* boot **2** FERR luggage rack

portaesquís *m inv* AUTO ski rack

portafolios *m inv* briefcase

portahelicópteros *m inv* MAR helicopter carrier

portal *m* **1** *de casa*, *pisos* foyer **2** (*entrada*) doorway **3** INFOR portal

portalámparas *m inv* EL (bulb) socket

portaligas *m inv Arg*, *Chi* garter belt, *Br* suspender belt

portamaletas *m inv* ☞ ***portaequipajes***

portaminas *m inv* automatic *o* mechanical pencil, *Br* propelling pencil

portamonedas *m inv* coin purse, *Br* purse

portante *m*: ***tomar el ~*** *fig* F clear off

portaobjeto, portaobjetos *m inv* (microscope) slide

portarrollos *m inv de papel higiénico* toilet-roll holder

portarse ⟨1a⟩ *v/r* behave

portátil *adj* portable

portatrajes *m inv* suit carrier

portavelas *m inv* candle holder

portavoz *m/f hombre* spokesman; *mujer* spokeswoman
◇ **portavoz del gobierno** government spokesperson

portazo *m*: ***dar un ~*** F slam the door

porte *m* **1** (*aspecto*) appearance, air **2** (*gasto de correo*) postage; ***a ~s debidos*** collect on delivery, *Br* cash on delivery; ***a ~s pagados*** freight paid, *Br* carriage paid **3**: ***de este ~*** about this big

porteador *m*,**~a** *f* porter, bearer

portear ⟨1a⟩ *v/t* carry, transport

portento *m* **1** (*fenómeno*) wonder **2** *persona* genius

portentoso *adj* incredible, prodigious

porteño *Arg* **I** *adj* of / from Buenos Aires, Buenos Aires *atr* **II** *m*,**-a** *f* native of Buenos Aires

portería *f* **1** (*conserjería*) reception **2** *ca-*

P

sa superintendent's apartment, *Br* caretaker's flat **3** DEP goal

portero *m* **1** doorman **2** *de edificio* superintendent, *Br* caretaker **3** DEP goalkeeper

◇ **portero automático** intercom, *Br* entryphone

portezuela *f* door

pórtico *m* portico

portilla *f* MAR porthole

portillo *m* **1** *de muralla* wicket (gate) **2** *entre dos montañas* defile

portón *m* large door

portorriqueño I *adj* Puerto Rican **II** *m*, **-a** *f* Puerto Rican

portuario *adj* port *atr*

Portugal *m* Portugal

portugués I *adj* Portuguese **II** *m*, **-esa** *f persona* Portuguese **III** *m idioma* Portuguese

porvenir *m* future

pos *adv*: ***en ~ de*** in pursuit of

pos(t)venta *adj inv* after-sales *atr*

posada *f* **1** *C.Am., Méx* Christmas party **2** (*fonda*) inn

posaderas *fpl* bottom *sg* F, backside *sg* F

posar ⟨1a⟩ *v/t mano* lay, place (***sobre*** on); ***~ la mirada en*** gaze at; **posarse** *v/r de ave, insecto*, AVIA land

posavasos *m inv* coaster

posdata *f* postscript

pose *f* pose

poseedor *m*, **~a** *f de acciones, licencia* holder; *de armas* owner

poseer ⟨2e⟩ *v/t* possess; (*ser dueño de*) own, possess

poseído I *adj* possessed (***de, por*** by) **II** *m*, **-a** *f*: ***gritar como un ~*** scream like one possessed

posesión *f* possession; ***tomar ~ (de un cargo)*** POL take up office; ***estar en ~ de la verdad*** know the truth; ***estar en ~ de las facultades*** be in possession of one's faculties

posesivo *adj* GRAM, *persona* possessive

poseso ☞ ***poseído***

posguerra *f* postwar period

posibilidad *f* possibility; ***vivir por encima de sus ~es*** live beyond one's means

posibilitar ⟨1a⟩ *v/t* make possible

posible I *adj* possible; ***en lo ~*** as far as possible; ***hacer ~*** make possible; ***hacer todo lo ~*** do everything possible; ***es ~ que ...*** perhaps ...; ***es muy ~ que*** it's very possible that; ***¿será ~?*** F I don't believe it! F **II** *mpl* **~s**: means *pl*; ***con ~s*** well-off, well-to-do

posiblemente *adv* possibly

posición *f* **1** *tb* MIL, *fig* position; ***en buena ~*** *en clasificación* in a good position, well-placed; ***en ~ de espera*** on standby **2** *social* standing, status; ***de ~*** of some standing

positivo I *adj* positive; ***dar ~*** *en test de alcoholemia* test positive (*on the breathalyzer test*) **II** *m* FOT print

posmodernidad *f* postmodernity

posmoderno *adj* postmodern

poso *m* dregs *pl*; ***los ~s del café*** the coffee grounds

posología *f* dosage

posoperatorio MED **I** *adj* postoperative **II** *m* postoperative period

posponer ⟨2r; *part* ***pospuesto***⟩ *v/t* postpone

pospuesto *part* ☞ ***posponer***

posta *f*: ***a ~*** on purpose

postal I *adj* mail *atr*, postal; ***tarjeta ~*** postcard **II** *f* postcard

postas *fpl L.Am.* relay race *sg*

poste *m* **1** post; ***~ alto / bajo*** *en baloncesto* high / low post **2** *en baloncesto*: *jugador* center, *Br* centre

◇ **poste kilométrico** distance marker

◇ **poste telegráfico** telegraph pole

póster *m* poster

postergar ⟨1a⟩ *v/t* postpone

posteridad *f* posterity; ***pasar a la ~*** go down in history

posterior *adj* **1** (*consecutivo*) later, subsequent **2** (*trasero*) rear *atr*, back *atr*

posterioridad *f*: ***con ~*** later, subsequently; ***con ~ a*** later than, subsequent to

posteriormente *adv* subsequently

postigo *m* shutter

postín *m*: ***de ~*** *comida* sumptuous; ***una vida de ~*** a life of ease; ***darse ~*** show off

postinero *adj* (*presuntuoso*) pretentious

postizo I *adj* false **II** *m* hairpiece

postor *m* bidder; ***al mejor ~*** to the highest bidder

postrar ⟨1a⟩ *v/t*: ***la gripe lo postró dos***

semanas he was laid up with flu for two weeks; **postrarse** *v/r* prostrate o.s.
postre *m* dessert; ***llegar a los ~s*** arrive very late; ***a la ~*** in the end
postrer(o) *adj* last
postrimerías *fpl* end *sg*, final years; ***en las ~ de*** *del reino* at the end of, in the final years of
postulado *m* postulate
postulante *m/f en una colecta* collector
postular ⟨1a⟩ *v/t hipótesis* put forward, advance
póstumo *adj* posthumous
postura *f tb fig* position
potabilizador *adj*: ***planta ~a de agua*** waterworks *sg*
potabilizadora *f* waterworks *sg*
potabilizar ⟨1f⟩ *v/t* make drinkable
potable *adj* **1** drinkable; ***agua ~*** drinking water **2** *fig* F passable
potaje *m* GASTR stew
potasa *f* potash
potasio *m* potassium
pote *m* **1** (*olla*) pot **2** GASTR stew **3** *fig* F: ***darse ~*** show off
potencia *f* power; ***en ~*** potential; ***elevar a la décima ~*** MAT raise to the power of ten
◇ **potencia nuclear** nuclear power
potencial *m/adj* potential
potenciar ⟨1b⟩ *v/t fig* foster, promote
potentado *m*, **-a** *f* tycoon
potente *adj* powerful
potestad *f* authority; ***patria ~*** parental authority
potingue *m* F *desp* lotion, cream
potito *m* jar of baby food
Potosí *m*: ***valer un ~*** *fig* be worth a fortune
potra *f* **1** ZO filly **2** F (*suerte*) luck; ***tener ~*** F be lucky
potranca *f* ZO filly
potranco *m* ZO colt
potrero *m L.Am.* pasture
potro *m* ZO colt
pozo *m* **1** *de agua* well; MIN shaft; ***un ~ sin fondo*** *fig* a bottomless pit; ***salir del ~*** *fig* F get out of the hole **2** *Rpl* pothole
◇ **pozo negro** cesspit
pozol *m C.Am.* corn liquor
pozole *m Méx* corn stew
PP *m abr* (= ***Partido Popular***) Popular Party
p.p. *abr* (= ***por poder***) by proxy
PPE *m abr* (= ***Partido Popular Europeo***) European Popular Party
práctica *f* practice; ***en la ~*** in practice; ***llevar a la ~, poner en ~*** put into practice; ***perder la ~*** get out of practice; ***tener ~ en algo*** have experience in sth; ***~s*** *pl* work experience *sg*; ***hacer ~s*** do a work placement
practicable *adj* **1** *tarea* feasible, practicable **2** *camino* passable
practicante **I** *adj* practicing, *Br* practising **II** *m/f* nurse (*who gives injections, does tests, dresses wounds, etc.*)
practicar ⟨1g⟩ *v/t* practice, *Br* practise; *deporte* play; ***~ la equitación / la esgrima*** ride / fence
práctico **I** *adj* practical **II** *m* MAR pilot
pradera *f* prairie, grassland
prado *m* meadow
Praga *f* Prague
pragmático **I** *adj* pragmatic **II** *m*, **-a** *f* pragmatist
pragmatismo *m* pragmatism
pral. *abr* (= ***principal***) first
preacuerdo *m* outline agreement
prealerta *f* initial alert
preámbulo *m* preamble; ***sin ~s*** without further ado
preaviso *m* notice; ***sin ~*** without notice *o* warning
prebenda *f* sinecure
preboste *m* HIST provost; *fig*: *de asociación, comunidad* leader
precalentamiento *m* DEP warm-up
precalentar ⟨1k⟩ *v/t* preheat
precariedad *f* **1** (*escasez*) poverty, deprivation **2** (*inseguridad*) precariousness
precario *adj* precarious
precaución *f* precaution; ***tomar precauciones*** take precautions
precaver ⟨2a⟩ *v/t* guard against; **precaverse** *v/r* take precautions (***contra*** against); ***~ de*** guard against
precavido *adj* cautious
precedencia *f* precedence, priority
precedente **I** *adj* previous **II** *m* precedent; ***sin ~s*** unprecedented, without precedent; ***sentar un ~*** set a precedent
preceder ⟨2a⟩ *v/t* precede
preceptiva *f* regulations *pl*
preceptivo *adj* compulsory, mandatory
precepto *m* precept
preceptor *m* (private) tutor

preciado *adj* precious
preciarse ⟨1b⟩ *v/r*: ***cualquier fontanero que se precie …*** any self-respecting plumber …
precintar ⟨1a⟩ *v/t paquete* seal; *lugar* seal off
precinto *m* seal
precio *m* price; ***~ por unidad*** unit price; ***a bajo ~*** at a low price; ***a mitad de ~*** at half price; ***estar bien de ~*** be reasonably priced; ***a buen ~*** at a good price; ***pagar a ~ de oro*** pay a fortune for; ***no tener ~*** *fig* be priceless
◇ **precio al contado** cash price;**precio de coste** cost price;**precio de lanzamiento** (special) introductory price; **precio al por mayor** wholesale price; **precio al por menor** retail price;**precio de venta** sale price;**precio de venta al público** recommended retail price
preciosidad *f*: ***esa casa / chica es una ~*** that house / girl is gorgeous *o* beautiful
precioso *adj* **1** (*de valor*) precious **2** (*hermoso*) beautiful
preciosura *f L.Am.* F ☞ ***preciosidad***
precipicio *m* precipice; ***estar al borde del ~*** *fig* be on the edge of the precipice
precipitación *f* **1** (*prisa*) hurry, haste **2**: ***precipitaciones*** *pl* rain *sg*
precipitado **I** *adj* hasty, sudden **II** *m* QUÍM precipitate
precipitar ⟨1a⟩ *v/t* **1** (*lanzar*) throw, hurl **2** (*acelerar*) hasten **3** QUÍM precipitate; **precipitarse** *v/r* **1** (*correr*) rush **2** *fig* be hasty
precisamente *adv* precisely
precisar ⟨1a⟩ *v/t* **1** (*aclarar*) specify **2** (*necesitar*) need
precisión *f* precision; ***de ~*** precision *atr*
preciso *adj* precise, accurate; ***ser ~*** be necessary
precocidad *f* precocity, precociousness
precocinado *adj* precooked
precolombino *adj* pre-Columbian
preconcebido *adj* preconceived; ***idea -a*** preconceived idea, preconception
preconizar ⟨1f⟩ *v/t* advocate
precontrato *m* precontract
precoz *adj* **1** (*anticipado*) early **2** *niño* precocious
precursor *m*,**~a** *f* precursor, forerunner
predador **I** ZO *adj* predatory **II** *m*,**~a** *f* (*saqueador*) predator
predecesor *m*,**~a** *f* predecessor
predecible *adj* predictable
predecir ⟨3p; *part* ***predicho***⟩ *v/t* predict
predestinación *f* predestination
predestinado **I** *adj* predestined **II** *m*,**-a** *f*: ***un ~ a algo*** a person who is predestined to sth
predestinar ⟨1a⟩ *v/t* predestine
predeterminar ⟨1a⟩ *v/t* predetermine
predicado *m* predicate
predicador *m*,**~a** *f* preacher
predicar ⟨1g⟩ *v/t* preach; ***~ con el ejemplo*** practice *o Br* practise what one preaches
predicativo *adj* GRAM predicative
predicción *f* prediction, forecast
◇ **predicción meteorológica** weather forecast
predicho *part* ☞ ***predecir***
predilección *f* predilection
predilecto *adj* favorite, *Br* favourite
predio *m L.Am* building
predisponer ⟨2r⟩ *v/t* **1** (*influir*) prejudice **2** MED predispose; **predisponerse** *v/r* be predisposed
predisposición *f* **1** MED predisposition **2** (*tendencia*) tendency; ***una ~ en contra de*** a prejudice against
predispuesto *adj* **1** (*proclive*) predisposed (***a*** to) **2** (*parcial*) bias(s)ed, prejudiced
predominante *adj* predominant
predominar ⟨1a⟩ *v/i* predominate
predominio *m* predominance
preelectoral *adj* pre-election *atr*
preeminencia *f* preeminence
preeminente *adj* preeminent
preescolar *adj* preschool
preestreno *m* preview
preexistente *adj* pre-existing
preexistir ⟨3a⟩ *v/i* pre-exist
prefabricado *adj* prefabricated
prefacio *m* preface, foreword
prefecto *m* REL prefect
preferencia *f* preference; ***de ~*** preferably; ***~ de paso*** AUTO right of way, *Br tb* priority
preferente *adj* preferential
preferentemente *adv* preferably
preferible *adj* preferable (***a*** to); ***es ~ que …*** it's better if …
preferiblemente *adv* preferably
preferido **I** *part* ☞ ***preferir*** **II** *adj* favor-

P

ite, *Br* favourite
preferir ⟨3i⟩ *v/t* prefer; ***prefiero hacerlo solo*** I'd rather do it on my own, I'd prefer to do it on my own
prefijar ⟨1a⟩ *v/t* arrange in advance
prefijo *m* **1** GRAM prefix **2** TELEC area code, *Br tb* dialling code
prefranqueado *adj* prefranked, prepaid
pregón *m* proclamation
pregonar ⟨1a⟩ *v/t* proclaim, make public
pregonero *m*,**-a** *f* HIST town crier
pregunta *f* question; ***hacer una ~*** ask a question
preguntar ⟨1a⟩ **I** *v/t* ask **II** *v/i* ask; ***~ por algo*** ask about sth; ***~ por alguien*** *paradero* ask for s.o.; *salud etc* ask about s.o.; **preguntarse** *v/r* wonder
preguntón **I** *adj* nosy **II** *m*,**-ona** *f* busybody, nosy parker
prehistoria *f* prehistory
prehistórico *adj* prehistoric
prejubilación *f* early retirement
prejuicio *m* prejudice
prejuzgar ⟨1h⟩ *v/t* prejudge
prelado *m* prelate
prelavado *m* prewash
preliminar **I** *adj* **1** *estudio, comentario* preliminary **2** DEP qualifying **II** *m L.Am.* qualifier
preludiar ⟨1b⟩ *v/t* MÚS, *fig* herald
preludio *m* prelude
premamá *adj* maternity *atr*
prematrimonial *adj* premarital
prematuro **I** *adj* premature **II** *m*,**-a** *f* premature baby
premeditación *f* premeditation; ***con ~*** deliberately
premeditado *adj* premeditated
premeditar ⟨1a⟩ *v/t* JUR premeditate
premiado **I** *adj* prizewinning **II** *m*, **-a** *f* prizewinner
premiar ⟨1b⟩ *v/t* award a prize to
premio *m* prize
◇ **premio de consolación** consolation prize
◇ **premio gordo** jackpot
premisa *f* premise
premonición *f* premonition
premonitorio *adj* premonitory
premura *f* haste; ***~ de tiempo*** pressure of time; ***hacer algo con ~ de tiempo*** be pressed for time when doing something
prenatal *adj* prenatal, *Br* antenatal; ***vestido ~*** maternity dress
prenavideño *adj* pre-Christmas
prenda *f* **1** *de vestir* item of clothing, garment; ***~s deportivas*** *pl* sportswear *sg* **2** *garantía* security **3** *en juegos* forfeit; ***juego de ~s*** forfeits *sg* **4**: ***no soltar ~*** not say a word (***sobre*** about); ***no me duelen ~s admitir que me equivoqué*** I don't mind admitting that I was wrong
prendar ⟨1a⟩ *v/t* captivate; **prendarse** *v/r*: ***~ de algo*** be captivated by sth; ***~ de alguien*** fall in love with s.o.
prender ⟨2a; *part* ***preso***⟩ **I** *v/t* **1** *a fugitivo* capture **2** *sujetar* pin up **3** *L.Am. fuego* light; *luz* switch on, turn on; ***~ fuego a*** set fire to **II** *v/i* **1** *de planta* take **2** (*empezar a arder*) catch **3** *de moda* catch on
prendería *f Esp* pawnbroker's, pawn shop
prensa *f* press; ***~ diaria*** daily newspapers *pl*, dailies *pl*; ***~ especializada*** specialist press; ***tener buena / mala ~*** *tb fig* have a good / bad press
◇ **prensa amarilla** gutter press
prensado *m* pressing
prensar ⟨1a⟩ *v/t* press
prensil *adj* ZO prehensile; ***cola ~*** prehensile tail
preñado *adj* **1** (*embarazada*) pregnant **2** *fig lit*: ***~ de*** filled with
preñar ⟨1a⟩ *v/t* impregnate, make pregnant
preocupación *f* worry, concern
preocupado *adj* worried (***por*** about), concerned (***por*** about)
preocupante *adj* worrying
preocupar ⟨1a⟩ *v/t* worry, concern; **preocuparse** *v/r* worry (***por*** about); ***~ de*** (*encargarse*) look after, take care of; ***¡no se preocupe!*** don't worry!
preparación *f* **1** (*preparativo*) preparation **2** (*educación*) education **3** *para trabajo* training
preparado **I** *adj* ready, prepared; ***¡~s, listos, ya!*** ready, set, go! **II** *m* preparation
preparador *m*,**~a** *f*: ***~ físico*** trainer
preparar ⟨1a⟩ *v/t* prepare, get ready; **prepararse** *v/r* **1** get ready (***para*** for), prepare o.s. (***para*** for) **2** *de tor-*

menta, crisis be brewing
preparativos *mpl* preparations
preparatorio *adj* preparatory; ***curso ~*** preparatory course
preponderancia *f* preponderance
preponderante *adj* predominant
preponderar ⟨1a⟩ *v/i* predominate
preposición *f* preposition
prepotencia *f* arrogance
prepotente *adj* arrogant
prepucio *m* ANAT foreskin, prepuce *fml*
prerrogativa *f* prerogative
presa *f* **1** (*dique*) dam **2** (*embalse*) reservoir **3** (*víctima*) prey; ***ser ~ del pánico*** be panic-stricken **4** *L.Am. para comer* bite to eat
presagiar ⟨1b⟩ *v/t* presage, forebode; ***no hacer ~ nada bueno*** not be a good omen, not augur well
presagio *m* **1** (*agüero*) omen, sign **2** (*premonición*) premonition
presbicia *f* MED farsightedness, longsightedness
presbiterio *m* presbytery
prescindir ⟨3a⟩ *v/i*: **~ *de*** **1** (*privarse de*) do without; ***no poder ~ de algo*** not be able to do without sth **2** (*omitir*) leave out, dispense with **3** (*no tener en cuenta*) disregard
prescribir ⟨3a; *part* ***prescrito***⟩ **I** *v/i* JUR prescribe **II** *v/t* MED prescribe
prescripción *f* JUR *de contrato* expiry, expiration
◇ **prescripción médica** prescription
prescrito *part* ☞ ***prescribir***
presencia *f* presence; ***en ~ de*** in the presence of; ***buena ~*** smart appearance; ***~ de ánimo*** presence of mind
presenciar ⟨1b⟩ *v/t* **1** *accidente* witness **2** (*estar presente en*) attend, be present at
presentable *adj* presentable
presentación *f* **1** presentation **2** COM launch **3** *entre personas* introduction
presentador *m*, **~a** *f* TV presenter
presentar ⟨1a⟩ *v/t* **1** TV present **2** *a alguien* introduce **3** *producto* launch **4** *solicitud* submit; **presentarse** *v/r* **1** *en sitio* show up **2** (*darse a conocer*) introduce o.s. **3** *a examen* take **4** *de problema, dificultad* arise **5** *a elecciones* run
presente I *adj* present; ***en el caso ~*** in the present case *o* situation; ***tener algo ~*** bear sth in mind; ***¡~!*** here!; ***mejorando lo ~*** just like you **II** *m tiempo* present **III** *m/f*: ***los ~s*** those present **IV** *f*: ***por la ~ le informamos que …*** we hereby wish to inform you that …
presentimiento *m* premonition; ***tengo el ~ que …*** I have a feeling that…
presentir ⟨3i⟩ *v/t* foresee; ***presiento que vendrá*** I have a feeling he'll come
preservación *f* (*protección*) preservation; *de naturaleza* preservation, conservation
preservar ⟨1a⟩ *v/t* protect; *naturaleza* preserve, conserve
preservativo *m* condom
presidencia *f de gobierno, organización* presidency; *de compañía* presidency, *Br* chairmanship; *de comité* chairmanship; ***bajo la ~ de …*** when … was president, under the presidency of …
presidenciable *m/f L.Am.* potential presidential candidate
presidencial *adj* presidential
presidente *m*, **-a** *f* president; *de gobierno* premier, prime minister; *de compañía* president, *Br* chairman, *Br mujer* chairwoman; *de comité* chair
◇ **presidente de honor, presidente honorífico** honorary president *o* chairman
presidiario *m*, **-a** *f* prisoner
presidio *m* prison
presidir ⟨3a⟩ *v/t organización* be president of; *reunión* chair, preside over
presión *f* **1** pressure; ***hacer ~ sobre*** put pressure on, pressure **2** *en baloncesto* press; ***~ en toda la cancha*** full-court press
◇ **presión arterial** blood pressure; **presión fiscal** tax burden; **presión sanguínea** blood pressure
presionar ⟨1a⟩ **I** *v/t* **1** *botón, en baloncesto* press **2** *fig* put pressure on, pressure **II** *v/i en baloncesto* press
preso I *part* ☞ ***prender*** **II** *adj*: ***hacer ~ a alguien*** take s.o. prisoner **III** *m*, **-a** *f* prisoner
◇ **preso preventivo** remand prisoner
prestación *f* provision
◇ **prestación por desempleo** unemployment benefit *o* compensation; **prestación social sustitutoria** MIL community service in lieu of military

service; **prestaciones sociales** welfare *sg*, *Br* social security *sg*
prestado *adj*: ***dejar algo ~ a alguien*** lend sth to s.o., lend s.o. sth; ***pedir ~ algo a alguien*** borrow sth from s.o.
prestamista *m/f* moneylender
préstamo *m* **1** *de dinero* loan; ***~ bancario*** bank loan; ***pedir un ~ para algo*** apply for a loan for sth **2** GRAM loanword
prestancia *f fml* distinction; ***tener ~*** be distinguished
prestar ⟨1a⟩ *v/t dinero* lend; *ayuda* give; *L.Am.* borrow; ***~ atención*** pay attention; **prestarse** *v/r* **1**: ***~ a*** give rise to **2**: ***~ a hacer algo*** volunteer to do sth
presteza *f* promptness
prestidigitación *f* conjuring
prestidigitador *m*, **~a** *f* conjurer
prestigiar ⟨1b⟩ *v/t* lend prestige to; ***~ algo con su presencia*** honor *o Br* honour sth with one's presence
prestigio *m* prestige; ***de ~*** prestigious; ***de ~ mundial*** respected worldwide
prestigioso *adj* prestigious
presumible *adj*: ***era ~ que ocurriera*** that was predictable
presumido **I** *adj* **1** (*creído*) conceited **2** (*coqueto*) vain **II** *m*, **-a** *f* bighead
presumir ⟨3a⟩ **I** *v/t* presume **II** *v/i* show off; ***~ de algo*** boast *o* brag about sth; ***presume de listo*** he thinks he's very clever
presunción *f* **1** (*vanidad*) presumptuousness **2** (*suposición*) presumption, supposition
presuntamente *adv* allegedly
presunto *adj* alleged, suspected
presuntuosidad *f* conceit, conceitedness
presuntuoso *adj* conceited
presuponer ⟨2r; *part* **presupuesto**⟩ *v/t* assume
presupuestal *adj L.Am.* budgetary
presupuestar ⟨1a⟩ *v/t* budget for
presupuestario *adj* budget *atr*
presupuesto **I** *part* ☞ **presuponer** **II** *m* POL budget
presurizado *adj*: ***cabina -a*** AVIA pressurized cabin
presurizar ⟨1f⟩ *v/t* AVIA pressurize
presuroso *adj* hurried
pretemporada *f* DEP pre-season
pretencioso *adj* pretentious
pretender ⟨2a⟩ *v/t*: ***~ hacer algo*** try to do sth
pretendiente **I** *m de mujer* suitor **II** *m/f*: ***~ al trono*** *o* ***a la corona*** pretender to the throne
pretensión *f L.Am.* (*arrogancia*) vanity; ***sin pretensiones*** unpretentious
pretensor *m*: ***cinturón con ~*** AUTO inertia-reel seatbelt
pretérito **I** *adj* past, bygone *lit* **II** *m* GRAM preterite
pretextar ⟨1a⟩ *v/t fml* claim
pretexto *m* pretext; ***con (el) ~, a ~ de*** under the pretext of
pretil *m* parapet
prevalecer ⟨2d⟩ *v/i* prevail (***sobre*** over)
prevaleciente *adj* prevailing
prevaricación *f* corruption
prevaricar ⟨1g⟩ *v/i* pervert the course of justice
prevención *f* prevention; ***tomar prevenciones*** take precautions
prevenido **I** *part* ☞ **prevenir** **II** *adj* well-prepared
prevenir ⟨3s⟩ *v/t* **1** (*evitar*) prevent; ***más vale ~ que curar*** prevention is better than cure **2** (*avisar*) warn (***contra*** against); **prevenirse** *v/r* (*prepararse*) prepare, get ready
preventiva *f Méx* yellow light, *Br* amber light
preventivo *adj* preventive, preventative; ***medicina -a*** preventive *o* preventative medicine
prever ⟨2v; *part* **previsto**⟩ *v/t* foresee
previamente *adv* previously
previo *adj* **1** previous; ***sin ~ aviso*** without (prior) warning **2** *fml*: ***~ pago de*** on payment of
previsible *adj* foreseeable
previsión *f* **1** (*predicción*) forecast; ***~ del tiempo*** weather forecast **2** (*preparación*) foresight
previsor *adj* farsighted
previsto **I** *part* ☞ **prever** **II** *adj* foreseen, expected; ***tener ~*** have planned
prieto *adj L.Am.* dark-skinned
prima *f* **1** *de seguro* premium **2** (*pago extra*) bonus
primacía *f* **1** (*supremacía*) supremacy, primacy **2** (*prioridad*) priority
primado *m* REL primate
primar ⟨1a⟩ **I** *v/i* take priority, take precedence (***sobre*** over) **II** *v/t* **1** (*priorizar*) give priority to **2** (*recompensar*) give a

bonus to
primario *adj* primary; ***elecciones -as*** POL primaries, primary elections
primate *m* ZO primate
primavera *f* **1** spring **2** BOT primrose
primaveral *adj* spring *atr*
primer *adj* first; ***~ piso*** second floor, *Br* first floor; *en edificio con piso principal* third floor, *Br* second floor
◇ **primer ministro** Prime Minister
primera *f* **1** first class; ***de ~*** *producto, pintor* first-class, first-rate **2** AUTO first (gear); ***poner la ~*** put the car in first (gear) **3** DEP first division **4**: ***a la ~*** first-time; ***a la ~ de cambio*** at the drop of a hat; ***me viene de ~*** F it's just what I needed
◇ **primera base** *f en béisbol* first base; *jugador* first baseman
primeriza *f* first-time mother, *fml* primigravida
primerizo **I** *adj* (*principiante*) inexperienced, green F; *madre* new, first-time **II** *m*,**-a** *f* novice, greenhorn F
primero **I** *adj* first **II** *m*,**-a** *f* first (one); ***a ~s de enero*** at the beginning of January; ***el ~ de mayo*** the first of May; ***ser el ~ de la clase*** be top of the class **III** *pron*: ***lo ~*** (*lo más importante*) the most important thing **IV** *adv* **1** *en posición* first **2** (*primeramente*) first of all
◇ **primeros auxilios** first aid *sg*
primicia *f* scoop
primitivo *adj* **1** (*prehistórico, rudimentario*) primitive **2** (*original*) original
primo **I** *adj número* prime **II** *m*,**-a** *f* cousin; ***~ hermano / prima hermana*** first cousin; ***hacer el ~*** *fig* F be taken for a ride F
primogénito **I** *adj* first **II** *m*,**-a** *f* first child
primor *m* skill; ***cocina que es un ~*** she's a wonderful cook; ***con ~*** finely, exquisitely
primordial *adj* fundamental
primoroso *adj* exquisite
prímula *f* BOT primrose
princesa *f* princess
principado *m* principality
principal **I** *adj* main, principal; ***lo ~*** the main *o* most important thing **II** *m* second floor, *Br* first floor
príncipe *m* prince
◇ **príncipe de Asturias** *heir to the Spanish throne*; **príncipe azul** *fig* Prince Charming; **príncipe consorte** prince consort; **príncipe de Gales** Prince of Wales; **príncipe heredero** crown prince
principesco *adj* princely
principiante **I** *adj* inexperienced **II** *m/f* beginner
principio *m* **1** *ley, moral* principle; ***en ~*** in principle; ***por ~*** on principle **2** *en tiempo* beginning; ***a ~s de abril*** at the beginning of April; ***al ~, en un ~*** at first; ***el ~ del fin*** the beginning of the end
pringar ⟨1h⟩ *v/t* **1** (*ensuciar*) get greasy **2** *fig* F get involved (***en*** in); ***~la*** P kick the bucket F; **pringarse** *v/r* **1** (*ensuciarse*) get greasy **2** *fig* F get mixed up (***en*** in)
pringoso *adj* greasy
pringue *m* (*also f*) grease
prior *m* prior
priora *f* prioress
prioridad *f* priority; ***~ de paso*** AUTO right of way, *Br* priority
prioritario *adj* priority *atr*
priorizar ⟨1f⟩ *v/t & v/i* prioritize
prisa *f* hurry, rush; ***darse ~*** hurry (up); ***tener ~*** be in a hurry *o* rush; ***a toda ~*** as fast *o* as quickly as possible; ***de ~*** fast, quickly; ***correr ~*** be urgent; ***meter ~ a alguien*** hurry s.o. along, make s.o. hurry
prisión *f* prison, jail
◇ **prisión de alta seguridad** high-security prison; **prisión incomunicada** solitary confinement, solitary F; **prisión preventiva** preventive detention
prisionero **I** *adj* captive **II** *m*,**-a** *f* prisoner; ***caer ~*** be taken prisoner
◇ **prisionero de guerra** prisoner of war, POW
prisma *m* prism
prismáticos *mpl* binoculars
prístino *adj* pristine
priva *f Esp* F booze F; ***dar a la ~*** hit the bottle
privacidad *f* privacy
privación *f acción* deprivation; ***sufrir privaciones*** sufffer privation(s) *o* hardship
privado **I** *part* ☞ ***privar*** **II** *adj* private; ***en ~*** in private
privar ⟨1a⟩ **I** *v/t*: ***~ a alguien de algo*** deprive s.o. of sth **II** *v/i* F: ***me priva la cer-***

veza I love beer; ***le privan los coches*** he's mad about cars F, he's car-mad F; **privarse** *v/r* deprive o.s.; ***~ de algo*** deprive o.s. of sth, go without sth
privatización *f* privatization
privatizar ⟨1f⟩ *v/t* privatize
privilegiado **I** *adj* **1** (*favorecido*) privileged **2** (*excelente*) exceptional **II** *m*, **-a** *f* privileged person; ***los ~s*** the privileged
privilegiar ⟨1b⟩ *v/t* **1** (*dar un privilegio a*) grant a privilege to **2** (*dar importancia a*) favor, *Br* favour
privilegio *m* privilege
pro **I** *prp* for, in aid of; ***en ~ de*** for **II** *m* pro; ***los ~s y los contras*** the pros and cons; ***hombre de ~*** worthy *o* upright man
proa *f* MAR bow, prow; ***poner ~ a*** set course for
probabilidad *f* probability
probable *adj* probable, likely; ***es ~ que venga*** she'll probably come
probador *m* fitting room
probar ⟨1m⟩ **I** *v/t* **1** *teoría* test, try out **2** (*comer un poco de*) taste, try; (*comer por primera vez*) try **3** (*justificar*) prove **II** *v/i* try; ***~ a hacer*** try doing; **probarse** *v/r* try on
probeta *f* test tube
problema *m* problem; ***sin ~*** without difficulty, without any problems
problemático *adj* problematic
procaz *adj* lewd, indecent
procedencia *f* origin, provenance
procedente *adj*: ***~ de*** from; ***el tren ~ de Bogotá*** the train from Bogota
proceder ⟨2a⟩ **I** *v/i* **1** (*venir*) come (***de*** from) **2** (*actuar*) proceed; ***~ a*** proceed to; ***~ contra alguien*** initiate proceedings against s.o. **3** (*ser conveniente*) be fitting **II** *m* conduct
procedimiento *m* **1** (*proceso*) procedure, method **2** JUR proceedings *pl*
procesado *m*, **-a** *f* accused, defendant
procesador *m* INFOR processor
◇ **procesador de textos** word processor
procesal *adj* JUR *costos* legal; *derecho* procedural
procesamiento *m* **1** INFOR processing **2** JUR prosecution
◇ **procesamiento de textos** word processing
procesar ⟨1a⟩ *v/t* **1** INFOR process **2** JUR prosecute
procesión *f* procession; ***la ~ va por dentro*** *fig* he's / she's putting on a brave front
procesionaria *f* ZO processionary moth
proceso *m* **1** (*procedimiento*) process; ***~ de paz*** peace process **2** JUR trial **3** INFOR: ***~ de datos / textos*** data / word processing
proclama *f* proclamation
proclamación *f* proclamation
proclamar ⟨1a⟩ *v/t* **1** (*decir públicamente*) proclaim **2** (*revelar*) show; **proclamarse** *v/r* (*anunciar públicamente*) proclaim o.s.; ***~ campeón del mundo*** be crowned world champion; ***~ vencedor*** achieve victory
proclive *adj* given (***a*** to)
procreación *f* breeding, procreation *fml*
procrear ⟨1a⟩ **I** *v/i* breed, procreate *fml* **II** *v/t* breed
procurador *m*, **-a** *f* JUR attorney, lawyer
procurador de justicia *Méx* attorney general
procurar ⟨1a⟩ *v/t* try; ***procura no llegar tarde*** try not to be late; **procurarse** *v/r* secure
prode *m Arg* sports lottery, *Br* football pools *pl*
prodigar ⟨1h⟩ *v/t* be generous with; ***~ algo a alguien*** *atenciones* lavish sth on s.o.; **prodigarse** *v/r* (*aparecer*) be seen in public; ***no se prodiga mucho por aquí*** you don't see much of him around here
prodigio *m* **1** *suceso* wonder, miracle **2** *persona* prodigy; ***niño ~*** child prodigy
prodigioso *adj* prodigious
pródigo **I** *adj* **1** (*generoso*) generous **2** (*derrochador*) extravagant; ***el hijo ~*** the prodigal son **II** *m*, **-a** *f* spendthrift
producción *f* production
◇ **producción en serie** mass production
producir ⟨3o⟩ *v/t* **1** (*crear*) produce **2** (*causar*) cause; **producirse** *v/r* happen, occur; ***se produjo un ruido tremendo*** there was a tremendous noise
productividad *f* productivity
productivo *adj* **1** *metodo*, *mañana* pro-

P

ductive **2** *empresa* profitable
producto *m* product; **~ *acabado*** finished product
◇ **producto bruto interno** *Rpl* gross domestic product; **producto bruto nacional** *Rpl* gross national product; **producto interior bruto** gross domestic product; **producto nacional bruto** gross national product
productor I *adj* producing *atr*; ***país ~ de petróleo / café*** oil-producing / coffee-producing country, oil / coffee producer **II** *m*, **~a** *f* producer
◇ **productos de belleza** beauty products; **productos manufacturados** manufactured goods, manufactures; **productos químicos** chemicals
produjo *vb* ☞ ***producir***
produzco *vb* ☞ ***producir***
proemio *m* (*prólogo*) preface
proeza *f* feat, exploit
profana *f* laywoman
profanación *f* desecration
profanar ⟨1a⟩ *v/t* defile, desecrate
profano I *adj fig* lay *atr* **II** *m* layman
profe *m/f* F teacher
profecía *f* prophecy
proferir ⟨3i⟩ *v/t* **1** *palabras, sonidos* utter **2** *insultos* hurl
profesar ⟨1a⟩ *v/t* **1** REL profess **2** *fig*: *admiración* feel, have
profesión *f* profession; ***la ~ más antigua del mundo*** the oldest profession in the world
◇ **profesión de fe** profession of faith
◇ **profesión liberal** profession
profesional I *adj* professional **II** *m/f* professional
◇ **profesional liberal** professional
profesionalidad *f* professionalism
profesionista *m/f Méx* professional
profesor *m*, **~a** *f* teacher; *de universidad* professor, *Br* lecturer; ***~ de educación infantil*** kindergarten teacher
◇ **profesor particular** private teacher *o* tutor
profesorado *m* faculty, *Br* staff *pl*
profeta *m* prophet; ***nadie es ~ en su tierra*** no-one is a prophet in his own country
profético *adj* prophetic
profetizar ⟨1f⟩ *v/t* prophesy
profiláctico I *adj* preventive, prophylactic *fml* **II** *m* condom
profilaxis *f* prophylaxis
prófugo *m*, **-a** *f* **1** JUR fugitive **2** MIL deserter
profundidad *f* depth; ***en ~*** *analizar* in depth; ***tener dos metros de ~*** be two meters deep
profundizar ⟨1f⟩ *v/i*: ***~ en algo*** go into sth in depth
profundo *adj cavidad* deep; *pensamiento, persona* profound, deep
profusión *f* profusion, abundance; ***con gran ~ de*** with an abundance of
profuso *adj* abundant, plentiful
progenitor *m*, **~a** *f* ancestor; ***~es*** *pl* parents
programa *m* **1** TV, RAD program, *Br* programme; ***~ de mano*** *de concierto* program, *Br* programme **2** INFOR program **3** EDU syllabus, curriculum
◇ **programa de estudios** syllabus, curriculum
programable *adj* programmable
programación *f* **1** RAD, TV programs *pl*, *Br* programmes *pl* **2** INFOR programming
programador *m*, **~a** *f* programmer
programar ⟨1a⟩ *v/t* **1** *aparato* program, *Br* programme **2** INFOR program **3** (*planear*) schedule
progre *adj* F trendy
progresar ⟨1a⟩ *v/i* progress, make progress
progresión *f* progression
progresista *m/f* & *adj* progressive
progresivamente *adv* progressively
progresivo *adj* progressive
progreso *m* progress
prohibición *f* ban (***de*** on)
prohibido *adj* forbidden
prohibir ⟨3a⟩ *v/t* forbid; *oficialmente* ban; ***~ a alguien hacer algo*** forbid s.o. to do sth; ***prohibido fumar*** no smoking
prohibitivo *adj precio* prohibitive
prohijar ⟨1a⟩ *v/t* adopt
prohombre *m* great man
prójimo *m* fellow human being
prolapso *m* MED prolapse
prole *f* offspring
prolegómeno *m fml* (*prefacio*) preface
proletariado *m* proletariat
proletario I *adj* proletarian **II** *m*, **-a** *f* proletarian
proliferación *f* proliferation

P

proliferar ⟨1a⟩ *v/i* proliferate
prolífico *adj* prolific
prolijidad *f* long-windedness, prolixity *fml*
prolijo *adj* **1** (*extenso*) long-winded, prolix *fml* **2** (*minucioso*) detailed **3** *Rpl*: *limpio* tidy
prologar ⟨1h⟩ *v/t* write the preface for
prólogo *m* preface
prolongación *f* extension; **~ *del plazo*** extension of the deadline
prolongado *adj* prolonged, lengthy
prolongar ⟨1h⟩ *v/t* extend, prolong; **prolongarse** *v/r* **1** *en tiempo* go *o* carry on **2** *en espacio* extend
promediar ⟨1a⟩ **I** *v/t* average out **II** *v/i* reach halfway; ***promediaba el año*** halfway *o* midway through the year
promedio *m* average; ***como** o **en ~*** on average; **~ *de bateo*** batting average
promesa *f* promise; **~ *electoral*** election promise
prometedor *adj* bright, promising
prometer ⟨2a⟩ *v/t* promise; **prometerse** *v/r* get engaged; **~ *algo*** promise o.s. sth; ***prometérselas (muy) felices*** F have high hopes
prometida *f* fiancée
prometido **I** *part* ☞ **prometer** **II** *adj* engaged **III** *m* fiancé
prominencia *f* prominence
prominente *adj* prominent
promiscuidad *f* promiscuity
promiscuo *adj* promiscuous
promoción *f* **1** *en empresa* promotion **2** EDU class, *Br* year **3** DEP play-offs *pl*
◇ **promoción de ventas** COM sales promotion
promocional *adj* promotional
promocionar ⟨1a⟩ *v/t* promote
promontorio *m* promontory
promotor *m*, **~a** *f* promoter
◇ **promotor inmobiliario** (property) developer
◇ **promotor de ventas** sales representative, sales rep F
promover ⟨2h⟩ *v/t* **1** (*fomentar*) promote **2** (*causar*) provoke, cause
promulgación *f* promulgation
promulgar ⟨1h⟩ *v/t* *ley* promulgate
pronombre *m* GRAM pronoun
◇ **pronombre demostrativo** demonstrative pronoun
pronominal *adj* GRAM pronominal
pronosticar ⟨1g⟩ *v/t* forecast
pronóstico *m* MED prognosis; ***sus heridas son de ~ reservado*** the hospital is making no statement about his injuries; **~ *del tiempo*** weather forecast; ***contra todo ~*** against all odds
prontitud *f* promptness
pronto **I** *adj* **1** prompt; ***por lo** o **de ~*** for now, for the moment **2** *Rpl*: *preparado* ready
II *adv* **1** (*dentro de poco*) soon; ***tan ~ como*** as soon as; ***lo más ~ posible*** as soon as possible; ***¡hasta ~!*** see you soon!; ***más ~ o más tarde*** sooner or later **2** (*temprano*) early; ***de ~*** suddenly; ***eso se dice ~*** that's easy for you / him *etc* to say, that's easily said
III *m* F: ***le dio un ~ y dejó el trabajo*** he left his job on impulse; ***tiene unos ~s de celos inaguantables*** he has fits of unbearable jealousy
pronunciación *f* pronunciation
pronunciamiento *m* **1** JUR *de sentencia* passing **2** (*rebelión*) military uprising
pronunciar ⟨1b⟩ *v/t* **1** *palabra* pronounce **2** (*decir*) say; **~ *un discurso*** give a speech; JUR **~ *sentencia*** pass judgment; **pronunciarse** *v/r* **1** (*rebelarse*) rise up, revolt **2** (*declararse*): **~ *a favor / en contra de algo*** declare o.s. *o* come out in favor of / against sth
propagación *f* spread
propaganda *f* **1** *de producto* advertising **2** POL propaganda
propagar ⟨1h⟩ *v/t* spread; **propagarse** *v/r* spread
propano *m* propane
propasarse ⟨1a⟩ *v/r* go too far
propensión *f* tendency (***a*** to); ***tiene ~ a la gripe*** he tends to catch flu easily
propenso *adj* prone (***a*** to); ***ser ~ a hacer*** be prone to do, have a tendency to do
propiamente *adv* exactly; **~ *dicho*** strictly speaking
propiciar ⟨1b⟩ *v/t* **1** (*favorecer*) promote **2** (*causar*) bring about
propicio *adj* favorable, *Br* favourable ***ser ~ para*** be favorable to
propiedad *f* property; ***ser ~ de alguien*** be s.o.'s property
◇ **propiedad horizontal** condominium; **propiedad industrial** industrial property; **propiedad intelectual** intel-

P

lectual property; **propiedad pública** public ownership
propietario *m*,**-a** *f* owner; ***ser ~ de*** be the owner of
propina *f* tip; ***de ~*** as a tip; *fig* (*por añadidura*) on top
propinar ⟨1a⟩ *v/t golpe*, *paliza* give
propio *adj* **1** (*de uno mismo*) own **2** (*característico*) characteristic (***de*** of), typical (***de*** of) **3** (*adecuado*) suitable (***para*** for); ***hacer lo ~*** do the right *o* appropriate thing **4**: ***la -a directora*** the director herself
proponer ⟨2r; *part* ***propuesto***⟩ *v/t* propose, suggest; ***el hombre propone y Dios dispone*** man proposes and God disposes;**proponerse** *v/r*: ***~ hacer algo*** decide to do sth, make up one's mind to do sth
proporción *f* proportion; ***en ~ a*** in proportion to
proporcionado *adj*: ***bien ~*** well-proportioned; ***~ a*** proportionate to
proporcional *adj* proportional
proporcionalmente *adv* proportionally
proporcionar ⟨1a⟩ *v/t* (*suministrar*) provide, supply; *satisfacción* give
proposición *f* proposal, suggestion; ***~ de matrimonio*** proposal of marriage
propósito *m* **1** (*intención*) intention **2** (*objetivo*) purpose **3**: ***a ~*** on purpose; (*por cierto*) by the way; ***a ~ de*** about; ***venir muy a ~*** *de comentario* be spot on, hit the nail on the head
propuesta *f* proposal; ***a ~ de*** at the suggestion of
propuesto *part* ☞ ***proponer***
propugnar ⟨1a⟩ *v/t* advocate
propulsar ⟨1a⟩ *v/t* TÉC propel; *fig* promote
propulsión *f* TÉC propulsion
◇ **propulsión a chorro, propulsión por reacción** jet propulsion
propulsor **I** *m* (*motor*) engine **II** *m*,**~a** *f* promoter
prorrata *f* share; ***a ~*** pro rata, on a pro rata basis
prórroga *f* DEP overtime, *Br* extra time
prorrogable *adj plazo* extendable
prorrogar ⟨1h⟩ *v/t plazo* extend
prorrumpir ⟨3a⟩ *v/i* burst (***en*** into)
prosa *f* prose
prosaico *adj* mundane, prosaic
proscenio *m* TEA proscenium
proscribir ⟨3a; *part* ***proscrito***⟩ *v/t* **1** (*prohibir*) ban, proscribe *fml* **2** (*desterrar*) banish, exile
proscrito *part* ☞ ***proscribir***
proseguir ⟨3d & 3l⟩ **I** *v/t* carry on, continue **II** *v/i* continue (***con*** with)
proselitismo *m* proselytism
prospección *f* **1** MIN prospecting **2** COM study, survey; ***~ de mercado*** market research
prospectar ⟨1a⟩ *v/t* **1** *terreno* prospect **2** *fig*: *mercado* research, test
prospectiva *f* forecast
prospectivo *adj* future *atr*, prospective
prospecto *m* **1** *de medicamento* directions for use *pl* **2** *de propaganda* leaflet
prosperar ⟨1a⟩ *v/i* prosper, thrive
prosperidad *f* prosperity; ***~ económica*** (economic) prosperity
próspero *adj* prosperous, thriving; ***¡ ~ año nuevo!*** Happy New Year!
próstata *f* prostate
prostíbulo *m* brothel
prostitución *f tb fig* prostitution; ***~ infantil*** child prostitution
prostituir ⟨3g⟩ *v/t* prostitute; **prostituirse** *v/r* prostitute o.s.
prostituta *f* prostitute
prostituto *m* male prostitute
protagonismo *m*: ***tener ~*** occupy center stage *o Br* centre stage; ***afán de ~*** longing to be in the limelight
protagonista *m/f* **1** *personaje* main character **2** *actor, actriz* star; ***papel de ~*** leading role **3** *de una hazaña* hero; *mujer* heroine
protagonizar ⟨1f⟩ *v/t* **1** *película* star in, play the lead in **2** *incidente* play a leading role in
protección *f* protection; ***~ solar*** suntan lotion *o* cream, sunblock
◇ **protección de datos** data protection;**protección del medio ambiente** environmental protection, protection of the environment; **protección de menores** child protection
proteccionismo *m* protectionism
protector **I** *adj* protective **II** *m*,**~a** *f* protector; ***~ labial*** lip salve
protectorado *m* protectorate
proteger ⟨2c⟩ *v/t* protect (***de*** from); **protegerse** *v/r* protect *o* defend o.s.
protegeslip *m* panty liner

protegida *f* protégée
protegido **I** *adj* protected **II** *m* protégé
proteico *adj* **1** BIO protein *atr* **2** *lit*: *persona* protean
proteína *f* protein
protésico *m*,**-a** *f*: **~ *dental*** dental technician
prótesis *f* prosthesis; **~ *auditiva*** hearing aid; **~ *dental*** *o* ***dentaria*** denture, false tooth / teeth
protesta *f* **1** protest **2** *Méx promesa* promise; ***cumplir con su* ~** keep one's promise
protestante *m/f* & *adj* Protestant
protestantismo *m* Protestantism
protestar ⟨1a⟩ **I** *v/t* protest **II** *v/i* **1** (*quejarse*) complain (***por, de*** about) **2** (*expresar oposición*) protest (***contra, por*** about, against)
protestón **I** *adj* grouchy **II** *m*, **-ona** *f* grouch
protocolario *adj* established by protocol; *como requiere* required by protocol
protocolo *m* protocol
protón *m* proton
protoplasma *m* BIO protoplasm
prototipo *m* TÉC prototype
protuberancia *f* protuberance
prov. *abr* (= ***provincia***) province
provecho *m* benefit; ***¡buen ~!*** enjoy (your meal)!; ***sacar ~ de*** benefit from; ***de ~*** useful
provechoso *adj* beneficial, useful
provecto *adj fml* advanced; ***edad -a*** advanced age
proveedor *m*,**~a** *f* supplier; **~ *de*** (***acceso a***) ***Internet*** Internet Service Provider, ISP
proveer ⟨2e; *part* ***provisto***⟩ *v/t* supply; **~ *a alguien de algo*** supply s.o. with sth; **proveerse** *v/r* equip o.s. (***de*** with)
provenir ⟨3s⟩ *v/i* come (***de*** from)
proverbial *adj* proverbial
proverbio *m* proverb
providencia *f* providence; ***tomar ~s*** take precautions
provincia *f* province
provincial **I** *adj* provincial **II** *m* REL provincial
provincianismo *m desp* provincialism, provincial attitudes *pl*
provinciano **I** *adj* provincial **II** *m*, **-a** *f* provincial
provisión *f* COM provision; **~ *de fondos*** provision of funds; ***provisiones*** *pl* (*alimentos*) provisions
provisional *adj* provisional, temporary
provisionalidad *f* provisional nature, temporary nature
provisorio *adj S.Am.* provisional
provisto **I** *part* ☞ ***proveer*** **II** *adj*: **~ *de*** equipped with
provocación *f* **1** (*incitación*) provocation **2** *de parto* induction
provocador **I** *adj* provocative **II** *m*,**~a** *f* agitator
provocar ⟨1g⟩ *v/t* **1** cause **2** *el enfado* provoke **3** *sexualmente* lead on **4** *parto* induce **5**: ***¿te provoca un café?*** *S.Am.* how about a coffee?
provocativo *adj* provocative
proxeneta *m* pimp
proxenetismo *m* procuring
próximamente *adv* shortly
proximidad *f* proximity
próximo *adj* **1** (*siguiente*) next; ***el ~ año*** next year; ***¡hasta la -a!*** see you next time! **2** (*cercano*) near, close (***a*** to)
◇ **Próximo Oriente** Near East
proyección *f* **1** MAT, PSI projection **2** *de película* showing
proyeccionista *m/f* projectionist
proyectar ⟨1a⟩ *v/t* **1** *luz, imagen* project **2** (*planear*) plan **3** *película* show **4** *sombra* cast
proyectil *m* missile
proyectista **I** *m/f* designer **II** *m* draftsman, *Br* draughtsman **III** *f* draftswoman, *Br* draughtswoman
proyecto *m* **1** (*plan*) plan; ***tener en ~ hacer algo*** plan to do sth **2** *trabajo* project
◇ **proyecto de ley** bill
proyector *m* projector; **~ *de transparencias*** slide projector
prudencia *f* caution, prudence; ***con ~*** cautiously, prudently
prudencial *adj* **1** (*aproximado*) rough, approximate **2** (*moderado*) modest
prudente *adj* careful, cautious
prueba *f* **1** *tb* TIP proof; ***en ~ de*** as proof of; ***dar ~s de*** prove, give proof of **2** JUR piece of evidence; ***por falta de ~s*** for lack of evidence **3** DEP event **4** EDU test; **~ *de acceso*** *o* ***admisión*** entrance exam **5** *resistencia*: ***a ~ de bala*** bulletproof; ***a ~ de agua*** waterproof; ***a ~ de aire*** airtight; ***a ~ de fuego*** fireproof; ***a ~ de choques*** shock-resistant; ***poner***

P

algo a ~ put sth to the test
◇ **prueba de alcoholemia** drunkometer test, *Br* Breathalyzer® test; **prueba de aptitud** aptitude test; **prueba nuclear** nuclear test
prurito *m* itching
P.S. *abr* (= ***postscriptum*** (***posdata***)) PS (= postscript)
pseudo... *pref* pseudo-
pseudónimo *m* pseudonym
psicoanálisis *f* (psycho)analysis
psicoanalista *m/f* (psycho)analyst
psicodélico *adj* psychedelic
psicodrama *m* psychodrama
psicofármaco *m* psychoactive drug
psicología *f* psychology
psicológico *adj* psychological
psicólogo *m*, **-a** *f* psychologist
psicópata *m/f* psychopath
psicopatía *f* psychopathy
psicosis *f inv* psychosis
◇ **psicosis colectiva** mass hysteria
◇ **psicosis maniacodepresiva** manic-depressive psychosis
psicosomático *adj* psychosomatic
psicoterapeuta *m/f* psychotherapist
psicoterapia *f* psychotherapy
psique *f* psyche
psiquiatra *m/f* psychiatrist
psiquiatría *f* psychiatry
psiquiátrico **I** *adj* psychiatric **II** *m* psychiatric hospital
psíquico *adj* psychic
PSOE *m abr* (= ***Partido Socialista Obrero Español***) Spanish Socialist Workers Party
psoriasis *f* MED psoriasis
P.V.P. *abr* (= ***precio de venta al público***) RRP (= recommended retail price)
pta *abr* (= ***peseta***) peseta
ptas *abr* (= ***pesetas***) pesetas
púa *f* **1** ZO spine, quill **2** MÚS plectrum, pick **3** *de alambre* barb
pub *m* bar
púber *adj* pubescent, adolescent
pubertad *f* puberty
pubiano, púbico *adj* ANAT pubic
pubis *m inv* ANAT pubis
publicación *f* publication
publicar ⟨1g⟩ *v/t* publish; **publicarse** *v/r* come out, be published
publicidad *f* **1** (*divulgación*) publicity **2** COM advertising; ***hacer ~*** advertise; ***dar ~ a algo*** publicize *o* advertise sth **3** (*anuncios*) advertisements *pl*
◇ **publicidad directa** direct advertising
◇ **publicidad encubierta** surreptitious advertising
publicista *m/f* advertising executive
publicitar ⟨1a⟩ *v/t* advertise, publicize
publicitario **I** *adj* advertising *atr* **II** *m*, **-a** *f* advertising executive
público **I** *adj* public; *escuela* public, *Br* state; ***hacer ~*** make public, announce; ***hacerse ~*** become public *o* known **II** *m* public; TEA audience; DEP spectators *pl*, crowd; ***el gran ~*** the general public; ***en ~*** in public
publirreportaje *m* advertorial, advertising feature
pucherazo *m* F vote rigging
puchero *m* GASTR (cooking) pot; ***hacer ~s*** *fig* pout
pucho *m S.Am.* P cigarette butt, *Br* fag end F; ***no valer un ~*** be completely worthless
pude *vb* ☞ ***poder***
pudendo *adj*: ***partes -as*** pudenda *pl*, private parts
pudibundez *f* prudishness
pudibundo *adj* prudish
púdico *adj* modest
pudiente *adj* (*poderoso*) powerful; (*rico*) wealthy
pudín *m* pudding
pudo *vb* ☞ ***poder***
pudor *m* modesty
pudoroso *adj* modest
pudrir ⟨3a⟩ *v/t* rot; **pudrirse** *v/r* rot; ***~ de envidia*** be green with envy
pueblerino *desp* **I** *adj* provincial, small-town **II** *m*, **-a** *f* hick *desp*, *Br* yokel *desp*
pueblero *m*, **-a** *f L.Am.* villager; *de pueblo más grande* townsperson
pueblo *m* village; *más grande* town; ***es de ~*** he's a country boy; *desp* he's a hick *o Br* yokel *desp*
puedo *vb* ☞ ***poder***
puente *m* bridge; ***hacer ~*** *have a day off between a weekend and a public holiday*; ***hacer el ~*** DEP do a bridge; ***hacer un ~ a un coche*** hot-wire a car; ***tender un ~*** *tb fig* build a bridge
◇ **puente aéreo** AVIA shuttle service; MIL airlift; **puente colgante** suspension bridge; **puente levadizo** drawbridge; **puente de mando** MAR bridge

puenting *m* bungee jumping
puerca *f* ZO sow; *fig* F slut F
puerco I *adj* dirty; *fig* filthy F **II** *m* **1** ZO pig; *fig persona* slob **2** *Méx: cerdo* pork
◇ **puerco espín** porcupine
puericultor *m*, **~a** *f* childcare specialist
puericultura *f* childcare
pueril *adj* childish, puerile
puerilidad *f* childishness, *fml* puerility
puerro *m* BOT leek
puerta *f* **1** *en pared* door; *en valla* gate; ***a ~ cerrada*** JUR in camera; ***por la ~ grande*** *fig* in triumph; ***estar a la ~*** *o* ***en ~s*** be very near; ***abrir la(s) ~(s) a algo*** *fig* open one's doors to sth; ***dar ~ a alguien*** F show s.o. the door; ***dar a alguien con la ~ en las narices*** *tb fig* slam the door in s.o.'s face; ***de ~ en ~*** *mendigando* door to door; ***de ~s (para) adentro*** in private, behind closed doors; ***de ~s (para) afuera*** in public
2 DEP goal; ***disparos a ~*** shots on goal
◇ **puerta atrás** *en baloncesto* backdoor play; **puerta corrediza** sliding door; **puerta de embarque** gate; **puerta falsa** secret door; **puerta giratoria** revolving door; **puerta de servicio** service entrance, *Br* tradesman's entrance; **puerta trasera** back door
puerto *m* **1** MAR port; ***tomar ~*** arrive in port; ***llegar a buen ~*** *tb fig* arrive safely **2** GEOG pass **3** INFOR port
◇ **puerto marítimo** seaport
◇ **puerto pesquero** fishing port
Puerto Rico *m* Puerto Rico
puertorriqueño I *adj* Puerto Rican **II** *m*, **-a** *f* Puerto Rican
pues *conj* **1** well; ***~ bien*** well; ***¡~ sí!*** of course! **2** *fml* (*porque*) as, since
puesta *f*: ***~ al día*** update; ***~ en libertad*** freeing
◇ **puesta en escena** TEA staging; **puesta en marcha** launch; *de central nuclear* commissioning; **puesta a punto** tune-up; **puesta de sol** sunset; **puesta en servicio** launch; *de central nuclear* commissioning
puestero *m*, **-a** *f L.Am.* market trader, *Br* stallholder
puesto I *part* ☞ ***poner***; ***bien ~*** well-dressed **II** *m* **1** *lugar* place **2** *en mercado* stand, stall **2** MIL post **III** *conj*: ***~ que*** since, given that
◇ **puesto de policía** police post; **puesto de socorro** first aid station; **puesto de trabajo** job
pufo *m* F con F, trick
púgil *m* boxer
pugilato *m* boxing
pugna *f* **1** (*oposición*) conflict; ***estar en ~ con*** be in conflict with **2** (*lucha*) struggle
pugnar ⟨1a⟩ *v/i* fight (***por*** for; ***por hacer*** to do)
puja *f* **1** (*lucha*) struggle **2** *en subasta* bid
pujante *adj empresa, economía* booming
pujanza *f de empresa, economía* strength
pujar ⟨1a⟩ *v/i* **1** (*luchar*) struggle **2** *en subasta* bid
pulcritud *f* **1** *apariencia* immaculate appearance **2** (*esmero*) extreme care
pulcro *adj* **1** (*aseado*) immaculate **2** (*esmerado*) extremely careful
pulga *f* ZO flea; ***tener malas ~s*** *fig* F be bad-tempered
pulgada *f* inch
pulgar *m* thumb
pulgón *m* ZO aphid, *Br* greenfly
pulido I *adj tb estilo* polished **II** *m acción* polishing; *efecto* polish
pulidora *f* buffer
pulimentar ⟨1a⟩ *v/t* polish
pulir ⟨3a⟩ *v/t* polish; *fig* F (*mejorar*) polish (up) F
pulla *f* gibe
pulmón *m* lung; ***respirar a pleno ~ en la montaña*** breathe in the clean mountain air
pulmonar *adj* pulmonary, lung *atr*
pulmonaria *f* BOT lungwort
pulmonía *f* MED pneumonia
pulpa *f* pulp
pulpería *f L.Am.* mom-and-pop store, *Br* corner shop
pulpero *m*, **-a** *f S.Am.* storekeeper, shopkeeper
púlpito *m* pulpit
pulpo *m* **1** ZO octopus **2** *m/f Esp* F (*persona pegajosa*) clingy person
pulque *m Méx* pulque (*alcoholic drink made from cactus*)
pulquería *f Méx* pulque bar
pulsación *f* **1** (*latido*) beat **2** *al escribir a máquina* key stroke
pulsador *m* TÉC button
pulsar ⟨1a⟩ *v/t botón, tecla* press

pulsera *f* bracelet
pulsión *f* drive, impulse
pulso *m* **1** pulse; ***tomar el ~ a alguien*** take s.o.'s pulse; ***tomar el ~ a algo*** *fig* take the pulse of sth **2** *fig* steady hand; ***tener buen ~*** have a steady hand **3**: ***echar un ~ a alguien*** *tb fig* armwrestle s.o.; ***ganarse algo a ~*** earn sth (by one's own efforts)
pulular ⟨1a⟩ *v/i* mill around
pulverización *f* **1** *de líquido* spraying **2** *de sólido* pulverization, crushing
pulverizador *m* spray
pulverizar ⟨1f⟩ *v/t* **1** *líquido* spray **2** (*convertir en polvo*) pulverize, crush **3** *argumentación* demolish
¡pum! *int* bang!
puma *m* ZO puma, mountain lion
¡pumba! *int* bang! crash!, kapow!
puna *f L.Am.* **1** GEOG high Andean plateau **2** MED altitude sickness
pundonor *m* pride
pundonoroso *adj* honorable, *Br* honourable
punible *adj* punishable; ***... es un acto ~*** ... calls for disciplinary action
punitivo *adj* punitive
punk I *adj* punk *atr* **II** *m/f* punk
punki *m/f* F punk
punta *f* **1** *de dedo, nariz, pie* tip **2** (*extremo*) end; ***de ~ a ~*** (*de principio a fin*) from beginning to end; (*de un extremo a otro*) from one extreme to the other **3** *de lápiz*, GEOG point; ***sacar ~ a*** sharpen **4** *L.Am.* (*grupo*) group **5**: ***a ~ de pistola*** at gunpoint; ***ir de ~ en blanco*** be dressed up **6** *en fútbol* forward
puntada *f* **1** *con aguja* stitch **2** (*indirecta*) hint
puntapié *m* kick; ***tratar a ~s*** *fig* treat badly
puntazo *m* TAUR jab; ***el concierto fue un ~*** P the concert was real cool P
puntera *f* toe
puntería *f* aim; ***tener buena / mala ~*** be a good / bad shot
puntero I *adj* leading **II** *m* pointer
puntiagudo *adj* pointed, sharp
puntilla *f*: ***de ~s*** on tippy-toe, *Br* on tip-toe; ***ponerse de ~s*** stand on tippy-toe
puntillismo *m* PINT pointillism
puntilloso *adj* particular, punctilious *fml*
punto *m* **1** point; ***~ por ~*** point by point; ***ganar por ~s*** win on points
2 *señal* dot; ***en ~*** on the dot; ***a las tres en ~*** at three sharp, at three on the dot
3 *signo de punctuación* period, *Br* full stop; ***dos ~s*** colon; ***~ y coma*** semicolon; ***con ~s y comas*** *fig* in full detail; ***poner ~ final a algo*** *fig* end sth, put an end to sth; ***y ~*** period; ***poner los ~s sobre las íes*** F make things crystal clear; ***empresa ~.com*** dot.com (company)
4 *en costura, sutura* stitch; ***hacer ~*** knit; ***de ~*** knitted
5: ***a ~*** (*listo*) ready; (*a tiempo*) in time ***llegar a ~ para ...*** arrive just in time to ...; ***estar a ~*** be ready; ***estar a ~ de*** be about to; ***el arroz está en su ~*** the rice is ready; ***poner a ~*** TÉC tune; ***puesta a ~*** tune-up
6 *alcance*: ***hasta cierto ~*** up to a point; ***hasta qué ~*** to what extent; ***me pregunto hasta qué ~ lo que dice es verdad o una exageración*** I wonder how much of what he says is true and how much is exaggeration; ***hasta tal ~ que*** to such an extent that
7: ***batir las claras a ~ de nieve*** beat the egg whites until they form stiff peaks
◇ **punto de congelación** freezing point; **punto de cruz** cross stitch; **punto débil** weak point; **punto fatídico** *en fútbol* penalty spot; **punto final** period, *Br* full stop; **punto flaco** weak point; **punto de fusión** melting point; **punto muerto** AUTO neutral; **punto de partida** starting point; **punto de recogida** pickup point; **punto de referencia** reference point; **punto de reunión** meeting place; **punto de sutura** stitch, suture; **punto de venta** point of sale; **punto de vista** point of view; **puntos suspensivos** suspension points
puntuación *f* punctuation; DEP score; EDU grade, mark
puntual *adj* punctual
puntualidad *f* punctuality
puntualización *f* clarification, further point
puntualizar ⟨1f⟩ *v/t* **1** (*señalar*) point out **2** (*aclarar*) clarify
puntuar ⟨1e⟩ *v/t* **1** GRAM punctuate **2** (*calificar*) grade, mark
punzada *f* sharp *o* stabbing pain
punzante *adj* stinging; *fig* (*mordaz*) biting, incisive

punzar ⟨1f⟩ *v/t fig* (*molestar*) torment
puñado *m* handful; ***a ~s*** by the handful; ***había … a ~s*** there were loads of … F
puñal *m* dagger; ***poner a alguien el ~ en el pecho*** *fig* put a gun to s.o.'s head
puñalada *f* stab wound; ***matar a ~s*** stab to death; ***ser una ~*** *fig* hurt; ***vaya ~*** that hurts
puñeta *f*: ***¡~(s)!*** F for heaven's sake! F; ***hacer la ~ a alguien*** F give s.o. a hard time F; ***en la quinta ~*** P in the boondocks F
puñetazo *m* punch; ***dar un ~*** punch
puñetero P **I** *adj* damn F, damned F, *Br* bloody P; ***no seas ~*** stop being such a damn pain F **II** *m*, **-a** *f* jerk F
puño *m* **1** *de mano* fist; ***de su ~ y letra*** in his / her very own handwriting **2** *de camisa* cuff **4** *de bastón, paraguas* handle; *de espada* hilt **5**: ***es una verdad como un ~*** F you never spoke a truer word
pupa *f* **1** ZO pupa **2** *en labio* cold sore; ***hacerse ~*** *lenguaje infantil* hurt o.s.
pupila *f* pupil
pupilente *m Méx* contact lens
pupilo *m*, **-a** *f* pupil
pupitre *m* desk
pupusa *f L.Am.* filled dumpling
puramente *adv* purely
purasangre *m* thoroughbred
puré *m* purée; *sopa* cream; ***~ de patatas*** *o* ***papas*** *L.Am.* mashed potatoes
pureza *f* purity
purga *f* POL purge
purgaciones *f pl* MED F gonorrh(o)ea
purgante *m/adj* purgative, laxative
purgar ⟨1h⟩ *v/t* MED, POL purge; **purgarse** *v/r* take a laxative
purgatorio *m* REL purgatory
puridad *f*: ***en ~*** (*claramente*) plainly; (*en realidad*) strictly speaking
purificación *f* purification
purificador I *adj* purifying **II** *m* purifier ◇ **purificador de aire** air filter, air purifier
purificar ⟨1g⟩ *v/t* purify
purista I *adj* purist **II** *m/f* purist
puritano I *adj* puritanical **II** *m*, **-a** *f* puritan
puro I *adj* **1** pure; ***la -a verdad*** the honest truth **2** *casualidad, coincidencia* sheer; ***de ~ miedo*** out of sheer fright **3** *Méx* (*único*) sole, only; ***te sirven la -a comida*** they just serve food **II** *m* cigar
púrpura I *adj*: (***de color***) ***~*** purple **II** *f* purple
purpúreo *adj* purple
pus *m* pus
puse *vb* ☞ ***poder***
pusilánime *adj* fainthearted
puso *vb* ☞ ***poder***
pústula *f* MED pustule
puta *f* P whore; ***ir(se) de ~s*** P go whoring
putada *f* P dirty trick; ***¡qué ~!*** shit! P
putativo *adj* putative
putear ⟨1a⟩ *v/t L.Am.* P swear at; ***~ alguien*** *Esp* give s.o. a hard time, make life difficult for s.o.
putero *m* P whoremonger
puticlub *m* red-light bar, pick up joint F
puto *adj* P goddamn F, *Br* bloody F; ***de -a madre*** P great F, fantastic F; ***las he pasado -as*** P I've been to hell and back F; ***no tener ni -a idea*** P not have a damned clue F
putrefacción *f* putrefaction
putrefacto, pútrido *adj* putrid
puya *f* **1** TAUR *point of the picador's lance* **2** *fig* gibe
puyazo *m* **1** TAUR *jab with the lance* **2** *fig* gibe
puzzle *m* jigsaw (puzzle)
PVC *m abr* (= ***cloruro de polivinilo***) PVC (= polyvinyl chloride)
PYMES *fpl abr* (= ***pequeñas y medianas empresas*** SMES (= small and medium-sized enterprises)
pza. *abr* (= ***plaza***) sq (= square)

P

Q

q.e.p.d. *abr* (= ***que en paz descanse***) RIP (= requiescat in pace, rest in peace)
qué I *adj & pron interr* what; ***¿~ pasó?*** what happened?; ***¿~ día es?*** what day is it?; ***¿~ vestido prefieres?*** which dress do you prefer?; ***¿de ~ estás hablando?*** what are you talking about?; ***¿~ hubo?*** *C.Am., Méx* how are things? **II** *adj & pron interj*: ***¡~ moto!*** what a motorbike!; ***¡~ de flores!*** what a lot of flowers! **III** *adv*: ***¡~ alto es!*** he's so tall!; ***¡~ bien!*** great!; ***¡~ ruido!*** what a noise!; ***¡y ~!*** so what?; ***¿a mí ~?*** so what?; ***un no sé ~*** a thingamajig; ***el ~ dirán*** what people say
que I *pron rel sujeto*: *persona* who, that; *cosa* which, that; *complemento*: *persona* that, whom *fml*; *cosa* that, which; ***el coche ~ ves*** the car you can see, the car that *o* which you can see; ***el ~*** the one that; ***la ~*** the one that; ***lo ~*** what **II** *conj* that; ***lo mismo ~ tú*** the same as you; ***¡~ entre!*** tell him to come in; ***¡~ descanses!*** sleep well; ***¡~ sí!*** I said yes; ***¡~ no!*** I said no; ***es ~ …*** the thing is …; ***yo ~ tú*** if I were you; ***¡~ no se repita!*** make sure it doesn't happen again!; ***¡~ me pase esto a mí!*** I can't believe this is happening to me!; ***eso sí ~ no*** definitely not!; ***alguno ~ otro*** the odd
quebrada *f L.Am.* stream
quebradero *m*: ***~s de cabeza*** *pl* F headaches
quebradizo *adj* brittle
quebrado I *adj* broken **II** *m* MAT fraction
quebrantahuesos *m inv* ZO lammergeier
quebrantamiento *m* breaking
quebrantar ⟨1a⟩ *v/t ley, contrato* break; *fig* break, undermine; **quebrantarse** *v/r* be broken, be undermined
quebranto *m* suffering
quebrar ⟨1k⟩ **I** *v/t* break **II** *v/i* COM go bankrupt; **quebrarse** *v/r* break
quedar ⟨1a⟩ *v/i* **1** (*permanecer*) stay; ***esto queda entre nosotros*** this is just between us; ***~ cerca*** be nearby **2** *en un estado* be; ***quedó sin resolver*** it remained unresolved, it wasn't sorted out; ***¿cómo quedó?*** how did it end up?; ***queda por hacer*** it still has *o* needs to be done **3** (*sentar*): ***te queda bien / mal*** *de estilo* it suits you / doesn't suit you; *de talla* it fits you / doesn't fit you **4** (*sobrar*) be left; ***¿queda mucho tiempo?*** is there much time left?; ***no queda nada*** *de tiempo* time's almost up; *distancia* it's not far now **5** (*encontrarse*): ***~ con alguien*** F arrange to meet (with) s.o.; ***¿dónde habíamos quedado?*** where had we arranged to meet? **6** (*acordar*): ***~ en algo*** agree to sth; ***¿en qué quedamos?*** what did we agree? **7**: ***por mí que no quede*** it's fine by me
quedarse *v/r* **1** stay **2** *en un estado*: ***~ ciego*** go blind; ***~ sin dinero*** run out of money; ***~ contento*** be happy; ***~ atrás*** be left behind **3** (*apropiarse*): ***~ con algo*** keep sth **4**: ***me quedé sin comer*** I ended up not eating
quedo *vb* ☞ ***quedar***
quehaceres *mpl* tasks
queja *f* complaint; ***no tener ~ de alguien*** have no complaints about s.o.
quejarse ⟨1a⟩ *v/r* **1** complain (***a*** to; ***de*** about) **2** *de dolor* moan, groan
quejica F **I** *adj* whining F **II** *m/f* crybaby
quejido *m* moan, groan
quejigo *m* BOT gall oak, dyer's oak
quejumbroso *adj* moaning
quema *f* burning
quemada *f Méx* burn
quemado *adj* **1** burnt; ***oler a ~*** smell of burning; ***~ por el sol*** sunburnt; ***estar ~*** *fig* be burned out **2** *Méx* (*desvirtuado*) discredited
quemador *m* TÉC burner
quemadura *f* burn
◇ **quemadura de sol, quemadura solar** sunburn
quemar ⟨1a⟩ **I** *v/t* **1** burn **2** *con agua* scald **3** F *recursos* use up; *dinero* blow F **II** *v/i* be very hot; **quemarse** *v/r* **1**

burn o.s.; *de tostada, papeles* burn; *fig* get burned out **2** *Méx* (*desvirtuarse*) become discredited
quemarropa: ***a ~*** *tb fig* point-blank
quemazón *f* burning
quena *f S.Am.* Indian flute
quepis *m* kepi
quepo *vb* ☞ ***caber***
queque *m L.Am.* cake
queratina *f* keratin
querella *f* JUR lawsuit
querellante *m/f* JUR plaintiff
querellarse ⟨1a⟩ *v/r* JUR bring a lawsuit (***contra*** against)
querer[1] ⟨2u⟩ *v/t* **1** (*desear*) want; ***quisiera …*** I would like …; ***quieras que no …*** like it or not …; ***sin ~*** unintentionally
2 (*amar*) love; ***~ bien a alguien*** be fond of s.o.; ***~ mal a alguien*** not care for s.o.; ***por lo que más quieras*** for pity's sake, for the love of God
3 (*esperar*): ***¡qué más quieres!*** what more do you want *o* expect!; ***¿qué quieres que*** (***le***) ***haga?*** what do you expect me to do?
4: ***~ decir*** mean; ***quiere decir*** it means; ***¡que si quieres!*** *irón* no way!
5: ***como quiera que*** however
querer[2] *m* love
querido I *part* ☞ ***querer* II** *adj* dear **III** *m*, **-a** *f* darling
querosén *m L.Am.* kerosene
queroseno *m* kerosene
querrá *vb* ☞ ***querer***
querría *vb* ☞ ***querer***
querubín *m* cherub
quesadilla *f* quesadilla (*folded tortilla*)
quesera *f* cheese dish
quesería *f* cheese store
quesero *m*, **-a** *f* cheese maker
queso *m* cheese; ***dársela a alguien con ~*** F fool s.o. F
◇ **queso azul** blue cheese; **queso de bola** *cheese similar to Edam*; **queso fundido** melted cheese; **queso rallado** grated cheese; **queso para untar** cheese spread
quetzal *m* FIN quetzal
quicio *m*: ***sacar de ~ a alguien*** F drive s.o. crazy F
quid *m*: ***el ~ de la cuestión*** the nub of the question
quiebra *f* COM bankruptcy; *fig* bankruptcy, failure; ***declararse en ~*** file for *o* declare bankruptcy
quiebro I *vb* ☞ ***quebrar* II** *m* feint
quien *pron rel sujeto* who, that; *objeto* who, whom *fml*, that; ***no soy ~ para hacerlo*** I'm not the right person to do it; ***hay ~*** there are people; ***no hay ~ lo haga*** nobody can do it; ***la mujer con ~ llegó*** the woman he arrived with; ***~ más*** (***y***) ***~ menos*** some more, (and) some less
quién *pron* who; ***¿~ es?*** who is it?; ***¿a ~ viste?*** who did you see?; ***¿~es son estas personas?*** who are those people?; ***¿de ~ es este libro?*** whose is this book?, who does this book belong to?; ***¿con ~ has hablado?*** who have you spoken to?
quienquiera *pron* whoever
quiero *vb* ☞ ***querer***
quieto *adj* still; ***¡estáte ~!*** keep still!
quietud *f* peacefulness
quihubo *interj C.Am., Méx* how are things?
quijada *f* ANAT jawbone
quijote *m* idealist
quijotesco *adj* quixotic
quilate *m* carat
quilla *f* keel
quilo *m* ☞ ***kilo***
quilombo *m* **1** *Arg* F whorehouse **2** *fig* mess F
quimera *f* pipe dream
quimérico *adj* chimerical
química *f* chemistry
químico I *adj* chemical; ***productos -s*** chemicals **II** *m*, **-a** *f* chemist
quimioterapia *f* MED chemotherapy
quimio *m* MED chemo, chemotherapy
quimono *m* kimono
quina *f* BOT cinchona bark; ***tragar ~*** F grin and bear it F
quincalla *f* junk
quince *adj* fifteen; ***dentro de ~ días*** in two weeks
quinceañero I *adj* teenage **II** *m*, **-a** *f* teenager
quincena *f* two weeks, *Br tb* fortnight
quincenal *adj* bimonthly, *Br tb* fortnightly
quincuagenario I *adj* fifty-year-old **II** *m*, **-a** *f person in his / her fifties*
quiniela *f lottery where the winners are decided by soccer results*, *Br* football

pools *pl*
quinielista *m/f person who plays the sports lottery*, *Br person who does the football pools*
quinientos *adj* five hundred
quinina *f* quinine
quinqué *m* kerosene lamp, *Br* oil lamp
quinquenal *adj* five-yearly
quinquenio *m* five-year period
quinta *f* MIL draft, *Br* call-up; ***es de mi ~*** he's my age
quintaesencia *f* quintessence
quintal *m* (short) hundredweight, *Br* a hundred pounds
◇ **quintal métrico** a hundred kilos
quinteto *m* MÚS quintet
quintillizos *mpl* quintuplets
quinto I *adj* fifth **II** *m* **1** fifth **2** MIL conscript **3** (*botellín*) bottle of beer
quintuplicar ⟨1g⟩ *v/t* quintuple
quíntuplo I *adj* quintuple **II** *m* quintuple; ***el ~ de algo*** five times sth
quiosco *m* kiosk; *de prensa* newsstand, *Br* newsagent's; *de flores* flower stall
quiosquero *m*, **-a** *f* newspaper vendor
quirófano *m* operating room, *Br* operating theatre
quiromancia, quiromancía *f* palmistry
quiromántico *m*, **-a** *f* palmist, palm reader
quiromasaje *m* massage
quiropráctica *f* chiropractic
quiropráctico *m*, **-a** *f* chiropractor
quirúrgico *adj* surgical
quise *vb* ☞ ***querer***
quisiera *vb* ☞ ***querer***
quiso *vb* ☞ ***querer***
quisque F: ***todo ~*** everyone and his brother F, *Br* the world and his wife F; ***cada ~*** everybody
quisquilla *f* ZO shrimp
quisquilloso *adj* touchy
quiste *m* MED cyst
quitaesmalte *m* nail varnish remover
quitamanchas *m inv* stain remover
quitamiedos *m inv* safety barrier
quitanieves *m* snowplow, *Br* snowplough
quitar ⟨1a⟩ **I** *v/t ropa* take off, remove; *obstáculos* remove; ***~ el polvo*** dust; ***~ algo a alguien*** take sth (away) from s.o.; ***~ la mesa*** clear the table; ***de quita y pon*** F removable **II** *v/i*: ***¡quita!*** get out of the way!; **quitarse** *v/r* **1** *ropa*, *gafas* take off **2** (*apartarse*) get out of the way; ***~ algo / a alguien de encima*** get rid of s.th / s.o.; ***¡quítate de en medio!*** F get out of the way!
quitasol *m* sunshade
quite *m* **1** TAUR *movement to draw the bull away* **2** *en esgrima* parry **3**: ***estar al ~*** *fig* be on hand to help
quiteño I *adj* of / from Quito, Quito *atr* **II** *m*, **-a** *f* native of Quito
quizá(s) *adv* perhaps, maybe
quórum *m* quorum; ***alcanzar el ~*** have a quorum

R

rabadilla *f* ANAT coccyx
rabanillo, rabanito *m* BOT wild radish
rábano *m* BOT radish; ***me importa un ~*** F I don't give a damn F
rabia *f* MED rabies *sg*; ***dar ~ a alguien*** make s.o. mad; ***¡qué ~!*** how annoying!; ***tener ~ a alguien*** have it in for s.o.
rabiar ⟨1b⟩ *v/i* **1**: ***~ de dolor*** be in agony; ***hacer ~ a alguien*** *fig* F jerk s.o.'s chain F, pull s.o.'s leg F; ***~ por*** be dying for **2** F: ***aplaudir a ~*** applaud like crazy F; ***me gusta a ~*** I'm crazy about him F
rabieta *f* tantrum
rabillo *m* **1** BOT stalk **2**: ***~ del ojo*** corner of one's eye; ***mirar con el ~ del ojo*** look out of the corner of one's eye
rabino *m* rabbi
rabioso *adj* **1** MED rabid **2** *fig* F furious; ***de -a actualidad*** highly topical
rabo *m* tail; ***irse** o **salir con el ~ entre las piernas*** F leave with one's tail between one's legs; ***queda el ~ por desollar*** *fig* F the worst is yet to come
rabón *adj L.Am. animal* short-tailed
rabona *f Rpl* F: ***hacerse la ~*** play hooky F, play truant
rabudo *adj* **1** F (*engreído*) bigheaded **2** *animal* long-tailed

racanear ⟨1a⟩ *v/i* F be a tightwad F *o* skinflint F
racanería *f* stinginess
rácano I *adj* F stingy F, mean **II** *m*, **-a** *f* tightwad F, skinflint F
RACE *m abr* (= ***Real Automóvil Club de España***) Royal Spanish Automobile Club
racha *f* spell; ***buena / mala ~*** F good / bad spell
racheado *adj* gusty
racial *adj* racial; ***odio ~*** racial hatred
racimo *m* bunch
raciocinio *m* reason
ración *f* **1** *de problemas, culpa etc* share **2** (*porción*) serving, portion
racional *adj* rational
racionalidad *f* rationality
racionalismo *m* rationalism
racionalista I *adj* rationalistic **II** *m/f* rationalist
racionalización *f* rationalization
racionalizar ⟨1f⟩ *v/t* rationalize
racionamiento *m* rationing
racionar ⟨1a⟩ *v/t* ration
racismo *m* racism
racista *m/f* & *adj* racist
rada *f* MAR roadstead
radar *m* radar; ***control por ~*** radar control; *de tráfico* radar check
radarista *m/f* radar operator
radiación *f* radiation; ***de baja ~*** low-radiation
◇ **radiación solar** solar radiation
radiactividad *f* radioactivity
radiactivo *adj* radioactive
radiador *m* radiator
radial *adj* radial
radiante *adj* radiant
radiar ⟨1b⟩ *v/t* radiate
radicación *f* **1** *de costumbre, vicio etc* roots *pl* **2** MAT extraction
radical I *adj* radical **II** *m/f persona* radical **III** *m* GRAM, MAT root
radicalismo *m* radicalism
radicalizar ⟨1f⟩ *v/t* radicalize
radicar ⟨1g⟩ *v/i* stem (***en*** from), lie (***en*** in); **radicarse** *v/r* settle
radiestesista *m/f* water dowser
radio I *m* **1** MAT radius; ***en un ~ de*** within a radius of **2** QUÍM radium **3** *L.Am.* radio **II** *f* radio
◇ **radio de acción** range; **radio despertador** clock radio; **radio de giro** AUTO lock, turning circle
radioaficionado *m*, **-a** *f* radio ham
radiobaliza *f* MAR, AVIA radio beacon
radiocasete *m* radio cassette player
radiocomunicación *f* radio communication
radiodespertador *m* radioalarm
radiodiagnóstico *m* X-ray diagnosis
radiodifusión *f* broadcasting
radioescucha *m/f* listener
radiofaro *m* MAR, AVIA radio beacon
radiofonía *f* radio
radiofónico *adj* radio *atr*
radiografía *f* X-ray
radiografiar ⟨1c⟩ *v/t* X-ray
radiología *f* radiology
radiológico *adj* radiological
radiólogo *m*, **-a** *f* radiologist
radiomensaje *m* radio message
radiopatrulla *f* radio patrol car
radioscopia *f* MED X-ray
radiosonda *f* radiosonde
radiotaxi *m* radio taxi
radiotecnia *f* radio technology
radiotécnico *m*, **-a** *f* radio technician
radiotelefonía *f* radio telephony
radioteléfono *m* radio telephone
radiotelegrafía *f* radio telegraphy
radiotelegrafista *m/f* radio operator
radiotelevisado *adj* broadcast
radioterapia *f* radiotherapy
radiotransmisor *m* radio transmitter
radioyente *m/f* listener
radón *m* radon
RAE *f abr* (= ***Real Academia Española***) Royal Spanish Academy
raedera *f utensilio* scraper
raedura *f* scraping
raer ⟨2z⟩ *v/t* scrape
ráfaga *f de viento* gust; *de balas* burst; ***~ de luz*** blaze of light
rafia *f* raffia
rafting *m* rafting
ragú *m* GASTR ragout
raído *adj* threadbare
raigambre *m* BOT, *fig* roots *pl*; ***de honda ~*** *fig* deep-rooted
rail, raíl *m* rail
raíz *f* **1** root; ***echar raíces*** *de persona* put down roots; *de costumbre* take root; ***arrancar de ~*** pull up by the root; ***cortar algo de ~*** *fig* nip sth in the bud; ***a ~ de*** as a result of **2** MAT: ***~ cuadrada / cúbica*** square / cube root

raja *f* **1** (*rodaja*) slice **2** (*corte*) cut **3** (*grieta*) crack
rajar ⟨1a⟩ **I** *v/t* **1** *fruta* cut, slice **2** *cerámica* crack **3** *neumático* slash **II** *v/i* F gossip; **rajarse** *v/r fig* F back out F
rajadura *f* crack
rajatabla: ***a ~*** strictly, to the letter
ralea *f desp*: ***de la misma ~*** as bad as each other
ralentí *m*: ***al ~*** AUTO idling; FOT in slow motion
ralentizar ⟨1f⟩ *v/t* slow down
rallador *m* grater
rallar ⟨1a⟩ *v/t* GASTR grate
ralladura *f*: ***~ de limón*** grated lemon rind
rally(e) *m* rally
rama *f* **1** branch; ***andarse por las ~s*** beat about the bush; ***canela en ~*** stick cinnamon **2** POL wing
ramaje *m* branches *pl*
ramal *m* branch
ramalazo *m* fit
rambla *f* **1** promenade, boulevard **2** *de río* dry riverbed
ramera *f* whore, prostitute
ramificación *f* ramification
ramificarse ⟨1g⟩ *v/r* branch out
ramillete *m* bunch
ramo *m* **1** COM sector **2**: ***~ de flores*** bunch of flowers
ramoso *adj* with a lot of branches
rampa *f* ramp
◇ **rampa de lanzamiento** launch pad
ramplón *adj* vulgar
ramplonería *f* vulgarity
rana *f* ZO frog; ***salir ~*** F be a let-down; ***cuando la(s) ~(s) críe(n) pelo*** *fig* not in a month of Sundays
ranchera *f typical Mexican song*
ranchero **I** *adj* **1**: ***canción -a*** romantic ballad; ***música -a*** *music of northern Mexico* **2** *Méx* F (*tímido*) shy **II** *m*, **-a** *f L.Am.* rancher
rancho *m* **1** *Méx* small farm **2** *L.Am.* (*barrio de chabolas*) shanty town **3**: ***hacer ~ aparte*** *fig* keep o.s. to o.s.
rancio *adj* rancid; *fig* ancient
rango *m* rank; ***de alto ~*** high-ranking
ranking *m* ranking
ranúnculo *m* BOT buttercup
ranura *f* slot
rapaces *fpl* ZO birds of prey, raptors
rapapolvo *m* F telling-off F; ***echar un ~ a alguien*** tell s.o. off
rapar ⟨1a⟩ *v/t pelo* crop
rapaz **I** *adj* predatory; ***ave ~*** bird of prey **II** *m*, **-a** *f* F kid F
rape *m pescado* anglerfish; ***al ~*** *pelo* cropped
rapé *m* snuff
rapel *m* DEP rappel; ***descender a*** *o* ***en ~*** rappel down
rapidez *f* speed, rapidity
rápido **I** *adj* quick, fast **II** *m* rapids *pl*
rapiña *f* pillage; ***ave de ~*** bird of prey
raposa *f* ZO vixen
rappel *m* ☞ ***rapel***
rapsodia *f* rhapsody
raptar ⟨1a⟩ *v/t* kidnap
rapto *m* kidnap
raptor *m*, **~a** *f* kidnapper
raqueta *f* **1** DEP racket **2** *de nieve* snowshoe
raquis *m* ANAT rachis, spine
raquítico *adj fig* rickety
raquitismo *m* MED rickets *sg*
raramente *adv* seldom, rarely
rareza *f* rarity
raro *adj* **1** rare **2** (*extraño*) strange; ***¡qué ~!*** how strange!
ras *m*: ***a ~ de tierra*** at ground level; ***a ~ de*** level with
rasante *adj vuelo* low; ***cambio de ~*** brow of a hill
rasca *f L.Am.* ***pegarse una ~*** F get plastered F
rascacielos *m inv* skyscraper
rascado *adj L.Am.* F plastered F
rascar ⟨1g⟩ *v/t* scratch; *superficie* scrape, scratch; ***~ el chelo*** scrape away at the cello; **rascarse** *v/r* **1** scratch o.s. **2** *L.Am.* (*emborracharse*) get drunk
rasero *m*: ***medir por el mismo ~*** treat equally
rasgado *adj boca* wide; ***ojos ~s*** almond-shaped eyes
rasgar ⟨1h⟩ *v/t* tear (up); **rasgarse** *v/r* scratch o.s.
rasgo *m* feature; ***a grandes ~s*** broadly speaking
rasgón *m* rip, tear
rasguear ⟨1a⟩ *v/t guitarra* strum
rasguñar ⟨1a⟩ *v/t* scratch
rasguño *m* scratch
raso **I** *adj* flat, level; ***soldado ~*** private **II** *m* **1** *material* satin **2**: ***al ~*** in the open air
raspa *f* **1** *de pescado* (fish)bone **2** *L.Am.*

(*reprimanda*) telling-off
raspado *m* **1** *Méx* water ice **2** MED D and C
raspadura *f* scrape; **~ *de limón*** grated lemon rind
raspar ⟨1a⟩ **I** *v/t* **1** *tb* MED scrape **2** *con lija* sand **II** *v/i* be scratchy
raspón, rasponazo *m* scratch, graze
rasposo *adj tejido* rough, scratchy
rasqueta *f* scraper
rastra *f*: ***entrar a ~s*** drag o.s. in, crawl in; ***llevar a ~s*** drag, drag along; ***sacar a alguien a ~s*** drag s.o. out
rastreador *adj*: ***perro ~*** tracker dog
rastrear ⟨1a⟩ **I** *v/t* **1** *persona* track **2** *bosque, zona* comb **II** *v/i* rake
rastrero *adj* mean, low; ***planta -a*** creeper
rastrillo *m* **1** *para jardín* rake **2** (*mercadillo*) flea market **3** *Méx*: *para rasurarse* razor
rastro *m* **1** street market **2** (*huella*) trace; ***desaparecer sin dejar ~*** vanish without trace; ***seguir el ~ a alguien*** follow s.o.'s trail
rastrojo *m* stubble
rasurado *m L.Am.* shave
rasurar ⟨1a⟩ *v/t L.Am.* shave; **rasurarse** *v/r* shave
rata I *f* ZO rat; ***más pobre que las ~s*** *o* ***una ~*** poor as a church mouse **II** *m/f* F rat F
ratear ⟨1a⟩ *v/t* F swipe, *Br tb* pinch F
ratero *m*, **-a** *f* petty thief
raticida *m* rat poison
ratificación *f* ratification
ratificar ⟨1g⟩ *v/t* POL ratify; **ratificarse** *v/r*: **~ *en*** reaffirm
rato *m* **1** time, while; ***~s libres*** spare time *sg*; ***al poco ~*** after a short time *o* while; ***todo el ~*** all the time; ***a ~s*** at times, from time to time; ***a ~s perdidos*** now and again; ***a cada ~*** always; ***un buen ~*** a good while, a pretty long time; ***pasar el ~*** pass the time; ***he pasado un buen / mal ~*** I've had a great / an awful time; ***¡hasta otro ~!*** see you later!
2 (*mucho*): ***hay para ~*** there is a lot to do; ***saber un ~ largo de algo*** know a lot about sth
ratón *m* ZO, INFOR mouse
◇ **ratón de biblioteca** *fig* F bookworm
ratonera *f* mouse trap; *fig* trap
raudal *m*: ***tienen dinero a ~es*** they've got loads of money F
raudo *adj* swift
raya *f* **1** line; ***a*** *o* ***de ~s*** striped; ***pasarse de la ~*** overstep the mark, go too far; ***mantener*** *o* ***tener a ~*** keep under control; ***poner alguien a ~*** make s.o. toe the line; ***tres en ~*** tic-tac-toe, *Br* noughts and crosses **2** GRAM dash **3** ZO ray **4** *de pelo* part, *Br* parting **5** *de pantalón* crease **6** *de droga* line
◇ **raya diplomática** pin stripe
rayado *adj disco, superficie* scratched
rayano *adj* bordering (***en*** on)
rayar ⟨1a⟩ **I** *v/t* **1** *coche* scratch **2** (*tachar*) cross out **3** *Méx cobrar*: **~ *a alguien*** pay s.o. **II** *v/i* **1** border (***en*** on), verge (***en*** on) **2** *Méx cobrar* get paid; **rayarse** *v/r* get scratched
rayo *m* **1** FÍS ray; **~ *de luz*** *de sol* ray of sunlight, sunbeam **2** METEO (bolt of) lightning; ***como un ~*** *fig* like a streak of lightning; ***echar ~s*** F fume, be furious; ***oler a ~s*** smell terrible, stink to high heaven
◇ **rayo láser** laser beam; **rayos ultravioleta** ultraviolet rays; **rayos X** X-rays
rayón *m* rayon
rayuela *f juego de niños* hopscotch
raza *f* **1** *humana* race **2** *de animal* breed; ***de ~*** pedigree *atr* **3** *Méx* F *gente* gang F
razón *f* **1** reason; ***sin ~*** for no reason; ***~ de más*** all the more reason; ***con mucha ~*** with good reason **2**: ***tener ~*** be right; ***dar la ~ a alguien*** admit that s.o. is right **3** (*sentido común*): ***entrar en ~*** see sense; ***hacer entrar a alguien en ~*** make s.o. see sense; ***perder la ~*** lose one's mind **4** (*causa*): ***en ~ a*** *o* ***de*** because of; ***por razones de edad*** on the grounds of age **5**: ***a ~ de*** *precio* at
◇ **razón de ser** raison d'être
◇ **razón social** registered name
razonable *adj precio* reasonable
razonado *adj* reasoned
razonamiento *m* reasoning
razonar ⟨1a⟩ **I** *v/i* reason **II** *v/t* think, reason
RDSI *abr* (= ***Red Digital de Servicios Integrados***) ISDN (= Integrated Services Digital Network)
reabierto *part* ☞ ***reabrir***
reabrir ⟨3a; *part* ***reabierto***⟩ *v/t tb* JUR

R

caso, *sesión etc* reopen
reacción *f* reaction (**a** to); ***avión a ~*** jet (aircraft)
◇ **reacción en cadena** chain reaction
reaccionar ⟨1a⟩ *v/i* react (**a** to)
reaccionario **I** *adj* reactionary **II** *m*, **-a** *f* reactionary
reacio *adj* reluctant (**a** to)
reactivación *f* COM revival, upturn
reactivar ⟨1a⟩ *v/t* COM revive
reactivo **I** *adj* reactive **II** *m* QUÍM reactant, reagent
reactor *m* **1** reactor **2** *motor* jet engine
◇ **reactor nuclear** nuclear reactor
readaptar ⟨1a⟩ *v/t* retrain; **readaptarse** *v/r* readapt, readjust
readmisión *f* readmission
readmitir ⟨3a⟩ *v/t* readmit
reafirmar ⟨1a⟩ *v/t* reaffirm; **reafirmarse** *v/r*: ***~ en** idea* reassert
reagrupación *f*, **reagrupamiento** *m* regrouping; ***~ familiar** tras guerra, exilio etc* family reunion
reagrupar ⟨1a⟩ *v/t* regroup
reajustar ⟨1a⟩ *v/t* readjust
reajuste *m* readjustment
◇ **reajuste ministerial** POL cabinet reshuffle
real **I** *adj* **1** (*regio*) royal **2** (*verdadero*) real **II** *m fig*: ***(a)sentar sus -es*** set up camp
realce *m*: ***dar ~ a algo*** highlight sth
realeza *f* royalty
realidad *f* reality; ***en ~*** in fact, in reality
◇ **realidad virtual** virtual reality
realismo *m* realism
realista **I** *adj* realistic **II** *m/f* realist
realimentación *f* ☞ ***retroalimentación***
realización *f* **1** *personal*, *de sueños* fulfillment, *Br* fulfilment **2** RAD, TV production
realizador *m*, **~a** *f de película* director; RAD, TV producer
realizar ⟨1f⟩ *v/t* **1** *tarea* carry out **2** RAD, TV produce **3** COM realize; **realizarse** *v/r de persona* fulfill o.s., *Br* fulfil o.s.
realmente *adv* really
realojamiento *m* rehousing
realojar ⟨1a⟩ *v/t* rehouse
realojo *m* rehousing
realquilado **I** *adj* sublet **II** *m* sublessee; ***ser un ~*** be subletting
realquilar ⟨1a⟩ *v/t* sublet
realzar ⟨1f⟩ *v/t* highlight
reanimación *f* revival
reanimar ⟨1a⟩ *v/t* revive; **reanimarse** *v/r* revive
reanudación *f* resumption
reanudar ⟨1a⟩ *v/t* resume
reaparecer ⟨2d⟩ *v/i* reappear
reaparición *f* reappearance
reapertura *f* reopening
rearme *m* rearming
reasegurar ⟨1a⟩ *v/t* reinsure
reaseguro *m* reinsurance
reasumir ⟨3a⟩ *v/t* reassume
reavivar ⟨1a⟩ *v/t* revive; **reavivarse** *v/r* be revived
rebaja *f* reduction; ***~s de verano / invierno*** summer / winter sale
rebajar ⟨1a⟩ *v/t precio* lower, reduce; *mercancías* reduce; *Rpl*: *peso* lose; **rebajarse** *v/r* **1** lower o.s., humble o.s. **2** *Rpl*: *adelgazar* lose weight; ***~ mucho*** lose a lot of weight
rebajamiento *m*: ***vaya ~ por su parte*** she has sunk pretty low
rebanada *f* slice
rebanar ⟨1a⟩ *v/t* slice
rebañar ⟨1a⟩ *v/t*: ***~ algo*** wipe sth clean
rebaño *m* flock
rebasar ⟨1a⟩ *v/t* **1** *Méx* AUTO pass, *Br* overtake **2** *límite* go beyond
rebatible *adj* refutable
rebatir ⟨3a⟩ *v/t razones* rebut, refute
rebato *m*: ***tocar a ~*** sound the alarm
rebeca *f* cardigan
rebeco *m* ZO chamois
rebelarse ⟨1a⟩ *v/r* rebel
rebelde **I** *adj* rebel *atr* **II** *m/f* rebel
rebeldía *f* rebelliousness; ***en ~*** JUR in absentia
rebelión *f* rebellion
reblandecer ⟨2d⟩ *v/t* soften; **reblandecerse** *v/r* go soft, soften
reblandecimiento *m* softening
rebobinar ⟨1a⟩ *v/t* rewind
rebosante *adj vaso*, *plato* overflowing, brimming; *fig* brimming
rebosar ⟨1a⟩ *v/i* overflow; ***(lleno) a ~*** full to the brim *o* to overflowing
rebotar ⟨1a⟩ **I** *v/t* **1** *pelota* bounce **2** (*disgustar*) annoy **II** *v/i* bounce, rebound
rebote *m* bounce; *contra poste etc* rebound; ***de ~*** on the rebound; ***~ defensivo / ofensivo** en baloncesto* defensive / offensive rebound
reboteador *m*, **~a** *f en baloncesto* re-

bounder
rebozar ⟨1f⟩ *v/t* GASTR coat
rebrotar ⟨1a⟩ *v/i* BOT produce new shoots; *fig* begin again
rebrote *m* BOT new shoot, *fig* new outbreak
rebujo *m* ball, mass
rebullicio *m* hubbub
rebullir ⟨3h⟩ *v/i* move; **rebullirse** *v/r* stir, move
rebuscado *adj* over-elaborate
rebuscamiento *m del lenguaje, concepto etc* overelaborate nature
rebuscar ⟨1g⟩ *v/t* AGR glean; *fig* search for
rebuznar ⟨1a⟩ *v/i* bray
rebuzno *m* bray, braying
recabar ⟨1a⟩ *v/t* gather, obtain
recadero *m*, **-a** *f* messenger
recado *m* **1** (*mensaje*) message; ***chico de los ~s*** errand boy; ***dejar un ~*** leave a message; ***dar un ~ a alguien*** give s.o. a message; ***hacer un ~*** run an errand **2** *Rpl* (*arnés*) harness
recaer ⟨2o⟩ *v/i* **1** *fig*: *de responsabilidad* fall (***en*** to) **2** MED have *o* suffer a relapse **3** JUR reoffend
recaída *f* MED relapse
recalar ⟨1a⟩ *v/i* MAR put in (***en*** at), call (***en*** at)
recalcar ⟨1g⟩ *v/t* stress, emphasize
recalcitrante *adj* recalcitrant
recalentamiento *m* overheating
recalentar ⟨1k⟩ *v/t comida* warm *o* heat up; **recalentarse** *v/r* overheat
recámara *f* **1** *de arma de fuego* chamber **2** *L.Am.* (*dormitorio*) bedroom
recambio *m* COM spare part; ***de ~*** spare; ***pieza de ~*** spare part
recapacitar ⟨1a⟩ *v/t* think over, reflect on
recapitular ⟨1a⟩ *v/t* recap
recargable *adj* rechargeable
recargado *adj* **1** *cuadro* overelaborate; *habitación* overfurnished **2** *texto* verbose
recargar ⟨1h⟩ *v/t* **1** *batería* recharge; *recipiente* refill **2**: ***~ un 5%*** charge 5% extra, add on 5%
recargo *m* surcharge
recatado *adj* **1** modest **2** (*cauto*) cautious
recato *m* **1** modesty **2** (*prudencia*) caution
recauchutado *m* retread
recauchutar ⟨1a⟩ *v/t neumáticos* retread
recaudación *f* **1** *acción* collection **2** *cantidad* takings *pl*; ***la ~ del día*** the day's takings
recaudador *m*, **~a** *f* collector
recaudar ⟨1a⟩ *v/t dinero* collect
recaudo *m*: ***poner a buen ~*** put in a safe place
recelar ⟨1a⟩ *v/t* suspect; ***~ de alguien*** not trust s.o.
recelo *m* mistrust; ***con ~*** suspiciously, warily
receloso *adj* suspicious
recensión *f* review
recepción *f* **1** *en hotel* reception **2** *en béisbol* catch
recepcionista *m/f* receptionist
receptáculo *m* receptacle
receptividad *f* receptiveness
receptivo *adj* receptive
receptor I *m* RAD,TV receiver **II** *m*, **~a** *f en béisbol* catcher
recesión *f* recession
receta *f* **1** GASTR recipe **2** MED prescription; ***sin ~*** without a prescription
recetar ⟨1a⟩ *v/t* MED prescribe
recetario *m* recipe book
rechace *m en fútbol* clearance
rechazar ⟨1f⟩ *v/t* reject; MIL repel
rechazo *m* rejection
rechifla *f* jeering, jeers *pl*
rechiflar ⟨1a⟩ *v/t* jeer; **rechiflarse** *v/r*: **~** (***de alguien***) jeer (s.o.)
rechinar ⟨1a⟩ **I** *v/i* creak, squeak **II** *v/t*: ***~ los dientes*** grind one's teeth
rechistar ⟨1a⟩ *v/i* protest; ***sin ~*** F without a murmur, without complaining
rechoncho *adj* F dumpy F
rechupete: ***de ~*** F delicious
recibidor *m* entrance hall
recibimiento *m* reception
recibir ⟨3a⟩ *v/t* receive; **recibirse** *v/r L.Am.* graduate
recibo *m* (sales) receipt; ***ser de ~*** be acceptable
reciclable *adj* recyclable
reciclado I *part* ☞ ***reciclar*** **II** *m* ☞ ***reciclaje***
reciclaje *m* recycling; ***curso de ~ profesional*** retraining course
reciclar ⟨1a⟩ *v/t tb concepto* recycle; **reciclarse** *v/r* retrain

recién *adv* **1** newly; **~ *casados*** newly-weds; **~ *nacido*** newborn; **~ *pintado*** wet paint **2** *L.Am.* (*hace poco*) recently, just; **~ *llegamos*** we only just arrived
reciente *adj* recent; ***de ~ publicación*** recently published
recientemente *adv* recently
recinto *m* **1** premises *pl* **2** *área* grounds *pl*
recio I *adj* sturdy, tough **II** *adv Méx*: ***hablar ~*** speak loudly, shout; ***no me hables ~*** don't shout at me
recipiente *m* container
reciprocidad *f* reciprocity
recíproco *adj* reciprocal; ***y a la -a*** and vice-versa
recitado *m* MÚS recital
recital *m* MÚS recital; *poético* poetry reading
recitar ⟨1a⟩ *v/t* recite
reclamación *f* **1** COM complaint **2** POL claim, demand
reclamar ⟨1a⟩ **I** *v/t* claim, demand **II** *v/i* complain
reclame *m L.Am.* advertisement
reclamo *m* **1** lure **2** *L.Am. queja* complaint **3** *L.Am. reivindicación* claim
reclinable *adj*: ***asiento ~*** reclining seat
reclinar ⟨1a⟩ *v/t* rest; **reclinarse** *v/r* lean, recline (***contra*** against)
recluir ⟨3g⟩ *v/t* imprison, confine; **recluirse** *v/r* become a recluse
reclusión *f* JUR imprisonment, confinement
◇ **reclusión perpetua** life imprisonment
recluso I *adj* reclusive; ***población -a*** prison population **II** *m*, **-a** *f* prisoner
recluta *m/f* recruit
reclutamiento *m* MIL recruitment
reclutar ⟨1a⟩ *v/t tb* COM recruit
recobrar ⟨1a⟩ *v/t* recover; **~ *el conocimiento*** regain consciousness, come around; **~ *las fuerzas*** get one's strength back; **recobrarse** *v/r* recover (***de*** from)
recodo *m* bend
recogedor *m* dustpan
recogepelotas *m/f inv* ball boy; *niña* ball girl
recoger ⟨2c⟩ *v/t* **1** pick up, collect; **~ *firmas*** collect signatures; **~ *las cartas*** collect one's mail **2** *habitación* tidy up; **~ *la mesa*** clear the table **3** AGR harvest **4** (*mostrar*) show **5**: **~ *las piernas*** lift up one's legs; **recogerse** *v/r* go home
recogida *f* **1** collection **2** AGR harvest
◇ **recogida de basuras** garbage collection, *Br* refuse collection
◇ **recogida de equipajes** AVIA baggage (re)claim
recogido *adj* **1** *habitación* tidy, neat **2** *modo de vida* quiet
recogimiento *m* meditation
recolección *f* harvest
recolectar ⟨1a⟩ *v/t* AGR harvest, bring in
recomendable *adj* recommendable
recomendación *f* recommendation; ***por ~ de*** on the recommendation of
recomendar ⟨1k⟩ *v/t* recommend
recomenzar ⟨1f & 1k⟩ *v/t* start again, begin again
recomerse *vb* ☞ ***reconcomerse***
recompensa *f* reward
recompensar ⟨1a⟩ *v/t* reward
recomponer ⟨2r; *part* ***recompuesto***⟩ *v/t* repair, mend
recompostura *f Am* repair
recompra *f* COM buyback, repurchase
recompuesto *part* ☞ ***recomponer***
reconciliación *f* reconciliation
reconciliar ⟨1b⟩ *v/t* reconcile; **reconciliarse** *v/r* make up (***con*** with), be reconciled (***con*** with)
reconcomerse ⟨2a⟩ *v/r* be consumed; **~ *de envidia*** be consumed by envy
recóndito *adj* remote
reconfortante *adj* comforting
reconfortar ⟨1a⟩ *v/t* comfort
reconocer ⟨2d⟩ *v/t* **1** recognize **2** *error* admit, acknowledge **3** *área* reconnoiter, *Br* reconnoitre **4** MED examine
reconocido *adj* grateful, obliged; ***te quedo muy ~ por …*** *fml* I am very grateful to you for…
reconocimiento *m* **1** recognition; ***en ~ a*** (*agradecimiento*) in recognition of **2** *de error* acknowledg(e)ment **3** MED examination, check-up **4** MIL reconnaissance
reconquista *f* reconquest
reconquistar ⟨1a⟩ *v/t* reconquer
reconsiderar ⟨1a⟩ *v/t* reconsider
reconstituir ⟨3g⟩ *v/t escena* reconstruct
reconstituyente *m* tonic

reconstrucción *f* reconstruction
reconstruir ⟨3g⟩ *v/t fig* reconstruct
reconvenir ⟨3s⟩ *v/i* JUR counterclaim
reconversión *f* COM restructuring
reconvertir ⟨3i⟩ *v/t* restructure
recopilación *f* compilation
recopilar ⟨1a⟩ *v/t* compile
récord I *adj* record(-breaking); ***en un tiempo ~*** in record time **II** *m* record; ***~ de taquilla*** box office record
recordar ⟨1m⟩ **I** *v/t* remember, recall; ***~ algo a alguien*** remind s.o. of sth **II** *v/i* **1**: ***si mal no recuerdo*** if my memory serves me right **2** *Méx* wake up; **recordarse** *v/r Arg, Méx* wake up
recordatorio *m* reminder
recorrer ⟨2a⟩ *v/t* **1** *distancia* cover, do; *a pie* walk; *territorio, país* go around, travel around; *camino* go along, travel along **2**: ***~ algo con la vista*** look sth over, run one's eyes over sth
recorrido *m* **1** route; ***tren de largo ~*** long-distance train **2** DEP round
recortable I *adj* cut-out-and-keep **II** *m* cutout
recortar ⟨1a⟩ *v/t* cut out; *fig* cut; *exceso* reduce, cut back on
recorte *m fig* cutback; ***~ de periódico*** cutting, clipping; ***~ salarial*** salary cut; ***~ de personal*** reduction in personnel, personnel cutback; ***~s sociales*** *pl* cutbacks in public services
recostar ⟨1m⟩ *v/t* lean
recostarse ⟨1m⟩ *v/r* lie down
recoveco *m* **1** *en casa, jardín* nook, cranny **2** *en camino* bend
recreación *f* recreation
recrear ⟨1a⟩ *v/t* recreate; **recrearse** *v/r* amuse o.s.
recreativo *adj* recreational; ***juegos ~s*** amusements; ***máquina -a*** slot machine; ***salón ~*** arcade, *Br* amusement arcade
recreo *m* **1** (*distracción*) recreation **2** EDU recess, *Br* break
recriminación *f* recrimination, reproach
recriminar ⟨1a⟩ *v/t* reproach
recrudecer ⟨2d⟩ *v/t* worsen; **recrudecerse** *v/r* intensify
recrudecimiento *m* worsening, intensification
recta *f* DEP straight; ***~ final*** *tb fig* home straight
rectal *adj* MED rectal
rectangular *adj* rectangular
rectángulo *m* rectangle; ***triángulo ~*** right-angled triangle
rectificación *f* **1** correction, rectification **2** *en baloncesto* double pump
rectificar ⟨1g⟩ *v/t* **1** *error* correct, rectify **2** *camino* straighten
rectilíneo *adj* rectilinear
rectitud *f* rectitude, probity
recto I *adj* **1** straight; ***ángulo ~*** right angle **2** (*honesto*) honest **II** *m* ANAT rectum **III** *adv*: ***seguir todo ~*** go straight ahead
rector *m* rector, *Br* vice-chancellor
rectorado *m* rector's office, *Br* vice--chancellor's office
rectoscopia *f* MED proctoscopy
recuadro *m* TIP inset, box
recubierto *part* ☞ ***recubrir***
recubrimiento *m* covering
recubrir ⟨3a; *part* **recubierto**⟩ *v/t* cover (**de** with)
recuento *m* count; ***~ de votos*** count; ***hacer el ~ de algo*** count sth
recuerdo *m* **1** memory, recollection; ***en ~ de*** in memory of **2**: ***da ~s a Luís*** give Luís my regards; ***mandar ~s a alguien*** send s.o. one's regards
recular ⟨1a⟩ *v/i* back up
recuperable *adj* recoverable
recuperación *f* **1** *tb fig* recovery **2** *en baloncesto* steal
recuperar ⟨1a⟩ *v/t* **1** *tiempo* make up **2** *algo perdido* recover, get back **3** *exámen* retake, *Br* re-sit **4** *en baloncesto* steal; **recuperarse** *v/r* recover (**de** from)
recurrente *adj* recurring, recurrent
recurrir ⟨3a⟩ **I** *v/t* JUR appeal against **II** *v/i*: ***~ a*** resort to, turn to
recurso *m* **1** JUR appeal; ***~ de apelación*** appeal **2** *material* resource; ***sin ~s*** with no means of support
◇ **recursos económicos** financial resources; **recursos energéticos** energy resources; **recursos humanos** human resources; **recursos naturales** natural resources
red *f* **1** *para pescar*, DEP *etc* net; ***echar la ~*** cast the net; ***caer en las ~es de*** *fig* fall into the clutches of **2** INFOR, *fig* network; ***la ~*** INFOR the Web; ***~ de transportes / comunicaciones*** transportation / communications network

R

◇ **red de arrastre** *en pesca* trawl net; **red barredera** trawl net; **red de carreteras** road network; **Red Digital de Servicios Integrados** Integrated Services Digital Network; **red de distribución** distribution network; **red de espionaje** spy ring; **red fija** TELEC land line network; **red ferroviaria** railroad *o Br* railway network; **red telefónica** telephone network; **red de telefonía móvil** cell phone *o Br* mobile phone network; **red vial, red viaria** road network
redacción *f* **1** *acto* writing **2** *de editorial* editorial department **3** EDU essay
redactar ⟨1a⟩ *v/t* write, compose
redactor *m*, **~a** *f* editor; **~ *jefe*** editor in chief; **~ *publicitario*** copy-writer
redada *f* raid
redaño *m* ANAT mesentery; ***tener* ~s** *fig* F have guts F
redecilla *f* hairnet
rededor *m*: ***al*** *o* ***en* ~** around; ***al* ~ *de la plaza*** around the square
redención *f* redemption
redentor *m*, **~a** *f* COM redeemer; ***el Redentor*** REL the Savior, *Br* the Saviour
redil *m* fold, enclosure; ***volver al* ~** *fig* return to the fold
redimir ⟨3a⟩ *v/t* redeem
redistribución *f* redistribution
redistribuir ⟨3g⟩ *v/t* redistribute
rédito *m* return, yield
redoblar ⟨1a⟩ *v/t* redouble; **redoblarse** *v/r* double
redoble *m* MÚS (drum)roll
redomado *adj* F total, out-and-out
redonda *f*: ***a la* ~** around, round about
redondear ⟨1a⟩ *v/t* **1** *para más* round up; *para menos* round down **2** (*rematar*) round off
redondel *m* ring
redondeo *m* rounding off
redondez *f* roundness
redondo *adj* **1** *forma* round **2** *negocio* excellent **3**: ***caer* ~** flop down; ***en* ~** *girar* around
reducción *f* **1** reduction; **~ *de empleo*** job cuts *pl*; **~ *de impuestos*** tax cut; **~ *de la jornada laboral*** shortening of the working day; **~ *de personal*** *o* ***plantilla*** cutbacks *pl*, job cuts *pl* **2** MED setting
reducido *adj precio* reduced; *espacio* small, confined
reducir ⟨3o⟩ *v/t* **1** reduce (***a*** to); *gastos* cut; **~ *personal*** cut jobs, reduce staff numbers; **~ *la marcha*** AUTO downshift, shift into a lower gear **2** MIL overcome; **reducirse** *v/r* come down (***a*** to)
reducto *m* redoubt
reductor I *adj* reducing; ***agente* ~** reducing agent **II** *m*: **~ *de velocidad*** AUTO differential
redujo *vb* → ***reducir***
redundancia *f* LING tautology
redundante *adj* redundant, tautologous
redundar ⟨1a⟩ *v/i* have an impact (***en*** on); **~ *en beneficio de*** be to the advantage of
reduplicar ⟨1g⟩ *v/t* reduplicate
reedición *f* TIP reprint
reedificación *f* rebuilding
reedificar ⟨1g⟩ *v/t* rebuild
reeditar ⟨1a⟩ *v/t* republish, reissue
reeducación *f* reeducation
reeducar ⟨1g⟩ *v/t* reeducate
reelección *f* reelection
reelegir ⟨3c & 3l⟩ *v/t* reelect
reembolsar ⟨1a⟩ *v/t* refund
reembolso *m* refund; ***contra* ~** collect on delivery, *Br* cash on delivery, COD
reemplazar ⟨1f⟩ *v/t diseño*, *máquina* replace; *persona* replace, stand in for; DEP substitute for; **~ *a alguien con alguien*** replace s.o. with s.o.
reemplazo I *m* **1** *acción* replacement **2** MIL recruit **II** *m/f persona* replacement, stand-in; DEP substitute
reencarnación *f* REL reincarnation
reencontrarse ⟨1m⟩ *v/r* meet again
reencuentro *m* reunion
reestrenar ⟨1a⟩ *v/t obra de teatro*, *película* re-release
reestreno *m* re-release
reestructuración *f* restructuring
reestructurar ⟨1a⟩ *v/t* restructure
reexpedir ⟨3l⟩ *v/t* forward
reexportación *f* reexport
reexportar ⟨1a⟩ *v/t* reexport
ref. *abr* (= ***referencia***) reference, Ref.
refacción *f L.Am.* **1** *de edificio* refurbishment **2** AUTO spare part
refectorio *m* refectory
referencia *f* **1** reference; ***hacer* ~ *a*** refer to, make reference to; ***con* ~ *a*** with reference to **2**: **~*s*** *pl* COM references
referéndum *m* referendum

referente *adj*: **~ *a*** referring to, relating to
referí *m/f L.Am.* referee
referir ⟨3i⟩ *v/t* tell, relate; **referirse** *v/r* refer (***a*** to)
refilón *m*: ***mirar de ~*** glance at
refinado I *adj tb fig* refined **II** *m* refining
refinamiento *m* refining
refinar ⟨1a⟩ *v/t* TÉC refine; **refinarse** *v/r* become more refined
refinería *f* TÉC refinery
reflectante *adj* reflecting, reflective
reflectar *vb* ☞ ***reflejar***
reflector *m* **1** *en prenda, bicicleta* reflector **2** EL spotlight
reflejar ⟨1a⟩ *v/t tb fig* reflect; **reflejarse** *v/r* be reflected
reflejo I *adj* reflex *atr* **II** *m* **1** *acción, movimiento* reflex; ***tener buenos ~s*** have good reflexes **2** *imagen* reflection
reflexión *f* reflection, thought
reflexionar ⟨1a⟩ *v/t* reflect on, ponder
reflexivo *adj* GRAM reflexive
reflexología *f* reflexology
reflexoterapia *f* reflexology
reflotar ⟨1a⟩ *v/t* COM refloat
reflujo *m* ebb
reforestación *f* reforestation
reforestar ⟨1a⟩ *v/t* reforest
reforma *f* **1** reform; ***~ educativa / tributaria*** education / tax reform **2**: ***~s*** *pl* (*obras*) refurbishment *sg*; (*reparaciones*) repairs
reformador I *adj* reform *atr* **II** *m*, **~a** *f* reformer
reformar ⟨1a⟩ *v/t* **1** *ley, organización* reform **2** (*reparar*) repair; *edificio* refurbish; **reformarse** *v/r* mend one's ways, reform
reformatorio *m* reform school, reformatory
reformismo *m* POL reformism
reformista I *adj* reformist, reform *atr* **II** *m/f* reformer
reforzamiento *m* reinforcement
reforzar ⟨1f & 1m⟩ *v/t estructura, idea* reinforce; *vigilancia* increase, step up; **reforzarse** *v/r* be reinforced
refracción *f* FÍS refraction
refractario *adj* TÉC heat-resistant, fireproof; *fig* ***ser ~ a algo*** be against sth
refrán *m* saying
refranero *m* book of sayings
refregar ⟨1h & 1k⟩ *v/t* scrub; ***~ algo en las narices de alguien*** *fig* F rub s.o.'s nose in sth
refrenar ⟨1a⟩ *v/t* restrain, contain
refrendar ⟨1a⟩ *v/t* **1** *documento* countersign **2** *decisión* approve
refrendo *m* **1** *firma* countersignature **2** *aprobación* approval
refrescante *adj* refreshing
refrescar ⟨1g⟩ **I** *v/t* **1** *tb fig* refresh **2** *conocimientos* brush up **II** *v/i* cool down; **refrescarse** *v/r* cool down
refresco *m* soda, *Br* soft drink
refriega *f* MIL clash, skirmish
refrigeración *f* **1** *de alimentos* refrigeration **2** *aire acondicionado* air-conditioning **3** *de motor* cooling
refrigerador *m* refrigerator
refrigerante *m para motor* coolant; *para frigorífico* refrigerant
refrigerar ⟨1a⟩ *v/t* **1** *alimentos* refrigerate **2** *motor* cool
refrigerio *m* snack
refrito *m* **1** GASTR: ***un ~ de pimiento y cebolla*** fried peppers and onions **2** *fig* rehash
refuerzo *m* reinforcement; ***~s*** *pl* MIL reinforcements
refugiado *m*, **-a** *f* refugee
refugiarse ⟨1b⟩ *v/r* take refuge
refugio *m* refuge; ***buscar ~*** look for shelter, seek refuge
◇ **refugio antiaéreo** air-raid shelter
◇ **refugio atómico** nuclear fallout shelter
refulgente *adj* dazzling
refunfuñar ⟨1a⟩ *v/i* grumble
refunfuñón I *adj* grouchy, grumpy **II** *m*, **-ona** *f* grouch, grump
refutar ⟨1a⟩ *v/t* refute
regable *adj* irrigable; ***zona ~*** irrigated land
regadera *f* **1** *para plantas* watering can; ***estar como una ~*** F be nuts F **2** *Méx* (*ducha*) shower
regadío *m*: ***tierra de ~*** irrigated land
regalado *adj* very cheap; ***a precio ~*** at giveaway prices
regalar ⟨1a⟩ *v/t*: ***~ algo a alguien*** give sth to s.o., give s.o. sth; ***~ el oído*** *o* ***los oídos con*** delight one's ears with
regaliz *m* BOT licorice, *Br* liquorice
regalo *m* gift, present; ***~ para los ojos*** sight for sore eyes; ***~ para los oídos*** delight to the ear; ***es un ~*** it's dead cheap;

~ *publicitario* free gift
regañadientes: ***a* ~** reluctantly
regañar ⟨1a⟩ **I** *v/t* tell off **II** *v/i* quarrel
regañina *f* F telling off
regaño *m* scolding, telling off
regar ⟨1h & 1k⟩ *v/t plantas* water; AGR irrigate; *fig* (*inundar*) flood; **~*la*** *Méx* F put one's foot in it
regata *f* **1** DEP regatta **2** (*reguera*) irrigation channel *o* ditch
regate *m* DEP sidestep, *Br* dummy
regatear ⟨1a⟩ **I** *v/t* **1** COM haggle over; ***no* ~ *esfuerzos*** spare no effort **2** DEP sidestep, *Br* dummy **II** *v/i* DEP sidestep, *Br* dummy
regatista *m/f* competitor (*in a sailing or rowing race*)
regazo *m* lap
regencia *f* regency
regeneración *f* regeneration
regenerar ⟨1a⟩ *v/t* regenerate; **regenerarse** *v/r* **1** *de persona* reform **2** *de zona* be regenerated
regentar ⟨1a⟩ *v/t* **1** *negocio* run, manage **2** *cargo* hold
regente *m/f* **1** regent **2** *Méx*: *de ciudad* mayor
regicida *m/f* regicide
regicidio *m* regicide
regidor I *adj* governing, ruling **II** *m*, **~*a*** *f* TEA stage manager
régimen *m* **1** POL regime **2** MED diet; ***estar a* ~** be on a diet; ***poner a* ~** put on a diet **3** (*programa*): ***preso en* ~ *abierto*** JUR prisoner in an open prison **4** (*normativa*): **~ *fiscal*** tax regime
regimiento *m* MIL regiment
regio *adj* **1** regal, majestic **2** *S.Am.* F (*estupendo*) great F, fantastic F
región *f* region; **~ *lumbar*** ANAT lumbar region
regional *adj* regional
regionalismo *m* regionalism
regionalista *m/f* regionalist
regir ⟨3l & 3c⟩ **I** *v/t* rule, govern **II** *v/i* apply, be in force; **regirse** *v/r* be guided (***por*** by)
registrador *adj* measuring
registrar ⟨1a⟩ *v/t* **1** (*inscribir*) register **2** *casa* search; (***a mí***) ***que me registren*** F search me! F; **registrarse** *v/r* be recorded; ***se registró un máximo de 45°C*** a high of 45°C was recorded
registro *m* **1** (*archivo*) register **2** *de casa* search **3**: ***tocar todos los* ~*s*** *fig* F pull out all the stops F
◇ **registro civil** register of births, marriages and deaths; **registro domiciliario** house search; **registro mercantil** register of companies; **registro de la propiedad inmobiliaria** land registry
regla *f* **1** (*norma*) rule; ***por* ~ *general*** as a rule; **~*s del juego*** *pl tb fig* rules of the game; ***en*** (***toda***) **~** in order **2** *para medir* ruler **3** MED period **4** MAT: ***las cuatro* ~*s*** addition, subtraction, multiplication and division
◇ **regla de cálculo** slide rule
◇ **regla de tres** MAT rule of three
reglaje *m* TÉC adjustment
reglamentación *f* regulations *pl*, rules *pl*
reglamentar ⟨1a⟩ *v/t* regulate
reglamentario *adj* regulation *atr*
reglamento *m* regulation
reglar ⟨1a⟩ *v/t* regulate
regleta *f* EL circuit board
regocijarse ⟨1a⟩ *v/r* rejoice (***de*** at), take delight (***de*** in)
regocijo *m* delight
regodearse ⟨1a⟩ *v/r* gloat (***con*** over), delight (***en*** in)
regoldar ⟨1m⟩ *v/i* F burp F
regordete *adj* F chubby
regresar ⟨1a⟩ **I** *v/i* return **II** *v/t Méx* return, give back; **regresarse** *v/r L.Am.* return
regresión *f* regression
regresivo *adj* regressive
regreso *m* return
regüeldo *m* F belch
reguero *m* trail; ***como un* ~ *de pólvora*** *fig* like wildfire
regulable *adj* adjustable; ***asiento* ~ *en altura*** adjustable-height seat
regulación *f* **1** regulation; **~ *de empleo*** *ley* reduction in the workforce **2** *de temperatura* control; **~ *del tráfico*** traffic control
regulador *m* TÉC regulator, control
regular[1] *adj* **1** *sin variar* regular **2** (*común*) ordinary **3** (*habitual*) regular, normal **4** (*no muy bien*) so-so
regular[2] ⟨1a⟩ *v/t* TÉC regulate; *temperatura* control, regulate
regularidad *f* regularity; ***con* ~** regularly
regularización *f* regularization

regularizar ⟨1f⟩ *v/t* regularize; **regularizarse** *v/r* be regularized
regularmente *adv* regularly
regurgitar ⟨1a⟩ *v/i* regurgitate
regusto *m* aftertaste; ***un ~ amargo*** a bitter aftertaste
rehabilitación *f* **1** MED, *fig* rehabilitation **2** ARQUI restoration
rehabilitar ⟨1a⟩ *v/t* **1** MED, *fig* rehabilitate **2** ARQUI restore
rehacer ⟨2s; *part* ***rehecho***⟩ *v/t* **1** *película, ropa, cama* remake **2** *trabajo, ejercicio* do over, do again **3** *casa, vida* rebuild; **rehacerse** *v/r*: ***~ de*** get over, overcome
rehago *vb* ☞ ***rehacer***
rehecho *part* ☞ ***rehacer***
rehén *m* hostage; ***toma de rehenes*** hostage taking
rehice *vb* ☞ ***rehacer***
rehizo *vb* ☞ ***rehacer***
rehogar ⟨1h⟩ *v/t* GASTR fry
rehuir ⟨3g⟩ *v/t* shy away from
rehusar ⟨1a⟩ *v/t* refuse, decline; **rehusarse** *v/r*: ***~ a hacer algo*** refuse to do sth
reimplantar ⟨1a⟩ *v/t* MED reimplant
reimpresión *f* reprinting
reimprimir ⟨3a⟩ *v/t* reprint
reina *f tb en naipes* queen
◇ **reina madre** queen mother
reinado *m* reign
reinante *adj tb fig* reigning
reinar ⟨1a⟩ *v/i tb fig* reign
reincidencia *f* JUR reoffending
reincidente I *adj* repeat **II** *m/f* repeat offender
reincidir ⟨3a⟩ *v/i* reoffend
reincorporación *f* return
reincorporar ⟨1a⟩ *v/t* reinstate, restore; **reincorporarse** *v/r* return (***a*** to)
reineta *f* BOT pippin
reingresar ⟨1a⟩ *v/i* return
reiniciar ⟨1b⟩ *v/t* restart; INFOR reboot, restart
reinicio *m* restart; INFOR reboot, restart
reino *m tb fig* kingdom
◇ **reino animal** animal kingdom; **reino de los cielos** kingdom of heaven; **reino mineral** mineral kingdom; **Reino Unido** United Kingdom; **reino vegetal** vegetable kingdom
reinserción *f*: ***~ social*** social rehabilitation
reinsertar ⟨1a⟩ *v/t* rehabilitate
reinstaurar ⟨1a⟩ *v/t* bring back
reintegración *f* reinstatement; *de dinero* refund
reintegrar ⟨1a⟩ *v/t* reinstate; *dinero* refund (***a*** to); **reintegrarse** *v/r* return (***a*** to)
reintegro *m* (*en lotería*) *prize in the form of a refund of the stake money*
reinversión *f* reinvestment
reinvertir ⟨3i⟩ *v/t* reinvest
reír ⟨3m⟩ **I** *v/i* laugh; ***hacer ~ a alguien*** make s.o. laugh; ***no me hagas ~*** *fig* F don't make me laugh F; ***quien ríe último, ríe mejor*** he who laughs last laughs longest **II** *v/t* laugh at; **reírse** *v/r* laugh (***de*** at)
reiteración *f* repetition, reiteration
reiteradamente *adv* repeatedly
reiterar ⟨1a⟩ *v/t* repeat, reiterate
reiterativo *adj* repetitive, reiterative
reivindicación *f* claim
reivindicar ⟨1g⟩ *v/t* claim; ***~ un atentado*** claim responsibility for an attack
reja *f* **1** AGR plowshare, *Br* ploughshare **2** (*barrote*) bar; ***meter entre ~s*** *fig* F put behind bars
rejilla *f* FERR luggage rack
rejón *m* lance
rejoneador *m bullfighter mounted on horseback*
rejuvenecer ⟨2d⟩ *v/t* rejuvenate
rejuvenecimiento *m* rejuvenation
relación *f* **1** relationship; ***la ~ calidad-precio es muy buena*** it's good value for money; ***~ causa-efecto*** cause and effect relationship; ***mantener relaciones (amorosas) con alguien*** have an affair with s.o. **2** (*conexión*) relation; ***no guardar ~ con*** bear no relation to; ***con*** *o* ***en ~ a*** with *o* in relation to
◇ **relación de pareja** relationship; **relaciones comerciales** trade relations; **relaciones diplomáticas** diplomatic relations; **relaciones públicas** *pl* public relations, PR *sg*; **relaciones sexuales** sexual relations
relacionado *adj* related (***con*** to); ***bien ~*** well connected
relacionar ⟨1a⟩ *v/t* relate (***con*** to), connect (***con*** with); **relacionarse** *v/r* **1** be connected (***con*** to), be related (***con*** to) **2** (*mezclarse*) mix
relajación *f* relaxation

relajado *adj* relaxed
relajamiento *m* relaxation
relajante *adj* relaxing
relajar ⟨1a⟩ *v/t* relax; **relajarse** *v/r* relax
relajo *m* **1** *C.Am.*, *Méx* uproar **2** (*relajación*) relaxation
relamer ⟨2a⟩ *v/t* lick; **relamerse** *v/r* lick one's lips
relamido *adj* F **1** (*persona*) smooth **2** (*adorno*) refined
relámpago *m* flash of lightning; ***viaje ~*** flying visit; ***como un ~*** *fig* like lightning
relampaguear ⟨1a⟩ *v/i*: ***relampagueó y tronó mucho*** there was a lot of thunder and lightning
relampagueo *m* lightning
relanzar ⟨1f⟩ *v/t fig* relaunch
relatar ⟨1a⟩ *v/t* tell, relate
relatividad *f* relativity
relativizar ⟨1f⟩ *v/t* put in context
relativo *adj* relative; ***~ a*** regarding, about; ***pronombre ~*** GRAM relative pronoun
relato *m* short story
relax *m* relaxation
relé *m* EL relay
releer ⟨2e⟩ *v/t* reread
relegar ⟨1h⟩ *v/t* relegate
relevancia *f* relevance
relevante *adj* relevant
relevar ⟨1a⟩ *v/t* MIL relieve; ***~ a alguien de algo*** relieve s.o. of sth
relevista *m/f* DEP relay runner
relevo *m* MIL change; (*sustituto*) relief, replacement; ***tomar el ~ de alguien*** take over from s.o., relieve s.o.; ***carrera de ~s*** DEP relay (race)
relicario *m* shrine
relieve *m* relief; ***alto / bajo ~*** high / bas relief; ***de ~*** *fig* important; ***poner de ~*** highlight; ***dar ~ a*** (*realzar*) highlight
religión *f* religion
religiosa *f* nun
religiosamente *adv* religiously
religiosidad *f* religiousness
religioso **I** *adj* religious **II** *m* monk
relinchar ⟨1a⟩ *v/i* neigh
relincho *m* neigh
reliquia *f* relic
rellamada *f*: ***~ (automática)*** TELEC automatic redial
rellano *m* landing
rellenar ⟨1a⟩ *v/t* fill; GASTR *pollo*, *pimientos* stuff; *formulario* fill out, fill in
relleno **I** *adj* **1** GASTR *pollo*, *pimientos* stuffed; *pastel* filled **2** *fig* F *persona* plump F **II** *m tb en cojín* stuffing; *en pastel* filling
reloj *m* clock; *de pulsera* watch, wristwatch; ***~ para fichar*** time clock; ***ser un ~*** F be as regular as clockwork F; ***ir*** *o* ***marchar como un ~*** go *o* run like clockwork; ***contra ~*** against the clock; ***carrera contra ~*** DEP race against the clock
◇ **reloj de arena** hourglass; **reloj de bolsillo** pocket watch; **reloj de cuarzo** quartz watch; **reloj de pared** wall clock; **reloj de pie** grandfather clock; **reloj de sol** sundial
relojería *f* watchmaker's
relojero *m*, **-a** *f* watchmaker
reluciente *adj* sparkling, glittering
relucir ⟨3f⟩ *v/i* sparkle, glitter; ***sacar a ~*** F bring up; ***salir a ~*** F come out
reluctante *adj* reluctant
relumbrar ⟨1a⟩ *v/i* shine brightly
relumbrón *m*: ***es un ~*** it's flashy; ***de ~*** fake
remachar ⟨1a⟩ *v/t* **1** *mesa*, *silla* rivet **2** *instrucción*, *orden* repeat
remache *m* rivet
remador *m*, **~a** *f* rower
remanente *m* remainder, surplus
remangar ⟨1h⟩ *v/t* roll up
remanso *m* backwater; ***~ de paz*** *fig* haven of peace
remar ⟨1a⟩ *v/i* row
remarcar ⟨1g⟩ *v/t* stress, emphasize
rematado *adj*: ***ser un loco ~*** F be completely crazy
rematar ⟨1a⟩ **I** *v/t* **1** (*acabar del todo*) finish off **2** *L.Am.* COM auction **II** *v/i en fútbol* shoot; ***~ de cabeza*** head the ball; ***~ a puerta*** shoot at goal, take a shot at goal
remate *m* **1** *L.Am.* COM auction, sale **2** *en fútbol* shot; ***~ de cabeza*** header **3** (*fin*): ***dar ~ a algo*** finish sth off; ***para ~ …*** to top it all off, … **4** *para enfatizar*: ***ser tonto de ~*** be a complete idiot; ***estar loco de ~*** be completely crazy
remedar ⟨1a⟩ *v/t* mimic, ape
remediar ⟨1b⟩ *v/t daños* repair; *error* remedy; ***no puedo ~lo*** I can't do anything about it
remedio *m* remedy; ***~ casero*** homemade remedy; ***sin ~*** hopeless; ***no tiene***

R

~ there's no solution; ***no hay más ~ que ...*** there's no alternative but to ...; ***poner ~ a algo*** remedy sth; ***¡qué ~!*** I have no choice
remedo *m* imitation, copy
rememoración *f* remembrance
rememorar ⟨1a⟩ *v/t* remember
remendar ⟨1k⟩ *v/t con parche* patch; (*zurcir*) darn
remera *f Rpl* T-shirt
remero *m* rower, oarsman
remesa *f* **1** (*envío*) shipment, consignment **2** *L.Am. dinero* remittance
remezón *m L.Am.* earth tremor
remiendo *m* (*parche*) patch; (*zurcido*) darn; ***hacer*** *o* ***echar un ~ a algo*** patch sth
remilgado *adj* fussy, finicky
remilgo *m*: ***tener*** *o* ***hacer ~s*** *pl* be fussy
reminiscencia *f* reminiscence
remisión *f* **1** REL, JUR, MED remission **2** *en texto* reference
remiso *adj* reluctant (***a*** to)
remite *m en carta* return address
remitente *m/f* sender
remitir ⟨3a⟩ **I** *v/t* **1** (*enviar*) send, ship **2** *en texto* refer (***a*** to) **II** *v/i* **1** MED go into remission **2** *de crisis* ease (off); **remitirse** *v/r* refer (***a*** to)
remo *m pala* oar; *deporte* rowing; ***meter el ~*** *fig* F put one's foot in it
remodelación *f de casa, edificio* remodeling
◇ **remodelación ministerial** cabinet reorganization *o Br* reshuffle
remodelar ⟨1a⟩ *v/t* remodel
remojar ⟨1a⟩ *v/t* **1** *en líquido* soak **2** *L.Am.* F *acontecimiento* celebrate; **remojarse** *v/r* (*bañarse*) go for a quick swim
remojo *m*: ***poner a*** *o* ***en ~*** leave to soak
remojón *m* drenching, soaking; ***darse un ~*** go for a dip
remolacha *f* beet, *Br* beetroot
◇ **remolacha azucarera** sugar beet
remolcador MAR **I** *adj* tug *atr* **II** *m* tug
remolcar ⟨1g⟩ *v/t* AUTO, MAR tow; ***~ a alguien*** *fig* drag s.o. along
remolino *m de aire* eddy; *de agua* whirlpool; ***~ de gente*** *fig* crowd of people
remolón F **I** *adj* idle, lazy **II** *m*, **-ona** *f* slacker; ***hacerse el ~*** slack (off)
remolque *m* AUTO trailer; ***llevar a ~*** to tow
remontada *f* comeback, recovery
remontar ⟨1a⟩ **I** *v/t* **1** *río* go up **2** *dificultad* overcome, surmount **II** *v/i* DEP stage a comeback, come from behind; **remontarse** *v/r en el tiempo* go back (***a*** to)
remonte *m* ski lift
remorder ⟨2h⟩ *v/t*: ***me remuerde la conciencia*** I have a guilty conscience
remordimiento *m* remorse; ***~s*** *pl* regrets, remorse *sg*
remotamente *adv* remotely; ***no se parecen ni ~*** they don't look even remotely alike
remoto *adj* remote; ***no tengo ni la más -a idea*** I haven't the faintest idea
remover ⟨2h⟩ *v/t* **1** (*agitar*) stir **2** *L.Am.* (*destituir*) dismiss **3** *C.Am., Méx* (*quitar*) remove; **removerse** *v/r* move around
remozar ⟨1f⟩ *v/t* renovate
remplazar ⟨1f⟩ *v/t* ☞ ***reemplazar***
remuneración *f* remuneration
remunerar ⟨1a⟩ *v/t* pay
renacentista *adj* Renaissance *atr*
renacer ⟨2d⟩ *v/i fig* be reborn
Renacimiento *m* Renaissance
renacuajo *m* **1** ZO tadpole **2** F *persona* shrimp F
renal *adj* ANAT renal, kidney *atr*
rencilla *f* fight, argument
rencor *m* resentment; ***guardar ~ a alguien*** bear s.o. a grudge
rencoroso *adj* resentful
rendición *f* surrender
rendido *adj* exhausted
rendija *f* (*raja*) crack; (*hueco*) gap
rendimiento *m* **1** performance; ***de alto ~*** *coche* high-powered, performance *atr* **2** (*producción*) output **3** FIN yield; ***de alto ~*** high-yield
rendir ⟨3l⟩ **I** *v/t* **1** *honores* pay, do **2** *beneficio* produce, yield **3**: ***~ las armas*** surrender one's weapons **4**: ***no tengo que ~ cuentas a nadie*** I don't have to explain myself to anyone **II** *v/i* perform; **rendirse** *v/r* surrender; ***~ a*** *o* ***ante la evidencia*** bow to the evidence; ***no te rindas*** don't give up
renegado I *adj* renegade *atr* **II** *m*, **-a** *f* renegade
renegar ⟨1h & 1k⟩ *v/i*: ***~ de alguien*** disown s.o.; ***~ de algo*** renounce sth
renegrido *adj* blackened

RENFE *f abr* (= ***Red Nacional de Ferrocarriles Españoles***) *Spanish rail operator*
renglón *m* line; ***a ~ seguido*** immediately after
rengo *adj CSur* lame
renguear ⟨1a⟩ *v/i CSur* limp, walk with a limp
renguera *f CSur* limp
reno *m* ZO reindeer
renombrado *adj* famous, renowned
renombre *m*: ***de ~*** famous, renowned; ***de ~ universal*** world-famous, known all over the world
renovable *adj* renewable
renovación *f* renewal
renovador *adj*: ***las fuerzas ~es*** the forces of renewal
renovar ⟨1m⟩ *v/t* renew
renquear ⟨1a⟩ *v/i* limp
renta *f* **1** (*ingresos*) income **2** *de casa* rent **3**: ***de ~ fija*** fixed-interest
◇ **renta per cápita** income per capita
◇ **renta vitalicia** life annuity, lifetime income
rentabilidad *f* profitability
rentabilizar ⟨1f⟩ *v/t* achieve a return on; *fig* make the most of
rentable *adj* profitable
rentar ⟨1a⟩ **I** *v/t* **1** (*arrendar*) rent out **2** (*alquiler*) rent **II** *v/i* be profitable
renuente *adj* reluctant, unwilling
renuncia *f* resignation
renunciar ⟨1b⟩ *v/i*: ***~ a*** *tabaco, alcohol etc* give up; *demanda* drop; *puesto* resign
reñido *adj batalla etc* hard fought, tough; ***estar ~ con alguien*** have fallen out with s.o.; ***estar ~ con algo*** be contrary to sth
reñir ⟨3h & 3l⟩ **I** *v/t* tell off **II** *v/i* quarrel, fight F
reo *m*, **-a** *f* accused
reojo: ***de ~*** out of the corner of one's eye; ***mirar de ~ a*** look out of the corner of one's eye at; *fig* look down on
reordenación *f* reorganization
reordenar ⟨1a⟩ *v/t* reorganize
reorganización *f* reorganization
reorganizar ⟨1f⟩ *v/t* reorganize
reorientación *f* reorientation
reorientar ⟨1a⟩ *v/t* reorientate
reóstato *m* rheostat
repantigarse ⟨1h⟩ *v/r* lounge, sprawl
reparación *f* repair; *fig* reparation
reparador *adj sueño etc* refreshing
reparar ⟨1a⟩ **I** *v/t* repair; ***~ fuerzas*** get one's strength back **II** *v/i*: ***~ en algo*** notice sth; ***no ~ en gastos*** not worry about the cost
reparo *m*: ***poner ~s a*** find problems with; ***no tener ~s en*** have no reservations about; ***sin ~*** without reservation *o* hesitation; ***me da ~ decirle*** I have qualms about telling him
repartición *f S.Am.* department
repartida *f L.Am.* ☞ ***repartición***
repartir ⟨3a⟩ *v/t* **1** (*dividir*) share out, divide up **2** *productos* deliver **3**: ***~ los papeles de*** *película, obra de teatro* cast; **repartirse** *v/r* share; ***~ algo*** share sth
repartidor *m* delivery man; ***~ de periódicos*** newspaper boy
reparto *m* **1** (*división*) share-out, distribution **2** TEA cast **3**: ***~ a domicilio*** home delivery
repasar ⟨1a⟩ *v/t* **1** *trabajo* go over again; EDU revise **2** TÉC *motor* service
repaso *m* **1** *de lección* review, revision; *de últimas novedades* review **2** TÉC *de motor* service **3**: ***dar un ~ a alguien*** tell s.o. off
repatear ⟨1a⟩ **I** *v/t*: ***me repatea que*** F it ticks me off that F **II** *v/i*: ***me repatea un montón*** F it really ticks me off F
repatriación *f* repatriation
repatriar ⟨1b⟩ *v/t* repatriate
repecho *m* steep slope
repelente I *adj* **1** *fig* repellent, repulsive **2** F *niño* horrible **II** *m* repellent
repeler ⟨2a⟩ *v/t* repel
repelús *m*: ***dar ~ a alguien*** F give s.o. the creeps F
repeluzno *m por frío, miedo etc* shiver, shudder; ***dar ~ a alguien*** give s.o. the shivers
repensar ⟨1k⟩ *v/t* reconsider
repente: ***de ~*** suddenly
repentino *adj* sudden
repera *f*: ***ser la ~*** F take the cake F
repercusión *f fig* repercussion
repercutir ⟨3a⟩ *v/i* have repercussions (***en*** on)
repertorio *m* TEA, MÚS repertoire
repesca *f* EDU *second chance at an exam*, *Br* resit
repescar ⟨1g⟩ *v/t* pass (*after a second test*)

R

repetible *adj* repeatable
repetición *f* repetition
repetido *adj* repeated; ***-as veces*** over and over again; ***lo tengo ~*** I have two of these
repetidor I *adj* TÉC booster *atr* **II** *m* TÉC booster **III** *m*, **~a** *f* EDU student repeating a year
repetir ⟨3l⟩ **I** *v/t* repeat **II** *v/i de comida* repeat; **repetirse** *v/r* **1** happen again **2** (*insistir*) repeat o.s
repetitivo *adj* repetitive
repicar ⟨1g⟩ **I** *v/t* **1** *campanas* ring **2** *castañuelas* click **II** *v/i* ring out
repintar ⟨1a⟩ *v/t* repaint; **repintarse** *v/r* put on make-up
repipi *adj* F (*afectado*) affected; ***es tan ~ niño*** he's such a know-it-all F
repique *m* **1** *de campanas* ringing **2** *de castañuelas* clicking
repiquetear ⟨1a⟩ *v/t* **1** *campanas* ring **2** *con los dedos* drum
repiqueteo *m* ringing
repisa *f* shelf
replantar ⟨1a⟩ *v/t* replant, transplant
replantear ⟨1a⟩ *v/t pregunta*, *problema* bring up again
replegarse ⟨1h & 1k⟩ *v/r* MIL fall back, withdraw
repleto *adj* full (***de*** of)
réplica *f* replica
replicar ⟨1g⟩ *v/t* reply
repliegue *m* **1** *de ejército* withdrawal **2** (*pliegue*) fold
repoblación *f* repopulation, restocking
◇ **repoblación forestal** reforestation
repoblar ⟨1m⟩ *v/t* repopulate
repollo *m* BOT cabbage
◇ **repollo morado** *L.Am.* red cabbage
reponer ⟨2r; *part* ***repuesto***⟩ *v/t* **1** *existencias* replace **2** TEA *obra* revive; ***~ una película*** rerun the original version of a movie **3**: ***~ fuerzas*** get one's strength back; **reponerse** *v/r* recover (***de*** from)
reportaje *m* story, report
◇ **reportaje gráfico** illustrated feature
◇ **reportaje publicitario** advertorial
reportar ⟨1a⟩ *v/t* **1** *beneficio*, *provecho* produce, bring **2** *L.Am. informar sobre* report
reporte *m L.Am.* report; ***el ~ metereológico*** the weather forecast
reportero *m*, **-a** *f* reporter
◇ **reportero gráfico** press photographer
reposabrazos *m inv* armrest
reposacabezas *m inv* AUTO headrest
reposado *adj* calm
reposapiés *m inv* footrest
reposar ⟨1a⟩ *v/i* **1** (*descansar*) rest **2** *de vino* settle; ***dejar ~ algo*** *té etc* let sth stand
reposera *f L.Am.* lounger
reposición *f* TEA revival; TV repeat
reposo *m* rest; ***hacer ~*** rest
repostar ⟨1a⟩ *v/i* refuel
repostería *f* pastries *pl*
reprender ⟨2a⟩ *v/t* scold, tell off F
reprensible *adj* reprehensible
represa *f* **1** (*dique*) dam **2** (*embalse*) reservoir
represalia *f* reprisal
represar ⟨1a⟩ *v/t agua* dam
representación *f* **1** representation **2** TEA performance **3** (*delegación*): ***en ~ de*** on behalf of
◇ **representación exclusiva** sole agency
representante *m/f tb* COM representative
representar ⟨1a⟩ *v/t* **1** (*simbolizar*) represent **2** *obra* put on, perform; *papel* play **3** (*aparentar*): ***~ menos años*** look younger
representativo *adj* representative
represión *f* repression
represivo *adj* repressive
represor I *adj* oppressive **II** *m*, **~a** *f* oppressor
reprimenda *f* reprimand
reprimir ⟨3a⟩ *v/t tb* PSI repress; **reprimirse** *v/r* repress one's feelings
reprobable *adj* reprehensible
reprobación *f* condemnation, disapproval
reprobador *adj* reproachful
reprobar ⟨1m⟩ *v/t* **1** *comportamiento*, *actitud* condemn **2** *L.Am.* EDU fail
reprobatorio *adj* ☞ ***reprobador***
reprocesamiento *m* reprocessing
reprocesar ⟨1a⟩ *v/t* reprocess
reprochable *adj* reproachable
reprochar ⟨1a⟩ *v/t* reproach
reproche *m* reproach
reproducción *f* **1** BIO reproduction **2** (*copia*) copy, reproduction
reproducir ⟨3o⟩ *v/t* **1** (*reflejar*), BIO re-

R

produce **2** (*copiar*) copy, reproduce; **reproducirse** *v/r* BIO reproduce, breed
reproductivo *adj* BIO reproductive; ***en edad -a*** *mujer* of child-bearing age
reproductor **I** *adj* breeding **II** *m*, **~a** *f* breeding animal
◇ **reproductor de discos compactos** compact disc player
reprografía *f* reprographics *sg*
reprogramar ⟨1a⟩ *v/t* reprogram
reptil *m* ZO reptile
república *f* republic
◇ **república bananera** *desp* banana republic; **república federal** federal republic; **República Dominicana** Dominican Republic
republicano **I** *adj* republican **II** *m*, **-a** *f* republican
repudiación *f* repudiation
repudiar ⟨1b⟩ *v/t* repudiate; *herencia* renounce
repuesto **I** *part* ☞ ***reponer*** **II** *m* spare part, replacement; ***de ~*** spare
repugnancia *f* disgust, repugnance
repugnante *adj* disgusting, repugnant
repugnar ⟨1a⟩ *v/t* disgust, repel
repujado *m* TÉC embossed
repujar ⟨1a⟩ *v/t metal* emboss
repulsa *f* condemnation, rejection
repulsión *f* repulsion
repulsivo *adj* repulsive, disgusting
repuntar ⟨1a⟩ *v/i* pick up, rally
repunte *m de valores*, *precios* rally, upturn; ***~ económico*** economic upturn
repuse *vb* ☞ ***reponerse***
reputación *f* reputation; ***de buena ~*** with a good reputation; ***tener buena / mala ~*** have a good / bad reputation
requemar ⟨1a⟩ *v/t* burn
requerimiento *m* request; ***a ~ de*** at the request of
requerir ⟨3i⟩ *v/t* **1** (*necesitar*) require **2** JUR summons
requesón *m* cottage cheese
requete *pref* F very, super F
requetebién *adv* F really well, brilliantly F
réquiem *m* requiem
requisa *f* MIL requisition
requisar ⟨1a⟩ *v/t* MIL requisition
requisición *f* MIL requisition
requisito *m* requirement
res *f L.Am.* animal; ***~es*** *pl* cattle *pl*; ***carne de ~*** beef
resabio *m* aftertaste
resaca *f* **1** MAR undertow, undercurrent **2** *de beber* hangover
resalado *adj* F witty, funny
resaltar ⟨1a⟩ **I** *v/t* highlight, stress **II** *v/i* ARQUI jut out; *fig* stand out
resarcimiento *m* compensation, reimbursement; ***~ de daños*** compensation for damages
resarcir ⟨3b⟩ *v/t* compensate (***de*** for), reimburse (***de*** for); **resarcirse** *v/r* make up (***de*** for)
resbaladizo *adj* **1** *superficie* slippery **2** *fig asunto*, *tema* tricky
resbalar ⟨1a⟩ *v/i* slide; *fig* slip up
resbalón *m* slip; *fig* F slip-up
resbaloso *adj L.Am.* slippery
rescatar ⟨1a⟩ *v/t persona*, *animal* rescue, save; *bienes* salvage, save
rescate *m* **1** *de peligro* rescue; ***equipo de ~*** rescue team **2** *en secuestro* ransom
rescindible *adj* which can be canceled *o Br* cancelled
rescindir ⟨3a⟩ *v/t* cancel; *contrato* terminate
rescisión *f* cancellation; *de contrato* termination
rescoldo *m* ember
reseco *adj* **1** (*seco*) parched **2** (*flaco*) skinny
resentido *adj* resentful
resentimiento *m* resentment
resentirse ⟨3i⟩ *v/r* **1** get upset; ***~ con alguien*** feel resentful toward s.o. **2** *de rendimiento*, *calidad* suffer; ***~ de algo*** suffer from the effects of sth
reseña *f* review
reseñar ⟨1a⟩ *v/t* review
reserva **I** *f* **1** reservation; ***~ de asiento*** FERR seat reservation; ***hacer una ~*** make a reservation **2** (*duda*): ***sin ~s*** without reservation **II** *m/f* DEP reserve, substitute
◇ **reserva natural** nature reserve
◇ **reservas hídricas** water reserves
reservación *f Méx* reservation
reservado **I** *adj* reserved **II** *m* private room
reservar ⟨1a⟩ *v/t* **1** (*guardar*) set aside, put by **2** *billete* reserve; ***~ mesa*** reserve a table; **reservarse** *v/r* save o.s. (***para*** for)
reservista *m/f* MIL reservist

resfriado I *adj*: ***estar ~*** have a cold **II** *m* cold
resfriarse ⟨1c⟩ *v/r* catch cold
resfrío *m L.Am.* cold
resguardar ⟨1a⟩ *v/t* protect (***de*** from); **resguardarse** *v/r* protect o.s. (***de*** from)
resguardo *m* **1** COM counterfoil **2** (*cobijo*): ***al ~ del frío*** sheltered from the cold
residencia *f* residence; ***segunda ~*** second home; ***~ habitual*** domicile
◇ **residencia de ancianos** retirement home; **residencia de estudiantes** dormitory, *Br* hall of residence; **residencia geriátrica** retirement home; **residencia para la tercera edad** retirement home
residencial I *adj* residential **II** *f Arg, Chi* rooming house
residente I *adj* resident **II** *m/f* resident; ***no ~*** non resident
residir ⟨3a⟩ *v/i* reside; ***~ en*** *fig* lie in
residual *adj* **1** *de restos* residual **2** *de desecho* waste *atr*
residuo *m* **1** (*resto*) residue **2**: ***~s*** waste *sg*
◇ **residuos nucleares** nuclear waste *sg*; **residuos orgánicos** organic waste *sg*; **residuos radiactivos** radioactive waste *sg*; **residuos tóxicos** toxic waste *sg*
resiembra *f* AGR resowing
resiento *vb* ☞ ***resentir***
resignación *f actitud* resignation
resignarse ⟨1a⟩ *v/r* resign o.s. (***a*** to)
resina *f* resin
resinoso *adj* resinous
resistencia *f* **1** (*oposición*) resistance **2** EL, TÉC *pieza* resistor
resistente *adj* **1** (*fuerte*) strong, tough **2** resistant (***a*** to); ***~ al calor*** heat-resistant; ***~ al fuego*** fireproof
resistir ⟨3a⟩ **I** *v/i* **1** resist **2** (*aguantar*) hold out; ***no resisto más*** I can't take any more **II** *v/t* **1** *tentación* resist **2** *frío, dolor etc* stand, bear; **resistirse** *v/r* be reluctant (***a*** to)
resollar ⟨1m⟩ *v/i* breathe heavily, puff
resoluble *adj* solvable
resolución *f* **1** *actitud* determination, decisiveness **2** *de problema* solution (***de*** to) **3** JUR ruling **4** (*decisión*): ***tomar una ~*** make *o* take a decision **5** TÉC: ***de alta ~*** high resolution **6**: ***en ~*** to sum up
resolver ⟨2h; *part* ***resuelto***⟩ *v/t problema* solve; **resolverse** *v/r* decide (***a*** to; ***por*** on); *de problema* be solved; *de conflicto* be resolved
resonancia *f* **1** TÉC resonance **2** *fig*: ***tener ~*** have an impact
◇ **resonancia magnética nuclear** nuclear magnetic resonance; MED MRI scan
resonar ⟨1m⟩ *v/i* echo
resoplar ⟨1a⟩ *v/i* snort
resoplido *m* snort
resorción *f* TEC reabsorption
resorte *m* spring; ***tocar todos los ~s*** *fig* pull all the strings one can
respaldar ⟨1a⟩ *v/t* back, support; **respaldarse** *v/r* sit back, lean back; ***~ en*** *fig* lean on, get support from
respaldo *m de silla* back; *fig* backing, support
respectar ⟨1a⟩ *v/i*: ***por lo que respecta a …*** as regards …, as far as … is concerned
respectivo *adj* respective
respectivamente *adv* respectively
respecto *m*: ***al ~*** on the matter; ***con ~ a*** regarding, as regards; ***a este ~*** with regard to this
respetabilidad *f* respectability
respetable I *adj* respectable **II** *m*: ***el ~*** F the audience, the crowd
respetar ⟨1a⟩ *v/t* respect; ***hacerse ~*** gain *o* win respect; **respetarse** *v/r* have self-respect
respeto *m* **1** respect; ***con todos los ~s*** with all due respect; ***falta de ~*** lack of respect; ***faltar el ~ a alguien*** not show s.o. the proper respect, lack respect for s.o. **2** (*saludos*): ***mis ~s a…*** my regards to…
respetuosidad *f* respect, respectfulness
respetuoso *adj* respectful; ***~ con el medio ambiente*** with respect for the environment
respingo *m* start, jump; ***dar un ~*** jump
respingón *adj*: ***nariz respingona*** turned-up nose
respirable *adj* breathable
respiración *f* breathing; ***me quedé sin ~*** I was breathless; *fig* it took my breath away; ***estar con ~ asistida*** MED be on a respirator
respiradero *m* vent
respirador *m* MED ventilator, respira-

tor
respirar ⟨1a⟩ *v/t & v/i* breathe; **~ hondo** breathe deeply; **no dejar ~ a alguien** *fig* not leave s.o. alone for a minute
respiratorio *adj* respiratory
respiro *m fig* breather, break; **darse** *o* **tomarse un ~** take a break
resplandecer ⟨2d⟩ *v/i* shine, gleam
resplandeciente *adj* shining
resplandor *m* shine, gleam
responder ⟨2a⟩ **I** *v/t* answer **II** *v/i* **1**: **~ a** answer, reply to; MED respond to; *descripción* fit, match; (*ser debido a*) be due to; **~ al nombre de …** answer to the name of … **2**: **~ de** take responsibility for **3**: **~ por alguien** vouch for s.o.
respondón F **I** *adj* mouthy, nervy, *Br* cheeky **II** *m*, **-ona** *f*: **es una respondona** she's always answering back
responsabilidad *f* responsibility
◇ **responsabilidad civil** civil liability
responsabilizar ⟨1f⟩ *v/t*: **~ a alguien** hold s.o. responsible (**de** for); **responsabilizarse** *v/r* take responsibility (**de** for)
responsable I *adj* responsible (**de** for) **II** *m/f* person responsible (**de** for); **los ~s del crimen** those responsible for the crime
respuesta *f* (*contestación*) reply, answer; *fig* response; **en ~ a** in reply to; *fig* following
resquebra(ja)dura *f* crack, split
resquebrajar ⟨1a⟩ *v/t* crack; **resquebrajarse** *v/r* crack
resquicio *m* gap
resta *f* MAT subtraction
restablecer ⟨2d⟩ *v/t* re-establish; *monarquía* restore; **restablecerse** *v/r* recover
restablecimiento *m* **1** re-establishment; *de monarquía* restoration **2** *de enfermo* recovery
restallar ⟨1a⟩ *v/i* crack
restallido *m* crack
restante I *adj* remaining **II** *m/fpl*: **los / las ~s** the rest *pl*, the remainder *pl*
restar ⟨1a⟩ **I** *v/t* subtract; **~ importancia a** play down the importance of **II** *v/i* remain, be left
restauración *f* restoration
restaurador *m*, **~a** *f* restorer
restaurant *m L.Am.* restaurant
restaurante *m* restaurant; **~ rápido** fast-food restaurant
restaurar ⟨1a⟩ *v/t* restore; **~ fuerzas** get one's strength back
restitución *f* **1** restitution; *de confianza, calma* restoration **2** *en cargo* reinstatement
restituir ⟨3g⟩ *v/t* **1** *confianza, calma* restore **2** *en cargo* reinstate
resto *m* rest, remainder; **los ~s mortales** the (mortal) remains; **echar el ~** go all out
restregar ⟨1h & 1k⟩ *v/t* scrub
restregón *m*: **dar un ~ a algo** give sth a scrub
restricción *f* restriction; **sin ~** with no restrictions
restrictivo *adj* restrictive
restringir ⟨3c⟩ *v/t* restrict, limit; **restringirse** *v/r* limit o.s.
resucitar ⟨1a⟩ **I** *v/t* resuscitate; *fig* revive **II** *v/i de persona* rise from *o* come back from the dead
resuello *m* puffing, heavy breathing
resuelto I *part* ☞ **resolver II** *adj* decisive, resolute
resulta *f*: **de ~s de** as a result of
resultado *m* **1** result; **~ final** *o* **total** DEP final score **2** (*rendimiento*): **dar buen ~** *de coche, zapatos* be a good buy **3**: **sin ~** *con sustantivo* unsuccessful; *con verbo* unsuccessfully
resultar ⟨1a⟩ *v/i* turn out; **~ caro** prove expensive, turn out to be expensive; **~ muerto** die, be killed; **resulta que …** it turns out that …
resumen *m* summary; **en ~** in short
resumir ⟨3a⟩ *v/t* summarize; **resumirse** *v/r* sum up (**en** as)
resurgimiento *m* resurgence
resurgir ⟨3c⟩ *v/i* reappear, come back
resurrección *f* REL resurrection; *fig* resurgence, revival
retablo *m* altarpiece
retaguardia *f* MIL rearguard
retahíla *f* string
retal *m* remnant
retama *f* BOT broom
retar ⟨1a⟩ *v/t* **1** challenge **2** *Rpl* (*regañar*) scold, tell off F
retardar ⟨1a⟩ *v/t* delay; **retardarse** *v/r* be late
retardo *m* delay
retazo *m fig* snippet, fragment
retén *m L.Am.* MIL patrol

retención *f* **1** MED retention **2** *de persona* detention

◇ **retención fiscal** tax deduction; **retención en origen** deduction at source; **retención de orina** MED urine retention

retener ⟨2l⟩ *v/t* **1** *dinero etc* withhold, deduct **2** *persona* detain, hold

reticencia *f* **1** reticence; ***sin ~s*** without hesitation **2** (*indirecta*): ***hablar con ~s*** insinuate things

reticente *adj* reticent

retina *f* ANAT retina

retintín *m*: ***con ~*** F sarcastically

retirada *f* **1** MIL retreat, withdrawal; ***batirse en ~*** beat a retreat **2**: ***~ del carnet de conducir*** suspension of one's driver's license

retirado *adj* **1** (*jubilado*) retired **2** (*alejado*) remote, out-of-the-way

retirar ⟨1a⟩ *v/t silla, obstáculo* take away, remove; *acusación, dinero* withdraw; **retirarse** *v/r* MIL withdraw

retiro *m* **1** *lugar* retreat **2** MIL retreat, withdrawal

reto *m* **1** challenge **2** *Rpl* (*regañina*) scolding, telling-off F

retobado *adj L.Am.* unruly

retocar ⟨1g⟩ *v/t* **1** FOT retouch, touch up **2** (*acabar*) put the finishing touches to

retomar ⟨1a⟩ *v/t*: ***~ algo*** *fig* take sth up again

retoñar ⟨1a⟩ *v/i* **1** BOT shoot **2** *fig* be rekindled

retoño *m* **1** BOT shoot **2** *fig* child; ***sus ~s*** their children *pl*, their offspring *pl*

retoque *m* **1** FOT touching-up **2** (*acabado*) finishing touch

retorcer ⟨2b & 2h⟩ *v/t* twist; **retorcerse** *v/r* writhe

retorcido *adj fig* twisted

retorcijón *m* cramps *pl*, *Br* stomach cramp

retorcimiento *m* twisting

retórica *f* rhetoric

retórico *adj* rhetorical

retornable *adj* returnable; ***no ~*** non-returnable

retornar ⟨1a⟩ *v/t & v/i* return

retorno *m* return

retortero *m*: ***andar al ~*** F be on the go; ***traer a alguien al ~*** F keep s.o. on the go

retortijón *m* cramps *pl*, *Br* stomach cramp

retozar ⟨1f⟩ *v/i* frolic, romp

retozo *m* frolicking

retracción *f* withdrawal

retractación *f* retraction, withdrawal

retractar ⟨1a⟩ *v/t* retract, withdraw; **retractarse** *v/r*: ***~ de algo*** withdraw sth

retráctil *adj* retractile, retractable

retraer ⟨2p; *part* ***retraído***⟩ *v/t* retract; **retraerse** *v/r* withdraw

retraído **I** *part* ☞ ***retraer*** **II** *adj* withdrawn

retranca *f* F crafty idea

retransmisión *f* RAD, TV transmission, broadcast; ***~ en diferido*** recorded transmission; ***~ en directo*** live broadcast

retransmitir ⟨3a⟩ *v/t* transmit, broadcast; ***~ en directo*** broadcast live

retrasado **I** *part* ☞ ***retrasar*** **II** *adj* **1** *tren, entrega* late **2** *con trabajo, pagos* behind; ***está ~ en clase*** he's lagging behind in class; ***~ mental*** mentally handicapped

retrasar ⟨1a⟩ **I** *v/t* **1** *proceso, movimiento* hold up, delay **2** *reloj* put back **3** *reunión* postpone, put back **4** *pelota* pass back **II** *v/i* **1** *de reloj* lose time **2** *en los estudios* be behind; **retrasarse** *v/r* **1** (*atrasarse*) be late **2** *de reloj* lose time **3** *con trabajo, pagos* get behind

retraso *m* delay; ***ir con ~*** be late; ***llegar con ~*** arrive late, be late *o* delayed; ***llevar ~*** be late *o* delayed

◇ **retraso mental** mental handicap

retratar ⟨1a⟩ *v/t* FOT take a picture of; *fig* depict

retratista *m/f* portrait artist

retrato *m* picture; ***~-robot*** composite photo, E-Fit®; ***ser el vivo ~ de alguien*** be the spitting image of s.o.

retreparse ⟨1a⟩ *v/r* lean back

retreta *f* **1** MIL retreat **2** *L.Am.* (*desfile*) parade

retrete *m* bathroom

retribución *f* salary

retribuir ⟨3g⟩ *v/t* **1** pay **2** (*recompensar*) reward

retro *adj* **1** old-fashioned, retro; ***moda ~*** retro fashion, retro look **2** POL reactionary

retroactivo *adj* retroactive

retroalimentación *f* feedback

retroceder ⟨2a⟩ *v/i* go back, move back;

fig back down
retroceso *m fig* backward step
retrógrado *adj* retrograde
retroproyector *m* overhead projector
retrospectiva *f* retrospective
retrospectivo *adj* retrospective
retrotraerse ⟨2p; *part* ***retrotraido***⟩ *v/r* go back (***a*** to)
retrovisor *m* AUTO rear-view mirror; **~ *exterior*** wing mirror
retumbar ⟨1a⟩ *v/i* boom
retuve *vb* ☞ ***retener***
reuma, reúma *m* MED rheumatism
reumático I *adj* rheumatic **II** *m*, **-a** *f* rheumatism sufferer
reumatismo *m* rheumatism
reumatólogo *m*, **-a** *f* rheumatologist
reunificación *f* POL reunification
reunificar ⟨1g⟩ *v/t* reunify, reunite
reunión *f* meeting; *de amigos* get-together
reunir ⟨3a⟩ *v/t* **1** *personas* bring together; ***estar reunido*** be in a meeting **2** *requisitos* meet, fulfill, *Br* fulfil **3** *datos* gather (together); **reunirse** *v/r de personas* meet up, get together; COM meet
reutilizable *adj* reusable
reutilización *f* re-use
reutilizar ⟨1f⟩ *v/t* re-use
reválida *f* final examination
revalidar ⟨1a⟩ *v/t examen* take
revalorización *f* appreciation, increase in value
revalorizar ⟨1f⟩ *v/t* revalue; **revalorizarse** *v/r* appreciate (***en*** by), increase in value (***en*** by)
revaluación *f* **1** *de una idea* re-assessment, re-evaluation **2** *de una moneda* appreciation; *por el gobierno* revaluation
revaluar ⟨1e⟩ *v/t* **1** *idea* re-assess, re-evaluate **2** *moneda* revalue; **revaluarse** *v/r* gain in value, appreciate
revancha *f* revenge; ***tomarse la ~*** take *o* get one's revenge
revelación *f* revelation
revelado *m* development
revelador I *adj* revealing **II** *m* FOT developer
revelar ⟨1a⟩ *v/t* FOT develop; **revelarse** *v/r* show o.s.
revendedor *m*, **~a** *f* scalper, *Br* ticket tout
revender ⟨2a⟩ *v/t ropa* resell; *entradas* scalp, *Br* tout
reventa *f* resale
reventado *adj* F beat F, shattered F
reventar ⟨1k⟩ **I 1** *v/i* burst; ***lleno a ~*** bursting at the seams, full to bursting; **~ *de risa*** burst out laughing; **~ *de orgullo*** be bursting with pride **2** (*molestar*): ***me revienta que …*** it really irritates me that … **3**: ***si no va revienta*** he'll be so disappointed if he doesn't go **II** *v/t puerta etc* break down; **reventarse** *v/r* **1** *de pelota* burst **2**: ***se reventó a trabajar*** *fig* he worked his butt off F
reventón *m* AUTO blowout; ***tener un ~*** have a blow-out
reverberación *f* **1** shimmering, reflection **2** *de sonido* reverberation
reverberar ⟨1a⟩ *v/i* **1** *de luz* shimmer, reflect **2** *de sonido* reverberate
reverdecer ⟨2d⟩ *v/t* revive
reverencia *f* **1** (*respeto*) reverence **2** *saludo*: *de hombre* bow; *de mujer* curtsy
reverencial *adj* reverential
reverenciar ⟨1b⟩ *v/t* revere
reverendísimo *adj* REL *tratamiento* most reverend
reverendo *m* REL reverend
reversa *f Méx* reverse (gear)
reversible *adj ropa* reversible
reverso *m* reverse, back; ***el ~ de la medalla*** *fig* the exact opposite
revertir ⟨3i⟩ *v/i*: **~ *en beneficio de alguien*** JUR benefit s.o.
revés *m* **1** (*contratiempo*) setback **2** *en tenis* backhand **3**: ***al*** *o* ***del ~*** back to front; *con el interior fuera* inside out; ***salir al ~*** *fig* go wrong
revestimiento *m* TÉC covering
revestir ⟨3l⟩ *v/t* **1** TÉC cover (***de*** with) **2**: **~ *gravedad*** be serious; **~ *importancia*** be important; **revestirse** *v/r*: **~ *de paciencia*** be patient; **~ *de valor*** pluck up courage
revientapisos *m/f inv* F burglar
revisación *f L.Am.* check-up
revisada *f L.Am.* ☞ ***revisión***
revisar ⟨1a⟩ *v/t* check, inspect
revisión *f* check, inspection; AUTO service
◇ **revisión médica** check-up
◇ **revisión técnica** roadworthiness test, *Br* MOT (test)
revisor *m*, **~a** *f* FERR (ticket) inspector

R

revista *f* **1** magazine **2**: ***pasar ~ a*** MIL inspect, review; *fig* review
revistero *m* magazine rack
revitalizar ⟨1f⟩ *v/t* revitalize; **revitalizarse** *v/r* be revitalized
revivificar ⟨1g⟩ *v/t* revive
revivir ⟨3a⟩ **I** *v/i* revive **II** *v/t* relive
revocable *adj* revocable
revocación *f* revocation
revocar ⟨1g⟩ *v/t* **1** *pared* render **2** JUR revoke
revocatoria *f L.Am.* revocation
revolcarse ⟨1g & 1m⟩ *v/r* roll around
revolcón *m* **1** *caída* tumble **2** F *de amantes* roll in the hay F; ***darse un ~*** have a roll in the hay F
revolotear ⟨1a⟩ *v/t* flutter
revoloteo *m* fluttering
revoltijo, revoltillo *m* mess, jumble
revoltoso I *adj niño* naughty **II** *m*, **-a** *f* naughty child
revolución *f* revolution
revolucionar ⟨1a⟩ *v/t* revolutionize
revolucionario I *adj* revolutionary **II** *m*, **-a** *f* revolutionary
revolver ⟨2h; *part* ***revuelto***⟩ **I** *v/t* **1** GASTR stir **2** *estómago* turn **3** (*desordenar*) mess up, turn upside down **II** *v/i* rummage (***en*** in); **revolverse** *v/r* **1** *del tiempo* worsen **2** (*rebelarse*) rebel **3**: ***se me revuelve el estómago*** *fig* my stomach turns
revólver *m* revolver
revuelo *m* stir; ***causar ~*** cause a stir
revuelta *f* uprising
revuelto I *part* ☞ ***revolver*** **II** *adj* **1** *mar* rough **2** *gente* restless **3** *pelo* disheveled, *Br* dishevelled **III** *m* GASTR: ***~ de gambas / setas*** scrambled eggs with shrimps / mushrooms
revulsivo *fig* **I** *adj* salutary **II** *m* lesson
rey *m* king; ***los ~es*** the king and queen; ***no quitar ni poner ~*** *fig* have no say
reyerta *f* fight
reyezuelo *m* ZO kinglet, *Br* goldcrest
rezagado I *adj* behind **II** *m*, **-a** *f* straggler
rezagarse ⟨1h⟩ *v/r* drop back, fall behind
rezar ⟨1f⟩ **I** *v/t oración* say **II** *v/i* **1** REL pray **2** *de texto* be worded
rezo *m* prayer
rezongar ⟨1h⟩ *v/i* grumble
rezongón *adj* F grumpy
rezumar ⟨1a⟩ *v/t & v/i* ooze
ría I *vb* ☞ ***reír*** **II** *f* estuary
riachuelo *m* stream
riada *f* flood
ribazo *m* bank, slope
ribera *f* shore, bank
riberano *L.Am.* **I** *adj* coastal; *de río* riverside *atr* **II** *m*, **-a** *f* person who lives by the sea / river
ribereño ☞ ***riberano***
ribete *m* trimming, edging; ***~s*** *pl fig* elements
ribetear ⟨1a⟩ *v/t* edge, border, trim
rica *f* rich woman
ricacho *m*, **-a** *f*, **ricachón** *m*, **-ona** *f desp* rich person
ricamente *adv* splendidly
ricino *m* BOT castor-oil plant
rico I *adj* **1** rich; ***~ en vitaminas*** rich in vitamins **2** *comida* delicious **3** F *niño* cute F **II** *m* rich man; ***nuevo ~*** nouveau riche
rictus *m* grin
ricura *f* F: ***es una ~ de niño*** he's a real cutie F
ridi *m* F: ***hacer el ~*** look dumb F
ridiculez *f* absurdity ***ser una ~*** be ridiculous
ridiculizar ⟨1f⟩ *v/t* ridicule
ridículo I *adj* ridiculous **II** *m* ridicule; ***hacer el ~, quedar en ~*** make a fool of o.s.; ***poner a alguien en ~*** make a fool of s.o., make s.o. look stupid
ríe *vb* ☞ ***reír***
riego I *vb* ☞ ***regar*** **II** *m* **1** AGR irrigation; ***~ por aspersión*** sprinkler irrigation **2** ANAT: ***~ sanguíneo*** blood flow
riel *m* **1** FERR rail **2**: ***~ para cortinas*** curtain rail
ríen *vb* ☞ ***reír***
rienda *f* rein; ***dar ~ suelta a*** give free rein to; ***a ~ suelta*** *fig* out of control; ***soltar las ~s*** slacken the reins; ***llevar las ~s*** *fig* be in charge; ***tomar las ~s*** (***de***) *fig* take charge (of)
riesgo *m* risk; ***a ~ de*** at the risk of; ***correr el ~*** run the risk (***de*** of); ***correr un ~*** to take a risk; ***de alto / bajo ~*** high / low risk; ***~ de desplome*** danger of collapse
riesgoso *adj L.Am.* risky
rifa *f* raffle
rifar ⟨1a⟩ *v/t* raffle; **rifarse** *v/r fig* fight over
rifirrafe *m* F fight, skirmish

rifle *m* rifle
rige *vb* ☞ ***regir***
rigidez *f* **1** *de material* rigidity **2** *de carácter* inflexibility; *fig* strictness
rígido *adj* **1** *material* rigid **2** *carácter* inflexible; *fig* strict
rigor *m* **1** rigor, *Br* rigour; ***ser de ~*** be a must, be obligatory **2** (*precisión*) rigor, *Br* rigour; ***~ científico*** scientific rigor; ***en ~*** strictly **3** (*dureza*) rigor, *Br* rigour; ***los ~es del invierno*** the rigors of winter; ***los ~es estivales*** the extremes of summer
rigurosidad *f* rigorousness, harshness
riguroso *adj* rigorous, harsh
rima *f* rhyme
rimar ⟨1a⟩ *v/i* rhyme (***con*** with)
rimbombancia *f* ostentation; *de estilo* elaborateness
rimbombante *adj* ostentatious; *estilo* very elaborate
rímel *m* mascara
rincón *m* corner
rinconera *f* corner unit, corner cupboard
rinde *vb* ☞ ***rendir***
ring *m* ring
rinitis *f* MED rhinitis
rinoceronte *m* ZO rhino, rhinoceros
rinoplastia *f* MED rhinoplasty
riña *f* quarrel, fight
◇ **riña de gallos** cockfight
riñe *vb* ☞ ***reñir***
riñón *m* ANAT kidney; ***dolor de riñones*** back pain; ***costar un ~*** F cost an arm and a leg F; ***tener el ~ bien cubierto*** *fig* be well-heeled
riñonera *f* fanny pack, *Br* bum bag
río I *m* river; ***~ abajo / arriba*** up / down river **II** *vb* ☞ ***reír***
◇ **Río de la Plata** River Plate
riojano *adj* of / from La Rioja, Rioja *atr*
rioplatense *adj* of / from the River Plate area, River Plate *atr*
ripio *m* **1** *en discurso etc* padding, waffle **2** *en edificio, pared* rubble **3**: ***no perder ~*** not miss a thing
riqueza *f* wealth
risa *f* laugh; ***~s*** *pl* laughter *sg*; ***dar ~*** be funny; ***morirse de ~*** kill o.s. laughing; ***tomar algo a ~*** treat sth as a joke; ***ser de ~*** *película* be funny; *irón* be a joke
risco *m* crag
risible *adj* laughable
risotada *f* guffaw
ristra *f* string
risueño *adj* cheerful
rítmico *adj* rhythmic(al)
ritmo *m* **1** rate, pace; ***a este ~*** at this rate **2** MÚS rhythm
rito *m* rite
ritual *m*/*adj* ritual
ritualizar ⟨1f⟩ *v/t* ritualize
rival *m/f* rival; ***no tener ~*** be unrivaled *o Br* unrivalled
rivalidad *f* rivalry
rivalizar ⟨1f⟩ *v/i*: ***~ con*** rival
rizado *adj* curly
rizar ⟨1f⟩ *v/t* curl; **rizarse** *v/r* curl
rizo *m* curl; ***rizar el ~*** *fig* loop the loop
rizoma *m* BOT rhizome
rizoso *adj pelo* curly
RNE *f abr* (= ***Radio Nacional de España***) Spanish National Radio
roano *adj caballo* roan
robar ⟨1a⟩ *v/t* **1** *persona, banco* rob; *objeto* steal **2** *naipe* take, pick up
roble *m* BOT oak; ***ser un ~*** *fig* be strong
robledal *m*, **robledo** *m* oak wood
robo *m de banco* robbery; *en casa* burglary; ***ser un ~*** *fig* be a rip-off F
robot *m* robot
◇ **robot de cocina** food processor
robótica *f* robotics *sg*
robotización *f* automation
robotizar ⟨1f⟩ *v/t* automate
robustecer ⟨2d⟩ *v/t* strengthen; **robustecerse** *v/r* become stronger
robustez *f* robustness, sturdiness
robusto *adj* robust, sturdy
roca *f* rock
rocalla *f* chunks of rock *pl*
rocambolesco *adj* bizarre
roce *m fig* friction; ***tener ~s con*** come into conflict with
rociada *f* **1** (*rocío*) dew **2** *de azúcar* sprinkling; *de agua* spraying
rociar ⟨1c⟩ **I** *v/t azúcar* sprinkle; *agua* spray **II** *v/i*: ***rociaba casi todas las noches*** dew fell almost every night
rocín *m* F nag F
rocío *m* dew
rock *m* MÚS rock
rockero I *adj* rock **II** *m*, **-a** *f* rock musician
rococó *adj* rococo
rocódromo *m* climbing wall
rocoso *adj* rocky

R

rocoto *m S.Am.* hot red pepper
rodaballo *m* ZO turbot
rodado *adj* **1** *caballo* pied **2** *tráfico* vehicular **3** *fig*: ***venir ~*** happen by chance
rodaja *f* slice
rodaje *m* **1** *de película* shooting, filming; ***estar de ~*** be shooting, be filming **2** AUTO breaking in, *Br* running in; ***en ~*** breaking in
rodamiento *m* TÉC bearing
◇ **rodamiento de bolas** ball bearing
rodapié *m* baseboard, *Br* skirting board
rodar ⟨1m⟩ **I** *v/i* **1** *de pelota* roll; ***rodarán cabezas*** *fig* heads will roll; ***echarlo todo a ~*** *fig* pack it all in **2** *de coche* go, travel (***a*** at) **3** *sin rumbo fijo* wander **II** *v/t* **1** *película* shoot, film **2** AUTO break in, *Br* run in
rodear ⟨1a⟩ *v/t* surround; **rodearse** *v/r* surround o.s. (***de*** with)
rodeo *m* **1** *en recorrido* detour; ***andarse con ~s*** beat about the bush; ***hablar sin ~s*** speak plainly, get straight to the point; ***dejarse de ~s*** stop beating about the bush **2** *con caballos y vaqueros etc* rodeo
rodilla *f* knee; ***de ~s*** kneeling, on one's knees; ***hincarse*** *o* ***ponerse de ~s*** kneel (down); ***hasta la ~*** *vestido, abrigo etc* knee-length
rodillera *f* DEP kneepad; *para las heridas* knee bandage
rodillo *m* **1** *para amasar* rolling pin **2** TÉC roller
rododendro *m* BOT rhododendron
rodrigón *m* stake, support
rodríguez: ***estar de ~*** be left on one's own
roedor *m* rodent
roedura *f* gnawing
roer ⟨2za⟩ *v/t* gnaw; *fig* eat away at
rogar ⟨1h & 1m⟩ *v/t* ask for; (*implorar*) beg for, plead for; ***hacerse de ~*** play hard to get
rogativa *f* REL rogation
rogatorio *adj* imploring, pleading
rojear ⟨1a⟩ *v/i* go red
rojez *f* redness
rojizo *adj* reddish
rojo **I** *adj* red; ***estar al ~ vivo*** *fig* be red hot; ***ponerse ~*** blush, go red **II** *m color* red **III** *m*, **-a** *f* POL red, commie F
rol *m* role
rolar ⟨1a⟩ *v/i del viento* come around
roleta *f L.Am. en béisbol* ground ball
roletazo *m L.Am. en béisbol* ground ball
rollista **I** *adj* cock and bull *atr* F **II** *m/f* bullshitter P
rollizo *adj* F chubby
rollo *m* **1** FOT roll **2** *fig* F drag F; ***¡qué ~!*** F what a drag! F **3** (*sermón*): ***¡corta el ~!*** F can it! F, shut up! F; ***soltar el ~*** F give a speech **4** (*lío*): ***tener un ~ con alguien*** have a thing with s.o. F **5** (*tema*): ***me va el ~ de la cocina mexicana / la pintura*** P I'm into Mexican cookery / painting F **6**: ***buen / mal ~*** P good / bad atmosphere
◇ **rollo de primavera** GASTR spring roll
Roma *f* Rome; ***mover ~ con Santiago*** *fig* move heaven and earth
romance *m* romance
romancero *m* collection of ballads
románico *m/adj* Romanesque
romano **I** *adj* Roman **II** *m*, **-a** *f* Roman **III**: ***a la -a*** GASTR in batter
romanticismo *m* romanticism
romántico **I** *adj* romantic **II** *m*, **-a** *f* romantic
romanza *f* MÚS romance
rombo *m* rhombus
romería *f* procession
romero *m* BOT rosemary
romo *adj* blunt
rompecabezas *m inv* puzzle
rompehielos *m inv* icebreaker
rompecorazones *m/f inv* F heartbreaker F
rompehuelgas *m inv L.Am.* strikebreaker
rompenueces *m inv L.Am.* nutcracker
rompeolas *m inv* breakwater
romper ⟨2a; *part* ***roto***⟩ **I** *v/t* **1** break; (*hacer añicos*) smash; *tela, papel* tear **2** *relación* break off **II** *v/i* **1** break; ***~ con alguien*** break up with s.o. **2**: ***~ a hacer algo*** start doing sth, start to do sth; ***~ a llorar*** burst into tears, start crying **3**: ***hombre de rompe y rasga*** strong-minded man; **romperse** *v/r* break
rompopo *m C.Am., Méx bebida* eggnog
ron *m* rum
roncador *m*, **~a** *f* snorer
roncar ⟨1g⟩ *v/i* snore
roncha *f* **1** MED bump, swelling; ***levantar ~s*** *fig* put people's backs up **2**

(*loncha*) slice

ronco *adj* hoarse; ***quedarse ~*** go hoarse

ronda *f* round; ***pagar una ~*** buy a round; ***~ de conversaciones*** round of discussions; ***~ negociadora*** round of negotiations

rondalla *f* group of minstrels

rondar ⟨1a⟩ **I** *v/t* **1** *zona* patrol **2**: ***me ronda una idea*** I have an idea going around in my head **3** *mujer* serenade **4**: ***~ los treinta*** be around thirty **II** *v/i* F hang around F

rondeño *adj* of / from Ronda, Ronda *atr*

rondón *m*: ***de ~*** without permission; ***entrar de ~*** gatecrash

ronquear ⟨1a⟩ *v/i* be hoarse

ronquera *f* hoarseness

ronquido *m* snore; ***~s*** *pl* snoring *sg*

ronronear ⟨1a⟩ *v/i de gato* purr

ronroneo *m* purring

roña *f* grime

roñería *f* grime

roñoso *adj* grimy, grubby

ropa *f* clothes *pl*; ***~ para el tiempo libre*** leisurewear; ***a quema ~*** ☞ ***quemarropa***

◇ **ropa blanca** whites *pl*; **ropa de calle** everyday clothes *pl*; **ropa de cama** bedclothes *pl*; **ropa de color** colors *pl*, *Br* coloureds *pl*; **ropa de confección** off-the-peg clothes *pl*; **ropa interior** underwear; **ropa íntima** *L.Am.* underwear; **ropa usada** secondhand clothes *pl*

ropaje *m* clothes *pl*, apparel *fml*

ropavejero *m*, **-a** *f* used clothes dealer, *Br* secondhand clothes dealer

ropero *m* closet, *Br* wardrobe

roque *m* **1** *en ajedrez* rook **2**: ***quedarse ~*** *fig* F drop *o* doze off F, fall asleep

roquedal *m* rocky area

roqueño *adj* rocky

roquero *adj* ☞ ***rockero***

rorcual *m* ZO finback whale

rorro *m* F baby

rosa I *adj* pink **II** *f* BOT rose; ***fresco como una ~*** fresh as a daisy; ***no hay ~ sin espinas*** there is no rose without a thorn **III** *m* pink; ***~ pálido*** pale pink; ***ver algo de color de ~*** see sth through rose-colored glasses; ***no es de color de ~*** *fig* it isn't a bed of roses

◇ **rosa náutica** compass rose; **rosa de té** BOT tea rose; **rosa de los vientos** compass rose

rosáceas *fpl* rosaceae *pl*

rosáceo *adj* pinkish

rosado I *adj* pink; *vino* rosé **II** *m* rosé

rosal *m* rosebush

rosaleda *f* rose garden

rosario *m* **1** REL rosary **2** *fig* string; ***acabar como el ~ de la aurora*** end badly

rosbif *m* GASTR roast beef

rosca *f* **1** TÉC thread; ***pasarse de ~*** *de tornillo* have its thread stripped; *fig* go too far, overstep the mark **2** GASTR F *pastry similar to a donut*; ***hacer la ~ a alguien*** butter s.o. up, sweet-talk s.o.; ***no comerse una ~*** F have no luck with the opposite sex

rosco *m* GASTR *pastry similar to a donut*; ***no comerse un ~*** F ☞ ***rosca***

roscón *m* GASTR *large ring-shaped cake*

◇ **roscón de Reyes** GASTR *large ring-shaped cake traditionally eaten at Epiphany*

roseta *f* rose window

rosetón *m* **1** ARQUI rose window **2** *de luz* ceiling rose

rosita *f*: ***irse de ~s*** (*sin ayudar*) be along for the ride

rosquilla *f pastry similar to a donut*; ***venderse como ~s*** F sell like hotcakes F

rosticería *f L.Am. type of deli that sells roast chicken*

rostro *m* face; ***tener mucho ~*** *fig* F have a lot of nerve F

rotación *f* rotation

◇ **rotación de cultivos** AGR crop rotation

rotar ⟨1a⟩ *v/i de personas* take turns

rotativa *f* TIP rotary press

rotativo *m* newspaper

rotatorio *adj* rotary

rotisería *f L.Am.* deli, delicatessen

roto I *part* ☞ ***romper*** **II** *adj pierna etc* broken; (*hecho añicos*) smashed; *tela, papel* torn **III** *m*, **-a** *f Chi* one of the urban poor **IV** *m en prenda de vestir* tear, rip; ***valer*** *o* ***servir lo mismo para un ~ que para un descosido*** *fig* F be useful for lots of things

rotonda *f* traffic circle, *Br* roundabout

rotor *m* TÉC rotor

rotoso *adj Rpl* scruffy

R

rótula *f* **1** ANAT knee cap, *fml* patella **2** TÉC ball-and-socket joint
rotulación *f* labeling, *Br* labelling
rotulador *m* fiber-tip, *Br* fibre-tip, felt-tip
rotular ⟨1a⟩ *v/t* label
rotulista *m/f* signwriter
rótulo *m* sign
rotundamente *adv* categorically, emphatically
rotundidad *f*: ***con ~*** flatly, categorically
rotundo *adj fig* categorical
rotura *f* breakage; ***una ~ de cadera*** MED a broken hip
roturación *f* AGR plowing, *Br* ploughing
roturar ⟨1a⟩ *v/t* AGR plow, *Br* plough
rozadura *f* chafing, rubbing
rozagante *adj* healthy
rozamiento *m* rubbing; FÍS friction
rozar ⟨1f⟩ **I** *v/t* **1** rub **2** (*tocar ligeramente*) brush; *fig* (*tener relación con*) touch on **3**: ***~ los sesenta*** be pushing 60 **F II** *v/i* rub; **rozarse** *v/r* **1** (*rasparse*) rub **2** (*desgastarse*) wear
r.p.m. *abr* (= ***revoluciones por minuto***) rpm (= revolutions per minute)
rte. *abr* (= ***remitente***) sender
RTVE *f abr* (= ***Radiotelevisión Española***) Spanish Radio and Television
ruana *f Ecuad* poncho
ruano *adj* ☞ ***roano***
rubeola, rubéola *f* MED German measles *sg*
rubí *m* ruby
rubiales *m/f inv* blonde guy; *mujer* blonde (woman)
rubicundo *adj* ruddy
rubio *adj* blonde; ***tabaco ~*** Virginia tobacco
◇ **rubio ceniza** ash blonde
◇ **rubio platino** platinum blonde
rublo *m* rouble
rubor *m* flush
ruborizar ⟨1f⟩ *v/t* blush; **ruborizarse** *v/r* go red, blush
ruboroso *adj*: ***estar ~*** be blushing; ***ser ~*** blush easily
rúbrica *f* **1** *de firma* flourish **2** *fml* (*epígrafe*) heading
rubricar ⟨1g⟩ *v/t* **1** *fml documento* sign **2** *fig* endorse, sanction
rubro *m L.Am.* category, heading
rudeza *f* roughness
rudimentario *adj* rudimentary
rudimento *m* rudiment, basic; ***~s*** *pl* rudiments, basics
rudo *adj* **1** *al tacto* rough **2** *persona* rude
rueca *f* distaff
rueda *f* wheel; ***ir*** *o* ***marchar sobre ~s*** *fig* go *o* run smoothly; ***hacer la ~*** *de pavón* display
◇ **rueda de auxilio** *Rpl* spare wheel; **rueda de Chicago** *Andes* Ferris wheel; **rueda dentada** cogwheel; **rueda gigante** *CSur* Ferris wheel; **rueda de prensa** press conference; **rueda de recambio** spare wheel; **rueda de reconocimiento** JUR line-up, *Br* ID parade
ruedo *m* TAUR bullring; ***dar la vuelta al ~*** do a lap of honor *o Br* honour
ruego I *vb* ☞ ***rogar* II** *m* request
rufián *m* rogue
rugby *m* rugby
rugido *m de león* roar; *de estómago* rumble, growl
rugir ⟨3c⟩ *v/i de león* roar; *de estómago* rumble, growl
rugosidad *f* roughness
rugoso *adj superficie* rough
ruibarbo *m* BOT rhubarb
ruido *m* noise; ***hacer ~*** make a noise; ***armar mucho ~*** make a lot of noise; *fig* make a fuss; ***mucho ~ y pocas nueces*** all talk and no action
◇ **ruido de fondo** background noise
◇ **ruido de sables** *fig* saber rattling
ruidoso *adj* noisy
ruin *adj* **1** (*despreciable*) despicable, mean **2** (*tacaño*) mean, miserly
ruina *f* **1** (*quiebra*) ruin; ***amenazar ~*** be on the point of collapse; ***llevar a alguien a la ~*** bankrupt s.o.; ***estar en la ~*** be in dire straits **2** *persona*: ***estar hecho una ~*** be a wreck **3** *de edificio*: ***~s*** *pl* ruins
ruinoso *adj* in ruins; ***estado ~*** dilapidated state
ruiseñor *m* ZO nightingale
ruleta *f* roulette
ruletero *m Méx* cab *o* taxi driver
rulo *m* roller
Rumania *f* Romania, Rumania
rumano I *adj* Romanian, Rumanian **II** *m*, **-a** *f* Romanian, Rumanian
rumbeador *m Rpl* tracker
rumbear ⟨1a⟩ *v/i L.Am.* head (***para*** for)
rumbo *m* course; ***tomar ~ a*** head for;

perder el ~ *fig* lose one's way; ***tomar otro ~*** *tb fig* take a different course
rumboso *adj* lavish
rumiante *m/adj* ruminant
rumiar ⟨1b⟩ *v/t fig* ponder
rumor *m* rumor, *Br* rumour
rumorearse ⟨1a⟩ *v/r* be rumored, *Br* be rumoured; ***se rumorea que*** it is rumored that
rumoreo *m* rumors *pl*, *Br* rumours *pl*
rumorología *f* F rumormongering, *Br* rumourmongering
runrún *m* F murmur
runrunear *vb* ☞ ***ronronear***
rupestre *adj*: ***pintura ~*** cave painting
rupia *f* rupee
ruptura *f de relaciones* breaking off; *de pareja* break-up
rural I *adj* rural **II** *m* **1** *Rpl* station wagon, *Br* estate car **2** *Méx*: ***~es*** *pl* (rural) police
Rusia *f* Russia
ruso I *adj* Russian **II** *m*, **-a** *f* Russian
rústico *adj* **1** *mueble, casa* rustic **2** (*tosco*) coarse **3**: ***en -a*** *libro* softcover *atr*
ruta *f* route
rutilante *adj* gleaming, twinkling
rutilar ⟨1a⟩ *v/i lit* gleam
rutina *f* routine
rutinario *adj* routine *atr*

S

S *abr* (= ***sur***) S (= South(ern))
s. *abr* (= ***siglo***) C (= century)
S.A. *abr* (= ***sociedad anónima***) inc (= incorporated), *Br* plc (= public limited company)
sábado *m* Saturday; ***Sábado Santo*** *o* ***de Gloria*** Easter Saturday
sábalo *m* ZO shad
sabana *f* savanna(h)
sábana *f* sheet; ***se le pegan las ~s*** he oversleeps
◇ **sábana ajustable** fitted sheet
◇ **sábana encimera** top sheet
sabandija *f* **1** bug F, *Br* creepy-crawly F **2** *fig persona* louse F
sabañón *m* chilblain
sabatino *adj* Saturday *atr*
sabedor *adj*: ***ser ~ de algo*** know about sth
sabelotodo *m* F know-it-all, *Br* know-all
saber ⟨2n⟩ **I** *v/t* **1** know; ***hacer ~ algo a alguien*** let s.o. know sth; ***¿cómo lo sabes?*** how do you know?; ***¡si lo sabré yo!*** don't I know it!; ***¡para que lo sepas!*** so there!; ***sabérselas todas*** F know every trick in the book
2 (*ser capaz de*): ***~ hacer algo*** know how to do sth, be able to do sth; ***sé nadar / leer*** I can swim / read; ***~ alemán*** know German
3 (*enterarse*) find out; ***lo supe ayer*** I found out yesterday
II *v/i* **1** know (***de*** about); ***¡vete a ~!, ¡vaya usted a ~!*** heaven knows; ***¡quién sabe!*** who knows!; ***¡qué sé yo!*** who knows?; ***que yo sepa*** as far as I know; ***no que yo sepa*** not as far as I know; ***hace mucho que no sé de ella*** I haven't heard from her for a long time
2 (*tener sabor*) taste (***a*** of); ***me sabe a quemado*** it tastes burnt to me; ***las vacaciones me han sabido a poco*** my vacation went much too quickly; ***me sabe mal*** *fig* it upsets me
III *m* knowledge, learning
IV: ***a ~*** namely
saberse *v/r*: ***nunca se sabe*** you never know
sabidillo *adj* F ☞ ***sabihondo***
sabido *adj* well-known; ***de todos es ~*** it is well known, everybody knows
sabiduría *f* wisdom; (*conocimientos*) knowledge
sabiendas *fpl*: ***a ~*** knowingly; ***a ~ que*** knowing full well that
sabihondo F **I** *adj*: ***es muy ~*** he's a real know-it-all, *Br* he's a real know-all **II** *m*, **-a** *f* know-it-all, *Br* know-all
sabio I *adj* **1** wise **2** (*sensato*) sensible **II** *m*, **-a** *f* **1** wise person **2** (*experto*) expert
sabiondo *adj* F ☞ ***sabihondo***
sablazo *m*: ***dar un ~ a alguien*** F scrounge money off s.o. F
sable *m* saber, *Br* sabre
sablear ⟨1a⟩ *v/t & v/i L.Am.* F scrounge

(***a*** from)
sablista *m/f* F scrounger F
sabor *m* flavor, *Br* flavour, taste; ***dejar mal ~ de boca*** *fig* leave a bad taste in the mouth
saborear ⟨1a⟩ *v/t* **1** *comida* savor, *Br* savour **2** *fig* relish
saborizante *m* flavoring, *Br* flavouring
sabotaje *m* sabotage
saboteador *m*, **~a** *f* saboteur
sabotear ⟨1a⟩ *v/t* sabotage
sabroso *adj* **1** *comida* tasty; *fig conversación* juicy **2** *L.Am.* (*agradable*) nice, pleasant
sabrosura *f L.Am.* tasty dish
sabueso *m* **1** ZO bloodhound **2** *fig* sleuth
saca *f* sack
sacacorchos *m inv* corkscrew
sacamuelas *m inv* F *desp* dentist
sacapuntas *m inv* pencil sharpener
sacar ⟨1g⟩ *v/t* **1** take out; ***~ de paseo*** take for a walk; ***~ a alguien a bailar*** ask s.o. to dance
2 *mancha* take out, remove
3 *disco*, *libro* bring out
4 *fotocopias* make; ***le sacó bien*** PINT, FOT that's a good picture of you
5 (*conseguir*) get; ***~ información*** get information; ***¿de dónde has sacado el dinero?*** where did you get the money from?; ***~ un buen sueldo*** make good money
6: ***~ a alguien de sí*** drive s.o. mad; ***~ algo en claro*** (*entender*) make sense of sth; ***me saca dos años*** he is two years older than me
sacarse *v/r* **1** *L.Am. ropa* take off **2**: ***se sacó el carnet de conducir el año pasado*** he got his license last year
sacarina *f* saccharin(e)
sacerdocio *m* priesthood
sacerdotal *adj* priestly
sacerdote *m* priest
sacerdotisa *f* priestess
saciar ⟨1b⟩ *v/t fig* satisfy, fulfill, *Br* fulfil; **saciarse** *v/r* be satisfied
saciedad *f* satiety; ***repetir algo hasta la ~*** *fig* repeat sth time and again, repeat sth ad nauseam
saco *m* **1** sack; ***mis consejos cayeron en ~ roto*** my advice fell on stony ground; ***tener algo / a alguien en el ~*** *fig* F have sth / s.o. in the bag **2** *L.Am. chaqueta* jacket **3**: ***entrar a ~ en*** F burst into, barge into F
◇ **saco de dormir** sleeping bag
◇ **saco de punta** *L.Am.* cardigan
sacramental *adj* sacramental
sacramento *m* sacrament; ***últimos ~s*** last rites
sacrificado *adj* self-sacrificing
sacrificar ⟨1g⟩ *v/t* **1** (*ofrecer*) sacrifice **2** (*matar*) slaughter; **sacrificarse** *v/r* make sacrifices (***por*** for)
sacrificio *m tb en béisbol* sacrifice
sacrilegio *m* sacrilege
sacrílego *adj* sacrilegious
sacristán *m* sexton
sacristía *f* vestry
sacro *adj* sacred, holy; ***música -a*** sacred music; ***hueso ~*** ANAT sacrum
sacrosanto *adj* sacrosanct
sacudida *f* **1** *a alfombra*, *de avión* shake **2** EL shock
sacudidor *m* duster
sacudimiento *m* **1** *a alfrombra*, *de avión* shake **2** EL shock
sacudir ⟨3a⟩ **I** *v/t* **1** *tb fig* shake **2** F *niño* beat, wallop F; **sacudirse** *v/r* shake off, shrug off; ***~ alguien*** (***de encima***) get rid of s.o.
sádico I *adj* sadistic **II** *m*, **-a** *f* sadist
sadismo *m* sadism
sadomasoquismo *m* sadomasochism
sadomasoquista I *adj* sadomasochistic **II** *m/f* sadomasochist
saeta *f* **1** (*flecha*) arrow; (*dardo*) dart **2** *de reloj* hand **3** REL: *verse sung at processions during Holy Week*
safari *m* safari; ***ir de ~*** go on safari
◇ **safari fotográfico** photo safari
saga *f* saga
sagacidad *f* shrewdness, sharpness
sagaz *adj* shrewd, sharp
sagitariano *L.Am.* ASTR **I** *adj* Sagittarian; ***soy ~*** I'm (a) Sagittarian, I'm (a) Sagittarius **II** *m*, **-a** *f* Sagittarian, Sagittarius
Sagitario ASTR **I** *adj* Sagittarian; ***soy ~*** I'm (a) Sagittarian, I'm (a) Sagittarius **II** *m/f inv* Sagittarius
sagrado *adj* sacred, holy
sagrario *m* tabernacle
Sahara *m* Sahara
sahariana *f* safari jacket
sahariano *adj* Saharan
SAI *m abr* (= ***sistema de alimentación***

ininterrumpible) UPS (= uninterruptible power supply)
sainete *m* TEA short farce, one-act play
sajar ⟨1a⟩ *v/t* MED cut open
sajón I *adj* Saxon **II** *m*, **-ona** *f* Saxon
sal I *f* **1** salt; ***sin ~*** salt-free, without salt; ***bajo en ~*** low in salt, low-salt *atr* **2** *fig* (*garbo, gracia*) wit; ***~ y pimienta*** spark, zest **3** *C.Am., Méx* bad luck **II** *vb* ☞ ***salir***
◇ **sal común** cooking salt; **sal gema** rock salt; **sal gorda, sal gruesa** cooking salt; **sal marina** sea salt; **sales de baño** bath salts
sala *f* room, hall; *de cine* screen; JUR court room
◇ **sala de lo civil** civil court; **sala de embarque** AVIA departure lounge; **sala de espera** waiting room; **sala de estar** living room; **sala de fiestas** night club; **sala de juntas** boardroom; **sala de máquinas** MAR engine room; **sala de lo penal** criminal court; **sala de sesiones** boardroom
saladero *m L.Am.* meat / fish salting factory
saladito *m Rpl* canapé
salado *adj* **1** (*con sal*) salted; (*con demasiada sal*) salty **2** (*no dulce*) savory, *Br* savoury **3** *fig* funny, witty **4** *C.Am., Chi, Rpl* F pricey F
saladura *f* salting
salamandra *f* **1** ZO salamander **2** *estufa* portable heater
salamanquesa *f* ZO gecko
salami *m* salami
salar ⟨1a⟩ **I** *v/t* add salt to, salt; *para conservar* salt **II** *m Arg* salt mine
salarial *adj* salary *atr*
salario *m* salary, wage
◇ **salario base** basic wage
◇ **salario mínimo** minimum wage
salazón *f* **1** *acto* salting; ***en ~*** salt *atr* **2**: ***salazones*** *pl carne* salted meat *sg*; *pescado* salted fish *sg*
salchicha *f* sausage
salchichería *f* pork butcher's (store), charcuterie
salchichón *m type of spiced sausage*
saldar ⟨1a⟩ *v/t* **1** *disputa* settle; *deuda* settle, pay **2** *géneros* sell off; **saldarse** *v/r* result (***con*** in)
saldo *m* **1** COM balance **2** (*resultado*) result **3**: ***~s*** *pl* clearance sale *sg*; ***de ~*** *artículo* reduced, on sale
◇ **saldo acreedor** credit balance
◇ **saldo deudor** debit balance
saldré *vb* ☞ ***salir***
saledizo ARQUI **I** *adj* projecting **II** *m* overhang, projection
salero *m* **1** *recipiente* salt cellar **2** *fig* wit
saleroso *adj* funny, witty
salesiano REL **I** *adj* Salesian **II** *m* Salesian
salga *vb* ☞ ***salir***
salgo *vb* ☞ ***salir***
salida *f* **1** *de edificio, zoo etc* exit, way out; *de autopista* exit **2** TRANSP departure **3** DEP *de carrera* start; ***tomar la ~*** start; ***dar la ~*** give the starting signal *o* the off **4** COM: ***tiene ~*** there's a market for it; ***~ a bolsa*** flotation **5** *fig* opportunity, opening; ***~ profesional*** career opportunity
◇ **salida de emergencia** emergency exit; **salida nula** DEP false start; **salida del sol** sunrise; **salida de tono** ill--judged remark
saliente I *adj* **1** *borde, moldura* projecting, protruding **2** *presidente* retiring, outgoing **II** *m* ARQUI projection
salina *f* salt mine; ***~s*** *pl* saltworks *sg*
salinidad *f* salinity
salino *adj* saline
salir ⟨3r⟩ *v/i* **1** leave, go out; ***~ de*** (*ir fuera de*) leave, go out of; (*venir fuera de*) leave, come out of; ***~ a Avda. América*** come out onto Avda. América; *de calle* lead to Avda. América; ***~ de apuros*** get out of difficulties; ***~ corriendo*** run off; ***~ con alguien*** date s.o., go out with s.o.
2 (*aparecer*) appear, come out
3: ***~ a bolsa*** float, be floated
4 DEP *en carrera* start; ***~ fuera*** *de pelota* go out
5 INFOR *de programa* quit, exit
6 (*parecerse a*): ***~ a alguien*** *de bebé* take after s.o.
7 (*resultar*): ***~ bien / mal*** turn out well / badly; ***salió caro*** *tb fig* it worked out expensive; ***~ ileso*** escape unharmed; ***~ perdiendo*** end up losing; ***~ a 1000 colones*** cost 1000 colons; ***a lo que salga*** any old how
8: ***¡ya salió aquello!*** F why did you have to bring that up?; ***~ con algo*** F come out with sth; ***¿y ahora me sales***

S

con que no tienes dinero? and you're telling me now that you don't have any money?
9 (*conseguir*): ***el dibujo no me sale*** F I can't get this drawing right; ***no me salió el trabajo*** I didn't get the job
10: ***~ por alguien*** stand up for s.o.
salirse *v/r* **1** *de líquido* overflow **2** (*dejar*) leave; ***~ de*** leave; ***~ de la carretera*** leave the road, go off the road **3**: ***~ con la suya*** get what one wants

salitre *m* saltpeter, *Br* saltpetre

saliva *f* saliva; ***gastar ~*** *fig* F waste one's breath; ***tragar ~*** *fig* F hold one's tongue

salivación *f* salivation

salival *adj* salivary; ***glándula ~*** ANAT salivary gland

salivar ⟨1a⟩ *v/i* **1** salivate **2** *L.Am. escupir* spit

salmantino *adj* of / from Salamanca, Salamanca *atr*

salmo *m* psalm

salmodia *f* F droning

salmón **I** *m* ZO salmon **II** *adj* salmon-pink; ***color ~*** salmon

salmonelosis *f* MED salmonella

salmonete *m* ZO red mullet

salmuera *f* pickle, brine

salobre *adj* salt; (*con demasiada sal*) salty

salomónico *adj* just, fair

salón *m* living room
◇ **salón de actos** auditorium, hall; **salón del automóvil** car show, *Br* motor show; **salón de baile** dance hall; **salón de belleza** beauty parlor, *Br* beauty parlour, beautician's; **salón de té** tearoom

salpicadera *f Méx* AUTO fender, *Br* mudguard

salpicadero *m* AUTO dash(board)

salpicadura *f* stain

salpicar ⟨1g⟩ **I** *v/t* **1** splash, spatter (***con*** with); *fig* sprinkle, pepper **2** (*afectar negativamente*) tarnish, touch **II** *v/i* splash; *de aceite* spit

salpicón *m* GASTR *vegetable salad with chopped meat or fish*

salpimentar ⟨1k⟩ *v/t* season (with salt and pepper)

salsa *f* **1** GASTR sauce; ***en su ~*** *fig* in one's element **2** *baile* salsa

salsera *f* sauce boat

salsifí *m* BOT salsify

saltador *m*, **~a** *f* DEP jumper
◇ **saltador de altura** high jumper; **saltador de esquí** ski jumper; **saltador de longitud** long jumper, broad jumper; **saltador de pértiga** pole-vaulter; **saltador de trampolín** diver

saltamontes *m inv* ZO grasshopper

saltar ⟨1a⟩ **I** *v/i* **1** jump, leap; ***~ a la comba*** jump rope, *Br* skip; ***andar*** *o* ***estar a la que salta*** never miss an opportunity **2** (*abalanzarse*): ***~ sobre*** pounce on; ***~ a la vista*** *fig* be obvious, be clear **3** *de fusible, plomos* blow; ***~ por los aires*** blow up, explode **4**: ***saltó con una sarta de estupideces*** he came out with one stupid thing after another
II *v/t* **1** *valla* jump **2**: ***~ la banca*** break the bank
saltarse *v/r* (*omitir*) miss, skip

saltarín *adj* fidgety, nervous

salteador *m*: **~ (*de caminos*)** highwayman

saltear ⟨1a⟩ *v/t* GASTR sauté

saltimbanqui *m* acrobat

salto *m* leap, jump; ***dar un ~*** jump; ***dar un ~ adelante*** jump forward; ***~ atrás*** *tb fig* step backwards; ***de un ~*** in one jump; ***dar ~s de alegría*** jump for joy; ***triple ~*** triple jump; ***concurso de ~s*** showjumping competition
◇ **salto de agua** waterfall; **salto alto** *L.Am.* high jump; **salto de altura** high jump; **salto de cama** negligee; **salto entre dos** *en baloncesto* jump ball; **salto con garrocha** DEP *L.Am.* pole vault; **salto inicial** *en baloncesto* tip-off; **salto largo** *L.Am.* long jump, broad jump; **salto de longitud** DEP long jump, broad jump; **salto mortal** somersault; **salto con pértiga** DEP pole vault; **salto de trampolín** DEP dive

saltón *adj*: ***ojos saltones*** bulging eyes

salubre *adj* healthy, salubrious *fml*

salubridad *f L.Am.* health; ***Salubridad*** Department of Health

salud *f* health; ***¡(a tu) ~!*** cheers!; ***~ de hierro*** iron constitution

saludable *adj* healthy

saludar ⟨1a⟩ *v/t* **1** say hello to, greet; ***salúdele de mi parte*** say hello to him for me **2** MIL salute

saludo *m* **1** greeting; ***mandar ~s a alguien*** send s.o. one's regards *o* one's

best wishes **2** *en carta*: **~s** best wishes; (**reciba**) **un cordial ~** regards, (with) best wishes **3** MIL salute
salva *f*: **~ de aplausos** round of applause
salvación *f* **1** REL salvation **2** (*rescate*) rescue
salvado *m* bran
salvador *m* REL savior, *Br* saviour
salvadoreño I *adj* Salvador(e)an **II** *m*, **-a** *f* Salvador(e)an
salvaguarda *f* ☞ **salvaguardia**
salvaguardar ⟨1a⟩ *v/t* safeguard, protect
salvaguardia *f* safeguard
salvajada *f* atrocity, act of savagery; **decir una ~** say something outrageous
salvaje I *adj* **1** *animal* wild **2** (*bruto*) brutal **II** *m/f* savage
salvajismo *m* savagery
salvamanteles *m inv* table mat
salvamento *m* rescue; **buque de ~** life boat
salvapantallas *m inv* INFOR screensaver
salvar ⟨1a⟩ *v/t* **1** *vida*, *matrimonio* save; **~ la vida a alguien** save s.o.'s life **2** *obstáculo* get round, get over **3** REL save; **salvarse** *v/r* **1** escape, get out; **sálvese quien pueda** *fig* every man for himself **2** REL be saved
salvaslip *m* panty liner
salvavidas I *adj*: **bote ~** lifeboat; **chaleco ~** life jacket **II** *m inv* **1** life belt; *chaleco* life jacket **2** *L.Am. socorrista* life guard
salvedad *f* (*excepción*) exception; **con la ~ de** with the exception of; **hacer una ~** make an exception
salvia *f* BOT sage
salvo I *adj*: **estar a ~** be safe (and sound); **ponerse a ~** reach safety **II** *adv* & *prp* except, save; **~ error u omisión** errors and omissions excepted; **~ que** unless
salvoconducto *m* safe-conduct
samaritano *m*, **-a** *f*: **el buen ~** the good Samaritan
sambenito *m*: **le han colgado el ~ de vago** F they've got him down as idle F
sambumbia *f L.Am. watery drink*
San *adj* Saint
sanable *adj* curable
sanalotodo *m* cure-all, panacea
sanar ⟨1a⟩ **I** *v/t* cure **II** *v/i de persona* get well, recover; *de herida* heal
sanatorio *m* sanitarium, clinic
San Bernardo *m/f perro* St Bernard
sanción *f* JUR penalty, sanction; **~ económica** economic sanction
sancionable *adj* punishable
sancionar ⟨1a⟩ *v/t* **1** penalize **2** (*multar*) fine
sancocho *m Carib type of stew*
sandalia *f* sandal
sándalo *m* BOT sandalwood
sandez *f* nonsense; **decir sandeces** talk nonsense; **una ~** a piece of nonsense
sandía *f* watermelon
sandunga *f* wit
sandwich *m tostado* toasted sandwich; *L.Am. sin tostar* sandwich
saneamiento *m* **1** *de terreno*, *edificio* cleaning up **2** COM restructuring, rationalization
sanear ⟨1a⟩ *v/t* **1** *terreno*, *edificio* clean up **2** COM restructure, rationalize
sangrar ⟨1a⟩ **I** *v/t*: **~ a alguien** *fig* F bleed s.o. dry **II** *v/i* bleed; **~ por la nariz** have a nosebleed
sangre *f* blood; **echaba ~ por la nariz** his nose was bleeding; **hacerse mala ~** get all worked up; **tener mala ~** be mean; **la ~ se le subió a la cabeza** the blood rushed to his head; **lo lleva en la ~** it's in his blood; **no tener ~ en las venas** *fig* be a cold fish; **no llegará la ~ al río** it won't come to that, it won't be that bad; **sudar ~** sweat blood; **a ~ y fuego** ruthlessly
◇ **sangre azul** blue blood
◇ **sangre fría** *fig* calmness, coolness; **a ~** in cold blood
sangría *f* **1** GASTR sangria **2** TIP indent
sangriento *adj* bloody
sangrigordo *adj Méx* tedious, boring
sanguijuela *f* ZO, *fig* leech
sanguina *adj*: **naranja ~** blood orange
sanguinario *adj* bloodthirsty
sanguíneo *adj* **1** MED blood *atr* **2** *temperamento* sanguine
sanguinolento *adj* **1** *herida*, *mancha* bleeding, bloody **2** *ojos* bloodshot
sanidad *f* health
sanitario I *adj* (public) health *atr* **II** *m*, **-a** *f Rpl* plumber
sanitarios *mpl* bathroom fittings
sano *adj* healthy; **~ y salvo** safe and well; **cortar por lo ~** take drastic mea-

sures
sánscrito *m* Sanskrit
sanseacabó: ***y ~*** F and that's that F
santanderino *adj* of / from Santander, Santander *atr*
santiagués *adj* of / from Santiago de Compostela, Santiago *atr*
santiaguino *adj* of / from Santiago de Chile, Santiago *atr*
santiamén *m*: ***en un ~*** F in an instant
santidad *f*: ***Su Santidad*** His Holiness
santificación *f* sanctification
santificar ⟨1g⟩ *v/t* sanctify
santiguar ⟨1i⟩ *v/t* bless; **santiguarse** *v/r* cross o.s., make the sign of the cross
santísimo I *adj sup* (most) holy **II** *m* REL: ***el Santísimo*** the Holy Sacrament
santo I *adj* holy
II *m*, **-a** *f* saint; ***¿a ~ de qué?*** F what on earth for? F; ***no es ~ de mi devoción*** F I don't like him very much, he isn't my favorite *o Br* favourite person; ***quedarse para vestir ~s*** F be left on the shelf; ***tener el ~ de cara*** be incredibly lucky, have the luck of the devil; ***tener el ~ de espaldas*** have no luck at all; ***fue llegar y besar el ~*** F everything fell into his lap; ***se me ha ido el ~ al cielo*** F it has gone right out of my head; ***dormir como un ~*** sleep like a baby *o* a log; ***Todos los Santos*** All Saints' (Day)
III *m* (*onomástica*) saint's day
◇ **santo y seña** F password
santón *m* holy man
santoral *m* hagiography
santuario *m fig* sanctuary
santurrón I *adj* sanctimonious **II** *m*, **-ona** *f* sanctimonious person, *Br tb* Holy Willie F
saña *f* viciousness
sapiencia *f* wisdom
sapo *m* ZO toad; ***echar ~s y culebras*** *fig* curse and swear; ***tragar(se) ~s*** *fig* F grin and bear it
saque *m* **1** *en fútbol* kick; *con las manos* throw; *en tenis* serve **2**: ***tener buen ~*** F have a big appetite
◇ **saque de banda** *en fútbol* throw-in; **saque de esquina** *en fútbol* corner (kick); **saque de fondo** *en fútbol* goal kick; **saque inicial** *en fútbol* kick-off; **saque lateral** *Rpl*: *en fútbol* throw-in; **saque de puerta** *en fútbol* goal kick; **saque de valla** *Rpl*: *en fútbol* goal kick
saqueador *m*, **~a** *f* looter
saquear ⟨1a⟩ *v/t* sack, ransack
S.A.R. *abr* (= ***Su Alteza Real***) HRH (= His / Her Royal Highness)
sarampión *m* MED measles *sg*
sarao *m* party
sarape *m Méx* poncho, blanket
sarasa *m* F fag V, *Br* poof F
sarcasmo *m* sarcasm
sarcástico *adj* sarcastic
sarcófago *m* sarcophagus
sarcoma *m* MED sarcoma
sardana *f* sardana (*traditional Catalan dance*)
sardina *f* sardine; ***como ~s en lata*** like sardines
sardinero I *adj* sardine *atr* **II** *m*, **-a** *f* sardine seller
sardónico *adj* sardonic
sargento *m* sergeant
◇ **sargento primero** sergeant 1st class, *Br* sergeant-major
sarna *f* MED scabies *sg*; ***más viejo que la ~*** as old as the hills
sarnoso *adj* scabby
sarpullido *m* MED rash
sarracina *f* brawl
sarraceno I *adj* Saracen **II** *m*, **-a** *f* Saracen
sarro *m* tartar
sarta *f* string, series *sg*; ***~ de mentiras*** pack of lies
sartén *f* frying pan; ***saltar de la ~ y dar en las brasas*** *fig* F jump out of the frying pan and into the fire; ***tener la ~ por el mango*** *fig* be the boss, be in the driving seat
sastra *f* tailor(ess)
sastre *m* tailor
sastrería *f* **1** *actividad* tailoring **2** (*taller*) tailor's shop
satán, satanás *m* Satan
satánico *adj* satanic
satélite *m* satellite; ***ciudad ~*** satellite town
◇ **satélite de comunicaciones** communications satellite; **satélite espía** spy satellite; **satélite meteorológico** weather satellite
satén *m*, **satín** *m* satin
satinado *adj papel*, *pintura* glossy
sátira *f* satire
satírico I *adj* satirical **II** *m*, **-a** *f* satirist
satirizar ⟨1f⟩ *v/t* satirize

S

sátiro *m* MYTH satyr; *fig* lecher
satisfacción *f* satisfaction; ***se acabó a mi ~*** it ended to my satisfaction, it ended satisfactorily; ***dar ~*** give satisfaction
satisfacer ⟨2s; *part* ***satisfecho***⟩ *v/t* **1** satisfy **2** *requisito*, *exigencia* meet, fulfill, *Br* fulfil **3** *deuda* settle, pay off; **satisfacerse** *v/r* be satisfied (***con*** with)
satisfactorio *adj* satisfactory
satisfecho I *part* ☞ ***satisfacer* II** *adj* **1** satisfied; ***darse por ~*** be satisfied (***con*** with) **2** (*lleno*) full
saturación *f* QUÍM *tb fig* saturation; ***~ del mercado*** COM market saturation
saturar ⟨1a⟩ *v/t* saturate
saturnismo *m* lead poisoning
sauce *m* BOT willow
◇ **sauce llorón** weeping willow
saúco *m* BOT elder
saudí *m/f & adj* Saudi
saudita *m/f* Saudi
sauna *f* sauna
saurio *m* ZO saurian
savia *f* BOT sap; *fig* vitality
saxo *m* sax
saxofón, saxófono *m* saxophone, sax
saxofonista *m/f* saxophonist
saya *f* **1** skirt **2** (*enagua*) petticoat
sayal *m coarse cloth made from wool*
sayo *m* smock
sazón *f* **1** *lit*: ***a la ~*** at that time **2**: ***estar en ~*** *fruta* be ripe
sazonado *adj* seasoned
sazonar ⟨1a⟩ *v/t* GASTR season
scooter *m* motor scooter
se 1 *pron complemento indirecto*: *a él* (to) him; *a ella* (to) her; *a usted*, *ustedes* (to) you; *a ellos* (to) them; ***~ lo daré*** I will give it to him / her / you / them **2** *reflexivo*: *con él* himself; *con ella* herself; *cosa* itself; *con usted* yourself; *con ustedes* yourselves; *con ellos* themselves; ***~ vistió*** he got dressed, he dressed himself; ***se lavó las manos*** she washed her hands; ***~ sentó*** he sat down; ***~ abrazaron*** they hugged each other
3 *oración impersonal*: ***~ cree*** it is thought; ***~ habla español*** Spanish spoken
SE *abr* (= ***sudeste***) SE (= Southeast)
S.E. *abr* (= ***Su Excelencia***) HE (= His / Her Excellency)

sé *vb* ☞ ***saber***
sea *vb* ☞ ***ser***
sebáceo *adj* sebaceous; ***glándula -a*** ANAT sebaceous gland
sebo *m* grease, fat
seboso *adj* greasy
secadero *m* drying shed
secado *m* drying; ***de ~ rápido*** *tejido* quick-dry
secador *m*: **~** (***de pelo***) hair dryer
secadora *f* dryer
secano *m* unirrigated land
secante I *m* blotting paper **II** *f* MAT secant
secar ⟨1g⟩ *v/t* dry; **secarse** *v/r* dry; *de planta* wither
sección *f* **1** GEOM section **2** BOT cutting **3** *de documento*, *organización* section **4** MIL platoon
seccionar ⟨1a⟩ *v/t* **1** (*cortar*) cut (off) **2** (*dividir en secciones*) divide into sections
secesión *f* POL secession
seco *adj* **1** dry; *planta* dried up; ***estar ~*** F (*tener sed*) be parched F **2** *fig* (*antipático*) curt, brusque **3**: ***dejar a alguien ~*** F kill s.o. stone dead; ***parar en ~*** stop dead **4**: ***llámala Carmen a -as*** just call her Carmen
secreción *f* secretion
secretar ⟨1a⟩ *v/t* secrete
secretaria *f* secretary; ***~ con idiomas*** bilingual / trilingual secretary
◇ **secretaria de dirección** executive secretary
secretaría *f de colegio* secretary's office; *de organización* secretariat
secretariado *m* **1** *estudios* secretarial studies *pl* **2** *puesto* secretaryship, post of secretary **3** *organismo* secretariat
secretario *m tb* POL secretary
◇ **secretario de Defensa** Defense Secretary, Secretary of Defense, *Br* Minister of Defence; **secretario de Estado** *Esp* under secretary, *Br* junior minister; **secretario general** POL secretary-general
secretear *v/i* F ⟨1a⟩ whisper
secreteo *m* F whispering
secreter *m mueble* writing desk
secretismo *m* secrecy
secreto I *adj* secret **II** *m* secret; ***un ~ a voces*** an open secret; ***en ~*** in secret
◇ **secreto bancario** client confidenti-

S

ality
◇ **secreto profesional** professional secrecy
secta *f* sect
sectario *adj* sectarian
sectarismo *m* sectarianism
sector *m* sector
◇ **sector (de) servicios** service sector
secuaz *m/f* follower
secuela *f* MED after-effect
secuencia *f* sequence
secuencial *adj* INFOR sequential
secuestrador *m*, **~a** *f* kidnapper, abductor
◇ **secuestrador aéreo** hijacker
secuestrar ⟨1a⟩ *v/t barco, avión* hijack; *persona* kidnap, abduct
secuestro *m de barco, avión* hijacking; *de persona* kidnapping, abduction
◇ **secuestro aéreo** hijacking
secular *adj* secular, lay
secularizar ⟨1f⟩ *v/t* secularize
secundar ⟨1a⟩ *v/t* support, back
secundario *adj* secondary
sed *f tb fig* thirst (***de*** for); ***tener ~*** be thirsty; ***~ de libertad*** thirst for freedom; ***~ de poder*** thirst for power
seda *f* silk; ***de ~*** silk *atr*; ***como una ~*** F as smooth as silk
◇ **seda artificial** artificial silk
sedación *f* MED sedation
sedal *m* fishing line
sedante *m/adj* MED sedative
sedar ⟨1a⟩ *v/t* MED sedate
sedativo *adj* sedative
sede *f* **1** *de organización* headquarters *sg o pl*; ***la Santa Sede*** the Holy See **2** *de acontecimiento* site
◇ **sede social** head office
sedentario *adj* sedentary
sedición *f* sedition
sedicioso *adj* seditious
sediento *adj* thirsty; ***estar ~ de*** *fig* thirst for; ***~ de venganza*** thirsting for vengeance
sedimentación *f* sedimentation
sedimentar ⟨1a⟩ *v/t* deposit; **sedimentarse** *v/r* settle
sedimento *m* sediment
sedoso *adj* silky
seducción *f* **1** (*enamoramiento*) seduction **2** (*atracción*) attraction
seducir ⟨3o⟩ *v/t* **1** (*enamorar*) seduce **2** (*atraer*) attract **3** (*cautivar*) captivate, charm
seductor I *adj* **1** (*conquistador*) seductive **2** (*atractivo*) attractive **3** *oferta* tempting **II** *m* seducer
seductora *f* seductress
sefardí I *adj* Sephardic **II** *m/f* Sephardi
sefardita *m/f* Sephardi
segada *f en fútbol* scything tackle
segador *m* reaper, harvester
segadora *f* **1** *máquina* harvester **2** *mujer* reaper, harvester
◇ **segadora-atadora** binder
◇ **segadora-trilladora** combine harvester
segar ⟨1h & 1k⟩ *v/t* **1** AGR reap, harvest **2** *vida* cut short
seglar I *adj* secular, lay *atr* **II** *m* layman **III** *f* laywoman
segmentar ⟨1a⟩ *v/t* segment
segmento *m* segment
segregación *f* **1** segregation **2** BIO secretion
◇ **segregación racial** racial segregation
segregar ⟨1h⟩ *v/t* **1** (*aislar*) segregate **2** BIO secrete
seguida *f*: ***en ~*** at once, immediately
seguidamente *adv* immediately afterward
seguidilla *f* seguidilla (*popular Spanish dance*)
seguido I *adj* **1** consecutive, successive; ***de ~*** in a row, one after another **2** (*recto*): ***ir todo ~*** go straight on **II** *adv L.Am.* often, frequently
seguidor *m*, **~a** *f* follower, supporter
seguimiento *m* **1** *de progreso, estudiante etc* monitoring **2** *de misil* tracking
seguir ⟨3l & 3d⟩ **I** *v/t* **1** *consejo, camino, moda etc* follow; ***~ a alguien*** follow s.o. **2** (*permanecer*): ***~ fiel a alguien*** remain faithful to s.o.
II *v/i* continue, carry on; ***~ con algo*** continue with sth, carry on with sth; ***~ haciendo algo*** go on doing sth, continue to do sth; ***sigue cometiendo los mismos errores*** he keeps on making the same mistakes; ***sigue enfadado conmigo*** he's still angry with me; ***¡a ~ bien!*** take care!, take it easy!
seguirse *v/r*: ***~ de algo*** follow from sth
según I *prp* according to; ***~ él*** according to him; ***~ eso*** which means; ***~ el tiempo*** depending on the weather; ***~ y como, ~***

y conforme vaya depending on how things pan out **II** *adv* **1** it depends; ***aceptaré o no, ~*** I might accept, it all depends **III** *conj* (*a medida que*): ***la tensión crecía ~ se acercaba el final*** the tension mounted as the end approached

segunda *f* **1**: ***de ~*** *fig* second-rate **2** *en fútbol* second division

◇ **segunda base** *f en béisbol* second base; *jugador* second baseman

segundero *m* second hand

segundo I *adj* second; ***prima -a*** second cousin **II** *m* **1** second; ***el ~ mejor*** the second best **2** *de tiempo* second **3** *de una comida* second course **4** *de edificio*: ***vivir en el ~*** live on the third *o Br* second floor

segundogénito *m*, **-a** *f*, **segundón** *m*, **-ona** *f* second child

seguramente *adv* surely, probably

seguridad *f* **1** *de tratamiento, puente* safety; ***cinturón de ~*** seatbelt **2** *contra crimen* security **3** (*certeza*) certainty; ***con toda ~*** for sure

◇ **Seguridad Social** *Esp* Social Security

◇ **seguridad vial** road safety

seguro I *adj* **1** *tratamiento, puente* safe; ***ir sobre ~*** be on the safe side **2** (*estable*) steady **3** (*cierto*) sure; ***es ~*** it's a certainty; ***dar algo por ~*** be sure about sth; ***no estoy tan ~*** I'm not so sure; ***a buen ~*** definitely **4** *persona*: ***~ de sí mismo*** self-confident, sure of o.s.
II *adv* for sure
III *m* **1** COM insurance **2** *de puerta, coche* lock; ***poner el ~*** lock the door **3** *L.Am. para ropa etc* safety pin

◇ **seguro de desempleo** unemployment benefit *o* compensation; **seguro de equipajes** baggage insurance; **seguro del hogar** household insurance; **seguro de jubilación** pension plan; **seguro médico** medical insurance; **seguro de paro** unemployment benefit *o* compensation; **seguro a todo riesgo** all-risks insurance; **seguro de vida** life insurance

seis *m/adj* six

seiscientos *adj* six hundred

seísmo *m* earthquake

selección *f* selection; ***~ de residuos*** waste separation

◇ **selección nacional** DEP national team

◇ **selección natural** BIO natural selection

seleccionador *m* DEP: ***~ nacional*** national team manager

seleccionar ⟨1a⟩ *v/t* choose, select

selectividad *f Esp* university entrance exam

selectivo *adj* selective

selecto *adj* select, exclusive

selector *m* TÉC *de temperatura, función* switch

selenio *m* QUÍM selenium

sellado *m* **1** *de documento* stamp **2** (*precinto*) seal

sellar ⟨1a⟩ *v/t* **1** *documento* stamp **2** (*precintar*) seal

sello *m* **1** stamp; ***~ de calidad*** stamp of quality **2** *fig* hallmark

◇ **sello discográfico** record label

selva *f* **1** (*bosque*) forest **2** (*jungla*) jungle

◇ **selva tropical** tropical rain forest

◇ **selva virgen** virgin forest

selvático *adj* forest *atr*

semáforo *m* traffic light; ***saltarse un ~ en rojo*** run *o* jump a red light

semana *f* week; ***entre ~*** during the week, midweek

◇ **semana inglesa** five-day week

◇ **Semana Santa** Holy Week, Easter

semanal *adj* weekly

semanario *m* weekly

semántica *f* semantics *sg*

semántico *adj* semantic

semblante *m* face

sembrado *m* sown field

sembrador *m* sower

sembradora *f* **1** *máquina* seed drill **2** *mujer* sower

sembrar ⟨1k⟩ *v/t* **1** sow **2** *fig*: *pánico, inquietud etc* spread

semejante I *adj* similar; ***jamás he oído ~ tontería*** I've never heard such nonsense **II** *m* fellow human being, fellow creature; ***mis ~s*** my fellow men

semejanza *f* similarity

semejar ⟨1a⟩ *v/t* resemble; **semejarse** *v/r* look alike, resemble each other

semen *m* BIO semen

semental *m toro* stud bull; *caballo* stallion

sementera *f* sowing

semestral *adj* six-monthly, half-yearly
semestre *m* **1** six-month period **2** EDU semester
semi *pref* semi
semibreve *f* MÚS whole note, *Br* semibreve
semicircular *adj* semicircular
semicírculo *m* semicircle
semiconductor *m* EL semiconductor
semidesnudo *adj* half-naked
semidiós *m* demigod
semiesfera *f* MAT hemisphere
semifinal *f* DEP semifinal
semifinalista *m/f* DEP semifinalist
semilla *f* seed
semillero *m* **1** seedbed **2** *fig*: *de disgustos, odio* breeding ground
seminal *adj* seminal
seminario *m* seminary
seminarista *m* seminarian
semiología *f* semiology
semiótica *f* semiotics *sg*
semita I *adj* Semitic **II** *m/f* Semite
semítico *adj* Semitic
semitono *m* MÚS semitone
sémola *f* semolina
sempiterno *adj* eternal
Sena: ***el ~*** the Seine
senado *m* senate
senador *m*, **~a** *f* senator
sencillamente *adv* simply
sencillez *f* simplicity
sencillo I *adj* simple; ***gente(s) -a(s)*** simple people **II** *m* **1** *L.Am.* small change **2** *en béisbol* base hit
senda *f* path, track
senderismo *m* trekking, hiking
senderista *m/f* walker, hiker
sendero *m* path, track
sendos, -as *adj pl*: ***les entregó ~ diplomas*** he presented each of them with a diploma; ***recibieron ~ regalos*** they each received a gift
senil *adj* senile
senilidad *f* senility
sénior *m/f* & *adj* senior
seno *m* **1** *tb fig* bosom; **~*s*** breasts **2** MAT sine **3** ANAT sinus
sensación *f* feeling, sensation; ***causar ~*** *fig* cause a sensation
sensacional *adj* sensational
sensacionalismo *m* sensationalism
sensacionalista *adj* sensationalist
sensatez *f* good sense
sensato *adj* sensible
sensibilidad *f* **1** *en parte del cuerpo* feeling **3** (*emotividad*) sensitivity
sensibilizar ⟨1f⟩ *v/t* make aware (***sobre*** of)
sensible *adj* **1** *persona, dispositivo* sensitive; ***~ al calor / a la luz*** heat- / light--sensitive **2** (*apreciable*) appreciable, noticeable
sensiblemente *adv* considerably
sensiblería *f* sentimentality, schmaltz F
sensiblero *adj* sentimental, schmaltzy F
sensitivo *adj* sensory
sensor *m* sensor
sensorial *adj* sensory
sensual *adj* sensual
sensualidad *f* sensuality
sentada *f* **1** *protesta* sit-down **2**: ***de una ~*** F in one sitting
sentado *adj* **1** sitting, seated; ***estar ~*** be sitting, be seated **2**: ***dar por ~*** *fig* take for granted, assume
sentar ⟨1k⟩ **I** *v/t fig* establish, create; ***~ las bases*** lay the foundations, pave the way **II** *v/i*: ***~ bien / mal*** *de propuesta* go down well / badly; ***~ bien a alguien*** *de comida* agree with s.o.; ***le sienta bien esa chaqueta*** that jacket suits her, she looks good in that jacket; **sentarse** *v/r* sit down
sentencia *f* JUR sentence; ***visto para ~*** ready for sentencing
sentenciar ⟨1b⟩ *v/t* JUR sentence
sentencioso *adj* sententious
sentido I *adj* heartfelt
II *m* **1** *oído etc* sense; ***el sexto ~*** the sixth sense
2 (*significado*) meaning; ***doble ~*** double meaning; ***en el ~ propio de la palabra*** in the true sense of the word; ***en todos los ~s de la palabra*** in every sense of the word; ***en un ~ más amplio*** in a wider sense; ***en cierto ~*** in a way
3 (*dirección*) direction; ***en el ~ de las agujas del reloj*** clockwise
4 consciousness; ***perder / recobrar el ~*** lose / regain consciousness
◇ **sentido común** common sense; **sentido del deber** sense of duty; **sentido del humor** sense of humor *o Br* humour
sentimental *adj* emotional; ***ser ~*** be sentimental

sentimentalismo *m* sentiment
sentimiento *m* feeling; ***lo acompaño en el ~*** my condolences
sentir I *m* feeling, opinion; ***en mi ~*** in my opinion **II** ⟨3i⟩ *v/t* **1** feel; ***siento calor*** I feel hot **2** (*percibir*) sense; ***sin ~lo llegar, acabar*** before I / we knew it **3** (*aparecer*): ***hacerse*** *o* ***dejarse ~*** make itself felt **4**: ***lo siento*** I'm sorry; **sentirse** *v/r* **1** feel **2** *L.Am.* (*ofenderse*) take offense *o Br* offence
seña *f* **1** gesture, sign; ***hacer ~s*** wave; ***me hizo una ~ para que entrara*** he gestured to me to go in **2**: ***~s*** *pl* address *sg* **3** (*detalles*): ***para*** *o* ***por más ~s*** to be exact
◇ **señas personales** *pl* description *sg*
señal *f* **1** signal; ***~ de prohibición*** prohibition disk **2** *fig* sign, trace; ***dar ~es de vida*** get in touch; ***en ~ de*** *amistad, amor* as a token of, as a mark of **3** COM deposit, downpayment; ***dejar una ~*** leave a deposit *o* downpayment **4** TELEC tone
◇ **señal de la cruz** REL sign of the cross; **señal horaria** RAD time signal; **señal de llamada** dial tone; **señal de ocupado** busy signal *o* tone; **señal de tráfico** traffic sign, road sign
señalado *adj* special
señalar ⟨1a⟩ *v/t* **1** indicate, point out; ***~ a alguien con el dedo*** *tb fig* point at s.o. **2** *con símbolo, línea etc* mark **3** (*fijar*) set, decide on; **señalarse** *v/r* distinguish o.s. (***por*** by)
señalero *m*, **-a** *f Arg* FERR signalman / signalwoman
señalización *f* **1** signposting **2** (*señales*) signs *pl*
señalizador *m Chi* turn signal, *Br* indicator
señalizar ⟨1f⟩ *v/t* signpost
señor I *m* **1** gentleman, man **2** *trato* sir **3** *antes de nombre* Mr; ***pase, ~ García*** come in, Mr García; ***el ~ López*** Mr López; ***los ~es López*** Mr and Mrs López; ***el ~ Juan López*** Mr Juan López **II** *adj* F huge, enormous; ***se ha comprado un ~ coche*** F he's bought a huge *o* enormous car
Señor *m* Lord
señora *f* **1** lady, woman; ***~s y señores*** ladies and gentlemen **2** *trato* ma'am, *Br* madam **3** *antes de nombre* Mrs; *casada o no casada* Ms; ***la ~ López*** Mrs Lopez; ***la ~ María López*** Miss María López; ***mi ~*** my wife
señoría *f* JUR: ***su ~*** your Honor *o Br* Honour
señorial *adj* lordly, noble
señorío *m* **1** HIST (feudal) estate **2** (*dominio*) rule
señorita *f* **1** young lady, young woman **2** *tratamiento* miss; *escrito* Miss; ***la ~ López*** Miss López; ***la ~ Ana López*** Ana López
señoritingo *m*, **-a** *f* F rich kid F
señorito *m* **1** F rich kid F **2** *tratamiento* young master
señuelo *m para aves* decoy; *fig* bait, lure
sepa *vb* ☞ ***saber***
sépalo *m* BOT sepal
separable *adj* separable
separación *f* separation
◇ **separación de bienes** JUR division of property
◇ **separación del cargo** dismissal
separado *adj* separated; ***por ~*** separately
separar ⟨1a⟩ *v/t* separate; **separarse** *v/r* separate, split up F
separatismo *m* separatism
separatista *m/f & adj* separatist
sepelio *m fml* burial
sepia *f* **1** ZO cuttlefish **2** (*color*) sepia
SEPLA *m abr* (= ***Sindicato Español de Pilotos de Líneas Aéreas***) Spanish Airline Pilots' Association
sept.e *abr* (= ***septiembre***) Sept. (= September)
septentrión *m* north
septentrional *adj* northern
septeto *m* MÚS septet
septicemia *f* MED septicemia
séptico *adj* MED septic
septiembre *m* September
séptima *f* MÚS seventh
séptimo *m/adj* seventh
septuagenario I *adj* septuagenarian **II** *m*, **-a** *f* septuagenarian, person in his / her seventies
septuagésimo *adj* seventieth
sepulcral *adj fig*: *silencio, frío* deathly; *voz* sepulchral
sepulcro *m* tomb
sepultar ⟨1a⟩ *v/t* bury
sepultura *f* **1** burial; ***dar ~ a alguien*** bury s.o. **2** (*tumba*) tomb; ***estar con***

S

un pie en la ~ *fig* have one foot in the grave
sepulturero *m* gravedigger
sequedad *f fig* curtness
sequía *f* drought
séquito *m* retinue, entourage
ser ⟨2w; *part* **sido**⟩ **I** *v/i* **1** be; ***¿quién es?*** who is it?; ***soy yo*** it's me; ***sea quien sea*** whoever it is; ***si yo fuera tú*** if I were you; ***yo soy de los que …*** I'm one of those people who …; ***si fuera por mí*** if I had my way; ***eso no es así*** that's not right; ***¿qué va a ser?*** *en bar etc* what's it going to be? **2** *origen, naturaleza*: ***~ de madera / plata*** be made of wood / silver; ***~ de Bogotá*** be from Bogotá **3** (*pertenecer*): ***es de Juan*** it's Juan's, it belongs to Juan; ***~ para*** be for **4** (*valer*): ***¿cuánto es?*** how much is it?; ***la entrada es diez dólares*** admission is 10 dollars **5** *para formar la pasiva*: ***~ vencido*** be defeated; ***fue vencido*** he was defeated **6** (*sumar*): ***dos y dos son cuatro*** two and two are *o* make four **7** (*suceder*): ***¿qué será de nosotros?*** what is going to become of us?; ***¿qué es de ti?*** how's life?, how're things? **8**: ***a no ~ que*** unless; ***de no ~ así*** otherwise; ***esto es*** that is; ***¡eso es!*** exactly!, that's right!; ***no sea que*** in case; ***es que …*** the thing is …; ***es de esperar*** it's to be hoped; ***o sea*** in other words; ***sea lo que sea, sea como sea*** be that as it may; ***siendo así*** the way things are; ***o lo que sea*** or whatever; ***¿cómo es eso?*** how come? **II** *m* being
◇ **ser humano** human being
◇ **ser vivo** living creature
SER *f abr* (= ***Sociedad Española de Radiodifusión***) network of independent Spanish radio stations
serafín *m* seraph
Serbia *f* Serbia
serbio I *adj* Serb(ian) **II** *m*, **-a** *f* Serb **III** *m idioma* Serb(ian)
serbocroata *adj* Serbo-Croat
serenar ⟨1a⟩ *v/t* calm; **serenarse** *v/r* **1** calm down **2** *del tiempo* clear up
serenata *f* MÚS serenade
serenidad *f* calmness, serenity
sereno I *m*: ***dormir al ~*** sleep outdoors **II** *adj* calm, serene
serial *m* TV, RAD series *sg*
seriamente *adv* seriously
serie *f* **1** *de acontecimientos, artículos etc* series *sg* **2**: ***fabricación en ~*** mass production; ***de ~*** *prestaciones en coche* standard; ***fuera de ~*** out of this world, extraordinary
◇ **Serie Mundial** *en béisbol* World Series *sg*
seriedad *f* seriousness
serigrafía *f* silk-screen printing
serio *adj* **1** serious; ***ésto va en ~*** this is serious; ***tomarse algo en ~*** take sth seriously **2** (*responsable*) reliable
sermón *m* sermon; F lecture, sermon; ***echar un ~ a alguien*** *fig* give s.o. a lecture
sermonear ⟨1a⟩ *v/i* preach; F lecture, preach
serología *f* serology
seropositivo *adj* MED HIV positive
serpentear ⟨1a⟩ *v/i de río, camino* wind, snake, meander
serpentín *m* TÉC coil
serpentina *f* streamer
serpiente *f* ZO snake
◇ **serpiente de cascabel** rattlesnake
serrado *adj* serrated
serraduras *fpl* sawdust *sg*
serranía *f* mountainous region
serrano I *adj* **1** mountain *atr* **2**: ***cuerpo ~*** shapely body **II** *m*, **-a** *f* mountain dweller
serrar ⟨1k⟩ *v/t* saw
serrería *f* sawmill
serrín *m* sawdust
serrote *m Méx* handsaw
serrucho *m* handsaw
servible *adj* us(e)able
servicial *adj* obliging, helpful
servicio *m* **1** service; ***estar al ~ de*** be at the service of; ***hacer un buen ~ a alguien*** do s.o. a great service; ***estar de ~*** be on duty; ***libre de ~*** off duty **2**: ***~s*** *pl* restroom *sg*, *Br* toilets **3** (*funcionamiento*): ***fuera de ~*** TÉC out of order; ***poner en ~*** put into service
◇ **servicio de atención al cliente** customer service; **servicio de averías** breakdown service; **servicio doméstico** domestic service; **servicio militar** military service; **servicio pos(t)venta**

S

after-sales service; **servicio religioso** church service; **servicio secreto** secret service; **servicio de urgencias** emergency service; **servicios mínimos** skeleton service *sg*
servidor *m* **1** INFOR server **2**: ***su atento, su seguro ~*** sincerely yours; ***no sé vosotros, pero ~ no piensa ir*** *hum* I don't know about you but yours truly is definitely not going
servidumbre *f* **1** (*criados*) servants *pl* **2** (*condición*) servitude
servil *adj* servile
servilismo *m* servility
servilleta *f* napkin, *Br tb* serviette
servilletero *m* napkin ring
servir ⟨3l⟩ **I** *v/t* serve; ***¿le sirven ya?*** are you being served?; ***¿en qué puedo ~le?*** what can I do for you?; ***¡para ~le!*** at your service!
II *v/i* **1** be of use; ***~ de*** serve as; ***esta habitación sirve de trastero*** we use this room as a junk room; ***~ para*** be (used) for; ***¿para qué sirve esto?*** what is this (used) for?; ***no ~ de nada*** be no use at all **2** MIL, DEP serve **3** *fig*: ***ir servido*** F have another think coming
servirse *v/r* **1**: ***~ de algo*** use sth, make use of sth **2** *comida* help o.s. to
servo *pref* power
servodirección *f* power steering
servofreno *m* servo-brake
sésamo *m* sesame
sesear ⟨1a⟩ *v/i pronounce Spanish 'c' before 'e', 'i' or 'z' as 's'*
sesenta *adj* sixty
sesentón I *adj* sexagenarian, in one's sixties **II** *m*, **-ona** *f* sexagenerian, person in his / her sixties
seseo *m pronunciation of Spanish 'c' before 'e' 'i' or 'z' as 's'*
sesera *f* F brains *pl*
sesgado *adj fig* skewed, biassed
sesgo *m fig* bias
sesión *f* **1** session **2** *en cine, teatro* show, performance
◇ **sesión golfa** *de cine* late show
◇ **sesión plenaria** plenary session
sesionar ⟨1a⟩ *v/i L.Am.* be in session
seso *m* **1** ANAT brain; *fig* brains *pl*, sense; ***sorber el ~ a alguien, tener sorbido el ~ a alguien*** have s.o. under one's spell **2** GASTR: ***~s*** *pl* brains
sestear ⟨1a⟩ *v/i* have a siesta
sesudo *adj* sensible
set *m tenis* set
seta *f* BOT mushroom; *venenosa* toadstool
setecientos *adj* seven hundred
setenta *adj* seventy
setentón I *adj* septuagenarian, in one's seventies **II** *m*, **-ona** *f* septuagenarian, person in his / her seventies
setiembre *m* September
seto *m*: **~ (*vivo*)** hedge
seudónimo I *adj* pseudonymous **II** *m* pseudonym
s.e.u.o. *abr* (= ***salvo error u omisión***) E & OE (= errors and omissions excepted)
severidad *f* severity
severo *adj* severe
sevillanas *fpl folk dance from Seville*
sevillano *adj* of / from Seville, Seville *atr*
sexagenario I *adj* sexagenarian, in one's sixties **II** *m*, **-a** *f* sexagenarian, person in his / her sixties
sexagésimo *adj* sixtieth
sexismo *m* sexism
sexista *m/f & adj* sexist
sexo *m* **1** sex **2** (*órganos sexuales*) sex(-ual) organs
◇ **sexo oral** oral sex
sexología *f* sexology
sexta *f* MÚS sixth
sextante *m* MAR sextant
sexteto *m* MÚS sextet
sexto *adj* sixth
sexual *adj* sexual
sexualidad *f* sexuality
sexy *adj inv* sexy
SGAE *f abr* (= ***Sociedad General de Autores y Editores***) Association of Authors and Editors
shock *m* MED: **~ (*nervioso*)** shock
short *m L.Am.* shorts *pl*
si I *conj* if; ***~ no*** if not; ***me pregunto ~ vendrá*** I wonder whether he'll come; ***como ~*** as if; ***por ~*** in case; ***¡~ no lo sabía!*** but I didn't know! **II** *m* MÚS B; ***~ bemol*** B flat
sí I *adv* yes; ***¡que ~!*** I said yes!
II *pron tercera persona*: *singular masculino* himself; *femenino* herself; *cosa, animal* itself; *plural* themselves; *usted* yourself; *ustedes* yourselves; ***es un asunto de por ~ complicado*** it's a

complex subject; ***ya es de por ~ bebedor como para que le alientes a beber más*** he drinks quite enough as it is without you egging him on; ***por ~ solo*** by himself / itself, on his / its own; ***entrar en ~*** come around, come to **III** *m* consent
siamés *adj* Siamese
sibarita *m/f* bon vivant, epicure
Siberia *f* Siberia
siberiano *adj* Siberian
sibila *f* MYTH sibyl
sibilante *f/adj* sibilant
sicario *m* hired assassin *o* killer
Sicilia *f* Sicily
siciliano I *adj* Sicilian **II** *m*, **-a** *f* Sicilian
sico *pref* ☞ ***psico***
sicómoro, sicomoro *m* BOT sycamore
SIDA *m abr* (= ***síndrome de inmunidad deficiente adquirida***) Aids (= acquired immune-deficiency syndrome)
sida *m* Aids; ***enfermo de ~*** person with Aids, Aids victim; ***prueba de ~*** Aids test
sidecar *m* sidecar
sideral *adj* **1** *viajes* space *atr*; ***espacio ~*** outer space **2** *Rpl* F *precio* astronomical
siderurgia *f* iron and steel making
siderúrgico *adj* iron and steel *atr*
sido *part* ☞ ***ser***
sidoso I *adj* Aids *atr* **II** *m*, **-a** *f* Aids sufferer, Aids victim
sidra *f* cider
siega *f* reaping, harvesting
siembra *f* sowing
siempre *adv* always; ***~ que*** providing that, as long as; ***de ~*** usual; ***sigue siendo la misma de ~*** she's still the same as always, she's just the same as ever; ***desde ~*** always, F for ever; ***lo de ~*** the same old story; ***para ~*** for ever; ***¡hasta ~!*** goodbye, farewell
siempreviva *f* BOT sempervivum
sien *f* ANAT temple
siendo *vb* ☞ ***ser***
siento *vb* ☞ ***sentir***
sierra *f* **1** *herramienta* saw **2** GEOG mountain range
◇ **sierra de calar** fretsaw; **sierra de cinta** band saw; **sierra circular** circular saw; **sierra mecánica** power saw
siervo *m*, **-a** *f* HIST serf
siesta *f* siesta, nap; ***dormir la ~*** have a siesta *o* nap
siete I *adj* seven **II** *m roto* tear
sietemesino I *adj bebé* born two months premature **II** *m*, **-a** *f* baby born two months premature
sífilis *f* MED syphilis
sifón *m* TÉC siphon
siga *vb* ☞ ***seguir***
sigilo *m* (*secreto*) secrecy; (*disimulo*) stealth
◇ **sigilo profesional** professional secrecy
◇ **sigilo sacramental** secrecy of the confessional
sigiloso *adj* stealthy
sigla *f* abbreviation, acronym
siglo *m* century; ***hace ~s*** *o* ***un ~ que no le veo*** *fig* I haven't seen him in a long long time; ***el Siglo de Oro*** the Golden Age; ***el Siglo de las Luces*** HIST the (Age of) Enlightenment
signar ⟨1a⟩ *v/t* sign; **signarse** *v/r* cross o.s., make the sign of the cross
signatario *m*, **-a** *f* signatory
significación *f*, **significado** *m* meaning
significar ⟨1g⟩ *v/t* mean, signify; **significarse** *v/r* distinguish o.s. (***por*** by)
significativo *adj* meaningful, significant
signo *m* sign
◇ **signo de admiración** exclamation mark; **signo de interrogación** question mark; **signo de puntuación** punctuation mark
sigo *vb* ☞ ***seguir***
siguiente I *adj* next, following **II** *pron* next (one); ***¡el ~!*** next!
sílaba *f* syllable
silabario *m* spelling book
silabear ⟨1a⟩ *v/t* pronounce syllable by syllable
silba *f* whistling
silbar ⟨1a⟩ *v/i* & *v/t* whistle
silbato *m* whistle
silbido *m* whistle
silbo *m* whistle
silenciador *m* AUTO muffler, *Br* silencer
silenciar ⟨1b⟩ *v/t* silence
silencio *m* **1** silence; ***en ~*** in silence, silently; ***el profesor impuso ~ a los alumnos*** the teacher made the students be quiet; ***guardar ~*** keep quiet **2** MÚS rest

S

silencioso *adj* silent
sílex *m* MIN flint, silex
sílfide *f* sylph
sílice *f* QUÍM silica
silicio *m* QUÍM silicon
silicona *f* silicone
silla *f* chair
◇ **silla eléctrica** electric chair; **silla giratoria** swivel chair; **silla de montar** saddle; **silla plegable** folding chair; **silla de ruedas** wheelchair
silleta *f* MED bedpan
sillín *m* saddle
sillón *m* armchair, easy chair
◇ **sillón orejero** wing chair
silo *m* silo
silueta *f* **1** silhouette **2** (*cuerpo*) figure
silvestre *adj* wild
silvicultor *m*, **~a** *f* forester
silvicultura *f* forestry
sima *f* chasm, abyss
simbiosis *f* symbiosis
simbólico *adj* symbolic
simbolismo *m* symbolism
simbolizar ⟨1f⟩ *v/t* symbolize
símbolo *m* symbol
simetría *f* symmetry
simétrico *adj* symmetrical
simiente *f* seed
simiesco *adj* simian, apelike
símil *m* comparison; *figura retórica* simile
similar *adj* similar; ***y ~es*** and the like
similitud *f* similarity
simio *m* ZO ape
simpatía *f* warmth, friendliness
simpático *adj* nice, lik(e)able
simpatizante *m/f* sympathizer, supporter
simpatizar ⟨1f⟩ *v/i* sympathize
simple I *adj* **1** (*fácil*) simple **2** (*mero*) ordinary **II** *m/f* simpleton
simplemente *adv* simply, just
simpleza *f* simple-mindedness
simplicidad *f* simplicity
simplificación *f tb* MAT simplification
simplificar ⟨1g⟩ *v/t tb* MAT simplify
simplista *adj* simplistic
simplón *m*, **-ona** *f* F sucker F
simposio *m* symposium
simulación *f* simulation
simulacro *m* **1** (*cosa falsa*) pretense, *Br* pretence, sham **2** (*simulación*) simulation
◇ **simulacro de incendio** fire drill
◇ **simulacro de salvamento** mock rescue
simulador *m* simulator
◇ **simulador de vuelo** flight simulator
simular ⟨1a⟩ *v/t* simulate
simultanear ⟨1a⟩ *v/t*: ***~ dos cargos*** hold two positions at the same time; ***~ el trabajo con los estudios*** combine work and study, work and study at the same time
simultaneidad *f* simultaneity
simultáneo *adj* simultaneous
sin *prp* without; ***~ preguntar*** without asking; ***~ decir nada*** without (saying) a word; ***~ paraguas*** without an umbrella; ***~ que*** without; ***y ~ más*** and without further ado; ***me lo dijo así, ~ más*** that's all he said to me, just that
sinagoga *f* synagogue
sincerarse ⟨1a⟩ *v/r* be honest (***con*** with), speak openly (***con*** to)
sinceridad *f* sincerity
sincero *adj* sincere
síncopa *f* MÚS syncopation
síncope *m* MED blackout
sincrónico *adj* synchronized
sincronismo *m* synchronism
sincronizar ⟨1f⟩ *v/t* synchronize
sindical *adj* (labor, *Br* trade) union *atr*
sindicalismo *m* (labor, *Br* trade) union movement
sindicalista I *adj* (labor, *Br* trade) union *atr* **II** *m/f* (labor, *Br* trade) union member
sindicalizar ⟨1f⟩, **sindicar** ⟨1g⟩ *v/t* unionize; **sindicalizarse** *v/r* form a (labor, *Br* trade) union
sindicato *m* (labor, *Br* trade) union
síndico *m* trustee
◇ **síndico de la quiebra** receiver
síndrome *m* syndrome
sinecura *f* sinecure
sinergia *f* BIO, *fig* synergy
sinfín *m*: ***un ~ de …*** no end of …
sinfonía *f* MÚS symphony
sinfónico *adj* symphonic; ***orquesta -a*** symphony orchestra
singladura *f* MAR day's run
singular I *adj* **1** (*raro*) strange, *fml* singular **2** (*único*) outstanding, extraordinary **II** *m* GRAM singular
singularidad *f* **1** (*rareza*) strangeness, *fml* singularity **2** (*carácter único*) out-

standing nature
singularizar ⟨1f⟩ *v/t* single out; **singularizarse** *v/r* stand out
singularmente *adv* singularly
sinhueso *f* F tongue; ***darle a la ~*** F talk, yap F
siniestrado *adj* wrecked
siniestralidad *f* accident rate
siniestro I *adj* sinister II *m* accident; (*catástrofe*) disaster
◇ **siniestro total** total wreck
sinnúmero *m*: ***un ~ de*** no end of
sino I *m* fate II *conj* **1** but; ***no cena en casa, ~ en el bar*** he doesn't have dinner at home, he has it in the bar; ***¿quién ~ ?*** who else but?; ***¿quién ~ tú?*** who else but you?; ***no sólo ... ~ también*** not only ... but also **2** (*salvo*) except; ***nadie ~ él pudo hacerlo*** nobody but him could do it
sínodo *m* synod
sinónimo I *adj* synonymous II *m* synonym
sinopsis *f inv* synopsis
sinóptico *adj* synoptic
sinovial *adj* ANAT synovial; ***líquido ~*** synovial fluid
sinrazón *f* injustice
sinsabores *mpl* troubles
sinsentido *m* nonsense
sintaxis *f* syntax
síntesis *f inv* synthesis; (*resumen*) summary; ***en ~*** in short, to sum up
sintético *adj* synthetic
sintetizador *m* MÚS synthesizer
sintetizar ⟨1f⟩ *v/t* synthesize
síntoma *m* symptom
sintomático *adj* symptomatic
sintonía *f* **1** *melodía* theme tune, signature tune **2** RAD tuning, reception; ***estar en la ~ de*** be tuned to; ***estar en ~ con*** *fig* be in tune with
sintonizador *m* tuner
sintonizar ⟨1f⟩ I *v/t radio* tune in II *v/i fig* be in tune (***con*** with)
sinuosidad *f* sinuosity
sinuoso *adj* winding
sinusitis *f* MED sinusitis
sinvergüenza I *adj* shameless, unscrupulous II *m/f* swine; ***¡qué ~!*** (*descarado*) what a nerve!
sionismo *m* Zionism
siquiatra *m/f*, **síquico** *adj* ☞ ***psiquiatra, psíquico***
siquiera I *adv*: ***ni ~*** not even; ***~ bebe algo*** *L.Am.* at least have a drink II *conj* even
sirena *f* **1** *pito* siren **2** MYTH mermaid
sirga *f* MAR towline
Siria *f* Syria
sirio I *adj* Syrian II *m*, **-a** *f* Syrian
sirlero *m*, **-a** *f Esp* mugger, robber *with a knife*
siroco *m* sirocco
sirope *m* syrup
sirve *vb* ☞ ***servir***
sirvienta *f* maid
sirviente *m* servant
sisal *m* BOT sisal
sisar ⟨1a⟩ *v/t* F pilfer
siseo *m* hiss, hissing
sísmico *adj* seismic
sismo *m* earthquake; *temblor* earth tremor
sismógrafo *m* seismograph
sismología *f* seismology
sistema *m* system
◇ **sistema digestivo** ANAT digestive system; **sistema inmunológico** ANAT immune system; **sistema métrico** metric system; **sistema monetario** monetary system; **sistema nervioso** ANAT nervous system; **sistema operativo** operating system; **sistema periódico** QUÍM periodic system *o* table
sistemático *adj* systematic
sistematizar ⟨1f⟩ *v/t* systemize, systematize
sístole *f* systole
sitiar ⟨1b⟩ *v/t* surround, lay siege to
sitio *m* **1** place; ***en ningún ~*** nowhere; ***poner las cosas en su ~*** *fig* straighten things out **2** (*espacio*) room; ***hacer ~*** make room; ***ocupar mucho ~*** take up a lot of room *o* space
◇ **sitio web** web site
sito *adj fml* situated, located
situación *f* situation; ***estar en ~ de*** be in a position to
situado *adj* situated; ***estar ~*** be situated; ***bien ~*** *fig* in a good position
situar ⟨1e⟩ *v/t* place, put; **situarse** *v/r* be
S.L. *abr* (= ***sociedad limitada***) Ltd (= limited)
slalom *m* slalom
slip *m* underpants *pl*
S.M. *abr* (= ***Su Majestad***) HM (=His / Her Majesty)

S

SMI *m abr* (= ***salario mínimo interprofesional***) minimum wage
s/n *abr* (= ***sin número***) not numbered
snowboard *m* snowboard
so I *prep* under; **~ *pena de muerte*** on pain of death **II** *interj* **1**: ***¡~!*** whoa! **2** *para enfatizar*: ***¡~ burro** o **idiota!*** you dumb idiot!
SO *abr* (= ***sudoeste***) SW *abr* (= Southwest)
soba *f* F beating; ***dar una ~ a alguien*** give s.o. a beating
sobaco *m* armpit
sobado *adj ropa* worn; *tema* old
sobaquina *f* body odor, BO
sobar ⟨1a⟩ *v/t* **1** *libro, tejido etc* handle, finger **2** F *sexualmente* grope F
soberanía *f* sovereignty
soberano I *adj* **1** sovereign **2** *fig* F tremendous **II** *m*, **-a** *f* sovereign
soberbia *f* pride, arrogance
soberbio *adj* **1** (*altivo*) proud, arrogant **2** *fig* superb
sobón I *adj*: ***es muy ~*** he's always touching you **II** *m person who is always touching others*
sobornable *adj* venal, bribable
sobornar ⟨1a⟩ *v/t* bribe
soborno *m* bribe
sobra *f* **1** surplus, excess; ***hay de ~*** there's more than enough; ***saber de ~*** know perfectly well, know full well; ***estar de ~*** not be wanted, not be needed **2**: ***~s*** *pl de comida* leftovers
sobradamente *adv conocido* well
sobrado I *adj*: ***estar** o **andar ~ de algo*** have plenty of sth; ***no andar muy ~ de algo*** not have much sth **II** *adv* easily; ***te conozco ~*** I know you well enough
sobrante *adj* remaining, left over
sobrar ⟨1a⟩ *v/t*: ***sobra comida*** there's food left over; ***me sobró pintura*** I had some paint left over; ***me sobra dinero*** (*soy rico*) I've got plenty of money; ***sobraba uno*** there was one left
sobrasada *f* GASTR spicy pork sausage
sobre I *m* envelope; ***sopa de ~*** packet soup **II** *prp* **1** on; ***~ la mesa*** on the table **2** (*acerca de*): ***~ esto*** about this **3** (*alrededor de*): ***~ las tres*** around three o'clock **4**: ***~ todo*** above all, especially ◇ **sobre acolchado** padded envelope; **sobre de dormir** *Urug* sleeping bag; **sobre ventana** window envelope
sobreabundancia *f* overabundance
sobreabundar ⟨1a⟩ *v/i*: ***sobreabundan ...*** there is an overabundance of ...
sobreactuar ⟨1e⟩ *v/i* TEA overact
sobrealimentación *f* overeating
sobrealimentar ⟨1a⟩ *v/t* overfeed
sobrecalentamiento *m* overheating
sobrecalentar ⟨1k⟩ *v/t* overheat
sobrecarga *f* overloading
sobrecargar ⟨1h⟩ *v/t* overload
sobrecargo *m/f* AVIA chief flight attendant, purser; MAR purser
sobrecogedor *adj* **1** (*que asusta*) horrific, shocking **2** (*que conmueve*) moving
sobrecoger ⟨2c⟩ *v/t* **1** (*asustar*) strike fear into **2** (*impresionar*) have an effect on; **sobrecogerse** *v/r* **1** (*asustarse*) be frightened **2** (*conmoverse*) be moved
sobrecubierta *f* dust jacket
sobredosis *f inv* overdose
sobreentender(se) ☞ ***sobrentender(se)***
sobreesfuerzo *m* overexertion
sobreestimar ⟨1a⟩ *v/i* overestimate
sobreexcitar ⟨1a⟩ *v/t* get overexcited
sobreexponer ⟨2r⟩ *v/t* FOT overexpose
sobrehumano *adj* superhuman
sobreimpresión *f* **1** TV superimposition **2** TIP overprinting
sobreimprimir ⟨3a⟩ *v/t* **1** TV superimpose **2** TIP overprint
sobrellevar ⟨1a⟩ *v/t* endure, bear
sobremanera *adv* exceedingly
sobremesa *f*: ***de ~*** afternoon *atr*
sobrenatural *adj* supernatural
sobrenombre *m* nickname
sobrentender ⟨2g⟩ *v/t* guess, understand; **sobrentenderse** *v/r*: ***se sobrentiende que ...*** needless to say ..., it goes without saying that ...
sobrentendido *m something that goes without saying*
sobrepasar ⟨1a⟩ *v/t* exceed, surpass; ***me sobrepasa en altura*** he is taller than me; **sobrepasarse** *v/r* go too far
sobrepesca *f* overfishing
sobrepeso *m* excess weight
sobreponer ⟨2r; *part* ***sobrepuesto***⟩ *v/t* superimpose; **sobreponerse** *v/r*: ***~ a*** overcome, get over
sobreproducción *f* overproduction
sobrepuesto I *part* ☞ ***sobreponerse*** **II** *adj* superimposed

sobresaliente I *adj* outstanding, excellent **II** *m* EDU top mark
sobresalir ⟨3r⟩ *v/t* stick out, protrude; *fig* excel; **~ *entre*** stand out among
sobresaltar ⟨1a⟩ *v/t* startle; **sobresaltarse** *v/r* jump, start
sobresalto *m* jump, start
sobreseer ⟨2e⟩ *v/t* JUR dismiss
sobreseimiento *m* JUR dismissal
sobrestimar ⟨1a⟩ *v/t* overestimate
sobresueldo *m* bonus
sobretasa *f* surcharge
sobretodo *m* overcoat
sobrevaloración *f* overvaluation
sobrevalorar ⟨1a⟩ *v/t* overrate
sobrevenir ⟨3s⟩ *v/i* happen; *de guerra* break out
sobreventa *f* overselling
sobreviviente I *adj* surviving **II** *m/f* survivor
sobrevivir ⟨3a⟩ *v/i* survive
sobrevolar ⟨1m⟩ *v/t* fly over, overfly
sobrexplotación *f* overexploitation
sobriedad *f* **1** soberness **2** *de comida, decoración* simplicity **3** (*moderación*) restraint
sobrina *f* niece
◇ **sobrina nieta** great-niece
sobrino *m* nephew
◇ **sobrino nieto** great-nephew
sobrio *adj* **1** sober **2** *comida, decoración* simple **3** (*moderado*) restrained
socaire *m* MAR lee; ***al ~ de*** sheltered by, in the lee of
socarrón *adj* sarcastic, snide F
socarronería *f* sarcasm
socavar ⟨1a⟩ *v/t tb fig* undermine
socavón *m* hollow
sociabilidad *f* sociability
sociable *adj* sociable
social *adj* social
socialdemocracia *f* POL social democracy
socialdemócrata I *adj* POL social democratic **II** *m/f* POL social democrat
socialismo *m* socialism
socialista *m/f & adj* socialist
socializar ⟨1f⟩ *v/t* socialize
sociedad *f* society; ***alta ~*** high society; ***presentar en ~*** present in society
◇ **sociedad anónima** public corporation, *Br* public limited company; **sociedad colectiva** collective; **sociedad comanditaria, sociedad en comandita** limited partnership; **sociedad de consumo** consumer society; **sociedad deportiva** sports club; **sociedad de la información** information society; **sociedad mercantil** trading company; **Sociedad de Naciones** HIST League of Nations; **sociedad de responsabilidad limitada** limited corporation, *Br* limited company; **sociedad protectora de animales** Society for the Prevention of Cruelty to Animals
socio *m*, **-a** *f* **1** *de club, asociación etc* member **2** COM partner
◇ **socio comanditario** partner with limited liability
◇ **socio de honor, socio honorario** honorary member
sociocultural *adj* sociocultural
socioeconómico *adj* socioeconomic
sociología *f* sociology
sociólogo *m*, **-a** *f* sociologist
sociopolítico *adj* sociopolitical
socorrer ⟨2a⟩ *v/t* help, assist
socorrido *adj fig* useful
socorrismo *m* life-saving
socorrista *m/f* lifeguard
socorro *m* help, assistance; ***¡~!*** help!; ***pedir ~*** ask for help
socucho *m L.Am.* tiny house, shoebox F
soda *f* soda (water)
sodio *m* sodium
sodomía *f* sodomy
soez *f* crude, coarse
sofá *m* sofa
◇ **sofá-cama** sofa bed
sofisma *m* sophism
sofisticación *f* sophistication
sofisticado *adj* sophisticated
sofocación *f* suffocation
sofocante *adj* suffocating
sofocar ⟨1g⟩ *v/t* **1** suffocate **2** *incendio* put out; **sofocarse** *v/r* **1** *fig* get embarrassed **2** (*irritarse*) get angry
sofoco *m* **1** *fig* embarrassment **2** (*disgusto*): ***me llevé un ~ tremendo*** I was terribly upset
sofocón *m* ☞ ***sofoco***
sofreír ⟨3m⟩ *v/t* sauté
sofrito *m* GASTR *mixture of fried onions, peppers etc*
software *m* INFOR software; ***~ de usuario*** user software
soga *f* rope; ***estar con la ~ al cuello*** F be

in big trouble F
sois *vb* ☞ ***ser***
soja *f* soy, *Br* soya; **~ *transgénica*** genetically modified soy
sojuzgar ⟨1h⟩ *v/t* subdue, subjugate
sol *m* **1** sun; ***al caer el* ~** at sunset; ***de* ~ *a* ~** from dawn to dusk; ***hace* ~** it's sunny; ***tomar el* ~** sunbathe; ***eres un* ~** *fig* F you're a darling; ***no dejar a alguien ni a* ~ *ni a sombra*** pester s.o. all the time *o* morning, noon and night **2** FIN sol
solamente *adv* only
solana *f* sunny spot
solapa *f de chaqueta* lapel; *de libro* flap
solapado *adj* sly
solapar ⟨1a⟩ *v/t* hide; **solaparse** *v/r* overlap; *fig* match, fit together
solar I *adj* solar **II** *m* lot, *Br* plot
solariego *adj*: ***casa -a*** family seat
solario, solárium *m* solarium
solazo *m* F hot sun
soldadesca *f* military life
soldado *m/f* soldier
soldador *m*, **~a** *f* welder
soldadura *f* welding, soldering
◇ **soldadura autógena** oxyacetylene welding
soldar ⟨1m⟩ *v/t* weld, solder; **soldarse** *v/r* knit together, knit
soleado *adj* sunny
soledad *f* solitude, loneliness
solemne *adj* solemn; ***una* ~ *tontería*** an absolutely stupid thing
solemnidad *f* solemnity; ***de* ~** extremely
solemnizar ⟨1f⟩ *v/t* solemnize
soler ⟨2h⟩ *v/i*: **~ *hacer algo*** usually do sth; ***suele venir temprano*** he usually comes early; ***como suele decirse*** as is usually *o* normally said; ***solía visitarme*** he used to visit me
solera *f* **1** tradition; ***de* ~** *fig* traditional **2** *Chi*: *de la acera* curb, *Br* kerb
solfa *f* (tonic) sol-fa; ***poner en* ~** F poke fun at
solfeo *m* (tonic) sol-fa
solicitante *m/f* applicant
◇ **solicitante de asilo** asylum-seeker
solicitar ⟨1a⟩ *v/t permiso* request; *empleo, beca* apply for
solícito *adj* attentive
solicitud *f* application, request
solidaridad *f* solidarity
solidario *adj* supportive, understanding
solidarizarse ⟨1f⟩ *v/r*: **~ *con alguien*** support s.o., back s.o.
solideo *m* REL cardinal's cap, biretta
solidez *f* solidity; *fig* strength
solidificación *f* solidification
solidificar ⟨1g⟩ *v/t* solidify; **solidificarse** *v/r* soldify, harden
sólido I *adj* solid; *fig*: *conclusion* sound **II** *m* FÍS solid
soliloquio *m* soliloquy
solista *m/f* soloist
solitaria *f* ZO tapeworm
solitario I *adj* **1** *persona* solitary; ***actuó en* ~** he acted alone **2** *lugar* lonely **II** *m juego* solitaire, *Br* patience
soliviantar ⟨1a⟩ *v/t* incite, stir up; **soliviantarse** *v/r* rise up, rebel
solla *f* ZO plaice
sollozar ⟨1f⟩ *v/i* sob
sollozo *m* sob
solo *adj* **1** single; ***estar* ~** be alone; ***sentirse* ~** feel lonely; ***a -as*** alone, by o.s.; ***más* ~ *que la una*** all alone, all by oneself; ***por sí* ~** by o.s. **2** *café* black **3** (*único*): ***un* ~ *día*** a single day **II** *m* MÚS solo
sólo *adv* only, just; ***tan* ~** just; ***no* ~ … *sino también*** not only … but also
solomillo *m* GASTR sirloin
solsticio *m* solstice
soltar ⟨1m⟩ *v/t* **1** let go of **2** (*librar*) release, let go **3** *olor* give off **4** *nudo, tuerca* undo **5** F *discurso* launch into **6**: **~ *una bofetada a alguien*** clobber s.o.; **soltarse** *v/r* **1** free o.s. **2**: **~ *a andar* / *hablar*** begin *o* start to walk / talk
soltera *f* single *o* unmarried woman
soltería *f* singledom; ***cansada de su* ~** tired of being single
soltero I *adj* single, not married **II** *m* bachelor, unmarried man
solterón *m* confirmed bachelor
solterona *f desp* old maid *desp*
soltura *f* fluency, ease; ***con* ~** *hablar* fluently; *desenvolverse* with ease, with aplomb
solubilidad *f* solubility
soluble *adj* **1** soluble; **~ *en agua*** water-soluble **2** *problema* solvable, soluble
solución *f* solution; ***no tener* ~** *fig* be hopeless
solucionar ⟨1a⟩ *v/t* solve
solvencia *f* **1** COM solvency **2** *de profesional* reliability

solventar ⟨1a⟩ *v/t* resolve, settle
solvente I *adj* **1** COM solvent **2** *profesional, artesano* reliable **II** *m* QUÍM solvent
somalí *m/f & adj* Somali
somanta *f* F beating
sombra *f* **1** shadow; ***a la ~ de un árbol*** in the shade of a tree; ***estar a la ~*** be in the shade; ***a la ~ de*** *fig* under the protection of; ***hacer ~ a alguien*** *fig* F to overshadow s.o., put s.o. in the shade; ***mantenerse en la ~*** *fig* stay behind the scenes; ***no es ni ~ de lo que era*** he bears no resemblance to his former self; ***tener mala ~*** be a nasty piece of work **2**: ***~s*** *pl* PINT shading *sg*
◇ **sombra de ojos** eye shadow
sombreado *m* PINT shading
sombrear ⟨1a⟩ *v/t* **1** PINT shade, shade in **2**: ***~ los ojos*** shade one's eyes
sombrerera *f* hat box
sombrerería *f* hat shop, milliner's
sombrerero *m* milliner, hatter
sombrero *m* hat; ***quitarse el ~ ante alguien / algo*** *fig* take one's hat off to s.o. / sth
◇ **sombrero de copa** top hat
◇ **sombrero de tres picos** three-cornered hat
sombrilla *f* sunshade, beach umbrella; ***me importa ~*** *Méx* F I couldn't *o* could care less, *Br* I couldn't care less
sombrío *adj fig* somber, *Br* sombre
somero *adj* superficial
someter ⟨2a⟩ *v/t* **1** subjugate **2**: ***~ a alguien a algo*** subject s.o. to sth **3**: ***~ algo a votación*** put sth to the vote; **someterse** *v/r* **1** yield (***a*** to) **2** *a ley* comply (***a*** with) **3** (*rendirse*) give in (***a*** to) **4**: ***~ a tratamiento*** undergo treatment
sometimiento *m de un país, tribu* subjection
somier *m* bed base
somnámbulo ☞ ***sonámbulo***
somnífero I *adj* soporific; ***pastilla -a*** sleeping pill **II** *m* sleeping pill
somnolencia *f* sleepiness, drowsiness
somnoliento *adj* sleepy, drowsy
somos *vb* ☞ ***ser***
son I *m* sound; ***al ~ de*** to the sound of; ***en ~ de broma*** jokingly; ***en ~ de paz*** in peace **II** *vb* ☞ ***ser***
sonado *adj* F famous, well-known
sonaja *f* rattle
sonajero *m* rattle
sonambulismo *m* sleepwalking
sonámbulo I *adj*: ***voy medio ~*** I'm half asleep **II** *m*, **-a** *f* sleepwalker
sonar ⟨1m⟩ **I** *v/i* **1** ring out **2** *de música* play; ***así, tal como suena*** *fig* as simple as that, just like that **3**: ***~ a*** sound like **4**: ***me suena esa voz*** I know that voice, that voice sounds familiar **II** *v/t la nariz* wipe; **sonarse** *v/r*: ***~ la nariz*** blow one's nose
sonata *f* MÚS sonata
sonda *f* MED catheter
◇ **sonda espacial** space probe
sondaje *m L.Am.* poll, survey
sondar ⟨1a⟩ *v/t* MED catheterize
sondear ⟨1a⟩ *v/t fig* survey, poll
sondeo *m*: ***~ (de opinión)*** survey, (opinion) poll; ***~ de mercado*** market survey
soneto *m* sonnet
sónico *adj* sonic
sonido *m* sound
◇ **sonido estereofónico** stereo sound
soniquete *m* droning
sonoridad *f* tone, sound
sonorizar ⟨1f⟩ *v/t película* add the soundtrack to
sonoro *adj voz, sonido* sonorous
sonreír ⟨3m⟩ *v/i* smile; ***~ a alguien*** smile at s.o.; ***la suerte le sonríe*** fortune smiles on him; **sonreírse** *v/r* smile
sonriente *adj* smiling
sonrisa *f* smile
sonrojar ⟨1a⟩ *v/t*: ***~ a alguien*** make s.o. blush; **sonrojarse** *v/r* blush
sonrojo *m* blush
sonrosado *adj* rosy, pink
sonsacar ⟨1g⟩ *v/t*: ***~ algo*** worm sth out (***a*** of), wheedle sth out (***a*** of)
sonso *adj L.Am.* silly
sonsonete *m* drone
soñación *f*: ***ni por ~*** *fig* F not in a million years F
soñador I *adj* dreamy **II** *m*, **~a** *f* dreamer
soñar ⟨1m⟩ **I** *v/t* dream (***con*** about) **II** *v/i* dream; ***~ despierto*** daydream; ***¡ni ~lo!*** dream on! F
soñolencia *f* ☞ ***somnolencia***
soñoliento *adj* ☞ ***somnoliento***
sopa *f* soup; ***estar hecho una ~*** F be sopping wet; ***hasta en la ~*** F all over the place F; ***dar ~s con honda*** F run rings around
◇ **sopa de sobre** packet soup

S

sopapo *m* F smack, slap
¡sopas! *interj Méx* F crash!, bang!, kapow!
sopera *f* soup tureen
sopero *adj* soup *atr*; ***ser muy ~*** F be a soup lover, be a big soup eater
sopesar ⟨1a⟩ *v/t fig* weigh up
sopetón *m*: ***de ~*** unexpectedly
soplado *m* blowing
◇ **soplado de vidrio** glassblowing
soplador *m* blower
◇ **soplador de vidrio** glassblower
soplagaitas *m/f inv* F twit F
soplamocos *m inv* F punch, slap
soplapollas *m/f inv* V cock-sucker V
soplar ⟨1a⟩ **I** *v/i del viento* blow **II** *v/t* **1** *vela* blow out **2** *polvo* blow away **3**: ***~ algo a la policía*** tip the police off about sth; **soplarse** *v/r* F *bebida* knock back F; *comida* put away F
soplete *m* welding torch
soplo *m*: ***en un ~*** F in an instant; ***~ de viento*** breath of wind
soplón *m*, **-ona** *f* F informer, stool pigeon F
soponcio *m*: ***le dio un ~*** F he passed out
sopor *m* drowsiness, sleepiness
soporífero I *adj* soporific **II** *m* sleeping pill
soportable *adj* bearable
soportal *m* **1** porch **2**: ***~es*** *pl* arcade *sg*
soportar ⟨1a⟩ *v/t fig* put up with, bear; ***no puedo ~ a José*** I can't stand José
soporte *m* **1** support, stand **2**: ***~ de sonido*** audio media
◇ **soporte físico** INFOR hardware
◇ **soporte lógico** INFOR software
soprano MÚS **I** *m* soprano **II** *m/f* soprano
sor *f* REL sister
sorber ⟨2a⟩ *v/t* sip
sorbete *m* **1** sorbet **2** *C.Am.* ice cream
sorbetería *f C.Am.* ice-cream parlor *o Br* parlour
sorbo *m* sip; ***tomar algo a ~s*** sip sth
sordera *f* deafness
sordidez *f* sordidness
sórdido *adj* sordid
sordina *f* MÚS mute, damper
sordo I *adj* **1** deaf **2** *sonido* dull **II** *m*, **-a** *f* deaf person; ***hacerse el ~*** turn a deaf ear; ***los ~s*** the deaf *pl*
sordomudo I *adj* deaf and dumb **II** *m*, **-a** *f* deaf-mute

sorna *f* sarcasm; ***con ~*** sarcastically, mockingly
sorocharse ⟨1a⟩ *v/r Pe, Bol* get altitude sickness
soroche *m Pe, Bol* altitude sickness
sorprendente *adj* surprising
sorprender ⟨2a⟩ *v/t* **1** surprise; ***me sorprende que …*** I'm surprised that … **2** (*descubrir*) catch; **sorprenderse** *v/r* be surprised
sorpresa *f* surprise; ***de** o **por ~*** by surprise; ***pillar a alguien de** o **por ~*** F take s.o. by surprise; ***llevarse una ~*** be surprised, get a surprise
sortear ⟨1a⟩ *v/t* **1** *premio* draw lots for **2** *obstáculo* get round
sorteo *m* (*lotería*) lottery, (prize) draw
sortija *f* ring
sortilegio *m* spell, charm
SOS *m* SOS
sosa *f* QUÍM: ***~ cáustica*** caustic soda
sosaina I *adj* dull **II** *m/f* dull person
sosegado *adj* calm
sosegar ⟨1h & 1k⟩ *v/t* calm; **sosegarse** *v/r* calm down
sosera *f* ☞ ***sosería***
soseras *m/f inv* F dull person
sosería *f* insipidness, dullness
sosia *m* double, look-alike
sosiego *m* calm, quiet; ***con ~*** calmly
soslayar ⟨1a⟩ *v/t* avoid, dodge
soslayo *adj*: ***de ~*** sideways; ***mirar de ~*** look sideways at; ***dejar de ~*** *fig* avoid
soso I *adj* tasteless, insipid; *fig* dull **II** *m*, **-a** *f* stick-in-the-mud F
sospecha *f* suspicion
sospechar ⟨1a⟩ **I** *v/t* suspect **II** *v/i* be suspicious; ***~ de alguien*** suspect s.o.
sospechoso I *adj* suspicious **II** *m*, **-a** *f* suspect
sostén *m* **1** brassiere, bra **2** *fig* pillar, mainstay
sostener ⟨2l⟩ **I** *v/t* **1** *familia* support **2** *opinión* hold; **sostenerse** *v/r* **1** support o.s. **2** *de pie* stand up **3** *en el poder* stay, remain
sostenido I *adj* sharp; ***fa ~*** MÚS F sharp **II** *m* MÚS sharp
sostenimiento *m* support
sota *f naipes* jack
sotabarba *f* double chin
sotana *f* REL cassock
sótano *m* basement, *Br* cellar
sotavento *m* MAR lee side, leeward

S

soterrado *adj recuerdo*, *objeto* buried
soterrar ⟨1k⟩ *v/t* bury
soto *m* grove, thicket
sotobosque *m* undergrowth
sotreta *f Arg*: *cosa* useless thing; *persona* useless person
soviético *adj* Soviet
soy *vb* ☞ ***ser***
soya *f L.Am.* soy, *Br* soya
SP *abr* (= ***Servicio Público***) Public Service
spot *m* TV commercial
spray *m* spray
sprint *m* sprint
◇ **sprint final** final sprint
sprintar ⟨1a⟩ *v/i* sprint
sprínter *m/f* sprinter
squash *m* DEP squash
Sr. *abr* (= ***Señor***) Mr.
Sra. *abr* (= ***Señora***) Mrs
Sres. *abr* (= ***Señores***) Messrs (= Messieurs)
Srta. *abr* (= ***Señorita***: Miss
SS.MM. *abr* (= ***Sus Majestades***) Your / Their Majesties
Sta. *abr* (= ***Santa***) St. (= Saint)
stand *m* COM stand
standing *m* standing; ***de alto ~*** *vivienda* luxury *atr*
status *m* status
stick *m* stick
Sto. *abr* (= ***Santo***) St. (= Saint)
stock *m* stock; ***tener en ~*** have in stock
su, sus *adj pos*: *de él* his; *de ella* her; *de cosa* its; *de usted*, *ustedes* your; *de ellos* their; *de uno* his, *Br* one's
suave *adj* **1** *al tacto* soft, smooth **2** *sabor*, *licor* mild
suavidad *f* **1** *al tacto* softness, smoothness **2** *de sabor*, *licor* mildness
suavizante *m de pelo*, *ropa* conditioner
suavizar ⟨1f⟩ *v/t tb fig* soften; **suavizarse** *v/r* become soft(er); *fig* become more amenable, soften
subacuático *adj* underwater
subalimentación *f* undernourishment
subalterno **I** *adj* subordinate **II** *m*, **-a** *f* subordinate
subarrendar ⟨1k⟩ *v/t* sublet
subarrendatario *m*, **-a** *f* sublessee
subarriendo *m* subletting
subasta *f* auction; ***sacar a ~*** put up for auction
subastador *m*, **~a** *f* auctioneer
subastar ⟨1a⟩ *v/t* auction (off)
subcampeón *m*, **-ona** *f* DEP runner-up
subclase *f* subclass
subcomisión *f* subcommittee
subconsciencia *f* subconscious
subconsciente *m/adj* subconscious
subcontinente *m* subcontinent
subcontrata(ción) *f* subcontracting
subcontratar ⟨1a⟩ *v/t* subcontract
subcontratista *m/f* subcontractor
subcultura *f* subculture
subcutáneo *adj* MED subcutaneous
subdesarrollado *adj* underdeveloped
subdesarrollo *m* underdevelopment
subdirector *m*, **~a** *f* deputy manager
súbdito *m* subject
subdividir ⟨3a⟩ *v/t* subdivide
subdivisión *f* subdivision
subempleo *m* underemployment
subespecie *f* BIO subspecies
subestimar ⟨1a⟩ *v/t* underestimate
subida *f* rise, ascent; ***~ de los precios*** rise in prices
subido **I** *part* ☞ ***subir*** **II** *adj*: ***~ de tono*** *fig* risqué, racy
subir ⟨3a⟩ **I** *v/t* **1** *cuesta*, *escalera* go up, climb; *montaña* climb **2** *objeto* raise, lift; *intereses*, *precio* raise
II *v/i* **1** *para indicar acercamiento* come up; *para indicar alejamiento* go up **2** *de precio* rise, go up **3** *a un tren*, *autobús* get on; *a un coche* get in **4**: ***~ al poder*** rise to power; ***~ al trono*** ascend to the throne
subirse *v/r* go up; *a un árbol* climb; ***~ a una silla*** get up onto a chair
súbito *adj*: ***de ~*** suddenly, all of a sudden
subjefe *m*, **-a** *f* deputy manager
subjetivo *adj* subjective
subjuntivo *m* GRAM subjunctive
sublevación *f* uprising, rebellion, revolt
sublevamiento *m* uprising, rebellion, revolt
sublevar ⟨1a⟩ *v/t* incite to revolt; *fig* infuriate, get angry; **sublevarse** *v/r* rise up, revolt
sublimación *f fig* sublimation
sublimado *m* QUÍM sublimate
sublimar ⟨1a⟩ *v/t* QUÍM, *fig* sublimate
sublime *adj* sublime
subliminal *adj* subliminal
submarinismo *m* scuba diving
submarinista *m/f* scuba diver

submarino I *adj* underwater **II** *m* submarine
subnormal I *adj* subnormal **II** *m/f desp* moron
suboficial *m* noncommissioned officer, NCO
suborden *m* BIO suborder
subordinación *f* subordination
subordinado I *adj* subordinate **II** *m*, **-a** *f* subordinate
subordinar ⟨1a⟩ *v/t* subordinate
subproducto *m* by-product
subrayar ⟨1a⟩ *v/t* underline; *fig* underline, emphasize
subrepticio *adj* surreptitious
subrogación *f* JUR transfer
subrogar ⟨1h⟩ *v/t* JUR transfer
subsanación *f de defecto, error* rectification; *de problema* resolution
subsanar ⟨1a⟩ *v/t defecto, error* rectify; *problema* resolve
subsecretario *m*, **-a** *f* undersecretary
subsecuente *adj* ☞ ***subsiguiente***
subsidiar ⟨1a⟩ *v/t L.Am.* subsidize
subsidiario *adj* subsidiary
subsidio *m* welfare, *Br* benefit
◇ **subsidio de desempleo, subsidio de paro** unemployment compensation *o Br* benefit
subsiguiente *adj* subsequent
subsistencia *f* subsistence, survival; *de pobreza, tradición* persistence
subsistente *adj which still exists*
subsistir ⟨3a⟩ *v/i* live, survive; *de pobreza, tradición* live on, persist
subsuelo *m* **1** subsoil **2** *Rpl: en edificio* basement
subte *m CSur* subway, *Br* underground
subteniente *m/f* second lieutenant
subterfugio *m* subterfuge
subterráneo I *adj* underground **II** *m L.Am.* subway, *Br* underground
subtitular ⟨1a⟩ *v/t* subtitle
subtítulo *m* subtitle
subtropical *adj* subtropical
suburbano *adj* suburban
suburbio *m* slum area
subvalorar ⟨1a⟩ *v/t* undervalue
subvención *f* subsidy
subvencionar ⟨1a⟩ *v/t* subsidize
subversión *f* subversion
subversivo *adj* subversive
subvertir ⟨3i⟩ *v/t* subvert
subyacente *adj* underlying
subyugar ⟨1h⟩ *v/t* subjugate
succión *f* suction
succionar ⟨1a⟩ *v/t* suck
sucedáneo *m* substitute
suceder ⟨2a⟩ *v/i* **1** happen, occur; ***¿qué sucede?*** what's going on? **2**: ***~ a*** follow; ***~ en el trono*** succeed to the throne
sucesión *f* **1** *de acontecimientos, problemas* succession **2**: ***~ al trono*** succession to the throne
sucesivamente *adv* successively; ***y así ~*** and so on
sucesivo *adj* successive; ***en lo ~*** from now on; ***tres días ~s*** three days in a row
suceso *m* event
sucesor *m*, **~a** *f* successor; ***~ al trono*** heir to the throne
sucesorio *adj* inheritance *atr*
suciedad *f* dirt
sucinto *adj* succint, concise
sucio *adj tb fig* dirty; ***en ~*** in rough; ***blanco ~*** off-white
sucre *m* FIN sucre
sucucho *m L.Am.* tiny house, shoebox F
suculento *adj* succulent
sucumbir ⟨3a⟩ *v/i* succumb, give in
sucursal *f* COM branch
sudaca *m/f desp* South American
sudadera *f* sweatshirt
sudado *adj* sweaty
Sudáfrica *f* South Africa
sudafricano I *adj* South African **II** *m*, **-a** *f* South African
Sudamérica *f* South America
sudamericano I *adj* South American **II** *m*, **-a** *f* South American
Sudán *m* Sudan
sudanés I *adj* Sudanese **II** *m*, **-esa** *f* Sudanese
sudar ⟨1a⟩ **I** *v/i* sweat; F (*trabajar duro*) work one's butt off F; ***~ la gota gorda*** *fig* sweat blood **II** *v/t* make sweaty
sudario *m* REL shroud
sudeste *m* southeast
sudoccidental *adj* southwestern, southwest *atr*
sudoeste *m* southwest
sudor *m* sweat
sudoración *f* perspiration
sudoriental *adj* southeastern, southeast *atr*

sudoriento *adj* sweaty
sudorífero *adj* sweat-producing
sudoríparo *adj*: ***glándulas -as*** ANAT sweat glands
sudoroso *adj* sweaty
Suecia *f* Sweden
sueco I *adj* Swedish **II** *m*, **-a** *f* Swede; ***hacerse el ~*** F pretend not to hear, act dumb F **III** *m idioma* Swedish
suegra *f* mother-in-law
suegro *m* father-in-law
suela *f de zapato* sole
sueldo *m* salary; ***asesino a ~*** hired killer
suelo *m* **1** *en casa* floor; *en el exterior* earth, ground; ***en el ~*** on the ground; ***estar por los ~s*** F be at rock bottom F; ***poner a alguien por los ~s*** run s.o. down; ***besar el ~*** *fig* fall flat on one's face; ***echar por los ~s*** *fig* F (*arruinar, frustrar*) ruin **2** AGR soil
suelta *f* release; ***dar ~ a alguien*** give s.o. permission to leave
suelto I *adj* **1** (*libre*) loose, free; ***estar*** *o* ***ir ~*** be *o* go free; ***andar ~*** be at large **2** (*separado*): ***un pendiente ~*** a single *o* an odd earring **II** *m* loose change **III** *part* ☞ ***soltar***
sueño *m* **1** (*estado de dormir*) sleep; ***tener ~*** be sleepy; ***echar un ~*** grab some sleep, take a nap; ***caerse de ~*** be dead tired, be out on one's feet; ***quitar el ~ a alguien*** keep s.o. awake **2** (*fantasía, imagen mental*) dream; ***ni en ~s*** *fig* not in a million years
suero *m* **1** MED saline solution **2** *sanguíneo* blood serum **3** *de la leche* whey
suerte *f* **1** luck; ***¡~!*** good luck!; ***buena ~*** good luck; ***mala ~*** bad luck; ***tener la ~ de cara*** be lucky; ***tener una ~ loca*** be *o* get incredibly lucky; ***probar ~*** try one's luck; ***por ~*** luckily **2** (*azar*): ***caer*** *o* ***tocar a alguien en ~*** fall to s.o.; ***echar a ~s*** toss for, draw lots for; ***la ~ está echada*** the die is cast **3** (*destino*): ***abandonar*** *o* ***dejar a alguien a su ~*** leave s.o. to their fate **4**: ***toda ~ de*** all kinds of; ***de ~ que*** so that
suertero ☞ ***suertudo***
suertudo *L.Am.* **I** *adj*: ***ser ~*** be lucky **II** *m*, **-a** *f* F lucky devil F
suéter *m* sweater
suficiencia *f* ability, aptitude; *fig* smugness; ***aire de ~*** smug air
suficiente I *adj* enough, sufficient; ***ser ~*** be enough **II** *m* EDU pass
sufragar ⟨1h⟩ **I** *v/t* COM meet, pay **II** *v/i L.Am.* vote
sufragio *m*: ***~ universal*** universal suffrage
sufrido *adj* **1** *persona* long-suffering **2** *material* tough, hard-wearing
sufrimiento *m* suffering
sufrir ⟨3a⟩ **I** *v/t fig* suffer, put up with **II** *v/i* suffer (***de*** from); ***sufre del estómago*** he has stomach problems
sugerencia *f* suggestion
sugerir ⟨3i⟩ *v/t* suggest
sugestión *f*: ***es pura ~*** it is all in the mind
sugestionable *adj* impressionable
sugestionar ⟨1a⟩ *v/t* influence
sugestivo *adj* suggestive
suicida I *adj* suicidal **II** *m/f* suicide victim
suicidarse ⟨1a⟩ *v/r* commit suicide
suicidio *m* suicide
suite *f tb* MÚS suite
Suiza *f* Switzerland
suizo I *adj* Swiss **II** *m*, **-a** *f* Swiss **III** *m* GASTR *sugar topped bun*
sujeción *f* holding, fixing
sujetador *m* brassiere, bra
sujetalibros *m inv* bookend
sujetapapeles *m inv* paperclip
sujetar ⟨1a⟩ *v/t* **1** (*fijar*) hold (down), keep in place **2** (*sostener*) hold; **sujetarse** *v/r* hold on
sujeto I *adj* **1** (*fijo*) secure **2**: ***~ a*** subject to **II** *m* **1** individual **2** GRAM subject
sulfamida *f* MED sulfonamide, *Br* sulphonamide
sulfatar ⟨1a⟩ *v/t* AGR sulfate, *Br* sulphate
sulfato *m* sulfate, *Br* sulphate
sulfurar ⟨1a⟩ *v/t* QUÍM sulfurize, *Br* sulphurize; ***~ a alguien*** *fig* F drive s.o. nuts F; **sulfurarse** *v/r fig* F blow one's top F
sulfuro *m* sulfur, *Br* sulphur
sulfuroso *adj* sulfurous, *Br* sulphurous
sultán *m* sultan
suma *f* sum; ***en ~*** in short
◇ **suma y sigue** COM balance carried forward
sumamente *adv* extremely, highly
sumar ⟨1a⟩ **I** *v/t* add; ***5 y 6 suman 11*** 5 and 6 make 11 **II** *v/i* add up; **sumarse** *v/r*: ***~ a*** join

sumario I *adj* brief **II** *m* **1** summary **2** JUR indictment
sumergible I *adj reloj* waterproof; *embarcación* submersible **II** *m* submersible
sumergir ⟨3c⟩ *v/t* submerge, immerse; **sumergirse** *v/r fig* immerse o.s. (***en*** in), throw o.s. (***en*** into)
sumersión *f* submersion
sumidero *m* drain
suministrador I *adj* supply *atr*; ***empresa ~a*** supplier, supply company **II** *m*, **~a** *f* supplier
suministrar ⟨1a⟩ *v/t* supply, provide
suministro *m* supply
sumir ⟨3a⟩ *v/t fig* plunge, throw (***en*** into); **sumirse** *v/r fig* sink (***en*** into)
sumisión *f* submission
sumiso *adj* submissive
sumo *adj* supreme; ***con ~ cuidado*** with the utmost care; ***a lo ~*** at the most
suntuario *adj* sumptuous
suntuosidad *f* sumptuousness, magnificence
suntuoso *adj* sumptuous
supe *vb* ☞ ***saber***
supeditar ⟨1a⟩ *v/t* make conditional (***a*** upon)
súper *adj* F super F, great F
superable *adj* surmountable
superabundancia *f* overabundance
superabundante *adj* overabundant
superabundar ⟨1a⟩ *v/i*: ***superabundan los …*** there's an overbundance of …
superación *f* overcoming, surmounting
superar ⟨1a⟩ *v/t persona* beat; *límite* go beyond, exceed; *obstáculo* overcome, surmount; **superarse** *v/r* surpass o.s., excel o.s.
superávit *m* surplus
superchería *f* trick, swindle
superdotado *adj* gifted
superestructura *f* superstructure
superficial *adj* superficial, shallow
superficialidad *f* superficiality, shallowness
superficie *f* surface; ***salir a la ~*** *del agua* come to the surface; ***grandes ~s (comerciales)*** large stores
superfluo *adj* superfluous
superhombre *m* superman
superintendente *m/f* superintendent
superior I *adj* **1** *labio, piso etc* upper **2** *en jerarquía* superior; ***ser ~ a*** be superior to **II** *m* superior
superiora *f* REL Mother Superior
superioridad *f* superiority
superlativo I *adj* superlative **II** *m* GRAM superlative
supermercado *m* supermarket
supermodelo *m/f* supermodel
superpoblación *f* overpopulation
superpoblado *adj* overpopulated
superponer ⟨2r⟩ *v/t* superimpose; **superponerse** *v/r* be superimposed; ***al miedo se superpone el sentido del deber*** fear becomes subordinate to a sense of duty
superposición *f* superimposition
superpotencia *f* POL superpower
superproducción *f* **1** COM overproduction **2** *película* blockbuster
superpuesto *adj* superimposed
supersónico *adj* supersonic
superstición *f* superstition
supersticioso *adj* superstitious
supervalorar ⟨1a⟩ *v/t* overvalue
supervisar ⟨1a⟩ *v/t* supervise
supervisión *f* supervision
supervisor *m*, **~a** *f* supervisor
supervivencia *f* survival
superviviente I *adj* surviving **II** *m/f* survivor
supiera *vb* ☞ ***saber***
supino *adj* **1** *posición* supine **2**: ***ignorancia -a*** crass ignorance
suplantación *f* **1** replacement **2** JUR impersonation
suplantar ⟨1a⟩ *v/t* **1** replace, take the place of **2** JUR impersonate
suplementario *adj* supplementary
suplemento *m* supplement; ***~ dominical*** *de periódico* Sunday supplement
suplencia *f* temporary job
suplente *m/f* substitute
supletorio I *adj* extra, additional **II** *m* TELEC extension
súplica *f* plea
suplicante I *adj* imploring, begging **II** *m* petitioner, supplicant
suplicar ⟨1g⟩ *v/t cosa* plead for, beg for; *persona* beg
suplicatorio *m* JUR request, petition
suplicio *m fig* torment, ordeal
suplir ⟨3a⟩ *v/t* **1** *carencia* make up for **2** (*sustituir*) substitute
supo *vb* ☞ ***saber***
suponer ⟨2r; *part* ***supuesto***⟩ *v/t* sup-

pose, assume; ***supongamos que …*** let's suppose *o* assume that …; ***supongo que sí*** I suppose so
suposición *f* supposition
supositorio *m* MED suppository
supranacional *adj* supranational
suprarrenal *adj* ANAT adrenal; ***glándula*** *o* ***cápsula ~*** adrenal gland
supremacía *f* supremacy
supremo *adj* supreme
supresión *f de rebelión* suppression; *de impuesto, ley* abolition; *de restricción* lifting; *de servicio* withdrawal; *en texto* deletion
suprimir ⟨3a⟩ *v/t rebelión* suppress, put down; *ley, impuesto* abolish; *restricción* lift; *servicio* withdraw; *puesto de trabajo* cut; *en texto* delete; ***suprimió algunos detalles*** she kept something back, she didn't give me / us the whole story
supuesto **I** *part* ☞ ***suponer*** **II** *adj* supposed, alleged; ***~ que*** (*ya que*) since; (*en caso de que*) if; ***por ~*** of course; ***dar algo por ~*** take sth as read **III** *m* assumption
supuración *f* weeping, oozing
supurar ⟨1a⟩ *v/i* weep, ooze
sur *m* south; ***al ~ de*** to the south of, south of
surafricano ☞ ***sudafricano***
suramericano ☞ ***sudamericano***
surcar ⟨1g⟩ *v/i* sail
surco *m* AGR furrow
surcoreano **I** *adj* South Korean **II** *m*, **-a** *f* South Korean
sureño *adj* southern
sureste *m* ☞ ***sudeste***
surf(ing) *m* surfing
surfista *m/f* surfer
surgimiento *m* emergence
surgir ⟨3c⟩ *v/i* **1** *fig* emerge; *de problema tb* come up **2** *de agua* spout
Suriname *m* Suriname
surinamés **I** *adj* Surinamese **II** *m*, **-esa** *f* Surinamese
suroccidental *adj* ☞ ***sudoccidental***
suroeste *m* ☞ ***sudoeste***
suroriental *adj* ☞ ***sudoriental***
surrealismo *m* surrealism
surrealista *m/f & adj* surrealist
surtido **I** *adj* **1** *galletas* assorted **2**: ***bien ~*** COM well stocked **II** *m* assortment, range
surtidor *m*: ***~ de gasolina*** *o* ***de nafta*** gas pump, *Br* petrol pump
surtir ⟨3a⟩ **I** *v/t* **1** supply **2**: ***~ efecto*** have the desired effect **II** *v/i* spout; **surtirse** *v/r* stock up (***de*** with)
susceptibilidad *f* touchiness
susceptible *adj* **1** *persona* touchy **2**: ***ser ~ de mejora*** leave room for improvement
suscitar ⟨1a⟩ *v/t enojo* arouse; *polémica* generate; *escándalo* provoke
suscribir ⟨3a; *part* ***suscrito***⟩ *v/t* **1** subscribe to; ***estar suscrito a un periódico*** have a subscription to a newspaper **2**: ***el que suscribe*** the undersigned; **suscribirse** *v/r* subscribe
suscripción *f* subscription
suscriptor *m*, **~a** *f* subscriber
suscrito **I** *part* ☞ ***suscribir*** **II** *m*, **-a** *f* undersigned
susodicho *adj* aforementioned, abovementioned
suspender ⟨2a⟩ **I** *v/t* **1** *empleado, alumno* suspend **2** *objeto* hang, suspend **3** *reunión* adjourn **4** *examen* fail **II** *v/i* EDU fail
suspense *m fig* suspense; ***película / novela de ~*** thriller
suspensión *f* **1** *de jugador, alumno* suspension **2** *de objeto* hanging, suspension **3** *de reunión* adjournment **4** *en baloncesto* jump
◇ **suspensión de pagos** COM suspension of salary payments
suspensivo *adj*: ***puntos ~s*** *pl* suspension points
suspenso **I** *adj* **1**: ***alumnos ~s*** students who have failed **2** (*aplazado*): ***en ~*** suspended **3**: ***dejar en ~*** keep in suspense **II** *m* **1** fail **2** *L.Am.* (*suspense*) suspense
suspensores *mpl L.Am.* suspenders, *Br* braces
suspensorio *m* MED athletic support, jockstrap F
suspicacia *f* suspicion; ***levantar ~s*** arouse suspicion
suspicaz *adj* suspicious
suspirar ⟨1a⟩ *v/i* **1** sigh **2**: ***~ por algo*** yearn for sth, long for sth
suspiro *m* sigh
sustancia *f* substance; ***sin ~*** *fig* insubstantial, lacking in substance
sustancial *adj* substantial
sustantivar ⟨1a⟩ *v/t* GRAM substantivize

sustantivo *m* GRAM noun
sustentación *f* AVIA lift
sustentamiento *m* **1** *comida etc* sustenance **2** *apoyo* base
sustentar ⟨1a⟩ *v/t* **1** sustain **2** *familia* support **3** *opinión* maintain; **sustentarse** *v/r* support o.s.
sustento *m* means of support
sustitución *f* DEP substitution
sustituible *adj* replaceable
sustituir ⟨3g⟩ *v/t*: ***~ X por Y*** replace X with Y, substitute Y for X
sustituto *m* substitute
sustitutorio *adj* substitute *atr*
susto *m* fright, scare; ***dar** o **pegar un ~ a alguien*** give s.o. a fright; ***no gano para ~s*** F nothing's going right for me, my world has gone haywire
sustracción *f* **1** (*robo*) theft **2** MAT subtraction
sustraendo *m* MAT subtrahend
sustraer ⟨2p; *part* ***sustraído***⟩ *v/t* subtract, take away; (*robar*) steal; **sustraerse** *v/r*: ***~ a*** avoid, resist
sustraído *part* ☞ ***sustraer***
sustrato *m* substrate, substratum
susurrar ⟨1a⟩ **I** *v/t* whisper **II** *v/i de viento* whisper
susurro *m* whisper
sutil *adj fig* subtle
sutileza *f fig* subtlety
sutura *f* MED suture
suturar ⟨1a⟩ *v/t* MED suture, stitch
suyo, suya *pron pos*: *de él* his; *de ella* hers; *de usted, ustedes* yours; *de ellos* theirs; ***los ~s*** his / her *etc* folks, his / her *etc* family; ***hacer ~ algo*** make sth one's own; ***hacer de las -as*** get up to one's old tricks; ***ir a lo ~*** think only of oneself; ***salirse con la -a*** get one's own way; ***ser muy ~*** keep to o.s.; ***de esto sabe lo ~*** he knows everything about this
switch *m L.Am.* switch

T

taba *f* ANAT ankle bone
tabacalero I *adj* tobacco *atr*; ***compañía -a*** cigarette company, tobacco company; ***industria -a*** tobacco industry **II** *m*, **-a** *f* tobacco grower
tabaco *m* tobacco
tábano *m* ZO horsefly
tabaquera *f para tabaco* tobacco tin; *para cigarillos* cigarette case
tabaquero ☞ ***tabacalero***
tabaquismo *m* nicotine poisoning
tabarra *f*: ***dar la ~ a alguien*** F bug s.o. F
taberna *f* bar
tabernario *adj* (*basto*) coarse
tabernero *m* bar owner, *Br* landlord; (*camarero*) bartender
tabicar ⟨1g⟩ *v/t* board up
tabique *m* partition, partition wall
tabla *f* **1** *de madera* board, plank **2** PINT panel; (*cuadro*) table **3** *en ajedrez*: ***acabar** o **quedar en ~s*** end in a tie **4**: ***tener ~s*** TEA be a natural actor
◇ **tabla de materias** table of contents; **tabla de multiplicar** multiplication table; **tabla de planchar** ironing board; **tabla de quesos** GASTR cheeseboard; **tabla rasa**: ***hacer ~ de algo*** disregard sth; **tabla de salvación** *fig* last resort; **tabla de surf** surf board; **Tablas de la Ley** Ten Commandments, Tables of the Law
tablado *m en un acto* platform; *de escenario* stage
tablear ⟨1a⟩ *v/t* **1** *madero* cut into planks **2** *tela* pleat
tablero *m* board, plank; *de juego* board; *en baloncesto* backboard
◇ **tablero de instrumentos, tablero de mandos** AUTO dashboard
tableta *f*: ***~ de chocolate*** chocolate bar
tableteo *m de ametralladora* rat-a-tat-tat, chatter; *de trueno* boom; *de madera* rattle
tabloide *m* tabloid
tablón *m* **1** plank **2**: ***llevar un ~*** F be plastered F
◇ **tablón de anuncios** bulletin board, *Br* noticeboard
tabú *m* taboo
tabulador *m tb* INFOR tab key
tabular[1] *adj* tabular
tabular[2] ⟨1a⟩ *v/t* tabulate

taburete *m* stool
tacada *f* shot; ***de una ~*** F in one shot
tacañería *f* F miserliness, stinginess F
tacaño I *adj* F miserly, stingy F **II** *m*, **-a** *f* F miser F, tightwad F
tacha *f* flaw, blemish; ***sin ~*** beyond reproach
tachadura *f* crossing out
tachar ⟨1a⟩ *v/t* **1** cross out; ***táchese lo que no proceda*** delete as applicable **2** (*tildar*): ***la tacharon de egoísta*** she was branded *o* labeled as selfish
tachero *m*, **-a** *f Rpl* F cabby F
tacho *m Rpl* **1** (*papelera*) wastepaper basket; *en la calle* garbage can, *Br* litter basket **2** *taxi* cab, taxi
tachón *m* **1** (*tachadura*) crossing out **2** (*tachuela*) ornamental stud
tachonado *adj* studded (***de*** with)
tachonar ⟨1a⟩ *v/t* stud
tachuela *f* thumbtack, *Br* drawing pin
tácito *adj* tacit
taciturno *adj* taciturn
taco *m* **1** F (*palabrota*) swearword; ***soltar*** *o* ***decir un ~*** swear, utter an oath **2** *L.Am. de zapato* heel **3** GASTR taco (*filled tortilla*) **4** DEP stud **5**: ***armar un ~*** F cause trouble
◇ **taco de salida** DEP starting block
tacógrafo *m* AUTO tachograph
tacómetro *m* AUTO tachometer
tacón *m de zapato* heel; ***zapatos de ~*** high-heeled shoes
◇ **tacón de aguja** spike heel
taconazo *m en fútbol* backheeler
taconear ⟨1a⟩ *v/i* stamp one's heels
taconeo *m* heel stamping
táctica *f* tactics *pl*
táctico *adj* tactical
táctil *adj* tactile
tacto *m* **1** (sense of) touch **2** *fig* tact, discretion; ***falta de ~*** tactlessness
TAE *f abr* (= ***tasa anual efectiva***) APR (= annual percentage rate)
tafetán *m* taffeta
tahona *f* bakery
tahúr *m* card sharp
taita *m S.Am.* **1** F dad, pop F **2** (*abuelo*) grandfather
Taiwán *m* Taiwan
taiwanés I *adj* of / from Taiwan, Taiwanese **II** *m*, **-esa** *f* Taiwanese
tajada *f* **1** GASTR slice; ***sacar ~*** F take a slice *o* cut F **2**: ***agarrar una ~*** F get drunk
tajamar *m S.Am.* (*dique*) dike
tajante *adj* categorical
tajo *m* **1** cut **2** (*trabajo*): ***ir al ~*** F go to work
tal I *adj* such; ***no dije ~ cosa*** I said no such thing; ***el gerente era un ~ Lucas*** the manager was someone called Lucas; ***el ~ abogado resultó ser su padre*** the lawyer (in question) turned out to be her father
II *adv* **1**: ***¿qué ~?*** how's it going?; ***¿qué ~ la película?*** what was the movie like? **2**: ***~ como*** such as; ***~ y como*** exactly as, just as; ***dejó la habitación ~ cual la encontró*** she left the room just as she found it; ***occurió así, ~ cual*** that was exactly how it happened; ***Marta está ~ cual*** Marta is the same as ever, Marta hasn't changed a bit; ***con ~ de que*** + *subj* as long as, provided that
III *pron*: ***~ y ~, ~ y cual*** and so on, and so forth; ***~ para cual*** two of a kind
◇ **tal vez** maybe, perhaps
tala I *f de árboles* felling **II** *m Arg*, *Bol* grazing
taladradora *f* drill
taladrar ⟨1a⟩ *v/t* drill
taladro *m* drill
tálamo *m* ANAT thalamus
talante *m* (*genio*, *humor*) mood; ***un ~ bonachón*** a kindly nature; ***estar de buen / mal ~*** be in a good / bad mood
talar ⟨1a⟩ *v/t árbol* fell, cut down
talasoterapia *f* MED seawater therapy, thalassotherapy
talco *m* talc, talcum; ***polvos de ~*** *pl* talcum powder *sg*
talega *f* sack
talego *m* P 1000 pesetas
talento *m* talent
TALGO *m abr* (= ***Tren Articulado Ligero Goicoechea Oriol***) TALGO (*Spanish long-distance train*)
talio *m* QUÍM thallium
talismán *m* talisman
talla *f* **1** size; ***de gran ~*** *fig* outstanding; ***dar la ~*** *fig* make the grade **2** (*estatura*) height **3** *C.Am.* (*mentira*) lie
tallado I *adj madera* carved; *piedra* sculpted; *piedra preciosa* cut **II** *m de madera* carving; *de piedra* sculpting; *de piedra preciosa* cutting
tallador *m*, **~a** *f L.Am. en naipes* banker

tallar ⟨1a⟩ *v/t* **1** *madera* carve; *piedra* sculpt; *piedra preciosa* cut **2** *Méx* rub; *al lavarse* scrub
tallarín *m* noodle
talle *m* waist
taller *m* workshop
◇ **taller mecánico** auto repair shop
◇ **taller de reparaciones** repair shop
tallo *m* BOT stalk, stem
talludo *adj* BOT tall
talón *m* **1** ANAT heel; ***pisar los talones a alguien*** be hot on s.o.'s heels **2** COM stub
◇ **talón de Aquiles** *fig* Achilles' heel
talonario *m*: **~ *de cheques*** checkbook, *Br* chequebook; **~ *de recibos*** receipt book
talud *m* slope
talvez *adv L.Am.* maybe, perhaps
tamal *m Méx, C.Am.* tamale (*meat wrapped in a leaf and steamed*)
tamaño I *adj*: **~ *fallo* / *problema*** such a great mistake / problem **II** *m* size; ***a ~ natural*** life-size
tamarindo *m* **1** BOT tamarind **2** *Méx* F traffic cop F
tamarisco *m* BOT tamarisk
tambalearse ⟨1a⟩ *v/r* stagger, lurch; *de coche* sway
tambarria *f C.Am., Pe, Bol* party
también *adv* also, too, as well; ***yo ~*** me too; ***él estudia inglés - yo ~*** he's studying English - me too *o* so am I; ***él ~ dice que …*** he also says that …
tambo *m* **1** *Rpl* dairy farm **2** *Méx*: *type of large container*
tambor *m* **1** drum; ***tocar el ~*** beat the drum; ***a ~ batiente*** (*triunfalmente*) in triumph **2** *persona* drummer
tamborear *vb* ☞ ***tamborilear***
tamboril *m* small drum
tamborilear ⟨1a⟩ *v/i* drum with one's fingers
tamborileo *m* drumming
tamborilero *m*, **-a** *f* drummer
tamiz *m* sieve; ***pasar por el ~*** *tb fig* sieve
tamizar ⟨1f⟩ *v/t* sieve, sift; *luz* filter; *información* sift
tampoco *adv* neither; ***él ~ va*** he's not going either; ***… ni ~ espero que lo haga*** … and I don't expect him to do it
tampón *m* **1** *higiénico* tampon **2** *de tinta* ink pad
tan *adv* so; ***era ~ grande que …*** it was so big that …; **~ *… como …*** as … as …; **~ *grande como …*** as big as …; **~ *sólo*** merely; **~ *siquiera*** at least
tanatorio *m* funeral home, funeral parlor
tanda *f* **1** series *sg*, batch; ***por ~s*** in batches **2** (*turno*) shift **3** *L.Am.* TV (commercial) break
◇ **tanda de penaltis** DEP penalty shootout
tándem *m* tandem
tanga *m* tanga
tangente *f* MAT tangent; ***salir*** *o* ***irse por la ~*** F sidestep the issue, duck the question F
tangible *adj fig* tangible
tango *m* tango
tanino *m* tannin
tano *m*, **-a** *f Rpl* F Italian
tanque *m tb* MIL tank
tanteador *m*, **~a** *f* DEP scorer
tantear ⟨1a⟩ *v/t* **1** feel **2** (*calcular a ojo*) work out roughly **3** *situación* size up; *persona* sound out; **~ *el terreno*** *fig* see how the land lies **4** (*probar*) try out
tanteo *m marcador* score
tantito *adv Méx* a little
tanto I *adj* so much; *igual cantidad* as much; **~s** *pl* so many; *igual número* as many; ***comí ~s pasteles que me puse malo*** I ate so many candies that I was ill; ***no vimos ~s pájaros como ayer*** we didn't see as many birds as we did yesterday
II *pron* so much; *igual cantidad* as much; ***un ~*** a little; **~s** *pl* so many; *igual número* as many; ***uno de ~s*** one of many; ***tienes ~*** you have so much; ***no hay ~s como ayer*** there aren't as many as yesterday; ***a las -as de la noche*** in the small hours
III *adv* so much; *igual cantidad* as much; *periodo* so long; ***tardó ~ como él*** she took as long as him; **~ *mejor*** so much the better; ***no es para ~*** it's not such a big deal; ***a ~ no llega*** things aren't as bad as that; **~ *es así que …*** so much so that…; **~ (*me*) *da*** I don't really care; ***¡y ~!*** yeah!, right on!
IV *en locuciones*: ***por lo ~*** therefore, so; ***entre ~*** meanwhile; ***ella trabajaba en ~ que él veía la televisión*** she was working while he was watching television
V *m* **1** point; ***apuntarse*** *o* ***marcar un ~***

T

DEP score a point; ***~ por ciento*** percentage **2**: ***estar al ~*** be informed (***de*** about) **3**: ***él es muy inteligente, y ella otro ~*** he is very intelligent and so is she *o* and she is too
Tanzania *f* Tanzania
tanzano I *adj* Tanzanian **II** *m*, **-a** *f* Tanzanian
tañer ⟨2f⟩ *v/t* MÚS: *instrumento* play; *campanas* ring
tapa *f* **1** *de tarro, cubo etc* lid; ***se voló la ~ de los sesos*** he blew his brains out **2** *de libro* cover; ***~ dura*** hardback **3**: ***~s*** *pl* GASTR tapas, bar snacks
tapabarros *m inv Andes* fender
tapacubos *m inv* AUTO hub cap
tapadera *f* lid; *fig* front
tapadillo *m*: ***de ~*** on the sly
tapado *adj nariz* blocked (up)
tapado *m Arg, Chi* coat
tapadura *f Chi*: *en diente* filling
tapar ⟨1a⟩ *v/t cara* cover; *fig*: *nerviosismo* cover up; *recipiente* put the lid on; **taparse** *v/r* wrap up; ***~ los ojos*** cover one's eyes
taparrabo *m* loincloth
tapear ⟨1a⟩ *v/i Esp* have some snacks
tapete *m* **1** tablecloth; ***~ (verde)*** card table; ***poner algo sobre el ~*** bring sth up for discussion **2** *L.Am. alfombra* carpet
tapia *f* wall; ***más sordo que una ~*** as deaf as a post
tapiar ⟨1b⟩ *v/t* **1** *terreno* wall in **2** *hueco* brick up
tapicería *f* **1** *de muebles* upholstery **2** (*tapiz*) tapestry; *arte* tapestry making
tapicero *m*, **-a** *f* **1** *de muebles* upholsterer **2** *arte* tapestry maker
tapioca *f* tapioca
tapir *m* tapir
tapiz *m* **1** tapestry **2** (*moqueta*) carpet
tapizar ⟨1f⟩ *v/t* upholster
tapón *m* **1** top, cap; *de baño* plug **2** *de tráfico* traffic jam; *de cera* blockage **3** *en baloncesto* block **4** *L.Am.* EL fuse
◇ **tapón de rosca** screw top
taponar ⟨1a⟩ *v/t* **1** *orificio* block **2** *herida* swab
tapujo *m*: ***sin ~s*** openly
taquicardia *f* MED tachycardia
taquigrafía *f* shorthand
taquigrafiar ⟨1c⟩ *v/t* take down in shorthand
taquigráfico *adj* shorthand *atr*
taquígrafo *m*, **-a** *f* stenographer, shorthand writer
taquilla *f* **1** FERR ticket office; TEA box-office **2** *C.Am.* (*bar*) small bar **3** *armario* locker; *para cartas* pigeonholes *pl*
taquillero I *adj cantante* popular; ***una película -a*** a hit movie, a box-office hit **II** *m*, **-a** *f* ticket clerk
taquillón *m* dresser
taquimecanógrafo *m*, **-a** *f* stenographer, *Br* shorthand typist
tara *f* **1** defect **2** COM tare
tarabilla *m/f* F *persona* chatterbox
taracea *f* inlay, marquetry
tarado *adj* F stupid, dumb F
tarambana *m/f* F scatterbrain F
tarántula *f* ZO tarantula
tararear ⟨1a⟩ *v/t* hum
tardanza *f* delay
tardar ⟨1a⟩ *v/i* **1** (*demorarse*) take a long time; ***tardamos dos horas*** we were two hours overdue *o* late; ***¡no tardes!*** don't be late; ***a más ~*** at the latest; ***sin ~*** without delay; ***no tardó en volver*** he soon came back, it wasn't long before he came back **2**: ***¿cuánto se tarda …?*** how long does it take to …?; **tardarse** *v/r Méx*: ***no te tardes*** don't be late
tarde I *adv* late; ***~ o temprano*** sooner or later; ***más vale ~ que nunca*** better late than never; ***llegar ~*** be late; ***se me hace ~*** it's getting late
II *f hasta las 5 ó 6* afternoon; *desde las 5 ó 6* evening; ***¡buenas ~s!*** good afternoon / evening; ***por la ~*** in the afternoon / evening; ***de ~ en ~*** from time to time; ***esta ~*** this afternoon / evening
tardío *adj fruto, primavera* late; *decisión* belated; ***es un escritor de vocación tardía*** he is a writer who found his calling late in life
tardón *adj* F **1** slow **2** (*impuntual*) late
tarea *f* task, job
◇ **tareas domésticas** housework *sg*
tarifa *f* rate; *de tren* fare; ***~s postales*** postal rates
◇ **tarifa plana, tarifa única** flat rate
tarima *f* platform; ***suelo de ~*** wooden floor
tarjeta *f* card
◇ **tarjeta amarilla** DEP yellow card; **tarjeta de crédito** credit card; **tarjeta de embarque** AVIA boarding pass *o* card;

tarjeta gráfica INFOR graphics card; **tarjeta inteligente** smart card; **tarjeta magnética** card with a magnetic strip; **tarjeta de memoria** INFOR memory card; **tarjeta postal** postcard; **tarjeta de prepago** prepaid card, *Br tb* prepayment card; **tarjeta roja** DEP red card; **tarjeta de sonido** INFOR sound card; **tarjeta telefónica** phone card; **tarjeta de visita** (business) card
tarjetero *m* **1** *caja* business card case **2** *cartera* credit card holder
tarrina *f de helado* tub
tarro *m* **1** jar **2** P (*cabeza*) nut F; ***comerse el ~*** F worry
tarso *m* ANAT tarsus
tarta *f* cake; *plana* tart
◇ **tarta helada** ice-cream cake
tartajear ⟨1a⟩ *v/i* F stammer, stutter
tartajoso *adj* F stammering, stuttering
tartamudear ⟨1a⟩ *v/i* stutter, stammer
tartamudez *f* stuttering, stammering
tartamudo I *adj* stuttering, stammering; ***ser ~*** stutter, stammer **II** *m*, **-a** *f* stutterer, stammerer
tartana *f* **1** (*carruaje*) light carriage, trap **2** (*coche*) jalopy F, *Br* old banger F
tartárico *adj*: ***ácido ~*** tartaric acid
tártaro *m* QUÍM tartar
tartera *f* lunch box
tarugo *m* F blockhead
tarumba *adj* F crazy F; ***volverse ~*** go crazy
tasa *f* **1** rate; ***~ de crecimiento*** rate of growth, growth rate **2** (*impuesto*) tax
◇ **tasa de capturas** fishing quota; **tasa de crecimiento** rate of growth, growth rate; **tasa de desempleo** unemployment rate; **tasa de inflación** rate of inflation, inflation rate; **tasa de paro** unemployment rate
tasación *f* valuation
tasador *m*, **~a** *f* valuer
tasar ⟨1a⟩ *v/t* fix a price for; (*valorar*) value
tasca *f* F bar
tata *m L.Am.* F (*abuelo*) grandpa F
tatarabuela *f* great-great-grandmother
tatarabuelo *m* great-great-grandfather
tataranieta *f* great-great-granddaughter
tataranieto *m* great-great-grandson
tate *interj* F **1** (*ahora caigo*) oh I see **2** (*cuidado*) look out!
ta-te-ti *m Rpl* tick-tack-toe, *Br* noughts and crosses *sg*
tatuador *m*, **~a** *f* tattooist
tatuaje *m* tattoo
tatuar ⟨1d⟩ *v/t* tattoo
taurino I *adj* **1** bullfighting *atr* **2** *L.Am.* ASTR Taurean; ***soy ~*** I'm Taurean, I'm (a) Taurus **II** *m*, **-a** *f L.Am.* ASTR Taurean, Taurus
Tauro ASTR **I** *adj* Taurean **II** *m*, **-a** *f* Taurean; ***soy ~*** I'm (a) Taurean, I'm (a) Taurus
tauromaquia *f* bullfighting
TAV *m abr* (= ***tren de alta velocidad***) high speed train
taxi *m* cab, taxi
taxidermia *f* taxidermy
taxidermista *m/f* taxidermist
taxímetro *m* meter
taxista *m/f* cab *o* taxi driver
taza *f* **1** cup **2** *del wáter* bowl **3** *Rpl*: *en vehículo* hub cap
tazón *m* bowl
TC *m abr* (= ***Tribunal Constitucional***) Constitutional Court
te *pron* **1** *directo* you; ***no ~ había visto*** I hadn't seen you **2** *indirecto* (to) you; ***~ doy el libro*** I'm giving you the book **3** *reflexivo* yourself
té *m* tea
tea *f* torch
teatral *adj fig* theatrical
teatro *m tb fig* theater, *Br* theatre
tebeo *m* children's comic
techado *m* roof
techar ⟨1a⟩ *v/t* roof
techo *m* ceiling; (*tejado*) roof; ***falso ~*** false ceiling; ***los sin ~*** homeless people, the homeless *pl*; ***tocar ~*** *fig* peak
◇ **techo corredizo, techo deslizante** AUTO sunroof
◇ **techo solar** AUTO sun-roof
techumbre *f* roof
tecla *f* key
◇ **tecla de borrado** INFOR delete key; **tecla de comando** INFOR command key; **tecla control** INFOR control key; **tecla cursor** INFOR arrow key, cursor key; **tecla de función** INFOR function key; **tecla de marcación rápida** TELEC speed-dial button; **tecla de mayúsculas** INFOR shift key; **tecla de movimiento del cursor** INFOR cursor control key, arrow key; **tecla de retroceso** INFOR backspace key

tecladista *m/f L.Am.* keyboard player
teclado *m* MÚS, INFOR keyboard
teclear ⟨1a⟩ *v/t* key; *fig* try to get
tecleteo *m* F keying
teclista *m/f* **1** INFOR keyboarder **2** MÚS keyboard player
técnica *f* **1** technique **2** *en baloncesto*: *infracción* technical foul
tecnicismo *m* technical nature; *término* technical term
técnico I *adj* technical **II** *m/f* **1** technician; *de televisor, lavadora etc* repairman; ***~ de sistemas*** INFOR systems technician **2** *en fútbol* coach, manager
tecnificación *f* increased use of technology
tecnificar ⟨1g⟩ *v/t* increase the use of technology in
tecno *m* MÚS techno
tecnología *f* technology; ***alta ~*** hi-tech
◇ **tecnología de la información** information technology
◇ **tecnología punta** state-of-the-art technology, leading-edge technology
tecnológico *adj* technological
tecolote *m Méx, C.Am.* (*búho*) owl
tedio *m* tedium
tedioso *adj* tedious
teja I *adj*: (***de color***) **~** terracotta *atr* **II** *f* roof tile; ***a toca ~*** in hard cash
tejado *m* roof
tejano I *adj* Texan, of / from Texas **II** *m*, **-a** *f* Texan
tejanos *mpl* jeans
tejar ⟨1a⟩ **I** *v/t* tile **II** *m* tile factory
Tejas *m* Texas
tejedor *m* weaver
tejedora *f* **1** knitting machine **2** *mujer* weaver
tejemanejes *mpl* F scheming *sg*, plotting *sg*
tejer ⟨2a⟩ **I** *v/t* weave; *tela de araña* spin; (*hacer punto*) knit; F *intriga* devise **II** *v/i L.Am.* plot, scheme
tejido *m* **1** (*tela*) fabric **2** ANAT tissue
tejo *m* **1** BOT yew **2**: ***tirar a alguien los ~s*** F hit on s.o. F, come on to s.o. F
tejón *m* ZO badger
Tel. *abr* (= ***teléfono***) Tel. (= telephone)
tela *f* fabric, material; ***poner en ~ de juicio*** call into question; ***hay ~ para rato*** F there's a lot to be done; ***tener ~*** (***marinera***) F be tricky F, be tough F; ***hay mucha ~ que cortar*** F there's plenty that could be said on the subject
◇ **tela de araña** spiderweb
◇ **tela metálica** wire netting
telar *m* loom
telaraña *f* spiderweb
tele *f* F TV, *Br* telly F
teleadicto *m*, **-a** *f* TV addict
telearrastre *m* drag lift
telebanca *f* telephone banking
telecabina *f* cable car
telecámara *f* TV camera
telecomedia *f* sitcom
telecompra *f* home shopping
telecomunicaciones *fpl* telecommunications
telediario *m* TV (television) news *sg*
teledirigido *adj* remote-controlled
teléf. *abr* (= ***teléfono***) tel. (= telephone)
telefax *m* fax
teleférico *m* cable car
telefilm(e) *m* TV movie
telefonazo *m* F call
telefonear ⟨1a⟩ *v/t & v/i* call, phone
telefonema *m L.Am.* (phone) message
telefonía *f* telephony
◇ **telefonía móvil** cell phone telephony, *Br* mobile telephony
telefónico *adj* (tele)phone *atr*
telefonista *m/f* (telephone) operator
teléfono *m* (tele)phone; ***hablar / llamar por ~*** make a phone call; ***le llaman al ~*** you're wanted on the phone; ***por ~*** by phone
◇ **teléfono fijo** fixed phone; **teléfono inalámbrico** cordless (phone); **teléfono de monedas** payphone; **teléfono monedero** *L.Am.* payphone; **teléfono móvil** cell phone, *Br* mobile (phone); **teléfono público** payphone, public telephone; **teléfono de tarjeta** card phone
telegénico *adj* telegenic
telegrafía *f* telegraphy
telegrafiar ⟨1c⟩ *v/t* telegraph
telegráfico *adj* telegraphic
telegrama *m* telegram
telekinesia, telekinesis *f* telekinesis
telele *m* F fit F; ***le dio un ~*** he had a fit
telemando *m* remote control
telemática *f* data comms *sg*
telenovela *f* soap (opera)
teleobjetivo *m* FOT telephoto lens
telepatía *f* telepathy
telescópico *adj* telescopic

telescopio *m* telescope
teleserie *f* (television) series *sg*
telesilla *f* chair lift
telespectador *m*, **~a** *f* (television) viewer
telesquí *m* drag lift
teletexto *m* teletext
teletienda *f* home shopping
teletipo *m* Teletype®, *Br* teleprinter
teletrabajador *m*, **~a** *f* teleworker
teletrabajo *m* teleworking
televidente *m/f* (television) viewer
televisar ⟨1a⟩ *v/t* televise
televisión *f* television
◇ **televisión por cable** cable (television); **televisión digital** digital television; **televisión de pago** pay-per-view television; **televisión vía satélite** satellite television
televisivo *adj* television *atr*
televisor *m* TV (set), television (set)
◇ **televisor en color** color TV
televisora *f L.Am.* television company
télex *m* telex
telón *m* TEA curtain; ***el ~ de acero*** POL the Iron Curtain; ***~ de fondo*** *fig* backdrop, background
telonero *m*, **-a** *f* supporting artist
telúrico *adj* GEOL of the earth, earth *atr*
tema *m de conversación* subject, topic; MÚS, *de novela* theme
temario *m* syllabus
temática *f* subject matter
temático *adj* thematic
temblar ⟨1k⟩ *v/i* tremble, shake; *de frío* shiver
tembleque *m* trembling, shaking; *de frío* shivering
temblor *m* **1** trembling, shaking; *de frío* shivering **2** *L.Am.* (*terremoto*) earthquake
◇ **temblor de tierra** earth tremor
tembloroso *adj* trembling, shaking; *de frío* shivering
temer ⟨2a⟩ *v/t* be afraid of; **temerse** *v/r* be afraid; ***me temo que no podrá venir*** I'm afraid he won't be able to come; ***~ lo peor*** fear the worst
temerario *adj* rash, reckless
temeridad *f* rashness, recklessness
temeroso *adj* fearful, frightened
temible *adj* terrifying
temor *m* fear; ***por ~ a*** for fear of
◇ **temor de Dios** REL fear of God
témpano *m* ice floe
temperamental *adj* temperamental
temperamento *m* temperament
temperante *adj Méx* teetotal
temperar ⟨1a⟩ *v/t* temper
temperatura *f* temperature; ***tener mucha ~*** have a high fever, *Br* have a high temperature
tempestad *f tb fig* storm
tempestuoso *adj tb fig* stormy
templado *adj* warm; *clima* temperate; *fig* moderate, restrained
templanza *f* restraint
templar ⟨1a⟩ *v/t ira, nervios etc* calm
temple *m* **1** mettle, courage; ***estar de buen / mal ~*** be in a good / bad mood **2**: ***pintura al ~*** tempera, distemper
Temple *m* HIST Temple
templete *m* pavilion; *de música* bandstand; *templo* small temple
templo *m* temple; ***es una verdad como un ~*** *fig* F it's absolutely true
tempo *m* MÚS tempo
temporada *f* season; ***una ~*** a time, some time; ***de ~*** seasonal
◇ **temporada alta** high season
◇ **temporada baja** low season
temporal I *adj* **1** (*limitado en el tiempo*) temporary **2** REL temporal **3** *bienes* worldly **II** *m* storm
temporalero *m*, **-a** *f Méx* temporary worker
temporalidad *f* temporary nature
temporalmente *adv* temporarily
temporero I *adj trabajador* seasonal **II** *m*, **-a** *f* seasonal worker
temporariamente *adv L.Am.* temporarily
temporario *adj L.Am.* temporary
temporizador *m* timer
tempranear ⟨1a⟩ *v/i L.Am.* get up early
tempranero *adj fruta* early; ***ser ~*** *persona* be early
temprano *adj & adv* early; ***a -a edad de*** at an early age; ***llegar ~*** be early
ten *vb* → ***tener***
tenacidad *f* tenacity
tenacillas *fpl* tongs; ***~ para rizar el pelo*** curling tongs
tenaz *adj* determined, tenacious
tenaza *f* pincer, claw; ***~s*** pincers; *para las uñas* pliers
tenca *f* ZO tench
tendedero *m* airer

tendencia *f* **1** tendency; ***tener ~ a*** have a tendency to **2** (*corriente*) trend; ***~ al alza / a la baja*** upward / downward trend
tendencioso *adj* tendentious
tendente *adj* tending (***a*** towards)
tender ⟨2g⟩ **I** *v/t* **1** *ropa* hang out **2** *cable* lay **3**: ***le tendió la mano*** he held out his hand to her **4** *L.Am. cama* make; *mesa* set **II** *v/i*: ***~ a*** tend to; **tenderse** *v/r* lie down
tenderete *m* stall
tendero *m*, **-a** *f* storekeeper, shopkeeper
tendido *m* EL: ***~ eléctrico*** power lines *pl*
tendinitis *f* MED tendinitis, tendonitis
tendón *m* ANAT tendon
◇ **tendón de Aquiles** Achilles' tendon
tenebrosidad *f* darkness, gloom
tenebroso *adj* dark, gloomy
tenedor I *m* fork **II** *m*, **~a** *f* JUR holder
◇ **tenedor de libros** bookkeeper
teneduría *f* accountancy
◇ **teneduría de libros** bookkeeping
tenencia *f* possession
◇ **tenencia ilícita de armas** illegal possession of weapons
tener ⟨2l⟩ *v/t* **1** have; ***~ 10 años*** be 10 (years old); ***~ un metro de ancho / largo*** be one meter wide / long *o* in width / length
2: ***ha tenido un niño*** she's had a little boy
3: ***~ a alguien por algo*** regard s.o. as sth, consider s.o. to be sth
4: ***tengo que madrugar*** I must get up early, I have to *o* I've got to get up early; ***tuve que madrugar*** I had to get up early
5: ***conque ¿esas tenemos?*** so that's how it is *o* things stand, eh?; ***no tuvo a bien saludarme*** he did not see fit to greet me; ***no las tengo todas conmigo*** F I'm not one hundred per cent sure; ***eso me tiene nervioso*** that makes me nervous
tenerse *v/r* **1** stand up; *fig* stand firm **2**: ***se tiene por atractivo*** he thinks he's attractive; ***me tengo por justa*** I regard myself as fair, I think I'm fair
tenga *vb* ☞ ***tener***
tengo *vb* ☞ ***tener***
tenia *f* ZO tapeworm
teniente *m/f* MIL lieutenant
◇ **teniente de alcalde** deputy mayor; **teniente coronel** lieutenant colonel; **teniente general** lieutenant general; **teniente de navío** lieutenant
tenis *m* tennis
◇ **tenis de mesa** table tennis
tenista *m/f* tennis player
tenor *m* MÚS tenor; ***a ~ de*** along the lines of
tenorio *m* lady-killer
tensar ⟨1a⟩ *v/t* tighten; *músculo* tense, tighten
tensión *f* **1** tension **2** EL voltage; ***alta ~*** high tension, high voltage **3** MED: ***~ (arterial)*** blood pressure; ***tener la ~ alta / baja*** have high / low blood pressure; ***tomarle la ~ a alguien*** take s.o.'s blood pressure
tenso *adj* tense; *cuerda, cable* taut
tensor *m/adj*: **(*músculo*) ~** ANAT tensor (muscle)
tentación *f* temptation
tentáculo *m* ZO, *fig* tentacle
tentador *adj* tempting
tentar ⟨1k⟩ *v/t* tempt, entice
tentativa *f* attempt
tentempié *m* F snack
tentetieso *m* tumbler
tenue *adj* faint
teñido *m* dyeing
teñir ⟨3h & 3l⟩ *v/t* dye; *fig* tinge; ***~ algo de rojo*** dye sth red; **teñirse** *v/r* dye
teocracia *f* theocracy
teodolito *m* theodolyte
teología *f* theology
teológico *adj* theological
teólogo *m*, **-a** *f* theologian
teorema *m* theorem
teoría *f* theory; ***en ~*** in theory
teórico I *adj* theoretical **II** *m*, **-a** *f* theorist
teorizar ⟨1f⟩ *v/i* theorize
tequila *m* tequila
terapeuta *m/f* therapist
terapéutica *f* therapeutics *sg*
terapéutico *adj* therapeutic
terapia *f* therapy
◇ **terapia génica** gene therapy; **terapia de grupo** group therapy; **terapia intensiva** *L.Am.* intensive care; **terapia ocupacional** occupational therapy
tercer *adj* third
◇ **Tercer Mundo** Third World
tercera *f* **1** AUTO third gear **2** (*clase*) third class
◇ **tercera base** *f en béisbol* third base;

jugador third baseman
tercerización *f L.Am.*COM outsourcing
tercerizar ⟨1f⟩ *v/t L.Am.* COM outsource
terciarización *f L.Am.* COM outsourcing
terciarizar ⟨1f⟩ *v/t L.Am.* COM outsource
tercermundista *adj* Third-World
tercero *m/adj* third
terceto *m* MÚS trio
terciar ⟨1b⟩ *v/i* intervene; **terciarse** *v/r de oportunidad* come up
terciario I *adj* tertiary **II** *m* GEOL Tertiary
tercio *m* third
terciopelo *m* velvet; ***de ~*** velvet *atr*
terco *adj* stubborn
tereré *m Arg, Parag*: *type of maté with lemon juice*
tergiversación *f* distortion, twisting
tergiversar ⟨1a⟩ *v/t* distort, twist
termal *adj* thermal; ***baño ~*** hot *o* thermal bath
termas *fpl* hot springs
termes *m inv* ZO termite
térmico *adj* heat *atr*
terminación *f* GRAM ending
terminal I *adj* terminal; ***estado ~*** MED terminal phase **II** *m* INFOR terminal **III** *f* AVIA terminal; ***~ de salidas*** AVIA departure terminal; ***~ de autobuses*** bus station, bus terminal
terminante *adj* categorical
terminantemente *adv* strictly; ***~ prohibido*** strictly prohibited *o* forbidden
terminar ⟨1a⟩ **I** *v/t* end, finish **II** *v/i* **1** end, finish; ***~ con algo / alguien*** finish with sth / s.o.; ***~ de hacer algo*** finish doing sth **2** (*parar*) stop **3**: ***~ por hacer algo*** end up doing sth; **terminarse** *v/r* **1** run out; ***se ha terminado la leche*** we've run out of milk, the milk's all gone **2** (*finalizar*) come to an end
término *m* **1** end, conclusion; ***poner ~ a algo*** put an end to sth; ***llevar a ~*** bring to an end **2** (*palabra*) term; ***en ~s generales*** in general terms **3**: ***~s*** *pl de contrato, acuerdo etc* terms **4**: ***por ~ medio*** on average; ***en primer ~*** in the foreground; ***en último ~*** as a last resort **5** (*periodo*): ***en el ~ de*** in the period of, in the space of
◇ **término municipal** municipal area
terminología *f* terminology
terminológico *adj* terminological
termita *f* ZO termite
termo *m* thermos® (flask)
termoaislante *adj* heat-insulating
termodinámica *f* thermodynamics *sg*
termómetro *m* thermometer
termostato *m* thermostat
termotécnia *f* heating technology
termoterapia *f* heat therapy
terna *f* short list of three
ternasco *m* sucking lamb, suckling lamb
ternera *f animal* calf; GASTR veal
ternero *m* calf
terno *m CSur* suit
ternura *f* tenderness
terquedad *f* stubbornness
terracota *f* terracotta
Terranova *f* Newfoundland
terraplén *m* embankment
terráqueo *adj*: ***globo ~*** globe
terrario *m* terrarium
terrateniente *m/f* landowner
terraza *f* **1** terrace **2** (*balcón*) balcony **3** (*café*) sidewalk café, *Br* pavement café
terremoto *m* earthquake
terrenal *adj* earthly, worldly
terreno I *adj* earthly, worldly **II** *m* land; *fig* field; ***un ~*** a lot, *Br* a plot *o* piece of land; ***sobre el ~*** in the field; ***ganar / perder ~*** *fig* gain / lose ground; ***tantear el ~*** *fig* see how the land lies; ***llevar a alguien a su ~*** get s.o. on one's home ground; ***pisar ~ resbaladizo*** *fig* be on slippery ground
◇ **terreno de juego** DEP field
terrero *adj* earthy; ***saco ~*** MIL sandbag
terrestre *adj animal* land *atr*; *transporte* surface *atr*; ***la atmósfera ~*** the earth's atmosphere
terrible *adj* terrible, awful
terrícola *m/f* earth dweller, earthling
terrífico *adj* ☞ ***terrorífico***
terrina *f* GASTR terrine
territorial *adj* territorial
territorialidad *f* territoriality
territorio *m* territory
terrón *m* lump, clod
◇ **terrón de azúcar** sugar lump
terror *m* terror
terrorífico *adj* terrifying, frightening
terrorismo *m* terrorism
terrorista I *adj* terrorist *atr*; ***organiza-***

T

***ción** ~* terrorist organization **II** *m/f* terrorist
◇ **terrorista suicida** suicide bomber
terruño *m* **1** (*patria*) home ground, native soil **2** *tierra* lot, *Br* plot of land
terso *adj* smooth
tertulia *f* TV debate, round table discussion; (*reunión*) discussion group
tertuliano *m*, **-a** *f participant in a debate or round table discussion*
tertuliar ⟨1b⟩ *v/i L.Am.* get together for a discussion
tesela *f* tessera, tile
tesina *f* dissertation
tesis *f inv* thesis
◇ **tesis doctoral** doctoral thesis
tesitura *f* situation
tesón *m* tenacity, determination
tesorería *f* **1** *oficio* post of treasurer; *oficina* treasury **2** (*activo disponsible*) liquid assets *pl*
tesorero *m*, **-a** *f* treasurer
tesoro *m* treasure
◇ **tesoro público** treasury
test *m* test; *~ **visual*** eye test
testa *f* head
◇ **testa coronada** crowned head
testador *m* testator
testadora *f* JUR testatrix
testaferro *m* front man
testamentario I *adj* testamentary **II** *m*, **-a** executor
testamento *m* JUR will; ***Antiguo / Nuevo Testamento*** REL Old / New Testament
testarazo *m* **1** bang *o* bump on the head **2** F *en fútbol* header
testarudez *f* stubbornness
testarudo *adj* stubborn
testear ⟨1a⟩ *v/t L.Am.* test
testículo *m* ANAT testicle
testificación *f* **1** testification **2** (*declaración*) testimony
testificar ⟨1g⟩ **I** *v/t* (*probar, mostrar*) be proof of; *~ **que*** JUR testify that, give evidence that **II** *v/i* testify, give evidence
testigo I *m/f* JUR witness; ***ser ~*** be a witness; *~ **de boda*** witness **II** *m* DEP baton
◇ **testigo de cargo** witness for the prosecution; **testigo de la defensa** defense *o Br* defence witness, witness for the defense *o Br* defence; **testigo de descargo** witness for the defense *o Br* defence; **testigo de Jehová** REL Jehovah's Witness; **testigo ocular** eye witness; **testigo presencial** eye witness
testimonial *adj presencia* token, symbolic
testimoniar ⟨1b⟩ **I** *v/t* (*testificar*) testify; (*demostrar*) testify to **II** *v/i* testify
testimonio *m* testimony, evidence; ***jurar en falso ~*** commit perjury, perjure o.s.; ***dar ~ de algo*** testify to sth
testosterona *f* testosterone
teta *f* **1** F boob F **2** ZO teat; ***niño de ~*** little baby
tétanos *m* MED tetanus
tetera *f* teapot
tetilla *f* **1** *de hombre* nipple **2**: ***queso de ~*** GASTR *type of soft cheese* **3** ☞ ***tetina***
tetina *f de biberón* nipple, teat
tetrabrik® *m* Tetra Pak®, tetrapack®
tetrapléjico I *adj* MED tetraplegic **II** *m*, **-a** *f* MED tetraplegic
tétrico *adj* gloomy
textil I *adj* textile *atr* **II** *mpl*: ***~es*** textiles
texto *m* text
◇ **texto completo** unabridged text
textual *adj* textual
textura *f* texture
tez *f* complexion
ti *pron* you; *reflexivo* yourself; ***¿y a ~ qué te importa?*** so what?, what's it to you?
tía *f* **1** aunt; ***¡no hay tu ~!*** F nothing doing!; ***cuéntaselo a tu ~*** come off it!, tell that to the marines! **2** F (*chica*) girl, chick F; ***¡~ buena!*** F hey gorgeous! F
◇ **tía abuela** great-aunt
tianguis *m inv Méx, C.Am.* market
tiara *f* REL tiara
tibetano I *adj* Tibetan **II** *m*, **-a** *f* Tibetan
tibia *f* ANAT tibia
tibieza *f* tepidness
tibio *adj tb fig* lukewarm, tepid; ***poner a alguien ~*** F lay into s.o. F
tiburón *m* **1** ZO, *fig* F shark **2** FIN raider
tic *m* MED tic; *~ **nervioso*** nervous tic
ticket *m* (sales) receipt
tico *L.Am.* F **I** *adj* Costa Rican **II** *m*, **-a** *f* Costa Rican
tictac *m* tick-tock
tiempo *m* **1** time; ***a ~*** in time; ***a un ~, al mismo ~*** at the same time; ***antes de ~*** *llegar* ahead of time, early; *celebrar victoria* too soon; ***a su*** (***debido***) *~* in due

course; ***cada cosa a su ~*** all in good time; ***con ~*** in good time, early; ***dar ~ al ~*** give things time; ***hacer ~*** while away the time; ***desde hace mucho ~*** for a long time; ***hace mucho ~*** a long time ago; ***de ~ en ~*** from time to time; ***de un ~ a esta parte*** for some time now; ***durante algún ~*** for some time; ***por poco ~*** for a short time; ***hace tanto ~*** it's so long ago; ***el ~ es oro*** time is money; ***con el ~, andando el ~*** with time, in time; ***trabajar a ~ completo / parcial*** work full / part time; ***le faltó ~ para ...*** *fig* he couldn't wait to...; ***poner al mal ~ buena cara*** *fig* look on the bright side; ***volver el ~ atrás*** *fig* turn the clock back
2 (*época*): ***en mis ~s*** in my day
3 (*clima*) weather; ***hace buen / mal ~*** the weather's fine / bad
4 GRAM tense
5 DEP *de juego* half; ***medio ~*** half time
6 (*edad*): ***¿qué ~ tiene?*** *de un niño* how old is he?
◇ **tiempo añadido** DEP overtime, *Br* extra time; **tiempo de descuento** DEP injury *o* stoppage time; **tiempo libre** spare time, free time; **tiempo muerto** DEP time-out; **tiempo real** INFOR real time; **tiempo reglamentario** DEP normal time

tienda *f* store, shop; ***ir de ~s*** go shopping
◇ **tienda de abarrotes** *L.Am.* grocery store, *Br* grocer's; **tienda de campaña** tent; **tienda de comestibles** grocery store, *Br* grocer's; **tienda de departamentos** *Méx* department store; **tienda libre de impuestos** duty-free shop; **tienda de productos naturales** health food store

tiene *vb* ☞ ***tener***

tientas *fpl*: ***andar a ~*** *fig* feel one's way

tiento *m*: ***con ~*** *fig* carefully

tierno *adj* soft; *carne* tender; *pan* fresh; *persona* tender-hearted; ***en mi -a edad*** at a tender age

tierra *f* **1** land; ***~ de labor, ~ cultivable*** arable land, farmland; ***~s altas*** highlands; ***~s bajas*** lowlands; ***poner ~ de por medio*** flee, make o.s. scarce F; ***por ~*** *viajar* by land; ***tomar ~*** AVIA land
2 *materia* soil, earth; ***echar ~ a algo*** *fig* hush sth up; ***echar por ~*** ruin, wreck; ***como si se lo hubiera tragado la ~*** as if he had vanished off the face of the earth
3 (*patria*) native land, homeland; ***de la ~*** locally produced, local
4 EL ground, *Br* earth
5: ***la Tierra*** the Earth
◇ **tierra firme** dry land, terra firma; **Tierra del Fuego** Tierra del Fuego; **tierra de nadie** no-man's land; **Tierra Santa** Holy Land

tieso *adj* stiff, rigid; ***quedarse ~*** *fig* be astonished; ***estar ~*** *fig* F be dead

tiesto *m* flowerpot; ***mear fuera del ~*** F put one's foot in it F

tifoideo *adj* MED: ***fiebre -a*** typhoid

tifón *m* typhoon

tifus *m* MED typhus

tigre *m* ZO tiger; *L.Am.* puma; *L.Am.* (*leopardo*) jaguar

tigresa *f* tigress

tijeras *fpl* scissors; ***~ de podar*** pruning shears

tijereta *f* **1** ZO earwig **2** DEP scissors kick, overhead kick

tijeretazo *m* DEP scissors kick, overhead kick

tila *f* lime blossom tea

tildar ⟨1a⟩ *v/t*: ***~ a alguien de*** *fig* brand s.o. as

tilde *f* **1** accent **2** *en ñ* tilde

tiliche *m Méx* F junk, things *pl*

tilín *m*: ***me hizo ~*** F I took an immediate liking to her

tilo *m* BOT lime (tree)

timador *m*, **~a** *f* cheat

timar ⟨1a⟩ *v/t* cheat

timba *f* F gambling den

timbal *m* MÚS kettle drum

timbrado *adj sobre* stamped

timbre *m* **1** *de puerta* bell; ***tocar el ~*** ring the bell **2** *Méx* (postage) stamp

timidez *f* shyness, timidity

tímido *adj* shy, timid

timo *m* confidence trick, swindle; ***dar el ~ a alguien*** con s.o.

timón *m* **1** MAR, AVIA rudder; ***tomar el ~*** *fig* take charge, take the helm **2** *Andes* AUTO steering wheel

timonel MAR **I** *m* helmsman **II** *f* helmswoman

timorato I *adj* **1** (*mojigato*) prudish **2** (*tímido*) gutless, spineless **II** *m*, **-a** *f* **1** (*mojigato*) prude **2** (*persona tímida*) wimp F, coward

T

tímpano *m* ANAT eardrum
tina *f* **1** large earthenware jar **2** (*cuba*) vat **3** *L.Am.* (*bañera*) (bath)tub
tinaco *m Méx* water tank
tinaja *f* large earthenware jar
tinerfeño *adj* of / from Tenerife, Tenerife *atr*
tinglado *m* **1** *fig* F mess **2** (*maquinación*) set-up, racket
tinieblas *fpl* darkness *sg*
tino *m* **1** aim, marksmanship **2** (*sensatez*) judg(e)ment; ***con mucho ~*** wisely, sensibly; ***sin ~*** immoderately
tinta *f* ink; ***sobre esto ha corrido ya mucha ~*** a lot has already been written about this; ***sudar ~*** sweat blood F; ***recargar las ~s*** exaggerate; ***de buena ~*** *fig* on good authority; ***medias ~s*** *fig* half measures
tintar ⟨1a⟩ *v/t* dye
tinte *m* **1** dye **2** *fig* veneer, gloss
tinterillo *m L.Am.* F shyster F
tintero *m* inkwell; ***dejarse algo en el ~*** leave sth unsaid, not mention sth
tintin(e)ar ⟨1a⟩ *v/t* jingle
tinto 1 *adj*: ***vino ~*** red wine **II** *m Col* black coffee
tintorería *f* dry cleaner's
tintorero *m*, **-a** *f* dry cleaner
tintorro *m* F cheap red wine
tintura *f* dye
tiña *f* MED ringworm; *fig* filth
tiñoso *adj* MED mangy; *fig* filthy
tío *m* **1** uncle **2** F (*tipo*) guy F; ***~ bueno*** good-looking guy F; ***¡hola, ~s!*** hi, guys! F **3** F *apelativo* pal F, man F
◇ **tío abuelo** great-uncle
tiovivo *m* carousel, merry-go-round
tipear *v/t & v/i L.Am.* type
tipejo *m*, **-a** *f* F **1** (*tonto*) moron F **2** (*antipático*) jerk F
típico *adj* typical (**de** of)
tipificar ⟨1g⟩ *v/t* **1** (*clasificar*) classify **2** (*representar*) typify
tiple *m/f* soprano
tipo *m* **1** type, kind; ***no es mi ~*** he's not my type **2** F *persona* guy F **3** COM rate **4**: ***tener buen ~*** *de hombre* be well built; *de mujer* have a good figure; ***jugarse el ~*** F risk one's neck; ***mantener*** *o* ***aguantar el ~*** F keep one's cool
◇ **tipo de cambio** exchange rate; **tipo de conversión** exchange *o* conversion rate; **tipo de descuento** discount rate; **tipo impositivo** tax rate; **tipo de interés** interest rate
tipografía *f* typography
tipográfico *adj* typographic(al); ***falta -a*** typo, typographical error
tipógrafo *m*, **-a** *f* printer
tíquet, tiquete *m L.Am.* receipt
tiquismiquis *m/f* F fuss-budget F, *Br* fusspot F
tira I *f* **1** strip **2**: ***la ~ de*** F loads of F, masses of F; ***hace la ~ que no hablo con ella*** F I haven't spoken to her in a long time **3** *Méx* F: ***la ~*** the cops *pl* **II** *m/f Méx* F cop
◇ **tira cómica** comic strip
◇ **tira y afloja** *fig* give and take
tirabuzón *m* **1** curl **2** (*sacacorchos*) corkscrew **3** *en béisbol* screwball
tirachinas *m inv* slingshot, *Br* catapult
tirada *f* **1** TIP print run **2**: ***de una ~*** in one shot **3** *Méx* F aim; ***no sé cuál es su ~*** I don't know what he is up to
tiradero *m Méx* dump
tirado *adj* P **1** (*barato*) dirt-cheap F **2** (*fácil*): ***estar ~*** F be a walkover F *o* a piece of cake F
tiradores *mpl Arg* suspenders, *Br* braces
tiraje *m L.Am.* print run
tiralíneas *m* ruling pen
tiranía *f* tyranny
tiránico *adj* tyrannical
tirano I *adj* tyrannical **II** *m*, **-a** *f* tyrant
tirante I *adj* taut; *fig* tense **II** *m* **1** strap **2**: ***~s*** *pl* suspenders, *Br* braces
tirantez *f fig* tension
tirar ⟨1a⟩ **I** *v/t* **1** throw; *edificio, persona* knock down; (*volcar*) knock over **2** *basura* throw away; *dinero* waste, throw away F **3** TIP print **4** F *en examen* fail **5** *foto* take **6** *tiro* fire
II *v/i* **1** *de coche* pull; ***~ de algo*** pull sth
2 (*disparar*) shoot
3 DEP *en fútbol*: ***~ a puerta*** shoot at goal; ***~ fuera*** shoot wide
4 (*atraer*) pull, attract; ***no me tira la música*** music doesn't turn me on
5: ***~ a*** tend toward; ***~ a conservador / verde*** have conservative / Green tendencies
6 (*girar*): ***~ a la derecha*** turn right, take a right
7: ***ir tirando*** F get by, manage
tirarse *v/r* **1** throw o.s. **2** F *en fútbol*

dive **3** F *tiempo* spend **4**: ***~ a alguien*** P screw s.o. P **5**: ***tirárselas de algo*** make out one is sth

tirita *f* MED Bandaid®, *Br* plaster

tiritar ⟨1a⟩ *v/i* shiver

tiro *m* **1** shot; *en fútbol tb* kick; *con las manos* throw; ***~ al aire*** shot in the air; ***a ~*** (with)in range; ***al ~*** *CSur* at once, right away; ***ni a ~s*** F for love nor money; ***le salió el ~ por la culata*** F it backfired on him; ***le sentó como un ~*** F he needed it like a hole in the head F; ***la noticia me cayó como un ~*** the news really shocked me; ***saber por dónde van los ~s*** *fig* know what's going on; ***estar a un ~ de piedra*** be a stone's throw away
2: ***de ~s largos*** F dressed up
◇ **tiro con arco** archery; **tiro al blanco** target practice; **tiro de campo** *en baloncesto* field goal; **tiro de dos** *en baloncesto* two-pointer; **tiro de esquina** *en fútbol* corner (kick); **tiro libre** DEP free kick; *en baloncesto* free throw; **tiro libre directo** DEP direct free kick; **tiro libre indirecto** DEP indirect free kick; **tiro al plato** trapshooting, clay pigeon shooting; **tiro en suspensión** *en baloncesto* jump shot; **tiro a tabla** *en baloncesto* bank shot; **tiro de tres** *en baloncesto* three-pointer

tiroides *m* ANAT thyroid (gland)

tirón *m* **1** tug, jerk; ***de un ~*** at a stretch, without a break; ***dormir de un ~*** sleep through; ***dar tirones*** *de pelo* pull, tug **2** MED: ***~ muscular*** pulled muscle

tirotear ⟨1a⟩ *v/t* fire on, shoot at

tiroteo *m* shooting

tirria *f*: ***tener ~ a alguien*** F have it in for s.o. F

tisana *f* herbal tea

tísico MED **I** *adj* consumptive **II** *m*, **-a** *f* consumptive

tisis *f* MED consumption

tisú *m* lamé

titán *m* titan

titánico *adj* titanic

titanio *m* QUÍM titanium

títere *m tb fig* puppet; ***teatro de ~s*** puppet show; ***no dejar ~ con cabeza*** F spare no-one

titiritero *m*, **-a** *f* acrobat

titubear ⟨1a⟩ *v/i* waver, hesitate

titubeo *m* wavering, hesitation

titulación *f* qualifications *pl*

titulado I *adj* qualified **II** *m*, **-a** *f* graduate, degree holder

titular[1] **I** *adj*: ***profesor ~*** *tenured professor* **II** *m/f* DEP first-team player **III** *m de periódico* headline

titular[2] ⟨1a⟩ *v/t* title, entitle; **titularse** *v/r* be entitled

título *m* **1** *nobiliario, de libro* title **2** *universitario* degree; ***tener muchos ~s*** be highly qualified **3** JUR title **4** COM bond **5**: ***a ~ de introducción*** as an introduction, by way of introduction; ***a ~ de representante*** as a representative
◇ **títulos de crédito** credits

tiza *f* chalk

tiznar ⟨1a⟩ *v/t* blacken

tizne *m* soot

tizón *m* ember

tlapalería *f Méx* hardware store

TLC *m abr* (= ***Tratado de Libre Comercio***) NAFTA (= North American Free Trade Agreement)

toalla *f* towel; ***tirar*** *o* ***arrojar la ~*** *fig* throw in the towel
◇ **toalla de baño** bath towel; **toalla femenina, toalla higiénica** *L.Am.* sanitary napkin, *Br* sanitary towel; **toalla de playa** beach towel

toallero *m* towel rail

toallita *f*: ***~ refrescante*** towelette

toar ⟨1a⟩ *v/t* MAR tow

tobillera *f* ankle support

tobillero *adj falda* ankle-length

tobillo *m* ankle

tobogán *m* **1** slide **2** (*trineo*) toboggan

toca *f* headdress; *de monja* wimple

tocadiscos *m inv* record player

tocado I *adj*: ***estar ~*** (***de la cabeza***) F be soft in the head F **II** *m* headdress

tocador *m* dressing table

tocamientos *mpl* touching *sg*

tocante: ***en lo ~ a …*** with regard to …

tocar ⟨1g⟩ **I** *v/t* **1** touch; ***~ el corazón*** touch one's heart; ***~ a alguien de cerca*** concern s.o. closely **2** MÚS play
II *v/i* **1** *L.Am. a la puerta* knock (on the door); *L.Am.* (*sonar la campanita*) ring the doorbell; ***las campanas de la iglesia tocaban a misa*** the church bells were ringing for mass; ***~ a muerto*** toll the death knell **2** (*ser hora de*): ***ya toca dar de comer al bebé*** it's time to feed the baby **3** (*ser el turno de*): ***te toca ju-***

gar it's your turn **4**: ***por lo que toca a ...*** as far as ... is concerned
tocarse *v/r* touch
tocateja: ***a ~*** in hard cash
tocayo *m*, **-a** *f* namesake
tocho I *adj* (*tosco, tonto*) stupid **II** *m* **1** brick, block **2** F *libro* great big book, weighty tome
tocino *m* bacon
◇ **tocino de cielo** GASTR *type of egg custard*
tocología *f* MED obstetrics *sg*
tocólogo *m*, **-a** *f* MED obstetrician
tocón *m* stump
todavía *adv* still, yet; ***~ no ha llegado*** he still hasn't come, he hasn't come yet; ***~ no*** not yet
todo I *adj* all; ***~s los domingos*** every Sunday; ***-a la clase*** the whole *o* the entire class
II *adv* all; ***estaba ~ sucio*** it was all dirty; ***con ~*** all the same; ***del ~*** entirely, absolutely
III *pron* all, everything; *pl* everybody, everyone; ***estaban ~s*** everybody was there; ***esto es ~ cuanto sé*** that's all I know
IV *en locuciones*: ***o ~ o nada*** all or nothing; ***de -as -as*** F without a shadow of a doubt; ***ir a por -as*** go all out; ***estar en ~*** be on top of things
todopoderoso *adj* omnipotent, all-powerful; ***el Todopoderoso*** the Almighty
todoterreno I *adj* AUTO four-wheel *atr* **II** *m* AUTO off-road *o* all-terrain vehicle **III** *m/f fig* jack-of-all trades
toga *f* toga
Togo *m* Togo
togolés I *adj* of / from Togo, Togolese **II** *m*, **-esa** *f* Togolese
toilette *m Rpl* toilet
toldo *m* **1** awning **2** *L.Am.* Indian hut
toledano *adj* of / from Toledo, Toledo *atr*
tolerable *adj* tolerable
tolerancia *f* tolerance
tolerante *adj* tolerant
tolerar ⟨1a⟩ *v/t* tolerate
toma *f* FOT shot, take
◇ **toma de agua** water outlet; **toma de conciencia** realization; **toma de corriente** outlet, *Br* socket; **toma del poder** seizure of power; **toma de posesión** POL taking office; *ceremonia* investiture; **toma de posición** (adoption of a) stance, position; **toma de tierra** EL ground (connection), *Br* earth (connection); AVIA landing
tomado *adj* **1** *voz* hoarse **2** *L.Am.* (*borracho*) drunk
tomador *m*, **~a** *f L.Am.* (*borracho*) drunkard, drinker
tomadura *f*: ***~ de pelo*** F joke
tomar ⟨1a⟩ **I** *v/t* take; *decisión tb* make; *bebida, comida* have; ***tenerla tomada*** *o* ***~la con alguien*** F have it in for s.o. F; ***~ el sol*** sunbathe; ***¡toma!*** here (you are); ***¡toma ya!*** serves you right!; ***¿por quién me toma?*** what do you take me for?; ***toma y daca*** give and take; ***~ las de Villadiego*** F hightail it F
II *v/i* **1** *L.Am.* drink **2**: ***~ por la derecha*** take a right, turn right
tomarse *v/r* **1** take; ***se lo tomó a pecho*** he took it to heart **2** *comida, bebida* have **3**: ***~ de las manos*** hold hands
tomate *m* **1** tomato; ***ponerse como un ~*** go bright red, turn as red as a beet, *Br* turn as red as a beetroot **2** *fig* mess
tomatera *f* tomato plant
tomavistas *m inv* movie camera, *Br* cinecamera
tómbola *f* tombola
tomillo *m* BOT thyme
tomo *m* volume, tome; ***de tres ~s*** three volume *atr*; ***un timador de ~ y lomo*** F an out-and-out conman
tomografía *f* MED tomography
ton *m*: ***sin ~ ni son*** for no particular reason
tonada *f* song
tonadilla *f popular song*
tonadillera *f* singer
tonal *adj* MÚS tonal
tonalidad *f* tonality
tonel *m* barrel, cask; ***ser un ~*** *fig* F be like a barrel
tonelada *f peso* ton
tonelaje *m* tonnage
tóner *m* toner
tongo *m* DEP: ***hubo ~*** it was fixed F *o* rigged F
tónica *f* **1** *bebida* tonic **2** (*tendencia*) trend, tendency **3** MÚS tonic
tonicidad *f* MED tonicity; ***~ muscular*** muscle tone
tónico *m* MED tonic

tonificar ⟨1g⟩ *v/t* tone up
tono *m* MÚS, MED, PINT tone; ***cambiar de ~*** *fig*: *al hablar* change one's tone; ***fuera de ~*** *comentario, respuesta* inappropriate; ***estar a ~ con algo*** be in harmony with sth; ***ponerse a ~*** get into the mood
◇ **tono de marcar** TELEC dial tone; **tono mayor** MÚS major key; **tono menor** MÚS minor key
tontada *f* ☞ ***tontería***
tontaina **I** *adj* silly **II** *m/f* F dimwit F
tontear ⟨1a⟩ *v/i* F **1** (*hacer el tonto*) act the fool **2** (*coquetear*) flirt
tontera *f*: ***llevar una ~ encima*** be feeling dopey
tontería *f fig* stupid *o* dumb F thing; ***~s*** *pl* nonsense *sg*
tonto **I** *adj* silly, foolish **II** *m*, **-a** *f* fool, idiot; ***~ del bote*** *o* ***haba*** F complete idiot; ***~ del pueblo*** village idiot; ***hacer el ~*** play the fool; ***hacerse el ~*** act dumb F; ***a tontas y a locas*** in a slapdash way
toña *f* **1** *Esp* (*borrachera*): ***coger una ~*** P get blitzed F **2** F (*excremento*) turd F; *de vaca* cowpat
top *m prenda* top
topacio *m* MIN topaz
topadora *f Rpl* bulldozer
toparse ⟨1a⟩ *v/r*: ***~ con alguien*** bump into s.o., run into s.o.
tope *m* **1** limit; ***edad ~*** upper age limit; ***estar hasta los ~s*** F be bursting at the seams F; ***pasarlo a ~*** F have a great time **2** *pieza* stop **3** *Méx*: *en la calle* speed bump
topetada *f* ☞ ***topetazo***
topetar ⟨1a⟩ *v/i* (*topar*) bump
topetazo *m* bump, bang
tópico **I** *adj* MED: ***de uso ~*** for external use **II** *m* cliché, platitude
topo *m* ZO mole; ***ver menos que un ~*** F be as blind as a bat F
topografía *f* topography
topográfico *adj* topographic(al)
topógrafo *m*, **-a** *f* topographer
topónimo *m* place name
toque *m* **1** tap; ***~ de atención*** warning **2** MÚS *de campana* chime **3**: ***dar los últimos ~s*** put the finishing touches (***a*** to); ***~ personal*** personal touch **4** DEP touch; *en béisbol* bunt
◇ **toque de diana** MIL reveille
◇ **toque de queda** MIL, *fig* curfew
toquetear ⟨1a⟩ *v/t* F fiddle with
toquilla *f* shawl
torácico *adj* ANAT thoracic; ***caja -a*** ANAT ribcage
tórax *m* ANAT thorax
torbellino *m* whirlwind
torcedura *f* twisting; MED sprain
torcer ⟨2b & 2h⟩ **I** *v/t* twist; (*doblar*) bend; (*girar*) turn **II** *v/i* turn; ***~ a la derecha*** turn right; **torcerse** *v/r* **1** twist, bend; ***~ un pie*** sprain one's ankle **2** *fig*: *de planes* go wrong
torcido *adj* twisted, bent
tordo *m* **1** *pájaro* thrush **2** *caballo* dapple-gray, *Br* dapple-grey
toreador *m*, **~a** *f esp L.Am.* bullfighter
torear ⟨1a⟩ **I** *v/i* fight bulls **II** *v/t* fight; *fig* dodge, sidestep
toreo *m* bullfighting
torera *f*: ***saltarse algo a la ~*** F flout sth, disregard sth
torero **I** *adj* bullfighting *atr*; ***chaqueta -a*** bolero **II** *m*, **-a** *f* bullfighter
tormenta *f* storm
tormento *m* torture
tormentoso *adj* stormy
torna *f* return; ***se han vuelto las ~s*** the shoe is on the other foot, *Br* the boot is on the other foot
tornado *m* tornado, twister F
tornar ⟨1a⟩ **I** *v/t* make **II** *v/i* return; ***~ a hacer algo*** do sth again; **tornarse** *v/r* *triste, difícil etc* become
tornasol *m* **1** BOT sunflower **2** QUÍM litmus
torneo *m* competition, tournament
tornillo *m* screw; *con tuerca* bolt; ***le falta un ~*** F he's got a screw loose F; ***apretarle a alguien los ~s*** F put the screws on s.o. F
◇ **tornillo de banco** vise, *Br* vice
torniquete *m* **1** *de entrada* turnstile **2** MED tourniquet
torno *m de alfarería* wheel; ***en ~ a*** around, about
toro *m* bull; ***ir a los ~s*** go to a bullfight; ***tomar al ~ por los cuernos*** take the bull by the horns
◇ **toro de lidia** fighting bull
toronja *f L.Am.* grapefruit
torpe *adj* clumsy; (*tonto*) dense, dim
torpedear ⟨1a⟩ *v/t* torpedo
torpedero *m* torpedo boat

torpedo *m* MIL torpedo
torpeza *f* **1** clumsiness **2** (*necedad*) stupidity
torpor *m* torpor
torrar ⟨1a⟩ *v/t* roast
torre *f* tower; ***~ de alta tensión*** EL high-voltage pylon
◇ **torre de control** AVIA control tower
◇ **torre de marfil** *fig* ivory tower
torrefacto *adj* roasted
torreja *f L.Am.* French toast
torrencial *adj* torrential
torrente *m fig* avalanche, flood
◇ **torrente circulatorio, torrente sanguíneo** bloodstream
torreón *m* tower
torrezno *m* GASTR fried slice *o Br* rasher of bacon
tórrido *adj* torrid
torrija *f* GASTR French toast
torsión *f* twisting; TÉC torsion
torso *m* ANAT, trunk, torso; *en artes plásticas* torso
torta *f* **1** cake; *plana* tart **2** F slap; ***le pegó una ~*** F I slapped him; ***darse una ~*** F have an accident **3**: ***no sabes ni ~ de fútbol*** F you don't know diddly-squat about soccer P; ***no ver ni ~*** F not be able to see in front of one's nose F
tortazo *m* F crash; (*bofetada*) punch
tortícolis *m* MED crick in the neck
tortilla *f* **1** omelet, *Br* omelette; ***se ha vuelto la ~*** the shoe is on the other foot, *Br* the boot is on the other foot **2** *L.Am.* tortilla
◇ **tortilla española** Spanish omelet *o Br* omelette
◇ **tortilla francesa** plain omelet *o Br* omelette
tortillera *f* V dyke F, lesbian
tórtola *f* ZO turtledove
tortuga *f* ZO tortoise; *marina* turtle; ***a paso de ~*** *fig* at a snail's pace
tortuosidad *f fml* tortuousness
tortuoso *adj fig* tortuous
tortura *f tb fig* torture
torturador *m*, **~a** *f* torturer
torturar ⟨1a⟩ *v/t* torture
torvo *adj* fierce
tos *f* cough
◇ **tos ferina** whooping cough
toscano *m Rpl* cigar
tosco *adj fig* rough, coarse
toser ⟨2a⟩ *v/i* cough
tosquedad *f* roughness, coarseness
tostada *f* piece of toast; ***~s*** *spl* toast *sg*
tostadero *m* roaster
tostado *adj* **1** (*moreno*) brown, tanned **2**: ***pan ~*** toast
tostador *m de pan* toaster; *de café* roaster
tostar ⟨1m⟩ **I** *v/t* toast; *café* roast; *al sol* tan; **tostarse** *v/r* tan, get brown
tostón *m* **1** F bore **2** GASTR crouton
total I *adj* total, complete; ***en ~*** altogether, in total **II** *m* total; ***un ~ de 50 personas*** a total of 50 people **III** *adv*: ***~, que no conseguí estudiar*** the upshot was that I didn't manage to get any studying done
totalidad *f* totality; ***la ~ de los Estados Unidos*** the whole of the United States
totalitario *adj* totalitarian
totalizar ⟨1f⟩ *v/t* total
totalmente *adv* totally, completely
tótem *m* totem
totémico *adj* totemic
toxicidad *f* toxicity
tóxico *adj* **I** toxic, poisonous **II** *m* toxin, poison
toxicomanía *f* drug addiction, drug dependency
toxicómano I *adj* addicted to drugs, drug-dependent **II** *m*, **-a** *f* drug addict
toxina *f* toxin
tozudez *f* obstinacy
tozudo *adj* obstinate
traba *f* obstacle; ***poner ~s*** raise objections; ***sin ~s*** without a hitch
trabajador I *adj* hard-working **II** *m*, **~a** *f* worker
◇ **trabajador eventual** casual worker
◇ **trabajador a tiempo parcial** part-time worker, part-timer
trabajar ⟨1a⟩ **I** *v/i* work; ***~ de camarero*** work as a waiter **II** *v/t* work; *tema, músculos* work on; ***~ media jornada*** work part-time
trabajo *m* work; (*tarea, puesto*) job; ***buscar ~*** be looking for work, be looking for a job; ***tengo un buen ~*** I have a good job; ***costar ~*** be hard *o* difficult; ***tomarse el ~ de*** take the trouble to
◇ **trabajo de campo** fieldwork; **trabajo a destajo** piece work; **trabajo en equipo** team work; **trabajo a jornada completa** full-time work; ***un ~*** a full-time job; **trabajo a media jornada**

part-time work; ***un** ~* a part-time job; **trabajo temporal** temporary work; ***un** ~* a temporary job; **trabajo a tiempo parcial** part-time work; ***un** ~* a part--time job; **trabajo por turnos** shift work; **trabajos forzados** hard labor *sg o Br* labour

trabajoso *adj* hard, laborious

trabalenguas *m inv* tongue twister

trabar ⟨1a⟩ *v/t conversación, amistad* strike up; **trabarse** *v/r* get tangled up

trabilla *f para cinturón* belt loop

trabucarse ⟨1g⟩ *v/r* get all mixed up

traca *f* string of firecrackers

tracción *f* TÉC traction

◇ **tracción en las cuatro ruedas** four--wheel drive; **tracción delantera** front--wheel drive; **tracción trasera** rear--wheel drive

tracoma *m* MED trachoma

tracto *m* ANAT tract; ***~ digestivo*** digestive tract

tractor *m* tractor

tractorista *m/f* tractor driver

tradición *f* tradition

tradicional *adj* traditional

tradicionalista *m/f & adj* traditionalist

traducción *f* translation; ***~ simultánea*** simultaneous translation

traducible *adj* translatable

traducir ⟨3o⟩ *v/t* translate; ***~ algo al / del alemán*** translate sth into / from German; **traducirse** *v/r* result (***en*** in); ***los cambios se tradujeron en mejoras*** the changes resulted in *o* led to improvements

traductor *m*, *~a f* translator

traer ⟨2p; *part* ***traído***⟩ *v/t* **1** bring; ***¿qué te trae por aquí?*** what brings you here? **2** (*acarrear*): ***~ consigo*** involve, entail **3**: ***~ a alguien de cabeza*** be driving s.o. mad; ***~ loco a alguien*** drive s.o. crazy **4**: ***este periódico la trae en portada*** this newspaper carries it on the front page

traerse *v/r*: ***este asunto se las trae*** F it's a very tricky matter

traficante *m/f* dealer

◇ **traficante de drogas** drug dealer

traficar ⟨1g⟩ *v/i* deal (***en*** in)

tráfico *m* traffic

◇ **tráfico aéreo** air traffic; **tráfico de armas** arms dealing *o* trafficking; **tráfico de drogas** drug trafficking; *en pequeña escala* drug dealing; **tráfico ferroviario** rail traffic; **tráfico fronterizo** cross-border traffic; **tráfico de influencias** influence-peddling; **tráfico de mercancías pesadas** freight traffic, *Br tb* heavy goods traffic; **tráfico rodado** road traffic

traga *m/f Rpl* F grind, *Br* swot

tragaderas *fpl* F gullet *sg*, throat *sg*; ***tener buenas ~*** *fig* have a good appetite

tragaldabas *m/f inv* F hog F, *Br* pig F

tragaluz *m* skylight

traganíqueles *f inv L.Am.* slot machine

tragaperras *f inv* slot machine

tragar ⟨1h⟩ **I** *v/t* **1** swallow; ***no lo trago*** I can't stand him *o* bear him **2** *Rpl* F *empollar* cram, *Br* swot **II** *v/i Rpl* F *empollar* cram, *Br* swot; **tragarse** *v/r tb fig* F swallow

tragasables *m inv* sword swallower

tragedia *f* tragedy

trágico *adj* tragic

tragicomedia *f* tragicomedy

tragicómico *adj* tragicomic

trago *m* **1** *de agua* mouthful **2** F *bebida* drink; ***echar*** *o* ***tomar un ~*** take a swig *o* drink; ***de un ~*** in one gulp; ***pasar un mal ~*** *fig* have a hard time

tragón **I** *adj* greedy **II** *m*, **-ona** *f* glutton, greedy person

traición *f* **1** treachery, betrayal; ***a ~*** treacherously **2** JUR treason; ***alta ~*** high treason

traicionar ⟨1a⟩ *v/t* betray

traicionero *adj* treacherous

traída *f* bringing

◇ **traída de aguas** water supply

traído **I** *adj vestido* worn; ***~ y llevado*** *fig* well-used **II** *part* ☞ ***traer***

traidor **I** *adj* treacherous **II** *m*, *~a f* traitor

traigo *vb* ☞ ***traer***

trailer *m Méx* trailer, *Br* caravan

tráiler *m* **1** *remolque* trailer **2** *de película* trailer, preview

traína *f*, **traíña** *f* MAR trawl net

trainera *f* MAR *small fishing boat used in northern Spain*

traje **I** *m* suit; ***~ a medida*** tailored suit **II** *vb* ☞ ***traer***

◇ **traje de baño** swimsuit; **traje de chaqueta** (woman's) two-piece suit; **traje de etiqueta** dress suit; **traje de luces** suit of lights, matador's outfit; **traje**

de noche evening dress; **traje de novia, traje nupcial** wedding dress; **traje-pantalón** pantsuit, *Br* trouser suit; **traje regional** regional costume; **traje sastre** (woman's) suit

trajeado *adj*: ***bien / mal ~*** well / badly dressed

trajín *m* hustle and bustle

trajinar ⟨1a⟩ *v/i* F rush around

trajo *vb* ☞ ***traer***

trallazo *m* **1** lash **2** F *en fútbol* thumping shot

trama *f* (*tema*) plot

tramar ⟨1a⟩ *v/t complot* hatch

tramitación *f* processing; ***el permiso se encuentra en ~*** the permit is being processed

tramitar ⟨1a⟩ *v/t documento*: *de persona* apply for; *de banco etc* process

trámite *m* formality

tramo *m* section, stretch; *de escaleras* flight

tramoya *f* TEA piece of stage machinery; *fig* trick, deception

tramoyista *m/f* TEA scene shifter; *fig* trickster

trampa *f* **1** trap; ***caer en la ~*** fall into the trap; ***tender una ~*** *tb fig* set *o* lay a trap **2** (*truco*) scam F, trick; ***hacer ~s*** cheat

trampero *m*, **-a** *f* trapper

trampilla *f* trapdoor

trampolín *m* diving board

tramposo I *adj* crooked **II** *m*, **-a** *f* cheat, crook

tranca *f* **1** *de puerta* bar; ***a ~s y barrancas*** with great difficulty **2** (*borrachera*): ***llevaba una ~ increíble*** F he was wasted F *o* smashed F

trancar ⟨1g⟩ *v/t puerta* bar

trancazo *m* F dose of flu

trance *m* **1** (*momento difícil*) tough time; ***pasar por un ~ amargo*** go through a terrible time; ***último ~*** final moment; ***a todo ~*** at all costs **2** *de médium*: ***en ~*** in a trance

tranco *m*: ***ir a grandes ~s*** stride along

tranqui *adj* P relaxed, laidback; ***¡~!*** relax!, cool it! F

tranquilidad *f* calm, quietness; ***para tu ~*** for your peace of mind

tranquilizador *adj* **1** *música* soothing **2** *noticia* reassuring

tranquilizante I *adj* tranquilizing, *Br* tranquillizing **II** *m* tranquilizer, *Br* tranquillizer

tranquilizar ⟨1f⟩ *v/t*: ***~ a alguien*** calm s.o. down

tranquillo *m*: ***pillar*** *o Esp tb* ***coger el ~ a algo*** F get the hang of sth F

tranquilo *adj* **1** *lugar, mañana, persona* calm, quiet **2** *sin preocupaciones*: ***¡~!*** don't worry; ***déjame ~*** leave me alone **3** (*fresco*): ***quedarse tan ~*** not bat an eyelid

transacción *f* COM deal, transaction

transalpino *adj* transalpine

transar ⟨1a⟩ *v/i L.Am.* (*ser vendido*) sell out

transatlántico I *adj* transatlantic **II** *m* liner

transbordador *m* ferry ◇ **transbordador espacial** space shuttle

transbordo *m*: ***hacer ~*** TRANSP transfer, change

transcendental *adj* ☞ ***trascendental***

transcribir ⟨3a; *part* ***transcrito***⟩ *v/t* transcribe

transcripción *f* transcription

transcrito *part* ☞ ***transcribir***

transcurrir ⟨3a⟩ *v/i de tiempo* pass, go by

transcurso *m* course; *de tiempo* passing; ***en el ~ del año*** in the course of the year

transeúnte *m/f* passer-by

transexual *m/f* & *adj* transsexual

transferencia *f* COM transfer; ***~ de datos*** data transfer

transferible *adj* transferable

transferir ⟨3i⟩ *v/t* transfer

transfiguración *f* transfiguration, transformation

transfigurar ⟨1a⟩ *v/t* transfigure, transform; **transfigurarse** *v/r* be transfigured, be transformed

transformación *f* transformation

transformador *m* EL transformer

transformar ⟨1a⟩ *v/t* **1** transform **2** DEP *penalti* score from

transformista *m/f* quick-change artist

transfronterizo *adj* cross-border

tránsfuga *m/f* POL defector

transfundir ⟨3a⟩ *v/t fml líquido* transfuse

transfusión *f*: **~ (*de sangre*)** (blood) transfusion

transgénico *adj* genetically modified

T

transgredir ⟨3a⟩ *v/t* infringe, transgress
transgresión *f* infringement, transgression
transgresor *m*, **~a** *f* transgressor
transición *f* transition; ***de ~*** transitional
transido *adj*: ***~ de*** racked with; ***~ de frío*** chilled to the bone
transigente *adj* accommodating
transigir ⟨3c⟩ *v/i* compromise, make concessions
transistor *m* transistor
transitable *adj* passable
transitar ⟨1a⟩ *v/i de persona* walk; *de vehículo* travel (***por*** along)
transitivo *adj* GRAM transitive
tránsito *m* **1** transit; ***de ~*** *mercancía, persona* in transit; ***pasajero en ~*** passenger in transit, transit passenger **2** *L.Am.* (*circulación*) traffic
transitorio *adj* transitory; ***periodo ~*** transitional period
translúcido *adj* translucent
transmigración *f* transmigration
transmisible *adj* transmissible
transmisión *f* **1** transmission; ***enfermedad de ~ sexual*** sexually transmitted disease; ***~ hereditaria*** hereditary transmission **2** RAD, TV broadcasting, transmission
◇ **transmisión de archivos** INFOR file transfer; **transmisión de datos** data transfer *o* transmission; **transmisión en diferido** TV recorded broadcast; **transmisión en directo** TV live broadcast; **transmisión de ficheros** INFOR file transfer
transmisor I *adj* transmitting **II** *m* transmitter
transmitir ⟨3a⟩ *v/t* **1** *enfermedad* spread, transmit; *noticia* spread; ***~ por herencia*** pass on in one's genes **2** RAD, TV broadcast; *señal* transmit
transmutación *f* transmutation
transmutar ⟨1a⟩ *v/t* transmute
transparencia *f* transparency; *para proyectar* transparency, slide
transparentar ⟨1a⟩ **I** *v/t* reveal **II** *v/i* be transparent; **transparentarse** *v/r* **1**: ***lleva un vestido que se transparenta*** she is wearing a see-through dress **2** *fig*: *nerviosismo, intenciones* be obvious
transparente *adj* transparent
transpiración *f* perspiration
transpirar ⟨1a⟩ *v/i* perspire
transpirenaico *adj* trans-Pyrenean
transplantar ⟨1a⟩ *v/t* transplant
transportable *adj* transportable
transportación *f Méx* transportation
transportador *m* **1** MAT protractor **2** TÉC conveyor
transportar ⟨1a⟩ *v/t* transport; **transportarse** *v/r* be transported
transporte *m* transport
◇ **transporte colectivo, transporte público** mass transit, public transportation, *Br* public transport
transportista *m/f* haulage contractor
transversal *adj* transverse, cross *atr*
tranvía *m* streetcar, *Br* tram
trápala I *f* (*embuste*) lie **II** *m/f persona* liar
trapatiesta *f* F: ***armar una ~*** make a racket F
trapear ⟨1a⟩ *v/t Méx* mop
trapecio *m* **1** *de circo* trapeze **2** MAT trapezium
trapecista *m/f* trapeze artist(e)
trapense *m* REL Trappist
trapero *m*, **-a** *f* junk dealer, ragman, *Br* rag-and-bone man
trapiche *m CSur* sugar mill *o* press
trapichear ⟨1a⟩ *v/i* F deal (illicitly) (***con*** in)
trapicheo *m* F shady deal F
trapo *m* **1** *para limpiar* cloth; *viejo* rag; ***poner a alguien como un ~*** F bad-mouth s.o. F; ***tratar a alguien como un ~*** F treat s.o. like dirt F; ***estar hecho un ~*** be worn out; ***sacar los ~s sucios a relucir*** *fig* reveal secrets **2**: ***~s*** *pl* F clothes **3** MAR sail; ***a todo ~*** *fig* F flat out F
trapujear ⟨1a⟩ *v/t & v/i C.Am.* smuggle
tráquea *f* ANAT windpipe, trachea
traqueotomía *f* MED tracheotomy
traquetear *v/i* ⟨1a⟩ rattle, clatter
traqueteo *m* rattle, clatter
tras *prp en el espacio* behind; *en el tiempo* after; ***ir*** *o* ***andar ~ alguien / algo*** be after s.o. / sth
trascendencia *f* significance
trascendental, trascendente *adj* momentous; *en filosofía* transcendental
trascender ⟨2g⟩ **I** *v/i* **1** *de noticia* get out **2**: ***~ de*** (*sobrepasar*) transcend **II** *v/t* transcend
trasero I *adj* rear *atr*, back *atr* **II** *m* F butt

F, *Br* rear end F

trasfondo *m* background; *fig* undercurrent

trasgo *m* goblin, imp

trashumancia *f* AGR transhumance, winter / summer migration

trasiego *m fig* bustle

traslación *f* AST movement

trasladar ⟨1a⟩ *v/t* move; *trabajador* transfer; **trasladarse** *v/r* move (***a*** to); ***se traslada*** *Méx*: *en negocio* under new management

traslado *m* move; *de trabajador* transfer; ***~ al aeropuerto*** airport transfer; ***~ de la producción*** transfer of production

traslúcido *adj* translucent

traslucir ⟨3f⟩ *v/t* reveal, show; **traslucirse** *v/r* be visible; *fig* be evident, show; ***su nerviosismo no se trasluce*** his nervousness is not evident *o* doesn't show

trasluz *m*: ***al ~*** against the light

trasnochado *adj* **1** *fig* outdated **2** (*persona*) *who has been awake all night*

trasnochar ⟨1a⟩ *v/i* (*acostarse tarde*) go to bed late, stay up late; (*no dormir*) stay up all night; *L.Am.* stay overnight, spend the night

traspapelar ⟨1a⟩ *v/t* mislay; **traspapelarse** *v/r* get mislaid

traspasar ⟨1a⟩ *v/t* **1** (*atravesar*) go through **2** COM transfer **3** (*exceder*) go beyond

traspaso *m* COM transfer

traspié *m* trip, stumble; ***dar un ~*** *fig* slip up, blunder

trasplantar ⟨1a⟩ *v/t* AGR, MED transplant

trasplante *m* AGR, MED transplant; ***~ cardiaco*** heart transplant

trasponer ⟨2r⟩ *v/t* **1** *fml* (*mover de sitio*) transfer **2** (*trasplantar*) transplant; **trasponerse** *v/r* doze off

traspuesto *adj*: ***quedarse ~*** doze off

traspunte *m/f* TEA prompter

trasquilar ⟨1a⟩ *v/t* shear

trastabillar, trastabillear ⟨1a⟩ *v/i* **1** stumble **2** *al hablar* stutter, stammer

trastada *f* F prank, trick; ***hacer ~s*** get up to mischief

trastazo *m* F bump

traste *m* **1**: ***irse al ~*** F fall through, go down the tubes F; ***dar al ~ con algo*** F ruin sth, trash sth F **2** *C.Am., Méx* dish; ***lavar los ~s*** do the dishes **3** *CSur* F *trasero* butt F, *Br* bottom

trastear ⟨1a⟩ **I** *v/t muebles* move around **II** *v/i* move things around

trastero I *adj*: ***cuarto ~*** lumber room **II** *m* lumber room

trastienda *f* back room (*of shop*)

trasto *m* **1** *desp* piece of junk; ***tirarse los ~s a la cabeza*** F have a big fight **2** *persona* good-for-nothing

trastocar *vb* ☞ ***trastrocar***

trastornar ⟨1a⟩ *v/t* **1** *plan* upset **2** (*molestar*) inconvenience **3** (*perturbar*): ***~ la mente de alguien*** affect s.o. mentally; **trastornarse** *v/r* **1** *de plan* be upset (***por*** by) **2** be affected mentally

trastorno *m* **1** inconvenience **2** MED disorder; ***~ alimentario*** eating disorder; ***~ circulatorio*** circulation problem

◇ **trastorno mental** mental disorder

trastrocar ⟨1g & 1m⟩ *v/t* change *o* switch around

trasvasar ⟨1a⟩ *v/t agua de río* transfer (*from one river to another*)

trasvase *m transfer of water from one river to another*

trata *f* trade

tratadista *m/f* author (*of a treatise*)

tratado *m esp* POL treaty

◇ **Tratado de Libre Comercio** North American Free Trade Agreement

◇ **tratado de paz** peace treaty

tratamiento *m* treatment

◇ **tratamiento de aguas residuales** sewage treatment; **tratamiento de datos** INFOR data processing; **tratamiento de residuos** waste treatment *o* processing; **tratamiento de textos** INFOR word processing

tratante *m/f* dealer, trader

◇ **tratante de ganado** cattle dealer

tratar ⟨1a⟩ **I** *v/t* **1** treat **2** (*manejar*) handle **3** (*dirigirse a*) address (***de*** as); ***~ a alguien de tú*** address s.o. informally, use the tú form with s.o.; ***~ a alguien de usted*** address s.o. formally, use the usted form with s.o. **4** *gente* come into contact with **5** *tema* deal with **II** *v/i*: **1**: ***~ con alguien*** deal with s.o. **2**: ***~ de*** (*intentar*) try to **3** COM: ***~ en*** deal in; **tratarse** *v/r*: ***¿de qué se trata?*** what's it about?

trato *m* **1** *de prisionero, animal* treat-

ment; ***malos ~s*** *pl* ill treatment *sg*, abuse *sg*; ***~ de favor*** favorable *o* preferential treatment **2** COM deal; ***hacer un ~*** make a deal; ***¡~ hecho!*** it's a deal; ***tener ~ con alguien*** have dealings with s.o.; ***estar en ~s con alguien*** be negotiating with s.o., be talking to s.o.
trauma *m* trauma
traumático *adj* traumatic
traumatismo *m* MED trauma, injury
◇ **traumatismo craneoencefálico** head injury, cranial trauma *fml*
traumatizar ⟨1f⟩ *v/t* traumatize
traumatología *f* trauma surgery
traumatólogo *m*, **-a** *f* trauma specialist, traumatologist
través *m*: ***a ~ de*** through; ***de ~*** diagonally, crosswise; ***mirar de ~*** look sideways at
travesaño *m en fútbol* crossbar
travesía *f* crossing
travesti, travestido *m* **1** *que se viste de mujer* transvestite **2** *artista* drag artist
travesura *f* bit of mischief, prank
traviesa *f* FERR tie, *Br* sleeper
travieso *adj niño* mischievous
trayecto *m* journey; ***10 dólares por ~*** 10 dollars each way
trayectoria *f fig* course, path
traza *f* **1** (*aspecto*): ***esta discusión lleva ~s de acabar mal*** this argument looks as if it will end badly *o* looks like ending badly; ***lleva ~s de llover*** it looks as though it's going to rain, it looks like rain F; ***por las ~s*** judging by appearances **2** (*maña*): ***darse (buena) ~ para*** to be good at
trazado *m* **1** *acción* drawing; (*diseño*) plan, design **2** *de canal, camino* route
trazar ⟨1f⟩ *v/t* **1** (*dibujar*) draw **2** *ruta* plot, trace **3** (*describir*) outline, describe
trazo *m* line
trébol *m* BOT clover
trece *adj* thirteen; ***mantenerse*** *o* ***seguir en sus ~*** stand firm, not budge
trecho *m* stretch, distance; ***de ~ en ~*** at intervals
tregua *f* truce, ceasefire; ***sin ~*** relentlessly; ***no dar ~*** give no respite
treinta *adj* thirty
treintena *f* thirty; ***una ~ de ...*** about thirty …
trekking *m* trekking
tremebundo *adj* horrendous, frightening
tremenda *f*: ***echar por la ~*** flip F, go crazy F; ***tomarse algo a la ~*** *fig* F make a big fuss about sth
tremendismo *m* sensationalism
tremendo *adj* **1** *susto, imagen* awful, dreadful **2** *éxito, alegría* tremendous
trementina *f* turpentine, turps F *sg*
trémolo *m* MÚS tremolo
trémulo *adj voz* tremulous, trembling; *luz* flickering
tren *m* FERR train; ***ir en ~*** go by train; ***perder el ~*** miss the train; *fig* miss the boat; ***vivir a todo ~*** F live in style; ***... (como) para parar un ~*** F loads of … F, masses of … F; ***estar como un ~*** F be absolutely gorgeous
◇ **tren de alta velocidad** high speed train; **tren de aterrizaje** AVIA undercarriage, landing gear; **tren de cercanías** local *o* suburban train; **tren de lavado** car wash; **tren de mercancías** freight train, *Br* goods train; **tren de pasajeros** pasenger train; **tren de vida** lifestyle
trena *f* P can P, slammer P
trenca *f* duffel coat
trencilla *f* **1** braid, *Br* plait **2** *en bordado* tassle **3** *m* F DEP ref F
trencito *m Urug* F *en examen* crib
trenza *f* plait; *de pelo* braid, *Br* plait
trenzado *m* plaiting; *de pelo* braiding, *Br* plaiting
trenzar ⟨1f⟩ *v/t* plait; *pelo* braid, *Br* plait
trepa *m/f* F *socialmente* social climber; *en el trabajo* careerist
trepador I *adj*: ***planta ~a*** BOT climber, climbing plant **II** *m* **1** climber, climbing plant **2** ZO: ***~ (azul)*** nuthatch **III** *m*, ***~a*** *f* social climber
trepar ⟨1a⟩ **I** *v/i* climb (***a*** up), scale (***a*** sth) **II** *v/t* climb (up), scale
trepidante *adj fig* frenetic
trepidar ⟨1a⟩ *v/i* vibrate, shake
tres I *adj* three; ***no funciona ni a la de ~*** there's no way it is going to work **II** *m* three
◇ **tres segundos** *en baloncesto* three-seconds violation
trescientos *adj* three hundred
tresillo *m* living-room suite, *Br* three-piece suite
treta *f* trick, ploy

tríada *f* triad
trial *m* DEP trials *pl*
triangular *adj* triangular
triángulo *m* triangle
◇ **triángulo de peligro** AUTO warning triangle
triásico *m* GEOL Triassic (period)
triatlón *m* DEP triathlon
tribal *adj* tribal
tribu *f* tribe
tribulaciones *fpl* tribulations
tribuna *f* **1** DEP grandstand **2**: ***~ de oradores*** speaker's platform
tribunal *m* court
◇ **tribunal de apelación** court of appeals, *Br* Court of Appeal; **Tribunal Constitucional** constitutional court; **tribunal de cuentas** National Audit Commission; **Tribunal Europeo de Justicia** European Court of Justice; **tribunal de menores** juvenile court; **Tribunal Supremo** Supreme Court
tributar ⟨1a⟩ **I** *v/t impuesto*, *fig* pay **II** *v/i* pay taxes
tributario I *adj* **1** COM tax *atr*; ***derecho / sistema ~*** tax law / system **2** GEOG tributary *atr* **II** *m* tributary
tributo *m* **1** tribute; ***rendir ~*** *fig* pay tribute **2** (*impuesto*) tax
tricampeón *m*, **-ona** *f* DEP three times champion, triple champion
tricentenario *m* tercentennial, tercentenary
triciclo *m* tricycle
tricolor *adj* tricolor, *Br* tricolour
tricornio *m* three-cornered hat
tricotar ⟨1a⟩ *v/i & v/t* knit
tricotosa *f* knitting machine
tridente *m* trident
tridimensional *adj* three-dimensional
trienal *adj* triennial, three-yearly
trienio *m* period of three years
trifásico *adj* EL three-phase
trifulca *f* F brawl, *Br tb* punch-up F
trigal *m* wheat field
trigo *m* wheat; ***no es ~ limpio*** F *comerciante, propuesta comercial* he's / it's a bit shady F
◇ **trigo negro, trigo sarraceno** buckwheat, Saracen corn
trigonometría *f* MAT trigonometry
trigueño *adj pelo* corn-colored, *Br* corn-coloured; *piel* olive
triguero *adj* wheat *atr*
trilingüe *adj* trilingual
trilla *f* AGR threshing
trillado *adj fig* hackneyed, clichéd
trillador *m* thresher
trilladora *f* threshing machine, thresher; *mujer* thresher
trillar ⟨1a⟩ *v/t* AGR thresh
trillizos *mpl* triplets
trillo *m* threshing machine, thresher
trillón *m* quintillion, *Br* trillion
trilogía *f* trilogy
trimestral *adj* quarterly
trimestre *m* quarter; *escolar* semester, *Br* term
trimotor *m* three-engined plane
trinar ⟨1a⟩ *v/i* trill, warble; ***está que trina*** *fig* F he's fuming F, he's hopping mad F
trincar ⟨1g⟩ F **I** *v/t criminal* catch **II** *v/i* drink, booze F
trinchar ⟨1a⟩ *v/t* GASTR carve
trinchera *f* MIL trench
trinchero *m* sideboard
trineo *m* sled, sleigh
trinidad *f* REL trinity
trino *m* trill, warble
trinquete *m* **1** MAR foremast **2** TÉC pawl
trío *m* trio
tripa *f* F belly F, gut F; ***hacer de ~s corazón*** *fig* pluck up courage; ***¿qué ~ se te ha roto?*** F what's so urgent?; ***echar las ~s*** *fig* F bust a gut; ***rascarse la ~*** *fig* F do nothing; ***se me revuelven las ~s*** my stomach turns
triple I *adj* triple **II** *m* **1**: ***el ~ que el año pasado*** three times as much as last year **2** *en baloncesto* three-pointer
triplicado *adj*: ***por ~*** in triplicate
triplicar ⟨1g⟩ *v/t* triple, treble
trípode *m* tripod
tríptico *m* triptych
tripudo *adj* F potbellied
tripulación *f* AVIA, MAR crew
tripulado *adj* crewed, manned
tripulante *m/f* crew member
tripular ⟨1a⟩ *v/t* crew
triquinosis *f* MED trichinosis
triquiñuela *f* F dodge F, trick
tris *m*: ***estuvo en un ~ de caerse*** F she came within an inch of falling
triste *adj* sad
tristeza *f* sadness
tristón *adj* gloomy, sad
tritón *m* **1** ZO newt **2** MYTH triton

T

trituradora *f de papel* shredder; *de hielo, roca etc* crusher; *de carne* grinder, *Br* mincer
◇ **trituradora de basuras** waste disposal unit
triturar ⟨1a⟩ *v/t papel* shred; *hielo, roca etc* crush; *carne* grind, *Br* mince
triunfador **I** *adj* winning **II** *m*, **~a** *f* winner, victor
triunfal *adj* **1** *arco, desfile* triumphal **2** *comportamiento, sonrisa* triumphant
triunfalismo *m* triumphalism
triunfante *adj* triumphant; ***salir ~*** emerge triumphant
triunfar ⟨1a⟩ *v/i* **1** triumph, win **2** *en naipes* ruff, trump
triunfo *m* **1** triumph, victory **2** *en naipes* trump
trivial *adj* trivial
trivialidad *f cualidad, cosa* triviality; *dicho* trivial remark, triviality
trivializar ⟨1f⟩ *v/t* trivialize
triza *f*: ***hacer ~s*** F *jarrón* smash to bits; *papel, vestido* tear to shreds; ***estar hecho ~s*** F be shattered
trocar ⟨1g & 1m⟩ *v/t* **1** (*intercambiar*) exchange **2** (*confundir*) mix up, confuse; **trocarse** *v/r* turn (***en*** into)
trocear ⟨1a⟩ *v/t* cut into pieces, cut up
troche: ***había errores a ~ y moche*** F there were mistakes galore F
trofeo *m* trophy
trófico *adj* BIO alimentary, food *atr*
trofología *f* BIO food science
troglodita *m/f* cave dweller; *fig* F redneck, *Br* yob
troj(e) *f* granary
trola *f* F fib
trolebús *m* trolley bus
trolero F **I** *adj* lying **II** *m*, **-a** *f* liar
tromba *f*: ***~ de agua*** downpour; ***entrar / pasar en ~*** rush in / past
trombo *m* MED clot
trombón *m* MÚS trombone
trombonista *m/f* trombonist, trombone player
trombosis *f* MED thrombosis
trompa **I** *adj* F wasted F **II** *f* **1** MÚS horn; *instrumentista* horn player **2** ZO trunk **III** *m* MÚS horn player
◇ **trompa de Falopio, trompa uterina** ANAT Fallopian tube
trompada *f*, **trompazo** *m L.Am.* F whack F; ***darse un ~ con algo*** F bang into sth
trompearse ⟨1a⟩ *L.Am.* F fight, lay into each other F
trompeta **I** *f* MÚS trumpet; *instrumentista* trumpet player, trumpeter **II** *m* trumpeter, trumpet player
trompetazo *m* trumpet blast
trompetilla *f* ear trumpet
trompetista *m/f* trumpeter, trumpet player
trompicar ⟨1g⟩ *v/i* stagger
trompicón *m*: ***a trompicones*** in fits and starts
trompo *m* spinning top
trona *f* high chair
tronada *f* thunderstorm
tronado *adj* crazy
tronar ⟨1m⟩ **I** *v/i* **1** thunder **2** *Méx*: *con persona* break up; ***~ con alguien*** break up with s.o. **II** *v/t Méx* F (*catear*) flunk
troncal *adj* main
troncha *f S.Am.* slice, piece
tronchante *adj* F sidesplitting
tronchar ⟨1a⟩ *v/t palo, rama etc* snap; *fig* (*truncar*) cut short; **troncharse** *v/r*: ***~ de risa*** F split one's sides laughing
troncho *m* stalk, stem
tronco *m* trunk; *cortado* log; ***dormir como un ~*** sleep like a log
tronío *m*: ***una mujer de ~*** extravagant woman
trono *m* throne; ***acceder** o **subir al ~*** ascend *o* come to the throne
tropa *f* MIL (*soldado raso*) ordinary soldier, enlisted man; ***~s*** troops; ***~s aerotransportadas*** airborne troops
tropecientos *adj* F hundreds of
tropel *m*: ***en ~*** in a mad rush; ***salir en ~*** pour out
tropelía *f* outrage
tropezar ⟨1f & 1k⟩ *v/i* **1** trip, stumble **2** (*chocar*): ***~ con*** *tb fig* bump into
tropezón *m* **1** trip, stumble; ***dar un ~*** trip, stumble; ***a tropezones*** in fits and starts **2**: ***tropezones*** *mpl pieces of meat or vegetable added to soup*
tropical *adj* tropical
trópico *m* tropic
◇ **Trópico de Cáncer** Tropic of Cancer
◇ **Trópico de Capricornio** Tropic of Capricorn
tropiezo *m fig* setback
tropilla *f L.Am.* herd
troqueladora *f* stamping press

trotacalles *m/f inv* F bum F
trotamundos *m/f inv* globetrotter
trotar ⟨1a⟩ *v/i* trot; *fig* gad around
trote *m* trot; F rush; ***ir al ~*** trot; ***ya no estoy para esos ~s*** I'm not up to it any more; ***para todo ~*** *prenda de vestir* everyday *atr*
trovador *m* troubadour, minstrel
Troya *f* HIST Troy; ***aquí*** *o* ***allí fue ~*** F it was chaos!; ***arda ~*** F to hell with it! F
trozo *m* piece
trucaje *m* fixing, rigging
trucar ⟨1g⟩ *v/t concurso* fix, rig; *motor* soup up F
trucha *f* ZO trout
truco *m* trick; ***pillar*** *o Esp tb* ***coger el ~ a algo*** F get the hang of sth F
truculento *adj* horrifying
trueno *m* thunder
trueque *m* barter; ***a ~ de*** in exchange for
trufa *f* BOT truffle
trufar ⟨1a⟩ *v/t* stuff with truffles
truhán *m* rogue
trullo *m* F can P, slammer P
truncar ⟨1g⟩ *v/t* **1** GEOM truncate **2** *vida, esperanzas* cut short; **truncarse** *v/r* be cut short
trunco *adj L.Am.* incomplete; *sin punta* truncated
trust *m* cartel
TS *m abr* (= ***Tribunal Supremo***) Supreme Court
Tte. *abr* (= ***Teniente***) Lieut. (= Lieutenant)
tú *pron sg* you; ***tratar de ~*** address as tú; ***tratar*** *o* ***hablar de ~ a ~ con alguien*** be on an equal footing with s.o., be on familiar terms with s.o.
tu, tus *adj pos* your
tuba *f* MÚS tuba
tubérculo *m* BOT tuber
tuberculosis *f* MED tuberculosis, TB
tuberculoso *adj* tubercular
tubería *f* pipe
tubo *m* **1** tube; ***había gente / cartas por un ~*** F there were masses of people / letters F; ***pasar por el ~*** F knuckle under **2** *Rpl* TELEC receiver
◇ **tubo digestivo** ANAT alimentary canal; **tubo de ensayo** test tube; **tubo de escape** AUTO exhaust (pipe); **tubo fluorescente** fluorescent tube
tubular *adj* tubular
tucán *m* ZO toucan
tuerca *f* TÉC nut; ***dar una vuelta de ~*** *fig* tighten the screw
◇ **tuerca mariposa** wing nut
tuerto I *adj (sin un ojo)* one-eyed; *(ciego de un ojo)* blind in one eye **II** *m*, **-a** *f (sin un ojo)* one-eyed person; *(ciego de un ojo) person who is blind in one eye*
tuétano *m*: ***hasta los ~s*** *fig* through and through
tufarada *f* F whiff F
tugurio *m* hovel, dive
tulipa *f* lampshade
tulipán *m* BOT tulip
tullido I *adj* crippled **II** *m*, **-a** *f* cripple
tumba *f* tomb, grave; ***revolverse en su ~*** *fig* turn in one's grave; ***estar con un pie en la ~*** have one foot in the grave; ***lanzarse a ~ abierta*** go headlong; ***ser una ~*** *fig* keep one's mouth shut
tumbar ⟨1a⟩ *v/t* knock down; **tumbarse** *v/r* lie down
tumbo *m* tumble; ***ir dando ~s*** stagger along
tumbona *f* (sun) lounger
tumefacto *adj* swollen, tumescent
tumor *m* MED tumor, *Br* tumour
túmulo *m* tumulus, burial mound
tumulto *m* uproar
tumultuario, tumultuoso *adj* uproarious
tuna *f* **1** MÚS *student musical group* **2** *Méx fruta* prickly pear
tunante *m*, **-a** *f* rogue
tunda *f* F beating
tundra *f* GEOG tundra
tunecino I *adj* Tunisian **II** *m*, **-a** *f* Tunisian
túnel *m* tunnel; ***hacer un ~ a alguien*** F *en fútbol* nutmeg s.o.
◇ **túnel aerodinámico** wind tunnel; **túnel de lavado** car wash; **túnel de viento** wind tunnel
Túnez *m país* Tunisia; *ciudad* Tunis
tungsteno *m* QUÍM tungsten
túnica *f* tunic
tuno *m*, **-a** *f* rogue
tuntún: ***decir algo al buen~*** say sth off the top of one's head
tupé *m* F quiff
tupido *adj pelo* thick; *vegetación* dense, thick
turba *f* **1** *(muchedumbre)* throng **2** *(carbón)* peat
turbado *adj* **1** *(emocionado)* upset **2**

T

(*avergonzado*) embarrassed
turbador *adj* **1** (*emocionante*) upsetting **2** *belleza* disturbing **3** (*avergonzante*) embarrassing
turbante *m* turban
turbar ⟨1a⟩ *v/t* **1** (*emocionar*) upset **2** *paz, tranquilidad* disturb **3** (*avergonzar*) embarrass; **turbarse** *v/r* **1** (*emocionarse*) get upset **2** *de paz, tranquilidad* be disturbed **3** (*avergonzarse*) get embarrassed
turbera *f* peat bog
turbina *f* turbine
turbio *adj* cloudy, murky; *fig* shady, murky
turbión *m* METEO downpour
turbo I *adj* turbocharged **II** *m* AUTO turbo
turbocompresor *m* turbocharger
turbopropulsor *m* AVIA turboprop
turborreactor *m* AVIA turbojet
turbulencia *f* turbulence
turbulento *adj* turbulent
turco I *adj* Turkish **II** *m*, **-a** *f* Turk **III** *m idioma* Turkish
turgente *adj* swollen
turismo *m* **1** tourism **2** *automóvil* sedan, *Br* saloon (car)
◇ **turismo de aventura** adventure tourism; **turismo de masas** mass tourism; **turismo rural** tourism in rural areas
turista *m/f* tourist
turístico *adj* tourist *atr*
turnarse ⟨1a⟩ *v/r* take it in turns
turno *m* **1** turn; ***por ~s*** in turns; ***es mi ~*** it's my turn **2** *de trabajo* shift; ***cambio de ~*** change of shift; ***trabajar por ~s*** work shifts; ***de ~*** on duty
◇ **turno de día** day shift
◇ **turno de noche** night shift
turolense *adj* **I** of / from Teruel, Teruel *atr* **II** *m/f* person from Teruel
turón *m* ZO polecat
turoperador *m* tour operator
turquesa I *adj*: ***azul ~*** turquoise **II** *f piedra preciosa* turquoise
Turquía *f* Turkey
turrón *m* nougat
turulato *adj* F stunned, dazed
tururú I *int* no way! **II** *adj*: ***estás ~*** F you're crazy
tus *adj pos* your
tute *m* **1** *juego*: *Spanish card game* **2**: ***darse un ~*** F work like a dog F, slave F
tutear ⟨1a⟩ *v/t* address as 'tú'; **tutearse** *v/r* be on familiar terms
tutela *f* **1** JUR guardianship, tutelage; ***bajo la ~ de*** under the guardianship *o* protection of **2** EDU tutorship
tutelar I *adj* tutelary **II** ⟨1a⟩ *v/t fig* supervise
tuteo *m* use of tú
tutiplén: ***había comida a ~*** F there was loads *o* masses to eat F
tutor *m*, **~a** *f* **1** JUR guardian **1** EDU tutor
tutoría *f* **1** *cargo* tutorship **2** *clase* tutorial **3** (*tutela*) guardianship
tutú *m* tutu
tuve *vb* ☞ ***tener***
tuvo *vb* ☞ ***tener***
tuya *f* BOT white cedar, thuja
tuyo, tuya *pron pos* yours; ***los ~s*** your folks, your family; ***este libro es ~*** this book is yours; ***un amigo ~*** a friend of yours
TV *abr* (= ***televisión***) TV (= television)
TVE *f abr* (= ***Televisión Española***) Spanish State Television

U

u *conj* (*instead of* ***o*** *before words starting with o*) or
ubicación *f* **1** *L.Am.* location **2** (*localización*) finding, location
ubicado *adj* located, situated
ubicar ⟨1g⟩ *v/t* **1** *L.Am.* place, put **2** (*localizar*) locate; **ubicarse** *v/r* **1** be located, be situated **2** *en un empleo* get a job
ubicuidad *f* ubiquity
ubicuo *adj* ubiquitous
ubre *f* udder
UCD *f abr* (= ***Unión de Centro Democrático***) Central Democratic Union
UCE *f abr* (= ***Unión de Consumidores***

de España) *Spanish consumers association*

UCI *f abr* (= ***unidad de cuidados intensivos***) ICU (= intensive care unit)

ucrani(an)o I *adj* Ukrainian **II** *m*, **-a** *f* Ukrainian

Ud. *pron* ☞ ***usted***

Uds. *pron* ☞ ***ustedes***

UE *f abr* (= ***Unión Europea***) EU (= European Union)

UEFA *f abr* (= ***Unión Europea de Fútbol Associación***): ***la ~*** UEFA (= Union of European Football Associations)

¡uf! *int* oof!

ufanarse ⟨1a⟩ *v/r* boast (***con, de*** of, about)

ufano *adj* **1** conceited **2** (*contento*) proud

ufología *f* study of UFOs, ufology

ugandés I *adj* Ugandan **II** *m*, **-esa** *f* Ugandan

UGT *f abr* (= ***Unión General de Trabajadores***) *Spanish trade union*

ujier *m* usher

ukelele *m* MÚS ukulele

úlcera *f* MED ulcer

◇ **úlcera duodenal** duodenal ulcer

◇ **úlcera gástrica** gastric ulcer

ulceración *f* ulceration

ulcerarse ⟨1a⟩ *v/r* MED become ulcerous, ulcerate

ulceroso *adj* ulcerous

ulterior *adj* subsequent

ulteriormente *adv fml* later, subsequently

ultimación *f de preparativos* completion

últimamente *adv* lately

ultimar ⟨1a⟩ *v/t* **1** *preparativos* finalize **2** *L.Am.* (*rematar*) finish off

ultimátum *m* ultimatum

último *adj* **1** last; ***ser el ~ en llegar*** be the last (one) to arrive; ***por ~*** finally; ***está en las -as*** he doesn't have long (to live); ***a ~s de mayo*** at the end of May **2** (*más reciente*) latest; ***-as noticias*** latest news *sg*; ***estar a la -a*** be right up to date; ***ir a la -a*** (***moda***) wear the latest fashions; ***es lo ~*** it's the latest thing **3** *piso* top *atr*

ultra *m* POL right-wing extremist

ultra- *pref* ultra-

ultracongelado I *adj* deep frozen **II** *m* deep frozen product

ultraconservador *adj* ultra-conservative

ultraderecha *f* POL extreme right

ultraderechista I *adj* extreme right wing *atr* **II** *m/f* right-wing extremist

ultraizquierda *f* POL far left

ultraizquierdista I *adj* extreme left wing *atr* **II** *m/f* left-wing extremist

ultrajante *adj fml* outrageous; *palabras* insulting

ultrajar ⟨1a⟩ *v/t fml* outrage; (*insultar*) insult

ultraje *m fml* outrage; (*insulto*) insult

ultraligero *m* AVIA microlight

ultramar *m*: ***de ~*** overseas, foreign

ultramarino *adj* overseas, foreign

ultramarinos *mpl* groceries; ***tienda de ~*** grocery store, *Br* grocer's (shop)

ultramoderno *adj* ultramodern

ultranza: ***a ~*** for all one is worth; ***un defensor a ~ de algo*** an ardent defender of sth

ultrasónico *adj* ultrasonic

ultrasonido *m* ultrasound

ultratumba *f*: ***la vida de ~*** life beyond the grave

ultravioleta *adj* ultraviolet

ulular ⟨1a⟩ *v/i de viento* howl; *de búho* hoot

umbilical *adj* ANAT umbilical

umbral *m fig* threshold; ***en el ~ de*** on the threshold of

umbrío, umbroso *adj* shady

un, una *art indet* a; *antes de vocal y h muda* an; ***~os coches / pájaros*** some cars / birds

unánime *adj* unanimous

unanimidad *f* unanimity; ***por ~*** unanimously

unción *f fig* unction

uncir ⟨3b⟩ *v/t* yoke

undécimo *adj* eleventh

UNED *f abr* (= ***Universidad Nacional de Educación a Distancia***) *Spanish distance-learning university*

ungir ⟨3c⟩ *v/t* REL anoint

ungüento *m* ointment

uni- *pref* uni-, one-

únicamente *adv* only

unicameral *adj* POL: ***sistema ~*** single-chamber system

unicelular *adj* BIO single-cell *atr*

unicidad *f fml* (*excepcionalidad*) uniqueness

único *adj* **1** only; ***hijo ~*** only child; ***su ~ hijo*** her only son; ***lo ~ que …*** the only thing that … **2** (*sin par*) unique; *fig* (*excelente*) outstanding, extraordinary; ***es ~*** it's unique
unicolor *adj* self-colored, *Br* self-colour *atr*
unicornio *m* MYTH unicorn
unidad *f* **1** unit; ***~ de máxima seguridad*** *en prisión* maximum security unit **2** (*cohesión*) unity
◇ **unidad de cuidados intensivos** MED intensive care unit; **unidad de disco** INFOR disk drive; **unidad monetaria** monetary unity; **unidad móvil** *de radio*, *TV* mobile unit, outside broadcast unit; **unidad de tratamiento intensivo** *CSur* MED intensive care unit; **unidad de vigilancia intensiva** MED intensive care unit
unidimensional *adj* one-dimensional
unidireccional *adj* unidirectional, one-directional
unido *adj* united; ***una familia -a*** a close-knit family; ***estar muy ~s*** be very close
unifamiliar *adj* single-family *atr*; ***vivienda ~*** single-family dwelling
unificación *f* unification
unificar ⟨1g⟩ *v/t* unify
uniformar ⟨1a⟩ *v/t fig* standardize
uniforme **I** *adj* uniform; *superficie* even **II** *m* uniform; ***ir de ~*** be in uniform
uniformidad *f* uniformity
unigénito **I** *adj hijo* only **II** *m* REL: ***el Unigénito*** the only begotten Son of God
unilateral *adj* unilateral
unión *f* **1** union; ***la ~ hace la fuerza*** united we stand **2** TÉC joint
Unión Americana *f Méx* United States of America
Unión Europea *f* European Union
unipartidista *adj* one-party *atr*
unipersonal *adj* individual, single
unir ⟨3a⟩ *v/t* **1** join **2** *personas* unite **3** *características* combine (***con*** with) **4** *ciudades* link; **unirse** *v/r* join together; ***~ a*** join
unisex *adj inv* unisex
unísono *m* MÚS unison; ***al ~*** in unison
unitario *adj* unitary; ***precio ~*** unit price
universal *adj* universal
universalidad *f* universality
universalizar ⟨1f⟩ *v/t* universalize
universidad *f* university; ***~ a distancia*** *university correspondence school*, *Br* Open University
universitario **I** *adj* university *atr* **II** *m*, **-a** *f estudiante* university student
universo *m* universe
unívoco *adj* univocal
uno **I** *pron* **1** one; ***es la -a*** it's one o'clock; ***~ a ~***, ***~ por ~***, ***de ~ en ~*** one by one; ***-a de dos*** one thing or the other
2 *personal en singular* someone, somebody; ***me lo dijo ~*** someone *o* somebody told me
3 *personal en plural*: ***~s cuantos*** a few, some; ***~s y otros*** everyone; ***~s niños*** some children; ***~s a otros*** one another, each other
4 *impersonal* you, one *fml*; ***¿qué puede ~ hacer?*** what can you *o* one *fml* do?
5 *aproximación*: ***-as mil pesetas*** about a thousand pesetas; ***~s 20 kilómetros*** about 20 kilometers, some 20 kilometers
6: ***a -a*** at the same time; ***-a y no más*** never again; ***no dar ni -a*** F not get anything right
7 *en baloncesto*: ***~ contra ~*** one on one; ***~ más ~*** one-and-one
II *art*: ***~s niños*** some children
III *m* one; ***el ~ de enero*** January first, the first of January
untar ⟨1a⟩ *v/t* **1** spread **2**: ***~ a alguien*** F (*sobornar*) grease s.o.'s palm; **untarse** *v/r* **1** smear o.s. (***con*** with) **2** *fig* take a cut F, get a rake-off F
untuosidad *f tb fig* oiliness
untuoso *adj tb fig* oily
uña *f* ANAT nail; ZO claw; ***comerse*** *o* ***morderse las ~s*** bite one's nails; ***defenderse con ~s y dientes*** *fig* F fight tooth and nail; ***ser ~ y carne*** *personas* be extremely close; ***enseñar*** *o* ***sacar las ~s*** *fig* show one's teeth; ***estar de ~s*** be at daggers drawn (***con*** with); ***ponerse de ~s*** F get upset
uñero *m inflamación* whitlow; *uña encarnada* ingrown toenail
uñeta *f L.Am.* plectrum
¡upa! *int* upsydaisy
upar ⟨1a⟩ *v/t* lift up
uperisado *adj*: ***leche -a*** UHT milk
uranio *m* uranium; ***~ enriquecido / empobrecido*** enriched / depleted uranium

urbanidad *f* civility
urbanismo *m* city planning, *Br* town planning
urbanista *m/f* city planner, *Br* town planner
urbanístico *adj* city planning *atr*, *Br* town planning *atr*
urbanita *m/f* F urbanite, city dweller
urbanizable *adj*: ***terreno ~*** building land
urbanización *f* (urban) development; (*colonia*) housing development, *Br* housing estate
urbanizar ⟨1f⟩ *v/t terreno* develop
urbano *adj* **1** urban; ***guardia ~*** local police officer **2** (*cortés*) courteous
urbe *f* city
urdir ⟨3a⟩ *v/t* **1** *complot* hatch **2** *hilos* warp
urea *f* urea
uremia *f* MED uremia
uréter *m* ANAT ureter
uretra *f* ANAT urethra
urgencia *f* **1** urgency; (*prisa*) haste; ***con la máxima ~*** with the utmost urgency **2** MED emergency; ***~s pl*** emergency room *sg*, A&E *sg*, *Br* casualty *sg*
urgente *adj* urgent
urgir ⟨3c⟩ *v/i* be urgent
urinario I *adj* urinary **II** *m* urinal
urna *f* urn
◇ **urna electoral** ballot box
urología *f* MED urology
urólogo *m*, **-a** *f* MED urologist
urraca *f* ZO magpie
URSS *f abr* (= ***Unión de Repúblicas Socialistas Soviéticas***) USSR (= Union of Soviet Socialist Republics)
urticaria *f* MED nettle rash, hives *sg*, urticaria *fml*
Uruguay *m* Uruguay
uruguayo I *adj* Uruguayan **II** *m*, **-a** *f* Uruguayan
usado *adj* **1** (*gastado*) worn **2** (*de segunda mano*) second-hand
usanza *f* usage, custom
usar ⟨1a⟩ **I** *v/t* **1** use **2** *ropa*, *gafas* wear **II** *v/i*: ***listo para ~*** ready to use; **usarse** *v/r* be used
◇ **usina eléctrica** *f Andes*, *Rpl* power station
◇ **usina nuclear** *f Andes*, *Rpl* nuclear power station
uso *m* **1** use; ***obligatorio el ~ de casco*** helmets must be worn; ***de ~ externo o tópico*** MED for external use; ***de ~ personal, para ~ propio*** for personal use, for one's own use; ***de un solo ~*** single-use *atr*, disposable; ***para ~ doméstico*** for domestic use; ***en buen ~*** still in use; ***fuera de ~*** *técnica*, *sistema etc* in disuse; ***hacer ~ de*** make use of; ***hacer ~ de la palabra*** *fml* speak; ***desde que tengo ~ de razón*** for as long as I can remember **2** (*costumbre*) custom; ***los trajes al ~ eran …*** the costumes of the time were …; ***no es un político al ~*** he is not your average politician
USO *f abr* (= ***Unión Sindical Obrera***) *Spanish trade union*
usted *pron* you; ***tratar de ~*** address as 'usted'; ***~es*** *pl* you; ***de ~ / ~es*** your; ***es de ~ / ~es*** it's yours
usual *adj* common, usual
usuario *m*, **-a** *f* INFOR user
usufructo *m* JUR usufruct
usufructuario *m*, **-a** *f* usufructuary
usura *f* usury
usurario *adj* usurious
usurero *m*, **-a** *f* usurer
usurpación *f* usurpation
usurpador *m*, **~a** *f* usurper
usurpar ⟨1a⟩ *v/t* usurp
utensilio *m* tool; *de cocina* utensil; ***~s*** *pl* equipment *sg*; ***~s de pesca*** *pl* fishing tackle *sg*
uterino *adj* ANAT uterine
útero *m* ANAT womb, uterus
UTI *f abr CSur* (= ***unidad de tratamiento intensivo***) ICU (= intensive care unit)
útil I *adj* useful; ***día ~*** working day **II** *m* tool; ***~es de pesca*** *pl* fishing tackle *sg*
utilería *f L.Am.* TEA props *pl*
utilero *m*, **-a** *f L.Am.* **1** TEA props manager **2** DEP boot boy
utilidad *f* **1** usefulness; ***ser de gran ~*** be very useful; ***de ~ pública*** of public benefit; ***una asociación de ~ pública*** a registered charity, a charitable organization **2**: ***~es*** *pl L.Am.* profits
utilitario I *adj* functional, utilitarian **II** *m* AUTO compact
utilitarismo *m* utilitarianism
utilizable *adj* usable
utilización *f* use
utilizar ⟨1f⟩ *v/t* use

utillaje *m* equipment, tools *pl*
utopía *f* utopia
utópico *adj* utopian
uva *f* BOT grape; ***estar de mala ~*** F be in a foul mood; ***tener mala ~*** F be a nasty piece of work F; ***de ~s a brevas*** *o* ***peras*** F once in a blue moon
uve *f* letter 'v'
◇ **uve doble** letter 'w'
UVI *f abr* (= ***unidad de vigilancia intensiva***) ICU (= intensive care unit)
úvula *f* ANAT uvula

V

va *vb* ☞ ***ir***
vaca *f* **1** cow; ***mal*** *o* ***enfermedad de las ~s locas*** F mad cow disease F; ***las ~s flacas / gordas*** the years of plenty / lean years **2** GASTR beef
◇ **vaca lechera** dairy cow; **vaca marina** manatee, sea cow; **vaca sagrada** sacred cow
vacacional *adj* vacation *atr*, *Br* holiday *atr*
vacaciones *fpl* vacation *sg*, *Br* holiday *sg*; ***~ escolares*** school vacation, *Br* school holiday(s); ***~ retribuidas*** paid vacation, *Br* paid holiday(s); ***estar de ~*** be on vacation *o Br* holiday; ***irse de ~*** go on vacation *o Br* holiday
vacacionar *v/i L.Am.* vacation, *Br* holiday
vacacionista *m/f L.Am.* vacationer, *Br* holiday-maker
vacante I *adj* vacant, empty **II** *f* job opening, position, *Br* vacancy; ***cubrir una ~*** fill a position
vaciado *m* emptying; *de madera* hollowing out; *en escultura* casting
vaciar ⟨1b⟩ *v/t* empty; *madera* hollow out; *en escultura* cast; **vaciarse** *v/r* empty
vacilación *f* hesitation, vacillation *fml*
vacilante *adj* **1** unsteady **2** (*dubitativo*) hesitant
vacilar ⟨1a⟩ **I** *v/i* **1** hesitate; *de fe, resolución* waver **2** *de objeto* wobble, rock; *de persona* stagger **3** *Méx* F (*divertirse*) have fun **II** *v/t* F make fun of
vacío I *adj* empty **II** *m* FÍS vacuum; *fig: espacio* void; ***dejar un ~*** *fig* leave a gap; ***envasado al ~*** vacuum-packed; ***hacer el ~ a alguien*** *fig* ostracize s.o.; ***caer en el ~*** *fig* fall on deaf ears F
◇ **vacío legal** (legal) loophole
◇ **vacío de poder** power vacuum
vacuidad *f fig* vacuity, vacuousness
vacuna *f* vaccine
vacunación *f* vaccination
vacunar ⟨1a⟩ *v/t* vaccinate
vacuno I *adj* bovine; ***ganado ~*** cattle *pl* **II** *m* cattle *pl*
vacuo *adj fig* vacuous
vadeable *adj* fordable
vadear ⟨1a⟩ *v/t* **1** *río* ford **2** *dificultad* get around
vademécum *m* handbook, vade mecum
vado *m* **1** ford **2** *en la calle* entrance ramp
◇ **vado permanente** *letrero* keep clear
vagabundear ⟨1a⟩ *v/i* drift around
vagabundeo *m* wandering
vagabundo I *adj perro* stray **II** *m*, **-a** *f* hobo, *Br* tramp
vagancia *f* laziness, idleness
vagar ⟨1h⟩ *v/i* wander
vagido *m de bebé* cry
vagina *f* ANAT vagina
vaginal *adj* vaginal
vago I *adj* **1** (*holgazán*) lazy; ***hacer el ~*** laze around **2** (*indefinido*) vague **II** *m*, **-a** *f* idler, *Br* layabout F
vagón *m de carga* wagon; *de pasajeros* car, *Br* coach
◇ **vagón cisterna** tank car, *Br* tank wagon
◇ **vagón restaurante** dining car, *Br tb* restaurant car
vagoneta *f* flatbed truck
vaguada *f* river bed
vaguear ⟨1a⟩ *v/i* laze around
vaguedad *f* vagueness; ***hablar sin ~es*** get right to the point
vahido *m* MED dizzy spell
vaho *m* **1** (*aliento*) breath **2** (*vapor*) steam
vaina *f* **1** BOT pod **2** *S.Am.* F (*molestia*)

drag F **3** *para armas* sheath
vainica *f* drawn-thread work
vainilla *f* vanilla
vais *vb* ☞ ***ir***
vaivén *m* to-and-fro; ***vaivenes*** *pl fig* ups and downs
vajilla *f* dishes *pl*; *juego* dinner service, set of dishes
vale *m* voucher, coupon; ***~ de comida*** lunch voucher
valedero *adj* valid
valedor I *m Méx* F guy; ***mi ~*** buddy, pal **II** *m*, **~a** *f* protector, defender
valencia *f* QUÍM valence, *Br* valency
valenciano *adj* Valencian, Valencia *atr*
valentía *f* bravery
valer ⟨2q⟩ **I** *v/t* **1** be worth **2** (*costar*) cost **II** *v/i* **1** *de billete, carné* be valid
2 (*estar permitido*) be allowed
3 (*tener valor*): ***vale mucho*** it's worth a lot
4 (*servir*) be of use; ***no ~ para algo*** be no good at sth; ***no ~ para nada*** *de objeto* be useless; ***sus consejos me valieron de mucho*** his advice was very useful to me
5 (*costar*): ***¿cuánto vale?*** how much is it?; ***vale más caro*** it's more expensive
6 (*emplear*): ***hacer ~*** *autoridad* assert; ***el presidente hizo valer su voto de calidad para ...*** the president used his casting vote to …
7: ***más vale ...*** it's better to …; ***más te vale ...*** *amenaza* you'd better …; *consejo* you'd be better to …
8: ***¡vale!*** okay, sure; ***¿vale?*** okay?; (*amenaza*) got it?; ***¡eso no vale!*** that's not fair!; ***¡vale ya!, ¡ya vale!*** that's enough!
valerse *v/r* **1** manage (by o.s.) **2**: ***~ de*** make use of
valeriana *f* BOT valerian
valeroso *adj* valiant
valga *vb* ☞ ***valer***
valgo *vb* ☞ ***valer***
valía *f* worth
validación *f* validation
validar ⟨1a⟩ *v/t* validate
validez *f* validity; ***tener ~*** be valid
válido *adj* valid; ***ser ~ hasta ...*** *pasaporte, garantía etc* be valid until…; ***no ser ~*** *firma* be invalid; *tanto* not count
valiente *adj* **1** brave **2** *irón* fine; ***¡~ sorpresa!*** a fine surprise this is!; ***¡en ~ lío te has metido!*** a fine mess you've gotten yourself into!; ***¡~s vacaciones!*** some vacation this is!
valija *f* (*maleta*) bag, suitcase, *Br tb* case
◇ **valija diplomática** diplomatic bag
valioso *adj* valuable
valla *f* **1** fence **2** DEP, *fig* hurdle; ***carrera de ~s*** hurdles
◇ **valla publicitaria** billboard, *Br* hoarding
vallado *m* fence
vallar ⟨1a⟩ *v/t* fence in
valle *m* valley
◇ **valle de lágrimas** *fig* vale of tears
vallisoletano *adj* of / from Valladolid, Valladolid *atr*
vallista *m/f* DEP hurdler
valor *m* **1** value; ***de gran ~*** very valuable; *fig* of great worth *o* value; ***objetos de ~*** valuables **2**: ***~es*** *pl* COM securities **3** (*valentía*) courage
◇ **valor agregado** *L.Am.* added value; **valor añadido** added value; **valor catastral** *local tax value*, *Br* rateable value; **valor nominal** *de acción* nominal value; *de título* par value; **valor nutritivo** nutritional value
valoración *f* **1** (*tasación*) valuation **2** *de situación* evaluation, assessment
valorar ⟨1a⟩ *v/t* **1** (*tasar*) value (***en*** at) **2** (*estimar*) appreciate, value
valorización *f* valuation
valorizar ⟨1f⟩ *v/t* value
vals *m* waltz
valuación *f* valuation
valuar ⟨1e⟩ *v/t* value
valva *f* BOT, ZO valve
válvula *f* ANAT, EL valve
◇ **válvula de escape** TÉC, *fig* safety valve; **válvula mitral** ANAT mitral valve; **válvula de seguridad** TÉC safety valve
vampiresa *f* vamp, femme fatale
vampiro *m*, **-a** *f* vampire
van *vb* ☞ ***ir***
vanagloria *f* boastfulness
vanagloriarse ⟨1b⟩ *v/r* boast (***de*** about), brag (***de*** about)
vanaglorioso *adj* boastful
vanamente *adv* in vain, vainly
vandálico *adj* destructive
vandalismo *m* vandalism
vándalo *m*, **-a** *f* vandal
vanguardia *f* **1** MIL vanguard **2** *cultural*

avant-garde; ***de ~*** avant-garde
vanguardista I *adj* avant-garde, modernist **II** *m/f* avant-gardist, modernist
vanidad *f* vanity
vanidoso *adj* conceited, vain
vano I *adj* futile, vain; ***en ~*** in vain **II** *m* ARQUI space, opening
vapor *m* vapor, *Br* vapour; *de agua* steam; ***cocinar al ~*** steam
vaporización *f* vaporization
vaporizador *m* vaporizer; *de parfume* spray
vaporizar ⟨1f⟩ *v/t* vaporize; *parfume* spray; **vaporizarse** *v/r* vaporize
vaporoso *adj* **1** vaporous **2** *fig*: *vestido* gauzy, filmy
vapulear ⟨1a⟩ *v/t* **1** beat up **2** (*reprender duramente*) tear a strip off
vapuleo *m* beating
vaquera *f* cowgirl
vaquero I *adj* **1** cattle-raising *atr* **2** *tela* denim *atr*; ***pantalones ~s*** jeans **II** *m* cowboy
vaqueta *f* calfskin
vaquilla *f* heifer
vaquita de San Antón *f Rpl* ladybug, *Br* ladybird
vara *f* **1** stick **2** TÉC rod **3** (*bastón de mando*) staff **4** TAUR lance **5** (*medida*): *measurement approximately equivalent to a yard*
varadero *m* MAR dry dock
varapalo *m* F (*contratiempo*) hitch F, setback
varar ⟨1a⟩ **I** *v/t barca* beach, run aground **II** *v/i de barca* run aground
varear ⟨1a⟩ *v/t* **1** *fruta* knock down; *alfombra* beat **2** *Arg*: *caballo* train
variabilidad *f* variability
variable I *adj* variable; *tiempo* changeable **II** *f* MAT variable
variación *f* variation
variado *adj* varied
variante *f* variant
variar ⟨1c⟩**I** *v/t* vary; (*cambiar*) change **II** *v/i* vary; (*cambiar*) change; ***para ~*** for a change
varice *f* MED varicose vein
varicela *f* MED chickenpox
varices *fpl* ☞ ***variz***
varicoso *adj* MED varicose
variedad *f* variety; ***~es*** *pl* vaudeville *sg*, *Br* variety *sg*
varilla *f* rod; *de paraguas* rib; *de gafas* side; *de sujetador* wire
variopinto *adj* varied, diverse
varios *adj* several
varita *f*: ***~ mágica*** magic wand
variz *f* varicose vein
varón *m* man, male; ***ser un santo ~*** F be a saint, be an angel
varonil *adj* manly, virile
vas *vb* ☞ ***ir***
vasallaje *m* HIST vassalage
vasallo *m* HIST vassal
vasco I *adj* Basque; ***País Vasco*** Basque country **II** *m idioma* Basque **III** *m*, **-a** *f* Basque
Vascongadas *fpl* Basque country *sg*
vascuence *m/adj* Basque
vascular *adj* ANAT vascular
vasectomía *f* MED vasectomy
vaselina *f* **1** Vaseline® **2** DEP lob
vasija *f* container, vessel
vaso *m* **1** glass; ***un ~ de vino*** a glass of wine; ***un ~ para vino*** a wine glass **2** ANAT vessel
◇ **vaso sanguíneo** blood vessel
vástago *m* **1** BOT shoot **2** TÉC rod **3** *lit* (*descendiente*) descendant
vastedad *f* vastness
vasto *adj* vast
váter *m* toilet, lavatory
Vaticano I *adj* Vatican *atr* **II** *m* Vatican
vaticinador *adj* prophetic
vaticinar ⟨1a⟩ *v/t* predict, forecast
vaticinio *m* prediction, forecast
vatio *m* EL watt
vaya *vb* ☞ ***ir***
V.B. *abr* (= ***visto bueno***) approved
Vd. *pron* ☞ ***usted***
Vda. *abr* (= ***viuda***) widow
Vds. *pron* ☞ ***usted***
ve I *vb* ☞ ***ir***, ***ver*** **II** *f L.Am.* ***~*** (***corta***) (letter) v
V.E. *abr* (= ***Vuestra Excelencia***) Your Excellency
vea *vb* ☞ ***ver***
veces *fpl* ☞ ***vez***
vecinal *adj* neighborhood *atr*, *Br* neighbourhood *atr*
vecindad *f Méx* poor area
vecindario *m* neighborhood, *Br* neighbourhood
vecino I *adj* neighboring, *Br* neighbouring; ***país ~*** neighboring country **II** *m*, **-a** *f* neighbor, *Br* neighbour
vector *m* FÍS, MAT vector

veda *f en caza* closed season, *Br* close season
vedado *m*: **~ *de caza*** game reserve
vedar ⟨1a⟩ *v/t* ban, prohibit
vedette *f* star
vega *f* plain
vegetación *f* **1** vegetation **2**: ***vegetaciones*** *pl* MED adenoids
vegetal I *adj* vegetable, plant *atr* **II** *m* vegetable
vegetar ⟨1a⟩ *v/i fig* vegetate
vegetarianismo *m* vegetarianism
vegetariano I *adj* vegetarian **II** *m*, **-a** *f* vegetarian
vegetativo *adj* **1** *estado* vegetative **2** BOT plant *atr*
vehemencia *f* vehemence
vehemente *adj* vehement
vehículo *m* **1** *tb fig* vehicle **2** MED carrier
◇ **vehículo espacial** spacecraft
◇ **vehículo todoterreno** four-wheel-drive (vehicle), 4 x 4
veinte *m/adj* twenty
veintena *f* twenty; ***una ~ de …*** about twenty …
vejación *f*, **vejamen** *m* humiliation
vejar ⟨1a⟩ *v/t* humiliate
vejatorio *adj* humiliating
vejestorio *m* F old fossil F, old relic F
vejete *m* F old guy F, old boy F
vejez *f* old age; ***a la ~, viruelas*** you're only as young / old as you feel
vejiga *f* ANAT bladder
vela *f* **1** *para alumbrar* candle; ***estar a dos ~s*** F be broke F; ***pasar la noche en ~*** stay up all night **2** DEP sailing; ***deportista de ~*** yachtsman; *mujer* yachtswoman **3** *de barco* sail; ***recoger ~s*** MAR take in sail; *fig* back down; ***a toda ~*** F flat out F, all out F
◇ **vela aromática** scented *o* perfumed candle
◇ **vela latina** MAR lateen sail
velada *f* evening
velador *m* **1** *L.Am. lámpara* bedlamp, *Br* bedside light **2** *Chi mueble* nightstand, *Br* bedside table
velamen *m* MAR sails *pl*
velar ⟨1a⟩ **I** *v/i*: ***~ por algo*** look after sth **II** *v/t* **1** *enfermo* sit up with, watch over; *cadáver* keep vigil over **2** FOT fog; ***velarse*** *v/r* FOT be exposed
velatorio *m* wake
velcro® *m* Velcro®
veleidad *f* fickleness
veleidoso *adj* fickle
velero *m* MAR sailing ship
veleta I *f* weathervane **II** *m/f fig* weathercock
vello *m* (body) hair
◇ **vello púbico, vello pubiano** pubic hair
vellocino, vellón *m* fleece
vellosidad *f* hairiness
velloso, velludo *adj* hairy
velo *m* veil; ***correr un tupido ~ sobre algo*** keep sth quiet; ***tomar el ~*** take the veil, become a nun
◇ **velo del paladar** ANAT soft palate
velocidad *f* **1** speed; ***a gran ~*** at high speed; ***ir a toda ~*** go at full speed; ***ganar ~*** pick up speed, gain momentum **2** (*marcha*) gear
◇ **velocidad de crucero** MAR, AVIA cruising speed
◇ **velocidad máxima, velocidad punta** top speed, maximum speed
velocímetro *m* speedometer
velocista *m/f* DEP sprinter
velódromo *m* velodrome
velomotor *m* moped
veloz *adj* fast, speedy
ven *vb* ☞ ***venir, ver***
vena *f* **1** ANAT vein; ***le dio la ~ y lo hizo*** F she just upped and did it F; ***estar en ~*** F be on form; ***tener ~ de algo*** have the makings of sth; ***tiene ~ de artista*** he has an artistic streak; ***lo lleva en las ~s*** it's in his blood **2** GEOL aquifer
◇ **vena cava** ANAT vena cava
venado *m* ZO deer
vencedor I *adj* winning **II** *m*, **~a** *f* winner
vencejo *m* ZO swift
vencer ⟨2b⟩ **I** *v/t* defeat; *fig* (*superar*) overcome **II** *v/i* **1** win **2** COM *de plazo etc* expire
vencido *adj*: ***darse por ~*** admit defeat, give in; ***a la tercera va la -a*** third time lucky
vencimiento *m* expiration, *Br* expiry; *de bono* maturity
venda *f* bandage; ***se le ha caído la ~ de los ojos*** *fig* the scales have fallen from his eyes; ***tener una ~ sobre los ojos*** *fig* be blind
vendaje *m* MED dressing
vendar ⟨1a⟩ *v/t* MED bandage, dress; ~

los ojos a alguien blindfold s.o.
vendaval *m* gale
vendedor *m*, **~a** *f* seller; ***~ ambulante*** peddler, street trader
vender ⟨2a⟩ *v/t* **1** sell; ***~ caro algo a alguien*** *fig* make s.o. pay dearly for sth **2** *fig* (*traicionar*) betray; **venderse** *v/r* sell o.s.; ***~ al enemigo*** sell out to the enemy
vendido *adj* sold
vendimia *f* grape harvest
vendimiador *m*, **~a** *f* grape picker
vendimiar ⟨1b⟩ *v/t uvas* harvest, pick
vendré *vb* ☞ ***venir***
veneno *m* poison
venenoso *adj* poisonous
venerable *adj* venerable
veneración *f* veneration, worship
venerar ⟨1a⟩ *v/t* venerate, worship
venéreo *adj* MED venereal
venezolano I *adj* Venezuelan **II** *m*, **-a** *f* Venezuelan
Venezuela *f* Venezuela
venga *vb* ☞ ***venir***
vengador I *adj* avenging **II** *m*, **~a** *f* avenger
venganza *f* vengeance, revenge
vengar ⟨1h⟩ *v/t* avenge; **vengarse** *v/r* take revenge (***de*** on; ***por*** for)
vengativo *adj* vengeful
vengo *vb* ☞ ***venir***
venia *f* consent, permission
venial *adj* venial
venida *f* (*llegada*) arrival, coming
venidero *adj* future
venir ⟨3s⟩ *v/i* **1** come; ***~ de Lima*** come from Lima; ***~ por*** *o* F ***a por algo*** come for sth, come to collect sth; ***viene a ser lo mismo*** it comes down to the same thing; ***~ a menos*** come down in the world; ***le vino una idea*** an idea occurred to him
2: ***~ bien / mal*** be convenient / inconvenient
3 (*sentar*): ***el vestido me viene estrecho*** this dress is too tight for me
4: ***viene en la página 3*** it's on page 3
5: ***¿a qué viene eso?*** why do you say that?; ***no me vengas ahora con …*** I don't want to hear your…
6: ***el año que viene*** next year, the coming year, the year to come
7: ***¡venga!*** *venga aquí, no seas pesado* come on!
venirse *v/r*: ***~ abajo*** collapse; *fig*: *de persona* fall apart, go to pieces; ***¡lo que se nos viene encima!*** things are going to be difficult!
venoso *adj* ANAT venous; *manos* veiny, veined
venta *f* sale; ***en ~*** for sale; ***estar / poner a la ~*** be / put on sale
◇ **venta ambulante** peddling, street trading; **venta anticipada** advance sales *pl*; **venta por catálogo** mail order; **venta al contado** cash sale; **venta por correo** mail order; **venta al detalle, venta al por menor** retail
ventaja *f* **1** advantage; ***sacar ~ de algo*** derive benefit from sth; ***ganar ~*** gain the advantage; ***llevar ~ a alguien*** have an advantage over s.o. **2** DEP *en carrera, partido* lead
◇ **ventaja fiscal** tax advantage
ventajista *m/f* opportunist
ventajoso *adj* advantageous
ventana *f* **1** window; ***echar*** *o* ***tirar por la ~*** throw out of the window; *fig* throw away **2** *de la nariz* nostril
ventanal *m* (large) window
ventanilla *f* AVIA, AUTO, FERR window; MAR porthole
ventano *m* small window
ventear ⟨1a⟩ *v/i* **1** *del viento* blow **2** *de un animal* sniff the air
ventilación *f* ventilation
ventilador *m* fan
ventilar ⟨1a⟩ *v/t* **1** air **2** *fig*: *problema* talk over; *opiniones* air
ventisca *f* blizzard
ventiscar ⟨1g⟩ *v/i* blow a blizzard
ventolera *f* gust of wind; ***le dio la ~ de …*** F he took it into his head to …
ventosa *f* ZO sucker
ventosear ⟨1a⟩ *v/i* F break wind
ventosidad *f* wind, flatulence
ventoso *adj* windy
ventrículo *m* ANAT ventricle
ventrílocuo *m*, **-a** *f* ventriloquist
ventura *f* **1** (*felicidad*) happiness **2** (*suerte*) good luck, good fortune **3** (*azar*) chance
venturoso *adj* fortunate
veo *vb* ☞ ***ver***
ver ⟨2v; *part* **visto**⟩ **I** *v/t* **1** *L.Am.* (*mirar*) look at; *televisión* watch
2 see; ***sin ser visto*** unseen, without being seen; ***la vi ayer en la reunión*** I saw her yesterday at the meeting; ***no***

puede verla *fig* he can't stand the sight of her; ***tengo un hambre que no veo*** F I'm starving *o* ravenous; ***me lo veía venir*** I could see it coming; ***te veo venir*** *fig* I know what you're after
3 (*visitar*): ***fui a ~ al médico*** I went to see the doctor
4 (*opinar*): ***¿cómo lo ves?*** what do you think?
5 (*entender*): ***me hizo ~ que estaba equivocado*** she made me see that I was wrong; ***¿(lo) ves?*** (do) you see?
6 JUR *pleito* hear
7: ***no tiene nada que ~ con*** it doesn't have anything to do with
II *v/i* **1** *L.Am.* (*mirar*) look; ***ve aquí dentro*** look in here
2 see; ***no veo bien sin gafas*** I don't see too well without my glasses
3 (*considerar*): ***está por ~*** that remains to be seen; ***ya veremos*** we'll see; ***vamos a ~*** let's see; ***a ~*** let's see, now then
4 *locuciones*: ***¡hay que ~!*** would you believe it!; ***¡para que veas!*** so there!
verse *v/r* **1** see o.s.; ***véase abajo*** see below **2** (*encontrarse*) see one another; ***~ con alguien*** see s.o., date s.o. **3** *locuciones*: ***¡habráse visto!*** would you believe it!; ***¡se las verá conmigo!*** F he'll have me to deal with!; ***se las vieron y desearon para salir del país*** they had a tough time getting out of the country
IV *m* **1**(*aspecto*): ***de buen ~*** good-looking **2**: ***a mi / tu ~*** as I / you see it, in my / your opinion

vera *f de río* bank; ***a la ~ del camino*** at the roadside, at the side of the road; ***estaba a la ~ de su madre*** he was at his mother's side

veracidad *f* truthfulness, veracity *fml*

veraneante *m/f* vacationer, *Br* holidaymaker

veranear ⟨1a⟩ *v/i* spend the summer vacation *o Br* holidays

veraneo *m* summer vacation *o Br* holidays; ***ir de ~*** go on one's summer vacation *o Br* holidays

veraniego *adj* summer *atr*

veranillo *m*: ***~ de San Martín*** Indian summer

verano *m* summer

veras *f*: ***de ~*** really, truly

veraz *adj* truthful

verbal *adj* GRAM verbal

verbalizar ⟨1f⟩ *v/t* verbalize, put into words

verbena *f* **1** (*fiesta*) party **2** BOT verbena

verbigracia *m* for example, e.g.

verbo *m* GRAM verb
◇ **verbo auxiliar** auxiliary verb
◇ **verbo pronominal** pronominal verb, *verb always used with a reflexive pronoun*

verborrea *f desp* verbosity, wordiness; *hum* F verbal diarrhea *o Br* diarrhoea

verbosidad *f* verbosity, wordiness

verboso *adj* verbose, wordy

verdad *f* **1** truth; ***a decir ~*** to tell the truth; ***en ~*** in truth; ***la ~ es que ...*** the truth (of the matter) is that ...; ***es ~*** it's true, it's the truth; ***faltar a la ~*** be untruthful; ***media ~, ~ a medias*** half truth; ***decir cuatro ~es a alguien*** tell s.o. a few home truths; ***ser una ~ de Perogrullo*** be blindingly obvious
2: ***de ~*** real, proper; ***es un amigo de ~*** he's a real friend
3: ***no te gusta, ¿~?*** you don't like it, do you?; ***vas a venir, ¿~?*** you're coming, aren't you?

verdaderamente *adv* really

verdadero *adj* true; (*cierto*) real

verde I *adj* **1** green; ***poner ~ a alguien*** F criticize s.o. **2** *fruta* unripe **3** F *chiste* blue, dirty; ***viejo ~*** dirty old man **II** *m* **1** green; ***~ botella / oliva*** bottle / olive green **2**: ***los ~s*** POL the Greens

verdear ⟨1a⟩ *v/i* (*parecer verde*) look green; (*volverse verde*) turn green

verdecer ⟨2d⟩ *v/i* turn green

verderón *m* ZO greenfinch

verdor *m* greenness

verdoso *adj* greenish

verdugo *m* executioner; *que ahorca* hangman

verdulería *f* fruit and vegetable store, *Br* greengrocer's

verdulero *m*, **-a** *f* (fruit and) vegetable seller, *Br* greengrocer

verdura *f*: **~(s)** (*hortalizas*) greens *pl*, (green) vegetables *pl*

verdusco *adj* dark green; *desp* dirty green

vereda *f S.Am.* sidewalk, *Br* pavement; ***meter alguien en ~*** *fig* put s.o. back on the straight and narrow, bring s.o. into line

veredicto *m* JUR, *fig* verdict

V

verga *f* rod
vergel *m* orchard
vergonzante *adj* disgraceful, shameful
vergonzoso *adj* **1** disgraceful, shameful **2** (*tímido*) shy
vergüenza *f* **1** shame; ***no sé cómo no se te cae la cara de ~*** you should be ashamed (of yourself); ***¿no te da ~?*** aren't you ashamed of yourself?; ***no tiene ~*** he has no shame, he's shameless **2** (*escándalo*) disgrace; ***es una ~*** it's a disgrace **3**: ***me da ~*** I'm embarrassed; ***sentir ~ ajena*** feel embarrassed for s.o. **4**: ***~s*** *pl* (*órganos sexuales*) private parts
vericuetos *mpl camino* rough track *sg*; *fig* twists and turns
verídico *adj* true
verificación *f* **1** (*autentificación*) verification **2** (*comprobación*) checking
verificar ⟨1g⟩ *v/t* **1** (*autentificar*) verify **2** (*comprobar*) check; **verificarse** *v/r* **1** (*tener lugar*) take place **2** (*realizarse*) come true
verja *f* **1** railing **2** (*puerta*) iron gate
vermú, vermut *m* vermouth
vernáculo *adj* vernacular; ***lengua -a*** vernacular
verónica *f* TAUR veronica, *pass in which the cape is moved away from the bull*
verosímil *adj* realistic; (*creíble*) plausible
verosimilitud *f* realistic nature; (*credibilidad*) plausibility
verraco *m* ZO boar
verruga *f* wart; *en el pie* verruca
verrugoso *adj* warty, covered in warts
versado *adj* well-versed (***en*** in)
versal *f/adj*: (***letra***) **~** capital (letter)
versalitas *fpl* TIP small capitals
versar ⟨1a⟩ *v/i*: ***~ sobre*** deal with, be about
versátil *adj* **1** (*voluble*) fickle **2** (*polivalente*) versatile
versatilidad *f* **1** (*volubilidad*) fickleness **2** (*polivalencia*) versatility
versículo *m* verse
versificar ⟨1g⟩ **I** *v/t* put into verse **II** *v/i* compose verse
versión *f* version; ***en ~ original*** *película* original language version
◇ **versión actualizada** INFOR update, updated version
verso *m* verse
◇ **verso blanco** blank verse
versus *esp* JUR versus
vértebra *f* ANAT vertebra
◇ **vértebra cervical** cervical vertebra
◇ **vértebra lumbar** lumbar vertebra
vertebrado *m/adj* ZO vertebrate
vertebral *adj* vertebral; *columna* spinal
vertebrar ⟨1a⟩ *v/t fig* give form to, structure
vertedero *m* dump, tip
vertedor *m* outlet
verter ⟨2g⟩ **I** *v/t* dump; (*derramar*) spill; *fig*: *opinión* voice; ***el Ebro vierte sus aguas en el Mediterráneo*** the Ebro flows into the Mediterranean **II** *v/i de un río* flow (***a*** into); **verterse** *v/r* spill
vertical I *adj* vertical **II** *f* vertical (line)
vértice *m de triángulo, cono* apex, vertex; *de ángulo* vertex
vertido *m* **1** dumping; ***~ incontrolado*** unauthorized dumping **2**: ***~s*** *pl* waste *sg*; ***~s tóxicos*** toxic waste
vertiente *f* **1** *L.Am.* (*cuesta*) slope **2** (*lado*) side
vertiginoso *adj* **1** dizzy **2** (*rápido*) frantic
vértigo *m* MED vertigo; ***darle a alguien ~*** make s.o. dizzy; ***de ~*** *fig* frenzied
vesícula *f* blister
◇ **vesícula biliar** ANAT gall bladder
vespa® *f* motorscooter
vespertino *adj* evening *atr*; ***periódico ~*** evening paper
vestíbulo *m de casa* hall; *de edifico público* lobby
vestido I *adj* dressed; ***bien ~*** well dressed **II** *m* **1** dress **2** *L.Am. de hombre* suit
◇ **vestido de cóctel** cocktail dress
vestidor *m* dressing room; *Méx* DEP locker room
vestiduras *fpl* **1** clothes, clothing *sg*; ***rasgarse las ~*** *fig* tear one's hair **2** REL vestments
vestigio *m* vestige, trace
vestimenta *f* clothes *pl*, clothing
vestir ⟨3l⟩ **I** *v/t* dress; (*llevar puesto*) wear; *fig* (*disimular*) hide **II** *v/i* dress; ***~ de negro*** wear black, dress in black; ***~ de uniforme*** wear a uniform; ***~ mucho*** *de traje* look good; **vestirse** *v/r* get dressed; (*disfrazarse*) dress up; ***~ de algo*** wear sth; (*disfrazarse*) dress up as sth

vestuario *m* **1** DEP locker room, *Br* changing room **2** TEA wardrobe
veta *f* MIN, *en mármol* vein; *en madera* grain
vetar ⟨1a⟩ *v/t* POL veto
veteado *adj madera* grained; *mármol* veined
veterano I *adj* veteran; (*experimentado*) experienced **II** *m*, **-a** *f* veteran
veterinaria *f* veterinary science, veterinary medicine
veterinario I *adj* veterinary **II** *m*, **-a** *f* veterinarian, vet
veto *m* veto; ***poner el ~ a ...*** veto ...
vetustez *f* great age
vetusto *adj* ancient
vez *f* **1** time; ***a la ~*** at the same time; ***¿cuántas veces?*** how many times?, how often?; ***esta ~*** this time; ***la otra ~*** the other time; ***otra ~ será*** some other time; ***cada ~ que*** every time that; ***de ~ en cuando*** from time to time; ***otra ~*** again; ***una ~*** once; ***érase una ~*** once upon a time, there was; ***una ~ no cuenta*** just once doesn't count *o* matter; ***una ~ más*** once again; ***una ~ que hayamos llegado ...*** once we've arrived ...; ***de una ~ para siempre*** once and for all; ***una y otra ~*** time and time again; ***a veces*** sometimes; ***muchas veces*** (*con frecuencia*) often; ***ninguna ~*** never; ***rara ~*** seldom, rarely; ***tantas veces*** so many times, so often; ***varias veces*** several times; ***de una sola ~*** in just one shot; ***por primera ~*** for the first time;
2 (*turno*): ***es mi ~*** it's my turn
3: ***hacer las veces de*** *de objeto* serve as; *de persona* act as; ***tal ~*** perhaps, maybe; ***a su ~*** for his / her part; ***en ~ de*** instead of
vi *vb* ☞ ***ver***
vía I *f* **1** FERR track; *de autopista* lane; ***~s públicas*** *pl* public roads; ***~ rápida*** fast route; ***darle ~ libre a alguien*** *fig* give s.o. a free hand **2** (*medio*): ***por ~ aérea*** by air; ***por ~ oral*** MED orally, by mouth; ***por ~ judicial*** through the courts **3**: ***en ~s de*** *fig* in the process of; ***en ~s de desarrollo*** developing **II** *prp* via
◇ **vía de agua** MAR leak; **vía estrecha** FERR narrow gauge; ***de ~*** narrow-gauge; **vía férrea** FERR railroad (track); **Vía Láctea** Milky Way; **vía lenta** slow lane; **vía marítima** sea route, sea way; **vía muerta** FERR siding; ***entrar en ~*** *fig* grind to a halt; **vías respiratorias** ANAT respiratory tract *sg*, airways; **vías urinarias** ANAT urinary tract *sg*
viabilidad *f* viability, feasibility
viable *adj plan, solución* viable, feasible
viaducto *m* viaduct
viajante *m/f* sales rep
viajar ⟨1a⟩ *v/i* travel
viaje *m* trip, journey; ***sus ~s por ...*** his travels in ...; ***irse*** *o* ***salir de ~*** go away; ***estar de ~*** be traveling *o Br* travelling; ***¡buen ~!*** have a good trip!; ***~ con todo incluido*** all inclusive trip
◇ **viaje de ida** outward journey; **viaje de negocios** business trip; **viaje de ida y vuelta** round trip, *Br* return; **viaje inaugural** MAR maiden voyage; **viaje de novios** honeymoon; **viaje organizado** package tour; **viaje de vuelta** return journey
viajero *m*, **-a** *f* traveler, *Br* traveller
vial I *adj* road *atr*; ***seguridad ~*** road safety **II** *m* MED vial, phial
vianda *f* food
viandante *m/f* pedestrian
viario *adj* road *atr*; ***educación -a*** instruction in road safety
víbora *f tb fig* viper; ***lengua de ~*** *fig* sharp tongue
vibración *f* vibration
vibrador *m* vibrator
vibráfono *m* MÚS vibraphone
vibrante *adj fig* exciting
vibrar ⟨1a⟩ *v/i* vibrate; *fig*: *de voz* quiver
vicaría *f* pastor's house, vicarage; ***pasar por la ~*** F get married in church
vicario *m* vicar; ***el ~ de Cristo*** the Vicar of Christ
vicealmirante *m/f* MAR vice-admiral
vicecanciller *m/f* **1** vice-chancellor **2** *L.Am. de asuntos exteriores* Under Secretary of State, *Br* Deputy Foreign Minister
vicecónsul *m/f* vice-consul
vicepresidente *m*, **-a** *f* **1** POL vice-president **2** COM vice-president, *Br* deputy chairman
vicerrector *m* vice-rector, *Br* deputy vice-chancellor
vicetiple *f* chorus girl
viceversa *adv*: ***y ~*** and vice versa

viciado *adj* **1** *aire* stuffy **2** *persona* hooked
viciar ⟨1b⟩ *v/t* **1** *objeto* twist **2** *sentido* distort **3** JUR invalidate **4**: **~ *a alguien con algo*** get s.o. addicted to sth, get s.o. hooked on sth; **viciarse** *v/r* **1** *de persona* fall into bad habits **2** *de aire* go stale
vicio *m* **1** vice; ***pasarlo de ~*** F have a great time **2** COM defect; **~ *oculto*** hidden defect
◇ **vicio de forma** JUR legal technicality
vicioso *adj* **1** vicious **2** (*corrompido*) depraved
vicisitudes *fpl* ups and downs
víctima *f* victim; **~ *mortal*** fatality; ***cobrarse muchas ~s*** *de incendio, terremoto etc* claim many victims, kill many people; ***ser ~ de alguien / algo*** fall victim to s.o. / sth
victimar ⟨1a⟩ *v/t L.Am.* kill
victoria *f* victory; ***cantar ~*** claim victory; **~ *en casa*** DEP home win
victorioso *adj* victorious
vicuña *f* ZO vicuna
vid *f* vine
vida *f* life; *esp* TÉC life span; ***de por ~*** for life; ***toda la ~*** all one's life; ***somos amigos de toda la ~*** we have been friends all our lives; ***en mi ~*** never (in my life); ***en ~*** in his / her *etc* lifetime; ***¿qué es de tu ~?*** how are things?; ***ganarse la ~*** earn a living; ***vivir su ~*** live one's own life; ***hacer la ~ imposible a alguien*** make s.o.'s life impossible; ***a ~ o muerte*** life-or-death; ***estar entre la ~ y la muerte*** be hovering between life and death, be fighting for life; ***darse buena ~*** *o* ***la gran ~*** live high on the hog F, live the life of Riley F; ***pasar a mejor ~*** pass away; ***quitarse la ~*** take one's own life, kill o.s.; ***perder la ~*** lose one's life; ***salir con ~*** come out alive; ***sin ~*** lifeless; ***la ~ y milagros de alguien*** s.o.'s life story; **~ *en pareja*** married life, life together; **~ *familiar / sentimental*** family / love life; **~ *interior*** inner self; ***así es la ~*** that's life; **~ *mía*** my love; ***mujer de la ~*** loose woman; ***dar ~ a*** TEA play the part of
vidente *m/f* seer, clairvoyant
vídeo, video *m L.Am.* video; ***grabar en ~*** video(tape)
videocámara *f* video camera
videocas(s)et(t)e *m* video cassette
videoclip *m* (pop) video
videoconferencia *f* video conference
videojuego *m* video game
videoteca *f* video library
videotex(to) *m* videotext
vidorra *f* F easy life, life of Riley F
vidriar ⟨1b⟩ *v/t* glaze
vidriera *f L.Am.* shop window
vidriería *f* glassworks *sg*
vidriero *m*, **-a** *f* glazier
vidrio *m* **1** *L.Am.* glass; ***pagar los ~s rotos*** *fig* take the blame **2** (*ventana*) window
vidrioso *adj* **1** *material* glass-like **2** *ojos, mirada* glassy **3** *cuestión* delicate, sensitive
vieira *f* ZO scallop
vieja *f* old woman
viejales *m* F old guy F
viejo I *adj* old **II** *m* old man; ***mis ~s*** *L.Am.* F my folks F
viendo *vb* ☞ ***ver***
viene *vb* ☞ ***venir***
viento *m* **1** wind; ***hacer ~*** be windy; **~ *en popa*** *fig* F splendidly; ***ir*** *o* ***marchar ~ en popa*** *fig* go extremely well; **~ *de cara*** *o* ***frente*** headwind; ***contra ~ y marea*** *fig* come what may; ***soplan*** *o* ***corren malos ~s*** times are bad; ***proclamar a los cuatro ~s*** *fig* shout from the rooftops; ***quien siembra ~s recoge tempestades*** they that sow the wind shall reap the whirlwind **2** MÚS wind instrument; ***los ~s*** the wind (section)
vientre *m* belly; ***bajo ~*** lower abdomen; ***hacer de ~*** have a bowel movement
viernes *m inv* Friday
◇ **Viernes Santo** Good Friday
Vietnam *m* Vietnam
vietnamita I *adj* Vietnamese **II** *m/f* Vietnamese **III** *m idioma* Vietnamese
viga *f de madera* beam, joist; *de metal* beam, girder
vigencia *f* validity; ***entrar en ~*** come into effect
vigente *adj legislación* in force
vigésimo *adj* twentieth
vigía I *f* watchtower **II** *m/f* lookout
vigilancia *f* watchfulness, vigilance
vigilante I *adj* watchful, vigilant **II** *m L.Am.* policeman
◇ **vigilante jurado** security guard
◇ **vigilante nocturno** night watchman

vigilar ⟨1a⟩ **I** *v/i* keep watch **II** *v/t* watch; *a un preso* guard

vigilia *f* **1** wakefulness **2** REL (*víspera*) vigil **3** REL (*abstinencia*) abstinence; (***día de***) **~** day of abstinence

vigor *m* vigor, *Br* vigour; ***en ~*** in force; ***estar en ~*** be in effect; ***entrar / poner en ~*** come / put into effect

vigorizar ⟨1f⟩ *v/t* invigorate

vigoroso *adj* vigorous

vigués *adj* of / from Vigo, Vigo *atr*

VIH *m abr* (= ***virus de inmunodeficiencia humana***) HIV (= human immunodeficiency virus)

vil *adj* vile, despicable

vileza *f* **1** vileness **2** *acción* despicable act

vilipendiar ⟨1b⟩ *v/t* insult, vilify *fml*; (*despreciar*) revile

villa *f* town

◇ **villa miseria** *Arg* shanty town

◇ **villa olímpica** Olympic village

villancico *m* (Christmas) carol

villanía *f* **1** villainy **2** *acción* villainous act

villano I *adj* villainous **II** *m*, **-a** *f* villain

vilo: ***en ~*** in the air; *fig* in suspense, on tenterhooks; ***tener a alguien en ~*** *fig* keep s.o. in suspense *o* on tenterhooks; ***levantar en ~*** lift off the ground

vinagre *m* vinegar

◇ **vinagre de vino** wine vinegar

vinagrera *f* **1** vinegar bottle; ***~s*** *pl* cruet *sg* **2** *S.Am.* (*indigestión*) indigestion

vinagreta *f* vinaigrette

vinatería *f* **1** wine merchant **2** *bar* wine bar

vinatero I *adj* wine *atr* **II** *m*, **-a** *f* vintner, *Br* wine merchant

vinazo *m* strong wine

vincha *f S.Am.* hairband

vinculación *f* links *pl*

vinculante *adj* binding

vincular ⟨1a⟩ *v/t* **1** link (***a*** to) **2** (*comprometer*) bind

vínculo *m* link; *fig* (*relación*) tie, bond

vindicación *f* vindication

vindicar ⟨1g⟩ *v/t* vindicate

vindicatorio *adj* vengeful, vindictive

vine *vb* ☞ ***venir***

vínico *adj* wine *atr*

vinícola *adj región, país* wine-growing *atr*; *industria* wine-making *atr*

vinicultor *m*, **~a** *f* wine producer, wine grower

vinicultura *f* wine growing

viniendo *vb* ☞ ***venir***

vinificación *f* vinification

vinilo *m* QUÍM vinyl

vino I *m* wine **II** *vb* ☞ ***venir***

◇ **vino blanco** white wine; **vino espumoso** sparkling wine; **vino de mesa** table wine; **vino de misa** communion wine; **vino del país** local wine; **vino rojo** *Andes* red wine; **vino tinto** red wine

viña *f* vineyard

viñatero *m*, **-a** *f S.Am.* wine grower

viñedo *m* vineyard

viñeta *f* TIP vignette

vio *vb* ☞ ***ver***

viola *f* MÚS viola

violáceo *adj* purplish

violación *f* **1** rape **2** *de derechos, en baloncesto* violation

violado *adj* violet

violador *m* rapist

violar ⟨1a⟩ *v/t* **1** rape **2** *derechos* violate

violencia *f* violence

violentar ⟨1a⟩ *v/t* **1** *puerta* force **2** (*incomodar*) embarrass

violento *adj* **1** violent; ***morir de muerte -a*** die a violent death **2** *situación* embarrassing; *persona* embarrassed

violeta I *f* BOT violet **II** *m/adj* violet

violín *m* violin

violinista *m/f* violinist

violista *m/f* viola player

violonc(h)elista *m/f* cellist

violonc(h)elo *m* cello

VIP *m/f* VIP

viperino *adj* malicious; ***lengua -a*** sharp tongue

virador *m* FOT toner

viraje *m* MAR tack; AVIA bank; AUTO swerve; *fig* change of direction

viral *adj* viral

virar ⟨1a⟩ **I** *v/i* MAR tack, go about; AVIA bank; AUTO swerve; *fig* change direction; *de orientación, procedimiento etc* change (completely) **II** *v/t* FOT tint

virgen I *adj* **1** virgin **2** *cinta* blank; ***lana ~*** pure new wool **II** *f* virgin; ***la Virgen*** the Virgin; ***ser un viva la ~*** F be unreliable

virginal *adj* virginal

virginiano *L.Am.* ASTR **I** *adj* Virgo; ***soy ~*** I'm (a) Virgo **II** *m*, **-a** *f* Virgo

virginidad *f* virginity

Virgo *m/f inv* ASTR Virgo
virguería *f*: ***hace ~s*** P he's a whizz F
vírgula *f* punctuation mark
vírico *adj* viral
viril *adj* virile, manly
virilidad *f* virility, manliness; *edad* manhood
virilizarse ⟨1f⟩ *v/r de mujer* become more masculine
virología *f* MED virology
virrey *m* viceroy
virtual *adj* virtual
virtualmente *adv* virtually
virtud *f* virtue; ***en ~ de*** by virtue of
virtuosismo *m* virtuosity
virtuoso I *adj* virtuous **II** *m*, **-a** *f* virtuoso
viruela *f* MED smallpox
virulé *adv*: ***a la ~*** F (*de medio lado*) crooked; ***ojo a la ~*** F black eye
virulencia *f* MED, *fig* virulence
virulento *adj* MED, *fig* virulent
virus *m inv* MED virus
◇ **virus informático** computer virus
◇ **virus del sida** Aids virus
viruta *f* shaving
vis *f*: ***~ cómica*** gift for comedy
visa *f L.Am.* visa
visado *m* visa
visaje *m* (funny) face; ***hacer ~s*** pull faces
visceral *adj fig* gut *atr*, visceral *fml*
vísceras *fpl* guts, entrails
viscosa *f* viscose
viscosidad *f* viscosity
viscoso *adj* viscous
visera *f de gorra* peak; *de casco* visor
visibilidad *f* visibility
visible *adj* visible; *fig* evident, obvious
visillo *m* sheer, *Br* net curtain
visión *f* **1** vision, sight; *fig* vision; ***ver visiones*** be seeing things **2** (*opinión*) view; ***tener ~ de futuro*** be forward-looking
visionar ⟨1a⟩ *v/t película* see, watch
visionario I *adj* visionary **II** *m*, **-a** *f* visionary
visir *m* HIST vizier
visita *f* visit; ***hacer una ~ a alguien*** visit s.o.; ***~ de(l) médico*** *fig* quick visit
◇ **visita de cumplido** courtesy call; **visita a domicilio** house call; **visita guiada** guided tour; **visita oficial** POL official visit
Visitación *f* REL Visitation

visitador *m*, **~a** *f* inspector
◇ **visitador médico** drugs company salesperson, pharmaceuticals rep
visitante I *adj* visiting; DEP *tb* away; ***victoria ~*** away win **II** *m/f* visitor
visitar ⟨1a⟩ *v/t* **1** visit **2**: ***el doctor no visita los lunes*** the doctor isn't on duty Mondays
vislumbrar ⟨1a⟩ *v/t* glimpse
visón *m* ZO mink; ***abrigo de ~*** mink coat
visor *m* **1** FOT viewfinder **2** *en arma de fuego* sight; ***~ nocturno*** night sight
visos *mpl*: ***tener ~ de*** show signs of
víspera *f* **1** eve; ***en ~s de*** on the eve of **2**: ***~s*** *pl* REL vespers
vista I *f* **1** (eye)sight; ***~ cansada*** MED tired eyes; ***tener buena / mala ~*** have good / bad eyesight; ***hacer la ~ gorda*** *fig* F turn a blind eye; ***tener ~ para algo*** *fig* have a good eye for sth
2 JUR hearing
3: ***a la ~*** COM at sight, on demand
4 (*panorámica*): ***la ciudad a ~ de pajaro*** a bird's eye view of the city, the city seen from above; ***~ aérea*** FOT aerial view
5 (*perspectiva*): ***con ~s a*** with a view to; ***en ~ de*** in view of
6: ***a simple ~*** with the naked eye; ***a primera ~*** at first sight; ***de ~*** by sight; ***estar a la ~*** be in sight; ***perder de ~*** lose sight of; ***no perder de ~*** *niño etc* not take one's eyes off; ***a la ~ de todos*** in full view of everyone; ***poner la ~ en alguien / algo*** look at s.o. / sth; *tener intención de conseguir algo* set one's sights on s.o. / sth; ***volver la ~ atrás*** *tb fig* look back; ***hasta la ~*** bye!, see you!
II *m/f*: ***~ (de aduanas)*** customs official *o* officer
◇ **vista oral** JUR hearing
vistazo *m* look; ***echar un ~ a*** take a (quick) look at
viste *vb* ☞ ***ver, vestir***
visto I *part* ☞ ***ver***
II *adj* **1**: ***está bien ~*** it's the done thing; ***está mal ~*** it's not done, it's not the done thing; ***estar muy ~*** be old hat, not be original; ***el espectáculo es lo nunca ~*** the show is like nothing I have ever seen in my life; ***~ y no ~*** in a flash **2** *en locuciones*: ***está ~ que*** it's obvious

that; ***por lo ~*** apparently **3**: ***~ que*** seeing that
III *m* check (mark), *Br* tick; ***dar el ~ bueno*** give one's approval
vistosidad *f* visual appeal
vistoso *adj* eye-catching
visual I *adj* visual **II** *f* line of sight
visualización *f* **1** visualization **2** *en pantalla* display
visualizar ⟨1f⟩ *v/t* **1** visualize **2** *en pantalla* display
vital *adj* **1** vital **2** *persona* lively
vitalicio *adj* life *atr*, for life; ***renta -a*** life annuity
vitalidad *f* vitality, liveliness
vitalizar ⟨1f⟩ *v/t* revitalize
vitamina *f* vitamin
vitaminado *adj* with added vitamins
vitamínico *adj* vitamin *atr*
vitícola *adj región, país* wine-growing *atr*
viticultor *m*, **~a** *f* wine grower
viticultura *f* wine growing
vitola *f* cigar band
vitorear ⟨1a⟩ *v/t* cheer
vítores *mpl* cheers, acclaim *sg*
vitoriano *adj* of / from Vitoria, Vitoria *atr*
vitral *m* stained glass window
vítreo *adj* vitreous
vitrificar ⟨1g⟩ *v/t* vitrify
vitrina *f* **1** *en museo* display cabinet **2** *L.Am. de tienda* shop window
vitriolo *m* vitriol
vitrocerámica *f* ceramic stove top, *Br* ceramic hob
vituallas *fpl* victuals, provisions
vituperable *adj* reprehensible
vituperar ⟨1a⟩ *v/t* condemn
vituperio *m* condemnation
viuda *f* widow
viudedad *f de mujer* widowhood; *de hombre* widowerhood; ***pensión de ~*** widow's pension
viudez *f de mujer* widowhood; *de hombre* widowerhood
viudo I *adj* widowed; ***quedarse ~*** be widowed **II** *m* widower
viva *interj* hurrah!; ***¡~ el rey!*** long live the king!
vivac *m* bivouac
vivacidad *f* liveliness, vivacity
vivales *m/f inv* F sharp operator
vivamente *adv desear* fervently; *recomendar* warmly; *describir* vividly; *interesado* deeply; ***lo siento ~*** I'm deeply sorry
vivaque *m* bivouac
vivaquear ⟨1a⟩ *v/i* bivouac
vivaracho *adj* lively
vivaz *adj* lively, vivacious
vivencia *f* experience
víveres *mpl* provisions
vivero *m para plantas* nursery; *para peces* hatchery; *para ostras, mejillones etc* bed
viveza *f* liveliness
vivido *adj persona* lively
vívido *adj* vivid
vividor *m*, **~a** *f* (*aprovechado*) freeloader
vivienda *f* **1** housing **2** (*casa*) house
◇ **vivienda de protección oficial** subsidized house / apartment
viviente *adj* living
vivificar ⟨1g⟩ *v/t* invigorate, energize
vivíparo *adj* ZO viviparous
vivir ⟨3a⟩ **I** *v/t* live through, experience **II** *v/i* live; ***~ de algo*** live on sth; ***no tienen con qué ~*** they don't have enough to live on; ***~ al día*** live from day to day; ***irse a ~ a*** go to live in; ***no dejar ~ a alguien*** *fig* not let s.o. breathe; ***¡~ para ver!*** who would have believed it!; ***¿quién vive?*** who goes there?; ***¡viva la república! - ¡viva!*** long live the republic! - hurrah! **III** *m* way of life
vivisección *f* vivisection
vivito: ***~ y coleando*** F alive and kicking
vivo I *adj* **1** alive; ***los seres ~*** living things; ***en ~*** *concierto* live **2** *fig* F sharp, smart **3** *color* bright **4** *ritmo* lively **II** *m*, **-a** *f* sharp operator
vizcaíno *adj* of / from Biscay, Biscay *atr*
Vizcaya *f* Biscay; ***Golfo de ~*** Bay of Biscay
vizconde *m* viscount
vizcondesa *f* viscountess
V.O., V.o. *abr* (= ***versión original***) original language version
vocablo *m* word
vocabulario *m* vocabulary
vocación *f* vocation; ***errar la ~*** get into the wrong line of work
vocacional *adj* vocational
vocal I *adj* vocal **II** *m/f* member **III** *f* vowel
vocalista *m/f* vocalist

vocalización *f* vocalization
vocalizar ⟨1f⟩ *v/i* vocalize
voceador *m*, **~a** *f Méx* newspaper vendor
vocear ⟨1a⟩ *v/t & v/i* shout (out)
vocerío *m* uproar
vocero *m*, **-a** *f esp L.Am.* spokesperson
voces *fpl* ☞ **voz**
vociferar ⟨1a⟩ *v/i* shout
vodka *m* vodka
vol. *abr* (= **volumen**) vol. (= volume)
voladizo ARQUI **I** *adj* projecting **II** *m* projection
volado I *adj* **1 estar ~** F (*colocado*) be high *o* stoned **2** TIP superior **II** *m* ☞ **voladizo**
volador I *adj* flying **II** *m* **1** (*cohete*) rocket **2** *pez* flying fish; *calamar*: *type of squid*
voladura *f* blowing up
volandas: **en ~** *fig* in the air
volante I *adj* flying **II** *m* **1** AUTO steering wheel; **ponerse al ~** take the wheel **2** *de vestido* flounce **3** MED referral (slip) **4** DEP shuttlecock
volantín *m Chi* kite
volar ⟨1m⟩ **I** *v/i* fly; *fig* vanish; **las horas pasaron volando** the hours flew past *o* by; **irse ~** rush off; **echarse a ~** fly away, fly off **II** *v/t* **1** fly **2** *edificio* blow up; **volarse** *v/r* **1** be blown away **2** *L.Am.* (*desaparecer*) disappear
volátil *adj tb fig* volatile
volatilizar ⟨1f⟩ *v/t* QUÍM volatilize; **volatilizarse** *v/r* QUÍM volatilize; *fig* vanish into thin air
volcán *m* volcano
volcánico *adj* volcanic; *fig*: *pasión* fiery
volcar ⟨1g & 1m⟩ **I** *v/t* **1** knock over **2** (*vaciar*) empty **3** *barco*, *coche* overturn **II** *v/i de coche*, *barco* overturn; **volcarse** *v/r* **1** tip over **2**: **~ por alguien** F bend over backward for s.o., go out of one's way for s.o.; **~ en algo** throw o.s. into sth
volea *f* DEP volley; **golpear de ~** volley
volear ⟨1a⟩ *v/t & v/i* DEP volley
voleibol *m* volleyball
voleo *m* **1**: **a ~** at random **2** AGR: **sembrar a ~** scatter seed
voley-playa *m* beach volleyball
volframio *m* QUÍM wolfram
volibol *m Méx* volleyball
volición *f* volition
volitivo *adj* volitional
volován *m* GASTR vol-au-vent
volquete *m* dump truck
vols. *abr* (= **volúmenes**) vols. (= volumes)
voltaje *m* EL voltage
voltear ⟨1a⟩ **I** *v/t* **1** *L.Am.* (*invertir*) turn over; **~ el jersey** turn the sweater inside out **2** *Rpl* (*tumbar*) knock over **3**: **~ la cabeza** turn one's head **II** *v/i* **1** roll over **2** *de campanas* ring out
voltereta *f* somersault; **dar una ~** do a somersault
voltímetro *m* EL voltmeter
voltio *m* **1** EL volt **2**: **darse un ~** *fig* F go for a stroll
volubilidad *f* erratic nature, unpredictability
voluble *adj* erratic, unpredictable
volumen *m* volume; **a todo ~** at full volume *o* blast; **en tres volúmenes** *diccionario* three-volume *atr*
◇ **volumen de negocios** COM turnover, volume of business
voluminoso *adj objeto*, *maleta* bulky; *vientre* ample; *historial* lengthy
voluntad *f* will; **buena / mala ~** good / ill will; **~ de hierro** *fig* iron will; **última ~** last wish; **por ~ propia** of one's own free will; **a ~** at will
voluntariado *m* **1** *actividad* voluntary work; (*voluntarios*) volunteers *pl* **2** MIL voluntary military service
voluntariedad *f* voluntariness, voluntary nature
voluntario I *adj* volunteer **II** *m*, **-a** *f* volunteer
voluntarioso *adj* willing, enthusiastic
voluptuosidad *f* voluptuousness
voluptuoso *adj* voluptuous
voluta *f* ARQUI scroll, volute
volver ⟨2h; *part* **vuelto**⟩ **I** *v/t* **1** *página*, *mirada etc* turn (**a** to; **hacia** toward); *tortilla*, *filete* turn (over); *vestido* turn inside outXXX; *boca abajo* turn upside down **2**: **~ loco** drive crazy; **el humo volvío negra la pared** the smoke turned the wall black, the smoke made the wall go black
II *v/i* **1** return, go / come back; **~ a casa** go / come back home; **¿cuándo vuelven?** when do they get back?; **~ sobre algo** return to sth, go back to sth; **~ a la normalidad** return to normality
2: **~ en sí** come to, come around

V

3: **~ *a hacer algo*** do sth again; **~ *a fumar*** start smoking again

volverse *v/r* **1** turn around; ***se volvió y me sonrió*** he turned around and smiled at me **2**: ***se volvió a preparar la cena*** he went *o* got back to fixing dinner **3**: **~ *contra alguien*** turn against s.o. **4**: **~ *loco*** go crazy

vomitar ⟨1a⟩ **I** *v/t* throw up; *lava* hurl, spew **II** *v/i* throw up, be sick; ***tengo ganas de*** **~** I feel nauseous, *Br* I feel sick

vomitivo *m* MED emetic

vómito *m* MED vomit

vomitona *f* F: ***tuvo una*** **~** she threw up all over the place F

voracidad *f* voracity; *de incendio* ferocity

vorágine *f* (*remolino*) whirlpool; *fig* whirl

voraz *adj* voracious; *incendio* fierce

vórtice *m* vortex

VOS *abr* (= ***versión original subtitulada***) original language version with subtitles

vos *pron pers sg Rpl, C.Am., Ven* you

vosear ⟨1a⟩ *v/t Rpl, C.Am., Ven* address as 'vos'

vosotros, vosotras *pron pers pl* you

votación *f* vote, ballot; **~ *a mano alzada*** show of hands

votante *m/f* voter

votar ⟨1a⟩ **I** *v/t* (*aprobar*) approve **II** *v/i* vote

voto *m* **1** POL vote **2**: **~*s*** *pl* REL vows **3**: ***hacemos*** **~*s por su recuperación*** *fml* we are hoping for his recovery

◇ **voto en blanco** spoiled ballot paper; **voto de calidad** casting vote, deciding vote; **voto de censura** vote of no confidence; **voto de confianza** vote of confidence; **voto por correo** absentee ballot; **voto nulo** spoiled ballot paper

voy *vb* ☞ ***ir***

voz *f* **1** voice; ***a media*** **~** in a hushed *o* low voice; ***a*** **~** ***en grito*** at the top of one's voice; ***en*** **~** ***alta*** aloud; ***en*** **~** ***baja*** in a low voice; ***levantar*** *o* ***alzar la*** **~** ***a alguien*** raise one's voice to s.o.; ***conocer a alguien en la*** **~** recognize s.o.'s voice; ***a una*** **~** with one voice, as one; ***quería contártelo de viva*** **~** he wanted to tell you in person; ***llevar la*** **~** ***cantante*** *fig* call the tune, call the shots; ***no tener*** **~** ***ni voto*** *fig* not have a say; ***tener*** **~** ***y voto*** POL have full voting rights; ***dar voces*** shout; ***estar pidiendo a voces algo*** be crying out for sth; ***hacer correr la*** **~** spread the word; ***a dos voces*** MÚS for two voices **2** *fig* rumor, *Br* rumour

◇ **voz activa** GRAM active voice; **voz de mando** MIL command; **voz en off** voice-over; **voz pasiva** GRAM passive voice

vozarrón *m* loud voice

vuelapluma: ***escribir unas líneas a*** **~** dash off a few lines

vuelco I *vb* ☞ ***volcar*** **II** *m* AUTO roll; MAR capsize; ***dar un*** **~** *fig* F take a dramatic turn; ***me dio un*** **~** ***el corazón*** my heart missed a beat

vuelo I *vb* ☞ ***volar*** **II** *m* **1** flight; ***en*** **~** in flight; ***cazar algo al*** **~** catch sth in midair; *fig* catch *o* latch on to sth quickly; ***de altos*** **~*s*** *boda, bautizo* big; *ceremonia* important; *restaurante* prestigious; *proyecto* big, prestigious **2**: ***una falda con*** **~** a full skirt

◇ **vuelo chárter** charter flight; **vuelo de conexión** connecting flight; **vuelo directo** direct flight; **vuelo sin escala** non-stop flight; **vuelo espacial** space flight; **vuelo internacional** international flight; **vuelo interplanetario** space flight; **vuelo de línea** scheduled flight; **vuelo sin motor** gliding; **vuelo nacional** domestic flight; **vuelo de reconocimiento** reconnaissance flight; **vuelo regular** scheduled flight; **vuelo a vela** gliding

vuelta *f* **1** (*regreso*) return; ***a la*** **~** on the way back; ***estar de*** **~** be back; ***estar de*** **~** ***de todo*** F have seen it all before; ***no tiene*** **~** ***atrás*** there is no turning back **2** (*devolución*): ***me dio de*** **~** ***tres dólares*** he gave me three dollars change **3** *en carrera* lap; ***dar la*** **~** ***a*** *llave etc* turn; ***dar media*** **~** turn round; ***dar una*** **~** ***de campana*** AUTO turn over; ***dar*** **~*s*** go to and fro; (*girar*) go around; ***la cabeza me da*** **~*s*** my head is spinning; ***dar*** **~** ***a una idea*** turn an idea over in one's mind; ***dar una*** **~** go for a walk; ***dar cien*** **~*s a alguien*** F be a hundred times better than s.o. F; ***poner a alguien de*** **~** ***y media*** F give s.o. a dressing-down **4**: ***a la*** **~** ***de la esquina*** *fig* just around the corner; ***a la*** **~** ***de pocos años*** a few

years later; ***buscarle las ~s a alguien*** F try to catch s.o. out; ***no tiene ~ de hoja*** there's no doubt about it
◇ **vuelta de carnero** *L.Am.* half-somersault
◇ **vuelta al mundo** round-the-world trip; ***dar la ~*** go around the world
vuelto I *part* ☞ ***volver*** **II** *m L.Am.* change
vuelvo *vb* ☞ ***volver***
vuestro I *adj pos* your **II** *pron* yours; ***¿es ~?*** is it yours?
vulcanizar ⟨1f⟩ *v/t* vulcanize
vulgar *adj* vulgar, common; *abundante* common
vulgaridad *f* vulgarity
vulgarizar ⟨1f⟩ *v/t* popularize; *desp* vulgarize
vulgarmente *adv* commonly, popularly; *desp* vulgarly
vulgo *m* lower classes *pl*, lower orders *pl*
vulnerabilidad *f* vulnerability
vulnerable *adj* vulnerable
vulnerar ⟨1a⟩ *v/t ley, norma* violate; *fig* damage, harm
vulva *f* vulva

W

w. *abr* (= ***watio***) w (= watt)
walkman *m* personal stereo, walkman®
wáter *m* bathroom, toilet
waterpolo *m* DEP water polo
WC *m abr* WC
western *m* western
whisky *m* whiskey, *Br* whisky
windsurf *m* **1** *tabla* sailboard, windsurfer **2** (*tb* ***~ing***) windsurfing; ***hacer ~*** go windsurfing
windsurfista *m/f* windsurfer
wolframio *m* QUÍM wolfram

X

xenofobia *f* xenophobia
xenófobo I *adj* xenophobic **II** *m*, **-a** *f* xenophobe
xilófago *adj* ZO wood-eating
xilófono *m* MÚS xylophone

Y

y *conj* and
ya *adv* **1** already; ***~ lo sé*** I know
2 (*ahora mismo*) now; ***~ viene*** she's coming now
3: ***¿lo puede hacer? - ¡~ lo creo!***; can she do it ? - you bet!; ***¡~!*** *incredulidad* oh, yeah!, sure!; *comprensión* I know, I understand; *asenso* OK, sure; *al terminar* finished!, done!; ***¡ah, ~!*** *al acordarse* oh, of course!
4 *en frases negativas*: ***~ no vive aquí*** he doesn't live here any more, he no longer lives here; ***~ no lo tengo*** I don't have it any more, I no longer have it
5: ***~ que*** since, as
6: ***~ … ~ …*** either … or …
yacaré *m L.Am.* ZO cayman
yacente *adj* reclining, recumbent
yacer ⟨2y⟩ *v/i* lie; ***aquí yace …*** here lies …
yachting *m* yachting
yacimiento *m* MIN deposit
yanqui *m/f & adj* F Yankee F
yantar ⟨1a⟩ *lit* **I** *v/i* eat **II** *m* food
yapa *f* **1** *L.Am.* bit extra (for free) **2** *Pe, Bol* (*propina*) tip
yarda *f medida* yard
yate *m* yacht

yatismo *m CSur* yachting
yaya *f* grandma
yayo *m* grandpa
yedra *f* BOT ivy
yegua *f* ZO mare
yeguada *f* herd of horses
yelmo *m* HIST helmet
yema *f* **1** yolk **2**: ~ ***del dedo*** fingertip
yemení, yemenita I *adj* Yemeni **II** *m/f* Yemeni
yendo *vb* ☞ ***ir***
yerba *f L.Am.* grass
◇ **yerba mate** maté
yerbal *m* maté plantation
yerbatero *m*, **-a** *f Rpl* herbalist
yerbear ⟨1a⟩ *v/i Rpl* drink maté
yerbero *m Méx* herbal healer
yergo *vb* ☞ ***erguir***
yermo I *adj* **1** *pueblo* uninhabited **2** *terreno* barren **II** *m* wasteland
yerno *m* son-in-law
yerro I *vb* ☞ ***errar*** **II** *m* error, mistake
yerto *adj* stiff, rigid; ~ ***de frío*** frozen stiff
yesca *f* tinder
yesera *f* plaster works *sg*
yesero *m*, **-a** *f* plasterer
yeso *m* plaster
yesoso *adj terreno* rich in gypsum
yeta *Rpl* F **I** *adj* jinxed **II** *m/f*: ***es un*** ~ he's jinxed, there's a jinx on him
yo *pron* I; ***soy*** ~ it's me; ~ ***que tú*** if I were you
yodado *adj* iodized
yodo *m* iodine
yoga *m* yoga
yogur *m* yog(h)urt
yogurtera *f* yog(h)urt maker
yonqui *m/f* F junkie F
yoquei, yóquey *m* ☞ ***jockey***
yoyó *m* yo-yo
yuca *f* BOT yucca
yudo *m* ☞ ***judo***
yugo *m* yoke; ***sacudir el*** ~ *fig* throw off the yoke
Yugoslavia *f* Yugoslavia
yugoslavo I *adj* Yugoslav(ian) **II** *m*, **-a** *f* Yugoslav(ian)
yugular I *adj* ANAT jugular; ***vena*** ~ jugular (vein) **II** ⟨1a⟩ *v/t* (*interrumpir bruscamente*): ~ ***algo*** cut sth short
yunque *m* anvil
yunta *f* yoke, team
yute *m* jute
yuxtaponer ⟨2r⟩ *v/t* juxtapose
yuxtaposición *f* juxtaposition
yuyo *m L.Am.* weed

Z

zacatal *m C.Am., Méx* pasture
zacate *m C.Am., Méx* fodder
zafarrancho *m*: ~ ***de combate*** call to action; ***¡~ de combate!*** action *o* battle stations!
zafarse ⟨1a⟩ *v/r* **1** get away (***de*** from) **2** (*soltarse*) come undone **3**: ~ ***de algo*** (*evitar*) get out of sth
zafio *adj* coarse
zafiro *m* sapphire
zafra *f C.Am., Cu, Méx* sugar-cane harvest
zaga *f*: ***a la*** ~ behind, in the rear; ***a la*** ~ ***del pelotón*** behind the pack; ***ir a la*** ~ bring up the rear; ***es perezoso y su hermano no le va a la*** ~ he's lazy and his brother isn't far behind
zagal *m* boy
zagala *f* girl
zaguán *m* hall(way)
zaguero *m*, **-a** *f* DEP back, defender
zahorí *m/f* dowser
zahúrda *f* **1** pigpen, *Br* pigsty **2** *vivienda* hovel
zaino, zaíno *adj caballo* chestnut; *res vacuna* black
zalamería *f* flattery, sweet talk
zalamero I *adj* **1** flattering **2** *empalagoso* syrupy, sugary **II** *m*, **-a** *f* flatterer, sweet talker
zamarra *f chaqueta* sheepskin jacket
zamba *f Arg* (*baile*) *Argentinian folk-dance*
Zambia *f* Zambia
zambiano I *adj* Zambian **II** *m*, **-a** *f* Zambian
zambo I *adj* knock-kneed, bandy-legged **II** *m*, **-a** *f L.Am. person of mixed black and Indian descent*
zambomba *f* MÚS *type of drum*

zambombazo *m* F **1** (*explosión*) bang, explosion **2**: ***me di un ~ contra la puerta*** I banged into the door
zambullida *f* dive
zambullir ⟨3h⟩ *v/t* plunge (***en*** into); **zambullirse** *v/r* dive (***en*** into); *fig* throw o.s. (***en*** into), immerse o.s. (***en*** in)
zamorano *adj* of / from Zamora, Zamora *atr*
zampabollos *m/f inv* F pig F, glutton F
zampar ⟨1a⟩ F *v/t* wolf down F; **zamparse** *v/r* wolf down F
zampón *m* F pig F, glutton F
zampoña *f* panpipes *pl*
zanahoria *f* carrot
zanca *f de ave* leg
zancada *f* stride; ***dar ~s*** stride; ***en dos ~s*** *fig* in a flash
zancadilla *f fig* obstacle; ***poner*** *o* ***echar la ~ a alguien*** trip s.o. up
zancadillear ⟨1a⟩ *v/t* trip up
zanco *m* stilt
zancudo I *adj* long-legged; ***aves -as*** *pl* waders **II** *m L.Am.* mosquito
zanfoña *f* MÚS hurdy-gurdy
zanganear ⟨1a⟩ *v/i* laze around
zángano *m* ZO drone; *fig* F lazybones *sg*
zanguango *L.Am.* F **I** *adj* lazy **II** *m* lazybones *sg*
zanja *f* ditch
zanjar ⟨1a⟩ *v/t fig* **1** *problemas* settle **2** *dificultades* overcome
zapa *f* (*pala*) spade
zapador *m* MIL sapper
zapallito *m Rpl* zucchini, *Br* courgette
zapallo *m CSur* zucchini, *Br* courgette; *calabaza* pumpkin
zapapico *m* pickax, *Br* pickaxe
zapata *f* TÉC brake shoe
zapateado *m Andalusian dance*
zapatear ⟨1a⟩ *v/i* tap one's feet
zapatería *f* shoe store, shoe shop
zapatero *m*, **-a** *f* shoemaker; ***~ a tus zapatos*** stick to what you know
◇ **zapatero remendón** shoe repairer
zapatiesta *f* F ☞ ***trapatiesta***
zapatilla *f* slipper; *de deporte* sneaker, *Br* trainer
Zapatista *m/f Méx*: *member or supporter of the Zapatista National Liberation Army*
zapato *m* shoe; ***no llegarle a alguien a la suela del ~*** F not be a patch on s.o.; ***sé dónde le aprieta el ~*** *fig* I know what his problem is
◇ **zapato de cordones** lace-up (shoe)
zapear ⟨1a⟩ *v/i* TV F channel-surf, *Br* channel-hop, *Br* zap
zapeo, zapping *m* TV F channel surfing, *Br* channel hopping, *Br* zapping
zapote *m árbol*, *fruta* sapodilla
Zaragoza *f* Saragossa
zaragozano *adj* of / from Zaragoza, Zaragoza *atr*
zarandajas *fpl* trifles; ***estas ~ de teatro*** this theater nonsense
zarandear ⟨1a⟩ *v/t* shake violently, buffet; ***~ a alguien*** *fig* give s.o. a hard time
zarandillo *m*: ***llevar a alguien como un ~*** F have s.o. running backward and forward
zarapito *m* ZO curlew
zarcillo *m* **1** earring **2** BOT tendril
zarco *adj esp ojos* pale-blue, light-blue
zarigüeya *f* ZO (o)possum
zarpa *f* paw; ***echar la ~ a algo*** F get one's hands on sth
zarpada *f* swipe
zarpar ⟨1a⟩ *v/i* MAR set sail (***para*** for)
zarpazo *m* swipe (with a paw); *fig* blow
zarrapastroso *adj* shabby
zarza *f* BOT bramble
zarzal *m* bramble patch
zarzamora *f* BOT blackberry
zarzaparrilla *f* BOT, *bebida* sarsaparilla
zarzo *m Col* attic
zarzuela *f* **1** MÚS *type of operetta* **2** GASTR *seafood casserole*
zas *int* splash!; *con la mano* thwack!
zascandil *m* F bum F, good-for-nothing
zascandilear ⟨1a⟩ *v/i* mess around
zeta *f* letter 'z'
zigzag *m* zigzag
zigzaguear ⟨1a⟩ *v/i* zigzag
Zimbabue *m* Zimbabwe
zimbabuo I *adj* Zimbabwean **II** *m*, **-a** *f* Zimbabwean
zinc *m* zinc
zipear ⟨1a⟩ *v/t* INFOR zip (up)
zíper *m C.Am.*, *Méx* zipper, *Br* zip
zipizape *m* F row, ruckus F
zócalo *m* **1** baseboard, *Br* skirting board **2** *Méx*: *plaza mayor* main square
zodical *adj*: ***signo ~*** sign of the zodiac, star sign
zodíaco, zodiaco *m* AST zodiac

zona *f* **1** area, zone **2** *en baloncesto*: *parte del campo* key; *violación* three-seconds violation
◇ **zona ajardinada** green space; **zona azul** meter zone; **zona catastrófica** disaster area; **zona euro** euro zone; **zona franca** duty-free zone; **zona de influencia** sphere of influence; **zona de libre cambio** free-trade area; **zona peatonal** pedestrian mall *o* area, *Br* pedestrian precinct; **zona residencial** residential area; **zona roja** *L.Am.* red light district; **zona de strike** *en béisbol* strike zone; **zona verde** green space
zoncería *f L.Am.* stupid thing
zonzo *adj L.Am.* stupid
zoo *m* zoo
zoología *f* zoology
zoológico I *adj* zoological; ***jardín*** *o* ***parque ~*** zoological garden, zoo **II** *m* zoo
zoólogo *m*, **-a** *f* zoologist
zoom *m* FOT zoom; ***usar el ~*** zoom in
zootecnia *f* animal husbandry
zopenco I *adj* stupid, idiotic **II** *m*, **-a** *f* F dummy F
zopilote *m L.Am.* ZO turkey buzzard
zoquete *m/f* F dimwit F
zorra *f* **1** ZO vixen **2** P whore P
zorrería *f* slyness, craftiness
zorrillo *m C.Am., Méx* skunk
zorrino *m Rpl* skunk
zorro I *adj* sly, crafty **II** *m* **1** ZO fox; *fig* old fox **2**: ***estar hecho unos ~s*** F be worn out
zorzal *m* ZO thrush
zote F **I** *adj* dim-witted, dumb F **II** *m/f* dimwit F
zozobra *f* **1** MAR overturning, capsizing; *de negocio* collapse **2** (*inquietud*) anxiety
zozobrar ⟨1a⟩ *v/i* **1** MAR overturn, capsize; *de negocio* go under **2** *fig* worry, be anxious
zueco *m* clog
zulo *m* hiding place
zumaque *m* BOT sumac(h)
zumba *f L.Am., Méx* (*paliza*) beating
zumbado *adj* F crazy
zumbador *m* buzzer
zumbar ⟨1a⟩ **I** *v/i* buzz; ***me zumban los oídos*** my ears are ringing; ***pasar zumbando*** shoot by, flash by; ***salir zumbando*** shoot off; *afuera* shoot out **II** *v/t golpe, bofetada* give; **zumbarse** *v/r Esp* P: ***~ de alguien*** make fun of s.o.
zumbido *m* buzzing; ***~ de oídos*** buzzing in one's ears
zumo *m* juice
zurcido *m de calcetines* darning; *de chaqueta, pantalones* patching
zurcir ⟨3b⟩ *v/t* **1** *calcetines* darn; *chaqueta, pantalones* patch **2**: ***¡que te zurzan!*** F get lost! F, go to hell! F
zurda *f* left hand; (*pie*) left foot
zurdo I *adj* left-handed **II** *m*, **-a** *f* left-hander
zurear ⟨1a⟩ *v/i* coo
zurra *f* TÉC tanning; *fig* F hiding F; ***dar una ~ a alguien*** beat s.o. up, give s.o. a beating *o* hiding
zurrapa *f* dregs *pl*; *del café* grounds *pl*
zurrar ⟨1a⟩ *v/t* TÉC tan; ***~ a alguien*** F tan s.o.'s hide F; **zurrarse** *v/r* P (*cascarse*) jerk off P
zurriagazo *m* lash, stroke
zurriburri *m* F ruckus F
zurrón *m* bag
zurrullo *m* **1** F *de lana* ball **2** P *excremento* piece of shit P, turd P
zutano *m*, **-a** *f* so-and-so; ***fulano, mengano y ~*** so-and-so and so-and-so

English-Spanish Dictionary
Vocabulario Inglés-Español

A

a [ə] *stressed* [eɪ] *art* un(a); ***an island*** una isla; ***$5 ~ ride*** 5 dólares por vuelta; ***he's ~ lawyer*** es abogado

A4 [eɪ'fɔːr] A4 *m*

a•back [ə'bæk] *adv*: ***taken ~*** desconcertado (***by*** por)

a•ban•don [ə'bændən] *v/t* abandonar

a•base [ə'beɪs] *v/t*: ***~ o.s.*** humillarse, postrarse

a•bashed [ə'bæʃt] *adj* avergonzado

a•bate [ə'beɪt] *v/i of storm, flood* amainar

ab•at•toir ['æbətwɑːr] matadero *m*

ab•bey ['æbɪ] abadía *f*

ab•bot ['æbət] abad *m*

ab•bre•vi•ate [ə'briːvɪeɪt] *v/t* abreviar

ab•bre•vi•a•tion [əbriːvɪ'eɪʃn] abreviatura *f*

ABC [eɪbiː'siː] abecedario *m*, abecé *m*; *fig* (*basics*) abecé *m*, nociones *fpl* básicas; ***the ~s*** el abecé *or* abecedario

ab•di•cate ['æbdɪkeɪt] *v/i* abdicar

ab•di•ca•tion [æbdɪ'keɪʃn] abdicación *f*

ab•do•men ['æbdəmən] abdomen *m*

ab•dom•i•nal [æb'dɑːmɪnl] *adj* abdominal

ab•duct [əb'dʌkt] *v/t* raptar, secuestrar

ab•duc•tion [əb'dʌkʃn] rapto *m*, secuestro *m*

ab•er•ra•tion [æbə'reɪʃn] aberración *f*

a•bet [ə'bet] *v/t* (*pret & pp* ***-ted***) LAW: ***aid and ~*** auxiliar

a•bey•ance [ə'beɪəns]: ***fall into ~*** caer en desuso; ***be in ~*** estar en suspenso

ab•hor [əb'hɔːr] *v/t* (*pret & pp* ***-red***) aborrecer

ab•hor•rence [əb'hɔːrəns] aborrecimiento *m* (***of*** de), antipatía *f* (***of*** por)

ab•hor•rent [əb'hɔːrənt] *adj crime, attitude* aborrecible, vergonzoso; ***be ~ to s.o.*** aborrecer a alguien

a•bide [ə'baɪd] *v/t*: ***I cannot ~ him / it*** no lo aguanto *or* soporto

◆ **abide by** *v/t* atenerse a

a•bid•ing [ə'baɪdɪŋ] *adj* duradero, inextinguible

a•bil•i•ty [ə'bɪlətɪ] capacidad *f*, habilidad *f*; ***~ to pay*** recursos *mpl* económicos; ***to the best of one's ~*** *perform, play* lo mejor posible

ab•ject ['æbdʒekt] *adj* **1** *poverty, misery* extremo; *failure* absoluto, total **2** *apology* abyecto

a•blaze [ə'bleɪz] *adj* en llamas; ***be ~*** estar en llamas; ***be ~ with light*** resplandecer de la luz; ***his eyes were ~ with anger*** le chispeaban los ojos de la ira

a•ble ['eɪbl] *adj* (*skillful*) capaz, hábil; ***be ~ to*** poder; ***I wasn't ~ to see / hear*** no conseguí *or* pude ver / escuchar

a•ble-bod•ied [eɪbl'bɑːdiːd] *adj* sano

a•ble 'sea•man NAUT marinero *m* de primera

ab•ne•ga•tion [æbnɪ'geɪʃn] abnegación *f*

ab•nor•mal [æb'nɔːrml] *adj* anormal

ab•nor•mal•ly [æb'nɔːrməlɪ] *adv* anormalmente; *behave* de manera anormal

a•board [ə'bɔːrd] **I** *prep* a bordo de **II** *adv* a bordo; ***be ~*** estar a bordo; ***go ~*** subir a bordo

a•bode [ə'boʊd]: ***place of ~*** LAW domicilio *m*, residencia *f*; ***of or with no fixed ~*** sin domicilio *or* residencia permanente

a•bol•ish [ə'bɑːlɪʃ] *v/t* abolir

ab•o•li•tion [æbə'lɪʃn] abolición *f*

'A-bomb bomba *f* atómica

a•bom•i•na•ble [ə'bɑːmɪnəbl] *adj* abominable, horroroso

a•bom•i•na•ble 'snow•man abominable hombre *m* de las nieves

a•bom•i•na•tion [əbɑːmɪ'neɪʃn] **1** (*disgust*) abominación *f* (***of*** de), repugnancia *f* (***of*** hacia) **2** *detestable thing* abominación *f*, infamia *f*

Ab•o•rig•i•nal [æbə'rɪdʒənl] **I** *adj* aborigen **II** *n* aborigen *m/f*
Ab•o•rig•i•ne [æbə'rɪdʒənɪ] ☞ ***Aboriginal II***
a•bort [ə'bɔːrt] *v/t mission, launch* suspender, cancelar; COMPUT cancelar
a•bor•tion [ə'bɔːrʃn] aborto *m* (*provocado*); ***have an ~*** abortar
a•bor•tion•ist [ə'bɔːrʃənɪst] abortista *m/f*
a•bor•tive [ə'bɔːrtɪv] *adj* fallido
a•bound [ə'baʊnd] *v/i* abundar; ***~ in** or* ***with sth*** abundar en *or* de algo
a•bout [ə'baʊt] **I** *prep* (*concerning*) acerca de, sobre; ***what's it ~?*** *of book, movie* ¿de qué trata? **II** *adv* (*roughly*) más o menos; ***be ~ to do sth*** *be going to* estar a punto de hacer algo; ***I'm not ~ to sign that*** no tengo la más minima intención de firmar eso
a•bove [ə'bʌv] **I** *prep* por encima de; ***500m ~ sea level*** 500 m sobre el nivel del mar; ***~ all*** por encima de todo, sobre todo **II** *adv*: ***on the floor ~*** en el piso de arriba; ***all those aged 15 and ~*** todos aquellos mayores de 15 años
a•bove 'board *adj* lícito, claro
a•bove-men•tioned [əbʌv'menʃnd] **I** *adj* arriba mencionado **II** *n*: ***the ~*** el arriba mencionado
ab•ra•sion [ə'breɪʒn] abrasión *f*
ab•ra•sive [ə'breɪsɪv] *adj personality* abrasivo
a•breast [ə'brest] *adv* de frente, en fondo; ***three ~*** tres juntos, tres uno al lado del otro; ***they were marching six ~*** marchaban en columna de seis en fondo; ***keep ~ of*** mantenerse al tanto de; ***keep ~ of the times*** manterse al día
a•bridge [ə'brɪdʒ] *v/t* abreviar, condensar
a•broad [ə'brɒːd] *adv live* en el extranjero; *go* al extranjero; ***from ~*** de fuera, del extranjero
ab•ro•gate ['æbrəgeɪt] *v/t fml* revocar, anular
a•brupt [ə'brʌpt] *adj* **1** *departure* brusco, repentino; ***come to an ~ halt*** parar bruscamente **2** *manner* brusco, rudo
a•brupt•ly [ə'brʌptlɪ] *adv* **1** (*suddenly*) repentinamente **2** (*curtly*) bruscamente
ABS [eɪbiː'es] *abbr* (= ***antilock braking system***) ABS *m* (= sistema *m* de frenos antibloqueo)
ab•scess ['æbsɪs] absceso *m*
ab•scond [əb'skɑːnd] *v/i* fugarse, evadirse (***from*** de)
ab•seil ['æbsaɪl] *v/i*: ***~ down a cliff*** bajar en rappel por un precipicio
ab•sence ['æbsəns] *of person* ausencia *f*; (*lack*) falta *f*; ***in the ~ of the President*** en ausencia del presidente; ***in the ~ of wine …*** a falta de vino …
ab•sent ['æbsənt] *adj* ausente
ab•sent [æb'sent] *v/t*: ***~ o.s.*** ausentarse, marcharse (***from*** de)
ab•sen•tee [æbsən'tiː] ausente *m/f*
ab•sen•tee 'bal•lot voto *m* por correo
ab•sen•tee•ism [æbsən'tiːɪzm] absentismo *m*
ab•sen•tee 'land•lord propietario *m* absentista
ab•sen•tee 'vot•er votante *m/f* ausente
ab•sent-'mind•ed *adj* distraído
ab•sent-mind•ed•ly [æbsənt'maɪndɪdlɪ] *adv* distraídamente
ab•sent-mind•ed•ness [æbsənt'maɪndɪdnɪs] descuido *m*, olvido *m*
ab•so•lute ['æbsəluːt] *adj power* absoluto; *idiot* completo; *mess* total
ab•so•lute•ly ['æbsəluːtlɪ] *adv* (*completely*) absolutamente, completamente; ***~ not!*** ¡en absoluto!; ***do you agree? – ~*** ¿estás de acuerdo? - ¡completamente!
ab•so•lu•tion [æbsə'luːʃn] REL absolución *f*
ab•solve [əb'zɑːlv] *v/t* absolver
ab•sorb [əb'sɔːrb] *v/t* absorber; ***~ed in*** absorto en
ab•sorb•en•cy [əb'sɔːrbənsɪ] absorbencia *f*
ab•sorb•ent [əb'sɔːrbənt] *adj* absorbente
ab•sorb•ent 'cot•ton algodón *m* hidrófilo
ab•sorb•ing [əb'sɔːrbɪŋ] *adj* absorbente
ab•stain [əb'steɪn] *v/i from voting* abstenerse
ab•ste•mi•ous [əb'stiːmɪəs] *adj* abstemio
ab•sten•tion [əb'stenʃn] *in voting* abstención *f*
ab•sti•nence ['æbstɪnəns] abstinencia *f*
ab•stract ['æbstrækt] *adj* abstracto
ab•strac•tion [æb'strækʃn] abstracción *f*

ab•struse [əb'struːs] *adj* abstruso
ab•surd [əb'sɜːrd] *adj* absurdo
ab•surd•i•ty [əb'sɜːrdətɪ] lo absurdo
a•bun•dance [ə'bʌndəns] abundancia *f*
a•bun•dant [ə'bʌndənt] *adj* abundante
a•buse[1] [ə'bjuːs] *n* **1** (*insults*) insultos *mpl* **2** *of thing* maltrato *m*; (**child**) ~ *physical* malos tratos *mpl* a menores; *sexual* agresión *f* sexual a menores; **drug and alcohol ~** consumo *m* de alcohol y drogas; **~ of power** abuso *m* de poder
a•buse[2] [ə'bjuːz] *v/t* **1** *physically* abusar de **2** *verbally* insultar
a•bu•sive [ə'bjuːsɪv] *adj language* insultante, injurioso; **he became ~ toward me** se puso a insultarme
a•bys•mal [ə'bɪʒml] *adj* F (*very bad*) desastroso F
a•byss [ə'bɪs] abismo *m*
AC ['eɪsiː] *abbr* (= **alternating current**) CA (= corriente *f* alterna)
a/c, A/C *abbr* (= **account**) cuenta *f*
a•ca•cia [ə'keɪʃə] BOT acacia *f*
ac•a•de•mi•a [ækə'diːmɪə] ámbito *m* académico
ac•a•dem•ic [ækə'demɪk] **I** *n* académico(-a) *m(f)*, profesor(a) *m(f)* **II** *adj* académico; **the exact reason is ~ now anyway** la razón exacta no tiene ya ninguna trascendencia
ac•a•dem•ic 'free•dom libertad *f* de cátedra
ac•a•dem•ic 'year año *m* escolar; *at university* año *m* académico
a•cad•e•my [ə'kædəmɪ] academia *f*
A•cad•e•my A'wards (cer•e•mo•ny) ceremonia *f* de los Oscar
ac•cel•e•rate [ək'seləreɪt] *v/t & v/i* acelerar
◆ **accelerate away** *v/i*: **he accelerated away** dio un acelerón y se marchó
ac•cel•e•ra•tion [əkselə'reɪʃn] aceleración *f*
ac•cel•e•ra•tor [ək'seləreɪtər] *of car* acelerador *m*
ac•cent ['æksənt] **1** *when speaking* acento *m* **2** (*emphasis*) énfasis *m*; **put the ~ on sth** poner énfasis en algo
ac•cen•tu•ate [ək'sentjuːeɪt] *v/t* acentuar
ac•cen•tu•a•tion [əksentjuː'eɪʃn] acentuación *f*
ac•cept [ək'sept] *v/t & v/i* aceptar
ac•cept•a•ble [ək'septəbl] *adj* aceptable
ac•cept•ance [ək'septəns] aceptación *f*; **gain ~** encontrar *or* tener aceptación
ac'cept•ance speech discurso *m* de envestidura
ac•cept•ed [ək'septɪd] *adj* corriente, generalizado
ac•cess ['ækses] **I** *n* acceso *m*; **have ~ to** *computer* tener acceso a; *child* tener derecho a visitar **II** *v/t also* COMPUT acceder a
'ac•cess code COMPUT código *m* de acceso
ac•ces•si•ble [ək'sesəbl] *adj* accesible
ac•ces•sion [ək'seʃn] acceso *m*
ac•ces•so•ry [ək'sesərɪ] **1** *for wearing* accesorio *m*, complemento *m* **2** LAW cómplice *m/f*
'ac•cess road carretera *f* de acceso
'ac•cess time COMPUT tiempo *m* de acceso
ac•ci•dent ['æksɪdənt] accidente *m*; **by ~** por casualidad; **it is no ~ that ...** no es una casualidad *or* coincidencia que ...; **~ report** parte *m* de incidentes
ac•ci•den•tal [æksɪ'dentl] *adj* accidental
ac•ci•den•tal•ly [æksɪ'dentlɪ] *adv* sin querer
ac•ci•dent 'black•spot punto *m* negro
'ac•ci•dent in•sur•ance seguro *m* de accidentes
'ac•ci•dent-prone *adj* patoso, con tendencia a sufrir accidentes
ac•claim [ə'kleɪm] **I** *n* alabanza *f*, aclamación *f*; **meet with ~** ser alabado *or* aclamado **II** *v/t* alabar, aclamar
ac•cla•ma•tion [əklə'meɪʃn] aclamación *f*
ac•cli•mate, ac•cli•ma•tize [ə'klaɪmət, ə'klaɪmətaɪz] *v/t* aclimatarse
ac•cli•ma•ti•za•tion [əklaɪmətaɪ'zeɪʃn] aclimatación *f*
ac•com•mo•date [ə'kɑːmədeɪt] *v/t* **1** (*have space for*) alojar **2** *requirements* satisfacer, hacer frente a
ac•com•mo•dat•ing [ə'kɑːmədeɪtɪŋ] *adj* considerado, benévolo
ac•com•mo•da•tion [əkɑːmə'deɪʃn] *Br* ☞ **accommodations**
ac•com•mo•da•tions [əkɑːmə'deɪʃnz] *npl* alojamiento *m*
ac•com•pa•ni•ment [ə'kʌmpənɪmənt]

MUS acompañamiento *m*

ac•com•pa•nist [ə'kʌmpənɪst] MUS acompañante *m/f*

ac•com•pa•ny [ə'kʌmpənɪ] *v/t* (*pret & pp* ***-ied***) *also* MUS acompañar

ac•com•plice [ə'kʌmplɪs] cómplice *m/f*

ac•com•plish [ə'kʌmplɪʃ] *v/t* **1** *task* realizar **2** *goal* conseguir, lograr

ac•com•plished [ə'kʌmplɪʃt] *adj* consumado

ac•com•plish•ment [ə'kʌmplɪʃmənt] **1** *of a task* realización *f* **2** (*talent*) habilidad *f*, (*achievement*) logro *m*

ac•cord [ə'kɔːrd] acuerdo *m*; ***of one's own ~*** de motu propio; ***be in ~ with*** estar de acuerdo con

ac•cord•ance [ə'kɔːrdəns]: ***in ~ with*** de acuerdo con

ac•cord•ing [ə'kɔːrdɪŋ] *adv*: ***~ to*** según

ac•cord•ing•ly [ə'kɔːrdɪŋlɪ] *adv* **1** (*consequently*) por consiguiente **2** (*appropriately*) como corresponde

ac•cor•di•on [ə'kɔːrdɪən] acordeón *m*

ac•cor•di•on•ist [ə'kɔːrdɪənɪst] acordeonista *m/f*

ac•cost [ə'kɑːst] *v/t* abordar

ac•count [ə'kaʊnt] **1** *financial* cuenta *f*; ***settle an ~ with s.o.*** *fig* ajustar cuentas con alguien
2 (*report*, *description*) relato *m*, descripción *f*; ***give an ~ of*** relatar, describir; ***by all ~s*** por lo que dicen todos; ***bring*** *or* ***call s.o. to ~*** hacer que alguien dé explicaciones
3: ***on no ~*** de ninguna manera, bajo ningún concepto; ***on ~ of*** a causa de; ***take sth into ~, take ~ of sth*** tener algo en cuenta, tener en cuenta algo
4 (*customer*) cuenta *f*, cliente *m*

◆ **account for** *v/t* **1** (*explain*) explicar; ***there's no accounting for tastes*** sobre gustos no hay nada escrito **2** (*make up*, *constitute*) suponer, constituir;

ac•count•a•bil•i•ty [əkaʊntə'bɪlətɪ] responsabilidad *f*

ac•count•a•ble [ə'kaʊntəbl] *adj* responsable (***to*** ante); ***be held ~*** ser considerado responsable

ac•count•an•cy [ə'kaʊntənsɪ] contabilidad *f*

ac•count•ant [ə'kaʊntənt] contable *m/f*, *L.Am.* contador(a) *m(f)*

ac'count di•rec•tor director(a) *m(f)* de cuentas

ac'count hold•er titular *m/f* de una cuenta

ac•count•ing [ə'kaʊntɪŋ] contabilidad *f*

ac'count•ing pe•ri•od periodo *m* contable

ac'count num•ber número *m* de cuenta

ac•counts [ə'kaʊnts] *npl* contabilidad *f*

ac'counts de•part•ment (sección *f* de) contabilidad *f*

ac'counts soft•ware software *m* de contabilidad

ac•cred•it [ə'kredɪt] *v/t ambassador*, *official* acreditar

ac•crue [ə'kruː] *v/i of interest* acumularse; ***the benefits will ~ to everyone in the community*** *fml* todos los ciudadanos se beneficiarán

ac•cu•mu•late [ə'kjuːmjʊleɪt] **I** *v/t* acumular **II** *v/i* acumularse

ac•cu•mu•la•tion [əkjuːmjʊ'leɪʃn] acumulación *f*

ac•cu•mu•la•tor [ə'kjuːmjʊleɪtər] ELEC acumulador *m*

ac•cu•ra•cy ['ækjʊrəsɪ] precisión *f*

ac•cu•rate ['ækjʊrət] *adj* preciso

ac•cu•rate•ly ['ækjʊrətlɪ] *adv* con precisión

ac•cu•sa•tion [ækjuː'zeɪʃn] acusación *f*

ac•cu•sa•tive [ə'kjuːzətɪv] LING **I** *n* acusativo *m* **II** *adj* acusativo

ac•cuse [ə'kjuːz] *v/t*: ***~ s.o. of sth*** acusar a alguien de algo; ***~ s.o. of doing sth*** acusar a alguien de hacer algo; ***be ~d of*** LAW ser acusado de; ***look, I'm not accusing you of anything*** yo no te estoy acusando de nada

ac•cused [ə'kjuːzd] *n* LAW acusado(-a) *m(f)*

ac•cus•ing [ə'kjuːzɪŋ] *adj* acusador

ac•cus•ing•ly [ə'kjuːzɪŋlɪ] *adv say* en tono acusador; ***he looked at me ~*** me lanzó una mirada acusadora

ac•cus•tom [ə'kʌstəm] *v/t* acostumbrar; ***get ~ed to*** acostumbrarse a; ***be ~ed to*** estar acostumbrado a

ace [eɪs] **I** *n in cards* as *m*; (*in tennis*: *shot*) ace *m*; ***the ~ of spades*** el as de espadas; ***have an ~ up one's sleeve*** *fig* tener un as escondido en la manga **II** *adj*: ***an ~ reporter*** un as como reportero

ac•e•tate ['æsɪteɪt] CHEM acetato *m*

a•ce•tic ac•id [əsiːtɪk'æsɪd] ácido *m* acético

a•cet•y•lene [ə'setɪli:n] acetileno *m*
ache [eɪk] **I** *n* dolor *m*; **~s and pains** achaques *mpl* **II** *v/i* doler
a•chieve [ə'ʧi:v] *v/t* conseguir, lograr
a•chieve•ment [ə'ʧi:vmənt] **1** *of ambition* consecución *f*, logro *m* **2** (*thing achieved*) logro *m*; **that's quite an ~** eso es todo un logro *or* una proeza
a•chiev•er [ə'ʧi:vər] *persona que tiene éxito y llega lejos en cualquier actividad*
A•chil•les heel [əkɪli:z'hi:l] *fig* talón *m* de Aquiles
A•chil•les 'ten•don ANAT tendón *m* de Aquiles
ac•id ['æsɪd] **I** *n* ácido *m* **II** *adj taste, comments* ácido
a•cid•i•ty [ə'sɪdətɪ] acidez *f*; *fig* sarcasmo *m*
ac•id 'rain lluvia *f* ácida
'ac•id test *fig* prueba *f* de fuego
ac•knowl•edge [ək'nɑ:lɪdʒ] *v/t* reconocer; **~ having done sth** reconocer haber hecho algo; **~ receipt of a letter** acusar recibo de una carta
ac•knowl•edg(e)•ment [ək'nɑ:lɪdʒmənt] reconocimento *m*; *of a letter* acuse *m* de recibo; **in ~ of** en reconocimiento a
ac•me ['ækmɪ] *fig* súmmum *m*
ac•ne ['æknɪ] MED acné *m*, acne *m*
a•corn ['eɪkɔ:rn] BOT bellota *f*
a•cous•tic [ə'ku:stɪk] *adj* acústico; **~ guitar** guitarra *f* acústica
a•cous•tics [ə'ku:stɪks] *npl* acústica *f*
ac•quaint [ə'kweɪnt] *v/t fml*: **be ~ed with** conocer; **we are already ~ed** ya nos conocemos; **become ~ed with s.o.** llegar a conocer a alguien; **become ~ed with sth** familiarizarse con algo
ac•quaint•ance [ə'kweɪntəns] *person* conocido(-a) *m*(*f*); **make s.o.'s ~** conocer a alguien
ac•qui•esce [ækwɪ'es] *v/i fml* acceder
ac•qui•es•cence [ækwɪ'esns] *fml* aquiescencia *f*
ac•quire [ə'kwaɪr] *v/t* adquirir; **it's an ~d taste** es un gusto adquirido
ac•qui•si•tion [ækwɪ'zɪʃn] adquisición *f*
ac•quis•i•tive [æ'kwɪzətɪv] *adj person* afanoso; **the ~ society** la sociedad consumista
ac•quis•i•tive•ness [æ'kwɪzətɪvnɪs] avaricia *f*, afán *m*
ac•quit [ə'kwɪt] *v/t* (*pret & pp* **-ted**) **1** LAW absolver **2**: **~ o.s. well** defenderse bien
ac•quit•tal [ə'kwɪtl] LAW absolución *f*
a•cre ['eɪkər] acre *m* (*4.047m2*)
ac•ri•mo•ni•ous [ækrɪ'moʊnɪəs] *adj* áspero, agrio
ac•ri•mo•ny ['ækrɪmənɪ] acrimonia *f*
ac•ro•bat ['ækrəbæt] acróbata *m/f*
ac•ro•bat•ic [ækrə'bætɪk] *adj* acrobático
ac•ro•bat•ics [ækrə'bætɪks] *npl* acrobacias *fpl*
ac•ro•nym ['ækrənɪm] acrónimo *m*
a•cross [ə'krɑ:s] **I** *prep* al otro lado de; **she lives ~ the street** vive al otro lado de la calle; **sail ~ the Atlantic** cruzar el Atlántico navegando **II** *adv* de un lado a otro; **it's too far to swim ~** está demasiado lejos como para cruzar a nado; **once you're ~** cuando hayas llegado al otro lado; **10m ~** 10 m de ancho
a•cross-the-'board *adj* general, total
a•cryl•ic [ə'krɪlɪk] **I** *adj* acrílico **II** *n* acrílico *m*
act [ækt] **I** *v/i* **1** THEA actuar **2** (*pretend*) hacer teatro **3**: **~ as** actuar *or* hacer de **II** *v/t*: **~ the fool** hacer el tonto **III** *n* **1** (*deed*), *of play* acto *m*; **~ of God** caso *m* fortuito; **catch s.o. in the** (**very**) **~** pillar a alguien in fraganti (**of doing sth** haciendo algo) **2** *in vaudeville* número *m*; **put on an ~** fingir, hacer teatro; **it's just an ~** (*pretense*) es puro teatro; **get one's ~ together** F ponerse las pilas F **3** (*law*) ley *f*
◆ **act on** *v/t advice* seguir; *information* actuar sobre la base de
◆ **act up** *v/i* F *of child* hacer de las suyas F, dar guerra F; *of machine, equipment* andar mal
act•ing ['æktɪŋ] **I** *n in a play* interpretación *f*; *as profession* teatro *m* **II** *adj* (*temporary*) en funciones
ac•tion ['ækʃn] acción *f*; **out of ~** *machine* sin funcionar; *person* fuera de combate; **take ~** actuar; **bring an ~ against** LAW demandar a; **man of ~** hombre *m* de acción; **put a plan into ~** poner un plan en marcha *or* acción; **killed in ~** matado en combate
'ac•tion mov•ie película *f* de acción;
'ac•tion-packed *adj* ajetreado, lleno

de acción; **ac•tion 're•play** TV repetición *f* (de la jugada)
ac•ti•vate ['æktɪveɪt] *v/t* activar
ac•tive ['æktɪv] *adj also* GRAM activo; *party member* en activo
ac•tiv•ism ['æktɪvɪzəm] POL activismo *m*
ac•tiv•ist ['æktɪvɪst] POL activista *m/f*
ac•tiv•i•ty [æk'tɪvətɪ] actividad *f*
Act of 'Con•gress ley *f* del Congreso
ac•tor ['æktər] actor *m*
ac•tress ['æktrɪs] actriz *f*
ac•tu•al ['ækʧʊəl] *adj* verdadero, real
ac•tu•al•ly ['ækʧʊəlɪ] *adv* (*in fact, to tell the truth*) en realidad; ***did you ~ see her?*** ¿de verdad llegaste a verla?; ***he ~ did it!*** ¡aunque parezca mentira lo hizo!; **~, *I do know him*** (*stressing converse*) pues sí, de hecho lo conozco; **~, *it's not finished yet*** el caso es que todavía no está terminado
ac•tu•ar•y ['ækʧuːerɪ] actuario(-a) *m(f)*
a•cu•men ['ækjʊmən] acumen *m*, agudeza *f*, ***financial ~*** olfato *m* financiero
ac•u•punc•ture ['ækjəpʌŋkʧər] acupuntura *f*
a•cute [ə'kjuːt] **I** *adj pain* agudo; *sense* muy fino **II** *n accent* acento *m* agudo
a•cute•ly [ə'kjuːtlɪ] *adv* (*extremely*) extremadamente; **~ *aware*** plenamente consciente
ad [æd] ☞ ***advertisement***
AD [eɪ'diː] *abbr* (= ***Anno Domini***) dC, d. de C. (= después de Cristo)
Ad•am ['ædəm]: ***I don't know him from ~*** F no tengo ni repajolera idea de quién es F
ad•a•mant ['ædəmənt] *adj* firme
ad•a•mant•ly ['ædəməntlɪ] *adv* firmemente
Ad•am's 'ap•ple nuez *f*
a•dapt [ə'dæpt] **I** *v/t* adaptar **II** *v/i of person* adaptarse
a•dapt•a•bil•i•ty [ədæptə'bɪlətɪ] adaptabilidad *f*
a•dapt•a•ble [ə'dæptəbl] *adj* adaptable
a•dap•ta•tion [ædæp'teɪʃn] *of play etc* adaptación *f*
a•dapt•er [ə'dæptər] *electrical* adaptador *m*
add [æd] **I** *v/t* añadir; MATH sumar **II** *v/i* MATH sumar
◆ **add on** *v/t 15% etc* sumar
◆ **add to** *v/t* incrementar, agrandar
◆ **add up I** *v/t* sumar **II** *v/i fig* cuadrar; ***it just doesn't add up*** no tiene sentido, no cuadra
◆ **add up to** *v/t* (*amount to*) sumar; *fig* (*mean*) equivaler
add•ed ['ædɪd] *adj* añadido, adicional
add•ed 'val•ue valor *m* añadido *or L.Am.* agregado
ad•den•dum [ə'dendəm] (*pl* ***addenda*** [ə'dendə]) apéndice *m*
ad•der ['ædər] víbora *f*
ad•dict ['ædɪkt] adicto(-a) *m(f)*; ***drug ~*** drogadicto(-a) *m(f)*; ***he's a terrible TV ~*** es un gran adicto a la televisión, es un teleadicto
ad•dic•ted [ə'dɪktɪd] *adj* adicto; ***be ~ to*** ser adicto a; ***you could easily get ~ to it*** eso podría crearte adicción facilmente
ad•dic•tion [ə'dɪkʃn] adicción *f*
ad•dic•tive [ə'dɪktɪv] *adj* adictivo
ad•di•tion [ə'dɪʃn] **1** MATH suma *f*; **~ *sign*** signo *m* más **2** *action: to list, company etc* incorporación *f*; *of new drive etc* instalación *f*; ***the latest ~ to the department / the family*** el nuevo miembro del departamento / de la familia **3**: ***in ~*** además; ***in ~ to*** además de
ad•di•tion•al [ə'dɪʃnl] *adj* adicional
ad•di•tive ['ædɪtɪv] aditivo *m*
add-on ['ædɑːn] extra *m*, accesorio *m*
ad•dress [ə'dres] **I** *n* dirección *f*, ***form of ~*** tratamiento *m* **II** *v/t letter* dirigir; *audience* dirigirse a; ***how do you ~ the judge?*** ¿qué tratamiento se le da al juez?
ad'dress book agenda *f* de direcciones
ad•dress•ee [ædre'siː] destinatario(-a) *m(f)*
ad'dress la•bel etiqueta *f* de dirección
ad•e•noids ['ædənɔɪdz] *npl* MED vegetaciones *fpl*
ad•ept ['ædept] *adj* experto; ***be ~ at*** ser un experto en
ad•e•qua•cy ['ædɪkwəsɪ] idoneidad *f*, suficiencia *f*
ad•e•quate ['ædɪkwət] *adj* suficiente; (*satisfactory*) aceptable; ***be ~ for*** ser suficiente *or* aceptable para
ad•e•quate•ly ['ædɪkwətlɪ] *adv* suficientemente; (*satisfactorily*) aceptablemente
ad•here [əd'hɪr] *v/i* adherirse
◆ **adhere to** *v/t surface* adherirse a;

rules cumplir
ad•her•ence [əd'hɪrəns] adhesión *f*, afiliación *f*
ad•her•ent [əd'hɪrənt] seguidor(a) *m(f)*
ad•he•sion [əd'hiːʒn] adherencia *f*
ad•he•sive [əd'hiːsɪv] adhesivo *m*
ad•he•sive 'plas•ter esparadrapo *m*
ad•he•sive 'tape cinta *f* adhesiva
ad hoc [æd'hɑːk] *adj* ad hoc, extraordinario; **~ committee** comité *m* extraordinario
ad in•fi•ni•tum [ædɪnfɪ'naɪtəm] *adv* infinitamente; ***and so on, ~*** y así hasta el infinito
ad•ja•cent [ə'dʒeɪsnt] *adj* adyacente
ad•jec•ti•val [ædʒɪk'taɪvl] *adj* adjetival
ad•jec•tive ['ædʒɪktɪv] adjetivo *m*
ad•join [ə'dʒɔɪn] *v/t* lindar con
ad•join•ing [ə'dʒɔɪnɪŋ] *adj* contiguo; ***in the ~ room*** en la habitación contigua *or* colindante
ad•journ [ə'dʒɜːrn] *v/i of court, meeting* aplazarse; ***let's ~ until tomorrow morning*** aplacémoslo hasta *or* dejémoslo para mañana por la mañana
ad•journ•ment [ə'dʒɜːrnmənt] aplazamiento *m*
ad•junct ['ædʒʌŋkt] adjunción *f*, agregación *f* (***to*** a)
ad•just [ə'dʒʌst] *v/t* ajustar, regular
ad•just•a•ble [ə'dʒʌstəbl] *adj* ajustable, regulable
ad•just•ment [ə'dʒʌstmənt] ajuste *m*; *psychological* adaptación *f*
ad•ju•tant ['ædʒʊtənt] MIL *oficial ayudante*
ad lib [æd'lɪb] **I** *adj* improvisado **II** *adv* improvisadamente **III** *v/i* (*pret & pp* ***-bed***) improvisar
ad•min ['ædmɪn] F administración *f*; *paperwork* papeleo *m* F
ad•min•is•ter [əd'mɪnɪstər] *v/t* administrar
ad•min•is•tra•tion [ədmɪnɪ'streɪʃn] administración *f*
ad•min•is•tra•tive [ədmɪnɪ'strətɪv] *adj* administrativo
ad•min•is•tra•tor [əd'mɪnɪstreɪtər] administrador(a) *m(f)*
ad•mi•ra•ble ['ædmərəbl] *adj* admirable
ad•mi•ra•bly ['ædmərəblɪ] *adv* admirablemente
ad•mi•ral ['ædmərəl] almirante *m*
ad•mi•ra•tion [ædmə'reɪʃn] admiración *f*; ***they were full of ~ for him*** sentían una gran adimiración por él
ad•mire [əd'maɪr] *v/t* admirar
ad•mir•er [əd'maɪrər] admirador(a) *m(f)*
ad•mir•ing [əd'maɪrɪŋ] *adj* de admiración
ad•mir•ing•ly [əd'maɪrɪŋlɪ] *adv* con admiración
ad•mis•si•ble [əd'mɪsəbl] *adj* admisible
ad•mis•sion [əd'mɪʃn] **1** (*confession*) confesión *f*; ***~ of guilt*** confesión de culpabilidad; ***by*** *or* ***on his own ~*** según sus propias palabras **2** *to a place* entrada *f*; *to organization* admisión *f*; *to hospital* ingreso *m*; ***~ free*** entrada gratis
ad'mis•sion fee entrada *f*
ad•mit [əd'mɪt] *v/t* (*pret & pp* ***-ted***) **1** *to a place* dejar entrar; *to school, organization* admitir; *to hospital* ingresar **2** (*confess*) confesar; ***~ doing sth / having done sth*** admitir *or* reconocer hacer algo / haber hecho algo **3** (*accept*) admitir
◆ **admit to** *v/t error* admitir, reconocer; ***she admitted to feeling guilty*** confesó sentirse culpable
ad•mit•tance [əd'mɪtəns] admisión *f*; ***no ~*** prohibido el paso
ad•mit•ted•ly [əd'mɪtedlɪ] *adv*: ***he didn't use those exact words, ~*** es verdad que no utilizó exactamente esas palabras
ad•mon•ish [əd'mɑːnɪʃ] *v/t fml* reprender
ad•mo•ni•tion [ædmɑː'nɪʃn] *fml* admonición *f fml*
ad nau•se•am [æd'nɔːzɪæm] *adv* hasta la saciedad
a•do [ə'duː]: ***without further ~*** sin más dilación
a•do•be house [ə'doubeɪ] casa *f* de adobe
ad•o•les•cence [ædə'lesns] adolescencia *f*
ad•o•les•cent [ædə'lesnt] **I** *n* adolescente *m/f* **II** *adj* de adolescente
a•dopt [ə'dɑːpt] *v/t child, plan* adoptar; ***~ed country*** país *m* adoptivo
a•dop•tion [ə'dɑːpʃn] *of child* adopción *f*; ***give a child up for ~*** dar a un niño en adopción
a•dop•tive par•ents [ədɑːptɪv 'perənts] *npl* padres *mpl* adoptivos

a•dor•a•ble [ə'dɔːrəbl] *adj* encantador
ad•o•ra•tion [ædə'reɪʃn] adoración *f*
a•dore [ə'dɔːr] *v/t* adorar; ***I ~ chocolate*** me encanta el chocolate
a•dor•ing [ə'dɔːrɪŋ] *adj expression* lleno de adoración; ***his ~ fans*** sus entregados fans
a•dorn [ə'dɔːrn] *v/t* adornar
a•dorn•ment [ə'dɔːrnmənt] adorno *m*
ad•ren•al•in [ə'drenəlɪn] adrenalina *f*; ***it really gets the ~ going*** pone la adrenalina a cien
A•dri•at•ic [eɪdrɪ'ætɪk] mar *m* Adriático
a•drift [ə'drɪft] *adj* a la deriva; *fig* perdido; ***our plans came ~*** nos salieron mal los planes
a•droit [ə'drɔɪt] *adj* hábil (***at*** en)
a•droit•ness [ə'drɔɪtnɪs] habilidad *f*
ad•u•la•tion [ædʊ'leɪʃn] adulación *f*
a•dult ['ædʌlt] **I** *n* adulto(-a) *m(f)* **II** *adj* adulto
a•dult ed•u'ca•tion educación *f* para adultos
a•dul•ter•ate [ə'dʌltəreɪt] *v/t* adulterar
a•dul•ter•er [ə'dʌltərər] adúltero *m*
a•dul•ter•ess [ə'dʌltərəs] adúltera *f*
a•dul•ter•ous [ə'dʌltərəs] *adj relationship* adúltero
a•dul•ter•y [ə'dʌltərɪ] adulterio *m*
'a•dult film *euph* película *f* para adultos
ad•vance [əd'væns] **I** *n* **1** *money* adelanto *m* **2** *in science*, MIL avance *m*; ***make ~s*** (*progress*) avanzar, progresar; *sexually* insinuarse **3**: ***in ~*** con antelación; *get money* por adelantado; ***in ~ of*** con anterioridad a, antes de; ***48 hours in ~*** con 48 horas de antelación
II *v/i* MIL avanzar; (*make progress*) avanzar, progresar
III *v/t* **1** *sum of money* adelantar **2** *human knowledge, a cause* hacer avanzar **3** *theory* presentar
ad•vance 'book•ing reserva *f* (anticipada)
ad•vanced [əd'vænst] *adj country, level, learner* avanzado
ad'vance man POL relaciones públicas *m* de un partido político; **ad•vance 'no•tice** aviso *m* previo; **ad•vance 'pay•ment** pago *m* por adelantado
ad•van•tage [əd'væntɪdʒ] ventaja *f*; ***there's no ~ to be gained*** no se gana nada; ***it's to your ~*** te conviene; ***take ~ of*** aprovecharse de; ***have the ~*** tener ventaja (***over*** sobre); ***~ law*** or ***rule*** SP ley *f* de la ventaja
ad•van•ta•geous [ædvən'teɪdʒəs] *adj* ventajoso
Ad•vent ['ædvent] REL Adviento *m*
ad•vent ['ædvent] *fig* llegada *f*
'ad•vent cal•en•dar calendario *m* de Adviento
ad•ven•ture [əd'ventʃər] aventura *f*
ad•ven•tur•er [əd'ventʃərər] **1** aventurero(-a) *m(f)* **2** *rogue* granuja *m/f*
ad•ven•tur•ous [əd'ventʃərəs] *adj person* aventurero; *investment* arriesgado
ad•verb ['ædvɜːrb] adverbio *m*
ad•ver•bi•al [əd'vɜːrbjəl] *adj* adverbial
ad•ver•sa•ry ['ædvərserɪ] adversario(-a) *m(f)*
ad•verse ['ædvɜːrs] *adj* adverso
ad•ver•si•ty [əd'vɜːrsətɪ] adversidad *f*
ad•vert ['ædvɜːrt] ☞ ***advertisement***
ad•ver•tise ['ædvərtaɪz] **I** *v/t* anunciar **II** *v/i* anunciarse, poner un anuncio
ad•ver•tise•ment [ədvɜːr'taɪsmənt] anuncio *m*
ad•ver•tis•er ['ædvərtaɪzər] anunciante *m/f*
ad•ver•tis•ing ['ædvərtaɪzɪŋ] publicidad *f*
'ad•ver•tis•ing a•gen•cy agencia *f* de publicidad; **'ad•ver•tis•ing budg•et** presupuesto *m* para publicidad; **'ad•ver•tis•ing cam•paign** campaña *f* publicitaria; **'ad•ver•tis•ing rev•e•nue** ingresos *mpl* por publicidad
ad•vice [əd'vaɪs] consejo *m*; ***he gave me some ~*** me dio un consejo; ***take s.o.'s ~*** seguir el consejo de alguien; ***take my ~ and ...*** hazme caso y ...; ***a piece*** or ***bit of ~*** un consejo; ***at*** or ***on s.o.'s ~*** por recomendación de alguien; ***seek medical / legal ~*** acudir a un médico / un abogado
ad•vis•a•ble [əd'vaɪzəbl] *adj* aconsejable
ad•vise [əd'vaɪz] *v/t person, caution* aconsejar; *government* asesorar; ***I ~ you to leave*** te aconsejo que te vayas; ***you would be well ~d to go*** es (muy) aconsejable que vayas
◆ **advise against** *v/t* desaconsejar
ad•vis•er, ad•vis•or [əd'vaɪzər] asesor(a) *m(f)*
ad•vi•so•ry [əd'vaɪzərɪ] *adj* asesor, consultivo; ***in an ~ capacity*** en calidad de

asesor
ad•vo•ca•cy ['ædvəkəsɪ] apoyo *m* (***of*** de)
ad•vo•cate ['ædvəkeɪt] *v/t* abogar por
ae•gis ['iːdʒɪs]: ***under the ~ of*** bajo los auspicios de
a•er•ate ['ereɪt] *v/t blood* oxigenar; *drink* gasificar
aer•i•al ['erɪəl] **I** *adj* aérea; ***~ game*** *in soccer* juego *m* aéreo **II** *n* antena *f*
aer•i•al 'pho•to•graph fotografía *f* aérea
aer•o•bics [e'roubɪks] *nsg* aerobic *m*
aer•o•drome ['erədroum] *Br* aeródromo *m*
aer•o•dy•nam•ic [eroudaɪ'næmɪk] *adj* aerodinámico
aer•o•foil ['eroufɔɪl] *on car* aleta *f*
aer•o•gram ['erəgræm] aerograma *m*
aer•o•nau•ti•cal [erou'nɒːtɪkl] *adj* aeronáutico
aer•o•plane ['erouplein] *Br* avión *m*
aer•o•sol ['erəsaːl] aerosol *m*
aer•o•space in•dus•try ['erəspeɪs] industria *f* aeroespacial
aes•thete *etc Br* ☞ ***esthete*** *etc*
a•far [ə'faːr] *adv*: ***from ~*** de lejos
af•fa•bil•i•ty [æfə'bɪlətɪ] afabilidad *f*, cortesía *f*
af•fa•ble ['æfəbl] *adj* afable
af•fair [ə'fer] **1** (*matter, business*) asunto *m*; ***foreign ~s*** asuntos *mpl* exteriores **2** (*love ~*) aventura *f*, lío *m*; ***have an ~ with*** tener una aventura *or* un lío con
af•fect [ə'fekt] *v/t also* MED afectar; ***be deeply ~ed by sth*** estar muy afectado por algo
af•fec•tion [ə'fekʃn] afecto *m*, cariño; ***win s.o.'s ~s*** ganarse el cariño de alguien
af•fec•tion•ate [ə'fekʃnət] *adj* afectuoso, cariñoso
af•fec•tion•ate•ly [ə'fekʃnətlɪ] *adv* con afecto, cariñosamente
af•fi•da•vit [æfə'deɪvɪt] LAW declaración *f* jurada
af•fil•i•ate [ə'fɪlɪeɪt] **I** *v/t*: ***be ~d to*** *or* ***with*** estar afiliado a; ***~d company*** COM compañía *f* afiliada *or* asociada **II** *v/i* afiliarse (***with*** a)
af•fil•i•a•tion [əfɪlɪ'eɪʃn] **1** *membership* afiliación *f* **2** *fig: belief* afiliación *f*, ideología *f*
af•fin•i•ty [ə'fɪnətɪ] afinidad *f*
af•firm [ə'fɜːrm] *v/t* afirmar, asegurar
af•fir•ma•tion [æfər'meɪʃn] afirmación *f*
af•fir•ma•tive [ə'fɜːrmətɪv] **I** *adj* afirmativo **II** *n*: ***answer in the ~*** responder afirmativamente
af•fix *v/t* [ə'fɪks] *notice* adherir (***to*** a); *signature* estampar (***to*** en)
af•flict [ə'flɪkt] *v/t* afectar; ***be ~ed with sth*** padecer de algo
af•flic•tion [ə'flɪkʃn] afección *f*, ***the ~s of old age*** los achaques de la vejez
af•flu•ence ['æfluəns] prosperidad *f*, riqueza *f*
af•flu•ent ['æfluənt] *adj* próspero, acomodado; ***~ society*** sociedad *f* opulenta
af•ford [ə'fɔːrd] *v/t* permitirse; ***be able to ~ sth*** *financially* poder permitirse algo; ***I can't ~ the time*** no tengo tiempo
af•ford•a•ble [ə'fɔːrdəbl] *adj* asequible
af•for•est [æ'faːrɪst] *v/t* reforestar
af•for•est•a•tion [æfaːrɪ'steɪʃn] reforestación *f*
af•front [ə'frʌnt] **I** *v/t* ofender, insultar **II** *n* insulto *m*
Af•ghan ['æfgæn] **I** *adj* afgano **II** *n* afgano(-a) *m(f)*
Af•ghan•i•stan [æf'gænɪstæn] Afganistán *m*
a•fi•cio•na•do [əfɪsjə'naːdou] aficionado(-a) *m(f)*
a•field [ə'fiːld] *adv*: ***further ~*** a lo lejos, más allá
a•fire [ə'faɪər] *adj*: ***be ~ with enthusiasm*** refulgir de entusiasmo
a•float [ə'flout] *adj boat* a flote; ***keep the company ~*** mantener la compañía a flote
a•foot [ə'fut] *adv*: ***what's ~?*** ¿qué se está planeando?; ***there's something strange ~ here*** aquí se está cociendo algo raro
a•fore•men•tioned [əfɔːr'menʃənd] **I** *adj* ya mencionado **II** *n*: ***the ~*** el susodicho(-a) *m(f)*
a•fore•said [ə'fɔːrsed] *adj* ☞ ***aforementioned***
a•fore•thought [ə'fɔːrθɔːt] *adj* LAW: ***with malice ~*** con malicia premeditada
a•fraid [ə'freɪd] *adj*: ***be ~*** tener miedo; ***be ~ of*** tener miedo de; ***I'm ~ of cats*** tengo miedo a los gatos; ***he's ~ of the dark*** le da miedo la oscuridad; ***I'm ~ of annoying him*** me da miedo

enfadarle; ***I'm ~ expressing regret*** me temo; ***he's very ill, I'm ~*** me temo que está muy enfermo; ***I'm ~ so*** (me) temo que sí; ***I'm ~ not*** (me) temo que no
a•fresh [ə'freʃ] *adv* de nuevo
Af•ri•ca ['æfrɪkə] África *f*
Af•ri•can ['æfrɪkən] **I** *adj* africano **II** *n* africano(-a) *m(f)*
Af•ri•can-A'mer•i•can I *adj* afroamericano **II** *n* afroamericano(-a) *m(f)*
Af•ri•kaans [æfrɪ'kɑːns] afrikaans *m*
Af•ri•kan•er [æfrɪ'kɑːnər] afrikáner *m/f*
Af•ro-A•mer•i•can [æfrouə'merɪkən] **I** *adj* afroamericano **II** *n* afroamericano(-a) *m(f)*
Af•ro-Car'ib•be•an I *adj* afrocaribeño **II** *n* afrocaribeño(-a) *m(f)*
aft [æft] *adv* NAUT a popa, en popa
af•ter ['æftər] **I** *prep* después de; ***~ all*** después de todo; ***~ that*** después de eso; ***it's ten ~ two*** son las dos y diez **II** *adv* después; ***the day ~*** el día siguiente
'af•ter•birth MED placenta *f*; **'af•ter•care** MED posoperatorio *m*; **'af•ter•ef•fects** *npl* efectos *mpl* secundarios, consecuencias *fpl*; **'af•ter•glow** recuerdo *m* placentero; **'af•ter•life** vida *f* después de la muerte
af•ter•math ['æftərmæθ] *time* periodo *m* posterior (***of*** a); *state of affairs* repercusiones *fpl*
af•ter•noon [æftər'nuːn] tarde *f*; ***in the ~*** por la tarde; ***this ~*** esta tarde; ***good ~*** buenas tardes
af•ters ['ɑːftərz] *sg Br* F postre *m*
'af•ter sales serv•ice servicio *m* posventa; **'af•ter•shave** loción *f* para después del afeitado, after shave *m*; **'af•ter•shock** réplica *f*; **'af•ter-sun cream** crema *f* para después del sol, aftersun *m*; **'af•ter•taste** *also fig* regusto *m*; **'af•ter-thought**: ***do / say sth as an ~*** hacer / decir algo en el último momento; ***their last child was an ~*** su último hijo no fue buscado; **'af•ter•treat•ment** MED tratamiento *m* ulterior
af•ter•ward ['æftərwərd] *adv* después
a•gain [ə'geɪn] *adv* otra vez; ***do sth ~*** volver a hacer algo; ***I never saw him ~*** no lo volví a ver; ***~ and ~*** una y otra vez; ***now and ~*** de vez en cuando; ***but then ~, …*** pero por otro lado …
a•gainst [ə'genst] *prep lean* contra; ***the USA ~ Brazil*** SP Estados Unidos contra Brasil; ***I'm ~ the idea*** estoy en contra de la idea; ***what do you have ~ her?*** ¿que tienes en contra de ella?; ***~ the law*** ilegal
a•gape [ə'geɪp] *adv* con sorpresa *or* asombro
ag•ate ['ægət] MIN ágata *f*
age [eɪdʒ] **I** *n* **1** *of person, object* edad *f*; ***at the ~ of ten*** a los diez años; ***under ~*** menor de edad; ***she's five years of ~*** tiene cinco años; ***what ~ is he?*** ¿cuántos años tiene?, ¿qué edad tiene?; ***when I was your ~*** cuando tenía tu edad; ***act your ~!*** ¡no seas crío!; ***come of ~*** cumplir la mayoría de edad; ***under ~*** menor de edad; ***be over ~ for the race*** ser demasiado mayor para participar en la carrera; ***old ~*** vejez *f* **2** (*era*) era *f*
II *v/i & v/t* envejecer
'age brack•et grupo *m* de edad
aged[1] [eɪdʒd] *adj*: ***~ 16*** con 16 años de edad
a•ged[2] ['eɪdʒɪd] **I** *adj*: ***her ~ parents*** sus ancianos padres **II** *npl*: ***the ~*** los ancianos
'age group grupo *m* de edades
age•ism ['eɪdʒɪzəm] ageísmo *m*
age•ist ['eɪdʒɪst] *adj* ageista
'age lim•it límite *m* de edad
a•gen•cy ['eɪdʒənsɪ] agencia *f*
a•gen•da [ə'dʒendə] orden *m* del día; ***on the ~*** en el orden del día
a•gent ['eɪdʒənt] agente *m/f*, representante *m/f*
'age-old *adj* ancestral, inmemorial
'age range grupo *m* de edad
ag•glom•er•a•tion [əglɑːmə'reɪʃn] aglomeración *f*, amalgama *f*
ag•gra•vate ['ægrəveɪt] *v/t* **1** *worsen* agravar **2** F (*annoy*) molestar
ag•gra•vat•ing ['ægrəveɪtɪŋ] *adj* **1** *factor* agravante **2** F (*annoying*) fastidioso, desagradable
ag•gra•va•tion [ægrə'veɪʃn] **1** (*worsening*) agravamiento *m* **2** F (*annoyance*) fastidio *m*, molestia *f*
ag•gre•gate ['ægrɪgət] **I** *n* SP: ***win on ~*** ganar en el total de la eliminatoria **II** *adj* final, total
ag•gres•sion [ə'greʃn] agresividad *f*
ag•gres•sive [ə'gresɪv] *adj* agresivo; (*dynamic*) agresivo, enérgico

ag•gres•sive•ly [ə'gresɪvlɪ] *adv* agresivamente
ag•gres•sive•ness [ə'gresɪvnɪs] agresividad *f*
ag•gres•sor [ə'gresər] *esp* MIL atacante *m/f*
ag•grieved [ə'gri:vd] *adj* agraviado; ***feel ~ about sth*** estar agraviado por algo
a•ghast [ə'gæst] *adj* horrorizado
ag•ile ['ædʒəl] *adj* ágil
a•gil•i•ty [ə'dʒɪlətɪ] agilidad *f*
ag•i•tate ['ædʒɪteɪt] *v/i*: ***~ for*** hacer campaña a favor de
ag•i•tat•ed ['ædʒɪteɪtɪd] *adj* agitado
ag•i•ta•tion [ædʒɪ'teɪʃn] agitación *f*
ag•i•ta•tor [ædʒɪ'teɪtər] agitador(a) *m(f)*
AGM [eɪdʒi:'em] *abbr Br* (= ***annual general meeting***) consejo *m* general anual
ag•nos•tic [æg'nɑ:stɪk] agnóstico(-a) *m(f)*
a•go [ə'goʊ] *adv*: ***2 days ~*** hace dos días; ***long ~*** hace mucho tiempo; ***how long ~?*** ¿hace cuánto tiempo?; ***how long ~ did he leave?*** ¿hace cuánto se marchó?
a•gog [ə'gɑ:g] *adj*: ***be ~ at sth*** estar emocionado con algo
ag•o•nize ['ægənaɪz] *v/i* atormentarse (***over*** por), angustiarse (***over*** por)
ag•o•niz•ing ['ægənaɪzɪŋ] *adj pain* atroz; *wait* angustioso
ag•o•ny ['ægənɪ] agonía *f*; ***he was in ~*** se retorcía de dolor
'ag•o•ny aunt F *consejero sentimental en un periódico o una revista*
'ag•o•ny col•umn *sección de consultas sentimentales en un periódico o una revista*
ag•o•ra•pho•bi•a [ægərə'foʊbɪə] agorafobia *f*
a•grar•i•an [ə'grerɪən] *adj* agrario
a•gree [ə'gri:] **I** *v/i* estar de acuerdo; *of figures* coincidir; (*reach agreement*) ponerse de acuerdo; ***I ~*** estoy de acuerdo; ***it doesn't ~ with me*** *of food* no me sienta bien; ***as ~d*** según lo acordado **II** *v/t price* acordar; ***~ that something should be done*** acordar que hay que hacer algo; ***~ to differ*** dejar por imposible
◆ **agree on** *v/t* ponerse de acuerdo en
◆ **agree to** *v/t suggestion, decision* aceptar; ***I cannot agree to him doing that*** no puedo aceptar que haga eso
a•gree•a•ble [ə'gri:əbl] *adj* **1** (*pleasant*) agradable **2**: ***be ~*** *fml* (*in agreement*) estar de acuerdo
a•gree•a•bly [ə'gri:əblɪ] *adv*: ***I was ~ surprised*** me sorprendió positivamente
a•greed [ə'gri:d] *adj* acordado, establecido; ***we are ~ that …*** estamos de acuerdo en que …
a•gree•ment [ə'gri:mənt] (*consent, contract*) acuerdo *m*; ***reach ~ on*** llegar a un acuerdo sobre
ag•ri•busi•ness ['ægrɪbɪznɪs] industria *f* agroalimentaria
ag•ri•cul•tur•al [ægrɪ'kʌltʃərəl] *adj* agrícola
ag•ri•cul•ture ['ægrɪkʌltʃər] agricultura *f*
a•ground [ə'graʊnd] *adv* NAUT: ***run ~*** encallar
ah [ɑ:] *int* ¡ah!, ¡alá!
a•ha [ɑ:'hɑ:] *int* ¡ah!
a•head [ə'hed] *adv position* delante; *movement* adelante; *in race* por delante, en cabeza; ***be ~ of*** estar por delante de; ***be ~ of one's competitors*** ir por delante de la competencia; ***plan ~*** planear con antelación; ***think ~*** pensar con anticipación
a•hoy [ə'hɔɪ] *int* NAUT ¡hola!
AI [eɪ'aɪ] *abbr* (= ***artificial intelligence***) inteligencia *f* artificial
aid [eɪd] **I** *n* ayuda *f*; ***come to s.o.'s ~*** acudir a ayudar a alguien; ***with the ~ of*** con (la) ayuda de; ***in ~ of*** en ayuda a; ***what's all this in ~ of?*** F ¿para qué es eso? **II** *v/t* ayudar
'aid do•nor donante *m/f* de ayuda
aide [eɪd] asistente *m/f*
Aids [eɪdz] *nsg* sida *m*
ail•ing ['eɪlɪŋ] *adj economy* débil, frágil
ail•ment ['eɪlmənt] achaque *m*
aim [eɪm] **I** *n in shooting* puntería *f*; (*objective*) objetivo *m*; ***take ~*** apuntar (***at*** a), poner la mira (***at*** en) **II** *v/i in shooting* apuntar; ***~ at doing sth, ~ to do sth*** tener como intención hacer algo **III** *v/t remark* dirigir; ***he ~ed the gun at me*** me apuntó con la pistola; ***be ~ed at*** *of remark etc* estar dirigido a; *of gun* estar apuntando a

aim•less ['eɪmlɪs] *adj* sin objetivos

ain't [eɪnt] F ***are not, am not, is not, have not, has not***

air[1] [er] **I** *n* **1** aire *m*; ***by ~*** *travel* en avión; *send mail* por correo aéreo; ***in the open ~*** al aire libre; ***I need to get a bit of ~*** necesito tomar un poco el aire *or* el fresco; ***on the ~*** RAD, TV en el aire **2** aire *m*; ***an ~ of importance*** un aire de importancia; ***put on ~s, give o.s. ~s*** darse aires **II** *v/t room* airear; *fig*: *views* airear, ventilar

air[2] [er] *n* MUS aire *m*

'air•bag airbag *m*, bolsa *f* de aire; **'air•base** base *f* aérea; **'air•bed** *Br* colchón *m* hinchable

'air•borne *adj*: ***be ~*** estar volando; ***I didn't relax until we were ~*** no me relajé hasta que despegamos

air•borne 'ra•dar radar *m* de a bordo

'air•borne troops *npl* MIL fuerzas *fpl* aerotransportadas

'air brake freno *m* neumático; **'air•brush** pistola *f* de aire comprimido; **'air•bus** AVIA aerobús *m*; **'air car•go** cargamento *m* aéreo; **'air-con•di•tioned** *adj* con aire acondicionado, climatizado; **'air-con•di•tion•ing** aire *m* acondicionado; **air-cooled** ['erku:ld] *adj* refrigerado por aire; **'air•craft** avión *m*, aeronave *f*; **'air•craft car•ri•er** portaaviones *m inv*; **'air cyl•in•der** *for diver* escafandra *f* autónoma; **'air•drop** *of supplies* lanzamiento *m* desde el aire; **'air fare** (precio *m* del) *Span* billete *m or L.Am.* boleto *m* de avión; **'air•field** aeródromo *m*, campo *m* de aviación; **'air force** fuerza *f* aérea; **'air freight** transporte *m* aéreo; **air fresh•en•er** ['erfreʃnər] ambientador *m*; **'air gun** pistola *f* / rifle *m* de aire comprimido; **'air•head** F cabeza hueca *m/f*; **'air host•ess** azafata *f*, *L.Am.* aeromoza *f*

air•ing ['erɪŋ]: ***give sth an ~*** *room* ventilar algo; *idea* airear algo

'air lane ruta *f* aérea

air•less ['erləs] *adj* cargado, viciado

'air let•ter aerograma *m*; **'air•lift I** *n* puente *m* aéreo **II** *v/t* transportar mediante puente aéreo; **'air•line** línea *f* aérea; **'air•lin•er** avión *m* de pasajeros; **'air•mail**: ***by ~*** por correo aéreo; **'air mar•shal** *Br* mariscal *m* del aire; **'air mile** milla *f*; ***collect ~s*** juntar millas; **'air•plane** avión *m*; **'air•pock•et** bolsa *f* de aire; **'air pol•lu•tion** contaminación *f* del aire; **'air•port** aeropuerto *m*; **'air•port ho•tel** hotel *m* de aeropuerto; **'air•port lounge** sala *f* de aeropuerto; **'air•port tax** tasas *fpl* de aeropuerto; **'air pres•sure** presión *f* de aire; **'air pump** bomba *f* de aire; **'air raid** MIL ataque *m* aéreo; **'air raid shel•ter** refugio *m* durante ataques aéreos; **air 'res•cue serv•ice** servicio *m* de rescate aéreo; **'air•ship** dirigible *m*; **'air•show** exhibición *f* aérea; **'air•sick**: ***get ~*** marearse (*en avión*); **'air•sick•ness** mareo *m*; **'air•space** espacio *m* aéreo; **'air•speed** velocidad *f* relativa al aire; **'air•strip** pista *f* de aterrizaje; **'air ter•mi•nal** terminal *f* aérea; **'air•tight** *adj container* hermético; **'air•time** tiempo *m* en antena; **'air traf•fic** tráfico *m* aéreo; **air-traf•fic con'trol** control *m* del tráfico aéreo; **air-traf•fic con'trol•ler** controlador(a) *m(f)* del tráfico aéreo; **'air vent** orificio *m* de ventilación; **'air•waves** *npl* ondas *fpl*; **air way•bill** ['erweɪbɪl] COM conocimiento *m* de embarque aéreo; **'air•wor•thy** *adj* AVIA aeronavegable

air•y ['erɪ] *adj room* aireado

air•y-'fair•y *adj* F fantasioso, poco realista

aisle [aɪl] pasillo *m*

'aisle seat asiento *m* de pasillo

a•jar [ə'dʒɑ:r] *adj*: ***be ~*** estar entreabierto

aka [eɪkeɪ'eɪ] *abbr* (= ***also known as***) también conocido como

a•kim•bo [ə'kɪmboʊ] *adv*: ***with arms ~*** con los brazos en jarras

a•kin [ə'kɪn] *adj* similar, afín (***to*** a)

al•a•bas•ter ['æləbɑ:stər] alabastro *m*

a•lac•ri•ty [ə'lækrətɪ] presteza *f*

a•larm [ə'lɑ:rm] **I** *n* alarma *f*; ***raise the ~*** dar la alarma **II** *v/t* alarmar

a'larm call *in hotel* llamada *f* para despertar

a'larm clock reloj *m* despertador

a•larm•ing [ə'lɑ:rmɪŋ] *adj* alarmante

a•larm•ing•ly [ə'lɑ:rmɪŋlɪ] *adv* de forma alarmante

a•larm•ist [ə'lɑ:rmɪst] alarmista *m/f*

a•las [ə'læs] *int* desafortunadamente, desgraciadamente

A•las•ka [ə'læskə] Alaska *f*
A•las•kan [ə'læskən] **I** *adj* de Alaska **II** *n* habitante *m/f* de Alaska
Al•ba•ni•a [æl'beɪnjə] Albania *f*
Al•ba•ni•an [æl'beɪnjən] **I** *adj* albanés **II** *n* **1** *person* albanés(-esa) *m(f)* **2** *language* albanés *m*
al•ba•tross ['ælbətrɑːs] ORN albatros *m*
al•be•it [ɔːl'biːɪt] *conj* aunque
al•bi•no [æl'biːnoʊ] BIO albino(-a) *m(f)*
al•bum ['ælbəm] *for photographs*, (*record*) álbum *m*
al•bu•men ['ælbjʊmən] BIO albumen *m*
al•che•my ['ælkəmɪ] alquimia *f*
al•co•hol ['ælkəhɑːl] alcohol *m*
al•co•hol•ic [ælkə'hɑːlɪk] **I** *n* alcohólico(-a) *m(f)* **II** *adj* alcohólico
al•co•hol•ism ['ælkəhɑːlɪzm] alcoholismo *m*
al•cove ['ælkoʊv] celdilla *f*, nicho *m*
al•der ['ɔːldər] BOT aliso *m*
ale [eɪl] cerveza *f*
a•lert [ə'lɜːrt] **I** *n signal* alerta *f*; ***be on the ~*** estar alerta **II** *v/t* alertar; ***~ s.o. to sth*** alertar *or* avisar a alguien de algo **III** *adj* alerta; ***be ~ to*** estar alerta de
A-lev•el ['eɪlevl] *Br*: *examen que se realiza en el último curso del bachillerato a la edad de 18 años*
al•fal•fa [æl'fælfə] alfalfa *f*
al•fres•co [æl'freskoʊ] *adj & adv* al aire libre
al•ga ['ælgə] (*pl* ***algae*** ['ældʒiː]) alga *f*
al•ge•bra ['ældʒɪbrə] álgebra *f*
al•ge•bra•ic ['ældʒɪbreɪɪk] *adj* algebraico
Al•ge•ri•a [æl'dʒɪərɪə] Argelia *f*
Al•ge•ri•an [æl'dʒɪərɪən] **I** *adj* argelino **II** *n* argelino(-a) *m(f)*
al•go•rithm ['ælgərɪðm] MATH algoritmo *m*
a•li•as ['eɪlɪəs] **I** *n* seudónimo *m* **II** *adv* alias
al•i•bi ['ælɪbaɪ] coartada *f*
al•ien ['eɪlɪən] **I** *n* **1** (*foreigner*) extranjero(-a) *m(f)* **2** *from space* extraterrestre *m/f* **II** *adj* **1** extraño **2**: ***be ~ to s.o.*** ser ajeno a alguien
al•ien•ate ['eɪlɪəneɪt] *v/t* alienar, provocar el distanciamiento de
al•ien•a•tion [eɪlɪən'eɪʃn] alienación *f*
a•light[1] [ə'laɪt] *adj* en llamas; ***set sth ~*** prender fuego a algo
a•light[2] [ə'laɪt] *v/i* **1** *from car, train etc* apearse, bajarse (***from*** de) **2** *of bird, butterfly etc* posarse (***on*** en)
a•lign [ə'laɪn] *v/t* alinear
a•lign•ment [ə'laɪnmənt] *of wheels* alineación *f*; *of policies* alianza *f*; ***in ~ with*** en concordancia con
a•like [ə'laɪk] **I** *adj*: ***be ~*** parecerse **II** *adv* igual; ***old and young ~*** viejos y jóvenes sin distinción
al•i•men•ta•ry ca•nal [ælɪ'mentərɪ] aparato *m* digestivo
al•i•mo•ny ['ælɪmənɪ] pensión *f* alimenticia
a•live [ə'laɪv] *adj* **1**: ***be ~*** estar vivo; ***be burnt ~*** ser quemado vivo; ***~ and kicking*** F vivito y coleando F **2** *fig*: ***be ~ to*** estar al tanto de, ser consciente de; ***be ~ with*** estar plagado de **3** *in basketball* en juego
al•ka•li ['ælkəlaɪ] CHEM álcali *m*
al•ka•line ['ælkəlaɪn] *adj* alcalino
all [ɒːl] **I** *adj* todo(s)
II *pron* todo; ***~ of us / them*** todos nosotros / ellos; ***he ate ~ of it*** se lo comió todo; ***that's ~, thanks*** eso es todo, gracias; ***for ~ I care*** para lo que me importa; ***for ~ I know*** por lo que sé
III *adv*: ***~ at once*** (*suddenly*) de repente; (*at the same time*) a la vez; ***~ but*** (*except*) todos menos; (*nearly*) casi; ***~ the better*** mucho mejor; ***~ the time*** todo el tiempo, desde el principio; ***it's ~ different*** es todo distinto; ***they're not at ~ alike*** no se parecen en nada; ***that's not at ~ funny*** eso no tiene nada de gracia, eso no es nada gracioso; ***not at ~!*** ¡en absoluto!; ***thank you - not at all*** gracias - de nada; ***two ~*** SP empate a dos; ***~ right*** ☞ ***alright***
all-A'mer•i•can *adj* típicamente americano
al•lay [ə'leɪ] *v/t* apaciguar
all-'clear: ***give sth the ~*** *fig* dar a algo el visto bueno
al•le•ga•tion [ælɪ'geɪʃn] acusación *f*
al•lege [ə'ledʒ] *v/t* alegar
al•leged [ə'ledʒd] *adj* presunto
al•leg•ed•ly [ə'ledʒɪdlɪ] *adv* presuntamente, supuestamente
al•le•giance [ə'liːdʒəns] lealtad *f*
al•le•gor•ic [ælɪ'gɑːrɪk], **al•le•gor•i•cal** [ælɪ'gɑːrɪkl] *adj* alegórico
al•le•go•ry ['ælɪgɔːrɪ] alegoría *f*
al•le•lu•ia [ælɪ'luːjə] aleluya *m*

al•len key ['ælən] llave *f* allen
al•ler•gen ['ælərdʒən] MED alergeno *m*
al•ler•gic [ə'lɜːrdʒɪk] *adj* alérgico; ***be ~ to*** ser alérgico a
al•ler•gist ['ælərdʒɪst] alergista *m/f*
al•ler•gy ['ælərdʒɪ] alergia *f*
al•le•vi•ate [ə'liːvɪeɪt] *v/t* aliviar
al•ley ['ælɪ] callejón *m*
al•li•ance [ə'laɪəns] alianza *f*
al•lied ['ælaɪd] *adj related* relacionado, afín; ***be ~ to s.o. / sth*** estar relacionado con alguien / algo
Al•lied ['ælaɪd] *adj* MIL HIST aliado
Al•lies ['ælaɪz] *npl* MIL HIST: ***the ~*** los Aliados
al•li•ga•tor ['ælɪgeɪtər] ZO aligátor *m*
'al•li•ga•tor clip pinza *f* cocodrilo
all-im'por•tant *adj* importantísimo, vital
'all-in *adj (inclusive)* final, total
all-in•clu•sive 'price precio *m* con todo incluido
all-in 'wres•tling lucha *f* libre
al•lit•er•a•tion [əlɪtə'reɪʃn] aliteración *f*
'all-night *adj party* nocturno, que dura toda la noche; *diner* abierto toda la noche
al•lo•cate ['æləkeɪt] *v/t* asignar
al•lo•ca•tion [ælə'keɪʃn] asignación *f*
al•lot [ə'lɑːt] *v/t (pret & pp **-ted**)* asignar
al•lot•ment [ə'lɑːtmənt] **1** *(portion)* cuota *f* **2** *Br: garden* huerta *f*, huerto *m*
'all-out *adj* F firme, que va a por todas F; ***an ~ effort*** un esfuerzo colosal
al•low [ə'laʊ] *v/t* **1** *(permit)* permitir; ***it's not ~ed*** no está permitido; ***he ~ed us to leave*** nos permitió salir; ***be ~ed to do sth*** tener permiso para hacer algo, poder hacer algo **2** *(calculate for)* calcular
◆ **allow for** *v/t* tener en cuenta
al•low•a•ble [ə'laʊəbl] *adj error* permisible
al•low•ance [ə'laʊəns] **1** *money* asignación *f*; *for kids* paga *f* **2**: ***make ~s for*** *weather etc* tener en cuenta; *person* disculpar
al•loy ['ælɔɪ] aleación *f*; ***~ wheels*** MOT llantas *fpl* de aleación
'all-pow•er•ful *adj* omnipotente; **'all-pur•pose** *adj* multiuso; **'all-round** *adj* completo; **all-risks in'sur•ance** seguro *m* a todo riesgo; **all-round•er** [ɒːl'raʊndər]: ***he's an ~*** *at sport* es un deportista completo; *at school* se le dan bien todas las asignaturas; **All 'Saints' Day** REL día *m* de Todos los Santos; **All 'Souls' Day** REL día *m* de Difuntos; **all-ter'rain** *adj* todoterreno; **'all-time**: ***be at an ~ high / low*** haber alcanzado un máximo / mínimo histórico; ***one of the ~ greats*** uno de los grandes de todos los tiempos
◆ **al•lude to** [ə'luːd] *v/t* aludir a
al•lure [ə'luːr] atractivo *m*, encanto *m*; ***lose its ~*** perder su atractivo *or* encanto
al•lur•ing [ə'luːrɪŋ] *adj* atractivo, seductor
al•lu•sion [ə'luːʒn] alusión *f* (***to*** a)
al•lu•vi•al [ə'luːvjəl] *adj* GEOL aluvial
'all-weath•er *adj* para cualquier condición atmosférica
all-wheel 'drive *adj* con tracción a las cuatro ruedas
al•ly ['ælaɪ] **1** *n* aliado(-a) *m(f)* **II** *v/t*: ***~ o.s. to*** aliarse con
al•might•y [ɒːl'maɪtɪ] **I** *adj* F potente, infernal **II** *n*: ***the Almighty*** el Todopoderoso
al•mond ['ɑːmənd] almendra *f*
al•most ['ɒːlmoʊst] *adv* casi
alms [ɑːmz] *npl* limosna *fsg*
al•oe ['æloʊ] BOT aloe *m*
a•loft [ə'lɑːft] *adv raise* en el aire
a•lone [ə'loʊn] *adj & adv* solo
a•long [ə'lɒːŋ] **I** *prep (situated beside)* a lo largo de; ***walk ~ this path*** sigue por esta calle **II** *adv*: ***would you like to come ~?*** ¿te gustaría venir conmigo / con nosotros?; ***he always brings the dog ~*** siempre trae al perro; ***~ with*** junto con; ***all ~*** *(all the time)* todo el tiempo, desde el principio
a•long•side [əlɒːŋ'saɪd] **I** *prep work* con, junto a; *exist, perform* junto con: *(parallel to)* al lado de **II** *adv*: ***a police car drew up ~*** un coche de policía se acercó *or* se aproximó al lado
a•loof [ə'luːf] *adj* distante, reservado; ***keep (o.s.) ~, stand ~*** mantenerse *or* quedarse al margen (***from*** de)
a•loud [ə'laʊd] *adv* en voz alta
al•pha•bet ['ælfəbet] alfabeto *m*
al•pha•bet•i•cal [ælfə'betɪkl] *adj* alfabético; ***~ order*** orden *m* alfabético
al•pha•nu•mer•ic [ælfənjuː'merɪk] *adj* COMPUT alfanumérico

al•pha•nu•mer•ic 'key•board COMPUT teclado *m* alfanumérico
al•pha•test ['ælfətest] test *m* alfa
al•pine ['ælpaɪn] *adj* alpino
Al•pine ['ælpaɪn] *adj* alpino, de los Alpes
Alps [ælps] *npl*: ***the*** ~ los Alpes
al•read•y [ɒːl'redɪ] *adv* ya
al•right [ɒːl'raɪt] *adj* (*not hurt, in working order*) bien; ***is it ~ to leave now?*** (*permitted*) ¿puedo irme / podemos irnos ahora?; ***is it ~ to take these out of the country?*** ¿se pueden sacar éstos del país?; ***is it ~ with you if I ...?*** ¿te importa si ...?; ***~, you can have one!*** de acuerdo, ¡puedes tomar uno!; ***~, I heard you!*** vale, ¡te he oído!; ***everything is ~ now between them*** vuelven a estar bien; ***that's ~*** (*don't mention it*) de nada; (*I don't mind*) no importa
Al•sa•tian [æl'seɪʃn] *Br* ZO pastor *m* alemán
al•so ['ɒːlsoʊ] *adv* también
'al•so-ran perdedor(a) *m*(*f*)
al•tar ['ɒːltər] altar *m*
al•ter ['ɒːltər] *v/t* alterar
al•ter•a•tion [ɒːltə'reɪʃn] alteración *f*; ***make ~s to*** *clothes* arreglar; *plan etc* modificar, cambiar
al•ter•ca•tion [ɒːltər'keɪʃn] altercado *m*
al•ter•nate I *v/i* ['ɒːltərneɪt] alternar **II** *adj* ['ɒːltərnət] alterno
al•ter•nate•ly [ɒːl'tərnətlɪ] *adv* alternativamente, alternadamente
al•ter•nat•ing ['ɒːltərneɪtɪŋ] *adj* alterno, alternativo
'al•ter•nat•ing cur•rent corriente *f* alterna
al•ter•na•tive [ɒːlt'ɜːrnətɪv] **I** *n* alternativa *f*; ***we had no ~ but to head back*** no tuvimos otra *or* más alternativa que regresar **II** *adj* alternativo
al•ter•na•tive•ly [ɒːlt'ɜːrnətɪvlɪ] *adv* si no
al•ter•na•tor ['ɒːltərneɪtər] ELEC alternador *m*
al•though [ɒːl'ðoʊ] *conj* aunque, si bien
al•tim•e•ter ['æltɪmiːtər] PHYS altímetro *m*
al•ti•tude ['æltɪtuːd] *of plane, city* altitud *f*; *of mountain* altura *f*
'al•ti•tude sick•ness mal *m* de las alturas
alt key ['ɒːltkiː] COMPUT tecla *f* alt
al•to ['æltoʊ] MUS *voice* contralto *m*; *singer* contralto *m/f*; ~ (***sax***) (saxo *m*) alto *m*
al•to•geth•er [ɒːltə'geðər] *adv* **1** (*completely*) completamente; ***on another matter ~, ...*** pasando a algo completamente diferente, ... **2** (*in all*) en total; ***~, this is a great movie*** en todos los sentidos, es una pelicula estupenda
al•tru•ism ['æltruːɪzm] altruismo *m*
al•tru•ist ['æltruːɪst] altruista *m/f*
al•tru•is•tic [æltruː'ɪstɪk] *adj* altruista
a•lu•mi•num [ə'luːmənəm], *Br* **a•lu•min•i•um** [æljʊ'mɪnɪəm] aluminio *m*
a•lum•ni [ə'lʌmnaɪ] *npl* antiguos *mpl* alumnos
al•ways ['ɒːlweɪz] *adv* siempre; ***you can ~ change your mind*** siempre puedes cambiar de opinión
Alz•hei•mer's (**dis•ease**) ['æltshaɪmərz] MED (enfermedad *f* de) Alzheimer *m*
am [æm] ☞ ***be***
a.m. ['eɪem] *abbr* (= ***ante meridiem***) a.m.; ***at 11 ~*** a las 11 de la mañana
a•mal•gam [ə'mælgəm] CHEM, TECH amalgamación *f*, amalgamamiento *m*
a•mal•gam•ate [ə'mælgəmeɪt] *v/i of companies* fusionarse
a•mal•ga•ma•tion [əmælgə'meɪʃn] **1** CHEM, TECH amalgama *f* **2** *mixture* amalgama *f*, unión *f*
a•mass [ə'mæs] *v/t* acumular
am•a•teur ['æmətʃʊr] *n unskilled* aficionado(-a) *m*(*f*); SP amateur *m/f*
am•a•teur•ish ['æmətʃʊrɪʃ] *adj pej* chapucero
a•maze [ə'meɪz] *v/t* asombrar
a•mazed [ə'meɪzd] *adj* asombrado; ***we were ~ to hear ...*** nos asombró oír ...; ***you'll be ~*** te vas a quedar pasmado F
a•maze•ment [ə'meɪzmənt] asombro *m*; ***in ~*** con (cara de) asombro; ***to my ~*** para mi asombro *or* sorpresa
a•maz•ing [ə'meɪzɪŋ] *adj* (*surprising*) asombroso; F (*very good*) alucinante F
a•maz•ing•ly [ə'meɪzɪŋlɪ] *adv* increíblemente
Am•a•zon ['æməzən]: ***the ~*** el Amazonas
Am•a•zon 'es•tu•a•ry Bocas *fpl* del Amazonas
Am•a•zo•ni•an [æmə'zoʊnɪən] *adj*

amazónico
am•bas•sa•dor [æm'bæsədər] embajador(a) *m(f)*
am•ber ['æmbər] *adj* ámbar; ***at ~*** en ámbar
am•bi•dex•trous [æmbɪ'dekstrəs] *adj* ambidiestro
am•bi•ence ['æmbɪəns] ambiente *m*
am•bi•gu•i•ty [æmbɪ'gju:ətɪ] ambigüedad *f*
am•big•u•ous [æm'bɪgjʊəs] *adj* ambiguo
am•bi•tion [æm'bɪʃn] *also pej* ambición *f*
am•bi•tious [æm'bɪʃəs] *adj* ambicioso; ***be ~ for s.o.*** desear lo mejor para alguien
am•biv•a•lence [æm'bɪvələns] ambivalencia *f*
am•biv•a•lent [æm'bɪvələnt] *adj* ambivalente
am•ble ['æmbl] *v/i* deambular
am•bu•lance ['æmbjʊləns] ambulancia *f*
am•bush ['æmbʊʃ] **I** *n* emboscada *f* **II** *v/t* tender una emboscada a
a•me•ba [ə'mi:bə] ZO ameba *f*
a•mel•io•rate [ə'mi:ljəreɪt] *v/t fml* mejorar, aliviar
a•men [eɪ'men] *int* amén
a•me•na•ble [ə'mi:nəbl] *adj person* manejable, fácil; *animal* dócil; ***be ~ to sth*** aceptar de buen grado algo, estar de acuerdo con algo
a•mend [ə'mend] *v/t* enmendar
a•mend•ment [ə'mendmənt] enmienda *f*
a•mends [ə'mendz] *npl*: ***make ~ for*** compensar
a•men•i•ties [ə'mi:nətɪz] *npl* servicios *mpl*
A•mer•i•ca [ə'merɪkə] **1** *continent* América **2** (*USA*) Estados *mpl* Unidos
A•mer•i•can [ə'merɪkən] **I** *adj* (*North ~*) estadounidense **II** *n* (*North ~*) estadounidense *m/f*
A•mer•i•can•ism [ə'merɪkənɪzm] LING americanismo *m*, angloamericanismo *m*
A•mer•i•can•ize [ə'merɪkənaɪz] *v/t* americanizar
A'mer•i•can plan pensión *f* completa
am•e•thyst ['æmɪθɪst] amatista *f*
a•mi•a•bil•i•ty [eɪmjə'bɪlətɪ] afabilidad *f*, amabilidad *f*
a•mi•a•ble ['eɪmɪəbl] *adj* afable, amable
a•mi•ca•ble ['æmɪkəbl] *adj* amistoso
a•mi•ca•bly ['æmɪkəblɪ] *adv* amistosamente
a•mid(st) [ə'mɪd(st)] *prep* entre, en medio de
a•miss [ə'mɪs] *adj & adv*: ***take sth ~*** tomarse algo a mal; ***there is something ~ with*** le pasa algo a; ***a bit of help wouldn't go ~*** un poco de ayuda no iría *or* no vendría mal
am•me•ter ['æmɪtər] ELEC amperímetro *m*
am•mo•ni•a [ə'moʊnjə] CHEM amoniaco *m*
am•mu•ni•tion [æmjʊ'nɪʃn] munición *f*; *fig* argumentos *mpl*
am•ne•si•a [æm'ni:zɪə] amnesia *f*
am•nes•ty ['æmnəstɪ] amnistía *f*
am•ni•o•cen•te•sis [æmnɪoʊsen'ti:sɪs] MED amniocentesis *f*
am•ni•ot•ic flu•id [æmnɪ'ɑ:tɪk] MED líquido *m* amniótico
a•moe•ba [ə'mi:bə] *Br* ZO ☞ ***ameba***
a•mok [ə'mɑ:k] ☞ ***amuck***
a•mong(st) [ə'mʌŋ(st)] *prep* entre; ***~ other things*** entre otras cosas
a•mor•al [eɪ'mɔ:rəl] *adj* amoral
am•o•rous ['æmərəs] *adj*: ***~ advances*** insinuaciones *fpl* amorosas; ***he started getting ~*** empezó a acaramelarse
a•mor•phous [ə'mɔ:fəs] *adj* amorfo
am•or•tize [ə'mɔ:taɪz] *v/t* FIN amortizar
a•mount [ə'maʊnt] cantidad *f*; (*sum of money*) cantidad *f*, suma *f*; ***to the ~ of*** por la cantidad de; ***a large ~ of work*** mucho trabajo
◆ **amount to** *v/t* ascender a; ***his contribution didn't amount to much*** su contribución no fue gran cosa; ***he'll never amount to much*** nunca llegará a mucho
amp [æmp] F ☞ ***ampere, amplifier***
am•pere ['æmper] ELEC amperio *m*
am•per•sand ['æmpərsænd] TIP *símbolo &*
am•phet•a•mine [æm'fetəmi:n] anfetamina *f*
am•phib•i•an [æm'fɪbɪən] anfibio *m*
am•phib•i•ous [æm'fɪbɪəs] *adj animal, vehicle* anfibio
am•phi•the•a•ter, *Br* **am•phi•the•a•tre**

['æmfɪθɪətər] anfiteatro *m*
am•ple ['æmpl] *adj* abundante; ***$4 will be ~*** 4 dólares serán más que suficientes
am•pli•fi•ca•tion [æmplɪfɪ'keɪʃn] amplificación *f*
am•pli•fi•er ['æmplɪfaɪr] amplificador *m*
am•pli•fy ['æmplɪfaɪ] *v/t* (*pret & pp* ***-ied***) *sound* amplificar
am•pli•tude ['æmplɪtjuːd] ELEC, PHYS amplitud *f*
am•pu•tate ['æmpjʊteɪt] *v/t* amputar
am•pu•ta•tion [æmpjʊ'teɪʃn] amputación *f*
am•pu•tee [æmpjʊ'tiː] amputado(-a) *m(f)*
Am•trak ['æmtræk] *empresa ferroviaria estadounidense*
a•muck [ə'mʌk] *adv*: ***run ~*** volverse loco, perder la cabeza
a•muse [ə'mjuːz] *v/t* **1** (*make laugh etc*) divertir; ***they weren't very ~d*** no les hizo mucha gracia; ***you'll be ~d to hear that …*** te va a hacer gracia escuchar que … **2** (*entertain*) entretener; ***the kids are well able to ~ themselves*** los niños pueden entretenerse *or* distraerse solos perfectamente
a•muse•ment [ə'mjuːzmənt] **1** (*merriment*) diversión *f*; ***to our great ~*** para nuestro regocijo; ***this caused a lot of ~*** esto hizo mucha gracia **2** (*entertainment*) entretenimiento *m*; ***~s*** (*games*) juegos *mpl*; ***what do you do for ~?*** ¿qué haces para entretenerte?
a'muse•ment ar•cade *Br* salón *m* de juegos recreativos
a'muse•ment park parque *m* de atracciones
a•mus•ing [ə'mjuːzɪŋ] *adj* divertido
an [æn] *unstressed* [ən] ☞ ***a***
an•a•bol•ic ster•oid [ænə'bɑːlɪk] esteroide *m* anabolizante
a•nach•ro•nism [ə'nækrənɪzəm] anacronismo *m*
a•nach•ro•nis•tic [ənækrə'nɪstɪk] *adj* anacrónico
an•a•con•da [ænə'kɑːndə] ZO anaconda *f*
a•nae•mi•a *etc Br* ☞ ***anemia*** *etc*
an•aes•thet•ic *etc Br* ☞ ***anesthetic*** *etc*
an•a•log ['ænəlɑːg] *adj* COMPUT analógico
a•nal•o•gous [ə'næləgəs] *adj* análogo, semejante
a•nal•o•gy [ə'nælədʒɪ] analogía *f*; ***by ~ with*** por analogía con
an•al•y•sis [ə'næləsɪs] (*pl* ***analyses*** [ə'næləsiːz]) **1** análisis *m inv* **2** PSYCH psicoanálisis *m inv*
an•a•lyst ['ænəlɪst] **1** analista *m/f* **2** PSYCH psicoanalista *m/f*
an•a•lyt•i•cal [ænə'lɪtɪkl] *adj* analítico
an•a•lyze ['ænəlaɪz] *v/t* **1** analizar **2** PSYCH psicoanalizar
an•arch•y ['ænərkɪ] anarquía *f*
a•nath•e•ma [ə'næθəmə] REL anatema *m*; ***it is ~ to the government*** *fig* le resulta aborrecible al gobierno
a•nat•o•my [ə'nætəmɪ] anatomía *f*
an•ces•tor ['ænsestər] antepasado(-a) *m(f)*
an•ces•tral [æn'sestrəl] *adj* ancestral; ***~ home*** casa solar
an•ces•try ['ænsestrɪ] descendencia *f*; ***I want to trace my ~*** quiero reconstruirme mi genealogía *or* mi árbol genealógico
an•chor ['æŋkər] **I** *n* **1** NAUT ancla *f* **2** TV presentador(a) *m(f)* **II** *v/i* NAUT anclar
an•chor•age ['æŋkərɪdʒ] ancladero *m*
'an•chor•man TV presentador *m*
an•cho•vy ['æntʃouvɪ] anchoa *f*
an•cient ['eɪnʃənt] *adj* antiguo
an•cil•lar•y [æn'sɪlərɪ] *adj staff* auxiliar
and [ənd] *stressed* [ænd] *conj* y; ***~ / or*** y / o; ***it's getting bigger ~ bigger*** se está haciendo cada vez mayor; ***they cried ~ cried*** no paraban de llorar
An•da•lu•si•a [ændæluː'sɪə] Andalucía *f*
An•da•lu•si•an [ændæluː'sɪən] *adj* andaluz
An•de•an ['ændɪən] *adj* andino
An•des ['ændiːz] *npl*: ***the ~*** los Andes
An•dor•ra [æn'dɔːrə] Andorra *f*
an•droid ['ændrɔɪd] androide *m*
an•ec•dot•al [ænek'doutl] *adj* anecdótico, circunstancial
an•ec•dote ['ænɪkdout] anécdota *f*
a•ne•mia [ə'niːmɪə] anemia *f*
a•ne•mic [ə'niːmɪk] *adj* anémico
an•e•mom•e•ter [ænɪ'mɑːmɪtər] PHYS anemómetro *m*
a•nem•o•ne [ə'nemənɪ] BOT anémona *f*
an•es•the•si•a [ænəs'θiːzɪə] anestesia *f*
an•es•the•si•ol•o•gist [ænəsθiːzɪ'ɑːlə-

dʒɪst] anestesista *m/f*
an•es•thet•ic [ænəs'θetɪk] anestesia *f*
an•es•the•tist [ə'niːsθətɪst] anestesista *m/f*
a•new [ə'njuː] *adv* de nuevo, otra vez; ***start ~*** empezar de nuevo, empezar desde cero
an•gel ['eɪndʒl] REL ángel *m*; *fig* ángel *m*, cielo *m*
an•gel•ic [æn'dʒelɪk] *adj* angelical
An•gel•i•no [ændʒə'liːnoʊ] **I** *adj* angelino **II** *n* angelino(-a) *m(f)*
an•ger ['æŋgər] **I** *n* enfado *m*, enojo *m* **II** *v/t* enfadar, enojar
an•gi•na [æn'dʒaɪnə] angina *f* (de pecho)
an•gle[1] ['æŋgl] *n* ángulo *m*; ***be at an ~*** estar torcido *or* en diagonal (***to*** con respecto a); ***see sth from a different ~*** *fig* ver algo desde otro punto de vista
an•gle[2] ['æŋgl] *v/i* pescar con caña
◆ **angle for** *v/t fig* ir detrás de, buscar
'an•gle brack•et paréntesis *m inv* angular
an•gler ['æŋglər] pescador(a) *m(f)* de caña
An•gli•can ['æŋglɪkən] REL **I** *adj* anglicano **II** *n* anglicano(-a) *m(f)*
An•gli•cism ['æŋglɪsɪzəm] LING anglicismo *m*
An•glo-A•mer•i•can [æŋgloʊə'merɪkən] **I** *n* angloamericano(-a) *m(f)* **II** *adj* angloamericano
An•glo-Sax•on [æŋgloʊ'sæksən] **I** *n* anglosajón(-ona) *m(f)* **II** *adj* anglosajón
An•go•la [æŋ'goʊlə] Angola *f*
An•go•lan [æŋ'goʊlən] **I** *n* angoleño(-a) *m(f)* **II** *adj* angoleño
an•go•ra [æŋ'gɔːrə] *wool* angora *f*; ***~ cat*** gato *m* de Angora
an•gry ['æŋgrɪ] *adj* enfadado, enojado; ***be ~ with s.o.*** estar enfadado *or* enojado con alguien; ***be ~ about sth*** estar enfadado por algo; ***get ~*** enfadarse; ***get ~ with s.o.*** enfadarse con alguien; ***get ~ about sth*** enfadarse por algo
an•guish ['æŋgwɪʃ] angustia *f*
an•gu•lar ['æŋgjulər] *adj* anguloso
an•i•mal ['ænɪml] animal *m*
'an•i•mal king•dom reino *m* animal; **'an•i•mal lov•er** amante *m/f* de los animales; **an•i•mal 'wel•fare** protección *f* de los animales
an•i•mate ['ænɪmeɪt] *v/t* animar, alegrar
an•i•mat•ed ['ænɪmeɪtɪd] *adj* animado
an•i•mat•ed car'toon dibujos *mpl* animados
an•i•mat•ed 'film película *f* de animación
an•i•ma•tion [ænɪ'meɪʃn] (*liveliness*), *of cartoon* animación *f*
an•i•ma•tor ['ænɪmeɪtər] *draws cartoons* animador(a) *m(f)*
an•i•mos•i•ty [ænɪ'mɑːsətɪ] animosidad *f*
an•ise [æ'nɪs] BOT anís *m*
an•i•seed ['ænɪsiːd] anís *m*, anisete *m*
an•kle ['æŋkl] tobillo *m*
an•klet ['æŋklət] **1** *jewellery* pulsera *f* para el tobillo **2** *clothing* calcetín *m* tobillero
an•nals ['ænlz] *npl* anales *mpl*; ***go down in the ~ of history*** incluirse en los anales de la historia
an•nex ['æneks] **I** *n building* edificio *m* anexo **II** *v/t state* anexionar
an•nex•a•tion [ænek'seɪʃn] anexión *f*, adhesión *f*
an•nexe ['æneks] *n Br* edificio *m* anexo
an•ni•hi•late [ə'naɪəleɪt] *v/t* aniquilar
an•ni•hi•la•tion [ənaɪə'leɪʃn] aniquilación *f*
an•ni•ver•sa•ry [ænɪ'vɜːrsərɪ] (*wedding ~*) aniversario *m*
An•no Do•mi•ni [ænoʊ'dɑːmɪnaɪ] *adv* después de Cristo
an•no•tate ['ænəteɪt] *v/t report* anotar
an•no•ta•tion [ænə'teɪʃn] anotación *f*, nota *f* explicativa
an•nounce [ə'naʊns] *v/t* anunciar
an•nounce•ment [ə'naʊnsmənt] anuncio *m*
an•nounc•er [ə'naʊnsər] TV, RAD presentador(a) *m(f)*
an•noy [ə'nɔɪ] *v/t* molestar, irritar; ***be ~ed*** estar molesto *or* irritado
an•noy•ance [ə'nɔɪəns] **1** (*anger*) irritación *f* **2** (*nuisance*) molestia *f*
an•noy•ing [ə'nɔɪɪŋ] *adj* molesto, irritante
an•nu•al ['ænʊəl] **I** *adj* anual **II** *n* **1** *book: libro que se publica anualmente* **2** BOT planta *f* de un año
an•nu•al 'earn•ings *npl* ganancias *fpl* anuales; **an•nu•al gen•e•ral 'meet•ing** *Br* consejo *m* general anual; **an•nu•al 'in•come** ingresos *mpl* anuales; **an•nu•al per'cen•tage rate** FIN tasa *f*

anual equivalente
an•nu•i•ty [ə'nu:ətɪ] anualidad *f*
an•nul [ə'nʌl] *v/t* (*pret & pp* **-led**) *marriage* anular
an•nul•ment [ə'nʌlmənt] anulación *f*
An•nun•ci•a•tion [ənʌnsɪ'eɪʃn] REL: ***the ~*** la Anunciación
an•ode ['ænoʊd] ELEC ánodo *m*
an•o•dyne ['ænoʊdaɪn] *adj* anodino, insubstancial
a•noint [ə'nɔɪnt] *v/t esp* REL ungir
a•nom•a•lous [ə'nɑ:mələs] *adj* anómalo, anormal
a•nom•a•ly [ə'nɑ:məlɪ] anomalía *f*, anormalidad *f*
an•o•nym•i•ty [ænə'nɪmətɪ] anonimato *m*; ***preserve one's ~*** permanecer en el anonimato
a•non•y•mous [ə'nɑ:nɪməs] *adj* anónimo
an•o•rak ['ænəræk] *Br* anorak *m*
an•o•rex•i•a [ænə'reksɪə] anorexia *f*
an•o•rex•ic [ænə'reksɪk] *adj* anoréxico
an•oth•er [ə'nʌðər] **I** *adj* otro **II** *pron* otro(-a) *m(f)*; ***they helped one ~*** se ayudaron (el uno al otro); ***do they know one ~?*** ¿se conocen?
ANSI ['ænsi:] *abbr* (= ***American National Standards Institute***) código ANSI *m*, ANSI *m*
an•swer ['ænsər] **I** *n* **1** *to letter, person, question* respuesta *f*, contestación *f*; ***in ~ to*** en respuesta a, para responder a **2** *to problem* solución *f* **II** *v/t letter, person, question* responder, contestar; ***~ the door*** abrir la puerta; ***~ the telephone*** responder *or Span* coger al teléfono
◆ **answer for** *v/t* responder de
◆ **answer to** *v/t* **1** *person* responder ante **2** *description* responder a
an•swer•a•ble ['ænsərəbl] *adj*: ***be ~ to s.o.*** tener que responder ante alguien; ***be ~ to s.o. for sth / s.o.*** ser responsable de algo / alguien ante alguien
an•swer•ing ma•chine ['ænsərɪŋ] TELEC contestador *m* (automático)
'an•swer•phone TELEC contestador *m* (automático)
ant [ænt] hormiga *f*
ant•ac•id ['æntæsɪd] antiácido *m*
an•tag•o•nism [æn'tægənɪzm] antagonismo *m*
an•tag•o•nist [æn'tægənɪst] antagonista *m/f*, contrincante *m/f*
an•tag•o•nis•tic [æntægə'nɪstɪk] *adj* hostil
an•tag•o•nize [æn'tægənaɪz] *v/t* antagonizar, enfadar
Ant•arc•tic [ænt'ɑ:rktɪk]: ***the ~*** el Antártico
Ant•arc•ti•ca [ænt'ɑ:rktɪkə] GEOG Antártida *f*
Ant•arc•tic 'Cir•cle círculo *m* polar antártico
Ant•arc•tic 'O•cean océano *m* Antártico
ant•eat•er ['ænti:tər] ZO oso *m* hormiguero
an•te•ced•ent [æntɪ'si:dənt] **1** (*forerunner*) predecesor(a) *m(f)*, antecesor(a) *m(f)* **2**: ***~s*** (*background*) antecedentes *mpl*
an•te•di•lu•vi•an [æntɪdaɪ'lu:vjən] *adj* antediluviano
an•te•lope ['æntɪloʊp] ZO antílope *m*
an•te•na•tal [æntɪ'neɪtl] *adj* prenatal; ***~ class*** clase *f* de preparación para el parto
an•ten•na [æn'tenə] *of insect, for TV* antena *f*
an•te•ri•or [æn'tɪərɪər] *adj* anterior
an•te•room ['æntɪrʊm] antesala *f*
an•them ['ænθəm] himno *m*
'ant•hill hormiguero *m*
an•thol•o•gy [æn'θɑ:lədʒɪ] antología *f*
an•thra•cite ['ænθrəsaɪt] MIN antracita *f*
an•thro•poid ['ænθrəpɔɪd] ZO **I** *adj* antropoide **II** *n* antropoide *m/f*
an•thro•po•log•i•cal [ænθrəpə'lɑ:dʒɪkl] *adj* antropológico
an•thro•pol•o•gist [ænθrə'pɑ:lədʒɪst] antropólogo(-a) *m(f)*
an•thro•pol•o•gy [ænθrə'pɑ:lədʒɪ] antropología *f*
an•ti... ['æntaɪ] *pref* anti ...
an•ti-a'bor•tion•ist antiabortista *m/f*
an•ti-'air•craft *adj* MIL antiaéreo
an•ti-'air•craft gun MIL cañón *m* antiaéreo
an•ti•bi•ot•ic [æntaɪbaɪ'ɑ:tɪk] antibiótico *m*
'an•ti•bod•y anticuerpo *m*
an•tic•i•pate [æn'tɪsɪpeɪt] *v/t* esperar, prever
an•tic•i•pa•tion [æntɪsɪ'peɪʃn] expectativa *f*, previsión *f*

an•tic•i•pa•to•ry [æntɪsɪ'peɪtərɪ] *adj* de anticipación
an•ti'cli•max *fig* anticlímax *m*, desilusión *f*
'an•ti-clock•wise *adv Br* en dirección contraria a las agujas del reloj
an•tics ['æntɪks] *npl* payasadas *fpl*
an•ti'cy•clone METEO anticiclón *m*
an•ti'daz•zle *adj* antirreflector
an•ti•de'pres•sant MED antidepresivo *m*
an•ti•dote ['æntɪdoʊt] antídoto *m*
an•ti'fas•cist I *n* antifascista *m/f* **II** *adj* antifascista
'an•ti•freeze anticongelante *m*
an•ti-'glare mir•ror espejo *m* antideslumbrante
an•ti•his•ta•mine [æntaɪ'hɪstəmi:n] MED antihistamínico *m*
An•til•les [æn'tɪli:z] *npl*: ***Greater / Lesser ~*** Grandes / Pequeñas Antillas *fpl*
an•ti-lock 'brak•ing sys•tem MOT sistema *m* de frenos antibloqueo
'an•ti•mat•ter antimateria *f*
an•tip•a•thy [æn'tɪpəθɪ] antipatía *f*
an•ti•per•spi•rant [æntaɪ'pɜ:rspərənt] antitranspirante *m*
An•tip•o•des [æn'tɪpədi:z] *npl Br*: ***the ~*** las Antípodas
an•ti•quar•i•an book•sell•er [æntɪkwerɪən'bʊkselər] librero(-a) *m(f)* especialista en libros antiguos
an•ti•quar•i•an 'book•store librería *f* de libros antiguos
an•ti•quat•ed ['æntɪkweɪtɪd] *adj* anticuado
an•tique [æn'ti:k] antigüedad *f*
an'tique deal•er anticuario(-a) *m(f)*
an•tiq•ui•ty [æn'tɪkwətɪ] antigüedad *f*
an•ti'rust *adj* antioxidante
an•ti-Sem•ite [æntaɪ'si:maɪt] antisemita *m/f*
an•ti-Se•mit•ic [æntaɪsə'mɪtɪk] *adj* antisemita, antisemítico
an•ti-Sem•i•tism [æntaɪ'semɪtɪzəm] antisemitismo *m*
an•ti•sep•tic [æntaɪ'septɪk] **I** *adj* antiséptico **II** *n* antiséptico *m*
an•ti-'smok•ing *adj campaign* anti-tabaco
an•ti'so•cial *adj* antisocial, poco sociable
an•ti-'theft de•vice dispositivo *m* antirrobo
an•tith•e•sis [æn'tɪθəsɪs] (*pl* ***antitheses*** [æn'tɪθəsi:z]) antítesis *f*
an•ti-'trust laws *npl* COM ley *f* antimonopolio *or* antimonopolista
an•ti'vi•rus pro•gram COMPUT (programa *m*) antivirus *m inv*
ant•lers ['æntlərz] *npl* cuernos *mpl*
an•to•nym ['æntoʊnɪm] antónimo *m*
a•nus ['eɪnəs] ANAT ano *m*
an•vil ['ænvɪl] yunque *m*
anx•i•e•ty [æŋ'zaɪətɪ] ansiedad *f*
anx•ious ['æŋkʃəs] *adj* **1** preocupado **2** (*eager*) ansioso; ***be ~ for*** *news etc* esperar ansiosamente
an•y ['enɪ] **I** *adj*: ***are there ~ diskettes / glasses?*** ¿hay disquetes / vasos?; ***is there ~ bread / improvement?*** ¿hay algo de pan / alguna mejora?; ***there aren't ~ diskettes / glasses*** no hay disquetes / vasos; ***there isn't ~ bread / improvement*** no hay pan / ninguna mejora; ***have you ~ idea at all?*** ¿tienes alguna idea?; ***~ one of them could win*** cualquiera de ellos podría ganar
II *pron* alguno(-a); ***do you have ~?*** ¿tienes alguno(s)?; ***there aren't ~ left*** no queda ninguno; ***there isn't ~ left*** no queda; ***~ of them could be guilty*** cualquiera de ellos podría ser culpable
III *adv*: ***is that ~ better / easier?*** ¿es mejor / más fácil así?; ***I don't like it ~ more*** ya no me gusta
an•y•bod•y ['enɪbɑ:dɪ] *pron* alguien; ***there wasn't ~ there*** no había nadie allí
an•y•how ['enɪhaʊ] *adv* en todo caso, de todos modos; ***if I can help you ~, please let me know*** si puedo ayudarte de alguna manera, por favor dímelo
an•y•one ['enɪwʌn] ☞ ***anybody***
an•y•thing ['enɪθɪŋ] *pron* algo; *with negatives* nada; ***I didn't hear ~*** no oí nada; ***~ but*** todo menos; ***~ else?*** ¿algo más?; ***I'll do absolutely ~ you want*** haría cualquier cosa que me pidieses; ***~ would be better than that*** cualquier cosa (es) mejor que eso
an•y•way ['enɪweɪ] ☞ ***anyhow***
an•y•where ['enɪwer] *adv* en alguna parte; ***is Peter around?*** ¿está Peter por ahí?; ***he never goes ~*** nunca va a ninguna parte; ***I can't find it ~*** no lo encuentro por ninguna parte

a•or•ta [eɪ'ɔːrtə] ANAT aorta *f*
a•part [ə'pɑːrt] *adv* aparte; ***the two cities are 250 miles ~*** las dos ciudades están a 250 millas la una de la otra; ***live ~ of people*** vivir separado; ***~ from*** aparte de
a•part•ment [ə'pɑːrtmənt] apartamento *m*, *Span* piso *m*
a'part•ment block bloque *m* de apartamentos *or Span* pisos; **a'part•ment ho•tel** apartahotel *m*; **a'part•ment house** bloque *m* de apartamentos *or Span* pisos
ap•a•thet•ic [æpə'θetɪk] *adj* apático
ap•a•thy ['æpəθɪ] apatía *f*
ape [eɪp] **I** simio *m* **II** *v/t* copiar, imitar
a•pe•ri•tif [ə'perɪtiːf] aperitivo *m*
ap•er•ture ['æpərtʃər] PHOT apertura *f*
a•pex ['eɪpeks] (*pl **apexes***) *also fig* cúspide *f*, cumbre *f*
a•phid ['eɪfɪd] ZO áfido *m*
aph•o•rism ['æfərɪzəm] aforismo *m*
aph•ro•dis•i•ac [æfroʊ'dɪzɪæk] **I** *n* afrodisiaco *m* **II** *adj* afrodisiaco
a•piece [ə'piːs] *adv* cada uno
a•poc•a•lypse [ə'pɑːkəlɪps] apocalipsis *f*
a•pol•o•get•ic [əpɑːlə'dʒetɪk] *adj letter* de disculpa; ***he was very ~ about …*** pedía constantes disculpas por …
a•pol•o•gize [ə'pɑːlədʒaɪz] *v/i* disculparse, pedir perdón
a•pol•o•gy [ə'pɑːlədʒɪ] disculpa *f*; ***owe s.o. an ~*** deber disculpas a alguien; ***in ~ for*** como disculpa por; ***make*** *or* ***offer s.o. an ~*** presentar *or* ofrecer disculpas a alguien (***for*** por); ***an ~ for a meal*** una lástima de comida
ap•o•plec•tic [æpə'plektɪk] *adj fig* encorajinado
ap•o•plex•y ['æpəpleksɪ] MED apoplejía *f*
a•pos•tle [ə'pɑːsl] REL apóstol *m*
a•pos•tro•phe [ə'pɑːstrəfɪ] GRAM apóstrofo *m*
a•poth•e•o•sis [əpɑːθɪ'oʊsɪs] apoteosis *f*
ap•pall [ə'pɒːl] *v/t* horrorizar, espantar; ***be ~ed*** horrorizarse (***at, by*** de, ante)
ap•pal•ling [ə'pɒːlɪŋ] *adj* horroroso
ap•pa•ra•tus [æpə'reɪtəs] aparatos *mpl*
ap•par•el [ə'pærəl] aparejo *m*, equipo *m*
ap•par•ent [ə'pærənt] *adj* aparente, evidente; ***become ~ that …*** hacerse evidente que …; ***be ~ from*** quedar claro (a juzgar) por; ***for no ~ reason*** sin motivo aparente, sin razón alguna
ap•par•ent•ly [ə'pærəntlɪ] *adv* al parecer, por lo visto
ap•pa•ri•tion [æpə'rɪʃn] (*ghost*) aparición *f*
ap•peal [ə'piːl] **I** *n* **1** (*charm*) atractivo *m* **2** *for funds etc* llamamiento *m* **3** LAW, *in sport* apelación *f*; ***file*** *or* ***lodge an ~*** entablar *or* presentar una apelación **II** *v/i* LAW, *in sport* apelar
◆ **appeal for** *v/t* solicitar
◆ **appeal to** *v/t* (*be attractive to*) atraer a
ap•peal•ing [ə'piːlɪŋ] *adj* **1** *idea, offer* atractivo **2** *glance* suplicante
ap•pear [ə'pɪr] *v/i* **1** aparecer; *in court* comparecer; ***~ in public / on television*** aparecer en público / en (la) televisión **2** (*look, seem*) parecer; ***it ~s to me that …*** me parece que …
ap•pear•ance [ə'pɪrəns] **1** aparición *f*, *in court* comparecencia *f*, ***put in an ~*** hacer acto de presencia; ***public ~*** aparición pública **2** (*look*) apariencia *f*, aspecto *m*; ***~s are deceptive*** las apariencias engañan; ***to all*** *or* ***from all ~s*** en apariencia; ***keep up ~s*** guardar las apariencias
ap•pease [ə'piːz] *v/t* apaciguar
ap•pease•ment [ə'piːzmənt] HIST contemporización *f*
ap•pend [ə'pend] *v/t* adjuntar (***to*** a)
ap•pend•age [ə'pendɪdʒ] adjunción *f*, añadidura *f*
ap•pen•dec•to•my [æpen'dektəmɪ] MED apendectomía *f*
ap•pen•di•ci•tis [əpendɪ'saɪtɪs] apendicitis *m*
ap•pen•dix [ə'pendɪks] MED, *of book* apéndice *m*
ap•per•tain [æpər'teɪn] *v/i fml* referirse (***to*** a)
ap•pe•tite ['æpɪtaɪt] *also fig* apetito *m*
ap•pe•tiz•er ['æpɪtaɪzər] aperitivo *m*
ap•pe•tiz•ing ['æpɪtaɪzɪŋ] *adj* apetitoso
ap•plaud [ə'plɒːd] **I** *v/i* aplaudir **II** *v/t also fig* aplaudir
ap•plause [ə'plɒːz] aplauso *m*
ap•ple ['æpl] manzana *f*, ***be the ~ of s.o.'s eye*** ser el ojito derecho de alguien
'ap•ple•cart: ***upset the ~*** *fig* hacer la pascua; **'ap•ple•jack** licor *m* de manza-

na; **'ap•ple juice** zumo *m* de manzana; **ap•ple 'pie** tarta *f* de manzana; **ap•ple--pie 'or•der**: ***in ~*** F en su sitio, como Dios manda F; **ap•ple pol•ish•er** ['æplpɑːlɪʃər] F pelotero(-a) *m(f)* F, pelotillero(-a) *m(f)* F; **ap•ple 'sauce** compota *f* de manzana; **'ap•ple tree** manzano *m*

ap•pli•ance [ə'plaɪəns] **1** aparato *m*; *household* electrodoméstico *m* **2**: ***by the ~ of a little logic*** siguiendo un razonamiento lógico

ap•plic•a•ble [ə'plɪkəbl] *adj* aplicable; ***it's not ~ to foreigners*** no se aplica a extranjeros; ***not ~*** no corresponde, no se aplica

ap•pli•cant ['æplɪkənt] solicitante *m/f*

ap•pli•ca•tion [æplɪ'keɪʃn] **1** *for job, passport etc* solicitud *f*; *for university* solicitud *f* (de admisión); ***details available on ~*** para más detalles, póngase en contacto con nosotros **2** *of rules, ointment, paint* aplicación *f* **3**: ***have no ~*** no tener relevancia (***to*** para), no tener relación (***to*** con)

ap•pli'ca•tion form *for passport* impreso *m* de solicitud; *for university, membership* impreso *m* de solicitud de admisión

ap•pli'ca•tion soft•ware software *m* de aplicaciones

ap•plied [ə'plaɪd] *adj* aplicado, práctico; ***~ sciences*** ciencias *fpl* aplicadas

ap•ply [ə'plaɪ] **I** *v/t* (*pret & pp* **-ied**) *rules, solution, ointment* aplicar; ***~ the brakes*** echar los frenos, frenar; ***~ one's mind to sth*** concentrarse *or* centrarse en algo; ***~ o.s. to sth*** concentrarse en algo, dedicarse a algo **II** *v/i* (*pret & pp* **-ied**) *of rule, law* aplicarse

◆ **apply for** *v/t job, passport* solicitar; *university* solicitar el ingreso en

◆ **apply to** *v/t* **1** (*contact*) dirigirse a **2** (*affect*) aplicarse a

ap•point [ə'pɔɪnt] *v/t to position* nombrar, designar

ap•point•ee [əpɔɪn'tiː] *persona nombrada para desempeñar un cargo*

ap•point•ment [ə'pɔɪntmənt] **1** *to position* nombramiento *m*, designación *f* **2** *meeting* cita *f*; ***make an ~ with the doctor*** pedir hora con el doctor; ***keep an ~*** acudir a una cita; ***by ~*** con cita previa

ap'point•ments di•a•ry agenda *f* de citas

ap•por•tion [ə'pɔːrʃn] *v/t* **1** *blame* atribuir, imputar (***to*** a) **2** *money* distribuir, repartir

ap•po•site ['æpəzɪt] *adj* apropiado, adecuado

ap•prais•al [ə'preɪz(ə)l] evaluación *f*

ap•praise [ə'preɪz] *v/t* evaluar, valorar

ap•pre•ci•a•ble [ə'priːʃəbl] *adj* apreciable

ap•pre•ci•ate [ə'priːʃɪeɪt] **I** *v/t* **1** (*value*) apreciar **2** (*be grateful for*) agradecer; ***thanks, I ~ it*** te lo agradezco **3** (*acknowledge*) ser consciente de **II** *v/i* FIN revalorizarse

ap•pre•ci•a•tion [əpriːʃɪ'eɪʃn] **1** *of kindness etc* agradecimiento *m* **2** *of music etc* aprecio *m*

ap•pre•ci•a•tive [ə'priːʃətɪv] *adj* agradecido

ap•pre•hend [æprɪ'hend] *v/t* **1** (*arrest*) arrestar, detener **2** *fml* (*understand*) aprehender

ap•pre•hen•sion [æprɪ'henʃn] **1** *arrest* arresto *m*, detención *f* **2** *fear* aprensión *f*, miedo *m*

ap•pre•hen•sive [æprɪ'hensɪv] *adj* aprensivo, temeroso

ap•pren•tice [ə'prentɪs] aprendiz(a) *m(f)*

ap•pren•tice•ship [ə'prentɪʃɪp] aprendizaje *m*

ap•proach [ə'proʊtʃ] **I** *n* **1** aproximación *f*; ***with the ~ of winter*** con la llegada del invierno **2** (*proposal*) propuesta *f*; ***make ~es to s.o.*** contactar con alguien, ponerse en contacto con alguien **3** *to problem* enfoque *m* **II** *v/t* **1** (*get near to*) aproximarse a **2** (*contact*) ponerse en contacto con **3** *problem* enfocar **III** *v/i of winter, Christmas etc* llegar; *of car etc* acercarse

ap•proach•a•ble [ə'proʊtʃəbl] *adj person* accesible

ap'proach lights *npl at aiport* luces *fpl* de aproximación

ap'proach path *of airplane* trayectoria *f* de aproximación

ap•pro•ba•tion [æproʊ'beɪʃn] aprobación *f*, conformidad *f*

ap•pro•pri•ate[1] [ə'proʊprɪət] *adj* apropiado, adecuado

ap•pro•pri•ate[2] [ə'proʊprɪeɪt] *v/t also euph* apropiarse de

ap•pro•pri•a•tion [əproʊprɪ'eɪʃn] apropiación *f*

ap•prov•al [ə'pruːvl] aprobación *f*; ***on ~*** COM de prueba, en periodo de prueba; ***meet with s.o.'s ~*** contar con el beneplácito de alguien

ap•prove [ə'pruːv] **I** *v/i*: ***my parents don't ~*** a mis padres no les parece bien **II** *v/t* aprobar

◆ **approve of** *v/t* aprobar; ***her parents don't approve of me*** no les gusto a sus padres

ap•prox•i•mate [ə'prɑːksɪmət] *adj* aproximado

ap•prox•i•mate•ly [ə'prɑːksɪmətlɪ] *adv* aproximadamente

ap•prox•i•ma•tion [əprɑːksɪ'meɪʃn] aproximación *f*

APR [eɪpiː'ɑːr] *abbr* (= ***annual percentage rate***) TAE *f* (= tasa *f* anual equivalente)

a•pri•cot ['æprɪkɑːt] albaricoque *m*, *L.Am.* damasco *m*

A•pril ['eɪprəl] abril *m*; ***~ Fool's Day*** día *m* de los (Santos) Inocentes (*1 de abril*)

a•pron ['eɪprən] **1** delantal *m* **2** AVIA área *m* de estacionamiento

'a•pron strings *npl*: ***be tied to one's mother's ~*** *fig* estar cosido a las faldas de la madre

apt [æpt] *adj* **1** *remark* oportuno **2**: ***be ~ to do sth*** ser propenso a hacer algo

ap•ti•tude ['æptɪtuːd] aptitud *f*; ***he has a natural ~ for ...*** tiene aptitudes naturales para ...

'ap•ti•tude test prueba *f* de aptitud

aq•ua•lung ['ækwəlʌŋ] escafandra *f* autónoma

aq•ua•ma•rine [ækwəmə'riːn] **1** MIN aguamarina *f* **2** *color* azul *m* verdoso

a•quar•i•um [ə'kwerɪəm] acuario *m*

A•quar•i•us [ə'kwerɪəs] ASTR Acuario *m/f inv*, *L.Am.* acuriano(-a) *m(f)*; ***be*** (***an***) ***~*** ser Acuariano, *L.Am.* ser acuariano

a•quat•ic [ə'kwætɪk] *adj* acuático

aq•ue•duct ['ækwɪdʌkt] acueducto *m*

Ar•ab ['ærəb] **I** *adj* árabe **II** *n* árabe *m/f*

ar•a•besque [ærə'besk] arabesco *m*

A•ra•bi•a [ə'reɪbɪə] Arabia *f*

A•ra•bi•an [ə'reɪbɪən] *adj* arábigo, árabe

Ar•a•bic ['ærəbɪk] **I** *adj* árabe; ***~ numerals*** números arábigos **II** *n* árabe *m*

ar•a•ble ['ærəbl] *adj*: ***~ land*** tierra *f* de cultivo

ar•bi•ter ['ɑːrbɪtər] árbitro(-a) *m(f)*, mediador(a) *m(f)*

ar•bi•tra•ry ['ɑːrbɪtrerɪ] *adj* arbitrario

ar•bi•trate ['ɑːrbɪtreɪt] *v/i* arbitrar

ar•bi•tra•tion [ɑːrbɪ'treɪʃn] arbitraje *m*; ***court of ~*** tribunal *m* arbitral *or* de arbitraje

ar•bi•tra•tor ['ɑːrbɪ'treɪtər] árbitro(-a) *m(f)*

ar•bor, *Br* **ar•bour** ['ɑːrbər] pérgola *f*

arc [ɑːrk] arco *m*, curva *f*

ar•cade [ɑːr'keɪd] **1** *of shops* pasaje *m or* galería *f* comercial **2** ARCHIT pasaje *m*, galería *f*

arch[1] [ɑːrʧ] **I** *n* arco *m* **II** *v/t*: ***~ one's back*** arquear *or* doblar la espalda

arch[2] [ɑːrʧ] *adj remark*, *expression* malintencionado, retorcido

arch[3] [ɑːrʧ] *adj enemy* malévolo

ar•chae•o•log•i•cal *etc Br* ☞ ***archeological*** *etc*

ar•cha•ic [ɑːr'keɪɪk] *adj* arcaico

arch•an•gel ['ɑːrkeɪndʒəl] arcángel *m*

arch'bish•op arzobispo *m*

arch•bish•op•ric [ɑːrʧ'bɪʃəprɪk] arzobispado *m*

arch'duch•y archiducado *m*

arch'duke archiduque *m*

ar•che•o•log•i•cal [ɑːrkɪə'lɑːdʒɪkl] *adj* arqueológico

ar•che•ol•o•gist [ɑːrkɪ'ɑːlədʒɪst] arqueólogo(-a) *m(f)*

ar•che•ol•o•gy [ɑːrkɪ'ɑːlədʒɪ] arqueología *f*

arch•er ['ɑːrʧər] arquero(-a) *m(f)*

arch•er•y ['ɑːrʧərɪ] arco *m*

ar•che•typ•al [ɑːrkɪ'taɪpl] *adj* arquetípico

ar•che•type ['ɑːrkɪtaɪp] arquetipo *m*, modelo *m*

ar•chi•pel•a•go [ɑːrkɪ'pelәgoʊ] (*pl* ***-go(e)s***) archipiélago *m*

ar•chi•tect ['ɑːrkɪtekt] arquitecto(-a) *m(f)*

ar•chi•tec•tur•al [ɑːrkɪ'tekʧərəl] *adj* arquitectónico

ar•chi•tec•ture ['ɑːrkɪtekʧər] arquitectura *f*

ar•chives ['ɑːrkaɪvz] *npl* archivos *mpl*

ar•chi•vist ['ɑːrkɪvɪst] historiador(a) *m(f)*

'arch•way arco *m*

Arc•tic ['ɑːrktɪk] **I** *n*: ***the*** **~** el Ártico **II** *adj* ártico
Arc•tic 'Cir•cle círculo *m* Polar Ártico
Arc•tic 'O•cean océano *m* Ártico
ar•dent ['ɑːrdənt] *adj* ardiente, ferviente
ar•dor, *Br* **ar•dour** ['ɑːrdər] ardor *m*, fervor *m*
ar•du•ous ['ɑːrdjʊəs] *adj* arduo
are [ɑːr] ☞ ***be***
ar•e•a ['erɪə] área *f*, zona *f*; *of activity, study etc* área *f*, ámbito *m*
'ar•e•a code TELEC prefijo *m*
ar•e•a 'man•ag•er gerente *m/f or* encargado(-a) *m(f)* de área
a•re•na [ə'riːnə] SP estadio *m*
aren't [ɑːrnt] F ***are not.***
Ar•gen•ti•na [ɑːrdʒən'tiːnə] Argentina *f*
Ar•gen•tin•i•an [ɑːrdʒən'tɪnɪən] **I** *adj* argentino **II** *n* argentino(-a) *m(f)*
ar•gu•a•ble ['ɑːrgjʊəbl] *adj* discutible; ***it is*** **~** ***that …*** es discutible que …
ar•gu•a•bly ['ɑːrgjʊəblɪ] *adv* posiblemente
ar•gue ['ɑːrgjuː] **I** *v/i* **1** (*quarrel*) discutir; ***don't*** **~*!*** ¡y a callar!, ¡sin rechistar! **2** (*reason*) argumentar **II** *v/t*: **~** ***that …*** argumentar que …
◆ **argue against** *v/t* criticar, condenar
◆ **argue for** *v/t* defender, sostener
ar•gu•ment ['ɑːrgjʊmənt] **1** (*quarrel*) discusión *f* **2** (*reasoning*) argumento *m*
ar•gu•men•ta•tion [ɑːrgjʊmen'teɪʃn] **1** argumentación *f* **2** (*reasoning*) argumento *m*
ar•gu•ment•a•tive [ɑːrgjʊ'mentətɪv] *adj* discutidor
a•ri•a ['ɑːrɪə] MUS aria *f*
ar•id ['ærɪd] *adj land* árido
Ar•ies ['eriːz] ASTR Aries *m/f inv*; ***be*** (***an***) **~** ser Aries
a•rise [ə'raɪz] *v/i* (*pret* ***arose***, *pp* ***arisen***) *of situation, problem* surgir
a•ris•en [ə'rɪzn] *pp* ☞ ***arise***
ar•is•toc•ra•cy [ærɪ'stɑːkrəsɪ] aristocracia *f*
a•ris•to•crat [ə'rɪstəkræt] aristócrata *m/f*
a•ris•to•crat•ic [ærɪstə'krætɪk] *adj* aristocrático
a•rith•me•tic [ə'rɪθmətɪk] aritmética *f*; ***some complicated*** **~** algunos cálculos complicados
a•rith•me•tic, ar•ith•met•i•cal [ærɪθ'metɪk, ærɪθ'metɪkl] *adj* aritmético
ark [ɑːrk]: ***Noah's*** **~** el arca de Noé
arm[1] [ɑːrm] *n of person, chair* brazo *m*; ***take s.o. in one's*** **~*s*** abrazar a alguien; ***welcome s.o. with open*** **~*s*** recibir a alguien con los brazos abiertos; ***within*** **~*'s reach*** al alcance de las manos; ***the long*** **~** ***of the law*** el brazo de la ley; ***keep s.o. at*** **~*'s length*** mantenerse alejado de alguien; F ***cost an*** **~** ***and a leg*** valer un riñón F; ***walk*** **~** ***in*** **~** ir del brazo
arm[2] [ɑːrm] *v/t* armar
Ar•ma•da [ɑːr'mɑːdə] HIST: ***the*** **~** la Armada Invencible
ar•ma•dil•lo [ɑːrmə'dɪloʊ] *n* ZO armadillo *m*
ar•ma•ments ['ɑːrməmənts] *npl* armamento *m*
'arm•band brazal *m*
'arm•chair sillón *m*; **~** ***traveler*** viajante *m/f* de sillón
armed [ɑːrmd] *adj* armado; **~** ***conflict*** conflicto *m* armado
armed 'forc•es *npl* fuerzas *fpl* armadas
armed 'rob•ber•y atraco *m* a mano armada
arm•ful ['ɑːrmfʊl] *quantity* brazado *m*
ar•mi•stice ['ɑːrmɪstɪs] armisticio *m*
ar•mor, *Br* **ar•mour** ['ɑːrmər] armadura *f*
ar•mored car, *Br* **ar•moured car** [ɑːrmərd'kɑːr] MIL coche *m* blindado
ar•mored 've•hi•cle, *Br* **ar•moured ve•hi•cle** vehículo *m* blindado
ar•mor-plat•ed, *Br* **ar•mour-plat•ed** ['pleɪtɪd] *adj* blindado
'arm•pit sobaco *m*
'arm•rest reposabrazos *m inv*
arms [ɑːrmz] *npl* (*weapons*) armas *fpl*
'arms•con•trol control *m* de armas; **'arms deal•er** traficante *m/f* de armas; **'arms race** carrera *f* armamentística
arm-twist•ing ['ɑːrmtwɪstɪŋ]: ***it took some*** **~** hubo que convencerlo
ar•my ['ɑːrmɪ] ejército *m*
a•ro•ma [ə'roʊmə] aroma *m*
a•ro•ma•ther•a•py [ə'roʊməθerəpɪ] aromatoterapia *f*
ar•o•mat•ic [æroʊ'mætɪk] *adj* aromático
a•rose [ə'roʊz] *pret* ☞ ***arise***
a•round [ə'raʊnd] **I** *prep* (*encircling*) al-

rededor de; ***it's ~ the corner*** está a la vuelta de la esquina
II *adv* **1** (*in the area*) por ahí; ***he lives ~ here*** vive por aquí; ***walk ~*** pasear; ***she has been ~*** (*has traveled, is experienced*) tiene mucho mundo; ***he's still ~*** F (*alive*) todavía está rondando por ahí F **2** (*encircling*) alrededor **3** (*roughly*) alrededor de, aproximadamente; (*with expressions of time*) en torno a
a•rouse [ə'rauz] *v/t* despertar; *sexually* excitar
ar•range [ə'reɪndʒ] *v/t* **1** (*put in order*) ordenar; *furniture* ordenar, disponer; *flowers, music* arreglar **2** *meeting, party etc* organizar; *time and place* acordar; ***I've ~d to meet her*** he quedado con ella
◆ **arrange for** *v/t*: ***I arranged for Jack to collect it*** quedé para que Jack lo recogiera
ar•range•ment [ə'reɪndʒmənt] **1** (*plan*) plan *m*, preparativo *m* **2** (*agreement*) acuerdo *m*; ***make ~s*** hacer los preparativos; ***I've made ~s for the neighbors to water my plants*** he quedado con los vecinos para que rieguen mis plantas **3** (*layout: of furniture etc*) orden *m*, disposición *f*; *of flowers, music* arreglo *m*
ar•ray [ə'reɪ] **I** *v/t* disponer, organizar **II** *n* selección *f*, conjunto *m*
ar•rears [ə'rɪərz] *npl* atrasos *mpl*; ***be in ~*** *of person* ir atrasado
ar•rest [ə'rest] **I** *n* detención *f*, arresto *m*; ***be under ~*** estar detenido *or* arrestado **II** *v/t* detener, arrestar
ar•riv•al [ə'raɪvl] llegada *f*; ***on your ~*** al llegar; ***~s*** *at airport* llegadas *fsg*
ar'riv•al time hora *f* de llegada
ar•rive [ə'raɪv] *v/i* llegar
◆ **arrive at** *v/t place, decision etc* llegar a
ar•ro•gance ['ærəgəns] arrogancia *f*
ar•ro•gant ['ærəgənt] *adj* arrogante
ar•ro•gant•ly ['ærəgəntlɪ] *adv* con arrogancia
ar•row ['æroʊ] flecha *f*
'ar•row•head punta *f or* cabeza *f* de flecha
'ar•row key COMPUT tecla *f* (de movimiento del) cursor
arse [ɑːrs] *Br* P culo *m* P
ar•se•nal ['ɑːrsənl] MIL arsenal *m*
ar•se•nic ['ɑːrsənɪk] arsénico *m*
ar•son ['ɑːrsn] incendio *m* provocado
ar•son•ist ['ɑːrsənɪst] pirómano(-a) *m*(*f*)
art [ɑːrt] arte *m*; ***the ~s*** las artes
'art crit•ic crítico *m/f* de arte
ar•te•ri•al [ɑːr'tɪərɪəl] *adj* ANAT arterial
ar•te•ri•o•scle•ro•sis [ɑːrtɪrɪoʊsklə'roʊsɪs] MED arteriosclerosis *f*
ar•te•ry ['ɑːrtərɪ] MED arteria *f*
ar•te•sian well [ɑːrtiːzjən'wel] pozo *m* artesiano
art•ful ['ɑːrtfʊl] *adj* astuto, hábil
'art gal•ler•y *public* museo *m*; *private* galería *f* de arte
art 'his•to•ry historia *f* del arte
ar•thrit•ic [ɑːr'θrɪtɪk] *adj* artrítico
ar•thri•tis [ɑːr'θraɪtɪs] artritis *f*
ar•ti•choke ['ɑːrtɪtʃoʊk] alcachofa *f*, *L.Am.* alcaucil *m*
ar•ti•cle ['ɑːrtɪkl] artículo *m*
ar•tic•u•late I *adj* [ɑːr'tɪkjʊlət] *person* elocuente **II** *v/t* [ɑːr'tɪkjʊleɪt] *idea, feelings* expresar, exteriorizar
ar•tic•u•lat•ed [ɑːr'tɪkjʊleɪtɪd] *adj* TECH articulado
ar•tic•u•la•tion [ɑːrtɪkjʊ'leɪʃn] *of idea, feelings* expresión *f*, exteriorización *f*
ar•ti•fice ['ɑːrtɪfɪs] artificio *m*
ar•ti•fi•cial [ɑːrtɪ'fɪʃl] *adj* artificial
ar•ti•fi•cial in•sem•i'na•tion inseminación *f* artificial; **ar•ti•fi•cial in'tel•li•gence** inteligencia *f* artificial; **ar•ti•fi•cial res•pi'ra•tion** respiración *f* artificial
ar•til•le•ry [ɑːr'tɪlərɪ] artillería *f*
ar•ti•san ['ɑːrtɪzæn] artesano(-a) *m*(*f*)
art•ist ['ɑːrtɪst] (*painter, artistic person*) artista *m/f*
ar•tis•tic [ɑːr'tɪstɪk] *adj* artístico
art•less ['ɑːrtlɪs] *adj* inocente, simple
'art school facultad *f* de Bellas Artes
'arts de•gree licenciatura *f* en letras
'arts fes•ti•val festival *f* cultural *or* de las artes
'art stud•ent estudiante *m/f* de Bellas Artes
'art•work ilustraciones *fpl*; ***a piece of ~*** una ilustración
as [æz] **I** *conj* **1** (*while, when*) cuando **2** (*because, like*) como **3**: ***~ if*** como si; ***~ usual*** como de costumbre; ***~ necessary*** como sea necesario
II *adv* como; ***~ high / pretty ~ …*** tan alto / guapa como …; ***~ much ~ that?***

¿tanto?
III *prep* como; ***work ~ a team*** trabajar en equipo; ***~ a child / schoolgirl*** cuando era un niño / una colegiala; ***work ~ a teacher / translator*** trabajar como profesor / traductor; ***~ for*** por lo que respecta a; ***~ Hamlet*** en el papel del Hamlet
asap ['eɪzæp] *abbr* (= ***as soon as possible***) cuanto antes
as•bes•tos [æz'bestɑːs] amianto *m*, asbesto *m*
as•cend [ə'send] **I** *v/i* ascender (***to*** a) **II** *v/t* subir, escalar
as•cend•an•cy [ə'sendənsɪ] superioridad *f*, dominio *m* (***over*** sobre); ***gain the ~ over*** ganar superioridad sobre
as•cend•ant [ə'sendənt]: ***in the ~*** *fig* en auge
as•cend•en•cy, as•cend•ent ☞ ***ascendancy, ascendant***
As•cen•sion [ə'senʃn] REL Ascensión *f*
As'cen•sion Day día *m* de la Ascensión
as•cent [ə'sent] ascenso *m*, subida *f*
as•cer•tain [æsər'teɪn] *v/t* determinar, establecer
as•cet•ic [ə'setɪk] *adj* ascético
as•cet•i•cism [ə'setɪsɪzəm] ascetismo *m*
ASCII ['æskiː] *abbr* (= ***American Standard Code for Information Interchange***) código *m* ASCII, ASCII *m*
a•scor•bic ac•id [əskɔːrbɪk'æsɪd] CHEM ácido *m* ascórbico
as•cribe [ə'skraɪb] *v/t*: ***~ sth to s.o.*** atribuir algo a alguien
a•sep•tic [eɪ'septɪk] *adj* MED aséptico
a•sex•u•al [eɪ'sekʃʊəl] *adj* **1** BIO asexual **2** *relationship* sin sexo
ash[1] [æʃ] ceniza *f*; ***~es*** *of person* cenizas *fpl*
ash[2] [æʃ] **1** *tree* fresno *m* **2** *wood* madera *f* de fresno
a•shamed [ə'ʃeɪmd] *adj* avergonzado, *L.Am.* apenado; ***be ~ of*** estar avergonzado *or L.Am.* apenado de; ***you should be ~ of yourself*** debería darte vergüenza *or L.Am.* pena; ***it's nothing to be ~ of*** no tienes por qué avergonzarte *or L.Am.* apenarte
'ash can cubo *m* de la basura
ash•en ['æʃn] *adj* pálido, blanco
a•shore [ə'ʃɔːr] *adv* en tierra; ***go ~*** desembarcar
'ash•tray cenicero *m*
Ash 'Wednes•day Miércoles *m* de Ceniza
A•sia ['eɪʃə] Asia *f*
A•sia 'Mi•nor GEOG Asia *f* Menor
A•sian ['eɪʃən] **I** *adj* asiático **II** *n* asiático(-a) *m(f)*
A•sian A'mer•i•can norteamericano(-a) *m(f)* de origen asiático
A•si•at•ic [eɪʃɪ'ætɪk] *adj* asiático
a•side [ə'saɪd] *adv* a un lado; ***move ~ please*** apártense, por favor; ***he took me ~*** me llevó aparte; ***~ from*** aparte de
as•i•nine ['æsɪnaɪn] *adj* ignorante, estúpido
ask [æsk] **I** *v/t* **1** *person* preguntar; *question* hacer; ***can I ~ you something?*** ¿puedo hacerte una pregunta?; ***he ~ed me to leave*** me pidió que me fuera; ***~ s.o. for sth*** pedir algo a alguien ***~ s.o. about sth*** preguntar por algo a alguien; ***~ a high price for sth*** pedir mucho dinero por algo; ***that is ~ing a lot*** eso es mucho pedir; ***don't ~ me*** yo qué sé F, (a mi) no me preguntes
2 (*invite*) invitar; *favor* pedir
II *v/i*: ***all you need to do is ~*** no tienes más que pedirlo
◆ **ask after** *v/t person* preguntar por
◆ **ask around** *v/i* preguntar (por ahí)
◆ **ask for** *v/t* pedir; *person* preguntar por; ***he was asking for it** or **trouble*** F se la estaba buscando F, se la tenía ganada F; ***don't get him to do it, that's asking for trouble*** no le pidas que lo haga o te causará problemas; ***well, you asked for that!*** ¡tú te lo has buscado!
◆ **ask in** *v/t*: ***ask s.o. in*** invitar a alguien a entrar *or* pasar
◆ **ask out** *v/t*: ***ask s.o. out*** pedir salir a alguien
a•skance [ə'skæns] *adv*: ***look ~ at s.o. / sth*** mirar a alguien / algo con recelo
a•skew [ə'skjuː] *adv* torcido; ***go ~*** *fig* salir torcido
ask•ing ['æskɪŋ]: ***it's yours for the ~*** es tuyo si lo quieres
'ask•ing price precio *m* de salida
a•sleep [ə'sliːp] *adj* dormido; ***be*** (***fast***) ***~*** estar (profundamente) dormido; ***fall ~*** dormirse, quedarse dormido
as•par•a•gus [ə'spærəgəs] espárragos *mpl*

as•pect ['æspekt] aspecto *m*
as•pen ['æspən] BOT álamo *m* alpino
as•per•i•ty [æ'sperətɪ] gravedad *f*, severidad *f*
as•per•sion [ə'spɜːrʒn]: ***cast ~s on sth*** echar *or* decir pestes de algo
as•phalt ['æsfælt] asfalto *m*
as•phyx•i•a [æs'fɪksɪə] MED asfixia *f*
as•phyx•i•ate [æ'sfɪksɪeɪt] *v/t* asfixiar
as•phyx•i•a•tion [əsfɪksɪ'eɪʃn] asfixia *f*
as•pic ['æspɪk] GASTR *gelatina a base de jugo de carne*; ***preserved in ~*** *fig* conservado tal cual, intacto
as•pi•rant [ə'spaɪərənt] aspirante *m/f*, candidato(-a) *m(f)*
as•pi•ra•tion [æspə'reɪʃn] aspiración *f*
◆ **as•pire to** [ə'spaɪər] *v/t* aspirar a
as•pi•rin ['æsprɪn] aspirina *f*
as•pir•ing [ə'spaɪərɪŋ] *adj*: ***she is an ~ writer*** es una escritora en ciernes
ass[1] [æs] (*idiot*) burro(-a) *m(f)*; ***make an ~ of o.s.*** ponerse en ridículo
ass[2] [æs] P (*backside*) culo *m* P; (*sex*) sexo *m*
as•sail [ə'seɪl] *v/t* **1** *fml*: *attack* asaltar **2** *fig* acometer, acosar; ***~ed by doubt*** acosado por las dudas
as•sai•lant [ə'seɪlənt] asaltante *m/f*
as•sas•sin [ə'sæsɪn] asesino(-a) *m(f)*
as•sas•sin•ate [ə'sæsɪneɪt] *v/t* asesinar
as•sas•sin•a•tion [əsæsɪ'neɪʃn] asesinato *m*
as•sault [ə'sɒːlt] **I** *n* agresión *f*, (*attack*) ataque *m*; ***~ course*** MIL campo *m* de entrenamiento, pista *f* americana; ***~ and battery*** LAW asalto y agresión; ***indecent ~*** agresión *f or* delito *m* sexual **II** *v/t* atacar, agredir
as•say [ə'seɪ] *of ore* ensayo *m*
as•sem•ble [ə'sembl] **I** *v/t parts* montar **II** *v/i of people* reunirse
as•sem•bler [ə'semblər] TECH ensamblador *m*
as•sem•bly [ə'semblɪ] **1** *of parts* montaje *m* **2** POL asamblea *f* **3** *in school*: reunión *f* de profesores y alumnos
as'sem•bly lan•guage COMPUT lenguaje *m* ensamblador; **as'sem•bly line** cadena *f* de montaje; **as'sem•bly plant** planta *f* de montaje
as•sent [ə'sent] **I** *v/i* asentir, dar el consentimiento **II** *n*: ***by common ~*** de común acuerdo, por consenso
as•sert [ə'sɜːrt] *v/t* afirmar, hacer valer; ***~ o.s.*** mostrarse firme
as•ser•tion [ə'sɜːrʃn] afirmación *f*, aseveración *f*
as•ser•tive [ə'sɜːrtɪv] *adj person* seguro y firme
as•ser•tive•ness [ə'sɜːrtɪvnɪs] seguridad *f*, aplomo *m*
as•sess [ə'ses] *v/t* **1** *situation* evaluar **2** *value* valorar
as•sess•ment [ə'sesmənt] evaluación *f*
as•set ['æset] **1** FIN activo *m*; ***~s and liabilities*** activo y pasivo **2** *fig* ventaja *f*; ***be a great ~*** ser de gran valor, ser una figura destacable; ***she's an ~ to the company*** es un gran valor para la compañía
'ass•hole V **1** ojete *m* V **2** (*idiot*) *Span* gilipollas *m/f inv* V, *L.Am.* pendejo(-a) *m(f)* V; ***make an ~ of o.s.*** ponerse en ridículo
as•sid•u•ous [ə'sɪdjʊəs] *adj fml* diligente, eficaz
as•sign [ə'saɪn] *v/t* asignar
as•sign•ment [ə'saɪnmənt] (*task, study*) trabajo *m*
as•sim•i•late [ə'sɪmɪleɪt] *v/t* **1** *information* asimilar **2** *person into group* integrar
as•sim•i•la•tion [əsɪmɪ'leɪʃn] **1** *of information* asimilación *f* **2** *into group* integración *f*
as•sist [ə'sɪst] **I** *v/t* ayudar **II** *n in basketball etc* asistencia *f*
as•sist•ance [ə'sɪstəns] ayuda *f*, asistencia *f*; ***come to s.o.'s ~*** ir *or* salir en ayuda de alguien
as•sis•tant [ə'sɪstənt] ayudante *m/f*, *Br*: *in store* dependiente(-a) *m(f)*
as•sis•tant di'rec•tor director(a) *m(f)* adjunto(-a); **as•sis•tant 'ed•i•tor** editor(a) *m(f)* adjunto(-a), co-editor(a) *m(f)*; **as•sis•tant 'man•ag•er** *of business* subdirector(a) *m(f)*; *of hotel, restaurant, store* subdirector(a) *m(f)*, subgerente *m/f*; **as•sis•tant pro'fes•sor** profesor(a) *m(f)* adjunto(-a); **as•sis•tant ref•er'ee** árbitro(-a) *m(f)* asistente
as•so•ci•ate I *v/t* [ə'soʊʃɪeɪt] asociar; ***he has long been ~d with the Ballet*** ha estado vinculado al Ballet durante mucho tiempo **II** *v/i* [ə'soʊʃɪeɪt]: ***~ with*** relacionarse con **III** *adj* [ə'soʊʃɪət] asociado **IV** *n* [ə'soʊʃɪət] colega *m/f*
as•so•ci•ate 'ed•i•tor editor(a) *m(f)*

asociado(-a), co-editor(a) *m(f)*
as•so•ci•ate pro'fes•sor profesor(a) *m(f)* adjunto(-a)
as•so•ci•a•tion [əsoʊsɪ'eɪʃn] asociación *f*; ***in ~ with*** conjuntamente con
as•sort•ed [ə'sɔːrtɪd] *adj* surtido, diverso
as•sort•ment [ə'sɔːrtmənt] *of food* surtido *m*; *of people* diversidad *f*
as•sume [ə'suːm] *v/t* (*suppose*) suponer; ***assuming that …*** suponiendo que …; ***I ~ so*** eso supongo
as•sump•tion [ə'sʌmpʃn] suposición *f*; ***on the ~ that*** suponiendo que
As'sump•tion (Day) REL (día *m* de) la Asunción
as•sur•ance [ə'ʃʊrəns] **1** garantía *f* **2** (*confidence*) seguridad *f*
as•sure [ə'ʃʊr] *v/t* **1** (*reassure*) asegurar; ***~ s.o. of sth*** garantizar a alguien algo, asegurar a alguien algo **2** *Br* FIN asegurar
as•sured [ə'ʃʊrd] *adj* (*confident*) seguro; ***you can rest ~ that …*** puedes estar tranquilo que …
as•sur•ed•ly [ə'ʃʊrədlɪ] *adv* claramente, sin lugar a dudas
as•ter•isk ['æstərɪsk] asterisco *m*
a•stern [ə'stɜːrn] *adv* NAUT hacia atrás
asth•ma ['æsmə] asma *f*; ***~ attack*** ataque *m* de asma
asth•mat•ic [æs'mætɪk] *adj* asmático; ***be ~*** padecer de asma
a•stig•ma•tism [ə'stɪgmətɪzəm] MED astigmatismo *m*
as•ton•ish [ə'stɑːnɪʃ] *v/t* asombrar, sorprender; ***be ~ed*** estar asombrado *or* sorprendido
as•ton•ish•ing [ə'stɑːnɪʃɪŋ] *adj* asombroso, sorprendente
as•ton•ish•ing•ly [ə'stɑːnɪʃɪŋlɪ] *adv* asombrosamente
as•ton•ish•ment [ə'stɑːnɪʃmənt] asombro *m*, sorpresa *f*; ***much to their ~*** para su gran asombro
as•tound [ə'staʊnd] *v/t* pasmar
as•tound•ing [ə'staʊndɪŋ] *adj* pasmoso
a•stray [ə'streɪ] *adv*: ***go ~*** extraviarse; *morally* descarriarse; ***lead s.o. ~*** *fig* descarriar a alguien, llevar a alguien por el mal camino
a•stride [ə'straɪd] **I** *adv* a horcajadas **II** *prep* a horcajadas sobre
as•trin•gent [ə'strɪndʒənt] **I** *adj liquid* astringente; *comment* mordaz, caústico **II** *n* astringente *m*
as•trol•o•ger [ə'strɑːlədʒər] astrólogo (-a) *m(f)*
as•tro•log•i•cal [æstrə'lɑːdʒɪkl] *adj* astrológico
as•trol•o•gy [ə'strɑːlədʒɪ] astrología *f*
as•tro•naut ['æstrənɒːt] astronauta *m/f*
as•tron•o•mer [ə'strɑːnəmər] astrónomo(-a) *m(f)*
as•tro•nom•ic [æstrə'nɑːmɪk] astronómico
as•tro•nom•i•cal [æstrə'nɑːmɪkl] *adj price etc* astronómico
as•tron•o•my [ə'strɑːnəmɪ] astronomía *f*
as•tro•phys•ics [æstroʊ'fɪzɪks] *nsg* astrofísica *f*
as•tute [ə'stuːt] *adj* astuto, sagaz
as•tute•ness [ə'stuːtnɪs] astucia *f*, sagacidad *f*
a•sy•lum [ə'saɪləm] **1** (*mental ~*) manicomio *m* **2** *political* asilo *m*; ***ask for ~*** solicitar asilo; ***grant s.o. ~*** conceder el asilo a alguien
a•sy•lum seek•er [ə'saɪləmsiːkər] solicitante *m/f* de asilo (político)
a•sym•met•ric, a•sym•met•ri•cal [eɪsɪ'metrɪk(l)] *adj* asimétrico
a•sym•me•try [eɪ'sɪmətrɪ] asimetría *f*
at [ət] *stressed* [æt] *prep with places* en; ***~ Joe's*** *house* en casa de Joe; *bar* en el bar de Joe; ***~ the door*** a la puerta; ***~ 10 dollars*** a 10 dólares; ***~ the age of 18*** a los 18 años; ***~ 5 o'clock*** a las 5; ***~ 150km/h*** a 150 km/h; ***be good / bad ~ sth*** ser bueno / malo haciendo algo
At•a•ca•ma de•sert [ætə'kɑːmə] desierto *m* Atacama
at•a•vis•tic [ætə'vɪstɪk] *adj* atávico, ancestral
ate [eɪt] *pret* ☞ ***eat***
a•the•ism ['eɪθɪɪzm] ateísmo *m*
a•the•ist ['eɪθɪɪst] ateo(-a) *m(f)*
a•the•is•tic [eɪθɪ'ɪstɪk] *adj* ateísta, ateo
Ath•ens ['æθənz] Atenas *f*
ath•lete ['æθliːt] atleta *m/f*
ath•lete's 'foot MED pie *m* de atleta
ath•let•ic [æθ'letɪk] *adj* atlético
ath•let•ics [æθ'letɪks] *nsg* atletismo *m*; ***~ field*** pista *f* de atletismo
At•lan•tic [ət'læntɪk]: ***the ~*** el Atlántico
at•las ['ætləs] atlas *m inv*

ATM [eɪtiː'em] *abbr* (= ***automated teller machine***) cajero *m* automático
at•mos•phere ['ætməsfɪr] **1** *of earth* atmósfera *f* **2** (*ambience*) ambiente *m*
at•mos•pher•ic pol•lu•tion [ætməsferɪkpə'luːʃn] contaminación *f* atmosférica
at•oll ['ætɑːl] GEOG atolón *m*
at•om ['ætəm] átomo *m*
'at•om bomb bomba *f* atómica
a•tom•ic [ə'tɑːmɪk] *adj* atómico
a•tom•ic 'bomb bomba *f* atómica; **a•tom•ic 'en•er•gy** energía *f* atómica *or* nuclear; **a•tom•ic pow•er** energía *f* atómica *or* nuclear; **a•tom•ic-pow•ered** [ətɑːmɪk'paʊərd] *adj* propulsado por energía nuclear; **a•tom•ic 'pow•er plant** central *f* nuclear; **a•tom•ic 'waste** desechos *mpl* radiactivos; **a•tom•ic 'weight** peso *m* atómico
a•tom•ize ['ætoʊmaɪz] *v/t* atomizar, pulverizar
a•tom•iz•er ['ætəmaɪzər] atomizador *m*
a•tone [ə'toʊn] *v/i*: ~ ***for*** expiar
a•top [ə'tɑːp] *prep* sobre
a•tro•cious [ə'troʊʃəs] *adj* atroz, terrible
a•troc•i•ty [ə'trɑːsətɪ] atrocidad *f*
at•ro•phy ['ætrəfɪ] *v/i also fig* atrofiarse
'at-sign arroba *f*
at•tach [ə'tætʃ] *v/t* **1** sujetar, fijar; *importance* atribuir; ~ ***a file to an e-mail*** adjuntar un archivo a un e-mail **2**: ***be ~ed to*** (*fond of*) tener cariño a
at•ta•ché [ə'tæʃeɪ] agregado(-a) *m*(*f*)
at'ta•ché case maletín *m*
at•tach•ment [ə'tætʃmənt] **1** (*fondness*) cariño *m* (***to*** por) **2** *to e-mail* archivo *m* adjunto
at•tack [ə'tæk] **I** *n* ataque *m* **II** *v/t* atacar
at•tack•er [ə'tækər] atacador(a) *m*(*f*)
at•tain [ə'teɪn] *v/t* conseguir, lograr
at•tain•a•ble [ə'teɪnəbl] *adj* realizable, posible
at•tain•ment [ə'teɪnmənt] **1** logro *m*, consecución *f* **2**: **~s** habilidades *fpl*
at•tempt [ə'tempt] **I** *n* intento *m*; ***an ~ on the world record*** un intento de batir el récord del mundo; ***make an ~ on s.o.'s life*** atentar contra la vida de alguien **II** *v/t* intentar
at•tempt•ed [ə'temptɪd] *adj* LAW: ~ ***murder / suicide*** asesinato *m* / suicidio *m* frustrado
at•tend [ə'tend] *v/t* acudir a
◆ **attend to** *v/t* ocuparse de; *customer* atender
at•tend•ance [ə'tendəns] asistencia *f*; ***in ~*** presente
at•tend•ant [ə'tendənt] *in museum etc* vigilante *m/f*
at•ten•dee [ətenˈdiː] *at conference etc* asistente *m/f*
at•ten•tion [ə'tenʃn] **1** atención *f*; ***bring sth to s.o.'s ~*** informar a alguien de algo; ***your ~ please*** atención, por favor; ***pay ~*** prestar atención; (***for the***) ***~ of*** a la atención de **2**: ***stand to ~*** MIL ponerse firme
at•ten•tion seek•ing [ə'tenʃnsiːkɪŋ] búsqueda *f* de atención
at'ten•tion span capacidad *f* de concentración
at•ten•tive [ə'tentɪv] *adj listener* atento
at•ten•u•ate [ə'tenjʊeɪt] *v/t fig* atenuar, amortiguar
at•test [ə'test] **I** *v/t* atestiguar, probar **II** *v/i*: ~ ***to sth*** dar testimonio de algo
at•tic ['ætɪk] ático *m*
at•tire [ə'taɪər] atuendo *m*, atavío *m*
at•ti•tude ['ætɪtuːd] actitud *f*; ***he has an ~ problem*** tiene un problema de actitud
attn *abbr* (= ***for the attention of***) atn (= a la atención de)
at•tor•ney [ə'tɜːrnɪ] abogado(-a) *m*(*f*); ***power of ~*** poder *m* (notarial)
at•tor•ney 'gen•er•al LAW fiscal *m/f* general
at•tract [ə'trækt] *v/t* atraer; ~ ***attention*** llamar la atención; ~ ***s.o.'s attention*** atraer la atención de alguien; ***be ~ed to s.o.*** sentirse atraído por alguien
at•trac•tion [ə'trækʃn] atracción *f*, atractivo *m*; *romantic* atracción *f*, ***the ~ of this solution is …*** el atractivo *or* lo llamativo de esta solución es …
at•trac•tive [ə'træktɪv] *adj* atractivo
at•trac•tive•ness [ə'træktɪvnɪs] atractivo *m*
at•trib•ute[1] [ə'trɪbjuːt] *v/t* atribuir(***to*** a)
at•trib•ute[2] ['ætrɪbjuːt] *n* atributo *m*
at•trib•u•tive [ə'trɪbjʊtɪv] LING *adj* atributivo
at•tri•tion [ə'trɪʃn] desgaste *m*, debilitamiento *m*; ***war of ~*** guerra *f* de desgaste
a•typ•i•cal [eɪ'tɪpɪkl] *adj* atípico

au•ber•gine ['oubərʒiːn] *Br* berenjena *f*
au•burn ['ɔːbərn] *adj* cobrizo
auc•tion ['ɒːkʃn] **I** *n* subasta *f*, *L.Am.* remate *m*; ***put sth up for ~*** sacar algo a subasta **II** *v/t* subastar, *L.Am.* rematar
◆ **auction off** *v/t* subastar, *L.Am.* rematar
auc•tion•eer [ɒːkʃə'nɪr] subastador(a) *m(f)*, *L.Am.* rematador(a) *m(f)*
au•da•cious [ɒː'deɪʃəs] *adj plan* audaz
au•dac•i•ty [ɒː'dæsətɪ] audacia *f*
au•di•ble ['ɒːdəbl] *adj* audible
au•di•ence ['ɒːdɪəns] *in theater, at show* público *m*, espectadores *mpl*; TV audiencia *f*
au•di•o ['ɒːdɪou] *adj* de audio
'au•di•o typ•ist audiomecanógrafo(-a) *m(f)*
au•di•o'vi•su•al *adj* audiovisual; ***~ aids*** herramientas *fpl* audiovisuales
au•dit ['ɒːdɪt] **I** *n* auditoría *f* **II** *v/t* **1** FIN auditar **2** *course* asistir de oyente a
au•di•tion [ɒː'dɪʃn] **I** *n* audición *f* **II** *v/i* hacer una prueba
au•di•tor ['ɒːdɪtər] auditor(a) *m(f)*
au•di•to•ri•um [ɒːdɪ'tɔːrɪəm] *of theater etc* auditorio *m*
aug•ment [ɔːg'ment] *v/t* agrandar, incrementar
au•gur ['ɔːgər] *v/i*: ***~ well / ill*** presentar buenos / malos augurios (***for*** para)
Au•gust ['ɒːgəst] agosto *m*
aunt [ænt] tía *f*
aunt•ie, aunt•y ['æntɪ] tía *f*
au pair [ou'per] au pair *m/f*
au•ra ['ɒːrə] aura *f*
au•ral ['ɔːrəl] *adj comprehension* auditivo
aus•pic•es ['ɒːspɪsɪz] *npl* auspicios *mpl*; ***under the ~ of*** bajo los auspicios de
aus•pi•cious [ɒː'spɪʃəs] *adj* propicio
Aus•sie ['ɑːzɪ] F **I** *n* australiano(-a) *m(f)* **II** *adj* australiano
aus•tere [ɒː'stiːr] *adj interior* austero
aus•ter•i•ty [ɒːs'terətɪ] *economic* austeridad *f*; ***~ program*** programa *m* de austeridad
Aus•tra•la•sia [ɒːstrəl'eɪʒə] Australasia *f*
Aus•tra•la•sian [ɒːstrəl'eɪʒən] *adj* australasiano
Aus•tra•li•a [ɒː'streɪlɪə] Australia *f*
Aus•tra•li•an [ɒː'streɪlɪən] **I** *adj* australiano **II** *n* australiano(-a) *m(f)*
Aus•tri•a ['ɒːstrɪə] Austria *f*
Aus•tri•an ['ɒːstrɪən] **I** *adj* austriaco **II** *n* austriaco(-a) *m(f)*
au•then•tic [ɒː'θentɪk] *adj* auténtico
au•then•ti•cate [ɒː'θentɪkeɪt] *v/t* autenticar, autentificar
au•then•ti•ca•tion [ɒː'θentɪkeɪʃn] autenticación *f*
au•then•tic•i•ty [ɒːθen'tɪsətɪ] autenticidad *f*
au•thor ['ɒːθər] **I** *n of story, novel* escritor(a) *m(f)*; *of text* autor(a) *m(f)* **II** *v/t story, novel* escribir
au•thor•i•tar•i•an [əθɑːrɪ'terɪən] *adj* autoritario
au•thor•i•ta•tive [ə'θɑːrɪtətɪv] *adj* autorizado
au•thor•i•ty [ə'θɑːrətɪ] **1** (*power*) autoridad *f*; ***the authorities*** las autoridades **2** (*permission*) autorización *f* **3**: ***be an ~ on sth*** ser una autoridad en algo; ***have sth on good ~*** saber algo de buena tinta
au•thor•i•za•tion [ɒːθəraɪ'zeɪʃn] autorización *f*
au•thor•ize ['ɒːθəraɪz] *v/t* autorizar; ***be ~d to do sth*** estar autorizado para hacer algo
au•thor•ized cap•i•tal ['ɑːθəraɪzd] FIN capital *m* autorizado
au•thor•ship ['ɔːθərʃɪp] *origin* autoría *f*
au•tism ['ɔːtɪzəm] MED autismo *m*
au•tis•tic [ɒː'tɪstɪk] *adj* autista
au•to... ['ɔːtou] *pref* auto...
au•to ['ɔːtou] F coche *m*, *L.Am.* carro *m*
au•to•bi•o•graph•i•cal [ɒːtəbaɪə'græfɪkl] *adj* autobiográfico
au•to•bi•og•ra•phy [ɒːtəbaɪ'ɑːgrəfɪ] autobiografía *f*
au•toc•ra•cy [ɔː'tɑːkrəsɪ] POL autocracia *f*
au•to•crat ['ɔːtəkræt] autócrata *m/f*
au•to•crat•ic [ɒːtə'krætɪk] *adj* autocrático
au•to•cue ['ɔːtəkjuː] TV autocue *m*, teleapuntador *m*
au•to•di•dact ['ɔːtoudaɪdækt] autodidacta *m/f*
au•to•di•dac•tic [ɔːtoudaɪ'dæktɪk] *adj* autodidáctico
au•to•graph ['ɒːtəgræf] autógrafo *m*; ***~ album*** álbum *m* de autógrafos
au•to•mate ['ɒːtəmeɪt] *v/t* automatizar

au•to•ma•ted tel•ler ma•chine [ɒːtəmeɪtəd'telərməʃiːn] cajero *m* automático
au•to•mat•ic [ɒːtə'mætɪk] **I** *adj* automático **II** *n car* (coche *m*) automático *m*; *gun* pistola *f* automática; *washing machine* lavadora *f* automática
au•to•mat•i•cal•ly [ɒːtə'mætɪklɪ] *adv* automáticamente
au•to•ma•tion [ɒːtə'meɪʃn] automatización *f*
au•tom•a•ton [ɒː'tɑːmətən] (*pl* ***automata*** [ɒː'tɑːmətə], ***-tons***) *fig* autómata *m/f*, robot *m/f*
au•to•mo•bile ['ɒːtəmoʊbiːl] automóvil *m*, coche *m*, *L.Am.* carro *m*, *Rpl* auto *m*
'au•to•mo•bile in•dus•try industria *f* automovilística
au•to•mo•tive [ɔːtə'moʊtɪv] *adj* automovilístico
au•ton•o•mous [ɒː'tɑːnəməs] *adj* autónomo
au•ton•o•my [ɒː'tɑːnəmɪ] autonomía *f*
au•to•pi•lot ['ɒːtoʊpaɪlət] piloto *m* automático; ***do sth on ~*** *fig* hacer algo sin pensar; *through force of habit* hacer algo por inercia
au•top•sy ['ɒːtɑːpsɪ] autopsia *f*
au•to-sug•ges•tion [ɒːtoʊsə'dʒestʃən] PSYCH autosugestión *f*
au•tumn ['ɒːtəm] *Br* otoño *m*; ***an ~ day*** un día otoñal; ***in*** (***the***) ***~*** en (el) otoño
au•tum•nal [ɔː'tʌmnəl] *adj* otoñal
aux•il•ia•ry [ɒːg'zɪljərɪ] *adj* auxiliar; ***~ verb*** verbo *m* auxiliar
a•vail [ə'veɪl] **I** *n*: ***to no ~*** en vano **II** *v/t fml*: ***~ o.s. of*** aprovechar
a•vail•a•bil•i•ty [əveɪlə'bɪlətɪ] disponibilidad *f*; ***subject to ~*** hasta agotar existencias
a•vai•la•ble [ə'veɪləbl] *adj* disponible; ***make sth ~ to s.o.*** poner algo a disposición de alguien; ***they're no longer ~*** *of product* ya no los venden
av•a•lanche ['ævəlænʃ] avalancha *f*, alud *m*
a•vant-garde [ævɑːn'gɑːd] *adj* vanguardista, progresista
av•a•rice ['ævərɪs] avaricia *f*
a•venge [ə'vendʒ] *v/t* vengar; ***~ o.s.*** vengarse (***on*** de)
av•e•nue ['ævənuː] avenida *f*; *fig* camino *m*
av•e•rage ['ævərɪdʒ] **I** *adj* **1** medio **2** (*of mediocre quality*) regular **II** *n* promedio *m*, media *f*; ***above / below ~*** por encima / por debajo del promedio; ***on ~*** como promedio, de media **III** *v/t*: ***I ~ six hours of sleep a night*** duermo seis horas cada noche como promedio *or* de media
◆ **average out** *v/t* calcular el promedio *or* la media de
◆ **average out at** *v/t* salir a
a•verse [ə'vɜːrs] *adj*: ***not be ~ to*** no ser reacio a
a•ver•sion [ə'vɜːrʃn] aversión *f*; ***have an ~ to*** tener aversión a
a•vert [ə'vɜːrt] *v/t one's eyes* apartar; *crisis* evitar
a•vi•a•tion [eɪvɪ'əɪʃn] aviación *f*
a•vi•a•tor ['eɪvɪeɪtər] aviador(a) *m*(*f*)
av•id ['ævɪd] *adj* ávido
av•o•ca•do [ɑːvə'kɑːdoʊ] (*pl* ***-o(e)s***) aguacate *m*, *S.Am.* palta *f*
a•void [ə'vɔɪd] *v/t* evitar; ***you've been ~ing me*** has estado huyendo de mí; ***~ doing sth*** evitar hacer algo
a•void•a•ble [ə'vɔɪdəbl] *adj* evitable, eludible
a•void•ance [ə'vɔɪdəns] evasión *f*
a•vow•al [ə'vaʊəl] declaración *f*, reconocimiento *m*
a•vowed [ə'vaʊd] *adj* declarado, reconocido
a•vun•cu•lar [ə'vʌŋkjʊlər] *adj* protector, paternalista
a•wait [ə'weɪt] *v/t* aguardar, esperar
a•wake [ə'weɪk] *adj* despierto; ***it kept me ~*** no me dejó dormir; ***be ~ to sth*** *fig* estar alerta de algo
a•wak•en•ing [ə'weɪkənɪŋ] aparición *f*, surgimiento *m*; ***then you're in for a rude ~*** entonces te vas a dar una bofetada F
a•ward [ə'wɔːrd] **I** *n* (*prize*) premio *m* **II** *v/t prize, damages* conceder
a'wards cer•e•mo•ny ceremonia *f* de entrega de premios
a'ward-win•ning *adj* galardonado, premiado
a•ware [ə'wer] *adj*: ***be ~ of sth*** ser consciente de algo; ***become ~ of sth*** darse cuenta de algo; ***make s.o. ~ of sth*** concienciar a alguien de algo
a•ware•ness [ə'wernɪs] conciencia *f*

a•wash [ə'wɑːʃ] *adj* ***be ~ with*** estar plagado de

a•way [ə'weɪ] *adv*: ***look ~*** mirar hacia otra parte; ***I'll be ~ until …*** *traveling* voy a estar fuera hasta …; *sick* no voy a ir hasta …; ***it's 2 miles ~*** está a 2 millas; ***Christmas is still six weeks ~*** todavía quedan seis semanas para Navidad; ***take sth ~ from s.o.*** quitar algo a alguien

a'way game SP partido *m* fuera de casa; **a'way team** SP equipo *m* visitante; **a'way win** SP victoria *f* visitante

AWB *abbr* (= ***air waybill***) conocimiento *m* de embarque aéreo

awe [ɒː] admiración *f*, respeto *m*; ***be in ~ of s.o.*** respetar a alguien; ***hold s.o. in ~*** tener respeto a alguien

awe-in•spir•ing ['ɒːɪnspaɪrɪŋ] *adj* abrumador, apabullante

awe•some ['ɒːsəm] *adj* F (*terrific*) alucinante F

'awe-struck *adj* estupefacto, anonadado

aw•ful ['ɒːfəl] *adj* horrible, espantoso; ***I feel ~*** me siento fatal

aw•ful•ly ['ɒːfəlɪ] *adv* F (*very*) tremendamente; ***~ bad*** malísimo

awk•ward ['ɒːkwərd] *adj* **1** (*clumsy*) torpe **2** (*embarrassing*) embarazoso; ***feel ~*** sentirse incómodo **3** (*difficult*) difícil; ***an ~ customer*** F una persona difícil

awl [ɒːl] TECH alesna *f*

awn•ing ['ɒːnɪŋ] toldo *m*

a•wry [ə'raɪ] *adv*: ***go ~*** *fig* salir mal, fracasar

ax, *Br* **axe** [æks] **I** *n* hacha *f* **II** *v/t project etc* suprimir; *budget*, *jobs* recortar

ax•es ['æksiːz] ☞ ***axis***

ax•i•om ['æksɪəm] axioma *m*

ax•i•o•mat•ic [æksɪə'mætɪk] *adj* axiomático

ax•is ['æksɪs] (*pl* **axes** ['æksiːz]) MATH, POL *etc* eje *m*

ax•le ['æksl] eje *m*

ay(**e**) [aɪ] PARL voto *m* a favor; ***the ~s have it*** ganan los síes

aye [aɪ] *int* NAUT: ***~ ~, captain!*** ¡sí, mi capitán!

a•za•le•a [ə'zeɪljə] BOT azalea *f*

Az•er•bai•jan [æzərbaɪ'dʒɑːn] Azerbaiyán *m*

Az•er•bai•ja•ni [æzərbaɪ'dʒɑːnɪ] **I** *adj* azerbaiyaní **II** *n* azerbaiyaní *m/f*

Az•tec ['æztek] **I** *adj* azteca **II** *n* azteca *m/f*

az•ure ['æʒər] *adj* azuloso, azulado

B

BA [biː'eɪ] *abbr* (= ***Bachelor of Arts***) licenciatura *f* en Filosofía y Letras

baa [bɑː] **I** *v/i* balar **II** *n* balido *m*

bab•ble ['bæbl] **I** *v/i* **1** *of water* borbotar **2** *of baby* balbucear; *of adult* mascullar; ***~ on about sth*** refunfuñar acerca de algo **II** *m* balbuceo *m*

babe [beɪb] **1** *lit* (*baby*) bebé *m* **2** F (*attractive woman*) bombón *m* F, encanto *m* F **3** *term of endearment* cariño *m/f*, cielo *m/f*

ba•bel ['beɪbl] babel *f*

ba•boon [bə'buːn] ZO babuino *m*

ba•by ['beɪbɪ] bebé *m*; ***have a ~*** tener un bebé; ***the ~ of the family*** el pequeño de la familia; ***don't be such a ~!*** ¡no seas niño! **II** *adj animal*, *vegetable* pequeño **III** *v/t* (*pret & pp* ***-ied***) tratar como un niño pequeño

'ba•by boom explosión *f* demográfica; **'ba•by bug•gy** cochecito *m or* silla *f* de bebé; **'ba•by car•riage** silla *f* de paseo; **'ba•by face** cara *f* de bebé

ba•by•hood ['beɪbɪhʊd] lactancia *f*

ba•by•ish ['beɪbɪɪʃ] *adj* infantil

'ba•by-mind•er *Br* niñera *f*; **'ba•by-sit** *v/i* (*pret & pp* ***-sat***) hacer de *Span* canguro *or L.Am.* babysitter (**for** de); **'ba•by-sit•ter** *Span* canguro *m/f*, *L.Am.* babysitter *m/f*; **'ba•by sit•ting** cuidado *m* de niños, *L.Am.* baby sitting *m*; **'ba•by talk** lenguaje *m* infantil

bach•e•lor ['bætʃələr] soltero *m*; ***Bachelor of Arts / Science*** licenciado(-a) *m*(*f*) en letras / ciencias

bach•e•lor•hood ['bætʃələrhʊd] soltería *f*

'bach•e•lor pad piso *m* de soltero

ba•cil•lus [bə'sɪləs] (*pl* **bacilli** [bə'sɪlaɪ]) MED bacilo *m*
back [bæk] **I** *n* **1** *of person, clothes* espalda *f*; *of car, bus, house* parte *f* trasera *or* de atrás; *of paper, book* dorso *m*; *of drawer* fondo *m*; *of chair* respaldo *m*; ***in ~*** *in store* en la trastienda; ***in the ~ (of the car)*** atrás (del coche); ***at the ~ of the bus*** en la parte trasera *or* de atrás del autobús; ***~ to front*** del revés; ***at the ~ of beyond*** en el quinto pino **2** SP defensa *m/f*
II *adj* trasero; ***~ road*** carretera *f* secundaria
III *adv* atrás; ***please stand ~*** pongase más para atrás **2** ***meters ~ from the edge*** a 2 metros del borde; ***~ in 1935*** allá por el año 1935; ***give sth ~ to s.o.*** devolver algo a alguien; ***she'll be ~ tomorrow*** volverá mañana; ***when are you coming ~?*** ¿cuándo volverás?; ***take sth ~ to the store*** *because unsatisfactory* devolver algo a la tienda; ***they wrote / phoned ~*** contestaron a la carta / a la llamada; ***he hit me ~*** me devolvió el golpe
IV *v/t* **1** (*support*) apoyar, respaldar **2** *horse* apostar por
V *v/i*: ***he ~ed into the garage*** entró en el garaje marcha atrás
◆ **back away** *v/i* alejarse (hacia atrás)
◆ **back down** *v/i* echarse atrás
◆ **back off** *v/i* echarse atrás
◆ **back onto** *v/t* dar por la parte de atrás a
◆ **back out** *v/i of commitment* echarse atrás
◆ **back up I** *v/t* **1** (*support*) respaldar **2** *file* hacer una copia de seguridad de **3**: ***traffic was backed up all the way to ...*** el atasco llegaba hasta ... **II** *v/i* **1** *in car* dar marcha atrás **2** *of drains* atascarse
'back•ache dolor *m* de espalda; **back 'al•ley** callejón *m*; **back•bench•er** [bæk'bentʃər] *Br* PARL *diputado que no forma parte del gabinete ministerial ni del fantasma*; **'back•bit•ing** cotilleo *m*, chismorreo *m*; **'back•board** *in basketball* tablero *m* de la canasta; **'back•bone** ANAT columna *f* vertebral, espina *f* dorsal; *fig* (*courage*) agallas *fpl*; *fig* (*mainstay*) columna *f* vertebral; **'back-break•ing** *adj* extenuante, deslomador; **back 'burn•er**: ***put sth on the ~*** aparcar algo; **'back•chat** *Br* insolencias *fpl*; **'back cloth** *Br* **1** THEA telón *m* de foro **2** *fig* contexto *m*, coyuntura *f*; **'back•comb** *v/t hair* cardar; **'back cop•y** *of newspaper* número *m* atrasado; **back•court vi•o'la•tion** *in basketball* campo *m* atrás; **'back•date** *v/t*: ***a raise ~d to 1st January*** una subida salarial con efecto retroactivo a partir del 1 de enero; **'back•door** puerta *f* trasera; **'back-door** *adj fig* clandestino, encubierto; ***~ play*** *in basketball* puerta *f* atrás; **'back drop 1** THEA telón *m* de foro **2** *fig* contexto *m*, coyuntura *f*
back•er ['bækər]: ***the ~s of the movie*** *financially* las personas que financiaron la película
back'fire *v/i* **1** MOT petardear **2** *fig*: ***it ~d on us*** nos salió el tiro por la culata; **'back for•ma•tion** LING derivación *f* regresiva; **'back•gam•mon** ['bækgæmən] backgammon *m*
'back•ground fondo *m*; *of person* origen *m*, historia *f* personal; *of situation* contexto *m*; ***she prefers to stay in the ~*** prefiere permanecer en un segundo plano; ***~ music*** música *f* de fondo; ***against the ~ of ...*** en el trasfondo de ...; ***~ information*** contexto *m*; ***educational ~*** formación *f* académica
'back•hand *in tennis* revés *m*
back•hand•ed ['bækhændɪd] *adj* **1** SP de revés **2** *compliment* ambiguo
back•hand•er ['bækhændər] (*bribe*) soborno *m*, *Andes*, *Rpl* coima *f*, *C.Am.*, *Mex* mordida *f*
back heel•er ['hiːlər] *in soccer* taconazo *m*
back•ing ['bækɪŋ] **1** (*support*) apoyo *m*, respaldo *m*; ***give sth one's ~*** apoyar *or* respaldar algo **2** MUS acompañamiento *m*
'back•ing group MUS grupo *m* de acompañamiento
'back•lash reacción *f* violenta; **'back•log** acumulación *f*; **'back•pack I** *n* mochila *f* **II** *v/i* viajar con la mochila a cuestas; **'back•pack•er** ['bækpækər] mochilero(-a) *m(f)*; **'back•pack•ing** viajes *mpl* con la mochila a cuestas; **'back pass** *to goalkeeper* cesión *f* al portero; **'back pay** pago *m* de atrasos; **'back•ped•al** *v/i* (*pret & pp* **-ed**, *Br* **-led**) *fig* echarse atrás, dar marcha atrás;

B

'back•room boys *npl* F *gente que realiza una labor importante y permanecen en el anonimato*; **'back seat** *of car* asiento *m* trasero *or* de atrás; **back-seat 'driv•er**: ***he's a terrible ~*** va siempre incordiando al conductor con sus comentarios; **'back•side** F trasero *m*, posaderas *fpl* F; **'back•slash** COMPUT barra *f* inversa *or* invertida; **'back•slide** *v/i* (*pret & pp* ***-slid***) retroceder, regresar; **back•slid•ing** ['bækslaɪdɪŋ] retroceso *m*, regresión *f*; **'back•space (key)** (tecla *f* de) retroceso *m*; **'back•spin** efecto *m* hacia atrás

'back•stage I *adv* **1** THEA entre bastidores **2** *fig* entre bastidores, confidencialmente **II** *adj* **1** THEA entre bastidores **2** *fig* clandestino

'back•stairs *npl* escalera *f* de servicio; **'back straight** SP recta *f* final; **'back-street** *adj*: ***~ abortion*** aborto *m* clandestino; ***~ abortionist*** abortista *m/f*; **'back streets** *npl* callejuelas *fpl*; *poorer, dirtier part of a city* zonas *fpl* deprimidas; **'back•stroke** SP espalda *f*; **'back talk** insolencias *fpl*; **'back•track** *v/i* volver atrás, retroceder

'back•up 1 (*support*) apoyo *m*, respaldo *m*; *for police* refuerzos *mpl* **2** COMPUT copia *f* de seguridad; ***take a ~*** hacer una copia de seguridad; ***~ copy*** copia *f* de seguridad

'back•up disk COMPUT disquete *m* con la copia de seguridad

back•ward ['bækwərd] **I** *adj* **1** *child* retrasado; *society* atrasado **2** *glance* hacia atrás **II** *adv* hacia atrás

'back•wash 1 NAUT corriente *f* de expulsión **2** *fig* repercusión *f*, efecto *m*; **'back•wa•ter 1** GEOG remanso *m* **2** *fig*: *isolated* lugar *m* apartado, enquilosamiento *m*; **'back•woods** *npl* monte *m*, alta montaña *f*

back'yard jardín *m* trasero; ***in s.o.'s ~*** *fig* en la misma puerta de alguien; ***the not-in-my-~ syndrome*** *apoyo de instalaciones, servicios etc sólo si no afectan directamente*

ba•con ['beɪkn] tocino *m*, *Span* bacon *m*; ***bring home the ~*** F *earn money* ganar el pan; *be successful* triunfar, conseguir los objetivos; ***save s.o.'s ~*** *Br* F salvar el pellejo a alguien F

bac•te•ri•a [bæk'tɪərɪə] *npl* bacterias *fpl*

bac•te•ri•al [bæk'tɪərɪəl] *adj* bacteriano

bac•te•ri•o•log•i•cal [bæktɪərɪə'lɑːdʒɪkl] *adj* bacteriológico

bac•te•ri•ol•o•gist [bæktɪərɪ'ɑːlədʒɪst] bacteriólogo(-a) *m(f)*

bac•te•ri•um [bæk'tɪərɪəm] (*pl* ***bacteria*** [bæk'tɪərɪə]) bacteria *f*

bac•tri•an cam•el ['bæktrɪən] camello *m*

bad [bæd] *adj* malo; *before singular masculine noun* mal; *cold, headache etc* fuerte; *mistake, accident* grave; ***I've had a ~ day*** he tenido un mal día; ***smoking is ~ for you*** fumar es malo; ***not ~*** (bastante) bien; ***it's not ~*** no está mal; ***that's really too ~*** (*shame*) es una verdadera pena; ***feel ~ about*** (*guilty*) sentirse mal por; ***I'm ~ at math*** se me dan mal las matemáticas; ***Friday's ~, how about Thursday?*** el viernes me viene mal, ¿qué tal el jueves?; ***that's too ~*** es una pena; ***go from ~ to worse*** ir de mal a peor; ***go ~*** pasarse, ponerse malo

bad 'debt deuda *f* incobrable

bad•die ['bædɪ] F: ***the ~*** el malo

badge [bædʒ] insignia *f*, chapa *f*; *of policeman* placa *f*; ***~ of office*** chapa *f* del cargo

bad•ger ['bædʒər] **I** ZO tejón *m* **II** *v/t* acosar, importunar; ***~ s.o. into doing sth*** machacar a alguien para que haga algo

bad 'lan•guage palabrotas *fpl*

bad•ly ['bædlɪ] *adv injured* gravemente; *damaged* seriamente; *work* mal; ***I did really ~ in the exam*** el examen me salió fatal; ***he hasn't done ~*** *in life, business etc* no le ha ido mal; ***you're ~ in need of a haircut*** necesitas urgentemente un corte de pelo; ***he is ~ off*** *poor* anda mal de dinero

bad-man•nered ['mænərd] *adj*: ***be ~*** tener malos modales

bad•min•ton ['bædmɪntən] bádminton *m*

'bad-mouth *v/t* F hablar mal de; **bad 'sec•tor** COMPUT sector *m* dañado; **bad-tem•pered** ['tempərd] *adj* malhumorado

baf•fle ['bæfl] *v/t* confundir, desconcertar; ***be ~d*** estar confundido *or* desconcertado; ***I'm ~d why she left*** no consigo entender por qué se fue

baf•fling ['bæflɪŋ] *adj mystery, software* desconcertante, incomprensible
bag [bæg] **I** *n* **1** bolsa *f*; *for school* cartera *f* **2** (*purse*) bolso *m*, *S.Am.* cartera *f*, *Mex* bolsa *f* **3** *in baseball* almohadilla *f* **II** *v/t* (*pret & pp* ***-ged***) *in hunting* matar
◆ **bag up** *v/t* embolsar, meter en bolsas
ba•gel ['beɪgəl] *panecillo en forma de rosquilla*
bag•gage ['bægɪdʒ] equipaje *m*
'bag•gage al•low•ance AVIA límite *m* de equipaje; **'bag•gage car** RAIL vagón *m* de equipajes; **'bag•gage check** *checkroom* consigna *f* equipajes; *for security* control *m* de equipajes; **'baggage claim** punto *m* de recolección de equipaje, recogida *f* de equipajes; **'bag•gage claim area** zona *f* de recogida de equipajes; **bag•gage han•dler** ['bægɪdʒhændlər] manipulador(-a) *m(f)* *or* mozo(-a) *m(f)* de equipajes; **'bag•gage lock•er** consigna *f* automática; **'bag•gage re•claim** AVIA punto *m* de recolección de equipaje; **'baggage room** consigna *f*
bag•gy ['bægɪ] *adj* ancho, holgado
'bag la•dy vagabunda *f*, mendiga *f*; **'bag•pip•er** gaitero(-a) *m(f)*; **'bagpipes** *npl* gaita *f*; **bag•snatch•er** ['bægsnætʃər] mangante *m/f* de bolsos
ba•guette [bæ'get] *bread* baguette *f*, barra *f* de pan
bah [bɑː] *int* ¡bah!, ¡bueno!
Ba•ha•mas [bə'hɑːməz] *npl*: ***the ~*** las Bahamas
Bah•rain [bɑː'reɪn] Bahrein *m*
Bah•rain•i [bɑː'reɪnɪ] **I** *adj* bahreiní **II** *n* bahreiní *m/f*
bail [beɪl] LAW libertad *f* bajo fianza; *money* fianza *f*; ***on ~*** bajo fianza; ***be out on ~*** estar libre bajo fianza; ***stand ~ for s.o.*** pagar la fianza a alguien
◆ **bail out I** *v/t* **1** LAW pagar la fianza de **2** *company, person* sacar de apuros (económicos) **II** *v/i* **1** *from airplane* tirarse en paracaídas **2** (*withdraw*) retirarse
'bail bond fianza *f*, caución *f*
bail•iff ['beɪlɪf] **1** *in courtroom* alguacil *m* **2** *Br* agente *m/f* judicial
bail•i•wick ['beɪlɪwɪk] territorio *m*, terreno *m*
bait [beɪt] cebo *m*; ***rise to*** *or* ***swallow*** *or* ***take the ~*** *fig* caer *or* picar en el anzuelo
baize [beɪz] tapete *m*
bake [beɪk] *v/t* hornear, cocer al horno
baked beans [beɪkt'biːnz] *npl judías blancas en salsa de tomate*
baked po'ta•to (*pl* ***-oes***) *L.Am.* papa *f* asada, *Span* patata *f* asada (*con piel*)
bak•er ['beɪkər] panadero(-a) *m(f)*
bak•er•y ['beɪkərɪ] panadería *f*
bak•ing hot ['beɪkɪŋ] *adj* achicharrante; ***it was ~*** hacía un calor asfixiante
'bak•ing pow•der levadura *f*
'baking sheet, 'baking tray bandeja *f* del horno
bal•a•cla•va [bælə'klɑːvə] *Br* pasamontañas *m*
bal•ance ['bæləns] **I** *n* **1** equilibrio *m*; ***lose one's ~*** perder el equilibrio **2** (*remainder*) resto *m* **3** *of bank account* saldo *m* **II** *v/t* **1** poner en equilibrio **2**: ***~ the books*** cuadrar las cuentas; ***~ a budget*** hacer que cuadre un presupuesto **III** *v/i* **1** mantenerse en equilibrio **2** *of accounts* cuadrar
bal•anced ['bælənst] *adj* **1** (*fair*) objetivo **2** *diet, personality* equilibrado
bal•ance of 'pay•ments balanza *f* de pagos; **bal•ance of 'trade** balanza *f* comercial; **'bal•ance sheet** balance *m*
bal•anc•ing act ['bælənsɪŋ] *fig* malabares *mpl*, pirueta *f*; ***do*** *or* ***perform a political ~*** hacer malabares políticos
bal•bo•a [bæl'boʊə] FIN balboa *m*
bal•co•ny ['bælkənɪ] **1** *of house* balcón *m* **2** *in theater* anfiteatro *m*
bald [bɒːld] *adj* calvo; *tire* desgastado ***he's going ~*** se está quedando calvo; ***~ spot*** calva *f*
bald 'ea•gle águila *f* de cabeza blanca
bal•der•dash ['bɔːldərdæʃ] bobadas *fpl*, sandeces *fpl*
bald-'head•ed *adj* calvo
bald•ing ['bɒːldɪŋ] *adj* medio calvo
bald•y ['bɒːldɪ] F calvorotas *m* F
bale [beɪl] **I** *n of hay, cotton* fardo *m* **II** *v/t* enfardar
Bal•e•ar•ics [bælɪ'ærɪks] *npl*: ***the ~*** las Baleares
bale•ful ['beɪlfʊl] *adj* maligno, mezquino
balk [bɔːk] **I** *v/i* **1** *of person* quejarse, rebelarse; ***~ at doing sth*** negarse a hacer algo **2** *of horse* echarse atrás (***at*** ante) **II** *n in baseball* balk *m*

B

Bal•kan ['bɒːlkən] *adj* balcánico
Bal•kans ['bɒːlkənz] *npl*: ***the ~*** los Balcanes
ball[1] [bɒːl] *tennis-ball size* pelota *f*; *football size* balón *m*, pelota *f*; *billiard-ball size, in baseball* bola *f*; ***on the ~*** *fig* despierto; ***play ~*** *fig* cooperar; ***the ~'s in his court*** le toca actuar a él, la pelota está en su tejado
ball[2] [bɒːl] *dance* baile *m* de salón *or* etiqueta; ***have a ~*** F pasárselo pipa *or* bomba F
bal•lad ['bæləd] balada *f*
ball-and-'sock•et joint ANAT, TECH articulación *f*
bal•last ['bæləst] NAUT lastre *m*, contrapeso *m*
ball 'bear•ing rodamiento *m* de bolas
ball•cock ['bɒːlkɑːk] válvula *f* de flotador
bal•le•ri•na [bælə'riːnə] bailarina *f*
bal•let [bæ'leɪ] ballet *m*
'bal•let danc•er bailarín(-ina) *m(f)*
'ball game (*baseball game*) partido *m* de béisbol; ***that's a different ~*** F esa es otra cuestión F
bal•lis•tic mis•sile [bə'lɪstɪk] misil *m* balístico
bal•lis•tics [bə'lɪstɪks] *nsg* balística *f*
bal•loon [bə'luːn] **I** *n* globo *m* **II** *v/i swell* hincharse, abombarse
bal•loon•ist [bə'luːnɪst] piloto *m/f* de globo aerostático
bal•lot ['bælət] **1** *n* voto *m* **2** *v/t members* consultar por votación
'bal•lot box urna *f*; **'bal•lot pa•per** papeleta *f*; **'bal•lot rig•ging** fraude *m* electoral
'ball•park *for baseball* campo *m* de béisbol; ***you're in the right ~*** F no vas descaminado; **'ball•park fig•ure** F cifra *f* aproximada; **'ball•point (pen)** bolígrafo *m*, *Mex* pluma *f*, *Rpl* birome *m*; **'ball•room** salón *m* de baile; **ball•room 'danc•ing** bailes *mpl* de salón
balls [bɒːlz] *npl* V *also fig* huevos *mpl* V; ***be going ~ out*** dejarse la piel F
'balls-up *Br* V: ***make a ~ of sth*** jorobar *or* joder algo V
bal•ly•hoo [bælɪ'huː] F revuelo *m*, alboroto *m*
balm [bɑːm] bálsamo *m*
balm•y ['bɑːmɪ] *adj* **1** *weather* templado, apacible **2** *Br* P (*crazy*) chiflado, tocado
ba•lo•ney [bə'lounɪ] F chorrada *f* F, memez *f* F
Bal•tic ['bɔːltɪk] **I** *adj* báltico; ***~ Sea*** mar *m* Báltico; ***the ~ states*** los estados bálticos **II** *n*: ***the ~*** el Báltico
bal•us•trade [bælə'streɪd] barandilla *f*, pasamanos *m*
bam•boo [bæm'buː] bambú *m*
bam•boo•zle [bæm'buːzl] *v/t* F apabullar F; ***~ s.o. into doing sth*** liar *or* confundir a alguien para que haga algo
ban [bæn] **1** *n* prohibición *f* **2** *v/t* (*pret & pp* ***-ned***) prohibir; ***~ s.o. from doing sth*** prohibir a alguien que haga algo
ba•nal [bə'næl] *adj* banal
ba•nal•i•ty [bə'nælɪtɪ] banalidad *f*, trivialidad *f*
ba•na•na [bə'nænə] plátano *m*, *Rpl* banana *f*; ***the audience went ~s*** P el público se puso como loco; ***he's completely ~s*** P está como una cabra F
ba'na•na re•pub•lic *pej* república *f* bananera
ba'na•na tree platanero *m*, *Rpl* banano *m*
band[1] [bænd] MUS banda *f*; *pop* grupo *m*
◆ **band together** *v/i* unirse, juntarse
band[2] [bænd] *of metal, cloth* tira *f*, cinta *f*
ban•dage ['bændɪdʒ] **1** *n* vendaje *m* **2** *v/t* vendar
'Band-Aid® *Span* tirita *f*, *L.Am.* curita *f*
ban•dan•a [bæn'dænə] bandana *f*, pañoleta *f*
B & B [biːənd'biː] *abbr* (= ***bed and breakfast***) *hostal familiar en el que está incluido el alojamiento y el desayuno*
ban•dit ['bændɪt] bandido *m*
'band•lead•er MUS líder *m/f* de un grupo musical; **'band•mas•ter** MUS director(a) *m(f)* de una banda de música; **'band•stand** MUS quiosco *m*; **'band•wag•on**: ***jump on the ~*** subirse al carro; **'band•width** ancho *m* de banda
ban•dy[1] ['bændɪ] *adj legs* arqueado
ban•dy[2] ['bændɪ] *v/t* intercambiar; ***~ blows*** pelear (***with*** con); ***~ words*** discutir (***with*** con)
◆ **bandy around** *v/t*: ***a name that has been bandied around a lot*** un nombre del que se ha hablado mucho

ban•dy-leg•ged ['bændılegd] *adj* estevado
bane [beın]: ***be the ~ of s.o.'s existence*** ser el tormento de alguien
bang [bæŋ] **I** *n* **1** *noise* estruendo *m*, estrépito *m m*; ***the door closed with a ~*** la puerta se cerró de un portazo; ***~ goes another $50*** F adiós a otros 50 dólares **2** (*blow*) golpe **II** *v/t* **1** *door* cerrar de un portazo **2** (*hit*) golpear; ***~ o.s. on the head*** golpearse la cabeza **III** *v/i* dar golpes; ***the door ~ed shut*** la puerta se cerró de un portazo
Ban•gla•desh [bæŋglə'deʃ] Bangladesh *m*
Ban•gla•desh•i [bæŋglə'deʃı] **I** *adj* bangladesí **II** *n* bangladesí *m/f*
ban•gle ['bæŋgl] brazalete *m*, pulsera *f*
bangs [bæŋz] *npl* flequillo *m*
'bang-up *adj* F genial F, súper F
ban•ish ['bænıʃ] *v/t* **1** *person* exiliar, desterrar **2** *worries*, *fears* desterrar, alejar
ban•ish•ment ['bænıʃmənt] exilio *m*, destierro *m*
ban•is•ters ['bænıstərz] *npl* barandilla *f*
ban•jo ['bændʒoʊ] banjo *m*
bank[1] [bæŋk] *n of river* orilla *f*
bank[2] [bæŋk] **I** *n* FIN banco *m* **II** *v/t money* ingresar, depositar
◆ **bank on** *v/t* contar con; ***don't bank on it*** no cuentes con ello
◆ **bank with** *v/t* tener una cuenta en
bank•a•ble ['bæŋkəbl] *adj fig* taquillero
'bank ac•count cuenta *f* (bancaria); **'bank bal•ance** saldo *m* bancario; **'bank bill** billete *m*; **'bank•book** cartilla *f or* libreta *f* (del banco); **'bank bor•row•ings** *npl* préstamos *mpl* bancarios; **'bank card 1** (*credit card*) tarjeta *f* de crédito **2** *for use in ATM* tarjeta *f* bancaria; **'bank charg•es** *npl* comisiones *fpl* bancarias; **'bank clerk** empleado(-a) *m*(*f*) de banco; **'bank de•tails** *npl* datos *mpl* bancarios; **'bank draft** giro *m* bancario
bank•er ['bæŋkər] banquero(-a) *m*(*f*)
'bank•er's card tarjeta *f* bancaria
bank 'hol•i•day *Br*: *día festivo en el que los bancos cierran*
bank•ing ['bæŋkıŋ] banca *f*
'bank loan préstamo *m* bancario; **'bank man•ag•er** director(a) *m*(*f*) de banco; **'bank note** *Br* billete *m*; **'bank raid** atraco *m* a un banco; **'bank rate** tipo *m* de interés bancario; **'bank rob•ber** atracador(a) *m*(*f*) de bancos; **'bank rob•ber•y** atraco *m* a un banco; **'bank•roll** *v/t* F financiar
bank•rupt ['bæŋkrʌpt] **I** *adj* en bancarrota *or* quiebra; ***go ~*** quebrar, ir a la quiebra; *of person* arruinarse **II** *v/t* llevar a la quiebra **III** *n* quebrado(-a) *m*(*f*)
bank•rupt•cy ['bæŋkrʌpsı] *of person*, *company* quiebra *f*, bancarrota *f*
'bank•shot *in basketball* tiro *m* a tabla; **bank 'sort code** código *m* identificador de banco; **'bank state•ment** extracto *m* bancario, extracto *m* de cuenta; **'bank trans•fer** transferencia *f* bancaria
ban•ner ['bænər] pancarta *f*
banns [bænz] *npl Br* amonestaciones *fpl*
ban•quet ['bæŋkwıt] banquete *m*
ban•quet•ing hall ['bæŋkwıtıŋ] sala *f* de banquetes
ban•quette [bæŋ'ket] banco *m*, bancada *f*
ban•tam•weight ['bæntəmweıt] SP **I** *adj* peso gallo **II** *n* peso *m/f* gallo
ban•ter ['bæntər] bromas *fpl*
bap•tism ['bæptızm] bautismo *m*
bap•tis•mal font [bæp'tızml] pila *f* bautismal
Bap•tist ['bæptıst] baptista *m/f*
bap•tize [bæp'taız] *v/t* bautizar
bar[1] [bɑːr] *n* **1** *of iron* barra *f*, *of chocolate* tableta *f*, *of soap* pastilla *f*, ***be behind ~s*** (*in prison*) estar entre barrotes **2** *for drinks* bar *m*; (*counter*) barra *f*
bar[2] [bɑːr] *v/t* (*pret & pp* **-red**) *from premises* prohibir la entrada a; ***~ s.o. from doing sth*** prohibir a alguien que haga algo
bar[3] [bɑːr] *prep* (*except*) excepto
barb [bɑːrb] **1** *on hook* lengüeta *f* **2** *remark* puyazo *m*, puya *f*
Bar•ba•dos [bɑːr'beıdɑːs] Barbados *m*
bar•bar•i•an [bɑːr'berıən] bárbaro(-a) *m*(*f*)
bar•ba•ric [bɑːr'bærık] *adj* brutal, inhumano
bar•bar•ism ['bɑːrbərızm] barbarie *f*, crueldad *f*
bar•bar•i•ty [bɑːr'bærıtı] **1** *act* atrocidad *f* **2** *cruelty* crueldad *f*, brutalidad *f*
'bar•ba•rous ['bɑːrbərəs] *adj* atroz,

bárbaro
bar•be•cue ['bɑːrbɪkjuː] **I** *n* barbacoa *f*, *RPl* asado *m* **II** *v/t* cocinar en la barbacoa; ***~d*** a la barbacoa
barbed [bɑːrbd] *adj* **1** *hook* con lengüeta **2** *remark* malicioso, malintencionado
barbed 'wire alambre *f* de espino
bar•bell ['bɑːrbel] SP pesas *f*
bar•ber ['bɑːrbər] barbero *m*
bar•bi•tu•rate [bɑːr'bɪtjərət] barbitúrico *m*
'bar chart *Br* diagrama *m or* gráfico *m* de barras; **'bar code** código *m* de barras; **'bar code read•er** lector *m* de código de barras
bare [ber] *adj* (*naked*) desnudo; (*empty*: *room*) vacío; *mountainside* pelado, raso; *floor* descubierto; ***in one's ~ feet*** descalzo
'bare•back *adv* sin silla de montar
'bare•boat chart•er flete *m* sin tripulación
bare•faced ['berfeɪst] *adj* sin vergüenza
'bare•foot *adj* descalzo
bare'head•ed *adj* sin sombrero
'bare•ly ['berlɪ] *adv* apenas; ***he's ~ five*** acaba de cumplir cinco años
barf [bɑːrf] *v/i* F devolver F, vomitar
bar•gain ['bɑːrgɪn] **1** *n* **1** (*deal*) trato *m*; ***into the ~*** además **2** (*good buy*) ganga *f* **2** *v/i* regatear, negociar
◆ **bargain for** *v/t* (*expect*) imaginarse, esperar; ***I got more than I bargained for*** me tocó más de lo que me esperaba
'bar•gain base•ment: ***at ~ prices*** a precio de saldo
'bar•gain hunt•er buscador(a) *m*(*f*) de gangas
bar•gain•ing ['bɑːrgɪnɪŋ] negociación *f*
'bar•gain•ing chip baza *f*
bar•gain 'of•fer oferta *m* especial; **'bar•gain price** precio *m* de ganga; **'bar•gain store** tienda *f* descuento
barge [bɑːrdʒ] NAUT barcaza *f*
◆ **barge into** *v/t person* tropezarse con; *room* irrumpir en
'barge pole *Br*: ***I wouldn't touch him / it with a ~!*** F *if I were you* yo lo dejaría estar
'bar graph diagrama *m* de barras
bar•i•tone ['bærɪtoʊn] barítono *m*
bark[1] [bɑːrk] **1** *n of dog* ladrido *m* **2** *v/i* ladrar; ***be ~ing up the wrong tree*** F estar en un error
bark[2] [bɑːrk] *n of tree* corteza *f*
'bar•keep•er camarero(-a) *m*(*f*), *L.Am.* mesero(-a) *m*(*f*), *Rpl* mozo(-a) *m*(*f*)
bar•ley ['bɑːrlɪ] cebada *f*
'bar•ley sug•ar *Br* azúcar *m* cande *or* candi
'bar•maid *Br* camarera *f*, *L.Am.* mesera *f*, *Rpl* moza *f*; **'bar•man** *Br* camarero *m*, *L.Am.* mesero *m*, *Rpl* mozo *m*; **'bar meal** *Br* comida *f* en un bar
bar mitz•vah [bɑːr'mɪtsvə] REL *ceremonia por la que el niño judío a los trece años entra en la edad adulta*
barm•y ['bɑːmɪ] *adj Br* P chiflado, tocado
barn [bɑːrn] granero *m*
bar•na•cle ['bɑːrnəkl] balano *m*
'barn dance *verbena de música tradicional*
'barn owl lechuza *f*
ba•rom•e•ter [bə'rɑːmɪtər] *also fig* barómetro *m*
bar•on ['bærən] barón *m*; ***press / steel ~*** magnate *m* de la prensa / del acero
bar•on•ess ['bærənes] baronesa *f*
Ba•roque [bə'rɑːk] *adj* barroco
bar•racks ['bærəks] *npl* MIL cuartel *m*
bar•ra•cu•da [bærə'kuədə] barracuda *f*
bar•rage [bə'rɑːʒ] MIL barrera *f* (de fuego); *fig* aluvión *m*
bar•rel ['bærəl] *container* tonel *m*, barril *m*; ***have s.o. over a ~*** F tener a alguien entre la espada y la pared
bar•ren ['bærən] *adj land* yermo, árido
bar•rette [bə'ret] pasador *m*
bar•ri•cade [bærɪ'keɪd] **I** *n* barricada *f* **II** *v/t* encerrar; ***~ o.s. in*** encerrarse
bar•ri•er ['bærɪər] *also fig* barrera *f*; ***language ~*** barrera lingüística
bar•ring ['bɑːrɪŋ] *prep* salvo, excepto; ***~ accidents*** salvo imprevistos
bar•ris•ter ['bærɪstər] *Br* abogado(-a) *m*(*f*) (*que aparece en tribunales*)
bar•row ['bæroʊ] carretilla *f*
'bar staff *npl* camareros *mpl*, *L.Am.* meseros *mpl*, *RPl* mozos *mpl*
'bar tend•er camarero(-a) *m*(*f*), *L.Am.* mesero(-a) *m*(*f*), *Rpl* mozo(-a) *m*(*f*)
bar•ter ['bɑːrtər] **I** *n* trueque *m* **II** *v/t* cambiar, trocar (***for*** por)
ba•salt ['bæsɔːlt] GEOL basalto *m*
base [beɪs] **1** *n bottom, center, in baseball* base *f*; ***~ on balls*** base por bolas

2 *v/t* basar (*on* en); ***be ~d in*** *of soldier* estar destinado en; *of company* tener su sede en **3** *adj fml* despreciable, vil
'base•ball *ball* pelota *f* de béisbol *or Cu, Mex* beisbol; *game* béisbol *m, Cu, Mex* beisbol, *L.Am.* pelota *f*
'base•ball bat bate *m* de béisbol; **'base•ball cap** gorra *f* de béisbol; **'base•ball play•er** jugador(a) *m(f)* de béisbol, *L.Am.* pelotero(-a) *m(f)*; **'base•board** rodapié *m*; **'base camp** campamento *m* base; **'base hit** *in baseball* sencillo *m*
base•less ['beɪslɪs] *adj* infundado
'base line SPORT línea *f* de saque
base•ment ['beɪsmənt] *of house, store* sótano *m*
'base met•al metal *m* base
'base rate FIN tipo *m* de interés básico, tasa *f* base
bash [bæʃ] F **1** *n* porrazo *m* F **2** *v/t* dar un porrazo a F
bash•ful ['bæʃfʊl] *adj* retraído, tímido
ba•sic ['beɪsɪk] *adj* (*rudimentary*) básico; *room* modesto, sencillo; *language skills* elemental; (*fundamental*) fundamental; ***~ salary*** sueldo *m* base
ba•sic•al•ly ['beɪsɪklɪ] *adv* básicamente
ba•sics ['beɪsɪks] *npl*: ***the ~*** lo básico, los fundamentos; ***get down to ~*** centrarse en lo esencial
bas•il ['bæzɪl] albahaca *f*
ba•sin ['beɪsn] *for washing* barreño *m*; *in bathroom* lavabo *m*
ba•sis ['beɪsɪs] (*pl* ***bases*** ['beɪsi:z]) base *f*; ***on the ~ of what you've told me*** de acuerdo con lo que me has dicho
bask [bæsk] *v/i* tomar el sol
bas•ket ['bæskɪt] cesta *f*; *in basketball* canasta *f*
'bas•ket•ball *game* baloncesto *m*, *L.Am.* básquetbol *m*; *ball* balón *m or* pelota *f* de baloncesto; ***~ player*** baloncestista *m/f*, *L.Am.* basquetbolista *m/f*
'bas•ket case F pirado(-a) *m(f)* F, chiflado(-a) *m(f)* F
Basque [bæsk] **I** *adj* vasco **II** *n* **1** *person* vasco(-a) *m(f)* **2** *language* vasco *m*
'Basque Coun•try: ***the ~*** el País Vasco
bass [beɪs] **1** *n part, singer* bajo *m*; *instrument* contrabajo *m*; *guitar* bajo *m* **2** *adj* bajo
bas•set hound ['bæsɪt] basset *m*
'bass gui•tar bajo *m*
'bass gui•tar•ist bajo *m/f*
bass•ist ['beɪsɪst] MUS *on double bass* contrabajo *m/f*; *on bass guitar* bajo *m/f*
bas•soon [bə'su:n] MUS fagot *m*
bas•soon•ist [bə'su:nɪst] MUS fagotista *m/f*
bas•tard ['bæstərd] **1** P cabrón(-ona) *m(f)* P; ***poor ~*** pobre desgraciado; ***stupid ~*** desgraciado **2** (*illegitimate child*) ilegítimo(-a) *m(f)*, bastardo(-a) *m(f)*
baste [beɪst] *v/t* GASTR *verter caldo o jugo*
bas•tion ['bæstɪən] *also fig* bastión *m*, baluarte *m*
bat[1] [bæt] **1** *n for baseball* bate *m*; *for table tennis* pala *f* **2** *v/i* (*pret & pp* ***-ted***) *in baseball* batear
bat[2] [bæt] *v/t* (*pret & pp* ***-ted***): ***he didn't ~ an eyelid*** no se inmutó
bat[3] [bæt] *n animal* murciélago *m*
batch [bætʃ] *of students* tanda *f*; *of data* conjunto *m*; *of bread* hornada *f*; *of products* lote *m*
'batch com•mand COMPUT comando *m* por lotes
ba•ted ['beɪtɪd] *adj*: ***with ~ breath*** con la respiración contenida
bath [bæθ] baño *m*; ***have a ~, take a ~*** darse *or* tomar un baño
bathe [beɪð] *v/i* (*swim, have a bath*) bañarse
bath•ing cap ['beɪðɪŋ] gorro *m* de baño; **'bath•ing suit** *of woman* traje *m* de baño, bañador *m*; **'bath•ing trunks** *npl of man* bañador *m*
'bath mat alfombra *f* de baño; **'bath-robe** albornoz *m*; **'bath•room** *for bath, washing hands* cuarto *m* de baño; (*toilet*) servicio *m*, *L.Am.* baño *m*; **'bath sheet**, **'bath tow•el** toalla *f* de baño; **'bath•tub** bañera *f*
ba•tik [bə'ti:k] batik *m*
bat•on [bə'tɑ:n] **1** *of conductor* batuta *f*; ***under the ~ of*** bajo la batuta de **2** SP testigo *m*
bat•tal•i•on [bə'tælɪən] MIL batallón *m*
◆ **bat•ten down** ['bætn] *v/t*: ***batten down the hatches*** NAUT cerrar las escotillas; *fig* estar sobre las armas
bat•ter[1] ['bætər] *n* GASTR masa *f*
bat•ter[2] ['bætər] *n in baseball* bateador(a) *m(f)*; ***~ runner*** bateador(a) corredor(a); ***~'s box*** cajón *m* del bateador

B

bat•ter[3] ['bætə] **I** *v/t* golpear, aporrear **II** *v/i*: ~ **(*away*) *at the door*** aporrear la puerta

◆ **batter down, batter in** *v/t* echar abajo

bat•tered ['bætərd] *adj* maltratado

bat•ter•ing ram ['bætərɪŋ] carnero *m*

bat•ter•y ['bætərɪ] **1** *in watch, flashlight* pila *f*; *in computer, car* batería *f* **2** *in baseball* batería *f*

'bat•ter•y charg•er cargador *m* de pilas / baterías; **'bat•ter•y farm•ing** AGR cría *f* intensiva; **'bat•ter•y hen** AGR gallina *f* de batería; **'bat•ter•y life** duración *f* de la batería / pila; **bat•tery 'low warn•ing** señal *f* de descarga de la batería / pila; **bat•ter•y-op•e•rat•ed** ['bætərɪɑ:pəreɪtɪd] *adj* que funciona con pilas

bat•ting ['bætɪŋ] *in baseball* bateo *m*; ~ ***order*** orden *m* de bateo

'bat•ting av•er•age promedio *m* de bateo

bat•tle ['bætl] **1** *n also fig* batalla *f* **2** *v/i against illness etc* luchar

'bat•tle-ax(e) F generala *f* F; **'bat•tle-field, 'bat•tle•ground** campo *m* de batalla; **'bat•tle•ship** acorazado *m*

bat•ty ['bætɪ] *adj Br* P grillado P, barrenado P

bau•ble ['bɔ:bl] joya *f* de bisutería, baratija *f*

baud rate ['bɒ:dreɪt] COMPUT velocidad *f* de transmisión

baulk ☞ ***balk***

baux•ite ['bɔ:ksaɪt] MIN bauxita *f*

bawd•y ['bɒ:dɪ] *adj* picante, subido de tono

bawl [bɒ:l] *v/i* **1** (*shout*) gritar, vociferar **2** (*weep*) berrear

◆ **bawl out** *v/t* F **1** *shout* gritar **2**: ***bawl s.o. out*** echar la bronca a alguien F

bay[1] [beɪ] *n* (*inlet*) bahía *f*

bay[2] [beɪ] *v/i of dogs etc* aullar

bay[3] [beɪ] *n*: ***hold*** *or* ***keep s.o. / sth at*** ~ mantener a alguien / algo alejado

'bay leaf hoja *f* de laurel

bay•o•net ['beɪənet] **I** *n* bayoneta *f* **II** *v/t* (*pret & pp* **-ed**, *Br* **-ted**) dar bayonetazos a

'bay tree laurel *m*

bay 'win•dow ventana *f* en saliente

ba•zaar [bə'zɑ:r] bazar *m*

ba•zoo•ka [bəzu:kə] MIL bazuka *f*

BC [bi:'si:] *abbr* (= ***before Christ***) a.C. (= antes de Cristo)

B/E *abbr* (= ***bill of exchange***) letra *f* de cambio

be [bi:] **1** *v/i* (*pret* **was / were**, *pp* **been**) *permanent characteristics, profession, nationality* ser; *position, temporary condition* estar; ***was she there?*** ¿estaba allí?; ***it's me*** soy yo; ***how much is / are …?*** ¿cuánto es / son …?; ***there is / are*** hay; ~ ***careful*** ten cuidado; ***don't ~ sad*** no estés triste

2: ***has the mailman been?*** ¿ha venido el cartero?; ***I've never been to Japan*** no he estado en Japón; ***I've been here for hours*** he estado aquí horas

3 *tags*: ***that's right, isn't it?*** eso es, ¿no?; ***she's Chinese, isn't she?*** es china, ¿verdad?

4 *as auxiliary*: ***I am thinking*** estoy pensando; ***he was running*** corría; ***you're ~ing stupid*** estás siendo un estúpido

5 *obligation*: ***you are to do what I tell you*** harás lo que yo te diga; ***I was to help him escape*** se suponía que le iba a ayudar a escaparse; ***you are not to tell anyone*** no debes decírselo a nadie

6 *passive*: ***he was arrested*** fue detenido, lo detuvieron; ***they have been sold*** se han vendido

◆ **be in for** *v/t*: ***he's in for a big disappointment*** se va a llevar una gran desilusión

beach [bi:tʃ] **I** *n* playa *f* **II** *v/t* NAUT hacer embarrancar en la orilla

'beach ball pelota *f* de playa; **'beach bug•gy** MOT buggy *m*; **'beach chair** tumbona *f*, hamaca *f*; **beach comb•er** ['bi:tʃkoumər] *persona que se dedica a buscar objetos de valor en las playas*; **'beach-head** MIL cabeza *f* de playa; **'beach•wear** ropa *f* playera

bea•con ['bi:kən] *fire* hoguera *f*; *light* baliza *f*

bead [bi:d] *of sweat* gota *f*

bead•ing ['bi:dɪŋ] ARCHIT moldura *f*

beads [bi:dz] *npl* cuentas *fpl*

bead•y ['bi:dɪ] *adj*: ***I've got my ~ eye on you*** te estoy vigilando

bea•gle ['bi:gl] beagle *m*

beak [bi:k] pico *m*

'be-all: ***the ~ and end-all*** lo más importante del mundo

beam [biːm] **I** *n in ceiling etc* viga *f* **II** *v/i* (*smile*) sonreír de oreja a oreja **III** *v/t* (*transmit*) emitir

bean [biːn] judía *f*, alubia *f*, *L.Am.* frijol *m*, *S.Am.* poroto *m*; ***green ~s*** judías *fpl* verdes, *Mex* ejotes *mpl*, *S.Am.* porotos *mpl* verdes; ***coffee ~s*** granos *mpl* de café; ***be full of ~s*** F estar lleno de vitalidad

'bean•bag *cojín relleno de bolitas*; **bean curd** ['biːnkɜːrd] tofu *m*; **'bean•pole** F palillo *m/f* F, fideo *m/f* F; **'bean•sprout** germen *m* de soja

bear[1] [ber] *n animal* oso(-a) *m(f)*

bear[2] [ber] **I** *v/t* (*pret* **bore**, *pp* **borne**) **1** *weight* resistir; *costs* correr con **2** (*tolerate*) aguantar, soportar **3** *child* dar a luz; ***she bore him six children*** le dio seis hijos **4**: ***~ interest*** devengar intereses **II** *v/i* (*pret* **bore**, *pp* **borne**): ***bring pressure to ~ on*** ejercer presión sobre

◆ **bear down on** *v/t*: ***he saw the truck bearing down on him*** vio el camión que se le venía encima

◆ **bear out** *v/t* (*confirm*) confirmar

bear•a•ble ['berəbl] *adj* soportable

beard [bɪrd] barba *f*

beard•ed ['bɪrdɪd] *adj* con barba

bear•er ['berər] **1** *of news* mensajero(-a) *m(f)*, avisador(a) *m(f)* **2** *of passport* titular *m/f* **3** *of coffin* portador(a) *m(f)*

'bear•er bond bono *m* al portador

'bear hug: ***give s.o. a ~*** dar a alguien un gran abrazo

bear•ing ['berɪŋ] **1** *in machine* rodamiento *m*, cojinete *m* **2**: ***that has no ~ on the case*** eso no tiene nada que ver con el caso

bear•ish ['berɪʃ] *adj* **1** *bad-tempered* malhumorado, arisco **2** FIN con tendencia a la baja

'bear mar•ket FIN mercado *m* a la baja

'bear•skin piel *f* de oso

beast [biːst] *animal* bestia *f*, *person* bestia *m/f*

beat [biːt] **I** *n of heart* latido *m*; *of music* ritmo *m*

II *v/i* (*pret* **beat**, *pp* **beaten**) *of heart* latir; *of rain* golpear; ***~ about the bush*** andarse por las ramas

III *v/t* (*pret* **beat**, *pp* **beaten**) **1** *in competition* derrotar, ganar a; *the defense* superar; ***it ~s me*** no logro entender; ***this certainly ~s sitting at home*** esto es mucho mejor que quedarse en casa **2** (*hit*) pegar a; (*pound*) golpear **3**: ***~ it!*** F ¡lárgate! F

◆ **beat back** *v/t flames*, *enemy* hacer retroceder

◆ **beat out** *v/t* **1** *flames* apagar a golpes **2** *rhythm* marcar

◆ **beat up** *v/t* dar una paliza a

beat•en ['biːtən] **1** *adj*: ***off the ~ track*** retirado **2** *pp* ☞ ***beat***

be•a•ti•fi•ca•tion [biːætɪfɪ'keɪʃən] REL beatificación *f*

be•a•ti•fy [biːætɪfaɪ] *v/t* REL beatificar

beat•ing ['biːtɪŋ] *physical* paliza *f*

'beat-up *adj* F destartalado F

beau•ti•cian [bjuː'tɪʃn] esteticista *m/f*

beau•ti•ful ['bjuːtəfəl] *adj woman*, *house*, *day*, *story*, *movie* bonito, precioso, *L.Am.* lindo; *smell*, *taste*, *meal* delicioso, *L.Am.* rico; *vacation* estupendo; ***thanks, that's just ~!*** ¡muchísimas gracias, está maravilloso!; ***the ~ game*** *soccer* el deporte rey

beau•ti•ful•ly ['bjuːtɪfəlɪ] *adv cooked*, *done* perfectamente, maravillosamente

beau•ti•fy ['bjuːtɪfaɪ] *v/t* embellecer

beau•ty ['bjuːtɪ] *of woman*, *sunset* belleza *f*, ***that's the ~ of this new way of doing it*** eso es lo bueno de esta nueva forma de hacerlo

'beau•ty con•test concurso *m* de belleza

'beau•ty par•lor salón *m* de belleza

bea•ver ['biːvər] ZO castor *m*

◆ **beaver away** *v/i* F trabajar como un burro F

be•came [bɪ'keɪm] *pret* ☞ ***become***

be•cause [bɪ'kɑːz] *conj* porque; ***~ it was too expensive*** porque era demasiado caro; ***~ of*** debido a, a causa de; ***~ of you, we can't go*** gracias a ti, no podemos ir

beck [bek]: ***be at s.o.'s ~ and call*** estar a la entera disposición de alguien

beck•on ['bekn] *v/i* hacer señas

be•come [bɪ'kʌm] *v/i* (*pret* **became**, *pp* **become**) hacerse, volverse; ***it became clear that …*** quedó claro que …; ***he became a priest*** se hizo sacerdote; ***she's becoming very forgetful*** cada vez es más olvidadiza; ***what's ~ of her?*** ¿qué fue de ella?

be•com•ing [bɪ'kʌmɪŋ] *adj* favorecedor,

B

apropiado

bed [bed] **1** cama *f*; ***go to ~*** ir a la cama; ***he's still in ~*** aún está en la cama; ***go to ~ with s.o.*** irse a la cama *or* acostarse con alguien; ***put a paper to ~*** finalizar la edición de un periódico **2** *of flowers* macizo *m* **3** *of sea* fondo *m*; *of river* cauce *m*, lecho *m*

bed and 'break•fast 1 *place*: *hostal familiar en el que está incluido el alojamiento y el desayuno* **2** *type of accommodations* alojamiento y desayuno

be•daub [bɪ'dɔːb] *v/t* pintarrajear

'bed•bug ZO chinche *m or f*; **'bed•clothes** *npl* ropa *f* de cama; **'bed•cov•er** cubierta *f*, colcha *f*

bed•ding ['bedɪŋ] ropa *f* de cama

be•deck [bɪ'dek] *v/t*: ***~ed with sth*** engalanado con algo

be•dev•il [bɪ'devl] *v/t* (*pret & pp* ***-ed***, *Br* ***-led***) acosar, plagar

bed•lam ['bedləm] F locura *f*, jaleo *m*

'bed lin•en ropa *f* blanca de cama; **'bed•pan** orinal *m*; **'bed•post** pilar *m* de la cama

be•drag•gled [bɪ'drægld] *adj* desaliñado, andrajoso

'bed rest reposo *m* en cama

bed•rid•den ['bedrɪdən] *adj*: ***be ~*** estar postrado en cama

'bed•rock GEOL estrato *m* de roca; *fig* cimiento *m*, fundamento *m*; ***get down to ~*** *fig* ir a las bases; **'bed•room** dormitorio *m*, *L.Am.* cuarto *m*; **'bed•side**: ***be at s.o.'s ~*** estar junto a la cama de alguien; **bed•side 'lamp** *Br* lámpara *f* de mesilla; **bed•side 'table** *Br* mesilla *f or* mesita *f* de noche; **'bed-sit, bed-sit•ter, bed-'sit•ting room** *Br habitación de alquiler que gen ralmente no incluye baño o cocina*; **'bed•sore** MED úlcera *f* de decúbito; **'bed•spread** colcha *f*

bed•stead ['bedsted] armazón *m* de la cama

'bed•time hora *f* de irse a la cama; ***~ reading*** libro *m* de cabecera; ***~ story*** cuento *m* para dormir

bee [biː] abeja *f*

beech [biːʧ] haya *f*

beef [biːf] **I** *n* **1** carne *f* de vaca *or* vacuna **2** F (*complaint*) queja *f*; ***what's his ~?*** ¿que le pasa? **II** *v/i* F (*complain*) quejarse

◆ **beef up** *v/t* reforzar, fortalecer

'beef tal•low sebo *m* de carne de vaca; **'beef•bur•ger** hamburguesa *f*; **'beef•steak** bistec *m*, filete *m* de ternera

beef•y ['biːfɪ] *adj* F cachas F, musculoso

'bee•hive colmena *f*

'bee•line: ***make a ~ for*** ir directamente a

been [bɪn] *pp* ☞ ***be***

beep [biːp] **I** *n* pitido *m* **II** *v/i* pitar **III** *v/t on pager* llamar con el buscapersonas

beep•er ['biːpər] buscapersonas *m inv*, *Span* busca *m*

beer [bɪr] cerveza *f*

'beer•mat posavasos *m inv*

beer•y ['bɪərɪ] *adj* a *or* de cerveza; ***~ breath*** aliento *m* a cerveza

'bees•wax cera *f* (de abeja)

beet [biːt] remolacha *f*

bee•tle ['biːtl] escarabajo *m*

beet•root ['biːtruːt] *Br* remolacha *f*

be•fall [bɪfɒːl] *v/i* (*pret* ***-fell***, *pp* ***-fallen***) ocurrir, suceder

be•fit [bɪ'fɪt] *v/t* (*pret & pp* ***-ted***) ajustarse a

be•fore [bɪ'fɔːr] **I** *prep* **1** *time* antes de; ***~ tax*** antes de impuestos **2** *space*, *order* antes de, delante de **II** *adv* antes; ***I've seen this movie ~*** ya he visto esta película; ***have you been to Japan ~?*** ¿habías estado antes *or* ya en Japón?; ***the week / day ~*** la semana / el día anterior **III** *conj* antes de que; ***~ we start*** antes de comenzar, antes de que empecemos

be•fore•hand [bɪ'fɔːrhænd] *adv* de antemano

be•friend [bɪ'frend] *v/t* hacerse amigo de

be•fud•dled [bɪ'fʌdld] *adj* confuso, aturdido

beg [beg] **1** *v/i* (*pret & pp* ***-ged***) mendigar, pedir **2** *v/t* (*pret & pp* ***-ged***): ***~ s.o. to do sth*** rogar *or* suplicar a alguien que haga algo

be•gan [bɪ'gæn] *pret* ☞ ***begin***

beg•gar ['begər] **I** *n* mendigo(-a) *m*(*f*); ***lucky ~*** F ¡qué chiripa F *or* suerte! **II** *v/t*: ***~ belief / description*** costar creer / describir

be•gin [bɪ'gɪn] **1** *v/i* (*pret* ***began***, *pp* ***begun***) empezar, comenzar; ***to ~ with*** (*at first*) en un primer momento, al principio; (*in the first place*) para empezar **2** *v/t* (*pret* ***began***, *pp* ***begun***) empezar,

comenzar; ~ ***to do sth, ~ doing sth*** empezar *or* comenzar a hacer algo
be•gin•ner [bɪ'gɪnər] principiante *m/f*; ~***'s luck*** suerte *f* del principiante
be•gin•ning [bɪ'gɪnɪŋ] principio *m*, comienzo *m*; (*origin*) origen *m*; ***in the*** ~ al principio
be•gon•ia [bɪ'goʊnjə] BOT begoña *f*
be•grudge [bɪ'grʌdʒ] *v/t* (*envy*) envidiar; (*give reluctantly*) dar a regañadientes
be•guile [bɪ'gaɪl] *v/t* **1** *enchant* encantar, cautivar **2** *deceive* engatusar, engañar
be•gun [bɪ'gʌn] *pp* ☞ **begin**
be•half [bɪ'hɑːf]: ***in ~ of, on ~ of*** en nombre de; *sign, accept* por; *more formally* en nombre de; ***in my / his ~*** en nombre mío / suyo
be•have [bɪ'heɪv] *v/i* comportarse, portarse; ~ (***o.s.***) comportarse *or* portarse bien; ~ (***yourself***)! ¡pórtate bien!
be•hav•ior [bɪ'heɪvɪər] comportamiento *m*, conducta *f*
be•hav•ior•al [bɪ'heɪvɪərəl] *adj* PSYCH del comportamiento, de la conducta; ~ ***disorder*** problema *m* de conducta
be•hav•ior•ism [bɪ'heɪvɪərɪzm] PSYCH behaviorismo *m*, conductismo *m*
be•hav•ior•ist [bɪ'heɪvɪərɪst] PSYCH **I** *adj* conductista **II** *n* conductista *m/f*
be•hav•iour *etc Br* ☞ **behavior** *etc*
be•head [bɪ'hed] *v/t* decapitar
be•hind [bɪ'haɪnd] **1** *prep in position, order* detrás de; *in progress* por detrás de; ***be ~ …*** (*responsible for*) estar detrás de …; (*support*) respaldar … **2** *adv* (*at the back*) detrás; ***be ~ with sth*** estar atrasado con algo; ***leave sth ~*** dejarse algo
be•hind•hand [bɪ'haɪndhænd] *adv*: ***be ~ with sth*** ir atrasado con algo
be•hold [bɪ'hoʊld] *v/t* (*pret & pp* **-held**) contemplar
be•hold•er [bɪ'hoʊldər]: ***beauty is in the eye of the ~*** todo depende del cristal con que se mire
be•hoove [bɪ'huːv] *v/t fml*: ***it ~s s.o. to do sth*** le corresponde a alguien hacer algo
beige [beɪʒ] *adj* beige, *Span* beis
Bei•jing [beɪ'ʒɪŋ] Beijing *m*
be•ing ['biːɪŋ] *existence, creature* ser *m*; ***come into ~*** surgir, aparecer
be•lat•ed [bɪ'leɪtɪd] *adj* tardío
belch [beltʃ] **I** *n* eructo *m* **II** *v/i* eructar
be•lea•guered [bɪ'liːgərd] *adj* maltrecho, desgraciado
bel•fry ['belfrɪ] campanario *m*
Bel•gian ['beldʒən] **I** *adj* belga **II** *n* belga *m/f*
Bel•gium ['beldʒəm] Bélgica *f*
be•lie [bɪ'laɪ] *v/t* contradecir
be•lief [bɪ'liːf] creencia *f*; ***it's my ~ that*** creo que
be•liev•a•ble [bɪ'liːvəbl] *adj* creíble, verosímil
be•lieve [bɪ'liːv] *v/t* creer
◆ **believe in** *v/t* creer en
be•liev•er [bɪ'liːvər] REL creyente *m/f*; *fig* partidario(-a) *m*(*f*) (***in*** de)
be•lit•tle [bɪ'lɪtl] *v/t* menospreciar
Be•lize [be'liːz] Belice *m*
Be•liz•e•an [bə'liːzɪən] **I** *adj* beliceño **II** *n* beliceño(-a) *m*(*f*)
bell [bel] *of bike, door, school* timbre *m*; *of church* campana *f*; ***does that ring a ~?*** ¿te suena (de algo)?
'bell•boy *Br* botones *m inv*; *for elevator* ascensorista *m*; **'bell cap•tain** jefe *m* de botones; **'bell•hop** botones *m inv*
bel•li•cose ['belɪkoʊs] *adj* belicoso, agresivo
bel•lig•er•ent [bɪ'lɪdʒərənt] *adj* beligerante
bel•low ['beloʊ] **I** *n* bramido *m* **II** *v/i* bramar
bel•lows ['beloʊz] *npl* fuelle *m*
'bell pep•per pimiento *m*
'bell push timbre *m*, botón *m*
bel•ly ['belɪ] *of person* estómago *m*, barriga *f*; (*fat stomach*) barriga *f*, tripa *f*; *of animal* panza *f*
'bel•ly•ache *v/i* F refunfuñar; **'bel•ly but•ton** F ombligo *m*; **'bel•ly danc•er** bailarina *f* de la danza del vientre; **'bel•ly•flop** panzada *f*, golpe *m* con la barriga
be•long [bɪ'lɒːŋ] *v/i*: ***where does this ~?*** ¿dónde va esto?; ***I don't ~ here*** no encajo aquí
◆ **belong to** *v/t of object, money* pertenecer a; *club* pertenecer a, ser socio de
be•long•ings [bɪ'lɒːŋɪŋz] *npl* pertenencias *fpl*
be•lov•ed [bɪ'lʌvɪd] *adj* querido
be•low [bɪ'loʊ] **1** *prep* debajo de; *in amount, rate, level* por debajo de **2** *adv* abajo; *in text* más abajo; ***see ~*** véase más abajo; ***10 degrees ~*** 10 grados

B

bajo cero
belt [belt] cinturón *m*; ***tighten one's ~*** *fig* apretarse el cinturón
'belt•way circunvalación *f*, cinturón *m*
be•moan [bɪ'moʊn] *v/t* deplorar, lamentar
be•mused [bɪ'mjuːzd] *adj* aturdido, confundido
bench [bentʃ] **1** *seat* banco *m*; *in soccer* banquillo *m* **2** (*work~*) mesa *f* de trabajo
'bench•mark punto *m* de referencia
'bench test ensayo *m* en banco de pruebas
bend [bend] **I** *n* curva *f* **II** *v/t* (*pret & pp* ***bent***) doblar **III** *v/i* (*pret & pp* ***bent***) torcer, girar; *of person* flexionarse
◆ **bend down** *v/i* agacharse
bend•er ['bendər] F parranda *f* F; ***go on a ~*** irse de juerga *or* parranda
bend•y ['bendɪ] *adj* F flexible, blando
be•neath [bɪ'niːθ] **I** *prep* debajo de; ***she thinks a job like that is ~ her*** cree que un trabajo como ése le supondría rebajarse **II** *adv* abajo; ***in the valley ~*** en el valle de abajo
ben•e•dic•tion [benɪ'dɪkʃn] REL bendición *f*
ben•e•fac•tor ['benɪfæktər] benefactor(a) *m(f)*
be•nef•i•cence [bɪ'nefɪsns] beneficencia *f*, bondad *f*
be•nef•i•cent [bɪ'nefɪsənt] *adj* benefactor, benévolo
ben•e•fi•cial [benɪ'fɪʃl] *adj* beneficioso
ben•e•fi•ci•a•ry [benɪ'fɪʃərɪ] beneficiario(-a) *m(f)*
ben•e•fit ['benɪfɪt] **I** *n* beneficio *m*; *of product, method, solution* ventaja *f* **II** *v/t* beneficiar **III** *v/i* beneficiarse
'ben•e•fit match partido *m* benéfico
Be•ne•lux coun•tries ['benɪlʌks] países *mpl* del Benelux
be•nev•o•lence [bɪ'nevələns] benevolencia *f*
be•nev•o•lent [bɪ'nevələnt] *adj* benevolente
Ben•ga•li [beŋgɔːlɪ] **I** *adj* bengalí **II** *n* **1** *person* bengalí *m/f* **2** *language* bengalí *m*
be•nign [bɪ'naɪn] *adj* **1** agradable **2** MED benigno
bent [bent] **I** *pret & pp* ☞ ***bend*** **II** *adj*: ***be ~ on doing sth*** estar empeñado en hacer algo
ben•zene ['benziːn] CHEM benceno *m*, benzol *m*
ben•zine ['benziːn] CHEM bencina *f*
be•queath [bɪ'kwiːð] *v/t also fig* legar; ***~ sth to s.o.*** legar *or* dejar algo a alguien
be•quest [bɪ'kwest] legado *m*
be•rate [bɪ'reɪt] *v/t* reprender, vituperar; ***~ s.o. for sth*** reprender a alguien por algo
be•reaved [bɪ'riːvd] *npl*: ***the ~*** los familiares del difunto
be•reave•ment [bɪ'riːvmənt] duelo *m*, luto *m*
be•reft [bɪ'reft] *adj*: ***~ of all hope*** despojado de toda esperanza
be•ret ['bereɪ] boina *f*
Ber•mu•da [bɜːr'mjuːdə] las Bermudas
Ber•mu•da 'shorts *npl* bermudas *fpl*
Ber•mu•da 'tri•an•gle triángulo *m* de las Bermudas
ber•ry ['berɪ] baya *f*
ber•serk [bər'zɜːrk] *adv*: ***go ~*** F volverse loco
berth [bɜːrθ] **1** *on ship* litera *f*; *on train* camarote *m* **2** *for ship* amarradero *m*; ***give s.o. a wide ~*** evitar a alguien; ***gain a ~ to the finals*** clasificarse para la final, hacerse con un puesto en la final
be•seech [bɪ'siːtʃ] *v/t* (*pret & pp* ***-ed*** *or* ***besought***): ***~ s.o. to do sth*** suplicar a alguien que haga algo
be•seech•ing [bɪ'siːtʃɪŋ] *adj* suplicante
be•seech•ing•ly [bɪ'siːtʃɪŋlɪ] *adv* de manera suplicante
be•set [bɪ'set] *v/t* (*pret & pp* ***-set***): ***be ~ with danger*** estar rodeado de peligros; ***be ~ by problems*** estar plagado de problemas
be•side [bɪ'saɪd] *prep* al lado de, junto a; ***be ~ o.s.*** estar fuera de sí; ***that's ~ the point*** eso no tiene nada que ver
be•sides [bɪ'saɪdz] **I** *adv* además **II** *prep* (*apart from*) aparte de, además de
be•siege [bɪ'siːdʒ] *v/t fig* asediar, cercar
be•smirch [bɪ'smɜːrtʃ] *v/t reputation* desacreditar, desprestigiar
be•sot•ted [bɪ'sɑːtɪd] *adj*: ***be ~ with*** *or* ***by s.o.*** estar encandilado con *or* por alguien
be•sought [bɪ'sɔːt] *pret & pp* ☞ ***beseech***
be•spec•ta•cled [bɪ'spektəkld] *adj* con gafas *fpl or L.Am.* anteojos *mpl*

be•spoke [bɪ'spoʊk] *adj Br clothes, furniture* a medida

best [best] **I** *adj* mejor

II *adv* mejor; ***which did you like ~?*** ¿cuál te gustó más?; ***it would be ~ if ...*** sería mejor si ...; ***I like her ~*** ella es la que más me gusta

III *n*: ***do one's ~*** hacer todo lo posible; ***the ~*** *person, thing* el / la mejor; ***we insist on the ~*** insistimos en lo mejor; ***we'll just have to make the ~ of it*** tendremos que arreglárnoslas; ***all the ~!*** ¡buena suerte!, ¡que te vaya bien!

IV *v/t* derrotar, vencer

best be'fore date fecha *f* de caducidad, fecha *f* límite de consumo

bes•tial ['bestjəl] *adj* bestial, inhumano

bes•ti•al•i•ty [bestɪ'ælətɪ] **1** *cruelty* bestialidad *f*, crueldad *f* **2** *sexual* zoofilia *f*

be•stir [bɪ'stɜːr] *v/t* (*pret & pp* ***-red***): ***~ o.s. to do sth*** ponerse a hacer algo

best man padrino *m* de la boda

be•stow [bɪ'stoʊ] *v/t title, honor* conceder, otorgar (***on*** a)

best 'sell•er bestseller *m*, éxito *m* de ventas

'best-sell•ing *adj*: ***~ novel*** novela *f* que es un éxito de ventas; ***~ author*** autor(a) *m(f)* de bestsellers

bet [bet] **1** *n* apuesta *f*; ***place a ~*** hacer una apuesta **2** *v/t & v/i* (*pret & pp* ***bet***) *also fig* apostar; ***I ~ he doesn't come*** apuesto a que no viene; ***you ~!*** ¡ya lo creo!

be•ta block•er ['biːtəblɑːkər] MED betabloqueante *m*

be•tray [bɪ'treɪ] *v/t* traicionar; *husband, wife* engañar

be•tray•al [bɪ'treɪəl] traición *f*; *of husband, wife* engaño *m*

be•trothed [bɪ'troʊðd] *adj fml* prometido (***to*** a)

bet•ter ['betər] **I** *adj* mejor; ***get ~*** *in skills, health* mejorar; ***he's ~*** *in health* está mejor **II** *adv* mejor; ***you'd ~ ask permission*** sería mejor que pidieras permiso; ***I'd really ~ not*** mejor no; ***all the ~ for us*** tanto mejor para nosotros; ***I like her ~*** me gusta más ella **III** *n*: ***the ~*** el mejor; ***get the ~ of s.o.*** tomar la delantera a alguien; ***my curiosity got the ~ of me*** mi curiosidad se apoderó de mí

bet•ter•ment ['betərmənt] mejora *f*

bet•ter 'off *adj* (*wealthier*) más rico; ***you're ~ without him*** estás mejor sin él

bet•ting ['betɪŋ] **I** *n* apuestas *fpl*; ***what's the ~ that it won't ever happen?*** ¿cuántas posibilidades hay de que no ocurra nunca?; ***~ office***, *Br* ***~ shop*** casa *f* de apuestas **II** *adj*: ***I'm not a ~ man*** no me gustan las apuestas

be•tween [bɪ'twiːn] *prep* entre; ***~ you and me*** entre tú y yo

bev•el ['bevl] **I** *n* bisel *m* **II** *v/t* (*pret & pp* ***-ed***, *Br* ***-led***) biselar

bev•eled, *Br* **bev•elled** ['bevld] *adj* biselado

bev•er•age ['bevərɪdʒ] *fml* bebida *f*

bev•y ['bevɪ] *of women* caterva *f*, pelotón *m*

be•wail [bɪ'weɪl] *v/t* maldecir, lamentar

be•ware [bɪ'wer] *v/t*: ***~ (of)*** tener cuidado con; ***~ of the dog*** (ten) cuidado con el perro

be•wil•der [bɪ'wɪldər] *v/t* desconcertar

be•wil•der•ing [bɪ'wɪldərɪŋ] *adj* desconcertante, abrumador

be•wil•der•ment [bɪ'wɪldərmənt] desconcierto *m*

be•witch [bɪ'wɪʧ] *v/t* encantar, hechizar

be•yond [bɪ'jɑːnd] **1** *prep in space* más allá de; ***she has changed ~ recognition*** ha cambiado tanto que es difícil reconocerla; ***it's ~ me*** (*don't understand*) no logro entender; (*can't do it*) me es imposible **2** *adv* más allá

bi•an•nu•al [baɪ'ænʊəl] *adj* bianual

bi•an•nu•al•ly [baɪ'ænʊəlɪ] *adv* dos veces al año

bi•as ['baɪəs] *against* prejuicio *m*; *in favor of* favoritismo *m*

bi•as(s)ed ['baɪəst] *adj* parcial

bib [bɪb] *for baby* babero *m*

Bi•ble ['baɪbl] Biblia *f*

bib•li•cal ['bɪblɪkl] *adj* bíblico

bib•li•o•graph•i•cal [bɪblɪoʊ'græfɪkl] *adj* bibliográfico

bib•li•og•ra•phy [bɪblɪ'ɑːgrəfɪ] bibliografía *f*

bib•li•o•phile ['bɪblɪ'oʊfaɪl] bibliófilo (-a) *m(f)*

bi•carb [baɪ'kɑːrb] F ☞ ***bicarbonate of soda***

bi•car•bon•ate [baɪ'kɑːrbəneɪt] CHEM bicarbonato *m*

bi'car•bon•ate of so•da bicarbonato *m* sódico

bi•cen•te•nar•y [baɪsen'tiːnərɪ] *Br* bi-

centenario *m*
bi•cen•ten•ni•al [baɪsen'tenɪəl] bicentenario *m*
bi•ceps ['baɪseps] *npl* bíceps *mpl*
bick•er ['bɪkər] *v/i* reñir, discutir
bick•er•ing ['bɪkərɪŋ] riñas *fpl*
bi•cy•cle ['baɪsɪkl] bicicleta *f*
bid [bɪd] **I** *n* **1** *at auction* puja *f*; COM oferta *f* **2** (*attempt*) intento *m* **II** *v/i* (*pret & pp* ***bid***) *at auction* pujar (***on, for*** por)
bid•der ['bɪdər] postor(a) *m(f)*
bid•ding[1] ['bɪdɪŋ] *at auction* puja *f*
bid•ding[2] ['bɪdɪŋ]: ***do s.o.'s ~*** actuar a la voluntad de alguien
bide [baɪd] *v/t* (*pret* ***bided*** *or* ***bode***): ***~ one's time*** esperar a que llegue el momento adecuado
bi•det ['bi:deɪ] bidé *m*
bi•en•ni•al [baɪ'enɪəl] *adj* bienal
bi•fo•cals [baɪ'foʊkəlz] *npl* gafas *fpl or L.Am.* lentes *mpl* bifocales
bi•fur•ca•tion [baɪfər'keɪʃən] bifurcación *f*
big [bɪg] **I** *adj* grande; *before singular nouns* gran; ***my ~ brother / sister*** mi hermano / hermana mayor; ***that's ~ of you*** *usu iron* qué generoso *or* espléndido eres **II** *adv*: ***talk ~*** alardear, fanfarronear
big•a•mist ['bɪgəmɪst] bígamo(-a) *m(f)*
big•a•mous ['bɪgəməs] *adj* bígamo
big•a•my ['bɪgəmɪ] bigamia *f*
big 'bang AST big bang *m*; **big dip•per** ['dɪpər] AST Osa *f* Mayor; **big 'end** MOT *of connecting rod* cabeza *f* de biela; **'big•head** F creído(-a) *m(f)* F; **big-'head•ed** *adj* F creído F; **big-heart•ed** ['hɑ:rtɪd] *adj* bondadoso; **'big•mouth** F bocazas *m/f inv* F; **'big name** famoso (-a) *m(f)*
big•ot ['bɪgət] fanático(-a) *m(f)*, intolerante *m/f*
big•ot•ed ['bɪgətɪd] *adj* intolerante
big•ot•ry ['bɪgətrɪ] intolerancia *f*
big 'pic•ture F situación *f* global; **'big screen** pantalla *f* grande; **'big shot** F pez gordo *m/f* F; **'big time**: ***make the ~*** F llegar a la cima del éxito; **big 'toe** dedo *m* gordo del pie; **'big top** (*circus tent*) carpa *f*; **'big•wig** F pez gordo *m/f* F
bike [baɪk] **I** *n* F bici *f* F; (*motor~*) moto *f* F **II** *v/i* ir en bici
bik•er ['baɪkər] **1** motero(-a) *m(f)* **2** F *courier* mensajero(-a) *m(f)*
bi•ki•ni [bɪ'ki:nɪ] biquini *m*
bi•lat•er•al [baɪ'lætərəl] *adj* bilateral
bil•ber•ry ['bɪlberɪ] BOT arándano *m*
bile [baɪl] **1** PHYSIO bilis *f* **2** *fig* mal carácter *m*, mal humor *m*
bilge [bɪldʒ] F *nonsense* tonterías *fpl*
bi•lin•gual [baɪ'lɪŋgwəl] *adj* bilingüe
bil•ious ['bɪljəs] *adj* **1** MED mareado, nauseabundo **2** *fig* bilioso, malhumorado
bilk [bɪlk] *v/t* F timar, estafar; ***~ s.o. of sth*** timar *or* estafar a alguien con algo
bill [bɪl] **I** *n* **1** *for phone, electricity* factura *f*, recibo *m* **2** *Br*: *in hotel, restaurant* cuenta *f* **3** *money* billete *m* **4** POL proyecto *m* de ley **5** (*poster*) cartel *m* **II** *v/t* (*invoice*) enviar la factura a
'bill•board valla *f* publicitaria
bil•let ['bɪlɪt] MIL **I** *n* campamento *m* **II** *v/t* albergar, aposentar (***with, on*** con)
'bill•fold cartera *f*, billetera *f*
bil•liards ['bɪljərdz] *nsg* billar *m*
bil•ling ['bɪlɪŋ] **1** COM facturación *f* **2** THEA: ***get top ~*** ser cabeza de cartel
bil•lion ['bɪljən] mil millones *mpl*
bill of ex'change FIN letra *f* de cambio; **Bill of 'Rights** declaración *f* de derechos; **bill of 'sale** escritura *f* de compraventa
billow [bɪloʊ] *v/i* ondear
'bill•post•er *persona que pone carteles en lugares públicos*
bil•ly (club) ['bɪlɪ] cachiporra *f*, porra *f*
'bil•ly goat cabro *m*, cabrón *m*
bim•bo ['bɪmboʊ] F *mujer guapa y tonta*
bi•month•ly [baɪ'mʌnθlɪ] **I** *adj* bimestral **II** *adv* bimestralmente
bin [bɪn] cubo *m*
bi•na•ry ['baɪnərɪ] *adj* binario
bind [baɪnd] **I** *v/t* (*pret & pp* ***bound***) **1** (*connect*) unir; (*tie*) atar; *pages* encuadernar **2** LAW (*oblige*) obligar **II** *n*: ***be in a ~*** F estar entre la espada y la pared
bind•er ['baɪndər] *cover* subcarpeta *f*, funda *f* archivadora
bind•ing ['baɪndɪŋ] **I** *adj agreement, promise* vinculante **II** *n of book* tapa *f*
binge [bɪndʒ] **I** *n* F: ***go on a ~*** *when drinking* beber en exceso; *when eating* comer en exceso **II** *v/i*: ***~ on sth*** atiborrarse de algo
bin•go ['bɪŋgoʊ] bingo *m*
bi•noc•u•lars [bɪ'nɑ:kjʊlərz] *npl* pris-

máticos *mpl*
bi•o•chem•i•cal [baɪoʊ'kemɪkl] **I** *adj* bioquímico **II** *n* bioquímico *m*
bi•o•chem•ist [baɪoʊ'kemɪst] bioquímico(-a) *m(f)*
bi•o•chem•is•try [baɪoʊ'kemɪstrɪ] bioquímica *f*
bi•o•de•gra•da•ble [baɪoʊdɪ'greɪdəbl] *adj* biodegradable
bi•o•di•ver•si•ty [baɪoʊdaɪ'vɜːrsɪtɪ] biodiversidad *f*
bi•o•dy•nam•ic [baɪoʊdaɪ'næmɪk] *adj* biodinámico
bi•o•en•gi•neer•ing [baɪoʊendʒɪ'nɪərɪŋ] bioingeniería *f*
bi•og•ra•pher [baɪ'ɑːgrəfər] biógrafo (-a) *m(f)*
bi•o•graph•i•cal [baɪoʊ'græfɪkl] *adj* biográfico
bi•og•ra•phy [baɪ'ɑːgrəfɪ] biografía *f*
bi•o•haz•ard ['baɪoʊhæzərd] peligro *m* para los seres vivos
bi•o•log•i•cal [baɪoʊ'lɑːdʒɪkl] *adj* biológico; ***~ parents*** padres *mpl* biológicos; ***~ detergent*** detergente *m* biológico ***~ clock*** reloj *m* biológico; ***my ~ clock is ticking*** se me está pasando el arroz
bi•ol•o•gist [baɪ'ɑːlədʒɪst] biólogo(-a) *m(f)*
bi•ol•o•gy [baɪ'ɑːlədʒɪ] biología *f*
bi•o•pic ['baɪoʊpɪk] *movie* biografía *f*
bi•op•sy ['baɪɑːpsɪ] MED biopsia *f*
bi•o•rythm ['baɪoʊrɪðm] biorritmo *m*
bi•o•sphere ['baɪəsfɪə] biosfera *f*
bi•o•tech•nol•o•gy [baɪoʊtek'nɑːlədʒɪ] biotecnología *f*
bi•par•ti•san [baɪpɑːrtɪ'zæn] *adj* POL bipartidista
birch [bɜːrʧ] BOT abedul *m*
bird [bɜːrd] ave *f*, pájaro *m*
'bird brain F cabeza *m/f* de chorlito F
'bird•cage jaula *f* para pájaros
bird•ie ['bɜːrdɪ] *in golf* birdie *m*
bird of 'prey ave *f* rapaz; **'bird sanc•tu•a•ry** reserva *f* de aves; **'bird•seed** alpiste *m*
bird's eye 'view vista *f* panorámica; ***get a ~ of sth*** ver algo a vista de pájaro
'bird's nest nido *m*
bird watch•ing ['bɜːrdwɑːʧɪŋ] observación *f* de aves; ***go ~*** ir a observar aves
bi•ro® ['baɪroʊ] *Br* bolígrafo *m*, *Mex* pluma *f*, *Rpl* birome *m*
birth [bɜːrθ] *also fig* nacimiento *m*; (*labor*) parto *m*; ***give ~ to*** *child* dar a luz; *of animal* parir; ***date of ~*** fecha *f* de nacimiento; ***the land of my ~*** mi tierra natal
'birth cer•tif•i•cate partida *f* de nacimiento; **'birth con•trol** control *m* de natalidad; **'birth•day** cumpleaños *m inv*; ***happy ~!*** ¡feliz cumpleaños!; **'birth•day cake** tarta *f* de cumpleaños; **'birth•mark** marca *f* de nacimiento, antojo *m*; **'birth•place** lugar *m* de nacimiento; **'birth•rate** tasa *f* de natalidad
bis•cuit ['bɪskɪt] **1** bollo *m*, panecillo *m* **2** *Br* galleta *f*
bi•sect [baɪ'sekt] *v/t* MATH bisecar
bi•sex•u•al ['baɪsekʃuəl] **1** *adj* bisexual **2** *n* bisexual *m/f*
bish•op ['bɪʃəp] obispo *m*
bi•son ['baɪsən] bisonte *m*
bis•tro ['biːstroʊ] *restaurante pequeño e informal*
bit[1] [bɪt] *n* **1** (*piece*) trozo *m*; (*part*) parte *f*; *of puzzle* pieza *f*; ***a ~*** (*a little*) un poco; ***let's sit down for a ~*** sentémonos un rato; ***you haven't changed a ~*** no has cambiado nada; ***a ~ of*** (*a little*) un poco de; ***a ~ of news*** una noticia; ***a ~ of advice*** un consejo; ***~ by ~*** poco a poco; ***I'll be there in a ~*** estaré allí dentro de un rato; ***I've done my ~*** yo ya he complido **2** COMPUT bit *m*
bit[2] [bɪt] *pret* ☞ ***bite***
bitch [bɪʧ] **I** *n* **1** *dog* perra *f* **2** F *woman* zorra *f* F **II** *v/i* F (*complain*) quejarse
bitch•y ['bɪʧɪ] *adj* F *person* malicioso; *remark* a mala leche F
bite [baɪt] **I** *n* **1** *of dog* mordisco *m*; *of spider*, *mosquito* picadura *f*, *of snake* mordedura *f*, picadura *f* **2** *of food* bocado *m*; ***let's have a ~ (to eat)*** vamos a comer algo
II *v/t* (*pret* ***bit***, *pp* ***bitten***) *of dog* morder; *of mosquito*, *flea* picar; *of snake* picar, morder; ***~ one's nails*** morderse las uñas
III *v/i* (*pret* ***bit***, *pp* ***bitten***) **1** *of dog* morder; *of mosquito*, *flea* picar; *of snake* morder, picar **2** *of fish* picar
bit•ing ['baɪtɪŋ] *adj* **1** *wind*, *cold* helador, gélido **2** *remark*, *sarcasm* incisivo, mordaz
bit-mapped ['bɪtmæpt] *adj* en mapa de bits; **'bit part** papel *m* secundario; **'bit part play•er** actor *m* / actriz *f* de pape-

les secundarios
bit•ten ['bɪtn] *pp* ☞ ***bite***
bit•ter ['bɪtər] *adj taste* amargo; *person* resentido; *weather* helador; *argument* agrio
bit•ter•ly ['bɪtərlɪ] *adv resent* amargamente; ***it's ~ cold*** hace un frío helador
bit•ter•ness ['bɪtərnɪs] **1** *taste* amargor *m* **2** *resentment* resentimiento *m*, amargura *f*
bit•ty ['bɪtɪ] *adj* F inconexo, incongruente
bi•tu•men ['bɪtjʊmɪn] MIN bitumen *m*
biv•ou•ac ['bɪvʊæk] **I** *n* campamento *m* **II** *v/i* acampar
biz [bɪz] F ☞ ***business***
bi•zarre [bɪ'zɑːr] *adj* extraño, peculiar
blab [blæb] *v/i* (*pret & pp* ***-bed***) F irse de la lengua F
blab•ber•mouth ['blæbərmaʊθ] F bocazas *m/f inv* F
black [blæk] **I** *adj* negro; *coffee* solo; *tea* sin leche; *fig* negro; *day* aciago **II** *n* **1** *color* negro *m*; ***be in the ~*** FIN no estar en números rojos, tener saldo positivo; ***in ~ and white*** en blanco y negro; *in writing* por escrito **2** *person* negro(-a) *m(f)*
◆ **black out** *v/i* perder el conocimiento
black-and-'white *adj illustration, movie, television* en blanco y negro; **'black•ball** *v/t* **1** votar en contra de **2** (*exclude*) aislar, excluir; **'black•ber•ry** mora *f*; **'black•bird** mirlo *m*; **'black•board** pizarra *f*, encerado *m*; **black 'box** caja *f* negra; **black 'cof•fee** café *m* solo; **'black•cur•rant** BOT grosella *f* negra; **black e'con•o•my** economía *f* sumergida
black•en ['blækn] *v/t fig*: *person's name* manchar
black 'eye ojo *m* morado; **black-eyed pea** ['blækaɪd] judía *f* carilla *or* de vaca; **'black•head** espinilla *f*, punto *m* negro; **black 'hole** AST agujero *m* negro; **'black ice** *on road* placa *f* de hielo; ***watch out for ~*** ten cuidado con las placas de hielo
black•ish ['blækɪʃ] *adj* negruzco
'black•jack blackjack *m*; **'black•list I** *n* lista *f* negra **II** *v/t* poner en la lista negra; **black 'mag•ic** magia *f* negra; **'black•mail I** *n* chantaje *m*; ***emotional ~*** chantaje emocional **II** *v/t* chantajear; **'black•mail•er** ['blækmeɪlər] chantajista *m/f*; **black 'mar•ket** mercado *m* negro; **black mar•ket•eer** [mɑːrkə'tɪr] comerciante *m/f* en el mercado negro
black•ness ['blæknɪs] oscuridad *f*
'black•out 1 ELEC apagón *m* **2** MED desmayo *m*; ***have a ~*** desmayarse; **black 'pud•ding** *Br* morcilla *f*; **Black 'Sea**: ***the ~*** el mar Negro; **black 'sheep** *fig* oveja *f* negra; **'black•smith** herrero *m*; **'black spot** punto *m* negro; **black 'tie**: ***a ~ dinner*** una cena de gala; **'black•top** carretera *f* asfaltada
blad•der ['blædər] vejiga *f*
blade [bleɪd] **1** *of knife, sword* hoja *f* **2** *of propeller, turbine* pala *f* **3** *of grass* brizna *f* **4** *of windshield wiper* escobilla *f*
blame [bleɪm] **I** *n* culpa *f*; ***I got the ~ for it*** me echaron la culpa **II** *v/t* culpar; ***~ s.o. for sth*** culpar a alguien de algo
blame•less ['bleɪmlɪs] *adj* inocente, sin culpa
blanch [blɑːntʃ] **I** *v/t* GASTR escaldar, hervir **II** *v/i* palidecer
bland [blænd] *adj* **1** *smile* insulso **2** *food* insípido, soso
blank [blæŋk] **I** *adj* **1** (*not written on*) en blanco; *tape* virgen; ***leave ~*** dejar en blanco **2** *look* inexpresivo **3** *cartridge* de fogueo **II** *n* **1** (*empty space*) espacio *m* en blanco; ***my mind's a ~*** tengo la mente en blanco **2** *cartridge* cartucho *m* de fogueo
blank 'check, *Br* **blank 'cheque** cheque *m* en blanco
blan•ket ['blæŋkɪt] manta *f*, *L.Am.* frazada *f*; ***a ~ of snow*** un manto de nieve
blare [bler] *v/i* retumbar
◆ **blare out I** *v/i* retumbar **II** *v/t* emitir a todo volumen
blar•ney ['blɑːrnɪ] coba *f*, lisonja *f*
bla•sé [blɑː'zeɪ] *adj* indiferente
blas•pheme [blæs'fiːm] *v/i* blasfemar
blas•phe•mous ['blæsfəməs] *adj* blasfemo
blas•phe•my ['blæsfəmɪ] blasfemia *f*
blast [blæst] **I** *n* **1** (*explosion*) explosión *f* **2** (*gust*) ráfaga *f* **II** *v/t* **1** *tunnel* abrir (con explosivos); *rock* volar **2**: ***~!*** F ¡mecachis! F
◆ **blast off** *v/i of rocket* despegar
'blast door puerta *f* blindada
blast•ed ['blæstɪd] *adj* F maldito F, condenado F

'blast fur•nace alto horno *m*; **'blast-off** despegue *m*; **'blast wave** onda *f* expansiva

bla•tant ['bleɪtənt] *adj* descarado

blaze [bleɪz] **1** *n* (*fire*) incendio *m*; ***a ~ of color*** una explosión de color **2** *v/i of fire* arder

◆ **blaze away** *v/i with gun* disparar sin parar

blaz•er ['bleɪzər] americana *f*

blaz•ing ['bleɪzɪŋ] *adj building* en llamas; ***be ~ hot*** hacer un calor achicharrante; ***a ~ row*** una discusión acalorada

bleach [bliːtʃ] **1** *n for clothes* lejía *f*, *for hair* decolorante *m* **2** *v/t hair* aclarar, desteñir

bleach•ers ['bliːtʃərz] *npl* SP gradas *fpl*

bleak [bliːk] *adj countryside* inhóspito; *weather* desapacible; *future* desolador

blear•y-eyed ['blɪrɪaɪd] *adj* con ojos de sueño

bleat [bliːt] *v/i of sheep* balar

bled [bled] *pret & pp* ☞ ***bleed***

bleed [bliːd] **1** *v/i* (*pret & pp* ***bled***) sangrar; ***he's ~ing internally*** tiene una hemorragia interna; ***~ to death*** desangrarse **2** *v/t* (*pret & pp* ***bled***) *fig* sangrar; ***he's ~ing me dry*** me está chupando la sangre

bleed•ing ['bliːdɪŋ] hemorragia *f*

bleep [bliːp] **I** *n* pitido *m* **II** *v/i* pitar **III** *v/t on pager* llamar con el buscapersonas

bleep•er ['bliːpər] *Br* buscapersonas *m inv*, *Span* busca *m*, *Mex* localizador *m*, *RPl* radiomensaje *m*

blem•ish ['blemɪʃ] **I** *n* imperfección *f* **II** *v/t reputation* manchar

blend [blend] **I** *n of coffee etc* mezcla *f*; *fig* combinación *f* **II** *v/t* mezclar

◆ **blend in 1** *v/i of person in environment* pasar desapercibido; *of animal with surroundings etc* confundirse; *of furniture etc* combinar **2** *v/t in cooking* añadir

blend•er ['blendər] *machine* licuadora *f*

bless [bles] *v/t* (*pret & pp* ***-ed*** *or* ***blest***) bendecir; ***(God) ~ you!*** ¡que Dios te bendiga!; *in response to sneeze* ¡Jesús!; ***be ~ed with*** tener la suerte de tener

bless•ed ['blesɪd] *adj also euph* bendito, sagrado; ***the Blessed Virgin*** la bendita Virgen María

bless•ing ['blesɪŋ] *also fig* bendición *f*; ***give s.o. / sth one's ~*** echar la bendición a algo / alguien

blest [blest] *pret & pp* ☞ ***bless***

blew [bluː] *pret* ☞ ***blow***

blight [blaɪt] **I** *n* **1** BOT plaga *f* **2** *fig* maldición *f*, desgracia *f* **II** *v/t* plagar

bli•mey ['blaɪmɪ] *int Br* F ¡vaya! F, ¡toma! F

blimp [blɪmp] zepelín *m*

blind [blaɪnd] **I** *adj* ciego; *corner* sin visibilidad; ***go ~*** quedarse ciego; ***be ~ to sth*** *fig* no ver algo; ***as ~ as a bat*** más ciego que un topo **II** *n* **1** *on window* estor *m*; (*roller ~*) persiana *f* **2** *pl*: ***the ~*** los ciegos, los invidentes **III** *v/t of sun* cegar; ***she was ~ed in an accident*** se quedó ciega a raíz de un accidente

blind 'al•ley callejón *m* sin salida

blind 'date cita *f* a ciegas

blind•ers ['blaɪndərz] *npl* antojeras *fpl*

'blind•fold I *n* venda *f* **II** *v/t* vendar los ojos a **III** *adv* con los ojos cerrados

blind•ing ['blaɪndɪŋ] *adj light* cegador; *headache* terrible

blind•ly ['blaɪndlɪ] *adv* a ciegas; *fig* ciegamente

blind•man's 'buff gallinita *f* ciega

blind•ness ['blaɪndnɪs] ceguera *f*

'blind spot 1 *in road* punto *m* sin visibilidad; *in driving mirror* ángulo *m* muerto **2** (*ability that is lacking*) punto *m* flaco

blink [blɪŋk] *v/i* parpadear

blink•ered ['blɪŋkərd] *adj fig* cerrado

blink•ers ['blɪŋkərz] *npl* **1** MOT (luces *fpl*) intermitentes *mpl* **2** *Br*: *for horse* antojeras *fpl*

blip [blɪp] *on radar screen* señal *f*, luz *f*; ***it's just a ~*** *fig* es algo momentáneo

bliss [blɪs] felicidad *f*; ***it was ~*** fue fantástico

bliss•ful ['blɪsfʊl] *adj* estupendo, fantástico

blis•ter ['blɪstər] **I** *n* ampolla *f* **II** *v/i* ampollarse; *of paint* hacer burbujas

'blis•ter pack blister *m*

blithe•ly ['blaɪðlɪ] *adv* alegremente, a la ligera

blitz [blɪts] *air attack* bombardeo *m*

blitzed [blɪtsd] *adj* P *on alcohol*, *drugs* colgado P

bliz•zard ['blɪzərd] ventisca *f*

bloat•ed ['bloʊtɪd] *adj* hinchado

blob [blɑːb] *of nail varnish*, *paint etc* goterón *m*

bloc [blɑːk] POL bloque *m*
block [blɑːk] **I** *n* **1** bloque *m*; *buildings* manzana *f*, *L.Am.* cuadra *f*; *of shares* paquete *m*; ***~ of seats*** grupo *m* de asientos **2** (*blockage*) bloqueo *m* **3** *in basketball* gorro *m*, tapón *m* **II** *v/t* bloquear; *sink* atascar
◆ **block in** *v/t with vehicle* bloquear el paso a
◆ **block out** *v/t* **1** *light* impedir el paso de **2** *memory* apartar de la mente
◆ **block up** *v/t sink etc* atascar; ***I'm feeling all blocked up*** tengo la nariz tapada
block•ade [blɑː'keɪd] **I** *n* bloqueo *m* **II** *v/t* bloquear
block•age ['blɑːkɪdʒ] obstrucción *f*
block and 'tack•le sistema *m* de poleas; **block 'book•ing** reserva *f* en grupo; **block•bust•er** ['blɑːkbʌstər] gran éxito *m*, exitazo *m*; **'block•bust•er mov•ie** exitazo *m* de película; **block 'cap•i•tals** *npl* (letras *fpl*) mayúsculas *fpl*; **'block-head** F cabeza hueca *or* vacía *m/f* F; **block 'let•ters** *npl* (letras *fpl*) mayúsculas *fpl*
bloke [blouk] *Br* F tipo *m* F, *Span* tío *m* F
blond [blɑːnd] *adj* rubio
blonde [blɑːnd] *woman* rubia *f*
blood [blʌd] sangre *f*; ***in cold ~*** a sangre fría
'blood al•co•hol lev•el nivel *m* de alcohol en la sangre; **'blood bank** banco *m* de sangre; **'blood bath** baño *m* de sangre; **'blood clot** MED coágulo *m*; **blood-curdling** ['blʌdkɜːrdlɪŋ] *adj* espantoso, horripilante; **'blood do•nor** donante *m/f* de sangre; **'blood group** grupo *m* sanguíneo; **'blood•hound** perro *m* sabueso
blood•less ['blʌdlɪs] *adj coup* incruento, pacífico
'blood or•ange naranja *f* de sangre; **'blood poi•son•ing** septicemia *f*; **'blood pres•sure** tensión *f* (arterial), presión *f* sanguínea; **'blood pud•ding** morcilla *f*; **'blood re•la•tion**: ***she's not a ~ of mine*** no nos unen lazos de sangre; **'blood sam•ple** muestra *f* de sangre; **blood•shed** ['blʌdʃed] derramamiento *m* de sangre; **'blood•shot** *adj* enrojecido; **'blood sport** *deporte en el que se matan animales*; **'blood•stain** mancha *f* de sangre; **'blood•stained** *adj* ensangrentado, manchado de sangre; **'blood•stream** flujo *m* sanguíneo; **'blood•suck•er** *also fig* sanguijuela *f*; **blood 'sug•ar lev•el** nivel *m* de azúcar en la sangre; **'blood test** análisis *m inv* de sangre; **'blood•thirst•y** *adj* sanguinario; *movie* macabro; **'blood trans-fu•sion** transfusión *f* sanguínea; **'blood type** grupo *m* sanguíneo; **'blood ves-sel** vaso *m* sanguíneo
blood•y ['blʌdɪ] *adj* **1** *hands etc* ensangrentado; *battle* sangriento **2** *Br* F maldito F, puñetero F
Blood•y 'Mar•y Bloody Mary *m* (*cocktail de vodka y zumo de tomate*)
blood•y-'mind•ed *adj* perverso, retorcido
bloom [bluːm] **I** *n* flor *f*; ***in ~*** en flor **II** *v/i also fig* florecer
bloom•ing ['bluːmɪŋ] *adj Br* F maldito F
blos•som ['blɑːsəm] **I** *n* flores *fpl* **II** *v/i also fig* florecer
blot [blɑːt] **1** *n* mancha *f*, borrón *m*; ***be a ~ on the landscape*** estropear el paisaje **2** *v/t* (*pret & pp* ***-ted***) (*dry*) secar
blotch [blɑːtʃ] *on skin* erupción *f*, mancha *f*
blotch•y ['blɑːtʃɪ] *adj skin* con erupciones
◆ **blot out** *v/t* **1** *sun, view* ocultar **2** *memory* borrar
blot•ting pa•per ['blɑːtɪŋ] papel *m* secante
blot•to ['blɑːtou] *adj* P pedo P, mamado P
blouse [blauz] blusa *f*
blow[1] [blou] *n* golpe *m*
blow[2] [blou] **I** *v/t* (*pret* ***blew***, *pp* ***blown***) *smoke* exhalar; *whistle* tocar; F (*spend*) fundir F; *opportunity* perder, desaprovechar; ***~ one's nose*** sonarse (la nariz) **II** *v/i* (*pret* ***blew***, *pp* ***blown***) *of wind, person* soplar; *of whistle* sonar; *of fuse* fundirse; *of tire* reventarse
◆ **blow away** *v/t* **1** *of wind* llevarse **2** P (*kill*) liquidar F, *Span* cargarse F
◆ **blow in** *v/i* F (*arrive*) aparecer
◆ **blow off I** *v/t* llevarse; ***blow off steam*** F desahogarse, *Span* desfogarse **II** *v/i of hat etc* salir volando
◆ **blow out I** *v/t candle* apagar; ***blow one's brains out*** volarse la tapa de

los sesos **II** *v/i of candle* apagarse

◆ **blow over I** *v/t* derribar, hacer caer **II** *v/i* **1** *because of wind* caerse, derrumbarse **2** *of storm* amainar; *of argument* calmarse

◆ **blow up I** *v/t* **1** *with explosives* volar **2** *balloon* hinchar **3** *photograph* ampliar **II** *v/i* **1** (*explode*) explotar **2** F (*become angry*) ponerse furioso

'blow-dry *v/t* (*pret & pp* **-ied**) secar (*con secador*)

blow•er ['blouər] TECH ventilador *m*, turbina *f*

'blow•fly ZO moscardón *m*; **'blow•job** V mamada *f* V; **'blow•lamp** TECH *Br* soplete *m*

blown [bloun] *pp* ☞ **blow**

'blow•out *of tire* reventón *m*; F (*big meal*) comilona *f* F; ***budget*** ~ desbordamiento *m* del presupuesto; **'blow-pipe** cebratana *f*, canuto *m*; **'blow-torch** TECH soplete *m*; **'blow-up** *of photo* ampliación *f*

blowz•y ['blauzɪ] *adj woman* dejada, desaliñada

blub•ber[1] ['blʌbər] *v/i cry* llorar, berrear

blub•ber[2] ['blʌbər] *n of whale* cetina *f*

bludg•eon ['blʌdʒən] *v/t* golpear, apalear; ~ ***s.o. to death*** matar a alguien a golpes; ~ ***s.o. into doing sth*** *fig* coaccionar *or* acosar a alguien para que haga algo

blue [bluː] **I** *adj* **1** azul **2** F *movie* porno *inv* F **3**: ***be feeling*** ~ F sentirse decaído *or* triste **II** *n* azul *m*

'blue•bell BOT campanilla *f*; **'blue•ber-ry** arándano *m*; **'blue•bird** ZO azulejo *m*; **blue-blood•ed** ['blʌdɪd] *adj* de sangre azul; **'blue•bot•tle** ZO mosca *f* azul; **blue 'chip** *adj* puntero, de primera fila; **blue-'col•lar work•er** trabajador(a) *m*(*f*) manual; **'blue-jacket** agente *m/f* de policía; **'blue jay** ZO arrendajo *m* americano; **'blue jeans** *npl Span* vaqueros *mpl*, *L.Am.* jeans *mpl*, jean *m*; **blue 'mov•ie** F película *f* porno F; **'blue•print** plano *m*; *fig* proyecto *m*, plan *m*; **'blue rinse** reflejos *mpl* azules

blues [bluːz] *npl* MUS blues *m inv*; ***have the*** ~ estar deprimido

'blues sing•er cantante *m/f* de blues

'blue•stock•ing F *pej* intelectual *f*

bluff [blʌf] **I** *n* (*deception*) farol *m* **II** *v/i* ir de farol **III** *v/t*: ***she*** ~***ed her way through the interview*** estuvo faroleando durante toda la entrevista

blu•ish ['bluːɪʃ] *adj* azulado

blun•der ['blʌndər] **1** *n* error *m* de bulto, metedura *f* de pata **2** *v/i* cometer un error de bulto, meter la pata

blunt [blʌnt] *adj* **1** *pencil* sin punta; *knife* desafilado **2** *person* franco

blunt•ly ['blʌntlɪ] *adv speak* francamente

blur [blɜːr] **1** *n* imagen *f* desenfocada; ***everything is a*** ~ todo está desenfocado **2** *v/t* (*pret & pp* **-red**) desdibujar

blurb [blɜːrb] *on book* nota *f* promocional

blurred [blɜːrd] *adj* borroso, desenfocado

◆ **blurt out** [blɜːrt] *v/t* soltar

blush [blʌʃ] **I** *n* rubor *m*, sonrojo *m* **II** *v/i* ruborizarse, sonrojarse

blush•er ['blʌʃər] *cosmetic* colorete *m*

blus•ter ['blʌstər] *v/i* protestar encolerizadamente

blus•ter•y ['blʌstərɪ] *adj* tempestuoso

BMI [biːem'aɪ] *abbr* (= ***body mass index***) IMC (= Índice *m* de Masa Corporal

'B-mov•ie película *f* de la serie B

BO [biː'ou] *abbr* (= ***body odor***) olor *m* corporal

bo•a con•strict•or [bouəkən'strɪktər] ZO boa *f*

boar [bɔːr] ZO jabalí *m*

board [bɔːrd] **I** *n* **1** tablón *m*, tabla *f*; *for game* tablero *m*; *for notices* tablón *m*; ***across the*** ~ de forma general **2**: ~ (***of directors***) consejo *m* de administración **3**: ***on*** ~ *on plane, boat, train* a bordo; ***take on*** ~ *comments etc* aceptar, tener en cuenta; (*fully realize truth of*) asumir **II** *v/t airplane etc* embarcar; *train* subir a **III** *v/i* **1** *of passengers* embarcar **2**: ~ ***with*** *as lodger* hospedarse con

◆ **board up** *v/t* cubrir con tablas

board•er ['bɔːrdər] huésped *m/f*

'board game juego *m* de mesa

board•ing card ['bɔːrdɪŋ] tarjeta *f* de embarque; **'board•ing house** hostal *m*, pensión *f*; **'board•ing pass** tarjeta *f* de embarque; **'board•ing school** internado *m*

'board meet•ing reunión *f* del consejo de administración; **'board room** sala *f* de reuniones *or* juntas; **'board•walk**

paseo *m* marítimo con tablas

boast [boʊst] **I** *n* presunción *f*, jactancia *f* **II** *v/i* presumir, alardear (***about*** de)

boast•er ['boʊstər] bravucón(-ona) *m(f)*

boast•ful ['boʊstfʊl] *adj* presuntuoso, pretencioso

boat [boʊt] barco *m*; *small*, *for leisure* barca *f*; ***go by ~*** ir en barco

'boat•house caseta *f* para barcas; **'boat peo•ple** *npl* refugiados *mpl* en barca; **'boat race** regata *f*

boat•swain ['boʊsn] NAUT contramaestre *m*

bob[1] [bɑːb] *n haircut* corte *m* a lo chico

bob[2] [bɑːb] *v/i* (*pret & pp* ***-bed***) *of boat etc* mecerse

◆ **bob up** *v/i* aparecer

bob•bin ['bɑːbɪn] bobina *f*, rollo *m*

bob•by ['bɑːbɪ] *Br* F agente *m* de policía

'bob•by pin pinza *f* de pelo

'bob cat ZO lince *m*

'bob•sled, 'bob•sleigh bobsleigh *m*

bode[1] [boʊd] *v/i*: ***~ ill*** ser un mal presagio; ***~ well*** ser un buen presagio

bode[2] [boʊd] *pret* ☞ ***bide***

bod•ice ['bɑːdɪs] cuerpo *m*

bod•i•ly ['bɑːdɪlɪ] **I** *adj* corporal; *needs* físico; *function* fisiológico **II** *adv eject* en volandas

bod•y ['bɑːdɪ] **1** cuerpo *m*; *dead* cadáver *m* **2** *of car* carrocería *f* **3**: ***~ of water*** masa *f* de agua

'bod•y bag bolsa *f* para cadáveres; **'bod•y build•er** culturista *m/f*; **'bod•y build•ing** culturismo *m*; **'bod•y•check** *v/t* SP blocar; **'bod•y•guard** guardaespaldas *m/f inv*; **'bod•y lan•guage** lenguaje *m* corporal; **'bod•y mass in•dex** índice *m* de masa corporal; **'bod•y o•dor** olor *m* corporal; **'bod•y pierc•ing** piercing *m*, perforaciones *fpl* corporales; **'bod•y search** cacheo *m*; **'bod•y•shop** MOT taller *m* de carrocería; **'bod•y stock•ing** malla *f*; **'bod•y suit** body *m*; **'bod•y•work** MOT carrocería *f*

bog [bɑːg] pantano *m*, ciénaga *f*

◆ **bog down** *v/i*: ***get bogged down*** *also fig* atascarse, atrancarse (***in*** en)

bo•gey 1 *worry* ☞ ***bogy* 2** *Br*: *in nose* ☞ ***booger***

bog•gle ['bɑːgl] *v/i*: ***it ~s the mind!*** ¡no quiero ni pensarlo!

bog•gy ['bɑːgɪ] *adj* pantanoso

bo•gus ['boʊgəs] *adj* falso

bo•gy ['boʊgɪ] temor *m*, miedo *m*

boil[1] [bɔɪl] *n swelling* forúnculo

boil[2] [bɔɪl] **I** *v/t liquid* hervir; *egg*, *vegetables* cocer **II** *v/i* hervir

◆ **boil down to** *v/t* reducirse a

◆ **boil over** *v/i of milk etc* salirse

boiled po•tat•oes [bɔɪldpə'teɪtoʊz] *npl L.Am.* papas *fpl or Span* patatas *fpl* hervidas

boil•er ['bɔɪlər] caldera *f*

'boil•er suit *Br* mono *m*, peto *m*

boil•ing point ['bɔɪlɪŋ] *of liquid* punto *m* de ebullición; ***reach ~*** *fig* perder la paciencia

bois•ter•ous ['bɔɪstərəs] *adj* escandaloso

bold [boʊld] **I** *adj* **1** valiente, audaz **2** *text* en negrita **II** *n print* negrita *f*; ***in ~*** en negrita

Bo•liv•i•a [bə'lɪvɪə] Bolivia *f*

Bo•liv•i•an [bə'lɪvɪən] **I** *adj* boliviano **II** *n* boliviano(-a) *m(f)*

Bo•liv•i•an 'pla•teau El Altiplano

bol•lard ['bɑːlɑːrd] **1** NAUT bolardo *m* **2** *Br*: *in road* baliza *f*

bol•locks ['bɑːləks] *pl Br* V: ***a load of ~*** un montón de gilipolleces V

bo•lo•ney [bə'loʊnɪ] F chorrada *f* F, memez *f* F

bo•lo tie ['boʊloʊtaɪ] corbata *f* de cordón con plaquita

bol•ster ['boʊlstər] *v/t confidence* reforzar

bolt [boʊlt] **I** *n* **1** *on door* cerrojo *m*, pestillo *m* **2** *with nut* perno *m* **3** *of lightning* rayo *m*; ***like a ~ from the blue*** de forma inesperada **II** *adv*: ***~ upright*** erguido **III** *v/t* **1** (*attach with bolts*) atornillar **2** *close* cerrar con cerrojo *or* pestillo **IV** *v/i* (*run off*) fugarse, escaparse

◆ **bolt down** *v/t food* engullirse

bomb [bɑːm] **I** *n* bomba *f* **II** *v/t* MIL bombardear; *of terrorist* poner una bomba en **III** *v/i* F *of play*, *movie etc* fracasar

bom•bard [bɑːm'bɑːrd] *v/t also fig* bombardear

bom•bard•ment [bɑːm'bɑːrdmənt] bombardeo *m*

bom•bast ['bɑːmbæst] grandilocuencia *f*

bom•bas•tic [bɑːm'bæstɪk] *adj* bombástico, grandilocuente

'bomb at•tack atentado *m* con bomba
'bomb dis•pos•al u•nit comando *m* de desarticulación de explosivos
bombed [bɑːmbd] *adj* P *on alcohol, drugs*: ***be ~*** ir ciego P
bomb•er ['bɑːmər] **1** *airplane* bombardero *m* **2** *terrorist* terrorista *m/f* (*que pone bombas*)
'bomb•er jack•et cazadora *f* de aviador
bomb•ing ['bɑːmɪŋ] bombardeo *m*
'bomb•proof *adj* a prueba de bombas; **'bomb scare** amenaza *f* de bomba; **'bomb•shell** *fig*: *news* bomba *f*; **'bomb threat** amenaza *f* de bomba
bo•na fi•de [bounə'fiːdeɪ] *adj* verdadero, genuino
bo•nan•za [bə'nænzə] **I** *n* bonanza *f*, prosperidad *f* **II** *adj* próspero
bond [bɑːnd] **I** *n* **1** (*tie*) unión *f* **2** FIN bono *m* **II** *v/i* **1** *of glue* adherirse **2** *of people* establecer vínculos
bond•age ['bɑːndɪdʒ] **1** *slavery* esclavitud *f* **2** *sexual practice* bondage *m*
bond•ed ware•house ['bɑːndɪd] depósito *m* franco
'bond•hold•er COM tenedor(a) *m*(*f*) de bonos *or* obligaciones
bond•ing ['bɑːndɪŋ]: ***male ~*** establecimiento *m* de vínculos *or* lazos entre hombres
bone [boun] **I** *n* hueso *m*; *of fish* espina *f* **II** *v/t meat* deshuesar; *fish* quitar las espinas a
◆ **bone up on** *v/t* F *subject* matarse estudiando, *Span* machacar F, *Mex* zambutirse F, *Chi* matearse en F, *Rpl* tragarse F
'bone-dry *adj* completamente seco; **'bone•head** F tonto(-a) *m*(*f*) F; **'bone-idle** *adj* holgazán, perezoso
bon•fire ['bɑːnfaɪr] hoguera *f*
bonk [bɑːŋk] *v/t* F *hit* golpear suavemente
bonk•ers ['bɑːŋkərz] *adj* P chiflado F; ***go ~*** volverse majara F
bon•net ['bɑːnɪt] *Br*: *of car* capó *m*
bo•nus ['bounəs] *money* plus *m*, bonificación *f*; (*something extra*) ventaja *f* adicional; ***a Christmas ~*** un plus por Navidad
bon•y ['bounɪ] *adj* **1** *body* huesudo, escuálido **2** *fish* espinoso
boo [buː] **I** *n* abucheo *m* **II** *v/t & v/i* abuchear
boob [buːb] P (*breast*) teta *f* P
boo•boo ['buːbuː] F metedura *f* de pata
boo•by ['buːbɪ] F memo(-a) *m*(*f*) F
'boo•by hatch P loquería *f* P; **'boo•by prize** premio *m* al perdedor; **'boo•by trap** **1** *bomb* bomba *f* lapa **2** *joke* broma *f* pesada
boo•ger ['buːgər] F moco *m*; ***he picked a ~ out of his nose*** se sacó un moco de la nariz
book [bʊk] **I** *n* **1** libro *m* **2** *of matches* caja *f* (*de solapa*) **II** *v/t* **1** (*reserve*) reservar **2** *of policeman* multar **III** *v/i* (*reserve*) reservar, hacer una reserva
'book•bind•er encuadernador(a) *m*(*f*); **'book•case** estantería *f*, librería *f*; **'book club** club *m* de lectores
booked up [bʊkt'ʌp] *adj* lleno, completo; *person* ocupado
'book end reposalibros *m inv*
book•ie ['bʊkɪ] *Br* F corredor(a) *m*(*f*) de apuestas
book•ing ['bʊkɪŋ] (*reservation*) reserva *f*
'book•ing clerk taquillero(-a) *m*(*f*); **'book•ing fee** suplemento *m* por reserva; **'book•ing of•fice** taquilla *f*, *L.Am.* boletería *f*
book•ish ['bʊkɪʃ] *adj* estudioso
'book•keep•er tenedor(a) *m*(*f*) de libros, contable *m/f*
'book•keep•ing contabilidad *f*
book•let ['bʊklɪt] folleto *m*
'book•mak•er corredor(a) *m*(*f*) de apuestas
'book•mark **I** *n* **1** marcapáginas *m inv* **2** COMPUT marcador *m*, favorito *m* **II** *v/t* COMPUT añadir a la lista de marcadores *or* favoritos
book•mo•bile ['bʊkmoubiːl] biblioteca *f* ambulante
books [bʊks] *npl* (*accounts*) contabilidad *f*; ***do the ~*** llevar la contabilidad
'book•sell•er librero(-a) *m*(*f*); **'book•shelf** estante *m*; **'book•shop** *Br* librería *f*; **'book•stall** *Br* puesto *m* de venta de libros; **'book•store** librería *f*; **'book to•ken** vale *m* para comprar libros; **'book val•ue** FIN valor *m* contable; **'book•worm** ratón *m* de biblioteca
Bool•e•an ['buːlɪən] *adj* booleano
boom[1] [buːm] **I** *n* boom *m* **II** *v/i of business* desarrollarse, experimentar un boom
boom[2] [buːm] *n noise* estruendo *m*

B

boom•er•ang ['bu:məræŋ] **I** *n* bumerán *m* **II** *v/i fig* salir el tiro por la culata; ***it ~ed on him*** le salió el tiro por la culata
'boom mi•cro•phone jirafa *f*
boon [bu:n] bendición *f*
boon•docks ['bu:ndɑ:ks], **boon•ies** ['bu:nɪz] *npl* F: ***they live out in the ~*** viven en el quinto pino F
boor [bʊr] basto *m*, grosero *m*
boor•ish ['bʊrɪʃ] *adj* basto, grosero
boost [bu:st] **I** *n to sales, economy* impulso *m*; ***your confidence needs a ~*** necesitas algo que te dé más confianza **II** *v/t production, economy* estimular, impulsar; *morale* levantar
boost•er ['bu:stər] **1** MED vacuna *f* de refuerzo **2** (*supporter*) entusiasta *m/f*
'boost•er ca•bles *npl* MOT cables *mpl* de arranque; **'boost•er rock•et** cohete *m* propulsor; **'boost•er seat** asiento *m* para niño; **'boost•er shot** MED vacuna *f* de refuerzo
boot [bu:t] **1** bota *f* **2** *Br. of car* maletero *m*, *C.Am.*, *Mex* cajuela *f*, *Rpl* baúl *m*
◆ **boot out** *v/t* F echar
◆ **boot up** *v/t & v/i* COMPUT arrancar
'boot•black limpiabotas *m inv*; **'boot-camp** F campo *m* de entrenamiento; **'boot disk** COMPUT disco *m* de arranque
boot•ee ['bu:ti:] patuco *m*
booth [bu:ð] *at market, fair* cabina *f*, *at exhibition* puesto *m*, stand *m*; (*in restaurant*) *mesa rodeada por bancos fijos*
boot•ie ['bu:ti:] ☞ ***bootee***
'boot•lace cordón *m*; **'boot•leg** *adj whiskey* clandestino; *recording*, *CD* pirata; **boot•lick•er** ['bu:tlɪkər] F pelota *m/f* F; **'boot•straps** *npl*: ***pull o.s. up by one's ~*** arreglárselas uno solo
boo•ty ['bu:tɪ] botín *m*
booze [bu:z] F bebida *f*, *Span* priva *f* F
bor•der ['bɔ:rdər] **I** *n* **1** *between countries* frontera *f* **2** (*edge*) borde *m*; *on clothing* ribete *m* **II** *v/t country* limitar con; *river* bordear
◆ **border on** *v/t* **1** *country* limitar con **2** (*be almost*) rayar en
'bor•der con•trols *npl* controles *mpl* fronterizos; **'bor•der cros•sing** paso *m* fronterizo; **'bor•der•guard** guardia *m/f* fronterizo(-a); **'bor•der•land** frontera *f*; **'bor•der•line** *adj*: ***a ~ case*** un caso dudoso; ***it's ~*** es algo intermedio
bore[1] [bɔ:r] **I** *v/t hole* taladrar; ***~ a hole in sth*** taladrar algo
bore[2] [bɔ:r] **I** *n person* pesado(-a) *m(f)*, pelma *m/f inv* F **II** *v/t* aburrir
bore[3] [bɔ:r] *pret* ☞ ***bear***[2]
bored [bɔ:rd] *adj* aburrido; ***I'm ~*** me aburro, estoy aburrido
bore•dom ['bɔ:rdəm] aburrimiento *m*
bor•ing ['bɔ:rɪŋ] *adj* aburrido
born [bɔ:rn] *adj*: ***be ~*** nacer; ***where were you ~?*** ¿dónde naciste?; ***be a ~ teacher*** haber nacido para ser profesor
'born-a•gain *adj*: ***~ Christian*** *persona convertida a un culto evangélico como resultado de una experiencia religiosa*
borne [bɔ:rn] *pp* ☞ ***bear***[2]
bor•ough ['bʌroʊ] municipio *m*
bor•row ['bɑ:roʊ] *v/t* tomar prestado (***from*** de)
◆ **borrow against** *v/t* avalar con
bor•row•er ['bɑ:roʊər] prestatario(-a) *m(f)*
bor•row•ings ['bɑ:roʊɪŋz] *npl* préstamos *mpl*
Bos•ni•a ['bɑ:znɪə] Bosnia *f*
Bos•ni•a-Her•ze•go•vi•na [bɑ:znɪəhɜ:rtsə'gɑ:vɪnə] Bosnia y Hercegovina *f*
Bos•ni•an ['bɑ:znɪən] **I** *adj* bosnio **II** *n person* bosnio(-a) *m(f)*
bos•om ['bʊzm] *of woman* pecho *m*
boss [bɑ:s] jefe(-a) *m(f)*
◆ **boss around** *v/t* dar órdenes a
boss•y ['bɑ:sɪ] *adj* mandón
Bos•to•ni•an [bɑ:s'toʊnjən] **I** *adj* de Boston **II** *n* abitante *m/f* de Boston
bo•tan•ic [bə'tænɪk] botánico
bo•tan•i•cal [bə'tænɪkl] *adj* botánico
bo'tan•i•cal gar•dens *npl* jardín *m* botánico
bot•a•nist ['bɑ:tənɪst] botánico(-a) *m(f)*
bot•a•ny ['bɑ:tənɪ] botánica *f*
botch [bɑ:tʃ] *v/t* arruinar, estropear
both [boʊθ] **I** *adj & pron* ambos, los dos; ***I know ~ (of the) brothers*** conozco a ambos hermanos, conozco a los dos hermanos; ***~ of them*** ambos, los dos **II** *adv*: ***~ my mother and I*** tanto mi madre como yo; ***he's ~ handsome and intelligent*** es guapo y además inteligente; ***is it business or pleasure? – ~*** ¿es de negocios o de placer? – las dos cosas
both•er ['bɑ:ðər] **I** *n* molestias *fpl*; ***it's no***

~ no es ninguna molestia **II** *v/t* **1** (*disturb*) molestar **2** (*worry*) preocupar **III** *v/i* preocuparse; ***don't ~!*** (*you needn't do it*) ¡no te preocupes!; ***you needn't have ~ed*** no deberías haberte molestado

both•er•some ['bɑːðərsʌm] *adj* molesto

bot•tle ['bɑːtl] **I** *n* botella *f*; *for baby* biberón *m*; ***hit the ~*** F darse a la bebida F **II** *v/t* embotellar

◆ **bottle up** *v/t feelings* reprimir, contener

'bot•tle bank contenedor *m* de vidrio

bot•tled wa•ter ['bɑːtld] agua *f* embotellada

'bot•tle•neck *in road* embotellamiento *m*, atasco *m*; *in production* cuello *m* de botella

'bot•tle-o•pen•er abrebotellas *m inv*

bot•tom ['bɑːtəm] **I** *adj* inferior, de abajo **II** *n* **1** *of drawer, case, pan* fondo *m*; *of hill, page* pie *m*; *of pile* parte *f* inferior; (*underside*) parte *f* de abajo; *of street* final *m*; *of garden* fondo *m*; ***at the ~ of the screen*** en la parte inferior de la pantalla; ***at the ~ of the page*** al pie de la página **2** (*buttocks*) trasero *m*

◆ **bottom out** *v/i* tocar fondo

bot•tom 'gear primera *f*

bot•tom•less ['bɑːtəmlɪs] *adj*: ***a ~ pit*** *fig* un pozo sin fondo

bot•tom 'line 1 (*financial outcome*) saldo *m* final **2** (*real issue*) realidad *f*

'bot•tom-of-the-range *adj* de gama baja

bot•u•lism ['bɑːtjʊlɪzm] MED botulismo *m*

bough [baʊ] *lit* rama *f*

bought [bɒːt] *pret & pp* ☞ ***buy***

bouil•lon cube ['buːjɑːnkjuːb] pastilla *f* de caldo

boul•der ['boʊldər] roca *f* redondeada

boul•e•vard ['buːləvɑːrd] bulevar *m*

bounce [baʊns] **I** *v/t ball* botar **II** *v/i of ball* botar, rebotar; *on sofa etc* saltar; *of rain* rebotar; *of check* ser rechazado; ***check that ~s*** cheque *m* sin fondos **III** *n* bote *m*

bounc•er ['baʊnsər] portero *m*, gorila *m*

bounc•ing ['baʊnsɪŋ] *adj baby* saludable

bounc•y ['baʊnsɪ] *adj ball* que bota bien; *cushion, chair* mullido

bound[1] [baʊnd] *adj*: ***be ~ to do sth*** (*obliged to*) estar obligado a hacer algo; ***she's ~ to call an election soon*** (*sure to*) seguro que convoca elecciones pronto

bound[2] [baʊnd] *adj*: ***be ~ for*** *of ship* llevar destino a

bound[3] [baʊnd] **I** *n* (*jump*) salto *m* **II** *v/i* saltar

bound[4] [baʊnd] *pret & pp* ☞ ***bind***

bound•a•ry ['baʊndərɪ] límite *m*; *between countries* frontera *f*

bound•less ['baʊndlɪs] *adj* ilimitado, infinito

boun•ti•ful ['baʊntɪfʊl] *adj* **1** *generous* generoso **2** *plentiful* abundante

boun•ty ['baʊntɪ] **1** *generosity* generosidad *f* **2** *prize* recompensa *f*

'boun•ty hunt•er cazarrecompensas *m/f inv*

bou•quet [bʊ'keɪ] **1** *flowers* ramo *m* **2** *of wine* bouquet *m*

bour•bon ['bɜːrbən] bourbon *m*

bour•geois ['bʊʒwɑː] *adj* burgués

bour•geoi•sie [bʊʒwɑː'ziː] burguesía *f*

bout [baʊt] **1** MED ataque *m* **2** *in boxing* combate *m*

bou•tique [buː'tiːk] boutique *f*

bo•vine ['boʊvaɪn] *adj* **1** ZO bovino **2** *stupid* bobo

bow[1] [baʊ] **I** *n as greeting* reverencia *f* **II** *v/i* saludar con la cabeza **III** *v/t head* inclinar

◆ **bow out** *v/i* retirarse

bow[2] [boʊ] *n* **1** (*knot*) lazo *m* **2** MUS, *for archery* arco *m*

bow[3] [baʊ] *n of ship* proa *f*

bowd•ler•ize ['baʊdləraɪz] *v/t text* censurar

bow•els ['baʊəlz] *npl* entrañas *fpl*

bowl[1] [boʊl] *n for rice, cereals etc* cuenco *m*; *for soup* plato *m* sopero; *for salad* ensaladera *f*, *for washing* barreño *m*, palangana *f*

bowl[2] [boʊl] SP **I** *n ball* bola *f* **II** *v/i* lanzar la bola

◆ **bowl over** *v/t fig* (*astonish*) impresionar, maravillar

bow•leg•ged ['boʊlegd] *adj* estevado

bow legs ['boʊlegz] *npl* piernas *fpl* estevadas

bowl•er ['boʊlər] **1** jugador(a) *m*(*f*) de bolos **2** *Br*: *in cricket* pitcher *m/f*, lanzador(a) *m*(*f*)

B

'bowl•er hat *Br* sombrero *m* de hongo
bowl•ing ['boʊlɪŋ] bolos *mpl*; ***Friday's his ~ night*** todos los viernes por la noche va a jugar a los bolos
'bowl•ing al•ley bolera *f*
bow•sprit ['boʊsprɪt] NAUT bauprés *m*
bow tie [boʊ'taɪ] pajarita *f*
box[1] [bɑːks] *n* **1** *container* caja *f* **2** *on form* casilla *f*; *in soccer* área *f*
◆ **box in** *v/t*: ***be boxed in*** *of driver, runner* estar encajonado; ***feel boxed in*** sentirse enjaulado
box[2] [bɑːks] *v/i* boxear
'box car RAIL vagón *m* de mercancías
box•er ['bɑːksər] boxeador(a) *m(f)*
'box•er shorts *npl* calzoncillos *mpl*, boxers *mpl*
box•ing ['bɑːksɪŋ] boxeo *m*
'Box•ing Day *Br*: *el 26 de diciembre, día festivo*; **'box•ing glove** guante *m* de boxeo; **'box•ing match** combate *m* de boxeo; **'box•ing ring** cuadrilátero *m*, ring *m*
'box lunch *almuerzo comprado en una tienda para llevar al colegio o al trabajo*; **'box num•ber** *at post office* apartado *m* de correos; **'box of•fice** taquilla *f*, *L.Am.* boletería *f*; **box-of•fice 'hit** éxito *m* de taquilla *or L.Am.* boletería
boy [bɔɪ] **1** niño *m*, chico *m* **2** *(son)* hijo *m* **3**: ***(oh) ~!*** ¡madre mía!
boy•cott ['bɔɪkɑːt] **I** *n* boicot *m* **II** *v/t* boicotear
'boy•friend novio *m*
boy•ish ['bɔɪɪʃ] *adj* varonil
boy'scout boy scout *m*
bo•zo ['boʊzoʊ] F memo(-a) *m(f)* F
bra [brɑː] sujetador *m*, sostén *m*
brace [breɪs] *on teeth* aparato *m*
brace•let ['breɪslɪt] pulsera *f*
bra•cer•o [brə'səroʊ] *temporero mejicano en EE.UU.*
brac•ing ['breɪsɪŋ] *adj* vigorizador, revitalizador
brack•en ['brækən] BOT helechos *fpl*
brack•et ['brækɪt] **1** *for shelf* escuadra *f*, soporte *m* **2**: ***(square) ~*** *in text* corchete *m* **3**: ***enter the ~s*** entrar en el campo de juego
brack•ish ['brækɪʃ] *adj* un poco salado
brag [bræg] *v/i* (*pret & pp* ***-ged***) presumir, fanfarronear
braid [breɪd] **1** *in hair* trenza *f* **2** *trimming* trenzado *m*
braille [breɪl] braille *m*
brain [breɪn] cerebro *m*; ***use your ~*** utiliza la cabeza
'brain•child creación *f*, invento *m*; **'brain dam•age** MED lesiones *fpl* cerebrales; **'brain dead** *adj* MED clínicamente muerto; **'brain death** MED muerte *f* cerebral; **'brain drain** fuga *f* de cerebros
brain•less ['breɪnlɪs] *adj* F estúpido
brains [breɪnz] *npl (intelligence)* inteligencia *f*; ***the ~ of the operation*** el cerebro de la operación; ***pick s.o.'s ~*** pedir consejo a alguien, preguntar a alguien
'brain•storm idea *f* genial; **brain-storm•ing** ['breɪnstɔːrmɪŋ] tormenta *f* de ideas; **'brain•storm•ing ses•sion** sesión *f* de brainstorming; **'brain surgeon** neurocirujano(-a) *m(f)*; **'brain sur•ger•y** neurocirugía *f*; **brain•teas•er** ['breɪntiːzər] rompecabezas *m inv*; **'brain trust** panel *m* de expertos; **'brain tu•mor** tumor *m* cerebral; **'brain•wash** *v/t* lavar el cerebro a; ***they were ~ed into believing that ...*** se les lavó el cerebro y se les hizo creer que ...; **'brain-wash•ing** lavado *m* de cerebro; **'brain•wave** *Br (brilliant idea)* idea *f* genial
brain•y ['breɪnɪ] *adj* F: ***be ~*** tener mucho coco F, ser una lumbrera
braise [breɪz] *v/t* GASTR estofar
brake [breɪk] **I** *n* freno *m*; ***put the ~s on public spending*** poner el freno al gasto público **II** *v/i* frenar
'brake flu•id MOT líquido *m* de frenos; **'brake light** MOT luz *f* de frenado; **brake 'horse•pow•er** potencia *f* de frenado; **'brake lin•ing** revestimiento *m* del freno; **'brake pad** *f* pastilla del freno; **'brake ped•al** MOT pedal *m* del freno; **'brake shoe** zapata *f* (del freno)
brak•ing dis•tance ['breɪkɪŋ] distancia *f* de frenado
bram•ble ['bræmbl] *Br* BOT zarza *f*
bran [bræn] salvado *m*
branch [bræntʃ] **1** *of tree* rama *f* **2** *of bank, company* sucursal *f*
◆ **branch off** *v/i of road* bifurcarse
◆ **branch out** *v/i* diversificarse; ***they've branched out into furniture*** han empezado a trabajar también con muebles

'branch line RAIL ramal *m*; **'branch man•ag•er** director(a) *m(f)* de sucursal; **'branch of•fice** sucursal *f*; **'branch wa•ter 1** *from stream* agua *m* mineral **2** *from faucet* agua *m* del grifo

brand [brænd] **I** *n* marca *f*; ***~ of humor*** sentido *m* del humor **II** *v/t* **1** *cattle* marcar **2**: ***be ~ed a liar*** ser tildado de mentiroso

brand a'ware•ness conocimiento *m* de marca

brand 'im•age imagen *f* de marca

bran•dish ['brændɪʃ] *v/t* blandir

brand 'lead•er marca *f* líder (del mercado); **brand 'loy•al•ty** lealtad *f* a una marca, fidelidad *f* a la marca; **'brand name** marca *f*, nombre *m* comercial; **brand-'new** *adj* nuevo; **brand re-cog'ni•tion** reconocimiento *m* de la marca

bran•dy ['brændɪ] brandy *m*, coñac *m*

'bran•dy glass copa *f* de coñac

brash [bræʃ] *adj* arrogante

brass [bræs] **1** *alloy* latón *m* **2** MUS: ***the ~*** los metales

brass 'band banda *f* de música

brass 'hat F MIL mandamás *m/f* F; *director etc also* jefe(-a) *m(f)*

bras•sière [brə'zɪr] sujetador *m*, sostén *m*

brass 'tacks *npl*: ***get down to ~*** F ir al grano

bras•sy ['brɑːsɪ] *adj* **1** *sound* estridente **2** F *woman* ordinario

brat [bræt] *pej* niñato(-a) *m(f)*

bra•va•do [brə'vɑːdoʊ] bravuconería *f*

brave [breɪv] *adj* valiente, valeroso; ***put on a ~ face*** guardar la compostura

brave•ly ['breɪvlɪ] *adv* valientemente, valerosamente

brav•er•y ['breɪvərɪ] valentía *f*, valor *m*

bra•vo ['brɑːvoʊ] **I** *int* bravo **II** *n* bravo *m*

brawl [brɒːl] **I** *n* pelea *f* **II** *v/i* pelearse

brawn [brɒːn] *physical strength* fuerza *f* bruta

brawn•y ['brɒːnɪ] *adj* fuerte, musculoso

bray [breɪ] *v/i* **1** *of donkey* rebuznar **2** *of person* carcajearse

bra•zen ['breɪzn] *adj* descarado

◆ **brazen out** *v/t*: ***brazen it out*** echarle cara

bra•zen-faced ['breɪznfeɪst] descarado

bra•zier ['breɪzɪər] brasero *m*

Bra•zil [brə'zɪl] Brasil *m*

Bra•zil•i•an [brə'zɪlɪən] **I** *adj* brasileño **II** *n* brasileño(-a) *m(f)*

Bra•zil•i•an 'high•lands Macizo *m* de Brasil

Bra'zil nut coquito *m* del Brasil

breach [briːtʃ] **1** (*violation*) infracción *f*, incumplimiento *m* **2** *in party* ruptura *f*

breach of 'con•tract LAW incumplimiento *m* de contrato

breach of 'trust abuso *m* de confianza

bread [bred] pan *m*; ***a loaf of ~*** un pan: ***I know which side my ~ is buttered on*** F sé lo que me conviene

'bread bas•ket *fig* granero *m*; **'bread bin** *Br* ☞ ***bread box***; **'bread board** tabla *f* para cortar el pan; **'bread box** panera *f*; **'bread•crumbs** *npl for cooking* pan *m* rallado; *for birds* migas *fpl*; **'bread knife** cuchillo *m* del pan; **'bread•line**: ***be on the ~*** vivir en la pobreza; **'bread roll** panecillo *m*

breadth [bredθ] *of road* ancho *m*; *of knowledge* amplitud *f*

'bread•win•ner: ***be the ~*** ser el que gana el pan

break [breɪk] **I** *n* **1** *in bone etc* fractura *f*, rotura *f* **2** (*rest*) descanso *m*; (*vacation*) vacaciones *fpl*; ***take a ~*** descansar; *vacation* ir de vacaciones; ***without a ~*** *work*, *travel* sin descanso **3** *in relationship* separación *f* temporal **4**: ***give s.o. a ~*** F (*opportunity*) ofrecer una oportunidad a alguien; ***give me a ~!*** ¡hazme el favor!

II *v/t* (*pret* ***broke***, *pp* ***broken***) **1** *device* romper, estropear; *stick* romper, partir; *arm*, *leg* fracturar, romper; *glass*, *egg* romper **2** *rules*, *law* violar, incumplir; *promise* romper **3** *news* dar **4** *record* batir **5**: ***~ a journey*** interrumpir un viaje

III *v/i* (*pret* ***broke***, *pp* ***broken***) **1** *of device* romperse, estropearse; *of glass*, *egg* romperse; *of stick* partirse, romperse **2** *of news* saltar; *of storm* estallar, comenzar **3** *of boy's voice* cambiar **4**: ***~ with tradition*** romper con la tradición

◆ **break away** *v/i* **1** (*escape*) escaparse **2** *from family* separarse; *from organization* escindirse

◆ **break down I** *v/i* **1** *of vehicle* averiarse, estropearse; *of machine* estropearse **2** *of talks* romperse **3** *in tears* romper a llorar; *mentally* venirse abajo **II** *v/t* **1** *door* derribar **2** *figures* detallar, desglo-

B

sar
◆ **break even** *v/i* COM cubrir gastos
◆ **break in I** *v/i* **1** (*interrupt*) interrumpir **2** *of burglar* entrar **II** *v/t horse* domar, amansar; F *person* formar, entrenar
◆ **break into** *v/t* **1** *house etc* entrar en, *L.Am.* entrar a **2**: ***break into a cold sweat*** empezar a sentir un sudor frío
◆ **break off I** *v/t* **1** partir **2** *relationship, negotiations* romper; ***they've broken it off*** han roto **II** *v/i* (*stop talking*) interrumpirse
◆ **break out** *v/i* **1** (*start up*) comenzar **2** *of fighting* estallar; *of disease* desatarse; ***he broke out in a rash*** le salió un sarpullido **3** *of prisoners* escaparse, darse a la fuga
◆ **break up I** *v/t* **1** *into component parts* descomponer; *company* dividir **2** *fight* poner fin a **II** *v/i of ice* romperse; *of couple* terminar, separarse; *of band* separarse; *of meeting* terminar
break•a•ble ['breɪkəbl] *adj* rompible, frágil
break•age ['breɪkɪdʒ] rotura *f*
'break•a•way escisión *f* (***from*** de); **'break•a•way group** grupo *m* disidente; **'break-dance** *v/i* bailar breakdance; **'break danc•er** bailarín(-ina) *m*(*f*) de breakdance; **'break danc•ing** breakdance *m*
'break•down 1 *of vehicle, machine* avería *f* **2** *of talks* ruptura *f* **3** (*nervous* ~) crisis *f inv* nerviosa **4** *of figures* desglose *m*
break•er ['breɪkər] *wave* ola *f* grande
break-'e•ven point punto *m* de equilibrio
break•fast ['brekfəst] desayuno *m*; ***have*** ~ desayunar
'break•fast meet•ing reunión *f* durante el desayuno
'break•fast tel•e•vi•sion televisión *f* matinal
'break-in entrada *f* (*mediante la fuerza*); *robbery* robo *m*; ***we've had a*** ~ han entrado a robar
break•ing and en•ter•ing [breɪkɪŋænd'entərɪŋ] LAW allanamiento *m* de morada; **break•ing 'bulk** COM carga *f* fraccionada; **'break•ing point**: ***reach*** ~ perder los estribos
'break•neck *adj*: ***at*** ~ ***speed*** a toda velocidad; **'break•out** *from prison* evasión *f*, fuga *f*; **'break•through** *in plan, negotiations* paso *m* adelante; *of science, technology* avance *m* **'break-up** *of marriage, partnership* ruptura *f*, separación *f*; **'break•wat•er** rompeolas *m inv*
breast [brest] **1** *of woman* pecho *m* **2** *of chicken* pechuga *f*
'breast•bone ANAT esternón *m*; **'breast•feed** *v/t* (*pret & pp* **-fed**) amamantar; **'breast pock•et** bolsillo *m* interior (*a la altura del pecho*); **'breast-stroke** braza *f*
breath [breθ] respiración *f*, aliento *m*; ***get your*** ~ ***back first*** primero, recobra la respiración *or* el aliento; ***be out of*** ~ estar sin respiración; ***she took a deep*** ~ respiró hondo
breath•a•lyze ['breθəlaɪz] *v/t* MOT hacer la prueba de la alcoholemia a
Breath•a•lyz•er® ['breθəlaɪzər] MOT alcoholímetro *m*
breathe [bri:ð] **I** *v/i* respirar **II** *v/t* **1** (*inhale*) aspirar, respirar **2** (*exhale*) exhalar, espirar
◆ **breathe in** *v/t & v/i* aspirar, inspirar
◆ **breathe out** *v/t & v/i* espirar
breath•er ['bri:ðər] F respiro *m*; ***have*** *or* ***take a*** ~ tomarse un respiro
breath•ing ['bri:ðɪŋ] respiración *f*; ~ ***space*** respiro *m*
breath•less ['breθlɪs] *adj*: ***arrive*** ~ llegar sin respiración, llegar jadeando
breath•less•ness ['breθlɪsnɪs] dificultad *f* para respirar
breath•tak•ing ['breθteɪkɪŋ] *adj* impresionante, sorprendente
'breath test prueba *f* de la alcoholemia
bred [bred] *pret & pp* → ***breed***
breed [bri:d] **I** *n* raza *f* **II** *v/t* (*pret & pp* ***bred***) criar; *plants* cultivar; *fig* causar, generar **III** *v/i* (*pret & pp* ***bred***) *of animals* reproducirse
breed•er ['bri:dər] *of animals* criador(a) *m*(*f*); *of plants* cultivador(a) *m*(*f*)
breed•ing ['bri:dɪŋ] **1** *of animals* cría *f*; *of plants* cultivo *m* **2** *of person* educación *f*
'breed•ing ground *fig* caldo *m* de cultivo
breeze [bri:z] brisa *f*; ***shoot the*** ~ F charlar F; ***be a*** ~ F estar chupado *or* tirado F
◆ **breeze in** *v/i* F entrar despreocupa-

damente
'breeze block *bloque de cemento ligero*
breez•i•ly ['bri:zɪlɪ] *adv fig* jovialmente, tranquilamente
breez•y ['bri:zɪ] *adj* **1** ventoso **2** *fig* jovial, tranquilo
bre•vi•ar•y ['bri:vjərɪ] REL breviario *m*
brev•i•ty ['brevətɪ] brevedad *f*
brew [bru:] **I** *v/t* **1** *beer* elaborar **2** *tea* preparar, hacer **II** *v/i of storm* avecinarse; *of trouble* fraguarse
brew•er ['bru:ər] fabricante *m/f* de cerveza
brew•er•y ['bru:ərɪ] fábrica *f* de cerveza
bribe [braɪb] **I** *n* soborno *m*, *Mex* mordida *f*, *S.Am.* coima *f* **II** *v/t* sobornar; ***~ s.o. to do sth*** sobornar a alguien para que haga algo
brib•er•y ['braɪbərɪ] soborno *m*, *Mex* mordida *f*, *S.Am.* coima *f*
bric-a-brac ['brɪkəbræk] baratijas *fpl*
brick [brɪk] ladrillo *m*
'brick•bat revés *m*; **'brick•lay•er** albañil *m/f*; **brick 'wall**: ***but I came up against a ~*** F pero me encontré con un obstáculo infranqueable; ***it's like talking to a ~!*** F ¡es como hablarle a la pared! F; **'brick•work** enladrillado *m*
brid•al suite ['braɪdl] suite *f* nupcial
bride [braɪd] novia *f* (*en boda*)
'bride•groom novio *m* (*en boda*)
'brides•maid dama *f* de honor
bridge[1] [brɪdʒ] **I** *n* **1** *also* NAUT puente *m*; ***burn one's ~s*** *fig* quemar las naves; ***we'll cross that ~ when we come to it*** *fig* cuando llegue el momento abordaremos el problema **2** *of nose* caballete *m* **II** *v/t gap* superar, salvar
bridge[2] [brɪdʒ] *n card game* bridge *m*
'bridge•head MIL cabeza *f* de puente
'bridge loan COM crédito *m* de puente
bridg•ing loan ['brɪdʒɪŋ] *Br* ☞ ***bridge loan***
bri•dle [braɪdl] **I** *n* brida *f* **II** *v/i*: ***~ at sth*** indignarse ante algo
brief[1] [bri:f] *adj* breve, corto; ***in ~*** en breve
brief[2] [bri:f] **I** *n* (*instructions*) misión *f*; *of designer etc* pautas *fpl* **II** *v/t*: ***~ s.o. on sth*** informar a alguien de algo
'brief•case maletín *m*
brief•ing ['bri:fɪŋ] sesión *f* informativa; ***give s.o. a ~ on sth*** informar a alguien de algo
brief•ly ['bri:flɪ] *adv* **1** (*for a short period of time*) brevemente **2** (*in a few words*) en pocas palabras **3** (*to sum up*) en resumen
brief•ness ['bri:fnɪs] brevedad *f*
briefs [bri:fs] *npl for women* bragas *fpl*; *for men* calzoncillos *mpl*
bri•gade [brɪ'geɪd] MIL brigada *f*
brig•a•dier [brɪgə'dɪər] MIL general *m* de brigada
bri•gand ['brɪgənd] bandito *m*
bright [braɪt] *adj* **1** *color* vivo; *smile* radiante; *future* brillante, prometedor; (*sunny*) soleado, luminoso **2** (*intelligent*) inteligente
◆ **bright•en up** ['braɪtn] **I** *v/t* alegrar **II** *v/i of weather* aclararse; *of face, person* alegrarse, animarse
bright•ly ['braɪtlɪ] *adv shine* intensamente, fuerte; *smile* alegremente
bright•ness ['braɪtnɪs] **1** *of light* brillo *m*; *of weather* luminosidad *f*; *of smile* alegría *f* **2** (*intelligence*) inteligencia *f*
'bright•ness con•trol control *m* de la luminosidad
bril•liance ['brɪljəns] **1** *of person* genialidad *f* **2** *of color* resplandor *m*
bril•liant ['brɪljənt] *adj* **1** *sunshine etc* resplandeciente, radiante **2** (*very good*) genial **3** (*very intelligent*) brillante
brim•ful ['brɪmfəl] *adj* rebosante
brim [brɪm] **I** *of container* borde *m*; *of hat* ala *f* **II** *v/i* (*pret & pp* ***-med***): ***his eyes ~med with tears*** tenía los ojos llenos de lágrimas; ***be ~ming with confidence*** rebosar (de) confianza
brine [braɪn] GASTR salmuera *f*
bring [brɪŋ] *v/t* (*pret & pp* ***brought***) traer; ***~ it here, will you*** tráelo aquí, por favor; ***can I ~ a friend?*** ¿puedo traer a un amigo?, ¿puedo venir con un amigo?; ***~ onto the market*** introducir en el mercado; ***~ an action against s.o.*** interponer una demanda contra alguien
◆ **bring about** *v/t* ocasionar; ***bring about peace*** traer la paz
◆ **bring around** *v/t* **1** *from a faint* hacer volver en sí **2** (*persuade*) convencer, persuadir
◆ **bring back** *v/t* **1** (*return*) devolver; *memories* traer **2** (*re-introduce*) reinstaurar

◆ **bring down** *v/t* **1** *fence, tree* tirar, echar abajo; *government* derrocar; *bird, airplane* derribar **2** *rates, inflation, price* reducir

◆ **bring forward** *v/t* **1** *in bookkeeping* pasar a cuenta nueva **2** *Br*: *meeting etc* adelantar

◆ **bring in** *v/t interest, income* generar; *legislation* introducir; *verdict* pronunciar; ***let's bring Bob in on the discussion*** que participe Bob en la discusión

◆ **bring off** *v/t deal* conseguir, lograr

◆ **bring on** *v/t illness* provocar; ***you brought it on yourself*** tú te lo buscaste

◆ **bring out** *v/t* **1** *book, video, new product* sacar **2** (*emphasize, highlight*) realzar, hacer resaltar

◆ **bring to** *v/t from a faint* hacer volver en sí

◆ **bring up** *v/t* **1** *child* criar, educar; ***I was brought up to believe in …*** desde niño, me enseñaron a creer en … **2** *subject* mencionar, sacar a colación **3** (*vomit*) vomitar

brink [brɪŋk] borde *m*; ***be on the ~ of doing sth*** *fig* estar a punto de hacer algo

brin•y ['braɪnɪ] *adj* salobre

brisk [brɪsk] *adj person, voice* enérgico; *walk* rápido; *trade* animado

bris•tle ['brɪsl] *v/i*: ***the streets are bristling with policemen*** las calles están atestadas de policías

brist•les ['brɪslz] *npl on chin* pelos *mpl*; *of brush* cerdas *fpl*

bris•tly ['brɪslɪ] *adj* hirsuto

Brit [brɪt] F británico(-a) *m(f)*

Brit•ain ['brɪtn] Gran Bretaña *f*

Brit•ish ['brɪtɪʃ] **I** *adj* británico **II** *npl*: ***the ~*** los británicos

Brit•ish•er ['brɪtɪʃər] británico(-a) *m(f)*

Brit•ish 'Isles *npl*: ***the ~*** las Islas Británicas

Brit•on ['brɪtn] británico(-a) *m(f)*

brit•tle ['brɪtl] *adj* frágil, quebradizo

broach [broʊtʃ] *v/t subject* sacar a colación

broad [brɒ:d] **I** *adj* ancho; *smile* amplio; (*general*) general; ***in ~ daylight*** a plena luz del día **II** *n* F (*woman*) tía *f* F

'broad•cast I *n* emisión *f*; ***a live ~*** una retransmisión en directo **II** *v/t* (*pret & pp* ***-cast***) emitir, retransmitir

'broad•cast•er presentador(a) *m(f)*

'broad•cast•ing emisiones *fpl*; (*TV*) televisión *f*; (*radio*) radiodifusión *f*

'broad•casting rights *npl* derechos *mpl* de emisión

broad•en ['brɒ:dn] **I** *v/i* ensancharse, ampliarse **II** *v/t* ensanchar; ***~ one's horizons*** ampliar los horizontes

'broad•jump salto *m* de longitud

'broad jump•er saltador(a) *m(f)* de longitud

broad•ly ['brɒ:dlɪ] *adv* en general; ***~ speaking*** en términos generales

broad'mind•ed *adj* tolerante, abierto

broad•mind•ed•ness [brɒ:d'maɪndɪdnɪs] mentalidad *f* abierta

'broad•sheet (news•pa•per) periódico *m* de formato grande

'broad•side NAUT andanada *f*; *fig* diatriba *f*; ***fire a ~ at s.o.*** *also fig* acometer contra alguien

bro•cade [broʊ'keɪd] brocado *m*

broc•co•li ['brɑ:kəlɪ] brécol *m*, brócoli *m*

bro•chure ['broʊʃər] folleto *m*

brogue[1] [broʊg] *tipo de zapato de piel*

brogue[2] [broʊg] *accent* acento *m* irlandés / escocés

broil [brɔɪl] *v/t* asar a la parrilla

broil•er ['brɔɪlər] **1** *on stove* parrilla *f* **2** *chicken* pollo *m* (para asar)

broke [broʊk] **I** *adj* F: ***be ~*** *temporarily* estar sin blanca F; *long term* estar arruinado; ***go ~*** (*go bankrupt*) arruinarse **II** *pret* ☞ ***break***

bro•ken ['broʊkn] **I** *adj* roto; *home* deshecho; ***they talk in ~ English*** chapurrean el inglés **II** *pp* ☞ ***break***

bro•ken-heart•ed ['hɑ:rtɪd] *adj* desconsolado, destrozado

bro•ker ['broʊkər] **I** *n* corredor(a) *m(f)*, agente *m/f* **II** *v/t deal* negociar

bro•ker•age ['broʊkərədʒ] **1** agencia *f* de bolsa **2** *fee* corretaje *m*

bron•chi•al ['brɑ:ŋkjəl] *adj* ANAT, MED bronquial

bron•chi•tis [brɑ:ŋ'kaɪtɪs] bronquitis *f*

Bronx cheer [brɑ:ŋks'tʃɪr] F pedorreta *f* F

bronze [brɑ:nz] bronce *m*

'Bronze Age Edad *f* del Bronce; **'bronze med•al** medalla *f* de bronce; **'bronze med•al•(l)ist** medallista *m/f* de bronce

brooch [broʊtʃ] broche *m*

brood [bruːd] **I** *v/i of person* darle vueltas a las cosas; **~ *about sth*** darle vueltas a algo **II** *n* ZO nidada *f*; F *children* prole *f* F

brood•y ['bruːdɪ] *adj*: ***be feeling ~*** F estar con ganas de tener hijos

brook[1] [brʊk] *n* barroyo *m*

brook[2] [brʊk] *v/t*: ***he will ~ no opposition*** no aceptará ninguna oposición

broom [bruːm] escoba *f*

'broom•stick palo *m* de escoba

broth [brɑːθ] **1** *soup* sopa *f* **2** *stock* caldo *m*

broth•el ['brɑːθl] burdel *m*

broth•er ['brʌðər] hermano *m*

broth•er•hood ['brʌðərhʊd] hermandad *f*

'broth•er-in-law (*pl* ***brothers-in-law***) cuñado *m*

broth•er•ly ['brʌðərlɪ] *adj* fraternal

brought [brɒːt] *pret & pp* ☞ ***bring***

brow [braʊ] **1** (*forehead*) frente *f* **2** *of hill* cima *f*

'brow•beat *v/t* (*pret* ***-beat***, *pp* ***-beaten***) intimidar; **~ *s.o. into doing sth*** intimidar a alguien para que haga algo

brown [braʊn] **I** *n* marrón *m*, *L.Am.* color *m* café **II** *adj* marrón; *eyes*, *hair* castaño; (*tanned*) moreno **III** *v/t in cooking* dorar **IV** *v/i in cooking* dorarse

'brown•bag *v/t* (*pret & pp* ***-ged***) F: **~ *it*** *llevar la comida al trabajo*

Brown•ie ['braʊnɪ] escultista *f*

brown•ie ['braʊnɪ] *cake* pastel *m* de chocolate y nueces

'Brown•ie points *npl* tantos *mpl*; ***earn ~*** anotarse tantos

brown•ish ['braʊnɪʃ] *adj* parduzco

'brown-nose P **I** *v/t* lamer el culo a P **II** *n* lameculos *m/f* P; **brown 'pa•per** papel *m* de estraza; **brown pa•per 'bag** bolsa *f* de cartón; **brown 'sug•ar** azúcar *m or f* moreno(-a)

browse [braʊz] **I** *v/i in store* echar una ojeada; COMPUT navegar **~ *through a book*** hojear un libro **II** *v/t the Web* navegar por

brows•er ['braʊzər] COMPUT navegador *m*

bruise [bruːz] **I** *n* magulladura *f*, cardenal *f*; *on fruit* maca *f* **II** *v/t arm*, *fruit* magullar; (*emotionally*) herir **III** *v/i of person* hacerse cardenales; *of fruit* macarse

bruis•ing ['bruːzɪŋ] *adj fig* doloroso

brunch [brʌnʧ] *combinación de desayuno y almuerzo*

bru•nette [bruː'net] morena *f*

brunt [brʌnt]: ***this area bore the ~ of the flooding*** esta zona fue la más castigada por la inundación; ***we bore the ~ of the layoffs*** fuimos los más perjudicados por los despidos

brush [brʌʃ] **I** *n* **1** cepillo *m* **2** *conflict* roce *m* **II** *v/t* **1** cepillar **2** (*touch lightly*) rozar; (*move away*) quitar

◆ **brush against** *v/t* rozar

◆ **brush aside** *v/t* hacer caso omiso a, no hacer caso a

◆ **brush off** *v/t* sacudir; *criticism* no hacer caso a

◆ **brush up** *v/t* repasar

'brush-off: ***give s.o. the ~*** darle calabazas a alguien; ***I got the ~*** me dieron calabazas

'brush•work PAINT pincelada *f*

brusque [brʊsk] *adj* brusco

Brus•sels ['brʌslz] Bruselas *f*

Brus•sels 'sprouts *npl* coles *fpl* de Bruselas

bru•tal ['bruːtl] *adj* brutal

bru•tal•i•ty [bruː'tælətɪ] brutalidad *f*

bru•tal•ize ['bruːtəlaɪz] *v/t* **1** *dehumanize* embrutecer **2** *mistreat* tratar brutalmente

bru•tal•ly ['bruːtəlɪ] *adv* brutalmente; ***be ~ frank*** ser de una sinceridad aplastante

brute [bruːt] bestia *m/f*

brute 'force fuerza *f* bruta

B.S. [biː'es] F ☞ ***bullshit***

B.Sc. [biːes'siː] *abbr* (= ***Bachelor of Science***) licenciatura *f* en Ciencias

BSE [biːes'iː] *abbr* (= ***bovine spongiform encephalopathy***) encefalopatía *f* espongiforme bovina

'B-side MUS cara *f* B

bub•ble ['bʌbl] burbuja *f*

◆ **bubble over with** *v/t*: ***be bubbling over with enthusiasm*** estar desbordante de entusiasmo

'bub•ble bath baño *m* de espuma; **'bub•ble gum** chicle *m*; **'bub•ble wrap** plástico *m* para embalar (*con burbujas*)

bub•bly ['bʌblɪ] **I** *n* F (*champagne*) champán *m* **II** *adj personality* alegre

buck[1] [bʌk] *n* F (*dollar*) dólar *m*

buck[2] [bʌk] *v/i of horse* corcovear

B

buck[3] [bʌk] *n*: ***pass the ~*** escurrir el bulto
buck[4] [bʌk] *v/t* F (*defy*) desafiar
◆ **buck for** *v/t*: ***be bucking for promotion*** estar agenciándose un ascenso F
buck•et ['bʌkɪt] cubo *m*
buck•et•ful ['bʌkɪtful] cubo *m* lleno
'buck•et seat MOT asiento *m* envolvente
buck•le[1] ['bʌkl] **I** *n* hebilla *f* **II** *v/t belt* abrochar
buck•le[2] ['bʌkl] *v/i of metal* combarse
◆ **buckle down** *v/i* ponerse a trabajar
'buck•skin piel *f* de ciervo; **'buck teeth** *npl* dientes *mpl* salidos; **'buck•wheat** BOT alforfón *m*
bud[1] [bʌd] BOT capullo *m*, brote *m*; ***nip sth in the ~*** *fig* cortar algo de raíz
bud[2] [bʌd] F ☞ ***buddy***
Bud•dhism ['budɪzəm] budismo *m*
Bud•dhist ['budɪst] **I** *adj* budista **II** *n* budista *m/f*
bud•ding ['bʌdɪŋ] *adj artist*, *musician* en ciernes
bud•dy ['bʌdɪ] F amigo(-a) *m(f)*, *Span* colega *m/f* F; *form of address Span* colega *m/f* F, *L.Am.* compadre *m/f* F
budge [bʌdʒ] **I** *v/t* mover; (*make reconsider*) hacer cambiar de opinión **II** *v/i* moverse; (*change one's mind*) cambiar de opinión
bud•ger•i•gar ['bʌdʒərɪgɑːr] periquito *m*
budg•et ['bʌdʒɪt] **I** *n* presupuesto *m*; ***be on a ~*** tener un presupuesto limitado **II** *v/i* administrarse **III** *adj* **1** (*inexpensive*) económico **2** (*relating to budgets*) presupuestario
◆ **budget for** *v/t* contemplar en el presupuesto; *fig* contar con
budg•et•ar•y ['bʌdʒɪterɪ] *adj* presupuestario
'budg•et def•i•cit déficit *m* presupuestario
'budg•et ho•tel hotel *m* económico
budg•et•ing ['bʌdʒɪtɪŋ] elaboración *f* del presupuesto
'budg•et sur•plus excedente *m* presupuestario
bud•gie ['bʌdʒɪ] F periquito *m*
Bue•nos Ai•res [bwenɑːs'erez] Buenos Aires *m*
buff[1] [bʌf] *adj color* marrón claro
buff[2] [bʌf] *n* aficionado(-a) *m(f)*; ***a movie ~*** un cinéfilo
buf•fa•lo ['bʌfəlou] búfalo *m*
'buf•fa•lo grass hierba *f* de búfalo
buff•er ['bʌfər] RAIL tope *m*; COMPUT búfer *m*; *fig* barrera *f*
buf•fet[1] ['bufeɪ] *n meal* bufé *m*
buf•fet[2] ['bʌfɪt] *v/t of wind* sacudir
buf•foon [bə'fuːn] payaso(-a) *m(f)*
bug [bʌg] **I** *n insect* bicho *m*; *virus* virus *m inv*; (*spying device*) micrófono *m* oculto; COMPUT error *m* **II** *v/t* (*pret & pp* **-ged**) **1** *room* colocar un micrófono en **2** F (*annoy*) fastidiar F, jorobar F
◆ **bug off** *v/i* P largarse F, *Chi*, *Col* mandarse a cambiar F, *Rpl* mandarse mudar F
'bug•bear motivo *m* de preocupación
bug•ger ['bʌgər] *Br* P: ***poor ~*** pobre cabroncete *m* P; ***silly ~*** berzotas *m/f inv* F
◆ **bugger off** *v/i Br* P pirárselas; ***bugger off!*** ¡vete a cascarla!
◆ **bugger up** *v/t Br* P cagar
bug•ging ['bʌgɪŋ] escucha *f or* intervención *f* telefónica
bug•gy ['bʌgɪ] *for baby* cochecito *m or* silla *f* de bebé
'bug•house F frenopático *m*
bu•gle [bjuːgl] corneta *f*, clarín *m*
bu•gler ['bjuːglər] corneta *m/f*, clarín *m/f*
build [bɪld] **I** *n of person* constitución *f*, complexión *f* **II** *v/t* (*pret & pp* **built**) construir, edificar
◆ **build on** *v/t* tomar como base
◆ **build up I** *v/t strength* aumentar; *relationship* fortalecer; *collection* acumular **II** *v/i of dirt* acumularse; *of pressure*, *excitement* aumentar
'build•er ['bɪldər] albañil *m/f*; *company* constructora *f*
'build•ing ['bɪldɪŋ] **1** edificio *m* **2** *activity* construcción *f*
'build•ing blocks *npl for child* piezas *fpl* de construcción; **'build•ing site** obra *f*; **'build•ing so•ci•e•ty** *Br* caja *f* de ahorros; **'build•ing trade** industria *f* de la construcción
'build-up 1 (*accumulation*) acumulación *f* **2**: ***after all the ~*** *publicity* después de tantas expectativas
built [bɪlt] *pret & pp* ☞ ***build***
'built-in *adj cupboard* empotrado; *flash* incorporado, integrado
built-up 'ar•e•a zona *f* urbanizada

bulb [bʌlb] **1** BOT bulbo *m* **2** (*light* ~) bombilla *f*, *Mex*, *RPl* foco *m*
bul•bous ['bʌlbəs] *adj nose* en forma de bulbo
Bul•gar•i•a [bʌl'gerɪə] Bulgaria *f*
Bul•gar•i•an [bʌl'gerɪən] **I** *adj* búlgaro **II** *n* **1** *person* búlgaro(-a) *m*(*f*) **2** *language* búlgaro *m*
bulge [bʌldʒ] **I** *n* bulto *m*, abultamiento *m* **II** *v/i of eyes* salirse de las órbitas; *of wall* abombarse
bu•lim•i•a [bʊ'lɪmɪə] bulimia *f*
bu•lim•ic [bʊ'lɪmɪk] *adj* bulímico
bulk [bʌlk]: ***the ~ of*** el grueso *or* la mayor parte de; ***in ~*** *merchandise* a granel; *buy* al por mayor
bulk buy•ing ['bʌlkbaɪɪŋ] compra *f* al por mayor; **'bulk•head** NAUT mamparo *m*; **'bulk or•der** pedido *m* al por mayor
bulk•y ['bʌlkɪ] *adj* voluminoso
bull [bʊl] *animal* toro *m*
'bull•dog bulldog *m*
'bull•dog clip pinza *f* sujetapapeles
bull•doze ['bʊldoʊz] *v/t* **1** (*demolish*) demoler, derribar **2**: ***~ s.o. into doing sth*** *fig* obligar a alguien a hacer algo
bull•doz•er ['bʊldoʊzər] bulldozer *m*
bul•let ['bʊlɪt] bala *f*; ***bite the ~*** apechugar
bul•le•tin ['bʊlɪtɪn] boletín *m*
'bul•le•tin board *on wall* tablón *m* de anuncios; COMPUT tablón *m* de anuncios, BBS *f*
'bul•let-proof *adj* antibalas *inv*
'bull fight corrida *f* de toros; **'bull fight•er** torero(-a) *m*(*f*); **'bull fight•ing** tauromaquia *f*, los toros; **'bull•horn** megáfono *m*
bul•lion ['bʊljən]: ***gold ~*** oro *m* en lingotes
bull•ish ['bʊlɪʃ] *adj* COM al alza; ***be ~ about sth*** *fig* ser optimista con respecto a algo
'bull mar•ket FIN mercado *m* al alza
bull•ock ['bʊlək] buey *m*
'bull•pen 1 *in police station* calabozo *m* **2** *in baseball* bullpen *m*; **'bull ring** plaza *f* de toros; **'bull's-eye** diana *f*, blanco *m*; ***hit the ~*** dar en el blanco
'bull•shit I *n* V *Span* gilipollez *f* V, *L.Am.* pendejada *f* V **II** *v/i* (*pret & pp* ***-ted***) V decir *Span* gilipolleces V *or L.Am.* pendejadas V
'bull ter•ri•er bulterrier *m*
bul•ly ['bʊlɪ] **I** *n* matón(-ona) *m*(*f*); *child* abusón(-ona) *m*(*f*) **II** *v/t* (*pret & pp* ***-ied***) intimidar
bul•ly•ing ['bʊlɪɪŋ] intimidación *f*
bul•rush ['bʊlrʌʃ] BOT junco *m*
bul•wark ['bʊlwək] *fig* bastión *m*
bum [bʌm] F **I** *n* **1** (*tramp*) vagabundo(-a) *m*(*f*) **2** (*worthless person*) inútil *m*/*f* **II** *adj* (*useless*) inútil **III** *v/t* (*pret & pp* ***-med***) *cigarette etc* gorronear
◆ **bum around** *v/i* F **1** (*travel*) vagabundear (***in*** por) **2** (*be lazy*) haraganear, *Span* aguear, *L.Am.* flojear F
bum•ble•bee ['bʌmblbiː] abejorro *m*
bum•bling ['bʌmblɪŋ] *adj*: ***a ~ fool*** un bobo
bum•mer ['bʌmər] F rollo *m* F, lata *f* F
bump [bʌmp] **I** *n* (*swelling*) chichón *m*; *on road* bache *m*; ***get a ~ on the head*** darse un golpe en la cabeza **II** *v/t* golpear
◆ **bump into** *v/t* **1** *table* chocar con **2** (*meet*) encontrarse con
◆ **bump off** *v/t* F (*murder*) liquidar F
◆ **bump up** *v/t* F *prices* aumentar
bump•er ['bʌmpər] **I** *n Br* MOT parachoques *m inv*; ***the traffic was ~ to ~*** el tráfico estaba colapsado **II** *adj* (*extremely good*) excepcional, extraordinario
'bump•er car auto *m* de choque
'bump•er stick•er adhesivo *m* para el parachoques
bump•kin ['bʌmpkɪn]: ***country ~*** paleto(-a) *m*(*f*)
'bump-start *v/t* **1**: ***~ a car*** arrancar un coche empujándolo **2** *fig*: *economy* reanimar
bump•tious ['bʌmpʃəs] *adj* F presuntuoso
bump•y ['bʌmpɪ] *adj* con baches; *flight* movido
bun [bʌn] **1** *hairstyle* moño *m* **2** *for eating* bollo *m*
bunch [bʌntʃ] *of people* grupo *m*; *of keys* manojo *m*; *of flowers* ramo *m*; *of grapes* racimo *m*; ***thanks a ~*** *iron* un millón de gracias
bun•dle ['bʌndl] **I** *n of clothes* fardo *m*; *of wood* haz *m* **II** *v/t*: ***~ sth with sth*** COM vender algo con algo
◆ **bundle up** *v/t* **1** liar **2** (*dress warmly*) abrigar

B

bung [bʌŋ] tapón *m*
◆ **bung up** *v/t* F tapar; ***I'm a bit bunged up*** tengo la nariz tapada
bun•gee jump•ing ['bʌndʒɪdʒʌmpɪŋ] puenting *m*
bun•gle ['bʌŋgl] *v/t* echar a perder
bun•gler ['bʌŋglər] chapucero(-a) *m(f)*
bun•gling ['bʌŋglɪŋ] *adj* chapucero
bun•ion ['bʌnjən] juanete *m*
bunk[1] [bʌŋk] *bed* litera *f*
bunk[2] [bʌŋk] F ☞ ***bunkum***
'bunk beds *npl* literas *fpl*
bunk•er ['bʌŋkər] MIL, *in golf* búnker *m*
bun•kum ['bʌŋkəm] bobadas *fpl*
bun•ny ['bʌnɪ] conejito *m*
bun•sen burn•er ['bʌnsən] mechero *m* Bunsen
bunt [bʌnt] *in baseball* toque *m*
bun•ting ['bʌntɪŋ] banderines *mpl*
buoy [bɔɪ] NAUT boya *f*
buoy•an•cy ['bɔɪənsɪ] **1** PHYS flotabilidad *f* **2** *cheerfulness* optimismo *m*
buoy•ant ['bɔɪənt] *adj* animado, optimista; *economy* boyante
bur [bɜːr] BOT erizo *m*
bur•ble ['bɜːrbəl] *v/i* & *v/t* mascullar
bur•den ['bɜːrdn] **I** *n also fig* carga *f*; ***the ~ of proof*** LAW la obligación de probar **II** *v/t*: ***~ s.o. with sth*** *fig* cargar a alguien con algo
bur•den•some ['bɜːrdnsəm] *adj* pesado
bu•reau ['bjʊroʊ] **1** (*chest of drawers*) cómoda *f* **2** (*office*) departamento *m*, oficina *f*; ***a translation ~*** una agencia de traducción
bu•reauc•ra•cy [bjʊ'rɑːkrəsɪ] burocracia *f*
bu•reau•crat ['bjʊrəkræt] burócrata *m/f*
bu•reau•crat•ic [bjʊrə'krætɪk] *adj* burocrático
bu•reauc•ra•tize [bjʊ'rɑːkrətaɪz] *v/t* burocratizar
bu•reau de change [bjʊroʊdə'ʃɑːnʒ] oficina *f* de cambio
burg [bɜːrg] P pueblucho *m* F
bur•geon ['bʌrdʒən] *v/i* crecer
bur•geon•ing ['bʌrdʒənɪŋ] *adj* creciente
bur•ger ['bɜːrgər] hamburguesa *f*
bur•glar ['bɜːrglər] ladrón(-ona) *m(f)*
'bur•glar a•larm alarma *f* antirrobo
bur•glar•ize ['bɜːrgləraɪz] *v/t* robar
'bur•glar•proof *adj* a prueba de ladrones
bur•glar•y ['bɜːrglərɪ] robo *m*; ***we've had a ~*** nos han entrado en casa, nos han robado
bur•gle ['bɜːrgl] *v/t Br* robar
bur•i•al ['berɪəl] entierro *m*
bur•lesque [bɜːr'lesk] revista *f*
bur•ly ['bɜːrlɪ] *adj* corpulento, fornido
Bur•ma ['bɜːrmə] Birmania *f*
Bur•mese [bɜːr'miːz] **I** *adj* birmano **II** *n* **1**: ***the ~*** los birmanos **2** *language* birmano *m*
burn [bɜːrn] **I** *n* quemadura *f* **II** *v/t* (*pret* & *pp* ***burnt***) quemar; ***be ~t to death*** morir abrasado **III** *v/i* (*pret* & *pp* ***burnt***) *of wood, meat, in sun* quemarse
◆ **burn down I** *v/t* incendiar **II** *v/i* incendiarse
◆ **burn out** *v/t*: ***burn o.s. out*** quemarse; ***a burned-out car*** un coche carbonizado
◆ **burn up I** *v/t energy* gastar **II** *v/i of space shuttle* desintegrarse por el calor
burn•er ['bɜːrnər] *on cooker* placa *f*
burn•ing ['bɜːrnɪŋ] *adj* en llamas; ***~ sensation*** sensación *f* de quemazón; ***take a ~ interest in sth*** estar muy interesado en algo
bur•nish ['bɜːrnɪʃ] *v/t* bruñir
'burn•out F (*exhaustion*) agotamiento *m*
burnt [bɜːrnt] *pret* & *pp* ☞ ***burn***
burp [bɜːrp] **I** *n* eructo *m* **II** *v/i* eructar **III** *v/t baby* hacer eructar
burr BOT ☞ ***bur***
bur•row ['bɜːroʊ] **I** *n* madriguera *f* **II** *v/i* cavar **III** *v/t*: ***~ a hole in sth*** cavar un agujero en algo
burst [bɜːrst] **I** *n in water pipe* rotura *f*; *of gunfire* ráfaga *f*; ***in a ~ of energy*** en un arrebato de energía
II *adj tire* reventado
III *v/t* (*pret* & *pp* ***burst***) *balloon* reventar
IV *v/i* (*pret* & *pp* ***burst***) *of balloon, tire* reventar; ***~ into a room*** irrumpir en una habitación; ***~ into tears*** echarse a llorar; ***~ out laughing*** echarse a reír; ***be ~ing to do sth*** F morirse de ganas de hacer algo
bur•y ['berɪ] *v/t* (*pret* & *pp* ***-ied***) enterrar; ***be buried under*** (*covered by*) estar sepultado por; ***~ o.s. in one's work*** meterse de lleno en el trabajo

bus[1] [bʌs] **I** *n local* autobús *m*, *Mex* camión *m*, *Arg* colectivo *m*, *C.Am.* guagua *f*; *long distance* autobús *m*, *Span* autocar **II** *v/t* (*pret & pp* ***-sed***) llevar en autobús
bus[2] [bʌs] *n* COMPUT bus *m*
'bus•boy ayudante *m/f* de camarero
'bus driv•er conductor(a) *m(f)* de autobús
bush [bʊʃ] **1** *plant* arbusto *m* **2** *type of countryside* monte *m*
bushed [bʊʃt] *adj* F (*tired*) molido F
bush•el ['bʊʃl] *medida de áridos equivalente a 35,2 litros en Estados Unidos y a 36,3 litros en el Reino Unido*
bush•y ['bʊʃɪ] *adj beard* espeso
busi•ness ['bɪznɪs] **1** negocios *mpl*; *as subject of study* empresariales *fpl*; ***on ~*** de negocios; ***do ~*** hacer negocios; ***they've been in ~ for 10 years*** la empresa lleva funcionando 10 años; ***go out of ~*** cerrar el negocio; ***~ is ~*** los negocios son los negocios **2** (*company*) empresa *f* **3** (*sector*) sector *m* **4** (*affair, matter*) asunto *m*; ***that's none of your ~!*** ¡no es asunto tuyo!; ***mind your own ~!*** ¡no te metas en lo que no te importa!
'busi•ness ad•dress dirección *f* comercial; **'busi•ness card** tarjeta *f* de visita; **'busi•ness class** clase *f* ejecutiva; **'busi•ness hours** *npl* horario *m* de oficina; **'busi•ness let•ter** carta *f* comercial; **'busi•ness•like** *adj* eficiente; **'busi•ness lunch** almuerzo *m* de negocios; **'busi•ness•man** hombre *m* de negocios, ejecutivo *m*; **'busi•ness meet•ing** reunión *f* de negocios; **'busi•ness peo•ple** hombres *mpl* de negocios; **'busi•ness plan** plan *m* económico; **'busi•ness re•la•tions** *npl* relaciones *fpl* comerciales; **'busi•ness school** escuela *f* de negocios; **'busi•ness stud•ies** *nsg course* empresariales *mpl*; **'busi•ness suit** traje *m* de ejecutivo; **'busi•ness tra•vel** viajes *mpl* de negocios; **'busi•ness trav•el•er** viajero(-a) *m(f)* de negocios; **'busi•ness trip** viaje *m* de negocios; **'busi•ness•wom•an** mujer *f* de negocios, ejecutiva *f*
busk•er ['bʌskər] *Br* músico(-a) *m(f)* callejero(-a)
'bus lane carril *m* bus; **bus•man's hol•i•day** ['bʌsmənz] *vacaciones que se pasan haciendo la misma cosa que se hace profesionalmente*; **'bus serv•ice** servicio *m* de autobús; **'bus shel•ter** marquesina *f*; **'bus sta•tion** estación *f* de autobuses; **'bus stop** parada *f* de autobús
bust[1] [bʌst] *n of woman* busto *m*
bust[2] [bʌst] **I** *adj* F **1** (*broken*) escacharrado F **2** ***go ~*** quebrar **II** *v/t* F escacharrar F
'bus tick•et billete *m or L.Am.* boleto *m* de autobús
◆ **bus•tle around** ['bʌsl] *v/i* trajinar
bus•tling ['bʌslɪŋ] *adj town* animado
'bust-up F corte *m* F
bust•y ['bʌstɪ] *adj* pechugona
bus•y ['bɪzɪ] **I** *adj* **1** *also* TELEC ocupado; ***the line was ~*** estaba ocupado, *Span* comunicaba; ***she leads a very ~ life*** lleva una vida muy ajetreada; ***be ~ doing sth*** estar ocupado *or* atareado haciendo algo **2** *full of people* abarrotado; *restaurant etc*: *making money* ajetreado **II** *v/t* (*pret & pp* ***-ied***): ***~ o.s. with*** entretenerse con
'bus•y•bod•y metomentodo *m/f*, entrometido(-a) *m(f)*
'bus•y sig•nal señal *f* de ocupado *or Span* comunicando
but [bʌt] *unstressed* [bət] **I** *conj* pero; ***it's not me ~ my father you want*** no me quieres a mí sino a mi padre; ***~ then*** (***again***) pero
II *prep*: ***all ~ him*** todos excepto él; ***the last ~ one*** el penúltimo; ***the next ~ one*** el próximo no, el otro; ***the next page ~ one*** la página siguiente a la próxima; ***~ for you*** si no hubiera sido por ti; ***nothing ~ the best*** sólo lo mejor
bu•tane ['bjuːteɪn] CHEM butano *m*
butch [bʊtʃ] *adj* F marimacho F
butch•er ['bʊtʃər] **I** *n* **1** carnicero(-a) *m(f)* **2** *murderer* asesino(-a) *m(f)* **II** *v/t kill* asesinar
butch•er•y ['bʊtʃərɪ] *preparation of meat, killing* carnicería *f*
but•ler ['bʌtlər] mayordomo *m*
butt [bʌt] **I** *n* **1** *of cigarette* colilla *f* **2** *of joke* blanco *m* **3** F (*buttocks*) trasero *m* F **II** *v/t* dar un cabezazo a; *of goat, bull* embestir
◆ **butt in** *v/i* inmiscuirse, entrometerse
◆ **butt out** *v/i* F no meterse
but•ter ['bʌtər] **I** *n* mantequilla *f*, *L.Am.*

B

manteca *f* ‖ *v/t* untar de mantequilla
◆ **butter up** *v/t* F hacer la pelota a F
'but•ter•cup BOT botón *m* de oro; **'but•ter dish** mantequera *f*; **'but•ter•fin•gers** *nsg* F: ***be a ~*** ser una manazas; ***~!*** ¡manazas!, ¡torpe!
'but•ter•fly 1 *insect* mariposa *f*; ***have butterflies in one's stomach*** F sentir un hormigueo en el estómago **2**: ***~ stroke*** (estilo *m*) mariposa *f*
'but•ter•milk suero *m* de leche
but•tocks ['bʌtəks] *npl* nalgas *fpl*
but•ton ['bʌtn] **I** *n* **1** *on shirt, machine* botón *m* **2** (*badge*) chapa *f* ‖ *v/t* abotonar
◆ **button up** *v/t* abotonar
'but•ton-down col•lar cuello *m* abrochado; **but•toned-down** [bʌtnd'daʊn] *adj* F convencional; **'but•ton•hole I** *n in suit* ojal *m* ‖ *v/t* acorralar; **'but•ton mush•room** champiñón *m* (pequeño)
but•tress ['bʌtrɪs] **I** *n* ARCHI contrafuerte *m* ‖ *v/t* respaldar
bux•om ['bʌksəm] *adj* de amplios senos
buy [baɪ] **I** *n* compra *f*, adquisición *f* ‖ *v/t* (*pret & pp* **bought**) comprar; ***can I ~ you a drink?*** ¿quieres tomar algo?; ***$5 doesn't ~ much*** con 5 dólares no se puede hacer gran cosa; ***I don't ~ that*** F no me lo trago *or* creo
◆ **buy forward** *v/i* FIN comprar a plazo fijo
◆ **buy off** *v/t* (*bribe*) sobornar
◆ **buy out** *v/t* COM comprar la parte de
◆ **buy up** *v/t* acaparar
'buy•back recompra *f*
buy•er ['baɪr] comprador(a) *m(f)*
'buyer's mar•ket mercado *m* favorable al comprador
'buy•out *by employees* adquisición *f* de la sociedad por los trabajadores; *by management* adquisición *f* de la sociedad por la dirección
buzz [bʌz] **I** *n* **1** *noise* zumbido *m* **2** F: ***she gets a real ~ out of it*** (*thrill*) le vuelve loca F, le entusiasma ‖ *v/i* **1** *of insect* zumbar **2** *with buzzer* llamar por el interfono **III** *v/t with buzzer* llamar por el interfono a
◆ **buzz off** *v/i* F largarse F, *Span* pirarse F, *Rpl* picar F
buz•zard ['bʌzərd] ZO (*turkey ~*) gallinazo *m*, guajalote *m*; (*honey ~*) abejero *m*; (*condor*) cóndor
buzz•er ['bʌzər] timbre *m*
'buzz•word palabra *f* de moda
by [baɪ] **I** *prep* **1** *to show agent* por; ***a play ~ …*** una obra de …
2 (*near, next to*) al lado de, junto a; ***side ~ side*** uno junto al otro
3 (*no later than*) no más tarde de; ***~ this time tomorrow*** mañana a esta hora; ***~ this time next year*** el año que viene por estas fechas
4 *mode of transport* en; ***~ bus / train*** en autobús / tren
5 *past*: ***she rushed ~ me*** pasó rápidamente por mi lado; ***as we drove ~ the church*** cuando pasábamos por la iglesia; ***go ~, pass ~*** pasar
6: ***~ day / night*** de día / noche; ***~ the dozen*** por docenas; ***~ the hour / ton*** por hora / por tonelada; ***~ my watch*** en mi reloj; ***~ nature*** por naturaleza; ***~ o.s.*** *without company* solo; ***I did it ~ myself*** lo hice yo solito; ***~ a couple of minutes*** por un par de minutos; ***2 ~ 4*** *measurement* 2 por 4
‖ *adv*: ***~ and ~*** (*soon*) dentro de poco
bye(-bye) [baɪ] adiós
'by-e•lec•tion *Br*: *elección parcial para reemplazar a un parlamentario que ha dimitido o ha muerto*
Bye•lo•rus•sian [bɪeloʊ'rʌʃn] **I** *adj* bielorruso ‖ *n* bielorruso(-a) *m(f)*
by•gones ['baɪgɑːnz]: ***let ~ be ~*** lo pasado, pasado está; **'by•law** *Br* ordenanza *f* municipal; **'by-line** *of article* pie *m* de autor; **'by•pass I** *n* **1** *road* circunvalación *f* **2** MED bypass *m* ‖ *v/t* sortear; **'by-prod•uct** subproducto *m*; **'by•road** carretera *f* secundaria; **by•stand•er** ['baɪstændər] transeúnte *m/f*
byte [baɪt] byte *m*
'by•way ☞ ***byroad***
'by•word: ***be a ~ for*** ser sinónimo de

C

c & f *abbr* (= ***cost and freight***) C&F (= costo y flete)
C/A *abbr* (= ***checking account***) cc (= cuenta *f* corriente)
cab [kæb] **1** (*taxi*) taxi *m* **2** *of truck* cabina *f*
cab•a•ret ['kæbəreɪ] cabaret *m*
cab•bage ['kæbɪdʒ] col *f*, repollo *m*
cab•bie, cab•by ['kæbɪ] F taxista *m/f*
'cab driv•er taxista *m/f*
cab•in ['kæbɪn] **1** *of plane* cabina *f* **2** *of ship* camarote *m*
'cab•in at•tend•ant auxiliar *m/f* de vuelo; **'cab•in bag•gage** equipaje *m* de mano; **'cab•in crew** personal *m* de a bordo; **'cab•in cruis•er** NAUT yate *m* a motor
cab•i•net ['kæbɪnɪt] **1** armario *m*; ***drinks ~*** mueble *m* bar; ***medicine ~*** botiquín *m*; ***display ~*** vitrina *f* **2** POL gabinete *m*
'cab•i•net mak•er ebanista *m/f*
'cab•in staff *npl* personal *m* de a bordo
'cab•in stew•ard *n* auxiliar *m/f* de vuelo
ca•ble ['keɪbl] cable *m*; **~ (*TV*)** televisión *f* por cable
'ca•ble car teleférico *m*; **'ca•ble channel** canal *m* de la televisión por cable; **'ca•ble com•pa•ny** TV cableoperadora *f*; **'ca•ble net•work** red *f* de cable; **'ca•ble tel•e•vi•sion** televisión *f* por cable
ca•bood•le [kə'buːdl]: ***the whole*** (***kit and***) **~** F todo el tinglado F
'cab rank, 'cab stand parada *f* de taxis
cache [kæʃ] **I** *n* **1** alijo *m* **2** COMPUT caché *m* **II** *v/t* esconder
cack•le ['kækl] **I** *v/i* **1** *of chicken* cacarear **2** (*laugh*) carcajearse **II** *n* (*laughter*) carcajada *f*
cac•tus ['kæktəs] cactus *m inv*
CAD [kæd] *abbr* (= ***computer assisted design***) CAD *m*, DAO *m* (= diseño asistido por computadora *or Span* ordenador)
ca•dav•er [kə'dævər] cadáver *m*
ca•dav•er•ous [kə'dævərəs] *adj* cadavérico, demacrado
cad•die ['kædɪ] **I** *n in golf* caddie *m/f* **II** *v/i* hacer de caddie
cad•dy ['kædɪ] *cajita de metal decorativa para guardar té*
ca•dence ['keɪdəns] cadencia *f*
ca•det [kə'det] cadete *m*
cadge [kædʒ] *v/t* F: **~ *sth from s.o.*** gorronear algo a alguien
cad•mi•um ['kædmɪəm] CHEM cadmio *m*
cad•re ['kɑːdər] MIL, POL brigada *f*, unidad *f*
Cae•sar•e•an *Br* ☞ ***Cesarean***
caf•é ['kæfeɪ] café *m*, cafetería *f*
caf•e•te•ri•a [kæfɪ'tɪrɪə] cafetería *f*, cantina *f*
caf•feine ['kæfiːn] cafeína *f*
cage [keɪdʒ] jaula *f*
ca•gey ['keɪdʒɪ] *adj* cauteloso, reservado; ***he's ~ about how old he is*** es muy reservado con respecto a su edad
ca•goule [kə'guːl] chubasquero *m* con capucha
ca•hoots [kə'huːts] *npl* F: ***be in ~ with*** estar conchabado con
cairn [kern] montículo *m* de piedras
ca•jole [kə'dʒoʊl] *v/t* engatusar, persuadir; **~ *s.o. into doing sth*** engatusar a alguien para que haga algo
cake [keɪk] **I** *n big* tarta *f*; *small* pastel *m*; ***be a piece of ~*** F estar chupado F **II** *v/i* endurecerse; ***he wants to have his ~ and eat it*** aspira a tenerlo todo
CAL [kæl] *abbr* (= ***computer-aided learning***) enseñanza *f* asistida por computadora *or Span* ordenador
ca•lam•i•tous [kə'læmɪtəs] *adj* penoso, fatal
ca•lam•i•ty [kə'læmətɪ] calamidad *f*
cal•ci•fy ['kælsɪfaɪ] **I** *v/t* calcificar **II** *v/i* calcificarse
cal•ci•um ['kælsɪəm] calcio *m*
cal•cu•la•ble ['kælkjʊləbl] *adj* calculable
cal•cu•late ['kælkjʊleɪt] *v/t* calcular; ***it was ~d to impress*** se preconcebió para impresionar
cal•cu•lat•ed ['kælkjʊleɪtɪd] *adj crime* premeditado, deliberado; ***take a ~ risk***

correr un riesgo calculado
cal•cu•lat•ing ['kælkjʊleɪtɪŋ] *adj* calculador
cal•cu•la•tion [kælkjʊ'leɪʃn] cálculo *m*
cal•cu•la•tor ['kælkjʊleɪtər] calculadora *f*
cal•cu•lus ['kælkjʊləs] (*pl* ***calculi*** ['kælkjʊlaɪ], ***calculuses***) MATH cálculo *m*
cal•en•dar ['kælɪndər] calendario *m*
'cal•en•dar year año *m* natural
calf[1] [kæf] (*pl* ***calves*** [kævz]) (*young of cow*) ternero(-a) *m*(*f*), becerro(-a) *m*(*f*)
calf[2] [kæf] (*pl* ***calves*** [kævz]) *of leg* pantorrilla *f*
'calf•skin piel *f* de becerro
cal•i•ber ['kælɪbər] *of gun* calibre *m*; ***a man of his ~*** un hombre de su calibre
cal•i•brate ['kælɪbreɪt] *v/t* TECH calibrar
cal•i•bra•tion [kælɪ'breɪʃn] calibración *f*
cal•i•bre *Br* ☞ ***caliber***
Cal•i•for•ni•an [kælɪ'fɔːnɪən] **I** *adj* californiano **II** *n* californiano(-a) *m*(*f*)
call [kɒːl] **I** *n* **1** TELEC llamada *f*; ***there's a ~ for you*** tienes una llamada, te llaman; ***I'll give you a ~ tomorrow*** te llamaré mañana; ***make a ~*** hacer una llamada; ***be on ~*** estar de guardia
2 (*shout*) llamada *f*; ***a ~ for help*** una llamada de socorro
3 (*appeal*: *to country etc*) llamamiento *m*
4 (*demand, request*) petición *f* (***for*** de); ***the ~ for a ban*** la petición de una prohibición
5 (*need*): ***there's no ~ to be aggressive*** no hay necesidad *or* motivo de ser agresivo
II *v/t* **1** *also* TELEC llamar; ***he ~ed him a liar*** le llamó mentiroso; ***what have they ~ed the baby?*** ¿qué nombre le han puesto al bebé?; ***but we ~ him Tom*** pero le llamamos Tom; ***~ s.o. names*** insultar a alguien; ***I ~ed his name*** lo llamé; ***and you ~ yourself unbiased!*** ¡y tú te consideras imparcial!; ***what time of night do you ~ this!*** ¡(crees que) estas son horas de llegar! **2** *meeting* convocar
III *v/i* **1** *also* TELEC llamar; ***can I tell him who's ~ing?*** ¿quién le llama?; ***~ for help*** pedir ayuda a gritos **2** (*visit*) pasarse
◆ **call at** *v/t* (*stop at*) pasarse por; *of train* hacer parada en
◆ **call away** *v/t*: ***he was called away on business*** tuvo que marcharse por negocios
◆ **call back I** *v/t* (*phone again*) volver a llamar; (*return call*) devolver la llamada; (*summon*) hacer volver **II** *v/i on phone* volver a llamar; (*make another visit*) volver a pasar
◆ **call for** *v/t* **1** (*collect*) pasar a recoger **2** (*demand*) pedir, exigir; (*require*) requerir; ***this calls for a celebration*** esto hay que celebrarlo
◆ **call in I** *v/t* (*summon*) llamar; ***call in a loan*** pedir la devolución de un préstamo **II** *v/i* (*phone*) llamar; ***he called in sick*** llamó para decir que estaba enfermo
◆ **call off** *v/t* (*cancel*) cancelar; *strike* desconvocar; ***let's call the whole thing off!*** ¡mejor que nos olvidemos de todo!
◆ **call on** *v/t* **1** (*urge*) instar **2** (*visit*) visitar **3** (*turn to*) recurrir a; ***he called on me for help*** recurrió a mí para que la ayudara
◆ **call out** *v/t* **1** (*shout*) gritar **2** (*summon*) llamar
◆ **call up** *v/t* **1** *on phone* llamar **2** COMPUT abrir, visualizar
'call box *Br* cabina *f* telefónica; **'call cen•ter** centro *m* de atención telefónica; **'call charg•es** *npl* costo *m or Span* coste *m* de llamadas
call•er ['kɒːlər] **1** *on phone* persona *f* que llama **2** (*visitor*) visitante *m/f*
call for 'ten•ders COM convocatoria *f* a la licitación; **call 'for•ward•ing** TELEC desvío *m* de llamada; **'call girl** prostituta *f* (*que concierta sus citas por teléfono*); **'call hold•ing** TELEC llamada *f* en espera
call•ing ['kɔːlɪŋ] (*profession, vocation*) vocación *f*
'call•ing card tarjeta *f* de visita
cal•lis•then•ics [kælɪs'θenɪks] *nsg* calistenia *f*
cal•lous ['kæləs] *adj* cruel, desalmado
cal•lous•ly ['kæləslɪ] *adv* cruelmente
cal•lous•ness ['kæləsnɪs] crueldad *f*
call 'trans•fer TELEC transferencia *f* de llamada
'call-up MIL llamada *f* a filas
cal•lus ['kæləs] callo *m*

calm [kɑːm] **I** *adj sea* tranquilo; *weather* apacible; *person* tranquilo, sosegado; ***please keep ~*** por favor mantengan la calma **II** *n* calma *f*; ***the ~ before the storm*** *also fig* la calma antes de la tormenta
◆ **calm down I** *v/t* calmar, tranquilizar **II** *v/i of sea, weather* calmarse; *of person* calmarse, tranquilizarse
calm•ly ['kɑːmlɪ] *adv* con calma, tranquilamente; ***you can't just ~ ignore it*** no puedes ignorarlo así como así
cal•o•rie ['kælərɪ] caloría *f*
cal•um•ny ['kæləmnɪ] calumnia *f*
calve [kæv] *v/i of cow* parir
calves [kævz] *pl* ☞ **calf**[1 & 2]
CAM [kæm] *abbr* (= ***computer-aided manufacture***) FAO *f* (= fabricación *f* asistida por ordenador)
cam [kæm] F cámara
cam•ber ['kæmbər] bache *f*
Cam•bo•di•a [kæm'boudɪə] Camboya *f*
Cam•bo•di•an [kæm'boudɪən] **I** *adj* camboyano **II** *n* **1** *person* camboyano(-a) *m(f)* **2** *language* camboyano *m*
cam•cor•der ['kæmkɔːrdər] videocámara *f*
came [keɪm] *pret* ☞ **come**
cam•el ['kæml] ZO camello *m*
'cam•el-hair *adj* de pelo de camello
cam•e•o ['kæmɪou] *in film* cameo *m*, *breve colaboración f de un artista famoso*; ***she had a ~ part in ...*** hizo un cameo en ...
cam•e•ra ['kæmərə] cámara *f*; ***on ~*** delante de las cámaras
'cam•e•ra crew equipo *m* de filmación; **'cam•e•ra•man** cámara *m*, camarógrafo *m*; **'cam•er•a-shy** *adj* tímido ante las cámaras
cam•i•sole ['kæmɪseʊl] camisola *f*
cam•o•mile ['kæməmaɪl] BOT camomila *f*, manzanilla *f*; ***~ tea*** infusión *f* de manzanilla
cam•ou•flage ['kæməflɑːʒ] **I** *n* camuflaje *m* **II** *v/t* camuflar
camp [kæmp] **I** *n* campamento *m*; *for refugees* campo *m*; ***make ~*** acampar **II** *v/i* acampar
◆ **camp out** *v/i* acampar al aire libre
cam•paign [kæm'peɪn] **I** *n* campaña *f* **II** *v/i* hacer campaña (***for*** a favor de)
cam•paign•er [kæm'peɪnər] defensor(a) *m(f)* (***for*** de); ***a ~ against racism*** una persona que hace campaña contra el racismo
'camp cot, *Br* **'camp bed** cama *f* plegable
camp•er ['kæmpər] **1** *person* campista *m/f* **2** *vehicle* autocaravana *f*
'camp•fire fuego *m*, fogata *f*
cam•phor ['kæmfər] CHEM alcanfor *m*
camp•ing ['kæmpɪŋ] acampada *f*; *on campsite* camping *m*; ***go ~*** ir de acampada *or* camping
'camp•site camping *m*
cam•pus ['kæmpəs] campus *m*
cam•shaft ['kæmʃæft] TECH árbol *m* de levas
can[1] [kæn] *unstressed* [kən] *v/aux* (*pret* ***could***) **1** (*ability*) poder; ***~ you swim?*** ¿sabes nadar?; ***~ you hear me?*** ¿me oyes?; ***I can't see*** no veo; ***~ you speak French?*** ¿hablas francés?; ***~ he call me back?*** ¿me podría devolver la llamada?; ***as fast / well as you ~*** tan rápido / bien como puedas; ***~ I help you?*** ¿te puedo ayudar?
2 (*permission*) poder; ***~ I have a beer / coffee?*** ¿me pones una cerveza / un café?; ***that can't be right*** debe haber un error
can[2] [kæn] **I** *n for drinks etc* lata *f* **II** *v/t* (*pret & pp* ***-ned***) enlatar
Can•a•da ['kænədə] Canadá *m*
Ca•na•di•an [kə'neɪdɪən] **I** *adj* canadiense **II** *n* canadiense *m/f*
ca•nal [kə'næl] *waterway* canal *m*
ca•nal•ize ['kænəlaɪz] *v/t fig* dirigir, concentrar
can•a•pé [kænə'peɪ] GASTR canapé *m*, aperitivo *m*
ca•nar•y [kə'nerɪ] canario *m*
Ca'nar•y Is•lands, Ca•nar•ies [kə'nerɪz] *npl*: ***the ~*** las Islas Canarias
can•cel ['kænsl] *v/t* (*prep & pp* ***-ed***, *Br* ***-led***) cancelar; ***no, ~ that*** no, olvídalo
◆ **cancel out** *v/t* neutralizar; ***they cancel each other out*** se neutralizan
can•cel•la•tion [kænsə'leɪʃn] cancelación *f*
can•cel'la•tion clause cláusula *f* de rescisión
can•cel'la•tion fee tarifa *f* de cancelación de reserva
Can•cer ['kænsər] ASTR Cáncer *m/f inv*, *L.Am.* canceriano(-a) *m(f)*; ***be (a) ~*** ser Cáncer, *L.Am.* ser canceriano

C

can•cer ['kænsər] cáncer *m*; **~ cells** células *fpl* cancerosas; **~ research** investigación *f* cancerológica
can•cer•ous ['kænsərəs] *adj* canceroso
can•de•la•bra [kændə'lɑ:brə] candelabro *m*
can•did ['kændɪd] *adj* sincero, franco
can•di•da•cy ['kændɪdəsɪ] candidatura *f*
can•di•date ['kændɪdət] *for position* candidato(-a) *m*(*f*); *in exam* candidato(-a) *m*(*f*), examinando(-a) *m*(*f*)
can•di•da•ture ['kændɪdətʃər] *Br* candidatura *f*
can•did•ly ['kændɪdlɪ] *adv* sinceramente, francamente
can•died ['kændi:d] *adj* confitado
can•dle ['kændl] vela *f*; ***burn the ~ at both ends*** trabajar de sol a sol; ***not be able to hold a ~ to s.o. / sth*** no admitir comparación con algo / alguien; ***the game is not worth the ~*** no merece la pena
'can•dle•light: ***by ~*** a la luz de las velas
'can•dle•lit *adj*: **~ *dinner*** cena *f* a la luz de las velas
Can•dle•mas ['kændlməs] REL fiesta *f* de la Candelaria
'can•dle•stick candelero *m*; *short* palmatoria *f*
can•dor, *Br* **can•dour** ['kændər] sinceridad *f*, franqueza *f*
can•dy ['kændɪ] (*sweet*) caramelo *m*; (*sweets*) dulces *mpl*; ***a box of ~*** una caja de caramelos *or* dulces
'can•dy•floss *Br* algodón *m* dulce
cane [keɪn] **I** *n* **1** caña *f* **2** *for walking* bastón *m* **II** *v/t* varear
'cane sug•ar azúcar *m* de caña
ca•nine ['keɪnaɪn] **I** *adj* canino **II** *n* **~** (***tooth***) diente *m* canino
can•is•ter ['kænɪstər] bote *m*
can•ker ['kæŋkər] **1** MED llaga *f* bucal **2** BOT cancro *m* **3** *fig* epidemia *f*
can•na•bis ['kænəbɪs] cannabis *m*, hachís *m*
canned [kænd] *adj* **1** *fruit, tomatoes* enlatado, en lata **2** (*recorded*) pregrabado; **~ *music*** F música *f* enlatada F **3** P (*drunk*) mamado P
can•ner•y ['kænərɪ] fábrica *f* de conservas
can•ni•bal ['kænɪbl] caníbal *m/f*
can•ni•bal•ism ['kænɪbəlɪzəm] canibalismo *m*
can•ni•bal•ize ['kænɪbəlaɪz] *v/t* canibalizar
can•non ['kænən] (*pl* **-non**(**s**)) MIL cañón *m*
'can•non•ball bala *f* de cañón
'can•non fod•der carne *f* de cañón
can•not ['kænɑ:t] ☞ ***can***[1]
can•ny ['kænɪ] *adj* (*astute*) astuto
ca•noe [kə'nu:] canoa *f*, piragua *f*; ***paddle one's own ~*** *fig* ser autosuficiente
ca•noe•ing [kə'nu:ɪŋ] piragüismo *m*
can•on ['kænən] REL **1** *priest* canónigo *m* **2** *rule* canon *m*
can•on•ize ['kænənaɪz] *v/t* canonizar
can•on 'law derecho *m* canónico
ca•noo•dle [kə'nu:dl] *v/i* F hacer manitas F
'can o•pen•er abrelatas *m inv*
can•o•py ['kænəpɪ] *over bed* dosel *m*; *in front of shop* toldo *m*
can't [kænt] ☞ ***can***
cant [kænt] *hypocrisy* hipocresía *f*
can•tan•ker•ous [kæn'tæŋkərəs] *adj* arisco, cascarrabias
can•teen [kæn'ti:n] *in factory* cantina *f*, cafetería *f*
can•ter ['kæntər] **I** *n* medio galope *m* **II** *v/i* ir *or* cabalgar a medio galope
can•ti•le•ver bridge ['kæntɪli:vər] puente *m* cantilever *or* voladizo
can•vas ['kænvəs] *for painting* lienzo *m*; *material* lona *f*
can•vass ['kænvəs] **I** *v/t* (*seek opinion of*) preguntar **II** *v/i* POL hacer campaña (***for*** en favor de)
can•vass•er ['kænvəsər] POL *persona que va de puerta en puerta haciendo campaña en favor de un partido político*
can•yon ['kænjən] cañón *m*
cap[1] [kæp] **I** *n* **1** *hat* gorro *m*; *with peak* gorra *f*; ***go ~ in hand to s.o.*** acudir a alguien con las orejas gachas **2** *of bottle, jar* tapón *m*; *of pen, lens* tapa *f* **3** *for tooth* funda *f* **II** *v/t* **1**: ***that ~s everything!*** ¡eso es el colmo!; ***to ~ it all*** para remate *or* colmo **2**: **~ *a tooth*** poner una funda a un diente
cap[2] [kæp] *n capital letter* mayúscula *f*
ca•pa•bil•i•ty [keɪpə'bɪlətɪ] capacidad *f*; ***it's beyond my capabilities*** no entra dentro de mis posibilidades
ca•pa•ble ['keɪpəbl] *adj* (*efficient*) capaz, competente; ***be ~ of*** ser capaz de

ca•pa•cious [kə'peɪʃəs] *adj* amplio, espacioso
ca•pac•i•tor [kə'pæsətər] ELEC condensador *m* eléctrico
ca•pac•i•ty [kə'pæsətɪ] **1** capacidad *f*; ***a ~ crowd*** un lleno absoluto; ***in my ~ as …*** en mi calidad de …; ***filled to ~*** hasta arriba, hasta los topes; ***that is beyond his ~*** eso va más allá de sus posibilidades **2** *of car engine* cilindrada *f*
cape[1] [keɪp] *clothing* capa *f*
cape[2] [keɪp] GEOG cabo *m*
ca•per[1] ['keɪpər] *n* GASTR alcaparra *f*
ca•per[2] ['keɪpər] **I** *n* F fechoría *f* **II** *v/i* retozar, brincar
cap•il•lar•y [kə'pɪlərɪ] ANAT capilar *m*
cap•i•tal ['kæpɪtl] *n* **1** *of country* capital *f* **2** (*~ letter*) mayúscula *f*; ***~ B*** B mayúscula **3** *money* capital *m*; ***make ~ (out) of*** aprovecharse de **4**: ***~ crime*** crimen con pena de muerte
cap•i•tal 'as•sets *npl* COM activo *m* fijo; **cap•i•tal 'cit•y** (ciudad *f*) capital *f*; **cap•i•tal con•tri'bu•tion** FIN aporte *m* de capital; **cap•i•tal ex'pend•i•ture** inversión *f* en activo fijo; **cap•i•tal 'gain** plusvalía *f*; **cap•i•tal 'gains tax** impuesto *m* sobre las plusvalías; **cap•i•tal 'goods** *npl* bienes *mpl* de capital; **cap•i•tal 'growth** crecimiento *m* del capital; **'cap•i•tal-in•ten•sive** *adj* con alta proporción de capital, con empleo intensivo de capital; **cap•i•tal in'vest•ment** inversión *f* de capital
cap•i•tal•ism ['kæpɪtəlɪzm] capitalismo *m*
'cap•i•tal•ist ['kæpɪtəlɪst] **I** *adj* capitalista **II** *n* capitalista *m/f*
cap•i•tal•ize ['kæpɪtəlaɪz] *v/t* **1** COM capitalizar **2** *word* escribir con (letras) mayúsculas
◆ **capitalize on** *v/t* aprovecharse de
cap•i•tal 'let•ter letra *f* mayúscula
cap•i•tal 'pun•ish•ment pena *f* capital, pena *f* de muerte
Cap•i•tol ['kæpɪtl] POL Capitolio *m*
ca•pit•u•late [kə'pɪtʊleɪt] *v/i* capitular
ca•pit•u•la•tion [kæpɪtʊ'leɪʃn] capitulación *f*
ca•pri•cious [kə'prɪʃəs] *adj* caprichoso, impredecible
Cap•ri•corn ['kæprɪkɔːrn] ASTR Capricornio *m/f inv*, *L.Am.* capricorniano(-a) *m(f)*; ***be (a) ~*** ser Capricornio, *L.Am.* ser capricorniano
cap•size [kæp'saɪz] **I** *v/i* volcar **II** *v/t* hacer volcar
cap•sule ['kæpsʊl] **1** *of medicine* cápsula *f* **2** (*space ~*) cápsula *f* espacial
cap•tain ['kæptɪn] **I** *n of ship*, *team*, MIL capitán(-ana) *m(f)*; *of aircraft* comandante *m/f*; ***~ of industry*** líder *m* industrial **II** *v/t ship* capitanear; *team* liderar, capitanear
cap•tion ['kæpʃn] *n* pie *m* de foto
cap•ti•vate ['kæptɪveɪt] *v/t* cautivar, fascinar
cap•tive ['kæptɪv] **I** *adj* prisionero; ***hold s.o. ~*** retener a alguien en cautiverio; ***take s.o. ~*** hacer cautivo *or* prisionero a alguien **II** *n* prisionero(-a) *m(f)*
cap•tive 'au•di•ence audiencia *f* cautiva
cap•tive 'mar•ket mercado *m* cautivo
cap•tiv•i•ty [kæp'tɪvətɪ] cautividad *f*
cap•ture ['kæptʃər] **I** *n of city* toma *f*; *of criminal*, *animal* captura *f* **II** *v/t* **1** *person*, *animal* capturar; *city*, *building* tomar; *market share* ganar **2** (*portray*) captar
car [kɑːr] **1** coche *m*, *L.Am.* carro *m*, *Rpl* auto *m*; ***by ~*** en coche **2** *of train* vagón *m*
ca•rafe [kə'ræf] garrafa *f*, jarra *f*
car•a•mel ['kærəmel] **1** *melted sugar* caramelo *m* **2** (*candy*) *caramelo a base de mantequilla, azúcar y leche*
car•at ['kærət] quilate *m*; ***18-~ gold*** oro de 18 quilates
car•a•van ['kærəvæn] **I** caravana *f* **II** *Br* MOT caravana *f*; ***~ site*** *or* ***park*** camping *m* para caravanas
car•a•way ['kærəweɪ] BOT alcaravea *f*; ***~ seeds*** carvis *mpl*
car•bine ['kɑːrbaɪn] carabina *f*
car•bo•hy•drate [kɑːrboʊ'haɪdreɪt] carbohidrato *m*
'car bomb coche *m* bomba
car•bon ['kɑːrbən] CHEM carbono *m*
car•bon•ate ['kɑːrbənɪt] CHEM carbonato *m*
car•bon•at•ed ['kɑːrbəneɪtɪd] *adj drink* con gas
car•bon 'co•py copia *f* con papel carbón
car•bon di'ox•ide dióxido *m* de carbono
car•bon•ize ['kɑːrbənaɪz] *v/t* carbonizar

car•bon mon'ox•ide monóxido *m* de carbono
'car•bon pa•per papel *m* carbón
car•bu•ret•er, car•bu•ret•or [kɑːrbʊ'retər] carburador *m*
car•cass ['kɑːrkəs] cadáver *m*
'car chase persecución *f* en coche
car•cin•o•gen [kɑːr'sɪnədʒen] agente *m* cancerígeno *or* carcinogéno
car•cin•o•genic [kɑːrsɪnə'dʒenɪk] *adj* cancerígeno, carcinogéno
car•ci•no•ma [kɑːrsɪ'noʊmə] carcinoma *m*
card [kɑːrd] **1** *to mark occasion*, COMPUT, *business* tarjeta *f* **2** (*post~*) (tarjeta *f*) postal *f* **3** (*playing ~*) carta *f*, naipe *m*; ***game of ~s*** partida *f* de cartas; ***have another ~ up one's sleeve*** *fig* tener un as escondido en la manga
'card•board cartón *m*; **card•board 'box** caja *f* de cartón; **'card game** juego *m* de cartas; **'card•hold•er** titular *m/f* de una tarjeta de crédito
car•di•ac ['kɑːrdɪæk] *adj* cardíaco
car•di•ac ar'rest paro *m* cardíaco
car•di•gan ['kɑːrdɪgən] cárdigan *m*
car•di•nal ['kɑːrdɪnl] *n* REL cardenal *m*; ***~ number*** número *m* cardinal; ***~ points*** puntos *mpl* cardinales
'card in•dex fichero *m*; **'card key** llave *f* tarjeta; **'card phone** teléfono *m* de tarjeta; **'card•sharp** estafador(a) *m(f)* profesional; **'card trick** truco *m* de cartas
care [ker] **I** *n* **1** cuidado *m*; (*medical ~*) asistencia *f* médica; ***~ of*** *on letter* en el domicilio de; ***take ~*** (*be cautious*) tener cuidado; ***take ~*** (***of yourself***)***!*** (*goodbye*) ¡cuídate!; ***take ~ of*** *dog, tool, house, garden* cuidar; *baby* cuidar (de); (*deal with*) ocuparse de; ***I'll take ~ of the bill*** yo pago la cuenta; (***handle***) ***with ~!*** *on label* frágil **2** (*worry*) preocupación *f*; ***be free from ~***(***s***) no tener preocupaciones
II *v/i* preocuparse; ***I don't ~!*** ¡me da igual!; ***I couldn't*** *or* ***could ~ less***, *Br* ***I couldn't ~ less*** ¡me importa un pimiento!; ***if you really ~d ...*** si de verdad te importara ...; ***a fat lot you ~!*** ¡no te importa lo más mínimo!, ¡te importa un pito! F
◆ **care about** *v/t* preocuparse por
◆ **care for** *v/t* **1** (*look after*) cuidar; ***he doesn't care for me the way he used to*** ya no le gusto como antes **2** (*like*): ***would you care for a drink?*** ¿le apetece tomar algo?; ***I don't care for that kind of language*** desapruebo esa clase de lenguaje
ca•reer[1] [kə'rɪr] *n* carrera *f*; ***~ prospects*** perspectivas *fpl* profesionales; ***make a ~ for o.s.*** labrarse una carrera; ***~ diplomat*** diplomatico(-a) *m(f)*; ***~ woman*** mujer *f* de carrera
ca•reer[2] [kə'rɪr] *v/i*: ***it went ~ing down the slope*** bajó por la pendiente a toda velocidad
ca'reers of•fi•cer asesor(a) *m(f)* de orientación profesional
'care•free *adj* despreocupado
care•ful ['kerfəl] *adj* (*cautious, thorough*) cuidadoso; ***be ~*** tener cuidado; (***be***) ***~!*** ¡(ten) cuidado!
care•ful•ly ['kerfəlɪ] *adv* (*with caution*) con cuidado; *worded etc* cuidadosamente
care•ful•ness ['kerfəlnɪs] cuidado *m*
care•less ['kerlɪs] *adj* descuidado; ***you are so ~!*** ¡qué descuidado eres!; ***~ driving*** conducción *f* temeraria; ***a ~ mistake*** un error por descuido
care•less•ly ['kerlɪslɪ] *adv* por descuido
care•less•ness ['kerlɪsnɪs] descuido *m*, negligencia *f*
car•er ['kerər] *persona que cuida de un familiar o enfermo*
ca•ress [kə'res] **I** *n* caricia *f* **II** *v/t* acariciar
'care•tak•er conserje *m*; ***~ government*** gobierno *m* provisional *or* temporal
'care•worn *adj* agobiado
'car fer•ry ferry *m*, transbordador *m*
car•go ['kɑːrgoʊ] (*pl* ***-o***(***e***)***s***) cargamento *m*
'car•go plane avión *m* de carga
'car•go ship carguero *m*
'car hire alquiler *m* de coches *or* automóviles
'car•hop *camarero(-a) que sirve a los clientes desde sus coches en un restaurante drive-in*
Car•ib•be•an [kə'rɪbɪən] **I** *adj* caribeño **II** *n*: ***the ~*** el Caribe
car•i•ca•ture ['kærɪkətʃər] **I** *n* caricatura *f* **II** *v/t* caricaturizar
car•i•ca•tur•ist ['kærɪkətʃʊrɪst] caricaturista *m/f*

car•ies ['keri:z] MED caries *f*
car•ing ['kerɪŋ] *adj person* afectuoso, bondadoso; *society* solidario
'car in•sur•ance seguro *m* del coche *or* automóvil
'car me•chan•ic mecánico(-a) *m(f)* de coches *or* automóviles
car•mine ['kɑ:rmaɪn] carmín *m*
car•nage ['kɑ:rnɪdʒ] matanza *f*, carnicería *f*
car•nal ['kɑ:rnl] *adj* carnal; ***have ~ knowledge of s.o.*** *fml*, *lit* tener relaciones sexuales con alguien
car•na•tion [kɑ:r'neɪʃn] clavel *m*
car•ni•val ['kɑ:rnɪvl] feria *f*
car•ni•vore ['kɑ:rnɪvɔr] ZO carnívoro (-a) *m(f)*
car•niv•o•rous [kɑ:r'nɪvərəs] *adj* carnívoro
car•ol ['kærəl] *n* villancico *m*
car•ou•sel [kærə'sel] **1** *at airport* cinta *f* transportadora de equipajes **2** *for slide projector* carro *m* **3** (*merry-go-round*) tiovivo *m*
'car own•er propietario(-a) *m(f)* de coche *or* automóvil
carp[1] [kɑ:rp] *n fish* carpa *f*
carp[2] [kɑ:rp] *v/i* refunfuñar, gruñir
'car park *Br* estacionamiento *m*, *Span* aparcamiento *m*
car•pen•ter ['kɑ:rpɪntər] carpintero(-a) *m(f)*; ***~'s bench*** banco *m* (de carpintero)
car•pet ['kɑ:rpɪt] *rug* alfombra *f*; *fitted* moqueta *f*; ***sweep sth under the ~*** *Br fig* echar tierra a algo, tapar algo **II** *v/t* **I** enmoquetar **II** *Br* F reprender, reñir
'car•pet•bag bolsa *f* de viaje
car•pet•ing ['kɑ:rpɪtɪŋ] enmoquetado *m*
'car•pet sweep•er limpiador *m* de alfombras *or* moqueta
'car phone teléfono *m* de coche; **'car-pool** *n acuerdo para compartir el vehículo entre varias personas que trabajan en el mismo sitio*; **'car port** estacionamiento *m* con techo; **car 'ra•di•o** autorradio *m*; **'car ren•tal** alquiler *m* de coches *or* automóviles
car•riage ['kærɪdʒ] **1** *vehicle* carruaje *m* **2** *Br* RAIL vagón *m* **3** COM *transportation* flete *m*; ***~ free*** *or* ***paid*** gastos de envío gratuitos *or* pagados **4** *of typewriter* carrete *m* **5** *bearing* porte *m*, presencia *f*
car•riage 'free *adv* porte franco; **carriage 'paid** *adv* porte pagado; **carriage re'turn** *at line end* retorno *m*
'car ride: ***it's just a short ~ away*** está a poca distancia en coche de aquí
car•ried for•ward [kærɪd'fɔ:rwərd] *adj in bookkeeping* suma y sigue
car•ri•er ['kærɪər] **1** *company* transportista *m/f*, empresa *f* de transportes; *airline* línea *f* aérea **2** *of disease* portador(a) *m(f)*
'car•ri•er bag *Br* bolsa *f* de plástico / papel
'car•ri•er pi•geon paloma *f* mensajera
car•ri•on ['kærɪən] carroña *f*
'car•ri•on crow cuervo *m* carroñero
car•rot ['kærət] zanahoria *f*
car•ry ['kærɪ] **I** *v/t* (*pret & pp* ***-ied***) **1** *of person* llevar; *disease* ser portador de; *of ship, plane, bus etc* transportar; ***be ~ing a child*** (*be pregnant*) estar embarazada; ***~ sth in one's head*** *fig* tener algo grabado en la cabeza; ***~ conviction*** ser convincente; ***~ weight*** producir efecto (***with*** en); ***a loan carrying interest of 10%*** un préstamo con un interés del 10%; ***~ sth too far*** *or* ***to excess*** pasarse (de la raya) con algo; ***~ 5*** MATH llevarse 5
2 *proposal* aprobar
II *v/i* (*pret & pp* ***-ied***) *of sound* oírse
◆ **carry about** *v/t* llevar; ***carry sth about with one*** llevar algo encima
◆ **carry away** *v/t* arrastrar, llevar; ***get carried away*** emocionarse, dejarse llevar por la emoción
◆ **carry forward** *v/t* COM pasar a la columna / página siguiente; *to next year* transferir al ejercicio siguiente; ***carried forward*** suma y sigue
◆ **carry off** *v/t* **1** *take away* quitar, arrebatar; *prize* ganar, llevarse **2** *fig*: ***carry sth off well*** afrontar algo con aplomo, llevar algo bien *or* con dignidad **3** *of disease* causar la muerte de, llevarse a la tumba
◆ **carry on I** *v/i* **1** (*continue*) seguir, continuar **2** (*make a fuss*) organizar un escándalo **3** (*have an affair*) tener un lío **II** *v/t* (*conduct*) mantener; *business* efectuar
◆ **carry out** *v/t survey etc* llevar a cabo;

threat llevar a cabo, cumplir; *promise* cumplir
◆ **carry over** *v/t* ☞ ***carry forward***
◆ **carry through** *v/t* llevar a cabo
'car•ry•all bolsa *f* de viaje; **'car•ry•cot** *Br* moisés *m*; **'car•ry-on** *Br* lío *m*, escándalo *m*; **'car•ry-on bag•gage** AVIA equipaje *m* de mano; **'car•ry•out** ☞ ***takeaway***
'car seat *for child* asiento *m* para niño; **'car•sick** *adj*: ***she gets ~ easily*** se marea en el coche con facilidad; **'car sick•ness** mareo *m*; **'car stick•er** pegatina *f* para el coche
cart [kɑːrt] carro *m*; *for shopping* carrito *m*; ***put the ~ before the horse*** *fig* empezar la casa por el tejado
car•tel [kɑːr'tel] cartel *m*
car•ti•lage ['kɑːrtɪlɪdʒ] ANAT cartílago *m*
car•tog•ra•pher [kɑːr'tɑːgrəfər] cartógrafo(-a) *m(f)*
car•tog•ra•phy [kɑːr'tɑːgrəfɪ] cartografía *f*
car•ton ['kɑːrtn] *for storage, transport* caja *f* de cartón; *for milk etc* cartón *m*, tetrabrik *m* ®; *for eggs, of cigarettes* cartón *m*
car•toon [kɑːr'tuːn] *in newspaper, magazine* tira *f* cómica; *on TV, movie* dibujos *mpl* animados
car•toon•ist [kɑːr'tuːnɪst] dibujante *m/f* de chistes
car'toon strip tira *f* cómica
car•tridge ['kɑːrtrɪdʒ] *for gun* cartucho *m*
'car•tridge case culote *m*
'cart•wheel: ***turn a ~*** dar una voltereta
carve [kɑːrv] *v/t meat* trinchar; *wood* tallar; ***~ sth out of stone*** tallar algo en piedra; ***she carved her name on a tree*** grabó su nombre en un árbol
◆ **carve out** *v/t*: ***she carved out a career for herself*** se labró un porvenir profesional
carv•ing ['kɑːrvɪŋ] *figure* talla *f*; ***~ knife*** trinchante *m*
'car wash lavado *m* de automóviles
cas•cade [kæ'skeɪd] cascada *f*
case¹ [keɪs] *container* funda *f*; *of scotch, wine* caja *f*; (*suitcase*) maleta *f*
case² [keɪs] *instance, criminal*, MED caso *m*; LAW causa *f*; ***I think there's a ~ for dismissing him*** creo que hay razones fundadas para despedirlo; ***the ~ for the prosecution*** (los argumentos jurídicos de) la acusación; ***make a ~ for sth*** defender algo; ***in ~ …*** por si …; ***in ~ of emergency*** en caso de emergencia; ***in any ~*** en cualquier caso; ***in that ~*** en ese caso; ***if that is the ~*** si así es; ***it's not the ~ that I didn't try*** no es que no lo intentara; ***as the ~ may be*** según sea el caso; ***it's a ~ of waiting to see what happens*** se trata de esperar y ver lo que pasa
'case his•to•ry MED historial *m* médico
'case•load número *m* de casos
case•ment ['keɪsmənt]: ***~ window*** ventana *f* de hojas
'case stud•y estudio *m* de caso
cash [kæʃ] **I** *n* (dinero *m* en) efectivo *m*; ***I'm a bit short of ~*** no tengo mucho dinero; ***~ down*** al contado; ***pay (in) ~*** pagar en efectivo; ***~ on delivery*** ☞ ***COD***; ***in ~*** en efectivo; ***~ in advance*** dinero por adelantado; ***be out of ~*** F estar sin blanca F **II** *v/t check* hacer efectivo
◆ **cash in** *v/t bonds etc* cobrar
◆ **cash in on** *v/t* F sacar provecho de
cash and 'car•ry tienda *f* al por mayor; **'cash bal•ance** saldo *m* de caja; **'cash cow** fuente *f* de ingresos; **'cash desk** caja *f*; **cash 'dis•count** descuento *m* por pago al contado; **'cash de•pos•it** depósito *m* de efectivo; **'cash dis•pens•er** *Br* cajero *m* automático; **'cash ex•pen•di•ture** gastos mpl de caja; **'cash flow** flujo *m* de caja, cash-flow *m*; ***~ problems*** problemas *mpl* de liquidez
cash•ier [kæ'ʃɪr] *n in store etc* cajero(-a) *m(f)*
cash•ier's 'check cheque *m* de caja
'cash in hand efectivo *m* disponible
cash•less ['kæʃlɪs] *adj* sin dinero en metálico
'cash ma•chine cajero *m* automático
cash•mere ['kæʃmɪr] *adj* cachemir *m*
'cash pay•ment pago *m* al contado *or* en efectivo; **'cash•point** cajero *m* automático; **'cash price** precio *m* al contado; **'cash pur•chase** compra *f* al contado *or* en efectivo; **'cash re•gis•ter** caja *f* registradora
cas•ing ['keɪsɪŋ] **1** *container* funda *f* **2** *of window, door* marco *m* **3** *of sausage* piel *f*

ca•si•no [kə'siːnoʊ] casino *m*
cask [kɑːsk] barrica *f*, tonel *m*
cas•ket ['kæskɪt] (*coffin*) ataúd *m*, féretro *m*
cas•sa•va [kə'sævə] fariña *f S.Am.*
cas•se•role ['kæsəroʊl] *n* **1** *meal* guiso *m* **2** *container* cacerola *f*, cazuela *f*
cas•sette [kə'set] cinta *f*, casete *f*
cas'sette deck platina *f* para casete
cas'sette play•er, cas'sette re•cord•er casete *m*
cas•sock ['kæsək] REL sotana *f*
cast [kæst] **I** *n* **1** *of play* reparto *m* **2** (*mold*) molde *m* **II** *v/t* (*pret & pp* ***cast***) **1** *doubt, suspicion* proyectar **2** *metal* fundir **3** *play* seleccionar el reparto de; ***they ~ Alan as ...*** le dieron a Alan el papel de ...; ***she was badly ~*** no acertaron dándole el papel **4** *vote* asignar
◆ **cast about for, cast around for** *v/t* rebuscar
◆ **cast aside** *v/t fear, prejudice* alejar, apartar; *friend* rechazar
◆ **cast down** *v/t*: ***be ~*** estar triste *or* alicaído
◆ **cast off** *v/i of ship* soltar amarras
'cast•a•way náufrago(-a) *m*(*f*)
caste [kæst] casta *f*
cast•er ['kæstər] *on chair etc* ruedecita *f*
cas•ti•gate ['kæstɪgeɪt] *v/t* vapulear
Cas•tile [kæs'tiːl] Castilla *f*
Cas•til•i•an [kæs'tɪlɪən] **I** *adj* castellano **II** *n* **1** *person* castellano(-a) *m*(*f*) **2** *language* castellano *m*
cast•ing ['kæstɪŋ] **1** TECH pieza *f* de fundición **2** *of actors* casting *m*
'cast•ing di•rec•tor director *m* de reparto
cast•ing 'vote voto *m* de calidad
cast 'i•ron hierro *m* fundido
cast-'i•ron *adj* de hierro fundido
cas•tle ['kæsl] castillo *m*
'cast•off *item of clothing* prenda *f* usada
'cast-off *adj clothing* viejo, usado
cast•or ['kæstər] ☞ ***caster***
'cast•or oil aceite *m* de ricino
cas•trate [kæ'streɪt] *v/t* castrar
cas•tra•tion [kæ'streɪʃn] castración *f*
cas•u•al ['kæʒʊəl] *adj* (*chance*) casual; (*offhand*) despreocupado; (*not formal*) informal; (*not permanent*) eventual; ***it was just a ~ remark*** no era más que un comentario hecho de pasada; ***he was very ~ about the whole thing*** parecía no darle mucha importancia al asunto; ***~ sex*** relaciones *fpl* sexuales (con parejas) ocasionales; ***~ laborer*** temporero(-a) *m*(*f*), jornalero(-a) *m*(*f*)
cas•u•al•ly ['kæʒʊəlɪ] *adv dressed* de manera informal; *say* a la ligera
cas•u•al•ty ['kæʒʊəltɪ] víctima *f*
'cas•u•al•ty de•part•ment *Br* urgencias *fpl*
'cas•u•al wear ropa *f* informal
cat [kæt] gato *m*; ***let the ~ out of the bag*** descubrir el pastel; ***play ~ and mouse with s.o.*** jugar al gato y el ratón con alguien; ***it's raining ~s and dogs*** está lloviendo a cántaros, están cayendo chuzos de punta
cat•a•comb ['kætəkuːm] catacumba *f*
Cat•a•lan ['kætəlæn] **I** *adj* catalán **II** *n* **1** *person* catalán(-ana) *m*(*f*) **2** *language* catalán *m*
cat•a•log, *Br* **cat•a•logue** ['kætəlɑːg] **I** *n* catálogo *m* **II** *v/t* catalogar
Cat•a•lon•i•a [kætə'loʊnɪə] Cataluña *f*
cat•a•lyst ['kætəlɪst] catalizador *m*
cat•a•lyt•ic con•vert•er [kætəlɪtɪkkən'vɜːrtər] catalizador *m*
cat-and-'dog *adj*: ***lead a ~ life*** estar siempre como el perro y el gato
cat•a•pult ['kætəpʌlt] **I** *v/t fig to fame, stardom* catapultar, lanzar **II** *n* catapulta *f*; *Br*: *toy* tirachinas *m inv*
cat•a•ract ['kætərækt] MED catarata *f*
ca•tarrh [kə'tɑːr] MED catarro *m*
ca•tas•tro•phe [kə'tæstrəfɪ] catástrofe *f*
cat•a•stroph•ic [kætə'strɑːfɪk] *adj* catastrófico
'cat bur•glar *ladrón*(*ona*) *que escala para robar en las casas*
'cat•call abucheo *m*
catch [kætʃ] **I** *n* **1** parada *f* (*sin que la pelota toque el suelo*); *in baseball* atrapada *f*, recepción *f*
2 *of fish* captura *f*, pesca *f*
3 (*locking device*) cierre *m*
4 (*problem*) pega *f*; ***there has to be a ~*** tiene que haber una trampa
II *v/t* (*pret & pp* ***caught***) **1** *ball* agarrar, *Span* coger
2 *animal* atrapar; *escaped prisoner* capturar; *fish* pescar; *in order to speak to* alcanzar, pillar; ***~ s.o. doing sth*** atrapar *or Span* coger a alguien haciendo

algo; **~ *s.o. lying*** pillar a alguien mintiendo; **~ *it*** F (*be punished*) cargársela F; ***my fingers got caught in the door*** me he pillado los dedos con la puerta; **~ *you later*** F nos vemos (luego)
3 *get on*: *bus*, *train*) tomar, *Span* coger; (*not miss*: *bus*, *train*) alcanzar, *Span* coger
4 (*hear*) oír
5 *illness* agarrar, *Span* coger; **~ (*a*) *cold*** agarrar *or Span* coger un resfriado, resfriarse
6: **~ *s.o.'s eye*** *of person*, *object* llamar la atención de alguien; **~ *sight of*, ~ *a glimpse of*** ver
◆ **catch at** *v/t* tratar de agarrar
◆ **catch on** *v/i* **1** (*become popular*) cuajar, ponerse de moda **2** (*understand*) darse cuenta; ***catch on to sth*** pillar *or* entender algo
◆ **catch out** *v/t*: ***catch s.o. out*** pillar *or* pescar a alguien
◆ **catch up** *v/i*: ***catch up with s.o.*** alcanzar a alguien; ***he's having to work hard to catch up*** tiene que trabajar muy duro para ponerse al día; ***be caught up in sth*** estar atrapado en algo
◆ **catch up on** *v/t*: ***catch up on one's sleep*** recuperar el sueño; ***there's a lot of work to catch up on*** hay mucho trabajo atrasado
catch-22 [kætʃtwentɪ'tu:]: ***it's a ~ situation*** es como la pescadilla que se muerde la cola
'catch-all term palabra *f* de sentido general
catch•er ['kætʃər] *in baseball* cácher *m*, cátcher *m*, receptor *m*; **~*'s box*** cajón *m* del receptor
catch•ing ['kætʃɪŋ] *adj also fig* contagioso
catch•ment ar•e•a ['kætʃmənt] **1** GEOL cuenca *f* fluvial **2** *of hospital*, *school* zona *f* de cobertura
'catch•phrase fórmula *f*; POL eslogan *m*
'catch•word eslogan *m*
catch•y ['kætʃɪ] *adj tune* pegadizo
cat•e•chism ['kætəkɪzəm] REL catequismo *m*
cat•e•gor•ic [kætə'gɑ:rɪk], **cat•e•gor•i•cal** [kætə'gɑ:rɪkl] *adj* categórico, contundente
cat•e•gor•i•cal•ly [kætə'gɑ:rɪklɪ] *adv* categóricamente
cat•e•go•rize ['kætəgɑ:raɪz] *vt* clasificar
cat•e•go•ry ['kætəgɔ:rɪ] categoría *f*
◆ **ca•ter for** ['keɪtər] *v/t* **1** (*meet the needs of*) cubrir las necesidades de **2** (*provide food for*) organizar la comida para
◆ **cater to** *v/t fig* satisfacer, complacer
ca•ter•er ['keɪtərər] hostelero(-a) *m*(*f*)
ca•ter•ing ['keɪtərɪŋ] catering *m*, hostelería *f*
'ca•ter•ing com•pa•ny empresa *f* de catering *or* hostelería
'ca•ter•ing in•dus•try sector *m* de la hostelería
ca•ter•pil•lar ['kætərpɪlər] oruga *f*
cat•er•waul ['kætəwɔ:l] *v/i* gemir, gañir
'cat•gut cuerda *f* de tripas
ca•the•dral [kə'θi:drl] catedral *f*
cath•e•ter ['kæθɪtər] MED catéter *m*
cath•ode ['kæθoʊd] ELEC cátodo *m*
cath•ode 'ray tube tubo *m* de rayos catódicos
Cath•o•lic ['kæθəlɪk] **I** *adj* católico **II** *n* católico(-a) *m*(*f*)
Ca•thol•i•cism [kə'θɑ:lɪsɪzm] catolicismo *m*
cat•kin ['kætkɪn] BOT amento *m*
'cat lit•ter arena *f* para gatos; **'cat•nap**: ***have*** *or* ***take a ~*** echarse una cabezada; **'cat's eyes** *on road* captafaros *mpl* (*en el centro de la calzada*); **'cat suit** body *m* entero
cat•sup ['kætsʌp] ketchup *m*, catchup *m*
cat•tle ['kætl] *npl* ganado *m*; ***ten head of ~*** diez cabezas de ganado
'cat•tle breed•ing cría *f* de ganado
'cat tray *to defecate in* bandeja *f* para gatos
cat•ty ['kætɪ] *adj* malintencionado
'cat•walk pasarela *f*
cau•cus ['kɒ:kəs] POL congreso *m* de partido
caught [kɒ:t] *pret & pp* ☞ **catch**
caul•dron ['kɒ:ldrən] caldera *f*
cau•li•flow•er ['kɒ:lɪflaʊər] coliflor *f*
caus•al ['kɒ:zl] *adj* causal
cau•sal•i•ty [kɒ:'zælətɪ] causalidad *f*
cause [kɒ:z] **I** *n* causa *f*; (*grounds*) motivo *m*, razón *f*; **~ *of death*** causa de muerte; ***have ~ for complaint*** tener

motivos para quejarse; ***make common ~ with*** hacer causa común con **II** *v/t* causar, provocar

'cause•way *over water, marshland* paso *m*

caus•tic ['kɒːstɪk] *adj fig* cáustico

cau•ter•ize ['kɒːtəraɪz] *v/t* MED cauterizar

cau•tion ['kɒːʃn] **I** *n* (*carefulness*) precaución *f*, prudencia *f* **II** *v/t* (*warn*) prevenir (***against*** contra); ***~ a player*** amonestar a un jugador

cau•tious ['kɒːʃəs] *adj* cauto, prudente

cau•tious•ly ['kɒːʃəslɪ] *adv* cautelosamente, con prudencia

cav•a•lier [kævə'lɪər] *adj attitude* despreocupado

cav•al•ry ['kævəlrɪ] caballería *f*

cave [keɪv] cueva *f*

◆ **cave in** *v/i* **1** *of roof* hundirse **2** *of person* ceder, transigir

'cave•man cavernícola *m*, troglodita *m*

cav•ern ['kævərn] caverna *f*

cav•i•ar ['kævɪɑːr] caviar *m*

cav•i•ty ['kævətɪ] *hole* cavidad *f*; *in tooth* caries *f inv*

ca•vort [kə'vɔːrt] *v/i* F corretear, juguetear

cay•enne pep•per [keɪen'pepər] cayena *f*

CB ra•di•o [siːbiː'reɪdɪoʊ] radio *f* de la BC *or* banda ciudadana

cc[1] [siː'siː] **I** *abbr* (= ***carbon copy***) copia *f* **II** *v/t* **1** *memo* enviar una copia de **2** *person* enviar una copia a

cc[2] [siː'siː] *abbr* **1** (= ***cubic centimeters***) cc (= centimetros *mpl* cúbicos) **2** (= ***cubic capacity***) MOT cilindrada *f*

CCTV [siːsiːtiː'viː] *abbr* (= ***closed circuit television***) CCTV (= circuito *m* cerrado de televisión)

CD [siː'diː] *abbr* (= ***compact disc***) CD *m*

C'D play•er (reproductor *m* de) CD *m*; **CD-'ROM** [siːdiː'rɑːm] CD-ROM *m*; **CD-'ROM drive** lector *m* de CD-ROM

cease [siːs] **I** *v/i* cesar **II** *v/t* suspender; ***~ doing sth*** dejar de hacer algo; ***~ trading*** dejar de operar

'cease-fire alto *m* el fuego

cede [siːd] *v/t* ceder, entregar; ***he ceded my point*** me dió la razón

cei•ling ['siːlɪŋ] *of room* techo *m*; (*limit*) tope *m*, límite *m*; ***he hit the ~*** F se puso como una fiera F

cel•e•brate ['selɪbreɪt] **I** *v/i*: ***let's ~ with a bottle of champagne*** celebrémoslo con una botella de champán **II** *v/t* **1** celebrar, festejar **2** (*observe*) celebrar

cel•e•brat•ed ['selɪbreɪtɪd] *adj* célebre; ***be ~ for*** ser célebre por

cel•e•bra•tion [selɪ'breɪʃn] celebración *f*

ce•leb•ri•ty [sɪ'lebrətɪ] (*fame*) celebridad *f*

cel•e•ry ['selərɪ] apio *m*

ce•les•tial [sɪ'lestjəl] *adj* celestial; ***~ body*** cuerpo *m* celeste

cel•i•ba•cy ['selɪbəsɪ] celibato *m*

cel•i•bate ['selɪbət] *adj* célibe

cell [sel] *for prisoner, in spreadsheet* celda *f*; BIO célula *f*

cel•lar ['selər] sótano *m*; *for wine* bodega *f*

'cell di•vi•sion BIO división *f* celular

cel•list ['tʃelɪst] violonchelista *m/f*

cel•lo ['tʃeloʊ] violonchelo *m*

cel•lo•phane ['seləfeɪn] celofán *m*

'cell phone (teléfono *m*) móvil *m*, *L.Am.* (teléfono *m*) celular *m*; ***you can get me on my ~*** puedes localizarme en el celular *or Span* el móvil

cel•lu•lar ['seljʊlər] *adj* celular

cel•lu•lar 'phone ☞ ***cell phone***

cel•lu•lite ['seljʊlaɪt] celulitis *f*

cel•lu•loid ['seljʊlɔɪd] celuloide *m*; ***on ~*** *fig* en celuloide

cel•lu•lose ['seljʊloʊs] celulosa *f*

Cel•si•us ['selsɪəs] *adj* centígrado; ***10 degrees ~*** 10 grados centígrados

Celt [kelt] celta *m/f*

Celt•ic ['keltɪk] *adj* celta

ce•ment [sɪ'ment] **I** *n* cemento *m* **II** *v/t* colocar con cemento; *friendship* consolidar

ce'ment mix•er hormigonera *f*

cem•e•ter•y ['semətərɪ] cementerio *m*

cen•o•taph ['senoʊtæf] cenotafio *m*

cen•sor ['sensər] **I** *n* censor(a) *m*(*f*) **II** *v/t* censurar

cen•so•ri•ous [sen'sɔːrɪəs] *adj* censurador, crítico; ***be ~ of s.o. / sth*** ser crítico con alguien / algo

cen•sor•ship ['sensɔːrʃɪp] censura *f*

cen•sure ['senʃər] **I** *n* censura *f*, condena *f*; ***vote of ~*** voto *m* de censura **II** *v/t* censurar, condenar

cen•sus ['sensəs] censo *m*

C

cent [sent] céntimo *m*
cen•te•nar•i•an [sentɪ'nerɪən] centenario(-a) *m(f)*
cen•te•na•ry [sen'ti:nərɪ] centenario *m*
cen•ten•ni•al [sen'tenjəl] **I** *adj* centenario **II** *n* centenario *m*
cen•ter ['sentər] **I** *n* **1** centro *m*; ***in the ~ of*** en el centro de; ***be the ~ of attention*** ser el centro de atención **2** *in basketball* pívot *m/f* **II** *v/t* centrar
◆ **center around, center on** *v/t* centrarse en
'cen•ter•back *in soccer* defensa *m* central; **'cen•ter field** *in baseball* exterior *m* central, *L.Am.* jardín *m* central; **'cen•ter field•er** *in baseball* exterior *m* centro; **cen•ter 'for•ward** *in soccer* delantero centro *m*
cen•ter•ing ['sentərɪŋ] *of text* centrado *m*
cen•ter of 'grav•i•ty centro *m* de gravedad
cen•ti•grade ['sentɪgreɪd] *adj* centígrado; ***10 degrees ~*** 10 grados centígrados
cen•ti•gram(me) ['sentɪgræm] centigramo *m*
cen•ti•me•ter, *Br* **cen•ti•me•tre** ['sentɪmi:ter] centímetro *m*
cen•tral ['sentrəl] *adj* central; *location, apartment* céntrico; ***~ Chicago*** el centro de Chicago; ***be ~ to sth*** ser el eje de algo; ***~ bank*** banco *m* central
Cen•tral A'mer•i•ca *n* Centroamérica, América *f* Central; **Cen•tral A'mer•i•can** **I** *adj* centroamericano, de (la) América Central **II** *n* centroamericano(-a) *m(f)*; **cen•tral 'heat•ing** calefacción *f* central
cen•tral•i•za•tion [sentrəlaɪ'zeɪʃn] *n* centralización *f*
cen•tral•ize ['sentrəlaɪz] *v/t* centralizar
cen•tral 'lock•ing [sentrəl'lɑ:kɪŋ] MOT cierre *m* centralizado; **cen•tral mid'field•er** *in soccer* interior *m*; **cen•tral 'nerv•ous sys•tem** PHYSIO sistema *m* nervioso central; **cen•tral 'pro•ces•sing u•nit** unidad *f* central de proceso; **cen•tral 'pur•chas•ing de•part•ment** COM central *f* de compras; **Cen•tral 'Stan•dard Time** *hora oficial en el centro de Norteamérica*
cen•tre *Br* ☞ ***center***
cen•trif•u•gal [sentrɪ'fjʊgl] *adj* PHYS centrífugo; ***~ force*** fuerza *f* centrífuga
cen•tri•fuge ['sentrɪfju:dʒ] TECH centrifugadora *f*
cen•tu•ry ['sentʃərɪ] siglo *m*; ***in the 21st ~*** en el siglo XXI
CEO [si:i:'oʊ] *abbr* (= ***Chief Executive Officer***) consejero(-a) *m(f)* delegado
ce•ram•ic [sɪ'ræmɪk] *adj* de cerámica
ce•ram•ics [sɪ'ræmɪks] **1** (*pl*: *objects*) objetos *mpl* de cerámica **2** (*sing*: *art*) cerámica *f*
ce•re•al ['sɪrɪəl] (*grain*) cereal *m*; (*breakfast ~*) cereales *mpl*
cer•e•bral ['serɪbrəl] *adj* ANAT cerebral
cer•e•bral pal•sy ['pɒ:lzɪ] parálisis *f* cerebral
cer•e•mo•ni•al [serɪ'moʊnɪəl] **I** *adj* ceremonial **II** *n* ceremonial *m*
cer•e•mo•ni•ous [serɪ'moʊnɪəs] *adj* ceremonioso
cer•e•mo•ny ['serɪmənɪ] (*event, ritual*) ceremonia *f*
cert [sɜ:rt] *Br* F: ***it's a dead ~*** es una apuesta segura
cer•tain ['sɜ:rtn] *adj* **1** (*sure*) seguro; ***I'm ~*** estoy seguro; ***make ~*** asegurarse (***of*** de); ***know / say for ~*** saber / decir con certeza; ***it is ~ to happen*** ocurrirá seguro, ocurrirá con toda seguridad **2** (*particular*) cierto; ***a ~ Mr. S.*** un cierto Sr. S.
cer•tain•ly ['sɜ:rtnlɪ] *adv* **1** (*definitely*) claramente **2** (*of course*) por supuesto; ***~ not!*** ¡por supuesto que no!
cer•tain•ty ['sɜ:rtntɪ] **1** (*confidence*) certeza *f*, certidumbre *f* **2** (*inevitability*) seguridad *f*; ***it's a ~*** es seguro; ***he's a ~ for the gold medal*** va a ganar seguro la medalla de oro
cer•tif•i•cate [sər'tɪfɪkət] (*qualification*) título *m*; (*official paper*) certificado *m*
cer•tif•i•cate of air•worth•i•ness [er'wɜ:rðɪnɪs] certificado *m* de estar en condiciones de navegar
cer•tif•i•cate of 'or•i•gin certificado *m* de origen
cer•ti•fied check ['sɜ:rtɪfaɪd] cheque *m* certificado; **'cer•ti•fied cop•y** copia *f* certificada *or* compulsada; **cer•ti•fied pub•lic ac'count•ant** censor(a) *m(f)* jurado(-a) de cuentas
cer•ti•fy ['sɜ:rtɪfaɪ] *v/t* (*pret & pp* **-ied**) certificar; ***this is to ~ that*** por la presente doy fe de que *or* certifico que
cer•vi•cal can•cer [sɜ:r'vaɪkl] MED

cáncer *m* de cuello de útero
cer•vi•cal 'smear MED citología *f*
Ce•sar•e•an (sec•tion) [sɪ'zerɪən] cesárea *f*; ***be born by ~ (section)*** nacer por cesárea
ces•sa•tion [se'seɪʃn] cese *m*
cess•pit ['sespɪt], **cess•pool** ['sespu:l] cloaca *f*
CFC [si:ef'si:] *abbr* (= ***chlorofluorocarbon***) CFC *m* (= clorofluorocarbono *m*)
chafe [ʧeɪf] *v/t rub* rozar
◆ **chafe against, chafe at** *v/t* indignarse por, soliviantarse por
chaff [ʧæf] *of wheat* ahechadura *f*, granza *f*
chain [ʧeɪn] **I** *n also of hotels etc* cadena *f*; ***~ of mountains*** cordillera *f* **II** *v/t* encadenar; ***~ sth / s.o. to sth*** encadenar algo / a alguien a algo
◆ **chain up** *v/t* encadenar
chain re'ac•tion reacción *f* en cadena; **'chain•saw** sierra *f* mecánica; **'chain-smoke** *v/i* fumar un cigarrillo tras otro, fumar como un carretero; **'chain-smok•er** *persona que fuma un cigarrillo tras otro*; **'chain store** *store* tienda *f* (de una cadena); *company* cadena *f* de tiendas
chair [ʧer] **I** *n* silla *f*, (*arm~*) sillón *m*; *at university* cátedra *f*; ***the ~*** (*electric ~*) la silla eléctrica; *at meeting* la presidencia; ***take the ~*** ocupar la presidencia; ***be in the ~*** ocupar la silla presidencial, presidir **II** *v/t meeting* presidir
'chair lift telesilla *f*;
'chair•man presidente *m*
chair•man e•mer•i•tus [e'merɪtəs] presidente *m* emérito
chair•man•ship ['ʧermənʃɪp] presidencia *f*; ***under the ~ of*** bajo la presidencia de
'chair•per•son presidente(-a) *m*(*f*)
'chair•wom•an presidenta *f*
cha•let ['ʃæleɪ] chalet *m*, chalé *m*
chal•ice ['ʧælɪs] REL cáliz *m*
chalk [ʧɒ:k] *for writing* tiza *f*; *in soil* creta *f*; ***be as different as ~ and cheese*** parecerse como un huevo a una castaña; ***not by a long ~*** ni muchísimo menos
◆ **chalk up** *v/t victory etc* apuntarse, anotarse
chal•lenge ['ʧælɪndʒ] **I** *n* **1** (*difficulty*) desafío *m*, reto *m* **2** *in race, competition* ataque *m* **II** *v/t* **1** desafiar, retar **2** (*call into question*) cuestionar
chal•len•ger ['ʧælɪndʒər] aspirante *m/f*
chal•len•ging ['ʧælɪndʒɪŋ] *adj job, undertaking* estimulante
cham•ber ['ʧeɪmbər] TECH, PARL *etc* cámara *f*
'cham•ber•maid camarera *f* (de hotel); **'cham•ber mu•sic** música *f* de cámara; **Cham•ber of 'Com•merce** Cámara *f* de Comercio; **'cham•ber pot** orinal *m*
cha•me•le•on [kə'mi:ljən] ZO camaleón *m*
cham•ois (leath•er) ['ʃæmɪ] ante *m*
champ[1] [ʧæmp] *v/i*: ***~ at the bit*** *fig* morirse de las ganas
champ[2] [ʧæmp] *n* F campeón(-ona) *m*(*f*)
cham•pagne [ʃæm'peɪn] champán *m*
cham•pi•on ['ʧæmpɪən] **I** *n* **1** SP campeón(-ona) *m*(*f*) **2** *of cause* abanderado(-a) *m*(*f*) **II** *v/t* (*cause*) abanderar
cham•pi•on•ship ['ʧæmpɪənʃɪp] campeonato *m*
chance [ʧæns] **I** *n* **1** (*possibility*) posibilidad *f*; ***there's not much ~ of that happening*** no es probable que ocurra; ***you don't stand a ~*** no tienes ninguna posibilidad
2 (*opportunity*) oportunidad *f*
3 (*risk*) riesgo *m*; ***take a ~*** correr el riesgo; ***I'm not taking any ~s*** no voy a correr ningún riesgo; ***game of ~*** juego *m* de azar; ***the ~s are that …*** lo más probable es que …
4 (*luck*) casualidad *f*, suerte *f*; ***leave nothing to ~*** no dejar nada a la improvisación; ***by ~*** por casualidad
II *v/i*: ***I chanced to meet her*** me la encontré de casualidad
III *v/t* arriesgarse a; ***I decided to ~ it*** F decidí probar fortuna *or* suerte
IV *adj* impensado, casual
◆ **chance on** *v/t* tropezar *or* dar con
chan•cel•lor ['ʧænsələr] POL canciller *m*; ***Chancellor of the Exchequer*** *Br* Ministro(-a) *m*(*f*) de Economía
chanc•y ['ʧænsɪ] *adj* F arriesgado, aventurado
chan•de•lier [ʃændə'lɪr] araña *f* (de luces)
change [ʧeɪndʒ] **I** *n* **1** cambio *m*; ***a ~ is as good as a rest*** a veces cambiar es lo mejor; ***that makes a nice ~*** eso es una

novedad bienvenida; ***for a ~*** para variar; ***a ~ of clothes*** una muda; ***~ of life*** (*menopause*) cambio *m* de edad, menopausia *f*
2 (*small coins*) suelto *m*; *from purchase* cambio *m*, *Span* vuelta *f*, *L.Am.* vuelto *m*; ***can you give me ~ for twenty dollars?*** ¿me puedes cambiar veinte dólares?
II *v/t* cambiar; ***~ trains*** hacer transbordo, cambiar de tren; ***~ planes*** hacer transbordo, cambiar de avión; ***~ one's clothes*** cambiarse de ropa; ***~ places with s.o.*** *fig* cambiarse por alguien; ***~ gear*** cambiar de marcha
III *v/i* **1** cambiar; ***the lights ~d to green*** el semáforo se puso verde **2** (*put on different clothes*) cambiarse **3** (*take different train / bus*) hacer transbordo
◆ **change down** *v/i* MOT cambiar a una marcha inferior
◆ **change over** *v/i* pasar, cambiar; *to different TV channel* cambiar de canal
◆ **change up** *v/i* MOT cambiar a una marcha superior

change•a•ble ['ʧeɪndʒəbl] *adj* variable, cambiante

'change•o•ver transición *f* (***to*** a); *in relay race* relevo *m*

chang•ing room ['ʧeɪndʒɪŋ] SP vestuario *m*; *in shop* probador *m*

chan•nel ['ʧænl] *on TV*, *at sea* canal *m*; ***switch*** *or* ***change ~s*** cambiar de canal; ***through official ~s*** por vías oficiales; ***~ of distribution*** canal de distribución; ***~s of communication*** canales de comunicación; ***go through ~s*** seguir los cauces apropiados

'chan•nel hop•ping TV zapping *m*

chant [ʧænt] **I** *n* **1** REL canto *m* **2** *of fans* cántico *m*; *of demonstrators* consigna *f* **II** *v/i* gritar **III** *v/t* corear

cha•os ['keɪɑːs] caos *m*; ***it was ~ at the airport*** el aeropuerto era un caos

cha•ot•ic [keɪ'ɑːtɪk] *adj* caótico

chap [ʧæp] *n Br* F tipo *m* F, *Span* tío *m* F

chap•el ['ʧæpl] capilla *f*

chap•er•on(e) ['ʃæpəroun] **I** *n* acompañante *m/f*, escolta *m/f* **II** *v/t* acompañar *or* escoltar a

chap•lain ['ʧæplɪn] capellán *m*

chapped [ʧæpt] *adj lips* cortado; *hands* agrietado

chap•ter ['ʧæptər] **1** *of book* capítulo *m* **2** *of organization* sección *f*

char [ʃɑːr] *v/i* quemarse, chamuscarse

char•ac•ter ['kærɪktər] *nature*, *personality*, *in printing* carácter *m*; *person*, *in book*, *play* personaje *m*; ***he's a real ~*** es todo un personaje; ***~ actor*** actor *m* de género; ***~ assassination*** difamación *f*, calumnia *f*

char•ac•ter•is•tic [kærɪktə'rɪstɪk] **I** *n* característica *f* **II** *adj* característico

char•ac•ter•is•ti•cal•ly [kærɪktə'rɪstɪklɪ] *adv* de modo característico; ***he was ~ rude*** fue grosero como de costumbre

char•ac•ter•ize ['kærɪktəraɪz] *v/t* (*be typical of*) caracterizar; (*describe*) describir, clasificar

cha•rade [ʃə'rɑːd] *fig* farsa *f*; ***play ~s*** jugar charadas (*acertijo en que se adivinan por medio de la mímica palabras*)

char•broiled ['ʧɑːrbrɔɪld] *adj* a la brasa

char•coal ['ʧɑːrkoul] **1** *for barbecue* carbón *m* vegetal **2** *for drawing* carboncillo *m*

charge [ʧɑːrdʒ] **I** *n* **1** (*fee*) tarifa *f*; ***free of ~*** gratis; ***bank ~s*** comisiones *fpl* bancarias
2: ***will that be cash or ~?*** ¿pagará en efectivo o con tarjeta?
3: ***the person in ~*** la persona responsable *or* encargada; ***be in ~*** estar a cargo; ***be in ~ of sth*** estar al cargo de algo, encargarse de algo; ***take ~*** hacerse cargo; ***take ~ of sth*** hacerse cargo de algo
4 LAW cargo *m*, acusación *f*; ***be on a ~ of murder*** estar acusado de asesinato; ***arrested on a ~ of …*** arrestado por …
II *v/t* **1** *sum of money* cobrar **2** (*put on account*) pagar con tarjeta; ***~ it to my account*** cárguelo a mi cuenta **3** LAW acusar (***with*** de) **4** *battery* cargar
III *v/i* (*attack*) cargar

'charge ac•count cuenta *f* de crédito

'charge card tarjeta *f* de compra

char•gé d'af•faires [ʃɑːrʒeɪdæ'fer] (*pl* ***chargés d'affaires*** [ʃɑːrʒeɪdæ'fer]) diplomático(-a) *m*(*f*) (*subordinado*)

charg•er ['ʧɑːrdʒər] ELEC cargador *m*

cha•ris•ma [kə'rɪzmə] carisma *m*

char•is•ma•tic [kærɪz'mætɪk] *adj* carismático

char•i•ta•ble ['ʧærɪtəbl] *adj institution*, *donation* de caridad; *person* caritativo

char•i•ty ['ʧærətɪ] **1** *assistance* caridad *f* **2** *organization* entidad *f* benéfica

char•la•tan ['ʃɑːrlətən] charlatán(-ana) *m(f)*
charm [ʧɑːrm] **I** *n* **1** (*appealing quality*) encanto *m* **2** *on bracelet etc* colgante *m* **II** *v/t* (*delight*) encantar
charm•er ['ʧɑːrmər] F: ***he's a real ~*** es encantador
charm•ing ['ʧɑːrmɪŋ] *adj* encantador; ***well, that's ~!*** *iron* ¡vaya, qué detalle!
charred [ʧɑːrd] *adj* carbonizado
chart [ʧɑːrt] **I** (*diagram*) gráfico *m*; (*map*) carta *f* de navegación; ***the ~s*** MUS las listas de éxitos **II** *v/t* hacer mapas de; ***~ s.o.'s progress*** describir el progreso de alguien
char•ter ['ʧɑːrtər] **I** *n* **1** *of institution* estatutos *mpl* **2** *of airplane etc* fletamiento *m* **II** *v/t* fletar
char•tered ac•count•ant [ʧɑːrtərdə'kaʊntənt] *Br* censor(a) *m(f)* jurado (-a) de cuentas
'char•ter flight vuelo *m* chárter
'char•ter plane avión *m* chárter
'char•wom•an *Br* señora *f* de la limpieza
char•y ['ʧerɪ] *adj*: ***be ~ of doing sth*** ser reticente a hacer algo
chase [ʧeɪs] **I** *n* persecución *f*; ***give ~ to*** perseguir **II** *v/t* perseguir
◆ **chase after** *v/t*: ***chase after s.o.*** correr detrás de alguien
◆ **chase away** *v/t* ahuyentar
◆ **chase up** *v/t payment, order* reclamar; ***chase s.o. up about sth*** meter prisa a alguien con algo
chas•er ['ʧeɪsər]: ***whiskey ~*** *vaso de whisky que se toma después de una cerveza*
cha•sm ['kæzəm] *also fig* abismo *m*
chas•sis ['ʃæsɪ] *of car* chasis *m inv*
chaste [ʧeɪst] *adj* casto
chas•ten ['ʧeɪsn] *v/t* escarmentar
chas•tise [ʧæ'staɪz] *v/t* reprender
chas•ti•ty ['ʧæstətɪ] castidad *f*
chat [ʧæt] **I** *n* charla *f*, *Mex* plática *f*; ***have a ~*** charlar, *Mex* platicar **II** *v/i* (*pret & pp* ***-ted***) charlar, *Mex* platicar
'chat show *Br* programa *m* de entrevistas
chat•tels ['ʧætlz] *npl* LAW bienes *mpl* muebles
chat•ter ['ʧætər] **I** *n* cháchara *f* **II** *v/i* **1** *talk* parlotear **2** *of teeth* castañetear
'chat•ter•box charlatán(-ana) *m(f)*
chat•ty ['ʧætɪ] *adj person* hablador
chauf•feur ['ʃoʊfər] *n* chófer *m*, *L.Am.* chofer *m*
'chauf•feur-driv•en *adj* con chófer *or* *L.Am.* chofer
chau•vin•ism ['ʃoʊvɪnɪzəm] chovinismo *m*; ***male ~*** machismo *m*
chau•vin•ist ['ʃoʊvɪnɪst] (*male ~*) machista *m*
chau•vin•ist•ic [ʃoʊvɪ'nɪstɪk] *adj* chovinista; (*sexist*) machista
cheap [ʧiːp] **I** *adj* (*inexpensive*) barato; (*nasty*) chabacano; (*mean*) tacaño; ***feel ~*** sentirse despreciable **II** *adv*: ***it was going ~*** estaba tirado; ***buy sth ~*** comprar algo barato; ***on the ~*** en plan barato
cheap•en ['ʧiːpən] *v/t* abaratar; ***~ o.s.*** rebajarse
cheap•ness ['ʧiːpnɪs] bajo precio *m*
cheap•o ['ʧiːpoʊ] F **I** *adj* tirado (de precio) F **II** *n* baratija *f* F
'cheap•skate F roñoso(-a) *m(f)*
cheat [ʧiːt] **I** *n person* tramposo(-a) *m(f)* **II** *v/t* engañar; ***~ s.o. out of sth*** estafar algo a alguien **III** *v/i in exam* copiar; *in cards etc* hacer trampa; ***~ on one's wife*** engañar a la esposa
Chech•ni•a ['ʧeʧnɪə] Chechenia *f*
check[1] [ʧek] **I** *adj shirt* a cuadros **II** *n* cuadro *m*
check[2] [ʧek] *n* **1** FIN cheque *m*; ***a ~ for $500*** un cheque de 500 dólares **2** *in restaurant etc* cuenta *f*; ***~ please*** la cuenta, por favor
check[3] [ʧek] **I** *n* **1** *to verify sth* comprobación *f*; ***keep a ~ on*** llevar el control de **2**: ***keep*** *or* ***hold in ~*** mantener bajo control; ***act as a ~ on sth*** actuar de contrapeso sobre algo **3** *checkmark* marca *f* de comprobado, tic *m*
II *v/t* **1** (*verify*) comprobar; *machinery* inspeccionar; ***I'll call to ~ what time we're needed*** llamaré para informarme *or* ver a que hora nos necesitan **2** (*restrain, stop*) contener, controlar **3** *with a ~mark* poner un tic en; ***~ the appropriate box*** marque la casilla apropiada **4** *coat* dejar en el guardarropa; *package* dejar en consigna
III *v/i* comprobar; ***~ for*** comprobar
◆ **check in I** *v/i at airport* facturar; *at hotel* registrarse **II** *v/t person* registrar; *luggage* facturar

C

◆ **check off** *v/t* marcar (*como comprobada*)
◆ **check on** *v/t* vigilar
◆ **check out I** *v/i* **1** *of hotel* dejar el hotel **2** F *of story etc* (*be true*) ser verdad(ero); (*make sense*) tener sentido **II** *v/t* (*look into*) investigar, *LAm* chequear, *Mex* checar; *club, restaurant etc* probar; ***check it out at your nearest store*** compruébelo en su tienda más cercana
◆ **check up on** *v/t* hacer averiguaciones sobre, investigar; ***Mom's always checking up on me*** mi madre siempre me está vigilando *or* controlando
◆ **check with** *v/t* **1** *of person* hablar con **2** (*tally: of information*) concordar con
'check•book talonario *m* de cheques, *L.Am.* chequera *f*
checked [ʧekt] *adj material* a cuadros
check•er ['ʧekər] *cashier* cajero(-a) *m*(*f*)
'check•er•board tablero *m* de ajedrez
check•ered ['ʧekərd] *adj* **1** *pattern* a cuadros **2** *career* accidentado
check•ers ['ʧekərz] *nsg* damas *fpl*
'check-in facturación *f*
'check-in clerk empleado(-a) *m*(*f*) en el mostrador de facturación
'check-in desk mostrador *m* de facturación
check•ing ac•count ['ʧekɪŋ] cuenta *f* corriente
'check-in time hora *f* de facturación; **'check•list** lista *f* de verificación; **'check mark** tic *m*; **'check•mate** jaque *m* mate; **'check-out** caja *f*; **'check-out time** *from hotel* hora *f* de salida; **'check•point** control *m*; **'check•room** *for coats* guardarropa *m*; *for baggage* consigna *f*; **'check•up** *medical* chequeo *m* (médico), revisión *f* (médica); *dental* revisión *f* (en el dentista); ***have a ~*** hacerse un chequeo, (ir a) hacerse una revisión
cheek [ʧi:k] **1** ANAT mejilla *f*; ***~ by jowl*** hombro con hombro **2** *Br* descaro *m*
'cheek•bone pómulo *m*
cheep [ʧi:p] **I** *v/i & v/t* piar **II** *n* piada *f*
cheer [ʧɪr] **I** *n* ovación *f*; ***~s!*** *toast* ¡salud!; ***the ~s of the fans*** los vítores de los aficionados; ***give three ~s for s.o.*** dar tres hurras por alguien **II** *v/t* ovacionar, vitorear **III** *v/i* lanzar vítores
◆ **cheer on** *v/t* animar
◆ **cheer up I** *v/i* animarse **II** *v/t* animar
cheer•ful ['ʧɪrfəl] *adj* alegre, contento; ***you're a ~ one, aren't you?*** *iron* ¿tu eres muy cuco *or* pillo, no? F
cheer•ing ['ʧɪrɪŋ] vítores *mpl*
cheer•i•o [ʧɪrɪ'oʊ] *Br* F ¡chao! F
'cheer•lead•er animadora *f*
cheer•less ['ʧɪərlɪs] *adj* sombrío
cheer•y ['ʧɪərɪ] *adj* alegre
cheese [ʧi:z] queso *m*; ***say ~!*** PHOT ¡sonríe!
'cheese•burg•er hamburguesa *f* de queso; **'cheese•cake** tarta *f* de queso; **cheese•par•ing** ['ʧi:zperɪŋ] tacañería *f*; **cheese 'spread** queso *m* para untar
chees•y ['ʧi:zɪ] *adj* **I** *flavor* a queso **II** F *fig* cutre F
chee•tah ['ʧi:tə] ZO guepardo *m*
chef [ʃef] chef *m*, jefe *m* de cocina
chem•i•cal ['kemɪkl] **I** *adj* químico **II** *n* producto *m* químico
chem•i•cal 'war•fare guerra *f* química
chem•ist ['kemɪst] **1** *in laboratory* químico(-a) *m*(*f*) **2** *Br*: *dispensing* farmacéutico(-a) *m*(*f*)
chem•is•try ['kemɪstrɪ] química *f*; *fig* sintonía *f*, química *f*
chem•o•ther•a•py [ki:moʊ'θerəpɪ] quimioterapia *f*
cheque *Br* ☞ ***check***[2]
'cheque card *tarjeta bancaria de aval para un cheque*
cheq•uered *Br* ☞ ***checkered***
cher•ish ['ʧerɪʃ] *v/t photo etc* apreciar mucho, tener mucho cariño a; *person* querer mucho; *hope* albergar
cher•ry ['ʧerɪ] **1** *fruit* cereza *f* **2** *tree* cerezo *m*
cher•ry 'bran•dy brandy *m* de cereza
cher•ry to'ma•to (*pl* ***-oes***) tomate *m* cereza
cher•ub ['ʧerəb] *in painting, sculpture* querubín *m*
chess [ʧes] ajedrez *m*
'chess•board tablero *m* de ajedrez
'chess•man, 'chess•piece pieza *f* de ajedrez
chest [ʧest] **1** *of person* pecho *m*; ***get sth off one's ~*** desahogarse **2** *box* cofre *m*
chest•nut ['ʧesnʌt] **1** castaña *f* **2** *tree* castaño *m*
chest of 'draw•ers cómoda *f*

chest•y ['ʧestɪ] *adj* F *woman* pechugona
chew [ʧuː] *v/t* mascar, masticar; *of dog, rats* mordisquear; *~ one's nails* morderse las uñas
◆ **chew on** *v/t* mordisquear
◆ **chew out** *v/t* F echar una bronca a F
chew•ing gum ['ʧuːɪŋ] chicle *m*
chic [ʃiːk] *adj* chic, elegante
chick [ʧɪk] **1** *young chicken* pollito *m*; *young bird* polluelo *m* **2** F *girl* nena *f* F
chick•en ['ʧɪkɪn] **I** *n* **1** gallina *f*; *food* pollo *m* **2** F (*coward*) gallina *f* F **II** *adj* F (*cowardly*) cobarde; *be ~* ser un(a) gallina F
◆ **chicken out** *v/i* F acobardarse
'chick•en broth sopa *f* de pollo; **'chick•en farm•er** avicultor(a) *m(f)*; **'chick•en•feed** F calderilla *f*; **'chick•en pox** MED varicela *f*
'chick•pea garbanzo *m*
chic•o•ry ['ʧɪkərɪ] achicoria *f*
chief [ʧiːf] **I** *n* jefe(-a) *m(f)*; *tribal ~* jefe de la tribu **II** *adj* principal
chief ex•ec•u•tive 'of•fi•cer consejero(-a) *m(f)* delegado
chief•ly ['ʧiːflɪ] *adv* principalmente
chif•fon ['ʃɪfɑːn] gasa *f*
chil•blain ['ʧɪlbleɪn] sabañón *m*
child [ʧaɪld] (*pl* ***children*** ['ʧɪldrən]) niño(-a) *m(f)*; *son* hijo *m*; *daughter* hija *f*; *pej* niño(-a) *m(f)*, crío(-a) *m(f)*; ***an only ~*** un hijo único; ***that's ~'s play*** *fig* es un juego de niños
'child a•buse malos tratos *mpl* a menores; **child a•bus•er** ['ʧaɪldəbjuːzər] *persona que maltrata a menores*; **'child•birth** parto *m*
child•hood ['ʧaɪldhʊd] infancia *f*; ***from ~*** desde la infancia
child•ish ['ʧaɪldɪʃ] *adj pej* infantil
child•ish•ly ['ʧaɪldɪʃlɪ] *adv pej* de manera infantil
child•ish•ness ['ʧaɪldɪʃnɪs] *pej* infantilismo *m*
child•less ['ʧaɪldlɪs] *adj* sin hijos
'child•like *adj* infantil
'child•mind•er niñero(-a) *m(f)*; **child•mind•ing** ['ʧaɪldmaɪndɪŋ]: ***do ~*** hacer de niñero; **child 'prod•i•gy** niño(-a) *m(f)* prodigio(-a); **'child•proof** *adj* a prueba de niños; ***~ lock*** MOT cierre *m* a prueba de niños
child•ren ['ʧɪldrən] *pl* ☞ ***child***; ***~'s TV*** programación *f* infantil
Chil•e ['ʧɪlɪ] Chile *m*
Chil•e•an ['ʧɪlɪən] **I** *adj* chileno **II** *n* chileno(-a) *m(f)*
Chil•e-Pe•ru 'Trench Golfo *m* de Arica
chill [ʧɪl] **I** *n* **1** *illness* resfriado *m*; ***catch a ~*** resfriarse **2**: ***there's a ~ in the air*** hace bastante fresco; ***take the ~ off sth*** templar algo **II** *adj* frío **III** *v/t wine* poner a enfriar; ***serve ~ed*** sírvase frío **IV** *v/i* enfriarse
◆ **chill out** *v/i* P relajarse; (*calm down*) tranquilizarse
chilled [ʧɪld] *adj* frío
chil•(l)i (pep•per) ['ʧɪlɪ] chile *m*, *Span* guindilla *f*
chill•y ['ʧɪlɪ] *adj weather, welcome* fresco; ***I'm feeling a bit ~*** tengo fresco
chime [ʧaɪm] **I** *v/i* dar campanadas *f* **II** *v/t*: ***the clock ~d three*** el reloj dio las tres **III** *n* campanada *f*; ***~s*** *pl* carillón *m*
◆ **chime in** *v/i* intervenir
chim•ney ['ʧɪmnɪ] chimenea *f*
'chim•ney sweep deshonillador(a) *m(f)*
chim•pan•zee [ʧɪm'pænziː] chimpancé *m*
chin [ʧɪn] barbilla *f*; (***keep your***) ***~ up!*** F ¡levanta esos ánimos!
chi•na ['ʧaɪnə] porcelana *f*
Chi•na ['ʧaɪnə] China *f*
'Chi•na•town barrio *m* chino
Chi•nese [ʧaɪ'niːz] **I** *adj* chino **II** *n* **1** *language* chino *m* **2** *person* chino(-a) *m(f)*; ***the ~*** *pl* los chinos
chink [ʧɪŋk] **I** *n* **1** *gap* resquicio *m* **2** *sound* tintineo *m* **II** *v/i* tintinear
chi•nos ['ʧiːnoʊz] *npl* chinos *mpl*
'chin•wag F charla *f*
chip[1] [ʧɪp] **I** *n* **1** *of wood* viruta *f*; *of stone* lasca *f*; *damage* mella *f*; ***~s*** patatas *fpl* fritas *or L.Am.* papas *fpl*; ***he's a ~ off the old block*** de tal palo, tal astilla; ***have a ~ on one's shoulder*** F estar acomplejado **2** *in gambling* ficha *f* **II** *v/t* (*pret & pp* ***-ped***) (*damage*) mellar
chip[2] [ʧɪp] *n* COMPUT chip *m*
◆ **chip away** *v/t* desconchar
◆ **chip in** *v/i* **1** (*interrupt*) interrumpir **2** *with money* poner dinero
◆ **chip off** *v/t* desconchar
'chip•board madera *f* prensada
chip•munk ['ʧɪpmʌŋk] ardilla *f* listada
chi•ro•prac•tor ['kaɪroʊpræktər] qui-

ropráctico(-a) *m(f)*
chirp [ʧɜːrp] *v/i* piar
chirp•y ['ʧɜːrpɪ] *adj* F alegre
chir•rup ['ʧɪrəp] *v/i* piar
chis•el ['ʧɪzl] **I** *n for stone* cincel *m*; *for wood* formón *m* **II** *v/t* (*pret & pp* **-eled**, *Br* **-elled**) tallar
chit [ʧɪt] *note* nota *f*
chit•chat ['ʧɪʧæt] charla *f*
chiv•al•rous ['ʃɪvlrəs] *adj* caballeroso
chiv•al•ry ['ʃɪvəlrɪ] caballerosidad *f*
chive [ʧaɪv] cebollino *m*
chlo•ric ac•id ['klɔːrɪk] CHEM ácido *m* clórico
chlor•ide ['klɔːraɪd] cloruro *m*
chlo•ri•nate ['klɔːrɪneɪt] *v/t* clorar
chlo•rine ['klɔːriːn] cloro *m*
chlo•ro•flu•o•ro•car•bon [klɔːroufluəroʊ'kɑːrbən] clorofluorocarbono *m*
chlo•ro•form ['klɔːrəfɔːrm] cloroformo *m*
chlo•ro•phyll ['klɔːrəfɪl] BOT clorofila *f*
choc•a•hol•ic [ʧɑːkə'hɑːlɪk] F adicto(-a) *m(f)* al chocolate
chock [ʧɑːk] calzo *m*
chock-a-'block *adj* abarrotado (***with*** de)
chock-'full *adj* F de bote en bote F
choc•o•late ['ʧɑːkələt] chocolate *m*; ***a ~*** un bombón; ***a box of ~s*** una caja de bombones
'choc•o•late bar chocolatina *f*
'choc•o•late cake pastel *m* de chocolate
choice [ʧɔɪs] **I** *n* elección *f*; (*selection*) selección *f*; ***you have a ~ of rice or potatoes*** puedes elegir entre arroz y patatas; ***the ~ is yours*** tú eliges; ***I had no ~*** no tuve alternativa; ***make a ~*** elegir; ***take one's ~*** elegir; ***the games software of ~*** el software de los juegos a elegir **II** *adj* (*top quality*) selecto; ***a few ~ words*** unas lindezas
choir [kwaɪr] coro *m*
'choir•boy niño *m* de coro
choke [ʧoʊk] **I** *n* MOT estárter *m* **II** *v/i* ahogarse; ***~ on sth*** atragantarse con algo **III** *v/t* estrangular; *screams* ahogar
◆ **choke back, choke down** *v/t tears, words* contener
◆ **choke off** *v/t supply, discussion* cortar
◆ **choke up** *v/t*: ***get choked up*** *of drain* atascarse
chol•er•a ['kɑːlərə] MED cólera *m*
chol•er•ic ['kɑːlərɪk] *adj* colérico
cho•les•te•rol [kə'lestərɔːl] colesterol *m*
choose [ʧuːz] *v/t & v/i* (*pret* **chose**, *pp* **chosen**) elegir, escoger; ***~ to do sth*** decidir hacer algo; ***there are three versions to ~ from*** puedes elegir entre tres versiones
choos•ey ['ʧuːzɪ] *adj* F exigente
chop [ʧɑːp] **I** *n* **1** *meat* chuleta *f* **2**: ***with one ~ of the ax*** con un hachazo **II** *v/t* (*pret & pp* **-ped**) *wood* cortar; *meat* trocear; *vegetables* picar **III** *v/i*: ***~ and change*** cambiar de idea constantemente
◆ **chop down** *v/t tree* talar
◆ **chop off** *v/t* cortar; ***chop s.o.'s head off*** cortar la cabeza a alguien
◆ **chop up** *v/t* cortar en trozos, trocear, *L.Am.* trozar
chop•per ['ʧɑːpər] F (*helicopter*) helicóptero *m*
chop•py ['ʧɑːpɪ] *adj* picado
'chop•sticks *npl* palillos *mpl* (chinos)
cho•ral ['kɔːrəl] *adj* coral; ***~ society*** coral *f*
chord [kɔːrd] MUS acorde *m*; ***strike the right ~*** estar en el punto justo; ***strike a ~ with s.o.*** calar hondo en alguien
chore [ʧɔːr] tarea *f*; ***do the ~s*** hacer las tareas
chor•e•o•graph ['kɔːrɪəgræf] *v/t* coreografiar
chor•e•og•ra•pher [kɔːrɪ'ɑːgrəfər] coreógrafo(-a) *m(f)*
chor•e•og•ra•phy [kɔːrɪ'ɑːgrəfɪ] coreografía *f*
chor•is•ter ['kɔːrɪstər] corista *m/f*
cho•rus ['kɔːrəs] **I** *singers* coro *m*; *of song* estribillo *m*; ***~ of protest*** coro de protestas; ***in ~*** *fig* a coro **II** *v/t* decir a coro
'cho•rus girl corista *f*
chose [ʧoʊz] *pret* ☞ **choose**
cho•sen ['ʧoʊzn] **I** *adj*: ***the ~ few*** los elegidos; ***the ~ people*** el pueblo elegido **II** *pp* ☞ **choose**
chow [ʧaʊ] **1** *dog* chow-chow *m* **2** F *food* papeo *m* F
◆ **chow down** *v/i* F comenzar a papear F
chow•der ['ʧaʊdər] GASTR *sopa espesa con marisco o pescado y verdura*

Christ [kraɪst] Cristo; ***~!*** ¡Dios mío!; ***before ~*** antes de Cristo
chris•ten ['krɪsn] *v/t* bautizar
chris•ten•ing ['krɪsnɪŋ] bautizo *m*
Chris•tian ['krɪstʃən] **I** *n* cristiano(-a) *m(f)* **II** *adj* cristiano; ***~ era*** era *f* cristiana
Chris•ti•an•i•ty [krɪstɪ'ænətɪ] cristianismo *m*
Chris•tian•ize ['krɪstʃənaɪz] *v/t* cristianizar
'Chris•tian name nombre *m* de pila
Christ•mas ['krɪsməs] Navidad(es) *f(pl)*; ***at ~*** en Navidad(es); ***Happy*** *or* ***Merry ~!*** ¡Feliz Navidad!; ***what did you get for ~?*** ¿qué te ha traído Papá Noel?
Christ•mas 'bo•nus aguinaldo *m*; **'Christ•mas card** crismas *m inv*, tarjeta *f* de Navidad; **'Christ•mas car•ol** villancico *m*; **Christ•mas 'Day** día *m* de Navidad; **Christ•mas 'Eve** Nochebuena *f*, **'Christ•mas pres•ent** regalo *m* de Navidad; **Christ•mas 'pud•ding** *pudin con ciruelas, pasas y especias*; **'Christ•mas•time** Navidad *f*, **'Christ•mas tree** árbol *m* de Navidad
chro•mat•ic [kroʊ'mætɪk] *adj* PHYS cromático
chrome, chro•mi•um [kroʊm, 'kroʊmɪəm] cromo *m*
chrome-plat•ed ['pleɪtɪd] *adj* cromado
chro•mo•some ['kroʊməsoʊm] cromosoma *m*
chron•ic ['krɑːnɪk] *adj* crónico
chron•i•cle ['krɑːnɪkl] **I** *n* crónica *f* **II** *v/t* relatar
chron•i•cler ['krɑːnɪklər] cronista *m/f*
chron•o•log•i•cal [krɑːnə'lɑːdʒɪkl] *adj* cronológico; ***in ~ order*** en orden cronológico
chron•o•log•i•cal•ly [krɑːnə'lɑːdʒɪklɪ] *adv* cronológicamente
chro•nol•o•gy [krə'nɑːlədʒɪ] cronología *f*
chrys•an•the•mum [krɪ'sænθəməm] crisantemo *m*
chub•by ['tʃʌbɪ] *adj* rechoncho; ***~ cheeks*** mofletes *mpl*
chuck[1] [tʃʌk] *v/t* **1** F tirar **2**: ***~ s.o. under the chin*** acariciar a alguien en la barbilla
chuck[2] [tʃʌk] *n* TECH mandril *m*
◆ **chuck away** *v/t* F tirar
◆ **chuck in** F *job* mandar a paseo F
◆ **chuck out** *v/t* F *object* tirar; *person* echar
◆ **chuck up** *v/t* F *vomit* potar F
chuck•le ['tʃʌkl] **I** *n* risita *f* **II** *v/i* reírse por lo bajo
chuffed [tʃʌft] *adj Br* F: ***be ~ about sth*** alegrarse un montón de algo
chug [tʃʌg] *v/i* (*pret & pp* **-ged**): ***~ along*** *of car, train* desplazarse cansinamente; ***he's still ~ging along*** *fig* sigue con la misma cosa
chum [tʃʌm] amigo(-a) *m(f)*; ***be great ~s*** ser grandes amigos; ***listen, ~*** escucha amigo *or* compadre
◆ **chum up with** *v/t* hacerse amigo de
chum•my ['tʃʌmɪ] *adj* F: ***be ~ with*** ser amiguete de F
chump [tʃʌmp] F (*fool*) tarugo *m* F; ***be off one's ~*** *Br* estar pirado F
chunk [tʃʌŋk] trozo *m*
chunk•y ['tʃʌŋkɪ] *adj sweater* grueso; *person, build* cuadrado, fornido
church [tʃɜːrtʃ] iglesia *f*, ***at*** *or* ***in ~*** en la iglesia; ***go to ~*** ir a misa
church•go•er ['tʃɜːrtʃgoʊər] practicante *m/f*, **church 'hall** *sala parroquial empleada para diferentes actividades*; **church 'serv•ice** oficio *m* religioso; **'church wed•ding** matrimonio *m* religioso; **'church•yard** cementerio *m* (al lado de iglesia)
churl•ish ['tʃɜːrlɪʃ] *adj* maleducado, grosero
churn [tʃɜːrn] **I** *n* **1** *for making butter* mantequera *f* **2** *Br*: *milk-container* lechera *f* **II** *v/t milk* batir **III** *v/i*: ***her stomach was ~ing*** tenía un nudo en el estómago
◆ **churn out** *v/t* producir como en serie
◆ **churn up** *v/t* agitar; ***be feeling all churned up*** tener un nudo en el estómago
chute [ʃuːt] rampa *f*, *for garbage* colector *m* de basura
chut•ney ['tʃʌtnɪ] GASTR *salsa fría hecha con frutas, vinagre, azúcar y especias, y que se come con carne o con queso*
CIA [siːaɪ'eɪ] *abbr* (= ***Central Intelligence Agency***) CIA *f* (= Agencia *f* Central de Inteligencia)
ci•ca•da [sɪ'keɪdə] ZO cigarra *f*
CID [siːaɪ'diː] *Br* (= ***Criminal Investiga-***

tion ***Department***) *cuerpo de detectives de la policía británica*
ci•der ['saɪdər] sidra *f*; ***hard ~*** sidra *f*; ***sweet ~*** zumo *m* de manzana
CIF [siːaɪ'ef] *abbr* (= ***cost, insurance, freight***) CIF (= costo, seguro y flete)
ci•gar [sɪ'gɑːr] (cigarro *m*) puro *m*
ci'gar cut•ter cortadora *f* de puros
cig•a•rette [sɪgə'ret] cigarrillo *m*
cig•a'rette case pitillera *f*; **cig•a'rette end** colilla *f*; **cig•a'rette hold•er** boquilla *f*; **cig•a'rette light•er** encendedor *m*, mechero *m*; **cig•a'rette pa•per** papel *m* de fumar; **cig•a'rette ma•chine** expendedor *m* de tabaco
cig•a•ril•lo [sɪgə'rɪloʊ] purito *m*
ci'gar light•er MOT encendedor *m*
ci•lan•tro [sɪ'læntroʊ] cilantro *m*
cinch [sɪntʃ] **1** *on saddle* cincha *f* **2** F: ***it was a ~*** estuvo chupado F
cin•der ['sɪndər]: ***~s*** cenizas *fpl*; ***burnt to a ~*** carbonizado
'cinder block *bloque de cemento ligero*
Cin•der•el•la [sɪndə'relə] Cenicienta
'cin•der track SP pista *f* de ceniza
cin•e•cam•er•a ['sɪnɪkæmərə] *Br* cámara *f* de cine
cin•e•film ['sɪnɪfɪlm] *Br* película *f*
cin•e•ma ['sɪnɪmə] cine *m*
cin•e•ma•go•er ['sɪnɪməgoʊər] *Br* ☞ ***moviegoer***
cin•e•mat•ic [sɪnɪ'mætɪk] *adj* cinematográfico
cin•na•mon ['sɪnəmən] canela *f*
ci•pher ['saɪfər] **1** *code* cifra *f*; ***in ~*** en clave **2** *fig person* marioneta *f*
cir•cle ['sɜːrkl] **I** *n* **1** *also of friends etc* círculo *m*; ***go*** *or* ***run round in ~s*** *fig* no avanzar **2** THEA piso *m*, anfiteatro *m* **II** *v/t* (*draw ~ around*) poner un círculo alrededor de; ***his name was ~d in red*** su nombre tenía un círculo rojo alrededor **III** *v/i of plane, bird* volar en círculo
cir•cuit ['sɜːrkɪt] **1** circuito *m* **2** (*lap*) vuelta *f*; ***make a ~ of*** hacer un recorrido por
'cir•cuit board COMPUT placa *f or* tarjeta *f* de circuitos
'cir•cuit break•er ELEC cortacircuitos *m inv*
cir•cu•i•tous [sər'kjuːɪtəs] *adj route, reasoning* tortuoso
'cir•cuit train•ing SP: ***do ~*** hacer circuitos de entrenamiento
cir•cu•lar ['sɜːrkjʊlər] **I** *n giving information* circular *f* **II** *adj* circular
cir•cu•lar 'saw TECH sierra *f* circular
cir•cu•late ['sɜːrkjʊleɪt] **I** *v/i* circular **II** *v/t memo* hacer circular
cir•cu•la•tion [sərkjʊ'leɪʃn] circulación *f*; ***~ problems*** MED problemas de circulación; ***be in ~*** estar en circulación; ***out of ~*** *fig* fuera de la circulación; ***~ figures*** cifras *fpl* de circulación
cir•cu•la•to•ry [sərkjʊ'leɪtərɪ] *adj* MED, PHYSIO circulatorio; ***~ system*** sistema *m* circulatorio
cir•cum•cise ['sɜːrkəmsaɪz] *v/t* circuncidar
cir•cum•ci•sion [sɜːrkəm'sɪʒn] circuncisión *f*; ***female ~*** ablación *f* del clítoris
cir•cum•fer•ence [sər'kʌmfərəns] circunferencia *f*
cir•cum•lo•cu•tion [sɜːrkəmlə'kjuːʃn] circunlocución *f*
cir•cum•nav•i•gate [sɜːrkəm'nævɪgeɪt] *v/t* circunnavegar
cir•cum•nav•i•ga•tion [sɜːrkəmnævɪ'geɪʃn]: ***~ of the globe*** circunnavegación *f* del globo
cir•cum•scribe ['sɜːrkəmskraɪb] *v/t delimit*, MATH circunscribir
cir•cum•spect ['sɜːrkəmspekt] *adj* circunspecto
cir•cum•stan•ces ['sɜːrkəmstænsɪs] *npl* circunstancias *fpl*; *financial* situación *f* económica; ***under no ~*** en ningún caso, de ninguna manera; ***under the ~*** dadas las circunstancias; ***live in easy ~s*** llevar una vida fácil
cir•cum•stan•tial ev•i•dence [sɜːrkəm'stænʃl] LAW pruebas *fpl* indiciarias
cir•cus ['sɜːrkəs] circo *m*
cir•rho•sis (of the liv•er) [sɪ'roʊsɪs] cirrosis *f* (hepática)
cis•tern ['sɪstɜːrn] cisterna *f*
cit•a•del ['sɪtədəl] MIL ciudadela *f*
ci•ta•tion [saɪ'teɪʃn] **1** *quotation* cita *f* **2** LAW citación *f*
cite [saɪt] *v/t* citar
cit•i•zen ['sɪtɪzn] ciudadano(-a) *m*(*f*)
cit•i•zen•ship ['sɪtɪznʃɪp] ciudadanía *f*
cit•ric ac•id [sɪtrɪk'æsɪd] CHEM ácido *m* cítrico
cit•rus ['sɪtrəs] *adj* cítrico; ***~ fruit*** cítrico *m*

cit•y ['sɪtɪ] ciudad *f*; ***the City*** la City londinense
cit•y 'cen•ter, *Br* **cit•y cen•tre** centro *m* de la ciudad; **cit•y 'fa•thers** *npl* ediles *mpl*; **cit•y 'hall** ayuntamiento *m*; **cit•y 'plan•ning** urbanismo *m*; **cit•y 'state** ciudad *f* estado
civ•ic ['sɪvɪk] *adj* cívico
civ•ics ['sɪvɪks] *nsg* educación *f* cívica
civ•il ['sɪvl] *adj* **1** civil; **~ *case*** causa *f* civil; **~ *marriage*** matrimonio *m* civil **2** (*polite*) cortés
Civ•il Aer•o•nau•tics Board [sɪvleroʊ'nɒːtɪks] *organización reguladora de la aviación civil*; **civ•il avi'a•tion** aviación *f* civil; **civ•il en•gi'neer** ingeniero(-a) *m*(*f*) civil; **civ•il en•gi'neer•ing** ingeniería *f* civil
ci•vil•ian [sɪ'vɪljən] **I** *n* civil *m*/*f* **II** *adj clothes* de civil
ci•vil•i•ty [sɪ'vɪlɪtɪ] cortesía *f*
civ•i•li•za•tion [sɪvəlaɪ'zeɪʃn] civilización *f*
civ•i•lize ['sɪvəlaɪz] *v/t person* civilizar
civ•i•lized ['sɪvəlaɪzd] *adj* civilizado
civ•il 'law derecho *m* civil
civ•il 'rights *npl* derechos *mpl* civiles; **~ *activist*** activista *m*/*f* por los derechos civiles; **~ *movement*** movimiento *m* por los derechos civiles
civ•il 'ser•vant funcionario(-a) *m*(*f*); **civ•il 'ser•vice** administración *f* pública; **civ•il 'war** guerra *f* civil
CJD [siːdʒeɪ'diː] (= ***Creutzfeld-Jakob disease***) enfermedad *f* de Creutzfeld-Jakob
clad [klæd] *adj*: **~ *in blue*** vestido de azul
claim [kleɪm] **I** *n* (*request*) reclamación *f* (***for*** de); (*right*) derecho *m*; (*assertion*) afirmación *f*; ***make a ~*** realizar una reclamación (***against*** contra); **~ *for damages*** reclamación por daños y perjuicios
II *v/t* (*ask for as a right*) reclamar; (*assert*) afirmar; *lost property* reclamar; ***they have ~ed responsibility for the attack*** se han atribuido la responsabilidad del ataque; **~ *damages*** reclamar compensación por daños y perjuicios
◆ **claim back** *v/t* reclamar
claim•ant ['kleɪmənt] reclamante *m*/*f*
clair•voy•ant [kler'vɔɪənt] clarividente *m*/*f*, vidente *m*/*f*
clam [klæm] almeja *f*
◆ **clam up** *v/i* (*pret & pp* **-med**) F callarse
clam•ber ['klæmbər] *v/i* trepar (***over*** por)
clam•my ['klæmɪ] *adj* húmedo
clam•or ['klæmər] *noise* griterío *m*; *outcry* clamor *m*
◆ **clamor for** *v/t justice* clamar por; *ice cream* pedir a gritos
clam•or•ous ['klæmərəs] *adj* ruidoso
clam•our *Br* ☞ **clamor**
clamp [klæmp] **I** *n fastener* abrazadera *f*, mordaza *f* **II** *v/t fasten* sujetar con abrazadera; *car* poner un cepo a
◆ **clamp down** *v/i* actuar contundentemente
◆ **clamp down on** *v/t* actuar contundentemente contra
clan [klæn] clan *m*
clan•des•tine [klæn'destɪn] *adj* clandestino
clang [klæŋ] **I** *n* sonido *m* metálico **II** *v/i* resonar; ***the metal door ~ed shut*** la puerta metálica se cerró con gran estrépito
clang•er ['klæŋər]: ***drop a ~*** *Br* F meter la pata F
clank [klæŋk] **I** *v/i*: ***the door ~ed shut*** la puerta se cerró con un sonido metálico **II** *n* sonido *m* metálico
clap[1] [klæp] **I** *v/i* (*pret & pp* **-ped**) (*applaud*) aplaudir **II** *v/t* (*pret & pp* **-ped**): **~ *one's hands*** aplaudir **III** *n*: ***a ~ of thunder*** un trueno
clap[2] [klæp] *n* P: ***the ~*** (*gonorrhea*) la gonorrea
clap•per ['klæpər] *of bell* badajo *m*
clap•trap ['klæptræp] F paridas *fpl* F
clar•et ['klærɪt] *wine* burdeos *m inv*
clar•i•fi•ca•tion [klærɪfɪ'keɪʃn] aclaración *f*
clar•i•fy ['klærɪfaɪ] *v/t* (*pret & pp* **-ied**) aclarar
clar•i•net [klærɪ'net] clarinete *m*
clar•i'net•(t)ist [klærɪ'netɪst] clarinetista *m*/*f*
clar•i•ty ['klærətɪ] claridad *f*
clash [klæʃ] **I** *n* choque *m*, enfrentamiento *m*; *of personalities* choque *m* **II** *v/i* chocar, enfrentarse; *of colors* desentonar; *of events* coincidir
clasp [klæsp] **I** *n* broche *m*, cierre *m* **II** *v/t in hand* estrechar; **~ *s.o.'s hand*** agarrar a alguien de la mano

C

'clasp knife navaja *f*
class [klæs] **I** *n lesson, students, in society* clase *f*; ***in ~*** en clase; ***attend ~es*** acudir a clase; ***not be in the same ~ as s.o. / sth*** *fig* no poder compararse a alguien / algo; ***be in a ~ of one's own*** *fig* constituir una clase aparte; ***have ~*** F tener clase **II** *v/t* clasificar (***as*** como); ***~ with*** clasificar junto con
'class-ac•tion law•suit pleito *m* de acción popular, acción *f* popular; **class 'con•flict** conflicto *m* de clases; **class-'con•scious** *adj* clasista
clas•sic ['klæsɪk] **I** *adj* clásico **II** *n* clásico *m*; ***~s*** EDU clásicas *fpl*
clas•si•cal ['klæsɪkl] *adj music* clásico
clas•si•fi•ca•tion [klæsɪfɪ'keɪʃn] clasificación *f*
clas•si•fied ['klæsɪfaɪd] *adj information* reservado
clas•si•fied ad('ver•tise•ment) anuncio *m* por palabras
clas•si•fy ['klæsɪfaɪ] *v/t* (*pret & pp* ***-ied***) clasificar
class•less ['klɑːslɪs] *adj society* sin clases
'class•mate compañero(-a) *m*(*f*) de clase; **class re'un•ion** reunión *f* de clase; **'class•room** clase *f*, aula *f*; **class 'strug•gle, class 'war•fare** lucha *f* de clases
class•y ['klæsɪ] *adj* F con clase
clat•ter ['klætər] **I** *n* estrépito *m* **II** *v/i* hacer ruido
◆ **clatter around** *v/i* moverse haciendo ruido
clause [klɒːz] **1** *in agreement* cláusula *f* **2** GRAM cláusula *f*, oración *f*
claus•tro•pho•bi•a [klɒːstrə'foubɪə] claustrofobia *f*
claus•tro•pho•bic [klɒːstrə'foubɪk] *adj* claustrofóbico
clav•i•cle ['klævɪkl] ANAT clavícula *f*
claw [klɒː] **I** *n also fig* garra *f*, *of lobster* pinza *f* **II** *v/t* (*scratch*) arañar
clay [kleɪ] arcilla *f*
'clay court SP pista *f* de tierra batida
clay•ey ['kleɪɪ] *adj* arcilloso
clay 'pi•geon shoot•ing tiro *m* al plato
clean [kliːn] **I** *adj* limpio; ***~ living*** vida *f* sana **II** *adv* F (*completely*) completamente; ***they got ~ away*** escaparon *or* se esfumaron sin dejar rastro **III** *v/t* limpiar; ***~ one's teeth*** limpiarse los dientes; ***I must have my coat ~ed*** tengo que llevar el abrigo a la tintorería
◆ **clean out** *v/t* **1** *room, closet* limpiar por completo **2** *fig* desplumar
◆ **clean up I** *v/t also fig* limpiar; *papers* recoger **II** *v/i* **1** limpiar; (*wash*) lavarse **2** *on stock market etc* ganar mucho dinero
clean-'cut *adj* sano
clean•er ['kliːnər] *person* limpiador(a) *m*(*f*); (***dry***) ***~*** tintorería *f*; ***take s.o. to the ~s*** F desplumar a alguien
clean•ing ['kliːnɪŋ]: ***do the ~*** hacer la limpieza
'clean•ing wom•an señora *f* de la limpieza
clean•li•ness ['klenlɪnɪs] limpieza *f*
clean•ly ['kliːnlɪ] *adv* limpiamente
clean•ness ['kliːnnɪs] limpieza *f*
cleanse [klenz] *v/t skin* limpiar
cleans•er ['klenzər] *for skin* loción *f* limpiadora
clean-'shav•en *adj* bien afeitado
cleans•ing cream ['klenzɪŋ] crema *f* limpiadora
clear [klɪr] **I** *adj* claro; *weather, sky* despejado; *water* transparente; ***I'm not ~ about it*** no lo tengo claro; ***I didn't make myself ~*** no me expliqué claramente; ***make sth ~*** dejar algo claro (***to*** a); ***for no ~ reason*** por ninguna razón aparente; ***he doesn't want to, that's ~*** él no quiere, eso está claro, está claro que él no quiere; ***~ of debt*** sin deudas; ***have a ~ conscience*** tener la conciencia tranquila; ***make a ~ profit*** tener un beneficio neto; ***a ~ win*** una victoria clara; ***~ soup*** GASTR consomé *m*
II *adv*: ***stand ~ of the doors*** apartarse de las puertas; ***steer ~ of*** evitar; ***get ~ of s.o.*** librarse de alguien
III *v/t* **1** *roads etc* despejar; ***~ one's throat*** carraspear; ***the guards ~ed everybody out of the room*** los guardias sacaron a todo el mundo de la habitación **2** (*acquit*) absolver **3** (*authorize*) autorizar; ***you're ~ed for takeoff*** tiene autorización *or* permiso para despegar **4** (*earn*) ganar, sacar **5**: ***~ customs*** pasar la aduana **6** *the ball* despejar
IV *v/i* **1** *of sky, mist* despejarse; *of face* alegrarse **2** *of check* compensarse

◆ **clear away** I *v/t* quitar II *v/i of fog, smoke, clouds* disiparse
◆ **clear off** *v/i* F largarse F
◆ **clear out** I *v/t closet* ordenar, limpiar II *v/i* marcharse
◆ **clear up** I *v/i* 1 ordenar 2 *of weather* despejarse 3 *of illness, rash* desaparecer II *v/t* (*tidy*) ordenar; *mystery, problem* aclarar
clear•ance ['klɪrəns] 1 *space* espacio *m* 2 (*authorization*) autorización *f* 3 *in sport* despeje *m*, rechace *m*
'clear•ance sale liquidación *f*
clear-'cut *adj* claro
clear-cut log•ging ['klɪrkʌtlɑːgɪŋ] tala *f* indiscriminada
clear-head•ed [klɪr'hedɪd] *adj* lúcido
clear•ing ['klɪrɪŋ] claro *m*
clear•ly ['klɪrlɪ] *adv* claramente; ***she is ~ upset*** está claro que está disgustada; ***~ we have to look at this again*** está claro que tenemos que echarle otro vistazo a ésto
clear•ness ['klɪrnɪs] claridad *f*
'clear•way MOT *tramo de carretera o calle en el que está prohibido parar o estacionar*
cleav•age ['kliːvɪdʒ] escote *m*
cleave [kliːv] *v/t* (*pret* **clove**, *pp* **cloven**): ***~ sth in two*** partir algo en dos
cleav•er ['kliːvər] cuchillo *m* de carnicero
clef [klef] MUS clave *f*
cleft [kleft] grieta *f*
cleft 'pal•ate MED fisura *f* de paladar
cleft 'stick: ***be (caught) in a ~*** estar en un callejón sin salida
clem•en•cy ['klemənsɪ] clemencia *f*
clem•ent ['klemənt] *adj weather* benigno
clem•en•tine ['klementaɪn] BOT clementina *f*
clench [klentʃ] *v/t teeth, fist* apretar
cler•gy ['klɜːrdʒɪ] clero *m*
'cler•gy•man clérigo *m*
cler•i•cal ['klerɪkl] *adj* 1 REL clerical 2 (*administrative: error, work*) administrativo; ***~ staff*** personal *m* de oficina
clerk [klɜːrk] 1 *administrative* oficinista *m/f* 2 *in store* dependiente(-a) *m/f*
clev•er ['klevər] *adj person, animal* listo; *idea, gadget* ingenioso; ***~ dick*** *Br* F listillo(-a) *m(f)* F
clev•er•ly ['klevərlɪ] *adv designed* ingeniosamente
clev•er•ness ['klevərnɪs] inteligencia *f*
cli•ché ['kliːʃeɪ] tópico *m*, cliché *m*
cli•chéd ['kliːʃeɪd] *adj* estereotipado
click [klɪk] I *n* COMPUT clic *m* II *v/i* 1 hacer clic; ***~ shut*** cerrarse con un clic 2: ***suddenly it ~ed*** *fig* de repente caí en la cuenta III *v/t* hacer clic con; ***~ one's fingers*** chasquear los dedos
◆ **click on** *v/t* COMPUT hacer clic en
cli•ent ['klaɪənt] cliente *m/f*; ***~ list*** lista *f* de clientes
cli•en•tele [kliːən'tel] clientela *f*
cliff [klɪf] acantilado *m*
'cliff•hang•er: ***the movie was a real ~*** la película era un suspense continuo
cli•mac•ter•ic [klaɪ'mæktərɪk] PHYSIO menopausia *f*
cli•mate ['klaɪmət] *also fig* clima *m*
'cli•mate change cambio *m* climático
cli•mat•ic [klaɪ'mætɪk] *adj* climático
cli•max ['klaɪmæks] I *n* 1 clímax *m*, punto *m* culminante; ***reach a ~*** llegar a un punto culminante 2 (*orgasm*) orgasmo *m* II *v/i* culminar
climb [klaɪm] I *n up mountain* ascensión *f*, escalada *f* II *v/t hill, ladder* subir; *mountain* subir, escalar; *tree* trepar a III *v/i* subir (***into*** a); *up mountain* subir, escalar; *of inflation etc* subir
◆ **climb down** *v/i* 1 *from ladder etc* bajar 2 *fig* retractarse. admitir un error
climb•er ['klaɪmər] *person* escalador(a) *m(f)*, alpinista *m/f*, *L.Am.* andinista *m/f*
climb•ing ['klaɪmɪŋ] escalada *f*, alpinismo *m*, *L.Am.* andinismo *m*
'climb•ing boots botas *fpl* de montaña; **'climb•ing frame** *estructura hecha con barras de hierro o metal para que los niños jueguen o se suban a ella*; **'climb•ing wall** rocódromo *m*
clinch [klɪntʃ] *v/t deal* cerrar; ***that ~es it*** ¡ahora sí que está claro!
cling [klɪŋ] *v/i* (*pret & pp* **clung**) *of clothes* pegarse al cuerpo
◆ **cling to** *v/t person, idea* aferrarse a
◆ **cling together** *v/i* apretarse uno contra otro
'cling•film plástico *m* transparente (para alimentos)
cling•y ['klɪŋɪ] *adj child, boyfriend* pegajoso; ***he is so ~*** es una lapa
clin•ic ['klɪnɪk] clínica *f*

C

clin•i•cal ['klɪnɪkl] *adj* clínico
clink[1] [klɪŋk] I *n noise* tintineo *m* II *v/i* tintinear III *v/t* hacer tintinear; ~ ***glasses*** brindar
clink[2] [klɪŋk] *n* P: ***in the*** ~ *prison* en chirona P
clip[1] [klɪp] I *n fastener* clip *m* II *v/t* (*pret & pp* **-ped**): ~ ***sth to sth*** sujetar algo a algo
clip[2] [klɪp] I *n extract* fragmento *m* II *v/t* (*pret & pp* **-ped**) *hair, grass* cortar; *hedge* podar
'clip•board 1 *for papers* carpeta *f* con sujetapapeles 2 COMPUT portapapeles *m inv*
'clip joint P garito *m* muy caro
clip•pers ['klɪpərz] *npl for hair* maquinilla *f*; *for nails* cortaúñas *m inv*; *for gardening* tijeras *fpl* de podar; ***pair of*** ~ *for nails* cortaúñas *m inv*; *for gardening* tijeras *fpl* de podar
clip•ping ['klɪpɪŋ] *from newspaper* recorte *m*
clique [kli:k] camarilla *f*
cliqu•ey ['kli:kɪ] *adj* exclusivista
clit•o•ris ['klɪtərɪs] ANAT clítoris *m inv*
cloak [kloʊk] I *n* capa *f*; ***under the*** ~ ***of darkness / friendship*** bajo el manto de la oscuridad / la amistad II *v/t*: ~***ed in secrecy*** rodeado de secreto
'cloak•room *Br* guardarropa *m*
clob•ber ['klɑ:bər] *v/t* F atizar F
clock [klɑ:k] reloj *m*; ***around the*** ~ día y noche; ***work off the*** ~ trabajar sin contabilizar las horas
◆ **clock in** *v/i* fichar al entrar
◆ **clock out** *v/i* fichar al salir
◆ **clock up** *v/t distance* acumular; *time* hacer
'clock•face esfera *f* del reloj; **'clock ra•di•o** radio *m* despertador; **clock-wise** ['klɑ:kwaɪz] *adv* en el sentido de las agujas del reloj; **'clock•work**: ***it went like*** ~ salió a la perfección
clod [klɑ:d] 1 *of earth* terrón *m* 2 F *idiot* memo(-a) *m(f)* F
◆ **clog up** [klɑ:g] I *v/i* (*pret & pp* **-ged**) bloquearse II *v/t* (*pret & pp* **-ged**) bloquear
clois•ter ['klɔɪstər] ARCHI claustro *m*
clone [kloʊn] I *n* clon *m* II *v/t* clonar
clon•ing ['kloʊnɪŋ] clonación *f*
close[1] [kloʊs] I *adj family* cercano; *friend* íntimo; ***bear a*** ~ ***resemblance to*** parecerse mucho a; ***the*** ~***st town*** la ciudad más cercana; ***be*** ~ ***to s.o.*** *emotionally* estar muy unido a alguien; ~ ***to tears*** a punto de llorar; ~ ***combat*** combate cuerpo a cuerpo II *adv* cerca; ~ ***to the school*** cerca del colegio; ~ ***at hand*** a mano; ~ ***by*** cerca; ***come*** ~ ***to doing sth*** estar a punto de hacer algo
close[2] [kloʊz] I *v/t* cerrar II *v/i of door, shop* cerrar; *of eyes* cerrarse III *n*: ***come or draw to a*** ~ llegar a su fin
◆ **close down** *v/t & v/i* cerrar
◆ **close in** *v/i of fog* echarse encima; *of troops* aproximarse, acercarse
◆ **close in on** *v/t enemy, prey* cercar, rodear
◆ **close up** I *v/t building* cerrar II *v/i* (*move closer*) juntarse
close-cap•tioned ['kloʊzkæpʃnd] *adj* con subtítulos codificados
closed [kloʊzd] *adj store, eyes* cerrado; ***behind*** ~ ***doors*** a puerta cerrada
closed 'cir•cuit ELEC circuito *m* cerrado
closed-cir•cuit 'tel•e•vi•sion circuito *m* cerrado de televisión
close-down ['kloʊzdaʊn] cierre *m*
closed 'shop COM *centro de trabajo en el que los trabajadores deben estar afiliados a un sindicato en particular*
close•fist•ed [kloʊs'fɪstɪd] *adj* roñoso; **close-fit•ting** [kloʊs'fɪtɪŋ] *adj* ajustado; **close-knit** ['kloʊsnɪt] *adj* muy unido
close•ly ['kloʊslɪ] *adv listen, watch* atentamente; *cooperate* de cerca
close sea•son ['kloʊzsi:zn] *in hunting* veda *f*; *in sport* temporada *f* de descanso
clos•et ['klɑ:zɪt] armario *m*
'clos•et queen F gay *m* que no ha salido del armario
close-up ['kloʊsʌp] primer plano *m*
clos•ing date ['kloʊzɪŋ] fecha *f* límite; **'clos•ing price** FIN cotización *f* de cierre; **'clos•ing time** hora *f* de cierre
clo•sure ['kloʊʒər] cierre *m*
clot [klɑ:t] I *n of blood* coágulo *m* II *v/i* (*pret & pp* **-ted**) *of blood* coagularse
cloth [klɑ:θ] 1 (*fabric*) tela *f*, tejido *m* 2 *for cleaning* trapo *m*
clothe [kloʊð] *v/t* vestir; ***fully*** ~***d*** completamente vestido
clothes [kloʊðz] *npl* ropa *f*, ***change***

C

one's ~ cambiarse de ropa
'clothes bas•ket cesta *f* de la ropa sucia; **'clothes brush** cepillo *m* para la ropa; **'clothes hang•er** percha *f*; **'clothes•horse** tendedero *m* plegable; **'clothes•line** cuerda *f* de tender la ropa; **'clothes peg, 'clothes•pin** pinza *f* (de la ropa)
cloth•ing ['kloʊðɪŋ] ropa *f*
clo•ture ['kloʊtʃər] POL: ***motion for ~*** moción *f* para proceder a una votación inmediata
cloud [klaʊd] **I** *n* nube *f*; ***a ~ of dust*** una nube de polvo; ***have one's head in the ~s*** *fig* estar en las nubes; ***be on ~ nine*** F estar más contento que unas castañuelas; ***cast a ~ on sth*** ensombrecer algo **II** *v/t*: ***~ the issue*** confundir las cosas; ***she allowed her feelings to ~ her judgment*** dejó que sus sentimientos la ofuscaran
◆ **cloud over** *v/i of sky* nublarse; *fig*: *of face* ensombrecerse
'cloud•burst chaparrón *m*
cloud-'cuck•oo land: ***live in ~*** estar en las nubes
cloud•less ['klaʊdlɪs] *adj sky* despejado
cloud•y ['klaʊdɪ] *adj* nublado
clout [klaʊt] **I** *n* **1** sopapo *m* **2** *fig* (*influence*) influencia *f* **II** *v/t* dar un sopapo a
clove[1] [kloʊv] *n* **1** *spice* clavo **2**: ***a ~ of garlic*** un diente de ajo
clove[2] [kloʊv] *pret* ☞ ***cleave***
clo•ven ['kloʊvən] **I** *pp* ☞ ***cleave*** **II** *adj*: ***~ hoof*** pezuña *f* hendida
clo•ver ['kloʊvər] BOT trébol *m*; ***be or live in ~*** *fig* vivir como un rey
clown [klaʊn] *also fig* payaso *m*
◆ **clown around** *v/i* payasear, *Span* hacer el payaso
clown•ish ['klaʊnɪʃ] *adj* de payaso
club [klʌb] *n* **1** *weapon* palo *m*, garrote *m* **2** *in golf* palo *m* **3** *organization* club *m* **4**: ***~s*** *in cards* tréboles *mpl*; *Spanish cards* bastos *mpl*
◆ **club together** *v/i* poner dinero
'club class clase *f* preferente; **club'foot** MED pie *m* deforme; **'club•house** *edificio en el que se reúnen los miembros de un club deportivo*
cluck [klʌk] *v/i* cacarear
clue [klu:] pista *f*; ***I haven't a ~*** F (*don't know*) no tengo idea F; ***he hasn't a ~*** F (*is useless*) no tiene ni idea F
◆ **clue in** *v/t* F poner al tanto F
clued-up [klu:d'ʌp] *adj* F puesto F; ***be ~ on sth*** F estar puesto sobre algo F
clump [klʌmp] *n* **1** *of earth* terrón *m* **2** *of flowers etc* grupo *m*
◆ **clump around** *v/i* andar ruidosamente
clum•si•ness ['klʌmzɪnɪs] torpeza *f*
clum•sy ['klʌmzɪ] *adj person* torpe
clung [klʌŋ] *pret & pp* ☞ ***cling***
clus•ter ['klʌstər] **I** *n* grupo *m* **II** *v/i of people* apiñarse; *of houses* agruparse
clutch [klʌtʃ] **I** *n* **1** MOT embrague *m* **2**: ***fall into s.o.'s ~es*** caer en las garras de alguien **II** *v/t* agarrar
◆ **clutch at** *v/t*: ***clutch at sth*** agarrarse a algo
'clutch ped•al (pedal *m* de) embrague *m*
clut•ter ['klʌtər] **I** *n* desorden *m*; ***all the ~ on my desk*** la cantidad de cosas que hay encima de mi mesa; ***in a ~*** patas arriba F **II** *v/t* (*also*: ***~ up***) abarrotar
CNN [si:en'en] *abbr* (= ***Cable News Network***) CNN *f*
Co. *abbr* (= ***Company***) Cía. (= Compañía *f*)
c/o *abbr* (= ***care of***) en el domicilio de
coach [koʊtʃ] **I** *n* **1** (*trainer*) entrenador(a) *m*(*f*); *of singer, actor* profesor(a) *m*(*f*) **2** *Br* (*bus*) autobús *m* **II** *v/t footballer* entrenar; *singer* preparar; ***~ s.o. in sth*** dar tutorías de algo a alguien
coach•ing ['koʊtʃɪŋ] entrenamiento *m*
'coach trip *Br* viaje *m* en autobús
co•ag•u•late [koʊ'ægjʊleɪt] *v/i of blood* coagularse
co•ag•u•la•tion [koʊægjʊ'leɪʃn] coágulo *m*
coal [koʊl] carbón *m*; ***haul or drag s.o. over the ~s*** *fig* poner de vuelta y media a alguien
co•a•li•tion [koʊə'lɪʃn] coalición *f*; ***form a ~*** formar *or* constituir una coalición; ***~ government*** gobierno *m* de coalición
'coal•mine mina *f* de carbón
'coal min•er minero(-a) *m*(*f*) del carbón
coarse [kɔ:rs] *adj* **1** áspero; *hair* basto **2** (*vulgar*) basto, grosero
coarse•ly ['kɔ:rslɪ] *adv* **1** (*vulgarly*) de manera grosera **2**: ***~ ground coffee*** café molido grueso
coast [koʊst] *n* costa *f*; ***at the ~*** en la cos-

ta; ***the ~ is clear*** *fig* no hay moros en la costa, vía libre **II** *v/i in car* ir en puento muerto; *on bicycle* ir sin pedalear
coast•al ['koustl] *adj* costero
coast•er ['koustər] posavasos *m inv*
'coast•guard *organization* servicio *m* de guardacostas; *person* guardacostas *m/f inv*
'coast•line litoral *m*, costa *f*
coat [kout] **I** *n* **1** chaqueta *f*, *L.Am.* saco *m*; (*over~*) abrigo *m* **2** *of animal* pelaje *m* **3** *of paint etc* capa *f*, mano *f* **II** *v/t* (*cover*) cubrir (***with*** de); ***sugar / chocolate-~ed*** recubierto de azúcar / chocolate
'coat•hang•er percha *f*
'coat hook perchero *m*
coat•ing ['koutɪŋ] capa *f*
coat of 'arms escudo *m* de armas
co-au•thor ['koʊɒ:θər] **I** *n* coautor(a) *m(f)* **II** *v/t*: ***~ a book*** escribir un libro conjuntamente
coax [kouks] *v/t* persuadir; ***~ sth out of s.o.*** sonsacar algo a alguien
cob [kɑ:b] *corn* mazorca *f*
co•balt ['koubɔ:lt] MIN cobalto *m*; ~ (***blue***) (azul) cobalto
cob•ble ['kɑ:bl] adoquín *m*
◆ **cobble together** *v/t* F improvisar
cob•bled ['kɑ:bld] *adj* adoquinado
cob•bler ['kɑ:blər] zapatero(-a) *m(f)*
'cob•ble•stone adoquín *m*
co•bra ['koubrə] ZO cobra *f*
cob•web ['kɑ:bweb] telaraía *f*
co•caine [kə'keɪn] cocaína *f*
cock [kɑ:k] **I** *n chicken* gallo *m*; (*any male bird*) macho *m* **II** *v/t gun* armar, cargar
cock-and-'bull sto•ry F cuento *m* chino F
cock•a•too [kɑ:kə'tu:] ORN cacatúa *f*
cock•er span•iel [kɑ:kər'spænjəl] ZO cocker spaniel *m*
cock•eyed [kɑ:k'aɪd] *adj* F *idea etc* ridículo
'cock•fight pelea *f* de gallos; **'cock-fight•ing** peleas *fpl* de gallos; **'cock•pit** *of plane* cabina *f*; **'cock•roach** cucaracha *f*; **cock'sure** *adj* engreído, arrogante; **'cock•tail** cóctel *m*; **'cock•tail bar** bar *m* de cócteles; **'cock•tail par•ty** cóctel *m*; **'cock•tail shak•er** coctelera *f*; **'cock-up** *Br* F chapucería *f* F
cock•y ['kɑ:kɪ] *adj* F creído, chulo
co•coa ['koukou] *drink* cacao *m*
co•co•nut ['koukənʌt] coco *m*
'co•co•nut palm cocotero *m*
co•coon [kə'ku:n] ZO capullo *m*
COD [si:ou'di:] *abbr* (= ***collect on delivery***) entrega *f* contra reembolso
cod [kɑ:d] bacalao *m*
cod•dle ['kɑ:dl] *v/t sick person* cuidar; *pej*: *child* mimar
code [koud] **I** *n* código *m*; ***in ~*** cifrado; ***~ of honor*** código de honor; ***~ of conduct*** código de conducta **II** *v/t* codificar
'code•word contraseña *f*
cod•i•fy ['koudɪfaɪ] *v/t* LAW codificar, compilar
cod•ing ['koudɪŋ]] codificación *f*
cod-liv•er 'oil aceite *m* de hígado de bacalao
co•ed [kou'ed] EDU F **I** *n student* alumno(-a) *m(f)* de un colegio mixto **II** *adj* mixto
co•ed•u•ca•tion•al [kouedu'keɪʃnl] *adj* mixto
co•ef•fi•cient [kouɪ'fɪʃnt] MATH coeficiente *m*
co•erce [kou'ɜ:rs] *v/t* coaccionar
co•er•cion [kou'ɜ:rʃn] coerción *f*, coacción *f*; ***by ~*** por la fuerza; ***under ~*** bajo coacción
co•er•cive [kou'ɜ:rsɪv] *adj* coercitivo, coactivo
co•ex•ist [kouɪg'zɪst] *v/i* coexistir
co•ex•ist•ence [kouɪg'zɪstəns] coexistencia *f*
cof•fee ['kɑ:fɪ] café *m*; ***a cup of ~*** un café
'cof•fee bar *Br* café *m*, cafetería *f*; **'cof-fee bean** grano *m* de café; **'cof•fee break** pausa *f* para el café; **'cof•fee cup** taza *f* de café; **'cof•fee grind•er** molinillo *m* de café; **'cof•fee grounds** *npl* cafetal *m*; **'cof•fee ma•chine** *in kitchen* cafetera *f*, *in cafeteria*, *hospital etc* máquina *f* del café; **'cof•fee mak•er** cafetera *f* (*para preparar*); **'cof•fee mill** molinillo *m* de café; **'cof•fee pot** cafetera *f* (*para servir*); **'cof•fee shop** café *m*, cafetería *f*; **'cof•fee ta•ble** mesa *f* de centro; **'cof•fee-ta•ble book** *libro de gran tamaño con numerosas ilustraciones*
cof•fin ['kɑ:fɪn] féretro *m*, ataúd *m*
cog [kɑ:g] diente *m*; ***be just a ~ in the machine*** *fig* ser un títere

co•gent ['koʊdʒənt] *adj* convincente
cog•i•tate ['kɑːdʒɪteɪt] *fml* **I** *v/t* meditar, cavilar **II** *v/i* reflexionar; **~ on** *or* **about** reflexionar sobre
co•gnac ['kɑːnjæk] coñac *m*
cog•ni•tion [kɑːg'nɪʃn] cognición *f*
cog•ni•tive ['kɑːgnətɪv] *adj* cognitivo
cog•ni•zance ['kɑːgnɪzəns] *fml* conocimiento *m*; ***take ~ of sth*** tomar algo en cuenta
'cog•wheel rueda *f* dentada
co•hab•it [koʊ'hæbɪt] *v/i* cohabitar
co•hab•i•ta•tion [koʊhæbɪ'teɪʃn] convivencia *f*
co•here [koʊ'hɪr] *v/i* ser coherente *or* congruente
co•her•ence, co•her•en•cy [koʊ'hɪrəns, koʊ'hɪrənsɪ] coherencia *f*
co•her•ent [koʊ'hɪrənt] *adj* coherente
co•he•sion [koʊ'hiːʒn] cohesión *f*
co•he•sive [koʊ'hiːsɪv] *adj* cohesivo
coil [kɔɪl] **I** *n of rope* rollo *m*; *of smoke* espiral *f*; *of snake* anillo *m* **II** *v/t*: **~ (*up*)** enrollar
coin [kɔɪn] moneda *f*; ***the other side of the ~*** *fig* la otra cara de la moneda
coin•age ['kɔɪnɪdʒ] **1** *money* moneda *f* **2** *phrase, word* acuñación *f*
co•in•cide [koʊɪn'saɪd] *v/i* coincidir
co•in•ci•dence [koʊ'ɪnsɪdəns] coincidencia *f*; ***by sheer ~*** por pura casualidad
co•in•ci•den•tal [koʊɪnsɪ'dəntl] *adj* casual, fortuito
coin-op•er•at•ed ['kɔɪnɑːpəreɪtɪd] *adj* a monedas
coke [koʊk] P (*cocaine*) coca *f*
Coke® [koʊk] Coca-Cola® *f*
col•an•der ['kʌləndər] escurridor *m*
cold [koʊld] **I** *adj also fig* frío; ***I'm (feeling) ~*** tengo frío; ***it's ~*** *of weather* hace frío; ***in ~ blood*** a sangre fría; ***a ~ snap*** una ola de frío; ***get ~ feet*** F echarse para atrás F; ***it left me ~*** no me dio ni frío ni calor
II *n* **1** frío *m*; ***I feel left out in the ~*** *fig* siento que se me deja de lado **2** MED resfriado *m*; ***I have a ~*** estoy resfriado, tengo un resfriado; ***catch a ~*** pillar un resfriado
cold-blood•ed [koʊld'blʌdɪd] *adj* de sangre fría; *fig*: *murder* a sangre fría
'cold call COM visita *f* sin avisar; *on telephone* llamada *f* sin avisar; **cold 'call•ing** COM *visitas o llamadas comerciales hechas sin cita previa*; **'cold cuts** *npl* fiambres *mpl*; **'cold drink** bebida *f* fresca; **cold-heart•ed** [koʊld'hɑːrtɪd] *adj* frío
cold•ish ['koʊldɪʃ] *adj* bastante frío
cold•ly ['koʊldlɪ] *adv* fríamente, con frialdad
cold•ness ['koʊldnɪs] frialdad *f*
'cold room cámara *f* frigorífica; **cold 'shoul•der** F: ***give s.o. the ~*** volver la espalda a alguien F; **'cold sore** calentura *f*; **cold 'start** COMPUT, MOT arranque *m* en frío; **cold 'stor•age** refrigeración *f*; **'cold store** almacén *m* frigorífico
cold 'tur•key P: ***go ~*** *of drug addict* limpiarse de la noche a la mañana P; ***give up smoking ~*** dejar de fumar de la noche a la mañana
cold 'war POL guerra *f* fría
cole•slaw ['koʊlslɒː] *ensalada de col, cebolla, zanahoria y mayonesa*
col•ic ['kɑːlɪk] cólico *m*
col•lab•o•rate [kə'læbəreɪt] *v/i* colaborar (***on*** en)
col•lab•o•ra•tion [kəlæbə'reɪʃn] colaboración *f*; ***in ~ with*** con la colaboración de
col•lab•o•ra•tor [kə'læbəreɪtər] colaborador(a) *m(f)*; *with enemy* colaboracionista *m/f*
col•lage [kə'lɑːʒ] colage *m*
col•lapse [kə'læps] **I** *v/i of roof, building* hundirse, desplomarse; *of person, the dollar* desplomarse **II** *n of roof, building* derrumbamiento *m*; *of the dollar* desplome *m*; ***nervous ~*** ataque *m* de nervios
col•lap•si•ble [kə'læpsəbl] *adj* plegable
col•lar ['kɑːlər] cuello *m*; *for dog* collar *m*
'col•lar-bone clavícula *f*
col•lat•er•al [kə'lætərəl] aval *m*
col•lat•er•al 'dam•age MIL daños *mpl* colaterales
col•league ['kɑːliːg] colega *m/f*
col•lect [kə'lekt] **I** *v/t* recoger; *taxes* recaudar; *as hobby* coleccionar **II** *v/i* **1** (*gather together*) reunirse **2**: ***we're collecting for charity*** estamos haciendo una colecta para una obra benéfica **III** *adv*: ***call ~*** llamar a cobro revertido
col'lect call llamada *f* a cobro revertido

C

col•lect•ed [kə'lektɪd] *adj* **1** *works, poems etc* completo **2** *person* sereno
col•lec•tion [kə'lekʃn] colección *f*, *in church* colecta *f*
col•lec•tive [kə'lektɪv] *adj* colectivo; **~ agreement** convenio *m* colectivo
col•lec•tive 'bar•gain•ing negociación *f* colectiva
col•lec•tive•ly [kə'lektɪvlɪ] *adv* colectivamente, conjuntamente
col•lec•tive 'noun nombre *m* colectivo
col•lec•tor [kə'lektər] coleccionista *m/f*; **~'s item** pieza *f* de coleccionista
col•lege ['kɑ:lɪdʒ] universidad *f*
col•le•gi•ate [kə'li:dʒɪət] *adj* universitario
col•lide [kə'laɪd] *v/i* chocar, colisionar (***with*** con *or* contra)
col•lie ['kɑ:lɪ] collie *m*
col•li•sion [kə'lɪʒn] choque *m*, colisión *f*; ***be on a ~ course*** *fig* estar en la antesala de un conflicto
col•lo•qui•al [kə'loʊkwɪəl] *adj* coloquial
col•lo•qui•al•ism [kə'loʊkwɪəlɪzəm] expresión *f* coloquial
col•lude [kə'lu:d] *v/i* confabularse; **~ *with s.o.*** colaborar clandestinamente con alguien
col•lu•sion [kə'lu:ʒn] confabulación *f*
Co•lom•bi•a [kə'lʌmbɪə] Colombia *f*
Co•lom•bi•an [kə'lʌmbɪən] **I** *adj* colombiano **II** *n* colombiano(-a) *m(f)*
co•lon ['koʊlən] **1** *punctuation* dos puntos *mpl* **2** ANAT colon *m* **3** FIN colón *m*
colo•nel ['kɜ:rnl] coronel *m*
co•lo•ni•al [kə'loʊnɪəl] *adj* colonial
co•lo•ni•al•ism [kə'loʊnɪəlɪzəm] POL colonialismo *m*
co•lo•ni•al 'split-lev•el casa *f* de estilo colonial de dos plantas
col•o•nist ['kɑ:lənɪst] *who lives in a colony* colono(-a) *m(f)*; *who helped found a colony* colonizador(a) *m(f)*
col•o•ni•za•tion [kɑ:lənaɪ'zeɪʃn] colonización *f*
col•o•nize ['kɑ:lənaɪz] *v/t country* colonizar
col•on•nade [kɑ:lə'neɪd] ARCHI columnata *f*
co•lo•ny ['kɑ:lənɪ] colonia *f*
col•or ['kʌlər] **I** *n* color *m*; ***in ~*** *movie etc* en color; **~*s*** MIL bandera *f*; ***what ~ is …?*** ¿de qué color es …?; ***paint sth in glowing ~s*** *fig* poner algo de color de rosa; ***pass an examination with flying ~s*** aprobar un exámen con muy buena nota; ***show one's true ~s*** *fig* mostrarse tal y como uno es **II** *v/t one's hair* teñir **III** *v/i* (*blush*) ruborizarse
Col•o•rad•o bee•tle [kɑ:lərɑ:doʊ'bi:tl] ZO escarabajo *m* de la patata
'col•or bar segregación *f* racial; **'col•or-blind** *adj* daltónico; **'col•or chart** muestrario *m* de colores; **col•or-cod•ed** ['kʌlərkoʊdɪd] *adj* codificado con colores; **'col•or cod•ing** código *m* de colores
col•ored ['kʌlərd] *adj person* de color; **~ *pencil*** lápiz *m* de color, pintura *f*
'col•or fast *adj* que no destiñe
col•or 'film PHOT película *f* en color
col•or•ful ['kʌlərfəl] *adj* lleno de colores; *account* colorido
col•or•ing ['kʌlərɪŋ] **1** color *m* **2**: **~ *book*** libro *m* para colorear
col•or•less ['kʌlərlɪs] *adj* **1** incoloro **2** *fig* aburrido, insípido
'col•or pho•to•graph fotografía *f* en color; **'col•or print•er** impresora *f* en color; **'col•or print•ing** impresión *f* en color; **'col•or scheme** combinación *f* de colores; **col•or 'sup•ple•ment** revista *f or* suplemento *m* a todo color; **col•or T'V** televisión *f* en color
co•los•sal [kə'lɑ:sl] *adj* colosal
co•los•sus [kə'lɑ:səs] (*pl* ***colossi*** [kə'lɑ:saɪ], ***-suses***) gigante *m/f*, coloso *m/f*
col•our *etc Br* ☞ ***color*** *etc*
colt [koʊlt] potro *m*
Co•lum•bus [kə'lʌmbəs] Colón
col•umn ['kɑ:ləm] *architectural, of text* columna *f*
col•um•nist ['kɑ:ləmnɪst] columnista *m/f*
co•ma ['koʊmə] coma *m*; ***be in a ~*** estar en coma
comb [koʊm] **I** *n* peine *m* **II** *v/t hair, area* peinar; **~ *one's hair*** peinarse
◆ **comb through** *v/t fig* buscar minuciosamente en
com•bat ['kɑ:mbæt] **I** *n* combate *m* **II** *v/t* combatir
com•bi•na•tion [kɑ:mbɪ'neɪʃn] combinación *f*
com•bi'na•tion lock cierre *m* de combinación

C

com•bine [kəm'baɪn] **I** *v/t* combinar; *ingredients* mezclar; **~ *business with pleasure*** combinar el placer con los negocios **II** *v/i* combinarse; ***everything ~d against him*** todo se volvió contra él **III** *n* ['kɑːmbaɪn] COM complejo *m* industrial

com•bined [kəm'baɪnd] *adj* combinado, coordinado

com•bine har•vest•er [kɑːmbaɪn'hɑːrvɪstər] cosechadora *f*

com•bus•ti•ble [kəm'bʌstɪbl] *adj* combustible

com•bus•tion [kəm'bʌstʃn] combustión *f*

com'bus•tion en•gine motor *m* de combustión

come [kʌm] **I** *v/i* (*pret* ***came***, *pp* ***come***) **1** *toward speaker* venir; *toward listener* ir; *of train, bus* llegar, venir; ***don't ~ too close*** no te acerques demasiado; ***he came to see us*** nos vino a ver; ***~ and go*** ir y venir; ***~ near to doing sth*** estar a punto de hacer algo; ***~ what may*** pase lo que pase; ***generations to ~*** las generaciones venideras *or* futuras; ***~ to think of it ...*** ahora que lo pienso ...; ***~ again?*** F ¿que has dicho?, ¿qué?, ¿qué qué?

2: ***you'll ~ to like it*** llegará a gustarte; ***how ~?*** F ¿y eso?; ***as I came to know him I realized that ...*** al irlo conociendo me di cuenta de que ...; ***~ to know sth*** descubrir algo; ***I have ~ to believe that...*** he llegado a la conclusión de que...; ***when it ~s to paying*** a la hora de pagar; ***~ true*** cumplirse, hacerse realidad; ***it doesn't ~ cheap*** no es ninguna ganga; ***how ~ you've stopped going to the club?*** ¿cómo es que has dejado de ir al club?

II *int*: ***~, ~!*** ¡venga!

◆ **come about** *v/i* (*happen*) pasar, suceder

◆ **come across I** *v/t* (*find*) encontrar **II** *v/i*: ***his humor comes across as ...*** su humor da la impresión de ser ...; ***she comes across as ...*** da la impresión de ser ...

◆ **come across with** *v/t* F *money* aflojar P, *Span* apoquinar F, *CSur* ponerse con P; *information* soltar P

◆ **come along** *v/i* **1** (*come too*) venir; ***why don't you come along?*** ¿por qué no te vienes conmigo / con nosotros? **2** (*turn up*) aparecer **3** (*progress*) marchar; ***come along!*** F ¡venga, vamos! F, ¡hala, hala! F

◆ **come apart** *v/i* **1** desmontarse **2** (*break*) romperse; *of alibi etc* venirse abajo

◆ **come around** *v/i* **1** *to s.o.'s home* venir, pasarse **2** (*regain consciousness*) volver en sí **3** *to a person's point of view* convencerse; ***I've come around to your way of thinking*** me he convencido de que tienes la razón

◆ **come at** *v/t* **1** *attack* atacar **2** *approach* acercarse a; *problem* abordar

◆ **come away** *v/i* (*leave*) salir; *of button etc* caerse

◆ **come back** *v/i* volver; *from losing position* recuperarse; ***it came back to me*** lo recordé; ***come back to sth*** retomar algo; *subject* volver a; ***can I come back to you on that later?*** ¿puedo darte una respuesta más tarde?

◆ **come between** *v/t people* interponerse entre

◆ **come by I** *v/i* pasarse **II** *v/t* (*acquire*) conseguir; ***how did you come by that bruise?*** ¿cómo te has dado ese golpe?

◆ **come down I** *v/i* bajar; *of rain, snow* caer; ***come down in the world*** venirse a menos **II** *v/t*: ***he came down the stairs*** bajó las escaleras

◆ **come down on** *v/t* (*reprimand*) reprender; ***come down hard on s.o.*** ser duro con alguien

◆ **come down to** *v/t factor, person* depender de

◆ **come down with** *v/t disease, illness* pillar

◆ **come for** *v/t* **1** (*attack*) atacar **2** (*collect thing*) venir a por; (*collect person*) venir a buscar a

◆ **come forward** *v/i* (*present o.s.*) presentarse

◆ **come from** *v/t* (*travel from*) venir de; (*originate from*) ser de; ***that's what comes from not paying attention*** eso es lo que pasa *or* sucede cuando no se presta atención; ***I see where you're coming from*** ya veo lo que te quieres decir

◆ **come in** *v/i* entrar; *of train* llegar; *of tide* subir; ***come in!*** ¡entre!, ¡adelante!; ***~ second*** quedar en segunda posición;

C

where do I come in? ¿cuál es mi papel en todo esto?, ¿qué pinto yo en todo esto? F
◆ **come in for** *v/t* recibir; ***come in for criticism*** recibir críticas
◆ **come in on** *v/t*: ***come in on a deal*** participar en un negocio
◆ **come into** *v/t* (*inherit*) heredar
◆ **come off** **I** *v/i* **1** *of handle etc* soltarse, caerse; *of paint etc* quitarse **2** *of plan etc* tener éxito, salir bien **II** *v/t*: ***come off it!*** F *expressing disbelief* ¡y qué más! F, ¡anda ya! F, *Span* ¡venga ya!; *expressing annoyance* ¡venga hombre! F
◆ **come on** *v/i* **1** (*progress*) marchar, progresar; ***come on!*** ¡vamos!; ***oh come on, you're exaggerating*** ¡vamos, hombre!, estás exagerando **2** *in play* aparecer, salir **3** (*start*) empezar, comenzar **4** (*behave*): ***come on tough with s.o.*** ser duro con algn; ***he tries to come on like a …*** quiere dar la impresión de ser …
◆ **come on to** *v/t* P (*make advances to*) insinuársele a, *Span* tirarle los tejos a P, *CSur* tirarse un lance con P
◆ **come out** *v/i* salir; *of book* publicarse; *of stain* irse, quitarse; *of secret, scandal* salir a la luz, descubrirse; *of gay* declararse homosexual públicamente; **~ *in a rash*** salir un sarpullido; **~ *against / for sth*** manifestarse *or* declararse en contra / a favor de algo
◆ **come out with** *v/t* F **1** (*say*) salir con, saltar con **2** (*disclose*) decir, soltar
◆ **come over** **I** *v/i* venir, pasarse; ***I came over all faint*** de repente me mareé; ***she came over very quiet*** se quedó muy callada de repente; ***he came over as being rather arrogant*** dio la impresión de ser bastante arrogante **II** *v/t*: ***what's come over you?*** ¿qué mosca te ha picado? F
◆ **come round** *v/i* **1** *visit* venir, pasarse **2** (*recover consciousness*) volver en sí **3** (*change opinion*) entrar en razón
◆ **come through** **I** *v/i arrive* llegar **II** *v/t* (*survive*) sobrevivir a; *test* pasar, aprobar
◆ **come to** **I** *v/t place* llegar a; *of hair, dress, water* llegar hasta; ***that comes to $70*** eso suma 70 dólares; ***it all comes to the same thing*** viene a ser lo mismo; ***when it comes to math …*** cuando se trata de las matemáticas …; ***is this what it has all come to?*** ¿cómo hemos podido llegar a esto? **II** *v/i* (*regain consciousness*) volver en sí
◆ **come together** *v/i of plan, scheme* tomar forma, *L.Am.* empezar a caminar
◆ **come under** *v/t* **1** (*be classified under*) entrar dentro de **2**: ***come under attack*** ser atacado
◆ **come up** *v/i* subir; *of sun* salir; ***something has come up*** ha surgido algo
◆ **come up against** *v/t* enfrentarse a, verse enfrentado a
◆ **come up for** *v/t*: ***come up for discussion*** sacarse a relucir
◆ **come upon** *v/t* (*find*) encontrar
◆ **come up to** *v/t* **1** (*approach*) acercarse a **2** (*be equal to*) equipararse a **3** (*reach*) llegar a; ***it's coming up to three weeks now*** ya van a ser tres semanas
◆ **come up with** *v/t solution* encontrar; ***John came up with a great idea*** a John se le ocurrió una idea estupenda

'come•back regreso *m*; ***make a ~*** regresar; *of team* remontar, hacer una remontada

co•me•di•an [kə'mi:dɪən] humorista *m/f*; *pej* payaso(-a) *m*(*f*)

'come•down gran decepción *f*

com•e•dy ['kɑ:mədɪ] comedia

come•ly ['kʌmlɪ] *adj fml* hermoso, bello

com•er ['kʌmər]: ***the competition is open to all ~s*** la competición está abierta a todos los aspirantes

com•et ['kɑ:mɪt] cometa *m*

come•up•pance [kʌm'ʌpəns] F: ***he'll get his ~*** tendrá su merecido

com•fort ['kʌmfərt] **I** *n* **1** comodidad *f*, confort *m*; ***live in ~*** vivir desahogadamente *or* con holgura **2** (*consolation*) consuelo *m*; ***that's cold ~*** eso no es ningún consuelo **II** *v/t* consolar

com•for•ta•ble ['kʌmfərtəbl] *adj chair* cómodo; *house, room* cómodo, confortable; ***be ~*** *of person* estar cómodo; *financially* estar en una situación holgada; ***make o.s. ~*** ponerse cómodo; ***feel ~*** sentirse cómodo *or* a gusto

com•for•ta•bly ['kʌmfərtəblɪ] *adv* cómodamente; ***they are ~ off*** viven holgadamente

com•fort•er ['kʌmfərtər] *bedcover* cubrecama *m*, colcha *f*

com•fort•ing ['kʌmfərtɪŋ] *adj* reconfortante

com•fort•less ['kʌmfərtlɪs] *adj* sin comodidades, poco confortable

'com•fort sta•tion servicios *mpl* públicos

com•fy ['kʌmfɪ] F cómodo

com•ic ['kɑːmɪk] **I** *n* **1** *to read* cómic *m* **2** (*comedian*) cómico(-a) *m*(*f*) **II** *adj* cómico

com•i•cal ['kɑːmɪkl] *adj* cómico

'com•ic book cómic *m*

com•ic 'op•er•a MUS opereta *f*

com•ics ['kɑːmɪks] *npl* tiras *fpl* cómicas

'com•ic strip tira *f* cómica

com•ing ['kʌmɪŋ] **I** *adj week, meeting* próximo, siguiente **II** *n* llegada *f*; **~s and goings** idas y venidas

com•ma ['kɑːmə] coma *f*

com•mand [kə'mænd] **I** *n* orden *f*, COMPUT comando *m*, instrucción *f*; ***have ~ of 500 men*** estar al cargo *or* frente de 500 soldados; ***his ~ of English*** sus conocimientos *or* su dominio de inglés; ***be in ~*** MIL estar al mando; ***the men under his ~*** los hombres bajo su mando
II *v/t* ordenar, mandar; ***~ s.o.'s admiration*** despertar la admiración de alguien; ***~ respect*** imponer respeto

com•man•dant ['kɑːməndænt] MIL comandante *m/f*

com•man•deer [kɑːmən'dɪr] *v/t* requisar

com•mand•er [kə'mændər] comandante *m/f*

com•mand•er-in-'chief comandante *m/f* en jefe

com•mand•ing of•fi•cer [kə'mændɪŋ] oficial *m/f* al mando

com•mand•ment [kə'mændmənt] mandamiento *m*: ***the Ten Commandments*** REL los Diez Mandamientos

com'mand mod•ule *of spacecraft* módulo *m* de mando

com•man•do [kə'mændoʊ] (*pl* ***-do(e)s***) MIL comando *m*

com•mem•o•rate [kə'meməreɪt] *v/t* conmemorar

com•mem•o•ra•tion [kəmemə'reɪʃn]: ***in ~ of*** en conmemoración de

com•mem•o•ra•tive [kə'memərətɪv] *adj* conmemorativo; ***~ plaque*** placa *f* conmemorativa

com•mence [kə'mens] *v/t & v/i* comenzar

com•mence•ment [kə'mensmənt] comienzo *m*

com•mend [kə'mend] *v/t* encomiar, elogiar

com•mend•a•ble [kə'mendəbl] *adj* encomiable

com•men•da•tion [kəmen'deɪʃn] *for bravery* mención *f*

com•mend•a•to•ry [kɑː'mendətɔːrɪ] *adj fml* comendatorio, de recomendación

com•men•su•rate [kə'menʃərət] *adj*: ***~ with*** acorde con

com•ment ['kɑːment] **I** *n* comentario *m*; ***no ~!*** ¡sin comentarios! **II** *v/i* hacer comentarios (***on*** sobre)

com•men•ta•ry ['kɑːmənterɪ] comentarios *mpl*

'com•men•ta•ry booth TV, RAD cabina *f* de comentaristas

com•men•tate ['kɑːmənteɪt] *v/i* hacer de comentarista

◆ **commentate on** *v/t* comentar

com•men•ta•tor ['kɑːmənteɪtər] comentarista *m/f*

com•merce ['kɑːmɜːrs] comercio *m*

com•mer•cial [kə'mɜːrʃl] **I** *adj* comercial **II** *n* (*advert*) anuncio *m* (publicitario)

com•mer•cial at'taché agregado *m* comercial; **com'mer•cial bank** banco *m* comercial; **com•mer•cial 'break** pausa *f* publicitaria

com•mer•cial•ize [kə'mɜːrʃlaɪz] *v/t Christmas* comercializar

com•mer•cial 'trav•el•er viajante *m/f* de comercio

com•mie ['kɑːmɪ] F *pej* rojo(-a) *m*(*f*) F

com•mis•er•ate [kə'mɪzəreɪt] *v/i*: ***she ~d with me on my failure to get the job*** me dijo cuánto sentía que no hubiera conseguido el trabajo

com•mis•er•a•tion [kəmɪzər'eɪʃn]: ***offer s.o. one's ~s*** compadecerse de alguien

com•mis•sion [kə'mɪʃn] **I** *n* (*payment, committee*) comisión *f*, (*job*) encargo *m*; ***paid on a ~ basis*** pagado a comisión **II** *v/t*: ***she has been commissioned ...*** se le ha encargado ...

com•mis•sion•aire [kəmɪʃə'ner] *Br* portero *m*

C

com•mis•sion•er [kə'mɪʃənər] **1** POL comisario(-a) *m(f)* **2** *police officer* comisario(-a) *m(f)* de policía

com•mis•sion•ing [kə'mɪʃənɪŋ] *of new plant etc* puesta *f* en funcionamiento

com•mit [kə'mɪt] *v/t* (*pret & pp* **-ted**) **1** *crime* cometer **2** *money* comprometer; **~ o.s.** comprometerse; **~ sth to paper** poner algo por escrito

com•mit•ment [kə'mɪtmənt] compromiso *m* (**to** con); **he's afraid of ~** tiene miedo de comprometerse; **without any ~** sin ningún compromiso

com•mit•ted [kə'mɪtɪd] *adj Christian, socialist* comprometido; **be ~ to sth** estar entregado *or* dedicado a algo; **he's ~ to getting the team into shape** se ha comprometido a poner en forma al equipo

com•mit•tee [kə'mɪtɪ] comité *m*; **be** *or* **sit on a ~** formar parte de un comité *or* una comisión

com'mit•tee meet•ing reunión *f* del comité

com'mit•tee mem•ber miembro *m* del comité

com•mode [kə'moʊd] **I** *chest of drawers* cómoda *f* **II** *Br toilet* asiento *m* con orinal

com•mo•di•ous [kə'moʊdjəs] *adj fml* espacioso, amplio

com•mod•i•ty [kə'mɑːdətɪ] *raw material* producto *m* básico; *product* bien *m* de consumo; **language skills are a rare ~** el conocimiento de idiomas es un bien escaso

com'mod•i•ty ex•change bolsa *f* de materias primas

com•mon ['kɑːmən] *adj* común; **in ~** al igual (**with** que); **have sth in ~ with s.o.** tener algo en común con alguien; **by ~ consent** por unanimidad; **it is ~ knowledge that …** es de todos sabido que …; **he was a ~ sight in town** se le veía a menudo por la ciudad; **~ or garden** F corriente y moliente F; **the ~ people** la gente corriente

com•mon•er ['kɑːmənər] plebeyo(-a) *m(f)*

com•mon 'law derecho *m* consuetudinario *or* angloamericano; **com•mon-law 'hus•band** esposo *m* de hecho; **com•mon-law 'mar•riage** matrimonio *m* consensual *or* de hecho; **com•mon law 'wife** esposa *f* de hecho

com•mon•ly ['kɑːmənlɪ] *adv* comúnmente

Com•mon 'Mar•ket Mercado *m* Común Europeo

'com•mon•place *adj* común

'com•mon room *Br* sala *f* de estudiantes / profesores

Com•mons ['kɑːmənz] *pl*: **the ~** PARL *Br* los Comunes

com•mon 'sense sentido *m* común; **it's only ~ to …** es de sentido común …

Com•mon•wealth ['kɑːmənwelθ]: **the ~ (of Nations)** la Comunidad Británica de las Naciones

com•mo•tion [kə'moʊʃn] alboroto *m*

com•mu•nal [kə'mjuːnl] *adj* comunal

com•mu•nal•ly [kəm'juːnəlɪ] *adv* en comunidad

com•mune[1] [kə'mjuːn] *v/i*: **~ with nature / God** estar en comunión con la naturaleza / Dios

com•mune[2] ['kɑːmjuːn] *n* comuna *f*

com•mu•ni•ca•ble [kə'mjuːnɪkəbl] *adj* MED contagioso

com•mu•ni•cate [kə'mjuːnɪkeɪt] **I** *v/i* comunicarse **II** *v/t* comunicar

com•mu•ni•ca•tion [kəmjuːnɪ'keɪʃn] comunicación *f*; **be in ~ with s.o.** estar en contacto con alguien; **have good / poor ~ skills** saber / no saber comunicarse

com•mu•ni'ca•tions *npl* comunicaciones *fpl*

com•mu•ni'ca•tions sat•el•lite satélite *m* de telecomunicaciones

com•mu•ni•ca•tive [kə'mjuːnɪkətɪv] *adj person* comunicativo

Com•mu•nion [kə'mjuːnjən] REL comunión *f*; **take ~** pasar a comulgar

com•mu•ni•qué [kə'mjuːnɪkeɪ] comunicado *m*

Com•mu•nism ['kɑːmjʊnɪzəm] comunismo *m*

Com•mu•nist ['kɑːmjʊnɪst] **I** *adj* comunista **II** *n* comunista *m/f*

com•mu•ni•ty [kə'mjuːnətɪ] comunidad *f*; **~ spirit** espíritu *m* de grupo

com'mu•ni•ty cen•ter centro *m* comunitario; **com'mu•ni•ty ra•di•o** radio *f* comunitaria; **com'mu•ni•ty serv•ice** servicios *mpl* a la comunidad (como pena)

com•mu•ta•tion [kɑːmjuː'teɪʃn] LAW

conmutación *f*
com•mute [kə'mju:t] **I** *v/i* viajar al trabajo; **~ *to work*** viajar al trabajo **II** *v/t* LAW conmutar
com•mut•er [kə'mju:tər] *persona que viaja al trabajo*
com'mut•er 'air•line línea *f* aérea de cercanías; **com'mut•er belt** *zona desde la que la gente viaja al trabajo*; **com'mut•er plane** avión *m* de cercanías; **com'mut•er town** ciudad *f* dormitorio; **com'mut•er traf•fic** *tráfico generado por los que se desplazan al trabajo*; **com'mut•er train** *tren de cercanías que utilizan los que se desplazan al trabajo*
comp [ka:mp] F indemnización *f*
com•pact I *adj* [kəm'pækt] compacto **II** *n* ['ka:mpækt] MOT utilitario *m* **III** *v/t* [kəm'pækt] comprimir
com•pact 'disc (disco *m*) compacto *m*
com•pact 'disc play•er reproductor *m* de (discos) compactos
com•pan•ion [kəm'pænjən] compañero(-a) *m(f)*
com•pan•ion•a•ble [kəm'pænjənəbl] *adj* sociable, simpático
com•pan•ion•ship [kəm'pænjənʃɪp] compañía *f*
com•pa•ny ['kʌmpənɪ] **1** COM empresa *f*, compañía *f*
2 (*companionship*, *guests*) compañía *f*; ***keep s.o. ~*** hacer compañía a alguien; ***in ~ with*** en compañía de, junto con; ***be in good ~*** estar en buena compañía; ***be good ~*** ser buena compañía; ***keep bad ~*** ir con malas compañías; ***part ~ with s.o.*** *separate* separarse de alguien; *fig* dejar de estar de acuerdo con alguien; ***present ~ excepted!*** ¡mejorando lo presente!
com•pa•ny 'car coche *m* de empresa; **com•pa•ny 'law** derecho *m* de sociedades; **com•pa•ny 'name** razón *f* social; **com•pa•ny 'pen•sion** *plan* plan *m* de jubilación de la empresa; *payment* pensión *f* de jubilación de la empresa; **com•pa•ny 'pro•file** perfil *m* de empresa; **com•pa•ny 'sec•ret•ary** secretario(-a) *m(f)* de la empresa
com•pa•ra•ble ['ka:mpərəbl] *adj* comparable
com•par•a•tive [kəm'pærətɪv] **I** *adj* (*relative*) relativo; *study* comparado, comparativo; GRAM comparativo; **~ *form*** GRAM comparativo *m* **II** *n* GRAM comparativo *m*
com•par•a•tive•ly [kəm'pærətɪvlɪ] *adv* relativamente
com•pare [kəm'per] **I** *v/t* comparar; ***~d with ...*** comparado con ...; ***you can't ~ them*** no se pueden comparar; ***this is not to be ~d with*** *or* ***to*** ésto no tiene ni punto de comparación con **II** *v/i* compararse; **~ *favorably with*** ser tan bueno como **III** *n*: ***beyond ~*** sin igual, inigualable
com•pa•ri•son [kəm'pærɪsn] comparación *f*; ***there's no ~*** no hay punto de comparación; ***by ~*** en comparación; ***in ~ with*** en comparación con
com•part•ment [kəm'pa:rtmənt] compartimento *m*
com•pass ['kʌmpəs] **1** brújula *f* **2** GEOM compás *m*
com•pas•sion [kəm'pæʃn] compasión *f*
com•pas•sion•ate [kəm'pæʃənət] *adj* compasivo
com•pas•sion•ate 'leave *permiso laboral por muerte o enfermedad grave de un familiar*
com•pat•i•bil•i•ty [kəmpætə'bɪlɪtɪ] compatibilidad *f*
com•pat•i•ble [kəm'pætəbl] *adj* compatible; ***be ~*** ser compatible (***with*** con)
com•pa•tri•ot [kəm'peɪtrɪət] compatriota *m/f*
com•pel [kəm'pel] *v/t* (*pret & pp* ***-led***) obligar; ***be ~led to do sth*** ser obligado a hacer algo
com•pel•ling [kəm'pelɪŋ] *adj argument* poderoso; *movie*, *book* fascinante
com•pen•di•um [kəm'pendɪəm] *book* compendio *m*
com•pen•sate ['ka:mpənseɪt] **I** *v/t with money* compensar **II** *v/i*: **~ *for*** compensar
com•pen•sa•tion [ka:mpən'seɪʃn] **1** *money* indemnización *f* **2** (*reward*, *comfort*) compensación *f*; ***in ~ for*** en compensación por
com•père, com•pere ['ka:mper] *Br* **I** *n* presentador(a) *m(f)* **II** *v/t* presentar
com•pete [kəm'pi:t] *v/i* competir (***for*** por, ***with*** con)
com•pe•tence ['ka:mpɪtəns] competencia *f*
com•pe•tent ['ka:mpɪtənt] *adj* compe-

tente; ***I'm not ~ to judge*** no estoy capacitado para juzgar

com•pe•tent•ly ['kɑːmpɪtəntlɪ] *adv* competentemente

com•pe•ti•tion [kɑːmpəˈtɪʃn] **1** (*contest*) concurso *m*; SP competición *f* **2** (*competitors*) competencia *f*; ***the government wants to encourage ~*** el gobierno quiere fomentar la competencia; ***unfair ~*** COM competición desleal

com•pet•i•tive [kəm'petətɪv] *adj* competitivo

com•pet•i•tive 'edge ventaja *f* competitiva

com•pet•i•tive•ly [kəm'petətɪvlɪ] *adv* competitivamente: ***~ priced*** con un precio muy competitivo

com•pet•i•tive•ness [kəm'petɪtɪvnɪs] **1** COM competitividad *f* **2** *of person* espíritu *m* competitivo

com•pet•i•tor [kəm'petɪtər] **1** *in contest* concursante *m/f*; SP competidor(a) *m(f)*, contrincante *m/f* **2** COM competidor(a) *m(f)*

com•pi•la•tion [kɑːmpɪ'leɪʃn] MUS recopilatorio *m*

com•pile [kəm'paɪl] *v/t* compilar

com•pla•cen•cy [kəm'pleɪsənsɪ] complacencia *f*

com•pla•cent [kəm'pleɪsənt] *adj* complaciente

com•plain [kəm'pleɪn] *v/i* **1** quejarse, protestar; *to shop, manager* quejarse; ***~ about sth*** quejarse de algo **2** MED: ***~ of*** estar aquejado de

com•plaint [kəm'pleɪnt] **1** queja *f*, protesta *f*; ***make*** *or* ***lodge a ~*** presentar una queja, hacer una reclamación; ***letter of ~*** carta *f* de protesta; *to hotel, shop, company* carta *f* de reclamación **2** MED dolencia *f*

com•ple•ment ['kɑːmplɪmənt] *v/t* complementar; ***they ~ each other*** se complementan

com•ple•men•ta•ry [kɑːmplɪ'mentərɪ] *adj* complementario; ***the two are ~*** los dos se complementan; ***be ~ to sth*** complementarse con algo

com•plete [kəm'pliːt] **I** *adj* (*total*) absoluto, total; (*full*) completo; (*finished*) finalizado, terminado **II** *v/t task, building etc* finalizar, terminar; *course* completar; *form* rellenar

com•plete•ly [kəm'pliːtlɪ] *adv* completamente

com•plete•ness [kəm'pliːtnɪs] lo completo

com•ple•tion [kəm'pliːʃn] finalización *f*, terminación *f*; ***bring sth to ~*** llevar a término algo; ***~ date*** fecha *f* de terminación

com•plex ['kɑːmpleks] **I** *adj* complejo **II** *n also* PSYCH complejo *m*

com•plex•ion [kəm'plekʃn] *facial* tez *f*; ***that puts a different ~ on the matter*** eso hace que el asunto tome un cariz diferente

com•plex•i•ty [kəm'pleksɪtɪ] complejidad *f*

com•pli•ance [kəm'plaɪəns] cumplimiento (***with*** de); ***in ~ with the regulations / the law*** de acuerdo a las normas / la ley; ***in ~ with my late aunt's wishes*** por voluntad de mi tía difunta

com•pli•ant [kəm'plaɪənt] *adj* sumiso, obediente

com•pli•cate ['kɑːmplɪkeɪt] *v/t* complicar

com•pli•cat•ed ['kɑːmplɪkeɪtɪd] *adj* complicado

com•pli•ca•tion [kɑːmplɪ'keɪʃn] complicación *f*; ***~s*** MED complicaciones *fpl*

com•plic•i•ty [kəm'plɪsətɪ] complicidad *f*

com•pli•ment ['kɑːmplɪmənt] **I** *n* cumplido *m*; ***pay s.o. a ~*** decir un cumplido a alguien; *by one's actions* hacer un cumplido a alguien; ***with the ~ of*** con saludos de **II** *v/t* hacer un cumplido a (***on*** por)

com•pli•men•ta•ry [kɑːmplɪ'mentərɪ] *adj* **1** elogioso **2** (*free*) de regalo, gratis; ***~ ticket*** entrada *f* gratuita

'com•pli•ments slip nota *f* de cortesia

com•ply [kəm'plaɪ] *v/i* (*pret & pp* ***-ied***) cumplir; ***~ with*** cumplir; ***~ with the law*** acatar la ley

com•po•nent [kəm'pounənt] pieza *f*, componente *m*; ***~ part*** pieza componente

com•pose [kəm'pouz] *v/t also* MUS componer; ***be ~d of*** estar compuesto de; ***~ o.s.*** serenarse

com•posed [kəm'pouzd] *adj* (*calm*) sereno

com•pos•er [kəm'pouzər] MUS compositor(a) *m(f)*

com•pos•ite ['kɑːmpəzɪt] combinación *f* (***of*** de)

com•po•si•tion [kɑːmpə'zɪʃn] **1** *also* MUS composición *f* **2** (*essay*) redacción *f*

com•pos•i•tor [kəm'pɑːzɪtər] (*typesetter*) cajista *m/f*

com•post ['kɑːmpɑːst] abono *m*, fertilizante *m*

'com•post heap *plantas y estiércol amontonados en el jardín para producir abono*

com•po•sure [kəm'poʊʒər] compostura *f*

com•pote ['kɑːmpɑːt] compota *f*

com•pound[1] ['kɑːmpaʊnd] *n* CHEM compuesto *m*

com•pound[2] [kəm'paʊnd] **I** *v/t* **1** CHEM combinar **2** *problem* empeorar, agravar **II** *adj* ['kɑːmpaʊnd] *eye*, *fracture* compuesto

com•pound[3] ['kɑːmpaʊnd] *n enclosure* recinto *m* cerrado

com•pound in•ter•est ['kɑːmpaʊnd] interés *m* compuesto *or* combinado

com•pre•hend [kɑːmprɪ'hend] *v/t fml* (*understand*) comprender

com•pre•hen•si•ble [kɑːmprɪ'hensɪbl] *adj* comprensible

com•pre•hen•sion [kɑːmprɪ'henʃn] comprensión *f*; ***beyond ~*** incomprensible *or* inexplicable

com•pre•hen•sive [kɑːmprɪ'hensɪv] *adj* detallado

com•pre•hen•sive in'sur•ance seguro *m* a todo riesgo

com•pre•hen•sive•ly [kɑːmprɪ'hensɪvlɪ] *adv* **1** (*in detail*) detalladamente **2** *beaten* totalmente

com•press I *n* ['kɑːmpres] MED compresa *f* **II** *v/t* [kəm'pres] *air*, *gas* comprimir; *information* condensar; ***~ed air*** aire *m* comprimido

com•pres•sion [kəm'preʃn] compresión *f*

com•pres•sor [kəm'presər] TECH compresor *m*

com•prise [kəm'praɪz] *v/t* comprender; ***be ~d of*** constar de

com•pro•mise ['kɑːmprəmaɪz] **I** *n* solución *f* negociada; ***I've had to make ~s all my life*** toda mi vida he tenido que hacer concesiones; ***reach a ~*** llegar a una solución de mutuo acuerdo; ***~ solution*** solución *f* negociada **II** *v/i* transigir, efectuar concesiones **III** *v/t principles* traicionar; (*jeopardize*) poner en peligro; ***~ o.s.*** ponerse en un compromiso

comp•trol•ler [kən'troʊlər] tesorero(-a) *m*(*f*)

com•pul•sion [kəm'pʌlʃn] **1** PSYCH compulsión *f* **2**: ***be under no ~ to do sth*** no tener la obligación de hacer algo

com•pul•sive [kəm'pʌlsɪv] *adj* **1** *behavior* compulsivo **2** *reading* absorbente

com•pul•so•ry [kəm'pʌlsərɪ] *adj* obligatorio

com•pu•ta•tion [kɑːmpjuː'teɪʃn] cómputo *m*, cálculo *m*

com•pu•ta•tion•al [kɑːmpjuː'teɪʃnl] *adj* computacional

com•pute [kəm'pjuːt] *v/t fml* computar, calcular

com•put•er [kəm'pjuːtər] *Span* ordenador *m*, *L.Am.* computadora *f*; ***have sth on ~*** tener algo en el *Span* ordenador *or L.Am.* computadora

com'put•er age era *f* de la informática *or L.Am.* las computadoras; **com•put•er-aid•ed** [kəmpjuːtər'eɪdɪd] *adj* asistido por *Span* ordenador *or L.Am.* computadora; **com•put•er-aid•ed de'sign** diseño *m* asistido por *Span* ordenador *or L.Am.* computadora; **com•put•er-aid•ed en•gi'neer•ing** ingeniería *f* asistida por *Span* ordenador *or L.Am.* computadora; **com•put•er-aid•ed 'learn•ing** enseñanza *f* asistida por *Span* ordenador *or L.Am.* computadora; **com•put•er-aid•ed man•u'fac•ture** fabricación *f* asistida por *Span* ordenador *or L.Am.* computadora; **com•put•er an•i'ma•tion** animación *f* por *Span* ordenador *or L.Am.* computadora; **com•put•er-as•sist•ed** [kəmpjuːtərə'sɪstɪd] ☞ ***computer-aided***; **com•put•er-con'trolled** *adj* controlado por *Span* ordenador *or L.Am.* computadora; **com'put•er game** juego *m* de *Span* ordenador *or L.Am.* computadora; **com'put•er ex•pert** experto(-a) *m*(*f*) en informática *or L.Am. also* computadoras; **com•put•er 'graphics** *npl* infografía *f*; **com•put•er 'hard•ware** hardware *m* (informático)

com•put•er•i•za•tion [kəmpjuːtəraɪ-

'zeɪʃn] informatización *f*, *L.Am. also* computerización *f*
com•put•er•ize [kəm'pju:təraɪz] *v/t* informatizar, *L.Am. also* computarizar
com'put•er lan•guage lenguaje *m* informático *or* de programación; **com•put•er 'lit•er•a•cy** conocimientos *mpl* de informática *or L.Am. also* computadoras; **com•put•er 'lit•er•ate** *adj* con conocimientos de informática *or L.Am. also* computación; **com•put•er 'net•work** red *f* informática *or L.Am also* de computadoras; **com'put•er op•er•a•tor** operador(a) *m*(*f*) informático *or L.Am. also* de computadoras; **com•put•er 'print•out** listado *m*; **com'put•er pro•gram** programa *m* informático; **com•put•er 'pro•gram•mer** programador(a) *m*(*f*) informático; **com•put•er 'sci•ence** informática *f*, *L.Am. also* computación *f*; **com•put•er 'sci•en•tist** informático(-a) *m*(*f*); **com•put•er 'sys•tem** sistema *m* informático; **com•put•er 'ter•min•al** terminal *m* de *Span* ordenador *or L.Am.* computadora; **com•put•er 'vi•rus** virus *m* informático
com•put•ing [kəm'pju:tɪŋ] informática *f*, *L.Am. also* computación *f*
com•rade ['kɑ:mreɪd] (*friend*) compañero(-a) *m*(*f*); POL camarada *m*/*f*
com•rade•ship ['kɑ:mreɪdʃɪp] camaradería *f*
con[1] [kɑ:n] F **I** *n* timo *m* **II** *v/t* (*pret & pp* **-ned**) timar; **~ s.o. out of sth** soplar *or* birlar a alguien algo F; **~ s.o. into doing sth** engañar *or* liar a alguien para que haga algo
con[2] [kɑ:n] *n*: **the pros and ~s of sth** los pros y los contras de algo
con•cave ['kɑ:ŋkeɪv] *adj* cóncavo
con•ceal [kən'si:l] *v/t* ocultar
con•ceal•ment [kən'si:lmənt] ocultación *f*
con•cede [kən'si:d] *v/t* **1** (*admit*) admitir, reconocer **2** *goal* encajar; *penalty* cometer
con•ceit [kən'si:t] engreimiento *m*, presunción *f*; **be full of ~** ser un engreído
con•ceit•ed [kən'si:tɪd] *adj* engreido, presuntuoso
con•ceiv•a•ble [kən'si:vəbl] *adj* concebible
con•ceive [kən'si:v] *v/i* **1** *of woman* concebir **2**: **~ of** (*imagine*) imaginar
con•cen•trate ['kɑ:nsəntreɪt] **I** *v/i* concentrarse **II** *v/t one's attention*, *energies* concentrar
con•cen•trat•ed ['kɑ:nsəntreɪtɪd] *adj juice etc* concentrado
con•cen•tra•tion [kɑ:nsən'treɪʃn] concentración *f*; **power of ~** capacidad *f* de concentración
con•cen'tra•tion camp campo *m* de concentración
con•cen•tric [kən'sentrɪk] *adj* concéntrico
con•cept ['kɑ:nsept] concepto *m*
con•cep•tion [kən'sepʃn] *of child* concepción *f*
con•cep•tu•al [kən'septʃuəl] *adj* conceptual
con•cern [kən'sɜ:rn] **I** *n* **1** (*anxiety*, *care*) preocupación *f*; **cause ~** preocupar, inquietar; **a matter of national ~** un problema a nivel nacional **2** (*business*) asunto *m*; **it's none of your ~** no es asunto tuyo; **that is no ~ of mine** eso no es asunto mío **3** (*company*) empresa *f*
II *v/t* **1** (*involve*) concernir, incumbir; *of story*, *report* tratar de **2** (*worry*) preocupar, inquietar; **~ o.s. with** preocuparse de
con•cerned [kən'sɜ:rnd] *adj* **1** (*anxious*) preocupado, inquieto (**about** por) **2** (*caring*) preocupado (**about** por) **3** (*involved*) en cuestión; **as far as I'm ~** por lo que a mí respecta
con•cern•ing [kən'sɜ:rnɪŋ] *prep* en relación con, sobre
con•cert ['kɑ:nsərt] **1** concierto *m* **2**: **in ~ with** en conjunción con
con•cert•ed [kən'sɜ:rtɪd] *adj* (*joint*) concertado, conjunto; **take ~ action** actuar de manera concertada
'con•cert hall auditorio *m*
'con•cert•mas•ter primer violín *m*/*f*
con•cer•to [kən'tʃertou] concierto *m*; **violin ~** concierto para violín
con•cert 'pi•an•ist pianista *m*/*f* de concierto
con•ces•sion [kən'seʃn] (*compromise*) concesión *f*
con•ces•sion•aire [kənseʃə'ner] COM concesionario(-a) *m*(*f*)
conch [kɑ:nʃ] ZO concha *f*, caracola *f*
con•cil•i•a•tion [kənsɪlɪ'eɪʃn] concilia-

ción *f*, reconciliación *f*
con•cil•i•a•to•ry [kənsɪlɪ'eɪtɔːrɪ] *adj* conciliador
con•cise [kən'saɪs] *adj* conciso
con•cise•ness, con•ci•sion [kən'saɪsnɪs, kən'sɪʒn] concisión *f*, brevedad *f*
con•clude [kən'kluːd] *v/t & v/i* **1** (*deduce*) concluir (***from*** de); ***~ that*** ir a la conclusión de que **2** (*end*) concluir
con•clud•ing [kən'kluːdɪŋ] *adj* conclusivo, final
con•clu•sion [kən'kluːʒn] **1** (*deduction*) conclusión *f*; ***come to*** *or* ***arrive at the ~ that*** llegar a la conclusión de que; ***draw a ~*** sacar una conclusión; ***jump to ~s*** sacar conclusiones antes de tiempo **2** (*end*) conclusión *f*; ***bring sth to a ~*** concluir algo, poner fin a algo; ***in ~*** en conclusión
con•clu•sive [kən'kluːsɪv] *adj* concluyente
con•coct [kən'kaːkt] *v/t meal, drink* preparar; *excuse, story* urdir
con•coc•tion [kən'kaːkʃn] *food* mejunje *m*; *drink* brebaje *m*, pócima *f*
con•cord ['kaːŋkɔːrd] *fml* concordia *f*
con•course ['kaːŋkɔːrs] *in station* hall *m*
con•crete ['kaːŋkriːt] **I** *adj* concreto; ***~ jungle*** jungla *f* de asfalto **II** *n* hormigón *m*, *L.Am.* concreto *m*
'con•crete mix•er hormigonera *f*
con•cur [kən'kɜːr] *v/i* (*pret & pp* ***-red***) coincidir; ***~ with s.o. that*** coincidir con alguien en que
con•cur•rent [kən'kɜːrənt] *adj* concurrente, simultáneo
con•cuss [kən'kʌs] *v/t* conmocionar; ***be ~ed*** sufrir una conmoción cerebral
con•cus•sion [kən'kʌʃn] conmoción *f* cerebral; ***have ~*** sufrir una conmoción cerebral
con•demn [kən'dem] *v/t* **1** condenar **2** *building* declarar en ruina
con•dem•na•tion [kaːndəm'neɪʃn] *of action* condena *f*
con•demned cell [kən'demd] celda *f* de los condenados a muerte
con•den•sa•tion [kaːnden'seɪʃn] *on walls, windows* condensación *f*
con•dense [kən'dens] **I** *v/t* (*make shorter*) condensar **II** *v/i of steam* condensarse
con•densed milk [kən'densd] leche *f* condensada
con•dens•er [kən'densər] TECH condensador *m*
con•de•scend [kaːndɪ'send] *v/i*: ***he ~ed to speak to me*** se dignó a hablarme
con•de•scend•ing [kaːndɪ'sendɪŋ] *adj* (*patronizing*) condescendiente
con•di•ment ['kaːndɪmənt] condimento *m*
con•di•tion [kən'dɪʃn] **I** *n* **1** (*state*) condiciones *fpl*; *of health* estado *m*; *illness* enfermedad *f*; ***~s*** (*circumstances*) condiciones; ***you're in no ~ to drive*** no estás en condiciones de conducir; ***out of ~*** en baja forma; ***I'm out of ~*** no estoy en forma; ***living ~s*** condiciones de vida; ***weather ~s*** condiciones atmosféricas
2 (*requirement, term*) condición *f*; ***on ~ that …*** a condición de que …; ***on no ~*** bajo ningún concepto, en ningún caso; ***make sth a ~*** poner algo como condición
II *v/t* PSYCH condicionar
con•di•tion•al [kən'dɪʃnl] **I** *adj acceptance* condicional; ***be ~ on*** depender de; ***make sth ~ on sth*** hacer que algo dependa de algo **II** *n* GRAM condicional *m*
con'di•tion•al clause GRAM oración *f* condicional
con•di•tioned re•sponse, con•di•tioned re•flex [kəndɪʃndrɪ'spaːns, kəndɪʃnd'riːfleks] PSYCH reacción *f* *or* respuesta *f* condicional
con•di•tion•er [kən'dɪʃnər] *for hair* suavizante *m*, acondicionador *m*; *for fabric* suavizante *m*
con•di•tion•ing [kən'dɪʃnɪŋ] PSYCH condicionamiento *m*
con•do ['kaːndoʊ] F *apartment* apartamento *m*, *Span* piso *m*; *building* bloque *m* de apartamentos
con•do•len•ces [kən'doʊlənsɪz] *npl* condolencias *fpl*; ***please accept my ~*** le expreso mi sincera condolencia
con•dom ['kaːndəm] condón *m*, preservativo *m*
con•do•min•i•um [kaːndə'mɪnɪəm] ☞ ***condo***
con•done [kən'doʊn] *v/t actions* justificar
con•dor ['kaːndɔːr] ORN cóndor *m*
con•du•cive [kən'duːsɪv] *adj*: ***~ to*** pro-

C

picio para

con•duct I *n* ['kɑːndʌkt] (*behavior*) conducta *f* **II** *v/t* [kən'dʌkt] **1** (*carry out*) realizar, hacer **2** ELEC conducir **3** MUS dirigir **4**: **~ *o.s.*** comportarse

con•duct•ed tour [kən'dʌktɪd] visita *f* guiada

con•duc•tion [kən'dʌkʃn] PHYS conducción *f*

con•duc•tor [kən'dʌktər] **1** MUS director(a) *m(f)* de orquesta **2** *on train* revisor(a) *m(f)* **3** PHYS conductor *m*

con•duit ['kɑːndʊɪt] **1** *for water, gas* conducto *m* **2** *fig* vía *f*, canal *m*; *person* contacto *m*

cone [koʊn] **1** GEOM, *on highway* cono *m* **2** *for ice cream* cucurucho *m* **3** *of pine tree* piña *f*

con•fec•tion [kən'fekʃn] *pastel o tarta minuciosamente decorado*

con•fec•tion•er [kən'fekʃənər] pastelero(-a) *m(f)*

con•fec•tion•ers' 'sug•ar azúcar *m or f* glas

con•fec•tion•e•ry [kən'fekʃənərɪ] (*candy*) dulces *mpl*

con•fed•er•a•cy [kən'fedərəsɪ] confederación *f*

con•fed•er•ate [kən'fedərət] **I** *adj* confederado **II** cómplice *m/f*

con•fed•er•a•tion [kənfedə'reɪʃn] confederación *f*

con•fer [kən'fɜːr] **1** *v/t* (*pret & pp* **-red**): **~ *sth on s.o.*** (*bestow*) conferir *or* otorgar algo a alguien **2** *v/i* (*pret & pp* **-red**) (*discuss*) deliberar

con•fer•ence ['kɑːnfərəns] congreso *m*; *discussion* conferencia *f*; ***be in ~*** estar reunido

'con•fer•ence room sala *f* de conferencias

con•fess [kən'fes] **1** *v/t* confesar **2** *v/i* confesar; REL confesarse; ***~ to a weakness for sth*** confesar una debilidad por algo; ***~ to having done sth*** confesar haber hecho algo

con•fessed [kən'fest] *adj* declarado

con•fes•sion [kən'feʃn] confesión *f*; ***I've a ~ to make*** tengo algo que confesar; ***make a full ~*** LAW realizar una confesión; ***go to ~*** REL confesarse

con•fes•sion•al [kən'feʃnl] REL confesionario *m*

con•fes•sor [kən'fesər] REL confesor *m*

con•fet•ti [kən'fetɪ] *sg* confeti *m*

con•fi•dant [kɑːnfɪ'dænt] confidente *m*

con•fi•dante [kɑːnfɪ'dænt] confidente *f*

con•fide [kən'faɪd] **I** *v/t* confiar (***to*** a) **II** *v/i*: ***~ in s.o.*** confiarse a alguien

con•fi•dence ['kɑːnfɪdəns] **1** confianza *f*; ***have ~ in s.o. / sth*** fiarse de alguien / algo; ***have ~ in o.s.*** tener confianza en sí mismo **2** (*secret*) confidencia *f*; ***take s.o. into one's ~*** confiarse a alguien; ***in ~*** en confianza, confidencialmente

'con•fi•dence man estafador *m*; **'con•fi•dence trick** estafa *f*; **'con•fi•dence trick•ster** estafador(a) *m(f)*

con•fi•dent ['kɑːnfɪdənt] *adj* **1** (*self-assured*) seguro de sí mismo **2** (*convinced*) seguro

con•fi•den•tial [kɑːnfɪ'denʃl] *adj* confidencial, secreto

con•fi•den•tial•ly [kɑːnfɪ'denʃlɪ] *adv* confidencialmente

con•fi•dent•ly ['kɑːnfɪdəntlɪ] *adv* con seguridad

con•fig•u•ra•tion [kənfɪgʊ'reɪʃn] COMPUT configuración *f*

con•fig•ure [kən'fɪgər] *v/t* COMPUT configurar

con•fine [kən'faɪn] *v/t* (*imprison*) confinar, recluir; (*restrict*) limitar; ***be ~d to one's bed*** tener que guardar cama

con•fined [kən'faɪnd] *adj space* limitado

con•fine•ment [kən'faɪnmənt] **1** (*imprisonment*) reclusión *f* **2** MED parto *m*

con•firm [kən'fɜːrm] *v/t* confirmar; ***be ~ed*** REL confirmarse, hacer la confirmación

con•fir•ma•tion [kɑːnfər'meɪʃn] *also* REL confirmación *f*

con•firmed [kɑːn'fɜːrmd] *adj* (*inveterate*) empedernido; ***I'm a ~ believer in ...*** creo firmemente en ...; ***a ~ bachelor*** un soltero empedernido

con•fis•cate ['kɑːnfɪskeɪt] *v/t* confiscar

con•fis•ca•tion [kɑːnfɪs'keɪʃn] confiscación *f*, embargo *m*

con•fla•gra•tion [kɑːnflə'greɪʃn] *fml* **1** *fire* incendio *m* **2** *conflict* conflicto *m*, lucha *f*

con•flict I *n* ['kɑːnflɪkt] conflicto *m*; ***come into ~ with*** entrar en conflicto con; ***~ of interests*** choque *m* de inte-

reses **II** *v/i* [kən'flɪkt] (*clash*) chocar
con•flict•ing [kən'flɪktɪŋ] *adj opinions* discrepante; **~ *loyalties*** lealtades *fpl* encontradas
con•form [kən'fɔːrm] *v/i* ser conformista; **~ *to*** *standards etc* ajustarse a
con•form•ist [kən'fɔːrmɪst] conformista *m/f*
con•form•i•ty [kən'fɔːrmətɪ] conformidad *f*; ***in* ~ *with*** en conformidad con, según
con•found [kən'faʊnd] *v/t surprise* sorprender; *overwhelm* confundir, desconcertar; **~ *it!*** ¡maldita sea!
con•found•ed [kən'faʊndɪd] *adj* maldito F
con•front [kən'frʌnt] *v/t* (*face*) hacer frente a, enfrentarse; (*tackle*) hacer frente a; ***be ~ed with a problem*** tener que afrontar un problema; **~ *s.o. with sth*** poner a alguien frente a frente con algo
con•fron•ta•tion [kɑːnfrən'teɪʃn] confrontación *f*, enfrentamiento *m*
con•fron•ta•tion•al [kɑːnfrən'teɪʃnl] *adj* agresivo
con•fuse [kən'fjuːz] *v/t* confundir; **~ *s.o. with s.o.*** confundir a alguien con alguien
con•fused [kən'fjuːzd] *adj person* confundido; *situation*, *piece of writing* confuso
con•fus•ing [kən'fjuːzɪŋ] *adj* confuso
con•fu•sion [kən'fjuːʒn] (*muddle*, *chaos*) confusión *f*; ***throw sth into* ~** desbaratar *or* desbarajustar algo
con•fute [kən'fjuːt] *v/t fml* refutar, rebatir
con•geal [kən'dʒiːl] *v/i of blood* coagularse; *of fat* solidificarse
con•gen•ial [kən'dʒiːnɪəl] *adj person* simpático, agradable; *occasion*, *place* agradable; ***be* ~ *to sth*** ser favorable *or* apropiado para algo
con•gen•i•tal [kən'dʒenɪtl] *adj* MED congénito; **~ *defect*** defecto *m* congénito; ***a* ~ *liar*** un mentiroso incorregible
con•gest•ed [kən'dʒestɪd] *adj roads* congestionado
con•ges•tion [kən'dʒestʃn] *also* MED congestión *f*; ***traffic* ~** congestión *f* circulatoria
con•glom•er•ate [kən'glɑːmərət] COM conglomerado *m*
con•glom•er•a•tion [kənglɑːmə'reɪʃn] conglomeración *f*
con•grats [kən'græts] *int Br* F felicidades, enhorabuena
con•grat•u•late [kən'grætʃuleɪt] *v/t* felicitar
con•grat•u•la•tions [kəngrætʃʊ'leɪʃnz] *npl* felicitaciones *fpl*; **~ *on …*** felicidades por …; ***let me offer my* ~** permita que le dé la enhorabuena
con•grat•u•la•to•ry [kəngrætʃʊ'leɪtərɪ] *adj* de felicitación
con•gre•gate ['kɑːŋgrɪgeɪt] *v/i* (*gather*) congregarse
con•gre•ga•tion [kɑːŋgrɪ'geɪʃn] REL congregación *f*
con•gress ['kɑːŋgres] (*conference*) congreso *m*
Con•gress ['kɑːŋgres] *in US* Congreso *m*
Con•gres•sion•al [kən'greʃnl] *adj* del Congreso
Con•gress•man ['kɑːŋgresmən] congresista *m*
'Con•gress•wo•man congresista *f*
con•i•cal ['kɑːnɪkl] *adj* cónico
con•i•fer ['kɑːnɪfər] conífera *f*
co•nif•er•ous [kə'nɪfərəs] *adj* conífero
con•jec•ture [kən'dʒektʃər] **I** *n* (*speculation*) conjetura *f* **II** *v/t*: **~ *that …*** especular que …
con•ju•gal ['kɑːndʒʊgl] *adj* conyugal; **~ *bliss*** felicidad *f* conyugal
con•ju•gate ['kɑːndʒʊgeɪt] GRAM **I** *v/t* conjugar **II** *v/i* conjugarse
con•ju•ga•tion [kɑːndʒʊ'geɪʃn] GRAM conjugación *f*
con•junc•tion [kən'dʒʌŋkʃn] **1** GRAM conjunción *f* **2**: ***in* ~ *with*** junto con
con•junc•ti•vi•tis [kəndʒʌŋktɪ'vaɪtɪs] conjuntivitis *f*
◆ **con•jure up** ['kʌndʒər] *v/t* **1** (*produce*) hacer aparecer **2** (*evoke*) evocar
con•jur•er, con•jur•or ['kʌndʒərər] (*magician*) prestidigitador(a) *m*(*f*)
con•jur•ing tricks ['kʌndʒərɪŋ] *npl* juegos *mpl* de manos
conk [kɑːŋk] *Br* P *nose* napias *fpl* P, trompa *f* P
◆ **conk out** *v/i* P **1** *fall asleep* quedarse frito *or* roque P **2** *stop working* escacharrarse P
'con man F timador *m*
con•nect [kə'nekt] **I** *v/t* conectar; (*link*)

relacionar, vincular; *to power supply* enchufar **II** *v/i* RAIL, AVIA enlazar, empalmar (***with*** con)

con•nect•ed [kə'nektɪd] *adj*: ***be well-~*** estar bien relacionado; ***be ~ with*** estar relacionado con; ***~ by marriage*** emparentado, entroncado

con•nect•ing [kə'nektɪŋ] *adj train, bus* de enlace *or* conexión

con•nect•ing 'door puerta *f* de paso

con•nect•ing 'flight vuelo *m* de conexión

con•nec•tion [kə'nekʃn] conexión *f*; *when traveling* conexión *f*, enlace *m*; (*personal contact*) contacto *m*; ***in ~ with*** en relación con; ***in this ~*** al respecto

con•nec•tive tis•sue [kənektɪv'tɪʃuː] ANAT tejido *m* conectivo *or* conjuntivo

con•nec•tor [kə'nektər] COMPUT conector *m*

con•nex•ion *Br* ☞ ***connection***

con•nois•seur [kɑːnə'sɜːr] entendido(-a) *m(f)*

con•no•ta•tion [kɑːnoʊ'teɪʃn] connotación *f*

con•note [kə'noʊt] *v/t fml* connotar, denotar

con•quer ['kɑːŋkər] *v/t* conquistar; *fig: fear etc* vencer

con•quer•or ['kɑːŋkərər] conquistador(a) *m(f)*

con•quest ['kɑːŋkwest] *of territory* conquista *f*

con•science ['kɑːnʃəns] conciencia *f*; ***a guilty ~*** un sentimiento de culpa; ***it was on my ~*** me remordía la conciencia; ***have a clear ~*** tener la conciencia tranquila

con•sci•en•tious [kɑːnʃɪ'enʃəs] *adj* concienzudo

con•sci•en•tious•ness [kɑːnʃɪ'enʃəsnəs] aplicación *f*

con•sci•en•tious ob'ject•or objetor(a) *m(f)* de conciencia

con•scious ['kɑːnʃəs] *adj* consciente; ***be ~ of*** ser consciente de

con•scious•ly ['kɑːnʃəslɪ] *adv* conscientemente

con•scious•ness ['kɑːnʃəsnɪs] **1** (*awareness*) conciencia *f* **2** MED con(s)ciencia *f*; ***lose ~*** quedar inconsciente; ***regain ~*** volver en sí

con•script MIL **I** *v/t* [kən'skrɪpt] reclutar **II** *n* ['kɑːnskrɪpt] recluta *m/f*

con•scrip•tion [kən'skrɪpʃn] MIL reclutamiento *m*

con•se•crate ['kɑːnsɪkreɪt] *v/t* REL *building* consagrar; *bishop* ordenar

con•se•cra•tion [kɑːnsɪ'kreɪʃn] REL *of building* consagración *f*; *of bishop* ordenación *f*

con•sec•u•tive [kən'sekjʊtɪv] *adj* consecutivo; ***for two ~ days*** durante dos días consecutivos

con•sec•u•tive•ly [kən'sekjʊtɪvlɪ] *adv* consecutivamente

con•sen•sus [kən'sensəs] consenso *m*; ***the ~ of opinion is that …*** la opinión generalizada es que…

con•sent [kən'sent] **I** *n* consentimiento *m*; ***the age of ~*** *edad a partir de la cual las relaciones sexuales son legales* **II** *v/i* consentir (***to*** en)

con•se•quence ['kɑːnsɪkwəns] (*result*) consecuencia *f*; ***as a ~ of*** como consecuencia de; ***in ~*** en *or* por consecuencia; ***accept the ~s*** asumir las consecuencias; ***his opinion is of no ~ to me*** me da igual su opinión, su opinión me es indiferente

con•se•quent ['kɑːnsɪkwənt] *adj* consiguiente

con•se•quent•ly ['kɑːnsɪkwəntlɪ] *adv* (*therefore*) por consiguiente

con•ser•va•tion [kɑːnsər'veɪʃn] (*preservation*) conservación *f*, protección *f*

con•ser'va•tion a•re•a zona *f* protegida

con•ser•va•tion•ist [kɑːnsər'veɪʃnɪst] ecologista *m/f*

con•ser•va•tive [kən'sɜːrvətɪv] **I** *adj* (*conventional*) conservador; *estimate* prudente; *Br* POL Conservador **II** *n* **1** ***Conservative*** *Br* POL Conservador(a) *m(f)*, Tory *m/f* **2** (*conventional person*) conservador(a) *m(f)*

con•ser•va•toire [kən'sɜːrvətwɑː] MUS conservatorio *m*

con•ser•va•to•ry [kən'sɜːrvətɔːrɪ] **1** MUS conservatorio *m* **2** *room cierro de cristales adjunto a la casa usado como sala de estar*

con•serve **I** *n* ['kɑːnsɜːrv] (*jam*) compota *f* **II** *v/t* [kən'sɜːrv] conservar; ***~ one's strength*** guardarse las fuerzas *or* energías

con•sid•er [kən'sɪdər] **I** *v/t* **1** (*regard*) considerar; ***it is ~ed to be …*** se considera que es …; **~ sth (to be) a mistake** considerar algo como un error, considerar algo ser un error **2** (*show regard for*) mostrar consideración por **3** (*think about*) considerar; **he wouldn't even ~ our suggestion** ni siquiera tendría en consideración nuestra sugerencia **II** *v/i* considerarse

con•sid•er•a•ble [kən'sɪdrəbl] *adj* considerable

con•sid•er•a•bly [kən'sɪdrəblɪ] *adv* considerablemente

con•sid•er•ate [kən'sɪdərət] *adj* considerado; **be ~ of** ser considerado con

con•sid•er•ate•ly [kən'sɪdərətlɪ] *adv* con consideración

con•sid•er•a•tion [kənsɪdə'reɪʃn] **1** (*thoughtfulness, concern*) consideración *f*; **out of ~ for** por consideración a **2** (*factor*) factor *m*; **money is no ~** el dinero no es problema
3: **take sth into ~** tomar algo en consideración; **after much ~** tras muchas deliberaciones; **your proposal is under ~** su propuesta está siendo estudiada; **in ~ of services rendered** *fml* en consideración a los servicios prestados

con•sid•er•ing [kən'sɪdərɪŋ] **I** *prep* teniendo en cuenta, considerando **II** *conj*: **~ that** teniendo en cuenta que, considerando que **III** *adv* F dentro de lo que cabe F

con•sign [kən'saɪn] *v/t* **1** (*entrust*) confiar **2**: **be ~ed to oblivion** quedar sepultado en el olvido

con•sign•ee [kɒnsaɪ'ni:] COM consignatario(-a) *m(f)*

con•sign•ment [kən'saɪnmənt] COM envío *m*

con'sign•ment note nota *f* de envío

con•sign•or [kən'saɪnər] COM expeditor(a) *m(f)*

◆ **con•sist in** [kən'sɪst] *v/t* consistir *or* basarse en

◆ **consist of** *v/t* consistir en

con•sis•ten•cy [kən'sɪstənsɪ] **1** (*texture*) consistencia *f* **2** (*unchangingness*) coherencia *f*, consecuencia *f*; *of player* regularidad *f*, constancia *f*

con•sis•tent [kən'sɪstənt] *adj person* coherente, consecuente; *improvement, change* constante

con•sis•tent•ly [kən'sɪstəntlɪ] *adv perform* con regularidad *or* constancia; *improve* continuamente; **he's ~ late** llega tarde sistemáticamente

con•so•la•tion [kɑːnsə'leɪʃn] consuelo *m*; **if it's any ~** si te sirve de consuelo

con•so'la•tion prize premio *m* de consolación

con•sol•a•to•ry [kən'soʊlətɔːrɪ] *adj* consolador, reconfortador

con•sole[1] [kən'soʊl] *v/t* consolar

con•sole[2] ['kɑːnsoʊl] *n control board* panel *m*; *for TV, hi-fi* mueble *m*, módulo *m*; **games ~** COMPUT consola *f* de videojuegos; **~ table** consola *f*

con•sol•i•date [kən'sɑːlɪdeɪt] *v/t* consolidar

con•sol•i•da•tion [kənsɑːlɪ'deɪʃn] consolidación *f*

con•som•mé [kɑːnsə'meɪ] consomé *m*

con•so•nant ['kɑːnsənənt] GRAM consonante *f*

con•sort ['kɑːnsɔːrt] consorte *m/f*; **prince ~** príncipe *m* consorte

◆ **consort with** [kən'sɔːrtwɪð] *v/t* relacionarse *or* asociarse con

con•sor•ti•um [kən'sɔːrtɪəm] consorcio *m*

con•spic•u•ous [kən'spɪkjʊəs] *adj* llamativo; **he felt very ~** sentía que estaba llamando la atención; **be ~** ser llamativo; **be ~ by one's / its absence** brillar por su ausencia; **make o.s. ~** hacerse notar, llamar la atención; **indulge in ~ consumption** permitirse gastar el dinero de manera ostentosa

con•spi•ra•cy [kən'spɪrəsɪ] conspiración *f*; **~ theory** teoría *f* de la conspiración

con•spi•ra•tor [kən'spɪrətər] conspirador(a) *m(f)*

con•spire [kən'spaɪr] **I** *v/i* conspirar **II** *v/t*: **~ to do sth** conspirar *or* confabularse para hacer algo

con•sta•ble ['kʌnstəbl] *Br* policía *m/f*

con•stab•u•lar•y [kən'stæbjʊlərɪ] *Br* cuerpo *m* de policía

con•stan•cy ['kɑːnstənsɪ] constancia *f*

con•stant ['kɑːnstənt] *adj* (*continuous*) constante

con•stant•ly ['kɑːnstəntlɪ] *adv* constantemente

con•stel•la•tion [kɑːnstə'leɪʃn] AST constelación *f*

con•ster•na•tion [kɑːnstər'neɪʃn] consternación *f*; **…, she said in ~** …, dijo consternada; ***to my ~*** para mi sorpresa y desgracia

con•sti•pate ['kɑːnstɪpeɪt] *v/t* estreñir

con•sti•pat•ed ['kɑːnstɪpeɪtɪd] *adj* estreñido

con•sti•pa•tion [kɑːnstɪ'peɪʃn] estreñimiento *m*

con•stit•u•en•cy [kən'stɪtjʊənsɪ] POL distrito *m* electoral

con•sti•tu•ent [kən'stɪtjʊənt] **I** *n* (*component*) elemento *m* constitutivo, componente *m* **II** *adj part, member* constitutivo, constituyente

con•sti•tu•ent as'sem•bly POL asamblea *f* constitucional

con•sti•tute ['kɑːnstɪtuːt] *v/t* constituir

con•sti•tu•tion [kɑːnstɪ'tuːʃn] constitución *f*

con•sti•tu•tion•al [kɑːnstɪ'tuːʃənl] *adj* POL constitucional

con•sti•tu•tion•al 'mon•ar•chy monarquía *f* constitucional

con•strain [kən'streɪn] *v/t* restringir, limitar; ***feel ~ed to do sth*** sentirse obligado a hacer algo

con•straint [kən'streɪnt] **1** (*restriction*) restricción *f*, límite *m* **2**: ***under ~*** a la fuerza

con•struct [kən'strʌkt] *v/t building etc* construir

con•struc•tion [kən'strʌkʃn] construcción *f*; ***under ~*** en construcción

con'struc•tion in•dus•try sector *m* de la construcción; **con'struc•tion site** obra *f*; **con'struc•tion work•er** obrero(-a) *m(f)* de la construcción

con•struc•tive [kən'strʌktɪv] *adj* constructivo

con•struc•tor [kən'strʌktər] *of cars, aircraft* constructor(a) *m(f)*

con•strue [kən'struː] *v/t* entender, interpretar

con•sul ['kɑːnsl] cónsul *m/f*

con•sul•ar ['kɑːnsʊlər] *adj* consular

con•su•late ['kɑːnsʊlət] consulado *m*

con•su•late 'gen•er•al consulado *m* general

con•sul 'gen•er•al cónsul *m/f* general

con•sult [kən'sʌlt] **I** *v/t* (*seek the advice of*) consultar **II** *v/i*: ***~ with s.o.*** consultarle a alguien

con•sult•an•cy [kən'sʌltənsɪ] *company* consultoría *f*, asesoría *f*; (*advice*) asesoramiento *m*

con•sult•ant [kən'sʌltənt] *n* **1** (*adviser*) asesor(a) *m(f)*, consultor(a) *m(f)* **2** *Br* MED médico *m/f* especialista

con•sul•ta•tion [kɑːnsl'teɪʃn] consulta *f*; ***have a ~ with*** consultar con; ***on or after ~ with*** tras consultar a

con•sult•ing en•gi•neer [kən'sʌltɪŋ] técnico(-a) *m(f)* asesor(a)

con'sult•ing room *Br* MED consulta *f*

con•sume [kən'suːm] *v/t* consumir; ***be ~d by fire*** ser pasto de las llamas; ***be ~d with hatred / jealousy*** estar consumido por el odio / la envidia

con•sum•er [kən'suːmər] (*purchaser*) consumidor(a) *m(f)*

con•sum•er ad'vice cen•ter centro *m* de asesoramiento al consumidor; **con•sum•er 'con•fi•dence** confianza *f* de los consumidores; **con'sum•er goods** *npl* bienes *mpl* de consumo; **con•sum•er 'price in•dex** índice *m* de precios al consumo; **con•sum•er pro'tec•tion** defensa *f* de los derechos del consumidor; **con•sum•er 're•search** investigación *f* del consumidor; **con•sum•er so'ci•e•ty** sociedad *f* de consumo; **con•sum•er 'sur•vey** encuesta *f* de consumidores

con•sum•mate I *v/t* ['kɑːnsəmeɪt] consumar **II** *adj* ['kɑːnsʌmət] (*skilled*) consumado; ***with ~ ease*** con una facilidad pasmosa

con•sump•tion [kən'sʌmpʃn] consumo *m*; ***unfit for human ~*** no apto para el consumo humano

con•tact ['kɑːntækt] **I** *n* contacto; ***keep in ~ with s.o.*** mantenerse en contacto con alguien; ***come into ~ with s.o.*** entrar en contacto con alguien; ***make / lose ~ with s.o.*** establecer / perder el contacto con alguien; ***business ~s*** contactos comerciales **II** *v/t* contactar con, ponerse en contacto con

'con•tact lens lentes *fpl* de contacto, *Span* lentillas *fpl*

'con•tact num•ber número *m* de contacto

con•ta•gion [kən'teɪdʒən] MED contagio *m*

con•ta•gious [kən'teɪdʒəs] *adj also fig* contagioso

con•tain [kən'teɪn] *v/t* (*hold, hold back*) contener; ***~ o.s.*** contenerse; ***the bag ~ed all my schoolbooks*** en la bolsa

llevaba todos mis libros de texto
con•tain•er [kən'teɪnər] **1** (*recipient*) recipiente *m* **2** COM contenedor *m*
con•tain•er•ize [kən'teɪnəraɪz] *v/t* COM poner en contenedores
con'tain•er ship buque *m* de transporte de contenedores
con•tam•i•nate [kən'tæmɪneɪt] *v/t* contaminar
con•tam•i•na•tion [kəntæmɪ'neɪʃn] contaminación *f*
con•tem•plate ['kɑːntəmpleɪt] *v/t* contemplar
con•tem•pla•tion [kɑːntəm'pleɪʃn] contemplación *f*, reflexión *f*
con•tem•pla•tive [kən'templətɪv] *adj* contemplativo, reflexivo
con•tem•po•ra•ne•ous [kəntempə'reɪnjəs] *adj fml* contemporáneo, coetáneo (***with*** de)
con•tem•po•ra•ry [kən'tempərerɪ] **I** *adj* contemporáneo **II** *n* contemporáneo(-a) *m(f)*
con•tempt [kən'tempt] desprecio *m*, desdén *m*; ***be beneath ~*** ser despreciable; ***feel ~ for s.o., hold s.o. in ~*** tener desprecio a alguien; ~ (***of court***) LAW desacato *m* (al tribunal)
con•tempt•i•ble [kən'temptəbl] *adj* despreciable
con•temp•tu•ous [kən'temptʃʊəs] *adj* despectivo; ***be ~ of sth*** despreciar *or* menospreciar algo
con•tend [kən'tend] *v/i*: ~ ***for*** competir por; ~ ***with*** enfrentarse a
con•tend•er [kən'tendər] SP, POL contendiente *m/f*; *against champion* aspirante *m/f*
con•tent[1] ['kɑːntent] *n* contenido *m*; ***fat ~*** contenido graso
con•tent[2] [kən'tent] **I** *adj* satisfecho; ***I'm quite ~ to sit here*** me contento con sentarme aquí; ***be ~ with sth*** conformarse con algo, darse por contento con algo; ***not ~ with ...*** no contento con ... **II** *v/t*: ***~ o.s. with*** contentarse con
con•tent•ed [kən'tentɪd] *adj* satisfecho
con•ten•tion [kən'tenʃn] (*assertion*) argumento *m*; ***be in ~ for*** tener posibilidades de ganar; ***my ~ is that ...*** a mi parecer, ...
con•ten•tious [kən'tenʃəs] *adj* polémico
con•tent•ment [kən'tentmənt] satisfacción *f*
con•tents ['kɑːntents] *npl* **1** *of house, letter, bag etc* contenido *m* **2** *list*: *in book* tabla *f or* lista *f* de contenidos
'con•tents page índice *m*, contenidos *mpl*
con•test[1] ['kɑːntest] *n* (*competition*) concurso *m*; (*struggle, for power*) lucha *f*
con•test[2] [kən'test] *v/t* **1** *leadership etc* presentarse como candidato a **2** *decision, will* impugnar; ***~ s.o.'s right to do sth*** cuestionar el derecho de alguien a hacer algo
con•test•ant [kən'testənt] concursante *m/f*; *in competition* competidor(a) *m(f)*
con•text ['kɑːntekst] contexto *m*; ***look at sth in ~ / out of ~*** examinar algo en contexto / fuera de contexto; ***in this ~*** bajo estas circunstancias
con•ti•nent ['kɑːntɪnənt] continente *m*
con•ti•nen•tal [kɑːntɪ'nentl] *adj* continental
con•ti•nen•tal 'break•fast desayuno *m* continental
con•ti•nen•tal 'quilt edredón *m*
con•tin•gen•cy [kən'tɪndʒənsɪ] contingencia *f*, eventualidad *f*
con'tin•gen•cy fund fondos *mpl* de imprevistos
con'tin•gen•cy plan plan *m* de emergencia
con•tin•gent [kən'tɪndʒənt] **I** *adj*: ***make sth ~ on sth*** hacer que algo dependa de algo **II** *n also* MIL contingente *m*
con•tin•u•al [kən'tɪnjʊəl] *adj* continuo
con•tin•u•al•ly [kən'tɪnjʊəlɪ] *adv* continuamente
con•tin•u•ance [kən'tɪnjʊəns] ☞ ***continuation***
con•tin•u•a•tion [kəntɪnjʊ'eɪʃn] continuación *f*
con•tin•ue [kən'tɪnjuː] **I** *v/t* continuar; ***to be ~d*** continuará; ***he ~d to drink*** continuó bebiendo **II** *v/i* continuar; ~ ***in office*** POL seguir en el poder
con•ti•nu•i•ty [kɑːntɪ'njuːətɪ] continuidad *f*; ~ ***girl*** secretaria *f* de rodaje
con•tin•u•ous [kən'tɪnjʊəs] *adj also* GRAM continuo
con•tin•u•ous 'cur•rent ELEC corriente *f* continua
con•tin•u•ous•ly [kən'tɪnjʊəslɪ] *adv* continuamente, ininterrumpidamente

C

con•tort [kən'tɔːrt] *v/t face* contraer; *body* contorsionar; ***be ~ed with pain*** retorcerse del dolor
con•tor•tion [kən'tɔːrʃn] contorsión *f*; ***go through all sorts of ~s*** *fig* hacer piruetas
con•tor•tion•ist [kən'tɔːrʃnɪst] contorsionista *m/f*
con•tour ['kɑːntʊr] contorno *m*
con•tra•band ['kɑːntrəbænd] (artículos *mpl* de) contrabando *m*; ***~ tobacco*** tabaco *m* de contrabando
con•tra•cep•tion [kɑːntrə'sepʃn] anticoncepción *f*
con•tra•cep•tive [kɑːntrə'septɪv] (*device, pill*) anticonceptivo *m*
con•tract[1] ['kɑːntrækt] **I** *n* contrato *m*; ***enter into a ~*** contraer obligaciones (***with*** con); ***by ~*** por contrato; ***be under ~*** estar bajo contrato (***to*** con); ***~ of employment*** contrato laboral, contrato de trabajo; ***~ of sale*** contrato de compraventa; ***~ work*** contrato temporal **II** *v/i*: ***I ~ed to do 15 hours a week*** me contrataron para trabajar 15 horas a la semana **III** *v/t illness* contraer
con•tract[2] [kən'trækt] **I** *v/i* (*shrink*) contraerse
con•trac•tion [kən'trækʃn] **1** *of material* contracción *f*; *of market, industry* reducción *f* **2** MED: ***have ~s*** tener contracciones
'con•tract kil•ler asesino(-a) *m(f)* de alquiler
con•trac•tor [kən'træktər] contratista *m/f*; ***building ~*** constructora *f*
con•trac•tu•al [kən'træktuəl] *adj* contractual
con•tra•dict [kɑːntrə'dɪkt] *v/t statement* desmentir; *person* contradecir
con•tra•dic•tion [kɑːntrə'dɪkʃn] contradicción *f*; ***be in ~ to*** contradecirse con; ***a ~ in terms*** una paradoja
con•tra•dic•to•ry [kɑːntrə'dɪktərɪ] *adj account* contradictorio
con•tra•flow sys•tem ['kɑːntrəfloʊ] MOT *sistema de circulación en sentido contrario*
con•tra•in•di•ca•tion [kɑːntrəɪndɪ'keɪʃn] MED contraindicación *f*
con•tral•to [kən'træltoʊ] MUS contralto *f*
con•trap•tion [kən'træpʃn] F artilugio *m* F
con•trar•y[1] ['kɑːntrerɪ] **I** *adj* contrario; ***~ to*** al contrario de; ***~ to expectations*** contra todo pronóstico; ***it runs ~ to ...*** esto va en contra de ... **II** *n*: ***the ~*** lo contrario; ***on the ~*** al contrario; ***in the absence of evidence to the ~*** si no se demuestra lo contrario
con•tra•ry[2] [kən'trerɪ] *adj* (*perverse*) difícil
con•trast I *n* ['kɑːntræst] contraste *m*; ***by ~*** por contraste; ***in ~ to*** *or* ***with*** a diferencia de **II** *v/t & v/i* [kən'træst] contrastar
con•trast•ing [kən'træstɪŋ] *adj* opuesto
con•tra•vene [kɑːntrə'viːn] *v/t* contravenir
con•tra•ven•tion [kɑːntrə'venʃn] contravención *f*; ***in ~ of*** en contravención a *or* de
con•trib•ute [kən'trɪbjuːt] **I** *v/i* **1** contribuir (***to*** a) **2**: ***~ to a newspaper*** colaborar con un periódico **II** *v/t money, time, suggestion* contribuir con, aportar
con•tri•bu•tion [kɑːntrɪ'bjuːʃn] **1** *money* contribución *f* (***to*** a); *to political party, church* donación *f*; *of time, effort, to debate* contribución *f*, aportación *f* **2** *to magazine* colaboración *f*
con•trib•u•tor [kən'trɪbjʊtər] **1** *of money* donante *m/f* **2** *to magazine* colaborador(a) *m(f)*
con•trive [kən'traɪv] *v/t* preparar, tramar; ***~ to do sth*** arreglárselas para hacer algo
con•trived [kən'traɪvd] *adj* artificial, irreal
con•trol [kən'troʊl] **I** *n* **1** control *m*; ***take / lose ~ of*** tomar / perder el control de; ***lose ~ of o.s.*** perder el control; ***circumstances beyond our ~*** circunstancias ajenas a nuestra voluntad; ***be in ~ of*** controlar; ***we're in ~ of the situation*** tenemos la situación controlada *or* bajo control; ***get out of ~*** descontrolarse; ***under ~*** bajo control; ***bring sth under ~*** controlar algo; ***be under s.o.'s ~*** ser responsabilidad *or* competencia de alguien
2: ***~s*** *of aircraft, vehicle* controles *mpl*; ***be at the ~s*** AVIA estar en los mandos *or* controles
3: ***~s*** (*restrictions*) controles *mpl*
4 COMPUT (tecla *f* de) control *m*
II *v/t* (*pret & pp* **-led**) (*govern*) contro-

lar, dominar; (*restrict, regulate*) controlar; ~ ***o.s.*** controlarse
con'trol cen•ter, *Br* **con'trol cen•tre** centro *m* de control; **con'trol desk** TV panel *m* de mandos; **con'trol freak** F *persona obsesionada con controlar todo*; **con'trol group** grupo *m* de control; **con'trol key** COMPUT tecla *f* de control
con•trolled [kən'trould] *adj environment, conditions* controlado, supervisado; *voice* controlado, moderado
con•trolled 'sub•stance estupefaciente *m*
con•trol•ling in•ter•est [kəntroulɪŋ'ɪntrəst] FIN participación *f* mayoritaria, interés *m* mayoritario
con'trol pan•el panel *m* de control; **con'trol room** TV control *m*, sala *f* de realización; **con'trol tow•er** torre *f* de control; **con'trol u•nit** COMPUT unidad *f* de control
con•tro•ver•sial [kɑːntrə'vɜːrʃl] *adj* polémico, controvertido
con•tro•ver•sy ['kɑːntrəvɜːrsɪ] polémica *f*, controversia *f*
con•tu•sion [kən'tuːʒn] MED contusión *f*
co•nun•drum [kə'nʌndrəm] enigma *m*; *guessing game* acertijo *m*
con•ur•ba•tion [kɑːnɜːr'beɪʃn] conurbación *f*
con•va•lesce [kɑːnvə'les] *v/i* convalecer
con•va•les•cence [kɑːnvə'lesns] convalecencia *f*
con•va•les•cent [kɑːnvə'lesnt] *adj* convaleciente
con•vect•or (heat•er) [kən'vektər] estufa *f* de aire caliente
con•vene [kən'viːn] *v/t* convocar
con•ve•ni•ence [kən'viːnɪəns] conveniencia *f*; ***at your / my*** ~ a su / mi conveniencia; ***the ~ of the location*** la comodidad de la localización; ***all (modern) ~s*** todas las comodidades; ***at your earliest ~*** *fml* tan pronto como le sea posible
con've•ni•ence food comida *f* preparada
con've•ni•ence store tienda *f* de barrio
con•ve•ni•ent [kən'viːnɪənt] *adj location, device* conveniente; *time, arrangement* oportuno; ***it's very ~ living so near the office*** vivir cerca de la oficina es muy cómodo; ***the apartment is ~ for the station*** el apartamento está muy cerca de la estación; ***I'm afraid Monday isn't ~*** me temo que el lunes no me va bien
con•ve•ni•ent•ly [kən'viːnɪəntlɪ] *adv* convenientemente; ***~ located for theaters*** situado cerca de los teatros
con•vent ['kɑːnvənt] convento *m*
con•ven•tion [kən'venʃn] **1** (*tradition*) convención *f* **2** (*conference*) congreso *m*
con•ven•tion•al [kən'venʃnl] *adj* convencional
con'ven•tion cen•ter, *Br* **con'vent•ion cen•tre** palacio *m* de congresos
con•ven•tion•eer [kən'venʃnɪr] congresista *m/f*
con•verge [kən'vɜːrdʒ] *v/i* converger
◆ **converge on** [kən'vɜːrdʒ] *v/t* converger en
con•ver•gence [kən'vɜːrdʒəns] convergencia *f*
con•ver•sant [kən'vɜːrsənt] *adj*: ***be ~ with*** estar familiarizado con
con•ver•sa•tion [kɑːnvər'seɪʃn] conversación *f*; ***make ~*** conversar; ***have a ~*** mantener una conversación; ***in ~ with*** hablando con; ***get into ~ with s.o.*** entablar una conversación con alguien
con•ver•sa•tion•al [kɑːnvər'seɪʃnl] *adj* coloquial; ***~ English*** inglés *m* coloquial; ***not be in a very ~ mood*** no tengo muchas ganas de conversación *or* charla
con•verse[1] [kən'vɜːrs] *v/i* conversar; ***~ with s.o. about sth*** conversar con alguien acerca de algo
con•verse[2] ['kɑːnvɜːrs] *n* (*opposite*): ***the ~*** lo opuesto
con•verse•ly [kən'vɜːrslɪ] *adv* por el contrario
con•ver•sion [kən'vɜːrʃn] conversión *f*
con'ver•sion ta•ble tabla *f* de conversión
con•vert I *n* ['kɑːnvɜːrt] converso(-a) *m(f)* (***to*** a) **II** *v/t* [kən'vɜːrt] convertir
con•vert•i•ble [kən'vɜːrtəbl] *car* descapotable *m*
con•vex [kɑːn'veks] *adj* convexo
con•vey [kən'veɪ] *v/t* **1** (*transmit*) trans-

mitir **2** (*carry*) transportar
con•vey•anc•ing [kən'veɪənsɪŋ] LAW traspaso *m*, cesión *f*
con•vey•or belt [kən'veɪər] cinta *f* transportadora
con•vict **I** *n* ['kɑːnvɪkt] convicto(-a) *m*(*f*) **II** *v/t* [kən'vɪkt] LAW: ***~ s.o. of sth*** declarar a alguien culpable de algo
con•vic•tion [kən'vɪkʃn] **1** LAW condena *f* **2** (*belief*) convicción *f*; ***out of ~*** por convicción; ***lack ~*** ser poco convincente
con•vince [kən'vɪns] *v/t* convencer: ***I'm ~d he's lying*** estoy convencido de que miente
con•vinc•ing [kən'vɪnsɪŋ] *adj* convincente
con•viv•i•al [kən'vɪvɪəl] *adj* (*friendly*) agradable
con•vo•lut•ed ['kɑːnvəluːtɪd] *adj* enrevesado, intrincado
con•voy ['kɑːnvɔɪ] *of ships*, *vehicles* convoy *m*
con•vulse [kən'vʌls] **I** *v/t*: ***be ~d with*** *laughter* retorcerse de, descoyuntarse de; *pain* retorcerse de
con•vul•sion [kən'vʌlʃn] MED convulsión *f*
con•vul•sive [kən'vʌlsɪv] *adj* convulsivo
coo [kuː] *v/i* arrullar
cook [kʊk] **I** *n* cocinero(-a) *m*(*f*); ***I'm a good ~*** soy un buen cocinero, cocino bien **II** *v/t* cocinar; ***a ~ed meal*** una comida caliente **III** *v/i* cocinar; ***what's ~ing?*** F ¿qué pasa? F, ¿qué hay de nuevo? F
◆ **cook up** *v/t* F *plan* maquinar
'cook•book libro *m* de cocina
cook•er ['kʊkər] *Br* (*stove*) cocina *f*, fogón *m*
cook•e•ry ['kʊkərɪ] cocina *f*
'cook•e•ry book *Br* libro *m* de cocina
cook•ie ['kʊkɪ] galleta *f*; ***he's a tough ~*** F es muy duro; ***she's a clever ~*** F esa es más lista que el hambre F
cook•ing ['kʊkɪŋ] *food* cocina *f*; ***Italian ~*** la cocina italiana
cool [kuːl] **I** *n*: ***keep one's ~*** F mantener la calma; ***lose one's ~*** F perder la calma **II** *adj* **1** *weather, breeze* fresco; *drink* frío **2** (*calm*) tranquilo, sereno; ***keep ~*** F mantener la calma **3** (*unfriendly*) frío **4** P (*great*) *L.Am.* chévere P, *Mex* padre P, *Rpl* copante P, *Span* guay P; ***a ~ thousand dollars*** la friolera de mil dólares F **III** *v/i of food*, *interest* enfriarse; *of tempers* calmarse **IV** *v/t*: ***~ it*** F cálmate
◆ **cool down I** *v/i* enfriarse; *of weather* refrescar; *fig*: *of tempers* calmarse, tranquilizarse **II** *v/t food* enfriar; *fig* calmar, tranquilizar
'cool bag *Br* bolsa *f* refrigerante; **'cool box** *Br* nevera *f* portátil; **cool-'head•ed** *adj* tranquilo, sosegado
cool•ing ['kuːlɪŋ] *adj* refrescante
cool•ing-'off pe•ri•od fase *f* de reflexión; **'cool•ing sys•tem** sistema *m* de refrigeración; **'cool•ing-tow•er** torre *f* de refrigeración *or* enfriamiento
cool•ness ['kuːlnɪs] frialdad *f*, frío *m*
◆ **coop up** [kuːp] *v/t*: ***be cooped up*** estar encerrado
co-op ['koʊɑːp] **1** COM cooperativa *f* **2** *apartment building* cooperativa *f* de apartamentos
co•op•e•rate [koʊ'ɑːpəreɪt] *v/i* cooperar
co•op•e•ra•tion [koʊɑːpə'reɪʃn] cooperación *f*
co•op•e•ra•tive [koʊ'ɑːpərətɪv] **I** *n* COM cooperativa *f* **II** *adj* COM conjunto; (*helpful*) cooperativo; ***~ society*** cooperativa *f*
co•or•di•nate I *v/t* [koʊ'ɔːrdɪneɪt] *activities* coordinar **II** *n* [koʊ'ɔːrdnət] MATH coordinada *f*
co•or•di•na•tion [koʊɔːrdɪ'neɪʃn] coordinación *f*
co•or•di•na•tor [koʊ'ɔːrdɪneɪtər] coordinador(a) *m*(*f*)
co-own•er [koʊ'oʊnər] co-propietario (-a) *m*(*f*)
co-own•er•ship [koʊ'oʊnərʃɪp] co-propiedad *f*
cop [kɑːp] F **I** *n* poli *m/f* F **II** *v/t Br* (*pret & pp* ***-ped***): ***~ it*** cargársela F
cope [koʊp] *v/i* arreglárselas; ***~ with*** poder con
cop•i•er ['kɑːpɪər] *machine* fotocopiadora *f*
co•pi•lot ['koʊpaɪlət] copiloto *m/f*
co•pi•ous ['koʊpɪəs] *adj* copioso
cop•per ['kɑːpər] *metal* cobre *m*
cop•per 'ore MIN mineral *m* de cobre
'cop•per•plate *adj handwriting* de letra redondilla

co•pro•duc•er ['kouprədu:sər] coproductor(a) *m(f)*
co•pro•duc•tion ['kouprədʌkʃn] coproducción *f*
'cop show TV serie *f* policial
cop•u•late ['kɑ:pjʊleɪt] *v/i* copular
cop•u•la•tion [kɑ:pjʊ'leɪʃn] copulación *f*
cop•y ['kɑ:pɪ] **I** *n* copia *f*; *of book* ejemplar *m*; (*written material*) texto *m*; ***make a ~ of a file*** COMPUT hacer una copia de un archivo; ***fair*** *or* ***clean ~*** copia en limpio; ***rough ~*** borrador *m* **II** *v/t* (*pret & pp* **-ied**) copiar
'cop•y cat F copión(-ona) *m(f)* F, copiota *m/f* F; **'cop•y•cat crime** *delito inspirado en otro*; **'cop•y•ed•i•tor** editor(a) *m(f)* de textos; **'cop•y•read•er** editor(a) *m(f)* de textos; **'cop•y•right I** *n* copyright *m*, derechos *mpl* de reproducción **II** *v/t* registrar el copyright de **III** *adj* protegido por el copyright; **'cop•y--writ•er** *in advertising* creativo(-a) *m(f)* (*de publicidad*)
cor•al ['kɑ:rəl] coral *m*
cord [kɔ:rd] (*string*) cuerda *f*, cordel *m*; (*cable*) cable *m*
cor•di•al ['kɔ:rdʒəl] **I** *adj* cordial **II** *n liqueur* licor *m*; *Br*: *soft drink* refresco *m*
cor•di•al•i•ty ['kɔ:rdɪ'ælətɪ] cordialidad *f*
cord•less phone ['kɔ:rdlɪs] teléfono *m* inalámbrico
cor•do•ba [kɔ:r'doubə] FIN córdoba *m*
cor•don ['kɔ:rdn] cordón *m*
◆ **cordon off** *v/t* acordonar
cords [kɔ:rdz] *npl pants* pantalones *mpl* de pana; ***a pair of ~s*** unos pantalones de pana
cor•du•roy ['kɔ:rdərɔɪ] pana *f*
core [kɔ:r] **I** *n of fruit* corazón *m*; *of problem* meollo *m*; *of organization, party* núcleo *m*; ***to the ~*** *fig* hasta la médula **II** *v/t fruit* sacar el corazón a **III** *adj issue, meaning* central
'core time horas *fpl* nucleares
co•ri•an•der ['kɑ:rɪændər] *Br* cilantro *m*
cork [kɔ:rk] **1** *in bottle* (tapón *m* de) corcho *m* **2** *material* corcho *m*
'cork•screw sacacorchos *m inv*
corn[1] [kɔ:rn] *grain* maíz *m*; *Br* trigo *m*
corn[2] [kɔ:rn] MED dureza *f*, callosidad *f*
'corn bread pan *m* de maíz
'corn•cob mazorca *f* de maíz
cor•ne•a ['kɔ:rnɪə] ANAT córnea *f*
corned beef ['kɔ:rndbi:f] fiambre *m* de carne de vaca
cor•ner ['kɔ:rnər] **I** *n of page, street* esquina *f*; *of room* rincón *m*; (*bend*: *on road*) curva *f*; *in soccer* córner *m*, saque *m* de esquina; ***in the ~*** en el rincón; ***I'll meet you on the ~*** te veré en la esquina; ***it's just around the ~*** está a la vuelta (de la esquina); ***take a ~*** *in car* tomar una curva; ***turn the ~*** volver la esquina; *of economy, sick person* sobreponerse, mejorarse; ***~ of the mouth*** comisura *f* de los labios; ***look at s.o. out of the ~ of one's eye*** mirar a alguien con el rabillo del ojo; ***force s.o. into a ~*** poner a alguien en un apuro; ***be in a tight ~*** estar en un apuro
II *v/t person* arrinconar; ***~ a market*** monopolizar un mercado
III *v/i of driver, car* girar; ***~ well*** MOT tomar bien las curvas
cor•ner•ing a•bil•i•ty ['kɔ:rnərɪŋ] MOT comportamiento *m* en curvas
'cor•ner kick *in soccer* saque *m* de esquina, córner *m*
'cor•ner•stone 1 ARCHI piedra *f* angular, primera piedra *f* **2** *fig* piedra *f* angular, base *f*
'corn•field maizal *m*; *Br* trigal *m*; **'corn•flakes** *npl* copos *mpl* de maíz; **'corn•flow•er** BOT aciano *m*
cor•nice ['kɔ:rnɪs] ARCHI cornisa *f*
'corn pop•py BOT amapola *f*
'corn•starch harina *f* de maíz
corn•y ['kɔ:rnɪ] *adj* F **1** (*sentimental*) cursi F **2** *joke* manido
cor•ol•lar•y ['kɑ:rələrɪ] consecuencia *f*, secuela *f*
cor•o•na•ry ['kɑ:rənerɪ] **I** *adj* coronario **II** *n* infarto *m* de miocardio
cor•o•na•ry 'heart dis•ease enfermedad *f* cardíaca coronaria
cor•o•na•tion [kɑ:rə'neɪʃn] coronamiento *m*
cor•o•ner ['kɑ:rənər] *oficial encargado de investigar muertes sospechosas*
cor•po•ral ['kɔ:rpərəl] cabo *m/f*
cor•po•ral 'pun•ish•ment castigo *m* corporal
cor•po•rate ['kɔ:rpərət] *adj* COM corporativo, de empresa; ***~ image*** imagen *f* corporativa; ***~ loyalty*** lealtad *f* a la em-

C

presa; ~ ***planning*** planificación *f* corporativa
cor•po•rate hos•pi'tal•i•ty hospitalidad *f* de empresa
cor•po•rate i'den•ti•ty identidad *f* corporativa
cor•po•ra•tion [kɔːrpə'reɪʃn] *business* sociedad *f* anónima
cor•po'ra•tion tax impuesto *m* sobre las sociedades
corps [kɔːr] *nsg* cuerpo *m*
corpse [kɔːrps] cadáver *m*
cor•pu•lence ['kɔːrpjʊləns] *fml* corpulencia *f*
cor•pu•lent ['kɔːrpjʊlənt] *adj* corpulento
cor•pus ['kɔːrpəs] corpus *m*
Cor•pus Chris•ti [kɔːrpəs'krɪstɪ] REL Corpus *m*, Corpus Christi *m*
cor•pus•cle ['kɔːrpʌsl] corpúsculo *m*
cor•ral [kə'ræl] **I** *n* corral *m* **II** *v/t horse, cattle* acorralar; *people* rodear, arrinconar
cor•rect [kə'rekt] **I** *adj* correcto; *time* exacto; ***you are*** ~ tiene razón **II** *v/t* corregir; ***I stand ~ed*** le doy la razón
cor•rec•tion [kə'rekʃn] corrección *f*
cor'rec•tion flu•id corrector *m* líquido, tippex *m*
cor•rec•tive [kə'rektɪv] *adj* correctivo
cor•rect•ly [kə'rektlɪ] *adv* correctamente
cor•rect•ness [kə'rektnɪs] corrección *f*
cor•re•late ['kɑːrəleɪt] *v/i* correlacionarse (***with*** con)
cor•re•la•tion [kɑːrə'leɪʃn] correlación *f*
cor•re•spond [kɑːrɪ'spɑːnd] *v/i* (*match*) corresponderse; ~ ***to*** corresponder a; ~ ***with*** corresponderse con; (*write letters*) mantener correspondencia con
cor•re•spon•dence [kɑːrɪ'spɑːndəns] **1** (*matching*) correspondencia *f*, relación *f* **2** (*letters*) correspondencia *f*; ***be in*** ~ mantener correspondencia (***with*** con)
cor•re'spon•dence course curso *m* por correspondencia, curso *m* a distancia
cor•re'spon•dence school escuela *f* de estudios por correspondencia, escuela *f* de estudios a distancia
cor•re•spon•dent [kɑːrɪ'spɑːndənt] *n* **1** (*reporter*) corresponsal *m/f*; ***foreign*** ~ corresponsal internacional **2** (*letter writer*) correspondiente *m/f*
cor•re•spon•ding [kɑːrɪ'spɑːndɪŋ] *adj* (*equivalent*) correspondiente
cor•ri•dor ['kɔːrɪdər] *in building* pasillo *m*
cor•rob•o•rate [kə'rɑːbəreɪt] *v/t* corroborar
cor•rode [kə'roʊd] **I** *v/t* corroer **II** *v/i* corroerse
cor•ro•sion [kə'roʊʒn] corrosión *f*
cor•ru•gat•ed card•board ['kɑːrəgeɪtɪd] cartón *m* ondulado
cor•ru•gat•ed 'i•ron chapa *f* ondulada
cor•rupt [kə'rʌpt] **I** *adj* corrupto; COMPUT corrompido **II** *v/t* corromper; (*bribe*) sobornar
cor•rup•tion [kə'rʌpʃn] corrupción *f*
cor•set ['kɔːrsɪt] corsé *m*
cor•ti•sone ['kɔːrtɪzoʊn] MED cortisona *f*
'cos [kɒz]F (*because*) porque
cosh [kɑːʃ] *Br* F porra *f*, cachiporra *f*
co•sig•na•to•ry [koʊ'sɪgnətɔːrɪ] firmante *m/f* conjunto(-a)
co•sine ['koʊsaɪn] MATH coseno *m*
co•si•ness ['koʊzɪnɪs] *Br* ☞ ***coziness***
cos•met•ic [kɑːz'metɪk] *adj* cosmético; *fig* superficial
cos•met•ics [kɑːz'metɪks] *npl* cosméticos *mpl*
cos•met•ic 'sur•geon especialista *m/f* en cirugía estética
cos•met•ic 'sur•ger•y cirugía *f* estética
cos•mic ['kɑːzmɪk] *adj* cósmico; ***of*** ~ ***proportions*** de dimensiones descomunales
cos•mo•naut ['kɑːzmənɒːt] cosmonauta *m/f*
cos•mo•pol•i•tan [kɑːzmə'pɑːlɪtən] **I** *adj city* cosmopolitano **II** *n* cosmopolita *m/f*
cos•mos ['kɑːzmɑːs] cosmos *m*
cost[1] [kɑːst] **I** *n also fig* costo *m*, *Span* coste *m*; ***at all ~s*** cueste lo que cueste; ***I've learnt to my*** ~ por desgracia he aprendido; ***at the ~ of her health*** a costa de su salud; ***at a heavy*** ~ a un precio muy alto; ***at*** ~ (***price***) al costo *or Span* coste; ***award ~s against s.o.*** LAW adjudicar los costos *or Span* costes a alguien; ~ ***inflation*** COM inflación *f* de costos *or Span* costes
II *v/t* (*pret & pp* ***cost***) *money, time* costar; ***how much does it ~?*** ¿cuánto

cuesta?; ***it ~ me ten dollars*** me costó diez dólares; ***it'll ~ you*** F te va a salir caro; ***it ~ him his life*** le costó la vida; ***it ~ me a lot of trouble*** me ocasionó muchos problemas, me fue muy difícil **III** *v/i* (*irr*): ***it ~ him dearly*** *fig* le salió caro

cost[2] [kɑːst] *v/t* (*pret & pp* ***-ed***) FIN *proposal, project* estimar el costo de

'cost an•al•y•sis análisis *m inv* de costos *or Span* costes

cost and 'freight COM costo *or Span* coste y flete

co-star ['koustɑːr] **I** *v/t* (*pret & pp* ***-red***): ***the film ~s Robin Williams*** la película está co-protagonizada por Robin Williams **II** *v/i* (*pret & pp* ***-red***): ***~ with s.o.*** actuar con alguien

Cos•ta Ri•ca [kɑːstə'riːkə] Costa Rica *f*

Cos•ta Ri•can [kɑːstə'riːkən] **I** *adj* costarricense **II** *n* costarricense *m/f*

cost-'ben•e•fit an•al•y•sis análisis *m* de costo-beneficio *or Span* coste-beneficio; **'cost-con•scious** *adj* consciente del costo *or Span* coste; **'cost-ef•fec•tive** *adj* rentable; **'cost es•ti•mate** estimación *f* de costos *or Span* costes

cost•ing ['kɑːstɪŋ] *n* cálculo *m* de costos *or Span* costes

'cost, in•sur•ance, freight COM costo *or Span* coste, seguro y flete

cost•ly ['kɑːstlɪ] *adj mistake* caro

cost of 'liv•ing costo *m or Span* coste *m* de la vida; **cost-of-'liv•ing al•low•ance** COM complemento *m* por carestía de vida; **cost 'price** precio *m* de costo *or Span* coste

cos•tume ['kɑːstuːm] *for actor* traje *m*

'cos•tume de•sign•er diseñador(a) *m(f)* de vestuario; **'cos•tume dra•ma** *movie* película *f* de época; *TV series* serie *f* de época; **cos•tume 'jew•el•ry,** *Br* **cos•tume 'jew•el•lery** bisutería *f*

'cos•y *Br* ☞ ***cozy***

cot [kɑːt] (*camp-bed*) catre *m*

'cot death (síndrome *m* de) muerte *f* súbita del lactante

cot•tage ['kɑːtɪdʒ] casa *f* de campo, casita *f*

cot•tage 'cheese queso *m* fresco

cot•tage 'in•dus•try industria *f* artesanal *or* familiar

cot•ton ['kɑːtn] **I** *n* algodón *m* **II** *adj* de algodón

◆ **cotton on** *v/i* F darse cuenta

◆ **cotton on to** *v/t* F darse cuenta de

◆ **cotton to** *v/t* F: ***I never cottoned to her*** nunca me cayó bien

'cot•ton bud *Br*: *for ears etc* bastoncillo *m*; **cot•ton 'can•dy** algodón *m* dulce; **'cot•ton•seed oil** aceite *m* de semillas de algodón; **'cot•ton•wood** álamo *m* de Virginia; **cot•ton 'wool** *Br* algodón *m* (hidrófilo)

couch [kaʊʧ] sofá *m*

cou•chette [kuː'ʃet] litera *f*

'couch po•ta•to F teleadicto(-a) *m(f)* F

cough [kɑːf] **I** *n* tos *f*; *to get attention* carraspeo *m*; ***have a ~*** tener tos **II** *v/i* toser; *to get attention* carraspear

◆ **cough up I** *v/t* **1** *blood etc* toser **2** F *money* soltar, *Span* apoquinar F **II** *v/i* F (*pay*) soltar dinero, *Span* apoquinar F

'cough drop pastilla *f* para la tos

cough•ing bout ['kɑːfɪŋ] ataque *m* de tos

'cough loz•enge ☞ ***cough drop***

'cough med•i•cine, 'cough syr•up jarabe *m* para la tos

could [kʊd] **I** *v/aux*: ***~ I have my key?*** ¿me podría dar la llave?; ***~ you help me?*** ¿me podrías ayudar?; ***this ~ be our bus*** puede que éste sea nuestro autobús; ***you ~ be right*** puede que tengas razón; ***I ~n't say for sure*** no sabría decirlo con seguridad; ***he ~ have got lost*** a lo mejor se ha perdido; ***you ~ have warned me!*** ¡me podías haber avisado!; ***that ~ be right*** puede que eso sea cierto
II *pret* ☞ ***can***

coun•cil ['kaʊnsl] **1** (*assembly*) consejo *m* **2**: (***municipal***) ~ autoridades *fpl* locales

'coun•cil es•tate *Br* urbanización *f* de protección oficial; **'coun•cil flat** *Br* piso *m* de protección oficial; **'coun•cil house** *Br* casa *f* de protección oficial; **'coun•cil•man** concejal *m*

coun•cil•or, *Br* **coun•cil•lor** ['kaʊnsələr] concejal(a) *m(f)*

'coun•cil tax *Br* contribución *f* urbana

coun•sel ['kaʊnsl] **I** *n* **1** (*advice*) consejo *m*; ***keep one's own ~*** ser muy reservado *or* callado **2** (*lawyer*) abogado(-a) *m(f)*; ***~ for the defense*** abogado(-a) *m(f)* defensor; ***~ for the prosecution***

acusador(a) *m(f)* **II** *v/t course of action* aconsejar; *person* ofrecer apoyo psicológico; **~ s.o. to do sth** aconsejar a alguien que haga algo

coun•sel•ing, *Br* **coun•sel•ling** ['kaʊnslɪŋ] apoyo *m* psicológico

coun•sel•or, *Br* **coun•sel•lor** ['kaʊnslər] **1** (*adviser*) consejero(-a) *m(f)*; *of student* orientador(a) *m(f)* **2** LAW abogado(-a) *m(f)*

count[1] [kaʊnt] **I** *n* (*number arrived at*) cuenta *f*; (*action of ~ing*) recuento *m*; *in baseball, boxing* cuenta *f*; ***what is your ~?*** ¿cuántos has contado?; ***keep ~ of*** llevar la cuenta de; ***lose ~ of*** perder la cuenta de; ***at the last ~*** en el último recuento; ***on all ~s*** LAW de todos los cargos

II *v/i to ten etc* contar; (*be important*) contar; (*qualify*) contar, valer; ***~ing from today*** contando desde hoy; ***it doesn't ~ for much*** no cuenta *or* vale mucho; ***doesn't that ~ for anything with you?*** ¿es que para ti eso no cuenta para nada?

III *v/t* **1** contar; ***not ~ing those present*** sin contar a los presentes; ***~ing those present*** contando a los presentes **2** (*consider*): ***~ o.s. lucky*** considerarse afortunado

◆ **count against** *v/t* desfavorecer, perjudicar

◆ **count down** *v/i* contar hacia atrás

◆ **count in** *v/t*: ***count me in*** cuenta conmigo, *CSur* yo me anoto

◆ **count on** *v/t* contar con

◆ **count out** *v/t* **1** contar; *in boxing* contar hasta diez, contar hasta out **2** (*exclude*): ***count me out!*** ¡no cuentes conmigo!

◆ **count up** *v/t* contar, recontar; *money* contar

count[2] [kaʊnt] *n nobleman* conde *m*

count•a•ble ['kaʊntəbl] *adj* GRAM contable

'count•down cuenta *f* atrás **~ *to the elections*** cuenta atrás para las elecciones

coun•te•nance ['kaʊntənəns] *fml* **I** *v/t* tolerar; **~ *doing sth*** contemplar *or* considerar hacer algo **II** *n face* semblante *m*, rostro *m*

coun•ter[1] ['kaʊntər] *n* **1** *in shop* mostrador *m*; *in café* barra *f*; ***under the ~*** *fig* por debajo de la mesa **2** *in game* ficha *f*

coun•ter[2] ['kaʊntər] **I** *v/t* contrarrestar **II** *v/i* (*retaliate*) responder

coun•ter[3] ['kaʊntər] *adv*: ***run ~ to*** estar en contra de

'coun•ter•act *v/t* contrarrestar

'coun•ter-ar•gu•ment refutación *f*, argumento *m* en contra

'coun•ter-at•tack **I** *n* contraataque *m* **II** *v/i* contraatacar

'coun•ter•bal•ance **I** *n* contrapeso *m* **II** *v/t* contrarrestar, contrapesar

'coun•ter•blast *fig* contraataque *m*

'coun•ter•charge LAW recriminación *f*

'coun•ter•claim COM, LAW contrapetición *f*

'coun•ter clerk cajero(-a) *m(f)*

'coun•ter•clock•wise *adv* en sentido contrario al de las agujas del reloj

'coun•ter•dem•on•stra•tion contramanifestación *f*

coun•ter-'es•pi•o•nage contraespionaje *m*

'coun•ter•ex•am•ple contraejemplo *m*

coun•ter•feit ['kaʊntərfɪt] **I** *v/t* falsificar **II** *adj* falso **III** falsificación *f*

coun•ter•feit•er ['kaʊntərfɪtər] falsificador(a) *m(f)*

'coun•ter•foil *Br* matriz *f*

coun•ter-in'tel•li•gence contrainteligencia *f*, contraespionaje *m*

coun•ter•mand ['kaʊntərmɑːnd] *v/t* contramandar

'coun•ter•meas•ure contramedida *f*

'coun•ter•move respuesta *f*

'coun•ter•of•fen•sive MIL contraofensiva *f*

'coun•ter-of•fer contraoferta *f*

coun•ter•pane ['kaʊntərpeɪn] colcha *f*, cubierta *f*

'coun•ter•part *person* homólogo(-a) *m(f)*

'coun•ter•point MUS contrapunto *m*

coun•ter•pro'duc•tive *adj* contraproducente

'coun•ter•pro•pos•al contraproposición *f*

coun•ter-rev•o'lu•tion POL contrarrevolución *f*

'coun•ter•sign *v/t* refrendar

coun•ter-'ter•ror•ism contraterrorismo *m*

'coun•ter•weight contrapeso *m*

coun•tess ['kaʊntes] condesa *f*

count•less ['kaʊntlɪs] *adj* incontables
coun•try ['kʌntrɪ] *n* **1** (*nation*) país *m*; **~ of birth** país de origen; **~ of origin** país de origen **2** *as opposed to town* campo *m*; **in the ~** en el campo; **flat / hilly ~** país *m* llano / con colinas; **~ life** vida *f* rural; **~ road** carretera *f* comarcal
coun•try and 'west•ern MUS música *f* country; **coun•try 'house** casa *f* de campo; **'coun•try•man** (*fellow ~*) compatriota *m*; **'coun•try mu•sic** MUS música *f* country; **'coun•try•side** campo *m*; **coun•try-'wide I** *adj* nacional **II** *adv* a nivel nacional; **'coun•try•wom•an** (*fellow ~*) compatriota *f*
coun•ty ['kaʊntɪ] condado *m*
coup [kuː] POL golpe *m* (de Estado); *fig* golpe *m* de efecto; **pull off a ~** *fig* dar un golpe maestro
coup d'é•tat [kuːdeɪ'tɑː] (*pl* **coups d'état** [kuːzdeɪ'tɑː]) golpe *m* (de Estado)
cou•pé ['kuːpeɪ] MOT cupé *m*
cou•ple ['kʌpl] **I** *n* pareja *f*; **just a ~** un par; **a ~ of** un par de; **it was all ~s at the party** en la fiesta sólo había parejitas **II** *v/t* RAIL empalmar, unir (**to** a)
cou•pon ['kuːpɑːn] cupón *m*
cour•age ['kʌrɪdʒ] valor *m*, coraje *m*; **lose ~** acobardarse; **pluck up one's ~** armarse de valor
cou•ra•geous [kə'reɪdʒəs] *adj* valiente
cou•ra•geous•ly [kə'reɪdʒəslɪ] *adv* valientemente
cour•gette [kɔːr'ʒet] BOT *Br* calabacín *m*
cou•ri•er ['kʊrɪər] **1** (*messenger*) mensajero(-a) *m(f)* **2** *with tourist party* guía *m/f*
course [kɔːrs] **1** (*series of lessons*) curso *m*; **English ~** curso de inglés; **~ of lectures** ciclo *m* de conferencias; **~ of study** programa *m* de estudios
2 (*part of meal*) plato *m*; **a three-~ meal** *una comida con primer plato, segundo plato y postre*
3 *of ship, plane* rumbo *m*; **change ~** cambiar de rumbo
4 *for horse race* circuito *m*; *for golf* campo *m*; *for skiing, marathon* recorrido *m*
5: **of ~** (*certainly*) claro, por supuesto; (*naturally*) por supuesto; **of ~ not** claro que no; **~ of action** táctica *f*; **~ of treatment** tratamiento *m*; **in the ~ of ...** durante ...; **in the ~ of time** con el tiempo, a la larga; **the ~ of events** el transcurso de los acontecimientos; **take *or* run its ~** tomar *or* seguir su curso
court [kɔːrt] **I** *n* **1** LAW tribunal *m*; (*courthouse*) palacio *m* de justicia; **take s.o. to ~** llevar a alguien a juicio; **in ~** en los tribunales; **come to ~** llevarse a los tribunales; **go to ~** ir a juicio; **settle out of ~** llegar a un acuerdo fuera de los tribunales **2** SP pista *f*, cancha *f* **3**: **pay ~ to s.o.** lisonjear a alguien **II** *v/t* cortejar a **III** *v/i* festejar; **~ing couple** pareja *f* de novios
'court case proceso *m*, causa *f*
cour•te•ous ['kɜːrtɪəs] *adj* cortés
cour•te•sy ['kɜːrtəsɪ] cortesía *f*; **by ~ of** por cortesía de; **~ visit** visita *f* de cortesía
'cour•te•sy car coche *m* de cortesía
'cour•te•sy light MOT luz *f* interior
'court•house palacio *m* de justicia; **court 'mar•tial I** *n* consejo *m* de guerra **II** *v/t* formar un consejo de guerra a; **he was ~ed** compareció ante un consejo de guerra; **'court or•der** orden *f* judicial; **'court•room** sala *f* de juicios
court•ship ['kɔːrtʃɪp] cortejo *m*, noviazgo *m*
'court•yard patio *m*
cous•in ['kʌzn] primo(-a) *m(f)*
cove [koʊv] (*small bay*) cala *f*
cov•er ['kʌvər] **I** *n* **1** *protective* funda *f*
2 *of book, magazine* portada *f*; **read sth from ~ to ~** leer algo de cabo a rabo
3 (*shelter*) protección *f*; **we took ~ from the rain** nos pusimos a cubierto de la lluvia; **take ~** cobijarse; **get under ~** ponerse a cubierto; **under (the) ~ of night** al abrigo *or* amparo de la noche
4 (*insurance*) cobertura *f*
5: **~s** *for bed* manta y sábanas *fpl*
6: **send sth under separate ~** enviar algo por separado; **under plain ~** en sobre sin membrete
II *v/t* cubrir
◆ **cover up I** *v/t* cubrir; *scandal* encubrir **II** *v/i* disimular; **cover up for s.o.** encubrir a alguien
cov•er•age ['kʌvərɪdʒ] *by media* cobertura *f* informativa
'cov•er charge cubierto *m*
'cov•er girl chica *f* de portada

cov•er•ing doc•tor ['kʌvrɪŋ] suplente *m/f*
cov•er•ing let•ter *Br* ☞ ***cover letter***
'cov•er let•ter carta *f*; **'cov•er note** certificado *m* provisional de cobertura; **'cov•er sto•ry** artículo *m* de portada
cov•ert ['koʊvɜːrt] *adj* encubierto
'cov•er-up encubrimiento *m*
cov•et ['kʌvɪt] *v/t* desear, ansiar
cov•et•ous ['kʌvɪtəs] *adj* codicioso, afanoso
cow [kaʊ] vaca *f*; ***wait till the ~s come home*** F esperar hasta que las ranas críen pelo F
cow•ard ['kaʊərd] cobarde *m/f*
cow•ard•ice ['kaʊərdɪs] cobardía *f*
cow•ard•ly ['kaʊərdlɪ] *adj* cobarde
'cow•boy vaquero *m*
cow•er ['kaʊər] *v/i* agacharse, amilanarse
'cow•girl vaquera *f*
'cow•hide piel *f* vacuna
cowl [kaʊl] (*monk's hood*) capucho *m*
co-work•er ['koʊwɜːrkər] compañero (-a) *m*(*f*) de trabajo, colega *m/f*
'cow•pat boñigo *m* de vaca; **'cow•shed** vaquería *f*; **'cow•skin** piel *f* vacuna
cox [kɑːks] *in rowing* timonel m
coy [kɔɪ] *adj* **1** (*evasive*) evasivo **2** (*flirtatious*) coqueto
coy•o•te [kɔɪ'oʊtɪ] coyote *m*
co•zi•ness ['koʊzɪnɪs] calidez *f*, comodidad *f*
co•zy ['koʊzɪ] *adj room* acogedor; *job* cómodo
CPA [siːpiː'eɪ] *abbr* (= ***certified public accountant***) censor(a) *m*(*f*) jurado (-a) de cuentas
CPU [siːpiː'juː] *abbr* (= ***central processing unit***) CPU *f* (= unidad *f* central de proceso)
crab[1] [kræb] cangrejo *m*
crab[2] [kræb] F (*bad-tempered person*) cascarrabias *m/fpl* F, gruñón(-ona) *m*(*f*) F
crab[3] [kræb] F (*pubic louse*) ladilla *f*
crab•bed ['kræbɪd] *adj* **1** *handwriting* enrevesado **2** (*bad-tempered*) gruñón
crab•by ['kræbɪ] *adj* gruñón
'crab louse ZO ladilla *f*
crack [kræk] **I** *n* **1** grieta *f*; *in cup, glass* raja *f*; ***at the ~ of dawn*** al despuntar el alba; ***give s.o. a fair ~ of the whip*** F dar a alguien una oportunidad; ***the door was open a ~*** la puerta estaba abierta una rendija **2** (*joke*) chiste *m* (malo); ***make ~s about*** burlarse *or* mofarse de **3**: ***have a ~ at sth*** intentar algo
II *v/t* **1** *cup, glass* rajar **2** *nut* cascar **3** *code* descifrar; F (*solve*) resolver **4**: ***~ a joke*** contar un chiste
III *v/i* **1** rajarse **2**: ***get ~ing*** F poner manos a la obra F
IV *adj* F (*skilled*): ***~ shot*** tirador *m* experto; ***~ troops*** tropas *fpl* de primera
◆ **crack down** *v/i* tomar medidas severas, actuar con dureza
◆ **crack down on** *v/t* tomar medidas severas contra
◆ **crack up** *v/i* **1** (*have breakdown*) sufrir una crisis nerviosa **2** F (*laugh*) desternillarse F
crack•brained ['krækbreɪnd] *adj* F chiflado F
'crack•down medidas *fpl* severas
cracked [krækt] *adj* **1** *cup, glass* rajado **2** F (*crazy*) chiflado F
crack•er ['krækər] *to eat* galleta *f* salada
crack•ers ['krækərz] *adj* F chalado, chiflado
crack•le ['krækl] **I** *v/i of fire* crepitar **II** *n* crepitación *f*
crack•ling ['kræklɪŋ] GASTR piel *f* de cerdo asada
crack•ly ['kræklɪ] *adj* chispeante, crujiente
'crack•pot F **I** *n* chalado(-a) *m*(*f*) F **II** *adj* disparatado
'crack-up F ataque *m* de nervios
cra•dle ['kreɪdl] **I** *n for baby* cuna *f*; ***from the ~ to the grave*** durante toda la vida **II** *v/t* acunar, mecer
craft[1] [kræft] NAUT embarcación *f*
craft[2] [kræft] **1** (*skill*) arte *m* **2** (*trade*) oficio *m*
craft•i•ness ['kræftɪnɪs] astucia *f*
crafts•man ['kræftsmən] artesano *m*
crafts•man•ship ['kræftsmənʃɪp] artesanía *f*
crafts•wom•an ['kræftswʊmən] artesana *f*
craft•y ['kræftɪ] *adj* astuto
crag [kræg] *rock* peñasco *m*, risco *m*
crag•gy ['krægɪ] *adj* **1** *mountain* escarpado **2** *features* anguloso
cram [kræm] (*pret & pp* **-med**) *v/t* embutir
cram-'full *adj* abarrotado

cramp[1] [kræmp] *n* calambre *m*; ***stomach ~*** retorcijón *m*
cramp[2] [kræmp] *v/t*: ***~ s.o.'s style*** cortar a alguien
cramped [kræmpt] *adj room, apartment* pequeño; ***we're a bit ~ed in here*** aquí estamos un poco apretujados
cram•pon ['kræmpɑːn] crampón *m*
cramps [kræmps] *npl* calambre *m*; ***stomach ~*** retorcijón *m*
cran•ber•ry ['krænbərɪ] arándano *m* agrio
cran•ber•ry 'sauce salsa *f* de arándanos agrios
crane [kreɪn] **I** *n machine* grúa *f* **II** *v/t*: ***~ one's neck*** estirar el cuello
◆ **crane forward** *v/i* asomarse
'crane driv•er conductor(a) *m(f)* de grúa
crank[1] [kræŋk] *person* maniático(-a) *m(f)*, persona *f* rara
crank[2] [kræŋk] TECH manivela *f*, manecilla *f*
◆ **crank out** *v/t* F producir en cadena F
◆ **crank up** *v/i* F *volume* subir
'crank•shaft cigüeñal *m*
crank•y ['kræŋkɪ] *adj* (*bad-tempered*) gruñón
cran•ny ['krænɪ] grieta *f*
crap [kræp] P **I** *n* (*excrement*) mierda *f* P; (*nonsense*) *L.Am.* pendejadas *fpl* P, *Rpl* boludeces *fpl* P, *Span* gilipolleces *fpl* P; (*poor quality item*) mierda *f* P **II** *v/i* (*pret & pp* **-ped**) (*defecate*) cagar V
crap•py ['kræpɪ] *adj* P cutre P, de mierda P
crash [kræʃ] **I** *n* **1** *noise* estruendo *m*, estrépito *m*; ***a ~ of thunder*** un trueno **2** *accident* accidente *m* **3** COM quiebra *f*, crac *m* **4** COMPUT bloqueo *m*
II *v/i* **1** *of car, airplane* estrellarse (***into*** con *or* contra) **2** *of thunder* sonar; ***the waves ~ed onto the shore*** las olas chocaban contra la orilla; ***the vase ~ed to the ground*** el jarrón se cayó con estruendo **3** COM *of market* hundirse, desplomarse **4** COMPUT bloquearse, colgarse **5** F (*sleep*) dormir, *Span* sobar F
III *v/t* **1** *car* estrellar **2**: ***~ a party*** colarse en una fiesta
◆ **crash out** *v/i* F (*fall asleep*) dormirse, *Span* quedarse sobado F

'crash bar•ri•er quitamiedos *m inv*; **'crash course** curso *m* intensivo; **'crash di•et** dieta *f* drástica; **'crash hel•met** casco *m* protector; **'crash-land** *v/i* realizar un aterrizaje forzoso; **'crash 'land•ing** aterrizaje *m* forzoso; **'crash-test** MOT test *m* de choque
crass [kræs] *adj* **1** *mistake* garrafal **2** *remark* irrespetuoso, grosero
crate [kreɪt] (*packing case*) caja *f*
cra•ter ['kreɪtər] *of volcano* cráter *m*
cra•vat [krə'væt] pañuelo *m* (*metido por el cuello de la camisa*)
crave [kreɪv] *v/t* ansiar
crav•ing ['kreɪvɪŋ] ansia *f*, deseo *m*; *of pregnant woman* antojo *m*; ***I have a ~ for …*** me apetece muchísimo …
craw•fish [krɒːfɪʃ] **I** *n freshwater* cangrejo *m* de río; *saltwater* langosta *f* **II** *v/i* P (*back out*) echarse atrás
crawl [krɒːl] **I** *n in swimming* crol *m*; ***at a ~*** (*very slowly*) muy lentamente **II** *v/i on floor* arrastrarse; *of baby* andar a gatas; (*move slowly*) avanzar lentamente; ***~ to s.o.*** *fig* arrastrarse a los pies de alguien; ***the sight made her flesh ~*** lo que vió le revolvió las tripas
◆ **crawl with** *v/t*: ***be crawling with*** estar abarrotado de
cray•fish ['kreɪfɪʃ] *freshwater* cangrejo *m* de río; *saltwater* langosta *f*
cray•on ['kreɪɑːn] lápiz *m* de color
craze [kreɪz] locura *f* (***for*** de); ***the latest ~*** la última locura *or* moda
cra•zi•ness ['kreɪzɪnɪs] locura *f*, disparate *m*
cra•zy ['kreɪzɪ] *adj* loco; ***be ~ about*** estar loco por; ***drive s.o. ~*** volver loco a alguien
'cra•zy bone húmero *m*
creak [kriːk] **I** *n of hinge, door* chirrido *m*; *of floor, shoes* crujido *m* **II** *v/i of hinge, door* chirriar; *of floor, shoes* crujir
creak•y ['kriːkɪ] *adj hinge, door* que chirria; *floor, shoes* que cruje
cream [kriːm] **I** *n* **1** *for skin* crema *f* **2** *for coffee, cake* nata *f*; ***whipped ~*** nata montada **3** (*color*) crema *m* **II** *adj* crema **II** *v/t* **1** (*purée*) hacer puré; *butter and sugar* mezclar **2** F (*defeat*) hacer papilla F
◆ **cream off** *v/t the best* quedarse con, llevarse

cream 'cheese queso *m* blanco para untar

'cream-col•ored, *Br* **'cream-col•oured** *adj* de color crema

cream•er ['kri:mər] **1** (*pitcher*) jarra *f* para la nata **2** *for coffee* leche *f* en polvo

cream•y ['kri:mɪ] *adj with lots of cream* cremoso

crease [kri:s] **I** *n accidental* arruga *f*; *deliberate* raya *f* **II** *v/t accidentally* arrugar

'crease-proof *adj* inarrugable

'crease-re•sist•ant *adj* resistente a las arrugas

cre•ate [kri:'eɪt] *v/t & v/i* crear

cre•a•tion [kri:'eɪʃn] creación *f*; ***the Creation*** REL la Creación

cre•a•tive [kri:'eɪtɪv] *adj* creativo; ***~ writing*** creación *f* literaria

cre•a•tiv•i•ty [kri:eɪ'tɪvɪtɪ] creatividad *f*

cre•a•tor [kri:'eɪtər] creador(a) *m*(*f*); (*founder*) fundador(a) *m*(*f*); ***the Creator*** REL el Creador

crea•ture ['kri:ʧər] *animal*, *person* criatura *f*; ***be a ~ of habit*** ser una persona de costumbres

crea•ture 'com•forts *npl* comodidades *fpl*, pequeños lujos *mpl*

crèche [kreʃ] **1** *for children* guardería *f* (infantil) **2** REL nacimiento *m*, belén *m*

cre•dence ['kri:dəns] ***give*** *or* ***attach ~ to*** dar *or* conceder crédito a

cre•den•tials [krɪ'denʃlz] *npl* (*abilities*) aptitudes *fpl*; ***establish one's ~*** demostrar que se vale; ***present one's ~*** presentar los credenciales

cred•i•bil•i•ty [kredə'bɪlətɪ] credibilidad *f*; ***~ gap*** falta *f* de credibilidad

cred•i•ble ['kredəbl] *adj* creíble

cred•it ['kredɪt] **I** *n* **1** FIN, crédito *m*; ***be in ~*** tener un saldo positivo; ***on ~*** a crédito; ***give s.o. ~ for $1,000*** abonar a alguien 1.000 dólares
2 (*honor*) credito *m*; ***get the ~ for sth*** recibir reconocimiento por algo; ***be a ~ to*** dar crédito *or* reputación a; ***be to s.o.'s ~*** hacer honor a alguien, decir mucho en favor de alguien; ***give s.o. ~ for sth*** reconocer el mérito a alguien por algo; ***to his ~ it has to be said that …*** en su favor hay que decir que …; ***~ where ~ is due*** para ser de justicia
II *v/t* **1** (*believe*) creer **2** FIN: ***~ an amount to an account*** abonar una cantidad en una cuenta **3**: ***~ s.o. with sth*** atribuir a alguien algo

cred•it•a•ble ['kredɪtəbl] *adj* estimable, honorable

'cred•it bal•ance haber *m*; **'cred•it card** tarjeta *f* de crédito; **'cred•it ceil•ing** límite *m* del crédito; **'cred•it con•trol** COM control *m* de crédito; **'cred•it lim•it** límite *m* de crédito; **'cred•it note** COM nota *f* de crédito

cred•i•tor ['kredɪtər] acreedor(a) *m*(*f*)

'cred•it rat•ing FIN clasificación *f* por grado de solvencia

cred•its ['kredɪts] *TV*, *movie* títulos *mpl* de crédito, créditos *mpl*

'cred•it squeeze estrechamiento *m* del crédito

'cred•it•wor•thy *adj* solvente

cre•du•li•ty [krɪ'du:lətɪ] credulidad *f*

cred•u•lous ['kredʊləs] *adj* crédulo

creed [kri:d] (*beliefs*) credo *m*

creek [kri:k] (*stream*) arroyo *m*; ***be up the ~*** (***without a paddle***) F estar en un aprieto F

creep [kri:p] **I** *n pej* asqueroso(-a) *m*(*f*) **II** *v/i* (*pret & pp* ***crept***) moverse sigilosamente; ***the sight made her flesh ~*** lo que vió le revolvió las tripas

◆ **creep in** *v/i of errors etc* manifestarse

◆ **creep up on** *v/t* acercarse sigilosamente a

creep•er ['kri:pər] BOT enredadera *f*

creep•ing ['kri:pɪŋ] *adj* gradual, progresivo

creeps [kri:ps] *npl* F: ***the house / he gives me the ~*** la casa / él me pone la piel de gallina F

creep•y ['kri:pɪ] *adj* F espeluznante F

cre•mate [krɪ'meɪt] *v/t* incinerar

cre•ma•tion [krɪ'meɪʃn] incineración *f*

cre•ma•to•ri•um [kremə'tɔ:rɪəm] crematorio *m*

cre•ma•to•ry ['kri:mətɔ:rɪ] ☞ ***crematorium***

crept [krept] *pret & pp* ☞ **creep**

cre•scen•do [krə'ʃendoʊ] MUS crescendo *m*; ***rise to*** *or* ***reach a ~*** *fig* alcanzar el punto culminante

cres•cent ['kresənt] *shape* medialuna *f*; ***~ moon*** cuarto *m* creciente

cress [kres] BOT berro *m*

crest [krest] *of hill* cima *f*, *of bird* cresta *f*; ***be riding on the ~ of a wave*** *fig* estar en la cresta de la ola

'crest•fal•len *adj* abatido
Creutz•feldt-Ja•kob dis•ease [krɔɪtsfelt'jækɑːb] MED enfermedad *f* de Creutzfeldt-Jakob
cre•vasse [krɪ'væs] hendidura *f*
crev•ice ['krevɪs] grieta *f*
crew [kruː] *n* **1** *of ship, airplane* tripulación *f* **2** *of repairmen etc* equipo *m* **3** (*crowd, group*) grupo *m*, pandilla *f*
'crew cut rapado *m*
'crew neck cuello *m* redondo
crib [krɪb] *for baby* cuna *f*
crick [krɪk]: ***have a ~ in the neck*** tener tortícolis
crick•et[1] ['krɪkɪt] *insect* grillo *m*
crick•et[2] ['krɪkɪt] *sport* cricket *m*
crick•et•er ['krɪkɪtər] jugador(a) *m(f)* de cricket
crime [kraɪm] (*offense*) delito *m*; *serious, also fig* crimen *m*
'crime•wave ola *f* de delincuencia
crim•i•nal ['krɪmɪnl] **I** *n* delincuente *m/f*, criminal *m/f* **II** *adj* **1** (*relating to crime*) criminal; (LAW: *not civil*) penal; *act* delictivo **2** (*shameful*) vergonzoso; ***it's ~*** es un crimen
crim•i•nal 'law ley *f* penal; **crim•i•nal pro'ceed•ings** *npl* procedimiento *m* penal; **crim•i•nal 'rec•ord** antecedentes *mpl* penales; ***have a ~*** tener antecedentes penales
crim•i•nol•o•gy [krɪmɪ'nɑːlədʒɪ] criminología *f*
crimp [krɪmp] *v/t* **1** *cloth, paper* doblar, plegar **2** *hair* rizar con tenacillas
crim•son ['krɪmzn] *adj* carmesí
cringe [krɪndʒ] *v/i with embarrassment* sentir vergüenza
crin•kle ['krɪŋkl] **I** *v/i* arrugarse **II** *v/t* arrugar **III** *n* arruga *f*
crip•ple ['krɪpl] **I** *n* (*disabled person*) inválido(-a) *m(f)* **II** *v/t person* dejar inválido; *fig*: *country, industry* paralizar
cri•sis ['kraɪsɪs] (*pl* ***crises*** ['kraɪsiːz]) crisis *f inv*
crisp [krɪsp] *adj weather, air* fresco; *lettuce, apple, bacon* crujiente; *new shirt, bills* flamante
'crisp•bread *pan dietético a base de centeno o trigo*
criss•cross ['krɪskrɑːs] **I** *n* cruz *f* **II** *v/t* atravesar, entrecruzar
cri•te•ri•on [kraɪ'tɪrɪən] (*pl* ***criteria*** [kraɪ'tɪrɪə]) (*standard*) criterio *m*
crit•ic ['krɪtɪk] crítico(-a) *m(f)*
crit•i•cal ['krɪtɪkl] *adj* (*making criticisms, serious*) crítico; *moment etc* decisivo; ***be ~ of s.o. / sth*** ser crítico con alguien / algo; ***he is in a ~ condition*** MED está en un estado crítico
crit•i•cal•ly ['krɪtɪklɪ] *adv speak etc* en tono de crítica; ***~ ill*** en estado crítico
crit•i•cism ['krɪtɪsɪzm] crítica *f*; ***be open to ~*** ofrecerse a críticas; ***above ~*** exento de críticas
crit•i•cize ['krɪtɪsaɪz] *v/t* criticar; ***~ s.o. for doing sth*** criticar a alguien por hacer algo
cri•tique [krɪ'tiːk] crítica *f*, análisis *m*
croak [kroʊk] **I** *n of frog* croar *m* **II** *v/i of frog* croar
Cro•at ['kroʊæt] **1** *person* croata *m/f* **2** *language* croata *m*
Cro•a•tia [kroʊ'eɪʃə] Croacia *f*
Cro•a•tian [kroʊ'eɪʃən] **I** *n* **1** *person* croata *m/f* **2** *language* croata *m* **II** *adj* croata
cro•chet ['kroʊʃeɪ] **I** *n* ganchillo *m* **II** *v/t* hacer a ganchillo
crock [krɑːk]: ***old ~*** F *vehicle* tastarro F *m*; *person* carca F *m*; ***that's a ~ of shit*** P eso es una chorrada *or* pijada P
crock•e•ry ['krɑːkərɪ] vajilla *f*
croc•o•dile ['krɑːkədaɪl] cocodrilo *m*
'croc•o•dile tears *npl* lágrimas *fpl* de cocodrilo
cro•cus ['kroʊkəs] azafrán *m*
cro•ny ['kroʊnɪ] F amiguete *m/f* F
crook [krʊk] **1** ladrón(-ona) *m(f)*; *dishonest trader* granuja *m/f* **2**: ***hold sth in the ~ of one's arm*** sostener algo con la parte interior del codo
crook•ed ['krʊkɪd] *adj* **1** (*not straight*) torcido **2** (*dishonest*) deshonesto
croon [kruːn] *v/t & v/i* cantar suavemente
croon•er ['kruːnər] cantante *m* de baladas
crop [krɑːp] **I** *n also fig* cosecha *f*; *plant grown* cultivo *m*; ***~ failure*** cosecha pésima **II** *v/t* (*pret & pp* ***-ped***) *hair* cortar; *photo* recortar
◆ **crop up** *v/i* salir
crop•per ['krɑːpər] *Br* F: ***come a ~*** *also fig* darse un batacazo F
cro•quet ['kroʊkeɪ] croquet *m*
cross [krɑːs] **I** *adj* (*angry*) enfadado, enojado

C

II *n* **1** cruz *f*; ***the Cross*** la Cruz; ***make the sign of the ~*** hacer la señal de la cruz **2** *in soccer* centro *m*, cruce *m*
III *v/t* **1** (*go across*) cruzar; ***~ o.s.*** REL santiguarse; ***~ one's arms / legs*** cruzar los brazos / las piernas; ***keep one's fingers ~ed*** cruzar los dedos; ***it never ~ed my mind*** no se me ocurrió; ***~ s.o.'s path*** *fig* cruzarse en el camino de alguien **2** *en fútbol* centrar
IV *v/i* **1** (*go across*) cruzar **2** *of lines* cruzarse, cortarse **3** *en fútbol* centrar
◆ **cross off, cross out** *v/t* tachar
◆ **cross over** *v/i* **1** POL pasarse (de bando) **2** *on road* cruzar
'cross•bar *of goal* larguero *m*; *of bicycle* barra *f*; *in high jump* listón *m*; **'cross-beam** TECH viga *f* transversal; **'cross-breed** BIO **I** *n* híbrido(-a) *m(f)* **II** *v/t* (*pret & pp* ☞ ***-bred***) cruzar; **cross-'check** **I** *n* comprobación *f* **II** *v/t* comprobar; **cross-coun•try 'ski•ing** esquí *m* de fondo; **'cross•cur•rent** contracorriente *f*; **cross-'dress•ing** travestismo *m*
crossed cheque *Br* [krɑːst'ʧek] cheque *m* cruzado
cross-ex•am•i'na•tion LAW interrogatorio *m*; **cross-ex'am•ine** *v/t* LAW interrogar; **cross-eyed** [krɑːs'aɪd] *adj* bizco; **'cross-fire** MIL fuego *m* cruzado; ***be caught in the ~*** *fig* estar entre dos fuegos
cross•ing ['krɑːsɪŋ] NAUT travesía *f*; ***~ point*** paso *m*
cross-leg•ged [krɑːs'legɪd] *adv*: ***sit ~*** sentarse con las piernas cruzadas
'cross•patch F refunfuñón(-ona) *m(f)* F; **cross-'pur•pos•es** *npl*: ***talk at ~*** hablar de dos cosas diferentes; **cross-'ref•er•ence** referencia *f*; **'cross•roads** *nsg also fig* encrucijada *f*; **'cross-sec•tion** *of people* muestra *f* representativa; **'cross•walk** paso *m* de peatones
'cross•ways, cross•wise ['krɑːswaɪz] *adv* al cruzado
'cross•word (puz•zle) crucigrama *m*
crotch [krɑːʧ] *of person, pants* entrepierna *f*
crotch•et ['krɑːʧɪt] *Br* MUS negra *f*
crotch•et•y ['krɑːʧətɪ] *adj* F renegón F
crouch [krauʧ] *v/i* agacharse
◆ **crouch down** *v/i* enroscarse

croup [kruːp] MED crup *m*
crou•pi•er ['kruːpɪər] crupier *m/f*
crow[1] [kroʊ] *n bird* corneja *f*; ***as the ~ flies*** en línea recta; ***eat ~*** F tragarse la soberbia F
crow[2] [kroʊ] *v/i* **1** *of rooster* cacarear **2**: ***~ with delight*** gorjear de placer; ***~ over sth*** presumir *or* alardear de algo
'crow•bar palanca *f*
crowd [kraʊd] **I** *n* multitud *f*, muchedumbre *f*; *at sports event* público *m*; ***~s of people*** montones *mpl* de gente; ***one of the ~*** uno más del montón; ***go with the ~*** hacer lo mismo que el resto de la gente; ***that ~ you hang around with*** esa gente con la que te juntas **II** *v/t* abarrotar
◆ **crowd around** **I** *v/t* apretujarse alrededor de **II** *v/i* arremolinarse alrededor
◆ **crowd into** *v/t* apiñarse en
crowd•ed ['kraʊdɪd] *adj* abarrotado (***with*** de)
crown [kraʊn] **I** *n on head, tooth* corona *f*; ***the Crown*** *Br* LAW la Corona **II** *v/t* *tooth* poner una corona a; ***the ~ed heads of Europe*** los monarcas europeos; ***to ~ it all*** para remate
crown•ing ['kraʊnɪŋ] *adj achievement* supremo; ***the city's ~ glory*** la joya de la ciudad
crown 'jew•els *npl* joyas *fpl* de la Corona; **crown 'prince** príncipe *m* heredero; **crown prin'cess** princesa *f* heredera
'crow's feet *npl* patas *fpl* de gallo
'crow's nest NAUT cofa *f* de vigilancia
CRT [siːɑːr'tiː] *abbr* (= ***cathode ray tube***) TRC *m* (= tubo *m* de rayos catódicos)
cru•cial ['kruːʃl] *adj* crucial
cru•ci•ble ['kruːsɪbl] crisol *m*
cru•ci•fix ['kruːsɪfɪks] crucifijo *m*
cru•ci•fix•ion [kruːsɪ'fɪkʃn] crucifixión *f*
cru•ci•fy ['kruːsɪfaɪ] *v/t* (*pret & pp* ***-ied***) *also fig* crucificar
crude [kruːd] **I** *adj* **1** (*vulgar*) grosero **2** (*unsophisticated*) primitivo **II** *n*: ***~ (oil)*** crudo *m*
crude•ly ['kruːdlɪ] *adv* **1** *speak* groseramente **2** *made* de manera primitiva
crude•ness, cru•di•ty ['kruːdnɪs, 'kruːdɪtɪ] **1** (*vulgarity*) ordinariez *f* **2** (*lack of sophistication*) simplicidad *f*

C

cru•el ['kru:əl] *adj* cruel (***to*** con)
cru•el•ty ['kru:əltɪ] crueldad *f* (***to*** con)
cru•et set, cru•et stand ['kru:ɪt] vinajera *f*
cruise [kru:z] **I** *n* crucero *m*; ***go on a ~*** ir de crucero **II** *v/i* **1** *of people* hacer un crucero **2** *of car* ir a velocidad de crucero; *of plane* volar
'cruise lin•er transatlántico *m*
cruise 'mis•sile MIL misil *m* de crucero
cruis•er ['kru:zər] **1** (*battleship*) crucero *m* de combate **2** (*police car*) coche *m* patrulla
cruis•ing speed ['kru:zɪŋ] *of vehicle* velocidad *f* de crucero; *fig*: *of project etc* ritmo *m* normal
crumb [krʌm] miga *f*; ***a few ~s of information*** unos cuantos fragmentos de información; ***~ of comfort*** pizca *f* de consuelo
crum•ble ['krʌmbl] **I** *v/t* desmigajar **II** *v/i of bread* desmigajarse; *of stonework* desmenuzarse; *fig*: *of opposition etc* desmoronarse
◆ **crumble away** *v/i* desmoronarse
crum•bly ['krʌmblɪ] *adj cookie* que se desmigaja; *stonework* que se desmenuza
crum•my ['krʌmɪ] *adj* F malo, penoso F
crum•ple ['krʌmpl] **I** *v/t* (*crease*) arrugar **II** *v/i* (*collapse*) desplomarse
◆ **crumple up** *v/t* arrugar; *into a ball* arrugar en una bola
crunch [krʌntʃ] **I** *n*: ***when it comes to the ~*** a la hora de la verdad **II** *v/i of snow, gravel* crujir
crunch•y ['krʌntʃɪ] *adj* crujiente
cru•sade [kru:'seɪd] **I** *n also fig* cruzada *f* **II** *v/i*: ***~ for / against sth*** luchar a favor / en contra de algo
cru•sad•er [kru:'seɪdər] HIST cruzado *m*
crush [krʌʃ] **I** *n* **1** (*crowd*) muchedumbre *f* **2**: ***have a ~ on*** estar loco por **II** *v/t* aplastar; (*crease*) arrugar; ***they were ~ed to death*** murieron aplastados **III** *v/i* (*crease*) arrugarse
'crush bar•ri•er *Br* barrera *f* de seguridad
crush•ing ['krʌʃɪŋ] *adj defeat* abrumador, aplastante; ***~ blow*** *fig* golpe *m* mortal; ***~ majority*** mayoría *f* aplastante
'crush-re•sist•ant *adj fabric* resistente a las arrugas
crust [krʌst] *on bread* corteza *f*
crust•y ['krʌstɪ] *adj bread* crujiente
crutch [krʌtʃ] *for injured person* muleta *f*
crux [krʌks]: ***the ~ of the matter*** el quid de la cuestión
cru•zei•ro [krʊ'seɪroʊ] FIN cruceiro *m*
cry [kraɪ] **I** *n* (*call*) grito *m*; ***have a ~*** llorar; ***~ for help*** *fig* grito de auxilio; ***be a far*** *or* ***long ~ from sth*** *fig* no tener nada que ver con algo **II** *v/t* (*pret & pp* ***-ied***) **1** (*call*) gritar **2**: ***~ o.s. to sleep*** llorar hasta quedarse dormido **III** *v/i* (*pret & pp* ***-ied***) **1** (*weep*) llorar **2**: ***~ for help*** gritar en busca de ayuda
◆ **cry off** *v/i Br* F arrepentirse, echarse para atrás
◆ **cry out** *v/t & v/i* gritar; ***cry out against sth*** protestar contra algo
◆ **cry out for** *v/t* (*need*) pedir a gritos
'cry•ba•by llorón(-ona) *m*(*f*)
cry•ing ['kraɪɪŋ] **I** *n* lloro *m* **II** *adj need* urgente, imperioso; ***it's a ~ shame*** es una verdadera lástima
crypt [krɪpt] ARCHI cripta *f*
cryp•tic ['krɪptɪk] *adj* críptico
crys•tal ['krɪstl] cristal *m*
crys•tal-'clear *adj water* claro, transparente; *explanation* claro, definido
crys•tal•li•za•tion [krɪstəlaɪ'zeɪʃn] cristalización *f*
crys•tal•lize ['krɪstəlaɪz] **I** *v/t* cristalizar **II** *v/i* cristalizarse
CS gas [si:es'gæs] gas *m* lacrimógeno
CST [si:es'ti:] *abbr* (= ***Central Standard Time***) *hora oficial en el centro de Norteamérica*
cub [kʌb] cachorro *m*; *of bear* osezno *m*
Cu•ba ['kju:bə] Cuba *f*
Cu•ban ['kju:bən] **I** *adj* cubano **II** *n* cubano(-a) *m*(*f*)
cube [kju:b] *shape* cubo *m*; ***~ root*** raíz *f* cúbica
cu•bic ['kju:bɪk] *adj* cúbico; ***~ meter*** metro *m* cúbico
cu•bic ca'pac•i•ty TECH cilindrada *f*
cu•bi•cle ['kju:bɪkl] (*changing room*) cubículo *m*
cuck•old ['kʌkoʊld] **I** *n* cornudo *m* **II** *v/t* poner los cuernos a
cuck•oo ['kʊku:] **I** *n* cuco *m* **II** *adj* F girado F, chalado F
'cuck•oo clock reloj *m* de cuco
cu•cum•ber ['kju:kʌmbər] pepino *m*;

(**as**) ***cool as a ~*** F con una pachorra increíble F
cud [kʌd]: ***chew the ~*** rumiar; *fig* rumiar, cavilar
cud•dle ['kʌdl] **I** *n* abrazo **II** *v/t* abrazar
◆ **cuddle up** *v/i* abrazarse; ***cuddle up to s.o.*** abrazarse a alguien
cud•dly ['kʌdlɪ] *adj kitten etc* tierno
cudg•el ['kʌdʒəl] **I** *n* garrote *m*, porra *f*; ***take up the ~s for s.o.*** / ***sth*** *fig* romper lanzas por alguien / algo **II** *v/t* (*pret & pp* ***-ed***, *Br* ***-led***) aporrear, apalear
cue [kjuː] **1** *for actor etc* pie *m*, entrada *f*; ***take one's ~ from s.o.*** *fig* tomar como ejemplo a alguien; ***she arrived right on ~*** llegó en el momento justo **2** *for pool* taco *m*
'**cue ball** bola *f* blanca
'**cue card** TV tarjeta *f* (*con los diálogos*)
cuff [kʌf] **I** *n* **1** *of shirt* puño *m*; *of pants* vuelta *f*; ***off the ~*** improvisado **2** (*blow*) cachete *m* **II** *v/t* (*hit*) dar un cachete a
'**cuff link** gemelo *m*
cui•sine [kwɪ'ziːn] cocina *f*
cul-de-sac ['kʌldəsæk] callejón *m* sin salida
cu•li•nar•y ['kʌlɪnerɪ] *adj* culinario
cull [kʌl] *v/t* **1** *animals* sacrificar **2** (*select*): ***~ sth from sth*** extraer *or* seleccionar algo de algo
cul•mi•nate ['kʌlmɪneɪt] *v/i* culminar (***in*** en)
cul•mi•na•tion [kʌlmɪ'neɪʃn] culminación *f*
cu•lottes [kuː'lɑːts] *npl* falda-pantalón *f*
cul•pa•ble ['kʌlpəbl] *adj* culpable
cul•prit ['kʌlprɪt] culpable *m/f*
cult [kʌlt] (*sect*) secta *f*; ***~ figure*** ídolo *m*
cul•ti•vate ['kʌltɪveɪt] *v/t also fig* cultivar
cul•ti•vat•ed ['kʌltɪveɪtɪd] *adj person* culto
cul•ti•va•tion [kʌltɪ'veɪʃn] *of land* cultivo *m*
cul•ti•va•tor ['kʌltɪveɪtər] motocultor *m*
cul•tu•ral ['kʌltʃərəl] *adj* cultural
cul•tu•ral ex'change intercambio *m* cultural
cul•tu•ral 'her•i•tage patrimonio *m* cultural
cul•ture ['kʌltʃər] *artistic* cultura *f*
cul•tured ['kʌltʃərd] *adj* **1** (*cultivated*) culto **2**: ***~ pearl*** perla *f* cultivada
'**cul•ture shock** choque *m* cultural
cum•ber•some ['kʌmbərsəm] *adj* engorroso
cu•mu•la•tive ['kjuːmjʊlətɪv] *adj* acumulativo
cu•mu•lus ['kjuːmjʊləs] (*pl* **cumuli** ['kjuːmjʊlaɪ]) METEO cúmulo *m*
cun•ni•lin•gus [kʌnɪ'lɪŋgəs] cunnilingus *m*
cun•ning ['kʌnɪŋ] **I** *n* astucia *f* **II** *adj* astuto
cunt [kʌnt] V coño *m* V, *L.Am.* concha *f* V
cup [kʌp] **I** *n* taza *f*; *trophy* copa *f*; ***that's not my ~ of tea*** *Br* F eso no me apasiona *or* gusta especialmente **II** *v/t* (*pret & pp* ***-ped***): ***~ one's hands*** ahuecar las manos (*para sostener algo*)
cup•board ['kʌbərd] armario *m*
'**cup fi•nal** *Br* final *f* de (la) copa
cup•ful ['kʌpfʊl] taza *f*
cu•po•la ['kjuːpələ] cúpula *f*
cu•ra•ble ['kjʊrəbl] *adj* curable
cu•ra•tor [kjʊ'reɪtər] conservador(a) *m*(*f*)
curb [kɜːrb] **I** *n* **1** *of street* bordillo *m* **2** *on powers etc* freno *m* **II** *v/t* frenar
'**curb•stone** bordillo *m*
curd [kɜːrd] cuajada *f*
cur•dle ['kɜːrdl] **I** *v/i of milk* cortarse; ***the sight made my blood ~*** lo que ví me heló la sangre **II** *v/t milk* cortar
cure [kjʊr] **I** *n* MED cura *f*; ***past ~*** incurable **II** *v/t* MED, *meat* curar
'**cure-all** panacea *f* universal
cur•few ['kɜːrfjuː] toque *m* de queda
cu•ri•o ['kjʊrɪoʊ] curiosidad *f*, rareza *f*
cu•ri•os•i•ty [kjʊrɪ'ɑːsətɪ] (*inquisitiveness*) curiosidad *f*
cu•ri•ous ['kjʊrɪəs] *adj* (*inquisitive*, *strange*) curioso; ***I am ~ to know if*** tengo curiosidad por saber si
cu•ri•ous•ly ['kjʊrɪəslɪ] *adv* **1** (*inquisitively*) con curiosidad **2** (*strangely*) curiosamente; ***~ enough*** curiosamente
curl [kɜːrl] **I** *n in hair* rizo *m*; *of smoke* voluta *f* **II** *v/t hair* rizar; (*wind*) enroscar **III** *v/i of hair* rizarse; *of leaf*, *paper etc* ondularse
◆ **curl up** *v/i of person* acurrucarse; *of cat* enroscarse; *of paper* rizarse
curl•er ['kɜːrlər] *for hair* rulo *m*
curl•ing ['kɜːrlɪŋ] SP curling *m*

C

curl•y ['kɜːrlɪ] *adj hair* rizado; *tail* enroscado
cur•rant ['kʌrənt] *dried fruit* pasa *f* de Corinto
cur•ren•cy ['kʌrənsɪ] **1** *money* moneda *f*; ***foreign ~*** divisas *fpl*; ***~ reform*** reforma *f* monetaria **2**: ***gain ~*** aceptarse, extenderse
cur•rent ['kʌrənt] **I** *n in sea*, ELEC corriente *f*; ***swim against the ~*** *fig* nadar *or* ir a contracorriente; ***~ of air*** corriente de aire **II** *adj* (*present*) actual; ***~ fiscal year*** año *m* fiscal en curso
'cur•rent ac•count *Br* cuenta *f* corriente; **cur•rent af'fairs, cur•rent e'vents** *npl* la actualidad; **cur•rent af'fairs pro•gram** programa *m* de actualidad;
cur•rent•ly ['kʌrəntlɪ] *adv* actualmente
cur•ric•u•lum [kə'rɪkjʊləm] plan *m* de estudios
cur•ric•u•lum vi•tae ['viːtaɪ] *Br* currículum *m* vitae
cur•ry[1] ['kʌrɪ] *n* curry *m*
cur•ry[2] ['kʌrɪ] *v/t*: ***~ favor with s.o.*** congraciarse con alguien
curse [kɜːrs] **I** *n* **1** (*spell*) maldición *f*; ***there is a ~ on the family*** ha caído una maldición sobre la familia **2** (*swearword*) palabrota *f* **II** *v/t* **1** maldecir; ***be ~d with*** cargar con la cruz de **2** (*swear at*) insultar **III** *v/i* (*swear*) decir palabrotas
cur•sor ['kɜːrsər] COMPUT cursor *m*
cur•so•ry ['kɜːrsərɪ] *adj* rápido, superficial
curt [kɜːrt] *adj* brusco, seco
cur•tail [kɜːr'teɪl] *v/t* acortar
cur•tain ['kɜːrtn] cortina *f*, THEA telón *m*
◆ **curtain off** *v/t* separar con cortinas
'cur•tain call llamada *f* a escena
cur•tain rais•er ['kɜːrtnreɪzər] *fig* preámbulo *m*
curt•s(e)y ['kɜːrtsɪ] **I** *n* reverencia *f* **II** *v/i* hacer una reverencia (***to*** a)
curve [kɜːrv] **I** *n* curva *f* **II** *v/i* (*bend*) curvarse
'curve ball *in baseball* bola *f* con curva
cush•ion ['kʊʃn] **I** *n for couch etc* cojín *m* **II** *v/t blow, fall* amortiguar
cush•y ['kʊʃɪ] *adj* F fácil, descansado
cuss [kʌs] F **I** *v/t* maldecir **II** *v/i* decir palabrotas **III** *n* **1** *swearword* palabrota *f* **2** *person* tipejo(-a) *m(f)*
cus•tard ['kʌstərd] natillas *fpl*
cus•to•di•al [kʌ'stoʊdjəl] *adj* LAW *sentence* de prisión
cus•to•di•an [kʌ'stoʊdjən] vigilante *m/f*, guardián(-ana) *m(f)*
cus•to•dy ['kʌstədɪ] *of children* custodia *f*; ***in ~*** LAW detenido; ***in s.o.'s ~*** bajo la custodia de alguien; ***take s.o. into ~*** detener *or* arrestar a alguien
cus•tom ['kʌstəm] **1** (*tradition*) costumbre *f*; ***it's the ~ in France*** es costumbre en Francia; ***as was his ~*** como era costumbre en él **2** COM clientela *f*; ***lose s.o.'s ~*** perder a alguien como cliente
cus•tom•a•ry ['kʌstəmerɪ] *adj* acostumbrado, de costumbre; ***it is ~ to ...*** es costumbre ...
cus•tom-'built *adj* hecho de encargo
cus•tom•er ['kʌstəmər] cliente(-a) *m(f)*
cus•tom•er 'loy•al•ty fidelidad *f* de clientes; **cus•tom•er re'la•tions** *npl* relaciones *fpl* con los clientes; **cus•tom•er sat•is'fac•tion** satisfacción *f* de los clientes; **cus•tom•er 'serv•ice** atención *f* al cliente
cus•tom•ize ['kʌstəmaɪz] *v/t* personalizar
cus•tom-'made *adj* hecho de encargo
cus•toms ['kʌstəmz] **I** *npl* aduana *f* **II** *adj* aduanero
'cus•toms clear•ance despacho *m* de aduanas; **'cus•toms dec•la•ra•tion** declaración *f* de aduana; **'cus•toms du•ties** *npl* derechos *mpl* aduaneros; **'cus•toms ex•am•i•na•tion** inspección *f* aduanera; **'cus•toms in•spec•tion** inspección *f* aduanera; **'cus•toms of•fi•cer** funcionario(-a) *m(f)* de aduanas
cut [kʌt] **I** *n with knife etc*, *of garment* corte *m*; (*reduction*) recorte *m* (***in*** de); F (*share*) parte *f*; ***~ in salary*** recorte salarial; ***he thinks he's a ~ above the others*** se cree superior a los demás **II** *v/t* (*pret & pp* ***cut***) **1** cortar; (*reduce*) recortar; *hours* acortar; ***get one's hair ~*** cortarse el pelo; ***I've ~ my finger*** me he cortado el dedo; ***~ s.o.'s hair*** cortar el pelo a alguien; ***~ sth to pieces*** cortar algo en pedazos; ***~ one's teeth*** *fig* hincar el diente; ***~ s.o. dead*** volver la cara a alguien; ***~ a deal with*** llegar a un acuerdo con **2** F *class*, *lecture* faltar a **III** *v/i*: ***that argument ~s both ways*** ese

C

argumento es aplicable a las dos partes **IV** *adj grass* recién cortada; **~ *flowers*** flores *fpl* cortadas

◆ **cut back I** *v/i in costs* recortar gastos **II** *v/t staff numbers* recortar

◆ **cut back on** *v/t* recortar, reducir

◆ **cut down on** *v/t*: ***cut down on the cigarettes*** fumar menos; ***cut down on chocolate*** comer menos chocolate

◆ **cut in I** *v/i* **1** (*interupt*) interrumpir, cortar **2** MOT: ***cut in on s.o.*** adelantar temerariamente a alguien **II** *v/t* F: ***cut s.o. in on a deal*** dejar que alguien se lleve una parte de un trato

◆ **cut into** *v/t cake etc* cortar; ***cut into s.o.'s time*** robar el tiempo de alguien; ***cut into s.o.'s savings*** hacer mella en los ahorros de alguien; ***cut into a conversation*** interrumpir una conversación

◆ **cut off** *v/t* **1** *with knife, scissors etc* cortar **2** (*isolate*) aislar **3**: ***I was cut off*** se me ha cortado la comunicación, *L.Am.* se cortó la comunicación; ***she had her electricity cut off*** le cortaron la luz

◆ **cut out I** *v/t* **1** *with scissors* recortar **2** (*eliminate*) eliminar; ***cut that out!*** F ¡ya está bien! F **3**: ***be cut out for sth*** estar hecho para algo **II** *v/i of engine* pararse, *Span* calarse

◆ **cut up** *v/t meat etc* trocear

'cut•back recorte *m*

cute [kjuːt] *adj* (*pretty*) guapo, lindo; (*sexually attractive*) atractivo; (*smart, clever*) listo; ***it looks really ~ on you*** eso te queda muy mono

cu•ti•cle ['kjuːtɪkl] cutícula *f*

cut•ler•y ['kʌtlərɪ] cubiertos *mpl*

cut•let ['kʌtlət] chuleta *f*

'cut-off date fecha *f* límite; **'cut•out** *shape* silueta *f*; **cut-'price** *adj goods* rebajado; *store* de productos rebajados; **cut-'rate** *adj* COM a precio reducido, rebajado; **~ *offer*** rebaja *f*

cut•ter ['kʌtər] **1** TECH alicates *mpl* **2** NAUT cúter *m*

'cut-throat *adj competition* despiadado

cut•ting ['kʌtɪŋ] **I** *n from newspaper etc* recorte *m* **II** *adj remark* hiriente; ***at the ~ edge*** a la cabeza; ***~ edge technology*** tecnología *f* puntera

CV [siː'viː] *abbr Br* (= ***curriculum vitae***) C.V. *m* (= currículum *m* vitae)

cy•a•nide ['saɪənaɪd] CHEM cianuro *m*

cy•ber•net•ics [saɪbər'netɪks] *nsg* cibernética *f*

cy•ber•space ['saɪbərspeɪs] ciberespacio *m*

cy•cla•men ['sɪkləmən] BOT ciclamen *m*

cy•cle ['saɪkl] **I** *n* **1** (*bicycle*) bicicleta *f*; ***~ race*** carrera *f* de bicicletas **2** (*series of events*) ciclo *m* **II** *v/i* ir en bicicleta

'cy•cle lane, 'cy•cle path vía *f* para bicicletas; *part of roadway* carril *m* bici

cy•cler ['saɪklər] ciclista *m/f*

'cy•cle•way ☞ ***cycle lane***

cy•clic, cy•cli•cal ['saɪklɪk(l)] *adj* cíclico

cy•cling ['saɪklɪŋ] ciclismo *m*

cy•clist ['saɪklɪst] ciclista *m/f*

cy•clone ['saɪkloʊn] ciclón *m*

cyl•in•der ['sɪlɪndər] cilindro *m*

cy•lin•dri•cal [sɪ'lɪndrɪkl] *adj* cilíndrico

cyn•ic ['sɪnɪk] escéptico(-a) *m(f)*, suspicaz *m/f*

cyn•i•cal ['sɪnɪkl] *adj* escéptico, suspicaz

cyn•i•cal•ly ['sɪnɪklɪ] *adv smile, remark* con escepticismo *or* suspicacia

cyn•i•cism ['sɪnɪsɪzm] escepticismo *m*, suspicacia *f*

cy•press ['saɪprəs] ciprés *m*

Cyp•ri•ot ['sɪprɪət] **I** *n* chipriota *m/f* **II** *adj* chipriota

Cy•prus ['saɪprəs] Chipre *f*

cyst [sɪst] quiste *m*

cys•ti•tis [sɪ'staɪtɪs] MED cistitis *f*

czar [zɑːr] HIST zar *m*

Czech [tʃek] **I** *adj* checo; ***the ~ Republic*** la República Checa **II** *n* **1** *person* checo(-a) *m(f)* **2** *language* checho *m*

D

DA [diː'eɪ] *abbr* (= ***district attorney***) fiscal *m/f* (del distrito)
dab [dæb] **I** *n small amount* pizca *f* **II** *v/t* (*pret & pp* ***-bed***) **1** (*remove*) quitar **2** (*apply*) poner
◆ **dab•ble in** ['dæbl] *v/t* ser aficionado a
dachs•hund ['dækshʊnd] perro(-a) *m(f)* salchicha
dad [dæd] *talking to him* papá *m*; *talking about him* padre *m*
dad•dy ['dædɪ] *talking to him* papi *m*; *talking about him* padre *m*
dad•dy 'long•legs (*pl* ***daddy long-legs***) ZO F **1** falangio *m* **2** *Br* típula *f*
daf•fo•dil ['dæfədɪl] narciso *m*
daft [dæft] *adj* F tonto F; ***be ~ about sth / s.o.*** estar loco por algo / alguien
dag•ger ['dægər] daga *f*; ***be at ~s drawn*** (***with s.o.***) estar de uñas (con alguien); ***look ~s at s.o.*** fulminar alguien con la mirada
da•go ['deɪgoʊ] (*pl* ***-go(e)s***) *palabra ofensiva para referirse a alguien de España, Italia, Portugal o Suramérica*
dahl•ia ['deɪljə] BOT daliadais *f*
dai•ly ['deɪlɪ] **I** *n* (*paper*) diario *m* **II** *adj* diario; ***~ newspaper*** diario *m*; ***be a ~ occurrence*** ser el pan nuestro de cada día
dain•ty ['deɪntɪ] *adj* grácil, delicado
dair•y ['derɪ] *on farm* vaquería *f*
'dair•y cat•tle ganado *m* vacuno; **'dair•y pro•duce** productos *mpl* lácteos; **'dair•y prod•ucts** *npl* productos *mpl* lácteos
da•is ['deɪɪs] tarima *f*
dai•sy ['deɪzɪ] margarita *f*; ***be pushing up the daisies*** P estar criando malvas P
'dai•sy wheel margarita *f*
dal•ly ['dælɪ] *v/i* distraerse
◆ **dally over** *v/t decision* demorar
◆ **dally with** *v/t person, idea* flirtear con
Dal•ma•tian [dæl'meɪʃn] ZO dálmata *m*
dam [dæm] **I** *n for water* presa *f* **II** *v/t* (*pret & pp* ***-med***) *river* embalsar
◆ **dam up** *v/t river* embalsar; *feelings* reprimir, contener
dam•age ['dæmɪdʒ] **I** *n* daños *mpl*; *fig: to reputation etc* daño *m* **II** *v/t also fig* dañar; ***you're damaging your health*** estás perjudicando tu salud; ***what's the ~?*** F ¿cuánto es la broma? F
dam•a•ges ['dæmɪdʒɪz] *npl* LAW daños *mpl* y perjuicios
dam•ag•ing ['dæmɪdʒɪŋ] *adj* perjudicial
dame [deɪm] F (*woman*) mujer *f*, *Span* tía *f* F
damn [dæm] **I** *int* F ¡mecachis! F
II *n* F: ***I don't give a ~!*** ¡me importa un pimiento! F; ***not be worth a ~*** no valer un carajo F
III *adj* F maldito F; ***~ fool*** imbécil; ***a ~ sight better*** mil veces mejor
IV *adv* F muy; ***a ~ stupid thing*** una tontería monumental; ***it's ~ cold*** hace un frío del demonio; ***he ~ well ought to know it*** lo debe de saber
V *v/t* (*condemn*) condenar; ***~ it!*** F ¡maldita sea! F; ***I'm ~ed if ...*** F ya lo creo que ... F; ***~ you!*** ¡maldito seas!; ***I'll be ~ed if I'm going to do that*** ya lo creo que voy a hacer eso F
dam•na•tion [dæm'neɪʃn] **I** *n* REL condena *f*, castigo *m* **II** *int* F ¡mecachis! F
damned [dæmd] **I** *adj, adv* ☞ **damn II** *npl* REL: ***the ~*** los condenados
damn•ing ['dæmɪŋ] *adj evidence* condenatorio; *report* crítico
damp [dæmp] *adj* húmedo
damp•en ['dæmpən] *v/t* humedecer; ***~ s.o.'s enthusiasm*** echar a perder el entusiasmo de alguien
damp•er ['dæmpər]: ***put a ~ on sth*** estropear algo; ***put a ~ on the celebrations*** aguar la fiesta
damp•ness ['dæmpnɪs] humedad *f*
dance [dæns] **I** *n* baile *m* **II** *v/i* bailar; ***would you like to ~?*** ¿le gustaría bailar?
'dance class clase *f* de baile
'dance floor pista *f* de baile
danc•er ['dænsər] bailarín(-ina) *m(f)*
'dance school academia *f or* escuela *f* de baile
danc•ing ['dænsɪŋ] baile *m*; ***~ partner*** pareja *f* de baile
dan•de•li•on ['dændɪlaɪən] diente *m* de

león

dan•der ['dændər] F: ***get s.o.'s ~ up*** poner de mal genio a alguien F, cabrear a alguien F

dan•druff ['dændrʌf] caspa *f*

dan•druff sham'poo champú *m* anticaspa

D

dan•dy ['dændɪ] **I** *n* dandi *m* **II** *adj* F genial, estupendo

Dane [deɪn] danés(-esa) *m(f)*

dang [dæŋ] ☞ ***damn*** *adj, adv*

dan•ger ['deɪndʒər] peligro *m*; ***be in ~*** estar en peligro; ***be out of ~*** *patient* estar fuera de peligro; ***be in no ~*** no estar en peligro; ***he was in ~ of his life*** su vida estaba en peligro

'dan•ger mon•ey *Br* prima *f* de peligrosidad

dan•ger•ous ['deɪndʒərəs] *adj* peligroso

dan•ger•ous 'driv•ing conducción *f* peligrosa *or* temeraria

dan•ger•ous•ly ['deɪndʒərəslɪ] *adv drive* peligrosamente; ***~ ill*** gravemente enfermo

'dan•ger pay prima *f* de peligrosidad

'dan•ger zone zona *f* peligrosa

dan•gle ['dæŋgl] **I** *v/t* balancear **II** *v/i* colgar; ***keep s.o. dangling*** F tener a alguien en vilo F; ***~ sth in front of s.o.*** *fig* tentar a alguien con algo

Da•nish ['deɪnɪʃ] **I** *adj* danés **II** *n* **1** *language* danés *m* **2** *npl*: ***the ~*** los daneses

Da•nish 'pas•try pastel *m* de hojaldre (*dulce*)

dank [dæŋk] *adj* húmedo

dap•per ['dæpər] *adj* pulcro, presumido

dare [der] **I** *v/i* atreverse; ***~ to do sth*** atreverse a hacer algo; ***how ~ you!*** ¡cómo te atreves! **II** *v/t*: ***~ s.o. to do sth*** desafiar a alguien para que haga algo; ***how ~ you say that?*** ¿cómo te atreves a decir eso?; ***don't (you) ~ touch it!*** ¡no te atrevas a tocarlo!; *Br* ***I ~ say he'll agree*** yo diría que estará de acuerdo

dare•dev•il ['derdevɪl] temerario(-a) *m(f)*

dar•ing ['derɪŋ] *adj* atrevido

dark [dɑːrk] **I** *n* oscuridad *f*; ***in the ~*** en la oscuridad; ***after ~*** después de anochecer; ***be in the ~*** *fig* no tener la menor idea; ***keep s.o. in the ~ about sth*** *fig* no revelar algo a alguien **II** *adj* oscuro; *hair* oscuro, moreno; ***~ green / blue*** verde / azul oscuro; ***get*** oscurecer, hacerse de noche; ***the country's ~est hour*** las horas bajas del país

'Dark Ag•es *npl* Alta Edad *f* Media; ***be in the ~*** *fig* estar en la edad de piedra

dark•en ['dɑːrkn] *v/i of sky* oscurecerse

dark 'glass•es *npl* gafas *fpl* oscuras, *L.Am.* lentes *fpl* oscuras

dark 'horse POL ganador(a) *m(f)* inesperado(-a)

dark•ness ['dɑːrknɪs] oscuridad *f*; ***in ~*** *house, office* a oscuras

'dark•room PHOT cuarto *m* oscuro

dark•skinned ['dɑːrkskɪnd] *adj* de piel morena *or* oscura

dar•ling ['dɑːrlɪŋ] **I** *n* cielo *m*; ***yes my ~*** sí cariño **II** *adj* encantador; ***~ Ann, how are you?*** querida Ann, ¿cómo estás?

darn[1] [dɑːrn] **I** *n mend* zurcido *m* **II** *v/t mend* zurcir

darn[2], **darned** [dɑːrn, dɑːrnd] ☞ ***damn*** *adj, adv*

dart [dɑːrt] **I** *n* **1** *for throwing* dardo *m* **2**: ***make a ~ for*** correr hacia **II** *v/i* lanzarse, precipitarse **III** *v/t*: ***~ a look at s.o.*** lanzar una mirada a alguien

darts [dɑːrts] *nsg* dardos *mpl*

'dart(s)•board diana *f*

dash [dæʃ] **I** *n* **1** *punctuation* raya *f* **2** (*small amount*) chorrito *m* **3** (MOT: *~board*) salpicadero *m* **4**: ***make a ~ for*** correr hacia **II** *v/i* correr; ***he ~ed downstairs*** bajó las escaleras corriendo **III** *v/t hopes* frustrar, truncar; ***be dashed to pieces*** hacerse pedazos

◆ **dash off I** *v/i* irse **II** *v/t* (*write quickly*) escribir rápidamente

'dash•board salpicadero *m*

dash•ing ['dæʃɪŋ] *adj* deslumbrante, impactante

da•ta ['deɪtə] datos *mpl*

'da•ta bank banco *m* de datos; **'da•ta•base I** *n* base *f* de datos **II** *v/t* introducir en una base de datos; **da•ta•base 'man•age•ment** gestión *f* de bases de datos; **da•ta 'cap•ture** captura *f* de datos; **'da•ta car•ri•er** soporte *m* de información; **da•ta comms** ['deɪtəkɑːmz] *nsg* transmisión *f* de datos; **da•ta 'pro•cess•ing** proceso *m or* tratamiento *m* de datos; **da•ta pro'tec•tion** protección *f* de datos; **da•ta 'stor•age** almacenamiento *m* de datos; **da•ta trans'mis•sion** transmisión *f* de datos

date[1] [deɪt] *n fruit* dátil *m*
date[2] [deɪt] **I** *n* **1** fecha *f*; ***what's the ~ today?*** ¿qué fecha es hoy?, ¿a qué fecha estamos?; ***out of ~*** *clothes* pasado de moda; *passport* caducado; ***go out of ~*** pasarse de moda; ***to ~*** hasta ahora, hasta la fecha; ***up to ~*** al día; ***bring sth up to ~*** actualizar algo, poner algo al día; ***bring s.o. up to ~*** poner a alguien al día (***about*** acerca de)
2 (*meeting*) cita *f*; (*person*) pareja *f*; ***have a ~ with s.o.*** tener una cita con alguien; ***make a ~*** concertar una cita **II** *v/t* **1** *letter, check* fechar; ***your letter ~d ...*** su carta del ...; ***~d this day*** a fecha de hoy **2** (*go out with*) salir con **3**: ***that ~s you*** (*shows your age*) eso demuestra lo viejo que eres
◆ **date back to** *v/t*: ***it dates back to the 18th century*** se remonta al siglo XVIII
◆ **date from** *v/t*: ***date from 1935*** proceder de 1935
dat•ed ['deɪtɪd] *adj* anticuado
'date line GEOG línea *f* horaria internacional; **date of 'birth** fecha *f* de nacimiento; **'date rape** *delito de violación perpetrado por un conocido de la víctima*; **'date stamp I** *n* sello *m* con la fecha **II** *v/t* fechar
dat•ing a•gen•cy ['deɪtɪŋ] agencia *f* de contactos
daub [dɒːb] *v/t* embadurnar
daugh•ter ['dɒːtər] hija *f*
'daugh•ter•board COMPUT placa *f* hija
'daugh•ter-in-law (*pl* ***daughters-in-law***) nuera *f*
daunt [dɒːnt] *v/t* acobardar, desalentar; ***nothing ~ed*** con gran determinación *or* valentía
daunt•less ['dɒːntlɪs] *adj* invencible, valeroso
dav•en•port ['dævnpɔːrt] sofá *m*
daw•dle ['dɒːdl] *v/i*: ***don't ~!*** ¡no te entretengas!; ***~ over a job*** tomarse mucho tiempo con un trabajo
◆ **dawdle away** *v/t afternoon* desperdiciar
dawn [dɒːn] **I** *n* amanecer *m*, alba *f*; *fig*: *of new age* albores *mpl*; ***at ~*** al amanecer **II** *v/i* **1** amanecer **2**: ***it ~ed on me that ...*** me di cuenta de que ...; ***has it never ~ed on you that ...?*** ¿nunca se te ha ocurrido pensar *or* pasado por la cabeza que ...?
day [deɪ] día *m*; ***what ~ is it today?*** ¿qué día es hoy?, ¿a qué día estamos?; ***~ off*** día de vacaciones; ***by ~*** durante el día; ***~ by ~*** día tras día; ***the ~ after*** el día siguiente; ***the ~ after tomorrow*** pasado mañana; ***the ~ before*** el día anterior; ***the ~ before yesterday*** anteayer; ***~ in ~ out*** un día sí y otro también; ***in those ~s*** en aquellos tiempos; ***one ~*** un día; ***the other ~*** (*recently*) el otro día; ***let's call it a ~!*** ¡dejémoslo!
'day•break amanecer *m*, alba *f*; ***at ~*** al amanecer; **'day care** servicio *m* de guardería; **'day•dream I** *n* fantasía *f* **II** *v/i* soñar despierto; **'day dream•er** soñador(a) *m(f)*
'day•light luz *f* del día; ***by*** *or* ***in ~*** a la luz del día, de día; ***in broad ~*** a plena luz del día; ***beat*** *or* ***knock the living ~s out of s.o.*** F sacudir el polvo a alguien F; ***that's ~ robbery*** F es un robo a mano armada F
day•light 'sav•ing time horario *m* de verano; **'day nurs•er•y** guardería *f* de día; **'day pu•pil** alumno(-a) *m(f)* externo(-a); **'day shift** turno *m* de día; ***be*** *or* ***work on the ~*** ir de turno de día; **'day-time**: ***in the ~*** durante el día; ***~ television*** programación *f* diurna; **'day trip** excursión *f* en el día
day-to-'day *adj* diario, cotidiano
daze [deɪz]: ***in a ~*** aturdido
dazed [deɪzd] *adj* aturdido
daz•zle ['dæzl] *v/t also fig* deslumbrar
DBMS [diːbiːem'es] *abbr* (= ***database management system***) COMPUT sistema *m* de gestión de bases de datos
DC [diː'siː] *abbr* **1** (= ***direct current***) corriente *f* continua **2** (= ***District of Columbia***) Distrito *m* de Columbia
'D-day HIST día *m* D; *fig* día *m* clave
dea•con ['diːkən] REL diácono *m*
dead [ded] **I** *adj* **1** *person, plant* muerto; *battery* agotado; *light bulb* fundido; F *place* muerto F; ***the phone is ~*** no hay línea; ***shoot s.o. ~*** matar a alguien de un tiro; ***~ ball*** *in basketball* balón *m* muerto; *in baseball* bola *f* muerta; ***she was ~ to the world*** F estaba profundamente dormida, no la despertaba ni un terremoto F
2 (*complete*): ***~ silence*** silencio *m* sepulcral; ***~ cert*** F apuesta *f* segura; ***be a ~ loss*** *tool etc* no valer para nada;

D

meeting etc ser una pérdida de tiempo; *person* ser una causa perdida
II *adv* **1**: **~ *slow*** lentísimo; ***be ~ set on sth*** estar empeñado en algo; ***stop ~ in one's tracks*** pararse en seco, pararse de golpe; ***be ~ against sth*** oponerse rotundamente a algo **2** F (*very*) la mar de F; ***~ beat, ~ tired*** hecho polvo; ***you're ~ right*** tienes toda la razón del mundo; ***~ drunk*** la mar de borracho, borracho perdido
III *n*: ***the ~*** (*~ people*) los muertos; ***in the ~ of night*** a altas horas de la madrugada; ***in the ~ of winter*** en puro invierno
dead 'cen•ter, *Br* **dead 'cen•tre**: ***hit sth ~*** dar a algo de lleno
dead•en ['dedn] *v/t pain, sound* amortiguar
dead 'end *street* callejón *m* sin salida; **dead-end 'job** trabajo *m* sin salidas; **dead 'heat** empate *m*; **'dead•line** fecha *f* tope; *for newspaper, magazine* hora *f* de cierre; ***meet a ~*** cumplir un plazo; **'dead•lock** *in talks* punto *m* muerto; **dead•locked** ['dedlɑːkt] *adj* en punto muerto
dead•ly ['dedlɪ] *adj* **1** (*fatal*) mortal; ***~ enemy*** enemigo *m* mortal; ***~ sin*** pecado *m* mortal **2** F (*boring*) mortal F
dead•ly 'night•shade BOT belladona *f*
'dead pan *adj* F **1** *expression* inexpresivo **2** *humor* con seriedad fingida; **Dead 'Sea** mar *m* Muerto; **'dead weight** peso *m* muerto; **'dead wood** *fig*: *people* personas *fpl* inservibles; *in text, thesis* material *m* inservible
deaf [def] **I** *adj* sordo; ***go ~*** quedarse sordo; ***be ~ in one ear*** estar sordo de un oído; ***as ~ as a post*** sordo como una tapia; ***be ~ to sth*** *fig* hacerse el sordo ante algo **II** *npl*: ***the ~*** los sordos
deaf-and-'dumb *adj* sordomudo
deaf•en ['defn] *v/t* ensordecer
deaf•en•ing ['defnɪŋ] *adj* ensordecedor
deaf-'mute I *adj* sordomudo **II** *n* sordomudo(-a) *m(f)*
deaf•ness ['defnɪs] sordera *f*
deal [diːl] **I** *n* **1** acuerdo *m*; ***I thought we had a ~?*** creía que habíamos hecho un trato; ***make a ~*** hacer un trato (***with*** con); ***it's a ~!*** ¡trato hecho! **2**: ***a good ~*** (*bargain*) una ocasión, un ofertón **3**: ***a good ~*** (*a lot*) mucho; ***a great ~ of*** (*lots of*) mucho(s) **4** *in cards*: ***it is my ~*** me toca repartir a mí **II** *v/t* (*pret & pp* ***dealt***) *cards* repartir; ***~ a blow to*** asestar un golpe a
◆ **deal in** *v/t* (*trade in*) comerciar con; ***deal in drugs*** traficar con drogas
◆ **deal out** *v/t cards* repartir
◆ **deal with** *v/t* **1** (*handle*) tratar; *situation* hacer frente a; *customer, applications* encargarse de **2** (*do business with*) hacer negocios con **3** *of book, movie etc* tratar de
deal•er ['diːlər] **1** (*merchant*) comerciante *m/f* **2** (*drug ~*) traficante *m/f*
deal•er•ship ['diːlərʃɪp] concesión *f*
deal•ing ['diːlɪŋ] (*drug ~*) tráfico *m*
deal•ings ['diːlɪŋz] *npl* (*business*) tratos *mpl*; ***have ~ with s.o.*** tener tratos con alguien
dealt [delt] *pret & pp* ☞ ***deal***
dean [diːn] *of college* decano(-a) *m(f)*
dear [dɪr] **I** *adj* querido; (*expensive*) caro; ***Dear Sir*** Muy Sr. Mío; ***Dear Richard / Margaret*** Querido Richard / Querida Margaret; (***oh***) ***~!, ~ me!*** ¡oh, cielos!; ***run for ~ life*** correr para ponerse a salvo **II** *adv*: ***it cost him ~*** le costó caro **III** *n*: ***he's such a ~*** es un encanto; ***be a ~ and get my slippers*** (anda) se bueno *or* amable y tráeme mis zapatillas
dear•ly ['dɪrlɪ] *adv love* muchísimo; ***I would ~ like see him try it*** me encantaría *or* gustaría mucho verle intentarlo
dearth [dɜːrθ] escasez *f*, falta *f*
death [deθ] muerte *f*; ***beat s.o. to ~*** matar a alguien de una paliza; ***put s.o. to ~*** dar la muerte a alguien; ***scare s.o. to ~*** dar a alguien un susto de muerte; ***catch one's ~*** (***of cold***) agarrar un resfriado de muerte; ***be at ~'s door*** estar con un pie en el hoyo; ***he'll be the ~ of me, that boy!*** ¡ese chico va a acabar conmigo!
'death•bed lecho *m* de muerte; ***be on one's ~*** estar en las últimas; **'death-blow** *fig* golpe *m* mortal; ***deal sth a ~*** propinar un golpe mortal a algo; **'death cell** celda *f* para los que van a ser ejecutados; **'death cer•tif•i•cate** certificado *m* de defunción; **death knell** ['deθnel]: ***sound the ~ for sth*** ser el principio del fin de algo
death•less ['deθlɪs] *adj iron* inmortal, inolvidable
death•ly ['deθlɪ] *adj* **1** (*fatal*) mortal **2**: ~

pallor palidez *f* de muerto; **~ *stillness*** calma *f* sepulcral
'death mask mascarilla *f*; **'death pen•al•ty** pena *f* de muerte; **'death rate** tasa *f* de mortalidad; **death 'row** corredor *m* de la muerte; **'death sen•tence** pena *f* de muerte; **'death's head** calavera *f*; **'death squad** escuadrón *m* de la muerte; **'death threat** amenaza *f* de muerte; **'death throes** *npl* coletazos *mpl*; ***the company is in its ~*** la compañía está dando los últimos coletazos; **'death toll** saldo *m* de víctimas mortales; **'death trap** peligro *m*; **'death war•rant** orden *f* de ejecución; ***sign one's own ~*** firmar su propia sentencia de muerte; **'death wish**: ***have a ~*** querer morirse
de•ba•cle [deɪ'bɑːkl] fiasco *m*, fracaso *m*
de•bar [dɪ'bɑːr] *v/t* (*pret & pp* ***-red***) prohibir; ***~ s.o. from doing sth*** impedir que alguien haga algo
de•base [dɪ'beɪs] *v/t* desvalorizar, depreciar; **~ *o.s.*** rebajarse
de•ba•ta•ble [dɪ'beɪtəbl] *adj* discutible
de•bate [dɪ'beɪt] **I** *n also* POL debate *m* **II** *v/i* debatir; ***I ~d with myself whether to go*** me debatía entre ir o no ir **III** *v/t* debatir
de•bauched [dɪ'bɔːtʃd] *adj* libertino, degenerado
de•bauch•er•y [dɪ'bɒːtʃərɪ] libertinaje *m*
de•ben•ture [dɪ'bentʃər] COM obligación *f*
de•bil•i•tate [dɪ'bɪlɪteɪt] *v/t* debilitar, resquebrajar
de•bil•i•ta•ting [dɪ'bɪlɪteɪtɪŋ] *adj* debilitante, erosivo
de•bil•i•ty [dɪ'bɪlɪtɪ] debilidad *f*
deb•it ['debɪt] **I** *n* cargo *m*; ***~ and credit*** débito y crédito; ***to the ~ of*** a cargo de **II** *v/t account* cargar en; *amount* cargar; ***~ $100 from*** *or* ***to s.o.'s account*** cargar 100 dólares a la cuenta de alguien
'deb•it ad•vice nota *f* de cargo *or* adeudo
'deb•it card tarjeta *f* de débito
deb•o•nair [debə'ner] *adj* galán
de•brief [diː'briːf] *v/t* interrogar
de•brief•ing [diː'briːfɪŋ] interrogatorio *m*
deb•ris ['debriː] *of building* escombros *mpl*; *of airplane, car* restos *mpl*
debt [det] deuda *f*; ***be in ~*** estar endeudado; ***be in s.o.'s ~, be in ~ to s.o.*** *fig* estar en deuda con alguien; ***be out of ~*** no tener deudas
'debt col•lec•tion cobro *m* de deudas; **'debt col•lec•tion a•gen•cy** agencia *f* de cobro de deudas; **'debt col•lec•tor** cobrador(a) *m*(*f*) de deudas
debt•or ['detər] deudor(a) *m*(*f*)
'debt ser•vic•ing servicio *m* de la deuda
de•bug [diː'bʌg] *v/t* (*pret & pp* ***-ged***) **1** *room* limpiar de micrófonos **2** COMPUT depurar
de•bunk [diː'bʌŋk] *v/t* F refutar, rebatir
dé•but ['deɪbjuː] debut *m*; ***make one's ~*** debutar
deb•u•tante ['deɪbjuːtɑːnt] debutante *f*
Dec. *abbr* (= ***December***) diciembre *m*
dec•ade ['dekeɪd] década *f*
dec•a•dence ['dekədəns] decadencia *f*
dec•a•dent ['dekədənt] *adj* decadente
de•caf ['diːkæf] F descafeinado *m*
de•caf•fein•at•ed [dɪ'kæfɪneɪtɪd] *adj* descafeinado
de•cal ['diːkæl] calcomanía *f*
de•camp [dɪ'kæmp] *v/i* F pirarse F, marcharse
de•cant [dɪ'kænt] *v/t* decantar
de•cant•er [dɪ'kæntər] licorera *f*
de•cap•i•tate [dɪ'kæpɪteɪt] *v/t* decapitar
de•cath•lete [dɪ'kæθliːt] atleta *m/f* de decatlón
de•cath•lon [dɪ'kæθlɑːn] decatlón *m*
de•cay [dɪ'keɪ] **I** *n of wood, plant* putrefacción *f*; *of civilization* declive *m*; *in teeth* caries *f inv* **II** *v/i of wood, plant* pudrirse; *of civilization* decaer; *of teeth* cariarse
de•ceased [dɪ'siːst]: ***the ~*** el difunto / la difunta
de•ceit [dɪ'siːt] engaño *m*, mentira *f*
de•ceit•ful [dɪ'siːtfəl] *adj* mentiroso
de•ceive [dɪ'siːv] *v/t* engañar; ***be ~d*** dejarse engañar; **~ *o.s.*** engañarse (a uno mismo)
de•cel•er•ate [diː'seləreɪt] *v/t & v/i* desacelerar
De•cem•ber [dɪ'sembər] diciembre *m*
de•cen•cy ['diːsənsɪ] decencia *f*; ***he had the ~ to …*** tuvo la delicadeza de …
de•cent ['diːsənt] *adj* **1** decente **2** (*adequately dressed*) presentable
de•cen•tral•i•za•tion [diːsentrəlaɪ-

'zeɪʃn] descentralización *f*
de•cen•tral•ize [diː'sentrəlaɪz] *v/t* descentralizar
de•cep•tion [dɪ'sepʃn] engaño *m*
de•cep•tive [dɪ'septɪv] *adj* engañoso; ***be ~*** ser engañoso; ***appearances can be ~*** las apariencias engañan
de•cep•tive•ly [dɪ'septɪvlɪ] *adv*: ***it looks ~ simple*** parece muy fácil
dec•i•bel ['desɪbel] decibelio *m*
'dec•i•bel lev•el nivel *m* de decibelios
de•cide [dɪ'saɪd] **I** *v/t* decidir; ***~ s.o. to do sth*** llevar *or* mover a alguien a hacer algo **II** *v/i* decidir; ***you ~*** decide tú; ***~ in favor of*** decidirse por, elegir; ***~ against*** descartar; ***~ against doing sth*** decidir no hacer algo
◆ **decide on** *v/t* decidirse por
de•cid•ed [dɪ'saɪdɪd] *adj* (*definite*) tajante
de•cid•er [dɪ'saɪdər]: ***this match will be the ~*** este partido será el que decida
de•cid•ing [dɪ'saɪdɪŋ] *adj* decisivo, crucial
de•cid•u•ous [dɪ'sɪduəs] *adj* de hoja caduca
dec•i•mal ['desɪml] decimal *m*
dec•i•mal 'fract•ion fracción *f* decimal
dec•i•mal•ize ['desɪmlaɪz] *v/t* convertir al sistema decimal
dec•i•mal 'point coma *f* (decimal)
dec•i•mal 'sys•tem sistema *m* decimal
dec•i•mate ['desɪmeɪt] *v/t* diezmar
de•ci•pher [dɪ'saɪfər] *v/t* descifrar
de•ci•sion [dɪ'sɪʒn] decisión *f*; ***come to a ~*** llegar a una decisión; ***make*** *or* ***take a ~*** tomar una decisión
de'ci•sion-mak•er: ***who's the ~ here?*** ¿quién toma aquí las decisiones?
de'ci•sion-mak•ing toma *f* de decisiones
de•ci•sive [dɪ'saɪsɪv] *adj* **1** decidido **2** (*crucial*) decisivo
deck [dek] **1** *of ship* cubierta *f*; ***on ~*** en la cubierta; ***hit the ~*** F tirarse *or* echarse al suelo; *of objects* caerse al suelo **2** *of cards* baraja *f*
◆ **deck out** *v/t* adornar, engalanar; ***deck o.s. out with sth*** arreglarse *or* acicalarse con algo
'deck•chair tumbona *f*
dec•la•ra•tion [deklə'reɪʃn] (*statement*) declaración *f*; ***make a ~*** hacer una declaración; ***~ of intent*** declaración de intenciones; ***~ of independence*** declaración de independencia; ***~ of war*** declaración de guerra
de•clare [dɪ'kler] *v/t* (*state*) declarar; ***~ sth open*** inaugurar algo; ***~ s.o. the winner*** proclamar a alguien ganador; ***~ war*** declarar la guerra (***on*** a); ***have you anything to ~?*** ¿tiene algo que declarar?
de•clared [dɪ'klerd] *adj* reconocido, admitido
de•clen•sion [dɪ'klenʃn] LING declinación *f*
de•cline [dɪ'klaɪn] **I** *n* (*fall*) descenso *m*; *in standards* caída *f*; *in health* empeoramiento *m*; ***be in ~, be on the ~*** estar en declive *or* decadencia **II** *v/t invitation* declinar; ***~ to comment*** declinar hacer declaraciones **III** *v/i* **1** (*refuse*) rehusar **2** (*decrease*) declinar; *of health* empeorar; ***~ in value*** devaluarse
de•clutch [diː'klʌtʃ] *v/i* desembragar
de•code [diː'koʊd] *v/t* descodificar
de•cod•er [diː'koʊdər] descodificador *m*
de•cod•ing [diː'koʊdɪŋ] descodificación *f*
de•com•mis•sion [diːkə'mɪʃn] *v/t* desmantelar
de•com•pose [diːkəm'poʊz] *v/i* descomponerse
de•com•po•si•tion [diːkɑːmpə'zɪʃn] descomposición *f*, putrefacción *f*
de•com•pres•sion cham•ber [diːkəm'preʃn] cámara *f* de descompresión
de•con•gest•ant [dɪ'kəndʒestənt] descongestionante *m*
de•con•struct [diːkən'strʌkt] *v/t* deconstruir
de•con•tam•i•nate [diːkən'tæmɪneɪt] *v/t* descontaminar
de•con•tam•i•na•tion [diːkəntæmɪ'neɪʃn] descontaminación *f*
dé•cor ['deɪkɔːr] decoración *f*
dec•o•rate ['dekəreɪt] *v/t* **1** *with paint* pintar; *with paper* empapelar **2** (*adorn*) decorar **3** *soldier* condecorar
dec•o•ra•tion [dekə'reɪʃn] **1** *paint* pintado *m*; *paper* empapelado *m* **2** (*ornament*) decoración *f* **3** *for soldier* condecoración *f*
dec•o•ra•tive ['dekərətɪv] *adj* decorativo
dec•o•ra•tor ['dekəreɪtər] **1** (*interior ~*)

decorador(a) *m(f)* **2** *with paint* pintor(a) *m(f)*; *with wallpaper* empapelador(a) *m(f)*
dec•o•rous ['dekərəs] *adj* decoroso, recatado
de•co•rum [dɪ'kɔːrəm] decoro *m*
de•coy ['diːkɔɪ] señuelo *m*
de•crease I *n* ['diːkriːs] disminución *f*, reducción *f* (**in** de); ***be on the ~*** estar en decadencia **II** *v/t* [dɪ'kriːs] disminuir, reducir **III** *v/i* [dɪ'kriːs] disminuir, reducirse; ***~ in value*** devaluarse
de•cree [dɪ'kriː] **I** *n* decreto *m* **II** *v/t* decretar
de•crep•it [dɪ'krepɪt] *adj car, coat, shoes* destartalado; *person* decrépito
de•crim•in•al•ize [diː'krɪmɪnəlaɪz] *v/t* despenalizar
de•cry [dɪ'kraɪ] *v/t* (*pret & pp* ***-ied***) condenar, denunciar
ded•i•cate ['dedɪkeɪt] *v/t book etc* dedicar; ***~ o.s. to.*** dedicarse a
ded•i•cat•ed ['dedɪkeɪtɪd] *adj* dedicado
ded•i•ca•tion [dedɪ'keɪʃn] **1** *in book* dedicatoria *f* **2** *to cause, work* dedicación *f*
de•duce [dɪ'duːs] *v/t* deducir
de•duct [dɪ'dʌkt] *v/t* descontar
de•duct•i•ble [dɪ'dʌktəbl] *adj* FIN desgravable
de•duc•tion [dɪ'dʌkʃn] *from salary*, (*conclusion*) deducción *f*
deed [diːd] **1** (*act*) acción *f*, obra *f* **2** LAW escritura *f*
deed of 'sale escritura *f* de venta
dee•jay ['diːdʒeɪ] F disk jockey *m/f*, *Span* pincha *m/f* F
deem [diːm] *v/t* estimar
deep [diːp] **I** *adj* **1** *water* profundo; *color* intenso; *voice* profundo, grave; ***be in ~ trouble*** estar metido en serios apuros; ***take a ~ breath*** respirar hondo; ***fall into a ~ sleep*** quedarse dormido profundamente; ***be in ~ water*** *fig* estar en un terreno pantanoso **2** (*complex*) profundo; ***that is too ~ for me*** eso es demasiado profundo para mí
II *adv*: ***people were standing three ~*** la gente formó tres filas; ***~ into the night*** bien entrada la noche; ***be ~ in thought*** estar absorto
III *n lit* profundidad *f*; ***in the ~ of night*** en mitad de la noche; ***in the ~ of winter*** en puro invierno
deep•en ['diːpn] **I** *v/t* profundizar **II** *v/i* hacerse más profundo; *of crisis, mystery* agudizarse
'deep end *of swimming pool* parte *f* profunda; ***throw s.o. in at the ~*** *fig* echar a alguien a los leones; **'deep-felt** *adj* sentido, sincero; **deep 'freeze** congelador *m*; **deep 'freeze cab•i•net** cámara *f* de ultracongelados; **deep 'freez•er** congelador *m*; **'deep-froz•en food** comida *f* congelada; **'deep-fry** *v/t* (*pret & pp* ***-ied***) freír (*en mucho aceite*); **deep 'fry•er** freidora *f*
deep•ly ['diːplɪ] *adv* profundamente, enormemente
deep-'root•ed *adj* arraigado; **deep-sea 'div•er** submarinista *m/f*; **deep-sea 'div•ing** buceo *m* de alta mar; **deep--sea 'fish•ing** pesca *f* de altura; **deep--'seat•ed** *adj* arraigado, inveterado; **'deep-set** *adj eyes* hundido; **deep 'South** *estados del sur de EE. UU.*
deer [dɪr] (*pl* ***deer***) ciervo *m*
de-es•ca•late [diː'eskəleɪt] *v/i* atenuarse
de•face [dɪ'feɪs] *v/t* desfigurar, dañar
de fac•to [deɪ'fæktoʊ] *adj* de hecho
def•a•ma•tion [defə'meɪʃn] difamación *f*
de•fam•a•to•ry [dɪ'fæmətɔːrɪ] *adj* difamatorio
de•fame [dɪ'feɪm] *v/t* difamar
de•fault ['diːfɒːlt] **I** *adj* COMPUT por defecto
II *n* **1** *on payment* incumplimiento *m*; *non-appearance in court* incomparecencia *f*; ***be in ~ with payments*** estar atrasado en pago **2**: ***win by ~*** ganar por incomparecencia del contrincante; ***be chosen by ~*** ser elegido automáticamente **3** COMPUT: ***this drive / font is the ~*** éste / ésta es el lector / la fuente por defecto
III *v/i* **1** ***~ on a payment*** incumplir un pago **2** COMPUT: ***it ~s to drive C*** utiliza la unidad C por defecto
'de•fault drive COMPUT unidad *f* por defecto
'de•fault set•ting COMPUT configuración *f* por defecto
de•feat [dɪ'fiːt] **I** *n* derrota *f* **II** *v/t* derrotar; *of task, problem* derrotar, vencer; ***admit ~*** darse por vencido
de•feat•ist [dɪ'fiːtɪst] *adj attitude* derrotista

def•e•cate ['defəkeɪt] *v/i* defecar
de•fect[1] ['di:fekt] *n* defecto *m*
defect[2] [dɪ'fekt] *v/i* POL desertar
de•fec•tion [dɪ'fekʃn] defección *f*
de•fec•tive [dɪ'fektɪv] *adj* defectuoso
de•fence *etc Br* ☞ ***defense*** *etc*
de•fend [dɪ'fend] *v/t* defender; ***~ s.o. against sth*** proteger a alguien de algo
de•fend•ant [dɪ'fendənt] acusado(-a) *m(f)*; *in civil case* demandado(-a) *m(f)*
de•fend•er [dɪ'fendər] **1** defensor(a) *m(f)* **2** SP defensa *m/f*, zaguero(-a) *m(f)*
de•fense [dɪ'fens] defensa *f*; ***come to s.o.'s ~*** salir en defensa de alguien; ***in ~ of*** en defensa de
de'fense budg•et POL presupuesto *m* de defensa; **de'fense coun•sel** abogado(-a) *m(f)* defensor(a); **de'fense law•yer** abogado(-a) *m(f)* defensor(a)
de•fense•less [dɪ'fenslɪs] *adj* indefenso
de'fense•man defensa *m*; **de'fense play•er** SP defensa *m/f*; **De'fense Se•cre•ta•ry** POL ministro(-a) *m(f)* de Defensa; *in USA* secretario(-a) *m(f)* de Defensa; **de'fense wit•ness** LAW testigo *m/f* de la defensa
de•fen•sive [dɪ'fensɪv] **I** *n*: ***on the ~*** a la defensiva; ***go on the ~*** ponerse a la defensiva **II** *adj weaponry* defensivo; ***stop being so ~!*** ¡no hace falta que te pongas tan a la defensiva!; ***~ rebound*** *in basketball* rebote *m* defensivo
de•fen•sive•ly [dɪ'fensɪvlɪ] *adv* a la defensiva
de•fer[1] [dɪ'fɜ:r] *v/t* (*pret & pp* ***-red***) (*postpone*) aplazar, diferir
de•fer[2] [dɪ'fɜ:r] *v/i* (*pret & pp* ***-red***): ***~ to s.o.*** deferirse a alguien
def•er•ence ['defərəns] deferencia *f*; ***out of*** *or* ***in ~ to*** por *or* en deferencia a
def•er•en•tial [defə'renʃl] *adj* deferente
de•fer•ment [dɪ'fɜ:rmənt] aplazo *m*, prórroga *f*
de•fi•ance [dɪ'faɪəns] desafío *m*; ***in ~ of*** desafiando
de•fi•ant [dɪ'faɪənt] *adj* desafiante
de•fi•cien•cy [dɪ'fɪʃənsɪ] **1** (*lack*) deficiencia *f*, carencia *f*; ***vitamin ~*** deficiencia vitamínica **2** (*weakness*) defecto *m*, debilidad *f*
de•fi•cient [dɪ'fɪʃənt] *adj* deficiente, carente; ***be ~ in ...*** carecer de ...
def•i•cit ['defɪsɪt] déficit *m*
de•fine [dɪ'faɪn] *v/t* **1** *word*, *objective* definir **2**: ***the building was clearly ~d against the sky*** el edificio se distinguía claramente en el cielo
def•i•nite ['defɪnɪt] *adj date*, *time*, *answer* definitivo; *improvement* claro; (*certain*) seguro; ***nothing ~ has been arranged*** no se ha acordado nada de forma definitiva
def•i•nite 'ar•ti•cle GRAM artículo *m* determinado *or* definido
def•i•nite•ly ['defɪnɪtlɪ] *adv* con certeza, sin lugar a dudas
def•i•ni•tion [defɪ'nɪʃn] definición *f*
def•i•ni•tive [dɪ'fɪnətɪv] *adj* definitivo
de•flate [dɪ'fleɪt] **I** *v/t* **1** *tire* desinflar **2** *person* desprestigiar **3** *currency* deflacionar **II** *v/i* desinflarse
de•fla•tion [dɪ'fleɪʃn] deflación *f*
de•fla•tion•ar•y [dɪ'fleɪʃnərɪ] *adj* deflacionario
de•flect [dɪ'flekt] *v/t* desviar; *criticism* distraer; ***be ~ed from*** desviarse de
de•flec•tion [dɪ'flekʃn] desviación *f*
de•fo•li•ant [di:'foʊlɪənt] defoliante *m*
de•fo•li•ate [di:'foʊlɪeɪt] *v/t* defoliar
de•for•est [di:'fɑ:rɪst] *v/t* deforestar
de•for•est•a•tion [dɪfɑ:rɪs'teɪʃn] deforestación *f*
de•form [dɪ'fɔ:rm] *v/t* deformar
de•for•ma•tion [di:fɔ:r'meɪʃn] deformación *f*
de•for•mi•ty [dɪ'fɔ:rmɪtɪ] deformidad *f*
de•fraud [dɪ'frɒ:d] *v/t* defraudar; ***~ s.o. of sth*** robar *or* desfalcar a alguien algo
de•fray [dɪ'freɪ] *v/t costs* sufragar
de•frost [di:'frɒ:st] *v/t food*, *fridge* descongelar
deft [deft] *adj* hábil, diestro
de•funct [dɪ'fʌŋkt] *adj* extinguido, inexistente
de•fuse [di:'fju:z] *v/t bomb* desactivar; *situation* calmar
de•fy [dɪ'faɪ] *v/t* (*pret & pp* ***-ied***) desafiar; ***~ description*** ser indescriptible; ***I ~ you to find a better solution*** te reto a que encuentres una solución mejor
de•gen•e•rate [dɪ'dʒenəreɪt] *v/i* degenerar; ***~ into*** degenerar en
de•gen•er•a•tion [dɪdʒenə'reɪʃn] degeneración *f*
deg•ra•da•tion [degrə'deɪʃn] degradación *f*
de•grade [dɪ'greɪd] *v/t* degradar

de•grad•ing [dɪ'greɪdɪŋ] *adj position, work* degradante
de•gree [dɪ'griː] **1** *from university* título *m*; ***get one's ~*** graduarse, *L.Am.* egresar; ***my brother's doing a ~ in law*** mi hermano esta haciendo la licenciatura de derecho, mi hermano está estudiando derecho
2 *of temperature, angle, latitude* grado *m*; ***there is a ~ of truth in that*** hay algo de verdad en eso; ***a ~ of compassion*** algo de compasión; ***by ~s*** gradualmente; ***to some** or **a certain ~*** en cierto modo, de alguna manera
de•hu•man•ize [diː'hjuːmənaɪz] *v/t* deshumanizar
de•hy•drate [diː'haɪdreɪt] *v/t* deshidratar
de•hy•drat•ed [diːhaɪ'dreɪtɪd] *adj* deshidratado; ***become ~*** deshidratarse
de-ice [diː'aɪs] *v/t* deshelar
de-ic•er [diː'aɪsər] *spray* descongelador *m*, descongelante *m*
de•i•fy ['deɪɪfaɪ] *v/t* deificar, exaltar
deign [deɪn] *v/i*: ***~ to*** dignarse a
de•i•ty ['diːɪtɪ] deidad *f*
dé•jà vu [deɪʒɑː'vuː]: ***a feeling of ~*** una sensación de déjà vu
de•jec•ted [dɪ'dʒektɪd] *adj* abatido, desanimado; ***get** or **become ~*** abatirse, desanimarse
de•jec•tion [dɪ'dʒekʃn] abatimiento *m*, desánimo *m*
de•lay [dɪ'leɪ] **I** *n* retraso *m*; ***without ~*** sin demora *or* dilación **II** *v/t* retrasar; ***be ~ed*** llevar retraso; ***be ~ed for two hours*** llevar un retraso de dos horas; ***~ doing sth*** retrasar *or* aplazar hacer algo **III** *v/i* retrasarse
de•lay•ing tac•tics [dɪ'leɪɪŋ] *npl* tácticas *fpl* dilatorias
del•ect•able [dɪ'lektəbl] *adj* deleitable, delicioso
del•e•gate ['delɪgət] **I** *n* delegado(-a) *m(f)* **II** ['delɪgeɪt] *v/t task* delegar; *person* delegar en; ***~ sth to s.o.*** delegar algo en alguien
del•e•ga•tion [delɪ'geɪʃn] delegación *f*
de•lete [dɪ'liːt] *v/t* borrar; (*cross out*) tachar; ***~ where not applicable*** táchese donde no corresponda; ***~ as appropriate*** táchese lo que no proceda
de'lete key COMPUT tecla *f* de borrado
de•le•tion [dɪ'liːʃn] *act* borrado *m*; *thing deleted* supresión *f*
del•i ['delɪ] ☞ ***delicatessen***
de•lib•e•rate I *adj* [dɪ'lɪbərət] deliberado, intencionado **II** *v/i* [dɪ'lɪbəreɪt] deliberar (***over*** sobre)
de•lib•e•rate•ly [dɪ'lɪbərətlɪ] *adv* deliberadamente, a propósito
de•lib•er•a•tion [dɪlɪbə'reɪʃn] deliberación *f*
del•i•ca•cy ['delɪkəsɪ] **1** delicadeza *f*; *of health* fragilidad *f* **2** *food* exquisitez *f*, manjar *m*
del•i•cate ['delɪkət] *adj fabric, problem* delicado; *health* frágil
del•i•ca•tes•sen [delɪkə'tesn] *tienda de productos alimenticios de calidad*
del•i•cious [dɪ'lɪʃəs] *adj* delicioso
de•light [dɪ'laɪt] placer *m*; ***to my ~*** para mi agrado; ***take ~ in sth*** disfrutar con algo
◆ **delight in** *v/t* disfrutar con
de•light•ed [dɪ'laɪtɪd] *adj* encantado; ***I'd be ~ to come*** me encantaría venir
de•light•ful [dɪ'laɪtfəl] *adj* encantador
de•lim•it [diː'lɪmɪt] *v/t* delimitar
de•lin•e•ate [dɪ'lɪnɪeɪt] *v/t* delinear
de•lin•quen•cy [dɪ'lɪŋkwənsɪ] delincuencia *f*
de•lin•quent [dɪ'lɪŋkwənt] **I** *adj* **1** delincuente **2** FIN *account* moroso **II** *n* delincuente *m/f*
de•lir•i•ous [dɪ'lɪrɪəs] *adj* **1** MED delirante **2** (*ecstatic*) entusiasmado; ***she's ~ about the new job*** está como loca con el nuevo trabajo; ***~ with joy*** loco de alegría
de•lir•i•ous•ly [dɪ'lɪrɪəslɪ] *adv*: ***~ happy*** loco de felicidad
de•lir•i•um [dɪ'lɪrɪəm] (*pl* ***-iums, deliria*** [dɪ'lɪrɪə]) *also fig* delirio *m*; ***~ tremens*** ['triːmenz] delirium *m* tremens
de•liv•er [dɪ'lɪvər] **I** *v/t* **1** entregar, repartir; *message* dar **2**: ***~ a baby*** ayudar a dar a luz **3** *speech* pronunciar **II** *v/i* (*fulfill a promise*) (ser capaz de) cumplir lo prometido
de•liv•er•y [dɪ'lɪvərɪ] **1** *of goods, mail* entrega *f*, reparto *m*; ***take ~ of sth*** recibir algo; ***on ~*** en el momento de la entrega **2** *of baby* parto *m*
de'liv•er•y charge gastos *mpl* de envío; **de'liv•er•y date** fecha *f* de entrega; **de'liv•er•y man** repartidor *m*; **de'liv•er•y note** nota *f* de entrega; **de'liv•er•y**

room *for babies* sala *f* de partos, paritorio *m*; **de'liv•er•y serv•ice** servicio *m* de reparto; **de'liv•er•y van** furgoneta *f* de reparto
dell [del] nava *f*
de•louse [diː'laʊs] *v/t* despiojar
del•ta ['deltə] GEOG delta *m*
de•lude [dɪ'luːd] *v/t* engañar; ***you're deluding yourself*** te estás engañando a ti mismo
de•luge ['deljuːdʒ] **I** *n* diluvio *m*; *fig* avalancha *f* **II** *v/t fig* inundar (***with*** de)
de•lu•sion [dɪ'luːʒn] engaño *m*; ***you're under a ~ if you think …*** te engañas si piensas que …; ***suffer from ~s of grandeur*** sufrir delirios de grandeza
de luxe [də'lʊks] *adj* de lujo
◆ **delve into** [delv] *v/t* rebuscar en
dem•a•gog•ic [demə'gɑːgɪk] *adj* demagógico
dem•a•gogue ['deməgɑːg] demagogo(-a) *m(f)*
dem•a•gog•y ['deməgɑːgɪ] demagogia *f*
de•mand [dɪ'mænd] **I** *n* exigencia *f*, *by union* reivindicación *f*, COM demanda *f*, ***in ~*** solicitado; ***on ~*** cuando así se requiera; ***make ~s on s.o.*** exigir mucho de alguien **II** *v/t* **1** exigir **2** (*require*) requirir
de•mand•ing [dɪ'mændɪŋ] *adj job* que exige mucho; *person* exigente
de•mar•cate ['diːmɑːrkeɪt] *v/t* demarcar
de•mar•ca•tion [diːmɑːr'keɪʃn] demarcación *f*
de•mar'ca•tion line línea *f* de demarcación
de•mean [dɪ'miːn] *v/t*: ***~ o.s.*** rebajarse
de•mean•ing [dɪ'miːnɪŋ] *adj* degradante
de•mean•or, *Br* **de•mean•our** [dɪ'miːnər] comportamiento *m*
de•men•ted [dɪ'mentɪd] *adj* demente
de•men•tia [dɪ'menʃə] MED demencia *f*
dem•e•rar•a sug•ar [demə'rerə] azúcar *m* moreno
dem•i•god ['demɪgɑːd] semidiós *m*
dem•i•john ['demɪdʒɑːn] damajuana *f*
de•mil•i•ta•rize [diː'mɪlɪtəraɪz] *v/t* desmilitarizar
de•mise [dɪ'maɪz] fallecimiento *m*; *fig* desaparición *f*
de•mist [diː'mɪst] *v/t Br* desempañar
dem•i•tasse ['demɪtæs] taza *f* de café
dem•o ['demoʊ] F **1** *protest* manifestación *f* **2** *of video etc* maqueta *f*
de•mo•bil•ize [dɪ'moʊbəlaɪz] *v/t* desmovilizar
de•moc•ra•cy [dɪ'mɑːkrəsɪ] democracia *f*
dem•o•crat ['deməkræt] demócrata *m/f*, ***Democrat*** POL Demócrata *m/f*
dem•o•crat•ic [demə'krætɪk] *adj* democrático
dem•o•crat•ic•al•ly [demə'krætɪklɪ] *adv* democráticamente
'dem•o disk disco *m* de demostración
de•mo•graph•ic [demoʊ'græfɪk] *adj* demográfico
de•mog•ra•phy [dɪ'mɑːgrəfɪ] demografía *f*
de•mol•ish [dɪ'mɑːlɪʃ] *v/t building* demoler; *argument* destruir, echar por tierra
dem•o•li•tion [demə'lɪʃn] *of building* demolición *f*, *of argument* destrucción *f*
de•mon ['diːmən] demonio *m*
de•mon•ic [dɪ'mɑːnɪk] *adj* demoniaco
de•mon•stra•ble [dɪ'mɑːnstrəbl] *adj* demostrable
de•mon•stra•bly [dɪ'mɑːnstrəblɪ] *adv*: ***the situation is ~ better*** se puede demostrar que la situación ha mejorado
dem•on•strate ['demənstreɪt] **I** *v/t* demostrar **II** *v/i politically* manifestarse
dem•on•stra•tion [demən'streɪʃn] **1** demostración *f*, ***~ car*** coche *f* de prueba **2** *protest* manifestación *f*
de•mon•stra•tive [dɪ'mɑːnstrətɪv] *adj* **1** *person* extrovertido, efusivo **2** GRAM demostrativo
de•mon•stra•tive 'pro•noun pronombre *m* demostrativo
dem•on•stra•tor ['demənstreɪtər] *protester* manifestante *m/f*
de•mor•al•ize [dɪ'mɔːrəlaɪz] *v/t* desmoralizar
de•mor•al•ized [dɪ'mɔːrəlaɪzd] *adj* desmoralizado; ***get*** *or* ***become ~*** desmoralizarse
de•mor•al•iz•ing [dɪ'mɔːrəlaɪzɪŋ] *adj* desmoralizador
de•mote [diː'moʊt] *v/t* degradar
de•mo•ti•vate [diː'moʊtɪveɪt] *v/t* desmotivar
de•mur [dɪ'mɜːr] *v/i* objetar

de•mure [dɪ'mjʊr] *adj* solemne, recatado

de•myst•i•fy [diː'mɪstɪfaɪ] *v/t* desmistificar

den [den] **1** ZO guarida *f* **2** (*study*) estudio *m* **3**: *~ of vice* antro *m* de perversión

de•na•tion•al•ize [diː'næʃnəlaɪz] *v/t* COM desnacionalizar

de•ni•al [dɪ'naɪəl] *of rumor, accusation* negación *f*; *of request* denegación *f*; *official* desmentido *m*; ***issue a ~*** emitir un desmentido; ***be in ~*** negarse a aceptarlo

den•i•grate ['denɪgreɪt] *v/t* menospreciar

den•im ['denɪm] tela *f* vaquera; ***~ jacket / skirt*** chaqueta / falda (de tela) vaquera

den•ims ['denɪmz] *npl* (*jeans*) vaqueros *mpl*

Den•mark ['denmɑːrk] Dinamarca *f*

de•nom•i•nate [dɪ'nɑːmɪneɪt] *v/t* denominar

de•nom•i•na•tion [dɪnɑːmɪ'neɪʃn] **1** *of money* valor *m* **2** *religious* confesión *f*

de•nom•in•a•tion•al [dɪnɑːmɪ'neɪʃənl] *adj* confesional

de•nom•i•na•tor [dɪ'nɑːmɪneɪtər] MATH denominador *m*

de•note [dɪ'noʊt] *v/t* denotar

dé•noue•ment [deɪ'nuːmɑ̃ː] desenlace *m*

de•nounce [dɪ'naʊns] *v/t* denunciar

dense [dens] *adj* **1** *smoke, fog* denso; *foliage* espeso; *crowd* compacto **2** F (*stupid*) corto

dense•ly ['denslɪ] *adv*: ***~ populated*** densamente poblado

den•si•ty ['densɪtɪ] *of population* densidad *f*; ***population ~*** densidad de población

dent [dent] **I** *n* abolladura *f* **II** *v/t also pride* abollar

den•tal ['dentl] *adj* dental; ***~ treatment*** tratamiento *m* dental

'den•tal floss hilo *m* dental; **den•tal 'hy•giene** higiene *f* dental; **den•tal hy•gien•ist** [haɪ'dziːnɪst] higienista *m/f* dental; **'den•tal nurse** enfermero(-a) *m(f)* de dentista; **'den•tal sur•geon** odontólogo(-a) *m(f)*

den•ted ['dentɪd] *adj* abollado

den•tist ['dentɪst] dentista *m/f*

'den•tist's of•fice dentista *m/f*

den•tist•ry ['dentɪstrɪ] odontología *f*

den•tures ['dentʃərz] *npl* dentadura *f* postiza

de•nude [dɪ'nuːd] *v/t*: ***~ sth of sth*** despojar algo de algo

de•nun•ci•a•tion [dɪnʌnsɪ'eɪʃn] denuncia *f*

Den•ver boot ['denvər] cepo *m*

de•ny [dɪ'naɪ] *v/t* (*pret & pp* ***-ied***) *charge, rumor* negar; *right, request* denegar; ***~ o.s. sth*** privarse de algo; ***there is no ~ing that ...*** no se puede negar que…

de•o•do•rant [diː'oʊdərənt] desodorante *m*

de•o•dor•ize [diː'oʊdəraɪz] *v/t* desodorizar

de•part [dɪ'pɑːrt] *v/i* salir; ***~ from*** (*deviate from*) desviarse de

de•part•ed [dɪ'pɑːrtɪd] *npl*: ***the ~*** los difuntos

de•part•ment [dɪ'pɑːrtmənt] departamento *m*; *of government* ministerio *m*

de•part•ment•al [diːpɑːrt'mentl] *adj* de departamento; ***~ manager*** gerente *m/f* de departamento, jefe(-a) *m(f)* de servicio

De•part•ment of 'De•fense Ministerio *m* de Defensa; **De•part•ment of the In'te•ri•or** Ministerio *m* del Interior; **De•part•ment of 'State** Ministerio *m* de Asuntos Exteriores

de'part•ment store grandes almacenes *mpl*

de•par•ture [dɪ'pɑːrtʃər] salida *f*; *of person from job* marcha *f*; (*deviation*) desviación *f*; ***a new ~*** *for government, organization* una innovación; *for company* un cambio; *for actor, artist, writer* una nueva experiencia

de'par•ture date fecha *f* de salida; **de'par•ture lounge** sala *f* de embarque; **de'par•ture time** hora *f* de salida

de•pend [dɪ'pend] *v/i* depender; ***that ~s*** depende; ***it ~s on the weather*** depende del tiempo; ***I ~ on you*** dependo de ti; ***~ing on whether ...*** dependiendo de si …

de•pen•da•ble [dɪ'pendəbl] *adj* fiable

de•pen•dant [dɪ'pendənt] ☞ ***dependent***

de•pen•dence, de•pen•den•cy [dɪ'pendəns, dɪ'pendənsɪ] dependencia *f*

de•pen•dent [dɪ'pendənt] **I** *n persona a*

cargo de otra; ***how many ~s do you have?*** ¿cuántas personas tiene a su cargo? **II** *adj* dependiente (***on*** de)
de•pict [dɪ'pɪkt] *v/t* describir
de•pic•tion [dɪ'pɪkʃn] descripción *f*
de•pil•a•to•ry [dɪ'pɪlətɔːrɪ] depilatorio *m*
de'pil•a•to•ry cream crema *f* depilatoria
de•plane ['diːpleɪn] *v/i* desembarcar del avión
de•plete [dɪ'pliːt] *v/t* agotar, mermar
de•plor•a•ble [dɪ'plɔːrəbl] *adj* deplorable
de•plore [dɪ'plɔːr] *v/t* deplorar
de•ploy [dɪ'plɔɪ] *v/t* **1** (*use*) utilizar **2** (*position*) desplegar
de•ploy•ment [dɪ'plɔɪmənt] despliegue *m*
de•pop•u•la•tion [diːpɑːpjə'leɪʃn] despoblación *f*
de•port [dɪ'pɔːrt] *v/t* deportar
de•por•ta•tion [diːpɔːr'teɪʃn] deportación *f*
de•por'ta•tion or•der orden *f* de deportación
de•port•ment [dɪ'pɔːrtmənt] porte *m*
de•pose [dɪ'poʊz] *v/t* deponer
de•pos•it [dɪ'pɑːzɪt] **I** *n in bank*, *of oil* depósito *m*; *of coal* yacimiento *m*; *on purchase* señal *f*, depósito *m*; ***make*** *or* ***pay a ~*** dar una entrada (***on*** para) **II** *v/t* **1** *money* depositar, *Span* ingresar **2** (*put down*) depositar
de'pos•it ac•count *Br* cuenta *f* de ahorro *or* de depósito
dep•o•si•tion [diːpoʊ'zɪʃn] LAW declaración *f*
de•pos•i•tor [dɪ'pɑːzɪtər] *of money* depositante *m/f*
de'pos•it slip comprobante *m* de ingreso
dep•ot ['diːpoʊ] **1** (*train station*) estación *f* de tren; (*bus station*) estación *f* de autobuses **2** *for storage* depósito *m*
de•prave [dɪ'preɪv] *v/t* depravar
de•praved [dɪ'preɪvd] *adj* depravado
de•prav•i•ty [dɪ'prævətɪ] depravación *f*
dep•re•cate ['deprɪkeɪt] *v/t* criticar
dep•re•ca•tion [deprɪ'keɪʃn] crítica *f*
dep•re•ca•to•ry ['deprɪkətɔːrɪ] *adj* crítico
de•pre•ci•ate [dɪ'priːʃɪeɪt] *v/i* FIN depreciarse
de•pre•ci•a•tion [dɪpriːʃɪ'eɪʃn] FIN depreciación *f*
de•pre•ci'a•tion pe•ri•od periodo *m* de amortización
de•pre•ci'a•tion rate coeficiente *m* de amortización
dep•re•da•tion [deprɪ'deɪʃn] estrago *m*
de•press [dɪ'pres] *v/t person* deprimir
de•pres•sant [dɪ'presənt] MED depresor *m*
de•pressed [dɪ'prest] *adj person* deprimido; ***get*** *or* ***become ~*** deprimirse
de•press•ing [dɪ'presɪŋ] *adj* deprimente
de•pres•sion [dɪ'preʃn] MED, *economic* depresión *f*, *meteorological* borrasca *f*
dep•ri•va•tion [deprɪ'veɪʃn] privación *f*
de•prive [dɪ'praɪv] *v/t* privar; ***~ s.o. of sth*** privar a alguien de algo
de•prived [dɪ'praɪvd] *adj* desfavorecido
depth [depθ] profundidad *f*, *of color* intensidad *f*; ***in ~*** (*thoroughly*) en profundidad; ***in the ~s of winter*** en pleno invierno; ***be out of one's ~*** *in water* no tocar el fondo; *fig*: *in discussion etc* saber muy poco; ***at a ~ of*** a una profundidad de; ***five meters in ~*** cinco metros de profundidad; ***with great ~ of feeling*** con mucho sentimiento
'depth charge NAUT carga *f* de profundidad
dep•u•ta•tion [depjʊ'teɪʃn] delegación *f*
◆ **dep•u•tize for** ['depjʊtaɪz] *v/t* sustituir
dep•u•ty ['depjʊtɪ] segundo(-a) *m*(*f*)
dep•u•ty 'head *Br in school* subdirector(a) *m*(*f*); **'dep•u•ty lead•er** vicelíder *m/f*; **'dep•u•ty she•riff** ayudante *m/f* del sheriff
de•rail [dɪ'reɪl] *v/t* hacer descarrilar; ***be ~ed*** *of train* descarrilar
de•ranged [dɪ'reɪndʒd] *adj* perturbado, trastornado
de•range•ment [dɪ'reɪndʒmənt]: (***mental***) **~** trastorno *m* mental
der•by 1 ['dɜːrbɪ] *hat* bombín *m* **2** ['dɑːbɪ] *Br* SP derby *m*, derbi *m*
de•reg•u•late [dɪ'regjʊleɪt] *v/t* liberalizar, desregular
de•reg•u•la•tion [dɪregjʊ'leɪʃn] liberalización *f*, desregulación *f*
der•e•lict ['derəlɪkt] *adj* en ruinas
de•ride [dɪ'raɪd] *v/t* ridiculizar, mofarse

de
de•ri•sion [dɪ'rɪʒn] burla *f*, mofa *f*
de•ri•sive [dɪ'raɪsɪv] *adj* burlón
de•ri•sive•ly [dɪ'raɪsɪvlɪ] *adv* burlonamente
de•ri•so•ry [dɪ'raɪsərɪ] *adj amount, salary* irrisorio
der•i•va•tion [derɪ'veɪʃn] origen *m*
de•riv•a•tive [dɪ'rɪvətɪv] *adj* (*not original*) poco original
de•rive [dɪ'raɪv] *v/t* obtener, encontrar; ***be ~d from*** *of word* derivar(se) de; ***~ pleasure from sth*** encontrar placer en algo
der•ma•ti•tis [dɜːrmə'taɪtɪs] MED dermatitis *f inv*
der•ma•tol•o•gist [dɜːrmə'tɑːlədʒɪst] dermatólogo(-a) *m*(*f*)
der•ma•tol•o•gy [dɜːrmə'tɑːlədʒɪ] dermatología *f*
de•rog•a•to•ry [dɪ'rɑːgətɔːrɪ] *adj* despectivo
der•rick ['derɪk] **1** *crane* grúa *f* **2** *above oil well* torre *f* de perforación
de•scend [dɪ'send] **I** *v/t* descender por; ***be ~ed from*** descender de **II** *v/i* descender; *of mood, darkness* caer; ***the country ~ed into civil war*** el país se vio sumido en una guerra civil
de•scen•dant [dɪ'sendənt] descendiente *m/f*
de•scent [dɪ'sent] **1** descenso *m* **2** (*ancestry*) ascendencia *f*
de•scribe [dɪ'skraɪb] *v/t* describir; ***~ sth as sth*** definir a algo como algo
de•scrip•tion [dɪ'skrɪpʃn] descripción *f*
de•scrip•tive [dɪ'skrɪptɪv] *adj* descriptivo
des•e•crate ['desɪkreɪt] *v/t* profanar
des•e•cra•tion [desɪ'kreɪʃn] profanación *f*
de•seg•re•gate [diː'segrəgeɪt] *v/t* acabar con la segregación racial en
de•seg•re•ga•tion [diːsegrə'geɪʃn] fin *m* de la segregación racial
de•sen•si•tize [diː'sensətaɪz] *v/t*: ***become ~d to sth*** insensibilizarse a algo
des•ert[1] ['dezərt] *n also fig* desierto *m*
de•sert[2] [dɪ'zɜːrt] **I** *v/t* (*abandon*) abandonar **II** *v/i of soldier* desertar
de•sert•ed [dɪ'zɜːrtɪd] *adj* desierto
de•sert•er [dɪ'zɜːrtər] MIL desertor(a) *m*(*f*)
de•ser•ti•fi•ca•tion [dezɜːrtɪfɪ'keɪʃn] desertización *f*
de•ser•tion [dɪ'zɜːrʃn] (*abandonment*) abandono *m*; MIL deserción *f*
des•ert 'is•land isla *f* desierta
de•serts [dɪ'zɜːrts] *npl*: ***get one's just ~*** recibir uno su merecido
de•serve [dɪ'zɜːrv] *v/t* merecer
de•serv•ed•ly [dɪ'zɜːrvɪdlɪ] *adv* merecidamente
de•serv•ing [dɪ'zɜːrvɪŋ] *adj* digno de ayuda; ***be ~ of sth*** ser merecedor de algo
des•ic•cat•ed ['desɪkeɪtɪd] *adj* desecado
des•ic•cat•ed 'co•co•nut coco *m* rallado
de•sign [dɪ'zaɪn] **I** *n* diseño *m*; (*pattern*) motivo *m*; ***by ~*** a propósito; ***have ~s on sth / s.o.*** tener las miras puestas en algo / alguien **II** *v/t* diseñar; ***~ed to do sth*** diseñado para hacer algo
des•ig•nate ['dezɪgneɪt] *v/t person* designar; *area* declarar; ***~d hitter*** *in baseball* bateador(a) *m*(*f*) designado(-a)
de•sign•er [dɪ'zaɪnər] diseñador(a) *m*(*f*)
de'sign•er clothes *npl* ropa *f* de diseño
de'sign•er la•bel marca *f* de diseñador conocido
de'sign fault defecto *m* de diseño
de'sign school escuela *f* de diseño
de•sir•a•ble [dɪ'zaɪrəbl] *adj* deseable; *house* apetecible, atractivo
de•sire [dɪ'zaɪr] **I** *n* deseo *m*; ***I have no ~ to see him*** no me apetece verlo **II** *v/t* desear; ***if ~d*** si así se desea; ***leave much / leave nothing to be ~d*** dejar mucho / no dejar nada que desear
de•sir•ous [dɪ'zaɪərəs] *adj fml*: ***be ~ of sth*** estar deseoso de algo
de•sist [dɪ'zɪst] *v/i* desistir (***from*** de)
desk [desk] *in classroom* pupitre *m*; *in home, office* mesa *f*; *in hotel* recepción *f*; ***pay at the ~*** pagar en caja
'desk clerk recepcionista *m/f*; **'desk di•a•ry** agenda *f*; **'desk•top** *also on screen* escritorio *m*; *computer L.Am.* computadora *f* de escritorio, *Span* ordenador *m* de escritorio; **desk•top 'cal•cu•la•tor** calculadora *f* de escritorio; **desk•top com'pu•ter** *L.Am.* computadora *f* de escritorio, *Span* ordenador *m* de escritorio; **desk•top 'pub•lish•ing** autoedición *f*

D

des•o•late ['desələt] *adj place* desolado
des•o•la•tion [desə'leɪʃn] desolación *f*
de•spair [dɪ'sper] **I** *n* desesperación *f*; ***in ~*** desesperado; ***a look of ~*** una mirada desesperada; ***drive s.o. to ~*** desesperar a alguien **II** *v/i* desesperarse; ***I ~ of finding something to wear*** he perdido la esperanza de encontrar algo para ponerme
des•pair•ing [dɪ'sperɪŋ] *adj* desesperado
de•spatch [dɪ'spætʃ] ☞ ***dispatch***
des•per•ate ['despərət] *adj* desesperado; ***be ~*** estar desesperado; ***be ~ for a drink / cigarette*** necesitar una bebida / un cigarrillo desesperadamente; ***get*** *or* ***become ~*** desesperarse; ***be ~ to do sth*** morirse de ganas de hacer algo
des•per•ate•ly ['despərətlɪ] *adv* extremadamente
des•per•a•tion [despə'reɪʃn] desesperación *f*; ***an act of ~*** un acto desesperado; ***out of*** *or* ***in ~*** por desesperación; ***drive s.o. to ~*** desesperar a alguien
des•pic•a•ble [dɪs'pɪkəbl] *adj* despreciable
de•spise [dɪ'spaɪz] *v/t* despreciar
de•spite [dɪ'spaɪt] *prep* a pesar de
de•spon•dent [dɪ'spɑːndənt] *adj* abatido, desanimado; ***get*** *or* ***become ~*** abatirse, desanimarse
des•pot ['despɑːt] déspota *m/f*
des•pot•ic [des'pɑːtɪk] *adj* despótico
des•sert [dɪ'zɜːrt] postre *m*; ***what's for ~?*** ¿qué hay de postre?
des'sert•spoon *Br* cuchara *f* de postre
des'sert wine vino *m* dulce
de•sta•bi•lize [diː'steɪbəlaɪz] *v/t* desestabilizar
des•ti•na•tion [destɪ'neɪʃn] destino *m*; ***country of ~*** país *m* de destino
des•tined ['destɪnd] *adj*: ***be ~ for*** *fig* estar destinado a; ***be ~ to do sth*** estar destinado a hacer algo
des•ti•ny ['destɪnɪ] destino *m*
des•ti•tute ['destɪtuːt] *adj* indigente; ***be ~*** estar en la miseria; ***become ~*** caer en la miseria
des•ti•tu•tion [destɪ'tuːʃn] indigencia *f*
de•stroy [dɪ'strɔɪ] *v/t* destruir
de•stroy•er [dɪ'strɔɪr] NAUT destructor *m*
de•struc•tion [dɪ'strʌkʃn] destrucción *f*
de•struc•tive [dɪ'strʌktɪv] *adj* destructivo; *child* revoltoso
de•struc•tive•ness [dɪ'strʌktɪvnɪs] capacidad *f* destructiva
des•ul•to•ry ['desəltɔːrɪ] *adj* sin ganas
de•tach [dɪ'tætʃ] *v/t* separar, soltar; *email attachment* abrir; ***become ~ed*** soltarse (***from*** de)
de•tach•a•ble [dɪ'tætʃəbl] *adj* desmontable, separable
de•tached [dɪ'tætʃt] *adj* **1** (*objective*) distanciado **2**: ***~ house*** casa *f* individual
de•tach•ment [dɪ'tætʃmənt] (*objectivity*) distancia *f*
de•tail ['diːteɪl] detalle *m*; ***in ~*** en detalle; ***go into ~*** entrar en detalles (***about*** sobre)
de•tailed ['diːteɪld] *adj* detallado
de•tain [dɪ'teɪn] *v/t* **1** (*hold back*) entretener **2** *as prisoner* detener
de•tain•ee [diːteɪn'iː] detenido(-a) *m(f)*
de•tect [dɪ'tekt] *v/t* percibir; *of device* detectar
de•tec•tion [dɪ'tekʃn] *of criminal, crime* descubrimiento *m*; *of smoke etc* detección *f*
de•tec•tive [dɪ'tektɪv] detective *m/f*
de'tec•tive mov•ie película *f* detectivesca
de'tec•tive nov•el novela *f* policiaca *or* de detectives
de•tec•tor [dɪ'tektər] detector *m*
dé•tente ['deɪtɑːnt] POL distensión *f*
de•ten•tion [dɪ'tenʃn] **1** (*imprisonment*) detención *f* **2** EDU *castigo por el que el alumno se queda en el colegio después de las clases*
de•ter [dɪ'tɜːr] *v/t* (*pret & pp* ***-red***) disuadir; ***~ s.o. from doing sth*** disuadir a alguien de hacer algo
de•ter•gent [dɪ'tɜːrdʒənt] detergente *m*
de•te•ri•o•rate [dɪ'tɪrɪəreɪt] *v/i* deteriorarse; *of weather* empeorar
de•te•ri•o•ra•tion [dɪtɪrɪə'reɪʃn] deterioro *m*; *of weather* empeoramiento *m*
de•ter•mi•na•tion [dɪtɜːrmɪ'neɪʃn] (*resolution*) determinación *f*
de•ter•mine [dɪ'tɜːrmɪn] *v/t* (*establish*) determinar
de•ter•mined [dɪ'tɜːrmɪnd] *adj* resuelto, decidido; ***I'm ~ to succeed*** estoy decidido a triunfar
de•ter•rence [dɪ'terəns] disuasión *f*

de•ter•rent [dɪ'terənt] elemento *m* disuasorio; ***act as a ~*** actuar como elemento disuasorio; ***nuclear ~*** disuasión *f* nuclear
de•test [dɪ'test] *v/t* detestar; ***~ having to do sth*** detestar tener que hacer algo
de•test•a•ble [dɪ'testəbl] *adj* detestable
de•tes•ta•tion [diːte'steɪʃn] odio *m* (***of*** a)
de•throne [diː'θroʊn] *v/t* destronar
de•to•nate ['detəneɪt] **I** *v/t* hacer detonar *or* explotar **II** *v/i* detonar, explotar
de•to•na•tion [detə'neɪʃn] detonación *f*, explosión *f*
de•to•na•tor ['detəneɪtər] detonador *m*
de•tour ['diːtʊr] rodeo *m*; (*diversion*) desvío *m*; ***make a ~*** dar un rodeo
de•tox•i•fi•ca•tion [diːtɑːksɪfɪ'keɪʃn] MED desintoxicación *f*
◆ **de•tract from** [dɪ'trækt] *v/t achievement* quitar méritos a; *beauty* quitar atractivo a
de•tract•or [dɪ'træktər] detractor(a) *m(f)*
de•tri•ment ['detrɪmənt]: ***to the ~ of*** en detrimento de
de•tri•men•tal [detrɪ'mentl] *adj* perjudicial (***to*** para)
deuce [duːs] **1** *in tennis* deuce *m* **2**: ***who / what the ~ … ?*** F ¿quién / qué rayos …?
Deutsch•mark ['dɔɪtʃmɑːrk] HIST marco *m* alemán
de•val•u•a•tion [diːvæljʊ'eɪʃn] *of currency* devaluación *f*
de•val•ue [diː'væljuː] *v/t currency* devaluar
dev•a•state ['devəsteɪt] *v/t crops*, *countryside*, *city* devastar; *fig*: *person* asolar; ***we were all ~d to hear that …*** estábamos todos destrozados *or* abatidos al oír que …
dev•a•stat•ing ['devəsteɪtɪŋ] *adj* devastador
dev•as•ta•tion [devə'steɪʃn] devastación *f*
de•vel•op [dɪ'veləp] **I** *v/t* **1** *film* revelar **2** *land*, *site* urbanizar; *activity*, *business* desarrollar **3** (*originate*) desarrollar; (*improve on*) perfeccionar **4** *illness*, *cold* contraer **II** *v/i* (*grow*) desarrollarse; ***~ into*** convertirse en
de•vel•oped coun•try [dɪ'veləpt] país *m* desarrollado
de•vel•op•er [dɪ'veləpər] **1** *of property* promotor(a) *m(f)* inmobiliario(-a) **2**: ***be a late ~*** desarrollarse tarde
de•vel•op•ing coun•try [dɪ'veləpɪŋ] país *m* en vías de desarrollo
de•vel•op•ment [dɪ'veləpmənt] **1** *of film* revelado *m* **2** *of land*, *site* urbanización *f*; *of business*, *country* desarrollo *m* **3** (*event*) acontecimiento *m* **4** (*origination*) desarrollo *m*; (*improving*) perfeccionamiento *m*
de'vel•op•ment aid ayuda *f* al desarrollo
de•vi•ant ['diːvɪənt] **1** *n* persona *f* anormal **2** *adj* desviado
de•vi•ate ['diːvɪeɪt] *v/i* desviarse (***from*** de)
de•vi•a•tion [diːvɪ'eɪʃn] desviación *f*
de•vice [dɪ'vaɪs] *tool* aparato *m*, dispositivo *m*
dev•il ['devl] *also fig* diablo *m*, demonio *m*; ***poor ~*** pobre diablo; ***be between the ~ and the deep blue sea*** estar entre la espada y la pared; ***go to the ~!*** ¡vete al infierno!; ***talk of the ~!*** hablando del rey de Roma; ***like the ~*** F como un poseso; ***who / what the ~ … ?*** F ¿quién / qué diablos …?
dev•il•ish ['devlɪʃ] *adj* **1** (*cruel*) diabólico **2** F (*difficult*) endemoniado
dev•il-may-'care *adj* despreocupado
dev•il•ry ['devlrɪ] brujería *f*
de•vi•ous ['diːvɪəs] *adj* **1** (*sly*) retorcido; ***by ~ means*** por *or* con métodos con engaños **2** *route* tortuoso
de•vise [dɪ'vaɪz] *v/t* idear
de•void [dɪ'vɔɪd] *adj*: ***be ~ of*** estar desprovisto de
dev•o•lu•tion [diːvə'luːʃn] POL traspaso *m* de competencias
de•volve [dɪ'vɑːlv] **I** *v/t* transferir (***on*** a) **II** *v/i* recaer (***on*** en)
de•vote [dɪ'voʊt] *v/t* dedicar (***to*** a); ***~ o.s. to sth*** dedicarse a algo
de•vot•ed [dɪ'voʊtɪd] *adj son etc* afectuoso; ***be ~ to s.o.*** tener mucho cariño a alguien
dev•o•tee [dɪvoʊ'tiː] entusiasta *m/f*
de•vo•tion [dɪ'voʊʃn] devoción *f*
de•vour [dɪ'vaʊər] *v/t food*, *book* devorar
de•vout [dɪ'vaʊt] *adj* devoto
dew [duː] rocío *m*
'dew•drop gota *f* de rocío

D

dew•y-eyed [duːɪ'aɪd] *adj*: ***go all ~ over sth*** ponerse sentimental por algo
dex•ter•i•ty [dek'sterətɪ] destreza *f*
dex•ter•ous ['dekstərəs] *adj* habilidoso
dex•trose ['dekstroʊs] dextrosa *f*
dex•trous ['dekstrəs] ☞ ***dexterous***
di•a•be•tes [daɪə'biːtiːz] *nsg* diabetes *f*
di•a•bet•ic [daɪə'betɪk] **I** *n* diabético(-a) *m(f)* **II** *adj* diabético; *foods* para diabéticos
di•a•bol•i•cal [daɪə'bɑːlɪkl] *adj* **1** diabólico **2** *Br* F horrible
di•a•dem ['daɪədem] diadema *f*
di•ag•nose ['daɪəgnoʊz] *v/t* diagnosticar; ***she has been ~d as having cancer*** se le ha diagnosticado un cáncer
di•ag•no•sis [daɪəg'noʊsɪs] (*pl* ***diagnoses*** [daɪəg'noʊsiːz]) diagnóstico *m*; ***give*** *or* ***make a ~*** emitir *or* realizar un diagnóstico
di•ag•nos•tic [daɪəg'nɑːstɪk] *adj* diagnóstico
di•ag•o•nal [daɪ'ægənl] *adj* diagonal
di•ag•o•nal•ly [daɪ'ægənlɪ] *adv* diagonalmente, en diagonal; ***~ opposite*** opuesto diagonalmente
di•a•gram ['daɪəgræm] diagrama *m*
di•al ['daɪl] **I** *n* **1** *of clock* esfera *f*; *of instrument* cuadrante *m* **2** TELEC disco *m* **II** *v/t & v/i* (*pret & pp* ***-ed***, *Br* ***-led***) TELEC marcar
di•a•lect ['daɪəlekt] dialecto *m*
di•al•ling code ['daɪlɪŋ] *Br* TELEC prefijo *m*
'di•al•ling tone *Br* ☞ ***dial tone***
di•a•log, *Br* **di•a•logue** ['daɪəlɑːg] diálogo *m*
'di•a•log box COMPUT ventana *f* de diálogo
'di•al tone tono *m* de marcar
di•al•y•sis [daɪ'æləsɪs] (*pl* ***dialyses*** [daɪ'æləsiːz]) MED diálisis *f inv*
di•am•e•ter [daɪ'æmɪtər] diámetro *m*; ***a circle 6 cms in ~*** un círculo de 6 cms. de diámetro
di•a•met•ri•cal•ly [daɪə'metrɪkəlɪ] *adv*: ***~ opposed*** diametralmente opuesto
di•a•mond ['daɪmənd] *also in cards, baseball* diamante *m*; *shape* rombo *m*
di•a•mond 'wed•ding bodas *fpl* de diamante
di•a•per ['daɪpər] pañal *m*
di•a•phragm ['daɪəfræm] ANAT, *contraceptive* diafragma *m*
di•ar•rhe•a, *Br* **di•ar•rhoe•a** [daɪə'riːə] diarrea *f*
di•a•ry ['daɪrɪ] **1** *for thoughts* diario *m* **2** *for appointments* agenda *f*
di•a•tribe ['daɪətraɪb] diatriba *f*
dice [daɪs] **I** *n* dado *m*; *pl* dados *mpl* **II** *v/t food* cortar en dados **III** *v/i*: ***~ with death*** jugarse el cuello
dic•ey ['daɪsɪ] *adj* F arriesgado
di•chot•o•my [daɪ'kɑːtəmɪ] dicotomía *f*
dick [dɪk] **1** P (*private detective*) sabueso *m* **2** V (*penis*) polla *f* V
dic•tate [dɪk'teɪt] **I** *v/t* dictar **II** *v/i*: ***~ to s.o.*** dar órdenes a alguien
dic•ta•tion [dɪk'teɪʃn] dictado *m*
dic•ta•tor [dɪk'teɪtər] POL dictador(a) *m(f)*
dic•ta•to•ri•al [dɪktə'tɔːrɪəl] *adj* dictatorial
dic•ta•tor•ship [dɪk'teɪtərʃɪp] dictadura *f*
dic•tion ['dɪkʃn] dicción *f*
dic•tion•a•ry ['dɪkʃənerɪ] diccionario *m*
did [dɪd] *pret* ☞ ***do***
di•dac•tic [dɪ'dæktɪk] *adj* didáctico
did•dle ['dɪdl] *v/t* F: ***~ s.o. out of sth*** timar algo a alguien
did•n't ['dɪdnt] = ***did not***
die[1] [daɪ] *v/i* morir; ***~ of cancer / Aids*** morir de cáncer / sida; ***I'm dying to know / leave*** me muero de ganas de saber / marchar; ***I was dying for something to drink*** me moría por beber algo, me moría de sed; ***never say ~!*** ¡no tires la toalla!; ***I just about ~d*** F *with embarrassment etc* me morí de (la) vergüenza
die[2] [daɪ] *n* (*pl* ***dice*** [daɪs]) dado *m*; ***the ~ is cast*** *fig* la suerte está echada
◆ **die away** *v/i of noise* desaparecer
◆ **die down** *v/i of noise* irse apagando; *of storm* amainar; *of fire* irse extinguiendo; *of excitement* calmarse
◆ **die out** *v/i of custom, species* desaparecer
die•sel ['diːzl] *fuel* gasoil *m*, gasóleo *m*
di•et ['daɪət] **I** *n* **1** (*regular food*) dieta *f* **2** *for losing weight, for health reasons* dieta *f*, régimen *m*; ***be on a ~*** estar a dieta *or* régimen **II** *v/i to lose weight* hacer dieta *or* régimen
di•e•ti•tian [daɪə'tɪʃn] experto(-a) *m(f)* en dietética
dif•fer ['dɪfər] *v/i* **1** (*be different*) ser dis-

tinto; ***the male ~s from the female in …*** el macho se diferencia de la hembra por … **2** (*disagree*) discrepar

dif•fe•rence ['dɪfrəns] diferencia *f*; ***it doesn't make any ~*** (*doesn't change anything*) no cambia nada; (*doesn't matter*) da lo mismo; ***~ of opinion*** diferencia de opiniones; ***~ in price, price ~*** diferencia de precio; ***with a ~*** diferente

dif•fe•rent ['dɪfrənt] *adj* diferente, distinto (***from, than*** de)

dif•fer•en•tial [dɪfə'renʃl] **I** *adj* diferencial **II** *n* diferencial *m*

dif•fer•en•tial 'cal•cu•lus cálculo *m* diferencial

dif•fe•ren•ti•ate [dɪfə'renʃɪeɪt] *v/i* **1** (*distinguish*) diferenciar, distinguir (***between*** entre) **2**: ***~ between*** (*treat differently*) establecer diferencias entre

dif•fer•en•ti•a•tion [dɪfərenʃɪ'eɪʃn] diferenciación *f*

dif•fe•rent•ly ['dɪfrəntlɪ] *adv* de manera diferente

dif•fi•cult ['dɪfɪkəlt] *adj* difícil; ***it was quite ~ for me to …*** me resultó bastante difícil …

dif•fi•cul•ty ['dɪfɪkəltɪ] dificultad *f*; ***with ~*** con dificultades; ***have ~ doing sth*** costar hacer algo; ***I had no ~ finding them*** no tuve problemas para encontrarlos; ***run into ~*** tropezar con dificultades; ***make difficulties for s.o.*** crear dificultades a alguien; ***get into difficulties*** empezar a tener problemas

dif•fi•dence ['dɪfɪdəns] retraimiento *m*

dif•fi•dent ['dɪfɪdənt] *adj* retraído

dif•fuse[1] [dɪ'fjuːz] **I** *v/t* difundir **II** *v/i* difundirse

dif•fuse[2] [dɪ'fjuːs] *adj* difuso

dig [dɪg] *v/t & v/i* (*pret & pp* ***dug***) cavar; ***~ s.o. in the ribs*** dar un codazo a alguien en las costillas

◆ **dig in** *v/i* F ponerse a comer

◆ **dig into** *v/t* F **1** *food* ponerse a zampar F **2** *person's past etc* indagar

◆ **dig out** *v/t* (*find*) encontrar

◆ **dig up** *v/t* levantar, cavar; *information* desenterrar

di•gest [daɪ'dʒest] *v/t also fig* digerir

di•gest•i•ble [daɪ'dʒestəbl] *adj food* digerible

di•ges•tion [daɪ'dʒestʃn] digestión *f*

di•ges•tive [daɪ'dʒestɪv] *adj* digestivo

di'ges•tive sys•tem aparato *m* digestivo

di•ges•tive 'tract tubo *m* digestivo

dig•ger ['dɪgər] *machine* excavadora *f*

di•git ['dɪdʒɪt] *number* dígito *m*; ***a 4 ~ number*** un número de 4 dígitos

di•gi•tal ['dɪdʒɪtl] *adj* digital

'di•gi•tal clock reloj *m* digital; **di•gi•tal dis'play** monitor *m* digital; **di•gi•tal 'read•out** lectura *f* digital; **di•gi•tal 'tel•e•vi•sion** televisión *f* digital; **di•gi•tal 'watch** reloj *m* digital

dig•i•tize ['dɪdʒɪtaɪz] *v/t* digitalizar

dig•ni•fied ['dɪgnɪfaɪd] *adj* digno

dig•ni•fy ['dɪgnɪfaɪ] *v/t* dignificar

dig•ni•ta•ry ['dɪgnɪterɪ] dignatario(-a) *m(f)*

dig•ni•ty ['dɪgnɪtɪ] dignidad *f*

di•gress [daɪ'gres] *v/i* divagar, apartarse del tema

di•gres•sion [daɪ'greʃn] digresión *f*

dike[1] [daɪk] *wall* dique *m*

dike[2] [daɪk] P *lesbian* tortillera *f* P

di•lap•i•dat•ed [dɪ'læpɪdeɪtɪd] *adj* destartalado

di•late [daɪ'leɪt] *v/i of pupils* dilatarse

◆ **dilate on** *v/t fml fig* explayarse sobre

dil•a•to•ry ['dɪlətɔːrɪ] *adj* dilatorio; ***be ~ in doing sth*** tardar mucho en hacer algo

di•lem•ma [dɪ'lemə] dilema *m*; ***be in a ~*** estar en un dilema; ***be on the horns of a ~*** estar entre la espada y la pared

dil•et•tante [dɪle'tæntɪ] diletante *m/f*

dil•i•gence ['dɪlɪdʒəns] diligencia *f*

dil•i•gent ['dɪlɪdʒənt] *adj* diligente

dill [dɪl] BOT eneldo *m*

dil•ly•dal•ly ['dɪlɪdælɪ] *v/i* F entretenerse

di•lute [daɪ'luːt] *v/t* diluir

di•lu•tion [daɪ'luːʃn] dilución *f*

dim [dɪm] **I** *adj room* oscuro; *light* tenue; *outline* borroso, confuso; (*stupid*) tonto; *prospects* remoto; *eyesight* borroso; ***take a ~ view of sth*** desaprobar algo **II** *v/t* (*pret & pp* ***-med***) atenuar; ***~ the headlights*** poner las luces cortas **III** *v/i* (*pret & pp* ***-med***) *of lights* atenuarse

dime [daɪm] *moneda de diez centavos*

'dime nov•el novela *f* barata

di•men•sion [daɪ'menʃn] (*measurement*) dimensión *f*

di•min•ish [dɪ'mɪnɪʃ] *v/t & v/i* disminuir; ***~ in value*** disminuir de valor

dim•i•nu•tion [dɪmɪ'njuːʃn] disminu-

ción *f*
di•min•u•tive [dɪ'mɪnʊtɪv] **I** *n* diminutivo *m* **II** *adj* diminuto
dim•ly ['dɪmlɪ] *adv*: **~ *lit*** con poca luz; ***I could ~ see …*** apenas veía …
dim•mer ['dɪmər] potenciómetro *m*, dimmer *m*
dim•ple ['dɪmpl] hoyuelo *m*
dim•wit•ted [dɪm'wɪtɪd] *adj* corto
din [dɪn] **I** *n* estruendo *m*; ***make a ~*** armar un estruendo **II** *v/t* (*pret & pp* ***-ned***): ***~ sth into s.o.*** intentar convencer a alguien de algo
dine [daɪn] *v/i fml* cenar, *L.Am.* comer
◆ **dine in** *v/i* cenar *or L.Am.* comer en casa
◆ **dine on** *v/t* cenar, *L.Am.* comer
◆ **dine out** *v/i* cenar *or L.Am.* comer fuera, *Rpl, Mex* cenar afuera
din•er ['daɪnər] **1** *person* comensal *m/f* **2** *restaurant* restaurante *m* barato
din•ghy ['dɪŋgɪ] (*small yacht*) bote *m* de vela; (*rubber boat*) lancha *f* neumática
din•gy ['dɪndʒɪ] *adj* sórdido; (*dirty*) sucio
din•ing car ['daɪnɪŋ] RAIL vagón *m* restaurante, coche *m* comedor; **'din•ing room** comedor *m*; **'din•ing ta•ble** mesa *f* de comedor
dink•y ['dɪŋkɪ] *adj* F **1** cutre **2** *Br* mono
din•ner ['dɪnər] *in the evening* cena *f*, *at midday* comida *f*, (*formal gathering*) cena *f* de gala; ***what's for ~?*** ¿qué hay de cena?, ¿ qué hay para cenar?
'din•ner guest invitado(-a) *m(f)* a cenar; **'din•ner jack•et** *Br* esmoquin *m*; **'din•ner par•ty** cena *f*, **'din•ner service, 'din•ner set** vajilla *f*, **'din•ner table**: ***at the ~*** en la mesa; **'din•ner time** hora *f* de la cena; *at midday* hora *f* de la comida
di•no•saur ['daɪnəsɔːr] dinosaurio *m*
dint [dɪnt]: ***by ~ of*** a fuerza de
di•ode ['daɪoʊd] ELEC diodo *m*
di•ox•ide [daɪ'ɑːksaɪd] CHEM dióxido *m*
di•ox•in [daɪ'ɑːksɪn] CHEM dioxina *f*
dip [dɪp] **I** *n* **1** (*slope*) inclinación *f*, pendiente *f*, (*depression*) hondonada *f* **2** (*swim*) baño *m*, zambullida *f*, ***go for a ~*** darse un baño *or* una zambullida **3** *for food* salsa *f* **II** *v/t* (*pret & pp* ***-ped***): ***~ sth into sth*** meter algo en algo; ***~ the headlights*** poner las luces cortas **III** *v/i* (*pret & pp* ***-ped***) *of road* bajar
◆ **dip into** *v/t* **1** *book* echar un vistazo a **2** *savings* echar mano de
diph•the•ri•a [dɪf'θɪrɪə] difteria *f*
diph•thong ['dɪfθɑːŋ] diptongo *m*
di•plo•ma [dɪ'ploʊmə] diploma *m*
di•plo•ma•cy [dɪ'ploʊməsɪ] *also fig* diplomacia *f*
di•plo•mat ['dɪpləmæt] diplomático(-a) *m(f)*
di•plo•mat•ic [dɪplə'mætɪk] *adj also fig* diplomático
dip•lo•mat•i•cal•ly [dɪplə'mætɪklɪ] *adv* de forma diplomática
di•plo•mat•ic 'bag valija *f* diplomática; **di•plo'mat•ic corps** cuerpo *m* diplomático; **dip•lo•mat•ic im'mu•ni•ty** inmunidad *f* diplomática
dip•py ['dɪpɪ] *adj* F tonto F, chiflado F
dip•so•man•i•ac [dɪpsə'meɪnɪæk] *adj* dipsomaníaco
'dip•stick MOT varilla *f* del aceite
dire [daɪr] *adj* terrible; ***be in ~ need of sth*** necesitar algo acuciantemente
di•rect [daɪ'rekt] **I** *adj* directo; ***the ~ opposite*** exactamente lo opuesto (***of*** de) **II** *v/t play, movie, attention* dirigir; ***can you ~ me to the museum?*** ¿me podría indicar cómo se va al museo?; ***~ sth to be done*** disponer que se haga algo
di•rect 'cur•rent ELEC corriente *f* continua
di•rect 'dis•course LING estilo *m* directo
di•rec•tion [dɪ'rekʃn] **1** dirección *f*, ***in the ~ of*** en dirección a, hacia; ***from all ~s*** de todas partes; ***sense of ~*** sentido de la orientación **2**: ***~s** to a place* indicaciones *fpl*; (*instructions*) instrucciones *fpl*; *for medicine* posología *f*; ***let's ask for ~s*** preguntemos cómo se va; ***~s for use*** modo *m* de empleo **3** *of movie* dirección *f*
di•rec•tion 'in•di•ca•tor MOT intermitente *m*
di•rec•tive [dɪ'rektɪv] directiva *f*
di•rect•ly [dɪ'rektlɪ] **I** *adv* (*straight*) directamente; (*soon*) pronto; (*immediately*) ahora mismo **II** *conj* en cuanto; ***~ I've finished this …*** en cuanto *or* tan pronto acabe esto …
di•rect mail 'ad•ver•tis•ing propaganda *f* por correo directo

di•rect 'ob•ject LING objeto *m* directo
di•rec•tor [dɪ'rektər] director(a) *m(f)*
di•rec•tor-'gen•e•ral COM director(a) *m(f)* general
di•rec•tor•ship [daɪ'rektərʃɪp] COM dirección *f*; ***be given a ~*** ser ascendido a director
di•rec•to•ry [dɪ'rektərɪ] *also* COMPUT directorio *m*; TELEC guía *f* telefónica
di•rec•to•ry en'qui•ries *nsg Br* TELEC servicio *m* de guía telefónica
di•rect 'speech *Br* LING estilo *m* directo
dirt [dɜːrt] suciedad *f*; ***treat s.o. like ~*** tratar a alguien como a un pelele *or* pingo
dirt 'cheap *adj* F tirado F; **dirt 'poor** *adj* F pordiosero F, desarrapado F; **'dirt road, 'dirt track** pista *f* (de tierra), camino *m*
dirt•y ['dɜːrtɪ] **I** *adj* sucio; (*pornographic*) pornográfico, obsceno; ***give s.o. a ~ look*** mirar a alguien con cara de pocos amigos F; ***have a ~ mind*** tener una mente pervertida *or* corrompida; ***~ old man*** viejo *m* verde; ***~ word*** obscenidad *f*, grosería *f*; ***do s.o.'s ~ work*** *fig* hacer el trabajo sucio por alguien **II** *v/t* (*pret & pp* ***-ied***) ensuciar; ***~ one's hands*** *fig* pringarse
dirt•y 'trick jugarreta *f*; ***play a ~ on s.o.*** hacer una jugarreta a alguien
dis•a•bil•i•ty [dɪsə'bɪlətɪ] discapacidad *f*, minusvalía *f*
dis•a•ble [dɪs'eɪbl] *v/t* **1** *person* dejar con una minusvalía **2** *machine* invalidar, estropear
dis•a•bled [dɪs'eɪbld] **I** *npl*: ***the ~*** los discapacitados *mpl* **II** *adj* discapacitado; ***~ access*** acceso *m* para discapacitados
dis•a•buse [dɪsə'bjuːz] *v/t*: ***~ s.o. of an idea*** desengañar a alguien de una idea
dis•ad•van•tage [dɪsəd'væntɪdʒ] (*drawback*) desventaja *f*; ***be at a ~*** estar en desventaja; ***to s.o.'s ~*** en perjuicio de alguien; ***put s.o. at a ~*** poner *or* dejar a alguien en desventaja
dis•ad•van•taged [dɪsəd'væntɪdʒd] *adj* desfavorecido
dis•ad•van•ta•geous [dɪsædvæn'teɪdʒəs] *adj* desventajoso, desfavorable
dis•af•fec•ted [dɪsə'fektɪd] *adj* descontento, insatisfecho
dis•a•gree [dɪsə'griː] *v/i of person* no estar de acuerdo, discrepar; ***let's agree to ~*** aceptemos que no nos vamos a poner de acuerdo
◆ **disagree with** *v/t* **1** *of person* no estar de acuerdo con, discrepar con **2** *of food* sentar mal; ***lobster disagrees with me*** la langosta me sienta mal
dis•a•gree•a•ble [dɪsə'griːəbl] *adj* desagradable
dis•a•gree•ment [dɪsə'griːmənt] **1** desacuerdo *m* **2** (*argument*) discusión *f*
dis•al•low [dɪsə'laʊ] *v/t* SP anular, pitar F
dis•ap•pear [dɪsə'pɪr] *v/i* desaparecer; ***now where has that boy ~ed to!*** ¡dónde se ha metido ahora ese chico!
dis•ap•pear•ance [dɪsə'pɪrəns] desaparición *f*
dis•ap•point [dɪsə'pɔɪnt] *v/t* desilusionar, decepcionar
dis•ap•point•ed [dɪsə'pɔɪntɪd] *adj* desilusionado, decepcionado
dis•ap•point•ing [dɪsə'pɔɪntɪŋ] *adj* decepcionante
dis•ap•point•ment [dɪsə'pɔɪntmənt] desilusión *f*, decepción *f*
dis•ap•prov•al [dɪsə'pruːvl] desaprobación *f*
dis•ap•prove [dɪsə'pruːv] *v/i* desaprobar, estar en contra; ***~ of*** desaprobar, estar en contra de
dis•ap•prov•ing [dɪsə'pruːvɪŋ] *adj* desaprobatorio, de desaprobación
dis•ap•prov•ing•ly [dɪsə'pruːvɪŋlɪ] *adv* con desaprobación
dis•arm [dɪs'ɑːrm] **I** *v/t* desarmar **II** *v/i* desarmarse
dis•ar•ma•ment [dɪs'ɑːrməmənt] desarme *m*
dis•arm•ing [dɪs'ɑːrmɪŋ] *adj* cautivador
dis•ar•range [dɪsə'reɪndʒ] *v/t* desordenar, revolver
dis•ar•ray [dɪsə'reɪ]: ***be in ~*** estar en desorden
dis•as•sem•ble [dɪsə'sembl] *v/t* desmantelar
dis•as•sem•bly [dɪsə'semblɪ] desmantelamiento *m*
dis•as•ter [dɪ'zæstər] desastre *m*
di'sas•ter ar•e•a zona *f* catastrófica; *fig*: *person* desastre *m*
di•sas•trous [dɪ'zæstrəs] *adj* desastroso

dis•band [dɪs'bænd] **I** *v/t* disolver **II** *v/i* disolverse
dis•be•lief [dɪsbə'liːf] incredulidad *f*; ***in ~*** con incredulidad
dis•be•lieve [dɪsbə'liːv] *v/t* descreer, cuestionar
dis•burse [dɪs'bɜːrs] *v/t* desembolsar
disc [dɪsk] *Br* ☞ ***disk***
dis•card [dɪ'skɑːrd] *v/t* desechar; *boyfriend* deshacerse de
'disc brake freno *m* de disco
di•scern [dɪ'sɜːrn] *v/t* distinguir, percibir
di•scern•i•ble [dɪ'sɜːrnəbl] *adj* perceptible
di•scern•ing [dɪ'sɜːrnɪŋ] *adj* entendido, exigente
dis•cern•ment [dɪ'sɜːrnmənt] discernimiento *m*, juicio *m*
dis•charge I *n* ['dɪstʃɑːrdʒ] **1** *from hospital* alta *f*; *from army* licencia *f* **2** (*pus*) emisión *f* **II** *v/t* [dɪs'tʃɑːrdʒ] **1** *from hospital* dar el alta a; *from army* licenciar; *from job* despedir **2** *pus* emitir
di•sci•ple [dɪ'saɪpl] *religious* discípulo *m*
dis•ci•pli•nar•y [dɪsɪ'plɪnərɪ] *adj* disciplinario
dis•ci•pline ['dɪsɪplɪn] **I** *n* disciplina *f* **II** *v/t child*, *dog* castigar; *employee* sancionar
dis•ci•plined ['dɪsɪplɪnd] *adj* disciplinado, ordenado
'disc jock•ey disc jockey *m/f*, *Span* pinchadiscos *m/f inv*
dis•claim [dɪs'kleɪm] *v/t* negar
dis•claim•er [dɪs'kleɪmər] *of rights* renuncia *f*; *of responsibility* descargo *m*
dis•close [dɪs'kloʊs] *v/t* revelar
dis•clo•sure [dɪs'kloʊʒər] revelación *f*
dis•co ['dɪskoʊ] discoteca *f*
dis•col•or, *Br* **dis•col•our** [dɪs'kʌlər] *v/i* decolorar
dis•com•fit [dɪs'kʌmfɪt] *v/t* avergonzar, turbar
dis•com•fi•ture [dɪs'kʌmfɪtʃər] vergüenza *f*, turbación *f*
dis•com•fort [dɪs'kʌmfərt] **1** (*pain*) molestia *f* **2** (*embarrassment*) incomodidad *f*
dis•con•cert [dɪskən'sɜːrt] *v/t* desconcertar
dis•con•cert•ed [dɪskən'sɜːrtɪd] *adj* desconcertado
dis•con•cert•ing [dɪskən'sɜːrtɪŋ] *adj* desconcertante
dis•con•nect [dɪskə'nekt] *v/t* desconectar
dis•con•so•late [dɪs'kɑːnsələt] *adj* desconsolado
dis•con•tent [dɪskən'tent] descontento *m*
dis•con•tent•ed [dɪskən'tentɪd] *adj* descontento; ***grow ~*** hartarse, disgustarse
dis•con•tin•ue [dɪskən'tɪnjuː] *v/t product* dejar de producir; *bus*, *train service* suspender; *magazine* dejar de publicar; ***~d line*** COM línea *f* discontinuada
dis•con•tin•u•ous [dɪskən'tɪnjʊəs] *adj* discontinuo
dis•cord ['dɪskɔːrd] **1** MUS discordancia *f* **2** *in relations* discordia *f*
dis•cord•ant [dɪs'kɔːrdənt] *adj* discorde, discordante; ***strike a ~ note*** *fig* ser la nota discordante
dis•co•theque ['dɪskətek] discoteca *f*
dis•count I *n* ['dɪskaʊnt] descuento *m*; ***at a ~*** a precio rebajado **II** *v/t* [dɪs'kaʊnt] **1** *goods* descontar **2** *theory* descartar
'dis•count rate tipo *m* de descuento
'dis•count store tienda *f* de saldos
dis•cour•age [dɪs'kʌrɪdʒ] *v/t* **1** (*dissuade*) disuadir (***from*** de) **2** (*dishearten*) desanimar, desalentar
dis•cour•age•ment [dɪs'kʌrɪdʒmənt] **1** disuasión *f* **2** (*being disheartened*) desánimo *m*, desaliento *m*
dis•cour•ag•ing [dɪs'kʌrɪdʒɪŋ] *adj* desalentador, desmoralizador
dis•course I *n* ['dɪskɔːrs] disquisición *f*, análisis *m* **II** *v/i* [dɪ'skɔːs] disertar, tratar (***on*** sobre)
dis•cour•te•ous [dɪs'kɜːrtjəs] *adj* descortés, desconsiderado
dis•cour•te•sy [dɪs'kɜːrtɪsɪ] descortesía *f*, desconsideración *f*
dis•cov•er [dɪ'skʌvər] *v/t* descubrir
dis•cov•er•er [dɪ'skʌvərər] descubridor(a) *m(f)*
dis•cov•e•ry [dɪ'skʌvərɪ] descubrimiento *m*
dis•cred•it [dɪs'kredɪt] **I** *v/t* desacreditar **II** *n*: ***bring sth into ~***, ***bring ~ on sth*** empañar la fama de algo, desprestigiar algo
di•screet [dɪ'skriːt] *adj* discreto

di•screet•ly [dɪ'skriːtlɪ] *adv* discretamente
di•screp•an•cy [dɪ'skrepənsɪ] discrepancia *f*
di•scre•tion [dɪ'skreʃn] discreción *f*; ***at your ~*** a discreción; ***use your ~*** usa tu criterio
di•scrim•i•nate [dɪ'skrɪmɪneɪt] *v/i* discriminar (***against*** contra); ***~ between*** (*distinguish*) distinguir entre
di•scrim•i•nat•ing [dɪ'skrɪmɪneɪtɪŋ] *adj* entendido, exigente
di•scrim•i•na•tion [dɪ'skrɪmɪneɪʃn] *sexual, racial etc* discriminación *f*
dis•crim•i•na•to•ry [dɪ'skrɪmɪnətɔːrɪ] *adj* discriminatorio
dis•cur•sive [dɪ'skɜːrsɪv] *adj* divagador, inconexo
dis•cus ['dɪskəs] SP *object* disco *m*; *event* lanzamiento *m* de disco
di•scuss [dɪ'skʌs] *v/t* discutir; *of article* analizar
di•scus•sion [dɪ'skʌʃn] discusión *f*; ***be under ~*** estar bajo consideración
dis'cus•sion pro•gram programa *m* de debate
'dis•cus throw•er lanzador(a) *m(f)* de disco
dis•dain [dɪs'deɪn] desdén *m*
dis•dain•ful [dɪs'deɪnfʊl] *adj* desdeñoso; ***be ~ of s.o.*** / ***sth*** menospreciar *or* despreciar a alguien / algo
dis•ease [dɪ'ziːz] enfermedad *f*
dis•em•bark [dɪsəm'bɑːrk] *v/i* desembarcar
dis•en•chant•ed [dɪsən'tʃæntɪd] *adj*: ***~ with*** desencantado con; ***become ~ with sth*** desencantarse con algo
dis•en•franch•ise [dɪsən'fræntʃaɪz] *v/t* negar el derecho al voto a
dis•en•gage [dɪsən'geɪdʒ] *v/t* soltar
dis•en•tan•gle [dɪsən'tæŋgl] *v/t* desenredar
dis•fa•vo(u)r [dɪs'feɪvər]: ***be in*** / ***fall into ~*** estar en / caer en desgracia (***with*** de)
dis•fig•ure [dɪs'fɪgər] *v/t* desfigurar
dis•gorge [dɪs'gɔːrdʒ] **I** *v/t* descargar, arrojar **II** *v/i* descargarse, arrojarse
dis•grace [dɪs'greɪs] **I** *n* vergüenza *f*, ***it's a ~!*** ¡qué vergüenza!; ***in ~*** desacreditado; ***bring ~ on*** desacreditar *or* deshonrar a **II** *v/t* deshonrar; ***~ o.s.*** degradarse
dis•grace•ful [dɪs'greɪsfəl] *adj behavior, situation* vergonzoso, lamentable
dis•grun•tled [dɪs'grʌntld] *adj* descontento
dis•guise [dɪs'gaɪz] **I** *n* disfraz *m*; ***in ~*** disfrazado **II** *v/t voice, handwriting* cambiar; *fear, anxiety* disfrazar; ***~ o.s. as*** disfrazarse de; ***he was ~d as …*** iba disfrazado de …
dis•gust [dɪs'gʌst] **I** *n* asco *m*, repugnancia *f*, ***in ~*** asqueado **II** *v/t* dar asco a, repugnar; ***I'm ~ed by*** *or* ***with*** *or* ***at …*** me da asco *or* me repugna …
dis•gust•ing [dɪs'gʌstɪŋ] *adj habit, smell, food* asqueroso, repugnante; ***it is ~ that …*** da asco que …, es repugnante que …
dish [dɪʃ] **1** (*part of meal, container*) plato *m*; ***wash*** *or* ***do the ~es*** fregar los platos **2** *for satellite TV* antena *f* parabólica
◆ **dish out** *v/t* F soltar F; *food* repartir
◆ **dish up** *v/t* servir
dis•har•mo•ny [dɪs'hɑːrmənɪ] tensión *f*, tirantez *f*
'dish•cloth paño *m* de cocina
dis•heart•en [dɪs'hɑːrtn] *v/t* descorazonar, desanimar
dis•heart•ened [dɪs'hɑːrtnd] *adj* desalentado, descorazonado; ***get*** *or* ***become ~*** descorazonarse, desanimarse
dis•heart•en•ing [dɪs'hɑːrtnɪŋ] *adj* descorazonador
di•shev•eled, *Br* **di•shev•elled** [dɪ'ʃevld] *adj hair, clothes* desaliñado; *person* despeinado
dis•hon•est [dɪs'ɑːnɪst] *adj* deshonesto
dis•hon•est•y [dɪs'ɑːnɪstɪ] deshonestidad *f*
dis•hon•or [dɪs'ɑːnər] **I** *n* deshonra *f*, ***bring ~ on*** deshonrar a **II** *v/t* deshonrar
dis•hon•o•ra•ble [dɪs'ɑːnərəbl] *adj* deshonroso
dis•hon•our *etc Br* ☞ ***dishonor*** *etc*
'dish tow•el paño *m* de cocina; **'dish•wash•er** *person* lavaplatos *m/f inv*; *machine* lavavajillas *m inv*, lavaplatos *m inv*; **'dish•wash•ing liq•uid** lavavajillas *m inv*; **'dish•wa•ter** agua *f* de lavar los platos
dish•y ['dɪʃɪ] *adj Br* F guapetón F, de buena facha F
dis•il•lu•sion [dɪsɪ'luːʒn] *v/t* desilusionar
dis•il•lu•sioned [dɪsɪ'luːʒnd] *adj* desi-

lusionado, desencantado; ***become ~ with sth*** desilusionarse con algo
dis•il•lu•sion•ment [dɪsɪ'lu:ʒnmənt] desilusión *f*
dis•in•cen•tive [dɪsɪn'sentɪv] inconveniente *m*, pega *f*
dis•in•cli•na•tion [dɪsɪnklɪ'neɪʃn] resistencia *f*
dis•in•clined [dɪsɪn'klaɪnd] *adj*: ***she was ~ to believe him*** no estaba inclinada a creerle
dis•in•fect [dɪsɪn'fekt] *v/t* desinfectar
dis•in•fec•tant [dɪsɪn'fektənt] desinfectante *m*
dis•in•fec•tion [dɪsɪn'fekʃn] desinfección *f*
dis•in•for•ma•tion [dɪsɪnfər'meɪʃn] desinformación *f*
dis•in•gen•u•ous [dɪsɪn'dʒenjʊəs] *adj* deshonesto, ruin
dis•in•her•it [dɪsɪn'herɪt] *v/t* desheredar
dis•in•te•grate [dɪs'ɪntəgreɪt] *v/i* desintegrarse; *of marriage* deshacerse
dis•in•te•gra•tion [dɪsɪntə'greɪʃn] desintegración *f*
dis•in•ter•est•ed [dɪs'ɪntərestɪd] *adj* (*unbiased*) desinteresado
dis•joint•ed [dɪs'dʒɔɪntɪd] *adj* deshilvanado
disk [dɪsk] *also* COMPUT disco *m*; ***on ~*** en disco
'disk drive COMPUT unidad *f* de disco
disk•ette [dɪs'ket] disquete *m*
dis•like [dɪs'laɪk] **I** *n* antipatía *f*; ***take a ~ to s.o.*** tomar manía a alguien **II** *v/t*: ***she ~s being kept waiting*** no le gusta que la hagan esperar; ***I ~ him*** no me gusta; ***get o.s. ~d*** ganarse la antipatía ajena
dis•lo•cate ['dɪsləkeɪt] *v/t shoulder* dislocar
dis•lo•ca•tion [dɪslou'keɪʃn] MED dislocación *f*
dis•lodge [dɪs'lɑ:dʒ] *v/t* desplazar, mover de su sitio
dis•loy•al [dɪs'lɔɪəl] *adj* desleal
dis•loy•al•ty [dɪs'lɔɪəltɪ] deslealtad *f*
dis•mal ['dɪzməl] *adj weather* horroroso, espantoso; *news*, *prospect* negro; *person* (*sad*) triste; *person* (*negative*) negativo; *failure* estrepitoso
dis•man•tle [dɪs'mæntl] *v/t* desmantelar
dis•may [dɪs'meɪ] **I** *n* (*alarm*) consternación *f*; (*disappointment*) desánimo *m*; ***in ~*** con pesar; ***I realized to my ~ that ...*** me dí cuenta, para mi desgracia, de que ... **II** *v/t* consternar
dis•mem•ber [dɪs'membər] *v/t* desmembrar, dividir
dis•miss [dɪs'mɪs] *v/t employee* despedir; *suggestion* rechazar; *idea*, *possibility* descartar
dis•miss•al [dɪs'mɪsl] *of employee* despido *m*
dis•mis•sive [dɪs'mɪsɪv] *adj*: ***be ~ of s.o.*** / ***sth*** mostrar desprecio por alguien / algo
dis•mount [dɪs'maʊnt] *v/i* desmontar
dis•o•be•di•ence [dɪsə'bi:dɪəns] desobediencia *f*
dis•o•be•di•ent [dɪsə'bi:dɪənt] *adj* desobediente
dis•o•bey [dɪsə'beɪ] *v/t* desobedecer
dis•o•blig•ing [dɪsə'blaɪdʒɪŋ] *adj* ineficiente
dis•or•der [dɪs'ɔ:rdər] **1** (*untidiness*) desorden *m*; ***in ~*** en desorden; ***throw sth into ~*** desbarajustar *or* revolucionar algo **2** (*unrest*) desórdenes *mpl* **3** MED dolencia *f*; ***mental ~*** enfermedad mental; ***stomach ~*** dolencia estomacal
dis•or•dered [dɪs'ɔ:rdərd] *adj* **1** *room*, *desk* desordenado **2** *mind* perturbado, desequilibrado
dis•or•der•ly [dɪs'ɔ:rdərlɪ] *adj* **1** *room*, *desk* desordenado **2** *mob* alborotado
dis•or•gan•ize [dɪs'ɔ:rgənaɪz] *v/t* desorganizar
dis•or•gan•ized [dɪs'ɔ:rgənaɪzd] *adj* desorganizado
dis•o•ri•ent, dis•o•ri•en•tate [dɪs'ɔ:rɪənt(eɪt)] *v/t* desorientar
dis•o•ri•ent•ed [dɪs'ɔ:rɪəntɪd] *adj* desorientado
dis•own [dɪs'oʊn] *v/t* repudiar, renegar de; ***if you do that, I'll ~ you*** si haces eso yo no te conozco
dis•par•age [dɪ'spærɪdʒ] *v/t* denigrar
dis•par•age•ment [dɪ'spærɪdʒmənt] desprecio *m*
dis•par•ag•ing [dɪ'spærɪdʒɪŋ] *adj* despreciativo
dis•pa•rate ['dɪspərət] *adj* dispar, diferente
dis•par•i•ty [dɪ'spærətɪ] disparidad *f*
dis•pas•sion•ate [dɪ'spæʃənət] *adj* (*objective*) desapasionado
dis•patch [dɪ'spætʃ] *v/t* (*send*) enviar

di•spatch•er [dɪ'spætʃər] *for taxi firm* coordinador(a) *m(f)* (de centralita de taxis)
dis•pel [dɪ'spel] *v/t* (*pret & pp* **-led**) *doubts*, *crowd* dispersar
dis•pen•sa•ble [dɪ'spensəbl] *adj* prescindible
dis•pen•sa•ry [dɪ'spensərɪ] *in pharmacy* dispensario *m*
dis•pen•sa•tion [dɪspen'seɪʃn] REL dispensa *f*
dis•pense [dɪ'spens] *v/t medicine* dispensar; *advice* dar; **~ *justice*** administrar justicia
◆ **dispense with** [dɪ'spens] *v/t* prescindir de
dis•pens•er [dɪ'spensər] máquina *f* expendedora
dis•pens•ing chem•ist [dɪ'spensɪŋ] *Br* farmacéutico(-a) *m(f)*
dis•per•sal [dɪ'spɜːrsl] esparcimiento *m*, difusión *f*
dis•perse [dɪ'spɜːrs] **I** *v/t* dispersar **II** *v/i of crowd* dispersarse; *of mist* disiparse
dis•pir•it•ed [dɪs'pɪrɪtɪd] *adj* desalentado, abatido; ***get* or *become* ~** desalentarse, abatirse
dis•place [dɪs'pleɪs] *v/t* (*supplant*) sustituir
dis•placed per•son ['dɪspleɪst] refugiado(-a) *m(f)*
dis•place•ment [dɪs'pleɪsmənt] desalojo *m*, evacuación *f*
dis•play [dɪs'pleɪ] **I** *n* muestra *f*; *in store window* objetos *mpl* expuestos; COMPUT pantalla *f*; ***be on* ~** estar expuesto **II** *v/t emotion*, *prices* mostrar; *at exhibition*, *for sale* exponer; COMPUT visualizar; ***a notice will be ~ed*** se pondrá un aviso
dis'play cab•i•net *in museum*, *shop* vitrina *f*; **dis'play case** vitrina *f*; **dis'play stand** expositor *m*; **dis'play unit** *in store* vitrina *f*
dis•please [dɪs'pliːz] *v/t* desagradar, disgustar; ***be ~d at* or *with*** estar descontento *or* disgustado con
dis•pleas•ing [dɪs'pliːzɪŋ] *adj* desagradable
dis•plea•sure [dɪs'pleʒər] desagrado *m*, disgusto *m*
dis•po•sa•ble [dɪ'spoʊzəbl] *adj* desechable; **~ *income*** ingreso(s) *m(pl)* disponible(s)
dis•pos•al [dɪ'spoʊzl] eliminación *f*; ***I am at your* ~** estoy a su disposición; ***put sth at s.o.'s* ~** poner algo a disposición de alguien
◆ **dis•pose of** [dɪ'spoʊz] *v/t* (*get rid of*) deshacerse de
dis•posed [dɪ'spoʊzd] *adj*: ***be* or *feel* ~ *to do sth*** (*willing*) estar dispuesto a hacer algo; ***be well* ~ *toward*** estar bien dispuesto hacia
dis•po•si•tion [dɪspə'zɪʃn] (*nature*) carácter *m*
dis•pos•sess [dɪspə'zes] *v/t* deshauciar, desposeer
dis•pro•por•tion•ate [dɪsprə'pɔːrʃənət] *adj* desproporcionado; ***be* ~ *to*** ser desproporcionado para
dis•prove [dɪs'pruːv] *v/t* refutar
dis•put•a•ble [dɪ'spjuːtəbl] *adj* cuestionable, discutible
dis•pu•ta•tion [dɪspjuː'teɪʃn] debate *m*, controversia *f*
dis•pu•ta•tious [dɪspjuː'teɪʃəs] *adj* discutidor
dis•pute [dɪ'spjuːt] **I** *n* disputa *f*, *industrial* conflicto *m* laboral **II** *v/t* discutir; (*fight over*) disputarse; ***I don't* ~ *that*** eso no lo discuto
dis•qual•i•fi•ca•tion [dɪskwɑːlɪfɪ'keɪʃn] descalificación *f*
dis•qual•i•fy [dɪs'kwɑːlɪfaɪ] *v/t* (*pret & pp* **-ied**) descalificar
dis•qui•et [dɪs'kwaɪət] inquietud *f*, preocupación *f*
dis•qui•et•ing [dɪs'kwaɪətɪŋ] *adj* inquietante, preocupante
dis•re•gard [dɪsrə'gɑːrd] **I** *n* indiferencia *f* **II** *v/t* no tener en cuenta
dis•re•pair [dɪsrə'per]: ***in a state of* ~** deteriorado; ***fall into* ~** deteriorarse
dis•rep•u•ta•ble [dɪs'repjʊtəbl] *adj* poco respetable; *area* de mala reputación
dis•re•pute [dɪsrɪ'pjuːt]: ***bring sth into* ~** desprestigiar algo; ***fall into* ~** adquirir mala reputación
dis•re•spect [dɪsrə'spekt] falta *f* de respeto
dis•re•spect•ful [dɪsrə'spektfəl] *adj* irrespetuoso
dis•rupt [dɪs'rʌpt] *v/t* **1** *train service* trastornar, alterar **2** *meeting*, *class* interrumpir
dis•rup•tion [dɪs'rʌpʃn] **1** *of train service* alteración *f* **2** *of meeting*, *class* in-

terrupción *f*
dis•rup•tive [dɪs'rʌptɪv] *adj* perjudicial; ***he's very ~ in class*** causa muchos problemas en clase
dis•sat•is•fac•tion [dɪssætɪs'fækʃn] insatisfacción *f*
dis•sat•is•fac•to•ry [dɪssætɪs'fæktərɪ] *adj* insatisfactorio
dis•sat•is•fied [dɪs'sætɪsfaɪd] *adj* insatisfecho
dis•sect [dɪ'sekt] *v/t* **1** MED diseccionar, disecar **2** *fig* diseccionar, analizar
dis•sec•tion [dɪ'sekʃn] MED disección *f*, disecación *f*
dis•sem•ble [dɪ'sembl] *v/t* ocultar, esconder
dis•sem•i•nate [dɪ'semɪneɪt] *v/t* propagar
dis•sem•in•a•tion [dɪsemɪ'neɪʃn] propagación *f*
dis•sen•sion [dɪ'senʃn] disensión *f*
dis•sent [dɪ'sent] **I** *n* discrepancia *f* **II** *v/i*: ***~ from*** disentir de
dis•sent•er [dɪ'sentər] disidente *m/f*
dis•ser•ta•tion [dɪsər'teɪʃn] EDU tesina *f*
dis•serv•ice [dɪs'sɜːrvɪs]: ***do s.o. a ~*** hacer un feo *or* desaire a alguien
dis•si•dent ['dɪsɪdənt] disidente *m/f*
dis•sim•i•lar [dɪs'sɪmɪlər] *adj* distinto
dis•sim•i•lar•i•ty [dɪssɪmɪ'lærətɪ] disimilitud *f*, diferencia *f*
dis•si•pate ['dɪsɪpeɪt] **I** *v/t* desvanecer **II** *v/i* desvanecerse
dis•si•pat•ed ['dɪsɪpeɪtɪd] *adj* disipado, libertino
dis•si•pa•tion [dɪsɪ'peɪʃn]: ***a life of ~*** una vida de excesos
dis•so•ci•ate [dɪ'soʊʃɪeɪt] *v/t* disociar; ***~ o.s. from*** disociarse de
dis•so•ci•a•tion [dɪsoʊsɪ'eɪʃn] disociación *f*
dis•so•lute ['dɪsəluːt] *adj* disoluto
dis•so•lu•tion ['dɪsəluːʃn] POL, COM disolución *f*
dis•solve [dɪ'zɑːlv] **I** *v/t substance, company* disolver **II** *v/i* **1** *of substance* disolverse **2**: ***~ into tears*** deshacerse en lágrimas
dis•so•nance ['dɪsənəns] **1** MUS disonancia *f* **2** *fig* discordancia *f*
dis•so•nant ['dɪsənənt] *adj* **1** MUS disonante **2** *fig* discordante
dis•suade [dɪ'sweɪd] *v/t* disuadir; ***~ s.o. from doing sth*** disuadir a alguien de hacer algo
dis•tance ['dɪstəns] **I** *n* distancia *f*; ***in the ~*** en la lejanía; ***at a ~*** desde *or* de lejos; ***from a ~*** desde *or* de lejos; ***keep one's ~*** permanecer alejado; ***go the ~*** *also fig* llegar hasta el final; ***at this ~ in time*** a estas alturas **II** *v/t* distanciar; ***~ o.s. from*** distanciarse de
'dis•tance run•ner SP corredor(a) *m(f)* de fondo
dis•tant ['dɪstənt] *adj place, time, relative* distante, lejano; *fig* (*aloof*) distante
dis•taste [dɪs'teɪst] desagrado *m*
dis•taste•ful [dɪs'teɪstfəl] *adj* desagradable; ***be ~ to s.o.*** resultar desagradable *or* ofensivo a alguien
dis•tend [dɪ'stend] **I** *v/t* distender **II** *v/i* distenderse
dis•till, *Br* **dis•til** [dɪ'stɪl] *v/t* destilar
dis•til•la•tion [dɪstɪ'leɪʃn] destilación *f*
dis•till•er•y [dɪs'tɪlərɪ] destilería *f*
dis•tinct [dɪ'stɪŋkt] *adj* **1** (*clear*) claro **2** (*different*) distinto; ***as ~ from*** a diferencia de
dis•tinc•tion [dɪ'stɪŋkʃn] (*differentiation*) distinción *f*; ***hotel / product of ~*** un hotel / producto destacado; ***draw*** *or* ***make a ~ between*** distinguir *or* diferenciar entre
dis•tinc•tive [dɪ'stɪŋktɪv] *adj* característico
dis•tinct•ly [dɪ'stɪŋktlɪ] *adv* **1** claramente, con claridad **2** (*decidedly*) verdaderamente
dis•tin•guish [dɪ'stɪŋgwɪʃ] *v/t* **1** distinguir (***from*** de; ***between*** entre) **2**: ***~ o.s.*** destacar, sobresalir
dis•tin•guished [dɪ'stɪŋgwɪʃt] *adj* distinguido
dis•tin•guish•ing mark [dɪ'stɪŋgwɪʃɪŋ] rasgo *m* característico *or* distintivo
dis•tort [dɪ'stɔːrt] *v/t* distorsionar
dis•tor•tion [dɪ'stɔːrʃn] distorsión *f*, deformación *f*
dis•tract [dɪ'strækt] *v/t* distraer; ***~ s.o.'s attention*** distraer *or* apartar la atención de alguien
dis•tract•ed [dɪ'stræktɪd] *adj* distraído, ensimismado; ***get*** *or* ***become ~*** distraerse
dis•trac•tion [dɪ'strækʃn] distracción *f*; ***drive s.o. to ~*** sacar a alguien de quicio
dis•traught [dɪ'strɒːt] *adj* angustiado,

consternado; ***become ~*** angustiarse, consternarse

dis•tress [dɪ'stres] **I** *n* sufrimiento *m*; ***in ~*** *ship*, *aircraft* en peligro **II** *v/t* (*upset*) angustiar

dis'tress call llamada *f* de socorro

dis•tressed [dɪ'stresd] *adj* angustiado; ***get*** *or* ***become ~*** angustiarse

dis•tress•ing [dɪ'stresɪŋ] *adj* angustiante

dis'tress sig•nal señal *m* de socorro

dis•trib•ute [dɪ'strɪbju:t] *v/t* distribuir, repartir; COM distribuir

dis•tri•bu•tion [dɪstrɪ'bju:ʃn] distribución *f*

dis•tri'bu•tion ar•range•ment COM acuerdo *m* de distribución

dis•tri'bu•tion net•work red *f* de distribución

dis•trib•u•tor [dɪs'trɪbju:tər] COM distribuidor(a) *m(f)*

dis•trict ['dɪstrɪkt] (*area*) zona *f*, (*neighborhood*) barrio *m*

dis•trict at'tor•ney fiscal *m/f* del distrito

dis•trict 'man•ag•er gerente *m/f* regional

dis•trust [dɪs'trʌst] **I** *n* desconfianza *f* **II** *v/t* desconfiar de

dis•trust•ful [dɪs'trʌstfʊl] *adj* sospechoso, receloso; ***be ~ of s.o.*** desconfiar de alguien

dis•turb [dɪ'stɜ:rb] *v/t* **1** (*interrupt*) molestar; ***do not ~*** no molestar **2** (*upset*) preocupar

dis•turb•ance [dɪ'stɜ:rbəns] (*interruption*) molestia *f*, ***~s*** (*civil unrest*) disturbios *mpl*; ***cause*** *or* ***create a ~*** causar *or* ocasionar molestias

dis•turbed [dɪ'stɜ:rbd] *adj* **1** (*concerned*, *worried*) preocupado, inquieto **2** *mentally* perturbado

dis•turb•ing [dɪ'stɜ:rbɪŋ] *adj* (*worrying*) inquietante; ***you may find some scenes ~*** algunas de las escenas pueden herir la sensibilidad del espectador

dis•u•nite [dɪsju:'naɪt] *v/t* desunir, dividir

dis•u•ni•ty [dɪs'ju:nətɪ] desunión *f*, división *f*

dis•use [dɪs'ju:s]: ***fall into ~*** caer en desuso

dis•used [dɪs'ju:zd] *adj* abandonado

ditch [dɪʧ] **I** *n* zanja *f* **II** *v/t* F (*get rid of*) deshacerse de; *boyfriend* plantar F; *plan* abandonar

dith•er ['dɪðər] **I** *v/i* vacilar **II** *n*: ***be all of a ~, be in a ~*** estar hecho un lío, estar en un mar de confusiones

dit•to ['dɪtoʊ] *adv* ídem

di•ur•nal [daɪ'ɜ:rnl] *adj* diurno

di•van [dɪ'væn] diván *m*; *Br* ***~ (bed)*** cama *f* turca

dive [daɪv] **I** *n* **1** salto *m* de cabeza; *underwater* inmersión *f*, *of plane* descenso *m* en picado; ***make a ~ for sth*** lanzarse *or* tirarse a por algo; ***take a ~*** F *of dollar etc* desplomarse **2** F *bar etc* antro *m* F **II** *v/i* (*pret also* ***dove***) tirarse de cabeza; *underwater* bucear; *of plane* descender en picado; ***~ for cover*** cobijarse, refugiarse

div•er ['daɪvər] *off board* saltador(a) *m(f)* de trampolín; *underwater* buceador(a) *m(f)*

di•verge [daɪ'vɜ:rdʒ] *v/i* bifurcarse

di•verg•ence [daɪ'vɜ:rdʒəns] divergencia *f*, discrepancia *f*

di•ver•gent [daɪ'vɜ:rdʒənt] *adj* divergente, discrepante

di•verse [daɪ'vɜ:rs] *adj* diverso

di•ver•si•fi•ca•tion [daɪvɜ:rsɪfɪ'keɪʃn] COM diversificación *f*

di•ver•si•fy [daɪ'vɜ:rsɪfaɪ] *v/i* (*pret & pp* ***-ied***) COM diversificarse (***into*** en)

di•ver•sion [daɪ'vɜ:rʃn] **1** *for traffic* desvío *m* **2** *to distract attention* distracción *f*

di•ver•si•ty [daɪ'vɜ:rsətɪ] diversidad *f*

di•vert [daɪ'vɜ:rt] *v/t* *traffic*, *attention* desviar

di•vest [daɪ'vest] *v/t*: ***~ s.o. of sth*** despojar a alguien de algo; ***~ o.s. of sth*** deshacerse de algo

di•vide [dɪ'vaɪd] *v/t also fig* dividir; ***~ 16 by 4*** dividir 16 entre 4; ***~ into two halves*** partir *or* dividir en dos mitades; ***opinion is ~d*** hay división de opiniones

di•vid•ed high•way [dɪvaɪdɪd'haɪweɪ] autovía *f*

div•i•dend ['dɪvɪdend] FIN dividendo *m*; ***pay ~s*** *fig* resultar beneficioso

di•vid•ers [dɪ'vaɪdərz] *npl*, *also* ***pair of ~*** compás *m* de puntas

di•vid•ing [dɪ'vaɪdɪŋ] *adj* divisorio

div•i•na•tion [dɪvɪ'neɪʃn] adivinación *f*, clarividencia *f*

D

di•vine [dɪ'vaɪn] *adj also* F divino
div•ing ['daɪvɪŋ] *from board* salto *m* de trampolín; (*scuba* ~) buceo *m*, submarinismo *m*
'div•ing bell campana *f* de buzo *or* inmersión; **'div•ing board** trampolín *m*; **'div•ing head•er** *in soccer* cabezazo *m* en plancha; **'div•ing hel•met** gorro *m* de buceo; **'div•ing mask** máscara *f* de buceo; **'div•ing suit** traje *m* de buceo
di•vin•i•ty [dɪ'vɪnətɪ] **1** REL divinidad *f* **2** UNIV teología *f*
di•vis•i•ble [dɪ'vɪzəbl] *adj* divisible (***by*** por)
di•vi•sion [dɪ'vɪʒn] división *f*
di•vorce [dɪ'vɔːrs] **I** *n* divorcio *m*; ***get a ~*** divorciarse **II** *v/t* divorciarse de; ***get ~d*** divorciarse **III** *v/i* divorciarse
di•vorced [dɪ'vɔːrst] *adj* divorciado
di•vor•cee [dɪvɔːr'siː] divorciado(-a) *m*(*f*)
di•vulge [daɪ'vʌldʒ] *v/t* divulgar; ***~ sth to s.o.*** desvelar *or* revelar algo a alguien
DIY [diːaɪ'waɪ] *abbr* (= ***do it yourself***) bricolaje *m*
DI'Y store tienda *f* de bricolaje
diz•zi•ness ['dɪzɪnɪs] mareo *m*
diz•zy ['dɪzɪ] *adj* mareado; ***feel ~*** estar mareado
DJ ['diːdʒeɪ] *abbr* **1** (= ***disc jockey***) disc jockey *m/f*, *Span* pinchadiscos *m/f inv* **2** (= ***dinner jacket***) esmoquin *m*
DNA [diːen'eɪ] *abbr* (= ***deoxyribonucleic acid***) AND *m* (= ácido desoxirribonucleico)
do¹ [duː] **I** *v/t* (*pret* ***did***, *pp* ***done***) hacer; *100 mph etc* ir a; ***~ one's hair*** peinarse; ***what are you ~ing tonight?*** ¿qué vas a hacer esta noche?; ***I don't know what to ~*** no sé qué hacer; ***~ it right now!*** hazlo ahora mismo; ***have one's hair done*** arreglarse el pelo; ***well done!*** ¡bien hecho!, ¡así se hace!; ***have done with sth*** acabar con algo, poner fin a algo
II *v/i* (*pret* ***did***, *pp* ***done***) (*be suitable, enough*): ***that'll ~ nicely*** eso bastará; ***that will ~!*** ¡ya vale!; ***~ well*** *of business* ir bien; ***he's ~ing well*** le van bien las cosas; ***how ~ you ~?*** encantado de conocerle
III *v/aux*: ***~ you know him?*** ¿lo conoces?; ***I don't know*** no sé; ***~ you like Des Moines? – yes I ~*** ¿te gusta Des Moines? - sí; ***he works hard, doesn't he?*** trabaja mucho, ¿verdad?; ***don't you believe me?*** ¿no me crees?; ***you ~ believe me, don't you?*** me crees, ¿verdad?; ***you don't know the answer, ~ you? – no, I don't*** no sabes la respuesta, ¿no es así? - no, no la sé
do² [duː] (*pl* ***dos, do's***) [duːz] *n*: ***~s and don'ts*** F lo que se debe y lo que no se debe hacer
◆ **do about** *v/t*: ***what are we going to do about him?*** ¿qué vamos a hacer con él?
◆ **do away with** *v/t* (*abolish*) abolir; ***do away with o.s.*** quitarse la vida
◆ **do down** *v/t* (*belittle*) menospreciar, hablar en términos despectivos de
◆ **do in** *v/t* F (*exhaust*) machacar F; ***I'm done in*** estoy hecho polvo F
◆ **do out of** *v/t*: ***do s.o. out of sth*** timar alguien a algo F
◆ **do over** *v/t* (*do again*) rehacer, volver a hacer
◆ **do up** **I** *v/t* **1** (*renovate*) renovar **2** *buttons, coat* abrocharse; *laces* atarse **II** *v/i of clothes* cerrarse; *with buttons* abrocharse
◆ **do with** *v/t*: ***I could do with …*** no me vendría mal …; ***he won't have anything to do with it*** (*won't get involved*) no quiere saber nada de ello
◆ **do without** **I** *v/i*: ***you'll have to do without*** te las tendrás que arreglar **II** *v/t* pasar sin
do•ber•man ['doʊbərmən] ZO doberman *m*
doc [dɑːk] F ☞ ***doctor***; ***thanks ~*** gracias doctor
do•cile ['doʊsəl] *adj* dócil
do•cil•i•ty [doʊ'sɪlətɪ] docilidad *f*
dock¹ [dɑːk] **I** *n* NAUT muelle *m* **II** *v/i of ship* atracar; *of spaceship* acoplarse
dock² [dɑːk] *n* LAW banquillo *m* (de los acusados)
dock³ [dɑːk] *v/t tail* descolar; ***~ $20 off*** *or* ***from s.o.'s wages*** descontar 20 dólares del salario de alguien
dock•er ['dɑːkər] *Br* cargador(a) *m*(*f*)
'dock•yard *Br* astillero *m*
doc•tor ['dɑːktər] MED médico(-a) *m*(*f*); *form of address* doctor(a) *m*(*f*); ***take one's ~'s degree*** hacer el docto-

rado
doc•tor•al the•sis ['dɑːktərəl] tesis *f* doctoral
doc•tor•ate ['dɑːktərət] doctorado *m*
doc•trine ['dɑːktrɪn] doctrina *f*
doc•u•dra•ma ['dɑːkjʊdrɑːmə] docudrama *m*
doc•u•ment ['dɑːkjʊmənt] **I** *n* documento *m* **II** *v/t* documentar
doc•u•men•ta•ry [dɑːkjʊ'mentərɪ] *program* documental *m*
doc•u•men•ta•tion [dɑːkjʊmen'teɪʃn] documentación *f*
dod•der ['dɑːdər] *v/i* F tambalearse
dod•der•er ['dɑːdərər] F: ***the old ~*** el viejo chocho F
dod•der•ing ['dɑːdərɪŋ] *adj* F tambaleante
dodge [dɑːdʒ] *v/t blow, person* esquivar; *issue, question* eludir
dodg•em ['dɑːdʒəm] *Br* ☞ ***bumper car***
doe [doʊ] *deer* cierva *f*
do•er ['duːər] hacedor(a) *m(f)*
does [dʌz] ☞ ***do***[1]
'doe•skin *leather* napa *f*
does•n't ['dʌznt] F = ***does not*** ☞ ***do***[1]
doff [dɑːf] *v/t*: ***~ one's hat to s.o.*** quitarse el sombrero ante alguien
dog [dɒːg] **I** *n* perro(-a) *m(f)*; ***go to the ~s*** ir de mal en peor; ***lead a ~'s life*** llevar una vida de perros; ***let sleeping ~s lie*** escurrir el bulto; ***dirty ~*** canalla F; ***lucky ~!*** ¡vaya suerte!; ***make a ~'s breakfast of sth*** F dejar algo hecho un desastre, liar un desaguisado **II** *v/t* (*pret & pp* **-ged**) *of bad luck* perseguir
'dog bis•cuit galleta *f* para perros; **'dog catch•er** perrero(-a) *m(f)*; **'dog col•lar 1** *for dog* collar *m* para perros **2** F *for priest* collarín *m*, alzacuello *m*
dog•eared ['dɒːgɪrd] *adj book* sobado, con las esquinas dobladas
dog-eat-'dog *adj* F: ***it's a ~ world*** éste es un mundo muy competitivo; **'dog•fight** MIL combate *m* aéreo; **'dog•fish** cazón *m*
dog•ged ['dɒːgɪd] *adj* tenaz
dog•ger•el ['dɒːgərəl] *pej* coplillas *fpl*
dog•gie ['dɒːgɪ] *in children's language* perrito *m*
dog•gy ['dɒːgɪ] F perrito *m* F
'dog•gy bag *bolsa para las sobras de la comida*
'dog•house: ***be in the ~*** F haber caído en desgracia
dog•ma ['dɒːgmə] dogma *m*
dog•mat•ic [dɒːg'mætɪk] *adj* dogmático
do-good•er ['duːgʊdər] *pej* buen(a) samaritano(-a) *m(f)*
dogs•bod•y ['dɒːgzbɑːdɪ] F: ***I'm not your ~*** no soy tu esclavo; **'dog tag** MIL chapa *f* de identificación; **'dog-tired** *adj* F hecho polvo F
doi•ly ['dɔɪlɪ] blonda *f*
do•ing ['duːɪŋ]: ***it was your ~*** lo hiciste tú, fuiste tú; ***that will take some ~!*** ¡eso será una odisea!
do-it-your•self [duːɪtjər'self] bricolaje *m*
dol•drums ['doʊldrəmz]: ***be in the ~*** *of economy* estar en un bache; *of person* estar deprimido
dole [doʊl] *Br* F: ***be on the ~*** estar en el paro
◆ **dole out** *v/t* repartir
dole•ful ['doʊlfʊl] *adj* triste, pesaroso
doll [dɑːl] **1** *toy* muñeca *f* **2** F *woman* muñeca *f* F
◆ **doll up** *v/t*: ***get dolled up*** F emperifollarse F
dol•lar ['dɑːlər] dólar *m*
'dol•lar ar•e•a área *f* del dólar; **'dol•lar di•plo•ma•cy** diplomacia *f* de dólar; **'dol•lar sign** signo *m* del dólar
'doll•house casita *f* de muñecas
dol•lop ['dɑːləp] F cucharada *f*
dol•ly ['dɑːlɪ] **1** *toy* muñeca *f* **2** *in film, TV studio* carro *m*
dol•phin ['dɑːlfɪn] delfín *m*
dolt [doʊlt] idiota *m/f*
do•main [doʊ'meɪn] competencia *f*, responsabilidad *f*
dome [doʊm] *of building* cúpula *f*
do•mes•tic [də'mestɪk] **I** *adj* **1** *chores* doméstico, del hogar **2** *news, policy* nacional **II** *n* empleado(-a) *m(f)* del hogar
do•mes•tic 'an•i•mal animal *m* doméstico
do•mes•tic a'p•pli•ance electrodoméstico *m*
do•mes•ti•cate [də'mestɪkeɪt] *v/t animal* domesticar; ***be ~d*** *of person* estar domesticado
do'mes•tic flight vuelo *m* nacional
do•mes•tic 'ser•vant empleado(-a) *m(f)* del hogar
dom•i•cile ['dɑːmɪsaɪl] **1** *n* LAW domici-

lio *m* **II** *v/t bill* domiciliar

dom•i•ciled ['dɑːmɪsaɪld] *adj*: ***be ~ in*** *of person* residir en; *of bill* estar domiciliado en

dom•i•nance ['dɑːmɪnəns] dominio *m*, control *m*

D

dom•i•nant ['dɑːmɪnənt] *adj* dominante

dom•i•nate ['dɑːmɪneɪt] *v/t* dominar

dom•i•na•tion [dɑːmɪ'neɪʃn] dominación *f*

dom•i•neer•ing [dɑːmɪ'nɪrɪŋ] *adj* dominante

Dom•i•ni•can Re•pub•lic [dəmɪnɪkənrɪ'pʌblɪk] República *f* Dominicana

do•min•ion [də'mɪnjən] autoridad *f*, poder *m*

dom•i•no ['dɑːmɪnoʊ] (*pl* ***-oes***) ficha *f* de dominó; ***play ~es*** jugar al dominó

don [dɑːn] *v/t* poner

do•nate [doʊ'neɪt] *v/t* donar

do•na•tion [doʊ'neɪʃn] donación *f*, donativo *m*; MED donación *f*

done [dʌn] *pp* ☞ ***do***; ***it isn't ~, it isn't the ~ thing*** es inaceptable, no está bien

don•key ['dɑːŋkɪ] burro *m*

do•nor ['doʊnər] *of money*, MED donante *m/f*

do•nut ['doʊnʌt] dónut *m*

doo•dle ['duːdl] *v/i* garabatear

doom [duːm] **1** (*fate*) destino *m* **2** (*ruin*) fatalidad *f*

doomed [duːmd] *adj project* condenado al fracaso; ***we are ~*** (*bound to fail*) estamos condenados al fracaso; (*going to die*) vamos a morir

dooms•day ['duːmzdeɪ] día *m* del juicio final

door [dɔːr] puerta *f*; ***there's someone at the ~*** hay alguien en la puerta; ***from ~ to ~*** a domicilio; ***out of ~s*** al aire libre; ***shut the ~ on sth*** *fig* cerrar la puerta a algo; ***lay sth at s.o.'s ~*** *fig* acusar a alguien de algo; ***show s.o. the ~*** *fig* poner a alguien de patitas en la calle; ***open the ~ for sth*** *fig* abrir las puertas *or* tener las puertas abiertas a algo

'door•bell timbre *m*; ***ring the ~*** llamar al timbre; **door-bel•ling** ['dɔːrbelɪŋ] visitas *fpl* de puerta en puerta (*haciendo campaña*); **'door han•dle** manilla *f* de la puerta; **'door•knob** pomo *m*; **'door-knock•er** aldaba *f*, llamador *m*; **'door-man** portero *m*; **'door•mat** felpudo *m*; **'door•post** jamba *f*; **'door•step** umbral *m*; ***on s.o.'s ~*** *fig* a la vuelta de la esquina; **door-to-door 'sales•man** vendedor *m* a domicilio; **door-to-door 'sel•ling** venta *f* a domicilio; **'door•way** puerta *f*

dope [doʊp] **I** *n* **1** (*drugs*) droga *f* **2** F (*idiot*) lelo(-a) *m*(*f*) **3** F (*information*) información *f* **II** *v/t* drogar

'dope test SP prueba *f* de dopaje

dop•ey ['doʊpɪ] *adj* F **1** (*stupid*) estúpido F **2** (*slow*) atontado F, alelado F **3** (*not awake*) casi *or* medio dormido, grogui F

dork [dɔːrk] F pardillo *m* F

dorm [dɔːrm] F ☞ ***dormitory***

dor•mant ['dɔːrmənt] *adj* **1** *plant* aletargado **2** *volcano* inactivo

dor•mer win•dow ['dɔːrmər] buhardilla *f*

dor•mi•to•ry ['dɔːrmɪtɔːrɪ] **1** dormitorio *m* (colectivo) **2** (*hall of residence*) residencia *f* de estudiantes

'dor•mi•to•ry sub•urb, 'dor•mi•to•ry town ciudad *f* dormitorio

dor•sal fin ['dɔːrsl] aleta *f* dorsal

dos•age ['doʊsɪdʒ] dosis *f inv*

dose [doʊs] dosis *f inv*; ***he's ok in small ~s*** se le puede soportar en pequeñas dosis

dos•si•er ['dɑːsɪeɪ] dossier *m*

dot [dɑːt] punto *m*; ***on the ~*** (*exactly*) en punto

dot•age ['doʊtɪdʒ]: ***be in one's ~*** ser un vejestorio

dot.com (**com•pa•ny**) [dɑːt'kɑːm] empresa *f* punto.com

◆ **dote on** [doʊt] *v/t* adorar a

dot•ing ['doʊtɪŋ] *adj*: ***my ~ aunt*** mi tía, que tanto me adora

dot 'ma•trix print•er impresora *f* de punteo, impresora *f* matricial

dot•ted line ['dɑːtɪd] línea *f* de puntos; ***sign on the ~*** F echar la firma F

dot•ty ['dɑːtɪ] *adj* F tocado F, chalado F

doub•le ['dʌbl] **I** *n* **1** *person* doble *m/f* **2** *room* habitación *f* doble **II** *adj* doble; ***inflation is now in ~ figures*** la inflación ha superado ya el 10% **III** *adv*: ***they offered me ~ what the others did*** me ofrecieron el doble que la otra gente; ***see ~*** ver doble **IV** *v/t* doblar, duplicar **V** *v/i* **1** doblarse, duplicarse **2**: ***it ~s as …*** hace también de …

◆ **double back** *v/i* (*go back*) volver sobre sus pasos

◆ **double up** *v/i* **1** *in pain* doblarse **2** (*share*) compartir habitación

◆ **double up with** *v/t* (*share*) compartir con

doub•le 'a•gent doble agente *m/f*; **doub•le-bar•relled name** [dʌbl-'bærəld] apellido *m* compuesto; **doub•le-bar•relled 'shot•gun** escopeta *f* de doble cañón; **doub•le 'bass** contrabajo *m*; **doub•le 'bed** cama *f* de matrimonio; **doub•le-'book** *v/t* reservar dos veces; **doub•le-breast•ed** [dʌbl-'brestɪd] *adj* cruzado; **doub•le'check** *v/t & v/i* volver a comprobar; **doub•le 'chin** papada *f*; **doub•le 'click** COMPUT **I** *n* doble clic *m* **II** *v/i* hacer doble clic (***on*** en); **doub•le-'cross I** *v/t* engañar, traicionar **II** *n* traición *f*, engaño *m*; **doub•le-'deal•ing I** *adj* engañoso, falso **II** *n* duplicidad *f*; **doub•le-deck•er** [dʌbl'dekər] *Br* autobús *m* de dos pisos; **doub•le 'drib•ble** *in basketball* dobles *mpl*; **doub•le-edged** [dʌbl'edʒd] *adj fig* ambiguo; **doub•le en•try 'book-keep•ing** contabilidad *f* por partida doble; **doub•le 'glaz•ing** doble acristalamiento *m*; **doub•le'park** *v/i* aparcar en doble fila; **'doub•le play** *in baseball* doble jugada *f*; **'doub•le pump** *in basketball* rectificación *f*; **'doub•le-quick** *adj*: ***in ~ time*** muy rápidamente; **'doub•le quotes** *npl* comillas *fpl*; **'doub•le room** habitación *f* doble

doub•les ['dʌblz] *in tennis* dobles *mpl*; ***a ~ match*** un partido de dobles; ***men's / women's ~*** dobles masculinos / femeninos

doub•le 'take: ***do a ~*** quedarse de una pieza, quedarse pasmado; **'doub•le team** *in basketball* dos contra uno; **doub•le 'time**: ***be paid ~*** cobrar el doble; **doub•le 'vi•sion**: ***suffer from ~*** ver doble

doubt [daʊt] **I** *n* duda *f*; (*uncertainty*) dudas *fpl*; ***be in ~*** ser incierto; ***not be in ~*** estar claro; ***no ~*** (*probably*) sin duda; ***cast*** *or* ***throw ~ on sth*** poner algo en duda; ***if*** *or* ***when in ~, …*** ante la duda, …; ***leave no ~s about sth*** dejar algo muy claro; ***there has to be no room for ~*** no puede caber la menor duda **II** *v/t* dudar; ***we never ~ed you*** nunca dudamos de ti

doubt•er ['daʊtər] esceptico(-a) *m*(*f*)

doubt•ful ['daʊtfəl] *adj remark*, *look* dubitativo; ***be ~*** *of person* tener dudas; ***it is ~ whether …*** es dudoso que …

doubt•ful•ly ['daʊtfəlɪ] *adv* lleno de dudas

doubt•less ['daʊtlɪs] *adv* sin duda, indudablemente

dough [doʊ] **1** masa *f* **2** F (*money*) *L.Am.* plata *f* F, *Span* pasta *f* F

dour [dʊər] *adj* severo, serio

dove[1] [dʌv] *n also fig* paloma *f*

dove[2] [doʊv] *pret* ☞ ***dive***

dow•dy ['daʊdɪ] *adj* poco elegante

Dow Jones Av•er•age [daʊ'dʒoʊnz] índice *m* Dow Jones

down[1] [daʊn] *n* (*feathers*) plumón *m*

down[2] [daʊn] **I** *adv* (*downward*) (hacia) abajo; ***pull the shade ~*** baja la persiana; ***put it ~ on the table*** ponlo en la mesa; ***when the leaves come ~*** cuando se caen las hojas; ***cut ~ a tree*** cortar un árbol; ***she was ~ on her knees*** estaba arrodillada; ***the plane was shot ~*** el avión fue abatido; ***~ there*** allá abajo; ***fall ~*** caerse; ***die ~*** amainar; ***$200 ~*** (*as deposit*) una entrada de 200 dólares; ***~ south*** hacia el sur; ***be ~*** *of price*, *rate* haber bajado; *of numbers*, *amount* haber descendido; (*not working*) no funcionar; F (*depressed*) estar deprimido *or* con la depre F
II *prep*: ***run ~ the stairs*** bajar las escaleras corriendo; ***the lava rolled ~ the hill*** la lava descendía por la colina; ***walk ~ the street*** andar por la calle; ***the store is halfway ~ Baker Street*** la tienda está a mitad de Baker Street; ***~ the corridor*** por el pasillo; ***the markings ~ its back*** las marcas en la espalda **III** *v/t* **1** (*swallow*) tragar **2** (*destroy*) derribar **3**: ***~ tools*** dejar de trabajar

'down-and-out vagabundo(-a) *m*(*f*); **down-at-'heel** *adj* desaliñado, andrajoso; **'down•beat** *adj* F pesimista, negativo; **'down•cast** *adj* (*dejected*) deprimido

down•er ['daʊnər] F *drug* barbitúrico *m*

'down•fall caída *f*; *of person* perdición *f*; **'down•grade** *v/t* degradar; ***the hurricane has been ~d to a storm*** el huracán ha sido reducido a la categoría de tormenta; **down•heart•ed** [daʊn-'hɑːrtɪd] *adj* abatido; **down'hill** *adv*

D

cuesta abajo; ***go ~*** *fig* ir cuesta abajo; **down•hill 'ski•ing** descenso *m*; **'down•load** *v/t* COMPUT descargar, bajar; **'down•mark•et** *adj* barato; **'down pay•ment** entrada *f*; ***make a ~ on sth*** pagar la entrada de algo; **'down•play** *v/t* quitar importancia a; **'down•pour** chaparrón *m*, aguacero *m*; **'down•right** **I** *adj lie* evidente; *idiot* completo **II** *adv dangerous* extremadamente; *stupid* completamente; **'down•side** (*disadvantage*) desventaja *f*, inconveniente *m*; **'down•size I** *v/t car* reducir el tamaño de; *company* reajustar la plantilla de **II** *v/i of company* reajustar la plantilla

Down's syn•drome ['daʊnzsɪndroʊm] MED síndrome *m* de Down

'down•stairs I *adj* del piso de abajo; ***my ~ neighbors*** los vecinos de abajo **II** *adv*: ***the kitchen is ~*** la cocina está en el piso de abajo; ***I ran ~*** bajé corriendo

down'stream *adv* río abajo; **'down-time** tiempo *m* de inactividad; **down--to-'earth** *adj approach*, *person* práctico, realista; **'down•town I** *n* centro *m* **II** *adj* del centro **III** *adv*: ***I'm going ~*** voy al centro; ***he lives ~*** vive en el centro; **down•trod•den** ['daʊntrɑːdn] *adj* maltratado, pisoteado; **'down•turn** *in economy* bajón *m*; **down 'un•der** F *Australia y Nueva Zelanda*

'down•ward ['daʊnwərd] **I** *adj* descendente; ***~ trend*** tendencia *f* bajista **II** *adv* a la baja

dow•ry ['daʊrɪ] dote *f*

doze [doʊz] **I** *n* cabezada *f*, sueño *m* **II** *v/i* echar una cabezada

◆ **doze off** *v/i* quedarse dormido

doz•en ['dʌzn] docena *f*; ***~s of*** F montonadas de F

doz•y ['doʊzɪ] *adj* somnoliento, adormilado

DP [diːpiː] *abbr* (= ***data processing***) COMPUT tratamiento *m* de datos

drab [dræb] *adj* gris

Dra•co•ni•an [drə'koʊnjən] *adj* draconiano, severo

draft [dræft] **I** *n* **1** *of air* corriente *f* **2** *of document* borrador *m* **3** MIL reclutamiento *m* **4**: ***~ (beer), beer on ~*** cerveza *f* de barril **II** *v/t* **1** *document* redactar un borrador de **2** MIL reclutar

'draft dodg•er prófugo(-a) *m*(*f*)

draft•ee [dræft'iː] recluta *m/f*

drafts•man ['dræftsmən] delineante *m/f*

draft•y ['dræftɪ] *adj*: ***it's ~ here*** hace mucha corriente aquí

drag [dræg] **I** *n* **1**: ***it's a ~ having to …*** F es un latazo tener que … F; ***he's a ~*** F es un peñazo F; ***what a ~!*** F ¡qué lata! F, ¡qué fastidio! F **2**: ***the main ~*** F la calle principal **3**: ***in ~*** vestido de mujer **II** *v/t* (*pret & pp* **-ged**) **1** (*pull*, *also with mouse*) arrastrar; ***~ s.o. into sth*** (*involve*) meter a alguien en algo; ***~ sth out of s.o.*** (*get information from*) arrancar algo de alguien ; ***~ one's feet*** *or* ***heels*** dar largas (***over*** a) **2** (*search*) dragar

III *v/i* (*pret & pp* **-ged**) *of time* pasar despacio; *of show*, *movie* ser pesado

◆ **drag along** *v/t* arrastrar

◆ **drag away** *v/t*: ***drag o.s. away from the TV*** despegarse de la TV

◆ **drag in** *v/t into conversation* introducir

◆ **drag on** *v/i* (*last long time*) alargarse

◆ **drag out** *v/t* (*prolong*) alargar

◆ **drag up** *v/t* F (*mention*) sacar a relucir

'drag co•ef•fi•cient MOT coeficiente *m* de resistencia *or* penetración aerodinámica

'drag•net red *f* barredera

drag•on ['drægn] dragón *m*; *fig* bruja *f*

'drag•on•fly libélula *f*

'drag queen drag queen *f*, travesti *m*

drain [dreɪn] **I** *n pipe* sumidero *m*, desagüe *m*; *under street* alcantarilla *f*; ***a ~ on resources*** una sangría en los recursos; ***it's money down the ~*** F es tirar el dinero **II** *v/t water*, *vegetables* escurrir; *land* drenar; *glass*, *tank*, *oil* vaciar; *person* agotar **III** *v/i of dishes* escurrir

◆ **drain away** *v/i* **1** *of liquid* desaparecer **2** *of strength*, *life* desvanecerse; ***his strength was draining away*** perdía las fuerzas, flaqueaba

◆ **drain off** *v/t water* escurrir

drain•age ['dreɪnɪdʒ] **1** (*drains*) desagües *mpl* **2** *of water from soil* drenaje *m*

drain•ing board ['dreɪnɪŋ] escurridero *m*

'drain•pipe *Br* tubo *m* de desagüe

drake [dreɪk] ORN pato *m*

dram [dræm] F chupito *m* F

DRAM ['di:ræm] *abbr* (= ***dynamic random access memory***) DRAM *f*, memoria *f* de acceso aleatorio dinámica

dra•ma ['drɑ:mə] **1** (*art form*) drama *m*, teatro *m* **2** (*excitement*) dramatismo *m* **3** (*play: on TV*) drama *m*, obra *f* de teatro

'dra•ma school academia *f or* escuela *f* de teatro

'dra•ma se•ries serie *f* dramática

dra•mat•ic [drə'mætɪk] *adj* dramático; *scenery* espectacular

dra•mat•i•cal•ly [drə'mætɪklɪ] *adv* **1** *say* con dramatismo, de manera dramática **2** *decline*, *rise*, *change etc* espectacularmente

dram•a•tist ['dræmətɪst] dramaturgo (-a) *m(f)*

dram•a•ti•za•tion [dræmətaɪ'zeɪʃn] (*play*) dramatización *f*

dram•a•tize ['dræmətaɪz] *v/t also fig* dramatizar

drank [dræŋk] *pret* ☞ ***drink***

drape [dreɪp] *v/t cloth* cubrir; ***~d in*** (*covered with*) cubierto con

drap•er•y ['dreɪpərɪ] ropajes *mpl*

drapes [dreɪps] *npl* cortinas *fpl*

dras•tic ['dræstɪk] *adj* drástico

drat [dræt] *int* ¡mecachis! F, ¡caramba! F

draught *Br* ☞ ***draft***

draw [drɒ:] **I** *n* **1** *in match*, *competition* empate *m*; ***end in a ~*** acabar en empate **2** *in lottery* sorteo *m* **3** (*attraction*) atracción *f*

II *v/t* (*pret* ***drew***, *pp* ***drawn***) **1** *picture*, *map* dibujar

2 *cart* tirar de; *curtain* correr; *in lottery* sortear

3 *gun*, *knife* sacar

4 (*attract*) atraer; ***feel ~n towards s.o.*** sentirse atraído por alguien; ***~ applause*** arrancar el aplauso

5 (*lead*) llevar; ***~ s.o. into sth*** *fig* conducir *or* arrastrar a alguien a algo; ***she refused to be ~n on the matter*** ella se negó a hacer comentarios sobre el asunto

6 *from bank account* sacar, retirar

7 (*derive*): ***~ inspiration from sth*** inspirarse con algo; ***she drew consolation from the fact that …*** le consoló el hecho de que …

III *v/i* (*pret* ***drew***, *pp* ***drawn***) **1** dibujar **2** *in match*, *competition* empatar **3**: ***~ near*** acercarse; ***~ ahead of s.o.*** tomar la delantera a alguien

◆ **draw apart** *v/i* distanciarse (***from*** de)

◆ **draw aside** *v/t* llevar a un lado

◆ **draw away** *v/i* apartarse, alejarse (***from*** de)

◆ **draw back I** *v/i* (*recoil*) echarse atrás **II** *v/t* (*pull back*) retirar

◆ **draw down** *v/t petroleum*, *water reserves* agotar

◆ **draw in** *v/i of nights* acortarse

◆ **draw on I** *v/i* (*approach*) aproximarse **II** *v/t* (*make use of*) utilizar

◆ **draw out** *v/t wallet*, *money from bank* sacar; ***draw s.o. out*** hacer que alguien hable

◆ **draw up I** *v/t* **1** *document* redactar **2** *chair* acercar **II** *v/i* **1** *of vehicle* parar **2**: ***draw o.s. up*** erguirse

'draw•back desventaja *f*, inconveniente *m*

'draw•bridge puente *m* levadizo

draw•ee [drɒ:'i:] COM librado(-a) *m(f)*

draw•er[1] [drɒ:r] *of desk etc* cajón *m*

draw•er[2] [drɒ:r]: ***she's a good ~*** dibuja muy bien

draw•ing ['drɒ:ɪŋ] dibujo *m*

'draw•ing board tablero *m* de dibujo; ***go back to the ~*** *fig* volver a empezar otra vez; **'draw•ing pin** *Br* chincheta *f*; **'draw•ing room** sala *f* de estar, salón *m*

drawl [drɒ:l] acento *m* arrastrado

drawn [drɒ:n] *pp* ☞ ***draw***

'draw•string agujeta *f*, cordón *m*

dread [dred] *v/t* tener pavor a; ***I ~ him ever finding out*** me da pavor pensar que lo pueda llegar a descubrir; ***I ~ going to the dentist*** me da pánico ir al dentista

dread•ed ['dredɪd] *adj* temible

dread•ful ['dredfəl] *adj* horrible, espantoso; ***it's a ~ pity you won't be there*** es una auténtica pena que no vayas a estar ahí

dread•ful•ly ['dredfəlɪ] *adv* F (*extremely*) terriblemente, espantosamente F; *behave* fatal

'dread•locks *npl* rastas *fpl*

dream [dri:m] **I** *n* sueño *m*; ***have a ~ about s.o. / sth*** soñar con alguien / algo; ***pleasant*** *or* ***sweet ~s!*** ¡felices *or* dulces sueños!; ***that's beyond my wildest ~s*** eso ni en mis mejores sueños; ***go like a ~*** ir como una seda, ir a la perfec-

ción; ***thanks darling, you're a ~*** F gracias cariño, eres un cielo *or* encanto **II** *adj*: ***win your ~ house!*** ¡gane la casa de sus sueños!
III *v/t* (*pret & pp* ***-t***) soñar; (*day~*) soñar (despierto)
IV *v/i* (*pret & pp* ***-t***) soñar; (*day~*) soñar (despierto); ***I ~t about you last night*** anoche soñé contigo; ***~ of doing sth*** soñar con hacer algo; ***I must be ~ing!*** ¡debo estar soñando!; ***I wouldn't ~ of upsetting you*** no *or* de ninguna manera se me ocurriría ofenderte; ***~ on!*** ¡deja de soñar!, ¡baja de las nubes!
◆ **dream away** *v/t* fantasear, soñar
◆ **dream up** *v/t* inventar
dream•er ['driːmər] (*day~*) soñador(a) *m(f)*
'dream•like *adj* irreal, fantástico
dreamt [dremt] *pret & pp* ☞ ***dream***
dream•y ['driːmɪ] *adj* **1** *voice, look* soñador **2** F (*super*) de ensueño
drear•y ['drɪrɪ] *adj* triste, deprimente
dredge[1] [dredʒ] *v/t harbor, canal* dragar
◆ **dredge up** *v/t fig* sacar a relucir
dredge[2] [dredʒ] *v/t* GASTR rebozar
dredg•er ['dredʒər] NAUT draga *f*
dregs [dregz] *npl of coffee* posos *mpl*; ***the ~ of society*** la escoria de la sociedad
drench [drentʃ] *v/t* empapar; ***get ~ed*** empaparse
dress [dres] **I** *n* **1** *for woman* vestido *m* **2** (*clothing*) traje *m*; ***he has no ~ sense*** no sabe vestir(se); ***the company has a ~ code*** la compañía tiene unas normas sobre la ropa que deben llevar los empleados **II** *v/t* **1** *person* vestir; ***get ~ed*** vestirse **2** *wound* vendar **III** *v/i* (*get ~ed*) vestirse; *well, in black etc* vestir(se) (***in*** de); ***~ to kill*** ir muy llamativo; ***~ well / badly*** vestir bien / mal
◆ **dress down** *v/i* vestir de manera informal
◆ **dress up** *v/i* **1** arreglarse, vestirse elegante **2** (*wear a disguise*) disfrazarse (***as*** de)
'dress cir•cle piso *m* principal
dress•er ['dresər] **1** (*dressing table*) tocador *m*; *Br in kitchen* aparador *m* **2** THEA ayudante *m/f* de camerino
dress•ing ['dresɪŋ] **1** *for salad* aliño *m*, *Span* arreglo *m* **2** *for wound* vendaje *m*
dress•ing 'down regaño *m*; ***give s.o. a ~*** regañar a alguien
'dres•sing gown *Br* bata *f*; **'dress•ing room** *in theater* camerino *m*; **'dress•ing ta•ble** *Br* tocador *m*
'dress•mak•er modisto(-a) *m(f)*
'dress re•hears•al ensayo *m* general
dress•y ['dresɪ] *adj* F elegante
drew [druː] *pret* ☞ ***draw***
drib•ble ['drɪbl] *v/i* **1** *of person, baby* babear **2** *of water* gotear **3** SP driblar
dribs and drabs [drɪbzən'dræbz] *pl*: ***in ~*** F gota a gota F, lentamente
dried [draɪd] *adj fruit etc* seco; ***~ milk*** leche *f* en polvo
dri•er [draɪr] ☞ ***dryer***
drift [drɪft] **I** *n of snow* ventisquero *m* **II** *v/i* **1** *of snow* amontonarse **2** *of ship* ir a la deriva; (*go off course*) desviarse del rumbo; *of person* vagar; ***let things ~*** dejar que ruede la bola
◆ **drift apart** *v/i of couple* distanciarse
drift•er ['drɪftər] vagabundo(-a) *m(f)*
'drift ice hielo *m* a la deriva; **'drift net** traína *f*; **'drift•wood** madera *f* a la deriva
drill [drɪl] **I** *n* **1** *tool* taladro *m* **2** *exercise* simulacro *m*; MIL instrucción *f* ***verb ~s*** ejercicios *mpl* para practicar los verbos, ejercicios de verbos **II** *v/t* **1** *hole* taladrar, perforar **2**: ***~ sth into s.o.*** *fig* inculcar algo a alguien **III** *v/i* **1** *for oil* hacer perforaciones **2** MIL entrenarse
dril•ling rig ['drɪlɪŋ] (*platform*) plataforma *f* petrolífera
dri•ly ['draɪlɪ] *adv remark* secamente, lacónicamente
drink [drɪŋk] **I** *n* bebida *f*; ***a ~ of ...*** un vaso de ...; ***go for a ~*** ir a tomar algo; ***take to ~*** darse a la bebida **II** *v/t* (*pret* ***drank***, *pp* ***drunk***) beber **III** *v/i* (*pret* ***drank***, *pp* ***drunk***) beber, *L.Am.* tomar; ***I don't ~*** no bebo; ***~ to s.o.*** beber a la salud de alguien
◆ **drink in** *v/t fig* absorber, empaparse de
◆ **drink up I** *v/i* (*finish drink*) acabarse la bebida **II** *v/t* (*drink completely*) beberse todo
drink•a•ble ['drɪŋkəbl] *adj* potable
drink-'driv•er conductor(a) *m(f)* ebrio(-a)
drink 'driv•ing *Br* conducción *f* bajo los efectos del alcohol
drink•er ['drɪŋkər] bebedor(a) *m(f)*

drink•ing ['drɪŋkɪŋ]: ***I'm worried about his ~*** me preocupa que beba tanto; ***a ~ problem*** un problema con la bebida
'drink•ing wa•ter agua *f* potable
'drinks ma•chine máquina *f* expendedora de bebidas
drip [drɪp] **I** *n* **1** gota *f* **2** MED gotero *m*, suero *m* **3** F *person* soso(-a) *m(f)*, insulso(-a) *m(f)* **II** *v/i* (*pret & pp* ***-ped***) gotear
'drip•dry *adj* que no necesita planchado
drip•ping ['drɪpɪŋ] *adv*: ***~ wet*** empapado
drive [draɪv] **I** *n* **1** *outing* vuelta *f*, paseo *m* (en coche); ***it's a short ~ from the station*** está a poca distancia en coche de la estación; ***with left- / right-hand ~*** MOT con el volante a la izquierda / a la derecha **2** (*energy*) energía *f* **3** COMPUT unidad *f* **4** (*campaign*) campaña *f*
II *v/t* (*pret* ***drove***, *pp* ***driven***) *vehicle* conducir, *L.Am.* manejar; (*own*) tener; (*take in car*) llevar (en coche); TECH impulsar; ***that noise / he is driving me mad*** ese ruido / él me está volviendo loco
III *v/i* (*pret* ***drove***, *pp* ***driven***) conducir, *L.Am.* manejar; ***don't drink and ~*** si bebes, no conduzcas; ***I ~ to work*** voy al trabajo en coche
◆ **drive at** *v/t*: ***what are you driving at?*** ¿qué insinúas?
◆ **drive away I** *v/t* **1** llevarse en un coche **2** (*chase off*) ahuyentar **II** *v/i* marcharse
◆ **drive back I** *v/i* volver en el coche, volver conduciendo, *L.Am.* volver manejando **II** *v/t* **1** *in car* llevar en coche **2** (*force to retreat*) hacer retroceder
◆ **drive in** *v/t nail* remachar
◆ **drive off** ☞ ***drive away***
◆ **drive out** *v/t* (*chase away*) ahuyentar
'drive-in *movie theater* autocine *m*; (*restaurant*) *restaurante en el que se pide desde el automóvil*
drive-in 'mov•ie the•a•ter autocine *m*
drive-in 'res•tau•rant *restaurante en el que se pide desde el automóvil*
driv•el ['drɪvl] tonterías *fpl*; ***talk ~*** decir tonterías
driv•en ['drɪvn] *pp* ☞ ***drive***
driv•er ['draɪvər] **1** conductor(a) *m(f)*; ***be in the ~'s seat*** *fig* estar al mando **2** COMPUT controlador *m*
'driv•er's li•cense carné *m* de conducir
drive•thru ['draɪvθruː] *restaurante / banco etc en el que se atiende al cliente sin que salga del coche*
'drive•way camino *m* de entrada
driv•ing ['draɪvɪŋ] **I** *n* conducción *f*; ***his ~ is appalling*** conduce *or L.Am.* maneja fatal **II** *adj rain* torrencial
driv•ing 'force fuerza *f* motriz; **'driv•ing in•struct•or** profesor(a) *m(f)* de autoescuela; **'driv•ing les•son** clase *f* de conducir; **'driv•ing li•cence** *Br* carné *m* de conducir; **'driv•ing school** autoescuela *f*; **'driv•ing test** examen *m* de conducir *or L.Am.* manejar
driz•zle ['drɪzl] **I** *n* llovizna *f* **II** *v/i* lloviznar
droll [droʊl] *adj* divertido
drom•e•dar•y ['drɑːmədərɪ] ZO dromedario *m*
drone[1] [droʊn] *noise* zumbido *m*
◆ **drone on** *v/i* hablar en tono monótono
drone[2] [droʊn] ZO zángano *m*
drool [druːl] *v/i* babear; ***~ over sth*** babear con algo
droop [druːp] *v/i of plant* marchitarse; ***her shoulders ~ed*** se encorvó
drop [drɑːp] **I** *n* **1** gota *f*; ***a ~ in the bucket*** *or* ***ocean*** *fig* un granito de arena; ***he has had a ~ too much*** se ha pasado de beber **2** *in price* caída *f*; *in temperature* caída *f*, descenso *m*
II *v/t* (*pret & pp* ***-ped***) **1** *object* dejar caer **2** *person from car* dejar; *person from team* excluir; (*stop seeing*) abandonar **3** *charges*, *demand etc* retirar; (*give up*) dejar; ***~ it!*** ¡basta ya!, ¡déjalo ya!; ***I ~ped everything and went to help her*** dejé lo que estaba haciendo y salí en su ayuda **4**: ***~ a line to*** mandar unas líneas a
III *v/i* (*pret & pp* ***-ped***) **1** caer, caerse; ***~ into a chair*** dejarse caer en una silla; ***let sth ~*** *fig* dejar de hablar de algo, dejar algo de lado; ***be ready to ~*** (***with fatigue***) estar a punto de desfallecer; ***~ dead*** caerse muerto; ***~ dead!*** ¡vete a paseo! F **2** (*decline*) caer; *of wind* amainar
◆ **drop away** *v/i* disminuir, menguar
◆ **drop back** *v/i* quedarse detrás
◆ **drop behind** *v/i in race* ir a la zaga
◆ **drop in** *v/i* (*visit*) pasar a visitar

◆ **drop off** **I** *v/t person from car* dejar; (*deliver*) llevar **II** *v/i* **1** (*fall asleep*) dormirse **2** (*decline*) disminuir
◆ **drop out** *v/i* (*withdraw*) retirarse; ***drop out of school*** abandonar el colegio

drop•let ['drɑ:plɪt] gotita *f*
'drop•out (*from school*) *alumno que ha abandonado los estudios*; *from society* marginado(-a) *m*(*f*)
drop•per ['drɑ:pər] cuentagotas *m*
drop•pings ['drɑ:pɪŋz] *npl* excrementos *mpl*, cagarrutas *fpl*
drops [drɑ:ps] *npl for eyes* gotas *fpl*
'drop shot SP dejada *f*
drought [draʊt] sequía *f*
drove[1] [droʊv] *pret* ☞ ***drive***
drove[2] [droʊv] *n* manada *f*, rebaño *m*; ***in ~s*** *fig* en manada
drown [draʊn] **I** *v/i* ahogarse **II** *v/t person, sound* ahogar; ***be ~ed*** ahogarse; ***~ one's sorrows*** ahogar las penas en alcohol
◆ **drown out** *v/t of sound* tapar, cubrir
drowse [draʊz] *v/i* adormilarse
drow•sy ['draʊzɪ] *adj* soñoliento(-a); ***get ~*** tener sueño
drudge [drʌdʒ] *person* burro *m* de carga
drudg•e•ry ['drʌdʒərɪ]: ***the job is sheer ~*** el trabajo es terriblemente pesado
drug [drʌg] **I** *n* MED, *illegal* droga *f*; ***be on ~s*** drogarse; ***be off ~s*** haber dejado las drogas; ***be a ~ on the market*** COM no ser rentable **II** *v/t* (*pret & pp* ***-ged***) drogar
'drug a•buse consumo *m* de drogas; **'drug ad•dict** drogadicto(-a) *m*(*f*); **'drug ad•dic•tion** drogodependencia *f*; **'drug clin•ic** clínica *f* de rehabilitación para drogodependientes; **'drug deal•er** traficante *m/f* (de drogas); **'drug de•pend•ency** drogodependencia *f*
drug•gist ['drʌgɪst] farmacéutico(-a) *m*(*f*)
'drug•push•er F camello *m/f* F; **'drug scene** mundo *m* de las drogas; **'drug squad** unidad *f* antidrogas de la policía; **'drug•store** *tienda en la que se venden medicinas, cosméticos, periódicos y que a veces tiene un bar*; **'drug test** SP control *m* antidoping; **'drug traf•fick•ing** tráfico *m* de drogas
drum [drʌm] **1** MUS tambor *m* **2** *container* barril *m*
◆ **drum into** *v/t* (*pret & pp* ***-med***): ***drum sth into s.o.*** meter algo en la cabeza de alguien
◆ **drum up** *v/t*: ***drum up support*** buscar apoyos
'drum•beat redoble *m* de tambor
'drum•kit batería *f*
drum•mer ['drʌmər] tambor *m*, tamborilero(-a) *m*(*f*)
'drum•stick **1** MUS baqueta *f* **2** *of poultry* muslo *m*
drunk [drʌŋk] **I** *n* borracho(-a) *m*(*f*) **II** *adj* borracho; ***get ~*** emborracharse; ***(as) ~ as a lord*** F borracho como una cuba F; ***~ with joy*** borracho *or* ebrio de alegría **III** *pp* ☞ ***drink***
drunk•ard ['drʌŋkəd] alcohólico(-a) *m*(*f*)
drunk 'driv•ing conducción *f* bajo los efectos del alcohol
drunk•en [drʌŋkn] *voices, laughter* borracho; *party* con mucho alcohol
drunk•en•ness ['drʌŋkənəs] ebriedad *f*, embriaguez *f*
dry [draɪ] **I** *adj* seco; *where alcohol is banned* donde está prohibido el consumo de alcohol; ***rub sth ~*** secar algo frotando; ***as ~ as a bone*** F muy seco, como un secadal; ***(as) ~ as dust*** F (*boring*) un rollo *or* aburrimiento **II** *v/t & v/i* (*pret & pp* ***-ied***) secar; ***~ o.s.*** secarse; ***~ one's hands*** secarse las manos
◆ **dry off** *v/i* secarse
◆ **dry out** *v/i* secarse; *of alcoholic* desintoxicarse
◆ **dry up** *v/i* **1** *of river* secarse **2** F (*be quiet*) cerrar el pico F **3** *of actor* quedarse en blanco
'dry bat•ter•y ELEC pila *f* seca; **'dry-clean** *v/t* limpiar en seco; **'dry clean•er** tintorería *f*; **'dry•clean•ing** *clothes*: ***would you pick up my ~ for me?*** ¿te importaría recogerme la ropa de la tintorería?; **dry 'dock** dique *m* seco
dry•er [draɪr] *machine* secadora *f*
dry 'goods *npl* COM prendas *fpl* textiles
dry 'ice CHEM nieve *f* carbónica
dry•ness ['draɪnɪs] sequedad *f*
dry 'rot carcoma *f*
DTP [di:ti:'pi:] *abbr* (= ***desk-top publishing***) autoedición *f*
du•al ['du:əl] *adj* doble
du•al 'car•riage•way *Br* MOT autovía *f*

dub[1] [dʌb] *v/t* (*pret & pp* **-bed**) *movie* doblar
dub[2] [dʌb] *v/t* (*pret & pp* **-bed**) (*name*) apodar
du•bi•ous ['du:bɪəs] *adj* dudoso; (*having doubts*) inseguro; ***I'm still ~ about the idea*** todavía tengo mis dudas sobre la idea; ***~ pleasure*** *iron* placer *m* cuestionable
duch•ess ['dʌtʃɪs] duquesa *f*
duch•y ['dʌtʃɪ] ducado *m*
duck [dʌk] **I** *n* pato *m*, pata *f*; ***he took to it like a ~ to water*** se sentía como el pez en el agua **II** *v/i* agacharse **III** *v/t* **1** *one's head* agachar **2** *question* eludir
◆ **duck out** *v/i*: ***duck out of sth*** escaquearse de algo
duck•ing ['dʌkɪŋ]: ***give s.o. a ~*** hacer a alguien una aguadilla
duck•ling ['dʌklɪŋ] patito *m*
duct [dʌkt] **1** TECH conducto *m*, tubo *m* **2** ANAT vaso *m*
duc•tile ['dʌktəl] *adj steel* dúctil
dud [dʌd] F (*false bill*) billete *m* falso
dude [du:d] F tipo *m* F, *Span* tío *m* F
due [du:] **I** *adj* **1** (*proper*) debido; ***after ~ consideration*** tras la debida deliberación; ***in ~ time*** dentro del plazo establecido; ***in ~ course*** en su debido momento
2: ***the money ~ me*** el dinero que se me debe; ***payment is now ~*** el pago se debe hacer efectivo ahora; ***fall or become ~*** vencer
3 *in time*: ***is there a train ~ soon?*** ¿va a pasar un tren pronto?; ***when is the baby ~?*** ¿cuándo está previsto que nazca el bebé?; ***he's ~ to meet him next month*** tiene previsto reunirse con él el próximo mes; ***when ~*** cuando venza el plazo
4: ***~ to*** (*because of*) debido a; ***be ~ to*** (*be caused by*) ser debido a
II *n*: ***give s.o. his ~*** ser justo con alguien
'**due date** fecha *f* de vencimiento
du•el ['du:əl] **I** *n* duelo *m* **II** *v/i* (*pret & pp* **-ed**, *Br* **-led**) enfrentarse en duelo
dues [du:z] *npl* cuota *f*
du•et [du:'et] MUS dúo *m*
duf•fle bag ['dʌflbæg] petate *m*, mochila *f*
duf•fle coat ['dʌflkoʊt] trenca *f*
dug [dʌg] *pret & pp* ☞ **dig**
'**dug•out 1** MIL trinchera *f* **2** (*canoe*) canoa *f* **3** *in sport* foso *m*, *Mex* dogaut *m*
duke [du:k] duque *m*
dull [dʌl] *adj* **1** *weather* gris **2** *sound*, *pain* sordo **3** (*boring*) aburrido, soso
dull•ness ['dʌlnɪs] *of book*, *movie* sosería *f*, hastío *m*
du•ly ['du:lɪ] *adv* **1** (*as expected*) tal y como se esperaba **2** (*properly*) debidamente
dumb [dʌm] *adj* **1** (*mute*) mudo; ***strike s.o. ~*** *fig* dejar a alguien de una pieza, dejar a alguien sin palabras **2** F (*stupid*) estúpido; ***a pretty ~ thing to do*** una tontería; ***just act ~*** tú hazte el tonto, tú actúa como si no supieses nada
◆ **dumb down** *v/t* F bajar el nivel intelectual de
'**dumb•bell 1** SP pesa *f* **2** F tonto(-a) *m*(*f*) F, idiota *m/f* F
dumb'found *v/t* dejar boquiabierto, anonadar
dumb•found•ed [dʌm'faʊndɪd] *adj* boquiabierto
dumb'wait•er montaplatos *m inv*, montacargas *m inv*
dum•found *etc* ☞ ***dumbfound*** *etc*
dum•my ['dʌmɪ] **I** *n* **1** *model* imitación *f*, copia *f* **2** *in clothes shop* maniquí *m* **3** *Br*: *for babies* chupete *m* **4** F (*idiot*) idiota *m/f* **5** SP amago *m* **II** *adj* falso **III** *v/i* SP amagar
dump [dʌmp] **I** *n* **1** *for garbage* vertedero *m*, basurero *m* **2** (*unpleasant place*) lugar *m* de mala muerte **II** *v/t* (*deposit*) dejar; (*dispose of*) deshacerse de; *toxic waste*, *nuclear waste* verter; COM hacer dumping con; COMPUT volcar; ***they ~ed the kids with gran and …*** le encasquetaron los niños a la abuela y … F
◆ **dump on** *v/t* P *with troubles* desahogarse con, descargarse con
dump•ing ['dʌmpɪŋ] **1** *of rubbish* vertido *m* **2** COM dumping *m*
'**dump•ing ground** *fig* receptáculo *m*, refugio *m*
dump•ling ['dʌmplɪŋ] *bola de masa dulce o salada*
dumps [dʌmps] *npl*: (***down***) ***in the ~*** F bajo de ánimos F
'**dump truck** volquete *m*
dump•y ['dʌmpɪ] *adj* rechoncho, achaparrado
dunce [dʌns] zoquete *m/f*
dune [du:n] duna *f*

'dune bug•gy MOT buggy *m*
dung [dʌŋ] estiércol *m*
dun•ga•rees [dʌŋgə'ri:z] *npl* pantalones *mpl* de trabajo
dun•geon ['dʌndʒən] calabozo *m*
'dung•hill montaña *f* de estiércol
dunk [dʌŋk] **I** *v/t in coffee etc* mojar **II** *n in basketball* machaque *m*, mate *m*
dun•no ['dʌnoʊ] F ☞ ***don't know***
du•o ['du:oʊ] MUS dúo *m*
du•o•de•num [du:ə'di:nəm] ANAT duodeno *m*
dupe [du:p] **I** *n* simplón(-ona) *m(f)* **II** *v/t* engañar; **~ *s.o. into doing sth*** engatusar *or* confundir a alguien para que haga algo
du•plex (a•part•ment) ['du:pleks] dúplex *m*
du•pli•cate I *n* ['du:plɪkət] duplicado *m*; ***in* ~** por duplicado **II** *v/t* ['du:plɪkeɪt] **1** (*copy*) duplicar, hacer un duplicado de **2** (*repeat*) repetir
du•pli•cate 'key llave *f* duplicada
du•plic•i•tous [du:'plɪsɪtəs] *adj* falso, deshonesto
du•plic•i•ty [du:'plɪsɪtɪ] duplicidad *f*, falsedad *f*
du•ra•bil•i•ty [dʊrə'bɪlətɪ] durabilidad *f*
du•ra•ble ['dʊrəbl] *adj material* duradero, durable; *relationship* duradero; **~ *goods*** bienes *mpl* duraderos
du•ra•tion [dʊ'reɪʃn] duración *f*; ***for the ~ of her visit*** mientras dure su visita
du•ress [dʊ'res]: ***under* ~** bajo coacción
Du•rex® ['dju:reks] *Br* condón *m*
dur•ing ['dʊrɪŋ] *prep* durante
dusk [dʌsk] crepúsculo *m*, anochecer *m*; ***at* ~** al anochecer
dust [dʌst] **I** *n* polvo *m*; ***once the* ~ *has settled*** *fig* cuando las aguas vuelvan a su cauce **II** *v/t* **1** quitar el polvo a **2** (*sprinkle*): **~ *sth with sth*** espolvorear algo con algo
'dust•bin *Br* contenedor *m* de basuras
'dust cov•er *of book* sobrecubierta *f*
dust•er ['dʌstər] *cloth* trapo *m* del polvo
'dust jack•et *Br of book* sobrecubierta *f*; **'dust•man** *Br* basurero(-a) *m(f)*; **'dust•pan** recogedor *m*; **'dust storm** tormenta *f* de arena; **'dust-up** *Br* F bronca *f* F, riña *f*
dust•y ['dʌstɪ] *adj* polvoriento
Dutch [dʌʧ] **I** *adj* holandés; ***go* ~** F pagar a escote F **II** *n* **1** *pl*: ***the* ~** los holandeses **2** (*language*) neerlandés *m*
Dutch 'cour•age F *valentía que resulta del consumo de alcohol*
Dutch•man ['dʌʧmən] holandés *m*
'Dutch•wom•an holandesa *f*
du•ti•a•ble ['du:tjəbl] *adj* COM imponible, gravable
du•ti•ful ['du:tɪfʊl] *adj* obediente
du•ty ['du:tɪ] **1** deber *m*; (*task*) obligación *f*, tarea *f*; ***be on* ~** estar de servicio; ***be off* ~** estar fuera de servicio; ***he did his* ~** cumplió con su deber *or* obligación; ***do* ~ *for*** servir como *or* de **2** *on goods* impuesto *m*
du•ty-'free I *adj* libre de impuestos **II** *n* productos *mpl* libres de impuestos; **du•ty-'free shop** tienda *f* libre de impuestos; **'du•ty of•fi•cer** MIL oficial *m/f* de servicio; **'du•ty ros•ter** calendario *m* de turnos
du•vet ['du:veɪ] *Br* edredón *m*
DVD [di:vi:'di:] *abbr* (= ***digital versatile disk***) DVD *m* (= disco *m* digital polivalente)
dwarf [dwɔ:rf] **I** *n* (*pl* ***dwarves*** [dwɔ:rvz]) enano *m* **II** *v/t* empequeñecer
dwarf•ish [dwɔ:rfɪʃ] *adj* diminuto, minúsculo
dwarves [dwɔ:rvz] *pl* ☞ ***dwarf***
◆ **dwell on** [dwel] *v/t* (*pret & pp* **dwelt**): ***dwell on the past*** pensar en el pasado; ***don't dwell on what he said*** no des demasiada importancia a lo que ha dicho
dwell•ing ['dwelɪŋ] alojamiento *m*
'dwell•ing house domicilio *m*, vivienda *f*
dwelt [dwelt] *pret & pp* ☞ ***dwell***
dwin•dle ['dwɪndl] *v/i* disminuir, menguar
dye [daɪ] **I** *n* tinte *m* **II** *v/t* teñir; **~ *one's hair*** teñirse el pelo
dyed-in-the-wool [daɪdɪnðə'wʊl] *adj* convencido, obstinado
dy•ing ['daɪɪŋ] *adj person* moribundo; *industry, tradition* en vías de desaparición; ***be* ~** estar moribundo; ***until my* ~ *day*** hasta que me muera; **~ *wish*** última voluntad *f*
dyke ☞ ***dike***[1 & 2]
dy•nam•ic [daɪ'næmɪk] *adj person* dinámico
dy•nam•ic 'RAM RAM *f* dinámica

dy•na•mism ['daɪnəmɪzm] dinamismo *m*
dy•na•mite ['daɪnəmaɪt] dinamita *f*
dy•na•mo ['daɪnəmoʊ] TECH dinamo *f*, dínamo *f*
dy•nas•ty ['daɪnəstɪ] dinastía *f*
dys•en•ter•y ['dɪsntrɪ] MED disentería *f*
dys•func•tion [dɪs'fʌŋkʃn] MED disfunción *f*
dys•func•tion•al [dɪs'fʌŋkʃnəl] *adj family* disfuncional
dys•lex•i•a [dɪs'leksɪə] dislexia *f*
dys•lex•ic [dɪs'leksɪk] **I** *adj* disléxico **II** *n* disléxico(-a) *m(f)*

E

each [iːʧ] **I** *adj* cada **II** *adv*: ***he gave us one ~*** nos dio uno a cada uno; ***they're $1.50 ~*** valen 1.50 dólares cada uno **III** *pron* cada uno; ***~ other*** el uno al otro; ***we love ~ other*** nos queremos
ea•ger ['iːgər] *adj* ansioso; *worker*, *competitor* entusiasta; ***she's always ~ to help*** siempre está deseando ayudar; ***they're ~ to get started*** estan ansiosos por empezar
ea•ger 'bea•ver F entusiasta *m/f*
ea•ger•ly ['iːgərlɪ] *adv* ansiosamente; *volunteer* con entusiasmo
ea•ger•ness ['iːgərnɪs] ansia *f*; *of worker*, *competitor etc* entusiasmo *m*
ea•gle ['iːgl] águila *f*
ea•gle-eyed [iːgl'aɪd] *adj* con vista de lince
ear[1] [ɪr] *of person*, *animal* oreja *f*; ***~, nose and throat specialist*** otorrinolaringólogo(-a) *m(f)*; ***be all ~s*** F ser todo oídos F; ***be up to the** or **one's ~s in debt / work*** estar hasta las orejas de deudas / trabajo F; ***keep one's ~ to the ground, keep one's ~s open*** *L.Am.* parar la(s) oreja(s), *Span* estar al tanto; ***it goes in one ~ and out the other*** F le entra por un oído y le sale por el otro F; ***he turned a deaf ~*** hizo oídos sordos; ***play sth by ~*** MUS tocar algo de oído; ***play it by ~*** *fig* improvisar
ear[2] [ɪr] *of corn* espiga *f*
'ear•ache dolor *m* de oídos; **'ear•drum** tímpano *m*; **'ear•lobe** lóbulo *m*
ear•ly ['ɜːrlɪ] **I** *adj* **1** (*not late*) temprano; (*ahead of time*) anticipado; ***let's have an ~ supper*** cenemos temprano; ***in the ~ hours of the morning*** a primeras horas de la madrugada; ***I'm an ~ riser*** soy madrugador; ***be ~*** (*arrive early*) llegar *L.Am.* temprano *or Span* pronto, llegar antes de la hora; ***it's never too ~ to start*** cuanto antes se empiece mejor; ***it's ~ days yet*** todavía es pronto; ***his ~ death*** su muerte prematura
2 (*farther back in time*) primero; *music* antiguo; ***an ~ Picasso*** un Picasso de su primera época
3 (*in the near future*) pronto
4 (*at the beginning of*): ***in ~ October*** a principios de octubre
II *adv* (*not late*) pronto, temprano; (*ahead of time*) antes de tiempo; ***it's too ~ to say*** es demasiado pronto como para poder decir nada; ***earlier than*** antes que; ***as ~ as May*** ya en mayo; ***at the (very) earliest*** como muy *Span* pronto *or L.Am.* temprano
ear•ly a•dopt•er [ɜːrlɪə'dɑːptər] *consumidor que compra rápidamente un producto nuevo*; **'ear•ly bird** madrugador(a) *m(f)*; ***the ~ catches the worm*** al que madruga Dios le ayuda; ***you're an ~*** *arriving before the others* llegas muy pronto; **ear•ly re'pay•ment** devolución *f* anticipada; **ear•ly re'tire•ment** jubilación *f* anticipada, prejubilación *f*; ***take ~*** jubilarse anticipadamente; **ear•ly 'warn•ing sys•tem** MIL sistema *m* de alerta inmediata *or* aviso inmediato
'ear•mark *v/t* destinar; ***~ sth for sth*** destinar algo a algo
ear•muff ['ɪrmʌf] orejera *f*
earn [ɜːrn] *v/t salary* ganar; *interest* devengar; *holiday*, *drink etc* ganarse; ***~ one's living*** ganarse la vida
ear•nest ['ɜːrnɪst] *adj* serio; ***in ~*** en serio
ear•nest•ness ['ɜːrnɪstnɪs] *of tone* seriedad *f*; *of belief* sinceridad *f*
earn•ings ['ɜːrnɪŋz] *npl* ganancias *fpl*

'ear•phones *npl* auriculares *mpl*; **'ear•piece** TELEC auricular *m*; **'ear-•pierc•ing** *adj* estrepitoso; **'ear•plug** tapón *m* para el oído; **'ear•ring** pendiente *m*; **ear•shot** ['ɪrʃɑːt]: ***within ~*** al alcance del oído; ***out of ~*** fuera del alcance del oído; **'ear•split•ting** *adj* estridente

earth [ɜːrθ] **1** (*soil*) tierra *f*; **2** (*world, planet*) Tierra *f*; ***where on ~ ...?*** F ¿dónde diablos ...? F; ***what / why on ~?*** ¿qué / por qué diablos *or* demonios?; ***cost the ~*** F costar un ojo de la cara F; ***it doesn't cost the ~*** F no cuesta una fortuna; ***come back or down to ~ (with a bang)*** *fig* bajar de las nubes, poner los pies sobre la tierra

earth•en ['ɜːrθn] *adj* **1** *floor* de tierra **2** *pot* de barro

earth•en•ware ['ɜːrθnwer] loza *f*; ***an ~ pot*** un tarro de loza

earth•ly ['ɜːrθlɪ] *adj* **1** terrenal **2** F ***it's no ~ use*** no sirve para nada; ***there's no ~ reason to think that ...*** no existe razón alguna para creer que ...; ***they don't have an ~ chance of winning*** no tienen la más mínima posibilidad de ganar

earth-mov•ing e'quip•ment maquinaria *f* (de excavaciones); **'earth•quake** terremoto *m*; **'earth•quake-proof** *adj* a prueba de terremotos; **'earth sci•en•ces** *npl* ciencias *fpl* de la tierra, ciencias *fpl* geológicas; **'earth-shat•ter•ing** *adj* extraordinario; **'earth trem•or** temblor *m* de tierra; **'earth•worm** lombriz *f* (de tierra)

earth•y ['ɜːrθɪ] *adj person, sense of humor* sencillo, directo

'ear•wig tijereta *f*

ease [iːz] **I** *n* **1** facilidad *f*; ***with ~*** con facilidad **2**: ***be at (one's) ~, feel at ~*** sentirse cómodo; ***feel ill at ~*** sentirse incómodo; ***live a life of ~*** vivir desahogadamente *or* cómodamente; ***at ~!*** MIL ¡descanse(n)! **II** *v/t* (*relieve*) aliviar; ***~ one's mind*** tranquilizarse **III** *v/i of pain* disminuir

◆ **ease off I** *v/t* (*remove*) quitar con cuidado **II** *v/i* **1** *of pain* disminuir; *of rain* amainar **2** *for health reasons* tomarse las cosas con calma

◆ **ease out** *v/t* (*remove gently*) sacar con cuidado; *employee* hacer dimitir

ea•sel ['iːzl] caballete *m*

eas•i•ly ['iːzəlɪ] *adv* **1** (*with ease*) fácilmente **2** (*by far*) con diferencia; ***this is ~ the best*** éste es el mejor con diferencia

east [iːst] **I** *n* este *m* **II** *adj* oriental, este; *wind* del este **III** *adv travel* hacia el este

'east•bound *adj* en dirección este

Eas•ter ['iːstər] Pascua *f*; *period* Semana *f* Santa; ***at ~*** en Semana Santa

Eas•ter 'Day Domingo *m* de Resurrección

'Eas•ter egg huevo *m* de pascua

eas•ter•ly ['iːstərlɪ] *adj* del este

Eas•ter 'Mon•day Lunes *m* Santo

east•ern ['iːstərn] *adj* del este; (*oriental*) oriental

east•er•ner ['iːstərnər] *habitante de la costa oeste estadounidense*

'east•ern•most *adj* más oriental, más al este

East•ern 'Stand•ard Time *hora oficial de la costa este estadounidense*

Eas•ter 'Sun•day Domingo *m* de Resurrección

east•ward ['iːstwərd] *adv* hacia el este

eas•y ['iːzɪ] **I** *adj* **1** fácil; ***it is ~ for him / you / them to talk*** se dice muy pronto; ***be ~ to please*** ser fácil de complacer; ***~ money*** dinero *m* fácil; ***be on ~ street*** F darse la gran vida F; ***on ~ terms*** con facilidades de pago **2** (*relaxed*) tranquilo; ***take things ~*** (*slow down*) tomarse las cosas con tranquilidad; ***take it ~!*** (*calm down*) ¡tranquilízate!; *don't rush* ¡no corras! ¡sin prisa!; *don't get worked up* ¡con tranquilidad!

II *adv*: ***go ~ on s.o.*** *not too demanding* ser poco exigente con alguien; *not too harsh* no ser duro con alguien; ***go ~ with or on the sugar*** no te pases con el azúcar F; ***that's easier said than done*** ¡eso se dice muy pronto!; ***~ come, ~ go*** tal como viene se va

'eas•y chair sillón *m*; **'eas•y•go•ing** *adj* tratable; **eas•y-peas•y** [iːzɪ'piːzɪ] *adj Br* F tirado F, pan comido F

eat [iːt] *v/t & v/i* (*pret* **ate**, *pp* **eaten**) comer; ***~ one's words*** tragarse las propias palabras; ***what's ~ing him?*** F ¿qué mosca *or* bicho le ha picado?

◆ **eat away** *v/t of rat* roer, corroer; *of acid* desgastar; *coastline* comerse, destruir

◆ **eat away at** *v/t fig confidence, self--esteem* acabar con
◆ **eat into** *v/t fig: reserves etc* corroer, reducir
◆ **eat out** *v/i* comer fuera
◆ **eat up** *v/t* comerse; *fig: use up* acabar con; ***be eaten up with jealousy*** *fig* consumirse *or* carcomerse de envidia
eat•a•ble ['i:təbl] *adj* comestible
'eat-by date fecha *f* de caducidad
eat•en ['i:tn] *pp* ☞ **eat**
eat•ing ['i:tɪŋ] **I** *n* el comer **II** *adj*: **~ *apple*** manzana *f* de mesa; **~ *disorder*** desorden *m* alimenticio; **~ *habits*** hábitos *mpl* alimentarios
eau de Co•logne [oudəkə'loun] agua *f* de colonia
eaves [i:vz] *npl* alero *m*
'eaves•drop *v/i* (*pret & pp* **-ped**) escuchar a escondidas (***on s.o.*** alguien)
ebb [eb] **I** *v/i of tide* bajar **II** *n*: ***be at a low ~*** estar de capa caída
◆ **ebb away** *v/i fig: of courage, strength* desvanecerse
'ebb tide marea *f* baja
eb•on•y ['ebənɪ] ébano *m*
e•bul•lience [ɪ'bʌljəns] entusiasmo *m*, animación *f*
e•bul•lient [ɪ'bʌljənt] *adj* entusiasta, animado
e-busi•ness ['i:bɪznɪs] comercio *m* electrónico
ec•cen•tric [ɪk'sentrɪk] **I** *adj* excéntrico **II** *n* excéntrico(-a) *m(f)*
ec•cen•tric•i•ty [ɪksen'trɪsɪtɪ] excentricidad *f*
ec•cle•si•as•ti•cal [ɪkli:zɪ'æstɪkl] *adj* eclesiástico
ECG [i:si:'dʒi:] *abbr* (= ***electrocardiogram***) electrocardiograma *m*
ech•o ['ekou] **I** *n* (*pl* **-oes**) eco *m* **II** *v/i* resonar **III** *v/t words* repetir; *views* mostrar acuerdo con
e•clair [ɪ'kleɪr] *pastelito de nata*
ec•lamp•si•a [ɪ'klæmpsɪə] MED eclampsia *f*
ec•lec•tic [ɪ'klektɪk] *adj* ecléctico
e•clipse [ɪ'klɪps] **I** *n* eclipse *m* **II** *v/t fig* eclipsar; ***be ~d by s.o. / sth*** quedar eclipsado *or* ensombrecido por alguien / algo
e•co•lo•gi•cal [i:kə'lɑ:dʒɪkl] *adj* ecológico; **~ *balance*** equilibrio *m* ecológico
e•co•lo•gi•cal•ly [i:kə'lɑ:dʒɪklɪ] *adv* ecológicamente; **~ *beneficial / harmful*** beneficioso / perjudicial desde el punto de vista ecológico
e•co•lo•gi•cal•ly 'friend•ly *adj* ecológico
e•col•o•gist [i:'kɑ:lədʒɪst] ecologista *m/f*
e•col•o•gy [i:'kɑ:lədʒɪ] ecología *f*
ec•o•nom•ic [i:kə'nɑ:mɪk] *adj* económico; **~ *aid*** ayuda *f* económica; **~ *migrant or refugee*** emigrante *m/f or* refugiado(-a) económico(-a); **~ *adviser*** asesor(a) *m(f)* económico(-a)
ec•o•nom•i•cal [i:kə'nɑ:mɪkl] *adj* (*cheap*) económico; (*thrifty*) cuidadoso; ***the car is very ~ to run*** este coche es muy económico; ***be ~ with the truth*** decir la verdad a medias
ec•o•nom•i•cal•ly [i:kə'nɑ:mɪklɪ] *adv* **1** (*in terms of economics*) económicamente **2** (*thriftily*) de manera económica
ec•o•nom•ic 'fore•cast previsiones *fpl* económicas; **ec•o•nom•ic 'growth** crecimiento *m* económico; **ec•o•nom•ic 'in•di•ca•tor** indicador *m* económico; **ec•o•nom•ic 'pol•i•cy** política *f* económica
ec•o•nom•ics [i:kə'nɑ:mɪks] **1** *nsg science* economía *f* **2** *npl* (*financial aspects*) aspecto *m* económico
e•con•o•mies of 'scale economías *fpl* de escala
e•con•o•mist [ɪ'kɑ:nəmɪst] economista *m/f*
e•con•o•mize [ɪ'kɑ:nəmaɪz] *v/i* economizar, ahorrar
◆ **economize on** *v/t* economizar, ahorrar
e•con•o•my [ɪ'kɑ:nəmɪ] **1** *of a country* economía *f* **2** (*saving*) ahorro *m*; ***we have to make economies*** tenemos que ahorrar *or* economizar
e'con•o•my brand marca *f* económica; **e'con•o•my class** clase *f* turista; **e'con•o•my drive** intento *m* de ahorrar; **e'con•o•my fare** tarifa *f* económica; **e'con•o•my pack** paquete *m* económico; **e'con•o•my price** precio *m* económico; **e'con•o•my size** tamaño *m* económico
e•co•sys•tem ['i:kousɪstm] ecosistema *m*
e•co•tour•ism ['i:kouturɪzm] ecoturis-

mo *m*, turismo *m* verde *or* ecológico

e•co•tour•ist ['i:koutʊrɪst] ecoturista *m/f*, turista *m/f* ecológico(-a)

ec•sta•sy ['ekstəsɪ] *also drug* éxtasis *m*; ***go into ecstasies over sth*** extasiarse *or* embelesarse con algo

ec•sta•tic [ɪk'stætɪk] *adj* muy emocionado, extasiado

ec•top•ic [ek'tɑ:pɪk] *adj*: ~ ***pregnancy*** embarazo *m* ectópico

Ec•ua•dor ['ekwədɔ:r] Ecuador *m*

Ec•ua•dor•e•an [ekwə'dɔ:rən] **I** *adj* ecuatoriano **II** *n* ecuatoriano(-a) *m(f)*

ec•u•men•i•cal [i:kju:'menɪkl] *adj* ecuménico

ec•ze•ma ['eksmə] eczema *m*

ed•dy ['edɪ] remolino *m*

edge [edʒ] **I** *n of knife* filo *m*; *of table, seat, road, cliff* borde *m*; *in voice* irritación *f*; ***on*** ~ tenso; ***take the*** ~ ***off*** *knife* mellar; ***take the*** ~ ***off one's hunger*** calmar el apetito; ***on the*** ~ ***of*** al borde *or* extremo de; ***set s.o.'s teeth on*** ~ *of sound, taste* dar dentera a alguien; ***have the*** ~ ***on s.o.*** llevar la delantera a alguien, aventajar a alguien

II *v/t* ribetear

III *v/i* (*move slowly*) ~ ***forward*** / ***back*** avanzar / retroceder poco a poco

◆ **edge away** *v/i* alejarse poco a poco (***from*** de)

edge•wise ['edʒwaɪz] *adv* de lado; ***I couldn't get a word in*** ~ no me dejó decir una palabra

edg•i•ness ['edʒɪnɪs] (estado *m* de) tensión *f*

edg•y ['edʒɪ] *adj* tenso

ed•i•ble ['edɪbl] *adj* comestible

ed•i•fy•ing ['edɪfaɪɪŋ] *adj* edificante

ed•it ['edɪt] *v/t text* corregir; *book* editar; *newspaper* dirigir; *TV program, movie* montar

e•di•tion [ɪ'dɪʃn] *also* SP edición *f*

ed•i•tor ['edɪtər] *of text, book* editor(a) *m(f)*; *of newspaper* director(a) *m(f)*; *of TV program, movie* montador(a) *m(f)*; ***sports*** / ***political*** ~ redactor(a) *m(f)* de deportes / política; ~ ***in chief*** director(a) *m(f)* editorial; ~***'s note*** nota *f* de la redacción

ed•i•to•ri•al [edɪ'tɔ:rɪəl] **I** *adj* editorial; ~ ***department*** (departamento *m* de) redacción *f* **II** *n in newspaper* editorial *m/f*

ed•i•to•ri•al di'rec•tor *of paper* jefe(-a) *m(f)* de redacción; *of publisher* director(a) *m(f)* editorial; **ed•i•to•ri•al 'pol•i•cy** política *f* editorial; **ed•i'to•ri•al staff** redacción *f*; **ed•i'to•ri•al writ•er** editorialista *m/f*

EDP [i:di:'pi:] *abbr* (= ***electronic data processing***) procesamiento *m* electrónico de datos

ed•u•cate ['edʒəkeɪt] *v/t child* educar; *consumers* concienciar; ***he was*** ~***d at*** ... estudió en ...

ed•u•cat•ed ['edʒəkeɪtɪd] *adj person* culto; ~ ***guess*** suposición *f* con fundamento

ed•u•ca•tion [edʒə'keɪʃn] educación *f*; ***the*** ~ ***system*** el sistema educativo

ed•u•ca•tion•al [edʒə'keɪʃnl] *adj* **1** educativo; ~ ***psychologist*** psico-pedagogo(-a) *m(f)* **2** (*informative*) instructivo

ed•u•ca•tion•al•ly [edʒə'keɪʃnəlɪ] *adv* educativamente hablando; ~ ***subnormal*** con dificultades de aprendizaje

ed•u•tain•ment [edju:'teɪnmənt] *software que entretiene y a la vez educa*

EEG [i:i:'dʒi:] *abbr* (= ***electroencephalogram***) electroencefalograma *m*

eel [i:l] anguila *f*

ee•rie ['ɪrɪ] *adj* escalofriante

ee•ri•ness ['ɪrɪnɪs] lo escalofriante

ef•fect [ɪ'fekt] **I** *n* efecto *m*; ***take*** ~ *of medicine, drug* hacer efecto; ***come into*** ~ *of law* entrar en vigor; ***have no*** ~ no producir ningún efecto; ***nothing I say has any*** ~ ***on him*** no hace caso a nada de lo que le digo; ***have an*** ~ ***on s.o.*** / ***sth*** afectar alguien / algo, hacer mella en alguien / algo; ***special*** ~***s*** efectos especiales; ***a letter to the*** ~ ***that ...*** una carta informando de que ...; ***I will inform him to that*** ~ *fml* le informaré al respecto *fml*; ***or words to that*** ~ o algo por el estilo; ***be in*** ~ *of law* estar vigente; ***with*** ~ ***from ...*** *date* a partir de...; ***he is, in*** ~***, the leader*** él es, de hecho, el líder

II *v/t* efectuar

ef•fec•tive [ɪ'fektɪv] *adj* **1** (*efficient*) efectivo **2** (*striking*) impresionante **3** (*real, actual*) real; ~ ***May 1*** a partir del 1 de mayo; ***become*** ~ *of law etc* entrar en vigor

ef•fec•tive•ly [ɪ'fektɪvlɪ] *adv* (*in reality*) en definitiva, de hecho

ef•fec•tive•ness [ɪ'fektɪvnɪs] eficacia *f*
ef•fem•i•nate [ɪ'femɪnət] *adj* afeminado
ef•fer•ves•cent [efər'vesnt] *adj* efervescente; *personality* chispeante
ef•fete [ɪ'fiːt] *adj person* amanerado; *nation, institution etc* decadente
ef•fi•cien•cy [ɪ'fɪʃənsɪ] *of person* eficiencia *f*; *of machine* rendimiento *m*; *of system* eficacia *f*
ef•fi•cient [ɪ'fɪʃənt] *adj person* eficiente; *machine* de buen rendimiento; *method* eficaz
ef•fi•cient•ly [ɪ'fɪʃəntlɪ] *adv* eficientemente
ef•fi•gy ['efɪdʒɪ] *on coin etc* efigie *f*; *dummy, model* monigote *m*; ***burn s.o. in ~*** quemar la efigie de alguien
ef•flu•ent ['efluənt] aguas *fpl* residuales
ef•fort ['efərt] (*struggle, attempt*) esfuerzo *m*; ***make an ~*** hacer un esfuerzo, esforzarse; ***make every ~ to do sth*** hacer todo lo posible por hacer algo; ***it was quite an ~*** costó mucho; ***it was well worth the ~*** mereció la pena hacer el esfuerzo
ef•fort•less ['efərtlɪs] *adj* fácil
ef•fort•less•ly ['efərtlɪslɪ] *adv* fácilmente, sin esfuerzo
ef•fron•te•ry [ɪ'frʌntərɪ] desvergüenza *f*
ef•fu•sive [ɪ'fjuːsɪv] *adj* efusivo
EFL [iːef'el] *abbr* (= ***English as a Foreign Language***) inglés *m* para extranjeros
EFTPOS ['eftpɑːs] *abbr* (= ***Electronic Funds Transfer at Point of Sale***) T.P.V. *f* (= transferencia *f* de fondos electrónica en el punto de venta)
e.g. [iː'dʒiː] p. ej.
e•gal•i•tar•i•an [ɪgælɪ'terɪən] *adj* igualitario
egg [eg] huevo *m*; *of woman* óvulo *m*; ***get ~ on one's face*** F quedar en ridículo; ***he had ~ all over his face*** *fig* quedó en ridículo
◆ **egg on** *v/t* incitar
'**egg•cup** huevera *f*; '**egg•head** F cerebrito(-a) *m(f)* F; '**egg•plant** berenjena *f*, '**egg•shell** cáscara *f* de huevo; '**egg tim•er** reloj *m* de arena; '**egg whisk** batidor *m* de huevos; '**egg white** clara *f* de huevo; '**egg yolk** yema *f* de huevo
e•go ['iːgoʊ] PSYCH ego *m*; (*self-esteem*) amor *m* propio; ***she's all ~*** tiene mucho ego *or* amor propio; ***boost s.o.'s ~, give s.o. an ~ boost*** alimentar el ego de alguien
e•go•cen•tric [iːgoʊ'sentrɪk] *adj* egocéntrico
e•go•ism ['iːgoʊɪzm] egoísmo *m*
e•go•ist ['iːgoʊɪst] egoísta *m/f*
e•go•is•tic [iːgoʊ'ɪstɪk] *adj* egoísta
e•go•tism ['iːgoʊtɪzəm] egoísmo *m*, egocentrismo *m*
e•go•tist ['iːgoʊtɪst] egocéntrico(-a) *m(f)*
e•go•tis•tic [iːgoʊ'tɪstɪk] *adj* egocéntrico
'**e•go trip**: ***be on an ~*** creerse el centro del universo; ***charity work is just a big ~ for him*** participa en obras benéficas sólo para sentirse superior
E•gypt ['iːdʒɪpt] Egipto *m*
E•gyp•tian [ɪ'dʒɪpʃn] **I** *adj* egipcio **II** *n* egipcio(-a) *m(f)*
ei•der•down ['aɪdərdaʊn] *quilt* edredón *m*
eight [eɪt] ocho
eigh•teen [eɪ'tiːn] dieciocho
eigh•teenth [eɪ'tiːnθ] *n & adj* decimoctavo
eighteen-'yard box *in soccer* área *f* grande
eighth [eɪtθ] *n & adj* octavo
eigh•ti•eth ['eɪtɪɪθ] *n & adj* octogésimo
eigh•ty ['eɪtɪ] ochenta; ***be in one's eighties*** tener ochenta y tantos; ***in the eighties*** en los (años) ochenta
Eir•e ['erə] República *f* de Irlanda
ei•ther ['aɪðər] **I** *adj* cualquiera de los dos; *with negative constructions* ninguno de los dos; (*both*) cada, ambos
II *pron* cualquiera de los dos; *with negative constructions* ninguno de los dos ***he wouldn't accept ~ of the proposals*** no quería aceptar ninguna de las dos propuestas
III *adv* tampoco; ***I won't go ~*** yo tampoco iré
IV *conj*: ***~ ... or*** *choice* o ... or; *with negative constructions* ni ... ni
e•jac•u•late [ɪ'dʒækjʊleɪt] *v/i* PHYSIO eyacular
e•jac•u•la•tion [ɪdʒækjʊ'leɪʃn] **1** PHYSIO eyaculación *f* **2** *exclamation* exclamación *f*
e•ject [ɪ'dʒekt] **I** *v/t* expulsar **II** *v/i from plane* eyectarse
e•jec•tor seat [ɪ'dʒektər] AVIA asiento

m de eyección

◆ **eke out** [iːk] *v/t* **1** (*make last*) hacer durar **2**: ***eke out a living*** ganarse la vida a duras penas

e•lab•o•rate I *adj* [ɪ'læbərət] elaborado **II** *v/t* [ɪ'læbəreɪt] elaborar **III** *v/i* [ɪ'læbəreɪt] dar detalles

◆ **elaborate on** *v/t* ampliar, explicar en detalle

e•lab•o•rate•ly [ɪ'læbəreɪtlɪ] *adv* elaboradamente

e•lapse [ɪ'læps] *v/i* pasar

e•las•tic [ɪ'læstɪk] **I** *adj* elástico; ~ ***band*** goma *f* elástica **II** *n* elástico *m*

e•las•ti•ca•ted [ɪ'læstɪkeɪtɪd] *adj* elástico

e•las•ti•ci•ty [ɪlæs'tɪsətɪ] elasticidad *f*

e•las•ti•cized [ɪ'læstɪsaɪzd] *adj* elástico

e•lat•ed [ɪ'leɪtɪd] *adj* eufórico

el•at•ion [ɪ'leɪʃn] euforia *f*

el•bow ['elbou] **I** *n* codo *m* **II** *v/t* dar un codazo a; ~ ***out of the way*** apartar a codazos; ~ ***one's way through the crowd*** abrirse paso a codazos entre la multitud

'el•bow grease F trabajo *m* duro F

'el•bow•room F espacio *m*, sitio *m* para moverse

el•der[1] ['eldər] **I** *adj* mayor **II** *n* mayor *m/f*; ***she's two years my*** ~ es dos años mayor que yo

el•der[2] ['eldər] *n* BOT saúco *m*

el•der•ly ['eldərlɪ] **I** *adj* mayor **II** *npl*: ***the*** ~ las personas mayores

el•dest ['eldəst] **I** *adj* mayor **II** *n*: ***the*** ~ el/la mayor

e•lect [ɪ'lekt] *v/t* elegir; ~ ***to do sth*** decidir hacer algo

e•lect•ed [ɪ'lektɪd] *adj* elegido

e•lec•tion [ɪ'lekʃn] elección *f*; ***call an*** ~ convocar elecciones; ~ ***promises*** promesas *fpl* electorales; ~ ***results*** resultados *mpl* electorales

e'lec•tion cam•paign campaña *f* electoral

e'lec•tion day día *m* de las elecciones

e•lec•tion•eer [ɪlekʃə'nɪər] *v/i* hacer campaña (electoral)

e•lec•tion•eer•ing [ɪlekʃə'nɪərɪŋ] campaña *f* electoral; ***that's just*** ~ eso es sólo hacer campaña electoral

e•lec•tive [ɪ'lektɪv] *adj* opcional; *subject*, *surgery* optativo

e•lec•tor [ɪ'lektər] elector(a) *m(f)*, votante *m/f*

e•lec•tor•al [ɪ'lektərəl] *adj* electoral

e•lec•tor•al 'col•lege colegio *m* electoral

e•lec•to•rate [ɪ'lektərət] electorado *m*

e•lec•tric [ɪ'lektrɪk] *adj* eléctrico; *fig atmosphere* electrizado

e•lec•tri•cal [ɪ'lektrɪkl] *adj* eléctrico

e•lec•tri•cal en•gi'neer ingeniero(-a) *m(f)* electrónico(-a)

e•lec•tri•cal en•gi'neer•ing ingeniería *f* electrónica

e•lec•tric 'blan•ket manta *f or L.Am.* cobija *f* eléctrica; **e•lec•tric 'chair** silla *f* eléctrica; **e•lec•tric gui'tar** guitarra *f* eléctrica

e•lec•tri•cian [ɪlek'trɪʃn] electricista *m/f*

e•lec•tri•ci•ty [ɪlek'trɪsətɪ] electricidad *f*

e•lec•tric 'ra•zor maquinilla *f* eléctrica

e•lec•trics [ɪ'lektrɪks]] *npl* MOT electricidad *f*

e•lec•tric 'shock descarga *f* eléctrica; ~ ***treatment*** MED tratamiento *m* por electrochoque

e•lec•tri•fy [ɪ'lektrɪfaɪ] *v/t* (*pret & pp* ***-ied***) electrificar; *fig* electrizar

e•lec•tri•fy•ing [ɪ'lektrɪfaɪɪŋ] *adj fig* electrizante

e•lec•tro•car•di•o•gram [ɪlektrou'kɑːrdɪougræm] MED electrocardiograma *m*

e•lec•tro•cute [ɪ'lektrəkjuːt] *v/t* electrocutar

e•lec•tro•cu•tion [ɪlektrə'kjuːʃn] *form of execution* electrocución *f*

e•lec•trode [ɪ'lektroud] electrodo *m*

e•lec•tro•lyte [ɪ'lektrəlaɪt] electrolito *m*

e•lec•tro•mag•net•ic [ɪlektroumæg'netɪk] *adj* electromagnético

e•lec•tron [ɪ'lektrɑːn] electrón *m*; ~ ***microscope*** microscopio *m* electrónico; ~ ***beam*** haz *m* de electrones

e•lec•tron•ic [ɪlek'trɑːnɪk] *adj* electrónico; ~ ***banking*** banca *f* electrónica *or* informatizada

e•lec•tron•ic da•ta 'pro•ces•sing procesamiento *m* electrónico de datos; **e•lec•tron•ic 'funds trans•fer** transferencia *f* electrónica de fondos; **e•lec•tron•ic 'mail** correo *m* electrónico; **e•lec•tron•ic 'mail•box** buzón *m* electrónico; **e•lec•tron•ic 'me•di•a** medios *mpl* de comunicación electrónicos; **e•lec•tron•ic 'pay•ment** pago *m* electrónico

e•lec•tron•ics [ɪlek'trɑːnɪks] **1** *nsg*: *subject* electrónica *f* **2** *npl*: ***the advanced ~ of the new car are …*** los modernos componentes electrónicos del coche nuevo son …

e•lec'tron•ics en•gi•neer ingeniero(-a) *m*(*f*) electrónico(-a)

e•lec•tron•ic 'trans•fer FIN transferencia *f* electrónica

e•lec•tro•ther•a•py [ɪlektroʊ'θerəpɪ] MED electroterapia *f*

el•e•gance ['elɪgəns] elegancia *f*

el•e•gant ['elɪgənt] *adj* elegante

el•e•gant•ly ['elɪgəntlɪ] *adv* elegantemente

el•e•ment ['elɪmənt] *also* CHEM elemento *m*; ***an ~ of uncertainty*** algo de inseguridad; ***~ of surprise*** factor *m* sorpresa; ***~ of risk*** factor de riesgo; ***be in one's ~*** estar en su elemento, estar como pez en el agua F; ***be out of one's ~*** estar fuera de su elemento

el•e•men•ta•ry [elɪ'mentərɪ] *adj* (*rudimentary*) elemental

el•e'men•ta•ry school escuela *f* primaria

el•e'men•ta•ry teacher maestro(-a) *m*(*f*)

el•e•phant ['elɪfənt] elefante *m*

el•e•vate ['elɪveɪt] *v/t* elevar

el•e•vat•ed rail•road [elɪveɪtɪd'reɪlroʊd] ferrocarril *m* elevado

el•e•va•tion [elɪ'veɪʃn] (*altitude*) altura *f*

el•e•va•tor ['elɪveɪtər] ascensor *m*; ***~ shaft*** hueco *m* del ascensor

el•e•ven [ɪ'levn] once

el•e•venth [ɪ'levnθ] *n & adj* undécimo; ***at the ~ hour*** justo en el último minuto

elf [elf] (*pl* ***elves*** [elvz]) duende *m*, elfo *m*

e•lic•it [ɪ'lɪsɪt] *v/t* **1** *truth* obtener (***from*** de) **2** *reaction*, *applause* suscitar, provocar (***from*** de)

el•i•gi•bil•i•ty [elɪdʒə'bɪlətɪ] *of candidate etc* elegibilidad *f*; ***there are doubts about their ~ to vote*** existen dudas acerca de que tengan derecho para votar

el•i•gi•ble ['elɪdʒəbl] *adj* que reúne los requisitos; ***be ~ to vote*** tener derecho al voto; ***be ~ to do sth*** tener derecho a hacer algo

el•i•gi•ble 'bach•e•lor buen partido *m*

e•lim•i•nate [ɪ'lɪmɪneɪt] *v/t* **1** eliminar; *poverty* acabar con **2** (*rule out*) descartar

e•lim•i•na•tion [ɪ'lɪmɪneɪʃn] eliminación *f*; ***by a process of ~*** por (un proceso de) eliminación

e•lite [eɪ'liːt] **I** *n* élite *f* **II** *adj* de élite

e•lit•ism [eɪ'liːtɪzəm] elitismo *m*

e•lit•ist [eɪ'liːtɪst] *adj* elitista

elk [elk] ciervo *m* canadiense

el•lipse [ɪ'lɪps] elipse *f*

elm [elm] olmo *m*

el•o•cu•tion [elə'kjuːʃn] dicción *f*, elocución *f*

e•lon•gate ['iːlɑːŋgeɪt] *v/t* alargar

e•lope [ɪ'loʊp] *v/i* fugarse con un amante

el•o•quence ['eləkwəns] elocuencia *f*

el•o•quent ['eləkwənt] *adj* elocuente

el•o•quent•ly ['eləkwəntlɪ] *adv* elocuentemente; ***very ~ put*** dicho de manera elocuente

El Sal•va•dor [el'sælvədɔːr] El Salvador *m*

else [els] *adv*: ***anything ~?*** ¿algo más?; ***if you have nothing ~ to do*** si no tienes nada más que hacer; ***no one ~*** nadie más; ***everyone ~ is going*** todos (los demás) van, va todo el mundo; ***who ~ was there?*** ¿quién más estaba allí?; ***someone ~*** otra persona; ***something ~*** algo más; ***let's go somewhere ~*** vamos a otro sitio; ***or ~*** si no

else•where ['elswer] *adv* en otro sitio

ELT [iːel'tiː] *abbr* (= ***English Language Teaching***) enseñanza *f* de inglés

e•lu•ci•date [ɪ'luːsɪdeɪt] *v/t* aclarar, esclarecer

e•lude [ɪ'luːd] *v/t* (*escape from*) escapar de; (*avoid*) evitar; ***the name ~s me*** no recuerdo el nombre

e•lu•sive [ɪ'luːsɪv] *adj* evasivo

elves [elvz] *pl* ☞ ***elf***

el [el] ☞ ***elevated railroad***

e•ma•ci•at•ed [ɪ'meɪsɪeɪtɪd] *adj* demacrado

e-mail ['iːmeɪl] **I** *n* correo *m* electrónico, e-mail *m* **II** *v/t person* mandar un correo electrónico a; ***~ sth to s.o.*** mandar algo por e-mail a alguien

'e-mail ad•dress dirección *f* de correo electrónico *or* de e-mail

em•a•nate ['emənet] *v/i of gas, light* emanar (***from*** de); *of reports, rumors* proceder, provenir (***from*** de)
e•man•ci•pat•ed [ɪ'mænsɪpeɪtɪd] *adj* emancipado
e•man•ci•pa•tion [ɪmænsɪ'peɪʃn] emancipación *f*
em•balm [ɪm'bɑːm] *v/t* embalsamar
em•bank•ment [ɪm'bæŋkmənt] **1** *of river* dique *m* **2** RAIL terraplén *m*
em•bar•go [em'bɑːrgoʊ] (*pl* ***-oes***) embargo *m*; ***place*** *or* ***put an ~ on sth*** imponer un embargo sobre algo
em•bar•ka•tion [embɑːr'keɪʃn] embarque *m*
em•bark [ɪm'bɑːrk] *v/i* embarcar
◆ **embark on** *v/t* embarcarse en
em•bar•rass [ɪm'bærəs] *v/t* avergonzar; ***he ~ed me in front of everyone*** me hizo pasar vergüenza delante de todos
em•bar•rassed [ɪm'bærəst] *adj* avergonzado; ***I was ~ to ask*** me daba vergüenza preguntar; ***don't be ~*** no te avergüences
em•bar•rass•ing [ɪm'bærəsɪŋ] *adj* embarazoso
em•bar•rass•ment [ɪm'bærəsmənt] embarazo *m*, apuro *m*; ***much to our ~*** para vergüenza nuestra; ***be an ~ to s.o.*** ser un motivo de vergüenza para alguien
em•bas•sy ['embəsɪ] embajada *f*; ***~ staff*** personal *m* de la embajada
em•bed [ɪm'bed] *v/t* (*pret & pp* ***-ded***) insertar, incrustar; *in mind* fijar, grabar; ***~ded in*** *concrete* incrustado en
em•bed•ded com•mand [ɪm'bedɪd] COMPUT comando *m* integrado
em•bel•lish [ɪm'belɪʃ] *v/t* adornar; *story* exagerar
em•bel•lish•ment [ɪm'belɪʃmənt] *also of story* adorno *m*
em•bers ['embərz] *npl* ascuas *fpl*
em•bez•zle [ɪm'bezl] *v/t* malversar
em•bez•zle•ment [ɪm'bezlmənt] malversación *f*
em•bez•zler [ɪm'bezlər] malversador(a) *m(f)*
em•bit•ter [ɪm'bɪtər] *v/t* amargar
em•blem ['embləm] emblema *m*
em•bod•i•ment [ɪm'bɑːdɪmənt] personificación *f*
em•bod•y [ɪm'bɑːdɪ] *v/t* (*pret & pp* ***-ied***) personificar
em•bo•lism ['embəlɪzm] embolia *f*
em•boss [ɪm'bɑːs] *v/t metal* repujar; *paper* grabar en relieve; ***~ed paper*** papel *m* gofrado; *wallpaper* papel *m* estampado en relieve
em•brace [ɪm'breɪs] **I** *n* abrazo *m* **II** *v/t* **1** (*hug*) abrazar **2** (*take in*) abarcar **III** *v/i of two people* abrazarse
em•broi•der [ɪm'brɔɪdər] *v/t* bordar; *fig* adornar
em•broi•der•y [ɪm'brɔɪdərɪ] bordado *m*; ***~ needle*** aguja *f* de bordar; ***do ~*** bordar
em•broil [ɪm'brɔɪl] *v/t*: ***be ~ed in sth*** estar envuelto *or* mezclado en algo
em•bry•o ['embrɪoʊ] embrión *m*; ***in ~*** en embrión
em•bry•on•ic [embrɪ'ɑːnɪk] *adj fig* embrionario
em•cee [em'siː] F **I** *n of show* presentador(a) *m(f)* **II** *v/t* presentar
em•e•rald ['emərəld] esmeralda *f*
e•merge [ɪ'mɜːrdʒ] *v/i* (*appear*) emerger, salir; *of truth* aflorar; ***it has ~d that*** se ha descubierto que; ***what ~s from this is that …*** lo que se desprende de esto es que…
e•mer•gence [ɪ'mɜːrdʒəns] *of truth, new state etc* aparición *f*, surgimiento *m*
e•mer•gen•cy [ɪ'mɜːrdʒənsɪ] emergencia *f*; ***in an ~*** en caso de emergencia; ***declare a state of ~*** declarar el estado de emergencia *or* excepción
e'mer•gen•cy call TELEC llamada *f* de emergencia; **e•mer•gen•cy 'ex•it** salida *f* de emergencia; **e'mer•gen•cy land•ing** aterrizaje *m* forzoso; ***make an ~*** hacer un aterrizaje forzoso; **e'mer•gen•cy light•ing** luz *f* de emergencia; **e•mer•gen•cy 'meet•ing** reunión *f* de emergencia; **e•mer•gen•cy 'num•ber** TELEC número *m* de emergencia; **e•mer•gen•cy op•er'a•tion** MED operación *f* de urgencia; **e•mer•gen•cy 'ra•tions** raciones *fpl* de reserva; **e'mer•gen•cy serv•i•ces** *npl* servicios *mpl* de urgencia; **e•mer•gen•cy 'stop** MOT parada *f* de emergencia; ***make*** *or* ***do an ~*** hacer una parada de emergencia; **e'mer•gen•cy tel•e•phone** teléfono *m* de emergencia
e•mer•gent [iː'mɜːrdʒənt] *adj fig nation* emergente, en vías de desarrollo
em•er•y board ['emərɪ] lima *f* de uñas

e•met•ic [ɪ'metɪk] emético *m*, vomitivo *m*
em•i•grant ['emɪgrənt] emigrante *m/f*
em•i•grate ['emɪgreɪt] *v/i* emigrar
em•i•gra•tion [emɪ'greɪʃn] emigración *f*
Em•i•nence ['emɪnəns] REL: ***His ~*** Su Eminencia
em•i•nent ['emɪnənt] *adj* eminente
em•i•nent•ly ['emɪnəntlɪ] *adv* sumamente
e•mis•sion [ɪ'mɪʃn] *of gases* emisión *f*
e•mis•sion-'free *adj* MOT que no emite gases contaminantes
e'mis•sion lim•it MOT límite *m* de emisiones
e•mit [ɪ'mɪt] *v/t* (*pret & pp* ***-ted***) emitir; *heat, odor* desprender
e•mo•tion [ɪ'moʊʃn] emoción *f*
e•mo•tion•al [ɪ'moʊʃənl] *adj* **1** *problems, development* sentimental **2** (*full of emotion*) emotivo; ***no need to get so ~ about it*** *start crying* no hay que ponerse tan sentimental; ***tired and ~*** *hum* alegre
e•mo•tion•al•ly [ɪ'moʊʃənlɪ] *adv* **1** emotivamente **2**: ***be ~ disturbed*** tener trastornos emocionales
e•mo•tive [ɪ'moʊtɪv] *adj* emotivo; ***~ term*** *or* ***word*** palabra *f* afectiva
em•pa•thize ['empəθaɪz] *v/i*: ***~ with*** identificarse con
em•pa•thy ['empəθɪ] empatía *f*
em•pe•ror ['empərər] emperador *m*
em•pha•sis ['emfəsɪs] *in word* acento *m*; *fig* énfasis *m*; ***place*** *or* ***put the ~ on sth*** poner énfasis *or* hacer hincapié en algo; ***with ~*** con énfasis
em•pha•size ['emfəsaɪz] *v/t syllable* acentuar; *fig* hacer hincapié en
em•phat•ic [ɪm'fætɪk] *adj* enfático; ***the response was an ~ no*** la respuesta fue un 'no' rotundo
em•phy•se•ma [emfɪ'siːmə] MED enfisema *m*
em•pire ['empaɪr] *also fig* imperio *m*
em•pir•i•cal [em'pɪrɪkl] *adj* empírico
em•ploy [ɪm'plɔɪ] *v/t* emplear; ***he's ~ed as a ...*** trabaja de ...
em•ploy•ee [emplɔɪ'iː] empleado(-a) *m(f)*
em•ploy•ee 'buy•out adquisición *f* de una empresa por los empleados
em•ploy•ee con•tri'bu•tions aportaciones *fpl or* cotizaciones *fpl* de los empleados
em•ploy•er [em'plɔɪər] empresario(-a) *m(f)*
em•ploy•er con•tri'bu•tions cuotas *fpl* patronales
em•ploy•er's li•a'bil•i•ty responsabilidad *f* patronal
em•ploy•ment [em'plɔɪmənt] empleo *m*; (*work*) trabajo *m*; ***be looking for ~*** buscar trabajo; ***be in ~*** tener empleo *or* trabajo; ***full ~*** pleno empleo; ***~ market*** mercado *m* laboral
em'ploy•ment a•gen•cy agencia *f* de colocaciones; **em'ploy•ment law** legislación *f* laboral; **em'ploy•ment tax** impuesto *m* sobre el empleo
em•pow•er [ɪm'paʊər] *v/t* **1** facultar, otorgar poderes a; ***~ s.o. to do sth*** autorizar a alguien para hacer algo **2** *the people, the user* dar poder a
em•press ['emprɪs] emperatriz *f*
emp•ti•ness ['emptɪnɪs] vacío *m*
emp•ty ['emptɪ] **I** *adj* **1** vacío **2** *promise, threat* vano; ***feel ~*** sentirse vacío **II** *v/t* (*pret & pp* ***-ied***) *drawer, pockets* vaciar; *glass, bottle* acabar; ***~ sth into sth*** vaciar algo en algo **III** *v/i* (*pret & pp* ***-ied***) *of room, street* vaciarse
◆ **empty out** *v/t drawers, closet* vaciar
emp•ty-hand•ed [emptɪ'hændɪd] *adj* con las manos vacías; ***return ~*** volver con las manos vacías
emp•ty-'head•ed *adj*: ***be ~*** ser un cabeza hueca
'emp•ty weight COM peso *m* en vacío
em•u•late ['emjʊleɪt] *v/t* emular
e•mul•sion [ɪ'mʌlʃn] *paint* emulsión *f*
en•a•ble [ɪ'neɪbl] *v/t* permitir; ***~ s.o. to do sth*** permitir a alguien hacer algo
en•act [ɪ'nækt] *v/t* **1** *law* promulgar **2** THEA representar
en•act•ment [ɪ'næktmənt] *of law* promulgación *f*
e•nam•el [ɪ'næml] esmalte *m*
en•am•or, *Br* **en•am•our** [ɪ'næmər] *v/t*: ***be ~ed of*** *idea etc* estar entusiasmado con
enc *abbr* (= ***enclosure(s)***) documento(s) *m(pl)* adjunto(s)
en•case [ɪn'keɪs] *v/t*: ***~d in*** revestido *or* recubierto de
en•chant•ed [ɪn'tʃɑːntɪd] *adj* **1** *forest etc* encantado **2**: ***be ~ed with sth*** quedar *or* estar encantado con algo

E

en•chant•ing [ɪnˈtʃæntɪŋ] *adj* encantador
en•cir•cle [ɪnˈsɜːrkl] *v/t* rodear
en•cir•cle•ment [ɪnˈsɜːrklmənt] MIL acorralamiento *m*
encl *abbr* (= ***enclosure(s)***) documento(s) *m(pl)* adjunto(s)
en•close [ɪnˈklouz] *v/t* **1** *in letter* adjuntar; ***please find ~d …*** remito adjunto … **2** *area* rodear
en•clo•sure [ɪnˈklouʒər] *with letter* documento *m* adjunto
en•code [ɪnˈkoud] *v/t text* codificar, cifrar
en•com•pass [ɪnˈkʌmpəs] *v/t fig fml* **1** (*include*) abarcar **2** (*surround*) rodear, cercar **3** (*bring about*) ocasionar
en•core [ˈɑːŋkɔːr] **I** *n* bis *m* **II** *int* ¡otra!
en•coun•ter [ɪnˈkauntər] **I** *n* encuentro *m* **II** *v/t person* encontrarse con; *problem*, *resistance* tropezar con
en•cour•age [ɪnˈkʌrɪdʒ] *v/t* animar; *violence* fomentar
en•cour•age•ment [ɪnˈkʌrɪdʒmənt] ánimo *m*; ***a few words of ~*** unas palabras de ánimo *or* aliento
en•cour•ag•ing [ɪnˈkʌrɪdʒɪŋ] *adj* alentador; ***that's ~*** eso es alentador, eso me da ánimos; ***it's ~ to see that …*** es alentador ver que …
◆ **en•croach on** [ɪnˈkroutʃ] *v/t land* invadir; *rights* usurpar; *time* quitar
en•crust•ed [ɪnˈkrʌstɪd] *adj*: ***~ with*** incrustado de
en•crypt [ɪnˈkrɪpt] *v/t* encriptar, codificar
en•cryp•tion [ɪnˈkrɪpʃn] encriptación *f*, codificación *f*
en•cy•clo•pe•di•a [ɪnsaɪkləˈpiːdɪə] enciclopedia *f*
en•cy•clo•pe•dic [ɪnsaɪkləˈpiːdɪk] *adj* enciclopédico
end [end] **I** *n* **1** (*conclusion*) fin *m*; *of journey*, *month* final *m*; ***come or draw to an ~*** acabar, llegar a su fin; ***it's not the ~ of the world!*** ¡no es el fin del mundo!, ¡no pasa nada!; ***in the ~*** al final; ***at the ~ of July*** a finales de julio; ***put an ~ to*** poner fin a
2 (*extremity*) extremo *m*; ***at the other ~ of town*** al otro lado de la ciudad; ***stand sth on ~*** poner de pie algo; ***make (both) ~s meet*** *fig* llegar a fin de mes; ***placed ~ to ~*** colocado uno tras otro; ***change ~s*** SP cambiar de lado; ***push it right up to the ~*** empújalo hasta el fondo
3 (*purpose*): ***the ~ justifies the means*** el fin justifica los medios; ***to this ~*** con *or* para este fin **4**: ***for hours on ~*** durante horas y horas; ***for three weeks on ~*** durante tres semanas seguidas
II *v/t* terminar, finalizar; ***the war to ~ all wars*** la guerra de las guerras
III *v/i* terminar; ***how does it ~?*** ¿cómo acaba?, ¿cuál es el final?; ***~ happily*** acabar bien; ***~ in disaster*** acabar mal; ***all's well that ~s well*** bien está lo que bien acaba
◆ **end up** *v/i* acabar; ***we ended up agreeing to it after all*** al final acabamos consintiéndolo
en•dan•ger [ɪnˈdeɪndʒər] *v/t* poner en peligro
en•dan•gered spe•cies [ɪnˈdeɪndʒərd] especie *f* en peligro de extinción
en•dear•ing [ɪnˈdɪrɪŋ] *adj* simpático
en•dear•ment [ɪnˈdɪrmənt]: ***term of ~*** palabra *f* cariñosa
en•deav•or, *Br* **en•deav•our** [ɪnˈdevər] **I** *n* esfuerzo *m*; ***make every ~ to do sth*** procurar por todos los medios hacer algo **II** *v/t*: ***~to do sth*** procurar hacer algo
en•dem•ic [ɪnˈdemɪk] *adj* endémico
end•ing [ˈendɪŋ] **1** final *m* **2** GRAM terminación *f*
en•dive [ˈendaɪv] BOT endibia *f*
end•less [ˈendlɪs] *adj* interminable
end•less ˈloop bucle *m* sin fin
ˈend line *in basketball* línea *f* de fondo
end-of-year ˈbo•nus paga *f* extra de fin de año
en•dorse [ɪnˈdɔːrs] *v/t* **1** *check* endosar **2** *candidacy* apoyar; *product* representar
en•dors•ee [ɪndɔːrˈsiː] FIN endosatario(-a) *m(f)*
en•dorse•ment [ɪnˈdɔːrsmənt] **1** *of check* endoso *m* **2** *of candidacy* apoyo *m*; *of product* representación *f*
en•dors•er [ɪnˈdɔːrsər] FIN endosante *m/f*
en•dow [ɪnˈdau] *v/t* **1** *financially* donar **2** *fig* (*equip*) dotar; ***be ~ed with …*** estar dotado de …; ***be well ~ed*** *hum* estar muy bien dotado P
en•dow•ment [ɪnˈdaumənt] **1** *financial* dotación *f* **2** *gift endowed* donación *f* **3** *talent* dote *f*, atributo *m*; ***because***

of his superior physical ~ gracias a sus dotes físicas superiores
en'dow•ment mort•gage hipoteca *f* de inversión
end 'prod•uct producto *m* final
end re'sult resultado *m* final
en•dur•a•ble [ɪn'dʊrəbl] *adj* tolerable, soportable
en•dur•ance [ɪn'dʊrəns] resistencia *f*; ***be beyond ~*** ser insoportable; ***~ test*** prueba *f* de resistencia
en•dure [ɪn'dʊər] **I** *v/t* resistir **II** *v/i* (*last*) durar
en•dur•ing [ɪn'dʊrɪŋ] *adj* duradero
end-'us•er usuario(-a) *m(f)* final
en•e•ma ['enəmə] MED enema *m*
en•e•my ['enəmɪ] enemigo(-a) *m(f)*; ***make an ~ of s.o.*** enemistarse con alguien; ***with friends like that, who needs enemies!*** F ¡con amigos así, uno ya no necesita enemigos!F
en•er•get•ic [enər'dʒetɪk] *adj* enérgico
en•er•get•ic•al•ly [enər'dʒetɪklɪ] *adv* enérgicamente
en•er•gy ['enərdʒɪ] energía *f*
en•er•gy 'cri•sis crisis *f* energética; **'en•er•gy-ef•fi•cient** *adj* que hace buen uso energético; **'en•er•gy-sav•ing** *adj device* que ahorra energía; **'en•er•gy sup•ply** suministro *m* de energía
en•force [ɪn'fɔːrs] *v/t* hacer cumplir
en•force•ment [ɪn'fɔːrsmənt] *of law* aplicación *f*
en'force•ment a•gen•cy organismo *m* de seguridad del estado
en•gage [ɪn'geɪdʒ] **I** *v/t* (*hire*) contratar **II** *v/i* TECH engranar
◆ **engage in** *v/t* dedicarse a
en•gaged [ɪn'geɪdʒd] *adj* **1** *to be married* prometido; ***get ~*** prometerse **2**: ***be ~ in doing sth*** *fml* estar ocupado haciendo algo **3** *Br* TELEC ocupado
en•gage•ment [ɪn'geɪdʒmənt] (*appointment, to be married*) compromiso *m*; MIL combate *m*; ***have a prior ~*** tener un compromiso previo
en'gage•ment ring anillo *m* de compromiso
en•gag•ing [ɪn'geɪdʒɪŋ] *adj smile, person* atractivo
en•gen•der [ɪn'dʒendər] *v/t hate, envy, emotions etc* engendrar, suscitar
en•gine ['endʒɪn] motor *m*
'en•gine block bloque *m* del motor; **en•gine 'brak•ing** MOT frenado *m* con el motor; **'en•gine com•part•ment** compartimento *m* del motor; **'en•gine driv•er** *Br* RAIL maquinista *m/f*
en•gi•neer [endʒɪ'nɪr] **I** *n* ingeniero(-a) *m(f)*; NAUT, RAIL maquinista *m/f* **II** *v/t fig*: *meeting etc* tramar
en•gi•neer•ing [endʒɪ'nɪrɪŋ] ingeniería *f*
'en•gine im•mo•bi•liz•er MOT inmovilizador *m*
'en•gine oil *for engine* aceite *m* para motor; *in engine* aceite *m* del motor
En•gland ['ɪŋglənd] Inglaterra *f*
En•glish ['ɪŋglɪʃ] **I** *adj* inglés(-esa) **II** *n* **1** *pl*: ***the ~*** los ingleses **2** *language* inglés *m*; ***in ~*** en inglés; ***in plain ~*** en el habla corriente
Eng•lish 'Chan•nel Canal *m* de la Mancha; **En•glish•man** ['ɪŋglɪʃmən] inglés *m*; **'En•glish•wom•an** inglesa *f*
en•grave [ɪn'greɪv] *v/t* grabar; ***it is ~d on his memory*** está grabado en su memoria
en•grav•ing [ɪn'greɪvɪŋ] grabado *m*
en•grossed [ɪn'groʊst] *adj* absorto (***in*** en)
en•gros•sing [ɪn'groʊsɪŋ] *adj* absorbente, fascinante
en•gulf [ɪn'gʌlf] *v/t* devorar
en•hance [ɪn'hæns] *v/t* realzar
e•nig•ma [ɪ'nɪgmə] enigma *m*
e•nig•mat•ic [enɪg'mætɪk] *adj* enigmático
en•joy [ɪn'dʒɔɪ] *v/t* disfrutar (de); ***~ o.s.*** divertirse; ***~ (your meal)!*** ¡que aproveche!; ***~ doing sth*** gustar hacer algo, disfrutar haciendo algo; ***I don't ~ doing this, you know*** no me gusta hacer ésto, sabes; ***I ~ dancing*** me gusta bailar; ***did you ~ the play?*** ¿te gustó la obra?; ***~ yourself!*** ¡que lo pases bien!; ***~ good health*** disfrutar *or* gozar de buena salud
en•joy•a•ble [ɪn'dʒɔɪəbl] *adj* agradable
en•joy•ment [ɪn'dʒɔɪmənt] diversión *f*; ***I don't get any ~ out of it*** no disfruto con ello
en•large [ɪn'lɑːrdʒ] *v/t* ampliar
en•large•ment [ɪn'lɑːrdʒmənt] ampliación *f*
en•light•en [ɪn'laɪtn] *v/t* educar
en•list [ɪn'lɪst] **I** *v/i* MIL alistarse **II** *v/t*: ***I ~ed his help*** conseguí que me ayudara

E

en•liv•en [ɪn'laɪvn] *v/t* animar
en•mi•ty ['enmətɪ] enemistad *f*
e•nor•mi•ty [ɪ'nɔːrmətɪ] magnitud *f*
e•nor•mous [ɪ'nɔːrməs] *adj* enorme; *satisfaction, patience* inmenso
e•nor•mous•ly [ɪ'nɔːrməslɪ] *adv* enormemente
e•nough [ɪ'nʌf] **I** *adj & pron* suficiente, bastante; ***will $50 be ~?*** ¿llegará con 50 dólares?; ***I've had ~!*** ¡estoy harto!; ***that's ~, calm down!*** ¡ya basta, tranquilízate!; ***I have had ~, thank you*** he tenido suficiente, gracias; ***~ of this foolishness!*** ¡basta de tonterías!; ***there's more than ~ to go around*** hay más que suficiente para todos **II** *adv* suficientemente, bastante; ***the bag isn't big ~*** la bolsa no es lo suficientemente *or* bastante grande; ***strangely ~*** curiosamente; ***would you be good ~ to ...?*** *fml* ¿le importaría…?; ***are you man ~ to admit it?*** ¿eres lo suficientemente hombre para admitirlo?, ¿eres tan hombre como para admitirlo?; ***are you warm ~?*** ¿tienes frío?
en•quire [ɪn'kwaɪr] ☞ ***inquire***
en•quiry [ɪn'kwaɪrɪ] ☞ ***inquiry***
en•raged [ɪn'reɪdʒd] *adj* enfurecido
en•rich [ɪn'rɪtʃ] *v/t* enriquecer
en•roll [ɪn'roʊl] *v/i* matricularse
en•roll•ment [ɪn'roʊlmənt] matrícula *f*
en•sign ['ensaɪn] NAUT **1** *flag* enseña *f* **2** *officer* alférez *m*
en•snare [ɪn'sner] *v/t* **1** atrapar; ***become ~d in*** quedar atrapado en **2** *fig* involucrar; ***become ~d in*** estar involucrado en
en•sue [ɪn'suː] *v/i* sucederse; ***the ensuing years*** los años subsiguientes
en suite ['ɑːnswiːt] **I** *n* habitación *f* con baño incorporado **II** *adj*: ***~ bathroom*** baño *m* incorporado
en•sure [ɪn'ʃʊər] *v/t* asegurar
ENT [iːen'tiː] *abbr* (= ***ear, nose and throat***) otorrinolaringología *f*
en•tail [ɪn'teɪl] *v/t* conllevar
en•tan•gle [ɪn'tæŋgl] *v/t in rope* enredar; ***become ~d in*** enredarse en; ***become ~d with*** *in love affair* liarse con
en•ter ['entər] **I** *v/t* **1** *room, house* entrar en ***it never ~ed my mind that ...*** jamás se me pasó por la cabeza que… **2** *competition* participar en; *person, horse in race* inscribir **3** (*write down*) escribir; COMPUT introducir **II** *v/i* **1** entrar; THEA entrar en escena **2** *in competition* inscribirse **III** *n* COMPUT intro *m*
◆ **enter into** *v/t agreement* llegar a; *discussion* entrar en; ***~ correspondence with*** cartearse con; ***~ negotiations*** entrar en negociaciones
'en•ter key COMPUT intro *m*, tecla *f* enter
en•ter•prise ['entərpraɪz] **1** (*initiative*) iniciativa *f* **2** (*venture*) empresa *f*
en•ter•pris•ing ['entərpraɪzɪŋ] *adj* con iniciativa; ***that's very ~ of you*** eso demuestra mucha iniciativa por tu parte
en•ter•tain [entər'teɪn] **I** *v/t* **1** (*amuse*) entretener **2** (*consider: idea*) considerar **II** *v/i* (*have guests*): ***we ~ a lot*** recibimos a mucha gente
en•ter•tain•er [entər'teɪnər] artista *m/f*
en•ter•tain•ing [entər'teɪnɪŋ] *adj* entretenido
en•ter•tain•ment [entər'teɪnmənt] entretenimiento *m*; ***much to his ~*** para su entretenimiento; ***~ industry*** industria *f* del entretenimiento
en•ter'tain•ment al•low•ance gastos *mpl* de representación
en•thrall [ɪn'θrɒːl] *v/t* cautivar
en•thrall•ing [ɪn'θrɒːlɪŋ] *adj* cautivador, embelesador
en•thuse [ɪn'θuːz] *v/i* entusiasmarse (***about, over*** con, por)
en•thu•si•asm [ɪn'θuːzɪæzm] entusiasmo *m*
en•thu•si•ast [ɪn'θuːzɪæst] entusiasta *m/f*; ***sailing ~*** entusiasta de la navegación
en•thu•si•as•tic [ɪnθuːzɪ'æstɪk] *adj* entusiasta; ***be ~ about sth*** estar entusiasmado con algo
en•thu•si•as•tic•al•ly [ɪnθuːzɪ'æstɪklɪ] *adv* con entusiasmo
en•tice [ɪn'taɪs] *v/t* atraer
◆ **entice away** *v/t*: ***entice s.o. away from sth / s.o.*** convencer a alguien para que deje algo / alguien
en•tice•ment [ɪn'taɪsmənt] incentivo *m*
en•tic•ing [ɪn'taɪsɪŋ] *adj* tentador, apetecible
en•tire [ɪn'taɪr] *adj* entero; ***the ~ school is going*** va a ir todo el colegio
en•tire•ly [ɪn'taɪrlɪ] *adv* completamente; ***that is ~ up to you*** como tú quieras; ***it's***

made ~ of ... es todo de ...; ***I ~ agree with you*** estoy completamente de acuerdo contigo

en•tire•ty [ɪn'taɪrətɪ]: ***in its ~*** en su totalidad

en•ti•tle [ɪn'taɪtl] *v/t*: ***~ s.o. to sth*** dar derecho a alguien a algo; ***be ~d to vote*** tener derecho al voto

en•ti•tled [ɪn'taɪtld] *adj book* titulado

en•ti•ty ['entətɪ] entidad *f*; ***legal ~*** persona *f* jurídica

en•to•mol•o•gist [entə'mɑːlədʒɪst] entomólogo(-a) *m(f)*

en•to•mol•o•gy [entə'mɑːlədʒɪ] entomología *f*

en•tou•rage ['ɑːntuːrɑːʒ] séquito *m*

en•trance[1] ['entrəns] *n* entrada *f*; THEA entrada *f* en escena; ***~ hall*** vestíbulo *m*, hall *m*; ***make one's ~*** THEA entrar en escena; ***make a dramatic ~*** THEA, *fig* hacer una entrada dramática en escena

en•trance[2] [ɪn'træns] *v/t* encantar, hechizar

en•tranced [ɪn'trænst] *adj* encantado

'en•trance ex•am(•i•na•tion) examen *m* de acceso

'en•trance fee (cuota *f* de) entrada *f*

en•trant ['entrənt] participante *m/f*

en•trap•ment [ɪn'træpmənt] *incitación por parte de los agentes de la ley a cometer un delito*

en•treat [ɪn'triːt] *v/t* suplicar; ***~ s.o. to do sth*** suplicar a alguien que haga algo

en•treat•y [ɪn'triːtɪ] súplica *f*, ruego *m*

en•trée ['ɑːntreɪ] (*main dish*) plato *m* principal

en•trenched [ɪn'trentʃt] *adj attitudes* arraigado

en•tre•pre•neur [ɑːntrəprə'nɜːr] empresario(-a) *m(f)*

en•tre•pre•neur•i•al [ɑːntrəprə'nɜːrɪəl] *adj* empresarial

en•tre•pre•neur•ship [ɑːntrəprə'nɜːrʃɪp] espíritu *m* emprendedor *or* empresarial

en•trust [ɪn'trʌst] *v/t* confiar; ***~ s.o. with sth, ~ sth to s.o.*** confiar algo a alguien

en•try ['entrɪ] **1** entrada *f*; ***no ~*** prohibida la entrada; ***gain ~*** *to building* conseguir entrar; ***make a forced ~*** entrar a la fuerza **2** *for competition* inscripción *f*; ***the winning ~ was painted by ...*** el cuadro ganador fue pintado por ... **3** *in diary etc* entrada *f*

'en•try form impreso *m* de inscripción; **'en•try-lev•el** *adj computer* de gama baja; **'en•try•phone** portero *m* automático; **'en•try vi•sa** visado *m*

en•twine [ɪn'twaɪn] *v/t* enroscar, entrelazar (***around*** alrededor de)

e•nu•me•rate [ɪ'nuːməreɪt] *v/t* enumerar

e•nun•ci•ate [ɪ'nʌnsɪeɪt] **I** *v/t* **1** *words* enunciar **2** *reasons* enumerar **II** *v/i speak clearly* vocalizar

en•vel•op [ɪn'veləp] *v/t* cubrir; ***~ed in mystery*** envuelto en misterio

en•ve•lope ['envəloʊp] sobre *m*

en•vi•a•ble ['envɪəbl] *adj* envidiable

en•vi•ous ['envɪəs] *adj* envidioso; ***be ~ of s.o.*** tener envidia de alguien

en•vi•ron•ment [ɪn'vaɪrənmənt] **1** (*nature*) medio *m* ambiente **2** (*surroundings*) entorno *m*, ambiente *m*; ***in an office ~*** en un ambiente de oficina

en•vi•ron•men•tal [ɪnvaɪrən'məntl] *adj* medioambiental; ***~ damage*** daño *m* medioambiental; ***~ impact*** impacto *m* medioambiental

en•vi•ron•men•tal•ist [ɪnvaɪrən'məntəlɪst] ecologista *m/f*

en•vi•ron•men•tal•ly friend•ly [ɪnvaɪrənməntəlɪ'frendlɪ] *adj* ecológico, que no daña el medio ambiente

en•vi•ron•men•tal pol'lu•tion contaminación *f* medioambiental

en•vi•ron•men•tal pro'tec•tion protección *f* medioambiental; ***~ group*** grupo *m* de protección del medio ambiente

en•vi•rons [ɪn'vaɪrənz] *npl* alrededores *mpl*

en•vis•age [ɪn'vɪzɪdʒ] *v/t* imaginar

en•vi•sion [ɪn'vɪʒn] *v/t* imaginar

en•voy ['envɔɪ] enviado(-a) *m(f)*

en•vy ['envɪ] **I** *n* envidia *f*; ***be the ~ of*** ser la envidia de **II** *v/t* (*pret & pp* ***-ied***) envidiar; ***~ s.o. sth*** envidiar a alguien por algo; ***I don't ~ you having to go out in this weather*** no te envidio por tener que salir (a la calle) con este tiempo

en•zyme ['enzaɪm] enzima *f*

e•phem•er•al [ɪ'femərəl] *adj* efímero

ep•ic ['epɪk] **I** *n* epopeya *f* **II** *adj journey* épico; ***a task of ~ proportions*** una tarea monumental

ep•i•cen•ter, *Br* **ep•i•cen•tre** ['epɪ-

sentər] epicentro *m*
ep•i•dem•ic [epɪ'demɪk] **I** *n* epidemia *f* **II** *adj*: ***the problem has reached ~ proportions*** el problema ha alcanzado dimensiones catastróficas
ep•i•du•ral [epɪ'dʊrəl] MED (anestesia *f*) epidural *f*
ep•i•lep•sy ['epɪlepsɪ] epilepsia *f*
ep•i•lep•tic [epɪ'leptɪk] epiléptico(-a) *m*(*f*)
ep•i•lep•tic 'fit ataque *m* epiléptico
ep•i•log, *Br* **ep•i•logue** ['epɪlɑːg] epílogo *m*
E•piph•a•ny [ɪ'pɪfənɪ] REL la Epifanía del Señor
e•pis•co•pal [ɪ'pɪskəpl] *adj* episcopal
ep•i•sode ['epɪsoʊd] *of story, soap opera* episodio *m*, capítulo *m*; (*happening*) episodio *m*; ***let's forget the whole ~*** olvidemos lo sucedido
e•pis•tle [ɪ'pɪsl] REL epístola *f*
ep•i•taph ['epɪtæf] epitafio *m*
ep•i•thet ['epɪθet] *fml* apelativo *m*
e•pit•o•me [ɪ'pɪtəmɪ] paradigma *m*, personificación *f*
e•pit•o•mize [ɪ'pɪtəmaɪz] *v/t* personificar, ser el paradigma de
e•poch ['iːpɑːk] época *f*
'e•poch-mak•ing *adj* que hace época
e•pon•y•mous [ɪ'pɑːnɪməs] *adj* epónimo
e•pox•y res•in [iː'pɑːksɪ] resina *f* epoxídica
eq•ua•ble ['ekwəbəl] *adj temperament, climate* estable, sereno
e•qual ['iːkwl] **I** *adj* igual; ***be ~ to** a task* estar capacitado para; ***~ opportunities*** igualdad *f* de oportunidades; ***be an ~ opportunities employer*** ser una empresa con una política de igualdad de oportunidades; ***~ pay for ~ work*** el mismo salario por el mismo trabajo; ***~ in size, of ~ size*** del mismo tamaño; ***all things being ~*** si no intervienen otros factores; ***be on ~ terms with*** estar en igualdad de condiciones con
II *n* igual *m/f*; ***your ~s*** tus iguales; ***he has no ~, he is without ~*** no tiene igual, no hay quien le iguale
III *v/t* (*pret & pp* **-ed**, *Br* **-led**) **1** (*with numbers*) equivaler; ***four times twelve ~s 48*** cuatro por doce, (igual a) cuarenta y ocho **2** (*be as good as*) igualar
e•qual•i•ty [ɪ'kwɑːlətɪ] igualdad *f*; ***~ of opportunity*** igualdad de oportunidades
e•qual•ize ['iːkwəlaɪz] **I** *v/t* igualar **II** *v/i Br* SP empatar, igualar
e•qual•iz•er ['iːkwəlaɪzər] *Br* SP gol *m* del empate; ***score** or **get the ~*** marcar el gol del empate
e•qual•ly ['iːkwəlɪ] *adv* igualmente; *share, divide* en partes iguales; ***~, you could say that …*** del mismo modo, podría decirse que…
e•qual 'rights *npl* igualdad *f* de derechos
'e•quals sign MATH signo *m* de igual
e•qua•nim•i•ty [ekwə'nɪmətɪ] ecuanimidad *f*
e•quate [ɪ'kweɪt] *v/t* equiparar
e•qua•tion [ɪ'kweɪʒn] MATH ecuación *f*
e•qua•tor [ɪ'kweɪtər] ecuador *m*; ***on the ~*** en el ecuador
e•qua•to•ri•al [ekwə'tɔːrɪəl] *adj* ecuatorial
e•ques•tri•an [ɪ'kwestrɪən] *adj sports, skills* ecuestre, hípico
e•qui•dis•tant [iːkwɪ'dɪstənt] *adj*: ***be ~ from two points*** ser equidistante de dos puntos
e•qui•lat•er•al [iːkwɪ'lætərəl] *adj* MATH *triangle* equilátero
e•qui•lib•ri•um [iːkwɪ'lɪbrɪəm] equilibrio *m*
e•qui•nox ['iːkwɪnɑːks] equinoccio *m*
e•quip [ɪ'kwɪp] *v/t* (*pret & pp* **-ped**) equipar; ***be intellectually ~ped for*** tener las cualidades intelectuales para; ***~ students for life*** preparar a los estudiantes para la vida
e•quip•ment [ɪ'kwɪpmənt] equipo *m*; ***a new piece of ~*** un nuevo equipamiento
eq•ui•ta•ble ['ekwɪtəbl] *adj solution* equitativo
eq•ui•ty ['ekwətɪ] FIN acciones *fpl* ordinarias
e•quiv•a•lence [ɪ'kwɪvələns] equivalencia *m*
e•quiv•a•lent [ɪ'kwɪvələnt] **I** *adj* equivalente; ***be ~ to*** equivaler a **II** *n* equivalente *m*
e•quiv•o•cal [ɪ'kwɪvəkl] *adj* equívoco
e•quiv•o•cate [ɪ'kwɪvəkeɪt] *v/i* hablar con evasivas
e•ra ['ɪrə] era *f*
e•rad•i•cate [ɪ'rædɪkeɪt] *v/t* erradicar
e•rad•i•ca•tion [ɪrædɪ'keɪʃn] erradica-

ción *f*

e•ras•a•ble [ɪ'reɪzəbl] *adj CD* regrabable

e•rase [ɪ'reɪz] *v/t* borrar

e'rase head COMPUT cabeza *f* de borrado

e•ras•er [ɪ'reɪzər] *for pencil* goma *f* (de borrar); *for chalk* borrador *m*

e•ras•ure [ɪ'reɪʒər] *on tape* borrado *m*; *on paper* tachadura *f*

e•rect [ɪ'rekt] **I** *adj* erguido **II** *v/t* levantar, erigir

e•rec•tion [ɪ'rekʃn] **1** *of building etc* construcción *f* **2** *of penis* erección *f*; ***have an ~*** tener una erección

er•go•nom•ic [ɜːrgoʊ'nɑːmɪk] *adj furniture* ergonómico

er•go•nom•i•cal•ly [ɜːrgoʊ'nɑːmɪklɪ] *adv*: ***~ designed*** de diseño ergonómico

er•go•nom•ics [ɜːrgoʊ'nɑːmɪks] *nsg or npl* ergonomía *f*

e•rode [ɪ'roʊd] *v/t also fig* erosionar

e•rog•e•nous [ɪ'rɑːdʒɪnəs] *adj* PHYSIO erógeno; ***~ zone*** zona *f* erógena

e•ro•sion [ɪ'roʊʒn] *also fig* erosión *f*

e•rot•ic [ɪ'rɑːtɪk] *adj* erótico

e•rot•i•cism [ɪ'rɑːtɪsɪzm] erotismo *m*

er•o•tism ['erətɪzəm] erotismo *m*

err [ɜːr] *v/i* errar, equivocarse; ***to ~ is human*** errar es de humanos; ***~ on the side of caution*** actuar con cautela; *be overcautious* pecar de cauteloso

er•rand ['erənd] recado *m*; ***run ~s*** hacer recados

'er•rand boy chico *m* de los recados

er•ra•ta [e'rætə] *npl* erratas *fpl*

er•rat•ic [ɪ'rætɪk] *adj* irregular; *course* errático

er•ro•ne•ous [ɪ'roʊnjəs] *adj fml* erróneo; ***in the ~ belief that …*** con la idea equivocada de que …

er•ro•ne•ous•ly [ɪ'roʊnjəslɪ] *adv* erróneamente

er•ror ['erər] error *m*; ***be in ~*** estar en un error, estar equivocado; ***do sth in ~*** hacer algo por equivocación; ***~ of judgment*** equivocación *f*, desacierto *m*; ***caused by pilot ~*** causado por un fallo del piloto; ***see the ~ of one's ways*** darse cuenta de sus errores; ***~s and omissions excepted*** salvo error u omisión

'er•ror mes•sage COMPUT mensaje *m* de error

er•u•dite ['erʊdaɪt] *adj* erudito

er•u•di•tion [erʊ'dɪʃn] erudición *f*

e•rupt [ɪ'rʌpt] *v/i of volcano* entrar en erupción; *of violence* brotar; *of person* explotar

e•rup•tion [ɪ'rʌpʃn] *of volcano* erupción *f*, *of violence* brote *m*

es•ca•late ['eskəleɪt] *v/i* intensificarse

es•ca•la•tion [eskə'leɪʃn] intensificación *f*

es•ca•la•tor ['eskəleɪtər] escalera *f* mecánica

es•ca•lope [e'skɑːləp] GASTR escalope *m*, filete *m*

es•ca•pade ['eskəpeɪd] aventura *f*

es•cape [ɪ'skeɪp] **I** *n* **1** *of prisoner, animal* fuga *f*, ***have a narrow ~*** escaparse por los pelos **2** *of gas* escape *m*, fuga *f* **II** *v/i of prisoner, animal, gas* escaparse; ***~ with one's life*** salir con vida; ***they were all affected, nobody ~d*** todos quedaron afectados, nadie se escapó **III** *v/t*: ***the word ~s me*** no consigo recordar la palabra; ***it didn't ~ his attention*** no se le pasó, no se le escapó; ***there is no escaping the fact that …*** no se puede negar que …

es'cape chute AVIA tobogán *m* de emergencia

es'cape key COMPUT tecla *f* de escape

es•cap•ism [ɪ'skeɪpɪzəm] escapismo *m*

es•cap•ist [ɪ'skeɪpɪst] *adj* escapista

es•cort **I** *n* ['eskɔːrt] **1** acompañante *m/f* **2** *guard* escolta *m/f*; ***under ~*** escoltado; ***motorcyle ~*** escolta de motocicletas **II** *v/t* [ɪ'skɔːrt] escoltar; *socially* acompañar; ***~ s.o. to the door*** acompañar *or* llevar a alguien hasta la puerta

'es•cort a•gen•cy agencia *f* de acompañantes

es•crow ac•count [es'kroʊ] FIN cuenta *f* de depósito en garantía

e-sig•na•ture ['iːsɪgnətʃər] firma *f* electrónica

Es•ki•mo ['eskɪmoʊ] esquimal *m/f*

ESL [iːes'el] *abbr* (= ***English as a second language***) inglés *m* como segundo idioma

e•soph•a•gus [iː'sɑːfəgəs] esófago *m*

es•o•ter•ic [esoʊ'terɪk] *adj* esotérico

es•pe•cial•ly [ɪ'speʃlɪ] *adv* especialmente

es•pe•cial [ɪ'speʃl] ☞ ***special***

es•pi•o•nage ['espɪənɑːʒ] espionaje *m*

es•pouse [ɪ'spaʊz] *v/t fig* apoyar, defender
es•pres•so [es'presoʊ] café *m* exprés
es•say ['eseɪ] *by author* ensayo *m*; *by student*: *creative* redacción *f*; *factual* trabajo *m*
es•sence ['esns] esencia *f*; ***in ~*** en esencia
es•sen•tial [ɪ'senʃl] **I** *adj* esencial; ***the ~ thing is ...*** lo esencial es ...; ***~ to life*** esencial para vivir; ***~ oil*** aceite *m* esencial
II *n*: ***we had only the bare ~s*** sólo teníamos lo imprescindible; ***the ~s of Spanish grammar*** los puntos esenciales de la gramática española
es•sen•tial•ly [ɪ'senʃlɪ] *adv* esencialmente
EST [iːes'tiː] *abbr* (= ***Eastern Standard Time***) *hora oficial de la costa este estadounidense*
es•tab•lish [ɪ'stæblɪʃ] *v/t* **1** *create* establecer; *company* fundar; ***~ o.s. as*** establecerse como; ***~ one's reputation as ...*** ganarse la fama de ... **2** (*determine*) establecer
es•tab•lished [ɪ'stæblɪʃt] *adj* **1** *business* establecido, consolidado; *method* establecido; *custom* arraigado **2** *fact* probado
es•tab•lish•ment [ɪ'stæblɪʃmənt] *firm, shop etc* establecimiento *m*; ***the Establishment*** el orden establecido
es•tate [ɪ'steɪt] (*area of land*) finca *f*; (*possessions of dead person*) patrimonio *m*
es'tate a•gen•cy *Br* agencia *f* inmobiliaria; **es'tate a•gent** *Br* agente *m/f* inmobiliario(-a); **es'tate car** *Br* coche *m* familiar
es•teem [ɪ'stiːm] **I** *v/t fml* valorar, estimar; ***we would ~ it an honor to ...*** lo consideraríamos un honor... **II** *n*: ***hold s.o. in*** (***high***) ***~*** tener a alguien en gran estima; ***rise / fall in s.o.'s ~*** ganar / perder valor ante los ojos de alguien
es•thete ['esθiːt] esteta *m/f*
es•thet•ic [es'θetɪk] *adj* estético
es•ti•mate ['estɪmət] **I** *n* estimación *f*; *for job* presupuesto *m*; ***rough ~*** estimación aproximada; ***at a rough ~*** aproximadamente
II *v/t* estimar; ***~d time of arrival*** hora *f* estimada *or* prevista de llegada; ***I would ~ the total at ...*** calculo que el total rondaría ...; ***~d value*** valor aproximado; ***an ~d 200 people were killed*** se estima que 200 personas murieron
es•ti•ma•tion [estɪ'meɪʃn] estima *f*; ***he has gone up / down in my ~*** le tengo en más / menos estima; ***in my ~*** (*opinion*) a mi parecer
es•tranged [ɪs'treɪndʒd] *adj wife, husband* separado
es•tro•gen ['estrədʒən] estrógeno *m*
es•tu•a•ry ['estʃəwerɪ] estuario *m*
ETA [iːtiː'eɪ] *abbr* (= ***estimated time of arrival***) hora *f* estimada de llegada
etc [et'setrə] *abbr* (= ***et cetera***) etc (= etcétera)
et cet•er•a [et'setrə] *adv* etcétera
etch [etʃ] *v/t also fig* grabar
etch•ing ['etʃɪŋ] aguafuerte *m*
e•ter•nal [ɪ'tɜːrnl] *adj* eterno; ***~ triangle*** triángulo *m* amoroso
e•ter•nal•ly [ɪ'tɜːrnəlɪ] *adv*: ***I shall be ~ grateful*** estaré eternamente agradecido
e•ter•ni•ty [ɪ'tɜːrnətɪ] eternidad *f*
e'ter•ni•ty ring anillo *m* de brillantes
e•ther ['iːθər] CHEM éter *m*
e•the•re•al [ɪ'θɪrɪəl] *adj lit* etéreo
eth•i•cal ['eθɪkl] *adj* ético; ***~ marketing*** márketing *m* ético
eth•ics ['eθɪks] **1** *nsg* ética *f*; ***code of ~*** código *m* ético **2** *npl* (*morality*) ética *f*
E•thi•o•pi•a [iːθɪ'oʊpjə] Etiopía *f*
E•thi•o•pi•an [iːθɪ'oʊpjən] **I** *adj* etíope **II** *n* etíope *m/f*
eth•nic ['eθnɪk] *adj* étnico
eth•nic 'cleans•ing limpieza *f* étnica; **eth•nic 'group** grupo *m* étnico; **eth•nic mi'nor•i•ty** minoría *f* étnica
e•thos ['iːθɑːs] espíritu *m*, escala *f* de valores
e-tick•et ['iːtɪkɪt] ticket *m* electrónico
et•i•quette ['etɪket] etiqueta *f*, protocolo *m*
et•y•mo•log•i•cal [etɪmə'lɑːdʒɪkl] *adj* etimológico
et•y•mol•o•gy [etɪ'mɑːlədʒɪ] etimología *f*
EU [iː'juː] *abbr* (= ***European Union***) UE *f* (=Unión *f* Europea)
eu•ca•lyp•tus [juːkə'lɪptəs] BOT eucalipto *m*

eu•lo•gy ['juːlədʒɪ] elogio *m*, encomio *m*
eu•nuch ['juːnək] eunuco *m*
eu•phe•mism ['juːfəmɪzm] eufemismo *m*
eu•phe•mis•tic [juːfə'mɪstɪk] *adj* eufemístico
eu•pho•ri•a [juː'fɔːrɪə] euforia *f*
eu•phor•ic [juː'fɑːrɪk] *adj* eufórico
eu•ro ['jʊroʊ] FIN euro *m*
Eu•rope ['jʊrəp] Europa *f*
Eu•ro•pe•an [jʊrə'pɪən] **I** *adj* europeo **II** *n* europeo(-a) *m(f)*
Eu•ro•pe•an Com'mis•sion Comisión *f* Europea; **Eu•ro•pe•an 'Par•lia•ment** Parlamento *m* Europeo; **Eu•ro'pe•an plan** media pensión *f*; **Eu•ro•pe•an 'Un•ion** Unión *f* Europea
'eu•ro zone zona *f* euro
eu•tha•na•si•a [juθə'neɪzɪə] eutanasia *f*
e•vac•u•ate [ɪ'vækjʊeɪt] *v/t* evacuar; ***the police ~ed the building*** la policía desalojó el edificio
e•vac•u•a•tion [ɪvækjʊ'eɪʃn] evacuación *f*
e•vac•u•ee [ɪvækjuː'iː] evacuado(-a) *m(f)*
e•vade [ɪ'veɪd] *v/t* evadir; ~ **(*answering*) *a question*** evadir una pregunta
e•val•u•ate [ɪ'væljʊeɪt] *v/t* evaluar
e•val•u•a•tion [ɪvæljʊ'eɪʃn] evaluación *f*
e•van•gel•i•cal [iːvæn'dʒelɪkl] *adj* evangélico
e•van•ge•lism [ɪ'vændʒəlɪzəm] evangelismo *m*
e•van•gel•ist [ɪ'vændʒəlɪst] evangelista *m/f*
e•van•ge•lize [ɪ'vændʒəlaɪz] **I** *v/t* evangelizar **II** *v/i* predicar el Evangelio
e•vap•o•rate [ɪ'væpəreɪt] *v/i of water* evaporarse; *of confidence* desvanecerse
e•vap•o•rat•ed milk [ɪvæpəreɪtɪd'mɪlk] leche *f* evaporada
e•vap•o•ra•tion [ɪvæpə'reɪʃn] *of water* evaporación *f*
e•va•sion [ɪ'veɪʒn] evasión *f*
e•va•sive [ɪ'veɪsɪv] *adj* evasivo; ***take ~ action*** adoptar tácticas evasivas
e•va•sive•ness [ɪ'veɪsɪvnɪs] *of person* esquivez *f*, carácter *m* evasivo
eve [iːv] víspera *f*; ***on the ~ of*** en la víspera de
e•ven ['iːvn] **I** *adj* **1** (*regular*) regular; (*level*) llano; *distribution* igualado; *voice* uniforme **2** *number* par **3**: ***I'll get ~ with him*** me las pagará; ***be ~ with s.o.*** estar en paz con alguien, estar a mano con alguien
II *adv* incluso; ***~ bigger / better*** incluso *or* aún mayor / mejor; ***~ as a child he was …*** incluso de niño era …; ***not ~*** ni siquiera; ***~ so*** aun así; ***~ though, ~ if*** aunque; ***~ I know that*** hasta yo sé eso; ***not ~ he could do that*** ni siquiera él pudo hacerlo; ***it's not ~ ten o'clock yet*** no son ni las diez todavía
III *v/t*: ***~ the score*** empatar, igualar el marcador
◆ **even out I** *v/i* **1** *of ground* allanarse **2** *of prices, of peaks and troughs* nivelarse **II** *v/t* **1** *surface* nivelar **2** *fluctuations, inequalities* nivelar, compensar
◆ **even up** *v/t*: ***… to even things up*** … para compensar
e•ven•hand•ed [iːvn'hændɪd] *adj person, treatment* imparcial, equitativo
eve•ning ['iːvnɪŋ] tarde *f*; *after dark* noche *f*; ***in the ~*** por la tarde / noche; ***this ~*** esta tarde / noche; ***yesterday ~*** anoche *f*; ***good ~*** buenas noches; ***on the ~ of the third of May*** en la noche del tres de mayo
'eve•ning class clase *f* nocturna; **'eve•ning dress** *for woman* traje *m* de noche; *for man* traje *m* de etiqueta; **eve•ning 'pa•per** periódico *m* de la tarde *or* vespertino; **eve•ning 'star** AST estrella *f* de Venus
e•ven•ly ['iːvnlɪ] *adv* (*regularly*) regularmente
e•ven•ness ['iːvnnɪs] **1** *of surface* lo llano *or* liso **2** *of breathing* regularidad *f* **3** *of distribution* uniformidad *f*
e•vent [ɪ'vent] acontecimiento *m*; SP prueba *f*; ***at all ~s*** en cualquier caso; ***in any ~*** en todo caso; ***in the ~ of*** en caso de; ***in that ~*** en ese caso; ***in the ~ that*** en caso de que; ***after the ~*** a posteriori
e•ven-tem•pered [iːvn'tempərd] *adj* ecuánime, apacible
e•vent•ful [ɪ'ventfəl] *adj* agitado, lleno de incidentes
e'vent man•age•ment organización *f* de espectáculos
e•ven•tu•al [ɪ'ventʃʊəl] *adj* final

E

e•ven•tu•al•i•ty [ɪventʃʊ'ælətɪ] eventualidad *f*
e•ven•tu•al•ly [ɪ'ventʃʊəlɪ] *adv* finalmente
ev•er ['evər] *adv* **1**: ***if I ~ hear you ...*** como te oiga ...; ***have you ~ been to Colombia?*** ¿has estado alguna vez en Colombia?; ***for ~*** siempre; ***~ since*** desde entonces; ***~ since she found out about it*** desde que se enteró de ello; ***~ since I've known him*** desde que lo conozco; ***nothing like this has ~ happened before*** nunca antes había ocurrido algo similar; ***I will never ~ do it again*** no volveré ha hacerlo nunca más
2 F: ***it was ~ so silly of me*** fue una (completa) tontería por mi parte; ***that's ~ so kind of you*** es muy amable *or* considerado por tu parte; ***am I ~ tired / mad!*** estoy cansadísimo / enfadadísimo
'ev•er•green árbol *m* de hoja perenne
ev•er'last•ing *adj love* eterno
ev•er•y ['evrɪ] *adj* cada; ***I see him ~ day*** lo veo todos los días; ***you have ~ reason to ...*** tienes razones para ...; ***one in ~ ten*** uno de cada diez; ***~ other day*** cada dos días; ***~ now and then*** de vez en cuando; ***~ few days*** cada dos o tres días; ***~ one of you*** cada uno de vosotros; ***he is ~ bit as much a sportsman as his father was*** tiene tanto de deportista como su padre; ***she's ~ bit as intelligent as her brother*** es tan inteligente como su hermano
ev•er•y•bod•y ['evrɪbɑːdɪ] ☞ ***everyone***
ev•er•y•day ['evrɪdeɪ] *adj* cotidiano; ***~ English*** inglés *m* corriente, inglés de uso común
ev•ery•one ['evrɪwʌn] *pron* todo el mundo; ***to ~'s amazement*** para sorpresa de todos
ev•er•y•place ['evrɪpleɪs] *adv* ☞ ***everywhere***
ev•er•y•thing ['evrɪθɪŋ] *pron* todo; ***and ~*** F y todo lo demás F; ***money isn't ~*** el dinero no lo es todo
ev•er•y•where ['evrɪwer] *adv* **1** en *or* por todos sitios **2** (*wherever*) dondequiera que; ***~ he goes*** dondequiera que va, allá donde va
e•vict [ɪ'vɪkt] *v/t* desahuciar
e•vic•tion [ɪ'vɪkʃn] deshaucio *m*, desalojo *m*; ***~ notice*** aviso *m* de deshaucio *or* desalojo
ev•i•dence ['evɪdəns] *also* LAW prueba(s) *f* (*pl*); ***give ~*** prestar declaración; ***he / it hasn't been in ~ much*** no se le ha visto mucho
ev•i•dent ['evɪdənt] *adj* evidente
ev•i•dent•ly ['evɪdəntlɪ] *adv* **1** (*clearly*) evidentemente **2** (*apparently*) aparentemente, al parecer
e•vil ['iːvl] **I** *adj* malo **II** *n* mal *m*; ***the lesser of two ~s*** el mal menor; ***it's a choice of ~s*** es una fatídica elección
e•vil-'mind•ed *adj* **1** (*suspicious*) malpensado **2** (*nasty*) malintencionado
e•voc•a•tive [ɪ'vɑːkətɪv] *adj* evocador; ***be ~ of*** evocar
e•voke [ɪ'voʊk] *v/t image* evocar
ev•o•lu•tion [iːvə'luːʃn] evolución *f*
e•volve [ɪ'vɑːlv] *v/i* evolucionar
ewe [juː] oveja *f*
ex- [eks] *pref* ex-
ex [eks] F (*former wife, husband*) ex *m/f* F
ex•ac•er•bate [ɪg'zæsərbeɪt] *v/t* **1** *situation, infection* agravar; *pain* exacerbar **2** (*annoy*) irritar
ex•act [ɪg'zækt] **I** *adj* exacto **II** *v/t obedience, money etc* exigir (**from** de)
ex•act•ing [ɪg'zæktɪŋ] *adj* exigente; *task* duro
ex•ac•ti•tude [ɪg'zæktɪtjuːd] exactitud *f*
ex•act•ly [ɪg'zæktlɪ] *adv* exactamente; ***not ~*** no exactamente
ex•act•ness [ɪg'zæktnɪs] exactitud *f*, precisión *f*
ex•ag•ge•rate [ɪg'zædʒəreɪt] *v/t & v/i* exagerar
ex•ag•ge•ra•tion [ɪgzædʒə'reɪʃn] exageración *f*; ***it is no ~ to say that ...*** no es una exageración decir que ...
ex•alt•ed [ɪg'zɔːltɪd] *adj rank, ideal* elevado
ex•am [ɪg'zæm] examen *m*; ***take an ~*** hacer un examen; ***pass / fail an ~*** aprobar / suspender un examen
ex•am•i•na•tion [ɪgzæmɪ'neɪʃn] **1** (*inspection*) examen *m*; *of patient* reconocimiento *m*; ***but on closer ~, ...*** pero mirándolo más de cerca, ...; ***be under ~*** estar bajo investigación **2** EDU examen *m*; ***~ paper*** preguntas *fpl* del examen; ***~ results*** notas *fpl* de los exámenes
ex•am•ine [ɪg'zæmɪn] *v/t* examinar; *pa-*

tient reconocer; ***~ sth for faults*** examinar algo en busca de imperfecciones
ex•am•i•nee [ɪgzæmɪ'niː] EDU examinando(-a) *m(f)*
ex•am•in•er [ɪg'zæmɪnər] EDU examinador(a) *m(f)*
ex•am•ple [ɪg'zæmpl] ejemplo *m*; ***for ~*** por ejemplo; ***set a good / bad ~*** dar buen / mal ejemplo; ***follow s.o.'s ~*** seguir el ejemplo de alguien; ***make an ~ of s.o.*** dar a alguien un castigo ejemplar; ***lead by ~*** dar ejemplo; ***this should serve as an ~ to you*** esto debería servirte de ejemplo
ex•as•per•ate [ɪg'zæspəreɪt] *v/t* exasperar
ex•as•pe•rat•ed [ɪg'zæspəreɪtɪd] *adj* exasperado
ex•as•pe•rat•ing [ɪg'zæspəreɪtɪŋ] *adj* exasperante
ex•as•per•at•ing•ly [ɪg'zæspəreɪtɪŋlɪ] *adv* que exaspera, que saca de quicio
ex•as•per•a•tion [ɪgzæspə'reɪʃn] exasperación *f*; ***in ~*** con exasperación
ex•ca•vate ['ekskəveɪt] *v/t* excavar
ex•ca•va•tion [ekskə'veɪʃn] excavación *f*
ex•ca•va•tor ['ekskəveɪtər] excavadora *f*
ex•ceed [ɪk'siːd] *v/t* (*be more than*) exceder; (*go beyond*) sobrepasar; ***it ~ed my expectations*** superó mis expectativas
ex•ceed•ing•ly [ɪk'siːdɪŋlɪ] *adj* sumamente
ex•cel [ɪk'sel] **I** *v/i* (*pret & pp* **-led**) sobresalir (***at*** en) **II** *v/t* (*pret & pp* **-led**): ***~ o.s.*** superarse a sí mismo
ex•cel•lence ['eksələns] excelencia *f*
ex•cel•lent ['eksələnt] *adj* excelente
ex•cel•lent•ly ['eksələntlɪ] *adv* muy bien, excelentemente
ex•cept [ɪk'sept] **I** *prep* excepto; ***~ for*** a excepción de; ***~ that*** sólo que **II** *conj* pero, si no fuera porque; ***~ I forgot it was election day*** pero se me olvidó que era el día de las elecciones **III** *v/t*: ***present company ~ed*** con exepción de los presentes
ex•cept•ing [ɪk'septɪŋ] *prep* excepto, salvo
ex•cep•tion [ɪk'sepʃn] excepción *f*; ***with the ~ of*** a excepción de; ***take ~ to*** molestarse por; ***by way of ~*** a modo de excepción; ***without ~*** sin excepción; ***make an ~*** hacer una excepción (***in s.o.'s case*** en el caso de alguien); ***the ~ proves the rule*** la excepción confirma la regla
ex•cep•tion•al [ɪk'sepʃnl] *adj* excepcional
ex•cep•tion•al•ly [ɪk'sepʃnlɪ] *adv* excepcionalmente
ex•cerpt ['eksɜːrpt] extracto *m* (***from*** de)
ex•cess [ɪk'ses] **I** *n* exceso *m*; ***eat / drink to ~*** comer / beber en exceso; ***in ~ of*** superior a **II** *adj* excedente; ***~ demand*** COM exceso *m* de demanda; ***~ postage*** franqueo *m* adicional; ***~ profit*** beneficio *m* extraordinario
ex•cess 'bag•gage exceso *m* de equipaje
ex•cess 'fare suplemento *m*
ex•ces•sive [ɪk'sesɪv] *adj* excesivo
ex•change [ɪks'ʧeɪndʒ] **I** *n* intercambio *m*; ***in ~*** a cambio (***for*** de); ***~ of letters*** carteo *m*; ***~ of shots*** tiroteo *m*; ***~ of views*** cambio *m* de impresiones; ***be on an ~*** (***visit***) estar de (visita de) intercambio; ***~ student*** estudiante *m/f* de intercambio **II** *v/t* cambiar (***for*** por); ***~ blows*** propinarse bofetadas; ***~ a few words*** intercambiar unas palabras
ex•change•a•ble [ɪks'ʧeɪndʒəbl] *adj goods purchased* cambiable; *commodity* canjeable
ex'change con•trols *npl* FIN control *m* de cambios; **ex'change gain** FIN beneficio *m* de cambio; **ex'change loss** FIN pérdida *f* de cambio; **ex'change rate** FIN tipo *m* de cambio; ***~ fluctuations*** fluctuaciones *fpl* del tipo de cambio
ex•ci•ta•ble [ɪk'saɪtəbl] *adj* excitable
ex•cite [ɪk'saɪt] *v/t* (*make enthusiastic*) entusiasmar
ex•cit•ed [ɪk'saɪtɪd] *adj* emocionado, excitado; *sexually* excitado; ***get ~*** emocionarse *or* excitarse (***about*** con); ***the new model is nothing to get ~ about*** el modelo nuevo no es para tanto F
ex•cite•ment [ɪk'saɪtmənt] emoción *f*, excitación *f*; ***their ~ grew as ...*** su entusiasmo crecía a medida que ...; ***in the ~ of the moment*** con la emoción del momento; ***sexual ~*** excitación sexual
ex•cit•ing [ɪk'saɪtɪŋ] *adj news, developments, product* emocionante, excitante; *actor, sportsman etc* interesante

E

ex•cit•ing•ly [ɪk'saɪtɪŋlɪ] *adv*: **~ *different*** apasionantemente diferente

ex•claim [ɪk'skleɪm] *v/t* exclamar

ex•cla•ma•tion [ekskləˈmeɪʃn] exclamación *f*

ex•cla'ma•tion point signo *m* de admiración

ex•clude [ɪk'sklu:d] *v/t* excluir; *possibility* descartar; ***feel ~ed*** sentirse excluido

ex•clud•ing [ɪk'sklu:dɪŋ] *prep* excluyendo

ex•clu•sion [ɪk'sklu:ʒn] exclusión *f* (***from*** de); ***to the ~ of everything else*** excluyendo todo lo demás

ex•clu•sive [ɪk'sklu:sɪv] **I** *adj* exclusivo; **~ *interview*** entrevista *f* exclusiva; **~ *of tax*** sin incluir impuestos; ***be ~ of sth*** no incluir algo; ***be mutually ~*** excluirse mutuamente **II** *n interview, report* exclusiva *f*

ex•clu•sive 'a•gent agente *m* exclusivo; **ex•clu•sive dis•tri'bu•tion** distribución *f* exclusiva; **ex•clu•sive 'li•cense** licencia *f* exclusiva

ex•clu•sive•ly [ɪk'sklu:sɪvlɪ] *adv* exclusivamente

ex•clu•sive 'rights *npl* derechos *mpl* exclusivos

ex•clu•siv•i•ty [ɪksklu:'sɪvɪtɪ] exclusividad *f*; **~ *arrangement*** acuerdo *m* de exclusividad

ex•com•mu•ni•cate [ekskəˈmju:nɪkeɪt] *v/t* REL excomulgar

ex•com•mu•ni•ca•tion [ekskəmju:nɪ'keɪʃn] excomunión *f*

ex•cre•ment ['ekskrɪmənt] excremento *m*

ex•crete [ɪk'skri:t] *v/t* excretar

ex•cre•tion [ɪk'skri:ʃn] excreción *f*

ex•cru•ci•at•ing [ɪk'skru:ʃɪeɪtɪŋ] *adj* **1** *pain* terrible **2** (*very embarrassing*) espantoso

ex•cru•ci•at•ing•ly [ɪk'skru:ʃɪeɪtɪŋlɪ] *adv* **1** *painful* terriblemente **2** *embarrassing* terriblemente, espantosamente

ex•cur•sion [ɪk'skɜ:rʃn] excursión *f*; ***go on an ~*** ir de excursión

ex•cus•a•ble [ɪk'skju:zəbl] *adj* perdonable, disculpable

ex•cuse I *n* [ɪk'skju:s] excusa *f*; ***make an ~*** poner una excusa; ***he's always making ~s*** siempre está poniendo excusas; ***stop making ~s for him!*** ¡deja de justificarlo!; ***without good ~*** sin una buena excusa; ***she offered no ~ for being late*** no se disculpó por llegar tarde; ***there's no ~ for it*** eso no admite disculpa alguna

II *v/t* [ɪk'skju:z] **1** (*forgive*) excusar, perdonar; **~ *me*** *to get past, interrupting, indignant* perdone; **~ *me for being late, ~ my being late*** disculpadme *or* perdonadme por llegar tarde; ***I do not wish to ~ his conduct*** no trato de justificar su conducta; ***if you will ~ the expression ...*** si me perdonas la expresión ...

2 (*allow to leave*) disculpar

3 (*exempt*): **~ *s.o. from sth*** dispensar a alguien de algo; ***he is ~d heavy work*** está exento de trabajos pesados

ex 'div•i•dend ex dividendo, sin derecho a dividendo

ex•e•cut•able file ['eksɪkju:təbl] COMPUT fichero *m* ejecutable

ex•e•cute ['eksɪkju:t] *v/t criminal, plan* ejecutar; ***~d on ...*** FIN ejecutado el...

'ex•e•cute file COMPUT fichero *m* ejecutable

ex•e•cu•tion [eksɪ'kju:ʃn] *of criminal, plan* ejecución *f*

ex•e•cu•tion•er [eksɪ'kju:ʃnər] verdugo *m*

ex•ec•u•tive [ɪg'zekjʊtɪv] **I** *n* **1** ejecutivo(-a) *m(f)*; ***senior ~*** alto(-a) ejecutivo(-a) **2** POL poder *m* ejecutivo; **II** *adj*: **~ *position*** puesto *m* directivo

ex•ec•u•tive 'brief•case maletín *m* de ejecutivo; **ex•ec•u•tive com'mit•tee** comité *m* ejecutivo; **ex•ec•u•tive de'ci•sion** *hum* decisión *f* de nivel ejecutivo; ***make an ~*** tomar una decisión de nivel ejecutivo; **ex•ec•u•tive di'rec•tor** director(a) *m(f)* ejecutivo(-a); **ex•ec•u•tive 'jet** jet *m* para ejecutivos; **ex•ec•u•tive pro'duc•er** TV *etc* productor(a) *m(f)* ejecutivo(-a); **ex•ec•u•tive 'sec•re•tar•y** secretario(-a) *m(f)* de dirección; **ex•ec•u•tive 'wash•room** aseo *m* para ejecutivos

ex•ec•u•tor [ɪg'zekjʊtər] LAW testamentario(-a) *m(f)*

ex•em•pla•ry [ɪg'zemplərɪ] *adj* ejemplar

ex•em•pli•fy [ɪg'zemplɪfaɪ] *v/t* ejemplificar, ilustrar

ex•empt [ɪg'zempt] *adj* exento; ***be ~ from*** estar exento de

ex•emp•tion [ɪg'zempʃn] exención *f* (***from*** de); ***tax ~*** exención fiscal; ***~ clause*** cláusula *f* de exención

ex•er•cise ['eksərsaɪz] **I** *n* ejercicio *m*; ***take ~*** hacer ejercicio; ***do one's ~s*** hacer los ejercicios **II** *v/t* **1** *muscle* ejercitar; *dog* pasear **2** *caution* proceder con; ***~ restraint*** controlarse **III** *v/i* hacer ejercicio

'ex•er•cise bike bicicleta *f* estática; **'ex•er•cise book** EDU cuaderno *m* de ejercicios; **'ex•er•cise price** FIN precio *m* de ejercicio

ex•er•cis•er ['eksərsaɪzər] aparato *m* de ejercicios

ex•ert [ɪg'zɜːrt] *v/t authority* ejercer; ***~ o.s.*** esforzarse

ex•er•tion [ɪg'zɜːrʃn] **1** esfuerzo *m* **2** *of influence* ejercicio *m*

ex gra•ti•a pay•ment [eks'greɪʃɪə] pago *m* voluntario

ex•hale [eks'heɪl] *v/t* exhalar

ex•haust [ɪg'zɒːst] **I** *n* **1** *fumes* gases *mpl* de la combustión **2** *pipe* tubo *m* de escape **II** *v/t* **1** (*tire*) cansar **2** (*use up*) agotar

ex•haust•ed [ɪg'zɒːstɪd] *adj* (*tired*) agotado

ex'haust e•mis•sion emisión *f* de gases de combustión; **ex'haust fumes** *npl* gases *mpl* de la combustión; **ex'haust gas** gas *f* de la combustión

ex•haust•ing [ɪg'zɒːstɪŋ] *adj* agotador

ex•haus•tion [ɪg'zɒːstʃn] agotamiento *m*

ex•haus•tive [ɪg'zɒːstɪv] *adj* exhaustivo

ex'haust man•i•fold colector *m* de escape; **ex'haust pipe** tubo *m* de escape; **ex'haust stroke** carrera *f* de escape

ex•hib•it [ɪg'zɪbɪt] **I** *n in exhibition* objeto *m* expuesto **II** *v/t of gallery* exhibir; *of artist* exponer; (*give evidence of*) mostrar

ex•hi•bi•tion [eksɪ'bɪʃn] exposición *f*; *of bad behavior, skill* exhibición *f*; ***be on ~*** estar expuesto; ***make an ~ of o.s.*** hacer el ridículo

ex•hi'bi•tion cen•ter, *Br* **ex•hi'bi•tion cen•tre** centro *m* de exposiciones

ex•hi•bi•tion•ist [eksɪ'bɪʃnɪst] exhibicionista *m/f*

ex•hib•i•tor [ɪg'zɪbɪtər] expositor(a) *m(f)*

ex•hil•a•rat•ed [ɪg'zɪləreɪtɪd] *adj* (*happy*) alegre; (*stimulated*) tonificado

ex•hil•a•rat•ing [ɪg'zɪləreɪtɪŋ] *adj* estimulante

ex•hil•a•ra•tion [ɪgzɪlə'reɪʃn] júbilo *m*, excitación *f*

ex•hort [ɪg'zɔːrt] *v/t* exhortar; ***~ s.o. to do sth*** exhortar a alguien a que haga algo

ex•hor•ta•tion [egzɔːr'teɪʃn] exhortación *f*

ex•hu•ma•tion [ekshjuː'meɪʃn] exhumación *f*

ex•hume [eks'hjuːm] *v/t body* exhumar

ex•ile ['eksaɪl] **I** *n* exilio *m*; *person* exiliado(-a) *m(f)*; ***go into ~*** exiliarse; ***live in ~*** vivir en el exilio; ***send s.o. into ~*** enviar a alguien al exilio, desterrar a alguien **II** *v/t* exiliar

ex•ist [ɪg'zɪst] *v/i* existir; ***~ on*** subsistir a base de

ex•ist•ence [ɪg'zɪstəns] existencia *f*; ***be in ~*** existir; ***come into ~*** crearse, nacer; ***go out of ~*** *species* desaparecer, extinguirse; *regulation, custom* desaparecer

ex•is•ten•tial [egzɪ'stenʃəl] *adj* existencial

ex•is•ten•tial•ism [egzɪ'stenʃəlɪzəm] *philosophy* existencialismo

ex•is•ten•tial•ist [egzɪ'stenʃəlɪst] **I** *adj* existencialista **II** *n* existencialista *m/f*

ex•ist•ing [ɪg'zɪstɪŋ] *adj* existente

ex•it ['eksɪt] **I** *n* **1** salida *f* **2** THEA salida *f*, mutis *m* **II** *v/i* **1** THEA hacer mutis, salir; ***~ stage left*** hacer mutis por la parte izquierda del escenario **2** COMPUT salir **III** *v/t highway* salir

ex•o•dus ['eksədəs] éxodo *m*

ex•on•e•rate [ɪg'zɑːnəreɪt] *v/t* exonerar de

ex•on•er•a•tion [ɪg'zɑːnəreɪʃn] exoneración *f*

ex•or•bi•tant [ɪg'zɔːrbɪtənt] *adj* exorbitante

ex•or•cism ['eksɔːrsɪzəm] exorcismo *m*

ex•or•cist ['eksɔːrsɪst] exorcista *m/f*

ex•or•cize ['eksɔːrsaɪz] *v/t* exorcizar

ex•ot•ic [ɪg'zɑːtɪk] *adj* exótico

ex•pand [ɪk'spænd] **I** *v/t* expandir; ***~ed memory*** COMPUT memoria *f* expandida **II** *v/i* expandirse; *of metal* dilatarse; ***~ing bracelet*** pulsera *f* extensible

◆ **expand on** *v/t* desarrollar

ex•panse [ɪk'spæns] extensión *f*

ex•pan•sion [ɪk'spænʃn] expansión *f*; *of*

E

metal dilatación *f*

ex'pan•sion card COMPUT tarjeta *f* de expansión; **ex'pan•sion slot** COMPUT ranura *f* de expansión; **ex'pan•sion tank** MOT caja *f* de dilatación; **ex'pan-sion valve** válvula *f* de expansión

ex•pan•sive [ɪk'spænsɪv] *adj person, mood* expansivo, sociable

ex•pat•ri•ate [eks'pætrɪət] **I** *adj* expatriado **II** *n* expatriado(-a) *m(f)*

ex•pect [ɪk'spekt] **I** *v/t* **1** esperar; ***they are ~ed to arrive around 3pm*** se espera que lleguen sobre las 3.00 de la tarde **2** (*suppose*) suponer, imaginar(se); ***am I ~ed to finish this by tomorrow?*** ¿se supone que tengo que acabar esto para mañana?; ***you are not ~ed to pay for yourselves*** no se espera que paguéis lo vuestro **3** (*demand*) exigir; ***~ s.o. to do sth*** esperar que alguien haga algo; ***~ sth of*** *or* ***from s.o.*** esperar algo de alguien **II** *v/i*: ***be ~ing*** (*be pregnant*) estar en estado; ***I ~ so*** eso espero, creo que sí

ex•pect•an•cy [ɪk'spektənsɪ] expectación *f*; ***the look of ~ on their faces*** la mirada expectante que tenían

ex•pec•tant [ɪk'spektənt] *adj crowd* expectante

ex•pec•tant 'moth•er futura madre *f*

ex•pec•ta•tion [ekspek'teɪʃn] expectativa *f*; ***it depends what your ~s are*** depende del concepto que tengas; ***in ~ of*** en espera de; ***beyond*** (***all***) ***~***(***s***) más allá de todo pronóstico; ***contrary to ~*** contra todo pronóstico; ***come up to ~*** estar a la altura de las expectativas; ***live up to s.o.'s ~s*** estar a la altura de lo que alguien se espera

ex•pe•di•ence, ex•pe•di•en•cy [ɪk'spiːdjəns(ɪ)] **1** *self-interest* conveniencia *f*, interés *m* personal **2** *advisability* conveniencia *f*

ex•pe•di•ent [ɪk'spiːdɪənt] *adj* oportuno, conveniente

ex•pe•dite ['ekspɪdaɪt] *v/t fml* acelerar

ex•pe•di•tion [ekspɪ'dɪʃn] expedición *f*

ex•pel [ɪk'spel] *v/t* (*pret & pp* **-led**) *person* expulsar (***from*** de)

ex•pend [ɪk'spend] *v/t energy* gastar

ex•pend•a•ble [ɪk'spendəbl] *adj person* prescindible

ex•pen•di•ture [ɪk'spendɪʧər] gasto *m*

ex•pense [ɪk'spens] gasto *m*; ***at great ~*** gastando mucho dinero; ***at the company's ~*** a cargo de la empresa; ***a joke at my ~*** una broma a costa mía; ***at the ~ of his health*** a costa de su salud; ***don't go to any ~*** no te metas en muchos gastos F

ex'pense ac•count cuenta *f* de gastos

ex•pen•ses [ɪk'spensɪz] *npl* gastos *mpl*

ex•pen•ses 'claim form formulario *m* para el reembolso de gastos

ex•pen•sive [ɪk'spensɪv] *adj* caro

ex•pe•ri•ence [ɪk'spɪrɪəns] **I** *n* experiencia *f*; ***from ~*** por experiencia; ***in my ~*** según mi (propia) experiencia; ***gain ~*** ganar experiencia; ***just put it down to ~*** considéralo como una experiencia más; ***what an ~!*** ¡menuda experiencia!,¡vaya experiencia! **II** *v/t* experimentar

ex•pe•ri•enced [ɪk'spɪrɪənst] *adj* experimentado

ex•per•i•ment [ɪk'sperɪmənt] **I** *n* experimento *m* **II** *v/i* experimentar; ***~ on*** *animals* experimentar con; ***~ with*** (*try out*) probar; ***~ with drugs*** experimentar con drogas

ex•per•i•men•tal [ɪksperɪ'mentl] *adj* experimental

ex•per•i•men•ta•tion [ɪksperɪmen'teɪʃn] experimentación *f*

ex•pert ['ekspɜːrt] **I** *adj* experto; ***~ advice*** / ***opinion*** opinión *f* de un experto *or* especialista **II** *n* experto(-a) *m(f)*

ex•pert•ise [ekspɜːr'tiːz] destreza *f*, pericia *f*

ex•pert 'sys•tem COMPUT sistema *m* experto

ex•pert 'wit•ness LAW perito(-a) *m/f*

ex•pi•ate ['ekspɪeɪt] *v/t sins* expiar

ex•pi•a•tion [ekspɪ'eɪʃn] expiación *f*

ex•pi•ra•tion [ɪkspɪ'reɪʃn] *of lease, contract* vencimiento *m*; *of passport, credit card* caducidad *f*; ***on the ~ of your passport*** cuando venza *or* caduque su pasaporte

ex•pi'ra•tion date *of food, passport, credit card* fecha *f* de caducidad; ***be past its ~*** haber caducado

ex•pire [ɪk'spaɪr] *v/i of lease, contract* vencer; *of passport, credit card* caducar

ex•pir•y date [ɪk'spaɪrɪ] *Br* fecha *f* de caducidad

ex•plain [ɪk'spleɪn] **I** *v/t* explicar; ***~ sth to s.o.*** explicarle algo a alguien; ***~***

o.s. explicarse, justificarse **II** *v/i* explicarse
◆ **explain away** *v/t* dar explicaciones convincentes de, justificar
ex•pla•na•tion [ekspləˈneɪʃn] explicación *f*
ex•plan•a•tor•y [ɪkˈsplænətɔːrɪ] *adj* explicativo
ex•ple•tive [ɪkˈspliːtɪv] (*swearword*) palabrota *f*
ex•pli•ca•ble [ɪkˈsplɪkəbl] *adj* explicable
ex•plic•it [ɪkˈsplɪsɪt] *adj instructions, sex scenes* explícito
ex•plic•it•ly [ɪkˈsplɪsɪtlɪ] *adv state* explícitamente; *forbid* terminantemente
ex•plode [ɪkˈsploʊd] **I** *v/i of bomb, in anger* explotar **II** *v/t bomb* hacer explotar
ex•ploit[1] [ˈeksplɔɪt] *n* hazaña *f*
ex•ploit[2] [ɪkˈsplɔɪt] *v/t person, resources* explotar
ex•ploi•ta•tion [eksplɔɪˈteɪʃn] *of person* explotación *f*
ex•plo•ra•tion [ekspləˈreɪʃn] exploración *f*
ex•plor•a•to•ry [ɪkˈsplɑːrətɔːrɪ] *adj surgery* exploratorio; ***~ talks*** conversaciones *fpl* preliminares
ex•plore [ɪkˈsplɔːr] **I** *v/t country etc* explorar; *possibility* estudiar **II** *v/i*: ***go exploring*** irse explorar
ex•plo•rer [ɪkˈsplɔːrər] explorador(a) *m(f)*
ex•plo•sion [ɪkˈsploʊʒn] *of bomb, in population* explosión *f*
ex•plo•sive [ɪkˈsploʊsɪv] **I** *n* explosivo *m* **II** *adj* **1** *device* explosivo **2** *fig*: *situation* delicado; *temperament* explosivo
ex•po•nent [ɪkˈspoʊnənt] **1** *of theory etc* defensor(a) *m(f)* **2** MATH exponente *m*
ex•po•nen•ti•al [ɪkˈspoʊnenʃl] *adj* exponencial
ex•port [ˈekspɔːrt] **I** *n action* exportación *f*, *item* producto *m* de exportación; ***~s*** *npl* exportaciones *fpl* **II** *v/t also* COMPUT exportar **III** *v/i* exportar
ˈex•port ban prohibición *f* de exportación; **ˈex•port cam•paign** campaña *f* de exportación; **ˈex•port com•pa•ny** empresa *f* exportadora; **ˈex•port cred•it guar•an•tee** garantía *f* de crédito a la exportación; **ˈex•port du•ty** derechos *mpl* de exportación
ex•port•er [ˈekspɔːrtər] exportador(a) *m(f)*
ex•port•ing coun•try [ˈekspɔːrtɪŋ] país *m* exportador
ex•port ˈli•cense permiso *m* de exportación; **ˈex•port mar•ket** mercado *m* de exportación; **ˈex•port re•stric•tions** *npl* restricciones *fpl* a las exportaciones; **ˈex•port sales** *npl* exportaciones *fpl*; **ˈex•port tax** impuesto *m* sobre la exportación; **ˈex•port trade** comercio *m* de exportación
ex•pose [ɪkˈspoʊz] *v/t* (*uncover*) exponer; *scandal* sacar a la luz; ***he's been ~d as a liar*** ha quedado como un mentiroso; ***~ s.o. / o.s. to*** *fig*: *the weather, danger, ridicule* exponer a alguien a / exponerse a; ***~ o.s.*** *indecently* hacer exhibicionismo
ex•po•sé [ekspoʊˈzeɪ] exposición *f*, revelación *f*; *in newspaper* artículo *m* de denuncia
ex•posed [ekˈspoʊzd] *adj also fig* desprotegido, expuesto
ex•po•si•tion [ekspoʊˈzɪʃn] *of theory etc* exposición *f*
ex•po•sure [ɪkˈspoʊʒər] exposición *f*; PHOT foto(grafía) *f*; ***die of ~*** morir de frío
exˈpo•sure me•ter PHOT exposímetro *m*
ex•pound [ɪkˈspaʊnd] *v/t theory* exponer
ex•press[1] [ɪkˈspres] **I** *adj* (*fast*) rápido **II** *n train* expreso *m*; *bus* autobús *m* directo **III** *adv mail* exprés, expreso
ex•press[2] [ɪkˈspres] *adj* (*explicit*) expreso
ex•press[3] [ɪkˈspres] *v/t* expresar; ***~ o.s. well / clearly*** expresarse bien / con claridad
ex•press deˈliv•er•y envío *m* urgente; ***send sth ~*** enviar algo por vía urgente; **exˈpress el•e•va•tor** *ascensor rápido que sólo para en algunos pisos*; **exˈpress freight** transporte *m* urgente
ex•pres•sion [ɪkˈspreʃn] *voiced* muestra *f*, *phrase, on face* expresión *f*; ***read with ~*** leer con sentimiento; ***give ~ to*** expresar, dar expresión a
ex•pres•sion•ism [ɪkˈspreʃnɪzəm] expresionismo *m*
ex•pres•sion•ist [ɪkˈspreʃnɪst] **I** *n* expresionista *m/f* **II** *adj* expresionista
ex•pres•sion•less [ɪkˈspreʃnləs] *adj*

inexpresivo, sin expresión
ex•pres•sive [ɪk'spresɪv] *adj* expresivo
ex•press•ly [ɪk'spreslɪ] *adv state* expresamente; *forbid* terminantemente
ex'press•way autopista *f*
ex•pro•pri•ate [eks'prouprɪeɪt] *v/t* LAW expropiar
ex•pro•pri•a•tion [eksprouprɪ'eɪʃn] expropiación *f*
ex•pul•sion [ɪk'spʌlʃn] *from school*, *of diplomat* expulsión *f*
ex•qui•site [ek'skwɪzɪt] *adj* (*beautiful*) exquisito
ex•tant ['ekstænt] *adj* existente
ex•tem•po•re [ek'stempərɪ] **I** *adj* improvisado **II** *adv* de improviso
ex•tem•po•rize [ek'stempəraɪz] *v/i* improvisar
ex•tend [ɪk'stend] **I** *v/t* **1** *house*, *investigation* ampliar; (*make wider*) ensanchar; (*make bigger*) agrandar; *runway*, *path* alargar **2** *contract*, *visa* prorrogar **3** *thanks*, *congratulations* extender **II** *v/i of garden etc* llegar
ex•tend•ed war•rant•y [ɪk'stendɪd] garantía *f* adicional
ex•ten•sion [ɪk'stenʃn] **1** *to house* ampliación *f* **2** *of contract*, *visa* prórroga *f* **3** TELEC teléfono *m* supletorio; *Br* (*local*) extensión *f*
ex'ten•sion cord cable *m* de extensión
ex•ten•sive [ɪk'stensɪv] *adj damage* cuantioso; *knowledge* considerable; *search* extenso, amplio
ex•ten•sive•ly [ɪk'stensɪvlɪ] *adv damaged*, *modified* ampliamente, considerablemente; *travel* mucho
ex•tent [ɪk'stent] alcance *m*; ***to such an ~ that*** hasta el punto de que; ***to a certain ~*** hasta cierto punto; ***to a large ~*** en gran medida *or* parte; ***~ of cover*** *in insurance* amplitud *f* de la cobertura
ex•ten•u•at•ing cir•cum•stan•ces [ɪk'stenʊeɪtɪŋ] *npl* circunstancias *fpl* atenuantes
ex•te•ri•or [ɪk'stɪrɪər] **I** *adj* exterior **II** *n* exterior *m*
ex•ter•mi•nate [ɪk'stɜːrmɪneɪt] *v/t* exterminar
ex•ter•mi•na•tion [ɪkstɜːrmɪ'neɪʃn] *of pests* exterminación *f*, *of people* exterminio *m*
ex•ter•nal [ɪk'stɜːrnl] *adj* (*outside*) exterior, externo
ex•ter•nal 'au•di•tor auditor(a) *m*(*f*) externo(-a)
ex'ter•nal drive COMPUT unidad *f* de disco externa
ex•ter•nal•ly [ɪk'stɜːrnəlɪ] *adv* externamente, exteriormente
ex•tinct [ɪk'stɪŋkt] *adj species* extinguido
ex•tinc•tion [ɪk'stɪŋkʃn] *of species* extinción *f*, ***be on the brink of ~*** estar en peligro de extinción; ***hunted to ~*** cazado hasta la extinción
ex•tin•guish [ɪk'stɪŋgwɪʃ] *v/t fire* extinguir, apagar; *cigarette* apagar
ex•tin•guish•er [ɪk'stɪŋgwɪʃər] extintor *m*
ex•tol [ɪk'stoul] *v/t* (*pret & pp* ***-led***) ensalzar, alabar
ex•tort [ɪk'stɔːrt] *v/t* obtener mediante extorsión; ***~ money from*** extorsionar a
ex•tor•tion [ɪk'stɔːrʃn] extorsión *f*
ex•tor•tion•ate [ɪk'stɔːrʃənət] *adj prices* desorbitado
ex•tra ['ekstrə] **I** *n* extra *m*; *in movie* extra *m/f*; ***be an ~*** hacer de extra; ***no hidden ~s*** sin extras escondidos
II *adj* extra; ***meals are ~*** las comidas se pagan aparte; ***that's $1 ~*** cuesta 1 dólar más; ***I need an ~ week*** necesito una semana más; ***~ pay*** paga *f* extraordinaria **III** *adv* super; ***~ strong*** extrafuerte; ***~ special*** muy especial; ***charge ~ for sth*** cobrar algo aparte
ex•tra 'charge recargo *m*
ex•tract[1] ['ekstrækt] *n* extracto *m*
ex•tract[2] [ɪk'strækt] *v/t* sacar (***from*** de); *coal*, *oil*, *tooth* extraer (***from*** de); *information* sonsacar (***from*** a)
ex•trac•tion [ɪk'strækʃn] *of oil*, *coal*, *tooth* extracción *f*, ***I have to have an ~*** me tienen que sacar un diente
ex•trac•tor fan [ɪk'stræktər] extractor *m* de humos
ex•tra•cur•ric•u•lar [ekstrəkə'rɪkjələr] *adj* EDU extracurricular, extraescolar
ex•tra•dite ['ekstrədaɪt] *v/t* extraditar
ex•tra•di•tion [ekstrə'dɪʃn] extradición *f*
ex•tra'di•tion re•quest petición *f* de extradición
ex•tra'di•tion trea•ty tratado *m* de extradición
ex•tra•mar•i•tal [ekstrə'mærɪtl] *adj* extramarital

ex•tra•ne•ous [ɪk'streɪnjəs] *adj*: ***be ~ to*** ser extrínseco *or* ajeno a

ex•tra•or•di•nar•i•ly [ekstrɔːrdɪn'erɪlɪ] *adv* extraordinariamente

ex•tra•or•di•na•ry [ɪk'strɔːrdɪnerɪ] *adj* extraordinario

ex•tra•sen•so•ry [ekstrə'sensərɪ] *adj*: ***~ perception*** percepción *f* extrasensorial

ex•tra•ter•res•tri•al [ekstrətə'restrɪəl] **I** *adj* extraterrestre **II** *n* extraterrestre *m/f*

ex•tra 'time *Br* SP prórroga *f*; ***the game went into ~*** hubo prórroga, jugaron la prórroga

ex•trav•a•gance [ɪk'strævəgəns] **1** *with money* despilfarro *m* **2** *of claim etc* extravagancia *f*

ex•trav•a•gant [ɪk'strævəgənt] *adj* **1** *with money* despilfarrador; ***that was rather ~ of you*** eso fue un derroche por tu parte **2** *claim* extravagante

ex•treme [ɪk'striːm] **I** *n* extremo *m*; ***in the ~*** en extremo; ***go to ~s*** tomar medidas extremas **II** *adj* extremo; *views* extremista

ex•treme•ly [ɪk'striːmlɪ] *adv* extremadamente, sumamente

ex•trem•ism [ɪk'striːmɪzəm] *esp* POL extremismo *m*

ex•trem•ist [ɪk'striːmɪst] **I** *adj* extremista **II** *n* extremista *m/f*

ex•trem•i•ty [ɪk'streməti] **1** *furthest point* extremo *m* **2**: ***I wouldn't go to that ~*** no llegaría hasta ese extremo; ***such were the extremities to which we were driven*** ese fue el extremo hasta el que tuvimos que llegar; ***extremities of love and hate*** los extremos del amor y el odio

ex•tri•cate ['ekstrɪkeɪt] *v/t* liberar

ex•tro•vert ['ekstrəvɜːrt] **I** *adj* extrovertido **II** *n* extrovertido(-a) *m(f)*

ex•u•ber•ance [ɪg'zuːbərəns] exuberancia *f*

ex•u•be•rant [ɪg'zuːbərənt] *adj* exuberante

ex•ude [ɪg'zuːd] *v/t* **1** *liquid etc* rezumar, supurar **2** *confidence, charm etc* rebosar, irradiar

ex•ult [ɪg'zʌlt] *v/i* exultar

ex•ult•ant [ɪg'zʌltənt] *adj* eufórico

ex 'ware•house *adv* franco en el almacén

ex 'works *adv* franco fábrica

eye [aɪ] **I** *n of person, needle* ojo *m*; ***keep an ~ on*** (*look after*) estar pendiente de; (*monitor*) vigilar; ***have an ~ for detail*** tener buen ojo para los detalles; ***they're up to their ~s in work*** están hasta los ojos de trabajo, estan hasta arriba de trabajo; ***see ~ to ~ with s.o. on sth*** estar de acuerdo con alguien en algo
II *v/t* mirar

◆ **eye up** *v/t* F devorar con los ojos F

'eye•ball globo *m* ocular; ***be up to the ~s in work*** estar hasta arriba de trabajo; **'eye•brow** ceja *f*; **'eye•brow pen•cil** lápiz *m* de cejas; **'eye-catch•ing** *adj* llamativo; **'eye con•tact** contacto *m* visual; ***make ~ with s.o.*** mirar a los ojos a alguien

eye•ful ['aɪfʊl]: ***get an ~*** F echar un vistazo F

'eye•glass•es *npl* gafas *fpl*, *L.Am.* anteojos *mpl*, *L.Am.* lentes *mpl*; **'eye•lash** pestaña *f*; **'eye lev•el**: ***at ~*** a la altura de los ojos; ***~ grill*** grill *m* alto; **'eye•lid** párpado *m*; **'eye•lin•er** lápiz *m* de ojos; **'eye-o•pen•er**: ***be an ~ for s.o.*** F ser una revelación para alguien, hacer abrir los ojos a alguien F; **'eye•pen•cil** lápiz *m* de ojos; **'eye•sha•dow** sombra *f* de ojos; **'eye•sight** vista *f*; **'eye•sore** engendro *m*, monstruosidad *f*; **'eye strain** vista *f* cansada; **'eye•wit•ness** testigo *m/f* ocular; **eye•wit•ness ac'count** declaración *f* del testigo ocular

E

F

F *abbr* (= ***Fahrenheit***) F
fab [fæb] *adj* F fabuloso, *L.Am.* chévere
fa•ble ['feɪbl] fábula *f*
fab•ric ['fæbrɪk] (*material*) tejido *m*
fab•ri•cate ['fæbrɪkeɪt] *v/t* **1** fabricar **2** *fig*: *story* inventar
fab•ri•ca•tion [fæbrɪ'keɪʃn] **1** fabricación *f* **2** *fig*: *lie* invención *f*
fab•u•lous ['fæbjʊləs] *adj* fabuloso, estupendo
fab•u•lous•ly ['fæbjʊləslɪ] *adv rich* tremendamente; *beautiful* increíblemente
fa•çade [fə'sɑːd] *of building*, *person* fachada *f*
face [feɪs] **I** *n* **1** cara *f*; ***~ to ~*** cara a cara; ***lose ~*** padecer una humillación; ***in the ~ of*** frente a, ante; ***say sth to s.o.'s ~*** decir algo a la cara a alguien; ***show one's ~*** dejarse ver; ***make** or **pull a ~*** hacer muecas; ***put a good ~ on it*** poner al mal tiempo buena cara; ***on the ~ of it*** a primera *or* simple vista; ***save ~*** guardar las apariencias; ***do one's ~*** F maquillarse, pintarse **2** *of mountain* cara *f*, pared *f*
II *v/t* **1** (*be opposite*) estar enfrente de **2** (*confront*) enfrentarse a; ***let's ~ it*** ¡reconozcámoslo!, ¡seamos realistas!; ***~ facts*** aceptar los hechos; ***be ~d with*** estar frente a; ***~ s.o. with sth / s.o.*** enfrentar a alguien con algo / alguien
◆ **face down** *v/t critics etc* plantar cara
◆ **face up to** *v/t* hacer frente a, afrontar
'face card figura *f*; **'face•cloth** toallita *f*; **'face cream** crema *f* para la cara
face•less ['feɪslɪs] *adj fig* anónimo, sin rostro
'face•lift: ***have a ~*** hacerse un lifting; ***the city's had a ~*** se han hecho mejoras a la ciudad; **'face mask** *for diving* máscara *f*; **'face pack** mascarilla *f* (*facial*)
fac•et ['fæsɪt] **1** *of jewel* faceta *f*, lado *m* **2** *fig* faceta *f*, aspecto *m*
fa•ce•tious [fə'siːʃəs] *adj* ocurrente, gracioso
face 'val•ue: ***take sth at ~*** tomarse algo literalmente
fa•cial ['feɪʃl] **I** *adj* facial **II** *n* limpieza *f* de cutis
fa•cil•i•tate [fə'sɪlɪteɪt] *v/t* facilitar
fa•cil•i•ties [fə'sɪlətɪz] *npl* instalaciones *fpl*
fa•cil•i•ty [fə'sɪlətɪ] (*ease*, *gift*) facilidad *f*
fac•sim•i•le [fæk'sɪmɪlɪ] **1** (*duplicate*) imitación *f* **2** *fml*: *fax* facsímil(e) *m*
fact [fækt] hecho *m*; ***in ~, as a matter of ~*** de hecho; ***know sth for a ~*** saber algo a ciencia cierta; ***tell s.o. the ~s of life*** decir a alguien los detalles de la reproducción humana; ***it's just a ~ of life*** así es la vida
fact-find•ing ['fæktfaɪndɪŋ] *adj* de investigación, de reconocimiento
fac•tion ['fækʃn] facción *f*
fac•tor ['fæktər] factor *m*
fac•to•ry ['fæktərɪ] fábrica *f*
'fac•to•ry farm•ing cría *f* intensiva; **'fac•to•ry hand, 'fac•to•ry work•er** obrero(-a) *m*(*f*) industrial; **'fac•to•ry out•let** *tienda que vende artículos de fábrica a precio reducido*; **'fac•to•ry ship** buque *m* factoría
'fact sheet hoja *f* informativa, informe *m*
fac•tu•al ['fæktʃʊəl] *adj* objetivo, basado en los hechos
fac•ul•ty ['fækəltɪ] (*hearing etc*), *at university* facultad *f*; (***mental***) ***faculties*** *pl* facultades mentales
fad [fæd] moda *f*
fad•dy ['fædɪ] *adj* caprichoso
fade [feɪd] *v/i of colors* desteñirse, perder color; *of memories* desvanecerse
◆ **fade away** *v/i* desvanecerse, apagarse gradualmente
◆ **fade in I** *v/t sound*, *picture* meter con un fundido **II** *v/i of sound*, *picture* entrar en fundido
◆ **fade out I** *v/t sound*, *picture* cerrar en fundido, apagar lentamente **II** *v/i of sound*, *picture* fundirse, apagarse
fad•ed ['feɪdɪd] *adj color*, *jeans* desteñido, descolorido
fae•ces ['fiːsiːz] *Br* ☞ ***feces***
fag[1] [fæg] F (*homosexual*) marica *m* F, maricón *m* F
fag[2] [fæg] *Br* F (*cigarette*) pitillo *m* F
fag•got ['fægət] F (*homosexual*) marica

m F, maricón *m* F
Fahr•en•heit ['færənhaɪt] *adj* Fahrenheit
fail [feɪl] **1** *v/i* fracasar; *of plan* fracasar, fallar; ***he ~ed in his attempt*** falló en su intentó; ***if all else ~s*** como último recurso; ***~ to do sth*** no hacer algo; ***I ~ to understand why …*** no logro entender porqué …; ***it never ~s to amaze me how …*** nunca deja de sorprenderme cómo …
II *v/t exam* suspender; ***his courage ~ed him*** le faltó valor; ***words ~ me!*** ¡no encuentro palabras!
III *n* **1**: ***without ~*** sin falta **2**: ***I got a ~ in biology*** tengo un suspenso en biología
fail•ing ['feɪlɪŋ] **I** *n* fallo *m* **II** *prep* a falta de; ***~ that*** si no
'fail-safe *adj* **1** (*won't fail*) infalible **2** (*safe if it fails*) de seguridad
fail•ure ['feɪljər] fracaso *m*; *in exam* suspenso *m*; ***I feel such a ~*** me siento un fracasado; ***~ to pay*** el (hecho de) no pagar
faint [feɪnt] **1** *adj line*, *smile* tenue; *smell*, *noise* casi imperceptible; *resemblance* ligero, leve: ***I haven't the ~est idea*** no tengo ni la menor idea **II** *v/i* desmayarse
faint•heart•ed [feɪnt'hɑːrtɪd] *adj* pusilánime, apocado
faint•ly ['feɪntlɪ] *adv* **1** *smile*, *smell* levemente **2** (*slightly*) ligeramente
fair[1] [fer] *n* **1** COM feria *f* **2** (*fun~*) parque *m* de atracciones
fair[2] [fer] *adj* **1** *hair* rubio; *complexion* claro **2** (*just*) justo; ***be ~ game*** ser un blanco justificado; ***everything is ~ and square*** todo está claro **II** *adv*: ***play ~*** jugar limpio; ***beat a team ~ and square*** vencer a un equipo con todas las de la ley; ***ok, ~ enough*** vale, está bien *or* de acuerdo
'fair ball *in baseball* bola *f* buena; **'fair-ground 1** COM recinto *m* ferial **2** *for fun~* parque *m* de atracciones; **fair-haired** [fer'herd] *adj* rubio
fair•ly ['ferlɪ] *adv* **1** *treat* justamente, con justicia **2** (*quite*) bastante; ***the time ~ flew past*** el tiempo pasó muy rápidamente
fair-'mind•ed *adj* imparcial, justo
fair•ness ['fernɪs] *of treatment* imparcialidad *f*, ***in ~ to him*** para ser justo con él
'fair•way 1 NAUT canalizo *m* **2** *in golf* calle *f*
'fair-weath•er *adj*: ***~ friend*** amigo(-a) *m*(*f*) en la prosperidad
fair•y ['ferɪ] **1** hada *f* **2** *pej* P *homosexual* maricón *m* F
fair•y 'god•moth•er hada *f* madrina
'fair•y sto•ry, 'fair•y tale cuento *m* de hadas
faith [feɪθ] **1** fe *f*, confianza *f*, ***have ~ in sth / s. o.*** tener fé en algo / alguien; ***in good / bad ~*** de buena / mala fé **2** REL fe *f*
faith•ful ['feɪθfəl] *adj* fiel; ***be ~ to one's partner*** ser fiel a la pareja
faith•ful•ly ['feɪθfəlɪ] *adv follow instructions* religiosamente; ***Yours ~*** (le saluda) atentamente
faith heal•er ['feɪθhiːlər] curandero(-a) *m*(*f*)
'faith heal•ing curación *f* por fé
fake [feɪk] **I** *n* falsificación *f*, *in basketball* finta *f*, *person* impostor(a) *m*(*f*); *with emotions etc* falso(-a) *m*(*f*) **II** *adj* falso **III** *v/t* **1** (*forge*) falsificar **2** (*feign*) fingir
fal•con ['fɔːlkən] halcón *m*
Falk•land Is•land•er ['fɒːlklənd] malvinense *m*/*f*, habitante *m*/*f* de las Islas Malvinas
'Falk•land Is•lands *npl*: ***the ~*** las Islas Malvinas
fall[1] [fɒːl] *n season* otoño *m*; ***in (the) ~*** en otoño
fall[2] [fɒːl] **I** *v/i* (*pret* **fell**, *pp* **fallen**) *of person* caerse; *of government*, *prices*, *temperature*, *night* caer; ***~ ill*** enfermar, caer enfermo; ***I fell off the wall*** me caí del muro; ***he fell to his death*** se cayó y se mató; ***her face fell*** puso cara larga **II** *n* caída *f*, ***have a ~*** sufrir una caída, caerse; ***~ in temperature*** descenso *m* de la temperatura
◆ **fall about** *v/i*: ***~ (laughing)*** F morirse *or* partirse de risa F
◆ **fall apart** *v/i* F *emotionally* desequilibrarse
◆ **fall away** *v/i* ☞ ***fall off***
◆ **fall back** *v/i of troops* replegarse
◆ **fall back on** *v/t* recurrir a
◆ **fall behind** *v/i with work*, *payments* retrasarse; *in race* quedarse atrás
◆ **fall down** *v/i* caerse; ***fall down on the***

job *fig* hacer un mal trabajo; ***that's where the proposal falls down*** es ahí donde la propuesta fracasa *or* se viene abajo

◆ **fall for** *v/t* **1** *person* enamorarse de **2** (*be deceived by*) dejarse engañar por; ***I'm amazed you fell for it*** me sorprende mucho que picaras

◆ **fall in** *v/i* **1** *of roof* desplomarse **2** MIL formar filas

◆ **fall into** *v/t bad habits* adquirir, incurrir en; *difficulties* entrar en

◆ **fall in with** *v/t* **1** *bad crowd* juntarse con **2** *rules, accepted procedures, what others want* aceptar, adherirse a

◆ **fall off** *v/i of business, attendances* decaer, empeorar

◆ **fall on** *v/t* **1** (*attack*) lanzarse sobre **2** (*encounter*): ***fall on hard times*** entrar en crisis **3**: ***his eyes fell on me*** dirigió su mirada hacia mí **4**: ***it falls on me to make the final decision*** me corresponde a mí tomar la última decisión **5**: ***it ~s on a Tuesday*** cae en martes

◆ **fall out** *v/i* **1** *of hair* caerse **2** (*argue*) pelearse

◆ **fall over I** *v/i* caerse; ***fall over backward to do sth*** F desvivirse por hacer algo **II** *v/t*: ***fall over sth*** tropezar con algo; ***be falling over o.s. to do sth*** F desvivirse por hacer algo

◆ **fall through** *v/i of plans* venirse abajo

◆ **fall to** *v/t*: ***it fell to him to make the casting vote*** le correspondió a él dar el voto decisivo

◆ **fall under** *v/t category etc* entrar en

fal•la•cious [fəˈleɪʃəs] *adj* (*incorrect*) erróneo; (*misleading*) engañoso

fal•la•cy [ˈfæləsɪ] falacia *f*

fal•len [ˈfɒːlən] *pp* ☞ ***fall***

ˈfall guy F **1** (*victim*) víctima *f* **2** (*scapegoat*) chivo *m* expiatorio, cabeza *f* de turco; ***make s.o. the ~ for sth*** convertir a alguien en el chivo expiatorio de algo

fal•li•ble [ˈfæləbl] *adj* falible

fall•ing star [fɔːlɪŋˈstɑːr] estrella *f* fugaz

Fal•lo•pi•an [fəˈloʊpɪən] *adj*: ***~ tube*** trompa *f* de Falopio

ˈfall•out 1 lluvia *f* radiactiva **2** *fig*: *from scandal, shake-up etc* secuelas *fpl*, repercusión *f*

ˈfall•out shel•ter refugio *m* nuclear *or* atómico

fal•low [ˈfæloʊ] *adj* AGR en barbecho; ***lie ~*** estar en barbecho

false [fɑːls] *adj* falso; ***raise ~ hopes*** alimentar falsas esperanzas; ***~ bottom*** doble fondo *m*

false aˈlarm falsa alarma *f*

false•hood [ˈfɑːlshʊd] **1** (*lie*) mentira *f* **2** *of statement etc* falsedad *f*

false•ly [ˈfɑːlslɪ] *adv argue, claim etc* falsamente, equivocadamente

false ˈmod•es•ty falsa modestia *f*

false•ness [ˈfɑːlsnəs] *of statement, theory* falsedad *f*; *of friend* deslealtad *f*

false ˈstart *in race* salida *f* nula; ***get off to a ~*** *fig* empezar mal

false ˈteeth *npl* dentadura *f* postiza

fal•si•fi•ca•tion [fɔːlsɪfɪˈkeɪʃn] falsificación *f*

fal•si•fy [ˈfɑːlsɪfaɪ] *v/t* (*pret & pp* **-ied**) falsificar

fal•ter [ˈfɔːltər] *v/i* titubear, vacilar

fame [feɪm] fama *f*; ***that team of World Cup 1994 ~*** ese equipo, famoso por los Mundiales de 1994

fa•mil•i•ar [fəˈmɪljər] *adj* familiar; ***get ~*** (*intimate*) tomarse demasiadas confianzas; ***be ~ with sth*** estar familiarizado con algo; ***that looks ~*** eso me resulta familiar; ***that sounds ~*** me suena; ***make o.s. ~ with sth, get ~ with sth*** familiarizarse con algo; ***be on ~ terms with s.o.*** tener confianza con alguien

fa•mil•i•ar•i•ty [fəmɪlɪˈærɪtɪ] familiaridad *f*

fa•mil•i•ar•ize [fəˈmɪljəraɪz] *v/t*: ***~ o.s. with*** familiarizarse con

fa•mil•i•ar•ly [fəˈmɪljərlɪ] *adv behave* con naturalidad; *address someone* con demasiada confianza; ***~ known as*** comúnmente conocido como; ***more ~ known as*** mejor conocido como

fam•i•ly [ˈfæməlɪ] familia *f*; ***do you have any ~?*** ¿tienes hijos?; ***from a good ~*** de buena familia; ***~ Bible*** Biblia *f* familiar; ***~ problems*** problemas *mpl* familiares

fam•i•ly ˈbusi•ness negocio *m* familiar; **ˈfam•i•ly car** *L.Am.* carro *m* familiar, *Span* coche *m* familiar; **fam•i•ly ˈdoc•tor** médico *m/f* de familia; **ˈfam•i•ly man** hombre *m* casero; **ˈfam•i•ly name** apellido *m*; **fam•i•ly ˈplan•ning** planificación *f* familiar; **fam•i•ly ˈplan•ning clin•ic** clínica *f* de planificación familiar; **ˈfam•i•ly pro•gram** programa

m familiar; **'fam•i•ly room** *in hotel* habitación *f* familiar; **'fam•i•ly-run** *adj hotel, restaurant* familiar; **fam•i•ly 'tree** árbol *m* genealógico
fam•ine ['fæmɪn] hambruna *f*
fam•ished ['fæmɪʃt] *adj* F: ***I'm ~*** estoy muerto de hambre F
fa•mous ['feɪməs] *adj* famoso; ***be ~ for*** ser famoso por
fa•mous•ly ['feɪməslɪ] *adv*: ***get along ~ with s.o.*** llevarse muy bien con alguien
fan[1] [fæn] *n* (*supporter*) seguidor(a) *m*(*f*); *of singer, band* admirador(a) *m*(*f*), fan *m/f*; ***I've always been a big ~ of yours*** siempre lo he admirado mucho
fan[2] [fæn] **I** *n electric* ventilador *m*; *handheld* abanico *m*; ***the shit will hit the ~*** F se irá al carajo F **II** *v/t* (*pret & pp* ***-ned***) abanicar; ***~ o.s.*** abanicarse
◆ **fan out** *v/i of searchers* desplegarse en abanico
fa•nat•ic [fə'nætɪk] fanático(-a) *m*(*f*)
fa•nat•i•cal [fə'nætɪkl] *adj* fanático
fa•nat•i•cal•ly [fə'nætɪklɪ] *adv* fanáticamente
fa•nat•i•cism [fə'nætɪsɪzm] fanatismo *m*
'fan belt MOT correa *f* del ventilador
fan•ci•ful ['fænsɪfʊl] *adj* (*unrealistic*) fantasioso, irrealista
'fan club club *m* de fans
fan•cy ['fænsɪ] *adj restaurant, prices* lujoso
fan•cy 'dress disfraz *m*
fan•cy-'dress par•ty fiesta *f* de disfraces
fan•fare ['fænfer] fanfarria *f*
fang [fæŋ] colmillo *m*
'fan heat•er estufa *f* eléctrica de aire caliente
'fan mail cartas *fpl* de los fans
fan•ny ['fænɪ] P **1** culo *m*, *CSur* traste *m* P **2** *Br* coño *m* V, *L.Am.* concha *f* V
'fan•ny pack riñonera *f*
fan•ta•size ['fæntəsaɪz] *v/i* fantasear (***about*** sobre)
fan•tas•tic [fæn'tæstɪk] *adj* **1** (*very good*) fantástico, excelente **2** (*very big*) inmenso
fan•tas•tic•al•ly [fæn'tæstɪklɪ] *adv* (*extremely*) sumamente, increíblemente
fan•ta•sy ['fæntəsɪ] fantasía *f*
fan•zine ['fænziːn] fanzine *m*
FAQ [efeɪ'kjuː] *abbr* (= ***frequently asked question***) pregunta *f* frecuente
far [fɑːr] **I** *adv* **1** lejos; ***~ away*** lejos; ***how ~ is it to ...?*** ¿a cuánto está ...?; ***as ~ as the corner / hotel*** hasta la esquina / el hotel; ***as ~ as the eye can see*** hasta donde alcanza la vista
2 *fig*: ***as ~ as I can see*** tal y como lo veo yo; ***as ~ as I know*** que yo sepa; ***you've gone too ~*** *in behavior* te has pasado; ***so ~ so good*** por ahora muy bien; ***~ from completed*** lejos de estar acabado; ***~ be it from me to criticize*** no es mi intención criticar; ***~ into the night*** (bien) adentrada la noche
3 (*much*) mucho; ***~ bigger / faster*** mucho más grande / rápido; ***she was by ~ the fastest*** fue sin lugar a dudas la más rápida; ***you're ~ too young*** eres demasiado joven; ***by ~, ~ and away*** con diferencia
II *adj* del extremo, del *or* al fondo; ***at the ~ end*** al otro extremo; ***from ~ and near*** *or* ***wide*** por todos los lados
'far•a•way *adj* **1** *places* lejano **2** *look* ausente, perdido
farce [fɑːrs] farsa *f*
far•ci•cal ['fɑːrsɪkl] *adj attempts, situation* ridículo, absurdo
fare [fer] **I** *n* tarifa *f*; *actual money* dinero *m*; ***what's the ~?*** ¿cuánto vale el billete *or L.Am.* boleto?; ***any more ~s please?*** ¿más billetes por favor? **II** *v/i esp fml*: ***how did you ~?*** ¿cómo te fue?; ***he didn't ~ very well*** no le fue bien
Far 'East Lejano Oriente *m*
fare•well [fer'wel] despedida *f*; ***make one's ~s*** despedirse
fare'well par•ty fiesta *f* de despedida
far•fetched [fɑːr'fetʃt] *adj* inverosímil, exagerado
far-'flung *adj* vasto, amplio
farm [fɑːrm] granja *f*
◆ **farm out** *v/t*: ***farm sth out*** mandar hacer algo (***to*** a)
farm•er ['fɑːrmər] granjero(-a) *m*(*f*), agricultor(a) *m*(*f*)
'farm•hand trabajador(a) *m*(*f*) del campo, jornalero(-a) *m*(*f*)
'farm•house granja *f*, alquería *f*
farm•ing ['fɑːrmɪŋ] agricultura *f*
'farm•land tierra *f* de cultivo; **'farm•work•er** trabajador(a) *m*(*f*) del campo,

agricultor(a) *m(f)*; **'farm•yard** corral *m*; **~ *animals*** animales *mpl* de corral
far-'off *adj* lejano; **far-'out** *adj* P **1** (*great*) sensacional, genial **2** (*wild, eccentric*) extravagante; **far-reach•ing** [fɑːr'riːʧɪŋ] *adj* trascendente, de magnitud; **far'see•ing** *adj fig* precabido, previsor; **far'sight•ed** *adj* previsor; *optically* hipermétrope
fart [fɑːrt] F **I** *n* **1** pedo *m* F **2 *he's a boring old ~*** es un pesado *or* un plasta F **II** *v/i* tirarse un pedo F

F

far•ther ['fɑːrðər] *adv* más lejos; **~ *away*** más allá, más lejos
far•thest ['fɑːrðəst] *adv travel etc* más lejos
fas•ci•nate ['fæsɪneɪt] *v/t* fascinar; ***be ~d by*** estar fascinado por
fas•ci•nat•ing ['fæsɪneɪtɪŋ] *adj* fascinante
fas•ci•na•tion [fæsɪ'neɪʃn] fascinación *f*; ***have a ~ for sth*** tener fascinación por algo; ***hold a ~ for s.o.*** resultar fascinante a alguien
fas•cism ['fæʃɪzm] fascismo *m*
fas•cist ['fæʃɪst] **I** *n* fascista *m/f* **II** *adj* fascista
fash•ion ['fæʃn] **1** moda *f*; ***in ~*** de moda; ***out of ~*** pasado de moda; ***come into ~*** ponerse de moda; ***go out of ~*** pasarse de moda **2** (*manner*) modo *m*, manera *f*; ***after*** *or* ***in a ~*** en cierto modo, en cierta manera
fash•ion•a•ble ['fæʃnəbl] *adj* de moda; ***be very ~*** estar muy de moda
fash•ion•a•bly ['fæʃnəblɪ] *adv dressed* a la moda
'fash•ion-con•scious *adj* que sigue la moda; **'fash•ion de•sign•er** modisto(-a) *m(f)*; **'fash•ion ed•i•tor** editor(a) *m(f)* de la sección de moda; **'fash•ion mag•a•zine** revista *f* de modas; **'fash•ion mod•el** modelo *m/f*; **'fash•ion show** desfile *m* de moda, pase *m* de modelos; **'fash•ion vic•tim** esclavo(-a) *m(f)* de la moda, fashion victim *m/f*
fast[1] [fæst] **I** *adj* rápido; ***be ~*** *of clock* ir adelantado; ***pull a ~ one on s.o.*** F jugarle una mala pasada a alguien F; ***you're a ~ worker!*** ¡no pierdes el tiempo ! **II** *adv* **1** rápido **2**: ***stuck ~*** atascado; ***~ asleep*** profundamente dormido
fast[2] [fæst] *n not eating* ayuno *m*
fast[3] [fæst] **I** *adj*: ***make ~*** agarrar fuerte, amarrar **II** *adv*: ***play ~ and loose with s.o. / s.o.'s feelings*** jugar con alguien / los sentimientos de alguien
'fast•back MOT fastback *m*; **'fast ball** *in baseball* bola *f* rápida; **fast 'breed•er, fast-breed•er re'ac•tor** PHYS reactor *m* reproductor rápido
fas•ten ['fæsn] **I** *v/t window, lid* cerrar (*poniendo el cierre*); *dress* abrochar; ***~ sth onto sth*** asegurar algo a algo **II** *v/i of dress etc* abrocharse
fas•ten•er ['fæsnər] *for dress, lid* cierre *m*
fast 'food comida *f* rápida; **fast•food 'res•tau•rant** restaurante *m* de comida rápida; **fast 'for•ward I** *n on video etc* avance *m* rápido **II** *v/i* avanzar
fas•tid•i•ous [fə'stɪdɪəs] *adj* escrupuloso, aprensivo (***about*** con)
'fast lane *on road* carril *m* rápido; ***in the ~*** *fig*: *of life* con un tren de vida acelerado
'fast train (tren *m*) rápido *m*
fat [fæt] **I** *adj* gordo; ***a ~ lot of good that is!*** F ¡eso no sirve para nada!; ***~ chance you have!*** F ¡ni de casualidad! F **II** *n on meat, for baking* grasa *f*; ***live off the ~ of the land*** vivir como un rey *or* señor
fa•tal ['feɪtl] *adj illness* mortal; *error* fatal
fa•tal•ism ['feɪtəlɪzəm] fatalismo *m*
fa•ta•list ['feɪtəlɪst] fatalista *m/f*
fa•tal•is•tic [feɪtə'lɪstɪk] *adj* fatalista
fa•tal•i•ty [fə'tælətɪ] víctima *f* mortal
fa•tal•ly ['feɪtəlɪ] *adv* mortalmente; ***~ injured*** herido mortalmente
'fat cat F pez *m* gordo F
fate [feɪt] destino *m*; ***he met his ~*** *died* encontró la muerte; **(*as*) *sure as ~*** con toda seguridad
fat•ed ['feɪtɪd] *adj*: ***be ~ to do sth*** estar predestinado a hacer algo
fate•ful ['feɪtfʊl] *adj encounter, decision, day* fatídico, fatal
'fat-free *adj* sin grasas
fa•ther ['fɑːðər] padre *m*; ***Father Martin*** REL el Padre Martin; ***like ~ like son*** de tal palo, tal astilla; ***the Holy ~*** REL el Papa
Fa•ther 'Christ•mas *Br* Papá Nöel *m*; **fa•ther con'fes•sor** REL confesor *m*, guía *m* espiritual; **'fa•ther fig•ure** PSYCH figura *f* paterna

fa•ther•hood ['fɑːðərhʊd] paternidad *f*
'fa•ther-in-law (*pl* ***fathers-in-law***) suegro *m*
'fa•ther•land país *m* de origen, patria *f*
fa•ther•less ['fɑːðərlɪs] *adj* huérfano(-a) *m(f)* de padre
fa•ther•ly ['fɑːðərlɪ] *adj* paternal
'Fa•ther's Day Día *m* del Padre
fath•om ['fæðəm] NAUT braza *f*
◆ **fathom out** *v/t fig* entender
fa•tigue [fə'tiːg] cansancio *m*, fatiga *f*
fat•so ['fætsoʊ] F gordinflón(-ona) *m(f)* F
fat•ten ['fætn] *v/t animal* engordar
fat•ten•ing ['fætnɪŋ] *adj* que engorda
fat•ty ['fætɪ] **I** *adj* graso **II** *n* F *person* gordinflón(-ona) *m(f)* F
fat•u•ous ['fætjʊəs] *adj* estúpido, tonto
fat•u•ous•ness ['fætjʊəsnəs] estupidez *f*, necedad *f*
fau•cet ['fɒːsɪt] *L.Am.* llave *f*, *Span* grifo *m*
fault [fɒːlt] **I** *n* (*defect*) fallo *m*; ***it's your / my ~*** es culpa tuya / mía; ***find ~*** encontrar defectos (***with*** a); ***you're the one who is at ~*** tú eres el que tiene la culpa; ***he's at ~ for not making it clear*** es su culpa no dejarlo claro **II** *v/t*: ***I can't ~ it*** no puedo decir nada en su contra
fault•find•er ['fɒːltfaɪndər] criticón (-ona) *m(f)* F
fault•find•ing ['fɒːltfaɪndɪŋ] **I** *n* criticqueo *m* F **II** *adj* criticón F
fault•less ['fɒːltlɪs] *adj* impecable
'fault line GEOL falla *f*
fault•y ['fɒːltɪ] *adj goods* defectuoso
fau•na ['fɔːnə] fauna *f*
fa•vor ['feɪvər] **I** *n* favor *m*; ***ask s.o. a ~*** pedir a alguien un favor; ***do s.o. a ~*** hacer un favor a alguien; ***do me a ~!*** (*don't be stupid*) ¡haz el favor!; ***in ~ of*** a favor de; ***be in ~ of*** estar a favor de; ***in my ~*** a mi favor; ***decide in s.o.'s ~*** decidir a favor de alguien; ***be in ~ with s.o.*** contar con la aceptación de alguien; ***be out of ~ with s.o.*** no contar con la aceptación de alguien **II** *v/t* (*prefer*) preferir
fa•vor•a•ble ['feɪvərəbl] *adj reply etc* favorable
fa•vor•a•bly ['feɪvərəblɪ] *adj*: ***I was ~ impressed with her*** me hizo una muy buena impresión
fa•vo•rite ['feɪvərɪt] **I** *n* favorito(-a) *m(f)*; *food* comida *f* favorita **II** *adj* favorito
fa•vor•it•ism ['feɪvrɪtɪzm] favoritismo *m*
fa•vour *etc Br* ☞ ***favor*** *etc*
fawn[1] [fɔːn] *deer* cervato *m*
fawn[2] [fɔːn] *adj color* pardo, castaño claro
◆ **fawn on** *v/t* halagar, hacer la pelota a F
fawn•ing ['fɔːnɪŋ] *adj* halagador
fax [fæks] **I** *n* fax *m*; ***send sth by ~*** enviar algo por fax **II** *v/t* enviar por fax; ***~ sth to s.o.*** enviar algo por fax a alguien; ***can you ~ me?*** ¿me puedes enviar un fax?
'fax ma•chine fax *m*, telefax *m*
'fax num•ber número *m* de fax
faze [feɪz] *v/t* desconcertar; *of physical hardship, danger etc* asustar
FBI [efbiː'aɪ] *abbr* (= ***Federal Bureau of Investigation***) FBI *m*
fear [fɪr] **I** *n* miedo *m*, temor *m*; ***for ~ that*** ... por miedo a que ...; ***for ~ of hurting him*** por miedo a hacerle daño; ***~ of God*** temor de Dios **II** *v/t* temer, tener miedo a
◆ **fear for** *v/t* temer por
fear•ful ['fɪrfʊl] *adj* **1** (*frightening*) espantoso, aterrador **2** F (*terrible*) monumental **3**: ***be ~ that ...*** *apprehensive* tener miedo de que ...
fear•less ['fɪrlɪs] *adj* valiente, audaz
fear•less•ly ['fɪrlɪslɪ] *adv* sin miedo
fea•si•bil•i•ty [fiːzə'bɪlətɪ] viabilidad *f*
fea•si'bil•i•ty stud•y estudio *m* de viabilidad
fea•si•ble ['fiːzəbl] *adj* factible, viable
feast [fiːst] **I** *n* banquete *m*, festín *m*; ***~ for the eyes*** regalo *m* para la vista **II** *v/t*: ***~ one's eyes on*** recrearse la vista con
'feast day REL fiesta *f*
feat [fiːt] hazaña *f*, proeza *f*; ***an amazing ~ of engineering*** un logro impresionante de la ingeniería; ***an amazing ~ of endurance*** un acto de resistencia impresionante
feath•er ['feðər] **I** *n* pluma *f*; ***birds of a ~ flock together*** Dios los cría y ellos se juntan; ***they're birds of a ~*** son harina del mismo costal; ***that is a ~ in his cap*** ese es un tanto a su favor **II** *v/t*: ***~ one's (own) nest*** hacer el agosto
feath•er•brained ['feðərbreɪnd] *adj*

scheme disparatado; ~ ***person*** cabeza *m/f* hueca

feath•er'dust•er plumero *m*

'feath•er-weight I *n* **1** *category* peso *m* pluma **2** *fig*: *person* minucia *f* **II** *adj champion etc* peso pluma

fea•ture ['fiːtʃər] **I** *n* **1** *on face* rasgo *m*, facción *f* **2** *of city, building, plan, style* característica *f*; ***make a ~ of*** destacar **3** *article in paper* reportaje *m* **4** *movie* largometraje *m* **II** *v/t*: ***a movie featuring …*** una película en la que aparece …

'fea•ture ar•ti•cle artículo *m* monográfico; **'fea•ture film** largometraje *m*; **'fea•ture-length mov•ie** largometraje *m*

Feb•ru•a•ry ['febrʊerɪ] febrero *m*

fe•ces ['fiːsiːz] *npl* heces *fpl*

feck•less ['feklɪs] *adj* insensato, irresponsable

fed[1] [fed] *pret & pp* ☞ ***feed***

fed[2] [fed] *n* F (*FBI agent*) federal *m/f*

fed•e•ral ['fedərəl] *adj* federal

fed•er•al•ism ['fedərəlɪzəm] federalismo *m*

fed•er•al•ist ['fedərəlɪst] **I** *adj* federalista **II** *n* federalista *m/f*

Fed•e•ral 'Trade Com•mis•sion Comisión *f* de Comercio Federal

fed•e•ra•tion [fedə'reɪʃn] federación *f*

fed 'up *adj* F harto, hasta las narices F; ***be ~ with*** estar harto *or* hasta las narices de F

fee [fiː] *of lawyer, doctor, consultant* honorarios *mpl*; *for entrance* entrada *f*; *for membership* cuota *f*

fee•ble ['fiːbl] *adj person, laugh* débil; *attempt* flojo; *excuse* pobre

fee•ble•ness ['fiːblnɪs] *of attempt* ineficacia *f*; *of joke, excuse* flojedad *f*, poca contundencia *f*

fee•bly ['fiːblɪ] *adv* débilmente, ineficazmente

feed [fiːd] **I** *v/t* (*pret & pp* ***fed***) **1** alimentar, dar de comer a **2** *reservoir* suministrar **3** *imagination* estimular, despertar **II** *v/i of animals* comer **III** *n for animals* pienso *m*; ***she gave us a good ~*** nos dio bien de comer

◆ **feed in** *v/t tape, wire etc* introducir, insertar

'feed•back reacción *f*; ***we'll give you some ~*** le daremos nuestra opinión

feed•er road ['fiːdər] ramal *m*

feed•ing bot•tle ['fiːdɪŋ] biberón *m*

'feed•lot AGR planta *f* de engorde de ganado

feel [fiːl] **I** *v/t* (*pret & pp* **felt**) (*touch*) tocar; (*sense*) sentir; (*think*) creer, pensar; ***you can ~ the difference*** se nota la diferencia

II *v/i* (*pret & pp* **felt**): ***it ~s like silk / cotton*** tiene la textura de la seda / algodón; ***your hand ~s hot*** tienes la mano caliente; ***I ~ hungry*** tengo hambre; ***I ~ tired*** estoy cansado; ***how are you ~ing today?*** ¿cómo te encuentras hoy?; ***how does it ~ to be rich?*** ¿qué se siente siendo rico?; ***do you ~ like a drink / meal?*** ¿te apetece beber / comer algo?; ***I ~ like going / staying*** me apetece ir / quedarme; ***I don't ~ like it*** no me apetece; ***how do you ~ about his decision?***¿qué te parece su decisión?

◆ **feel out** *v/t*: ***feel s.o. out*** tantear a alguien

◆ **feel up** *v/t sexually* manosear

◆ **feel up to** *v/t* sentirse con fuerzas para

feel•er ['fiːlər] *of insect* antena *f*; ***put out ~s*** *fig* tantear el terreno

'feel•good fac•tor sensación *f* positiva

feel•ing ['fiːlɪŋ] **1** sentimiento *m*; ***what are your ~s about it?*** ¿qué piensas sobre ello?; ***play / sing with ~*** tocar / cantar con sentimiento *or* pasión **2** (*sensation*) sensación *f*; ***I have this ~ that …*** tengo el presentimiento de que …

'fee-pay•ing *adj school* de pago

feet [fiːt] *pl* ☞ ***foot***

feign [feɪn] **I** *v/t interest, illness etc* fingir **II** *v/i* fingir

feint [feɪnt] SP finta *f*

feist•y ['faɪstɪ] *adj* F luchador, de armas tomar

fe•line ['fiːlaɪn] *adj* felino

fell[1] [fel] *pret* ☞ ***fall***

fell[2] [fel] *v/t* **1** *tree* talar, cortar **2** *opponent* tumbar, derribar

fel•low ['feloʊ] (*man*) tipo *m*; ***listen ~, if you …*** escucha hombre, si tú …

fel•low 'cit•i•zen conciudadano(-a) *m(f)*; **fel•low 'coun•try•man** compatriota *m/f*; **fel•low 'man** prójimo *m*; **fel•low 'stu•dent** compañero(-a) *m(f)*

fel•o•ny ['felənɪ] delito *m* grave

felt [felt] **I** *n* fieltro *m* **II** *pret & pp* ☞ ***feel***
felt 'tip, felt-tip 'pen rotulador *m*
fe•male ['fiːmeɪl] **I** *adj* **1** *animal, plant* hembra **2** *relating to people* femenino; ***~ executive*** ejecutiva *f* **II** *n* **1** *of animals, plants* hembra *f* **2** *person* mujer *f*
fem•i•nine ['femɪnɪn] **I** *adj also* GRAM femenino **II** *n* GRAM femenino *m*
fem•i•nin•i•ty [femɪ'nɪnɪtɪ] feminidad *f*
fem•i•nism ['femɪnɪzm] feminismo *m*
fem•i•nist ['femɪnɪst] **I** *n* feminista *m/f* **II** *adj* feminista
fe•mur ['fiːmər] ANAT fémur *m*
fence [fens] **1** *around garden etc* cerca *f*, valla *f*; ***sit on the ~*** *fig* nadar entre dos aguas **2** F *criminal* perista *m/f*
◆ **fence in** *v/t* **1** *land* cercar, vallar **2** *with rules* limitar, restringir (***with*** por)
fenc•er ['fensər] SP esgrimidor(a) *m(f)*, *L.Am.* esgrimista *m/f*
fenc•ing ['fensɪŋ] SP esgrima *f*
fend [fend] *v/i*: ***~ for o.s.*** valerse por sí mismo
◆ **fend off** *v/t blow, attacker* esquivar, evitar
fend•er ['fendər] MOT aleta *f*
fend•er-bend•er ['fendərbendər] MOT F golpe *m*
fen•nel ['fenl] BOT hinojo *m*
fer•ment[1] [fər'ment] *v/i of liquid* fermentar
fer•ment[2] ['fɜːrment] *n* (*unrest*) agitación *f*
fer•men•ta•tion [fɜːrmen'teɪʃn] fermentación *f*
fern [fɜːrn] helecho *m*
fe•ro•cious [fə'roʊʃəs] *adj* feroz
fe•roc•i•ty [fə'rɑːsɪtɪ] ferocidad *f*, furia *f*
fer•ret ['ferɪt] hurón *m*
◆ **ferret around** *v/i* hurgonear, rebuscar (***among*** entre; ***for*** por)
◆ **ferret out** *v/t truth, secret* averiguar, dar con F
fer•rous ['ferəs] *adj* ferroso
fer•ry ['ferɪ] **I** *n* ferry *m*, transbordador *m* **II** *v/t* transportar
'fer•ry•boat ferry *m*, transbordador *m*; **fer•ry•man** ['ferɪmən] barquero *m*; **'fer•ry serv•ice** servicio *m* de transporte (de mercancías, pasajeros)
fer•tile ['fɜːrtəl] *adj* fértil
fer•til•i•ty [fɜːr'tɪlətɪ] fertilidad *f*
fer'til•i•ty drug medicamento *m* para el tratamiento de la infertilidad
fer•til•i•za•tion [fɜːrtɪlaɪ'zeɪʃn] *of egg* fertilización *f*
fer•ti•lize ['fɜːrtəlaɪz] *v/t* fertilizar
fer•ti•liz•er ['fɜːrtəlaɪzər] *for soil* fertilizante *m*
fer•vent ['fɜːrvənt] *adj admirer* ferviente
fer•vent•ly ['fɜːrvəntlɪ] *adv* fervientemente
fer•vor ['fɜːrvər] fervor *m*, entusiasmo *m*
fes•ter ['festər] *v/i of wound* enconarse; *of hatred, resentment* exarcerbarse, enconarse
fes•ti•val ['festɪvl] festival *m*
fes•tive ['festɪv] *adj* festivo; ***the ~ season*** la época navideña, las Navidades
fes•tiv•i•ties [fe'stɪvətɪz] *npl* celebraciones *fpl*
fes•toon [fe'stuːn] *v/t* engalanar
fe•tal ['fiːtl] *adj* fetal
'fe•tal po•si•tion posición *f* fetal
fetch [fetʃ] *v/t* **1** *person* recoger; *thing* traer, ir a buscar **2** *price* alcanzar; ***how much did it ~?*** ¿qué precio alcanzó?
fetch•ing ['fetʃɪŋ] *adj dress, smile* cautivador, atractivo
fet•id ['fetɪd] *adj* fétido
fet•ish ['fetɪʃ] fetiche *m*
fet•ish•ism ['fetɪʃɪzəm] fetichismo *m*
fet•ish•ist ['fetɪʃɪst] fetichista *m/f*
fet•ish•ist•ic [fetɪ'ʃɪstɪk] *adj* fetichista
fet•ters ['fetərz] *npl* grilletes *mpl*; *fig* cadenas *fpl*, ataduras *fpl*
fet•tle ['fetl]: ***in fine ~*** en buena forma
fe•tus ['fiːtəs] feto *m*
feud [fjuːd] **I** *n* enemistad *f* **II** *v/i* estar enemistado
feu•dal ['fjuːdl] *adj* feudal
feu•dal•ism ['fjuːdəlɪzəm] feudalismo *m*
fe•ver ['fiːvər] fiebre *f*; ***have a ~*** tener fiebre; ***they were in a ~ of excitement*** les embargaba una emoción febril
fe•ver•ish ['fiːvərɪʃ] *adj* con fiebre; *fig*: *excitement* febril
few [fjuː] **I** *adj* (*not many*) pocos; ***a ~*** *things* unos pocos; ***quite a ~, a good ~*** (*a lot*) bastantes **II** *pron* (*not many*) pocos(-as); ***a ~*** (*some*) unos pocos; ***quite a ~, a good ~*** (*a lot*) bastantes; ***~ of them could speak English*** de ellos muy pocos hablaban inglés

few•er ['fju:ər] *adj* menos; **~ than** menos que; *with numbers* menos de
fi•an•cé [fɪ'ɑ:nseɪ] prometido *m*, novio *m*
fi•an•cée [fɪ'ɑ:nseɪ] prometida *f*, novia *f*
fi•as•co [fɪ'æskoʊ] fiasco *m*
fib [fɪb] F bola *f* F
fi•ber ['faɪbər] fibra *f*
'fi•ber•board fibra *f* vulcanizada; **'fi•ber•glass I** *n* fibra *f* de vidrio **II** *adj* de fibra de vidrio; **fi•ber-'op•tic** *adj* de fibra óptica; **~ cable** cable *m* de fibra óptica; **fi•ber 'op•tics** *nsg* tecnología *f* de la fibra óptica
fi•bre *Br* ☞ **fiber**
fib•u•la ['fɪbjʊlə] ANAT peroné *m*
fick•le ['fɪkl] *adj* inconstante, mudable
fic•tion ['fɪkʃn] **1** (*novels*) literatura *f* de ficción **2** (*made-up story*) ficción *f*
fic•tion•al ['fɪkʃnl] *adj* de ficción
fic•ti•tious [fɪk'tɪʃəs] *adj* ficticio
fid•dle ['fɪdl] **I** *n* (*violin*) violín *m* **II** *v/i*: **~ around with** enredar con **III** *v/t* F *accounts*, *result* amañar
fid•dler ['fɪdlər] F **1** MUS violinista *m/f* **2** F *cheat* tramposo(-a) *m(f)*, fullero(-a) *m(f)*
fid•dly ['fɪdlɪ] *adj job* complicado, laborioso; *little details* dificultoso
fi•del•i•ty [fɪ'delətɪ] fidelidad *f*
fid•get ['fɪdʒɪt] *v/i* moverse; **stop ~ing!** ¡estáte quieto!
fid•get•y ['fɪdʒɪtɪ] *adj* inquieto
field [fi:ld] **I** *n* **1** *also of research etc* campo *m* **2** *for sport* campo *m*, *L.Am.* cancha *f*, (*competitors in race*) participantes *mpl* **II** *v/t & v/i in baseball* fildear
'field day: **have a ~** *be successful* tener un día de suerte; *have fun* disfrutar
field•er ['fi:ldər] *in baseball* fildeador(-a) *m(f)*; **~'s choice** jugada *f* de elección
'field e•vents *npl* pruebas *fpl* de salto y lanzamiento; **'field goal** *in basketball* tiro *m* de campo; **'field hock•ey** hockey *m* sobre hierba; **'field mar•shal** MIL mariscal *m* de campo; **'field•stone** peña *f or* piedra *f* viva; **'field stud•y** estudio *m* de campo; **'field-test** *v/t* probar sobre el terreno; **'field tri•als** *npl* pruebas *fpl* sobre el terreno; **'field trip** viaje *m* de estudio(s); **'field•work** trabajo *m* de campo; *of scientist*, *market researcher* investigación *f* de campo; **'field work•er** *for relief organization* trabajador(a) *m(f)* de campo; *for market research etc* investigador(a) *m(f)* de campo
fiend [fi:nd] **1** (*devil*) demonio *m* **2** F: **she's a real fresh-air ~** (*likes the outdoors*) le encanta estar al aire libre; **opera ~** incondicional *m/f* de la ópera
fiend•ish ['fi:ndɪʃ] *adj* **1** *appearance*, *laugh*, *cunning* perverso **2** F *complexity*, *heat* endemoniado
fierce [fɪrs] *adj animal* feroz; *wind*, *storm* violento
fierce•ly ['fɪrslɪ] *adv* ferozmente
fi•er•y ['faɪrɪ] *adj* fogoso, ardiente
fif•teen [fɪf'ti:n] quince
fif•teenth [fɪf'ti:nθ] *n & adj* decimoquinto
fifth [fɪfθ] *n & adj* quinto
fif•ti•eth ['fɪftɪɪθ] *n & adj* quincuagésimo
fif•ty ['fɪftɪ] cincuenta
fif•ty-'fif•ty *adv* a medias; **go ~ with s.o.** ir a medias con alguien
fig [fɪg] higo *m*
fight [faɪt] **I** *n* **1** lucha *f*, pelea *f*; *fig*: *for survival*, *championship etc* lucha *f* **2** (*argument*) pelea *f*; **have a ~** pelearse **3** *in boxing* combate *m* **II** *v/t* (*pret & pp* **fought**) **1** *enemy*, *person* luchar contra, pelear contra; *in boxing* pelear contra **2** *disease*, *injustice* luchar contra, combatir **III** *v/i* (*pret & pp* **fought**) **1** luchar, pelear **2** (*argue*) pelearse
◆ **fight back I** *v/i* defenderse **II** *v/t scream*, *tears etc* contener, ahogar
◆ **fight for** *v/t one's rights*, *a cause* luchar por
◆ **fight off** *v/t attackers*, *fans* apartar, quitarse de encima; *infection* vencer
◆ **fight on** *v/i* seguir luchando
fight•er ['faɪtər] **1** combatiente *m/f*; **she's a ~** tiene espíritu combativo **2** *airplane* caza *m* **3** (*boxer*) púgil *m*
fight•ing ['faɪtɪŋ] *physical*, *verbal* peleas *fpl*; MIL luchas *fpl*, combates *mpl*
fight•ing 'chance: **have a ~** tener posibilidades
fight•ing 'fit *adj* en plena forma
fig•ment ['fɪgmənt]: **~ of the imagination** producto *m* de la imaginación
'fig tree higuera *f*
fig•u•ra•tive ['fɪgjərətɪv] *adj* figurado
fig•ure ['fɪgər] **I** *n* **1** figura *f*; **have a**

good ~ tener buen tipo **2** (*digit*) cifra *f* **II** *v/t* F (*think*) imaginarse, pensar

◆ **figure on** *v/t* F (*plan*) pensar; ***I was figuring on going to ...*** estaba pensando en ir a ...

◆ **figure out** *v/t* (*understand*) entender; *calculation* resolver; ***figure it out for yourself*** averígualo por tí mismo

'fig•ure•head **1** NAUT mascarón *m* de proa **2** *fig* monigote *m/f*; **'fig•ure skat•er** patinador(a) *m(f)* artístico(-a); **'fig•ure skat•ing** patinaje *m* artístico

filch [fɪltʃ] *v/t* F mangar, soplar F

file[1] [faɪl] **I** *n* **1** *of documents* expediente *m* **2** COMPUT archivo *m*, fichero *m* **II** *v/t* **1** *documents* archivar **2** LAW: ***~ a petition in bankruptcy*** presentar una declaración de bancarrota

◆ **file away** *v/t documents* archivar

file[2] [faɪl] *n for wood, fingernails* lima *f*

'file cab•i•net archivador *m*; **'file clerk** archivero(-a) *m(f)*; **'file man•age•ment** COMPUT gestión *f* de archivos; **'file man•ag•er** COMPUT administrador *m* de archivos; **'file name** COMPUT nombre *m* de archivo

fi•li•al ['fɪlɪəl] *adj* filial

fil•i•bus•ter ['fɪlɪbʌstər] POL **I** *n* **1** *speech* obstruccionismo *m* **2** *person* obstruccionista *m/f* **II** *v/i* practicar el obstruccionismo

fil•i•bus•ter•er ['fɪlɪbʌstərər] POL obstruccionista *m/f*

fil•i•bus•ter•ing ['fɪlɪbʌstərɪŋ] POL tácticas *fpl* obstruccionistas

fil•i•gree ['fɪlɪgriː] filigrana *f*

fil•ing cab•i•net ['faɪlɪŋ] *Br* ☞ ***file cabinet***

fil•ings ['faɪlɪŋz] *npl* limaduras *fpl*

fill [fɪl] **I** *v/t* **1** llenar **2** *tooth* empastar, *L.Am.* emplomar **3** *prescription* despachar **II** *n*: ***eat one's ~*** hincharse

◆ **fill in** *v/t* **1** *form, hole* rellenar **2**: ***fill s.o. in*** poner a alguien al tanto; ***can you fill me in on what's been happening?*** ¿me podrías poner al tanto de lo que ha pasado?

◆ **fill in for** *v/t* sustituir a

◆ **fill out I** *v/t form* rellenar **II** *v/i* (*get fatter*) engordar

◆ **fill up I** *v/t* llenar (hasta arriba) **II** *v/i of stadium, theater* llenarse

fill•er ['fɪlər] *for filling holes* masilla *f*

'fill•er cap MOT tapa *f* del depósito

fil•let ['fɪlɪt] filete *m*

fill•ing ['fɪlɪŋ] **I** *n* **1** *in sandwich* relleno *m* **2** *in tooth* empaste *m*, *L.Am.* emplomadura *f* **II** *adj*: ***be ~*** *of food* llenar mucho

'fill•ing sta•tion estación *f* de servicio, gasolinera *f*

fil•ly ['fɪlɪ] potra *f*

film [fɪlm] **I** *n* **1** *for camera* carrete *m* **2** (*movie*) película *f* **II** *v/t person, event* filmar

'film di•rec•tor director(a) *m(f)* de cine; **'film fes•ti•val** festival *m* de cine; **'film-mak•er** cineasta *m/f*; **'film star** estrella *f* de cine; **'film stu•di•o** estudio *m* de cine

Fi•lo•fax® ['faɪləfæks] filofax® *m*, agenda *f* de anillas

fil•ter ['fɪltər] **I** *n* filtro *m* **II** *v/t coffee, liquid* filtrar

◆ **filter through** *v/i of news reports* filtrarse

'fil•ter pa•per papel *m* de filtro

'fil•ter tip *cigarette* cigarrillo *m* con filtro

filth [fɪlθ] **1** suciedad *f*, mugre *f* **2** *pej*: *people* bazofia *f*, (*pornography*) porquerías *fpl*

filth•y ['fɪlθɪ] *adj* sucio, mugriento; *language, movie etc* obsceno; ***~ weather*** tiempo *m* asqueroso F

fin [fɪn] *of fish* aleta *f*

fi•nal ['faɪnl] **I** *adj* (*last*) último; *decision* final, definitivo; ***~ four*** *in basketball* final *f* a cuatro **II** *n* SP final *f*; ***get through to the ~*** llegar a la final

fi•nal ac'cept•ance COM recepción *f* definitiva

fi•nal de'mand FIN demanda *f* final

fi•na•le [fɪ'nælɪ] final *m*

fi•nal e'di•tion *of newspaper* última *f* edición

fi•nal•ist ['faɪnəlɪst] finalista *m/f*

fi•nal•i•ty [faɪ'nælətɪ] *of decision* irreversibilidad *f*, *of tone* rotundidad *f*

fi•nal•ize ['faɪnəlaɪz] *v/t plans, design* ultimar

fi•nal•ly ['faɪnəlɪ] *adv* **1** finalmente, por último **2** (*at last*) finalmente, por fin

fi•nal 'of•fer oferta *f* final

fi•nance ['faɪnæns] **I** *n* finanzas *fpl* **II** *v/t* financiar

fi•nan•ces ['faɪnænsɪz] *npl* finanzas *fpl*

fi•nan•cial [faɪ'nænʃl] *adj* financiero

fi•nan•cial ad•vis•er asesor(a) *m(f)* financiero(-a)
fi•nan•cial•ly [faɪˈnænʃəlɪ] *adv* económicamente
fiˈnan•cial mar•ket mercado *m* financiero; **fiˈnan•cial pag•es** *npl of newspaper* sección *f* de economía; **fi•nan•cial ˈyear** *Br* ejercicio *m* económico, año *m* fiscal
fi•nan•cier [faɪˈnænsɪr] financiero(-a) *m(f)*
fi•nanc•ing plan [ˈfaɪnænsɪŋ] plan *m* de financiación
finch [fɪntʃ] pinzón *m*
find [faɪnd] *v/t* (*pret & pp* **found**) encontrar, hallar; ***if you ~ it too hot / cold*** si te parece demasiado caliente / frío; ***~ s.o. innocent / guilty*** LAW declarar a alguien inocente / culpable; ***I ~ it strange that ...*** me sorprende que ...; ***how did you ~ the hotel?*** ¿qué te pareció el hotel?
◆ **find out I** *v/t* descubrir, averiguar **II** *v/i* (*discover*) descubrir; ***can you try to find out?*** ¿podrías enterarte?; ***what's he like? – you'll find out*** ¿cómo es? – ya lo verás
◆ **find out about** *v/t secret, goings-on* descubrir, enterarse de
find•ings [ˈfaɪndɪŋz] *npl of report* conclusiones *fpl*
fine[1] [faɪn] *adj* **1** *day, weather* bueno; *wine, performance, city* excelente; ***how's that? – that's ~*** ¿qué tal está? – bien; ***that's ~ by me*** por mí no hay ningún problema; ***how are you? – ~*** ¿cómo estás? – bien **2** *distinction, line* fino
fine[2] [faɪn] **I** *n* multa *f* **II** *v/t* multar, poner una multa a; ***you'll get ~d*** te van a multar
fine ˈarts *npl* bellas artes *fpl*
fine•ly [ˈfaɪnlɪ] *adv* **1** *made, crafted* con maestría, elegantemente **2** *sliced* muy fino
fine ˈprint letra *f* pequeña
fi•nesse [fɪˈnes] (*skill*) delicadeza *f*, tacto *m*
fine-ˈtooth comb: ***go through sth with a ~*** revisar algo minuciosamente
fine-ˈtune *v/t engine, fig* afinar, hacer los últimos ajustes a
fin•ger [ˈfɪŋgər] **I** *n* dedo *m*; ***I can't quite put my ~ on it*** *fig* no sé exactamente de qué se trata; ***they didn't lift a ~ (to help)*** no movieron ni un dedo (para ayudar); ***point the ~ at s.o.*** *fig* señalar con el dedo a alguien; ***give s.o. the ~*** *obscene gesture* hacer a alguien un corte de mangas **II** *v/t* tocar
ˈfin•ger•board *of guitar* diapasón *m*; **ˈfin•ger-food** *comida para la que no se necesitan cubiertos*; **ˈfin•ger•mark** marca *f* dactilar; **ˈfin•ger•nail** uña *f*; **ˈfin•ger•print I** *n* huella *f* digital *or* dactilar **II** *v/t* tomar las huellas digitales *or* dactilares a; **ˈfin•ger•tip** punta *f* del dedo; ***have sth at one's ~s*** saberse algo al dedillo
fin•i•cky [ˈfɪnɪkɪ] *adj* **1** *person* quisquilloso **2** *design* enrevesado
fin•ish [ˈfɪnɪʃ] **I** *v/t* acabar, terminar; ***~ doing sth*** acabar *or* terminar de hacer algo **II** *v/i* acabar, terminar **III** *n* **1** *of product* acabado *m* **2** *of race* final *m*; ***he has a strong ~*** *of runner* siempre remata bien las carreras
◆ **finish off** *v/t* **1** acabar, terminar **2** (*kill*) acabar con, matar
◆ **finish up I** *v/t food* acabar, terminar; ***he finished up liking it*** acabó gustándole **II** *v/i*: ***we finished up at Paula's place*** acabamos en casa de Paula
◆ **finish with** *v/t* **1** *boyfriend etc* cortar con **2**: ***can I have that when you've finished with it?*** ¿me lo puedes dejar cuando hayas acabado?
fin•ished [ˈfɪnɪʃt] *adj* **1** *goods* terminado, acabado **2**: ***be ~*** *of person, job* estar acabado; *of food, beer etc* estar terminado *or* acabado; ***he's ~ as a politician*** como político está acabado; ***it's all ~ between us*** todo ha acabado entre nosotros
ˈfin•ished goods *npl* producto *m* final
ˈfin•ished pro•duct producto *m* final
fin•ish•ing [ˈfɪnɪʃɪŋ] *adj*: ***put the ~ touches to sth*** dar los últimos retoques a algo
ˈfin•ish•ing line línea *f* de meta
fi•nite [ˈfaɪnaɪt] *adj* limitado, definido
fink [fɪŋk] P **1** (*strikebreaker*) esquirol *m/f* P **2** (*unpleasant person*) cabrón(-ona) *m(f)*
Fin•land [ˈfɪnlənd] Finlandia *f*
Finn•ish [ˈfɪnɪʃ] **I** *adj* finlandés **II** *n language* finés *m*
Finn [fɪn] finlandés(-esa) *m(f)*

fir [fɜːr] abeto *m*
'fir cone piña *f*
fire [faɪr] **I** *n* fuego *m*; *electric, gas* estufa *f*; (*blaze*) incendio *m*; (*bonfire, campfire etc*) hoguera *f*; ***be on ~*** estar ardiendo; ***catch ~*** prender; ***set sth on ~, set ~ to sth*** prender fuego a algo **II** *v/i* (*shoot*) disparar (***on*** sobre; ***at*** a) **III** *v/t* F (*dismiss*) despedir; ***you're ~d*** estás despedido
◆ **fire away** *v/i with questions*: ***fire away!*** ¡adelante!, ¡dispara!
'fire a•larm alarma *f* contra incendios; **'fire•arm** arma *f* de fuego; **'fire•bug** F pirómano(-a) *m(f)*; **'fire•crack•er** petardo *m*; **'fire de•part•ment** (cuerpo *m* de) bomberos *mpl*; **'fire door** puerta *f* contra incendios; **'fire drill** simulacro *m* de incendio; **'fire en•gine** coche *m* de bomberos; **'fire es•cape** salida *f* de incendios; **'fire ex•tin•guish•er** extintor *m*; **'fire•fight** MIL tiroteo *m*; **'fire fight•er** bombero(-a) *m(f)*; **'fire•guard** pantalla *f*, parachispas *m inv*; **'fire house** estación *f or Span* parque *m* de bomberos; **'fire hy•drant** hidrante *m* de incendios, boca *f* de incendios; **'fire in•sur•ance** seguro *m* contra incendios; **'fire•light** luz *f* de la lumbre; *of camp fire* luz *f* del fuego; **'fire•man** bombero *m*; **'fire•place** chimenea *f*, hogar *m*; **'fire•plug** hidrante *m* de incendios, boca *f* de incendios; **'fire pre•ven•tion** prevención *f* de incendios; **'fire•proof** *adj* ignífugo, resistente al fuego; **'fire•side**: ***by the ~*** junto al hogar, al calor de la lumbre; **'fire station** estación *f or Span* parque *m* de bomberos; **'fire truck** coche *m* de bomberos; **'fire•wood** leña *f*; **'fire•work dis•play** fuegos *mpl* artificiales
'fire•works *npl* fuegos *mpl* artificiales; ***there'll be ~ if he finds out*** F se va a armar una buena si se entera F
fir•ing line ['faɪrɪŋ]: ***be in the ~*** *fig* estar en la línea de fuego; **'fir•ing par•ty** pelotón *m* de fusilamiento; **'fir•ing range** MIL **1** *for exercises* campo *m* de tiro **2**: ***within ~*** al alcance de tiro; **'fir•ing squad** pelotón *m* de fusilamiento
firm[1] [fɜːrm] *adj* firme; ***a ~ deal*** un acuerdo en firme
firm[2] [fɜːrm] *n* COM empresa *f*
firm•ness ['fɜːrmnɪs] firmeza *f*, fortaleza *f*
firm•ware ['fɜːrmwer] COMPUT firmware *m*, microprograma *m*
first [fɜːrst] **I** *adj* primero; ***who's ~ please?*** ¿quién es el primero, por favor? **II** *n* primero(-a) *m(f)* **III** *adv* primero; ***~ of all*** (*for one reason*) en primer lugar; ***at ~*** al principio
first 'aid primeros auxilios *mpl*; **first-'aid box, first-'aid kit** botiquín *m* de primeros auxilios; **first aid•er** [fɜːrst'eɪdər] persona *f* que presta primeros auxilios ; **'first base** *in baseball* primera base *f*, *player* inicialista *m/f*; **'first base•man** *in baseball* jugador(a) *m(f)* de primera base; **'first•born** *adj* primogénito; **'first class I** *adj* **1** *ticket, seat* de primera (clase) **2** (*very good*) excelente **II** *adv travel* en primera (clase); **first 'cous•in** primo(-a) *m(f)* hermano(-a); **first-de'gree** *adj burns* de primer grado; **first 'floor** planta *f* baja, *Br* primer piso *m*; **first'hand** *adj* de primera mano; **First 'La•dy** *of US* primera dama *f*
first•ly ['fɜːrstlɪ] *adv* en primer lugar
first 'name nombre *m* (de pila); **first 'night** estreno *m*; **first of'fend•er** delincuente *m/f* sin antecedentes; **first of'fense** primer delito *m*; **first-'rate** *adj* excelente; **first-time 'buy•er** persona *f* que compra por primera vez
fis•cal ['fɪskl] *adj* fiscal
fis•cal 'pe•ri•od ejercicio *m* fiscal
fis•cal 'year año *m* fiscal
fish [fɪʃ] **I** *n* (*pl* ***fish***) pez *m*; *to eat* pescado *m*; ***drink like a ~*** F beber como un cosaco F; ***feel like a ~ out of water*** F sentirse fuera de lugar; ***they're after the big ~*** *fig* están buscando al pez gordo **II** *v/i* pescar; ***go ~ing*** ir de pesca
◆ **fish for** *v/t compliment, information* ir detrás de, ir buscando
◆ **fish out** *v/t*: ***he fished it out of his pocket*** lo sacó de su bolsillo; ***they fished him out of the water*** lo sacaron del agua
'fish•bone espina *f* (de pescado); **'fish bowl** pecera *f*; **'fish cake** *pastel individual de pescado*
fish•er•man ['fɪʃərmən] pescador *m*
'fish farm piscifactoría *f*
fish 'fin•ger *Br* ☞ ***fish stick***
fish•ing ['fɪʃɪŋ] pesca *f*

'**fish•ing boat** (barco *m*) pesquero *m*; '**fish•ing grounds** *npl* caladero *m*; '**fish•ing line** sedal *m*; '**fish•ing net** red *f* de pescar; '**fish•ing rod** caña *f* de pescar; '**fish•ing tack•le** abalorios *mpl* de pesca; '**fish•ing vil•lage** pueblo *m* pesquero

fish•mon•ger ['fɪʃmʌŋgər] *esp Br* pescadero(-a) *m(f)*

'**fish stick** croqueta *f or* palito *m* de pescado

'**fish tank** *in home* pecera *f*

fish•y ['fɪʃɪ] *adj* F (*suspicious*) sospechoso

fis•sion ['fɪʃn] fisión *f*

fis•sure ['fɪʃər] fisura *f*

fist [fɪst] puño *m*

fit[1] [fɪt] *n* MED ataque *m*; ***a ~ of rage / jealousy*** un arrebato de cólera / un ataque de celos; ***she'll have a ~*** F le va a dar un ataque

fit[2] [fɪt] *adj* **1** *physically* en forma; ***are you ~ to drive?*** ¿estás *or* te encuentras en condiciones de conducir?; ***keep ~*** mantenerse en forma **2** *morally* adecuado; ***he's not ~ to be President*** no es la persona apta para ser Presidente **3**: ***he was laughing ~ to burst*** se desternillaba *or* se moría de risa

fit[3] [fɪt] **I** *v/t* (*pret & pp* ***-ted*** *or* ***fit***) **1** (*attach*) colocar; ***the doors are ~ted with a special alarm*** las puertas están equipadas con una alarma especial **2**: ***these pants don't ~ me any more*** estos pantalones ya no me entran; ***it ~s you perfectly*** te queda perfectamente **3** *description etc* ajustarse a, coincidir con **II** *v/i* (*pret & pp* ***-ted*** *or* ***fit***) *of clothes* quedar bien; *of piece of furniture etc* caber

III *n*: ***it's a good ~*** *of coat etc* queda bien; *of piece of furniture* cabe bien; ***it's a tight ~*** *of coat ect* me / te *etc* queda ajustado; *of furniture* no hay mucho espacio

◆ **fit in I** *v/i of person in group, with plans* encajar; ***it fits in perfectly with the color scheme*** va a la perfección con la combinación de colores **II** *v/t*: ***fit s.o. in*** *into schedule etc* hacer un hueco a alguien

fit•ful ['fɪtfəl] *adj sleep* intermitente

fit•ness ['fɪtnɪs] *physical* buena forma *f*

'**fit•ness cen•ter**, *Br* '**fit•ness cen•tre** gimnasio *m*

fit•ted kitch•en [fɪtɪd'kɪʧɪn] cocina *f* a medida

fit•ted 'sheet sábana *f* ajustable

fit•ter ['fɪtər] técnico(-a) *m(f)*

fit•ting ['fɪtɪŋ] *adj* apropiado

fit•tings ['fɪtɪŋz] *npl* equipamiento *m*

five [faɪv] cinco

fix [fɪks] **I** *n* **1** (*solution*) solución *f* **2**: ***be in a ~*** F estar en un lío F **II** *v/t* **1** (*attach*) fijar; ***~ sth onto sth*** fijar algo a algo **2** (*repair*) arreglar, reparar **3** *arrange*: *meeting etc*) organizar **4** *lunch* preparar; ***I'll ~ you a drink*** te prepararé una bebida **5** *dishonestly*: *match etc* amañar

◆ **fix on** *v/t* **1** (*decide on*) fijar, decidir **2**: ***I was fixing on coming out to see you*** estaba pensando en ir a verte

◆ **fix up** *v/t meeting* organizar

fix•ate [fɪk'seɪt] *v/t*: ***be ~d on*** PSYCH tener fijación por

fix•a•tion [fɪk'seɪʃn] PSYCH fijación *f*

fixed [fɪkst] *adj* fijo

fixed 'as•sets *npl* activos *mpl* fijos; **fixed 'costs** *npl* FIN costos *mpl* fijos; '**fixed-in•ter•est** *adj loan* a interés fijo

fix•ed•ly ['fɪksɪdlɪ] *adv stare* fijamente

fix•er ['fɪksər] F amañador(a) *m(f)*

fix•ings ['fɪkɪŋz] *npl* guarnición *f*; ***roast beef with all the ~*** ternera *f* al horno con guarnición

fix•ture ['fɪksʧər] (*in room*) *parte fija del mobiliario o la decoración de una habitación*

fizz [fɪz] *v/i of champagne etc* burbujear, hacer burbujas

◆ **fiz•zle out** ['fɪzl] *v/i* F quedarse en nada

fiz•zy ['fɪzɪ] *adj Br* con burbujas

flab [flæb] *on body* grasa *f*

flab•ber•gast ['flæbərgæst] *v/t* F: ***be ~ed*** quedarse estupefacto *or Span* alucinado F

flab•by ['flæbɪ] *adj muscles etc* fofo

flac•cid ['flæsɪd] *fml* ☞ ***flabby***

flag[1] [flæg] *v/i* (*pret & pp* ***-ged***) (*tire*) desfallecer

flag[2] [flæg] *n* bandera *f*

◆ **flag down** *v/t driver, taxi* parar

◆ **flag up** *v/t* señalar, indicar

flag of con've•ni•ence pabellón *m or* bandera *f* de conveniencia

'**flag•pole** asta *f* (de bandera)

fla•grant ['fleɪgrənt] *adj* flagrante
'flag•ship *fig* estandarte *m*; **'flag•staff** asta *f* (de bandera); **'flag•stone** losa *f*
flail [fleɪl] **I** *v/i* agitarse **II** *v/t*: **~ *one's arms*** agitar los brazos
flair [fler] (*talent*) don *m*; ***have a natural ~ for*** tener dotes para
flake [fleɪk] **1** *of snow* copo *m*; *of skin* escama *f*; *of plaster* desconchón *m* **2** F *person* bicho *m* raro
◆ **flake off** *v/i of skin* descamarse; *of plaster, paint* desconcharse
flak•y ['fleɪkɪ] *adj* **1** *skin* con escamas; *paint* desconchado **2** F *behavior* excéntrico
flak•y 'pas•try hojaldre *m*
flam•boy•ance [flæm'bɔɪəns] *of personality, dress* extravagancia *f*, exuberancia *f*
flam•boy•ant [flæm'bɔɪənt] *adj personality* extravagante
flam•boy•ant•ly [flæm'bɔɪəntlɪ] *adv dressed* extravagantemente
flame [fleɪm] **1** llama *f*; ***go up in ~s*** ser pasto de las llamas **2**: ***an old ~ of his*** un viejo amorío suyo
fla•men•co [flə'meŋkoʊ] flamenco *m*
fla'men•co danc•er bailaor(a) *m*(*f*)
flam•ma•ble ['flæməbl] *adj* inflamable
flan [flæn] tarta *f*
flange [flændʒ] TECH pestaña *f*, reborde *m*
flank [flæŋk] **I** *n* **1** *of horse etc* costado *m* **2** MIL flanco *m* **II** *v/t* flanquear
flap [flæp] **I** *n* **1** *of envelope, pocket* solapa *f* **2** *of table* hoja *f* **3**: ***be in a ~*** F estar histérico F **II** *v/t* (*pret & pp* **-ped**) *wings* batir **III** *v/i* (*pret & pp* **-ped**) *of flag etc* ondear
flap•jack ['flæpdʒæk] *galleta a base de avena, mantequilla y azúcar*
flare [fler] **I** *n* **1** (*distress signal*) bengala *f* **2** *in dress* vuelo *m* **II** *v/t*: **~ *one's nostrils*** hinchar las narices resoplando
◆ **flare up** *v/i of violence* estallar; *of illness, rash* brotar; *of fire* llamear; (*get very angry*) estallar
flared [flerd] *adj pants, skirt* acampanado
'flare-up *of violence, rash* brote *m*
flash [flæʃ] **I** *n* **1** *of light* destello *m*; PHOT flash *m*; ***in a ~*** F en un abrir y cerrar de ojos; ***have a ~ of inspiration*** tener una inspiración repentina; ***a ~ of lightning*** un relámpago **2** (*~light*) linterna *f* **II** *v/i of light* destellar **III** *v/t*: **~ *one's headlights*** echar las luces
'flash•back *in movie* flash-back *m*, escena *f* retrospectiva
'flash bulb PHOT flash *m*
flash•er ['flæʃər] **1** MOT intermitente *m* **2** F exhibicionista *m*/*f*
'flash-freeze *v/t* congelar ultrarrápidamente
'flash•light 1 linterna *f* **2** PHOT flash *m*
flash•y ['flæʃɪ] *adj pej* ostentoso, chillón
flask [flæsk] **1** (*hip ~*) petaca *f* **2** *in laboratory* matraz *m*
flat[1] [flæt] **I** *adj* **1** *surface, land* llano, plano **2** *beer* sin gas **3** *battery* descargado **4** *tire* desinflado **5** *shoes* bajo **6** MUS bemol **7**: ***and that's ~*** F y sanseacabó F **II** *adv* **1** MUS demasiado bajo **2**: **~ *out*** *work, run, drive* a tope **III** *n* (*~ tire*) pinchazo *m*
flat[2] [flæt] *n Br* apartamento *m*, *Span* piso *m*
'flat•bed truck camión *m* con remolque de plataforma; **flat-chest•ed** [flæt'tʃestɪd] *adj* plana de pecho; **'flat•foot** P *policeman* madero *m* F
flat•ly ['flætlɪ] *adv refuse, deny* rotundamente
'flat•mate *Br* compañero(-a) *m*/*f* de apartamento *or Span* piso
flat•ness ['flætnəs] *of ground, surface* lisura *f*, lo llano
'flat rate tarifa *f* única
flat•ten ['flætn] *v/t* **1** *land, road* allanar, aplanar **2** *by bombing, demolition* arrasar
flat•ter ['flætər] *v/t* halagar, adular
flat•ter•er ['flætərər] adulador(a) *m*(*f*)
flat•ter•ing ['flætərɪŋ] *adj* **1** *comments* halagador **2** *color, clothes* favorecedor
flat•ter•y ['flætərɪ] halagos *mpl*, adulación *f*; **~ *will get you nowhere*** no vas a conseguir nada con halagos
flat•u•lence ['flætjʊləns] flatulencia *f*
flat•ware ['flætwer] (*cutlery*) cubertería *f*
flaunt [flɒːnt] *v/t* hacer ostentación de, alardear de
flau•tist ['flɒːtɪst] flautista *m*/*f*
fla•vor ['fleɪvər] **I** *n* sabor *m*; ***what ~ (of) ice cream do you want?*** ¿de qué sabor quieres el helado?; ***it gives you the ~ of what life was like then*** eso te da una

F

idea *or* visión de cómo era la vida antes; ***she's not exactly ~ of the month around here*** F no es muy popular por aquí que digamos **II** *v/t food* condimentar
fla•vor•ing ['fleɪvərɪŋ] aromatizante *m*
fla•vor•ist ['fleɪvərɪst] creador(a) *m(f)* de aromatizantes
fla•vour *etc Br* ☞ ***flavor*** *etc*
flaw [flɒː] defecto *m*, fallo *m*
flawed [flɒːd] *adj* defectuoso, erróneo; *beauty* imperfecto; ***the plan was fatally ~*** el plan contenía errores mayúsculos
flaw•less ['flɒːlɪs] *adj* impecable
flax•en ['flæksən] *adj hair* rubio claro
flay [fleɪ] *v/t animal* despellejar, desollar
flea [fliː] pulga *f*
'flea mar•ket mercadillo *m*, rastro *m*
fleck [flek] mota *f*
fled [fled] *pret & pp* ☞ ***flee***
fledg•ling ['fledʒlɪŋ] **1** *bird* pajarito *m* **2** *fig* principiante *m/f*
flee [fliː] (*pret & pp* ***fled***) **I** *v/i* escapar, huir **II** *v/t the country* escapar de, huir de
fleece[1] [fliːs] *v/t* F desplumar F
fleece[2] [fliːs] *n* **1** *of sheep* lana *f* **2** *jacket* forro *m* polar
fleec•y ['fliːsɪ] *adj material*, *lining* lanoso
fleet [fliːt] NAUT, *of vehicles* flota *f*
fleet•ing ['fliːtɪŋ] *adj visit etc* fugaz; ***catch a ~ glimpse of*** vislumbrar fugazmente a
flesh [fleʃ] carne *f*, *of fruit* pulpa *f*; ***meet / see s.o. in the ~*** conocer / ver a alguien en persona
'flesh-col•ored *adj* de color carne, rosado; **flesh-press•er** ['fleʃpresər] relaciones públicas *m/f*; **'flesh wound** herida *f* superficial
flew [fluː] *pret* ☞ ***fly***
flex [fleks] *v/t muscles* flexionar
flex•i•bil•i•ty [fleksə'bɪlətɪ] flexibilidad *f*
flex•i•ble ['fleksəbl] *adj* flexible
flex•time ['flekstaɪm] horario *m* flexible
flick [flɪk] *v/t tail* sacudir; ***he ~ed a fly off his hand*** espantó una mosca que tenía en la mano; ***she ~ed her hair out of her eyes*** se apartó el pelo de los ojos
◆ **flick through** *v/t book*, *magazine* hojear
flick•er ['flɪkər] *v/i of light*, *screen* parpadear
flick•er-'free *adj screen* sin parpadeo
fli•er[1] [flaɪr] **1** (*aviator*) aviador(a) *m(f)* **2**: ***rewards for frequent ~s*** recompensas para los que más vuelan
fli•er[2] [flaɪr] (*circular*) folleto *m*
flies [flaɪz] *npl Br*: *on pants* bragueta *f*
flight [flaɪt] **1** *in airplane* vuelo *m*; ***not capable of ~*** incapaz de volar; ***in ~*** *in baseball* en vuelo **2** (*fleeing*) huida *f* **3**: ***~ of stairs*** tramo *m* (de escaleras); ***two ~s up*** dos tramos de escaleras arriba
'flight at•tend•ant auxiliar *m/f* de vuelo; **'flight bag** bolsa *f* de viaje; **flight con•trol•ler** ['flaɪtkəntroulər] controlador(a) *m(f)* aéreo(-a); **'flight crew** tripulación *f*; **'flight deck** AVIA **1** cabina *f* del piloto **2** *of aircraft carrier* cubierta *f* de despegue / aterrizaje; **'flight en•gi•neer** ingeniero(-a) *m(f)* de vuelo; **'flight num•ber** número *m* de vuelo; **'flight path** ruta *f* de vuelo; **'flight re•cord•er** caja *f* negra; **'flight time 1** *departure* hora *f* del vuelo **2** *duration* duración *f* del vuelo; **'flight sim•u•la•tor** simulador *m* de vuelo
flight•y ['flaɪtɪ] *adj* inconstante
flim•sy ['flɪmzɪ] *adj structure*, *furniture* endeble; *dress*, *material* débil; *excuse* pobre
flinch [flɪntʃ] *v/i* encogerse
fling [flɪŋ] **I** *v/t* (*pret & pp* ***flung***) arrojar, lanzar; ***~ o.s. into a chair*** dejarse caer en una silla **II** *n* F (*affair*) aventura *f*; ***have a ~ with s.o.*** tener una aventura con alguien
◆ **fling back** *v/t one's head* echar para atrás
flint [flɪnt] piedra *f*; GEOL sílex *m*
◆ **flip over** [flɪp] *v/i* (*pret & pp* ***-ped***) volcar
◆ **flip through** *v/t magazine* hojear
'flip chart flip chart *m* (*pizarra con hojas de papel que se usa para escribir gráficos, etc en reuniones y conferencias*)
'flip-flops *npl* chancletas *fpl*
flip•pan•cy ['flɪpənsɪ] frivolidad *f*
flip•pant ['flɪpənt] *adj* frívolo, superficial
flip•per ['flɪpər] *for swimming* aleta *f*
'flip side *of record* cara *f* B

flirt [flɜːrt] **I** *v/i* flirtear, coquetear **II** *n* ligón(-ona) *m(f)*

flir•ta•tion [flɜːr'teɪʃn] flirteo *m*, coqueteo *m*

flir•ta•tious [flɜːr'teɪʃəs] *adj* provocador

flit [flɪt] *v/i* (*pret & pp* ***-ted***) revolotear

float [floʊt] **I** *v/i also* FIN flotar **II** *v/t* **1** *on stock market* sacar a bolsa, comenzar a cotizar **2** *currency* hacer fluctuar

float•ing vot•er ['floʊtɪŋ] votante *m/f* indeciso(-a)

flock [flɑːk] **I** *n of sheep* rebaño *m* **II** *v/i* acudir en masa

flog [flɑːg] *v/t* (*pret & pp* ***-ged***) (*whip*) azotar

flood [flʌd] **I** *n* inundación *f* **II** *v/t of river* inundar; *carburetor, engine* ahogar

◆ **flood in** *v/i* llegar en grandes cantidades

flood•ing ['flʌdɪŋ] inundaciones *fpl*

'flood•light foco *m*; **'flood•lit** *adj game* con luz artificial; **'flood plain** llanura *f* alrededor de un río (*expuesta a inundaciones*); **'flood wa•ters** *npl* crecida *f*

floor [flɔːr] **1** suelo *m* **2** (*story*) piso *m*; ***on the fifteenth ~*** en el piso decimocuarto, *Br* en el piso decimoquinto

'floor•board tabla *f* del suelo; **'floor cloth** trapo *m* del suelo;; **'floor ex•er•cis•es** *npl* ejercicios *mpl* de suelo

floor•ing ['flɔːrɪŋ] *material* suelo *m*

'floor lamp lámpara *f* de pie; **'floor lead•er** POL *persona dentro de un partido político encargada de organizar las actividades*; **'floor plan** plano *m* de planta; **'floor show** espectáculo *m*, show *m*; **'floor wait•er** *in hotel* camarero(-a) *m(f)* de planta

floo•zy ['fluːzɪ] *pej* P fresca *f*

flop [flɑːp] **I** *v/i* (*pret & pp* ***-ped***) **1** dejarse caer **2** F (*fail*) pinchar F **II** *n* F (*failure*) pinchazo *m* F

flop•py ['flɑːpɪ] *adj* **1** *ears* caído; *hat* blando **2** (*weak*) flojo

flop•py 'disk disquete *m*

flop•py-'disk drive unidad *f* de disquete

flo•ra ['flɔːrə] BOT flora *f*

flo•ral ['flɔːrəl] *adj* floral; ***~ pattern*** estampado *m* floral

flor•id ['flɑːrɪd] *adj complexion* rubicundo

flor•ist ['flɔːrɪst] florista *m/f*

floss [flɑːs] **I** *n for teeth* hilo *m* dental **II** *v/t*: ***~ one's teeth*** limpiarse los dientes con hilo dental

flot•sam ['flɑːtsəm] NAUT restos *mpl* de un naufragio; ***the ~ and jetsam*** *fig* la sociedad marginal

flounce [flaʊns] *v/i* moverse mostrando irritación; ***she ~d out of the room*** salió de la habitación con aires de indignación

floun•der[1] ['flaʊndər] *n fish* platija

floun•der[2] ['flaʊndər] *v/i* **1** *through swamp etc* avanzar con dificultad **2** *in speech, exam* vacilar

flour [flaʊr] harina *f*

flour•ish ['flʌrɪʃ] *v/i of plant* crecer rápidamente; *of business, civilization* florecer, prosperar

flour•ish•ing ['flʌrɪʃɪŋ] *adj business, trade* floreciente, próspero

flout [flaʊt] *v/t s.o.'s wishes, convention* desobedecer; *law* infringir

flow [floʊ] **I** *v/i* fluir **II** *n* flujo *m*

'flow•chart diagrama *m* de flujo

flow•er [flaʊr] **I** *n* **1** flor *f* **2**: ***be in ~*** estar en flor **II** *v/i* florecer

'flow•er ar•range•ment decoración *f* floral; **'flow•er•bed** parterre *m*; **'flow•er girl 1** *selling* chica *f* de las flores **2** (*at wedding*) *niña que lleva un ramo de flores*; **'flow•er•pot** tiesto *m*, maceta *f*; **'flow•er pow•er** paz y amor; **'flow•er show** exposición *f* floral

flow•er•y ['flaʊrɪ] *adj pattern* floreado; *style of writing* florido

flown [floʊn] *pp* ☞ ***fly***

flu [fluː] gripe *f*

fluc•tu•ate ['flʌktjʊeɪt] *v/i* fluctuar

fluc•tu•a•tion [flʌktjʊ'eɪʃn] fluctuación *f*

flu•en•cy ['fluːənsɪ] *in a language* fluidez *f*

flu•ent ['fluːənt] *adj*: ***he speaks ~ Spanish*** habla español con soltura

flu•ent•ly ['fluːəntlɪ] *adv speak, write* con soltura

fluff [flʌf] *material* pelusa *f*

fluff•y ['flʌfɪ] *adj* esponjoso; ***~ toy*** juguete *m* de peluche

fluid ['fluːɪd] fluido *m*

fluke [fluːk] F chiripa *f* F; ***by a ~*** de chiripa *or* casualidad

flung [flʌŋ] *pret & pp* ☞ ***fling***

flunk [flʌŋk] *v/t & v/i* F suspender, *Span*

catear F

flu•o•res•cent [flʊ'resnt] *adj light* fluorescente

flu•o•ride ['flʊəraɪd] CHEM fluoruro *m*

flu•o•ride 'tooth•paste pasta *f* dentífrica con flúor

flur•ry ['flʌrɪ] *of snow* torbellino *m*

flush [flʌʃ] **I** *v/t*: **~ the toilet** tirar de la cadena; **~ sth down the toilet** tirar algo por el retrete **II** *v/i* **1** *(go red in the face)* ruborizarse **2**: **the toilet won't ~** la cisterna no funciona **III** *adj (level)*: **be ~ with** estar a la misma altura que **IV** *n*: **in the first ~ of youth** *esp lit* en la flor de la vida **V** *adv*: **~ left / right** alineado a la izquierda / derecha

◆ **flush away** *v/t*: **flush sth away** *down toilet* tirar algo por el retrete

◆ **flush out** *v/t rebels etc* hacer salir

flus•ter ['flʌstər] *v/t*: **get ~ed** ponerse nervioso; **don't ~ me!** ¡no me pongas nervioso!

flute [flu:t] **1** MUS flauta *f* **2** *glass* copa *f* de champán

flut•ist ['flu:tɪst] flautista *m/f*

flut•ter ['flʌtər] *v/i of bird, wings* aletear; *of flag* ondear; *of heart* latir con fuerza

flux [flʌks]: **in (a state of) ~** en continuo estado de cambio

fly[1] [flaɪ] *n insect* mosca *f*

fly[2] [flaɪ] *n on pants* bragueta *f*

fly[3] [flaɪ] **I** *v/i (pret* **flew**, *pp* **flown**) **1** *of bird, airplane* volar; *in airplane* volar, ir en avión; **2** *of flag* ondear **3**: **~ into a rage** enfurecerse; **she flew out of the room** salió a toda prisa de la habitación; **doesn't time ~!** ¡el tiempo vuela! **II** *v/t (pret* **flew**, *pp* **flown**) *airplane* pilotar; *airline* volar con; *(transport by air)* enviar por avión

◆ **fly away** *v/i of bird* salir volando; *of airplane* alejarse

◆ **fly back** *v/i travel back* volver en avión

◆ **fly in I** *v/i of passengers* llegar en avión **II** *v/t supplies etc* transportar en avión

◆ **fly off** *v/i in airplane* volar, irse en avión; *of hat etc* salir volando

◆ **fly out** *v/i* **I** irse *(en avión)*; **when do you fly out?** ¿cuándo os vais? **II** *v/t troops, supplies* trasladar en avión

◆ **fly past** *v/i in formation* pasar volando en formación; *of time* volar

'fly ball *in baseball* englobado *m*, fly *m*

fly•er ☞ **flier**[1 & 2]

fly•ing ['flaɪɪŋ] volar *m*

fly•ing 'sau•cer platillo *m* volante

'fly•ing save *in soccer* estirada *f*

fly-on-the-'wall doc•u•men•ta•ry *documental hiperrealista con una presencia discreta de la cámara*; **'fly•o•ver** *Br* paso *m* elevado; **'fly spray** matamoscas *m*; **'fly•swat•ter** matamoscas *m*; **'fly•weight I** *n* peso *m* mosca**II** *adj champion etc* peso mosca

FM [ef'em] *abbr* (= **frequency modulation**) FM *f* (= frecuencia modulada)

FO [ef'oʊ] *abbr Br* (= **Foreign Office**) Ministerio *m* de Asuntos Exteriores, *L.Am.* Ministerio *m* de Relaciones Exteriores

foal [foʊl] potro *m*; **be in ~** estar preñada

foam [foʊm] **I** *n on liquid* espuma *f* **II** *v/i of liquid* espumar, hacer espuma; **~ at the mouth** sacar espuma por la boca

'foam bath baño *m* de burbujas

foam 'rub•ber gomaespuma *f*

FOB [efoʊ'bi:] *abbr* (= **free on board**) franco a bordo

fob [fɑ:b] *v/t*: **~ sth off on s.o.** encajar algo a alguien F; **~ s.o. off with sth** dar largas a alguien con algo

fo•cal ['foʊkl] *adj*: **~ length** PHOT distancia *f* focal; **~ point** *fig* punto *m* focal

fo•cus ['foʊkəs] **I** *n of attention*, PHOT foco *m*; **be in ~ / out of ~** PHOT estar enfocado / desenfocado **II** *v/t*: **~ one's attention on** concentrar la atención en **III** *v/i* enfocar

◆ **focus on** *v/t problem, issue* concentrarse en; PHOT enfocar

fo•cused ['foʊkəst] *adj person, approach* concentrado, enfocado

'fo•cus group *in marketing* grupo *m* analizado

fod•der ['fɑ:dər] forraje *m*

foe•tal *Br* ☞ **fetal**

foe•tus *Br* ☞ **fetus**

fog [fɑ:g] niebla *f*

◆ **fog up** *v/i (pret & pp* **-ged**) empañarse

'fog•bound *adj airport* paralizado por la niebla; *person* atrapado por la niebla

fo•gey ['foʊgɪ]: **old ~** F viejo *m* testarudo *or* carcamal F

fog•gy ['fɑ:gɪ] *adj* neblinoso, con niebla; **it's ~** hay niebla; **I haven't the foggiest**

idea no tengo la más remota idea
'fog•horn sirena *f* de niebla
'fog lamps, 'fog lights *npl* luces *fpl* antiniebla
foi•ble ['fɔɪbl] manía *f*
foil[1] [fɔɪl] *n* papel *m* de aluminio
foil[2] [fɔɪl] *v/t* (*thwart*) frustrar
fold[1] [fould] **I** *v/t paper etc* doblar; ***~ one's arms*** cruzarse de brazos **II** *v/i* F *of business* quebrar **III** *n in cloth etc* pliegue *m*
◆ **fold up I** *v/t* plegar **II** *v/i of chair, table* plegarse
fold[2] [fould] *n for sheep etc* redil *m*
'fold•a•way *adj chairs etc* plegable
fold•er ['fouldər] *for documents*, COMPUT carpeta *f*
fold•ing ['fouldɪŋ] *adj* plegable; ***~ chair*** silla *f* plegable
fo•li•age ['foulɪɪdʒ] follaje *m*
folk [fouk] *npl* (*people*) gente *f*, ***my ~s*** (*family*) mi familia; ***evening, ~s*** F buenas noches, gente F
'folk dance baile *m* popular; **'folk•lore** folklore *m*, cultura *f* popular; **'folk mu•se•um** museo *m* antropológico; **'folk mu•sic** música *f* folk *or* popular; **'folk sing•er** cantante *m/f* de folk; **'folk song** canción *m/f* folk *or* popular
folk•sy ['fouksɪ] *adj* tradicional, artesanal
fol•low ['fɑːlou] **I** *v/t* **1** seguir; ***~ me*** sígueme **2** (*understand*) entender **II** *v/i* **1** seguir; ***you go first and I'll ~*** tú ve primero que yo (te) sigo; ***the requirements are as ~s*** los requisitos son los siguientes **2** *logically* deducirse; ***it ~s from this that …*** de esto se deduce que …; ***that doesn't ~*** no es así
◆ **follow through** *v/i with tennis shot etc* acompañar (el golpe)
◆ **follow up** *v/t letter, inquiry* hacer el seguimiento de
fol•low•er ['fɑːlouər] seguidor(a) *m(f)*
fol•low•ing ['fɑːlouɪŋ] **I** *adj* siguiente **II** *n people* seguidores(-as) *mpl(fpl)*; ***the ~*** lo siguiente
'fol•low-up seguimiento *m*; **'fol•low-up meet•ing** reunión *f* de seguimiento; **'fol•low-up vis•it** *to doctor etc* visita *f* de seguimiento
fol•ly ['fɑːlɪ] **1** (*madness*) locura *f* **2** *architectural* fantasía *f*
fond [fɑːnd] *adj* (*loving*) cariñoso; *memory* entrañable; ***he's ~ of travel / music*** le gusta viajar / la música; ***I'm very ~ of him*** le tengo mucho cariño
fon•dle ['fɑːndl] *v/t* acariciar
fond•ly ['fɑːndlɪ] *adv look, speak, remember* cariñosamente, con afectividad
fond•ness ['fɑːndnɪs] *for s.o.* cariño *m* (***for*** por); *for wine, food* afición *f* (***for*** por)
font [fɑːnt] **1** *for printing* tipo *m* **2** *in church* pila *f* bautismal
food [fuːd] comida *f*; ***I wouldn't mind some ~*** no me vendría mal comer algo; ***that's ~ for thought*** eso es material de reflexión
'food chain cadena *f* alimentaria
food•ie ['fuːdɪ] F gourmet *m/f*
'food mix•er robot *m* de cocina; **'food poi•son•ing** intoxicación *f* alimentaria; **'food pro•cess•or** robot *m* de cocina; **'food•serv•ice** hostelería *f*; **'food•stuff** producto *m* alimenticio
fool [fuːl] **I** *n* tonto(-a) *m(f)*, idiota *m/f*; ***you stupid ~!*** ¡estúpido!; ***make a ~ of o.s.*** ponerse en ridículo; ***make a ~ of s.o.*** dejar a alguien en mal lugar *or* en ridículo **II** *v/t* engañar; ***ha, that ~ed you, didn't it!*** te lo has tragado, ¿eh? F, te lo has creído, ¿verdad?
◆ **fool around** *v/i* **1** hacer el tonto **2** *sexually* tener un lío
◆ **fool around with** *v/t* **1** *knife, drill etc* enredar con **2** *sexually* tener un lío con
fool•har•dy ['fuːlhɑːrdɪ] *adj* temerario
fool•ish ['fuːlɪʃ] *adj* tonto
fool•ish•ly ['fuːlɪʃlɪ] *adv*: ***I ~ …*** cometí la tontería de …
'fool•proof *adj* infalible
foot [fʊt] (*pl* ***feet*** [fiːt]) **I** *n also measurement* pie *m*; *of animal* pata *f*; ***on ~*** a pie, caminando, andando; ***I've been on my feet all day*** llevo todo el día de pie; ***be back on one's feet*** estar recuperado; ***at the ~ of the page / hill*** al pie de la página / de la colina; ***put one's ~ in it*** F meter la pata F; ***put one's ~ down*** (*be firm*) ponerse firme; (*accelerate*) pisarle (al acelerador); ***put one's feet up*** descansar; ***we'll let him find his feet first*** dejaremos que se asiente primero; ***fall on one's feet*** caer de pie; ***not put a ~ wrong*** *of gymnast etc* no cometer errores; *fig* no meter nunca

la pata
II *v/t*: **~ *the bill*** correr con *or* pagar la cuenta

foot•age ['fʊtɪdʒ] secuencias *fpl*, imágenes *fpl*

foot-and-'mouth dis•ease fiebre *f* aftosa

'foot•ball *Br* (*soccer*) fútbol *m*; *American style* fútbol *m* americano; *ball* balón *m or* pelota *f* (de fútbol)

'foot•ball boots *npl* zapatillas *fpl* de fútbol; **'foot•ball coach** entrenador *m* de fútbol; **'foot•ball-cra•zy** *adj* fanático del fútbol

foot•bal•ler ['fʊtbɒːlər] *American style* jugador(a) *m*(*f*) de fútbol americano; *Br in soccer* jugador(a) *m*(*f*) de fútbol, futbolista *m*/*f*

'foot•ball game partido *m* (de fútbol); **'foot•ball pitch** *Br* campo *m* de fútbol; **'foot•ball play•er** *American style* jugador(a) *m*(*f*) de fútbol americano; *Br*: *in soccer* jugador(a) *m*(*f*) de fútbol, futbolista *m*/*f*; **'foot•ball sta•di•um** estadio *m* de fútbol; **'foot•bridge** puente *m* peatonal

foot•er ['fʊtər] *in document* pie *m* de página

'foot•fall paso *m*; **'foot•hills** *npl* estribaciones *fpl*; **'foot•hold** *in climbing* punto *m* de apoyo; ***gain a* ~** *fig* introducirse

foot•ing ['fʊtɪŋ] (*basis*): ***put the business back on a secure* ~** volver a afianzar la empresa; ***lose one's* ~** perder el equilibrio; ***be on the same / a different* ~** estar / no estar en igualdad de condiciones; ***be on a friendly* ~ *with*** tener relaciones de amistad con

'foot•lights *npl* candilejas *fpl*

foo•tling ['fuːtlɪŋ] *adj* F *little details* insignificante, banal

'foot•loose *adj*: **~ *and fancy-free*** libre como el viento; **'foot•mark** pisada *f*; **'foot•note** nota *f* a pie de página; **'foot pas•sen•ger** pasajero(-a) *m*(*f*) de pie; **'foot•path** sendero *m*; **'foot•print** pisada *f*; *of computer, machine* perfil *m*; **'foot•rest** reposapiés *m inv*

foot•sie ['fʊtsɪ]: ***play* ~** F hacer piececitos F

'foot•sore *adj* con dolor de pies; **'foot•step** paso *m*; *footprint* pisada *f*; ***follow in s.o.'s* ~*s*** seguir los pasos de alguien; **'foot•stool** escabel *m*; **'foot•wear** calzado *m*; **'foot•work** *in football, boxing etc* juego *m* de pies

for [fər, fɔːr] **I** *prep* **1** *purpose, destination etc* para; ***a train* ~ ...** un tren para *or* hacia ...; ***clothes* ~ *children*** ropa para niños; ***it's too big / small* ~ *you*** te queda demasiado grande / pequeño; ***this is* ~ *you*** esto es para ti; ***what's* ~ *lunch?*** ¿qué hay para comer?; ***the steak is* ~ *me*** el filete es para mí; ***what is this* ~*?*** ¿para qué sirve esto?; ***it's good* ~ *coughs*** es bueno para la tós; ***what* ~*?*** ¿para qué?

2 *time* durante; **~ *three days / two hours*** durante tres días / dos horas; ***it lasts* ~ *two hours*** dura dos horas; ***please get it done* ~ *Monday*** por favor tenlo listo (para) el lunes; ***I've been waiting* ~ *an hour*** llevo una hora esperando

3 *distance*: ***I walked* ~ *a mile*** caminé una milla; ***it stretches for 100 miles*** se extiende 100 millas

4 (*in favor of*): ***I am* ~ *the idea*** estoy a favor de la idea

5 (*instead of, in behalf of*): ***let me do that* ~ *you*** déjame que te lo haga; ***we are agents* ~** somos representantes de

6 (*in exchange for*) por; ***I bought it* ~ *$25*** lo compré por 25 dólares: ***how much did you sell it* ~*?*** ¿por cuánto lo vendiste?

II *conj* porque; **~ *there was no food*** porque no había comida

for•ay ['fɑːreɪ] **1** MIL incursión *f* **2** *into the unknown, new subject area* aproximación *f*, acercamiento *m*

for•bade [fər'bæd] *pret* ☞ **forbid**

for•bear•ance [fɔːr'berəns] *fml* paciencia *f*, tolerancia *f*

for•bear•ing [fɔːr'berɪŋ] *adj fml* comprensivo, paciente

for•bid [fər'bɪd] *v/t* (*pret* **forbade**, *pp* **forbidden**) prohibir; **~ *s.o. to do sth*** prohibir a alguien hacer algo

for•bid•den [fər'bɪdn] **I** *adj* prohibido; ***smoking / parking* ~** prohibido fumar / aparcar **II** *pp* ☞ **forbid**

for•bid•ding [fər'bɪdɪŋ] *adj person, tone, look* amenazador; *rockface* imponente; *prospect* intimidador

force [fɔːrs] **I** *n* fuerza *f*; ***come into* ~** *of law etc* entrar en vigor; ***the* ~*s*** MIL las fuerzas **II** *v/t door, lock* forzar; **~ *s.o. to***

do sth forzar a alguien a hacer algo; **~ sth open** forzar algo
◆ **force back** *v/t tears* contener
forced [fɔːrst] *adj* forzado
forced 'land•ing aterrizaje *m* forzoso
'force-feed *v/t* hacer comer a la fuerza
force•ful ['fɔːrsfəl] *adj argument* poderoso; *speaker* vigoroso; *character* enérgico
force•ful•ly ['fɔːrsfəlɪ] *adv* de manera convincente
for•ceps ['fɔːrseps] *npl* MED fórceps *m inv*; ***~ delivery*** parto *m* con fórceps
for•ci•ble ['fɔːrsəbl] *adj entry* por la fuerza
for•ci•bly ['fɔːrsəblɪ] *adv* por la fuerza
ford [fɔːrd] **I** *n* vado *m* **II** *v/t river* vadear
fore [fɔːr]: ***come to the ~*** salir a la palestra; ***an idea which is very much to the ~ at present*** una idea que está en el candelero actualmente
'fore•arm antebrazo *m*; **fore•bears** ['fɔːrberz] *npl* antepasados *mpl*; **fore-bod•ing** [fɔːr'boudɪŋ] premonición *f*; **'fore•cast I** *n* pronóstico *m*; *of weather* pronóstico *m* (del tiempo) **II** *v/t* (*pret & pp* **forecast**) pronosticar; **fore'clo-sure** FIN ejecución *f*; **'fore•court** (*of garage*) *explanada en la parte de delante*; **'fore•fa•thers** *npl* ancestros *mpl*; **'fore•fin•ger** (dedo *m*) índice *m*; **'fore•front**: ***be in the ~ of*** estar a la vanguardia de; **'fore•gone** *adj*: ***that's a ~ conclusion*** eso ya se sabe de antemano; **'fore•ground** primer plano *m*; ***be in the ~*** *of painting etc* estar en primer plano; *fig*: *be prominent* resaltar; **'fore•hand** *in tennis* derecha *f*; **'fore-head** frente *f*
for•eign ['fɑːrən] *adj* extranjero; ***a ~ holiday*** unas vacaciones en el extranjero
for•eign af'fairs *npl* asuntos *mpl* exteriores; **for•eign 'aid** ayuda *f* al exterior; **for•eign 'bod•y** cuerpo *m* extraño; **for•eign cor•re'spon•dent** corresponsal *m/f* en el extranjero; **for•eign 'cur-ren•cy** divisas *fpl* extranjeras
for•eign•er ['fɑːrənər] extranjero(-a) *m(f)*
for•eign ex'change divisas *fpl*; **for-eign ex'change con•trols** *npl* controles *mpl* de cambio de divisas; **for•eign ex'change mar•ket** mercado *m* de divisas; **for•eign 'lan•guage** idioma *m* extranjero; **'For•eign Of•fice** *in UK* Ministerio *m* de Asuntos Exteriores, *L.Am.* Ministerio *m* de Relaciones Exteriores; **for•eign 'pol•i•cy** política *f* exterior; **For•eign 'Sec•re•ta•ry** *in UK* Ministro(-a) *m(f)* de Asuntos Exteriores; **for•eign se'cu•ri•ties** *npl* valores *mpl* extranjeros; **for•eign 'trav•el** viajes *mpl* al extranjero
'fore•man 1 capataz *m* **2** *of jury* presidente *m*
'fore•most I *adj* principal **II** *adv*: ***first and ~ we must ...*** lo primordial es que ...; ***an issue which has been ~ in our minds*** un asunto que ha sido nuestra mayor preocupación
fo•ren•sic med•i•cine [fə'rensɪk] medicina *f* forense; **fo•ren•sic 'sci•ence** ciencia *f* forense; **fo•ren•sic 'sci•en-tist** forense *m/f*
'fore•play *sexual* jugueteo *m* erótico; **'fore•run•ner** predecesor(a) *m(f)*; **fore'see** *v/t* (*pret* **-saw**, *pp* **-seen**) prever; **fore•see•a•ble** [fɔːr'siːəbl] *adj* previsible; ***in the ~ future*** en un futuro próximo; **fore'shad•ow** *v/t* augurar; **'fore•sight** previsión *f*; ***have the ~ to do sth*** tener la precaución de hacer algo; **'fore•skin** ANAT prepucio *m*
for•est ['fɑːrɪst] bosque *m*
fore•stall [fɔːr'stɒːl] *v/t person*, *event* anticiparse; *objection* impedir, obstruir
for•est•er ['fɑːrɪstər] guarda *m/f* forestal
for•est•ry ['fɑːrɪstrɪ] silvicultura *f*
'fore•taste anticipo *m*; ***a ~ of things to come*** un anticipo de lo que sucederá; **fore'tell** *v/t* (*pret & pp* **-told**) predecir; **'fore•thought** premeditación *f*
for•ev•er [fə'revər] *adv* siempre; ***I will remember this day ~*** no me olvidaré nunca de ese día
fore'warn *v/t* advertir, avisar; **'fore-wom•an** LAW presidenta *f* del jurado; **'fore•word** prólogo *m*
for•feit ['fɔːrfət] *v/t* **1** (*lose*) perder **2** (*give up*) renunciar a
for•fei•ture ['fɔːrfətʃər] pérdida *f*
for•gave [fər'geɪv] *pret* ☞ **forgive**
forge [fɔːrdʒ] *v/t* falsificar
◆ **forge ahead** *v/i* progresar rápidamente; *of runner* tomar la delantera
forg•er ['fɔːrdʒər] falsificador(a) *m(f)*

forg•er•y ['fɔːrdʒərɪ] falsificación *f*
for•get [fər'get] **I** *v/t* (*pret* ***forgot***, *pp* ***forgotten***) olvidar; ***I forgot his name*** se me olvidó su nombre; ***~ to do sth*** olvidarse de hacer algo; ***you can ~ that vacation for a start*** te puedes ir olvidando de esas vacaciones, para empezar; ***you might as well ~ it*** te puedes ir olvidando; ***thanks – ~ it, my pleasure*** gracias - olvídalo, es un placer
II *v/i* (*pret* ***forgot***, *pp* ***forgotten***) olvidar; ***I never ~*** nunca me olvido
◆ **forget about** *v/t* olvidarse de
for•get•ful [fər'getfəl] *adj* olvidadizo
for'get-me-not *flower* nomeolvides *m inv*
for•get•ta•ble [fər'getəbl] *adj* **1** que se puede olvidar **2** corriente, normal; ***an eminently ~ movie*** una película sumamente corriente
for•give [fər'gɪv] *v/t & v/i* (*pret* ***forgave***, *pp* ***forgiven***) perdonar; ***~ s.o. sth*** perdonar a alguien algo; ***let's ~ and forget*** borrón y cuenta nueva; ***you could be ~n for thinking that …*** se te podría disculpar por creer que …
for•giv•en [fər'gɪvn] *pp* ☞ ***forgive***
for•give•ness [fər'gɪvnɪs] perdón *m*; ***the ~ of sins*** REL el perdón de los pecados
for•giv•ing [fər'gɪvɪŋ] *adj toward lover, friend, child* indulgente; *in broader religious sense* piadoso
for•go [fɔːr'goʊ] *v/t* (*pret* ***forwent***, *pp* ***forgone***) sacrificar, renunciar a
for•got [fər'gɑːt] *pret* ☞ ***forget***
for•got•ten [fər'gɑːtn] *pp* ☞ ***forget***
fork [fɔːrk] **1** *for eating* tenedor *m* **2** *for garden* horca *f* **3** *in road* bifurcación *f*
◆ **fork out** *v/t & v/i* F (*pay*) apoquinar F
forked [fɔːrkt] *adj tongue* bífido; *stick* bifurcado
fork•lift 'truck carretilla *f* elevadora
for•lorn [fər'lɔːrn] *adj* **1** *deserted*: *person, place* desolado **2** *desperate*: *attempt* desesperado; ***~ hope*** esperanza *f* inútil
form [fɔːrm] **I** *n* **1** *shape* forma *f*; ***it's beginning to take ~*** está empezando a tomar *or* cobrar forma; ***a response in the ~ of an email*** una respuesta por email; ***recognition in the ~ of a medal*** reconocimiento con una medalla **2** (*document*) formulario *m*, impreso *m* **3**: ***be on / off ~*** estar / no estar en forma **4**: ***know the ~*** conocer las normas, conocer el procedimiento
II *v/t in clay etc* moldear; *friendship* establecer; *opinion* formarse; *past tense etc* formar; (*constitute*) formar, constituir
III *v/i* (*take shape, develop*) formarse
form•al ['fɔːrml] *adj* formal; *recognition etc* oficial; *dress* de etiqueta
for•mal•ism ['fɔːrməlɪzəm] formalismo *m*
for•mal•i•ty [fər'mælətɪ] formalidad *f*; ***it's just a ~*** es pura formalidad
for•mal•ize ['fɔːrməlaɪz] *v/t agreement etc* formalizar
for•mal•ly ['fɔːrməlɪ] *adv speak, behave* formalmente; *accepted, recognized* oficialmente
for•mat ['fɔːrmæt] **I** *v/t* (*pret & pp* **-ted**) *diskette, document* formatear **II** *n of paper, program etc* formato *m*
for•ma•tion [fɔːr'meɪʃn] formación *f*; ***~ flying*** vuelo *m* en formación
for•ma•tive ['fɔːrmətɪv] *adj* formativo; ***in his ~ years*** en sus años de formación
for•mer ['fɔːrmər] *adj* antiguo; ***the ~*** el primero; ***the ~ arrangement*** la situación de antes
for•mer•ly ['fɔːrmərlɪ] *adv* antiguamente
For•mi•ca® [fɔːr'maɪkə] formica® *f*
for•mi•da•ble ['fɔːrmɪdəbl] *adj personality* formidable; *opponent, task* terrible
'form let•ter carta *f* estándar
for•mu•la ['fɔːrmjʊlə] MATH, CHEM, *fig* fórmula *f*; ***Formula 1 racing*** carreras de Fórmula 1
for•mu•late ['fɔːrmjʊleɪt] *v/t* (*express*) formular
for•mu•la•tion [fɔːrmjʊ'leɪʃn] formulación *f*; *of chemical* fórmula *f*
for•ni•cate ['fɔːrnɪkeɪt] *v/i fml* fornicar
for•ni•ca•tion [fɔːrnɪ'keɪʃn] *fml* fornicación *f*
for•sake [fər'seɪk] *v/t* (*pret* ***forsook*** [fər'sʊk], *pp* ***forsaken*** [fər'seɪkn]) *lit* **1** *person* abandonar **2** *old ways etc* abandonar, renunciar
fort [fɔːrt] MIL fuerte *m*; ***hold the ~*** hacerse cargo de la situación
for•te ['fɔːrteɪ] fuerte *m*
forth [fɔːrθ] *adv*: ***back and ~*** de un lado

para otro; ***and so ~*** y así sucesivamente; ***from that day ~*** desde ese día en adelante

'forth•com•ing *adj* **1** (*future*) próximo **2** *personality* comunicativo; **'forth•right** *adj* directo; **forth'with** *adv fml* inmediatamente

for•ti•eth ['fɔːrtɪɪθ] *n & adj* cuadragésimo

for•ti•fi•ca•tion [fɔːrtɪfɪ'keɪʃn] MIL fortificación *f*; ***~s** pl* fortificaciones *fpl*

for•ti•fy ['fɔːrtɪfaɪ] *v/t* MIL fortificar

for•ti•tude ['fɔːrtɪtjuːd] *lit* fortaleza *f*, coraje *m*

fort•night ['fɔːrtnaɪt] *Br* quincena *f*

for•tress ['fɔːrtrɪs] MIL fortaleza *f*

for•tu•i•tous [fɔːr'tjuːɪtəs] *adj* fortuito

for•tu•nate ['fɔːrtʃnət] *adj* afortunado

for•tu•nate•ly ['fɔːrtʃnətlɪ] *adv* afortunadamente; ***~ for you ...*** afortunadamente *or* por suerte para tí ...

for•tune ['fɔːrtʃən] (*fate, money*) fortuna *f*; (*luck*) fortuna *f*, suerte *f*; ***tell s.o.'s ~*** decir a alguien la buenaventura

'for•tune hunt•er cazafortunas *m/f*

'for•tune-tell•er adivino(-a) *m(f)*

for•ty ['fɔːrtɪ] cuarenta; ***have ~ winks*** F echarse una siestecilla F

fo•rum ['fɔːrəm] *fig* foro *m*; ***a discussion ~*** un foro de debate

for•ward ['fɔːrwərd] **I** *adv* hacia delante **II** *adj pej*: *person* atrevido **III** *n* SP delantero(-a) *m(f)*; *in basketball* ala *m/f*, alero(-a) *m(f)* **IV** *v/t letter* reexpedir

'for•ward buy•ing FIN compra *f* a plazo

for•ward•er ['fɔːrwərdər] COM transitario(-a) *m(f)*

for•ward•er and con•sol•i•da•tor [kən'sɑːlɪdeɪtər] COM embarcador(a) *m(f)* y agrupador(a) *m(f)*

for•ward•ing ad•dress ['fɔːrwərdɪŋ] *dirección a la que reexpedir correspondencia*

'for•ward•ing a•gent COM transitario(-a) *m(f)*

'for•ward rate FIN cambio *m* a plazo

for•wards ['fɔːrwədz] ☞ ***forward* I**

for•ward 'slash barra *f*

fos•sil ['fɑːsəl] fósil *m*

fos•sil•ized ['fɑːsəlaɪzd] *adj* fosilizado

fos•ter ['fɑːstər] *v/t* **1** *child* acoger, adoptar (temporalmente) **2** *attitude, belief* fomentar

'fos•ter child niño(-a) *m(f)* en régimen de acogida; **'fos•ter home** hogar *m* de acogida; **'fos•ter par•ents** *npl* familia *f* de acogida

fought [fɒːt] *pret & pp* ☞ ***fight***

foul [faʊl] **I** *n* SP falta *f*; ***commit a ~*** hacer una falta **II** *adj smell, taste* asqueroso; *weather* terrible **III** *v/t* SP hacer (una) falta a

'foul ball *in baseball* foul *m*; **foul-mouthed** ['faʊlmaʊðd] *adj* malhablado; **foul-smel•ling** ['faʊlsmelɪŋ] *adj* maloliente

found[1] [faʊnd] *v/t school etc* fundar

found[2] [faʊnd] *pret & pp* ☞ ***find***

foun•da•tion [faʊn'deɪʃn] **1** *of theory etc* fundamento *m* **2** *organization* fundación *f*

foun•da•tions [faʊn'deɪʃnz] *npl of building* cimientos *mpl*; ***lay the ~ for sth*** *fig* sentar las bases de algo

foun'da•tion stone ARCHIT primera piedra *f*

found•er ['faʊndər] fundador(a) *m(f)*

found•ing ['faʊndɪŋ] fundación *f*

'Founding Fathers Padres *mpl* Fundadores

foun•dry ['faʊndrɪ] fundición *f*

foun•tain ['faʊntɪn] fuente *f*; *jet of water* manantial *m*

'foun•tain pen pluma *f* (estilográfica)

four [fɔːr] cuatro; ***on all ~s*** a gatas, a cuatro patas

four-'door mod•el MOT cuatro puertas *m inv*; **four-leaf 'clo•ver** BOT trébol *m* de cuatro hojas; **four-leg•ged** ['fɔːrlegɪd] *adj* cuadrúpedo, de cuatro patas; ***our ~ friends*** nuestros amigos cuadrúpedos; **four-let•ter 'word** palabrota *f*; **four-post•er 'bed** cama *f* de dosel; **'four-star** *adj hotel etc* de cuatro estrellas; **'four-speed gear•box** cambio *m* de cuatro velocidades; **'four-star ho•tel** hotel *m* de cuatro estrellas

four•teen [fɔːr'tiːn] catorce

four•teenth [fɔːr'tiːnθ] *n & adj* decimocuarto

fourth [fɔːrθ] *n & adj* cuarto

four-wheel 'drive MOT **1** *vehicle* vehículo *m* con tracción a las cuatro ruedas **2** *type of drive* tracción *f* a las cuatro ruedas

fowl [faʊl] ave *f* de corral

fox [fɑːks] **I** *n* zorro *m* **II** *v/t* (*puzzle*) dejar perplejo

F

'fox cub cachorro *m* (de zorro); **'fox·glove** BOT dedalera *f*; **'fox·hole** MIL foso *m* de atrincheramiento; **'fox hunting** caza *f* del zorro; **fox 'ter·ri·er** ZO foxterrier *m*; **'fox·trot** foxtrot *m*
fox·y ['fɑːksɪ] *adj* F *woman* atractiva, sexy F
foy·er ['fɔɪəɪ] vestíbulo *m*
fra·cas ['frækɑː] *noise* jaleo *m*; *fuss* riña *f*, contienda *f*
frac·tal ['fræktəl] fractal *f*
frac·tion ['frækʃn] fracción *f*; MATH fracción *f*, quebrado *m*; ***just a ~ bigger*** sólo una pizca *or* un poco más grande
frac·tion·al ['frækʃnəl] *adj slight, small* muy pequeño, ligero
frac·tion·al·ly ['frækʃnəlɪ] *adv* ligeramente
frac·tious ['frækʃəs] *adj* irritable
frac·ture ['fræktʃər] **I** *n* fractura *f* **II** *v/t* fracturar; ***he ~d his arm*** se fracturó el brazo
fra·gile ['frædʒəl] *adj* frágil
fra·gil·i·ty [frə'dʒɪlətɪ] fragilidad *f*
frag·ment ['frægmənt] fragmento *m*
frag·men·tar·y [fræg'məntərɪ] *adj* fragmentario
fra·grance ['freɪgrəns] fragancia *f*
fra·grant ['freɪgrənt] *adj* fragante
frail [freɪl] *adj* frágil, delicado
frail·ty ['freɪltɪ] *of health* debilidad *f*, fragilidad *f*; ***the frailties of human nature*** las debilidades del ser humano
frame [freɪm] **I** *n of picture, window* marco *m*; *of eyeglasses* montura *f*; *of bicycle* cuadro *m*; *of film, video* fotograma *m*; ***~ of mind*** estado *m* de ánimo **II** *v/t* **1** *picture* enmarcar **2** F *person* tender una trampa a
'frame house casa *f* de madera
fram·er ['freɪmər]: ***the ~s*** *of constitution* los artífices
'frame-up F trampa *f*
'frame·work estructura *f*; *for agreement* marco *m*
France [fræns] Francia *f*
fran·chise ['fræntʃaɪz] *for business* franquicia *f*
fran·chised ['fræntʃaɪzd] *adj* franquiciado
fran·chi·see [fræntʃaɪ'ziː] franquiciado(-a) *m(f)*, concesionario(-a) *m(f)*
'fran·chise hold·er franquiciado(-a) *m(f)*, concesionario(-a) *m(f)*
fran·chis·ing ['fræntʃaɪzɪŋ] franquicia *f*
fran·chi·sor [fræntʃaɪ'zɔːr] franquiciador(a) *m(f)*
frank [fræŋk] *adj* franco
frank·furt·er ['fræŋkfɜːrtər] salchicha *f* de Fráncfort
frank·ly ['fræŋklɪ] *adv* francamente
frank·ness ['fræŋknɪs] franqueza *f*
fran·tic ['fræntɪk] *adj* frenético
fran·ti·cal·ly ['fræntɪklɪ] *adv* frenéticamente
fra·ter·nal [frə'tɜːrnl] *adj* fraternal
fra·ter·ni·ty [frə'tɜːrnətɪ] **1** *brotherliness* fraternidad *f* **2** EDU hermandad *f* **3**: ***the medical / legal ~*** los médicos / abogados
frat·er·ni·za·tion [frætərnaɪ'zeɪʃn] fraternización *f*
frat·er·nize ['frætərnaɪz] *v/i* fraternizar (***with*** con)
fraud [frɒːd] fraude *m*; *person* impostor(a) *m(f)*; ***you're not hurt at all, you big ~*** no te has hecho ningún daño, mentiroso *or* farsante
fraud·u·lence ['frɒːdjʊləns] fraudulencia *f*, fraude *m*
fraud·u·lent ['frɒːdjʊlənt] *adj* fraudulento
fraud·u·lent·ly ['frɒːdjʊləntlɪ] *adv* fraudulentamente
frayed [freɪd] *adj cuffs* deshilachado; ***~ nerves*** *pl* nervios *mpl* crispados
fraz·zle ['fræzl]: ***worn to a ~*** *exhausted* hecho polvo; ***burnt to a ~*** chamuscado
freak [friːk] **I** *n unusual event* fenómeno *m* anormal; *two-headed person, animal etc* monstruo *m*, monstruosidad *f*, F *strange person* bicho *m* raro F; ***a movie / jazz ~*** F un fanático del cine / jazz F **II** *adj wind, storm etc* anormal
◆ **freak out** *v/i* P flipar P
freak·y ['friːkɪ] *adj* P raro, freaky P
freck·le ['frekl] peca *f*
free [friː] **I** *adj* **1** libre; ***are you ~ this afternoon?*** ¿estás libre esta tarde?; ***~ and easy*** relajado; ***I'm not ~ to tell you that*** me temo que eso no puedo decírtelo; ***~ movement of goods / people*** libre circulación *f* de mercancías / personas; ***~ of customs duty*** franco de aduanas; ***~ of tax*** libre de impuestos **2** *no cost* gratis, gratuito; ***for ~*** *travel, get sth* gratis **II** *v/t prisoners* liberar

free•bie ['fri:bɪ] F regalo *m*; ***as a ~*** de regalo
free•dom ['fri:dəm] libertad *f*
'free•dom fight•er guerrillero(-a) *m(f)*; **free•dom of 'speech** libertad *f* de expresión; **free•dom of the 'press** libertad *f* de prensa
free 'en•ter•prise empresa *f* libre; **'free fall** AVIA, PHYS caída *f* libre; ***the economy is in ~*** la economía está en (profunda) crisis; **free 'kick** *in soccer* falta *f*, golpe *m* franco; **free•lance** ['fri:læns] **I** *adj* autónomo, free-lance **II** *adv*: ***work~*** trabajar como autónomo(-a) *or* free-lance; **free•lanc•er** ['fri:lænsər] autónomo(-a) *m(f)*, free-lance *m/f*; **'free-load** *v/i* F gorronear, *Rpl* garronear; **free•load•er** ['fri:loʊdər] F gorrón (-ona) *m(f)*, *Rpl* garronero(-a) *m(f)*
free•ly ['fri:lɪ] *adv admit* libremente
free mar•ket e'con•o•my economía *f* de libre mercado; **'free•ma•son** masón(-ona) *m(f)*; **free on 'board** *adv* COM franco a bordo; **free on 'rail** *adv* COM franco en estación, libre sobre vagón; **'free port** puerto *m* franco; **free-range 'chick•en** pollo *m* de corral; **free-range 'eggs** *npl* huevos *mpl* de corral; **free 'sam•ple** muestra *f* gratuita; **free 'speech** libertad *f* de expresión; **'free•style** SP **I** *n* estilo *m* libre **II** *adj events*, *swimming* de estilo libre; **'free throw** SP tiro *m* libre; ***~ line*** *in basketball* línea *f* de tiro libre; **free 'trade** libre comercio *m*; ***~ agreement*** acuerdo *m* de libre comerio; **free-'trade ar•e•a** área *f* de libre comercio, área *f* de libre cambio; **'free•way** autopista *f*; **free'wheel** *v/i on bicycle* ir sin pedalear; **free 'will** libre albedrío *m*; ***he did it of his own ~*** lo hizo por propia iniciativa
freeze [fri:z] **I** *v/t* (*pret* **froze**, *pp* **frozen**) *food*, *wages*, *video* congelar; *river* congelar, helar **II** *v/i* (*pret* **froze**, *pp* **frozen**) **1** *of water* congelarse, helarse **2** *of computer*, *screen* bloquear, congelar; ***~!*** (*don't move*) ¡alto!
◆ **freeze out** *v/t* F hacer el vacío a, aislar
◆ **freeze over** *v/i of river* helarse
'freeze-dried *adj* liofilizado; **'freeze-dry** *v/t* liofilizar; **'freeze frame** imagen *f* congelada
freez•er ['fri:zər] congelador *m*
'freez•er com•part•ment congelador *m*
freez•ing ['fri:zɪŋ] **I** *adj* muy frío; ***it's ~ (cold)*** *of weather* hace mucho frío; *of water* está muy frío; ***I'm ~ (cold)*** tengo mucho frío **II** *n*: ***10 degrees below ~*** diez grados bajo cero
'freez•ing com•part•ment congelador *m*
'freez•ing point punto *m* de congelación
freight [freɪt] **1** transporte **2** *costs* flete *m*
'freight car *on train* vagón *m* de mercancías
freight con•sol•i•da•tor [kən'sɑ:lɪdeɪtər] COM agrupador(a) *m(f)*
freight•er ['freɪtər] *ship* carguero *m*; *airplane* avión *m* de carga
freight 'for•ward•er transitario(-a) *m(f)*; **'freight plane** avión *m* de carga; **'freight train** tren *m* de mercancías
French [frentʃ] **I** *adj* francés **II** *n* **1** *language* francés *m* **2**: *pl* ***the ~*** los franceses
French 'bread pan *m* de barra; **French 'doors** *npl* puerta *f* cristalera; **French 'dress•ing** vinagreta *f*; **'French fries** *npl L.Am.* papas *fpl or Span* patatas *fpl* fritas; **French 'kiss** beso *m* con lengua; **French•man** ['frentʃmən] francés *m*; **'French•wom•an** francesa *f*
fre•net•ic [frə'netɪk] *adj activity*, *pace*, *life* frenético, loco
fren•zied ['frenzɪd] *adj attack*, *activity* frenético; *mob* desenfrenado
fren•zy ['frenzɪ] frenesí *m*; ***whip s.o. into a ~*** poner a alguien frenético
fre•quen•cy ['fri:kwənsɪ] *also* RAD frecuencia *f*
'fre•quen•cy band RAD banda *f* de frecuencia
fre•quent[1] ['fri:kwənt] *adj* frecuente; ***how ~ are the trains?*** ¿con qué frecuencia pasan trenes?
fre•quent[2] [frɪ'kwent] *v/t bar* frecuentar
fre•quent 'fly•er pro•gram programa *m* de fidelización de pasajeros
fre•quent•ly ['fri:kwentlɪ] *adv* con frecuencia
fres•co ['freskoʊ] fresco *m*
fresh [freʃ] *adj* **1** fresco; *start* nuevo **2**

cool fresco **3** (*impertinent*) fresco; ***don't you get ~ with your mother!*** ¡no seas descarado con tu madre!
fresh 'air aire *m* fresco; ***get some ~*** tomar *or* respirar aire fresco
fresh•en ['freʃn] *v/i of wind* refrescar
◆ **freshen up I** *v/i* refrescarse **II** *v/t room, paintwork* renovar, revivir
fresh•ly ['freʃlɪ] *adv* (*recently*) recién
'fresh•man estudiante *m/f* de primer año
fresh•ness ['freʃnɪs] frescura *f*
'fresh•wa•ter *adj* de agua dulce
fret [fret] *v/i* (*pret & pp* **-ted**) ponerse nervioso, inquietarse
fret•ful ['fretfʊl] *adj* **1** (*anxious*) nervioso **2** (*irritable*) irritable
Freud•i•an ['frɔɪdɪən] *adj* freudiano; ***~ slip*** lapsus *m* (linguae)
FRG [efɑː'dʒiː] *abbr* (= ***Federal Republic of Germany***) RFA *f* (= República Federal de Alemania)
fric•a•tive ['frɪkətɪv] LING fricativo(-a) *m*(*f*)
fric•tion ['frɪkʃn] PHYS rozamiento *m*; *between people* fricción *f*
'fric•tion tape cinta *f* aislante
Fri•day ['fraɪdeɪ] viernes *m inv*
fridge [frɪdʒ] nevera *f*, frigorífico *m*
fried egg [fraɪd'eg] huevo *m* frito
fried po'ta•toes *npl L.Am.* papas *fpl or Span* patatas *fpl* fritas
friend [frend] amigo(-a) *m*(*f*); ***make ~s*** *of one person* hacer amigos; *of two people* hacerse amigos; ***make ~s with s.o.*** hacerse amigo de alguien
friend•li•ness ['frendlɪnɪs] simpatía *f*
friend•ly ['frendlɪ] *adj atmosphere* agradable; *person* agradable, simpático; (*easy to use*) fácil de usar; *argument, match, relations* amistoso; ***be ~ with s.o.*** (*be friends*) ser amigo de alguien; ***~ fire*** MIL fuego *m* amigo
'friend•ship ['frendʃɪp] amistad *f*
fries [fraɪz] *npl L.Am.* papas *fpl or Span* patatas *fpl* fritas
frieze [friːz] ARCHIT friso *m*
frig•ate ['frɪgət] NAUT fragata *f*
frig•ging ['frɪgɪŋ] P **I** *adj* puto P **II** *adv*: ***because it's too ~ hot*** porque hace un calor de cojones P; ***they're so ~ stupid*** joder que tontos que son P
fright [fraɪt] susto *m*; ***give s.o. a ~*** dar un susto a alguien, asustar a alguien; ***scream with ~*** gritar asustado
fright•en ['fraɪtn] *v/t* asustar; ***be ~ed*** estar asustado, tener miedo; ***don't be ~ed*** no te asustes, no tengas miedo; ***be ~ed of*** tener miedo de
◆ **frighten away** *v/t* ahuyentar, espantar
fright•en•ing ['fraɪtnɪŋ] *adj noise, person, prospect* aterrador, espantoso
fright•en•ing•ly ['fraɪtnɪŋlɪ] *adv fast, complex* terriblemente, horrorosamente
fright•ful ['fraɪtfʊl] *adj* horroroso, terrible
fright•ful•ly ['fraɪtfʊlɪ] *adv* F (*very*) tremendamente, horrorosamente
fri•gid ['frɪdʒɪd] *adj sexually* frígido
fri•gid•i•ty [frɪ'dʒɪdətɪ] *sexual* frigidez *f*
frill [frɪl] **1** *on dress etc* volante *m* **2** (*fancy extra*) extra *m*
frill•y ['frɪlɪ] *adj* de volantes
fringe [frɪndʒ] **1** *on dress, curtains etc* flecos *mpl* **2** *Br in hair* flequillo *m* **3** (*edge*) margen *m*
'fringe ben•e•fits *npl* ventajas *fpl* adicionales
'fringe group grupo *m* marginal
fris•bee® ['frɪzbiː] frisbee® *m*, disco *m* volador
frisk [frɪsk] *v/t* F (*search*) cachear
frisk•y ['frɪskɪ] *adj puppy etc* juguetón
◆ **frit•ter away** ['frɪtər] *v/t time* desperdiciar; *fortune* despilfarrar
fri•vol•i•ty [frɪ'vɑːlətɪ] frivolidad *f*
friv•o•lous ['frɪvələs] *adj* frívolo
friz•zy ['frɪzɪ] *adj hair* crespo
fro [froʊ] *adv* ☞ **to**
frog [frɑːg] rana *f*
'frog•man hombre *m* rana
frol•ic ['frɑːlɪk] *v/i* (*pret & pp* **-ked**) jugar, corretear
from [frɑːm] *prep* **1** *in time* desde; ***~ 9 to 5 (o'clock)*** de 9 a 5; ***~ the 18th century*** desde el siglo XVIII; ***~ today on*** a partir de hoy; ***~ next Tuesday*** a partir del próximo martes
2 *in space* de, desde; ***~ here to there*** de *or* desde aquí hasta allí; ***we drove here ~ Las Vegas*** vinimos en coche desde Las Vegas
3 *origin* de; ***a letter ~ Jo*** una carta de Jo; ***it doesn't say who it's ~*** no dice de quién es; ***I am ~ New Jersey*** soy de Nueva Jersey; ***the next flight ~ Cara-***

cas el próximo vuelo (procedente) de Caracas; ***made ~ bananas*** hecho con plátanos
4 (*because of*): ***tired ~ the journey*** cansado del viaje; ***it's ~ overeating*** es por comer demasiado; ***he suffers ~ eczema*** padece de eczema
front [frʌnt] **I** *n* **1** *of building*, *book* portada *f* **2** (*cover organization*) tapadera *f* **3** MIL, *of weather* frente *m* **4**: ***in ~*** delante; *in a race* en cabeza; ***the car in ~*** el coche de delante; ***in ~ of*** delante de; ***at the ~ of*** en la parte de delante de **II** *adj wheel*, *seat* delantero **III** *v/t TV program* presentar
front•age ['frʌntɪdʒ] *of building* fachada *f*
front 'cov•er portada *f*; **front 'door** puerta *f* principal; **front 'en•trance** entrada *f* principal
fron•tier ['frʌntɪr] frontera *f*, *fig*: *of knowledge*, *science* límite *m*
front 'line MIL línea *f* del combate; ***be in the ~*** *fig* estar al pie del cañón; **front 'page** *of newspaper* portada *f*, primera plana *f*; **front page 'news** *nsg* noticia *f* de portada *or* de primera plana; **front 'row** primera fila *f*; **front-'run•ner** *in race*, *election etc* favorito(-a) *m*(*f*); **front-seat 'pas•sen•ger** *in car* pasajero(-a) *m*(*f*) de delante; **front-wheel 'drive** tracción *f* delantera
frost [frɑːst] escarcha *f*; ***there was a ~ last night*** anoche cayó una helada
'frost•bite congelación *f*
'frost•bit•ten *adj* congelado
frost•ed glass ['frɑːstɪd] vidrio *m* esmerilado
frost•ing ['frɑːstɪŋ] *on cake* glaseado *m*
frost•y ['frɑːstɪ] *adj weather* gélido; *fig*: *welcome* glacial
froth [frɑːθ] espuma *f*
froth•y ['frɑːθɪ] *adj cream etc* espumoso
frown [fraʊn] **I** *n*: ***what's that ~ for?*** ¿por qué frunces el ceño? **II** *v/i* fruncir el ceño
◆ **frown on** *v/t* rechazar, desaprobar
froze [froʊz] *pret* ☞ ***freeze***
fro•zen ['froʊzn] **I** *adj ground* congelado; *wastes* helado; ***I'm ~*** F estoy helado *or* congelado F **II** *pp* ☞ ***freeze***
fro•zen 'food comida *f* congelada
fru•gal ['fruːgl] *adj person* comedido, prudente; *meal* frugal
fruit [fruːt] **1** fruta *f*; ***the ~s of our labors*** los frutos de nuestros sudores; ***bear ~*** *of tree* dar fruta; *fig*: *of discussions etc* dar frutos **2** P *homosexual* maricón *m* P, mariquita *m* P
'fruit•bowl bol *m* para la fruta
'fruit cake 1 bizcocho *m* de frutas **2** P *eccentric* chiflado(-a) *m*(*f*) F, locatis *m*/*f* P
fruit•ful ['fruːtfəl] *adj discussions etc* fructífero
fru•i•tion [fruː'ɪʃn]: ***bring sth to ~*** llevar algo a (buen) término; ***come to ~*** materializarse
'fruit juice *L.Am.* jugo *m or Span* zumo *m* de fruta
fruit•less ['fruːtlɪs] *adj attempt*, *search* vano, inútil
'fruit ma•chine *Br* (máquina *f*) tragaperras *f*; **fruit 'sal•ad** macedonia *f*; **'fruit tree** árbol *m* frutal
fruit•y ['fruːtɪ] *adj* **1** *taste*, *wine* afrutado **2** *voice* profundo, armonioso **3** P *homosexual* amanerado
frump [frʌmp]: ***old ~*** vieja *f* anticuada
frump•ish ['frʌmpɪʃ], **frump•y** ['frʌmpɪ] *adj* a la antigua
frus•trate [frʌ'streɪt] *v/t person*, *plans* frustrar
frus•trat•ed [frʌ'streɪtɪd] *adj* frustrado
frus•trat•ing [frʌ'streɪtɪŋ] *adj* frustrante
frus•trat•ing•ly [frʌ'streɪtɪŋlɪ] *adv* que produce frustración, que desespera
frus•tra•tion [frʌ'streɪʃn] frustración *f*
fry [fraɪ] **I** *v/t* (*pret & pp* ***-ied***) freír **II** *n* patata *f* frita
'fry com•pa•ny fabricante *m* de patatas fritas
'fry•pan sartén *f*
f-stop ['efstɑːp] PHOT posición *f* del número f
FTC [eftiː'siː] *abbr* (= ***Federal Trade Commission***) Comisión *f* de Comercio Federal
fuck [fʌk] *v/t* V *L.Am.* coger V, *Span* follar con V; ***~!*** ¡joder! V; ***~ him!*** ¡que se joda! V; ***we're ~ed*** estamos jodidos V
◆ **fuck around** V **I** *v/t* putear V **II** *v/i* enredar F
◆ **fuck off** *v/i* V: ***fuck off!*** ¡vete a la mierda! V
◆ **fuck up** V **I** *v/t job*, *mission etc* echar a perder; ***a fucked-up kid*** un chaval jodi-

do V **II** *v/i*: ***you've fucked up again*** la has vuelto a joder otra vez V

fuck•ing ['fʌkɪŋ] **I** *adj* V puto V **II** *adv* V: ***it's ~ crazy*** es una estupidez ¡coño!; ***it was ~ brilliant!*** ¡estuvo de puta madre! V; ***~ hell!*** ¡joder! V, ¡coño! V

fud•dy-dud•dy ['fʌdɪdʌdɪ] F carca *m/f* F

fu•el ['fjʊəl] **I** *n* combustible *m* **II** *v/t* (*pret & pp* **-ed**, *Br* **-led**) **1**: ***be ~ed by*** *of machine, engine* utlizar como combustible **2** *fig* avivar

fu•el / 'air mix•ture mezcla *f* de aire / combustible; **'fu•el cell** compartimento *m* de combustible; **'fu•el con•sump•tion** consumo *m* de combustible; **'fu•el ef•fi•cien•cy** eficiencia *f* del combustible; **'fu•el gauge** indicador *m* del nivel de combustible; **fu•el-in•ject•ed engine** ['fjʊəlɪndʒektɪd] motor *m* a inyección; **'fu•el in•jec•tion** MOT injección *f* (de combustible); **'fu•el pump** bomba *f* de combustible; **'fu•el tank** *of car, airplane* tanque *m* del carburante, depósito *m* de combustible

fug [fʌg] atmósfera *f* cargada

fu•gi•tive ['fju:dʒətɪv] fugitivo(-a) *m(f)*

ful•fill, *Br* **ful•fil** [fʊl'fɪl] *v/t dream* cumplir, realizar; *task* realizar; *contract* cumplir; ***feel ~ed*** *in job, life* sentirse realizado

ful•fill•ing [fʊl'fɪlɪŋ] *adj*: ***I have a ~ job*** mi trabajo me llena

ful•fill•ment, *Br* **ful•fil•ment** [fʊl'fɪlmənt] *of contract etc* cumplimiento *m*; *moral, spiritual* satisfacción *f*

full [fʊl] *adj* lleno; *account, schedule* completo; *life* pleno; ***~ of*** *water etc* lleno de; ***~ up*** *hotel etc, with food* lleno; ***pay in ~*** pagar al contado

'full•back *in soccer* defensa *m/f*; **full--blood•ed** [fʊl'blʌdɪd] *adj onslaught, critique* vehemente, enardecido; **full--'blown** *adj theory, scandal* verdadero, genuino; *lawyer, doctor* auténtico; ***~ Aids*** sida *m* en su última fase; **full--bod•ied** [fʊl'bɑ:dɪd] *adj wine* con *or* de mucho cuerpo; **full-'court press** *in basketball* presión *f* en toda la cancha; **full 'cov•er•age insurance** seguro *m* a todo riesgo; **full em'ploy•ment** pleno empleo *m*; **full-fledged** [fʊl'fledʒd] *adj* **1** *bird* que puede volar **2** *doctor, architect* auténtico, con todas las de la ley; **full-front•al** [fʊl'frʌntəl] *adj nudity* integral; *photograph* de cuerpo entero; **'full-grown** *adj* completamente desarrollado; **'full-length** *adj dress* de cuerpo entero; ***~ movie*** largometraje *m*; **full 'moon** luna *f* llena

full•ness ['fʊlnɪs] *of sound* riqueza *f*, carácter *m*

'full-page *adj advertisement* de una página; **full 'pay•ment** pago *m* completo; **'full price** precio *m* completo; **'full--scale** *adj* **1** *model* a escala natural **2** *attack, redesign etc* decisivo, de magnitud; **full 'stop** *Br* punto *m*; **full 'time 1** *adj worker, job* a tiempo completo **2** *adv work* a tiempo completo

full•y ['fʊlɪ] *adv* completamente; *describe* en detalle

full•y-'fledged *Br* ☞ ***full-fledged***

ful•some ['fʊlsəm] *adj praise* desproporcionado, desmesurado

fum•ble ['fʌmbl] *v/t ball* dejar caer

◆ **fumble around** *v/i* rebuscar

fume [fju:m] *v/i*: ***be fuming*** F *with anger* echar humo F

fumes [fju:mz] *npl* humos *mpl*

fu•mi•gate ['fju:mɪgeɪt] *v/t* fumigar

fun [fʌn] diversión *f*; ***it was great ~*** fue muy divertido; ***bye, have ~!*** ¡adiós, que lo paséis bien!; ***for ~*** para divertirse; ***make ~ of*** burlarse de; ***he's good ~*** es muy divertido; ***you're no ~!*** ¡eres un aburrido *or* soso!; ***it's no ~ having to do it all by yourself*** no tiene nada de divertido tener que hacerlo solo; ***they were just having a bit of ~ with him*** sólo estaban de broma con él; ***say sth in ~*** decir algo de broma; ***it takes all the ~ out of it*** le quita toda la gracia

func•tion ['fʌŋkʃn] **I** *n* **1** (*purpose*) función *f* **2** (*reception etc*) acto *m* **II** *v/i* funcionar; ***~ as*** hacer de

func•tion•al ['fʌŋkʃnl] *adj* funcional

func•tion•ar•y ['fʌŋkʃnrɪ] *esp* POL funcionario(-a) *m(f)*

'func•tion key COMPUT tecla *f* de función

fund [fʌnd] **I** *n* fondo *m* **II** *v/t project etc* financiar

fun•da•men•tal [fʌndə'mentl] *adj* **1** fundamental (***to*** para) **2** (*crucial*) esencial

fun•da•men•tal•ism [fʌndə'mentl-

ɪzəm] fundamentalismo *m*
fun•da•men•tal•ist [fʌndə'mentlɪst] fundamentalista *m/f*
fun•da•men•tal•ly [fʌndə'mentlɪ] *adv* fundamentalmente
fund•ing ['fʌndɪŋ] *money* fondos *mpl*, financiación *f*
fu•ne•ral ['fju:nərəl] funeral *m*
'fu•ne•ral di•rec•tor encargado(-a) *m(f)* de una funeraria
'fu•ne•ral home funeraria *f*
'fun•fair parque *m* de atracciones, feria *f*
fun•gal ['fʌŋgəl] *adj*: **~ infection** infección *f* de hongos
fun•gus ['fʌŋgəs] (*pl* **fungi** ['fʌŋgaɪ]) **1** (*mold*) hongos *mpl* **2** *mushroom etc* hongo *m*
fu•nic•u•lar [fju:'nɪkjʊlər], **fu•nic•u•lar 'rail•way** funicular *m*
funk•y ['fʌŋkɪ] *adj* P guay P, *Span* molón
fun•nel ['fʌnl] *of ship* chimenea *f*
fun•nies ['fʌnɪz] *npl* F *sección de humor*
fun•ni•ly ['fʌnɪlɪ] *adv* **1** (*oddly*) de modo extraño; **~ enough** curiosamente **2** (*comically*) de forma divertida
fun•ny ['fʌnɪ] *adj* **1** (*comical*) divertido, gracioso; **that's not ~** eso no tiene gracia; **are you trying to be ~, pal?** ¿te estás haciendo el gracioso, amigo?; **don't get ~ with me** no te hagas el gracioso conmigo **2** (*odd*) curioso, raro
'fun•ny bone hueso *m* de la risa
fur [fɜ:r] **1** piel *f* **2** *on tongue* saburra *f*
fu•ri•ous ['fjʊrɪəs] *adj* **1** (*angry*) furioso **2** (*intense*) furioso, feroz; *effort* febril; **at a ~ pace** a un ritmo vertiginoso
fur•lough ['fɜ:rloʊ] MIL permiso *m*; **be on ~** estar de permiso
fur•nace ['fɜ:rnɪs] horno *m*
fur•nish ['fɜ:rnɪʃ] *v/t* **1** *room* amueblar **2** (*supply*) suministrar
fur•nish•ings ['fɜ:rnɪʃɪŋz] *npl* mobiliario *m*
fur•ni•ture ['fɜ:rnɪtʃər] mobiliario *m*, muebles *mpl*; **a piece of ~** un mueble; **she just treats him like part of the ~** F lo trata con indiferencia *or* desgana
fur•row ['fʌroʊ] *in field* surco *m*
fur•rowed ['fʌroʊd] *esp lit*: *brow* arrugado, fruncido
fur•ry ['fɜ:rɪ] *adj* **1** *animal* peludo **2** *tongue* saburroso
fur•ther ['fɜ:rðər] **I** *adj* **1** (*additional*) adicional; **there's been a ~ development** ha pasado algo nuevo; **until ~ notice** hasta nuevo aviso; **have you anything ~ to say?** ¿tiene algo más que añadir? **2** (*more distant*) más lejano **II** *adv* **1** *walk*, *drive* más lejos **2** (*additionally*): **~, I want to say ...** además, quiero decir ...; **two miles ~ (on)** dos millas más adelante **III** *v/t cause etc* promover
fur•ther'more *adv* es más
'fur•ther•most *adj* más lejano, remoto
fur•thest ['fɜ:rðɪst] **I** *adj*: **the ~ point north** el punto más al norte; **the ~ stars** las estrellas más lejanas **II** *adv* más lejos; **this is the ~ north I've ever been** nunca había estado tan al norte
fur•tive ['fɜ:rtɪv] *adj glance* furtivo
fur•tive•ly ['fɜ:rtɪvlɪ] *adv* furtivamente
fu•ry ['fjʊrɪ] (*anger*) furia *f*, ira *f*
fuse [fju:z] ELEC **I** *n* fusible *m* **II** *v/i* fundirse; **the lights have ~d** se han fundido los plomos **III** *v/t* fundir
'fuse•box caja *f* de fusibles
fu•se•lage ['fju:zəlɑ:ʒ] fuselaje *m*
'fuse wire fusible *m*
fu•sion ['fju:ʒn] fusión *f*
fuss [fʌs] escándalo *m*; **make a ~** (*complain*, *behave in exaggerated way*) armar un escándalo; **make a ~ of** (*be very attentive to*) deshacerse en atenciones con
fuss•budg•et ['fʌsbʌdʒɪt] F protestón(-ona) *m(f)* F, puntilloso(-a) *m(f)* F
fuss•y ['fʌsɪ] *adj person* quisquilloso; *design etc* recargado; **be a ~ eater** ser un quisquilloso a la hora de comer
fus•ty ['fʌstɪ] *adj smell* rancio
fu•tile ['fju:tl] *adj* inútil, vano
fu•til•i•ty [fju:'tɪlətɪ] inutilidad *f*
fu•ture ['fju:tʃər] **I** *n also* GRAM futuro *m*; **in ~** en el futuro **II** *adj* futuro
fu•tures ['fju:tʃərz] *npl* FIN futuros *mpl*
'fu•tures mar•ket FIN mercado *m* de futuros
'fu•tures trad•ing FIN compraventa *f* de futuros
fu•tur•is•tic [fju:tʃə'rɪstɪk] *adj design* futurista
fu•tur•ol•o•gy [fju:tʃər'ɑ:lədʒɪ] futurología *f*
fuze [fju:z] ☞ **fuse**
fuzz [fʌz] *on chin*, *fruit* pelusa *f*, pelusi-

lla *f*
fuzz•y ['fʌzɪ] *adj* **1** *hair* crespo **2** (*out of focus*) borroso
fuzz•y 'lo•gic lógica *f* difusa

G

gab [gæb] F **I** *n*: ***have the gift of the ~*** tener labia F **II** *v/i* (*pret & pp* ***-bed***) largar (***about*** de)
gab•ar•dine [gæbər'diːn] ☞ ***gaberdine***
gab•ble ['gæbl] *v/i* farfullar
gab•by ['gæbɪ] *adj* F charlatán
gab•er•dine [gæbər'diːn] *fabric, coat* gabardina *f*
ga•ble ['geɪbl] hastial *m*
ga•ble 'win•dow ventana *f* en el hastial
Ga•bon [gæ'bain] Gabón *m*
Ga•bon•ese [gæbə'niːz] **I** *adj* gabonés **II** *n* gabonés(-esa) *m(f)*
◆ **gad about, gad around** [gæd] *v/i* (*pret & pp* ***-ded***) pendonear
gad•get ['gædʒɪt] artilugio *m*, chisme *m*
gadg•et•ry ['gædʒɪtrɪ] utensilios *mpl*
gaff [gæf] *hook* garfio *m*
gaffe [gæf] metedura *f* de pata
gaf•fer ['gæfər] *Br* F jefe *m*
gag [gæg] **I** *n* **1** *over mouth* mordaza *f* **2** (*joke*) chiste *m* **II** *v/t* (*pret & pp* ***-ged***) *also fig* amordazar
ga•ga ['gɑːgɑː] *adj* P chocho; ***go ~*** comenzar a chochear
gage [geɪdʒ] **I** *n* indicador *m* **II** *v/t pressure* medir, calcular; *opinion* estimar, evaluar
gag•gle ['gægl] bandada *f*; F horda *f*
'gag writ•er escritor(a) *m(f)* de chistes
gai•e•ty ['geɪətɪ] alegría *f*
gai•ly ['geɪlɪ] *adv* alegremente
gain•ful ['geɪnfʊl] *adj* remunerado
gain [geɪn] *v/t* (*acquire*) ganar; *victory* obtener; ***~ speed*** cobrar velocidad; ***~ 10 pounds*** engordar 10 libras; ***~ entrance*** entrar; ***~ weight*** ganar peso
◆ **gain on** *v/t* ganar terreno a
gait [geɪt] paso *m*
gal [gæl] F moza *f*
ga•la ['gælə] gala *f*
ga•lac•tic [gə'læktɪk] *adj* AST galáctico
gal•ax•y ['gæləksɪ] AST galaxia *f*
gale [geɪl] vendaval *m*
gall [gɔːl] **I** *n* **1** MED bilis *f inv* **2**: ***have the ~ to do sth*** tener el valor de hacer algo **II** *v/t* enfadar
gal•lant ['gælənt] *adj* galante
gal•lan•try ['gæləntrɪ] valor *m*
'gall blad•der vesícula *f* biliar
gal•le•on ['gælɪən] galeón *m*
gal•le•ry ['gælərɪ] **1** *for art* museo *m* **2** *in theater* galería *f*
gal•ley ['gælɪ] *on ship* cocina *f*
Gal•lic ['gælɪk] *adj* galo
gall•ing ['gɔːlɪŋ] *adj* irritante
◆ **gal•li•vant around** ['gælɪvænt] *v/i* pendonear
gal•lon ['gælən] galón *m* (*en EE.UU. 3,785 litros, en GB 4,546*); ***~s of tea*** F toneladas de té F
gal•lop ['gæləp] **I** *v/i* galopar **II** *n*: ***at a ~*** al galope
gal•lows ['gælouz] *npl* horca *f*; ***~ humor*** humor *m* negro
gall•stone ['gɒːlstoʊn] cálculo *m* biliar
Gal•lup poll® ['gæləppoʊl] encuesta *f* de opinión de Gallup
ga•lore [gə'lɔːr] *adj*: ***apples / novels ~*** manzanas / novelas a montones
gal•va•nize ['gælvənaɪz] *v/t* TECH galvanizar; ***~ s.o. into activity*** hacer que alguien se vuelva más activo
gal•van•ized ['gælvənaɪzd] *adj* galvanizado
Gam•bi•a ['gæmbɪə] Gambia *f*
Gam•bi•an ['gæmbɪən] **I** *n* gambiano(-a) *m(f)* **II** *adj* gambiano
gam•bit ['gæmbɪt] gambito *m*
gam•ble ['gæmbl] **I** *v/i* jugar **II** *n* apuesta *f*; ***it was a ~, but it paid off*** fue un riesgo pero valió la pena; ***I'm taking a ~ here*** me voy a arriesgar aquí
gam•bler ['gæmblər] jugador(a) *m(f)*
gam•bling ['gæmblɪŋ] juego *m*
gam•bol ['gæmbl] *v/i* (*pret & pp* ***-ed***, *Br* ***-led***) retozar
game[1] [geɪm] partido *m*; *children's* juego *m*; *in tennis* juego *m*; COMPUT: ***~s console*** consola *f* de videojuegos
game[2] [geɪm] *animals* caza *f*
'game•keep•er *Br* guarda *m/f* forestal;

'game park coto *m* de caza; **'game plan** estrategia *f*; **'game re•serve** coto *m* de caza; **'game show** concurso *m*; **'game war•den** guarda *m/f* de caza
gam•ing ['geɪmɪŋ] COMPUT juegos *mpl* de ordenador
gam•ma rays ['gæməreɪz] *npl* PHYS rayos *mpl* gamma
gam•ut ['gæmət] gama *f*
gan•der ['gændər] ORN ganso *m*
gang [gæŋ] *of friends* cuadrilla *f*, pandilla *f*; *of criminals* banda *f*
◆ **gang up on** *v/t* compincharse contra
gan•gling ['gæŋglɪŋ] *adj* larguirucho
gan•gli•on ['gæŋglɪən] MED ganglio *m*
'gang rape I *n* violación *f* colectiva **II** *v/t* violar colectivamente
gan•grene ['gæŋgriːn] MED gangrena *f*
gang•ster ['gæŋstər] gángster *m*
'gang war•fare lucha *f* entre bandas
'gang•way pasarela *f*
gan•net ['gænɪt] ORN alcatraz *m*
gap [gæp] *in wall* hueco *m*; *for parking, in figures* espacio *m*; *in time* intervalo *m*; *in conversation* interrupción *f*; *between two people's characters* diferencia *f*
gape [geɪp] *v/i of person* mirar boquiabierto
◆ **gape at** *v/t* mirar boquiabierto a
gap•ing ['geɪpɪŋ] *adj hole* enorme
gar•age [gə'rɑːʒ] *for parking* garaje *m*; *Br*: *for gas* gasolinera *f*, *for repairs* taller *m*
gar•bage ['gɑːrbɪdʒ] basura *f*, *fig* (*nonsense*) tonterías *fpl*; (*poor quality goods*) basura *f*, porquería *f*
'gar•bage bag bolsa *f* de la basura; **'gar•bage can** cubo *m* de la basura; *in street* papelera *f*, **'gar•bage chute** vertedor *m* de basura; **'gar•bage col•lec•tion** recogida *f* de basuras; **'gar•bage col•lec•tor, 'gar•bage man** basurero *m*; **'gar•bage time** *in basketball* minutos *mpl* de la basura; **'gar•bage truck** camión *m* de la basura
gar•ble ['gɑːrbl] *v/t* distorsionar
gar•bled ['gɑːrbld] *adj message* confuso
gar•den ['gɑːrdn] jardín *m*
'gar•den cen•ter, *Br* **'gar•den cen•tre** vivero *m*, centro *m* de jardinería
gar•den•er ['gɑːrdnər] aficionado(-a) *m*(*f*) a la jardinería; *professional* jardinero(-a) *m*(*f*)
gar•den•ing ['gɑːrdnɪŋ] jardinería *f*
gar•gan•tu•an [gɑːr'gæntjʊən] *adj* pantagruélico
gar•gle ['gɑːrgl] *v/i* hacer gárgaras
gar•goyle ['gɑːrgɔɪl] ARCHI gárgola *f*
gar•ish ['gerɪʃ] *adj color* chillón; *design* estridente
gar•land ['gɑːrlənd] guirnalda *f*
gar•lic ['gɑːrlɪk] ajo *m*
gar•lic 'bread pan *m* con ajo
gar•ment ['gɑːrmənt] prenda *f* (de vestir)
gar•ner ['gɑːrnər] *v/t* recopilar
gar•net ['gɑːrnɪt] MIN granate *m*
gar•nish ['gɑːrnɪʃ] *v/t* guarnecer (***with*** con)
gar•ret ['gærət] buhardilla *f*
gar•ri•son ['gærɪsn] *place* plaza *f*, *troops* guarnición *f*
gar•rotte [gə'rɑːt] *v/t* ejecutar con garrote vil a
gar•ru•lous ['gærələs] *adj* charlatán
gar•ter ['gɑːrtər] liga *f*
'gar•ter belt liguero *m*
'gar•ter snake ZO serpiente *f* de jarretera
gas [gæs] gas *m*; (*gasoline*) gasolina *f*, *Rpl* nafta *f*
'gas•bag F parlanchín(-ina) *m*(*f*) F; **'gas cham•ber** cámara *f* de gas; **gas chro•mat•o•graph** [kroʊ'mætoʊgræf] cromatógrafo *m* de gases; **gas 'cook•er** cocina *f* de gas
gas•e•ous ['gæsjəs] *adj* gaseoso
gas 'fire estufa *f* de gas; **gas-fired cen•tral heat•ing** ['gæsfaɪrd] calefacción *f* central a gas; **gas guz•zler** ['gæsgʌzlər]: ***it's a ~*** F gasta mucha gasolina
gash [gæʃ] corte *m* profundo
gas•ket ['gæskɪt] junta *f*, ***blow a ~*** *fig* subirse por las paredes
'gas main tubería *f* del gas; **'gas•man** empleado *m* de la compañía suministradora del gas; **'gas mask** máscara *f* antigás; **'gas me•ter** contador *m* del gas
gas•o•line ['gæsəliːn] gasolina *f*, *Rpl* nafta *f*
'gas ov•en horno *m* a gas
gasp [gæsp] **I** *n* grito *m* apagado **II** *v/i* lanzar un grito apagado; ***~ for breath*** luchar por respirar
'gas ped•al acelerador *m*; **'gas pipe•line** gasoducto *m*; **'gas pump** surtidor

m (de gasolina); '**gas stove** cocina *f* de gas; '**gas sta•tion** gasolinera *f*, *S.Am.* bomba *f*

gas•sy ['gæsɪ] *adj* con demasiado gas

'**gas tank** depósito *m* de gasolina

gas•tric ['gæstrɪk] *adj* MED gástrico

gas•tric 'flu MED gripe *f* gastrointestinal; **gas•tric 'juices** *npl* jugos *mpl* gástricos; **gas•tric 'ul•cer** MED úlcera *f* gástrica

gas•tri•tis [gæ'straɪtɪs] MED gastritis *f inv*

gas•tro•en•ter•i•tis [gæstroʊentə'raɪtɪs] MED gastroenteritis *f inv*

gas•tro•nom•ic [gæstrə'nɑːmɪk] *adj* gastronómico

gas•tron•o•my [gæ'strɑːnəmɪ] gastronomía *f*

gas 'tur•bine turbina *f* de gas; ~ ***engine*** motor *m* de turbina de gas

'**gas•works** *nsg* fábrica *f* de gas

gate [geɪt] *of house, at airport* puerta *f*; *made of iron* verja *f*

ga•teau ['gætoʊ] tarta *f*

'**gate•crash** *v/t*: ~ ***a party*** colarse en una fiesta; **gate-crash•er** ['geɪtkræʃər] colón(-ona) *m(f)*; '**gate•house** casa *f* del guarda; '**gate•keep•er** guarda *m/f*; **gate-leg(ged) ta•ble** [geɪtleg(d)'teɪbl] mesa *f* plegable; '**gate mon•ey** recaudación *f*; '**gate•post** poste *m* (de puerta); '**gate•way** *also fig* entrada *f*

gath•er ['gæðər] **I** *v/t facts, information* reunir; ***am I to ~ that ...?*** ¿debo entender que ...?; ~ ***speed*** ganar velocidad **II** *v/i of crowd* reunirse

◆ **gather up** *v/t possessions* recoger

gath•er•ing ['gæðərɪŋ] (*group of people*) grupo *m* de personas

GATT [gæt] *abbr* (= ***General Agreement on Tariffs and Trade***) GATT *m* (Acuerdo *m* General sobre Aranceles y Comercio)

gauche [goʊʃ] *adj* torpe

gau•dy ['gɒːdɪ] *adj* chillón, llamativo

gauge [geɪdʒ] *Br* **I** *n* indicador *m* **II** *v/t pressure* medir, calcular; *opinion* estimar, evaluar

gaunt [gɒːnt] *adj* demacrado

gaunt•let ['gɔːntlɪt] *fig*: ***fling*** *or* ***throw down the ~*** arrojar el guante (***to*** a); ***pick*** *or* ***take up the ~*** recoger el guante; ***run the ~ of*** exponerse a

gauze [gɒːz] gasa *f*

gave [geɪv] *pret* ☞ ***give***

gav•el ['gævl] martillo *m*

gawk [gɔːk] *v/i* mirar boquiabierto; ~ ***at s.o. / sth*** mirar boquiabierto a alguien / algo

gaw•ky ['gɒːkɪ] *adj* desgarbado

gawp [gɒːp] *v/i* F mirar boquiabierto; ***don't just stand there ~ing!*** ¡no te quedes ahí boquiabierto!

gay [geɪ] **I** *n* (*homosexual*) homosexual *m*, gay *m* **II** *adj* homosexual, gay

gaze [geɪz] **I** *n* mirada *f* **II** *v/i* mirar fijamente

ga•zelle [gə'zel] gacela *f*

ga•zette [gə'zet] *Br* boletín *m* oficial

GB [dʒiː'biː] *abbr* **1** (= ***Great Britain***) GB (= Gran Bretaña) **2** (= ***Gigabyte***) GB (= gigabyte)

GDP [dʒiːdiː'piː] *abbr* (= ***gross domestic product***) PIB *m* (= producto *m* interior bruto)

gear [gɪr] **1** *n* (*equipment*) equipo *m* **2** *in vehicles* marcha *f*; ***move into second ~*** poner la segunda (marcha)

◆ **gear toward** *v/t*: ***be geared toward s.o. / sth*** estar orientado a alguien / algo

'**gear•box** MOT caja *f* de cambios

'**gear change** cambio *m* de marcha

gear•ing ['gɪrɪŋ] FIN apalancamiento *m*, relación *f* endeudamiento-capital propio

'**gear le•ver,** '**gear shift,** '**gear•stick** MOT palanca *f* de cambios

geck•o ['gekoʊ] ZO geco *m*

gee [dʒiː] *int* F ¡anda!; ~, ***I'm sorry*** oye, lo siento; ~, ***that's kind of you*** oye, muy amable por tu parte

geek [giːk] F colgado(-a) *m(f)* F

geese [giːs] *pl* ☞ ***goose***

Gei•ger count•er ['gaɪgər] contador *m* Geiger

gel [dʒel] **1** *n for hair* gomina *f*, *for shower* gel *m* **2** *v/t* (*prep & pp* ***-led***): ~ ***one's hair*** echarse gomina en el pelo

gel•a•tine ['dʒelətiːn] gelatina *f*

gel•ig•nite ['dʒelɪgnaɪt] gelignita *f*

gem [dʒem] gema *f*; *fig*: *book etc* joya *f*, *person* cielo *m*

Gem•i•ni ['dʒemɪnaɪ] ASTR Géminis *m/f inv*; ***be (a) ~*** ser Géminis

gen•der ['dʒendər] género *m*

'**gen•der-bend•er** P **1** travestí *m* **2** COMPUT adaptador *m* macho-hembra

'gen•der gap diferencia *f* entre los sexos
gene [dʒiːn] gen *m*; ***it's in his ~s*** lo lleva en los genes
ge•ne•a•log•i•cal [dʒiːnjə'lɑːdʒɪkl] *adj* genealógico
ge•ne•al•o•gist [dʒiːnɪ'ælədʒɪst] genealogista *m/f*
ge•ne•al•o•gy [dʒiːnɪ'ælədʒɪ] genealogía *f*
'gene pool acervo *m* genético
gen•er•a ['dʒenərə] *pl* ☞ ***genus***
gen•er•al ['dʒenrəl] **I** *n* MIL general *m*; ***in ~*** en general, por lo general **II** *adj* general
gen•er•al an•(a)es'thet•ic anestesia *f* general; **gen•er•al de'liv•er•y I** *n* lista *f* de correos **II** *adv send* para la lista de correos; **gen•er•al e'lec•tion** elecciones *fpl* generales
gen•er•al•i•za•tion [dʒenrəlaɪ'zeɪʃn] generalización *f*; ***that's a ~*** eso es generalizar
gen•er•al•ize ['dʒenrəlaɪz] *v/i* generalizar
gen•er•al 'know•ledge cultura *f* general
gen•er•al•ly ['dʒenrəlɪ] *adv* generalmente, por lo general; ***~ speaking*** en términos generales
gen•er•al 'o•ver•head gastos *mpl* generales; **gen•er•al prac•ti•tion•er** ['dʒenrəlpræk'tɪʃnər] *Br* médico(-a) *m(f)* de familia; **gen•er•al 'pub•lic** gran público *m*; **gen•er•al 'staff** MIL estado *m* mayor; **gen•er•al 'store** tienda *f*; **gen•er•al 'strike** huelga *f* general
gen•e•rate ['dʒenəreɪt] *v/t* generar; *feeling* provocar
gen•e•ra•tion [dʒenə'reɪʃn] generación *f*
gen•e'ra•tion gap conflicto *m* generacional
gen•er•a•tive ['dʒenərətɪv] *adj* generativo
gen•e•ra•tor ['dʒenəreɪtər] generador *m*
ge•ner•ic [dʒə'nerɪk] *adj* genérico
ge'ner•ic drug MED medicamento *m* genérico
gen•e•ros•i•ty [dʒenə'rɑːsətɪ] generosidad *f*
gen•e•rous ['dʒenərəs] *adj* generoso
gen•e•sis ['dʒenəsɪs] génesis *f inv*
'gene ther•a•py terapia *f* génica
ge•net•ic [dʒɪ'netɪk] *adj* genético
ge•net•i•cal•ly [dʒɪ'netɪklɪ] *adv* genéticamente; ***~ modified*** *organism* modificado genéticamente; *crops* transgénico; ***be ~ modified*** estar modificado genéticamente
ge•net•ic 'code código *m* genético; **ge•net•ic en•gi'neer•ing** ingeniería *f* genética; **ge•net•ic 'fin•ger•print** identificación *f* genética
ge•net•i•cist [dʒɪ'netɪsɪst] genetista *m/f*, especialista *m/f* en genética
ge•net•ics [dʒɪ'netɪks] *nsg* genética *f*
Ge•ne•va [dʒɪ'niːvə] Ginebra *f*
ge•ni•al ['dʒiːnjəl] *adj* afable, cordial
ge•ni•al•i•ty [dʒiːnɪ'ælətɪ] afabilidad *f*, cordialidad *f*
ge•nie ['dʒiːnɪ] genio *m*
gen•i•tals ['dʒenɪtlz] *npl* genitales *mpl*
gen•i•tive ['dʒenətɪv] LING genitivo *m*
ge•ni•us ['dʒiːnjəs] genio *m*
gen•o•ci•dal [dʒenə'saɪdl] *adj* genocida
gen•o•cide ['dʒenəsaɪd] genocidio *m*
ge•nome ['dʒiːnoʊm] genoma *m*
gen•o•type ['dʒenoʊtaɪp] genotipo *m*
gen•re ['ʒɑːnrə] género *m*
gent [dʒent] **1** F caballero *m* **2** *Br*: ***~s*** *sg* servicio *m* de caballeros
gen•teel [dʒen'tiːl] *adj* fino
gen•tile ['dʒentaɪl] REL gentil *m/f*
gen•tle ['dʒentl] *adj person* tierno, delicado; *touch*, *detergent* suave; *breeze* suave, ligero; *slope* poco inclinado; ***be ~ with it, it's fragile*** ten mucho cuidado con él, es frágil
gen•tle•man ['dʒentlmən] caballero *m*; ***he's a real ~*** es todo un caballero; ***a ~'s agreement*** un pacto entre caballeros; ***gentlemen, shall we start?*** ¿podemos comenzar caballeros *or* señores?
gen•tle•man•ly ['dʒentlmənlɪ] *adj* caballeroso
gen•tle•ness ['dʒentlnɪs] *of person* ternura *f*, delicadeza; *of touch*, *detergent*, *breeze* suavidad *f*, *of slope* poca inclinación *f*
gen•tly ['dʒentlɪ] *adv touch*, *kiss etc* con delicadeza; *slope* poco a poco; ***a breeze blew ~*** sopla una ligera *or* suave brisa
gen•tri•fi•ca•tion [dʒentrɪfɪ'keɪʃən] aburguesamiento *m*
gen•try ['dʒentrɪ] *in town* alta burguesía

f, in country terratenientes *mpl*

gen•u•ine ['dʒenʊɪn] *adj* **1** *antique etc* genuino, auténtico **2** (*sincere*) sincero

gen•u•ine•ly ['dʒenʊɪnlɪ] *adv* realmente, de verdad

ge•nus ['dʒi:nəs] (*pl* **genera** ['dʒenərə]) BOT, ZO género *m*

ge•og•ra•pher [dʒɪ'ɑ:grəfər] geógrafo(-a) *m(f)*

ge•o•graph•i•cal [dʒɪə'græfɪkl] *adj features* geográfico

ge•og•ra•phy [dʒɪ'ɑ:grəfɪ] geografía *f*

ge•o•log•i•cal [dʒɪə'lɑ:dʒɪkl] *adj* geológico

ge•ol•o•gist [dʒɪ'ɑ:lədʒɪst] geólogo(-a) *m(f)*

G

ge•ol•o•gy [dʒɪ'ɑ:lədʒɪ] geología *f*

ge•o•met•ric, ge•o•met•ri•cal [dʒɪə'metrɪk(l)] *adj* geométrico

ge•om•e•try [dʒɪ'ɑ:mətrɪ] geometría *f*

ge•o•phys•i•cist [dʒɪoʊ'fɪzɪsɪst] geofísico(-a) *m(f)* .

ge•o•phys•ics [dʒɪoʊ'fɪzɪks] *nsg* geofísica *f*

ge•o•sta•tion•ar•y [dʒɪoʊ'steɪʃənərɪ] *adj*: ***in ~ orbit*** en órbita geoestacionaria; ***~ satellite*** satélite *m* geoestacionario

ge•ra•ni•um [dʒə'reɪnɪəm] geranio *m*

ger•bil ['dʒɜ:rbɪl] jerbo *m*

ger•i•at•ric [dʒerɪ'ætrɪk] **I** *adj* geriátrico **II** *n* anciano(-a) *m(f)*

germ [dʒɜ:rm] *also fig* germen *m*

Ger•man ['dʒɜ:rmən] **I** *adj* alemán **II** *n* **1** *person* alemán(-ana) *m(f)* **2** *language* alemán *m*

Ger•man•ic [dʒɜ:r'mænɪk] *adj* germánico

Ger•man 'mea•sles *nsg* rubeola *f*

Ger•man 'shep•herd pastor *m* alemán

Ger•man•y ['dʒɜ:rmənɪ] Alemania *f*

'germ-free *adj* libre de gérmenes

ger•mi•nate ['dʒɜ:rmɪneɪt] *v/i of seed* germinar

germ 'war•fare guerra *f* bacteriológica

ger•on•tol•o•gist [dʒerən'tɑ:lədʒɪst] gerontólogo(-a) *m(f)*

ger•on•tol•o•gy [dʒerən'tɑ:lədʒɪ] MED gerontología *f*

ger•und ['dʒerənd] LING gerundio *m*

ges•ta•tion [dʒe'steɪʃn] gestación *f*; ***~ period*** periodo *m* de gestación

ges•tic•u•late [dʒe'stɪkjʊleɪt] *v/i* gesticular

ges•tic•u•la•tion [dʒestɪkjʊ'leɪʃn] gesticulación *f*

ges•ture ['dʒestʃər] *also fig* gesto *m*

get [get] *v/t* (*pret* ***got***, *pp* ***got*** *or* ***gotten***)

1 (*obtain*) conseguir; ***you can ~ them at the corner store*** los puedes comprar en la tienda de la esquina

2 (*fetch*) traer; ***can I ~ you something to drink?*** ¿quieres tomar algo?

3 (*receive: letter, knowledge, respect*) recibir

4 (*catch: bus, train etc*) tomar, *Span* coger

5 (*understand*) entender

6 (*become*): ***~ tired*** cansarse; ***~ drunk*** emborracharse; ***I'm ~ting old*** me estoy haciendo mayor

7: ***~ the TV fixed*** hacer que arreglen la televisión; ***~ s.o. to do sth*** hacer que alguien haga algo; ***~ one's hair cut*** cortarse el pelo

8: ***~ to do sth*** (*have opportunity*) llegar a hacer algo; ***~ to know*** llegar a conocer; ***~ sth ready*** preparar algo

9: ***~ going*** (*leave*) marcharse, irse

10: ***have got*** tener; ***he's got a lot of money*** tiene mucho dinero; ***I have got to study / see him*** tengo que estudiar / verlo; ***I don't want to, but I've got to*** no quiero, pero tengo que hacerlo

◆ **get across I** *v/i over road* cruzar, atravesar **II** *v/t*: ***he got his argument across well*** se hizo entender muy bien; ***get sth across to s.o.*** hacer entender algo a alguien

◆ **get along** *v/i* **1** (*come to party etc*) ir **2** *with s.o.* llevarse bien; ***how are you getting along at school?*** ¿cómo te van las cosas en el colegio?; ***the patient is getting along nicely*** el paciente está progresando satisfactoriamente

◆ **get around I** *v/i* **1** (*travel*) viajar, ver mundo **2** (*be mobile*) desplazarse **3** *of rumor* circular **4** *socially* hacer vida social **5**: ***I just never got around to fixing it*** nunca encontré el momento *or* tiempo para arreglarlo; ***you really should get around to taking more exercise*** deberías (plantearte el) hacer más ejercicio

II *v/t* **1** *obstacle, problem* sortear, evitar; ***there's no getting around it*** es imposible escaquearse **2** (*get to agree*) camelar

◆ **get at** *v/t* **1** (*reach*) llegar a; ***get at the truth*** averiguar la verdad **2** (*criticize*) meterse con **3** (*imply, mean*) querer decir **4** P *witness* untar P

◆ **get away I** *v/i* **1** (*escape*) escaparse **2** (*leave*) marcharse, irse **II** *v/t*: ***get sth away from s.o.*** quitar algo a alguien

◆ **get away with** *v/t of thief* llevarse, escaparse con; *fig* salir impune de; ***get away with it*** salirse con la suya; ***she lets him get away with anything*** le permite todo; ***I'll let you get away with it this time*** por esta vez te perdonaré

◆ **get back I** *v/i* **1** (*return*) volver; ***I'll get back to you on that tomorrow*** le responderé a eso mañana **2** (*move back*) retroceder; ***get back!*** ¡(échense) atrás! **II** *v/t* (*obtain again*) recuperar

◆ **get by** *v/i* **1** (*pass*) pasar **2** (*cope*) apañarse; *financially* arreglárselas

◆ **get down I** *v/i from ladder etc* bajarse (**from** de); (*duck etc*) agacharse **II** *v/t* **1** *object from a high place* bajar **2** (*depress*) desanimar, deprimir

◆ **get down to** *v/t* (*start*: *work*) ponerse a; ***get down to the facts*** ir a los hechos

◆ **get in I** *v/i* **1** (*arrive*) llegar **2** *to car etc* subir(se), meterse; ***how did they get in?*** *of thieves, mice etc* ¿cómo entraron?; ***we couldn't get in*** *to disco etc* no pudimos entrar; ***he applied for college but didn't get in*** mandó la solicitud para la universidad pero no le aceptaron **3** (*be elected*) ganar unas elecciones **II** *v/t to suitcase etc* meter

◆ **get into** *v/t house* entrar en, meterse en; *car* subir(se) a, meterse en; *computer system* introducirse en; *clothes* ponerse; ***what's gotten into you?*** ¿qué mosca te ha picado?

◆ **get off I** *v/i* **1** *from bus, train etc* bajarse **2** (*finish work*) salir **3** (*not be punished*) librarse **II** *v/t* **1** (*remove*) quitar; *clothes, hat, footgear* quitarse; ***get off my bike!*** ¡bájate de mi bici!; ***get off the grass!*** ¡no pises la hierba! **2**: ***get s.o. off*** *of lawyer* librar a alguien de un castigo

◆ **get off with** *v/t*: ***get off with a small fine*** tener que pagar sólo una pequeña multa

◆ **get on I** *v/i* **1** *to bike, bus, train* montarse, subirse **2** (*be friendly*) llevarse bien **3** (*advance*: *of time*) hacerse tarde; (*become old*) hacerse mayor; ***it's getting on*** *getting late* se está haciendo tarde; ***he's getting on*** se está haciendo mayor; *Br* ***he's getting on for 50*** está a punto de cumplir 50 **4** (*make progress*) progresar; ***how did you get on at school today?*** ¿qué tal te ha ido hoy en el colegio? **II** *v/t* **1**: ***get on the bus / one's bike*** montarse en el autobús / la bici **2** *shoes etc* ponerse; *lid etc* poner; ***I can't get these pants on*** estos pantalones no me entran

◆ **get onto** *v/t* **1** *subject* empezar a hablar de **2** (*contact*) ponerse en contacto con

◆ **get on with** *v/t* **1** (*continue*) seguir con; (*progress*) avanzar con **2**: ***I don't get on with him*** no me llevo bien con él, no me entiendo con él

◆ **get out I** *v/i of car, prison etc* salir; ***get out!*** ¡vete!, ¡fuera de aquí!; ***let's get out of here*** ¡salgamos de aquí!; ***how do you get out?*** *of this building* ¿por dónde se sale?; ***I don't get out much these days*** últimamente no salgo mucho; ***if word gets out that I …*** si alguien se entera de que … **II** *v/t nail, sth jammed* sacar, extraer; *stain* quitar; *gun, pen* sacar; ***get that dog out of here!*** ¡llévate *or* saca a ese perro de aquí!

◆ **get out of** *v/t* **1** *the city* salir de **2** *task* librarse de **3**: ***I don't see what they get out of it*** no sé que sacan *or* ganan con esto **4** *habit* perder, quitarse

◆ **get over** *v/t* **1** *fence etc* franquear **2** *disappointment* superar; *lover etc* olvidar; ***he never got over it*** nunca lo superó

◆ **get over with** *v/t* terminar con; ***let's get it over with*** quitémonoslo de encima

◆ **get through** *v/i* **1** *on telephone* conectarse **2**: ***get through to s.o.*** (*make self understood*) comunicarse con alguien; ***obviously I'm just not getting through*** está claro que no me estoy haciendo entender **3** (*finish*) acabar

◆ **get to** *v/t* (*annoy*) molestar, ofender; *have emotional effect on* afectar; ***these late nights must be getting to you*** es-

G

tas trasnochadas deben estar haciendo mella en tí

◆ **get together** I *v/i of people* reunirse, juntarse II *v/t* 1 *objects* reunir, recoger 2: ***he's really got it all together*** F lo tiene todo y es feliz

◆ **get up** I *v/i* levantarse II *v/t* (*climb*) subir

◆ **get up to** *v/t mischief* hacer; ***what have those two been getting up to?*** ¿qué han estado haciendo esos dos?; ***what are you getting up to these days?*** ¿qué haces ahora?

'get•a•way *from robbery* fuga *f*, huida *f*; **'get•a•way car** coche *m* utilizado en la fuga; **'get-to•geth•er** reunión *f*; **'get-up** F indumentaria *f*

G

gey•ser ['gaɪzər] GEOL géiser *m*

ghast•ly ['gæstlɪ] *adj* terrible

gher•kin ['gɜːrkɪn] pepinillo *m*

ghet•to ['getoʊ] (*pl* ***-o(e)s***) gueto *m*

ghost [goʊst] fantasma *m*

ghost•ly ['goʊstlɪ] *adj* fantasmal

'ghost sto•ry historia *f* de fantasmas; **'ghost town** ciudad *f* fantasma; **'ghost train** tren *m* fantasma; **'ghost writ•er** negro(-a) *m*(*f*)

ghoul [guːl] macabro(-a) *m*(*f*), morboso(-a) *m*(*f*)

ghoul•ish ['guːlɪʃ] *adj* macabro, morboso

gi•ant ['dʒaɪənt] I *n* gigante *m* II *adj* gigantesco, gigante

'gi•ant kil•lers *npl* matagigantes *m inv*

gib•ber ['dʒɪbər] *v/i* farfullar

gib•ber•ish ['dʒɪbərɪʃ] F memeces *fpl* F, majaderías *fpl* F; ***talk ~*** decir memeces

gib•bon ['gɪbən] gibón *m*

gibe [dʒaɪb] pulla *f*

gib•lets ['dʒɪblɪts] *npl* menudillos *mpl*

gid•di•ness ['gɪdɪnɪs] mareo *m*

gid•dy ['gɪdɪ] *adj* mareado; ***feel ~*** estar mareado; ***become ~*** marearse

gift [gɪft] regalo *m*; ***have a ~ for sth*** tener un don para algo

'gift cer•ti•fi•cate vale *m* de regalo

gift•ed ['gɪftɪd] *adj* con talento

'gift shop tienda *f* de artículos de regalo; **'gift to•ken** vale *m* de regalo; **'gift-wrap** I *n* papel *m* de regalo II *v/t* (*pret & pp* ***-ped***) envolver para regalo

gig [gɪg] F concierto *m*, actuación *f*

gi•ga•byte ['gɪgəbaɪt] COMPUT gigabyte *m*

gi•gan•tic [dʒaɪ'gæntɪk] *adj* gigantesco

gig•gle ['gɪgl] I *v/i* soltar risitas II *n* risita *f*; ***get the ~s*** tener un ataque de risa

gig•gly ['gɪglɪ] *adj* que suelta risitas

gild [gɪld] *v/t* dorar

gill [gɪl] *of fish* branquia *f*

gilt [gɪlt] dorado *m*; ***~s*** FIN valores *mpl* del Estado

gilt-edged se•cur•i•ties [gɪltedʒdsɪ'kjuːrɪtɪz] *npl* FIN valores *mpl* a plazo fijo

gim•crack ['dʒɪmkræk] *adj* de tres al cuarto

gim•mick ['gɪmɪk] truco *m*, reclamo *m*

gim•mick•y ['gɪmɪkɪ] *adj* superficial, artificioso

gin [dʒɪn] ginebra *f*; ***~ and tonic*** gin-tonic *m*

gin•ger ['dʒɪndʒər] *spice* jengibre *m*

gin•ger 'ale ginger ale *m*

'gin•ger•bread pan *m* de jengibre

gin•ger•ly ['dʒɪndʒərlɪ] *adv* cuidadosamente, delicadamente

ging•ham ['gɪŋəm] guinga *f*

gin•gi•vi•tis [dʒɪndʒɪ'vaɪtɪs] MED gingivitis *f inv*

gip•sy ['dʒɪpsɪ] *Br* gitano(-a) *m*(*f*)

gi•raffe [dʒɪ'ræf] jirafa *f*

gir•der ['gɜːrdər] viga *f*

gir•dle ['gɜːrdl] faja *f*

girl [gɜːrl] 1 chica *f*; (***young***) ~ niña *f*, chica *f* 2 *daughter* niña *f*, hija *f*

'girl•friend *of boy* novia *f*; *of girl* amiga *f*

girl•hood ['gɜːrlhʊd] niñez *f*

girl•ie mag•a•zine ['gɜːrlɪ] revista *f* porno

girl•ish ['gɜːrlɪʃ] *adj* de niñas

girl 'scout escultista *f*, scout *f*

girth [gɜːrθ] 1 *of tree etc* circunferencia *f* 2 *for horse* cincha *f*

gist [dʒɪst] esencia *f*; ***catch the ~ of sth*** captar la esencia de algo

give [gɪv] I *v/t* (*pret* ***gave***, *pp* ***given***) dar; *as present* regalar; (*supply*: *electricity etc*) proporcionar; *talk*, *lecture* dar, pronunciar; *cry*, *groan* soltar; ***~ her my love*** dale recuerdos (de mi parte); ***~ s.o. a present*** hacer un regalo a alguien; ***~n the fact that he …*** dado que; … ***don't ~ me that!*** F ¡no me vengas con esas!

II *v/i of structure*, *bridge etc* ceder, remitir

◆ **give away** *v/t* **1** *as present* regalar **2** (*betray*) traicionar; ***give o.s. away*** descubrirse, delatarse
◆ **give back** *v/t* devolver (***to*** a)
◆ **give in I** *v/i* (*surrender*) rendirse **II** *v/t* (*hand in*) entregar
◆ **give off** *v/t smell*, *fumes* emitir, despedir
◆ **give onto** *v/t* (*open onto*) dar a
◆ **give out I** *v/t* **1** *leaflets etc* repartir **2** *heat* despedir **II** *v/i of supplies*, *strength* agotarse
◆ **give up I** *v/t smoking etc* dejar de; *hope* perder; ***give o.s. up to the police*** entregarse a la policía **II** *v/i* (*stop making effort*) rendirse; ***I find it hard to give up*** me cuesta mucho dejarlo
◆ **give up on** *v/t person* perder la fe en
◆ **give way** *v/i* **1** *of bridge etc* hundirse **2** *esp Br*. *of traffic* ceder el paso
◆ **give way to** *v/t* dar paso a
give-and-'take toma *m* y daca
'give•a•way I 1 *n*: ***it's a dead ~*** salta a la vista **2** COM regalo *m* **II** *adj*: ***~ price*** precio *m* de ganga
giv•en ['gɪvn] *pp* ☞ ***give***
'giv•en name nombre *m* de pila
giv•er ['gɪvər] donante *m/f*
giz•mo ['gɪzmoʊ] F cacharro *m*
giz•zard ['gɪzərd] molleja *f*
gla•cé ['glæseɪ] *adj* confitado
gla•cial ['gleɪʃəl] *adj also fig* gélido
gla•cier ['gleɪʃər] glaciar *m*
glad [glæd] *adj* contento, alegre; ***I was ~ to see you*** me alegré de verte
glad•den ['glædn] *v/t* alegrar
glade [gleɪd] claro *m*
glad•i•a•tor ['glædɪeɪtər] gladiador *m*
glad•i•o•lus [glædɪ'oʊləs] (*pl* ***gladoli*** [glædɪ'oʊlaɪ]) BOT gladiolo *m*
glad•ly ['glædlɪ] *adv* con mucho gusto
glad•ness ['glædnɪs] alegría *f*
glam•or ['glæmər] atractivo *m*, glamour *m*
glam•or•ize ['glæməraɪz] *v/t* hacer atractivo, ensalzar
glam•or•ous ['glæmərəs] *adj* atractivo, glamoroso
glam•our *Br* ☞ ***glamor***
glance [glæns] **I** *n* ojeada *f*, vistazo *m*; ***I could tell at a ~ that ...*** con sólo (echar) un vistazo me di cuenta de que ... **II** *v/i* echar una ojeada *or* vistazo
◆ **glance at** *v/t* echar una ojeada *or* vistazo a
gland [glænd] glándula *f*
glan•du•lar 'fe•ver ['glændʒələr] mononucleosis *f inv* infecciosa
glare [gler] **I** *n of sun*, *headlights* resplandor *m* **II** *v/i of headlights* resplandecer
◆ **glare at** *v/t person* mirar con furia a
glar•ing ['glerɪŋ] *adj mistake* garrafal
glar•ing•ly ['glerɪŋlɪ] *adv*: ***it's ~ obvious*** está clarísimo
glass [glæs] **1** *material* vidrio *m* **2** *for drink* vaso *m*
'glass blow•er soplador(a) *m*(*f*) de vidrio; **glass 'case** vitrina *f*; **glass 'ceil•ing** *fig barreras que impiden a la mujer alcanzar altos cargos*
glass•es ['glæsɪz] *npl* gafas *fpl*, *L.Am.* lentes *mpl*, *L.Am.* anteojos *mpl*
glass•ful ['glæsfʊl] vaso *m*
'glass•house invernadero *m*
glass•ware ['glæswer] cristalería *f*
glass•y ['glæsɪ] *adj* **1** *surface* cristalino **2** *stare* vidrioso
glau•co•ma [glɒː'koʊmə] MED glaucoma *m*
glazed [gleɪzd] *adj expression* vidrioso
glaze [gleɪz] vidriado *m*
◆ **glaze over** *v/i of eyes* vidriarse
gla•zi•er ['gleɪzɪr] cristalero(-a) *m*(*f*), vidriero(-a) *m*(*f*)
glaz•ing ['gleɪzɪŋ] cristales *mpl*, vidrios *mpl*
gleam [gliːm] **I** *n* resplandor *m*, brillo *m* **II** *v/i* resplandecer, brillar
glean [gliːn] *v/t fig* averiguar; ***~ from*** extraer de
glee [gliː] júbilo *m*, regocijo *m*
glee•ful ['gliːfəl] *adj* jubiloso
glib [glɪb] *adj* fácil
glib•ly ['glɪblɪ] *adv* con labia
glide [glaɪd] *v/i of bird*, *plane* planear; *of piece of furniture* deslizarse
glid•er ['glaɪdər] planeador *m*
glid•ing ['glaɪdɪŋ] *sport* vuelo *m* sin motor
glim•mer ['glɪmər] **I** *n of light* brillo *m* tenue; ***~ of hope*** rayo *m* de esperanza **II** *v/i* brillar tenuamente
glimpse [glɪmps] **I** *n* vistazo *m*; ***catch a ~ of*** vislumbrar **II** *v/t* vislumbrar
glint [glɪnt] **I** *n* destello *m*; *in eyes* centelleo *m* **II** *v/i of light* destellar; *of eyes* centellear
glis•ten ['glɪsn] *v/i* relucir, centellear

G

glitch [glɪʧ] *F* fallo *m* técnico
glit•ter ['glɪtər] *v/i* resplandecer, destellar
glit•ter•a•ti [glɪtər'ɑ:tɪ] *npl* famosos *mpl*
glit•ter•ing ['glɪtərɪŋ] *adj* **1** resplandeciente **2** *fig* rutilante
glitz [glɪts] F glamour *m*
glitz•y ['glɪtsɪ] *adj* F glamoroso
gloat [gloʊt] *v/i* regodearse
◆ **gloat over** *v/t* regodearse de
glo•bal ['gloʊbl] *adj* global
glo•bal e'con•o•my economía *f* global
glob•al•i•za•tion [gloʊbəlaɪ'zeɪʃn] COM globalización *f*
glob•al•ly ['gloʊbəlɪ] *adv* globalmente
glo•bal 'mar•ket mercado *m* global
glo•bal warm•ing ['wɔ:rmɪŋ] calentamiento *m* global
globe [gloʊb] **1** (*the earth*) globo *m* **2** (*model of earth*) globo *m* terráqueo
globe•trot•ter ['gloʊbtrɑ:tər] trotamundos *m/f inv*
glob•ule ['glɑ:bju:l] gota *f*
gloom [glu:m] **1** (*darkness*) tinieblas *fpl*, oscuridad *f* **2** *mood* abatimiento *m*, melancolía *f*
gloom•i•ly ['glu:mɪlɪ] *adv* con abatimiento, melancólicamente
gloom•y ['glu:mɪ] *adj* **1** *room* tenebroso, oscuro **2** *mood*, *person* abatido, melancólico
glo•ri•fi•ca•tion [glɔ:rɪfɪ'keɪʃn] glorificación *f*
glo•ri•fied ['glɔ:rɪfaɪd] *adj* F con aires de grandeza
glo•ri•fy ['glɔ:rɪfaɪ] *v/t* glorificar
glo•ri•ous ['glɔ:rɪəs] *adj weather*, *day* espléndido, maravilloso; *victory* glorioso
glo•ry ['glɔ:rɪ] gloria *f*
◆ **glory in** *v/t* deleitarse con
gloss [glɑ:s] **1** (*shine*) lustre *m*, brillo *m* **2** (*general explanation*) glosa *f*
◆ **gloss over** *v/t* pasar por alto
glos•sa•ry ['glɑ:sərɪ] glosario *m*
'gloss paint pintura *f* brillante
gloss•y ['glɑ:sɪ] **I** *adj paper* cuché, satinado **II** *n magazine* revista *f* en color (*en papel cuché or satinado*)
glove [glʌv] guante *m*
'glove box, 'glove com•part•ment *in car* guantera *f*
'glove pup•pet marioneta *f* de guiñol (*de guante*)
glow [gloʊ] **I** *n of light*, *fire* resplandor *m*, brillo *m*; *in cheeks* rubor *m* **II** *v/i of light*, *fire* resplandecer, brillar; *of cheeks* ruborizarse
glow•er [glaʊr] *v/i* fruncir el ceño
glow•ing ['gloʊɪŋ] *adj description* entusiasta
glow•ing•ly ['gloʊɪŋlɪ] *adv*: ***speak ~ of s.o. / sth*** hablar elogiosamente de alguien / algo
'glow•worm ZO luciérnaga *f*
glu•cose ['glu:koʊs] glucosa *f*
glue [glu:] **I** *n* pegamento *m*, cola *f* **II** *v/t* pegar, encolar; ***~ sth to sth*** pegar *or* encolar algo a algo; ***be ~d to the radio / TV*** F estar pegado a la radio / televisión F
glue-sniff•ing ['glu:snɪfɪŋ] inhalación *f* de pegamento
glu•ey ['glu:ɪ] *adj* pegajoso
glum [glʌm] *adj* sombrío, triste; ***get** or **become ~*** entristecerse
glum•ly ['glʌmlɪ] *adv* con tristeza
glut [glʌt] exceso *m*, superabundancia *f*
glu•ten ['glu:tən] gluten *m*
glu•ti•nous ['glu:tənəs] *adj* glutinoso
glut•ton ['glʌtən] glotón(-ona) *m(f)*; ***she's a ~ for punishment*** es masoquista
glut•ton•ous ['glʌtənəs] *adj* glotón
glut•ton•y ['glʌtənɪ] gula *f*, glotonería *f*
glyc•er•in(e) ['glɪsəri:n] CHEM glicerina *f*
GMO [dʒi:em'oʊ] *abbr* (= ***genetically modified organism***) organismo *m* modificado genéticamente
GMT [dʒi:em'ti:] *abbr* (= ***Greenwich Mean Time***) hora *f* del meridiano de Greenwich
gnarled [nɑ:rld] *adj* nudoso
gnash [næʃ] *v/t*: ***~ one's teeth*** rechinar los dientes
gnat [næt] *tipo de mosquito*
gnaw [nɒ:] *v/t bone* roer
gnome [noʊm] gnomo *m*
GNP [dʒi:en'pi:] *abbr* (= ***gross national product***) PNB *m* (= producto *m* nacional bruto)
go [goʊ] **I** *n*: ***on the ~*** en marcha
II *v/i* (*pret* ***went***, *pp* ***gone***) **1** ir (***to*** a); (*leave*) irse, marcharse; (*come out*: *of stain etc*) irse; (*cease*: *of pain etc*) pasarse; ***~ shopping / jogging*** ir de compras / a hacer footing; ***I must be ~ing***

me tengo que ir; ***let's ~!*** ¡vamos!; ***~ for a walk*** ir a pasear *or* a dar un paseo; ***~ to bed*** ir(se) a la cama; ***~ to school*** ir al colegio; ***hamburger to ~*** hamburguesa para llevar; ***be all gone*** (*finished*) haberse acabado; ***where do the knives ~?*** ¿dónde van los cuchillos?
2 (*work, function*) funcionar; ***how's the work ~ing?*** ¿cómo va el trabajo?; ***how does the tune ~?*** ¿cómo es la música?; ***five into three won't ~*** (*fit*) tres (dividido) entre cinco no cabe; (*be divisible*) tres no es divisible por cinco
3 (*match*: *of colors etc*) ir bien, pegar
4: ***they're ~ing for $50*** (*being sold at*) se venden por 50 dólares
5: ***~ green*** ponerse verde
6: ***be ~ing to do sth*** ir a hacer algo
◆ **go ahead** *v/i and do sth* seguir adelante; ***can I? – sure, go ahead*** ¿puedo? - por supuesto, adelante
◆ **go after** *v/t person* perseguir; *job, opportunity* ir detrás de
◆ **go ahead with** *v/t plans etc* seguir adelante con
◆ **go along with** *v/t suggestion* aceptar; (*agree with*) estar de acuerdo con
◆ **go around** *v/i of virus, rumor* circular; ***there isn't enough food to go around*** no hay comida suficiente para todos
◆ **go at** *v/t* (*attack*) atacar
◆ **go away** *v/i of person* irse, marcharse; *of rain, pain, clouds* desaparecer
◆ **go back** *v/i* **1** (*return*) volver; ***go back to sleep*** volver a dormirse **2** (*date back*) remontarse; ***we go back a long way*** nos conocemos desde hace tiempo
◆ **go back on** *v/t one's word* faltar a
◆ **go by** *v/i of car, time* pasar
◆ **go down** *v/i* bajar; *of sun* ponerse; *of ship* hundirse; ***go down well / badly*** *of suggestion etc* sentar bien / mal
◆ **go for** *v/t* **1** (*attack*) atacar **2** (*like*): ***I don't much go for gin*** no me va mucho la ginebra **3** (*apply to*): ***does that go for me too?*** ¿eso también va por mí?
◆ **go in** *v/i* **1** *to room, house* entrar **2** *of sun* ocultarse **3** (*fit*: *of part etc*) ir, encajar
◆ **go in for** *v/t competition, race* tomar parte en; ***I used to go in for badminton quite a lot*** antes jugaba mucho al bádminton; ***I don't go in for that kind of music*** no me llama ese tipo de música
◆ **go into** *v/t* **1** *room, building* entrar en **2** *profession* meterse en **3** (*discuss*) entrar en
◆ **go off I** *v/i* **1** (*leave*) marcharse **2** *of bomb* explotar, estallar; *of gun* dispararse; *of alarm* saltar **3** *of milk etc* echarse a perder **II** *v/t*: ***I've gone off whiskey*** ya no me gusta el whisky
◆ **go on** *v/i* **1** (*continue*) continuar; ***the play goes on for three hours*** la obra dura tres horas; ***go on, do it!*** (*encouraging*) ¡venga, hazlo! **2** (*happen*) ocurrir, pasar; ***what's going on?*** ¿qué pasa? **3** (*talk, complain*): ***I wish you wouldn't go on so*** podrías dejarlo ya; ***he does go on, doesn't he?*** podía dejarlo ya
◆ **go on at** *v/t* (*nag*) meterse con
◆ **go out 1** *v/i of person* salir; *of tide* bajar; ***go out for dinner*** ir a cenar fuera **2** *of light, fire* apagarse
◆ **go out with** *v/t romantically* salir con
◆ **go over I** *v/t* **1** (*check*) examinar; ***I went over and over it again in my mind*** le di mil vueltas a la cabeza **2** (*do again*) repasar **3** (*discuss*) hablar de, discutir **II** *v/i*: ***go over to s.o.*** acercarse a alguien
◆ **go through I** *v/t* **1** *illness, hard times* atravesar **2** (*check*) revisar, examinar **3** (*read through*) estudiar **4** (*search*) buscar por, registrar **5**: ***he goes through one pair of socks a week*** destroza un par de calcetines cada semana **II** *v/i* **1** (*be accepted*) aprobarse **2**: ***it's gone through at the elbows*** está desgastado por los codos
◆ **go through with** *v/t threat* llevar a cabo; ***I couldn't go through with it*** me eché para atrás
◆ **go together** *v/i of colors etc* combinar, pegar
◆ **go under** *v/i* (*sink*) hundirse; *of company* ir a la quiebra
◆ **go up** *v/i* **1** subir **2** (*explode*) saltar en pedazos
◆ **go without I** *v/t food etc* pasar sin **II** *v/i* pasar privaciones

goad [goud] *v/t* pinchar; ***~ s.o. into doing sth*** pinchar a alguien para que haga algo

'go-a•head I *n* luz *f* verde; ***when we get the ~*** cuando nos den la luz verde **II** *adj*

(*enterprising, dynamic*) dinámico
goal [goʊl] **1** (*objective*) objetivo *m*, meta *f* **2** SP *target* portería *f*, *L.Am.* arco *m*; *point* gol *m*; ***shot on ~*** tiro *m* a portería
goal•ie ['goʊlɪ] F portero(-a) *m(f)*, *L.Am.* arquero(-a) *m(f)*
'goal•keep•er portero(-a) *m(f)*, guardameta *m/f*, *L.Am.* arquero(-a) *m(f)*; **'goal kick** saque *m* de puerta *or Rpl* de valla; **'goal line** línea *f* de gol; **'goal•mouth** portería *f*; **'goal•post** poste *m*; **'goal•scor•er** goleador(a) *m(f)*
goat [goʊt] cabra *f*; ***it really gets my ~!*** F ¡me pone del hígado! F
goa•tee [goʊ'tiː] perilla *f*
gob•ble•dy•gook ['gɑːbldɪguːk] F jerigonza *f* F
gob•ble ['gɑːbl] *v/t* engullir
◆ **gobble up** *v/t* engullir
'go-be•tween intermediario(-a) *m(f)*
gob•let ['gɑːblət] copa *f*
gob•lin ['gɑːblɪn] duende *m*
'go-cart kart *m*
god [gɑːd] dios *m*; ***thank God!*** ¡gracias a Dios!; ***oh God!*** ¡Dios mío!
'god-aw•ful *adj* F terrible; **'god•child** ahijado(-a) *m(f)*; **god•dam•mit** [gɑːd'dæmɪt] *int* F ¡maldita sea!; **goddamned** ['gɑːddæmd] *adj* F maldito; **'god•daugh•ter** ahijada *f*
god•dess ['gɑːdɪs] diosa *f*
'god•fa•ther *also in mafia* padrino *m*; **God-fear•ing** ['gɑːdfɪrɪŋ] *adj* temeroso de Dios; **'god•for•sak•en** *adj place* dejado de la mano de Dios
god•less ['gɑːdlɪs] *adj* impío
god•like ['gɑːdlaɪk] *adj* divino
god•ly ['gɑːdlɪ] *adj* piadoso
'god•moth•er madrina *f*; **'god•pa•rent** *man* padrino *m*; *woman* madrina *f*; **'god•send** regalo *m* del cielo; **'god•son** ahijado *m*
go•fer ['goʊfər] F recadero(-a) *m(f)*
go-get•ter ['goʊgetər] F ambicioso(-a) *m(f)*
gog•gle ['gɑːgl] *v/i*: **~ *at s.o.*** mirar a alguien con los ojos abiertos de par en par
gog•gle-eyed [gɑːgl'aɪd] *adj* F *in amazement* con los ojos desorbitados
gog•gles ['gɑːglz] *npl* gafas *fpl*
'go-go danc•er gogó *f*
go•ing ['goʊɪŋ] **I** *adj price etc* vigente; **~ *concern*** empresa *f* en marcha **II** *n*: ***the path was hard ~*** el camino estaba en mal estado; ***the book isn't very easy ~*** el libro es bastante pesado
go•ings-on [goʊɪŋz'ɑːn] *npl* actividades *fpl*
goi•ter, *Br* **goi•tre** ['gɔɪtər] MED bocio *m*
go-kart ['goʊkɑːrt] *Br* kart *m*
gold [goʊld] **I** *n* oro *m* **II** *adj* de oro
'gold dig•ger F cazafortunas *f inv*
'gold dust oro *m* en polvo; ***be like ~*** ser difícil de encontrar
gold•en ['goʊldn] *adj sky, hair* dorado; ***a ~ opportunity*** una oportunidad de oro
'gold•en age edad *f* de oro; **gold•en ag•er** ['eɪðʒər] pensionista *m/f*; **gold•en 'ea•gle** águila *f* real; **'gold•en goal** *in soccer* gol *m* de oro; **gold•en 'hand•shake** *gratificación entregada tras la marcha de un directivo*; **gold•en 'hel•lo** prima *f* de contratación; **gold•en re'triev•er** retriever *m* dorado; **gold•en 'wed•ding (an•ni•ver•sa•ry)** bodas *fpl* de oro
'gold•field yacimiento *m* de oro; **'gold•fish** pez *m* de colores; **'gold med•al** medalla *f* de oro; **'gold mine** *fig* mina *f*; **gold-plat•ed** [goʊld'pleɪtɪd] *adj* bañado en oro; **'gold•smith** orfebre *m/f*
golf [gɑːlf] golf *m*
'golf ball pelota *f* de golf; **'golf club** *organization* club *m* de golf; *stick* palo *m* de golf; **'golf course** campo *m* de golf
golf•er ['gɑːlfər] golfista *m/f*
golf•ing ['gɑːlfɪŋ]: ***go ~*** jugar a golf
'golf links *npl* campo *m* de golf (*al lado del mar*)
Go•li•ath [gə'laɪəθ] *fig* gigante *m*
go•nad ['goʊnæd] ANAT gónada *f*
gon•do•la ['gɑːndələ] **1** *of cable car* (coche *m* de) teleférico *m* **2** *in Italy* góndola *f*
gone [gɑːn] **1** *pp* ☞ ***go*** **2** *prep*: ***it is ~ six (o'clock)*** acaban de dar las seis
go•ner ['gɑːnər] F: ***she's a ~*** tiene un pie en la tumba
gong [gɑːŋ] gong *m*
gon•na ['gɔːnə] F ☞ ***go***
gon•or•rhe•a, *Br* **gon•or•rhoe•a** [gɑːnə'rɪə] MED gonorrea *f*
goo [guː] F **1** pringue *m* **2** *fig* sensiblería *f*
good [gʊd] *adj* bueno; *food* bueno, rico;

a ~ many muchos; ***he's ~ at chess*** se le da muy bien el ajedrez; ***be ~ for s.o.*** ser bueno para alguien; ***~ morning*** buenos días; ***~ afternoon*** buenas tardes; ***~ evening*** buenas tardes / noches; ***~ night*** buenas noches; ***it was as ~ as finished*** estaba prácticamente terminado *or* acabado; ***it's no ~ keeping on asking*** no sirve de nada pedir tanto; ***that's no ~, we can't have that*** es inaceptable; ***how about tomorrow? – no, that's no ~*** ¿qué tal mañana? no, no me viene bien; ***it's no ~, I can't do it*** imposible, no puedo

good•bye [gʊd'baɪ] adiós *m*, despedida *f*; ***say ~ to s.o., wish s.o. ~*** decir adiós a alguien, despedirse de alguien

'good-for-no•thing inútil *m/f*; **Good 'Fri•day** Viernes *m inv* Santo; **good-‑heart•ed** [gʊd'hɑːrtɪd] *adj* bondadoso; **good-hu•mored**, *Br* **good-hu•moured** [gʊd'hjuːmərd] *adj* jovial, afable; **good-look•ing** [gʊd'lʊkɪŋ] *adj woman, man* guapo; **good-na•tured** [gʊd'neɪʧərd] bondadoso

good•ness ['gʊdnɪs] *moral* bondad *f*; *of fruit etc* propiedades *fpl*, valor *m* nutritivo; ***thank ~!*** ¡gracias a Dios!; ***for ~ sake!*** ¡por el amor de Dios!

goods [gʊdz] *npl* COM mercancías *fpl*, productos *mpl*

good-tem•pered [gʊd'tempərd] *adj* afable

good'will buena voluntad *f*

good•y-good•y ['gʊdɪgʊdɪ] F: ***she's a real ~*** es una buenaza F

goo•ey ['guːɪ] *adj* **1** *sticky* pegajoso **2** *sentimental* sentimentaloide

goof [guːf] *v/i* F meter la pata F

◆ **goof off** *v/i* F eludir obligaciones

goon [guːn] F matón *m*

goose [guːs] (*pl* ***geese*** [giːs]) ganso *m*, oca *f*

goose•ber•ry ['gʊzberɪ] grosella *f*; **'goose bumps** *npl* carne *f* de gallina; **'goose pim•ples** *npl* carne *f* de gallina; **'goose step** paso *m* de la oca

go•pher ['goʊfər] ZO taltuza *f*

Gor•di•an ['gɔːrdjən] *adj*: ***cut the ~ knot*** cortar el nudo gordiano

gore[1] [gɔːr] *n* sangre *f*; ***the movie is full of blood and ~*** la película tiene mucha casquería

gore[2] [gɔːr] *v/t* cornear, dar una cornada a

gorge [gɔːrdʒ] **I** *n* garganta *f*, desfiladero *m* **II** *v/t*: ***~ o.s. on sth*** comer algo hasta hartarse

gor•geous ['gɔːrdʒəs] *adj weather* maravilloso; *dress, hair* precioso; *woman, man* buenísimo; *smell* estupendo

go•ril•la [gə'rɪlə] gorila *m*

gor•y ['gɔːrɪ] *adj* sangriento; ***she gave me all the ~ details*** me contó hasta los detalles más escabrosos

gosh [gɑːʃ] *int* ¡caramba!, ¡vaya!

gos•ling ['gɑːzlɪŋ] ORN ansarón *m*

go-'slow huelga *f* de celo

gos•pel ['gɑːspl] *in Bible* evangelio *m*; ***it's the ~ truth*** es la pura verdad

gos•sa•mer ['gɑːsəmər] *fabric* gasa *f*

gos•sip ['gɑːsɪp] **I** *n* cotilleo *m*; *person* cotilla *m/f* **II** *v/i* cotillear

'gos•sip col•umn ecos *mpl* de sociedad

'gos•sip col•um•nist escritor(a) *m(f)* de los ecos de sociedad

gos•sip•y ['gɑːsɪpɪ] *adj letter* lleno de cotilleos

got [gɑːt] *pret & pp* ☞ ***get***

Goth•ic ['gɑːθɪk] **I** *adj* gótico; ***~ novel*** novela *f* gótica **II** *n* ARCHI gótico *m*

got•ta ['gɑːtə] ☞ ***have*** (***got***) ***to***

got•ten ['gɑːtn] *pp* ☞ ***get***

gouge [gaʊdʒ] *v/t* **1** cavar; ***~ s.o.'s eyes out*** arrancar los ojos a alguien **2** F *customers* timar

gou•lash ['guːlæʃ] GASTR gulasch *m*

gourd [gʊrd] BOT calabaza *f*

gour•met ['gʊrmeɪ] gastrónomo(-a) *m(f)*, gourmet *m/f*

gout [gaʊt] MED gota *f*

gov•ern ['gʌvərn] *v/t country* gobernar

gov•ern•ing ['gʌvərnɪŋ] *adj* gobernante; ***~ body*** órgano *m* rector

gov•ern•ment ['gʌvərnmənt] gobierno *m*

gov•ern•ment 'spend•ing gasto *m* público

gov•er•nor ['gʌvərnər] gobernador(a) *m(f)*

gown [gaʊn] **1** *long dress* vestido *m*; *wedding dress* traje *m* **2** *of academic, judge* toga *f* **3** *of surgeon* bata *f*

grab [græb] **I** *v/t* (*pret & pp* ***-bed***) agarrar; *food* tomar; ***~ some sleep*** dormir; ***it doesn't ~ me*** F no me emociona **II** *n*: ***make a ~ for sth*** intentar agarrar algo; ***be up for ~s*** F estar disponible

grace [greɪs] **1** *of dancer etc* gracia *f*, elegancia *f*; ***he didn't even have the ~ to say sorry!*** ¡no tuvo ni siquiera la delicadeza de pedir perdón! **2** *at meal*: ***say ~*** bendecir la mesa **3** COM: ***period of ~*** periodo *m* de gracia
grace•ful ['greɪsfəl] *adj* elegante
grace•ful•ly ['greɪsfəlɪ] *adv move* con gracia *or* elegancia
gra•cious ['greɪʃəs] *adj person* amable; *style, living* elegante; ***good ~!*** ¡Dios mío!
gra•da•tion [grə'deɪʃn] gradación *f*
grade [greɪd] **I** *n* **1** *quality* grado *m* **2** EDU curso *m*; (*mark*) nota *f* **II** *v/t* clasificar
'grade cross•ing paso *m* a nivel
'grade school escuela *f* primaria
gra•di•ent ['greɪdɪənt] pendiente *f*
grad•u•al ['grædʒʊəl] *adj* gradual
grad•u•al•ly ['grædʒʊəlɪ] *adv* gradualmente, poco a poco
grad•u•ate ['grædʒʊət] **I** *n* licenciado(-a) *m*(*f*); *from high school* bachiller *m/f* **II** *v/i from university* licenciarse, *L.Am.* egresarse; *from high school* sacar el bachillerato
'grad•u•ate school escuela *f* de posgrado
grad•u•a•tion [grædʒʊ'eɪʃn] graduación *f*
grad•u'a•tion cer•e•mon•y ceremonia *f* de graduación
graf•fi•ti [grə'fi:ti:] graffiti *m*
graft [græft] **I** *n* **1** BOT, MED injerto *m* **2** F *corruption* corrupción *f* **II** *v/t* BOT, MED injertar
grain [greɪn] **1** grano *m* **2** *in wood* veta *f*; ***go against the ~*** ir contra la naturaleza de alguien
gram [græm] gramo *m*
gram•mar ['græmər] gramática *f*
gram•mat•i•cal [grə'mætɪkl] *adj* gramatical
gram•mat•i•cal•ly [grə'mætɪklɪ] *adv* gramaticalmente
gran•ar•y ['grænərɪ] granero *m*
grand [grænd] **I** *adj* grandioso; F (*very good*) estupendo, genial **II** *n* F (*$1000*) mil dólares
gran•dad *Br* ☞ **granddad**; **Gran 'Can•yon** Gran Cañon *m*; **'grand•child** nieto(-a) *m*(*f*); **grand•dad** ['grændæd] abuelito *m*; **'grand•daugh•ter** nieta *f*
gran•deur ['grændʒər] grandiosidad *f*; ***suffer from delusions of ~*** sufrir delirios de grandeza
'grand•fa•ther abuelo *m*
'grand•fa•ther clock reloj *m* de pie
gran•di•ose ['grændɪoʊs] *adj* grandioso
grand 'jur•y jurado *m* de acusación, gran jurado; **'grand•ma** F abuelita *f*, yaya *f* F; **'grand•moth•er** abuela *f*; **'grand•pa** F abuelito *m*, yayo *m* F; **'grand•par•ents** *npl* abuelos *mpl*; **grand pi'an•o** piano *m* de cola; **grand 'slam** gran slam *m*; **'grand•son** nieto *m*; **'grand•stand** tribuna *f*
gran•ite ['grænɪt] granito *m*
gran•ny ['grænɪ] F abuelita *f*, yaya *f* F
grant [grænt] **I** *n money* subvención *f*; EDU beca *f* **II** *v/t* conceder; ***take sth for ~ed*** dar algo por sentado; ***take s.o. for ~ed*** no apreciar a alguien lo suficiente
grant-in-'aid subvención *f*
gran•u•lar ['grænjʊlər] *adj* granuloso
gran•u•lat•ed sug•ar ['grænʊleɪtɪd] azúcar *m or f* granulado(-a)
gran•ule ['grænju:l] gránulo *m*
grape [greɪp] uva *f*
'grape•fruit pomelo *m*, *L.Am.* toronja *f*; **'grape•fruit juice** *L.Am.* jugo *m* de toronja, *Span* zumo *m* de pomelo; **'grape•vine**: ***I've heard through the ~ that …*** me ha contado un pajarito que …
graph [græf] gráfico *m*, gráfica *f*
graph•ic ['græfɪk] **I** *adj* (*vivid*) gráfico **II** *n* COMPUT gráfico *m*
graph•ic•al•ly ['græfɪklɪ] *adv describe* gráficamente
graph•ic 'art•ist artista *m/f* gráfico(-a); **graph•ic de'sign** diseño *m* gráfico; **graph•ic de'sign•er** diseñador(a) *m*(*f*) gráfico(-a); **graph•ic 'e•qual•iz•er** equalizador *m* gráfico
'graph•ics card COMPUT tarjeta *f* gráfica
graph•ite ['græfaɪt] MIN grafito *m*
graph•ol•o•gy [græ'fɑ:lədʒɪ] grafología *f*
'graph pap•er papel *m* cuadriculado
◆ **grap•ple with** ['græpl] *v/t attacker* forcejear con; *problem etc* enfrentarse a
grasp [græsp] **I** *n* **1** *physical* asimiento *m* **2** *mental* comprensión *f* **II** *v/t* **1** *physi-*

cally agarrar **2** *mentally* comprender
grasp•ing ['græspɪŋ] *adj* codicioso
grass [græs] *also drug* hierba *f*
'grass cloth fibra *f* natural; **grass-hop•per** ['græshɑːpər] saltamontes *m inv*; **grass 'roots** *npl people* bases *fpl*; **'grass snake** ZO culebra *f* de collar; **grass 'wid•ow** *mujer cuyo marido está a menudo ausente durante largos periodos de tiempo*; **grass 'wid•ow•er** *hombre cuya mujer está a menudo ausente durante largos periodos de tiempo*
grass•y ['græsɪ] *adj* lleno de hierba
grate[1] [greɪt] *n metal* parrilla *f*, reja *f*
grate[2] [greɪt] **I** *v/t in cooking* rallar **II** *v/i of sound* rechinar
◆ **grate on** *v/t* atacar
grate•ful ['greɪtfəl] *adj* agradecido; ***we are ~ for your help*** (le) agradecemos su ayuda; ***I'm ~ to him*** le estoy agradecido
grate•ful•ly ['greɪtfəlɪ] *adv* con agradecimiento
grat•er ['greɪtər] rallador *m*
grat•i•fi•ca•tion [grætɪfɪ'keɪʃn] satisfacción *f*
grat•i•fy ['grætɪfaɪ] *v/t* (*pret & pp* **-ied**) satisfacer, complacer
grat•i•fy•ing ['grætɪfaɪɪŋ] *adj* gratificante
grat•ing ['greɪtɪŋ] **I** *n* reja *f* **II** *adj sound, voice* chirriante
gra•tis ['greɪtɪs] *adv* gratis
grat•i•tude ['grætɪtuːd] gratitud *f*
gra•tu•i•tous [grə'tuːɪtəs] *adj* gratuito
gra•tu•i•ty [grə'tuːətɪ] *fml* propina *f*, gratificación *f*
grave[1] [greɪv] *n* tumba *f*, sepultura *f*
grave[2] [greɪv] *adj* grave
'grave dig•ger sepulturero(-a) *m*(*f*)
grav•el ['grævl] gravilla *f*
grave•ly ['greɪvlɪ] *adv* gravemente; ***be ~ ill*** estar gravemente enfermo
'grave•stone lápida *f*
'grave•yard cementerio *m*
◆ **grav•i•tate toward** ['grævɪteɪt] *v/t* verse atraído por
grav•i•ta•tion [grævɪ'teɪʃn] PHYS gravitación *f*
grav•i•ta•tion•al [grævɪ'teɪʃnl] *adj* PHYS gravitatorio
grav•i•ta•tion•al 'field PHYS campo *m* gravitatorio
grav•i•ty ['grævətɪ] PHYS gravedad *f*
gra•vy ['greɪvɪ] jugo *m* (de la carne)
gray [greɪ] *adj* gris; ***be going ~*** encanecer; ***~ hairs*** canas *fpl*
'gray area *fig* área *f* poco clara
gray-haired [greɪ'herd] *adj* canoso
gray•ish ['greɪɪʃ] *adj* grisáceo
gray 'mat•ter materia *f* gris
gray 'squir•rel ardilla *f* gris
graze[1] [greɪz] *v/i of cow etc* pastar, pacer
graze[2] [greɪz] **I** *v/t arm etc* rozar, arañar **II** *n* rozadura *f*, arañazo *m*
grease [griːs] **I** *n* grasa *f* **II** *v/t* engrasar
'grease•paint maquillaje *m* de teatro
grease•proof 'pa•per papel *m* de cera *or* parafinado
greas•y ['griːsɪ] *adj food, hands, plate* grasiento; *hair, skin* graso
greas•y 'spoon F restaurante *m* barato
great [greɪt] *adj* **1** grande, *before singular noun* gran **2** F (*very good*) estupendo, genial; ***how was it? – ~!*** ¿cómo fue? – ¡estupendo *or* genial!; ***~ to see you again!*** ¡me alegro de volver a verte!
great-'aunt tía *f* abuela; **Great 'Brit•ain** Gran Bretaña *f*; **great-'grand•child** bisnieto(-a) *m*(*f*); **great-'grand-daugh•ter** bisnieta *f*; **great-'grand-fa•ther** bisabuelo *m*; **great-'grand-moth•er** bisabuela *f*; **great-'grand-par•ents** *npl* bisabuelos *mpl*; **great--'grandson** bisnieto *m*
great•ly ['greɪtlɪ] *adv* muy
great•ness ['greɪtnɪs] grandeza *f*
great-'un•cle tío *m* abuelo
Greece [griːs] Grecia *f*
greed [griːd] *for money* codicia *f*; *for food* gula *f*, glotonería *f*
greed•i•ly ['griːdɪlɪ] *adv* con codicia; *eat* con gula *or* glotonería
greed•i•ness ['griːdɪnɪs] *for money* codicia *f*, *for food* gula *f*, glotonería *f*
greed•y ['griːdɪ] *adj for food* glotón; *for money* codicioso; ***be ~ for power / success*** estar ávido de poder / éxito; ***can I be ~ and have another?*** si no te importa, voy a tomar otro más; ***you ~ pig!*** F ¡mira que eres glotón *or* tragón!
Greek [griːk] **I** *adj* griego **II** *n* **1** *person* griego(-a) *m*(*f*) **2** *language* griego *m*; ***it's all ~ to me!*** F ¡me suena a chino!
green [griːn] **I** *adj* verde; *environmen-*

tally ecologista, verde **II** *n* **1** *in golf* green *m* **2** P *money* plata *f* F, *Span* pasta *f* F

'green•back F billete *m*, dólar *m*; **green 'beans** *npl* judías *fpl* verdes, *L.Am.* porotos *mpl* verdes, *Mex* ejotes *mpl*; **'green belt** cinturón *m* verde; **'green card** (*work permit*) permiso *m* de trabajo; **'green chan•nel** *at airport etc* pasillo *m* de nada que declarar

green•er•y ['gri:nərɪ] vegetación *f*

'green•field site terreno *m* edificable en el campo; **'green•fly** pulgón *m*; **green•gro•cer's** ['gri:ngrousərz] *Br* verdulería *f*; **'green•horn** F novato(-a) *m(f)* F; **'green•house** invernadero *m*; **'green•house ef•fect** efecto *m* invernadero; **'green•house gas** gas *m* invernadero

green•ish ['gri:nɪʃ] *adj* verdoso

Green•land ['gri:nlənd] Groenlandia *f*; **green 'light** luz *f* verde; ***give sth the ~*** dar la luz verde a algo; **green 'pep•per** pimiento *m* verde

greens [gri:nz] *npl* verduras *f*

green 'thumb: ***have a ~*** tener buena mano con la jardinería

Green•wich Mean Time [grenɪdʒ'mi:ntaɪm] hora *f* del meridiano de Greenwich

greet [gri:t] *v/t* saludar

greet•ing ['gri:tɪŋ] saludo *m*

'greet•ing card tarjeta *f* de felicitación

gre•gar•i•ous [grɪ'gerɪəs] *adj person* sociable

grem•lin ['gremlɪn] duende *m*

gre•nade [grɪ'neɪd] granada *f*

grew [gru:] *pret* ☞ ***grow***

grey *Br* ☞ ***gray***

'grey•hound galgo *m*

grid [grɪd] reja *f*, rejilla *f*

grid•dle ['grɪdl] plancha *f*

'grid•i•ron SP *campo de fútbol americano*; **'grid•lock** *in traffic* paralización *f* del tráfico; **grid•locked** ['grɪdlɑ:kt] *adj* paralizado

grief [gri:f] dolor *m*, aflicción *f*

'grief-strick•en *adj* afligido

griev•ance ['gri:vəns] queja *f*; ***have a ~ against s.o.*** tener un resentimiento contra alguien

grieve [gri:v] *v/i* sufrir; ***~ for s.o.*** llorar por alguien

griev•ous ['gri:vəs] *adj* grave

grill [grɪl] **I** *n on window* reja *f* **II** *v/t* F (*interrogate*) interrogar

grille [grɪl] reja *f*

gril•ling ['grɪlɪŋ]: ***give s.o. a ~*** F acribillar a alguien a preguntas

'grill•room asador *m*

grim [grɪm] *adj face* severo; *prospects* desolador; *surroundings* lúgubre

gri•mace ['grɪməs] **I** *n* gesto *m*, mueca *f* **II** *v/i* hacer una mueca

grime [graɪm] mugre *f*

grim•ly ['grɪmlɪ] *adv speak* en tono grave

grim•y ['graɪmɪ] *adj* mugriento

grin [grɪn] **I** *n* sonrisa *f* (amplia) **II** *v/i* (*pret & pp **-ned***) sonreír abiertamente

grind [graɪnd] *v/t* (*pret & pp **ground***) *coffee* moler; *meat* picar; ***~ one's teeth*** hacer rechinar los dientes

grind•er ['graɪndər] *for coffee, spices* molinillo *m*; *for meat* picadora *f*

grind•ing ['graɪndɪŋ] *adj*: ***~ poverty*** pobreza *f* absoluta

'grind•stone piedra *f* de afilar; ***keep*** *or* ***have one's nose to the ~*** *fig* trabajar como un esclavo

grip [grɪp] **I** *n*: ***he lost his ~ on the rope*** se le escapó la cuerda; ***be losing one's ~*** (*losing one's skills*) estar volviéndose majara F **II** *v/t* (*pret & pp **-ped***) agarrar

gripe [graɪp] F **I** *n* queja *f* **II** *v/i* quejarse

grip•ping ['grɪpɪŋ] *adj* apasionante

gris•ly ['grɪzlɪ] *adj* horripilante

grist [grɪst]: ***it's all ~ to the mill*** *fig* todo se puede aprovechar

gris•tle ['grɪsl] cartílago *m*

gris•tly ['grɪslɪ] *adj* con muchos cartílagos

grit [grɪt] **I** *n dirt* arenilla *f*; *for roads* gravilla *f* **II** *v/t* (*pret & pp **-ted***): ***~ one's teeth*** apretar los dientes

grit•ty ['grɪtɪ] *adj* F *book, movie etc* duro F, descarnado

griz•zle ['grɪzl] *v/i Br* F **1** *cry* lloriquear **2** *complain* refunfuñar

griz•zly bear [grɪzlɪ'ber] ZO oso *m* pardo

groan [groun] **I** *n* gemido *m* **II** *v/i* gemir

gro•cer ['grousər] tendero(-a) *m(f)*

gro•cer•ies ['grousərɪz] *npl* comestibles *mpl*

gro•cer•y store ['grousərɪ] tienda *f* de comestibles *or Mex* abarrotes

grog•gy ['grɑ:gɪ] *adj* F grogui F

groin [grɔɪn] ANAT ingle *f*
groom [gruːm] **I** *n* **1** *for bride* novio *m* **2** *for horse* mozo *m* de cuadra **II** *v/t horse* almohazar; (*train, prepare*) preparar; ***well ~ed*** *in appearance* bien arreglado
groove [gruːv] ranura *f*
groov•y ['gruːvɪ] *adj* F dabuti
grope [groʊp] **I** *v/i in the dark* caminar a tientas **II** *v/t sexually* manosear
◆ **grope for** *v/t door handle, the right word* intentar encontrar
gross [groʊs] *adj* **1** (*coarse, vulgar*) grosero **2** *exaggeration* tremendo; *error* craso; ***~ negligence*** LAW negligencia *f* grave **3** FIN bruto
◆ **gross out** *v/t* P: ***gross s.o. out*** asquear a alguien
gross do•mes•tic 'prod•uct producto *m* interior bruto; **gross 'earn•ings** *npl of company* beneficio *m* bruto; **gross 'in•come** ingreso *m* bruto
gross•ly ['groʊslɪ] *adv*: ***~ exaggerated*** exageradísimo, desmesurado ***~ overweight*** exageradamente gordo; ***~ unfair*** sumamente injusto
gross na•tion•al 'prod•uct producto *m* nacional bruto; **gross 'prof•it margin** margen *m* de beneficio bruto; **gross reg•is•ter•ed ton•nage** [groʊsredʒɪstərd'tʌnɪdʒ] *of ship* tonelaje *m* bruto registrado
gro•tesque [groʊ'tesk] *adj* grotesco
grot•to ['grɑːtoʊ] (*pl* ***-to(e)s***) gruta *f*
grot•ty ['grɑːtɪ] *adj Br* F cutre
grouch [graʊtʃ] F **I** *v/i* refunfuñar (***about*** sobre) **II** *n* gruñón(-ona) *m(f)*
grouch•y ['graʊtʃɪ] *adj* F gruñón
ground[1] [graʊnd] **I 1** *n* suelo *m*, tierra *f*; ***on the ~*** en el suelo **2** (*reason*) motivo *m* **3** ELEC tierra *f* **II** *v/t* ELEC conectar a tierra
ground[2] [graʊnd] *pret & pp* ☞ ***grind***
'ground ball *in baseball* roleta *f*, roletazo *m*; **ground 'beef** carne *f* picada; **'ground•break•ing** *adj* innovador; **'ground ca•ble** ELEC cable *m* de toma de tierra; **'ground con•trol** control *m* de tierra; **'ground crew** personal *m* de tierra; **'ground for•ces** *npl* MIL fuerzas *fpl* terrestres; **'ground frost** escarcha *f*; **'ground•hog** ZO marmota *f*
ground•ing ['graʊndɪŋ] *in subject* fundamento *m*; ***he's had a good ~ in electronics*** tiene buenos fundamentos de electrónica
ground•less ['graʊndlɪs] *adj* infundado
ground 'meat carne *f* picada; **'groundnut** cacahuete *m*, *L.Am.* maní *m*, *Mex* cacahuate *m*; **'ground plan** plano *m*; **'ground rules** *npl* normas *fpl* básicas; **'ground squir•rel** ZO ardilla *f* terrestre; **'ground staff** SP personal *m* de mantenimiento; *at airport* personal *m* de tierra; **'ground•swell**: ***a ~ of opinion*** una corriente de opinión; **'ground wa•ter** agua *m* subterránea *or* freática; **'ground-wa•ter lev•el** nivel *m* de agua subterránea *or* freática; **'ground•work** trabajos *mpl* preliminares; **Ground 'Ze•ro** nivel *m* cero
group [gruːp] **I** *n* grupo *m*; ***~ dynamics*** *pl* dinámica *f* de grupo **II** *v/t* agrupar
group•ie ['gruːpɪ] F grupi *m/f* F
group•ing ['gruːpɪŋ] grupo *m*
group 'ther•a•py terapia *f* de grupo
grouse[1] [graʊs] F **I** *n* queja *f* **II** *v/i* quejarse, refunfuñar
grouse[2] [graʊs] *n* ORN lagópodo *m*
grove [groʊv] arboleda *f*
grov•el ['grɑːvl] *v/i* (*pret & pp* ***-ed***, *Br* ***-led***) *fig* arrastrarse
grov•el•er, *Br* **grov•el•ler** ['grɑːvələr] persona *f* servil
grov•el•ing, *Br* **grov•el•ling** ['grɑːvəlɪŋ] *adj* servil
grow [groʊ] **I** *v/i* (*pret* ***grew***, *pp* ***grown***) crecer; *of number, amount* crecer, incrementarse; ***~ old / tired*** envejecer / cansarse **II** *v/t* (*pret* ***grew***, *pp* ***grown***) *flowers* cultivar
◆ **grow apart** *v/i* distanciarse
◆ **grow out of** *v/t clothes, shoes* no caber en; *habit, friend etc* dejar atrás
◆ **grow up** *v/i of person, city* crecer; ***grow up!*** ¡no seas crío!
grow•er ['groʊər] cultivador(a) *m(f)*; ***potato ~s*** cultivadores de patatas
growl [graʊl] **I** *n* gruñido *m* **II** *v/i* gruñir
grown [groʊn] *pp* ☞ ***grow***
'grown-up I *n* adulto(-a) *m(f)* **II** *adj* maduro
growth [groʊθ] *of person, economy* crecimiento *m*; (*increase*) incremento *m*; MED bulto *m*
'growth in•dus•try COM industria *f* en expansión
'growth rate COM tasa *f* de crecimiento
grub [grʌb] *of insect* larva *f*, gusano *m*

◆ **grub around** *v/i* (*pret & pp* **-bed**) rebuscar; ~ ***for sth*** buscar algo
grub•by ['grʌbɪ] *adj* mugriento *m*
grudge [grʌdʒ] **I** *n* rencor *m*; ***bear s.o. a ~*** guardar rencor a alguien **II** *v/t*: ***~ s.o. sth*** *feel envy* envidiar algo a alguien
grudg•ing ['grʌdʒɪŋ] *adj* rencoroso
grudg•ing•ly ['grʌdʒɪŋlɪ] *adv* de mala gana
gru•el ['gruəl] gachas *fpl*
gru•el•ing, *Br* **gru•el•ling** ['gru:əlɪŋ] *adj* agotador
grue•some ['gru:səm] *adj* espantoso
gruff [grʌf] *adj* seco, brusco
grum•ble ['grʌmbl] *v/i* murmurar, refunfuñar
grum•bler ['grʌmblər] quejica *m/f*
grump•y ['grʌmpɪ] *adj* cascarrabias; ***get*** *or* ***become ~*** ponerse de mal humor
grunt [grʌnt] **I** *n* gruñido *m* **II** *v/i* gruñir
GSOH [dʒi:esoʊ'eɪtʃ] *abbr* (= ***good sense of humor***) gran sentido *m* del humor
G-string ['dʒi:strɪŋ] *of dancer* tanga *m*
gua•ra•ní [gwə'rɑ:nɪ] FIN guaraní *m*
guar•an•tee [gærən'ti:] **I** *n* garantía *f*; ***~ period*** periodo *m* de garantía **II** *v/t* garantizar
guar•an•tor [gærən'tɔ:r] garante *m/f*
guard [gɑ:rd] **I** *n* (*security ~*) guardia *m/f*, guarda *m/f*; MIL guardia *f*; *in prison* guardián(-ana) *m(f)*; *in basketball* base *m/f*; ***be on one's ~ against*** estar en guardia contra **II** *v/t* guardar, proteger
◆ **guard against** *v/t* evitar
'guard dog perro *m* guardián
'guard du•ty guardia *f*; ***be on ~*** estar de guardia
guard•ed ['gɑ:rdɪd] *adj reply* cauteloso
'guard house cuartel *m*
guard•i•an ['gɑ:rdɪən] LAW tutor(a) *m(f)*
guard•i•an 'an•gel ángel *m* de la guardia
guard•i•an•ship ['gɑ:rdɪənʃɪp] LAW custodia *f*
guard of 'hon•or, *Br* **guard of 'hon•our** guardia *f* de honor
'guard•rail barandilla *f*, MOT barrera *f* de protección
guards•man ['gɑ:rdzmən] MIL soldado *m* de la Guardia Real; *in National Guard* guardia *m* nacional
Gua•te•ma•la [gwætə'mɑ:lə] Guatemala *f*
Gua•te•ma•la 'Cit•y [gwætə'mɑ:lə] Ciudad *f* de Guatemala
Gua•te•ma•lan [gwætə'mɑ:lən] **I** *adj* guatemalteco **II** *n* guatemalteco(-a) *m(f)*
Guy•a•na [gɪ'ɑ:nə] Guyana *f*
Guy•a•nese [gaɪə'ni:z] **I** *adj* guyanés **II** *n* guyanés(-esa) *m(f)*
gu•ber•na•tor•i•al [gu:bərnə'tɔ:rɪəl] *adj* del gobernador; *elections* para gobernador
guer•ril•la [gə'rɪlə] guerrillero(-a) *m(f)*
guer•ril•la 'war•fare guerra *f* de guerrillas
guess [ges] **I** *n* conjetura *f*, suposición *f* **II** *v/t the answer* adivinar **III** *v/i* adivinar; ***I ~ so*** me imagino *or* supongo que sí; ***I ~ not*** me imagino *or* supongo que no
guess•ti•mate ['gestɪmət] F cálculo *m* a ojo
'guess•work conjeturas *fpl*; ***it was a bit of inspired ~*** era una mera conjetura *or* suposición
guest [gest] invitado(-a) *m(f)*; ***be my ~*** F por supuesto, claro (que sí)
'guest•house casa *f* de huéspedes
'guest•room habitación *f* para invitados
guf•faw [gʌ'fɒ:] **I** *n* carcajada *f*, risotada *f* **II** *v/i* carcajearse
Gui•a•na [gɪ'ɑ:nə] las Guayanas
guid•ance ['gaɪdəns] orientación *f*, consejo *m*
'guid•ance teach•er orientador(a) *m(f)*
guide [gaɪd] **I** *n person* guía *m/f*; *book* guía *f* **II** *v/t* guiar
'guide•book guía *f*
guid•ed mis•sile [gaɪdɪd'mɪsəl] misil *m* teledirigido
'guide dog *Br* perro *m* lazarillo
guid•ed 'tour visita *f* guiada
'guide•lines *npl* directrices *fpl*, normas *fpl* generales
guid•ing ['gaɪdɪŋ] *adj*: ***~ principle*** principio *m* rector
guild [gɪld] gremio *m*
guile [gaɪl] astucia *f*
guile•less ['gaɪlləs] *adj* ingenuo
guil•lo•tine ['gɪləti:n] **I** *n* guillotina *f* **II** *v/t* guillotinar
guilt [gɪlt] culpa *f*, culpabilidad *f*, LAW

culpabilidad *f*
guilt•i•ly ['gɪltɪlɪ] *adv* con aire culpable
guilt•y ['gɪltɪ] *adj also* LAW culpable; ***be ~ of sth*** ser culpable de algo; ***have a ~ conscience*** tener remordimientos de conciencia
guin•ea pig ['gɪnɪ] conejillo *m* de Indias, cobaya *f*; *fig* conejillo *m* de Indias
guise [gaɪz] apariencia *f*; ***under the ~ of*** bajo la apariencia de
gui•tar [gɪ'tɑːr] guitarra *f*
gui'tar case estuche *m* de guitarra
gui•tar•ist [gɪ'tɑːrɪst] guitarrista *m/f*
gui'tar play•er guitarrista *m/f*
gulch [gʌltʃ] garganta *f*
gulf [gʌlf] golfo *m*; *fig* abismo *m*; ***the Gulf*** el Golfo
Gulf of Cal•i'for•ni•a Golfo *m* de California, Mar *m* Bermejo
Gulf of 'Mex•i•co Golfo *m* de México
gull [gʌl] ORN gaviota *f*
gul•let ['gʌlɪt] ANAT esófago *m*
gul•li•bil•i•ty [gʌlɪ'bɪlətɪ] credulidad *f*, ingenuidad *f*
gul•li•ble ['gʌlɪbl] *adj* crédulo, ingenuo
gul•ly ['gʌlɪ] barranco *m*
gulp [gʌlp] **I** *n of water etc* trago *m* **II** *v/i in surprise* tragar saliva
◆ **gulp down** *v/t drink* tragar; *food* engullir
gum[1] [gʌm] *in mouth* encía *f*
gum[2] [gʌm] **1** (*glue*) pegamento *m*, cola *f* **2** (*chewing ~*) chicle *m*
'gum•ball chicle *m* de bola
'gum•ball ma•chine máquina *f* de chicles en forma de bola
gum•bo ['gʌmboʊ]: ***chicken ~*** *sopa espesa a base de kimbombo y pollo*
gump•tion ['gʌmpʃn] coraje *m*
'gum•shoe P (*private detective*) detective *m/f* privado
gun [gʌn] *pistol*, *revolver* pistola *f*; *rifle* rifle *m*; *cannon* cañón *m*; ***stick to one's ~s*** *fig* no dar el brazo a torcer
◆ **gun down** *v/t* (*pret & pp* ***-ned***) matar a tiros
'gun•boat cañonera *f*; **'gun•fight** tiroteo *m*; **'gun•fire** disparos *mpl*
gung-ho [gʌŋ'hoʊ] *adj* F belicoso
'gun li•cense licencia *f* de armas; **gun•man** ['gʌnmən] hombre *m* armado; **'gun•point**: ***at ~*** a punta de pistola; **'gun•pow•der** pólvora *f*; **'gun•run•ner** contrabandista *m/f* de armas; **'gun•run•ning** contrabando *m* de armas; **'gun•shot** disparo *m*, tiro *m*; **'gun•shot wound** herida *f* de bala; **'gun•smith** armero(-a) *m(f)*
gur•gle ['gɜːrgl] *v/i of baby* gorjear; *of drain* gorgotear
gu•ru ['guːruː] *fig* gurú *m*
gush [gʌʃ] *v/i of liquid* manar, salir a chorros
gush•y ['gʌʃɪ] *adj* F (*enthusiastic*) efusivo, exagerado
gus•set ['gʌsɪt] *in garment* escudete *m*
gust [gʌst] ráfaga *f*
gus•to ['gʌstoʊ] entusiasmo *m*
gust•y ['gʌstɪ] *adj weather* ventoso, con viento racheado; ***~ wind*** viento *m* racheado
gut [gʌt] **I** *n* **1** intestino *m* **2** F (*stomach*) tripa *f* F **II** *v/t* (*pret & pp* ***-ted***) (*destroy*) destruir
gut•less ['gʌtlɪs] *adj* F cobarde
guts [gʌts] *npl* F (*courage*) agallas *fpl* F; ***have the ~ to do sth*** tener agallas para hacer algo
guts•y ['gʌtsɪ] *adj* F (*brave*) valiente, con muchas agallas F
gut•ter ['gʌtər] *on sidewalk* cuneta *f*; *on roof* canal *m*, canalón *m*
gut•ter•ing ['gʌtərɪŋ] canalones *mpl*
gut•ter 'press prensa *f* amarilla
gut•tur•al ['gʌtərəl] *adj* gutural
guy [gaɪ] F tipo *m* F, *Span* tío *m* F; ***hey, you ~s*** eh, gente
guz•zle ['gʌzl] *v/t* tragar, engullir
gym [dʒɪm] gimnasio *m*
gym•na•si•um [dʒɪm'neɪzɪəm] gimnasio *m*
gym•nast ['dʒɪmnæst] gimnasta *m/f*
gym•nas•tics [dʒɪm'næstɪks] *nsg* gimnasia *f*; ***mental ~*** gimnasia mental
'gym shoes *npl Br* zapatillas *fpl* de gimnasia
gy•nae•col•o•gist *etc Br* ☞ ***gynecologist*** *etc*
gy•ne•col•o•gist [gaɪnɪ'kɑːlədʒɪst] ginecólogo(-a) *m(f)*
gy•ne•col•o•gy [gaɪnɪ'kɑːlədʒɪ] ginecología *f*
gyp•sum ['dʒɪpsəm] MIN yeso *m*
gyp•sy ['dʒɪpsɪ] gitano(-a) *m(f)*
gy•rate [dʒaɪ'reɪt] *v/i* girar
gy•ra•tion [dʒaɪ'reɪʃn] giro *m*

H

ha [hɑː] *int* ¡ah!; **~, ~!** ¡ja, ja!
ha•be•as cor•pus [heɪbjəs'kɔːrpəs]: ***writ of ~*** LAW auto *m* de habeas corpus
hab•er•dash•ery ['hæbərdæʃərɪ] **1** boutique *f* para caballeros **2** *Br* mercería *f*
hab•it ['hæbɪt] hábito *m*, costumbre *f*; ***get into the ~ of doing sth*** adquirir el hábito de hacer algo
hab•it•a•ble ['hæbɪtəbl] *adj* habitable
hab•i•tat ['hæbɪtæt] hábitat *m*
hab•i•ta•tion [hæbɪ'teɪʃn] habitación *f*; ***unfit for human ~*** no habitable
hab•it-form•ing ['hæbɪtfɔːrmɪŋ] *adj* adictivo
ha•bit•u•al [hə'bɪtʊəl] *adj* habitual
ha•bit•u•al•ly [hə'bɪtjʊəlɪ] *adv*: ***be ~ late*** llegar tarde habitualmente *or* normalmente
ha•bit•u•at•ed [hə'bɪtjʊeɪtɪd] *adj*: ***become ~ to sth*** habituarse a algo
hack[1] [hæk] *n* (*poor writer*) gacetillero(-a) *m(f)*
hack[2] [hæk] **I** *v/t*: **~ *sth to pieces*** hacer algo pedazos *or* trizas **II** *v/i*: **~ *at sth*** cortar algo a machetazos *or* tajos
◆ **hack into** *v/t* COMPUT piratear
hack•er ['hækər] COMPUT pirata *m/f* informático(-a)
hack•le ['hækl]: ***get s.o.'s ~ up*** enfurecer a alguien; ***his ~s rose*** frunció el ceño, puso mala cara
hack•neyed ['hæknɪd] *adj* manido
'hack•saw *for metal* serreta *f*
had [hæd] *pret & pp* ☞ ***have***
had•dock ['hædək] eglefino *m*
had•n't ['hædnt] ☞ ***had not***
haem•a•tol•o•gy *etc Br* ☞ ***hematology etc***
haem•or•rhage *Br* ☞ ***hemorrhage***
haft [hɑːft] mango *m*, puño *m*
hag [hæg] bruja *f*, espantajo *m*
hag•gard ['hægərd] *adj* demacrado
hag•gle ['hægl] *v/i* regatear; **~ *over sth*** regatear algo
hail[1] [heɪl] *n* granizo *m*; ***a ~ of bullets*** una lluvia de balas; ***a ~ of criticism*** una avalancha de críticas
hail[2] [heɪl] *v/t greet* proclamar; **~ *s.o. as sth*** proclamar a alguien algo; **~ *sth as*** ... proclamar algo ...
◆ **hail from** *v/i* (*originate from*) ser de
'hail•stone piedra *f* de granizo
'hail•storm granizada *f*
hair [her] pelo *m*, cabello *m*; *single* pelo *m*; (*body* **~**) vello *m*; ***have short / long ~*** tener el pelo corto / largo
'hair•band goma *f* de pelo; **'hair•brush** cepillo *m*; **'hair•cut** corte *m* de pelo; ***have a ~*** cortarse el pelo; **'hair•do** F peinado *m*; **'hair•dress•er** peluquero(-a) *m(f)*; ***at the ~*** en la peluquería; **'hair•dress•ing** peluquería *f*; **'hair•dress•ing sal•on** (salón *m* de) peluquería *f*; **'hair•dri•er, 'hair•dry•er** secador *m* (de pelo); **'hair gel** gomina *f* para el pelo; **'hair grip** pinza *f* para el pelo; **'hair lac•quer** laca *f*
hair•less ['herlɪs] *adj* sin pelo
'hair•line 1 nacimiento *m* del pelo **2**: **~ *crack*** TECH grieta *f* muy fina; **~ *fracture*** MED fractura *f* muy delgada; **'hair•net** redecilla *f*; **'hair•piece** postizo *m*; **'hair•pin** horquilla *f*; **hair•pin 'turn** curva *f* muy cerrada; **hair-rais•ing** ['hereɪzɪŋ] *adj* espeluznante; **hair re•mov•er** [rɪ'muːvər] depilatorio *m*; **hair's breadth** ['herz] *fig*: ***by a ~*** por un pelo; **'hair slide** *Br* pasador *m*; **'hair-split•ting** sutilezas *fpl*; **'hair spray** laca *f*; **'hair•style** peinado *m*; **'hair•styl•ist** estilista *m/f*, peluquero(-a) *m(f)*
hair•y ['herɪ] *adj* **1** *arm*, *animal* peludo **2** F (*frightening*) espeluznante
hake [heɪk] merluza *f*
hal•cy•on days ['hælsɪəndeɪz] *npl*: ***the ~*** los días felices
hale [heɪl] *adj*: **~ *and hearty*** como una rosa
half [hæf] **I** *n* (*pl* ***halves*** [hævz]) **1** mitad *f*; **~ *past ten*** las diez y media; **~ *after ten*** las diez y media; **~ *an hour*** media hora; **~ *a pound*** media libra; ***go halves with s.o. on sth*** ir a medias con alguien en algo; **~ *of the class was*** *or* ***were late*** la mitad de la clase llegó tarde **2** SP: ***first / second ~*** primer / segundo tiempo *m*

II *adj* medio; ***at ~ price*** a mitad de precio
III *adv* a medias; ***~ finished*** a medio acabar
half-and-'half *mezcla de nata y leche que se echa en el café*; **half-assed** ['hæfæst] *adj* P *idea, plan* chapucero F, torpe F; **half-'baked** *adj* F mal pensado; **half 'board** *Br* media pensión *f*; **'half-breed** mestizo(-a) *m(f)*; **'half broth•er** hermanastro *m*; **'half-caste** mestizo(-a) *m(f)*; **half 'dol•lar** medio dólar *m*; **half-heart•ed** [hæf'hɑːrtɪd] *adj* desganado; **half-'hour** media hora *f*; **'half-life** PHYS vida *f* media; **'half light** penumbra *f*; **half 'mar•a•thon** media maratón *f*; **'half-mast** ***fly at ~*** ondear a media asta; **half 'meas•ure** remedio *m* ineficaz; **'half-moon** media luna *f*; **'half note** MUS blanca *f*; **half-'price** *adj & adv* a mitad de precio; **'half sis•ter** hermanastra *f*; **'half staff** ☞ ***half mast***; **half 'term** *Br días de vacaciones a mitad del trimestre escolar*; **half 'time I** *n* SP descanso *m*; ***at ~*** en el descanso **II** *adj*: ***~ score*** marcador *m* en el descanso; **'half-truth** verdad *f* a medias; **half'way I** *adj stage, point* intermedio **II** *adv* a mitad de camino; **half•way 'house 1** *for ex-prisoners, drug addicts etc* centro *m* de reinserción social **2** *fig compromise* amalgama *f*; **'half-wit** lelo(-a) *m(f)*, bobo(-a) *m(f)*; **half-wit•ted** ['hɑːfwɪtɪd] *adj* lerdo, bobo; **half-'year•ly** *adj & adv* semestral
hal•i•but ['hælɪbət] halibut *m*
hal•i•to•sis [hælɪ'toʊsɪs] halitosis *f*
hall [hɒːl] **1** *large room* sala *f* **2** (*hallway in house*) vestíbulo *m*
hal•le•lu•jah [hælɪ'luːjə] *int* aleluya
'hall•mark I *n* **1** *Br* sello *m* de contraste **2** *fig* sello *m* distintivo, característica *f* **II** *v/t Br* sellar, grabar
hal•lo [hə'loʊ] *Br* ☞ ***hello***
hal•lowed ['hæloʊd] *adj* venerable, sagrado
Hal•low•e'en [hæloʊ'iːn] *víspera de Todos los Santos*
'hall por•ter *Br* botones *m inv*
hal•lu•ci•nate [hə'luːsɪneɪt] *v/i* alucinar
hal•lu•ci•na•tion [hə'luːsɪneɪʃn] alucinación *f*; ***have ~s*** tener alucinaciones, alucinar
hal•lu•ci•no•gen•ic [həluːsɪnə'dʒenɪk] *adj* alucinógeno
'hall•way vestíbulo *m*
ha•lo ['heɪloʊ] (*pl* ***-o(e)s***) halo *m*
hal•o•gen ['hælədʒen] CHEM halógeno *m*; ***~ lamp*** lámpara *f* halógena
halt [hɒːlt] **I** *v/i* detenerse **II** *v/t* detener **III** *n* alto *m*; ***come to a ~*** detenerse
hal•ter ['hɔːltər] ronzal *m*, cabestro *m*
'hal•ter neck *neckline*: ***dress / top with a ~*** vestido / camiseta sin espalda
halt•ing ['hɔːltɪŋ] *adj speech* titubeante, vacilante; *progress* intermitente
halve [hæv] *v/t input, costs, effort* reducir a la mitad; *apple* partir por la mitad
ham [hæm] jamón *m*
◆ **ham up** *v/t* F: ***ham it up*** actuar haciendo aspavientos
ham•burg•er ['hæmbɜːrgər] hamburguesa *f*
'ham•burg•er joint F hamburguesería *f*
ham•burg•er 'pat•ty hamburguesa *f* (*antes de freírla*)
ham-fist•ed [hæm'fɪstɪd] *adj Br* F patoso F
ham-hand•ed [hæm'hændɪd] *adj* F torpe, patoso F
ham•let ['hæmlɪt] aldea *f*
ham•mer ['hæmər] **I** *n* martillo *m* **II** *v/i*: ***~ at the door*** golpear la puerta **III** *v/t* martillar
◆ **hammer home** *v/t nail* clavar hasta adentro; *argument* remachar
◆ **hammer out** *v/t* **1** *dent* desabollar con un martillo **2** *agreement* negociar
ham•mock ['hæmək] hamaca *f*
ham•per[1] ['hæmpər] *n for food* cesta *f*
ham•per[2] ['hæmpər] *v/t* (*obstruct*) estorbar, obstaculizar
ham•ster ['hæmstər] hámster *m*
'ham•string I *n* ANAT ligamento *m* de la corva **II** *v/t* (*pret & pp* ***-strung***) *fig* limitar, restringir
hand [hænd] **I 1** *n* mano *f*; ***at ~, to ~*** a mano; ***at first ~*** de primera mano, directamente; ***by ~*** a mano; ***on the one ~ ..., on the other ~*** por una parte ..., por otra parte; ***the work is in ~*** el trabajo se está llevando a cabo; ***on your right ~*** a mano derecha; ***~s off!*** ¡fuera las manos!; ***~s up!*** ¡arriba las manos!; ***change ~s*** cambiar de manos; ***give s.o. a ~*** echar un a mano a alguien **2** *of clock* manecilla *f*

3 (*worker*) brazo *m*
II *v/t* **1**: **~ sth to s.o.** pasarle *or* acercarle algo a alguien **2**: ***you've got to ~ it to her*** tienes que reconocérselo
◆ **hand back** *v/t* devolver
◆ **hand down** *v/t* **1** *values* transmitir; *clothes* pasar **2** *findings* hacer público
◆ **hand in** *v/t* entregar
◆ **hand on** *v/t* pasar
◆ **hand out** *v/t* repartir
◆ **hand over I** *v/t* entregar; ***we now hand you over to …*** TV, RAD ahora pasamos la conexión a … **II** *v/i of outgoing president, executive etc* ceder el puesto (***to*** a)
'**hand•bag** *Br* bolso *m*, *L.Am.* cartera *f*; '**hand bag•gage** equipaje *m* de mano; '**hand•ball** *game* balonmano *m*; '**hand•book** manual *m*; '**hand•brake** *Br* MOT freno *m* de mano; **hand--carved** [hænd'kɑːrvd] *adj* tallado a mano; '**hand cream** crema *f* hidratante de manos; '**hand•cuff** ['hæn(d)kʌf] *v/t* esposar; **hand•cuffs** *npl* esposas *fpl*
hand•ful ['hændfʊl] **1** puñado *m* **2**: ***he's a real ~*** F es un demonio F *or* terremoto F; ***having three daughters is quite a ~*** tres hijas dan bastante trabajo
'**hand gre•nade** MIL granada *f* de mano; '**hand gun** pistola *f*; **hand-'held** *adj* portátil
hand•i•cap ['hændɪkæp] desventaja *f*
hand•i•capped ['hændɪkæpt] *adj physically* minusválido, disminuido; ***~ by lack of funds*** en desventaja por carecer de fondos
hand•i•craft ['hændɪkræft] artesanía *f*
hand•i•work ['hændɪwɜːrk] manualidades *fpl*
hand•ker•chief ['hæŋkərtʃɪf] pañuelo *m*
han•dle ['hændl] **I** *n of door* manilla *f*; *of suitcase* asa *f*; *of pan, knife* mango *m* **II** *v/t goods, difficult person* manejar; *case, deal* llevar, encargarse de; ***let me ~ this*** deja que me ocupe yo de esto; ***~ o.s. well*** *in fight, hostile situation* saber defenderse
han•dle•bars ['hændlbɑːrz] *npl* manillar *m*, *L.Am.* manubrio *m*
hand•ling charg•es ['hændlɪŋ] *npl* gastos *mpl* de manipulación; *administrative* gastos *mpl* de administración
'**hand lug•gage** equipaje *m* de mano; **hand•made** [hæn(d)'meɪd] *adj* hecho a mano; **hand-o•per•at•ed** [hænd-'ɑːpəreɪtɪd] *adj* de manejo manual; '**hand-out 1** *money, food* donativo *m* **2** EDU hoja *f*; '**hand•o•ver** transferencia *f*, traspaso *m*; **hand•picked** [hænd'pɪkt] *adj* selecto, escogido; '**hand•rail** barandilla *f*; **hand•script•ed** ['hændskrɪptɪd] *adj* escrito a a mano; '**hand•set** TELEC auricular *m* (del teléfono); '**hand•shake 1** apretón *m* de manos **2** TELEC diálogo *m* de establecimiento de comunicación; **hands-off** [hændz'ɑːf] *adj* no intervencionista
hand•some ['hænsəm] *adj* guapo, atractivo; ***make a ~ profit*** sacar buen provecho
hands-on [hændz'ɑːn] *adj* práctico; ***he has a ~ style of management*** le gusta implicarse en todos los aspectos de la gestión
'**hand•stand** pino *m*; ***do a ~*** hacer el pino, *L.Am.* pararse de cabeza; **hand-to--'hand** *adj fighting* cuerpo a cuerpo; **hand-to-'mouth** *adj*: ***lead a ~ existence*** llevar una vida precaria; '**hand tow•el** toalla *f* de tocador; '**hand-writ•ing** caligrafía *f*; '**hand•writ•ten** *adj* escrito a mano
hand•y ['hændɪ] *adj tool, device* práctico; ***it might come in ~*** nos puede venir muy bien
hand•y•man ['hændɪmæn] manitas *m/f inv* F
hang [hæŋ] **I** *v/t* **1** (*pret & pp* **hung**) *picture* colgar **2** (*pret & pp* **-ed**) *person* colgar, ahorcar; ***~ o.s.*** ahorcarse, colgarse **II** *v/i* (*pret & pp* **hung**) colgar; *of dress, hair* caer, colgar **III** *n*: ***get the ~ of sth*** F agarrarle el tranquillo a algo F
◆ **hang around** *v/i*: ***he's always hanging around on the street corner*** siempre está rondando por la esquina
◆ **hang in** *v/i*: ***hang in there!*** P ¡aguanta un poco más!, ¡resiste!
◆ **hang on I** *v/i* **1** agarrarse; ***hang on tight!*** ¡agárrate fuerte! **2** (*wait*) esperar **II** *v/t* (*depend on*) depender de
◆ **hang on to** *v/t* **1** (*cling to*) aferrarse a **2** (*keep*) conservar; ***do you mind if I hang on to it for a while?*** ¿te importa si me lo quedo durante un tiempo?
◆ **hang out** *v/i* P **1** (*be idle*) pasar el rato F **2** (*spend time*): ***where does he hang***

out? ¿por dónde suele estar?
◆ **hang up** I *v/i* TELEC colgar II *v/t hat, coat etc* colgar
han•gar ['hæŋər] hangar *m*
hang•er ['hæŋər] *for clothes* percha *f*
'hang glid•er *person* piloto *m* de ala delta; *device* ala *f* delta
'hang glid•ing ala *f* delta
hang•ing ['hæŋɪŋ] *execution* ahorcamiento *m*
hang•ing 'bas•ket maceta *f* colgante
'hang•nail padrastro *m*; **'hang•out** F lugar *m* favorito; **'hang•o•ver** resaca *f*; **'hang-up** F complejo *m*, inhibición *f*; ***have a ~ about sth*** estar acomplejado *or* inhibido por algo
◆ **han•ker after** ['hæŋkər] *v/t* anhelar
han•ker•ing ['hæŋkərɪŋ]: ***have a ~ for sth*** tener antojo de algo
han•kie, han•ky ['hæŋkɪ] F pañuelo *m*
han•ky-pan•ky [hæŋkɪ'pæŋkɪ] F **1** *sexual* manitas *fpl* F **2** *corrupt* chanchullo *m* F
hap•haz•ard [hæp'hæzərd] *adj* descuidado
hap•less ['hæplɪs] *adj* desafortunado
hap•pen ['hæpn] *v/i* ocurrir, pasar, suceder; ***if you ~ to see him*** si por casualidad lo vieras; ***what has ~ed to you?*** ¿qué te ha pasado?
◆ **happen across** *v/t* encontrar por casualidad
◆ **happen along** *v/i* aparecer por casualidad
hap•pen•ing ['hæpnɪŋ] suceso *m*
hap•pi•ly ['hæpɪlɪ] *adv* **1** alegremente; ***~ married*** felizmente casado(s) **2** (*luckily*) afortunadamente
hap•pi•ness ['hæpɪnɪs] felicidad *f*
hap•py ['hæpɪ] *adj* **1** feliz, contento **2** *coincidence* afortunado
hap•py-go-'luck•y *adj* despreocupado
'hap•py hour *franja horaria en la que las bebidas se venden más baratas*
ha•rangue [hə'ræŋ] I *n* arenga *f*, discurso *m* II *v/t* arengar
har•ass [hə'ræs] *v/t* acosar; *enemy* asediar, hostigar
har•assed [hə'ræst] *adj* agobiado
har•ass•ment [hə'ræsmənt] acoso *m*
har•bin•ger ['hɑːrbɪndʒər] auspicio *m*, agüero *m*; ***~ of doom*** mal agüero
har•bor, *Br* **har•bour** ['hɑːrbər] I *n* puerto *m* II *v/t criminal* proteger; *grudge* albergar
hard [hɑːrd] *adj* duro; (*difficult*) difícil; *facts, evidence* real; ***be ~ of hearing*** ser duro de oído
'hard•back libro *m* de tapas duras; **'hard•ball**: ***play ~*** *fig* ir en serio; **'hard•board** panel *m* de madera; **hard-'boiled** *adj egg* duro; **hard 'cash** dinero *m* en efectivo; **'hard cop•y** copia *f* impresa; **'hard core** I *adj fan, supporter* incondicional II (*pornography*) porno *m* duro; **'hard•cov•er** ☞ ***hardback***; **hard 'cur•ren•cy** divisa *f* fuerte; **hard 'disk** disco *m* duro; **'hard drug** droga *f* dura; **hard-earned** [hɑːrd'ɜːrnd] *adj money* sudado
hard•en ['hɑːrdn] I *v/t* endurecer II *v/i of glue, attitude* endurecerse
hard•ened ['hɑːrdnd] *adj*: ***become ~ to sth*** hacerse insensible a algo; ***a ~ criminal*** un criminal despiadado
'hard hat casco *m*; (*construction worker*) obrero(-a) *m*(*f*) (de la construcción); **hard'head•ed** *adj* pragmático; **hard•heart•ed** [hɑːrd'hɑːrtɪd] *adj* insensible; **hard-hit•ting** [hɑːrd'hɪtɪŋ] *adj* contundente; **hard 'line** línea *f* dura; ***take a ~ on*** adoptar una línea dura en cuanto a; **hard'lin•er** partidario(-a) *m*(*f*) de la línea dura; **hard 'liq•uor** licor *m*, bebida *f* fuerte
hard•ly ['hɑːrdlɪ] *adv* apenas; ***did you agree? – ~!*** ¿estuviste de acuerdo? - ¡en absoluto!
hard•ness ['hɑːrdnɪs] **1** dureza *f* **2** (*difficulty*) dificultad *f*
hard-nosed [hɑːrd'noʊzd] *adj* F realista, práctico; **hard-pressed** [hɑːrd'presd] *adj* apurado, agobiado; ***be ~ to do sth*** tener dificultades para hacer algo; **hard 'sell** venta *f* agresiva
hard•ship ['hɑːrdʃɪp] penuria *f*
hard 'shoul•der MOT *Br* arcén *m*; **'hard•top** MOT coche *m* no descapotable; **hard 'up** *adj*: ***be ~*** andar mal de dinero; **'hard•ware** **1** ferretería *f* **2** COMPUT hardware *m*; **'hard•ware store** ferretería *f*; **'hard•wood** madera *f* dura; **hard-'work•ing** *adj* trabajador
har•dy ['hɑːrdɪ] *adj* resistente
hare [her] liebre *f*
'hare•bell BOT campánula *f*; **hare-brained** ['herbreɪnd] *adj* alocado; **hare'lip** MED labio *m* partido

ha•rem ['hɑːriːm] harén *m*
◆ **hark back to** [hɑːrk] *v/t* **1** (*date back to*) remontarse a **2** *remember* rememorar
harm [hɑːrm] **I** *n* daño *m*; ***it wouldn't do any ~ to buy two*** por comprar dos no pasa nada **II** *v/t* hacer daño a, dañar; **~ *o.s.*** hacerse daño
harm•ful ['hɑːrmfəl] *adj* dañino, perjudicial
harm•less ['hɑːrmlɪs] *adj* inofensivo; *fun* inocente
har•mon•ic [hɑːr'mɑːnɪk] *adj* armónico
har•mon•i•ca [hɑːr'mɑːnɪkə] MUS armónica *f*
har•mo•ni•ous [hɑːr'moʊnɪəs] *adj* armonioso
har•mo•ni•um [hɑːr'moʊnjəm] MUS armonio *m*
har•mo•ni•za•tion [hɑːrmənaɪ'zeɪʃn] armonización *f*
har•mo•nize ['hɑːrmənaɪz] *v/i* armonizar
har•mo•ny ['hɑːrmənɪ] MUS, *fig* armonía *f*, ***live in ~*** vivir en armonía (***with*** con)
har•ness ['hɑːrnɪs] **I** *n* arnés *m*; ***die in ~*** *fig* morir antes de jubilarse **II** *v/t horse* poner los arneses a
harp [hɑːrp] arpa *f*
◆ **harp on about** *v/t* F dar la lata con F
harp•ist ['hɑːrpɪst] arpista *m/f*
har•poon [hɑːr'puːn] arpón *m*
harp•si•chord ['hɑːrpsɪkɔːrd] MUS clavicordio *m*
har•row ['hæroʊ] AGR arado *m*
har•row•ing ['hæroʊɪŋ] *adj* estremecedor
har•ry ['hærɪ] *v/t* (*pret & pp* **-ied**) acosar, hostigar
harsh [hɑːrʃ] *adj words* duro, severo; *color* chillón; *light* potente
harsh•ly ['hɑːrʃlɪ] *adv* con dureza *or* severidad
harsh•ness ['hɑːrʃnɪs] dureza *f*, severidad *f*
har•um-scar•um [herəm'skerəm] *adj* alocado, atolondrado
har•vest ['hɑːrvɪst] cosecha *f*
has [hæz] ☞ ***have***
'has-been F celebridad *f* del pasado
hash[1] [hæʃ] GASTR *estofado de carne y patatas*; ***make a ~ of*** F fastidiar
hash[2] [hæʃ] F (*hashish*) chocolate *m* F
hash browns ['braʊnz] *npl* papas *fpl or Span* patatas *fpl* fritas
hash•ish ['hæʃiːʃ] hachís *m*
'hash mark almohadilla *f*, *el signo '#'*
has•n't ['hæznt] ☞ ***has not***
has•sle ['hæsl] F **I** *n* lata *f* F; ***it was a real ~*** F fue una lata de aquí te espero F; ***give s.o. ~*** dar la lata a alguien **II** *v/t* dar la lata a
has•sock ['hæsək] escabel *m*, taburete *m*
haste [heɪst] prisa *f*; ***more ~, less speed*** vísteme despacio, que tengo prisa
has•ten ['heɪsn] *v/i*: **~ *to do sth*** apresurarse en hacer algo
hast•i•ly ['heɪstɪlɪ] *adv* precipitadamente
hast•y ['heɪstɪ] *adj* precipitado
hat [hæt] sombrero *m*
hatch[1] [hætʃ] *n* **1** *for serving food* trampilla *f* **2** *on ship* escotilla *f*
hatch[2] [hætʃ] **I** *v/t eggs* incubar; **~ *a plan*** trazar un plan **II** *v/i of eggs* romperse; *of chicks* salir del cascarón
◆ **hatch out** *v/i of eggs* romperse; *of chicks* salir del cascarón
'hatch•back MOT **1** *vehicle* tres puertas *m inv*; cinco puertas *m inv* **2** *actual door* puerta *f* trasera
hatch•et ['hætʃɪt] hacha *f*; ***bury the ~*** enterrar el hacha de guerra
hate [heɪt] **I** *n* odio *m* **II** *v/t* odiar
hate•ful ['heɪtfʊl] *adj* odioso, detestable
'hate mail correspondencia *f* intimidatoria
'hat pin aguja *f* de sombrero
ha•tred ['heɪtrɪd] odio *m*
'hat stand perchero *m* para sombreros
hat•ter ['hætər]: (***as***) ***mad as a ~*** como una cabra F *or* regadera F
'hat trick (*in soccer*) *tres goles en el mismo partido*; ***a ~ of victories*** tres victorias consecutivas
haugh•ty ['hɒːtɪ] *adj* altanero
haul [hɒːl] **I** *n* **1** *of fish* captura *f* **2** *from robbery* botín *m* **II** *v/t* (*pull*) arrastrar
haul•age ['hɒːlɪdʒ] transporte *m*
haul•er ['hɒːlər], *Br* **haul•i•er** ['hɒːljər] transportista *m/f*
haunch [hɒːntʃ] *of person* trasero *m*; *of animal* pierna *f*
haunt [hɒːnt] **I** *v/t*: ***this place is ~ed*** en este lugar hay fantasmas **II** *n* lugar *m*

favorito
haunt•ing ['hɒːntɪŋ] *adj tune* fascinante
Ha•van•a [hə'vænə] La Habana
have [hæv] **I** *v/t* (*pret & pp* **had**) **1** (*own*) tener; ***I don't ~ a TV*** no tengo televisión **2** *breakfast*, *lunch* tomar
3: ***can I ~ a coffee?*** ¿me da un café?; ***can I ~ more time?*** ¿me puede dar más tiempo?
4 *must*: **~ (*got*) *to*** tener que; ***I ~ to do it, I've got to do it*** tengo que hacerlo
5 *causative*: ***I'll ~ it faxed to you*** te lo mandaré por fax; ***I'll ~ it repaired*** haré que lo arreglen; ***I had my hair cut*** me corté el pelo
II *v/aux*: ***I ~ eaten*** he comido; ***~ you seen her?*** ¿la has visto?
◆ **have around** *v/t*: ***he's a useful person to have around*** viene bien tenerlo a mano
◆ **have back** *v/t*: ***when can I have it back?*** ¿cuándo me lo devolverá?
◆ **have in** *v/t*: ***have it in for s.o.*** tenerla tomada con alguien
◆ **have on** *v/t* **1** (*wear*) llevar puesto **2**: ***do you have anything on for tonight?*** *have planned* ¿tenéis algo planeado para esta noche?
◆ **have out** *v/t*: ***have it out with s.o.*** decirle cuatro cosas a alguien
ha•ven ['heɪvn] *fig* refugio *m*
have-'nots *npl*: ***the ~*** los necesitados *or* pobres
have•n't ['hævnt] ☞ ***have not***
hav•oc ['hævək] estragos *mpl*; ***play ~ with*** hacer estragos en
hawk [hɒːk] *also fig* halcón *m*
haw•ser ['hɔːzər] NAUT amarra *f*
haw•thorn ['hɔːθɔːrn] BOT espino *m*
hay [heɪ] heno *m*
'hay fe•ver fiebre *f* del heno; **'hay•stack** pajar *m*; **'hay•wire** *adj* F: ***the printer went ~*** la impresora se volvió loca
haz•ard ['hæzərd] riesgo *m*, peligro *m*
'haz•ard lights *npl* MOT luces *fpl* de emergencia
haz•ard•ous ['hæzərdəs] *adj* peligroso, arriesgado; ***~ waste*** residuos *mpl* peligrosos
haze [heɪz] neblina *f*
ha•zel ['heɪzl] *tree* avellano *m*
'ha•zel•nut avellana *f*
haz•y ['heɪzɪ] *adj image*, *memories* confuso, vago; ***I'm a bit ~ about it*** no lo tengo muy claro
H-bomb ['eɪtʃbɑːm] MIL bomba *f* de hidrógeno
he [hiː] *pron* él; ***~ is French / a doctor*** es francés / médico; ***you're funny, ~'s not*** tú tienes gracia, él no
head [hed] **I** *n* **1** cabeza *f*; *on beer* espuma *f*; *of nail*, *line* cabeza *f*; ***$15 a ~*** 15 dólares por cabeza; ***~s or tails?*** ¿cara o cruz?; ***at the ~ of the list*** encabezando la lista; ***~ over heels*** *fall* rodando; *fall in love* locamente **2** (*boss*, *leader*) jefe(-a) *m*(*f*); *Br*: *of school* director(a) *m*(*f*)
II *v/t* **1** (*lead*) estar a la cabeza de **2** *ball* cabecear
III *v/i*: ***where are you ~ing?*** ¿hacia dónde vas?, ¿hacia dónde te diriges?; ***you should ~ downtown*** deberías dirigirte al *or* tirar F para el centro (de la ciudad)
◆ **head for** *v/t* dirigirse a *or* hacia; ***she's heading for trouble*** se está buscando problemas
◆ **head off** *v/t person* cerrar el paso a
◆ **head up** *v/t committee etc* encabezar
'head•ache dolor *m* de cabeza; **'head•band** cinta *f* para la cabeza; **'head•butt** *v/t* topetar; **'head•case** F pirado(-a) *m*(*f*) F, chiflado(-a) *m*(*f*) F; **'head•dress** tocado *m*
head•ed note•pa•per ['hedɪd] papel *m* con membrete
head•er ['hedər] **1** *in soccer* cabezazo *m* **2** *in document* encabezamiento *m*
head'first *adv fall* de cabeza; **'head•hunt** *v/t* COM buscar, captar; ***she's been headhunted*** la descubrió un cazatalentos; **'head•hunt•er** COM cazatalentos *m/f inv*
head•ing ['hedɪŋ] *in list* encabezamiento *m*
'head•lamp faro *m*; **head•land** ['hedlənd] GEOG cabo *m*; **'head•light** faro *m*; **'head•line** *in newspaper* titular *m*; ***make the ~s*** saltar a los titulares; **'head•long** *adv fall* de cabeza; ***rush ~ into sth*** *fig* lanzarse a algo; **head'mas•ter** *Br* director *m*; **head'mis•tress** *Br* directora *f*; **head 'of•fice** *of company* central *f*; **head of 'state** jefe *m* de Estado; **head-'on I** *adv crash* de frente **II** *adj crash* frontal; **'head•phones** *npl* auriculares *mpl*;

H

'**head-quar•ters** *npl of party, organization* sede *f*; *of army* cuartel *m* general; '**head•rest** reposacabezas *f inv*; '**headroom** *under bridge* gálibo *m*; *in car* altura *f* de la cabeza al techo; '**headscarf** pañuelo *m* (para la cabeza); '**head•set** auriculares *mpl*; **headshrink•er** ['hedʃrɪŋkər] F loquero(-a) *m(f)* F; **head 'start**: ***have a ~ on s.o.*** sacar ventaja a alguien; ***give s.o. a ~*** dar ventaja a alguien; '**head•stone** lápida *f*; '**head•strong** *adj* cabezudo, testarudo; **head 'teach•er** *Br* director(a) *m(f)*; **head 'wait•er** maître *m*; '**head•way**: ***make ~*** hacer progreso, progresar; '**head•wind** viento *m* contrario; '**head•word** lema *m*

head•y ['hedɪ] *adj drink, wine etc* que se sube a la cabeza

heal [hi:l] *v/t* curar

◆ **heal up** *v/i* curarse

heal•ing ['hi:lɪŋ] **I** *n* curación *f* **II** *adj* curativo, terapeútico; ***~ process*** proceso *m* de recuperación

health [helθ] salud *f*; ***your ~!*** ¡a tu salud!; ***be in good ~*** gozar de buena salud; ***~ and safety*** sanidad *f*; ***~ and safety regulations*** normativa *f* de sanidad

'**health care** asistencia *f* sanitaria; '**health club** gimnasio *m* (*con piscina, pista de tenis, sauna etc*); '**health-con•scious** *adj* cuidadoso con la salud; '**health farm** *complex* balneario *m*; '**health food** comida *f* integral; '**health food store** tienda *f* de comida integral; '**health in•su•rance** seguro *m* de enfermedad; '**health re•sort** centro *m* de reposo

health•y ['helθɪ] *adj person* sano; *food, lifestyle, influence, relationship* saludable; *economy* saneado

heap [hi:p] montón *m*

◆ **heap up** *v/t* amontonar

hear [hɪr] *v/t & v/i* (*pret & pp* **heard**) oír

◆ **hear about** *v/t*: ***have you heard about Mike?*** ¿te has enterado de lo de Mike?; ***they're bound to hear about it sooner or later*** se van a enterar tarde o temprano

◆ **hear from** *v/t* (*have news from*) tener noticias de

◆ **hear of** *v/t*: ***have you heard of ...?*** ¿has oído hablar de ...?; ***I won't hear of it!*** ¡ni hablar!, ¡de ninguna manera!

◆ **hear out** *v/t* escuchar con atención; ***hear me out*** atiende

heard [hɜ:rd] *pret & pp* ☞ **hear**

hear•ing ['hɪrɪŋ] **1** *sense* oído *m*; ***his ~ is not so good now*** ahora ya no oye tan bien; ***she was within ~ / out of ~*** estaba / no estaba lo suficientemente cerca como para oírlo **2** LAW vista *f*; ***give s.o. a fair ~*** permitir explicarse a alguien

'**hear•ing aid** audífono *m*

'**hear•say** rumores *mpl*; ***by ~*** de oídas

hearse [hɜ:rs] coche *m* fúnebre

heart [hɑ:rt] *also fig* corazón *m*; *of problem* meollo *m*; ***know sth by ~*** saber algo de memoria; ***~s*** *in cards* corazones *mpl*; ***take sth to ~*** tomarse algo a pecho; ***lose ~*** desanimarse

'**heart•ache** tristeza *f*, dolor *m*; '**heart at•tack** infarto *m*; '**heart•beat** latido *m*; '**heart•break•ing** *adj* desgarrador; '**heart•brok•en** *adj* descorazonado; '**heart•burn** acidez *f* (de estómago); '**heart con•di•tion** MED condición *f* cardíaca; '**heart dis•ease** MED enfermedad *f* cardíaca

heart•en ['hɑ:rtn] *v/t* animar, alentar

heart•en•ing ['hɑ:rtnɪŋ] *adj* alentador

'**heart fail•ure** paro *m* cardíaco

'**heart•felt** *adj sympathy* sincero

hearth [hɑ:rθ] chimenea *f*

heart•i•ly ['hɑ:rtɪlɪ] *adv* animadamente

heart•less ['hɑ:rtlɪs] *adj* despiadado

heart•rend•ing ['hɑ:rtrendɪŋ] *adj plea, sight* desgarrador; '**heart throb** F rompecorazones *m inv*; **heart-to-'heart** **I** *adj* de corazón, sincero **II** *n* conversación *f* con el corazón en la mano; '**heart trans•plant** transplante *m* de corazón

heart•y ['hɑ:rtɪ] *adj appetite* voraz; *meal* copioso; *person* cordial, campechano

heat [hi:t] calor *m*

◆ **heat up I** *v/t* calentar **II** *v/i* calentarse; *fig*: *of situation* caldearse

heat•ed ['hi:tɪd] *adj* **1** *swimming pool* climatizado **2** *discussion* acalorado

heat•er ['hi:tər] *in room* estufa *f*; ***turn on the ~*** *in car* enciende la calefacción

heat ex•chang•er ['hi:tɪkstʃeɪndʒər] cambiador *m* de calor

hea•then ['hi:ðn] pagano(-a) *m(f)*

heat•ing ['hi:tɪŋ] calefacción *f*

'**heat•proof** *adj* resistente al calor; '**heat rash** MED sarpullido *m*; '**heat-re•sis-**

tant *adj* resistente al calor; **'heat·stroke** insolación *f*; **'heat·wave** ola *f* de calor

heave [hi:v] *v/t* (*pret & pp* ***-ed*** *or* ***hove***) **1** (*lift*) subir **2**: ***~ a sigh*** lanzar un suspiro

heav·en ['hevn] cielo *m*; ***good ~s!*** ¡Dios mío!

heav·en·ly ['hevənlı] *adj* F divino F

heav·y ['hevı] *adj* pesado; *cold, rain, accent, loss* fuerte; *smoker, drinker* empedernido; *loss of life* grande; *bleeding* abundante; ***there's ~ traffic*** hay mucho tráfico

heav·y 'cream nata *f* para montar; **heav·y-'du·ty** *adj* resistente; **heav·y 'goods ve·hi·cle** *Br* vehículo *m* pesado; **heav·y-hand·ed** [hevı'hændıd] *adj* **1** (*cruel*) implacable, severo **2** (*tactless*) descortés; **heav·y 'met·al** MUS heavy metal *m*; **'heav·y·weight** *also fig* peso *m* pesado

He·brew ['hi:bru:] *language* hebreo *m*

heck [hek] *int* F: ***who / what the ~ ... ?*** ¿quién / qué demonios F *or* narices F ...?; ***a ~ of a lot*** una barbaridad F; ***oh ~!*** ¡maldita sea!

heck·le ['hekl] *v/t* interrumpir (*molestando*)

heck·ler ['heklər] *persona que interrumpe a un intérprete u orador para molestar*

hec·tic ['hektık] *adj* vertiginoso, frenético

hec·to·li·ter, *Br* **hec·to·li·tre** ['hektoʊli:tər] hectolitro *m*

he'd [hi:d] F ☞ ***he had***; ***he would***

hedge [hedʒ] **I** *n* seto *m* **II** *v/t*: ***~ one's bets*** no jugárselo todo

hedge·hog ['hedʒhɑ:g] erizo *m*

he·don·ism ['hedənızm] hedonismo *m*

he·don·ist ['hedənıst] hedonista *m/f*

he·do·nist·ic [hedə'nıstık] *adj* hedonista

heed [hi:d]: ***pay ~ to*** hacer caso de

heed·ful ['hi:dfʊl] *adj*: ***be ~ of*** hacer caso de

heed·less ['hi:dlıs] *adj*: ***be ~ of*** hacer caso omiso de

heel [hi:l] *of foot* talón *m*; *of shoe* tacón *m*

'heel bar zapatería *f*

hef·ty ['heftı] *adj weight, suitcase* pesado; *person* robusto

he·gem·o·ny ['hedʒemoʊnı] POL hegemonía *f*

heif·er ['hefər] ZO vaquilla *f*

height [haıt] altura *f*; ***at the ~ of the season*** en plena temporada

height-ad'just·a·ble *adj* de altura regulable

height·en ['haıtn] *v/t effect, tension* intensificar

hei·nous ['heınəs] *adj* atroz, inhumano

heir [er] heredero *m*

heir·ess ['erıs] heredera *f*

heir·loom ['eırlu:m] reliquia *f* familiar

heist [haıst] F (*robbery*) golpe *m* F

held [held] *pret & pp* ☞ ***hold***

hel·i·cop·ter ['helıkɑ:ptər] helicóptero *m*

hel·i·cop·ter 'gun·ship helicóptero *m* de ataque

hel·i·port ['helıpɔ:rt] helipuerto *m*

he·li·um ['hi:lıəm] CHEM helio *m*

hell [hel] infierno *m*; ***what the ~ are you doing / do you want?*** F ¿qué demonios estás haciendo / quieres? F; ***go to ~!*** F ¡vete a paseo! F; ***a ~ of a lot*** F un montonazo F; ***one ~ of a nice guy*** F un tipo muy simpático *or Span* legal F

he'll [hi:l] F ☞ ***he will***

hell'bent *adj* F: ***be ~ on*** (***doing***) ***sth*** estar empeñado en (hacer) algo

'hell·hole F antro *m* F, cuchitril *m* F

hell·ish ['helıʃ] *adj* F horrendo, infernal

hel·lo [hə'loʊ] hola; TELEC ¿sí?, *S. Am.* ¿alo?, *Rpl* ¿oigo?, *Mex* ¿bueno?, *Span* ¿diga?; ***say ~ to s.o.*** saludar a alguien

Hell's 'An·gels los Ángeles del Infierno

hell·uv·a ['heləvə] *F* ☞ ***hell of a***

helm [helm] NAUT timón *m*; ***at the ~*** *fig* al mando

hel·met ['helmıt] casco *m*

helms·man ['helmzmən] NAUT timonel *m*

help [help] **I** *n* ayuda *f*; ***~!*** ¡socorro! **II** *v/t* ayudar; ***just ~ yourself*** *to food* toma lo que quieras; ***I can't ~ it*** no puedo evitarlo; ***I couldn't ~ laughing*** no pude evitar reírme

help·er ['helpər] ayudante *m/f*

help·ful ['helpfəl] *adj advice* útil; *person* servicial

help·ing ['helpıŋ] *of food* ración *f*

help·less ['helplıs] *adj* **1** (*unable to*

H

cope) indefenso **2** (*powerless*) impotente

help•less•ly ['helplɪslɪ] *adv* impotentemente

help•less•ness ['helplɪsnɪs] impotencia *f*

'help line TELEC teléfono *m* de información y ayuda; **'help men•u** COMPUT menú *m* de ayuda; **'help screen** COMPUT pantalla *f* de ayuda

hel•ter-skel•ter [heltər'skeltər] **I** *adv* alocadamente, desenfrenadamente **II** *adj* alocado, desenfrenado **III** *n Br* tobogán *m* en espiral

hem [hem] *of dress etc* dobladillo *m*

'he-man F machote *m* F

he•ma•tol•o•gy [hiːmə'tɑːlədʒɪ] MED hematología *f*

hem•i•sphere ['hemɪsfɪr] hemisferio *m*

'hem•line bajo *m*

he•mo•glo•bin [hiːmə'gloʊbɪn] PHYSIO hemoglobina *f*

he•mo•phil•i•a [hiːmə'fɪlɪə] MED hemofilia *f*

he•mo•phil•i•ac [hiːmə'fɪlɪæk] MED hemofílico(-a) *m*(*f*)

hem•or•rhage ['hemərɪdʒ] **I** *n* hemorragia *f* **II** *v/i* sangrar

hem•or•rhoids ['hemərɔɪdz] *pl* MED hemorroides *fpl*

hemp [hemp] cáñamo *m*

hen [hen] gallina *f*

hence [hens] *adv* **1** *therefore* por (lo) tanto **2**: ***a week ~*** dentro de una semana, de hoy en una semana; ***it's still a long time ~*** todavía falta mucho tiempo

hence'forth, hence'for•ward(s) *adv* desde ese / este momento en adelante

hench•man ['hentʃmən] *pej* sicario *m*

'hen par•ty despedida *f* de soltera

hen•pecked ['henpekt] *adj*: ***~ husband*** calzonazos *m inv*

hep•a•ti•tis [hepə'taɪtɪs] MED hepatitis *f*

hep•ta•gon ['heptəgɑːn] heptágono *m*

hep•tag•o•nal [hep'tægənl] *adj* heptagonal

hep•tath•lon [hep'tæθlən] SP heptalón *m*

her [hɜːr] **I** *adj* su; *to distinguish* de ella; ***~ ticket*** su entrada; la entrada de ella; ***~ books*** sus libros **II** *pron direct object* la; *indirect object* le; *after prep* ella; ***I know ~*** la conozco; ***I gave ~ the keys*** le di las llaves; ***I sold it to ~*** se lo vendí; ***this is for ~*** esto es para ella; ***who do you mean? – ~*** ¿a quién te refieres? – a ella

her•ald ['herəld] **I** *n* heraldo *m* **II** *v/t* marcar, significar

herb [ɜːrb] hierba *f*

herb•al tea ['ɜːrbəl] infusión *f*

herb•al 'med•i•cine medicina *f* naturista

'herb gar•den plantel *m* de hierbas

her•bi•cide ['ɜːrbɪsaɪd] herbicida *m*

her•bi•vore ['ɜːrbɪvɔːr] ZO herbívoro(-a) *m*(*f*)

her•biv•o•rous [ɜːr'bɪvərəs] *adj* ZO herbívoro

herd [hɜːrd] **I** *n* rebaño *m*; *of elephants* manada *f* **II** *v/t also fig* guiar, conducir

'herd in•stinct *fig* instinto *m* gregario

herds•man ['hɜːrdzmən] pastor *m*

here [hɪr] *adv* aquí; ***over ~*** aquí; ***~'s to you!*** *as toast* ¡a tu salud!; ***~ you are*** *giving sth* ¡aquí tienes!; ***~ we are!*** *finding sth* ¡aquí está!

here•a'bouts *adv* (por) aquí

here'af•ter I *adv in document* de ahora en adelante **II** *n*: ***the ~*** el más allá

here'by *adv* por el presente (documento)

he•red•i•ta•ry [hə'redɪterɪ] *adj disease* hereditario

he•red•i•ty [hə'redɪtɪ] herencia *f*

here'in *adv fml* incluso, en el presente (documento)

here'of *adv fml* del presente, de esto

her•e•sy ['herəsɪ] herejía *f*

her•e•tic ['herətɪk] hereje *m/f*

he•ret•i•cal [hɪ'retɪkl] *adj* herético

here•up'on *adv* **1** *at this* en este momento **2** *fml agree* en este respecto

here'with *adv fml* con este documento

her•it•a•ble ['herɪtəbl] *adj* hereditable

her•i•tage ['herɪtɪdʒ] patrimonio *m*

her•maph•ro•dite [hɜːr'mæfrədaɪt] BIO hermafrodita *m/f*

her•met•ic [hɜːr'metɪk] *adj* hermético

her•met•i•cal•ly [hɜːr'metɪklɪ] *adv*: ***~ sealed*** cerrado herméticamente

her•mit ['hɜːrmɪt] ermitaño(-a) *m*(*f*)

her•mit•age ['hɜːrmɪtɪdʒ] ermita *f*

her•ni•a ['hɜːrnɪə] MED hernia *f*

he•ro ['hɪroʊ] (*pl* ***-o(e)s***) héroe *m*

he•ro•ic [hɪ'roʊɪk] *adj* heroico

he•ro•i•cal•ly [hɪ'roʊɪklɪ] *adv* heroica-

mente
her•o•in ['heroʊɪn] heroína *f*
'her•o•in ad•dict heroinómano(-a) *m(f)*
her•o•ine ['heroʊɪn] heroína *f*
her•o•ism ['heroʊɪzm] heroísmo *m*
her•on ['herən] garza *f*
her•pes ['hɜːrpiːz] MED herpes *m*
her•ring ['herɪŋ] arenque *m*
'her•ring•bone (*also* ~ ***pattern***) espiguilla *f*
hers [hɜːrz] *pron* el suyo, la suya; ~ ***are red*** los suyos son rojos; ***that book is*** ~ ese libro es suyo; ***a cousin of*** ~ un primo suyo
her•self [hɜːr'self] *pron reflexive* se; *emphatic* ella misma; ***she hurt*** ~ se hizo daño; ***when she saw*** ~ ***in the mirror*** cuando se vio en el espejo; ***she saw it*** ~ lo vio ella misma; ***by*** ~ (*alone*) sola; (*without help*) ella sola, ella misma
he's [hiːz] F ☞ ***he is***; ***he has***
hes•i•tant ['hezɪtənt] *adj* indeciso
hes•i•tant•ly ['hezɪtəntlɪ] *adv* con indecisión
hes•i•tate ['hezɪteɪt] *v/i* dudar, vacilar; ~ ***to do sth*** dudar en hacer algo
hes•i•ta•tion [hezɪ'teɪʃn] vacilación *f*; ***without*** ~ sin dudarlo (un momento)
het•er•o•ge•ne•ous [hetəroʊ'dʒiːnɪəs] *adj* heterogéneo
het•er•o•sex•u•al [hetəroʊ'sekʃʊəl] *adj* heterosexual
het up [het'ʌp] *adj* F: ***be*** ~ (***about sth***) estar alterado *or* inquieto (por algo) F; ***get*** ~ ***about sth*** alterarse *or* disgustarse por algo
hew [hjuː] *v/t* (*pp* ***hewed, hewn***) cortar a tajos
hewn [hjuːn] *pp* ☞ ***hew***
hex•a•gon ['heksəgən] hexágono *m*
hex•ag•o•nal [hek'sægənl] *adj* hexagonal
hey [heɪ] *int* ¡eh!
hey•day ['heɪdeɪ] apogeo *m*
hi [haɪ] *int* ¡hola!
hi•ber•nate ['haɪbərneɪt] *v/i* hibernar
hi•ber•na•tion [haɪbər'neɪʃn] hibernación *f*; ***go into*** ~ hibernar
hi•bis•cus [hɪ'bɪskəs] BOT hibisco *m*
hic•cough ['hɪkʌp] ☞ ***hiccup***
hic•cup ['hɪkʌp] **1** hipo *m*; ***have the*** ~***s*** tener hipo **2** (*minor problem*) tropiezo *m*, traspié *m*
hick [hɪk] *pej* F palurdo(-a) *m(f)* F, pueblerino(-a) *m(f)* F
'hick town *pej* F ciudad *f* provinciana
hid [hɪd] *pret* ☞ ***hide***
hid•den ['hɪdn] **I** *adj meaning, treasure* oculto **II** *pp* ☞ ***hide***
hid•den a'gen•da *fig* objetivo *m* secreto
hide[1] [haɪd] **I** *v/t* (*pret* ***hid***, *pp* ***hidden***) esconder, ocultar **II** *v/i* (*pret* ***hid***, *pp* ***hidden***) esconderse, ocultarse
◆ **hide out** *v/i* esconderse
hide[2] *n of animal* piel *f*
hide-and-'seek escondite *m*
'hide•a•way escondite *m*
'hide•bound *adj* conservador, cerrado
hid•e•ous ['hɪdɪəs] *adj* espantoso, horrendo; *person* repugnante
'hide-out escondite *m*, refugio *m*
hid•ing[1] ['haɪdɪŋ] (*beating*) paliza *f*
hid•ing[2] ['haɪdɪŋ]: ***be in*** ~ estar escondido; ***go into*** ~ esconderse
'hid•ing place escondite *m*
hi•er•arch•i•cal [haɪər'ɑːrkɪkl] *adj* jerárquico
hi•er•ar•chy ['haɪərɑːrkɪ] jerarquía *f*
hi•er•o•glyph•ic [haɪəroʊ'glɪfɪk] *adj handwriting* indescifrable
hi•er•o•glyph•ics [haɪəroʊ'glɪfɪks] *npl* jeroglíficos *mpl*
hi-fi ['haɪfaɪ] equipo *m* de alta fidelidad
high [haɪ] **I** *adj* alto; *wind* fuerte; F *on drugs* colocado P; ***have a very*** ~ ***opinion of*** tener muy buena opinión de; ***it is*** ~ ***time you understood*** ya va siendo hora de que entiendas
II *n* **1** MOT directa *f* **2** *in statistics* máximo *m* **3** EDU escuela *f* secundaria, *Span* instituto *m*
III *adv*: ~ ***in the sky*** en lo alto; ***that's as*** ~ ***as we can go*** eso es lo máximo que podemos ofrecer
high 'al•tar altar *m* mayor; **high-'al•ti•tude** *adj* de altitud; **high and 'dry** *adj*: ***leave s.o.*** ~ dejar a alguien tirado *or* colgado F; **high and 'might•y** *adj* F: ***act all*** ~ darse (muchos) aires; **'high•ball** *whisky con soda*; **'high beams** MOT luces *fpl* largas; **'high•brow** *adj* intelectual; **'high•chair** trona *f*; **'high-class** *adj* de categoría; **'high-den•si•ty disk** disquete *m* de alta densidad; **high 'div•ing** salto *m* de trampolín
high•er ed•u•ca•tion [haɪəredjʊ'keɪʃn]

enseñanza *f* superior *or* universitaria
high•est bid•der [haɪəst'bɪdər] mejor postor *m*
high ex'plo•sive explosivo *m*; **high-fi'del•i•ty** *adj* de alta fidelidad; **high-'fli•er** promesa *m/f*, portento *m/f*; **high-flown** ['haɪfloʊn] *adj* extravagante, pomposo; **high-'fre•quen•cy** *adj* de alta frecuencia; **high-'grade** *adj* de calidad superior; **high-hand•ed** [haɪ'hændɪd] *adj* despótico; **high-heeled** [haɪ'hi:ld] *adj* de tacón alto; **'high jump** salto *m* de altura; ***he's for the ~*** *fig* F le va caer una buena F; **'high jump•er** saltador(a) *m(f)* de altura; **'high•lands** *npl* tierras *fpl* altas; **high-'lev•el** *adj* de alto nivel; **~ (*pro-gramming*) *language*** lenguage *m* de alto nivel; **'high life** buena vida *f*; **'high•light I** *n* **1** (*main event*) momento *m* cumbre **2** *in hair* reflejo *m* **II** *v/t with pen* resaltar; COMPUT seleccionar, resaltar; **'high•light•er** *pen* fluorescente *m*
high•ly ['haɪlɪ] *adv desirable*, *likely* muy; ***be ~ paid*** estar muy bien pagado; ***think ~ of s.o.*** tener una buena opinión de alguien
high-necked [haɪ'nekt] *adj* de cuello alto
High•ness ['haɪnɪs]: ***His / Your ~*** Su Alteza
high-'oc•tane fu•el combustible *m* de alto octanaje; **high per'form•ance** *adj drill*, *battery* de alto rendimiento; **high-'pitched** *adj* agudo; **'high point** *of life*, *career* punto *m* culminante; **'high post** *in basketball* poste *m* alto; **high-pow•ered** [haɪ'paʊərd] *adj engine* potente; *intellectual* de alto(s) vuelo(s); *salesman* enérgico; **high 'pres•sure I** *n weather* altas presiones *fpl* **II** *adj* TECH a gran presión; *salesman* agresivo; *job*, *lifestyle* muy estresante; **high 'priest** sumo sacerdote *m*; **high-'qual•i•ty** *adj* de calidad suprema; **high-'rank•ing** *adj* de alto rango; **high-res•o'lu•tion** *adj* de alta resolución; **'high-rise** edificio *m* alto; **'high school** escuela *f* secundaria, *Span* instituto *m*; **high 'seas** *npl* aguas *fpl* internacionales; **high 'sea•son** temporada *f* alta; **high so-'ci•e•ty** alta sociedad *f*; **'high-speed** *adj printer etc* rápido; **high-speed 'train** tren *m* de alta velocidad; **high-'spir•it•ed** *adj* ilusionado, animado; **'high street** *Br* calle *f* principal; ***high-street bank*** banco *m* comercial; ***high-street store*** tienda *f* del centro; **high-'strung** *adj* muy nervioso; **high tech I** ['haɪtek] *n* alta *f* tecnología **II** *adj* de alta tecnología; **high-tech'nol•o•gy** alta *f* tecnología; **high-'ten•sion** *adj* de alta tensión; **high 'tide** marea *f* alta; **high 'trea•son** alta traición *f*; **'high val•ue ad•ded** *adj* de alto valor añadido; **high 'volt•age** alta tensión *f*, alto voltaje *m*; **high 'wa•ter**: ***at ~*** con la marea alta; **'high-way** autopista *f*; **'high•way di•vid•er** barrera *f* de protección; **'high wire** *in circus* cuerda *f* floja
hi•jack ['haɪdʒæk] **I** *v/t plane*, *bus* secuestrar **II** *n of plane*, *bus* secuestro *m*
hi•jack•er ['haɪdʒækər] *of plane*, *bus* secuestrador(a) *m(f)*
hike[1] [haɪk] **I** *n* caminata *f* **II** *v/i* caminar
hike[2] [haɪk] F *in prices* subida *f*
hik•er ['haɪkər] senderista *m/f*
hik•ing ['haɪkɪŋ] senderismo *m*
'hik•ing boots *npl* botas *fpl* de senderismo
hi•lar•i•ous [hɪ'lerɪəs] *adj* divertidísimo, graciosísimo
hi•lar•i•ty [hɪ'lærətɪ] gracia *f*, risa *f*
hill [hɪl] **1** colina *f* **2** (*slope*) cuesta *f*
hill•bil•ly ['hɪlbɪlɪ] F *rústico montañés*
hill•ock ['hɪlək] collado *m*
'hill•side ladera *f*; **'hill•top** cumbre *f*; **'hill•walk•er** senderista *m/f*, montañero(-a) *m(f)*; **'hill•walk•ing** senderismo *m*, montañismo *m*; ***go ~*** hacer senderismo *or* montañismo
hill•y ['hɪlɪ] *adj* con colinas
hilt [hɪlt] puño *m*
him [hɪm] *pron direct object* lo; *indirect object* le; *after prep* él; ***I know ~*** lo conozco; ***I gave ~ the keys*** le di las llaves; ***I sold it to ~*** se lo vendí; ***this is for ~*** esto es para él; ***who do you mean? – ~*** ¿a quién te refieres? - a él
him•self [hɪm'self] *pron reflexive* se; *emphatic* él mismo; ***he hurt ~*** se hizo daño; ***when he saw ~ in the mirror*** cuando se vio en el espejo; ***he saw it ~*** lo vio él mismo; ***by ~*** (*alone*) solo; (*without help*) él solo, él mismo
hind [haɪnd] *adj* trasero

hin•der ['hɪndər] *v/t* obstaculizar, entorpecer
Hin•di ['hɪndɪ] *language* hindi *m*
hind•most ['haɪndmoʊst] *adj* anterior, trasero
'hind•quart•ers *npl* cuartos *mpl* traseros
hin•drance ['hɪndrəns] estorbo *m*, obstáculo *m*
'hind•sight: ***with ~*** a posteriori
Hin•du [hɪn'duː]**I** *n* hindú *m/f* **II** *adj* hindú
Hin•du•ism ['hɪnduːɪzəm] hinduismo *m*
hinge [hɪndʒ] bisagra *f*
◆ **hinge on** *v/t* depender de
hint [hɪnt] **1** *n* **1** (*clue*) pista *f* **2** (*advice*) consejo *m* **3** (*implied suggestion*) indirecta *f* **4** *of red, sadness etc* rastro *m* **II** *v/t*: ***~ that ...*** dar a entender que ...
hin•ter•land ['hɪntərlænd] interior *m*
hip[1] [hɪp] *n* cadera *f*
hip[2] [hɪp] *int*: ***~, ~, hooray!*** ¡viva!, ¡hip, hip, hurra!
hip[3] [hɪp] *adj* F *C.Am* chévere, *Rpl* macanudo, *Span* guay *inv*
'hip•bone ANAT hueso *m* de la cadera; **'hip flask** petaca *f*; **'hip joint** ANAT articulación *f* de la cadera
hip•pie ['hɪpɪ] hippy *m/f*
hip 'pock•et bolsillo *m* trasero
hip•po ['hɪpoʊ] F hipopótamo *m*
hip•po•pot•a•mus [hɪpə'pɑːtəməs] hipopótamo *m*
hip•py ☞ ***hippie***
hire [haɪr] *v/t* alquilar; ***be on ~*** estar alquilado; ***for ~*** se alquila
'hire car *Br* coche *m* de alquiler
hire 'pur•chase *Br* compra *f* a plazos; ***buy sth on ~*** comprar algo a plazos
his [hɪz] **I** *adj* su; *to distinguish* de él; ***~ ticket*** su entrada; la entrada de él; ***~ books*** sus libros **II** *pron* el suyo, la suya; ***~ are red*** los suyos son rojos; ***that ticket is ~*** esa entrada es suya; ***a cousin of ~*** un primo suyo
His•pan•ic [hɪ'spænɪk] **I** *n* hispano(-a) *m(f)* **II** *adj* hispano, hispánico
hiss [hɪs] *v/i of snake, audience* silbar
his•to•gram ['hɪstoʊgræm] histograma *m*
his•to•ri•an [hɪ'stɔːrɪən] historiador(a) *m(f)*
his•tor•ic [hɪ'stɑːrɪk] *adj* histórico
his•tor•i•cal [hɪ'stɑːrɪkl] *adj* histórico
his•to•ry ['hɪstərɪ] historia *f*
hit [hɪt] **I** *v/t* (*pret & pp* ***hit***) golpear; (*collide with*) chocar contra; ***he was ~ by a bullet*** le alcanzó una bala; ***it suddenly ~ me*** (*I realized*) de repente me di cuenta; ***~ town*** (*arrive*) llegar a la ciudad
II *n* **1** (*blow*) golpe *m*; *in baseball* batazo *m*, hit *m* **2** MUS, (*success*) éxito *m*; ***the new teacher is a big ~ with most of the school*** F el nuevo profesor es muy popular en el colegio
◆ **hit back** *v/i physically* devolver el golpe; *verbally, with actions* responder
◆ **hit off** *v/t*: ***hit it off*** F hacer buenas migas F
◆ **hit on** *v/t* **1** *idea* dar con **2** (*flirt with*) intentar ligar con
◆ **hit out at** *v/t* (*criticize*) atacar
hit-and-'run *adj*: ***~ accident*** *accidente en el que el vehículo causante se da a la fuga*
hitch [hɪtʃ] **I** *n* (*problem*) contratiempo *m*; ***without a ~*** sin ningún contratiempo **II** *v/t* **1** (*fix*) enganchar **2**: ***~ a ride*** hacer autoestop; ***can I ~ a ride with you tomorrow?*** ¿me puedes llevar en tu coche mañana? **III** *v/i* (*hitchhike*) hacer autoestop
◆ **hitch up** *v/t wagon, trailer* enganchar
'hitch•hike *v/i* hacer autoestop; **'hitch•hik•er** autoestopista *m/f*, **'hitch•hik•ing** autoestop *m*
hi-tech I ['haɪtek] *n* alta tecnología *f* **II** *adj* de alta tecnología
hith•er ['hɪðər] *adv* (hacia) aquí
hith•er'to *adv* hasta el momento
'hit•list lista *f* de blancos; **'hit•man** asesino *m* a sueldo; **hit-or-'miss** *adj* a la buena ventura; **'hit squad** grupo *m* de intervención especial
HIV [eɪtʃaɪ'viː] *abbr* (= ***human immunodeficiency virus***) VIH *m* (= virus *m inv* de la inmunodeficiencia humana); ***~-positive*** seropositivo
hive [haɪv] *for bees* colmena *f*
◆ **hive off** *v/t* COM (*separate off*) desprenderse de
hives [haɪvz] *npl* MED urticaria *f*
hoard [hɔːrd] **I** *n* reserva *f* **II** *v/t* hacer acopio de; *money* acumular
hoard•er ['hɔːrdər] acaparador(a) *m(f)*
hoar•frost [hɔːr'frɑːst] escarcha *f*
hoarse [hɔːrs] *adj* ronco

hoarse•ness ['hɔːrsnɪs] ronquedad *f*
hoar•y ['hɔːrɪ] *adj*: ***a ~ old joke*** un chiste viejo viejísimo
hoax [hoʊks] bulo *m*, engaño *m*; ***bomb ~*** amenaza *f* falsa de bomba
hoax•er ['hoʊksər] farsante *m/f*, gracioso(-a) *m(f)*
hob [hɑːb] *on cooker* fuegos *mpl*, quemadores *mpl*
hob•ble ['hɑːbl] *v/i* cojear
hob•by ['hɑːbɪ] hobby *m*, afición *f*
hob•gob•lin ['hɑːbgɑːblɪn] duende *m*, geniecillo *m*
hob•nob ['hɑːbnɑːb] *v/i*: ***~ with s.o.*** hacer buenas migas con alguien
ho•bo ['hoʊboʊ] (*pl* ***-o(e)s***) F vagabundo(-a) *m(f)*
Hob•son's choice [hɑːbsnz'tʃɔɪs]: ***it was (a case of) ~*** no hubo otra alternativa
hock [hɑːk] F: ***be in ~ to s.o.*** estar endeudado con alguien; ***get out of ~*** pagar las deudas; ***get sth out of ~*** desempeñar algo
hock•ey ['hɑːkɪ] hockey *m*; *Br* (*field ~*) hockey sobre hierba
ho•cus-po•cus [hoʊkəs'poʊkəs] engaño *m*, embrollo *m*
hodge•podge ['hɑːdʒpɑːdʒ] batiburrillo *m* F, revoltijo *m* F
hoe [hoʊ] **I** *n* azada *f* **II** *v/t* entrecavar
hog [hɑːg] (*pig*) cerdo *m*, *L.Am.* chancho *m*
'hog•wash F tonterías *fpl*, sandeces *fpl*
hoi pol•loi [hɔɪpə'lɔɪ]: ***the ~*** la gente de a pie
hoist [hɔɪst] **I** *n* montacargas *m inv*; *manual* elevador *m* **II** *v/t* (*lift*) levantar, subir; *flag* izar
hoi•ty-toi•ty [hɔɪtɪ'tɔɪtɪ] *adj* F estirado, altanero; ***he got all ~*** se le subió el humo a las narices
ho•kum ['hoʊkəm] F **1** (*nonsense*) tonterías *fpl* **2** (*sentimental stuff*) cursilería *f*
hold [hoʊld] **I** *v/t* (*pret & pp* ***held***) *in hand* llevar; (*support, keep in place*) sostener; *passport, license* tener; *prisoner, suspect* retener; (*contain*) contener; *job, post* ocupar; *course* mantener; *views* tener, mantener; ***~ my hand*** dame la mano; ***~ one's breath*** aguantar la respiración; ***he can ~ his drink*** sabe beber; ***~ s.o. responsible*** hacer a alguien responsable; ***~ that ...*** (*believe, maintain*) mantener que ...; ***~ the line, please*** TELEC espere, por favor **II** *n* **1** *in ship, plane* bodega *f* **2**: ***take ~ of sth*** agarrar algo; ***lose one's ~ on*** *rope* soltar; *reality* perder el contacto con; ***wait till I get ~ of him!*** ¡espera a que lo pille!, ¡(ya) verás cuando lo pille!
◆ **hold against** *v/t*: ***hold sth against s.o.*** tener algo contra alguien
◆ **hold back I** *v/t* **1** *crowds* contener **2** *facts, information* guardar **II** *v/i* (*not tell all*): ***I'm sure he's holding back*** estoy seguro de que no dice todo lo que sabe
◆ **hold down** *v/t* **1** *person* reducir **2** *interest rates* rebajar **3** *job* conservar
◆ **hold on** *v/i* **1** (*wait*) esperar; ***now hold on a minute!*** ¡un momento! **2**: ***hold on tight!*** ¡agárrate *or* sujétate fuerte!
◆ **hold on to** *v/t* **1** (*keep*) guardar **2** *belief* aferrarse a
◆ **hold out I** *v/t* **1** *hand* tender **2** *prospect* ofrecer **II** *v/i* **1** *of supplies* durar **2** (*survive*) resistir, aguantar
◆ **hold out on** *v/t not tell all* engañar a
◆ **hold up** *v/t* **1** *hand* levantar; ***hold s.o. up as an example*** poner a alguien como ejemplo **2** *bank etc* atracar **3** (*make late*) retrasar; ***I was held up by the traffic*** he llegado tarde por culpa del tráfico
◆ **hold with** *v/t* (*approve of*): ***I don't hold with that sort of behavior*** no me parece bien ese tipo de comportamiento
'hold-all *Br* bolsa *f* de viaje
hold•er ['hoʊldər] **1** (*container*) receptáculo *m* **2** *of passport, ticket etc* titular *m/f*; *of record* poseedor(a) *m(f)*
hold•ing ['hoʊldɪŋ] COM acción *f*
'hold•ing com•pa•ny holding *m*
'hold•o•ver vestigio *m*
'hold•up 1 (*robbery*) atraco *m* **2** (*delay*) retraso *m*
hole [hoʊl] **1** *in sleeve, wood, bag* agujero *m* **2** *in ground* hoyo *m*; ***be half a million dollars in the ~*** F tener una deuda *or* agujero de medio millón de dólares
◆ **hole up** *v/i* F esconderse
hol•i•day ['hɑːlədeɪ] **1** *single day* día *m* de fiesta **2** *Br period* vacaciones *fpl*; ***take a ~*** tomarse vacaciones
'hol•i•day a•part•ment *Br* apartamen-

to *m* de veraneo; **'hol•i•day camp** *Br* colonia *f* de verano; **'hol•i•day des•ti•na•tion** *Br* destino *m* vacacional; **'hol•i•day home** *Br* casa *f* de veraneo; **'hol•i•day-mak•er** *Br* veraneante *m/f*, turista *m/f*

Ho•li•ness ['hoʊlɪnɪs]: ***His ~*** Su Santidad

Hol•land ['hɑːlənd] Holanda *f*

hol•ler ['hɑːlər] F **I** *v/t* gritar, chillar **II** *v/i* gritar, chillar (***at*** a); ***~ for help*** gritar en busca de ayuda

hol•low ['hɑːloʊ] **I** *adj object* hueco; *cheeks* hundido; *promise* vacío **II** *n in ground* hoyo *m*

◆ **hollow out** *v/t tree trunk* vaciar

hol•ly ['hɑːlɪ] acebo *m*

hol•o•caust ['hɑːləkɒːst] holocausto *m*

hol•o•gram ['hɑːləgræm] holograma *m*

hol•ster ['hoʊlstər] pistolera *f*

ho•ly ['hoʊlɪ] *adj* santo

Ho•ly 'Fa•ther Papa *m*; **Ho•ly 'Ghost** Espíritu *m* Santo; **Ho•ly 'Scrip•ture** Sagradas Escrituras *fpl*; **Ho•ly 'Spir•it** Espíritu *m* Santo; **ho•ly 'war** guerra *f* santa; **ho•ly 'wa•ter** agua *m* bendita; **'Ho•ly Week** Semana *f* Santa

hom•age ['hɑːmɪdʒ] homenaje *m*; ***do*** *or* ***pay ~ to s.o.*** dedicar *or* rendir un homenaje a alguien

home [hoʊm] **I** *n* **1** casa *f*; (*native country*) tierra *f*; ***New York is my ~*** Nueva York es mi hogar; ***at ~*** *also* SP en casa; (*in country*) en mi / su / nuestra tierra; ***make yourself at ~*** ponte cómodo; ***at ~ and abroad*** en el país y en el extranjero; ***work from ~*** trabajar desde casa **2** *for old people* residencia *f* **3** *in baseball* meta *f*, home *m*

II *adv* a casa; ***go ~*** ir a casa; *to country* ir a mi / tu / su tierra; *to town, part of country* ir a mi / tu / su ciudad

◆ **home in on** *v/t of missile* apuntar hacia; *mistake* centrarse en

'home ad•dress domicilio *m*; **home 'bank•ing** telebanca *f*, banca *f* electrónica; **'home•com•ing** vuelta *f* a casa; **home com'put•er** *L.Am.* computadora *f* doméstica, *Span* ordenador *m*; **home 'de•liv•er•y** entrega *f* a domicilio; **home ec•o'nom•ics** *nsg* ciencias *fpl* del hogar; **'home game** partido *m* en casa; **home-'grown** *adj vegetables* de cosecha propia, casero; *fig* nacional; **home 'help** *Br* asistente *m/f* doméstico; **'home•land** país *m* de origen

home•less ['hoʊmlɪs] **I** *adj* sin casa **II** *npl* ***the ~*** los sin casa

'home•lov•ing *adj* hogareño

home•ly ['hoʊmlɪ] *adj* **1** (*homeloving*) hogareño **2** (*not good-looking*) feúcho

home-'made *adj* casero; **'home•mak•er** ama *f* de casa; **home 'mov•ie** película *f* casera; **'Home Of•fice** *Br* POL Ministerio *m* del Interior

ho•me•o•path ['hoʊmɪoʊpæθ] MED homeópata *m/f*

ho•me•o•path•ic [hoʊmɪoʊ'pæθɪk] *adj* homeopático

ho•me•op•a•thy [hoʊmɪ'ɑːpəθɪ] homeopatía *f*

'home•own•er propietario(-a) *m*(*f*) de vivienda; **home'own•er•ship** propiedad *f* de vivienda; **'home page** *web site* página *f* personal; *on web site* página *f* inicial; **'home plate** *in baseball* goma *f*, plato *m*

hom•er ['hoʊmər], **home 'run** *in baseball* carrera *f* completa, cuadrangular *m*

'home shop•ping telecompra *f*; **'home•sick** *adj* nostálgico; ***be ~*** tener morriña; **'home•sick•ness** morriña *f*, nostalgia *f*; **home•stead•er** ['hoʊmstedər] colono(-a) *m*(*f*); **'home town** ciudad *f* natal; **home 'truth**: ***tell s.o. a few ~s*** decir a alguien cuatro cosas *or* verdades; **home 'vid•e•o** video *m* *or Span* vídeo *m* doméstico

home•ward ['hoʊmwərd] *adv to own house* a casa; *to own country* a su país

'home•work EDU deberes *mpl*, tareas *fpl*; ***what ~ do you have?*** ¿qué tienes que hacer de tareas?, ¿qué tareas tienes?; **'home•work•er** COM teletrabajador(a) *m*(*f*); **'home•work•ing** COM teletrabajo *m*

hom•i•cide ['hɑːmɪsaɪd] *crime* homicidio *m*; *police department* brigada *f* de homicidios

hom•i•ly ['hɑːmɪlɪ] sermón *m*

ho•mo•ge•ne•ous [hoʊmə'dʒiːnɪəs] *adj* homogéneo

ho•mog•e•nize [hə'mɑːdʒənaɪz] *v/t* homogeneizar

hom•o•graph ['hɑːməgræf] homógrafo *m*

ho•mo ['hoʊmoʊ] F marica *m* F

H

hom•o•nym ['hɑːmənɪm] LING homónimo *m*

ho•mo•phobe ['hoʊməfoʊb] homófobo(-a) *m(f)*

ho•mo•pho•bi•a [hoʊmə'foʊbɪə] homofobia *f*

ho•mo•pho•bic [hoʊmə'foʊbɪk] *adj* homofóbico

hom•o•phone ['hɑːməfoʊn] LING homófono *m*

ho•mo•sex•u•al [hoʊmə'sekʃʊəl] **I** *adj* homosexual **II** *n* homosexual *m/f*

ho•mo•sex•u•al•i•ty [hoʊməsekʃʊ'ælətɪ] homosexualidad *f*

hom•y ['hoʊmɪ] *adj* F acogedor, cálido

Hon•du•ran [hɑːn'dʊrən] **I** *adj* hondureño **II** *n* hondureño(-a) *m(f)*

Hon•du•ras [hɑːn'dʊrəs] Honduras *f*

hone [hoʊn] *v/t sharpen* afilar; *skills* perfeccionar, pulir

hon•est ['ɑːnɪst] *adj* honrado

hon•est•ly ['ɑːnɪstlɪ] *adv* honradamente; **~!** ¡desde luego!

hon•es•ty ['ɑːnɪstɪ] honradez *f*

hon•ey ['hʌnɪ] **1** miel *f* **2** F (*darling*) cariño *m*, vida *f* mía

'hon•ey•bee abeja *f* de panal; **'hon•ey•comb** panal *m*; **hon•ey•dew 'mel•on** *melón de corteza amarilla*; **'hon•ey•moon** luna *f* de miel; **hon•ey•moon•er** ['hʌnɪmuːnər] novio(-a) *m(f)* en luna de miel; **'hon•ey•suck•le** BOT madreselva *f*

honk [hɑːŋk] *v/t horn* tocar

hon•ky ['hɑːŋkɪ] P *pej* blanco(-a) *m(f)*

hon•or ['ɑːnər] **I** *n* honor *m* **II** *v/t* honrar

hon•or•a•ble ['ɑːnrəbl] *adj* honorable

hon•or•ar•y ['ɑːnərərɪ] *adj* honorario

hon•our *etc Br* ☞ ***honor*** *etc*

hooch [huːtʃ] F licor *m* de contrabando

hood [hʊd] **1** *over head* capucha *f*; *over cooker* campana *f* extractora; MOT capó *m* **2** F (*gangster*) matón(-ona) *m(f)*

hood•lum ['huːdləm] matón(-ona) *m(f)*

'hood•wink *v/t* engañar; **~ *s.o. into doing sth*** liar *or* embarullar a alguien para que haga algo

hoo•ey ['huːɪ] P chorrada *f* P

hoof [huːf] (*pl* ***hooves***) casco *m*

hook [hʊk] gancho *m*; *to hang clothes on* colgador *m*; *for fishing* anzuelo *m*; ***off the* ~** TELEC descolgado

hooked [hʊkt] *adj* enganchado (***on*** a); ***get* ~ *on sth*** engancharse a algo

hook•er ['hʊkər] F fulana *f* F

hook•ey ['hʊkɪ] F: ***play* ~** hacer novillos, *Mex* irse de pinta, *S.Am.* hacerse la rabona

hoo•li•gan ['huːlɪgən] gamberro(-a) *m(f)*

hoo•li•gan•ism ['huːlɪgənɪzm] gamberrismo *m*

hoop [huːp] aro *m*

hoo•ray [hʊ'reɪ] ☞ ***hurray***

hoot [huːt] **I** *v/t horn* tocar **II** *v/i* **1** *of car* dar bocinazos **2** *of owl* ulular **III** *n*: ***there were* ~*s of laughter*** hubo carcajadas; ***I don't care a* ~** F me importa un comino *or* bledo F

hoot•er ['huːtər] *Br* sirena *f*; MOT claxon *m*, bocina *f*

hoo•ver® ['huːvər] *Br* **I** *n* aspiradora *f* **II** *v/t* pasar la aspiradora por **III** *v/i* pasar la aspiradora

◆ **hoover up** *v/t Br* limpiar con la aspiradora

hooves [huːvz] *pl* ☞ ***hoof***

hop[1] [hɑːp] *n plant* lúpulo *m*

hop[2] [hɑːp] *v/i* (*pret & pp* ***-ped***) saltar

hope [hoʊp] **I** *n* esperanza *f* **II** *v/i* esperar; **~ *for sth*** esperar algo; ***we all* ~ *for peace*** todos ansiamos la paz; ***I* ~ *so*** eso espero; ***I* ~ *not*** espero que no **III** *v/t*: ***I* ~ *you like it*** espero que te guste

hope•ful ['hoʊpfəl] *adj* prometedor; ***I'm* ~ *that ...*** espero que ...

hope•ful•ly ['hoʊpfəlɪ] *adv* **1** *say, wait* esperanzadamente **2**: **~ *he hasn't forgotten*** esperemos que no se haya olvidado

hope•less ['hoʊplɪs] *adj* **1** *position, prospect* desesperado **2** (*useless: person*) inútil

hop•ping ['hɑːpɪŋ] *adv*: ***be* ~ *mad*** F echar chispas F

horde [hɔːrd] horda *f*

ho•ri•zon [hə'raɪzn] horizonte *m*

hor•i•zon•tal [hɑːrɪ'zɑːntl] *adj* horizontal

hor•mone ['hɔːrmoʊn] hormona *f*

hor•mone re'place•ment ther•a•py terapia *f* de sustitución hormonal

horn [hɔːrn] **1** *of animal* cuerno *m* **2** MOT bocina *f*, claxon *m*

hor•net ['hɔːrnɪt] avispón *m*

horn-rimmed spec•ta•cles ['hɔːrnrɪmd] *npl* gafas *fpl* de concha

horn•y ['hɔːrnɪ] *adj* F *sexually* cachondo

F

hor•o•scope ['hɑːrəskoʊp] horóscopo *m*

hor•ren•dous [hɔː'rendəs] *weather, accident, experience* horroroso, espantoso; *noise* horroroso, tremendo

hor•ri•ble ['hɑːrɪbl] *adj* horrible; *person* muy antipático

hor•rid ['hɑːrɪd] *adj* horrendo; *person, experience* desagradable, repugnante

hor•rif•ic [hɑː'rɪfɪk] *adj* horrible, aterrador

hor•ri•fy ['hɑːrɪfaɪ] *v/t* (*pret & pp* ***-ied***) horrorizar; ***I was horrified*** me quedé horrorizado

hor•ri•fy•ing ['hɑːrɪfaɪɪŋ] *adj* horroroso

hor•ror ['hɑːrər] horror *m*

'hor•ror mov•ie película *f* de terror; **'hor•ror sto•ry** historia *f* de miedo; **'hor•ror-strick•en, 'hor•ror-struck** *adj* horrorizado, espantado

hors d'oeu•vre [ɔːr'dɜːrv] entremés *m*

horse [hɔːrs] caballo *m*; ***hold your ~s*** F un momento, frena (un poco)

'horse•back: ***on ~*** a caballo; **horse 'chest•nut** castaño *m* de Indias; **'horse•fly** tábano *m*; **horse•man** ['hɔːrsmən] jinete *m*; **'horse•pow•er** caballo *m* (de vapor); **'horse race** carrera *f* de caballos; **'horse•rad•ish** BOT rábano *m* picante; **'horse rid•ing** equitación *f*; ***go ~*** ir a montar a caballo; **'horse sense** F sentido *m* común; **'horse•shoe** herradura *f*; **'horse trad•ing** *esp* POL F regateo *m* F, trapicheo *m* F; **'horse•wom•an** amazona *f*

hor•ti•cul•tur•al [hɔːrtɪ'kʌltʃərəl] *adj* agrícola

hor•ti•cul•ture ['hɔːrtɪkʌltʃər] horticultura *f*

hose [hoʊz] *for water* manguera *f*

ho•sier•y ['hoʊzɪərɪ] medias *fpl*; *in shop* sección *f* de medias

hos•pice ['hɑːspɪs] hospital *m* para enfermos terminales

hos•pi•ta•ble [hɑː'spɪtəbl] *adj* hospitalario

hos•pi•tal ['hɑːspɪtl] hospital *m*; ***go into the ~*** ir al hospital

hos•pi•tal•i•ty [hɑːspɪ'tælətɪ] hospitalidad *f*

hos•pi'tal•i•ty in•dus•try sector *m* hotelero

hos•pi•tal•ize ['hɑːspɪtlaɪz] *v/t* hospitalizar

host[1] [hoʊst] **I** *n at party, reception* anfitrión *m*; *of TV program* presentador(a) *m(f)* **II** *v/t TV program* presentar, conducir; *website* albergar, hospeder

host[2] [hoʊst] *n* (*vast number*) sinfín *m*, multitud *f*; ***a ~ of questions*** un montón de preguntas

Host[3] [hoʊst] REL hostia *f* sagrada

hos•tage ['hɑːstɪdʒ] rehén *m/f*; ***take s.o. ~*** tomar a alguien como rehén

'hos•tage tak•er *persona que toma rehenes*

hos•tel ['hɑːstl] **1** *for students* residencia *f* **2** (*youth ~*) albergue *m*

host•ess ['hoʊstɪs] *at party, reception* anfitriona *f*; *on airplane* azafata *f*; *in bar* cabaretera *f*

hos•tile ['hɑːstl] *adj* hostil

hos•til•i•ty [hɑː'stɪlətɪ] **1** *of attitude* hostilidad *f* **2**: ***hostilities*** hostilidades *fpl*

hot [hɑːt] **1** *adj weather* caluroso; *object, water, food* caliente; ***it's ~*** *of weather* hace calor; ***I'm ~*** tengo calor **2** (*spicy*) picante **3**: ***she's pretty ~ at math*** F (*good*) es una fenómena con las matemáticas F

◆ **hot up** *v/i fig* F caldearse

hot 'air F cuento *m* F, charlatanería *f* F; ***she talks a lot of ~*** tiene mucho cuento; **'hot•bed** *fig* núcleo *m*, foco *m*; **hot-blood•ed** [hɑːt'blʌdɪd] *adj* apasionado, impetuoso; **hot 'choc•o•late** *drink* chocolate *m* caliente

hotch•potch ['hɑːtʃpɑːtʃ] *Br* batiburrillo *m* F, revoltijo *m* F

hot 'desk•ing *uso de diferentes terminales de trabajo*

'hot dog perrito *m* caliente

ho•tel [hoʊ'tel] hotel *m*

ho•tel•ier [hoʊ'telɪeɪ] hotelero(-a) *m(f)*

ho'tel keep•er hotelero(-a) *m(f)*

'hot•foot F *v/t*: ***~ it*** salir volando F *or* pitando F; **'hot•head** majadero(-a) *m(f)*; **hot•'head•ed** *adj* insensato, alocado; **'hot•house** invernadero *m*; **'hot line** POL teléfono *m* rojo; COM línea *f* telefónica

hot•ly ['hɑːtlɪ] *adv* contundentemente, vehementemente

'hot•plate placa *f*; **hot po'ta•to** *fig* patata *f* caliente; **'hot spot** *military, political* punto *m* caliente; **hot-'wa•ter bot•tle** bolsa *f* de agua caliente; **hot-'wire** *v/t*

car hacer un puente a
hound [haʊnd] **I** *n* perro *m* rastrero **II** *v/t* perseguir, acosar
hour [aʊr] hora *f*
hour•ly ['aʊrlɪ] *adj*: ***at ~ intervals*** a intervalos de una hora; ***an ~ bus*** un autobús que pasa cada hora
house [haʊs] casa *f*; ***at your ~*** en tu casa; ***this one is on the ~*** esto corre a cuenta de la casa; ***clean ~*** hacer la limpieza de la casa
'house ar•rest arresto *m* domiciliario; ***be under ~*** estar bajo arresto domiciliario; **'house•boat** barco-vivienda *f*; **'house•bound** *adj due to illness, bad weather etc* encerrado *or* inmovilizado en casa; **'house•break•ing** allanamiento *m* de morada; **'house•bro•ken** *adj* adiestrado, amaestrado; **'house•fly** mosca *f* común; **'house•hold** hogar *m*; **house•hold 'name** nombre *m* conocido; **'house-hunt•ing**: ***go ~*** ir en busca de casa; **'house hus•band** amo *m* de casa; **'house•keep•er** ama *f* de llaves; **'house•keep•ing 1** *activity* tareas *fpl* domésticas **2** *money* dinero *m* para gastos domésticos
house mar•tin ['haʊsmɑːrtɪn] ORN avión *m* común
House of 'Com•mons *Br* Cámara *f* de los Comunes; **House of 'Lords** *Br* Cámara *f* de los Lores; **House of Rep•re'sent•a•tives** *npl* Cámara *f* de Representantes; **'house plant** planta *f* de interior; **'house-proud** *adj orgulloso del orden y de la limpieza en la casa*; **house-to-house 'search** búsqueda *f* casa por casa; **house-trained** ['haʊstreɪnd] *adj Br* adiestrado, amaestrado; **house•warm•ing (par•ty)** ['haʊswɔːrmɪŋ] fiesta *f* de estreno de una casa; **'house•wife** ama *f* de casa; **'house•work** tareas *fpl* domésticas
hous•ing ['haʊzɪŋ] vivienda *f*; TECH cubierta *f*
'hous•ing de•vel•op•ment urbanización *f*; **'hous•ing mar•ket** mercado *m* inmobiliario; **'hous•ing short•age** escasez *f* de viviendas; **'hous•ing con•di•tions** *npl* condiciones *fpl* de la vivienda
hove [hoʊv] *pret & pp* ☞ ***heave***
hov•el ['hɑːvl] chabola *f*
hov•er ['hɑːvər] *v/i of bird* cernerse; *of helicopter* permanecer inmóvil en el aire
'hov•er•craft aerodeslizador *m*, hovercraft *m*
how [haʊ] *adv* cómo; ***~ are you?*** ¿cómo estás?; ***~'s your bad leg?*** ¿cómo tienes la pierna?; ***~ about …?*** ¿qué te parece …?; ***~ about a drink?*** ¿te apetece tomar algo?; ***~ much?*** ¿cuánto?; ***~ much is it?*** *of cost* ¿cuánto vale *or* cuesta?; ***~ many?*** ¿cuántos?; ***~ often?*** ¿con qué frecuencia?; ***~ funny / sad!*** ¡qué divertido / triste!
how'ev•er *adv* **1** sin embargo **2**: ***~ big / rich / small they are*** independientemente de lo grandes / ricos / pequeños que sean
howl [haʊl] *of dog* aullido *m*; *of person in pain* alarido *m*; *with laughter* risotada *f*
howl•er ['haʊlər] F gazapo *m* F
howl•ing ['haʊlɪŋ] *adj*: ***a ~ gale*** un vendaval espantoso; ***~ success*** F éxito *m* rotundo *or* aplastante
HP [eɪtʃ'piː] *abbr Br* (= ***hire purchase***) compra *f* a plazos
HQ [eɪtʃ'kjuː] *abbr* (= ***headquarters***) *of party, organization* sede *f*, *of army* cuartel *m* general
HRT [eɪtʃɑːr'tiː] *abbr* (= ***hormone replacement therapy***) terapia *f* de sustitución hormonal
hub [hʌb] *of wheel* cubo *m*
hub•bub ['hʌbʌb] algarabía *f*, griterío *m*
'hub•cap tapacubos *m inv*
hud•dle ['hʌdl] **1** corrillo *m*; ***go into a ~*** hacer corrillo **2** *in football* timbac *m*, jol *m*
◆ **huddle together** ['hʌdl] *v/i* apiñarse, acurrucarse
hue [hjuː] tonalidad *f*
huff [hʌf]: ***be in a ~*** estar enfurruñado
huff•y ['hʌfɪ] *adj* enfurruñado, picado
hug [hʌg] **I** *v/t* (*pret & pp* ***-ged***) abrazar **II** *n* abrazo *m*
huge [hjuːdʒ] *adj* enorme
huge•ly ['hjuːdʒlɪ] *adv* enormemente
hulk [hʌlk] *person* grandullón(-ona) *m(f)*; *thing* mole *f*
hulk•ing ['hʌlkɪŋ] *adj person* corpulento, fornido; *thing, animal* grandote
hull [hʌl] *of ship* casco *m*
hul•la•ba•loo [hʌləbə'luː] alboroto *m*
hum [hʌm] **I** *v/t* (*pret & pp* ***-med***) *song,*

tune tararear **II** *v/i* (*pret & pp* **-med**) *of person* tararear; *of machine* zumbar
hu•man ['hju:mən] **I** *n* humano *m* **II** *adj* humano; ~ ***error*** error *m or* fallo *m* humano
hu•man 'be•ing ser *m* humano
hu•mane [hju:'meɪn] *adj* humano
hu•man•ism ['hju:mənɪzəm] humanismo *m*
hu•man•ist ['hju:mənɪst] humanista *m/f*
hu•man•is•tic ['hju:mənɪstɪk] *adj* humanístico
hu•man•i•tar•i•an [hju:mænɪ'terɪən] *adj* humanitario
hu•man•i•ty [hju:'mænətɪ] humanidad *f*
hu•man•kind [hju:mən'kaɪnd] la humanidad
hu•man•ly ['hju:mənlɪ] *adv*: ***do everything ~ possible*** hacer todo lo humanamente posible
hu•man 'na•ture la naturaleza humana; **hu•man 'race** raza *f* humana; **hu•man re'sour•ces** *npl* recursos *mpl* humanos; ~ ***management*** gestión *f* de recursos humanos; **hu•man 'rights** *npl* derechos *mpl* humanos
hum•ble ['hʌmbl] **I** *adj* humilde **II** *v/t* empequeñecer, achicar
hum•bug ['hʌmbʌg] (*hypocrisy*) teatro *m*, doblez *f*
hum•ding•er [hʌm'dɪŋər] F preciosidad *f*, encanto *m*
hum•drum ['hʌmdrʌm] *adj* monótono, anodino
hum•er•us ['hju:mərəs] ANAT húmero *m*
hu•mid ['hju:mɪd] *adj* húmedo
hu•mid•i•fi•er [hju:'mɪdɪfaɪr] humidificador *m*
hu•mid•i•fy [hju:'mɪdɪfaɪ] *v/t* (*pret & pp* **-ied**) humidificar
hu•mid•i•ty [hju:'mɪdətɪ] humedad *f*
hu•mil•i•ate [hju:'mɪlɪeɪt] *v/t* humillar
hu•mil•i•at•ing [hju:'mɪlɪeɪtɪŋ] *adj* humillante
hu•mil•i•a•tion [hju:mɪlɪ'eɪʃn] humillación *f*
hu•mil•i•ty [hju:'mɪlətɪ] humildad *f*
hum•ming•bird ['hʌmɪŋbɜ:rd] ORN colibrí *m*
hu•mor ['hju:mər] humor *m*; ***sense of*** ~ sentido *m* del humor
hu•mor•ist ['hju:mərɪst] humorista *m/f*
hu•mor•less ['hju:mərlɪs] serio, severo
hu•mor•ous ['hju:mərəs] *adj* gracioso
hu•mour *Br* ☞ **humor**
hump [hʌmp] **I** *n of camel, person* joroba *f*; *on road* bache *m* **II** *v/t* F (*carry*) acarrear
hump•back 'whale ballena *f* jorobada
hunch [hʌntʃ] (*idea*) presentimiento *m*, corazonada *f*; ***I've got a ~ he'll be back*** tengo la corazonada de que volverá
hun•dred ['hʌndrəd] cien *m*; ***a ~ dollars*** cien dólares; ***~s of birds*** cientos *or* centenares de aves; ***a ~ and one*** ciento uno; ***two ~*** doscientos
hun•dred•fold ['hʌndrədfould] **I** *adj*: ***there has been a ~ increase in …*** …se ha multiplicado por cien **II** *adv*: ***increase a ~*** multiplicarse cien veces
hun•dredth ['hʌndrədθ] *n & adj* centésimo
'hun•dred•weight *43 kilogramos*
hung [hʌŋ] *pret & pp* ☞ **hang**
Hun•gar•i•an [hʌŋ'gerɪən] **I** *adj* húngaro **II 1** *n person* húngaro(-a) *m(f)* **2** *language* húngaro *m*
Hun•ga•ry ['hʌŋgərɪ] Hungría *f*
hun•ger ['hʌŋgər] hambre *f*
'hun•ger strike huelga *f* de hambre; ***go on*** (***a***) ~ hacer (una) huelga de hambre
hung-'o•ver *adj*: ***be ~*** tener resaca
hun•gry ['hʌŋgrɪ] *adj* hambriento; ***I'm ~*** tengo hambre; ***she was getting ~*** le estaba entrando hambre, estaba empezando a tener hambre
hunk [hʌŋk] **1** *of bread, cheese* cacho *m*, pedazo *m* **2** F *man* cachas *m inv* F
hun•ky-dor•y [hʌŋkɪ'dɔ:rɪ] *adj* F: ***everything's ~*** todo va de perlas
hunt [hʌnt] **I** *n* caza *f*, búsqueda *f* **II** *v/t animal* cazar
◆ **hunt down** *v/t* (*look for*) buscar; (*find*) encontrar
◆ **hunt for** *v/t* buscar
hunt•er ['hʌntər] *person* cazador(a) *m(f)*
hunt•ing ['hʌntɪŋ] caza *f*
'hunt•ing ground *fig*: ***a popular ~ for*** un paraíso para
hur•dle ['hɜ:rdl] SP valla *f*; *fig* obstáculo *m*
hur•dler ['hɜ:rdlər] SP vallista *m/f*
hur•dles *npl* SP vallas *fpl*

hurl [hɜːrl] *v/t* lanzar
hurl•y-burl•y [hɜːrlɪˈbɜːrlɪ] jaleo *m*, barullo *m*
hur•ray [hʊˈreɪ] *int* ¡hurra!
hur•ri•cane [ˈhʌrɪkən] huracán *m*
hur•ried [ˈhʌrɪd] *adj* apresurado
hur•ry [ˈhʌrɪ] **I** *n* prisa *f*; ***be in a ~*** tener prisa; ***there's no ~*** no hay prisa **II** *v/i* (*pret & pp* ***-ied***) darse prisa
◆ **hurry along** *v/t* meter prisa a; *delivery etc* agilizar, aligerar
◆ **hurry up I** *v/i* darse prisa; ***hurry up!*** ¡date prisa! **II** *v/t* meter prisa a; ***hurry things up*** acelerar las cosas
hurt [hɜːrt] **I** *v/i* (*pret & pp* **hurt**) doler; ***does it ~?*** ¿te duele? **II** *v/t* (*pret & pp* **hurt**) *physically* hacer daño a; *emotionally* herir; ***I've ~ my hand*** me he hecho daño en la mano; ***did he ~ you?*** ¿te hizo daño?; ***~ o.s.*** hacerse daño
hurt•ful [ˈhɜːrtfʊl] *adj* hiriente
hur•tle [ˈhɜːrtl] *v/i* lanzarse, dispararse
hus•band [ˈhʌzbənd] marido *m*
hush [hʌʃ] silencio *m*; ***~!*** ¡silencio!
◆ **hush up** *v/t scandal etc* acallar
hush-ˈhush *adj* F confidencial
ˈhush mon•ey F soborno *m*; ***pay s.o. ~*** sobornar a alguien
husk [hʌsk] *of peanuts etc* cáscara *f*
husk•y[1] [ˈhʌskɪ] *adj voice* áspero
hus•ky[2] [ˈhʌskɪ] *n* ZO husky *m*
hus•sy [ˈhʌsɪ] mujerzuela *f*, fresca *f*
hus•tle [ˈhʌsl] **I** *n* agitación *f*; ***~ and bustle*** ajetreo *m* **II** *v/t person* empujar
hus•tler [ˈhʌslər] F timador(-a) *m*(*f*)
hut [hʌt] cabaña *f*, refugio *m*; *workman's* cobertizo *m*
hutch [hʌtʃ] *for rabbits* jaula *f* para conejos
hy•a•cinth [ˈhaɪəsɪnθ] jacinto *m*
hy•brid [ˈhaɪbrɪd] híbrido *m*
hy•drant [ˈhaɪdrənt] hidrante *m or* boca *f* de incendios
hy•draul•ic [haɪˈdrɒːlɪk] *adj* hidráulico; ***~ brake*** freno *m* hidráulico
hy•dro•car•bon [haɪdrəˈkɑːrbən] CHEM hidrocarbono *m*
hy•dro•chlo•ric a•cid [haɪdrəklɔːrɪkˈæsɪd] CHEM ácido *m* clorhídrico
hy•dro•e•lec•tric [haɪdroʊɪˈlektrɪk] *adj* hidroeléctrico
hy•dro•foil [ˈhaɪdrəfɔɪl] *boat* hidroplaneador *m*
hy•dro•gen [ˈhaɪdrədʒən] hidrógeno *m*
ˈhy•dro•gen bomb bomba *f* de hidrógeno
hy•dro•pho•bi•a [haɪdrəˈfoʊbɪə] hidrofobia *f*, rabia *f*
hy•dro•plane [ˈhaɪdrəpleɪn] AVIA hidroavión *m*
hy•e•na [haɪˈiːnə] ZO hiena *f*
hy•giene [ˈhaɪdʒiːn] higiene *f*
hy•gien•ic [haɪˈdʒiːnɪk] *adj* higiénico
hymn [hɪm] himno *m*
ˈhymn•book libro *m* de himnos
hype [haɪp] F bombo *m*
◆ **hype up** *v/t* F anunciar a bombo y platillos F
hy•per [ˈhaɪpər] *adj* F alterado F, alborotado F
hy•perˈac•tive *adj* hiperactivo
hy•per•bo•le [haɪˈpɜːrbəlɪ] hipérbole *f*
hy•perˈcrit•i•cal *adj* hipercrítico
hy•per•inˈfla•tion hiperinflación *f*
ˈhy•per•link COMPUT vínculo *m*
ˈhy•per•mar•ket *Br* hipermercado *m*
hy•perˈsen•si•tive *adj* hipersensible
hy•perˈten•sion hipertensión *f*
ˈhy•per•text COMPUT hipertexto *m*
hy•perˈven•ti•late *v/i* MED hiperventilar
hy•phen [ˈhaɪfn] guión *m*
hy•phen•ate [ˈhaɪfəneɪt] *v/t* escribir con guión
hyp•no•sis [hɪpˈnoʊsɪs] hipnosis *f*
hyp•no•ther•a•py [hɪpnoʊˈθerəpɪ] hipnoterapia *f*
hyp•not•ic [hɪpˈnɑːtɪk] *adj* hipnótico
hyp•no•tism [ˈhɪpnətɪzm] hipnotismo *m*
hyp•no•tist [ˈhɪpnətɪst] hipnotizador(a) *m*(*f*)
hyp•no•tize [ˈhɪpnətaɪz] *v/t* hipnotizar
hy•po•chon•dri•a [haɪpəˈkɑːndrɪə] hipocondria *f*
hy•po•chon•dri•ac [haɪpəˈkɑːndrɪæk] hipocondríaco(-a) *m*(*f*)
hy•poc•ri•sy [hɪˈpɑːkrəsɪ] hipocresía *f*
hyp•o•crite [ˈhɪpəkrɪt] hipócrita *m/f*
hyp•o•crit•i•cal [hɪpəˈkrɪtɪkl] *adj* hipócrita
hy•po•der•mic [haɪpəˈdɜːrmɪk] *adj* MED hipodérmico
hy•po•ther•mi•a [haɪpoʊˈθɜːrmɪə] hipotermia *f*
hy•poth•e•sis [haɪˈpɑːθəsɪs] (*pl* ***hypotheses*** [haɪˈpɑːθəsiːz]) hipótesis *f inv*

hy•po•thet•i•cal [haɪpəˈθetɪkl] *adj* hipotético
hys•ter•ec•to•my [hɪstəˈrektəmɪ] histerectomía *f*
hys•te•ri•a [hɪˈstɪrɪə] histeria *f*
hys•ter•i•cal [hɪˈsterɪkl] *adj* **1** *person, laugh* histérico; ***become ~*** ponerse histérico **2** F (*very funny*) tronchante F
hys•ter•ics [hɪˈsterɪks] *npl* **1** ataque *m* de histeria **2** (*laughter*) ataque *m* de risa

I

I[1] [aɪ] *pron* yo; ***~ am English / a student*** soy inglés / estudiante; ***you're crazy, ~'m not*** tú estás loco, yo no
I[2] *abbr* (= ***interstate***) interestatal *f*
IATA *abbr* (= ***International Air Transport Association***) IATA *f*
ice [aɪs] *in drink, on road* hielo *m*; ***break the ~*** *fig* romper el hielo; ***be (skating) on thin ~*** *fig* pisar (un) terreno resbaladizo; ***cut no ~ with s.o.*** F no impresionar a alguien; ***your excuses cut no ~ with me*** tus excusas me dejan tal cual; ***put on ~*** *fig* F aplazar, posponer
◆ **ice over** *v/i of river, lake* helarse
◆ **ice up** *v/i of engine, wings* helarse
'Ice Age GEOL edad *f* de hielo, era *f* glaciar; **'ice ax(e)** piqueta *f*; **'ice bag** MED bolsa *f* de hielo; **ice•berg** [ˈaɪsbɜːrg] iceberg *m*; ***the tip of the ~*** *fig* la punta del iceberg; **'ice•bound** *adj* paralizado por el hielo; **'ice•box** nevera *f*, *Rpl* heladera *f*; **'ice•break•er** *ship* rompehielos *m inv*; **'ice buck•et** cubo *m* de hielo; **ice-'cold** *adj* helado, gélido; **'ice cream** helado *m*; ***chocolate ~*** helado de chocolate; **'ice cream par•lor** heladería *f*; **'ice cube** cubito *m* de hielo
iced [aɪst] *adj drink* helado
'ice danc•er patinador(a) *m*(*f*) artístico(-a)
'ice danc•ing baile *m* sobre hielo
iced 'cof•fee café *m* helado
iced 'tea té *m* helado
ice floe [ˈaɪsfloʊ] témpano *m* de hielo
'ice hock•ey hockey *m* sobre hielo
Ice•land [ˈaɪslənd] Islandia *f*
Ice•land•er [ˈaɪsləndər] islandés(-esa) *m*(*f*)
Ice•lan•dic [aɪsˈlændɪk] **I** *adj* islandés **II** *n* islandés *m*
'ice lol•ly *Br* polo *m*; **'ice pack** compresa *f* de hielo; **'ice rink** pista *f* de hielo; **'ice skate** patín *m* de cuchilla; **'ice skat•er** patinador(a) *m*(*f*); **'ice skat•ing** patinaje *m* sobre hielo; **'ice wa•ter** agua *m* con hielo
i•ci•cle [ˈaɪsɪkl] carámbano *m*
i•ci•ly [ˈaɪsɪlɪ] *adv fig* con frialdad
i•ci•ness [ˈaɪsɪnɪs] **1** *of road* lo hielo **2** *fig* frialdad *f*
ic•ing [ˈaɪsɪŋ] *Br* GASTR glaseado *m*; ***~ sugar*** *Br* azúcar *m/f* glasé
i•con [ˈaɪkɑːn] *also* COMPUT icono *m*
ICU [aɪsiːˈjuː] *abbr* (= ***intensive care unit***) UCI *f* (= unidad *f* de cuidados intensivos), UVI *f* (= unidad *f* de vigilancia intensiva)
i•cy [ˈaɪsɪ] *adj road* con hielo; *surface* helado; *welcome* frío
ID [aɪˈdiː] *abbr* (= ***identity***) documentación *f*; ***got any ~ on you?*** ¿lleva algún tipo de documentación?
I'd [aɪd] F ☞ ***I had***; ***I would***
i•de•a [aɪˈdiːə] idea *f*; ***good ~!*** ¡buena idea!; ***I have no ~*** no tengo ni idea; ***it's not a good ~ to ...*** no es buena idea ...; ***put ~s into s.o.'s head*** meter a alguien ideas en la cabeza; ***the ~ is ...*** la idea es ...; ***the ~ never entered my mind*** nunca se me ha pasado esa idea por la cabeza; ***this will give us some ~ of what is needed*** esto nos dará una idea de lo que se necesita; ***it's not my ~ of a good night out*** no es precisamente lo que yo llamaría una noche divertida; ***I have an ~ that*** sospecho que; ***yeah, that's the general ~*** sí, esa es la idea (general); ***ok, I get the general ~*** vale, ya me hago una idea (general)
i•de•al [aɪˈdiːəl] **I** *adj* (*perfect*) ideal **II** *n* ideal *m*
ide•al•ism [aɪˈdɪːəlɪzəm] idealismo *m*
ide•al•ist [aɪˈdiːəlɪst] idealista *m/f*

i•de•al•is•tic [aɪdiːə'lɪstɪk] *adj* idealista
ide•al•ize [aɪ'diːəlaɪz] *v/t* idealizar
i•de•al•ly [aɪ'diːəlɪ] *adv*: **~ *situated*** en una posición ideal; **~, *we would do it like this*** lo ideal sería que lo hiciéramos así
i•den•ti•cal [aɪ'dentɪkl] *adj* idéntico; **~ *twins*** gemelos(-as) *mpl*(*fpl*) idénticos(-as)
i•den•ti•fi•ca•tion [aɪdentɪfɪ'keɪʃn] identificación *f*; *papers etc* documentación *f*; **~ *papers*** documentación *f*, papeles *mpl*; **~ *parade*** LAW *Br* rueda *f* de reconocimiento
i•den•ti•fy [aɪ'dentɪfaɪ] *v/t* (*pret & pp* ***-ied***) identificar; **~ *o.s.*** identificarse
◆ **identify with** *v/i* identificarse con
i•den•ti•ty [aɪ'dentətɪ] identidad *f*; **~ *card*** carné *m* de identidad; ***prove one's*** **~** probar *or* acreditar la identidad
i'den•ti•ty cri•sis crisis *f* de identidad
i•de•o•log•i•cal [aɪdɪə'lɑːdʒɪkl] *adj* ideológico
i•de•ol•o•gy [aɪdɪ'ɑːlədʒɪ] ideología *f*
id•i•o•cy ['ɪdɪəsɪ] idiotez *f*, necedad *f*
id•i•om ['ɪdɪəm] *saying* modismo *m*
id•i•o•mat•ic [ɪdɪə'mætɪk] *adj English, Spanish etc* idiomático
id•i•o•syn•cra•sy [ɪdɪə'sɪŋkrəsɪ] peculiaridad *f*, rareza *f*
id•i•ot ['ɪdɪət] idiota *m/f*, estúpido(-a) *m/f*
id•i•ot•ic [ɪdɪ'ɑːtɪk] *adj* idiota, estúpido
i•dle ['aɪdl] **I** *adj not working* desocupado; (*lazy*) vago; *threat* vano; *machinery* inactivo; ***in an*** **~ *moment*** en un momento libre; **~ *gossip*** cotilleo *m* sin fundamento **II** *v/i of engine* funcionar al ralentí
◆ **idle away** *v/t the time etc* pasar ociosamente
i•dler ['aɪdlər] perezoso(-a) *m*(*f*), vago(-a) *m*(*f*)
i•dly ['aɪdlɪ] *adv*: ***stand*** **~ *by*** quedarse de brazos cruzados
i•dol ['aɪdl] ídolo *m*
i•dol•a•try [aɪd'ɑːlətrɪ] idolatría *f*
i•dol•ize ['aɪdəlaɪz] *v/t* idolatrar
i•dyll ['ɪdɪl] idilio *m*
i•dyl•lic [ɪ'dɪlɪk] *adj* idílico
i.e. [aɪ'iː] *abbr* es decir
if [ɪf] **I** *conj* si; **~ *only I hadn't shouted at her*** ojalá no le hubiera gritado; ***he was asking*** **~ *you could help*** preguntó que si podrías ayudarle; **~ *I were you*** si (yo) fuese tú, yo en tu lugar; ***as*** **~** como si; **~ *so*** en tal caso, si es así; ***see*** **~ *you can do it*** a ver si tú puedes hacerlo **II** *n*: ***no*** **~*s or buts*** no hay peros que valgan; ***if … and it's a big*** **~** si … y recalco esto *or* y lo recalco
if•fy ['ɪfɪ] *adj* F dudoso, incierto
ig•nite [ɪg'naɪt] *v/t* inflamar
ig•ni•tion [ɪg'nɪʃn] *in car* encendido *m*; **~ *key*** llave *f* de contacto
ig•no•min•i•ous [ɪgnə'mɪnɪəs] *adj* ignominioso, denigrante
ig•no•ra•mus [ɪgnə'reɪməs] ignorante *m/f*, inculto(-a) *m*(*f*)
ig•no•rance ['ɪgnərəns] ignorancia *f*; ***out of*** *or* ***through*** **~** por ignorancia, por desconocimiento
ig•no•rant ['ɪgnərənt] *adj* **1** ignorante; ***be*** **~ *of sth*** desconocer *or* ignorar algo **2** (*rude*) maleducado
ig•nore [ɪg'nɔːr] *v/t* ignorar; COMPUT omitir
i•gua•na [ɪ'gwɑːnə] ZO iguana *f*
I'll [aɪl] F ☞ ***I will***
ill [ɪl] **I** *adj* enfermo; ***fall*** **~, *be taken*** **~** caer enfermo, enfermar; ***feel*** **~ *at ease*** no sentirse a gusto, sentirse incómodo **II** *adv* mal; ***speak / think*** **~ *of*** hablar / pensar mal de
ill-ad•vised [ɪləd'vaɪzd] *adj comment* desacertado; *decision, choice* desafortunado; ***it was*** **~ *of her to tell him*** decírselo no fue un acierto
ill-'bred *adj* maleducado
ill-con•ceived [ɪlkən'siːvd] *adj* inadecuado, inoportuno
ill-de•fined [ɪldɪ'faɪnd] *adj* poco definido
ill-dis'posed *adj*: ***be*** **~ *toward*** tener mala disposición *or* actitud hacia
il•le•gal [ɪ'liːgl] *adj* ilegal
il•le•gal•i•ty [ɪlɪ'gælətɪ] ilegalidad *f*
il•le•gi•ble [ɪ'ledʒəbl] *adj* ilegible
il•le•git•i•ma•cy [ɪlɪ'dʒɪtɪməsɪ] ilegitimidad *f*
il•le•git•i•mate [ɪlɪ'dʒɪtɪmət] *adj child* ilegítimo
ill-e•quipped [ɪlɪ'kwɪpt] *adj* mal equipado; *fig* ***be*** **~ *to do sth*** estar mal preparado para hacer algo
ill-'fat•ed *adj* infortunado
il•li•cit [ɪ'lɪsɪt] *adj* ilícito

il•lit•er•a•cy [ɪ'lɪtərəsɪ] analfabetismo *m*
il•lit•er•ate [ɪ'lɪtərət] *adj* analfabeto
ill-judged [ɪl'dʒʌdʒd] mal enjuiciado, mal juzgado
ill-man•nered [ɪl'mænərd] *adj* maleducado
ill-matched [ɪl'mætʃd] *adj* incompatible
ill-na•tured [ɪl'neɪtʃərd] *adj* malhumorado
ill•ness ['ɪlnɪs] enfermedad *f*
il•log•i•cal [ɪ'lɑːdʒɪkl] *adj* ilógico
ill-suit•ed [ɪl'suːtɪd] *adj*: ***be ~ to sth*** no ser indicado para algo; ***be ~ to s.o.*** ser incompatible con alguien
ill-tem•pered [ɪl'tempərd] *adj* malhumorado
ill-timed [ɪl'taɪmd] *adj* inoportuno, improcedente
ill'treat *v/t* maltratar
il•lu•mi•nate [ɪ'luːmɪneɪt] *v/t building etc* iluminar
il•lu•mi•nat•ing [ɪ'luːmɪneɪtɪŋ] *adj remarks etc* iluminador, esclarecedor
il•lu•min•a•tion [ɪluːmɪn'eɪʃn] iluminación *f*
il•lu•sion [ɪ'luːʒn] ilusión *f*; ***be under the ~ that*** hacerse ilusiones de que; ***have no ~s*** no hacerse ilusiones (***about*** sobre)
il•lu•so•ry [ɪ'luːsərɪ] *adj* ilusorio, engañoso; ***~ hopes of peace*** vanas esperanzas *fpl* de paz
il•lus•trate ['ɪləstreɪt] *v/t* ilustrar
il•lus•tra•tion [ɪlə'streɪʃn] ilustración *f*; ***by way of ~*** a modo de ejemplo, a modo ilustrativo
il•lus•tra•tive ['ɪləstrətɪv] *adj* ilustrativo
il•lus•tra•tor [ɪlə'streɪtər] ilustrador(a) *m(f)*
il•lus•tri•ous [ɪ'lʌstrɪəs] *adj* ilustre, glorioso
ill 'will rencor *m*
I'm [aɪm] F ☞ ***I am***
im•age ['ɪmɪdʒ] imagen *f*; ***he's the ~ of his father*** es la viva imagen de su padre
'im•age-con•scious *adj* preocupado por la imagen
i•ma•gi•na•ble [ɪ'mædʒɪnəbl] *adj* imaginable; ***the smallest size ~*** la talla más pequeña que se pueda imaginar
i•ma•gi•na•ry [ɪ'mædʒɪnərɪ] *adj* imaginario
i•ma•gi•na•tion [ɪmædʒɪ'neɪʃn] imaginación *f*; ***it's all in your ~*** son (todo) imaginaciones tuyas
i•ma•gi•na•tive [ɪ'mædʒɪnətɪv] *adj* imaginativo
i•ma•gine [ɪ'mædʒɪn] *v/t* imaginar, imaginarse; ***I can just ~ it*** me lo imagino, me lo puedo imaginar; ***you're imagining things*** son imaginaciones tuyas; ***I ~ him as a tall man*** me lo imagino un hombre alto; ***don't ~ that …*** no te vayas a pensar que …, no te creas que … **II** *v/i*: ***I ~ so*** eso creo, creo que sí
im•bal•ance [ɪm'bæləns] desproporción *f*
im•be•cile ['ɪmbəsiːl] imbécil *m/f*
im•bue [ɪm'bjuː] *v/t fig*: ***~ s.o. with sth*** imbuir a alguien de algo
IMF [aɪem'ef] *abbr* (= ***International Monetary Fund***) FMI *m* (= Fondo *m* Monetario Internacional)
im•i•tate ['ɪmɪteɪt] *v/t* imitar
im•i•ta•tion [ɪmɪ'teɪʃn] **I** *n* imitación *f*; ***learn by ~*** aprender imitando **II** *adj* de imitación
im•i•ta•tor ['ɪmɪteɪtər] imitador(a) *m(f)*
im•mac•u•late [ɪ'mækjʊlət] *adj* inmaculado
im•ma•te•ri•al [ɪmə'tɪrɪəl] *adj (not relevant)* irrelevante
im•ma•ture [ɪmə'tʃʊər] *adj* inmaduro
im•ma•tu•ri•ty [ɪmə'tʃʊərətɪ] inmadurez *f*
im•meas•ur•a•ble [ɪ'meʒərəbl] *adj* inconmesurable, incalculable
im•me•di•ate [ɪ'miːdɪət] *adj* inmediato; ***the ~ family*** los familiares más cercanos; ***in the ~ neighborhood*** en las inmediaciones; ***in the ~ future*** en el futuro inmediato
im•me•di•ate•ly [ɪ'miːdɪətlɪ] **I** *adv* inmediatamente; ***~ after the bank / church*** justo después del banco / la iglesia **II** *conj*: ***~ you said that …*** justo cuando dijiste que …
im•me•mo•ri•al [ɪmə'mɔːrɪəl] *adj*: ***since time ~*** desde tiempos inmemoriables *or* remotos
im•mense [ɪ'mens] *adj* inmenso
im•men•si•ty [ɪ'mensɪtɪ] inmensidad *f*, magnitud *f*
im•merse [ɪ'mɜːrs] *v/t* sumergir; ***~ o.s. in*** sumergirse en; ***~d in thought*** inmerso *or* sumido en sus / mis *etc* pensamientos

im•mer•sion [ɪ'mɜːrʃn] *in liquid, culture* inmersión *f*; **~ course** curso *m* de inmersión
im'mer•sion heat•er calentador *m* de agua eléctrico
im•mi•grant ['ɪmɪgrənt] inmigrante *m/f*
im•mi•grate ['ɪmɪgreɪt] *v/i* inmigrar
im•mi•gra•tion [ɪmɪ'greɪʃn] inmigración *f*; ***Immigration*** *government department* (Departamento *m* de) Inmigración *f*; **~ *officer*** oficial *m/f or* agente *m/f* de inmigración
im•mi•nent ['ɪmɪnənt] *adj* inminente
im•mo•bile [ɪ'moʊbaɪl] *adj* inmóvil
im•mo•bil•i•ty [ɪmə'bɪlətɪ] inmovilidad *f*
im•mo•bi•lize [ɪ'moʊbɪlaɪz] *v/t factory* paralizar; *person*, *car* inmovilizar
im•mo•bi•liz•er [ɪ'moʊbɪlaɪzər] *on car* inmovilizador *m*
im•mod•e•rate [ɪ'mɑːdərət] *adj* desmedido, exagerado
im•mod•est [ɪ'mɑːdɪst] *adj* inmodesto, presuntuoso
im•mor•al [ɪ'mɔːrəl] *adj* inmoral
im•mor•al•i•ty [ɪmɔː'rælɪtɪ] inmoralidad *f*
im•mor•tal [ɪ'mɔːrtl] *adj* inmortal
im•mor•tal•i•ty [ɪmɔːr'tælɪtɪ] inmortalidad *f*
im•mor•tal•ize [ɪ'mɔːrtəlaɪz] *v/t* inmortalizar
im•mov•a•ble [ɪ'muːvəbl] *adj opposition* inamovible
im•mune [ɪ'mjuːn] *adj to illness, infection* inmune; *from ruling, requirement* con inmunidad
im'mune sys•tem MED sistema *m* inmunológico
im•mu•ni•ty [ɪ'mjuːnətɪ] inmunidad *f*
im•mu•nize ['ɪmjʊnaɪz] *v/t* inmunizar
im•mu•no•de•fi•cien•cy [ɪmjuːnoʊdɪ'fɪʃənsɪ] immunodeficiencia *f*
im•mu•nol•o•gist [ɪmjʊ'nɑːlədʒɪst] inmunólogo(-a) *m(f)*
im•mu•nol•o•gy [ɪmjʊ'nɑːlədʒɪ] inmunología *f*
imp [ɪmp] *also fig* diablillo *m*
im•pact ['ɪmpækt] impacto *m*; ***the warning had no ~ on him*** el aviso no le hizo cambiar lo más mínimo
◆ **impact on** *v/t* impactar en
im•pair [ɪm'per] *v/t* dañar
im•paired [ɪm'perd] *adj*: ***with ~ hearing / sight*** con problemas auditivos / visuales
im•pale [ɪm'peɪl] *v/t* atravesar (***on*** con)
im•part [ɪm'pɑːrt] *v/t* transmitir (***to*** a)
im•par•tial [ɪm'pɑːrʃl] *adj* imparcial
im•par•ti•al•i•ty [ɪmpɑːrʃɪ'ælətɪ] imparcialidad *f*
im•pass•a•ble [ɪm'pæsəbl] *adj road* intransitable
im•passe ['ɪmpæs] *in negotations etc* punto *m* muerto
im•pas•sioned [ɪm'pæʃnd] *adj speech, plea* apasionado
im•pas•sive [ɪm'pæsɪv] *adj* impasible
im•pa•tience [ɪm'peɪʃəns] impaciencia *f*
im•pa•tient [ɪm'peɪʃənt] *adj* impaciente; ***be ~ to do sth*** estar impaciente por hacer algo
im•pa•tient•ly [ɪm'peɪʃəntlɪ] *adv* impacientemente
im•peach [ɪm'piːʧ] *v/t President* iniciar un proceso de destitución contra
im•peach•ment [ɪm'piːʧmənt] proceso *m* de destitución
im•pec•ca•ble [ɪm'pekəbl] *adj* impecable
im•pec•ca•bly [ɪm'pekəblɪ] *adv* impecablemente
im•pede [ɪm'piːd] *v/t* dificultar
im•ped•i•ment [ɪm'pedɪmənt] *in speech* defecto *m* del habla
im•pel [ɪm'pel] *v/t* (*prep & pp* ***-led***) impeler; **~ *s.o. to do sth*** arrastrar *or* empujar a alguien a hacer algo
im•pend•ing [ɪm'pendɪŋ] *adj* inminente
im•pen•e•tra•ble [ɪm'penɪtrəbl] *adj* impenetrable
im•per•a•tive [ɪm'perətɪv] **I** *adj* imprescindible **II** *n* GRAM imperativo *m*
im•per•cep•ti•ble [ɪmpɜːr'septɪbl] *adj* imperceptible
im•per•fect [ɪm'pɜːrfekt] **I** *adj* imperfecto **II** *n* GRAM imperfecto *m*
im•per•fec•tion [ɪmpər'fekʃn] imperfección *f*
im•pe•ri•al [ɪm'pɪrɪəl] *adj* imperial
im•pe•ri•al•ism [ɪm'pɪrɪəlɪzəm] POL imperialismo *m*
im•pe•ri•al•ist [ɪm'pɪrɪəlɪst] **I** *n* imperialista *m/f* **II** *adj* imperialista
im•per•il [ɪm'perəl] *v/t* (*prep & pp* ***-led***) hacer peligrar, poner en peligro
im•pe•ri•ous [ɪm'pɪrɪəs] *adj* imperioso

im•per•ma•nent [ɪm'pɜːrmənənt] *adj* transitorio, pasajero
im•per•me•a•ble [ɪm'pɜːrmjəbl] *adj* impermeable, aislante
im•per•son•al [ɪm'pɜːrsənl] *adj* impersonal
im•per•son•ate [ɪm'pɜːrsəneɪt] *v/t as a joke* imitar; *illegally* hacerse pasar por
im•per•son•a•tion [ɪmpɜːrsən'eɪʃn] *as a joke* imitación *f*
im•per•son•a•tor [ɪm'pɜːrsəneɪtər] imitador(a) *m(f)*
im•per•ti•nence [ɪm'pɜːrtɪnəns] impertinencia *f*
im•per•ti•nent [ɪm'pɜːrtɪnənt] *adj* impertinente
im•per•tur•ba•ble [ɪmpər'tɜːrbəbl] *adj* imperturbable
im•per•vi•ous [ɪm'pɜːrvɪəs] *adj*: ***~ to*** inmune a
im•pe•tu•ous [ɪm'petʃʊəs] *adj* impetuoso
im•pe•tus ['ɪmpɪtəs] *of campaign etc* ímpetu *m*; ***give ~ to*** dar ímpetu a
im•pinge [ɪm'pɪndʒ] *v/i*: ***~ on s.o.'s freedoms / rights*** vulnerar las libertades / derechos de alguien
imp•ish ['ɪmpɪʃ] *adj* cuco, pillo
im•pla•ca•ble [ɪm'plækəbl] *adj* implacable
im•plant I *v/t* [ɪm'plænt] **1** MED implantar (***in, into*** en) **2** *fig* implantar, establecer (***in, into*** en) **II** *n* ['ɪmplænt] MED implante *m*
im•plau•si•ble [ɪm'plɔːzəbl] *adj* inverosímil, insólito
im•ple•ment I *n* ['ɪmplɪmənt] utensilio *m* **II** *v/t* ['ɪmplɪment] *measures etc* poner en práctica
im•ple•men•ta•tion [ɪmplɪmen'teɪʃn] implementación *f*, puesta *f* en práctica
im•pli•cate ['ɪmplɪkeɪt] *v/t* implicar; ***~ s.o. in sth*** implicar a alguien en algo
im•pli•ca•tion [ɪmplɪ'keɪʃn] consecuencia *f*; ***the ~ is that ...*** implica que ...; ***what are the ~s of this for our school?*** ¿qué supone esto para nuestra escuela?
im•plic•it [ɪm'plɪsɪt] *adj* implícito; *trust* inquebrantable
im•plic•it•ly [ɪm'plɪsɪtlɪ] *adv* **1** *by implication* implícitamente **2**: ***trust s.o. ~*** confiar incondicionalmente *or* plenamente en alguien

im•plied [ɪm'plaɪd] *adj* insinuado, aludido
im•plode [ɪm'ploʊd] *v/i* PHYS implosionar
im•plore [ɪm'plɔːr] *v/t* implorar; ***~ s.o. not to do sth*** implorar a alguien que no haga algo
im•ply [ɪm'plaɪ] *v/t* (*pret & pp **-ied***) implicar; ***are you ~ing I lied?*** ¿insinúas que mentí?
im•po•lite [ɪmpə'laɪt] *adj* maleducado
im•pon•der•a•ble [ɪm'pɑːndərəbl] *adj* imponderable, inestimable
im•port ['ɪmpɔːrt] **I** *n* importación *f*; ***~ trade*** comercio *m* de importación **II** *v/t* importar
im•por•tance [ɪm'pɔːrtəns] importancia *f*; ***attach ~ to*** darle importancia a; ***be of no ~*** no ser importante (***to*** para), no tener importancia (***to*** para); ***a matter of some ~*** una cuestión de cierta importancia
im•por•tant [ɪm'pɔːrtənt] *adj* importante
im•por•tant•ly [ɪm'pɔːrtəntlɪ] *adv*: ***more ~, ...*** y lo que es (aún) más importante, ...
'im•port du•ty derechos *mpl* de importación
im•por•ter [ɪm'pɔːrtər] importador(a) *m(f)*
im•port-'ex•port importación-exportación *f*
'im•port quo•tas *npl* cuotas *fpl* de importación
'im•port re•stric•tions *npl* restricciones *fpl* a la importación
im•por•tune [ɪmpɔːr'tjuːn] *v/t* importunar, molestar
im•pose [ɪm'poʊz] **I** *v/t tax* imponer; ***~ o.s. on s.o.*** molestar a alguien; ***~ one's will on s.o.*** imponer la voluntad sobre alguien **II** *v/i*: ***~ on s.o.*** abusar de alguien
im•pos•ing [ɪm'poʊzɪŋ] *adj* imponente
im•po•si•tion [ɪmpə'zɪʃn] *of punishment, taxes* imposición *f*
im•pos•si•bil•i•ty [ɪmpɑːsɪ'bɪlɪtɪ] imposibilidad *f*
im•pos•si•ble [ɪm'pɑːsɪbəl] *adj* imposible; ***it is ~ for me to come*** me es imposible venir
im•pos•si•bly [ɪm'pɑːsɪblɪ] *adv expensive, beautiful* increíblemente

I

im•pos•tor [ɪm'pɑːstər] impostor(a) *m(f)*
im•po•tence ['ɪmpətəns] impotencia *f*
im•po•tent ['ɪmpətənt] *adj* impotente
im•pov•e•rished [ɪm'pɑːvərɪʃt] *adj* empobrecido
im•prac•ti•ca•ble [ɪm'præktɪkəbl] *adj* impracticable, irrealizable
im•prac•ti•cal [ɪm'præktɪkəl] *adj* poco práctico
im•preg•nate ['ɪmpregneɪt] *v/t* **1** BIO impregnar **2** *with liquid* impregnar, empapar
im•pre•sa•ri•o [ɪmprə'sɑːrɪoʊ] empresario(-a) *m(f)* teatral
im•press [ɪm'pres] *v/t* impresionar; ***be ~ed by s.o. / sth*** quedar impresionado por alguien / algo; ***I'm not ~ed*** no me parece nada bien; ***she ~ed me as being quite serious*** me dio la impresión de que es bastante seria
im•pres•sion [ɪm'preʃn] **1** impresión *f*; ***make a good / bad ~ on s.o.*** causar a alguien buena / mala impresión; ***I get the ~ that*** me da la impresión de que; ***give s.o. the wrong ~*** dar a alguien una impresión equivocada; ***be under the ~ that*** tener la impresión de que **2** (*impersonation*) imitación *f*
im•pres•sion•a•ble [ɪm'preʃənəbl] *adj* influenciable
im•pres•sion•ism [ɪm'preʃənɪzəm] impresionismo *m*
im•pres•sion•ist [ɪm'preʃənɪst] **I** *n* **1** *artist* impresionista *m/f* **2** *comedian* imitador(a) *m(f)* **II** *adj* impresionista
im•pres•sion•is•tic [ɪmpreʃə'nɪstɪk] *adj* impresionista
im•pres•sive [ɪm'presɪv] *adj* impresionante
im•print I *n* ['ɪmprɪnt] *of credit card* impresión *f* **II** *v/t* [ɪm'prɪnt] imprimir, estampar (***on*** en); ***it was ~ed in my memory*** se me quedó grabado en la memoria
im•pris•on [ɪm'prɪzn] *v/t* encarcelar
im•pris•on•ment [ɪm'prɪznmənt] encarcelamiento *m*
im•prob•a•bil•i•ty [ɪmprɑːbə'bɪlətɪ] improbabilidad *f*
im•prob•a•ble [ɪm'prɑːbəbəl] *adj* improbable
im•promp•tu [ɪm'prɑːmptjuː] *adj* improvisado
im•prop•er [ɪm'prɑːpər] *adj behavior* incorrecto
im•pro•pri•e•ty [ɪmprə'praɪətɪ] impropiedad *f*
im•prove [ɪm'pruːv] *v/t & v/i* mejorar; ***he*** *or* ***his health is improving*** está mejorando, su salud mejora
◆ **improve on** *v/t marks, score* mejorar
im•prove•ment [ɪm'pruːvmənt] mejora *f*, mejoría *f*; ***there has been a slight ~ in his work / health*** su trabajo / salud ha mejorado ligeramente; ***that's an ~ on what you did last time!*** ¡has mejorado desde la última vez que lo hiciste!
im•prov•i•sa•tion [ɪmprəvaɪ'zeɪʃn] improvisación *f*
im•pro•vise ['ɪmprəvaɪz] *v/i* improvisar
im•pru•dence [ɪm'pruːdəns] imprudencia *f*
im•pru•dent [ɪm'pruːdənt] *adj* imprudente
im•pu•dence ['ɪmpjʊdəns] insolencia *f*, desfachatez *f*
im•pu•dent ['ɪmpjʊdənt] *adj* insolente, desvergonzado
im•pulse ['ɪmpʌls] impulso *m*; ***do sth on (an) ~*** hacer algo impulsivamente
'im•pulse buy compra *f* impulsiva
im•pul•sive [ɪm'pʌlsɪv] *adj* impulsivo
im•pu•ni•ty [ɪm'pjuːnətɪ] impunidad *f*; ***with ~*** impunemente
im•pure [ɪm'pjʊr] *adj* impuro
im•pu•ri•ty [ɪm'pjʊrətɪ] impureza *f*
im•pute [ɪm'pjuːt] *v/t*: ***~ sth to s.o.*** imputar algo a alguien
in [ɪn] **I** *prep* **1** *place* en; ***~ Washington*** en Washington; ***~ the street*** en la calle; ***put it ~ your pocket*** mételo en el bolsillo; ***wounded ~ the leg / arm*** herido en la pierna / el brazo ***~ his novel*** en su novela; ***~ Faulkner*** en Faulkner
2 *time* en; ***~ 1999*** en 1999; ***~ two hours*** *from now* dentro de dos horas; ***~ the morning*** por la mañana; ***~ the summer*** en verano; ***~ August*** en agosto
3 *manner* en; ***~ English / Spanish*** en inglés / español; ***~ a loud voice*** en voz alta; ***~ his style*** en su estilo; ***~ yellow*** de amarillo
4: ***~ crossing the road*** (*while*) al cruzar la calle; ***~ agreeing to this*** (*by virtue of*) al expresar acuerdo con esto
5: ***three ~ all*** tres en total; ***one ~ ten*** uno de cada diez

II *adv* **1**: ***is he ~?*** *at home* ¿está en casa?; ***is the express ~ yet?*** ¿ha llegado ya el expreso?; ***when the diskette is ~*** cuando el disquete está dentro; ***~ here*** aquí dentro **2**: ***she was ~ for a surprise / disappointment*** se iba a llevar una sorpresa / decepción **3**: ***be ~ on a plan / a joke*** tomar parte *or* participar en un plan / una broma

III *adj* (*fashionable*, *popular*) de moda; ***the ~ crowd*** el grupo de moda

IV *n*: ***know the ~s and outs of*** conocer los intríngulis de

in•a•bil•i•ty [ɪnə'bɪlɪtɪ] incapacidad *f*

in•ac•ces•si•ble [ɪnək'sesɪbl] *adj* inaccesible

in•ac•cu•ra•cy [ɪn'ækjʊrəsɪ] imprecisión *f*

in•ac•cu•rate [ɪn'ækjʊrət] *adj* inexacto

in•ac•tion [ɪn'ækʃn] inacción *f*, inactividad *f*

in•ac•tive [ɪn'æktɪv] *adj* inactivo

in•ac•tiv•i•ty [ɪnæk'tɪvɪtɪ] inactividad *f*

in•ad•e•quate [ɪn'ædɪkwət] *adj* insuficiente, inadecuado

in•ad•mis•si•ble [ɪnəd'mɪsəbl] *adj* inadmisible

in•ad•vert•ent [ɪnəd'vɜːrtənt] *adj* involuntario, inconsciente

in•ad•vert•ent•ly [ɪnəd'vɜːrtəntlɪ] *adv* inconscientemente

in•ad•vis•a•ble [ɪnəd'vaɪzəbl] *adj* poco aconsejable

in•al•ien•a•ble [ɪn'eɪljənəbl] *adj* inalienable, inajenable

in•ane [ɪ'neɪn] *adj* tonto, estúpido

in•an•i•mate [ɪn'ænɪmət] *adj* inanimado

in•ap•pli•ca•ble [ɪnə'plɪkəbl] *adj* inaplicable

in•ap•pro•pri•ate [ɪnə'proupriət] *adj* *remark*, *thing to do* inadecuado, improcedente; *choice* inapropiado

in•ar•tic•u•late [ɪnɑːr'tɪkjʊlət] *adj*: ***be ~*** expresarse mal

in•as•much as [ɪnəz'mʌtʃæz] *conj* puesto que, ya que

in•at•ten•tion [ɪnə'tenʃn] desatención *f*, falta *f* de atención

in•at•ten•tive [ɪnə'tentɪv] *adj* desatento, distraído

in•au•di•ble [ɪn'ɒːdəbl] *adj* inaudible

in•au•gu•ral [ɪ'nɒːgjʊrəl] *adj* *speech* inaugural

in•au•gu•rate [ɪ'nɒːgjʊreɪt] *v/t* inaugurar

in•au•gu•ra•tion [ɪnɒːgjʊ'reɪʃn] inauguración *f*

In•au•gu'ra•tion Day POL *día en que el presidente de los Estados Unidos toma posesión del cargo*

in•aus•pi•cious [ɪnɒː'spɪʃəs] *adj* poco prometedor, desfavorable

in•board 'mo•tor motor *m* de a bordo

'in•born *adj* innato

in'bred *adj* **1** *innate* innato **2** BIO endogámico

'in•breed•ing endogamia *f*

inc. *abbr* (= ***incorporated***) S.A. (= sociedad *f* anónima)

In•ca ['ɪŋkə] inca *m/f*

In•can ['ɪŋkən] **I** *adj* inca, incaico **II** *n* inca, incaico(-a) *m(f)*

in•cal•cu•la•ble [ɪn'kælkjʊləbl] *adj* *damage* incalculable

in•ca•pa•bil•i•ty [ɪnkeɪpə'bɪlətɪ] incapacidad *f*

in•ca•pa•ble [ɪn'keɪpəbl]] *adj* incapaz; ***be ~ of doing sth*** ser incapaz de hacer algo

in•ca•pac•i•tate [ɪnkə'pæsɪteɪt] *v/t* incapacitar, inhabilitar

in•ca•pac•i•ty [ɪnkə'pæsətɪ] incapacidad *f*

in•car•cer•ate [ɪn'kɑːrsəreɪt] *v/t* encarcelar

in•car•cer•a•tion [ɪnkɑːrsə'reɪʃn] encarcelación *f*

in•car•nate [ɪn'kɑːrnət] *adj* en persona, personificado

in•car•na•tion [ɪnkɑːr'neɪʃn] encarnación *f*

in•cen•di•ar•y [ɪn'sendɪərɪ] *adj* incendiario

in'cen•di•a•ry de•vice artefacto *m* incendiario

in•cense[1] ['ɪnsens] *n* incienso *m*

in•cense[2] [ɪn'sens] *v/t* encolerizar

in•cen•tive [ɪn'sentɪv] incentivo *m*

in'cen•tive scheme plan *m* de incentivos

in'cen•tive trav•el viajes *mpl* como incentivo

in•ces•sant [ɪn'sesnt] *adj* incesante

in•ces•sant•ly [ɪn'sesntlɪ] *adv* incesantemente

in•cest ['ɪnsest] incesto *m*

in•ces•tu•ous [ɪn'sestjʊəs] *adj* incestuoso

inch [ɪntʃ] **I** *n* pulgada *f*; **~ by ~** poco a poco; ***every ~*** *fig* de pies a cabeza, de arriba abajo; ***come within an ~ of doing sth*** estar a punto de hacer algo **II** *v/i*: **~ *forward*** avanzar poco a poco

in•ci•dence ['ɪnsɪdəns] **1** (*rate*) índice *m*; ***the high ~ of …*** el alto índice de … **2** PHYS incidencia *f*

in•ci•dent ['ɪnsɪdənt] incidente *m*

in•ci•den•tal [ɪnsɪ'dentl] **I** *adj* secundario; **~ *costs*** gastos *mpl* imprevistos **~ *expenses*** gastos *mpl* varios **II** *npl*: **~*s*** gastos *mpl* imprevistos

in•ci•den•tal•ly [ɪnsɪ'dentlɪ] *adv* a propósito

in•ci'den•tal mu•sic música *f* de acompañamiento

in•cin•er•ate [ɪn'sɪnəreɪt] *v/t* incinerar

in•cin•e•ra•tor [ɪn'sɪnəreɪtər] incinerador *m*

in•ci•sion [ɪn'sɪʒn] incisión *f*

in•ci•sive [ɪn'saɪsɪv] *adj* incisivo

in•ci•sor [ɪn'saɪzər] ANAT incisivo *m*

in•cite [ɪn'saɪt] *v/t* incitar; **~ *s.o. to do sth*** incitar a alguien a que haga algo

in•cite•ment [ɪn'saɪtmənt] LAW incitación *f*, instigación *f* (***to*** a)

in•clem•ent [ɪn'klemənt] *adj* inclemente

in•cli•na•tion [ɪnklɪ'neɪʃn] (*tendency, liking*) inclinación *f*; ***I have no ~ to sympathize*** no tiendo a compadecerme; ***he's always had an ~ to be lazy*** siempre ha tendido a ser vago

in•cline [ɪn'klaɪn] *v/t*: ***be ~d to do sth*** tender a hacer algo

in•close, in•clos•ure ☞ ***enclose, enclosure***

in•clude [ɪn'klu:d] *v/t* incluir; ***service ~d*** servicio incluido

in•clud•ing [ɪn'klu:dɪŋ] *prep* incluyendo; ***not ~ me*** sin incluirme a mí

in•clu•sion [ɪn'klu:ʒn] inclusión *f*, incorporación *f*

in•clu•sive [ɪn'klu:sɪv] **I** *adj price* total, global **II** *prep*: **~ *of*** incluyendo, incluido; ***be ~ of sth*** incluir algo **III** *adv*: ***from Monday to Thursday ~*** de lunes al jueves, ambos inclusive; ***it costs $1000 ~*** cuesta 1.000 dólares todo incluido

in•cog•ni•to [ɪnkɑ:g'ni:toʊ] *adv* de incógnito

in•co•her•ence [ɪnkoʊ'hɪərəns] incoherencia *f*

in•co•her•ent [ɪnkoʊ'hɪərənt] *adj* incoherente

in•come ['ɪnkəm] ingresos *mpl*

'in•come brack•et, 'in•come group grupo *m* económico; **in•come sup•'port** *Br* subsidio *m*; ***be on ~*** recibir subsidio; **'in•come tax** impuesto *m* sobre la renta; **'in•come tax re•turn** declaración *f* de la renta

'in•com•ing *adj tide* que sube; **~ *flight*** vuelo *m* que llega; **~ *mail*** correo *m* recibido; **~ *calls*** llamadas *fpl* recibidas

in•com•mu•ni•ca•do [ɪnkəmju:nɪ'kɑ:doʊ] *adj*: ***be ~*** F estar incomunicado *or* confinado

in•com•pa•ra•ble [ɪn'kɑ:mpərəbl] *adj* incomparable

in•com•pat•i•bil•i•ty [ɪnkəmpætɪ'bɪlɪtɪ] incompatibilidad *f*

in•com•pat•i•ble [ɪnkəm'pætɪbl] *adj* incompatible

in•com•pe•tence [ɪn'kɑ:mpɪtəns] incompetencia *f*

in•com•pe•tent [ɪn'kɑ:mpɪtənt] *adj* incompetente

in•com•plete [ɪnkəm'pli:t] *adj* incompleto

in•com•pre•hen•si•ble [ɪnkɑ:mprɪ'hensɪbl] *adj* incomprensible

in•com•pre•hen•si•bly [ɪnkɑ:mprɪ'hensɪblɪ] *adv* incomprensiblemente, de manera incomprensible

in•com•pre•hen•sion [ɪnkɑ:mprɪ'henʃn] incomprensión *f*

in•con•cei•va•ble [ɪnkən'si:vəbl] *adj* inconcebible; ***it is ~ to me that*** para mí es inconcebible que

in•con•clu•sive [ɪnkən'klu:sɪv] *adj* no concluyente

in•con•gru•i•ty [ɪnkɑ:ŋ'gru:ətɪ] incongruencia *f*

in•con•gru•ous [ɪn'kɑ:ŋgruəs] *adj* incongruente

in•con•se•quen•tial [ɪnkɑ:nsɪ'kwənʃəl] *adj* intrascendente, insubstancial

in•con•sid•er•a•ble [ɪnkən'sɪdərəbl] *adj*: ***a not ~ amount*** una cantidad nada despreciable

in•con•sid•er•ate [ɪnkən'sɪdərət] *adj* desconsiderado

in•con•sis•ten•cy [ɪnkən'sɪstənsɪ] inconsistencia *f*

in•con•sis•tent [ɪnkən'sɪstənt] *adj ar-*

gument, behavior incoherente, inconsecuente; *player* irregular; ***be ~ with sth*** no ser consecuente con algo
in•con•so•la•ble [ɪnkən'souləbl] *adj* inconsolable, desconsolado
in•con•spic•u•ous [ɪnkən'spɪkjuəs] *adj* discreto
in•con•test•a•ble [ɪnkən'testəbl] *adj* irrebatible, indiscutible
in•con•ti•nence [ɪn'kɑːntɪnəns] MED incontinencia *f*
in•con•ti•nent [ɪn'kɑːntɪnənt] *adj* MED incontinente
in•con•tro•vert•i•ble [ɪnkɑːntrə'vɜːrtəbl] *adj* irrebatible, innegable
in•con•ve•ni•ence [ɪnkən'viːnɪəns] inconveniencia *f*; ***put s.o. to ~, be an ~ to s.o.*** causar molestias a alguien
in•con•ve•ni•ent [ɪnkən'viːnɪənt] *adj* inconveniente, inoportuno; ***at an ~ time*** en un momento inoportuno
in•con•ve•ni•ent•ly [ɪnkən'viːnɪəntlɪ] *adv*: ***~ located*** mal situado
in•cor•po•rate [ɪn'kɔːrpəreɪt] *v/t* incorporar
in•cor•po•rat•ed [ɪn'kɔːrpəreɪtɪd] *adj* COM: ***ABC Incorporated*** ABC, sociedad *f* anónima; ***~ company*** sociedad *f* anónima
in•cor•por•a•tion [ɪnkɔːrpər'eɪʃn] **1** incorporación *f* **2** COM constitución *f* en sociedad
in•cor•rect [ɪnkə'rekt] *adj* incorrecto
in•cor•rect•ly [ɪnkə'rektlɪ] *adv* incorrectamente
in•cor•ri•gi•ble [ɪn'kɑːrɪdʒəbl] *adj* incorregible
in•cor•rupt•i•ble [ɪnkə'rʌptəbl] *adj* incorruptible
in•crease I *v/t & v/i* [ɪn'kriːs] aumentar (***in*** de) **II** *n* ['ɪnkriːs] aumento *m* (***in*** de); ***be on the ~*** estar *or* ir en aumento
in•creas•ing [ɪn'kriːsɪŋ] *adj* creciente
in•creas•ing•ly [ɪn'kriːsɪŋlɪ] *adv* cada vez más; ***we're getting ~ concerned*** cada vez estamos más preocupados
in•cred•i•ble [ɪn'kredɪbl] *adj (amazing, very good)* increíble
in•cred•u•lous [ɪn'kredjuləs] *adj* incrédulo
in•cre•ment ['ɪnkrɪmənt] COM incremento *m*
in•crim•i•nate [ɪn'krɪmɪneɪt] *v/t* incriminar; ***~ o.s.*** incriminarse
in•crim•i•nat•ing *adj* [ɪn'krɪmɪneɪtɪŋ] incriminatorio
in•cu•bate ['ɪŋkjubeɪt] *v/t* incubar
in•cu•ba•tion [ɪŋkjʊ'beɪʃn] incubación *f*
in•cu'ba•tion pe•ri•od periodo *m* de incubación
in•cu•ba•tor ['ɪŋkjubeɪtər] incubadora *f*
in•cur [ɪn'kɜːr] *v/t (pret & pp* ***-red****) costs* incurrir en; *debts* contraer; *s.o's anger* provocar; *losses* sufrir
in•cu•ra•ble [ɪn'kjurəbl] *adj* incurable
in•cur•sion [ɪn'kɜːrʒn] incursión *f* (***into*** en)
in•debt•ed [ɪn'detɪd] *adj*: ***be ~ to s.o.*** estar en deuda con alguien
in•de•cen•cy [ɪn'diːsnsɪ] indecencia *f*; LAW atentado *m* contra la moral pública
in•de•cent [ɪn'diːsnt] *adj* indecente; ***~ exposure*** exhibicionismo *m*
in•de•ci•pher•a•ble [ɪndɪ'saɪfərəbl] *adj* indescifrable
in•de•ci•sion [ɪndɪ'sɪʒn] indecisión *f*
in•de•ci•sive [ɪndɪ'saɪsɪv] *adj* indeciso
in•de•ci•sive•ness [ɪndɪ'saɪsɪvnɪs] indecisión *f*
in•dec•o•rous [ɪn'dekərəs] *adj* indecoroso
in•deed [ɪn'diːd] *adv (in fact)* ciertamente, efectivamente; *yes, agreeing* ciertamente, en efecto; ***very much ~*** muchísimo; ***thank you very much ~*** muchísimas gracias; ***did you ~?*** ¿de veras?, ¿en serio?
in•de•fat•i•ga•ble [ɪndɪ'fætɪgəbl] *adj* infatigable, incansable
in•de•fen•si•ble [ɪndɪ'fensəbl] *adj* inexcusable, injustificable
in•de•fi•na•ble [ɪndɪ'faɪnəbl] *adj* indefinible
in•def•i•nite [ɪn'defɪnɪt] *adj* indefinido; ***~ article*** GRAM artículo *m* indefinido; ***~ pronoun*** GRAM pronombre *m* indefinido
in•def•i•nite•ly [ɪn'defɪnɪtlɪ] *adv* indefinidamente
in•del•i•ble [ɪn'deləbl] *adj also fig* imborrable, indeleble
in•del•i•cate [ɪn'delɪkət] *adj* poco delicado, desaprensivo
in•dem•ni•fy [ɪn'demnɪfaɪ] *v/t (pret & pp* ***-ied****)* **1** *(reimburse)* indemnizar, compensar (***for*** por) **2** *insure* asegurar

(***from, against*** contra)
in•dem•ni•ty [ɪn'demnɪtɪ] indemnidad *f*
in•dent I *n* ['ɪndent] *in text* sangrado *m* **II** *v/t* [ɪn'dent] *line* sangrar
in•den•ta•tion [ɪnden'teɪʃn] incisión *f*, hendidura *f*
in•de•pen•dence [ɪndɪ'pendəns] independencia *f*
In•de'pen•dence Day Día *m* de la Independencia
in•de•pen•dent [ɪndɪ'pendənt] *adj* independiente
in•de•pen•dent•ly [ɪndɪ'pendəntlɪ] *adv* *deal with* por separado; **~ *of*** al margen de
in-'depth *adj* en profundidad, a fondo
in•de•scri•ba•ble [ɪndɪ'skraɪbəbl] *adj* indescriptible
in•de•scrib•a•bly [ɪndɪ'skraɪbəblɪ] *adv* indescriptiblemente
in•de•struc•ti•ble [ɪndɪ'strʌktəbl] *adj* indestructible
in•de•ter•mi•nate [ɪndɪ'tɜːrmɪnət] *adj* indeterminado
in•dex ['ɪndeks] (*pl* ***indices*** ['ɪndɪsiːz]) *for book* índice *m*
'in•dex card ficha *f*; **'in•dex fin•ger** (dedo *m*) índice *m*; **in•dex-linked** [ɪndeks'lɪŋkt] *adj Br* indexado; **in•dex--link•ing** [ɪndeks'lɪŋkɪŋ] *Br* indexación *f*
In•di•a ['ɪndɪə] (la) India
In•di•an ['ɪndɪən] **I** *adj* indio **II** *n* **1** *from India* indio(-a) *m(f)*, hindú *m/f* **2** *American* indio(-a) *m(f)*
In•di•an 'corn maíz *m*; **In•di•an 'O•cean** (océano *m*) índico *m*; **In•di•an 'sum•mer** *in northern hemisphere* veranillo *m* de San Martín; *in southern hemisphere* veranillo *m* de San Juan
in•di•cate ['ɪndɪkeɪt] **I** *v/t* indicar; ***this does seem to ~ that*** esto parece indicar que; ***I think a meeting is ~d*** creo que es recomendable celebrar una reunión **II** *v/i when driving* poner el intermitente
in•di•ca•tion [ɪndɪ'keɪʃn] indicio *m*; ***there is every ~ that*** todo indica que, todos los indicios apuntan a que
in•dic•a•tive [ɪn'dɪkətɪv] **I** *adj* **1** LING indicativo **2**: ***be ~ of*** ser indicativo de **II** *n* LING indicativo *m*
in•di•ca•tor ['ɪndɪkeɪtər] *Br*: *on car* intermitente *m*
in•dict [ɪn'daɪt] *v/t* acusar
in•dict•ment [ɪn'daɪtmənt] acusación *f*, procesamiento *m*
in•die ['ɪndɪ] MUS F indie *m* F
in•dif•fer•ence [ɪn'dɪfrəns] indiferencia *f*
in•dif•fer•ent [ɪn'dɪfrənt] *adj* **1** indiferente; ***are you totally ~ to the way I feel?*** ¿no te importa lo más mínimo lo que sienta yo?; ***he is ~ to it*** le es indiferente **2** (*mediocre*) mediocre
in•dig•e•nous [ɪn'dɪdʒənəs] *adj* **1** indígena, natural (***to*** de); BOT, ZO autóctono **2** *qualities* innato, propio (***to*** de)
in•di•ges•ti•ble [ɪndɪ'dʒestɪbl] *adj* indigesto
in•di•ges•tion [ɪndɪ'dʒestʃn] indigestión *f*
in•dig•nant [ɪn'dɪgnənt] *adj* indignado; ***become ~*** indignarse
in•dig•na•tion [ɪndɪg'neɪʃn] indignación *f*; ***to my ~*** para mi indignación
in•dig•ni•ty [ɪn'dɪgnɪtɪ] indignidad *f*, infamia *f*
in•di•rect [ɪndɪ'rekt] *adj* indirecto; ***by ~ means*** indirectamente, de modo indirecto; **~ *object*** LING objeto *m or* complemento *m* indirecto; **~ *discourse*** LING estilo *m* indirecto
in•di•rect•ly [ɪndɪ'rektlɪ] *adv* indirectamente
in•dis•cern•i•ble [ɪndɪ'sɜːrnəbl] *adj* imperceptible
in•dis•creet [ɪndɪ'skriːt] *adj* indiscreto
in•dis•cre•tion [ɪndɪ'skreʃn] indiscreción *f*
in•dis•crim•i•nate [ɪndɪ'skrɪmɪnət] *adj* indiscriminado
in•dis•pen•sa•ble [ɪndɪ'spensəbl] *adj* indispensable, imprescindible
in•dis•posed [ɪndɪ'spoʊzd] *adj* **1** (*not well*) indispuesto; ***be ~*** hallarse indispuesto **2**: ***be ~ to do sth*** no estar dispuesto a hacer algo
in•dis•pu•ta•ble [ɪndɪ'spjuːtəbl] *adj* indiscutible
in•dis•pu•ta•bly [ɪndɪ'spjuːtəblɪ] *adv* indiscutiblemente
in•dis•tinct [ɪndɪ'stɪŋkt] *adj* indistinto, impreciso
in•dis•tin•guish•a•ble [ɪndɪ'stɪŋgwɪʃəbl] *adj* indistinguible
in•di•vid•u•al [ɪndɪ'vɪdʒʊəl] **I** *n* individuo *m* **II** *adj* individual
in•di•vid•u•al•ism [ɪndɪ'vɪdʒʊəlɪzəm]

individualismo *m*
in•di•vid•u•al•ist [ɪndɪ'vɪdʒʊəlɪst] *adj* individualista
in•di•vid•u•al•is•tic [ɪndɪvɪdʒʊəl'ɪstɪk] *adj* individualista
in•di•vid•u•al•i•ty [ɪndɪvɪdʒʊ'ælətɪ] individualidad *f*
in•di•vid•u•al•ize [ɪndɪ'vɪdʒʊəlaɪz] *v/t* individualizar
in•di•vid•u•al•ly [ɪndɪ'vɪdʒʊəlɪ] *adv* individualmente
in•di•vis•i•ble [ɪndɪ'vɪzɪbl] *adj* indivisible
in•doc•tri•nate [ɪn'dɑːktrɪneɪt] *v/t* adoctrinar
in•doc•trin•a•tion [ɪndɑːktrɪ'neɪʃn] adoctrinamiento *m*, aleccionamiento *m*
in•do•lence ['ɪndələns] indolencia *f*
in•do•lent ['ɪndələnt] *adj* indolente
in•dom•i•ta•ble [ɪn'dɑːmɪtəbl] *adj* indomable
In•do•ne•sia [ɪndə'niːʒə] Indonesia *f*
In•do•ne•sian [ɪndə'niːʒən] **I** *adj* indonesio **II** *n person* indonesio(-a) *m*(*f*)
in•door ['ɪndɔːr] *adj activities* de interior; *sport* de pista cubierta; *arena, swimming pool* cubierto; *athletics* en pista cubierta
in•doors [ɪn'dɔːrz] *adv* dentro; *go* adentro
in•dorse ☞ ***endorse***
in•du•bi•ta•ble [ɪn'duːbɪtəbl] *adj* indudable, inequívoco
in•duce [ɪn'duːs] *v/t* **1**: **~ *s.o. to do sth*** inducir *or* mover a alguien a hacer algo **2** MED *labor* provocar
in•duce•ment [ɪn'duːsmənt] aliciente *m*, incentivo *m*
in•duc•tion [ɪn'dʌkʃn] *in job* introducción *f*
in•dulge [ɪn'dʌldʒ] **I** *v/t o.s., one's tastes* satisfacer **II** *v/i*: **~ *in a pleasure*** entregarse a un placer; ***if I might ~ in a little joke*** si se me permite contar un chiste
in•dul•gence [ɪn'dʌldʒəns] **1** (*luxury*) lujo *m* **2** (*permissiveness*) indulgencia *f*
in•dul•gent [ɪn'dʌldʒənt] *adj* indulgente
in•dus•tri•al [ɪn'dʌstrɪəl] *adj* industrial; **~ *action*** acciones *fpl* reivindicativas; **~ *accident*** accidente *m* laboral; **~ *dispute*** conflicto *m* laboral; **~ *espionage*** espionaje *m* industrial; **~ *relations*** relaciones *fpl* laborales; **~ *revolution*** revolución *f* industrial; **~ *waste*** residuos *mpl* industriales
in•dus•tri•al•ist [ɪn'dʌstrɪəlɪst] industrial *m/f*
in•dus•tri•al•i•za•tion [ɪndʌstrɪəlaɪ'zeɪʃn] industrialización *f*
in•dus•tri•al•ize [ɪn'dʌstrɪəlaɪz] **I** *v/t* industrializar **II** *v/i* industrializarse
in•dus•tri•ous [ɪn'dʌstrɪəs] *adj* trabajador, aplicado
in•dus•try ['ɪndəstrɪ] industria *f*; ***the advertising ~*** la industria de la publicidad; ***steel ~*** industria del acero, industria acerera
in•e•bri•at•ed [ɪn'iːbrɪeɪtɪd] *adj* ebrio, embriagado
in•ed•i•ble [ɪn'edəbl] *adj* incomestible, indigestible
in•ef•fec•tive [ɪnɪ'fektɪv] *adj* ineficaz
in•ef•fec•tu•al [ɪnɪ'fektʃʊəl] *adj person* inepto, incapaz
in•ef•fi•cient [ɪnɪ'fɪʃənt] *adj* ineficiente
in•el•e•gant [ɪn'elɪgənt] *adj* poco elegante
in•eli•gi•ble [ɪn'elɪdʒɪbl] *adj*: ***be ~*** no reunir las condiciones
in•ept [ɪ'nept] *adj* inepto
in•ep•ti•tude [ɪn'eptɪtuːd] ineptitud *f*, incapacidad *f*
in•e•qual•i•ty [ɪnɪ'kwɑːlɪtɪ] desigualdad *f*
in•eq•ui•ta•ble [ɪn'ekwɪtəbl] *adj* no equitativo, desigual
in•ert [ɪ'nɜːrt] *adj* inerte
in•er•ti•a [ɪ'nɜːrʃə] inercia *f*
in•es•ca•pa•ble [ɪnɪ'skeɪpəbl] *adj conclusion* inevitable; *fact* ineludible
in•es•sen•tial [ɪnɪ'senʃl] *adj* innecesario, superfluo
in•es•ti•ma•ble [ɪn'estɪməbl] *adj* inestimable
in•ev•i•ta•bil•i•ty [ɪnevɪtə'bɪlɪtɪ]: ***the ~ of the decision*** lo inevitable de la decisión
in•ev•i•ta•ble [ɪn'evɪtəbl] *adj conclusion* inevitable; *fact* ineludible
in•ev•i•ta•bly [ɪn'evɪtəblɪ] *adv* inevitablemente
in•ex•act [ɪnɪg'zækt] *adj* inexacto, impreciso
in•ex•cu•sa•ble [ɪnɪk'skjuːzəbl] *adj* inexcusable, injustificable
in•ex•haus•ti•ble [ɪnɪg'zɒːstəbl] *adj*

supply inagotable
in•ex•o•ra•ble [ɪn'eksərəbl] *adj* inexorable, implacable
in•ex•pen•sive [ɪnɪk'spensɪv] *adj* barato, económico
in•ex•pe•ri•ence [ɪnɪk'spɪərɪəns] inexperiencia *f*, falta *f* de experiencia
in•ex•pe•ri•enced [ɪnɪk'spɪrɪənst] *adj* inexperto
in•ex•pert [ɪn'ekspɜːrt] *adj* inexperto, poco habilidoso
in•ex•plic•a•ble [ɪnɪk'splɪkəbl] *adj* inexplicable
in•ex•pres•si•ble [ɪnɪk'spresɪbl] *adj joy* indescriptible
in•ex•tri•ca•ble [ɪneks'trɪkəbl] *adj also fig* inseparable (***from*** de)
in•ex•tri•ca•bly [ɪneks'trɪkəblɪ] *adv*: ***~ linked*** íntimamente *or* acérrimamente ligado
in•fal•li•bil•i•ty [ɪnfælə'bɪlətɪ] *also* REL infalibilidad *f*
in•fal•li•ble [ɪn'fælɪbl] *adj* infalible
in•fa•mous ['ɪnfəməs] *adj* infame
in•fa•my ['ɪnfəmɪ] infamia *f*
in•fan•cy ['ɪnfənsɪ] infancia *f*; ***be still in its ~*** *fig* estar todavía en pañales
in•fant ['ɪnfənt] bebé *m*; ***~ class*** *Br* clase *f* infantil (*para niños de entre cinco y siete años*); ***~ mortality*** mortalidad *f* infantil; ***~ prodigy*** niño(-a) *m(f)* prodigio(-a)
in•fan•ti•cide [ɪn'fæntɪsaɪd] infanticidio *m*
in•fan•tile ['ɪnfəntaɪl] *adj pej* infantil, pueril
in•fan•try ['ɪnfəntrɪ] infantería *f*
in•fan•try•man ['ɪnfəntrɪmən] soldado *m* de infantería
'in•fan•try sol•dier soldado *m/f* de infantería, infante *m/f*
'in•fant school *Br* escuela *f* del primer ciclo de primaria (*para niños de entre cinco y siete años*)
in•fat•u•at•ed [ɪn'fætʃʊeɪtɪd] *adj*: ***be ~ with s.o.*** estar encaprichado de alguien
in•fat•u•a•tion [ɪnfætʃʊ'eɪʃn] infatuación *f*, emperramiento *m*
in•fect [ɪn'fekt] *v/t* infectar; ***he ~ed everyone with his cold*** contagió el resfriado a todo el mundo; ***become ~ed*** *of wound* infectarse; *of person* contagiarse
in•fec•tion [ɪn'fekʃn] infección *f*
in•fec•tious [ɪn'fekʃəs] *adj disease* infeccioso; *laughter* contagioso
in•fe•lic•i•tous [ɪnfɪ'lɪsɪtəs] *adj* infeliz, desdichado
in•fer [ɪn'fɜːr] *v/t* (*pret & pp* ***-red***) inferir, deducir (***from*** de)
in•fer•ence ['ɪnfərəns] deducción *f*; ***draw an ~*** sacar una conclusión
in•fe•ri•or [ɪn'fɪrɪər] *adj* inferior (***to*** a)
in•fe•ri•or•i•ty [ɪnfɪrɪ'ɑːrətɪ] *in quality* inferioridad *f*
in•fe•ri'or•i•ty com•plex complejo *m* de inferioridad
in•fer•nal [ɪn'fɜːrnl] *adj* infernal, maldito
in•fer•no [ɪn'fɜːrnoʊ] infierno *m*
in•fer•tile [ɪn'fɜːrtl] *adj woman, plant* estéril; *soil* estéril, yermo
in•fer•til•i•ty [ɪnfər'tɪlɪtɪ] esterilidad *f*
in•fest [ɪn'fest] *v/t* infestar (***with*** de)
in•fi•del ['ɪnfɪdəl] REL infiel *m/f*
in•fi•del•i•ty [ɪnfɪ'delɪtɪ] infidelidad *f*
'in•fight•ing luchas *fpl* internas
in•fil•trate ['ɪnfɪltreɪt] *v/t* infiltrarse en
in•fil•tra•tion [ɪnfɪl'treɪʃn] infiltración *f*
in•fi•nite ['ɪnfɪnət] *adj* infinito
in•fi•nite•ly ['ɪnfɪnətlɪ] *adv fig* infinitamente
in•fin•i•tes•i•mal [ɪnfɪnɪ'tesɪml] *adj* infinitesimal, mínimo
in•fin•i•tive [ɪn'fɪnətɪv] GRAM infinitivo *m*
in•fin•i•ty [ɪn'fɪnətɪ] infinidad *f*
in•firm [ɪn'fɜːrm] *adj* enfermo, achacoso
in•fir•ma•ry [ɪn'fɜːrmərɪ] enfermería *f*
in•fir•mi•ty [ɪn'fɜːrmətɪ] debilidad *f*
in•flame [ɪn'fleɪm] *v/t* despertar; ***become ~d*** inflamarse; ***~d with rage*** ciego de ira
in•flam•ma•ble [ɪn'flæməbl] *adj* inflamable
in•flam•ma•tion [ɪnflə'meɪʃn] MED inflamación *f*
in•flam•ma•to•ry [ɪn'flæmətɔːrɪ] *adj* **1** MED inflamatorio **2** *fig* incendiario
in•flat•a•ble [ɪn'fleɪtəbl] *adj dinghy* hinchable, inflable
in•flate [ɪn'fleɪt] *v/t* **1** *tire, dinghy* hinchar, inflar **2** *economy* inflar **3**: ***he has an ~d opinion of himself*** se cree muy importante
in•fla•tion [ɪn'fleɪʃən] inflación *f*; ***rate of ~*** tasa *f* de inflación

in•fla•tion•a•ry [ɪn'fleɪʃənərɪ] *adj* inflacionario, inflacionista
in'fla•tion-proof *adj* revisable de acuerdo con la inflación
in•flec•tion [ɪn'flekʃn] inflexión *f*
in•flex•i•ble [ɪn'fleksɪbl] *adj* inflexible
in•flict [ɪn'flɪkt] *v/t* infligir (***on*** a); ***~ o.s. on s.o.*** pegarse *or* acoplarse a alguien F
in•flic•tion [ɪn'flɪkʃn] imposición *f*, coacción *f*
'in-flight *adj*: ***~ entertainment*** entretenimiento *m* durante el vuelo
in•flu•ence ['ɪnfluəns] **I** *n* influencia *f*; ***be a good / bad ~ on s.o.*** tener una buena / mala influencia en alguien; ***be under s.o.'s ~*** estar bajo la influencia de alguien; ***under the ~ of alcohol*** bajo los efectos del alcohol **II** *v/t* influir en, influenciar
in•flu•en•tial [ɪnflʊ'enʃl] *adj* influyente
in•flu•en•za [ɪnflʊ'enzə] gripe *f*
in•flux ['ɪnflʌks] flujo *m*, oleada *f*; ***an ~ of visitors / tourists*** una afluencia de visitantes / turistas
in•fo ['ɪnfoʊ] F ☞ ***information***
in•fo•mer•cial ['ɪnfoʊmɜːrʃl] publirreportaje *m*
in•form [ɪn'fɔːrm] **I** *v/t* informar; ***~ s.o. about sth*** informar a alguien de algo; ***please keep me ~ed*** por favor mantenme informado; ***~ s.o. that*** informar a alguien que **II** *v/i*: ***~ on s.o.*** delatar a alguien
in•for•mal [ɪn'fɔːrməl] *adj* informal
in•for•mal•i•ty [ɪnfɔːr'mælɪtɪ] informalidad *f*
in•for•mal•ly [ɪn'fɔːrməlɪ] *adv* informalmente, de manera informal
in•form•ant [ɪn'fɔːrmənt] confidente *m/f*
in•for•ma•tion [ɪnfər'meɪʃn] información *f*, TELEC servicio *m* de guía telefónica; ***a piece of ~*** una información; ***well, for your ~, I did check first but ...*** bien, para tu información, que sepas que consulté primero pero…; ***for your ~*** para tu información, para que lo sepas
in•for'ma•tion desk (ventanilla *f* de) información *f*; **in•for'ma•tion re•triev•al** recuperación *f* de información; **in•for•ma•tion 'sci•ence** informática *f*; **in•for•ma•tion 'sci•en•tist** informático(-a) *m(f)*; **in•for•ma•tion 'su•per•high•way** COMPUT autopista *f* de la información; **in•for•ma•tion tech'nol•o•gy** tecnologías *fpl* de la información
in•for•ma•tive [ɪn'fɔːrmətɪv] *adj* informativo; ***you're not being very ~*** no estás dando mucha información
in•formed [ɪn'fɔːrmd] *adj*: ***make an ~ decision*** tomar una decisión fundada
in•form•er [ɪn'fɔːrmər] confidente *m/f*
in•fra-red [ɪnfrə'red] *adj* infrarrojo
in•fra•struc•ture ['ɪnfrəstrʌktʃər] infraestructura *f*
in•fre•quent [ɪn'friːkwənt] *adj* poco frecuente
in•fringe [ɪn'frɪndʒ] *v/t* LAW infringir; *rights* violar
◆ **infringe on** *v/t* LAW infringir; *rights* violar
in•fringe•ment [ɪn'frɪndʒmənt] LAW infracción *f* (***of*** de); *of rights* violación *f* (***of*** de)
in•fu•ri•ate [ɪn'fjʊrɪeɪt] *v/t* enfurecer, exasperar
in•fu•ri•at•ing [ɪn'fjʊrɪeɪtɪŋ] *adj* exasperante
in•fuse [ɪn'fjuːz] *v/i of tea* infundir
in•fu•sion [ɪn'fjuːʒn] (*herb tea*) infusión *f*
in•ge•ni•ous [ɪn'dʒiːnɪəs] *adj* ingenioso
in•ge•nu•i•ty [ɪndʒɪ'nuːətɪ] lo ingenioso
in•gen•u•ous [ɪn'dʒenjʊəs] *adj* ingenuo
in•glo•ri•ous [ɪn'glɔːrɪəs] *adj* denigrante, deshonroso
in•got ['ɪŋgət] lingote *m*
in•grained [ɪn'greɪnd] *adj dirt* incrustado; *habit*, *belief* arraigado
in•gra•ti•ate [ɪn'greɪʃɪeɪt] *v/t*: ***~ o.s. with s.o.*** congraciarse con alguien
in•gra•ti•at•ing [ɪn'greɪʃɪeɪtɪŋ] *adj* complaciente, halagador
in•grat•i•tude [ɪn'grætɪtuːd] ingratitud *f*
in•gre•di•ent [ɪn'griːdɪənt] *also fig* ingrediente *m*
in•grown 'toe•nail uñero *m*
in•hab•it [ɪn'hæbɪt] *v/t* habitar
in•hab•it•a•ble [ɪn'hæbɪtəbl] *adj* habitable
in•hab•i•tant [ɪn'hæbɪtənt] habitante *m/f*
in•hab•it•ed [ɪn'hæbɪtɪd] *adj* habitado, poblado
in•hale [ɪn'heɪl] **I** *v/t* inhalar **II** *v/i when*

smoking tragarse el humo
in•hal•er [ɪn'heɪlər] inhalador *m*
in•her•ent [ɪn'hɪərənt] *adj* inherente, intrínseco
in•her•ent•ly [ɪn'hɪərəntlɪ] *adv* intrínsecamente
in•her•it [ɪn'herɪt] *v/t* heredar
in•her•i•tance [ɪn'herɪtəns] herencia *f*; **~ *tax*** impuesto *m* sobre la herencia, impuesto *m* sobre sucesiones
in•hib•it [ɪn'hɪbɪt] *v/t growth* impedir; *conversation* inhibir, cohibir
in•hib•it•ed [ɪn'hɪbɪtɪd] *adj* inhibido, cohibido
in•hi•bi•tion [ɪnhɪ'bɪʃn] inhibición *f*
in•hos•pi•ta•ble [ɪnhɑː'spɪtəbl] *adj person* inhospitalario; *city, climate* inhóspito
'in-house I *adj facilities* en el lugar de trabajo; **~ *team*** equipo *m* en plantilla; **~ *magazine*** revista *f* interna **II** *adv work* en la empresa
in•hu•man [ɪn'hjuːmən] *adj* inhumano
in•hu•mane [ɪnhjuː'meɪn] *adj* inhumano, infrahumano
in•hu•man•i•ty [ɪnhjuː'mænətɪ] inhumanidad *f*, impiedad *f*
i•nim•i•cal [ɪ'nɪmɪkl] *adj climate* hostil; *decision, restrictions etc* contrario (***to*** a)
in•im•i•ta•ble [ɪ'nɪmɪtəbl] *adj* inimitable
in•iq•ui•tous [ɪ'nɪkwɪtəs] *adj* inicuo, injusto
in•iq•ui•ty [ɪ'nɪkwɪtɪ] inicuidad *f*, injusticia *f*
i•ni•tial [ɪ'nɪʃl] **I** *adj* inicial **II** *n* inicial *f* **III** *v/t* (*pret & pp* ***-ed***, *Br* ***-led***) (*write* **~*s on***) poner las iniciales en
i•ni•tial•ly [ɪ'nɪʃlɪ] *adv* inicialmente, al principio
i•ni•ti•ate [ɪ'nɪʃɪeɪt] *v/t* iniciar
i•ni•ti•a•tion [ɪnɪʃɪ'eɪʃn] iniciación *f*; **~ *ceremony*** ceremonia *f* de iniciación
i•ni•ti•a•tive [ɪ'nɪʃətɪv] iniciativa *f*; ***do sth on one's own*** **~** hacer algo por iniciativa propia; ***take the*** **~** tomar la iniciativa
i•ni•ti•a•tor [ɪ'nɪʃɪeɪtər] iniciador(a) *m(f)*
in•ject [ɪn'dʒekt] *v/t drug, fuel, capital* inyectar; **~ *s.o. with sth*** inyectar a alguien algo
in•jec•tion [ɪn'dʒekʃn] *of drug, fuel, capital* inyección *f*; ***give s.o. an*** **~** poner a alguien una inyección
'in-joke: ***it's an*** **~** es un chiste que entendemos nosotros / ellos *etc*
in•junc•tion [ɪn'dʒʌŋkʃn] LAW orden *f* judicial; ***take out an*** **~** obtener una orden judicial (***against*** contra)
in•jure ['ɪndʒər] *v/t* lesionar; ***he*** **~*d his leg*** se lesionó la pierna
in•jured ['ɪndʒərd] **I** *adj leg* lesionado; *feelings* herido **II** *npl*: ***the*** **~** los heridos
in•jur•y ['ɪndʒərɪ] lesión *f*; *wound* herida *f*; **~ *to the head*** herida en la cabeza
'in•jur•y time SP tiempo *m* de descuento
in•jus•tice [ɪn'dʒʌstɪs] injusticia *f*; ***do s.o. an*** **~** no hacer justicia a alguien, ser injusto con alguien
ink [ɪŋk] tinta *f*
'ink•jet, ink•jet 'print•er impresora *f* de chorro de tinta
ink•ling ['ɪŋklɪŋ]: ***have no*** **~** ***of sth*** no tener ni la más remota idea de algo
'ink•pad tampón *m* de tinta
'ink•stain mancha *f* de tinta
in•land ['ɪnlənd] *adj* interior; *mail* nacional
In•land 'Rev•e•nue *Br* Hacienda *f*, *Span* Agencia *f* Tributaria
in-laws ['ɪnlɒːz] *npl* familia *f* política
in•lay I *n* ['ɪnleɪ] incrustación *f* **II** *v/t* [ɪn'leɪ] (*pret & pp* ***-laid***) incrustar (***with*** de); ***inlaid design*** incrustaciones *fpl*
in•let ['ɪnlet] **1** *of sea* ensenada *f* **2** *in machine* entrada *f*
in•line skates ['ɪnlaɪnskeɪts] *npl* patines *mpl* en línea
in•mate ['ɪnmeɪt] *of prison* recluso(-a) *m(f)*; *of mental hospital* paciente *m/f*
in•most ['ɪnmoʊst] *adj* más íntimo
inn [ɪn] posada *f*, mesón *m*
in•nards ['ɪnərdz] *npl* F tripas *fpl*
in•nate [ɪ'neɪt] *adj* innato
in•ner ['ɪnər] *adj* interior; ***the*** **~** ***ear*** el oído interno
in•ner 'cit•y *barrios degradados del centro de la ciudad*; **~ *decay*** degradación *f* del centro de la ciudad
'in•ner•most *adj feelings* más íntimo; *recess* más recóndito
in•ner 'tube cámara *f* (de aire)
in•ning ['ɪnɪŋ] *in baseball* entrada *f*
'inn•keep•er mesonero(-a) *m(f)*, posadero(-a) *m(f)*
in•no•cence ['ɪnəsəns] inocencia *f*; ***lose one's*** **~** perder la inocencia

in•no•cent ['ɪnəsənt] *adj* inocente
in•no•cu•ous [ɪ'nɑːkjʊəs] *adj* inocuo
in•no•vate ['ɪnəveɪt] *v/i* innovar
in•no•va•tion [ɪnə'veɪʃn] innovación *f*
in•no•va•tive [ɪnə'veɪtɪv] *adj* innovador
in•no•va•tor ['ɪnəveɪtər] innovador(a) *m(f)*
in•nu•en•do [ɪnjuː'endoʊ] (*pl* ***-do(e)s***) insinuación *f*, indirecta *f* (***about*** sobre, acerca de)
in•nu•me•ra•ble [ɪ'nuːmərəbl] *adj* innumerable
i•noc•u•late [ɪ'nɑːkjʊleɪt] *v/t* inocular; ***be ~d against polio*** estar vacunado contra la polio
i•noc•u•la•tion [ɪ'nɑːkjʊ'leɪʃn] inoculación *f*
in•of•fen•sive [ɪnə'fensɪv] *adj* inofensivo
in•op•er•a•ble [ɪn'ɑːpərəbl] *adj* MED inoperable
in•op•er•a•tive [ɪn'ɑːpərətɪv] *adj* **1** *machine* no operativo **2** LAW inoperante
in•op•por•tune [ɪnɑːpər'tuːn] *adj* inoportuno
in•or•di•nate [ɪn'ɔːrdɪnət] *adj* desorbitado
in•or•gan•ic [ɪnɔːr'gænɪk] *adj* inorgánico
'in-pa•tient paciente *m/f* interno(-a)
in•put ['ɪnpʊt] **I** *n into project etc* contribución *f*, aportación *f*; COMPUT entrada *f* **II** *v/t* (*pret & pp* ***-ted*** *or* ***input***) *into project* contribuir, aportar; COMPUT introducir
in•quest ['ɪnkwest] investigación *f* (***into*** sobre)
in•quire [ɪn'kwaɪr] **I** *v/i* preguntar; ***~ into sth*** investigar algo; ***~ within*** razón aquí, infórmese aquí **II** *v/t*: ***~ what / when / where*** preguntar qué / cuándo / dónde
in•quir•y [ɪn'kwaɪrɪ] **1** consulta *f*, pregunta *f*; ***on ~*** al preguntar; ***make inquiries*** hacer preguntas (***about*** sobre, acerca de) **2** *into rail crash etc* investigación *f*
in•qui•si•tion [ɪnkwɪ'zɪʃn] **1** inquisición *f*, averiguación *f* **2** ***Inquisition*** REL Inquisición *f*
in•quis•i•tive [ɪn'kwɪzətɪv] *adj* curioso, inquisitivo
in•quis•i•tive•ness [ɪn'kwɪzətɪvnɪs] curiosidad *f*
in•quis•i•tor [ɪn'kwɪzɪtər] *fig* inquisidor(a) *m(f)*, indagador(a) *m(f)*
in•roads ['ɪnroʊdz]: ***make ~ into sth*** hacer avances en algo
INS [aɪen'es] *abbr* (= ***Immigration and Naturalization Service***) Servicio *m* de Inmigración y Nacionalización
in•sa•lu•bri•ous [ɪnsə'luːbrɪəs] *adj* insalubre
in•sane [ɪn'seɪn] *adj person* loco, demente; *idea* descabellado
in•sane•ly [ɪn'seɪnlɪ] *adv* como loco, rematadamente; ***be ~ jealous*** estar como loco de celos
in•san•i•ta•ry [ɪn'sænɪterɪ] *adj* antihigiénico
in•san•i•ty [ɪn'sænɪtɪ] locura *f*, demencia *f*
in•sa•ti•a•ble [ɪn'seɪʃəbl] *adj* insaciable
in•scribe [ɪn'skraɪb] *v/t* inscribir (***on*** en)
in•scrip•tion [ɪn'skrɪpʃn] inscripción *f*
in•scru•ta•ble [ɪn'skruːtəbl] *adj* inescrutable
in•sect ['ɪnsekt] insecto *m*
in•sec•ti•cide [ɪn'sektɪsaɪd] insecticida *f*
'in•sect re•pel•lent repelente *m* contra insectos
in•se•cure [ɪnsɪ'kjʊr] *adj* inseguro
in•se•cu•ri•ty [ɪnsɪ'kjʊrɪtɪ] inseguridad *f*
in•sem•i•nate [ɪn'semɪneɪt] *v/t* inseminar
in•sem•i•na•tion [ɪnsemɪ'neɪʃn] inseminación *f*
in•sen•si•tive [ɪn'sensɪtɪv] *adj* insensible (***to*** a)
in•sen•si•tiv•i•ty [ɪnsensɪ'tɪvɪtɪ] insensibilidad *f*
in•sep•a•ra•ble [ɪn'seprəbl] *adj* inseparable
in•sert I *n* ['ɪnsɜːrt] *in magazine etc* encarte *m* **II** *v/t* [ɪn'sɜːrt] *coin, finger, diskette* introducir, meter; *extra text* insertar
in•ser•tion [ɪn'sɜːrʃn] *act* introducción *f*, inserción *f*; *of text* inserción *f*
in•shore [ɪn'ʃɔːr] *adj* costero
in•side [ɪn'saɪd] **I** *n of house, box* interior *m*; ***from the ~*** desde dentro; ***pass s.o. on the ~*** adelantar a alguien por la derecha; *in UK* adelantar a alguien por la izquierda; ***somebody on the ~*** alguien de dentro; ***~ out*** del revés; ***turn sth ~ out*** dar la vuelta a algo (*de dentro*

a fuera); ***know sth ~ out*** saberse algo al dedillo

II *prep* **1** dentro de; ***~ the house*** dentro de la casa **2**: ***~ of 2 hours*** dentro de 2 horas

III *adv stay, remain* dentro; *go, carry* adentro; ***we went ~*** entramos

IV *adj*: ***~ information*** información *f* confidencial; ***~ lane*** SP calle *f* de dentro; *on road* carril *m* de la derecha; *in UK* carril *m* de la izquierda; ***~ pocket*** bolsillo *m* interior; ***it was an ~ job*** F el golpe fue organizado por alguien de dentro

in•sid•er [ɪn'saɪdər] *persona con acceso a información confidencial*

in•sid•er 'trad•ing FIN uso *m* de información privilegiada

in•sides [ɪn'saɪdz] *npl* tripas *fpl*

in•sid•i•ous [ɪn'sɪdɪəs] *adj* insidioso

in•sight ['ɪnsaɪt]: ***this film offers an ~ into local customs*** esta película permite hacerse una idea de las costumbres locales; ***full of ~*** muy perspicaz

in•sig•ni•a [ɪn'sɪgnɪə] *npl* insignias *fpl*

in•sig•nif•i•cant [ɪnsɪg'nɪfɪkənt] *adj* insignificante

in•sin•cere [ɪnsɪn'sɪr] *adj* poco sincero, falso

in•sin•cer•i•ty [ɪnsɪn'serɪtɪ] falta *f* de sinceridad

in•sin•u•ate [ɪn'sɪnʊeɪt] *v/t* (*imply*) insinuar

in•sin•u•a•tion [ɪnsɪnjʊ'eɪʃn] insinuación *f*; ***by ~ this meant ...*** esto insinuaba que ...

in•sip•id [ɪn'sɪpɪd] *adj flavor, food* insípido; *fig* insulso, soso

in•sist [ɪn'sɪst] *v/i* insistir; ***please keep it, I ~*** por favor, insisto en que te lo quedes

◆ **insist on** *v/t* insistir en; ***he will insist on making the same mistakes*** sigue cometiendo los mismos errores

in•sist•ence [ɪn'sɪstəns] insistencia *f*; ***at s.o.'s ~*** por insistencia de alguien, a petición de alguien

in•sis•tent [ɪn'sɪstənt] *adj* insistente; ***she was quite ~*** insistió bastante; ***be ~ that*** insistir en que

in•so•far [ɪnsoʊ'fɑːr] *adv*: ***~ as*** en la medida en que

in•sole ['ɪnsoʊl] plantilla *f*

in•so•lence ['ɪnsələns] insolencia *f*

in•so•lent ['ɪnsələnt] *adj* insolente

in•sol•u•ble [ɪn'sɑːljʊbl] *adj* **1** *problem* irresoluble **2** *substance* insoluble

in•sol•ven•cy [ɪn'sɑːlvənsɪ] COM insolvencia *f*

in•sol•vent [ɪn'sɑːlvənt] *adj* insolvente

in•som•ni•a [ɪn'sɑːmnɪə] insomnio *m*

in•som•ni•ac [ɪn'sɑːmnɪæk] persona *f* que padece insomnio

in•spect [ɪn'spekt] *v/t* inspeccionar

in•spec•tion [ɪn'spekʃn] inspección *f*; ***on ~*** tras inspeccionar; ***for ~*** COM para inspección

in'spec•tion pit *in garage* foso *m*

in•spec•tor [ɪn'spektər] *in factory, of police* inspector(a) *m(f)*; *on buses* revisor(a) *m(f)*

in•spi•ra•tion [ɪnspə'reɪʃn] inspiración *f*; ***be s.o.'s ~, be an ~ to s.o.*** ser la inspiración de alguien, ser una inspiración para alguien; ***she should be an ~ to us all*** nos debería servir de inspiración a todos

in•spire [ɪn'spaɪr] *v/t respect etc* inspirar; ***be ~d by s.o. / sth*** estar inspirado por alguien / algo

in•sta•bil•i•ty [ɪnstə'bɪlɪtɪ] *of character, economy* inestabilidad *f*

in•stall [ɪn'stɒːl] *v/t* instalar

in•stal•la•tion [ɪnstə'leɪʃn] instalación *f*; ***military ~*** instalación *f* militar

in•stall•ment, *Br* **in•stal•ment** [ɪn'stɒːlmənt] *of story, TV drama etc* episodio *m*; *payment* plazo *m*; ***by*** *or* ***in ~s*** a plazos; ***monthly ~s*** plazos *mpl* mensuales, mensualidades *fpl*; ***publish sth in ~s*** publicar algo en entregas

in'stall•ment plan compra *f* a plazos; ***buy on the ~*** comprar a plazos

in•stance ['ɪnstəns] (*example*) ejemplo *m*; ***for ~*** por ejemplo; ***in this ~*** en esta ocasión; ***in the first ~*** en primer lugar

in•stant ['ɪnstənt] **I** *adj* instantáneo, inmediato; ***~ camera*** PHOT cámara *f* (de fotos) instantánea **II** *n* instante *m*; ***in an ~*** en un instante; ***come here this ~!*** ¡ven aquí ahora mismo!

in•stan•ta•ne•ous [ɪnstən'teɪnɪəs] *adj* instantáneo

in•stan•ta•ne•ous•ly [ɪnstən'teɪnɪəslɪ] *adv* instantáneamente

in•stant 'cof•fee café *m* instantáneo

in•stant•ly ['ɪnstəntlɪ] *adv* al instante

in•stant 're•play SP repetición *f* (de la

jugada); *in slow motion* repetición *f* a cámara lenta
in•stead [ɪn'sted] *adv*: ***I'll take that one ~*** me llevaré mejor ese otro; ***would you like coffee ~?*** ¿preferiría mejor café?; ***I'll have coffee ~ of tea*** tomaré café en vez de té; ***he went ~ of me*** fue en mi lugar; ***~ of going*** en vez *or* lugar de ir
in•step ['ɪnstep] empeine *m*
in•sti•gate ['ɪnstɪgeɪt] *v/t* instigar
in•sti•ga•tion [ɪnstɪ'geɪʃn] instigación *f*; ***at s.o.'s ~*** a instancias de alguien
in•stil(l) [ɪn'stɪl] *v/t* inculcar (***into*** a)
in•stinct ['ɪnstɪŋkt] instinto *m*; ***by or from ~*** por instinto
in•stinc•tive [ɪn'stɪŋktɪv] *adj* instintivo
in•stinc•tive•ly [ɪn'stɪŋktɪvlɪ] *adv* instintivamente
in•sti•tute ['ɪnstɪtu:t] **I** *n* instituto *m*; *for elderly* residencia *f* de ancianos; *for mentally ill* psiquiátrico *m* **II** *v/t new law* establecer; *inquiry* iniciar
in•sti•tu•tion [ɪnstɪ'tu:ʃn] **1** institución *f* **2** (*setting up*) iniciación *f*
in•sti•tu•tion•al [ɪnstɪ'tu:ʃənl] *adj* institucional
in•sti•tu•tion•al•ize [ɪnstɪ'tu:ʃənəlaɪz] *v/t* institucionalizar; ***become ~d*** pasar a depender de las instituciones
in•struct [ɪn'strʌkt] *v/t* **1** (*order*) dar instrucciones a; ***~ s.o. to do sth*** ordenar a alguien que haga algo; ***you should do what you were ~ed to do*** deberías hacer lo que se te ordenó que hicieras **2** (*teach*) instruir
in•struc•tion [ɪn'strʌkʃn] instrucción *f*; ***~s for use*** instrucciones *fpl* de uso
in'struc•tion man•u•al manual *m* de instrucciones
in•struc•tive [ɪn'strʌktɪv] *adj* instructivo
in•struc•tor [ɪn'strʌktər] instructor(a) *m(f)*
in•stru•ment ['ɪnstrumənt] MUS, *tool* instrumento *m*
in•stru•men•tal [ɪnstru'mentl] *adj* **1** MUS instrumental **2**: ***be ~ in sth*** jugar un papel en algo
'in•stru•ment pan•el panel *m or* tablero *m* de mandos
in•sub•or•di•nate [ɪnsə'bɔ:rdɪnət] *adj* insubordinado
in•sub•or•di•na•tion [ɪnsəbɔ:rdɪ'neɪʃn] insubordinación *f*
in•sub•stan•tial [ɪnsəb'stænʃl] *adj* insubstancial
in•suf•fer•a•ble [ɪn'sʌfərəbl] *adj* insufrible, intolerable
in•suf•fi•cien•cy [ɪnsə'fɪʃnsɪ] *also* MED insuficiencia *f*
in•suf•fi•cient [ɪnsə'fɪʃnt] *adj* insuficiente
in•su•lar ['ɪnsələr] *adj fig* cerrado
in•su•lar•i•ty [ɪnsə'lærɪtɪ] *fig* cerrazón *f*, obcecación *f*
in•su•late ['ɪnsəleɪt] *v/t also* ELEC aislar
in•su•la•tion [ɪnsə'leɪʃn] ELEC aislamiento *m*; *against cold* aislamiento *m* (térmico)
in•su•lin ['ɪnsəlɪn] insulina *f*
in•sult I *n* ['ɪnsʌlt] insulto *m* **II** *v/t* [ɪn'sʌlt] insultar
in•su•per•a•ble [ɪn'su:pərəbl] *adj* insuperable
in•sur•ance [ɪn'ʃurəns] seguro *m*
in'sur•ance a•gent agente *m/f* de seguros; **in'sur•ance bro•ker** corredor(a) *m(f)* de seguros; **in'sur•ance claim** reclamación *f* al seguro; **in'sur•ance com•pa•ny** compañía *f* de seguros, aseguradora *f*; **in'sur•ance cov•er** cobertura *f* del seguro; **in'sur•ance num•ber** número *m* de póliza; **in'sur•ance pol•i•cy** póliza *f* de seguros; **in'sur•ance pre•mi•um** prima *f* (del seguro)
in•sure [ɪn'ʃur] *v/t* asegurar (***for*** por)
in•sured [ɪn'ʃurd] **I** *adj* asegurado; ***~ value*** valor *m* asegurado **II** *n*: ***the ~*** el asegurado, la asegurada
in•sur•er [ɪn'ʃurər] *person* asegurador(a) *m(f)*; *company* compañía *f* de seguros, compañía *f* aseguradora
in•sur•moun•ta•ble [ɪnsər'maʊntəbl] *adj* insuperable
in•sur•rec•tion [ɪnsə'rekʃn] insurrección *f*
in•tact [ɪn'tækt] *adj* (*not damaged*) intacto
'in•take 1 *of college etc* remesa *f*; ***we have an annual ~ of 300 students*** cada año admitimos a 300 alumnos **2**: ***he reacted with a sharp ~ of breath*** se quedó sin respiración
in•tan•gi•ble [ɪn'tændʒəbl] *adj fig* intangible
in'tan•gi•ble as•sets *npl* activos *mpl* intangibles
in•te•ger ['ɪntɪdʒər] MATH (número *m*)

entero *m*
in•te•gral ['ɪntɪgrəl] *adj* integral; **~ to sth** vital *or* esencial para algo
in•te•grate ['ɪntɪgreɪt] *v/t* integrar (**into** en) **II** *v/i*: **~ with sth** integrarse con algo
in•te•grat•ed cir•cuit [ɪntɪgreɪtɪd'sɜːrkɪt] circuito *m* integrado
in•te•gra•tion [ɪntɪ'greɪʃn] integración *f*
in•teg•ri•ty [ɪn'tegrətɪ] (*honesty*) integridad *f*; **a man of ~** un hombre íntegro
in•tel•lect ['ɪntəlekt] intelecto *m*
in•tel•lec•tual [ɪntə'lektʃuəl] **I** *adj* intelectual **II** *n* intelectual *m/f*
in•tel•li•gence [ɪn'telɪdʒəns] **1** inteligencia *f* **2** (*information*) información *f* secreta
in'tel•li•gence of•fi•cer agente *m/f* del servicio de inteligencia; **in'tel•li•gence quo•tient** cociente *m* intelectual; **in'tel•li•gence serv•ice** servicio *m* de inteligencia; **in'tel•li•gence test** test *m* de inteligencia
in•tel•li•gent [ɪn'telɪdʒənt] *adj* inteligente
intel•li•gent•si•a [ɪntelɪ'dʒentsɪə] intelectualidad *f*
in•tel•li•gi•ble [ɪn'telɪdʒəbl] *adj* inteligible
in•tem•per•ate [ɪn'tempərət] *adj* inmoderado
in•tend [ɪn'tend] *v/t*: **~ to do sth** tener la intención de hacer algo; **that's not what I ~ed** esa no era mi intención; **was this ~ed?** ¿esto fue intencionado *or* a propósito?; **it was ~ed for you** iba dirigido a tí; **it was ~ed as a compliment** se dijo como un cumplido, fue un cumplido
in•tend•ed [ɪn'tendɪd] *adj* esperado, deseado
in•tense [ɪn'tens] *adj sensation*, *pleasure*, *heat*, *pressure* intenso; *personality* serio
in•ten•si•fi•ca•tion [ɪntensɪfɪ'keɪʃn] intensificación *f*
in•ten•si•fy [ɪn'tensɪfaɪ] **I** *v/t* (*pret & pp* **-ied**) *effect*, *pressure* intensificar **II** *v/i* (*pret & pp* **-ied**) intensificarse
in•ten•si•ty [ɪn'tensətɪ] intensidad *f*
in•ten•sive [ɪn'tensɪv] *adj study*, *training*, *treatment* intensivo
in•ten•sive 'care (u•nit) MED (unidad *f* de) cuidados *mpl* intensivos
in•ten•sive 'course *of language study* curso *m* intensivo
in•tent [ɪn'tent] **I** *adj*: **be ~ on doing sth** *determined* estar decidido a hacer algo; *concentrating* estar concentrado haciendo algo **II** *n* intención *f*; **with ~** LAW con premeditación; **with ~ to do sth** LAW con intención de hacer algo
in•ten•tion [ɪn'tenʃn] intención *f*; **I have no ~ of ...** (*refuse to*) no tengo intención de ...; **with the best (of) ~s** con la mejor intención
in•ten•tion•al [ɪn'tenʃənl] *adj* intencionado
in•ten•tion•al•ly [ɪn'tenʃnlɪ] *adv* a propósito, adrede
in•ter•act [ɪntər'ækt] *v/i* interactuar; **~ with s.o.** relacionarse con alguien
in•ter•ac•tion [ɪntər'ækʃn] interacción *f*
in•ter•ac•tive [ɪntər'æktɪv] *adj* interactivo
in•ter•ac•tive 'learn•ing aprendizaje *m* interactivo
in•ter•breed [ɪntər'briːd] (*pret & pp* **-bred**) BIO **I** *v/t* cruzar **II** *v/i* cruzarse
in•ter•cede [ɪntər'siːd] *v/i* interceder
in•ter•cept [ɪntər'sept] *v/t* interceptar
in•ter•cep•tion [ɪntər'sepʃn] intercepción *f*
in•ter•ces•sion [ɪntər'seʃn] mediación *f*, intervención *f*
in•ter•change I *n* ['ɪntərtʃeɪndʒ] *of highways* nudo *m* vial **II** *v/t* [ɪntər'tʃeɪndʒ] intercambiar (**with** con)
in•ter•change•a•ble [ɪntər'tʃeɪndʒəbl] *adj* intercambiable
in•ter•com ['ɪntərkɑːm] *in office*, *ship* interfono *m*; *for front door* portero *m* automático
in•ter•com•mu•ni•cate [ɪntərkə'mjuːnɪkeɪt] *v/i* comunicarse
in•ter•con•ti•nen•tal [ɪntərkɑːntɪ'nentl] *adj* intercontinental; **~ ballistic missile** misíl *m* balístico intercontinental
in•ter•course ['ɪntərkɔːrs] *sexual* coito *m*; **have ~** tener relaciones sexuales
in•ter•de•nom•in•a•tion•al [ɪntərdɪnɑːmɪ'neɪʃənl] *adj* REL interconfesional
in•ter•de•part•men•tal [ɪntərdiːpɑːrt'mentl] *adj* interdepartamental
in•ter•de•pend•ence [ɪntər'dɪpendəns] interdependencia *f*
in•ter•de•pend•ent [ɪntərdɪ'pendənt] *adj* interdependiente

in•ter•dis•ci•plin•ar•y [ɪntər'dɪsəplɪnerɪ] *adj* interdisciplinar
in•ter•est ['ɪntrəst] **I** *n also* FIN interés *m*; ***take an ~ in sth*** interesarse por algo; ***is that of any ~ to you?*** ¿te interesa?; ***be of ~*** ser de interés (***to*** para); ***of great / little ~*** de gran / poco interés; ***have an ~ in sth*** tener interés en algo, estar interesado en algo; ***be in s.o.'s ~*** ser en *or* por el interés de alguien; ***it is not in your ~ to protest*** no te conviene protestar; ***bear ~*** dar un interés (***at 4%*** del 4%)
II *v/t* interesar
'in•ter•est-bear•ing *adj* con interés
'in•ter•est charg•es *npl* gastos *mpl* de intereses
in•ter•est•ed ['ɪntrəstɪd] *adj* interesado; ***be ~ in sth*** estar interesado en algo; ***thanks, but I'm not ~*** gracias, pero no me interesa; ***I'd be ~ to see her reaction*** me gustaría ver su reacción
in•ter•est-free 'loan préstamo *m* sin intereses
in•ter•est•ing ['ɪntrəstɪŋ] *adj* interesante
in•ter•est•ing•ly ['ɪntrestɪŋlɪ] *adv*: ***~ enough*** curiosamente, casualmente
'in•ter•est rate tipo *m* de interés
in•ter•face ['ɪntərfeɪs] **I** *n* interface *m or f*, interfaz *m or f*; ***the pupil / teacher ~*** la relación alumno / profesor **II** *v/i* relacionarse
in•ter•fere [ɪntər'fɪr] *v/i* interferir, entrometerse; ***he's an interfering old busybody*** es un viejo entrometido
◆ **interfere with** *v/t* afectar a; ***the lock had been interfered with*** alguien había manipulado la cerradura
in•ter•fer•ence [ɪntər'fɪrəns] intromisión *f*; *on radio*, *in baseball* interferencia *f*
in•ter•im ['ɪntərɪm] **I** *n*: ***in the ~*** en el ínterim *or* intervalo **II** *adj* provisional; ***~ government*** gobierno *m* provisional
in•ter•im 'div•i•dend FIN dividendo *m* a cuenta
in•te•ri•or [ɪn'tɪrɪər] **I** *adj* interior **II** *n* interior *m*; ***Department of the Interior*** Ministerio *m* del Interior
in•te•ri•or 'dec•o•ra•tor interiorista *m/f*, decorador(a) *m(f)* de interiores; **in•te•ri•or de'sign** interiorismo *m*; **in•te•ri•or de'sign•er** interiorista *m/f*
in•ter•ject [ɪntər'dʒekt] *v/t* interrumpir, objetar
in•ter•jec•tion [ɪntər'dʒekʃn] LING interjección *f*
in•ter•lace [ɪntər'leɪs] *v/t fig* entrelazar (***with*** con)
in•ter•lop•er ['ɪntərloupər] intruso(-a) *m(f)*
in•ter•lude ['ɪntərlu:d] *at theater* entreacto *m*, intermedio *m*; *at concert* intermedio *m*; (*period*) intervalo *m*; ***a brief ~ of peace*** un intervalo breve de paz
in•ter•mar•riage [ɪntər'mærɪdʒ] matrimonio *m* mixto
in•ter•mar•ry [ɪntər'mærɪ] *v/i* (*pret & pp* ***-ied***) casarse (*con miembros de otra raza, religión o grupo*); ***the two tribes intermarried*** las dos tribus se casaron entre sí
in•ter•me•di•ar•y [ɪntər'mi:dɪərɪ] intermediario *m*
in•ter•me•di•ate [ɪntər'mi:dɪət] *adj* intermedio *m*
in•ter•mi•na•ble [ɪn'tɜ:rmɪnəbl] *adj* interminable
in•ter•min•gle [ɪntər'mɪŋgl] *v/i* entremezclarse
in•ter•mis•sion [ɪntər'mɪʃn] *in theater* entreacto *m*, intermedio *m*; *in movie theater* intermedio *m*, descanso *m*
in•ter•mit•tent [ɪntər'mɪtənt] *adj* intermitente
in•tern [ɪn'tɜ:rn] *v/t* recluir
in•ter•nal [ɪn'tɜ:rnl] *adj* interno; ***~ injury*** herida *f* interna; ***~ affairs*** asuntos *mpl* internos
in•ter•nal com'bus•tion en•gine motor *m* de combustión interna
in•ter•nal•ize [ɪn'tɜ:rnəlaɪz] *v/t* interiorizar
in•ter•nal•ly [ɪn'tɜ:rnəlɪ] *adv* internamente; ***he was bleeding ~*** tenía una hemorragia interna
In•ter•nal 'Rev•e•nue (Serv•ice) Hacienda *f*, *Span* Agencia *f* Tributaria
in•ter•na•tion•al [ɪntər'næʃnl] **I** *adj* internacional; ***~ law*** derecho *m* internacional **II** *n game* partido *m* internacional; *player* internacional *m/f*
In•ter•na•tion•al Court of 'Jus•tice Tribunal *m* Internacional de Justicia
in•ter•na•tion•al•ize [ɪntər'næʃnəlaɪz] *v/t* internacionalizar
in•ter•na•tion•al•ly [ɪntər'næʃnəlɪ] *adv*

internacionalmente
In•ter•na•tion•al 'Mon•e•tar•y Fund Fondo *m* Monetario Internacional; **In•ter•na•tion•al 'Stan•dards Or•gan•i•za•tion** Organización *f* Internacional de Normalización; **in•ter•na•tion•al 'wa•ters** *npl* aguas *fpl* internacionales
in•ter•ne•cine [ɪntər'niːsaɪn] *adj* fratricidal
in•tern•ee [ɪntɜːr'niː] interno(-a) *m(f)*, prisionero(-a) *m(f)*
In•ter•net ['ɪntərnet] Internet *f*; ***on the ~*** en Internet
'In•ter•net caf•é cybercafé *m*
'In•ter•net ser•vice pro•vid•er proveedor *m* de (acceso a) Internet
in•ter•nist [ɪn'tɜːrnɪst] internista *m/f*
in•tern•ment [ɪn'tɜːrnmənt] internamiento *m*; ***~ camp*** campo *m* de internamiento
in•ter•per•son•al [ɪntər'pɜːrsənl] *adj* interpersonal
in•ter•phone ['ɪntərfoun] ☞ ***intercom***
in•ter•plan•e•tar•y [ɪntər'plænəteri] *adj* interplanetario
in•ter•play ['ɪntərpleɪ] interacción *f*
in•ter•pret [ɪn'tɜːrprɪt] *v/t & v/i* interpretar
in•ter•pre•ta•tion [ɪntɜːrprɪ'teɪʃn] interpretación *f*
in•ter•pret•er [ɪn'tɜːrprɪtər] intérprete *m/f*
in•ter•ra•cial [ɪntər'reɪʃl] *adj* interracial
in•ter•re•lat•ed [ɪntərɪ'leɪtɪd] *adj facts* interrelacionado
in•ter•re•la•tion [ɪntərɪ'leɪʃn] interrelación *f*
in•ter•ro•gate [ɪn'terəgeɪt] *v/t* interrogar
in•ter•ro•ga•tion [ɪnterə'geɪʃn] **1** interrogatorio *m* **2** GRAM: ***~ mark*** *or* ***point*** signo *m* de interrogación
in•ter•rog•a•tive [ɪntər'rɑːgətɪv] GRAM (forma *f*) interrogativa *f*; ***~ pronoun*** pronombre *m* interrogativo
in•ter•ro•ga•tor [ɪn'terəgeɪtər] interrogador(a) *m(f)*
in•ter•rog•a•to•ry [ɪntər'rɑːgətɔːrɪ] *adj* interrogativo
in•ter•rupt [ɪntər'rʌpt] **I** *v/t speaker* interrumpir **II** *v/i* interrumpir; ***stop interrupting*** ¡deja de interrumpir!
in•ter•rup•tion [ɪntər'rʌpʃn] interrupción *f*; ***without ~*** sin interrupción, ininterrumpidamente
in•ter•sect [ɪntər'sekt] **I** *v/t* cruzar **II** *v/i* cruzarse
in•ter•sec•tion ['ɪntərsekʃn] *(crossroads)* intersección *f*
in•ter•sperse [ɪntər'spɜːrs] *v/t* intercalar (***with*** con)
in•ter•state ['ɪntərsteɪt] *road* autopista *f* interestatal
in•ter•stice [ɪn'tɜːrstɪs] grieta *f*
in•ter•twine [ɪntər'twaɪn] **I** *v/t* entrecruzar, entrelazar **II** *v/i* entrecruzarse, entrelazarse
in•ter•ur•ban [ɪntər'ɜːrbən] *adj* interurbano
in•ter•val ['ɪntərvl] intervalo *m*; *in theater* entreacto *m*, intermedio *m*; *at concert* intermedio *m*; ***there will be sunny intervals*** habrá intervalos de sol; ***an ~ of peace*** un intervalo de paz; ***at regular ~s*** a intervalos regulares
in•ter•vene [ɪntər'viːn] *v/i of person, police etc* intervenir
in•ter•ven•tion [ɪntər'venʃn] intervención *f*
in•ter•view ['ɪntərvjuː] **I** *n* entrevista *f*; ***give s.o. an ~*** conceder una entrevista a alguien **II** *v/t* entrevistar
in•ter•view•ee [ɪntərvjuː'iː] *on TV* entrevistado(-a) *m(f)*; *for job* candidato(-a) *m(f)*
in•ter•view•er ['ɪntərvjuːər] entrevistador(a) *m(f)*
in•ter•weave [ɪntər'wiːv] *v/t also fig* (*pret* ***-wove***, *pp* ***-woven***) combinar, intercalar (***with*** con)
in•tes•tate [ɪn'testeɪt] *adj*: ***die ~*** LAW morir intestado, morir sin dejar testamento
in•tes•tine [ɪn'testɪn] intestino *m*; ***~s*** intestinos *mpl*; ***large / small ~*** intestino grueso / delgado
in•ti•ma•cy ['ɪntɪməsɪ] *of friendship* intimidad *f*; *sexual* relaciones *fpl* íntimas
in•ti•mate[1] ['ɪntɪmət] *adj* íntimo; ***be on ~ terms*** mantener relaciones íntimas (***with*** con)
in•ti•mate[2] ['ɪntɪmeɪt] *v/t* insinuar, dar a entender; ***~ to s.o. that*** insinuar a alguien que
in•ti•mate•ly ['ɪntɪmətlɪ] *adv* íntimamente

in•tim•i•date [ɪn'tɪmɪdeɪt] *v/t* intimidar; ***~ s.o. into doing sth*** intimidar a alguien para que haga algo
in•tim•i•da•tion [ɪntɪmɪ'deɪʃn] intimidación *f*
in•to ['ɪntʊ] *prep* **1** en; ***he put it ~ his suitcase*** lo puso en su maleta; ***translate ~ English*** traducir al inglés; ***6 ~ 12 goes*** *or* ***is 2*** 12 dividido entre *or* por 6 es 2; ***turn water ~ ice*** transformar agua en hielo
2 F: ***he's ~ classical music*** (*likes*) le gusta*or Span* le va mucho la música clásica; ***he's ~ local politics*** (*is involved with*) está muy metido en el mundillo de la política local; ***when you're ~ the job*** cuando te hayas metido en el trabajo
in•tol•er•a•ble [ɪn'tɑːlərəbl] *adj* intolerable
in•tol•er•ance [ɪn'tɑːlərəns] intolerancia *f*
in•tol•er•ant [ɪn'tɑːlərənt] *adj* intolerante; ***be ~ of sth*** ser intolerante con algo
in•to•na•tion [ɪntə'neɪʃn] entonación *f*
in•tox•i•cant [ɪn'tɑːksɪkənt] estupefaciente *m*
in•tox•i•cate [ɪn'tɑːksɪkeɪt] *v/t* intoxicar
in•tox•i•cat•ed [ɪn'tɑːksɪkeɪtɪd] *adj* ebrio, embriagado
in•tox•i•ca•tion [ɪntɑːksɪ'keɪʃn] intoxicación *f*
in•trac•ta•ble [ɪn'træktəbl] *adj* incorregible, incurable
in•tra•net ['ɪntrənet] COMPUT intranet *m or f*
in•tran•si•gent [ɪn'trænsɪdʒənt] *adj* intransigente
in•tran•si•tive [ɪn'trænsɪtɪv] *adj* GRAM intransitivo
in•tra•u•ter•ine de•vice [ɪntrəjuːtəraɪn dɪ'vaɪs] MED dispositivo *m* intrauterino
in•tra•ve•nous [ɪntrə'viːnəs] *adj* intravenoso
'in-tray bandeja *f* de entrada
in•trep•id [ɪn'trepɪd] *adj* intrépido
in•tri•ca•cy ['ɪntrɪkəsɪ] complejidad *f*
in•tri•cate ['ɪntrɪkət] *adj* intrincado, complicado
in•trigue I *n* ['ɪntriːg] intriga *f* **II** *v/t* [ɪn'triːg] intrigar; ***I would be ~d to know*** tendría curiosidad por saber **II** *v/i* conspirar (***against*** contra)
in•trigu•ing [ɪn'triːgɪŋ] *adj* intrigante
in•trin•sic [ɪn'trɪnsɪk] *adj* intrínseco
in•trin•si•cal•ly [ɪn'trɪnsɪklɪ] *adv* intrínsecamente
in•tro•duce [ɪntrə'duːs] *v/t* presentar; *new technique etc* introducir; ***may I ~ ...?*** permítame presentarle a ...; ***~ s.o. to a new sport*** iniciar a alguien en un deporte nuevo
in•tro•duc•tion [ɪntrə'dʌkʃn] *to person* presentación *f*; *to a new food, sport etc* iniciación *f*; *in book, of new techniques etc* introducción *f*
in•tro•duc•to•ry [ɪntrə'dʌktərɪ] *adj* introductorio; ***~ price*** precio *m* de lanzamiento
in•tro•spec•tion [ɪntrə'spekʃn] introspección *f*
in•tro•spec•tive [ɪntrə'spektɪv] *adj* introspectivo
in•tro•vert ['ɪntrəvɜːrt] introvertido(-a) *m(f)*
in•tro•vert•ed ['ɪntrəvɜːrtɪd] *adj* PSYCH introvertido, tímido
in•trude [ɪn'truːd] *v/i* molestar
in•trud•er [ɪn'truːdər] intruso(-a) *m(f)*
in•tru•sion [ɪn'truːʒn] intromisión *f*
in•tru•sive [ɪn'truːsɪv] *adj* entrometido
in•tu•i•tion [ɪntuː'ɪʃn] intuición *f*
in•tu•i•tive [ɪn'tuːɪtɪv] *adj* intuitivo
in•un•date ['ɪnʌndeɪt] *v/t* inundar, saturar (***with*** de)
in•ure [ɪ'njʊər] *v/t* amoldar, acostumbrar (***to*** a); ***become ~d to sth*** habituarse a algo
in•vade [ɪn'veɪd] *v/t* invadir
in•vad•er [ɪn'veɪdər] invasor(a) *m(f)*
in•val•id[1] [ɪn'vælɪd] *adj* nulo
in•va•lid[2] ['ɪnvəlɪd] *n* MED minusválido(-a) *m(f)*
in•val•i•date [ɪn'vælɪdeɪt] *v/t claim, theory* invalidar
in•val•i•da•tion [ɪnvælɪ'deɪʃn] invalidación *f*
in•va•lid•i•ty pen•sion [ɪnvə'lɪdətɪ] *Br* pensión *f* de *or* por invalidez
in•val•u•a•ble [ɪn'væljʊbl] *adj help, contributor* inestimable; ***be ~ to s.o.*** tener un valor inestimable para alguien
in•var•i•a•ble [ɪn'verɪəbl] *adj* invariable
in•var•i•a•bly [ɪn'veɪrɪəblɪ] *adv* (*always*) invariablemente, siempre
in•va•sion [ɪn'veɪʒn] invasión *f*; ***an ~ of***

I

my privacy una invasión de mi intimidad
in•vec•tive [ɪn'vektɪv] injuria *f*
in•veigh [ɪn'veɪ] *v/i* embestir, arremeter (***against*** contra)
in•vei•gle [ɪn'veɪgl] *v/t*: **~ *s.o. into doing sth*** inducir a alguien a que haga algo
in•vent [ɪn'vent] *v/t* inventar
in•ven•tion [ɪn'venʃn] **1** *action* invención *f* **2** *thing invented* invento *m*
in•ven•tive [ɪn'ventɪv] *adj* inventivo, imaginativo
in•ven•tive•ness [ɪn'ventɪvnɪs] inventiva *f*
in•ven•tor [ɪn'ventər] inventor(a) *m(f)*
in•ven•to•ry ['ɪnvəntɔːrɪ] inventario *m*; ***take an ~ of*** hacer un inventario de
'in•ven•to•ry con•trol control *m* de inventario; **'in•ven•to•ry lev•el** nivel *m* de existencias; **'in•ven•to•ry turn•o•ver** rotación *f* de existencias
in•verse [ɪn'vɜːrs] *adj order* inverso; ***in ~ proportion to*** en proporción inversa a
in•ver•sion [ɪn'vɜːrʒn] inversión *f*
in•vert [ɪn'vɜːrt] *v/t* invertir
in•ver•te•brate [ɪn'vɜːrtɪbrət] **I** *n* invertebrado *m* **II** *adj* invertebrado
in•vert•ed com•mas [ɪnvɜːrtɪd'kɑːməz] *npl Br* comillas *fpl*
in•vest [ɪn'vest] **I** *v/t* invertir **II** *v/i* invertir (***in*** en)
in•ves•ti•gate [ɪn'vestɪgeɪt] *v/t* investigar
in•ves•ti•ga•tion [ɪnvestɪ'geɪʃn] investigación *f*; ***be under ~*** estar bajo investigación
in•ves•ti•ga•tive jour•nal•ism [ɪn'vestɪgətɪv] periodismo *m* de investigación
in•ves•ti•ga•tive 'jour•nal•ist periodista *m/f* de investigación
in•ves•ti•ga•tor [ɪn'vestɪgeɪtər] investigador(a) *m(f)*
in•vest•ment [ɪn'vestmənt] inversión *f*
in'vest•ment an•a•lyst analista *m/f* de inversiones; **in'vest•ment bank** banco *m* de inversiones; **in'vest•ment income** renta *f* de inversiones; **in'vest•ment trust** fondo *m* de inversiones
in•ves•tor [ɪn'vestər] inversor(a) *m(f)*
in•vet•er•ate [ɪn'vetərət] *adj* empedernido
in•vid•i•ous [ɪn'vɪdɪəs] *adj* odioso, desagradable
in•vig•i•late [ɪn'vɪdʒɪleɪt] *v/i Br* supervisar un examen
in•vig•or•ate [ɪn'vɪgəreɪt] *v/t* vigorizar
in•vig•or•at•ing [ɪn'vɪgəreɪtɪŋ] *adj climate* vigorizante
in•vin•ci•ble [ɪn'vɪnsəbl] *adj* invencible
in•vis•i•ble [ɪn'vɪzɪbl] *adj* invisible; **~ *imports*** *npl* importaciones *fpl* invisibles
in•vi•ta•tion [ɪnvɪ'teɪʃn] invitación *f*; ***at the ~ of*** a *or* por invitación de
in•vite [ɪn'vaɪt] **I** *v/t* invitar **II** *n* F ☞ ***invitation***
◆ **invite in** *v/t*: ***invite s.o. in*** invitar a alguien a que entre
in•vit•ing [ɪn'vaɪtɪŋ] *adj room* apetecible; *prospect*, *smile*, *smell* tentador
in vi•tro fer•til•i•za•tion [ɪnviːtroʊfɜːrtɪlaɪ'zeɪʃn] fecundación *f* in vitro
in•voice ['ɪnvɔɪs] **I** *n* factura *f* **II** *v/t customer* enviar la factura a
'in•voice date fecha *f* de facturación
'in•voice price precio *m* facturado
in•voke [ɪn'voʊk] *v/t* invocar
in•vol•un•ta•ry [ɪn'vɑːlənterɪ] *adj* involuntario
in•volve [ɪn'vɑːlv] *v/t hard work*, *expense* involucrar, entrañar; ***it would ~ emigrating*** supondría emigrar; ***this doesn't ~ you*** esto no tiene nada que ver contigo; ***what does it ~?*** ¿en qué consiste?; ***the police didn't want to get ~d*** la policía no quería intervenir; ***get ~d with s.o.*** *emotionally*, *romantically* tener una relación sentimental con alguien; ***get ~d with sth*** involucrarse *or* meterse en algo; ***he got involved with the school play*** participó en la obra de teatro del colegio; ***~d in an accident*** envuelto *or* involucrado en un accidente; ***the people ~d*** las personas involucradas
in•volved [ɪn'vɑːlvd] *adj* (*complex*) complicado
in•volve•ment [ɪn'vɑːlvmənt] *in a project*, *crime etc* participación *f*, intervención *f*
in•vul•ne•ra•ble [ɪn'vʌlnərəbl] *adj* invulnerable
in•ward ['ɪnwərd] **I** *adj feeling*, *smile* interior **II** *adv* hacia dentro
in•ward•ly ['ɪnwərdlɪ] *adv* por dentro
in•wards ['ɪnwərdz] *adv* hacia dentro
i•o•dine ['aɪoʊdiːn] yodo *m*

i•on ['aɪən] CHEM, PHYS ión *m*
i•o•ta [aɪ'oʊtə] ápice m, pizca *f*; ***not an ~ of truth*** ni un ápice de verdad
IOU [aɪoʊ'juː] *abbr* (= ***I owe you***) pagaré *m*
IQ [aɪ'kjuː] *abbr* (= ***intelligence quotient***) cociente *m* intelectual
I•ran [ɪ'rɑːn] Irán *m*
I•ra•ni•an [ɪ'reɪnɪən] **I** *adj* iraní **II** *n* iraní *m/f*
I•raq [ɪ'ræːk] Iraq *m*, Irak *m*
I•ra•qi [ɪ'rækɪ] **I** *adj* iraquí **II** *n* iraquí *m/f*
i•ras•ci•ble [ɪ'ræsəbl] *adj* irascible
i•rate [aɪ'reɪt] *adj* furioso, colérico
Ire•land ['aɪrlənd] Irlanda *f*
ir•i•des•cent [ɪrɪ'desnt] *adj* iridiscente
i•ris ['aɪrɪs] **1** *of eye* iris *m inv* **2** *flower* lirio *m*
I•rish ['aɪrɪʃ] **I** *adj* irlandés; ***~ coffee*** café *m* irlandés **II** *n* **1** *language* irlandés *m* **2** *pl*: ***the ~*** los irlandeses
I•rish•man ['aɪrɪʃmən] irlandés *m*
'I•rish•wom•an irlandesa *f*
irk [ɜːrk] *v/t* molestar, fastidiar
irk•some ['ɜːrksəm] *adj* irritante
i•ron ['aɪərn] **I** *n* **1** *substance* hierro *m*; ***strike while the ~ is hot*** *fig* aprovechar la oportunidad; ***will of ~*** voluntad *f* de hierro **2** *for clothes* plancha *f* **II** *adj* de hierro; ***~ ore*** MIN mineral *m* de hierro **III** *v/t shirts etc* planchar
◆ **iron out** *v/t* **1** *creases* planchar **2** *problem* resolver
I•ron 'Cur•tain POL telón *m* de acero
i•ron•i•c, i•ron•i•cal [aɪ'rɑːnɪk(l)] *adj* irónico
i•ron•ing ['aɪərnɪŋ] planchado *m*; ***do the ~*** planchar
'i•ron•ing board tabla *f* de planchar
i•ron•mon•ger ['aɪərnmʌŋgər] *Br* ferretero(-a) *m(f)*
'i•ron•works fundición *f*
i•ron•y ['aɪrənɪ] ironía *f*; ***the ~ of it all is that ...*** lo irónico del tema es que ...
ir•ra•di•ate [ɪ'reɪdɪeɪt] *v/t* irradiar
ir•ra•di•a•tion [ɪreɪdɪ'eɪʃn] irradiación *f*
ir•ra•tion•al [ɪ'ræʃənl] *adj* irracional
ir•rec•on•ci•la•ble [ɪrekən'saɪləbl] *adj* irreconciliable
ir•re•cov•e•ra•ble [ɪrɪ'kʌvərəbl] *adj* irrecuperable
ir•re•deem•a•ble [ɪrɪ'diːməbl] *adj weakness etc* irremediable
ir•ref•u•ta•ble [ɪrɪ'fjuːtəbl] irrefutable *f*
ir•reg•u•lar [ɪ'regjʊlər] *adj* irregular
ir•reg•u•lar•i•ty [ɪregjʊ'lærətɪ] irregularidad *f*
ir•rel•e•vance, ir'rel•e•van•cy [ɪ'reləvəns(ɪ)] irrelevancia *f*
ir•rel•e•vant [ɪ'reləvənt] *adj* irrelevante
ir•re•me•di•a•ble [ɪrɪ'miːdjəbl] *adj* irremediable
ir•rep•a•ra•ble [ɪ'repərəbl] *adj* irreparable
ir•re•place•a•ble [ɪrɪ'pleɪsəbl] *adj object, person* irreemplazable
ir•re•pres•si•ble [ɪrɪ'presəbl] *adj sense of humor* incontenible; *person* irreprimible
ir•re•proach•a•ble [ɪrɪ'proʊtʃəbl] *adj* irreprochable
ir•re•sis•ti•ble [ɪrɪ'zɪstəbl] *adj* irresistible
ir•res•o•lute [ɪ'rezəluːt] *adj* irresoluto
ir•re•spec•tive [ɪrɪ'spektɪv] *adv*: ***~ of*** independientemente de
ir•re•spon•si•ble [ɪrɪ'spɑːnsəbl] *adj* irresponsable
ir•re•trie•va•ble [ɪrɪ'triːvəbl] *adj* irrecuperable
ir•rev•er•ence [ɪ'revərəns] falta *f* de respeto
ir•rev•e•rent [ɪ'revərənt] *adj* irreverente
ir•re•vers•i•ble [ɪrɪ'vɜːrsəbl] *adj* irreversible, irrevocable
ir•rev•o•ca•ble [ɪ'revəkəbl] *adj* irrevocable
ir•ri•gate ['ɪrɪgeɪt] *v/t* regar
ir•ri•ga•tion [ɪrɪ'geɪʃn] riego *m*
ir•ri•ga•tion ca'nal acequia *f*
ir•ri•ta•bil•i•ty [ɪrɪtə'bɪlɪtɪ] irritabilidad *f*
ir•ri•ta•ble ['ɪrɪtəbl] *adj* irritable
ir•ri•tate ['ɪrɪteɪt] *v/t* irritar; ***be ~d at*** *or* ***with*** irritarse por
ir•ri•tat•ing ['ɪrɪteɪtɪŋ] *adj* irritante
ir•ri•ta•tion [ɪrɪ'teɪʃn] irritación *f*
IRS [aɪɑːr'es] *abbr* (= ***Internal Revenue Service***) Hacienda *f*, *Span* Agencia *f* Tributaria
is [ɪz] ☞ ***be***
ISDN [aɪesdiː'en] *abbr* (= ***Integrated Services Digital Network***) RDSI *f*
Is•lam ['ɪzlɑːm] (el) Islam
Is•lam•ic [ɪz'læmɪk] *adj* islámico; ***~ fundamentalist*** fundamentalista *m/f or*

I

integrista *m/f* islámico(-a)
is•land ['aɪlənd] isla *f*
is•land•er ['aɪləndər] isleño(-a) *m(f)*
ISO [aɪes'oʊ] *abbr* (= ***International Standards Organization***) ISO *f*
i•so•late ['aɪsəleɪt] *v/t* aislar
i•so•lat•ed ['aɪsəleɪtɪd] *adj* aislado; ~ ***case*** caso *m* aislado
i•so•la•tion [aɪsə'leɪʃn] *of a region* aislamiento *m*; ***in*** ~ *prisoner, patient* aislado; *consider sth* aisladamente
i•so'la•tion ward pabellón *m* de enfermedades infecciosas
i•so•tope ['aɪsətoʊp] PHYS isótopo *m*
ISP [aɪes'piː] *abbr* (= ***Internet service provider***) proveedor *m* de (acceso a) Internet
Is•ra•el ['ɪzreɪl] Israel *m*
Is•rae•li [ɪz'reɪlɪ] **I** *adj* israelí **II** *n person* israelí *m/f*
is•sue ['ɪʃuː] **I** *n* **1** (*matter*) tema *m*, asunto *m*; ***the point at*** ~ el tema que se debate; ***take*** ~ ***with s.o.*** / ***sth*** discrepar de alguien / algo; ***your honesty is not at*** ~ no se cuestiona tu honestidad **2** *of magazine* número *m* **II** *v/t coins* emitir; *passports, visa* expedir; *warning* dar; ~ ***s.o. with sth*** entregar algo a alguien
isth•mus ['ɪsməs] istmo *m*
IT [aɪ'tiː] *abbr* (= ***information technology***) tecnologías *fpl* de la información; ~ ***department*** departamento *m* de informática
it [ɪt] *pron as object* lo *m*, la *f*, ***what color is*** ~***?*** – ~ ***is red*** ¿de qué color es? - es rojo; ~***'s raining*** llueve; ~***'s me / him*** soy yo / es él; ~***'s Charlie here*** TELEC soy Charlie; ~***'s your turn*** te toca; ***that's*** ~***!*** (*that's right*) ¡eso es!; (*finished*) ¡ya está!; ~ ***is to him that you should turn*** es a él a quien deberías dirigirte
I•tal•ian [ɪ'tæljən] **I** *adj* italiano **II** *n* **1** *person* italiano(-a) *m(f)* **2** *language* italiano *m*
i•tal•ic [ɪ'tælɪk] *adj* cursiva
i•tal•i•cize [ɪ'tælɪsaɪz] *v/t* poner en cursiva
i•tal•ics [ɪ'tælɪks] *npl* cursiva *f*; ***in*** ~ en cursiva
It•a•ly ['ɪtəlɪ] Italia *f*
itch [ɪʧ] **I** *n* picor *m* **II** *v/i* picar; ***be*** ~***ing for sth*** F estar deseando algo, morirse por algo; ***they're*** ~***ing to get home*** F se mueren por llegar a casa
itch•y ['ɪʧɪ] *adj* que pica; ***have*** ~ ***feet*** *fig* F tener el gusanillo de viajar
i•tem ['aɪtəm] *in list, accounts*, (*article*) artículo *m*; *on agenda* punto *m*; *of news* noticia *f*; ~ ***of clothing*** prenda *f* de vestir; ***they're an*** ~ F *of couple* son pareja
i•tem•ize ['aɪtəmaɪz] *v/t invoice* detallar
i•tin•er•ant [ɪ'tɪnərənt] *adj* itinerante
i•tin•e•ra•ry [aɪ'tɪnərerɪ] itinerario *m*
it'll ['ɪtl] F ☞ ***it will***
it's [ɪts] ☞ ***it is***; ***it has***
its [ɪts] *poss adj* su; ***where is*** ~ ***box?*** ¿dónde está su caja?; ***the dog has hurt*** ~ ***leg*** el perro se ha hecho daño en la pata
it•self [ɪt'self] *pron reflexive* se; ***the dog hurt*** ~ el perro se hizo daño; ***the hotel*** ~ ***is fine*** el hotel en sí (mismo) está bien; ***by*** ~ (*alone*) aislado, solo; (*automatically*) solo
IUD [aɪjuː'diː] *abbr* (= ***intrauterine device***) DIU *m* (= dispositivo *m* intrauterino)
I've [aɪv] F ☞ ***I have***
IVF [aɪviː'ef] *abbr* (= ***in vitro fertilization***) fecundación *f* in vitro, FIV *f*
i•vo•ry ['aɪvərɪ] **I** *n* marfil *m* **II** *adj* de marfil; ***live in an*** ~ ***tower*** *fig* vivir en una torre de marfil
I•vo•ry 'Coast Costa *f* de Marfil
i•vy ['aɪvɪ] hiedra *f*
I•vy 'League *grupo de ocho universidades americanas de gran prestigio*

J

jab [dʒæb] *v/t* (*pret & pp* ***-bed***) clavar
jab•ber ['dʒæbər] *v/i* parlotear
jack [dʒæk] **1** MOT gato *m* **2** *in cards* jota *f*
◆ **jack up** *v/t* **1** MOT levantar con el gato **2** F *prices, salaries* subir
jack•al ['dʒækəl] chacal *m*
jack•ass ['dʒækæs] *fig* memo(-a) *m(f)*
jack•daw ['dʒækdɔː] grajilla *f*
jack•et ['dʒækɪt] **1** (*coat*) chaqueta *f* **2** *of book* sobrecubierta *f*
jack•et po'ta•to (*pl* ***-o(e)s***) *Span* patata *f or L.Am.* papa *f* asada (*con piel*)
'jack-in-the-box caja *f* de sorpresas
'jack-knife *v/i* derrapar (*por la parte del remolque*); **jack-of-'all-trades**: ***be a ~ of*** *teacher, secretary etc* hacer un poco de todo; **'jack plug** ELEC enchufe *m* de clavija; **'jack•pot** gordo *m*; ***he hit the ~*** le tocó el gordo
ja•cuz•zi® [dʒə'kuːzɪ] jacuzzi *m*
jade [dʒeɪd] jade *m*
jad•ed ['dʒeɪdɪd] *adj* harto; *appetite* hastiado
jag•ged ['dʒægɪd] *adj* accidentado
jag•u•ar ['dʒægʊər] jaguar *m*
jail [dʒeɪl] cárcel *f*; ***he's in ~*** está en la cárcel; ***go to ~*** ir a la cárcel; ***put s.o. in ~*** encarcelar a alguien, meter a alguien en la cárcel
'jail•bird F delincuente *m/f* habitual
'jail•break F fuga *f*, evasión *f*
jail•er ['dʒeɪlər] carcelero(-a) *m(f)*, celador(a) *m(f)*
ja•lop•y [dʒə'lɑːpɪ] F chatarra *f* F, cacharro *m* F
jam[1] [dʒæm] *n for bread* mermelada *f*
jam[2] [dʒæm] **I** *n* **1** MOT atasco *m* **2** F (*difficulty*) aprieto *m*; ***be in a ~*** estar en un aprieto
II *v/t* (*pret & pp* ***-med***) (*ram*) meter, embutir; (*cause to stick*) atascar; *broadcast* provocar interferencias en; ***be ~med*** *of roads* estar colapsado; *of door, window* estar atascado; ***he got his finger ~med in the door*** se pilló el dedo en la puerta
III *v/i* (*pret & pp* ***-med***) **1** *of printer, window* atascarse **2**: ***all ten of us managed to ~ into the car*** nos las arreglamos para meternos los diez en el coche
◆ **jam in** *v/t* apretujar; ***we were all jammed in*** estábamos apretujados
◆ **jam on** *v/t*: ***jam on the brakes*** dar un frenazo
Ja•mai•ca [dʒə'meɪkə] Jamaica *f*
Ja•mai•can [dʒə'meɪkən] **I** *adj* jamaicano, *L.Am.* jamaiquino **II** *n person* jamaicano(-a) *m(f)*, *L.Am.* jamaiquino(-a) *m(f)*
jamb [dʒæm] jamba *f*
jam•bo•ree [dʒæmbə'riː] **1** F fiesta *f*, juerga *f* **2** *of Scouts* congreso *m*
jam-'packed *adj* F abarrotado (***with*** de)
jan•gle ['dʒæŋgl] **I** *v/i* tintinear, sonar **II** *v/t* hacer tintinear
jan•i•tor ['dʒænɪtər] portero(-a) *m(f)*, conserje *m/f*
Jan•u•a•ry ['dʒænʊerɪ] enero *m*
Ja•pan [dʒə'pæn] Japón *m*
Jap•a•nese [dʒæpə'niːz] **I** *adj* japonés **II** *n* **1** *person* japonés(-esa) *m(f)*; ***the ~*** los japoneses **2** *language* japonés *m*
jar[1] [dʒɑːr] *n container* tarro *m*
jar[2] [dʒɑːr] *v/i* (*pret & pp* ***-red***) *of noise* rechinar; ***~ on*** rechinar en
jar•gon ['dʒɑːrgən] jerga *f*
jas•min(e) ['dʒæzmɪn] BOT jazmín *m*
jaun•dice ['dʒɒːndɪs] ictericia *f*
jaun•diced ['dʒɒːndɪst] *adj fig* resentido
jaunt [dʒɒːnt] excursión *f*; ***go on a ~*** ir de excursión
jaunt•y ['dʒɒːntɪ] *adj* desenfadado
jav•e•lin ['dʒævlɪn] (*spear*) jabalina *f*; *event* (lanzamiento *m* de) jabalina *f*
jaw [dʒɒː] mandíbula *f*
'jaw•bone mandíbula *f*, maxilar *m*
jay [dʒeɪ] arrendajo *m*
'jay•walk•er peatón(-ona) *m(f)* imprudente
'jay•walk•ing *cruzar la calle de manera imprudente*
jazz [dʒæz] jazz *m*; ***~ band*** banda *f* de jazz; ***and all that ~*** F y todo ese rollo
◆ **jazz up** *v/t* F animar; *décor, dress* alegrar, dar vida a F
jazz•y ['dʒæzɪ] *adj* **1** MUS de jazz, jazzístico **2** F *colors, design* llamativo, visto-

so

jeal•ous ['dʒeləs] *adj* celoso; **be ~ of** *in love* tener celos de; *of riches etc* tener envidia de

jeal•ous•ly ['dʒeləslɪ] *adv* celosamente; *relating to possessions* con envidia

jeal•ous•y ['dʒeləsɪ] celos *mpl*; *of possessions* envidia *f*

jeans [dʒi:nz] *npl* vaqueros *mpl*, jeans *mpl*

jeep [dʒi:p] jeep *m*

jeer [dʒɪr] **I** *n* abucheo *m* **II** *v/i* abuchear; **~ at** burlarse de

jeer•ing ['dʒɪrɪŋ] abucheo *m*

Je•ho•vah's Wit•ness [dʒɪhoʊvəz'wɪtnɪs] REL testigo *m/f* de Jehová

jell [dʒel] *v/i fig of plans* concretarse

Jel•lo® ['dʒeloʊ] gelatina *f*

jel•ly ['dʒelɪ] mermelada *f*

'jel•ly bean gominola *f*

'jel•ly•fish medusa *f*

jem•my ['dʒemɪ] *Br* ☞ **jimmy**

jeop•ar•dize ['dʒepərdaɪz] *v/t* poner en peligro

jeop•ar•dy ['dʒepərdɪ]: **be in ~** estar en peligro

jerk[1] [dʒɜ:rk] **I** *n* sacudida *f* **II** *v/t* dar un tirón a

◆ **jerk off** *v/i* P hacerse una paja P

jerk[2] [dʒɜ:rk] *n* F imbécil *m/f*, *Span* gilipollas *m/f inv* F

jerk•y ['dʒɜ:rkɪ] *adj movement* brusco

jer•ry-built ['dʒerɪbɪlt] *adj* chapucero, mal construido

jer•sey ['dʒɜ:rzɪ] (*sweater*) suéter *m*, *Span* jersey *m*

jest [dʒest] **I** *n* broma *f*; **in ~** en broma **II** *v/i* bromear

jest•er ['dʒestər] HIST bufón *m*

Jes•u•it ['dʒezjʊɪt] REL jesuita *m*

Je•sus ['dʒi:zəs] Jesús; **~!** F ¡por Dios!, ¡por el amor de Dios!

jet [dʒet] **I** *n* **1** *of water* chorro *m* **2** (*nozzle*) boquilla *f* **3** (*airplane*) reactor *m*, avión *m* a reacción **II** *v/i* (*pret & pp* **-ted**) *travel* viajar en avión

jet-'black *adj* azabache; **'jet en•gine** reactor *m*; **'jet fight•er** AVIA, MIL caza *m* reactor, caza *m*; **'jet•lag** desfase *m* horario, jet lag *m*; **jet-lagged** [dʒet'lægd] *adj*: **be ~** tener jet lag *or* desfase horario; **'jet plane** avión *m* reactor; **jet-pro•pelled** [dʒetprə'peld] *adj esp* AVIA a reacción

jet•sam ['dʒetsəm] NAUT ☞ **flotsam**

'jet set jet *f* set

jet•ti•son ['dʒetɪsn] *v/t also fig* tirar por la borda

jet•ty ['dʒetɪ] malecón *m*

Jew [dʒu:] judío(-a) *m(f)*

jew•el ['dʒu:əl] joya *f*, alhaja *f*, *fig*: *person* joya *f*

'jew•el case *for CD* carcasa *f*

jew•el•er, *Br* **jew•el•ler** ['dʒu:lər] joyero(-a) *m(f)*

jew•el•lery *Br*, **jew•el•ry** ['dʒu:lrɪ] joyas *fpl*, alhajas *fpl*; **piece of ~** joya *f*, alhaja *f*

Jew•ish ['dʒu:ɪʃ] *adj* judío

jib [dʒɪb] **1** NAUT foque *m* **2** TECH brazo *m*

◆ **jib at** *v/t* (*pret & pp* **-bed**) **1** *fence* plantarse ante **2** *fig expense etc* resistirse a

jif•fy [dʒɪfɪ] F: **in a ~** en un periquete F

jig•gle ['dʒɪgl] *v/t* sacudir

jig•saw (puz•zle) ['dʒɪgsɒ:] rompecabezas *m inv*, puzzle *m*

jilt [dʒɪlt] *v/t* dejar plantado

Jim Crow [dʒɪm'kroʊ] *adj* F racista; *school* para negros

jim•my ['dʒɪmɪ] palanca *f*, palanqueta *f*

jin•gle ['dʒɪŋgl] **I** *n song* melodía *f* publicitaria **II** *v/i of keys, coins* tintinear

jin•go•ism ['dʒɪŋgoʊɪzm] patrioterismo *m*, patriotería *f*

jin•go•is•tic [dʒɪŋgoʊ'ɪstɪk] *adj* jingoísta

jinks [dʒɪŋks] *npl*: **high ~** jarana *f*, parranda *f*; **they were having high ~** estaban de juerga

jinx [dʒɪŋks] gafe *m*; **there's a ~ on this project** este proyecto está gafado

JIT [dʒeɪaɪ'ti:] *abbr* (= **just in time**) COM justo a tiempo

jit•ters ['dʒɪtərz] *npl* F: **I got the ~** me entró el pánico *or Span* canguelo F

jit•ter•y ['dʒɪtərɪ] *adj* F nervioso

job [dʒɑ:b] (*employment*) trabajo *m*, empleo *m*; (*task*) tarea *f*, trabajo *m*; **it's not my ~ to answer the phone** no me corresponde a mí contestar el teléfono; **it's not my ~ to clean up your mess** no es mi obligación recoger tu desorden; **I have a few ~s to do around the house** tengo que hacer unas cuantas cosas en la casa; **out of a ~** sin trabajo *or* empleo; **it's a good ~ you warned me** menos mal que me avisaste; ***you'll have a ~*** (*it'll be difficult*) te va a costar Dios y ayuda; ***it was a real ~ but we managed it*** fue una odisea pero al final lo conseguimos; ***make a good / bad ~ of sth*** hacer algo bien / mal; ***on the ~*** en el trabajo; ***make the best of a bad ~*** apechugar y hacer lo que se pueda; ***~ interview*** entrevista *f* de trabajo

'job de•scrip•tion (descripción *f* de las) responsabilidades *fpl* del puesto

'job hunt *v/i*: ***be ~ing*** buscar trabajo

job•less ['dʒɑːblɪs] *adj* desempleado, *Span* parado

job los•ses ['dʒɑːblɔːsɪs] *npl* pérdidas *fpl* de puestos de trabajo; **'job of•fer** oferta *f* de trabajo *or* empleo; **'job o•pen•ing** vacante *f*; **job sat•is'fac•tion** satisfacción *f* con el trabajo; **'job se•cu•ri•ty** seguridad *f* profesional; **job seek•er** ['dʒɑːbsiːkər] persona *f* que busca empleo; **job-shar•ing** ['dʒɑːbʃeɪrɪŋ] sistema *m* de trabajo compartido

jock [dʒɑːk] F *sporting type* deportista *m*

jock•ey ['dʒɑːkɪ] jockey *m/f*

◆ **jockey for** *v/t*: ***jockey for position*** *fig* disputarse el puesto, rivalizar por el puesto

'jock•strap vendaje *m* suspensorio, suspendedor *m*

joc•u•lar ['dʒɑːkjʊlər] *adj* jocoso, ocurrente

jog ['dʒɑːg] **I** *n*: ***go for a ~*** ir a hacer jogging *or* footing **II** *v/i* (*pret & pp* ***-ged***) *as exercise* hacer jogging *or* footing **III** *v/t* (*pret & pp* ***-ged***): ***~ s.o.'s memory*** refrescar la memoria de alguien; ***somebody ~ged my elbow*** alguien me dio en el codo

◆ **jog along** *v/i* F ir tirando F

jog•ger ['dʒɑːgər] *person* persona *f* que hace jogging *or* footing; *shoe* zapatilla *f* de jogging *or* footing; *trousers* pantalones *mpl* de deporte

jog•ging ['dʒɑːgɪŋ] jogging *m*, footing *m*; ***go ~*** ir a hacer jogging *or* footing

'jog•ging suit chándal *m*

jog•gle ['dʒɑːgl] *v/t* sacudir, balancear

john [dʒɑːn] P (*toilet*) baño *m*, váter *m*; ***in the ~*** en el váter

John Han•cock [dʒɑːn'hænkɑːk] P firma *f*

join [dʒɔɪn] **I** *n* juntura *f* **II** *v/i of roads, rivers* juntarse; (*become a member*) hacerse socio **III** *v/t* (*connect*) unir; *person* unirse a; *club* hacerse socio de; (*go to work for*) entrar en; *of road* desembocar en; ***I'll ~ you at the theater*** me reuniré contigo en el teatro; ***~ hands*** agarrarse *or* cogerse de la mano

◆ **join in** *v/i* participar

◆ **join up I** *v/i* **1** *of two groups of walkers etc* juntarse **2** *Br* MIL alistarse **II** *v/t parts etc* unir, juntar

join•er ['dʒɔɪnər] carpintero(-a) *m*(*f*)

join•er•y ['dʒɔɪnərɪ] carpintería *f*

joint [dʒɔɪnt] **I** *n* **1** ANAT articulación *f*; *in woodwork* junta *f*; *of meat* pieza *f* **2** F (*place*) garito *m* F **3** F *of cannabis* porro *m* F, canuto *m* F **II** *adj* (*shared*) conjunto; ***take ~ action*** actuar conjuntamente

joint ac'count cuenta *f* conjunta

joint and 'sev•er•al *adj guarantor, liability* solidario

joint•ly and sev•er•al•ly [dʒɔɪntlɪənd'sevrəlɪ] *adv* mancomunada y solidariamente

joint 'ven•ture empresa *f* conjunta

joist [dʒɔɪst] ARCHI viga *f*

joke [dʒoʊk] **I** *n story* chiste *m*; (*practical ~*) broma *f*; ***play a ~ on*** gastar una broma a; ***it's no ~*** no tiene ninguna gracia; ***in the end the ~ was on him*** al final le salió el tiro por la culata; ***it was only a ~, sir*** sólo era una broma, señor; ***Mr. Stroud can't take a ~*** al Sr Stroud no se le puede hacer *or* gastar una broma; ***oh come on, take a ~!*** ¡venga, que iba en broma!; ***our football team is a ~*** nuestro equipo de fútbol es un desastre; ***they were just having a ~*** sólo estaban de broma; ***crack a ~*** contar un chiste; ***for a ~*** en *or* de broma

II *v/i* bromear; ***I'm not joking*** no bromeo; ***you must be joking!*** ¡no hablas en serio!

jok•er ['dʒoʊkər] *person* bromista *m/f*, F *pej* payaso(-a) *m*(*f*); *in cards* comodín *m*

jok•ey ['dʒoʊkɪ] *adj movie* ameno; *style* gracioso; *person* guasón

jok•ing ['dʒoʊkɪŋ]: ***~ apart*** bromas aparte

jok•ing•ly ['dʒoʊkɪŋlɪ] *adv* en broma

jol•ly ['dʒɑːlɪ] *adj* **1** alegre **2** *Br* F (*very*) super- (superinteresante), -ísimo (dificilísimo)

J

Jol•ly 'Rog•er bandera *f* pirata

jolt [dʒoʊlt] **I** *n* (*jerk*) sacudida *f*; ***give s.o. a ~*** *fig* dar un susto a alguien **II** *v/t* (*push*): ***somebody ~ed my elbow*** alguien me dio en el codo; ***~ s.o. out of*** (*shock*) hacer salir a alguien de

Jor•dan ['dʒɔːrdn] Jordania *f*

Jor•da•ni•an [dʒɔːr'deɪnɪən] **I** *adj* jordano **II** *n* jordano(-na) *m(f)*

josh [dʒɑːʃ] *v/t* F tomarle el pelo a

joss stick ['dʒɑːsstɪk] varilla *f* de incienso

jos•tle ['dʒɑːsl] *v/t* empujar

jot [dʒɑːt] *fig*: ***not a ~ of*** ni un ápice de, ni pizca de; ***it doesn't make a ~ of difference*** da exactamente igual

◆ **jot down** [dʒɑːt] *v/t* (*pret & pp* ***-ted***) apuntar, anotar

jot•ter ['dʒɑːtər] *Br* bloc *m*

joule [dʒuːl] PHYS julio *m*

jour•nal ['dʒɜːrnl] **1** (*magazine*) revista *f* **2** (*diary*) diario *m*

'jour•nal en•try *in accounts* asiento *m* en el libro diario

jour•nal•ism ['dʒɜːrnəlɪzm] periodismo *m*

jour•nal•ist ['dʒɜːrnəlɪst] periodista *m/f*

jour•ney ['dʒɜːrnɪ] viaje *m*; ***the daily ~ to school*** el camino diario al colegio; ***go on*** *or* ***make a ~*** hacer un viaje

jo•vi•al ['dʒoʊvɪəl] *adj* jovial

jowls [dʒaʊlz] *npl* carillos *mpl*, papada *f*

joy [dʒɔɪ] alegría *f*, gozo *m*; ***for ~*** de alegría; ***tears of ~*** lágrimas *fpl* de alegría; ***to s.o.'s ~*** para alegría *or* gozo de alguien

joy•ful ['dʒɔɪfʊl] *adj* alegre, contento

joy•less ['dʒɔɪlɪs] *adj* triste, alicaído

joy•ous ['dʒɔɪəs] → ***joyful***

'joy rid•er F *persona que roba coches para darse una vuelta y luego los abandona*; **'joy rid•ing** F *robo de un coche para darse una vuelta y luego abandonarlo*; **'joy•stick** COMPUT joystick *m*

ju•bi•lant ['dʒuːbɪlənt] *adj* jubiloso

ju•bi•la•tion [dʒuːbɪ'leɪʃn] júbilo *m*

ju•bi•lee [dʒuːbɪ'liː] aniversario *m*

judge [dʒʌdʒ] **I** *n* LAW juez *m/f*, jueza *f*; *in competition* juez *m/f*, miembro *m* del jurado; ***be a good ~ of wine / people*** tener buen ojo para el vino / las personas **II** *v/t* **1** juzgar **2** (*estimate*) calcular **III** *v/i* juzgar; ***~ for yourself*** júzgalo por ti mismo; ***judging by his words*** a juzgar por sus palabras

judg(e)•ment ['dʒʌdʒmənt] LAW fallo *m*; (*opinion*) juicio *m*; ***an error of ~*** una equivocación; ***he showed good ~*** mostró tener criterio; ***against my better ~*** a pesar de no estar convencido; ***the Last Judgment*** REL el Juicio Final; ***it shows a lack on ~ on his part*** muestra una falta de criterio por su parte; ***in my ~*** a mi juicio; ***form a ~ on sth*** formarse una opinión sobre algo; ***pass ~ on s.o.*** juzgar a alguien, opinar de alguien

judg•men•tal [dʒʌdʒ'mentl] *adj* sentencioso, crítico

'Judg(e)•ment Day Día *m* del Juicio Final

ju•di•cial [dʒuː'dɪʃl] *adj* judicial

ju•di•ci•ar•y [dʒuː'dɪʃərɪ] LAW judicatura *f*

ju•di•cious [dʒuː'dɪʃəs] *adj* juicioso

ju•do ['dʒuːdoʊ] judo *m*

jug [dʒʌg] jarra *f*

jug•ger•naut ['dʒʌgərnɔːt] MOT *Br* camión *m* grande

jug•gle [dʒʌgl] *v/t also fig* hacer malabarismos con

jug•gler ['dʒʌglər] malabarista *m/f*

'jug wine morapio *m*

juice [dʒuːs] *L.Am.* jugo *m*, *Span* zumo *m*; ***let s.o. stew in his own ~*** F dejar sufrir a alguien

juic•er ['dʒuːsər] exprimidor *m*

juic•y ['dʒuːsɪ] *adj* jugoso; *news, gossip* jugoso, sabroso

ju•jit•su [dʒuː'dʒɪtsuː] SP jiujitsu *m*

juke•box ['dʒuːkbɑːks] máquina *f* de discos

Ju•ly [dʒʊ'laɪ] julio *m*

jum•ble ['dʒʌmbl] revoltijo *m*

◆ **jumble together** *v/t* mezclar

◆ **jumble up** *v/t* revolver

'jum•ble sale *Br*: *mercadillo de beneficencia donde se suelen vender artículos de segunda mano*

jum•bo (jet) ['dʒʌmboʊ] jumbo *m*

jum•bo, jum•bo-sized [dʒʌmboʊ'saɪzd] *adj* gigante

jump [dʒʌmp] **I** *n* salto *m*; (*increase*) incremento *m*, subida *f*; ***give a ~ of surprise*** dar un salto **II** *v/i* saltar; (*increase*) dispararse; ***you made me ~!*** ¡me diste un susto!; ***~ to one's feet*** ponerse de pie de un salto;

~ to conclusions sacar conclusiones precipitadas; **~ off** *bus* bajarse de; *bridge* saltar de; **~ for joy** saltar de alegría
III *v/t fence etc* saltar; F (*attack*) asaltar; **~ the lights** saltarse el semáforo, pasarse un semáforo en rojo; **~ the gun** *fig* precipitarse, apresurarse; *Br* **~ the queue** colarse
◆ **jump at** *v/t opportunity* no dejar escapar
◆ **jump on** *v/t* F (*reprimand*) regañar
◆ **jump up** *v/i out of chair* ponerse de pie de un salto
'jump ball *in basketball* lucha *f*, salto *m* entre dos
jumped-up [dʒʌmpt'ʌp] *adj Br* F presuntuoso
jump•er[1] ['dʒʌmpər] *dress* pichi *m*
jump•er[2] ['dʒʌmpər] SP saltador(a) *m(f)*; *horse* caballo *m* de saltos
'jump•er ca•bles *npl* MOT cables *mpl* de arranque
'jump leads *npl Br* ☞ **jumper cables**; **'jump-rope** comba *f*, cuerda *f* de saltar; **'jump shot** *in basketball* tiro *m* en suspensión; **'jump-start** *v/t* **1** *car*: *with cables* hacer un puente a; *by pushing* empujar **2** *fig*: *economy* impulsar; **'jump suit** mono *m*
jump•y ['dʒʌmpɪ] *adj* nervioso; **get ~** ponerse nervioso
junc•tion ['dʒʌŋkʃn] *Br*: *of roads* cruce *m*
junc•ture ['dʒʌŋktʃər] *fml*: **at this ~** en esta coyuntura
June [dʒu:n] junio *m*
jun•gle ['dʒʌŋgl] selva *f*, jungla *f*; **it's a ~ out there** es my peligroso ahí fuera
'jun•gle gym *estructura hecha con barras de hierro o metal para que los niños jueguen o se suban a ella*
ju•ni•or ['dʒu:njər] **I** *adj subordinate* de rango inferior; *younger* más joven; **~ athletics** atletismo *m* junior *or* infantil; **~ fashions** moda *f* infantil; **~ partner** COM socio(-a) *m(f)* comanditario(-a) *m(f)*; **~ school** *Br* escuela *f* de primaria (*para niños de 7 a 11 años*); **Michael Harrison ~** Michael Harrison Junior *or* hijo
II *n in rank* subalterno(-a) *m(f)*; **she is ten years my ~** es diez años menor *or* más joven que yo
ju•ni•or 'high (school) escuela *f* secundaria (*para alumnos de entre 12 y 15 años*)
ju•ni•per ['dʒu:nɪpər] BOT enebro *m*
junk [dʒʌŋk] trastos *mpl*; **don't eat ~ like that** no comas porquerías de esas, no comas esa porquería
'junk bond bono *m* basura
junk•et ['dʒʌŋkət] *feast etc* banquete *m* con todo pagado; *trip* viaje *m* con todos los gastos pagados
'junk fax anuncio *m* por fax
'junk food comida *f* basura
junk•ie ['dʒʌŋkɪ] F drogata *m/f* F
'junk mail propaganda *f* postal; **'junk shop** cacharrería *f*; **'junk•yard** depósito *m* de chatarra
jun•ta ['dʒʌntə] POL junta *f* militar
jur•is•dic•tion [dʒʊrɪs'dɪkʃn] LAW jurisdicción *f*; **come** *or* **fall under the ~ of** estar dentro de la jurisdicción de; **have ~ over** tener jurisdicción *or* competencia sobre
ju•ris•pru•dence [dʒʊrɪs'pru:dəns] jurisprudencia *f*
ju•ror ['dʒʊrər] miembro *m* del jurado
ju•ry ['dʒʊrɪ] jurado *m*
'ju•ry serv•ice: **do ~** ser miembro de un jurado
just [dʒʌst] **I** *adj law, cause* justo
II *adv* **1** (*barely*) justo; **it's ~ past Gardner Street** está justo al lado de Gardner Street
2 (*exactly*) justo, justamente; **~ as** (*exactly*) justo cuando, en el preciso momento en que; (*equally*) tan; **that is ~ like you** eso es (muy) propio de ti
3 (*only*) sólo, solamente; **have ~ done sth** acabar de hacer algo; **I've ~ seen her** la acabo de ver; **~ about** (*almost*) casi; **I was ~ about to leave when ...** estaba a punto de salir cuando ...; **~ like that** (*abruptly*) de repente; **~ now** (*at the moment*) ahora mismo; **I saw her ~ now** (*a few moments ago*) la acabo de ver; **~ you wait!** ¡ya verás!; **~ be quiet!** ¡cállate de una vez!; **it was ~ too much** fue demasiado
jus•tice ['dʒʌstɪs] justicia *f*; **bring s.o. to ~** hacer pagar a alguien (por lo que ha hecho); **do ~ to** hacer justicia a; **you didn't do yourself ~** no estuviste a tu altura, no rendiste acorde con tu capacidad

K

jus•tice of the 'peace juez(a) *m(f)* de paz

jus•ti•fi•a•ble [dʒʌstɪ'faɪəbl] *adj* justificable

jus•ti•fi•a•bly [dʒʌstɪ'faɪəblɪ] *adv* justificadamente

jus•ti•fi•ca•tion [dʒʌstɪfɪ'keɪʃn] justificación *f*; ***there's no ~ for behavior like that*** ese comportamiento es injustificable *or* no tiene justificación

jus•ti•fy ['dʒʌstɪfaɪ] *v/t* (*pret & pp* **-ied**) *also text* justificar; ***be justified in doing sth*** tener motivos (justificados) para hacer algo; ***left / right justified*** justificado a la izquierda / derecha

'just-in-time *adj* COM justo a tiempo

just•ly ['dʒʌstlɪ] *adv* **1** (*fairly*) con justicia **2** (*rightly*) con razón

◆ **jut out** [dʒʌt] *v/i* (*pret & pp* **-ted**) sobresalir

jute [dʒu:t] yute *m*

ju•ve•nile ['dʒu:vənl] **I** *adj* **1** *crime* juvenil; *court* de menores **2** *pej* infantil **II** *n fml* menor *m/f*

ju•ve•nile de'lin•quen•cy delincuencia *f* juvenil

ju•ve•nile de'lin•quent delincuente *m/f* juvenil

jux•ta•pose [dʒʌkstə'pouz] *v/t* yuxtaponer

jux•ta•po•si•tion [dʒʌkstəpə'zɪʃn] yuxtaposición *f*

K

k [keɪ] *abbr* **1** (= ***kilobyte***) k (= kilobyte *m*) **2** (= ***thousand***) mil

kale [keɪl] BOT col *f* rizada

ka•lei•do•scope [kə'laɪdəskoup] calidoscopio *m*, caleidoscopio *m*

kan•ga•roo [kæŋgə'ru:] canguro *m*

ka•put [kæ'put] *adj* F *kettle, photocopier etc* cascado F

ka•ra•o•ke [kærɪ'oukɪ] karaoke *m*

ka•ra•te [kə'rɑ:tɪ] kárate *m*

ka'ra•te chop golpe *m* de kárate

kay•ak ['kaɪæk] kayak *m*

KB [keɪ'bi:] *abbr* (= ***kilobyte***) kb (= kilobyte *m*)

ke•bab [kɪ'bæb] pincho *m*, brocheta *f*

keel [ki:l] NAUT quilla *f*; ***be back on an even ~*** *fig* estabilizarse

◆ **keel over** *v/i of structure* desplomarse; *of person* desmayarse

keen [ki:n] *adj interest* gran; *competition* reñido

keen•ness ['ki:nnɪs] entusiasmo *m*, fervor *m*

keep [ki:p] **I** *n* **1** (*maintenance*) manutención *f* **2**: ***for ~s*** F para siempre
II *v/t* (*pret & pp* **kept**) **1** guardar; (*not lose*) conservar; (*detain*) entretener; ***you can ~ it*** (*it's for you*) te lo puedes quedar; ***~ a promise*** cumplir una promesa; ***~ s.o. company*** hacer compañía a alguien; ***~ s.o. waiting*** hacer esperar a alguien; ***he can't ~ anything to himself*** no sabe guardar un secreto; ***~ sth from s.o.*** ocultar algo a alguien; ***~ s.o. busy*** mantener a alguien ocupado; ***keep the twins quiet!*** ¡haz que se callen los gemelos!; ***~ sth a secret from s.o.*** ocultar algo a alguien; ***can you ~ a secret?*** ¿sabes *or* puedes guardar un secreto?; ***~ your seats, please*** permanezcan sentados por favor, por favor permanezcan en sus asientos
2 *family* mantener; *animals* tener, criar
3: ***~ doing sth*** seguir haciendo algo, no parar de hacer algo; ***~ trying!*** ¡sigue intentándolo!; ***don't ~ interrupting!*** ¡deja de interrumpirme!
III *v/i* (*pret & pp* **kept**) **1** *of food, milk* aguantar, conservarse **2**: ***~ calm!*** ¡tranquilízate!; ***~ quiet!*** ¡cállate!; ***~ still!*** ¡estate quieto!

◆ **keep at** *v/t math etc* machacar; ***just keep at it until you find a solution*** no pares hasta que encuentres una solución; ***keep at it!*** ¡no te rindas!

◆ **keep away I** *v/i*: ***keep away from that building*** no te acerques a ese edificio **II** *v/t*: ***keep the children away from the stove*** no dejes que los niños se acerquen a la cocina

◆ **keep back** *v/t* **1** (*hold in check*) contener **2** *information* ocultar

◆ **keep down** *v/t* **1** *voice* bajar; *costs, inflation etc* reducir; ***tell the kids to keep***

the noise down diles a los niños que no hagan tanto ruido **2** *food* retener; ***I can't keep anything down*** devuelvo todo lo que como

◆ **keep from** *v/t* ocultar, esconder; ***we kept the news from him*** no le contamos la noticia; ***keep s.o. from doing sth*** *of person, noise* no dejar a alguien hacer algo; ***I couldn't keep him from leaving*** no pude convencerle para que se quedara; ***I could hardly ~ from laughing*** casi no *or* apenas podía aguantar la risa

◆ **keep in** *v/t in school* castigar (*a quedarse en clase*); ***the hospital's keeping her in*** la tienen en observación

◆ **keep in with** *v/t* mantener buenas relaciones con

◆ **keep off I** *v/t* (*avoid*) evitar; ***keep off the grass!*** ¡prohibido pisar el césped!; ***just you keep your hands off!*** ¡quita las manos de encima! **II** *v/i*: ***if the rain keeps off*** si no llueve

◆ **keep on I** *v/i* continuar; ***if you keep on interrupting me*** si no dejas de interrumpirme; ***keep on trying!*** ¡sigue intentándolo!; ***it keeps on breaking*** no para de romperse **II** *v/t*: ***the company kept them on*** la empresa los mantuvo en el puesto; ***keep your coat on!*** ¡no te quites el abrigo!; ***keep on (going) until the next traffic light*** sigue (conduciendo) hasta el próximo semáforo

◆ **keep on at** *v/t* (*nag*): ***my parents keep on at me to get a job*** mis padres no dejan de decirme que busque un trabajo

◆ **keep out I** *v/t*: ***it keeps the cold out*** protege del frío; ***they must be kept out*** no pueden entrar **II** *v/i*: ***I told you to keep out!*** *of a place* ¡te dije que no entraras!; ***I would keep out of it if I were you*** *of discussion etc* yo en tu lugar no me metería; ***keep out*** *as sign* prohibida la entrada, prohibido el paso

◆ **keep to** *v/t path* seguir; *rules* cumplir, respetar; ***keep to the left / right*** seguir por la izquierda / derecha; ***keep sth to a minimum*** mantener algo al mínimo; ***keep sth to o.s.*** guardarse algo; ***I kept the news of the accident to myself*** no dije nada sobre el accidente

◆ **keep together I** *v/t* mantener unido **II** *v/i* no separarse

◆ **keep up I** *v/i when walking, running etc* seguir *or* mantener el ritmo (***with*** de); ***keep up with s.o.*** (*stay in touch with*) mantener contacto con alguien; ***~ with the Joneses*** F no ser menos que los demás

II *v/t* **1** *pace* seguir, mantener; *payments* estar al corriente de **2** *bridge, pants* sujetar **3** *in good condition* cuidar, atender **4** (*maintain*): ***keep up a pretence*** seguir fingiendo, mantener la fachada; ***~ the good work!*** ¡sigue así!

keep•er ['kiːpər] *n in zoo* cuidador(a) *m(f)*, guarda *m/f*; *in museum* conservador(a) *m(f)*

keep-'fit *adj* de mantenimiento

keep•ing ['kiːpɪŋ]: ***be in ~ with*** *decor* combinar con; ***in ~ with*** *promises* de acuerdo con; ***put sth in s.o.'s ~*** poner *or* depositar algo al cuidado de alguien

keep•sake ['kiːpseɪk] recuerdo *m*

keg [keg] barril *m*

ken•nel ['kenl] caseta *f* del perro

ken•nels ['kenlz] *npl* residencia *f* canina

Ken•ya ['kenjə] Kenia *f*

Ken•yan ['kenjən] **I** *adj* keniata **II** *n* keniata *m/f*

kept [kept] *pret & pp* ☞ **keep**

kerb [kɜːrb] *Br of street* bordillo *m*

ker•nel ['kɜːrnl] almendra *f*

ker•o•sene ['kerəsiːn] queroseno *m*

ketch•up ['ketʃʌp] ketchup *m*

ket•tle ['ketl] hervidor *m*; ***that's a different ~ of fish*** eso es harina de otro costal, eso es otro cantar *or* baile

'ket•tle•drum MUS timbal *m*

key [kiː] **I** *n* **1** *to door, drawer, fig* llave *f*; ***the ~ to success*** la clave del éxito **2** *on keyboard, piano* tecla *f*; *of piece of music* clave *f*; ***major / minor ~*** clave *f* mayor / menor; ***off ~*** desafinado **3** *on map* leyenda *f* **4** *in basketball* bombilla *f*, botella *f* **II** *adj* (*vital*) clave, crucial **III** *v/t & v/i* COMPUT teclear; ***~ to disk*** pasar a computadora *or Span* ordenador

◆ **key in** *v/t data* introducir, teclear

◆ **key up** *v/t text* pasar a computadora *or Span* ordenador

'key•board COMPUT, MUS teclado *m*

'key•board•er COMPUT operador(a) *m(f)*, *persona que introduce datos en la computador(a) o el ordenador*, *L.Am.* digitador(a) *m(f)*

K

'key•board lay•out COMPUT disposición *f* del teclado; **'key•board op•e•ra•tor** COMPUT operador(a) *m(f)*, teclista *m/f*; **'key•card** tarjeta *f* llave, tarjeta-llave *f*
keyed-up [kiːd'ʌp] *adj* nervioso; *psyched-up* mentalizado
'key•hole ojo *m* de la cerradura
key•ing er•ror ['kiːɪŋ] error *m* de teclado
key•note 'speech discurso *m* central; **'key•pad** COMPUT teclado *m*; **'key•ring** llavero *m*; **'key•stone** ARCHI clave *f*; *fig* piedra *f* angular
kha•ki ['kækɪ] *adj* caqui
kick [kɪk] **I** *n* **1** patada *f*; ***give s.o. a ~*** dar una patada a alguien; **2** *fig* F: ***he got a ~ out of watching them suffer*** disfrutó viéndoles sufrir; ***(just) for ~s*** por diversión
II *v/t* **1** dar una patada a; ***I could have ~ed myself*** me daba cabezazos contra la pared; ***~ the bucket*** F palmar F, estirar la pata F **2** F *habit* dejar
III *v/i of person* patalear; *of horse, mule* cocear; ***he can't ~*** no sabe chutar (el balón)
◆ **kick around I** *v/t* **1** *ball* dar patadas a; F *(discuss)* comentar **2** F *person*: *physically* maltratar **II** *v/i* F *(lie about)* estar tirado; ***it's kicking around somewhere*** está muerto de risa en alguna parte F
◆ **kick in** F **I** *v/t money* apoquinar F **II** *v/i of fridge, furnace etc* ponerse en marcha
◆ **kick off** *v/i* SP comenzar, sacar de centro; F *(start)* empezar
◆ **kick out** *v/t of bar, company* echar; *of country, organization* expulsar
◆ **kick over** *v/t* tirar *or* volcar (de una patada)
◆ **kick up** *v/t*: ***kick up a fuss*** montar un numerito
'kick•back F *(bribe)* soborno *m*
'kick•off SP saque *m* inicial; ***for a ~*** F para empezar
kid [kɪd] F **I** *n (child)* crío *m* F, niño *m*; ***when I was a ~*** cuando era pequeño; ***~ brother*** hermano *m* pequeño; ***~ sister*** hermana *f* pequeña; ***a bunch of college ~s*** un grupo de colegiales **II** *v/t (pret & pp **-ded**)* tomar el pelo a F; ***I ~ you not*** no estoy de broma, no bromeo **III** *v/i (pret & pp **-ded**)* bromear; ***I was only ~ding*** estaba bromeando; ***no kidding!*** ¡te lo juro!, ¡no me digas!
kid•der ['kɪdər] F vacilón *m* F
kid 'gloves: ***handle s.o. with ~*** tratar a alguien con guante de seda
kid•nap ['kɪdnæp] *v/t (pret & pp **-ped**)* secuestrar
kid•nap•(p)er ['kɪdnæpər] secuestrador(a) *m(f)*
'kid•nap•(p)ing ['kɪdnæpɪŋ] secuestro *m*
kid•ney ['kɪdnɪ] ANAT riñón *m*; *in cooking* riñones *mpl*
'kid•ney bean alubia *f* roja de riñón; **'kid•ney ma•chine** MED riñón *m* artificial, máquina *f* de diálisis; **'kid•ney stone** MED cálculo *m* renal; **'kid•ney trans•plant** MED transplante *m* de riñón
kill [kɪl] *v/t* matar; ***the drought ~ed all the plants*** las plantas murieron como resultado de la sequía; ***I had six hours to ~*** tenía seis horas sin nada que hacer; ***be ~ed in an accident*** matarse en un accidente, morirse en un accidente; ***be ~ed in action*** morir en combate; ***~ o.s.*** suicidarse; ***~ o.s. laughing*** F morirse de risa F; ***I could ~ him*** F le mataba; ***~ the ball*** *football* parar el balón; *tennis* matar la pelota; ***~ that noise!*** *of CD player etc* ¡apaga esa música!; ***if looks could ~*** si las miradas matasen; ***~ two birds with one stone*** *fig* matar dos pájaros de un tiro; ***my feet are ~ing me*** F los pies me están matando; ***dressed to ~*** F vestido para deslumbrar
◆ **kill off** *v/t* matar, acabar con
kil•ler ['kɪlər] *(murderer)* asesino *m*; ***be a ~*** *of disease, question* ser mortal
'kil•ler whale ZO orca *f*
kil•ling ['kɪlɪŋ] asesinato *m*; ***make a ~*** F *(lots of money)* forrarse F
kil•ling•ly ['kɪlɪŋlɪ] *adv* F: ***~ funny*** para morirse de risa
'kill•joy aguafiestas *m/f inv*
kiln [kɪln] horno *m*
ki•lo ['kiːloʊ] kilo *m*
ki•lo•byte ['kɪloʊbaɪt] COMPUT kilobyte *m*
ki•lo•gram ['kɪloʊgræm] kilogramo *m*
ki•lo•me•ter, *Br* **ki•lo•me•tre** [kɪ'lɑːmɪtər] kilómetro *m*

ki•lo•watt ['kɪloʊwɑːt] ELEC kilovatio *m*, kilowatio *m*
kilt [kɪlt] falda *f* escocesa
ki•mo•no [kɪ'moʊnoʊ] kimono *m*, quimono *m*
kin [kɪn] ☞ ***kinfolk***
kind[1] [kaɪnd] *adj* agradable, amable; ***that's very ~ of you*** gracias por tu amabilidad
kind[2] [kaɪnd] *n* (*sort*) tipo *m*; (*make, brand*) marca *f*; ***all ~s of people*** toda clase de personas; ***I did nothing of the ~!*** ¡no hice nada parecido!; ***~ of ...*** *sad, lonely, etc* un poco ...; ***did you miss me? - yeah, ~ of*** ¿me echaste de menos? - digamos que sí; ***I've ~ of promised*** de alguna manera lo he prometido; ***in ~*** *repay* de la misma manera, con la misma moneda; *pay* en especie
kind•a ['kaɪndə] F ☞ ***kind of***
kin•der•gar•ten ['kɪndərgɑːrtn] guardería *f*, jardín *m* de infancia
kind-heart•ed [kaɪnd'hɑːrtɪd] *adj* agradable, amable
kin•dle ['kɪndl] *v/t fire* encender; *fig: hope* crear, avivar
kin•dling ['kɪndlɪŋ] ramajes *mpl or* astillas *fpl* para encender el fuego
kind•ly ['kaɪndlɪ] **I** *adj* amable, agradable **II** *adv* con amabilidad; ***~ don't interrupt*** por favor, no me interrumpa; ***~ lower your voice*** ¿le importaría hablar más bajo?
kind•ness ['kaɪndnɪs] amabilidad *f*
kin•dred ['kɪndrəd] *adj*: ***~ spirit*** alma *f* gemela
ki•net•ic [kɪ'netɪk] PHYS *adj* cinético
ki•net•ic 'en•er•gy energía *f* cinética
'kin•folk *npl* familia *f*
king [kɪŋ] rey *m*; ***~ of hearts*** *in cards* rey de corazones
king•dom ['kɪŋdəm] reino *m*; ***animal / mineral / vegetable ~*** reino animal / mineral / vegetal
'king•pin F cerebro *m*; **king 'prawn** *Br* ZO langostino *m* tigre; **'king-size** *adj* F *cigarettes* extralargo; ***~ bed*** cama *f* de matrimonio grande
kink [kɪŋk] *in hose etc* doblez *f*
kink•y ['kɪŋkɪ] *adj* F vicioso
kin•ship ['kɪnʃɪp] parentesco *m*
ki•osk ['kiːɑːsk] quiosco *m*
kip•per ['kɪpər] arenque *m* ahumado
kiss [kɪs] **I** *n* beso *m*; ***~ of death*** *fig* golpe *m* de gracia **II** *v/t* besar; ***~ s.o. good night*** dar a alguien un beso de buenas noches; ***~ sth goodbye*** F despedirse de algo, decir adiós a algo **III** *v/i* besarse
kiss•er ['kɪsər]: ***he's a good ~*** besa muy bien
kiss of 'life *Br* boca a boca *m*, respiración *f* artificial; ***give s.o. the ~*** hacer a alguien el boca a boca
kit [kɪt] **I** *n* (*equipment*) equipo *m*; ***tool ~*** juego *m* de herramientas **II** *v/t* (*prep & pp* ***-ted***): ***~ s.o. out*** equipar a alguien (***with*** de)
'kit bag MIL petate *m*
kitch•en ['kɪtʃɪn] cocina *f*; ***~ knife*** cuchillo *m* de cocina; ***~ table*** mesa *f* de cocina; ***~ foil*** papel *m* de aluminio, papel *m* albal®
kitch•en•ette [kɪtʃɪ'net] *cocina pequeña*
kitch•en 'sink: ***you've got everything but the ~*** F llevas la casa a cuestas F
kite [kaɪt] *for flying* cometa *f*
kit•ten ['kɪtn] gatito *m*
kit•ty ['kɪtɪ] *money* fondo *m*
Ki•wi ['kiːwiː] F (*New Zealander*) neozelandés(-esa) *m(f)*
ki•wi ['kiːwiː] ORN, BOT kiwi *m*
'ki•wi fruit kiwi *m*
Klee•nex® ['kliːneks] kleenex® *m*, pañuelo *m* de papel
klep•to•ma•ni•a [kleptə'meɪnɪə] PSYCH cleptomanía *f*
klep•to•ma•ni•ac [kleptə'meɪnɪæk] cleptómano(-a) *m(f)*
klutz [klʌts] F (*clumsy person*) manazas *m/f inv* F
knack [næk] habilidad *f*; ***have a ~ of doing sth*** arreglárselas siempre para hacer algo, tener la habilidad de hacer algo; ***he has a ~ of upsetting people*** *irón* tiene la habilidad de disgustar a la gente; ***I soon got the ~ of the new machine*** le pillé el truco a la nueva máquina rápidamente; ***there's a ~ to it*** tiene su truco
knack•ered ['nækərd] *adj Br* F hecho polvo F, reventado F
knap•sack ['næpsæk] mochila *f*
knave [neɪv] *in cards* sota *f*
knead [niːd] *v/t dough* amasar
knee [niː] rodilla *f*; ***bring s.o. to his ~s*** abatir *or* doblegar a alguien; ***go down on one's ~s*** ponerse de rodillas, arrodillarse; *fig* suplicar, implorar

'knee•cap rótula *f*; **knee-'deep** *adj* hasta la(s) rodilla(s); **knee-jerk re'ac•tion** reacción *f* instintiva, acto *m* reflejo
kneel [ni:l] *v/i* (*pret & pp* ***knelt***) arrodillarse
'knee-length *adj* hasta la(s) rodilla(s)
'knee•pad rodillera *f*
knelt [nelt] *pret & pp* ☞ ***kneel***
knew [nu:] *pret* ☞ ***know***
knick•ers ['nɪkərz] *npl esp Br* bragas *fpl*; ***get one's ~ in a twist*** *Br* F ponerse nervioso, exaltarse
knick-knacks ['nɪknæks] *npl* F baratijas *fpl*
knife [naɪf] **I** *n* (*pl* ***knives*** [naɪvz]) *for food* cuchillo *m*; *carried outside* navaja *f*; ***he's got his ~ into me*** me la tiene jurada **II** *v/t* acuchillar, apuñalar
'knife-edge: ***be balanced on a ~*** *fig* pender de un hilo
'knife point: ***I was robbed at ~*** me robaron amenazándome con un cuchillo
knight [naɪt] caballero *m*
knit [nɪt] **I** *v/t* (*pret & pp* ***-ted***) tejer **II** *v/i* (*pret & pp* ***-ted***) tricotar
◆ **knit together** *v/i of broken bone* soldarse
knit•ting ['nɪtɪŋ] punto *m*
'knit•ting nee•dle aguja *f* para hacer punto
'knit•wear prendas *fpl* de punto
knives [naɪvz] *pl* ☞ ***knife***
knob [nɑ:b] **1** *on door* pomo *m*; *on drawer* tirador *m* **2** *of butter* nuez *f*, trocito *m*
knob•bly ['nɑ:blɪ] *adj* huesudo
knock [nɑ:k] **I** *n on door*, (*blow*) golpe *m*; ***there was a ~ on the door*** llamaron a la puerta **II** *v/t* **1** (*hit*) golpear; ***he was ~ed to the ground*** le tiraron al suelo **2** F (*criticize*) criticar, meterse con F **III** *v/i on the door* llamar; ***~ on wood!*** ¡toca madera!
◆ **knock around I** *v/t* F (*beat*) pegar a **II** *v/i* F (*travel*) viajar; ***it's knocking around here somewhere*** tiene que estar por aquí; ***knock around with*** ir con
◆ **knock back** *v/t* F *drink* trincarse F
◆ **knock down** *v/t* **1** *of car* atropellar; *building* tirar; *object* tirar al suelo **2** F (*reduce the price of*) rebajar
◆ **knock off I** *v/t* **1** P (*steal*) mangar P **2** F: ***knock it off!*** ¡déjalo ya!, ¡para ya! **II** *v/i* F (*stop work for the day*) acabar, *Span* plegar F
◆ **knock out** *v/t* **1** (*make unconscious*) dejar K.O.; *of medicine* dejar para el arrastre F **2** *power lines etc* destruir **3** F (*eliminate*) eliminar; ***be knocked out*** *of tournament* quedarse fuera *or* eliminado **4** (*exhaust*) dejar molido F **5** (*delight*) dejar flipado P
◆ **knock over** *v/t* **1** tirar; *of car* atropellar **2** P (*rob*) atracar
◆ **knock up** *v/t* **1** *assemble* improvisar **2** P (*make pregnant*) preñar a P; ***get knocked up*** quedarse embarazada *or* preñada P
'knock•down *adj*: ***at a ~ price*** tirado
knock•er ['nɑ:kər] *on door* llamador *m*, aldaba *f*
knock-kneed [nɑ:k'ni:d] *adj* patizambo; **knock-'knees** *npl*: ***have ~*** ser patizambo; **'knock•out 1** *in boxing* K.O. *m*; ***win by a ~*** ganar por K.O. **2**: ***it's a ~*** F *fantastic* es una maravilla
knot [nɑ:t] **I** *n* nudo *m*; ***tie a ~*** atar un nudo; ***tie the ~*** *fig* casarse, contraer matrimonio **II** *v/t* (*pret & pp* ***-ted***) anudar
'knot•ty ['nɑ:tɪ] *adj problem* complicado
know [noʊ] **I** *v/t* (*pret* ***knew***, *pp* ***known***) *fact*, *language*, *how to do sth* saber; *person*, *place* conocer; (*recognize*) reconocer; ***will you let him ~ that …?*** ¿puedes decirle que …?; ***~ how to do sth*** saber hacer algo
II *v/i* (*pret* ***knew***, *pp* ***known***) saber; ***I don't ~*** no (lo) sé; ***yes, I ~*** sí, lo sé; ***you never ~*** nunca se sabe; ***it was sort of, you ~, …*** digamos que, ya sabes, …
III *n*: ***people in the ~*** los enterados; ***be in the ~ about*** estar al corriente de
◆ **know of** *v/t place* conocer; *solution* saber; ***not that I know of*** no que yo sepa
'know-all *Br* F sabiondo F
'know•how pericia *f*
know•ing ['noʊɪŋ] *adj* cómplice
know•ing•ly ['noʊɪŋlɪ] *adv* **1** (*wittingly*) deliberadamente **2** *smile etc* con complicidad
'know-it-all F sabiondo F
knowl•edge ['nɑ:lɪdʒ] conocimiento *m*; ***to the best of my ~*** por lo que sé; ***have a good ~ of*** tener buenos conocimientos de; ***not to my ~*** que yo sepa no; ***without my ~*** sin yo saberlo, sin mi co-

nocimiento

knowl•edge•a•ble ['nɑːlɪdʒəbl] *adj*: ***she's very ~ about music*** sabe mucho de música

known [noʊn] **1** *pp* ☞ ***know*** **2** *adj*: ***~ to the police*** conocido por la policía; ***make sth ~*** hacer saber algo; ***a ~ militant*** un militante reconocido

knuck•le ['nʌkl] nudillo *m*

◆ **knuckle down** *v/i* F aplicarse F

◆ **knuckle under** *v/i* F pasar por el aro F

'knuck•le-dust•er nudillera *f* de metal

KO [keɪ'oʊ] (*knockout*) K.O.

ko•a•la (bear) [koʊ'ɑːlə(ber)] ZO koala *m*

kohl [koʊl] kajal *m*; ***~ pencil*** lápiz *m* de ojos

kook [kuːk] F chiflado(-a) *m(f)* F

Ko•ran [kə'ræn] Corán *m*

Ko•re•a [kə'riːə] Corea *f*

Ko•re•an [kə'riːən] **I** *adj* coreano **II** *n* **1** coreano(-a) *m(f)* **2** *language* coreano *m*

ko•sher ['koʊʃər] *adj* REL kosher; F legal F

◆ **kow•tow to** ['kaʊtaʊ] *v/t* doblar el espinazo ante

kph [keɪpiː'eɪtʃ] *abbr* (= ***kilometres per hour***) km/h (= kilómetros por hora)

Krem•lin ['kremlɪn] Kremlin *m*

ku•dos ['kjuːdɑːs] reconocimiento *m*, prestigio *m*

Ku•wait [kʊ'weɪt] Kuwait *m*

Ku•wai•ti [kʊ'weɪtɪ] **I** *adj* kuwaití **II** *n* kuwaití *m/f*

L

L.A. [el'eɪ] *abbr* (= ***Los Angeles***)

lab [læb] laboratorio *m*

la•bel ['leɪbl] **I** *n* etiqueta *f*; ***you're just paying for the ~*** estás pagando la marca **II** *v/t* (*pret & pp* ***-ed***, *Br* ***-led***) *baggage* etiquetar; ***~ s.o. a liar*** etiquetar *or* tachar a alguien de mentiroso; ***be ~ed a …*** *become known as* ser etiquetado *or* catalogado de…

la•bi•al ['leɪbɪəl] LING labial *f*

la•bor ['leɪbər] **I** *n* **1** (*work*) trabajo *m*; ***a ~ of love*** un trabajo hecho con amor **2** *in pregnancy* parto *m*; ***be in ~*** estar de parto **II** *v/i* (*work*) trabajar; ***~ over sth*** sudar con algo **III** *v/t*: ***~ a point*** extenderse demasiado en un punto

la•bor•a•to•ry ['læbərətɔːrɪ] laboratorio *m*

la•bor•a•to•ry tech'ni•cian técnico(-a) *m(f)* de laboratorio

'la•bor camp campo *m* de trabajos forzados

'La•bor Day *primer lunes de septiembre, festivo en el que se celebra el día del trabajador en los Estados Unidos*

la•bored ['leɪbərd] *adj style, speech* elaborado

la•bor•er ['leɪbərər] obrero(-a) *m(f)*

'la•bor-in•ten•sive *adj* que requiere de mucha mano de obra

la•bo•ri•ous [lə'bɔːrɪəs] *adj* laborioso

la•bo•ri•ous•ly [lə'bɔːrɪəslɪ] *adv* laboriosamente

'la•bor laws *npl* derecho *m* laboral; **'la•bor mar•ket** mercado *m* de trabajo; **la•bor-sav•ing de'vice** aparato *m or* mecanismo *m* que ahorra esfuerzo; **'la•bor un•ion** sindicato *m*; **'la•bor ward** MED sala *f* de partos

la•bour *etc Br* ☞ ***labor*** *etc*

lab•ra•dor ['læbrədɔːr] ZO labrador *m*

la•bur•num [lə'bɜːrnəm] BOT codeso *m*, laburnum *m*

lab•y•rinth ['læbərɪnθ] laberinto *m*

lab•y•rin•thine [læbə'rɪnθaɪn] *adj* laberíntico

lace [leɪs] **I** *n* **1** *material* encaje *m* **2** *for shoe* cordón *m* **II** *v/t*: ***~ s.o.'s drink with sth*** añadir algo en la bebida de alguien, aderezar la bebida de alguien con algo

◆ **lace up** *v/t shoes* atar

lac•er•ate ['læsəreɪt] *v/t* desgarrar

lac•er•a•tion [læsə'reɪʃn] desgarro *m*

lack [læk] **I** *n* falta *f* carencia *f* (***of*** de) **II** *v/t* carecer de; ***he ~s confidence*** le falta confianza **III** *v/i*: ***be ~ing*** faltar

lack•a•dai•si•cal [lækə'deɪzɪkl] *adj* apático

lack•ey ['lækɪ] *fig* lacayo(-a) *m(f)*, sirviente(-a) *m(f)*

lack•ing ['lækɪŋ] *adj Br* F falto, desprovisto; ***be found ~*** sucumbir, desplomarse
lack•lus•ter, *Br* **lack•lus•tre** ['læklʌstər] *adj* deficiente, poco brillante
la•con•ic [lə'kɑːnɪk] *adj* lacónico
lac•quer ['lækər] **I** *n for hair* laca *f* **II** *v/t*: ***~ one's hair*** ponerse *or* echarse laca en el pelo
la•crosse [lə'krɑːs] lacrosse *m*
lad [læd] muchacho *m*, chico *m*
lad•der ['lædər] **1** escalera *f* (de mano) **2** *Br in pantihose* carrera *f*
la•den ['leɪdn] *adj* cargado (***with*** de)
la-di-da [lɑːdɪ'dɑː] *adj* F cursi F, repipi F
la•dies' man ['leɪdiːz] mujeriego *m*, faldero *m*
'la•dies' room servicio *m* de señoras
la•dle ['leɪdl] cucharón *m*, cazo *m*
◆ **ladle out** *v/t* servir; *fig*: *advice* ofrecer a diestro y siniestro
la•dy ['leɪdɪ] señora *f*
'la•dy•boy chica *f* de alterne; **'la•dy•bug** mariquita *f*; **'la•dy-kill•er** F donjuán *m*, seductor *m*; **'la•dy•like** *adj* femenino
lag[1] [læg] *v/t* (*pret & pp* ***-ged***) *pipes* revestir con aislante
lag[2] [læg] *n* intervalo *m*
◆ **lag behind** *v/i* (*pret & pp* ***-ged***) quedarse atrás
la•ger ['lɑːgər] cerveza *f* rubia
lag•gard ['lægərd] rezagado(-a) *m*(*f*), remolón(-ona) *m*(*f*)
lag•ging ['lægɪŋ] TECH revestimiento *m*
la•goon [lə'guːn] laguna *f*
laid [leɪd] *pret & pp* ☞ ***lay***
laid'back *adj* tranquilo, despreocupado
laid-'up: *adj*: ***be ~ with flu*** estar en cama con gripe
lain [leɪn] *pp* ☞ ***lie***
lair [ler] ZO madriguera *f*, guarida *f*
la•i•ty ['leɪətɪ] laicado *m*
lake [leɪk] lago *m*
lam [læm] *v/i* (*pret & pp* ***-med***) F: ***~ into s.o.*** arremeter *or* acometer contra alguien
lamb [læm] *animal*, *meat* cordero *m*
lamb 'chop chuleta *f* de cordero; **'lamb•skin** borreguito *m*; **lamb's wool** ['læmzwʊl] lana *f* de borrego
lame [leɪm] *adj person*, *horse* cojo; *excuse* pobre; ***go ~*** quedarse cojo
lame 'duck F POL lame duck *m*, pato *m* cojo (*para referirse a un presidente a punto de ser cedido del cargo*)
la•ment [lə'ment] **I** *n* lamento *m* **II** *v/t* lamentar
lam•en•ta•ble ['læməntəbl] *adj* lamentable
lam•en•ta•tion [læmen'teɪʃn] lamentación *f*
lam•i•nate ['læmɪneɪt] *v/t* laminar
lam•i•nat•ed ['læmɪneɪtɪd] *adj surface* laminado; *paper* plastificado
lam•i•nat•ed 'glass cristal *m* laminado
lamp [læmp] lámpara *f*
'lamp•light luz *f* de lámpara
lam•poon [læm'puːn] **I** *n* sátira *f* **II** *v/t* satirizar
'lamp•post farola *f*
'lamp•shade pantalla *f* (*de lámpara*)
LAN [læn] *abbr* COMPUT (= ***local area network***) red *f* de área local
lance [lɑːns] **I** *n* lanza *f* **II** *v/t* MED sajar
lan•cet ['lɑːnsɪt] MED lanceta *f*
land [lænd] **I** *n* tierra *f*; ***by ~*** por tierra; ***on ~*** en tierra; ***work on the ~*** *as farmer* trabajar la tierra **II** *v/t* **1** *airplane* aterrizar **2** F *job* conseguir; ***get ~ed with a problem*** cargar *or* apechugar con un problema **3**: ***he ~ed him one*** F le encajó una **III** *v/i of airplane* aterrizar; *of capsule on the moon* alunizar; *of ball*, *sth thrown* caer
◆ **land up** *v/i* ir a parar (***in*** a), acabar (***in*** en)
land•ed ['lændɪd] *adj* hacendado; ***~ gentry*** terratenientes *mpl*
'land•fill site *for waste* vertedero *m* de basuras
'land forc•es *npl* MIL fuerzas *fpl* terrestres *or* de tierra
land•ing ['lændɪŋ] **1** *of airplane* aterrizaje *m*; *on moon* alunizaje *m* **2** *of staircase* rellano *m*
'land•ing field pista *f* de aterrizaje; **'land•ing gear** tren *m* de aterrizaje; **'land•ing strip** pista *f* de aterrizaje
'land•la•dy *of hostel etc* dueña *f*; *of rented room* casera *f*; *Br*: *of bar* patrona *f*; **land•locked** ['lændlɑːkt] *adj* de interior; **'land•lord** *of hostel etc* dueño *m*; *of rented room* casero *m*; *Br*: *of bar* patrón *m*; **land•lub•ber** ['lændlʌbər] F marinero *f* de agua dulce; **'land•mark** punto *m* de referencia; *fig* hito *m*; **'land•mine** mina *f* terrestre; **'land own•er** terrateniente *m/f*

land•scape ['lændskeɪp] **I** *n also painting* paisaje *m* **II** *adv print* en formato apaisado
'land•scape gar•den•er jardinero(-a) *m(f)* de paisajes
'land•slide corrimiento *m* de tierras; **~ *victory*** victoria *f* arrolladora
land•ward ['lændwərd] *adv look* hacia *or* a tierra
lane [leɪn] *in country* camino *m*, vereda *f*; (*alley*) callejón *m*; MOT carril *m*; ***get in ~*** *on sign* únase al carril
lan•guage ['læŋgwɪdʒ] lenguaje *m*; *of nation* idioma *f*, lengua *f*; (***watch your***) **~*!*** ¡no digas palabrotas!
'lan•guage bar•ri•er barrera *f* idiomática *or* del idioma; **'lan•guage course** curso *m* de idiomas; **'lan•guage lab** laboratorio *m* de idiomas; **'lan•guage lab•o•ra•to•ry** laboratorio *m* de idiomas; **'lan•guage school** academia *f* de idiomas
lan•guid ['læŋgwɪd] *adj* lánguido
lan•guish ['læŋgwɪʃ] *v/i* languidecer, perder vigor
lan•guor ['læŋgər] languidez *f*
lan•guor•ous ['læŋgərəs] *adj* lánguido
lank [læŋk] *adj hair* lacio
lank•y ['læŋkɪ] *adj person* larguirucho
lan•tern ['læntərn] farol *f*
La•os [laʊs] Laos *m*
La•o•tian ['laʊʃɪən] **I** *adj* laosiano **II** *n* **1** *person* laosiano(-a) *m(f)* **2** *language* laosiano *m*
lap[1] [læp] *of track* vuelta *f*
lap[2] [læp] *of person* regazo *m*; ***it's in the ~ of the gods*** está de la mano de Dios, es cosa del azar; ***live in the ~ of luxury*** vivir por todo lo alto, vivir a lo grande
lap[3] [læp] *of water* chapoteo *m*
◆ **lap up** *v/t* (*pret & pp* **-ped**) *drink, milk* beber a lengüetadas; *flattery* deleitarse con
'lap dog perrito *m* faldero
la•pel [lə'pel] solapa *f*
lapse [læps] **I** *n* **1** (*mistake, slip*) desliz *m*; ***a ~ of attention*** un momento de distracción; ***a ~ of memory*** un olvido **2** *of time* lapso *m* **II** *v/i* **1** *of membership* vencer **2**: ***~ into silence / despair*** sumirse en el silencio / la desesperación; ***she ~d into English*** empezó a hablar en inglés
'lap•top COMPUT computadora *f* portátil, *Span* ordenador *m* portátil
lap•wing ['læpwɪŋ] ORN avefría *f*
lar•ce•ny ['lɑːrsənɪ] latrocinio *m*
larch [lɑːrtʃ] BOT alerce *m*
lard [lɑːrd] manteca *f* de cerdo
lar•der ['lɑːrdər] despensa *f*
large [lɑːrdʒ] **I** *adj* **1** grande **2**: ***be at ~*** *of criminal, wild animal* andar suelto **II** *adv*: ***by and ~*** en general, por lo general
large•ly ['lɑːrdʒlɪ] *adv* (*mainly*) en gran parte, principalmente
large•ness ['lɑːrdʒnɪs] grandeza *f*
'large-scale *adj* en *or* a gran escala
'large-scale in•te•gra•tion integración *f* a larga escala
lar•gesse [lɑːr'dʒes] generosidad *f*
lark[1] [lɑːrk] ORN alondra *f*; ***rise*** *or* ***be up with the ~*** levantarse al alba, levantarse con el canto del gallo
lark[2] [lɑːrk] F: ***for a ~*** en *or* de broma
◆ **lark around** *v/i* hacer el tonto *or* ganso
lar•va ['lɑːrvə] larva *f*
lar•yn•gi•tis [lærɪn'dʒaɪtɪs] laringitis *f*
lar•ynx ['lærɪŋks] laringe *f*
las•civ•i•ous [lə'sɪvɪəs] *adj* lascivo
la•ser ['leɪzər] láser *m*
'la•ser beam rayo *m* láser; **'la•ser gun** pistola *f* láser; **'la•ser print•er** impresora *f* láser; **'la•ser sur•ger•y** cirugía *f* con láser
lash[1] [læʃ] *n* (*eye~*) pestaña *f*
lash[2] [læʃ] *v/t with whip* azotar
◆ **lash down** *v/t with rope* amarrar
◆ **lash out** *v/i with fists, words* atacar (***at*** a), arremeter (***at*** contra)
lash•ing ['læʃɪŋ]: ***~s of cream*** *Br* montones de crema
las•si•tude ['læsɪtuːd] lasitud *f*, desfallecimiento *m*
las•so [læ'suː] **I** (*pl* **-so(e)s**) *n* lazo *m* **II** *v/t* enlazar
last[1] [læst] **I** *adj in series* último; (*preceding*) anterior; ***~ Friday*** el viernes pasado; ***~ but one*** penúltimo; ***~ night*** anoche; ***~ but not least*** por último, pero no por ello menos importante **II** *adv*: ***at ~*** por fin, al fin
last[2] [læst] **I** *v/i* durar **II** *v/t*: ***two kilos should ~ us a week*** con dos kilos deberíamos tener para una semana
◆ **last out** *v/i* (*survive*) sobrevivir; *of supplies* durar
'last-ditch *adj* desesperado; ***~ attempt***

L

último intento *m* desesperado
last•ing ['læstɪŋ] *adj* duradero
last•ly ['læstlɪ] *adv* por último, finalmente
last-'min•ute *adj* de último momento; **'last name** apellido *m*; **last 'rites** *npl* extremaunción *f*; **last 'straw** *fig*: ***the ~*** la gota que colma el vaso
latch [lætʃ] pestillo *m*
◆ **latch onto** *v/t* engancharse, agarrarse
'latch key llave *f* de la casa; ***~ child*** *niño que permanece solo en casa a la vuelta del colegio dado que sus padres trabajan*
late [leɪt] **I** *adj*: ***the bus is ~ again*** el autobús vuelve a llegar tarde; ***don't be ~!*** ¡no llegues tarde! ***it's ~*** es tarde; ***it's getting ~*** se está haciendo tarde; ***of ~*** últimamente, recientemente; ***the ~ 19th century*** la última parte del siglo XIX; ***in the ~ 19th century*** a finales del siglo XIX; ***your ~ wife*** su difunta esposa **II** *adv arrive, leave* tarde
'late•com•er persona *m/f* que llega tarde
late•ly ['leɪtlɪ] *adv* últimamente, recientemente
late•ness ['leɪtnɪs] tardanza *f*
la•tent ['leɪtənt] *adj* latente
late 'pay•ment pen•al•ty indemnización *f* por pago tardío
lat•er ['leɪtər] *adv* más tarde; ***see you ~!*** ¡hasta luego!; ***~ on*** más tarde
lat•er•al ['lætərəl] *adj* lateral; ***~ thinking*** pensamiento *m* lateral
lat•er•al•ly ['lætərəlɪ] *adv* lateralmente
lat•est ['leɪtɪst] *adj news, girlfriend* último
lat•ex ['leɪteks] látex *m*
lathe [leɪð] torno *m*
la•ther ['lɑːðər] *from soap* espuma *f*; ***in a ~*** (*sweaty*) empapado de sudor
Lat•in ['lætɪn] **I** *adj* latino **II** *n* latín *m*
Lat•in A'mer•i•ca Latinoamérica *f*, América *f* Latina
Lat•in A'mer•i•can I *n* latinoamericano(-a) *m(f)* **II** *adj* latinoamericano
La•ti•no [læ'tiːnoʊ] **I** *adj* latino **II** *n* latino(-a) *m(f)*
lat•i•tude ['lætɪtuːd] **1** *geographical* latitud *f* **2** (*freedom to act*) libertad *f*
la•trine [lə'triːn] letrina *f*
lat•ter ['lætər] **I** *adj* último **II** *n*: ***Mr. Brown and Mr. White, of whom the ~ was …*** el Señor Brown y el Señor White, de quien el segundo *or* este último era …
lat•tice ['lætɪs] enrejado *m*
Lat•vi•a ['lætvɪə] Letonia *f*
Lat•vi•an ['lætvɪən] **I** *adj* letón **II** *n* **1** *person* letón(-ona) *m(f)* **2** *language* letón *m*
laud•a•ble ['lɔːdəbl] *adj* loable, ejemplar
laugh [læf] **I** *n* risa *f*; ***it was a ~*** F fue genial **II** *v/i* reírse (***about*** de)
◆ **laugh at** *v/t* reírse de
◆ **laugh off** *v/t* tomarse a risa
laugh•a•ble ['læfəbl] *adj* de risa, absurdo
laugh•ing gas ['læfɪŋ] CHEM gas *m* hilarante
'laugh•ing stock: ***make o.s. a ~*** ponerse en ridículo; ***become a ~*** ser el hazmerreír
laugh•ter ['læftər] risas *fpl*
launch [lɒːntʃ] **I** *n* **1** *small boat* lancha *f* **2** *of ship* botadura *f*, *of rocket, new product* lanzamiento *m* **II** *v/t rocket, new product* lanzar; *ship* botar **III** *v/i of new product* lanzarse
'launch cer•e•mo•ny ceremonia *f* de lanzamiento
launch•ing pad ['lɒːntʃɪŋ] ☞ ***launch pad***
'launch pad plataforma *f* de lanzamiento; **'launch par•ty** fiesta *f* de presentación *or* lanzamiento; **'launch site** lugar *m* de lanzamiento
laun•der ['lɒːndər] *v/t* **1** *clothes* lavar (y planchar) **2** *money* blanquear
laun•der•ette [lɒːn'dret] *Br* lavandería *f*
laun•dro•mat ['lɒːndrəmæt] lavandería *f*
laun•dry ['lɒːndrɪ] **1** *place* lavadero *m* **2** *dirty clothes* ropa *f* sucia; *clean clothes* ropa *f* lavada; ***do the ~*** lavar la ropa, *Span* hacer la colada
'laun•dry bas•ket cesta *f or* cesto *m* de la ropa
lau•rel ['lɑːrəl] laurel *m*; ***rest on one's ~s*** dormirse en los laureles
la•va ['lɑːvə] lava *f*
lav•a•to•ry ['lævətɔːrɪ] **1** *room* cuarto *m* de baño, lavabo *m*; ***go to the ~*** ir al baño *or* servicio **2** *Br*: *equipment* retrete *m*
lav•en•der ['lævəndər] espliego *m*, la-

vanda *f*
lav•ish ['lævɪʃ] *adj* espléndido
law [lɒː] **1** ley *f*; ***be against the ~*** estar prohibido, ser ilegal; ***be above the ~*** estar por encima de la ley; ***break the ~*** infringir la ley **2** *subject* derecho *m* **3**: ***~ and order*** orden *m* público
'law-a•bid•ing *adj* respetuoso con la ley; **'law•break•er** infractor(a) *m(f)* de la ley; **'law court** juzgado *m*
law•ful ['lɒːfəl] *adj* legal; *wife* legítimo
law•less ['lɒːlɪs] *adj* sin ley
'law•mak•er político(-a) *m(f)*, legislador(a) *m(f)*
lawn [lɒːn] césped *m*
'lawn chair silla *f* de jardín
'lawn mow•er cortacésped *m*
'law•suit pleito *m*
law•yer ['lɒːjər] abogado(-a) *m(f)*
lax [læks] *adj* poco estricto
lax•a•tive ['læksətɪv] laxante *m*
lax•i•ty ['læksɪtɪ], **lax•ness** ['læksnɪs] relajación *f*
lay[1] [leɪ] *v/t* (*pret & pp* **laid**) **1** (*put down*) dejar, poner **2** *eggs* poner **3** V *sexually* tirarse a V; ***he wants to get laid*** quiere coger V *or Span* follar V
◆ **lay aside** *v/t* **1** dejar a un lado **2** (*keep*) apartar, guardar
◆ **lay down** *v/t* dejar; ***~ the law to s.o.*** decir a alguien lo que tiene que hacer; ***~ one's life*** dar la vida
◆ **lay in** *v/t supplies* recoger
◆ **lay into** *v/t* (*attack*) arremeter contra
◆ **lay off** *v/t* **1** *workers* despedir **2** F: ***lay off him, will you!*** ¡déjale en paz!; ***lay off it!*** ¡basta ya!
◆ **lay on** *v/t* (*provide*) organizar
◆ **lay out** *v/t objects* colocar, disponer; *page* diseñar, maquetar
◆ **lay up** *v/t*: ***be laid up with*** (*sick*) guardar cama por
lay[2] [leɪ] *pret* ☞ ***lie***
'lay•a•bout *Br* F vago(-a) *m(f)*, maula *m/f*
'lay-by *Br*: *on road* área *f* de descanso
lay•er ['leɪər] estrato *m*; *of soil*, *paint* capa *f*
lay•ette [leɪ'et] canastilla *f* (de bebé)
'lay•man laico *m*; **'lay-off** despido *m*; **'lay-out** diseño *m*; **'lay•o•ver** escala *f*, alto *m*; **'lay-up** *in basketball* bandeja *f*
laze [leɪz] *v/i* hacer el vago, remolonear
◆ **laze around** [leɪz] *v/i* holgazanear; ***laze around in the sun*** tumbarse al sol sin hacer nada
◆ **laze away** *v/t weekend* desperdiciar, malemplear
la•zi•ness ['leɪzɪnɪs] pereza *f*, holgazanería *f*
la•zy ['leɪzɪ] *adj person* holgazán, perezoso; *day* ocioso
'la•zy•bones *nsg* F holgazán(-ana) *m(f)*, vago(-a) *m(f)*
la•zy Susan ['suːzn] *bandeja giratoria en el centro de la mesa para servirse comida*
lb *abbr* (= ***pound***) libra *f* (*de peso*)
LCD [elsiː'diː] *abbr* (= ***liquid crystal display***) LCD, pantalla *f* de cristal líquido
lead[1] [liːd] *n for dog* correa *f*
lead[2] [led] *n substance* plomo *m*
lead[3] [liːd] **I** *v/t* (*pret & pp* **led**) **1** *procession*, *race* ir al frente de; *company*, *team* dirigir **2** (*guide*, *take*) conducir; *life* llevar
II *v/i* (*pret & pp* **led**) *in race*, *competition* ir en cabeza; (*provide leadership*) tener el mando; ***a street ~ing off the square*** una calle que sale de la plaza; ***where is this ~ing?*** ¿adónde nos lleva esto?
III *n in race* ventaja *f*; ***be in the ~*** estar en cabeza; ***take the ~*** ponerse en cabeza; ***lose the ~*** perder la cabeza
◆ **lead on I** *v/i* (*go in front*) ir delante **II** *v/t* (*incite*) provocar, incitar; ***she's just leading him on*** le está tomando el pelo
◆ **lead up to** *v/t* preceder a; ***I wonder what she's leading up to*** me pregunto a dónde quiere ir a parar
lead•ed ['ledɪd] *adj gas* con plomo
lead•en ['ledn] *adj sky* plomizo; *conversation*, *performance* aburrido
lead•er ['liːdər] líder *m*; ***he's up with the ~s*** *in a race* va a la cabeza
lead•er•ship ['liːdərʃɪp] *of party etc* liderazgo *m*
'lead•er•ship con•test pugna *f* por el liderazgo
'lead•er writ•er editorialista *m/f*
lead-free ['ledfriː] *adj gas* sin plomo
'lead gui•tar•ist guitarrista *m/f* principal
lead•ing ['liːdɪŋ] *adj runner* en cabeza; *company*, *product* puntero
lead•ing 'ar•ti•cle artículo *m* de opinión; **'lead•ing-edge** *adj company* en

la vanguardia; *technology* de vanguardia; **lead•ing 'la•dy** protagonista *f*, actriz *f* principal; **'lead•ing light** *fig* líder *m/f*, *of stage, movies* estrella *m/f*; **'lead•ing man** protagonista *m*, actor *m* principal; **lead•ing 'ques•tion** *pregunta parafraseada para generar la respuesta deseada*; **'lead•ing strings** *npl* rienda *f*, *fig* riendas *fpl*; ***keep s.o. in ~*** mantener a alguien a raya

leaf [li:f] (*pl* **leaves** [li:vz]) hoja *f*; ***take a ~ out of s.o.'s book*** seguir el ejemplo de alguien; ***turn over a new ~*** pasar página, hacer borrón y cuenta nueva

◆ **leaf through** *v/t* hojear

leaf•let ['li:flət] folleto *m*

leaf•y ['li:fɪ] *adj* frondoso

league [li:g] liga *f*; ***be in a different ~*** no tener (punto de) comparación, no tener igual

'league game *in soccer* partido *m* ligero

leak [li:k] **I** *n in roof* gotera *f*, *in pipe* agujero *m*; *of air, gas* fuga *f*, escape *m*; *of information* filtración *f* **II** *v/i of boat* hacer agua; *of pipe* tener un agujero; *of liquid, gas* fugarse, escaparse

◆ **leak out** *v/i of air, gas* fugarse, escaparse; *of news* filtrarse

leak•age ['li:kɪdʒ] ☞ **leak**

leak•y ['li:kɪ] *adj pipe* con agujeros; *boat* que hace agua

lean[1] [li:n] **I** *v/i* (*pret & pp* **leant**) (*be at an angle*) estar inclinado; ***~ against sth*** apoyarse en algo; ***I can't work with you ~ing over me*** no puedo trabajar contigo aquí encima **II** *v/t* (*pret & pp* **leant**) apoyar

◆ **lean back** *v/i* reclinarse

◆ **lean forward** *v/i* inclinarse, asomarse

◆ **lean on** *v/t* **1** F (*put pressure on*) hacer presión sobre **2** (*depend on*) depender de

◆ **lean toward** *v/t* (*favour, prefer*) inclinarse por

lean[2] [li:n] *adj meat* magro; *style, prose* pobre, escueto; ***~ mixture*** MOT mezcla *f* con alta proporción de aire

lean•ing ['li:nɪŋ] tendencia *f*, inclinación *f*

leant [lent] *Br pret & pp* ☞ **lean**[1]

lean-to ['li:ntu:] soportal *m*, porche *m*

leap [li:p] **I** *n* salto *m*; ***a great ~ forward*** un gran salto adelante; ***he's coming on by ~s and bounds*** viene volando **II** *v/i* (*pret & pp* **-ed** *or* **leapt**) saltar; ***he ~t over the fence*** saltó la valla; ***they ~t into the river*** se tiraron al río; ***~ at an opportunity*** no dejar pasar una oportunidad

◆ **leap out** *v/i* **1** *of car* bajarse de un salto **2** (*stand out*) saltar a la vista; ***it really leaps out at you*** salta a la vista

◆ **leap up** *v/i* **1** *from chair* ponerse en pie de un salto **2** *of prices, temperature* subir bruscamente, dispararse

'leap•frog I *n* salto *m* al potro (*juego infantil*) **II** *v/i* (*pret & pp* **-ged**): ***~ over s.o.*** *fig* pasar por encima de alguien

leapt [lept] *pret & pp* ☞ **leap**

'leap year año *m* bisiesto

learn [lɜ:rn] **I** *v/t* (*pret & pp* **-ed** *or* **learnt**) aprender; (*hear*) enterarse de; ***~ how to do sth*** aprender a hacer algo; ***~ one's lesson*** aprender la lección **II** *v/i* (*pret & pp* **-ed** *or* **learnt**) aprender; ***you just never ~, do you!*** ¡nunca aprendes!; ***you live and ~*** se aprende con la experiencia

learn•er ['lɜ:rnər] estudiante *m/f*; ***be a quick / slow ~*** aprender con rapidez / lentitud

learn•ing ['lɜ:rnɪŋ] **1** (*knowledge*) conocimientos *mpl* **2** *act* aprendizaje *m*

'learn•ing curve curva *f* de aprendizaje; ***be on the ~*** tener que aprender cosas nuevas; ***it's a steep ~*** hay mucho que aprender en poco tiempo

'learn•ing dif•fi•cul•ties *npl* dificultades *fpl* de aprendizaje

lease [li:s] **I** *n* (contrato *m* de) arrendamiento *m*; ***give s.o. / sth a new ~ of life*** insuflar nueva vida a alguien / algo **II** *v/t apartment, equipment* arrendar

◆ **lease out** *v/t apartment, equipment* arrendar

'lease•hold•er inquilino(-a) *m(f)*, arrendatario(-a) *m(f)*

lease 'pur•chase arrendamiento *m* con opción de compra

leash [li:ʃ] *for dog* correa *f*

least [li:st] **I** *adj* (*slightest*) menor; ***the ~*** *amount, money, baggage* menos; ***there's not the ~ reason to …*** no hay la más mínima razón para que … **II** *adv* menos **III** *n* lo menos; ***he drank the ~*** fue el que menos bebió; ***not in the ~ surprised*** en absoluto sorprendido; ***at ~*** por lo menos

leath•er ['leðər] **I** *n* piel *f*, cuero **II** *adj* de piel, de cuero
leath•er 'belt cinturón *m* de piel *or* cuero; **leath•er 'jack•et** chaqueta *f* de piel *or* cuero; **'leath•er neck** MIL P marine *m*
leath•er•y ['leðərɪ] *adj* curtido; *meat* duro
leave [liːv] **I** *n* (*vacation*) permiso *m*; ***on ~*** de permiso
II *v/t* (*pret & pp* ***left***) *city*, *place* marcharse de, irse de; *person*, *food*, *memory*, (*forget*) dejar; ***let's ~ things as they are*** dejemos las cosas tal y como están; ***how did you ~ things with him?*** ¿cómo quedaron las cosas con él?; ***~ s.o. / sth alone*** (*not touch*, *not interfere with*) dejar a alguien / algo en paz; ***be left*** quedar; ***there is nothing left*** no queda nada; ***I only have one left*** sólo me queda uno
III *v/i* (*pret & pp* ***left***) *of person* marcharse, irse; *of plane*, *train*, *bus* salir
◆ **leave behind** *v/t intentionally* dejar; (*forget*) dejarse
◆ **leave on** *v/t hat*, *coat* dejar puesto; *TV*, *computer* dejar encendido
◆ **leave out** *v/t word*, *figure* omitir; (*not put away*) no guardar; ***leave me out of this*** a mí no me metas en esto
leav•er ['liːvər] *in school* joven *m/f* que termina el colegio
leaves [liːvz] *pl* ☞ ***leaf***
leav•ing par•ty ['liːvɪŋ] fiesta *f* de despedida
Leb•a•nese [lebə'niːz] **I** *adj* libanés **II** *n* libanés(-esa) *m(f)*
Leb•a•non ['lebənɑːn] Líbano *m*
lech•er ['letʃər] lascivo *m*, libidinoso *m*
lech•er•ous ['letʃərəs] *adj* lujurioso, lascivo
lec•tern ['lektərn] atril *m*
lec•ture ['lektʃər] **I** *n* clase *f*; *to general public* conferencia *f* **II** *v/i at university* dar clases (***in*** de); *to general public* dar una conferencia
'lec•ture hall sala *f* de conferencias
'lec•tur•er ['lektʃərər] profesor(a) *m(f)*
LED [eliː'diː] *abbr* (= ***light-emitting diode***) LED *m*, diodo *m* emisor de luz
led [led] *pret & pp* ☞ ***lead***[1]
ledge [ledʒ] *of window* alféizar *f*; *on rock face* saliente *m*
ledg•er ['ledʒər] COM libro *m* mayor
lee [liː] NAUT sotavento *m*
leech [liːtʃ] *also fig* sanguijuela *f*
leek [liːk] puerro *m*
leer [lɪr] **I** *n sexual* mirada *f* impúdica; *evil* mirada *f* maligna **II** *v/i* mirar lascivamente; ***~ at s.o.*** lanzarle una mirada lasciva a alguien
lees [liːz] *npl* posos *mpl*
lee•ward ['liːwərd] *adv* NAUT a sotavento *m*
'lee•way *fig* margen *m*; ***give s.o. some ~*** dar margen a alguien
left[1] [left] **I** *adj* izquierdo **II** *n also* POL izquierda *f*; ***on the ~*** a la izquierda; ***to the ~*** *turn*, *look* a la izquierda; ***take a ~*** girar a la izquierda **III** *adv turn*, *look* a la izquierda
left[2] [left] *pret & pp* ☞ ***leave***
'left-hand *adj* de la izquierda; ***on your ~ side*** a tu izquierda; **left-hand 'drive**: ***this car is ~*** este coche tiene el volante a la izquierda; **left-hand•ed** [left'hændɪd] *adj* zurdo
left•ist ['leftɪst] *adj* POL izquierdista, de izquierdas
left 'lug•gage (of•fice) *Br* consigna *f*; **'left-overs** *npl food* sobras *fpl*; **'left-wing** *adj* POL izquierdista, de izquierdas; **left-'wing•er** POL izquierdista *m/f*, persona *m/f* de izquierdas
leg [leg] **1** *of person* pierna *f*; *of animal* pata *f*; ***pull s.o.'s ~*** tomar el pelo a alguien **2** SP: ***first ~*** partido *m* de ida
leg•a•cy ['legəsɪ] legado *m*
le•gal ['liːgl] *adj* legal
le•gal ad'vis•er asesor(a) *m(f)* jurídico(-a)
le•gal 'en•ti•ty persona *f* jurídica
le•gal•i•ty [lɪ'gælətɪ] legalidad *f*
le•gal•i•za•tion [liːgəlaɪ'zeɪʃn] legalización *f*
le•gal•ize ['liːgəlaɪz] *v/t* legalizar
le•gal•ly ['liːgəlɪ] *adv* legalmente
le•ga•tion [lɪ'geɪʃn] legación *f*
le•gend ['ledʒənd] leyenda *f*
le•gen•da•ry ['ledʒəndrɪ] *adj* legendario
leg•gings ['legɪnz] *npl* mallas *fpl*
leg•gy ['legɪ] *adj* de piernas largas, zancudo
le•gi•ble ['ledʒəbl] *adj* legible
le•gion ['liːdʒən] legión *f*
le•gion•ar•y ['liːdʒənərɪ] legionario *m*
leg•is•late ['ledʒɪsleɪt] *v/i* legislar

(***against*** contra)
leg•is•la•tion [ledʒɪs'leɪʃn] legislación *f*
leg•is•la•tive ['ledʒɪslətɪv] *adj* legislativo
leg•is•la•tor ['ledʒɪsleɪtər] legislador(a) *m(f)*
leg•is•la•ture ['ledʒɪslətʃər] POL legislativo *m*
le•git•i•ma•cy [lɪ'dʒɪtɪməsɪ] legitimidad *f*
le•git•i•mate [lɪ'dʒɪtɪmət] *adj* legítimo
le•git•i•mize [lɪ'dʒɪtəmaɪz] *v/t* legitimar
'leg room espacio *m* para las piernas
leg•ume ['legju:m] BOT legumbre *f*
leg warm•ers ['legwɒ:rmərz] *npl* calentadores *mpl*
lei•sure ['li:ʒər] ocio *m*; ***I look forward to having more ~*** estoy deseando tener más tiempo libre; ***do it at your ~*** tómate tu tiempo para hacerlo
'lei•sure cen•ter, *Br* **'lei•sure cen•tre** centro *m* recreativo
'lei•sure in•dus•try sector *m* del ocio
lei•sure•ly ['li:ʒərlɪ] *adj pace, lifestyle* tranquilo, relajado
'lei•sure time tiempo *m* libre
lem•ming ['lemɪŋ] ZO lemming *m*; ***they rushed into it like ~s*** se precipitaron como borregos
le•mon ['lemən] limón *m*
le•mon•ade [lemə'neɪd] limonada *f*
'le•mon juice zumo *m* de limón, *L.Am.* jugo *m* de limón
le•mon 'tea té *m* con limón
lem•pi•ra [lem'pi:rə] FIN lempira *m*
lend [lend] *v/t* (*pret & pp* ***lent***) prestar; ***~ s.o. a hand*** echar una mano a alguien, ayudar a alguien; ***~ support to s.o.*** prestar *or* dar apoyo a alguien
lend•er ['lendər] prestamista *m/f*; ***banks and other ~s*** bancos y otras entidades de crédito
lend•ing li•bra•ry ['lendɪŋ] biblioteca *f* pública (*con servicio de préstamo de libros*)
length [leŋθ] longitud *f*; (*piece: of material etc*) pedazo *m*; ***at ~*** *describe, explain* detalladamente; (*finally*) finalmente; ***go to the ~ of doing sth*** llegar al extremo de hacer algo; ***go to great ~s to do sth*** hacer todo lo posible para conseguir algo
length•en ['leŋθən] *v/t* alargar
length•ways ['lenθweɪz], **length•wise** ['lenθwaɪz] *adv* longitudinalmente, a lo largo
length•y ['leŋθɪ] *adj speech, stay* largo
le•ni•ence, le•ni•en•cy ['li:nɪəns(ɪ)] indulgencia *f*; *of prison sentence, judge* indulto *m*
le•ni•ent ['li:nɪənt] *adj* indulgente, poco severo
lens [lenz] *of camera* objetivo *m*, lente *f*; *of eyeglasses* cristal *m*; *of eye* cristalino *m*; (*contact* ~) lente *m* de contacto, *Span* lentilla *f*
'lens cov•er *of camera* tapa *f* del objetivo
Lent [lent] REL Cuaresma *f*
lent [lent] *pret & pp* ☞ ***lend***
len•til ['lentl] lenteja *f*
len•til 'soup sopa *f* de lentejas
Le•o ['li:oʊ] ASTR Leo *m/f inv*; ***be (a) ~*** ser Leo
leop•ard ['lepərd] leopardo *m*
le•o•tard ['li:oʊtɑ:rd] malla *f*
lep•er ['lepər] leproso(-a) *m(f)*; *fig* paria *m/f*
lep•ro•sy ['leprəsɪ] MED lepra *f*
les•bi•an ['lezbɪən] **I** *n* lesbiana *f* **II** *adj* lésbico, lesbiano
le•sion ['li:ʒn] lesión *f*
Le•sot•ho [le'soʊθoʊ] Lesoto *m*
less [les] *adv* menos; ***it costs ~*** cuesta menos; ***~ than $200*** menos de 200 dólares
les•see [le'sɪ:] inquilino(-a) *m(f)*, arrendatario(-a) *m(f)*
les•sen ['lesn] **I** *v/t* disminuir **II** *v/i* reducirse, disminuir
less•er ['lesər] *adj* menor; ***the ~ of two evils*** el mal menor
les•son ['lesn] **1** lección *f*; ***~s start at 9.15*** las clases empiezan a las 9:15; ***teach s.o. a ~*** *fig* darle una lección *or* un escarmiento a alguien; ***I've learnt my lesson*** *fig* he aprendido la lección; ***that should be a ~ to them*** *fig* eso debería enseñarles una lección **2** REL lectura *f*
les•sor [le'sɔ:r] arrendador(a) *m(f)*
lest [lest] *conj* para que no
let[1] [let] *n in tennis* red *f*
let[2] [let] *v/t* (*pret & pp* ***let***) **1** (*allow*) dejar, permitir; ***~ s.o. do sth*** dejar a alguien hacer algo; ***~ me go!*** ¡déjame!; ***~ him come in!*** ¡déjale entrar!; ***~'s go / stay*** vamos / quedémonos; ***~'s***

not argue no discutamos; **~ *alone*** mucho menos; **~ *go of*** *rope, handle etc* soltar; **~ *go of me!*** ¡suéltame! **2**: ***room to ~*** *Br* se alquila habitación

◆ **let down** *v/t* **1** *hair* soltarse; *shades* bajar **2** *dress, pants* alargar **3** *(disappoint)* decepcionar, defraudar **4** *tires* desinflar

◆ **let in** *v/t person, rain* dejar pasar

◆ **let off** *v/t* **1** *(not punish)* perdonar; ***the court let him off with a small fine*** el tribunal sólo le impuso una pequeña multa **2** *from car* dejar **3** *smoke, fumes etc* despedir; **~ *steam*** *fig* desahogarse

◆ **let on** *v/i*: ***don't let on*** *(don't tell)* no se lo digas a nadie; ***he didn't let on*** *let it show* no se le notó

◆ **let out** *v/t* **1** *from room, building* dejar salir **2** *jacket etc* agrandar **3** *groan, yell* soltar **4** *from prison* poner en libertad **5** *Br (rent)* alquilar, *Mex* rentar

◆ **let up** *v/i (stop)* amainar

'let•down decepción *f*

le•thal ['li:θl] *adj* letal

le•thar•gic [lɪ'θɑ:rdʒɪk] *adj* aletargado, apático

leth•ar•gy ['leθərdʒɪ] sopor *m*, apatía *f*

let's [lets] F ☞ ***let us***

let•ter ['letər] **1** *of alphabet* letra *f* **2** *in mail* carta *f*

'let•ter bomb carta *f* bomba; **'let•ter-box** *Br* buzón *m*; **'let•ter•car•ri•er** cartero(-a) *m(f)*; **'let•ter•head** *(heading)* membrete *m*; *(headed paper)* papel *m* con membrete; **let•ter of 'cred•it** COM carta *f* de crédito; **'let•ter o•pen•er** abrecartas *m*

let•tuce ['letɪs] lechuga *f*

'let•up: ***without a ~*** sin interrupción

leu•ke•mi•a [lu:'ki:mɪə] MED leucemia *f*

leu•ko•cyte ['lu:kousaɪt] MED leucocito *m*

lev•el ['levl] **I** *adj field, surface* nivelado, llano; *in competition, scores* igualado; ***draw ~ with s.o.*** *in race* ponerse a la altura de alguien **II** *n on scale, in hierarchy, (amount)* nivel *m*; ***on the ~*** F *(honest)* honrado

◆ **level out** *v/i (pret & pp **-ed**, Br **-led**) of prices, road* nivelarse; *of airplane* enderezarse

lev•el-'head•ed *adj* ecuánime, sensato

le•ver ['levər] **I** *n* palanca *f* **II** *v/t*: **~ *sth open*** abrir algo haciendo palanca

lev•er•age ['levrɪdʒ] **1** apalancamiento *m* **2** *(influence)* influencia *f*

lev•er•aged buy-out ['levrɪdʒd] COM adquisición *f* apalancada

lev•i•tate ['levɪteɪt] *v/i* levitar

lev•y ['levɪ] *v/t (pret & pp **-ied**) taxes* imponer

lewd [lu:d] *adj* obsceno

lewd•ness ['lu:dnɪs] lascivia *f*

lex•i•cog•ra•pher [leksɪ'kɑ:grəfər] lexicógrafo(-a) *m(f)*

lex•i•cog•ra•phy [leksɪ'kɑ:grəfɪ] lexicografía *f*

li•a•bil•i•ty [laɪə'bɪlətɪ] **1** *(responsibility)* responsabilidad *f* **2** *(likeliness)* propensión *f* (***to*** a)

li•a'bil•i•ty in•sur•ance seguro *m* a terceros

li•a•ble ['laɪəbl] *adj* **1** *(responsible)* responsable (***for*** de) **2**: ***be ~ to*** *(likely: of person)* ser propenso a; ***the computer's ~ to crash if you …*** es probable que la computadora se bloquee si …

◆ **li•aise with** [lɪ'eɪz] *v/t* actuar de enlace con

li•ai•son [lɪ'eɪzɑ:n] *(contacts)* contacto *m*, enlace *m*

li•ar [laɪr] mentiroso(-a) *m(f)*

li•bel ['laɪbl] **I** *n* calumnia *f*, difamación *f* **II** *v/t (pret & pp **-ed**, Br **-led**)* calumniar, difamar

li•bel•(l)ous ['laɪbələs] *adj* calumnioso, difamatorio

lib•er•al ['lɪbərəl] *adj (broad-minded)*, POL liberal; *(generous: portion etc)* abundante

lib•er•al•ism ['lɪbərəlɪzəm] liberalismo *m*

lib•er•al•i•ty [lɪbə'rælətɪ] liberalidad *f*

lib•er•al•ize ['lɪbərəlaɪz] *v/t* liberalizar

lib•er•ate ['lɪbəreɪt] *v/t* liberar

lib•er•at•ed ['lɪbəreɪtɪd] *adj* liberado

lib•er•a•tion [lɪbə'reɪʃn] liberación *f*

Li•ber•i•a [laɪ'bɪrɪə] Liberia *f*

Li•ber•i•an [laɪ'bɪrɪən] **I** *adj* liberiano **II** *n* liberiano(-a)

lib•er•tar•i•an [lɪbər'terɪən] *adj* libertario

lib•er•tine ['lɪbərti:n] libertino(-a) *m(f)*

lib•er•ty ['lɪbərtɪ] libertad *f*; ***at ~*** *prisoner etc* en libertad; ***be at ~ to do sth*** tener libertad para hacer algo

li•bi•do [lɪ'bi:dou] líbido *f*

Li•bra ['li:brə] ASTR Libra *m/f inv*,

L

L.Am. libr(i)ano(-a) *m(f)*; ***be (a) ~*** ser Libra, *L.Am.* ser libr(i)ano
li•brar•i•an [laɪ'brerɪən] bibliotecario(-a) *m(f)*
li•bra•ry ['laɪbrerɪ] biblioteca *f*
li•bret•tist [lɪ'bretɪst] libretista *m/f*
li•bret•to [lɪ'bretoʊ] (*pl* ***-tos, libretti*** [lɪ'bretɪ]) libreto *m*
Lib•y•a ['lɪbɪə] Libia *f*
Lib•y•an ['lɪbɪən] **I** *adj* libio **II** *n* libio(-a) *m(f)*
lice [laɪs] *pl* ☞ ***louse***
li•cence *Br* ☞ ***license*** *n*
li•cense ['laɪsns] **I** *n* permiso *m*, licencia *f* **II** *v/t* autorizar; ***be ~d*** tener permiso *or* licencia
'**li•cense a•gree•ment** acuerdo *m* de licencia; '**li•cense num•ber** (número *m* de) matrícula *f*; '**li•cense plate** *of car* (placa *f* de) matrícula *f*
li•cen•tious [laɪ'senʃəs] *adj* licencioso
li•chen ['laɪkən] BOT liquen *m*
lick [lɪk] **I** *n* lamedura *f* **II** *v/t* lamer; ***~ one's lips*** relamerse; ***we've got it ~ed*** F está bajo control
lick•ing ['lɪkɪŋ] F (*defeat*): ***we got a ~*** nos dieron una paliza F
li•co•rice ['lɪkərɪs] regaliz *m*
lid [lɪd] (*top*) tapa *f*
lie[1] [laɪ] **I** *n* (*untruth*) mentira *f*; ***tell a ~*** decir *or* contar una mentira; ***give the ~ to sth*** desmentir *or* contradecir algo **II** *v/i* mentir
lie[2] [laɪ] *v/i* (*pret* ***lay***, *pp* ***lain***) *of person* estar tumbado; *of object* estar; (*be situated*) estar, encontrarse; ***~ on your stomach*** túmbate boca abajo
◆ **lie around** *v/i* dejar botado *or Span* tendido
◆ **lie down** *v/i* tumbarse
'**lie de•tec•tor** detector *m* de mentiras; ***~ test*** prueba *f* con el detector de mentiras; **lie-'down**: ***have a ~*** echarse un rato (a descansar); **lie-'in** *Br* F: ***have a ~*** (*sleep late*) quedarse un rato más en la cama
lieu [lu:]: ***in ~ of*** en lugar de
lieu•ten•ant [lʊ'tenənt] teniente *m/f*
lieu•ten•ant 'colo•nel teniente *m/f* coronel
life [laɪf] (*pl* ***lives*** [laɪvz]) vida *f*; *of machine* vida *f*, duración *f*; ***that's ~!*** ¡así es la vida!; ***all her ~*** durante toda su vida ***how many lives were lost?*** ¿cuántas víctimas hubo?; ***it put a bit of ~ into the party*** animó la fiesta un poco; ***he's doing ~*** F está condenado a cadena perpetua; ***it's not a matter of ~ and death*** no es una cuestión de vida o muerte; ***get a ~!*** P ¡no seas patético!
life an'nu•i•ty renta *f* vitalicia; '**life as•sur•ance** *Br* seguro *m* de vida; '**life belt** salvavidas *m inv*; '**life•boat** *from ship* bote *m* salvavidas; *from land* lancha *f* de salvamento; '**life cy•cle** ciclo *m* vital; '**life ex•pect•an•cy** esperanza *f* de vida; '**life•guard** socorrista *m/f*; '**life his•to•ry** historia *f* de la vida; **life im'pris•on•ment** cadena *f* perpetua; '**life in•sur•ance** seguro *m* de vida; '**life in•ter•est** renta *f* vitalicia; '**life jack•et** chaleco *m* salvavidas
life•less ['laɪflɪs] *adj* sin vida
'**life•like** *adj* realista
'**life•line**: ***throw s.o. a ~*** *fig* echar *or* tender una mano a alguien; '**life•long** *adj* de toda la vida; **life 'mem•ber** miembro *m/f* vitalicio; **life 'peer•age** *Br* título *m* (nobiliario) vitalicio; **life pre•serv•er** ['laɪfprɪzɜ:rvər] salvavidas *m inv*
lif•er ['laɪfər] LAW F condenado(-a) *m(f)* a cadena perpetua
'**life raft** NAUT balsa *f* de salvamento; '**life•sav•er 1** socorrista *m/f* **2** *fig* salvación *f*; '**life-sav•ing** *adj medical equipment*, *drug* que salva vidas; '**life sen•tence** LAW cadena *f* perpetua; **life--sized** ['laɪfsaɪzd] *adj* de tamaño natural; '**life•style** estilo *m* de vida; **life sup'port ma•chine** máquina *f* de respiración artificial; ***be on a ~*** estar con una máquina de respiración artificial; '**life--threat•en•ing** *adj* que puede ser mortal; '**life•time** vida *f*; ***in my ~*** durante mi vida
lift [lɪft] **I** *v/t* levantar **II** *v/i of fog* disiparse **III** *n* **1** *in car*: ***give s.o. a ~*** llevar a alguien (en coche); ***thanks for the ~*** gracias por traerme (en coche) **2** (*encouragement*): ***it gave us all a ~*** nos levantó el ánimo **3** *Br* (*elevator*) ascensor *m*
◆ **lift off** *v/i of rocket* despegar
'**lift-off** *of rocket* despegue *m*
lig•a•ment ['lɪgəmənt] ligamento *m*
lig•a•ture ['lɪgətʃər] TIP, MUS ligadura *f*
light[1] [laɪt] **I** *n* luz *f*; ***in the ~ of*** a la luz de; ***have you got a ~?*** ¿tienes fuego?;

set ~ to sth prender fuego a algo **II** *v/t* (*pret & pp* ***-ed*** *or* ***lit***) **1** *fire, cigarette* encender **2** (*illuminate*) iluminar **III** *adj color, sky* claro; *room* luminoso

◆ **light up I** *v/t* (*illuminate*) iluminar **II** *v/i* **1** *of face* iluminarse **2** *start to smoke* encender un cigarrillo

light[2] [laɪt] **I** *adj* (*not heavy*) ligero **II** *adv*: ***travel ~*** viajar ligero de equipaje

'light bulb bombilla *f*

light-e•mit•ting di•ode [laɪtɪmɪtɪŋ 'daɪoʊd] diodo *m* emisor de luz

light•en[1] ['laɪtn] *v/t color* aclarar

light•en[2] ['laɪtn] *v/t load* aligerar

◆ **lighten up** *v/i of person* alegrarse; ***come on, lighten up*** venga, no te tomes las cosas tan en serio

light•er ['laɪtər] *for cigarettes* encendedor *m*, *Span* mechero *m*

light-fin•gered [laɪt'fɪŋgərd] *adj* largo *or* suelto de manos; **light-'head•ed** *adj* (*dizzy*) mareado; **light-heart•ed** [laɪt'hɑːrtɪd] *adj* alegre; **'light•house** faro *m*

light•ing ['laɪtɪŋ] iluminación *f*

light•ly ['laɪtlɪ] *adv touch* ligeramente; ***get off ~*** salir bien parado; ***and I don't say this ~*** y no digo esto a la ligera

light•ness[1] ['laɪtnɪs] *of room, color* claridad *f*

light•ness[2] ['laɪtnɪs] *in weight* ligereza *f*

light•ning ['laɪtnɪŋ]: ***a flash of ~*** un relámpago; ***they were struck by ~*** les cayó un rayo

'light•ning con•duc•tor pararrayos *m inv*

'light•ning rod ELEC pararrayos *mpl*

'light pen lápiz *m* óptico; **'light•proof** *adj* resistente a la luz; **'light•ship** NAUT buque *m* faro; **'light•weight** *in boxing* peso *m* ligero; **'light year** año *m* luz; ***it's ~s away from what we used to have*** no tiene absolutamente nada que ver con lo que teníamos antes

lik•a•ble ['laɪkəbl] *adj* agradable, simpático

like[1] [laɪk] **I** *prep* como; ***be ~ s.o.*** ser como alguien; ***what is she ~?*** ¿cómo es?; ***it's not ~ him*** (*not his character*) no es su estilo; ***that's more ~ it*** ¡eso es otra cosa!; ***there's nothing ~ a good ...*** no hay nada como un buen ... **II** *conj* F (*as*) como; ***~ I said*** como dije

like[2] [laɪk] *v/t*: ***I ~ it / her*** me gusta; ***I would ~ ...*** querría ...; ***I would ~ to ...*** me gustaría ...; ***would you ~ ...?*** ¿querrías ...?; ***would you ~ to ...?*** ¿querrías ...?; ***she ~s to swim*** le gusta nadar; ***if you ~*** si quieres

like•a•ble ['laɪkəbl] *adj* agradable, simpático

like•li•hood ['laɪklɪhʊd] probabilidad *f*; ***in all ~*** con toda probabilidad

like•ly ['laɪklɪ] **I** *adj* (*probable*) probable; ***not ~!*** ¡ni hablar!; ***the most ~ candidates*** los candidatos con más posibilidades; ***he's a ~ winner*** es un posible ganador; ***are you ~ to see him tomorrow?*** ¿crees que le verás mañana?; ***I'm not ~ to have time*** lo más seguro es que no tenga tiempo; ***a ~ story!*** ¡menudo cuento! **II** *adv* probablemente

like-'mind•ed *adj* afín, semejante

lik•en ['laɪkən] *v/t* comparar (***to*** con), equiparar (***to*** a)

like•ness ['laɪknɪs] (*resemblance*) parecido *m*

like•wise ['laɪkwaɪz] *adv* igualmente; ***pleased to meet you – ~!*** encantado de conocerle – ¡lo mismo digo!

lik•ing ['laɪkɪŋ] afición *f* (***for*** a); ***to your ~*** a su gusto; ***take a ~ to s.o.*** tomar cariño a alguien

li•lac ['laɪlək] *flower* lila *f*; *color* lila *m*

lilt [lɪlt] tonillo *m*, sonsonete *m*

li•ly ['lɪlɪ] lirio *m*

li•ly-liv•ered ['lɪlɪlɪvərd] *adj* cobarde, pusilánime

li•ly of the 'val•ley lirio *m* de los valles

limb [lɪm] miembro *m*

lim•ber ['lɪmbər] *adj* flexible, ágil

◆ **limber up** *v/i* entrar en calor, calentarse

lime[1] [laɪm] *fruit, tree* lima *f*

lime[2] [laɪm] *substance* cal *f*

lime'green *adj* verde lima

'lime•light: ***be in the ~*** estar en el candelero

lim•er•ick ['lɪmərɪk] quinteto *m* humorístico

'lime•stone GEOL caliza *f*

lim•ey ['laɪmɪ] F británico(-a) *m*(*f*) (*palabra despectiva usada en EE.UU.*)

lim•it ['lɪmɪt] **I** *n* límite *m*; ***within ~s*** dentro de un límite; ***be off ~s*** *of place* ser zona prohibida; ***that's the ~!*** F ¡es el colmo! F; ***~ warranty*** garantía *f* limitada **II** *v/t* limitar (***to*** a)

L

lim•i•ta•tion [lɪmɪ'teɪʃn] limitación *f*; ***know one's ~s*** ser consciente de las limitaciones propias
lim•it•ed ['lɪmɪtɪd] *adj* limitado
lim•it•ed 'com•pa•ny *Br* sociedad *f* limitada; **lim•it•ed li•a'bil•i•ty** responsabilidad *f* limitada; **lim•it•ed li•a'bil•i•ty com•pa•ny** *Br* sociedad *f* de responsabilidad limitada
lim•o ['lɪmoʊ] F limusina *f*
lim•ou•sine ['lɪməziːn] limusina *f*
limp[1] [lɪmp] *adj* flojo
limp[2] [lɪmp] **I** *n*: ***he has a ~*** cojea **II** *v/i* cojear
limp•et ['lɪmpɪt] ZO lapa *f*; ***stick to s.o. like a ~*** pegarse a alguien como una lapa
lim•pid ['lɪmpɪd] *adj* cristalino
linch•pin ['lɪntʃpɪn] TECH pasador *m* de bloqueo; *fig* base *f*, fundamento *m*
lin•den ['lɪndən] BOT tilo *m*
line[1] [laɪn] *n of text, on road*, TELEC línea *f*; *of trees* fila *f*, hilera *f*; *of people* fila *f*, cola *f*; *of business* especialidad *f*; ***what ~ are you in?*** ¿a qué te dedicas?; ***the ~ is busy*** está ocupado, *Span* está comunicando; ***hold the ~*** no cuelgue; ***draw the ~ at sth*** no estar dispuesto a hacer algo; ***~ of inquiry*** línea de investigación; ***~ of reasoning*** argumentación *f*; ***stand in ~*** hacer cola; ***in ~ with*** (*conforming with*) en las mismas líneas que
◆ **line up I** *v/i* hacer cola **II** *v/t* (*arrange*) *objects* poner en fila; *interview etc* preparar, organizar
line[2] [laɪn] *v/t with lining* forrar
lin•e•age ['lɪnɪɪdʒ] linaje *m*
lin•e•al ['lɪnɪəl] *adj* lineal
lin•e•ar ['lɪnɪər] *adj* lineal
'line•back•er *in football* defensa *m/f*
'line drive *in baseball* batazo *m* de línea
lin•en ['lɪnɪn] **1** *material* lino *m* **2** (*sheets etc*) ropa *f* blanca
line of 'cred•it linea *f* de crédito
lin•er ['laɪnər] *ship* transatlántico *m*
lines•man ['laɪnzmən] SP juez *m* de línea, linier *m*
'line•up 1 SP alineación *f* **2** *for police* rueda *f* de reconocimiento **3**: ***the ~ for tonight's gig*** los componentes del grupo que toca esta noche
lin•ge•rie ['lænʒəriː] lencería *f*
lin•ger•ing ['lɪŋgərɪŋ] *adj feelings* persistente; *sunset* paulatino
lin•ger ['lɪŋgər] *v/i of person* entretenerse; *of pain* persistir
◆ **linger on** *v/i* perdurar
lin•go ['lɪŋgoʊ] F **1** *jargon* argot *m* **2** (*language*): ***I don't speak the ~*** no hablo el idioma
lin•guist ['lɪŋgwɪst] lingüista *m/f*; ***she's a good ~*** se le dan bien los idiomas
lin•guis•tic [lɪŋ'gwɪstɪk] *adj* lingüístico
lin•i•ment ['lɪnɪmənt] MED linimento *m*
lin•ing ['laɪnɪŋ] *of clothes* forro *m*; *of brakes, pipe* revestimiento *m*
link [lɪŋk] **I** *n* (*connection*) conexión *f*; *between countries* vínculo *m*; *in chain* eslabón *m* **II** *v/t* conectar; ***they're ~ing her with the robbery*** la relacionan con el robo
◆ **link up** *v/i* encontrarse; TV conectar; ***~ with sth*** enlazarse *or* unirse con algo
links [lɪŋks] *npl* SP campo *m* de golf (*al lado del mar*)
'link•up conexión *f*
li•no•le•um [lɪ'noʊlɪəm] linóleo *m*
lin•seed ['lɪnsiːd] BOT linaza *f*
'lin•seed oil aceite *m* de linaza
lin•tel ['lɪntl] ARCHI lintel *m*
li•on ['laɪən] león *m*
'li•on cub cachorro(-a) *m*(*f*) de león
li•on•ess ['laɪənes] leona *f*
lip [lɪp] labio *m*
'lip gloss brillo *m* de labios, lip gloss *m*
lip•o•suc•tion ['lɪpoʊsʌkʃn] liposucción *f*
'lip•read *v/i* (*pret & pp* ***-read*** [red]) leer los labios; **lip salve** ['lɪpsælv] bálsamo *m* para labios; **'lip serv•ice**: ***he was only paying ~*** sólo lo decía de boquilla; **'lip•stick** barra *f* de labios
li•queur [lɪ'kjʊr] licor *m*
liq•uid ['lɪkwɪd] **I** *n* líquido *m* **II** *adj* líquido
liq•ui•date ['lɪkwɪdeɪt] *v/t* **1** *assets* liquidar **2** F (*kill*) cepillarse a F
liq•ui•da•tion [lɪkwɪ'deɪʃn] liquidación *f*; ***go into ~*** ir a la quiebra
liq•uid crys•tal 'dis•play pantalla *f* de cristal líquido
liq•uid crys•tal 'screen pantalla *f* de cristal líquido
liq•ui•di•ty [lɪ'kwɪdɪtɪ] FIN liquidez *f*
liq•uid•ize ['lɪkwɪdaɪz] *v/t* licuar
liq•uid•iz•er ['lɪkwɪdaɪzər] licuadora *f*
liq•uor ['lɪkər] bebida *f* alcohólica

liq•uo•rice ['lɪkərɪʃ] *esp Br* regaliz *m*
'liq•uor store tienda *f* de bebidas alcohólicas
lisp [lɪsp] **I** *n* ceceo *m* **II** *v/i* cecear
list[1] [lɪst] **I** *n* lista *f*; ***is the name on your ~?*** ¿aparece el nombre en tu lista? **II** *v/t* enumerar; COMPUT listar
list[2] [lɪst] *v/i* NAUT escorar
lis•ten•er ['lɪsnər] *to radio* oyente *m/f*; ***he's a good ~*** sabe escuchar
lis•ten ['lɪsn] *v/i* escuchar; ***I tried to persuade him, but he wouldn't ~*** intenté convencerle, pero no me hizo ningún caso
◆ **listen in** *v/i* escuchar
◆ **listen to** *v/t radio*, *person* escuchar
lis•ter•i•a [lɪs'tɪrɪə] listeria *f*
list•ings mag•a•zine ['lɪstɪŋz] guía *f* de espectáculos
list•less ['lɪstlɪs] *adj* apático, lánguido
'list price precio *m* de catálogo
lit [lɪt] *pret & pp* ☞ ***light***
lit•a•ny ['lɪtənɪ] REL letanía *f*; ***a ~ of complaints*** una letanía *or* retahíla de quejas
li•ter ['li:tər] litro *m*
lit•er•a•cy ['lɪtərəsɪ] alfabetización *f*
lit•er•al ['lɪtərəl] *adj* literal
lit•er•al•ly ['lɪtərəlɪ] *adv* literalmente
lit•er•ar•y ['lɪtərerɪ] *adj* literario
lit•er•ate ['lɪtərət] *adj* culto; ***be ~*** saber leer y escribir
lit•er•a•ture ['lɪtrətʃər] literatura *f*; *about a product* folletos *mpl*, prospectos *mpl*
lithe [laɪð] *adj* flexible, ágil
lith•o•graph ['lɪθəgræf] litografía *f*
Lith•u•a•ni•a [lɪθu:'eɪnɪə] Lituania *f*
Lith•u•a•ni•an [lɪθu:'eɪnɪən] **I** *adj* lituano **II** *n* **1** *person* lituano(-a) *m(f)* **2** *language* lituano
lit•i•gant ['lɪtɪgənt] LAW litigante *m/f*, pleiteador(a) *m(f)*
lit•i•gate ['lɪtɪgeɪt] *v/i & v/t* litigar
lit•i•ga•tion [lɪtɪ'geɪʃn] litigación *f*
li•ti•gious [lɪ'tɪdʒəs] *adj* litigioso
lit•mus test ['lɪtməs] *fig* prueba *f* de fuego
li•tre *Br* ☞ ***liter***
lit•ter ['lɪtər] **1** basura *f* **2** *of animal* camada *f*
'lit•ter bas•ket *Br* papelera *f*; **'lit•ter bin** cubo *m* de la basura; **'lit•ter bug** F *persona que tira basura en lugares públicos*
lit•tle ['lɪtl] **I** *adj* pequeño; ***the ~ ones*** los pequeños **II** *n* poco *m*; ***the ~ I know*** lo poco que sé; ***a ~*** un poco; ***a ~ bread / wine*** un poco de pan / vino; ***a ~ is better than nothing*** más vale poco que nada **III** *adv* poco; ***~ by ~*** poco a poco; ***a ~ better / bigger*** un poco mejor / más grande; ***a ~ before 6*** un poco antes de las 6
lit•ur•gy ['lɪtərdʒɪ] REL liturgia *f*
live[1] [lɪv] *v/i* vivir
◆ **live down** *v/t*: ***he's trying to live down his past*** intenta que se olvide su pasado
◆ **live for** *v/t* vivir para
◆ **live off** *v/t salary* vivir de; *person* vivir a costa de
◆ **live on I** *v/t rice*, *bread* sobrevivir a base de **II** *v/i* (*continue living*) sobrevivir, vivir
◆ **live together** *v/i* vivir juntos
◆ **live through** *v/t* (*experience*) vivir, pasar por
◆ **live up**: ***live it up*** pasarlo bien
◆ **live up to** *v/t expectations* responder a; *s.o.'s reputation* estar a la altura de
◆ **live with** *v/t with person* vivir con
live[2] [laɪv] *adj broadcast* en directo; *ammunition* real; *wire* con corriente; ***a real ~ movie star*** F una estrella de cine en carne y hueso
live•li•hood ['laɪvlɪhʊd] vida *f*, sustento *m*; ***earn one's ~*** ganarse la vida
live•li•ness ['laɪvlɪnɪs] *of person*, *music* vivacidad *f*; *of debate* lo animado
live•ly ['laɪvlɪ] *adj* animado
◆ **liv•en up** ['laɪvn] **I** *v/t* animar **II** *v/i* animarse
liv•er ['lɪvər] MED, *food* hígado *m*
liv•er 'sau•sage *embutido de pate de higado*
'liv•er spot mancha *f* (*por la edad*)
liv•er•wurst ['lɪvərwɜ:rst] *embutido de pate de higado*
lives [laɪvz] *pl* ☞ ***life***
live•stock ['laɪvstɑ:k] ganado *m*
liv•id ['lɪvɪd] *adj* (*angry*) enfurecido, furioso
liv•ing ['lɪvɪŋ] **I** *adj* vivo **II** *n* vida *f*; ***what do you do for a ~?*** ¿en qué trabajas?; ***earn one's ~*** ganarse la vida; ***standard of ~*** estándar *m* de vida
'liv•ing room sala *f* de estar, salón *m*
liv•ing 'will voluntad *f* anticipada

L

liz•ard ['lɪzərd] lagarto *m*
lla•ma ['lɑːmə] ZO llama *f*
load [loud] **I** *n also* ELEC carga *f*; **~*s of*** F montones de F; ***you've got ~s*** F tienes un montón F; ***that's a ~ off my mind*** eso me quita un peso de encima **II** *v/t car, truck, gun* cargar; *camera* poner el carrete a; COMPUT: *software* cargar (en memoria)
◆ **load up** *v/t car, truck* cargar
load•ed ['loudɪd] *adj* F **1** (*very rich*) forrado F **2** (*drunk*) como una cuba F
load•ing dock ['loudɪŋ] *at factory* plataforma *f* de carga
loaf•er[1] ['loufər] *shoe* mocasín *m*
loaf•er[2] ['loufər] F gandul(a) *m*(*f*), manta *m/f* F
loaf [louf] (*pl **loaves*** [louvz]) pan *m*; ***a ~ of bread*** una barra de pan, un pan; ***use your ~*** F usa el coco F
◆ **loaf around** *v/i* F gandulear F
loam [loum] tierra *f* vegetal, limo *m*
loan [loun] **I** *n* préstamo *m*; ***on ~*** prestado; ***~ application*** solicitud *f* de préstamo **II** *v/t* prestar; ***~ s.o. sth*** prestar algo a alguien
'**loan shark** F usurero(-a) *m*(*f*) F
'**loan•word** LING préstamo *m* lingüístico
loath [louθ] *adj*: ***be ~ to do sth*** ser reacio a hacer algo
loathe [louð] *v/t* detestar, aborrecer; ***I ~ having to stay in*** detesto *or* odio tenerme que quedar
loath•ing ['louðɪŋ] odio *m*, aborrecimiento *m*
loath•some ['louðsʌm] *adj* detestable, insufrible
loaves [louvz] *pl* ☞ ***loaf***[1]
lob [lɑːb] SP **I** *n* lob *m*, globo *m* **II** *v/t* (*pret & pp* ***-bed***) *throw* arrojar por lo alto; ***~ a ball*** *in tennis* hacer un lob *or* globo
lob•by ['lɑːbɪ] **I** *n* **1** *in hotel, theater* vestíbulo *m* **2** POL lobby *m*, grupo *m* de presión **II** *v/t* hacer lobby a, presionar; ***~ s.o. for sth*** ejercer presión sobre alguien para algo
lobe [loub] *of ear* lóbulo *m*
lob•ster ['lɑːbstər] langosta *f*
lo•cal ['loukl] **I** *adj* local; ***the ~ people*** la gente del lugar; ***I'm not ~*** no soy de aquí **II** *n*: ***the ~s*** los del lugar; ***are you a ~?*** ¿eres de aquí?
lo•cal an•es'thet•ic anestesia *f* local; '**lo•cal ar•e•a net•work** red *f* de área local; '**lo•cal call** TELEC llamada *f* local; **lo•cal e'lec•tions** *npl* elecciones *fpl* municipales; **lo•cal 'gov•ern•ment** administración *f* municipal
lo•cal•i•ty [lou'kælətɪ] localidad *f*
lo•cal•i•za•tion [loukəlaɪzeɪʃn] localización *f*
lo•cal•ize ['loukəlaɪz] *v/t* localizar
lo•cal•ly ['loukəlɪ] *adv live, work* cerca, en la zona; ***it's well known ~*** es muy conocido en la zona; ***they are grown ~*** son cultivados en la región
lo•cal 'pro•duce productos *mpl* del lugar
'**lo•cal time** hora *f* local
lo•cate [lou'keɪt] *v/t* **1** *new factory etc* emplazar, ubicar **2** (*identify position of*) situar; ***be ~d*** encontrarse
lo•ca•tion [lou'keɪʃn] **1** (*siting*) emplazamiento *m* **2** (*identifying position of*) localización *f* **3**: ***on ~*** *movie* en exteriores
lock[1] [lɑːk] *n of hair* mechón *m*
lock[2] [lɑːk] **I** *n on door* cerradura *f* **II** *v/t door* cerrar (con llave)
◆ **lock away** *v/t* guardar bajo llave
◆ **lock in** *v/t person* encerrar
◆ **lock onto** *v/t target* seguir
◆ **lock out** *v/t of house* dejar fuera; ***I locked myself out*** me dejé las llaves dentro
◆ **lock up I** *v/t in prison* encerrar **II** *v/i* cerrar
lock•er ['lɑːkər] taquilla *f*
'**lock•er room** vestuario *m*
lock•et ['lɑːkɪt] guardapelo *m*
'**lock•jaw** MED tétano *m*; '**lock•out** COM lockout *m*, paro *m* forzoso; **lock•smith** ['lɑːksmɪθ] cerrajero(-a) *m*(*f*); '**lock•up** calabozo *m*
lo•co ['loukou] P locomotora *f*
lo•co•mo•tion [loukə'mouʃn] locomoción *f*
lo•co•mo•tive [loukə'moutɪv] **I** *adj* locomotriz **II** *n* RAIL locomotora *f*
lo•cum ['loukəm] *Br* suplente *m/f*
lo•cust ['loukəst] langosta *f*
lo•cu•tion [lou'kjuːʃn] locución *f*
lodge [lɑːdʒ] **I** *v/t complaint* presentar **II** *v/i* **1** *of bullet* alojarse **2**: ***~ with s.o.*** alojarse con alguien
lodg•er ['lɑːdʒər] húesped *m/f*
lodg•ing ['lɑːdʒɪŋ] alojamiento *m*

loft [lɑːft] buhardilla *f*, desván *m*
loft•y ['lɑːftɪ] *adj heights, ideals* elevado
log [lɑːg] **1** *wood* tronco *m* **2** *written record* registro *m*
◆ **log off** *v/i* (*pret & pp* **-ged**) salir
◆ **log on** *v/i* entrar
◆ **log on to** *v/t* entrar a
log•a•rithm ['lɑːgərɪðəm] MATH logaritmo *m*
'log•book *captain's* cuaderno *m* de bitácora; *driver's* documentación *f* del vehículo
log 'cab•in cabaña *f*
log•ger•heads ['lɑːgərhedz]: ***be at ~*** estar enfrentado
lo•gic ['lɑːdʒɪk] lógica *f*
lo•gic•al ['lɑːdʒɪkl] *adj* lógico
lo•gic•al•ly ['lɑːdʒɪklɪ] *adv* lógicamente
'lo•gic cir•cuit circuito *m* lógico
'lo•gic di•a•gram diagrama *m* lógico
lo•gis•tics [lə'dʒɪstɪks] *npl* logística *f*
lo•go ['lougou] logotipo *m*
'log•roll•ing *fig* apoyo *m* recíproco
loin [lɔɪn] **1**: ***~s*** *pl* ANAT entrañas *fpl* **2** GASTR lomo *m*
'loin•cloth taparrabos *mpl*
loi•ter ['lɔɪtər] *v/i* holgazanear
lol•li•pop ['lɑːlɪpɑːp] piruleta *f*
loll [lɑːl] **I** *v/i* repantigarse
◆ **loll around** *v/i* repantigarse
Lon•don ['lʌndən] Londres *m*
Lon•don•er ['lʌndənər] londinense *m/f*
lone [loun] *adj* solitario
lone•li•ness ['lounlɪnɪs] *of person, place* soledad *f*
lone•ly ['lounlɪ] *adj person* solo; *place* solitario
lon•er ['lounər] solitario(-a) *m(f)*
lone•some ['lounsəm] *adj* solo
long[1] [lɒːŋ] **I** *adj* largo; ***it's a ~ way*** hay un largo camino; ***it's two feet ~*** mide dos pies de largo; ***the movie is three hours ~*** la película dura tres horas **II** *adv* mucho tiempo; ***don't be ~*** no tardes mucho; ***5 weeks is too ~*** 5 semanas son mucho tiempo; ***will it take ~?*** ¿llevará mucho tiempo?; ***that was ~ ago*** eso fue hace mucho tiempo; ***~ before then*** mucho antes; ***before ~*** al poco tiempo; ***we can't wait any ~er*** no podemos esperar más tiempo; ***she no ~er works here*** ya no trabaja aquí; ***so ~ as*** (*provided*) siempre que; ***so ~!*** ¡hasta la vista!
long[2] [lɒːŋ] *v/i*: ***~ for** home* echar en falta; *change etc* anhelar, desear; ***be ~ing to do sth*** anhelar *or* desear hacer algo
long-a•wait•ed ['lɒːŋəweɪtɪd] *adj* esperado, deseado; **long-'dis•tance** *adj race* de fondo; *flight* de larga distancia; ***a ~ phonecall*** una llamada de larga distancia, una conferencia interurbana; **long-dis•tance 'run•ner** corredor(a) *m(f)* de fondo; **long di'vi•sion** MATH división *f* (por escrito)
lon•gev•i•ty [lɑːn'dʒevɪtɪ] longevidad *f*
long•haired ['lɒːŋherd] *adj* con melena, con pelo largo
long•ing ['lɒːŋɪŋ] anhelo *m*, deseo *m*
long•ish ['lɒːŋɪʃ] *adj* bastante largo
lon•gi•tude ['lɑːŋgɪtuːd] longitud *f*
long johns ['lɒːŋdʒɑːnz] *npl* F marianos *mpl* F, calzas *fpl*; **'long jump** *Br* salto *m* de longitud; **'long jump•er** *Br* saltador(-a) de longitud *m(f)*; **long-life 'milk** leche *f* uperizada; **long-lived** [lɒːŋ'lɪvd] *adj* longevo, duradero; **long-play•ing 're•cord** LP *m*, disco *m* de larga duración; **'long-range** *adj* **1** *missile* de largo alcance **2** *forecast* a largo plazo; **long•shore•man** ['lɒːŋʃɔːrmən] cargador *m*; **'long shot**: ***it's a ~ but maybe*** dudo que funcione pero; **long-'sight•ed** *adj* hipermétrope; **long-sleeved** [lɒːŋ'sliːvd] *adj* de manga larga; **long-'stand•ing** *adj* antiguo; **'long-term** *adj* a largo plazo; ***~ unemployment*** desempleo *m or Span* paro *m* de larga duración; **'long wave** RAD onda *f* larga; **long•wind•ed** [lɒːŋ'wɪndɪd] *adj* prolijo
loo [luː] *Br* F baño *m*, servicio *m*
look [lʊk] **I** *n* **1** (*appearance*) aspecto *m*; ***~s*** (*beauty*) atractivo *m*, guapura *f* **2** (*glance*) mirada *f*; ***give s.o. / sth a ~*** mirar a alguien / mirar algo; ***have a ~ at sth*** (*examine*) echar un vistazo a algo; ***can I have a ~?*** ¿puedo echarle un vistazo?; ***can I have a ~ around?*** *in store etc* ¿puedo echar un vistazo? **II** *v/i* **1** mirar; ***it depends how you ~ at it*** depende de cómo lo mires; ***~, I've explained it three times*** a ver, te lo expliqué tres veces **2** (*search*) buscar **3** (*seem*) parecer; ***you ~ tired / different*** pareces cansado / diferente; ***he ~s about 25*** aparenta 25 años; ***how do things ~ to you?*** ¿qué te parece cómo

están las cosas?; ***that ~s good*** tiene buena pinta
III *v/t*: ***~ where you're going!*** ¡cuida por dónde vas!; ***he couldn't ~ me in the face*** no me podía mirar a la cara
◆ **look after** *v/t children* cuidar (de); *property, interests* proteger
◆ **look ahead** *v/i fig* mirar hacia el futuro
◆ **look around I** *v/i* mirar **II** *v/t museum, city* dar una vuelta por
◆ **look at** *v/t* **1** mirar **2** (*examine*) estudiar; (*consider*) considerar; ***it depends how you look at it*** depende de cómo lo mires **3** F (*be faced with*) afrontar
◆ **look back** *v/i* mirar atrás
◆ **look down on** *v/t* mirar por encima del hombro a
◆ **look for** *v/t* buscar
◆ **look forward to** *v/t* estar deseando; ***I'm looking forward to the vacation*** tengo muchas ganas de empezar las vacaciones
◆ **look in on** *v/t* (*visit*) hacer una visita a
◆ **look into** *v/t* (*investigate*) investigar
◆ **look on I** *v/i* (*watch*) quedarse mirando **II** *v/t*: ***look on s.o. / sth as*** (*consider*) considerar a alguien / algo como
◆ **look onto** *v/t garden, street* dar a
◆ **look out** *v/i* **1** *from window etc* mirar **2** (*pay attention*) tener cuidado; ***look out!*** ¡cuidado!
◆ **look out for** *v/t* **1** buscar **2** (*be on guard against*) tener cuidado con **3** (*take care of*) cuidar, proteger
◆ **look out of** *v/t window* mirar por
◆ **look over** *v/t translation* revisar, repasar; *house* inspeccionar
◆ **look through** *v/t magazine, notes* echar un vistazo a, hojear
◆ **look to** *v/t* (*rely on*): ***we look to you for help*** acudimos a usted en busca de ayuda
◆ **look up I** *v/i* **1** *from paper etc* levantar la mirada **2** (*improve*) mejorar **II** *v/t* **1** *word, phone number* buscar **2** (*visit*) visitar
◆ **look up to** *v/t* (*respect*) admirar
'look-a•like doble *m/f*
look•er ['lʊkər]: ***she's a real ~*** F es un bombón F
look•er-'on, *pl* **look•ers-'on** mirón (-ona) *m(f)*, curioso(-a) *m(f)*
'look-in F: ***I don't get a ~*** no puedo meter baza F
look•ing glass ['lʊkɪŋ] espejo *m*
'look•out 1 *person* centinela *m*, vigía *m* **2**: ***be on the ~ for*** estar buscando
loom [lu:m] telar *m*
◆ **loom up** *v/i* aparecer (***out of*** de entre)
loon•y ['lu:nɪ] F **I** *n* chalado(-a) *m(f)* F **II** *adj* chalado F
'loon•y bin P loquería *f* P
loop [lu:p] **I** *n* bucle *m* **II** *v/t*: ***~ sth around sth*** pasar algo alrededor de algo
'loop•hole *in law etc* resquicio *m or* vacío *m* legal
loop•y ['lu:pɪ] *adj* F loco, tocado F
loose [lu:s] *adj connection, button* suelto; *clothes* suelto, holgado; *morals* disoluto, relajado; *wording* impreciso; ***~ change*** suelto *m*, *L.Am.* sencillo *m*; ***~ ends*** *of problem, discussion* cabos *mpl* sueltos; ***be at a ~ end*** no tener nada que hacer
loose•ly ['lu:slɪ] *adv worded* vagamente
loos•en ['lu:sn] *v/t collar, knot* aflojar
◆ **loosen up I** *v/t muscles, person* relajar, aflojar; *fig* relajar, distender **II** *v/i fig*: *of person* largar P
loot [lu:t] **I** *n* botín *m* **II** *v/i* saquear
loot•er ['lu:tər] saqueador(a) *m(f)*
◆ **lop off** [lɑ:p] *v/t* (*pret & pp* ***-ped***) *branch* cortar; podar
lop-sid•ed [lɑ:p'saɪdɪd] *adj* torcido; *balance of committee* desigual
lo•qua•cious [loʊ'kweɪʃəs] *adj fml* locuaz
lord [lɔ:rd] lord *m*, aristócrata *m*
Lord [lɔ:rd] (*God*) Señor *m*; ***good ~!*** ¡Dios mío!
Lord's 'Prayer padrenuestro *m*
lore [lɔ:r] sabiduría *f* popular
lor•ry ['lɑ:rɪ] *Br* camión *m*
lose [lu:z] **I** *v/t* (*pret & pp* ***lost***) *object, match* perder; ***have nothing to ~*** no tener nada que perder; ***I'm lost*** me he perdido; ***get lost!*** F ¡vete a paseo! F; ***you've lost me there*** me he perdido **II** *v/i* (*pret & pp* ***lost***) **1** SP perder **2** *of clock* retrasarse
◆ **lose out** *v/i* salir perdiendo
los•er ['lu:zər] perdedor(-a) *m(f)*; F *in life* fracasado(-a) *m(f)*
los•ing ['lu:zɪŋ] *adj*: ***fight a ~ battle*** *fig* luchar en vano

loss [lɑːs] pérdida *f*; ***make a ~*** tener pérdidas; ***I'm at a ~ what to say ~*** no sé qué decir
loss ad•just•er ['lɑːsədʒʌstər] *in insurance* tasador(a) *m(f)* de pérdidas; **'loss lead•er** COM artículo *m* de reclamo; **loss of 'earn•ings** pérdida *f* de ganancias
lost [lɑːst] **I** *adj* perdido; ***be ~ in thought*** estar absorto **II** *pret & pp* ☞ ***lose***
lost-and-'found, *Br* **lost 'prop•er•ty (of•fice)** oficina *f* de objetos perdidos
lot[1] [lɑːt]: ***a ~, ~s*** mucho, *pl* muchos; ***a ~ of books, ~s of books*** muchos libros; ***a ~ of butter, ~s of butter*** mucha mantequilla; ***a ~ better / easier*** mucho mejor / más fácil
lot[2] [lɑːt] *n*: ***draw ~s*** echar a suertes
lo•tion ['loʊʃn] loción *f*
lot•te•ry ['lɑːtərɪ] lotería *f*
'lot•te•ry tick•et boleto *m or* número *m* de lotería
lo•tus ['loʊtəs] BOT loto *m*; ***~ position*** postura *f* de loto
loud [laʊd] *adj voice*, *noise* fuerte; *music* fuerte, alto; *color* chillón
loud hail•er [laʊd'heɪlər] megáfono *m*; **'loud•mouth** F boceras *m/f inv* F, bocazas *m/f inv*; **loud'speak•er** altavoz *m*, *L.Am.* altoparlante *m*
lounge [laʊndʒ] *in house* salón *m*
◆ **lounge around** *v/i* holgazanear
'lounge suit *Br* traje *m* de calle
louse [laʊs] (*pl* ***lice*** [laɪs]) piojo *m*
◆ **louse up** *v/t* P estropear, echar a perder F
lous•y ['laʊzɪ] *adj* F asqueroso F; ***I feel ~*** me siento de pena F
lout [laʊt] gamberro *m*
lout•ish ['laʊtɪʃ] *adj* gamberro, desconsiderado
lov•a•ble ['lʌvəbl] *adj* adorable, encantador
love [lʌv] **I** *n* amor *m*; *in tennis* nada *f*; ***be in ~*** estar enamorado (***with*** de); ***fall in ~*** enamorarse (***with*** de); ***make ~*** hacer el amor; ***make ~*** hacer el amor (***to*** con); ***yes, my ~*** sí, amor **II** *v/t person*, *country*, *wine* amar; ***she ~s to watch tennis*** le encanta ver tenis
'love af•fair aventura *f* amorosa; **'love bite** F muerdo *m* F, chupón *m* F; **love-'hate re•la•tion•ship** relación *f* de amor y odio
love•less ['lʌvlɪs] *adj* desamorado, sin amor
'love let•ter carta *f* de amor
'love•life vida *f* amorosa
love•ly ['lʌvlɪ] *adj face*, *hair*, *color*, *tune* precioso, lindo; *person*, *character* encantador; *holiday*, *weather*, *meal* estupendo; ***we had a ~ time*** nos lo pasamos de maravilla
'love•mak•ing sexo *m*, vida *f* sexual; ***his idea of ~ is …*** su idea de hacer el amor es …
'love po•em poema *m* de amor
lov•er ['lʌvər] amante *m/f*
'love scene escena *f* de amor; **'love-sick** *adj*: ***be ~*** tener mal de amores; **'love song** canción *f* de amor; **'love sto•ry** historia *f* de amor, romance *m*
lov•ing ['lʌvɪŋ] *adj* cariñoso
lov•ing•ly ['lʌvɪŋlɪ] *adv* con cariño
low[1] [loʊ] **I** *adj bridge*, *salary*, *price*, *voice*, *quality* bajo; ***be feeling ~*** estar deprimido; ***we're ~ on gas / tea*** nos queda poca gasolina / poco té **II** *n* **1** *in weather* zona *f* de bajas presiones, borrasca *f* **2** *in sales*, *statistics* mínimo *m*; ***be at an all-time ~*** estar en su punto más bajo
low[2] [loʊ] *v/i of cows* mugir
'low•brow *adj* poco intelectual, popular; **low-'cal•o•rie** *adj* bajo en calorías; **'low-cost** *adj* de bajo coste; **'low-cut** *adj dress* escotado; **'low•down** F **I** *adj* rastrero, deshonesto **II** *n*: ***give s.o. the ~*** poner al tanto a alguien (***on*** de); ***get the ~*** quedar al tanto (***on*** de); **low-e'mis•sion** *adj* MOT de baja emisión
low•er ['loʊər] *v/t to the ground*, *hemline*, *price* bajar; *flag* arriar; *pressure* reducir
Low•er Cal•i•forn•i•a Baja California *f*
'low-fat *adj* de bajo contenido graso; **'low-fly•ing** *adj* volando bajo; **low-'in•come** *adj* de renta baja; **'low•key** *adj* discreto, mesurado; **'low•lands** *npl* tierras *fpl* bajas; **'low post** *in basketball* poste *m* bajo; **low-'pres•sure ar•e•a** zona *f* de bajas presiones, borrasca *f*; **'low sea•son** temporada *f* baja; **low-'ly•ing** *adj* bajo; **low-'spir•it•ed** *adj* desanimado, deprimido; **'low tide** marea *f* baja
lox [lɑːks] salmón *m* ahumado

loy•al ['lɔɪəl] *adj* leal, fiel (***to*** a)
loy•al•ist ['lɔɪəlɪst] (*government supporter*) seguidor(a) *m(f)* del régimen; *in Northern Ireland* unionista *m/f*; *in Spanish Civil War* republicano(-a) *m(f)*
loy•al•ly ['lɔɪəlɪ] *adv* lealmente, fielmente
loy•al•ty ['lɔɪəltɪ] lealtad *f* (***to*** a)
loz•enge ['lɑːzɪndʒ] **1** *shape* rombo *m* **2** *tablet* pastilla *f*
LP [el'piː] *abbr* (= ***long-playing record***) LP *m*, disco *m* de larga duración
L-plate ['elpleɪt] (placa *f* de la) L *f*
LSD [eles'diː] *abbr* (= ***lysergic acid diethylamide***) LSD *m*
Ltd *abbr* (= ***limited*** S.L. (= sociedad *f* limitada)
LTR [eltiː'ɑːr] *abbr* (= ***long-term relationship***) relación *f* sentimental estable
lu•bri•cant ['luːbrɪkənt] lubricante *m*
lu•bri•cate ['luːbrɪkeɪt] *v/t* lubricar
lu•bri•ca•tion [luːbrɪ'keɪʃn] lubricación *f*
lu•cid ['luːsɪd] *adj* (*clear, sane*) lúcido
luck•i•ly ['lʌkɪlɪ] *adv* afortunadamente, por suerte
luck•less ['lʌklɪs] *adj* desafortunado
luck [lʌk] suerte *f*; ***bad ~*** mala suerte; ***good ~!*** ¡buena suerte!; ***wish s.o. ~*** desear a alguien (buena) suerte; ***be in ~*** estar de suerte, tener suerte; ***be out of ~*** no tener suerte; ***that's just my ~!*** ¡qué (mala) suerte que tengo!
◆ **luck out** *v/i* F tener mucha suerte
luck•y ['lʌkɪ] *adj person, coincidence* afortunado; *day, number* de la suerte; ***you were ~*** tuviste suerte; ***she's ~ to be alive*** tiene suerte de estar con vida; ***that's ~!*** ¡qué suerte!
lu•cra•tive ['luːkrətɪv] *adj* lucrativo
lu•cre ['luːkər]: ***filthy ~*** cochino dinero *m*
Lud•dite ['lʌdaɪt] ludita *m/f*
lu•di•crous ['luːdɪkrəs] *adj* ridículo
lug [lʌg] *v/t* (*pret & pp* ***-ged***) arrastrar
lug•gage ['lʌgɪdʒ] equipaje *m*
'lug•gage al•low•ance AVIA límite *m* de equipaje; **'lug•gage lock•er** consigna *f* automática; **'lug•gage trol•ley** carro *m* para el equipaje
luke•warm ['luːkwɔːrm] *adj water* tibio, templado; *reception* indiferente
lull [lʌl] **I** *n in storm, fighting* tregua *f*; *in conversation* pausa *f* **II** *v/t*: ***~ s.o. into a false sense of security*** dar a alguien una falsa sensación de seguridad; ***~ s.o. to sleep*** adormecer a alguien
lul•la•by ['lʌləbaɪ] canción *f* de cuna, nana *f*
lum•ba•go [lʌmbeɪgoʊ] lumbago *m*
lum•ber[1] ['lʌmbər] **I** *n* (*timber*) madera *f* **II** *v/t Br*: ***get ~ed with sth*** F tener que cargar con algo
lum•ber[2] ['lʌmbər] *v/i* moverse torpemente
'lum•ber•jack leñador(a) *m(f)*; **'lum•ber•mill** aserradero *m*; **'lum•ber•room** *Br* trastero *m*
lu•mi•nar•y ['luːmɪnərɪ] lumbrera *m/f*
lu•mi•nos•i•ty [luːmɪ'nɑːsətɪ] luminosidad *f*
lu•mi•nous ['luːmɪnəs] *adj* luminoso
lump [lʌmp] **1** *of sugar, earth* terrón *m* **2** (*swelling*) bulto *m*
◆ **lump together** *v/t* agrupar
lump 'sum pago *m* único
lump•y ['lʌmpɪ] *adj liquid, sauce* grumoso; *mattress* lleno de bultos
lu•na•cy ['luːnəsɪ] locura *f*
lu•nar ['luːnər] *adj* lunar
lu•na•tic ['luːnətɪk] lunático(-a) *m(f)*, loco(-a) *m(f)*
lunch [lʌntʃ] almuerzo *m*, comida *f*; ***have ~*** almorzar, comer
'lunch box fiambrera *f*
'lunch break pausa *f* para el almuerzo
lunch•eon meat ['lʌntʃən] fiambre *m* enlatado
'lunch hour hora *f* del almuerzo
'lunch•time hora *f* del almuerzo
lung [lʌŋ] pulmón *m*; ***shout at the top of one's ~s*** gritar a pleno pulmón
'lung can•cer cáncer *m* de pulmón
lunge [lʌndʒ] arremetida *f*, ***make a ~ for sth*** abalanzarse sobre algo
◆ **lunge at** *v/t* arremeter contra
lurch[1] [lɜːrtʃ] *v/i of drunk* tambalearse; *of ship* dar sacudidas
lurch[2] [lɜːrtʃ] *n*: ***leave s.o. in the ~*** dejar a alguien tirado
lure [lʊr] **I** *n* atractivo *m* **II** *v/t* atraer; ***he was ~d into a trap*** le hicieron caer en una trampa; ***she ~d him into her hotel room*** lo sedujo para llevarlo a su habitación del hotel

◆ **lure away** *v/t from TV etc* apartar (***from*** de); *from another company* hacer salir (***from*** de)

lu•rid ['lʊrɪd] *adj color* chillón; *details* espeluznante

lurk [lɜːrk] *v/i of person* estar oculto, estar al acecho

lus•cious ['lʌʃəs] *adj* **1** *fruit, dessert* jugoso, exquisito **2** F *woman, man* cautivador

lush [lʌʃ] *adj vegetation* exuberante

lust [lʌst] lujuria *f*

◆ **lust after** *v/t person* desear; *object* anhelar

lus•ter ['lʌstər] lustre *m*; *fig* lustre *m*, esplendor *m*

lust•ful ['lʌstfʊl] *adj* lujurioso

lus•tre *Br* ☞ ***luster***

lute [luːt] MUS laúd *m*

Lux•em•bourg ['lʌksəmbɜːrg] Luxemburgo *m*

Lux•em•bourg•er ['lʌksəmbɜːrgər] luxemburgués(-esa) *m(f)*

lux•u•ri•ant [lʌg'ʒʊrɪənt] *adj* exuberante

lux•u•ri•ate [lʌg'ʒʊrɪeɪt] *v/i in bath, bed* relajarse

lux•u•ri•ous [lʌg'ʒʊrɪəs] *adj* lujoso

lux•u•ri•ous•ly [lʌg'ʒʊrɪəslɪ] *adv* lujosamente

lux•u•ry ['lʌkʃərɪ] **I** *n* lujo *m* **II** *adj* de lujo

ly•chee [laɪ'ʧɪ] BOT lichi *m*

lye [laɪ] CHEM lejía *f*

ly•ing ['laɪɪŋ] **I** *present participle* ☞ ***lie***[2] **II** *adj* mentiroso

lymph gland ['lɪmfglænd] ganglio *m* linfático

lymph node ['lɪmfnoʊd] ANAT nódulo *m* linfático

lynch [lɪnʧ] *v/t* linchar

lynx [lɪŋks] ZO lince *m*

lynx-eyed ['lɪŋksaɪd] *adj fig* con ojos de lince

lyr•ic ['lɪrɪk] *adj* lírico

lyr•i•cal ['lɪrɪkl] *adj* **1** lírico **2**: ***wax ~ about sth*** ensalzar algo

lyr•i•cist ['lɪrɪsɪst] letrista *m/f*

lyr•ics ['lɪrɪks] *npl* letra *f*

M

MA [em'eɪ] *abbr* (= ***Master of Arts***) Máster *m* en Humanidades

ma'am [mæm] señora *f*

mac [mæk] F (*mackintosh*) impermeable *m*

ma•ca•bre [mə'kɑːbrə] *adj* macabro

mac•a•ro•ni [mækə'roʊnɪ] macarrones *mpl*

mac•a•ro•ni and 'cheese macarrones *mpl* con queso

mace [meɪs] *of mayor* maza *f*

Mach [mæk]: ***fly at ~ two*** volar a Mach 2

ma•che•te [mə'ʃetɪ] machete *m*

ma•chine [mə'ʃiːn] **I** *n* máquina *f* **II** *v/t with sewing machine* coser a máquina; TECH trabajar a máquina

ma'chine gun ametralladora *f*

ma•chine-'read•a•ble *adj* legible por la computadora *or Span* el ordenador

ma•chin•e•ry [mə'ʃiːnərɪ] *also of government* maquinaria *f*

ma'chine tool máquina *f* herramienta; **ma•chine trans'la•tion** traducción *f* automática; **ma•chine 'wash•a•ble** *adj* lavable a máquina

ma•chis•mo [mə'kɪzmoʊ] machismo *m*

mach•o ['mæʧoʊ] *adj* macho; ***stop being so ~*** deja de hacerte el macho

mack•er•el ['mækrəl] caballa *f*

mack•in•tosh ['mækɪntɑːʃ] impermeable *m*

mac•ro ['mækroʊ] COMPUT macro *m*

mac•ro•bi•ot•ic [mækroʊbaɪ'ɑːtɪk] *adj* macrobiótico

mac•ro•cosm ['mækroʊkɑːzəm] macrocosmos *m inv*

macro•ec•o•nom•ics [mækroʊiːkə'nɑːmɪks] *nsg* macroeconomía *f*

mad [mæd] *adj* **1** (*insane*) loco; ***a ~ idea*** una idea disparatada; ***be ~ about*** F estar loco por; ***drive s.o. ~*** volver loco a alguien; ***go ~*** (*become insane, with enthusiasm*) volverse loco; ***like ~*** F *run, work* como un loco F **2** F (*angry*) enfadado; ***Pa got real ~ when I told him*** papá se puso hecho una furia cuando se lo conté

'mad•cap *adj* disparatado

mad 'cow dis•ease enfermedad *f or* mal *m* de las vacas locas
mad•den ['mædən] *v/t* (*infuriate*) sacar de quicio
mad•den•ing ['mædnɪŋ] *adj* exasperante
mad•den•ing•ly ['mædnɪŋlɪ] *adv* exasperantemente
made [meɪd] *pret & pp* ☞ ***make***
made-to-'meas•ure *adj clothes* hecho a medida; **made-to-'or•der** *adj fig* a medida; **'made-up** *adj* **1** *story etc* inventado **2** *with make-up on* maquillado
'mad•house *fig* casa *f* de locos
mad•ly ['mædlɪ] *adv* como loco; ***~ in love*** locamente enamorado
mad•man ['mædmən] loco *m*
mad•ness ['mædnɪs] locura *f*; ***that's sheer ~*** eso es una auténtica locura
Ma•don•na [mə'dɑːnə] madona *f*
'mad•wom•an loca *f*
Ma•fi•a ['mɑːfɪə]: ***the ~*** la mafia
ma•fi•o•so [mɑːfɪ'oʊsoʊ] (*pl* ***-sos, mafiosi*** [mɑːfɪ'oʊsɪ]) mafioso *m*
mag•a•zine [mægə'ziːn] *printed* revista *f*
mag•a'zine rack revistero *m*
Ma•gel•lan straits [məgelən'streɪts] *npl* Estrecho *m* de Magallanes
ma•gen•ta [mə'dʒentə] *adj* magenta
mag•got ['mægət] gusano *m*
Ma•gi ['meɪdʒaɪ] REL: ***the ~*** los Reyes Magos
mag•ic ['mædʒɪk] **I** *n* magia *f*; ***as if by ~, like ~*** como por arte de magia **II** *adj* mágico; ***there's nothing ~ about it*** no tiene nada de mágico
mag•i•cal ['mædʒɪkl] *adj* mágico
mag•i•cal•ly ['mædʒɪklɪ] *adv* mágicamente
mag•ic 'car•pet alfombra *f* mágica
ma•gi•cian [mə'dʒɪʃn] *performer* mago(-a) *m(f)*
mag•ic 'spell hechizo *m*; **mag•ic 'trick** truco *m* de magia; **mag•ic 'wand** varita *f* mágica
mag•is•trate ['mædʒɪstreɪt] LAW juez *m/f* de primera instancia
mag•na•nim•i•ty [mægnə'nɪmətɪ] magnanimidad *f*
mag•nan•i•mous [mæg'nænɪməs] *adj* magnánimo
mag•nate ['mægneɪt] magnate *m/f*
mag•ne•sia [mæg'niːʃə] CHEM magnesia *f*
mag•ne•si•um [mæg'niːzɪəm] CHEM magnesio *m*
mag•net ['mægnət] imán *m*
mag•net•ic [mæg'netɪk] *adj* magnético; *fig*: *personality* cautivador
mag•net•ic 'stripe banda *f* magnética
mag•net•ism ['mægnətɪzəm] *of person* magnetismo *m*
mag•net•ize ['mægnətaɪz] *v/t* magnetizar
mag•ni•fi•ca•tion [mægnɪfɪ'keɪʃn] ampliación *f*
mag•nif•i•cence [mæg'nɪfɪsəns] magnificencia *f*
mag•nif•i•cent [mæg'nɪfɪsənt] *adj* magnífico
mag•nif•i•cent•ly [mæg'nɪfɪsəntlɪ] *adv* magníficamente
mag•ni•fy ['mægnɪfaɪ] *v/t* (*pret & pp* ***-ied***) aumentar; *difficulties* magnificar
mag•ni•fy•ing glass ['mægnɪfaɪɪŋ] lupa *f*
mag•ni•tude ['mægnɪtuːd] magnitud *f*
mag•no•li•a [mæg'noʊlɪə] BOT magnolia *f*
mag•num ['mægnəm] *botella de un litro y medio*
mag•num 'o•pus obra *f* maestra
mag•pie ['mægpaɪ] urraca *f*
ma•hog•a•ny [mə'hɑːgənɪ] caoba *f*
maid [meɪd] *servant* criada *f*; *in hotel* camarera *f*
maid•en name ['meɪdn] apellido *m* de soltera
maid•en 'voy•age viaje *m* inaugural
mail [meɪl] **I** *n* correo *m*; ***put sth in the ~*** echar algo al correo **II** *v/t letter* enviar (por correo)
'mail•box *also* COMPUT buzón *m*
'mail car•ri•er cartero(-a) *m(f)*
mail•ing list ['meɪlɪŋlɪst] lista *f* de direcciones
'mail•man cartero *m*; **'mail•merge program** programa *m* de fusión de correo; **mail-'or•der cat•a•log**, *Br* **mail-'or•der cat•a•logue** catálogo *m* de venta por correo; **mail-'or•der firm** empresa *f* de venta por correo; **'mail•shot** mailing *m*
maim [meɪm] *v/t* mutilar
main [meɪn] *adj* principal; ***she's alive, that's the ~ thing*** está viva, que es lo principal

M

'main course plato *m* principal; **main 'en•trance** entrada *f* principal; **'main-frame** computadora *f* central, *Span* ordenador *m* central; **'main•land** tierra *f* firme; ***on the ~*** en el continente; **'main•line I** *n* RAIL línea *f* principal **II** *adj* tradicional **III** *v/t* P picarse

main•ly ['meɪnlɪ] *adv* principalmente

main 'road carretera *f* general

mains ['meɪnz] *for electricity* red *f* eléctrica; *for gas* conducción *f* general; ***run a machine off the ~*** funcionar una máquina por conexión a la red

'mains a•dapt•er ELEC adaptador *m*

'main•stay *fig* pilar *m*; **'main•stream I** *n*: ***the ~*** la corriente principal **II** *adj* predominante, convencional; **'main street** calle *f* principal

main•tain [meɪn'teɪn] *v/t* mantener

main•te•nance ['meɪntənəns] **1** *of building, machine* mantenimiento *m* **2** *after divorce* pensión *f* alimenticia

'main•te•nance costs *npl* gastos *mpl* de mantenimiento

'main•te•nance staff personal *m* de mantenimiento

mai•tre d' [meɪtər'di:] maître *m/f*

maize [meɪz] *esp Br* maíz *m*

ma•jes•tic [mə'dʒestɪk] *adj* majestuoso

ma•jes•ty ['mædʒestɪ] majestuosidad *f*; ***Her Majesty*** Su Majestad

ma•jor ['meɪdʒər] **I** *adj* (*significant*) importante, principal; ***in C ~*** MUS en C mayor **II** *n* MIL comandante *m*

◆ **major in** *v/t* especializarse en

Ma•jor•ca [mə'jɔːrkə] Mallorca *f*

Ma•jor•can [mə'jɔːrkən] *adj* mallorquín

ma•jor•ette [meɪdʒə'ret] majorette *f*

ma•jor•i•ty [mə'dʒɑːrətɪ] *also* POL mayoría *f*; ***be in the ~*** ser mayoría

ma•jor•i•ty de'ci•sion decisión *f* por mayoría, decisión *f* mayoritaria

ma'jor•i•ty hold•ing participación *f* mayoritaria

ma•jor-league ['meɪdʒərli:g] *adj* SP de la liga mayor *or* principal; *fig* de primera línea

make [meɪk] **I** *n* (*brand*) marca *f* **II** *v/t* (*pret & pp* ***made***) **1** hacer; *cars* fabricar, producir; *movie* rodar; ***made in Japan*** hecho en Japón; ***~ a decision*** tomar una decisión; ***~ it*** (*catch bus, train*) llegar a tiempo; (*come*) ir; (*succeed*) tener éxito; (*survive*) sobrevivir; *Br* ***what time do you ~ it?*** ¿qué hora llevas?; ***~ believe*** imaginarse; ***~ do with*** conformarse con; ***what do you ~ of it?*** ¿qué piensas?; ***they were made for each other*** estaban hechos el uno para el otro; ***you're just made for this job*** es el trabajo perfecto para ti; ***it made him a hero*** lo convirtió en heroe; ***he's got it made*** F lo tiene todo resuelto
2 *speech* pronunciar
3 (*earn*) ganar
4 MATH hacer; ***two and two ~ four*** dos y dos son cuatro
5: ***~ s.o. do sth*** (*force to*) obligar a alguien a hacer algo; (*cause to*) hacer que alguien haga algo; ***you can't ~ me do it!*** ¡no puedes obligarme a hacerlo!; ***~ s.o. happy*** hacer feliz a alguien; ***~ s.o. angry*** enfadar a alguien

◆ **make for** *v/t* **1** (*go toward*) dirigirse hacia **2**: ***it doesn't make for a good working atmosphere*** esto no contribuye a crear una buena atmósfera de trabajo

◆ **make off** *v/i* escaparse

◆ **make off with** *v/t* (*steal*) llevarse

◆ **make out I** *v/t* **1** *list* hacer, elaborar **2** *check* extender **3** (*see*) distinguir **4** (*imply*) pretender; ***you're making me out to be something I'm not*** estás dando una imagen de mí que no es cierta **II** *v/i* **1** (*manage*) apañarse, arreglarse **2** P *kiss etc* meterse mano

◆ **make over** *v/t* (*transfer*) ceder (***to*** a)

◆ **make up I** *v/i* **1** *of woman, actor* maquillarse **2** *after quarrel* reconciliarse **II** *v/t* **1** *story, excuse* inventar **2** *face* maquillar **3** (*constitute*) suponer, formar; ***be made up of*** estar compuesto de **4**: ***make up one's mind*** decidirse; ***make it up*** *after quarrel* reconciliarse

◆ **make up for** *v/t* compensar por

◆ **make up to** *v/t* (*be nice to*) hacer la pelota a

'make-be•lieve ficción *f*, fantasía *f*

'make•o•ver *of person* transformación *f*, *of building* renovación *f*, ***give s.o. a ~*** hacer una transformación a alguien; ***give sth a ~*** renovar algo

mak•er ['meɪkər] (*manufacturer*) fabricante *m*; ***go to meet one's ~*** *hum* irse al otro barrio; ***Our Maker*** nuestro Creador, nuestro Dios

make•shift ['meɪkʃɪft] *adj* improvisado;

'make-up (*cosmetics*) maquillaje *m*; ***she doesn't use ~*** no se maquilla, no se pinta; **'make-up bag** bolsa *f* del maquillaje; **'make-up re•mo•ver** desmaquillador *m*

mak•ing ['meɪkɪŋ] (*manufacture*) fabricación *f*; (*of movie*) realización *f*, rodaje *m*; ***it was twelve years in the ~*** llevó doce años hacerlo; ***have the ~s of*** *of person* tener madera de; ***it'll be the ~ of him*** eso le acabará de formar como persona; ***we're watching history in the ~ here*** se está haciendo historia; ***these problems are of your own ~*** tú mismo te has buscado estos problemas

mal•ad•just•ed [mælə'dʒʌstɪd] *adj* inadaptado

mal•a•prop•ism ['mæləprɑːpɪzəm] gazapo *m*

ma•lar•i•a [mə'lerɪə] malaria *f*

mal•con•tent ['mælkəntent] insatisfecho(-a) *m/f*

Mal•dives ['mældiːvz]: ***the ~*** *pl* las Maldivas

male [meɪl] **I** *adj* (*masculine*) masculino; *animal*, *bird*, *fish* macho; ***~ bosses*** los jefes varones; ***a ~ teacher*** un profesor **II** *n man* hombre *m*, varón *m*; *animal*, *bird*, *fish* macho *m*

male 'chau•vin•ism machismo *m*; **male chau•vin•ist 'pig** machista *m*; **male 'mod•el** modelo *m*; **male 'nurse** enfermero *m*; **male 'pros•ti•tute** prostituto *m*

ma•lev•o•lence [mə'levələns] malevolencia *f*

ma•lev•o•lent [mə'levələnt] *adj* malévolo

mal•for•ma•tion [mælfɔː'meɪʃn] *esp* MED malformación *f*

mal•func•tion [mæl'fʌŋkʃn] **I** *n* fallo *m* (***in*** de) **II** *v/i* fallar

mal•ice ['mælɪs] malicia *f*; ***I bear him no ~*** no pretendo hacerle daño

ma•li•cious [mə'lɪʃəs] *adj* malicioso

ma•lig•nant [mə'lɪgnənt] *adj tumor* maligno; *attitude*, *remark* perjudicial

ma•lin•ger [mə'lɪŋgər] *v/i* fingir una enfermedad

mall [mɒːl] (*shopping ~*) centro *m* comercial

mal•lard ['mælɑːrd] ánade *m* real

mal•le•a•ble ['mælɪəbl] *adj material*; *personality* maleable

mal•let ['mælɪt] mazo *m*

mal•nour•ished [mæl'nʌrɪʃt] *adj* desnutrido

mal•nu•tri•tion [mælnuː'trɪʃn] desnutrición *f*

mal•prac•tice [mæl'præktɪs] negligencia *f*

malt [mɔːlt] malta *f*

Mal•ta ['mɔːltə] Malta *f*

Mal•tese [mɔːl'tiːz] **I** *adj* maltés **II** *n* maltés(-esa) *m*(*f*)

mal•treat [mæl'triːt] *v/t* maltratar

mal•treat•ment [mæl'triːtmənt] maltrato *m*

malt 'whis•key whisky *m* de malta

mam•mal ['mæml] mamífero *m*

mam•moth ['mæməθ] **I** *n* ZO mamut *m* **II** *adj* enorme; *building* mastodóntico

man [mæn] **I** *n* (*pl* ***men*** [men]) **1** hombre *m*; ***be one's own ~*** ser dueño de sí mismo; ***he took it like a ~*** se lo tomó como un hombre; ***the ~ of the match*** el mejor jugador del partido; ***be ~ and wife*** ser marido y mujer; ***~ about town*** hombre socialmente muy activo **2** (*humanity*) el hombre **3** *in checkers* ficha *f* **II** *v/t* (*pret & pp* ***-ned***) *telephones*, *front desk* atender; *spacecraft* tripular **III** *int*: ***hey ~, that's fantastic!*** ¡eh tío, eso es genial!

man•age ['mænɪdʒ] **I** *v/t* **1** *business* dirigir; *money* gestionar **2** *suitcase*, *stairs*, *three eggs* poder con; ***~ to do sth*** conseguir hacer algo; ***could you ~ next week?*** ¿puedes la semana que viene? **II** *v/i* (*cope*) arreglárselas

man•age•a•ble ['mænɪdʒəbl] *adj* **1** (*easy to handle*) manejable **2** (*feasible*) factible

man•age•ment ['mænɪdʒmənt] **1** (*managing*) gestión *f*, administración *f* **2** (*managers*) dirección *f*

man•age•ment 'buy•out *compra de una empresa por sus directivos*; **man•age•ment by ob'jec•tives** administración *f* por objetivos; **man•age•ment con'sult•an•cy** consultoría *f* en administración de empresas; **man•age•ment con'sult•ant** consultor(a) *m*(*f*) en administración de empresas; **'man•age•ment fee** tarifa *f* de gestion *or* administración; **'man•age•ment stud•ies** *npl* estudios *mpl* de administración de

empresas; **'man•age•ment style** estilo *m* de dirección; **'man•age•ment team** equipo *m* directivo; **'man•age•ment tool** herramienta *f* de dirección
man•ag•er ['mænɪdʒər] *of hotel, company* director(a) *m(f)*; *of shop, restaurant* encargado(-a) *m(f)*
man•ag•er•ess [mænɪdʒə'res] *of hotel, company* directora *f*; *of shop, restaurant* encargada *f*
man•a•ge•ri•al [mænɪ'dʒɪrɪəl] *adj* de gestión; ***a ~ post*** un puesto directivo
man•ag•ing di•rec•tor [mænɪdʒɪŋdaɪ'rektər] director(a) *m(f)* gerente
man•ag•ing 'ed•i•tor director(a) *m(f)* gerente
man•da•rin or•ange [mændərɪn'ɔːrɪndʒ] mandarina *f*
man•date ['mændeɪt] **I** *n* (*authority*) mandato *m*; (*task*) tarea *f* **II** *v/t*: ***be ~d to do sth*** recibir el mandato de hacer algo
man•da•to•ry ['mændətɔːrɪ] *adj* obligatorio
mane [meɪn] *of horse* crines *fpl*
man-eat•er ['mæniːtər] *tiger etc* devorador(a) *m(f)* de hombres; F *hum*: *woman* devoradora *f* de hombres
ma•neu•ver [mə'nuːvər] **I** *n* maniobra *f*; ***this leaves us no room for ~*** *fig* esto no nos deja margen de maniobra; ***be on ~s*** MIL estar de maniobras **II** *v/t* maniobrar; ***she ~ed him into giving her the assignment*** consiguió convencerle para que le diera el trabajo
man•ful•ly ['mænfəlɪ] *adv* como un hombre
man•ga•nese ['mæŋgəniːz] CHEM manganeso *m*
man•ger ['meɪndʒər] pesebre *m*
mange•tout [mɑːnʒ'tuː] *Br* tirabeque *m*
man•gle ['mæŋgl] *v/t* (*crush*) destrozar
man•go ['mæŋgoʊ] (*pl* ***-go(e)s*** ['mæŋgoʊz]) *fruit, tree* mango *m*
man•grove ['mæŋgroʊv] mangle *m*
man•gy ['meɪndʒɪ] *adj dog etc* sarnoso; *dirty* raído; *hotel* cochambroso
'man•han•dle *v/t* mover a la fuerza; ***he was ~d into a truck*** lo metieron a la fuerza en un camión
'man•hole boca *f* de alcantarilla; ***~ cover*** tapa *f* de alcantarilla
man•hood ['mænhʊd] **1** (*maturity*) madurez *f* **2** (*virility*) virilidad *f*
'man-hour hora-hombre *f*
'man•hunt persecución *f*
ma•ni•a ['meɪnɪə] (*craze*) pasión *f*
ma•ni•ac ['meɪnɪæk] F chiflado(-a) *m(f)* F
man•ic-de•pres•sive [mænɪkdɪ'presɪv] PSYCH **I** *adj* maniaco-depresivo **II** *n* maniaco(-a)-depresivo(-a) *m(f)*; ***be a ~*** ser maniaco-depresivo
man•i•cure ['mænɪkjʊr] manicura *f*; ***have a ~*** hacerse la manicura
man•i•fest ['mænɪfest] **I** *adj* manifiesto **II** *n of airplane, ship* manifiesto *m* **III** *v/t* manifestar; ***~ itself*** manifestarse
man•i•fes•ta•tion [mænɪfes'teɪʃn] manifestación *f*
man•i•fest•ly ['mænɪfestlɪ] *adv* manifiestamente
man•i•fes•to [mænɪ'festoʊ] (*pl* ***-to(e)s*** [mænɪ'festoʊz]) manifiesto *m*
man•i•fold ['mænɪfoʊld] **I** *adj* múltiple **II** *n* TECH colector *m*
ma•nip•u•late [mə'nɪpjəleɪt] *v/t person, bones* manipular
ma•nip•u•la•tion [mənɪpjə'leɪʃn] *of person, bones* manipulación *f*
ma•nip•u•la•tive [mə'nɪpjələtɪv] *adj* manipulador
man'kind la humanidad
man•ly ['mænlɪ] *adj* (*brave*) de hombres; (*strong*) varonil
'man-made *adj fibers, materials* sintético; *crater, structure* artificial
man•ne•quin ['mænɪkɪn] *in store window* maniquí *m*
man•ner ['mænər] *of doing sth* manera *f*, modo *m*; (*attitude*) actitud *f*; ***in a ~ of speaking*** en cierta manera
man•ner•ism ['mænərɪzəm] *of person* peculiaridad *f*
man•ners ['mænərz] *npl* modales *mpl*; ***good / bad ~*** buena / mala educación; ***have no ~*** ser un maleducado
ma•noeu•vre *Br* ☞ ***maneuver***
man•or ['mænər] *Br*: **~ (*house*)** casa *f* solariega
'man•pow•er (*workers*) mano *f* de obra; *for other tasks* recursos *mpl* humanos
man•sion ['mænʃn] mansión *f*
'man•slaugh•ter *Br* homicidio *m* sin premeditación
man•tel•piece ['mæntlpiːs] repisa *f* de chimenea
man-to-'man *adj talk* de hombre a

hombre; ~ ***defense*** *in basketball* defensa *f* al hombre

man•u•al ['mænjʊəl] **I** *adj* manual **II** *n* manual *m*

man•u•al•ly ['mænjʊəlɪ] *adv* a mano

man•u•fac•ture [mænjʊ'fæktʃər] **I** *n* fabricación *f* **II** *v/t equipment* fabricar

man•u•fac•tur•er [mænjʊ'fæktʃərər] fabricante *m/f*

man•u•fac•tur•ing [mænjʊ'fæktʃərɪŋ] *adj industry* manufacturero

man•u'fac•tur•ing com•pa•ny industria *f*

ma•nure [mə'nʊr] estiércol *m*

man•u•script ['mænjʊskrɪpt] manuscrito *m*

man•y ['menɪ] **I** *adj* muchos; ***take as ~ apples as you like*** toma todas las manzanas que quieras; ***not ~ people / taxis*** no mucha gente / muchos taxis; ***too ~ problems / beers*** demasiados problemas / demasiadas cervezas **II** *pron* muchos; ***a great ~, a good ~*** muchos; ***how ~ do you need?*** ¿cuántos necesitas?; ***as ~ as 200 are still missing*** hay hasta 200 desaparecidos

'man-year año-hombre *m*

man•y-sid•ed [menɪ'saɪdɪd] *adj person*, polifacético; *problem* con muchas derivaciones

map [mæp] mapa *m*; ***put a town on the ~*** *fig* dar a conocer una ciudad

◆ **map out** *v/t* (*pret & pp* ***-ped***) proyectar

ma•ple ['meɪpl] arce *m*

ma•ple 'syr•up jarabe *m* de arce

mar [mɑːr] *v/t* (*pret & pp* ***-red***) empañar

mar•a•thon ['mærəθɑːn] *race* maratón *m or f*

'mar•a•thon run•ner corredor(a) *m*(*f*) de maratón

ma•raud•er [mə'rɔːdər] merodeador(a) *m*(*f*)

mar•ble ['mɑːrbl] **1** *material* mármol *m* **2** *for child's game* canica *f*

March [mɑːrtʃ] marzo *m*

march [mɑːrtʃ] **I** *n* marcha *f* **II** *v/i* marchar

◆ **march off I** *v/i* MIL emprender la marcha; *of person* irse a toda marcha **II** *v/t*: ***march s.o. off*** llevarse a alguien

march•er ['mɑːrtʃər] manifestante *m/f*

march•ing or•ders ['mɑːrtʃɪŋɔːrdərz]: ***get one's ~*** *fig* F ser mandado a paseo

Mar•di Gras ['mɑːrdɪgrɑː] martes *m inv* de Carnaval

mare [mer] yegua *f*

mar•ga•rine [mɑːrdʒə'riːn] margarina *f*

mar•gin ['mɑːrdʒɪn] *also* COM margen *m*

mar•gin•al ['mɑːrdʒɪnl] *adj* (*slight*) marginal

mar•gin•al•ize ['mɑːrdʒɪnəlaɪz] *v/t* marginar; ***feel ~d*** sentirse marginado

mar•gin•al•ly ['mɑːrdʒɪnlɪ] *adv* (*slightly*) ligeramente

mar•i•hua•na, mar•i•jua•na [mærɪ'hwɑːnə] marihuana *f*

ma•ri•na [mə'riːnə] puerto *m* deportivo

mar•i•nade [mærɪ'neɪd] adobo *m*

mar•i•nate ['mærɪneɪt] *v/t* adobar, marinar

ma•rine [mə'riːn] **I** *adj* marino **II** *n* MIL marine *m/f*, infante *m/f* de marina; ***tell that to the ~s!*** F ¡cuéntaselo a tu abuela!

ma•rine bill of lad•ing ['leɪdɪŋ] conocimiento *m* de embarque marítimo

mar•i•o•nette [mærɪə'net] marioneta *f*

mar•i•tal ['mærɪtl] *adj* marital

mar•i•tal 'sta•tus estado *m* civil

mar•i•time ['mærɪtaɪm] *adj* marítimo

mar•jo•ram ['mɑːrdʒərəm] mejorana *f*

mark[1] [mɑːrk] **I** *n* **1** señal *f*, marca *f*; (*stain*) marca *f*, mancha *f*; (*trace*) señal *f*; ***leave one's ~*** dejar huella; ***be wide of the ~*** equivocarse por mucho; ***be up to the ~*** *meet required standards* estar a la altura; *in health* encontrarse bien; ***on your ~s!*** SP ¡preparados!, en sus marcas; ***be quick / slow off the ~*** *starting to do sth* salir rápido / despacio; *understand* ser rápido / despacio **2** (*sign, token*) signo *m*, señal *f*; ***as a ~ of our appreciation*** como muestra de nuestro aprecio
3 EDU *esp Br* nota *f*
II *v/t* **1** (*stain*) manchar **2** EDU *esp Br* calificar **3** (*indicate, commemorate*) marcar **4** *in soccer* marcar
III *v/i of fabric* mancharse

◆ **mark down** *v/t goods* rebajar

◆ **mark out** *v/t with a line etc* marcar; *fig* (*set apart*) distinguir

◆ **mark up** *v/t price* subir; *goods* subir de precio

mark[2] [mɑːrk] *n* FIN marco *m*

marked [mɑːrkt] *adj* (*definite*) marcado, notable

mark•ed•ly ['mɑːrkədlɪ] *adv* notablemente

mark•er ['mɑːrkər] (*highlighter*) rotulador *m*

mar•ket ['mɑːrkɪt] **I** *n* mercado *m*; (*stock* ~) bolsa *f*; ***on the ~*** en el mercado; ***there's no ~ for …*** no hay mercado para…; ***bring a product to ~*** introducir un producto en el mercado, sacar un producto al mercado; ***put one's house on the ~*** poner la casa a la venta **II** *v/t* comercializar

mar•ket•a•ble ['mɑːrkɪtəbl] *adj* comercializable

mar•ket 'an•a•lyst analista *m/f* de mercados; **'mar•ket day** día *m* de mercado; **mar•ket e'con•o•my** economía *f* de mercado; **'mar•ket for•ces** *npl* fuerzas *fpl* del mercado

mar•ket•ing ['mɑːrkɪtɪŋ] marketing *m*

'mar•ket•ing cam•paign campaña *f* de marketing; **'mar•ket•ing de•part•ment** departamento *m* de marketing; **'mar•ket•ing mix** marketing mix *m*, *el producto*, *el precio*, *la distribución y la promoción*; **'mar•ket•ing strat•e•gy** estrategia *f* de marketing

mar•ket 'lead•er líder *m* del mercado; **mar•ket 'mak•er** creador(a) *m*(*f*) de mercado; **'mar•ket•place** *in town* plaza *f* del mercado; *for commodities* mercado *m*; **mar•ket re'search** investigación *f* de mercado; **mar•ket 're•search com•pa•ny** empresa *f* de estudio de mercados; **mar•ket 'share** cuota *f* de mercado; **mar•ket 'sur•vey** estudio *m* de mercado ; **mar•ket 'val•ue** valor *m* de mercado

mark•ing ['mɑːrkɪŋ] **1** EDU *esp Br* corrección *f* **2** *in soccer* marcaje *m*

mark•ings ['mɑːrkɪŋz] *on animal* manchas *fpl*; *on airplane* distintivo *m*

marks•man ['mɑːrksmən] tirador *m*

'mark-up margen *m*

mar•lin ['mɑːrlɪn] aguja *f*

mar•ma•lade ['mɑːrməleɪd] mermelada *f* de naranja

ma•roon [mə'ruːn] *adj* granate

ma•rooned [mə'ruːnd]: ***be ~*** quedarse aislado

mar•quee [mɑːr'kiː] carpa *f*

mar•riage ['mærɪdʒ] matrimonio *m*; *event* boda *f*

'mar•riage cer•tif•i•cate certificado *m* de matrimonio; **mar•riage 'guid•ance coun•se•lor** consejero(-a) *m*(*f*) matrimonial; **'mar•riage vows** *pl* votos *mpl* matrimoniales

mar•ried ['mærɪd] *adj* casado; ***be ~ to*** estar casado con

mar•ried 'cou•ple matrimonio *m*

mar•ried 'life vida *f* matrimonial

mar•row ['mæroʊ] ANAT médula *f*; *Br* ***be frozen to the ~*** estar helado hasta los tuétanos

mar•ry ['mærɪ] *v/t* (*pret & pp* ***-ied***) casarse con; *of priest* casar; ***get married*** casarse (***to*** con); ***~ me*** cásate conmigo

◆ **marry into** *v/t*: ***marry into a rich family*** casarse con alguien de una familia adinerada

◆ **marry off** *v/t* casar

marsh [mɑːrʃ] pantano *m*, ciénaga *f*

mar•shal ['mɑːrʃl] *in police* jefe(-a) *m*(*f*) de policía; *in security service* miembro *m* del servicio de seguridad

'marsh•land zona *f* pantanosa

marsh•mal•low [mɑːrʃ'mæloʊ] *dulce de consistencia blanda*

marsh•y ['mɑːrʃɪ] *adj* pantanoso

mar•su•pi•al [mɑːr'suːpɪəl] marsupial *m*

mar•ten ['mɑːrtɪn] ZO marta *f*

mar•tial arts [mɑːrʃl'ɑːrts] *npl* artes *fpl* marciales

mar•tial 'law ley *f* marcial

Mar•tian ['mɑːrʃn] marciano(-a) *m*(*f*)

mar•ti•ni [mɑːr'tiːnɪ] martini *m*

mar•tyr ['mɑːrtər] mártir *m/f*; ***make a ~ of o.s.*** *fig* hacerse el martir

mar•tyr•dom ['mɑːrtərdəm] martirio *m*

mar•tyred ['mɑːrtərd] *adj fig* de mártir

mar•vel ['mɑːrvl] maravilla *f*

◆ **marvel at** *v/t* (*pret & pp* ***-ed***, *Br* ***-led***) maravillarse de

mar•ve•lous, *Br* **mar•vel•lous** ['mɑːrvələs] *adj* maravilloso

Marx•ism ['mɑːrksɪzm] marxismo *m*

Marx•ist ['mɑːrksɪst] **I** *adj* marxista **II** *n* marxista *m/f*

mar•zi•pan ['mɑːrzɪpæn] mazapán *m*

mas•ca•ra [mæ'skærə] rímel *m*

mas•cot ['mæskət] mascota *f*

mas•cu•line ['mæskjʊlɪn] *adj* masculino

mas•cu•lin•i•ty [mæskjʊ'lɪnətɪ] (*viri-*

lity) masculinidad *f*

mash [mæʃ] *v/t* hacer puré de, majar

mashed po'ta•toes [mæʃt] *npl* puré *m* de patatas *or L.Am.* papas

mask [mæsk] **I** *n* máscara *f*; *to cover mouth, nose* mascarilla *f* **II** *v/t feelings* enmascarar

mask•ing tape ['mæskɪŋ] cinta *f* adhesiva de pintor

mas•o•chism ['mæsəkɪzm] masoquismo *m*

mas•o•chist ['mæsəkɪst] masoquista *m/f*

mas•o•chis•tic [mæsə'kɪstɪk] *adj* masoquista

ma•son ['meɪsn] *craftsman* cantero *m*

ma•son•ic [mə'sɑːnɪk] *adj* masón

ma•son•ry ['meɪsnrɪ] albañilería *f*

mas•que•rade [mæskə'reɪd] **I** *n fig* mascarada *f* **II** *v/i*: **~ as** hacerse pasar por

mass[1] [mæs] **I** *n* (*great amount*) gran cantidad *f*; (*body*) masa *f*; ***the ~es*** las masas; ***~es of*** F un montón de F **II** *v/i* concentrarse

mass[2] [mæs] *n* REL misa *f*; ***go to ~*** ir a misa; ***say ~*** decir misa

mas•sa•cre ['mæsəkər] **I** *n* masacre *f*, matanza *f*; F *in sport* paliza *f* **II** *v/t* masacrar; F *in sport* dar una paliza a

mas•sage ['mæsɑːʒ] **I** *n* masaje *m* **II** *v/t* dar un masaje en; *figures* maquillar

'mas•sage par•lor, *Br* **'mas•sage par•lour** salón *m* de masajes

mas•seur [mæ'sɜːr] masajista *m*

mas•seuse [mæ'sɜːrz] masajista *f*

mas•sive ['mæsɪv] *adj* enorme; *heart attack* muy grave

mas•sive•ly ['mæsɪvlɪ] *adv* enormemente

mass 'mar•ket mercado *m* de masas; **mass 'me•di•a** *npl* medios *mpl* de comunicación; **mass 'mur•der** matanza *f*; **mass 'mur•der•er** asesino(-a) *m(f)* múltiple; **mass-pro'duce** *v/t* fabricar en serie; **mass pro'duc•tion** fabricación *f* en serie; ***go into ~*** empezar a ser fabricado en serie; **mass 'tran•sit, mass-trans•por'ta•tion** transporte *m* público; **mass un•em'ploy•ment** desempleo *m* masivo

mast [mæst] **1** *of ship* mástil *m* **2** *for radio signal* torre *f*

mas•ter ['mæstər] **I** *n of dog* dueño *m*, amo *m*; *of ship* patrón *m*; ***be a ~ of*** ser un maestro de; ***be one's own ~*** ser dueño de sí mismo **II** *v/t skill, language, situation* dominar

'mas•ter bed•room dormitorio *m* principal

'mas•ter cop•y copia *f* maestra

mas•ter•ful ['mɑːstərfʊl] *adj* magistral

'mas•ter fuse ELEC fusible *m* principal

'mas•ter key llave *f* maestra

mas•ter•ly ['mæstərlɪ] *adj* magistral

'mas•ter•mind I *n* cerebro *m* **II** *v/t* dirigir, organizar; **Mas•ter of 'Arts** Máster *m* en Humanidades; **mas•ter of 'cer•e•mo•nies** maestro *m* de ceremonias; **'mas•ter•piece** obra *f* maestra; **'mas•ter's (de•gree)** máster *m*; **'mas•ter•stroke** golpe *m* maestro; **'mas•ter•switch** interruptor *m* principal

mas•ter•y ['mæstərɪ] dominio *m*

mas•ti•cate ['mæstɪkeɪt] *v/t* masticar

mas•ti•ca•tion [mæstɪ'keɪʃn] masticación *f*

mas•tiff ['mæstɪf] ZO mastín *m*

mas•tur•bate ['mæstərbeɪt] *v/i* masturbarse

mas•tur•ba•tion [mæstər'beɪʃn] masturbación *f*

mat [mæt] **1** *for floor* estera *f* **2** *for table* salvamanteles *m inv*

match[1] [mæʧ] *n for cigarette* cerilla *f*, fósforo *m*

match[2] [mæʧ] **I** *n* SP partido *m*; *in chess* partida *f*; ***be no ~ for s.o.*** no estar a la altura de alguien; ***meet one's ~*** encontrar la horma de su zapato **II** *v/t* (*be the same as*) coincidir con; (*be in harmony with*) hacer juego con; (*equal*) igualar **III** *v/i of colors, patterns* hacer juego

◆ **match up to** estar a la altura de

'match•box caja *f* de cerillas

match•ing ['mæʧɪŋ] *adj* a juego

match•less ['mæʧlɪs] *adj* sin igual

'match•mak•er casamentero(-a) *m(f)*; **match 'point** *in tennis* punto *m* de partido; **'match•stick** cerilla *f*, fósforo *m*

mate[1] [meɪt] ☞ ***checkmate***

mate[2] [meɪt] **I** *n* **1** *of animal* pareja *f* **2** NAUT oficial *m/f* **II** *v/i* aparearse; ***these birds ~ for life*** estas aves viven con la misma pareja toda la vida

ma•te•ri•al [mə'tɪrɪəl] **I** *n* **1** (*fabric*) tejido *m* **2** (*substance*) material *m*; ***~s*** materiales *mpl* **II** *adj* material

ma•te•ri•al•ism [mə'tɪrɪəlɪzm] materia-

lismo *m*
ma•te•ri•al•ist [mə'tɪrɪəlɪst] materialista *m/f*
ma•te•ri•al•is•tic [mətɪrɪə'lɪstɪk] *adj* materialista
ma•te•ri•al•ize [mə'tɪrɪəlaɪz] *v/i* **1** (*appear*) aparecer **2** (*come into existence*) hacerse realidad
ma•ter•nal [mə'tɜːrnl] *adj* maternal
ma•ter•ni•ty [mə'tɜːrnətɪ] maternidad *f*
ma'ter•ni•ty clothes *npl* ropa *f* premamá; **ma'ter•ni•ty dress** vestido *m* premamá; **ma'ter•ni•ty leave** baja *f* por maternidad; ***be on ~*** estar de baja *or* tener la baja por maternidad; **ma'ter•ni•ty ward** pabellón *m* de maternidad
mat•ey ['meɪtɪ] *adj Br* F: ***be ~ with s.o.*** ser muy amigo de alguien
math [mæθ] matemáticas *fpl*
math•e•mat•i•cal [mæθə'mætɪkl] *adj* matemático
math•e•ma•ti•cian [mæθmə'tɪʃn] matemático(-a) *m(f)*
math•e•mat•ics [mæθ'mætɪks] *nsg* matemáticas *fpl*
maths *Br* ☞ ***math***
mat•i•née ['mætɪneɪ] sesión *f* de tarde
mat•ing ['meɪtɪŋ] ZO apareamiento *m*
'mat•ing rit•u•al ritual *m* de apareamiento
'mat•ing sea•son época *f* de celo
ma•tri•arch ['meɪtrɪɑːrk] matriarca *f*
ma•tri•arch•al [meɪtrɪ'ɑːrkəl] matriarcal
ma•tri•arch•y ['meɪtrɪɑːrkɪ] matriarcado *m*
ma•tri•ces ['meɪtrɪsiːz] *pl* ☞ ***matrix***
ma•tric•u•late [mə'trɪkjʊleɪt] *v/i* matricularse
ma•tric•u•la•tion [mətrɪkjʊ'leɪʃn] matriculación *f*
mat•ri•mo•ni•al [mætrə'moʊnɪəl] *adj* matrimonial
mat•ri•mo•ny ['mætrəmoʊnɪ] matrimonio *m*
ma•trix ['meɪtrɪks] (*pl* ***matrices*** ['meɪtrɪsiːz], ***matrixes*** ['meɪtrɪksəz]) TECH, MATH matriz *f*
ma•tron ['meɪtrən] *Br in hospital* enfermera *f* jefe
ma•tron•ly ['meɪtrənlɪ] *adj* matronil
ma•tron of 'hon•or, *Br* **ma•tron of 'hon•our** dama *f* de honor
matt [mæt] *adj* mate
mat•ter ['mætər] **I** *n* **1** (*affair*) asunto *m*; ***you're only making ~s worse*** sólo estás empeorando las cosas; ***as a ~ of course*** automáticamente; ***as a ~ of fact*** de hecho; ***what's the ~?*** ¿qué pasa?; ***is there anything the ~ with that?*** ¿hay algo malo en eso?; ***no ~ what she says*** diga lo que diga; ***no ~ how hard I try*** por mucho que lo intente; ***no ~*** no importa; ***that's a ~ of opinion*** eso es una cuestión de opinión; ***it's just a ~ of time*** es sólo cuestión de tiempo; ***I'll raise the ~ with him*** hablaré con él del asunto; ***it took a ~ of seconds*** llevó unos pocos segundos; ***as ~s stand*** tal y como están las cosas **2** PHYS materia *f*
II *v/i* importar; ***it doesn't ~*** no importa
mat•ter-of-'fact *adj* tranquilo
mat•tress ['mætrɪs] colchón *m*
ma•ture [mə'ʧʊr] **I** *adj* maduro **II** *v/i* **1** *of person* madurar **2** *of insurance policy etc* vencer
ma•tu•ri•ty [mə'ʧʊrətɪ] **1** *of person* madurez *f* **2** *of insurance policy etc* vencimiento *m*
ma'tu•ri•ty date FIN fecha *f* de vencimiento
maud•lin ['mɔːdlɪn] *adj person* llorón; *novel* lacrimógeno
maul [mɒːl] *v/t of lion, tiger* atacar; *of critics* destrozar
mau•so•le•um [mɔːsə'lɪəm] mausoleo *m*
mauve [moʊv] *adj* malva
mav•er•ick ['mævərɪk] *person* inconformista *m/f*
max•im ['mæksɪm] máxima *f*
max•i•mi•za•tion [mæksɪmaɪ'zeɪʃn] maximización *f*
max•i•mize ['mæksɪmaɪz] *v/t* maximizar
max•i•mum ['mæksɪməm] **I** *adj* máximo; ***it will cost $500 ~*** costará 500 dólares como máximo **II** *n* máximo *m*
may [meɪ] *v/aux* **1** *possibility*: ***it ~ rain*** puede que llueva; ***you ~ be right*** puede que tengas razón; ***it ~ not happen*** puede que no ocurra **2** *permission* poder; ***~ I help / smoke?*** ¿puedo ayudar / fumar?
May [meɪ] mayo *m*
Ma•yan ['maɪən] **I** *adj* maya **II** *n* maya *m/f*

M

may•be ['meɪbiː] *adv* quizás, tal vez; ***try some – yes, ~ I will*** prueba algunos – sí, puede que los pruebe; ***there were 50, ~ 70, people there*** había allí 50, puede que 70 personas
'may bee•tle, 'may bug ZO melolonta *f*; **'May Day** el Primero de Mayo; **'may-day** *int* AVIA, NAUT ¡SOS!; **'may•fly** ZO efímera *f*
may•hem ['meɪhem] caos *m inv*; ***cause ~*** provocar el caos
may•o ['meɪoʊ] F, **may•on•naise** [meɪə'neɪz] mayonesa *f*
may•or [mer] alcalde *m*
maze [meɪz] laberinto *m*
MB *abbr* (= ***megabyte***) MB (= megabyte *m*)
MBA [embiː'eɪ] *abbr* (= ***Master of Business Administration***) MBA *m* (= Máster *m* en Administración de Empresas)
MBO [embiː'oʊ] *abbr* **1** (= ***management buyout***) *compra de una empresa por sus directivos* **2** (= ***management by objectives***) administración *f* por objetivos
MC [em'siː] *abbr* (= ***master of ceremonies***) maestro *m* de ceremonias
Mc•Coy [mə'kɔɪ]: ***the real ~*** el auténtico
MD [em'diː] *abbr* **1** (= ***Doctor of Medicine***) Doctor(a) *m(f)* en Medicina **2** (= ***managing director***) director(a) *m(f)* gerente
me [miː] *pron direct & indirect object* me; *after prep* mí; ***he knows ~*** me conoce; ***he gave ~ the keys*** me dio las llaves; ***he sold it to ~*** me lo vendió; ***this is for ~*** esto es para mí; ***who do you mean, ~?*** ¿a quién te refieres?, ¿a mí?; ***with ~*** conmigo; ***it's ~*** soy yo; ***taller than ~*** más alto que yo
mead•ow ['medoʊ] prado *m*
mea•ger, *Br* **mea•gre** ['miːgər] *adj* escaso, exiguo
meal[1] [miːl] comida *f*; ***enjoy your ~*** ¡que aproveche!; ***take s.o. out for a ~*** invitar a alguien a salir a comer; ***did you enjoy your ~?*** ¿estaba buena la comida?; *Br* ***don't make a ~ it*** no te compliques la vida
meal[2] [miːl] *grain* harina *f*
'meal•time hora *f* de comer
meal•y-mouthed ['miːlɪmaʊðd] *adj* evasivo
mean[1] [miːn] *adj* **1** *with money* tacaño **2** (*nasty*) malo, cruel; ***that was a ~ thing to say*** ha estado fatal que dijeras eso
mean[2] [miːn] **I** *v/t* (*pret & pp* **meant**) (*intend to say*) querer decir; (*signify*) querer decir, significar; ***you weren't ~t to hear that*** no era mi / su *etc* intención que oyeras eso; ***you are ~t to have it done for tomorrow*** se supone que tienes que tenerlo hecho *or* acabado para mañana; ***~ to do sth*** tener la intención de hacer algo; ***be ~t for*** ser para; *of remark* ir dirigido a; ***doesn't it ~ anything to you?*** (*doesn't it matter?*) ¿no te importa para nada?; ***what do you ~ it won't be ready for another two weeks!*** ¿qué dices, que no estará listo hasta dentro de otras dos semanas?
II *v/i* (*pret & pp* **meant**): ***~ well*** tener buena intención
mean[3] [miːn] *n* (*average*) media *f*
me•an•der [mɪ'ændər] *v/i* serpentear
mean•ing ['miːnɪŋ] *of word* significado *m*; ***what's the ~ of this!*** ¿esto qué es?; ***do you get my ~?*** ¿entiendes lo que digo?
mean•ing•ful ['miːnɪŋfəl] *adj* (*comprehensible*) con sentido; (*constructive*), *glance* significativo
mean•ing•less ['miːnɪŋlɪs] *adj* sin sentido
mean•ing•less•ness ['miːnɪŋlɪsnɪs] falta *f* de sentido
mean•ness ['miːnnɪs] **1** *with money* tacañería *f* **2** *of behavior* maldad *f*
means [miːnz] **1** *npl financial* medios *mpl* **2** *nsg* (*way*) medio *m*; ***a ~ of transportation*** un medio de transporte; ***by all ~*** (*certainly*) por supuesto; ***by all ~ check my figures*** comprueba mis cifras, faltaría más; ***by no ~ rich / poor*** ni mucho menos rico / pobre; ***by ~ of*** mediante
meant [ment] *pret & pp* ☞ **mean**[2]
mean•time ['miːntaɪm] **I** *adv* mientras tanto **II** *n*: ***in the ~*** mientras tanto
mean•while ['miːnwaɪl] ☞ ***meantime***
mea•sles ['miːzlz] *nsg* sarampión *m*
meas•ly ['miːzlɪ] *adj* F rídiculo
meas•ur•a•ble ['meʒərəbl] *adj* medible
meas•ur•a•bly ['meʒərəblɪ] *adv* apreciablemente
meas•ure ['meʒər] **I** *n* (*step*) medida *f*;

we've had a ~ of success (*certain amount*) hemos tenido cierto éxito; ***happiness beyond ~*** felicidad *f* immesurable **II** *v/t* medir **III** *v/i* medir; ***it ~s 7 by 15*** mide 7 por 25

◆ **measure out** *v/t area, drink, medicine* medir; *sugar, flour, ingredients* pesar

◆ **measure up** *v/i* estar a la altura (***to*** de)

meas•ure•ment ['meʒɜrmənt] medida *f*; ***system of ~*** sistema *m* de medidas

meas•ur•ing jug ['meʒɜrɪŋ] jarra *f* graduada

'meas•ur•ing tape cinta *f* métrica

meat [miːt] carne *f*

'meat•ball albóndiga *f*; **meat•eat•er** ['miːtiːtər] *person* persona *f* que come carne; *animal* carnívoro(-a) *m(f)*; **'meat•loaf** *masa de carne cocinada en forma de barra de pan*; **meat•pack•er** ['miːtpækər] *firm* empresa *f* de productos cárnicos; **'meat•pack•ing in•dus•try** industria *f* cárnica, industria *f* de productos cárnicos

Mec•ca ['mekə] La Meca

mec•ca ['mekə] *fig* meca *f*

me•chan•ic [mɪ'kænɪk] mecánico(-a) *m(f)*

me•chan•i•cal [mɪ'kænɪkl] *adj also fig* mecánico

me•chan•i•cal en•gi'neer ingeniero(-a) *m(f)* industrial

me•chan•i•cal en•gi'neer•ing ingeniería *f* industrial

me•chan•i•cal•ly [mɪ'kænɪklɪ] *adv also fig* mecánicamente

me•chan•i•cal 'pen•cil portaminas *m inv*

mech•a•nism ['mekənɪzm] mecanismo *m*

mech•a•ni•za•tion [mekənaɪ'zeɪʃn] mecanización *f*

mech•a•nize ['mekənaɪz] *v/t* mecanizar

med•al ['medl] medalla *f*

med•a•list, *Br* **med•al•list** ['medəlɪst] medallista *m/f*

me•dal•lion [mɪ'dæliən] *around neck* medallón *m*

med•dle ['medl] *v/i* entrometerse; ***don't ~ with the TV*** no enredes con la televisión

me•di•a ['miːdɪə] *npl*: ***the ~*** los medios de comunicación; ***a lot of ~ people were there*** había mucha gente del mundo de la comunicación

'me•di•a cov•er•age cobertura *f* informativa

me•di•ae•val *Br* ☞ ***medieval***

'me•di•a e•vent acontecimiento *m* informativo

me•di•a 'hype revuelo *m* informativo

me•di•an strip [miːdɪən'strɪp] mediana *f*

'me•d•ia stud•ies ciencias *fpl* de la información

me•di•ate ['miːdɪeɪt] *v/i* mediar

me•di•a•tion [miːdɪ'eɪʃn] mediación *f*

me•di•a•tor ['miːdɪeɪtər] mediador(a) *m(f)*

med•ic ['medɪk] F médico(-a) *m(f)*

med•i•cal ['medɪkl] **I** *adj* médico **II** *n* reconocimiento *m* médico

'med•i•cal cer•tif•i•cate certificado *m* médico; **'med•i•cal ex•am•i•na•tion** reconocimiento *m* médico; **'med•i•cal ex•am•in•er** médico *m/f* forense; **'med•i•cal his•to•ry** historial *m* médico; **'med•i•cal in•sur•ance** seguro *m* médico; **'med•i•cal pro•fes•sion** profesión *f* médica; (*doctors*) médicos *mpl*; **'med•i•cal rec•ord** ficha *f* médica

Med•i•care ['medɪker] *seguro de enfermedad para los ancianos en Estados Unidos*

med•i•cat•ed ['medɪkeɪtɪd] *adj* medicinal; ***~ shampoo*** champú *m* medicinal

med•i•ca•tion [medɪ'keɪʃn] medicamento *m*, medicina *f*; ***are you on any ~?*** ¿está tomando algún medicamento?

me•di•ci•nal [mɪ'dɪsɪnl] *adj* medicinal

med•i•cine ['medsən] **1** *science* medicina *f* **2** (*medication*) medicina *f*, medicamento *m*; ***give s.o. a taste of his own ~*** pagar a alguien con su misma moneda; **'med•i•cine ball** SP balón *m* medicinal; **'med•i•cine cab•i•net** botiquín *m*; **'med•i•cine chest** botiquín *m*; **'med•i•cine man** curandero *m*

med•i•e•val [medɪ'iːvl] *adj* medieval

me•di•o•cre [miːdɪ'oʊkər] *adj* mediocre

me•di•oc•ri•ty [miːdɪ'ɑːkrətɪ] *of work etc, person* mediocridad *f*

med•i•tate ['medɪteɪt] *v/i* meditar

med•i•ta•tion [medɪ'teɪʃn] meditación *f*

Med•i•ter•ra•ne•an [medɪtə'reɪnɪən] **I** *adj* mediterráneo **II** *n*: ***the ~*** el Mediterráneo

me•di•um ['miːdɪəm] **I** *adj* **1** (*average*) medio **2** *steak* a punto **II** *n* **1** *size* talla *f* media **2** (*means*) medio *m* **3** (*spiritualist*) médium *m/f*

me•di•um-priced ['miːdɪəmpraɪst] *adj* de precio medio; **'me•di•um-range** *adj*: ***~ missile*** MIL misil *m* de alcance medio; **me•di•um-'rare** *adj steak* poco hecho; **me•di•um-sized** ['miːdɪəmsaɪzd] *adj* de tamaño medio; **me•di•um 'term**: ***in the ~*** a medio plazo; **'me•di•um wave** RAD onda *f* media

med•ley ['medlɪ] (*assortment*) mezcla *f*; ***4x100 meters ~*** *in swimming* 4x100 metros estilos

meek [miːk] *adj* manso, dócil

meet [miːt] **I** *v/t* (*pret & pp* **met**) **1** *by appointment* encontrarse con, reunirse con; *by chance*, *of eyes* encontrarse con; (*get to know*) conocer; (*collect*) ir a buscar; *in competition* enfrentarse con; ***pleased to ~ you*** encantado de conocerle; ***we could ~ you halfway*** *fig* podríamos llegar a una solución de compromiso; ***he refused to ~ my gaze*** se negó a mirarme a la cara
2 (*satisfy*) satisfacer; ***~ a deadline*** cumplir un plazo
II *v/i* (*pret & pp* **met**) encontrarse; *in competition* enfrentarse; *of committee etc* reunirse; ***have you two met?*** ¿os conocíais?
III *n* SP reunión *f*

◆ **meet up** *v/i* encontrarse

◆ **meet with** *v/t person*, *opposition*, *approval* encontrarse con; ***my attempts met with failure*** mis intentos fracasaron

meet•ing ['miːtɪŋ] *by chance* encuentro *m*; *of committee*, *in business* reunión *f*; ***he's in a ~*** está reunido

'meet•ing place lugar *m* de encuentro

meg•a ['megə] *adj* F (*very*) súper; (*very big*) gigantesco

'meg•a•bucks *npl* F una fortuna

meg•a•byte ['megəbaɪt] COMPUT megabyte *m*

meg•a•lo•ma•ni•a [megəloʊ'meɪnɪə] megalomanía *f*

meg•a•lo•ma•ni•ac [megəloʊ'meɪnɪæk] *adj* megalómano *m*

meg•a•phone ['megəfoʊn] megáfono *m*

mel•an•chol•y ['melənkəlɪ] *adj* melancólico

mel•a•no•ma [melə'noʊmə] MED melanoma *m*

me•lee ['meleɪ] enjambre *m*

mel•low ['meloʊ] **I** *adj* suave **II** *v/i of person* suavizarse, sosegarse

me•lod•ic [mə'lɑːdɪk] *adj* melódico

me•lo•di•ous [mə'loʊdɪəs] *adj* melodioso

mel•o•dra•ma ['meloʊdrɑːmə] melodrama *m*

mel•o•dra•mat•ic [melədrə'mætɪk] *adj* melodramático

mel•o•dy ['melədɪ] melodía *f*

mel•on ['melən] melón *m*

melt [melt] **I** *v/i* fundirse, derretirse **II** *v/t* fundir, derretir

◆ **melt away** *v/i fig* desvanecerse

◆ **melt down** *v/t metal* fundir

'melt•down fusión *f* del núcleo; *fig* colapso *m*

melt•ing point ['meltɪŋpɔɪnt] PHYS punto *m* de fusión

'melt•ing pot *fig* crisol *m*

mem•ber ['membər] miembro *m*

Mem•ber of 'Con•gress diputado(-a) *m*(*f*)

Mem•ber of 'Par•lia•ment *Br* diputado(-a) *m*(*f*)

mem•ber•ship ['membərʃɪp] afiliación *f*; (*number of members*) número *m* de miembros; ***he applied for ~ in the club*** solicitó ser admitido en el club

'mem•ber•ship card tarjeta *f* de socio

'mem•ber•ship fee cuota *f* de socio

mem•brane ['membreɪn] membrana *f*

me•men•to [me'mentoʊ] recuerdo *m*

mem•o ['memoʊ] nota *f*

mem•oirs ['memwɑːrz] *npl* memorias *fpl*

'mem•o pad bloc *m* de notas

mem•o•ra•bil•i•a [memərə'bɪlɪə] *npl* recuerdos *mpl*

mem•o•ra•ble ['memərəbl] *adj* memorable

mem•o•ran•dum [memə'rændəm] (*pl* ***memoranda*** [memə'rændə], ***-dums***) *fml* memorándum *m*

me•mo•ri•al [mɪ'mɔːrɪəl] **I** *adj* conmemorativo **II** *n* monumento *m* conmemorativo

Me'mo•ri•al Day Día *m* de los Caídos

me'mo•ri•al ser•vice funeral *m*; *Catho-*

lic also misa *f* de difuntos
mem•o•rize ['meməraɪz] *v/t* memorizar
mem•o•ry ['memərɪ] (*recollection*) recuerdo *m*; (*power of recollection*), COMPUT memoria *f*; ***I have no ~ of the accident*** no recuerdo el accidente; ***have a good / bad ~*** tener buena / mala memoria; ***in ~ of*** en memoria de; ***that brings back memories*** eso me trae recuerdos
'mem•o•ry ca•pac•i•ty capacidad *f* de memoria; **'mem•o•ry chip** chip *m* de memoria; **mem•o•ry ex'pan•sion card** tarjeta *f* de expansión de memoria
men [men] *pl* ☞ ***man***
men•ace ['menɪs] **I** *n* (*threat*) amenaza *f*; *person* peligro *m* **II** *v/t* amenazar
men•ac•ing ['menɪsɪŋ] *adj* amenazador
mend [mend] **I** *v/t* reparar; *clothes* coser, remendar; *shoes* remendar **II** *n*: ***be on the ~*** *after illness* estar recuperándose
men•da•cious [men'deɪʃəs] *adj fml* mendaz
'men•folk *npl* hombres *mpl*
me•ni•al ['miːnɪəl] *adj* ingrato, penoso
men•in•gi•tis [menɪn'dʒaɪtɪs] meningitis *f*
men•o•pause ['menəpɒːz] menopausia *f*
'men's room servicio *m* de caballeros
men•stru•ate ['menstrʊeɪt] *v/i* menstruar
men•stru•a•tion [menstrʊ'eɪʃn] menstruación *f*
men•tal ['mentl] *adj* **1** mental **2** F (*crazy*) chiflado F, pirado F
men•tal a'rith•me•tic cálculo *m* mental; **men•tal 'cru•el•ty** crueldad *f* mental; **men•tal 'hand•i•cap** minusvalía *f* psíquica; **'men•tal hos•pi•tal** hospital *m* psiquiátrico; **men•tal 'ill•ness** enfermedad *f* mental
men•tal•i•ty [men'tælətɪ] mentalidad *f*
men•tal•ly ['mentəlɪ] *adv* (*inwardly*) mentalmente
men•tal•ly 'hand•i•capped *adj* con minusvalía psíquica
men•tal•ly 'ill *adj*: ***be ~*** sufrir una enfermedad mental
men•thol ['menθɑːl] CHEM mentol *m*
men•tion ['menʃn] **I** *n* mención *f*; ***she made no ~ of it*** no lo mencionó, no hizo mención de eso **II** *v/t* mencionar; ***don't ~ it*** (*you're welcome*) no hay de qué; ***not to ~ …*** por no mencionar…
men•tor ['mentɔːr] mentor(a) *m*(*f*)
men•u ['menuː] *for food*, COMPUT menú *m*
'men•u bar COMPUT barra *f* de menús
mer•can•tile ['mɜːrkəntaɪl] *adj* mercantil; ***~ law*** derecho *m* mercantil
mer•ce•na•ry ['mɜːrsɪnərɪ] **I** *adj* mercenario **II** *n* MIL mercenario(-a) *m*(*f*)
mer•chan•dise ['mɜːrtʃəndaɪz] mercancías *fpl*, *L.Am.* mercadería *f*
mer•chan•dis•ing ['mɜːrtʃəndaɪzɪŋ] merchandising *m*, comercialización *f*
mer•chant ['mɜːrtʃənt] comerciante *m/f*
mer•chant 'bank *Br* banco *m* mercantil
mer•chant 'bank•er *Br* banquero(-a) *m*(*f*) comercial
mer•ci•ful ['mɜːrsɪfəl] *adj* compasivo, piadoso
mer•ci•ful•ly ['mɜːrsɪfəlɪ] *adv* (*thankfully*) afortunadamente
mer•ci•less ['mɜːrsɪlɪs] *adj* despiadado
mer•ci•less•ly ['mɜːrsɪlɪslɪ] *adv* despiadadamente, sin piedad
Mer•cu•ry ['mɜːrkjʊrɪ] AST, MYTH Mercurio *m*
mer•cu•ry ['mɜːrkjʊrɪ] mercurio *m*
mer•cy ['mɜːrsɪ] clemencia *f*, compasión *f*; ***be at s.o.'s ~*** estar a merced de alguien
'mer•cy kill•ing eutanasia *f*
mere [mɪr] *adj* mero, simple
mere•ly ['mɪrlɪ] *adv* meramente, simplemente
merge [mɜːrdʒ] *v/i* **1** *of two lines etc* juntarse, unirse **2** *of companies* fusionarse
merg•er ['mɜːrdʒər] COM fusión *f*
me•rid•i•an [mə'rɪdɪən] GEOG meridiano *m*
mer•it ['merɪt] **I** *n* **1** (*worth*) mérito *m*; ***she got the job on ~*** consiguió el trabajo por méritos propios **2** (*advantage*) ventaja *f* **II** *v/t* merecer
mer•i•toc•ra•cy [merɪ'tɑːkrəsɪ] meritocracia *f*
mer•maid ['mɜːrmeɪd] sirena *f*
mer•ri•ment ['merɪmənt] diversión *f*; ***sounds of ~*** risas *fpl*; ***there was some ~ at this suggestion*** esta sugerencia fue recibida con algunas risas
mer•ry ['merɪ] *adj* alegre; ***Merry Christmas!*** ¡Feliz Navidad!
'mer•ry-go-round tiovivo *m*
mesh [meʃ] malla *f*

mess[1] [mes] (*untidiness*) desorden *m*; (*trouble*) lío *m*; ***I'm in a bit of a ~*** estoy metido en un lío; ***be a ~*** *of room, desk* estar desordenado; *of hair* estar revuelto; *of situation, s.o.'s life* ser un desastre

◆ **mess around I** *v/i* enredar **II** *v/t person* jugar con

◆ **mess around with** *v/t* enredar con; *s.o.'s wife* tener un lío con

◆ **mess up** *v/t room, papers* desordenar; *task* convertir en una chapuza; *plans, marriage* estropear, arruinar

mess[2] [mes] MIL comedor *m*; ***officers' ~*** comedor de oficiales

mes•sage ['mesɪdʒ] *also of movie etc* mensaje *m*; ***can I take a ~ for him?*** ¿quiere dejarle un recado?; ***he got the ~*** F lo captó

mes•sen•ger ['mesɪndʒər] (*courier*) mensajero(-a) *m*(*f*)

Mes•si•ah [mə'saɪə] REL Mesías *m*

'mess-up lío *m*

mess•y ['mesɪ] *adj room, person* desordenado; *job* sucio; *divorce, situation* desagradable

met [met] *pret & pp* ☞ ***meet***

met•a•bol•ic [metə'bɑːlɪk] *adj* PHYSIO metabólico

me•tab•o•lism [mə'tæbəlɪzm] metabolismo *m*

met•al ['metl] **I** *n* metal *m* **II** *adj* metálico

'met•al de•tec•tor detector *m* de metales

'met•al fa•tigue fatiga *f* del metal

me•tal•lic [mɪ'tælɪk] *adj* metálico

me•tal•lic 'paint pintura *f* metalizada

met•al•lur•gy [met'ælədʒɪ] metalurgia *f*

'met•al•work 1 objetos *mpl* de metal **2** EDU metalistería *f*

met•a•mor•pho•sis [metə'mɔːrfəsɪs] (*pl* ***metamorphoses*** [metə'mɔːrfəsiːz]) metamorfosis *f inv*

met•a•phor ['metəfər] metáfora *f*

met•a•phor•i•cal [metə'fɑːrɪkl] *adj* metafórico

met•a•phor•i•cal•ly *adv* [metə'fɑːrɪkl] metafóricamente; ***~ speaking*** metafóricamente hablando

met•a•phys•i•cal [metə'fɪzɪkl] *adj* metafísico

met•a•phys•ics [metə'fɪzɪks] *nsg* metafísica *f*

me•tas•ta•sis [mə'tæstəsɪs] (*pl* ***metastases*** [mə'tæstəsiːz]) MED metástasis *f inv*

me•te•or ['miːtɪər] meteoro *m*

me•te•or•ic [miːtɪ'ɑːrɪk] *adj fig* meteórico

me•te•or•ite ['miːtɪəraɪt] meteorito *m*

me•te•or•o•log•i•cal [miːtɪrə'lɑːdʒɪkl] *adj* meteorológico

me•te•or•ol•o•gist [miːtɪə'rɑːlədʒɪst] meteorólogo(-a) *m*(*f*)

me•te•o•rol•o•gy [miːtɪə'rɑːlədʒɪ] meteorología *f*

me•ter[1] ['miːtər] **1** *for gas, electricity* contador *m* **2** (*parking ~*) parquímetro *m*

me•ter[2] ['miːtər] *unit of length* metro *m*

'met•er maid F vigilante *f* de aparcamiento; **'met•er read•er** lector(a) *m*(*f*) del contador; **'me•ter read•ing** lectura *f* del contador

meth•a•done ['meθədoʊn] MED metadona *f*

meth•ane ['miːθeɪn] metano *m*

meth•od ['meθəd] método *m*

me•thod•i•cal [mɪ'θɑːdɪkl] *adj* metódico

me•thod•i•cal•ly [mɪ'θɑːdɪklɪ] *adv* metódicamente

Meth•od•ist ['meθədɪst] **I** *adj* metodista **II** *n* metodista *m/f*

meth•yl ['meθɪl] CHEM metilo *m*

meth•yl•a•ted spir•its ['meθɪleɪtəd] alcohol *m* de quemar

me•tic•u•lous [mə'tɪkjʊləs] *adj* meticuloso, minucioso

me•tic•u•lous•ly [mə'tɪkjʊləslɪ] *adv* meticulosamente

me•tre *Br* ☞ ***meter***[2]

met•ric ['metrɪk] *adj* métrico

me•trop•o•lis [mɪ'trɑːpəlɪs] metrópolis *f inv*

met•ro•pol•i•tan [metrə'pɑːlɪtən] *adj* metropolitano

mew [mjuː] ☞ ***miaow***

Mex•i•can ['meksɪkən] **I** *adj* mexicano, mejicano **II** *n* mexicano(-a) *m*(*f*), mejicano(-a) *m*(*f*)

Mex•i•can 'wave *Br* ola *f* (mexicana)

Mex•i•co ['meksɪkoʊ] México *m*, Méjico *m*

Mex•i•co 'Cit•y Ciudad *f* de México, *Mex* México *m*, *Mex* el Distrito Federal, *Mex* el D.F.

mez•za•nine (floor) ['mezəniːn] entresuelo *m*

MIA [emaɪ'eɪ] *abbr* (= ***missing in action***) desaparecido en combate
mi•aow [mɪaʊ] **I** *n* maullido *m* **II** *v/i* maullar
mice [maɪs] *pl* ☞ ***mouse***
mick•ey ['mɪkɪ]: ***take the ~ out of s.o.*** *esp Br* F cachondearse de alguien
mick•ey 'mouse *adj* P *pej course, qualification* de tres al cuarto P
mi•cro... ['maɪkroʊ] *pref* micro...
mi•crobe ['maɪkroʊb] BIO microbio *m*
mi•cro•bi•al ['maɪkroʊb] *adj* BIO microbiano
mi•cro•bi'ol•o•gy microbiología *f*; **'mi•cro•chip** microchip *m*; **'mi•cro•cli•mate** microclima *m*; **'mi•cro•com•put•er** microcomputador *m*, microcomputadora *f*, *Span* microordenador *m*
mi•cro•cosm ['maɪkroʊkɑːzm] microcosmos *m inv*
mi•cro•eco'nom•ics *nsg* microeconomía *f*; **'mi•cro•e•lec•tron•ics** *nsg* microelectrónica *f*; **mi•cro•fiche** ['maɪkroʊfiːʃ] microficha *f*; **'mi•cro•film** microfilm *m*; **'micro•light** *esp Br* ultraligero *m*; **'mi•cro-or•gan•ism** microorganismo *m*; **'mi-cro•phone** micrófono *m*; **mi•cro'pro-ces•sor** microprocesador *m*; **'mi•cro-scope** microscopio *m*; **mi•cro•scop•ic** [maɪkrə'skɑːpɪk] *adj* microscópico; **'mi•cro•sur•ger•y** microcirugía *f*; **'mi-cro•wave** *oven* microondas *m inv*
mid [mɪd]: ***a man in his ~ forties*** un hombre de unos cuarenta años; ***in the ~ 19th century*** a mediados del siglo XIX; ***he stopped in ~ sentence*** se paró a mitad de frase
mid'air: ***in ~*** en pleno vuelo
mid'day mediodía *m*
mid•dle ['mɪdl] **I** *adj* del medio; ***the ~ child of five*** el tercero de cinco hermanos **II** *n* medio *m*; ***it's the ~ of the night!*** ¡estamos en plena noche!; ***in the ~ of*** *floor, room* en medio de; *period of time* a mitad *or* mediados de; ***in the ~ of winter*** en pleno invierno; ***be in the ~ of doing sth*** estar ocupado haciendo algo; ***in this photo, I'm the one in the ~*** en esta foto soy el del medio
'mid•dle-aged *adj* de mediana edad; **'Mid•dle A•ges** *npl* Edad *f* Media; **mid•dle-age 'spread** F curva *f* de la felicidad; **mid•dle 'class** *adj* de clase media; **'mid•dle class(•es)** clases *fpl* medias; **mid•dle 'dis•tance run•ner** mediofondista *m/f*; **Mid•dle 'East** Oriente *m* Medio; **'mid•dle fin•ger** (dedo *m*) corazón *m*; **'mid•dle•man** intermediario *m*; ***cut out the ~*** evitar al intermediario; **mid•dle 'man•age•ment** mandos *mpl* intermedios; **middle manager** mando *m* intermedio; **mid•dle 'name** segundo nombre *m*; **mid•dle-of-the--'road** *adj* **1** *politician, views* moderado **2** *music* para el gran público; **'mid•dle-weight** *boxer* peso *m* medio
mid•dling ['mɪdlɪŋ] *adj* regular; ***fair to ~*** regular
mid'field centro *m* del campo
mid'field•er centrocampista *m/f*
midg•et ['mɪdʒɪt] *adj* en miniatura
'mid•life cri•sis PSYCH crisis *f inv* de los cuarenta; **'mid•night** ['mɪdnaɪt] medianoche *f*; ***at ~*** a medianoche; ***burn the ~ oil*** quedarse trabajando hasta muy tarde; **'mid•point** punto *m* medio; **'mid-sum•mer** pleno verano *m*; **'mid•way** *adv*: ***we'll stop for lunch ~*** pararemos para comer a mitad de camino; ***~ through the meeting*** a mitad de la reunión; **'mid•week** *adv* a mitad de semana; **'Mid•west** Medio Oeste *m* (de Estados Unidos); **'mid•wife** comadrona *f*; **'mid•win•ter** pleno invierno *m*
might[1] [maɪt] *v/aux* poder, ser posible que; ***I ~ be late*** puede *or* es posible que llegue tarde; ***it ~ never happen*** puede *or* es posible que no ocurra nunca; ***he ~ have left*** a lo mejor se ha ido; ***you ~ have told me!*** ¡me lo podías haber dicho!
might[2] [maɪt] *n* (*power*) poder *m*, fuerza *f*
might•y ['maɪtɪ] **I** *adj* poderoso **II** *adv* F (*extremely*) muy, cantidad de F
mi•graine ['miːgreɪn] migraña *f*
mi•grant ['maɪgrənt] **I** *n* emigrante *m/f* **II** *adj* emigrante
mi•grant 'work•er trabajador(a) *m(f)* itinerante
mi•grate [maɪ'greɪt] *v/i* emigrar
mi•gra•tion [maɪ'greɪʃn] emigración *f*
mi•gra•to•ry ['maɪgrətərɪ] *adj* migratorio: ***~ bird*** ave *f* migratoria
mike [maɪk] F micro *m* F
mild [maɪld] *adj weather, climate* apaci-

M

ble; *cheese, voice* suave; *chili* no muy picante; *person* afable, apacible

mil•dew ['mɪldu:] moho *m*; *on plants* añublo *m*

mild•ly ['maɪldlɪ] *adv say sth* con suavidad; *spicy* ligeramente; ***to put it ~*** por no decir algo peor

mild-man•nered [maɪld'mænərd] *adj* apacible

mild•ness ['maɪldnɪs] *of weather, voice* suavidad *f*; *of person* afabilidad *f*

mile [maɪl] milla *f*; ***be ~s better / easier*** F ser mil veces mejor / más fácil F; ***I was ~s away*** F estaba en la inopia; ***he was ~s ahead of the others*** *in race, study etc* llevaba la delantera a los otros; ***go the extra ~*** *fig* hacer un esfuerzo adicional

mile•age ['maɪlɪdʒ] millas *fpl* recorridas; ***unlimited ~*** kilometraje *m* ilimitado

'mile•age al•low•ance dieta *f* de kilometraje

mile 'high club F *personas que han mantenido relaciones sexuales en un vuelo*

mile•om•e•ter [maɪ'lɑ:mɪtər] *Br* MOT cuentakilómetros *m inv*

'mile•stone *fig* hito *m*

mil•i•tant ['mɪlɪtənt] **I** *adj* militante **II** *n* militante *m/f*

mil•i•ta•rism ['mɪlɪtərɪzəm] militarismo *m*

mil•i•ta•rist ['mɪlɪtərɪst] militarista

mil•i•ta•ris•tic [mɪlɪtər'ɪstɪk] *adj* militarista

mil•i•ta•ry ['mɪlɪterɪ] **I** *adj* militar **II** *n*: ***the ~*** el ejército, las fuerzas armadas

mil•i•ta•ry a'cad•e•my academia *f* militar; **mil•i•ta•ry 'cem•e•ter•y** cementerio *m* militar; **mil•i•ta•ry dic'ta•tor•ship** dictadura *f* militar; **mil•i•ta•ry po'lice** policía *f* militar; **mil•i•tar•y 'serv•ice** servicio *m* militar

mi•li•tia [mɪ'lɪʃə] milicia *f*

mi•li•tia•man [mɪ'lɪʃəmən] miliciano *m*

milk [mɪlk] **I** *n* leche *f* **II** *v/t* ordeñar

milk 'choc•o•late chocolate *m* con leche; **'milk jug** jarra *f* de leche; **milk of mag'ne•sia** leche *f* de magnesia; **milk•man** ['mɪlkmən] lechero *m*; **'milk•shake** batido *m*; **'milk tooth** diente *m* de leche

milk•y ['mɪlkɪ] *adj with lots of milk* con mucha leche; *made with milk* con leche

Milk•y 'Way Vía *f* Láctea

mill [mɪl] *for grain* molino *m*; *for textiles* fábrica *f* de tejidos; ***put s.o. through the ~*** hacérselas pasar canutas a alguien

◆ **mill around** *v/i* pulular

Mil•len•ni•um [mɪ'lenɪəm] milenio *m*

mil•le•pede ☞ ***millipede***

mill•er ['mɪlər] molinero(-a) *m(f)*

mil•let ['mɪlɪt] BOT mijo *m*

mil•li•gram, *Br* **mil•li•gramme** ['mɪlɪgræm] miligramo *m*

mil•li•me•ter, *Br* **mil•li•me•tre** ['mɪlɪmi:tər] milímetro *m*

mil•lion ['mɪljən] millón *m*; ***three ~ dollars*** tres millones de dólares; ***never in a ~ years*** F nunca jamás; ***feel like a ~ dollars*** F sentirse genial; ***thanks a ~*** F un millón de gracias; ***you're one in a ~*** F eres uno entre un millón, no hay dos como tú

mil•lion•aire [mɪljə'ner] millonario(-a) *m(f)*

mil•li•pede ['mɪlɪpi:d] ZO milpiés *m inv*

'mill•stone rueda *f* de molino; ***be a ~ around s.o.'s neck*** *fig* ser una cruz para alguien

mime [maɪm] **I** *v/t* representar con gestos **II** *v/i of singer* hacer mímica

mim•ic ['mɪmɪk] **I** *n* imitador(a) *m(f)* **II** *v/t* (*pret & pp* **-ked**) imitar

mim•ic•ry ['mɪmɪkrɪ] **1** imitación *f* **2** ZO mimetismo *m*

mi•mo•sa [mɪ'moʊzə] BOT mimosa *f*

min•a•ret [mɪnə'ret] ARCHI minarete *m*

mince [mɪns] *v/t* picar

'mince•meat carne *f* picada; ***make ~ out of s.o.*** F hacer picadillo a alguien

mince 'pie *empanada de carne picada*

minc•er ['mɪnsər] *esp Br* picadora *f*

min•cing ['mɪnsɪŋ] *adj* afectado

mind [maɪnd] **I** *n* mente *f*; ***it's uppermost in my ~*** es lo que más me preocupa; ***it's all in your ~*** son imaginaciones tuyas; ***be out of one's ~*** haber perdido el juicio; ***bear** or **keep sth in ~*** recordar algo; ***I've a good ~ to ...*** estoy considerando seriamente ...; ***change one's ~*** cambiar de opinión; ***it didn't enter my ~*** no se me ocurrió; ***give s.o. a piece of one's ~*** cantarle a alguien las cuarenta; ***make up one's ~*** decidirse; ***have something on one's***

~ tener algo en la cabeza; ***what do you have in ~ for the weekend?*** ¿qué tienes pensado para el fin de semana?; ***keep one's ~ on sth*** concentrarse en algo
II *v/t* **1** (*look after*) cuidar (de)
2 (*heed*) prestar atención a; *Br* ***~ the step!*** ¡cuidado con el escalón!; ***~ your own business!*** ¡métete en tus asuntos!; ***~ you, he wasn't always like that*** ojo, no siempre ha sido así
3 *object to*: ***I don't ~ what we do*** no me importa lo que hagamos; ***do you ~ if I smoke?, do you ~ my smoking?*** ¿le importa que fume?; ***would you ~ opening the window?*** ¿le importaría abrir la ventana?
III *v/i*: ***~!*** ¡ten cuidado!; ***never ~!*** ¡no importa!; ***I don't ~*** no me importa, me da igual

mind-bog•gling ['maɪndbɑːglɪŋ] *adj* increíble

mind•ed ['maɪndɪd] *adj*: ***I am ~ to ...*** estoy considerando ...; ***if you are so ~*** si eso deseas; ***be very independently ~*** ser muy independiente

mind•er ['maɪndər] **1** *for child* baby-sitter *f*, *Span* canguro *m/f* **2** *for popstar etc* guardaespaldas *m/f inv*

mind-ex•pand•ing ['maɪndekspændɪŋ] *adj* psicodélico

mind•ful ['maɪndfʊl] *adj*: ***be ~ of*** tener en cuenta

mind•less ['maɪndlɪs] *adj violence* gratuito

'mind read•er adivinador(a) *m(f)* del pensamiento; ***I'm not a ~*** F no soy adivino

mine[1] [maɪn] *pron* el mío, la mía; ***~ are red*** los míos son rojos; ***that book is ~*** eso libro es mío; ***a cousin of ~*** un primo mío

mine[2] [maɪn] **I** *n for coal etc* mina *f* **II** *v/i*: ***~ for*** extraer

mine[3] [maɪn] **I** *n* (*explosive*) mina *f* **II** *v/t* minar

'mine clear•ance limpieza *f* de minas; **'mine de•tec•tor** detector *m* de minas; **'mine•field** MIL campo *m* de minas; *fig* campo *m* minado

min•er ['maɪnər] minero(-a) *m(f)*

min•e•ral ['mɪnərəl] mineral *m*

min•er•al•og•i•cal [mɪnərə'lɑːdʒɪkl] *adj* mineralógico

min•er•al•o•gist [mɪnə'rælədʒɪst] mineralogista *m/f*

min•er•al•o•gy [mɪnə'rælədʒɪ] mineralogía *f*

'min•e•ral rights *npl* derechos *mpl* de explotación

'min•e•ral wa•ter agua *f* mineral

'mine•sweep•er NAUT dragaminas *m inv*

min•gle ['mɪŋgl] *v/i* **1** *of sounds, smells* mezclarse **2** *at party* alternar

min•i ['mɪnɪ] *skirt* minifalda *f*

min•i•a•ture ['mɪnɪʧər] *adj* en miniatura

min•i•a•tur•i•za•tion [mɪnɪʧəraɪ'zeɪʃn] miniaturización *f*

min•i•a•tur•ize ['mɪnɪʧəraɪz] *v/t* miniaturizar

'min•i•bar minibar *m*; **'min•i•bas•ket** SP minibasket *m*; **'min•i•bus** microbús *m*

min•im ['mɪnɪm] *Br* MUS blanca *f*

min•i•ma ['mɪnɪmə] *pl* ☞ ***minimum***

min•i•mal ['mɪnɪməl] *adj* mínimo

min•i•mal•ism ['mɪnɪməlɪzm] minimalismo *m*

min•i•mize ['mɪnɪmaɪz] *v/t* **1** *risk, delay* minimizar, reducir al mínimo **2** (*downplay*) minimizar, quitar importancia a

min•i•mum ['mɪnɪməm] **I** *adj* mínimo **II** *n* (*pl* **-ma** ['mɪnɪmə]) mínimo *m*; ***keep sth to a ~*** mantener algo al mínimo

min•i•mum 'wage salario *m* mínimo

min•ing ['maɪnɪŋ] minería *f*

'min•ing en•gi•neer ingeniero(-a) *m(f)* de minas

min•ion ['mɪnɪən] lacayo *m*

'min•i•se•ries *nsg* TV miniserie *f*

'min•i•skirt minifalda *f*

min•is•ter ['mɪnɪstər] **1** POL ministro(-a) *m(f)* **2** REL ministro(-a) *m(f)*, pastor(a) *m(f)*

min•is•te•ri•al [mɪnɪ'stɪrɪəl] *adj* ministerial

min•is•try ['mɪnɪstrɪ] POL ministerio *m*

'min•i•van furgoneta *f* (pequeña)

mink [mɪŋk] *animal, fur* visón *m*; *coat* abrigo *m* de visón

mi•nor ['maɪnər] **I** *adj problem, setback* menor, pequeño; *operation, argument* de poca importancia; *aches and pains* leve; ***in D ~*** MUS en D menor **II** *n* LAW menor *m/f* de edad

◆ **minor in** *v/t* EDU estudiar como especialidad optativa

M

Mi•nor•ca [mɪ'nɔːrkə] Menorca *f*
Mi•nor•can [mɪ'nɔːrkən] **I** *adj* menorquín **II** *n* menorquín(-ina) *m(f)*
mi•nor•i•ty [maɪ'nɑːrətɪ] minoría *f*; ***be in the ~*** ser minoría
'mi•nor-league *adj* SP de la liga menor; *fig* de segunda
mint [mɪnt] *herb* menta *f*, *chocolate* pastilla *f* de chocolate con sabor a menta; *hard candy* caramelo *m* de menta; ***in ~ condition*** como nuevo
mi•nus ['maɪnəs] **I** *n* (*~ sign*) (signo *m* de) menos *m* **II** *prep* menos; ***temperatures of ~ 18*** temperaturas de 18 grados bajo cero
mi•nus•cule ['mɪnəskjuːl] *adj* minúsculo
min•ute[1] ['mɪnɪt] **I** *n of time* minuto *m*; ***in a ~*** (*soon*) en un momento; ***just a ~*** un momento **II** *v/t record in the minutes* hacer constar en acta
mi•nute[2] [maɪ'nuːt] *adj* **1** (*tiny*) diminuto, minúsculo **2** (*detailed*) minucioso; ***in ~ detail*** minuciosamente
min•ute hand ['mɪnɪt] minutero *m*
mi•nute•ly [maɪ'nuːtlɪ] *adv* **1** *in detail* minuciosamente **2** (*very slightly*) mínimamente
min•utes ['mɪnɪts] *npl of meeting* acta(s) *f(pl)*
'min•ute steak filete *m* fino
mir•a•cle ['mɪrəkl] milagro *m*; ***we can't work ~s!*** ¡no podemos hacer milagros!
mi•rac•u•lous [mɪ'rækjʊləs] *adj* milagroso
mi•rac•u•lous•ly [mɪ'rækjʊləslɪ] *adv* milagrosamente
mi•rage [mɪ'rɑːʒ] espejismo *m*
mire ['maɪər] lodo *m*; ***drag s.o. through the ~*** *fig* poner verde a alguien
mir•ror ['mɪrər] **I** *n* espejo *m*; MOT (espejo *m*) retrovisor *m* **II** *v/t* reflejar
mir•ror 'im•age *exact image* reflejo *m* exacto; *inverse* imagen *f* invertida
mirth [mɜːrθ] regocijo *m*
mirth•less ['mɜːrθlɪs] *adj* frío
mis•ad•ven•ture [mɪsəd'ventʃər]: ***death by ~*** muerte *f* accidental
mis•an•throp•ic [mɪsən'θrɑːpɪk] *adj* misantrópico
mis•an•thro•pist [mɪ'sænθrəpɪst] misántropo(-a) *m(f)*
mis•an•thro•py [mɪ'sænθrəpɪ] misantropía *f*
mis•ap•pre•hend [mɪsæprɪ'hend] *v/t fml* malinterpretar
mis•ap•pre•hen•sion [mɪsæprɪ'henʃn]: ***be under a ~*** estar equivocado
mis•ap•pro•pri•ate [mɪsə'proʊprɪeɪt] *v/t funds* malversar
mis•ap•pro•pri•a•tion [mɪsəproʊprɪ'eɪʃn] *of funds* malversación *f*
mis•be•have [mɪsbə'heɪv] *v/i* portarse mal
mis•be•hav•ior, *Br* **mis•be•hav•iour** [mɪsbə'heɪvɪər] mal comportamiento *m*
mis•cal•cu•late [mɪs'kælkjʊleɪt] *v/t & v/i* calcular mal
mis•cal•cu•la•tion [mɪs'kælkjʊleɪʃn] error *m* de cálculo
mis•car•riage ['mɪskærɪdʒ] MED aborto *m* (espontáneo); ***have a ~*** abortar (espontáneamente); ***~ of justice*** error *m* judicial
mis•car•ry ['mɪskærɪ] *v/i* (*pret & pp* ***-ied***) **1** *fml*: *of plan* fracasar **2** *of pregnant woman* abortar (espontáneamente)
mis•cel•la•ne•ous [mɪsə'leɪnɪəs] *adj* diverso; ***the file marked ~*** la carpeta de varios
mis•chance [mɪs'tʃæns]: ***by ~*** por desgracia
mis•chief ['mɪstʃɪf] (*naughtiness*) travesura *f*, trastada *f*
'mis•chief-mak•er travieso(-a) *m(f)*
mis•chie•vous ['mɪstʃɪvəs] *adj* **1** (*naughty*) travieso **2** (*malicious*) malicioso
mis•chie•vous•ly ['mɪstʃɪvəslɪ] *adv* **1** (*naughtily*) traviesamente **2** (*maliciously*) maliciosamente
mis•con•ceived [mɪskən'siːvd] *adj* mal concebido
mis•con•cep•tion [mɪskən'sepʃn] idea *f* equivocada
mis•con•duct [mɪs'kɑːndʌkt] mala conducta *f*
mis•con•struc•tion [mɪskən'strʌkʃn] *fml* (*misinterpretation*) interpretación *f* errónea
mis•con•strue [mɪskən'struː] *v/t* malinterpretar
mis•count [mɪs'kaʊnt] *v/t & v/i* contar mal
mis•deal [mɪs'diːl] *v/t & v/i* (*pret & pp* ***-dealt***): ***~*** (***the cards***) repartir mal (las

M

cartas)
mis•deed [mɪs'diːd] fechoría *f*
mis•de•mea•nor, *Br* **mis•de•mea•nour** [mɪsdə'miːnər] falta *f*, delito *m* menor
mis•di•ag•nose [mɪsdaɪəg'noʊs] *v/t* diagnosticar erróneamente
mis•di•rect [mɪs'daɪrekt] *v/t* **1** *letter etc* enviar a una dirección equivocada **2** *jury* dar instrucciones erróneas a **3** (*give false directions to*) indicar mal la dirección a
mi•ser ['maɪzər] avaro(-a) *m(f)*
mis•er•a•ble ['mɪzrəbl] *adj* **1** (*unhappy*) triste, infeliz **2** *weather*, *performance* horroroso
mis•er•a•bly ['mɪzrəblɪ] *adv* miserablemente; *look*, *say* con tristeza
mi•ser•ly ['maɪzərlɪ] *adj person* avaro; ***a ~ $150*** 150 míseros dólares
mis•e•ry ['mɪzərɪ] **1** (*unhappiness*) tristeza *f*, infelicidad *f* **2** (*wretchedness*) miseria *f*
mis•fire [mɪs'faɪr] *v/i* **1** *of joke*, *scheme* salir mal **2** *of engine* fallar
mis•fit ['mɪsfɪt] *in society* inadaptado (-a) *m(f)*
mis•for•tune [mɪs'fɔːrʧən] desgracia *f*
mis•giv•ings [mɪs'gɪvɪŋz] *npl* recelo *m*, duda *f*
mis•gov•ern [mɪs'gʌvərn] *v/t* gobernar mal
mis•guid•ed [mɪs'gaɪdɪd] *adj person* equivocado; *attempt*, *plan* desacertado
mis•han•dle [mɪs'hændl] *v/t situation* llevar mal
mis•hap ['mɪshæp] contratiempo *m*
mis•hear [mɪs'hɪr] (*pret & pp* ***-heard***) *v/t & v/i* entender mal
mis•hit I *v/t* [mɪs'hɪt] (*pret & pp* ***-hit***) dar mal a **II** *n* ['mɪshɪt] error *m*
mish•mash ['mɪʃmæʃ] batiburrillo *m*
mis•in•form [mɪsɪn'fɔːrm] *v/t* informar mal
mis•in•for•ma•tion [mɪsɪnfər'meɪʃn] información *f* errónea
mis•in•ter•pret [mɪsɪn'tɜːrprɪt] *v/t* malinterpretar
mis•in•ter•pre•ta•tion [mɪsɪntɜːrprɪ'teɪʃn] mala interpretación *f*
mis•judge [mɪs'dʒʌdʒ] *v/t person*, *situation* juzgar mal
mis•lay [mɪs'leɪ] *v/t* (*pret & pp* ***-laid***) perder
mis•lead [mɪs'liːd] *v/t* (*pret & pp* ***-led***) engañar
mis•lead•ing [mɪs'liːdɪŋ] *adj* engañoso
mis•man•age [mɪs'mænɪdʒ] *v/t* gestionar mal
mis•man•age•ment [mɪs'mænɪdʒmənt] mala gestión *f*
mis•match ['mɪsmæʧ]: ***there's a ~ between the two sets of figures*** los dos grupos de cifras no se corresponden
mis•no•mer [mɪs'noʊmər] impropriedad *f*; ***it's a ~ to call it a …*** … no es el término correcto
mi•sog•y•nist [mɪ'sɑːdʒɪnɪst] misógino(-a) *m(f)*
mi•sog•y•ny [mɪ'sɑːdʒɪnɪ] misoginia *f*
mis•place [mɪs'pleɪs] *v/t* (*lose*) perder
mis•placed ['mɪspleɪst] *adj loyalty* inmerecido; *enthusiasm* inoportuno
mis•print ['mɪsprɪnt] errata *f*
mis•pro•nounce [mɪsprə'naʊns] *v/t* pronunciar mal
mis•pro•nun•ci•a•tion [mɪsprənʌnsɪ'eɪʃn] pronunciación *f* incorrecta
mis•quo•ta•tion [mɪskwoʊ'teɪʃn] cita *f* errónea
mis•quote [mɪs'kwoʊt] *v/t* citar erróneamente
mis•read [mɪs'riːd] *v/t* (*pret & pp* ***-read*** [red]) *word*, *figures* leer mal; *situation* malinterpretar
mis•rep•re•sent [mɪsreprɪ'zent] *v/t* deformar, tergiversar
mis•rep•re•sen•ta•tion [mɪsreprɪzen'teɪʃn] deformación *f*, distorsión *f*
mis•rule [mɪs'ruːl] desgobierno *m*
miss[1] [mɪs] *n*: ***Miss Smith*** la señorita Smith; ***~!*** ¡señorita!
miss[2] [mɪs] **I** *n* SP fallo *m*; ***give sth a ~*** *meeting*, *party etc* no ir a algo
II *v/t* **1** *target* no dar en; ***I ducked and he ~ed me*** me agaché y no me dio
2 *emotionally* echar de menos; ***I ~ you so much*** te echo tanto de menos
3 *bus*, *train*, *airplane* perder; ***you just ~ed her*** (*she's just left*) se acaba de marchar
4 (*not notice*) pasar por alto; ***we must have ~ed the turnoff*** nos hemos debido pasar el desvío; ***you don't ~ much!*** ¡no se te escapa una!; ***sorry, am I ~ing something?*** ¿(es que) me he perdido algo?; ***I ~ed what he said*** no me enteré de lo que dijo

M

5 (*not be present at*) perderse; **~ a class** faltar a una clase
III *v/i* fallar
◆ **miss out I** *v/t* dejarse, saltarse F **II** *v/i* F: ***oh, you really missed out*** vaya la que te has perdido F
◆ **miss out on** *v/t* F perderse F
mis•shap•en [mɪs'ʃeɪpən] *adj* deforme
mis•sile ['mɪsəl] misil *m*; (*sth thrown*) arma *f* arrojadiza
mis•sile launch•er ['mɪsəllɔːnʧər] lanzadera *f* de misiles, lanzamisiles *m inv*
miss•ing ['mɪsɪŋ] *adj* desaparecido; ***be ~ of person, plane*** haber desaparecido; ***go ~*** *of objects* perderse; *of climbers* desaparecer; ***the ~ money*** el dinero que falta; ***~ in action*** MIL desaparecido en combate
miss•ing 'link *in human evolution* eslabón *m* perdido
miss•ing 'per•sons *npl* desaparecidos(-as) *mpl* (*fpl*)
mis•sion ['mɪʃn] *task* misión *f*; *people* delegación *f*
mis•sion•a•ry ['mɪʃənerɪ] REL misionero(-a) *m*(*f*)
'mis•sion•a•ry po•si•tion *hum* postura *f* del misionero
mis•sion con'trol centro *m* de control
'mis•sion state•ment declaración *f* de la misión
mis•spell [mɪs'spel] *v/t* escribir incorrectamente
mis•spell•ing [mɪs'spelɪŋ] falta *f* de ortografía
mis•spent ['mɪsspent] *adj*: ***~ youth*** juventud *f* malgastada
mis•state [mɪs'steɪt] *v/t* tergiversar
mis•state•ment [mɪs'steɪtmənt] tergiversación *f*
mist [mɪst] neblina *f*
◆ **mist over** *v/i of eyes* empañarse
◆ **mist up** *v/i of mirror, window* empañarse
mis•take [mɪ'steɪk] **I** *n* error *m*, equivocación *f*; ***make a ~*** cometer un error *or* una equivocación, equivocarse; ***by ~*** por error *or* equivocación **II** *v/t* (*pret* ***mistook***, *pp* ***mistaken***) confundir; ***~ X for Y*** confundir X con Y
mis•tak•en [mɪ'steɪkən] **I** *adj* erróneo, equivocado; ***be ~*** estar equivocado; ***unless I am very much ~*** a no ser que esté muy equivocado; ***a case of ~ identity*** un caso de identificación errónea **II** *pp* ☞ ***mistake***
mis•tak•en•ly [mɪ'steɪkənlɪ] *adv* erróneamente
mis•ter ['mɪstər] ☞ ***Mr.***
mis•time [mɪs'taɪm] *v/t* hacer a destiempo
mis•tle•toe ['mɪsltoʊ] BOT muérdago *m*
mis•took [mɪ'stʊk] *pret* ☞ ***mistake***
mis•trans•late [mɪstrænz'leɪt] *v/t* traducir erróneamente
mis•trans•la•tion [mɪstrænz'leɪʃn] error *m* de traducción
mis•treat [mɪs'triːt] *v/t* maltratar
mis•treat•ment [mɪs'triːtmənt] malos *mpl* tratos
mis•tress ['mɪstrɪs] **1** *lover* amante *f*, querida *f* **2** *of servant* ama *f*; *of dog* dueña *f*, ama *f*
mis•tri•al ['mɪstraɪəl] juicio *m* nulo; ***declare a ~*** declarar el juicio nulo
mis•trust [mɪs'trʌst] **I** *n* desconfianza *f* (***of*** en) **II** *v/t* desconfiar de
mis•trust•ful [mɪs'trʌstfʊl] *adj* desconfiado (***of*** de)
mist•y ['mɪstɪ] *adj weather* neblinoso; *eyes* empañado; *color* borroso
mis•un•der•stand [mɪsʌndər'stænd] *v/t* (*pret & pp* ***-stood***) entender mal; ***don't ~ me*** no me malinterpretes
mis•un•der•stand•ing [mɪsʌndər'stændɪŋ] **1** (*mistake*) malentendido *m*; ***let there be no ~*** que no haya malentendidos **2** (*argument*) desacuerdo *m*
mis•use I *n* [mɪs'juːs] uso *m* indebido **II** *v/t* [mɪs'juːz] usar indebidamente
mite[1] [maɪt] *n* ZO ácaro *m*
mite[2] [maɪt] **I** *n* (*little child*) criatura *f* **II** *adv*: ***a ~*** F un poquitín
mit•i•gate ['mɪtɪgeɪt] *v/t punishment, seriousness of offense* mitigar, atenuar
miti•gat•ing cir•cum•stan•ces [mɪtɪgeɪtɪŋ'sɜːrkəmstænsɪs] *npl* circunstancias *fpl* atenuantes
mit•i•ga•tion [mɪtɪ'geɪʃn] atenuación *f*; ***say sth in ~ of sth*** decir algo como atenuante de algo
mitt [mɪt] *in baseball* guante *m* de béisbol
mit•ten ['mɪtən] mitón *m*
mix [mɪks] **I** *n* (*mixture*) mezcla *f*; *cooking*: *ready to use* preparado *m* **II** *v/t* mezclar; *cement* preparar; ***~ the flour in***

well mezclar la harina bien **III** *v/i socially* relacionarse

◆ **mix up** *v/t* (*confuse*) confundir (***with*** con); (*put in wrong order*) revolver, desordenar; ***be mixed up*** *emotionally* tener problemas emocionales; *of figures* estar confundido; *of papers* estar revuelto *or* desordenado; ***be mixed up in*** estar metido en; ***get mixed up with*** verse liado con

◆ **mix with** *v/t* (*associate with*) relacionarse con

mixed [mɪkst] *adj feelings* contradictorio; *reactions*, *reviews* variado

mixed 'bag: ***the budget is something of a ~*** el presupuesto contiene un poco de todo; **mixed 'bless•ing**: ***it's a ~*** tiene sus ventajas y sus inconvenientes; **mixed 'dou•bles** *nsg in tennis* dobles *mpl* mixtos; ***a ~*** (***match***) un partido de dobles mixtos; **mixed e'con•o•my** economía *f* mixta; **mixed 'mar•riage** matrimonio *m* mixto

mix•er ['mɪksər] **1** *for food* batidora *f* **2** *drink* refresco *m* (*para mezclar con bebida alcohólica*) **3**: ***she's a good ~*** es muy sociable

mix•ing bowl ['mɪksɪŋboʊl] cuenco *m*

mix•ture ['mɪkstʃər] mezcla *f*, *medicine* preparado *m*

mix-up ['mɪksʌp] confusión *f*

mne•mon•ic [niː'mɑːnɪk] recurso *m* mnemotécnico

MO [em'oʊ] *abbr* **1** (= ***medical officer***) médico(-a) *m*(*f*) militar **2** F (= ***modus operandi***) modus *m inv* operandi

mo [moʊ] F segundo *m*

moan [moʊn] **I** *n of pain* gemido *m* **II** *v/i in pain* gemir

moat [moʊt] foso *m*

mob [mɑːb] **I** *n* muchedumbre *f* **II** *v/t* (*pret & pp* ***-bed***) asediar, acosar

mo•bile ['moʊbəl] **I** *adj person* con movilidad; (*that can be moved*) móvil; ***she's a lot less ~ now*** ahora tiene mucha menos movilidad; ***when will I be ~ again?*** ¿cuándo podré volver a moverme? **II** *n* **1** *Br* TELEC móvil *m* **2** *in art* movible *m*

mo•bile 'home casa *f* caravana

mo•bile 'phone *Br* teléfono *m* móvil, *L.Am.* celular *m*

mo•bil•i•ty [mə'bɪlətɪ] movilidad *f*

mo•bi•li•za•tion [moʊbɪlaɪ'zeɪʃn] *of help*, *resources*, MIL movilización *f*

mo•bi•lize ['moʊbɪlaɪz] **I** *v/t help*, *resources*, MIL movilizar **II** *v/i* MIL movilizarse

mob•ster ['mɑːbstər] gángster *m*

moc•ca•sin ['mɑːkəsɪn] mocasín *m*

mo•cha ['moʊkə] moca *f*

mock [mɑːk] **I** *adj* fingido, simulado; ***~ exams / elections*** exámenes *mpl* / elecciones *fpl* de prueba **II** *v/t* burlarse de

mock•er•y ['mɑːkərɪ] **1** (*derision*) burlas *fpl* **2** (*travesty*) farsa *f*

mock•ing ['mɑːkɪŋ] *adj* burlón

'mock•ing bird sinsonte *m*

mock•ing•ly ['mɑːkɪŋlɪ] *adv* burlonamente

mock-up ['mɑːkʌp] (*model*) maqueta *f*, modelo *m*

mod•al ['moʊdl]: **~** (***auxiliary***) (auxiliar *m*) modal *m*

mo•dal•i•ty [moʊ'dælətɪ] modalidad *f*

mod cons [mɑːd'kɑːnz] *abbr pl* (= ***modern conveniences***): ***all ~*** todas las comodidades

mode [moʊd] (*form*), COMPUT modo *m*; ***~ of transportation*** medio *m* de transporte

mod•el ['mɑːdl] **I** *adj employee*, *husband* modélico, modelo; ***~ boat / plane*** maqueta *f* de un barco / avión **II** *n* **1** *miniature* maqueta *f*, modelo *m* **2** (*pattern*) modelo *m* **3** (*fashion* **~**) modelo *m/f*; ***male ~*** modelo *m* **III** *v/t* **1**: ***~ clothes*** trabajar de modelo; ***she ~s swimsuits*** trabaja de modelo de bañadores **2**: ***~ o.s. on s.o.*** tomar a alguien como modelo; ***a building ~ed on …*** un edificio que imita a … **IV** *v/i for designer* trabajar de modelo; *for artist*, *photographer* posar

mod•el•(l)ing ['mɑːdəlɪŋ] **1** *making models* modelismo *m* **2** *of clothes*, *for artist*, *photographer* trabajo *m* de modelo; ***do some ~*** hacer de modelo

'mod•el•(l)ing a•gen•cy agencia *f* de modelos

mo•dem ['moʊdem] módem *m*

mod•e•rate I *adj* ['mɑːdərət] moderado **II** *n* ['mɑːdərət] POL moderado(-a) *m*(*f*) **III** *v/t* ['mɑːdəreɪt] moderar

mod•e•rate•ly ['mɑːdərətlɪ] *adv* medianamente, razonablemente

mod•e•ra•tion [mɑːdə'reɪʃn] (*restraint*)

M

moderación *f*; ***in ~*** con moderación; ***show a degree of ~*** mostrar moderación

mod•er•a•tor ['mɑːdəreɪtər] *of discussion* moderador(a) *m(f)*

mod•ern ['mɑːdərn] *adj* moderno; ***in the ~ world*** en el mundo contemporáneo

'mod•ern-day *adj* de hoy en día

mod•ern 'his•to•ry historia *f* contemporánea

mod•ern•is•tic [mɑːdərn'ɪstɪk] *adj* modernista

mo•der•ni•ty [mɑː'dɜːrnɪtɪ] modernidad *f*

mod•ern•i•za•tion [mɑːdənaɪ'zeɪʃn] modernización *f*

mod•ern•ize ['mɑːdənaɪz] **I** *v/t* modernizar **II** *v/i of business, country* modernizarse

mod•ern 'lan•gua•ges *npl* lenguas *fpl* modernas

mod•est ['mɑːdɪst] *adj* modesto

mod•es•ty ['mɑːdɪstɪ] modestia *f*

mod•i•cum ['mɑːdɪkəm]: ***a ~ of sense*** un mínimo de sentido común

mod•i•fi•a•ble ['mɑːdɪfaɪəbl] *adj* modificable

mod•i•fi•ca•tion [mɑːdɪfɪ'keɪʃn] modificación *f*

mod•i•fy ['mɑːdɪfaɪ] *v/t* (*pret & pp* ***-ied***) modificar

mod•u•lar ['mɑːdʒələr] *adj furniture* por módulos

mod•u•late ['mɑːdʒəleɪt] *v/t & v/i* MUS *etc* modular

mod•u•la•tion [mɑːdʒə'leɪʃn] MUS modulación *f*

mod•ule ['mɑːdʒʊl] módulo *m*

mo•dus o•pe•ran•di [moʊdəsɑːpə'rændaɪ] modus *m inv* operandi

mog•gy ['mɑːgɪ] F *cat* minino *m*

mo•gul ['moʊgəl] magnate *m*; ***movie ~*** magnate del cine

mo•hair ['moʊher] mohair *m*

mo•hi•can [moʊ'hiːkən] *hairstyle* cresta *f*

moist [mɔɪst] *adj* húmedo

moist•en ['mɔɪsn] *v/t* humedecer

mois•ture ['mɔɪstʃər] humedad *f*

mois•tur•iz•er ['mɔɪstʃəraɪzər] *for skin* crema *f* hidratante

mo•lar ['moʊlər] muela *f*, molar *m*

mo•las•ses [mə'læsɪz] *nsg* melaza *f*; ***as slow as ~*** más lento que una tortuga

mold[1] [moʊld] *n on food* moho *m*

mold[2] [moʊld] **I** *n* molde *m* **II** *v/t clay, character* moldear

mold•y ['moʊldɪ] *adj food* mohoso

mole[1] [moʊl] *on skin* lunar *m*

mole[2] [moʊl] *animal, spy* topo *m*

mole[3] [moʊl] (*breakwater*) espigón *m*

mo•lec•u•lar [mə'lekjʊlər] *adj* molecular

mol•e•cule ['mɑːlɪkjuːl] molécula *f*

'mole•hill topera *f*; ***make a mountain out of a ~*** hacer una montaña de un grano de arena

mo•lest [mə'lest] *v/t child, woman* abusar sexualmente de

moll [mɑːl] P chica *f* (*de un gángster*)

mol•li•fy ['mɑːlɪfaɪ] *v/t* apaciguar

mol•lusc, mol•lusk ['mɑːləsk] ZO molusco *m*

mol•ly•cod•dle ['mɑːlɪkɑːdl] *v/t* F mimar, consentir

Mol•o•tov cock•tail [mɑːlətɔːf'kɑːkteɪl] cóctel *m* molotov

molt [moʊlt] *v/i* mudar el pelo

mol•ten ['moʊltən] *adj* fundido

mom [mɑːm] F mamá *f*

mom-and-'pop store F tienda *f* familiar

mo•ment ['moʊmənt] momento *m*; ***at the ~*** en estos momentos, ahora mismo; ***for the ~*** por el momento, por ahora; ***live for the ~*** vivir el momento *or* presente; ***he could arrive at any ~*** podría llegar en cualquier momento; ***now hold on a ~!*** ¡espera un momento!; ***and not a ~ too soon!*** ¡y ya iba siendo hora!

mo•men•tar•i•ly [moʊmən'terɪlɪ] *adv* **1** (*for a moment*) momentáneamente **2** (*in a moment*) de un momento a otro

mo•men•ta•ry ['moʊmənterɪ] *adj* momentáneo

mo•men•tous [mə'mentəs] *adj* trascendental, muy importante

mo•men•tum [mə'mentəm] impulso *m*

Mo•na•co ['mɑːnəkoʊ] Monaco *m*

mon•arch ['mɑːnərk] monarca *m/f*

mo•nar•chic [mə'nɑːrkɪk] *adj* monárquico

mon•ar•chist ['mɑːnərkɪst] monárquico(-a) *m(f)*

mon•ar•chy ['mɑːnərkɪ] monarquía *f*

mon•as•tery ['mɑːnəsterɪ] monasterio *m*

mo•nas•tic [mə'næstɪk] *adj* monástico
Mon•day ['mʌndeɪ] lunes *m inv*
mon•e•tar•ism ['mɑːnɪtərɪzəm] monetarismo *m*
mon•e•tar•ist ['mɑːnɪtərɪst] *adj* monetarista
mon•e•ta•ry ['mɑːnɪterɪ] *adj* monetario
mon•ey ['mʌnɪ] dinero *m*; ***be in the ~*** estar forrado; ***I'm not made of ~*** F a mí también me cuesta ganar el dinero; ***~ talks*** poderoso caballero es don dinero; ***I don't feel I got my ~'s worth*** lo que he comprado no vale lo que he pagado; ***we like the customer to feel that he has got his ~'s worth*** nos gusta que el cliente sienta que ha empleado bien su dinero; ***he should put his ~ where his mouth is*** F debería transformar en dinero sus promesas; ***~ isn't everything*** el dinero no lo es todo
'mon•ey•bags *nsg* F ricachón(-ona) *m(f)*; **'mon•ey belt** faltriquera *f*; **'mon•ey box** hucha *f*; **mon•ey-•chang•er** ['mʌnɪʧeɪndʒər] *person* cambista *m/f*; *machine* máquina *f* de cambio
mon•eyed ['mʌnɪd] *adj* adinerado
'mon•ey•lend•er prestamista *m/f*; **'mon•ey•mak•er**: ***it's a ~*** *scheme etc* es muy rentable; **'mon•ey mar•ket** mercado *m* monetario; **'mon•ey or•der** giro *m* postal; **'mon•ey prob•lems** problemas *mpl* de dinero; **mon•ey-spin•ner** ['mʌnɪspɪnər] F *Br* ☞ ***money-maker***
mon•gol•ism ['mɑːŋgəlɪzəm] MED mongolismo *m*
mon•gol•oid ['mɑːŋgəlɔɪd] *adj* MED mongoloide
mon•grel ['mʌŋgrəl] perro *m* cruzado
mon•i•tor ['mɑːnɪtər] **I** *n* COMPUT monitor *m* **II** *v/t* controlar
monk [mʌŋk] monje *m*
mon•key ['mʌŋkɪ] mono *m*; F *child* diablillo *m* F; ***don't make a ~ out of me*** F no me tomes el pelo; ***I don't give a ~'s*** P me importa un rábano *or* un pito F
◆ **monkey around with** *v/t* F enredar con
'mon•key busi•ness F **1** (*fooling around*) barrabasadas *fpl* **2** (*cheating*) trucos *mpl*; **'mon•key nut** cacahuete *m*; **'mon•key wrench** llave *f* inglesa
monk•fish ['mʌŋkfɪʃ] rape *m*
mon•o ['mɑːnoʊ] **1** *not stereo* mono **2** *not color* monocromo
mon•o•chrome ['mɑːnəkroʊm] *adj* monocromo
mon•o•cle ['mɑːnəkl] monóculo *m*
mo•nog•a•mous [mə'nɑːgəməs] *adj* monógamo
mo•nog•a•my [mə'nɑːgəmɪ] monogamia *f*
mon•o•gram ['mɑːnəgræm] monograma *m*
mon•o•grammed ['mɑːnəgræmd] *adj* con monograma
mon•o•lith ['mɑːnəlɪθ] monolito *m*
mon•o•lith•ic [mɑːnə'lɪθɪk] *adj* monolítico
mon•o•log, *Br* **mon•o•logue** ['mɑːnəlɑːg] monólogo *m*
mon•o•nu•cle•o•sis [mɑːnoʊnuːklɪ'oʊsɪs] mononucleosis *f inv*
mo•nop•o•lis•tic [mənɑːpə'lɪstɪk] *adj* monopolístico
mo•nop•o•lize [mə'nɑːpəlaɪz] *v/t* monopolizar
mo•nop•o•ly [mə'nɑːpəlɪ] monopolio *m*
mon•o•rail ['mɑːnoʊreɪl] monorraíl *m*
mon•o•so•di•um glu•ta•mate [mɑːnoʊsoʊdɪəm'gluːtəmeɪt] glutamato *m* monosódico
mon•o•syl•lab•ic [mɑːnoʊsɪ'læbɪk] *adj* LING monosilábico; ***he was rather ~*** era muy lacónico
mon•o•the•is•tic [mɑːnoʊθeɪ'ɪstɪk] *adj* monoteísta
mo•not•o•nous [mə'nɑːtənəs] *adj* monótono
mo•not•o•ny [mə'nɑːtənɪ] monotonía *f*
mon•ox•ide [mə'nɑːksaɪd] CHEM monóxido *m*
mon•soon [mɑːn'suːn] monzón *m*
mon•ster ['mɑːnstər] monstruo *m*
mon•stros•i•ty [mɑːn'strɑːsətɪ] monstruosidad *f*
mon•strous ['mɑːnstrəs] *adj* (*frightening, huge*) monstruoso; (*shocking*) escandaloso
mon•strous•ly ['mɑːnstrəslɪ] *adv* monstruosamente, terriblemente
mon•tage [mɑːn'tɑːʒ] montaje *m*
month [mʌnθ] mes *m*; ***how much do you pay a ~?*** ¿cuánto pagas al mes?; ***you'll never do it, not in a ~ of Sun-***

days F no lo conseguirás, ni aunque vivas cien años

month•ly ['mʌnθlɪ] **I** *adj* mensual **II** *adv* mensualmente **III** *n magazine* revista *f* mensual

mon•u•ment ['mɑːnʊmənt] monumento *m*

mon•u•ment•al [mɑːnʊ'mentl] *adj fig* monumental

moo [muː] **I** *v/i* mugir **II** *n* mugido *m*

mood[1] [muːd] (*frame of mind*) humor *m*; (*bad* ~) mal humor *m*; *of meeting, country* atmósfera *f*; ***be in a good / bad ~*** estar de buen / mal humor; ***I'm in the ~ for a pizza*** me apetece una pizza; ***I'm not in the ~*** no estoy de humor; ***she's in one of her ~s again*** vuelve a estar de mal humor; ***~ swings*** cambios *mpl* de humor

mood[2] [muːd] LING modo *m*

mood•i•ly ['muːdɪlɪ] *adv* malhumoradamente

mood•y ['muːdɪ] *adj* temperamental; (*bad-tempered*) malhumorado

moon [muːn] luna *f*; ***once in a blue ~*** de Pascuas a Ramos

◆ **moon around** *v/i* F estar pensando en las musarañas

'moon•beam rayo *m* de luna; **'moon land•ing** alunizaje *m*; **'moon•light I** *n* luz *f* de luna **II** *v/i* F estar pluriempleado irregularmente; ***he's ~ing as a barman*** tiene un segundo empleo de camarero; **'moon•light•er** F pluriempleado(-a) *m(f)* (irregularmente); **'moon-light•ing** F pluriempleo *m* (irregular)

'moon•lit *adj* iluminado por la luna; **'moon•shine 1** luz *f* de luna **2** F *nonsense* paridas *fpl* **3** F *illegal liquor*: *bebida destilada ilegalmente*

moor [mʊr] *v/t boat* atracar

moor•ing ['mʊrɪŋ] atracadero *m*

moose [muːs] alce *m* americano

moot [muːt] *adj*: ***it's a ~ point*** es algo discutible

mop [mɑːp] **I** *n for floor* fregona *f*; *for dishes* estropajo *m* (*con mango*); ***his ~ of ginger hair*** su mata de pelo pelirrojo **II** *v/t* (*pret & pp* **-ped**) *floor* fregar; *eyes, face* limpiar

◆ **mop up** *v/t* limpiar; MIL acabar con

mope [moʊp] *v/i* estar abatido

mo•ped ['moʊped] *Br* ciclomotor *m*

mo•raine [mə'reɪn] GEOL morrena *f*

mor•al ['mɔːrəl] **I** *adj* moral; *person, behavior* moralista; ***take the ~ high ground*** aparecer como moralmente superior **II** *n* **1** *of story* moraleja *f*; **2** *pl*: ***~s*** moral *f*, moralidad *f*

mo•rale [mə'ræl] moral *f*

mor•al•ist ['mɔːrəlɪst] moralista *m/f*

mor•al•is•tic [mɔːrə'lɪstɪk] *adj* moralista

mo•ral•i•ty [mə'rælətɪ] moralidad *f*

mor•al•ize ['mɔːrəlaɪz] *v/i* moralizar (***about*** sobre)

mor•al•ly ['mɔːrəlɪ] *adv* moralmente

mor•a•to•ri•um [mɔːrə'tɔːrɪəm] (*pl* ***moratoria*** [mɔːrə'tɔːrɪə] *or* ***-riums***) COM, POL moratoria *f*, ***have a ~ on sth*** tener moratoria en algo

mor•bid ['mɔːrbɪd] *adj* morboso

mor•bid•i•ty [mɔːr'bɪdɪtɪ] morbosidad *f*

mor•dant ['mɔːrdənt] *adj fig* mordaz

more [mɔːr] **I** *adj* más; ***there are no ~ eggs*** no quedan huevos; ***some ~ tea?*** ¿más té?; ***one ~ glass, please*** una *or* otra (copa más) por favor; ***~ and ~ students / time*** cada vez más estudiantes / tiempo

II *adv* más; ***~ important*** más importante; ***~ often*** más a menudo; ***~ and ~*** cada vez más; ***~ or less*** más o menos; ***once ~*** una vez más; ***he paid ~ than $100 for it*** pagó más de 100 dólares por él; ***he earns ~ than I do*** gana más que yo; ***I don't live there any ~*** ya no vivo allí

III *pron* más; ***do you want some ~?*** ¿quieres más?; ***a little ~*** un poco más

more•ish ['mɔːrɪʃ] *adj* delicioso, cautivador

mo•rel•lo [mə'reloʊ]: ~ (***cherry***) BOT guinda *f*

more•o•ver [mɔː'roʊvər] *adv* además, lo que es más

morgue [mɔːrg] depósito *m* de cadáveres

Mor•mon ['mɔːrmən] mormón(-ona) *m(f)*

morn•ing ['mɔːrnɪŋ] mañana *f*, ***in the ~*** por la mañana; ***this ~*** esta mañana; ***tomorrow ~*** mañana por la mañana; ***good ~*** buenos días; ***it's four o'clock in the ~!*** ¡son las cuatro de la mañana!; ***I'm not at my best in the ~*** la mañana no es mi mejor momento del día

morn•ing-'af•ter pill píldora *f* del día siguiente

'morn•ing sick•ness náuseas *fpl* matutinas (*típicas del embarazo*)
Mo•roc•can [mə'rɑːkən] **I** *adj* marroquí **II** *n* marroquí *m/f*
Mo•roc•co [mə'rɑːkoʊ] Marruecos *m*
mo•ron ['mɔːrɑːn] F imbécil *m/f* F, subnormal *m/f* F
mo•ron•ic [mə'rɑːnɪk] *adj* imbécil
mo•rose [mə'roʊs] *adj* hosco, malhumorado
mor•pheme ['mɔːrfiːm] LING morfema *m*
mor•phine ['mɔːrfiːn] morfina *f*
mor•pho•log•i•cal [mɔːrfə'lɑːdʒɪkl] *adj* morfológico
mor•phol•o•gy [mɔːr'fɑːlədʒɪ] morfología *f*
Morse code [mɔːrs'koʊd] código *m* morse
mor•sel ['mɔːrsl] pedacito *m*
mor•tal ['mɔːrtl] **I** *adj* mortal **II** *n* mortal *m/f*
mor•tal 'com•bat combate *m* a muerte; **mor•tal 'dan•ger** peligro *m* de muerte; **mor•tal 'en•e•my** enemigo *m* mortal
mor•tal•i•ty [mɔːr'tælətɪ] mortalidad *f*
mor'tal•i•ty rate índice *m* de mortalidad
mor•tal•ly ['mɔːrtəlɪ] *adv wounded etc* de muerte; ***be ~ offended*** sentirse ultrajado
mor•tal 'sin pecado *m* mortal
mor•tar[1] ['mɔːrtər] MIL mortero *m*
mor•tar[2] ['mɔːrtər] (*cement*) mortero *m*, argamasa *f*
mort•gage ['mɔːrgɪdʒ] **I** *n* hipoteca *f*, préstamo *m* hipotecario **II** *v/t* hipotecar
mor•ti•cian [mɔːr'tɪʃn] encargado(-a) *m(f)* de una funeraria
mor•ti•fi•ca•tion [mɔːrtɪfɪ'keɪʃn]: ***to my ~*** para bochorno mío
mor•ti•fy ['mɔːrtɪfaɪ] *v/t*: ***~ the flesh*** mortificar el cuerpo; ***I was mortified to hear that …*** me sentí abochornado cuando oí que…
mor•tu•a•ry ['mɔːrtʊerɪ] depósito *m* de cadáveres
mo•sa•ic [moʊ'zeɪɪk] mosaico *m*
Mos•cow ['mɑːskaʊ] Moscú *m*
Mos•lem ['mʊzlɪm] **I** *adj* musulmán **II** *n* musulmán(-ana) *m(f)*
mosque [mɑːsk] mezquita *f*
mos•qui•to [mɑːs'kiːtoʊ] (*pl* ***-o(e)s***) mosquito *m*
mos'qui•to net mosquitera *f*
moss [mɑːs] musgo *m*
moss•y ['mɑːsɪ] *adj* cubierto de musgo
most [moʊst] **I** *adj* la mayoría de **II** *adv* (*very*) muy, sumamente; ***the ~ beautiful / interesting*** el más hermoso / interesante; ***that's the one I like ~*** ése es el que más me gusta; ***~ of all*** sobre todo **III** *pron* la mayoría de; ***~ of her novels / friends*** la mayoría de sus novelas / amigos; ***~ of his time / money*** la mayor parte de su tiempo / dinero; ***at (the) ~*** como mucho; ***make the ~ of*** aprovechar al máximo
most•ly ['moʊstlɪ] *adv* principalmente, sobre todo
MOT [emoʊ'tiː] *Br* (*test*): *inspección anual de vehículos*, *Span* ITV *f*; (*certificate*): *certificado de haber pasado la inspección anual*, *Span* ITV *f*
mo•tel [moʊ'tel] motel *m*
moth [mɑːθ] mariposa *f* nocturna; (*clothes ~*) polilla *f*
'moth•ball bola *f* de naftalina
'moth-eat•en *adj* apolillado
moth•er ['mʌðər] **I** *n* madre *f* **II** *v/t* mimar
'moth•er•board COMPUT placa *f* madre
moth•er•hood ['mʌðərhʊd] maternidad *f*
Moth•er•ing Sun•day [mʌðərɪŋ'sʌndeɪ] ☞ ***Mother's Day***
'moth•er-in-law (*pl* ***mothers-in-law***) suegra *f*
'moth•er•land tierrra *f* natal
moth•er•less ['mʌðərlɪs] *adj* huérfano (*de madre*)
moth•er•ly ['mʌðərlɪ] *adj* maternal
Moth•er 'Na•ture la madre naturaleza; **moth•er-of-'pearl** nácar *m*; **'Moth•er's Day** Día *m* de la Madre; **moth•er-to-'be** (*pl* ***mothers-to-be***) futura madre *f*; **'moth•er tongue** lengua *f* materna
mo•tif [moʊ'tiːf] motivo *m*
mo•tion ['moʊʃn] **I** *n* **1** (*movement*) movimiento *m*; ***put or set things in ~*** poner las cosas en marcha; ***he's just going through the ~s*** está haciendo las cosas mecánicamente **2** (*proposal*) moción *f* **II** *v/t*: ***he ~ed me forward*** me indicó con un gesto que avanzara
'mo•tion de•tect•or detector *m* de movimientos
mo•tion•less ['moʊʃnlɪs] *adj* inmóvil

M

mo•tion 'pic•ture película *f*
mo•ti•vate ['moʊtɪveɪt] *v/t person* motivar
mo•ti•va•tion [moʊtɪ'veɪʃn] motivación *f*
mo•tive ['moʊtɪv] motivo *m*
mo•tive•less ['moʊtɪvlɪs] *adj crime* sin motivo
mot•ley ['mɑːtlɪ] *adj* heterogéneo
mo•tor ['moʊtər] motor *m*
'mo•tor•bike moto *f*; **'mo•tor•boat** lancha *f* motora; **mo•tor•cade** ['moʊtərkeɪd] caravana *f*, desfile *m* de coches; **'mo•tor•cy•cle** motocicleta *f*; **'mo•tor•cy•clist** motociclista *m/f*; **'mo•tor home** autocaravana *f*; **'mo•tor in•dus•try** *Br* industria *f* automovilística
mo•tor•ing ['moʊtərɪŋ] automovilismo *m*
mo•tor•ist ['moʊtərɪst] conductor(a) *m(f)*, automovilista *m/f*
'mo•tor me•chan•ic mecánico(-a) *m(f)* (de automóviles); **'mo•tor•mouth** F charlatán(-ana) *m(f)*; **mo•tor 'neu•rone dis•ease** enfermedad *f* neurona motora; **'mo•tor rac•ing** carreras *fpl* de coches; **'mo•tor•scoot•er** vespa® *f*; **'mo•tor ve•hi•cle** vehículo *m* de motor; **'mo•tor•way** *Br* autopista *f*
mot•tled ['mɑːtld] *adj* moteado
mot•to ['mɑːtoʊ] (*pl* **-o(e)s**) lema *m*
mould *etc Br* ☞ ***mold*** *etc*
moult *Br* ☞ ***molt***
mound [maʊnd] *also baseball* montículo *m*
mount [maʊnt] **I** *n* **1** (*mountain*) monte *m*; ***Mount McKinley*** el Monte McKinley **2** (*horse*) montura *f* **II** *v/t* **1** *steps* subir; *horse*, *bicycle* montar en **2** *campaign*, *photo* montar **III** *v/i* aumentar, crecer
◆ **mount up** *v/i* **1** *of bills etc* acumularse **2** *get on horse* montar
moun•tain ['maʊntɪn] montaña *f*
'moun•tain bike bicicleta *f* de montaña
'moun•tain chain cadena *f* montañosa
moun•tain•eer [maʊntɪ'nɪr] montañero(-a) *m(f)*, alpinista *m/f*, *L.Am.* andinista *m/f*
moun•tain•eer•ing [maʊntɪ'nɪrɪŋ] montañismo *m*, alpinismo *m*, *L.Am.* andinismo *m*
'moun•tain goat cabra *f* montés
'moun•tain li•on puma *m*
moun•tain•ous ['maʊntɪnəs] *adj* montañoso
'moun•tain range cordillera *f*, cadena *f* montañosa
'moun•tain•side ladera *f*
mount•ed ['maʊntɪd] *adj* montado
mount•ed po'lice policía *f* montada
Moun•tie ['maʊntɪ] (*in Canada*): *agente de la policía montada*
mount•ing ['maʊntɪŋ] *adj* creciente
mourn [mɔːrn] **I** *v/t* llorar **II** *v/i*: ***~ for s.o.*** llorar la muerte de alguien
mourn•er ['mɔːrnər] doliente *m/f*
mourn•ful ['mɔːrnfəl] *adj voice*, *face* triste
mourn•ing ['mɔːrnɪŋ] luto *m*, duelo *m*; ***be in ~*** estar de luto; ***wear ~*** vestir de luto
mouse [maʊs] (*pl* **mice** [maɪs]) *also* COMPUT ratón *m*
'mouse•hole ratonera *f*; **'mouse mat** COMPUT alfombrilla *f*; **'mouse•trap** cepo *m*
mousse [muːs] **1** *to eat* mousse *m* **2**: (***styling***) ~ espuma *f*
mous•tache *Br* ☞ ***mustache***
mous•y ['maʊsɪ] *adj color*, *hair* pardo
mouth[1] [maʊθ] *n of person* boca *f*; *of river* desembocadura *f*; ***be down in the ~*** F estar con la depre F; ***you took the words right out of my ~*** me lo has quitado de la punta de la lengua; ***you keep your ~ shut!*** F ¡cierra el pico!
mouth[2] [maʊð] *v/t* decir moviendo los labios
◆ **mouth off** *v/i* P **1** (*be fresh*) rebotarse P, contestar F **2** (*be indiscreet*) irse de la boca P **3** (*boast*) farolear P, fardar P
mouth•ful ['maʊθfəl] *of food* bocado *m*; *of drink* trago *m*
'mouth•or•gan armónica *f*; **'mouth•piece 1** *of instrument* boquilla *f* **2** (*spokesperson*) portavoz *m/f*; **mouth-to-mouth re•sus•ci'ta•tion** respiración *f* boca a boca; **'mouth•wash** enjuague *m* bucal, elixir *m* bucal; **'mouth•wa•ter•ing** *adj* apetitoso
move [muːv] **I** *n* **1** *in chess*, *checkers* movimiento *m*; *in soccer* jugada *f*; ***make the first ~*** dar el primer paso; ***get a ~ on!*** F ¡espabílate! F; ***don't make a ~!*** ¡ni te muevas!; ***it's your ~*** *in chess*, *fig* te toca **2** (*step*, *action*) paso *m* **3** (*change of house*) mudanza *f*

II *v/t* **1** *object* mover; **~ *those papers out of your way*** aparta esos papeles **2** (*transfer*) trasladar; **~ *house*** mudarse de casa **3** *emotionally* conmover
III *v/i* **1** moverse **2** (*transfer*) trasladarse; (~ *house*) mudarse
◆ **move along** *v/i*: ***move along there please!*** ¡muévanse!, ¡apártense!; ***it's time to be moving along*** ya va siendo hora de marcharse
◆ **move around** *v/i in room* andar; *from place to place* trasladarse, mudarse
◆ **move away** *v/i* **1** alejarse, apartarse **2** (*move house*) mudarse
◆ **move in** *v/i to house, neighborhood* mudarse; *to office* trasladarse
◆ **move in on** *v/t* MIL avanzar sobre
◆ **move in with** *v/t* irse a vivir con
◆ **move on** *v/i to another town* mudarse; *to another job* cambiarse; *to another subject* pasar a hablar de
◆ **move out** *v/i of house* mudarse; *of area* marcharse
◆ **move over** *v/i* (*make room*) correrse
◆ **move up I** *v/i* **1** *in league* ascender, subir **2** (*make room*) correrse **II** *v/t meeting, trip* anticipar
move•ment ['muːvmənt] *also organization*, MUS movimiento *m*
mov•ers ['muːvərz] *npl firm* empresa *f* de mudanzas; *men* empleados *mpl* de una empresa de mudanzas
mov•ie ['muːvɪ] película *f*; ***go to a ~*** *or* ***the ~s*** ir al cine; ***be in the ~s*** trabajar en el cine
'mov•ie cam•er•a cámara *f* de cine; **mov•ie•go•er** ['muːvɪgoʊər] aficionado(-a) *m/f* al cine; **'mov•ie star** estrella *f* de cine; **'mov•ie thea•ter** cine *m*, sala *f* de cine
mov•ing ['muːvɪŋ] *adj* **1** (*that can move*) movible **2** *emotionally* conmovedor
mow [moʊ] *v/t grass* cortar
◆ **mow down** *v/t* segar la vida de
mow•er ['moʊər] cortacésped *m*
MP [em'piː] *abbr* **1** (= ***Member of Parliament***) *Br* diputado(-a) *m(f)* **2** (= ***Military Policeman***) policía *m* militar
mpg [empiː'dʒiː] *abbr* (= ***miles per gallon***) millas por galón (*medición del consumo de un coche*)
mph [empiː'eɪtʃ] *abbr* (= ***miles per hour***) millas *fpl* por hora
MPV [empiː'viː] *abbr* (= ***multi-purpose vehicle***) vehículo *m* polivalente, monovolúmen *m*
Mr. ['mɪstər] Sr.
Mrs ['mɪsɪz] Sra.
Ms [mɪz] Sra. (*casada o no casada*)
much [mʌtʃ] **I** *adj* mucho; ***so ~ money*** tanto dinero; ***as ~ ... as ...*** tanto ... como
II *adv* mucho; ***I don't like him ~*** no me gusta mucho; ***he's ~ more intelligent than ...*** es mucho más inteligente que ...; ***the house is ~ too large for one person*** la casa es demasiado grande para una sola persona; ***~ admired*** muy admirado; ***very ~*** mucho; ***thank you very ~*** muchas gracias; ***I love you very ~*** te quiero muchísimo; ***too ~*** demasiado
III *pron* mucho; ***what did she say? – nothing ~*** ¿qué dijo? – no demasiado; ***as ~ as ...*** tanto como ...; ***it may cost as ~ as half a million dollars*** puede que haya malversado hasta medio millón de dólares; ***I thought as ~*** eso es lo que pensaba; ***I'm not ~ of a dancer*** no se me da muy bien bailar; ***he's not ~ of a party-goer*** no es muy dado a ir de fiesta, no le gusta mucho salir de fiesta; ***there's not ~ of a difference*** no hay mucha diferencia; ***~ as I would like to*** a pesar de lo que me gustaría
muck [mʌk] (*dirt*) suciedad *f*
◆ **muck around** *v/i* F enredar
◆ **muck around with** *v/t* F enredar con
'muck•rake *v/i* desenterrar escándalos
muck•y ['mʌkɪ] *adj* F mugriento
mu•cous ['mjuːkəs] *adj* mucoso; ***~ membrane*** ANAT mucosa *f*
mu•cus ['mjuːkəs] mocos *mpl*, mucosidad *f*
mud [mʌd] barro *m*
'mud•bath baño *m* de barro
mud•dle ['mʌdl] **I** *n* lío *m*; ***get into a ~ with sth*** armarse *or* montarse un lío con algo **II** *v/t person* liar; ***you've gotten the story all ~d*** te has hecho un lío con la historia
◆ **muddle through** *v/i* arreglárselas
◆ **muddle up** *v/t* desordenar; (*confuse*) liar
mud•dy ['mʌdɪ] *adj* embarrado
'mud•flap guardabarros *m inv*; **'mud•flat** marisma *f*, **'mud•guard** guardaba-

rros *m inv*; **'mud pack** mascarilla *f* de barro; **mud•sling•ing** ['mʌdslɪŋɪŋ] descalificaciones *fpl*
mues•li ['mju:zlɪ] muesli *m*
muf•fin ['mʌfɪn] magdalena *f*
muf•fle ['mʌfl] *v/t* ahogar, amortiguar
◆ **muffle up** *v/i* abrigarse
muf•fler ['mʌflər] **1** MOT silenciador *m* **2** *thick scarf* bufanda *f*
muf•ti ['mʌftɪ] F: ***in ~*** de paisano
mug[1] [mʌg] **1** *for tea, coffee* taza *f* **2** F (*face*) jeta *f* F *Span* careto *m* F **3** F (*fool*) tonto(-a) *m*(*f*)
mug[2] [mʌg] *v/t* (*pret & pp* ***-ged***) (*attack*) atracar
mug•ger ['mʌgər] atracador(a) *m*(*f*)
mug•ging ['mʌgɪŋ] atraco *m*
mug•gy ['mʌgɪ] *adj* bochornoso
'mug•shot P foto *f* (*para ficha policial*)
mule [mju:l] **1** *animal* mulo(-a) *m*(*f*); ***as stubborn as a ~*** terco como una mula **2** *slipper* pantufla *f*
◆ **mull over** [mʌl] *v/t* reflexionar sobre
mulled [mʌld] *adj*: ***~ wine*** *vino con especias que se bebe caliente*
mul•ti... ['mʌltɪ] multi...
mul•ti'col•ored *adj* multicolor
mul•ti'cul•tur•al *adj* multicultural
mul•ti•fac•et•ed [mʌltɪ'fæsɪtɪd] *adj personality, issue* múltiple
mul•ti•far•i•ous [mʌltɪ'ferɪəs] *adj* múltiple
mul•ti'func•tion•al *adj* multifuncional
mul•ti•lat•e•ral [mʌltɪ'lætərəl] *adj* POL multilateral
mul•ti•lin•gual [mʌltɪ'lɪŋgwəl] *adj* multilingüe
mul•ti'me•di•a **I** *n* multimedia *f* **II** *adj* multimedia
mul•ti•mil•lion'aire multimillonario (-a) *m*(*f*)
mul•ti'na•tion•al **I** *adj* multinacional **II** *n* COM multinacional *f*
mul•ti•ple ['mʌltɪpl] *adj* múltiple
mul•ti•ple 'choice ques•tion pregunta *f* tipo test
mul•ti•ple scle•ro•sis [skle'roʊsɪs] esclerosis *f* múltiple
mul•ti•plex ['mʌltɪpleks] *movie theater* (cine *m*) multisalas *m inv*, multicines *mpl*
mul•ti•pli•ca•tion [mʌltɪplɪ'keɪʃn] multiplicación *f*
mul•ti•pli'ca•tion sign signo *m* de multiplicar
mul•ti•plic•i•ty [mʌltɪ'plɪsətɪ] multiplicidad *f*
mul•ti•pli•er ['mʌltɪplaɪər] MATH multiplicador *m*
mul•ti•ply ['mʌltɪplaɪ] **I** *v/t* (*pret & pp* ***-ied***) multiplicar **II** *v/i* (*pret & pp* ***-ied***) multiplicarse
mul•ti'pur•pose *adj* multiuso
mul•ti'ra•cial *adj* multirracial
mul•ti'ra•cial•ism carácter *m* multirracial
mul•ti-screen 'mov•ie the•a•ter multicine *m*
mul•ti-sto•rey 'car park *Br* aparcamiento *m* de varias plantas
mul•ti-task•ing ['mʌltɪtæskɪŋ] multitarea *f*
mul•ti•tude ['mʌltɪtju:d] multitud *f*; ***for a ~ of reasons*** por numerosas razones
mul•ti-'us•er *adj system* multiusuario
mum[1] [mʌm]: ***~'s the word*** no diré ni mu; ***keep ~ about sth*** no decir ni mu sobre algo
mum[2] [mʌm] *esp Br* F mamá *f*
mum•ble ['mʌmbl] **I** *n* murmullo *m* **II** *v/t* farfullar **III** *v/i* hablar entre dientes
mum•bo jum•bo [mʌmboʊ'dʒʌmboʊ] palabrería *f*; ***the usual management ~*** las galimatías típicas de los directivos
mum•mi•fy ['mʌmɪfaɪ] *v/t* momificar
mum•my ['mʌmɪ] *Br* mamá *f*
mumps [mʌmps] *nsg* paperas *fpl*
munch [mʌntʃ] *v/t & v/i* mascar
mun•dane [mʌn'deɪn] *adj* (*everyday*) rutinario
mu•ni•ci•pal [mju:'nɪsɪpl] *adj* municipal
mu•ni•ci•pal•i•ty [mju:nɪsɪ'pælətɪ] municipio *m*
mu•ni•tions [mju:'nɪʃənz] *npl* municiones *mpl*
mu•ral ['mjʊrəl] mural *m*
mur•der ['mɜ:rdər] **I** *n* asesinato *m*; ***she lets him get away with ~*** F le consiente todo; ***scream blue ~*** poner el grito en el cielo; ***the traffic was ~*** P el tráfico era criminal **II** *v/t* **1** *person* asesinar, matar **2** F *song* destrozar
mur•der•er ['mɜ:rdərər] asesino(-a) *m*(*f*)
mur•der•ess ['mɜ:rdəres] asesina *f*
mur•der•ous ['mɜ:rdrəs] *adj rage, look* asesino

'mur•der weap•on arma *f* homicida
murk•y ['mɜːrkɪ] *adj water* turbio, oscuro; *fig*: *past* turbio
mur•mur ['mɜːrmər] **I** *n* murmullo *m*; **... he said in a ~** ... murmulló; **accept without a ~** aceptar sin rechistar **II** *v/t* murmurar
Mur•phy bed ['mɜːrfɪ] mueble *m* cama
mus•cle ['mʌsl] músculo *m*
◆ **muscle in** *v/i* F meterse a la fuerza
◆ **muscle in on** *v/t* F meterse a la fuerza en
mus•cle•man ['mʌslmæn] forzudo *m*
mus•cu•lar ['mʌskjʊlər] *adj* **1** *pain, strain* muscular **2** *person* musculoso
mus•cu•lar dys•troph•y [mʌskjʊlər'dɪstrəfɪ] MED distrofia *f* muscular
muse [mjuːz] *v/i* meditar, reflexionar
mu•se•um [mjuː'zɪəm] museo *m*
mush [mʌʃ] puré *m*
mush•room ['mʌʃrʊm] **I** *n* seta *f*, hongo *m*; (*button* ~) champiñón *m* **II** *v/i* crecer rápidamente
'mush•room cloud hongo *m* atómico
mush•y ['mʌʃɪ] *adj* blando; F *too sentimental* sentimentaloide
mu•sic ['mjuːzɪk] música *f*; *in written form* partitura *f*; **set sth to ~** poner música a algo; **that's ~ to my ears** F me suena a música celestial, eso es música para mis oídos
mu•sic•al ['mjuːzɪkl] **I** *adj* **1** musical **2** *person* con talento para la música **II** *n* musical *m*
'mu•sic(•al) box caja *f* de música
mu•sic•al 'in•stru•ment instrumento *m* musical
mu•si•cian [mjuː'zɪʃn] músico(-a) *m(f)*
mu•si•col•o•gy [mjuːzɪ'kɑːlədzɪ] musicología *f*
'mu•sic stand atril *m*
'mu•sic stool taburete *m* (*para un músico*)
musk [mʌsk] *cosmetic* almizcle *m*
Mus•lim ['mʊzlɪm] ☞ **Moslem**
◆ **muss up** [mʌs'ʌp] *v/t* F revolver
mus•sel ['mʌsl] mejillón *m*
must [mʌst] **I** *v/aux* **1** *necessity* tener que, deber; **I ~ be on time** tengo que *or* debo llegar a la hora; **do you have to leave now? – yes, I ~** ¿tienes que marcharte ahora? - sí, debo marcharme; **I ~n't be late** no tengo que llegar tarde, no debo llegar tarde
2 *probability* deber de; **it ~ be about 6 o'clock** deben de ser las seis; **they ~ have arrived by now** ya deben de haber llegado
II *n*: **be a ~** *proper clothing, clean water etc* ser imprescindible; **the Grand Canyon is a ~** el Gran Cañón es una visita obligada
mus•tache [mə'stæʃ] bigote *m*
mus•tard ['mʌstərd] mostaza *f*
'mus•tard gas gas *m* mostaza
mus•ter ['mʌstər] **I** *v/t troops, resources* reunir **II** *n*: **pass ~** ser pasable
◆ **muster up** *v/t courage* armarse de
must•n't ['mʌsnt] = **must not**
must•y ['mʌstɪ] *adj room* que huele a humedad; *smell* a humedad
mu•tant [mjuː'tənt] **I** *adj* mutante **II** *n* mutante *m/f*
mu•tate [mjuː'teɪt] *v/i* mutar (**into** en)
mu•ta•tion [mjuː'teɪʃn] mutación *f*
mute [mjuːt] **I** *adj animal* mudo **II** *n* MUS sordina *f*
mut•ed ['mjuːtɪd] *adj color* apagado; *criticism* débil
mu•ti•late ['mjuːtɪleɪt] *v/t* mutilar
mu•ti•la•tion [mjuːtɪ'leɪʃn] mutilación *f*
mu•ti•neer [mjuːtɪ'nɪər] **I** *n* amotinado(-a) *m(f)* **II** *v/i* amotinarse
mu•ti•nous ['mjuːtɪnəs] *adj* rebelde
mu•ti•ny ['mjuːtɪnɪ] **I** *n* motín *m* **II** *v/i* (*pret & pp* **-ied**) amotinarse
mut•ter ['mʌtər] *v/t & v/i* murmurar
mut•ton ['mʌtn] carnero *m*
mu•tu•al ['mjuːʧʊəl] *adj* mutuo; **the feeling's ~** el sentimiento es mutuo
mu•tu•al•ly ['mjuːʧʊəlɪ] *adv* mutuamente; **the two are ~ exclusive** se excluyen mutuamente
mu•zak® ['mjuːzæk] música *f* ambiental
muz•zle ['mʌzl] **I** *n* **1** *of animal* hocico *m* **2** *for dog* bozal *m* **3** *of rifle* boca *f* **II** *v/t* poner un bozal a; **~ the press** amordazar a la prensa
my [maɪ] *adj* mi; **~ house** mi casa; **~ parents** mis padres
my•o•pi•a [maɪ'oʊpɪə] MED, *fig* miopía *f*
my•op•ic [maɪ'ɑːpɪk] *adj* miope
myr•i•ad ['mɪrɪəd]: **a ~ ...** miles de...
myrrh [mɜːr] BOT mirra *f*
myr•tle ['mɜːrtl] BOT mirto *m*
my•self [maɪ'self] *pron reflexive* me; *emphatic* yo mismo(-a); **when I saw**

~ in the mirror cuando me vi en el espejo; **I saw it ~** lo vi yo mismo; **by ~** (*alone*) solo; (*without help*) yo solo, yo mismo

mys•te•ri•ous [mɪ'stɪrɪəs] *adj* misterioso

mys•te•ri•ous•ly [mɪ'stɪrɪəslɪ] *adv* misteriosamente

mys•te•ry ['mɪstərɪ] misterio *m*; **~** (**story**) relato *m* de misterio; **tonight's ~ guest is …** nuestro invitado sorpresa de esta noche es …

mys•tic ['mɪstɪk] **I** *adj* místico **II** *n* místico(-a) *m*(*f*)

mys•ti•cism ['mɪstɪsɪzəm] misticismo *m*

mys•ti•fy ['mɪstɪfaɪ] *v/t* (*pret & pp* **-ied**) dejar perplejo

mys•ti•fy•ing ['mɪstɪfaɪɪŋ] *adj* desconcertante

mys•tique [mɪ'stiːk] aureola *f* de misterio

myth [mɪθ] *also fig* mito *m*

myth•i•cal ['mɪθɪkl] *adj* mítico

myth•o•log•i•cal [mɪθə'lɑːdʒɪkl] *adj* mitológico

my•thol•o•gy [mɪ'θɑːlədʒɪ] mitología *f*

N

n/a [en'eɪ] *abbr* (= **not applicable**) no corresponde

nab [næb] *v/t* (*pret & pp* **-bed**) F (*take for o.s.*) pescar F, agarrar

na•dir ['neɪdɪr] AST nadir *m*; *fig* punto *m* más bajo

naff [næf] *adj Br* F hortera

NAFTA ['næftə] *abbr* (= **North American Free Trade Agreement**) ALCA *m* (= Acuerdo *m* de Libre Comercio de las Américas)

nag [næg] **I** *v/i* (*pret & pp* **-ged**) *of person* dar la lata **II** *v/t* (*pret & pp* **-ged**): **~ s.o. to do sth** dar la lata a alguien para que haga algo **III** *n* (*person*) pesado(-a) *m*(*f*)

nag•ger ['nægər] pesado(-a) *m*(*f*)

nag•ging ['nægɪŋ] *adj person* quejica; *doubt* persistente; *pain* continuo

nail [neɪl] **I 1** *n for wood* clavo *m*; **as hard as ~s** muy duro **2** *on finger, toe* uña *f* **II** *v/t*: **~ sth to sth** clavar algo a algo;

◆ **nail down** *v/t lid etc* cerrar con clavos; *fig* **nail s.o. down to a decision / price etc** hacer que alguien tome una decisión / se comprometa a un precio

'nail-bit•ing *adj suspense etc* de infarto

'nail brush cepillo *m* de uñas; **'nail clip•pers** *npl* cortaúñas *m inv*; **'nail file** lima *f* de uñas; **'nail pol•ish** esmalte *m* de uñas; **'nail pol•ish re•mov•er** quitaesmaltes *m inv*; **'nail scis•sors** *npl* tijeras *fpl* de manicura; **'nail var•nish** esmalte *m* de uñas

na•ive [naɪ'iːv] *adj* ingenuo

na•ive•ty [naɪ'iːvtɪ] ingenuidad *f*

na•ked ['neɪkɪd] *adj* desnudo; **to the ~ eye** a simple vista

name [neɪm] **I** *n* nombre *m*; **what's your ~?** ¿cómo te llamas?; **call s.o. ~s** insultar a alguien; **make a ~ for o.s.** hacerse un nombre; **have a bad ~** tener mala fama; **you'll get yourself a bad ~** te ganarás mala fama; **Forsyth by ~** de nombre Forsyth; **he's the leader in ~ only** es el líder sólo de nombre; **the house is in my wife's ~** la casa está a nombre de mi esposa; **put one's ~ down for sth** apuntarse a algo; **in the ~ of peace / of progress** en el nombre de la paz / del progreso; **one of the big ~s in …** una de las figuras de … **II** *v/t*: **they ~d him Ben** le llamaron Ben; **~d** llamado

◆ **name for** *v/t*: **name s.o. for s.o.** poner a alguien el nombre de alguien

'name day santo *m*

name-drop•per ['neɪmdrɑːpər] F: **he's a terrible ~** le encanta presumir de conocer a mucha gente famosa

name•ly ['neɪmlɪ] *adv* a saber

'name plate placa *f* con el nombre; **name•sake** ['neɪmseɪk] tocayo(-a) *m*(*f*), homónimo(-a) *m*(*f*); **'name•tag** *on clothing etc* etiqueta *f*

nan•ny ['nænɪ] niñera *f*

'nan•ny goat cabra *f*

nap [næp] **I** *n* cabezada *f*; **have a ~** echar una cabezada **II** *v/i* (*pret & pp* **-ped**):

N

catch s.o. ~ping *fig* sorprender a alguien desprevenido
na•palm ['neɪpɑːm] napalm *m*
nape [neɪp]: ***~ of the neck*** nuca *f*
nap•kin ['næpkɪn] **1** (*table ~*) servilleta *f* **2** (*sanitary ~*) compresa *f*
nap•py ['næpɪ] *Br* pañal *m*
nar•cis•sism ['nɑːrsɪsɪzəm] PSYCH narcisismo *m*
nar•cis•sus [nɑːr'sɪsəs] (*pl* ***-uses*** [nɑːr'sɪsəsəs], ***narcissi*** [nɑːr'sɪsaɪ]) BOT narciso *m*
nar•cot•ic [nɑːr'kɑːtɪk] narcótico *m*, estupefaciente *m*
nar'cot•ics a•gent agente *m/f* de la brigada de estupefacientes
nar•rate [nə'reɪt] *v/t* narrar
nar•ra•tion [nə'reɪʃn] (*telling*) narración *f*
nar•ra•tive ['nærətɪv] **I** *n* (*story*) narración *f* **II** *adj poem, style* narrativo
nar•ra•tor [nə'reɪtər] narrador(a) *m(f)*
nar•row ['næroʊ] **I** *adj street, bed, victory* estrecho; *views, mind* cerrado; ***in the ~est sense of the word*** en el sentido más estricto de la palabra; ***by a ~ margin*** por un estrecho margen **II** *v/i of river, road* estrecharse
◆ **narrow down I** *v/t fig* reducir (***to*** a) **II** *v/i* reducirse
nar•row•ly ['næroʊlɪ] *adv win* por poco; ***~ escape sth*** escapar por poco de algo
nar•row-'mind•ed *adj* cerrado
NASA ['næsə] *abbr* (= ***National Aeronautics and Space Administration***) NASA *f*
na•sal ['neɪzl] *adj voice* nasal
nas•ty ['næstɪ] *adj person, smell* desagradable, asqueroso; *thing to say* malintencionado; *weather* horrible; *cut, wound* feo; *disease* serio; ***turn ~*** *of person* ponerse agresivo; *of situation* ponerse feo
na•tion ['neɪʃn] nación *f*
na•tion•al ['næʃənl] **I** *adj* nacional; ***~ costume*** traje *m* típico; ***~ dish*** plato *m* nacional; ***~ service*** servicio *m* militar; ***~ team*** equipo *m* nacional **II** *n* ciudadano(-a) *m(f)*
na•tion•al 'an•them himno *m* nacional; **na•tion•al 'coach** *in soccer* seleccionador *m* (nacional); **na•tion•al 'debt** deuda *f* pública; **Na•tion•al 'Guard** Guardia *f* Nacional; **Na•tion•al 'Health Serv•ice** *in UK sistema público de salud británico*
na•tion•al•ism ['næʃənəlɪzm] nacionalismo *m*
na•tion•al•is•tic [næʃənə'lɪstɪk] *adj* nacionalista
na•tion•al•i•ty [næʃə'nælətɪ] nacionalidad *f*; ***what ~ is she?*** ¿de qué nacionalidad es?
na•tion•al•i•za•tion [næʃənəlaɪ'zeɪʃn] nacionalización *f*
na•tion•al•ize ['næʃənəlaɪz] *v/t industry etc* nacionalizar
na•tion•al 'park parque *m* nacional
'na•tion•wide I *adj* de todo el país **II** *adv* por todo el país
na•tive ['neɪtɪv] **I** *adj* nativo; ***~ language*** lengua *f* materna **II** *n* **1** nativo(-a) *m(f)*, natural *m/f*; ***he's a ~ of New York*** es natural de Nueva York **2** *tribesman* nativo(-a) *m(f)*, indígena *m/f*
'Na•tive A•mer•i•can indio(-a) *m(f)* americano(-a); **na•tive 'coun•try** país *m* natal; **na•tive 'speak•er** hablante *m/f* nativo(-a)
Na•tiv•i•ty [nə'tɪvətɪ] Natividad *f*; ***~ play*** auto *m* navideño
NATO ['neɪtoʊ] *abbr* (= ***North Atlantic Treaty Organization***) OTAN *f* (= Organización *f* del Tratado del Atlántico Norte)
nat•ty ['nætɪ] *adj* F **1** (*stylish*) elegante **2** (*clever and useful*) ingenioso
nat•u•ral ['nætʃrəl] **I** *adj* natural; *conclusion, thing to think* natural, lógico; ***a ~ yoghurt*** un yogur de sabor natural; ***a ~ blonde*** una rubia natural; ***die a ~ death*** morir de muerte natural **II** *n*: ***she's a ~*** tiene talento natural
nat•u•ral di'sas•ter desastre *m* natural; **nat•u•ral 'gas** gas *m* natural; **nat•u•ral 'his•to•ry** historia *f* natural
nat•u•ral•ist ['nætʃrəlɪst] naturalista *m/f*
nat•u•ral•is•tic [nætʃrə'lɪstɪk] *adj* naturalista
nat•u•ral•i•za•tion [nætʃrəlaɪ'zeɪʃn] naturalización *f*
nat•u•ral•ize ['nætʃrəlaɪz] *v/t*: ***become ~d*** naturalizarse, nacionalizarse
nat•u•ral•ly ['nætʃərəlɪ] *adv* (*of course*) naturalmente; *behave, speak* con naturalidad; (*by nature*) por naturaleza; ***substances which occur ~*** sustancias que se encuentran en la naturaleza; ***it***

N

doesn't come ~ to him no tiene un don natural, no le sale por naturaleza
nat•u•ral re'sour•ces *npl* recursos *mpl* naturales; **nat•u•ral 'sci•ence** ciencias *fpl* naturales; **nat•u•ral 'sci•en•tist** experto(-a) *m(f)* en ciencias naturales; **nat•u•ral 'wast•age** reducción *f* de plantilla por jubilación
na•ture ['neɪʧər] naturaleza *f*; ***by ~*** por naturaleza; ***it is (in) her ~*** es característico suyo; ***it's not in her ~ to be ...*** no es de las que ...; ***of a serious ~*** de naturaleza seria
na•ture re'serve reserva *f* natural
'na•ture trail sendero *m* natural
na•tur•ism ['neɪʧərɪzm] *Br* naturismo *m*
naugh•ty ['nɒːtɪ] *adj* travieso, malo; *photograph*, *word etc* picante; ***you ~ little boy!*** ¡malo!, ¡pillo!; ***that was a very ~ thing to do*** eso estuvo mal
nau•se•a ['nɒːzɪə] náusea *f*
nau•se•ate ['nɒːzɪeɪt] *v/t* (*disgust*) dar náuseas a
nau•se•at•ing ['nɒːzɪeɪtɪŋ] *adj smell*, *taste* nauseabundo; *person* repugnante
nau•seous ['nɒːʃəs] *adj* nauseabundo; ***feel ~*** tener náuseas
nau•ti•cal ['nɒːtɪkl] *adj* náutico
'nau•ti•cal mile milla *f* náutica
na•val ['neɪvl] *adj* naval; ***~ officer*** oficial *m/f* de marina; ***~ battle*** batalla *f* naval
'na•val base base *f* naval
nave [neɪv] ARCHI nave *f* central
na•vel ['neɪvl] ombligo *m*
nav•i•ga•ble ['nævɪgəbl] *adj river* navegable
nav•i•gate ['nævɪgeɪt] *v/i in ship*, *airplane*, COMPUT navegar; *in car* hacer de copiloto
nav•i•ga•tion [nævɪ'geɪʃn] navegación *f*; *in car* direcciónes *fpl*; ***thanks to her brilliant ~*** gracias a lo bien que indicaba direcciones
nav•i•ga•tor ['nævɪgeɪtər] *on ship* oficial *m/f* de derrota; *in airplane* navegante *m/f*, *in car* copiloto *m/f*
na•vy ['neɪvɪ] armada *f*, marina *f* (de guerra)
na•vy 'blue I *n* azul *m* marino **II** *adj* azul marino
nay [neɪ] PARL no *m*; ***the ~s have it*** ganan los noes
Na•zi ['nɑːtsɪ] **I** *adj* nazi **II** *n* nazi *m/f*
Na•zism ['nɑːtsɪzəm] nazismo *m*
NBA [enbiː'eɪ] *abbr* (= ***National Basketball Association***) NBA *f* (= Asociación Nacional de Baloncesto)
near [nɪr] **I** *adv* **1** cerca; ***come a bit ~er*** acércate un poco más; ***Christmas is getting ~er*** se acerca la Navidad; ***she came ~ to tears*** casi lloró **2** (*almost*) casi; ***~ impossible*** casi imposible
II *prep* cerca de; ***~ the bank*** cerca del banco
III *adj* cercano, próximo; *relative* cercano; ***the ~est bus stop*** la parada de autobús más cercana *or* próxima; ***in the ~ future*** en un futuro próximo; ***~ miss*** AVIA incidente *m* en el que casi se produce una colisión; ***that was a ~ miss*** *or* ***thing*** F le faltó muy poco
IV *v/t* acercarse a; ***be ~ing completion*** estar próximo a acabarse
near•by [nɪr'baɪ] *adv live* cerca
near•ly ['nɪrlɪ] *adv* casi; ***not ~ as good / fast*** ni de lejos tan bueno / rápido; ***that's not ~ enough*** eso no es ni con mucho suficiente; ***very ~*** casi; ***I very ~ changed my mind*** me faltó poco para cambiar de idea
near'sight•ed *adj* miope
near•sight•ed•ness [nɪr'saɪtɪdnɪs] miopía *f*
neat [niːt] *adj* **1** ordenado; *handwriting* claro **2** *whiskey* solo, seco **3** *solution* ingenioso **4** F (*terrific*) genial F, estupendo F
ne•ces•sar•i•ly ['nesəserəlɪ] *adv* necesariamente
ne•ces•sar•y ['nesəserɪ] *adj* necesario, preciso; ***it is ~ to ...*** es necesario ..., hay que ...; ***a ~ evil*** un mal necesario; ***if ~*** si fuera necesario
ne•ces•si•tate [nɪ'sesɪteɪt] *v/t* exigir, hacer necesario
ne•ces•si•ty [nɪ'sesɪtɪ] **1** (*being necessary*) necesidad *f*; ***of ~*** por fuerza; ***~ is the mother of invention*** *proverb* la necesidad agudiza el ingenio **2** (*something necessary*) necesidad *f*, requisito *m* imprescindible; ***necessities pl of life*** necesidades *fpl*; ***be a ~ of life*** ser algo muy necesario
neck [nek] **I** *n* cuello *m*; ***be ~ and ~*** ir igualadísimo; ***be up to one's ~ in debt*** estar hasta el cuello de deudas; ***risk one's ~*** jugarse el pellejo; ***save one's***

~ salvar el pellejo; ***stick one's ~ out*** arriesgarse; ***get it in the ~*** F recibir un buen rapapolvo F **II** *v/i* meterse mano

neck•lace ['neklɪs] collar *m*; **'neck•line** *of dress* escote *m*; **'neck•tie** corbata *f*

nec•tar ['nektər] BOT néctar *m*

nec•tar•ine ['nektəri:n] BOT nectarina *f*

née [neɪ] *adj* de soltera

need [ni:d] **I** *n* necesidad *f*; ***if ~ be*** si fuera necesario; ***in ~*** necesitado; ***be in ~ of sth*** necesitar algo; ***those in ~*** los (más) necesitados; ***there's no ~ to be rude / upset*** no hace falta ser grosero / que te enfades
II *v/t* necesitar
III *v/aux*: ***you'll ~ to buy one*** tendrás que comprar uno; ***you don't ~ to wait*** no hace falta que esperes; ***I ~ to talk to you*** tengo que *or* necesito hablar contigo; ***~ I say more?*** ¿hace falta que añada algo?; ***you ~ not have come*** no hacía falta que vinieras

nee•dle ['ni:dl] **I** *n for sewing, injection, on dial* aguja *f*; ***a ~ in a haystack*** *fig* una aguja en un pajar **II** *v/t* F (*annoy*) pinchar F

need•less ['ni:dlɪs] *adj* innecesario; ***~ to say*** ni que decir tiene

need•less•ly ['ni:dlɪslɪ] *adv* innecesariamente

'nee•dle•work costura *f*

need•y ['ni:dɪ] **I** *adj* necesitado **II** *npl*: ***the ~*** los necesitados

neg [neg] PHOT F negativo *m*

ne•gate [nɪ'geɪt] *v/t* **1** GRAM *sentence etc* poner en la negativa **2** *effect etc* invalidar

ne•ga•tion [nɪ'geɪʃn] **1** GRAM *of sentence etc* anulación *f* **2** *of effect etc* invalidación *f*

neg•a•tive ['negətɪv] *adj* negativo; ***answer in the ~*** dar una respuesta negativa

neg•a•tive 'eq•ui•ty patrimonio *m* negativo neto

ne•glect [nɪ'glekt] **I** *n* abandono *m*, descuido *m*; ***be in a state of ~*** estar abandonado; ***~ of duty*** incumplimiento *m* del deber **II** *v/t* **1** *garden, one's health* descuidar, desatender **2**: ***~ to do sth*** no hacer algo

ne•glect•ed [nɪ'glektɪd] *adj garden* abandonado, descuidado; *author* olvidado; ***feel ~*** sentirse abandonado

ne•glect•ful [nɪ'glektfʊl] ☞ ***negligent***

neg•li•gee ['neglɪʒeɪ] salto *m* de cama

neg•li•gence ['neglɪdʒəns] negligencia *f*

neg•li•gent ['neglɪdʒənt] *adj* negligente

neg•li•gi•ble ['neglɪdʒəbl] *adj quantity, amount* insignificante

ne•go•ti•a•ble [nɪ'goʊʃəbl] *adj salary, contract* negociable

ne•go•ti•a•ble pa•per FIN efecto *m* negociable

ne•go•ti•ate [nɪ'goʊʃɪeɪt] **I** *v/i* negociar; ***negotiating skills*** *pl* habilidades *fpl* para negociar; ***negotiating table*** mesa *f* de negociaciones **II** *v/t deal, settlement* negociar; *obstacles* franquear, salvar; *bend in road* tomar

ne•go•ti•a•tion [nɪgoʊʃɪ'eɪʃn] negociación *f*; ***be under ~*** estar siendo negociado; ***be in ~s with*** estar en negociaciones con

ne•go•ti•a•tor [nɪ'goʊʃɪeɪtər] negociador(a) *m(f)*

Ne•gro ['ni:groʊ] negro(-a) *m(f)*

neigh [neɪ] *v/i* relinchar

neigh•bor ['neɪbər] vecino(-a) *m(f)*; ***next-door ~*** vecino de al lado

neigh•bor•hood ['neɪbərhʊd] *in town* vecindario *m*, barrio *m*; ***in the ~ of ...*** *fig* alrededor de ...

neigh•bor•ing ['neɪbərɪŋ] *adj house, state* vecino, colindante

neigh•bor•ly ['neɪbərlɪ] *adj* amable

neigh•bour *etc Br* ☞ ***neighbor*** *etc*

nei•ther ['ni:ðər] **I** *adj* ninguno; ***~ applicant was any good*** ninguno de los candidatos era bueno **II** *pron* ninguno(-a) *m(f)* **III** *adv*: ***~ ... nor ...*** ni ... ni ... **IV** *conj*: ***~ do I*** yo tampoco; ***~ can I*** yo tampoco

ne•o•clas•si•cal [ni:oʊ'klæsɪkəl] *adj* neoclásico

ne•o•lith•ic [ni:ə'lɪθɪk] *adj* neolítico

ne•ol•o•gism [ni:'ɑ:lədʒɪzəm] LING neologismo *m*

ne•o-na•zi [ni:oʊ'nɑ:tsɪ] **I** *adj* neonazi **II** *n* neonazi *m/f*

ne•on light [ni:ɑ:n'laɪt] luz *f* de neón

Ne•pal [nə'pɔ:l] Nepal *m*

Nep•a•lese [nepə'li:z] **I** *adj* nepalés, nepalí **II** *n* nepalés(-esa) *m(f)*, nepalí *m/f*

neph•ew ['nefju:] sobrino *m*

nerd [nɜ:rd] F petardo(-a) *m(f)* F; ***he's a***

real computer ~ está obsesionado con las computadoras *or Span* ordenadores
nerve [nɜːrv] nervio *m*; (*courage*) valor *m*; (*impudence*) descaro *m*, cara *f*; ***it's bad for my ~s*** me pone de los nervios; ***get on s.o.'s ~s*** sacar de quicio a alguien; ***he's got a ~*** F ¡qué cara tiene!; ***have ~s of steel*** tener nervios de acero; ***a bag*** *or* ***bundle of ~s*** F un manojo de nervios; ***be suffering from ~s*** estar muy nervioso; ***have the ~ to do sth*** tener el valor / descaro de hacer algo; ***have lost one's ~*** *of racing driver etc* tener miedo; ***hit a ~*** poner el dedo en la llaga
'nerve cell neurona *f*; **'nerve cen•ter**, *Br* **nerve cen•tre** *fig* centro *m* neurálgico; **'nerve gas** gas *m* nervioso; **nerve-rack•ing** ['nɜːrvrækɪŋ] *adj* angustioso, exasperante
ner•vous ['nɜːrvəs] *adj person* nervioso, inquieto; *twitch* nervioso; ***I'm ~ about meeting them*** la reunión con ellos me pone muy nervioso
ner•vous 'break•down crisis *f inv* nerviosa
ner•vous 'en•er•gy energía *f*
ner•vous•ly ['nɜːrvəslɪ] *adv* nerviosamente
ner•vous•ness ['nɜːrvəsnɪs] nerviosismo *m*
ner•vous 'wreck manojo *m* de nervios
nerv•y ['nɜːrvɪ] *adj* (*fresh*) descarado
nest [nest] **I** *n* nido *m* **II** *v/i* anidar
'nest egg *fig* ahorros *mpl*
nes•tle ['nesl] *v/i* acomodarse; ***a village nestling in the hills*** un pueblecito enclavado en las montañas
◆ **nestle up to** *v/t* recostarse en
Net [net] COMPUT: ***the ~*** la Red; ***on the ~*** en Internet
net[1] [net] *n for fishing, tennis etc* red *f*
net[2] [net] **I** *adj price, weight* neto **II** *v/t* (*pret & pp* **-ted**) *profit, salary* embolsarse
net as•sets *npl* FIN activos mpl netos
net 'cur•tain visillo *m*
Neth•er•lands ['neðərləndz] *npl* Países *mpl* Bajos
net•i•quette ['netɪket] COMPUT netiqueta *f*
'net play *in tennis* juego *m* en la red; **net 'pro•fit** beneficio *m* neto; **net re'turn** beneficio *m* neto; **'Net surf•er** internauta *m/f*
net•tle ['netl] ortiga *f*; ***grasp the ~*** *fig* coger el toro por los cuernos
'net•work I *n of contacts, cells*, COMPUT red *f* **II** *v/t computers* conectar en red; **'net•work driv•er** COMPUT controlador *m* de red; **'net•work•ing** (*building contacts*) establecimiento *m* de contactos; **net 'worth** activo *m* neto
neu•ral ['nʊrəl] *adj* neural
neu•ral•gi•a [nʊ'rældʒə] MED neuralgia *f*
neu•ral•gic [nʊr'ældʒɪk] *adj* neurálgico
neu•ro•log•i•cal [nʊrə'lɑːdʒɪkl] *adj* MED neurológico
neu•rol•o•gist [nʊ'rɑːlədʒɪst] neurólogo(-a) *m(f)*
neu•rol•o•gy [nʊ'rɑːlədʒɪ] neurología *f*
neu•ron(e) ['nʊrɑːn] neurona *f*
neu•ro•sis [nʊ'roʊsɪs] (*pl* **neuroses** [nʊ'roʊsiːz]) neurosis *f inv*
neu•ro•sur•geon ['nʊroʊsɜːrdʒən] neurocirujano(-a) *m(f)*
neu•rot•ic [nʊ'rɑːtɪk] *adj* neurótico
neu•ter ['nuːtər] *v/t animal* castrar
neu•tral ['nʊtrl] **I** *adj country* neutral; *color* neutro **II** *n gear* punto *m* muerto; ***in ~*** en punto muerto
neu•tral•i•ty [nʊ'trælətɪ] neutralidad *f*
neu•tral•ize ['nʊtrəlaɪz] *v/t* neutralizar; ***~ each other*** neutralizarse
neu•tron ['nuːtrɑːn] PHYS neutrón *m*; ***~ bomb*** bomba *f* de neutrones
nev•er ['nevər] *adv* nunca; ***you're ~ going to believe this*** no te vas a creer esto; ***you ~ promised, did you?*** no lo llegaste a prometer, ¿verdad?; ***I have ~ ever seen …*** nunca jamás había visto…; ***~ again will I trust them*** no volveré a confiar en ellos nunca más
nev•er-'end•ing *adj* interminable
nev•er•the•less [nevərðə'les] *adv* sin embargo, no obstante
new [nuː] *adj* nuevo; ***this system is still ~ to me*** todavía no me he hecho con este sistema; ***I'm ~ to the job*** soy nuevo en el trabajo; ***that's nothing ~*** no es nada nuevo; ***feel a ~ man*** sentirse como nuevo; ***the ~ boys and girls*** los nuevos
'new•born *adj* recién nacido
'new•com•er recién llegado(-a) *m(f)*; ***I'm a ~ to this sort of approach*** este enfoque me resulta nuevo
new•fan•gled ['nuːfæŋgld] *adj pej* mo-

derno
new'found *adj* nuevo; **New•found-land** ['nu:faʊndlænd] Terranova *f*; **New Guin•ea** [nu:'gɪnɪ] Nueva Guinea *f*; **New Jer•sey** Nueva Jersey *f*
new•ly ['nu:lɪ] *adv* (*recently*) recientemente, recién
new•ly-weds ['nu:lɪwedz] *npl* recién casados *mpl*
new 'moon luna *f* nueva
news [nu:z] *nsg* noticias *fpl*; *on TV* noticias *fpl*, telediario *m*; *on radio* noticias *fpl*; ***that's ~ to me*** no sabía eso; ***this is good / bad ~*** son buenas / malas noticias; ***a bit** or **piece of ~*** una noticia; ***is there any ~ ?*** ¿ha habido alguna noticia?; ***is there any ~ of Jim ?*** ¿hay noticias de Jim?; ***break the ~ to s.o.*** dar la noticia a alguien; ***have ~ from s.o.*** recibir noticias de alguien; ***I heard it on the ~*** lo escuché en las noticias; ***he's always in the ~*** siempre sale en las noticias; ***the good / bad ~ is ...*** la buena / mala noticia es ...
'news a•gen•cy agencia *f* de noticias; **'news•a•gent** *Br* vendedor(a) *m(f)* de periódicos; **'news black•out** prohibición *f* de informar; ***impose a ~*** imponer censura informativa; **'news•cast** TV noticias *fpl*, telediario *m*; *on radio* noticias *fpl*; **'news•cast•er** TV presentador(a) *m(f)* de informativos; **'news-deal•er** quiosquero(-a) *m(f)*; **'news flash** flash *m* informativo, noticia *f* de última hora; **'news chan•nel** canal *m* de noticias; **'news•let•ter** hoja *f* informativa; **'news•pa•per** periódico *m*; **'news•read•er** TV *etc* presentador(a) *m(f)* de informativos; **'news re•lease** comunicado *m* de prensa; **'news report** reportaje *m*; **'news•sheet** hoja *f* informativa; **'news•stand** quiosco *m*; **'news•vend•or** vendedor(a) *m(f)* de periódicos; **'news•wor•thy** *adj* de interés informativo
newt [nu:t] ZO tritón *m*; ***as drunk as a ~*** borracho como una cuba
New 'Tes•ta•ment Nuevo Testamento *m*; **New 'World** Nuevo Mundo *m*; **'New Year** año *m* nuevo; ***Happy New Year!*** ¡Feliz Año Nuevo!; **New Year's 'Day** Día *m* de Año Nuevo; **New Year's 'Eve** Nochevieja *f*; **New 'York** [jɔ:rk] **I** *adj* neoyorquino **II** *n*: **~ (City)** Nueva York *f*; **New York•er** ['jɔ:rkər] neoyorquino(-a) *m(f)*; **New Zea•land** ['zi:lənd] Nueva Zelanda *f*; **New Zea-land•er** ['zi:ləndər] neozelandés(-esa) *m(f)*, neocelandés(-esa) *m(f)*
next [nekst] **I** *adj in time* próximo, siguiente; *in space* siguiente, de al lado; ***~ week*** la próxima semana, la semana que viene; ***the ~ week he came back again*** volvió a la semana siguiente; ***who's ~?*** ¿quién es el siguiente? **II** *adv* luego, después; ***~, we're going to study ...*** a continuación, vamos a estudiar ...; ***~ to*** (*beside*) al lado de; (*in comparison with*) en comparación con; ***wearing ~ to nothing*** llevando apenas nada (de ropa)
next 'door I *adj neighbor* de al lado **II** *adv live* al lado
next of 'kin pariente *m* más cercano
NHS [eneɪtʃ'es] *abbr* (= ***National Health Service***) *Br sistema público de salud británico*
nib•ble ['nɪbl] *v/t* mordisquear
Nic•a•ra•gua [nɪkə'rɑ:gwə] Nicaragua *f*
Nic•a•ra•guan [nɪkə'rɑ:gwən] **I** *adj* nicaragüense **II** *n* nicaragüense *m/f*
nice [naɪs] *adj trip, house, hair* bonito, *L.Am.* lindo; *person* agradable, simpático; *weather* bueno, agradable; *meal, food* bueno, rico; ***be ~ to your sister!*** ¡trata bien a tu hermana!; ***that's very ~ of you*** es muy amable de tu parte
nice•ly ['naɪslɪ] *adv written, presented* bien; (*pleasantly*) amablemente; ***that will do ~*** eso me viene perfecto; ***she is doing ~*** le va muy bien
ni•ce•ties ['naɪsətɪz] *npl* sutilezas *fpl*, refinamientos *mpl*; ***social ~*** cumplidos *mpl*
niche [ni:ʃ] **1** *in market* hueco *m*, nicho *m* **2** (*special position*) hueco *m*
'niche mar•ket nicho m; **'niche mar-ket•ing** márketing *m* de nichos; **'niche prod•uct** producto *m* con un nicho
nick [nɪk] **I** *n* (*cut*) muesca *f*, mella *f*; ***in the ~ of time*** justo a tiempo **II** *v/t* F: ***~ s.o. for $100*** estafar 100 dólares a alguien
nick•el ['nɪkl] **1** *metal* níquel *m* **2** *coin*: *moneda de cinco centavos*
'nick•el-plate *v/t* niquelar
'nick•name apodo *m*, mote *m*
nic•o•tine ['nɪkəti:n] nicotina *f*

N

'nic•o•tine poi•son•ing nicotinismo *m*
niece [niːs] sobrina *f*
niff [nɪf] *Br* F (*stink*) peste *f*
nif•ty ['nɪftɪ] *adj* F *gadget, idea* ingenioso
Ni•ger•i•a [naɪ'dʒɪrɪə] Nigeria *f*
Ni•ger•i•an [naɪ'dʒɪrɪən] **I** *adj* nigeriano **II** *n* nigeriano(-a) *m(f)*
nig•gard•ly ['nɪgərdlɪ] *adj amount, person* mísero
nig•gle ['nɪgl] **I** *v/i* quejarse (***about, over*** de) **II** *v/t* (*worry*) preocupar
nig•gling ['nɪglɪŋ] *adj doubt* inquietante; *ache* molesto; ***all the ~ little details*** todos los detalles insignificantes
night [naɪt] noche *f*; ***tomorrow ~*** mañana por la noche; ***11 o'clock at ~*** las 11 de la noche; ***travel by ~*** viajar de noche; ***during the ~*** por la noche; ***last ~*** ayer por la noche; ***the ~ before last*** anteanoche; ***on the ~ of May 5th*** en la noche del 5 de mayo; ***stay the ~*** quedarse a dormir; ***work ~s*** trabajar de noche; ***good ~*** buenas noches; ***~ and day*** noche y día; ***have a good / bad ~*** pasar una buena / mala noche; ***have a ~ out*** salir por la noche
'night bird ave *f* nocturna; *fig* trasnochador(a) *m(f)*; **'night blind•ness** MED ceguera *f* nocturna; **'night•cap** *drink* copa *f* (*tomada antes de ir a dormir*); **'night•club** club *m* nocturno, discoteca *f*; **'night•dress** camisón *m*; **'night•fall**: ***at ~*** al anochecer; ***after ~*** después del anochecer; **'night flight** vuelo *m* nocturno; **'night•gown** camisón *m*
night•ie ['naɪtɪ] F camisón *m*
night•in•gale ['naɪtɪŋgeɪl] ruiseñor *m*
'night•life vida *f* nocturna
night•ly ['naɪtlɪ] **I** *adj*: ***a ~ event*** algo que sucede todas las noches **II** *adv* todas las noches
night•mare ['naɪtmer] *also fig* pesadilla *f*
night•mar•ish ['naɪtmerɪʃ] *adj* de pesadilla
'night nurse enfermero(-a) *m(f)* de noche; **'night owl** F trasnochador(a) *m(f)*; **'night por•ter** portero *m* de noche; **'night school** escuela *f* nocturna; **'night shift** turno *m* de noche; **'night•shirt** camisa *f* de dormir; **'night•spot** local *m* nocturno; **'night•stick** porra *f*; **'night•time**: ***at ~, in the ~*** por la noche; **night 'watch•man** vigilante *m* nocturno
ni•hil•ism ['naɪɪlɪzəm] nihilismo *m*
ni•hil•ist ['naɪɪlɪst] nihilista *m/f*
ni•hil•is•tic [naɪɪ'lɪstɪk] *adj* nihilista
nil [nɪl] *Br* cero
Nile [naɪl] Nilo *m*
nim•ble ['nɪmbl] *adj person, mind* ágil
nim•by ['nɪmbɪ] *adj* F *que apoya un proyecto etc mientras no le afecte directamente*
nin•com•poop ['nɪnkəmpuːp] tarugo(-a) *m(f)*
nine [naɪn] nueve; ***~ times out of ten*** *fig* nueve de cada diez veces; ***~ of hearts*** nueve de corazones; ***be dressed up to the ~s*** F ir de punta en blanco
nine•teen [naɪn'tiːn] diecinueve
nine•teenth [naɪn'tiːnθ] *n & adj* decimonoveno
nine•ti•eth ['naɪntɪɪθ] *n & adj* nonagésimo
nine-to-'five I *adj*: ***a ~ job*** un trabajo de oficina **II** *adv*: ***work ~*** trabajar en una oficina
nine•ty ['naɪntɪ] noventa; ***be in one's nineties*** tener noventa y tantos años; ***in the nineties*** en los noventa
nin•ny ['nɪnɪ] F bobo(-a) *m(f)*, besugo(-a) *m(f)*
ninth [naɪnθ] *n & adj* noveno
nip[1] [nɪp] **I** *n* (*pinch*) pellizco *m*; (*bite*) mordisco *m*; ***there's a ~ in the air today*** hoy hace bastante fresco **II** *v/t* (*pret & pp* ***-ped***) (*pinch*) pellizcar; ***~ sth in the bud*** cortar algo de raíz
◆ **nip in** *v/i Br* F *to house, shop etc* entrar un momento
◆ **nip out** *v/i Br* F *of house, office etc* salir un momento
nip[2] [nɪp] *n of whiskey etc* copita *f*
nip•ple ['nɪpl] pezón *m*; *on valve etc* engrasador *m*
nip•py ['nɪpɪ] *adj* F **1** (*cold*) fresco **2** *Br* (*fast*) rápido
nit [nɪt] *in hair* piojo *m*
nit•pick•er ['nɪtpɪkər] F quisquilloso(-a) *m(f)*
nit•pick•ing *adj* ['nɪtpɪkɪŋ] F quisquilloso
ni•trate ['naɪtreɪt] CHEM nitrato *m*
ni•tric ac•id [naɪtrɪk'æsɪd] CHEM ácido *m* nítrico

N

ni•tro•gen ['naɪtrədʒn] nitrógeno *m*
ni•tro•glyc•er•in(e) [naɪtroʊ'glɪsəri:n] CHEM nitroglicerina *f*
nit•ty-grit•ty [nɪtɪ'grɪtɪ]: ***get down to the ~*** F ir al grano
nit•wit ['nɪtwɪt] F bobo(-a) *m(f)*, percebe *m/f*
no [noʊ] **I** *adv* no; ***they ~ longer live here*** ya no viven aquí **II** *adj*: ***there's ~ coffee / tea left*** no queda café / té; ***I have ~ family / money*** no tengo familia / dinero; ***I'm ~ linguist / expert*** no soy un lingüista / experto; ***~ smoking / parking*** prohibido fumar / aparcar; ***in ~ time*** en un abrir y cerrar de ojos **III** *int* no; ***say ~ to*** decir no a **IV** *n* (*pl* ***noes***): ***a clear ~*** un claro no
No•bel 'peace prize premio *m* Nobel de la Paz; **No•bel 'prize** premio *m* Nobel; **No•bel 'prize win•ner** premio *m/f* Nobel
no•bil•i•ty [noʊ'bɪlətɪ] nobleza *f*
no•ble ['noʊbl] *adj* noble
no•bod•y ['noʊbədɪ] *pron* nadie; ***~ knows*** nadie lo sabe; ***there was ~ at home*** no había nadie en casa
no-claims bo•nus [noʊ'kleɪmzboʊnəs] descuento *m* por no haber sufrido ningún siniestro
noc•tur•nal [nɑ:k'tɜ:rnl] *adj* nocturno
nod [nɑ:d] **I** *n* movimiento *m* de la cabeza; ***give a ~*** *in agreement* asentir con la cabeza **II** *v/i* (*pret & pp* ***-ded***) asentir con la cabeza; ***~ to s.o.*** hacer un gesto de asentimiento a alguien; *greeting* saludar a alguien con la cabeza; ***have a ~ding acquaintance with s.o.*** conocer un poco a alguien **III** *v/t* (*pret & pp* ***-ded***): ***~ one's head*** asentir con la cabeza
◆ **nod off** *v/i* (*fall asleep*) quedarse dormido
nod•ule ['nɑ:dju:l] BOT, MED nódulo *m*
no-'fault in•sur•ance seguro *m* a todo riesgo; **no-'go ar•e•a** zona *f* prohibida; **no-hop•er** [noʊ'hoʊpər] F inútil *m/f* F
noise [nɔɪz] ruido *m*
noise•less ['nɔɪzlɪs] *adj* silencioso
nois•y ['nɔɪzɪ] *adj* ruidoso
no•mad ['noʊmæd] nómada *m/f*
no•mad•ic [noʊ'mædɪk] *adj* nómada
no man's land ['noʊmænzlænd] tierra *f* de nadie
no•men•cla•ture [nə'menklətʃər] *name* nombre *m*; *system of naming* nomenclatura *f*
nom•i•nal ['nɑ:mɪnl] *adj amount* simbólico; *leader* nominal; ***~ income*** ingreso *m* nominal; ***~ value*** FIN valor *m* nominal
nom•i•nate ['nɑ:mɪneɪt] *v/t* (*appoint*) nombrar; ***~ s.o. for a post*** (*propose*) proponer a alguien para un puesto
nom•i•na•tion [nɑ:mɪ'neɪʃn] (*appointment*) nombramiento *m*; (*proposal*) nominación *f*; ***who was your ~?*** ¿a quién propusiste?
nom•i•nee [nɑ:mɪ'ni:] candidato(-a) *m(f)*
non ... [nɑ:n] no ...
non•ac'cept•ance rechazo *m*
non•ag'gres•sion pact POL pacto *m* de no agresión
non•al•co'hol•ic *adj* sin alcohol
non•a'ligned *adj* no alineado
non•ap'pear•ance incomparecencia *f*
non•be'liev•er no creyente *m/f*
non•cha•lance ['nɑ:nʃələns] indiferencia *f*
non•cha•lant ['nɑ:nʃəlɑ:nt] *adj* despreocupado
non•com•mis•sioned 'of•fi•cer suboficial *m/f*
non•com'mit•tal *adj person*, *response* evasivo; ***be ~*** responder con evasivas
non•com'pli•ance incumplimiento *m* (***with*** de)
non•con'form•ist **I** *n* inconformista *m/f* **II** *adj* inconformista
non•co•op•er'a•tion falta *f* de cooperación
non'core *adj activities*, *business* secundario, periférico
non•de•script ['nɑ:ndɪskrɪpt] *adj* anodino
none [nʌn] *pron*: ***~ of the students*** ninguno de los estudiantes; ***~ of the water*** nada de agua; ***there are ~ left*** no queda ninguno; ***there is ~ left*** no queda nada; ***~ too soon*** justo a tiempo
non'en•ti•ty nulidad *f*
non•es'sen•tial *adj* prescindible (***to*** para)
none•the•less [nʌnðə'les] *adv* sin embargo, no obstante
non•e'vent chasco *m*
non•ex'ist•ence inexistencia *f*
non•ex'ist•ent *adj* inexistente

N

non'fic•tion no ficción *f*
non•ful'fill•ment, *Br* **non•ful'fil•ment** incumplimiento *m*
non(•in)'flam•ma•ble *adj* incombustible, no inflamable
non•in•ter'fer•ence, non•in•ter'vention no intervención *f*
non-'i•ron *adj shirt* que no necesita plancha
'non•mem•ber no socio(-a) *m(f)*
'no-no: ***that's a ~*** F de eso nada; ***lying in the sun all day is a definite ~*** ni hablar de estar todo el día tumbados al sol
non•ob'serv•ance incumplimiento *m*
no-'non•sense *adj approach* directo
non•par•ti'san *adj* imparcial
non'pay•ment impago *m*
non•plussed [nɑːn'plʌst] *adj* desconcertado
non•pol•lut•ing [nɑːnpə'luːtɪŋ] *adj* que no contamina
non'prof•it altruista, sin ánimo de lucro
non'prof•it-mak•ing *adj* sin ánimo de lucro
non•pro•lif•er'a•tion POL no proliferación *f*; ***~ treaty*** tratado *m* de no proliferación
non'res•i•dent no residente *m/f*
non•re•turn•a•ble [nɑːnrɪ'tɜːrnəbl] *adj* no retornable
non•sense ['nɑːnsəns] disparate *m*, tontería *f*; ***don't talk ~*** no digas disparates *or* tonterías; ***~, it's easy!*** tonterías, ¡es fácil!; ***make (a) ~ of*** echar por tierra; ***stand no ~*** no tolerar tonterías
non•sen•si•cal [nɑːn'sensɪkl] *adj* absurdo
non'skid *adj tires* antideslizante
non'slip *adj surface* antideslizante
non'smok•er *person* no fumador(a) *m(f)*
non'smok•ing *adj* de no fumadores; ***~ car*** RAIL vagón *m* de no fumadores
non'stand•ard *adj* no estándar
non'start•er: ***be a ~*** *of idea, project etc* ser inviable; ***he's a ~*** no se le puede tomar en consideración
non'stick *adj pans* antiadherente
non'stop I *adj flight, train* directo, sin escalas; *chatter* ininterrumpido **II** *adv fly, travel* directamente; *chatter, argue* sin parar
non'swim•mer: ***be a ~*** no saber nadar
non'tox•ic *adj* no tóxico
non'u•nion *adj* no sindicado
non'vi•o•lence no violencia *f*
non'vi•o•lent *adj* no violento
noo•dles ['nuːdlz] *npl* tallarines *mpl* (chinos)
nook [nʊk] rincón *m*; ***search for sth in every ~ and cranny*** buscar algo por todos los recovecos
noo•kie ['nʊkɪ] P polvo *m* P; ***no ~ for two weeks*** nada de polvos durante dos semanas P
noon [nuːn] mediodía *m*; ***at ~*** al mediodía
'no one → ***nobody***
noose [nuːs] lazo *m* corredizo
nope [noʊp] *int* F no
nor [nɔːr] *conj* ni; ***~ do I*** yo tampoco, ni yo
norm [nɔːrm] norma *f*
nor•mal ['nɔːrml] *adj* normal; ***be back to ~*** volver a la normalidad; ***go back*** *or* ***return to ~*** volver a la normalidad; ***be above / below ~*** estar por encima / debajo de lo normal
nor•mal•i•ty [nɔːr'mælətɪ] normalidad *f*
nor•mal•ize ['nɔːrməlaɪz] *v/t relationships* normalizar
nor•mal•ly ['nɔːrməlɪ] *adv* **1** (*usually*) normalmente **2** (*in a normal way*) normalmente, con normalidad
'nor•mal time *in soccer* tiempo *m* reglamentario
north [nɔːrθ] **I** *n* norte *m*; ***to the ~ of*** al norte de **II** *adj* norte **III** *adv travel* al norte; ***~ of*** al norte de
North A'mer•i•ca América *f* del Norte, Norteamérica *f*; **North A'mer•i•can I** *n* norteamericano(-a) *m(f)* **II** *adj* norteamericano; **north'east** nordeste *m*, noreste *m*; **'north•bound** *adj* en dirección norte
north•er•ly ['nɔːrðərlɪ] *adj* norte, del norte
north•ern ['nɔːrðərn] norteño, del norte
north•ern•er ['nɔːrðərnər] norteño(-a) *m(f)*
North•ern 'Ire•land Irlanda *f* del Norte
north•ern•most ['nɔːrðərnmoʊst] *adj* más al norte
North Ko're•a Corea *f* del Norte; **North Ko're•an I** *adj* norcoreano **II** *n* norcoreano(-a) *m(f)*; **North 'Pole** Polo *m* Norte; **North 'Sea** Mar *m* del Norte;

North 'Star Estrella *f* Polar
north•ward ['nɔːrðwərd] *adv travel* hacia el norte
north•west [nɔːrð'west] noroeste *m*
Nor•way ['nɔːrweɪ] Noruega *f*
Nor•we•gian [nɔːr'wiːdʒn] **I** *adj* noruego **II** *n* **1** *person* noruego(-a) *m(f)* **2** *language* noruego *m*
nose [noʊz] nariz *m*; *of animal* hocico *m*; ***it was right under my ~!*** ¡lo tenía delante de mis narices!; ***cut off one's ~ to spite one's face*** tirar piedras contra su propio tejado; ***follow one's ~*** (*go straight ahead*) seguir todo recto; ***lead s.o. by the ~*** manejar a alguien con facilidad; ***look down one's ~ at s.o.*** mirar a alguien por encima del hombro; ***poke*** *or* ***stick one's ~ into sth*** meter las narices en algo; ***put s.o.'s ~ out of joint*** hacer que alguien se moleste *or* se ofenda
◆ **nose around** *v/i* F husmear
'nose•bleed: ***I have a ~*** me sangra la nariz, sangro por la nariz; **'nose dive** AVIA picado *m*; **'nose-dive** *v/i of airplane* descender en picado; F *of prices etc* caer en picado; **'nose drops** *npl* MED gotas *fpl* para la nariz
no-'smok•ing *adj* ☞ ***nonsmoking***
nos•tal•gia [nɑː'stældʒə] nostalgia *f*
nos•tal•gic [nɑː'stældʒɪk] *adj* nostálgico
nos•tril ['nɑːstrəl] ventana *f* de la nariz
nos•y ['noʊzɪ] *adj* F entrometido
nos•y par•ker [noʊzɪ'pɑːrkər] F cotilla *m/f* F
not [nɑːt] *adv* no; ***~ this one, that one*** éste no, ése; ***~ now*** ahora no; ***~ there*** no allí; ***~ like that*** así no; ***~ before Tuesday / next week*** no antes del martes / de la próxima semana; ***~ for me, thanks*** para mí no, gracias; ***~ a lot*** no mucho; ***it's ~ ready / allowed*** no está listo / permitido; ***I don't know*** no lo sé; ***he didn't help*** no ayudó; ***there was ~ a shop in sight*** no se veía ninguna tienda; ***~ that I have to do it*** no es que yo tenga que hacerlo; ***she's so beautiful ... ~*** es guapísima ... ¡qué va!
no•ta•ble ['noʊtəbl] *adj* notable
no•ta•bly ['noʊtəblɪ] *adv* notablemente
no•ta•ry ['noʊtərɪ] notario(-a) *m(f)*
notch [nɑːʧ] muesca *f*, mella *f*; ***be a ~ above the others*** estar por encima de los demás
◆ **notch up** *v/t* F *victory etc* hacerse con
note [noʊt] **I** *n written*, MUS nota *f*; ***take ~s*** tomar notas; ***take ~ of sth*** prestar atención a algo; ***make a ~ of sth*** apuntar algo; ***I made a mental ~ to speak to him*** traté de acordarme de hablar con él; ***speak without ~s*** hablar sin utilizar notas; ***strike the right ~*** *fig* acertar con el tono **II** *v/t* (*observe*) notar; (*pay special attention to*) tomar nota de
◆ **note down** *v/t* anotar
'note•book 1 cuaderno *m*, libreta *f* **2** COMPUT *L.Am.* computadora *f* portátil, *Span* ordenador *m* portátil
not•ed ['noʊtɪd] *adj* destacado; ***be ~ for sth*** destacar por algo
'note•pad bloc *m* de notas; **'note•paper** papel *m* de carta; **'note•wor•thy** *adj* digno de mención
not-for-'pro•fit *adj* sin ánimo de lucro
noth•ing ['nʌθɪŋ] *pron* nada; ***~ but*** sólo; ***~ much*** no mucho; ***for ~*** (*for free*) gratis; (*for no reason*) por nada; ***I'd like ~ better*** me encantaría
noth•ing•ness ['nʌθɪŋnɪs] nada *f*
no•tice ['noʊtɪs] **I** *n* **1** *on bulletin board, in street* cartel *m*, letrero *m*; *in newspaper* anuncio *m*
2 (*advance warning*) aviso *m*; ***four weeks' ~*** cuatro semanas de preaviso; ***at short ~*** con poca antelación; ***until further ~*** hasta nuevo aviso; ***give s.o. his / her ~*** *to quit job* despedir a alguien; *to leave house* comunicar a alguien que tiene que abandonar la casa; ***hand in one's ~*** *to employer* presentar la dimisión
3: ***escape ~*** pasar desapercibido; ***escape s.o.'s ~*** pasar desapercibido a alguien; ***it escaped her ~*** se le pasó; ***take ~ of sth*** observar algo, prestar atención a algo; ***take no ~ of s.o. / sth*** no hacer caso de alguien / algo
II *v/t road sign etc* ver, advertir; *change, difference* notar, fijarse en; ***~ s.o. doing sth*** ver a alguien hacer algo; ***did you ~ anyone talking to him?*** ¿viste si alguien hablaba con él?; ***what do you ~ about this new design?*** ¿qué es lo que te llama la atención de este nuevo diseño?; ***I didn't ~ what he was wearing*** no me fijé en lo que llevaba

no•tice•a•ble ['noʊtɪsəbl] *adj* apreciable, evidente; ***the stain is still very ~*** todavía se nota mucho la mancha
no•tice•a•bly ['noʊtɪsəblɪ] *adv* apreciablemente, claramente
'no•tice board *Br* tablón *m* de anuncios
no•ti•fi•a•ble ['noʊtɪfaɪəbl] *adj disease* notificable
no•ti•fi•ca•tion [noʊtɪfɪ'keɪʃn] notificación *f*
no•ti•fy ['noʊtɪfaɪ] *v/t* (*pret & pp* ***-ied***) notificar, informar
no•tion ['noʊʃn] noción *f*, idea *f*
no•tion•al ['noʊʃənl] *adj* hipotético
no•tions ['noʊʃnz] *npl* artículos *mpl* de costura
no•to•ri•e•ty [noʊtə'raɪətɪ] mala fama *f*
no•to•ri•ous [noʊ'tɔːrɪəs] *adj* de mala fama
no•to•ri•ous•ly [noʊ'tɔːrɪəslɪ] *adv*: ***be ~ unreliable*** ser muy poco fiable
not•with•stand•ing [nɑːtwɪθ'stændɪŋ] **I** *prep* a pesar de **II** *adv* no obstante
nou•gat ['nuːgət] *especie de turrón*
nought [nɔːt] *Br* cero *m*
noun [naʊn] nombre *m*, sustantivo *m*
nou•rish ['nʌrɪʃ] *v/t person* nutrir, alimentar
nou•rish•ing ['nʌrɪʃɪŋ] *adj* nutritivo
nou•rish•ment ['nʌrɪʃmənt] alimento *m*, alimentación *f*
nou•veau riche [nuːvoʊ'riːʃ] (*pl* ***nouveaux riches*** [nuːvoʊ'riːʃ]) nuevo(-a) rico(-a) *m(f)*
nov•el ['nɑːvl] **I** *n* novela *f* **II** *adj* novedoso
nov•el•ist ['nɑːvlɪst] novelista *m/f*
nov•el•ty ['nɑːvəltɪ] **1** (*being new*) lo novedoso **2** (*something new*) novedad *f*
No•vem•ber [noʊ'vembər] noviembre *m*
nov•ice ['nɑːvɪs] principiante *m/f*
no•vi•ci•ate *Br*, **no•vi•ti•ate** [nɑː'vɪsɪət] REL noviciado *m*
now [naʊ] *adv* ahora; ***~ and again, ~ and then*** de vez en cuando; ***by ~*** ya; ***from ~ on*** de ahora en adelante; ***right ~*** ahora mismo; ***just ~*** (*at this moment*) en este momento; (*a little while ago*) hace un momento; ***~, ~!*** ¡vamos!, ¡venga!; ***~, where did I put it?*** ¿y ahora dónde lo he puesto?; ***up to ~*** hasta ahora; ***~ that*** ahora que; ***it's ~ or never*** (es) ahora o nunca
now•a•days ['naʊədeɪz] *adv* hoy en día
no•where ['noʊwer] *adv* en ningún lugar; ***it's ~ near finished*** no está acabado ni mucho menos; ***he was ~ to be seen*** no se le veía en ninguna parte; ***get ~*** (***fast***) no ir a ninguna parte; ***this is getting us ~*** (***fast***) con esto no vamos a ninguna parte
no-win sit•u'a•tion callejón *m* sin salida
nox•ious ['nɑːkʃəs] *adj* nocivo; ***~ substance*** sustancia *f* nociva
noz•zle ['nɑːzl] boquilla *f*
nu•ance ['nuːɑːns] matiz *m*
nu•bile ['nuːbaɪl] *adj attractive* bien parecido
nu•cle•ar ['nuːklɪər] *adj* nuclear
nu•cle•ar 'en•er•gy energía *f* nuclear; **nu•cle•ar 'fis•sion** fisión *f* nuclear; **'nu•cle•ar-free** *adj* desnuclearizado; **nu•cle•ar 'phys•ics** *nsg* física *f* nuclear; **nu•cle•ar 'pow•er** energía *f* nuclear; POL potencia *f* nuclear; **nu•cle•ar-pow•ered** ['nuːklɪərpaʊərd] nuclear; **nu•cle•ar 'pow•er sta•tion** central *f* nuclear; **nu•cle•ar re'ac•tor** reactor *m* nuclear; **nu•cle•ar 'sci•en•tist** científico(-a) *m(f)* en energía nuclear; **nu•cle•ar 'sub•ma•rine** submarino *m* nuclear; **nu•cle•ar 'test** prueba *f* nuclear; **nu•cle•ar 'war(•fare)** guerra *f* nuclear; **nu•cle•ar 'war•head** cabeza *f* nuclear; **nu•cle•ar 'waste** residuos *mpl* nucleares; **nu•cle•ar 'weap•on** arma *f* nuclear; **nu•cle•ar 'win•ter** invierno *m* nuclear
nu•cle•us ['nuːklɪəs] (*pl* ***nuclei*** ['nuːklɪaɪ]) *also fig* núcleo *m*
nude [nuːd] **I** *adj* desnudo **II** *n* **1** *painting* desnudo *m* **2**: ***in the ~*** desnudo
nudge [nʌdʒ] *v/t* dar un toque con el codo a
nud•ism ['nuːdɪzəm] nudismo *m*
nud•ist ['nuːdɪst] nudista *m/f*; ***~ beach*** playa *f* nudista
nu•di•ty ['nuːdɪtɪ] desnudez *f*
nug•get ['nʌgət] *of gold etc* pepita *f*; ***these ~s of information*** estos datos valiosos
nui•sance ['nuːsns] incordio *m*, molestia *f*; ***make a ~ of o.s.*** dar la lata; ***what a ~!*** ¡qué incordio!; ***public ~*** LAW alteración *f* del orden público; ***cause a public ~*** LAW alterar el orden público

nuke [nuːk] *v/t* F atacar con armas nucleares
null and 'void [nʌl] *adj* nulo y sin efecto
nul•li•fy ['nʌlɪfaɪ] *v/t esp* LAW anular
numb [nʌm] *adj* entumecido; *emotionally* insensible; ***go ~ physically*** entumecerse; *emotionally* paralizarse
num•ber ['nʌmbər] **I** *n* número *m*; ***look after ~ one*** F cuidar de uno mismo; ***it's not a ~s game*** F no es una lotería; ***five in ~*** cinco; ***a ~ of times*** unas cuantas veces; ***a ~ of people*** un cierto número de personas; ***in large ~s*** en grandes cantidades; ***there are quite a ~ of things wrong*** hay bastantes cosas que estan mal *or* que son erróneas; ***I still have a fair ~ of questions*** todavía tengo un buen número de preguntas *or* bastantes preguntas; ***I've tried any ~ of different methods*** he intentado varios métodos diferentes
II *v/t* **1** (*put a ~ on*) numerar **2**: ***his days are ~ed*** tiene los días contados; ***~ s.o. among one's friends*** contar a alguien entre los amigos de uno
num•ber•ing ['nʌmbərɪŋ] numeración *f*
'num•ber•ing sys•tem sistema *m* de numeración
'num•ber•plate MOT *Br* placa *f* de la matrícula
numb•ness ['nʌmnɪs] entumecimiento *m*; *emotional* parálisis *f inv*
numb•skull ['nʌmskʌl] F percebe *m/f*
nu•mer•a•cy ['nuːmərəsɪ] conocimientos *m* de aritmética
nu•mer•al ['nuːmərəl] número *m*
nu•mer•ate ['nuːmərət] *adj* que sabe sumar y restar
nu•mer•i•cal [nuː'merɪkl] *adj system, superiority* numérico
nu•mer•ic key•pad [njuː'merɪk] teclado *m* numérico
nu•mer•ous ['nuːmərəs] *adj* numeroso; ***on ~ occasions*** en numerosas ocasiones
nun [nʌn] monja *f*
nup•tial ['nʌpʃl] *adj* nupcial
nurse [nɜːrs] **I** *n* enfermero(-a) *m(f)* **II** *v/t* **1** *baby* amamantar **2** *patient* cuidar; ***~ s.o. back to health*** cuidar a alguien hasta que se cura
nur•se•ry ['nɜːrsərɪ] **1** *for children* guardería *f* **2** *for plants* vivero *m*
'nur•se•ry rhyme canción *f* infantil; **'nur•se•ry school** parvulario *m*, jardín *m* de infancia; **'nur•se•ry school teach•er** profesor(a) *m(f)* de parvulario
nurs•ing ['nɜːrsɪŋ] enfermería *f*
'nurs•ing bot•tle biberón *m*
'nurs•ing home *for old people* residencia *f*
nut [nʌt] **1** nuez *f*; ***~s*** F (*testicles*) pelotas *fpl* F **2** *for bolt* tuerca *f*
nut•crack•ers ['nʌtkrækərz] *npl* cascanueces *m inv*
nut•meg ['nʌtmeg] BOT nuez *f* moscada
nu•tri•ent ['nuːtrɪənt] nutriente *m*
nu•tri•tion [nuː'trɪʃn] nutrición *f*
nu•tri•tion•al [nuː'trɪʃnl] *adj* nutritivo; ***~ value*** valor *m* nutritivo
nu•tri•tion•ist [nuː'trɪʃnɪst] nutricionista *m/f*
nu•tri•tious [nuː'trɪʃəs] *adj* nutritivo
nuts [nʌts] *adj* F (*crazy*) chalado F, pirado F; ***be ~ about s.o.*** estar coladito por alguien F
'nut•shell: ***in a ~*** en una palabra
nut•ter ['nʌtər] *Br* F pirado(-a) *m(f)* F
nut•ty ['nʌtɪ] **1** *adj taste* a nuez **2** F (*crazy*) chalado F, pirado F
ny•lon ['naɪlɑːn] **I** *n* nylon *m* **II** *adj* de nylon
nymph [nɪmf] ninfa *f*
nym•pho•ma•ni•ac [nɪmfə'meɪnɪæk] ninfómana *f*

O

O

oaf [oʊf] zopenco *m*
oaf•ish ['oʊfɪʃ] *adj* bruto
oak [oʊk] *tree, wood* roble *m*
OAP [oʊeɪ'piː] *abbr Br* (= ***old age pensioner***) pensionista *m/f*, jubilado(-a) *m(f)*
oar [ɔːr] remo *m*; ***put*** *or* ***stick one's ~s in*** F meter las narices
oars•man ['ɔːrzmən] remero *m*
o•a•sis [oʊ'eɪsɪs] (*pl* ***oases*** [oʊ'eɪsiːz])

also fig oasis *m inv*
oath [ouθ] LAW, (*swearword*) juramento *m*; ***on ~*** bajo juramento; ***~ of office*** juramento de toma de posesión; ***swear*** *or* ***take an ~*** jurar (***to*** a, ante)
'oat•meal harina *f* de avena
oats [outs] *npl* copos *mpl* de avena
ob•du•ra•cy ['ɑːbdərəsɪ] obstinación *f*
ob•du•rate ['ɑːbdərət] *adj* obstinado
o•be•di•ence [ou'biːdɪəns] obediencia *f*
o•be•di•ent [ou'biːdɪənt] *adj* obediente
o•be•di•ent•ly [ou'biːdɪəntlɪ] *adv* obedientemente
ob•e•lisk ['ɑːbəlɪsk] obelisco *m*
o•bese [ou'biːs] *adj* obeso
o•bes•i•ty [ou'biːsɪtɪ] obesidad *f*
o•bey [ou'beɪ] *v/t* obedecer
o•bit•u•a•ry [ə'bɪtuerɪ] necrología *f*, obituario *m*
ob•ject[1] ['ɑːbdʒɪkt] *n* **1** (*thing*) objeto *m* **2** (*aim*) objetivo *m* **3** GRAM objeto *m* **4**: ***money is no ~*** el dinero no es ningún inconveniente
ob•ject[2] [əb'dʒekt] *v/i* oponerse
◆ **object to** *v/t* oponerse a
ob•jec•tion [əb'dʒekʃn] objeción *f*; ***if you have no ~s*** si no tienes ninguna objeción; ***I have no ~ to him*** no tengo nada que objetar con respecto a él
ob•jec•tion•a•ble [əb'dʒekʃnəbl] *adj* (*unpleasant*) desagradable
ob•jec•tive [əb'dʒektɪv] **I** *adj* objetivo **II** *n* objetivo *m*
ob•jec•tive•ly [əb'dʒektɪvlɪ] *adv* objetivamente
ob•jec•tiv•i•ty [əbdʒek'tɪvətɪ] objetividad *f*
ob•jec•tor [əb'dʒektər] objetor(a) *m*(*f*), opositor(a) *m*(*f*)
ob•li•gate ['ɑːblɪgeɪt] *v/t*: ***feel ~d to do sth*** sentirse obligado a hacer algo
ob•li•ga•tion [ɑːblɪ'geɪʃn] obligación *f*; ***be under an ~ to s.o.*** tener una obligación para con alguien; ***be under an ~ to do sth*** estar obligado a hacer algo; ***meet one's ~s*** hacer frente a sus obligaciones; ***with no ~ to buy*** sin obligación de compra; ***without ~*** sin obligación
ob•lig•a•to•ry [ə'blɪgətɔːrɪ] *adj* obligatorio
o•blige [ə'blaɪdʒ] *v/t* obligar; ***much ~d!*** muy agradecido; ***be ~d to do sth*** estar obligado a hacer algo; ***feel ~d to do sth*** sentirse obligado a hacer algo
o•blig•ing [ə'blaɪdʒɪŋ] *adj* atento, servicial
o•blig•ing•ly [ə'blaɪdʒɪŋlɪ] *adv* amablemente
o•blique [ə'bliːk] **I** *adj reference* indirecto **II** *n in punctuation* barra *f* inclinada
ob•lit•er•ate [ə'blɪtəreɪt] *v/t city* destruir, arrasar; *memory* borrar
ob•lit•er•a•tion [əblɪtər'eɪʃn] eliminación *f*
o•bliv•i•on [ə'blɪvɪən] olvido *m*; ***fall into ~*** caer en el olvido
o•bliv•i•ous [ə'blɪvɪəs] *adj*: ***be ~ of sth*** no ser consciente de algo
ob•long ['ɑːblɒːŋ] *adj* rectangular
ob•nox•ious [əb'nɑːkʃəs] *adj person* detestable, odioso; *smell* repugnante
o•boe ['oubou] MUS oboe m
o•bo•ist ['oubouɪst] oboe *m*/*f*
ob•scene [ɑːb'siːn] *adj* obsceno; *salary, poverty* escandaloso
ob•scen•i•ty [əb'senətɪ] obscenidad *f*
ob•scure [əb'skjʊr] **I** *adj* oscuro; ***for some ~ reason*** por alguna razón incomprensible **II** *v/t intentions* ocultar; *view* oscurecer; ***~ the issue*** complicar las cosas
ob•scu•ri•ty [əb'skjʊrətɪ] oscuridad *f*
ob•se•qui•ous [əb'siːkwɪəs] *adj* servil
ob•se•qui•ous•ness [əb'siːkwɪəsnɪs] servilismo *m*
ob•ser•va•ble [əb'zɜːrvəbl] *adj* apreciable
ob•ser•vance [əb'zɜːrvns] *of festival* práctica *f*
ob•ser•vant [əb'zɜːrvnt] *adj* observador
ob•ser•va•tion [ɑːbzə'veɪʃn] **1** *of nature, stars* observación *f*; ***keep s.o. under ~*** tener a alguien bajo *or* en observación **2** (*comment*) observación *f*, comentario *m*
ob•ser•va•to•ry [əb'zɜːrvətɔːrɪ] observatorio *m*
ob•serve [əb'zɜːrv] *v/t* observar
ob•serv•er [əb'zɜːrvər] observador(a) *m*(*f*)
ob•sess [ɑːb'ses] **I** *v/t* obsesionar; ***be ~ed by / with*** estar obsesionado con / por **II** *v/i*: ***~ about sth*** obsesionarse con algo
ob•ses•sion [ɑːb'seʃn] obsesión *f*
ob•ses•sive [ɑːb'sesɪv] *adj* obsesivo

ob•so•les•cence [ɑːbsəˈlesəns] obsolescencia *f*

ob•so•les•cent [ɑːbsəˈlesnt] *adj*: ***be ~*** quedarse obsoleto

ob•so•lete [ˈɑːbsəliːt] *adj* obsoleto

ob•sta•cle [ˈɑːbstəkl] obstáculo *m*; ***be an ~ to sth*** ser un obstáculo para algo; ***put ~s in s.o.'s way*** poner obstáculos en el camino de alguien

'ob•sta•cle course carrera *f* de obstáculos

ob•ste•tri•cian [ɑːbstəˈtrɪʃn] obstetra *m/f*, tocólogo(-a) *m(f)*

ob•stet•rics [ɑːbˈstetrɪks] *nsg* obstetricia *f*, tocología *f*

ob•sti•na•cy [ˈɑːbstɪnəsɪ] obstinación *f*

ob•sti•nate [ˈɑːbstɪnət] *adj* obstinado

ob•sti•nate•ly [ˈɑːbstɪnətlɪ] *adv* obstinadamente

ob•strep•er•ous [əbˈstrepərəs] *adj* alborotado

ob•struct [ɑːbˈstrʌkt] *v/t road* obstruir; *investigation, police* obstaculizar

ob•struc•tion [əbˈstrʌkʃn] *on road etc* obstrucción *f*; ***you're causing an ~, please move your car*** mueva su coche por favor, está obstruyendo el paso

ob•struc•tion•ism [əbˈstrʌkʃənɪzəm] POL obstruccionismo *m*

ob•struc•tive [əbˈstrʌktɪv] *adj behavior, tactics* obstruccionista

ob•tain [əbˈteɪn] **I** *v/t* obtener, lograr **II** *v/i fml*: *of conditions, circumstances, rules* prevalecer

ob•tain•a•ble [əbˈteɪnəbl] *adj products* disponible

ob•tru•sive [əbˈtruːsɪv] *adj* molesto; ***the plastic chairs are rather ~*** las sillas de plástico desentonan por completo

ob•tuse [əbˈtuːs] *adj fig* duro de mollera

ob•vi•ate [ˈɑːbvɪeɪt] *v/t fml* evitar; ***~ the need for*** evitar la necesidad de

ob•vi•ous [ˈɑːbvɪəs] *adj* obvio, evidente; *lacking subtlety* poco sutil; ***that's stating the ~*** eso es decir lo evidente; ***it was the ~ thing to do*** era evidente que era eso lo que había que hacer; ***he was the ~ choice for the job*** era el candidato más obvio; ***am I being too ~?*** ¿se me está notando demasiado?

ob•vi•ous•ly [ˈɑːbvɪəslɪ] *adv* obviamente; ***~!*** ¡por supuesto!

oc•ca•sion [əˈkeɪʒn] ocasión *f*; ***on this ~*** en esta ocasión; ***on the ~ of*** con ocasión de; ***rise to the ~*** estar a la altura de las circunstancias; ***have ~ to do sth*** *fml* tener la necesidad de hacer algo

oc•ca•sion•al [əˈkeɪʒənl] *adj* ocasional, esporádico; ***I like the ~ Scotch*** me gusta tomarme un whisky de vez en cuando

oc•ca•sion•al•ly [əˈkeɪʒnlɪ] *adv* ocasionalmente, de vez en cuando

oc•ci•den•tal [ɑːksɪˈdentl] *adj* occidental

oc•cult [əˈkʌlt] **I** *adj* oculto **II** *n*: ***the ~*** lo oculto

oc•cu•pant [ˈɑːkjʊpənt] ocupante *m/f*

oc•cu•pa•tion [ɑːkjʊˈpeɪʃn] ocupación *f*

oc•cu•pa•tion•al [ɑːkjʊˈpeɪʃənl] *adj* profesional

oc•cu•pa•tion•al dis'ease enfermedad *f* profesional; **oc•cu•pa•tion•al 'haz•ard** gaje *m* del oficio; **oc•cu•pa•tion•al health and 'safe•ty** salud *f* y seguridad laboral; **oc•cu•pa•tion•al 'ther•a•pist** terapeuta *m/f* ocupacional; **oc•cu•pa•tion•al 'ther•a•py** terapia *f* ocupacional

oc•cu•pi•er [ˈɑːkjʊpaɪər] ☞ ***occupant***

oc•cu•py [ˈɑːkjʊpaɪ] *v/t* (*pret & pp* **-ied**) ocupar; ***the building is no longer occupied*** el edificio está deshabitado *or* abandonado; ***keep the kids occupied*** mantener ocupados a los niños

oc•cur [əˈkɜːr] *v/i* (*pret & pp* **-red**) ocurrir, suceder; ***it ~red to me that …*** se me ocurrió que …

oc•cur•rence [əˈkʌrəns] acontecimiento *m*; ***be an everyday ~*** ser cosa de todos los días

o•cean [ˈoʊʃn] océano *m*; ***~s of*** F montones de F

o•cean 'floor fondo *m* oceánico; **'o•cean•go•ing** *adj* transatlántico; **o•cean 'lin•er** transatlántico *m*

o•ce•an•og•ra•phy [oʊʃnˈɑːgrəfɪ] oceanografía *f*

o•cher, *Br* **o•chre** [ˈoʊkər] **I** *n* MIN ocre *m* **II** *adj* ocre

o'clock [əˈklɑːk]: ***at five / six ~*** a las cinco / seis

OCR [oʊsiːˈɑːr] (= ***optical character recognition***) OCR *m*

oc•ta•gon [ˈɑːktəgən] octógono *m*

oc•tag•o•nal [ɑːkˈtægənl] *adj* octagonal

oc•tane ['ɑːkteɪn] CHEM octano *m*; **~ number** *or* **rating** octanaje *m*
oc•tave ['ɑːktɪv] MUS octava *f*
Oc•to•ber [ɑːk'toʊbər] octubre *m*
oc•to•ge•nar•i•an [ɑːktoʊdʒə'nerɪən] octogenario(-a) *m(f)*
oc•to•pus ['ɑːktəpəs] pulpo *m*
oc•u•lar ['ɑːkjʊlər] *adj* ocular
oc•u•list ['ɑːkjʊlɪst] oculista *m/f*
OD [oʊ'diː] (= **overdose**) **I** *v/i* F: **~ on** *drug* tomar una sobredosis de **II** *n* sobredosis *f inv*
odd [ɑːd] *adj* **1** (*strange*) raro, extraño **2** (*not even*) impar; **the ~ one out** el bicho raro; **50 ~** cerca de 50
'odd•ball F bicho *m* raro F
odd•i•ty ['ɑːdɪtɪ] *thing* rareza *f*, *person* bicho *m* raro
odd-'job man manitas *m inv*
odd•ly ['ɑːdlɪ] *adv* extrañamente; **~ enough** aunque parezca raro
odds [ɑːdz] *npl*: **be at ~ with sth** no concordar con algo; **be at ~ with s.o.** estar peleado con alguien; **the ~ are 10 to one** las apuestas están en 10 a 1; **the ~ are that ...** lo más probable es que ...; **against all the ~** contra lo que se esperaba; **the ~ are in our favor / against us** tenemos todo a favor / en contra
odds and 'ends *npl objects* cacharros *mpl*; *things to do* cosillas *fpl*
'odds-on *adj favorite* indiscutible; **it's ~ that he'll come** es bastante seguro que venga
o•di•ous ['oʊdɪəs] *adj* odioso
o•dom•e•ter [oʊ'dɑːmətər] cuentakilómetros *m inv*
o•dor, *Br* **o•dour** ['oʊdər] olor *m*
od•ys•sey ['ɑːdɪsɪ] odisea *f*
Oed•i•pus com•plex ['iːdɪpəs] PSYCH complejo *m* de Edipo
OEM [oʊiː'em] *abbr* (= **own equipment manufacturer**) COMPUT fabricante *m* de su proprio equipo
oe•soph•a•gus ☞ **esophagus**
oes•tro•gen ☞ **estrogen**
of [ɑːv] *unstressed* [əv] *prep* de; **the name ~ the street / the hotel** el nombre de la calle / del hotel; **the color ~ the car** el color del coche; **five / ten (minutes) ~ twelve** las doce menos cinco / diez, *L.Am.* cinco / diez para las doce; **die ~ cancer** morir de cáncer; **love ~ money / adventure** amor por el dinero / la aventura; **~ the three this is ...** de los tres éste es ...
off [ɑːf] **I** *prep*: **~ the main road** (*away from*) apartado de la carretera principal; (*leading off*) saliendo de la carretera principal; **$20 ~ the price** una rebaja en el precio de 20 dólares; **he's ~ his food** no come nada, está desganado
II *adv*: **be ~** *of light, TV, machine* estar apagado; *of brake, lid, top* no estar puesto; *not at work* faltar; *on vacation* estar de vacaciones; (*canceled*) estar cancelado; **we're ~ tomorrow** (*leaving*) nos vamos mañana; **I'm ~ to New York** me voy a Nueva York; **with his pants / hat ~** sin los pantalones / el sombrero; **take a day ~** tomarse un día de fiesta *or* un día libre; **it's 3 miles ~** está a tres millas de distancia; **it's a long way ~** *in distance* está muy lejos; *in future* todavía queda mucho tiempo; **he got into his car and drove ~** se subió al coche y se marchó; **~ and on** de vez en cuando
III *adj*: **the ~ switch** el interruptor de apagado
'off•beat *adj* F original
off-'cen•ter, *Br* **off-'cen•tre** *adj* descentrado; *definition* descabellado
off-'col•o(u)r *adj* **1** *unwell* indispuesto **2** *comments, joke* fuera de tono
of•fence *Br* ☞ **offense**
of•fend [ə'fend] *v/t* (*insult*) ofender; *sense of justice etc* delinquir
of•fend•er [ə'fendər] LAW delincuente *m/f*
of•fend•ing [ə'fendɪŋ] *adj* (*causing the problem*) problemático
of•fense [ə'fens] **1** LAW delito *m* **2**: **take ~ at sth** ofenderse por algo; **give** *or* **cause ~** ofender (**to** a); **be quick to take ~** ofenderse fácilmente; **no ~ (meant** *or* **intended)** no quería ofender **3** SP ataque *m*; **~ is the best defense** el ataque es la mejor defensa; **~ foul** falta *f* en ataque
of•fen•sive [ə'fensɪv] **I** *adj behavior, remark, also* SP ofensivo; *smell* repugnante; **there's no need to get ~** no hace falta ofender; **find sth ~** encontrar algo ofensivo; **~ weapon** arma *f* ofensiva **II** *n* (*attack*) ofensiva *f*, **go on(to) the ~** pa-

O

sar a la ofensiva
of•fer ['ɑːfər] **I** *n* oferta *f*; ***make s.o. an ~ of sth*** ofrecer algo a alguien; ***on ~*** de oferta; ***a contract extension was not on ~ for them*** no podían aspirar a una extensión del contrato; ***$100 or nearest ~*** 100 dólares negociables; ***our house is under ~*** nos han hecho una oferta
II *v/t* ofrecer; ***~ s.o. sth*** ofrecer algo a alguien; ***he ~ed to help*** se ofreció a ayudar
III *v/i*: ***if the opportunity ~s*** si surge la oportunidad; ***you need more people to lift that – are you ~ing?*** hace falta más gente para levantar eso – ¿te estás ofreciendo para ayudar?
off'hand *adj*: ***... he replied in an ~ way*** ... respondió mostrando falta de interés
of•fice ['ɑːfɪs] **1** *building* oficina *f* **2** *room* oficina *f*, despacho *m* **3** *position* cargo *m*
of•fice au•to•ma•tion ofimática *f*; **'of•fice block** bloque *m* de oficinas; **'of•fice boy** chico *m* de los recados; **'of•fice girl** chica *f* de los recados; **'of•fice-hold•er** alto cargo *m*; **'of•fice hours** *npl* horas *fpl* de oficina; **'of•fice job** trabajo *m* de oficina *or* despacho; **of•fice 'jun•ior** *Br* auxiliar *m/f* de oficina
of•fi•cer ['ɑːfɪsər] MIL oficial *m/f*; *in police* agente *m/f*; ***excuse me, ~*** perdone, (señor) agente
'of•fice sup•plies *npl* material *m* de oficina
'of•fice work•er oficinista *m/f*
of•fi•cial [ə'fɪʃl] **I** *adj* oficial **II** *n* **1** *civil servant* funcionario(-a) *m(f)* **2** *at sports event* organizador(a) *m(f)*; *referee, umpire* juez *m*, árbitro *m*
of•fi•cial•dom [ə'fɪʃldəm] la administración
of•fi•cial•ese [əfɪʃə'liːz] jerga *f* administrativa
of•fi•cial•ly [ə'fɪʃlɪ] *adv* oficialmente
of•fi•ci•ate [ə'fɪʃɪeɪt] *v/i*: ***with X officiating*** con X celebrando la ceremonia
of•fi•cious [ə'fɪʃəs] *adj* entrometido
off•ing ['ɑːfɪŋ]: ***be in the ~*** ser inminente
'off-li•cence *Br* tienda *f* de bebidas alcohólicas
off-'line *adv work* fuera de línea; ***be ~*** *of printer etc* estar desconectado; ***go ~*** desconectarse
off-'peak *adj rates* en horas valle, fuera de las horas punta; ***~ ticket*** billete *m* en hora valle
off-put•ting ['ɑːfpʌtɪŋ] *adj Br* F desagradable
'off•ramp *from highway* carril *m or* vía *f* de salida
off-road 've•hi•cle MOT vehículo *m* todoterreno
'off-sea•son I *adj rates, vacation* de temporada baja **II** *n* temporada *f* baja
'off•set *v/t* (*pret & pp* ***-set***) *losses, disadvantage* compensar
'off•shoot *fig* filial *f*
'off•shore I *adj drilling rig* cercano a la costa; *investment* en el exterior **II** *adv* cerca de la costa
'off•side I *adj* **1** *wheel etc* del lado del conductor **2** SP: ***be ~*** estar fuera de juego; ***~ trap*** trampa *f* del fuera de juego **II** *adv* SP fuera de juego
'off•spring *of person* vástagos *mpl*, hijos *mpl*; *of animal* crías *fpl*
off-street 'park•ing aparcamiento *m* fuera de las calles
off-the-'cuff *adj* espontáneo
off-the-'rec•ord *adj* confidencial
off-the-'wall *adj* F *sense of humor* estrafalario
'off-white *adj* blancuzco
of•ten ['ɑːfn] *adv* a menudo, frecuentemente; ***how ~ did it happen?*** ¿cada cuánto ocurría?; ***no, not so ~*** no, con tanta frecuencia no; ***it's not ~ you get a chance like this*** no se encuentran oportunidades así muy a menudo; ***he annoyed her once too ~*** la enfadó demasiadas veces; ***more ~ than not they would disagree*** muchas veces no estaban de acuerdo; ***sometimes as ~ as three times a day*** a veces hasta tres veces al día; ***as ~ as not*** la mitad de las veces
o•gle ['oʊgl] *v/t* comerse con los ojos
o•gre ['oʊgr] ogro *m*
oh [oʊ] *int* ¡oh!
oil [ɔɪl] **I** *n* **1** *for machine, food, skin* aceite *m*; ***painted in ~s*** al óleo **2** *petroleum* petróleo *m*; ***strike ~*** descubrir petróleo **II** *v/t hinges, bearings* engrasar; ***~ the wheels*** *fig* allanar el terreno

'oil can lata *f* de aceite; **'oil change** cambio *m* del aceite; **'oil com•pa•ny** compañía *f* petrolera; **'oil cri•sis** crisis *f inv* del petróleo; **'oil•field** yacimiento *m* petrolífero; **'oil-fired** *adj central heating* de gasóleo *or* fuel; **'oil lamp** lámpara *f* de aceite; **'oil lev•el** MOT nivel *m* del aceite; **'oil paint** pintura *f* al óleo; **'oil paint•ing** óleo *m*; **'oil pipe•line** oleoducto *m*; **oil-pro•duc•ing coun•try** [ɔılprəduːsıŋ'kʌntrı] país *m* productor de petróleo; **'oil re•fin•e•ry** refinería *f* de petróleo; **'oil rig** plataforma *f* petrolífera; **oil•seed 'rape** colza *f*; **'oil sheik(h)** jeque *m* del petróleo; **'oil-skins** *npl* ropa *f* impermeable; **'oil slick** marea *f* negra; **'oil sump** cárter *m* de aceite; **'oil tank•er** petrolero *m*; **'oil well** pozo *m* petrolífero

oil•y ['ɔılı] *adj* grasiento

oint•ment ['ɔıntmənt] ungüento *m*, pomada *f*

ok [oʊ'keı] **I** *adj & adv* F: ***can I? – ~*** ¿puedo? - de acuerdo *or Span* vale; ***is it ~ with you if …?*** ¿te parece bien si …?; ***that's ~ by me*** por mí, ningún problema; ***are you ~?*** (*well, not hurt*) ¿estás bien?; ***are you ~ for Friday?*** ¿te va bien el viernes?; ***he's ~*** (*is a good guy*) es buena persona; ***does that look ~?*** ¿queda bien?; ***is this bus ~ for …?*** ¿este autobús va a …?; ***I can afford it ~, I'm just not interested*** no es que no me lo pueda permitir, es que no me interesa; ***he'll come back ~, don't worry*** volverá bien, no te preocupes; ***~, ~, don't get angry!*** ¡vale, vale, no te enfades!; ***~, it was a difficult task but …*** sí, fue difícil, pero…; ***~, it's not the best ever, but still …*** de acuerdo *or* es cierto que no es lo mejor pero todavía …

II *n* aprobación *f*

old [oʊld] **I** *adj* **1** viejo; ***an ~ man / woman*** un anciano / una anciana, un viejo / una vieja; ***how ~ are you / is he?*** ¿cuántos años tienes / tiene?; ***he's getting ~*** está haciéndose mayor **2** (*previous*) anterior, antiguo; ***in the ~ days*** antiguamente **3**: ***any ~ disk*** cualquier disquete; ***he is not just any ~ designer*** no es un diseñador cualquiera **II** *npl*: ***the ~*** los ancianos

old 'age vejez *f*; ***in one's ~*** en la vejez; ***die of or from ~*** morirse de viejo

old-age 'pen•sion *Br* pensión *f* de jubilación; **old-age 'pen•sion•er** *Br* pensionista *m/f*, jubilado(-a) *m(f)*; **old--'fash•ioned** *adj clothes, style, ideas* anticuado, pasado de moda; *word* anticuado; **old 'flame** viejo amor *m*; **old 'guard** vieja guardia *f*; **old 'hand** experto(-a) *m(f)*

old•ie ['oʊldı] *person* viejo(-a) *m(f)*; *joke* chiste *m* viejo; *song* canción *f* antigua

old 'maid vieja *f* solterona; **old 'mas•ter** *painter* clasico *m*; **Old 'Test•a•ment** Antiguo Testamento *m*; **old 'wives' tale** cuento *m* de viejas

ol•fac•to•ry [ɑːl'fæktɔːrı] *adj* olfativo

ol•i•gar•chy ['ɑːlıgɑːrkı] oligarquía *f*

ol•ive ['ɑːlıv] aceituna *f*, oliva *f*; ***hold out an ~ branch*** *fig* hacer un gesto de paz

'ol•ive oil aceite *m* de oliva

O•lym•pi•ad [ə'lımpıæd] Olimpiada *f*

O•lym•pic [ə'lımpık] *adj* olímpico; ***~ champion*** campeón(-ona) *m(f)* olímpico(-a)

O•lym•pic 'Games *npl* Juegos *mpl* Olímpicos

O•lym•pics [ə'lımpıks] *npl* Juegos *mpl* Olímpicos

OMB [oʊem'biː] *abbr* (= ***Office of Management and Budget***) Ministerio *m* de Economía

om•buds•man ['ɑːmbʊdzmən] POL defensor *m* del pueblo

om•e•let, *Br* **om•e•lette** ['ɑːmlıt] tortilla *f* (francesa)

om•i•nous ['ɑːmınəs] *adj* siniestro

om•i•nous•ly ['ɑːmınəslı] *adv* siniestramente

o•mis•sion [oʊ'mıʃn] omisión *f*

o•mit [ə'mıt] *v/t* (*pret & pp* **-*ted***) omitir; ***~ to do sth*** no hacer algo

om•nip•o•tence [ɑːm'nıpətəns] omnipotencia *f*

om•nip•o•tent [ɑːm'nıpətənt] *adj* omnipotente

om•nis•ci•ence [ɑːm'nısıəns] omnisciencia *f*

om•nis•ci•ent [ɑːm'nısıənt] *adj* omnisciente

on [ɑːn] **I** *prep* en; ***~ the table / wall*** en la mesa / la pared; ***~ the bus / train*** en el autobús / el tren; ***~ TV / the radio*** en la televisión / la radio; ***~ Sunday*** el domingo; **~ the 1st of ...** el uno de ...; **this is ~ me** (*I'm paying*) invito yo; **have you any money ~ you?** ¿llevas dinero encima?; **what's he ~!** ¿se ha metido algo? F; **~ his arrival / departure** cuando llegue / se marche; **~ hearing this** al escuchar esto

II *adv*: **be ~** *of light, TV, computer etc* estar encendido *or L.Am.* prendido; *of brake, lid, top* estar puesto; *of meeting etc: be scheduled to happen* haber sido acordado; **it's ~ at 5am** *of TV program* lo dan *or Span* ponen a las cinco; **what's ~ tonight?** *on TV etc* ¿qué dan *or Span* ponen esta noche?; (*what's planned?*) ¿qué planes hay para esta noche?; **with his hat ~** con el sombrero puesto; **you're ~** (*I accept your offer etc*) trato hecho; **~ you go** (*go ahead*) adelante; **walk / talk ~** seguir caminando / hablando; **and so ~** etcétera; **~ and ~** *talk etc* sin parar

III *adj*: **the ~ switch** el interruptor de encendido

once [wʌns] **I** *adv* (*one time, formerly*) una vez; **~ again, ~ more** una vez más; **at ~** (*immediately*) de inmediato, inmediamente; **all at ~** (*suddenly*) de repente; **(all) at ~** (*together*) al mismo tiempo; **~ upon a time there was ...** érase una vez ...; **~ in a while** de vez en cuando; **~ and for all** de una vez por todas; **for ~** por una vez; **~ or twice** una o dos veces; **not ~** ni una sola vez; **this ~** por esta vez

II *conj* una vez que; **~ you have finished** una vez que hayas acabado

'once-o•ver: **give sth a ~** *look at, check* examinar algo de arriba a abajo; *clean* dar un repaso a algo

'on•com•ing *adj*: **~ traffic** tráfico que viene de frente

one [wʌn] **I** *n number* uno *m* **II** *adj* un(a); **~ day** un día; **he's ~ good runner** es un corredor fenómeno **III** *pron* uno(-a); **which ~?** ¿cuál?; **~ by ~** *enter, deal with* uno por uno; **we help ~ another** nos ayudamos mutuamente; **what can ~ say / do?** ¿qué puede uno decir / hacer?; **the little ~s** los pequeños; **I for ~** yo personalmente

one-and-'one *in basketball* uno más uno *m*

one-eyed [wʌn'aɪd] *adj* tuerto; **one-horse 'town** F ciudad *f* de mala muerte; **one-leg•ged** [wʌn'legɪd] *adj* cojo; **one-man 'band** hombre *m* orquesta; *fig: business* empresa *f* de una sola persona; **one-man 'show** espectáculo *m* en solitario

one•ness ['wʌnnɪs] (*concord, union*) unidad *f*

one-night 'stand 1 THEA representación *f* única **2** F *sexual relationship* relación *f* de una noche; **one-'off 1** (*unique event, person*) hecho *m* aislado **2** (*exception*) excepción *f*; **one-on-'one I** *adj* de uno a uno **II** *n in basketball* uno contra uno *m*; **one-par•ent 'fam•i•ly** familia *f* monoparental

on•er•ous ['ɑːnərəs] *adj* oneroso (**to** para)

one'self *pron* uno(-a) mismo(-a) *m(f)*; **do sth by ~** hacer algo sin ayuda; **look after ~** cuidarse; **be by ~** estar solo

one-sid•ed [wʌn'saɪdɪd] *adj discussion, fight* desigual; **'one•time** *adj* antiguo; **one-to-'one** *adj correspondence* de uno a uno; **one-track 'mind** *hum*: **have a ~** ser un obseso; **one-'two** *in soccer* pared *f*; **'one-way street** calle *f* de sentido único; **'one-way tick•et** billete *m* de ida

'on•go•ing *adj* en curso

on•ion ['ʌnjən] cebolla *f*

'on-line *adv* en línea; **go ~ to** conectarse a

'on-line serv•ice COMPUT servicio *m* en línea

'on•look•er espectador(a) *m(f)*, curioso(-a) *m(f)*

on•ly ['oʊnlɪ] **I** *adv* sólo, solamente; **he was here ~ yesterday** estuvo aquí ayer mismo; **not ~ ... but also ...** no sólo *or* solamente ... sino también ...; **~ just** por poco; **I've ~ just arrived** acabo de llegar ahora mismo; **it ~ just fitted** entró justísimo **II** *adj* único; **~ son** hijo *m* único

o.n.o. *abbr* (= **or nearest offer**): **$50 ~** 50 dólares negociables

'on-ramp *to highway* carril *m* de aceleración

'on-screen *adj instructions etc* en pantalla

'on•set comienzo *m*

'on•shore *adj* en tierra firme

'on•side *adv* SP en posición reglamentaria

on•slaught ['ɑːnslɔːt] acometida *f*

on-the-job 'train•ing formación *f* continua

on•to ['ɑːntuː] *prep* **1**: ***put sth ~ sth*** *on top of* poner algo encima de algo **2**: ***the police are ~ him*** la policía le sigue la pista; ***the tenants have been ~ him about getting the pipe fixed*** los inquilinos han estado persiguiéndole para que les arregle la tubería; ***how did we get ~ that subject?*** ¿cómo hemos llegado a este tema?; ***they are already ~ the next chapter*** ya van por el capítulo siguiente

o•nus ['oʊnəs]: ***the ~ is on you to prove it*** te incumbe a ti probarlo

on•ward ['ɑːnwərd] *adv* hacia adelante; ***from ... ~*** de ... en adelante

oo•dles ['uːdlz] *npl* F montonadas *fpl* (***of*** de)

oomph [ʊmf] F (*dynamism*) garra *f*

ooze [uːz] **I** *v/i of liquid*, *mud* rezumar **II** *v/t* rezumar; ***he ~s charm*** rezuma *or* rebosa encanto

◆ **ooze out** *v/i of liquid* rezumar

o•pal ['oʊpəl] ópalo *m*

o•paque [oʊ'peɪk] *adj glass* opaco; *fig*: *style*, *prose* oscuro

OPEC ['oʊpek] *abbr* (= ***Organization of Petroleum Exporting Countries***) OPEP *f* (= Organización *f* de Países Exportadores de Petróleo)

O

o•pen ['oʊpən] **I** *adj* abierto; (*honest*) abierto, franco; ***in the ~ air*** al aire libre; ***hold the door ~ for s.o.*** abrir la puerta a alguien; ***keep one's eyes ~*** *fig* mantener los ojos abiertos; ***keep an ~ mind about sth*** no tener prejuicios con respecto a algo; ***~ to the public*** abierto al público; ***we're ~ to suggestions*** estamos abiertos a sugerencias; ***on the ~ market*** en el mercado libre; ***~ to question*** cuestionable; ***that is ~ to argument*** eso es discutible

II *v/t* abrir

III *v/i of door*, *shop* abrir; *of flower* abrirse; ***we ~ at the City Lights on Monday*** THEA estrenamos la obra en el City Lights el lunes

IV *n* **1** *in golf*, *tennis* open *m*, abierto *m* **2**: ***in the ~*** (*in the ~ air*) al aire libre; ***bring sth into the ~*** *fig* sacar algo a la luz; ***come out into the ~ about sth*** *fig* revelar algo, hacer público algo

◆ **open out I** *v/t map etc* desplegar **II** *v/i of countryside* abrirse

◆ **open up** *v/i of person*, *market* abrirse; *of artillery* abrir fuego; *of new business*, *storekeeper* abrir

o•pen-'air *adj meeting*, *concert* al aire libre; *pool* descubierto; **o•pen'cast** *adj* a cielo abierto; **'o•pen day** *Br* jornada *f* de puertas abiertas; **o•pen-'end•ed** *adj contract etc* abierto

o•pen•er ['oʊpnər] **1** *for cans* abrelatas *m inv* **2** (*opening number*) primer número *m*

o•pen-eyed [oʊpən'aɪd] *adj* con los ojos abiertos; ***look at s.o. in ~ amazement*** mirar a alguien con los ojos abiertos de asombro; **o•pen•hand•ed** [oʊpən'hændɪd] *adj* generoso; **o•pen-heart 'sur•ger•y** cirugía *f* a corazón abierto; **o•pen 'house 1** jornada *f* de puertas abiertas **2**: ***it's ~ here*** aquí la puerta está abierta a todo el mundo

o•pen•ing ['oʊpənɪŋ] **1** *in wall etc* abertura *f* **2** (*beginning*: *of film*, *novel etc*) comienzo *m* **3** (*job*) puesto *m* vacante

'o•pen•ing hours *npl* horario *m* de apertura

o•pen 'let•ter carta *f* abierta

o•pen•ly ['oʊpənlɪ] *adv* (*honestly*, *frankly*) abiertamente

o•pen-'mind•ed *adj* de mentalidad abierta; **o•pen-mouthed** [oʊpən'maʊðd] *adj* boquiabierto; **o•pen-necked** [oʊpən'nekt] *adj shirt* desabrochada

o•pen•ness ['oʊpənnɪs] *of countryside*, *layout* lo abierto; *frankness* franqueza *f*; ***her ~ to new ideas*** lo abierta que es a nuevas ideas

o•pen 'plan of•fice oficina *f* de planta abierta; **'o•pen sea•son** temporada *f* de caza; **o•pen 'se•cret** secreto *m* a voces; **'o•pen tick•et** billete *m* abierto; **'o•pen tour•na•ment** (torneo *m*) abierto *m*; **O•pen U•ni'ver•si•ty** *Br universidad a distancia británica*

op•e•ra ['ɑːpərə] ópera *f*

op•er•a•ble ['ɑːpərəbl] *adj* MED operable

'op•e•ra glass•es *npl* gemelos *mpl*, prismáticos *mpl*; **'op•e•ra house** (teatro *m* de la) ópera *f*; **'op•e•ra sing•er** cantante *m/f* de ópera

op•er•ate ['ɑːpəreɪt] **I** *v/i of company* operar, actuar; *of airline*, *bus service*, MED operar; *of machine* funcionar (**on** con) **II** *v/t machine* manejar
◆ **operate on** *v/t* MED operar; ***they operated on his leg*** le operaron de la pierna
op•er•at•ic [ɑːpə'rætɪk] *adj* MUS operístico
op•er•at•ing costs ['ɑːpəreɪtɪŋ] *pl* costos *mpl or Span* costes *mpl* de explotación; **'op•er•at•ing in•struc•tions** *npl* instrucciones *fpl* de funcionamiento; **'op•er•at•ing mar•gin** margen *m* de explotación; **'op•er•at•ing prof•it** beneficio *m* de explotación; **'op•er•ating room** MED quirófano *m*; **'op•er•at•ing sys•tem** COMPUT sistema *m* operativo; **'op•er•at•ing ta•ble** mesa *f* de operaciones; **'op•er•at•ing the•a•tre** *Br* quirófano *m*
op•er•a•tion [ɑːpə'reɪʃn] MED operación *f*, *of machine* manejo *m*; ***~s** of company* operaciones *fpl*, actividades *fpl*; ***have an ~*** MED ser operado; ***I have to have an ~ on my hip*** me tienen que operar de la cadera
op•er•a•tion•al [ɑːpər'eɪʃənl] *adj*: ***be ~*** estar operativo
op•er•a•tive ['ɑːpərətɪv] *adj* vigente; ***become ~*** *esp* LAW entrar en vigor; ***the ~ word*** la palabra clave
op•er•a•tor ['ɑːpəreɪtər] TELEC operador(a) *m(f)*; *of machine* operario(-a) *m(f)*; (*tour ~*) operador *m* turístico; ***he's a clever*** *or* ***smooth ~*** F consigue lo que quiere
op•er•et•ta [ɑːpə'retə] MUS opereta *f*
oph•thal•mic [ɑːf'θælmɪk] *adj* oftálmico
oph•thal•mol•o•gist [ɑːfθæl'mɑːlədʒɪst] oftalmólogo(-a) *m(f)*
o•pin•ion [ə'pɪnjən] opinión *f*, ***in my ~*** en mi opinión; ***have a high / low ~ of s.o.*** tener buena / mala opinión de alguien, tener un mal / buen concepto de alguien
o•pin•ion•at•ed [ə'pɪnjəneɪtɪd] *adj* dogmático
o'pin•ion poll encuesta *f* de opinión
o'pin•ion poll•ster encuestador(a) *m(f)*
o•pi•um ['oʊpjəm] opio *m*
o•pos•sum [ə'pɑːsəm] ZO zarigüeya *f*
op•po•nent [ə'poʊnənt] oponente *m/f*, adversario(-a) *m(f)*
op•por•tune ['ɑːpərtuːn] *adj fml* oportuno
op•por•tun•ism [ɑːpər'tuːnɪzəm] oportunismo *m*
op•por•tun•ist [ɑːpər'tuːnɪst] oportunista *m/f*
op•por•tun•is•tic [ɑːpərtuːn'ɪstɪk] *adj* oportunista
op•por•tu•ni•ty [ɑːpər'tuːnətɪ] oportunidad *f*, ***take the ~ to do sth*** aprovechar la oportunidad para hacer algo
op•pose [ə'poʊz] *v/t* oponerse a; ***be ~d to*** estar en contra de; ***John, as ~d to George ...*** John, al contrario que George ...
op•pos•ing [ə'poʊzɪŋ] *adj team*, *views* contrario
op•po•site ['ɑːpəzɪt] **I** *adj* contrario; *views*, *characters*, *meaning* opuesto; ***the ~ side of town / end of the road*** el otro lado de la ciudad / extremo de la calle; ***the ~ sex*** el sexo opuesto **II** *n*: ***the ~ of*** lo contrario de; ***they are complete ~s*** son dos polos opuestos **III** *prep* enfrente de; ***they live ~ me*** viven enfrente mío **IV** *adv* enfrente
op•po•site 'num•ber homólogo(-a) *m(f)*
op•po•si•tion [ɑːpə'zɪʃn] *to plan*, POL oposición *f*
op•po'si•tion par•ty partido *m* de la oposición
op•press [ə'pres] *v/t the people* oprimir
op•pres•sion [ə'preʃn] opresión *f*
op•pres•sive [ə'presɪv] *adj* **1** *rule*, *dictator* opresor **2** *weather* agobiante
op•pres•sor [ə'presər] opresor(a) *m(f)*
opt [ɑːpt] *v/t*: ***~ to do sth*** optar por hacer algo
op•tic ['ɑːptɪk] *adj* óptico
op•ti•cal ['ɑːptɪkl] *adj* óptico
op•ti•cal 'char•ac•ter re•cog•ni•tion reconocimento *m* óptico de caracteres; **op•ti•cal 'fi•ber**, *Br* **op•ti•cal fi•bre** fibra *f* óptica; **op•ti•cal il'lu•sion** ilusión *f* óptica
op•tic 'fi•ber ca•ble cable *m* de fibra óptica
op•ti•cian [ɑːp'tɪʃn] óptico(-a) *m(f)*
op•tics ['ɑːptɪks] *nsg* óptica *f*
op•ti•mal ['ɑːptɪml] *adj* óptimo
op•ti•mism ['ɑːptɪmɪzm] optimismo *m*

op•ti•mist ['ɑːptɪmɪst] optimista *m/f*
op•ti•mist•ic [ɑːptɪ'mɪstɪk] *adj* optimista
op•ti•mist•ic•al•ly [ɑːptɪ'mɪstɪklɪ] *adv* con optimismo
op•ti•mize ['ɑːptɪmaɪz] *v/t* optimizar
op•ti•mum ['ɑːptɪməm] **I** *adj* óptimo **II** *n*: ***the ~*** lo ideal
op•tion ['ɑːpʃn] opción *f*; *at university* optativa *f*; ***keep one's ~s open*** tener abiertas varias opciones; ***I had no ~ but to …*** no tuve otra opción que…; ***~ to buy*** opción de compra
op•tion•al ['ɑːpʃnl] *adj* optativo
op•tion•al 'ex•tras *npl* accesorios *mpl* opcionales
op•tions mar•ket ['ɑːpʃnz] mercado *m* de opciones
op•u•lence ['ɑːpjʊləns] opulencia *f*
op•u•lent ['ɑːpjʊlənt] *adj* opulento
o•pus ['oʊpəs] *esp* MUS opus *m inv*
or [ɔːr] *conj* or; *before a word beginning with the letter o* u
or•a•cle ['ɑːrəkl] oráculo *m*
o•rac•u•lar [ə'rækjʊlər] *adj* del oráculo
o•ral ['ɔːrəl] **I** *adj exam, sex* oral; *hygiene* bucal **II** *n exam* examen *m* oral
o•ral•ly ['ɔːrəlɪ] *adv* **1** *examine student* oralmente **2** *take medicine* por vía oral
or•ange ['ɔːrɪndʒ] **I** *adj color* naranja **II** *n* **1** *fruit* naranja *f* **2** *color* naranja *m*
or•ange•ade ['ɔːrɪndʒeɪd] naranjada *f*
'or•ange juice *Span* zumo *m or L.Am.* jugo *m* de naranja
o•rang-u•tan [ɔːræŋuː'tæn] ZO orangután *m*
o•ra•tion [ɔː'reɪʃn] discurso *m*
or•a•tor ['ɔːrətər] orador(a) *m(f)*
or•a•tor•i•cal [ɔːrə'tɔːrɪkl] *adj* oratorio
or•a•to•ri•o [ɔːrə'tɔːrɪoʊ] MUS oratorio *m*
or•bit ['ɔːrbɪt] **I** *n of earth* órbita *f*; ***put sth into ~*** poner algo en órbita **II** *v/t the earth* girar alrededor de
or•chard ['ɔːrtʃərd] huerta *f* (de frutales)
or•ches•tra ['ɔːrkɪstrə] **1** MUS orquesta *f* **2** THEA platea *f*
or•ches•tral [ɔːr'kestrəl] *adj* orquestal
'or•ches•tra pit foso *m* de la orquesta
or•ches•trate ['ɔːrkɪstreɪt] *v/t* orquestar
or•chid ['ɔːrkɪd] orquídea *f*
or•dain [ɔːr'deɪn] *v/t* ordenar
or•deal [ɔːr'diːl] calvario *m*, experiencia *f* penosa

or•der ['ɔːrdər] **I** *n* **1** (*command*) orden *f*; ***by ~ of the city council*** por orden del ayuntamiento; ***be under ~s to do sth*** tener órdenes de hacer algo; ***take ~s*** aceptar órdenes; ***that's a tall ~*** va ser dificilísimo
2 (*sequence, being well arranged*) orden *m*; ***in ~ of importance*** en orden de importancia; ***in ~*** (*in the right ~*) en orden; ***out of ~*** (*not in sequence*) desordenado
3 *for goods* pedido *m*; ***take s.o.'s ~*** *in restaurant* preguntar a alguien lo que va a tomar; ***an ~ of French fries*** unas patatas fritas
4: ***out of ~*** (*not functioning*) estropeado; ***in good working ~*** en buen estado de funcionamiento
5: ***in ~ to*** para
6: ***on the ~ of*** (*approximately*) del orden de
7: ***is it in ~ for me to leave now?*** *permissible* ¿me podría ir ahora?
8 REL orden *f*
II *v/t* **1** (*put in sequence, proper layout*) ordenar **2** *goods* pedir, encargar; *meal* pedir **3**: ***~ s.o. to do sth*** ordenar a alguien hacer algo *or* que haga algo
III *v/i in restaurant* pedir
◆ **order around** *v/t* dar órdenes continuamente a
'or•der book libro *m* de pedidos; ***the ~s are full*** el libro de pedidos está lleno
'or•der form hoja *f* de pedido
or•der•ly ['ɔːrdəlɪ] **I** *adj lifestyle* ordenado, metódico **II** *n in hospital* celador(a) *m(f)*
or•di•nal num•ber ['ɔːrdɪnl] (número *m*) ordinal *m*
or•di•nar•i•ly [ɔːrdɪ'nerɪlɪ] *adv* (*as a rule*) normalmente
or•di•nar•y ['ɔːrdɪnerɪ] **1** *adj* común, normal **II** *n*: ***out of the ~*** extraordinario; ***nothing out of the ~*** nada extraordinario
ore [ɔːr] mineral *m*, mena *f*
or•gan ['ɔːrgən] ANAT, MUS órgano *m*
'or•gan grind•er organillero(-a) *m(f)*
or•gan•ic [ɔːr'gænɪk] *adj* **1** *food* ecológico, biológico **2** *fertilizer* orgánico; ***~ chemistry*** química *f* orgánica
or•gan•i•cal•ly [ɔːr'gænɪklɪ] *adv grown* ecológicamente, biológicamente
or•gan•ism ['ɔːrgənɪzm] organismo *m*
or•gan•ist ['ɔːrgənɪst] MUS organista *m/*

f
or•gan•i•za•tion [ɔːrgənaɪ'zeɪʃn] organización *f*
or•gan•i'za•tion chart organigrama *m*
or•gan•ize ['ɔːrgənaɪz] *v/t* organizar; *essay etc* estructurar
or•gan•ized 'crime crimen *m* organizado
or•gan•iz•er ['ɔːrgənaɪzər] *person* organizador(a) *m(f)*; *electronic* organizador *m*, agenda *f* electrónica
or•gas•m ['ɔːrgæzm] orgasmo *m*; ***have an ~*** tener un orgasmo; ***he was having ~s*** P estaba muy exaltado *or* emocionado
or•gy ['ɔːrdʒɪ] orgía *f*; ***an ~ of color*** un festival de color
O•ri•ent ['ɔːrɪənt] Oriente *m*
o•ri•ent ['ɔːrɪənt] *v/t* (*direct*) orientar; ***~ o.s.*** (*get bearings*) orientarse
O•ri•en•tal [ɔːrɪ'entl] **I** *adj* oriental **II** *n* oriental *m/f*
o•ri•en•tate ['ɔːrɪenteɪt] ☞ ***orient***
o•ri•en•ta•tion [ɔːrɪen'teɪʃn] orientación *f*; ***political / sexual ~*** orientación política / sexual
or•i•fice ['ɑːrɪfɪs] orificio *m*
or•i•gin ['ɑːrɪdʒɪn] origen *m*; ***country of ~*** país *m* de origen
o•rig•i•nal [ə'rɪdʒənl] **I** *adj* (*not copied, first*) original **II** *n painting etc* original *m*; ***she can read it in the ~*** puede leerlo en el idioma original
o•rig•i•nal•i•ty [ərɪdʒən'ælətɪ] originalidad *f*
o•rig•i•nal•ly [ə'rɪdʒənəlɪ] *adv* originalmente; (*at first*) originalmente, en un principio
o•rig•i•nal 'sin pecado *m* original
o•rig•i•nate [ə'rɪdʒɪneɪt] **I** *v/t scheme, idea* crear **II** *v/i of idea, belief* originarse; *of family* proceder
o•rig•i•na•tor [ə'rɪdʒɪneɪtər] *of scheme etc* creador(a) *m(f)*; ***he's not an ~*** no es un creador nato
Ork•neys ['ɔːrknɪz] *npl* Orcadas *fpl*
or•na•ment ['ɔːrnəmənt] adorno *m*
or•na•men•tal [ɔːrnə'mentl] *adj* ornamental
or•na•men•ta•tion [ɔːrnəmen'teɪʃn] ornamentación *f*
or•nate [ɔːr'neɪt] *adj style, architecture* recargado
or•ni•thol•o•gist [ɔːrnɪ'θɑːlədʒɪst] ornitólogo(-a) *m(f)*
or•ni•thol•o•gy [ɔːrnɪ'θɑːlədʒɪ] ornitología *f*
or•phan ['ɔːrfn] **I** *n* huérfano(-a) *m(f)* **II** *v/t*: ***be ~ed*** quedar huérfano
or•phan•age ['ɔːrfənɪdʒ] orfanato *m*
or•tho•don•tist [ɔːrθə'dɑːntɪst] ortodontista *m/f*
or•tho•dox ['ɔːrθədɑːks] *adj* REL, *fig* ortodoxo
or•tho•pe•dic [ɔːrθə'piːdɪk] *adj* ortopédico
or•tho•pe•dics [ɔːrθə'piːdɪks] *nsg* ortopedia *f*
or•tho•pe•dist [ɔːrθə'piːdɪst] ortopeda *m/f*
os•cil•late ['ɑːsɪleɪt] *v/i* PHYS, *fig* oscilar (***between*** entre)
os•cil•la•tion [ɑːsɪ'leɪʃn] *esp* PHYS oscilación *f*
OSHA ['oʊʃə] *abbr* (= ***Occupational Safety and Health Administration***) Sanidad *f* y Seguridad Laboral
os•mo•sis [ɑːz'moʊsɪs] ósmosis *f inv*
os•ten•si•ble [ɑː'stensəbl] *adj* aparente
os•ten•si•bly [ɑː'stensəblɪ] *adv* aparentemente
os•ten•ta•tion [ɑːsten'teɪʃn] ostentación *f*
os•ten•ta•tious [ɑːsten'teɪʃəs] *adj* ostentoso
os•ten•ta•tious•ly [ɑːsten'teɪʃəslɪ] *adv* de forma ostentosa
os•te•o•ar•thri•tis [ɑːstɪoʊɑːr'θraɪtɪs] osteoartritis *f inv*
os•te•o•path ['ɑːstɪəpæθ] osteópata *m/f*
os•te•op•a•thy [ɑːstɪ'ɑːpəθɪ] osteopatía *f*
os•te•o•po•ro•sis [ɑːstɪoʊpə'roʊsɪs] osteoporosis *f inv*
os•tra•cism ['ɑːstrəsɪzəm] ostracismo *m*
os•tra•cize ['ɑːstrəsaɪz] *v/t* condenar al ostracismo
os•trich ['ɑːstrɪtʃ] ORN avestruz *f*
oth•er ['ʌðər] **I** *adj* **1** otro; ***~ people might not agree*** puede que otros no estén de acuerdo; ***the ~ day*** (*recently*) el otro día; ***every ~ day / person*** cada dos días / personas
2: ***~ than*** aparte de; ***do you have anything ~ than these red ones?*** ¿tiene otros además de los rojos?; ***I'd do anything ~ than go back there again*** haría

O

cualquier otra cosa antes de volver ahí otra vez; ***it was none ~ than the president himself who …*** fue nada más y nada menos que el propio presidente quien …

II *n*: ***the ~*** el otro; ***the ~s*** los otros

oth•er•wise ['ʌðərwaɪz] **I** *conj* de lo contrario, si no **II** *adv* (*differently*) de manera diferente; ***be ~ engaged*** *fml* tener otros asuntos que abordar; ***think ~*** pensar de otra manera; ***X, ~ known as Y*** X, conocido también como Y

ot•ter ['ɑːtər] nutria *f*

ouch [aʊʧ] ¡ay!

ought [ɒːt] *v/aux*: ***I / you ~ to know*** debo / debes saberlo; ***you ~ to have done it*** deberías haberlo hecho

ounce [aʊns] onza *f*

our [aʊr] *adj* nuestro *m*, nuestra *f*; ***~ brother*** nuestro hermano; ***~ books*** nuestros libros

ours [aʊrz] *pron* el nuestro, la nuestra; ***~ are red*** los nuestros son rojos; ***that book is ~*** ese libro es nuestro; ***a friend of ~*** un amigo nuestro

our•selves [aʊr'selvz] *pron reflexive* nos; *emphatic* nosotros mismos *mpl*, nosotras mismas *fpl*; ***we hurt ~*** nos hicimos daño; ***when we saw ~ in the mirror*** cuando nos vimos en el espejo; ***we saw it ~*** lo vimos nosotros mismos; ***by ~*** (*alone*) solos; (*without help*) nosotros solos, nosotros mismos

oust [aʊst] *v/t from office* derrocar

out [aʊt] **I** *adv*: ***be ~*** *of light, fire* estar apagado; *of flower* estar en flor; (*not at home, not in building*), *of sun* haber salido; *of calculations* estar equivocado; (*be published*) haber sido publicado; (*no longer in competition*) estar eliminado; (*no longer in fashion*) estar pasado de moda; ***the secret is ~*** el secreto ha sido revelado; ***~ here in Dallas*** aquí en Dallas; ***he's ~ in the garden*** está en el jardín; (***get***) ***~!*** ¡vete!; ***that's ~!*** (*~ of the question*) ¡eso es imposible!; ***he's ~ to win*** (*fully intends to*) va a por la victoria

II *v/t homosexual* revelar la homosexualidad de

out-and-'out *adj lie* como una casa; *liar* redomado; *disgrace* total

out'bid *v/t* (*pret & pp* ***-bid***) hacer mejor oferta que

out•board 'mo•tor motor *m* de fueraborda

'out•break *of violence, war* estallido *m*

'out•build•ing edificio *m* anexo

'out•burst *emotional* arrebato *m*, arranque *m*

'out•cast paria *m/f*

out'class *v/t* superar con creces

'out•come resultado *m*

'out•cry protesta *f*

out'dat•ed *adj* anticuado

out'dis•tance *v/t* dejar atrás

out'do *v/t* (*pret* ***-did***, *pp* ***-done***) superar

out'door *adj toilet, activities, life* al aire libre; ***~ shoes*** *pl* zapatos *mpl* para el aire libre; ***~ shot*** PHOT foto *f* en exteriores

out'doors *adv* fuera; *go* afuera

out•er ['aʊtər] *adj wall etc* exterior; ***~ garments*** *pl* prendas *fpl* exteriores

out•er 'space espacio *m* exterior

'out•field *in baseball* jardín *m* exterior

'out•field•er *in baseball* jardinero(-a) *m(f)*

'out•fit 1 *clothes* traje *m*, conjunto *m* **2** *company, organization* grupo *m*

'out•flow salida *f*

out'fox *v/t* aventajar en astucia

'out•go•ing I *adj* **1** *flight, mail* saliente **2** *personality* extrovertido **II** *npl* FIN gastos *mpl*

out'grow *v/t* (*pret* ***-grew***, *pp* ***-grown***) *old ideas* dejar atrás; ***he's outgrown his pants*** se le han quedado pequeños los pantalones

'out•house dependencia *f*

out•ing ['aʊtɪŋ] **1** (*trip*) excursión *f* **2** *of homosexual* revelación *f* de la homosexualidad

out•land•ish [aʊt'lændɪʃ] *adj* estrafalario

out'last *v/t* durar más que

'out•law I *n* proscrito(-a) *m(f)* **II** *v/t activity* prohibir; *person* declarar fuera de la ley

'out•lay desembolso *m* (***on*** en; ***for*** para)

'out•let 1 *of pipe* desagüe *m* **2** *for sales* punto *m* de venta **3** ELEC enchufe *m*

'out•line I *n* **1** *of person, building etc* perfil *m*, contorno *m* **2** *of plan, novel* resumen *m* **II** *v/t plans etc* resumir

out'live *v/t* sobrevivir a

'out•look (*prospects*) perspectivas *fpl*

'out•ly•ing *adj areas* periférico

out•ma'neu•ver, *Br* **out•ma'noeu•vre** *v/t* MIL, *fig* superar estratégicamente
out•mod•ed [aʊt'moʊdɪd] *adj* anticuado
'out•most: ***at the ~*** como mucho
out'num•ber *v/t* superar en número; ***we were ~ed*** nos superaban en número
out of *prep* **1** *motion* fuera de; ***(get) ~ my room!*** ¡fuera de mi habitación!; ***run ~ the house*** salir corriendo de la casa; ***it fell ~ the window*** se cayó por la ventana
2 *position*: ***20 miles ~ Detroit*** a 20 millas de Detroit
3 *cause* por; ***~ jealousy / curiosity*** por celos / curiosidad
4 *without*: ***we're ~ gas / beer*** no nos queda gasolina / cerveza
5 *from a group* de cada; ***5 ~ 10*** 5 de cada 10
out-of-'date *adj* anticuado, desfasado
out-of-the-'way *adj* apartado
'out•pa•tient paciente *m/f* externo(-a)
'out•pa•tients' (clin•ic) clínica *f* ambulatoria
'out•per•form *v/t* superar a
out'play *v/t* jugar mejor que
'out•post MIL enclave *m*; *fig* reducto *m*
out•pour•ing ['aʊtpɔːrɪŋ] manifestación *f* desbordada
'out•put I *n* **1** *of factory* producción *f* **2** COMPUT salida *f* **II** *v/t* (*pret & pp* ***-ted*** *or* ***-put***) (*produce*) producir
'out•put de•vice COMPUT periférico *m* de salida
'out•rage I *n* **1** *feeling* indignación *f* **2** *act* ultraje *m*, atrocidad *f* **II** *v/t* indignar, ultrajar; ***I was ~d to hear that …*** me indignó escuchar que …
out•ra•geous [aʊt'reɪdʒəs] *adj acts* atroz; *prices* escandaloso
out'rank *v/t* superar en rango a
'out•right I *adj* **1** *winner* absoluto **2** *lie, disaster* total, absoluto; *nonsense* rotundo, claro **II** *adv* **1** *win* completamente **2** *kill, buy sth* en el acto
out'run *v/t* (*pret* ***-ran***, *pp* ***-run***) correr más que
out'sell *v/t* (*pret & pp* ***-sold***) vender más que
'out•set principio *m*, comienzo *m*; ***from the ~*** desde el principio *or* comienzo
out'shine *v/t* (*pret & pp* ***-shone***) eclipsar
'out•side I *adj surface, wall* exterior; *lane* de fuera; ***~ chance*** posibilidad *f* remota **II** *adv sit, go* fuera **III** *prep* **1** fuera de **2** (*apart from*) aparte de **IV** *n* **1** *of building, case etc* exterior *m* **2**: ***at the ~*** a lo sumo
out•side 'broad•cast emisión *f* desde exteriores
out•side 'left *in soccer* extremo(-a) *m(f)* izquierdo(-a)
out•sid•er [aʊt'saɪdər] *in life* forastero (-a) *m(f)*; ***be an ~*** *in election, race* no ser uno de los favoritos
out•side 'right *in soccer* extremo(-a) *m(f)* derecho(-a)
'out•size *adj clothing* de talla especial
'out•skirts *npl* afueras *fpl*
out'smart ☞ ***outwit***
'out•source *v/t* subcontratar
out'spo•ken *adj* abierto
out'stand•ing *adj* **1** *success, quality* destacado, sobresaliente; *writer, athlete* excepcional **2** FIN: *invoice, sums* pendiente
out'stay *v/t*: ***~ one's welcome*** quedarse alguien más tiempo del debido
out•stretched ['aʊtstretʃt] *adj hands* extendido
out'strip *v/t* (*pret & pp* ***-ped***) superar
'out-tray bandeja *f* de salida
out'vote *v/t*: ***be ~d*** perder la votación
out•ward ['aʊtwərd] *adj* **1** *appearance* externo **2**: ***~ journey*** viaje *m* de ida
out•ward•ly ['aʊtwərdlɪ] *adv* aparentemente
out'weigh *v/t* pesar más que
out'wit *v/t* (*pret & pp* ***-ted***) mostrarse más listo que
o•va ['oʊvə] *pl* ☞ ***ovum***
o•val ['oʊvl] *adj* oval, ovalado
o•var•i•an [oʊ'verɪən] *adj* ovárico
o•va•ry ['oʊvərɪ] ovario *m*
o•va•tion [oʊ'veɪʃn] ovación *f*; ***give s.o. a standing ~*** aplaudir a alguien de pie
ov•en ['ʌvn] horno *m*
'ov•en glove, 'ov•en mitt manopla *f* para el horno; **'ov•en•proof** *adj* refractario; **'ov•en-read•y** *adj* listo para el horno
o•ver ['oʊvər] **I** *prep* **1** (*above*) sobre, encima de **2** (*across*) al otro lado de; ***she walked ~ the street*** cruzó la calle; ***travel all ~ Brazil*** viajar por todo Brasil **3** (*more than*) más de; ***~ and above***

además de **4** (*during*) durante; ***let's talk ~ a drink / meal*** hablemos mientras tomamos una bebida / comemos **5**: ***we're ~ the worst*** lo peor ya ha pasado
II *adv*: ***be ~*** (*finished*) haber acabado; ***there were just 6 ~*** sólo quedaban seis; ***~ to you*** (*your turn*) te toca a ti; ***~ in Japan*** allá en Japón; ***~ here / there*** por aquí / allá; ***it hurts all ~*** me duele por todas partes; ***painted white all ~*** pintado todo de blanco; ***it's all ~*** se ha acabado; ***~ and ~ again*** una y otra vez; ***do sth ~ (again)*** volver a hacer algo

o•ver'act *v/i* sobreactuar

o•ver•all ['oʊvərɒːl] **I** *adj length* total **II** *adv* (*in general*) en general; ***it measures six feet ~*** mide en total seis pies

o•ver•alls ['oʊvərɒːlz] *npl* overol *m*, *Span* mono *m*

o•ver'anx•ious *adj* excesivamente ansioso

o•ver'awe *v/t* intimidar; ***be ~d by s.o. / sth*** sentirse intimidado por alguien / algo

o•ver'bal•ance *v/i* perder el equilibrio

o•ver'bear•ing *adj* dominante, despótico

'o•ver•board *adv* por la borda; ***man ~!*** ¡hombre al agua!; ***go ~ for s.o. / sth*** entusiasmarse muchísimo con alguien / algo

o•ver'book *v/t*: ***the flight is ~ed*** el vuelo tiene overbooking

'o•ver•cast *adj day* nublado; *sky* cubierto

o•ver'charge *v/t customer* cobrar de más a

'o•ver•coat abrigo *m*

o•ver'come *v/t* (*pret* ***-came***, *pp* ***-come***) *difficulties*, *shyness* superar, vencer; ***be ~ by emotion*** estar embargado por la emoción

o•ver'cook *v/t* cocinar demasiado

o•ver'crowd•ed *adj train* atestado; *city* superpoblado

o•ver'do *v/t* (*pret* ***-did***, *pp* ***-done***) **1** (*exaggerate*) exagerar **2** *in cooking* recocer, cocinar demasiado; ***you're ~ing things*** te estás excediendo

o•ver'done *adj meat* demasiado hecho

'o•ver•dose sobredosis *f inv*

'o•ver•draft descubierto *m*; ***have an ~*** tener un descubierto

'o•ver•draft fa•cil•i•ty facilidad *f* de descubierto

o•ver'draw *v/t* (*pret* ***-drew***, *pp* ***-drawn***) *account* dejar al descubierto; ***be $800 ~n*** tener un descubierto de 800 dólares

o•ver'dressed *adj* demasiado trajeado

'o•ver•drive MOT superdirecta *f*; ***go into ~*** *fig* alcanzar un buen ritmo, F agilizarse

o•ver'due *adj*: ***his apology was long ~*** se debía haber disculpado hace tiempo

o•ver'eat *v/i* (*pret* ***-ate***, *pp* ***-eaten***) comer demasiado

o•ver'es•ti•mate *v/t abilities*, *value* sobreestimar

o•ver•ex'cit•ed *adj* sobreexcitado; ***get ~*** sobreexcitarse

o•ver'ex•pose *v/t photograph* sobreexponer

o•ver'fish•ing sobrepesca *f*

'o•ver•flow[1] *n pipe* desagüe *m*, rebosadero *m*; ***~ valve*** válvula *f* de desagüe

o•ver'flow[2] *v/i of water* desbordarse

o•ver'grown *adj garden* abandonado, cubierto de vegetación; ***he's an ~ baby*** es como un niño

'o•ver•hang *on rock face* saliente *m*

o•ver'haul *v/t engine*, *plans* revisar

'o•ver•head I *adj lights*, *railroad* elevado **II** *n* FIN gastos *mpl* generales; ***travel ~*** gastos de viaje **III** *adv* en lo alto

'o•ver•head kick *in soccer* chilena *f*

'o•ver•head pro•jec•tor retroproyector *m*

o•ver'hear *v/t* (*pret & pp* ***-heard***) oír por casualidad

o•ver'heat *v/i* TECH, *of economy* recalentarse

o•ver'heat•ed *adj* recalentado

o•ver•in'dulge I *v/t person* consentir; *own preferences* dejarse arrastrar por **II** *v/i in food*, *drink* empacharse

o•ver•joyed [oʊvər'dʒɔɪd] *adj* contentísimo, encantado

'o•ver•kill: ***that's ~*** eso es exagerar

'o•ver•land I *adj route* terrestre **II** *adv travel* por tierra

o•ver'lap *v/i* (*pret & pp* ***-ped***) *of tiles etc* solaparse; *of periods of time* coincidir; *of theories* tener puntos en común

o•ver'leaf *adv*: ***see ~*** véase al dorso

o•ver'load *v/t vehicle*, ELEC sobrecargar

o•ver'look *v/t* **1** *of tall building etc* dominar **2** (*not see*) pasar por alto
o•ver•ly ['oʊvərlɪ] *adv* excesivamente, demasiado
o•ver'much *adv* excesivamente
'o•ver•night *adv travel* por la noche; ***stay*** ~ quedarse a pasar la noche
o•ver•night 'bag bolso *m* de viaje
o•ver'paid *adj*: ***be*** ~ cobrar demasiado
'o•ver•pass paso *m* elevado
o•ver•pop•u•lat•ed [oʊvə'pɑːpjʊleɪtɪd] *adj* superpoblado
o•ver'pow•er *v/t physically* dominar
o•ver•pow•er•ing [oʊvər'paʊrɪŋ] *adj smell* fortísimo; *sense of guilt* insoportable
o•ver•priced [oʊvər'praɪst] *adj* demasiado caro
o•ver•pro'duc•tion superproducción *f*
o•ver•rat•ed [oʊvə'reɪtɪd] *adj* sobrevalorado
o•ver'reach *v/t*: ~ ***o.s.*** extralimitarse
o•ver•re'act *v/i* reaccionar exageradamente (***to*** ante)
o•ver•re'ac•tion reacción *f* exagerada (***to*** ante)
o•ver'ride *v/t* (*pret* ***-rode***, *pp* ***-ridden***) anular
o•ver'rid•ing *adj concern* primordial
o•ver'rule *v/t decision* anular
o•ver'run *v/t* (*pret* ***-ran***, *pp* ***-run***) **1** *country* invadir; ***be*** ~ ***with*** estar plagado de **2** *time* superar
o•ver'seas I *adv live*, *work* en el extranjero; *go* al extranjero **II** *adj* extranjero
o•ver'see *v/t* (*pret* ***-saw***, *pp* ***-seen***) supervisar
o•ver•sexed [oʊvər'sekst] *adj* libidinoso
o•ver'shad•ow *v/t fig* eclipsar
o•ver'shoot *v/t* (*pret & pp* ***-shot***) **1** *runway* salirse de **2** *production target* pasarse de
'o•ver•sight descuido *m*
o•ver•sim•pli•fi'ca•tion simplificación *f* excesiva
o•ver'sim•pli•fy *v/t* (*pret & pp* ***-ied***) simplificar en exceso
o•ver•size(d) ['oʊvərsaɪz(d)] *adj* enorme
o•ver'sleep *v/i* (*pret & pp* ***-slept***) quedarse dormido
o•ver'spend *v/i* (*pret & pp* ***-spent***) gastar de más
o•ver•staffed [oʊvər'stæft] *adj* con demasiado personal
o•ver'state *v/t* exagerar
o•ver'state•ment exageración *f*
o•ver'stay *v/t*: ~ ***one's welcome*** quedarse alguien más tiempo del debido
o•ver'step *v/t* (*pret & pp* ***-ped***) *fig* traspasar; ~ ***the mark*** propasarse, pasarse de la raya
o•vert [oʊ'vɜrt] *adj* ostensible, claro
o•ver'take *v/t* (*pret* ***-took***, *pp* ***-taken***) *in work*, *development* adelantarse a; *Br* MOT adelantar
o•ver'tax *v/t* **1** FIN cobrar más impuestos de los debidos a **2** *patience*, *strength etc* poner a prueba
o•ver'throw[1] *v/t* (*pret* ***-threw***, *pp* ***-thrown***) derrocar
'o•ver•throw[2] *n* derrocamiento *m*
'o•ver•time I *n* **1** SP: ***in*** ~ en la prórroga; ***the game went into*** ~ hubo que jugar una prórroga **2** *at work* horas *fpl* extra **II** *adv*: ***work*** ~ hacer horas extras; ***my imagination was working*** ~ mi imaginación se disparó
o•vert•ly [oʊ'vɜrtlɪ] *adv* ostensiblemente, claramente
o•ver•tones *npl* tono *m*; ***there were*** ~ ***of disbelief in his remark*** su comentario tenía un tono de incredulidad
o•ver•ture ['oʊvərtʃʊr] MUS obertura *f*; ***make*** ~***s to*** establecer contactos con
o•ver'turn I *v/t* **1** *vehicle* volcar; *object* dar la vuelta a **2** *government* derribar **II** *v/i of vehicle* volcar
o•ver•use I *v/t* [oʊvər'juːz] abusar de **II** *n* [oʊvər'juːs] abuso *m*
'o•ver•view visión *f* general
o•ver'weight *adj* con sobrepeso; ***be*** ~ estar demasiado gordo
o•ver'whelm [oʊvər'welm] *v/t with work* abrumar, inundar; *with emotion* abrumar; ***be*** ~***ed by*** *response* estar abrumado por
o•ver•whelm•ing [oʊvər'welmɪŋ] *adj feeling* abrumador; *majority* aplastante
o•ver•whelm•ing•ly [oʊvər'welmɪŋlɪ] *adv vote* en su (inmensa) mayoría
o•ver'work I *n* exceso *m* de trabajo **II** *v/i* trabajar en exceso **III** *v/t* hacer trabajar en exceso
o•ver'write *v/t* (*pret* ***-wrote***, *pp* ***-written***) COMPUT sobreescribir
ov•u•late ['ɑːvjʊleɪt] *v/i* ovular

ov•u•la•tion [ɑːvjʊ'leɪʃn] ovulación *f*
o•vum ['oʊvəm] (*pl* ***ovums*** *or* ***ova*** ['oʊvə]) BIO óvulo *m*
owe [oʊ] *v/t* deber; ***~ s.o. $500*** deber a alguien 500 dólares; ***how much do I ~ you?*** ¿cuánto te debo?
ow•ing to ['oʊɪŋ] *prep* debido a
owl [aʊl] búho *m*
own[1] [oʊn] *v/t* poseer; ***who ~s the restaurant?*** ¿de quién es el restaurante?, ¿quién es el propietario del restaurante?
own[2] [oʊn] **I** *adj* propio **II** *pron*: ***a car / an apartment of my ~*** mi propio coche / apartamento; ***on my / his ~*** yo / él solo **III** *n*: ***come into one's ~*** demostrar lo que vale uno
◆ **own up** *v/i* confesar
own 'brand marca *f* propia
own•er ['oʊnər] dueño(-a) *m(f)*, propietario(-a) *m(f)*
own•er-'oc•cu•pi•er *Br* ocupante *m/f* propietario(-a)
own•er•ship ['oʊnərʃɪp] propiedad *f*
own 'goal gol *m* en propia meta *or* puerta, autogol *m*; ***score an ~*** marcar en propia meta; *fig* tirar piedras contra su propio tejado
ox [ɑːks] (*pl* ***oxen*** ['ɑːksn]) buey *m*
Ox•bridge ['ɑːksbrɪdʒ] *universidades de Oxford y Cambridge*
ox•en ['ɑːksn] *pl* ☞ ***ox***
ox•ide ['ɑːksaɪd] óxido *m*
ox•i•dize ['ɑːksɪdaɪz] **I** *v/t* oxidar **II** *v/i* oxidarse
ox•y•gen ['ɑːksɪdʒən] oxígeno *m*
'ox•y•gen mask MED mascarilla *f* de oxígeno
'ox•y•gen tent MED tienda *f* de oxígeno
oys•ter ['ɔɪstər] ostra *f*; ***the world's your ~*** el mundo es tuyo, tienes el mundo a tus pies
'oys•ter bed criadero *m* de ostras
oz *abbr* (= ***ounce(s)***) onza(s) *f(pl)*
o•zone ['oʊzoʊn] ozono *m*
'o•zone lay•er capa *f* de ozono

P

PA [piː'eɪ] *abbr* (= ***personal assistant***) secretario(-a) *m(f)* personal
pace [peɪs] **I** *n* **1** (*step*) paso *m* **2** (*speed*) ritmo *m* **II** *v/i*: ***~ up and down*** pasear de un lado a otro
'pace•mak•er 1 MED marcapasos *m inv* **2** SP liebre *f*
Pa•cif•ic [pə'sɪfɪk]: ***the ~ (Ocean)*** el (Océano) Pacífico
pac•i•fi•er ['pæsɪfaɪər] chupete *m*
pac•i•fism ['pæsɪfɪzm] pacifismo *m*
pac•i•fist ['pæsɪfɪst] pacifista *m/f*
pac•i•fy ['pæsɪfaɪ] *v/t* (*pret & pp* ***-ied***) tranquilizar; *country* pacificar
pack [pæk] **I** *n* **1** (*back~*) mochila *f* **2** *of cereal, food, cigarettes* paquete *m* **3** *of cards* baraja *f* **II** *v/t item of clothing etc* meter en la maleta; *goods* empaquetar; *groceries* meter en una bolsa; ***~ one's bag / suitcase*** hacer la bolsa / la maleta **III** *v/i* hacer la maleta
◆ **pack in** *v/t* F *job, girlfriend* dejar; ***pack it in, will you!*** *stop that* ¡para ya! *or* ¡ya vale!(, ¿no?)
◆ **pack off** *v/t to bed, school etc* mandar
◆ **pack up** *v/i* hacer las maletas
pack•age ['pækɪdʒ] **I** *n* paquete *m* **II** *v/t* **1** *in packs* embalar **2** *idea, project* presentar
'pack•age deal *for holiday* paquete *m*; **'pack•age hol•i•day** *Br* viaje *m* organizado; **'pack•age store** tienda *f* de bebidas alcohólicas; **'pack•age tour** viaje *m* organizado
pack•ag•ing ['pækɪdʒɪŋ] **1** *of product* embalaje *m* **2** *of idea, project* presentación *f*; ***it's all ~*** *fig* es sólo imagen
'pack an•i•mal bestia *f* de carga
packed [pækt] *adj* (*crowded*) abarrotado
packed lunch [pækt'lʌntʃ] *Br* almuerzo *m* para llevar
pack•et ['pækɪt] paquete *m*; ***it'll cost you a ~*** *Br* F te va a costar un dineral *or* una fortuna
pack•et switch•ing ['pækɪtswɪtʃɪŋ] TELEC conmutación *f* de paquetes
'pack horse caballo *m* de carga
'pack ice banco *m* de hielo
pack•ing ['pækɪŋ] **1** *act* empaquetado

m; ***do one's ~*** hacer el equipaje **2** *material* embalaje *m*
'pack•ing case cajón *m* para embalar
pact [pækt] pacto *m*
pad[1] [pæd] **I** *n* **1** *for protection* almohadilla *f* **2** *for absorbing liquid* compresa *f* **3** *for writing* bloc *m* **II** *v/t* (*pret & pp* **-ded**) **1** *with material* acolchar **2** *speech, report* meter paja en
◆ **pad out** *v/t essay* rellenar, meter paja en F
pad[2] *v/i* (*pret & pp* **-ded**) (*move quietly*) caminar silenciosamente
pad•ded shoul•ders ['pædɪd] hombreras *fpl*
pad•ding ['pædɪŋ] **1** *material* relleno *m* **2** *in speech etc* paja *f*
pad•dle ['pædəl] **I** *n for canoe* canalete *m*, remo *m* **II** *v/i* **1** *in canoe* remar **2** *in water* chapotear
'pad•dle steam•er barco *m* de vapor de ruedas
pad•dling pool ['pædlɪŋpu:l] *Br* piscina *f* hinchable
pad•dock ['pædək] potrero *m*
pad•dy ['pædɪ] *for rice* arrozal *m*
'pad•dy wag•on F furgón *m* policial
pad•lock ['pædlɑ:k] **I** *n* candado *m* **II** *v/t gate* cerrar con candado; ***I ~ed my bike to the railings*** até mi bicicleta a la verja con candado
pa•gan ['peɪgən] **I** *n* pagano(-a) *m(f)* **II** *adj* pagano
pa•gan•ism ['peɪgənɪzəm] paganismo *m*
page[1] [peɪdʒ] *n of book etc* página *f*; ***~ number*** número *m* de página
page[2] [peɪdʒ] *v/t* (*call*) llamar; *by PA* llamar por megafonía; *by beeper* llamar por el buscapersonas *or Span* busca
'page•boy 1 paje *m* **2** *haircut* corte *m* estilo paje
'page proof prueba *f*
pag•er ['peɪdʒər] buscapersonas *m inv*, *Span* busca *m*
pag•i•nate ['pædʒɪneɪt] *v/t* paginar
pag•i•na•tion [pædʒɪ'neɪʃn] paginación *f*
paid [peɪd] *pret & pp* ☞ **pay**
paid em'ploy•ment empleo *m* remunerado
paid-up 'share cap•i•tal capital *m* descubierto desembolsado
pail [peɪl] cubo *m*
pain [peɪn] dolor *m*; ***be in ~*** sentir dolor; ***take ~s to do sth*** tomarse muchas molestias por hacer algo; ***a ~ (in the neck)*** F *person* un(-a) pesado(-a) F; *thing, situation* una lata F; ***he's a ~ in the butt*** P es un coñazo V
pain•ful ['peɪnfəl] *adj* **1** dolorido; *blow, condition, subject* doloroso; ***my arm is still very ~*** me sigue doliendo mucho el brazo **2** (*laborious*) difícil
pain•ful•ly ['peɪnfəlɪ] *adv* (*extremely, acutely*) extremadamente
pain•kill•er ['peɪnkɪlər] analgésico *m*
pain•less ['peɪnlɪs] *adj* indoloro; ***be completely ~*** doler nada
pains•tak•ing ['peɪnzteɪkɪŋ] *adj* meticuloso
pains•tak•ing•ly ['peɪnzteɪkɪŋlɪ] *adv* meticulosamente
paint [peɪnt] **I** *n* pintura *f* **II** *v/t* pintar
'paint•box caja *f* de acuarelas
'paint•brush brocha *f*, *small* pincel *m*
paint•er ['peɪntər] **1** *decorator* pintor(a) *m(f)* (de brocha gorda) **2** *artist* pintor(a) *m(f)*
'pain thresh•old umbral *m* del dolor
paint•ing ['peɪntɪŋ] **1** *activity* pintura *f* **2** *picture* cuadro *m*
'paint strip•per decapante *m*
'paint•work pintura *f*
pair [per] *of shoes, gloves, objects* par *m*; *of people, animals* pareja *f*
◆ **pair off** *v/i* emparejarse
pa•ja•ma jack•et [pədʒɑ:mə'dʒækɪt] camisa *f* de pijama
pa•ja•ma 'pants *npl* pantalón *m* de pijama
pa•ja•mas [pə'dʒɑ:məz] *npl* pijama *m*
Pa•ki•stan [pɑ:kɪ'stɑ:n] Paquistán *m*, Pakistán *m*
Pa•ki•sta•ni [pɑ:kɪ'stɑ:nɪ] **I** *n* paquistaní *m/f*, pakistaní *m/f* **II** *adj* paquistaní, pakistaní
pal [pæl] F (*friend*) amigo(-a) *m(f)*, *Span* colega *m/f* F; ***hey ~, got a light?*** oye amigo *or Span* tío, ¿tienes fuego?
pal•ace ['pælɪs] palacio *m*
pal•at•a•ble ['pælətəbl] *adj food* apetitoso; *proposal etc* aceptable; ***make sth ~ to s.o.*** hacer algo más aceptable para alguien
pal•a•tal ['pælətl] LING **I** *n* sonido *m* palatal **II** *adj* palatal

P

pal•ate ['pælət] paladar *m*
pa•la•tial [pə'leɪʃl] *adj* palaciego
pa•lav•er [pə'lɑːvər] F follón *m*
pale [peɪl] *adj person* pálido; ***she went ~*** palideció; ***~ pink / blue*** rosa / azul claro
pale•ness ['peɪlnɪs] palidez *f*
pa•le•o•lith•ic [pælɪoʊ'lɪθɪk] *adj* paleolítico
pa•le•on•tol•o•gy [pælɪɑːn'tɑːlədʒɪst] paleontología *f*
Pal•e•stine ['pæləstaɪn] Palestina *f*
Pal•e•stin•i•an [pælə'stɪnɪən] **I** *n* palestino(-a) *m(f)* **II** *adj* palestino
pall[1] [pɔːl] *n on coffin* paño *m* mortuorio; ***a ~ of smoke*** una cortina de humo
pall[2] [pɔːl] *v/i* desvanecerse
'pall•bear•er portador(a) *m(f)* del féretro
pal•let ['pælɪt] palé *m*
'pal•let truck carretilla *f* elevadora
pal•li•a•tive ['pælɪətɪv] MED paliativo *m*
pal•lid ['pælɪd] *adj* pálido
pal•lor ['pælər] palidez *f*
pal•ly ['pælɪ] *adj* F: ***they are very ~*** se han hecho muy amigos; ***get ~ with s.o.*** hacerse amigo de alguien
palm [pɑːm] **1** *of hand* palma *f* **2** *tree* palmera *f*
◆ **palm off** *v/t*: ***palm sth off on s.o.*** endosar algo a alguien
palm•ist ['pɑːmɪst] quiromántico(-a) *m(f)*
palm•is•try ['pɑːmɪstrɪ] quiromancia *f*
Palm 'Sun•day REL Domingo *m* de Ramos
'palm tree BOT palmera *f*
'palm•top computadora *f* de mano, *Span* ordenador *m* de mano
pa•lo•mi•no [pælə'miːnoʊ] alazán *m* de crin blanca
pal•pa•ble ['pælpəbl] *adj fig: clear, obvious* claro
pal•pa•bly ['pælpəblɪ] *adv (manifestly)* claramente
pal•pi•tate ['pælpɪteɪt] *v/i* palpitar
pal•pi•ta•tions [pælpɪ'teɪʃnz] *npl* MED palpitaciones *fpl*
pal•try ['pɒːltrɪ] *adj* miserable
pam•pas ['pæmpəs] *npl* pampa *f*
'pam•pas grass hierba *f* de las pampas
pam•per ['pæmpər] *v/t* mimar
pam•phlet ['pæmflɪt] *for information* folleto *m*; *political* panfleto *m*
pan[1] [pæn] **I** *n for cooking* cacerola *f*; *for frying* sartén *f*; ***have s.o. on the ~*** F poner a alguien de vuelta y media F **II** *v/t* (*pret & pp* ***-ned***) F (*criticize*) poner por los suelos F
◆ **pan out** *v/i* F (*develop*) salir
pan[2] [pæn] **I** *n in filming* plano *m* general **II** *v/i* hacer un plano general
pan•a•ce•a [pænə'sɪə] panacea *f*
pa•nache [pə'næʃ] gracia *f*, salero *m*
Pan•a•ma ['pænəmɑː] Panamá *m*
Pan•a•ma Ca'nal: ***the ~*** el Canal de Panamá
Pan•a•ma 'Cit•y Ciudad *f* de Panamá
Pan•a•ma•ni•an [pænə'meɪnɪən] **I** *adj* panameño **II** *n* panameño(-a) *m(f)*
Pan-A'mer•i•can *adj* panamericano
pan•a•tel•la [pænə'telə] panatela *f*
'pan•cake crepe *m*, *L.Am.* panqueque *m*
pan•cre•as ['pæŋkrɪəs] ANAT páncreas *m inv*
pan•da ['pændə] (oso *m*) panda *m*
pan•de•mo•ni•um [pændɪ'moʊnɪəm] pandemónium *m*, pandemonio *m*
◆ **pan•der to** ['pændər] *v/t* complacer
pane [peɪn] *of glass* hoja *f*
pan•el ['pænl] **1** panel *m* **2** *people* grupo *m*, panel *m*
pan•el•ist, *Br* **pan•el•list** ['pænəlɪst] miembro *m* de un panel
pan•el•ing ['pænəlɪŋ] paneles *mpl*; *of ceiling* artesonado *m*
pang [pæŋ]: ***~s of hunger*** retortijones *mpl*; ***~s of remorse*** remordimientos *mpl*
'pan•han•dle *v/i* F mendigar
pan•ic ['pænɪk] **I** *n* pánico *m*; ***I was in a real ~*** me entró el pánico **II** *v/i* (*pret & pp* ***-ked***) ser preso del pánico; *get agitated* perder la calma; ***don't ~!*** ¡tranquilo! **III** *v/t* (*pret & pp* ***-ked***) entrarle el pánico a alguien; ***don't let them ~ you in making a decision*** no dejes que te hagan tomar una decisión precipitada
pan•ic buy•ing ['pænɪkbaɪɪŋ] FIN compra *f* provocada por el pánico
pan•ick•y ['pænɪkɪ] *adj* F de pánico; ***he got ~*** le entró el pánico
'pan•ic sel•ling FIN venta *f* provocada por el pánico
'pan•ic sta•tions: ***it was ~ all around*** F

P

cundió el pánico
'pan•ic-strick•en *adj* preso del pánico
pan•nier ['pænɪər] alforja *f*
pan•o•ra•ma [pænə'rɑːmə] panorama *m*
pa•no•ra•mic [pænə'ræmɪk] *adj view* panorámico
pan•sy ['pænzɪ] *flower* pensamiento *m*
pant [pænt] *v/i* jadear
pan•the•is•tic [pænθɪ'ɪstɪk] *adj* panteísta *m/f*
pan•ther ['pænθər] ZO pantera *f*
pan•ties ['pæntɪz] *npl Span* bragas *fpl*, *L.Am.* calzones *mpl*
pan•ti•hose ☞ ***pantyhose***
pan•to•mime ['pæntəmaɪm] **1** pantomima *f* **2** *Br*: *comedia musical navideña basada en los cuentos de hada*
pan•try ['pæntrɪ] despensa *f*
pants [pænts] *npl* pantalones *mpl*
'pant•suit traje *m* pantalón
pant•y•hose ['pæntɪhouz] *npl* medias *fpl*, pantis *mpl*
'pant•y lin•er protege-slip *m*, salva-slip *m*
pap [pæp] papilla *f*
pa•pa•cy ['peɪpəsɪ] papado *m*
pa•pal ['peɪpəl] *adj* papal
pa•pa•ya [pə'paɪə] BOT papaya *f*
pa•per ['peɪpər] **I** *n* **1** papel *m*; ***a piece of ~*** un trozo de papel **2** (*news~*) periódico *m* **3** *academic* estudio *m*; *at conference* ponencia *f*; (*examination ~*) examen *m* **4**: ***~s*** (*documents*) documentos *mpl*; *of vehicle*, (*identity ~s*) papeles *mpl*, documentación *f* **II** *adj* de papel **III** *v/t room, walls* empapelar
◆ **paper over** *v/t fig* tapar, camuflar
'pa•per•back libro *m* en rústica; **pa•per 'bag** bolsa *f* de papel; **'pa•per boy** repartidor *m* de periódicos; **'pa•per clip** clip *m*; **pa•per 'cup** vaso *m* de papel; **'pa•per feed** alimentador *m* de papel; **pa•per 'hand•ker•chief** pañuelo *m* de papel; **pa•per 'mon•ey** papel *m* moneda; **pa•per 'plate** plato *m* de papel; **'pa•per prof•it** ganancias *fpl* por realizar; **'pa•per round** ronda *f* de reparto a domicilio del periódico; **'pa•per-thin** *adj* finísimo; **pa•per 'tis•sue** pañuelo *m* de papel; **'pa•per•weight** pisapapeles *m inv*; **'pa•per•work** papeleo *m*
pa•pier-mâ•ché [pæpjeɪ'mæʃeɪ] cartón *m* piedra
pa•pri•ka ['pæprɪkə] pimentón *m*
par [pɑːr] *in golf* par *m*; ***be on a ~ with*** ser comparable a; ***feel below ~*** sentirse en baja forma
para ['pærə] MIL paracaidista *m/f*
par•a•ble ['pærəbl] parábola *f*
pa•rab•o•la [pə'ræbələ] MATH parábola *f*
par•a•bol•ic [pærə'bɑːlɪk] *adj* MATH parabólico
par•a•cet•a•mol [pærə'siːtəmɑːl] paracetamol *m*
par•a•chute ['pærəʃuːt] **I** *n* paracaídas *m inv* **II** *v/i* saltar en paracaídas **III** *v/t troops, supplies* lanzar en paracaídas
par•a•chut•ist ['pærəʃuːtɪst] paracaidista *m/f*
pa•rade [pə'reɪd] **I** *n procession* desfile *m* **II** *v/i* **1** desfilar **2** (*walk about*) pasearse **III** *v/t knowledge, new car* hacer ostentación de
pa'rade ground MIL patio *m* de armas
par•a•digm ['pærədaɪm] paradigma *m*
par•a•dise ['pærədaɪs] paraíso *m*
par•a•dox ['pærədɑːks] paradoja *f*
par•a•dox•i•cal [pærə'dɑːksɪkl] *adj* paradójico
par•a•dox•i•cal•ly [pærə'dɑːksɪklɪ] *adv* paradójicamente
par•af•fin ['pærəfɪn] **1** *wax* parafina **2** *Br* queroseno *m*
pa•ra•glid•ing ['pærəglaɪdɪŋ] parapente *m*
par•a•gon ['pærəgən]: ***~ of virtue*** dechado *m* de virtudes
par•a•graph ['pærəgræf] párrafo *m*
Par•a•guay ['pærəgwaɪ] Paraguay *m*
Par•a•guay•an [pærə'gwaɪən] **I** *adj* paraguayo **II** *n* paraguayo(-a) *m*(*f*)
par•a•keet ['pærəkiːt] periquito *m*
par•al•lel ['pærəlel] **I** *n* GEOM paralela *f*, GEOG paralelo *m*; *fig* paralelismo *m*; ***draw a ~*** establecer un paralelismo; ***do two things in ~*** hacer dos cosas al mismo tiempo; ***an event without ~*** un acontecimiento sin paralelo *or* comparación **II** *adj also fig* paralelo **III** *v/t* (*match*) equipararse a
par•al•lel 'bars (barras *fpl*) paralelas *fpl*
par•al•lel•ism ['pærəlelɪzəm] paralelismo *m*
par•al•lel•o•gram [pærəl'eləgræm] MATH paralelogramo *m*
par•al•lel 'port COMPUT puerto m para-

lelo
Par•a•lym•pics [pærə'lɪmpɪks] *npl* juegos *mpl* paraolímpicos
pa•ral•y•sis [pə'ræləsɪs] (*pl* **paralyses** [pə'ræləsi:z]) parálisis *f*
par•a•lyt•ic [pærə'lɪtɪk] *adj* **1** MED paralítico **2** *Br* F (*drunk*) pedo, mamado
par•a•lyze ['pærəlaɪz] *v/t also fig* paralizar
par•a•med•ic [pærə'medɪk] auxiliar *m/f* sanitario(-a)
pa•ram•e•ter [pə'ræmɪtər] parámetro *m*
par•a•mil•i•tar•y [pærə'mɪlɪterɪ] **I** *adj* paramilitar **II** *n* paramilitar *m/f*
par•a•mount ['pærəmaʊnt] *adj* supremo, extremo; **be ~** ser de importancia capital
par•a•noi•a [pærə'nɔɪə] paranoia *f*
par•a•noid ['pærənɔɪd] *adj* paranoico
par•a•nor•mal [pærə'nɔ:rməl] *adj* paranormal
par•a•pet ['pærəpet] parapeto *m*
par•a•pher•na•li•a [pærəfər'neɪlɪə] parafernalia *f*
par•a•phrase ['pærəfreɪz] *v/t* parafrasear
par•a•ple•gi•a [pærə'pli:dʒə] MED paraplejia *f*
par•a•ple•gic [pærə'pli:dʒɪk] parapléjico(-a) *m(f)*
par•a•psy•chol•o•gy [pærəsaɪ'kɑ:lədʒɪ] parapsicología *f*
par•as•cend•ing ['pærəsendɪŋ] parapente *m* con lancha motora
par•a•site ['pærəsaɪt] *also fig* parásito *m*
par•a•sit•ic [pærə'sɪtɪk] *adj* parásito
par•a•sol ['pærəsɑ:l] sombrilla *f*
par•a•troop•er ['pærətru:pər] paracaidista *m/f* (*militar*)
par•a•troops ['pærətru:ps] *npl* tropas *fpl* paracaidistas
par•boil ['pɑ:rbɔɪl] *v/t* cocer a medias
par•cel ['pɑ:rsl] paquete *m*
◆ **parcel up** *v/t* empaquetar
'par•cel bomb paquete *m* bomba
'par•cel post servicio *m* de paquete postal
parch [pɑ:rtʃ] *v/t* secar; **be ~ed** F *of person* estar muerto de sed F
parch•ment ['pɑ:rtʃmənt] pergamino *m*
par•don ['pɑ:rdn] **I** *n* **1** LAW indulto *m* **2**: ***I beg your ~?*** (*what did you say?*) ¿cómo ha dicho?; ***I beg your ~*** (*I'm sorry*) discúlpeme **II** *v/t* **1** perdonar; ***~ me?*** ¿perdón?, ¿qué?; ***~ me for saying so, but ...*** perdóneme pero ..., permítame que le diga que ... **2** LAW indultar
par•don•a•ble ['pɑ:rdnəbl] *adj* perdonable
pare [per] *v/t* (*peel*) pelar
◆ **pare down** *v/t* recortar
par•ent ['perənt] *father* padre *m*; *mother* madre *f*; ***my ~s*** mis padres; ***each ~ must ...*** todos los padres deben...
par•ent•age ['perəntɪdʒ] origen *m*
pa•ren•tal [pə'rentl] *adj* de los padres
'par•ent com•pa•ny empresa *f* matriz
pa•ren•the•sis [pə'renθəsɪs] (*pl* ***parentheses*** [pə'renθəsi:z]) paréntesis *m inv*; ***in ~*** entre paréntesis
par•ent•hood ['perənthʊd] paternidad *f*
par•ent•ing ['perəntɪŋ]: ***what can they learn about ~?*** ¿qué pueden aprender sobre cómo ser buenos padres?; ***their ~ skills*** su capacidad para ser padres
par•ent•less ['perəntlɪs] *adj* sin padres
'par•ents' eve•ning reunión *f* de padres
'par•ents-in-law *npl* padres *mpl* políticos
par•ent-'teach•er as•so•ci•a•tion asociación *f* de padres de alumnos
Par•is ['pærɪs] París *m*
par•ish ['pærɪʃ] parroquia *f*
pa•rish•ion•er [pə'rɪʃənər] REL feligrés (-esa) *m(f)*
par•i•ty ['pærətɪ] igualdad *f* (***with*** con)
park[1] [pɑ:rk] *n* parque *m*
park[2] [pɑ:rk] *v/t & v/i* MOT estacionar, *Span* aparcar
par•ka ['pɑ:rkə] parka *f*
par•king ['pɑ:rkɪŋ] MOT estacionamiento *m*, *Span* aparcamiento *m*; ***no ~*** prohibido aparcar; ***there's plenty of ~ around here*** hay muchos sitios para aparcar por aquí
'par•king brake freno *m* de mano; **'par•king disc** disco *m* de estacionamiento *or Span* aparcamiento; **'par•king fee** tarifa *f* del párking; **'par•king ga•rage** párking *m*, *Span* aparcamiento *m*; **'par•king lot** estacionamiento *m*, *Span* aparcamiento *m* (*al aire libre*); **'par•king me•ter** parquímetro *m*; **par•king of'fense** estacionamiento *m* indebido; **'par•king place, par•king**

P

space (plaza *f* de) estacionamiento *m or Span* aparcamiento *m*, sitio *m* para estacionar *or Span* aparcar; **'par-king tick•et** multa *f* de estacionamiento

Par•kin•son's dis•ease ['pɑːrkɪnsnz] MED enfermedad *f* de Parkinson

'park•keep•er guarda *m/f* del parque

par•lance ['pɑːrləns]: ***in common ~*** en el habla común; ***in legal ~*** en la jerga legal

par•lia•ment ['pɑːrləmənt] parlamento *m*

par•lia•men•tar•i•an [pɑːrləmen'terɪən] parlamentario(-a) *m(f)*

par•lia•men•ta•ry [pɑːrlə'mentərɪ] *adj* parlamentario

par•lor, *Br* **par•lour** ['pɑːrlər] **1** *in house* salón *m* **2** (*beauty ~*) salón de belleza **3** (*ice-cream ~*) heladería *f*

'par•lor game juego *m* de salón

Par•me•san ['pɑːrməzæn] parmesano *m*

pa•ro•chi•al [pə'roʊkjəl] *adj* parroquial; *fig* provinciano

par•o•dy ['pærədɪ] **I** *n* parodia *f* (***of*** de) **II** *v/t* parodiar

pa•role [pə'roʊl] **I** *n* libertad *f* condicional; ***be on ~*** estar en libertad condicional **II** *v/t* poner en libertad condicional; ***be ~d*** salir en libertad condicional

par•quet ['pɑːrkeɪ] **1** parqué *m* **2** THEA platea *f*

par•quet 'floor suelo *m* de parqué

par•rot ['pærət] **I** *n* loro *m* **II** *v/t* repetir como un loro

'par•rot-fash•ion *adv learn, repeat* como un loro

par•ry ['pærɪ] *v/t* (*pret & pp* **-ied**) *blow* desviar; *question* esquivar

par•si•mo•ni•ous [pɑːrsɪ'moʊnjəs] *adj* mezquino

par•si•mo•ny ['pɑːrsəmoʊnɪ] mezquindad *f*

pars•ley ['pɑːrslɪ] perejil *m*

pars•nip ['pɑːrsnɪp] BOT pastinaca *f*

par•son ['pɑːrsn] párroco *m*

part [pɑːrt] **I** *n* **1** (*portion, area*) parte *f* **2** (*episode*) parte *f*, episodio *m* **3** *of machine* pieza *f* (de repuesto) **4** *in play, film* papel *m* **5** *in hair* raya *f* **6**: ***take ~ in*** tomar parte en
II *adv* (*partly*) en parte; ***~ American, ~ Spanish*** medio americano medio español; ***~ fact, ~ fiction*** con una parte de realidad y una parte de ficción
III *v/i* separarse; ***we ~ed good friends*** quedamos como amigos
IV *v/t*: ***~ one's hair*** hacerse la raya

◆ **part with** *v/t* desprenderse de

'part ex•change: ***take sth in ~*** llevarse algo como parte del pago

par•tial ['pɑːrʃl] *adj* **1** (*incomplete*) parcial **2**: ***be ~ to*** tener debilidad por

par•ti•al•i•ty [pɑːrʃɪ'ælətɪ] **1** (*bias*) parcialidad *f* **2** (*liking*) afición *f* (***for*** por)

par•tial•ly ['pɑːrʃəlɪ] *adv* parcialmente

par•ti•ci•pant [pɑːr'tɪsɪpənt] participante *m/f*

par•ti•ci•pate [pɑːr'tɪsɪpeɪt] *v/i* participar

par•ti•ci•pa•tion [pɑːrtɪsɪ'peɪʃn] participación *f*

par•ti•ci•ple ['pɑːrtɪsɪpl] GRAM participio *m*

par•ti•cle ['pɑːrtɪkl] **1** PHYS partícula *f* **2** (*small amount*) pizca *f*

par•tic•u•lar [pər'tɪkjələr] *adj* **1** (*specific*) particular, concreto; ***this ~ morning*** precisamente esta mañana; ***in ~*** en particular; ***it's a ~ favorite of mine*** es uno de mis preferidos **2** (*demanding*) exigente; *about friends, employees* selectivo; *pej* especial, quisiquilloso; ***you know how ~ she is*** ya sabes lo especial que es

par•tic•u•lar•ly [pər'tɪkjələrlɪ] *adv* particularmente, especialmente

par•tic•u•late e•mis•sions [pɑːrtɪkjʊlətɪ'mɪʃnz] *npl* emisión *f* de partículas

part•ing ['pɑːrtɪŋ] **I 1** partida *f* **2** *Br*: *in hair* raya *f* **II** *adj*: ***~ kiss*** beso *m* de despedida

'part•ing shot *remark* comentario *m* desagradable

par•ti•san ['pɑːrtɪzæn] **I** *n* **1** partidario(-a) *m(f)* **2** MIL partisano(-a) *m(f)* **II** *adj* **1** parcial **2** MIL partisano

par•ti•tion [pɑːr'tɪʃn] **I** *n* **1** (*screen*) tabique *m* **2** *of country* partición *f*, división *f* **II** *v/t country* dividir

◆ **partition off** *v/t* dividir con tabiques

part•ly ['pɑːrtlɪ] *adv* en parte

part•ner ['pɑːrtnər] COM socio(-a) *m(f)*; *in relationship* compañero(-a) *m(f)*; *in tennis, dancing* pareja *f*

part•ner•ship ['pɑːrtnərʃɪp] COM sociedad *f*; *in particular activity* colabora-

P

ción *f*
part of 'speech (*pl* ***parts of speech***) parte *f* de la oración
'part own•er copropietario(-a) *m*(*f*)
par•tridge ['pɑːrtrɪdʒ] perdiz *f*
'part-time I *adj* a tiempo parcial **II** *adv* *work* a tiempo parcial
part-'tim•er: ***be a ~*** trabajar a tiempo parcial
par•ty ['pɑːrtɪ] **I** *n* **1** (*celebration*) fiesta *f*; ***have*** *or* ***give a ~*** hacer *or* dar una fiesta; ***I met her at a ~*** la conocí en una fiesta **2** POL partido *m* **3** (*group of people*) grupo *m* **4**: ***be a ~ to*** tomar parte en **II** *v/i* (*pret & pp* ***-ied***) F salir de marcha F
par•ty 'line POL línea *f* del partido; **par•ty poop•er** ['pɑːrtɪpuːpər] F aguafiestas *m/f inv*; **par•ty 'wall** pared *f* medianera
pass [pæs] **I** *n* **1** *for entry*, SP pase *m* **2** *in mountains* desfiladero *m* **3**: ***make a ~ at*** tirarle los tejos a
II *v/t* **1** (*hand*) pasar **2** (*go past*) pasar por delante de; (*go beyond*) sobrepasar **3** (*overtake*) adelantar **4** (*approve*) aprobar **5**: ***~ an exam*** aprobar un examen; ***~ sentence*** LAW dictar sentencia; ***~ the time*** pasar el tiempo
III *v/i* **1** *of time*, SP pasar; ***I'll just mention in ~ing that …*** sólo mencionaré de pasada que … **2** *in exam* aprobar **3** (*go away*) pasarse
◆ **pass around** *v/t* repartir
◆ **pass away** *v/i euph* fallecer, pasar a mejor vida
◆ **pass by I** *v/t* (*go past*) pasar por **II** *v/i* (*go past*) pasarse
◆ **pass for** *v/t*: ***he could pass for 40*** podría pasar por alguien de 40 años
◆ **pass off I** *v/t* hacer pasar, colar (***as*** como) **II** *v/i* (*take place*) tener lugar
◆ **pass on I** *v/t information*, *book* pasar; ***~ the savings to …*** *of supermarket etc* revertir el ahorro en … **II** *v/i* (*euph*: *die*) fallecer, pasar a mejor vida
◆ **pass out I** *v/i* **1** (*faint*) desmayarse **2** *from police or military academy* graduarse **II** *v/t* (*distribute*) pasar
◆ **pass over** *v/t person* pasar por encima
◆ **pass through** *v/t town* pasar por
◆ **pass up** *v/t* F *opportunity* dejar pasar
pass•a•ble ['pæsəbl] *adj* **1** *road* transitable **2** (*acceptable*) aceptable
pas•sage ['pæsɪdʒ] **1** (*corridor*) pasillo *m* **2** *from poem*, *book* pasaje *m* **3** *of time* paso *m*
'pas•sage•way pasillo *m*
pas•sen•ger ['pæsɪndʒər] pasajero(-a) *m*(*f*)
'pas•sen•ger seat asiento *m* de pasajero
'pas•sen•ger train tren *m* de pasajeros
pas•ser-by [pæsər'baɪ] (*pl* ***passers-by***) transeúnte *m/f*
pass•ing ['pɑːsɪŋ] **I** *n of an era* paso *m*; (*death*) fallecimiento *m*; ***with the ~ of time*** con el paso del tiempo; ***in ~*** de pasada **II** *adj thought*, *glance* de pasada
pas•sion ['pæʃn] pasión *f*; ***a crime of ~*** un crimen pasional
pas•sion•ate ['pæʃnət] *adj* **1** *lover* apasionado **2** (*fervent*) fervoroso
pas•sion•ate•ly ['pæʃnətlɪ] *adv* apasionadamente
'pas•sion fruit BOT fruta *f* de la pasión, maracuyá *f*
pas•sive ['pæsɪv] **I** *adj* pasivo **II** *n* GRAM (voz *f*) pasiva *f*; ***in the ~*** en pasiva
'pas•sive smok•ing (el) fumar pasivamente
pas•siv•i•ty [pæs'ɪvətɪ] pasividad *f*
'pass•key llave *f* maestra; **'pass mark** EDU nota *f* mínima para aprobar; **'Pass•o•ver** REL Pascua *f* de los hebreos; **pass•port** ['pæspɔːrt] pasaporte *m*; **'pass•port con•trol** control *m* de pasaportes; **'pass•word** contraseña *f*
past [pæst] **I** *adj* (*former*) pasado; ***his ~ life*** su pasado; ***the ~ few days*** los últimos días; ***that's all ~ now*** todo eso es agua pasada
II *n* pasado; ***in the ~*** antiguamente
III *prep in position* después de; ***it's half ~ two*** son las dos y media; ***it's ~ seven o'clock*** pasan de las siete; ***it's ~ your bedtime*** hace rato que tenías que haberte ido a la cama
IV *adv*: ***run / walk ~*** pasar
pas•ta ['pæstə] pasta *f*
paste [peɪst] **I** *n* (*adhesive*) cola *f* **II** *v/t* (*stick*) pegar
pas•tel ['pæstl] **I** *n color* pastel *m* **II** *adj* pastel
pas•teur•ize ['pɑːstʃəraɪz] *v/t* pasteurizar
pas•tille [pæ'stiːl] pastilla *f*
pas•time ['pæstaɪm] pasatiempo *m*

pas•tor ['pæstər] vicario *m*
pas•to•ral ['pæstərəl] *adj* **1** pastoril **2** REL pastoral
past par'ti•ci•ple GRAM participio *m* pasado
pas•tra•mi [pæ'strɑːmɪ] pastrami *m*, *carne de vaca ahumada con especias*
pas•try ['peɪstrɪ] **1** *for pie* masa *f* **2** *small cake* pastel *m*
'past tense GRAM (tiempo *m*) pasado *m*
pas•ture ['pæstʃər] pasto *m*
pas•ty ['peɪstɪ] *adj complexion* pálido
pat[1] [pæt] **I** *n* palmadita *f*; ***give s.o. a ~ on the back*** *fig* dar una palmadita a alguien en la espalda **II** *v/t* (*pret & pp* ***-ted***) dar palmaditas a
pat[2] [pæt] *adv*: ***have*** *or* ***know sth off ~*** saber algo de memoria
Pat•a•gon•i•a [pætə'goʊnɪə] Patagonia *f*
Pat•a•gon•i•an [pætə'goʊnɪən] *adj* patagónico
patch [pætʃ] **I** *n* **1** *on clothing* parche *m*; ***not be a ~ on*** *fig* no tener ni punto de comparación con **2** (*area*) mancha *f*; ***a bad ~*** (*period of time*) un mal momento, una mala racha; ***~es of fog*** zonas *fpl* de niebla **II** *v/t clothing* remendar
◆ **patch up** *v/t* (*repair temporarily*) hacer un remiendo a, arreglar a medias; *quarrel* solucionar
patch•work ['pætʃwɜːrk] **I** *n needlework* labor *f* de retazo **II** *adj hecho de remiendos*
patch•y ['pætʃɪ] *quality* desigual; *work*, *performance* irregular
pã•té [pɑː'teɪ] paté *m*
pa•tent ['peɪtnt] **I** *adj* patente, evidente **II** *n for invention* patente *f* **III** *v/t invention* patentar
pa•tent 'leath•er charol *m*
pa•tent•ly ['peɪtntlɪ] (*clearly*) evidentemente, claramente
pa•ter•nal [pə'tɜːrnl] *relative* paterno; *pride*, *love* paternal
pa•ter•nal•ism [pə'tɜːrnlɪzm] paternalismo *m*
pa•ter•nal•is•tic [pətɜːrnl'ɪstɪk] *adj* paternalista
pa•ter•ni•ty [pə'tɜːrnɪtɪ] paternidad *f*
pa'ter•ni•ty leave baja *f* por paternidad; ***be on ~*** estar de baja *or* tener la baja por paternidad
pa'ter•ni•ty suit LAW litigio *m or* querella *f* por paternidad
path [pæθ] *also fig* camino *m*
pa•thet•ic [pə'θetɪk] *adj* **1** *invoking pity* patético; **2** F (*very bad*) lamentable F
path•o•gen ['pæθədʒən] patógeno *m*
path•o•log•i•cal [pæθə'lɑːdʒɪkl] *adj* patológico
pa•thol•o•gist [pə'θɑːlədʒɪst] patólogo(-a) *m*(*f*)
pa•thol•o•gy [pə'θɑːlədʒɪ] patología *f*
pa•thos ['peɪθɑːs] patetismo *m*
path•way ['pæθweɪ] camino *m*
pa•tience ['peɪʃns] paciencia *f*
pa•tient ['peɪʃnt] **I** *n* paciente *m/f* **II** *adj* paciente; ***just be ~!*** ¡ten paciencia!
pa•tient•ly ['peɪʃntlɪ] *adv* pacientemente
pat•i•na ['pætɪnə] pátina *f*
pat•i•o ['pætɪoʊ] patio *m*
pa•tri•arch ['peɪtrɪɑːrk] patriarca *m*
pa•tri•ar•chal [peɪtrɪ'ɑːrkl] *adj* patriarcal
pa•tri•ot ['peɪtrɪət] patriota *m/f*
pa•tri•ot•ic [peɪtrɪ'ɑːtɪk] *adj* patriótico
pa•tri•ot•ism ['peɪtrɪətɪzm] patriotismo *m*
pa•trol [pə'troʊl] **I** *n* patrulla *f*; ***be on ~*** estar de patrulla **II** *v/t* (*pret & pp* ***-led***) *streets*, *border* patrullar
pa'trol car coche *m* patrulla; **pa'trol•man** policía *m*, patrullero *m*; **pa'trol wag•on** furgón *m* policial
pa•tron ['peɪtrən] **1** *of store*, *movie theater* cliente *m/f* **2** *of artist*, *charity etc* patrocinador(a) *m*(*f*)
pa•tron•age ['pætrənɪdʒ] *support* patronazgo *m*; *of artist etc* patrocinio *m*; ***under the ~ of*** bajo el patronazgo de
pa•tron•ize ['pætrənaɪz] *v/t person* tratar con condescendencia *or* como a un niño
pa•tron•iz•ing ['pætrənaɪzɪŋ] condescendiente
pa•tron 'saint santo(-a) *m*(*f*) patrón(-ona), patrón(-ona) *m*(*f*)
pat•ter ['pætər] **I** *n* **1** *of rain etc* repiqueteo *m*; *of feet* golpeteo *m*; ***soon there'll be the ~ of tiny feet*** *hum* pronto habrá pasitos de niño **2** F *of salesman* parloteo *m* F **II** *v/i* repiquetear
pat•tern ['pætərn] **I** *n* **1** *on wallpaper*, *fabric* estampado *m* **2** *for knitting*, *sewing* diseño *m*; (*model*) modelo *m* **3** *in*

P

behavior, events pauta *f* **II** *v/t*: ***~ sth on sth*** hacer algo tomando como modelo algo

pat•terned ['pætərnd] *adj* estampado

pat•ty ['pætɪ] empanadilla *f*

paunch [pɒːntʃ] barriga *f*

pau•per ['pɔːpər] pobre *m/f*

pause [pɒːz] **I** *n* pausa *f* **II** *v/i* parar; *when speaking* hacer una pausa **III** *v/t tape* poner en pausa

'pause but•ton (botón *m* de) pausa *f*

pave [peɪv] *with concrete* pavimentar; *with slabs* adoquinar; ***~ the way for*** *fig* preparar el terreno para

pave•ment ['peɪvmənt] **1** (*roadway*) calzada *f* **2** *Br* (*sidewalk*) acera *f*

pav•ing stone ['peɪvɪŋ] losa *f*

paw [pɒː] **I** *n of animal* pata *f*; F (*hand*) pezuña *f* F; ***keep your ~s off, you!*** F ¡oye tú, mantén lejos tus manazas *or* zarpas! **II** *v/t* F sobar F

pawn[1] [pɒːn] *n in chess* peón *m*; *fig* títere *m*

pawn[2] [pɒːn] *v/t* empeñar

'pawn•bro•ker prestamista *m/f*

'pawn•shop casa *f* de empeños

pay [peɪ] **I** *n* paga *f*, sueldo *m*; ***in the ~ of*** a sueldo de **II** *v/t* (*pret & pp* ***paid***) *employee, sum, bill* pagar; ***~ attention*** prestar atención; ***~ s.o. a compliment*** hacer un cumplido a alguien **III** *v/i* (*pret & pp* ***paid***) **1** pagar; ***~ for*** *purchase* pagar; ***you'll ~ for this!*** *fig* ¡me las pagarás! **2** (*be profitable*) ser rentable; ***it doesn't ~ to ...*** no conviene ...

◆ **pay back** *v/t person* devolver el dinero a; *loan* devolver

◆ **pay in** *v/t to bank* ingresar

◆ **pay off I** *v/t* **1** *debt* liquidar **2** (*bribe*) sobornar **3** *employee* despedir **II** *v/i* (*be profitable*) valer la pena

◆ **pay up** *v/i* pagar

pay•a•ble ['peɪəbl] *adj* pagadero

'pay check cheque *m* del sueldo; **'pay-day** día *m* de paga; **'pay•dirt**: ***hit ~*** F encontrar un chollo, tocar la lotería

pay•ee [peɪ'iː] beneficiario(-a) *m*(*f*)

'pay en•ve•lope sobre *m* con la paga

pay•er ['peɪər] pagador(a) *m*(*f*); ***they are good ~s*** pagan puntualmente

pay•ing ['peɪɪŋ] *adj* **1** (*profitable*) rentable **2**: ***~ guest*** huésped *m/f* de pago

pay-'in slip resguardo *m* de ingreso

pay•load ['peɪloud] carga *f* útil

pay•ment ['peɪmənt] pago *m*

'pay•ment ad•vice aviso *m* de pago

'pay•off 1 (*bribe*) soborno *m* **2** (*final outcome*) desenlace *m* **3** *of joke* desenlace *m*; **'pay•out** pago *m*; **'pay pack•et** *Br* sobre *m* con la paga; **pay-per-view T'V** televisión *f* de pago por visión; **'pay phone** teléfono *m* público; **'pay rise** *Br* subida *f* de sueldo; **'pay•roll** *money* salarios *mpl*; *employees* nómina *f*; ***be on the ~*** estar en nómina; **'pay•slip** nómina *f* (*papel*); **'pay sta•tion** TELEC teléfono *m* de monedas; **pay T'V** televisión *f* de pago

PC [piː'siː] *abbr* **1** (= ***personal computer***) PC *m*, *Span* ordenador *m or L.Am.* computadora *f* personal **2** (= ***politically correct***) políticamente correcto

PCB *abbr* (= ***printed circuit board***) placa *f* impresa

pda [piːdiː'eɪ] *abbr* (= ***personal digital assistant***) pda *m*, organizador *m* personal

PE [piː'iː] *abbr* (= ***physical education***) educación *f* física

pea [piː] arveja *f*, *Mex* chícharo *m*, *Span* guisante *m*

peace [piːs] **1** paz *f* **2** (*quietness*) tranquilidad; ***can we have a bit of ~!*** ¡silencio, por favor!

peace•a•ble ['piːsəbl] *adj person* pacífico

'Peace Corps *organización gubernamental estadounidense de ayuda al desarrollo*

peace•ful ['piːsfəl] *adj* tranquilo; *demonstration* pacífico

peace•ful•ly ['piːsfəlɪ] *adv* pacíficamente

'peace•keep•ing *adj*: ***~ force*** fuerza *f* de pacificación; **'peace-lov•ing** *adj* pacifista; **'peace•time** tiempo *m* de paz

peach [piːtʃ] *fruit* melocotón *m*, *L.Am.* durazno *m*; *tree* melocotonero *m*, *L.Am.* duraznero *m*

pea•cock ['piːkɑːk] pavo *m* real

peak [piːk] **I** *n of mountain* cima *f*; *mountain* pico *m*; *fig* clímax *m*; ***when the crisis was at its ~*** cuando la crisis estaba en su punto culminante *or* álgido **II** *v/i* alcanzar el máximo; ***it has ~ed*** lo peor ya ha pasado

peaked [piːkt] *adj*: ***~ cap*** gorra *f* con vi-

sera
'peak hours *npl* horas *fpl* punta
peal [piːl]: **~*of bells*** repique *m* de campanas; **~ *of thunder*** trueno *m*; **~ *of laughter*** carcajadas *fpl*
pea•nut ['piːnʌt] cacahuete *m*, *L.Am.* maní *m*, *Mex* cacahuate *m*; ***get paid ~s*** F cobrar una miseria F; ***that's ~s to him*** F eso es calderilla para él F
pea•nut 'but•ter crema *f* de cacahuete
pear [per] pera *f*
pearl [pɜːrl] perla *f*; ***~s of wisdom*** perlas de sabiduría
pearl 'bar•ley cebada *f* perlada
'pearl div•er pescador(a) *m(f)* de perlas
pearl•y 'gates ['pɜːrlɪ] *npl* F puertas *fpl* del cielo
pear-shaped ['perʃeɪpt] *adj*: ***go~*** F salir mal, torcerse
peas•ant ['peznt] campesino(-a) *m(f)*
peat [piːt] turba *f*
peb•ble ['pebl] guijarro *m*
pe•can ['piːkən] pacana *f*
pe•can 'pie tarta *f* de pacana
pec•ca•dil•lo [pekə'dɪloʊ] (*pl* **-lo(*e*)*s*** [pekə'dɪloʊz]) desliz *m*
peck [pek] **I** *n* **1** *bite* picotazo *m* **2** *kiss* besito *m* **II** *v/t* **1** *bite* picotear **2** *kiss* dar un besito a
◆ **peck at** *v/t*: ***peck at one's food*** picotear la comida
pec•to•ral ['pektərəl] *adj* pectoral
pe•cu•liar [pɪ'kjuːljər] *adj* **1** (*strange*) raro **2**: **~ *to*** (*special*) característico de
pe•cu•li•ar•i•ty [pɪkjuːlɪ'ærətɪ] **1** (*strangeness*) rareza *f* **2** (*special feature*) peculiaridad *f*, característica *f*
pe•cu•li•ar•ly [pɪ'kjuːljərlɪ] *adv* (*especially*) particularmente
pe•cu•ni•ar•y [pɪ'kjuːnjərɪ] *adj* pecuniario; **~ *difficulties*** dificultades *fpl* económicas
ped•a•gog•i•cal [pedə'gɑːdʒɪkl] *adj* pedagógico
ped•al ['pedl] **I** *n of bike* pedal *m* **II** *v/i* **1** (*pret & pp* **-ed**, *Br* **-led**) (*turn **~s***) pedalear **2** (*cycle*) recorrer en bicicleta
'ped•al bin cubo *m* de basura con pedal
ped•ant ['pedənt] puntilloso(-a) *m(f)*
pe•dan•tic [pɪ'dæntɪk] *adj* puntilloso
ped•ant•ry ['pedəntrɪ] meticulosidad *f*
ped•dle ['pedl] *v/t drugs* traficar *or* trapichear con
ped•er•ast ['pedəræst] pederasta *m/f*
ped•es•tal ['pedəstl] *for statue* pedestal *m*
pe•des•tri•an [pɪ'destrɪən] **I** *n* peatón (-ona) *m(f)* **II** *adj* pedestre
pe•des•tri•an 'cros•sing *Br* paso *m* de peatones
pe•des•tri•a•nize [pɪ'destrɪənaɪz] *v/t* hacer peatonal
pe•des•tri•an 'pre•cinct zona *f* peatonal
pe•di•at•ric [piːdɪ'ætrɪk] *adj* pediátrico
pe•di•a•tri•cian [piːdɪə'trɪʃn] pediatra *m/f*
pe•di•at•rics [piːdɪ'ætrɪks] *nsg* pediatría *f*
ped•i•cure ['pedɪkjʊr] pedicura *f*
ped•i•gree ['pedɪgriː] **I** *n* pedigrí *m*; *of person* linaje *m* **II** *adj* con pedigrí
pe•do•phile ['piːdəfaɪl] pedófilo(-a) *m(f)*, pederasta *m/f*
pe•do•phil•i•a [piːdə'fɪlɪə] pedofilia *f*, pederastia *f*
pee [piː] *v/i* F hacer pis F, mear F
peek [piːk] **I** *n* ojeada *f*, vistazo *m* **II** *v/i* echar una ojeada *or* vistazo
peel [piːl] **I** *n* piel *f* **II** *v/t fruit*, *vegetables* pelar **III** *v/i of nose*, *shoulders* pelarse; *of paint* levantarse
◆ **peel off I** *v/t wrapper etc* quitar; *jacket etc* quitarse **II** *v/i of wrapper* quitarse
peel•er ['piːlər] *for potatoes* pelapatatas *m inv*
peel•ings ['piːlɪŋz] *npl* peladuras *fpl*
peep [piːp] ☞ ***peek***
peep•ers ['piːpərz] *npl* F (*eyes*) ojos *mpl*
peep•hole ['piːphoʊl] mirilla *f*
Peep•ing Tom [piːpɪŋ'tɑːm] mirón (-ona) *m(f)*
'peep show peepshow *m*, espectáculo *m* pornográfico
peer¹ [pɪr] *n* (*equal*) igual *m*
peer² [pɪr] *v/i* mirar; **~ *through the mist*** buscar con la mirada entre la niebla; **~ *at*** forzar la mirada para ver
peer•age ['pɪrɪdʒ] *Br* título *m* de par; ***be raised to the ~*** obtener el título de par
'peer group grupo *m* paritario
peer•less ['pɪrlɪs] *adj* sin igual
'peer pres•sure la influencia de las compañías
peeved [piːvd] F mosqueado F
pee•vish ['piːvɪʃ] *adj* malhumorado
peg [peg] *for hat*, *coat* percha *f*; *for tent* clavija *f*; ***off the ~*** de confección

pe•jo•ra•tive [pɪ'dʒɑːrətɪv] *adj* peyorativo

pe•kin•ese [piːkə'niːz] (*pl* ***pekinese***) pequinés *m*

pel•i•can ['pelɪkən] pelícano *m*

pel•let ['pelɪt] **1** pelotita *f* **2** (*bullet*) perdigón *m*

pelt[1] [pelt] **I** *v/t*: **~ *s.o. with sth*** tirar algo a alguien **II** *v/i*: ***they ~ed along the road*** F fueron a toda mecha por la carretera F; ***it's ~ing down*** F está diluviando F

pelt[2] [pelt] *n* piel *f*

pel•vic ['pelvɪk] *adj* ANAT, MED pélvico

pel•vis ['pelvɪs] pelvis *f*

pen[1] [pen] (*ballpoint ~*) bolígrafo *m*; (*fountain ~*) pluma *f* (estilográfica)

pen[2] [pen] (*enclosure*) corral *m*

pen[3] [pen] ☞ ***penitentiary***

pe•nal ['piːnl] *adj* penal; ***~ reform*** reforma *f* penal

'pe•nal code código *m* penal

pe•nal•ize ['piːnəlaɪz] *v/t* penalizar

pen•al•ty ['penəltɪ] sanción *f*; SP penalti *m*; ***take the ~*** *in soccer* lanzar el penalti; ***award*** *or* ***give a ~*** SP señalar *or* pitar penalti; ***score a ~*** marcar de penalti; ***win on penalties*** ganar por penalties

'pen•al•ty ar•e•a SP área *f* de castigo; **'pen•al•ty clause** LAW cláusula *f* de penalización; **'pen•al•ty kick** SP (lanzamiento *m* de) penalti *m*; **pen•al•ty 'shoot-out** SP tanda *f* de penaltis; **'pen•al•ty spot** SP punto *m* de penalti, punto *m* fatídico

pen•ance ['penəns] REL penitencia *f*; ***do ~ for sth*** hacer penitencia por algo

pen-and-'ink draw•ing dibujo *m* a pluma

pence [pens] *pl* ☞ ***penny***

pen•chant ['penʃənt] inclinación *f* (***for*** a, por)

pen•cil ['pensɪl] lápiz *m*

◆ **pencil in** *v/t* apuntar provisionalmente

'pen•cil case estuche *m*, plumier *m*

'pen•cil sharp•en•er sacapuntas *m inv*

pen•dant ['pendənt] *necklace* colgante *m*

pend•ing ['pendɪŋ] **I** *prep* en espera de **II** *adj* pendiente; ***be ~*** *awaiting a decision* estar pendiente; *about to happen* ser inminente

pen•du•lum ['pendjʊləm] péndulo *m*

pen•e•trate ['penɪtreɪt] *v/t* (*pierce*) penetrar; *market* penetrar en

pen•e•trat•ing ['penɪtreɪtɪŋ] *adj stare, scream* penetrante; *analysis* exhaustivo

pen•e•tra•tion [penɪ'treɪʃn] penetración *f*; *of defenses* incursión *f*; *of market* entrada *f*

'pen friend amigo(-a) *m*(*f*) por correspondencia

pen•guin ['peŋgwɪn] pingüino *m*

pen•i•cil•lin [penɪ'sɪlɪn] penicilina *f*

pe•nin•su•la [pə'nɪnsʊlə] península *f*

pe•nin•su•lar [pə'nɪnsʊlər] *adj* peninsular

pe•nis ['piːnɪs] pene *m*

pen•i•tence ['penɪtəns] (*remorse*) arrepentimiento *m*

pen•i•tent ['penɪtənt] *adj* arrepentido

pen•i•tent•ia•ry [penɪ'tenʃərɪ] prisión *f*, cárcel *f*

'pen name seudónimo *m*

pen•nant ['penənt] banderín *f*

pen•ni•less ['penɪlɪs] *adj* sin un centavo

pen•ny ['penɪ] (*pl* ***-ies***, ***pence*** [pens]) penique *m*; ***at last the ~ has dropped*** F al final se dio cuenta / me di cuenta *etc*; ***a ~ for your thoughts*** F ¿en qué estabas pensando?

pen•ny-pinch•ing ['penɪpɪntʃɪŋ] *adj* F rácano

'pen pal amigo(-a) *m*(*f*) por correspondencia

'pen push•er *pej* chupatintas *m/f inv*

pen•sion ['penʃn] pensión *f*

◆ **pension off** *v/t* jubilar

pen•sion•a•ble ['penʃənəbl] *adj*: ***of ~ age*** en edad de jubilación

pen•sion•er ['penʃənər] pensionista *m/f*, jubilado(-a) *m*(*f*)

'pen•sion fund fondo *m* de pensiones

'pen•sion scheme plan *m* de jubilación

pen•sive ['pensɪv] *adj* pensativo

Pen•ta•gon ['pentəgɑːn]: ***the ~*** el Pentágono

pen•tag•o•nal [pen'tægənl] *adj* pentagonal

pen•tath•lete [pen'tæθliːt] pentatleta *m/f*

pen•tath•lon [pen'tæθlən] pentatlón *m*

Pen•te•cost ['pentɪkɑːst] Pentecostés *m*

pent•house ['penthaʊs] ático *m* (*de lujo*)

pent-up ['pentʌp] *adj* reprimido
pe•nul•ti•mate [pe'nʌltɪmət] *adj* penúltimo
pe•o•ny ['pɪənɪ] BOT peonía *f*
peo•ple ['pi:pl] **1** *npl* gente *f*; (*individuals*) personas *fpl*; ***the ~*** (*citizens*) el pueblo, los ciudadanos; ***a lot of ~ think ...*** muchos piensan que ...; ***~ say ...*** se dice que ..., dicen que ... **2** *nsg* (*race, tribe*) pueblo *m*; ***the Spanish ~*** los españoles
pep [pep] F energía *f*
◆ **pep up** *v/t* (*pret & pp* **-ped**) F *person* animar; *food* alegrar; ***pep things up*** animar las cosas
pep•per ['pepər] **1** *spice* pimienta *f* **2** *vegetable* pimiento *m*
'pep•per•corn grano *m* de pimienta; **pep•per•corn 'rent** alquiler *m* simbólico; **'pep•per•mill** molinillo *m* de pimienta; **'pep•per•mint** *candy* caramelo *m* de menta
pep•per•o•ni ['pepərounɪ] pepperoni *m*
'pep•per pot pimentero *m*
pep•per•y ['pepərɪ] *adj taste* a pimienta
'pep pill F estimulante *m*
'pep talk ***give a ~*** decir unas palabras de aliento
pep•tic ['peptɪk] *adj*: ***~ ulcer*** MED úlcera *f* péptica
per [pɜ:r] *prep* por; ***~ annum*** al año, por año
per cap•i•ta [pər'kæpɪtə] *adj & adv* per cápita
per•ceive [pər'si:v] *v/t* **1** *with senses* percibir **2** (*view, interpret*) interpretar; ***how do you ~ your role in this?*** ¿cuál consideras que es tu papel en esto?
per•cent [pər'sent] *adv* por ciento; ***a 5 ~ increase*** un incremento del 5 por ciento
per•cen•tage [pər'sentɪdʒ] porcentaje *m*, tanto *m* por ciento
per•cep•ti•ble [pər'septəbl] *adj* perceptible
per•cep•ti•bly [pər'septəblɪ] *adv* visiblemente
per•cep•tion [pər'sepʃn] **1** *through senses, of situation etc* percepción *f* **2** (*insight*) perspicacia *f*
per•cep•tive [pər'septɪv] *adj* perceptivo
perch[1] [pɜ:rtʃ] **I** *n for bird* percha *f* **II** *v/i of bird* posarse; *of person* sentarse
perch[2] [pɜ:rtʃ] *n fish* perca *f*
per•co•late ['pɜ:rkəleɪt] *v/i of coffee* filtrarse
per•co•la•tor ['pɜ:rkəleɪtər] cafetera *f* de filtro
per•cus•sion [pər'kʌʃn] percusión *f*
per'cus•sion in•stru•ment instrumento *m* de percusión
per•cus•sion•ist [pər'kʌʃnɪst] percusionista *m/f*
per'cus•sion sec•tion sección *f* de percusión
per•emp•to•ry [pə'remptərɪ] *adj person* autoritario; *tone of voice, command* perentorio
pe•ren•ni•al [pə'renɪəl] **I** *n* BOT árbol *m* de hoja perenne **II** *adj* **1** BOT perenne **2** (*endless*) eterno
per•fect I *n* ['pɜ:rfɪkt] GRAM pretérito *m* perfecto **II** *adj* perfecto; ***I was a ~ stranger to them*** era un completo extraño para ellos **III** *v/t* [pər'fekt] perfeccionar
per•fec•tion [pər'fekʃn] perfección *f*; ***do sth to ~*** hacer algo a la perfección
per•fec•tion•ism [pər'fekʃnɪzəm] perfeccionismo *m*
per•fec•tion•ist [pər'fekʃnɪst] perfeccionista *m/f*
per•fect•ly ['pɜ:rfɪktlɪ] **1** perfectamente **2** (*totally*) completamente
per•fid•i•ous [pər'fɪdɪəs] *adj* pérfido
per•fi•dy ['pɜ:rfɪdɪ] perfidia *f*
per•fo•rate ['pɜ:rfəreɪt] *v/t* perforar
per•fo•rat•ed ['pɜ:rfəreɪtɪd] *adj line* perforado
per•fo•ra•tions [pɜ:rfə'reɪʃnz] *npl* perforaciones *fpl*
per•form [pər'fɔ:rm] **I** *v/t* **1** (*carry out*) realizar, llevar a cabo **2** *of actor, musician etc* interpretar, representar **II** *v/i of actor, musician, dancer* actuar; *of machine* funcionar
per•form•ance [pər'fɔ:rməns] *by actor, musician etc* actuación *f*, interpretación *f*; *of play* representación *f*; *of employee* rendimiento *m*; *of official, company, in sport* actuación *f*; *of machine* rendimiento *m*
per'form•ance car coche *m* de gran rendimiento
per•form•er [pər'fɔ:rmər] intérprete *m/f*
per•form•ing arts [pərfɔ:rmɪŋ'ærts] *npl* artes *fpl* escénicas *or* interpretati-

P

vas
per•fume ['pɜːrfjuːm] perfume *m*
per•func•to•ry [pər'fʌŋktərɪ] *adj* superficial
per•haps [pər'hæps] *adv* quizá(s), tal vez; ~ ***it's not too late*** puede que no sea demasiado tarde
per•il ['perəl] peligro *m*
per•il•ous ['perələs] *adj* peligroso
pe•rim•e•ter [pə'rɪmɪtər] perímetro *m*
pe'rim•e•ter fence cerca *f*
pe•ri•od ['pɪrɪəd] **1** periodo *m*, período *m*; ~ ***of grace*** periodo de gracia **2** (*menstruation*) periodo *m*, regla *f*; ***have one's*** ~ tener el periodo; ~ ***pains*** dolores *mpl* menstruales **3** *punctuation mark* punto *m*; ***I don't want to,*** ~***!*** F ¡no me da la gana y punto! F
pe•ri•od•ic [pɪrɪ'ɑːdɪk] *adj* periódico
pe•ri•od•i•cal [pɪrɪ'ɑːdɪkl] publicación *f* periódica
pe•ri•od•i•cal•ly [pɪrɪ'ɑːdɪklɪ] *adv* periódicamente, con periodicidad
pe•riph•e•ral [pə'rɪfərəl] **I** *adj* (*not crucial*) secundario **II** *n* COMPUT periférico *m*
pe•riph•e•ry [pə'rɪfərɪ] periferia *f*
pe•ri•scope ['perɪskoup] periscopio *m*
per•ish ['perɪʃ] *v/i* **1** *of rubber* estropearse, picarse **2** *of person* perecer
per•ish•a•ble ['perɪʃəbl] *adj food* perecedero
per•i•to•ni•tis [perɪtə'naɪtɪs] MED peritonitis *f inv*
per•jure ['pɜːrdʒər] *v/t*: ~ ***o.s.*** perjurar
per•ju•ry ['pɜːrdʒərɪ] perjurio *m*
perk [pɜːrk] *of job* ventaja *f*
◆ **perk up** F **I** *v/t* animar **II** *v/i* animarse
perk•y ['pɜːrkɪ] F (*cheerful*) animado
perm [pɜːrm] **I** *n* permanente *f* **II** *v/t* hacer la permanente; ***she had her hair*** ~***ed*** se hizo la permanente
per•ma•nence ['pɜːrmənəns] permanencia *f*
per•ma•nent ['pɜːrmənənt] *adj* permanente; ~ ***contract*** contrato *m* fijo *or* indefinido
per•ma•nent•ly ['pɜːrmənəntlɪ] *adv* permanentemente
per•me•a•ble ['pɜːrmɪəbl] *adj* permeable
per•me•ate ['pɜːrmɪeɪt] *v/t* impregnar
per•mis•si•ble [pər'mɪsəbl] *adj* permisible
per•mis•sion [pər'mɪʃn] permiso *m*; ***ask s.o.'s*** ~ ***to do sth*** pedir permiso a alguien para hacer algo; ***give s.o.*** ~ ***to do sth*** dar a alguien permiso para que haga algo
per•mis•sive [pər'mɪsɪv] *adj* permisivo
per•mit ['pɜːrmɪt] **I** *n* licencia *f* **II** *v/t* (*pret & pp* ***-ted***) [pər'mɪt] permitir; ~ ***s.o. to do sth*** permitir a alguien que haga algo
per•ni•cious [pər'nɪʃəs] *adj* pernicioso
per•nick•et•y [pər'nɪkətɪ] *adj* F quisquilloso
per•pen•dic•u•lar [pɜːrpən'dɪkjʊlər] *adj* perpendicular
per•pe•trate ['pɜːrpətreɪt] *v/t crime* perpetrar
per•pe•tra•tor ['pɜːrpətreɪtər] autor(a) *m*(*f*)
per•pet•u•al [pər'petʃʊəl] *adj* perpetuo; *interruptions* continuo
per•pet•u•al•ly [pər'petʃʊəlɪ] *adv* constantemente
per•pet•u•ate [pər'petʃʊeɪt] *v/t* perpetuar
per•pe•tu•i•ty [pɜːrpə'tjuːətɪ]: ***in*** ~ a perpetuidad
per•plex [pər'pleks] *v/t* dejar perplejo
per•plexed [pər'plekst] *adj* perplejo
per•plex•i•ty [pər'pleksɪtɪ] perplejidad *f*
per•se•cute ['pɜːrsɪkjuːt] *v/t* perseguir; (*hound*) acosar
per•se•cu•tion [pɜːrsɪ'kjuːʃn] persecución *f*; (*harassment*) acoso *m*
per•se•cu•tor [pɜːrsɪ'kjuːtər] perseguidor(a) *m*(*f*)
per•se•ver•ance [pɜːrsɪ'vɪrəns] perseverancia *f*
per•se•vere [pɜːrsɪ'vɪr] *v/i* perseverar
Per•sian Gulf ['pɜːrʃən] Golfo *m* Pérsico
per•sist [pər'sɪst] *v/i* persistir; ~ ***in*** persistir en; ***if you will*** ~ ***in doing it that way*** si insistes en hacerlo así *or* de esa forma
per•sis•tence [pər'sɪstəns] **1** (*perseverance*) perseverancia *f* **2** (*continuation*) persistencia *f*
per•sis•tent [pər'sɪstənt] *adj* **1** *person, questions* perseverante **2** *rain, unemployment etc* persistente
per•sis•tent•ly [pər'sɪstəntlɪ] *adv* (*continually*) constantemente
per•son ['pɜːrsn] persona *f*; ***in*** ~ en persona

per•son•a•ble ['pɜːrsənəbl] *adj* agradable

per•son•age ['pɜːrsənɪdʒ] personaje *m*

per•son•al ['pɜːrsənl] *adj* (*private*) personal; *life* privado; ***don't make ~ remarks*** no hagas comentarios personales

per•son•al ap'pear•ance: ***make a ~*** aparecer en persona; **per•son•al as'sist•ant** secretario(-a) *m*(*f*) personal; **'per•son•al col•umn** sección *f* de anuncios personales; **per•son•al com'put•er** *Span* ordenador *m* personal, *L.Am.* computadora *f* personal; **'per•son•al foul** *in basketball* falta *f* personal, personal *f*; **per•son•al 'hy-giene** higiene *f* personal

per•son•al•i•ty [pɜːrsə'nælətɪ] **1** personalidad *f* **2** (*celebrity*) personalidad *f*, personaje *m*

per•son•al•ize ['pɜːrsənəlaɪz] *v/t* personalizar

per•son•al 'loan préstamo *m* personal

per•son•al•ly ['pɜːrsənəlɪ] *adv* **1** (*for my part*) personalmente **2** (*in person*) en persona **3**: ***don't take it ~*** no te lo tomes como algo personal

per•son•al 'or•gan•iz•er organizador *m* personal; **per•son•al 'pro•noun** pronombre *m* personal; **per•son•al 'ster-e•o** walkman *m* ®

per•son•i•fi•ca•tion [pərsɑːnɪfɪ'keɪʃn] personificación *f*

per•son•i•fy [pɜːr'sɑːnɪfaɪ] *v/t* (*pret & pp* ***-ied***) *of person* personificar

per•son•nel [pɜːrsə'nel] *employees, department* personal *m*

per•son'nel man•a•ger director(a) *m*(*f*) de personal

per•spec•tive [pər'spektɪv] PAINT perspectiva *f*; ***get sth into ~*** poner algo en perspectiva; ***try to keep things in ~*** trata de no sacar las cosas de su contexto

per•spi•ra•tion [pɜːrspɪ'reɪʃn] sudor *m*, transpiración *f*

per•spire [pɜːr'spaɪr] *v/i* sudar, transpirar

per•suade [pər'sweɪd] *v/t person* persuadir; ***~ s.o. to do sth*** persuadir a alguien para que haga algo; ***he didn't need much persuading*** no hubo que insistirle mucho

per•sua•sion [pər'sweɪʒn] persuasión *f*

per•sua•sive [pər'sweɪsɪv] persuasivo

pert [pɜːrt] *adj* coqueto

per•tain [pər'teɪn] *v/i fml*: ***~ to sth*** pertenecer a algo

per•ti•nent ['pɜːrtɪnənt] *adj fml* pertinente

per•turb [pər'tɜːrb] *v/t* perturbar

per•turb•ing [pər'tɜːrbɪŋ] *adj* perturbador

Pe•ru [pə'ruː] Perú *m*

pe•ruse [pə'ruːz] *v/t fml* leer atentamente

Pe•ru•vi•an [pə'ruːvɪən] **I** *adj* peruano **II** *n* peruano(-a) *m*(*f*)

per•vade [pər'veɪd] *v/t* impregnar

per•va•sive [pər'veɪsɪv] *adj influence, ideas* dominante

per•verse [pər'vɜːrs] *adj* (*awkward*) terco; *sense of humor* retorcido; ***just to be ~*** sólo para llevar la contraria

per•ver•sion [pər'vɜːrʃn] *sexual* perversión *f*

per•vert I *n* ['pɜːrvɜːrt] *sexual* pervertido(-a) *m*(*f*) **II** *v/t* [pər'vɜːrt] **1** (*deprave*) pervertir **2** (*distort*) distorsionar; ***~ the course of justice*** obstaculizar el curso de la justicia

pe•se•ta [pe'seɪtə] peseta *f*

pes•ky ['peskɪ] *adj* F pesado

pe•so ['peɪsoʊ] FIN peso *m*

pes•sa•ry ['pesərɪ] MED pesario *m*

pes•si•mism ['pesɪmɪzm] pesimismo *m*

pes•si•mist ['pesɪmɪst] pesimista *m/f*

pes•si•mist•ic [pesɪ'mɪstɪk] *adj* pesimista

pest [pest] plaga *f*, F *person* tostón *m* F

pes•ter ['pestər] *v/t* acosar; ***~ s.o. to do sth*** molestar *or* dar la lata a alguien para que haga algo

'pes•ter pow•er *in advertising* táctica *f* del machaqueo

pes•ti•cide ['pestɪsaɪd] pesticida *f*

pet [pet] **I** *n* **1** *animal* animal *m* doméstico *or* de compañía **2** (*favorite*) preferido(-a) *m*(*f*); ***teacher's ~*** el ojito derecho de la maestra **II** *adj* preferido, favorito **III** *v/t* (*pret & pp* ***-ted***) *animal* acariciar **IV** *v/i* (*pret & pp* ***-ted***) *of couple* magrearse F

pet•al ['petl] pétalo *m*

◆ **pe•ter out** ['piːtər] *v/i of rain* amainar; *of rebellion* irse extinguiendo; *of path* ir desapareciendo

'pet food comida *f* para mascotas

pet 'hate: ***it's one of his ~s*** es una de las

cosas que más odia
pe•tite [pə'ti:t] *adj* chiquito; *size* menudo
pe•ti•tion [pə'tɪʃn] petición *f*
pe•ti•tion in 'bank•rupt•cy notificación *f* de bancarrota
'pet name nombre *m* cariñoso
pet•ri•fied ['petrɪfaɪd] *adj person* petrificado; *scream*, *voice* aterrorizado
pet•ri•fy ['petrɪfaɪ] *v/t* (*pret & pp* ***-ied***) dejar petrificado
pet•ro•chem•i•cal [petrou'kemɪkl] *adj* petroquímico
pet•rol ['petrl] *Br* gasolina *f*, *Rpl* nafta *f*
'pet•rol bomb cóctel *m* Molotov
pe•tro•le•um [pɪ'troulɪəm] petróleo *m*
'pet•rol sta•tion *Br* gasolinera *f*
'pet shop pajarería *f*, tienda *f* de animales
pet•ti•coat ['petɪkout] enaguas *fpl*
pet•ting ['petɪŋ] magreo *m* F
pet•ty ['petɪ] *adj* **1** *person*, *behavior* mezquino **2** *details*, *problem* sin importancia
pet•ty 'cash dinero *m* para gastos menores
pet•u•lant ['petʃələnt] *adj* caprichoso
pe•tu•ni•a [pə'tu:nɪə] BOT petunia *f*
pew [pju:] banco *m* (*de iglesia*)
pew•ter ['pju:tər] peltre *m*
pha•lanx ['fælæŋks] (*pl* ***-lanxes*** ['fælæŋksɪs], ***-langes*** [fæ'lændʒi:z]) ANAT, MIL falange *f*
phal•li ['fælaɪ] *pl* ☞ ***phallus***
phal•lic ['fælɪk] *adj* fálico; ~ ***symbol*** símbolo *m* fálico
phal•lus ['fæləs] (*pl* ***phalli*** ['fælaɪ]) falo *m*
phan•tom ['fæntəm] fantasma *m*; ~ ***pain*** dolor *m* fantasma; ~ ***pregnancy*** embarazo *m* psicológico; ~ ***withdrawal*** *from bank account* reintegro *m* ficticio
phar•i•see ['færɪsi:] fariseo(-a) *m(f)*
phar•ma•ceu•ti•cal [fɑ:rmə'su:tɪkl] *adj* farmacéutico
phar•ma•ceu•ti•cals [fɑ:rmə'su:tɪklz] *npl* fármacos *mpl*
phar•ma•cist ['fɑ:rməsɪst] *in store* farmacéutico(-a) *m(f)*
phar•ma•cy ['fɑ:rməsɪ] *store* farmacia *f*
phar•yn•gi•tis [færɪn'dʒaɪtɪs] MED faringitis *f inv*
phase [feɪz] fase *f*; ***go through a difficult*** ~ atravesar una mala etapa
◆ **phase in** *v/t* introducir gradualmente
◆ **phase out** *v/t* eliminar gradualmente
pH-bal•anced [pi:eɪtʃ'bælənsd] *adj* con el pH neutro
PhD [pi:eɪtʃ'di:] *abbr* (= ***Doctor of Philosophy***) doctorado *m*
pheas•ant ['feznt] ORN faisán *m*
phe•nom•e•na [fɪ'nɑ:mɪnə] *pl* ☞ ***phenomenon***
phe•nom•e•nal [fɪ'nɑ:mɪnl] *adj* fenomenal
phe•nom•e•nal•ly [fɪ'nɑ:mɪnlɪ] *adv* extraordinariamente; *stupid* increíblemente
phe•nom•e•non [fɪ'nɑ:mɪnɑ:n] (*pl* ***phenomena***) fenómeno *m*
phew [fju:] *int* uf
pH fac•tor [pi:eɪtʃ'fæktər] pH *m*
phi•al ['faɪəl] vial *m*
Phi Be•ta Kap•pa [faɪbi:tə'kæpə] *sociedad de universitarios estadounidenses distinguidos*
phi•lan•der•er [fɪ'lændərər] mujeriego *m*
phil•an•throp•ic [fɪlən'θrɑ:pɪk] *adj* filantrópico
phi•lan•thro•pist [fɪ'lænθrəpɪst] filántropo(-a) *m(f)*
phi•lan•thro•py [fɪ'lænθrəpɪ] filantropía *f*
phi•lat•e•list [fɪ'lætəlɪst] filatélico(-a) *m(f)*
phi•lat•e•ly [fɪ'lætəlɪ] filatelia *f*
Phil•ip•pines ['fɪlɪpi:nz] *npl*: ***the*** ~ las Filipinas
phil•is•tine ['fɪlɪstaɪn] **I** *n* filisteo(-a) *m(f)* **II** *adj* filisteo
Phil•lips screw ['fɪlɪps] tornillo *m* de cruz
'Phil•lips screw•driv•er destornillador *m* de cruz
phil•o•log•i•cal [fɪlə'lɑ:dʒɪkl] *adj* filológico
phi•lol•o•gist [fɪ'lɑ:lədʒɪst] filólogo(-a) *m(f)*
phi•lol•o•gy [fɪ'lɑ:lədʒɪ] filología *f*
phi•los•o•pher [fɪ'lɑ:səfər] filósofo(-a) *m(f)*
phil•o•soph•i•cal [fɪlə'sɑ:fɪkl] *adj* filosófico
phi•los•o•phize [fɪ'lɑ:səfaɪz] *v/i* filosofar (***about, on*** sobre)
phi•los•o•phy [fɪ'lɑ:səfɪ] filosofía *f*
phlegm [flem] PHYSIO, *fig* flema *f*

phleg•mat•ic [fleg'mætɪk] *adj* flemático

pho•bi•a ['foʊbɪə] fobia *f*; ***have a ~ about sth*** tener fobia a algo

phone [foʊn] **I** *n* teléfono *m*; ***be on the ~*** *have a ~* tener teléfono; *be talking* estar hablando por teléfono **II** *v/t* llamar (por teléfono) a **III** *v/i* llamar (por teléfono)

'phone book guía *f* (de teléfonos); **'phone booth** cabina *f* (de teléfonos); **'phone call** llamada *f* (telefónica); **'phone card** *Br* tarjeta *f* telefónica; **'phone-in** *Br* programa *m* con llamadas

pho•neme ['foʊni:m] LING fonema *m*

'phone num•ber número *m* de teléfono

pho•net•ic [fə'netɪk] *adj* fonético

pho•net•ics [fə'netɪks] *nsg* fonética *f*

pho•n(e)y ['foʊnɪ] F **I** *adj* falso **II** *n person* farsante *m/f*; *thing* falsificación *f*

phos•phate ['fɑ:sfeɪt] CHEM fosfato *m*

phos•pho•res•cent [fɑ:sfə'resnt] *adj* fosforescente

phos•pho•rus ['fɑ:sfərəs] CHEM fósforo *m*

pho•to ['foʊtoʊ] foto *f*

'pho•to al•bum álbum *m* de fotos; **'pho•to•cell** ELEC célula *f* fotoeléctrica; **'pho•to•cop•i•er** fotocopiadora *f*; **'pho•to•cop•y I** *n* fotocopia *f* **II** *v/t* (*pret & pp* ***-ied***) fotocopiar; **pho•to 'fin•ish** SP fotofinish *f*; **'Pho•to-fit®** retrato *m* robot

pho•to•gen•ic [foʊtoʊ'dʒenɪk] *adj* fotogénico

pho•to•graph ['foʊtəgræf] **I** *n* fotografía *f* **II** *v/t* fotografiar

pho•tog•ra•pher [fə'tɑ:grəfər] fotógrafo(-a) *m(f)*

pho•to•graph•ic [foʊtə'græfɪk] *adj* fotográfico; ***~ studio*** estudio *m* fotográfico

pho•tog•ra•phy [fə'tɑ:grəfɪ] fotografía *f*

pho•to'jour•nal•ist reportero(-a) *m/f* gráfico(-a)

pho•to•mon'tage fotomontaje *m*

pho•ton ['foʊtɑ:n] PHYS fotón *m*

pho•to'sen•si•tive *adj* fotosensible; **'pho•to•shoot** sesión *f* de fotografías; **pho•to'syn•the•sis** BIO fotosíntesis *f inv*

phras•al ['freɪzl] *adj*: ***~ verb*** LING verbo *m* con partícula

phrase [freɪz] **I** *n* frase *f* **II** *v/t* expresar

'phrase•book guía *f* de conversación

phra•se•ol•o•gy [freɪzɪ'ɑ:lədʒɪ] fraseología *f*

phys•i•cal ['fɪzɪkl] **I** *adj* físico **II** *n* MED reconocimiento *m* médico

phys•i•cal ed•u'ca•tion educación *f* física; **phys•i•cal 'hand•i•cap** minusvalía *f* física; **'phys•i•cal in•ven•to•ry** inventario *m* físico

phys•i•cal•ly ['fɪzɪklɪ] *adv* físicamente; ***~ impossible*** físicamente imposible

phys•i•cal•ly 'hand•i•cap•ped *npl*: ***the ~*** los disminuídos físicos

phy•si•cian [fɪ'zɪʃn] médico(-a) *m(f)*

phys•i•cist ['fɪzɪsɪst] físico(-a) *m(f)*

phys•ics ['fɪzɪks] *nsg* física *f*

phys•i•og•no•my [fɪzɪ'ɑ:nəmɪ] fisonomía *f*, fisionomía *f*

phys•i•o•log•i•cal [fɪzɪə'lɑ:dʒɪkl] *adj* fisiológico

phys•i•ol•o•gy [fɪzɪ'ɑ:lədʒɪ] fisiología *f*

phys•i•o•ther•a•pist [fɪzɪoʊ'θerəpɪst] fisioterapeuta *m/f*

phys•i•o•ther•a•py [fɪzɪoʊ'θerəpɪ] fisioterapia *f*

phy•sique [fɪ'zi:k] físico *m*

pi•a•nist ['pɪənɪst] pianista *m/f*

pi•an•o [pɪ'ænoʊ] piano *m*

pi•an•o ac'cor•de•on acordeón *m*

pi'an•o play•er pianista *m/f*

pi'an•o stool taburete *m* (para el piano)

pick [pɪk] **I** *n*: ***take your ~*** elige el que prefieras **II** *v/t* **1** (*choose*) escoger, elegir **2** *flowers*, *fruit* recoger; ***~ one's nose*** meterse el dedo en la nariz **III** *v/i*: ***~ and choose*** ser muy exigente

◆ **pick at** *v/t*: ***pick at one's food*** comer como un pajarito

◆ **pick on** *v/t* **1** (*treat unfairly*) meterse con **2** (*select*) elegir

◆ **pick out** *v/t* **1** (*identify*) identificar **2** *tune* tocar de oído

◆ **pick over** *v/t* triar

◆ **pick up I** *v/t* **1** *object* recoger, *Span* coger; *telephone* descolgar; ***pick up the tab*** F pagar **2** *illness* contraer, *Span* coger **3** *habit* adquirir, *Span* coger; *language*, *skill* aprender **4** *in car*, *from ground*, *from airport etc* recoger **5** (*buy*) comprar **6** *criminal* detener **7**: ***pick s.o. up*** *sexually* ligar con alguien **8** RAD sintonizar; *hear* entender, pillar F

P

II *v/i* (*improve*) mejorar
◆ **pick up on** *v/t* **1** *details*, *what s.o. said etc* darse cuenta de **2**: ***pick s.o. up on sth*** corregir algo a alguien
pick•a•back ['pɪkəbæk] **I** *adv*: ***carry s.o. ~*** llevar a alguien a cuestas **II** *n*: ***give s.o. a ~*** llevar a alguien a cuestas
'pick•ax(e) pico *m*
pick•er ['pɪkər] recolector(a) *m(f)*
pick•et ['pɪkɪt] **I** *n of strikers* piquete *m* **II** *v/t* hacer piquete delante de
'pick•et fence valla *f* de estacas
'pick•et line piquete *m*
pick•ings ['pɪkɪŋz] *npl*: ***there are easy ~ in this job*** en este trabajo es muy fácil obtener beneficios
pick•le ['pɪkl] *v/t* encurtir; *fish* poner en escabeche; *meat* poner en adobo
pick•led ['pɪkld] *adj* **1** en vinagre **2** F (*drunk*) bolinga
pick•les ['pɪklz] *npl* (*dill ~*) encurtidos *mpl*
'pick-me-up F reconstituyente *m*; **'pick•pock•et** carterista *m/f*; **'pick•up** *of car* aceleración *f*; **'pick•up (truck)** camioneta *f*
'pick-up game juego *m* callejero
pick•y ['pɪkɪ] *adj* F tiquismiquis F
pic•nic ['pɪknɪk] **I** *n* picnic *m* **II** *v/i* (*pret & pp* ***-ked***) ir de picnic
pic•to•gram ['pɪktəgræm] pictograma *m*
pic•to•ri•al [pɪk'tɔːrɪəl] *adj* gráfico
pic•ture ['pɪkʧər] **I** *n* **1** (*photo*) fotografía *f*, (*painting*) cuadro *m*; (*illustration*) dibujo *m* **2** (*movie*) película *f* **3** *on TV* imagen *f* **4**: ***keep s.o. in the ~*** mantener a alguien al día; ***be in the ~*** *know what's going on* estar al tanto de lo que pasa; ***ok, I get the ~*** vale, ya me doy cuenta, vale, ya lo capto; ***her face was a ~!*** ¡vaya cara que puso!; ***he's not exactly the ~ of health*** no es exactamente la viva imagen de la salud **II** *v/t* imaginar; ***I can just ~ it*** me lo puedo imaginar perfectamente
'pic•ture book libro *m* ilustrado; **'pic•ture frame** marco *m*; **'pic•ture gal•ler•y** pinacoteca *f*; **pic•ture 'post•card** postal *f*
pic•tur•esque [pɪkʧə'resk] *adj* pintoresco
'pic•ture win•dow ventanal *m*
pid•dle ['pɪdl] *v/i* F hacer pis
pid•dling ['pɪdlɪŋ] *adj* F mísero
pidg•in Eng•lish ['pɪdʒɪn] *inglés mezclado con un dialecto local*
pie [paɪ] pastel *m*
piece [piːs] (*fragment*) fragmento *m*; *component*, *in board game* pieza *f*; ***a ~ of pie / bread*** un trozo de pastel / una rebanada de pan; ***a ~ of advice*** un consejo; ***go to ~s*** derrumbarse; ***take to ~s*** desmontar
◆ **piece together** *v/t broken plate* recomponer; *facts*, *evidence* reconstruir
piece•meal ['piːsmiːl] *adv* poco a poco
'piece•work trabajo *m* a destajo
'pie chart gráfico *m* circular *or* de sectores
pied-a-terre [pjeɪdɑː'ter] *segunda vivienda en la ciudad*
pie-eyed [paɪ'aɪd] *adj* F (*drunk*) ciego
pier [pɪr] *at seaside* malecón *m*
pierce [pɪrs] *v/t* **1** (*penetrate*) perforar **2** *ears* agujerear
pierc•ing ['pɪrsɪŋ] **1** *adj scream* desgarrador; *gaze* penetrante; *wind* cortante **II** *n of lips*, *nose etc* piercing *m*
pi•e•ty ['paɪətɪ] piedad *f*
pif•fle ['pɪfl] F bobadas *fpl*
pig [pɪg] *also fig* cerdo *m*; ***make a ~ of o.s.*** ponerse como un cerdo
◆ **pig out** *v/i* ponerse como un cerdo
◆ **pig out on** *v/t* ponerse como un cerdo comiendo
pi•geon ['pɪdʒɪn] paloma *f*
'pi•geon•hole I *n* casillero *m* **II** *v/t* **1** *person* encasillar **2** *proposal* archivar
pi•geon-toed [pɪdʒɪn'toʊd] *adv*: ***walk ~*** caminar con las puntas de los pies hacia dentro
pig•gish ['pɪgɪʃ] *adj* cerdo
pig•gy•back ['pɪgɪbæk] ☞ ***pickaback***
pig•gy•bank ['pɪgɪbæŋk] hucha *f*
pig'head•ed *adj* F cabezota F
'pig i•ron arrabio *m*
pig•let ['pɪglɪt] cerdito *m*
pig•ment ['pɪgmənt] pigmento *m*
pig•my ☞ ***pygmy***
'pig•pen *also fig* pocilga *f*; **'pig•skin** piel *f* de cerdo; **'pig swill** bazofia *f*; **'pig•tail** coleta *f*
pike[1] [paɪk] *fish* lucio *m*
pike[2] [paɪk] ☞ ***turnpike***
pil•chard ['pɪlʧərd] sardina *f*
pile[1] [paɪl] montón *m*, pila *f*; ***a ~ of work*** F un montón de trabajo F

P

◆ **pile up I** *v/i of work, bills* acumularse **II** *v/t* amontonar
pile[2] [paɪl] *stake, in ground* estaca *f*
pile[3] [paɪl] *of carpet* pelo *m*
'pile driv•er martinete *m*
piles [paɪlz] *nsg* MED hemorroides *fpl*
'pile-up MOT choque *m* múltiple
pil•fer ['pɪlfər] *v/t & v/i* hurtar
pil•fer•ing ['pɪlfərɪŋ] hurtos *mpl*
pil•grim ['pɪlgrɪm] peregrino(-a) *m(f)*
pil•grim•age ['pɪlgrɪmɪdʒ] peregrinación *f*
pill [pɪl] pastilla *f*; *contraceptive* píldora *f*; ***be on the ~*** tomar la píldora
pil•lage ['pɪlɪdʒ] **I** *v/t & v/i* saquear **II** *n* saqueo *m*, pillaje *m*
pil•lar ['pɪlər] pilar *m*; ***a ~ of society*** uno de los pilares de la sociedad
pil•lion ['pɪljən] *of motor bike* asiento *m* trasero; ***ride ~*** ir de paquete
pil•lo•ry ['pɪlərɪ] **I** *n* HIST picota *f* **II** *v/t fig* vituperar
pil•low ['pɪloʊ] almohada *f*
'pill•ow•case, 'pil•low•slip funda *f* de almohada; **'pil•low fight** pelea *f* de almohadas; **'pil•low talk** secretos *mpl* de alcoba
pi•lot ['paɪlət] **I** *n of airplane* piloto *m/f*; *for ship* práctico *m* **II** *v/t airplane* pilotar
'pi•lot light piloto *m*; **'pi•lot plant** planta *f* piloto; **'pi•lot scheme** plan *m* piloto; **'pi•lot stud•y** estudio *m* piloto
pi•men•to [pɪ'mentoʊ] pimiento *m* morrón
pimp [pɪmp] proxeneta *m*, *Span* chulo *m* F
pim•ple ['pɪmpl] grano *m*
pim•ply ['pɪmplɪ] *adj* con muchos granos
PIN [pɪn] (= ***personal identification number***) PIN *m*, número *m* de identificación personal
pin [pɪn] **I** *n* **1** *for sewing* alfiler *m* **2** *in bowling* bolo *m* **3** *badge* pin *m* **4** ELEC clavija *f* **II** *v/t* (*pret & pp* ***-ned***) **1** (*hold down*) mantener **2** (*attach*) sujetar
◆ **pin down** *v/t reason, exact nature of sth* precisar; ***pin s.o. down to a date*** forzar a alguien a concretar una fecha; ***be pinned down*** *trapped* estar atrapado
◆ **pin up** *v/t notice* sujetar con chinchetas
pin•a•fore ['pɪnəfɔːr] **1** delantal *m* **2** *Br*: **~** (***dress***) pichi *m*
'pin•ball flíper *m*; ***play ~*** jugar al flíper
'pin•ball ma•chine flíper *m*
'pin•cer move•ment *also fig* movimiento *m* de tenaza
pin•cers ['pɪnsərz] *npl of crab* pinzas *fpl*; *tool* tenazas *fpl*; ***a pair of ~*** unas tenazas
pinch [pɪntʃ] **I** *n* pellizco *m*; *of salt, sugar etc* pizca *f*; ***at a ~*** si no queda otro remedio; *with numbers* como máximo **II** *v/t* pellizcar **III** *v/i of shoes* apretar
'pin•cush•ion acerico *m*
pine[1] [paɪn] *n tree* pino *m*; *wood* (madera *f* de) pino *m*
pine[2] [paɪn] *v/i*: **~ *for*** echar de menos
'pine•ap•ple piña *f*, *L.Am.* ananá(s) *f*
'pine mar•ten marta *f*; **'pine nee•dle** aguja *f* de pino; **'pine tree** pino *m*
ping [pɪŋ] **I** *n* sonido *m* metálico **II** *v/i* hacer un sonido metálico
ping-pong ['pɪŋpɑːŋ] pimpón *m*, ping-pong *m*
pin•ion ['pɪnjən] TECH piñón *m*
pink [pɪŋk] **I** *adj* rosa **II** *v/i of engine* atascarse
pin•kie ['pɪŋkɪ] F meñique *m*
'pin•kie ring anillo *m* para el meñique
'pin mon•ey dinero *m* extra
pin•na•cle ['pɪnəkl] *fig* cima *f*
'pin•point I *v/t* determinar **II** *adj*: ***with ~ accuracy*** con precisión milimétrica
pins and 'nee•dles *npl* hormigueo *m*
'pin•stripe *adj* a rayas
pint [paɪnt] pinta *f*, *medida equivalente a 0,473 litros en Estados Unidos o a 0,568 litros en Gran Bretaña*
'pin ta•ble flíper *m*
'pin-up modelo *m/f* de revista
pi•o•neer [paɪə'nɪr] **I** *n fig* pionero(-a) *m(f)* **II** *v/t* ser pionero en
pi•o•neer•ing [paɪə'nɪrɪŋ] *adj work* pionero
pi•ous ['paɪəs] piadoso
pip [pɪp] *of fruit* pepita *f*
pipe [paɪp] **I** *n* **1** *for smoking* pipa *f* **2** *for water, gas, sewage* tubería *f* **II** *v/t* conducir por tuberías
◆ **pipe down** *v/i* F cerrar el pico F
◆ **pipe up** *v/t* F *of person* soltar
'pipe clean•er desatascador *m*
piped mu•sic [paɪpt'mjuːzɪk] hilo *m* musical
'pipe dream sueño *m* imposible

'pipe•line *for oil* oleoducto *m*; *for gas* gasoducto *m*; ***in the ~*** *fig* en trámite
pip•er ['paɪpər] gaitero(-a) *m(f)*
'pipe smok•er fumador(a) *m(f)* en pipa
pip•ing hot [paɪpɪŋ'hɑːt] *adj* muy caliente
pi•quant ['piːkənt] *adj* picante
pique [piːk] **I** *v/t* molestar; ***be ~d*** estar molesto (***at*** por) **II** *n*: ***in a fit of ~*** en una rabieta
pi•ra•cy ['paɪrəsɪ] *also of software etc* piratería *f*
pi•rate ['paɪrət] **I** *n* pirata *m/f* **II** *v/t software* piratear
'pi•rate cop•y copia *f* pirata
pi•rat•ed cop•y ['paɪrətɪdkɑːpɪ] copia *f* pirata
'pi•rate e•di•tion edición *f* pirata; **pi•rate 'rad•i•o sta•tion** radio *f* pirata; **'pi•rate ship** barco *m* pirata
pir•ou•ette [pɪrʊ'et] pirueta *f*; ***do a ~*** hacer una pirueta
Pis•ces ['paɪsiːz] ASTR Piscis *m/f inv*; ***be (a) ~*** ser Piscis
piss [pɪs] **I** *v/i* P (*urinate*) mear P **II** *n* P (*urine*) meada *f* P; ***take the ~ out of s.o.*** *Br* P tomar el pelo a alguien
◆ **piss off** P **I** *v/t* (*annoy*) cabrear **II** *v/i* *Br* largarse
piss•ant [pɪsænt] P **I** *adj* maldito, puñetero F **II** *n* canalla *m/f* F
pissed [pɪst] *adj* P **1** (*annoyed*) cabreado P **2** *Br* (*drunk*) borracho, pedo F
piss•poor ['pɪspʊr] *adj* P chapucero
pis•tach•i•o [pɪ'stɑːʃɪoʊ] BOT pistacho *m*
piste [piːst] pista *f*
pis•til ['pɪstɪl] BOT pistilo *m*
pis•tol ['pɪstl] pistola *f*
'pis•tol-whip *v/t* (*pret & pp* ***-ped***) golpear con una pistola a
pis•ton ['pɪstən] pistón *m*
'pis•ton ring anillo *m* de pistón
'pis•ton rod biela *f* del pistón
pit [pɪt] **1** (*hole*) hoyo *m* **2** (*coal mine*) mina *f* **3** *in fruit* hueso *m*
pit•bull 'ter•ri•er pitbull *m* terrier
pitch[1] [pɪʧ] *n* **1** MUS tono *m* **2** *of roof* pendiente *f* **3** (*throw*) lanzamiento *m* **4** SP *field* campo *m* **5**: ***the tension had reached such a ~ that ...*** la tensión había crecido tanto que... **6** *when trying to sell sth etc* charla *f*, discurso *m*
pitch[2] [pɪʧ] **I** *v/i in baseball* lanzar la pelota **II** *v/t* **1** *tent* montar **2** *ball* lanzar
◆ **pitch in** *v/i* echar una mano
'pitch-black *adj* negro como el carbón
'pitch-dark *adj* oscuro como boca de lobo
pitched bat•tle [pɪʧt'bætl] batalla *f* campal
pitch•er[1] ['pɪʧər] *baseball player* lanzador(a) *m(f)*, pí(t)cher *m/f*
pitch•er[2] ['pɪʧər] *container* jarra *f*
'pitch•fork I *n* horca *f* **II** *v/t hay etc* aventar; ***be ~ed into sth*** *fig* verse metido de repente en algo
pit•e•ous ['pɪtɪəs] *adj* patético
'pit•fall dificultad *f*, peligro *m*
pith [pɪθ] *of citrus fruit* piel *f* blanca
pith•y ['pɪθɪ] *adj remark* sucinto
pit•i•a•ble ['pɪtɪəbl] ☞ ***pitiful***
pit•i•ful ['pɪtɪfəl] *adj sight* lastimoso; *excuse, attempt* lamentable
pit•i•ful•ly ['pɪtɪflɪ] *adv* lastimosamente
pit•i•less ['pɪtɪləs] *adj* despiadado
pit•i•less•ly ['pɪtɪləslɪ] *adv* despiadadamente
pits [pɪts] *npl* **1** *in motor racing* boxes *mpl* **2**: ***this is the ~*** P esto es de pena *or* de lo peor
'pit stop *in motor racing* parada *f* en boxes
pit•ta bread ['pɪtə] pan *m* pitta
pit•tance ['pɪtns] miseria *f*
pi•tu•i•tar•y (gland) [pɪ'tjʊɪterɪ] ANAT glándula *f* pituitaria
pit•y ['pɪtɪ] **I** *n* pena *f*, lástima *f*; ***it's a ~ that*** es una pena *or* lástima que; ***what a ~!*** ¡qué pena!; ***take ~ on*** compadecerse de **II** *v/t* (*pret & pp* ***-ied***) *person* compadecerse de
pit•y•ing ['pɪtɪɪŋ] *adj* compasivo
piv•ot ['pɪvət] *v/i* pivotar
piv•ot•al ['pɪvətl] *adj role etc* central
'piv•ot foot *in baseball* pie *m* de pivote
pix•el ['pɪksl] TYP, COMPUT píxel *m*
pix•ie, pix•y ['pɪksɪ] duende *m*
piz•za ['piːtsə] pizza *f*
piz•ze•ri•a [piːtsə'riːə] pizzería *f*
plac•ard ['plækɑːrd] pancarta *f*
pla•cate [plə'keɪt] *v/t* aplacar
place [pleɪs] **I** *n* sitio *m*, lugar *m*; *in race, competition* puesto *m*; (*seat*) sitio *m*, asiento *m*; ***I've lost my ~*** *in book* no sé por dónde iba; ***at my / his ~*** en mi / su casa; ***in ~ of*** en lugar de; ***feel out of ~*** sentirse fuera de lugar; ***take***

~ tener lugar, llevarse a cabo; ***in the first ~*** (*firstly*) en primer lugar; (*in the beginning*) en principio; ***I know my ~*** sé cuál es mi sitio; ***he needs putting in his ~*** necesita que alguien lo ponga en su sitio
II *v/t* (*put*) poner, colocar; ***I know you but I can't quite ~ you*** te conozco pero no recuerdo de qué; ***~ an order*** hacer un pedido
pla•ce•bo [plə'siːbou] (*pl* ***-bo(e)s*** [plə'siːbouz]) MED placebo *m*
'place card tarjeta *f* con el nombre
'place mat mantel *m* individual
place•ment ['pleɪsmənt] *for training* colocación *f* en prácticas
'place name topónimo *m*
pla•cen•ta [plə'sentə] placenta *f*
plac•id ['plæsɪd] *adj* apacible
pla•gia•rism ['pleɪdʒərɪzm] plagio *m*
pla•gia•rist ['pleɪdʒərɪst] plagiario(-a) *m(f)*
pla•gia•rize ['pleɪdʒəraɪz] *v/t* plagiar
plague [pleɪg] **I** *n* plaga *f* **II** *v/t* (*bother*) molestar
plaice [pleɪs] (*pl* ***plaice***) platija *f*
plaid [plæd] tela *f* escocesa
plain[1] [pleɪn] *n* llanura *f*
plain[2] [pleɪn] **I** *adj* **1** (*clear, obvious*) claro **2** (*not elaborate*) simple; (*not patterned*) liso; ***~ chocolate*** chocolate *m* amargo; ***it's all ~ sailing from here on*** a partir de ahora todo va a ser pan comido **3** (*not pretty*) feíllo **4** (*blunt*) directo **II** *adv* verdaderamente; ***it's ~ crazy*** es una verdadera locura
'plain-clothes: ***in ~*** de paisano; ***~ policeman*** policía *m/f* de paisano
plain•ly ['pleɪnlɪ] *adv* **1** (*clearly*) evidentemente; ***he's ~ upset*** está claro que está enfadado **2** (*simply*) con sencillez **3** (*bluntly*) directamente
plain•ness ['pleɪnnɪs] **1** (*obviousness*) claridad *f* **2** (*simplicity*) sencillez *f* **3** (*unattractiveness*) falta *f* de atractivo
plain 'spo•ken *adj* directo
plain•tiff ['pleɪntɪf] demandante *m/f*
plain•tive ['pleɪntɪv] *adj* quejumbroso
plait [plæt] **I** *n* trenza *f* **II** *v/t* trenzar
plan [plæn] **I** *n* (*project, intention*) plan *m*; (*drawing*) plano *m*; ***what are your ~s for the future?*** ¿qué planes tienes para el futuro?; ***wedding ~s*** preparaciones *fpl* para la boda; ***there are no ~s to change anything*** no está previsto cambiar nada
II *v/t* (*pret & pp* ***-ned***) (*prepare*) planear; (*design*) hacer los planos de; ***~ to do sth, ~ on doing sth*** planear hacer algo
III *v/i* (*pret & pp* ***-ned***) hacer planes
plane[1] [pleɪn] AVIA avión *m*; ***we went by ~*** fuimos en avión
plane[2] [pleɪn] *tool* cepillo *m*
plan•et ['plænɪt] planeta *f*
plan•e•tar•i•um [plænɪ'terɪəm] (*pl* ***-iums, planetaria*** [plænɪ'terɪə]) planetario *m*
plan•e•tar•y ['plænɪterɪ] *adj* planetario
plank [plæŋk] *of wood* tablón *m*; *fig*: *of policy* punto *m*
plank•ing ['plæŋkɪŋ] tablas *fpl*
plank•ton ['plæŋktən] ZO plancton *m*
plan•ner ['plænər] responsable *m/f* de la planificación
plan•ning ['plænɪŋ] planificación *f*; ***at the ~ stage*** en fase de estudio
'plan•ning per•mis•sion licencia *f* de obras
plant[1] [plænt] BOT **I** *n* planta *f* **II** *v/t* plantar
plant[2] [plænt] *n* **1** (*factory*) fábrica *f*, planta *f* **2** (*equipment*) maquinaria *f*
plan•ta•tion [plæn'teɪʃn] plantación *f*; *sugar* cañaveral *m*; ***~ worker*** *sugar* cañero(-a) *m(f) L.Am.*
plant•er ['plɑːntər] **1** *machine* sembradora *f* **2** *pot* maceta *f*
plaque [plæk] *on wall, teeth* placa *f*
plas•ma ['plæzmə] plasma *m*
plas•ter ['plæstər] **I** *n on wall, ceiling* yeso *m* **II** *v/t wall, ceiling* enyesar; ***be ~ed with*** estar recubierto de
'plas•ter works *sg* yesera *f*
'plas•ter cast escayola *f*
plas•tered ['plæstərd] *adj* F ciego; ***get ~*** ponerse ciego
plas•tic ['plæstɪk] **I** *n* **1** plástico *m* **2** F (*credit card*) tarjeta *f* **II** *adj* (*made of ~*) de plástico
plas•tic 'bag bolsa *f* de plástico; **plas•tic 'bul•let** bala *f* de plástico; **plas•tic ex'plo•sive** explosivo *m* plástico; **'plas•tic mon•ey** plástico *m*, tarjetas *fpl* de pago
'plas•tics in•dus•try industria *f* del plástico
plas•tic 'sur•geon cirujano(-a) *m(f)*

P

plástico(-a)
plas•tic 'sur•ge•ry cirugía *f* estética
plate [pleɪt] **1** *for food* plato *m*; ***have a lot on one's ~*** F llevar un montón de cosas entre manos; ***he had it handed to him on a ~*** F se lo puso en bandeja **2** (*sheet of metal*) chapa *f* **3** PHOT placa *f*
pla•teau ['plætoʊ] meseta *f*
'plate rack escurreplatos *m inv*
plat•form ['plætfɔːrm] **1** (*stage*) plataforma *f*; *fig*: *political* programa *m* **2** *of railroad station* andén *m*
plat•i•num ['plætɪnəm] **I** *n* platino *m* **II** *adj* de platino
plat•i•num 'blonde rubia *f* platino
plat•i•tude ['plætɪtuːd] tópico *m*
pla•ton•ic [plə'tɑːnɪk] *adj relationship* platónico
pla•toon [plə'tuːn] *of soldiers* sección *f*
plat•ter ['plætər] *for meat, fish* fuente *f*
plau•si•ble ['plɒːzəbl] *adj* plausible
play [pleɪ] **I** *n* **1** *in theater, on TV* obra *f* (de teatro) **2** *of children, in match* juego *m*; **3** TECH juego *m* **4**: ***the different forces at ~ here*** las diferentes fuerzas que intervienen aquí; ***that's where your idea comes into ~*** ahí es dónde tu idea entra en juego
II *v/i* **1** jugar **2** *of musician* tocar
III *v/t* **1** *musical instrument* tocar; *piece of music* intepretar, tocar **2** *game* jugar; *tennis, football* jugar a; *opponent* jugar contra; ***~ a joke on*** gastar una broma a; ***the game on Sunday is being ~ed at home*** el partido del domingo se juega en casa **3** (*perform*: *Macbeth etc*) representar; *particular role* interpretar, hacer el papel de
◆ **play along I** *v/i* seguir la corriente **II** *v/t* (*deceive*) tomar el pelo
◆ **play around** *v/i* F (*be unfaithful*) acostarse con otras personas
◆ **play at** *v/t* jugar a; ***what do you think you're playing at?*** F ¿a qué juegas?
◆ **play back** *v/t tape etc* volver a poner
◆ **play down** *v/t* quitar importancia a
◆ **play off** *v/t*: ***play one person off against another*** enfrentar a dos personas
◆ **play on** *v/i* continuar el juego, seguir *or* continuar jugando
◆ **play up** *v/i of machine* dar problemas; *of child* dar guerra
◆ **play up to** *v/t* hacer la pelota a
play•a•ble ['pleɪəbl] *adj* SP en condiciones de ser jugado
'play•act *v/i* (*pretend*) fingir; **'play•back** playback *m*; **'play•boy** playboy *m*
play•er ['pleɪr] **1** SP jugador(a) *m*(*f*) **2** (*musician*) intérprete *m/f* **3** (*actor*) actor *m*, actriz *f*
play•ful ['pleɪfəl] *adj punch etc* de broma
'play•ground zona *f* de juegos; **'play•group** guardería *f*; **'play•house** *for children* casita *f* de juguete
play•ing card ['pleɪɪŋkɑːrd] carta *f*
'play•ing field campo *m* de deportes
'play•mak•er SP base *m/f*; **'play•mate** compañero(-a) *m*(*f*) de juego; **'play-off** SP play-off *m*, eliminatoria *f*; **'play•pen** parque *m*; **'play•room** cuarto *m* de juegos; **'play•school** guardería *f*; **'play•thing** *also fig* juguete *m*; **'play•time** *Br* EDU recreo *m*; ***at ~*** en el recreo, en la hora del recreo; **play•wright** ['pleɪraɪt] autor(a) *m*(*f*)
pla•za ['plɑːzə] *for shopping* centro *m* comercial
plc [piːel'siː] *abbr Br* (= ***public limited company***) S.A. *f* (= sociedad *f* anónima)
plea [pliː] súplica *f*; ***make a ~ for help*** suplicar *or* implorar ayuda
plead [pliːd] *v/i* (*pret & pp* **-ed, pled**): ***~ for mercy*** pedir clemencia; ***~ guilty / not guilty*** declararse culpable / inocente; ***she ~ed with me not to go*** me suplicó que no fuera
pleas•ant ['pleznt] *adj* agradable
please [pliːz] **I** *adv* por favor; ***more tea? – yes, ~*** ¿más té? – sí, por favor; ***~ do*** claro que sí, por supuesto **II** *v/t* complacer; ***~ yourself!*** ¡haz lo que quieras!; ***there's no pleasing him*** es imposible complacerle; ***he's easy to ~*** se contenta con cualquier cosa **III** *v/i* **1** agradar **2**: ***and then, if you ~, they demand …*** y después, para que veas, piden que …
pleased [pliːzd] *adj* contento; (*satisfied*) satisfecho; ***~ to meet you*** encantado de conocerle; ***I'm very ~ to be here*** estoy muy contento de estar aquí
pleas•ing ['pliːzɪŋ] *adj* agradable
pleas•ur•a•ble ['pleʒərəbl] *adj* agradable
pleas•ure ['pleʒər] (*happiness, satisfac-*

P

tion, *delight*) satisfacción *f*; *as opposed to work* placer *m*; ***it's a ~*** (*you're welcome*) no hay de qué; ***with ~*** faltaría más

'pleas•ure boat barco *m* de recreo; **'pleas•ure prin•ci•ple** PSYCH principio *m* del placer; **'pleas•ure trip** viaje *m* de placer

pleat [pliːt] *in skirt* tabla *f*

pleat•ed skirt ['pliːtɪd] falda *f* de tablas

pleb [pleb] F ordinario(-a) *m*(*f*)

ple•be•ian [plə'biːən] **I** *adj* plebeyo **II** *n* plebeyo(-a) *m*(*f*)

pleb•i•scite ['plebɪsɪt] plebiscito *m*

plec•trum ['plektrəm] púa *f*

pled [pled] *pret & pp* ☞ ***plead***

pledge [pledʒ] **I** *n* **1** (*promise*) promesa *f*; ***Pledge of Allegiance*** *juramento de lealtad a la bandera estadounidense* **2** (*guarantee*) compromiso *m* **3** (*money*) donación *f* **II** *v/t* **1** (*promise*) prometer **2** (*guarantee*) comprometerse **3** *money* donar

ple•na•ry ['pliːnərɪ] *adj*: ***~ session*** sesión *f* plenaria; ***~ powers*** plenos poderes *mpl*

plen•ti•ful ['plentɪfəl] *adj* abundante

plen•ty ['plentɪ] **1** (*abundance*) abundancia *f*; ***that's ~*** es suficiente; ***there's ~ for everyone*** hay (suficiente) para todos **2**: ***~ of books / food*** muchos libros / mucha comida; ***we have ~ of room*** tenemos espacio más que suficiente

pleth•o•ra ['pleθərə]: ***a ~ of*** una plétora de

pleu•ri•sy ['plʊrəsɪ] MED pleuresía *f*

pli•a•ble ['plaɪəbl] *adj* flexible

pli•ers ['plaɪərz] *npl* alicates *mpl*; ***a pair of ~*** unos alicates

plight [plaɪt] situación *f* difícil

plinth [plɪnθ] pedestal *m*

plod [plɑːd] *v/i* (*pret & pp* ***-ded***) (*walk*) arrastrarse

◆ **plod on** *v/i with a job* avanzar laboriosamente

plod•der ['plɑːdər] *at work*, *school*: *persona no especialmente lista pero muy trabajadora*

plonk[1] [plɑːŋk] *v/t* ☞ ***plunk***

plonk[2] [plɑːŋk] *n Br* F vino *m* peleón

plot[1] [plɑːt] *n land* terreno *m*

plot[2] [plɑːt] **I** *n* (*conspiracy*) complot *m*; *of novel* argumento *m*; ***lose the ~*** F *fig* perder el hilo **II** *v/t* (*pret & pp* ***-ted***) tramar **III** *v/i* (*pret & pp* ***-ted***) conspirar

plot•ter ['plɑːtər] **1** conspirador(a) *m*(*f*) **2** COMPUT plóter *m*

plow, *Br* **plough** [plaʊ] **I** *n* arado *m* **II** *v/t & v/i* arar

◆ **plow back** *v/t profits* reinvertir

ploy [plɔɪ] estratagema *f*

pluck [plʌk] *v/t eyebrows* depilar; *chicken* desplumar

◆ **pluck up** *v/t*: ***pluck up courage to do sth*** reunir el valor para hacer algo

pluck•y ['plʌkɪ] *adj* valiente

plug [plʌg] **I** *n* **1** *for sink*, *bath* tapón *m* **2** *electrical* enchufe *m* **3** (*spark ~*) bujía *f* **4**: ***give a book a ~*** dar publicidad a un libro **II** *v/t* (*pret & pp* ***-ged***) **1** *hole* tapar **2** *new book etc* hacer publicidad de

◆ **plug away at** *v/t* F trabajar con esfuerzo en

◆ **plug in** *v/t* enchufar

'plug•hole desagüe *m*

plum [plʌm] **I** *n fruit* ciruela *f*, *tree* ciruelo *m* **II** *adj* F: ***a ~ job*** un chollo de trabajo

plum•age ['pluːmɪdʒ] plumaje *m*

plumb [plʌm] *adj* vertical

◆ **plumb in** *v/t washing machine* conectar a la red del agua

plumb•er ['plʌmər] *Span* fontanero(-a) *m*(*f*), *L.Am.* plomero(-a) *m*(*f*)

plumb•ing ['plʌmɪŋ] *pipes* tuberías *fpl*

'plumb line plomada *f*

plume [pluːm] (*feather*) pluma *f*; *of smoke* nube *f*

plum•met ['plʌmɪt] *v/i of airplane*, *prices* caer en picado

plump [plʌmp] *adj* rellenito

◆ **plump for** *v/t* F decidirse por

◆ **plump up** *v/t cushions* ahuecar

plum 'pud•ding pudin *m* de pasas

plun•der ['plʌndər] *v/t* saquear

plun•der•er ['plʌndərər] saqueador(a) *m*(*f*)

plunge [plʌndʒ] **I** *n* salto *m*; *in prices* caída *f*; ***take the ~*** dar el paso **II** *v/i* precipitarse; *of prices* caer en picado **III** *v/t* hundir; *into water* sumergir; ***the city was ~d into darkness*** la ciudad quedó inmersa en la oscuridad; ***the news ~d him into despair*** la noticia lo hundió en la desesperación

plung•er ['plʌndʒər] *for drains* desatascador *m*

P

plung•ing ['plʌndʒɪŋ] *adj neckline* escotado
plunk [plʌŋk] F *v/t* poner; ***she ~ed herself right in front of the TV*** se apalancó *or* apoltronó delante de la tele
◆ **plunk down** *v/t* F dejar de golpe
plu•per•fect ['plu:pɜ:rfɪkt] GRAM pluscuamperfecto *m*
plu•ral ['plʊrəl] **I** *n* plural *m*; ***in the ~*** en plural **II** *adj* plural
plu•ral•ism ['plʊrəlɪzəm] pluralismo *m*
plu•ral•is•tic [plʊrəl'ɪstɪk] *adj* pluralista
plus [plʌs] **I** *prep* más; ***I want John ~ two other volunteers*** quiero a John y a otros dos voluntarios **II** *adj* más de; ***$500 ~*** más de 500 dólares **III** *n* **1** *symbol* signo *m* más **2** (*advantage*) ventaja *f* **IV** *conj* (*moreover, in addition*) además
plush [plʌʃ] *adj* F lujoso
'plus sign signo *m* más
plu•to•ni•um [plu:'toʊnɪəm] CHEM plutonio *m*
ply [plaɪ] **I** *v/i* (*pret & pp* **-ied**) *of ship, ferry* realizar la ruta (***between*** entre) **II** *v/t* (*pret & pp* **-ied**): ***~ s.o. with drink*** ofrecer bebida constantemente a alguien
ply•wood ['plaɪwʊd] madera *f* contrachapada
PM [pi:'em] *abbr Br* (= ***Prime Minister***) Primer(a) *m(f)* Ministro(-a)
p.m. [pi:'em] *abbr* (= ***post meridiem***) p.m.; ***at 3 ~*** a las 3 de la tarde; ***at 11 ~*** a las 11 de la noche
pneu•mat•ic [nu:'mætɪk] *adj* neumático
pneu•mat•ic 'drill martillo *m* neumático
pneu•mo•ni•a [nu:'moʊnɪə] pulmonía *f*, neumonía *f*
poach[1] [poʊtʃ] *v/t* (*cook*) hervir
poach[2] [poʊtʃ] *v/t & v/i* (*hunt*) cazar furtivamente; *fish* pescar furtivamente
poached egg [poʊtʃt'eg] huevo *m* escalfado
poach•er ['poʊtʃər] *of game* cazador(a) *m(f)* furtivo(-a); *of fish* pescador(a) *m(f)* furtivo(-a)
P.O. Box [pi:'oʊbɑ:ks] apartado *m* de correos
pock•et ['pɑ:kɪt] **I** *n* bolsillo *m*; ***line one's own ~s*** llenarse los bolsillos; ***be $10 out of ~*** salir perdiendo 10 dólares; ***a ~ of resistance*** un foco de resistencia **II** *adj radio, dictionary* de bolsillo **III** *v/t* meter en el bolsillo
'pock•et•book 1 (*purse*) bolso *m*; (*billfold*) cartera *f* **2** *book* libro *m* de bolsillo; **pock•et 'cal•cu•la•tor** calculadora *f* de bolsillo; **'pock•et•knife** navaja *f*; **'pock•et mon•ey** *Br. for kids* paga *f*; **'pock•et ve•to** *veto por la falta de la firma presidencial para la aprobación de una ley antes de la disolución del Congreso*
pock•mark ['pɑ:kmɑ:rk] marca *f* de viruela
pock•marked ['pɑ:kmɑ:rkd] *adj* con marcas de viruela
pod [pɑ:d] **1** BOT vaina *f* **2** AVIA *for fuel* tanque *m*
po•di•um ['poʊdɪəm] podio *m*
po•em ['poʊɪm] poema *m*
po•et ['poʊɪt] poeta *m/f*, poetisa *f*
po•et•ic [poʊ'etɪk] *adj* poético
po•et•ic 'jus•tice justicia *f* divina
po•et•ic 'li•cense licencia *f* poética
po•et•ry ['poʊɪtrɪ] poesía *f*
poign•ant ['pɔɪnjənt] *adj* conmovedor
poin•set•ti•a [pɔɪn'setɪə] BOT flor *f* de Pascua
point [pɔɪnt] **I** *n* **1** *of pencil, knife* punta *f* **2** *in competition, argument* punto *m*; ***the ~ I'm trying to make ...*** lo que estoy intentando decir ...; ***that's beside the ~*** eso no viene a cuento; ***I take your ~*** entiendo lo que quieres decir; ***get to the ~*** ir al grano; ***the ~ is ...*** la cuestión es que ...
3 (*purpose*) objetivo *m*; ***what's the ~ of telling him?*** ¿qué se consigue diciéndoselo?; ***there's no ~ in waiting / trying*** no vale la pena esperar / intentarlo; ***make a ~ of doing sth*** considerar importante hacer algo
4 (*moment*) momento *m*; ***at one ~*** en un momento dado
5 *in decimals* coma *f*
6: ***be on the ~ of*** estar a punto de
II *v/i* señalar con el dedo
III *v/t*: ***he ~ed the gun at me*** me apuntó con la pistola
◆ **point out** *v/t sights* indicar; *advantages etc* destacar
◆ **point to** *v/t with finger* señalar con el dedo; *fig* (*indicate*) indicar
'point-blank I *adj refusal, denial* categórico; ***at ~ range*** a quemarropa **II** *adv re-*

fuse, deny categóricamente
point•ed ['pɔɪntɪd] *adj remark* mordaz
point•er ['pɔɪntər] **1** *for teacher* puntero *m* **2** (*hint*) consejo *m* **3** (*sign, indication*) indicador *m*
point•less ['pɔɪntləs] *adj* inútil; ***it's ~ trying*** no sirve de nada intentarlo
'point of sale 1 *place* punto *m* de venta **2** *promotional material* material *m* promocional; **'point-of-sale dis•play** expositor *m* en el punto de venta; **'point-of-sale pro•mo•tion** promoción *f* en el punto de venta; **'point of view** punto *m* de vista
poise [pɔɪz] confianza *f*
poised [pɔɪzd] *adj person* con aplomo
poi•son ['pɔɪzn] **I** *n* veneno *m* **II** *v/t* envenenar
poi•son 'gas gas *m* tóxico
poi•son•ing ['pɔɪzənɪŋ] envenenamiento *m*, intoxicación *f*
poi•son 'i•vy zumaque *m* venenoso
poi•son•ous ['pɔɪznəs] *adj* venenoso
poke [poʊk] **I** *n* empujón *m* **II** *v/t* (*prod*) empujar; (*stick*) clavar; ***he ~d his head out of the window*** asomó la cabeza por la ventana; ***~ fun at*** reírse de; ***~ one's nose into*** F meter las narices en F
◆ **poke around** *v/i* F husmear
pok•er[1] ['poʊkər] *card game* póquer *m*
pok•er[2] ['poʊkər] *for fire* atizador *m*
pok•er-faced ['poʊkərfeɪst] *adj* con cara de póquer
pok•y ['poʊkɪ] *adj* F (*cramped*) enano, minúsculo
Po•land ['poʊlənd] Polonia *f*
po•lar ['poʊlər] *adj* polar
po•lar 'bear oso *m* polar *or* blanco
po•lar•i•za•tion [poʊləraɪ'ʒeɪʃn] polarización *f*
po•lar•ize ['poʊləraɪz] *v/t* polarizar
pole[1] [poʊl] *for support* poste *m*; *for tent, pushing things* palo *m*
pole[2] [poʊl] *of earth* polo *m*; ***they're ~s apart*** están en polos opuestos
Pole [poʊl] polaco(-a) *m(f)*
'pole•cat ZO turón *m*
po•lem•ic [pə'lemɪk] *adj* polémico
'pole po•si•tion pole-position *f*; **'pole star** estrella *f* polar; **'pole•vault** salto *m* con pértiga; **'pole-vault•er** saltador(a) *m(f)* de pértiga
po•lice [pə'li:s] **I** *n* policía *f* **II** *v/t area* vigilar, patrullar; *measures* supervisar
po'lice car coche *m* de policía; **po'lice dog** perro *m* policía; **po'lice force** cuerpo *m* de policía; **po'lice•man** policía *m*; **po'lice of•fi•cer** agente *m/f* de policía; **po•lice pro'tec•tion** protección *f* policial; **po'lice rec•ord** ficha *f* policial; **po'lice state** estado *m* policial; **po'lice sta•tion** comisaría *f* (de policía); **po'lice•wo•man** (mujer *f*) policía *f*
pol•i•cy[1] ['pɑ:lɪsɪ] política *f*; ***you should make it a ~ always to check*** deberías acostumbrarte a comprobar
pol•i•cy[2] ['pɑ:lɪsɪ] (*insurance* ~) póliza *f*
'pol•i•cy hold•er asegurado(-a) *m(f)*
po•li•o ['poʊlɪoʊ] polio *f*
po•li•o•my•e•li•tis [poʊlɪoʊmaɪə'laɪtɪs] MED poliomelitis *f inv*
Pol•ish ['poʊlɪʃ] **I** *adj* polaco **II** *n* polaco *m*
pol•ish ['pɑ:lɪʃ] **I** *n* abrillantador *m*; (*nail* ~) esmalte *m* de uñas **II** *v/t* dar brillo a; *speech* pulir
◆ **polish off** *v/t food* acabar, comerse
◆ **polish up** *v/t skill* perfeccionar
pol•ished ['pɑ:lɪʃt] *adj performance* brillante
po•lite [pə'laɪt] *adj* educado
po•lite•ly [pə'laɪtlɪ] *adv* educadamente
po•lite•ness [pə'laɪtnɪs] educación *f*
po•lit•i•cal [pə'lɪtɪkl] *adj* político
po•lit•i•cal a'sy•lum asilo *m* político; ***ask for ~*** pedir asilo político
po•lit•i•cal e'con•o•my economía *f* política
po•lit•i•cal•ly cor•rect [pəlɪtɪklɪkə'rekt] políticamente correcto
po•lit•i•cal 'pris•on•er preso(-a) *m(f)* político(-a); **po•lit•i•cal 'sci•ence** ciencias *fpl* políticas; **po•lit•i•cal 'sci•en•tist** politólogo(-a) *m(f)*
pol•i•ti•cian [pɑ:lɪ'tɪʃn] político(-a) *m(f)*
po•lit•i•cize [pə'lɪtɪsaɪz] *v/t* politizar
po•lit•i•co [pə'lɪtɪkoʊ] F politicastro(-a) *m(f)*
pol•i•tics ['pɑ:lətɪks] **1** *nsg* política *f*; ***I'm not interested in ~s*** no me interesa la política **2** *npl*: ***what are his ~?*** ¿cuáles son sus ideas políticas?
pol•ka ['pɑ:lkə] MUS polka *f*
'pol•ka-dot *adj* con lunares
poll [poʊl] **I** *n* **1** (*survey*) encuesta *f*, son-

deo *m* **2**: ***the ~s*** (*election*) las elecciones; ***go to the ~s*** (*vote*) acudir a las urnas **II** *v/t* **1** *people* sondear **2** *votes* obtener
pol•len ['pɑːlən] polen *m*
'**pol•len count** concentración *f* de polen en el aire
pol•li•nate ['pɑːləneɪt] *v/t* polinizar
poll•ing booth ['poulɪŋ] cabina *f* electoral; '**poll•ing day** día *m* de las elecciones; '**poll•ing place** colegio *m* electoral
poll•ster ['pɑːlstər] encuestador(a) *m(f)*
pol•lu•tant [pə'luːtənt] contaminante *m*
pol•lute [pə'luːt] *v/t* contaminar
pol•lut•er [pə'luːtər] contaminador(a) *m(f)*
pol•lu•tion [pə'luːʃn] contaminación *f*
po•lo ['poulou] SP polo *m*
'**po•lo neck** *sweater* suéter *m* de cuello alto
'**po•lo shirt** polo *m*
pol•y•es•ter [pɑːlɪ'estər] poliéster *m*
pol•y•eth•yl•ene [pɑːlɪ'eθɪliːn] polietileno *m*
po•lyg•a•mous [pə'lɪgəməs] *adj* polígamo
po•lyg•a•my [pə'lɪgəmɪ] poligamia *f*
pol•y•glot ['pɑːlɪglɑːt] *adj* políglota
pol•y•gon ['pɑːlɪgɑːn] MATH polígono *m*
pol•y•graph ['pɑːlɪgræf] detector *m* de mentiras; ~ ***test*** prueba *f* con un detector de mentiras
pol•y•mer ['pɑːlɪmər] polímero *m*
Pol•y•ne•sia [pɑːlɪ'niːʒə] Polinesia *f*
pol•yp ['pɑːlɪp] MED, ZO pólipo *m*
pol•y•sty•rene [pɑːlɪ'staɪriːn] poliestireno *m*
pol•y•syl•lab•ic [pɑːlɪsɪ'læbɪk] *adj* LING polisílabo
pol•y•tech•nic [pɑːlɪ'teknɪk] *Br* escuela *f* politécnica
pol•y•thene ['pɑːlɪθiːn] *Br* polietileno *m*; ~ ***bag*** bolsa *f* de plástico
pol•y•un•sat•u•rat•ed [pɑːlɪʌn'sætjəreɪtɪd] *adj* poliinsaturado
pol•y•u•re•thane [pɑːlɪ'jʊrəθeɪn] poliuterano *m*
pol•y•va•lent [pɑːlɪ'veɪlənt] *adj* CHEM polivalente
po•made [pə'meɪd] pomada *f*
po•me•gran•ate ['pɑːmɪgrænɪt] BOT granada *f*
pomp [pɑːmp] pompa *f*
pom•pous ['pɑːmpəs] *adj* pomposo
pond [pɑːnd] estanque *m*
pon•der ['pɑːndər] *v/i* reflexionar
pon•der•o•sa (pine) [pɑːndər'ousə] pino *m* ponderosa
pon•der•ous ['pɑːndərəs] *adj* **1** *prose* pesado **2** *decision-making* lento
pone [poun] pan *m* de maíz
pong [pɑːŋ] *Br* F peste *f*
pon•tiff ['pɑːntɪf] pontífice *m*
pon•toon [pɑːn'tuːn] pontón *m*
pon•toon 'bridge puente *m* de pontones
pon•y ['pounɪ] poni *m*
'**pon•y•tail** coleta *f*
poo•dle ['puːdl] caniche *m*
poof, poof•ter [pʊf, pʊftər] *Br pej* maricón *m*
pooh [puː] *int* puaj
pooh-'pooh *v/t* burlarse de
pool[1] [puːl] *n* **1** (*swimming* ~) piscina *f*, *L.Am.* pileta *f*, *Mex* alberca *f* **2** *of water, blood* charco *m*
pool[2] [puːl] *n game* billar *m* americano
pool[3] [puːl] **I** *n* (*common fund*) bote *m*, fondo *m* común **II** *v/t resources* juntar
'**pool hall** sala *f* de billares
'**pool table** mesa *f* de billar americano
poop [puːp] F **I** *n* caca *f* **II** *v/i* hacer caca
'**poop deck** NAUT toldilla *f*
poop•ed [puːpt] *adj* F hecho polvo F
poop•er-scoop•er ['puːpərskuːpər] F *utensilio para recoger los excrementos de los perros*
poor [pʊr] **I** *adj* pobre; (*not good*) malo; ***be in ~ health*** estar enfermo; ***~ old Tony!*** ¡pobre(cito) Tony! **II** *npl*: ***the ~*** los pobres
poor•ly ['pʊlɪ] **I** *adv* mal **II** *adj* (*unwell*): ***feel ~*** encontrarse mal
pop[1] [pɑːp] **I** *n noise* pequeño ruido *m* **II** *v/i* (*pret & pp* **-ped**) *of balloon etc* estallar **III** *v/t* (*pret & pp* **-ped**) *cork* hacer saltar; *balloon* pinchar
pop[2] [pɑːp] **I** *n* MUS pop *m* **II** *adj* pop
pop[3] [pɑːp] *n* F (*father*) papá *m* F
pop[4] [pɑːp] *v/t* (*pret & pp* **-ped**) F (*put*) meter; ***he finally ~ed the question*** finalmente le pidió que se casara con él
◆ **pop up** *v/i* F (*appear suddenly*) aparecer
'**pop con•cert** concierto *m* (de música) pop

'pop•corn palomitas *fpl* de maíz
Pope [poʊp] papa *m*
Pope•mo•bile ['poʊpməbiːl] papamóvil *m*
'pop group grupo *m* (de música) pop
'pop•gun pistola *f* de juguete con corchos
pop•py ['pɑːpɪ] amapola *f*
Pop•sicle® ['pɑːpsɪkl] polo *m* (*helado*)
'pop sing•er cantante *m/f* pop; **'pop song** canción *f* pop; **'pop star** estrella *f* del pop; **'pop tune** canción *f* pop
pop•u•lar ['pɑːpjʊlər] *adj* popular; ***contrary to ~ belief*** contrariamente a lo que se piensa
pop•u•lar 'front frente *m* popular
pop•u•lar•i•ty [pɑːpjʊ'lærətɪ] popularidad *f*
pop•u•lar•ize ['pɑːpjʊləraɪz] *v/t* **1** popularizar **2** (*make understandable*) divulgar
pop•u•lar•iz•er ['pɑːpjʊləraɪzər] divulgador(a) *m*(*f*)
pop•u•lar•ly ['pɑːpjʊlərlɪ] *adv* (*generally*) popularmente
pop•u•lar 'mu•sic música *f* popular
pop•u•lar 'press prensa *f* de masas
pop•u•late ['pɑːpjʊleɪt] *v/t* poblar
pop•u•la•tion [pɑːpjʊ'leɪʃn] población *f*
pop•u•list ['pɑːpjʊlɪst] populista *m/f*
pop•u•lous ['pɑːpjʊləs] *adj* populoso
porce•lain ['pɔːrsəlɪn] **I** *n* porcelana *f* **II** *adj* de porcelana
porch [pɔːrʧ] porche *m*
por•cu•pine ['pɔːrkjʊpaɪn] puercoespín *m*
pore [pɔːr] *of skin* poro *m*
◆ **pore over** *v/t* estudiar detenidamente
pork [pɔːrk] cerdo *m*
pork 'chop chuleta *f* de cerdo; **pork 'cut•let** chuleta *f* de cerdo; **pork 'pie** empanada *f* de cerdo; **pork 'rinds** *npl* cortezas *fpl* de cerdo
porn [pɔːrn] F **I** *adj* porno F **II** *n* porno *m* F
por•no ['pɔːrnoʊ] *adj* F porno F
por•no•graph•ic [pɔːrnə'græfɪk] *adj* pornográfico
porn•og•ra•phy [pɔːr'nɑːgrəfɪ] pornografía *f*
po•rous ['pɔːrəs] *adj* poroso
por•poise ['pɔːrpəs] ZO marsopa *f*
por•ridge ['pɔrɪdʒ] gachas *fpl* de avena

port[1] [pɔːrt] *n town, area* puerto *m*
port[2] [pɔːrt] *adj* (*left-hand*) a babor
port[3] [pɔːrt] *n wine* oporto *m*
port[4] [pɔːrt] *n* COMPUT puerto *m*
port•a•ble ['pɔːrtəbl] **I** *adj* portátil **II** *n* COMPUT portátil *m*; *TV* televisión *f* portátil
por•tal ['pɔːrtl] **1** *gate* pórtico *m* **2** COMPUT portal *m*
por•tent ['pɔːrtənt] augurio *m*
por•ter ['pɔːrtər] *for luggage* mozo(-a) *m*(*f*)
port•fo•li•o [pɔːrt'foʊlɪoʊ] **1** (*briefcase*) cartera *f* **2** *of artist, designer* carpeta *f* **3**: ***investment ~*** cartera *f* de inversiones; ***~ of shares*** cartera de valores
port'fo•li•o man•age•ment administración *f* de carteras
port•hole ['pɔːrthoʊl] NAUT portilla *f*
por•ti•co ['pɔːrtɪkoʊ] (*pl* ***-co(e)s*** ['pɔːrtɪkoʊz]) pórtico *m*
por•tion ['pɔːrʃn] parte *f*; *of food* ración *f*
◆ **portion out** *v/t* racionar
port•ly ['pɔːrtlɪ] *adj* corpulento
por•trait ['pɔːrtreɪt] **I** *n* retrato *m* **II** *adv print* en formato vertical
por•trait•ist ['pɔːrtreɪtɪst] retratista *m/f*
por•trai•ture ['pɔːrtrəʧər] retrato *m*
por•tray [pɔːr'treɪ] *of artist, photographer* retratar; *of actor* interpretar; *of author* describir
por•tray•al [pɔːr'treɪəl] *by actor* interpretación *f*, representación *f*; *by author* descripción *f*
Por•tu•gal ['pɔːrʧʊgl] Portugal *m*
Por•tu•guese [pɔːrʧʊ'giːz] **I** *adj* portugués **II** *n* **1** *person* portugués(-esa) *m*(*f*) **2** *language* portugués *m*
pose [poʊz] **I** *n* (*pretense*) pose *f*; ***it's all a ~*** no es más que una pose **II** *v/i for artist, photographer* posar; ***~ as*** hacerse pasar por **III** *v/t*: ***~ a problem / a threat*** representar un problema / una amenaza
pos•er ['poʊzər] F *pej*: *person* presumido(-a) *m*(*f*)
posh [pɑːʃ] *adj Br* F elegante; *pej* pijo
po•si•tion [pə'zɪʃn] **I** *n* **1** posición *f*; (*stance, point of view*) postura *f*; (*status*) posición *f* (social); ***what would you have done in my ~?*** ¿qué hubieses hecho tú en mi situación *or* lugar? **2** (*job*) puesto *m*, empleo *m* **II** *v/t* situar, colocar

P

pos•i•tive ['pɑːzətɪv] *adj* positivo; ***test ~ for drugs / Aids*** dar positivo en una prueba antidopaje / del sida; ***be ~*** (*sure*) estar seguro; ***it was a ~ disaster*** fue un auténtico *or* verdadero desastre

pos•i•tive•ly ['pɑːzətɪvlɪ] *adv* **1** (*decidedly*) verdaderamente, sin lugar a dudas **2** (*definitely*) claramente

pos•sess [pə'zes] *v/t* poseer

pos•ses•sion [pə'zeʃn] posesión *f*; ***~s*** posesiones *fpl*; ***be in ~ of sth*** tener algo; ***be in full ~ of one's faculties*** estar en posesión de sus facultades; ***take ~ of sth*** tomar posesión de algo

pos•ses•sive [pə'zesɪv] *adj person*, GRAM posesivo

pos•si•bil•i•ty [pɑːsə'bɪlətɪ] posibilidad *f*; ***there is a ~ that …*** cabe la posibilidad de que …; ***as a proposal, it has possibilities*** como propuesta, tiene potencial

pos•si•ble ['pɑːsəbl] *adj* posible; ***the shortest / quickest route ~*** la ruta más corta / rápida posible; ***the best ~ …*** el mejor …

possibly ['pɑːsəblɪ] *adv* (*perhaps*) puede ser, quizás; ***that can't ~ be right*** no puede ser; ***they're doing everything they ~ can*** están haciendo todo lo que pueden; ***could you ~ tell me …?*** ¿tendría la amabilidad de decirme …?

pos•sum ['pɑːsəm] F ☞ ***opossum***; ***play ~*** (*pretend to be dead*) hacerse el muerto

post[1] [poʊst] **I** *n of wood, metal* poste *m* **II** *v/t notice* pegar; *on notice board* poner; *profits* presentar; ***keep s.o. ~ed*** mantener a alguien al corriente

post[2] [poʊst] **I** *n* (*place of duty*) puesto *m* **II** *v/t* **1** *soldier, employee* destinar **2** *guards* apostar

post[3] [poʊst] *Br* **I** *n* (*mail*) correo *m* **II** *v/t letter* echar al correo

post•age ['poʊstɪdʒ] franqueo *m*

'post•age stamp *fml* sello *m*, *L.Am.* estampilla *f*, *Mex* timbre *m*

post•al ['poʊstl] *adj* postal

'post•box *Br* buzón *m*; **'post•card** (tarjeta *f*) postal *f*; **'post•code** *Br* código *m* postal; **'post•date** *v/t* posfechar

post•er ['poʊstər] póster *m*, *L.Am.* afiche *m*

poste res•tante [poʊstres'tɑːnt] *Br* **I** *n* lista *f* de correos **II** *adv send* para la lista de correos

pos•te•ri•or [pɑː'stɪrɪər] (*hum*: *buttocks*) trasero *m*

pos•ter•i•ty [pɑː'sterətɪ] posteridad *f*; ***for ~*** para la posteridad

post•grad•u•ate ['poʊstgrædʒʊət] **I** *n* posgraduado(-a) *m*(*f*) **II** *adj* de posgrado

post•hu•mous ['pɑːstʊməs] *adj* póstumo

post•hu•mous•ly ['pɑːstʊməslɪ] *adv* póstumamente

post•ing ['poʊstɪŋ] (*assignment*) destino *m*

post•man ['poʊstmən] *Br* cartero *m*

'post•mark matasellos *m inv*

post•mod•ern•ism [poʊst'mɑːdərnɪzəm] posmodernismo *m*

post•mod•ern•ist [poʊst'mɑːdərnɪst] **I** *adj* posmoderno **II** *n* posmoderno(-a) *m*(*f*)

post-mor•tem [poʊst'mɔːrtəm] autopsia *f*, *fig* análisis *m*

post•na•tal [poʊst'neɪtl] *adj* posparto; ***~ depression*** depresión *f* posparto

'post of•fice oficina *f* de correos

post•pone [poʊst'poʊn] *v/t* posponer, aplazar

post•pone•ment [poʊst'poʊnmənt] aplazamiento *m*

post•script ['poʊstskrɪpt] posdata *f*; *to a speech* epílogo *m*

post•struc•tur•al•ism [poʊst'strʌktʃərəlɪzəm] posestructuralismo *m*

post•struc•tur•al•ist [poʊst'strʌktʃərəlɪst] **I** *adj* posestructuralista **II** *n* posestructuralista *m/f*

pos•tu•late I *v/t* ['pɑːstjʊleɪt] postular **II** *n* ['pɑːstjʊlət] postulado *m*

pos•ture ['pɑːstʃər] postura *f*

'post-war *adj* de posguerra

pot[1] [pɑːt] **1** *for cooking* olla *f* **2** *for coffee* cafetera *f*; *for tea* tetera *f* **3** *for plant* maceta *f*

pot[2] [pɑːt] F (*marijuana*) maría *f* F

po•tas•si•um [pə'tæsɪəm] CHEM potasio *m*

po•ta•to [pə'teɪtoʊ] (*pl* **-oes**) *Span* patata *f*, *L.Am.* papa *f*

po'ta•to bee•tle, po'ta•to bug ZO escarabajo *m* de la patata; **po'ta•to chips**, *Br* **po•ta•to 'crisps** *npl Span* patatas *fpl* fritas, *L.Am.* papas *fpl* fritas; **po'ta•to peel•er** *Span* pelapatatas *f inv*,

P

L.Am. pelapapas *f inv*; **po•ta•to 'sal•ad** ensalada *f* de *Span* patatas *or L.Am.* papas
pot•bel•ly ['pɑːtbelɪ] barriga *f*
po•ten•cy ['poutənsɪ] potencia *f*; PHYSIO fuerza *f*
po•tent ['poutənt] *adj* potente
po•ten•tate ['poutənteɪt] soberano *m* absoluto
po•ten•tial [pə'tenʃl] **I** *adj* potencial **II** *n* potencial *m*
po•ten•tial•ly [pə'tenʃəlɪ] *adv* potencialmente
'pot•hole 1 *in road* bache *m* **2** *underground* sima *f*; **pot•hol•er** ['pɑːthoulər] espeleólogo(-a) *m(f)*; **pot•hol•ing** ['pɑːthoulɪŋ] espeleología *f*
po•tion ['pouʃn] poción *f*
pot'luck: ***take ~*** aceptar lo que haya; **'pot plant** planta *f* de interior; **'pot•roast** estofado *m* de carne; **'pot shot**: ***take a ~ at*** disparar al azar contra
pot•ted plant [pɑːtɪd'plænt] planta *f* en una maceta
pot•ter[1] ['pɑːtər] *v/i* entretenerse
◆ **potter around** *v/i* entretenerse
pot•ter[2] ['pɑːtər] *n* alfarero(-a) *m(f)*
pot•ter•y ['pɑːtərɪ] alfarería *f*
pot•ty[1] ['pɑːtɪ] *adj esp Br* F majareta
pot•ty[2] ['pɑːtɪ] *n for baby* orinal *m*
pot•ty-trained ['pɑːtɪtreɪnd] *adj* que ya no necesita pañales
pouch [pautʃ] *bag* bolsa *f*; *for tobacco* petaca *f*; *for amunition* cartuchera *f*; *for mail* saca *f*
poul•tice ['poultɪs] MED cataplasma *f*
poul•try ['poultrɪ] *birds* aves *fpl* de corral; *meat* carne *f* de ave
pounce [pauns] *v/i of animal* saltar; *fig* echarse encima
pound[1] [paund] *n weight* libra *f* (*453,6 gr*)
pound[2] [paund] *n for strays* perrera *f*; *for cars* depósito *m*
pound[3] [paund] *v/i of heart* palpitar con fuerza; ***~ on*** (*hammer on*) golpear en
pound•ing ['paundɪŋ]: ***the ~ of the waves*** el embate de la mar; ***the ship took a ~*** el barco sufrió el embate de la mar; ***the dollar took a ~*** el dólar sufrió un fuerte descenso
pound 'ster•ling libra *f* esterlina
pour [pɔːr] **I** *v/t into a container* verter; *spill* derramar; ***~ s.o. some coffee*** servir café a alguien; ***~ yourself a drink*** sírvete *or* ponte algo de beber **II** *v/i*: ***it's ~ing*** (***with rain***) está lloviendo a cántaros
◆ **pour out** *v/t liquid* servir; *troubles* contar
pout [paut] *v/i* hacer un mohín
pov•er•ty ['pɑːvərtɪ] pobreza *f*
'pov•er•ty line umbral *f* de la pobreza
'pov•er•ty-strick•en depauperado
POW [piːou'dʌbljuː] *abbr* (= ***prisoner of war***) prisionero(-a) *m(f)* de guerra
pow•der ['paudər] **I** *n* polvo *m*; *for face* polvos *mpl*, colorete *m*; *snow* nieve *f* en polvo **II** *v/t face* empolvarse
'pow•der keg *fig* polvorín *m*; **'pow•der puff** borla *f*; **'pow•der room** servicio *m* de señoras
pow•der•y ['paudərɪ] *adj* arenoso; *snow* en polvo
pow•er ['pauər] **I** *n* (*strength*) fuerza *f*; *of engine* potencia *f*; (*authority*) poder *m*; ***in ~*** POL en el poder; ***fall from ~*** POL perder el poder; ***he did everything within his ~ to help us*** hizo todo lo que estuvo en su mano para ayudarnos; ***it is beyond our ~s of imagination*** rebasa los límites de nuestra imaginación **2** (*energy*) energía *f*; (*electricity*) electricidad *f*
II *v/t*: ***be ~ed by*** estar impulsado por
'pow•er-as•sist•ed steer•ing dirección *f* asistida; **'pow•er cut** apagón *m*; **'pow•er fail•ure** apagón *m*; **'pow•er•boat** lancha *f* motora; **'pow•er dress•ing** *estilo de vestir que comunica profesionalidad y seguridad*; **'pow•er for•ward** *in basketball* ala *m/f* pívot
pow•er•ful ['pauərfəl] *adj* poderoso; *car* potente; *drug* fuerte
pow•er•less ['pauərlɪs] *adj* impotente; ***be ~ to do sth*** ser incapaz de hacer algo
'pow•er line línea *f* de conducción eléctrica; **pow•er of at'tor•ney** poder *m* (notarial); **pow•er out•age** ['pauərautɪdʒ] apagón *m*; **'pow•er pack 1** ELEC transformador *m* **2** *engine* motor *m*; **'pow•er plant** central *f* eléctrica; **'pow•er point** *Br* ELEC toma *f* de corriente; **pow•er 'serve** *in tennis* servicio *m* potente; **'pow•er show•er** ducha *f* de hidromasaje; **'pow•er sta•tion** central *f* eléctrica; **'pow•er steer•ing** direc-

ción *f* asistida; **'pow•er tool** herramienta *f* eléctrica; **'pow•er u•nit** fuente *f* de alimentación; **'pow•er walk•ing** marcha *f* atlética

pow•wow ['paʊwaʊ] F asamblea *f*; *chat* charla *f*

pox [pɑːks] MED (*syphillis*) sífilis *f inv*

PR [piː'ɑːr] *abbr* (= ***public relations***) relaciones *fpl* públicas

prac•ti•ca•ble ['præktɪkəbl] *adj* viable

prac•ti•cal ['præktɪkl] *adj* práctico; *layout* funcional

prac•ti•cal 'joke broma *f* (*que se gasta*)

prac•tic•al•ly ['præktɪklɪ] *adv* **1** *behave, think* de manera práctica **2** (*almost*) prácticamente, casi

prac•tice ['præktɪs] **I** *n* práctica *f*; (*rehearsal*) ensayo *m*; (*custom*) costumbre *f*; ***in ~*** (*in reality*) en la práctica; ***be out of ~*** estar desentrenado; ***~ makes perfect*** la práctica hace al maestro **II** *v/i* practicar; *of musician* ensayar; *of footballer* entrenarse **III** *v/t* practicar; *law, medicine* ejercer

prac•ticed ['præktɪsd] *adj* experto

prac•tise *Br* ☞ ***practice*** *v/i & v/t*

prac•tised *Br* ☞ ***practiced***

prag•mat•ic [præg'mætɪk] *adj* pragmático

prag•ma•tism ['prægmətɪzm] pragmatismo *m*

prag•ma•tist ['prægmətɪst] pragmático(-a) *m*(*f*)

Prague [prɑːg] Praga *f*

prai•rie ['prerɪ] pradera *f*

'prai•rie dog perro *m* de las praderas

'prai•rie schoon•er carromato *m*

praise [preɪz] **I** *n* elogio *m*, alabanza *f* **II** *v/t* elogiar

'praise•wor•thy *adj* elogiable

prance [præns] *v/i* (*walk proudly*) caminar dando saltitos; (*jump*) dar saltos

prank [præŋk] travesura *f*

prat•tle ['prætl] *v/i* F parlotear F

prawn [prɔːn] ZO gamba *f*

pray [preɪ] *v/i* rezar

prayer [prer] oración *f*; ***not have a ~*** *fig* F no tener ninguna posibilidad (de tener éxito)

'prayer book devocionario *m*

pray•ing man•tis [preɪɪŋ'mæntɪs] mantis *f inv* religiosa

preach [priːʧ] **I** *v/i in church* predicar; (*moralize*) sermonear **II** *v/t sermon* predicar

preach•er ['priːʧər] predicador(a) *m*(*f*)

pre•am•ble [priː'æmbl] preámbulo *m*

pre•ar•range [priːə'reɪndʒ] *v/t* acordar de antemano

pre•car•i•ous [prɪ'kerɪəs] *adj* precario

pre•car•i•ous•ly [prɪ'kerɪəslɪ] *adv* precariamente

pre•cau•tion [prɪ'kɒːʃn] precaución *f*; ***as a ~*** como precaución

pre•cau•tion•a•ry [prɪ'kɒːʃnrɪ] *adj measure* preventivo

pre•cede [prɪ'siːd] *v/t* **1** *in time* preceder **2** (*walk in front of*) ir delante de

prec•e•dence ['presɪdəns] prioridad *f*; ***take ~ over s.o. / sth*** tener prioridad sobre alguien / algo

prec•e•dent ['presɪdənt] precedente *m*

pre•ced•ing [prɪ'siːdɪŋ] *adj week, chapter* anterior

pre•cinct ['priːsɪŋkt] (*district*) distrito *m*

pre•cious ['preʃəs] *adj* preciado; *gem* precioso

prec•i•pice ['presɪpɪs] precipicio *m*

pre•cip•i•tate [prɪ'sɪpɪteɪt] *v/t crisis* precipitar

pre•cip•i•ta•tion [prəsɪpɪ'teɪʃn] *rainfall etc* precipitación *f*

pre•cip•i•tous [prə'sɪpɪtəs] *adj* **1** *cliffs* empinado **2** *action* precipitado

pré•cis ['preɪsiː] resumen *m*

pre•cise [prɪ'saɪs] *adj* preciso

pre•cise•ly [prɪ'saɪslɪ] *adv* exactamente

pre•ci•sion [prɪ'sɪʒn] precisión *f*

pre•clude [prɪ'kluːd] *v/t* excluir; ***~ s.o. from doing sth*** impedir a alguien que haga algo

pre•co•cious [prɪ'koʊʃəs] *adj child* precoz

pre•co•cious•ness [prɪ'koʊʃəsnɪs] precocidad *f*

pre•con•ceived ['priːkənsiːvd] *adj idea* preconcebido

pre•con•cep•tion [priːkən'sepʃn] idea *f* preconcebida

pre•con•di•tion [priːkən'dɪʃn] condición *f* previa

pre•cook [priː'kʊk] *v/t* precocinar

pre•cur•sor [priː'kɜːrsər] precursor(a) *m*(*f*)

pre•date [priː'deɪt] *v/t* anteceder a

pred•a•tor ['predətər] *animal* depredador(a) *m*(*f*)

pred•a•to•ry ['predətɔːrɪ] *adj* depredador

pre•de•ces•sor ['pri:dɪsesər] *in job* predecesor(a) *m(f)*; *of machine* modelo *m* anterior

pre•des•ti•na•tion [pri:destɪ'neɪʃn] predestinación *f*

pre•des•tined [pri:'destɪnd] *adj*: ***be ~ to*** estar predestinado a

pre•dic•a•ment [prɪ'dɪkəmənt] apuro *m*

pred•i•cate ['predɪkət] LING predicado *m*

pred•i•ca•tive [prɪ'dɪkətɪv] *adj* predicativo

pre•dict [prɪ'dɪkt] *v/t* predecir, pronosticar

pre•dict•a•ble [prɪ'dɪktəbl] *adj* predecible

pre•dic•tion [prɪ'dɪkʃn] predicción *f*, pronóstico *m*

pre•di•gest [pri:daɪ'dʒest] *v/t food* digerir de antemano; *information* simplificar

pred•i•lec•tion [pri:dɪ'lekʃn] predilección *f* (***for*** por)

pre•dis•pose [pri:dɪ'spoʊz] *v/t* predisponer (***in favor of*** a favor de)

pre•dis•po•si•tion [pri:dɪspə'zɪʃn] predisposición *f* (***to*** a)

pre•dom•i•nance [prɪ'dɑ:mɪnəns] predominio *m*

pre•dom•i•nant [prɪ'dɑ:mɪnənt] *adj* predominante

pre•dom•i•nant•ly [prɪ'dɑ:mɪnəntlɪ] *adv* predominantemente

pre•dom•i•nate [prɪ'dɑ:mɪneɪt] *v/i* predominar

pre•em•i•nent [pri:'emɪnənt] *adj* preeminente

pre•empt [pri:'empt] *v/t* adelantarse a

pre•emp•tive [pri:'emptɪv] *adj*: ***~ strike*** MIL ataque *m* preventivo

preen [pri:n] *v/t*: ***~ o.s.*** *of bird* arreglarse las plumas; *of person* acicalarse

pre•fab•ri•cat•ed [pri:'fæbrɪkeɪtɪd] *adj* prefabricado

pref•ace ['prefɪs] **I** *n* prólogo *m*, prefacio *m* **II** *v/t speech etc* comenzar

pre•fer [prɪ'fɜ:r] *v/t* (*pret & pp* ***-red***) preferir; ***~ X to Y*** preferir X a Y; ***~ to do*** preferir hacer

pref•e•ra•ble ['prefərəbl] *adj* preferible; ***anywhere is ~ to this*** cualquier sitio es mejor que éste

pref•e•ra•bly ['prefərəblɪ] *adv* preferentemente

pref•e•rence ['prefərəns] preferencia *f*; ***I'll take this one in ~ to that one*** prefiero este antes que ese otro

pref•er•en•tial [prefə'renʃl] *adj* preferencial; ***get ~ treatment*** recibir tratamiento preferencial; ***~ rate*** tasa *f* preferencial

pre•ferred cred•i•tor [prɪ'fɜ:rdkredɪtər] FIN acreedor(a) *m(f)* privilegiado(-a)

pre•fix ['pri:fɪks] prefijo *m*

preg•nan•cy ['pregnənsɪ] embarazo *m*

preg•nant ['pregnənt] *adj woman* embarazada; *animal* preñada; ***make s.o. ~*** dejar a alguien embarazada *or* preñada F

pre•heat ['pri:hi:t] *v/t oven* precalentar

pre•his•tor•ic [pri:hɪs'tɑ:rɪk] *adj* prehistórico

pre•in•stalled [pri:ɪn'stɒ:ld] *adj software* preinstalado

pre•judge [pri:'dʒʌdʒ] *v/t* prejuzgar, juzgar de antemano

prej•u•dice ['predʒʊdɪs] **I** *n* prejuicio *m* **II** *v/t person* predisponer, influir; *chances* perjudicar

prej•u•diced ['predʒʊdɪst] *adj* parcial, predispuesto

prej•u•di•cial [predʒʊ'dɪʃl] *adj* perjudicial; ***be ~ to sth*** ser perjudicial para algo

pre•lim•i•na•ry [prɪ'lɪmɪnerɪ] *adj* preliminar

prel•ude ['prelju:d] MUS, *fig* preludio *m* (***to*** a)

pre•mar•i•tal [pri:'mærɪtl] *adj* prematrimonial

pre•ma•ture ['pri:mətʊr] *adj* prematuro

pre•ma•ture 'ba•by bebé *m* prematuro

pre•ma•ture•ly [pri:mə'tʊrlɪ] *adv* prematuramente

pre•med•i•tat•ed [pri:'medɪteɪtɪd] *adj* premeditado

pre•men•stru•al ten•sion [pri:menstrʊəl'tenʃn] tensión *f* premenstrual

prem•i•er ['premɪr] (*prime minister*) primer(a) ministro(-a) *m(f)*

prem•i•ère ['premɪer] estreno *m*

pre•mise ['premɪs] *of an argument* premisa *f*

prem•is•es ['premɪsɪz] *npl* local *m*

pre•mi•um ['pri:mɪəm] *in insurance* prima *f*; ***be at a ~*** escasear; ***put a ~ on sth*** conceder mucho valor a algo

pre•mo•ni•tion [premə'nɪʃn] premonición *f*, presentimiento *m*

pre•na•tal [priː'neɪtl] *adj* prenatal

pre•oc•cu•pa•tion [priːɑːkjʊ'peɪʃn] preocupación *f* (***with*** con)

pre•oc•cu•pied [prɪ'ɑːkjʊpaɪd] *adj* preocupado

pre•or•dain [priːɔːr'deɪn] *v/t* predestinar

pre-owned ['priːoʊnd] *adj euph* usado, de segunda mano

pre•paid [priː'peɪd] *adj*: ***~ envelope*** sobre *m* franqueado

prep•a•ra•tion [prepə'reɪʃn] preparación *f*; ***in ~ for*** como preparación a; ***~s*** preparativos *mpl*

pre•par•a•to•ry [prɪ'pærətɔːrɪ] *adj* preparatorio; ***~ to*** en preparación para; ***~ to doing sth*** antes de hacer algo

pre'par•a•to•ry school *colegio privado de secundaria*; *Br*: *colegio privado para niños de entre 7 y 12 años*

pre•pare [prɪ'per] **I** *v/t* preparar; ***be ~d to do sth*** (*willing*) estar dispuesto a hacer algo; ***be ~d for sth*** (*be expecting*, *ready*) estar preparado para algo; ***~ yourself for a shock*** prepárate **II** *v/i* prepararse

pre•pon•der•ance [prɪ'pɑːndərəns] preponderancia *f*

prep•o•si•tion [prepə'zɪʃn] preposición *f*

pre•pos•sess•ing [priːpə'zesɪŋ] *adj* atractivo

pre•pos•ter•ous [prɪ'pɑːstərəs] *adj* ridículo, absurdo

P

pre•pro•gram [priː'proʊgræm] *v/t* (*pret & pp* ***-med***) preprogramar; ***be ~med to do sth*** estar programado para hacer algo

prep school ['prepskuːl] F ☞ ***preparatory school***

pre•re•cord•ed [priːrɪ'kɔːrdɪd] *adj* pregrabado

pre•req•ui•site [priː'rekwɪzɪt] requisito *m* previo

pre•rog•a•tive [prɪ'rɑːgətɪv] prerrogativa *f*, ***that's your ~*** está en su derecho

Pres•by•te•ri•an [prezbɪ'tɪrɪən] **I** *adj* presbiteriano **II** *n* presbiteriano(-a) *m*(*f*)

pre•school ['priːskuːl] **I** *adj* preescolar; ***of ~ age*** en edad preescolar **II** *n* preescolar *m*

pre•scribe [prɪ'skraɪb] *v/t of doctor* recetar

pre•scrip•tion [prɪ'skrɪpʃn] MED receta *f*

pres•ence ['prezns] presencia *f*; ***in the ~ of*** en presencia de, delante de

pres•ence of 'mind presencia *f* de ánimo

pres•ent[1] ['preznt] **I** *adj* (*current*) actual; ***be ~*** estar presente **II** *n*: ***the ~*** *also* GRAM el presente; ***at ~*** en este momento

pres•ent[2] ['preznt] *n* (*gift*) regalo *m*

pre•sent[3] [prɪ'zent] *v/t also* TV, RAD presentar; *award* entregar; ***~ s.o. with sth, ~ sth to s.o.*** entregar algo a alguien

pre•sent•a•ble [prɪ'zentəbl] *adj* presentable; ***make o.s. ~*** ponerse presentable

pre•sen•ta•tion [prezn'teɪʃn] *to audience* presentación *f*; *of prizes* entrega *f*

pres•ent-day [preznt'deɪ] *adj* actual

pre•sent•er [prɪ'zentər] presentador(a) *m*(*f*)

pre•sen•ti•ment [prɪ'zentɪmənt] presentimiento *m*

pres•ent•ly ['prezntlɪ] *adv* **1** (*at the moment*) actualmente **2** (*soon*) pronto

'pres•ent tense tiempo *m* presente

pres•er•va•tion [prezər'veɪʃn] conservación *f*; *of standards*, *peace* mantenimiento *m*

pre•ser•va•tive [prɪ'zɜːrvətɪv] conservante *m*

pre•serve [prɪ'zɜːrv] **I** *n* **1** (*domain*) dominio *m* **2** *to eat* conserva *f* **II** *v/t* **1** *standards*, *peace etc* mantener **2** *food*, *wood* conservar

pre•side [prɪ'zaɪd] *v/i at meeting* presidir; ***~ over*** *meeting* presidir

pres•i•den•cy ['prezɪdənsɪ] presidencia *f*

pres•i•dent ['prezɪdnt] POL, *of company* presidente(-a) *m*(*f*); ***yes, Mr President*** sí, señor presidente

pres•i•den•tial [prezɪ'denʃl] *adj* presidencial

press [pres] **I** *n* **1**: ***the ~*** la prensa **2** *in basketball* presión *f* **II** *v/t* **1** *button* pulsar, presionar **2** (*urge*), *in basketball* presionar **3** (*squeeze*) apretar **4** *clothes* planchar **III** *v/i* presionar; ***~ for*** presionar para obtener

◆ **press on** *v/i* proseguir
'press a•gen•cy agencia *f* de prensa; **'press box** tribuna *f* de prensa; **'press card** carnet *m* de prensa; **'press clip-ping** recorte *m* de prensa; **'press con-fer•ence** rueda *f or* conferencia *f* de prensa
press•ing ['presɪŋ] *adj* urgente
'press of•fice oficina *f* de prensa; **'press of•fi•cer** jefe(-a) *m(f)* de pren-sa; **'press pho•tog•ra•pher** reporte-ro(-a) *m(f)* gráfico(-a); **'press re•lease** nota *f* de prensa; **'press-up** *Br* flexión *f* (de brazos)
pres•sure ['preʃər] **I** *n* presión *f*; ***be un-der ~*** estar sometido a presión; ***he is under ~ to resign*** lo están presionando para que dimita **II** *v/t* presionar; ***~ s.o. into doing sth*** presionar a alguien para que haga algo
'pres•sure cook•er olla *f* a presión; **pres•sure gauge** manómetro *m*; **pres•sure group** POL grupo *m* de pre-sión; **'pres•sure-sen•si•tive** *adj* MED *etc* sensible a la presión; **'pres•sure suit** traje *m* presurizado
pres•sur•ize ['preʃəraɪz] *v/t* **1** *fig esp Br* presionar (***to do sth*** para hacer algo) **2**: ***~d cabin*** AVIA cabina *f* presurizada
pres•tige [pre'stiːʒ] prestigio *m*
pres•ti•gious [pre'stɪdʒəs] *adj* presti-gioso
pres•to ['prestoʊ] *adv*: ***hey ~*** y ya está
pre•sum•a•ble [prɪ'zjuːməbl] *adj* pre-sumible
pre•sum•a•bly [prɪ'zuːməblɪ] *adv* pre-sumiblemente, probablemente
pre•sume [prɪ'zuːm] *v/t* **1** suponer; ***they were ~d dead*** los dieron por muertos **2**: ***~ to do sth*** *fml* tomarse la libertad de hacer algo
pre•sump•tion [prɪ'zʌmpʃn] *of inno-cence, guilt* presunción *f*
pre•sump•tu•ous [prɪ'zʌmptʊəs] *adj* presuntuoso
pre•sup•pose [priːsə'poʊs] *v/t* presupo-ner
pre•sup•po•si•tion [priːsʌpə'zɪʃn] su-posición *f*
pre-tax ['priːtæks] *adj* antes de impues-tos
pre•tence *Br* ☞ ***pretense***
pre•tend [prɪ'tend] **I** *v/t* **1** fingir, hacer como si; ***~ to be s.o.*** hacerse pasar por alguien; ***the children are ~ing to be spacemen*** los niños están jugando a que son astronautas **2** *claim* preten-der **II** *v/i* fingir
pre•tense [prɪ'tens] farsa *f*
pre•ten•tious [prɪ'tenʃəs] *adj* preten-cioso
pre•ten•tious•ness [prɪ'tenʃəsnɪs] pre-tenciosidad *f*
pret•er•ite ['pretərət] LING pretérito *m*
pre•text ['priːtekst] pretexto *m*; ***under the ~ of being ill*** con el pretexto de estar enfermo
pret•ty ['prɪtɪ] **I** *adj village, house, fabric etc* bonito, lindo; *child, woman* guapo, lindo **II** *adv* (*quite*) bastante; ***it's ~ much finished*** está prácticamente acabado; ***are they the same? – yeah, ~ much*** ¿son lo mismo? – sí, casi, casi
pre•vail [prɪ'veɪl] *v/i* (*triumph*) prevale-cer (***over*** sobre)
pre•vail•ing [prɪ'veɪlɪŋ] *adj* predomi-nante
prev•a•lence ['prevələns] predominio *m*
prev•a•lent ['prevələnt] *adj* frecuente
pre•var•i•cate [prɪ'værɪkeɪt] *v/i* dar ro-deos
pre•var•i•ca•tion [prɪværɪ'keɪʃn] ro-deos *mpl*
pre•var•i•ca•tor [prɪ'værɪkeɪtər]: ***he's a terrible ~*** siempre se anda con rodeos
pre•vent [prɪ'vent] *v/t* impedir, evitar; ***~ s.o. (from) doing sth*** impedir que al-guien haga algo
pre•vent•a•tive [prɪ'ventətɪv] *adj* ☞ ***preventive***
pre•ven•tion [prɪ'venʃn] prevención *f*
pre•ven•tive [prɪ'ventɪv] *adj* preventivo
pre•view ['priːvjuː] **I** *n of movie, exhibi-tion* preestreno *m* **II** *v/t* hacer la presen-tación previa de
pre•vi•ous ['priːvɪəs] *adj* anterior, pre-vio; ***have a ~ engagement*** tener un compromiso previo
pre•vi•ously ['priːvɪəslɪ] *adv* anterior-mente, antes
pre-war ['priːwɔːr] *adj* de preguerra, de antes de la guerra
prey [preɪ] presa *f*; ***~ to*** presa de
◆ **prey on** *v/t* atacar; *fig*: *of con man etc* aprovecharse de; ***it is preying on my mind*** me preocupa, no paro de darle vueltas F

prez•zie ['prezɪ] F regalo *m*
price [praɪs] **I** *n* precio *m*; ***go up / down in ~*** subir / bajar de precio; ***that's the ~ you have to pay*** *fig* ése es el precio que hay que pagar; ***he achieved his ambition, but at a ~*** consiguió su ambición, pero pagó un precio muy caro **II** *v/t* COM poner precio a; ***it was ~d at $9.99*** valía $9.99
'price-con•scious *adj* ahorrador; **'price cut** bajada *f* de precios; **price / 'earn•ings ra•tio** FIN proporción *f* precio-beneficio; **price fix•ing** ['praɪsfɪksɪŋ] fijación *f* de precios; **'price freeze** congelación *f* de precios; **'price in•fla•tion** inflación *f* de precios
price•less ['praɪslɪs] *adj* **1** que no tiene precio **2** F *amusing* divertidísimo
'price list lista *f* de precios; **'price range** escala *f* de precios; ***that's out of my ~*** se sale de mi presupuesto; **'price tag** etiqueta *f* del precio; **'price tick•et** etiqueta *f* del precio; **'price war** guerra *f* de precios
price•y ['praɪsɪ] *adj* F carillo F
prick[1] [prɪk] **I** *n pain* punzada *f* **II** *v/t (jab)* pinchar
prick[2] [prɪk] *n* V **1** *(penis)* polla *f* V, carajo *m* V **2** *person Span* gilipollas *m inv* P, *L.Am.* pendejo *m* V
◆ **prick up** *v/t*: ***prick up one's ears*** *of dog* aguzar las orejas; *of person* prestar atención
prick•le ['prɪkl] *on plant* espina *f*
prick•ly ['prɪklɪ] *adj* **1** *beard, plant* que pincha **2** *(irritable)* irritable
'pri•cy ☞ ***pricey***
pride [praɪd] **I** *n* **1** *in person, achievement* orgullo *m* **2** *(self-respect)* amor *m* propio **II** *v/t*: ***~ o.s. on*** enorgullecerse de
priest [priːst] sacerdote *m*; *(parish ~)* cura *m*
priest•ess ['priːstes] sacerdotisa *f*
priest•hood ['priːsthʊd] sacerdocio *m*
prig [prɪg] puritano(-a) *m(f)*
prig•gish ['prɪgɪʃ] *adj* puritano
prim [prɪm] *adj*: ***~ (and proper)*** remilgado
pri•ma•cy ['praɪməsɪ] **1** primacía *f* ***(over*** sobre) **2** REL primado *m*
pri•ma don•na [priːmə'dɑːnə] diva *f*; *fig* persona *f* quisquillosa
pri•mae•val [praɪm'iːvl] *esp Br* ☞ ***primeval***
pri•ma fa•cie [praɪmə'feɪʃɪ] *adv* a primera vista
pri•mal ['praɪml] *adj* primario
pri•ma•ri•ly [praɪ'merɪlɪ] *adv* principalmente
pri•ma•ry ['praɪmerɪ] **I** *adj (main)* principal **II** *n* POL elecciones *fpl* primarias
'pri•ma•ry col•or color *m* primario
'pri•ma•ry school *Br* escuela *f* primaria
prime [praɪm] **I** *n*: ***be in one's ~*** estar en la flor de la vida **II** *adj example, reason* primordial; ***of ~ importance*** de suprema importancia
prime 'min•is•ter primer(a) ministro(-a) *m(f)*
prime 'num•ber número *m* primo
prim•er ['praɪmər] **1** *paint* tapaporos *m inv* **2** *for explosive* cebo *m*
prime 'sus•pect principal sospechoso(-a) *m(f)*
'prime time TV horario *m* de mayor audiencia
pri•me•val [praɪ'miːvl] *adj* primigenio
prim•i•tive ['prɪmɪtɪv] *adj* primitivo
pri•mor•di•al [praɪ'mɔːrdɪəl] *adj* primigenio
prim•rose ['prɪmroʊs] BOT primavera *f*
prim•u•la ['prɪmjʊlə] BOT prímula *f*
prince [prɪns] príncipe *m*
prince•ly ['prɪnslɪ] *adj* magnífico; ***the ~ sum of ...*** la bonita suma de…
prin•cess [prɪn'ses] princesa *f*
prin•ci•pal ['prɪnsəpl] **I** *adj* principal **II** *n of school* director(a) *m(f)*; *of university* rector(a) *m(f)*
prin•ci•pal•i•ty [prɪnsɪ'pælətɪ] principado *m*
prin•ci•pal•ly ['prɪnsəplɪ] *adv* principalmente
prin•ci•ple ['prɪnsəpl] principio *m*; ***on ~*** por principios; ***in ~*** en principio
print [prɪnt] **I** *n* **1** *in book, newspaper etc* letra *f*; ***out of ~*** agotado **2** *(photograph)* grabado *m* **3** *of painting* lámina *f* **II** *v/t* **1** imprimir **2** *use block capitals* escribir en mayúsculas
◆ **print out** *v/t* imprimir
print•ed cir•cuit board [prɪntɪd'sɜːrkɪtbɔːrd] placa *f* impresa
'print•ed mat•ter impresos *mpl*
print•er ['prɪntər] *person* impresor(a) *m(f)*; *machine* impresora *f*; *company* imprenta *f*

print•ing press ['prɪntɪŋpres] imprenta *f*
'print•ing works imprenta *f*
'print•out copia *f* impresa; **'print run** tirada *f*; **'print•shop** imprenta *f*
pri•or [praɪr] **I** *adj* previo **II** *prep*: **~ *to*** antes de
pri•or•i•tize [praɪ'ɔːrətaɪz] *v/t* **1** (*put in order of priority*) ordenar atendiendo a las prioridades **2** (*give priority to*) dar prioridad a
pri•or•i•ty [praɪ'ɑːrətɪ] prioridad *f*; ***have ~*** tener prioridad
prism ['prɪzəm] MATH, PHYS *etc* prisma *m*
pris•on ['prɪzn] prisión *f*, cárcel *f*
'pris•on camp campo *m* de prisioneros
'pris•on cell celda *f*
pris•on•er ['prɪznər] prisionero(-a) *m(f)*; ***take s.o. ~*** hacer prisionero a alguien
pris•on•er of 'war prisionero(-a) *m(f)* de guerra
pris•on 'guard carcelero(-a) *m(f)*
'pris•on sen•tence pena *f* de prisión
pris•sy ['prɪsɪ] *adj* F remilgado
pris•tine ['prɪstiːn] *adj*: ***be in ~ condition*** estar en un estado inmaculado
priv•a•cy ['prɪvəsɪ] intimidad *f*
pri•vate ['praɪvət] **I** *adj* privado **II** *n* **1** MIL soldado *m/f* raso **2**: ***in ~*** en privado
pri•vate 'en•ter•prise empresa *f* privada
'pri•vate life vida *f* privada
pri•vate•ly ['praɪvətlɪ] *adv* (*in private*) en privado; *with one other* a solas; (*inwardly*) para sí; **~ *owned*** en manos privadas
'pri•vate sec•tor sector *m* privado
pri•va•tion [praɪ'veɪʃn] privación *f*
pri•va•ti•za•tion [praɪvətaɪz'eɪʃn] privatización *f*
pri•va•tize ['praɪvətaɪz] *v/t* privatizar
priv•i•lege ['prɪvəlɪdʒ] **1** (*special treatment*) privilegio *m* **2** (*honor*) honor *m*; ***it's a ~ to be invited*** es un honor haber sido invitado
priv•i•leged ['prɪvəlɪdʒd] *adj* privilegiado
priv•y ['prɪvɪ] *adj*: ***be ~ to sth*** estar enterado de algo
prize [praɪz] **I** *n* premio *m* **II** *v/t* apreciar, valorar
◆ **prize off** *v/t lid* arrancar
◆ **prize open** *v/t* forzar
'prize•fight•er boxeador *m* profesional; **'prize•fight•ing** boxeo *m* profesional; **prize•giv•ing** ['praɪzgɪvɪŋ] *Br* entrega *f* de premios; **'prize mon•ey** premio *m* (*dinero*); **'prize•win•ner** premiado(-a) *m(f)*; **'prize•win•ning** *adj* premiado
pro[1] [proʊ] *n*: ***the ~s and cons*** los pros y los contras
pro[2] [proʊ] ☞ ***professional***
pro[3] [proʊ] *prep*: ***be ~ ...*** estar a favor de; ***the ~ Clinton Democrats*** los demócratas partidarios de Clinton
pro•ac•tive [proʊ'æktɪv] *adj* proactivo
pro-am [proʊ'æm] *adj golf* de profesionales y aficionados
prob•a•bil•i•ty [prɑːbə'bɪlətɪ] probabilidad *f*; ***in all ~*** con toda probabilidad
prob•a•ble ['prɑːbəbl] *adj* probable
prob•a•bly ['prɑːbəblɪ] *adv* probablemente
pro•ba•tion [prə'beɪʃn] **1** *in job* periodo *m* de prueba **2** LAW libertad *f* condicional; ***be given ~*** ser puesto en libertad condicional
pro•ba•tion•ar•y [prə'beɪʃnrɪ] *adj*: **~ *period*** *in job* periodo *m* de prueba
pro•ba•tion•er [prə'beɪʃnər] persona *f* en periodo de prueba; LAW condenado(-a) *m(f)* en libertad provisional
pro'ba•tion of•fi•cer *oficial encargado de la vigilancia de los que están en libertad condicional*
pro'ba•tion pe•ri•od *in job* periodo *m* de prueba
probe [proʊb] **I** *n* (*investigation*) investigación *f*, *scientific* sonda *f* **II** *v/t* examinar; (*investigate*) investigar **III** *v/i*: ***you should ~ a little deeper*** escarba un un poco más; **~ *into a person's past*** hurgar en el pasado de alguien
prob•ing ['proʊbɪŋ] *adj question* perspicaz; *gaze* escrutinador
pro•bi•ty ['proʊbɪtɪ] probidad *f*
prob•lem ['prɑːbləm] problema *m*; ***no ~!*** ¡claro!; ***I'll fix it, that's no ~*** lo arreglaré, por supuesto; ***I have no ~ with that*** (*don't object*) para mí eso no es ningún problema; ***have a drink ~*** tener un problema de alcoholismo
prob•lem•at•ic [prɑːblə'mætɪk] *adj* problemático
pro•ce•dur•al [prə'siːdʒərəl] *adj* de pro-

P

cedimiento; LAW procesal
pro•ce•dure [prə'siːdʒər] procedimiento *m*
pro•ceed [prə'siːd] *v/i* (*go: of people*) dirigirse; *of work etc* proseguir, avanzar; ***~ to do sth*** pasar a hacer algo
pro•ceed•ings [prə'siːdɪŋz] *npl* (*events*) actos *mpl*
pro•ceeds ['prɑːsiːdz] *npl* recaudación *f*
pro•cess ['prɑːses] **I** *n* proceso *m*; ***in the ~*** (*while doing it*) al hacerlo **II** *v/t food* tratar; *raw materials, data* procesar; *application* tramitar
pro•cess•ing ['prɑːsesɪŋ] procesado *m*; ***~ industry*** industria *f* de procesado
pro•ces•sion [prə'seʃn] desfile *m*; *religious* procesión *f*
pro•ces•sor ['prɑːsesər] procesador *m*
pro-choice [proʊ'tʃɔɪs] *adj* con derecho a decidir (*sobre el embarazo*)
pro•claim [prə'kleɪm] *v/t* declarar, proclamar
proc•la•ma•tion [prɑːklə'meɪʃn] proclamación *f*
pro•cliv•i•ty [prə'klɪvətɪ] propensión *f*
pro•cras•ti•nate [proʊ'kræstɪneɪt] *v/i* andarse con dilaciones
pro•cras•ti•na•tion [proʊkræstɪ'neɪʃn] dilaciones *fpl*
pro•cre•ate ['prɑːkrɪeɪt] *v/i* procear
pro•cre•a•tion [prɑːkrɪ'eɪʃn] procreación *f*
pro•cure [prə'kjʊr] *v/t* conseguir
pro•cure•ment [prə'kjʊrmənt] *of supplies etc* obtención *f*
prod [prɑːd] **I** *n* empujoncito *m*; ***he needs a little ~ now and again*** necesita que lo espoleen de vez en cuando **II** *v/t* (*pret & pp* ***-ded***) dar un empujoncito a; *with elbow* dar un codazo a
prod•i•gal son [prɑːdɪgl'sʌn] hijo *m* pródigo
pro•di•gious [prə'dɪdʒəs] *adj* prodigioso
prod•i•gy ['prɑːdɪdʒɪ]: (***infant***) **~** niño(-a) *m*(*f*) prodigio(-a)
prod•uce[1] ['prɑːduːs] *n* productos *mpl* del campo
pro•duce[2] [prə'duːs] *v/t* **1** producir; (*manufacture*) fabricar **2** (*take out*) sacar
pro•duc•er [prə'duːsər] productor(a) *m*(*f*); (*manufacturer*) fabricante *m/f*
prod•uct ['prɑːdʌkt] producto *m*
pro•duc•tion [prə'dʌkʃn] producción *f*
pro'duc•tion ca•pac•i•ty capacidad *f* de producción; **pro'duc•tion costs** *npl* costos *mpl* de producción; **pro'duc•tion di•rect•or** director(a) *m*(*f*) de producción; **pro'duc•tion line** cadena *f* de producción; **pro'duc•tion man•ag•er** jefe(-a) *m*(*f*) de producción
pro•duc•tive [prə'dʌktɪv] *adj* productivo
pro•duc•tiv•i•ty [prɑːdʌk'tɪvətɪ] productividad *f*
'prod•uct man•ag•er jefe(-a) *m*(*f*) de producto; **'prod•uct mix** combinación *f* de estrategias de productos; **'prod•uct range** gama *f* de productos
prof [prɑːf] F ☞ ***professor***
pro•fane [prə'feɪn] *adj language* profano
pro•fan•i•ty [prə'fænətɪ] grosería *f*
pro•fess [prə'fes] *v/t* manifestar
pro•fessed [prə'fesd] *adj* declarado
pro•fes•sion [prə'feʃn] profesión *f*; ***what's your ~?*** ¿a qué se dedica?
pro•fes•sion•al [prə'feʃnl] **I** *adj* profesional; ***turn ~*** hacerse profesional **II** *n* profesional *m/f*
pro•fes•sion•al•ism [prə'feʃənəlɪzəm] profesionalismo *m*
pro•fes•sion•al•ly [prə'feʃnlɪ] *adv* **1** *play sport* profesionalmente **2** (*well, skillfully*) con profesionalidad
pro•fes•sor [prə'fesər] catedrático(-a) *m*(*f*)
pro•fes•sor•ship [prə'fesərʃɪp] cátedra *f*
prof•fer ['prɑːfər] *v/t fml*: ***~ sth to s.o.*** ofrecer algo a alguien
pro•fi•cien•cy [prə'fɪʃnsɪ] competencia *f*
pro•fi•cient [prə'fɪʃnt] competente; (*skillful*) hábil
pro•file ['proʊfaɪl] **I** *n* **1** *of face* perfil *m*; ***see sth in ~*** ver algo de perfil **2** *biographical* reseña *f* **II** *v/t in newspaper article etc* hacer un monográfico sobre
prof•it ['prɑːfɪt] **I** *n* beneficio *m*; ***make a ~*** obtener beneficios (***on*** con); ***sell sth at a ~*** vender algo con beneficios **II** *v/i*: ***~ by, ~ from*** beneficiarse de
prof•it•a•bil•i•ty [prɑːfɪtə'bɪlətɪ] rentabilidad *f*; ***~ ratio*** proporción *f* de rentabilidad

prof•i•ta•ble ['prɑːfɪtəbl] *adj* rentable
prof•it and 'loss state•ment cuenta *f* de resultados
'prof•it cen•ter centro *m* de beneficios
prof•it•eer•ing [prɑːfɪt'ɪrɪŋ] especulación *f*
'prof•it mar•gin margen *m* de beneficios
prof•it shar•ing ['prɑːfɪtʃerɪŋ] participación *f* en los beneficios
prof•li•gate ['prɑːflɪgət] *adj* derrochador
pro for•ma (in•voice) [proʊ'fɔːrmə] factura *f* proforma
pro•found [prə'faʊnd] *adj* profundo
pro•found•ly [prə'faʊndlɪ] *adv* profundamente, enormemente
pro•fuse [prə'fjuːs] *adj* profuso; *apologies* efusivo
pro•fuse•ly [prə'fjuːslɪ] *adv bleed* profusamente; *thank*, *apologize* efusivamente
pro•fu•sion [prə'fjuːʒn] profusión *f* (**of** de)
prog•no•sis [prɑːg'noʊsɪs] pronóstico *m*
pro•gram ['proʊgræm] **I** *n* programa *m* **II** *v/t* (*pret & pp* **-med**) COMPUT programar; ***be ~med to do sth*** estar programado para hacer algo
pro•gram•er, pro•gram•ing ☞ ***programmer, programming***
programme *Br* ☞ ***program***
pro•gram•mer ['proʊgræmər] COMPUT programador(a) *m(f)*
pro•gram•ming ['proʊgræmɪŋ] programación *f*
'pro•gram•ming lang•uage lenguaje *m* de programación
pro•gress I *n* ['prɑːgres] progreso *m*; ***make ~*** hacer progresos; ***in ~*** en curso **II** *v/i* [prə'gres] (*advance in time*) avanzar; (*move on*) pasar; (*make ~*) progresar; ***how is the work ~ing?*** ¿cómo avanza el trabajo?
pro•gres•sion [prə'greʃn] evolución *f*; MATH progresión *f*
pro•gres•sive [prə'gresɪv] *adj* **1** (*enlightened*) progresista **2** (*which progresses*) progresivo
pro•gres•sive•ly [prə'gresɪvlɪ] *adv* progresivamente
pro•hib•it [prə'hɪbɪt] *v/t* prohibir
pro•hi•bi•tion [proʊhɪ'bɪʃn] prohibición *f*; ***during Prohibition*** durante la ley seca
pro•hib•i•tive [prə'hɪbɪtɪv] *adj prices* prohibitivo
proj•ect[1] ['prɑːdʒekt] *n* **1** (*plan, undertaking*) proyecto *m* **2** EDU trabajo *m* **3** *housing area* barriada *f* de viviendas sociales
pro•ject[2] [prə'dʒekt] **I** *v/t* **1** *movie* proyectar **2** *figures, sales* prever, estimar; ***~ed sales revenue*** ingresos *mpl* por ventas previstos **II** *v/i* (*stick out*) sobresalir
pro•jec•tile [prə'dʒektəl] proyectil *m*
pro•jec•tion [prə'dʒekʃn] (*forecast*) previsión *f*
pro•jec•tion•ist [prə'dʒekʃnɪst] proyeccionista *m/f*
pro•ject 'lead•er director(a) *m(f)* de proyecto; **pro•ject 'man•age•ment** dirección *f* de proyecto; **proj•ect 'man•ag•er** director(a) *m(f)* de proyecto
pro•jec•tor [prə'dʒektər] *for slides* proyector *m*
pro•le•tar•i•an [proʊlə'terɪən] **I** *adj* proletario **II** *n* proletario(-a) *m(f)*
pro•le•tar•i•at [proʊlə'terɪət] proletariado *m*
pro-'life *adj* pro vida
pro•lif•er•ate [prə'lɪfəreɪt] *v/i* proliferar
pro•lif•er•a•tion [prəlɪfər'eɪʃn] proliferación *f*
pro•lif•ic [prə'lɪfɪk] *adj writer, artist* prolífico
pro•log, *Br* **pro•logue** ['proʊlɑːg] prólogo *m*
pro•long [prə'lɒːŋ] *v/t* prolongar
prom [prɑːm] (*school dance*) *baile de fin de curso*
prom•e•nade deck [prɑːme'neɪddek] NAUT cubierta *f* de paseo
prom•i•nence ['prɑːmɪnəns] *also hill* prominencia *f*; ***come to ~*** empezar a destacar
prom•i•nent ['prɑːmɪnənt] *adj* **1** *nose, chin* prominente **2** (*significant*) destacado; ***play a ~ part in sth*** desempeñar un papel destacado en algo
prom•i•nent•ly ['prɑːmɪnəntlɪ] *adv positioned* en un lugar prominente
prom•is•cu•i•ty [prɑːmɪ'skjuːətɪ] promiscuidad *f*
pro•mis•cu•ous [prə'mɪskjʊəs] *adj* promiscuo

prom•ise ['prɑːmɪs] **I** *n* promesa *f*; ***it's a ~*** lo prometo; ***~s!, ~s!*** F ¡promesas, promesas! **II** *v/t* prometer; ***she ~d to help*** prometió ayudar; ***~ sth to s.o.*** prometer algo a alguien **III** *v/i*: ***do you ~?*** ¿lo prometes?
prom•is•ing ['prɑːmɪsɪŋ] *adj* prometedor
prom•is•so•ry note ['prɑːmɪsɔːrɪ] COM pagaré *m*
prom•on•to•ry ['prɑːməntɔːrɪ] promontorio *m*
pro•mote [prə'moʊt] *v/t* **1** *employee* ascender **2** (*encourage, foster*) promover; COM promocionar
pro•mot•er [prə'moʊtər] *of sports event* promotor(a) *m*(*f*)
pro•mo•tion [prə'moʊʃn] **1** *of employee* ascenso *m*; ***~ prospects*** perspectivas *fpl* de ascenso **2** *of scheme, idea*, COM promoción *f*
pro•mo•tion•al [prə'moʊʃənl] *adj* promocional
prompt [prɑːmpt] **I** *adj* **1** (*on time*) puntual **2** (*speedy*) rápido **II** *adv*: ***at two o'clock ~*** a las dos en punto **III** *v/t* **1** (*cause*) provocar **2** *actor* apuntar **IV** *n* COMPUT mensaje *m*; ***go to the c ~*** ir a c:\
prompt•er ['prɑːmptər] THEA apuntador(a) *m*(*f*)
prompt•ly ['prɑːmptlɪ] *adv* **1** (*on time*) puntualmente **2** (*immediately*) inmediatamente
prone [proʊn] *adj*: ***be ~ to*** ser propenso a
prong [prɑːŋ] diente *m*; ***three-~ed*** con tres dientes
pro•noun ['proʊnaʊn] pronombre *m*
pro•nounce [prə'naʊns] *v/t* **1** *word* pronunciar **2** (*declare*) declarar
pro•nounced [prə'naʊnst] *adj accent* marcado; *views* fuerte
pro•nounce•ment [prə'naʊnsmənt] declaración *f*
pron•to ['prɑːntoʊ] *adv* F ya, en seguida
pro•nun•ci•a•tion [prənʌnsɪ'eɪʃn] pronunciación *f*
proof [pruːf] **1** prueba(s) *f*(*pl*); ***~ of identity*** documento *m* de identidad; ***~ of purchase*** justificante *m* de compra **2** *of book* prueba *f* **3**: ***8% ~*** *alcohol* de 8 grados
'proof•read•er corrector(a) *m*(*f*) de pruebas
prop [prɑːp] **I** *v/t* (*pret & pp* **-ped**) apoyar **II** *n* THEA accesorio *m*
◆ **prop up** *v/t* apoyar
prop•a•gan•da [prɑːpə'gændə] propaganda *f*
prop•a•gate ['prɑːpəgeɪt] *v/t species, views etc* propagar
prop•a•ga•tion [prɑːpə'geɪʃn] propagación *f*
pro•pane ['proʊpeɪn] CHEM propano *m*
pro•pel [prə'pel] *v/t* (*pret & pp* **-led**) propulsar
pro•pel•lant [prə'pelənt] *in aerosol* propelente *m*
pro•pel•ler [prə'pelər] *of boat* hélice *f*
pro•pen•si•ty [prə'pensətɪ] propensión (***for*** a); ***have a ~ for doing sth*** tener propensión a hacer algo
prop•er ['prɑːpər] *adj* **1** (*real*) de verdad; ***he's not a ~ doctor*** no es un doctor de verdad; ***put it back in its ~ place*** vuelve a ponerlo en su sitio; ***that's not the ~ cover for this*** esta no es la tapa adecuada; ***in Mexico City ~*** en la Ciudad de México propiamente dicha **2** (*fitting*) adecuado; ***it's not ~*** no está bien; ***it's the ~ thing to do*** es lo que se hace en estos casos
prop•er•ly ['prɑːpərlɪ] *adv* **1** (*correctly*) bien **2** (*fittingly*) adecuadamente
prop•er•ty ['prɑːpərtɪ] **1** propiedad *f* **2** (*land*) propiedad(es) *f*(*pl*)
'prop•er•ty de•vel•op•er promotor(a) *m*(*f*) inmobiliario(-a); **'prop•er•ty mar•ket** mercado *m* inmobiliario; **'prop•er•ty tax** impuesto *m* sobre la propiedad
proph•e•cy ['prɑːfəsɪ] profecía *f*
proph•e•sy ['prɑːfəsaɪ] *v/t* (*pret & pp* **-ied**) profetizar
proph•et ['prɑːfɪt] profeta *m*; ***~ of doom*** agorero *m*
pro•phet•ic [prə'fetɪk] *adj* profético
pro•phy•lac•tic [prɑːfɪ'læktɪk] **I** *adj esp* MED profiláctico **II** *n* MED, *condom* profiláctico *m*
pro•po•nent [prə'poʊnənt] partidario(-a) *m*(*f*) (***of*** de)
pro•por•tion [prə'pɔːrʃn] proporción *f*; ***a large ~ of North Americans*** gran parte de los norteamericanos; ***~s*** (*dimensions*) proporciones; ***the reaction was out of all ~*** la reacción fue despropor-

cionada
pro•por•tion•al [prə'pɔːrʃnl] *adj* proporcional
pro•por•tion•al rep•re•sen'ta•tion POL representación *f* proporcional
pro•por•tion•ate [prə'pɔːrʃnət] *adj* proporcional (***to*** a)
pro•pos•al [prə'pouzl] **1** (*suggestion*) propuesta *f* **2** *of marriage* proposición *f*
pro•pose [prə'pouz] **I** *v/t* **1** (*suggest*) sugerir, proponer **2** (*plan*) proponerse **II** *v/i* (*make offer of marriage*) pedir la mano (***to*** a)
prop•o•si•tion [prɑːpə'zɪʃn] **I** *n* propuesta *f*; ***I've got a ~ to put to you*** quiero proponerte algo **II** *v/t woman* hacer proposiciones a
pro•pri•e•tar•y [prə'praɪəterɪ] *adj brand, goods* registrado, de marca registrada
pro•pri•e•tor [prə'praɪətər] propietario(-a) *m(f)*
pro•pri•e•tress [prə'praɪətrɪs] propietaria *f*
pro•pri•e•ty [prə'praɪətɪ] decoro *m*; ***the proprieties*** *pl* las convenciones
pro•pul•sion [prə'pʌlʃn] TECH propulsión *f*
pro ra•ta [prou'rɑːtə] **I** *adj* prorrateado **II** *adv* de forma prorrateada
pro•rogue [prou'roug] *v/t* posponer
pro•sa•ic [prou'zeɪɪk] *adj* prosaico
pro•scribe [prə'skraɪb] *v/t* (*forbid, exile*) proscribir
pro•scrip•tion [prə'skrɪpʃn] proscripción *f*
prose [prouz] prosa *f*
pros•e•cute ['prɑːsɪkjuːt] *v/t* LAW procesar
pros•e•cu•tion [prɑːsɪ'kjuːʃn] LAW procesamiento *m*; *lawyers* acusación *f*; ***he's facing ~*** lo van a procesar
pros•e•cu•tor ☞ ***public prosecutor***
pros•pect ['prɑːspekt] **I** *n* **1** (*chance, likelihood*) probabilidad *f* **2** (*thought of something in the future*) perspectiva *f*; ***~s*** perspectivas (de futuro) **II** *v/i*: ***~ for*** *gold* buscar
pro•spec•tive [prə'spektɪv] *adj* potencial
pros•pec•tor ['prɑːspektər] buscador(a) *m(f)*
pros•per ['prɑːspər] *v/i* prosperar
pros•per•i•ty [prɑː'sperətɪ] prosperidad *f*
pros•per•ous ['prɑːspərəs] *adj* próspero
pros•tate (gland) ['prɑːsteɪt] ANAT próstata *f*
pros•the•sis [prɑːs'θiːsɪs] prótesis *f inv*
pros•ti•tute ['prɑːstɪtuːt] prostituta *f*; ***male ~*** prostituto *m*
pros•ti•tu•tion [prɑːstɪ'tuːʃn] prostitución *f*
pros•trate ['prɑːstreɪt] *adj* postrado; ***be ~ with grief*** estar postrado por el dolor
pro•tag•o•nist [prə'tægənɪst] THEA *etc* protagonista *m/f*
pro•tect [prə'tekt] *v/t* proteger
pro•tec•tion [prə'tekʃn] protección *f*
pro•tec•tion•ism [prə'tekʃnɪzəm] proteccionismo *m*
pro'tec•tion mon•ey *dinero pagado a delincuentes a cambio de obtener protección*; *paid to terrorists* impuesto *m* revolucionario
pro'tec•tion rack•et red *f* de extorsión
pro•tec•tive [prə'tektɪv] *adj* protector
pro•tec•tive 'cloth•ing ropa *f* protectora
pro•tec•tive 'cus•to•dy prisión *f* preventiva
pro•tec•tor [prə'tektər] protector(a) *m(f)*
pro•tec•tor•ate [prə'tektərət] POL protectorado *m*
pro•té•gé(e) ['prɑːtəʒeɪ] protegido(-a) *m(f)*
pro•tein ['proutiːn] proteína *f*
pro•test I *n* ['proutest] protesta *f*; ***in ~ at these changes*** en (señal de) protesta por estos cambios **II** *v/t* [prə'test] protestar, quejarse de; (*object to*) protestar contra **III** *v/i* [prə'test] protestar
Prot•es•tant ['prɑːtɪstənt] **I** *n* protestante *m/f* **II** *adj* protestante
Prot•es•tant•ism ['prɑːtɪstəntɪzəm] protestantismo *m*
prot•es•ta•tion [prɑːtes'teɪʃn] proclamación *f*; ***~s*** *pl* ***of innocence*** declaración *f* de inocencia
pro•test•er [prə'testər] manifestante *m/f*
pro•to•col ['proutəkɑːl] protocolo *m*
pro•ton ['proutɑːn] PHYS protón *m*
pro•to•type ['proutətaɪp] prototipo *m*

pro•tract [prə'trækt] *v/t* prolongar
pro•tract•ed [prə'træktɪd] *adj* prolongado, largo
pro•trac•tor [prə'træktər] MATH transportador *m*
pro•trude [prə'tru:d] *v/i* sobresalir
pro•trud•ing [prə'tru:dɪŋ] *adj* saliente; *ears, teeth* prominente
pro•tru•sion [prə'tru:ʒn] protuberancia *f*
pro•tu•ber•ance [proʊ'tu:bərəns] protuberancia *f*
pro•tu•ber•ant [proʊ'tu:bərənt] *adj* protuberante
proud [praʊd] *adj* orgulloso; ***be ~ of*** estar orgulloso de
proud•ly ['praʊdlɪ] *adv* con orgullo, orgullosamente; ***we ~ present*** tenemos el orgullo de presentar
prov•a•ble ['pru:vəbl] *adj* que se puede probar
prove [pru:v] *v/t* demostrar, probar
prov•en ['pru:vn] **I** *pp* ☞ ***prove*** **II** *adj* probado
prov•erb ['prɑ:vɜ:rb] proverbio *m*, refrán *m*
pro•ver•bi•al [prə'vɜ:rbɪəl] *adj* proverbial
pro•vide [prə'vaɪd] *v/t* proporcionar; ***~ sth to s.o., ~ s.o. with sth*** proporcionar algo a alguien
◆ **provide for** *v/t* **1** *family* mantener **2** *of law etc* prever
pro•vid•ed (that) [prə'vaɪdɪd] *conj* (*on condition that*) con la condición de que, siempre que
prov•i•dence ['prɑ:vɪdəns] providencia *f*
prov•i•den•tial [prɑ:vɪ'denʃl] *adj* providencial
pro•vid•er [prə'vaɪdər] proveedor(a) *m(f)*; (*Internet service ~*) proveedor *m*
pro•vid•ing [prə'vaɪdɪŋ] *conj* siempre que
prov•ince ['prɑ:vɪns] provincia *f*
pro•vin•cial [prə'vɪnʃl] *adj city* provincial; *pej*: *attitude* de pueblo, provinciano
pro•vi•sion [prə'vɪʒn] **1** (*supply*) suministro *m* **2** *of law, contract* disposición *f*
pro•vi•sion•al [prə'vɪʒnl] *adj* provisional
pro•vi•sion•al•ly [prə'vɪʒənlɪ] *adv* provisionalmente
pro•vi•so [prə'vaɪzoʊ] condición *f*
prov•o•ca•tion [prɑ:və'keɪʃn] provocación *f*
pro•voc•a•tive [prə'vɑ:kətɪv] *adj* provocador; *sexually* provocativo
pro•voke [prə'voʊk] *v/t* (*cause, annoy*) provocar
prow [praʊ] NAUT proa *f*
prow•ess ['praʊɪs] proezas *fpl*
prowl [praʊl] *v/i of tiger, burglar* merodear
'prowl car coche *m* patrulla
prowl•er ['praʊlər] merodeador(a) *m(f)*
prox•im•i•ty [prɑ:k'sɪmətɪ] proximidad *f*
prox•y ['prɑ:ksɪ] *authority* poder *m*; *person* apoderado(-a) *m(f)*
prude [pru:d] mojigato(-a) *m(f)*
pru•dence ['pru:dns] prudencia *f*
pru•dent ['pru:dnt] *adj* prudente
pru•dent•ly ['pru:dntlɪ] *adv* prudentemente
prud•er•y ['pru:dərɪ] mojigatería *f*
prud•ish ['pru:dɪʃ] *adj* mojigato
prune[1] [pru:n] *n* ciruela *f* pasa
prune[2] [pru:n] *v/t plant* podar; *fig* reducir
pru•ri•ence ['prʊrɪəns] lascivia *f*
pru•ri•ent ['prʊrɪənt] *adj* lascivo
prus•sic ac•id [prʌsɪk'æsɪd] CHEM ácido *m* prúsico
pry[1] [praɪ] *v/i* (*pret & pp* ***-ied***) entrometerse
◆ **pry into** *v/t* entrometerse en
pry[2] [praɪ] *v/t* (*pret & pp* ***-ied***) ☞ ***prize***
pry•ing ['praɪɪŋ] *adj* fisgón
PS ['pi:es] *abbr* (= ***postscript***) PD (= posdata *f*)
psalm [sɑ:m] salmo *m*
pseud [su:d] F pretencioso(-a) *m(f)*
pseu•do•nym ['su:dənɪm] pseudónimo *m*
pso•ri•a•sis [sə'raɪəsɪs] soriasis *f*
◆ **psych out** [saɪk] *v/t* F poner nervioso
◆ **psych up** *v/t* F mentalizar
psy•che ['saɪkɪ] psique *f*
psy•che•del•ic [saɪkə'delɪk] *adj drug, color* psicodélico
psy•chi•at•ric [saɪkɪ'ætrɪk] *adj* psiquiátrico
psy•chi•a•trist [saɪ'kaɪətrɪst] psiquiatra *m/f*
psy•chi•a•try [saɪ'kaɪətrɪ] psiquiatría *f*

psy•chic ['saɪkɪk] *adj research* paranormal; ***I'm not ~*** no soy vidente
psy•cho•a•nal•y•sis [saɪkouən'æləsɪs] psicoanálisis *m*
psy•cho•an•a•lyst [saɪkou'ænəlɪst] psicoanalista *m/f*
psy•cho•an•a•lyze [saɪkou'ænəlaɪz] *v/t* psicoanalizar
psy•cho•bab•ble ['saɪkoubæbl] F charla *fpl* pseudopsicológica
psy•cho•log•i•cal [saɪkə'lɑːdʒɪkl] *adj* psicológico
psy•cho•log•i•cal•ly [saɪkə'lɑːdʒɪklɪ] *adv* psicológicamente
psy•chol•o•gist [saɪ'kɑːlədʒɪst] psicólogo(-a) *m(f)*
psy•chol•o•gy [saɪ'kɑːlədʒɪ] psicología *f*
psy•cho•met•ric [saɪkə'metrɪk] *adj*: ***~ testing*** pruebas *fpl* psicométricas
psy•cho•path ['saɪkoupæθ] psicópata *m/f*
psy•cho•sis [saɪ'kousɪs] (*pl* ***psychoses*** [saɪ-'kousiːz]) MED psicosis *f inv*
psy•cho•so•mat•ic [saɪkousə'mætɪk] *adj* psicosomático
psy•cho•ther•a•pist [saɪkou'θerəpɪst] psicoterapeuta *m/f*
psy•cho•ther•a•py [saɪkou'θerəpɪ] psicoterapia *f*
psy•chot•ic [saɪ'kɑːtɪk] *adj* psicótico
PTA [piːtiː'eɪ] *abbr* (= ***parent-teacher association***) APA *f* (= asociación *f* de padres de alumnos)
PTO [piːtiː'ou] *abbr* (= ***please turn over***) véase al dorso
pub [pʌb] *Br* bar *m*
'pub crawl: ***go on a ~*** *Br* F salir de copas
pu•ber•ty ['pjuːbərtɪ] pubertad *f*
pu•bic ['pjuːbɪk] *adj* ANAT púbico
'pu•bic hair vello *m* púbico
pub•lic ['pʌblɪk] **I** *adj* público **II** *n*: ***the ~*** el público; ***in ~*** en público
pub•lic-ad'dress sys•tem sistema *m* de megafonía
pub•li•ca•tion [pʌblɪ'keɪʃn] publicación *f*
pub•lic ex'pen•di•ture gasto *m* público
pub•lic 'hol•i•day día *m* festivo
pub•li•cist ['pʌblɪsɪst] publicista *m/f*
pub•lic•i•ty [pʌb'lɪsətɪ] publicidad *f*
pub'lic•i•ty cam•paign campaña *f* publicitaria; **pub'lic•i•ty de•part•ment** departamento *m* de publicidad; **pub'lic•i•ty ma•te•ri•al** material *m* publicitario; **pub'lic•i•ty of•fi•cer** publicista *m/f*, publicitario(-a) *m(f)*; **pub'lic•i•ty stunt** truco *m* publicitario
pub•li•cize ['pʌblɪsaɪz] *v/t* (*make known*) publicar, hacer público; COM dar publicidad a
pub•lic li•a'bil•i•ty in•sur•ance seguro *m* de responsabilidad civil; **pub•lic 'li•bra•ry** biblioteca *f* pública; **pub•lic lim•it•ed 'com•pa•ny** *Br* sociedad *f* anónima
pub•lic•ly ['pʌblɪklɪ] *adv* públicamente
pub•lic o'pin•ion opinión *f* pública; **pub•lic 'pros•e•cu•tor** fiscal *m/f*; **pub•lic re'la•tions** *npl* relaciones *fpl* públicas; **'pub•lic school 1** colegio *m* público **2** *Br* colegio *m* privado; **'pub•lic sec•tor** sector *m* público; **pub•lic-'spir•it•ed** *adj* cívico; **pub•lic 'trans•port** *Br* transporte *m* público; **pub•lic u'til•i•ty** empresa *f* de servicios públicos
pub•lish ['pʌblɪʃ] *v/t* publicar
pub•lish•er ['pʌblɪʃər] *person* editor(a) *m(f)*; *company* editorial *f*
pub•lish•ing ['pʌblɪʃɪŋ] industria *f* editorial
'pub•lish•ing com•pa•ny editorial *f*
puce [pjuːs] *adj* morado oscuro
puck [pʌk] *in ice hockey* disco *m*
puck•er ['pʌkər] *v/t lips* fruncir
pud•ding ['pʊdɪŋ] **1** budin *m* **2** *Br* postre *m*
pud•dle ['pʌdl] charco *m*
pu•er•ile ['pjuːrɪl] *adj* pueril
Puer•to Ri•can [pwertou'riːkən] **I** *adj* portorriqueño, puertorriqueño **II** *n* portorriqueño(-a) *m(f)*, puertorriqueño(-a) *m(f)*
Puer•to Ri•co [pwertou'riːkou] Puerto Rico *m*
puff [pʌf] **I** *n* **1** *of wind* racha *f* **2** *from cigarette* calada *f* **3** *of smoke* bocanada *f* **II** *v/i* **1** (*pant*) resoplar **2**: ***~ on a cigarette*** dar una calada a un cigarrillo
puffed [pʌft] *adj* F (*out of breath*) sin aliento
puf•fin ['pʌfɪn] frailecillo *m*
puff 'paste, puff 'pas•try *Br* hojaldre *m*
puff•y ['pʌfɪ] *adj eyes, face* hinchado

pug [pʌg] *dog* dogo *m*
pug•na•cious [pʌg'neɪʃəs] *adj* combativo
pug•nac•i•ty [pʌg'næsətɪ] combatividad *f*
puke [pju:k] P **I** *n substance* vomitona *f* P **II** *v/i* echar la pota P
pull [pʊl] **I** *n on rope etc* tirón *m*; ***she gave the door a good ~*** dió un buen portazo **2** F *(appeal)* gancho *m* F **3** F *(influence)* enchufe *m* F
II *v/t* **1** *(drag)* arrastrar **2** *(tug)* tirar de; *tooth* sacar; ***~ a muscle*** sufrir un tirón en un músculo **3**: ***~ a face*** hacer una mueca; ***not ~ one's punches, ~ no punches*** no andarse con chiquitas
III *v/i* tirar
◆ **pull ahead** *v/i in race, competition* adelantarse
◆ **pull apart** *v/t* **1** *(separate)* separar **2** *(criticize)* hacer trizas
◆ **pull away I** *v/t* apartar **II** *v/i of vehicle* apartarse; *in race* escaparse (***from*** de)
◆ **pull down** *v/t* **1** *(lower)* bajar **2** *(demolish)* derribar
◆ **pull for** *v/t (cheer on)* animar a
◆ **pull in** *v/i of bus, train* llegar
◆ **pull off** *v/t* **1** quitar; *item of clothing* quitarse **2** F conseguir; ***he finally pulled it off*** al final lo consiguió
◆ **pull on** *v/t item of clothing* ponerse
◆ **pull out I** *v/t* sacar; *troops* retirar **II** *v/i* retirarse; *of ship* salir
◆ **pull over** *v/i* parar en el arcén
◆ **pull through** *v/i from an illness* recuperarse
◆ **pull together I** *v/i (cooperate)* cooperar **II** *v/t*: ***pull o.s. together*** tranquilizarse
◆ **pull up I** *v/t (raise)* subir; *item of clothing* subirse; *plant, weeds* arrancar **II** *v/i of car etc* parar
pul•ley ['pʊlɪ] polea *f*
pull•o•ver ['pʊloʊvər] suéter *m*, *Span* jersey *m*
'pull-up flexión *f (en barra)*
pul•mo•nar•y ['pʌlmənerɪ] *adj* ANAT, MED pulmonar
pulp [pʌlp] *of fruit* pulpa *f*; *for papermaking* pasta *f*; ***beat s.o. to a ~*** hacer papilla a alguien
'pulp fic•tion literatura *f* barata
pul•pit ['pʊlpɪt] púlpito *m*
'pulp nov•el novela *f* barata
pul•sate [pʌl'seɪt] *v/i of heart, blood* palpitar; *of music* vibrar
pulse [pʌls] pulso *m*
pul•ver•ize ['pʌlvəraɪz] *v/t* pulverizar
pu•ma ['pju:mə] ZO puma *m*
pum•ice ['pʌmɪs]: ***~ stone*** piedra *f* pómez
pum•mel ['pʌml] *v/t (pret & pp* ***-ed****, Br* ***-led****)* aporrear
pump [pʌmp] **I** *n* bomba *f*; *(gas ~)* surtidor *m* **II** *v/t* bombear; ***~ money into*** *fig* inyectar dinero en; ***~ s.o.'s stomach*** MED hacer a alguien un lavado de estómago; ***~ s.o. for information*** F tratar de sonsacar *or* sacar información a alguien
◆ **pump up** *v/t* inflar
pump•kin ['pʌmpkɪn] calabaza *f*
pun [pʌn] juego *m* de palabras
punch[1] [pʌntʃ] **I** *n* **1** *blow* puñetazo *m* **2** *implement* perforadora *f* **II** *v/t* **1** *with fist* dar un puñetazo a **2** *ticket* agujerear; ***~ a hole in sth*** agujerear algo
punch[2] [pʌntʃ] *n drink* ponche *m*
'punch•bag saco *m* de boxeo; **'punch card** tarjeta *f* perforada; **'punch line** golpe *m*, punto *m* culminante; **'punch-up** *Br* F pelea *f*
punc•til•i•ous [pʌŋk'tɪlɪəs] *adj* puntilloso
punc•tu•al ['pʌŋktʃʊəl] *adj* puntual
punc•tu•al•i•ty [pʌŋktʃʊ'ælətɪ] puntualidad *f*
punc•tu•al•ly ['pʌŋktʃʊəlɪ] *adv* puntualmente
punc•tu•ate ['pʌŋktʃʊeɪt] *v/t* puntuar
punc•tu•a•tion [pʌŋktʃʊ'eɪʃn] puntuación *f*
punc•tu'a•tion mark signo *m* de puntuación
punc•ture ['pʌŋktʃər] **I** *n* perforación *f* **II** *v/t* perforar
pun•dit ['pʌndɪt] experto(-a) *m(f)*
pun•gen•cy ['pʌndʒənsɪ] fuerza *f*
pun•gent ['pʌndʒənt] *adj* fuerte
pun•ish ['pʌnɪʃ] *v/t person* castigar
pun•ish•a•ble ['pʌnɪʃəbl] *adj* punible; ***~ offense*** delito *m* punible; ***murder is ~ by death*** el asesianto está castigado con la pena de muerte
pun•ish•ing ['pʌnɪʃɪŋ] *adj schedule* exigente; *pace* fuerte
pun•ish•ment ['pʌnɪʃmənt] castigo *m*
pu•ni•tive ['pju:nətɪv] *adj* punitivo; ~

damages daños *mpl* punitivos
punk ['pʌŋk], **'punk rock** MUS (música *f*) punk *m*
punk 'rock•er MUS punki *m/f*
pun•ster ['pʌnstər] *persona a la que gusta hacer juegos de palabras*
punt [pʌnt] *boat* batea *f*
pu•ny ['pju:nɪ] *adj person* enclenque
pup [pʌp] cachorro *m*
pu•pil[1] ['pju:pl] *of eye* pupila *f*
pu•pil[2] ['pju:pl] (*student*) alumno(-a) *m*(*f*)
pup•pet ['pʌpɪt] *also fig* marioneta *f*
pup•pet•eer [pʌpɪ'tɪr] marionetista *m/f*
'pup•pet gov•ern•ment gobierno *m* títere
'pup•pet show espectáculo *m* de guiñol
pup•py ['pʌpɪ] cachorro *m*
'pup•py love F amor *m* de adolescente
pur•chas•a•ble ['pɜ:rtʃəsəbl] *adj* adquirible
pur•chase[1] ['pɜ:rtʃəs] **I** *n* adquisición *f*, compra *f* **II** *v/t* adquirir, comprar
pur•chase[2] ['pɜ:rtʃəs] *n* (*grip*) agarre *m*; ***I can't get any ~ on it*** no consigo agarrarme a ello
'pur•chase in•voice factura *f* de compra; **'pur•chase ledg•er** libro *m* mayor de cuentas; **'pur•chase or•der** orden *f* de compra; **'pur•chase price** precio *m* de compra
pur•chas•er ['pɜ:rtʃəsər] comprador(a) *m*(*f*)
pur•chas•ing (de•part•ment) ['pɜ:rtʃəsɪŋ] departamento *m* de compras
'pur•chas•ing power COM poder *m* de compra
pure [pjʊr] *adj* puro; ***~ new wool*** pura lana *f* virgen
'pure•bred I *adj* purasangre **II** *n* purasangre *m*
pu•ree ['pjʊreɪ] **I** *n* puré *m* **II** *v/t* hacer puré
pure•ly ['pjʊrlɪ] *adv* puramente
pur•ga•to•ry ['pɜ:rgətɔ:rɪ] purgatorio *m*
purge [pɜ:rdʒ] **I** *n of political party* purga *f* **II** *v/t* purgar *f*
pu•ri•fi•ca•tion [pjʊrɪfɪ'keɪʃn] purificación *f*
pu•ri•fy ['pjʊrɪfaɪ] *v/t* (*pret & pp* ***-ied***) *water* depurar
pur•ism ['pjʊrɪzəm] purismo *m*
pur•ist ['pjʊrɪst] purista *m/f*
Pu•ri•tan ['pjʊrɪtən] **I** *adj* puritano **II** *n* puritano(-a) *m*(*f*)
pu•ri•tan ['pjʊrɪtən] puritano(-a) *m*(*f*)
pu•ri•tan•i•cal [pjʊrɪ'tænɪkl] *adj* puritano
Pu•ri•tan•ism ['pjʊrɪtənɪzəm] puritanismo *m*
pu•ri•ty ['pjʊrɪtɪ] pureza *f*
pur•loin [pɜ:r'lɔɪn] *v/t* sustraer
pur•ple ['pɜ:rpl] *adj* morado; ***he went ~*** *with embarrassment* se puso rojo; *with anger* se puso encendido
Pur•ple 'Heart MIL *medalla concedida a los soldados heridos en combate*
pur•port [pɜ:r'pɔ:rt] *v/t*: ***~ to be*** pretender ser
pur•port•ed•ly [pɜ:r'pɔ:rtɪdlɪ] *adv* supuestamente
pur•pose ['pɜ:rpəs] (*aim, object*) propósito *m*, objeto *m*; ***on ~*** a propósito; ***what is the ~ of your visit?*** ¿cuál es el objeto de su visita?
pur•pose•ful ['pɜ:rpəsfəl] *adj* decidido
pur•pose•ly ['pɜ:rpəslɪ] *adv* decididamente
purr [pɜ:r] *v/i of cat* ronronear; *of engine* zumbar
purse [pɜ:rs] **1** (*pocketbook*) bolso *m* **2** *Br for money* monedero *m*
purs•er ['pɜ:rsər] NAUT, AVIA sobrecargo *m*
pur•su•ance [pər'sʊəns]: ***in (the) ~ of one's duty*** en el cumplimiento del deber
pur•sue [pər'su:] *v/t person* perseguir; *career* ejercer; *course of action* proseguir
pur•su•er [pər'su:ər] perseguidor(a) *m*(*f*)
pur•suit [pər'su:t] **1** (*chase*) persecución *f*; *of happiness etc* búsqueda *f*; ***those in ~*** los perseguidores **2** (*activity*) actividad *f*
pus [pʌs] pus *m*
push [pʊʃ] **I** *n* (*shove*) empujón *m*; ***at the ~ of a button*** apretando un botón; ***give s.o. a ~*** dar un empujón a alguien; *in car* empujar el coche de alguien; ***she got the ~*** *Br* F *from job, in relationship* la pusieron / la puso de patitas en la calle; ***when it comes to the ~*** F, ***when ~ comes to shove*** F cuando las cosas se ponen feas; ***at a ~*** F apurando **II** *v/t* **1** (*shove*) empujar; *button* apretar,

pulsar; ***the reporter ~ed a microphone into his face*** el periodista le metió un micrófono en la cara; ***~ one's way through*** abrirse paso a empujones
2 (*pressurize*) presionar; ***he was ~ed into it*** *into job etc* le hicieron hacerlo; ***~ s.o. to do sth*** presionar a alguien para que haga algo
3 F *drugs* pasar F, mercadear con
4: ***be ~ed for cash*** F estar pelado F, estar sin un centavo; ***be ~ed for time*** F ir mal de tiempo F; ***be ~ing 40*** F rondar los 40
III *v/i* empujar
◆ **push ahead** *v/i* seguir adelante
◆ **push along** *v/t cart etc* empujar
◆ **push around** *v/t* F (*boss around*) abusar de, mangonear a
◆ **push away** *v/t* apartar
◆ **push for** *v/t* (*try to get*) insistir en
◆ **push in** *v/i* colarse
◆ **push off I** *v/t lid* destapar **II** *v/i* largarse; ***push off!*** ¡lárgate!
◆ **push on** *v/i* (*continue*) continuar
◆ **push past** *v/t*: ***push past s.o.*** adelantar a alguien a empujones
◆ **push up** *v/t prices* hacer subir

'push but•ton botón *m*

'push-but•ton *adj* de botones; ***~ telephone*** teléfono *m* de botones

'push•cart carro *m*

push•er ['pʊʃər] F *of drugs* camello *m* F

'push•o•ver F: ***it was a ~*** era pan comido F; ***I'm a ~ for …*** no sé decir que no a…; **'push-start** *v/t* arrancar empujando; **'push-up** flexión *f* (de brazos)

push•y ['pʊʃɪ] *adj* F avasallador, agresivo

puss, pus•sy (cat) [pʊs, 'pʊsɪ] F minino *m* F

◆ **pus•sy•foot around** ['pʊsɪfʊt] *v/i* F andarse con rodeos

put [pʊt] **I** *v/t* (*pret & pp* **put**) **1** poner; ***~ the cost at …*** estimar el costo en …; ***stay ~*** no moverse; ***~ sth before sth*** *fig* poner algo antes que algo; ***~ a tax on sth*** poner un impuesto sobre algo
2 (*say*) poner, decir; *question* hacer; ***let me ~ it this way*** pongámoslo así; ***and that's ~ting it mildly*** y eso por decirlo suavemente; ***~ it to s.o. that …*** proponer a alguien que … **II** *v/i*: ***~ to sea*** NAUT zarpar
◆ **put about** *v/i* NAUT cambiar de rumbo
◆ **put across** *v/t idea etc* hacer llegar
◆ **put ahead** *v/t in competition* poner por delante
◆ **put aside** *v/t money* apartar, ahorrar; *work* dejar a un lado
◆ **put away** *v/t* **1** *in closet etc* guardar; *in institution* encerrar; F (*consume*) consumir, cepillarse F; *money* apartar, ahorrar **2** *animal* sacrificar
◆ **put back** *v/t* **1** (*replace*) volver a poner **2** *clocks* retrasar, atrasar
◆ **put by** *v/t money* apartar, ahorrar
◆ **put down** *v/t* **1** dejar; *deposit* entregar; ***put one's foot down*** *in car* apretar el acelerador; (*be firm*) plantarse; ***put one's name down for sth*** apuntarse a algo **2** F (*belittle*) dejar en mal lugar **3** *rebellion* reprimir **4**: ***put down in writing*** poner por escrito **5** (*attribute*): ***put sth down to sth*** atribuir algo a algo
◆ **put forward** *v/t idea etc* proponer, presentar
◆ **put in** *v/t* meter; *time* dedicar; *request, claim* presentar
◆ **put in for** *v/t* (*apply for*) solicitar
◆ **put off** *v/t* **1** *light, radio, TV* apagar **2** (*postpone*) posponer, aplazar **3** (*deter*) desalentar **4** (*repel*) desagradar; ***I was put off by the smell*** el olor me quitó las ganas; ***that put me off shellfish for life*** me quitó las ganas de volver a comer marisco
◆ **put on** *v/t* **1** *light, radio, TV* encender, *L.Am.* prender; *tape, music* poner; ***put on make-up*** maquillarse; ***put on the brake*** frenar; ***put on weight*** engordar **2** *jacket, shoes, eye glasses* ponerse **3** (*perform*) representar **4** (*assume*) fingir; ***she's just putting it on*** está fingiendo
◆ **put out** *v/t* **1** *hand* extender **2** *fire, light* apagar **3**: ***don't put yourself out on my account*** por mí no te molestes, no te tomes ninguna molestia por mí
◆ **put over** ☞ ***put across***
◆ **put past** *v/t*: ***I wouldn't put it past him*** sería muy capaz de hacerlo
◆ **put through** *v/t*: ***put s.o. through to s.o.*** *on phone* poner a alguien con alguien; ***I'll put you through*** le paso
◆ **put together** *v/t* (*assemble, organize*)

montar
◆ **put up** *v/t* **1** *hand, fence, building* levantar; ***put your hands up!*** ¡arriba las manos! **2** *person* alojar **3** (*erect*) levantar **4** *prices* subir **5** *poster, notice* colocar **6** *money* aportar **7**: ***put up for sale*** poner en venta
◆ **put up with** *v/t* (*tolerate*) aguantar
pu•ta•tive ['pju:tətɪv] *adj fml* presunto
'put-down F comentario *m* (*para dejar en ridículo*)
'put-on F fingimiento *m*
put-'out *adj* molesto, contrariado
pu•tre•fy ['pju:trɪfaɪ] *v/i* pudrirse
pu•trid ['pju:trɪd] *adj* putrefacto; F horrible
putsch [pʊtʃ] POL pronunciamiento *m*
putt [pʌt] SP **I** *v/i* golpear con el putter **II** *n* putt *m*
putt•er ['pʌtər] *in golf* putter *m*
◆ **put•ter around** *v/i* entretenerse
put•ty ['pʌtɪ] masilla *f*; ***she is (like) ~ in his hands*** es una marioneta en sus manos
'put-up job F apaño *m*
'put-up•on *adj*: ***feel ~*** sentirse utilizado
puz•zle ['pʌzl] **I** *n* (*mystery*) enigma *m*; *game* pasatiempos *mpl*; (*jigsaw ~*) puzzle *m*; (*crossword ~*) crucigrama *m* **II** *v/t* desconcertar; ***one thing ~s me*** hay algo que no acabo de entender
◆ **puzzle out** *v/t* averiguar
puz•zler ['pʌzlər] F *problem* enigma *m*
puz•zling ['pʌzlɪŋ] *adj* desconcertante
PVC [pi:vi:'si:] *abbr* (= ***polyvinyl chloride***) PVC *m* (= cloruro *m* de polivinilo)
pyg•my ['pɪgmɪ] pigmeo(-a) *m*(*f*)
py•ja•mas *Br* → ***pajamas***
py•lon ['paɪlən] torre *f* de alta tensión
pyr•a•mid ['pɪrəmɪd] pirámide *f*
'pyr•a•mid sell•ing ventas *fpl* piramidales
pyre ['paɪər] pira *f*
py•ro•ma•ni•ac [paɪroʊ'meɪnɪæk] pirómano(-a) *m*(*f*)
py•ro•tech•nics [paɪroʊ'teknɪks] *npl* pirotecnia *f*
Pyr•rhic vic•to•ry [pɪrɪk'vɪktərɪ] victoria *f* pírrica
py•thon ['paɪθɑ:n] pitón *f*

Q

quack[1] [kwæk] **I** *n of duck* graznido *m* **II** *v/i* graznar
quack[2] [kwæk] *n* F (*bad doctor*) medicucho(-a) *m*(*f*) F; *hum* (*doctor*) matasanos *m/f inv* F
quad•ran•gle ['kwɑ:dræŋgl] **1** *figure* cuadrángulo *m* **2** *courtyard* patio *m*
quad•ran•gu•lar [kwɑ:d'ræŋgjʊlər] *adj* cuadrangular
quad•rat•ic e•qua•tion [kwɑ:drætɪkɪ'kweɪʃn] ecuación *f* de segundo grado
quad•ru•ped ['kwɑ:drʊped] cuadrúpedo *m*
quad•ru•ple ['kwɑ:drʊpl] *v/i* cuadruplicarse
quad•ru•plets ['kwɑ:drʊplɪts] *npl* cuatrillizos(-as) *mpl*(*fpl*)
quads [kwɑ:dz] *npl* F cuatrillizos(-as) *mpl*(*fpl*)
quag•mire ['kwɑ:gmaɪr] *fig* atolladero *m*
quail [kweɪl] *v/i* temblar (***at*** ante)
quaint [kweɪnt] *adj* **1** *cottage* pintoresco **2** (*slightly eccentric: ideas etc*) extraño
quake [kweɪk] **I** *n* (*earth~*) terremoto *m* **II** *v/i of earth, with fear* temblar
Quak•er ['kweɪkər] REL cuáquero(-a) *m*(*f*)
qual•i•fi•ca•tion [kwɑ:lɪfɪ'keɪʃn] **1** *from university etc* título *m*; ***have the right ~s for a job*** estar bien cualificado para un trabajo **2**: ***I'd like to add one ~ to that remark*** me gustaría matizar ese comentario
qual•i•fied ['kwɑ:lɪfaɪd] *adj* **1** *doctor, engineer, plumber etc* titulado; ***I am not ~ to judge*** no estoy en condiciones de poder juzgar **2** (*restricted*) limitado
qual•i•fi•er ['kwɑ:lɪfaɪər] SP **1** eliminatoria *f* **2** *person, team* clasificado(-a) *m*(*f*)
qual•i•fy ['kwɑ:lɪfaɪ] **I** *v/t* (*pret & pp -ied*) **1** *of degree, course etc* habilitar **2** *remark etc* matizar **II** *v/i* (*pret & pp -ied*) **1** (*get degree etc*) titularse, *L.Am.* egresar; *in competition* calificar-

Q

se **2**: ***that doesn't ~ as ...*** eso no cuenta como ...

qual•i•ta•tive ['kwɑːlɪtətɪv] *adj* cualitativo

qual•i•ty ['kwɑːlətɪ] **1** calidad *f*; ***~ of life*** calidad de vida; ***~ wine*** vino de calidad **2** (*characteristic*) cualidad *f*

'qual•i•ty as•sur•ance garantía *f* de calidad; **qual•i•ty con'trol** control *m* de calidad; **'qual•i•ty goods** *pl* productos *mpl* de calidad; **'qual•i•ty news•pa•per** periódico *m* no sensacionalista; **'qual•i•ty time** *tiempo de disfrute de familia, amigos etc*

qualm [kwɑːm]: ***have no ~s about doing sth*** no tener reparos en hacer algo

quan•da•ry ['kwɑːndərɪ] dilema *m*; ***be in a ~ about what to do*** estar en un dilema sobre qué hacer

quan•go ['kwæŋgoʊ] *Br organismo público independiente del gobierno*

quan•ti•fy ['kwɑːntɪfaɪ] *v/t* (*pret & pp* ***-ied***) cuantificar

quan•ti•ta•tive ['kwɑːntɪtətɪv] *adj* cuantitativo

quan•ti•ty ['kwɑːntətɪ] cantidad *f*; ***in small quantities*** en pequeñas cantidades

quan•tum leap [kwɑːntəm'liːp] paso *m* gigante

quan•tum 'phys•ics *nsg* física *f* cuántica

quar•an•tine ['kwɑːrəntiːn] cuarentena *f*; ***put in ~*** poner en cuarentena

quark [kwɑːrk] PHYS quark *m*

quar•rel ['kwɑːrəl] **I** *n* pelea *f*; ***have no ~ with sth*** no tener nada en contra de algo **II** *v/i* (*pret & pp* ***-ed***, *Br* ***-led***) pelearse (***with*** con)

quar•rel•some ['kwɑːrəlsʌm] *adj* peleón

quar•ry¹ ['kwɑːrɪ] *in hunt* presa *f*

quar•ry² ['kwɑːrɪ] *for mining* cantera *f*

quart [kwɔːrt] cuarto *m* de galón; ***you can't put a ~ into a pint pot*** F no pidas peras al olmo

quar•ter ['kwɔːrtər] **1** cuarto *m*; (*25 cents*) cuarto *m* de dólar; ***a ~ of an hour*** un cuarto de hora; ***a ~ of 5*** las cinco menos cuarto, *L.Am.* un cuarto para las cinco; ***a ~ after 5*** las cinco y cuarto **2** (*part of town*) barrio *m*; ***from all ~s*** de todas partes; ***from official ~s*** de fuentes oficiales

'quar•ter•back SP quarterback *m*, *en fútbol americano, jugador que dirige el juego de ataque*; **'quar•ter•deck** NAUT cubierta *f* de popa; **quar•ter-'fi•nal** cuarto *m* de final; **quar•ter-'fi•nal•ist** cuartofinalista *m/f*

quar•ter•ly ['kwɔːrtərlɪ] **I** *adj* trimestral **II** *adv* trimestralmente

'quar•ter•note MUS negra *f*

quar•ters ['kwɔːrtərz] *npl* MIL alojamiento *m*

quar•tet [kwɔːr'tet] MUS cuarteto *m*

quar•tile ['kwɔːrtaɪl] cuartil *m*

quartz [kwɔːrts] cuarzo *m*

quartz 'clock reloj *m* de cuarzo

quash [kwɑːʃ] *v/t rebellion* aplastar, sofocar; *court decision* revocar

qua•ver ['kweɪvər] **I** *n* **1** *in voice* temblor *m* **2** *Br* MUS corchea *f* **II** *v/i of voice* temblar

quay [kiː] NAUT muelle *m*

quea•sy ['kwiːzɪ] *adj* mareado; ***get ~*** marearse; ***I feel ~*** estoy mareado

queen [kwiːn] **1** reina *f*; ***~ of hearts*** reina de corazones **2** F *homosexual* loca *f*

queen 'bee abeja *f* reina

queen•ly ['kwiːnlɪ] *adj* de reina

queen 'moth•er reina *f* madre

queer [kwɪr] *adj* (*peculiar*) raro, extraño

queer•ly ['kwɪrlɪ] *adv* de manera extraña

quell [kwel] *v/t protest*, *crowd* acallar; *riot* aplastar, sofocar

quench [kwentʃ] *v/t thirst* apagar, saciar; *flames* apagar

que•ry ['kwɪrɪ] **I** *n* duda *f*, pregunta *f* **II** *v/t* (*pret & pp* ***-ied***) (*express doubt about*) cuestionar; (*check*) comprobar; ***~ sth with s.o.*** preguntar algo a alguien

quest [kwest] busca *f* (***for*** de)

ques•tion ['kwestʃn] **I** *n* **1** pregunta *f*; ***raise a ~*** plantear una pregunta **2** (*matter*) cuestión *f*, asunto *m*; ***in ~*** (*being talked about*) en cuestión; (*in doubt*) en duda; ***it's a ~ of money / time*** es una cuestión de dinero / tiempo; ***that's out of the ~*** eso es imposible; ***that's not the point in ~*** no se trata de eso; ***there is no ~ that ..., it is beyond ~ that ...*** no hay duda que…; ***without ~*** sin duda; ***call into ~*** poner en duda **II** *v/t person* preguntar a; LAW interro-

Q

gar; (*doubt*) cuestionar, poner en duda
ques•tion•a•ble ['kwestʃnəbl] *adj* cuestionable, dudoso
ques•tion•er ['kwestʃənər] interrogador(a) *m*(*f*)
ques•tion•ing ['kwestʃnɪŋ] **I** *adj look, tone* inquisitivo **II** *n* interrogatorio *m*
'ques•tion mark signo *m* de interrogación; ***there's a big ~ over the future of the organization*** el futuro de la organización está en el aire
ques•tion•naire [kwestʃə'ner] cuestionario *m*
quet•zal ['ketzəl] FIN quetzal *m*
queue [kjuː] *Br* **I** *n* cola *f*; ***there was a big ~ for tickets*** había mucha cola *or* fila para los billetes **II** *v/i* hacer cola
◆ **queue up for** *v/t Br* hacer cola para
quib•ble ['kwɪbl] *v/i* discutir (*por algo insignificante*); ***now you're just quibbling*** ahora estás discutiendo por discutir
quick [kwɪk] **I** *adj* rápido; ***be ~!*** ¡date prisa!; ***let's have a ~ drink*** vamos a tomarnos algo rápidamente; ***can I have a ~ look?*** ¿me dejas echarle un vistazo?; ***that was ~!*** ¡qué rápido!; ***how about a ~ swim?*** ¿qué tal si nos damos un chapuzón?; ***be ~ to learn*** aprender rápidamente **II** *n*: ***cut s.o. to the ~*** herir a alguien en donde más duele
'quick-act•ing *adj* de efecto rápido
quick•en ['kwɪkən] *v/i* acelerarse
'quick-fire *adj questions* rápido
quick•ie ['kwɪkɪ] F *drink* copa *f* rápida; *sex* polvo *m* rápido; *question* pregunta *f* rápida
quick•ly ['kwɪklɪ] *adv* rápidamente, rápido, deprisa
'quick•sand arenas *fpl* movedizas; **'quick•sil•ver** azogue *m*; **quick-tem•pered** [kwɪk'tempərd] *adj* irascible; **quick-wit•ted** [kwɪk'wɪtɪd] *adj* agudo
quid [kwɪd] *Br* F libra *f*
qui•et ['kwaɪət] *adj* tranquilo; *engine* silencioso; ***keep ~ about sth*** guardar silencio sobre algo; ***~!*** ¡silencio!; ***on the ~*** F a escondidas
◆ **qui•et•en down** ['kwaɪətn] **I** *v/t children, class* tranquilizar, hacer callar **II** *v/i of children* tranquilizarse, callarse; *of political situation* calmarse
quiet•ly ['kwaɪətlɪ] *adv* (*not loudly*) silenciosamente; (*without fuss*) discretamente; (*peacefully*) tranquilamente; ***speak ~*** hablar en voz baja
quiet•ness ['kwaɪətnɪs] *of voice* suavidad *f*; *of night, street* silencio *m*, calma *f*
quilt [kwɪlt] *on bed* edredón *m*
quilt•ed ['kwɪltɪd] *adj* acolchado
quince [kwɪns] BOT membrillo *m*
quin•ine ['kwɪniːn] quinina *f*
quint•es•sen•tial [kwɪntɪ'senʃəl] *adj* prototípico
quin•tet [kwɪn'tet] MUS quinteto *m*
quin•tu•plets ['kwɪntjʊpləts] quintillizos(-as) *mpl*(*fpl*)
quip [kwɪp] **I** *n joke* broma *f*; *remark* salida *f* **II** *v/i* (*pret & pp* ***-ped***) bromear
quirk [kwɜːrk] peculiaridad *f*, rareza *f*; ***by some ~ of fate*** por un capricho del destino
quirk•y ['kwɜːrkɪ] *adj* peculiar, raro
quit [kwɪt] **I** *v/t* (*pret & pp* ***quit***) *job* dejar, abandonar; ***~ doing sth*** dejar de hacer algo **II** *v/i* (*pret & pp* ***quit***) (*leave job*) dimitir; COMPUT salir
quite [kwaɪt] *adv* **1** (*fairly*) bastante; ***that's ~ nice*** está bastante bien; ***it was only ~ hot*** hacía calor pero no demasiado; ***I ~ like it*** me gusta algo
2 (*completely*) completamente; ***you're ~ right*** tienes toda la razón; ***these two are ~ different*** estas dos son totalmente diferentes; ***not ~ ready*** no listo del todo; ***not ~ the same*** no exactamente lo mismo; ***I didn't ~ understand*** no entendí bien; ***you haven't ~ understood*** no lo acabas de entender; ***is that right? – not ~*** ¿es verdad? – no exactamente; ***are you ready? – not ~*** ¿estás listo? – no del todo; ***~ !*** ¡exactamente!
3: ***~ a lot*** bastante; ***~ a few*** bastantes; ***it was ~ a surprise*** fue toda una sorpresa; ***$500 is ~ a lot to pay*** 500 dólares son muchos dólares; ***it was ~ a sight*** era todo un espectáculo; ***she's ~ a girl*** es toda una niña; ***she looks ~ the New York socialite*** es todo un personaje de la vida neoyorquina
quits [kwɪts] *adj*: ***be ~ with s.o.*** estar en paz con alguien; ***let's call it ~*** quedemos en paz
quit•ter ['kwɪtər] F: ***he's no ~*** no es de los que abandona
quiv•er[1] ['kwɪvər] *v/i* estremecerse
quiv•er[2] ['kwɪvər] *n for arrows* carcaj *m*

Q

quix•ot•ic [kwɪk'sɑːtɪk] *adj* quijotesco
quiz [kwɪz] **I** *n* concurso *m* (*de preguntas y respuestas*) **II** *v/t* (*pret & pp* **-zed**) interrogar (***about*** sobre)
'quiz mas•ter presentador *m* (*de un concurso de preguntas y respuestas*)
'quiz pro•gram, *Br* **'quiz pro•gramme** programa *m* concurso (*de preguntas y respuestas*)
quiz•zi•cal ['kwɪzɪkl] *adj* dubitativo
quo•rum ['kwɔːrəm] quórum *m inv*; ***have a ~*** haber quórum
quo•ta ['kwoʊtə] cuota *f*
quo•ta•ble ['kwoʊtəbl] *adj remark* reproducible
quo•ta•tion [kwoʊ'teɪʃn] **1** *from author* cita *f* **2** (*price*) presupuesto *m*
quo'ta•tion marks *npl* comillas *fpl*
quote [kwoʊt] **I** *n* **1** *from author* cita *f* **2** (*quotation mark*) comilla *f*; ***in ~s*** entre comillas **3** (*price*) presupuesto *m* **II** *v/t* **1** *text* citar; ***he was ~d as saying that*** se le atribuye haber dicho que; ***don't ~ me on this, but ...*** no me hagas mucho caso, pero … **2** *price* dar **3** FIN: ***be ~d on the stock market*** cotizar en bolsa; ***be ~d at*** cotizar a **III** *v/i*: ***~ from an author*** citar de un autor; ***he is ~ ... unquote*** es … entre comillas; ***it was described as, and I ~, ...*** lo describieron como, y cito textualmente,… **2**: ***~ for a job*** dar un presupuesto para un trabajo
'quote marks *npl* comillas *fpl*; ***put sth in ~*** poner algo entre comillas
quo•tient ['kwoʊʃnt] MATH cociente *m*

R

rab•bi ['ræbaɪ] rabino *m*
rab•bit ['ræbɪt] conejo *m*
'rab•bit punch colleja *f*
rab•ble ['ræbl] chusma *f*, multitud *f*
rab•ble-rous•er ['ræblraʊzər] agitador(a) *m*(*f*)
'rab•ble-rous•ing *adj* inflamatorio
rab•id ['ræbɪd] *adj* (*fanatical*) furibundo
ra•bies ['reɪbiːz] *nsg* rabia *f*
rac•coon [rə'kuːn] mapache *m*
race[1] [reɪs] *n of people* raza *f*
race[2] [reɪs] **I** *n* SP carrera *f*; ***the ~s*** *horses* las carreras; ***take your time, it's not a ~*** tómate el tiempo que necesites, ésto no es una carrera a contrarreloj **II** *v/i* (*run fast*) correr; ***he ~d through his meal / work*** acabó su comida / trabajo a toda velocidad **III** *v/t* correr contra; ***I'll ~ you*** te echo una carrera
'race•course *Br* hipódromo *m*; **'race•horse** caballo *m* de carreras; **'race meet•ing** *Br* carreras *fpl* de caballos
rac•er ['reɪsər] *horse* caballo *m* de carreras; *car* coche *m* de carreras; *bicycle* bicicleta *f* de carreras; *motorbike* moto *f* de carreras; *runner* corredor(a) *m*(*f*)
'race ri•ot disturbios *mpl* raciales
'race•track circuito *m*; *for horses* hipódromo *m*
ra•cial ['reɪʃl] *adj* racial
ra•cial dis•crim•i'na•tion discriminación *f* racial
ra•cial e'qual•i•ty igualdad *f* racial
ra•cial•ism ['reɪʃəlɪzəm] racismo *m*
ra•cial seg•re'ga•tion segregación *f* racial
rac•ing ['reɪsɪŋ] carreras *fpl*
'rac•ing bi•cy•cle bicicleta *f* de carreras; **'rac•ing car** coche *m* de carreras; **'rac•ing driv•er** piloto *m* de carreras
rac•ism ['reɪsɪzm] racismo *m*
ra•cist ['reɪsɪst] **I** *n* racista *m/f* **II** *adj* racista
rack[1] [ræk] **I** *n for bikes*: *barras para aparcar bicicletas*; *for bags on train* portaequipajes *m inv*; *for CDs* mueble *m* **II** *v/t*: ***~ one's brains*** devanarse los sesos
rack[2] [ræk] *n*: ***go to ~ and ruin*** arruinarse
rack•et[1] ['rækɪt] SP raqueta *f*
rack•et[2] ['rækɪt] **1** (*noise*) jaleo *m*; ***make a ~*** armar mucho jaleo **2** *criminal activity* negocio *m* sucio
rack•et•eer [rækə'tɪr] extorsionista *m/f*, mafioso(-a) *m/f*
rack•et•eer•ing [rækə'tɪrɪŋ] extorsión *f*
'rack rate *in hotel* tarifa *f* oficial
ra•coon [rə'kuːn] ZO mapache *m*
rac•y ['reɪsɪ] *adj* atrevido

R

ra•dar ['reɪdɑːr] radar *m*
'ra•dar screen pantalla *f* de radar; **ra•dar 'speed check** control *m* de velocidad por radar; **'ra•dar trap** control *m* de velocidad por radar
ra•di•al ['reɪdɪəl] neumático *m* radial
ra•di•al 'tire, *Br* **ra•di•al 'tyre** neumático *m* radial
ra•di•ance ['reɪdɪəns] esplendor *m*, brillantez *f*
ra•di•ant ['reɪdɪənt] *adj smile, appearance* resplandeciente, brillante
ra•di•ate ['reɪdɪeɪt] *v/i of heat, light* irradiar
ra•di•a•tion [reɪdɪ'eɪʃn] PHYS radiación *f*
ra•di•a•tor ['reɪdɪeɪtər] *in room, car* radiador *m*
'ra•di•a•tor core núcleo *m* del radiador
rad•i•cal ['rædɪkl] **I** *adj* radical **II** *n* POL radical *m/f*
rad•i•cal•ism ['rædɪkəlɪzm] POL radicalismo *m*
rad•i•cal•ize ['rædɪklaɪz] *v/t* radicalizar
rad•i•cal•ly ['rædɪklɪ] *adv* radicalmente
ra•di•i ['reɪdɪaɪ] *pl* ☞ ***radius***
ra•di•o ['reɪdɪoʊ] radio *f*; ***on the ~*** en la radio; ***by ~*** por radio
ra•di•o'ac•tive *adj* radiactivo; **ra•di•o•ac•tive 'waste** residuos *mpl* radiactivos; **ra•di•o•ac'tiv•i•ty** radiactividad *f*; **ra•di•o a'larm** radiodespertador *m*; **'ra•di•o bul•le•tin** boletín *m* radiofónico; **'ra•di•o cab** radiotaxi *m*; **ra•di•o 'cas•sette play•er** radiocasete *m*; **'ra•di•o con•tact** contacto *m* por radio; ***be in ~ with*** estar en contacto por radio con; ***lose ~ with*** perder el contacto por radio con; **ra•di•o-controlled** [reɪdɪoʊkən'troʊld] *adj* teledirigido; **'ra•di•o dra•ma** drama *m* radiofónico
ra•di•og•ra•pher [reɪdɪ'ɑːgrəfər] técnico(-a) *m(f)* de rayos X
ra•di•og•ra•phy [reɪdɪ'ɑːgrəfɪ] radiografía *f*
'ra•di•o ham radioaficionado(-a) *m(f)*
'ra•di•o link enlace *m* por radio
ra•di•ol•o•gist [reɪdɪ'ɑːlədʒɪst] radiólogo(-a) *m(f)*
ra•di•ol•o•gy [reɪdɪ'ɑːlədʒɪ] radiología *f*
'ra•di•o mes•sage mensaje *m* por radio; **'ra•di•o op•er•a•tor** operador(a) *m(f)* de radio; **'ra•di•o pro•duc•er** productor(a) *m(f)* de radio; **'ra•di•o pro•gram**, *Br* **'ra•di•o pro•gramme** programa *m* de radio; **'ra•di•o re•port•er** periodista *m/f* radiofónico(-a); **'ra•di•o sat•el•lite** satélite *m* radiofónico; **'ra•di•o sig•nal** señal *f* de radio; **'ra•di•o sta•tion** emisora *f* de radio; **'ra•di•o tax•i** radiotaxi *m*; **ra•di•o-'ther•a•py** radioterapia *f*; **ra•di•o 'tel•e•phone** radioteléfono *m*; **'ra•di•o traf•fic** tráfico *m* radiofónico; **'ra•di•o wave** onda *f* de radio
rad•ish ['rædɪʃ] rábano *m*
ra•di•us ['reɪdɪəs] (*pl* ***radii***) radio *m*
raf•fle ['ræfl] rifa *f*
raft [ræft] **1** balsa *f* **2** F: ***a whole ~ of ...*** una colección *or* caterva de ...
raf•ter ['ræftər] viga *f*
rag [ræg] *for cleaning etc* trapo *m*; ***in ~s*** con harapos
rag•bag ['rægbæg] F batiburrillo *m*
rage [reɪdʒ] **I** *n* ira *f*, cólera *f*; ***be in a ~*** estar encolerizado; ***be all the ~*** F estar arrasando F **II** *v/i of storm* bramar
rag•ged ['rægɪd] *adj* andrajoso
raid [reɪd] **I** *n* **1** *by troops* incursión *f*; *by police* redada *f* **2** *by robbers* atraco *m* **3** FIN ataque *m*, incursión *f* **II** *v/t* **1** *of troops* realizar una incursión en; *of police* realizar una redada en **2** *of robbers* atracar; *fridge, orchard* saquear
raid•er ['reɪdər] *on bank etc* atracador(a) *m(f)*; ***corporate ~*** tiburón *m* de bolsa
rail[1] [reɪl] *n* **1** *on track* riel *m*, carril *m*; ***by ~*** en tren **2** (*hand~*) pasamanos *m inv*, baranda *f* **3** *for towel* barra *f*
rail[2] [reɪl] *v/i* protestar airadamente (***against, at*** contra)
'rail•freight: ***send sth ~*** enviar algo por vía férrea
rail•ings ['reɪlɪŋz] *npl around park etc* verja *f*
'rail pass abono *m* de tren; **rail•road** ['reɪlroʊd] ferrocarril *m*; **'rail•road sta•tion** estación *f* de ferrocarril *or* de tren; **rail•way** ['reɪlweɪ] *Br* ferrocarril *m*
rain [reɪn] **I** *n* lluvia *f*; ***in the ~*** bajo la lluvia; ***the ~s*** *pl* las lluvias; ***come ~ or shine*** pase lo que pase **II** *v/i* llover; ***it's ~ing*** llueve **III** *v/t*: ***~ blows on s.o*** hacer llover golpes sobre alguien
◆ **rain down on** *v/t of blows* llover sobre
◆ **rain off** *v/t*: *Br*: ***be rained off*** suspen-

R

derse por la lluvia
◆ **rain out** *v/t*: ***be rained out*** suspenderse por la lluvia
'rain•bow arco *m* iris; **'rain•check**: ***can I take a ~ on that?*** F ¿lo podríamos aplazar para algún otro momento?; **'rain•coat** impermeable *m*; **'rain•drop** gota *f* de lluvia; **'rain•fall** pluviosidad *f*, precipitaciones *fpl*; **'rain for•est** selva *f*; **'rain•proof** *adj fabric* impermeable; **'rain•storm** tormenta *f*, aguacero *m*; **'rain•wa•ter** agua *f* de lluvia
rain•y ['reɪnɪ] *adj* lluvioso; ***it's ~*** llueve mucho
'rain•y sea•son estación *f* de las lluvias
raise [reɪz] **I** *n in salary* aumento *m* de sueldo **II** *v/t* **1** *shelf etc* levantar **2** *offer* incrementar **3** *children* criar **4** *question* plantear **5** *money* reunir
rai•sin ['reɪzn] pasa *f*
rake [reɪk] *for garden* rastrillo *m*
◆ **rake in** *v/t* F *huge profits* amasar; ***he's raking it in*** se está forrando
◆ **rake up** *v/t leaves* rastrillar; *fig* sacar a la luz
'rake-off F tajada *f*
rak•ish ['reɪkɪʃ] *adj behavior*, *grin* licencioso
ral•ly ['rælɪ] **1** (*meeting*, *reunion*) concentración *f*; *political* mitin *m* **2** MOT rally *m* **3** *in tennis* peloteo *m*
◆ **rally round I** *v/i* (*pret & pp* ***-ied***) acudir a ayudar **II** *v/t* (*pret & pp* ***-ied***): ***rally round s.o.*** acudir a ayudar a alguien
RAM [ræm] *abbr* (= ***random access memory***) COMPUT RAM *f* (= memoria *f* de acceso aleatorio)
ram [ræm] **I** *n* carnero *m* **II** *v/t* (*pret & pp* ***-med***) *ship*, *car* embestir
ram•ble ['ræmbl] **I** *n walk* caminata *f*, excursión *f* **II** *v/i* **1** *walk* caminar **2** *in speaking* divagar; *of sick person* delirar
ram•bler ['ræmblər] *walker* senderista *m/f*, excursionista *m/f*
ram•bling ['ræmblɪŋ] **I** *n* **1** *walking* senderismo *m* **2** *in speech* divagaciones *fpl* **II** *adj speech* inconexo
ram•i•fi•ca•tion [ræmɪfɪ'keɪʃn] ramificación *f*
ram•i•fy ['ræmɪfaɪ] *v/i* ramificarse
ramp [ræmp] rampa *f*; *for raising vehicle* elevador *m*
ram•page ['ræmpeɪdʒ] **I** *v/i* pasar arrasando con todo **II** *n*: ***go on the ~*** pasar arrasando con todo
ramp•ant ['ræmpənt] *adj inflation* galopante
ram•part ['ræmpɑːrt] muralla *f*
'ram raid *irrupción de un vehículo en una tienda para cometer un robo*
ram•shack•le ['ræmʃækl] *adj* destartalado, desvencijado
ran [ræn] *pret* ☞ ***run***
ranch [ræntʃ] rancho *m*
ranch•er ['ræntʃər] ranchero(-a) *m*(*f*)
ranch•lands *npl* dehesa *f*
ran•cid ['rænsɪd] *adj* rancio
ran•cor ['rænkər] rencor
ran•cor•ous ['ræŋkərəs] *adj* rencoroso
R & D [ɑːrən'diː] *abbr* (= ***research and development***) I+D *f* (= investigación *f* y desarrollo)
ran•dom ['rændəm] **I** *adj* al azar; ***~ sample*** muestra *f* aleatoria **II** *n*: ***at ~*** al azar
ran•dom ac•cess 'mem•o•ry memoria *f* de acceso aleatorio
ran•dy ['rændɪ] *adj Br* F cachondo F; ***it makes me ~*** me pone cachondo
rang [ræŋ] *pret* ☞ ***ring***
range [reɪndʒ] **I** *n* **1** *of products* gama *f* **2** *of gun*, *airplane* alcance *m*; *of voice* registro *m*; ***at close ~*** de cerca **3** *of mountains* cordillera *f* **II** *v/i*: ***~ from X to Y*** ir desde X a Y
range find•er ['reɪndʒfaɪndər] PHOT *etc* telémetro *m*
rang•er ['reɪndʒər] guardabosques *m/f inv*
rank[1] [ræŋk] **I** *n* MIL, *in society* rango *m*; ***the ~s*** MIL la tropa; ***the ~ and file*** MIL la tropa; *fig*: *of political party* las bases; ***close ~s*** *also fig* cerrar filas; ***break ~s*** *also fig* romper filas; ***top ~*** *fig*: *hotel*, *player*, *company* de primera línea *or* clase; ***join the ~s of the unemployed*** engrosar las filas del paro; ***pull ~ on s.o.*** F aprovecharse de alguien (*por estar en un puesto superior*); ***rise from the ~s*** pasar de soldado raso a oficial **II** *v/t* clasificar **III** *v/i* clasificarse
◆ **rank among** *v/t* figurar entre
rank[2] [ræŋk] *adj* **1** (*foul-smelling*) pestilente **2** *outsider*, *beginner*, *nonsense* total
rank•ing ['ræŋkɪŋ] *adj officer* de mayor rango
rank•ings ['ræŋkɪŋz] *npl* SP clasifica-

R

ción *f*
ran•kle ['ræŋkl] *v/i* doler; ***it still ~s*** (***with him***) todavía le duele
ran•sack ['rænsæk] *v/t* saquear
ran•som ['rænsəm] rescate *m*; ***hold s.o. to ~*** pedir un rescate por alguien
'ran•som mon•ey (dinero *m* del) rescate *m*
rant [rænt] *v/i*: ***~ and rave*** despotricar
rap[1] [ræp] **I** *n* **1** *at door etc* golpe *m*; ***give s.o. a ~ over the knuckles*** *fig* echar un rapapolvo a alguien **2** MUS rap *m* **II** *v/t* (*pret & pp* ***-ped***) *table etc* golpear
◆ **rap at** *v/t window etc* golpear
rap[2] [ræp] *n* P: ***take the ~ for sth*** cargar con las culpas por algo; ***I had to take the ~ for him*** yo tuve que cargar con las culpas
rap[3] [ræp] *n*: ***I don't care a ~*** me importa un pimiento
rape[1] [reɪp] **I** *n* violación *f* **II** *v/t* violar
rape[2] [reɪp] *n* BOT colza *f*
'rape•seed oil aceite *m* de colza
'rape vic•tim víctima *m/f* de una violación
rap•id ['ræpɪd] *adj* rápido
'rap•id-fire *adj* MIL, *fig*: *questioning* rápido
ra•pid•i•ty [rə'pɪdətɪ] rapidez *f*
rap•id•ly ['ræpɪdlɪ] *adv* rápidamente
rap•ids ['ræpɪdz] *npl* rápidos *mpl*
rap•ist ['reɪpɪst] violador(a) *m*(*f*)
rap•port [ræ'pɔːr] relación *f*, ***we have a good ~*** nos entendemos muy bien
rap•proche•ment [ræprəʃ'mɑːn] POL acercamiento *m* (***between*** entre)
rapt [ræpt] *adj*: ***with ~ attention*** absorto
rap•ture ['ræptʃər]: ***go into ~s over*** extasiarse con
rap•tur•ous ['ræptʃərəs] *adj* clamoroso
rare [rer] *adj* **1** (*not common*) raro **2** *steak* poco hecho
rar•e•fied ['rerəfaɪd] *adj also fig* enrarecido
rare•ly ['rerlɪ] *adv* raramente, raras veces
rar•ing ['rerɪŋ] *adj*: ***be ~ to do s.th.*** F estar muerto de ganas de hacer algo; ***we're all ~ to go*** F nos morimos por empezar
rar•i•ty ['rerətɪ] rareza *f*
ras•cal ['ræskl] pícaro(-a) *m*(*f*)
rash[1] [ræʃ] *n* MED sarpullido *m*, erupción *f* cutánea
rash[2] [ræʃ] *adj action*, *behavior* precipitado
rash•er ['ræʃər] *Br* loncha *f*
rash•ly ['ræʃlɪ] *adv* precipitadamente
rasp [rɑːsp] *noise* chirrido *m*
rasp•ber•ry ['ræzberɪ] frambuesa *f*
rasp•ing ['rɑːspɪŋ] *adj noise*, *voice* áspero
Ras•ta•far•i•an [ræstə'ferɪən] rastafari *m/f*
rat [ræt] rata *f*; ***smell a ~*** *fig* intuir *or* olerse algo sospechoso
◆ **rat on** *v/t* (*pret & pp* ***-ted***) F chivarse de
rate [reɪt] **I** *n* **1** *of exchange* tipo *m*; *of pay* tarifa *f*; ***~ of interest*** FIN tipo *m* de interés **2** (*price*) tarifa *f*, precio *m* **3** (*speed*) ritmo *m*; ***at this ~*** (*at this speed*) a este ritmo; (*if we carry on like this*) si seguimos así **4**: ***at any ~*** (*anyway*) en todo caso; (*at least*) por lo menos
II *v/t*: ***~ s.o. as ...*** considerar a alguien (como) ...; ***~ s.o. highly*** tener buena opinión de alguien
rate of re'turn tasa *f* de rentabilidad
rather ['ræðər] *adv* **1** (*fairly, quite*) bastante **2**: ***I would ~ stay here*** preferiría quedarme aquí; ***or would you ~ ...?*** ¿o preferiría ...?; ***I'd do anything ~ than stay home*** haría cualquier cosa antes que quedarme en casa
rat•i•fi•ca•tion [rætɪfɪ'keɪʃn] ratificación *f*
rat•i•fy ['rætɪfaɪ] *v/t* (*pret & pp* ***-ied***) ratificar
rat•ings ['reɪtɪŋz] *npl* índice *m* de audiencia
'rat•ings war guerra *f* de audiencia
ra•tio ['reɪʃɪoʊ] proporción *f*
ra•tion ['ræʃn] **I** *n* ración *f* **II** *v/t supplies* racionar
ra•tion•al ['ræʃənl] *adj* racional
ra•tion•ale [ræʃə'nɑːl] lógica *f* (***for, behind*** de)
ra•tion•al•ism ['ræʃnəlɪzəm] racionalismo *m*
ra•tion•al•ist ['ræʃnəlɪst] **I** *n* racionalista *m/f* **II** *adj* racionalista
ra•tion•al•i•ty [ræʃə'nælɪtɪ] racionalidad *f*
ra•tion•al•i•za•tion [ræʃənəlaɪ'zeɪʃn] racionalización *f*
ra•tion•al•ize ['ræʃənəlaɪz] **I** *v/t* raciona-

R

lizar **II** *v/i* buscar una explicación racional
ra•tion•al•ly ['ræʃənlɪ] *adv* racionalmente
'rat poi•son matarratas *m inv*
'rat race *vida frenética y competitiva*
rat•tle ['rætl] **I** *n* **1** *noise* traqueteo *m*, golpeteo *m* **2** *toy* sonajero *m* **II** *v/t* **1** *chains etc* entrechocar **2** *person* inquietar; ***he looks a bit ~d*** parece un poco inquieto **III** *v/i of chains etc* entrechocarse; *of crates* traquetear
◆ **rattle off** *v/t poem, list of names* decir rápidamente
◆ **rattle on** *v/i* parlotear
◆ **rattle through** *v/t* hacer rápidamente
'rat•tle•snake serpiente *f* de cascabel
'rat•trap *also fig* ratonera *f*
rat•ty ['rætɪ] *adj* F **1** (*irritable*) susceptible; (*annoyed*) mosqueado **2** *sweater etc* sobado, gastado
rau•cous ['rɒːkəs] *adj laughter, party* estridente
raun•chy ['rɒːntʃɪ] *adj novel, style* picante; *person, laugh* provocativo
rav•age ['rævɪdʒ] **I** *n*: ***the ~s of time*** los estragos del tiempo **II** *v/t* arrasar; ***~d by war*** arrasado por la guerra
rave [reɪv] **I** *v/i* (*talk deliriously*) delirar; (*talk wildly*) desvariar; ***~ about sth*** (*be very enthusiastic*) estar muy entusiasmado con algo **II** *n party* fiesta *f* tecno
ra•ven ['reɪvn] cuervo *m*
rav•e•nous ['rævənəs] *adj* (*very hungry*) famélico; ***have a ~ appetite*** tener un hambre canina
rav•e•nous•ly ['rævənəslɪ] *adv* con voracidad
rave re'view crítica *f* muy entusiasta
ra•vine [rə'viːn] barranco *m*
rav•ing ['reɪvɪŋ] *adv*: ***~ mad*** chalado
ra•vi•o•li [rævɪ'oʊlɪ] ravioli *m*
rav•ish ['rævɪʃ] *v/t* (*rape*) forzar
rav•ish•ing ['rævɪʃɪŋ] *adj* encantador, cautivador
raw [rɒː] *adj meat, vegetable* crudo; *sugar* sin refinar; *iron* sin tratar; ***get a ~ deal*** F no ser tratado con justicia
raw ma'te•ri•als *npl* materias *fpl* primas
ray[1] [reɪ] *of sun, light etc* rayo *m*; ***a ~ of hope*** un rayo de esperanza
ray[2] [reɪ] *fish* raya *f*
ray•on ['reɪɑːn] rayón *m*
raze [reɪz] *v/t*: ***~ to the ground*** arrasar *or* asolar por completo
ra•zor ['reɪzər] maquinilla *f* de afeitar
'ra•zor blade cuchilla *f* de afeitar; **'ra•zor edge**: ***be on a ~*** *fig* pender de un hilo; **'ra•zor-sharp** *adj blade* afilado; *mind* agudo
raz•zle ['ræzl]: ***go on the ~*** F salir de marcha
razz•ma•tazz [ræzmə'tæz] F parafernalia *f*
re [riː] *prep* COM con referencia a
reach [riːtʃ] **I** *n*: ***within ~*** al alcance; ***out of ~*** fuera del alcance **II** *v/t* llegar a; *decision, agreement, conclusion* alcanzar, llegar a; ***can you ~ it?*** ¿alcanzas?, ¿llegas?
◆ **reach out** *v/i* extender el brazo
re•act [rɪ'ækt] *v/i* reaccionar
re•ac•tion [rɪ'ækʃn] reacción *f*
re•ac•tion•ar•y [rɪ'ækʃnrɪ] **I** *n* POL reaccionario(-a) *m(f)* **II** *adj* POL reaccionario
re•ac•ti•vate [rɪ'æktɪveɪt] *v/t* reactivar
re•ac•tive [rɪ'æktɪv] *adj* CHEM reactivo
re•ac•tor [rɪ'æktər] *nuclear* reactor *m*
read[1] [riːd] **I** *v/t* (*pret & pp **read*** [red]) *also* COMPUT leer **II** *v/i* (*pret & pp **read*** [red]) leer; ***~ to s.o.*** leer a alguien; ***your essay ~s well*** tu trabajo está bien escrito
◆ **read into** *v/t*: ***read sth into sth*** interpretar algo a partir de algo
◆ **read out** *v/t aloud* leer en voz alta
◆ **read through** *v/t* leer
◆ **read up on** *v/t* leer mucho sobre, estudiar
read[2] [red] *pret & pp* ☞ ***read***[1]
rea•da•ble ['riːdəbl] *adj* **1** *handwriting* legible **2** *book* ameno
read•er ['riːdər] *person* lector(a) *m(f)*
'read er•ror COMPUT error *m* de lectura
read•er•ship ['riːdərʃɪp] lectores *mpl*
'read head COMPUT cabeza *f* lectora
read•i•ly ['redɪlɪ] *adv admit, agree* de buena gana
read•i•ness ['redɪnɪs]: ***in a state of ~*** preparado par actuar; ***their ~ to help*** la facilidad con la que ayudaron
read•ing ['riːdɪŋ] *activity* lectura *f*; ***take a ~ from the meter*** leer el contador
'read•ing glass•es gafas *fpl* para leer; **'read•ing lamp** lámpara *f* para leer; **'read•ing mat•ter** lectura *f*; **'read•ing**

room sala *f* de lectura
re•ad•just [riːəˈdʒʌst] **I** *v/t equipment, controls* reajustar **II** *v/i to conditions* volver a adaptarse
re•ad•just•ment [riːəˈdʒʌstmənt] reajuste *m*
ˈread-me doc•u•ment COMPUT documento *m* léeme; **read-ˈon•ly file** COMPUT archivo *m* sólo de lectura; **read-ˈon•ly mem•o•ry** COMPUT memoria *f* sólo de lectura; **ˈread•out** COMPUT visualización *f*; **ˈread-through** *of script* lectura *f*; **read-ˈwrite head** COMPUT cabeza *f* lectora-grabadora
read•y [ˈredɪ] *adj* **1** (*prepared*) listo, preparado; ***get (o.s.) ~*** prepararse; ***get sth ready*** preparar algo **2** (*willing*) dispuesto
read•y ˈcash dinero *m* contante y sonante; **read•y-cooked** [redɪˈkʊkt] *adj* precocinado; **read•y-ˈmade** *adj stew etc* precocinado; *solution* ya hecho; **read•y-to-ˈwear** *adj* de confección
re•af•firm [riːəˈfɜːrm] *v/t* reafirmar
re•af•fir•ma•tion [riːæfərˈmeɪʃn] reafirmación *f*
re•af•for•est [riːəˈfɑːrɪst] *v/t* reforestar
re•af•for•est•a•tion [riːəfɑːrɪsˈteɪʃn] reforestación *f*
re•a•gent [riːˈeɪdʒənt] CHEM reactivo *m*
real [riːl] **I** *adj* real; *surprise, genius* auténtico; ***he's a ~ idiot*** es un auténtico idiota; ***get ~!*** F ¡abre los ojos!, ¡baja de las nubes! **II** *adv* F **1** muy; ***I'm ~ sorry*** lo siento muchísimo **2**: ***this time it's for ~*** esta vez va en serio *or* es de verdad
ˈreal es•tate bienes *mpl* inmuebles
ˈreal es•tate a•gent agente *m/f* inmobiliario(-a)
re•al•ism [ˈrɪəlɪzəm] realismo *m*
re•al•ist [ˈrɪəlɪst] realista *m/f*
re•al•is•tic [rɪəˈlɪstɪk] *adj* realista
re•al•is•tic•al•ly [rɪəˈlɪstɪklɪ] *adv* realísticamente
re•al•i•ty [rɪˈælətɪ] realidad *f*
ˈre•al•i•ty show reality show *m*
re•al•i•za•tion [rɪəlaɪˈzeɪʃn]: ***the ~ dawned on me that …*** me di cuenta de que …
re•al•ize [ˈrɪəlaɪz] *v/t* **1** darse cuenta de; ***I ~ now that …*** ahora me doy cuenta de que … **2** FIN (*yield*) producir; (*sell*) realizar, liquidar
real-ˈlife *adj story etc* de la vida real
real•ly [ˈrɪəlɪ] *adv* **1** *in truth* de verdad; ***I am ~ ~ sorry*** lo siento en el alma; ***~?*** ¿de verdad?; ***not ~*** *as reply* la verdad es que no **2** *big, small* muy
realm [relm] *of monarch* reino *m*; *fig* ámbito *m*; ***be within the ~s of possibility*** entrar dentro de lo posible
ˈreal time COMPUT tiempo *m* real
ˈreal-time *adj* COMPUT en tiempo real
re•al•tor [ˈriːltər] agente *m/f* inmobiliario(-a)
re•alty [ˈriːltɪ] bienes *mpl* inmuebles
reap [riːp] *v/t* cosechar; ***~ the benefits of sth*** cosechar los beneficios de algo
re•ap•pear [riːəˈpɪr] *v/i* reaparecer
re•ap•pear•ance [riːəˈpɪrəns] reaparición *f*
re•ap•prais•al [riːəˈpreɪzl] revaluación *f*
re•ap•praise [riːəˈpreɪz] *v/t* reconsiderar
rear[1] [rɪr] **I** *n* parte *f* de atrás **II** *adj legs* de atrás; *seats, wheels, lights* trasero
rear[2] [rɪr] *v/t* **1** *children, animals* criar **2** *head* levantar; ***~ its ugly head*** *fig* aparecer
◆ **rear up** *v/i of horse* encabritarse
rear ˈax•le eje *m* trasero; **rear ˈend I** *n* F *of person* trasero *m* **II** *v/t* MOT F dar un golpe por atrás a; **rear ˈex•it** salida *f* trasera; **ˈrear•guard** MIL retaguardia *f*; ***fight a ~ action*** MIL luchar en la retaguardia; *fig* hacer un último esfuerzo desesperado; **rear ˈlight** *of car* luz *f* trasera
re•arm [riːˈɑːrm] **I** *v/t* rearmar **II** *v/i* rearmarse
re•ar•ma•ment [rɪˈɑːrməmənt] rearme *m*
ˈrear•most *adj* último
rear-mount•ed ˈen•gine motor *m* trasero
re•ar•range [riːəˈreɪnʒ] *v/t flowers* volver a colocar; *furniture* reordenar; *schedule, meetings* cambiar
rear-view ˈmir•ror espejo *m* retrovisor
rear•ward [ˈrɪrwərd] **I** *adj* trasero **II** *adv* hacia atrás
rear-wheel ˈdrive tracción *f* trasera
rea•son [ˈriːzn] **I** *n* **1** *faculty* razón *f*; ***see / listen to ~*** atender a razones **2** (*cause*) razón *f*, motivo *m*; ***I don't know the ~ why*** desconozco el porqué **II** *v/i*: ***~ with s.o.*** razonar con alguien
rea•son•a•ble [ˈriːznəbl] *adj* **1** *person*

R

razonable **2**: ***a ~ number of people*** un buen número de personas
rea•son•a•bly ['ri:znəblɪ] *adv* **1** *act, behave* razonablemente **2** (*quite*) bastante
rea•son•ing ['ri:znɪŋ] razonamiento *m*
re•as•sem•ble [ri:ə'sembl] *v/t* TECH volver a montar
re•as•sur•ance [ri:ə'ʃɔ:rəns] garantía *f*
re•as•sure [ri:ə'ʃʊr] *v/t* tranquilizar; ***she ~d us of her continued support*** nos aseguró que continuábamos contando con su apoyo
re•as•sur•ing [ri:ə'ʃʊrɪŋ] *adj* tranquilizador
re•bate ['ri:beɪt] *money back* reembolso *m*
reb•el[1] ['rebl] *n* rebelde *m/f*; ***~ troops*** tropas *fpl* rebeldes
re•bel[2] [rɪ'bel] *v/i* (*pret & pp* ***-led***) rebelarse
reb•el•lion [rɪ'belɪən] rebelión *f*
reb•el•lious [rɪ'belɪəs] *adj* rebelde
reb•el•lious•ly [rɪ'belɪəslɪ] *adv* con rebeldía
reb•el•lious•ness [rɪ'belɪəsnɪs] rebeldía *f*
re•birth [ri:'bɜ:rθ] resurgimiento *m*
re•boot [ri:'bu:t] **I** *v/t & v/i* reinicializar **II** *n* reinicio *m*
re•bound [rɪ'baʊnd] **I** *v/i of ball etc* rebotar **II** *n* rebote *m*
re•bound•er [rɪ'baʊndər] *in basketball* reboteador(a) *m(f)*
re•buff [rɪ'bʌf] **1** *n* desaire *m*, rechazo *m* **II** *v/t* rechazar
re•build ['ri:bɪld] *v/t* (*pret & pp* ***-built***) reconstruir
re•buke [rɪ'bju:k] *v/t* reprender
re•but [rɪ'bʌt] *v/t* (*pret & pp* ***-ted***) refutar
re•but•tal [rɪ'bʌtl] refutación *f*
re•cal•ci•trant [rɪ'kælsɪtrənt] *adj fml* recalcitrante
re•call [rɪ'kɒ:l] *v/t* **1** *goods* retirar del mercado **2** (*remember*) recordar
re•cap ['ri:kæp] *v/i* (*pret & pp* ***-ped***) recapitular
re•ca•pit•u•late [ri:kə'pɪtjʊleɪt] *v/t & v/i* recapitular
re•ca•pit•u•la•tion [ri:kəpɪtjʊ'leɪʃn] recapitulación *f*
re•cap•ture [ri:'kæptʃər] *v/t* **1** MIL reconquistar; *criminal* volver a detener **2** *mood, atmosphere* recobrar, recuperar
re•cast [ri:'kɑ:st] *v/t* (*pret & pp* ***-cast***) **1** (*restructure*) reestructurar **2** THEA volver a realizar el reparto de
re•cede [rɪ'si:d] *v/i of flood waters* retroceder
re•ced•ing [rɪ'si:dɪŋ] *adj forehead, chin* hundido; ***have a ~ hairline*** tener entradas
re•ceipt [rɪ'si:t] **1** *for purchase* recibo *m*; ***acknowledge ~ of sth*** acusar recibo de algo **2**: ***~s*** FIN ingresos *mpl*
re•ceive [rɪ'si:v] *v/t* recibir
re•ceiv•er[1] [rɪ'si:vər] **1** *of letter* destinatario(-a) *m(f)* **2** TELEC auricular *m*; *for radio* receptor *m*
re•ceiv•er[2] [rɪ'si:vər] FIN administrador(a) *m(f)* judicial
re•ceiv•er•ship [rɪ'si:vərʃɪp]: ***be in ~*** estar en suspensión de pagos
re•ceiv•ing [rɪ'si:vɪŋ] **1** *of stolen goods* receptación *f* **2**: ***be on the ~ end of sth*** F ser víctima de algo
re•cent ['ri:snt] *adj* reciente
re•cent•ly ['ri:sntlɪ] *adv* recientemente
re•cep•ta•cle [rɪ'septəkl] receptáculo *m*
re•cep•tion [rɪ'sepʃn] recepción *f*; (*welcome*) recibimiento *m*
re'cep•tion desk recepción *f*
re•cep•tion•ist [rɪ'sepʃnɪst] recepcionista *m/f*
re•cep•tive [rɪ'septɪv] *adj*: ***be ~ to sth*** ser receptivo a algo
re•cess ['ri:ses] **1** *in wall etc* hueco *m* **2** EDU recreo *m*; *of legislature* periodo *m* vacacional
re•ces•sion [rɪ'seʃn] *economic* recesión *f*
re•charge [ri:'tʃɑ:rdʒ] *v/t battery* recargar; ***~ one's batteries*** *fig* recargar las pilas
re•charge•a•ble [ri:'tʃɑ:rdʒəbl] *adj* recargable
re•cid•i•vist [rɪ'sɪdɪvɪst] reincidente *m/f*
re•ci•pe ['resəpɪ] receta *f*
're•ci•pe book libro *m* de cocina, recetario *m*
re•cip•i•ent [rɪ'sɪpɪənt] *of parcel etc* destinatario(-a) *m(f)*; *of payment* receptor(a) *m(f)*
re•cip•ro•cal [rɪ'sɪprəkl] *adj* recíproco
re•cip•ro•cate [rɪ'sɪprəkeɪt] **I** *v/t* invita-

tion, affections corresponder a **II** *v/i* corresponder
re•cip•ro•ca•tion [rɪsɪprə'keʃn] correspondencia *f*
re•cit•al [rɪ'saɪtl] MUS recital *m*
rec•i•ta•tion [resɪ'teɪʃn] recitación *f*
rec•i•ta•tive [resɪtə'tiːv] MUS recitativo *m*
re•cite [rɪ'saɪt] *v/t* **1** *poem* recitar **2** *details, facts* enumerar
reck•less ['reklɪs] *adj* imprudente; *driving* temerario
reck•less•ly ['reklɪslɪ] *adv* con imprudencia; *drive* con temeridad
reck•less•ness ['reklɪsnɪs] imprudencia *f*; *of driving* temeridad *f*
reck•on ['rekən] *v/t* (*think, consider*) estimar, considerar; ***I ~ it won't happen*** creo que no va a pasar
◆ **reckon on** *v/t* contar con
◆ **reckon with** *v/t*: ***have s.o. / sth to reckon with*** tener que vérselas con alguien / algo
reck•on•ing ['rekənɪŋ] estimaciones *fpl*, cálculos *mpl*; ***by my ~*** según mis cálculos
re•claim [rɪ'kleɪm] *v/t* **1** *land from sea* ganar, recuperar **2** *lost property, rights* reclamar
rec•la•ma•tion [reklə'meɪʃn] recuperación *f*
re•cline [rɪ'klaɪn] *v/i* reclinarse
re•clin•er [rɪ'klaɪnər] *chair* sillón *m* reclinable
re•cluse [rɪ'kluːs] solitario(-a) *m(f)*
re•clu•sive [rɪ'kluːsɪv] *adj* solitario
rec•og•ni•tion [rekəg'nɪʃn] *of state, s.o.'s achievements* reconocimiento *m*; ***in ~ of*** en reconocimiento a; ***be changed beyond ~*** estar irreconocible
rec•og•niz•a•ble [rekəg'naɪzəbl] *adj* reconocible
rec•og•nize ['rekəgnaɪz] *v/t* reconocer; ***it can be ~d by …*** se le reconoce por …
re•coil [rɪ'kɔɪl] *v/i* echarse atrás, retroceder
rec•ol•lect [rekə'lekt] *v/t* recordar
rec•ol•lec•tion [rekə'lekʃn] recuerdo *m*; ***I have no ~ of the accident*** no me acuerdo del accidente
rec•om•mend [rekə'mend] *v/t* recomendar
rec•om•mend•a•ble [rekə'mendəbl] *adj* recomendable
rec•om•men•da•tion [rekəmen'deɪʃn] recomendación *f*
rec•om•mend•ed re•tail price [rekəmendɪd'riːteɪlpraɪs] precio *m* de venta al público recomendado
rec•om•pense ['rekəmpens] **I** *n* recompensa *f* **II** *v/t*: ***~ s.o. for sth*** recompensar a alguien por algo
rec•on•cile ['rekənsaɪl] *v/t people* reconciliar; *differences, facts* conciliar; ***~ o.s. to …*** hacerse a la idea de …; ***be ~d*** *of two people* haberse reconciliado
rec•on•cil•i•a•tion [rekənsɪlɪ'eɪʃn] *of people* reconciliación *f*; *of differences, facts* conciliación *f*
rec•on•dite ['rekəndaɪt] *adj* abstruso
re•con•di•tion [riːkən'dɪʃn] *v/t* reacondicionar
re•con•di•tioned en•gine [riːkəndɪʃnd'endʒɪn] MOT motor *m* reacondicionado
re•con•nais•sance [rɪ'kɑːnɪsns] MIL reconocimiento *m*
re'con•nais•sance flight vuelo *m* de reconocimiento
re'con•nais•sance plane avión *m* de reconocimiento
rec•on•noi•ter, *Br* **rec•on•noi•tre** [rekə'nɔɪtər] *v/t* MIL reconocer
re•con•quer [riː'kɑːŋkər] *v/t* reconquistar
re•con•quest [riː'kɑːŋkwest] reconquista *f*
re•con•sid•er [riːkən'sɪdər] **I** *v/t offer, one's position* reconsiderar **II** *v/i*: ***won't you please ~?*** ¿por qué no lo reconsideras, por favor?
re•con•sid•er•a•tion [riːkənsɪdər'eɪʃn] reconsideración *f*
re•con•struct [riːkən'strʌkt] *v/t* reconstruir
re•con•struc•tion [riːkən'strʌkʃn] reconstrucción *f*; ***~ of a crime*** reconstrucción de un crimen
rec•ord[1] ['rekɔːrd] *n* **1** MUS disco *m* **2** SP *etc* récord *m* **3** *written document etc* registro *m*, documento *m*; *in database* registro *m*; ***~s*** archivos *mpl*; ***say sth off the ~*** decir algo oficiosamente; ***have a criminal ~*** tener antecedentes penales; ***have a good ~ for sth*** tener un buen historial en materia de algo
re•cord[2] [rɪ'kɔːrd] *v/t electronically* gra-

bar; *in writing* anotar
'rec•ord-break•ing *adj* récord
re•cord•ed high•lights [rɪkɔːrdɪd 'haɪlaɪts] *npl* TV momentos *mpl* más destacados
re•cor•der [rɪ'kɔːrdər] MUS flauta *f* dulce
'rec•ord hold•er plusmarquista *m/f*
re•cord•ing [rɪ'kɔːrdɪŋ] grabación *f*
re'cord•ing en•gi•neer ingeniero(-a) *m(f)* de grabación; **re'cord•ing head** cabeza *f* grabadora; **re'cord•ing stu•di•o** estudio *m* de grabación
'rec•ord play•er tocadiscos *m inv*
re•count [rɪ'kaʊnt] *v/t (tell)* relatar
re-count ['riːkaʊnt] **I** *n of votes* segundo recuento *m* **II** *v/t (count again)* volver a contar
re•coup [rɪ'kuːp] *v/t financial losses* resarcirse de
re•course [rɪ'kɔːrs]: ***have ~ to*** recurrir a
re•cov•er [rɪ'kʌvər] **I** *v/t sth lost, stolen goods* recuperar; *composure* recobrar **II** *v/i from illness* recuperarse
re•cov•er•y [rɪ'kʌvərɪ] recuperación *f*; ***he has made a good ~*** se ha recuperado muy bien
rec•re•a•tion [rekrɪ'eɪʃn] ocio *m*
rec•re•a•tion•al [rekrɪ'eɪʃnl] *adj done for pleasure* recreativo; ***~ drug*** droga *f* recreativa
re•crim•in•a•tion [rɪkrɪmɪn'eɪʃn] recriminación *f*
re•cruit [rɪ'kruːt] **I** *n* MIL recluta *m/f*; *to company* nuevo(-a) trabajador(a) **II** *v/t new staff* contratar
re•cruit•ment [rɪ'kruːtmənt] MIL reclutamiento *m*; *to company* contratación *f*
re'cruit•ment drive MIL campaña *f* de reclutamiento; *to company* campaña *f* de contratación
rec•tan•gle ['rektæŋgl] rectángulo *m*
rec•tan•gu•lar [rek'tæŋgjulər] *adj* rectangular
rec•ti•fi•ca•tion [rektɪfɪ'keɪʃn] rectificación *f*
rec•ti•fy ['rektɪfaɪ] *v/t (pret & pp* ***-ied****)* rectificar
rec•ti•lin•e•ar [rektɪ'lɪnɪər] *adj* rectilíneo
rec•ti•tude ['rektɪtjuːd] rectitud *m*
rec•tor ['rektər] **1** REL párroco *m* **2** *of school* rector(a) *m(f)*
rec•to•ry ['rektərɪ] rectoría *f*
rec•tum ['rektəm] ANAT recto *m*
re•cu•pe•rate [rɪ'kuːpəreɪt] *v/i* recuperarse
re•cur [rɪ'kɜːr] *v/i (pret & pp* ***-red****) of error, event* repetirse; *of symptoms* reaparecer
re•cur•rence [rɪ'kʌrəns] *of error, event* repetición *f*, *of symptoms* reaparición *f*
re•cur•rent [rɪ'kʌrənt] *adj* recurrente
re•cy•cla•ble [riː'saɪkləbl] *adj* reciclable
re•cy•cle [riː'saɪkl] *v/t* reciclar
re•cy•cling [riː'saɪklɪŋ] reciclado *m*
re'cy•cling plant planta *f* de reciclado
red [red] **I** *adj* rojo; ***~ alert*** alerta *f* roja; ***go ~*** ponerse rojo, ruborizarse **II** *n* rojo *m*; ***in the ~*** FIN en números rojos; ***see ~*** ponerse furioso
red 'card tarjeta *f* roja; ***he got a ~*** le sacaron la tarjeta roja; **red 'car•pet**: ***give s.o. the ~ treatment*** tratar a alguien a cuerpo de rey; **Red 'Cross** Cruz *f* Roja; **red'cur•rant** BOT grosella *f* roja
red•den ['redn] *v/i (blush)* ponerse colorado
red•dish ['redɪʃ] *adj* rojizo
re•dec•o•rate [riː'dekəreɪt] *v/t with paint* volver a pintar; *with paper* volver a empapelar
re•deem [rɪ'diːm] *v/t* **1** *debt* amortizar **2** REL redimir
Re•deem•er [rɪ'diːmər] REL Redentor *m*
re•deem•ing fea•ture [rɪdiːmɪŋ'fiːʧər]: ***his one ~ is that …*** lo único que lo salva es que …
re•de•fine [riːdɪ'faɪn] redefinir
re•demp•tion [rɪ'dempʃn] REL redención *f*
re•de•ploy [riːdɪ'plɔɪ] *v/t* redistribuir
re•de•ploy•ment [riːdɪ'plɔɪmənt] redistribución *f*
re•de•sign [riːdɪ'zaɪn] *v/t* rediseñar
re•de•vel•op [riːdɪ'veləp] *v/t part of town* reedificar
re•de•vel•op•ment [riːdɪ'veləpmənt] *of part of town* reconversión *f*
'red eye PHOT ojos *mpl* rojos; **'red-eye (flight)** F vuelo *m* nocturno; **red-hand•ed** [red'hændɪd] *adj*: ***catch s.o. ~*** coger a alguien con las manos en la masa; **'red•head** pelirrojo(-a) *m(f)*; **'red-head•ed** *adj* pelirrojo; **red 'her•ring** *fig* señuelo *m*; **'red-hot** *adj* **1** al rojo vivo **2**: ***be ~ at sth*** F ser un(a) fiera en

R

algo
re•di•al [riː'daɪəl] *v/t & v/i* volver a marcar
re•di•rect [riːdɪ'rekt] *v/t letter* reexpedir; *phone call* desviar
re•dis•cov•er [riːdɪ'skʌvər] *v/t* redescubrir
re•dis•cov•er•y [riːdɪ'skʌvərɪ] redescubrimiento *m*
re•dis•trib•ute [riːdɪ'strɪbjuːt] *v/t* redistribuir
re•dis•trib•u•tion [riːdɪstrɪ'bjuːʃn] redistribución *f*
red-'let•ter day día *m* señalado; **red 'light** *at traffic light* semáforo *m* (en) rojo; **red 'light dis•trict** zona *f* de prostitución; **red 'meat** carne *f* roja; **'red-neck** F *individuo racista y reaccionario, normalmente de clase trabajadora*
red•ness ['rednɪs] rojez *f*
re•do [riː'duː] *v/t* (*pret* ***-did***, *pp* ***-done***) volver a hacer
re•dou•ble [riː'dʌbl] *v/t*: ***~ one's efforts*** redoblar los esfuerzos
re•doubt•a•ble [rɪ'daʊtəbəl] *adj* formidable
red 'pep•per *vegetable* pimiento *m* rojo
red 'tape F burocracia *f*, papeleo *m*
re•duce [rɪ'duːs] *v/t* reducir; *price* rebajar
re•duced-e•mis•sion [rɪduːsdɪ'mɪʃn] *adj* MOT de emisión reducida
re•duc•tion [rɪ'dʌkʃn] reducción *f*; *in price* rebaja *f*
re•dun•dan•cy [rɪ'dʌndənsɪ] **1** redundancia *f* **2** *Br.* *at work* despido *m* (*por falto de trabajo*)
re•dun•dant [rɪ'dʌndənt] *adj* **1** (*unnecessary*) innecesario **2** *Br.* ***be made ~*** *at work* ser despedido
re•du•pli•cate [rɪ'duːplɪkeɪt] *v/t* repetir
red 'wine vino *m* tinto
re-ech•o [riː'ekoʊ] *v/i* resonar (***with*** con)
reed [riːd] **1** BOT junco *m* **2** MUS lengüeta *f*
re-ed•u•cate [riː'edʒʊkeɪt] *v/t* reeducar
reed•y ['riːdɪ] *adj voice*, *note* agudo
reef [riːf] *in sea* arrecife *m*
'reef knot *Br* nudo *m* de rizos, nudo *m* marinero
reek [riːk] *v/i* apestar (***of*** a)
reel[1] [riːl] *n of film* rollo *m*; *of thread* carrete *m*
◆ **reel off** *v/t* soltar
reel[2] [riːl] *v/i*: ***my head ~ed*** me daba vueltas la cabeza; ***the room ~ed before my eyes*** la habitación me daba vueltas
re-e•lect [riː'ɪlekt] *v/t* reelegir
re-e•lec•tion [riː'ɪlekʃn] reelección *f*
reel-to-reel 'tape re•cord•er casete *m* de carretes
re-en•ter [riː'entər] *v/t building*, *earth's atmosphere* volver a entrar en
re-en•try [riː'entrɪ] *of spacecraft* reentrada *f*
ref [ref] F árbitro(-a) *m*(*f*), trencilla *m* F
ref. [ref] *abbr* (= ***in*** *or* ***with reference to***) ref.
re•fec•to•ry [rɪ'fektərɪ] EDU comedor *m*
re•fer [rɪ'fɜːr] *v/t* (*pret & pp* ***-red***): ***~ a decision / problem to s.o.*** remitir una decisión / un problema a alguien
◆ **refer to** *v/t* **1** (*allude to*) referirse a **2** *dictionary etc* consultar
ref•er•ee [refə'riː] **I** *n* **1** SP árbitro(-a) *m*(*f*), *L.Am.* referí *m* **2** (*for job*) *persona que pueda dar referencias* **II** *v/t* SP arbitrar
ref•er•ee•ing [refə'riːɪŋ] SP arbitraje *m*
ref•er•ence ['refərəns] referencia *f*; ***with ~ to*** con referencia a
'ref•er•ence book libro *m* de consulta; **'ref•er•ence li•bra•ry** biblioteca *f* de consulta; **'ref•er•ence num•ber** número *m* de referencia
ref•e•ren•dum [refə'rendəm] (*pl* ***referenda*** [mɔːrə'tɔːrɪə] *or* ***-dums***) referéndum *m*
re•fill ['riːfɪl] *v/t tank*, *glass* volver a llenar
're•fill pack paquete *m* de recambio
re•fi•nance [riː'faɪnæns] *v/t* refinanciar
re•fine [rɪ'faɪn] *v/t* **1** *oil*, *sugar* refinar **2** *technique* perfeccionar
re•fined [rɪ'faɪnd] *adj manners*, *language* refinado
re•fine•ment [rɪ'faɪnmənt] *to process*, *machine* mejora *f*
re•fin•e•ry [rɪ'faɪnərɪ] refinería *f*
re•fla•tion ['riːfleɪʃn] reflación *f*
re•flect [rɪ'flekt] **I** *v/t light* reflejar; ***be ~ed in*** reflejarse en **II** *v/i* (*think*) reflexionar
re•flec•tion [rɪ'flekʃn] **1** *in water*, *glass etc* reflejo *m* **2** (*consideration*) reflexión *f*

re•flec•tive [rɪ'flektɪv] *adj surface* reflectante

re•flec•tor [rɪ'flektər] reflectante *m*

re•flex ['riːfleks] *in body* reflejo *m*

're•flex ac•tion acto *m* reflejo

're•flex cam•er•a cámara *f* réflex

re•flex•ive [rɪ'fleksɪv] *adj* GRAM reflexivo; ~ ***pronoun*** pronombre *m* reflexivo; ~ ***verb*** verbo *m* reflexivo

re•flex•ol•o•gy [riːflek'sɑːlədʒɪ] MED reflexología *f*

re•flex re'ac•tion acto *m* reflejo

re•for•est [riː'fɑːrɪst] ☞ ***reafforest***

re•for•est•a•tion [riːfɑːrɪs'teɪʃn] ☞ ***reafforestation***

re•form [rɪ'fɔːrm] **I** *n* reforma *f* **II** *v/t* reformar

re•for•mat [riː'fɔːrmæt] *v/t* (*pret & pp* ***-ted***) *disk* volver a formatear; *page* volver a diseñar; *TV program* cambiar el formato de

ref•or•ma•tion [refər'meɪʃn] reforma *f*; ***the Reformation*** REL la Reforma

re•form•er [rɪ'fɔːrmər] reformador(a) *m*(*f*)

re•fract [rɪ'frækt] *v/t* PHYS refractar

re•frac•tion [rɪ'frækʃn] PHYS refracción *f*

re•frac•to•ry [rɪ'fræktɔːrɪ] *adj* (*stubborn*) obstinado

re•frain[1] [rɪ'freɪn] *v/i fml* abstenerse; ***please ~ from smoking*** se ruega no fumar

re•frain[2] [rɪ'freɪn] *n in song, poem* estribillo *m*

re•fresh [rɪ'freʃ] *v/t person* refrescar; ***feel ~ed*** sentirse fresco

re•fresh•er course [rɪ'freʃər] curso *m* de actualización *or* reciclaje

re•fresh•ing [rɪ'freʃɪŋ] *adj* **1** *drink* refrescante **2** *experience* reconfortante

re•fresh•ing•ly [rɪ'freʃɪŋlɪ] *adv*: ~ ***honest*** con una honestidad que da gusto

re•fresh•ments [rɪ'freʃmənts] *npl* refrigerio *m*

re'fresh rate COMPUT velocidad *f* de refresco

re•frig•er•ate [rɪ'frɪdʒəreɪt] *v/t* refrigerar; ***keep ~d*** conservar refrigerado

re•frig•er•a•tion [rɪfrɪdʒər'eɪʃn] refrigeración *f*

re•frig•er•a•tor [rɪ'frɪdʒəreɪtər] frigorífico *m*, refrigerador *m*

re•fu•el [riːf'juəl] **I** *v/t* (*pret & pp* ***-led***) *airplane* reabastecer de combustible a **II** *v/i* (*pret & pp* ***-led***) *of airplane* repostar

ref•uge ['refjuːdʒ] refugio *m*; ***take ~*** *from storm etc* refugiarse

ref•u•gee [refjʊ'dʒiː] refugiado(-a) *m*(*f*)

ref•u'gee camp campo *m* de refugiados

re•fund I *n* ['riːfʌnd] reembolso *m*; ***give s.o. a ~*** devolver el dinero a alguien **II** *v/t* [rɪ'fʌnd] reembolsar

re•fur•bish [riː'fɜːrbɪʃ] *v/t* renovar

re•fur•bish•ment [riː'fɜːrbɪʃmənt] renovación *f*

re•fus•al [rɪ'fjuːzl] negativa *f*

re•fuse[1] [rɪ'fjuːz] **I** *v/i* negarse **II** *v/t help, food* rechazar; ~ ***s.o. sth*** negar algo a alguien; ~ ***to do sth*** negarse a hacer algo

ref•use[2] ['refjuːs] *n* basura *f*

ref•use dump ['refjuːsdʌmp] vertedero *m*

ref•use skip ['refjuːsskɪp] *Br* contenedor *m* de basuras

re•fut•a•ble [rɪ'fjuːtəbl] *adj* refutable

ref•u•ta•tion [refjʊ'teɪʃn] refutación *f*

re•fute [rɪ'fjuːt] *v/t* **1** refutar **2** (*deny*) negar

re•gain [rɪ'geɪn] *v/t* recuperar

re•gal ['riːgl] *adj* regio

re•ga•li•a [rɪ'geɪlɪə] *npl* galas *fpl*

re•gard [rɪ'gɑːrd] **I** *n*: ***have great ~ for s.o.*** sentir gran estima por alguien; ***in this ~*** en este sentido; ***with ~ to*** con respecto a; (***kind***) ***~s*** saludos; ***give my ~s to Paula*** dale saludos *or* recuerdos a Paula de mi parte; ***with no ~ for*** sin tener en cuenta **II** *v/t*: ~ ***sth / s.o. as sth*** considerar algo / a alguien como algo; ***I ~ it as an honor*** para mí es un honor; ***as ~s*** con respecto a

re•gard•ing [rɪ'gɑːrdɪŋ] *prep* con respecto a

re•gard•less [rɪ'gɑːrdlɪs] *adv* a pesar de todo; ~ ***of*** sin tener en cuenta; ***they just carried on ~*** a pesar de todo, siguieron adelante

re•gat•ta [rɪ'gætə] SP regata *f*

re•gen•cy ['riːdʒənsɪ] regencia *f*

re•gen•er•ate [rɪ'dʒenəreɪt] *v/t* regenerar

re•gen•er•a•tion [rɪdʒenər'eɪʃn] regeneración *f*

re•gent ['riːdʒənt] regente *m/f*

reg•gae ['regeɪ] MUS reggae *m*
re•gime [reɪ'ʒiːm] (*government*) régimen *m*
re•gi•ment ['redʒɪmənt] **I** *n* regimiento *m* **II** *v/t* controlar estrictamente
reg•i•men•tal [redʒɪ'mentl] *adj* MIL de regimiento
reg•i•men•ta•tion [redʒɪmen'teɪʃn] control *m* estricto
re•gion ['riːdʒən] región *f*; ***in the ~ of*** del orden de
re•gion•al ['riːdʒənl] *adj* regional
reg•is•ter ['redʒɪstər] **I** *n* registro *m*; *at school* lista *f* **II** *v/t* **1** *birth, death* registrar; *vehicle* matricular; *letter* certificar; ***send a letter ~ed*** enviar una carta por correo certificado **2** *emotion* mostrar **III** *v/i at university, for a course* matricularse; *with police* registrarse
reg•is•tered let•ter [redʒɪstərd'letər] carta *f* certificada; **reg•is•tered 'of•fice** domicilio *m* social; **reg•is•tered 'trade•mark** marca *f* registrada
reg•is•trar [redʒɪ'strɑːr] *Br* doctor(a) *m(f)*
re•gis•tra•tion [redʒɪ'streɪʃn] registro *m*; *at university, for course* matriculación *f*
re•gis'tra•tion num•ber *Br* MOT (número *m* de) matrícula *f*
reg•is•try ['redʒɪstrɪ] registro *m*
'reg•is•try of•fice *Br* registro *m* civil; ***get married at a ~*** casarse por lo civil
re•gress [rɪ'gres] *v/i* involucionar
re•gres•sion [rɪ'greʃn] regresión *f*
re•gres•sive [rɪ'gresɪv] *adj* regresivo
re•gret [rɪ'gret] **I** *v/t* (*pret & pp* ***-ted***) lamentar, sentir **II** *n* arrepentimiento *m*, pesar *m*
re•gret•ful [rɪ'gretfəl] *adj* arrepentido
re•gret•ful•ly [rɪ'gretfəlɪ] *adv* lamentablemente
re•gret•ta•ble [rɪ'gretəbl] *adj* lamentable
re•gret•ta•bly [rɪ'gretəblɪ] *adv* lamentablemente
re•group [riː'gruːp] *v/i* reagruparse
reg•u•lar ['regjʊlər] **I** *adj* **1** regular; ***be in ~ employment*** tener un trabajo regular **2** (*normal, ordinary*) normal **II** *n at bar etc* habitual *m/f*
reg•u•lar 'cus•tom•er cliente *m/f* habitual
reg•u•lar 'gas•o•line gasolina *f* súper
reg•u•lar•i•ty [regjʊ'lærətɪ] regularidad *f*
reg•u•lar•ize ['regjʊləraɪz] *v/t* regularizar
reg•u•lar•ly ['regjʊlərlɪ] *adv* regularmente
reg•u•late ['regjʊleɪt] *v/t* regular
reg•u•la•tion [regjʊ'leɪʃn] (*rule*) regla *f*, norma *f*
reg•u•la•tor ['regjʊleɪtər] TECH, FIN regulador *m*
reg•u•la•to•ry [regjʊ'leɪtərɪ] *adj* regulador
re•hab ['riːhæb] F rehabilitación *f*
re•ha•bil•i•tate [riːhə'bɪlɪteɪt] *v/t ex-criminal* rehabilitar
re•ha•bil•i•ta•tion [riːhəbɪlɪ'teɪʃn] rehabilitación *f*; ***~ center*** centro *m* de rehabilitación
re•hash I *v/t* [riː'hæʃ] *old data etc* reutilizar **II** *n* ['riːhæʃ] refrito *m* F
re•hears•al [rɪ'hɜːrsl] ensayo *m*
re•hearse [rɪ'hɜːrs] *v/t & v/i* ensayar
reign [reɪn] **I** *n* reinado *m* **II** *v/i* reinar
re•im•burse [riːɪm'bɜːrs] *v/t* reembolsar
re•im•burse•ment [riːɪm'bɜːrsmənt] reembolso *m*
rein [reɪn] rienda *f*; ***keep a tight ~ on*** *fig* controlar de cerca; ***take the ~s*** *fig* tomar las riendas; ***give free ~ to one's imagination*** *fig* dar rienda suelta a la imaginación
◆ **rein in** *v/t horse* frenar; *emotions* controlar; *budget deficit* tirar las riendas de
re•in•car•nate [riː'ɪnkɑːrneɪt] *v/t*: ***be ~ed*** reencarnarse
re•in•car•na•tion [riːɪnkɑːr'neɪʃn] reencarnación *f*
rein•deer ['reɪndɪr] (*pl* ***reindeer***) ZO reno *m*
re•in•force [riːɪn'fɔːrs] *v/t structure* reforzar; *belief* reafirmar
re•in•forced con•crete [riːɪn'fɔːrst] hormigón *m* armado
re•in•force•ments [riːɪn'fɔːrsmənts] *npl* MIL refuerzos *mpl*
re•in•state [riːɪn'steɪt] *v/t person in office* reincorporar; *paragraph in text* volver a colocar
re•in•sur•ance [riːɪn'ʃʊrəns] COM reaseguro *m*
re•in•sure [riːɪn'ʃʊr] *v/t* reasegurar
re•in•vent [riːɪn'vent] *v/t*: ***~ o.s.*** reinventarse

re•is•sue [riːˈɪʃuː] *v/t recording* reeditar; *stamps etc* volver a emitir; *warning* volver a lanzar

re•it•er•ate [riːˈɪtəreɪt] *v/t fml* reiterar

re•ject [rɪˈdʒekt] *v/t* rechazar

re•jec•tion [rɪˈdʒekʃn] rechazo *m*; ***he felt a sense of ~*** se sintió rechazado

ˈre•ject shop tienda *f* de productos defectuosos

re•joice [rɪˈdʒɔɪs] *v/i* alegrarse (***at, over*** de); ***~!*** REL ¡alegría!

re•joic•ing [rɪˈdʒɔɪsɪŋ] alegría *f*

re•join [riːˈdʒɔɪn] *v/t* volver a unirse a; *regiment* reincorporarse a

re•join•der [riːˈdʒɔɪndər] réplica *f*

re•ju•ve•nate [rɪˈdʒuːvəneɪt] *v/t* rejuvenecer

re•ju•ve•na•tion [rɪdʒuːvəˈneɪʃn] rejuvenecimiento *m*

re•key *v/t text* volver a escribir

re•kin•dle [riːˈkɪndl] *v/t fig passions, interest etc* reavivar

re•lapse [ˈriːlæps] MED recaída *f*; ***have a ~*** sufrir una recaída

re•late [rɪˈleɪt] **I** *v/t* **1** *story* relatar, narrar **2** *connect*: ***~ sth to sth*** relacionar algo con algo **II** *v/i*: ***~ to*** *be connected with* estar relacionado con; ***he doesn't ~ to people*** no se relaciona fácilmente con la gente

re•lat•ed [rɪˈleɪtɪd] *adj by family* emparentado; *events, ideas etc* relacionado; ***are you two ~?*** ¿sois parientes?

re•la•tion [rɪˈleɪʃn] *in family* pariente *m/f*; (*connection*) relación *f*; ***business / diplomatic ~s*** relaciones *fpl* comerciales / diplomáticas

re•la•tion•al da•ta•base [rɪˈleɪʃnl] base *f* de datos relacional

re•la•tion•ship [rɪˈleɪʃnʃɪp] relación *f*; ***have a good ~ with*** tener una buena relación con

rel•a•tive [ˈrelətɪv] **I** *n* pariente *m/f* **II** *adj* **1** (*comparative*) relativo **2**: ***X is ~ to Y*** X está relacionado con Y

rel•a•tive•ly [ˈrelətɪvlɪ] *adv* relativamente

rel•a•tiv•i•ty [reləˈtɪvɪtɪ] relatividad *f*; ***theory of ~*** PHYS teoría *f* de la relatividad

re•launch [ˈriːlɒːntʃ] **I** *v/t product* relanzar **II** *n* relanzamiento *m*

re•lax [rɪˈlæks] **I** *v/i* relajarse; ***~!, don't get angry*** ¡tranquilízate!, no te enfades **II** *v/t muscle, pace* relajar

re•lax•a•tion [riːlækˈseɪʃn] relajación *f*; ***what do you do for ~?*** ¿qué haces para relajarte?

re•laxed [rɪˈlækst] *adj* relajado

re•lax•ing [rɪˈlæksɪŋ] *adj* relajante

re•lay [ˈriːleɪ] **I** *v/t message* pasar; *radio, TV signals* retransmitir **II** *n*: **~ (*race*)** carrera *f* de relevos

re-lay [riːˈleɪ] *v/t* (*pret & pp* ***-laid***) *cable, carpet* volver a colocar

re•lease [rɪˈliːs] **I** *n* **1** *from prison* liberación *f*, puesta *f* en libertad **2** *of CD etc* lanzamiento *m*; *CD, record* trabajo *m*; ***be on general ~*** *of movie* estar en cartelera

II *v/t* **1** *prisoner* liberar, poner en libertad; ***~ s.o. from a contract*** librar a alguien de las obligaciones de un contrato **2** *parking brake* soltar **3** *information* hacer público; *CD etc* sacar

rel•e•gate [ˈrelɪgeɪt] *v/t* relegar; ***be ~d*** *Br* SP descender

rel•e•ga•tion [relɪˈgeɪʃn] *Br* SP descenso *m*

re•lent [rɪˈlent] *v/i* ablandarse, ceder

re•lent•less [rɪˈlentlɪs] *adj* (*determined*) implacable; *rain etc* que no cesa

re•lent•less•ly [rɪˈlentlɪslɪ] *adv* implacablemente; *rain* sin cesar

rel•e•vance [ˈreləvəns] pertinencia *f*

rel•e•vant [ˈreləvənt] *adj* pertinente

re•li•a•bil•i•ty [rɪlaɪəˈbɪlətɪ] fiabilidad *f*

re•li•a•ble [rɪˈlaɪəbl] *adj* fiable; *information* fiable, fidedigna

re•li•a•bly [rɪˈlaɪəblɪ] *adv*: ***I am ~ informed that*** sé de buena fuente que

re•li•ance [rɪˈlaɪəns] confianza *f*, dependencia *f*; ***~ on s.o. / sth*** confianza en alguien / algo, dependencia de alguien / algo

re•li•ant [rɪˈlaɪənt] *adj*: ***be ~ on*** depender de

rel•ic [ˈrelɪk] reliquia *f*

re•lief [rɪˈliːf] **1** alivio *m*; ***pain ~*** alivio del dolor; ***that's a ~*** qué alivio; ***to my great ~*** para alivio mío **2**: ***in ~*** *in art* en relieve

reˈlief bus autobús *m* de apoyo; **reˈlief fund** fondo *m* de ayuda; **reˈlief map** mapa *m* de relieve; **reˈlief road** carretera *f* auxiliar; **reˈlief staff** personal *m* de apoyo; **reˈlief train** tren *m* de apoyo

re•lieve [rɪˈliːv] *v/t* **1** *pressure, pain* aliviar; ***be ~d*** *at news etc* sentirse aliviado

2 *(take over from)* relevar
re•li•gion [rɪ'lɪdʒən] religión *f*
re•li•gious [rɪ'lɪdʒəs] *adj* religioso
re•li•gious•ly [rɪ'lɪdʒəslɪ] *adv* *(conscientiously)* religiosamente
re•lin•quish [rɪ'lɪŋkwɪʃ] *v/t* renunciar a
rel•ish ['relɪʃ] **I** *n* **1** *sauce* salsa *f* **2** *(enjoyment)* goce *m* **II** *v/t idea, prospect* gozar con; ***I don't ~ the idea*** la idea no me entusiasma
re•live [riː'lɪv] *v/t the past, an event* revivir
re•load [riː'loʊd] **I** *v/t gun, camera* recargar **II** *v/i* recargarse
re•lo•cate [riːlə'keɪt] *v/i of business, employee* trasladarse
re•lo•ca•tion [riːlə'keɪʃn] *of business, employee* traslado *m*
re•lo'ca•tion al•low•ance subsidio *m* por traslado
re•luc•tance [rɪ'lʌktəns] reticencia *f*; ***because of his ~ to change his mind*** ya que era reacio a cambiar de opinión
re•luc•tant [rɪ'lʌktənt] *adj* reticente, reacio; ***be ~ to do sth*** ser reacio a hacer algo
re•luc•tant•ly [rɪ'lʌktəntlɪ] *adv* con reticencia; ***he finally ~ accepted*** al final, aceptó a regañadientes
◆ **re•ly on** [rɪ'laɪ] *v/t (pret & pp* ***-ied****)* depender de; ***rely on s.o. to do sth*** contar con alguien para hacer algo
re•main [rɪ'meɪn] *v/i* **1** *(be left)* quedar **2** *(stay)* permanecer
re•main•der [rɪ'meɪndər] **I** *n also* MATH resto *m* **II** *v/t* vender como saldo
re•main•ing [rɪ'meɪnɪŋ] *adj* restante
re•mains [rɪ'meɪnz] *npl of body* restos *mpl* (mortales)
re•make ['riːmeɪk] *of movie* nueva versión *f*
re•mand [rɪ'mænd] **I** *v/t*: ***~ s.o. in custody*** poner a alguien en prisión preventiva **II** *n*: ***be on ~*** *in prison* estar en prisión preventiva; *on bail* estar en libertad bajo fianza
re•mark [rɪ'mɑːrk] **I** *n* comentario *m*, observación *f* **II** *v/t* comentar, observar
re•mark•a•ble [rɪ'mɑːrkəbl] *adj* notable, extraordinario
re•mark•a•bly [rɪ'mɑːrkəblɪ] *adv* extraordinariamente
re•mar•ket [rɪ'mɑːrkɪt] *v/t* lanzar de nuevo
re•mar•riage [riː'mærɪdʒ] nuevo *m* matrimonio
re•mar•ry [riː'mærɪ] *v/i (pret & pp* ***-ied****)* volver a casarse
re•mas•ter [riː'mæstər] *v/t recording* remasterizar
re•me•di•al [rɪ'miːdɪəl] *adj* corrector; ***~ classes*** *pl* clases *fpl* especiales; ***~ exercises*** *pl* ejercicios *mpl* de rehabilitación
rem•e•dy ['remədɪ] MED, *fig* remedio *m*
re•mem•ber [rɪ'membər] **I** *v/t s.o., sth* recordar, acordarse de; ***~ doing sth*** acordarse de hacer algo; ***~ to lock the door*** acuérdate de cerrar la puerta; ***~ me to her*** dale recuerdos de mi parte; ***~, I'll be watching*** no te olvides de que te estoy vigilando **II** *v/i* recordar, acordarse; ***I don't ~*** no recuerdo, no me acuerdo
re•mem•brance [rɪ'membrəns] recuerdo *m* (***of*** de); ***in ~ of*** en recuerdo de; ***Remembrance Day*** *or* ***Sunday*** *Br domingo de homenaje a los caídos en las guerras mundiales*
re•mind [rɪ'maɪnd] *v/t*: ***~ s.o. of sth*** recordar algo a alguien; ***~ s.o. of s.o.*** recordar alguien a alguien; ***you ~ me of your father*** me recuerdas a tu padre; ***that ~s me, I have to …*** eso me recuerda que tengo que…
re•mind•er [rɪ'maɪndər] recordatorio *m*; *for payment* recordatorio *m* de pago
rem•i•nisce [remɪ'nɪs] *v/i* contar recuerdos
rem•i•nis•cence [remɪ'nɪsns] recuerdo *m*
rem•i•nis•cent [remɪ'nɪsənt] *adj*: ***be ~ of sth*** recordar a algo, tener reminiscencias de algo
re•miss [rɪ'mɪs] *adj fml* negligente, descuidado
re•mis•sion [rɪ'mɪʃn] remisión *f*; ***go into ~*** MED remitir
re•mit [rɪ'mɪt] *v/t (pret & pp* ***-ted****)* **1** *sins* perdonar **2** COM *(pay)* remitir (***to*** a)
re•mit•tance [rɪ'mɪtəns] COM pago *m*
re'mit•tance ad•vice COM notificación *f* de pago
rem•nant ['remnənt] resto *m*
re•mod•el [riː'mɑːdl] *v/t (pret & pp* ***-eled****, Br* ***-elled****)* remodelar; ***~ sth on sth*** rediseñar algo tomando como modelo algo
re•mon•strance [rɪ'mɑːnstrəns] queja *f*

re•mon•strate ['remənstreɪt] *v/i* discutir (***with*** con)
re•morse [rɪ'mɔːrs] remordimientos *mpl*
re•morse•ful [rɪ'mɔːrsfʊl] *adj* lleno de remordimientos
re•morse•less [rɪ'mɔːrsləs] *adj person* despiadado; *pace, demands* implacable
re•morse•less•ly [rɪ'mɔːrsləslɪ] *adv* implacablemente
re•mote [rɪ'moʊt] *adj* **1** *village, possibility* remoto; *ancestor* lejano **2** *(aloof)* distante
re•mote 'ac•cess COMPUT acceso *m* remoto; **re•mote con'trol** control *m* remoto; *for TV* mando *m* a distancia; **re•mote-con'trolled** *adj* teledirigido; **re'mote da•ta en•try** COMPUT introducción *f* remota de datos
re•mote•ly [rɪ'moʊtlɪ] *adv related, connected* remotamente; ***it's just ~ possible*** es una posibilidad muy remota
re•mote•ness [rɪ'moʊtnəs]: ***the ~ of the house*** la lejanía *or* lo aislado de la casa
re•mount [riː'maʊnt] *v/t horse, bike* volver a montarse en
re•mov•a•ble [rɪ'muːvəbl] *adj* de quita y pon
re•mov•al [rɪ'muːvl] eliminación *f*
re•move [rɪ'muːv] *v/t* eliminar; *top, lid* quitar; *coat etc* quitarse; *doubt, suspicion* despejar; *growth, organ* extirpar
re•mu•ner•ate [rɪ'mjuːnəreɪt] *v/t* remunerar
re•mu•ner•a•tion [rɪmjuːnə'reɪʃn] remuneración *f*
re•mu•ner•a•tive [rɪ'mjuːnərətɪv] *adj* bien remunerado
Ren•ais•sance [rə'neɪsəns] Renacimiento *m*
Ren•ais•sance 'man renacentista *m*
re•nal ['riːnl] *adj* ANAT renal; ***~ failure*** MED insuficiencia *f* renal
re•name [riː'neɪm] *v/t* cambiar el nombre a
ren•der ['rendər] *v/t* **1** *service* prestar **2**: ***~ s.o. helpless / unconscious*** dejar a alguien indefenso / inconsciente **3** *wall* enyesar
ren•der•ing ['rendərɪŋ] *of piece of music* interpretación *f*
ren•dez-vous ['rɑːndeɪvuː] *romantic* cita *f*; MIL encuentro *m*
ren•di•tion [ren'dɪʃn] interpretación *f*
ren•e•gade ['renɪgeɪd] **I** *n* renegado(-a) *m(f)* **II** *adj* renegado
re•nege [rɪ'neɪg] *v/i*: ***~ on sth*** incumplir algo
re•new [rɪ'nuː] *v/t contract, license* renovar; *discussions* reanudar; ***feel ~ed*** sentirse como nuevo
re•new•a•ble [rɪ'nuːəbl] *adj* renovable; ***~ resources*** recursos *mpl* renovables
re•new•al [rɪ'nuːəl] *of contract etc* renovación *f*, *of discussions* reanudación *f*
re'new•al clause cláusula *f* de renovación
re•nounce [rɪ'naʊns] *v/t title, rights* renunciar a
ren•o•vate ['renəveɪt] *v/t* renovar
ren•o•va•tion [renə'veɪʃn] renovación *f*
re•nown [rɪ'naʊn] renombre *m*
re•nowned [rɪ'naʊnd] *adj* renombrado; ***be ~ for sth*** ser célebre por algo
rent [rent] **I** *n* alquiler *m*; ***for ~*** se alquila **II** *v/t apartment, car, equipment* alquilar, *Mex* rentar
'rent-a-car (serv•ice) alquiler *m* de coches
rent•al ['rentl] *for apartment, TV* alquiler *m*, *Mex* renta *f*
'rent•al a•gree•ment acuerdo *m* de alquiler; **'rent•al a•part•ment** apartmento *or Span* piso arrendado; **'rent•al car** coche *m* de alquiler
rent•er ['rentər] arrendatario(-a) *m(f)*
rent-'free *adv* sin pagar alquiler
re•nun•ci•a•tion [rɪnʌnsɪ'eɪʃn] renuncia *f*
re•o•pen [riː'oʊpn] **I** *v/t* reabrir; *negotiations* reanudar **II** *v/i of theater etc* volver a abrir
re•or•gan•i•za•tion [riːɔːrgənaɪz'eɪʃn] reorganización *f*
re•or•gan•ize [riː'ɔːrgənaɪz] *v/t* reorganizar
rep[1] [rep] COM representante *m/f*, comercial *m/f*
rep[2] [rep] *fabric* canalé *m*; ***~ tie*** corbata *f* de canalé
re•pack•age ['riːpækɪdʒ] *v/t product* reempaquetar
re•paint [riː'peɪnt] *v/t* repintar
re•pair [rɪ'per] **I** *v/t fence, TV* reparar; *shoes* arreglar **II** *n to fence, TV* reparación *f*, *of shoes* arreglo *m*; ***in a good / bad state of ~*** en buen / mal estado
re'pair•man técnico *m*

rep•a•ra•tion [repər'eɪʃn] compensación *f*; ***make ~s for sth*** compensar por algo
rep•ar•tee [repɑːr'tiː] respuestas *fpl* ingeniosas
re•pa•tri•ate [riː'pætrɪeɪt] *v/t* repatriar
re•pa•tri•a•tion [riː'pætrɪ'eɪʃn] repatriación *f*
re•pay [riː'peɪ] *v/t* (*pret & pp* ***-paid***) *money* devolver; *person* pagar
re•pay•a•ble [riː'peɪəbl] *adj* pagadero
re•pay•ment [riː'peɪmənt] **1** *of money* devolución *f* **2** *installment* plazo *m*
re•peal [rɪ'piːl] *v/t law* revocar
re•peat [rɪ'piːt] **I** *v/t* repetir; ***am I ~ing myself?*** ¿me estoy repitiendo? **II** *n TV program etc* repetición *f*
re'peat busi•ness COM negocio *m* que se repite
re•peat•ed [rɪ'piːtɪd] *adj* repetido
re•peat•ed•ly [rɪ'piːtɪdlɪ] *adv* repetidamente, repetidas veces
re•peat 'or•der COM pedido *m* repetido
re•peat pur•chase compra *f* persistente
re•pel [rɪ'pel] *v/t* (*pret & pp* ***-led***) **1** *invaders, attack* rechazar; *insects* repeler, ahuyentar **2** (*disgust*) repeler, repugnar
re•pel•lent [rɪ'pelənt] **I** *n* (*insect ~*) repelente *m* **II** *adj* repelente, repugnante
re•pent [rɪ'pent] *v/i* arrepentirse
re•per•cus•sions [riːpər'kʌʃnz] *npl* repercusiones *fpl*
rep•er•toire ['repərtwɑːr] repertorio *m*
rep•e•ti•tion [repɪ'tɪʃn] repetición *f*
re•pet•i•tive [rɪ'petɪtɪv] *adj* repetitivo
re•pet•i•tive 'strain in•ju•ry lesión *f* por movimiento repetitivo
re•phrase [rɪ'freɪs] *v/t* reformular; ***sorry, I'll ~ that*** perdón, lo diré de otra manera
re•place [rɪ'pleɪs] *v/t* **1** (*put back*) volver a poner **2** (*take the place of*) reemplazar, sustituir
re•place•ment [rɪ'pleɪsmənt] *person* sustituto(-a) *m*(*f*); *thing* recambio *m*, reemplazo *m*
re•place•ment 'part (pieza *f* de) recambio *m*
re'place•ment val•ue in•sur•ance seguro *m* por el valor de reposición
re•plant [riː'plænt] *v/t* replantar
re•play ['riːpleɪ] **I** *n* **1** *recording* repetición *f* (de la jugada) **2** *match* repetición *f* (del partido) **II** *v/t match* repetir
re•plen•ish [rɪ'plenɪʃ] *v/t container* rellenar; *supplies* reaprovisionar
re•plete [rɪ'pliːt] *adj* **1** *after eating* repleto **2**: ***~ with*** *fml* repleto de
rep•li•ca ['replɪkə] réplica *f*
re•ply [rɪ'plaɪ] **I** *n* respuesta *f*, contestación *f* **II** *v/t & v/i* (*pret & pp* ***-ied***) responder, contestar
re•ply-'paid en•ve•lope sobre *m* con el franqueo pagado
re•port [rɪ'pɔːrt] **I** *n* (*account*) informe *m*; *by journalist* reportaje *m* **II** *v/t* **1** *facts* informar; ***~ one's findings to s.o*** dar a conocer a alguien los hallazgos de algo; ***he is ~ed to be in Washington*** se dice que está en Washington **2** *to authorities* informar de, dar parte de; ***~ s.o. to the police*** denunciar a alguien a la policía **III** *v/i* **1** *of journalist* informar **2** (*present o.s.*) presentarse (***to*** ante)
◆ **report to** *v/t in business* trabajar a las órdenes de
re'port card boletín *m* de evaluación
re•port•er [rɪ'pɔːrtər] reportero(-a) *m*(*f*)
re'port form COMPUT informe *m*
re•pose [rɪ'pouz] *lit* **I** *n* reposo *m* **II** *v/i* reposar
re•pos•sess [riːpə'zes] *v/t* COM embargar
rep•re•hen•si•ble [reprɪ'hensəbl] *adj* recriminable
rep•re•sent [reprɪ'zent] *v/t* representar
re-pres•ent [riːprɪ'zent] *v/t* FIN *check* volver a presentar
rep•re•sen•ta•tion [reprɪzen'teɪʃn] **1** representación *f* **2**: ***make ~s to*** *fml* presentar una protesta a (***about*** por)
rep•re•sen•ta•tion•al [reprɪzen'teɪʃənl] *adj art* figurativo
rep•re•sen•ta•tive [reprɪ'zentətɪv] **I** *n* representante *m/f*, POL representante *m/f*, diputado(-a) *m*(*f*) **II** *adj* (*typical*) representativo
re•press [rɪ'pres] *v/t revolt* reprimir; *feelings, laughter* reprimir, controlar
re•pres•sion [rɪ'preʃn] POL represión *f*
re•pres•sive [rɪ'presɪv] *adj* POL represivo
re•prieve [rɪ'priːv] **I** *n* LAW indulto *m*; *fig* aplazamiento *m* **II** *v/t prisoner* indultar

R

rep•ri•mand ['reprɪmænd] *v/t* reprender
re•print ['ri:prɪnt] **I** *n* reimpresión *f* **II** *v/t* reimprimir
re•pri•sal [rɪ'praɪzl] represalia *f*; ***take ~s*** tomar represalias; ***in ~ for*** en represalia por
re•proach [rɪ'proʊʧ] **I** *n* reproche *m*; ***be beyond ~*** ser irreprochable **II** *v/t*: ***~ s.o. for sth*** reprochar algo a alguien
re•proach•ful [rɪ'proʊʧfəl] *adj* de reproche
re•proach•ful•ly [rɪ'proʊʧfəlɪ] *adv look* con una mirada de reproche; *say* con tono de reproche
re•proc•ess [ri:'proʊses] *v/t* reprocesar
re•proc•ess•ing plant [ri:'proʊsesɪŋplænt] planta *f* de reprocesado
re•pro•duce [ri:prə'du:s] **I** *v/t atmosphere, mood* reproducir **II** *v/i* BIO reproducirse
re•pro•duc•tion [ri:prə'dʌkʃn] reproducción *f*
re•pro•duc•tion 'fur•ni•ture reproducciones *mpl* de muebles antiguos
re•pro•duc•tive [rɪprə'dʌktɪv] *adj* reproductivo
re•pro•gram *v/t* (*pret & pp* ***-med***) reprogramar
re•prove [rɪ'pru:v] *v/t* reprobar (***for*** por)
rep•tile ['reptaɪl] reptil *m*
re•pub•lic [rɪ'pʌblɪk] república *f*
re•pub•li•can [rɪ'pʌblɪkn] **I** *n* republicano(-a) *m*(*f*); ***Republican*** POL Republicano(-a) *m*(*f*) **II** *adj* republicano
re•pu•di•ate [rɪ'pju:dɪeɪt] *v/t* (*deny*) rechazar
re•pug•nance [rɪ'pʌgnəns] repugnancia *f*
re•pug•nant [rɪ'pʌgnənt] *adj* repugnante
re•pulse [rɪ'pʌls] *v/t fml*: *attack, enemy* rechazar
re•pul•sion [rɪ'pʌlʃn] repulsión *f*
re•pul•sive [rɪ'pʌlsɪv] *adj* repulsivo
re•pur•chase [ri:'pɜ:rʧəs] **I** *v/t* recomprar **II** *n* recompra *f*
rep•u•ta•ble ['repjʊtəbl] *adj* reputado, acreditado
rep•u•ta•tion [repjʊ'teɪʃn] reputación *f*; ***have a good / bad ~*** tener una buena / mala reputación; ***she has a ~ for being rather difficult*** tiene fama de ser una persona bastante difícil
re•pute [rɪ'pju:t]: ***of ~*** de prestigio; ***be held in high ~*** estar muy bien considerado
re•put•ed [rep'jʊtəd] *adj*: ***be ~ to be*** tener fama de ser
re•put•ed•ly [rep'jʊtədlɪ] *adv* según se dice
re•quest [rɪ'kwest] **I** *n* petición *f*, solicitud *f*; ***on ~*** por encargo **II** *v/t* pedir, solicitar
re'quest pro•gram, *Br* **re'quest programme** *programa de petición de canciones, música etc*
re•quiem ['rekwɪəm] MUS réquiem *m*
re•quire [rɪ'kwaɪr] *v/t* (*need*) requerir, necesitar; ***it ~s great care*** se requiere mucho cuidado; ***as ~d by law*** como estipula la ley; ***guests are ~d to ...*** se ruega a los invitados que ...; ***~ s.o. to do sth*** requerir a alguien que haga halgo
re•quired [rɪ'kwaɪrd] *adj* (*necessary*) necesario; ***if ~d*** si fuera necesario
re•quired 'read•ing lectura *f* obligatoria
re•quire•ment [rɪ'kwaɪrmənt] (*need*) necesidad *f*; (*condition*) requisito *m*
req•ui•site ['rekwɪzɪt] **I** *adj* necesario (***for*** para) **II** *usu pl* requisito *m*
req•ui•si•tion [rekwɪ'zɪʃn] *v/t* requisar
re-route [ri:'ru:t] *v/t airplane etc* desviar
re•run ['ri:rʌn] **I** *n of TV program* reposición *f* **II** *v/t* (*pret* ***-ran***, *pp* ***-run***) *tape* volver a poner
re•sale ['ri:seɪl]: ***not for ~*** prohibida su venta
're•sale val•ue valor m de reventa
re•sched•ule [ri:'ʃedu:l] *v/t* volver a programar
re•scind [rɪ'sɪnd] *v/t* LAW derogar
res•cue ['reskju:] **I** *n* rescate *m*; ***come to s.o.'s ~*** acudir al rescate de alguien **II** *v/t* rescatar
'res•cue op•er•a•tion FIN operación *f* de rescate; **'res•cue pack•age** FIN paquete *m* de rescate; **'res•cue par•ty** equipo *m* de rescate
res•cu•er ['reskjʊər] salvador(a) *m*(*f*)
re•search [rɪ'sɜ:rʧ] **I** *n* investigación *f* **II** *v/t* investigar; ***a well ~ed thesis*** una tesis bien documentada
◆ **research into** *v/t* investigar
re•search and de'vel•op•ment investigación *f* y desarrollo
re'search as•sist•ant ayudante *m/f* de investigación

re•search•er [rɪ'sɜːrʧər] investigador(a) *m(f)*
re'search proj•ect proyecto *m* de investigación
re•sem•blance [rɪ'zembləns] parecido *m*, semejanza *f*
re•sem•ble [rɪ'zembl] *v/t* parecerse a
re•sent [rɪ'zent] *v/t* estar molesto por; ***I ~ the implication*** me molesta *or* ofende la implicancia; ***I ~ that remark*** me ofende ese comentario
re•sent•ful [rɪ'zentfəl] *adj* resentido
re•sent•ful•ly [rɪ'zentfəlɪ] *adv* con resentimiento
re•sent•ment [rɪ'zentmənt] resentimiento *m*
res•er•va•tion [rezər'veɪʃn] reserva *f*; ***I have a ~*** *in hotel, restaurant* tengo una reserva
re•serve [rɪ'zɜːrv] **I** *n* reserva *f*; SP reserva *m/f*; **~s** FIN reservas *fpl*; ***keep sth in ~*** tener algo en la reserva **II** *v/t seat, table* reservar; *judgment* reservarse
re'serve cur•ren•cy moneda *f* de reserva
re•served [rɪ'zɜːrvd] *adj table, manner* reservado
re•serv•ist [rɪ'zɜːrvɪst] MIL reservista *m/f*
res•er•voir ['rezərvwɑːr] *for water* embalse *m*, pantano *m*
re•set [riː'set] *v/t* (*pret & pp* ***-set***) **1** *jewel* volver a engastar **2** *clock* ajustar; *counter etc* poner a cero **3** (*re-typeset*) volver a componer
re•set•tle•ment [riː'setlmənt] *of refugees etc* reasentamiento *m*
re•shuf•fle ['riːʃʌfl] POL **I** *n* remodelación *f* **II** *v/t* remodelar
re•side [rɪ'zaɪd] *v/i fml* residir
res•i•dence ['rezɪdəns] **1** (*fml: house etc*) residencia *f* **2** (*stay*) estancia *f*
'res•i•dence per•mit permiso *m* de residencia
'res•i•dent ['rezɪdənt] **I** *n* residente *m/f* **II** *adj* (*living in a building*) residente
res•i•den•tial [rezɪ'denʃl] *adj district* residencial
re•sid•u•al [rɪ'zɪdjʊəl] *adj* residual
res•i•due ['rezɪduː] residuo *m*
re•sign [rɪ'zaɪn] **I** *v/t* **1** *position* dimitir de **2**: **~ *o.s. to*** resignarse a **II** *v/i from job* dimitir
res•ig•na•tion [rezɪg'neɪʃn] **1** *n from job* dimisión *f* **2** *mental* resignación *f*
re•signed [re'zaɪnd] *adj* resignado; ***we have become ~ to the fact that …*** nos hemos resignado a aceptar que …
re•sil•i•ence [rɪ'zɪlɪəns] *of personality* fortaleza *f*; *of material* resistencia *f*
re•sil•ient [rɪ'zɪlɪənt] *adj personality* fuerte; *material* resistente
res•in ['rezɪn] resina *f*
res•in•ous ['rezɪnəs] *adj* resinoso
re•sist [rɪ'zɪst] **I** *v/t* resistir; *new measures* oponer resistencia a **II** *v/i* resistir
re•sist•ance [rɪ'zɪstəns] resistencia *f*
re•sis•tant [rɪ'zɪstənt] *adj material* resistente; ***~ to heat / rust*** resistente al calor / a la oxidación
re•sis•tor [rɪ'zɪstər] ELEC resistencia *f*
re•sit *Br* EDU **I** *v/t* (*pret & pp* ***-sat***) [riː'sɪt] *exam* presentarse de nuevo a **II** *n* ['riːsɪt] repesca *f*, exámen *m* de recuperación
re•sole [riː'soʊl] *v/t* poner suela a
res•o•lute ['rezəluːt] *adj* resuelto
res•o•lu•tion [rezə'luːʃn] **1** resolución *f* **2** *made at New Year etc* propósito *m*
re•solve [rɪ'zɑːlv] *v/t* **1** *problem, mystery* resolver **2**: ***~ to do sth*** resolver hacer algo
res•o•nance ['rezənəns] resonancia *f*
res•o•nant ['rezənənt] *adj* **1** PHYS, *voice, sound* resonante **2**: ***be ~ of sth*** *lit* recordar a algo
re•sort [rɪ'zɔːrt] **1** *place* centro *m* turístico **2**: ***as a last ~*** como último recurso
◆ **resort to** *v/t violence, threats* recurrir a
◆ **re•sound with** [rɪ'zaʊnd] *v/t* resonar con
re•sound•ing [rɪ'zaʊndɪŋ] *adj success, victory* clamoroso
re•source [rɪ'sɔːrs] recurso *m*
re•source•ful [rɪ'sɔːrsfəl] *adj person* lleno de recursos; *attitude, approach* ingenioso
re•spect [rɪ'spekt] **I** *n* **1** respeto *m*; ***show ~ to*** mostrar respeto hacia; ***have ~ for*** respetar; ***have no ~ for*** no respetar en absoluto; ***out of ~ for*** por respeto hacia; ***pay one's last ~s to s.o.*** decir el último adiós a alguien
2: ***with ~ to*** con respecto a; ***in this / that ~*** en cuanto a esto / eso, en este / ese respecto; ***in some / many ~s*** en algunos / muchos aspectos

II *v/t* respetar
re•spect•a•bil•i•ty [rɪspektə'bɪlətɪ] respetabilidad *f*
re•spect•a•ble [rɪ'spektəbl] *adj* respetable
re•spect•a•bly [rɪ'spektəblɪ] *adv* respetablemente
re•spect•ful [rɪ'spektfəl] *adj* respetuoso
re•spect•ful•ly [rɪ'spektfəlɪ] *adv* respetuosamente, con respeto
re•spec•tive [rɪ'spektɪv] *adj* respectivo
re•spec•tive•ly [rɪ'spektɪvlɪ] *adv* respectivamente
res•pi•ra•tion [respɪ'reɪʃn] respiración *f*
res•pi•ra•tor [respɪ'reɪtər] MED respirador *m*
res•pi•ra•to•ry [rɪ'spɪrətɔːrɪ] *adj* respiratorio; **~ *tract*** ANAT vía *f* respiratoria; **~ *failure*** MED insuficiencia *f* respiratoria
res'pi•ra•to•ry sys•tem aparato *m* respiratorio
re•spite ['respaɪt] respiro *m*; ***without ~*** sin respiro
re•splend•ent [rɪ'splendənt] *adj* resplandeciente
re•spond [rɪ'spɑːnd] *v/i* responder
re•spond•ent [rɪ'spɑːndənt] **1** LAW demandado(-a) *m(f)* **2** *to questionnaire* encuestado(-a) *m(f)*
re•sponse [rɪ'spɑːns] respuesta *f*; ***in ~ to your letter of*** en respuesta a su carta de
re•spon•si•bil•i•ty [rɪspɑːnsɪ'bɪlətɪ] responsabilidad *f*; ***accept ~ for*** aceptar responsabilidad de; ***a job with more ~*** un trabajo con más responsabilidad
re•spon•si•ble [rɪ'spɑːnsəbl] *adj* reponsable (***for*** de); *job* de responsabilidad
re•spon•sive [rɪ'spɑːnsɪv] *adj brakes* que responde bien; ***a ~ audience*** una audiencia que muestra interés
re•spray [riː'spreɪ] *v/t* volver a pintar
rest[1] [rest] **I** *n* descanso *m*; ***he needs a ~*** necesita descansar; ***set s.o.'s mind at ~*** tranquilizar a alguien **II** *v/i* **1** descansar; **~ *on*** *of theory*, *box* apoyarse en **2**: ***it all ~s with him*** todo depende de él **III** *v/t* (*lean, balance*) apoyar
rest[2] [rest] *n*: ***the ~*** el resto
re•start [riː'stɑːrt] **I** *v/t computer, talks* reiniciar; *engine* volver a arrancar **II** *v/i* reiniciarse; *of engine* volver a arrancar
res•tau•rant ['restrɑːnt] restaurante *m*
'res•tau•rant car vagón *m or* coche *m* restaurante
res•tau•ra•teur [restɔːræ'tɜːr] hostelero(-a) *m(f)*
'rest cure cura *f* de reposo *or* descanso
rest•ful ['restfəl] *adj* tranquilo, relajante
'rest home residencia *f* de ancianos
rest•ing place ['restɪŋ]: (***last***) **~** última morada *f*
res•ti•tu•tion [restɪ'tjuːʃn] restitución *f*
res•tive ['restɪv] *adj* inquieto
res•tive•ness ['restɪvnɪs] inquietud *f*
rest•less ['restlɪs] *adj* inquieto; ***have a ~ night*** pasar una mala noche
rest•less•ly ['restlɪslɪ] *adv* sin descanso
re•stock [riː'stɑːk] *v/t farm* llenar de reservas; *shelves, store* reabastecer
res•to•ra•tion [restə'reɪʃn] restauración *f*
re•store [rɪ'stɔːr] *v/t* **1** *building etc* restaurar **2** (*bring back*) devolver
re•stor•er [rɪ'stɔːrər] **1** *of painting, building* restaurador(a) *m(f)* **2** *for hair* regenerador *m*
re•strain [rɪ'streɪn] *v/t* contener; **~ *o.s.*** contenerse
re•strained [rɪ'streɪnd] *adj behavior* comedido; *color* sobrio
re•straint [rɪ'streɪnt] (*moderation*) moderación *f*, comedimiento *m*
re•strict [rɪ'strɪkt] *v/t* restringir, limitar; ***I'll ~ myself to ...*** me limitaré a ...
re•strict•ed [rɪ'strɪktɪd] *adj view* limitado
re•strict•ed 'ar•e•a MIL zona *f* de acceso restringido
re•stric•tion [rɪ'strɪkʃn] restricción *f*, limitación *f*; ***place ~s on s.o.*** imponer restricciones *or* limitaciones a alguien
re•stric•tive [rɪ'strɪktɪv] *adj* restrictivo
'rest room aseo *m*, servicios *mpl*
re•struc•ture [riː'strʌktʃər] *v/t* reestructurar
re•struc•tur•ing [riː'strʌktʃərɪŋ] reestructuración *f*
re•sult [rɪ'zʌlt] *n* **1** resultado *m*; ***as a ~ of this*** como resultado de esto **2** *in exam* nota *f*; ***she got good ~s*** ha sacado buenas notas
◆ **result from** *v/t* resultar de
◆ **result in** *v/t* tener como resultado
re•sume [rɪ'zuːm] **I** *v/t* reanudar **II** *v/i* continuar

ré•su•mé ['rezʊmeɪ] currículum *m* (vitae)
re•sump•tion [rɪ'zʌmpʃn] reanudación *f*
re•sur•face [riː'sɜːrfɪs] **I** *v/t roads* volver a asfaltar **II** *v/i* (*reappear*) reaparecer
re•sur•gence [rɪ'sɜːrdʒəns] resurgimiento *m*
re•sur•gent [rɪ'sɜːrdʒənt] *adj* resurgente
res•ur•rect [rezə'rekt] *v/t custom, old problem etc* resucitar
res•ur•rec•tion [rezə'rekʃn] REL resurrección *f*
re•sus•ci•tate [rɪ'sʌsɪteɪt] *v/t* resucitar, revivir
re•sus•ci•ta•tion [rɪsʌsɪ'teɪʃn] resucitación *f*
re•tail ['riːteɪl] **I** *adv*: ***sell sth ~*** vender algo al por menor **II** *v/i*: ***it retails at ...*** su precio de venta al público es de ...
re•tail•er ['riːteɪlər] minorista *m/f*
're•tail out•let punto *m* de venta; **'re•tail park** *Br* centro *m* comercial; **'re•tail price** precio *m* de venta al público; **re•tail 'price in•dex** índice *m* de precios al consumo
re•tain [rɪ'teɪn] *v/t* conservar; *heat* retener
re•tain•er [rɪ'teɪnər] FIN anticipo *m*
re•take [riː'teɪk] **I** *v/t* (*pret* ***-took***, *pp* ***-taken***) **1** MIL recuperar **2** *TV etc*: *scene etc* volver a filmar **3** EDU: *exam* volver a presentarse a **II** *n of scene* toma *f* nueva
re•tal•i•ate [rɪ'tælɪeɪt] *v/i* tomar represalias
re•tal•i•a•tion [rɪtælɪ'eɪʃn] represalias *fpl*; ***in ~ for*** como represalia por
re•tal•i•a•to•ry [rɪ'tælɪətɔːrɪ] *adj* en represalia
re•tard•ed [rɪ'tɑːrdɪd] *adj mentally* retrasado mental
retch [retʃ] *v/i* tener arcadas
re•ten•tion [rɪ'tenʃn] (*keeping*) conservación *f*; *of information, body fluids* retención *f*; ***powers*** *pl* ***of ~*** poder *m* de retención
re•ten•tive [rɪ'tentɪv] *adj memory* retentivo
re•think [riː'θɪŋk] *v/t* (*pret & pp* ***-thought***) replantear
re•ti•cence ['retɪsns] reserva *f*
re•ti•cent ['retɪsnt] *adj* reservado
ret•i•na ['retɪnə] ANAT retina *f*
ret•i•nue ['retɪnjuː] comitiva *f*
re•tire [rɪ'taɪr] *v/i* **1** *from work, with pension* jubilarse; *of soldier, admiral, sportsman, from politics* retirarse **2** *from race* retirarse **3** *fml*: *to bed* retirarse
re•tired [rɪ'taɪrd] *adj with pension* jubilado; *soldier, sportsman etc* retirado
re•ti•ree [rɪtaɪ'riː] jubilado(-a) *m(f)*, pensionista *m/f*
re•tire•ment [rɪ'taɪrmənt] *with pension* jubilación *f*; *of soldier, admiral etc* retiro *m*; *of sportsman, from politics etc* retirada *f*
re'tire•ment age edad *f* de jubilación
re•tir•ing [rɪ'taɪrɪŋ] *adj* retraído, reservado
re•tort[1] [rɪ'tɔːrt] **I** *n* réplica *f* **II** *v/t* replicar
re•tort[2] [rɪ'tɔːrt] *n* CHEM retorta *f*
re•touch [riː'tʌtʃ] *v/t* PHOT retocar
re•trace [rɪ'treɪs] *v/t*: ***they ~d their footsteps*** volvieron sobre sus pasos
re•tract [rɪ'trækt] *v/t* **1** *claws* retraer; *undercarriage* replegar **2** *statement* retirar
re•tract•a•ble [rɪ'træktəbl] *adj undercarriage* replegable
re•trac•tion [rɪ'trækʃn] **1** *of claws* retracción *f*, *of undercarriage* repliegue *m* **2** *of statement* retractación *f*
retrain [riː'treɪn] *v/i* reciclarse
re•train•ing [riː'treɪnɪŋ] reciclaje *m*; ***~ course*** curso *m* de reciclaje
re•tread ['riːtred] neumático *m* recauchutado
re•treat [rɪ'triːt] **I** *v/i* retirarse **II** *n* **1** MIL retirada *f* **2** *place* retiro *m*
re•trench [rɪ'trentʃ] *v/i* recortar gastos
re•tri•al ['riːtraɪəl] LAW nuevo juicio *m*
ret•ri•bu•tion [retrɪ'bjuːʃn] represalias *fpl*
re•triev•al [rɪ'triːvl] recuperación *f*; ***beyond ~*** *situation, work* irreparable
re•trieve [rɪ'triːv] *v/t* recuperar
re•triev•er [rɪ'triːvər] *dog* perro *m* cobrador
ret•ro•ac•tive [retroʊ'æktɪv] *adj law etc* retroactivo
ret•ro•ac•tive•ly [retroʊ'æktɪvlɪ] *adv* con retroactividad
ret•ro•grade ['retrəgreɪd] *adj move, decision* retrógrado
ret•ro•gres•sive [retrə'gresɪv] *adj* re-

trógrado
ret•ro•spect ['retrəspekt]: ***in ~*** en retrospectiva
ret•ro•spec•tive [retrə'spektɪv] **I** *n* retrospectiva *f* **II** *adj* retrospectivo
ret•ro•spec•tive•ly [retrə'spektɪvlɪ] *adv* retrospectivamente
ret•ro•vi•rus ['retroʊvaɪrəs] MED retrovirus *m inv*
re•try [riː'traɪ] **I** *v/t* LAW volver a juzgar **II** *v/i* COMPUT intentar de nuevo
re•turn [rɪ'tɜːrn] **I** *n* **1** *to a place* vuelta *f*, regreso *m*; ***on his ~*** a su vuelta
2 (*giving back*) devolución *f*; ***in ~ for*** a cambio de; ***by ~*** (***of post***) a vuelta de correo
3 COMPUT retorno *m*
4 *in tennis* resto *m*
5 (*profit*) rendimiento *m*; ***~ on capital / on investment*** rendimiento del capital / de la inversión
6 *Br ticket* billete *m or L.Am.* boleto *m* de ida y vuelta
7: ***many happy ~s*** (***of the day***) feliz cumpleaños
II *v/t* devolver; (*put back*) volver a colocar; ***~ to sender*** devolver al remitente
III *v/i* (*go back*, *come back*) volver, regresar; *of good times*, *doubts etc* volver
re•turn•a•ble [rɪ'tɜːrnəbl] *adj*: ***the books are ~ within …*** hay que devolver los libros en …
re•turn 'flight vuelo *m* de vuelta; **re•turn 'jour•ney** viaje *m* de vuelta; **re'turn key** COMPUT tecla *f* (de) retorno
re•u•ni•fi•ca•tion [riːjuːnɪfɪ'keɪʃn] reunificación *f*
re•u•ni•fy [riː'juːnɪfaɪ] *v/t* (*pret & pp* ***-ied***) reunificar
re•u•nion [riː'juːnjən] reunión *f*
re•u•nite [riːjuː'naɪt] *v/t* reunir
re•us•a•ble [riː'juːzəbl] *adj* reutilizable
re•use [riː'juːz] *v/t* reutilizar
rev [rev] revolución *f*; ***~s per minute*** revoluciones por minuto
◆ **rev up** *v/t* (*pret & pp* ***-ved***) *engine* revolucionar
re•val•u•a•tion [riːvæljʊ'eɪʃn] revaluación *f*
re•vamp ['riːvæmp] *v/t* renovar
re•veal [rɪ'viːl] *v/t* (*make visible*) revelar; (*make known*) revelar, desvelar
re•veal•ing [rɪ'viːlɪŋ] *adj remark* revelador; *dress* insinuante, atrevido
◆ **rev•el in** ['revl] *v/t* (*pret & pp* ***-ed***, *Br* ***-led***) deleitarse con; ***like it?, he revels in it*** ¿que si le gusta?, le encanta
rev•e•la•tion [revə'leɪʃn] revelación *f*
rev•el•er ['revələr] juerguista *m/f*
rev•el•ry ['revlrɪ] jolgorio *m*
re•venge [rɪ'vendʒ] venganza *f*, ***take one's ~*** vengarse; ***in ~ for*** como venganza por
re•venge•ful [rɪ'vendʒfʊl] *adj* vengativo
rev•e•nue ['revənuː] ingresos *mpl*
re•ver•ber•ate [rɪ'vɜːrbəreɪt] *v/i of sound* reverberar
re•ver•ber•a•tion [rɪvɜːrbə'reɪʃn] reverberación *f*
re•vere [rɪ'vɪr] *v/t* reverenciar
rev•er•ence ['revərəns] reverencia *f*
Rev•er•end ['revərənd] REL Reverendo *m*
rev•er•ent ['revərənt] *adj* reverente
rev•er•en•tial [revə'renʃl] *adj* reverente
rev•er•ie ['revərɪ] ensoñación *f*
re•ver•sal [rɪ'vɜːrsl] *of decision* revocación *f*, *of sequence* inversión *f*, ***suffer a ~*** sufrir un revés
re•verse [rɪ'vɜːrs] **I** *adj sequence* inverso; ***in ~ order*** en orden inverso **II** *n* **1** (*back*) dorso *m* **2** MOT marcha *f* atrás **3**: ***the ~*** (*the opposite*) lo contrario **III** *v/t* **1** *sequence* invertir **2**: ***~ a vehicle*** hacer marcha atrás con un vehículo **IV** *v/i* MOT hacer marcha atrás
◆ **reverse out** *v/t in printing* invertir
re•vers•i•ble [rɪ'vɜːrsəbl] *adj* **1** *n garment* reversible **2** *decision* revocable
re•vert [rɪ'vɜːrt] *v/i*: ***~ to*** volver a
re•view [rɪ'vjuː] **I** *n* **1** *of book*, *movie* reseña *f*, crítica *f* **2** *of troops* revista *f* **3** *of situation etc* revisión *f* **II** *v/t* **1** *book*, *movie* reseñar, hacer una crítica de **2** *troops* pasar revista a **3** *situation etc* revisar; EDU repasar
re•view•er [rɪ'vjuːər] *of book*, *movie* crítico(-a) *m*(*f*)
re•vise [rɪ'vaɪz] *v/t opinion*, *text* revisar
re•vi•sion [rɪ'vɪʒn] *of opinion*, *text* revisión *f*
re•vi•tal•ize [riː'vaɪtəlaɪz] *v/t* revitalizar
re•viv•al [rɪ'vaɪvl] **1** *of custom*, *old style etc* resurgimiento *m* **2** *of patient* reanimación *f*
re•vive [rɪ'vaɪv] **I** *v/t* **1** *custom*, *old style etc* hacer resurgir **2** *patient* reanimar **II**

R

v/i of business, exchange rate etc reactivarse
rev•o•ca•ble let•ter of cred•it [rɪ'voukəbəl] carta *f* de crédito revocable
re•voice [riː'vɔɪs] *v/t movie* doblar
re•voke [rɪ'vouk] *v/t law* derogar; *license* revocar
re•volt [rɪ'voult] **I** *n* rebelión *f* **II** *v/i* rebelarse
re•volt•ing [rɪ'voultɪŋ] *adj* (*disgusting*) repugnante
rev•o•lu•tion [revə'luːʃn] **1** POL revolución *f* **2** (*turn*) vuelta *f*, revolución *f*
rev•o•lu•tion•ar•y [revə'luːʃnerɪ] **I** *n* POL revolucionario(-a) *m*(*f*) **II** *adj* revolucionario
rev•o•lu•tion•ize [revə'luːʃnaɪz] *v/t* revolucionar
re•volve [rɪ'vɑːlv] *v/i* girar (***around*** en torno a)
re•volv•er [rɪ'vɑːlvər] revólver *m*
re•volv•ing door [rɪ'vɑːlvɪŋ] puerta *f* giratoria
re•volv•ing let•ter of cred•it carta *f* de crédito renovable
re•vue [rɪ'vjuː] THEA revista *f*
re•vul•sion [rɪ'vʌlʃn] repugnancia *f*
re•ward [rɪ'wɔːrd] **I** *n* recompensa *f* **II** *v/t financially* recompensar
re•ward•ing [rɪ'wɔːrdɪŋ] *adj experience* gratificante
re•wind [riː'waɪnd] *v/t* (*pret & pp* ***-wound***) *film, tape* rebobinar
re•wire [riː'waɪər] *v/t* cambiar la instalación eléctrica de
re•word [riː'wɜːrd] *v/t* reformular
re•write [riː'raɪt] *v/t* (*pret* ***-wrote***, *pp* ***-written***) reescribir, volver a escribir
re•write•a•ble [riː'raɪtəbl] *adj CD etc* regrabable
rhap•so•dy ['ræpsədɪ] MUS rapsodia *f*; ***go into rhapsodies*** *fig* deshacerse en elogios (***about, over*** sobre)
rhe•sus fac•tor ['riːsəs] MED factor *m* Rh
rhe•to•ric ['retərɪk] retórica *f*
rhe•to•ric•al ques•tion [rɪ'tɑːrɪkl] pregunta *f* retórica
rheu•mat•ic [ruː'mætɪk] *adj* reumático; ***~ fever*** fiebre *f* reumática
rheu•ma•tism ['ruːmətɪzm] reumatismo *m*
rhi•no ['raɪnou] rinoceronte *m*
rhi•no•ce•ros [raɪ'nɑːsərəs] rinoceronte *m*
rhi•no•plas•ty ['raɪnouplæstɪ] rinoplastia *f*
rho•do•den•dron [roudə'dendrən] BOT rododendro *m*
rhom•bus ['rɑːmbəs] (*pl* ***-buses, rhombi*** ['rɑːmbaɪ]) MATH rombo *m*
rhu•barb ['ruːbɑːrb] ruibarbo *m*
rhyme [raɪm] **I** *n* rima *f*; ***do sth without ~ or reason*** hacer algo sin venir a cuento; ***there's no ~ or reason to it*** no tiene ni pies ni cabeza **II** *v/i* rimar
rhythm ['rɪðm] ritmo *m*; ***~ and blues*** MUS rhythm and blues *m*
rhyth•mic, rhyth•mi•cal ['rɪðmɪk(l)] *adj* rítmico
rib [rɪb] ANAT costilla *f*
rib•bon ['rɪbən] cinta *f*
'rib cage ANAT caja *f* torácica
rice [raɪs] arroz *m*
'rice pad•dy arrozal *m*; **'rice pa•per** papel *m* de arroz; **rice 'pud•ding** *Br* arroz *m* con leche
rich [rɪʧ] **I** *adj* **1** (*wealthy*) rico **2** *food*: *con mucha grasa o azúcar*; ***it's too ~*** es muy pesado **3**: ***~ in vitamin C*** rico en vitamina C **4** F: ***that's ~!*** ¡genial!; ***it's ~ that they are now …*** tiene gracia que ahora sean ellos los que … **II** *npl*: ***the ~*** los ricos
rich•es ['rɪʧɪz] *npl* riquezas *fpl*
rich•ly ['rɪʧlɪ] *adv*: ***be ~ deserved*** ser muy merecido
rich•ness ['rɪʧnɪs] (*wealth*) riqueza *f*
rick•ets ['rɪkɪts] *nsg* MED raquitismo *m*
rick•et•y ['rɪkətɪ] *adj* desvencijado
ric•o•chet ['rɪkəʃeɪ] *v/i* rebotar
rid [rɪd]: ***get ~ of*** deshacerse de
rid•dance ['rɪdns] F: ***good ~ to her!*** ¡espero no volver a verla nunca!
rid•den ['rɪdn] *pp* ☞ ***ride***
rid•dle ['rɪdl] **I** *n* acertijo *m* **II** *v/t*: ***be ~d with*** estar lleno de
ride [raɪd] **I** *n on horse, in vehicle* paseo *m*, vuelta *f*, (*journey*) viaje *m*; ***do you want a ~ into town?*** ¿quieres que te lleve al centro?; ***take s.o. for a ~*** F tomar el pelo a alguien
II *v/t* (*pret* ***rode***, *pp* ***ridden***) *horse* montar a; *bike* montar en
III *v/i* (*pret* ***rode***, *pp* ***ridden***) **1** *on horse* montar; ***can you ~?*** ¿sabes montar?; ***those who were riding at the back of the bus*** los que iban en la parte

R

de atrás del autobús **2**: ***let sth ~*** dejar algo estar; ***there's a lot riding on this*** hay muchas cosas que dependen de ello

◆ **ride up** *v/i of skirt etc* subirse

rid•er ['raɪdər] *on horse* jinete *m*, amazona *f*; *on bicycle* ciclista *m/f*; *on motorbike* motorista *m/f*

ridge [rɪdʒ] *raised strip* borde *m*; *of mountain* cresta *f*; *of roof* caballete *m*

rid•i•cule ['rɪdɪkjuːl] **I** *n* burlas *fpl* **II** *v/t* ridiculizar, poner en ridículo

ri•dic•u•lous [rɪ'dɪkjʊləs] *adj* ridículo

ri•dic•u•lous•ly [rɪ'dɪkjʊləslɪ] *adv expensive, difficult* terriblemente; ***it's ~ easy*** es facilísimo

rid•ing ['raɪdɪŋ] *on horseback* equitación *f*

'rid•ing boots *npl* botas *fpl* de montar; **rid•ing breech•es** ['raɪdɪŋbrɪtʃəs] *npl* pantalones *mpl* de montar; **'rid•ing school** escuela *f* de equitación

rife [raɪf] *adj*: ***~ with*** *disease, corruption, in-fighting* plagado de; ***crime is ~*** impera el crimen

riff [rɪf] MUS riff *m*

riff•raff ['rɪfræf] gentuza *f*

ri•fle ['raɪfl] rifle *m*

◆ **rifle through** *v/t* rebuscar en

'ri•fle range campo *m* de tiro

rift [rɪft] **1** *in earth* grieta *f* **2** *in party etc* escisión *f*

rig [rɪg] **I** *n* **1** (*oil ~*) plataforma *f* petrolífera **2** (*truck*) camión *m* **II** *v/t* (*pret & pp* ***-ged***) *elections* amañar

◆ **rig up** *v/t* montar

rig•ging ['rɪgɪŋ] NAUT cordaje *m*

right [raɪt] **I** *adj* **1** (*correct*) correcto; ***it's not ~ to treat people like that*** no está bien tratar así a la gente; ***it's the ~ thing to do*** es lo que hay que hacer; ***be ~*** *of answer* estar correcto; *of person* tener razón; *of clock* ir bien; ***put things ~*** arreglar las cosas; ***that's ~!*** ¡eso es!
2 (*suitable*) adecuado, apropiado
3 (*not left*) derecho
4: ***that's all ~*** *doesn't matter* no te preocupes; *when s.o. says thank you* de nada; *is quite good* está bastante bien; ***I'm all ~*** *not hurt* estoy bien; *have got enough* no, gracias; ***all ~, that's enough!*** ¡ahora sí que ya está bien! ☞ ***alright***
II *adv* **1** (*directly*) justo; ***~ now*** ahora mismo; ***they arrived ~ after me*** llegaron justo después de mí; ***I'll be ~ back*** vuelvo ahora mismo; ***it broke ~ down the middle*** se rompio justo por la mitad
2 (*correctly*) correctamente
3 (*not left*) a la derecha
4 (*completely*) completamente; ***he broke it ~ off*** lo rompió por completo; ***it goes ~ around the house*** va alrededor de toda la casa; ***~ back in 1982*** allá en 1982; ***~!, that does it!*** ¡hasta aquí hemos llegado!
III *n* **1** *civil, legal etc* derecho *m* **2** *not left*, POL derecha *f*; ***on the ~*** *also* POL a la derecha; ***turn to the ~, take a ~*** gira a la derecha **3**: ***be in the ~*** tener razón; ***know ~ from wrong*** distinguir lo que está bien de lo que está mal

right-'an•gle ángulo *m* recto; ***at ~s to*** en *or* formando ángulo recto con

right-an•gled ['raɪtæŋgld] *adj* rectángulo

◆ **right-click on** *v/t* cliquear con el botón derecho en

right•eous ['raɪtʃəs] *adj* **1** *person* honrado **2** *anger* justificado

right•ful ['raɪtfəl] *adj heir, owner etc* legítimo

'right-hand *adj*: ***on the ~ side*** a mano derecha; **right-hand 'drive** MOT vehículo *m* con el volante a la derecha; **right-hand•ed** [raɪt'hændɪd] *adj person* diestro; **right-hand•er** [raɪt'hændər] diestro(-a) *m*(*f*); **right-hand 'man** mano *f* derecha

right•ly ['raɪtlɪ] *adv* (*correctly*) correctamente; (*justifiably*) justificadamente; *accuse, complain* con (toda la) razón; *assume* con toda seguridad; ***~ or wrongly*** para bien o para mal; ***I don't ~ know*** F no sé muy bien; ***I can't ~ say*** F no puedo decir

right of 'way *in traffic* preferencia *f*; *across land* derecho *m* de paso

'rights is•sue FIN emisión *f* con derechos para los accionistas

right 'wing POL derecha *f*; SP banda *f* derecha; **right-'wing** *adj* POL de derechas; **right-'wing•er** POL derechista *m/f*; **right-wing ex'trem•ism** POL extremismo *m* de derechas

rig•id ['rɪdʒɪd] *adj* rígido

ri•gid•i•ty [rɪ'dʒɪdɪtɪ] rigidez *f*

rig•ma•role ['rɪgmərooul] F engorro *m*
rig•or ['rɪgər] *of discipline* rigor *m*; ***the ~s of the winter*** los rigores del invierno
rig•or mor•tis [rɪgər'mɔːrtɪs] MED rigor *m* mortis
rig•or•ous ['rɪgərəs] *adj* riguroso
rig•or•ous•ly ['rɪgərəslɪ] *adv check, examine* rigurosamente
rig•our *Br* ☞ ***rigor***
rile [raɪl] *v/t* F fastidiar, *Span* mosquear F
rim [rɪm] *of wheel* llanta *f*; *of cup* borde *m*; *of eye glasses* montura *f*
rind [raɪnd] *on bacon, cheese* corteza *f*
ring[1] [rɪŋ] *n* **1** (*circle*) círculo *m* **2** *on finger* anillo *m* **3** *in boxing* cuadrilátero *m*, ring *m*; *at circus* pista *f*
ring[2] [rɪŋ] **I** *n of bell* timbrazo *m*; *of voice* tono *m*; ***give s.o. a ~*** *Br* TELEC dar un telefonazo a alguien; ***that has a familiar ~ to it*** me suena; ***have a hollow ~*** no sonar muy convincente
II *v/t* (*pret* ***rang***, *pp* ***rung***) *bell* hacer sonar, tocar; *doorbell* tocar
III *v/i* (*pret* ***rang***, *pp* ***rung***) *of bell* sonar; ***please ~ for attention*** toque el timbre para que lo atiendan; ***~ing tone*** TELEC tono *m* de llamada
◆ **ring back** *v/t & v/i Br* llamar más tarde, volver a llamar
◆ **ring in** *v/i Br* llamar
◆ **ring off** *v/i Br* colgar
◆ **ring out** *v/i of bell, voice* resonar
◆ **ring up** *v/t & v/i Br* llamar (por teléfono)
'ring bind•er bloc *m* de anillas; **'ring-fence** *v/t fig: make secure* proteger; **'ring fin•ger** dedo *m* anular; **'ring-lead•er** cabecilla *m/f*; **'ring-pull** anilla *f*; **'ring road** *Br* carretera *f* de circunvalación; **'ring•side**: ***at the ~*** *in boxing* en primera fila; ***~ seat*** asiento *m* de primera fila
rink [rɪŋk] pista *f* de patinaje
rinse [rɪns] **I** *n for hair color* reflejo *m* **II** *v/t* aclarar
ri•ot ['raɪət] **I** *n* disturbio *m*; ***read s.o. the ~ act*** cantar a alguien las cuarenta; ***run ~*** *of kids, the imagination* desbocarse **II** *v/i* causar disturbios
ri•ot•er ['raɪətər] alborotador(a) *m(f)*
ri•ot•ous ['raɪətəs] *adj* **1** *behavior, crowd* descontrolado **2**: ***we had a ~ time*** nos lo pasamos de maravilla
ri•ot•ous•ly ['raɪətəslɪ] *adv*: ***it was ~ funny*** era desternillante
'ri•ot po•lice policía *f* antidisturbios
rip [rɪp] **I** *n in cloth etc* rasgadura *f* **II** *v/t* (*pret & pp* ***-ped***) *cloth etc* rasgar; ***~ sth open*** romper algo rasgándolo
◆ **rip apart** *v/t also fig* destrozar
◆ **rip off** *v/t* F *customers* robar F, clavar F; (*cheat*) timar
◆ **rip up** *v/t letter, sheet* hacer pedazos
'rip cord cordón *m* de apertura
ripe [raɪp] *adj fruit* maduro
rip•en ['raɪpn] *v/i of fruit* madurar
ripe•ness ['raɪpnɪs] *of fruit* madurez *f*
'rip-off F **1** *n* robo *m* F; ***the concert was a ~*** el concierto fue un timo **II** *adj*: ***~ prices*** precios *mpl* escandalosos
rip•ple ['rɪpl] *on water* onda *f*
rise [raɪz] **I** *v/i* (*pret* ***rose***, *pp* ***risen***) **1** *from chair etc* levantarse **2** *of sun* salir; *of rocket* ascender, subir **3** *of price, temperature, water* subir **II** *n* **1** *in price, temperature* subida *f*, aumento *m*; *in water level* subida *f*, *Br*: *in salary* aumento *m* **2**: ***give ~ to*** dar pie a
ris•en ['rɪzn] *pp* ☞ ***rise***
ris•er ['raɪzər]: ***be an early ~*** ser un madrugador; ***be a late ~*** levantarse tarde
ris•ing ['raɪzɪŋ] **I** *n* (*rebellion*) revuelta *f* **II** *adj* **1** *generation* venidera **2** *politician etc* en alza; ***a ~ star in the company*** un valor en alza en la empresa
risk [rɪsk] **I** *n* riesgo *m*, peligro *m*; ***take a ~*** arriesgarse; ***put sth at ~*** poner algo en peligro; ***run the ~ of doing sth*** correr el riesgo de hacer algo **II** *v/t* arriesgar; ***let's ~ it*** arriesguémonos
'risk a•nal•y•sis análisis *m inv* de riesgos; **'risk man•age•ment** gestión *f* de riesgos; **'risk-tak•er**: ***he's a ~*** le gusta tomar riesgos
risk•y ['rɪskɪ] *adj* arriesgado
ri•sot•to [rɪ'zɑːtoʊ] risotto *m*
ris•qué [rɪ'skeɪ] *adj* subido de tono
ris•sole ['rɪsoʊl] GASTR *bola frita de carne o pescado*
rite [raɪt] rito *m*; ***perform the last ~s over s.o.*** REL administrar la extrema unción a alguien
rit•u•al ['rɪtʃʊəl] **I** *n* ritual *m* **II** *adj* ritual
rit•u•al•ist•ic [rɪtʃʊə'lɪstɪk] *adj* ritualista
ritz•y ['rɪtsɪ] *adj* F lujoso
ri•val ['raɪvl] **I** *n* rival *m/f* **II** *v/t* (*pret & pp*

-ed**, Br **-led**)* rivalizar con; ***I can't ~ that no puedo rivalizar con eso
ri•val•ry ['raɪvlrɪ] rivalidad *f*
riv•er ['rɪvər] río *m*
'riv•er•bank ribera *f*; **'riv•er•bed** lecho *m*; **Riv•er 'Plate**: ***the ~*** el Río de la Plata; **'riv•er•side I** *adj* a la orilla del río **II** *n* ribera *f*, orilla *f* del río
riv•et ['rɪvɪt] **I** *n* remache *m* **II** *v/t* remachar; ***~ sth to sth*** unir algo a algo con remaches
riv•et•ing ['rɪvɪtɪŋ] *adj* fascinante
RNA [ɑːren'eɪ] *abbr* (= ***ribonucleic acid***) ARN *m* (= ácido *m* ribonucleico)
roach [roʊʧ] F *insect* cucaracha *f*
road [roʊd] *in country* carretera *f*; *in city* calle *f*; ***it's just down the ~*** está muy cerca; ***be on the ~*** *traveling* estar de viaje; *of theater group* estar de gira; ***when we get our car back on the ~*** cuando el coche vuelva a funcionar; ***the car's been off the ~ for a year*** hace un año que no conducimos el coche; ***let's get this project on the ~*** F pongamos este proyecto en marcha; ***on the ~ to recovery*** en vías de recuperación; ***and one more for the ~*** F y la penúltima (copa); ***be on the right ~*** *fig* ir por el bueno camino; ***hit the ~*** F largarse
'road ac•ci•dent accidente *m* de carretera; **'road•block** control *m* de carretera; **'road hog** *conductor(a) temerario(-a)*; **'road-hold•ing** *of vehicle* adherencia *f*, agarre *m*; **'road•house** taberna *f* (*al lado de la carretera*); **'road map** mapa *m* de carreteras; **'road noise** MOT ruido *m* de la carretera; **'road rage** *Br* cólera *f* al volante, agresividad *f* en la carretera; **'road re•pairs** *npl* obras *fpl*; **road 'safe•ty** seguridad *f* vial; **'road•show** exhibición *f* itinerante; **'road•side**: ***at the ~*** al borde de la carretera; **'road•sign** señal *f* de tráfico; **'road tax** impuesto *m* de circulación; **'road test** MOT prueba *f* en carretera; **'road-test** *v/t car* probar en carretera; **'road toll** peaje *m*; **road 'traf•fic ac•ci•dent** accidente *m* de tráfico por carretera; **'road us•er** usuario(-a) *m(f)* de las carreteras; **'road•way** calzada *f*; **'road•wor•thy** *adj* en condiciones de circular
roam [roʊm] *v/i* vagar
roar [rɔːr] **I** *n of traffic, engine* estruendo *m*; *of lion* rugido *m*; *of person* grito *m*, bramido *m* **II** *v/i of engine, lion* rugir; *of person* gritar, bramar; ***~ with laughter*** reírse a carcajadas
roar•ing ['rɔːrɪŋ] *adj*: ***~ success*** F éxito *m* clamoroso; ***~ drunk*** F borracho como una cuba F
roast [roʊst] **I** *n of beef etc* asado *m* **II** *v/t* asar **III** *v/i of food* asarse; ***we're ~ing*** nos estamos asando
roast 'beef rosbif *m*
roast•ing ['roʊstɪŋ] *adj* F *day, weather* abrasador; ***I'm ~*** me estoy asando
'roast•ing dish plato *m* para asar
roast 'pork cerdo *m* asado
rob [rɑːb] *v/t* (*pret & pp* **-bed**) *person* robar a; *bank* atracar, robar; ***I've been ~bed*** me han robado
rob•ber ['rɑːbər] atracador(a) *m(f)*
rob•ber•y ['rɑːbərɪ] atraco *m*, robo *m*
robe [roʊb] **1** *of judge* toga *f*; *of priest* sotana *f* **2** (*bath~*) bata *f*
rob•in ['rɑːbɪn] petirrojo *m*
ro•bot ['roʊbɑːt] robot *m*
ro•bust [roʊ'bʌst] *adj person, structure* robusto; *material* resistente; *defense* sólido; *attitude* firme; ***be in ~ health*** tener una salud de hierro
rock [rɑːk] **I** *n* **1** roca *f*; ***on the ~s*** *of drink* con hielo; ***their marriage is on the ~s*** su matrimonio está en crisis **2** MUS rock *m* **II** *v/t* **1** *baby* acunar; *cradle* mecer **2** (*surprise*) sorprender, impactar **III** *v/i on chair* mecerse; *of boat* balancearse
rock-and-'roll MUS rock and roll *m*; **'rock band** grupo *m* de rock; **rock 'bot•tom**: ***reach ~*** tocar fondo; **'rock-bot•tom** *adj prices* mínimo; **'rock climb•er** escalador(a) *m(f)*; **'rock climb•ing** escalada *f* (en roca)
rock•er ['rɑːkər] **1** (*rocking chair*) mecedora *f* **2** *Br*: *person* roquero(-a) *m(f)* **3**: ***off one's ~*** F pirado F
'rock•er arm MOT balancín *m*
rock•er•y ['rɑːkərɪ] jardín *m* de rocalla
rock•et ['rɑːkɪt] **I** *n* cohete *m*; ***give s.o. a ~*** F echar la bronca a alguien **II** *v/i of prices etc* dispararse
'rock•et sci•ence F: ***it's hardly ~!*** ¡no hace falta ser un genio!
'rock•et sci•en•tist F listillo(-a) *m(f)*, sabiondo(-a) *m(f)*

'rock face pared *f*; **'rock•fall** caída *f* de rocas; **'rock gar•den** jardín *m* de rocalla; **'rock-hard** *adj* duro como una piedra

rock•ing chair ['rɑːkɪŋ] mecedora *f*

'rock•ing horse caballito *m* de juguete

'rock mu•sic música *f* rock; **rock 'n' roll** [rɑːkn'roʊl] rock and roll *m*; **'rock salt** sal *f* gema; **rock-'sol•id** *adj structure*, *fig*: *support etc* sólido como una piedra; **'rock star** estrella *f* del rock

rock•y[1] ['rɑːkɪ] *adj beach*, *path* pedregoso

rock•y[2] ['rɑːkɪ] *adj* (*unsteady*) inestable

ro•co•co [rə'koʊkoʊ] rococó *m*

rod [rɑːd] **1** vara *f* **2** *for fishing* caña *f*

rode [roʊd] *pret* ☞ ***ride***

ro•dent ['roʊdnt] roedor *m*

ro•de•o ['roʊdɪoʊ] rodeo *m*

roe[1] [roʊ] *of fish* huevas *fpl*

roe[2] [roʊ] *deer* corzo *m*

'roe•buck corzo *m*

'roe deer corzo *m*

rog•er ['rɑːdʒər] *int* RAD recibido

rogue [roʊg] granuja *m/f*, bribón(-ona) *m(f)*

ROI *abbr* (= ***return on investment***) rendimiento *m* de la inversión

role [roʊl] papel *m*

'role mod•el ejemplo *m*; ***be a ~ for*** ser un modelo a seguir para; **'role play** juego *m* de roles; **role re'ver•sal** cambio *m* de papeles; **role-swap•ping** ['roʊlswɑːpɪŋ] intercambio *m* de papeles

roll [roʊl] **I** *n* **1** (*bread ~*) panecillo *m* **2** *of film* rollo *m* **3** *of thunder* retumbo *m* **4** (*list*, *register*) lista *f* **II** *v/i* **1** *of ball etc* rodar **2** *of boat* balancearse **III** *v/t* **1**: ***~ sth into a ball*** hacer una bola con algo **2**: ***~ sth along the ground*** hacer rodar algo por el suelo **3**: ***~ one's own*** liarse los cigarrillos

◆ **roll around** *v/i*: ***they were rolling around laughing*** F se desternillaban de risa

◆ **roll back** *v/t carpet etc* enrollar; ***if we could roll back the years*** si pudiéramos retroceder en el tiempo

◆ **roll down** *v/t shades* bajar

◆ **roll in** *v/i of contributions*, *letters* llover; F *of person* llegar

◆ **roll out** *v/t* **1** *pastry* extender **2** *new product* introducir

◆ **roll over I** *v/i* darse la vuelta **II** *v/t* **1** *person*, *object* dar la vuelta a **2** (*renew*) renovar; (*extend*) refinanciar

◆ **roll up I** *v/t sleeves* remangar **II** *v/i* F (*arrive*) llegar

'roll bar MOT barra *f* antivuelco

'roll call lista *f*; ***have a ~*** pasar lista

roll•er ['roʊlər] *for hair* rulo *m*

'roll•er blade® patín *m* en línea; **'roll•er blind** *Br* persiana *f*; **'roll•er coast•er** montaña *f* rusa; **'roll•er skate** patín *m* (de ruedas); **'roll•er-skate** *v/i* patinar (*sobre ruedas*); **'roll•er skat•er** patinador(a) *m(f)* (*sobre ruedas*); **'roll•er--skat•ing** patinaje *m* sobre ruedas; **'roll•er tow•el** toalla *f* de rodillo

roll•ing mill ['roʊlɪŋ] TECH laminadora *f*, laminador *m*; **'roll•ing pin** rodillo *m* de cocina; **'roll•ing stock** RAIL material *m* rodante

ROM [rɑːm] *abbr* (= ***read only memory***) COMPUT ROM *f* (= memoria *f* de sólo lectura)

Ro•man ['roʊmən] **I** *adj* romano **II** *n* romano(-a) *m(f)*

Ro•man 'Cath•o•lic I *n* REL católico(-a) *m(f)* romano(-a) **II** *adj* católico romano

ro•mance[1] [rə'mæns] *n* **1** (*affair*) aventura *f* (amorosa) **2** *novel* novela *f* rosa; *movie* película *f* romántica

Ro•mance[2] [rə'mæns] *adj language* romance, románico

Ro•man•esque [roʊmə'nesk] *adj* románico

Ro•ma•ni•a [ruː'meɪnɪə] Rumanía *f*

Ro•ma•ni•an [ruː'meɪnjən] **I** *adj* rumano **II** *n* **1** rumano(-a) *m(f)* **2** *language* rumano *m*

ro•man•tic [roʊ'mæntɪk] *adj* romántico

ro•man•tic•al•ly [roʊ'mæntɪklɪ] *adv*: ***be ~ involved with s.o.*** tener un romance con alguien

ro•man•ti•cism [roʊ'mæntɪsɪzəm] romanticismo *m*

ro•man•ti•cize [roʊ'mæntɪsaɪz] *v/t* idealizar

Rom•a•ny ['roʊmənɪ] **1** (*gypsy*) romaní *m/f* **2** *language* romaní *m*

Rome [roʊm] Roma *f*; ***~ was not built in a day*** Zamora no se ganó en una hora; ***all roads lead to ~*** todos los caminos llevan a Roma; ***when in ~ (do as the Romans do)*** allá donde fueres, haz lo que vieres

romp [rɑːmp] **I** *v/i* juguetear; **~ around** juguetear; **~ through** F *exam etc* pasar con mucha facilidad **II** *n*: **have a ~** juguetear

roof [ruːf] techo *m*, tejado *m*; **have a ~ over one's head** tener un techo donde dormir

'roof box caja *f* portaequipajes para baca; **'roof gar•den** azotea *f* con jardín; **'roof-rack** MOT baca *f*; **'roof•top** tejado *m*; **scream** *or* **shout sth from the ~s** *fig* proclamar algo a los cuatro vientos

rook[1] [rʊk] *v/t* F (*cheat*) camelar F

rook[2] [rʊk] *n in chess* torre *f*

rook•ie ['rʊkɪ] F novato(-a) *m(f)*

room [ruːm] **1** habitación *f* **2** (*space*) espacio *m*, sitio *m*; **there's no ~ for ...** no hay sitio para ..., no cabe ...; **leave little ~ for doubt as to ...** no dejar lugar a dudas de que ...

'room clerk recepcionista *m/f*

room•er ['ruːmər] húesped *m/f*

room•ing house ['ruːmɪŋ] pensión *f*

'room•mate *sharing room* compañero(-a) *m(f)* de habitación; *sharing apartment* compañero(-a) *m(f)* de apartamento; **'room ser•vice** servicio *m* de habitaciones; **room 'tem•per•a•ture** temperatura *f* ambiente

room•y ['ruːmɪ] *adj house, car etc* espacioso; *clothes* holgado

roost [ruːst] **I** *n* percha *f* **II** *v/i of bird* posarse; **his mistakes have come home to ~** ahora está pagando sus errores

roost•er ['ruːstər] gallo *m*

root [ruːt] raíz *f*; **~s** *of person* raíces *fpl*

◆ **root around** *v/i* rebuscar

◆ **root for** *v/t* F apoyar

◆ **root out** *v/t* **1** (*get rid of*) cortar de raíz **2** (*find*) encontrar

'root beer *bebida efervescente no alcohólica hecha a partir de hierbas y especias*; **'root crop** tubérculo *m*; **'root di•rec•to•ry** COMPUT directorio *m* raíz

root•ed ['ruːtɪd] *adj*: **be ~ in** *fig* tener raíces en; **stand** *or* **be ~ to the spot** quedarse de una pieza

rope [roʊp] cuerda *f*, *thick* soga *f*; **show s.o. the ~s** F poner a alguien al tanto; **he doesn't know the ~s yet** F todavía no está al tanto; **jump ~** saltar a la combapara; **give s.o. plenty of ~** *fig* dar libertad de acción a alguien

◆ **rope off** *v/t* acordonar

'rope lad•der escalera *f* de cuerda

rop•(e)y ['roʊpɪ] *adj Br* F flojo; **I'm still feeling a bit ~** estoy pachucho

ro•sa•ry ['roʊzərɪ] REL rosario *m*

rose[1] [roʊz] *n* BOT rosa *f*

rose[2] [roʊz] *pret* ☞ **rise**

ro•sé [roʊ'zeɪ] rosado *m*

'rose•bud BOT capullo *m*; **'rose•bush** BOT rosal *m*; **rose-col•ored**, *Br* **rose-col•oured** ['roʊzkʌlərd] *adj* rosado; **see things through ~ glasses** *fig* ver las cosas de color de rosa; **'rose•hip** BOT escaramujo *m*; **rose•ma•ry** ['roʊzmerɪ] romero *m*

ro•sette [roʊ'zet] *worn* escarapela *f*

ros•in ['rɑːzɪn] colofonia *f*

ros•ter ['rɑːstər] lista *f*

ros•trum ['rɑːstrəm] estrado *m*

ros•trum cam•er•a•man TV cámara *m* de primeros planos

ros•y ['roʊzɪ] *adj cheeks* sonrosado; *future* de color de rosa

rot [rɑːt] **I** *n in wood* putrefacción *f* **II** *v/i* (*pret & pp* **-ted**) *of food, wood* pudrirse; *of teeth* cariarse

ro•ta ['roʊtə] turnos *mpl*; *actual document* calendario *m* con los turnos

ro•ta•ry ['roʊtərɪ] **I** *adj* rotatorio **II** *n* MOT rotonda *f*

ro•tate [roʊ'teɪt] **I** *v/i of blades, earth* girar **II** *v/t* **1** hacer girar **2** *crops* rotar

ro•ta•tion [roʊ'teɪʃn] *around the sun etc* rotación *f*; **do sth in ~** hacer algo por turnos rotatorios

rote [roʊt]: **learn sth by ~** aprender algo de memoria

ro•tor ['roʊtər] TECH, ELEC rotor *m*

'ro•tor blade pala *f* del rotor

rot•ten ['rɑːtn] *adj food, wood etc* podrido; F *weather, luck* horrible; F **that was a ~ trick** ¡qué mala idea!

rott•weil•er ['rɑːtwaɪlər] rottweiler *m*

ro•tund [roʊ'tʌnd] *adj* rollizo

rouge [ruːʒ] colorete *m*

rough [rʌf] **I** *adj* **1** *surface, ground* accidentado; *hands, skin* áspero; *voice* ronco

2 (*violent*) bruto; *crossing* movido; *seas* bravo; **be ~ with s.o.** ser duro con alguien

3 (*approximate*) aproximado; **~ draft** borrador *m*; **~ estimate** cálculo *m* aproximado; **at a ~ guess** a ojo; **I have a ~ idea where it is** tengo una vaga idea

R

de dónde está

II *adv*: ***sleep ~*** dormir a la intemperie; ***play*** (***it***) ~ SP jugar duro

III *n* **1** *in golf* rough *m* **2**: ***take the ~ with the smooth*** estar a las duras y a las maduras

IV *v/t*: ~ ***it*** apañárselas

◆ **rough up** *v/t* F dar una paliza a

rough•age ['rʌfɪdʒ] *in food* fibra *f*

rough-and-'read•y *adj estimate, method, repair job* rudimentario; **rough-and-'tum•ble** rifirrafe *m*; ***have a ~*** tener un rifirrafe; **'rough•cast** ARCHI mortero *m* grueso; **rough 'di•a•mond**: ***be a ~*** ser buena persona aunque se tengan malos modales

rough•ly ['rʌflɪ] *adv* **1** (*approximately*) aproximadamente; ~ ***speaking*** aproximadamente **2** (*harshly*) brutalmente

'rough•neck F matón(-ona) *m*(*f*)

rough•shod ['rʌfʃɑːd] *adv*: ***ride ~ over sth*** / ***s.o.*** pisotear algo / a alguien

rou•lette [ruː'let] ruleta *f*

round [raʊnd] **I** *adj* redondo; ***in ~ figures*** en números redondos

II *n* **1** *of mailman, doctor, drinks, competition* ronda *f*; *in championship* jornada *f*; *in boxing match* round *m*, asalto *m*; ***go the ~s*** *of rumor, illness* correr; ***the daily ~*** *fig* las tareas cotidianas; ***it's my ~*** me toca pagar a mí **2** *of toast* rebanada *f*

III *v/t corner* doblar

IV *adv, prep* ☞ ***around***

◆ **round down** *v/t sum* redondear a la baja

◆ **round off** *v/t* **1** *edges* redondear **2** *meeting, night out* concluir

◆ **round up** *v/t* **1** *figure* redondear (hacia la cifra más alta) **2** *suspects, criminals* detener

round•a•bout ['raʊndəbaʊt] **I** *adj route, way of saying sth* indirecto; ***in a ~ way*** *fig* dando muchos rodeos **II** *n Br*: *on road* rotonda *f*, *Span* glorieta *f*

round•ly ['raʊndlɪ] *adv criticize, condemn* rotundamente

'round-ta•ble *adj*: ~ ***discussion*** mesa *f* redonda; **'round-the-clock** *adj & adv* 24 horas al día; **'round-the-world** *adj* alrededor del mundo; **round 'trip** viaje *m* de ida y vuelta; **round trip 'tick•et** billete *m or L.Am.* boleto *m* de ida y vuelta; **'round-up 1** *of cattle* rodeo *m*; *of suspects, criminals* redada *f* **2** *of news* resumen *m*

rouse [raʊz] *v/t* **1** *from sleep* despertar **2** *interest, emotions* excitar, provocar

rous•ing ['raʊzɪŋ] *adj speech, finale* emocionante

rout [raʊt] MIL **I** *n* debacle *f* **II** *v/t* aplastar

route [raʊt] ruta *f*, recorrido *m*; ***is this his normal ~ home?*** ¿es éste el camino que toma normalmente para ir a casa?

rou•tine [ruː'tiːn] **I** *adj* habitual **II** *n* rutina *f*; ***as a matter of ~*** como rutina

rou•tine•ly [ruː'tiːnlɪ] *adv* habitualmente

row[1] [roʊ] *n* (*line*) hilera *f*; ***5 days in a ~*** 5 días seguidos

row[2] [roʊ] **I** *v/t boat* llevar remando **II** *v/i* remar

row[3] [raʊ] F *Br* **I** *n* **1** *noise* follón *m* **2** (*quarrel*) bronca *f* **II** *v/i* (*quarrel*) pelearse

RoW [ɑːroʊ'dʌbljuː] *abbr* (= ***Rest of World***) resto *m* del mundo

row•boat ['roʊboʊt] bote *m* de remos

row•dy ['raʊdɪ] *adj* alborotador, *Span* follonero

row house ['roʊhaʊs] casa *f* adosada

roy•al [rɔɪəl] *adj* real

roy•al•ist ['rɔɪəlɪst] **I** *adj* monárquico **II** *n* monárquico(-a) *m*(*f*)

roy•al•ty ['rɔɪəltɪ] **1** *royal persons* realeza *f* **2** *on book, recording* derechos *mpl* de autor

RSI [ɑːres'aɪ] *abbr* (= ***repetitive strain injury***) lesión *f* por movimiento repetitivo

RSVP [ɑːresviː'piː] *abbr* (= ***répondez s'il vous plaît***) se ruega contestación

RTA [ɑːrtiː'eɪ] *abbr* (= ***road traffic accident***) accidente *m* de tráfico por carretera

rub [rʌb] *v/t* (*pret & pp* **-bed**) frotar; ~ ***sth dry*** secar algo (frotándolo); ~ ***one's hands*** (***together***) frotarse las manos; ~ ***one's hands with glee*** frotarse las manos; ~ ***s.o.'s nose in sth*** F restregarle a alguien algo por las narices; ~ ***shoulders with*** F codearse con

◆ **rub down** *v/t to clean* lijar

◆ **rub in** *v/t cream, ointment* extender, frotar; ***don't rub it in!*** *fig* ¡no me lo restriegues por las narices!

◆ **rub off I** *v/t dirt* limpiar frotando; *paint etc* borrar **II** *v/i*: ***it rubs off on***

you se te contagia
◆ **rub up** *v/t*: ***rub s.o. up the wrong way*** F caer mal a alguien
rub•ber ['rʌbər] **I** *n* **1** *material* goma *f*, caucho *m* **2** P (*condom*) goma *f* P **II** *adj* de goma *or* caucho
rub•ber 'band goma *f* elástica; **rub•ber 'bul•let** bala *f* de goma; **rub•ber 'din-ghy** lancha *f* neumática; **rub•ber gloves** [rʌbər'glʌvz] *npl* guantes *mpl* de goma; **'rub•ber•neck** F **I** *n* curioso(-a) *m(f)* **II** *v/i* curiosear; **'rub•ber plant** BOT ficus *m inv*; **rub•ber 'stamp** sello *m* de caucho; **rub•ber-'stamp** *v/t* sellar; *fig* F dar el visto bueno a
rub•ber•y ['rʌbərɪ] *adj* correoso
rub•bish ['rʌbɪʃ] *Br* **1** *garbage, poor quality* basura *f* **2** (*nonsense*) tonterías *fpl*
rub•ble ['rʌbl] escombros *mpl*
ru•bel•la [rʊ'belə] MED rubeola *f*
ru•by ['ru:bɪ] *jewel* rubí *m*
ruck•sack ['rʌksæk] mochila *f*
ruck•us ['rʌkəs] F trifulca *f*
ruc•tions ['rʌkʃnz] *npl* F jaleo *m*
rud•der ['rʌdər] timón *m*
rud•dy ['rʌdɪ] *adj complexion* rubicundo
rude [ru:d] *adj person, behavior* maleducado, grosero; *language* grosero; ***it is ~ to ...*** es de mala educación ...; ***I didn't mean to be ~*** no pretendía faltar al respeto; ***~ awakening*** sorpresa *f* desagradable
rude•ly ['ru:dlɪ] *adv* (*impolitely*) groseramente
rude•ness ['ru:dnɪs] mala *f* educación, grosería *f*
ru•di•men•ta•ry [ru:dɪ'mentərɪ] *adj* rudimentario
ru•di•ments ['ru:dɪmənts] *npl* rudimentos *mpl*
rue [ru:] *v/t*: ***~ the day ...*** *lit* lamentar el día ...
rue•ful ['ru:fəl] *adj* arrepentido, compungido
rue•ful•ly ['ru:fəlɪ] *adv* con arrepentimiento
ruff [rʌf] golilla *f*
ruf•fi•an ['rʌfɪən] rufián *m*
ruf•fle ['rʌfl] **I** *n on dress* volante *m* **II** *v/t* **1** *hair* despeinar; *clothes* arrugar **2** *person* alterar, enfadar; ***get ~d*** alterarse
rug [rʌg] **1** alfombra *f*; ***pull the ~ (out) from under s.o.*** *fig* ponerle la zancadilla a alguien; ***sweep sth under the ~*** *fig* ocultar algo **2** (*blanket*) manta *f* (de viaje)
rug•by ['rʌgbɪ] rugby *m*
'rug•by match partido *m* de rugby; **'rug•by play•er** jugador(a) *m(f)* de rugby; **'rug•by-tack•le** *v/t* hacer un placaje a
rug•ged ['rʌgɪd] *adj* **1** *scenery, cliffs* escabroso, accidentado **2** *face* de rasgos duros; *resistance* decidido; *build, equipment* resistente
ru•in ['ru:ɪn] **I** *n* ruina *f*, ***~s*** ruinas *fpl*; ***in ~s*** *city, building* en ruinas; *plans, marriage* arruinado; ***fall into ~*** quedarse en ruinas **II** *v/t* arruinar; ***be ~ed*** *financially* estar arruinado *or* en la ruina; ***~ one's eyesight*** arruinarse la vista
ru•in•a•tion [ru:ɪn'eɪʃn]: ***be the ~ of s.o.*** ser la ruina de alguien
ru•in•ous ['ru:ɪnəs] *adj* ruinoso
ru•in•ous•ly ['ru:ɪnəslɪ] *adv*: ***~ expensive*** increíblemente caro
rule [ru:l] **I** *n* **1** *of club, game* regla *f*, norma *f*; ***as a ~*** por regla general; ***make it a ~ to do sth*** tener por norma hacer algo; ***against the ~s*** contra las normas; ***work to ~*** *esp Br* hacer huelga de celo **2** *of monarch* reinado *m* **3** *for measuring* regla *f*; ***as a ~ of thumb*** por regla general
II *v/t* **1** *country* gobernar; ***he's ~d by self-interest*** se deja llevar por su propio interés **2**: ***the judge ~d that ...*** el juez dictaminó que ... **3**: ***~ the roost*** *fig* ser el amo del cottaro
III *v/i of monarch* reinar
◆ **rule out** *v/t* descartar; ***I wouldn't rule it out*** no lo descartaría
rul•er ['ru:lər] **1** *for measuring* regla *f* **2** *of state* gobernante *m/f*
rul•ing ['ru:lɪŋ] **I** *n* fallo *m*, decisión *f* **II** *adj party* gobernante, en el poder
rum [rʌm] *drink* ron *m*
Ru•ma•ni•a *etc* ☞ ***Romania***
rum•ble ['rʌmbl] *v/i of stomach* gruñir; *of train in tunnel* retumbar
'rum•ble strip MOT banda *f* sonora
rum•bus•tious [rʌm'bʌstʃəs] *adj* bullicioso
ru•mi•nant ['ru:mɪnənt] ZO rumiante *m*
ru•mi•nate ['ru:mɪneɪt] *v/i of animal* rumiar; ***~ over sth*** *fig* rumiar algo

◆ **rum•mage around** ['rʌmɪdʒ] *v/i* buscar revolviendo
'rum•mage sale rastrillo *m* benéfico
ru•mor ['ru:mər] **I** *n* rumor *m* **II** *v/t*: ***it is ~ed that ..., ~ has it that ...*** se rumorea que ...
ru•mor•mon•ger ['ru:mərmʌŋgər]: ***he's a ~*** le gusta hacer correr rumores
ru•mor•mon•ger•ing ['ru:mərmʌŋgərɪŋ] rumorología *f*
rump [rʌmp] *of animal* cuartos *mpl* traseros
rum•ple ['rʌmpl] *v/t clothes, paper* arrugar
rump 'steak filete *m* de lomo
run [rʌn] **I** *n* **1** *on foot, in baseball* carrera *f*, *in car* viaje *m*; ***go for a ~*** ir a correr; ***go for a ~ in the car*** ir a dar una vuelta en el coche; ***at a ~*** corriendo; ***make a ~ for it*** salir corriendo; ***a criminal on the ~*** un criminal fugado; ***have the ~ of a place*** moverse libremente por un sitio
2 *in pantihose* carrera *f*
3 THEA: *of play* temporada *f*, ***it has had a three year ~*** *of play* lleva tres años en cartel; ***~ of good / bad luck*** racha *f* de buena / mala suerte
4: ***in the short / long ~*** a corto / largo plazo
5: ***a ~ on the dollar*** un movimiento especulativo contra el dólar
6: ***have the ~s*** *Br* F tener cagalera
II *v/i* (*pret* ***ran***, *pp* ***run***) **1** *of person, animal* correr
2 *of river* correr, discurrir; ***don't leave the water ~ning*** no dejes el grifo abierto; ***his nose is ~ning*** le moquea la nariz; ***her eyes are ~ning*** le lloran los ojos
3 *of paint, make-up* correrse
4 *of play* estar en cartel
5 *of engine, machine, software* funcionar; ***with the engine ~ning*** con el motor en marcha; ***the trains ~ every ten minutes*** pasan trenes cada diez minutos; ***this train doesn't ~ on Saturdays*** no hay servicio de este tren los sábados; ***it runs on electricity*** va con electricidad
6 *in election* presentarse; ***~ for President*** presentarse a las elecciones presidenciales
7: ***it ~s in the family*** *fig* es cosa de familia, viene de familia
III *v/t* (*pret* ***ran***, *pp* ***run***) **1** *race* correr
2 *business, hotel, project etc* dirigir
3 *software* usar; (*start*) ejecutar
4 *car* tener; (*use*) usar
5: ***can I ~ you to the station?*** ¿te puedo llevar hasta la estación?; ***he ran his eye down the page*** echó una ojeada a la página
6: ***~ an errand*** hacer un recado; ***~ a temperature*** tener fiebre; ***~ s.o. a bath*** preparar un baño a alguien
◆ **run across** *v/t* (*meet*) encontrarse con; (*find*) encontrar
◆ **run after** *v/t* **1** correr detrás de **2** *look after a lot* ir detrás de; ***you won't have me to run after you all the time*** F no me vas a tener pendiente de tí todo el tiempo
◆ **run against** *v/t* POL enfrentarse contra
◆ **run along** *v/i*: ***run along!*** ¡marchaos!
◆ **run around with** *v/t* andar con
◆ **run away** *v/i* salir corriendo, huir; *from home* escaparse
◆ **run away with** *v/t*: ***don't run away with the idea that ...*** no te pienses que...
◆ **run back I** *v/i* volver corriendo **II** *v/t tape, film* rebobinar
◆ **run down I** *v/t* **1** (*knock down*) atropellar **2** (*criticize*) criticar **3** *stocks* reducir **II** *v/i of battery* agotarse
◆ **run for** *v/t*: ***run for it!*** ¡corre!; ***run for one's life*** poner pies en polvorosa
◆ **run into** *v/t* (*meet*) encontrarse con; *difficulties* tropezar con
◆ **run off I** *v/i* salir corriendo **II** *v/t* **1** (*print off*) tirar **2**: ***run another car off the road*** sacar a un coche de la carretera
◆ **run out** *v/i of contract* vencer; *of supplies* agotarse; ***time has run out*** se ha acabado el tiempo
◆ **run out of** *v/t time, supplies* quedarse sin; ***I ran out of gas*** me quedé sin gasolina; ***I'm running out of patience*** se me está acabando la paciencia
◆ **run over I** *v/t* **1** (*knock down*) atropellar **2**: ***can we run over the details again?*** ¿podríamos repasar los detalles otra vez? **II** *v/i of water etc* desbordarse
◆ **run through** *v/t* **1** (*rehearse, go over*) repasar **2**: ***run through s.o.'s mind*** pa-

sar por la cabeza de alguien
◆ **run up** *v/t* **1** *debts, large bill* acumular **2** *clothes* coser
'run•a•bout MOT coche *m* pequeño; **'run•a•round**: ***give s.o. the ~*** F tomar el pelo a alguien, jugar con alguien; **'run•a•way I** *n persona que se ha fugado de casa* **II** *adj*: ***~ child*** niño *m* fugado; ***~ inflation*** COM inflación *f* galopante; **run-'down** *adj person* débil, apagado; *part of town, building* ruinoso; **'run-down** *in baseball* corre-corre *m*
rung[1] [rʌŋ] *n of ladder* peldaño *m*
rung[2] [rʌŋ] *pp* ☞ **ring**
'run-in: ***have a ~ with s.o.*** F tener un encontronazo con alguien
run•ner ['rʌnər] *athlete* corredor(a) *m(f)*
run•ner 'beans *npl* judías *fpl* verdes, *L.Am.* porotos *mpl* verdes, *Mex* ejotes *mpl*
run•ner-'up subcampeón(-ona) *m(f)*
run•ning ['rʌnɪŋ] **I** *n* **1** SP el correr; (*jogging*) footing *m*; ***make the ~*** SP, *fig* ir en primera posición; ***be out of the ~*** *fig* no tener posibilidades de ganar; ***be still in the ~*** *fig* tener todavía posibilidades de ganar **2** *of business* gestión *f* **II** *adj*: ***for two days ~*** durante dos días seguidos
run•ning 'bat•tle: ***be fighting a ~ against disease / inflation*** mantener una lucha incesante contra la enfermedad / inflación; **'run•ning costs** *npl* gastos *mpl* de mantenimiento; **running 'head** *on page* folio *m*; **'run•ning mate** candidato(-a) *m(f)* a la vicepresidencia; **'run•ning shoes** *npl* zapatillas *fpl* de deporte; **run•ning 'wa•ter** agua *f* corriente
run•ny ['rʌnɪ] *adj* **1** *mixture* fluido, líquido **2** *nose* que moquea
'run-off eliminatoria *f*
run-of-the-'mill *adj usu pej* corriente; **'run-up** SP carrerilla *f*; ***in the ~ to*** en el periodo previo a; **'run•way 1** AVIA pista *f* (de aterrizaje / despegue) **2** *for models* pasarela *f*
rup•ture ['rʌptʃər] **I** *n* ruptura *f* **II** *v/i of pipe etc* romperse
ru•ral ['rʊrəl] *adj* rural; ***~ population*** población *f* rural; ***~ exodus*** éxodo *m* rural
ruse [ruːz] artimaña *f*
rush[1] [rʌʃ] **I** *n* prisa *f*; ***do sth in a ~*** hacer algo con prisas; ***be in a ~*** tener prisa; ***what's the big ~?*** ¿qué prisa tenemos? **II** *v/t person* meter prisa a; *meal* comer a toda prisa; ***~ s.o. to the hospital*** llevar a alguien al hospital a toda prisa; ***be ~ed off one's feet*** no parar ni un instante **III** *v/i* darse prisa; ***~ into sth*** *fig* precipitarse a algo
◆ **rush at** *v/t* **1** *job, task* precipitarse en **2** (*attack*) *person* atacar
◆ **rush through** *v/t*: ***rush a bill through*** aprobar un proyecto de ley a toda prisa
rush[2] [rʌʃ] *n* BOT junco *m*
rush•es ['rʌʃɪz] *npl of movie* primeras pruebas *fpl*
'rush hour hora *f* punta; ***~ traffic*** tráfico *m* de hora punta
rusk [rʌsk] *galleta seca y crujiente*
Rus•sia ['rʌʃə] Rusia *f*
Rus•sian ['rʌʃən] **I** *adj* ruso **II** *n* ruso(-a) *m(f)*; *language* ruso *m*
Rus•sian rou'lette ruleta *f* rusa
rust [rʌst] **I** *n* óxido *m* **II** *v/i* oxidarse
rus•tic ['rʌstɪk] **I** *adj* rústico; ***~ furniture*** mobiliario *m* rústico **II** *n* campesino(-a) *m(f)*
rus•tle ['rʌsl] **I** *n of silk, leaves* susurro *m* **II** *v/i of silk, leaves* susurrar **III** *v/t cattle* robar
◆ **rustle up** *v/t* F *meal* improvisar
rus•tler ['rʌslər] ladrón(-ona) *m(f)* de ganado
'rust-proof *adj* inoxidable
rust re•mov•er ['rʌstrɪmuːvər] desoxidante *m*
rust•y ['rʌstɪ] *adj* oxidado; ***my French is pretty ~*** tengo el francés muy abandonado; ***I'm a little ~*** estoy un poco falto de forma
rut[1] [rʌt] *n in road* rodada *f*; ***be in a ~*** *fig* estar estancado; ***get into a ~*** apalancarse
rut[2] [rʌt] ZO **I** *n* celo *m* **II** *v/i* estar en celo
ru•ta•ba•ga [ruːtə'beɪgə] nabo *m* sueco
ruth•less ['ruːθlɪs] *adj* implacable, despiadado
ruth•less•ly ['ruːθlɪslɪ] *adv* sin compasión, despiadadamente
ruth•less•ness ['ruːθlɪsnɪs] falta *f* de compasión
RV [ɑːr'viː] *abbr* (= ***recreational vehicle***) autocaravana *f*
rye [raɪ] centeno *m*
'rye bread pan *m* de centeno; **'rye grass** centeno *m*; **rye 'whis•key** whisky *m* de centeno

R

S

Sab•bath ['sæbəθ] REL *Jewish* sábado *m*; *Christian* domingo *m*
sab•bat•i•cal [sə'bætɪkl] *year* año *m* sabático; ***a 6 month ~*** 6 meses de excedencia; ***be on ~*** estar en excedencia
sa•ber ['seɪbər] sable *m*
sab•o•tage ['sæbətɑːʒ] **I** *n* sabotaje *m* **II** *v/t* sabotear
sab•o•teur [sæbə'tɜːr] saboteador(a) *m(f)*
sa•bre *Br* ☞ ***saber***
sac•cha•rin ['sækərɪn] sacarina *f*
sa•chet [sæ'ʃeɪ] *of shampoo, cream etc* sobrecito *m*
sack[1] [sæk] **I** *n bag* saco *m*; *for groceries* bolsa *f*; ***hit the ~*** F irse a la piltra, irse a planchar la oreja; ***he got the ~*** *Br* F le echaron F **II** *v/t Br* F echar
sack[2] [sæk] *v/t city* saquear
sac•ra•ment ['sækrəmənt] REL sacramento *m*
sa•cred ['seɪkrɪd] *adj* sagrado; ***be a ~ cow*** *fig* ser sagrado *or* intocable
sac•ri•fice ['sækrɪfaɪs] **I** *n* sacrificio *m*; ***make ~s*** *fig* hacer sacrificios **II** *v/t* sacrificar
'sac•ri•fice hit *in baseball* batazo *m* de sacrificio
sac•ri•fi•cial [sækrɪ'fɪʃl] *adj* expiatorio; ***~ lamb*** *fig* chivo *m* expiatorio
sac•ri•lege ['sækrɪlɪdʒ] sacrilegio *m*
sac•ri•le•gious [sækrɪ'lɪdʒəs] *adj* sacrílego
sac•ris•ty ['sækrɪstɪ] REL sacristía *f*
sad [sæd] *adj person, face, song* triste; *state of affairs* lamentable, desgraciado; ***~ to say*** lamentablemente, desgraciadamente; ***you ~ man*** F que patético, eres patético
sad•den ['sædn] *v/t* entristecer; ***we were all ~ed to hear of the death of …*** estábamos todos apenados al enterarnos de la muerte de …
sad•dle ['sædl] **I** *n* silla *f* de montar; ***be in the ~*** *fig* estar al mando **II** *v/t horse* ensillar; ***~ s.o. with sth*** *fig* endilgar algo a alguien; ***be ~d with sth*** *fig* tener que apechugar *or* cargar con algo
◆ **saddle up I** *v/t* ensillar **II** *v/i* ensillar el caballo
'sad•dle bag *on bike, horse* alforja *f*
'sad•dle soap grasa *f* de caballo
sa•dism ['seɪdɪzm] sadismo *m*
sa•dist ['seɪdɪst] sádico(-a) *m(f)*
sa•dis•tic [sə'dɪstɪk] *adj* sádico
sad•ly ['sædlɪ] *adv* **1** *look, say etc* con tristeza **2** (*regrettably*) lamentablemente; ***be ~ mistaken*** estar muy equivocado
sad•ness ['sædnɪs] tristeza *f*
sad•o•mas•o•chism [seɪdou'mæsəkɪzəm] sadomasoquismo *m*
sad•o•mas•o•chis•tic [seɪdoumæsə'kɪstɪk] *adj* sadomasoquista
s.a.e. [eseɪ'iː] *abbr* (= ***stamped addressed envelope***) sobre *m* franqueado a nombre del destinatario
sa•fa•ri [sə'fɑːrɪ] safari *m*; ***go on ~*** ir de safari, hacer un safari
sa'fa•ri park safari-park *m*
safe [seɪf] **I** *adj* seguro; *driver* prudente; (*not in danger*) a salvo; ***is it ~ to walk here?*** ¿se puede andar por aquí sin peligro?; ***be in ~ hands*** estar en buenas manos; ***~ sex*** sexo *m* seguro; ***to be on the ~ side, just to be ~*** para mayor seguridad, por si acaso; ***it is ~ to say that …*** se puede decir con toda seguridad que …; ***keep sth in a ~ place*** guardar algo en (un) lugar seguro
II *n* caja *f* fuerte
'safe•break•er, 'safe•crack•er ladrón(-ona) *m(f)* de cajas fuertes; **safe-de'pos•it box** *in bank, hotel* caja *f* de seguridad; **'safe•guard I** *n* garantía *f*; ***as a ~ against*** como garantía contra **II** *v/t* salvaguardar; **safe 'ha•ven** lugar *m* seguro, cobijo *m*; **'safe•keep•ing**: ***give sth to s.o. for ~*** dar algo a alguien para que lo custodie
safe•ly ['seɪflɪ] *adv arrive* sin percances; (*successfully*) sin problemas; *drive* prudentemente; *assume* con certeza
safe•ty ['seɪftɪ] seguridad *f*; ***jump / swim to ~*** saltar / nadar para salvarse *or* ponerse a salvo; ***there's ~ in numbers*** es más seguro en grupo
'safe•ty belt cinturón *m* de seguridad;

'safe•ty catch *on gun* seguro *m*; **'safe•ty-con•scious** *adj*: ***be ~*** tener en cuenta la seguridad; **'safe•ty curtain** *in theater* telón *m* de seguridad; **safe•ty 'first** prevención *f* de accidentes; **'safe•ty glass** cristal *m or* vidrio *m* de seguridad; **'safe•ty is•land** *on road* isla *f*; **'safe•ty lock** cierre *m* de seguridad; **'safe•ty mar•gin** margen *m* de seguridad; **'safe•ty meas•ure** medida *f* de seguridad, medida *f* preventiva; **'safe•ty net** *at circus* red *f* de seguridad; **'safe•ty pin** imperdible *m*; **'safe•ty pre•cau•tion** precaución *f* de seguridad; **'safe•ty ra•zor** maquinilla *f* (de afeitar); **'safe•ty valve 1** TECH válvula *f* de seguridad **2** *fig* válvula *f* de escape

saf•fron ['sæfrən] azafrán *m*

sag [sæg] **I** *n in ceiling etc* combadura *f* **II** *v/i* (*pret & pp* **-ged**) *of ceiling* combarse; *of rope* destensarse; *of tempo* disminuir; *of spirits* decaer, flaquear

sa•ga ['sægə] saga *f*

sage [seɪdʒ] *herb* salvia *f*

'sage•brush artemisa *f*

Sa•git•tar•i•us [sædʒɪ'terɪəs] ASTR Sagitario *m/f inv*, *L.Am.* sagitariano(-a) *m*(*f*); ***be*** (***a***) ***~*** ser Sagitario, *L.Am.* ser sagitariano

Sa•ha•ra [sə'hɑːrə]: ***the ~*** el Sáhara

said [sed] *pret & pp* ☞ ***say***

sail [seɪl] **I** *n* **1** *of boat* vela *f* **2** *trip* viaje *m* (en barco); ***go for a ~*** salir a navegar **II** *v/t yacht* manejar **III** *v/i* **1** navegar **2** *depart* zarpar, hacerse a la mar **3** *fig*: ***she ~ed into the room*** entró en la habitación con mucha seguridad; ***~ through an examination*** aprobar un examen fácilmente; ***my cigar went ~ing out the window*** mi cigarro salió volando por la ventana

'sail•board I *n* tabla *f* de windsurf **II** *v/i* hacer windsurf; **'sail•board•er** windsurfista *m/f*; **'sail•board•ing** windsurf *m*; **'sail•boat** barco *m* de vela, velero *m*

sail•ing ['seɪlɪŋ] **1** SP vela *f*; ***go ~*** ir *or* salir a navegar; ***everything was plain ~*** *fig* fue todo muy fácil, (todo) fue pan comido **2** *departure* salida *f*; ***when is the next ~ to ...?*** ¿cuándo sale el próximo barco para ...?

'sail•ing boat *Br* barco *m* de vela, velero *m*

'sail•ing ship buque *m* de vela

sail•or ['seɪlər] *in the navy* marino *m/f*, *in the merchant navy*, SP marinero(-a) *m*(*f*); ***I'm a good / bad ~*** no me mareo / me mareo con facilidad

'sail•or's knot nudo *m* marinero

'sail•plane planeador *m*

saint [seɪnt] santo *m*; ***he has the patience of a ~*** tiene más paciencia que un santo

saint•ly ['seɪntlɪ] *adj* angelical, cándido

'saint's day REL (día *m* del) santo *m*

sake [seɪk]: ***for my ~*** por mí; ***for the ~ of peace*** por la paz; ***for God's*** *or* ***heaven's ~*** F ¡por (el amor de) Dios!; ***for the ~ of simplicity*** para simplificar las cosas

sal•a•ble ['seɪləbl] *adj* vendible

sal•ad ['sæləd] ensalada *f*; ***ham / cheese ~*** ensalada *f* de jamón / queso

'sal•ad cream *aliño para ensalada muy parecido a la mayonesa pero con un sabor más avinagrado*

'sal•ad dress•ing aliño *m or* aderezo *m* para ensalada

sal•a•man•der ['sæləmændər] salamandra *f*

sa•la•mi [sə'lɑːmɪ] salami *m*

sal•a•ried ['sælərɪd] *adj*: ***~ employee*** trabajador(a) *m*(*f*) asalariado(-a)

sal•a•ry ['sælərɪ] sueldo *m*, salario *m*

'sal•a•ry scale escala *f* salarial

sale [seɪl] venta *f*; *reduced prices* rebajas *fpl*; ***be on ~*** estar a la venta; *at reduced prices* estar de rebajas; ***for ~*** *sign* se vende; ***is this for ~?*** ¿está a la venta?; ***it's not for ~*** no está a la venta; ***be up for ~*** estar en venta; ***~ price*** *reduced* precio *m* rebajado *or* de rebaja

'sale•a•ble ['seɪləbl] *adj* ☞ ***salable***

'sale a•gree•ment acuerdo *m* de venta

sales [seɪlz] *npl also department* ventas *fpl*

'sales clerk *in store* vendedor(a) *m*(*f*), dependiente(-a) *m*(*f*); **'sales en•gi•neer** ingeniero(-a) *m*(*f*) de ventas; **'sales fig•ures** *npl* cifras *fpl* de ventas; **'sales force** plantilla *f or* personal *m* de ventas; **'sales•girl** dependienta *f*; **'sales•man** vendedor *m*; **'sales man•ag•er** jefe(-a) *m*(*f*) de ventas

sales•man•ship ['seɪlzmənʃɪp] habilidad *f* para la venta

'sales meet•ing reunión *f* del departamento de ventas; **'sales pitch** F charla *f*, discurso *m*; **'sales pro•mo•tion** promoción *f* de ventas; **'sales rep•re•sent•a•tive** representante *m/f* de ventas; **'sales slip** *from store* tique *m* (de compra); **'sales tax** impuesto *m* de ventas; **'sales team** equipo *m* de ventas; **'sales tech•ni•cian** vendedor(a) *m(f)* técnico(-a)-comercial; **'sales•wo•man** vendedora *f*

sa•lient ['seɪlɪənt] *adj* sobresaliente, destacado

sa•line ['seɪliːn] *adj* salino; ***~ solution*** solución *f* salina

sa•li•va [sə'laɪvə] saliva *f*

sal•i•var•y ['sæləverɪ] *adj*: ***~ gland*** glándula *f* salivar

sal•i•vate ['sælɪveɪt] *v/i* salivar; *at sight of food* hacerse la boca agua; *at sight of pretty girl etc* babear

sal•low ['sæloʊ] *adj complexion* amarillento, pajizo

salm•on ['sæmən] (*pl* ***salmon***) salmón *m*

sal•mo•nel•la [sælmə'nelə] MED salmonela *f*, salmonelosis *f*

sal•on ['sælɑːn] *of hairdresser, beautician etc* salón *m* de belleza

sa•loon [sə'luːn] **1** (*bar*) bar *m* **2** *Br* MOT turismo *m*

sal•sa ['sælsə] MUS, GASTR salsa *f*

salt [sɒːlt] **I** *n* sal *f*; ***take sth with a pinch of ~*** *fig* no tomarse algo al pie de la letra; ***no composer worth his ~ ...*** ningún compositor que se precie ... **II** *v/t food* salar

◆ **salt away** *v/t* F *money* guardar, poner a buen recaudo

'salt•cel•lar salero *m*;

'salt-free *adj* sin sal; **'salt•shak•er** salero *m*; **salt 'wa•ter** agua *f* salada; **'salt-wa•ter fish** pez *m* de agua salada

salt•y ['sɒːltɪ] *adj* salado

sa•lu•bri•ous [sə'luːbrɪəs] *adj district, neighborhood* salubre

sal•u•tar•y ['sæljʊterɪ] *adj experience* beneficioso

sal•u•ta•tion [sæljuː'teɪʃn] *also in letter* saludo *m*

sa•lute [sə'luːt] **I** *n* MIL saludo; ***take the ~*** presidir un desfile; ***a 21-gun ~*** una salva de 21 cañonazos **II** *v/t* saludar; *fig* (*hail*) elogiar **III** *v/i* MIL saludar

Sal•va•dor(e)•an [sælvə'dɔːrən] **I** *adj* salvadoreño **II** *n* salvadoreño(-a) *m(f)*

sal•vage ['sælvɪdʒ] *v/t from wreck* rescatar

'sal•vage ves•sel barco *m* de salvamento

sal•va•tion [sæl'veɪʃn] *also fig* salvación *f*

Sal•va•tion 'Ar•my Ejército *m* de Salvación

sal•ver ['sælvər] bandeja *f*, *C.Am.*, *Mex* charola *f*

sal•vo ['sælvoʊ] salva *f*, saludo *m*

Sa•mar•i•tan [sə'mærɪtən]: ***good ~*** buen(a) *m(f)* samaritano(-a)

sam•ba ['sæmbə] **I** *n* samba *f* **II** *v/i* bailar la samba

same [seɪm] **I** *adj* mismo; ***amount*** *or* ***come to the ~ thing*** venir a ser lo mismo

II *pron*: ***the ~*** lo mismo; ***Happy New Year – the ~ to you*** Feliz Año Nuevo – igualmente; ***he's not the ~ any more*** ya no es el mismo; ***life isn't the ~ without you*** la vida es distinta sin ti; ***all the ~*** (*even so*) aun así; ***men are all the ~*** todos los hombres son iguales; ***it's all the ~ to me*** me da lo mismo, me da igual; ***(the) ~ again, please*** lo mismo por favor

III *adv*: ***the ~*** igual; ***~ as*** F lo mismo que, igual que

'same-day de•liv•er•y entrega *f* en el mismo día

same•y ['seɪmɪ] *adj Br* F muy parecido

sam•ple ['sæmpl] **I** *n* muestra *f*; ***~ bottle*** frasco *m* de muestra **II** *v/t* probar, degustar; *fig* descubrir

sam•pling ['sæmplɪŋ] muestreo *m*

sanc•ti•mo•ni•ous [sæŋktɪ'moʊnɪəs] *adj* mojigato

sanc•tion ['sæŋkʃn] **I** *n* **1** (*approval*) consentimiento *m*, aprobación *f* **2** (*penalty*) sanción *f*; ***impose ~s on a country*** imponer sanciones a un país **II** *v/t* (*approve*) sancionar

sanc•ti•ty ['sæŋktətɪ] carácter *m* sagrado

sanc•tu•a•ry ['sæŋktʃuerɪ] santuario *m*

sand [sænd] **I** *n* arena *f* **II** *v/t with ~paper* lijar

◆ **sand down** *v/t* lijar, pulimentar

san•dal ['sændl] sandalia *f*

'sand•bag saco *m* de arena; **'sand•bank** banco *m* de arena; **'sand•blast** *v/t* arenar; **'sand box** caja *f* de arena;

'sand-cas•tle castillo *m* de arena; **'sand dune** duna *f*
sand•er ['sændər] *tool* lijadora *f*
'sand•pa•per I *n* lija *f* **II** *v/t* lijar; **'sand-stone** arenisca *f*; **'sand storm** tormenta *f* de arena
sand•wich ['sænwɪʧ] **I** *n Span* bocadillo *m*, *L.Am.* sandwich *m* **II** *v/t*: ***be ~ed between two ...*** estar encajonado entre dos ...
sand•y ['sændɪ] *adj* **1** *soil* arenoso; *feet, towel etc* lleno de arena; ***~ beach*** playa *f* de arena **2** *hair* rubio oscuro
sane [seɪn] *adj* cuerdo
sang [sæŋ] *pret* ☞ ***sing***
san•gri•a [sæŋ'gri:ə] sangría *f*
san•guine ['sæŋgwɪn] *adj fml* optimista
san•i•tar•i•um [sænɪ'terɪəm] sanatorio *m*
san•i•ta•ry ['sænɪterɪ] *adj conditions* salubre, higiénico; ***~ installations*** instalaciones *fpl* sanitarias
'san•i•ta•ry nap•kin compresa *f*, *L.Am.* toalla *f* femenina
san•i•ta•tion [sænɪ'teɪʃn] (*sanitary installations*) instalaciones *fpl* sanitarias; (*removal of waste*) saneamiento *m*
san•i'ta•tion de•part•ment servicio *m* de limpieza
san•i•tize ['sænɪtaɪz] *v/t* **1** *make hygienic* higienizar **2** *make less offensive* expurgar
san•i•ty ['sænətɪ] razón *f*, juicio *m*; ***he started to doubt his own ~*** comenzó a tener dudas sobre su propia cordura
sank [sæŋk] *pret* ☞ ***sink***
San•ta Claus ['sæntəklɒ:z] Papá Noel *m*, Santa Claus *m*
sap [sæp] **I** *n in tree* savia *f* **II** *v/t* (*pret & pp* ***-ped***) *s.o.'s energy* consumir
sap•ling ['sæplɪŋ] BOT árbol *m* joven
sap•phire ['sæfaɪr] *jewel* zafiro *m*
sar•cas•m ['sɑ:rkæzm] sarcasmo *m*
sar•cas•tic [sɑ:r'kæstɪk] *adj* sarcástico
sar•cas•tic•al•ly [sɑ:r'kæstɪklɪ] *adv* sarcásticamente
sar•coph•a•gus [sɑ:r'kɑ:fəgəs] (*pl* ***sarcophagi*** [sɑ:r'kɑ:fəgaɪ], ***-guses*** [sɑ:r-'kɑ:fəgəsəz]) sarcófago *m*
sar•dine [sɑ:r'di:n] sardina *f*; ***be packed in like ~s*** F estar (apiñados) como sardinas en lata
Sar•din•i•a [sɑ:r'dɪnɪə] Cerdeña *f*
Sar•din•i•an [sɑ:r'dɪnɪən] **I** *adj* sardo **II** *n* sardo(-a) *m*(*f*)
sar•don•ic [sɑ:r'dɑ:nɪk] *adj* sardónico
sar•don•ic•al•ly [sɑ:r'dɑ:nɪklɪ] *adv* sardónicamente
sark•y ['sɑ:rkɪ] *Br* F ☞ ***sarcastic***
sash [sæʃ] *on dress* faja *f*, *on uniform* fajín *m*
sash 'win•dow ventana *f* corredera *or* de guillotina
sass•y ['sæsɪ] *adj* F *person* atrevido, insolente; *dress* atrevido
sat [sæt] *pret & pp* ☞ ***sit***
SAT [eseɪ'ti:] *abbr* (= ***scholastic aptitude test***) test *m* de aptitud escolar
Sa•tan ['seɪtn] Satán, Satanás
sa•tan•ic [sə'tænɪk] *adj* satánico
satch•el ['sætʃəl] cartera *f* (de colegio)
sat•el•lite ['sætəlaɪt] satélite *m*
'sat•el•lite dish antena *f* parabólica; **'sat•el•lite state** estado *m* satélite; **sat•el•lite T'V** televisión *f* por satélite
sa•ti•ate ['seɪʃɪeɪt] *v/t fml* saciar
sat•in ['sætɪn] **I** *adj* satinado **II** *n* satín *m*
sat•ire ['sætaɪr] sátira *f*
sa•tir•i•cal [sə'tɪrɪkl] *adj* satírico
sat•i•rist ['sætərɪst] escritor(a) *m*(*f*) de sátiras
sat•ir•ize ['sætəraɪz] *v/t* satirizar
sat•is•fac•tion [sætɪs'fækʃn] satisfacción *f*; ***to s.o.'s ~*** para satisfacción de alguien; ***is everything to your ~, sir?*** *fml* ¿está todo a su gusto señor?; ***I get great ~ out of listening to this music*** disfruto mucho escuchando esta música
sat•is•fac•to•ry [sætɪs'fæktərɪ] *adj* **1** satisfactorio **2** (*just good enough*) suficiente
sat•is•fy ['sætɪsfaɪ] *v/t* (*pret & pp* ***-ied***) satisfacer; *conditions* cumplir; ***I am satisfied*** (*had enough to eat*) estoy lleno; ***be satisfied with sth*** estar satisfecho con algo; ***I am satisfied that ...*** (*convinced*) estoy convencido *or* satisfecho de que ...; ***I hope you're satisfied!*** ¡estarás contento!; ***a satisfied smile*** una sonrisa de satisfacción
sat•su•ma [sæt'su:mə] (naranja *f*) mandarina *f*
sat•u•rate ['sætʃəreɪt] *v/t* **1** saturar (***with*** con); ***be absolutely ~d*** *soaking wet* estar calado hasta los huesos **2** *fig*: ***~ o.s. in a subject*** empaparse *or* imbuirse de un tema

S

sat•u•ra•tion [sætʃə'reɪʃn] *also fig* saturación *f*; ***reach ~ point*** alcanzar el punto de saturación
Sat•ur•day ['sætərdeɪ] sábado *m*; ***on ~*** el sábado; ***on ~s*** los sábados
Sat•urn ['sætərn] ASTR Saturno *m*
sauce [sɒːs] salsa *f*
'sauce•pan cacerola *f*
sau•cer ['sɒːsər] plato *m* (*de taza*)
sauc•y ['sɒːsɪ] *adj person, dress* descarado
Sa•u•di A•ra•bi•a [saʊdɪə'reɪbɪə] Arabia *f* Saudí *or* Saudita
Sa•u•di A•ra•bi•an [saʊdɪə'reɪbɪən] **I** *adj* saudita, saudí **II** *n* saudita *m/f*, saudí *m/f*
sau•na ['sɒːnə] sauna *f*; ***have a ~*** tomar una sauna
saun•ter ['sɒːntər] *v/i* andar sin prisas; ***she ~ed up to me*** se acercó tranquilamente hacia mí, se me acercó tranquilamente
saus•age ['sɒːsɪdʒ] salchicha *f*; ***~ roll*** *rollito de hojaldre con una salchicha dentro*
sau•té [soʊ'teɪ] *v/t* saltear; ***~d potatoes*** patatas *fpl* salteadas
sav•age ['sævɪdʒ] **I** *adj animal, attack* salvaje; *criticism* feroz **II** *n* salvaje *m/f* **III** *v/t of lion etc* atacar ferozmente *or* salvajemente
sav•age•ry ['sævɪdʒrɪ] crueldad *f*
save [seɪv] **I** *v/t* **1** (*rescue*) rescatar, salvar; REL salvar; ***~ s.o.'s life*** salvarle la vida a alguien
2 *money, time, effort* ahorrar; ***~ sth for s.o.*** guardarle algo a alguien; ***~ s.o. doing sth*** evitar a alguien (tener que) hacer algo; ***~ one's strength*** guardar las fuerzas; ***you can ~ your excuses*** puedes guardarte tus excusas
3 (*collect*) guardar
4 COMPUT guardar
5 *goal* parar
II *v/i* **1** (*put money aside*) ahorrar **2** SP hacer una parada
III *n* SP parada *f*
◆ **save on** *v/t electricity, gas etc* ahorrar, economizar
◆ **save up for** *v/t* ahorrar para
sav•er ['seɪvər] *person* ahorrador(a) *m(f)*; ***be a real time ~*** ser un verdadero ahorro de tiempo
savi•ng ['seɪvɪŋ] *amount saved, activity* ahorro *m*
sav•ing 'grace: ***his only ~*** lo único que le salva
sav•ings ['seɪvɪŋz] *npl* ahorros *mpl*
'sav•ings ac•count cuenta *f* de ahorros; **sav•ings and 'loan** caja *f* de ahorros; **'sav•ings bank** caja *f* de ahorros
sa•vior, *Br* **sa•viour** ['seɪvjər] REL salvador *m*
sa•vor ['seɪvər] *v/t* saborear
sa•vor•y ['seɪvərɪ] *adj not sweet* salado
sa•vour *etc Br* ☞ ***savor*** *etc*
sav•vy ['sævɪ] F **I** *n* cabeza *f* F, sentido *f* comun **II** *adj* astuto **III** *v/t & v/i* entender
saw[1] [sɒː] **I** *n tool* serrucho *m*, sierra *f* **II** *v/t* (*pret* ***-ed***, *pp* ***sawn***) aserrar
◆ **saw off** *v/t* cortar (con un serrucho)
saw[2] [sɒː] *pret* ☞ ***see***
'saw•dust serrín *m*, aserrín *m*
'saw•mill aserradero *m*, serrería *f*
sawn [sɔːn] *pp* ☞ ***saw***[1]
sax [sæks] F saxo *m* F
sax•o•phone ['sæksəfoʊn] saxofón *m*
sax•o•phon•ist [sæks'ɑːfənɪst] saxofonista *m/f*
say [seɪ] **I** *v/t* (*pret & pp* ***said***) decir; *poem* recitar; ***that is to ~*** es decir; ***what do you ~ to that?*** ¿qué opinas de eso?; ***what does the note ~?*** ¿qué dice la nota?, ¿qué pone en la nota?; ***they ~ he is rich, he is said to be rich*** dicen que es rico, se dice que es rico; ***what does your watch ~?*** ¿qué hora tienes tú?; ***you can ~ that again!*** ¡y que lo digas!; ***~, isn't that Carlos?*** F oye, ¿no es ése Carlos?; (***let's***) ***~ this happens*** digamos *or* supongamos que ocurre esto; ***a sum of, ~, $500*** una suma de, digamos *or* vamos a suponer, 500 dólares **II** *v/i* (*tell*) decir; ***it's hard to ~*** es difícil de decir; ***I can't ~*** no lo sé; ***I couldn't ~*** no sabría decir; ***you don't ~!*** ¡no me digas!, ¡qué me dices!; ***it goes without ~ing*** ni que decir tiene
III *n*: ***have one's ~*** expresar una opinión; ***they have no ~ in the matter*** no tienen nada que decir *or* opinar sobre este asunto; ***have a ~ in sth*** tener voz y voto en algo
say•ing ['seɪɪŋ] dicho *m*; ***as the ~ goes*** como dice *or* reza el dicho
'say-so F: ***just on his ~*** sólo porque él lo dice *or* diga; ***on his ~*** *with his permission* con su permiso *or* aprobación

scab [skæb] *on skin* costra *f*
sca•bies ['skeɪbiːz] MED sarna *f*
scaf•fold•ing ['skæfəldɪŋ] *on building* andamiaje *m*
scal•a•wag ['skæləwæg] F (*rascal*) granuja *m/f*
scald [skɒːld] *v/t* escaldar
scald•ing ['skɒːldɪŋ] *adj* ardiendo, hirviendo
scale[1] [skeɪl] *n on fish, reptile* escama *f*
scale[2] [skeɪl] **I** *n* (*size*) escala *f*, tamaño *m*; *on thermometer, map*, MUS escala *f*; ***on a larger ~*** a gran escala; ***on a smaller ~*** a pequeña escala; ***drawn to ~*** (hecho) a escala **II** *v/t cliffs etc* escalar
◆ **scale down** *v/t* disminuir, reducir
scale 'draw•ing dibujo *m* a escala
scale 'mo•del maqueta *f* a escala
scales [skeɪlz] *npl for weighing* báscula *f*, peso *m*; ***pair of ~*** báscula *f*, peso *m*
scal•lion ['skælɪən] cebollino *m*
scal•lop ['skæləp] *shellfish* vieira *f*
scal•ly•wag ['skælɪwæg] *Br* F granuja *m/f*
scalp [skælp] **I** *n* cuero *m* cabelludo **II** *v/t* arrancar la cabellera a
scal•pel ['skælpl] bisturí *m*
scalp•er ['skælpər] *for tickets etc* revendedor(a) *m(f)*
scam [skæm] F chanchullo *m* F
scamp [skæmp] granuja *m/f*, pillue-lo(-a) *m(f)*
scam•per ['skæmpər] *v/i of children, mice* corretear
scam•pi ['skæmpɪ] gambas *fpl* rebozadas
scan [skæn] **I** *v/t* (*pret & pp* ***-ned***) *horizon* otear; *page* ojear; COMPUT escanear **II** *n of brain* escáner *m*; *of fetus* ecografía *f*; ***have a ~*** *when pregnant* hacerse una ecografía; ***have a quick ~ of the newspapers*** echar un vistazo a los periódicos
◆ **scan in** *v/t* COMPUT escanear
scan•dal ['skændl] escándalo *m*
scan•dal•ize ['skændəlaɪz] *v/t* escandalizar; ***he was ~d to hear ...*** se escandalizó al oír ...
scan•dal•mon•ger ['skændlmʌŋgər] cotilla *m/f*, chismoso(-a) *m(f)*
scan•dal•ous ['skændələs] *adj affair, prices* escandaloso
Scan•di•na•vi•a [skændɪ'neɪvɪə] Escandinavia *f*
Scan•di•na•vi•an [skændɪ'neɪvɪən] **I** *n* escandinavo(-a) *m(f)* **II** *adj* escandinavo
scan•ner ['skænər] MED, COMPUT escáner *m*; *for fetus* ecógrafo *m*
scant [skænt] *adj* escaso
scant•i•ly ['skæntɪlɪ] *adv*: ***be ~ clad*** andar ligero de ropa
scant•y ['skæntɪ] *adj skirt* cortísimo; *bikini* mínimo
scape•goat ['skeɪpgoʊt] cabeza *f* de turco, chivo *m* expiatorio
scar [skɑːr] **I** *n* cicatriz *f* **II** *v/t* (*pret & pp* ***-red***) cicatrizar; ***he was ~red for life by the experience*** esta experiencia le dejó cicatrices de por vida
scarce [skers] *adj in short supply* escaso; ***make o.s. ~*** desaparecer
scarce•ly ['skerslɪ] *adv*: ***he had ~ said it when ...*** apenas lo había dicho cuando ...; ***there was ~ anything left*** no quedaba casi nada; ***I ~ know her*** apenas la conozco
scarce•ness ['skersnɪs] escasez *f*
scar•ci•ty ['skersətɪ] escasez *f*
scare [sker] **I** *v/t* asustar, atemorizar; ***be ~d of*** tener miedo de **II** *v/i*: ***he doesn't ~ easily*** no se asusta fácilmente *or* con facilidad **III** *n* (*panic, alarm*) miedo *m*, temor *m*; ***give s.o. a ~*** dar a alguien un susto; ***you gave me such a ~*** me diste un buen susto; ***new typhoid ~*** *headline* nuevo temor de una fiebre tifoidea
◆ **scare away** *v/t* ahuyentar
'scare•crow espantapájaros *m inv*
scare•mon•ger ['skermʌŋgər] alarmista *m/f*
scarf [skɑːrf] (*pl* ***scarves***) *around neck, over head* pañuelo *m*; *woollen* bufanda *f*
scar•let ['skɑːrlət] *adj* escarlata
scar•let 'fe•ver escarlatina *f*
scarred [skɑːrd] *adj* con cicatrices
scarves [skɑːvz] *pl* ☞ ***scarf***
scar•y ['skerɪ] *adj sight* espeluznante; ***~ music / movie*** música *f* / película *f* de miedo
scath•ing ['skeɪðɪŋ] *adj* feroz; ***they were ~ in their comments*** fueron muy mordaces en *or* con sus comentarios
scat•ter ['skætər] **I** *v/t leaflets* esparcir; *seeds* diseminar; ***be ~ed all over the room*** estar esparcido por toda la habi-

tación **II** *v/i of people* dispersarse
'scat•ter•brain F despistado(-a) *m(f)*, cabeza *m/f* de chorlito F
scat•ter•brained ['skætərbreınd] *adj* despistado
scat•tered ['skætərd] *adj showers, family, villages* disperso
scat•ter•ing ['skætərıŋ]: ***a ~ of houses*** unas cuantas casas dispersas
scav•enge ['skævındʒ] *v/i* rebuscar; ***~ for sth*** rebuscar en busca de algo
scav•eng•er ['skævındʒər] *animal, bird* carroñero *m*; *(person) persona que busca comida entre la basura*
sce•na•ri•o [sı'nɑːrıoʊ] situación *f*
scene [siːn] **1** escena *f*; *of accident, crime etc* lugar *m*; ***~s*** THEA decorados *mpl*; ***change of ~*** cambio *m* de decorado; *fig* cambio *m* de aires; ***behind the ~s*** entre bastidores; ***be on the ~*** llegar al lugar de los hechos; ***come on the ~*** aparecer, entrar en escena; ***a ~ of destruction met our eyes*** ante nuestros ojos se hallaba una escena de destrucción; ***jazz / rock ~*** mundo *m* del jazz / rock; ***... isn't my ~*** F ... no es lo mío **2** *(argument)* escena *f*, número *m*; ***make a ~*** hacer una escena, montar un número
sce•ne•ry ['siːnərı] THEA escenario *m*
sce•nic ['siːnık] *adj countryside* pintoresco; ***~ route*** ruta *f* pintoresca
scent [sent] olor *m*; *(perfume)* perfume *m*, fragancia *f*; ***be on the ~ of*** *fig* seguir la pista a
scep•ter ['septər] cetro *m*
scep•tic *etc Br* ☞ ***skeptic*** *etc*
scep•tre *Br* ☞ ***scepter***
sched•ule ['skedʒuːl] **I** *n of events, work* programa *m*; *of exams* calendario *m*; *for train, work, of lessons* horario *m*; ***be on ~*** *of work* ir según lo previsto; *of train* ir a la hora prevista; ***be behind ~*** *of work, train etc* ir con retraso; ***be three months ahead of ~*** *of builders, project* llevar tres meses de adelanto **II** *v/t (put on ~)* programar; ***it's ~d for completion next month*** está previsto que se complete el próximo mes; ***~d departure*** hora *f* de salida prevista
sched•uled flight ['skedʒuːld] vuelo *m* regular
sche•mat•ic [skı'mætık] *adj* esquemático
scheme [skiːm] **I** *n (plan)* plan *m*, proyecto *m*; *(plot)* confabulación *f* **II** *v/i (plot)* confabularse
schem•er ['skiːmər] maquinador(a) *m(f)*
schem•ing ['skiːmıŋ] *adj* maquinador
schiz•oid ['skıtsɔıd] *adj* esquizoide
schiz•o•phre•ni•a [skıtsə'friːnıə] esquizofrenia *f*
schiz•o•phren•ic [skıtsə'frenık] **I** *n* esquizofrénico(-a) *m(f)* **II** *adj* esquizofrénico
schlep [ʃlep] *v/t (pret & pp **-ped**)* F llevar a rastras F
schmal(t)z [ʃmɑːlts] F sentimentalismo *m*, sensiblería *f*
schmal(t)z•y ['ʃmɑːltsı] *adj* F sentimental, sensiblón
schmooze [ʃmuːz] *v/i* F charlotear, cotorrear
schmuck [ʃmʊk] P subnormal *m/f* F, gilipollas *m/f inv* P
schnit•zel ['ʃnıtsl] GASTR escalope *m*, *L.Am.* escalopa *f*
schnoz•zle ['ʃnɑːzl] P *(nose)* tocha *f* P, napia *f*
schol•ar ['skɑːlər] erudito(-a) *m(f)*
schol•ar•ly ['skɑːlərlı] *adj* erudito
schol•ar•ship ['skɑːlərʃıp] **1** *scholarly work* estudios *mpl* **2** *financial award* beca *f*
school[1] [skuːl] **I** *n* escuela *f*, colegio *m*; *(university)* universidad *f*; ***in ~*** en la escuela / universidad; ***go to ~*** ir a la escuela / universidad; ***there is no ~ today*** hoy no hay escuela **II** *v/t person* formar, instruir (***in*** en)
school[2] [skuːl] *n of dolphins etc* grupo *m*, banco *m*
'school age edad *f* escolar; ***be of ~*** estar en edad escolar; **'school-age** *adj* de *or* en edad escolar; **'school bag** *(satchel)* cartera *f*; **'school•boy** escolar *m*; **'school bus** autobús *m* escolar; **'school•chil•dren** *npl* escolares *mpl*; **'school days** *npl*: ***do you remember your ~?*** ¿te acuerdas de cuándo ibas al colegio?; **'school dis•trict** distrito *m* escolar; **'school friend** amigo(-a) *m(f)* del colegio; **'school•girl** escolar *f*
school•ing ['skuːlıŋ] educación *f* escolar
'school kid colegial(a) *m(f)*; **'school•mate** *Br* compañero *m* de colegio;

S

'school•teach•er maestro(-a) *m(f)*, profesor(a) *m(f)*; **'school•work** trabajo *m* escolar; **'school yard** patio *m* del colegio, recreo *m*
schoon•er ['sku:nər] NAUT goleta *f*
sci•at•i•ca [saɪ'ætɪkə] ciática *f*
sci•ence ['saɪəns] ciencia *f*
sci•ence 'fic•tion ciencia *f* ficción
'sci•ence park parque *m* tecnológico, parque *m* científico
sci•en•tif•ic [saɪən'tɪfɪk] *adj* científico
sci•en•tist ['saɪəntɪst] científico(-a) *m(f)*
sci-fi ['saɪfaɪ] F ciencia *f* ficción
scin•til•lat•ing ['sɪntɪleɪtɪŋ] *adj wit, conversation* chisposo, brillante
scis•sors ['sɪzərz] *npl* tijeras *fpl*; ***a pair of ~*** unas tijeras
'scis•sors kick *in soccer* chilena *f*
scle•ro•sis [sklə'roʊsɪs] MED esclerosis *f*
scoff[1] [skɑ:f] *v/t* F *(eat fast)* zamparse F
scoff[2] [skɑ:f] *v/i (mock)* burlarse, mofarse
◆ **scoff at** *v/t* burlarse de, mofarse de
scold [skoʊld] *v/t child, husband* regañar
scold•ing ['skoʊldɪŋ] regañina *f*, sermoneo *m*; ***give s.o. a ~*** echar a alguien un rapapolvo F
scone [skɑ:n] *bollito pequeño, a veces con frutas secas, que se suele comer untado con mantequilla o mermelada*
scoop [sku:p] **I** *n* **1** *implement* cuchara *f*; *for mud* pala *f* **2** *(story)* exclusiva *f* **II** *v/t*: ***~ sth into sth*** recoger algo para meterlo en algo
◆ **scoop up** *v/t* recoger
scoot [sku:t] *v/i* F largarse, salir zumbando
scoot•er ['sku:tər] **1** *with motor* escúter *m* **2** *child's* patinete *m*
scope [skoʊp] alcance *m*; *(freedom, opportunity)* oportunidad *f*; *of enquiry* límites *mpl*; ***he wants more ~ to do his own thing*** quiere más libertad para hacer lo que quiere; ***be within / beyond the ~ of*** *issue etc* estar dentro / más allá del alcance de
scorch [skɔ:rtʃ] *v/t* quemar
scorch•er ['skɔ:rtʃər] F día *m* abrasador
scorch•ing ['skɔ:rtʃɪŋ] *adj* abrasador
score [skɔ:r] **I** *n* **1** SP resultado *m*; *in competition* puntuación *f*; ***what's the ~?*** SP ¿cómo van?; ***keep (the) ~*** llevar el tanteo; ***the ~ was 2-1 when …*** iban 2 a 1 cuando …; ***the final ~*** el resultado final
2 *matter*: ***on that ~*** a ese respecto, en ese sentido; ***have a ~ to settle with s.o.*** tener una cuenta pendiente con alguien
3 *(written music)* partitura *f*; *of movie etc* banda *f* sonora, música *f*
4 *twenty* veintena *f*; ***~s of …*** montones de …
II *v/t* **1** *goal* marcar; *point* anotar; *in basketball* encestar **2** *(cut: line)* marcar
III *v/i* **1** SP marcar; *in basketball* encestar; ***~ from a free kick*** marcar de falta **2** *(keep the ~)* llevar el tanteo **3**: ***that's where he ~s*** ése es su punto fuerte; ***~ with a girl*** ligarse a una chica F
◆ **score off** *v/t* **1** *from list* borrar (***from*** de) **2**: ***score points off s.o.*** poner por los suelos a alguien
◆ **score out** *v/t* tachar
'score•board marcador *m*
'score•line resultado *m* final
scor•er ['skɔ:rər] **1** *of goal* goleador(a) *m(f)*; *of point* marcador(a) *m(f)*; *in basketball* encestador(a) *m(f)* **2** *(official score-keeper) encargado del marcador*
scorn [skɔ:rn] **I** *n* desprecio *m*; ***pour ~ on sth*** despreciar algo, menospreciar algo **II** *v/t idea, suggestion* despreciar
scorn•ful ['skɔ:rnfəl] *adj* despreciativo
scorn•ful•ly ['skɔ:rnfəlɪ] *adv* con desprecio
Scor•pi•o ['skɔ:rpɪoʊ] ASTR Escorpio *m/f inv*; ***be (a) ~*** ser Escorpio
scor•pi•on ['skɔ:rpɪən] escorpión *m*
Scot [skɑ:t] escocés(-esa) *m(f)*
Scotch [skɑ:tʃ] *(whiskey)* whisky *m* (escocés)
Scotch 'tape® celo *m*, *L.Am.* Durex® *m*
scot-'free *adv*: ***get off ~*** salir impune
Scot•land ['skɑ:tlənd] Escocia *f*
Scots•man ['skɑ:tsmən] escocés *m*
Scots•wom•an ['skɑ:tswʊmən] escocesa *f*
Scot•tish ['skɑ:tɪʃ] *adj* escocés
scoun•drel ['skaʊndrəl] canalla *m/f*
scour[1] ['skaʊər] *v/t (search)* rastrear, peinar
scour[2] ['skaʊər] *v/t pans* fregar

scourge [skɜːrdʒ] *fig* tormento *m*, martirio *m*
scout [skaʊt] **1** (*boy* ~) boy-scout *m* **2** *for talent* ojeador(a) *m*(*f*)
◆ **scout around** *v/i* hacer un reconocimiento
◆ **scout around for** *v/t* buscar, rebuscar
scowl [skaʊl] **I** *n* ceño *m* **II** *v/i* fruncir el ceño
◆ **scowl at** *v/t* mirar con el ceño fruncido
scrab•ble ['skræbl]*v/i* hurgar, escarbar
scrag•gy ['skrægɪ] *adj* escuálido, raquítico
scram [skræm] *v/i* (*pret & pp* **-med**) F largarse F; **~!** ¡largo!
scram•ble ['skræmbl] **I** *n* (*rush*) prisa *f*; ***in the ~ to sell off stocks*** en el barullo para liquidar existencias **II** *v/t message* cifrar, codificar **III** *v/i* (*climb*) trepar; ***he ~d to his feet*** se levantó de un salto
scram•bled eggs [skræmbld'egz] *npl* huevos *mpl* revueltos
scram•bler ['skræmblər] *for messages* aleatorizador *m*, mezclador *m*
scrap[1] [skræp] **I** *n* **1** *metal* chatarra *f*; ***sell sth for ~*** vender algo a la chatarra **2** *of food* trocito *m*; *of common sense* pizca *f*; ***there is not a ~ of evidence*** no existe el más mínimo indicio; ***there is not a ~ of truth in it*** no hay ni un ápice de verdad en esto **II** *v/t* (*pret & pp* **-ped**) *plan*, *project* abandonar; *paragraph* borrar
scrap[2] [skræp] *n* F *fight* pelea *f*
'scrap•book álbum *m* de recortes
scrape [skreɪp] **I** *n on paintwork etc* arañazo *m*; ***be in a ~*** F estar en un lío **II** *v/t paintwork* rayar; ***~ a living*** apañarse, ir tirando **III** *v/i* rozar (***against*** con, contra); ***~ along the ground*** arrastrarse por el suelo
◆ **scrape along, scrape by** *v/i fig* arreglárselas, subsistir
◆ **scrape off** *v/t* raspar
◆ **scrape through** *v/i in exam* aprobar por los pelos
◆ **scrape together** *v/t money* juntar (con dificultad)
scrap•er ['skreɪpər] espátula *f*, raspador *m*
'scrap heap: ***be good for the ~*** *of person* estar para el arrastre; *of object* estar para tirar; **scrap 'met•al** chatarra *f*; **scrap 'pa•per** papel *m* usado
scrap•py ['skræpɪ] *adj work*, *writing* desorganizado
'scrap val•ue precio *m* como chatarra
'scrap•yard desguace *m*, chatarrería *f*
'scratch pad bloc *m* de notas
'scratch pa•per papel *m* de *or* para borrador
scratch [skrætʃ] **I** *n mark* marca *f*; ***have a ~*** *to stop itching* rascarse; ***start from ~*** empezar desde cero; ***your work isn't up to ~*** tu trabajo es insuficiente **II** *v/t* (*mark*: *skin*) arañar; (*mark*: *paint*) rayar; *because of itch* rascarse; ***~ one's arm on a nail*** arañarse el brazo con un clavo; ***~ one's head*** *because of itch* rascarse la cabeza; *in puzzlement* comerse la cabeza **III** *v/i of cat etc* arañar; *because of itch* rascarse
◆ **scratch off** *v/t* rascar
scratch•y ['skrætʃɪ] *adj* **1** *noise* chirriante; *old record* rayado **2** *wool* que pica
scrawl [skrɒːl] **I** *n* garabato *m* **II** *v/t* garabatear
scraw•ny ['skrɒːnɪ] *adj* escuálido
scream [skriːm] **I** *n* grito *m*; ***~s of laughter*** carcajadas *fpl*; ***be a ~*** F ser graciosísimo(-a), ser un punto F **II** *v/i* gritar; *of jet plane* rugir; ***~ with laughter*** reírse a carcajadas, reírse a mandíbula batiente
◆ **scream down** *v/t*: ***scream the place down*** F chillar *or* gritar hasta desgañitarse
◆ **scream out** *v/t orders etc* vocear
scree [skriː] peñascal *m*
screech [skriːtʃ] **I** *n of tires* chirrido *m*; (*scream*) chillido *m* **II** *v/i of tires* chirriar; (*scream*) chillar; ***~ to a halt*** parar en seco con un chirrido
screed [skriːd] rollo *m*; ***she writes ~s and ~s*** escribe hojas y hojas
screen [skriːn] **I** *n* **1** *in room*, *hospital* mampara *f*; *protective* cortina *f*; *in basketball* bloqueo *m* **2** *in movie theater* pantalla *f*; COMPUT monitor *m*, pantalla *f*; ***adapt a novel for the ~*** adaptar una novela para la gran pantalla **II** *v/t* **1** (*protect*, *hide*) ocultar; *in basketball* bloquear **2** *movie* proyectar **3** *for security reasons* investigar
◆ **screen off** *v/t part of room* separar, dividir

'screen dis•play COMPUT pantalla *f*; **'screen i•dol** ídolo *m* de la pantalla; **'screen•play** guión *m*; **'screen sav•er** COMPUT salvapantallas *m inv*; **'screen test** *for movie* prueba *f*; **'screen-writ•er** guionista *m/f*

screw [skru:] **I** *n* **1** tornillo *m*; ***he has a ~ loose*** F le falta un tornillo F; ***put the ~s on s.o.*** *fig* apretarle las tuercas a alguien **2** V (*sex*) polvo *m* V **II** *v/t* **1**: ***~ sth to sth*** atornillar algo a algo **2** V (*have sex with*) echar un polvo con V **3** F (*cheat*) timar F **III** *v/i* V echar un polvo

◆ **screw up I** *v/t* **1** *eyes* cerrar **2** *piece of paper* arrugar **3** F (*make a mess of*) fastidiar F **II** *v/i* F (*make a bad mistake*) meter la pata F

'screw•ball 1 F excéntrico(-a) *m(f)*, chiflado(-a) *m(f)* F **2** *in baseball* tirabuzón *m*

'screw•driv•er destornillador *m*

screwed up [skru:d'ʌp] *adj* F *psychologically* acomplejado

'screw top *on bottle* tapón *m* de rosca

screw•y ['skru:ɪ] *adj* F chiflado F; *idea, film* descabellado F

scrib•ble ['skrɪbl] **I** *n* garabato *m* **II** *v/t & v/i* garabatear

scrib•bler ['skrɪblər] *hum, pej* escritorzuelo(-a) *m(f)*

scrim•mage ['skrɪmɪdʒ] *in football* melé *f*

scrimp [skrɪmp] *v/i*: ***~ and scrape*** pasar apuros, pasar estrecheces

scrip [skrɪp] *representing stock* bono *m* social

script [skrɪpt] **1** *for movie, play* guión *m*, *L.Am.* libreto *m* **2** *form of writing* caligrafía *f*

'script girl *in the movies* chica *f* del guión

scrip•ture ['skrɪptʃər] escritura *f*; ***the (Holy) Scriptures*** las Sagradas Escrituras

S

'script•writ•er guionista *m/f*, *L.Am.* libretista *m/f*

scroll [skroul] (*manuscript*) manuscrito *m*

◆ **scroll down** *v/i* COMPUT avanzar

◆ **scroll up** *v/i* COMPUT retroceder

'scroll bar COMPUT barra *f* de desplazamiento

scrooge [skru:dʒ] F agarrado(-a) *m(f)*, tacaño(-a) *m(f)*

scro•tum ['skroutəm] (*pl* ***-tums, scrota*** ['skroutə]) ANAT escroto *m*

scrounge [skraundʒ] *v/t* gorronear (***from*** de)

scroung•er ['skraundʒər] gorrón(-ona) *m(f)*

scrub[1] [skrʌb] *n type of countryside* matorral *m*

scrub[2] [skrʌb] **I** *v/t* (*pret & pp* ***-bed***) *floors* fregar; *hands* frotar **II** *n*: ***give sth a ~*** dar un fregado a algo

scrub•bing brush ['skrʌbɪŋ] cepillo *m* para fregar

scrub•by ['skrʌbɪ] *adj countryside* de matorrales, cubierto de maleza

scruff [skrʌf]: ***grab s.o. by the ~ of the neck*** agarrar a alguien del pescuezo

scruff•y ['skrʌfɪ] *adj* andrajoso, desaliñado

scrum [skrʌm] *in rugby* melé *f*

scrump•tious ['skrʌmpʃəs] *adj* F de muerte *or* rechupete F

◆ **scrunch up** [skrʌntʃ] *v/t plastic cup etc* estrujar

scru•ples ['skru:plz] *npl* escrúpulos *mpl*; ***have no ~s about doing sth*** no tener escrúpulos a la hora de hacer algo

scru•pu•lous ['skru:pjələs] *adj* **1** *with moral principles* escrupuloso **2** (*thorough*) meticuloso; *attention to detail* minucioso

scru•pu•lous•ly ['skru:pjələslɪ] *adv* (*meticulously*) minuciosamente

scru•ti•nize ['skru:tɪnaɪz] *v/t* (*examine closely*) estudiar, examinar

scru•ti•ny ['skru:tɪnɪ] escrutinio *m*; ***come under ~*** ser objeto de investigación

scu•ba div•er ['sku:bə] submarinista *m/f*

'scu•ba div•ing submarinismo *m*

scuff [skʌf] *v/t shoes, paintwork* raspar, arañar

scuf•fle ['skʌfl] riña *f*

sculpt [skʌlpt] *v/t* esculpir

sculp•tor ['skʌlptər] escultor(a) *m(f)*

sculp•ture ['skʌlptʃər] escultura *f*

scum [skʌm] **1** *on liquid* película *f* de suciedad **2** (*pej*: *people*) escoria *f*; ***the ~ of the earth*** la escoria del mundo

scur•ri•lous ['skʌrələs] *adj* (*defamatory*) difamatorio

scur•ry ['skʌrɪ] *v/i of mice* corretear; *of*

people salir corriendo, apresurarse
scythe [saɪð] guadaña *f*
scyth•ing tack•le ['saɪðɪŋ] *in soccer* segada *f*
sea [siː] mar *m or f*; ***by the ~*** junto al mar; ***at ~*** en el mar; ***be all at ~*** *fig* estar totalmente desorientado *or* perdido; ***by ~*** en barco; ***go to ~*** *of person* hacerse marinero; ***put to ~*** hacerse a la mar; ***a ~ of faces*** un mar de caras
'sea an•i•mal animal *m* marino; **'sea•bed** fondo *m* marino; **'sea•bird** ave *f* marina; **'sea•board** costa *f*, ensenada *f*; **'sea breeze** brisa *f* marina; **sea•far•ing** ['siːferɪŋ] *adj nation* marinero; **'sea•food** marisco *m*; **'sea•front** paseo *m* marítimo; **'sea•go•ing** *adj vessel* de altura; **'sea•gull** gaviota *f*; **'sea horse** caballito *m* de mar
seal[1] [siːl] *n animal* foca *f*
seal[2] [siːl] **I** *n on document* sello *m*; TECH junta *f*, sello *m*; ***~ of approval*** *fig* aprobación *f*, visto *m* bueno **II** *v/t container* sellar; ***~ed envelope*** sobre *m* sellado; ***~ed bid*** COM oferta *f* en sobre cerrado; ***my lips are ~ed*** mis labios están sellados, no diré nada; ***~ s.o.'s fate*** decidir irrevocablemente el futuro de alguien
◆ **seal off** *v/t area* aislar
seal•ant ['siːlənt] material *m* de sellado, pasta *f* para sellar
'sea lev•el: ***above ~*** sobre el nivel del mar; ***below ~*** bajo el nivel del mar
'sea li•on león *m* marino
seam [siːm] **1** *on garment* costura *f*; ***be bursting at the ~s*** *fig* estar a reventar, estar hasta los topes **2** *of ore* filón *m*
sea•man ['siːmən] marinero *m*
seam•stress ['siːmstrɪs] modista *f*
seam•y ['siːmɪ] *adj area, bar* sórdido, sucio; ***the ~ side of life*** el lado sórdido de la vida, la cara miserable de la vida
'sea•plane hidroavión *m*; **'sea•port** puerto *m* marítimo; **'sea pow•er** *nation* potencia *f* marítima
search [sɜːrʧ] **I** *n* búsqueda *f*; ***be in ~ of*** estar en busca de; ***do a ~*** COMPUT hacer una búsqueda, buscar; ***do a ~ and replace*** COMPUT buscar y sustituir **II** *v/t baggage, person* registrar; ***~ a place for s.o.*** buscar a alguien en un lugar; ***~ me!*** F ¡(y) yo qué sé!, ¡(y) a mí que me cuentas!
◆ **search for** *v/t* buscar
◆ **search through** *v/t desk, papers, files* buscar entre
search•ing ['sɜːrʧɪŋ] *adj look* escrutador; *question* difícil
'search•light reflector *m*; **'search par•ty** grupo *m* de rescate; **'search war•rant** orden *f* de registro
'sea•shore orilla *f*; **'sea•sick** *adj* mareado; ***get ~*** marearse; **'sea•sick•ness** mareo *m*; **'sea•side** costa *f*, playa *f*; ***at*** *or* ***by the ~*** en la costa *or* playa; ***go to the ~*** ir a la costa *or* playa; ***~ resort*** centro *m* de veraneo costero
sea•son ['siːzn] **I** *n* (*winter, spring etc*) estación *f*; *for tourism etc* temporada *f*; ***plums aren't in ~ at the moment*** ahora no es temporada de ciruelas; ***Season's Greetings!*** ¡Felices Pascuas!, ¡Felices Fiestas! **II** *v/t* **1** *food* condimentar **2** *wood* curar
sea•son•al ['siːznl] *adj fruit, vegetables* del tiempo; *employment* temporal
sea•soned ['siːznd] *adj* **1** *wood* seco **2** *traveler, campaigner* experimentado
sea•son•ing ['siːznɪŋ] condimento *m*
'sea•son tick•et abono *m*
seat [siːt] **I** *n in room, bus, airplane* asiento *m*; *in theater* butaca *f*; *of pants* culera *f*; POL escaño *m*, *Mex* curul *m*; ***please take a ~*** por favor, siéntese; ***do sth by the ~ of one's pants*** F hacer algo sobre la marcha
II *v/t* **1** (*have seating for*): ***the hall can ~ 200 people*** la sala tiene capacidad para 200 personas **2**: ***please remain ~ed*** *fml* por favor, permanezcan sentados; ***please be ~ed*** *fml* por favor tome asiento
'seat belt cinturón *m* de seguridad; ***fasten one's ~*** abrocharse el cinturón de seguridad
seat•ing ['siːtɪŋ] **I** *n* aforo *m* **II** *adj*: ***a ~ capacity of 200*** un aforo de 200 personas
'sea ur•chin erizo *m* de mar; **sea 'wall** espigón *m*, escollera *f*; **'sea•weed** alga(s) *f(pl)*; **'sea•wor•thy** *adj* en condiciones para navegar
sec [sek] F ☞ ***second***[1] **I 1**
SEC [esiː'siː] *abbr* (= ***Securities and Exchange Commission***) Comisión *f* de Valores y Bolsas
sec•a•teurs [sekə'tɜːrz] *npl Br* tijeras

fpl de podar
se•cede [sɪ'si:d] *v/i* POL separarse (***from*** de)
se•ces•sion [sɪ'seʃn] POL secesión *f* (***from*** de)
se•clud•ed [sɪ'klu:dɪd] *adj* apartado
se•clu•sion [sɪ'klu:ʒn] aislamiento *m*
sec•ond[1] ['sekənd] **I** *n* **1** *of time* segundo *m*; ***just a ~*** un segundo; ***I won't be a ~*** no tardaré nada, no tardaré ni un segundo; ***do you have a ~?*** ¿tienes un segundo? **2** *in sequence* segundo(-a) *m(f)* **3**: ***~s out!*** *in boxing* ¡segundos fuera!
II *adj* segundo; ***he's going through a ~ childhood*** está pasando por una segunda infancia; ***~ home*** segunda vivienda *f*; ***it has become a ~ home to me*** es como mi segunda casa; ***it has become ~ nature for him*** se ha convertido en una costrumbre para él; ***a ~ Lorca*** otro Lorca; ***be ~ to none*** ser insuperable *or* inigualable
III *adv come in* en segundo lugar
IV *v/t motion* apoyar
se•cond[2] [sɪ'kɑ:nd] *v/t*: ***be ~ed to*** ser asignado a
sec•ond•a•ry ['sekənderɪ] *adj* secundario; ***of ~ importance*** de menor importancia
sec•ond•a•ry ed•u'ca•tion educación *f* secundaria
'sec•ond base segunda base *f*; **'sec•ond base•man** segunda base *m/f*, jugador(a) *m(f)* de segunda base; **sec•ond 'best** *adj*: ***be ~*** ser el segundo mejor; *inferior* ser un segundón; ***come off ~*** quedar segundo; **sec•ond 'big•gest** *adj*: ***it is the ~ company in the area*** es la segunda empresa más grande de la zona; **sec•ond-'class** *adj ticket* de segunda clase; **sec•ond 'cous•in** primo(-a) *m(f)* segundo(-a); **sec•ond-de'gree** *adj burns* de segundo grado; **sec•ond 'floor** primer piso *m*, *Br* segundo piso *m*; **sec•ond-'guess** *v/t* adelantar, anticipar; **'sec•ond hand** *on clock* segundero *m*; **sec•ond-'hand** **I** *adj* de segunda mano; ***~ bookstore*** tienda *f* de libros usados *or* libros de segunda mano **II** *adv buy* de segunda mano
sec•ond•ly ['sekəndlɪ] *adv* en segundo lugar
sec•ond-'rate *adj* inferior
sec•ond 'thoughts: ***I've had ~*** he cambiado de idea; ***on ~ …*** pensándolo mejor …
se•cre•cy ['si:krəsɪ] secretismo *m*; ***in or amid great ~*** entre *or* en medio de un gran secretismo; ***~ of the confessional*** REL secreto *m* de confesión
se•cret ['si:krət] **I** *n* secreto *m*; ***in ~*** en secreto; ***have no ~s from s.o.*** no tener secretos con alguien; ***make no ~ of sth*** no guardar algo en secreto **II** *adj* secreto; ***keep sth ~*** mantener *or* guardar algo en secreto; ***keep sth ~ from s.o.*** ocultar algo a alguien
se•cret 'a•gent agente *m/f* secreto(-a)
sec•re•tar•i•al [sekrə'terɪəl] *adj tasks, job* de secretario
sec•re•tar•y ['sekrəterɪ] **1** secretario(-a) *m(f)* **2** POL ministro(-a) *m(f)*
sec•re•tar•y-'gen•er•al secretario(-a) *m(f)* general
Sec•re•tar•y of 'State *in USA* Secretario(-a) *m(f)* de Estado
se•crete [sɪ'kri:t] *v/t* **1** (*give off*) segregar **2** (*hide away*) esconder
se•cre•tion [sɪ'kri:ʃn] secreción *f*
se•cre•tive ['si:krətɪv] *adj* reservado (***about*** acerca de)
se•cret•ly ['si:krətlɪ] *adv* en secreto
se•cret po'lice policía *f* secreta
se•cret 'ser•vice servicio *m* secreto
sect [sekt] secta *f*
sec•tar•i•an [sek'terɪən] *adj fighting, violence, attitudes* sectario
sec•tion ['sekʃn] *of book, company, text* sección *f*; *of building* zona *f*; *of apple* parte *f*
sec•tor ['sektər] sector *m*
sec•u•lar ['sekjələr] *adj* laico
sec•u•lar•ize ['sekjələraɪz] *v/t* secularizar
se•cure [sɪ'kjʊr] **I** *adj shelf etc* seguro; *job, contract* fijo; ***financially ~*** seguro económicamente **II** *v/t* **1** *shelf etc* asegurar **2** *s.o.'s help* conseguir
se'cured cred•i•tor acreedor(a) *m(f)* asegurado(-a); **se'cured debt** deuda *f* garantizada; **se'cured loan** préstamo *m* garantizado
se'cu•ri•ties mar•ket FIN mercado *m* de valores
se•cu•ri•ty [sɪ'kjʊrətɪ] **1** seguridad *f*; ***go through ~*** *at airport etc* pasar por segu-

ridad; ***will you call ~?*** ¿va a llamar a seguridad?; ***for ~ reasons*** por razones de seguridad **2** *for investment* garantía *f*
se'cu•ri•ty a•lert alerta *f*; **se'cu•ri•ty check** control *m* de seguridad; **se'cu•ri•ty-con•scious** *adj* consciente de la seguridad; **Se'cu•ri•ty Coun•cil** *of UN* Consejo *m* de Seguridad; **se'cu•ri•ty forces** *npl* fuerzas *fpl* de seguridad; **se'cu•ri•ty guard** guardia *m/f* de seguridad; **se'cu•ri•ty risk** *person* peligro *m* (para la seguridad)
se•dan [sɪ'dæn] MOT turismo *m*
se•date[1] [sɪ'deɪt] *v/t* sedar
se•date[2] [sɪ'deɪt] *adj person, tempo* tranquilo, pausado
se•da•tion [sɪ'deɪʃn]: ***be under ~*** estar sedado; ***put s.o. under ~*** sedar a alguien, dar un sedante a alguien
sed•a•tive ['sedətɪv] sedante *m*
sed•en•ta•ry ['sedənterɪ] *adj job* sedentario
sed•i•ment ['sedɪmənt] sedimento *m*
se•duce [sɪ'du:s] *v/t* seducir
se•duc•tion [sɪ'dʌkʃn] seducción *f*
se•duc•tive [sɪ'dʌktɪv] *adj dress* seductor; *offer* tentador
see [si:] **I** *v/t* (*pret* ***saw***, *pp* ***seen***) ver; (*understand*) entender, ver; *romantically* ver, salir con; ***can I ~ the manager?*** ¿puedo ver al encargado?; ***you should ~ a doctor*** deberías ir a que te viera un médico; ***~ s.o. home*** acompañar a alguien a casa; ***~ you!*** F ¡hasta la vista!, ¡chao! F; ***I don't ~ that working*** no veo que eso vaya a funcionar; ***what do you ~ in him?*** ¿qué es lo que ves en él?; ***I saw him arrive*** *or* ***arriving*** lo ví llegar; ***as I ~ it*** tal y como yo lo veo *or* entiendo
II *v/i* ver; ***you'll ~*** (ya) verás; ***you ~*** ves, sabes; ***I ~*** ya veo; ***let me ~*** déjame ver; ***we'll ~*** ya veremos; ***~!, I told you it wouldn't work*** ¡ves!, te dije que no funcionaría
◆ **see about** *v/t* (*look into*): ***I'll see about getting it repaired*** me encargaré de que lo arreglen; ***we'll see about that!*** F ¡eso ya lo veremos! F
◆ **see in** *v/i to room etc* ver (dentro)
◆ **see off** *v/t* **1** *at airport etc* despedir **2** (*chase away*) espantar
◆ **see out** *v/t*: ***see s.o. out*** acompañar a alguien a la puerta; ***I'll see myself out*** no hace falta que me acompañes
◆ **see over** *v/t new house* visitar, echar un vistazo a
◆ **see through** *v/t* **1** *person* conocer **2**: ***see s.o. through a difficult time*** ayudar *or* apoyar a alguien en un momento difícil
◆ **see to** *v/t*: ***see to sth*** ocuparse de algo; ***see to it that something gets done*** asegurarse de que algo se haga
seed [si:d] **1** semilla *f*; ***go to ~*** *of person* descuidarse; *of district* empeorarse **2** *in tennis* cabeza *f* de serie
seed•ed ['si:dɪd] *adj player* cabeza de serie; ***he is ~ 15th in the world*** ocupa el puesto decimoquinto a nivel mundial
seed•less ['si:dlɪs] *adj* sin semillas *or* pipas
seed•ling ['si:dlɪŋ] planta *f* de semillero
seed•y ['si:dɪ] *adj bar, district* de mala calaña
see•ing (that) ['si:ɪŋ] *conj* dado que, ya que
see•ing 'eye dog perro *m* lazarillo
seek [si:k] *v/t* (*pret & pp* ***sought***) buscar
seem [si:m] *v/i* parecer; ***it ~s that …*** parece que …; ***it ~s as if*** *or* ***though*** parece como si; ***strange as it may ~*** por extraño que parezca *or* pueda parecer; ***it seems like it*** eso (es lo que) parece; ***how does she ~ to you?*** ¿cómo la encuentras?, ¿cómo la vés?
seem•ing ['si:mɪŋ] *adj* aparente
seem•ing•ly ['si:mɪŋlɪ] *adv* aparentemente
seen [si:n] *pp* ☞ ***see***
seep [si:p] *v/i of liquid* filtrarse
◆ **seep out** *v/i of liquid* filtrarse
see•saw ['si:sɒ:] subibaja *m*, balancín *m*
seethe [si:ð] *v/i*: ***be seething with anger*** estar a punto de estallar (de cólera)
'see-through *adj dress, material* transparente
seg•ment ['segmənt] segmento *m*
seg•ment•ed [seg'məntɪd] *adj* segmentado, dividido
seg•re•gate ['segrɪgeɪt] *v/t* segregar
seg•re•ga•tion [segrɪ'geɪʃn] segregación *f*
seis•mic ['saɪzmɪk] *adj* **1** sísmico **2** *fig*: *consequences, significance* colosal, cuantioso

seis•mo•graph ['saɪzməgrɑːf] sismógrafo *m*

seis•mol•o•gy [saɪz'mɑːlədʒɪ] sismología *f*

seize [siːz] *v/t s.o., s.o.'s arm* agarrar; *opportunity* aprovechar; *of Customs, police etc* incautarse de

◆ **seize on** *v/t idea, opportunity* aferrarse a, aprovecharse de

◆ **seize up** *v/i of engine* atascarse

sei•zure ['siːʒər] **1** MED ataque *m* **2** *of drugs etc* incautación *f*, *amount seized* alijo *m*

sel•dom ['seldəm] *adv* raramente, casi nunca; ***~, if ever, has there been ...*** pocas veces, si es que alguna vez ha habido ...

se•lect [sɪ'lekt] **I** *v/t* seleccionar **II** *adj* (*exclusive*) selecto

se•lec•tion [sɪ'lekʃn] selección *f*; (*choosing*) elección *f*

se'lec•tion pro•cess proceso *m* de selección

se•lec•tive [sɪ'lektɪv] *adj* selectivo

self [self] (*pl* ***selves*** [selvz]) ego *m*; ***my other ~*** mi otro yo; ***his / my true ~*** su / mi verdadero yo; ***he's back to his old ~ again*** ya ha vuelto a ser el de antes

self-ad•dressed en•ve•lope [selfədrest'envəloʊp]: ***send us a ~*** envíenos un sobre con sus datos; **self-ad'he•sive** *adj stamps* autoadhesivo; **self-ap•point•ed** [selfə'pɔɪntɪd] *adj* autoproclamado, autoeregido; **self-as'sur•ance** confianza *f* en sí mismo; **self-as'sured** *adj* seguro de sí mismo; **self-'ca•ter•ing a•part•ment** *Br* apartamento *m or Span* piso *m* sin servicio de comidas; **self-'cen•tered**, *Br* **self-'cen•tred** [self'sentərd] *adj* egoísta; **self-'clean•ing** *adj oven* con autolimpieza; **self-con'fessed** *adj*: ***he's a ~ megalomaniac*** se confiesa megalómano; **self-'con•fi•dence** confianza *f* en sí mismo; **self-'con•fi•dent** *adj* seguro de sí mismo; **self-'con•scious** *adj* tímido; **self-'con•scious•ness** timidez *f*, **self-con•tained** [selfkən'teɪnd] *adj apartment* independiente; **self con'trol** autocontrol *m*; **self-'crit•i•cal** *adj* autocrítico; **self-'crit•i•cism** autocrítica *f*; **self-de'fense**, *Br* **self-de'fence** autodefensa *f*; ***in ~*** en defensa propia; **self-de•struct** [selfdɪ'strʌkt] *v/i* autodestruirse, destruirse automáticamente; **self-de•ter•mi'na•tion** POL autodeterminación *f*, **self-'dis•ci•pline** autodisciplina *f*, **self-'doubt** inseguridad *f*; **self-'ed•u•cat•ed** *adj*: ***~ person*** persona *f* autodidacta; **self-ef•fac•ing** [selfɪ'feɪsɪŋ] *adj* recatado, modesto; **self-em•ployed** [selfɪm'plɔɪd] *adj* autónomo, *L.Am.* cuentapropista; **self-es'teem** autoestima *f*, **self-'ev•i•dent** *adj* obvio, evidente; **self-ex'pres•sion** autoexpresión *f*, **self-ex'tract•ing archive** COMPUT archivo *m* autoextraíble; **self-'gov•ern•ment** autogobierno *m*; **self-'help** autoayuda *f*, **self-im'por•tance** soberbia *f*, humos *mpl*; **self-im'por•tant** *adj* soberbio, engreído; **self-in'dul•gent** *adj* excesivo, sin moderación; **self-'in•terest** interés *m* propio

self•ish ['selfɪʃ] *adj* egoísta

self•less ['selflɪs] *adj* desinteresado

self-made 'man hombre *m* hecho a sí mismo; **self-'pit•y** autocompasión *f*, **self-'por•trait** autorretrato *m*; **self-pos•sessed** [selfpə'zest] *adj* sereno; **self-pres•er'va•tion** supervivencia *f*, **self-pro•claimed** [selfprə'kleɪmd] *adj* autoproclamado; **self-re'li•ant** *adj* autosuficiente; **self-re'spect** amor *m* propio; **self-re•spect•ing** [selfrɪ'spektɪŋ] *adj*: ***no ~ businessman ...*** ningún hombre de negocios con amor propio ...; **self-'right•eous** *adj pej* santurrón, intolerante; **self-'ris•ing** *adj flour* con levadura; **self-'rule** POL autogobierno *m*; **self-'sac•ri•fice** autosacrificio *m*; ***in a spirit of ~*** haciendo un autosacrificio, como autosacrificio; **self-sat•is•fied** [self'sætɪsfaɪd] *adj pej* pagado de sí mismo; **self-seal•ing** [self'siːlɪŋ] *adj envelope* con auto-pegado, autoadhesivo; **self-'ser•vice** *adj* de autoservicio; **self-ser•vice 'res•tau•rant** (restaurante *m*) autoservicio *m*; **self-suf'fi•cient** *adj* autosuficiente, independiente; ***be ~ in oil*** autoabastercerse de petróleo; **self-sup'port•ing** *adj* **1** FIN independiente, autónomo **2** *structure* independiente, aparte; **self-'taught** *adj* autodidacta

sell [sel] (*pret & pp* ***sold***) **I** *v/t* vender; ***~ o.s.*** venderse (a sí mismo); ***you'll never manage to ~ them that idea*** nunca

S

conseguirás venderles esa idea; ***be completely sold on sth*** *enthusiastic about* estar absolutamente entusiasmado *or* emocionado con algo

II *v/i* (*pret & pp* ***sold***) vender; *of goods* venderse; **~ *by …*** *on label* vender antes de …; ***they are ~ing at $5 each*** se venden a 5 dólares cada uno

◆ **sell off** *v/t* liquidar, deshacerse de

◆ **sell out** *v/i* **1** *of product* agotarse; ***we've*** *or* ***we are sold out*** se nos ha(n) agotado **2** *of idealist* venderse

◆ **sell out of** *v/t* agotar las existencias de

◆ **sell up I** *v/i* vender todo **II** *v/t business etc* vender, liquidar

'sell-by date fecha *f* límite de venta; ***be past its ~*** haber pasado la fecha límite de venta; ***she's well past her ~*** F hace tiempo que se le pasó el arroz

sell•er ['selər] *person* vendedor(a) *m(f)*; ***it's a ~'s market*** es un mercado favorable para el vendedor; ***be a good ~*** *of product* venderse muy bien

sell•ing ['selıŋ] COM ventas *fpl*

'sell•ing point COM ventaja *f*

Sel•lo•tape® ['selәteıp] *Br* celo *m*, *L.Am.* Durex® *m*

'sell•out *success* éxito *m* de taquilla

selves [selvz] *pl* ☞ ***self***

se•man•tic [sı'mæntık] *adj* semántico

se•man•tics [sı'mæntıks] *nsg*: *subject* semántica *f*; ***that's just ~*** eso es pura palabrería

sem•blance ['sembləns] indicio *m*, atisbo *m*; ***without the slightest ~ of fear*** sin el mínimo indicio de miedo

se•men ['si:mən] semen *m*

se•mes•ter [sı'mestər] semestre *m*

sem•i ['semı] *truck* camión *m* semirremolque

sem•i•breve ['semıbri:v] *Br* MUS semibreve *f*; **'sem•i•cir•cle** semicírculo *m*; **sem•i'cir•cu•lar** *adj* semicircular; **sem•i-'co•lon** punto *m* y coma; **sem•i•con'duc•tor** ELEC semiconductor *m*; **sem•i•de•tached 'house** *casa unida a la casa contigua por un mismo muro*; **sem•i'fi•nal** semifinal *f*; **sem•i-'fi•nal•ist** semifinalista *m/f*; **sem•i-man•u'fac•tured prod•uct** producto *m* semimanufacturado

sem•i•nar ['semına:r] seminario *m*

sem•i•nar•y ['semınerı] REL seminario *m* (conciliar)

sem•i•of'fi•cial *adj* semioficial; **sem•i•pre•cious 'stone** piedra *f* semipreciosa; **sem•i'skilled** *adj* semicualificado; **sem•i•skimmed 'milk** *Br* leche *f* semidesnatada

'sem•i•tone MUS semitono *m*

'sem•i•trail•er MOT semitráiler *m*

sem•o•li•na [semə'li:nə] sémola *f*

Sem•tex® ['semteks] Semtex *m*

sen•ate ['senət] senado *m*

sen•a•tor ['senətər] senador(a) *m(f)*; ***Senator George Schwarz*** el Senador George Schwarz

sen•a•to•ri•al [senə'tɔ:rıəl] *adj* senatorial

send [send] *v/t* (*pret & pp* ***sent***) **1** enviar, mandar; ***~ her my best wishes*** dale recuerdos de mi parte; ***~ s.o. after s.o.*** mandar a alguien en busca a alguien **2**: ***~ s.o. mad*** volver a alguien loco; ***the news sent him into fits of laughter*** las noticias le hicieron partirse de la risa; ***the explosion sent the car flying through the air*** la explosión hizo volar el coche por los aires

◆ **send away** *v/t* **1** *person* despedir, echar **2** *letter etc* enviar, mandar

◆ **send away for** *v/t*: ***send away for sth*** escribir solicitando algo

◆ **send back** *v/t* devolver

◆ **send down** *v/t* **1** *prices, stock values* hacer bajar **2** *Br* EDU expulsar (***from*** de)

◆ **send for** *v/t* mandar buscar

◆ **send in** *v/t troops, application* enviar, mandar; *next interviewee* hacer pasar

◆ **send off** *v/t* **1** *letter, fax etc* enviar, mandar **2** *Br* SP expulsar

◆ **send on** *v/t* **1** *baggage in advance* enviar con antelación **2** *letter* reenviar, reexpedir

◆ **send out I** *v/t* **1** *invitations, application forms* mandar, echar **2** *heat etc* despedir, echar **3** *person*: *to a place, country* mandar, enviar **II** *v/i*: ***send out for a pizza*** pedir una pizza (por teléfono)

◆ **send up** *v/t* **1** *rocket* lanzar **2** *prices, temperature* hacer subir **3** *Br* F (*satirize*) caricaturizar

send•er ['sendər] *of letter* remitente *m/f*

send•ing-off [sendıŋ'a:f] *Br*: *in soccer* expulsión *f*

'send-off despedida *f*; ***give s.o. a good***

~ dar a alguien una buena despedida

se•nile ['si:naɪl] *adj* senil

se•nil•i•ty [sɪ'nɪlətɪ] senilidad *f*

se•ni•or ['si:njər] **I** *adj* (*older*) mayor; *in rank* superior; ~ ***partner*** COM socio(-a) *m*(*f*) principal; ~ ***high*** (***school***) instituto *m* de bachillerato **II** *n* **1** (*older person*) persona *f* más mayor; ***he is my ~ by two years, he is two years my ~*** me lleva dos años, es dos años más mayor que yo **2** *at school* estudiante *m*/*f* de último año

se•ni•or 'cit•i•zen persona *f* de la tercera edad

se•ni•or•i•ty [si:nj'ɑ:rətɪ] *in job* antigüedad *f*

sen•sa•tion [sen'seɪʃn] sensación *f*; ***a burning ~*** una sensación de calor; ***cause*** *or* ***create a ~*** causar *or* producir una sensación

sen•sa•tion•al [sen'seɪʃnl] *adj* sensacional

sen•sa•tion•al•ism [sen'seɪʃnəlɪzəm] *of press*, *reports* sensacionalismo *m*

sen•sa•tion•al•ize [sen'seɪʃnəlaɪz] *v/t* tratar con sensacionalismo

sense [sens] **I** *n* **1** (*hearing etc*) sentido *m*; ~ ***of hearing*** / ***smell*** sentido del oído / olfato; ~ ***of direction*** sentido de la orientación; ~ ***of duty*** / ***of humor*** sentido de la obligación / del humor; ***come to one's ~s*** entrar en razón; ***bring s.o. to his ~s*** hacer que entre alguien en razón

2 (*meaning, point etc*) sentido *m*; ***it doesn't make ~*** no tiene sentido; ***there's no ~ in waiting*** no tiene sentido que esperemos; ***in a ~*** en cierto sentido

3 (*feeling*) sentimiento *m*; ~ ***of security*** sensación *f* de seguridad

4 (*common sense*) sentido *m* común, sensatez *f*; ***talk ~, man!*** ¡no digas tonterías!; ***have the ~ to do sth*** tener cabeza para hacer algo; ***I couldn't make any ~ of it*** no hubo manera de entenderlo; ***where's the ~ in that?*** ¿qué sentido tiene eso?; ***it makes good economic ~*** es aconsejable desde el punto de vista económico

II *v/t s.o.'s presence* sentir, notar; ***I could ~ that something was wrong*** tenía la sensación de que algo no iba bien

sense•less ['senslɪs] *adj* (*pointless*) absurdo

'sense or•gan órgano *m* sensorial

sen•si•bil•i•ty [sensɪ'bɪlətɪ] sensibilidad *f*

sen•si•ble ['sensəbl] *adj* sensato; *clothes*, *shoes* práctico, apropiado

sen•si•bly ['sensəblɪ] *adv* con sensatez; ***she wasn't ~ dressed*** no llevaba ropa apropiada

sen•si•tive ['sensətɪv] *adj skin*, *person* sensible; ***be ~ to the cold*** / ***to criticism*** ser sensible al frío / a las críticas; ***heat-*** / ***light-~*** sensible al calor / a la luz; ***it's a rather ~ issue at the moment*** es un asunto bastante delicado en estos momentos

sen•si•tiv•i•ty [sensə'tɪvətɪ] *of skin*, *person* sensibilidad *f* (***to*** a); ~ ***to heat*** / ***light*** sensibilidad al calor / a la luz

sen•si•tize ['sensɪtaɪz] *v/t material*, *person* sensibilizar

sen•sor ['sensər] sensor *m*

sen•so•ry ['sensərɪ] *adj* sensorial

sen•su•al ['senʃʊəl] *adj* sensual

sen•su•al•i•ty [senʃʊ'ælətɪ] sensualidad *f*

sen•su•al•ly ['senʃʊəlɪ] *adv* sensualmente

sen•su•ous ['senʃʊəs] *adj* sensual

sent [sent] *pret & pp* ☞ ***send***

sen•tence ['sentəns] **I** *n* **1** GRAM oración *f* **2** LAW sentencia *f*; ***pass ~*** pronunciar sentencia (***on*** a) **II** *v/t* LAW sentenciar, condenar; ***he was ~d to 6 months*** / ***to death*** se le condenó a 6 meses / a pena de muerte

sen•ten•tious [sen'tenʃəs] *adj* sentencioso

sen•ti•ment ['sentɪmənt] **1** (*sentimentality*) sentimentalismo *m* **2** (*opinion*) opinión *f*

sen•ti•ment•al [sentɪ'mentl] *adj* sentimental; ~ ***value*** valor *m* sentimental

sen•ti•men•tal•i•ty [sentɪmen'tælətɪ] sentimentalismo *m*

sen•try ['sentrɪ] centinela *m*

'sen•try box puesto *m* de vigilancia

'sen•try du•ty servicio *m* de vigilancia; ***be on ~*** estar de servicio *or* guardia

sep•a•rate[1] ['sepərət] *adj* separado; ***keep sth ~ from sth*** guardar algo separado de algo

separate[2] ['sepəreɪt] **I** *v/t* separar; ~ ***sth***

from sth separar algo de algo **II** *v/i of couple* separarse
sep•a•rat•ed ['sepəreɪtɪd] *adj couple* separado
sep•a•rate•ly ['sepərətlɪ] *adv pay, treat* por separado
sep•a•ra•tion [sepə'reɪʃn] separación *f*
sep•a•ra•tism ['sepərətɪzəm] POL separatismo *m*
sep•a•ra•tist ['sepərətɪst] POL **I** *n* separatista *m/f* **II** *adj* separatista
Sep•tem•ber [sep'tembər] septiembre *m*
sep•tic ['septɪk] *adj* séptico; ***go ~*** *of wound* infectarse
'sep•tic tank, pozo *m* séptico *or* negro
se•quel ['siːkwəl] continuación *f*
se•quence ['siːkwəns] secuencia *f*; ***in ~*** en orden; ***out of ~*** en desorden; ***the ~ of events*** la secuencia de hechos
se•quen•tial [sɪ'kwenʃl] *adj* secuencial
se•quen•tial•ly [sɪ'kwenʃəlɪ] *adv* secuencialmente
se•quin ['siːkwɪn] lentejuela *f*
se•quoi•a [sɪ'kwɔɪə] BOT secuoya *f*, secoya *f*
Serb [sɜːrb] serbio(-a) *m(f)*
Ser•bi•a ['sɜːrbɪə] Serbia *f*
Ser•bi•an ['sɜːrbɪən] **I** *adj* serbio **II** *n* serbio(-a) *m(f)*
ser•e•nade [serə'neɪd] **I** *n* serenata *f* **II** *v/t person* dar una serenata a
se•rene [sɪ'riːn] *adj* sereno
se•ren•i•ty [sə'renətɪ] serenidad *f*, tranquilidad *f*
ser•geant ['sɑːrdʒənt] sargento *m/f*
se•ri•al ['sɪrɪəl] *on TV, radio* serie *f*, serial *m*; *in magazine* novela *f* por entregas
'se•ri•al in•ter•face COMPUT interfaz *m* de serie
se•ri•al•ize ['sɪrɪəlaɪz] *v/t novel on TV* emitir en forma de serie; *in newspaper* publicar por entregas
'se•ri•al kill•er asesino(-a) *m(f)* en serie; **'se•ri•al num•ber** *of product* número *m* de serie; **'se•ri•al port** COMPUT puerto *m* (en) serie; **'se•ri•al print•er** impresora *f* en serie
se•ries ['sɪriːz] *nsg* serie *f*
se•ri•ous ['sɪrɪəs] *adj* **1** *situation, damage, illness* grave **2** (*earnest: person, company*) serio; ***I'm ~*** lo digo en serio; ***we'd better take a ~ look at it*** deberíamos examinarlo seriamente; ***be ~ about doing sth*** hablar en serio de hacer algo; ***you can't be ~!*** ¿estás de broma?
se•ri•ous•ly ['sɪrɪəslɪ] *adv* **1** *injured* gravemente; ***~ ill*** enfermo de gravedad **2**: ***~ intend to …*** tener intenciones firmes de …; ***~?*** ¿en serio?; ***take s.o. ~*** tomar a alguien en serio
se•ri•ous•ness ['sɪrɪəsnɪs] **1** *of person* seriedad *f*; ***in all ~*** en serio, de verdad **2** *of situation* seriedad *f*, gravedad *f*; *of illness* gravedad *f*
ser•mon ['sɜːrmən] sermón *m*
ser•rat•ed [sə'reɪtɪd] *adj edge, knife* serrado, dentellado
se•rum ['siːrəm] suero *m*
ser•vant ['sɜːrvənt] sirviente(-a) *m(f)*
serve [sɜːrv] **I** *n in tennis* servicio *m*, saque *m* **II** *v/t food, meal* servir; *customer in shop* atender; *one's country, the people* servir a; ***it ~s you right*** ¡te lo mereces!; ***are you being ~d?*** *in store* ¿le atienden? **III** *v/i* servir; *in tennis* servir, sacar; ***~ on a committee*** servir en un comité; ***the crate ~d as a table*** la caja sirvió *or* hizo de mesa; ***that simply ~s to prove that …*** eso sólo sirve para demostrar que …
◆ **serve up** *v/t meal* servir
serv•er ['sɜːrvər] **1** *in tennis* jugador(a) *m(f)* al servicio **2** COMPUT servidor *m* **3**: ***salad ~s*** *pl* paletas *fpl* para servir ensalada
ser•vice ['sɜːrvɪs] **I** *n* **1** *to customers, community* servicio *m*; ***can I be of ~ to you?*** *fml* ¿te puedo ayudar en algo?; ***do s.o. a ~*** hacer un favor a alguien; ***have given good ~*** *of machine* haber sido de mucho provecho; ***the elevator is out of ~*** el ascensor no funciona **2** *for vehicle, machine* revisión *f*; ***put one's car in for a ~*** hacer una revisión *or* puesta a punto al coche **3** *in tennis* servicio *m*, saque *m* **4**: ***~s*** *pl* (*~ sector*) el sector servicios; ***the ~s*** MIL las fuerzas armadas **II** *v/t vehicle, machine* revisar; ***my car is being ~d*** me están revisando el coche
ser•vice•a•ble ['sɜːrvɪsəbl] *adj* (*usable*) servible
'ser•vice ar•e•a área *f* de servicio; **'ser•vice charge** *in restaurant* servicio *m* (*tarifa*); **'ser•vice con•tract** contrato

S

m de mantenimiento; **'ser•vice en•gi-neer** técnico(-a) *m(f)* de mantenimiento; **'ser•vice in•dus•try** industria *f* de servicios; **'ser•vice•man** MIL militar *m*; **'ser•vice man•u•al** manual *m* de mantenimiento; **'ser•vice pro•vid-er** COMPUT proveedor *m* de servicios; **'ser•vice sec•tor** sector *m* servicios; **'ser•vice sta•tion** estación *f* de servicio
ser•vi•ette [sɜːrvɪ'et] *esp Br* servilleta *f*
ser•vile ['sɜːrvəl] *adj pej* servil
serv•ing ['sɜːrvɪŋ] *of food* ración *f*
ser•vo-brake ['sɜːrvoʊbreɪk] servofreno *m*
ses•a•me ['sesəmɪ] sésamo *m*; ***~ seeds*** semillas *fpl* de sésamo
ses•sion ['seʃn] sesión *f*; ***be in ~*** *of committee etc* estar reunido (en sesión); ***I had a three-hour ~ on the Net*** estuve metido en Internet tres horas
set [set] **I** *n* **1** *of tools* juego *m*; *of books* colección *f*; (*group of people*) grupo *m*; MATH conjunto *m*; ***a ~ of dishes*** una vajilla; ***a ~ of glasses*** una cristalería **2** (THEA: *scenery*) decorado *m*; *where a movie is made* plató *m* **3** *in tennis* set *m* **4**: ***television ~*** televisor *m*, televisión *f*
II *adj* **1** *views*, *ideas* fijo; ***be very ~ in one's ways*** ser de ideas fijas; ***~ meal*** menú *m* (del día); ***~ books*** EDU libros *mpl* de texto obligatorios **2** (*ready*) preparado; ***we were all ~ to leave*** estábamos todos listos para irnos **3**: ***be dead ~ on doing sth*** estar empeñado en hacer algo; ***be dead ~ against sth*** oponerse rotundamente a algo
III *v/t* (*pret & pp* **set**) **1** (*place*) colocar; *movie*, *novel etc* ambientar
2 *date*, *time*, *limit* fijar
3 *mechanism*, *alarm* poner; *clock* poner en hora; *broken limb* recomponer; ***~ the table*** poner la mesa
4 *jewel* engastar
5 (*type~*) componer
6: ***~ s.o. free*** liberar a alguien, dejar libre a alguien; ***~ sth in motion*** poner algo en marcha; ***~ s.o. thinking*** hacer pensar a alguien, dar a alguien que pensar
IV *v/i* (*pret & pp* **set**) **1** *of sun* ponerse **2** *of glue* solidificarse
◆ **set about** *v/t task* empezar; ***~ doing sth*** empezar a hacer algo

◆ **set against** *v/t*: ***set s.o. against s.o.*** enemistar a alguien con alguien; ***set two countries against each other*** enemistar a dos países
◆ **set apart** *v/t* distinguir
◆ **set aside** *v/t material*, *food* apartar; *money* ahorrar
◆ **set back** *v/t* **1** *in plans etc* retrasar **2**: ***it set me back $400*** me salió por 400 dólares
◆ **set down** *v/t* **1** *load*, *bags* colocar, dejar en el suelo **2** *of cab driver* dejar, parar **3** *in writing* redactar, poner por escrito
◆ **set forth** *v/t* exponer
◆ **set in** *v/i of winter* establecerse, afincarse
◆ **set off I** *v/i on journey* salir **II** *v/t explosion* provocar; *bomb* hacer explotar; *chain reaction* desencadenar; *alarm* activar
◆ **set out I** *v/i on journey* salir (**for** hacia) **II** *v/t* **1** *ideas*, *goods* exponer **2**: ***set out to do sth*** (*intend*) tener la intención de hacer algo
◆ **set to** *v/i* (*start on a task*) empezar a trabajar
◆ **set up I** *v/t* **1** *new company* establecer; *equipment*, *machine* instalar; *market stall* montar; ***set o.s. up in business as ...*** montarse un negocio de ... **2** *meeting* organizar **3** F (*frame*) tender una trampa a; ***I've been set up*** F se me ha tendido una trampa **II** *v/i in business* emprender un negocio
'set•back contratiempo *m*; **'set de-sign•er** THEA escenógrafo(-a) *m(f)*; **set 'piece** SP jugada *f* a balón parado; **set 'point** *in tennis* punto *m* de set; **'set square** escuadra *f*
set•tee [se'tiː] (*couch*, *sofa*) sofá *m*
'set the•o•ry MATH teoría *f* de los conjuntos
set•ting ['setɪŋ] *of novel etc* escenario *m*; *of house* ubicación *f*
set•tle ['setl] **I** *v/i of bird*, *dust* posarse; *of building* hundirse; *to live* establecerse **II** *v/t dispute*, *uncertainty* resolver, solucionar; *debts* saldar; *nerves*, *stomach* calmar; ***that ~s it!*** ¡está decidido!
◆ **settle back** *v/i* sentarse, repantingarse
◆ **settle down I** *v/i* (*stop being noisy*) tranquilizarse; (*stop wild living*) sentar

S

la cabeza; *in an area* establecerse **II** *v/t* ***settle o.s. down*** (*calm down*) tranquilizarse, calmarse

◆ **settle for** *v/t* (*take, accept*) conformarse con; ***we'll settle for nothing less*** no nos conformaremos con menos

◆ **settle in** *v/i to new apartment, new area* adaptarse, acostumbrarse

◆ **settle on** *v/t* (*decide on*) ponerse de acuerdo en

◆ **settle up** *v/i* (*pay*) pagar; ***settle up with*** sacar cuentas con

set•tled ['setld] *adj weather, life* estable

set•tle•ment ['setlmənt] **1** *of claim* resolución *f*; *of debt* liquidación *f*; *of dispute* acuerdo *m*; ***reach a ~*** alcanzar un acuerdo **2** (*payment*) suma *f* **3** *of building* hundimiento *m* **4** *village etc* asentamiento *m*

set•tler ['setlər] *in new country* colono(-a) *m(f)*

'set-to F *argument, fight* pelea *f*, riña *f*

'set-up 1 (*structure*) estructura *f*; (*relationship*) relación *f* **2** F (*frameup*) trampa *f*

sev•en ['sevn] siete

sev•en•teen [sevn'tiːn] diecisiete

sev•en•teenth [sevn'tiːnθ] *n & adj* décimoséptimo

sev•enth ['sevnθ] *n & adj* séptimo

sev•en•ti•eth ['sevntɪɪθ] *n & adj* septuagésimo

sev•en•ty ['sevntɪ] setenta

sev•er ['sevər] *v/t* cortar; *relations* romper

sev•er•al ['sevrl] **I** *adj* varios **II** *pron* varios(-as) *mpl(fpl)*; ***~ of you*** varios de vosotros

sev•er•ance ['sevərəns] *of relations* ruptura *f*

'sev•er•ance pay indemnización *f* por despido

se•vere [sɪ'vɪr] *adj illness* grave; *penalty, winter, weather* severo; *teacher* estricto

se•vere•ly [sɪ'vɪrlɪ] *adv punish, speak* con severidad; *injured, disrupted* gravemente

se•ver•i•ty [sɪ'verətɪ] severidad *f*; *of illness* gravedad *f*

Se•ville [sə'vɪl] Sevilla *f*

sew [soʊ] *v/t & v/i* (*pret* ***-ed***, *pp* ***sewn***) coser

◆ **sew on** *v/t button* coser

◆ **sew up** *v/t* **1** *hem etc* remendar, coser **2** *fig* F: ***we've got it all sewn up*** lo tenemos en el bote

sew•age ['suːɪdʒ] aguas *fpl* residuales

'sew•age plant planta *f* de tratamiento de aguas residuales, depuradora *f*

sew•er ['suːər] alcantarilla *f*, cloaca *f*

sew•er•age ['suːərɪdʒ] *system* (sistema *m* de) alcantarillado *m*

sew•ing ['soʊɪŋ] *skill* costura *f*; *that being sewn* labor *f*

'sew•ing ma•chine máquina *f* de coser

sewn [soʊn] *pp* ☞ ***sew***

sex [seks] (*act, gender*) sexo *m*; ***have ~ with*** tener relaciones sexuales con, acostarse con; ***the opposite ~*** el sexo opuesto

'sex ap•peal atractivo *m*, sex appeal *m*; **'sex change** cambio *m* de sexo; **'sex change op•er•a•tion** operación *f* de cambio de sexo; **'sex crime** delito *m* sexual; **sex ed•u'ca•tion** educación *f* sexual

sex•ism ['seksɪzəm] sexismo *m*

sex•ist ['seksɪst] **I** *adj* sexista **II** *n* sexista *m/f*

'sex life vida *f* sexual; **'sex ma•ni•ac** maníaco(-a) *m(f)* sexual; **'sex ob•ject** objeto *m* sexual; **'sex of•fend•er** delincuente *m/f or* agresor(a) *m(f)* sexual; **'sex or•gan** órgano *m* sexual; **'sex shop** sex shop *f*; **'sex sym•bol** sex symbol *m/f*

sex•tant ['sekstənt] NAUT sextante *m*

'sex tour•ism turismo *m* sexual

sex•tu•plet [seks'tuːplət] sextillizo(-a) *m(f)*

sex•u•al ['sekʃʊəl] *adj* sexual

sex•u•al as'sault agresión *f* sexual; **sex•u•al ha'rass•ment** acoso *m* sexual; **sex•u•al 'in•ter•course** relaciones *fpl* sexuales

sex•u•al•i•ty [sekʃʊ'ælətɪ] sexualidad *f*

sex•u•al•ly ['sekʃʊlɪ] *adv* sexualmente; ***~ transmitted disease*** enfermedad *f* de transmisión sexual

sex•y ['seksɪ] *adj* sexy *inv*

SF [es'ef] *abbr* (= ***science fiction***) ciencia *f* ficción

shab•bi•ly ['ʃæbɪlɪ] *adv* **1** *dressed* con desaliño **2** *treat* muy mal, de manera muy injusta

shab•by ['ʃæbɪ] *adj* **1** *coat etc* desgastado, raído **2** *treatment* malo, muy injusto

shack [ʃæk] choza *f*
◆ **shack up** *v/i* F: ***they shacked up together*** se arrejuntaron F
◆ **shack up with** *v/t* F arrejuntarse con F
shack•les ['ʃæklz] *pl chains* cadenas *fpl*, grillos *mpl*; *fig* cadenas *fpl*, ataduras *fpl*
shade [ʃeɪd] **I** *n* **1** *for lamp* pantalla *f*; *on window* persiana *f* **2** *of color* tonalidad *f*; ***~ of meaning*** matiz *m*; ***a ~ lower / higher*** un poco más arriba / abajo **3**: ***in the ~*** a la sombra; ***put s.o. / sth in the ~*** *fig* hacer sombra a alguien / algo **II** *v/t from sun, light* proteger de la luz
shad•ow ['ʃædoʊ] **I** *n* sombra *f*; ***be only a ~ of one's former self*** ser sólo la sombra de lo que se era; ***cast a ~ over sth*** *fig* estropear *or* deslustrar algo; ***there isn't a ~ of doubt about it*** no existe ni la menor duda sobre eso **II** *v/t person* seguir, rastrear
shad•ow 'cab•i•net *Br* POL gabinete *m* fantasma
shad•ow•y ['ʃædoʊɪ] *adj* **1** *spot* oscuro, tenebroso **2** *blurred*: *outline* borroso **3** *character* triste, lánguido
shad•y ['ʃeɪdɪ] *adj* **1** *spot* umbrío **2** *character, dealings* sospechoso
shaft [ʃæft] TECH eje *m*, árbol *m*; *of mine* pozo *m*
shag•gy ['ʃægɪ] *adj hair, dog* greñudo
shake[1] [ʃeɪk] **I** *n* sacudida *f*; ***give sth a good ~*** agitar algo bien; ***he declined with a ~ of his head*** dijo que no moviendo la cabeza; ***he's got the ~s*** F le dan tembleques F, tiene temblores **II** *v/t* (*pret* ***shook***, *pp* ***shaken***) agitar; *emotionally* conmocionar; ***he shook his head*** negó con la cabeza; ***~ hands*** estrechar *or* darse la mano; ***~ hands with s.o.*** estrechar *or* dar la mano a alguien; ***~ one's fist at s.o.*** levantar el puño a alguien
III *v/i* (*pret* ***shook***, *pp* ***shaken***) **1** *of voice, building, person* temblar; ***~ with fear*** temblar del miedo **2**: ***let's ~ on it*** zanjémoslo con un apretón de manos
◆ **shake down** F **I** *v/i of people, new system* arreglárselas **II** *v/t* **1** (*rip off*) sacar, limpiar **2** *search, frisk* cachear, registrar
◆ **shake off** *v/t dust* sacudir; *pursuers* escapar, librarse de; *cold, fever* curar, librarse de
◆ **shake out** *v/t rug, blankets etc* sacudir
◆ **shake up** *v/t* **1** *bottle etc* agitar **2** *upset* conmover, impresionar **3** *jolt out of complacency* despabilar, despertar
shake[2] [ʃeɪk] *n wood for building* tablilla *f* de madera
'shake•down F **1** *bed, place to sleep* piltra *f*, catre *m* **2** (*rip-off, extortion*) robo *m*, timo *m* **3** *search* rastreo *m*
shak•en ['ʃeɪkən] **I** *adj emotionally* conmocionado **II** *pp* ☞ ***shake***
'shake•out *in company, department* reestructuración *f*
shak•er ['ʃeɪkər] *for drinks* coctelera *f*
'shake-up 1 *in company, department* reestructuración *f* **2**: ***it gave her a bit of a ~*** le produjo una cierta impresión
'shak•y ['ʃeɪkɪ] *adj table etc* inestable; *after illness* débil; *after shock* conmocionado; *grasp of sth, grammar etc* flojo; *voice, hand* tembloroso
shale [ʃeɪl] GEOL esquisto *m*
shall [ʃæl] *v/aux* **1** *future*: ***I ~ do my best*** haré todo lo que pueda **2** *suggesting*: ***~ we go?*** ¿nos vamos?
shal•low ['ʃæloʊ] **I** *adj water* poco profundo; *person* superficial **II** *npl*: ***~s*** aguas *fpl* poco profundas, banco *m*
sham [ʃæm] **I** *n* (*pretense*) farsa *f*, patraña *f*; *person* farsante *m/f*, hipócrita *m/f* **II** *adj emotions* fingido, falso; *jewels* falso
sham•bles ['ʃæmblz] *nsg* caos *m*; ***the room was*** (***in***) ***a ~*** la habitación era un caos
shame [ʃeɪm] **I** *n* vergüenza *f*, *Col, Mex, Ven* pena *f*; ***bring ~ on*** avergonzar, *Col, Mex, Ven* apenar; ***~ on you!*** ¡debería darte vergüenza!; ***have you no ~?*** ¿no tienes vergüenza?; ***put s.o. to ~*** poner a alguien en evidencia; ***what a ~!*** ¡qué pena *or* lástima!; ***it's a ~ you can't make it tomorrow*** es una pena que no puedas mañana
II *v/t* avergonzar, *Col, Mex, Ven* apenar; ***~ s.o. into doing sth*** avergonzar a alguien para que haga algo
shame•faced ['ʃeɪmfeɪst] *adj* avergonzado
shame•ful ['ʃeɪmfəl] *adj* vergonzoso
shame•ful•ly ['ʃeɪmfəlɪ] *adv* vergonzosamente

S

shame•less ['ʃeɪmlɪs] *adj* desvergonzado
shame•less•ly ['ʃeɪmlɪslɪ] *adv* descaradamente, tranquilamente
sham•poo [ʃæm'pu:] **I** *n* champú *m* **II** *v/t customer* lavar la cabeza a; *hair* lavar
shan•dy gaff ['ʃændɪgæf] cerveza *f* con limón
shan't [ʃɑ:nt] ☞ ***shall not***
shan•ty town ['ʃæntɪ] *Span* barrio *m* de chabolas, *L.Am.* barriada *f*, *Arg* villa *f* miseria, *Chi* callampa *f*, *Mex* ciudad *f* perdida, *Urug* cantegril *m*
shape [ʃeɪp] **I** *n* forma *f*; ***in the ~ of*** consistente en; ***triangular in ~*** con forma triangular; ***out of ~*** *object* deforme; *person*: *not fit* en baja forma; ***take ~*** *fig*: *of new play*, *plan etc* concretarse, tomar forma; ***be in good / bad ~*** *of person*, *boxer etc* estar en forma / baja forma; *of building*, *machine* estar en buenas / malas condiciones, estar en buen / mal estado
II *v/t clay* modelar; *person's life*, *character* determinar; *the future* dar forma a; ***~d like a ...*** con forma de ...
◆ **shape up** *v/i* F: ***how's the new guy shaping up?*** ¿como va el nuevo?; ***he's shaping up well*** va bien; ***if you don't shape up*** como no espabiles; ***things are shaping up nicely*** las cosas marchan bien
shape•less ['ʃeɪplɪs] *adj dress etc* amorfo
shape•ly ['ʃeɪplɪ] *adv figure* esbelto
share [ʃer] **I** *n* **1** parte *f*; ***I did my ~ of the work*** hice la parte del trabajo que me correspondía **2** FIN acción *f* **II** *v/t feelings*, *opinions* compartir; ***they ~d second place*** compartieron el segundo puesto **III** *v/i* compartir
◆ **share out** *v/t* repartir
'share cap•i•tal capital *m* en acciones; **'share cer•tif•i•cate** bono *m* social; **'share•crop•per** aparcero(-a) *m*(*f*), colono(-a) *m*(*f*)
shared [ʃerd] *adj kitchen*, *shower etc* comunitario
'share•hold•er accionista *m/f*; ***~s' equity*** capital *m* contable; **'share is•sue** emisión *f* de acciones; **'share-out** reparto *m*; **'share own•er•ship** accionariado *m*; **'share price in•dex** índice *m* de cotización; **'share•ware** COMPUT shareware *m*, programa *m* compartido
shark [ʃɑ:rk] **1** *fish* tiburón *m* **2** F *crook* ladrón(-a) *m/f*, timador(a) *m/f*
sharp [ʃɑ:rp] **I** *adj* **1** *knife* afilado **2** *mind* vivo; ***that was pretty ~ of him*** eso fue muy perspicaz por su parte **3** *pain*, *tone of voice* agudo; *taste* ácido **4** *curve* pronunciado, acentuado **II** *adv* **1** MUS demasiado alto **2**: ***at 3 o'clock ~*** a las tres en punto **3**: ***look ~*** F darse prisa
sharp•en ['ʃɑ:rpn] *v/t* **1** *knife* afilar; *pencil* sacar punta a **2** *skills* perfeccionar
sharp•en•er ['ʃɑ:rpnər] afilador *m*, sacapuntas *mpl*
sharp•ly ['ʃɑ:rplɪ] *adv* **1** *say* tajantemente, de manera arisca **2** *brake* bruscamente; *curve*: *of road* acentuadamente
sharp•ness ['ʃɑ:rpnɪs] **1** *of knife* agudeza *f* **2** *of mind* perspicacia *f* **3** *of taste* acidez *f*, intensidad *f*; *of tone of voice* agudeza *f* **4** *of curve in road* lo pronunciado, brusquedad *f*
sharp 'prac•tice triquiñuelas *fpl*, tejemanejes *mpl*
sharp•shoot•er ['ʃɑ:rpʃu:tər] tirador(a) *m*(*f*) de primera
shat [ʃæt] *pret & pp* ☞ ***shit***
shat•ter ['ʃætər] **I** *v/t glass* hacer añicos; *illusions* destrozar; *silence* romper **II** *v/i of glass* hacerse añicos
shat•tered ['ʃætərd] *adj* F (*exhausted*) destrozado F, hecho polvo F; (*very upset*) destrozado F
shat•ter•ing ['ʃætərɪŋ] *adj news*, *experience* demoledor, sorprendente
'shat•ter•proof *adj* irrompible
shave [ʃeɪv] **I** *v/t* afeitar **II** *v/i* afeitarse **III** *n* afeitado *m*; ***have a ~*** afeitarse; ***that was a close ~*** ¡le faltó un pelo!
◆ **shave off** *v/t beard* afeitar; *from piece of wood* rebajar
shav•en ['ʃeɪvn] *adj head* afeitado
shav•er ['ʃeɪvər] *electric* máquinilla *f* de afeitar (eléctrica)
shav•ing brush ['ʃeɪvɪŋ] brocha *f* de afeitar; **'shav•ing foam** espuma *f* de afeitar; **'shav•ing soap** jabón *m* de afeitar
shawl [ʃɒ:l] chal *m*
she [ʃi:] *pron* ella; ***~ is German / a student*** es alemana / estudiante; ***you're funny, ~'s not*** tú tienes gracia, ella no
sheaf [ʃi:f] (*pl* ***sheaves*** [ʃi:vz]) **1** AGR paca *f* **2** *of paper* fajo *m*

S

shear [ʃɪr] *v/t* (*pret* **-ed**, *pp* **shorn**) *sheep* esquilar

◆ **shear off** *v/i* (*break off*) ceder, romperse

shears [ʃɪrz] *npl for gardening* tijeras *fpl* (de podar); *for sewing* tijeras *fpl* (*grandes*)

sheath [ʃiːθ] **1** *for knife* funda *f* **2** *contraceptive* condón *m*

'sheath knife cuchillo *m* de monte

sheaves [ʃiːvz] *pl* ☞ **sheaf**

she•bang [ʃɪ'bæŋ]: **the whole ~** F todo el asunto *m*, todo el tinglado F

'she-bear osa *f*

shed[1] [ʃed] *v/t* (*pret & pp* **shed**) *blood, tears* derramar; *leaves* perder; **~ light on** *fig* arrojar luz sobre; **~ its skin** mudar su piel; **~ a few pounds** perder unos kilos

shed[2] [ʃed] *n* cobertizo *m*

she'd [ʃiːd] ☞ **she had**; **she would**

sheen [ʃiːn] brillo *m*

sheep [ʃiːp] (*pl* **sheep**) oveja *f*

'sheep•dog perro *m* pastor

sheep-herd•er ['ʃiːphɜːrdər] pastor *m*

sheep•ish ['ʃiːpɪʃ] *adj* avergonzado

'sheep•skin *adj lining* (de piel) de borrego

sheer [ʃɪr] *adj* **1** *madness, luxury* puro, verdadero; *hell* verdadero; **by ~ coincidence** de pura casualidad **2** *drop, cliffs* escarpado

sheet [ʃiːt] **1** *for bed* sábana *f*; **(as) white as a ~** (tan) blanco como el papel **2** *of paper* hoja *f*; *of metal* chapa *f*, plancha *f*; *of glass* hoja *f*, lámina *f*; **the rain was coming down in ~s** llovía a raudales, cayó una sábana de agua

'sheet light•ning relámpago *m* difuso

'sheet mu•sic partitura *f*

sheik(h) [ʃeɪk] jeque *m*

'sheik(h)•dom ['ʃeɪkdəm] *tierra gobernada por un jeque*

shelf [ʃelf] (*pl* **shelves** [ʃelvz]) estante *m*; **shelves** estanterías *fpl*; **she has been left on the ~** *fig* F se ha quedado para vestir santos F; **buy sth off the ~** comprar algo en el acto

'shelf life (*of food product*) *duración de un producto perecedero*

shell [ʃel] **I** *n* **1** *of mussel etc* concha *f*, *of egg* cáscara *f*, *of tortoise* caparazón *m*; **come out of one's ~** *fig* salir del caparazón **2** MIL proyectil *m* **II** *v/t* **1** *peas* pelar **2** MIL bombardear (*con artillería*)

◆ **shell out** F **I** *v/t* soltar F, enterar *Mex* **II** *v/i* soltar F, enterar *Mex*

she'll [ʃiːl] ☞ **she will**

'shell•fire fuego *m* de artillería; **come under ~** sufrir un bombardeo; **'shell-fish** marisco *m*; **'shell suit** *Span* chándal *m*, *Arg* buzo *m*, *Mex* pants *mpl*

shel•ter ['ʃeltər] **I** *n* refugio *m*; (*bus ~*) marquesina *f*; **provide ~ for** dar cobijo a; **run for ~** ir en busca de refugio; **take ~** refugiarse **II** *v/i from rain, bombing etc* refugiarse **III** *v/t* (*protect*) proteger

shel•tered ['ʃeltərd] *adj place* resguardado; **lead a ~ life** llevar una vida protegida

shelve [ʃelv] *v/t fig* posponer

shelves [ʃelvz] *pl* ☞ **shelf**

shelv•ing ['ʃelvɪŋ] estanterías *fpl*

she•nan•i•gans [ʃɪ'nænɪgənz] *npl* F artimañas *fpl*, triquiñuelas *fpl* F

shep•herd ['ʃepərd] **I** *n* pastor *m* **II** *v/t people* guiar, acompañar

sher•iff ['ʃerɪf] sheriff *m/f*

sher•ry ['ʃerɪ] jerez *m*

shield [ʃiːld] **I** *n* escudo *m*; *sports trophy* trofeo *m* (*en forma de escudo*); TECH placa *f* protectora; *of policeman* placa *f* **II** *v/t* (*protect*) proteger

shift [ʃɪft] **I** *n* **1** cambio *m* **2** *period of work* turno *m*; **be on night ~** trabajar en el turno de noche **II** *v/t* (*move*) mover; *stains etc* eliminar **III** *v/i* (*move*) moverse; (*change*) trasladarse, desplazarse; *of wind* cambiar; **he was ~ing!** F iba a toda mecha F

'shift key COMPUT tecla *f* de mayúsculas; **'shift work** trabajo *m* por turnos; **'shift work•er** trabajador(a) *m(f)* por turnos

shift•y ['ʃɪftɪ] *adj pej* sospechoso

shil•ly-shal•ly ['ʃɪlɪʃælɪ] *v/i* vacilar

shim•mer ['ʃɪmər] *v/i* brillar; *of roads in heat* reverberar

shin [ʃɪn] espinilla *f*

◆ **shin up** *v/t* (*pret & pp* **-ned**) *tree etc* trepar

'shin•bone tibia *f*

shine [ʃaɪn] **I** *v/i* (*pret & pp* **shone**) brillar; *fig*: *of student etc* destacar (**at** en) **II** *v/t* (*pret & pp* **shone**): **could you ~ a light in here?** ¿podrías alumbrar aquí?; **the cop shone a flashlight in my face** el policía me deslumbró con

S

una linterna en la cara **III** *n* **1** *on shoes etc* brillo *m*; ***give one's shoes a ~*** limpiarse los zapatos **2**: ***the kids took a ~ to her*** F a los niños les cayó bien

shin•gle[1] ['ʃɪŋgl] *on beach* guijarros *mpl*; ***~ beach*** playa *f* de guijarros *or* piedras

shin•gle[2] ['ʃɪŋgl] **1** *for roof etc* lámina *f* de madera **2** (*sign*) placa *f*; ***he put up his ~*** (***as a dentist***) abrió una consulta (de dentista)

shin•gles ['ʃɪŋglz] *nsg* MED herpes *m*

shin•gly ['ʃɪŋglɪ] *adj beach* de guijarros *or* piedras

'shin pad espinillera *f*

shin•y ['ʃaɪnɪ] *adj surface* brillante

ship [ʃɪp] **I** *n* barco *m*, buque *m*; ***by ~*** en barco **II** *v/t* (*pret & pp* ***-ped***) (*send*) enviar; *by sea* enviar por barco **III** *v/i of product* distribuirse

'ship•build•er (*shipyard*) astillero *m*; *person* constructor(a) *m(f)* de barcos

'ship•build•ing industria *f* astillera

ship•ment ['ʃɪpmənt] (*consignment*) envío *m*

'ship•own•er naviero(-a) *m(f)*, armador(a) *m(f)*

ship•per ['ʃɪpər] COM consignador *m*

ship•ping ['ʃɪpɪŋ] **1** (*sea traffic*) navíos *mpl*, buques *mpl* **2** (*sending*) envío *m*; (*sending by sea*) envío *m* por barco

'ship•ping a•gent agente *m/f* marítimo; **'ship•ping com•pa•ny** (compañía *f*) naviera *f*; **'ship•ping costs** *npl* gastos *mpl* de envío; **'ship•ping fore•cast** parte *m* de navegación; **'ship•ping lane** ruta *f* de navegación

ship'shape *adj* ordenado, organizado; **'ship•wreck I** *n* naufragio *m* **II** *v/t*: ***be ~ed*** naufragar; **'ship•yard** astillero *m*

shirk [ʃɜːrk] *v/t* eludir

shirk•er ['ʃɜːrkər] vago(-a) *m(f)*

shirt [ʃɜːrt] camisa *f*; ***in his ~ sleeves*** en mangas de camisa; ***keep your ~ on!*** F ¡tranquilo, hombre!, ¡no te piques! F

shirt•y ['ʃɜːrtɪ] *adj Br* F: ***get ~ with s.o.*** enfadarse con alguien

shish ke•bab ['ʃɪʃkəbæb] *pincho de carne con verduras asado en el grill*

shit [ʃɪt] P **I** *n* **1** mierda *f* P; ***I need a ~*** tengo que cagar P; ***be in the ~*** *fig* estar jodido; ***talk a load of ~*** decir muchas gilipolleces F; ***don't give me that ~!*** ¡sí hombre! F, ¡y una mierda! V; ***piece of ~*** *person* hijo(-a) *m(f)* de puta V, *Mex* hijo(-a) *m(f)* de la chingada V **2**: ***he's a real ~*** es un mierda V
II *int* mierda P
III *v/i* (*pret & pp* ***shat***) cagar P
IV *v/t* (*pret & pp* ***shat***): ***~ o.s.*** cagarse encima P; ***they were ~ting themselves*** *with fear* se estaban cagando de miedo P

shit•ty ['ʃɪtɪ] *adj* F asqueroso F; ***I feel ~*** me encuentro de pena F

shiv•er ['ʃɪvər] **I** *v/i* tiritar **II** *n* escalofrío *m*; ***the sight sent ~s down my spine*** lo que ví me dio escalofríos

shoal[1] [ʃoʊl] *of fish* banco *m*

shoal[2] [ʃoʊl] *shallow water* banco *m*

shock[1] [ʃɑːk] **I** *n* shock *m*, impresión *f*; ELEC descarga *f*; ***be in ~*** MED estar en estado de shock; ***come as a ~ to s.o.*** impresionar a alguien, dejar sin respiración a alguien
II *v/t* impresionar, dejar boquiabierto; ***I was ~ed by the news*** la noticia me impresionó *or* dejó boquiabierto; ***an artist who tries to ~ his public*** un artista que intenta escandalizar a su público

shock[2] [ʃɑːk] *n*: ***~ of hair*** mata *f* de pelo

shock ab•sorb•er ['ʃɑːkəbsɔːrbər] MOT amortiguador *m*

shock•ing ['ʃɑːkɪŋ] *adj behavior, poverty* impresionante, escandaloso; F *prices* escandaloso; F *weather, spelling* terrible

shock•ing•ly ['ʃɑːkɪŋlɪ] *adv behave* escandalosamente

'shock•proof *adj* resistente, a prueba de golpes

'shock wave *from explosion* onda *f* expansiva; *fig* impacto *m*, consecuencia *f*; ***send ~s through*** *fig* impactar, conmocionar

shod [ʃɑːd] *pret & pp* ☞ ***shoe***

shod•dy ['ʃɑːdɪ] *adj goods* de mala calidad; *behavior* vergonzoso

shoe [ʃuː] **I** zapato *m*; ***I wouldn't like to be in your ~s*** no me gustaría estar en tu pellejo *or* situación **II** *v/t* (*pret & pp* ***shod***) *horse* herrar

'shoe•box caja *f* de zapatos; **'shoe•horn** calzador *m*; **'shoe-lace** cordón *m*; **'shoe•mak•er** zapatero(-a) *m(f)*; **shoe mend•er** ['ʃuːmendər] zapatero(-a) *m(f)*, remendón(-ona) *m(f)*; **'shoe-shine boy** (chico *m*) limpiabotas *m* *inv*; **'shoe•store** zapatería *f*; **'shoe•string**: ***do sth on a ~*** hacer algo con cuatro duros; **'shoe•tree** horma *f* de zapatos

shone [ʃɑːn] *pret & pp* ☞ ***shine***

◆ **shoo away** [ʃuː] *v/t* espantar

shook [ʃuːk] *pret* ☞ ***shake***

shoot [ʃuːt] **I** *n* BOT brote *m*
II *v/t* (*pret & pp* ***shot***) **1** disparar; *and kill* matar de un tiro; ***~ s.o. in the leg*** disparar a alguien en la pierna; ***~ s.o. dead*** matar a alguien de un disparo *or* tiro, matar a alguien a disparos *or* tiros; ***~ o.s.*** *deliberately* pegarse un tiro; ***he accidentally shot himself*** se le disparó la pistola accidentalmente
2 *movie* rodar
3: ***~ a glance at s.o.*** lanzar una mirada a alguien; ***~ questions at s.o.*** bombardear con preguntas a alguien
III *v/i* **1** *with gun* disparar **2** *in soccer* chutar, rematar; ***~ at goal*** SP tirar *or* rematar a puerta **3** *go quickly* dispararse; ***~ to fame*** saltar a la fama

◆ **shoot down** *v/t airplane* derribar; *fig*: *suggestion* echar por tierra

◆ **shoot off I** *v/i* (*rush off*) irse deprisa **II** *v/t* F: ***shoot one's mouth off*** irse de la boca F

◆ **shoot up** *v/i* **1** *of prices* dispararse; *of children* crecer mucho; *of new suburbs, buildings etc* aparecer de repente **2** F *of drug addict* chutarse F

shoot•ing ['ʃuːtɪŋ] **1** disparos *mpl* **2** *murder* tiroteo *m* **3** *of movie* rodaje *m*

'shoot•ing gal•ler•y *for guns* galería *f* de tiro; **'shoot•ing guard** *in basketball* escolta *m/f*; **'shoot•ing match**: ***the whole ~*** F todo el asunto *m*, todo el tenderete F; **'shoot•ing range** campo *m* de tiro; **shoot•ing 'star** estrella *f* fugaz

'shoot-out 1 tiroteo *m* **2** *in soccer* tiro *m* de penalti

shop [ʃɑːp] **I** *n* tienda *f*; ***talk ~*** hablar del trabajo; ***shut up ~*** F cerrar **II** *v/i* (*pret & pp* ***-ped***) comprar; ***go ~ping*** ir de compras **III** *v/t esp Br* P delatar

◆ **shop around** *v/i* buscar y comparar

◆ **shop around for** *v/t* tantear, indagar

'shop as•sist•ant *Br* dependiente(-a) *m(f)*; **shop 'floor** *workers* trabajadores *mpl*; ***the reaction on the ~*** la reacción de los trabajadores; **'shop•keep•er** tendero(-a) *m(f)*; **shop•lift•er** ['ʃɑːplɪftər] ladrón(-ona) *m(f)* (*en tienda*); **shop•lift•ing** ['ʃɑːplɪftɪŋ] hurtos *mpl* (*en tiendas*)

shop•per ['ʃɑːpər] *person* comprador(a) *m(f)*

shop•ping ['ʃɑːpɪŋ] *items* compra *f*; ***I hate ~*** odio hacer la compra; ***do one's ~*** hacer la compra

'shop•ping bag bolsa *f* de la compra; **'shop•ping bas•ket** cesta *f* de la compra; **'shop•ping cart** carro *m* de la compra; **'shop•ping cen•ter**, *Br* **'shop•ping cen•tre** centro *m* comercial; **'shop•ping list** lista *f* de la compra; **'shop•ping mall** centro *m* comercial; **shop 'stew•ard** representante *m/f* sindical; **shop 'win•dow** escaparate *m*; **'shop•worn** manoseado

shore [ʃɔːr] orilla *f*; ***on ~*** (*not at sea*) en tierra; ***~ leave*** permiso *m* para bajar a tierra

◆ **shore up** *v/t building* apuntalar; *fig*: *economy, currency* fortalecer, reanimar

shorn [ʃɔːrn] *pp* ☞ ***shear***

short [ʃɔːrt] **I** *adj* **1** corto; ***it's just a ~ walk away*** está a poca distancia a pie; ***time is ~*** hay poco tiempo; ***a ~ time ago*** no hace mucho tiempo; ***well that was ~ and sweet*** F lo bueno si breve, dos veces bueno F; ***Jo is ~ for ...*** Jo es la forma corta de ...; ***be in ~ supply*** COM escasear
2 *in height* bajo
3: ***we're ~ of fuel*** nos queda poco combustible; ***he's not ~ of ideas*** no le faltan ideas
II *adv* **1**: ***cut ~*** *vacation, meeting* interrumpir; ***stop a person ~*** hacer pararse a una persona; ***in ~*** en resumen; ***sell s.o. ~*** no hacer justicia a alguien; ***run ~*** *of commodity* escasear, agotarse; ***he is called Brin for ~*** le llaman Brin para abreviar
2: ***go ~ of*** pasar sin; ***stop ~ of doing sth*** no llegar a hacer algo; ***fall ~ of the target*** *of shell* quedarse corto; *of production* quedarse por debajo del objetivo; ***three miles ~ of the airport*** a tres millas del aeropuerto; ***we are running ~ of bread*** nos estamos quedando sin pan; ***we are running ~ of ideas*** se nos agotan las ideas; ***~ of selling up I don't know what to do*** aparte de ven-

derlo todo, no sé qué hacer
III *v/t* ELEC F producir un cortocircuito
short•age ['ʃɔːrtɪdʒ] escasez *f*, falta *f*; ***he has no ~ of ideas*** no le faltan ideas
'short•bread *galleta a base de harina, azúcar y mucha mantequilla*; **short--'change** *v/t in store* sisar; **short 'cir-cuit I** *n* cortocircuito *m* **II** *v/t* **1** ELEC producir un cortocircuito **2** *fig*: *bypass* eludir, evadir **III** *v/i* ELEC producirse un cortocircuito; **short•com•ing** ['ʃɔːrt-kʌmɪŋ] defecto *m*; **'short•cut** atajo *m*; ***take a ~*** tomar un atajo; COMPUT utilizar un shortcut *or* un acceso directo; **'short-dat•ed bill** COM letra *f* a corto plazo
short•en ['ʃɔːrtn] *v/t dress, hair, vacation* acortar; *chapter, article* abreviar; *work day* reducir
short•en•ing ['ʃɔːrtnɪŋ] *grasa utilizada para hacer masa de pastelería*
'short•fall déficit *m*; **short-haired** ['ʃɔːrtherd] *adj* de pelo corto; **'short-hand** taquigrafía *f*; ***take sth down in ~*** escribir algo taquigráficamente; **short-hand•ed** [ʃɔːrt'hændɪd] *adj* falto de personal
short•ie ['ʃɔːrtɪ] F *person* persona *f* bajita; ***hey, ~!*** ¡tú enano! F
'short list *Br* lista *f* de preseleccionados; ***be on the ~*** estar en la lista de preseleccionados
short-lived ['ʃɔːrtlɪvd] *adj* efímero
short•ly ['ʃɔːrtlɪ] *adv* (*soon*) pronto; ***~ before / after*** justo antes / después
short 'mes•sage sys•tem COMPUT servicio *m* de mensajes cortos
short•ness ['ʃɔːrtnɪs] **1** *of visit* brevedad *f* **2** *in height* baja *f* estatura
'short or•der cook *cocinero(-a) de platos sencillos*
'short-range *adj* **1** MIL, AVIA de corto alcance **2** *forecast* a corto plazo
shorts [ʃɔːrts] *npl* **1** pantalones *mpl* cortos, shorts *mpl*; ***a pair of ~*** un par de pantalones cortos **2** *underwear* calzoncillos *mpl*
short'sight•ed *adj* miope; *fig* corto de miras; **short-sleeved** ['ʃɔːrtsliːvd] *adj* de manga corta; **short-staffed** [ʃɔːrt-'stæft] *adj* falto de personal; **'short-stop** *in baseball* shortstop *m*; **short 'sto•ry** relato *m or* cuento corto; **short-tem•pered** [ʃɔːrt'tempərd] *adj* irascible; **'short-term** *adj* a corto plazo; **'short time**: ***be on ~*** *of workers* trabajar a jornada reducida; **'short wave** onda *f* corta
shot[1] [ʃɑːt] *n* **1** *from gun* disparo *m*; ***he accepted like a ~*** aceptó al instante; ***he ran off like a ~*** se fue como una bala; ***it was just a ~ in the dark*** *fig* solo fue una suposición; ***call the ~s*** F llevar la voz cantante F, mangonear F **2** (*photograph*) fotografía *f* **3** (*injection*) inyección *f* **4**: ***be a good / poor ~*** tirar bien / mal **5** SP tiro *m*; ***~s on goal*** disparos *mpl* a puerta **6** (*attempt*) intento *m*; ***at the first ~*** en el primer intento; ***it's my ~*** me toca a mí; ***I'll have a ~ at it*** lo probaré *or* intentaré
shot[2] [ʃɑːt] **I** *pret & pp* ☞ ***shoot*** **II** *adj Br*: ***be / get ~ of s.o. / sth*** F librarse de alguien / algo, quitarse de encima a alguien / algo
'shot•gun escopeta *f*; **'shot•gun wed-ding** F boda *f* de penalti; **'shot put** *sports event* lanzamiento *m* de peso; **shot-put•ter** ['ʃɑːtpʊtər] lanzador(a) *m(f)* de peso
should [ʃʊd] *v/aux*: ***what ~ I do?*** ¿qué debería hacer?; ***you ~n't do that*** no deberías hacer eso; ***that ~ be long enough*** debería ser lo suficientemente largo; ***you ~ have heard him!*** ¡tendrías que haberle oído!; ***he ~ be home by then*** debería estar en casa para entonces; ***I ~ think so!*** ¡espero *or* creo que sí!
shoul•der ['ʃoʊldər] **I** *n* ANAT hombro *m*; ***a ~ to cry on*** un paño de lágrimas; ***give s.o. the cold ~*** volver a alguien la espalda; ***put one's ~ to the wheel*** *fig* arrimar el hombro **II** *v/t fig costs, responsibility* asumir
'shoul•der bag bolso *m* (de bandolera); **'shoul•der blade** omóplato *m*, omoplato *m*; **'shoul•der-length** *adj hair* por los hombros; **'shoul•der pad** hombrera *f*; **'shoul•der strap** *of brassiere, dress* tirante *m*; *of bag* correa *f*
should•n't ['ʃʊdnt] ☞ ***should not***
shout [ʃaʊt] **I** *n* grito *m*; ***give me a ~ when we get there*** avísame cuando lleguemos **II** *v/t & v/i* gritar; ***~ o.s. hoarse*** gritar hasta quedarse ronco; ***if you want anything, just ~*** F si quieres algo, lo dices
◆ **shout at** *v/t* gritar a

S

◆ **shout down** *v/t speaker* callar, arrumbar

shout•ing ['ʃaʊtɪŋ] griterío *m*; ***it's all over bar the ~*** *Br* F está decidido

shove [ʃʌv] **I** *n* empujón *m* **II** *v/t & v/i* empujar; ***when push comes to ~*** cuando las cosas se ponen feas

◆ **shove in** *v/i in line* meterse empujando

◆ **shove off** *v/i* F (*go away*) largarse F

shov•el ['ʃʌvl] **I** *n* pala *f* **II** *v/t* (*pret & pp* **-ed**, *Br* **-led**): ***~ snow off the path*** retirar a paladas la nieve del camino; ***~ food into one's mouth*** atiborrarse de comida

show [ʃoʊ] **I** *n* **1** THEA espectáculo *m*; TV programa *m*; ***steal the ~*** robar el protagonismo (***from*** a); ***run the ~*** *be the boss* dirigir el cotarro F, mandar; ***put up a poor ~*** no desenvolverse bien **2** *of emotion* muestra *f*; ***on ~*** *at exhibition* expuesto, en exposición; ***on a ~ of hands*** por votación a mano alzada; ***make a ~ of being interested*** fingir interés
II *v/t* (*pret* **-ed**, *pp* **shown**) *passport etc* enseñar, mostrar; *interest*, *emotion* mostrar; *at exhibition* exponer; *movie* proyectar; ***~ s.o. sth, ~ sth to s.o.*** enseñar *or* mostrar algo a alguien; ***~ s.o. how to do sth*** enseñar a alguien a hacer algo; ***I'll ~ him!*** ¡se va a enterar!; ***I'll show him who's the boss!*** ¡se va a enterar quién manda!; ***~ o.s. to be sth*** demostrar que se es algo
III *v/i* (*pret* **-ed**, *pp* **shown**) **1** (*be visible*) verse **2**: ***what's ~ing at ...?*** *at movie theater* qué ponen en el ...?

◆ **show around** *v/t* enseñar; ***he showed us around*** nos enseñó la casa / el edificio *etc*

◆ **show in** *v/t* hacer pasar

◆ **show off I** *v/t skills* mostrar **II** *v/i pej* presumir, alardear

◆ **show out** *v/t visitor etc* acompañar a la salida

◆ **show up I** *v/t shortcomings etc* poner de manifiesto; ***don't show me up in public*** (*embarrass*) no me avergüences en público **II** *v/i* **1** (*be visible*) verse **2** F (*arrive*, *turn up*) aparecer

show biz ['ʃoʊbɪz] F el mundo del espectáculo; **'show busi•ness** el mundo del espectáculo; **'show•case** vitrina *f*; *fig* escaparate *m*; **'show•down** enfrentamiento *m*

show•er ['ʃaʊər] **I** *n* **1** *of rain* chaparrón *m*, chubasco *m* **2** *to wash* ducha *f*, *Mex* regadera *f*; ***take a ~*** ducharse **3** (*party*) *fiesta con motivo de un bautizo, una boda etc., en la que los invitados llevan obsequios* **II** *v/i* ducharse **III** *v/t*: ***~ s.o. with compliments / praise*** colmar a alguien de cumplidos / alabanzas

'show•er cap gorro *m* de baño; **'show•er cur•tain** cortina *f* de ducha; **'show•er gel** gel *m* de ducha; **'show•er•proof** *adj* impermeable

'show•girl cabaretera *f*; **'show jump•er** *person*, *horse* jinete *m/f* de saltos; **show•jump•ing** ['ʃoʊdʒʌmpɪŋ] concurso *m* de saltos; **show•man** ['ʃoʊmən] **1** *who puts on shows* representante *m*, empresario *m* **2** *who does things for effect* entretenedor *m*, showman *m*

show•man•ship ['ʃoʊmənʃɪp] **1** *of person*, *act* espectáculo *m*, entretenimiento *m* **2** *fig pej*: ***it's all ~*** es puro teatro

shown [ʃoʊn] *pp* ☞ ***show***

'show-off *pej* fanfarrón(-ona) *m*(*f*); **'show•piece** modelo *m*, tesoro *m*; **'show•room** sala *f* de exposición *f*; ***in ~ condition*** como nuevo

show•y ['ʃoʊɪ] *adj jacket*, *behavior* llamativo

shrank [ʃræŋk] *pret* ☞ ***shrink***

shrap•nel ['ʃræpnəl] metralla *f*; ***~ wound*** herida *f* de metralla

shred [ʃred] **I** *n of paper etc* trozo *m*; *of fabric* jirón *m*; ***there isn't a ~ of evidence*** no hay prueba alguna; ***there's not a ~ of truth in the story*** la historia no tiene nada de verdadera; ***be in ~s*** estar malogrado; *fig*: *of reputation*, *theory* estar por los suelos; ***tear to ~s*** *fig*: *argument* poner por los suelos
II *v/t* (*pret & pp* **-ded**) *paper* hacer trizas; *in cooking* cortar en tiras

shred•der ['ʃredər] *for documents* trituradora *f* (de documentos)

shrewd [ʃruːd] *adj person* astuto; *judgement*, *investment* inteligente

shrewd•ness ['ʃruːdnɪs] *of person* astucia *f*, *of decision* inteligencia *f*

shriek [ʃriːk] **I** *n* alarido *m*, chillido *m*; ***~ of terror*** grito *m* de terror; ***~s pl of laughter*** carcajadas *fpl* de risa **II** *v/i* chi-

S

llar; **~ with laughter** reírse a carcajadas
shrift [ʃrɪft]: **give s.o. short ~** no hacer caso a alguien
shrill [ʃrɪl] *adj* estridente, agudo
shrimp [ʃrɪmp] **1** gamba *f*; *larger*: *Span* langostino *m*, *L.Am.* camarón *m* **2** F *little person* enano(-a) *m(f)*
shrine [ʃraɪn] santuario *m*
shrink[1] [ʃrɪŋk] *v/i* (*pret* **shrank**, *pp* **shrunk**) **1** *of material* encoger(se); *of level of support etc* reducirse **2**: **~ from doing sth** acobardarse de hacer algo
shrink[2] [ʃrɪŋk] *n* F (*psychiatrist*) psiquiatra *m/f*
shrink•age [ˈʃrɪŋkɪdʒ] COM *through pilferage* merma *f*
shrink•ing [ˈʃrɪŋkɪŋ] *adj*: **be a ~ violet** F ser poquita cosa F *or* un infeliz F
ˈshrink-wrap *v/t* (*pret & pp* **-ped**) envolver en plástico adherente
ˈshrink-wrap•ping *material plástico adherente para envolver*
shriv•el [ˈʃrɪvl] *v/i* (*pret & pp* **-ed**, *Br* **-led**) *of skin* arrugarse; *of leaves* marchitarse
shroud [ʃraʊd] **I** *n for corpse* sudario *m* **II** *v/t*: **be ~ed in mist** estar cubierto de neblina; **be ~ed in mystery / secrecy** estar envuelto en el misterio / secretismo
shrub [ʃrʌb] arbusto *m*
shrub•ber•y [ˈʃrʌbərɪ] arbustos *mpl*
shrug [ʃrʌg] **I** *n*: **... he said with a ~ ...** dijo encogiendo los hombros **II** *v/i* (*pret & pp* **-ged**) encoger los hombros **III** *v/t* (*pret & pp* **-ged**): **~ one's shoulders** encoger los hombros
◆ **shrug off** *v/t fig* ignorar, restar importancia a
shrunk [ʃrʌŋk] *pp* ☞ **shrink**
shuck [ʃʌk] **I** *n of peas, corn etc* vaina *f*, cáscara *f* **II** *v/t peas, corn* pelar, descascarar
shucks [ʃʌks] F *mild annoyance* ¡caramba!F; **~, it was nothing** ¡huy!, no era nada
shud•der [ˈʃʌdər] **I** *n of fear, disgust* escalofrío *m*; *of earth, building* temblor *m* **II** *v/i with fear, disgust* estremecerse; *of earth, building* temblar; **I ~ to think what ...** me entran escalofríos sólo de pensar que ...
shuf•fle [ˈʃʌfl] **I** *v/t cards* barajar **II** *v/i in walking* arrastrar los pies
shun [ʃʌn] *v/t* (*pret & pp* **-ned**) rechazar
shut [ʃʌt] *v/t & v/i* (*pret & pp* **shut**) cerrar
◆ **shut away** *v/t in closet etc* encerrar, guardar; **shut o.s. away** encerrarse, recluirse
◆ **shut down I** *v/t business* cerrar; *computer* apagar **II** *v/i of business* cerrarse; *of computer* apagarse
◆ **shut off** *v/t* cortar
◆ **shut out** *v/t light, sunshine, view*: *of trees, clouds* bloquear, tapar; *thoughts* apartar, ahuyentar; **it will help to shut out the noise / the light** ayudará a no dejar pasar el ruido / la luz
◆ **shut up** *v/i* F (*be quiet*) callarse; **shut up!** ¡cállate!
ˈshut•down *of factory, mine* cierre *m*; *of computer* apagamiento *m*
ˈshut-eye F sueñecito *m* F; **get some ~** echarse un sueñecito F
shut•ter [ˈʃʌtər] **1** *on window* contraventana *f* **2** PHOT obturador *m*
ˈshut•ter speed PHOT tiempo *m* de exposición
shut•tle [ˈʃʌtl] *v/i*: **~ between** *of bus* conectar; *of airplane* hacer el puente aéreo entre
ˈshut•tle•bus *at airport* autobús *m* de conexión; **ˈshut•tle•cock** SP volante *m*; **ˈshut•tle ser•vice** servicio *m* de conexión
shy [ʃaɪ] **1** *adj* tímido **2**: **fight ~ of sth** evitar algo; **fight ~ of doing sth** evitar hacer algo
◆ **shy away** *v/i* (*pret & pp* **shied**) *fig* evadir, eludir; **~ from doing sth** evadir hacer algo
shy•ness [ˈʃaɪnɪs] timidez *f*
shy•ster [ˈʃaɪstər] F *crook* ladrón(-ona) *m(f)*, sinvergüenza *m/f*; *crooked lawyer* granuja *m/f*
Si•a•mese twins [saɪəmiːzˈtwɪnz] *npl* siameses *mpl* (*fpl*)
Si•ber•i•a [saɪˈbɪrɪə] Siberia *f*
Si•ber•i•an [saɪˈbɪrɪən] *adj* siberiano
sib•ling [ˈsɪblɪŋ] *esp fml* hermano(-a) *m(f)*
Si•cil•i•an [sɪˈsɪlɪən] **I** *adj* siciliano **II** *n* siciliano(-a) *m(f)*
Sic•i•ly [ˈsɪsɪlɪ] Sicilia *f*
sick [sɪk] **I** *adj* **1** enfermo; **be off ~** estar de baja; **call in ~** telefonear al trabajo para avisar de que se está enfermo; **be**

worried ~ estar preocupadísimo **2** *Br*: ***be ~*** (*vomit*) vomitar **3** F *sense of humor* morboso, macabro; *society* enfermo **4**: ***be ~ of*** (*fed up with*) estar harto de; ***it makes me ~*** F me pone enfermo *or* malo **II** *npl*: ***the ~*** los enfermos *mpl*

'sick bag *in airplane* bolsa *f* para el mareo

'sick bay MIL, NAUT enfermería *f*

sick•en ['sɪkn] **I** *v/t* **1** (*disgust*) poner enfermo **2** (*make ill*) hacer enfermar, hacer caer enfermo **II** *v/i*: ***be ~ing for sth*** estar incubando algo

sick•en•ing ['sɪknɪŋ] *adj stench* nauseabundo; *behavior*, *crime* repugnante

sick•le ['sɪkl] AGR hoz *f*

'sick leave baja *f* (por enfermedad); ***be on ~*** estar de baja

sick•ly ['sɪklɪ] *adj person* enfermizo; *color* pálido

sick•ness ['sɪknɪs] **1** enfermedad *f* **2** (*vomiting*) vómitos *mpl*

'sick pay subsidio *m* por enfermedad

side [saɪd] **1** *of box*, *house*, *field* lado *m*; *of mountain* ladera *f*, vertiente *f*; *of person* costado *m*; ***at the ~ of the road*** al lado de la carretera; ***at*** *or* ***by s.o.'s ~*** al lado de alguien, con alguien; ***~ by ~*** juntos, uno al lado del otro; ***on the ~*** *earn extra money* aparte; *have an affair* en secreto; ***his ~ of the story*** su versión de la historia; ***there are two ~s to every story*** siempre hay dos versiones de una misma historia; ***be on the wrong ~ of 50*** tener más de 50 años; ***put to one ~*** *money* apartar, reservar; ***take s.o. to one ~*** llevar a alguien a un lado

2 SP equipo *m*; ***take ~s*** (*favor one ~*) tomar partido (***with*** por); ***I'm on your ~*** estoy de parte tuya

3: ***on the big*** / ***small ~*** un poco grande / pequeño

◆ **side with** *v/t* tomar partido por

'side•board aparador *m*; **'side•burns** *npl* patillas *fpl*; **'side•car** sidecar *m*; **'side dish** plato *m* de acompañamiento; **'side door** puerta *f* secundaria; **'side ef•fect** efecto *m* secundario; **'side im•pact pro•tec•tion** MOT protección *f* lateral; **'side is•sue** asunto *m* secundario; **'side•light** MOT luz *f* de posición; **'side•line I** *n* actividad *f* complementaria **II** *v/t*: ***feel ~d*** sentirse marginado; **'side•long** *adj*: ***~ glance*** mirada *f* de reojo; ***take a ~ glance at s.o.*** / ***sth*** mirar de reojo a alguien / algo; **'side road** carretera *f* secundaria; **'side•sad•dle I** *n* silla *f* de amazona *or* mujer **II** *adv ride* a la amazona, a mujeriegas; **'side show** barracón *m* de feria, atracción *f*; **side--split•ting** ['saɪdsplɪtɪŋ] *adj* desternillante, gracioso; **'side•step I** *v/t* (*pret & pp* **-ped**) SP regatear; *fig* evadir **II** *n* regate *m*; **'side street** bocacalle *f*; **'side•swipe I** *n*: ***take a ~ at*** F meterse de pasada con F **II** *v/t* MOT arañar; **'side•track** *v/t* distraer; ***get ~ed*** distraerse; **'side•walk** acera *f*, *Rpl* vereda *f*, *Mex* banqueta *f*; **side•walk 'caf•é** terraza *f*

'side•ways *adv* de lado

sid•ing ['saɪdɪŋ] **1** RAIL vía *f* muerta **2** TECH revestimiento *m*

◆ **si•dle up** ['saɪdl] *v/i*: ***sidle up to s.o.*** abordar discretamente a alguien

SIDS [esaɪdiː'es] *abbr* (= ***sudden infant death syndrome***) síndrome *m* de muerte súbita del lactante

siege [siːdʒ] sitio *m*; ***lay ~ to*** sitiar

si•es•ta [sɪ'estə] siesta *f*; ***have*** *or* ***take a ~*** echarse una siesta

sieve [sɪv] **I** *n* tamiz *m*; ***he has a memory like a ~*** F es flaco de memoria F **II** *v/t flour* tamizar

sift [sɪft] *v/t flour* tamizar; *data* examinar a fondo

◆ **sift out** *v/t fig* seleccionar (***from*** de)

◆ **sift through** *v/t details*, *data* pasar por el tamiz

sigh [saɪ] **I** *n* suspiro *m*; ***heave a ~ of relief*** suspirar de alivio **II** *v/i* suspirar

sight [saɪt] **I** *n* **1** vista *f*, (*power of seeing*) vista *f*, visión *f*; ***~s*** *of city* lugares *mpl* de interés; ***he can't stand the ~ of blood*** no aguanta ver sangre; ***I caught ~ of him just as ...*** lo vi justo cuando ...; ***know by ~*** conocer de vista; ***be*** (***with***)***in ~*** estar a la vista; ***within ~ of*** a la vista de; ***come into ~*** aparecer, dejarse ver; ***lose ~ of*** *objective etc* olvidarse de; ***at the ~ of*** al ver a; ***at first ~*** a primera vista; ***what a ~ you look!*** ¡qué pintas llevas!; ***you're a ~ for sore eyes*** F dichosos los ojos que te ven F; ***hate the ~ of sth*** / ***s.o.*** odiar algo / a alguien a muerte; ***buy sth ~ unseen*** COM comprar algo sin verlo antes; ***there wasn't***

a soul in ~ no había ni un alma; ***I disliked her on ~*** me cayó mal desde el primer momento en que la vi; ***keep out of ~!*** ¡escóndete!; ***let s.o. out of one's ~*** perder a alguien de vista; ***be out of ~*** F (*unattainable*) ser un imposible; ***once we're out of his ~*** cuando ya no pueda vernos; ***as soon as the car was out of ~*** en cuanto se dejó de ver el coche; ***get out of my ~!*** ¡fuera de mi vista!
2 *of gun, also **~s*** mirilla *f*; ***set one's ~s on sth*** *fig* marcarse algo como meta **II** *v/t submarine, rhinoceros, missing child etc* ver

'sight bill COM efecto *m* a la vista

sight•ed ['saɪtɪd] *adj* vidente

sight•ing ['saɪtɪŋ] avistamiento *m*

'sight-read MUS *v/t & v/i* (*pret & pp **-read*** [red]) repentizar; **'sight•see•ing**: ***we like ~*** nos gusta hacer turismo; ***go ~*** hacer turismo; **'sight•see•ing bus** bus *m* turístico; **'sight•see•ing tour** visita *f* turística

sight•seer ['saɪtsiːər] turista *m/f*

sign [saɪn] **I** *n* señal *f*, *outside shop, on building* cartel *m*, letrero *m*; ***it's a ~ of the times*** es un signo de los tiempos que corren; ***~s of the zodiac*** signos *mpl* del zodíaco; ***all the ~s are that ...*** todo indica que ...; ***there was no ~ of him*** no había rastro de él; ***be showing ~s of sth*** presentar indicios de algo; ***at midnight they were still showing no ~s of leaving*** a medianoche aún no parecían tener ninguna prisa por irse
II *v/t* firmar
III *v/i* **1** firmar **2** (*use sign language*) emplear el lenguaje de signos
◆ **sign away** *v/t rights, inheritance* renunciar a
◆ **sign for** *v/t*: ***I signed for it*** firmé yo
◆ **sign in** *v/i* registrarse
◆ **sign off** *v/i* **1** RAD hacer el cierre **2** *in letter writing* despedirse
◆ **sign over** *v/t possessions* ceder (***to*** a)
◆ **sign up I** *v/i* (*join the army*) alistarse **II** *v/t player* fichar

sig•nal ['sɪgnl] **I** *n* señal *f*, ***send out all the wrong ~s*** dar a una impresión equivocada **II** *v/i* (*pret & pp **-ed**, Br **-led***) **1** *of car driver* poner el intermitente **2**: ***~ to s.o. to do sth*** hacer señas a alguien para que haga algo **III** *v/t* (*pret & pp **-ed**, Br **-led***) *of driver: intentions* señalar, indicar; *readiness* avisar

sig•na•to•ry ['sɪgnətɔːrɪ] signatario(-a) *m*(*f*), firmante *m/f*; ***the signatories to the treaty*** los firmantes del tratado

sig•na•ture ['sɪgnətʃər] firma *f*

sig•na•ture 'tune sintonía *f*

sig•net ring ['sɪgnɪt] sello *m* (*anillo*)

sig•nif•i•cance [sɪg'nɪfɪkəns] importancia *f*, relevancia *f*; ***be of great ~ to*** ser de suma importancia para

sig•nif•i•cant [sɪg'nɪfɪkənt] *adj* **1** *event etc* importante, relevante **2** (*quite large*) considerable

sig•nif•i•cant•ly [sɪg'nɪfɪkəntlɪ] *adv larger, more expensive* considerablemente

sig•ni•fy ['sɪgnɪfaɪ] *v/t* (*pret & pp **-ied***) significar, suponer

sign•ing ['saɪnɪŋ] *for soccer team etc* fichaje *m*

'sign lan•guage lenguaje *m* por señas

'sign•post señal *f*

si•lence ['saɪləns] **I** *n* silencio *m*; ***in ~*** *work, march* en silencio; ***observe a one-minute ~*** guardar un minuto de silencio; ***buy s.o.'s ~*** comprar el silencio de alguien **II** *v/t* hacer callar

si•lenc•er ['saɪlənsər] *on gun, Br: on car* silenciador *m*

si•lent ['saɪlənt] *adj* silencioso; *movie* mudo; ***stay ~*** (*not comment*) permanecer callado; ***the ~ majority*** la mayoría que no expresa sus opiniones públicamente; ***they watched in ~ admiration as ...*** miraban pasmados con gran admiración cómo ...

si•lent 'part•ner COM socio(-a) *m*(*f*) capitalista

sil•hou•ette [sɪluː'et] **I** *n* silueta *f* **II** *v/t*: ***be ~d against*** perfilarse *or* recortarse sobre

sil•i•con ['sɪlɪkən] silicio *m*

sil•i•con 'chip chip *m* de silicio

sil•i•cone ['sɪlɪkoun] silicona *f*; ***~ breast implants*** implantes *mpl* de silicona para pechos

Sil•i•con 'Val•ley Silicon Valley *m*

sil•i•co•sis [sɪlɪ'kousɪs] MED silicosis *f*

silk [sɪlk] **I** *n* seda *f* **II** *adj shirt etc* de seda

'silk•worm ZO gusano *m* de seda

silk•y ['sɪlkɪ] *adj hair, texture* sedoso

sill [sɪl] **1** *of window* repisa *f* **2** *of car chassis* umbral *m* de la puerta

S

sil•li•ness ['sɪlɪnɪs] tontería *f*, estupidez *f*
sil•ly ['sɪlɪ] *adj* tonto, estúpido
si•lo ['saɪloʊ] *for grain, missiles* silo *m*
silt [sɪlt] cieno *m*
◆ **silt up** *v/i* encenagarse
sil•ver ['sɪlvər] **I** *n metal, medal* plata *f*; (*~ objects*) (objetos *mpl* de) plata *f* **II** *adj* **1** *ring* de plata; ***be born with a ~ spoon in one's mouth*** ser de familia rica **2** *hair* canoso
sil•ver 'foil papel *m* de plata; **sil•ver-haired** ['sɪlvərherd] *adj* canoso; **sil•ver 'ju•bi•lee** vigésimoquinto aniversario *m*; **sil•ver 'med•al** medalla *f* de plata; **sil•ver 'med•a•list**, *Br* **sil•ver 'med•al•list** medallista *m/f* de plata; **'sil•ver mine** mina *f* de plata; **sil•ver 'pa•per** papel *m* plateado; **sil•ver-plat•ed** [sɪlvər'pleɪtɪd] *adj* plateado; **sil•ver 'screen** séptimo arte *m*; *actual screen* pantalla *f* grande; **'sil•ver smith** platero(-a) *m*(*f*); **sil•ver•ware** ['sɪlvərwer] plata *f*; **sil•ver 'wed•ding** bodas *fpl* de plata
Sim card ['sɪmkɑːrd] tarjeta *f* Sim
sim•i•lar ['sɪmɪlər] *adj* parecido, similar; ***be ~ to*** ser parecido a, parecerse a
sim•i•lar•i•ty [sɪmɪ'lærətɪ] parecido *m*, similitud *f*; ***there are similarities between the two cases*** los dos casos presentan analogías
sim•i•lar•ly ['sɪmɪlərlɪ] *adv* de la misma manera
sim•i•le ['sɪmɪlɪ] símil *m*
sim•mer ['sɪmər] *v/i* **1** *in cooking* cocer a fuego lento **2**: ***be ~ing*** (***with rage***) estar a punto de explotar
◆ **simmer down** *v/i* tranquilizarse
sim•per ['sɪmpər] *v/i* soltar risitas
sim•ple ['sɪmpl] *adj* (*easy, not elaborate*) sencillo; *person* simple; ***for the ~ reason that ...*** simplemente porque ...; ***wouldn't it be ~r to start again?*** ¿no sería más fácil empezar de nuevo?
sim•ple-'mind•ed *adj pej* simplón
sim•pli•ci•ty [sɪm'plɪsətɪ] *of task, design* sencillez *f*, simplicidad *f*; ***it's ~ itself*** es facilísimo
sim•pli•fi•ca•tion [sɪmplɪfɪ'keɪʃn] simplificación *f*
sim•pli•fy ['sɪmplɪfaɪ] *v/t* (*pret & pp* ***-ied***) simplificar
sim•plis•tic [sɪm'plɪstɪk] *adj* simplista
sim•ply ['sɪmplɪ] *adv* sencillamente; ***it is ~ the best*** es sin lugar a dudas el mejor; ***to put it ~*** en un lenguaje más sencillo; ***I was ~ trying to help*** sólo trataba de ayudar
sim•u•late ['sɪmjʊleɪt] *v/t* simular
sim•u•la•tion [sɪmjʊ'leɪʃn] simulación *f*
sim•u•la•tor ['sɪmjʊleɪtər] TECH simulador *m*
si•mul•cast ['saɪmlkæst] **I** *n* retransmisión *f* simultánea por radio y televisión **II** *v/t* (*pret & pp* ***-cast***) retransmitir por radio y televisión simultáneamente
sim•ul•ta•ne•ous [saɪml'teɪnɪəs] *adj* simultáneo; ***~ translator*** intérprete *m/f* simultáneo
sim•ul•ta•ne•ous•ly [saɪml'teɪnɪəslɪ] *adv* simultáneamente
sin [sɪn] **I** *n* pecado *m*; ***live in ~*** *hum* vivir en pecado; ***as ugly as ~*** más feo que Picio **II** *v/i* (*pret & pp* ***-ned***) pecar
'sin bin I *n* banquillo *m* **II** *v/t* (*pret & pp* ***-ned***) mandar al banquillo
since [sɪns] **I** *prep* desde; ***~ last week*** desde la semana pasada **II** *adv* desde entonces; ***I haven't seen him ~*** no lo he visto desde entonces **III** *conj* **1** *in expressions of time* desde que; ***~ you left*** desde que te marchaste; ***~ I have been living here*** desde que vivo acquí **2** (*seeing that*) ya que, dado que; ***~ you don't like it*** ya que *or* dado que no te gusta
sin•cere [sɪn'sɪr] *adj* sincero
sin•cere•ly [sɪn'sɪrlɪ] *adv* sinceramente; ***I ~ hope he appreciates it*** espero de verdad que lo aprecie; ***Sincerely yours***, *Br* ***Yours ~*** atentamente
sin•cer•i•ty [sɪn'serətɪ] sinceridad *f*; ***in all ~*** con el corazón en la mano
sine [saɪn] MATH seno *m*
si•ne qua non [sɪneɪkwɑː'noʊn] *fml* condición *f* sine qua non
sin•ew ['sɪnjuː] ANAT tendón *m*
'sin•ew•y *adj* (*strong, muscular*) fibroso
sin•ful ['sɪnfəl] *adj person* pecador; *things* pecaminoso; ***it is ~ to ...*** es pecado ...
sing [sɪŋ] *v/t & v/i* (*pret* ***sang***, *pp* ***sung***) cantar; ***~ s.o. sth*** cantar algo a alguien; ***~ a baby to sleep*** acunar *or* mecer a un bebé; ***~ s.o.'s praises*** elogiar a alguien
◆ **sing along** *v/i* cantar (***with*** con)
Sin•ga•pore ['sɪŋəpɔːr] Singapur *m*
singe [sɪndʒ] *v/t* chamuscar

sing•er ['sɪŋər] cantante *m/f*
sing•er-'song•writ•er cantautor(a) *m(f)*
sing•ing ['sɪŋɪŋ] **I** *n* canto *m*; ***we could hear ~ coming from …*** oímos a gente cantando en … **II** *adj*: ***~ lesson*** clase *f* de canto; ***~ voice*** voz *f* para cantar
sin•gle ['sɪŋgl] **I** *adj* **1** (*sole*) único, solo; ***there wasn't a ~ mistake*** no había ni un solo error; ***every ~ day*** absolutamente todos los días; ***~ currency*** moneda única **2** (*not double*) único; ***in ~ file*** en fila india **3** (*not married*) soltero *m*
II *n* **1** MUS sencillo *m* **2** (*~ room*) habitación *f* individual **3** *person* soltero(-a) *m(f)*; ***holidays for ~s*** vacaciones *fpl* para gente sin pareja **4** *Br*: *ticket* billete *m or L.Am.* boleto *m* de ida **5**: ***~s*** *in tennis* individuales *mpl*; ***a ~s match*** un partido de individuales; ***men's ~s*** individuales *mpl* masculinos
◆ **single out** *v/t* **1** (*choose*) seleccionar **2** (*distinguish*) distinguir
sin•gle-breast•ed [sɪŋgl'brestɪd] *adj* recto, con una fila de botones; **sin•gle 'file**: ***in ~*** en fila india; **sin•gle-'hand•ed** [sɪŋgl'hændɪd] *adj & adv* en solitario; **sin•gle-'mind•ed** *adj* determinado, resuelto; **Sin•gle 'Mar•ket** *in Europe* Mercado *m* Único; **sin•gle 'moth•er** madre *f* soltera; **sin•gle 'pa•rent** padre *m* / madre *f* soltero(-a); **sin•gle pa•rent 'fam•i•ly** familia *f* monoparental; **sin•gle 'room** habitación *f* individual
'sin•gles bar *bar para los que buscan pareja*
sin•gu•lar ['sɪŋgjʊlər] GRAM **I** *adj* singular **II** *n* singular *m*; ***in the ~*** en singular
sin•gu•lar•ly ['sɪŋgjʊlərlɪ] *adv* extraordinariamente
sin•is•ter ['sɪnɪstər] *adj* siniestro; *sky* amenazador
sink [sɪŋk] **I** *n in kitchen* fregadero *m*; *in bathroom* lavabo *m*
II *v/i* (*pret* **sank**, *pp* **sunk**) *of ship, object* hundirse; *of sun* ponerse; *of interest rates, pressure etc* descender, bajar; ***he sank onto the bed*** se tiró a la cama; ***leave s.o. to ~ or swim*** *fig* dejar que alguien se las arregle como pueda; ***how could you ~ so low as to …?*** *also iron* ¿cómo pudiste caer tan bajo como para …?; ***my heart sank*** me dio un vuelco el corazón
III *v/t* (*pret* **sank**, *pp* **sunk**) **1** *ship* hundir; ***we're sunk!*** F ¡nos vamos a pique! F **2** *funds* investir **3** SP *golfball, snooker ball* meter **4**: ***~ one's teeth into sth*** hincar los dientes en algo
◆ **sink in** *v/i* **1** *of liquid* penetrar **2**: ***it gradually sank in that …*** *I realized* me di cuenta de que …; ***it still hasn't really sunk in*** *of realization* todavía no lo he asumido
sink•ing ['sɪŋkɪŋ] *adj*: ***I got that ~ feeling when …*** F se me puso mal cuerpo cuando …
sin•ner ['sɪnər] pecador(a) *m(f)*
si•nus ['saɪnəs] seno *m* (*nasal*)
si•nus•i•tis [saɪnə'saɪtɪs] MED sinusitis *f*
sip [sɪp] **I** *n* sorbo *m*; ***take a ~ of wine*** tomar un sorbo de vino **II** *v/t* (*pret & pp* **-ped**) sorber
◆ **sip at** *v/t* beber a sorbos; ***he ~ped at his wine*** tomó un sorbo de vino
si•phon ['saɪfn] *also soda ~* sifón *m*
◆ **siphon off** *v/t liquid* extraer a presión; *fig*: *profits, personnel* desviar furtivamente
sir [sɜːr] **1** señor *m*; ***excuse me, ~*** perdone, caballero; *to teacher* perdone, profesor **2**: ***Sir*** *Br* Caballero Británico, Sir
si•ren ['saɪrən] sirena *f*
sir•loin ['sɜːrlɔɪn] solomillo *m*
sis [sɪs] F tata *f* F, hermana *f*
sis•sy ['sɪsɪ] F llorica *m* F
sis•ter ['sɪstər] **1** hermana *f* **2** *in movement* compañera *f*, camarada *f* **3** REL: ***Sister Mary*** la Hermana María, Sor María **II** *adj* gemelo; ***~ company*** compañía *f* afiliada; ***~ ship*** buque *m* gemelo
sis•ter•hood ['sɪstərhʊd] **1** *togetherness of women* fraternidad *f* **2** *other women* hermandad *f*, sociedad *f*
'sis•ter-in-law (*pl* ***sisters-in-law***) cuñada *f*
sis•ter•ly ['sɪstərlɪ] *adj* fraternal
sit [sɪt] *v/i* (*pret & pp* **sat**) **1** estar sentado **2** (*~ down*) sentarse
◆ **sit around** *v/i* estar sentado sin hacer nada
◆ **sit back** *v/i* **1** sentarse **2** *fig*: ***now we***

S

can all sit back and relax ahora ya podemos sentarnos y relajarnos; ***you can't just sit back and do nothing!*** ¡no te puedes quedar ahí de brazos cruzados!

◆ **sit by** *v/i*: ***I am not going to ~ while …*** no me voy a quedar de brazos cruzados mientras …

◆ **sit down I** *v/i* sentarse; ***eat sitting down*** comer sentado; ***they won't take that sitting down*** *fig* opondrán resistencia a eso; ***sit down and discuss sth*** sentarse y hablar algo **II** *v/t*: ***sit s.o. down*** invitar a alguien sentarse

◆ **sit for** *v/t painter* posar para; ***sit for one's portrait*** posar para hacerse un retrato

◆ **sit in for** *v/t* hacer de suplente de

◆ **sit in on** *v/t* acudir de oyente a

◆ **sit on** *v/t* **1** *fig* (*not deal with*) *documents etc* evitar despachar **2** (*suppress*) *facts, idea etc* reprimir; *person* hacer callar **3**: ***sit on a committee*** ser miembro de un comité

◆ **sit out** *v/t* **1** *dance* no bailar **2** *crisis etc* esperar el fin de

◆ **sit up I** *v/i* **1** *in bed* incorporarse **2** (*straighten back*) sentarse derecho; ***make s.o. sit up*** (***and take notice***) F llamar la atención de alguien; ***sit up at table*** sentarse a la mesa **3** (*wait up at night*) esperar levantado **II** *v/t patient in bed* incorporar

sit•com ['sɪtkɑːm] telecomedia *f*, comedia *f* de situación

'sit-down 1: ~ (***protest***) sentada *f* **2**: ***have a ~*** sentarse para descansar

site [saɪt] **I** *n* emplazamiento *m*; *of battle* lugar *m* **II** *v/t new offices etc* situar; ***be ~d*** estar emplazado *or* colocado

sit•ter ['sɪtər] (*baby ~*) **1** *Span* canguro *m/f*, *L.Am.* babysitter *m/f* **2** *for painter* modelo *m/f*

sit•ting ['sɪtɪŋ] *of committee, court, for artist* sesión *f*; *for meals* turno *m*; ***read sth at a single ~*** leer algo de una sentada

sit•ting 'duck *fig* blanco *m* fácil

'sit•ting room sala *f* de estar, salón *m*

sit•u•at•ed ['sɪtʊeɪtɪd] *adj* situado; ***be well ~ to do sth*** estar en buena situación para hacer algo

sit•u•a•tion [sɪtʊ'eɪʃn] situación *f*

sit•u•a•tion 'com•e•dy ☞ ***sitcom***

sit-ups ['sɪtʌps] abdominales *fpl*

six [sɪks] seis; ***be all at ~es and sevens*** F *of person* estar confundido; *of place* estar patas arriba F

'six-pack *of beer* pack *m* de seis

six•teen [sɪks'tiːn] dieciséis

six•teenth [sɪks'tiːnθ] *n & adj* decimosexto

sixth [sɪksθ] *n & adj* sexto; ***~ sense*** *fig* sexto sentido *m*; ***the ~ of May, May the ~*** el seis de mayo

six•ti•eth ['sɪkstɪɪθ] *n & adj* sexagésimo

six•ty ['sɪkstɪ] sesenta; ***be in one's sixties*** tener sesenta y tantos; ***in the sixties*** en los (años) sesenta

six-'yard box *in soccer* área *f* pequeña

size [saɪz] tamaño *m*; *of loan* importe *m*; *of jacket, dress, shirt etc* talla *f*; *of shoes* número *m*; ***what ~ is your room?*** ¿cómo es de grande tu habitación; ***what ~ do you take?*** ¿qué talla / número lleva?; ***I'll cut him down to ~*** F le voy a parar los pies F; ***that's about the ~ of it*** *fig* eso parece; ***the only building of any ~*** el único edificio de un tamaño considerable

◆ **size up** *v/t* evaluar, examinar

size•a•ble ['saɪzəbl] *adj house, order* considerable; *meal* copioso

siz•zle ['sɪzl] *v/i* chisporrotear

skate [skeɪt] **I** *n* patín *m*; ***get your ~s on!*** F ¡ponte las pilas! F, ¡date prisa! **II** *v/i* patinar

◆ **skate around, skate over** *v/t fig* evitar, esquivar

'skate•board monopatín *m*; **'skate•board•er** skater *m/f*; **'skate•board•ing** patinaje *m* en monopatín

skat•er ['skeɪtər] patinador(a) *m(f)*

skat•ing ['skeɪtɪŋ] patinaje *m*

'skat•ing rink pista *f* de patinaje

ske•dad•dle [skɪ'dædl] *v/i* F pirarse F, abrirse F

skeet shoot•ing ['skiːtʃuːtɪŋ] tiro *m* al plato

skel•e•tal ['skelətl] *adj* (*emaciated*) esquelético, raquítico

skel•e•ton ['skelɪtn] esqueleto *m*; ***have a ~ in the closet*** *fig* tener algo que ocultar; ***~ service*** / ***crew*** servicio *m* / personal *m* mínimo

'skel•e•ton key llave *f* maestra

skep•tic ['skeptɪk] escéptico(-a) *m(f)*

skep•ti•cal ['skeptɪkl] *adj* escéptico; ***be***

~ about sth ser escéptico acerca de algo
skep•ti•cism ['skeptɪsɪzm] escepticismo *m*
sketch [sketʃ] **I** *n* **1** boceto *m*, esbozo *m* **2** THEA sketch *m* **II** *v/t* bosquejar
◆ **sketch in** *v/t fig* añadir, adjuntar
◆ **sketch out** *v/t fig* bosquejar
'sketch•book cuaderno *m* de dibujo
'sketch pad cuaderno *m* de dibujo
sketch•y ['sketʃɪ] *adj knowledge etc* básico, superficial; *description, memory etc* incompleto, fragmentario
skew [skju:] *v/t* torcer; *fig*: *data, facts* desvirtuar, manipular
skew•er ['skjʊər] **I** *n* brocheta *f* **II** *v/t fish* espetar
ski [ski:] **I** *n* esquí *m* **II** *v/i* esquiar; ***we ~ed down to the chalet*** bajamos esquiando hasta la cabaña
'ski boots *npl* botas *fpl* de esquí
skid [skɪd] **I** *n of car* patinazo *m*; *of person* resbalón *m*; ***~ marks*** *pl* MOT marcas *fpl* de patinazo; ***he's on the ~s*** F va de mal en peor F **II** *v/i* (*pret & pp* ***-ded***) *of car* patinar; *of person* resbalar
ski•doo® [skɪ'du:] ☞ ***snowmobile***
skid 'row [skɪd'roʊ] calles *fpl* de mala muerte; ***finish up on ~*** acabar en la miseria
ski•er ['ski:ər] esquiador(a) *m(f)*
skiff [skɪf] NAUT esquife *m*
ski gog•gles ['ski:gɑ:glz] *npl* gafas *fpl* de esquiar
ski•ing ['ski:ɪŋ] esquí *m*
'ski in•struc•tor monitor(a) *m(f)* de esquí
'ski jump salto *m*; *structure* pista *f* de salto
skil•ful *etc Br* ☞ ***skillful*** *etc*
'ski lift remonte *m*
skill [skɪl] destreza *f*, habilidad *f*; ***game of ~*** juego *m* de destreza; ***learn a new ~*** aprender una habilidad nueva
skilled [skɪld] *adj* capacitado, preparado; *worker* cualificado; *work* especializado
skilled 'work•er trabajador(a) *m(f)* cualificado
skil•let ['skɪlɪt] sartén *f*
'skill•ful ['skɪlfəl] *adj* hábil, habilidoso
skill•ful•ly ['skɪlfəlɪ] *adv* con habilidad *or* destreza
skim [skɪm] *v/t* (*pret & pp* ***-med***) **1** *surface* rozar; *document* leer por encima **2** *milk* desnatar, descremar
◆ **skim off** *v/t the best* escoger
◆ **skim through** *v/t text* leer por encima
'ski mask pasamontañas *mpl*
'skim milk, 'skimmed milk [skɪmd] leche *f* desnatada *or* descremada
◆ **skimp on** [skɪmp] *v/t* escatimar
skimp•y ['skɪmpɪ] *adj account etc* superficial; *dress* cortísimo; *bikini* mínimo
skin [skɪn] **I** *n* piel *f*; ***by the ~ of one's teeth*** F por los pelos F; ***be all ~ and bone(s)*** estar en los huesos; ***it's no ~ off my nose*** F no es de mi incumbencia; ***be drenched or soaked to the ~*** estar calado hasta los huesos; ***get under s.o.'s ~*** F (*annoy*) sacar a alguien de quicio F; (*fascinate*) hechizar a alguien; ***save one's ~*** F salvar el pellejo F
II *v/t* (*pret & pp* ***-ned***) despellejar, desollar; ***keep one's eyes ~ned*** F estar con cien ojos F
'skin can•cer cáncer *m* de piel; **'skin care** cuidado *m* de la piel; **skin-'deep** *adj fig* superficial, fútil; **'skin div•er** buceador(a) *m(f)* en bañador; **'skin div•ing** buceo *m* (en bañador); **'skin flick** F peli *f* porno F
skin•flint ['skɪnflɪnt] F agarrado(-a) *m(f)* F, roñoso(-a) *m(f)*
skin•ful ['skɪnfʊl]: ***he's had a ~*** F lleva una buena castaña F
'skin game F engañifa *f* F, timo *m*; **'skin graft** injerto *m* de piel; **'skin•head** skinhead *m/f*, cabeza rapada *m/f*
skin•ny ['skɪnɪ] **I** *adj* escuálido **II** *n* canijo(-a) *m(f)*
skin•ny-dip•ping ['skɪnɪdɪpɪŋ] F: ***go ~*** bañarse en pelotas F
'skin test prueba *f* del parche, prueba *f* epicutánea
'skin-tight *adj* ajustado
skip [skɪp] **I** *n* (*little jump*) brinco *m*, saltito *m* **II** *v/i* (*pret & pp* ***-ped***) brincar **III** *v/t* (*pret & pp* ***-ped***) (*omit*) pasar por alto; *lunch, lecture etc* saltarse; ***~ it!*** ¡no pasa nada!, ¡no importa!
◆ **skip off** *v/i* F largarse F, pirarse F
'ski pants *npl* mallas *fpl* de esquiar
'ski pole bastón *m* de esquí
skip•per ['skɪpər] NAUT patrón(-ona) *m(f)*, capitán(-ana) *m(f)*; *of team* ca-

pitán(-ana) *m(f)*
skip•ping rope ['skɪpɪŋ] *Br* comba *f*
'ski re•sort estación *f* de esquí
skir•mish ['skɜːrmɪʃ] MIL contienda *f*
skirt [skɜːrt] **I** *n* falda *f* **II** *v/t* **1** (*border*) bordear, rodear **2** *in order to avoid* esquivar
◆ **skirt around** *v/t fig* esquivar, evitar
'skirt•ing board *Br* rodapié *m*
'ski run pista *f* de esquí
skit [skɪt] sketch *m* (cómico); ***do a ~ on*** hacer un sketch (cómico) de
'ski tow telesquí *m*
◆ **skive off** [skaɪv] *v/t Br* F: ***skive off school*** hacer novillos F *or* pellas F
skiv•vies ['skɪvɪz] *npl* F calzoncillos *mpl*
skul•dug•ger•y [skʌl'dʌgərɪ] F chanchullo *m*, trapicheo *m*
skulk [skʌlk] *v/i* esconderse, rondar
◆ **skulk off** *v/i* esconderse
skull [skʌl] cráneo *m*; ***the ~ and crossbones*** las dos tibias y la calavera; ***can't you get it into that thick ~ of yours that ...?*** F ¿no te entra en esa cabezota que ...? F
skunk [skʌŋk] mofeta *f*
sky [skaɪ] cielo *m*; ***in the ~*** en el cielo; ***the ~'s the limit*** F no hay límites, no hay nada imposible
sky-'blue *adj* azul cielo; **'sky•cap** mozo(-a) *m(f)* de equipajes; **'sky•div•er** paracaidista *m/f*; **'sky-div•ing** paracaidismo *m*; **sky-'high** *adv*: ***blow ~*** *building* volar por los aires; *theory, argument* echar por tierra; **'sky•light** claraboya *f*; **'sky•line** horizonte *m*; ***the New York ~*** la silueta de los edificios de Nueva York en el horizonte; **'sky•scrap•er** rascacielos *m inv*
slab [slæb] *of stone* losa *f*; *of cake etc* trozo *m* grande
slack [slæk] *adj rope* flojo; *work* descuidado; *period* tranquilo; ***discipline is very ~*** no hay disciplina
slack•en ['slækn] *v/t rope, pace* aflojar
◆ **slacken off** *v/i of trading, pace* disminuir
slack•er ['slækər] holgazán(-ana) *m(f)*, vago(-a) *m(f)*
slacks [slæks] *npl* pantalones *mpl*
slag [slæg] *in furnace* escoria *f*
◆ **slag off** *v/t* (*pret & pp* **-ged**) *Br* F meterse con F, echar pestes de F

slain [sleɪn] *pp* ☞ ***slay***
slake [sleɪk] *v/t*: ***~ one's thirst*** apagar la sed
sla•lom ['slɑːləm] slalom *m*, carrera *f* de obstáculos
slam [slæm] **I** *v/t* (*pret & pp* **-med**) **1** *door* cerrar de un golpe **2** F *criticize* triturar, vapulear **II** *v/i* (*pret & pp* **-med**) *of door* cerrarse de golpe
◆ **slam down** *v/t* estampar; *phone* colgar de golpe
◆ **slam on** *v/t*: ***slam on the brakes*** frenar bruscamente
'slam-dunk *v/t* rematar
slam•mer ['slæmər] P trena *f* P
slan•der ['slændər] **I** *n* difamación *f* **II** *v/t* difamar
slan•der•ous ['slændərəs] *adj* difamatorio
slang [slæŋ] argot *m*, jerga *f*; *of a specific group* jerga *f*
'slang•ing match: ***they had a ~*** *Br* F se tiraron los trastos a la cabeza F
slant [slænt] **I** *v/i* inclinarse **II** *v/t* **1** *line, post* torcer **2** *story, report* desvirtuar; ***be ~ed toward sth*** ser parcial acerca de algo **III** *n* **1** inclinación *f* **2** *given to a story* enfoque *m*
slant•ing ['slæntɪŋ] *adj* **1** *roof* inclinado **2** *eyes* rasgado
slap [slæp] **I** *n* (*blow*) bofetada *f*, cachete *m*; ***a ~ in the face*** una bofetada en la cara; *fig* una bofetada, un golpe; ***a ~ on the wrist*** *fig* un toque de atención **II** *v/t* (*pret & pp* **-ped**) dar una bofetada *or* un cachete a; ***~ s.o. in the face*** dar una bofetada a alguien; ***just ~ a bit of paint on it!*** ¡dale un poco de pintura a eso!; ***the company was ~ped with a fine / a lawsuit*** a la empresa le encasquetaron una multa / un pleito **III** *adv* F de plano F, de sopetón F; ***I walked ~ into him*** me di de sopetón con él
◆ **slap around** *v/t* F zurrar a F
slap-'bang *adv Br* F de plano F, de sopetón F
'slap•dash *adj* chapucero
'slap•stick *comedia de humor básico consistente en caídas, bofetadas, etc*
slash [slæʃ] **I** *n* **1** *cut* corte *m*, raja *f* **2** *in punctuation* barra *f* **II** *v/t* **1** *skin etc* cortar; ***~ one's wrists*** cortarse las venas **2** *prices, costs* recortar drástica-

S

mente

slat [slæt] *in blinds* tablilla *f*

slate [sleɪt] **I** *n* **1** pizarra *f*; ***put sth on the ~*** *Br* F *fig* poner algo en cuenta; ***wipe the ~ clean*** *fig* hacer borrón y cuenta nueva **2** POL (*list of candidates*) lista *f* de candidatos **II** *v/t* **1** (*designate*) designar *or* elegir como candidato **2** (*schedule*) programar **3** *Br* F (*criticize*) poner verde F

slaugh•ter ['slɒːtər] **I** *n of animals* sacrificio *m*; *of people, troops* matanza *f* **II** *v/t animals* sacrificar; *people, troops* masacrar

'slaugh•ter•house *for animals* matadero *m*

Slav [slɑːv] *adj* eslavo

slave [sleɪv] esclavo(-a) *m*(*f*)

◆ **slave away** *v/i* sudar sangre

◆ **slave away at** *v/t* sudar sangre con

'slave-driv•er F negrero(-a) *m*(*f*) F

slave 'la•bor *also fig* **1** esclavos *mpl* **2** *work* explotación *f*

slav•er•y ['sleɪvərɪ] esclavitud *f*; ***be sold into ~*** ser vendido como esclavo

'slave trade, 'slave traf•fic tráfico *m* de esclavos

slav•ish ['sleɪvɪʃ] *adj* exacto, al pie de la letra

Sla•von•ic [slə'vɑːnɪk] *adj* eslavo

slaw [slɔː] *ensalada de col, cebolla, zanahoria y mayonesa*

slay [sleɪ] *v/t* (*pret* **slew**, *pp* **slain**) asesinar

slay•er ['sleɪər] asesino(-a) *m*(*f*)

slay•ing ['sleɪɪŋ] (*murder*) asesinato *m*

sleaze [sliːz] POL corrupción *f*

slea•zy ['sliːzɪ] *adj bar* sórdido; *person* de mala calaña

sled, sledge [sled, sledʒ] trineo *m*

'sledge ham•mer mazo *m*

sleek [sliːk] *adj* **1** *lines, profile* elegante, armonioso **2** *hair, animal's coat* lustroso

sleep [sliːp] **I** *n* sueño *m*; ***go to ~*** dormirse; ***I need a good ~*** necesito dormir bien; ***I couldn't get to ~*** no pude dormirme; ***in one's ~*** mientras se duerme; ***I wouldn't lose any ~ over it if I were you*** si yo fuera tú no dejaría que eso me quitara el sueño; ***put an animal to ~*** sacrificar a un animal; ***my leg has gone to ~*** se me ha dormido la pierna **II** *v/i* (*pret & pp* **slept**) dormir; ***~ late*** dormir hasta tarde; ***~ like a log*** dormir como un lirón *or* tronco **III** *v/t* (*pret & pp* **slept**): ***this tent ~s four*** en esta tienda de campaña pueden dormir cuatro

◆ **sleep around** *v/i* F acostarse con otras personas F

◆ **sleep in** *v/i Br* (*sleep late*) dormir hasta tarde

◆ **sleep off** *v/t*: ***sleep it off*** dormirla

◆ **sleep on** *v/t*: ***sleep on sth*** *decision* consultar algo con la almohada

◆ **sleep over** *v/i* quedarse a dormir

◆ **sleep through** *v/t* dormir sin enterarse de

◆ **sleep together** *v/i* acostarse

◆ **sleep with** *v/t* (*have sex with*) acostarse con

sleep•er ['sliːpər] **1** *Br* RAIL *on track* traviesa *f* **2** *Br* RAIL (*sleeping car*) coche *m* cama **3**: ***be a light / heavy ~*** tener el sueño ligero / pesado

sleep•i•ly ['sliːpɪlɪ] *adv*: ***say sth ~*** decir algo medio dormido

sleep•ing bag ['sliːpɪŋ] saco *m* de dormir; **'sleep•ing car** RAIL coche *m* cama; **'sleep•ing part•ner** *Br* COM socio(-a) *m*(*f*) capitalista; **'sleep•ing pill** somnífero *m*, pastilla *f* para dormir; **'sleep•ing sick•ness** MED enfermedad *f* del sueño

sleep•less ['sliːplɪs] *adj*: ***have a ~ night*** pasar la noche en blanco

'sleep•o•ver: ***have a ~ at s.o.'s house*** quedarse a dormir en casa de alguien; **'sleep•walk** *v/i* andar sonámbulo; **'sleep•walk•er** sonámbulo(-a) *m*(*f*); **'sleep walk•ing** sonambulismo *m*

sleep•y ['sliːpɪ] *adj* adormilado, somnoliento; *town* tranquilo; ***I'm ~*** tengo sueño

'sleep•y•head F dormilón(-ona) *m*(*f*) F

sleet [sliːt] aguanieve *f*

sleeve [sliːv] *of jacket etc* manga *f*; ***have sth up one's ~*** *fig* tener algo planeado en secreto

sleeve•less ['sliːvlɪs] *adj* sin mangas

sleigh [sleɪ] trineo *m*

sleight of 'hand [slaɪt] juegos *mpl* de manos

slen•der ['slendər] *adj figure, arms* esbelto; *income, margin* escaso; *chance* remoto

slept [slept] *pret & pp* ☞ ***sleep***
sleuth [slu:θ] F detective *m/f*
slew[1] [slu:] *pret* ☞ ***slay***
slew[2] [slu:] *n*: ***a (whole) ~ of*** F un montón de F, una caterva de F
slice [slaɪs] **I** *n of bread* rebanada *f*; *of cake* trozo *m*; *of salami*, *cheese* loncha *f*; *fig*: *of profits etc* parte *f* **II** *v/t loaf etc* cortar (en rebanadas)
◆ **slice off** *v/t* cortar
◆ **slice up** *v/t* cortar (en rebanadas, trozos, lonchas etc)
sliced bread [slaɪst'bred] pan *m* de molde en rebanadas; ***it's not exactly the greatest thing since ~*** F no es la octava maravilla F
slick [slɪk] **I** *adj performance* muy logrado; (*pej*: *cunning*) con mucha labia **II** *n of oil* marea *f* negra
slick•er ['slɪkər] *coat* chaquetón *m* impermeable
slid [slɪd] *pret & pp* ☞ ***slide***
slide [slaɪd] **I** *n* **1** *for kids* tobogán *m* **2** PHOT diapositiva *f* **II** *v/i* (*pret & pp* ***slid***) deslizarse; *of exchange rate etc* descender; ***let things ~*** *fig* dejar que las cosas vayan a la deriva **III** *v/t* (*pret & pp* ***slid***) deslizar
'slide pro•jec•tor proyector *m* de diapositivas
slid•ing door [slaɪdɪŋ'dɔ:r] puerta *f* corredera; **slid•ing 'scale** escala *f* móvil; **'slid•ing tack•le** *in soccer* entrada *f* en plancha
slight [slaɪt] **I** *adj* **1** *person*, *figure* menudo **2** (*small*) pequeño; *accent* ligero; ***I have a ~ headache*** me duele un poco la cabeza; ***no, not in the ~est*** no, en absoluto; ***I haven't the ~est idea*** no tengo ni la más remota idea **II** *n* desaire *m* **III** *v/t* desestimar; ***feel ~ed*** sentirse menospreciado
slight•ly ['slaɪtlɪ] *adv* un poco
slim [slɪm] **I** *adj* delgado; *chance* remoto **II** *v/i* (*pret & pp* **-med**): ***I'm ~ming*** estoy a dieta
◆ **slim down I** *v/t fig*: *administration*, *bureaucracy etc* reducir, recortar **II** *v/i of person* adelgazar
slime [slaɪm] (*mud*) lodo *m*; *of slug etc* baba *f*
'slime•ball *pej* P granuja *m/f* P, bribón(-ona) *m(f)* P
slim•ming ['slɪmɪŋ] **I** *n* adelgazamiento *m* **II** *adj*: ***that dress is very ~*** ese vestido estiliza mucho
slim•y ['slaɪmɪ] *adj* **1** *liquid* viscoso; *river bed* lleno de lodo **2** *pej* F *person*, *grin* pillo F
sling [slɪŋ] **I** *n for arm* cabestrillo *m*; *for baby* canguro *m* **II** *v/t* (*pret & pp* ***slung***) F (*throw*) tirar
◆ **sling out** *v/t garbage* arrojar, lanzar; *drunk from bar* echar a patadas
'sling•backs *npl zapatos con el talón abierto y con tira*
slink [slɪŋk] *v/i* (*pret & pp* ***slunk***) moverse a hurtadillas
slink•y ['slɪŋkɪ] *adj little dress* ceñido
slip [slɪp] **I** *n* **1** *on ice etc* resbalón *m*; **2** (*mistake*) desliz *m*; ***a ~ of the tongue*** un lapsus **3**: ***a ~ of paper*** un trozo de pape **4**: ***give s.o. the ~*** dar esquinazo a alguien **5** *woman's undergarment* combinación *f*
II *v/i* (*pret & pp* **-ped**) **1** *on ice etc* resbalar; MOT *of clutch* patinar; ***let an opportunity ~ (through one's fingers)*** dejar escapar una oportunidad **2** *of quality etc* empeorar **3**: ***he ~ped out of the room*** se fue de la habitación sigilosamente **4**: ***he let ~ that …*** *fig* dejó caer que…
III *v/t* (*pret & pp* **-ped**) **1** (*put*): ***he ~ped it into his briefcase*** lo metió en su maletín sigilosamente; ***~ s.o. $10*** dar a alguien 10 dólares con disimulo **2**: ***it ~ped my mind*** se me olvidó; ***it may have ~ped your attention, but …*** puede que no te hayas dado cuenta, pero … **3**: ***he has ~ped a disk*** MED tiene una hernia discal
◆ **slip away** *v/i* **1** *of time* pasar; *of opportunity* esfumarse **2** (*die quietly*) morir tranquilamente
◆ **slip by** *v/i of time* pasar volando
◆ **slip in** *v/i to a room* entrar (sigilosamente)
◆ **slip off** *v/t jacket etc* quitarse
◆ **slip on** *v/t jacket etc* ponerse
◆ **slip out** *v/i* **1** (*go out*) salir (sigilosamente) **2**: ***it just slipped out*** me ha salido sin pensarlo
◆ **slip up** *v/i* (*make mistake*) equivocarse
'slip•cov•er funda *f*
slip-ons ['slɪpɑ:nz] *npl shoes* zapatos *mpl or* zapatillas *fpl* sin cordones

slip•page ['slɪpɪdʒ] atraso *m*
slipped disc [slɪpt'dɪsk] hernia *f* discal
slip•per ['slɪpər] zapatilla *f (de estar por casa)*
slip•per•y ['slɪpərɪ] *adj surface, road* resbaladizo; *fish* escurridizo; ***be a ~ customer*** ser muy escurridizo; ***you're on a ~ slope*** *fig* estás perdido
'slip road *Br* vía *f* de acceso; *exit* salida *f*
'slip•shod *adj* chapucero
'slip•stream I *n of runner, vehicle* estela *f*, rastro *m* **II** *v/t* pisar los talones a
'slip-up *(mistake)* error *m*
slit [slɪt] **I** *n (tear)* raja *f*; *(hole)* rendija *f*; *in skirt* corte *m* **II** *v/t (pret & pp* ***slit****)* abrir; ***~ s.o.'s throat*** degollar a alguien
slith•er ['slɪðər] *v/i* deslizarse
sliv•er ['slɪvər] *of soap, garlic* trocito *m*; *of wood, glass* astilla *f*
slob [slɑːb] *pej* dejado(-a) *m(f)*, guarro(-a) *m(f)*
slob•ber ['slɑːbər] *v/i* babear
slog [slɑːg] **1** *effort, hard work* paliza *f* **2** *walk*: ***the long ~ back to town*** la larga caminata de vuelta a la ciudad
◆ **slog away at** *v/t (pret & pp* ***-ged****)* sudar la gota gorda con
slo•gan ['slougən] eslogan *m*
slop [slɑːp] *v/t (pret & pp* ***-ped****)* derramar
slope [sloup] **I** *n of roof, handwriting* inclinación *f*; *of mountain* ladera *f*; ***built on a ~*** construido en una pendiente **II** *v/i* inclinarse; ***the road ~s down to the sea*** la carretera baja hasta el mar
slop•py ['slɑːpɪ] *adj* **1** descuidado **2** *too sentimental* sensiblero
sloshed [slɑːʃt] *adj Br* F borracho, pedo F
slot [slɑːt] ranura *f*; *in schedule* hueco *m*
◆ **slot in I** *v/t (pret & pp* ***-ted****)* introducir; ***I can slot you in at 2pm*** te puedo dar cita a las 2 de la tarde **II** *v/i (pret & pp* ***-ted****)* encajar
'slot ma•chine 1 *for cigarettes, food* máquina *f* expendedora **2** *for gambling* máquina *f* tragaperras
slouch [slaʊtʃ] *v/i*: ***don't ~*** ponte derecho
◆ **slough off** [slʌf] *v/t skin* mudar
Slo•vak ['slouvæk] **I** *adj* eslovaco **II** *n* eslovaco(-a) *m(f)*
Slo•va•ki•a [slə'vækɪə] Eslovaquia *f*
Slo•vene ['slouviːn] ☞ ***Slovenian***
Slo•ve•ni•a [slə'viːnɪə] Eslovenia *f*
Slo•ve•ni•an [slə'viːnɪən] **I** *adj* esloveno **II** *n* **1** *person* esloveno(-a) *m(f)* **2** *language* esloveno *m*
slov•en•ly ['slʌvnlɪ] *adj* descuidado
slow [slou] *adj* lento; ***be ~*** *of clock* ir retrasado; *mentally* ser torpe; ***be five minutes ~*** ir cinco minutos retrasado; ***be ~ to do sth*** tardar mucho tiempo en hacer algo; ***he wasn't ~ to accept*** aceptó en seguida; ***business is very ~ at the moment*** en estos momentos hay muy poca actividad en el negocio; ***I was doing a ~ burn*** se me estaba encendiendo la sangre
◆ **slow down I** *v/t work, progress* restrasar; *traffic, production* ralentizar **II** *v/i in walking, driving* reducir la velocidad; *of production etc* relantizarse; ***you need to slow down*** *in lifestyle* tienes que tomarte las cosas con calma; ***she's slowed down a lot*** *because of age, illness* se ha entorpecido bastante
'slow•coach *Br* F tortuga *f* F; **'slow-down** *in production* ralentización *f*; **'slow lane** MOT carril *m* lento
slow•ly ['sloulɪ] *adv* despacio, lentamente; ***~ but surely*** sin prisa pero sin pausa
slow 'mo•tion: ***in ~*** a cámara lenta; **slow-mo•tion 're•play** repetición *f* en cámara lenta; **'slow-mov•ing** *adj traffic, movie* lento
slow•ness ['slounɪs] lentitud *f*
'slow•poke F tortuga *f* F
sludge [slʌdʒ] *(mud)* limo *m*
slug[1] [slʌg] *n animal* babosa *f*
slug[2] [slʌg] F **1** *(bullet)* bala *f* **2** *of whiskey etc* lingotazo *m* F, trago *m*; ***he took another ~ from the bottle*** se echó otro trago de la botella
slug[3] [slʌg] **I** *v/t (pret & pp* ***-ged****) hit* dar un puñetazo a **II** *n punch* puñetazo *m*
◆ **slug out** *v/t*: ***slug it out*** pelearse, enzarzarse
slug•gish ['slʌgɪʃ] *adj* lento
sluice [sluːs] canal *m*
◆ **sluice down** *v/t* lavar con agua
◆ **sluice out** *v/t* lavar con abundante agua
'sluice gate compuerta *f*
slum [slʌm] *area* suburbio *m*, arrabal *m*; *house* cuchitril *m*
slum•ber par•ty ['slʌmbər] *fiesta en la*

que los invitados acaban pasando la noche el la casa del anfitrión

slump [slʌmp] **I** *n in trade* desplome *m*; **~ *in prices*** caída *f* de los precios **II** *v/i* **1** *economically* desplomarse, hundirse **2** (*collapse*: *of person*) desplomarse; ***he ~ed into a chair*** se dejó caer en una silla; ***he sat ~ed over the keyboard*** estaba postrado sobre el teclado

slung [slʌŋ] *pret & pp* ☞ ***sling***

slunk [slʌŋk] *pret & pp* ☞ ***slink***

slur [slɜːr] **I** *n on s.o.'s character* difamación *f* **II** *v/t* (*pret & pp* ***-red***) *words* arrastrar

slurp [slɜːrp] *v/t* sorber

slurred [slɜːrd] *adj*: ***his speech was ~*** habló arrastrando las palabras

slush [slʌʃ] **1** nieve *f* derretida **2** (*pej*: *sentimental stuff*) sensiblería *f*

'slush fund fondo *m* para corruptelas

slush•y ['slʌʃɪ] *adj* **1** *snow* derretido **2** *movie*, *novel* sensiblero

slut [slʌt] *pej* fulana *f*

sly [slaɪ] **I** *adj* ladino; ***you're a ~ one!*** ¡estás hecho un zorro! **II** *n*: ***on the ~*** a escondidas

smack[1] [smæk] **I** *n*: ***a ~ on the bottom*** un azote; ***a ~ in the face*** una bofetada **II** *v/t child* pegar; *bottom* dar un azote en; ***~ one's lips*** lamerse los labios **III** *adv* F justamente, justo; ***the ball landed ~ on top of the ...*** la pelota cayó justo encima de ...

◆ **smack of** *v/t fig* oler a

smack[2] [smæk] *n* P *heroin* caballo *m* P

smack•er ['smækər] F **1** *big kiss* besazo *m* **2** *dollar* pavo *m* F

smack•ing ['smækɪŋ] *Br* azotaina *f*; ***get a ~*** llevarse una azotaina

small [smɒːl] **I** *adj* pequeño, *L.Am.* chico; ***feel ~*** *of person* sentirse insignificante *or* poca cosa **II** *n*: ***~ of the back*** riñones *mpl*

'small arms *pl* armas *fpl* ligeras; **small 'bus•i•ness** pequeño negocio *m*; **small 'caps** *npl in printing* letra *f* versalita; **small 'change** cambio *m*, suelto *m*, *L.Am.* sencillo *m*; **small 'hours** *npl* madrugada *f*; ***in the ~*** a altas horas de la madrugada; **small-'mind•ed** *adj narrow*, *petty* cerrado, mezquino; **'small•pox** viruela *f*; **'small print** letra *f* pequeña; **'small talk**: ***make ~*** hablar de banalidades *or* trivialidades; **'small-time** *adj crook* de poca monta; *operation*, *outfit* de poca importancia; **'small-town** *adj* provincial

smarm•y ['smɑːrmɪ] *adj Br pej* F halagador, zalamero

smart[1] [smɑːrt] *adj* (*elegant*) elegante; (*intelligent*) inteligente; *pace* rápido; ***get ~ with*** hacerse el listillo con

smart[2] [smɑːrt] *v/i* (*hurt*) escocer

smart al•eck [smɑːrt'ælɪk] F, **'smart ass** F sabelotodo *m/f* F; **'smart bomb** bomba *f* inteligente; **'smart card** tarjeta *f* inteligente

◆ **smart•en up** ['smɑːrtn] *v/t appearance* mejorar; *room* arreglar

smart•ly ['smɑːrtlɪ] *adv dressed* con elegancia

smash [smæʃ] **I** *n* **1** *noise* estruendo *m* **2** (*car crash*) choque *m* **3** *in tennis* smash *m*, mate *m* **II** *v/t break* hacer pedazos *or* añicos; ***he ~ed the toys against the wall*** estrelló los juguetes contra la pared; ***~ sth to pieces*** hacer algo añicos **III** *v/i* **1** *break* romperse **2**: ***the driver ~ed into ...*** el conductor se estrelló contra ...

◆ **smash down** *v/t door* echar abajo; *fig*: *barriers* derribar

◆ **smash up** *v/t place* destrozar

smashed [smæʃt] *adj* F ciego F, pedo F; ***get ~ on sth*** ponerse ciego con algo F

smash 'hit F exitazo *m* F; ***be a ~ with s.o.*** ser todo un éxito con alguien

smash•ing ['smæʃɪŋ] *adj esp Br* F genial F, estupendo

smat•ter•ing ['smætərɪŋ]: ***have a ~ of English*** saber muy poco de inglés

smear [smɪr] **I** *n* **1** *of ink* borrón *m*; *of paint*, *on window*, *glass* mancha *f* **2** MED citología *f* **3** *on character* difamación *f* **II** *v/t* **1** *character* difamar **2**: ***~ X over Y*** untar *or* embadurnar Y de X; ***~ed with blood*** manchado de sangre

'smear cam•paign campaña *f* de difamación

'smear test MED citología *f*, *L.Am.* papanicolau *m*

smell [smel] **I** *n* olor *m*; ***it has no ~*** no huele a nada; ***sense of ~*** sentido *m* del olfato; ***there's a ~ of gas*** huele a gas; ***there's a ~ of garlic in here*** aquí huele a ajo; ***have a ~ of sth*** oler a algo; *sniff at* oler algo **II** *v/t* (*pret & pp* ***-ed*** *or* ***smelt***) oler; **~**

trouble olerse *or* barruntar problemas **III** *v/i* (*pret & pp* **-ed** *or* **smelt**) **1** *have a smell* oler; ***you ~ of beer*** hueles a cerveza; ***it ~s good*** huele bien; ***his breath ~s*** le huele el aliento **2** (*sniff*) olfatear
smell•y ['smelɪ] *adj* apestoso; ***she had ~ feet*** le olían los pies
smelt[1] [smelt] *pret & pp* ☞ **smell**
smelt[2] [smelt] *v/t ore* fundir
smile [smaɪl] **I** *n* sonrisa *f*; ***give a ~*** sonreír; ***give s.o. a ~*** sonreír a alguien; ***they're all ~s again*** todos estan de buenas otra vez **II** *v/i* sonreír
◆ **smile at** *v/t* sonreír a
smirk [smɜːrk] **I** *n* sonrisa *f* maligna **II** *v/i* sonreír malignamente
smith [smɪθ] ☞ **blacksmith**
smith•er•eens [smɪðə'riːnz] *npl*: ***smash sth to ~*** hacer algo añicos
smith•y ['smɪðɪ] herrería *f*
smit•ten ['smɪtn]: ***she has been ~ with flu*** le ha aquejado la gripe; ***be ~ with s.o.*** estar perdidamente enamorado de alguien
smog [smɑːg] niebla *f* tóxica
smoke [smoʊk] **I** *n* **1** humo *m*; ***go up in ~*** *of building, objects* quedar reducido a cenizas; ***all our plans have gone up in ~*** todos nuestros planes se han quedado en agua de borrajas **2**: ***have a ~*** fumarse un cigarrillo **II** *v/t* **1** *cigarettes* fumar **2** *bacon* ahumar **III** *v/i of person* fumar
◆ **smoke out** *v/t person in hiding* hacer aparecer
'smoke a•larm detector *m* de humo
smoked [smoʊkt] *adj* **1** *meat* ahumado **2**: ***~ glass*** cristal *m* esmerilado
'smoke de•tec•tor ☞ ***smoke alarm***; **smoke-'free** *adj zone* de no fumadores; **'smoke gre•nade** granada *f* de humo; **'smoke jump•er** bombero *m/f* paracaidista
smok•er ['smoʊkər] *person* fumador(a) *m(f)*; ***~'s cough*** tos *f* de fumador
'smoke•screen *fig* tapadera *f*
'smoke•stack chimenea *f*; ***~ industries*** industria *f* pesada
smok•ing ['smoʊkɪŋ]: ***~ is bad for you*** fumar es malo; ***no ~*** *sign* prohibido fumar
'smok•ing com•part•ment RAIL compartimento *m* de fumadores
smok•ing 'gun *fig* pruebas *fpl* concluyentes
smok•y ['smoʊkɪ] *adj room, air* lleno de humo
smol•der ['smoʊldər] *v/i* **1** *of fire* arder (*sin llama*); ***the fire was still ~ing*** todavía ardían los rescoldos **2** *fig*: *with anger* arder de rabia; *with desire* arder en deseos
smooch [smuːtʃ] *v/i* F besuquearse F
smooth [smuːð] **I** *adj surface, skin* liso, suave; *sea* en calma; (*peaceful*) tranquilo; *ride, drive* sin vibraciones; *transition* sin problemas; *pej*: *person* meloso **II** *v/t hair* alisar
◆ **smooth down** *v/t with sandpaper etc* alisar
◆ **smooth out** *v/t paper, cloth* alisar
◆ **smooth over** *v/t*: ***smooth things over*** suavizar las cosas
smooth•ie ['smuːðɪ] *pej* F *hombre elegantemente vestido y con mucha labia*
smooth•ly ['smuːðlɪ] *adv without any problems* sin incidentes
'smooth-talk•ing *adj* con mucha labia
smoth•er ['smʌðər] *v/t flames* apagar, sofocar; *person* asfixiar; *opposition, dissent* acallar, contener; ***be ~ed in sth*** estar cubierto *or* inundado de algo; ***~ s.o. with kisses*** comerse a alguien a besos
smoul•der *v/i Br* ☞ **smolder**
SMS [esem'es] *abbr* (= ***short message system***) SMS *m*
smudge [smʌdʒ] **I** *n of paint* mancha *f*; *of ink* borrón *m* **II** *v/t ink* emborronar; *paint* difuminar
smug [smʌg] *adj* engreído
smug•gle ['smʌgl] *v/t* pasar de contrabando; ***the kids had ~d a rabbit into class*** los niños habían metido un conejo en la clase a escondidas; ***they ~d him out of the country*** le sacaron clandestinamente del país
smug•gler ['smʌglər] contrabandista *m/f*
smug•gling ['smʌglɪŋ] contrabando *m*
smug•ly ['smʌglɪ] *adv* con engreimiento *or* suficiencia
smut [smʌt] *fig* obscenidades *fpl*
smut•ty ['smʌtɪ] *adj joke, sense of humor* obsceno
snack [snæk] tentempié *m*, aperitivo *m*; ***have a ~*** tomar un tentempié
'snack bar cafetería *f*

sna•fu ['snæfu:] F *mess* chapuza *f*
snag [snæg] **I** *n* (*problem*) inconveniente *m*, pega *f* **II** *v/t* (*pret & pp* **-ged**) *sweater*, *pantyhose* enganchar
snail [sneɪl] caracol *m*; ***at a ~'s pace*** a paso de tortuga
'snail mail F: ***send sth by ~*** enviar algo por correo tradicional *or* por snail-mail
snake [sneɪk] **I** *n* serpiente *f*; ***~ in the grass*** *fig* traidor(a) *m(f)* **II** *v/t*: ***~ its way through the jungle*** avanzar haciendo eses por la selva
'snake•bite mordedura *f* de serpiente; **'snake charm•er** encantador(a) *m(f)* de serpientes; **'snake•skin** piel *f* de serpiente
snap [snæp] **I** *n* **1** chasquido *m* **2** PHOT foto *f*
II *v/t* (*pret & pp* **-ped**) **1** *break* romper **2**: ***none of your business, she ~ped*** no es asunto tuyo, saltó **3**: ***~ one's fingers*** dar un chasquido con los dedos
III *v/i* (*pret & pp* **-ped**) **1** *break* romperse; F *crack up* perder los papeles F; ***my patience ~ped*** se me acabó la paciencia **2**: ***~ at s.o.*** chillar a alguien, hablar bruscamente a alguien **3**: ***~ shut*** cerrarse de golpe; ***~ out of it!*** F ¡anímate! F; ***the guards ~ped to attention*** los guardias se cuadraron
IV *adj decision*, *judgement* rápido, súbito
◆ **snap off** *v/t twig etc* arrancar; ***snap s.o.'s head off*** F echar un rapapolvo a alguien F
◆ **snap up** *v/t bargains* llevarse
'snap fast•en•er automático *m*, corchete *m*
snap•py ['snæpɪ] *adj* **1** *person*, *mood* irascible **2** *decision*, *response* rápido; ***make it ~!*** F ¡acelera! F, ¡los he visto más rápidos! F **3** (*elegant*) elegante; *title*, *phrase* ingenioso, con chispa
'snap•shot foto *f*
snare [sner] cepo *m*, lazo *m*; *fig* trampa *f*
snarl[1] [snɑ:rl] **I** *n of dog* gruñido *m* **II** *v/i* gruñir; ***~ at s.o.*** renegar a alguien
snarl[2] [snɑ:rl] **I** *n in hair*, *wool* enredo *m* **II** *v/t hair*, *wool* enredar
◆ **snarl up** *v/t*: ***the traffic was completely snarled up*** el tráfico estaba totalmente inmovilizado
'snarl-up embotellamiento *m*, congestión *f*
snatch [snætʃ] **I** *v/t* **1** arrebatar; ***~ sth from s.o.*** arrebatar algo a alguien **2** (*steal*) robar; (*kidnap*) secuestrar **II** *v/i*: ***don't ~*** no lo agarres **III** *n* **1**: ***make a ~ at sth*** intentar arrebatar algo **2**: ***~es of conversation*** trozos *mpl* de conversación **3** F *kidnap* secuestro *m* **4** P *female genitals* coño *m* P
◆ **snatch at** *v/t* intentar agarrar
snaz•zy ['snæzɪ] *adj* F vistoso, *Span* chulo F
sneak [sni:k] (*pret & pp* **-ed** *or* F **snuck**) **I** *v/t* (*remove*, *steal*) llevarse; ***~ a glance at*** mirar con disimulo **II** *v/i*: ***~ into the room*** entrar disimuladamente en la habitación; ***I snuck out the back way*** salí sigilosamente por detrás
◆ **sneak up on** *v/t* pillar por sorpresa a
sneak•ers ['sni:kərz] *npl* zapatillas *fpl* de deporte
sneak•ing ['sni:kɪŋ] *adj*: ***have a ~ suspicion that …*** sospechar que …; ***have a ~ admiration for s.o.*** admirar con reticiencia a alguien
sneak 'pre•view *of film*, *exhibition* preestreno *m*; *of TV*, *radio program* adelanto *m*; ***have a ~ of sth*** tener un avance *or* anticipo de algo
sneak•y ['sni:kɪ] *adj* F (*crafty*) ladino, cuco F
sneer [sni:r] **I** *n* mueca *f* desdeñosa **II** *v/i* burlarse (***at*** de)
sneeze [sni:z] **I** *n* estornudo *m* **II** *v/i* estornudar; ***it's not to be ~d at*** F no es moco de pavo F
snick•er ['snɪkər] **I** *n* risita *f* **II** *v/i* reírse (*en voz baja*)
snide [snaɪd] *adj comments* malicioso, rebuscado
sniff [snɪf] **I** *v/i* **1** *to clear nose* sorberse los mocos **2** *of dog* olfatear **II** *v/t* (*smell*) oler; *of dog* olfatear
snif•fer dog ['snɪfər] perro *m* policía
snif•fle ['snɪfl] F *light cold* resfriado *m* leve; ***he's got a ~*** *or* ***the ~s*** tiene un catarro
snif•fy ['snɪfɪ] *adj* F despectivo, desdeñoso
snif•ter ['snɪftər] copa *f* de coñac
snig•ger ['snɪgər] ☞ ***snicker***
snip [snɪp] *Br* F (*bargain*) ganga *f*
◆ **snip off** *v/t* (*pret & pp* **-ped**) tijeretear
◆ **snipe at** [snaɪp] *v/t* MIL disparar (*desde un lugar escondido*)

snip•er ['snaɪpər] francotirador(a) *m(f)*
snip•pet ['snɪpɪt]: *~ of conversation* fragmento *m* de conversación
snip•py ['snɪpɪ] *adj* F (*rude*) borde F, grosero
snitch [snɪtʃ] F **I** *n* (*telltale*) chivato(-a) *m(f)* **II** *v/i* chivarse
sniv•el ['snɪvl] *v/i* (*pret & pp* **-ed**, *Br* **-led**) gimotear
snob [snɑ:b] presuntuoso(-a) *m(f)*
snob•ber•y ['snɑ:bərɪ] presuntuosidad *f*
snob•bish ['snɑ:bɪʃ] *adj* presuntuoso
snog [snɑ:g] *Br* F **I** *v/i* (*pret & pp* **-ged**) besuquearse F **II** *v/t* (*pret & pp* **-ged**) besuquear F, *Span* liarse con F
snook•er ['snu:kər] **I** *n* billar *m* inglés **II** *v/t* F (*deceive*, *cheat*) timar; *Br* **be ~ed** *in a difficult situation* estar en un aprieto F
snoop [snu:p] *person* fisgón(-ona) *m(f)*
◆ **snoop around** *v/i* fisgonear
snoot•y ['snu:tɪ] *adj* presuntuoso
snooze [snu:z] **I** *n* cabezada *f*; ***have a ~*** echar una cabezada **II** *v/i* echar una cabezada
snore [snɔ:r] *v/i* roncar
snor•ing ['snɔ:rɪŋ] ronquidos *mpl*
snor•kel ['snɔ:rkl] snorkel *m*, tubo *m* para buceo
snor•kel•ing, *Br* **snor•kel•ling** ['snɔ:rklɪŋ] buceo *m* con snorkel; ***go ~*** hacer buceo con snorkel
snort [snɔ:rt] **I** *v/i of bull*, *person* bufar, resoplar **II** *v/t* F *cocaine* esnifar **III** *n* F *of whiskey* trago *m*
snot [snɑ:t] F mocos *mpl*
snot•ty ['snɑ:tɪ] *adj* F **1** *nose*, *handkerchief* mocoso **2** (*stuck-up*) estirado
snot•ty-nosed ['snɑ:tɪnoʊzd] *adj*: ***~ kid*** *also fig* mocoso(-a) *m(f)*, crío(-a) *m(f)*
snout [snaʊt] *of pig*, *dog* hocico *m*
snow [snoʊ] **I** *n* nieve *f* **II** *v/i* nevar
◆ **snow in** *v/t*: ***be snowed in*** estar aislado por la nieve
◆ **snow under** *v/t*: ***be snowed under*** estar desbordado
'**snow•ball I** bola *f* de nieve **II** *v/i fig* agrandarse, intensificarse; '**snow•ball fight** pelea *f or* lucha *f* de bolas de nieve; '**Snow Belt** *área de Estados Unidos desde la frontera con Canadá hasta el Medio Oeste*; '**snow•bird** F *persona del norte que pasa los inviernos en zonas cálidas*; **snow blow•er** ['snoʊbloʊər] máquina *f* quitanieves; '**snow•board** snowboard *m*; '**snow•board•er** *persona que hace snowboard*; '**snow•bound** *adj* aislado por la nieve; **snow-capped** ['snoʊkæpt] *adj* coronado de nieve; '**snow chains** *npl* MOT cadenas *fpl* para la nieve; '**snow•drift** nevero *m*; '**snow•drop** campanilla *f* de invierno; '**snow•fall**: ***the average ~ in April*** la media de nieve en abril; ***a heavy ~*** una buena nevada; '**snow•flake** copo *m* de nieve; '**snow job** F tomadura *f* de pelo; '**snow line** límite *m* de las nieves perpetuas; '**snow•man** muñeco *m* de nieve; **snow•mo•bile** ['snoʊməbi:l] moto *f* de nieve; '**snow•plow**, *Br* '**snow•plough** quitanieves *f inv*; '**snow•shoe** raqueta *f* de nieve; '**snow•storm** tormenta *f* de nieve; '**snow tires** *npl* ruedas *fpl* antideslizantes; '**Snow White** Blancanieves *f*
snow•y ['snoʊɪ] *adj weather* de nieve; *roads*, *hills* nevado
snub [snʌb] **I** *n* desaire **II** *v/t* (*pret & pp* **-bed**) desairar
snub-nosed ['snʌbnoʊzd] *adj person* con la nariz respingona
snuck [snʌk] F *pret & pp* ☞ ***sneak***
snuff [snʌf] *v/t candle* apagar; ***~ it*** *Br* P diñarla P
'**snuff mov•ie** película *f* snuff (*película porno en la que se asesina a alguien*)
snug [snʌg] *adj* **1** (*tight-fitting*) ajustado; ***be a ~ fit*** ajustarse *or* adaptarse al cuerpo; *too tight* ser demasiado ceñido **2**: ***we are nice and ~ in here*** aquí se está muy a gusto
◆ **snug•gle down** ['snʌgl] *v/i* acurrucarse
◆ **snuggle up to** *v/t* acurrucarse contra
so [soʊ] **I** *adv* **1** tan; ***it was ~ easy*** fue tan fácil; ***I'm ~ cold*** tengo tanto frío; ***that was ~ kind of you*** fue muy amable de tu parte; ***not ~ much*** no tanto; ***~ much easier*** mucho más fácil; ***you shouldn't eat / drink ~ much*** no deberías comer / beber tanto; ***I miss you ~*** te echo tanto de menos
2: ***~ am / do I*** yo también; ***~ is she / does she*** ella también
3 *like this* así, de esta manera; ***and ~ on*** etcétera
4: ***~ what?*** F ¿y qué? F; ***is that ~?*** ¿y qué? F

II *pron*: ***I hope / think ~*** eso espero / creo; ***you didn't tell me – I did ~*** no me lo dijiste – sí que lo hice; ***50 or ~*** unos 50; ***a mile or ~*** una milla más o menos
III *conj* **1** *for that reason* así que; ***I got up late and ~ I missed the train*** me levanté tarde así que perdí el tren **2** *in order that* para que; ***~ (that) I could come too*** para que yo también pudiera venir; ***I did it ~ as to make things easier for you*** lo hice para facilitarte las cosas

soak [souk] **I** *v/t* (*steep*) poner en remojo; *of water, rain* empapar **II** *v/i*: ***~ in the tub*** darse un baño
◆ **soak up** *v/t liquid* absorber; *atmosphere* empaparse de; ***soak up the sun*** tostarse al sol

soaked [soukt] *adj* empapado; ***be ~ to the skin*** estar calado hasta los huesos

soak•ing (**wet**) ['soukɪŋ] *adj* empapado

so-and-so ['souənsou] F (*unknown person*) fulanito *m*; (*euph*: *annoying person*) canalla *m/f*

soap [soup] **1** *for washing* jabón *m* **2** (*~ opera*) telenovela *f*

'soap dish jabonera *f*; **'soap op•e•ra** telenovela *f*; **'soap pow•der** detergente *m* para la ropa; **'soap•suds** *npl* espuma *f* de jabón

soap•y ['soupɪ] *adj water* jabonoso

soar [sɔːr] *v/i of rocket etc* elevarse; *of prices* dispararse

sob [sɑːb] **I** *n* sollozo *m* **II** *v/i* (*pret & pp* **-bed**) sollozar

sob, SOB [esou'biː] *abbr* F (= ***son of a bitch***) hijo *m* de puta V, *Mex* hijo *m* de la chingada V

so•ber ['soubər] *adj* **1** (*not drunk*) sobrio **2** (*serious*) serio
◆ **sober up I** *v/i*: ***he sobered up*** se le pasó la borrachera **II** *v/t* despejar, espabilar

so•ber•ing ['soubərɪŋ] *adj*: ***have a ~ effect on s.o.*** *fig* hacer reflexionar a alguien, impactar a alguien

'sob sto•ry F desgracias *fpl*, tragedia *f*

so-'called *adj* (*referred to as*) así llamado; (*incorrectly referred to as*) mal llamado

soc•cer ['sɑːkər] fútbol *m*

'soc•cer hoo•li•gan hincha *m* violento

so•cia•ble ['souʃəbl] *adj* sociable

so•cial ['souʃl] *adj* social; ***be a ~ drinker*** beber (alcohol) sólo en ocasiones especiales

so•cial 'climb•er arribista *m/f*

so•cial 'dem•o•crat socialdemócrata *m/f*

so•cial•ism ['souʃəlɪzm] socialismo *m*

so•cial•ist ['souʃəlɪst] **I** *adj* socialista **II** *n* socialista *m/f*

so•cial•ite ['souʃəlaɪt] *persona de la alta sociedad*

so•cial•i•za•tion [souʃəlaɪ'zeɪʃn]] *of children* socialización *f*

so•cial•ize ['souʃəlaɪz] **I** *v/i* socializar (**with** con); ***I don't ~ much*** no hago mucha vida social **II** *v/t child* socializar

'so•cial life vida *f* social; ***have a busy ~*** tener una gran vida social

so•cial•ly ['souʃəlɪ] *adv*: ***I don't know him ~*** sólo le conozco del trabajo

so•cial 'sci•ence ciencia *f* social; **so•cial se'cur•i•ty** *Br* seguridad *f* social; **so•cial ser•vi•ces** *pl* asistencia *f* social; **'so•cial work** trabajo *m* social; **'so•cial work•er** asistente(-a) *m*(*f*) social

so•ci•e•ty [sə'saɪətɪ] sociedad *f*

so•ci•o•e•co•nom•ic [sousjouiːkə'nɑːmɪk] *adj* socioeconómico

so•ci•o•log•i•cal [sousɪə'lɑːdʒɪkl] *adj* sociológico

so•ci•ol•o•gist [sousɪ'ɑːlədʒɪst] sociólogo(-a) *m*(*f*)

so•ci•ol•o•gy [sousɪ'ɑːlədʒɪ] sociología *f*

sock[1] [sɑːk] *n for wearing* calcetín *m*; ***pull one's ~s up*** *Br* F espabilarse F, esforzarse; ***put a ~ in it!*** *Br* P ¡cierra el pico! F

sock[2] [sɑːk] **I** *n* (*punch*) puñetazo *m* **II** *v/t* (*punch*) dar un puñetazo a; ***~ s.o. on the jaw*** dar un puñetazo a alguien en la mandíbula; ***~ it to him!*** F ¡déjaselo todo bien clarito!

sock•et ['sɑːkɪt] **1** *for light bulb* casquillo *m* **2** *of arm* cavidad *f*; *of eye* cuenca *f* **3** *Br* ELEC enchufe *m*

sod [sɑːd] *Br* P **I** *n* (*bastard*) cabrón (-ona) *m*(*f*) P; ***poor ~*** pobre infeliz *m/f* **II** *v/t*: ***~ it!*** ¡mierda! P

so•da ['soudə] **1** (*~ water*) soda *f*; ***two whiskey ~s*** dos whiskies con soda **2** (*soft drink*) refresco *m*; (*ice-cream ~*) *refresco con helado*

'so•da foun•tain *mostrador de refrescos y helados*; **'so•da jerk** *persona que tra-*

baja en una 'soda fountain'; **'so•da wa•ter** soda *f*
sod•den ['sɑːdn] *adj* empapado
so•di•um ['soʊdɪəm] CHEM sodio *m*
so•do•my ['sɑːdəmɪ] sodomía *f*
so•fa ['soʊfə] sofá *m*
'so•fa-bed sofá cama *m*
soft [sɑːft] *adj voice, light, color, skin* suave; *pillow, attitude, water* blando; ***have a ~ spot for*** tener una debilidad por; ***be ~ in the head*** F ser un memo F; ***be a ~ touch*** ser un blando; ***get ~*** *of fruit etc* reblandecerse; ***be ~ on*** *crime, terrorism etc* no tener mano dura con; ***be ~ on s.o.*** (*be lenient with*) ser poco severo con alguien; (*have a crush on*) estar loco por alguien
'soft•ball *game* softball *m* (*tipo de béisbol que se juega en campo más pequeño y con pelota más blanda*); **soft-boiled** ['sɑːftbɔɪld] *adj egg* pasado por agua; **'soft cur•ren•cy** divisa *f* débil; **'soft drink** refresco *m*; **'soft drug** droga *f* blanda
soft•en ['sɑːfn] **I** *v/t* **1** *position* ablandar **2** *impact, blow* amortiguar **II** *v/i of butter, ice cream* ablandarse, reblandecerse
◆ **soften up** *v/t* F ablandar
soft•en•er ['sɑːfnər] *for fabrics* suavizante *m*
soft•heart•ed ['sɑːfthɑːrtɪd] *adj* sensible
soft•ie ['sɑːftɪ] F **1** (*crybaby*) quejica *m/f* F **2** (*softhearted person*) blanducho(-a) *m(f)*
'soft loan préstamo *m* a interés reducido
soft•ly ['sɑːftlɪ] **1** *adv* suavemente **II** *adj*: ***a ~-~ approach*** *in a hostage taking incident etc* una aproximación con tiento
'soft-ped•al *v/t* (*pret & pp* ***-ed***, *Br* ***-led***) F quitar importancia a; **'soft porn** porno *m* blando; **'soft porn mov•ie** película *f* erótica; **'soft sell** venta *f* no agresiva; **'soft-soap** *v/t* F hacer la pelota a F; **'soft-spo•ken** *adj* de voz suave; **soft 'toy** peluche *m*; **soft•ware** ['sɑːftwer] software *m*; **'soft•ware pack•age** paquete *m* de software; **'soft wood** madera *f* blanda
soft•y F ☞ ***softie***
sog•gy ['sɑːgɪ] *adj* empapado
SOH [esoʊ'eɪtʃ] *abbr* (= ***sense of humor***) sentido *m* del humor
soil [sɔɪl] **I** *n* (*earth*) tierra *f* **II** *v/t* ensuciar
sol [sɑːl] FIN sol *m*
sol•ace ['sɑːləs] consuelo *m*
so•lar cell [soʊlər'sel] placa *f* solar; **solar e'clipse** eclipse *m* de sol; **so•lar 'en•er•gy** energía *f* solar
so•lar•i•um [sə'lerɪəm] (*pl* ***solaria*** [sə'lerɪə], ***-iums***) solarium *m*
'so•lar pan•el panel *m* solar; **so•lar plex•us** [soʊlər'pleksəs] ANAT plexo *m* solar; **'so•lar sys•tem** sistema *m* solar
sold [soʊld] *pret & pp* ☞ ***sell***
sol•der ['sɑːldər] *v/t* soldar
sol•dier ['soʊldʒər] soldado *m*
◆ **soldier on** *v/i* seguir adelante; ***we'll have to soldier on without her*** nos las tendremos que arreglar sin ella
sole[1] [soʊl] *n of foot* planta *f*; *of shoe* suela *f*
sole[2] [soʊl] *adj* único
sole[3] [soʊl] *n fish* lenguado *m*
'sole a•gen•cy representación *f* exclusiva
'sole a•gent agente *m/f* exclusivo(-a)
sole•ly ['soʊllɪ] *adv* únicamente
sol•emn ['sɑːləm] *adj* solemne; ***I give you my ~ word that*** te doy mi palabra de honor de que
so•lem•ni•ty [sə'lemnətɪ] solemnidad *f*
sol•emn•ly ['sɑːləmlɪ] *adv* solemnemente
so•lic•it [sə'lɪsɪt] **I** *v/i of prostitute* abordar clientes **II** *v/t help* solicitar
so•lic•i•tor [sə'lɪsɪtər] *Br* abogado(-a) *m(f)* (*que no aparece en tribunales*)
so•lic•i•tous [sə'lɪsɪtəs] *adj* solícito, atento
sol•id ['sɑːlɪd] **I** *adj* sólido; (*without holes*) compacto; *gold, silver, oak* macizo; ***a ~ hour*** una hora seguida; ***a ~ gold watch*** un reloj de oro macizo **II** *n* **1** MATH cuerpo *m* sólido **2**: ***~s*** *pl* comida *f* sólida
sol•i•dar•i•ty [sɑːlɪ'dærətɪ] solidaridad *f*; ***in ~ with*** en solidaridad con
so•lid•i•fy [sə'lɪdɪfaɪ] *v/i* (*pret & pp* ***-ied***) solidificarse
sol•id•ly ['sɑːlɪdlɪ] *adv* **1** *built* sólidamente **2** *in favor of sth* unánimente
so•lil•o•quy [sə'lɪləkwɪ] soliloquio *m*
sol•i•taire [sɑːlɪ'ter] *card game* solitario *m*; ***play ~*** jugar al solitario

sol•i•ta•ry ['sɑːlɪterɪ] *adj* **1** *life, activity* solitario **2** (*single*) único
sol•i•ta•ry con'fine•ment prisión *f* incomunicada
sol•i•tude ['sɑːlɪtuːd] soledad *f*
so•lo ['soʊloʊ] **I** *n* MUS solo *m* **II** *adj flight, voyage* en solitario **III** *adv* MUS, *fly, sail* en solitario
so•lo•ist ['soʊloʊɪst] solista *m/f*
sol•stice ['sɑːlstɪs] AST solsticio *m*
sol•u•ble ['sɑːljʊbl] *adj substance, problem* soluble
so•lu•tion [sə'luːʃn] *also mixture* solución *f*
solv•a•ble ['sɑːlvəbl] *adj problem* resoluble
solve [sɑːlv] *v/t problem* solucionar, resolver; *mystery* resolver; *crossword* resolver, sacar
sol•ven•cy ['sɑːlvənsɪ] COM solvencia *f*
sol•vent ['sɑːlvənt] **I** *adj financially* solvente **II** *n* CHEM disolvente *m*; **~ abuse** adicción *f* a los disolventes
som•ber, *Br* **som•bre** ['sɑːmbər] *adj* **1** (*dark*) oscuro **2** (*serious*) sombrío
som•bre•ro [sɑːm'breroʊ] sombrero *m* mejicano
some [sʌm] **I** *adj*: ***would you like ~ water / cookies?*** ¿quieres agua / galletas?; ***~ countries*** algunos países; ***I gave him ~ money*** le di (algo de) dinero; ***~ people say that …*** hay quien dice …; ***have ~ more*** toma (un poco) más; ***would you like ~ more cake?*** ¿quieres más tarta?; ***~ more coffee?*** ¿más café? **II** *pron*: ***~ of the group*** parte del grupo; ***would you like ~?*** ¿quieres?; ***milk? – no thanks, I already have ~*** ¿leche? – gracias, ya tengo
III *adv* (*a bit*): ***we'll have to wait ~*** tendremos que esperar algo *or* un poco; ***~ 30 people*** alrededor de 30 personas
some•bod•y ['sʌmbədɪ] *pron* **1** alguien **2**: ***be ~*** ser alguien importante *or* destacable
'some•day *adv* algún día
'some•how *adv* **1** (*by one means or another*) de alguna manera **2** (*for some unknown reason*) por alguna razón; ***I've never liked him ~*** por alguna razón u otra nunca me cayó bien
'some•one *pron* ☞ ***somebody***
'some•place *adv* ☞ ***somewhere***
som•er•sault ['sʌmərsɒːlt] **I** *n* voltereta *f*; *in the air* salto *m* mortal; ***do a ~*** dar una voltereta / un salto mortal **II** *v/i* dar una voltereta; *in the air* dar un salto mortal; *of vehicle* dar una vuelta de campana
'some•thing **I** *pron* algo; ***would you like ~ to drink / eat?*** ¿te gustaría beber / comer algo?; ***is ~ wrong?*** ¿pasa algo?; ***~ funny / sad*** algo divertido / triste; ***or ~*** F o algo así F; ***he really thinks he's ~*** se cree que es alguien (especial); ***that was really ~!*** eso estuvo muy bien *or* genial; ***the price of gas in Europe is ~ else*** F el precio de la gasolina en Europa está por las nubes F; ***your brother is ~ else*** F tu hermano es de lo que no hay F
II *adv*: ***~ like $5,000 / six months*** algo así como 5.000 dólares / seis meses; ***look ~ like*** parecerse algo a; ***~ over $200*** poco más de 200 dólares; ***be ~ of a pianist*** tener bastante talento como pianista; ***it was ~ of a shock*** fue un shock de alguna manera; ***he's ~ of a local hero here*** aquí se le considera *or* es considerado un héroe
III *n*: ***a little ~*** una chuchería *or* tontería; ***a certain ~*** ese no sé qué
'some•time *adv*: ***let's have lunch ~*** quedemos para comer un día de éstos; ***~ last year*** en algún momento del año pasado
'some•times ['sʌmtaɪmz] *adv* a veces
'some•way *adv* de alguna manera
'some•what *adv* un tanto; ***it was ~ of a shock*** fue un shock en cierto modo
'some•where **I** *adv* en alguna parte *or* algún lugar; ***~ between 30 and 40 people*** entre 30 y 40 personas; ***we're finally getting ~!*** ¡por fin parece que avanzamos!; ***~ in the region of $ 100 dollars*** alrededor de los 100 dólares
II *pron*: ***let's go ~ quiet*** vamos a algún sitio tranquilo; ***I was looking for ~ to park*** buscaba un sitio donde aparcar
son [sʌn] hijo *m*
so•nar ['soʊnɑːr] NAUT sonar *m*
so•na•ta [sə'nɑːtə] MUS sonata *f*
song [sɒːŋ] canción *f*; ***I got it for a ~*** F me ha salido tirado de precio F; ***make a ~ and dance about sth*** F armar un follón *or* pitote por algo F
'song•bird pájaro *m* cantor
'song•writ•er cantautor(a) *m(f)*

S

son•ic ['sɑːnɪk] *adj* PHYS sonoro; **~ bang** *or* **boom** AVIA bang *m or* estampido *m* supersónico
'son-in-law (*pl* **sons-in-law**) yerno *m*
'son•net ['sɑːnɪt] soneto *m*
son of a 'bitch V hijo *m* de puta V, *Mex* hijo *m* de la chingada V
son of a 'gun F sinvergüenza *m/f* F, granuja *m/f* F
so•no•rous ['sɑːnərəs] *adj lit* sonoro, resonante
soon [suːn] *adv* pronto; ***how ~ can you be ready to leave?*** ¿cuándo estarás listo para salir?; ***he left ~ after I arrived*** se marchó al poco de llegar yo; ***can't you get here any ~er?*** ¿no podrías llegar antes?; ***as ~ as*** tan pronto como; ***as ~ as possible*** lo antes posible; ***~er or later*** tarde o temprano; ***the ~er the better*** cuanto antes mejor; ***I don't want to speak too ~*** no quiero adelantarme a los acontecimientos; ***I wouldn't speak too ~ if I was you*** yo que tú no estaría tan seguro; ***no ~er had he mentioned her name than she appeared*** antes le llega a nombrar y antes aparece; ***no ~er said than done*** dicho y hecho; ***I would ~er go to the movies than ...*** antes iba al cine que ...
soot [sʊt] hollín *m*
soothe [suːð] *v/t* calmar
soot•y ['sʊtɪ] *adj ceiling, walls* cubierto de hollín
sop [sɑːp]: ***as a ~ to*** para apaciguar *or* tranquilizar
so•phis•ti•cat•ed [sə'fɪstɪkeɪtɪd] *adj* sofisticado
so•phis•ti•ca•tion [sə'fɪstɪkeɪʃn] sofisticación *f*
soph•o•more ['sɑːfəmɔːr] estudiante *m/f* de segundo año
sop•o•rif•ic [sɑːpə'rɪfɪk] *adj*: ***the ~ effect of ...*** el efecto soporífero de ...
sop•ping ['sɑːpɪŋ] *adj or adv*: **~ (*wet*)** F ensopado, empapado
sop•py ['sɑːpɪ] *adj* F sensiblero
so•pra•no [sə'prænoʊ] *singer* soprano *m/f*, *voice* voz *f* de soprano
sor•bet ['sɔːrbeɪ] sorbete *m*
sor•cer•er ['sɔːrsərə] brujo *m*
sor•cer•y ['sɔːrsərɪ] brujería *f*
sor•did ['sɔːrdɪd] *adj affair, business* sórdido
sore [sɔːr] **I** *adj* **1** (*painful*) dolorido; ***is it ~?*** ¿duele?; ***I'm ~ all over*** me duele todo el cuerpo; ***my legs are ~*** tengo las piernas cansadas; ***I have a ~ stomach*** me duele estómago; ***stick out like a ~ thumb*** F destacar mucho, *Span* dar el cante F; ***it's a ~ point with him*** eso es ponerle el dedo en la llaga **2** F (*angry*) enojado, *Span* mosqueado F **II** *n* llaga *f*
sore•ly ['sɔːrlɪ] *adv*: ***you'll be ~ missed*** se te echará muchísimo de menos; ***you're ~ needed*** se te necesita desesperadamente
so•ror•i•ty [sə'rɑːrətɪ] *in college* fraternidad *f* femenina
sor•row ['sɑːroʊ] pena *f*
sor•row•ful ['sɑːroʊfʊl] *adj* apenado, consternado
sor•ry ['sɑːrɪ] *adj* **1** *day* triste; ***be a ~ sight*** ofrecer un espectáculo lamentable; ***I was so ~ to hear of her death*** me dio mucha pena oír lo de su muerte; ***I won't be ~ to leave here*** no me arrepentiré de irme de aquí; ***you'll be ~*** te arrepentirás; ***I feel ~ for her*** siento pena *or* lástima por ella; ***I am ~ to say that he is neglecting his work*** siento tener que decir que está descuidando su trabajo
2: **(*I'm*) *~!*** *apologizing* ¡lo siento!; ***I'm ~ (that) I didn't tell you sooner*** lamento no habértelo dicho antes; ***(I'm) ~ but I can't help*** lo siento pero no puedo ayudar; ***say ~*** pedir perdón, disculparse
sort [sɔːrt] **I** *n* **1** clase *f*, tipo *m*; ***all ~s of things*** muchas cosas; ***some ~ of virus*** una especie de virus; ***I said nothing of the ~*** no dije nada por el estilo; ***what ~ of (a) man is he?*** ¿qué clase de hombre es?; ***he's my ~ of drummer*** es la clase de batería que me gusta; ***I had a ~ of (a) feeling that*** presentí como que
2: ***be out of ~s*** F estar para pocas fiestas F; ***he's a poet of ~s*** es un poeta de poca monta; ***make a curtain of ~s*** confeccionar una especie de cortina
3 COMPUT: ***do a ~*** ordenar
II *adv*: **~ *of*** F un poco, algo; ***is it finished? – ~ of*** F ¿está acabado? – más o menos; ***I ~ of expected it*** F más bien me lo esperaba F; ***I feel ~ of lonely*** me siento algo solo
III *v/t* ordenar, clasificar; COMPUT ordenar
◆ **sort out** *v/t papers* ordenar, clasificar;

S

problem resolver, arreglar; ***sort oneself out*** organizarse; ***I'll sort him out!*** *Br* F ¡ya lo arreglo yo!

◆ **sort through** *v/t* organizar, ordenar

sort•a ['sɔːrtə] F ☞ ***sort of***

sor•tie ['sɔːrtiː] MIL incursión *f*, AVIA combate *m* aéreo

SOS [esoʊ'es] SOS *m*; *fig* llamada *f* de auxilio; **~ *message*** mensaje *m* de socorro

so-'so *adv* F así así F

souf•flé ['suːfleɪ] suflé *m*

sought [sɒːt] *pret & pp* ☞ ***seek***

'sought-af•ter *adj* solicitado

soul [soʊl] REL, *fig*: *of a nation etc* alma *f*, *character* personalidad *f*; ***the poor ~*** el pobrecillo; ***I didn't see a ~*** no vi ni un alma; ***be the ~ of kindness*** ser la amabilidad en persona

soul-de•stroy•ing ['soʊldɪstrɔɪɪŋ] *adj* tedioso, pesado

soul•less ['soʊlləs] *adj* deprimente

'soul mate alma *f* gemela; **'soul mu•sic** soul *m*, música *f* soul; **'soul-search•ing** reflexión *f*, meditación *f*

sound[1] [saʊnd] **I** *adj* **1** (*sensible*) sensato **2** (*healthy*) sano **3** *sleep* profundo **II** *adv*: ***be ~ asleep*** estar profundamente dormido

sound[2] [saʊnd] **I** *n* sonido *m*; (*noise*) ruido *m*; ***I don't like the ~ of it*** *fig* no me gusta ni un pelo; ***by the ~ of things*** *fig* por lo visto **II** *v/t* **1** (*pronounce*) pronunciar **2** MED auscultar **3**: **~ *one's horn*** tocar la bocina; **~ *a warning*** dar un aviso **III** *v/i* parecer; ***that ~s interesting*** parece interesante

◆ **sound off** *v/i* F (*complain*) protestar (***about*** por)

◆ **sound out** *v/t*: ***I sounded her out about the idea*** sondeé a ver qué le parecía la idea

'sound bar•ri•er PHYS barrera *f* del sonido; **'sound bite** *frase breve pero expresiva extraída de un discurso político*; **'sound card** COMPUT tarjeta *f* de sonido; **'sound ef•fects** *npl* efectos *mpl* sonoros

sound•ing board ['saʊndɪŋ]: ***use s.o. as a ~*** pedir consejo *or* asesoramiento a alguien

sound•ly ['saʊndlɪ] *adv* **1** *sleep* profundamente **2** *beaten* rotundamente

sound•ness ['saʊndnɪs] sensatez *f*

'sound•proof I *adj* insonorizado **II** *v/t* insonorizar; **sound•proof•ing** ['saʊndpruːfɪŋ] insonorización *f*; **'sound sys•tem** equipo *m or* sistema *m* de sonido; **'sound•track** banda *f* sonora

soup [suːp] sopa *f*; ***be in the ~*** F estar en un lío F

◆ **soup up** *v/t* F trucar F

'soup bowl cuenco *m*

souped-up ['suːptʌp] *adj* F trucado

'soup kitch•en comedor *m* de la caridad; **'soup plate** plato *m* sopero; **'soup spoon** cuchara *f* sopera

sour [saʊr] *adj apple*, *orange* ácido, agrio; *milk* cortado; *comment* agrio; ***go ~*** *of milk* cortarse; *fig* echarse a perder

source [sɔːrs] **I** *n* fuente *f*, *of river* nacimiento *m*; ***from a reliable ~*** de una fuente veraz **II** *v/t* (*obtain*) obtener

'source file COMPUT archivo *m* fuente

'source lan•guage LING lengua *f* de origen

sour 'cream, *Br* **soured 'cream** nata *f* agria; **sour 'grapes** *npl*: ***that's just ~*** las uvas están verdes: ***it's just ~ on his part*** está disimulando que se muere de la envidia; **'sour•puss** F cascarrabias *m/f* F

south [saʊθ] **I** *adj* sur, del sur **II** *n* sur *m*; ***to the ~ of*** al sur de; ***in the ~ of*** en el sur de; ***the South*** *of the US* el Sur **III** *adv* al sur; **~ *of*** al sur de

South 'Af•ric•a Sudáfrica *f*; **South 'Af•ri•can I** *adj* sudafricano **II** *n* sudafricano(-a) *m(f)*; **South A'mer•i•ca** Sudamérica *f*, América *f* del Sur; **South A'mer•i•can I** *adj* sudamericano **II** *n* sudamericano(-a) *m(f)*; **'south•bound** *adj* hacia el sur, en dirección al sur; **south'east I** *n* sudeste *m*, sureste *m* **II** *adj* sudeste, sureste **III** *adv* al sudeste *or* sureste; **~ *of*** al sudeste *or* sureste de; **South•east 'A•sia** sudeste *m* de Asia; **south'east•ern** *adj* del sudeste *or* sureste

south•er•ly ['sʌðərlɪ] *adj wind* sur, del sur; *direction* sur

south•ern ['sʌðərn] *adj* sureño

south•ern•er ['sʌðərnər] sureño(-a) *m(f)*

South•ern 'Hem•i•sphere hemisferio *m* sur

'south•ern•most *adj* más al sur

'south•paw F zurdo(-a) *m(f)*
South 'Pole Polo *m* Sur
south•ward ['saʊθwərd] *adv* hacia el sur
south'west I *n* sudoeste *m*, suroeste *m* **II** *adj* sudoeste, suroeste **III** *adv* al sudoeste *or* suroeste; **~ of** al sudoeste *or* suroeste de
south'west•ern *adj* del sudoeste *or* suroeste
sou•ve•nir [suːvə'nɪr] recuerdo *m*
sov•er•eign ['sɑːvrɪn] *adj state* soberano
sov•er•eign•ty ['sɑːvrɪntɪ] *of state* soberanía *f*
So•vi•et ['soʊvɪət] HIST **I** *adj* soviético **II** *npl*: ***the ~s*** los soviéticos
So•vi•et 'U•nion HIST Unión *f* Soviética
sow[1] [saʊ] *n* (*female pig*) cerda *f*, puerca *f*
sow[2] [soʊ] *v/t* (*pret* ***sowed***, *pp* ***sown***) *seeds* sembrar; *suspicion* infundir; ***~ doubt in s.o.'s mind*** *fig* sembrar la duda en alguien; ***~ the seeds of sth*** *fig* sembrar algo
sown [soʊn] *pp* ☞ ***sow***[2]
'soy bean [sɔɪ] semilla *f* de soja
'soy sauce salsa *f* de soja
soz•zled ['sɑːzəld] *adj* F bebido F, mamado F
spa [spɑː] *in hotel* balneario *m*
space [speɪs] **I** *n* espacio *m*; ***stare into ~*** tener la mirada perdida **II** *v/t* espaciar, separar; ***~ the chairs two feet apart*** separar las sillas dos pies las unas de las otras
◆ **space out** *v/t* espaciar
'space age I *n* futuro *m* **II** *adj* futurista; **'space bar** COMPUT barra *f* espaciadora; **'space ca•det** F colgado(-a) *m(f)* F; **'space cap•sule** cápsula *f* espacial; **'space•craft** nave *f* espacial
spaced-out [speɪst'aʊt] *adj* F colgado F; ***look ~*** parecer un zombi
'space•flight vuelo *m* espacial; **'space heat•er** estufa *f* eléctrica; **'space•lab** laboratorio *m* espacial; **space•man** ['speɪsmæn] astronauta *m*; **'space probe** sonda *f* espacial; **'space•ship** nave *f* espacial; **'space shut•tle** transbordador *m* espacial; **'space sta•tion** estación *f* espacial; **'space•suit** traje *m* espacial; **'space trav•el** viajes *mpl* espaciales; **'space•walk** paseo *m* espacial
spac•ing ['speɪsɪŋ] espacio *m*
spa•cious ['speɪʃəs] *adj* espacioso
spade [speɪd] *for digging* pala *f*; ***~s*** *in card game* picas *fpl*; ***call a ~ a ~*** *fig* llamar al pan, pan, y al vino, vino; ***in ~s*** F de sobra F, para dar y vender F
'spade•work *fig* trabajo *m* preliminar
spa•ghet•ti [spə'getɪ] *nsg* espaguetis *mpl*
spa•ghet•ti 'west•ern spaghetti western *m*
Spain [speɪn] España *f*
spam [spæm] COMPUT propaganda *f* electrónica
span [spæn] **I** *v/t* (*pret & pp* ***-ned***) abarcar; *of bridge* cruzar **II** *n* **1** AVIA, ORN envergadura *f* **2** *of time* periodo *m*
span•gle ['spæŋgl] **I** *v/t* recamar con lentejuelas; ***be ~d with stars*** estar plagado de estrellas **II** *n* lentejuela *f*
Spang•lish ['spæŋglɪʃ] F espanglés *m*
Span•iard ['spænɪərd] español(a) *m(f)*
span•iel ['spænɪəl] ZO spaniel *m*
Span•ish ['spænɪʃ] **I** *adj* español **II** *n* **1** *language* español *m* **2** *npl*: ***the ~*** los españoles
spank [spæŋk] *v/t* azotar
spank•ing ['spæŋkɪŋ] **I** *n* azotaina *f* **II** *adj pace* rápido, veloz **III** *adv* F: ***~ clean*** como los chorros del oro F, como una patena F; ***~ new*** completamente nuevo
span•ner ['spænər] *Br* llave *f*
spar [spɑːr] **I** *v/i* (*pret & pp* ***-red***) SP entrenarse (***with*** con); *fig* pelearse (***with*** con) **II** *n of wood* poste *m*
spare [sper] **I** *v/t* **1**: ***can you ~ me $50?*** ¿me podrías dejar 50 dólares?; ***we can't ~ a single employee*** no podemos prescindir ni de un solo trabajador; ***can you ~ the time?*** ¿tienes tiempo?; ***I have time to ~*** me sobra el tiempo; ***there were five to ~*** sobraban cinco; ***can you ~ me a cigarette / 10 minutes?*** ¿me das un cigarrillo / 10 minutos?; ***~ s.o. sth*** evitarle *or* ahorrarle a alguien algo; ***~ me the details*** ahórrate (contarme) los detalles
2: ***~ s.o.'s life*** perdonar la vida a alguien
II *adj pair of glasses, set of keys* de repuesto; ***do you have any ~ cash?*** ¿no te sobrará algo de dinero?
III *n* recambio *m*, repuesto *m*

S

spare 'part pieza *f* de recambio *or* repuesto; **spare 'ribs** *npl* costillas *fpl* de cerdo; **spare 'room** habitación *f* de invitados; **spare 'time** tiempo *m* libre; **spare 'tire**, *Br* **spare 'tyre** MOT rueda *f* de recambio *or* repuesto

spar•ing ['sperɪŋ] *adj* moderado; ***be ~ with*** no derrochar

spar•ing•ly ['sperɪŋlɪ] *adv* con moderación

spark [spɑːrk] **I** *n* chispa *f*; ***the ~s fly*** *fig* saltan chispas **II** *v/i* resplandecer **III** *v/t* despertar

◆ **spark off** *v/t* desatar, desencadenar

spar•kle ['spɑːrkl] **I** *v/i* destellar; *fig* brillar, sobresalir **II** *n* brillo *m*; *fig* gracia *f*, duende *m*

spar•kler ['spɑːrklər] **1** *firework* bengala *f* **2**: ***~s*** *pl* F (*diamonds*) pedruscos *mpl* F

spar•kling ['spɑːrklɪŋ] *adj* **1** resplandeciente **2** *fig* brillante, sobresaliente

spar•kling 'wine vino *m* espumoso

'spark plug bujía *f*

spar•ring ['spɑːrɪŋ] *adj*: ***~ partner*** SP compañero(-a) *m(f)* de entrenamiento; *fig* adversario(-a) *m(f)*

spar•row ['spæroʊ] gorrión *m*

sparse [spɑːrs] *adj vegetation* escaso

sparse•ly ['spɑːrslɪ] *adv*: ***~ populated*** poco poblado

spar•tan ['spɑːrtn] *adj room* espartano

spasm ['spæzəm] MED espasmo *m*

spas•mod•ic [spæz'mɑːdɪk] *adj* intermitente

spat[1] [spæt] *pret & pp* ☞ ***spit***

spat[2] [spæt] *n* F *argument* rebote *m* F

spate [speɪt] *fig* oleada *f*

spa•tial ['speɪʃl] *adj* espacial

spat•ter ['spætər] *v/t*: ***the car ~ed mud all over me*** el coche me salpicó de barro

spat•u•la ['spætjʊlə] espátula *f*, paleta *f*

spawn [spɔːn] **I** *n* ZO huevos *mpl* **II** *v/i* ZO desovar **III** *v/t fig* engendrar

spay [speɪ] *v/t* extirpar los ovarios a

speak [spiːk] **I** *v/i* (*pret* **spoke**, *pp* **spoken**) hablar (**to**, **with** con); (*make a speech*) dar una charla; ***we're not ~ing*** (***to each other***) (*we've quarreled*) no nos hablamos; ***~ing*** TELEC al habla; ***so to ~*** digamos, (por decirlo) de alguna manera; ***no-one / nothing to ~ of*** nadie / nada que merezca la pena destacar

II *v/t* (*pret* **spoke**, *pp* **spoken**) *foreign language* hablar; ***she spoke her mind*** dijo lo que pensaba

◆ **speak for** *v/t on behalf of* hablar en nombre de; ***speak for yourself!*** ¡habla por ti!; ***it speaks for itself*** habla por sí solo, lo dice todo

◆ **speak out** *v/i*: ***speak out against injustice*** denunciar la injusticia

◆ **speak up** *v/i* (*speak louder*) hablar más alto

◆ **speak up for** *v/t* defender

'speak-eas•y F *lugar donde se podía comprar alcohol ilegalmente durante los años 20 y 30 en EE.UU.*

speak•er ['spiːkər] **1** *at conference* conferenciante *m/f* **2** *of language* hablante *m/f*; ***an English ~*** un anglohablante **3** (*orator*) orador(a) *m(f)* **4** *of sound system* altavoz *m*, *L.Am.* altoparlante *m*

speak•ing ['spiːkɪŋ] *adj*: ***we are not on ~ terms*** no nos hablamos; ***~ tour*** gira *f* de conferencias

spear [spɪr] **I** *n* **1** *weapon* lanza *f* **2** *of asparagus* punta *f* **II** *v/t piece of food* pinchar

spear•head ['spɪrhed] *v/t also fig* ir al frente de, encabezar

spear•mint ['spɪrmɪnt] hierbabuena *f*

spec [spek]: ***on ~*** F a la aventura F

spe•cial ['speʃl] *adj* especial; ***~ offer*** COM oferta *f* especial; ***be on ~ offer*** estar de oferta

spe•cial ef'fects *npl* efectos *mpl* especiales

spe•cial•ist ['speʃlɪst] especialista *m/f*

spe•ci•al•i•ty [speʃɪ'ælətɪ] *Br* ☞ ***specialty***

spe•cial•i•za•tion [speʃəlaɪ'zeɪʃn] *subject* especialidad *f*

spe•cial•ize ['speʃəlaɪz] *v/i* especializarse (**in** en)

spe•cial•ly ['speʃlɪ] *adv* ☞ ***especially***

spe•cial•ty ['speʃəltɪ] especialidad *f*; ***the house ~*** la especialidad de la casa

spe•cies ['spiːʃiːz] *nsg* especie *f*

spe•cif•ic [spə'sɪfɪk] **I** *adj* específico; ***~ gravity*** gravedad *f* específica **II** *npl*: ***the ~s*** las particularidades

spe•cif•i•cal•ly [spə'sɪfɪklɪ] *adv* específicamente

spec•i•fi•ca•tions [spesɪfɪ'keɪʃnz] *npl of machine etc* especificaciones *fpl*

spe•ci•fy ['spesɪfaɪ] *v/t* (*pret & pp* **-ied**) especificar
spe•ci•men ['spesɪmən] muestra *f*
'spe•ci•men sig•na•ture muestra *f* de firma
spe•cious ['spiːʃəs] *adj* especioso, engañoso; *argument* capcioso
speck [spek] *of dust, soot* mota *f*
speck•led ['spekld] *adj egg* moteado
specs [speks] *npl* F **1** *Br* (*spectacles*) gafas *fpl*, *L.Am.* lentes *mpl* **2** (*specifications*) especificaciones *fpl*
spec•ta•cle ['spektəkl] **1** (*sight*) espectáculo *m*; ***make a ~ of o.s.*** dar el espectáculo **2**: (***a pair of***) **~*s*** unas gafas, *L.Am.* unos lentes
spec•tac•u•lar [spek'tækjʊlər] **I** *adj* espectacular **II** *n movie* megaproducción *f*; *on TV* gala *f*
spec•ta•tor [spek'teɪtər] espectador(a) *m(f)*
spec'ta•tor sport deporte *m* espectáculo
spec•ter ['spektər] *tb fig* espectro *m*, fantasma *m*
spec•tral ['spektrəl] *adj* **1** *figure* espectral **2** PHYS espectral
spec•tre *Br* ☞ ***specter***
spec•trum ['spektrəm] PHYS, *fig* espectro *m*; ***a broad ~ of opinion*** una amplia gama de opiniones
spec•u•late ['spekjʊleɪt] *v/i also* FIN especular
spec•u•la•tion [spekjʊ'leɪʃn] *also* FIN especulación *f*; ***idle ~*** conjeturas *fpl*
spec•u•la•tive ['spekjʊlətɪv] *adj* **1** FIN especulativo **2** *look* reflexivo
spec•u•la•tor ['spekjʊleɪtər] FIN especulador(a) *m(f)*
sped [sped] *pret & pp* ☞ ***speed***
speech [spiːtʃ] **1** (*address*) discurso *m*; *in play* parlamento *m*; ***give a ~*** dar un discurso (***to*** a) **2** (*ability to speak*) habla *f*, dicción *f*; (*way of speaking*) forma *f* de hablar
'speech de•fect, 'speech im•ped•i•ment defecto *m* del habla
speech•less ['spiːtʃlɪs] *adj with shock, surprise* sin habla; ***I was left ~*** me quedé sin habla
'speech rec•og•ni•tion reconocimiento *m* del habla; **'speech syn•the•siz•er** sintetizador *m* de voz; **'speech ther•a•pist** logopeda *m/f*; **'speech ther•a•py** logopedia *f*; **'speech writ•er** redactor(a) *m(f)* de discursos
speed [spiːd] **I** *n* **1** velocidad *f*; (*promptness*) rapidez *f*; ***at a ~ of 150 mph*** a una velocidad de 150 millas por hora; ***at full or top speed*** a toda velocidad; ***five-~ gearbox*** caja *f* de cambios de cinco velocidades **2** F *drug* speed *m*
II *v/i* (*pret & pp* ***sped***) **1** *run* correr; ***we were ~ing along*** íbamos a toda velocidad **2** *drive too quickly* sobrepasar el límite de velocidad
◆ **speed by** *v/i* pasar a toda velocidad
◆ **speed up I** *v/i of car, driver* acelerar; *when working* apresurarse **II** *v/t process* acelerar
'speed•boat motora *f*, planeadora *f*
'speed bump resalto *m* (*para reducir la velocidad del tráfico*), *Arg* despertador *m*, *Mex* tope *m*
speed•i•ly ['spiːdɪlɪ] *adv* con rapidez
speed•ing ['spiːdɪŋ]: ***fined for ~*** multado por exceso de velocidad
'speed•ing fine multa *f* por exceso de velocidad
'speed lim•it *on roads* límite *m* de velocidad
speed•om•e•ter [spiː'dɑːmɪtər] velocímetro *m*
'speed trap control *m* de velocidad por radar
speed•y ['spiːdɪ] *adj* rápido
speed•y Gon•za•lez [gɑːn'zɑːlez] F: ***he's a real ~*** es (como) una bala F
spe•le•ol•o•gy [spiːliː'ɑːlədʒɪ] espeleología *f*
spell[1] [spel] **I** *v/t word* deletrear; ***how do you ~ …?*** ¿cómo se escribe …? **II** *v/i* deletrear
◆ **spell out** *v/t*: ***spell sth out*** explicar algo con pelos y señales (***for s.o.*** a alguien)
spell[2] [spel] *n* (*period of time*) periodo *m*, temporada *f*; ***I'll take a ~ at the wheel*** te relevaré un rato al volante; ***I'll wait a ~*** esperaré un ratito F; ***cold ~*** METEO periodo de frío
spell[3] [spel] *n* encantamiento *m*, hechizo *m*; *fig* hechizo *m*, embrujo *m*; ***be under s.o.'s ~*** *fig* estar bajo el hechizo de alguien; ***cast a ~ on s.o.*** hechizar *or* encantar a alguien; *fig* cautivar a alguien
'spell•bind•ing *adj* cautivador
'spell•bound *adj* hechizado; ***hold s.o. ~***

embelesar a alguien; **'spell•check** COMPUT: ***do a ~ on*** pasar el corrector ortográfico a; **'spell•check•er** COMPUT corrector *m* ortográfico
spell•er ['spelər]: ***be a good / bad ~*** ser bueno / malo en ortografía
spell•ing ['spelɪŋ] ortografía *f*; ***~ mistake*** falta *f* de ortografía
spend [spend] *v/t* (*pret & pp* ***spent***) *money* gastar; *time* pasar; ***~ an hour doing sth*** pasar *or* estar una hora haciendo algo
spend•er ['spendər]: ***he's a big ~*** es un gastador
spend•ing ['spendɪŋ] gastos *mpl*; ***public ~*** gasto *m* público; ***~ cut*** recorte *m* de gastos
'spend•ing mon•ey dinero *m* para gastos personales
'spend•thrift *pej* derrochador(a) *m(f)*
spent [spent] *pret & pp* ☞ ***spend***
sperm [spɜːrm] espermatozoide *m*; (*semen*) esperma *f*
'sperm bank banco *m* de esperma; **'sperm count** recuento *m* espermático; **'sperm whale** cachalote *m*
spew [spjuː] *v/i* P (*vomit*) potar P
◆ **spew out I** *v/t* arrojar, expulsar **II** *v/i* salir violentamente (***from*** de)
sphere [sfɪr] *also fig* esfera *f*; ***~ of influence*** ámbito *m* de influencia; ***in the ~ of*** en el campo de
spher•i•cal ['sferɪkl] *adj* esférico, redondo
sphinc•ter ['sfɪŋktər] ANAT esfínter *m*
spice [spaɪs] (*seasoning*) especia *f*
◆ **spice up** *v/t food* especiar; *fig*: *story*, *speech* aderezar
'spice rack especiero *m*
spick-and-span [spɪkən'spæn] *adj* como los chorros del oro
spic•y ['spaɪsɪ] *adj food* con especias; (*hot*) picante
spi•der ['spaɪdər] araña *f*
'spi•der•web telaraña *f*, tela *f* de araña
spiel [ʃpiːl] F sermón *m* F, parrafada *f* F
spike [spaɪk] **I** *n* pincho *m*; *on running shoe* clavo *m* **II** *v/t*: ***~ s.o.'s drink*** adulterar la bebida de alguien
'spike heel tacón *m* de aguja; ***~s*** *shoes* zapatos *mpl* de tacón de aguja
spikes [spaɪks] *npl* zapatillas *fpl* de correr
spik•y ['spaɪkɪ] *adj* **1** pinchudo **2** *Br* F irritable
spill [spɪl] **I** *v/t* derramar; ***I've ~ed coffee over my pants*** me he tirado café por los pantalones **II** *v/i* derramarse **III** *n* **1** *of oil* derrame *m* **2**: ***have a ~*** sufrir una caída
◆ **spill out** *v/i of liquid* derramarse
◆ **spill over** *v/i of liquid* desparramarse; ***spill over into*** *of war* extenderse *or* propagarse hasta
'spill•way *of dam* canal *m* desagüe
spin[1] [spɪn] **I** *n* **1** (*turn*) giro *m*; ***put ~ on a ball*** SP hacer girar una pelota **2** *given by ~ doctor* enfoque *m* arbitrario; ***put a different ~ on sth*** darle la vuelta a algo **II** *v/t* (*pret & pp* ***spun***) **1** *turn* hacer girar **2**: ***~ s.o. a yarn*** tomar el pelo a alguien **III** *v/i* (*pret & pp* ***spun***) *of wheel* girar, dar vueltas; ***my head is ~ning*** me da vueltas la cabeza
◆ **spin around** *v/i of person*, *car* darse la vuelta
spin[2] [spɪn] *v/t wool*, *cotton* hilar; *web* tejer
◆ **spin out** *v/t* alargar
spin•ach ['spɪnɪdʒ] espinacas *fpl*
spin•al ['spaɪnl] *adj* de la columna vertebral
spin•al 'col•umn columna *f* vertebral
spin•al 'cord médula *f* espinal
spin•dle ['spɪndl] TECH eje *m*
spin•dly ['spɪndlɪ] *adj person*, *legs*, *tree* escúalido; *chair* endeble
'spin doc•tor F *asesor encargado de dar la mejor prensa posible a un político o asunto*; **'spin-dry** *v/t* centrifugar; **spin-'dry•er** centrifugadora *f*
spine [spaɪn] **1** *of person*, *animal* columna *f* vertebral; *of book* lomo *m* **2** *on plant*, *hedgehog* espina *f*
spine-chill•ing ['spaɪntʃɪlɪŋ] *adj* espeluznante
spine•less ['spaɪnlɪs] *adj* (*cowardly*) débil
spin•na•ker ['spɪnəkər] NAUT spinnaker *m*
spin•ning wheel ['spɪnɪŋwiːl] rueca *f*
'spin-off producto *m* derivado
spin•ster ['spɪnstər] solterona *f*
spin•ster•ish ['spɪnstərɪʃ] *adj* melindroso
spin•y ['spaɪnɪ] *adj* espinoso
spi•ral ['spaɪrəl] **I** *n* espiral **II** *v/i* (*rise quickly*) subir vertiginosamente; ***and***

inflation ~s out of control again y la inflacción se dispara de nuevo desmesuradamente
spi•ral 'stair•case escalera *f* de caracol
spire [spaɪr] aguja *f*
spir•it ['spɪrɪt] espíritu *m*; (*courage*) valor *m*; ***in a ~ of cooperation*** con espíritu de cooperación; ***I'll be with you in ~*** estaré contigo en mis pensamientos; ***get into the ~ of things*** ambientarse
◆ **spirit away** *v/t* retirar disimuladamente
spir•it•ed ['spɪrɪtɪd] *adj* (*energetic*) enérgico
'spir•it lev•el nivel *m* de burbuja
spir•its [spɪrɪts] *pl* (*morale*) la moral; ***be in good*** *or* ***high / poor ~*** tener la moral alta / baja; ***lift*** *or* ***raise s.o.'s ~*** levantar los ánimos a alguien, animarse a alguien
spir•it•u•al ['spɪrɪʧʊəl] **I** *adj* espiritual **II** *n* MUS espiritual *m*
spir•it•u•al•ism ['spɪrɪʧəlɪzm] espiritismo *m*
spir•it•u•al•ist ['spɪrɪʧəlɪst] espiritista *m/f*
spit[1] [spɪt] **I** *v/i* (*pret & pp* ***spat***) *of person* escupir; ***it's ~ting with rain*** está chispeando; ***~ at s.o.*** escupir a alguien; ***"get out!" she spat at him*** "¡fuera!" le gritó enfurecida **II** *v/t* escupir
◆ **spit out** *v/t food, liquid* escupir; ***spit it out!*** *fig* F ¡suéltalo! F
spit[2] [spɪt] *n* **1** *for meat* pincho *m*, brocheta *f* **2** GEOG lengua *f*
spite [spaɪt] **1** rencor *m*; ***out of pure ~*** por pura malicia **2**: ***in ~ of*** a pesar de **II** *v/t* fastidiar
spite•ful ['spaɪtfəl] *adj* malo, malicioso
spite•ful•ly ['spaɪtfəlɪ] *adv* con maldad *or* malicia
'spit•fire furia *f*
spit•ting ['spɪtɪŋ] *adj*: ***be within ~ distance*** F estar a un paso F
spit•ting 'im•age: ***be the ~ of s.o.*** ser el vivo retrato de alguien
spit•tle ['spɪtl] babas *fpl*
splash [splæʃ] **I** *n small amount of liquid* chorrito *m*; *of color* mancha *f*; ***make (quite) a ~*** F causar sensación F **II** *v/t person* salpicar; ***~ cold water over one's face*** refrescarse la cara con agua fría; ***it was ~ed all over the newspapers*** *fig* fue noticia de primera plana en todos los periódicos **III** *v/i* chapotear; *of water* salpicar
◆ **splash about** *v/t*: ***splash one's money about*** *Br* F malgastar el dinero F
◆ **splash down** *v/i of spacecraft* amerizar
◆ **splash out** *v/i Br* F: *in spending* gastarse una fortuna
◆ **splash out on** *v/t Br* F derrochar en F
'splash•down amerizaje *m*
splat [splæt] *adv*: ***go ~*** hacer chof
splat•ter ['splætər] ☞ ***spatter***
splay [spleɪ] *v/t* abrir, extender
◆ **splay out** *v/t* ☞ ***splay***
spleen [spliːn] ANAT bazo *m*
splen•did ['splendɪd] *adj* espléndido
splen•dor, *Br* **splen•dour** ['splendər] esplendor *m*
splice [splaɪs] *v/t* **1** empalmar **2** F: ***get ~d*** casarse
spliff [splɪf] *cannabis joint* porro *m*
splint [splɪnt] MED tablilla *f*
splin•ter ['splɪntər] **I** *n* astilla *f* **II** *v/i* astillarse
'splin•ter group grupo *m* escindido
split [splɪt] **I** *n* **1** *damage* raja *f* **2** (*disagreement*) escisión *f* **3** (*division, share*) reparto *m* **4**: ***do the ~s*** hacer el spagat **II** *v/t* (*pret & pp* ***split***) **1** *damage* rajar; *logs* partir en dos; ***~ one's sides*** F partirse de risa F **2** (*cause disagreement in*) escindir; ***be ~*** *fig* discrepar (***on*** sobre) **3** (*share*) repartir; ***~ sth three ways*** dividir algo para tres; ***~ the difference*** partir la diferencia
III *v/i* (*pret & pp* ***split***) **1** (*tear*) rajarse **2** (*disagree*) escindirse **3** F (*leave*) largarse F
◆ **split up I** *v/i of couple* separarse **II** *v/t* (*divide*) dividir
split 'ends *npl* puntas *fpl* abiertas; **split-'lev•el** casa *f* de dos plantas; **split-lev•el co•lo•ni•al** casa *f* de estilo colonial de dos plantas; **split per•son'al•i•ty** PSYCH doble personalidad *f*; **split 'screen** COMPUT pantalla *f* dividida; **split 'sec•ond** F instante *m*
split•ting ['splɪtɪŋ] *adj*: ***~ headache*** dolor *m* de cabeza atroz
splodge [splɑːdʒ] *esp Br*, **splotch** [splɑːʧ] pegote *m*, mancha *f*
splurge [splɜːrdʒ] F **I** *n*: ***have a ~*** tirar la

casa por la ventana (***on*** en) F II *v/i* despilfarrar (***on*** en)
splut•ter ['splʌtər] *v/i* farfullar
spoil [spɔɪl] I *v/t* (*pret & pp* ***spoiled*** *or* ***spoilt***) 1 estropear, arruinar 2 *child* consentir, mimar II *v/i* 1 echarse a perder 2: ***be ~ing for a fight*** estar buscando bronca III *npl*: ***the ~s*** (***of war***) el botín de guerra
spoil•er ['spɔɪlər] MOT alerón *m*
'spoil•sport F aguafiestas *m/f inv* F
spoilt [spɔɪlt] I *adj child* consentido, mimado; ***be ~ for choice*** tener mucho donde elegir; ***~ ballot*** (***paper***) POL papeleta *f* inválida II *pret & pp* ☞ ***spoil***
spoke[1] [spoʊk] *n of wheel* radio *m*; ***put a ~ in s.o.'s wheel*** *fig* poner la zancadilla a alguien
spoke[2] [spoʊk] *pret* ☞ ***speak***
spo•ken ['spoʊkən] I *pp* ☞ ***speak*** II *adj*: ***in ~ English*** en inglés hablado
spokes•man ['spoʊksmən] portavoz *m*
spokes•per•son ['spoʊkspɜːrsən] portavoz *m/f*
spokes•wom•an ['spoʊkswʊmən] portavoz *f*
sponge [spʌndʒ] esponja *f*; ***throw in the ~*** *fig* tirar la toalla
◆ **sponge down** *v/t* humedecer
◆ **sponge off, sponge on** *v/t* F vivir a costa de
'sponge cake bizcocho *m*
spong•er ['spʌndʒər] F gorrón(-ona) *m(f)* F
spong•y ['spʌndʒɪ] *adj* 1 (*waterlogged*) anegado 2 *in texture* esponjoso; *pej: bread etc* abizcochado
spon•sor ['spɑːnsər] I *n* patrocinador(a) *m(f)* II *v/t* patrocinar
spon•sor•ship ['spɑːnsərʃɪp] patrocinio *m*
spon•ta•ne•i•ty [spɑːntə'neɪətɪ] espontaneidad *f*
spon•ta•ne•ous [spɑːn'teɪnɪəs] *adj* espontáneo
spon•ta•ne•ous•ly [spɑːn'teɪnɪəslɪ] *adv* espontáneamente
spoof [spuːf] F parodia *f* (***of*** de; ***on*** sobre)
spook [spuːk] F I *n* 1 (*ghost*) fantasma *m* 2 (*spy*) espía *m/f* II *v/t* asustar
spook•y ['spuːkɪ] *adj* F espeluznante, terrorífico
spool [spuːl] carrete *m*
spoon [spuːn] cuchara *f*
'spoon•feed *v/t* (*pret & pp* ***-fed***) *fig* dar todo mascado a
spoon•ful ['spuːnfʊl] cucharada *f*
spo•rad•ic [spə'rædɪk] *adj* esporádico
spo•rad•i•cal•ly [spə'rædɪklɪ] *adv* esporádicamente
spore [spɔːr] BIO espora *f*
sport [spɔːrt] 1 deporte *m* 2: ***be a good ~*** F ser buena gente F; ***be a ~ and let me borrow your car*** no seas aguafiestas y déjame el coche
sport•ing ['spɔːrtɪŋ] *adj* deportivo; ***a ~ gesture*** un gesto deportivo; ***give s.o. a ~ chance*** dar ventaja a alguien
'sports car [spɔːrts] (coche *m*) deportivo *m*; **'sports•cast** noticias *fpl* deportivas; **'sports cen•ter**, *Br* **'sports cen•tre** polideportivo *m*; **'sports•coat**, *Br* **'sports jack•et** chaqueta *f* de sport; **sports 'jour•nal•ist** periodista *m/f* deportivo(-a); **'sports•man** deportista *m*
sports•man•like ['spɔːrtsmənlaɪk] *adj* deportivo, correcto
sports•man•ship ['spɔːrtsmənʃɪp] deportividad *f*
'sports med•i•cine medicina *f* deportiva; **'sports news** *nsg* noticias *fpl* deportivas; **'sports page** página *f* de deportes; **'sports•wear** ropa *f* de deporte; **'sports•wom•an** deportista *f*
sport•y ['spɔːrtɪ] *adj person* deportista; *clothes* deportivo
spot[1] [spɑːt] *n* (*pimple etc*) grano *m*; (*part of pattern*) lunar *m*; ***a ~ of …*** (*a little*) algo de …, un poco de …
spot[2] [spɑːt] *n* (*place*) lugar *m*, sitio *m*; ***on the ~*** (*in the place in question*) en el lugar; (*immediately*) en ese momento; ***put s.o. on the ~*** F poner a alguien en un aprieto F; ***be in a ~*** F estar en un apuro *or* aprieto F; ***that hit the ~!*** ¡era justo lo que necesitaba!; ***earn a ~ on the team*** hacerse con un puesto en el equipo
spot[3] [spɑːt] *v/t* (*pret & pp* ***-ted***) (*notice*) ver; (*identify*) ver, darse cuenta de
'spot buy•ing FIN compra *f* al contado
spot 'check control *m* al azar; ***carry out ~s*** llevar a cabo controles al azar
spot•less ['spɑːtlɪs] *adj* inmaculado, impecable
'spot•light foco *m*; ***be in the ~*** *fig* estar en el candelero; **spot-'on** *adj Br*: ***he***

was ~ dio en el clavo; **'spot price** FIN precio *m* al contado
spot•ted ['spɑːtɪd] *adj fabric* de lunares
spot•ty ['spɑːtɪ] *adj with pimples* con granos
spouse [spaʊs] *fml* cónyuge *m/f*
spout [spaʊt] **I** *n* pitorro *m*; ***be up the ~*** *Br* F *machine* estar en las últimas; *person, company* estar en la cuerda floja F; ***she's up the ~*** *Br* P (*pregnant*) está preñada P **II** *v/i of liquid* chorrear **III** *v/t* F soltar F
sprain [spreɪn] **I** *n* esguince *m* **II** *v/t* hacerse un esguince en
sprang [spræŋ] *pret* ☞ **spring**
sprawl [sprɒːl] *v/i* despatarrarse; *of city* expandirse; ***send s.o. ~ing*** *with punch* derribar alguien de un golpe
sprawl•ing ['sprɒːlɪŋ] *adj city* extendido
spray [spreɪ] **I** *n of sea water, from fountain* rociada *f*; *for hair* spray *m*; *container* aerosol *m*, spray *m* **II** *v/t* rociar; *crops* fumigar; ***~ sth with sth*** rociar algo de algo
'spray can aerosol *m*
'spray•gun pistola *f* pulverizadora
spread [spred] **I** *n* **1** *of disease, religion etc* propagación *f* **2** F (*big meal*) comilona *f* F **II** *v/t* (*pret & pp* ***spread***) **1** (*lay*) extender; *butter, jelly* untar **2** *news, rumor* difundir; *disease* propagar **3** *arms, legs* extender **III** *v/i* (*pret & pp* ***spread***) **1** *of disease, fire* propagarse; *of rumor, news* difundirse **2** *of butter* extenderse, untarse
◆ **spread around** *v/t news etc* extender; ***don't spread this around, but …*** no lo cuentes por ahí, pero …
◆ **spread out I** *v/t* abrir, extender **II** *v/i of people* distribuirse, separarse
spread-ea•gled [spred'iːgld] *adj* con las manos y las piernas abiertas
'spread•sheet COMPUT hoja *f* de cálculo
spree [spriː] F: ***go*** (***out***) ***on a ~*** ir de juerga; ***go on a shopping ~*** salir a comprar a lo loco
sprig [sprɪg] ramita *f*
spright•ly ['spraɪtlɪ] *adj* lleno de energía
spring[1] [sprɪŋ] **I** *n season* primavera *f*; ***in*** (***the***) ***~*** en (la) primavera **II** *adj* de primavera
spring[2] [sprɪŋ] *n device* muelle *m*
spring[3] [sprɪŋ] **I** *n* **1** (*jump*) brinco *m*, salto *m* **2** (*stream*) manantial *m*
II *v/i* (*pret* ***sprang***, *pp* ***sprung***) brincar, saltar; ***~ from*** proceder de; ***he sprang to his feet*** se levantó de un salto; ***~ into action*** ponerse manos a la obra de inmediato; ***~ open*** *of lid etc* abrirse de golpe
III *v/t* (*pret* ***sprang***, *pp* ***sprung***) **1**: ***~ sth on s.o.*** F soltar algo a alguien de buenas a primeras F **2**: ***~ a leak*** agrietarse **3**: ***~ s.o.*** (***from prison***) F sacar a alguien de la cárcel
◆ **spring from** *v/t* originarse en; ***where did you spring from?*** ¿de dónde sales?
◆ **spring up** *v/i of wind* levantarse; *of coffee shops, new houses etc* multiplicarse
'spring•board *also fig* trampolín *m*; **spring 'chick•en** *hum*: ***she's no ~*** no es ninguna niña; **spring-'clean** *v/t & v/i* limpiar a fondo; **spring-'clean•ing** limpieza *f* a fondo; **spring 'on•ion** *Br* cebollino *m*; **spring 'roll** GASTR rollito *m* de primavera; **spring 'tide** marea *f* viva; **'spring•time** primavera *f*
spring•y ['sprɪŋɪ] *adj mattress, ground* mullido; *walk* ligero; *piece of elastic* elástico
sprin•kle ['sprɪŋkl] *v/t* espolvorear; ***~ sth with sth*** espolvorear algo con algo
sprin•kler ['sprɪŋklər] *for garden* aspersor *m*; *in ceiling* rociador *m* contra incendios
sprin•kling ['sprɪŋklɪŋ]: ***a ~ of*** un poco de; *people* un puñado de
sprint [sprɪnt] **I** *n* esprint *m*; SP carrera *f* de velocidad **II** *v/i* (*run fast*) correr a toda velocidad; *of runner* esprintar
sprint•er ['sprɪntər] SP esprínter *m/f*, velocista *m/f*
spritz [sprɪts] *v/t* (*spray*) rociar
spritz•er ['sprɪtsər] *vino blanco con soda*
sprog [sprɑːg] *Br* F pequeño(-a) *m*(*f*) F
sprout [spraʊt] **I** *v/i of seed* brotar **II** *n*: (***Brussels***) ***~s*** coles *fpl* de Bruselas **III** *v/t*: ***~ a beard*** F dejarse barba
◆ **sprout up** *v/i* surgir
spruce[1] [spruːs] *adj* pulcro
◆ **spruce up** *v/t house etc* dejar como una patena; ***spruce o.s. up*** F recomponerse F, arreglarse F

spruce[2] [spruːs] *n* BOT picea *f*
sprung [sprʌŋ] *pp* ☞ ***spring***
spry [spraɪ] *adj* lleno *m* de energía
spud [spʌd] F patata *f*
spun [spʌn] *pret & pp* ☞ ***spin***
spunk [spʌŋk] F (*courage*) valor *m*
spunk•y ['spʌŋkɪ] *adj* F valiente
spur [spɜːr] **I** *n* espuela *f*; *fig* incentivo; ***on the ~ of the moment*** sin pararse a pensar **II** *v/t* (*pret & pp* ***-red***): ***~ s.o. into action*** empujar a alguien a actuar
◆ **spur on** *v/t* (*encourage*) espolear
spu•ri•ous ['spjʊrɪəs] *adj emotion* fingido; *argument* falaz
spurn [spɜːrn] *v/t* rechazar; ***a ~ed lover*** un amante repudiado
spur-of-the-'mo•ment *adj* repentino
spurt [spɜːrt] **I** *n in race* arrancada *f*; ***put on a ~*** acelerar **II** *v/i of liquid* chorrear
sput•ter ['spʌtər] *v/i of engine* chisporrotear
spy [spaɪ] **I** *n* espía *m/f* **II** *v/i* (*pret & pp* ***-ied***) espiar **III** *v/t* (*pret & pp* ***-ied***) (*see*) ver
◆ **spy on** *v/t* espiar
'spy mov•ie película *f* de espías
squab•ble ['skwɑːbl] **I** *n* riña *f* **II** *v/i* reñir
squad [skwɑːd] **1** MIL pelotón *m* **2** *in police* brigada *f*; ***the vice ~*** la brigada antivicio **3** SP plantilla *f*
'squad car coche *m* patrulla
squad•ron ['skwɑːdrən] MIL, AVIA escuadrón *m*; NAUT escuadra *f*
squal•id ['skwɒːlɪd] *adj* inmundo, miserable
squall[1] [skwɔːl] **I** *v/i* berrear **II** *n* berreo *m*
squall[2] [skwɔːl] *n* ráfaga *f*
squall•y ['skwɔːlɪ] *adj day, weather* ventoso
squal•or ['skwɒːlər] inmundicia *f*; ***live in ~*** vivir en la inmundicia *or* miseria
squan•der ['skwɒːndər] *v/t money* despilfarrar
square [skwer] **I** *adj* **1** *in shape* cuadrado; ***~ miles*** millas *fpl* cuadradas **2**: ***be*** (***all***) ***~*** F estar en paz F
II *n* **1** *also* MATH cuadrado *m* **2** *in town* plaza *f*, *in board game* casilla *f*; ***we're back to ~ one*** volvemos al punto de partida
III *v/t* **1** *number* elevar al cuadrado; ***4 ~d*** 4 al cuadrado **2** F: ***~ sth with one's conscience*** no tener cargo de conciencia por algo; ***I'll need to ~ it with the boss first*** necesitaré primero el visto bueno del jefe
◆ **square up** *v/i* (*pay*) hacer cuentas
◆ **square up to** *v/t opponent* plantar cara a; *problem* hacer frente a
'square dance *baile típico estadounidense en grupos de cuatro parejas*
squared 'pa•per [skwerd] papel *m* cuadriculado
square•ly ['skwerlɪ] *adv*: ***face a problem ~*** afrontar un problema directamente
square 'meal comida *f* substanciosa
square 'root raíz *f* cuadrada
squash[1] [skwɑːʃ] *n vegetable* calabacera *f*
squash[2] [skwɑːʃ] *n game* squash *m*
squash[3] [skwɑːʃ] *v/t* (*crush*) aplastar; ***~ flat*** chafar
'squash court pista *f* de squash
'squash rack•et raqueta *f* de squash
squash•y ['skwɑːʃɪ] *adj* blando, maduro
squat [skwɑːt] **I** *adj person, build* chaparro; *figure, buildings* bajo **II** *v/i* (*pret & pp* ***-ted***) *sit* agacharse; ***~ in a building*** ocupar ilegalmente un edificio **III** *n building* casa *f* okupa *Span* F
◆ **squat down** *v/i* acuclillarse
squat•ter ['skwɑːtər] ocupante *m/f* ilegal, *Span* okupa *m/f* F
squaw [skwɔː] nativa *f* norteamericana
squawk [skwɔːk] *v/i* F refunfuñar F (***about*** por)
squeak [skwiːk] **I** *n of mouse* chillido *m*; *of hinge* chirrido *m*; ***I don't want to hear a ~ from you guys*** no quiero oíros ni respirar; ***that was a narrow ~!*** F ¡por los pelos! F **II** *v/i of mouse* chillar; *of hinge* chirriar; *of shoes* crujir
◆ **squeak through** *v/i* F aprobar por los pelos
squeak•y ['skwiːkɪ] *adj hinge* chirriante; *shoes* que crujen; *voice* chillón
'squeak•y clean *adj* F *hair* bien limpio; *fig*: *politician* honesto
squeal [skwiːl] **I** *n* chillido; ***there was a ~ of brakes*** se oyó una frenada estruendosa **II** *v/i* **1** chillar; *of brakes* armar un estruendo **2** F *of informant* chivarse F; ***~ on s.o.*** F delatar a alguien
squeam•ish ['skwiːmɪʃ] *adj* aprensivo
squee•gee ['skwiːdʒiː] limpiacristales

m de goma

squeeze [skwi:z] **I** *n of hand, shoulder* apretón *m*; ***give sth a ~*** apretujar algo; ***put the ~ on s.o.*** F apretarle los tornillos a alguien F **II** *v/t* **1** (*press*) apretar **2** (*remove juice from*) exprimir

◆ **squeeze in I** *v/i to a car etc* meterse a duras penas **II** *v/t* hacer hueco para

◆ **squeeze out** *v/t* exprimir

◆ **squeeze up** *v/i to make space* apretarse

squelch [skweltʃ] *v/i* chapotear

squib [skwɪb] petardo *m*

squid [skwɪd] calamar *m*

squig•gle ['skwɪgl] (*scribble*) garabato *m*

squint [skwɪnt]: ***she has a ~*** es estrábica, tiene estrabismo

squirm [skwɜ:rm] *v/t* retorcerse

squir•rel ['skwɪrl] ardilla *f*

squir•rel•ly ['skwɪrəlɪ] *adj* F majareta F

squirt [skwɜ:rt] **I** *v/t* lanzar un chorro de **II** *n* F *pej* canijo(-a) *m(f)* F, mequetrefe *m/f* F

Sri Lan•ka [sri:'læŋkə] Sri Lanka *m*

St *abbr* **1** (= ***saint***) *male* Sto; *female* Sta (= santo *m*; santa *f*) **2** (= ***street***) c / (= calle *f*)

stab [stæb] **I** *n* **1** puñalada *f*; ***~ wound*** puñalada *f*; ***~ in the back*** *fig* puñalada por la espalda; ***feel a ~ of pain / remorse*** sufrir un ataque de dolor / remordimientos **2** F intento *m*; ***have a ~ at sth*** intentar algo **II** *v/t* (*pret & pp* ***-bed***) *person* apuñalar; ***he was ~bed in the stomach*** recibió una puñalada en el estómago; ***~ s.o. in the back*** *fig* clavar a alguien un puñal por la espalda

stab•bing ['stæbɪŋ] **I** *adj pain* punzante **II** *n* puñalada *f*

sta•bil•i•ty [stə'bɪlətɪ] estabilidad *f*

sta•bi•li•za•tion [steɪbəlaɪ'zeɪʃn] estabilización *f*

sta•bi•lize ['steɪbəlaɪz] **I** *v/t prices, boat* estabilizar **II** *v/i of prices etc* estabilizarse

sta•bi•liz•er ['steɪbəlaɪzər] TECH estabilizador *m*

sta•ble[1] ['steɪbl] *n for horses* establo *m*

sta•ble[2] ['steɪbl] *adj* estable; *patient's condition* estacionario

stack [stæk] **I** *n* **1** (*pile*) pila *f*; ***be in the ~*** *of airplane* estar en espera de recibir permiso para aterrizar; ***~s of*** F montones de F **2** (*smoke~*) chimenea *f* **3** *for CDs* estantería *f* **II** *v/t* apilar; ***the odds are ~ed against us*** el viento no sopla a nuestro favor

◆ **stack up** *v/t* ☞ ***stack*** **II**

◆ **stack up against** *v/t* F comparar con

sta•di•um ['steɪdɪəm] (*pl* ***stadia*** ['steɪdɪə], ***-ums***) estadio *m*

staff [stæf] *npl* (*employees*) personal *m*; (*teachers*) profesorado *m*; ***~ are not allowed to ...*** los empleados no tienen permitido ...; ***be on the ~*** formar parte de la plantilla **II** *v/t* proporcionar personal a

staf•fer ['stæfər] empleado(-a) *m(f)*

'staff of•fi•cer MIL oficial *m* del Estado Mayor

'staff•room *in school* sala *f* de profesores

stag [stæg] ciervo *m*

stage[1] [steɪdʒ] *n in life, project etc* etapa *f*; ***in*** (***easy***) ***~s*** por partes; ***at a later ~*** posteriormente

stage[2] [steɪdʒ] **I** *n* THEA escenario *m*; ***go on ~*** salir a escena; ***go on the ~*** *become an actor* hacerse actor / actriz; ***set the ~ for*** ultimar los preparativos para **II** *v/t* **1** *play* escenificar, llevar a escena **2** *demonstration* llevar a cabo; ***it was all specially ~d*** *not spontaneous* no fue algo espontáneo

'stage di•rec•tion acotación *f*; **stage 'door** entrada *f* de artistas; **'stage fright** miedo *m* escénico; **'stage hand** tramoyista *m/f*; **'stage-man•age** *v/t* organizar entre bastidores; **'stage man•ag•er** director(a) *m(f)* de escena; **'stage name** nombre *m* artístico; **'stage-struck** *adj* apasionado de la interpretación

stage•y ['steɪdʒɪ] *adj gesture* teatral, exagerado

stag•ger ['stægər] **I** *v/i* tambalearse **II** *v/t* **1** (*amaze*) dejar anonadado; ***I was ~ed to see so many people*** me quedé estupefacto al ver a tanta gente **2** *coffee breaks etc* escalonar

stag•ger•ing ['stægərɪŋ] *adj* asombroso

stag•nant ['stægnənt] *adj also fig* estancado

stag•nate [stæg'neɪt] *v/i fig* estancarse

stag•na•tion [stæg'neɪʃn] estancamiento *m*

'stag par•ty despedida *f* de soltero
staid [steɪd] *adj* aburrido, soso
stain [steɪn] **I** *n* **1** (*dirty mark*) mancha *f* **2** *for wood* tinte *m* **II** *v/t* **1** (*dirty*) manchar **2** *wood* teñir **III** *v/i* **1** *of wine etc* manchar, dejar mancha **2** *of fabric* mancharse
stained-glass 'win•dow [steɪnd] vidriera *f*
stain•less steel ['steɪnlɪssti:l] acero *m* inoxidable
stain re•mov•er ['steɪnrɪmu:vər] quitamanchas *m inv*
stair [ster] escalón *m*; ***the ~s*** la(s) escalera(s); ***two flights of ~s*** dos tramos de escalera
'stair car•pet alfombra *f* para escaleras
'stair•case, 'stair•way escalera(s) *f(pl)*
stake [steɪk] **I** *n* **1** *of wood* estaca *f* **2** *when gambling* apuesta *f*; ***be at ~*** estar en juego; ***play for high ~s*** jugarse mucho **3** (*investment*) participación *f*; ***have a ~ in sth*** tener intereses en algo **II** *v/t* **1** *tree* arrodrigar **2** *money* apostar; *reputation* jugarse **3** *person* ayudar (*económicamente*) **4**: ***~ a** or **one's claim to sth*** *fig* reclamar el derecho sobre algo
◆ **stake out** *v/t* F vigilar
'stake•out F vigilancia *f*
sta•lac•tite ['stæləktaɪt] GEOL estalactita *f*
sta•lag•mite ['stæləgmaɪt] GEOL estalagmita *f*
stale [steɪl] *adj bread* rancio; *air* viciado; *fig: news* viejo
'stale•mate *in chess* tablas *fpl* (*por rey ahogado*); *fig* punto *m* muerto; ***end in ~*** quedar tablas
stalk[1] [stɒ:k] *n of fruit, plant* tallo *m*
stalk[2] [stɒ:k] *v/t* (*follow*) acechar; *person* seguir
stalk•er ['stɒ:kər] *persona que sigue a otra obsesivamente*
stall[1] [stɒ:l] *n* **1** *at market* puesto *m* **2** *for cow, horse* casilla *f*
stall[2] [stɒ:l] **I** *v/i* **1** *of vehicle, engine* calarse; *of plane* entrar en pérdida **2** (*play for time*) intentar ganar tiempo **II** *v/t* **1** *engine* calar **2** *person* retener
stal•li•on ['stæljən] semental *m*
stalls [stɒ:lz] *npl* THEA patio *m* de butacas
stal•wart ['stɒ:lwərt] *adj support, supporter* incondicional
stam•i•na ['stæmɪnə] resistencia *f*
stam•mer ['stæmər] **I** *n* tartamudeo *m*; ***have a ~, speak with a ~*** tartamudear **II** *v/i* tartamudear
◆ **stammer out** *v/t* mascullar
stam•mer•er ['stæmərər] tartamudo(-a) *m(f)*
stamp[1] [stæmp] **I** *n* **1** *for letter* sello *m*, *L.Am.* estampilla *f*, *Mex* timbre *m* **2** *device* tampón *m*; *mark made with device* sello *m* **II** *v/t* sellar; ***~ed addressed envelope*** sobre *m* franqueado con la dirección
stamp[2] [stæmp] *v/t*: ***~ one's feet*** patear
◆ **stamp out** *v/t* (*eradicate*) terminar con
'stamp al•bum álbum *m* filatélico; **'stamp col•lect•ing** filatelia *f*; **'stamp col•lec•tion** collección *f* de sellos *or L.Am.* estampillas *or Mex* timbres; **'stamp col•lec•tor** coleccionista *m/f* de sellos *or L.Am.* estampillas *or Mex* timbres
stam•pede [stæm'pi:d] **I** *n of cattle etc* estampida *f*, *of people* desbandada *f* **II** *v/i of cattle etc* salir de estampida; *of people* salir en desbandada **III** *v/t cattle, horses* hacer salir de estampida; ***~ s.o. into doing sth*** presionar a alguien para que haga algo
stamp•ing ground ['stæmpɪŋ] *fig* F lugar *m* favorito
stance [stæns] (*position*) postura *f*
stand [stænd] **I** *n* **1** *at exhibition* puesto *m*, stand *m* **2** (*witness ~*) estrado *m*; ***take the ~*** subir al estrado **3** (*support, base*) soporte *m* **4**: ***~s*** *pl* SP graderío *m* **5**: ***make** or **take a ~*** adoptar una postura **6** MIL resistencia *f*
II *v/i* (*pret & pp* ***stood***) **1** *as opposed to sit* estar de pie; (*rise*) ponerse de pie **2** *of building* encontrarse, hallarse; ***there was a large box ~ing in the middle of the floor*** había una caja muy grande en mitad del suelo; ***the house ~s at the corner of …*** la casa se encuentra en la esquina de …; ***~ still*** *of person* quedarse quieto; ***don't just ~ there, do something!*** ¡no te quedes ahí parado *or* quieto, haz algo!
3: ***where do you ~ with Liz?*** ¿cual es tu situación con Liz?; ***where do you ~ on this?*** ¿de qué lado estás?; ***at least I***

know now where I ~ al menos sé a que atenerme; ***as things ~*** tal y como están las cosas; ***my offer still ~s*** mi oferta todavía está en pie; ***it ~s at 5%*** asciende al 5%
4 *for election etc* presentarse
III *v/t* (*pret & pp* ***stood***) **1** (*put*) colocar **2** (*tolerate*) aguantar, soportar **3**: ***you don't ~ a chance*** no tienes ninguna posibilidad; ***~ one's ground*** mantenerse firme; ***~ s.o. a drink*** F invitar a alguien a tomar algo F
◆ **stand around** *v/i*: ***just standing around on the corner*** rondando por la esquina
◆ **stand back** *v/i* echarse atrás
◆ **stand by I** *v/i* **1** (*not take action*) quedarse sin hacer nada; ***stand idly by*** quedarse de brazos cruzados **2** (*be ready*) estar preparado **II** *v/t person* apoyar; *decision* atenerse a
◆ **stand down** *v/i* (*withdraw*), LAW retirarse
◆ **stand for** *v/t* **1** (*tolerate*) aguantar **2** (*represent*) significar **3**: ***stand for election*** *Br* presentarse como candidato a unas elecciones
◆ **stand in for** *v/t* sustituir
◆ **stand on** *v/t* **1** subirse a; ***stand on one's hands / head*** *L.Am.* pararse de cabeza, *Span* hacer el pino con las manos / la cabeza; ***be able to do sth standing on one's head*** F poder hacer algo con los ojos cerrados F
◆ **stand out** *v/i* destacar
◆ **stand out against** *v/t* **1** (*resist*) oponerse a **2** (*be silhouetted against*) resaltar sobre
◆ **stand over** *v/t* estar encima de
◆ **stand up I** *v/i* **1** levantarse **2** *fig*: *of argument, claim* estimarse **II** *v/t* F plantar F
◆ **stand up for** *v/t* defender; ***stand up for yourself!*** ¡defiéndete!
◆ **stand up to** *v/t* hacer frente a; *use, pressure* aguantar
'stand-a•lone *adj computer, workstation* independiente
stan•dard[1] ['stændərd] **I** *adj* **1** *size etc* estándar; ***it is ~ for applicants to …*** por norma los solicitantes deben … **2** (*usual*) habitual
II *n* (*level of excellence*) nivel *m*; TECH estándar *m*; ***be up to ~*** cumplir el nivel exigido; ***not be up to ~*** estar por debajo del nivel exigido; ***my parents set very high ~s*** mis padres exigen mucho; ***by present-day ~s*** según los criterios de hoy en día
stan•dard[2] ['stændərd] *n flag* estandarte *m*
stan•dard de•vi'a•tion desviación *f* típica
stan•dard•i•za•tion [stændərdaɪ'zeɪʃn] estandarización *f*
stan•dard•ize ['stændərdaɪz] *v/t* normalizar
◆ **standardize on** *v/t* estandarizar
'stan•dard lamp *Br* lámpara *f* de pie
stan•dard of 'liv•ing nivel *m* de vida
'stand•by I *n* **1** AVIA *ticket* billete *m* stand-by; ***be on ~*** estar en stand-by *or* en lista de espera **2**: ***be on ~*** *to deal with crisis* estar en alerta **3**: ***canned tomatoes are a useful ~*** los tomates en lata son un recurso muy socorrido **II** *adv fly* con un billete stand-by
'stand•by pas•sen•ger pasajero(-a) *m(f)* en stand-by *or* en lista de espera
'stand-in sustituto(-a) *m(f)*
stand•ing ['stændɪŋ] *in society etc* posición *f*; (*repute*) reputación *f*; ***a musician / politician of some ~*** un reputado músico / político; ***a relationship of long ~*** una relación establecida hace mucho tiempo
'stand•ing com•mit•tee comisión *f* permanente; **stand•ing 'or•der** *Br* FIN orden *f* de pago; **'stand•ing room**: ***~ only*** no quedan asientos
'stan•dings *npl* SP tabla *f* de clasificación, clasificación *f*
'stand•off punto *m* muerto
stand•off•ish [stænd'ɑːfɪʃ] *adj* distante
'stand•point punto *m* de vista; **'stand•still**: ***be at a ~*** estar paralizado; ***bring to a ~*** paralizar; **stand-up 'com•ic** cómico(-a) *m(f)*; **stand-up 'fight** pelea *f* en toda regla
stank [stæŋk] *pret* → ***stink***
stan•za ['stænzə] estrofa *f*
sta•ple[1] ['steɪpl] *n foodstuff* alimento *m* básico
sta•ple[2] ['steɪpl] **I** *n fastener* grapa *f* **II** *v/t* grapar
sta•ple 'di•et dieta *f* básica
'sta•ple gun grapadora *f* industrial
sta•pler ['steɪplər] grapadora *f*

star [stɑːr] **I** *n also person* estrella *f*; ***see ~s*** ver las estrellas; ***thank one's lucky ~s*** F dar las gracias a la providencia; ***the ~ of the show*** la estrella del espectáculo
II *adj player etc* estrella
III *v/t* (*pret & pp* ***-red***) *of movie* estar protagonizado por
IV *v/i* (*pret & pp* ***-red***) *in movie*: ***Tom Hanks ~red in …*** Tom Hanks protagonizó …

'star•board *adj* de estribor

starch [stɑːrʧ] *in foodstuff* fécula *f*

starch•y ['stɑːrʧɪ] *adj* **1** *foodstuff* feculento **2** *fig* F rígido, recto

star•dom ['stɑːrdəm] estrellato *m*

stare [ster] **I** *n* mirada *f* fija **II** *v/i* mirar fijamente; ***~ at*** mirar fijamente **II** *v/t*: ***it's staring you in the face!*** *fig*: *object* ¡lo tienes justo delante!; *situation* ¡está más claro que el agua!

'star•fish estrella *f* de mar

stark [stɑːrk] **I** *adj landscape* desolado; *reminder, picture etc* desolador; ***in ~ contrast to*** en marcado contraste con **II** *adv*: ***~ naked*** completamente desnudo; ***be ~ staring*** *or* ***raving mad*** estar como una cabra F

star•let ['stɑːrlət] *pej* actriz *f* de cine principiante

'star•light luz *f* de las estrellas

star•ling ['stɑːrlɪŋ] estornino *m*

'star•lit *adj* iluminado por las estrellas

star•ry ['stɑːrɪ] *adj night* estrellado

star•ry-eyed [stɑːrɪ'aɪd]] *adj person* cándido, ingenuo

Stars and 'Stripes *la bandera estadounidense*; **'star•sign** signo *m* del zodiaco; **Star-Span•gled Ban•ner** [stɑːr-spæŋgld'bænər] **1** *song* himno *m* nacional estadounidense **2** *flag* bandera *f* estadounidense

start[1] [stɑːrt] **I** *n* (*beginning*) comienzo *m*, principio *m*; *of race* salida *f*; ***get off to a good / bad ~*** empezar bien / mal; ***well, it's a ~!*** bueno, ¡algo es algo!; ***it's a good ~*** es un buen comienzo; ***at the ~*** al principio; *of race* a la salida; ***for a ~*** para empezar; ***from the ~*** desde el principio; ***from ~ to finish*** de principio a fin; ***we want to make an early ~*** queremos salir temprano *or* pronto; ***make a fresh ~*** (***in life***) empezar desde cero; ***make a ~ on sth*** emprender algo
II *v/i* empezar, comenzar; *of engine, car* arrancar; ***if you ~ from city hall and head …*** si sales del ayuntamiento y te diriges a …; ***~ing from tomorrow*** a partir de mañana; ***don't you ~!*** ¡no empieces!; ***to ~ with*** (*for a start*) en primer lugar; (*in the beginning*) al principio; ***~ back for home*** volver para casa
III *v/t* empezar, comenzar; *engine, car* arrancar; *business* montar; ***~ to do sth, ~doing sth*** empezar *or* comenzar a hacer algo; ***he ~ed to cry, he ~ed crying*** se puso a llorar
◆ **start in on** *v/t* meterse con F
◆ **start off I** *v/i* **1** empezar, comenzar **2** *on journey* salir (***for*** hacia) **II** *v/t* **1** *proceedings* empezar, iniciar **2**: ***don't start him off again!*** ¡no le des cuerda otra vez!
◆ **start out** *v/i* partir, salir
◆ **start up I** *v/t engine, machine* arrancar; *business* montar, abrir **II** *v/i of storm* empezar, comenzar; *of business* poner en marcha, montar

start[2] [stɑːrt] *n of fright, surprise* sobresalto *m*; ***wake up with a ~*** despertarse dando un bote

start•er ['stɑːrtər] **1** *part of meal* entrada *f*, entrante *m*; ***and that's just for ~s*** F y eso es sólo para empezar **2** *of car* motor *m* de arranque **3** *of race* juez *m/f* de salida

start•ing blocks ['stɑːrtɪŋblɑːks] *npl* SP tacos *mpl* de salida; **'start•ing gate** parrilla *f* de salida; **'start•ing line** línea *f* de salida; **'start•ing point** punto *m* de partida; **'start•ing sal•a•ry** sueldo *m* inicial

start•le ['stɑːrtl] *v/t* sobresaltar

start•ling ['stɑːrtlɪŋ] *adj* sorprendente, asombroso

'start-up cap•i•tal capital *m* inicial

'start-up costs *npl of company* costes *mpl or Span* costos *mpl* de puesta en marcha

star•va•tion [stɑːr'veɪʃn] inanición *f*, hambre *f*; ***die of ~*** morir de inanición; ***~ diet*** dieta *f* deficiente y escasa; ***~ wage*** sueldo *m* ínfimo

starve [stɑːrv] **I** *v/i* pasar hambre; ***~ to death*** morir de inanición *or* hambre; ***I'm starving*** F me muero de hambre F **II** *v/t* hacer pasar hambre; ***~ s.o. to death*** hacer morir de hambre a al-

guien; ***she ~d herself to death*** se mataba de hambre; ***be ~d of*** *fig* estar necesitado de; ***~ the enemy into surrender*** hacer pasar hambre al enemigo hasta que se rinda
'Star Wars MIL F la Guerra *f* de las Galaxias
stash [stæʃ] **I** *n* reserva *f* secreta **II** *v/t* ocultar, esconder
◆ **stash away** *v/t* ☞ ***stash***
state[1] [steɪt] **I** *n* (*condition, country*) estado *m*; ***the States*** (los) Estados Unidos; ***~ of affairs*** situación *f*, coyuntura *f*; ***~ of mind*** estado *m* de ánimo; ***be in a ~ of war with ...*** estar en guerra abierta con ...; ***get in(to) a ~*** F perder los estribos; ***turn ~'s evidence*** testificar en contra de los otros reos **II** *adj capital etc* estatal, del estado; *banquet etc* de estado
state[2] [steɪt] *v/t* declarar; ***on the ~d date*** en la fecha establecida
'State De•part•ment Departamento *m* de Estado, *Ministerio de Asuntos Exteriores*
state•less ['steɪtlɪs] *adj* POL sin patria
state•ly ['steɪtlɪ] *adj* armonioso, elegante; ***~ home*** *Br* palacio *m*, mansión *f*
state•ment ['steɪtmənt] **1** declaración *f*; ***make a ~*** hacer una declaración (***to*** ante) **2** (*bank ~*) extracto *m*
state•ment of ac'count extracto *m* de cuenta
Stat•en Is•land [stætn'aɪlənd] la Isla Staten
state of e'mer•gen•cy estado *m* de emergencia; **state-of-'play re•port** informe *m* de la situación; **state-of--the-'art** *adj* modernísimo; **state-of--the-art tech'no•lo•gy** tecnología *f* punta; **State of the 'Un•ion Mes•sage** discurso *m* al Congreso sobre el estado de la nación; **'state•side** *adv* F *go, travel* a Estados Unidos
states•man ['steɪtsmən] hombre *m* de estado
states•man•like ['steɪtsmənlaɪk] *adj* de hombre de estado
state 'troop•er policía *m/f* estatal
state 'vis•it visita *f* de estado
stat•ic ['stætɪk] **I** *adj* **1** PHYS estático **2** *fig*: *image* fijo; *amount* invariable **II** *n* **1** ELEC electricidad *f* estática **2**: ***take a lot of ~ about sth*** F recibir duras críticas por algo F
stat•ic e•lec'tric•i•ty electricidad *f* estática
sta•tion ['steɪʃn] **I** *n* **1** RAIL estación *f* **2** RAD emisora *f*; TV canal *m* **II** *v/t guard etc* apostar; ***be ~ed in*** *of soldier* estar destinado en
sta•tion•a•ry ['steɪʃnerɪ] *adj* parado
sta•tion•er ['steɪʃənər] papelería *f*
sta•tion•er•y ['steɪʃənerɪ] artículos *mpl* de papelería
'sta•tion house *for policemen* comisaría *f* de policía; *for firefighters* parque *m* de bomberos; **sta•tion 'man•ag•er, 'sta•tion mas•ter** RAIL jefe *m* de estación; **'sta•tion wag•on** ranchera *f*
sta•tis•tic [stə'tɪstɪk]: ***we're just another ~ to them*** para ellos sólo somos otro número más
sta•tis•ti•cal [stə'tɪstɪkl] *adj* estadístico
sta•tis•ti•cal•ly [stə'tɪstɪklɪ] *adv* estadísticamente
sta•tis•ti•cian [stætɪs'tɪʃn] estadístico(-a) *m(f)*
sta•tis•tics [stə'tɪstɪks] **1** *nsg science* estadística *f* **2** *npl*: *figures* estadísticas *fpl*
stat•ue ['stætʃuː] estatua *f*
Stat•ue of 'Lib•er•ty Estatua *f* de la Libertad
stat•ure ['stætʃər] **1** *physical* estatura *f* **2** *fig* prestigio *m*, mérito *m*
sta•tus ['steɪtəs] categoría *f*, posición *f*; ***women want equal ~ with men*** las mujeres quieren igualdad con los hombres
'sta•tus bar COMPUT barra *f* de estado; **sta•tus quo** [steɪtəs'kwoʊ] statu quo *m*; **'sta•tus re•port** informe *m* de la situación; **'sta•tus sym•bol** símbolo *m* de estatus
stat•ute ['stætuːt] estatuto *m*; ***~ of limitations*** ley *f* de prescripción
'stat•ute book código *m* fundamental
stat•u•to•ry ['stætjʊtɔːrɪ] *adj* **1** (*fixed by statute*) establecido por la ley, estatutario **2** *offense* normalizado
stat•u•to•ry re'serves reservas *fpl* estatutarias
stat•u•to•ry 'rights *npl* derechos *mpl* estatutarios
staunch [stɒːntʃ] *adj supporter* incondicional; *friend* fiel
◆ **stave off** [steɪv] *v/t* evitar, esquivar
stay [steɪ] **I** *n* estancia *f*, *L.Am.* estadía *f*; ***~ in the hospital*** estancia en el hospi-

tal; ***he was given*** *or* ***granted a ~ of execution*** se suspendió su ejecución
II *v/i in a place* quedarse; *in a condition* permanecer; **~ *in a hotel*** alojarse en un hotel; **~ *right there!*** ¡quédate ahí!; **~ *put*** no moverse; **~ *for*** *or* ***to lunch*** quedarse a comer; **~ *home*** (*not go out*) quedarse en casa; *of wife*, *mother* dedicarse a sus labores
III *v/t*: **~ *the course*** SP, *fig* aguantar hasta el final
◆ **stay away** *v/i*: ***tell the children to stay away*** diles a los niños que no se acerquen
◆ **stay away from** *v/t* no acercarse a
◆ **stay behind** *v/i* quedarse
◆ **stay down** *v/i in school* repetir (curso)
◆ **stay in** *v/i at home* quedarse en casa
◆ **stay on** *v/i*: ***stay on as chairman*** seguir de presidente; ***stay on for another year*** *at school* quedarse un año más
◆ **stay out** *v/i at night* salir
◆ **stay out of** *v/t argument etc* mantenerse al margen de; ***you stay out of this!*** ¡no te metas en esto! F, ¡mantente al margen!
◆ **stay up** *v/i* (*not go to bed*) quedarse levantado
'stay-at-home casero, hogareño
stay•ing pow•er ['steɪɪŋ] resistencia *f*
STD [esti:'di:] *abbr* (= ***sexually transmitted disease***) ETS *f* (= enfermedad *f* de transmisión sexual)
stead [sted]: ***in s.o.'s ~*** en lugar de alguien
stead•fast ['stedfæst] *adj* tenaz, perseverante
stead•i•ly ['stedɪlɪ] *adv improve etc* constantemente
stead•y ['stedɪ] **I** *adj* **1** (*not shaking*) firme **2** (*continuous*) continuo; *beat* regular; *boyfriend* estable **II** *adv*: ***they've been going ~ for two years*** llevan saliendo dos años; ***~ on!*** ¡un momento! **III** *v/t* (*pret & pp* ***-ied***) afianzar; *voice* calmar
steak [steɪk] filete *m*
'steak•house asador *m*
'steak knife cuchillo *m* de sierra
steal [sti:l] **I** *v/t* (*pret* ***stole***, *pp* ***stolen***) **1** *money etc* robar; *in basketball* recuperar; ***~ s.o.'s girlfriend*** quitarle la novia a alguien **2**: ***~ a glance at s.o.*** echar una mirada furtiva a alguien **II** *v/i* (*pret* ***stole***, *pp* ***stolen***) **1** (*be a thief*) robar **2**: ***he stole into the bedroom*** entró sigilosamente en la habitación **III** *n in basketball* recuperación *f*
stealth [stelθ] sigilo *m*; ***by ~*** a escondidas
'stealth bomb•er bombardero *m* invisible
stealth•y ['stelθɪ] *adj* sigiloso
steam [sti:m] **I** *n* vapor *m*; ***full ~ ahead!*** NAUT ¡a toda máquina!; ***under one's own ~*** *fig* por sí mismo, por medios propios; ***let off ~*** *fig* desahogarse; *by taking exercise etc* desfogarse; ***run out of ~*** *fig* quedarse sin gas **II** *v/t food* cocinar al vapor; **~ *open*** *letter* abrir con vapor
◆ **steam up** *v/i of window* empañarse
steamed up [sti:md'ʌp] *adj* F (*angry*) enojado, *Span* mosqueado F
'steam en•gine máquina *f* de vapor
steam•er ['sti:mər] *for cooking* olla *f* para cocinar al vapor
'steam i•ron plancha *f* de vapor
'steam roll•er *v/t*: ***~ s.o. into doing sth*** *fig* forzar a alguien a que haga algo; ***~ a bill through*** conseguir que se apruebe un proyecto de ley a la fuerza
'steam ship barco *m* de vapor
steam•y ['sti:mɪ] *adj fig* F tórrido
steel [sti:l] **I** *n* acero *m* **II** *adj* (*made of ~*) de acero **III** *v/t*: ***~ o.s. for*** armarse de coraje para
steel 'band *banda de instrumentos de percusión del Caribe*; **steel 'wool** estropajo *m* de acero; **'steel•work•er** trabajador(a) *m(f)* del acero; **'steel•works** *nsg* acería *f*
steel•y ['sti:lɪ] *adj* **1** *blue*, *gray* acero **2** *look* duro; *refusal*, *determination* acerado, firme
steep[1] [sti:p] *adj* **1** *hill etc* empinado **2** F: *prices* caro
steep[2] [sti:p] *v/t* (*soak*) poner en remojo; ***~ed in history*** rebosante de historia
stee•ple ['sti:pl] torre *f*
'stee•ple•chase *in athletics* carrera *f* de obstáculos
'stee•ple•jack *persona encargada del mantenimiento de torres, chimeneas, etc.*
steep•ly ['sti:plɪ] *adv*: ***climb ~*** *of path* subir pronunciadamente; *of prices* dis-

S

pararse

steer[1] [stɪr] *n animal* buey *m*

steer[2] [stɪr] *v/t car* conducir, *L.Am.* manejar; *boat* gobernar; *person* guiar; *conversation* llevar

steer•age ['stɪrɪdʒ] HIST: ***travel ~*** viajar en tercera clase

steer•ing ['stɪrɪŋ] MOT dirección *f*

'steer•ing col•umn MOT columna *f* de dirección

'steer•ing wheel volante *m*, *S.Am.* timón *m*

stel•lar ['stelər] *adj fig* (*excellent*) estelar, magnífico

stem[1] [stem] *n* **1** *of plant* tallo *m* **2** *of glass* pie *m*; *of pipe* tubo *m* **3** *of word* raíz *f*

◆ **stem from** *v/t* (*pret & pp **-med***) derivarse de

stem[2] [stem] *v/t* (*pret & pp **-med***) (*block*) contener

'stem•ware ['stemwer] cristalería *f*

stench [stentʃ] peste *f*, hedor *m*

sten•cil ['stensɪl] **I** *n* plantilla *f* **II** *v/t* (*pret & pp **-ed**, Br **-led***) *pattern* estarcir

ste•nog•ra•pher [stə'nɑːgrəfər] taquígrafo(-a) *m*(*f*)

step [step] **I** *n* **1** (*pace*), *of dance* paso *m*; ***~ by ~*** paso a paso; ***take a ~*** dar un paso; ***be one ~ ahead of s.o.*** *fig* adelantarse a alguien; ***fight s.o. / sth every ~ of the way*** oponerse a alguien / algo infatigablemente; ***a ~ in the right direction*** un paso adelante; ***watch one's ~*** tener cuidado de dónde se pisa; *fig* andarse con cuidado; ***be in / out of ~*** MIL seguir / no seguir el paso; *of chorus dancer* seguir / no seguir el ritmo; ***be out of ~ with*** *fig* no armonizar con
2 (*stair*) escalón *m*; ***~s*** *Br pl*, ***pair of ~s*** ☞ ***stepladder***
3 (*measure*) medida *f*; ***take ~s to do sth*** tomar medidas para hacer algo
II *v/i* (*pret & pp **-ped***): ***~ on sth*** pisar algo; ***~ into a puddle*** pisar un charco; ***I ~ped back*** di un paso atrás; ***~ forward*** dar un paso adelante; ***~ on it*** MOT F meterle (gas) F

◆ **step aside** *v/i* **1** apartarse **2** *fig* renunciar (***in favor of*** en favor de)

◆ **step down** *v/i from post etc* dimitir

◆ **step forward** *v/i fig*: *of witness etc* ofrecerse voluntario

◆ **step in** *v/i fig* intervenir

◆ **step out** *v/i* (*go out for a short time*) salir un momento

◆ **step up** *v/t* (*increase*) incrementar; ***step up the pace*** acelerar el paso

'step•broth•er hermanastro *m*; **'step•child•ren** *pl* hijastros *mpl*; **'step•daugh•ter** hijastra *f*; **'step•fa•ther** padrastro *m*; **'step•lad•der** escalera *f* de tijera; **'step•moth•er** madrastra *f*

step•ping stone ['stepɪŋ] pasadera *f*, *fig* trampolín *m*

'step•sis•ter hermanastra *f*

'step•son hijastro *m*

ster•e•o ['sterɪoʊ] **I** *n* (*sound system*) equipo *m* de música; ***in ~*** en estéreo **II** *adj* estéreo; ***~ unit*** equipo *m* de música

ster•e•o•type ['sterɪoʊtaɪp] estereotipo *m*

ster•e•o•typed ['sterɪoʊtaɪpt], **ster•e•o•typ•i•cal** [sterɪoʊ'tɪpɪkl] *adj* estereotipado

ster•ile ['sterəl] *adj* estéril

ste•ril•i•ty [stə'rɪlətɪ] esterilidad *f*

ster•i•li•za•tion [sterəlaɪ'zeɪʃn] MED esterilización *f*

ster•i•lize ['sterəlaɪz] *v/t woman*, *equipment* esterilizar

ster•ling ['stɜːrlɪŋ] **I** *n* FIN libra *f* esterlina **II** *adj* formidable

ster•ling 'sil•ver plata *f* de ley

stern[1] [stɜːrn] *adj* severo

stern[2] [stɜːrn] *n* NAUT popa *f*

stern•ly ['stɜːrnlɪ] *adv* con severidad

ster•num ['stɜːrnəm] ANAT esternón *m*

ster•oids ['sterɔɪdz] *npl* esteroides *mpl*

steth•o•scope ['steθəskoʊp] fonendoscopio *m*, estetoscopio *m*

Stet•son® ['stetsn] sombrero *m* de vaquero

ste•ve•dore ['stiːvədɔːr] estibador *m*

stew [stuː] **I** *n* guiso *m* **II** *v/t meat* guisar; *fruit* confitar **III** *v/i of meat* guisar; *of fruit* confitar; ***let s.o. ~ in their own juice*** dejar que alguien se saque las castañas del fuego

stew•ard ['stuːərd] *on plane* auxiliar *m* de vuelo; *on ship* camarero *m*; *at demonstration*, *meeting* miembro *m* de la organización

stew•ard•ess [stuːər'des] *on plane* auxiliar *f* de vuelo; *on ship* camarera *f*

stew•ard•ship ['stuːərdʃɪp] intendencia *f*, gobierno *m*

stewed [stuːd] *adj apples, plums* en compota

stick[1] [stɪk] *n* **1** palo *m*; *of policeman* porra *f*; (*walking* ~) bastón *m*; ***get hold of the wrong end of the ~*** F entender al revés **2** *of celery, rhubarb* tallo *m*; *of dynamite* cartucho *m*; ***~ of butter*** *barra de mantequilla de dos onzas de peso*; ***~ of furniture*** F trasto *m* F **3**: ***live out in the ~s*** F vivir en el quinto pino F, vivir en el campo

stick[2] [stɪk] **I** *v/t* (*pret & pp* **stuck**) **1** *with adhesive* pegar **2** F (*put*) meter **II** *v/i* (*pret & pp* **stuck**) **1** (*jam*) atascarse **2** (*adhere*) pegarse; ***~ in s.o.'s mind*** *fig* quedarse grabado en la memoria de alguien

◆ **stick at** *v/t* **1**: ***stick at nothing*** hacer cualquier cosa **2** (*persevere*): ***stick at sth*** persistir en algo

◆ **stick around** *v/i* F quedarse

◆ **stick by** *v/t* F apoyar, no abandonar

◆ **stick out** *v/i* (*protrude*) sobresalir; (*be noticeable*) destacar; ***his ears stick out*** tiene las orejas salidas **II** *v/t* **1**: ***stick one's tongue out*** sacar la lengua (***at*** a); ***stick one's head out of the window*** sacar la cabeza por la ventana **2**: ***stick sth out*** *until the end* aguantar *or* sobrellevar algo

◆ **stick out for** *v/t* insistir en

◆ **stick to** *v/t* **1** *of sth sticky* pegarse a **2** F *plan etc* seguir; (*trail, follow*) pegarse a F

◆ **stick together** *v/i* mantenerse unidos; *when lost* seguir juntos

◆ **stick up** *v/t poster, leaflet* pegar; ***stick 'em up!*** F ¡manos arriba! F

◆ **stick up for** *v/t* F defender

◆ **stick with** *v/t* F quedarse *or* seguir con

stick•er ['stɪkər] *label* pegatina *f*

'stick•er price precio *m* de venta recomendado

stick•ing plas•ter ['stɪkɪŋ] *Span* tirita *f*, *L.Am.* curita *f*

'stick•ing point *fig* inconveniente *m*, traba *f*

'stick-in-the-mud F aburrido(-a) *m(f)* F, soso(-a) *m(f)*

stick•ler ['stɪklər]: ***be a ~ for*** estar obsesionado con

'stick-on *adj*: ***~ label*** etiqueta *f* adhesiva; **'stick•pin** *for man* pisacorbatas *m* *inv*; *for woman* prendedor *m*; **'stick shift** MOT palanca *f* de cambios

stick-to-it-ness [stɪk'tuːɪtnɪs] F persistencia *f*, empeño *m*

'stick•up F atraco *m* a mano armada

stick•y ['stɪkɪ] *adj hands, surface, weather* pegajoso; *label* adhesivo; ***have ~ fingers*** F tener las manos largas F; ***he'll come to a ~ end*** acabará mal

stiff [stɪf] **I** *adj* **1** *cardboard, manner* rígido; *brush* duro; *muscle, body* agarrotado; *mixture, paste* consistente; ***beat until ~*** batir a punto de nieve; ***have a ~ neck*** tener tortícolis **2** *competition, penalty* duro **3** *drink* cargado

II *adv*: ***be scared ~*** F estar muerto de miedo F; ***be bored ~*** F aburrirse como una ostra F; ***be frozen ~*** F estar helado **III** *n* P *corpse* fiambre *m* P; ***a working ~*** F un(a) trabajador(a)

IV *v/t* P tomar el pelo a F

stiff•en ['stɪfn] *v/i of person* agarrotarse

◆ **stiffen up** *v/i of muscle* agarrotarse

stiff•ly ['stɪflɪ] *adv* con rigidez; *fig* forzadamente

stiff•ness ['stɪfnəs] *of muscles* agarrotamiento *m*; *fig*: *of manner* rigidez *f*

sti•fle ['staɪfl] *v/t yawn, laugh* reprimir, contener; *criticism, debate* reprimir

sti•fling ['staɪflɪŋ] *adj* sofocante; ***it's ~ in here*** hace un calor sofocante aquí dentro

stig•ma ['stɪgmə] estigma *m*

stig•ma•ta [stɪg'mɑːtə] REL estigmas *mpl*

stig•ma•tize ['stɪgmətaɪz] *v/t fig*: ***they were ~d as …*** los tacharon *or* tildaron de …

sti•let•to heel [stɪletoʊ'hiːl] *Br* tacón *m* de aguja

sti•let•tos [stɪ'letoʊz] *npl Br shoes* zapatos *mpl* de tacón de aguja

still[1] [stɪl] **I** *adj* (*not moving*) quieto; *with no wind* sin viento; ***it was very ~*** *no wind* no soplaba nada de viento **II** *adv*: ***keep ~!*** ¡estáte quieto!; ***stand ~!*** ¡no te muevas!

still[2] [stɪl] *adv* **1** (*yet*) todavía, aún; ***do you ~ want it?*** ¿todavía *or* aún lo quieres?; ***she ~ hasn't finished*** todavía *or* aún no ha acabado; ***I ~ don't understand*** sigo sin entenderlo; ***she might ~ come*** puede que aún venga; ***~ more*** (*even more*) todavía más **2** (*neverthe-*

less) de todas formas; ***they are ~ my parents*** siguen siendo mis padres

still[3] [stɪl] *n* CHEM alambique *m*

'still•birth *nacimiento de un bebé muerto*; **'still•born** *adj*: ***be ~*** nacer muerto; **still 'life** naturaleza *f* muerta, bodegón *m*

stilt•ed ['stɪltɪd] *adj* forzado

stilts [stɪlts] *npl* **1** zancos *mpl* **2** ARCHI pilotes *mpl*

stim•u•lant ['stɪmjʊlənt] estimulante *m*

stim•u•late ['stɪmjʊleɪt] *v/t person* estimular; *growth*, *demand* estimular, provocar

stim•u•lat•ing ['stɪmjʊleɪtɪŋ] *adj* estimulante

stim•u•la•tion [stɪmjʊ'leɪʃn] estimulación *f*

stim•u•lus ['stɪmjʊləs] (*pl* ***stimuli*** ['stɪmjʊlaɪ], ***-uses***) (*incentive*) estímulo *m*

sting [stɪŋ] **I** *n from bee*, *jellyfish* picadura *f*; ***take the ~ out of sth*** *fig* quitar hierro a algo; ***have a ~ in the tail*** tener un final insospechado **II** *v/t* (*pret & pp* ***stung***) **1** *of bee*, *jellyfish* picar **2**: ***they stung me for $95*** F me clavaron *or* sangraron 95 dólares F **III** *v/i* (*pret & pp* ***stung***) *of eyes*, *scratch* escocer

sting•ing ['stɪŋɪŋ] *adj remark*, *criticism* punzante

sting•y ['stɪndʒɪ] *adj* F agarrado F, rácano F; ***be ~ with sth*** racanear con algo

stink [stɪŋk] **I** *n* **1** (*bad smell*) peste *f*, hedor *m*; ***there's a ~ of garlic in here*** aquí apesta a ajo **2** F (*fuss*) escándalo F; ***make a ~*** F armar un escándalo F **II** *v/i* (*pret* ***stank***, *pp* ***stunk***) **1** (*smell bad*) apestar; ***~ to high heaven*** oler a rayos **2** F (*be very bad*) dar asco

◆ **stink up** *v/t* F *room* apestar

stink•ing ['stɪŋkɪŋ] **I** *adj* F espantoso, apestoso F **II** *adv*: ***~ rich*** F asquerosamente rico F

stint [stɪnt] temporada *f*; ***do a ~ in the army*** pasar una temporada en el ejército

◆ **stint on** *v/t* F racanear F

stip•u•late ['stɪpjʊleɪt] *v/t* estipular

stip•u•la•tion [stɪpjʊ'leɪʃn] estipulación *f*

stir [stɜːr] **I** *n*: ***give the soup a ~*** darle vueltas a la sopa; ***cause a ~*** causar revuelo **II** *v/t* (*pret & pp* ***-red***) remover, dar vueltas a **III** *v/i* (*pret & pp* ***-red***) *of sleeping person* moverse; ***don't ~ from this spot*** no te muevas de aquí

◆ **stir up** *v/t* **1** *crowd* agitar **2** *bad memories* traer a la memoria

stir-'cra•zy *adj* F majareta F

'stir-fry *v/t* (*pret & pp* ***-ied***) freír rápidamente y dando vueltas

stir•ring ['stɜːrɪŋ] *adj music*, *speech* conmovedor

stir•rup ['stɪrəp] estribo *m*

stitch [stɪʧ] **I** *n* **1** *in sewing* puntada *f*; *in knitting* punto *m*; ***~es*** MED puntos *mpl*; ***be in ~es*** *laughing* partirse de risa; ***he had his ~es out*** le quitaron los puntos; ***drop a ~*** perder un punto; ***he hadn't got a ~ on*** F iba en cueros F **2** *in the side*: ***have a ~*** tener flato **II** *v/t sew* coser

◆ **stitch up** *v/t wound* coser, suturar

stitch•ing ['stɪʧɪŋ] (*stitches*) cosido *m*

stock [stɑːk] **I** *n* **1** (*reserves*) reservas *fpl*; COM *of store* existencias *fpl*; *animals* ganado *m*; ***in ~*** en existencias; ***out of ~*** agotado; ***have sth in ~*** tener algo en existencias; ***take ~*** hacer balance **2** FIN acciones *fpl* **3** *for soup etc* caldo *m* **II** *v/t* COM (*have*) tener en existencias; (*sell*) vender; ***be well ~ed with*** *fish*, *game* estar lleno de; *goods*, *preserves* estar bien provisto de

◆ **stock up on** *v/t* aprovisionarse de

'stock•breed•er ganadero(-a) *m*(*f*); **'stock•breed•ing** ganadería *f*; **'stock•brok•er** corredor(a) *m*(*f*) de bolsa; **'stock car** *coche reforzado para carreras de choque*; **'stock cer•tif•i•cate** COM título *m* de acciones; **'stock com•pa•ny** COM sociedad *f* anónima; **'stock con•trol** control *m* de inventario; **'stock cube** *Br* pastilla *f* de caldo concentrado; **'stock ex•change** bolsa *f* (de valores); **'stock•hold•er** accionista *m/f*

stock•ing ['stɑːkɪŋ] media *f*

'stock•ing cap gorro *m* con pompón

'stock•ing mask media *f* de ladrón

stock in 'trade: ***be part of s.o.'s ~*** *fig* ser típico de alguien

stock•ist ['stɑːkɪst] distribuidor(a) *m*(*f*)

'stock mar•ket mercado *m* de valores; **'stock•mar•ket crash** crack *m* bursátil; **'stock•mar•ket trans•ac•tion** opera-

ción *f* bursátil; **stock•mar•ket 'val•ue** valor *m* en bolsa; **stock out•age** ['stɑːkaʊtɪdʒ] agotamiento *m* de existencias; **'stock•pile I** *n of food, weapons* reservas *fpl* **II** *v/t* acumular; **'stock-room** almacén *m*; **'stock shrink•age** pérdida *f* de existencias; **stock-'still** *adv*: ***stand ~*** quedarse inmóvil; **stock-tak•ing** ['stɑːkteɪkɪŋ] inventario *m*
'stock•y ['stɑːkɪ] *adj* bajo y robusto
stodg•y ['stɑːdʒɪ] *adj food* pesado
sto•i•cal ['stoʊɪkl] *adj* estoico
sto•i•cism ['stoʊɪsɪzm] estoicismo *m*
stoke [stoʊk] *v/t* ☞ ***stoke up***
◆ **stoke up** *v/t fire* avivar; *fig* encender, estimular
stole[1] [stoʊl] *pret* ☞ ***steal***
stole[2] [stoʊl] *n* piel *m*
stol•en ['stoʊlən] *pp* ☞ ***steal***
'stol•en base *in baseball* base *f* robada
stol•id ['stɑːlɪd] *adj* apático, desapasionado
stom•ach ['stʌmək] **I** *n* estómago *m*, tripa *f*; ***on an empty ~*** con el estómago vacío; ***turn s.o.'s ~*** revolver el estómago a alguien **II** *v/t* (*tolerate*) soportar
'stom•ach-ache dolor *m* de estómago
◆ **stomp on** [stɑːmp] *v/t* pisotear
◆ **stomp off** *v/t* F salir violentamente
stone [stoʊn] **I** *n* **1** piedra *f*; ***it's only a ~'s throw (away) from ...*** está a tiro de piedra de ...; ***have a heart of ~*** no tener corazón; ***leave no ~ unturned*** *fig* remover el cielo y la tierra; ***throw ~s at*** apedrear **2** *Br unidad de peso* (= *6,35kg*) **II** *v/t*: ***~ (to death)*** matar a pedradas
'Stone Age Edad *f* de Piedra; **stone--'broke** F sin blanca F; **stone-'cold I** *adj* helado **II** *adv*: ***~ sober*** F completamente sereno
stoned [stoʊnd] *adj* F (*on drugs*) colocado F
stone-'deaf *adj*: ***be ~*** estar más sordo que una tapia; **'stone•ma•son** picapedrero(-a) *m(f)*, cantero(-a) *m(f)*; **'stone•wall** *v/i* F andarse con evasivas; **'stone•work** estructura *f* de piedra
ston•y ['stoʊnɪ] *adj ground, path* pedregoso
ston•y-'broke *adj Br* F ☞ ***stone-broke***
stood [stuːd] *pret & pp* ☞ ***stand***
stooge [stuːdʒ] F **1** (*of comedian*) *personaje cómico del que los otros se ríen en el escenario* **2** *pej* (*underling*) monigote *m/f*
stool [stuːl] *seat* taburete *m*
stool•ie [stuːlɪ] F, **'stool pi•geon** F soplón(-ona) *m(f)* F
stoop[1] [stuːp] **I** *n*: ***have a ~*** estar encorvado **II** *v/i* (*bend down*) agacharse
◆ **stoop down** *v/i* ☞ ***stoop***
◆ **stoop to** *v/t fig* rebajarse *or* degradarse a; ***stoop to doing sth*** rebajarse a hacer algo
stoop[2] [stuːp] *n* (*porch*) porche *m*
stop [stɑːp] **I** *n* **1** *for train, bus* parada *f*; ***come to a ~*** detenerse; ***put a ~ to*** poner fin a **2** *on organ* registro *m*; ***pull out all the ~s*** *fig* tocar todos los registros **3** *in soccer* parada *f*
II *v/t* (*pret & pp* ***-ped***) (*put an end to*) poner fin a; (*prevent*) impedir; (*cease*) parar; *person in street* parar; *car, bus, train, etc*: *of driver* detener; *check* bloquear; ***~ doing sth*** dejar de hacer algo; ***it has ~ped raining*** ha parado *or* dejado de llover; ***I ~ped her from leaving*** impedí que se fuera
III *v/i* (*pret & pp* ***-ped***) (*come to a halt*) pararse, detenerse; *in a particular place*: *of bus, train* parar; ***~ at nothing*** hacer cualquier cosa (***to do sth*** por hacer algo)
◆ **stop by** *v/i* (*visit*) pasarse
◆ **stop off** *v/i* hacer una parada
◆ **stop over** *v/i* hacer escala
◆ **stop up** *v/t sink* atascar
'stop•cock TECH llave *f* de paso; **'stop-gap** solución *f* intermedia; **'stop•light** (*traffic light*) semáforo *m*; (*brake light*) luz *f* de freno; **'stop•o•ver** parada *f*; *in air travel* escala *f*
stop•page ['stɑːpɪdʒ] **1** (*strike*) paro *m* **2** TECH (*blockage*) obstrucción *f*
stop•per ['stɑːpər] *for bath, bottle* tapón *m*
stop•ping ['stɑːpɪŋ]: ***no ~*** *sign* prohibido estacionar
'stop sign (señal *f* de) stop *m*
'stop•watch cronómetro *m*
stor•age ['stɔːrɪdʒ] almacenamiento *m*; ***put sth in ~*** almacenar algo; ***be in ~*** estar almacenado
'stor•age ca•pac•i•ty COMPUT capacidad *f* de almacenamiento; **'stor•age heat•er** estufa *f* de acumulación; **'stor•age space** espacio *m* para guar-

dar cosas

store [stɔːr] **I** *n* **1** tienda *f* **2** (*stock*) reserva *f*; ***there was a shock in ~ for us*** nos esperaba una buena sorpresa; ***have a surprise in ~ for s.o.*** tener preparada una sorpresa a alguien **3** (*~house*) almacén *m* **4**: ***set great ~ by*** *fig* dar valor a **II** *v/t* almacenar; COMPUT guardar

◆ **store up** *v/t* acumular

'store•card tarjeta *f* de compra; **'store de•tec•tive** vigilante *m/f* de seguridad; **'store•front** fachada *f* de tienda; **'store•house** almacén *m*; **'store-keep•er** tendero(-a) *m(f)*; **'store•room** almacén *m*; **store 'win•dow** escaparate *m*, *L.Am.* vidriera *f*, *Mex* aparador *m*

sto•rey *Br* ☞ ***story***[2]

stork [stɔːrk] cigüeña *f*

storm [stɔːrm] **I** *n* **1** tormenta *f*; ***a ~ of protest*** un aluvión de quejas; ***a ~ in a teapot*** *or Br* ***a teacup*** *fig* una tempestad en un vaso de agua **2**: ***take by ~*** MIL asaltar; *fig* conquistar **II** *v/t* MIL tomar **III** *v/i* **1** *speak* bramar **2**: ***~ into / out of a room*** entrar / salir violentamente de una habitación

'storm cloud nubarrón *m*; ***the ~s are gathering*** *fig* se está preparando una tormenta; **'storm drain** canal *m* de desagüe; **'storm warn•ing** aviso *m* de tormenta; **'storm win•dow** contraventana *f*

storm•y ['stɔːrmɪ] *adj weather*, *relationship* tormentoso

sto•ry[1] ['stɔːrɪ] (*tale*) cuento *m*; (*account*) historia *f*; (*newspaper article*) artículo *m*; F (*lie*) cuento *m*; ***it's the same old ~*** es la historia de siempre; ***to cut a long ~ short*** en resumidas cuentas; ***tell s.o. a ~*** contar un cuento / una historia a alguien; ***it's a long ~*** es una larga historia; ***a hard-luck ~*** una tragedia

sto•ry[2] ['stɔːrɪ] *of building* piso *m*, planta *f*; ***a six-~ building*** un edificio de seis pisos

'sto•ry book I *n* libro *m* de cuentos **II** *adj* de cuento de hadas

'sto•ry line argumento *m*

stout [staʊt] *adj person* relleno, corpulento; *boots* resistente; *defender* valiente

stove [stoʊv] *for cooking* cocina *f*, *Col*, *Mex*, *Ven* estufa *f*; *for heating* estufa *f*

stow [stoʊ] *v/t* guardar

◆ **stow away** *v/i* viajar de polizón

'stow•a•way polizón *m/f*

strad•dle ['strædl] *v/t river*, *wall* cruzar, extenderse por; *chair* sentarse a horcajadas en; *fig* abarcar

strag•gle ['strægl] *v/i*: ***~ in*** llegar poco a poco

strag•gler ['stræglər] rezagado(-a) *m(f)*

strag•gly ['stræglɪ] *adj hair* despeinado

straight [streɪt] **I** *adj* **1** *line*, *back* recto; *hair* liso; ***keep a ~ face*** contener la risa; ***let's get this ~*** a ver si nos aclaramos; ***set*** *or* ***put s.o. ~ about sth*** *fig* dejar algo claro a alguien
2 (*honest*, *direct*) franco
3 *whiskey* solo
4 (*tidy*) en orden
5 (*conservative*) serio
6 (*not homosexual*) heterosexual
7: ***be a ~ A student*** sacar sobresaliente en todas las asignaturas; ***win / lose in ~ sets*** *tennis* ganar / perder los dos / tres sets seguidos; ***his third ~ win*** su tercera victoria consecutiva
II *adv* **1** (*in a straight line*) recto; ***stand up ~!*** ¡ponte recto!; ***go ~*** F *of criminal* reformarse; ***give it to me ~*** F dímelo sin rodeos; ***~ ahead*** *be situated* todo derecho; *walk*, *drive* todo recto; *look* hacia delante; ***carry ~ on*** *of driver etc* seguir recto
2 (*directly*, *immediately*) directamente; ***look s.o. ~ in the eye*** mirar a los ojos de alguien; ***~ away*** *or* ***off*** en seguida; ***~ out*** directamente
3 (*clearly*) con claridad
4: ***~ up*** *without ice* solo
III *n* **1** SP recta *f* **2**: ***keep to the ~ and narrow*** ir por el buen camino

straight•en ['streɪtn] *v/t* enderezar; *hair* alisar

◆ **straighten out I** *v/t situation* resolver; F *person* poner por el buen camino **II** *v/i of road* hacerse recto

◆ **straighten up** *v/i* ponerse derecho

straight'for•ward *adj* **1** (*honest*, *direct*) franco **2** (*simple*) simple

'straight•line de•pre•ci•a•tion FIN amortización *f* constante

'straight man *personaje del que el cómico principal se burla*

strain[1] [streɪn] **I** *n on rope* tensión *f*; *on engine*, *heart* esfuerzo *m*; *on person* agobio *m*; ***take the ~*** *on rope* aguantar el peso; ***put a great ~ on s.o.*** someter a alguien a gran estrés emocional; ***be under a lot of ~*** soportar mucha tensión **II** *v/t fig*: *finances*, *budget* crear presión en; ***~ one's back*** hacerse daño en la espalda; ***~ one's eyes*** forzar la vista; ***~ one's ears*** aguzar las orejas; ***~ a muscle*** distenderse un músculo

◆ **strain at** *v/t*: ***strain at the leash to do sth*** *fig* no ver la hora de hacer algo

strain[2] [streɪn] *v/t vegetables* escurrir; *oil*, *fat etc* colar

strain[3] [streɪn] *n of virus* cepa *f*

strained [streɪnd] *adj relations* tirante; ***look ~*** parecer tenso *or* estresado

strain•er ['streɪnər] *for vegetables etc* colador *m*

strait [streɪt] GEOG estrecho *m*; ***be in dire ~s*** *fig*: *financially* andar apurado

'strait•jack•et camisa *f* de fuerza

strait•laced [streɪt'leɪst] *adj* mojigato

strand[1] [strænd] *n of wool*, *thread* hebra *f*; ***a ~ of hair*** un pelo

strand[2] [strænd] *v/t* abandonar; ***be ~ed*** quedarse atrapado *or* tirado

strange [streɪndʒ] *adj* **1** (*odd*, *curious*) extraño, raro **2** (*unknown*, *foreign*) extraño

strange•ly ['streɪndʒlɪ] *adv* (*oddly*) de manera extraña; ***~ enough*** aunque parezca extraño

strang•er ['streɪndʒər] **1** (*person you don't know*) extraño(-a) *m*(*f*), desconocido(-a) *m*(*f*) **2**: ***I'm a ~ here myself*** yo tampoco soy de aquí; ***be no ~ to*** *fig* estar hecho a

stran•gle ['stræŋgl] *v/t person* estrangular

'stran•gle•hold agarrón *m* por el cuello; ***have a ~ on sth*** *fig* tener control absoluto sobre algo

stran•gu•la•tion [stræŋgjʊ'leɪʃn] estrangulamiento *m*

strap [stræp] *of purse*, *watch* correa *f*; *of brassiere*, *dress* tirante *m*; *of shoe* tira *f*

◆ **strap in** *v/t* (*pret & pp* **-ped**) poner el cinturón de seguridad a

◆ **strap on** *v/t* ponerse

◆ **strap up** *v/t Br ankle etc* vendar

'strap•hang•er F *usuario del transporte público que permanece de pie*

strap•less ['stræplɪs] *adj* sin tirantes

strapped [stræpt] *adj* F: **~ (*for cash*)** escaso de dinero

stra•ta ['strɑːtə] *pl* ☞ ***stratum***

strat•a•gem ['strætədʒəm] estratagema *f*

stra•te•gic [strə'tiːdʒɪk] *adj* estratégico

strat•e•gist ['strætədʒɪst] estratego(-a) *m*(*f*)

strat•e•gy ['strætədʒɪ] estrategia *f*

strat•i•fied ['strætɪfaɪd] *adj society* estratificado

strat•o•sphere ['strætəsfɪr] METEO estratrosfera *f*

stra•tum ['streɪtəm] (*pl* ***strata*** ['streɪtə]) estrato *m*

straw[1] [strɒː] *material* paja *f*; ***that's the last ~!*** ¡es la gota que colma el vaso!; ***clutch at ~s*** *fig* forjarse ilusiones en vano

straw[2] [strɒː] *for drink* pajita *f*

straw•ber•ry ['strɒːberɪ] *fruit* fresa *f*, *S.Am.* frutilla *f*

'straw•ber•ry mark marca *f* de nacimiento

straw 'hat sombrero *m* de paja; **'straw man** *of little importance* don nadie *m*; **straw 'poll** POL sondeo *m* informal

stray [streɪ] **I** *adj animal* callejero; *bullet* perdido **II** *n dog* perro *m* callejero; *cat* gato *m* callejero **III** *v/i of animal*, *child* extraviarse, perderse; *fig*: *of eyes*, *thoughts* desviarse

streak [striːk] **I** *n of dirt*, *paint* raya *f*; *in hair* mechón *m*; *fig*: *of nastiness etc* vena *f*; ***like a ~ of lightning*** como un rayo; ***be on a winning / losing ~*** estar de buena / mala racha; ***be on a lucky ~*** estar de suerte **II** *v/i move quickly* pasar disparado

streak•er ['striːkər] *persona que corre desnuda en actos públicos*

streak•y ['striːkɪ] *adj* veteado

stream [striːm] **I** *n* riachuelo *m*; *fig*: *of people*, *complaints* oleada *f*; ***come on ~*** entrar en funcionamiento **II** *v/i*: ***there were tears ~ing down my face*** me bajaban ríos de lágrimas por la cara; ***people ~ed out of the building*** la gente salía en masa; ***his face was ~ing with sweat*** el sudor corría a chorros por su cara

stream•er ['striːmər] serpentina *f*

stream•ing ['striːmɪŋ] *adj*: ***he's got a ~ cold*** tiene un buen catarro

'stream•line *v/t fig* racionalizar

'stream•lined *adj car*, *plane* aerodiná-

mico; *fig*: *organization* racionalizado
street [striːt] calle *f*; ***on the ~***, *Br* ***in the ~*** en la calle; ***be right up s.o.'s ~*** *fig* venir como anillo al dedo a alguien; ***I'm ~s ahead of him*** F le doy mil vueltas F; ***walk the ~s*** vagar por las calles; ***live on the ~s*** vivir en la calle
'street•car tranvía *f*; **street cred** ['striːtkred] F *buena imágen de acuerdo a la cultura urbana*; **'street kid** niño *m* / niña *f* de la calle; **'street lamp, 'street light** farola *f*; **'street light•ing** alumbrado *m* público; **'street map** plano *m*; **'street mu•si•cian** músico(-a) *m(f)* callejero(-a); **'street peo•ple** *npl* los sin techo; **'street val•ue** *of drugs* valor *m* en la calle; **'street vend•or** vendedor(a) *m(f)* callejero(-a); **'street-walk•er** F prostituta *f*; **'street•wise** *adj* espabilado
strength [streŋθ] **1** fuerza *f*; *of friendship etc* solidez *f*; *of emotion* intensidad *f*; *of currency* fortaleza *f*; ***~ of character*** entereza *f*; ***on the ~ of*** en virtud de; ***go from ~ to ~*** ir viento en popa; ***show of ~*** alarde *m* de poder; ***in ~*** *be present* a raudales; ***be at full ~*** contar con todo el personal; ***be below ~*** no disponer de todo el personal **2** *fig* (*strong point*) punto *m* fuerte
strength•en ['streŋθn] **I** *v/t muscles, currency* fortalecer; *bridge* reforzar; *country, ties, relationship* consolidar; ***~ s.o.'s resolve*** afianzar la decisión de alguien **II** *v/i of bonds, ties* consolidarse; *of currency* fortalecerse
stren•u•ous ['strenjʊəs] *adj* agotador
stren•u•ous•ly ['strenjʊəslɪ] *adv deny* tajantemente
strep throat [strep'θroʊt] F infección *f* de garganta
stress [stres] **I** *n* **1** (*emphasis*) énfasis *m*; *on syllable* acento *m*; ***put the ~ on*** *fig* hacer hincapié en **2** (*tension*) estrés *m*; ***be under ~*** estar estresado; ***the ~es and strains of modern life*** el estrés y la tensión de la vida moderna; ***~-related illnesses*** enfermedades *fpl* relacionadas con el estrés **II** *v/t* (*emphasize*: *syllable*) acentuar; *importance etc* hacer hincapié en; ***I must ~ that …*** quiero hacer hincapié en que …
stressed [strest], **stressed out** [strest'aʊt] *adj* F estresado
'stress-free *adj* relajado, sin estrés
stress•ful ['stresfəl] *adj* estresante
stretch [stretʃ] **I** *n* **1** *of land, water* extensión *f*; *of road* tramo *m*; ***at a ~*** (*non-stop*) de un tirón; ***do a three-year ~*** F *in prison* estar tres años entre rejas **2**: ***have a ~*** estirarse; ***be at full ~*** *fig* estar saturado (de trabajo); ***not by any ~ of the imagination*** de ninguna de las maneras
II *adj fabric* elástico
III *v/t material, income* estirar; F *rules* ser flexible con; ***my job ~es me*** mi trabajo me obliga a esforzarme; ***be fully ~ed*** *fig unable to take on more work* estar saturado (de trabajo)
IV *v/i* **1** *to relax muscles, reach sth* estirarse **2** (*spread*) extenderse **3** *of fabric* estirarse, dar de sí
◆ **stretch out I** *v/i* **1** *to reach something* estirarse **2** (*lie down*) tumbarse **II** *v/t hand etc* estirar
stretch•er ['stretʃər] camilla *f*
'stretch lim•o F limusina *f* grande
'stretch marks *npl* estrías *fpl*
stretch•y ['stretʃɪ] *adj* elástico
strick•en ['strɪkən] *adj parents, face* desolado; *country, city* asolado; ***~ with*** arrasado por
strict [strɪkt] *adj* estricto; ***in ~ confidence*** en total confianza
strict•ly ['strɪktlɪ] *adv* con rigor; ***it is ~ forbidden*** está terminantemente prohibido; ***~ speaking*** propiamente hablando
strid•den ['strɪdn] *pp* ☞ ***stride***
stride [straɪd] **I** *n* zancada *f*; ***take sth in one's ~*** *fig* tomarse algo con tranquilidad; ***make great ~s*** *fig* avanzar a pasos agigantados; ***get into one's ~, hit one's ~*** *fig* coger la marcha **II** *v/i* (*pret* **strode**, *pp* **stridden**) caminar dando zancadas
stri•dent ['straɪdnt] *adj also fig* estridente
strife [straɪf] conflicto *m*, polémica *f*
strike [straɪk] **I** *n* **1** *of workers* huelga *f*; ***be on ~*** estar en huelga; ***go on ~*** ir a la huelga **2** *in baseball* strike *m*, *L.Am.* ponche *m* **3** *of oil* descubrimiento *m* **II** *v/i* (*pret & pp* **struck**) **1** *of workers* hacer huelga **2** (*attack*) atacar; *of disaster* sobrevenir **3** *of clock* dar las horas; ***the clock struck three*** el reloj dio las tres

S

III *v/t* (*pret & pp* **struck**) **1** (*hit*) golpear **2** *fig*: *of disaster* sacudir **3** *match* encender **4** *oil* descubrir **5**: ***didn't it ever ~ you that …?*** ¿no se te ocurrió que …?; ***she struck me as being …*** me dio la impresión de ser …; ***I was struck by …*** me impactó …; ***how does the house ~ you?*** ¿qué te parece la casa?
◆ **strike back** *v/i* contraatacar
◆ **strike down** *v/t fig* golpear, sacudir
◆ **strike off** *v/t Br* suspender
◆ **strike out I** *v/t* **1** (*delete*) tachar **2** *in baseball* eliminar, *L.Am.* ponchar; ***be struck out*** estroquear *L.Am.* **II** *v/i* **1** *in baseball* quedar eliminado, *L.Am.* poncharse **2** F (*fail*) fracasar **3**: ***strike out on one's own*** *fig* irse por libre; ***strike out in a new direction*** tomar otro rumbo
◆ **strike through** *v/t* tachar
◆ **strike up I** *v/t* **1** entablar (***with*** con) **2** MUS empezar a tocar **II** *v/i* MUS empezar a tocar
'strike bal•lot *votación por la que un sindicato convoca una huelga*; **'strike-bound** *adj* cerrado (*por acciones reivindicativas*); **'strike•break•er** esquirol(a) *m(f)*; **'strike•out** *in baseball* strikeout *m*; **'strike pay** subsidio *m* de huelga
strik•er ['straɪkər] **1** (*person on strike*) huelguista *m/f* **2** *in soccer* delantero(-a) *m(f)*
'strike zone *in baseball* zona *f* de strike
strik•ing ['straɪkɪŋ] *adj* **1** (*marked*) sorprendente, llamativo; (*eye-catching*) deslumbrante **2**: ***be within ~ distance of*** *fig* estar muy cerca de
string [strɪŋ] **I** *n also of violin, racket etc* cuerda *f*; ***the ~s*** *musicians* la sección de cuerda; ***pull ~s*** mover hilos; ***pull the ~s*** *fig* tirar de la manta; ***a ~ of*** (*series*) una serie de; ***with no ~s attached*** *fig* sin compromiso alguno; ***he has more than one ~ to his bow*** *fig* es muy polifacético; *with girlfriends* tiene muchas novias
II *adj* MUS de cuerda
III *v/t* (*pret & pp* **strung**) **1** *beads* engarzar **2** *tennis racket* encordar
◆ **string along I** *v/i* F apuntarse F **II** *v/t* F: ***string s.o. along*** dar falsas esperanzas a alguien
◆ **string out** *v/t* **1** *make last longer* alargar **2**: ***the crowd was strung out the whole length of the course*** el público se extendía a lo largo de todo el circuito
◆ **string together** *v/t* articular
◆ **string up** *v/t* F colgar
string 'bean BOT judía *f* verde, *L.Am.* poroto *m* verde, *Mex* ejote *m*
stringed in•stru•ment [strɪŋd'ɪnstrʊmənt] instrumento *m* de cuerda
strin•gent ['strɪndʒnt] *adj* riguroso
'string play•er instrumentista *m/f* de cuerda
string•y ['strɪŋɪ] *adj* hebroso, fibroso
strip [strɪp] **I** *n* **1** *of land* franja *f*; *of cloth* tira *f* **2** (*comic ~*) tira *f* cómica **3**: ***do a ~*** hacer un striptease **II** *v/t* (*pret & pp* **-ped**) **1** (*remove*) quitar; ***~ s.o. of sth*** despojar a alguien de algo **2** (*undress*) desnudar **III** *v/i* (*pret & pp* **-ped**) (*undress*) desnudarse; *of stripper* hacer striptease; ***~ to the waist*** quitarse la parte de arriba
◆ **strip down** *v/t* desmontar
◆ **strip off** *v/i* desvestirse, desnudarse
strip car'toon *Br* tira *f* cómica
'strip club club *m* de striptease
stripe [straɪp] **1** raya *f* **2** *indicating rank* galón *m*
striped [straɪpt] *adj* a rayas
'strip joint F ☞ ***strip club***; **'strip light•ing** fluorescentes *mpl*; **'strip mall** *calle comercial a las afueras de la ciudad*; **'strip min•ing** explotación *f* a cielo abierto
strip•per ['strɪpər] artista *m/f* de striptease
strip 'pok•er strip poker *m*; **'strip-search** *v/t* registrar sin ropa; **'strip show** espectáculo *m* de striptease; **strip'tease** striptease *m*
strive [straɪv] *v/i* (*pret* **strove**, *pp* **striven**) esforzarse; ***~ to do sth*** esforzarse por hacer algo; ***~ for*** luchar por
striv•en ['strɪvn] *pp* ☞ ***strive***
strobe [stroʊb], **'strobe light** luz *f* estroboscópica
strode [stroʊd] *pret* ☞ ***stride***
stroke [stroʊk] **I** *n* **1** MED derrame *m* cerebral
2 *in writing* trazo *m*; *in painting* pincelada *f*; ***with a ~ of the pen*** de un plumazo
3 (*style of swimming*) estilo *m*

4: ~ ***of luck*** golpe de suerte; ***she never does a*** ~ (***of work***) no pega ni golpe; ***a*** ~ ***of genius*** *fig* un momento de inspiración; ***at a*** (***single***) ~ *fig* de (un) golpe; ***on the*** ~ ***of ten*** a las diez en punto; ***put s.o. off their*** ~ desconcentrar a alguien **II** *v/t cat etc* acariciar

stroll [stroul] **I** *n* paseo *m*; ***go for a*** ~, ***take a*** ~ ir a dar un paseo, dar un paseo **II** *v/i* caminar

stroll•er ['stroulər] *for baby* silla *f* de paseo

strong [strɒ:ŋ] **I** *adj* **1** fuerte; *structure* resistente; *candidate* claro, con muchos posibilidades; *support, supporter, views, objection* firme; *tea, coffee* cargado, fuerte **2**: ~ ***language*** lenguaje *m* enérgico; (*swearing*) palabrotas *fpl* **3**: ***a twenty-~ expedition*** una expedición de veinte miembros; ***an 8,000-~ community*** una comunidad de 8.000 personas
II *adv*: ***be still going*** ~ seguir en buen estado; *of person* seguir en buena forma

'strong•box caja *f* fuerte

'strong•hold *fig* baluarte *m*

strong•ly ['strɒ:ŋlɪ] *adv* fuertemente, rotundamente; ***I*** ~ ***advised him against it*** se lo desaconsejé contundentemente

strong-'mind•ed *adj* decidido; **'strong point** (punto *m*) fuerte *m*; **'strong-room** cámara *f* acorazada; **strong--willed** [strɒ:ŋ'wɪld] *adj* tenaz

stron•ti•um ['strɑ:ntɪəm] CHEM estroncio *m*

strop•py ['strɑ:pɪ] *adj Br* F: ***get*** ~ ponerse impertinente F

strove [strouv] *pret* ☞ ***strive***

struck [strʌk] *pret & pp* ☞ ***strike***

struc•tur•al ['strʌktʃərl] *adj* estructural

struc•tur•al•ly ['strʌktʃərəlɪ] *adv* estructuralmente; ***be*** ~ ***sound*** tener una estructura sólida

struc•ture ['strʌktʃər] **I** *n* (*something built*) construcción *f*; *of novel, society etc* estructura *f* **II** *v/t* estructurar

strug•gle ['strʌgl] **I** *n* lucha *f*; ~ ***for survival*** lucha por la supervivencia **II** *v/i with a person* forcejear; (*have a hard time*) luchar; ***he was struggling with the door*** tenía problemas con la puerta; ~ ***to do sth*** luchar por hacer algo; ***he was struggling for words*** le costó expresarse; ~ ***to one's feet*** ponerse en pie con mucho esfuerzo

◆ **struggle on** *v/i* proseguir con dificultad

strum [strʌm] *v/t* (*pret & pp* ***-med***) *guitar* rasguear

strung [strʌŋ] *pret & pp* ☞ ***string***

strung 'out *adj* P **1** *through drugs* colgado P **2** *exhausted* reventado P **3** *nervous* alterado F

strut[1] [strʌt] **I** *v/i* (*pret & pp* ***-ted***) pavonearse **II** *v/t* (*pret & pp* ***-ted***) F: ~ ***one's stuff*** lucirse F

strut[2] [strʌt] *n* TECH montante *m*

strych•nine ['strɪkni:n] CHEM, PHARM estricnina *f*

stub [stʌb] **I** *n* **1** *of cigarette* colilla *f* **2** *of check* matriz *f*, *of ticket* resguardo *m* **II** *v/t* (*pret & pp* ***-bed***): ~ ***one's toe*** darse un golpe en el dedo (del pie)

◆ **stub out** *v/t* apagar (apretando)

stub•ble ['stʌbl] *on man's face* barba *f* incipiente

stub•bly ['stʌblɪ] *adj* con barba incipiente

stub•born ['stʌbərn] *adj person* testarudo, terco; *defense, refusal, denial* tenaz, pertinaz

stub•by ['stʌbɪ] *adj* regordete

stuc•co ['stʌkou] ARCHI estuco *m*

stuck [stʌk] **I** *pret & pp* ☞ ***stick***
II *adj*: ***be*** ~ *of door, drawer* estar atrancado; *of person in elevator etc* estar atrapado; *fig* F estar atascado F; ***be*** ~ ***on s.o.*** F estar colado por alguien F; ***get*** ~ *in elevator etc* quedarse atrapado; *fig* F atascarse F; ***be*** ~ ***with*** *not be able to get away from* F no poderse librar de; ***get*** ~ ***into*** *Br* F *task* ponerse (las pilas) con F

stuck-'up *adj* F engreído

stud[1] [stʌd] **I** *n* **1** *metal knob* tachuela *f* **2** *earring etc* pendiente *m* de bolita **3** *on boot* taco *m* **II** *v/t* (*pret & pp* ***-ded***): ***be*** ~***ded with*** estar cubierto de

stud[2] [stʌd] *n* **1** *for horses* cuadra *f* **2** F *man* semental *m* F

stu•dent ['stu:dnt] estudiante *m/f*, *at high school* alumno(-a) *m(f)*

stu•dent 'driv•er *persona que está aprendiendo a conducir*; **stu•dent 'loan** préstamo *m* para estudiantes; **stu•dent 'nurse** estudiante *m/f* de enfermería;

stu•dent 'teach•er profesor(a) *m*(*f*) en prácticas
'stud farm cuadra *f*
stud•ied ['stʌdɪd] *adj* estudiado, artificial
stu•di•o ['stu:dɪoʊ] **1** *of artist, sculptor* estudio *m*; (*film* ~, *TV* ~) estudio *m*, plató *m* **2** ☞ ***studio apartment***
'stu•di•o apart•ment estudio *m*; **stu•di•o 'au•di•ence** público *m* en el plató; **'stu•di•o couch** sofá cama *m*; **'stu•di•o flat** *Br* estudio *m*
stu•di•ous ['stu:dɪəs] *adj* estudioso
stud•y ['stʌdɪ] **I** *n* **1** estudio *m*; ***make*** *or* ***carry out a ~ of*** realizar un estudio sobre **2** (*room*) despacho *m* **3**: ***she's a quick ~*** es capaz de aprender de memoria rápidamente **II** *v/t & v/i* (*pret & pp* ***-ied***) estudiar; ***~ to be a doctor*** estudiar medicina
'stud•y hall sala *f* de estudio; *period* hora *f* de estudio
stuff [stʌf] **I** *n* (*things*) cosas *fpl*; ***be good ~*** ser de calidad; ***once you've done your ~*** cuando hayas hecho la parte que a ti te corresponde; ***know one's ~*** saber lo que se hace / dice; ***I have to get ready and ~*** P me tengo que preparar y tal F
II *v/t turkey* rellenar; ***~ sth into sth*** meter algo dentro de algo; ***~ed full of*** repleto de; ***~ o.s.*** F atiborrarse F; ***get ~ed!*** *Br* P ¡piérdete! P, ¡vete a paseo! P
◆ **stuff up** *v/t hole* rellenar; ***I'm ~ed up*** tengo la nariz tapada
stuffed [stʌft] *adj*: ***~ shirt*** F persona *f* pomposa F
stuffed 'toy muñeco *m* de peluche
stuff•ing ['stʌfɪŋ] relleno *m*; ***knock the ~ out of s.o.*** F dejar hecho polvo a alguien F
stuff•y ['stʌfɪ] *adj* **1** *room* cargado **2** *person* anticuado, estirado
stum•ble ['stʌmbl] *v/i* tropezar
◆ **stumble across** *v/t* toparse con
◆ **stumble over** *v/t* tropezar con; *words* trastrabillarse con
◆ **stumble through** *v/t* hacer a trompicones F
stum•bling-block ['stʌmblɪŋ] escollo *m*
stump [stʌmp] **I** *n* **1** *of tree* tocón *m* **2** POL F: ***be on the ~*** hacer campaña **II** *v/t of question, questioner* dejar perplejo; ***I'm ~ed, you've got me ~ed*** no sé que responder, me has dejado sin respuesta
◆ **stump up** *v/t* F aflojar, *Span* apoquinar F
stump•y ['stʌmpɪ] *adj* achaparrado, rechoncho
stun [stʌn] *v/t* (*pret & pp* ***-ned***) *of blow* dejar sin sentido; *of news* dejar atonito *or* de piedra; ***there was a ~ned silence*** hubo un silencio total por el shock
stung [stʌŋ] *pret & pp* ☞ ***sting***
'stun gun pistola *f* paralizante
stunk [stʌŋk] *pp* ☞ ***stink***
stun•ner ['stʌnər]: ***be a real ~*** ser una verdadera preciosidad *or* belleza
stun•ning ['stʌnɪŋ] *adj* **1** (*amazing*) increíble, sorprendente **2** (*very beautiful*) imponente
stunt[1] [stʌnt] *n for publicity* truco *m*; *in movie* escena *f* peligrosa; ***pull a ~*** hacer una estupidez
stunt[2] [stʌnt] *v/t* ralentizar el crecimiento de; ***~ed*** desmirriado
stunt•man ['stʌntmæn] *in movie* doble *m*, especialista *m*
'stunt wom•an *in movie* doble *f*, especialista *f*
stu•pe•fy ['stu:pɪfaɪ] *v/t* (*pret & pp* ***-ied***) dejar perplejo
stu•pen•dous [stu:'pendəs] *adj* extraordinario
stu•pid ['stu:pɪd] *adj* estúpido; ***what a ~ thing to say / do!*** ¡qué estupidez!
stu•pid•i•ty [stu:'pɪdətɪ] estupidez *f*
stu•por ['stu:pər] aturdimiento *m*; ***in a drunken ~*** en estado de estupor a causa del alcohol
stur•dy ['stɜ:rdɪ] *adj person* robusto; *table, plant* resistente
stut•ter ['stʌtər] **I** *v/i* tartamudear **II** *v/t* tartamudear **III** *n* tartamudeo *m*
stut•ter•er ['stʌtərər] tartamudo(-a) *m*(*f*)
sty [staɪ] *for pig* pocilga *f*
style [staɪl] **I** *n* estilo *m*; (*fashion*) moda *f*; ***go out of ~*** pasarse de moda; ***~ of leadership*** tipo *m or* forma *f* de liderazgo; ***in ~*** a lo grande; ***that's not my ~*** F eso no va conmigo F; ***she has ~*** tiene estilo; ***cramp s.o.'s ~*** cohibir a alguien **II** *v/t hair* peinar

styl•ing mousse ['staɪlɪŋ] espuma *f* moldeadora
styl•ish ['staɪlɪʃ] *adj* elegante
styl•ist ['staɪlɪst] (*hair* ~) estilista *m/f*
sty•lis•tic [staɪ'lɪstɪk] *adj* estilístico
styl•ize ['staɪlaɪz] *v/t* estilizar
sty•lus ['staɪləs] aguja *f*
sty•mie ['staɪmɪ] *v/t* F frustar
Sty•ro•foam® ['staɪrəfoʊm] poliestireno *m*
suave [swɑːv] *adj person* cortés, sofisticado; *pej* zalamero
sub [sʌb] F **1** (*submarine*) submarino *m* **2** (*subscription*) suscripción *f* **3** SP suplente *m/f* **II** *v/i* ☞ ***substitute* III**
sub•a•tom•ic [sʌbə'tɑːmɪk] *adj* subatómico
sub•com•mit•tee ['sʌbkəmɪtɪ] subcomité *m*
sub•com•pact (**car**) [sʌb'kɑːmpækt] *utilitario de pequeño tamaño*
sub•con•scious [sʌb'kɑːnʃəs] *adj* subconsciente; ***the ~*** (***mind***) el subconsciente
sub•con•scious•ly [sʌb'kɑːnʃəslɪ] *adv* inconscientemente
sub•con•ti•nent [sʌb'kɑːntɪnənt] subcontinente *m*
sub•con•tract [sʌbkɑːn'trækt] *v/t* subcontratar
sub•con•trac•tor [sʌbkɑːn'træktər] subcontratista *m/f*
sub•cul•ture ['sʌbkʌltʃər] subcultura *f*
sub•cu•ta•ne•ous [sʌbkjuː'teɪnɪəs] *adj* subcutáneo
sub•di•vide [sʌbdɪ'vaɪd] *v/t* subdividir
sub•di•vi•sion ['sʌbdɪvɪʒn] subdivisión *f*
sub•due [səb'duː] *v/t rebellion, mob* someter, contener
sub•dued [səb'duːd] *adj* apagado
sub•ed•i•tor ['sʌbedɪtər] *Br* redactor(a) *m(f)*
sub•head•ing ['sʌbhedɪŋ] subtítulo *m*
sub•hu•man [sʌb'hjuːmən] *adj* inhumano
sub•ject I *n* ['sʌbdʒɪkt] **1** (*topic*) tema *m*; (*branch of learning*) asignatura *f*, materia *f*; ***change the ~*** cambiar de tema; ***on the ~ of*** (*about*) sobre; ***be the ~ of*** ser objeto de; ***that's a ~ for the specialists*** eso es materia de especialista **2** GRAM sujeto *m* **3** *of monarch* súbdito(-a) *m(f)*
II *adj* ['sʌbdʒɪkt]: ***be ~ to*** *have tendency to* ser propenso a; *be regulated by* estar sujeto a; ***~ to availability*** *goods* promoción válida hasta fin de existencias; ***prices ~ to change*** precios con tendencia al cambio
III *v/t* [səb'dʒekt] someter (***to*** a)
sub•jec•tion [səb'dʒekʃn] **1** (*subjugation*) subyugación *f*, sometimiento *m* **2**: ***~ to*** (*exposure to*) exposición *f* a
sub•jec•tive [səb'dʒektɪv] *adj* subjetivo
'sub•ject mat•ter tema *m*
sub•ju•gate ['sʌbdʒʊgeɪt] *v/t* subyugar, someter
sub•junc•tive [səb'dʒʌŋktɪv] GRAM subjuntivo *m*
sub•lease [sʌb'liːs] *v/t to s.o.* realquilar (***to*** a); *from s.o.* realquilar (***from*** de)
sub•let [sʌb'let] *v/t* (*pret & pp* ***-let***) ☞ ***sublease***
sub•lime [sə'blaɪm] *adj iron*: *disregard, ignorance* sumo, supremo
sub•lim•i•nal [sʌb'lɪmɪnl] *adj* PSYCH subliminal
sub•ma•chine gun [sʌbmə'ʃiːngʌn] metralleta *f*
sub•ma•rine ['sʌbməriːn] **I** *n* submarino *m* **II** *adj world, life* submarino
sub•ma•rin•er [sʌb'mærɪnər] submarinista *m/f*
sub•merge [səb'mɜːrdʒ] **I** *v/t* sumergir **II** *v/i of submarine* sumergirse
sub•mis•sion [səb'mɪʃn] **1** (*surrender*) sumisión *f* **2** *to committee etc* propuesta *f*
sub•mis•sive [səb'mɪsɪv] *adj* sumiso
sub•mit [səb'mɪt] **I** *v/t* (*pret & pp* ***-ted***) *plan, proposal* presentar; ***I ~ that …*** sostengo *or* mantengo que … **II** *v/i* (*pret & pp* ***-ted***) someterse
sub•nor•mal [sʌb'nɔːrml] *adj* subnormal
sub•or•di•nate [sə'bɔːrdɪneɪt] **I** *adj employee, position* subordinado (***to*** a); ***~ clause*** LING oración *f* subordinada **II** *n* subordinado(-a) *m(f)*
sub•plot ['sʌbplɑːt] trama *f* secundaria
sub•poe•na [sə'piːnə] **I** *n* citación *f* **II** *v/t person* citar
sub•rou•tine ['sʌbruːtiːn] COMPUT subrutina *f*
◆ **sub•scribe to** [səb'skraɪb] *v/t* **1** *magazine etc* suscribirse a **2** *theory* suscribir

sub•scribed cap•i•tal [səb'skraɪbd] capital *m* suscrito
sub•scrib•er [səb'skraɪbər] *to magazine* suscriptor(a) *m(f)*
sub•scrip•tion [səb'skrɪpʃn] suscripción *f*; ***take out a ~ to*** suscribirse a
sub•sec•tion ['sʌbsekʃn] subapartado *m*
sub•se•quent ['sʌbsɪkwənt] *adj* posterior
sub•se•quent•ly ['sʌbsɪkwəntlɪ] *adv* posteriormente
sub•ser•vi•ence [səb'sɜːrvɪəns] servilismo *m*
sub•ser•vi•ent [səb'sɜːrvɪənt] *adj* **1** *person* servil **2**: ***be ~ to*** (*less important than*) estar por debajo de
sub•side [səb'saɪd] *v/i* **1** *of flood waters* bajar; *of high winds* amainar; *of fears, panic* calmarse **2** *of building* hundirse
sub•sid•ence ['səbsaɪdəns] hundimiento *m*
sub•sid•i•a•ry [səb'sɪdɪerɪ] filial *f*; ***~ company*** empresa *f* filial
sub•si•dize ['sʌbsɪdaɪz] *v/t* subvencionar
sub•si•dy ['sʌbsɪdɪ] subvención *f*
◆ **sub•sist on** [sʌb'sɪst] *v/t* subsistir a base de
sub•sist•ence [səb'sɪstəns] subsistencia *f*
sub'sist•ence farm•er agricultor(a) *m(f)* de subsistencia; **sub'sist•ence farm•ing** agricultura *f* de autoabastecimiento; **sub'sist•ence lev•el** nivel *m* mínimo de subsistencia
sub•spe•cies ['sʌbspiːʃiːz] *nsg* subespecie *f*
sub•stance ['sʌbstəns] (*matter*) sustancia *f*; ***in ~*** en esencia
sub•stan•dard [sʌb'stændərd] *adj performance* deficiente; *shoes, clothes* con tara
sub•stan•tial [səb'stænʃl] *adj* sustancial, considerable
sub•stan•tial•ly [səb'stænʃlɪ] *adv* **1** (*considerably*) considerablemente **2** (*in essence*) sustancialmente, esencialmente
sub•stan•ti•ate [səb'stænʃɪeɪt] *v/t* probar
sub•stan•tive [səb'stæntɪv] *adj* significativo
sub•sti•tute ['sʌbstɪtuːt] **I** *n for person* sustituto(-a) *m(f)*; SP suplente *m/f*; *for commodity* sustituto *m*; ***there's no ~ for …*** no hay nada como …; ***~s' bench*** SP banquillo *m* **II** *v/t* sustituir, reemplazar; ***~ X for Y*** sustituir Y por X **III** *v/i*: ***~ for s.o.*** sustituir a alguien
sub•sti•tu•tion [sʌbstɪ'tuːʃn] (*act*) sustitución *f*; ***make a ~*** SP hacer un cambio *or* una sustitución
sub•struc•ture ['sʌbstrʌktʃər] ARCHI infraestructura *f*
sub•ten•ant [sʌb'tenənt] subarrendatario(-a) *m(f)*
sub•ter•fuge ['sʌbtərfjuːdʒ] subterfugio *m*, escapatoria *f*
sub•ter•ra•ne•an [sʌbtə'reɪnɪən] *adj* subterráneo
sub•ti•tle ['sʌbtaɪtl] subtítulo *m*
sub•tle ['sʌtl] *adj* sutil
sub•tle•ty ['sʌtltɪ] sutileza *f*
sub•to•tal ['sʌbtoʊtl] subtotal *m*
sub•tract [səb'trækt] *v/t number* restar
sub•trac•tion [səb'trækʃn] sustracción *f*, resta *f*
sub•trop•i•cal [sʌb'trɑːpɪkl] *adj* subtropical
sub•urb ['sʌbɜːrb] zona *f* residencial de la periferia; ***live in the ~s*** vivir en las afueras
sub•ur•ban [sə'bɜːrbən] *adj housing* de la periferia; *attitudes, lifestyle* aburguesado
sub•ur•bi•a [sə'bɜːrbɪə] (*suburbs*) zona *f* residencial de la periferia
sub•ver•sion [səb'vɜːrʃn] POL subversión *f*
sub•ver•sive [səb'vɜːrsɪv] **I** *adj* subversivo **II** *n* subversivo(-a) *m(f)*
sub•way ['sʌbweɪ] metro *m*
sub 'ze•ro [sʌb'zɪroʊ] *adj* bajo cero
suc•ceed [sək'siːd] **I** *v/i* **1** (*be successful*) tener éxito; ***~ in doing sth*** conseguir hacer algo **2** *to throne* suceder en el trono; ***~ to a position*** suceder en un puesto **II** *v/t* (*come after*) suceder; ***~ s.o. as*** suceder a alguien como
suc•ceed•ing [sək'siːdɪŋ] *adj* siguiente
suc•cess [sək'ses] éxito *m*; ***be a ~*** *of book, play, idea* ser un éxito; *of person* tener éxito; ***without ~*** sin éxito, en vano
suc•cess•ful [sək'sesfəl] *adj person* con éxito; ***be ~ in business*** tener éxito en los negocios; ***be ~ in doing sth*** lograr hacer algo

S

suc•cess•ful•ly [sək'sesfəlɪ] *adv* con éxito
suc•ces•sion [sək'seʃn] sucesión *f*; ***three days in ~*** tres días seguidos; ***in quick ~*** uno detrás de otro, sin parar
suc•ces•sive [sək'sesɪv] *adj* sucesivo; ***on three ~ days*** en tres días consecutivos
suc•ces•sor [sək'sesər] sucesor(a) *m(f)*
suc'cess sto•ry éxito *m*, triunfo *m*
suc•cinct [sək'sɪŋkt] *adj* sucinto
suc•cu•lent ['ʃʌkjʊlənt] *meat, fruit* suculento
suc•cumb [sə'kʌm] *v/i* (*give in*) sucumbir
such [sʌtʃ] **I** *adj* **1** (*of that kind*) tal; ***~ men are dangerous*** los hombres así son peligrosos; ***I know of many ~ cases*** conozco muchos casos así
2: ***don't make ~ a fuss*** no armes tanto alboroto; ***I never thought it would be ~ a success*** nunca imaginé que sería un éxito tal
3: ***~ as*** como; ***there is no ~ word as …*** no existe la palabra …; ***there is no ~ thing as …*** … no existe
II *adv* tan; ***as ~*** como tal; ***~ a nice day*** un día tan bueno; ***~ a long time*** tanto tiempo
III *pron* tal; ***~ is life*** así es la vida
'such•like **I** *adj* parecido, por el estilo **II** *pron* cosas por el estilo
suck [sʌk] **I** *v/t candy etc* chupar; ***~ one's thumb*** chuparse el dedo **II** *v/i* P: ***it ~s*** (*is awful*) es una mierda P
◆ **suck under** *v/t* absorber
◆ **suck up** **I** *v/t* absorber **II** *v/i* F: ***suck up to s.o.*** hacer la pelota a alguien
suck•er ['sʌkər] F **1** *person* primo(-a) *m(f)* F, ingenuo(-a) *m(f)*; ***be a ~ for*** tener debilidad por **2** *candy* piruleta *f*
suck•le ['sʌkl] *v/t young* dar de mamar a
suck•ling pig [sʌklɪŋ'pɪg] lechón *m*
su•cre ['suːkreɪ] FIN sucre *m*
suc•tion ['sʌkʃn] succión *f*
'suc•tion pump TECH bomba *f* aspirante
Su•dan [suː'dɑːn]: ***the ~*** el Sudán
sud•den ['sʌdn] *adj* repentino; ***all of a ~*** de repente; ***be very ~*** ser muy súbito
sud•den death 'play-off desempate *m*
sud•den in•fant 'death syn•drome síndrome *m* de muerte súbita del lactante
sud•den•ly ['sʌdnlɪ] *adv* de repente
suds [sʌdz] *npl* (*soap ~*) espuma *f*
sue [suː] *v/t & v/i* demandar (***for*** por)
suede [sweɪd] ante *m*; ***~ shoes / jacket*** zapatos *mpl* / chaqueta *f* de ante
Su•ez Ca•nal [suːezkə'næl]: ***the ~*** el canal de Suez
suf•fer ['sʌfər] **I** *v/i* (*be in great pain*) sufrir; (*deteriorate*) deteriorarse; ***be ~ing from*** sufrir **II** *v/t loss, setback, heart attack* sufrir
suf•fer•er ['sʌfərər]: ***migraine / rheumatism ~s*** aquellos que padecen de migraña / reumatismo
suf•fer•ing ['sʌfərɪŋ] sufrimiento *m*
suf•fice [sə'faɪs] **I** *v/i* ser suficiente (***for*** para) **II** *v/t*: ***~ it to say that…*** basta con decir que …
suf•fi•cient [sə'fɪʃnt] *adj* suficiente
suf•fi•cient•ly [sə'fɪʃntlɪ] *adv* suficientemente
suf•fix ['sʌfɪks] LING sufijo *m*
suf•fo•cate ['sʌfəkeɪt] **I** *v/i* asfixiarse **II** *v/t* asfixiar
suf•fo•ca•tion [sʌfə'keɪʃn] asfixia *f*
suf•frage ['sʌfrɪdʒ] POL sufragio *m*
suf•fuse [sə'fjuːz] *v/t*: ***be ~d with*** estar bañado en *or* teñido de
sug•ar ['ʃʊgər] **I** *n* azúcar *m or f*; ***how many ~s?*** ¿cuántas cucharadas de azúcar? **II** *v/t* echar azúcar a; ***is it ~ed?*** ¿lleva azúcar? **III** *int euph* cariño, cielo
'sug•ar bowl azucarero *m*; **'sug•ar cane** caña *f* de azúcar; **'sug•ar cube** terrón *m* de azúcar; **'sug•ar dad•dy** F *hombre rico que mantiene a una amante más joven*; **'sug•ar plan•ta•tion** cañaveral *m*
sug•ar•y ['ʃʊgərɪ] *adj* **1** *drink, breakfast cereal* dulce **2** *fig*: *person, smile* sentimental, dulzón
sug•gest [sə'dʒest] *v/t* sugerir; ***I ~ going home, I suggest that we go home*** propongo ir a casa, sugiero que vayamos a casa; ***~ that*** *of evidence, event, situation* dar a entender que; ***I'm not ~ing that you're to blame*** no estoy insinuando que la culpa sea tuya
sug•gest•i•ble [sə'dʒestəbl] *adj* influenciable
sug•ges•tion [sə'dʒestʃən] sugerencia *f*; ***at José's ~*** a sugerencia de José; ***make a ~*** hacer una sugerencia; ***be open to***

~s admitir sugerencias

sug•ges•tive [sə'dʒestɪv] *adj* **1** *remark* provocativo **2**: **be ~ of** sugerir

su•i•ci•dal [suɪ'saɪdl] *adj* suicida, temerario; **be feeling ~** pensar en el suicidio

su•i•cide ['suːɪsaɪd] suicidio *m*; **commit ~** suicidarse; **~ attempt** intento *m* de suicidio

'su•i•cide bomb•er terrorista *m/f* suicida

'su•i•cide pact *pacto de suicidio colectivo entre dos o más personas*

suit [suːt] **I** *n* **1** traje *m* **2** *in cards* palo *m*; **follow ~** *fig* hacer lo mismo, hacer otro tanto **II** *v/t of clothes, color* sentar bien a; **~ yourself!** F ¡haz lo que quieras!; **be ~ed for** *or* **to sth** estar hecho para algo; **that ~s me fine** eso me viene bien; **they are well ~ed (to each other)** están hechos el uno para el otro

suit•a•ble ['suːtəbl] *adj partner, words, clothing* apropiado, adecuado; *time* apropiado

suit•a•bly ['suːtəblɪ] *adv* apropiadamente, adecuadamente

'suit•case maleta *f*, *L.Am.* valija *f*

suite [swiːt] *of rooms*, MUS suite *f*; *furniture* tresillo *m*

sul•fate ['sʌlfeɪt] sulfato *m*

sul•fide ['sʌlfaɪd] sulfuro *m*

sul•fur ['sʌlfər] azufre *m*

sul•fur di'ox•ide dióxido *m* de azufre

sul•fu•ric ac•id [sʌlfjuːrɪk'æsɪd] ácido *m* sulfúrico

sul•fu•rous ['sʌlfərəs] *adj* sulfuroso, sulfúreo

sulk [sʌlk] **I** *v/i* enfurruñarse; **be ~ing** estar enfurruñado **II** *npl*: **have the ~s** estar de morros

sulk•y ['sʌlkɪ] *adj* enfurruñado

sul•len ['sʌlən] *adj* malhumorado, huraño

sul•phate, sul•phide, sul•phur *Br* ☞ **sulfate** *etc*

sul•try ['sʌltrɪ] *adj* **1** *climate* sofocante, bochornoso **2** *sexually* sensual

sum [sʌm] **1** (*total*) total *m*, suma *f*; **the ~ total of his efforts** la suma de sus esfuerzos **2** (*amount*) cantidad *f*; **a large ~ of money** una gran cantidad de dinero; **~ insured** suma *f* asegurada **3** *in arithmetic* suma *f*; **do ~s** sumar, hacer sumas

◆ **sum up I** *v/t* (*pret & pp* **-med**) **1** (*summarize*) resumir **2** (*assess*) catalogar **II** *v/i* (*pret & pp* **-med**) LAW recapitular

sum•mar•ize ['sʌməraɪz] *v/t* resumir

sum•ma•ry ['sʌmərɪ] **I** *n* resumen *m* **II** *adj justice* sumario

sum•mer ['sʌmər] **I** *n* verano *m*; **in (the) ~** en (el) verano **II** *adj* estival, veraniego

'sum•mer camp campamento *m* de verano; **sum•mer 'hol•i•days** *npl Br* ☞ **summer vacation**; **'sum•mer house** cenador *m*; **'sum•mer school** curso *m* de verano; **'sum•mer•time** *season* (estación *f* de) verano *m*; **in (the) ~** en (el) verano; **sum•mer va'ca•tion** vacaciones *fpl* de verano

sum•mer•y ['sʌmərɪ] *adj* veraniego

sum•ming-up [sʌmɪŋ'ʌp] *by judge* sumario *m*

sum•mit ['sʌmɪt] **1** *of mountain* cumbre *f*, cima *f* **2** POL cumbre *f*

'sum•mit meet•ing cumbre *f*

sum•mon ['sʌmən] *v/t staff, ministers* llamar; *meeting* convocar

◆ **summon up** *v/t*: **he summoned up his strength** hizo acopio de fuerzas; **summon up the courage to do sth** armarse de valor para hacer algo

sum•mons ['sʌmənz] *nsg* LAW citación *f*

sump [sʌmp] *for oil* cárter *m*

sump•tu•ous ['sʌmptʃuəs] *adj* espléndido, suntuoso

sun [sʌn] sol *m*; **in the ~** al sol; **out of the ~** a la sombra; **he has had too much ~** le ha dado demasiado el sol **II** *v/t*: **~ o.s.** tomar el sol

'sun•bathe *v/i* tomar el sol; **'sun•bed** cama *f* de rayos UVA; **'Sun Belt** *estados del sur y suroeste de EE.UU.*; **'sun•block** crema *f* solar de alta protección; **'sun•burn** quemadura *f* (del sol); **'sun•burnt** *adj* quemado (por el sol); **'sun•cream** crema *f* bronceadora

sun•dae ['sʌndeɪ] helado *m* en copa (*con frutas, jarabe, etc.*)

Sun•day ['sʌndeɪ] domingo *m*; **on ~** el domingo; **on ~s** los domingos

Sun•day 'best: **I was dressed in my ~** llevaba puestas mis mejores galas

'Sun•day school *catequismo dominical para niños*

'sun•dial reloj *m* de sol; **'sun•down** ☞ **sunset**; **'sun-dried** *adj* secado al sol

sun•dries ['sʌndrɪz] *npl* varios *mpl*

sun•dry ['sʌndrɪ] *adj*: **all and ~** todo el

S

mundo
'sun•flow•er BOT girasol *m*
sung [sʌŋ] *pp* ☞ ***sing***
'sun•glass•es *npl* anteojos *mpl or Span* gafas *fpl* de sol; ***a pair of ~*** unos anteojos *or Span* unas gafas de sol; **'sun god** dios *m* solar; **'sun hat** sombrero *m* para el sol
sunk [sʌŋk] *pp* ☞ ***sink***
sunk•en ['sʌŋkn] *adj ship, cheeks* hundido
'sun•lamp lámpara *f* de rayos UVA; **'sun•light** luz *f* solar; **'sun•lit** *adj* iluminado por el sol
sun•ny ['sʌnɪ] *adj* **1** *day* soleado; ***it is ~*** hace sol; ***~ side up*** frito sólo por un lado **2** *disposition* alegre, optimista
'sun•rise amanecer *m*; ***at ~*** al amanecer; **'sun•roof** MOT techo *m* solar *or* correrizo; **'sun•screen** pantalla *f* solar; **'sun•set** atardecer *m*, puesta *f* de sol; ***at ~*** al atardecer; **'sun•shade** sombrilla *f*; **'sun•shine** sol *m*; **'sun•spot** AST mancha *f* solar; **'sun•stroke** insolación *f*; **'sun•tan** bronceado *m*; ***get a ~*** broncearse; **'sun•tan lo•tion** bronceador *m*; **'sun•tanned** *adj* bronceado, moreno; **'sun•tan oil** aceite *m* bronceador; **'sun•trap** *sitio resguardado donde da el sol de lleno*; **'sun•up** ☞ ***sunrise***; **'sun vi•sor** MOT visera *f* antideslumbrante
su•per ['su:pər] **I** *adj* F genial F, estupendo F **II** *n* (*janitor*) portero(-a) *m*(*f*)
su•per•a'bun•dant *adj* superabundante
su•perb [sʊ'pɜ:rb] *adj* excelente
'su•per•bug F súper virus *m*
su•per•cil•i•ous [su:pər'sɪlɪəs] *adj* altivo, soberbio
su•per•con'duc•tor superconductor *m*
su•per•fi•cial [su:pər'fɪʃl] *adj* superficial
su•per•fi•ci•al•i•ty [su:pərfɪʃɪ'ælətɪ] superficialidad *f*
su•per•fine 'sug•ar azúcar *m* extrafino
su•per•flu•ous [sʊ'pɜ:rfluəs] *adj* superfluo
'su•per•glue® superglue *m*
su•per'hu•man *adj efforts* sobrehumano
su•per•im'pose *v/t* superponer (***on*** sobre)
su•per•in•tend•ent [su:pərɪn'tendənt] *of apartment block* portero(-a) *m*(*f*)
su•pe•ri•or [su:'pɪrɪər] **I** *adj* (*better, greater*) superior; *pej*: *attitude* arrogante; ***be ~ to*** ser superior a **II** *n in organization* superior *m*
su•pe•ri•or•i•ty [su:pɪrɪ'ɑ:rətɪ] **1** superioridad *f*, ***numerical ~*** superioridad en número **2** *pej* superioridad *f*, arrogancia *f*
su•per•la•tive [su:'pɜ:rlətɪv] **I** *adj superb* excelente **II** *n* GRAM superlativo *m*
'su•per•man supermán *m*, superhombre *m*
'su•per•mar•ket supermercado *m*; ***~ trolley*** *Br* carrito *m*
'su•per•mod•el supermodelo *m*/*f*
su•per'nat•u•ral I *adj powers* sobrenatural **II** *n*: ***the ~*** lo sobrenatural
'su•per•pow•er POL superpotencia *f*
su•per•sede [su:pər'si:d] *v/t* reemplazar
su•per•son•ic [su:pər'sɑ:nɪk] *adj flight, aircraft* supersónico
'su•per•star superestrella *f*
su•per•sti•tion [su:pər'stɪʃn] superstición *f*
su•per•sti•tious [su:pər'stɪʃəs] *adj person* supersticioso
'su•per•struc•ture ARCHI, NAUT superestructura *f*
'su•per•tank•er NAUT superpetrolero *m*
su•per•vise ['su:pərvaɪz] *v/t class* vigilar; *workers* supervisar; *activities* dirigir
su•per•vi•sion [su:pər'vɪʒn] supervisión *f*, vigilancia *f*; ***under s.o.'s ~*** bajo la supervisión de alguien
su•per•vi•sor ['su:pərvaɪzər] *at work* supervisor(a) *m*(*f*)
su•per•vi•so•ry [su:pər'vaɪzərɪ] *adj* de supervisión
sup•per ['sʌpər] cena *f*, *L.Am.* comida *f*; ***have ~*** cenar, *L.Am.* comer
sup•plant [sə'plɑ:nt] *v/t* reemplazar, sustituir
sup•ple ['sʌpl] *adj person* ágil; *limbs, material* flexible
sup•ple•ment I *n* ['sʌplɪmənt] (*extra payment*), *in newspaper* suplemento *m* **II** *v/t* ['sʌplɪment] *income* complementar (***with*** con)
sup•ple•men•ta•ry [sʌplɪ'mentərɪ] *adj* adicional, complementario

sup•pli•er [sə'plaɪər] COM proveedor(a) *m(f)*

sup•ply [sə'plaɪ] **I** *n* suministro *m*, abastecimiento *m*; **~ *and demand*** la oferta y la demanda; ***supplies*** *of food* provisiones *fpl*; ***office supplies*** material *f* de oficina **II** *v/t* (*pret & pp* **-*ied***) *goods* suministrar; **~ *s.o. with sth*** suministrar algo a alguien; ***be supplied with*** venir con

sup'ply teach•er *Br* profesor(a) *m(f)* suplente

sup'ply volt•age tensión *f* de alimentación

sup•port [sə'pɔːrt] **I** *n* **1** *for structure* soporte *m* **2** (*backing*) apoyo *m*; ***in ~ of*** en apoyo *or* defensa de **II** *v/t* **1** *building, structure* soportar, sostener **2** *financially* mantener **3** (*back*) apoyar; *soccer team* ser de

sup•port•er [sə'pɔːrtər] partidario(-a) *m(f)*; *of football team etc* seguidor(a) *m(f)*

sup'port group asociación *f*, grupo *m* de apoyo (***for*** de)

sup•port•ing [sə'pɔːrtɪŋ] *adj* **1**: **~ *actor*** actor *m* secundario ; **~ *actress*** actriz *f* secundaria; **~ *role*** papel *m* secundario **2**: **~ *wall*** pared *f* maestra

sup•port•ive [sə'pɔːrtɪv] *adj* comprensivo; ***be ~*** apoyar (***toward, of*** a)

sup'port ser•vi•ces *npl* servicios *mpl* de apoyo

sup'port staff personal *m* de apoyo

sup•pose [sə'poʊz] *v/t* **1** (*imagine*) suponer; ***I ~ so*** supongo (que sí); ***I ~ I must have fallen asleep*** supongo que me he quedado dormido **2**: ***you are not ~d to …*** (*not allowed to*) no deberías …; ***it is ~d to be delivered today*** (*is meant to be*) se supone que lo van a entregar hoy; ***aren't you ~d to be at work?*** ¿no tendrías que estar trabajando?; ***it's ~d to be very beautiful*** (*is said to be*) se supone que es hermosísimo; ***what's that ~d to mean?*** ¿qué se supone que quiere decir eso? **II** *conj*: **~ *we went home?*** ¿y si nos vamos a casa?

sup•posed [sə'poʊzd] *adj* supuesto, presunto

sup•pos•ed•ly [sə'poʊzɪdlɪ] *adv* supuestamente

sup•pos•ing [sə'poʊzɪŋ] *conj* ☞ ***suppose* II**

sup•po•si•tion [sʌpə'zɪʃn] suposición *f*, presunción *f*

sup•pos•i•to•ry [sə'pɑːzɪtɔːrɪ] MED supositorio *m*

sup•press [sə'pres] *v/t rebellion etc* reprimir, sofocar

sup•pres•sion [sə'preʃn] represión *f*

su•prem•a•cy [suː'preməsɪ] supremacía *f*

su•preme [suː'priːm] *adj* supremo

Su'preme Court Tribunal *m* Supremo, *L.Am.* Corte *f* Suprema

su•preme•ly [suː'priːmlɪ] *adv* extremadamente

sur•charge ['sɜːrtʃɑːrdʒ] recargo *m*

sure [ʃʊr] **I** *adj* seguro; ***I'm not ~*** no estoy seguro; ***be ~ about sth*** estar seguro de algo; ***make ~ that …*** asegurarse de que …; ***make ~ of sth*** asegurarse de algo; **~ *of o.s.*** seguro de sí mismo; **~ *thing!*** F ¡claro! F; ***be a ~ thing*** estar asegurado *or* garantizado; ***you're ~ to like this play*** seguro que te gusta esta obra; ***be ~ to lock the door!*** ¡asegúrate de cerrar bien la puerta!; ***I can't say for ~*** no lo puedo decir con seguridad; ***one thing's for ~*** una cosa es segura; ***and to be ~, he …*** y, por supuesto, … **II** *adv*: **~ *enough*** efectivamente; ***it ~ is hot today*** F vaya calor que hace F; **~*!*** F ¡claro!

'sure-fire *adj* F seguro, infalible

sure-foot•ed [ʃʊr'fʊtɪd] *adj* con los pies firmes

sure•ly ['ʃʊrlɪ] *adv* **1** (*gladly*) claro que sí **2**: **~ *you don't mean that!*** ¡ no lo dirás en serio!; **~ *somebody knows*** alguien tiene que saberlo

sur•e•ty ['ʃʊrətɪ] *for loan* aval *m*, fianza *f*; ***stand ~ for s.o.*** avalar a alguien

surf [sɜːrf] **I** *n on sea* surf *m* **II** *v/t*: **~ *the Net*** navegar por Internet **III** *v/i on sea* hacer surf

sur•face ['sɜːrfɪs] **I** *n of table, object, water* superficie *f*; ***on the ~*** *fig* a primera vista; **~ *tension*** PHYS tensión *f* de superficie **II** *v/i* **1** *of swimmer, submarine* salir a la superficie **2** (*appear*) aparecer **III** *v/t roads* revestir

'sur•face mail correo *m* terrestre; **sur•face-to-'air** *adj* tierra-aire; **sur•face-to-'sur•face** *adj* tierra-tierra; **'sur•face trans•port** transporte *m* por superficie

sur•fac•tant [sɜːr'fæktənt] CHEM tensioactivo *m*
'surf•board tabla *f* de surf
sur•feit ['sɜːrfɪt] exceso (***of*** de)
surf•er ['sɜːrfər] *on sea* surfista *m/f*
surf•ing ['sɜːrfɪŋ] surf *m*; ***go ~*** ir a hacer surf
surge [sɜːrdʒ] **I** *n in electric current* sobrecarga *f*; *in demand etc* incremento *m* repentino; ***there was a sudden ~ forward*** la gente se abalanzó de repente **II** *v/i*: ***the mob ~d toward the palace*** la muchedumbre se precipitó hacia el palacio
◆ **surge forward** *v/i of crowd* avanzar atropelladamente
◆ **surge up** *v/i*: ***anger surged up in her*** la rabia se adueñó de ella
sur•geon ['sɜːrdʒən] cirujano(-a) *m(f)*
Sur•geon 'Gen•e•ral (*in government*) *máximo responsable de la sanidad pública*
sur•ge•ry ['sɜːrdʒərɪ] **1** cirugía *f*; ***undergo ~*** ser intervenido quirúrgicamente; ***he needs ~*** requiere una operación **2** *Br*: *doctor's office* consulta *f*; ***~ hours*** *pl* horas *fpl* de consulta
sur•gi•cal ['sɜːrdʒɪkl] *adj* quirúrgico; ***~ stocking*** media *f* ortopédica
sur•gi•cal•ly ['sɜːrdʒɪklɪ] *adv* quirúrgicamente
Su•ri•name ['sʊrɪnæm] Suriname *m*
Su•ri•nam•ese [sʊrɪnæm'iːz] **I** *adj* surinamés **II** *n* surinamés(-esa) *m(f)*
sur•ly ['sɜːrlɪ] *adj* arisco, hosco
sur•mise [sɜːr'maɪz] *v/t* inferir, deducir
sur•mount [sər'maʊnt] *v/t difficulties* superar
sur•mount•a•ble [sər'maʊntəbl] *adj* superable
sur•name ['sɜːrneɪm] apellido *m*
sur•pass [sər'pæs] *v/t* superar
sur•plus ['sɜːrpləs] **I** *n* excedente *m* **II** *adj* excedente; ***be ~ to requirements*** ser superfluo *or* prescincible
sur•prise [sər'praɪz] **I** *n* sorpresa *f*; ***it came as no ~*** no me sorprendió; ***in ~*** sorprendido; ***take s.o. by ~*** pillar a alguien por sorpresa **II** *v/t* sorprender; ***be / look ~d*** quedarse / parecer sorprendido (***at*** ante; ***by*** por); ***I wouldn't be ~d if*** no me sorprendería si
sur•prise 'par•ty fiesta *f* sorpresa
sur•pris•ing [sər'praɪzɪŋ] *adj* sorprendente; ***it's not ~ that ...*** no me sorprende que ...
sur•pris•ing•ly [sər'praɪzɪŋlɪ] *adv* sorprendentemente; ***~ (enough)*** sorprendentemente, aunque parezca sorprendente
sur•re•al• [sə'riːəl] *adj* surrealista, extraño
sur•re•al•ism [sə'riːəlɪzəm] *in art* surrealismo *m*
sur•re•al•ist [sə'riːəlɪst] **I** *adj* surrealista **II** *n* surrealista *m/f*
sur•re•al•is•tic [səriːəl'ɪstɪk] *adj* surrealista
sur•ren•der [sə'rendər] **I** *v/i of army* rendirse; *to police* entregarse **II** *v/t weapons, passport etc* entregar **III** *n* **1** rendición *f* **2** (*handing in*) entrega *f*
sur•rep•ti•tious [sʌrəp'tɪʃəs] *adj* furtivo, disimulado
sur•rep•ti•tious•ly [sʌrəp'tɪʃəslɪ] *adv* furtivamente, disimuladamente
sur•ro•ga•cy ['sʌrəgəsɪ] *embarazo por encargo de terceros*
sur•ro•gate moth•er [sʌrəgət'mʌðər] madre *f* de alquiler
sur•round [sə'raʊnd] **I** *v/t* rodear; ***~ed by*** rodeado de *or* por **II** *n of picture etc* marco *m*
sur•round•ing [sə'raʊndɪŋ] *adj* circundante
sur•round•ings [sə'raʊndɪŋz] *npl* **1** *of village* alrededores *mpl* **2** (*environment*) entorno *m*
sur'round sound sonido *m* surround
sur•veil•lance [sɜːr'veɪləns] vigilancia *f*; ***be / keep under ~*** *person, premises* estar / mantener bajo vigilancia
sur•vey ['sɜːrveɪ] **I** *n* ['sɜːrveɪ] **1** *of modern literature etc* estudio *m* **2** *of building* tasación *f*, peritaje **3** (*poll*) encuesta *f* **II** *v/t* [sər'veɪ] **1** (*look at*) contemplar **2** *building* tasar, peritar
sur•vey•or [sɜːr'veɪr] tasador(a) *m(f)* *or* perito(-a) *m(f)* de la propiedad
sur•viv•al [sər'vaɪvl] supervivencia *f*; ***~ of the fittest*** la ley del más fuerte; ***~ suit*** traje *m* de supervivencia; ***~ training course*** curso *m* de supervivencia
sur•vive [sər'vaɪv] **I** *v/i* sobrevivir; ***how are you? – I'm surviving*** ¿cómo estás? – voy tirando; ***his two surviving daughters*** las dos hijas que aún viven **II** *v/t accident, operation* sobrevivir a;

(*outlive*) sobrevivir; ***he is ~d by his second wife*** le survive su segunda esposa
sur•vi•vor [sər'vaɪvər] superviviente *m/f*; ***he's a ~*** *fig* es incombustible
sus•cep•ti•ble [sə'septəbl] *adj emotionally* sensible, susceptible; ***be ~ to the cold / heat*** ser sensible al frío / calor
su•shi ['su:ʃɪ] sushi *m*
sus•pect I *n* ['sʌspekt] sospechoso(-a) *m(f)* II *v/t* [sə'spekt] 1 *person* sospechar de; ***~ s.o. of doing sth*** sospechar que alguien ha hecho algo; ***be ~ed of sth / doing sth*** ser sospechoso de algo / haber hecho algo 2 (*suppose*) sospechar III *adj* ['sʌspekt] dudoso; ***a ~ package*** un paquete sospechoso; ***his motives are ~*** sus motivos son sospechosos
sus•pect•ed [sə'spektɪd] *adj murderer* presunto; *cause, heart attack etc* supuesto
sus•pend [sə'spend] *v/t* 1 (*hang*) colgar 2 *from office, duties* suspender; ***he was given a two-year ~ed sentence*** recibió una condena condicional de dos años; ***~ed animation*** animación *f* suspendida
sus•pend•er belt [sə'spendər] *Br* liguero *m*
sus•pend•ers [sə'spendərz] *npl* 1 *for pants* tirantes *mpl*, *S.Am.* suspensores *mpl* 2 *Br: for stockings* ligas *fpl*
sus•pense [sə'spens] *Span* suspense *m*, *L.Am.* suspenso *m*; ***keep s.o. in ~*** dejar a alguien en vilo
sus'pense ac•count cuenta *f* provisional
sus•pen•sion [sə'spenʃn] MOT, *from duty* suspensión *f*; ***he received a two-game ~*** le han penalizado con dos partidos sin jugar
sus'pen•sion bridge puente *m* colgante
sus•pi•cion [sə'spɪʃn] sospecha *f*; ***be above ~*** estar libre de toda sospecha; ***be under ~ of murder*** ser sospechoso de asesinato; ***with ~*** con desconfianza
sus•pi•cious [sə'spɪʃəs] *adj* 1 (*causing suspicion*) sospechoso 2 (*feeling suspicion*) receloso, desconfiado; ***be ~ of*** sospechar de
sus•pi•cious•ly [sə'spɪʃəslɪ] *adv* 1 *behave* de manera sospechosa 2 *ask* con recelo *or* desconfianza

sus•tain [sə'steɪn] *v/t* sostener
sus•tain•a•ble [sə'steɪnəbl] *adj* sostenible
sus•tain•a•ble de'vel•op•ment desarrollo *m* sostenible
sus•tained [sə'steɪnd] *adj* sostenido
sus•te•nance ['sʌstənəns] sustento *m*
su•ture ['su:tʃər] MED I *n* sutura *f* II *v/t wound* suturar
SUV [esju:'vi:] *abbr* (= ***sport utility vehicle***) SUV *m*, todoterreno *m* ligero
svelte [svelt] *adj* elegante, estiloso
SVGA [esvi:dʒi:'eɪ] *abbr* (= ***Super Video Graphics Array***) SVGA *m*, super adaptador *m* de gráficos de vídeo
swab [swɑ:b] 1 *n material* torunda *f* 2 *test* muestra *f*; ***take a ~*** extraer una muestra (***from*** de) II *v/t* (*pret & pp* ***-bed***) *wound* limpiar
swag•ger ['swægər] I *n*: ***walk with a ~*** caminar pavoneándose II *v/i* caminar pavoneándose
swal•low[1] ['swɑ:loʊ] I *v/t* 1 *liquid, food* tragar, tragarse; ***~ one's words*** desdecirse 2 F *story, lie* tragar, tragarse F; ***find sth hard to ~*** F no tragarse algo F II *v/i* tragar III *n* trago *m*
◆ **swallow up** *v/t* absorber; (*engulf*) devorar
swal•low[2] ['swɑ:loʊ] *n bird* golondrina *f*
swam [swæm] *pret* ☞ ***swim***
swamp [swɑ:mp] I *n* pantano *m* II *v/t*: ***be ~ed with*** estar inundado de
swamp•y ['swɑ:mpɪ] *adj* pantanoso
swan [swɑ:n] cisne *m*
swank•y ['swæŋkɪ] *adj* F pijo F
'swan song *fig* canto *m* del cisne
swap [swɑ:p] I *v/t* (*pret & pp* ***-ped***) cambiar (de); ***~ sth for sth*** cambiar algo por algo; ***~ places*** cambiarse el sitio; ***~ places with s.o.*** cambiarse por alguien II *v/i* (*pret & pp* ***-ped***) hacer un cambio III *n* intercambio *m*; ***do a ~*** cambiar
◆ **swap around, swap over** *v/i* (*exchange seats*) cambiar
'swap meet *feria en la que se intercambian objetos*
swarm [swɔ:rm] I *n of bees* enjambre *m* II *v/i*: ***the town was ~ing with ...*** la ciudad estaba abarrotada de ...
swar•thy ['swɔ:rðɪ] *adj face, complexion* moreno

swash•buck•ling ['swɑːʃbʌklɪŋ] *adj hero, movie* de capa y espada
swat [swɑːt] *v/t* (*pret & pp* **-ted**) *insect, fly* aplastar, matar
swatch [swɑːʧ] muestra *f* de tela
swat•ter ['swɑːtər] (*fly~*) matamoscas *m inv*
sway [sweɪ] **I** *n* (*influence, power*) dominio *m* **II** *v/i* tambalearse
swear [swer] **I** *v/i* (*pret* **swore**, *pp* **sworn**) **1** (*use ~word*) decir palabrotas *or* tacos; ***~ at s.o.*** insultar a alguien **2** LAW, *fig* jurar; ***I ~*** lo juro; ***I couldn't ~ to it*** no estoy seguro del todo **II** *v/t* (*pret* **swore**, *pp* **sworn**) (*promise*), LAW jurar; ***~ sth to s.o.*** jurar a alguien algo; ***I was sworn to secrecy*** se me hizo prometer que no diría nada
◆ **swear by** *v/t fig* F tener mucha fe en
◆ **swear in** *v/t witnesses etc* tomar juramento a
◆ **swear off** *v/t* prometerse dejar
'swear•word palabrota *f*, taco *m*
sweat [swet] **I** *n* sudor *m*; ***covered in ~*** empapado de sudor; ***break out in a cold ~*** dar sudores fríos; ***no ~!*** F ¡nada hombre! F, ¡no importa! F; ***I can do that, no ~*** F puedo hacerlo, no te preocupes; ***get in(to) a ~*** *fig* F estar agobiado (***about*** por) F
II *v/i* sudar; ***let them ~ for a bit*** F déjales que sufran un poco
III *v/t*: ***~ blood*** F sudar sangre F
◆ **sweat out** *v/t*: ***sweat it out*** F esperar, aguantar
'sweat•band banda *f* (en la frente); *on wrist* muñequera *f*
sweat•er ['swetər] suéter *m*, *Span* jersey *m*
'sweat gland ANAT glándula *f* sudorípara
sweats [swets] *npl* chándal *m*
'sweat•shirt sudadera *f*
'sweat•shop *taller donde se explota a los trabajadores*
sweat•y ['swetɪ] *adj hands* sudoroso
Swede [swiːd] sueco(-a) *m(f)*
Swe•den ['swiːdn] Suecia *f*
Swe•dish ['swiːdɪʃ] **I** *adj* sueco **II** *n* sueco *m*
sweep [swiːp] **I** *v/t* (*pret & pp* **swept**) *floor, leaves* barrer; ***~ the board*** *in competition* arrasar; ***~ a woman off her feet*** *fig* hacer perder la cabeza a una mujer; ***be swept to power*** llegar al poder por un margen de votos amplio
II *v/i* (*pret & pp* **swept**) **1** barrer **2**: ***~ past s.o.*** *of person* pasar por delante de alguien con aires de grandeza
III *n* **1** barrida *f*; ***give the floor a ~*** dar una barrida al suelo **2** (*long curve*) curva *f* **3**: ***make a clean ~*** *in competition* arrasar
◆ **sweep along** *v/t of wind, tide* arrastrar
◆ **sweep aside** *v/t objections* desoír, ignorar
◆ **sweep away** *v/t* **1** *boat, swimmer* arrastrar; ***be swept away by*** *fig* ser arrastrado por **2** *obstacles, restrictions* eliminar
◆ **sweep up** *v/t mess, crumbs* barrer
sweep•er ['swiːpər] **1** *person* barrendero(-a) *m(f)* **2** *machine* cepillo *m* (mecánico) **3** *in soccer* líbero *m/f*
sweep•ing ['swiːpɪŋ] *adj statement* demasiado generalizado; *changes* radical
sweet [swiːt] *adj* **1** *taste, tea, smile* dulce; ***whisper ~ nothings to each other*** decirse cosas románticas al oído; ***revenge is ~*** la venganza es dulce; ***have a ~ tooth*** ser laminero *or* goloso; ***keep s.o. ~*** F tener a alguien contento F **2** F (*kind*) amable **3** F (*cute*) mono **II** *n Br* **1** (*piece of candy*) caramelo *m* **2** (*dessert*) postre *m*
sweet and 'sour *adj* agridulce
'sweet•corn maíz *m*, *S.Am.* choclo *m*
sweet•en•er ['swiːtnər] *for drink* edulcorante *m*; *fig* (*incentive*) soborno *m*, incentivo *m*
sweet•en ['swiːtn] *v/t drink, food* endulzar
◆ **sweeten up** *v/t* F *person* camelar F
'sweet•heart **1** novio(-a) *m(f)* **2**: ***hi, ~!*** ¡hola cielo!; ***be a ~ and get me a beer*** anda cariño, traeme una cerveza
sweet•ie ['swiːtɪ] F **1** ☞ ***sweetheart*** **2** *Br* caramelo *m*
sweet•ly ['swiːtlɪ] *adv smile* dulcemente
sweet 'pea arvejo *m*, *CSur* arveja *f*; **sweet po'ta•to** BOT boniato *m*, *Andes, C.Am., Mex* camote *m*; **'sweet talk** halagos *mpl*, adulación *f*; **'sweet-talk** *v/t* F: ***~ s.o. into doing sth*** pelotear *or* embelesar a alguien para que haga algo
swell [swel] **I** *v/i* (*pret* **-ed**, *pp* **swollen**)

S

of wound, limb hincharse **II** *v/t* (*pret* **-ed**, *pp* **swollen**) *numbers* aumentar **III** *adj* F (*good*) genial F, fenomenal F **IV** *n of the sea* oleaje *m*; ***a heavy ~*** una marejada
◆ **swell up** *v/i* MED hincharse
swell•ing ['swelɪŋ] MED hinchazón *f*
swel•ter ['sweltər] *v/i* asarse de calor
swel•ter•ing ['sweltərɪŋ] *adj heat, day* sofocante
swept [swept] *pret & pp* ☞ ***sweep***
swerve [swɜːrv] **I** *v/i of car, person walking* girar *or* apartarse bruscamente; *of driver* dar un volantazo; *of football player* regatear **II** *n of car, person walking* giro *m* brusco; *of driver* volantazo *m*; *of football player* regateo *m*
swift[1] [swɪft] *adj* rápido; ***be ~ to do sth*** no tardar en hacer algo
swift[2] [swɪft] *n bird* vencejo *m* común
swift•ly ['swɪftlɪ] *adv* rápidamente
swift•ness ['swɪftnɪs] rapidez *f*
swig [swɪg] F **I** *v/t* (*pret & pp* **-ged**) *drink* beber a tragos **II** *n*: ***take a ~ from the bottle*** echarse un trago de la botella
swill [swɪl] *v/t pej*: *drink* pimplar F, *L.Am.* tomar
swim [swɪm] **I** *v/i* (*pret* **swam**, *pp* **swum**) nadar; ***go ~ming*** ir a nadar; ***my head is ~ming*** me da vueltas la cabeza **II** *n* baño *m*; ***go for a ~*** ir a darse un baño
swim•mer ['swɪmər] nadador(a) *m(f)*
swim•ming ['swɪmɪŋ] natación *f*
'swim•ming cap gorro *m* de natación; **'swim•ming hole** *lugar apto para el baño en un río*; **'swim•ming pool** piscina *f*, *Mex* alberca *f*, *Rpl* pileta *f*; **'swim•ming trunks** *npl esp Br* bañador *m* (*para caballero*)
'swim•suit traje *m* de baño, bañador *m*
'swim•wear trajes *mpl* de baño, bañadores *mpl*
swin•dle ['swɪndl] **I** *n* timo *m*, estafa *f* **II** *v/t* timar, estafar; ***~ s.o. out of sth*** estafar algo a alguien
swin•dler ['swɪndlər] timador(a) *m(f)*, estafador(a) *m(f)*
swine [swaɪn] F *person* cerdo(-a) *m(f)* F
swing [swɪŋ] **I** *n* **1** oscilación *f* **2** *for child* columpio *m* **3**: ***~ to the Democrats*** giro *m* favorable a los Demócratas **4**: ***be in full ~*** estar en pleno apogeo; ***get into the ~ of things*** coger el ritmo *or* la marcha **II** *v/t* (*pret & pp* **swung**) balancear; *hips* menear **III** *v/i* (*pret & pp* **swung**) **1** balancearse; ***~ shut*** cerrarse **2** (*turn*) girar; *of public opinion etc* cambiar
◆ **swing around** *v/i* girarse de golpe
swing-'door puerta *f* basculante *or* de vaivén
swing•ing ['swɪŋɪŋ] *adj* F **1** *party, city* animado **2** *having casual sex* que va de flor en flor
swipe [swaɪp] F **I** *n physical* golpe *m*; *verbal* crítica *f*; ***take a ~ at*** *physically* dar un golpe a; *verbally* criticar F **II** *v/t* **1** *credit card* pasar por el lector **2** F (*steal*) robar **III** *v/i of credit card* pasar por el lector
◆ **swipe at** *v/t physically* dar un golpe a; *verbally* criticar F
swirl [swɜːrl] **I** *v/i* hacer remolinos **II** *n* remolino *m*; *of cream* espiral *f*
swish [swɪʃ] **I** *v/i of silk* crujir; *of tires* rechinar **II** *v/t tail* agitar, menear **III** *n of silk* crujido *m*; *of tires* rechinamiento *m*; *of curtains* roce *m* **IV** *adj esp Br* F elegante, fino F
Swiss [swɪs] **I** *adj* suizo **II** *n person* suizo(-a) *m(f)*; ***the ~*** los suizos
switch [swɪʧ] **I** *n* **1** *for light* interruptor *m* **2** (*change*) cambio *m* **II** *v/t* (*change*) cambiar (de); ***~ places with s.o.*** cambiarse por alguien **III** *v/i* (*change*) cambiar
◆ **switch around** *v/t* cambiar de sitio
◆ **switch off** **I** *v/t lights, engine, PC, TV* apagar **II** *v/i* F *of person* desconectar
◆ **switch on** *v/t lights, engine, PC, TV* encender, *L.Am.* prender
◆ **switch over** *v/i* cambiarse (***to*** a)
'switch•blade navaja *f* automática; **'switch•board** centralita *f*, *L.Am.* conmutador; ***~ operator*** telefonista *m/f*; **'switch•o•ver** *to new system* cambio *m* (***to*** a)
Swit•zer•land ['swɪtsərlənd] Suiza *f*
swiv•el ['swɪvl] *v/i* (*pret & pp* **-ed**, *Br* **-led**) *of chair, monitor* girar
◆ **swivel around** *v/i* girar
'swiv•el chair silla *f* giratoria
swol•len ['swoulən] **I** *pp* ☞ ***swell*** **II** *adj* hinchado
swol•len-head•ed [swoulən'hedɪd] *adj fig* engreido
swoon [swuːn] *v/i* perder el sentido

(*over* por)
swoop [swuːp] *v/i of bird* volar en picado
◆ **swoop down on** *v/t prey* caer en picado sobre
◆ **swoop on** *v/t of police etc* hacer una redada contra
swop ☞ ***swap***
sword [sɔːrd] espada *f*; ***cross ~s*** *fig* ponerse a mal (***with*** con)
'**sword•fish** pez *f* espada
swore [swɔːr] *pret* ☞ ***swear***
sworn [swɔːrn] **I** *pp* ☞ ***swear*** **II** *adj* **1**: ***~ enemies*** *pl* enemigos *mpl* encarnizados **2** LAW jurado
swot [swɑːt] *Br* F **I** *v/i* (*pret & pp* ***-ted***) empollar F **II** *n* empollón(-ona) *m(f)* F
swum [swʌm] *pp* ☞ ***swim***
swung [swʌŋ] *pret & pp* ☞ ***swing***
syc•a•more ['sɪkəmɔːr] plátano *m*
syc•o•phan•tic [sɪkə'fæntɪk] *adj* halagador
syl•la•ble ['sɪləbl] sílaba *f*
syl•la•bus ['sɪləbəs] plan *m* de estudios
sym•bi•o•sis [sɪmbaɪ'oʊsɪs] BIO simbiosis *f*
sym•bi•ot•ic [sɪmbaɪ'ɑːtɪk] *adj* BIO simbiótico
sym•bol ['sɪmbəl] símbolo *m*
sym•bol•ic [sɪm'bɑːlɪk] *adj* simbólico; ***be ~ of sth*** ser el símbolo de algo, simbolizar algo
sym•bol•i•cal•ly [sɪm'bɑːlɪklɪ] *adv* simbólicamente
sym•bol•ism ['sɪmbəlɪzm] simbolismo *m*
sym•bol•ist ['sɪmbəlɪst] simbolista *m/f*
sym•bol•ize ['sɪmbəlaɪz] *v/t* simbolizar
sym•met•ric, sym•met•ri•cal [sɪ'metrɪk(l)] *adj* simétrico
sym•me•try ['sɪmətrɪ] simetría *f*
sym•pa•thet•ic [sɪmpə'θetɪk] *adj* (*showing pity*) compasivo; (*understanding*) comprensivo; ***be ~ toward a person / an idea*** simpatizar con una persona / idea
◆ **sym•pa•thize with** ['sɪmpəθaɪz] *v/t person, views* comprender
sym•pa•thiz•er ['sɪmpəθaɪzər] POL simpatizante *m/f*
sym•pa•thy ['sɪmpəθɪ] **1** (*pity*) compasión *f*; ***in ~*** mis condolencias; *go on strike* en solidaridad; ***I have no ~ for him*** no me da ninguna pena; ***don't expect any ~ from me*** no esperes que te compadezca **2** (*understanding*) comprensión *f*; ***be in ~ with*** simpatizar con **3**: ***my sympathies lie with*** mis simpatías están con
'**sym•pa•thy strike** huelga *f* por solidaridad
sym•phon•ic [sɪm'fɑːnɪk] *adj* MUS sinfónico
sym•pho•ny ['sɪmfənɪ] sinfonía *f*
'**sym•pho•ny or•ches•tra** orquesta *f* sinfónica
sym•po•si•um [sɪm'poʊzɪəm] (*pl* ***-siums***, ***symposia*** [sɪm'poʊzɪə]) *conference* simposio *m*, congreso *m*
symp•tom ['sɪmptəm] *also fig* síntoma *f*
symp•to•mat•ic [sɪmptə'mætɪk] *adj*: ***be ~ of*** *fig* ser sintomático de
syn•a•gogue ['sɪnəgɑːg] sinagoga *f*
syn•chro•nize ['sɪŋkrənaɪz] *v/t* sincronizar
syn•chro•nized swim•ming [sɪŋkrənaɪzd'swɪmɪŋ] natación *f* sincronizada
syn•di•cate ['sɪndɪkət] COM corporación *f*, consorcio *m*
syn•drome ['sɪndroʊm] MED síndrome *m*
syn•er•gy ['sɪnərdʒɪ] sinergia *f*
syn•o•nym ['sɪnənɪm] sinónimo *m*
sy•non•y•mous [sɪ'nɑːnɪməs] *adj* sinónimo; ***be ~ with*** *fig* ser sinónimo de
syn•op•sis [sɪ'nɑːpsɪs] (*pl* ***synopses*** [sɪ-'nɑːpsiːz]) sinopsis *f*
syn•tac•tic [sɪn'tæktɪk] *adj* LING sintáctico
syn•tax ['sɪntæks] sintaxis *f inv*
syn•the•sis ['sɪnθəsɪs] (*pl* ***syntheses*** ['sɪnθəsiːz]) síntesis *f*
syn•the•size ['sɪnθəsaɪz] *v/t* CHEM sintetizar
syn•the•siz•er ['sɪnθəsaɪzər] MUS sintetizador *m*
syn•thet•ic [sɪn'θetɪk] *adj* sintético
syph•i•lis ['sɪfɪlɪs] *nsg* sífilis *f*
sy•phon ☞ ***siphon***
Syr•i•a ['sɪrɪə] Siria *f*
Syr•i•an ['sɪrɪən] **I** *adj* sirio **II** *n* sirio(-a) *m(f)*
sy•ringe [sɪ'rɪndʒ] jeringuilla *f*
syr•up ['sɪrəp] almíbar *m*
syr•up•y ['sɪrəpɪ] *adj* **1** almibarado **2** *fig* empalagoso
sys•tem ['sɪstəm] *also* COMPUT sistema *m*; ***the braking ~*** el sistema de frenado;

the digestive ~ el aparato digestivo; ***~ of government*** sistema de gobierno; ***~ crash*** COMPUT bloqueo *m* del sistema; ***~ error*** COMPUT error *m* del sistema; ***~ failure*** fracaso *m* del sistema; ***~s engineer*** ingeniero(-a) *m(f)* de sistemas; ***get sth out of one's ~*** *fig* sacarse una espina

sys•tem•at•ic [sɪstə'mætɪk] *adj* sistemático

sys•tem•at•i•cal•ly [sɪstə'mætɪklɪ] *adv* sistemáticamente

sys•tem•a•tize ['sɪstəmətaɪz] *v/t* sistematizar

sys•tems 'an•a•lyst COMPUT analista *m/f* de sistemas

T

T [tiː]: ***that's him to a ~*** F ése es justamente él

tab [tæb] **1** *for pulling* lengüeta *f* **2** *in text* tabulador *m* **3** *bill* cuenta *f*; ***pick up the ~*** pagar (la cuenta) **4**: ***keep ~s on s.o.*** F seguir la pista a alguien

'tab key tecla *f* de tabulación

ta•ble ['teɪbl] **I** *n* **1** mesa *f*; ***at the ~*** a la mesa; ***put sth on the ~*** *fig* poner algo sobre el tapete; ***set the ~*** poner la mesa; ***turn the ~s on s.o.*** *fig* volver las tornas a alguien; ***drink s.o. under the ~*** aguantar bebiendo mucho más que alguien **2** *of figures* cuadro *m* **II** *v/t* **1** *bill, amendment* posponer, aplazar **2** *Br. bill, amendment* presentar

'ta•ble•cloth mantel *m*; **'ta•ble lamp** lámpara *f* de mesa; **'ta•ble man•ners** *npl* modales *mpl*; **'ta•ble•mat** salvamanteles *m inv*; **ta•ble of 'con•tents** índice *m* (de contenidos); **'ta•ble•spoon** *object* cuchara *f* grande; *quantity* cucharada *f* grande

tab•let ['tæblɪt] MED pastilla *f*

'ta•ble ten•nis tenis *m* de mesa

ta•ble•ware ['teɪblwer] vajilla *f*

'ta•ble wine vino *m* de mesa

tab•loid ['tæblɔɪd] *newspaper* periódico *m* sensacionalista (*de tamaño tabloide*)

tab•loid 'press prensa *f* sensacionalista

ta•boo [tə'buː] **I** *adj* tabú *inv* **II** *n* tabú *m*

tab•u•lar ['tæbjʊlər] *adj* tabular; ***in ~ form*** en forma tabular

tab•u•late ['tæbjʊleɪt] *v/t* tabular

tach•o•graph ['tækəgræf] MOT tacógrafo *m*

ta•chom•e•ter [tæk'ɑːmɪtər] MOT tacómetro *m*

tac•it ['tæsɪt] *adj* tácito

tac•i•turn ['tæsɪtɜːrn] *adj* taciturno

tack [tæk] **I** *n* **1** (*nail*) tachuela *f* **2**: ***change ~*** *fig* cambiar de táctica **II** *v/t* (*sew*) hilvanar **III** *v/i of yacht* dar bordadas

◆ **tack on** *v/t* añadir posteriormente (***to*** a)

tack•le ['tækl] **I** *n* **1** (*equipment*) equipo *m*; ***fishing ~*** aparejos *mpl* de pesca **2** SP entrada *f*, placaje *m*; ***make a ~ on s.o.*** hacer una entrada a alguien **II** *v/t* SP entrar a, placar; *problem* abordar; *intruder* hacer frente a

tack•y ['tækɪ] *adj* **1** *paint, glue* pegajoso **2** F (*cheap, poor quality*) chabacano, *Span* hortera F; *behavior* impresentable

tact [tækt] tacto *m*

tact•ful ['tæktfəl] *adj* diplomático

tact•ful•ly ['tæktfəlɪ] *adv* diplomáticamente

tac•ti•cal ['tæktɪkl] *adj* táctico

tac•ti•cian [tæk'tɪʃn] táctico(-a) *m(f)*

tac•tics ['tæktɪks] *npl* táctica *f*

tact•less ['tæktlɪs] *adj* indiscreto

tad•pole ['tædpoʊl] renacuajo *m*

taf•fe•ta ['tæfɪtə] tafetán *m*

taf•fy ['tæfɪ] caramelo *m* de melaza

tag[1] [tæg] **I** *n* (*label*) etiqueta *f* **II** *v/t* (*pret & pp* ***-ged***) (*label*), COMPUT etiquetar

◆ **tag along** *v/i* pegarse; ***tag along behind s.o.*** pegarse a alguien

◆ **tag on** *v/t* añadir posteriormente (***to*** a)

tag[2] [tæg] *n*: ***play ~*** jugar al corre que te pillo

ta•glia•tel•le [tæljə'telɪ] tallarines *mpl*

tail [teɪl] **I** *n* **1** *of bird, fish* cola *f*; *of mammal* cola *f*, rabo *m* **2**: ***put a ~ on s.o.*** F hacer seguir alguien de cerca **II** *v/t* F (*follow*) seguir por todas partes

◆ **tail back** *v/i* MOT *esp Br*: ***traffic was tailed back all the way to the bridge*** el tapón de tráfico llegaba hasta el puente
◆ **tail off** *v/i* disminuir
'tail•back MOT *esp Br* caravana *f*; **'tail coat** frac *m*; **'tail end** final *m*; **'tail•gate** MOT **I** *n* puerta *f* trasera **II** *v/t* conducir pegado a; **'tail light** luz *f* trasera
tai•lor ['teɪlər] **I** *n* sastre *m* **II** *v/t fig* adaptar (***to*** a)
tai•lor-'made *adj suit, solution* hecho a medida
'tail•pipe *of car* tubo *m* de escape
'tail•wind viento *m* de cola
taint•ed ['teɪntɪd] *adj food* contaminado; *reputation* empañado
Tai•wan [taɪ'wɑːn] Taiwán *m*
Tai•wan•ese [taɪwɑːn'iːz] **I** *adj* taiwanés **II 1** taiwanés(-esa) *m(f)* **2** *dialect* taiwanés *m*
take [teɪk] **I** *v/t* (*pret* ***took***, *pp* ***taken***) **1** llevarse, *Span* coger; ***I'll ~ it*** *when shopping* me lo llevo; ***~ s.o. by the arm*** agarrar *or Span* coger a alguien del brazo; ***be ~n*** *of seat, table* estar ocupado
2 (*steal*) llevarse
3 (*transport, accompany*) llevar
4 (*accept*: *money, gift, credit cards*) aceptar; ***you can ~ it from me that …*** hazme caso cuando te digo que…
5 (*study*: *maths, French*) hacer, estudiar
6 *photograph, photocopy* hacer, sacar; *exam, degree* hacer; *shower* darse; *stroll* dar
7 *medicine, s.o.'s temperature, taxi* tomar
8 (*endure*) aguantar
9 *with expressions of time*: ***it took him two hours to do it*** le costó *or* llevó dos horas hacerlo; ***how long does it ~?*** ¿cuánto tiempo lleva?
10 (*require*) requerir; ***it ~s a lot of courage*** se requiere *or* necesita mucho valor; ***he's got what it ~s*** F tiene lo que hay que tener
11: ***be ~n by*** *or* ***with*** quedarse encantado con
II *n in movies* toma *f*
◆ **take after** *v/t* parecerse a
◆ **take along** *v/t* llevar
◆ **take apart** *v/t* **1** (*dismantle*) desmontar **2** F (*criticize*) hacer pedazos; F (*reprimand*) echar una bronca a F **3** F *in physical fight* machacar F
◆ **take aside** *v/t* llevar a un lado
◆ **take away** *v/t* **1** *pain* hacer desaparecer; (*remove*: *object*) quitar; ***take sth away from s.o.*** quitar algo a alguien; ***… to take away*** *Br* … para llevar **2** MATH restar (***from*** a); ***15 take away 5*** 15 menos 5
◆ **take back** *v/t* **1** (*return*: *object*) devolver; *person* llevar de vuelta **2** (*accept back*: *husband etc*) dejar volver **3** *in time*: ***that takes me back*** *of music, thought etc* me trae recuerdos
◆ **take down** *v/t* **1** *from shelf* bajar; *scaffolding* desmontar; *trousers* bajarse **2** (*write down*) anotar, apuntar
◆ **take in** *v/t* **1** (*take indoors*) recoger; (*give accommodation to*) acoger **2** (*make narrower*) meter **3** (*deceive*) engañar; ***be ~n in by*** ser engañado por **4** (*include*) incluir
◆ **take for** *v/t*: ***what do you take me for?*** ¿por quién me tomas?
◆ **take off I** *v/t* **1** *clothes, hat* quitarse; *10% etc* descontar **2** (*mimic*) imitar **3** (*cut off*) cortar **4**: ***take a day / week off*** tomarse un día / una semana de vacaciones **II** *v/i* **1** *of airplane* despegar, *L.Am.* decolar **2** (*become popular*) empezar a cuajar
◆ **take on** *v/t job* aceptar; *staff* contratar
◆ **take out** *v/t* **1** *from bag, pocket, money from bank* sacar; *tooth* sacar, extraer; *word from text* quitar, borrar; ***he took her out to dinner*** la llevó a cenar; ***take the dog out*** sacar al perro a pasear; ***take the kids out to the park*** llevar a los niños al parque; ***take s.o. out of himself*** animar a alguien **2** *insurance policy* suscribir **3**: ***don't take it out on me!*** ¡no la pagues conmigo!
◆ **take over I** *v/t company etc* absorber, adquirir; ***tourists took over the town*** los turistas invadieron la ciudad **II** *v/i of new management etc* asumir el cargo; *of new government* asumir el poder; (*do sth in s.o.'s place*) tomar el relevo
◆ **take to** *v/t* **1** (*like*): ***how did they take to the new idea?*** ¿qué les pareció la nueva idea?; ***I took to him immediately*** me cayó bien de inmediato **2**: ***he has taken to getting up early*** le ha dado por levantarse temprano; ***she took to drink*** se dio a la bebida; ***take to one's bed*** meterse en la

cama

◆ **take up** *v/t* **1** *carpet etc* levantar; (*carry up*) subir **2** (*shorten*: *dress etc*) acortar **3** *hobby* empezar a hacer; *subject* empezar a estudiar **4** *offer* aceptar; *new job* comenzar; ***I'll take you up on your offer*** aceptaré tu oferta **5** *space, time* ocupar

◆ **take up with** *v/t* entablar amistad con

'take•a•way *Br* ☞ ***takeout***; **'take-home pay** salario *m* neto; **'take•off 1** *of airplane* despegue *m*, *L.Am.* decolaje *m* **2** (*impersonation*) imitación *f*;

tak•en ['teɪkən] *pp* ☞ ***take***

'take•out 1 *restaurant* restaurante *m* de comida para llevar **2** *meal* comida *f* para llevar; **'take•o•ver** COM absorción *f*, adquisición *f*; **'take•o•ver bid** oferta pública de adquisición, OPA *f*

tak•er ['teɪkər]: ***there weren't many ~s*** no había mucha gente interesada

'take•up *of offer, share issue etc* nivel *m* de aceptación

tak•ings ['teɪkɪŋz] *npl* recaudación *f*

talc [tælk] ☞ ***talcum powder***

tal•cum pow•der ['tælkəmpaudər] polvos *mpl* de talco

tale [teɪl] cuento *m*, historia *f*; ***tell ~s*** (*lie*) contar mentiras

tal•ent ['tælənt] talento *m*; ***have a great ~ for music*** tener mucho talento para la música

tal•ent•ed ['tæləntɪd] *adj* con talento; ***she's very ~*** tiene mucho talento

'tal•ent scout cazatalentos *m/f inv*

talk [tɒːk] **I** *v/i* hablar; ***can I talk to …?*** ¿podría hablar con …?; ***I'll ~ to him about it*** hablaré del tema con él; ***~ about sth*** hablar de algo; ***you're getting yourself ~ed about*** estás haciendo que la gente hable de ti; ***~ing of …*** hablando de…; ***you can ~!, look who's ~ing!, you're a fine one to ~!*** F ¡quién fue a hablar!; ***now you're ~ing*** así se habla

II *v/t English etc* hablar; ***~ business / politics*** hablar de negocios / de política; ***~ s.o. into sth*** persuadir a alguien para que haga algo; ***~ s.o. out of sth*** persuadir a alguien para que no haga algo; ***~ one's way out of sth*** salir con palabras de algo; ***and we're ~ing big money here*** y hablamos *or* estamos hablando aquí de mucho dinero

III *n* **1** (*conversation*) charla *f*, *C.Am., Mex* plática *f*; ***I had a long ~ with him about it*** hablé con él un buen rato sobre ello **2** (*lecture*) conferencia *f*; ***give a ~ on sth*** dar una conferencia sobre algo **3**: ***~s*** *pl* negociaciones *fpl* **4**: ***there has been a lot of ~ about it*** se ha hablado mucho de eso; ***he's all ~*** *pej* habla mucho y no hace nada; ***be the ~ of the town*** ser la comidilla local

◆ **talk back** *v/i* responder, contestar

◆ **talk down** *v/t airplane* dar instrucciones para el aterrizaje

◆ **talk down to** *v/t* hablar con aires de superioridad a

◆ **talk over** *v/t* hablar de, discutir

◆ **talk around** *v/t* persuadir (***to*** para)

◆ **talk through** *v/t problem etc* discutir (***with*** con); ***talk me through it*** enséñamelo

talk•a•tive ['tɒːkətɪv] *adj* hablador

talk•er ['tɒːkər]: ***be a good ~*** ser un buen conversador

talk•ing ['tɒːkɪŋ] **I** *n*: ***let me do the ~*** déjame hablar a mí **II** *adj*: ***~ doll*** muñeca *f* habladora

'talk•ing point tema *m* de conversación

'talk•ing-to sermón *m*, rapapolvo *m*; ***give s.o. a good ~*** echar a alguien un buen sermón *or* rapapolvo

'talk show programa *m* de entrevistas

tall [tɒːl] *adj* alto; ***it is ten meters ~*** mide diez metros de alto

tall 'or•der: ***that's a ~*** eso es muy difícil

tal•low ['tæloʊ] sebo *m*

tall 'sto•ry cuento *m* chino

tal•ly ['tælɪ] **I** *n* cuenta; ***keep a ~ of*** llevar la cuenta de **II** *v/i* (*pret & pp* ***-ied***) cuadrar, encajar

◆ **tally with** *v/t* cuadrar con, encajar con

tal•on ['tælən] ORN garra *f*

tam•bou•rine [tæmbə'riːn] MUS pandereta *f*

tame [teɪm] **I** *adj* **1** *animal* manso, domesticado **2** *joke etc* soso **II** *v/t animal* domesticar

◆ **tam•per with** ['tæmpər] *v/t lock* intentar forzar; *brakes* tocar

'tam•per-proof *adj lock etc* imposible de manipular

tam•pon ['tæmpɑːn] tampón *m*

tan [tæn] **I** *n* **1** *from sun* bronceado *m*; ***get a ~*** ponerse moreno **2** *color* marrón claro **II** *v/i* (*pret & pp* ***-ned***) *in sun* bron-

cearse **III** *v/t* (*pret & pp* **-ned**) *leather* curtir
tan•dem ['tændəm] **1** *bike* tándem *m* **2**: ***in ~ with*** conjuntamente con
tang [tæŋ] *taste* sabor *m* fuerte
tan•gent ['tændʒənt] MATH tangente *f*; ***go off at a ~*** *fig* irse por las ramas
tan•ge•rine [tændʒə'ri:n] mandarina *f*
tan•gi•ble ['tændʒɪbl] *adj* tangible
'tan•gi•ble as•sets *npl* activos *mpl* materiales
tan•gle ['tæŋgl] lío *m*, maraña *f*
◆ **tangle up**: ***get tangled up*** *of string etc* quedarse enredado
◆ **tangle with** *v/t* F meterse en líos con
tan•go ['tæŋgou] **I** *n* tango *m* **II** *v/i* bailar el tango; ***it takes two to ~*** *fig* es cosa de dos
tank [tæŋk] *for water* depósito *m*, tanque *m*; *for fish* pecera *f*, MOT depósito *m*; MIL, *for skin diver* tanque *m*
tank•er ['tæŋkər] *truck* camión *m* cisterna; *ship* buque *m* cisterna; *for oil* petrolero *m*
'tank top camiseta *f* sin mangas
tan•ned [tænd] *adj* moreno, bronceado
Tan•noy® ['tænɔɪ] megafonía *f*
tan•ta•liz•ing ['tæntəlaɪzɪŋ] *adj* sugerente
tan•ta•mount ['tæntəmaʊnt] *adj*: ***be ~ to*** equivaler a
tan•trum ['tæntrəm] rabieta *f*, ***have or throw a ~*** coger una rabieta
Tan•za•nia [tænzə'nɪə] Tanzania *f*
Tan•za•ni•an [tænzə'nɪən] **I** *adj* tanzano **II** *n* tanzano(-a) *m*(*f*)
tap [tæp] **I** *n* (*faucet*) grifo *m*, *L.Am.* llave; ***have sth on ~*** *fig* tener algo disponible **II** *v/t* (*pret & pp* **-ped**) **1** (*knock*) dar un golpecito en; ***~ s.o. on the shoulder*** dar un toque en el hombro a alguien **2** *phone* intervenir
◆ **tap into** *v/t resources* explotar
'tap dance claqué *m*
'tap-danc•ing claqué *m*
tape [teɪp] **I** *n* cinta **II** *v/t* **1** *conversation etc* grabar **2** *with sticky tape* pegar con cinta adhesiva
◆ **tape up** *v/t ankle*, *knee* vendar
'tape deck pletina *f*, **'tape drive** COMPUT unidad *f* de cinta; **'tape meas•ure** cinta *f* métrica
ta•per ['teɪpər] *v/i* estrecharse
◆ **taper off** *v/i of production*, *figures* disminuir
'tape-re•cord *v/t* grabar en cinta; **'tape re•cor•der** magnetofón *m*, *L.Am.* grabador *m*; **'tape re•cord•ing** grabación *f* (magnetofónica)
ta•pes•try ['tæpɪstrɪ] **1** *cloth* tapiz *m* **2** *art* tapicería *f*
'tape•worm tenia *f*, solitaria *f*
'tap wa•ter agua *f* del grifo
tar [tɑ:r] alquitrán *m*
ta•ran•tu•la [tə'ræntjʊlə] ZO tarántula *f*
tar•dy ['tɑ:rdɪ] *adj* tardío
tare [ter] COM tara *f*
tar•get ['tɑ:rgɪt] **I** *n in shooting* blanco *m*; *for sales*, *production* objetivo *m*; ***set o.s. a ~ of doing sth*** proponerse como objetivo hacer algo; ***meet a ~*** alcanzar un objetivo **II** *v/t market* apuntar a; ***be ~ed at*** *fig* estar dirigido a
tar•get 'au•di•ence audiencia *f* a la que está orientado el programa; **'tar•get date** fecha *f* fijada; **tar•get 'fig•ure** cifra *f* objetivo; **'tar•get group** COM grupo *m* estratégico; **'tar•get lan•guage** lengua *f* de destino; **'tar•get mar•ket** mercado *m* objetivo
tar•iff ['tærɪf] **1** *price* tarifa *f* **2** *tax* arancel *m*
'tar•iff bar•ri•er barrera *f* arancelaria
tar•mac ['tɑ:rmæk] **1** *for road surface* asfalto *m* **2** *at airport* pista *f*
tar•nish ['tɑ:rnɪʃ] **I** *v/t metal* deslucir, deslustrar; *reputation* empañar **II** *v/i metal* empañarse
ta•rot ['tɑ:roʊ] tarot *m*
tar•pau•lin [tɑ:r'pɒ:lɪn] lona *f* (*impermeable*)
tar•ra•gon ['tærəgɑ:n] BOT estragón *m*
tar•ry ['tærɪ] *v/i lit* demorarse
tart[1] [tɑ:rt] *n* tarta *f*, pastel *m*
tart[2] [tɑ:rt] *adj fig* agrio
◆ **tart up** *v/t Br* F remodelar
tar•tan ['tɑ:rtn] tartán *m*
tar•tar ['tɑ:rtər] CHEM sarro *m*
tar•tar(e) sauce [tɑ:rtər'sɔ:s] GASTR salsa *f* tártara
task [tæsk] **1** tarea *f* **2**: ***take s.o. to ~*** *fig* reprender a alguien (***for*** por)
'task force *for a special job* equipo *m* de trabajo; MIL destacamento *m*
'task mas•ter: ***be a hard ~*** ser muy exigente
tas•sel ['tæsl] borla *f*
taste [teɪst] **I** *n* **1** gusto *m*; ***he has no ~***

tiene mal gusto; ***be in bad** or **poor** ~* ser de mal gusto **2** *of food etc* sabor *m*; ***it has no** ~* no sabe a nada; ***leave a bad** ~ **in s.o.'s mouth*** *fig* dejar un mal sabor de boca; ***would you like to have a** ~ **of …?*** ¿quieres probar un poco de …?; ***a** ~ **of her temper*** una muestra de su mal genio; ***a** ~ **of things to come*** un anticipo de lo que va a pasar
II *v/t also fig* probar
III *v/i* saber
◆ **taste of** *v/t* saber a
'taste buds *npl* papilas *fpl* gustativas
taste•ful ['teɪstfəl] *adj* de buen gusto
taste•ful•ly ['teɪstfəlɪ] *adv* con buen gusto
taste•less ['teɪstlɪs] *adj* **1** *food* insípido **2** *remark* de mal gusto
tast•ing ['teɪstɪŋ] *of wine* cata *f*, degustación *f*
tast•y ['teɪstɪ] *adj* sabroso, rico
ta-ta [tæ'tɑː] *int Br* F chao F, hasta luego
tat•tered ['tætərd] *adj clothes* andrajoso; *book* destrozado
tat•ters ['tætərz]: ***in** ~ clothes* hecho jirones; *reputation*, *career* arruinado
tat•too [tə'tuː] tatuaje *m*
tat•ty ['tætɪ] *adj Br* F sobado, gastado
taught [tɒːt] *pret & pp* ☞ ***teach***
taunt [tɒːnt] **I** *n* pulla **II** *v/t* mofarse de
Tau•rus ['tɔːrəs] ASTR Tauro *m/f inv*, *L.Am.* taurino(-a) *m(f)*; ***be*** (***a***) ~ ser Tauro, ser taurino
taut [tɒːt] *adj* tenso
taut•en ['tɒːtn] **I** *v/t* tensar **II** *v/i* tensarse
taw•dry ['tɒːdrɪ] *adj* barato, cursi
taw•ny ['tɔːnɪ] *adj* leonado
tax [tæks] **I** *n* impuesto *m*; ***before / after** ~* sin descontar / descontando impuestos **II** *v/t people* cobrar impuestos a; *product* gravar
tax•a•ble 'in•come ingresos *mpl* gravables
'tax al•low•ance desgravación *f* fiscal
'tax as•sess•ment determinación *f* del impuesto
tax•a•tion [tæk'seɪʃn] **1** (*act of taxing*) imposición de impuestos **2** (*taxes*) fiscalidad *f*, impuestos *mpl*
'tax au•thor•i•ties *npl* administración *f* fiscal; **'tax a•void•ance** elusión *f* legal de impuestos; **'tax ben•e•fit** beneficio *m* fiscal; **'tax brack•et** banda *f* impositiva; **'tax break** ventaja *f* fiscal; **'tax bur•den** carga *f* fiscal; **'tax col•lec•tion** recaudación *f* de impuestos; **'tax con•sult•ant** asesor(a) *m(f)* fiscal; **'tax de•duct•i•ble** *adj* desgravable; **'tax disc** *Br* justificante *m* del impuesto de circulación; **'tax eva•sion** evasión *f* fiscal; **'tax ex•empt** *adj* libre de impuestos; **'tax ex•ile** exiliado(-a) *m(f)* fiscal; **'tax ex•pert** experto(-a) *m(f)* fiscal; **'tax-free** *adj* libre de impuestos; **'tax haven** paraíso *m* fiscal
tax•i ['tæksɪ] **I** *n* taxi *m* **II** *v/i of airplane* rodar
'tax•i driv•er taxista *m/f*
tax•ing ['tæksɪŋ] *adj* difícil, arduo
'tax in•spect•or inspector(a) *m(f)* de Hacienda
'tax•i rank, 'tax•i stand parada *f* de taxis
'tax law derecho *m* fiscal; **'tax loop•hole** vacío *m* fiscal; **tax•man** ['tæksmæn] F Hacienda *f*; **'tax pay•er** contribuyente *m/f*; **'tax re•bate** devolución *f* de impuestos; **'tax re•duc•tion** reducción *f* fiscal; **'tax re•fund** devolución *f* de impuestos; **'tax re•lief** desgravación *f* fiscal; **'tax re•turn** *form* declaración *f* de la renta; **'tax rev•e•nue** ingresos *mpl* fiscales; **'tax year** año *m* fiscal
TB [tiː'biː] *abbr* (= ***tuberculosis***) tuberculosis *f*
T-bone steak [tiːboʊn'steɪk] chuletón *f* (*en forma de T*)
tea [tiː] **1** *drink* té *m* **2** *meal* merienda *f*
'tea•bag bolsita *f* de té
teach [tiːʧ] **I** *v/t* (*pret & pp* ***taught***) *person*, *subject* enseñar; ~ ***s.o. to do sth*** enseñar a alguien a hacer algo; ~ ***s.o. a lesson*** *fig* dar una lección a alguien; ***that'll** ~ **him!*** ¡eso le enseñará!, ¡así aprenderá!; ***that'll** ~**you to be so aggressive*** eso te enseñará a no ser tan agresivo
II *v/i* (*pret & pp* ***taught***): ***I taught at that school*** di clases en ese. colegio; ***he always wanted to** ~* siempre quiso ser profesor
teach•er ['tiːʧər] *at elementary school* maestro(-a) *m(f)*; *at secondary school*, *university* profesor(a) *m(f)*
teach•er 'train•ing formación *f* pedagógica, magisterio *m*
teach•ing ['tiːʧɪŋ] *profession* enseñanza *f*, docencia *f*

T

'teach•ing aid material *m* didáctico
'tea•cloth paño *m* de cocina; **'tea•co•zy,** *Br* **'tea• co•sy** cubretetera *m*; **'tea•cup** taza *f* de té; **'tea drink•er** bebedor(a) *m(f)* de té
teak [ti:k] teca *f*
'tea leaf hoja *f* de té
team [ti:m] equipo *m*
◆ **team up** *v/i* unirse (***with*** a)
team 'ef•fort trabajo *m* de equipo; **'team game** juego *m* de equipo; **'team•mate** compañero(-a) *m(f)* de equipo; **team 'spirit** espíritu *m* de equipo
team•ster ['ti:mstər] camionero(-a) *m(f)*
'team•work trabajo *m* en equipo
'tea par•ty *Br* té *m* (*de media tarde*)
'tea•pot tetera *f*
tear[1] [ter] **I** *n in cloth etc* desgarrón *m*, rotura *f* **II** *v/t* (*pret* ***tore***, *pp* ***torn***) *paper, cloth* rasgar; ***be torn between two alternatives*** debatirse entre dos alternativas; ***~ a muscle*** desgarrarse un músculo **III** *v/i* (*pret* ***tore***, *pp* ***torn***) (*run fast, drive fast*) ir a toda velocidad
◆ **tear away** *v/t* arrancar (***from*** de)
◆ **tear down** *v/t poster* arrancar; *building* derribar
◆ **tear into** *v/t* F (*verbally*) arremeter contra
◆ **tear off** *v/t* arrancar
◆ **tear out** *v/t* arrancar
◆ **tear up** *v/t paper* romper, rasgar; *agreement* romper
tear[2] [tɪr] *n in eye* lágrima *f*; ***burst into ~s*** echarse a llorar; ***be in ~s*** estar llorando; ***~s of joy*** lágrimas de alegría
tear•a•way ['terəweɪ] *Br* F alborotador(a) *m(f)*
tear•drop ['tɪrdrɑ:p] lágrima *f*
tear•ful ['tɪrfəl] *adj* lloroso
'tear gas gas *m* lacrimógeno
tear•ing ['terɪŋ] *adj*: ***be in a ~ hurry*** F tener muchísima prisa
tear-jerk•er ['tɪrdʒɜ:rkər] F dramón *m*
tear•off ['terɑ:f] *adj*: ***~ calendar*** calendario *m* de taco
'tea•room salón *m* de té
tease [ti:z] **I** *v/t person* tomar el pelo a, burlarse de; *animal* hacer rabiar **II** *v/i*: ***he is only teasing*** está bromeando **III** *n* bromista *m/f*
'tea ser•vice, 'tea set servicio *m* de té
'tea•spoon 1 *object* cucharilla *f* **2** *quantity* cucharadita *f*
teat [ti:t] teta *f*
'tea•tow•el *Br* paño *m* de cocina
'tea trol•ley *Br*, **'tea wag•on** carrito *m*
tech•ie ['tekɪ] F COMPUT entendido(-a) *m/f* en informática; *technical expert* técnico(-a) *m(f)*
tech•ni•cal ['teknɪkl] *adj* técnico; ***he got too ~ for me*** hablaba con demasiados tecnicismos (para yo entenderlo); ***~ foul*** *in basketball* falta *f* técnica, técnica *f*; ***~ knockout*** *in boxing* K.O. *m* técnico; ***~ term*** término *m* técnico
tech•ni•cal•i•ty [teknɪ'kælətɪ] **1** (*technical nature*) tecnicismo *m* **2** LAW detalle *m* técnico
tech•ni•cal•ly ['teknɪklɪ] *adv* técnicamente
tech•ni•cian [tek'nɪʃn] técnico(-a) *m(f)*
tech•nique [tek'ni:k] técnica *f*
tech•no ['teknoʊ] MUS tecno *m*
tech•no•crat ['teknəkræt] tecnócrata *m/f*
'tech•no•junk tecnología *f* obsoleta
tech•no•log•i•cal [teknə'lɑ:dʒɪkl] *adj* tecnológico
tech•no•lo•gy [tek'nɑ:lədʒɪ] tecnología *f*
tech'no•lo•gy park parque *m* tecnológico
tech'no•lo•gy trans•fer transferencia *f* de tecnología
tech•no•phobe ['teknəfoʊb]: ***he's a ~*** rechaza la tecnología
tech•no'phob•i•a rechazo *m* de las nuevas tecnologías
ted•dy bear ['tedɪber] osito *m* de peluche
te•di•ous ['ti:dɪəs] *adj* tedioso
te•di•um ['ti:dɪəm] tedio *m*
tee [ti:] *in golf* tee *m*
◆ **tee off** *v/i* salir del primer tee
teem [ti:m] *v/i*: ***be ~ing with rain*** llover a cántaros; ***be ~ing with tourists / ants*** estar abarrotado de turistas / lleno de hormigas
teen•age ['ti:neɪdʒ] *adj fashions* adolescente, juvenil; ***a ~ boy / girl*** un adolescente / una adolescente
teen•ag•er ['ti:neɪdʒər] adolescente *m/f*
teens [ti:nz] *npl* adolescencia *f*; ***be in one's ~*** ser un adolescente; ***reach one's ~*** alcanzar la adolescencia

T

tee•ny ['ti:nɪ] *adj* F chiquitín F
tee•ny-bop•per ['ti:nɪbɑ:pər] niña *f* en la edad del pavo
tee•ny-wee•ny [ti:nɪ'wi:nɪ] *adj* F pequeñín
'tee shirt camiseta *f*
tee•ter ['ti:tər] *v/i* tambalearse
'tee•ter-tot•ter balancín *m*
teeth [ti:θ] *pl* ☞ ***tooth***
teethe [ti:ð] *v/i* echar los dientes
teeth•ing prob•lems ['ti:ðɪŋ] *npl* problemas *mpl* iniciales
tee•to•tal•er, *Br* **tee•to•tal•ler** [ti:'toʊtlər] abstemio(-a) *m (f)*
tel•e•cast ['telɪkɑ:st] emisión *f* televisiva
tel•e•com•mu•ni•ca•tions [telɪkəmju:nɪ'keɪʃnz] telecomunicaciones *fpl*
tel•e•com•mu•ni'ca•tions link enlace *m* de telecomunicaciones
tel•e•com•mu•ni'ca•tions sat•el•lite satélite *m* de telecomunicaciones
tel•e•com•mute ['telɪkəmju:t] *v/i* teletrabajar
tel•e•com•mut•er ['telɪkəmju:tər] teletrabajador(a) *m(f)*
tel•e•com•mut•ing ['telɪkəmju:tɪŋ] teletrabajo *m*
tel•e•gram ['telɪgræm] telegrama *m*
tel•e•graph pole ['telɪgræf] poste *m* telegráfico
tel•e•path•ic [telɪ'pæθɪk] *adj* telepático; ***you must be ~!*** ¡debes tener telepatía!
te•lep•a•thy [tɪ'lepəθɪ] telepatía *f*
tel•e•phone ['telɪfoʊn] **I** *n* teléfono *m*; ***be on the ~*** (*be speaking*) estar hablando por teléfono; (*possess a phone*) tener teléfono; ***by ~*** por teléfono **II** *v/t person* telefonear, llamar por teléfono **III** *v/i* telefonear, llamar por teléfono
'tel•e•phone bank•ing banca *f* telefónica; **'tel•e•phone bill** factura *f* del teléfono; **'tel•e•phone book** guía *f* telefónica, listín *m* telefónico; **'tel•e•phone booth** cabina *f* telefónica; **'tel•e•phone call** llamada *f* telefónica; **'tel•e•phone con•ver•sa•tion** conversación *f* por teléfono *or* telefónica; **'tel•e•phone di•rec•to•ry** guía *f* telefónica, listín *m* telefónico; **'tel•e•phone ex•change** central *f* telefónica, centralita *f*; **'tel•e•phone mes•sage** mensaje *m* telefónico; **'tel•e•phone num•ber** número *m* de teléfono; **'tel•e•phone sell•ing** venta *f* por teléfono
tel•e•phon•ist [tə'lefənɪst] *Br* telefonista *m/f*
te•leph•o•ny [tə'lefənɪ] telefonía *f*
tel•e•pho•to lens [telɪ'foʊtoʊ] teleobjetivo *m*
tel•e•pro•cess•ing [telɪ'proʊsesɪŋ] COMPUT teleprocesado *m*
tel•e•sales ['telɪseɪlz] televentas *fpl*
tel•e•scope ['telɪskoʊp] telescopio *m*
tel•e•scop•ic [telɪ'skɑ:pɪk] *adj* telescópico
tel•e•scop•ic an'ten•na antena *f* telescópica; **tel•e•scop•ic 'sight** mira *f* telescópica; **tel•e•scop•ic um'brel•la** paraguas *m inv* telescópico
tel•e•shop•ping ['telɪshɑ:pɪŋ] telecompra *f*
tel•e•text ['telɪtekst] teletexto *m*
tel•e•thon ['telɪθɑ:n] maratón *m* benéfico televisivo
tel•e•vise ['telɪvaɪz] *v/t* televisar
tel•e•vi•sion ['telɪvɪʒn] televisión *f*, *set* televisión *f*, televisor *m*; ***on ~*** en *or* por (la) televisión; ***what's on ~ tonight?*** ¿qué hay *or* ponen esta noche en la televisión?; ***watch ~*** ver la televisión; ***work in ~*** trabajar en la televisión
'tel•e•vi•sion au•di•ence audiencia *f* televisiva; **'tel•e•vi•sion mov•ie** telefilm *m*; **'tel•e•vi•sion net•work** red *f* televisiva; **'tel•e•vi•sion news** *nsg* noticiario *m* televisivo, telediario *m*; **'tel•e•vi•sion pro•gram** programa *m* televisivo; **'tel•e•vi•sion set** televisión *f*, televisor *m*; **'tel•e•vi•sion stu•di•o** estudio *m* de televisión
tel•e•work•er ['telɪwɜ:rkər] teletrabajador(a) *m(f)*
tel•e•work•ing ['telɪwɜ:rkɪŋ] teletrabajo *m*
tel•ex ['teleks] télex *m inv*
tell [tel] **I** *v/t* (*pret & pp* **told**) **1**: *story* contar; *lie* decir, contar; ***~ s.o. sth*** decir algo a alguien; ***don't ~ Mom*** no se lo digas a mamá; ***could you ~ me the way to ... ?*** ¿me podría decir por dónde se va a ...?; ***you're ~ing me!*** F ¡a mí me lo vas a contar!; ***I can't ~ you how relieved*** ... no te puedes imaginar el alivio...; ***I told you so*** te lo dije; ***to ~ you the truth*** para decirte la verdad
2: ***I can't ~ the difference*** no veo la diferencia; ***I can't ~ one from the other, I***

T

can't ~ them apart no los distingo; ***be able to ~ the time*** saber *or* ser capaz de decir la hora; ***it's hard to ~ what will happen*** es difícil decir que pasará **3**: ***~ s.o. to do sth*** decir a alguien que haga algo
II *v/i* (*pret & pp* **told**) **1**: ***who can ~?*** ¿quién sabe?; ***you can never ~, you never can ~*** nunca se sabe **2** (*have effect*) hacerse notar; ***time will ~*** el tiempo lo dirá; ***~ against*** perjudicar
◆ **tell off** *v/t* F echar la bronca F (***for*** por)
◆ **tell on** *v/t* **1** *to teacher etc* chivarse de **2**: ***the heat is ~ing on him*** el calor está empezando a afectarle
tell•er ['telər] *in bank* cajero(-a) *m(f)*
tell•ing ['telɪŋ] *adj* contundente
tell•ing-'off F regañina *f* F; ***give s.o. a (good) ~*** F echar una bronca a alguien (***for*** por) F
tell•tale ['telteɪl] **I** *adj signs* revelador **II** chivato(-a) *m(f)*
tel•ly ['telɪ] *Br* F tele *f*
te•mer•i•ty [tə'merətɪ] osadía *f*; ***he had the ~ to …*** tuvo la osadía de…
temp [temp] **I** *n employee* trabajador(a) *m(f)* temporal **II** *v/i* hacer trabajo temporal
tem•per ['tempər] **1** (***bad ~***) mal humor *m*; ***be in a ~*** estar de mal humor; ***lose one's ~*** perder los estribos; ***have a quick*** *or* ***terrible ~*** tener mal genio; ***fly into a ~*** ponerse hecho una furia; ***~, ~!*** F ¡cálmate!, ¡no te sulfures! **2**: ***keep one's ~*** mantener la calma **II** *v/t* TECH *steel* templar
tem•per•a•ment ['temprəmənt] temperamento *m*
tem•per•a•men•tal [temprə'mentl] *adj* (*moody*) temperamental
tem•per•a•men•tal•ly [temprə'mentəlɪ] *adv* temperamentalmente; ***be ~ unsuited to the job*** no tener el temperamento adecuado para el trabajo
tem•per•ate ['tempərət] *adj* templado
tem•per•a•ture ['temprətʃər] **1** temperatura *f*; ***take s.o.'s ~*** tomar la temperatura a alguien **2** (*fever*) fiebre *f*; ***have a ~*** tener fiebre
'tem•per•a•ture gauge calibrador *m* de temperatura
tem•pest ['tempɪst] tempestad *f*; ***a ~ in a teapot*** una tormenta en un vaso de agua
tem•pes•tu•ous [tem'pestjʊəs] *adj fig* tempestuoso
tem•pi ['tempɪ] *pl* ☞ **tempo**
tem•plate ['templeɪt] COMPUT, TECH plantilla *f*
tem•ple[1] ['templ] REL templo *m*
tem•ple[2] ['templ] ANAT sien *f*
tem•po ['tempoʊ] tempo *m*
tem•po•ral[1] ['tempərəl] *adj of this world* temporal
tem•po•ral[2] ['tempərəl] *adj* ANAT temporal
tem•po•rar•i•ly [tempə'rerɪlɪ] *adv* temporalmente
tem•po•ra•ry ['tempərerɪ] *adj* temporal; ***~ replacement*** suplencia *f*
tempt [tempt] *v/t* tentar; ***be ~ed to do sth*** sentirse tentado de hacer algo; ***~ s.o. into doing sth*** tentar a alguien para que haga algo; ***~ fate*** tentar a la suerte
temp•ta•tion [temp'teɪʃn] tentación *f*
tempt•er ['temptər] tentador *m*
tempt•ing ['temptɪŋ] *adj* tentador
tempt•ress ['temptres] seductora *f*
ten [ten] diez; ***~s of thousands*** decenas *fpl* de miles
ten•a•ble ['tenəbl] *adj* sostenible
te•na•cious [tɪ'neɪʃəs] *adj* tenaz
te•nac•i•ty [tɪ'næsɪtɪ] tenacidad *f*
ten•an•cy ['tenənsɪ] tenencia *f*
ten•ant ['tenənt] *of building* inquilino(-a) *m(f)*; *of farm, land* arrendatario(-a) *m(f)*
tend[1] [tend] *v/t* (*look after*) cuidar (de)
tend[2] [tend] *v/i*: ***~ to do sth*** soler hacer algo; ***~ toward sth*** tender hacia algo
ten•den•cy ['tendənsɪ] tendencia *f*; ***have a ~ to*** *or* ***toward sth*** ser propenso a algo; ***have a ~ to do sth*** tener tendencia a hacer algo
ten•den•tious [ten'denʃəs] *adj* tendencioso
ten•der[1] ['tendər] *adj* **1** (*sore*) sensible, delicado **2** (*affectionate*) cariñoso, tierno **3** *steak* tierno
ten•der[2] ['tendər] **I** *n* COM oferta *f* **II** *v/i* COM hacer una oferta (***for*** para) **III** *v/t*: ***~ one's resignation*** presentar la dimisión
'ten•der doc•u•ments *npl* documentos *mpl* de oferta
ten•der•er licitador(a) *m(f)*; ***success-***

T

ful ~ adjudicatario(-a) *m(f)*
'ten•der•foot F novato(-a) *m(f)*
ten•der•heart•ed [tendər'hærtɪd] *adj* bondadoso
ten•der•ize ['tendəraɪz] *v/t meat* ablandar
'ten•der•loin solomillo *m*
ten•der•ness ['tendərnɪs] **1** *(soreness)* dolor *m* **2** *of kiss* cariño *m*, ternura *f*
ten•don ['tendən] tendón *m*
ten•dril ['tendrəl] BOT zarcillo *m*
ten•e•ment ['tenəmənt] bloque *m* de viviendas
ten•fold ['tenfould] **I** *adj* multiplicado por diez **II** *adv increase* diez veces
ten-foot 'pole: ***I wouldn't touch him / it with a ~!*** F *if I were you* yo lo dejaría estar
'ten-gallon hat sombrero *m* jarano *or* de cowboy
ten•ner ['tenər] F *Br* diez libras
ten•nis ['tenɪs] tenis *m*
'ten•nis ball pelota *f* de tenis; **'ten•nis court** pista *f* de tenis, cancha *f* de tenis; **ten•nis 'el•bow** MED codo *m* de tenista; **'ten•nis play•er** tenista *m/f*; **'ten•nis rack•et** raqueta *f* de tenis; **'ten•nis shoe** zapatilla *f* de tenis
ten•or ['tenər] MUS tenor *m*
ten•pin 'bowl•ing *Br* bolos *mpl*
tense[1] [tens] *n* GRAM tiempo *m*
tense[2] [tens] *adj muscle, moment* tenso; *voice, person* tenso, nervioso
◆ **tense up** *v/i* ponerse tenso
ten•sile ['tensəl] *adj*: ***~ strength*** resistencia *f* a la tracción
ten•sion ['tenʃn] **1** *of rope* tensión *f* **2** *fig: in atmosphere, voice* tensión *f*, tirantez *f*; *in film, novel* tensión *f*
tent [tent] tienda *f*
ten•ta•cle ['tentəkl] tentáculo *m*
ten•ta•tive ['tentətɪv] *adj move, offer* provisional
ten•ta•tive•ly ['tentətɪvlɪ] *adv suggest etc* con precaución, cautelosamente; ***he ~ put his hand on ...*** puso la mano encima ... para probar
ten•ter•hooks ['tentərhʊks]: ***be on ~*** estar sobre ascuas; ***keep s.o. on ~*** tener a alguien sobre ascuas
tenth [tenθ] **I** *adj* décimo **II** *n* décimo *m*, décima parte *f*; *of second, degree* décima *f*; ***the ~ of May*** el diez de mayo
'tent•peg clavija *f*
'tent•pole mástil *m*
ten•u•ous ['tenjʊəs] *adj* **1** *thread etc* delgado **2** *fig: connection* tenue; *proof etc* poco sólido, poco convincente
ten•ure ['tenjər] *of office* ocupación *f*; ***during his ~*** *of president* durante su presidencia
tep•id ['tepɪd] *adj water, reaction* tibio
term [tɜːrm] **I** *n* **1** *in office etc* mandato *m*; ***~ of imprisonment*** LAW periodo *m* de reclusión; ***~ of office*** mandato *m*; ***in the long / short ~*** a largo / corto plazo
2 *Br* EDU trimestre *m*
3 *(condition)* término *m*, condición *f*; ***~s of payment*** COM condiciones *fpl* de pago; ***I accept the offer, but on my own ~s*** acepto la oferta, pero pongo yo las condiciones; ***be on good / bad ~s with s.o.*** llevarse bien / mal con alguien; ***come to ~s with sth*** llegar a aceptar algo
4 *(word)* término *m*; ***~ of abuse*** insulto *m*; ***in no uncertain ~s*** en términos claros
5: ***in ~s of*** en lo referente a; ***a good movie in ~s of storyline*** una buena película en cuanto al argumento se refiere
II *v/t (describe as)* llamar
'term de•pos•it FIN depósito *m* a plazo
ter•mi•nal ['tɜːrmɪnl] **I** *n* **1** *at airport, for buses, for containers* terminal *f* **2** ELEC, COMPUT terminal *m*; *of battery* polo *m* **II** *adj illness* terminal
ter•mi•nal•ly ['tɜːrmɪnəlɪ] *adv*: ***~ ill*** en la fase terminal de una enfermedad
ter•mi•nate ['tɜːrmɪneɪt] **I** *v/t contract* rescindir; *pregnancy* interrumpir **II** *v/i* finalizar; ***this train ~s here*** éste es el final del recorrido de este tren
ter•mi•na•tion [tɜːrmɪ'neɪʃn] *of contract* rescisión *f*; *of pregnancy* interrupción *f*
ter•mi'na•tion clause cláusula *f* de rescisión
ter•mi•nol•o•gy [tɜːrmɪ'nɑːlədʒɪ] terminología *f*
ter•mi•nus ['tɜːrmɪnəs] *for buses* final *m* de trayecto; *for trains* estación *f* terminal
ter•mite ['tɜːrmaɪt] ZO termita *f*
ter•race ['terəs] terraza *f*
ter•raced house ['terəsd] *Br* casa *f* adosada

T

ter•ra cot•ta [terə'kɑːtə] *adj* de terracota

ter•ra fir•ma [terə'fɜːrmə] tierra *f* firme

ter•rain [te'reɪn] terreno *m*

ter•ra•pin ['terəpɪn] tortuga *f* acuática

ter•res•tri•al [te'restrɪəl] **I** *n* terrestre *m/f* **II** *adj television* por vía terrestre; **~ broadcasting** emisión *f* por vía terrestre

ter•ri•ble ['terəbl] *adj* terrible, horrible

ter•ri•bly ['terəblɪ] *adv* (*very*) tremendamente

ter•ri•er ['terɪər] ZO terrier *m*

ter•rif•ic [tə'rɪfɪk] *adj* estupendo

ter•rif•i•cal•ly [tə'rɪfɪklɪ] *adv* (*very*) tremendamente

ter•ri•fy ['terɪfaɪ] *v/t* (*pret & pp* **-ied**) aterrorizar; **be terrified** estar aterrorizado; **spiders ~ me, I'm terrified of spiders** me dan terror las arañas

ter•ri•fy•ing ['terɪfaɪɪŋ] *adj* aterrador

ter•rine [tə'riːn] terrina *f*

ter•ri•to•ri•al [terɪ'tɔːrɪəl] *adj* territorial; **~ claims** reivindicaciones *fpl* territoriales

ter•ri•to•ri•al•i•ty [terɪtɔːrɪ'ælɪtɪ] territorialidad *f*

ter•ri•to•ri•al 'wa•ters *npl* aguas *fpl* territoriales

ter•ri•to•ry ['terɪtɔːrɪ] territorio *m*; *fig* ámbito *m*, territorio *m*

ter•ror ['terər] terror *m*; **in ~** aterrorizado; **I have a ~ of ...** ... me da terror; **she's a little ~** F es un pequeño diablo, es un diablillo

ter•ror•ism ['terərɪzm] terrorismo *m*

ter•ror•ist ['terərɪst] terrorista *m/f*

'ter•ror•ist at•tack atentado *m* terrorista

'ter•ror•ist or•gan•i•za•tion organización *f* terrorista

ter•ror•ize ['terəraɪz] *v/t* aterrorizar

ter•ry (cloth) ['terɪ(klɑːθ)] toalla *f* de rizo

terse [tɜːrs] *adj* tajante, seco

ter•ti•ar•y sec•tor ['tɜːrʃerɪ] sector *m* terciario

test [test] **I** *n* prueba *f*; *academic*, *for driving* examen *m*; **take a ~** hacer una prueba; **put sth / s.o. to the ~** poner algo / a alguien a prueba; **stand the ~ of time** resistir la prueba del tiempo; **pass / fail a ~** superar / no superar una prueba; **carry out ~s on sth** efectuar pruebas en algo **II** *v/t* probar, poner a prueba (**on** con)

tes•ta•ment ['testəmənt] *to s.o.'s life etc* testimonio *m*; **Old / New Testament** REL Viejo / Nuevo Testamento *m*

'test case LAW juicio *m* que sienta jurisprudencia

'test-drive **I** *v/t* (*pret* **-drove**, *pp* **-driven**) *car* probar en carretera **II** *n* prueba *f* de conducción; **go for a ~** ir a hacer una prueba de conducción

tes•ti•cle ['testɪkl] testículo *m*

tes•ti•fy ['testɪfaɪ] *v/i* (*pret & pp* **-ied**) LAW testificar, prestar declaración; **~ to** atestiguar **II** *v/t*: **~ that** LAW, *fig* testificar que

tes•ti•mo•ni•al [testɪ'moʊnɪəl] **1** referencias *fpl* **2** *for sportsman etc* partido *m* de homenaje

tes•ti•mo•ny ['testɪmənɪ] LAW testimonio *m*; **be ~ of** *fig* ser testimonio de

test•ing ['testɪŋ] *adj*: **~ times** tiempos *mpl* difíciles

'test pi•lot AVIA piloto *m/f* de pruebas; **'test tube** tubo *m* de ensayo, probeta *f*; **'test-tube ba•by** niño(-a) *m(f)* probeta

tes•ty ['testɪ] *adj* irritable

te•ta•nus ['tetənəs] tétanos *m*

tetch•y ['tetʃɪ] *adj* irritable

teth•er ['teðər] **I** *v/t horse* atar **II** *n* correa *f*; **be at the end of one's ~** estar al punto de perder la paciencia

Teu•ton•ic [tjuː'tɑːnɪk] *adj* teutón

text [tekst] **I** *n* **1** texto *m* **2** (**~** *message*) mensaje *m* **II** *v/t* mandar un mensaje a

'text•book **I** *n* libro de texto **II** *adj*: **~ example** ejemplo *m* de libro

tex•tile ['tekstəl] **I** *n* textil *m*; **~s** industria *f* textil **II** *adj* textil

'text mes•sage mensaje *m* de texto

text mes•sag•ing ['tekstmesədʒɪŋ] envío *m* de mensajes de texto

tex•tu•al ['tekstjʊəl] *adj* textual

tex•tu•al an'al•y•sis LING comentario *m* de texto

tex•ture ['tekstʃər] textura *f*

Thai [taɪ] **I** *adj* tailandés **II** **1** *person* tailandés(-esa) *m(f)* **2** *language* tailandés *m*

Thai•land ['taɪlænd] Tailandia *f*

tha•lid•o•mide [θə'lɪdəmaɪd] PHARM talidomida *f*

Thames [temz]: **the ~** el Támesis

than [ðæn] *adv* que; ***bigger / faster ~ me*** más grande / más rápido que yo; ***more than 50*** más de 50

thank [θæŋk] *v/t* dar las gracias a; ***~ you*** gracias; ***no, ~ you*** no, gracias; ***he's only got himself to ~*** es culpa suya

thank•ful ['θæŋkfəl] *adj* agradecido; ***we have to be ~ that …*** tenemos que dar gracias de que …

thank•ful•ly ['θæŋkfəlɪ] *adv* (*luckily*) afortunadamente

thank•less ['θæŋklɪs] *adj task* ingrato

thanks [θæŋks] *npl* gracias *fpl*; ***~!*** ¡gracias!; ***~ to*** gracias a; ***many ~, ~ very much*** muchas gracias; ***no, ~*** no, gracias; ***with ~*** con agradecimiento

Thanks•giv•ing (Day) [θæŋks'gɪvɪŋ] Día *m* de Acción de Gracias

'thank-you gracias

'thank-you let•ter carta *f* de agradecimiento

that [ðæt] **I** *adj* ese *m*, esa *f*; *more remote* aquel *m*, aquella; ***~ one*** ése
II *pron* ése *m*, ésa *f*; *more remote* aquél *m*, aquella *f*; ***what is ~?*** ¿qué es eso?; ***who is ~?*** ¿quién es ése?; ***~'s mine*** ése es mío; ***~'s tea*** es té; ***~'s very kind*** qué amable; ***~ is (to say)*** es decir; ***at ~*** además; ***just let it go at ~*** F déjalo estar F; ***and ~'s ~*** ¡y ya está!
III *rel pron* que; ***the person / car ~ you see*** la persona / el coche que ves
IV *adv* (*so*) tan; ***~ big / expensive*** tan grande / caro
V *conj* que; ***I think ~ …*** creo que …

thatch [θætʃ] paja *f*; ***a ~ of red hair*** una mata de pelo rojizo

thatched [θætʃt] *adj cottage* con techo de paja; *roof* de paja

thaw [θɒː] **I** *v/i of snow* derretirse, fundirse; *of frozen food* descongelarse **II** *n also fig* deshielo *m*

the [ðə] *stressed* [ðiː] el *m*, la *f*, *plural* los *m*, las *f*; ***~ sooner ~ better*** cuanto antes, mejor; ***it's ~ place to go*** es el sitio de moda

the•a•ter ['θɪətər] **1** teatro *m*; ***be in the ~*** trabajar en el teatro **2**: ***~ of war*** escenario *m* de guerra

'the•a•ter crit•ic crítico(-a) *m*(*f*) teatral

the•a•ter•go•er ['θɪətərgoʊər] aficionado(-a) *m*(*f*) al teatro

the•a•tre *etc Br* ☞ ***theater*** *etc*

the•at•ri•cal [θɪ'ætrɪkl] *adj also fig* teatral

theft [θeft] robo *m*

their [ðer] *adj* su; (*his or her*) su; ***~ brother*** su hermano; ***~ books*** sus libros

theirs [ðerz] *pron* el suyo *m*, la suya *f*; ***~ are red*** los suyos son rojos; ***that book is ~*** ese libro es suyo; ***a friend of ~*** un amigo suyo

them [ðem] *pron direct object* los *mpl*, las *fpl*; *indirect object* les; *after prep* ellos *mpl*, ellas *fpl*; ***I know ~*** los / las conozco; ***I gave ~ the keys*** les di las llaves; ***I sold it to ~*** se lo vendí; ***he lives with ~*** vive con ellos / ellas; ***they looked behind ~*** miraron detrás suyo; ***we are younger than ~*** somos más jóvenes que ellos; ***if a person asks for help, you should help ~*** *him / her* si una persona pide ayuda, hay que ayudarla

theme [θiːm] tema *m*

'theme mu•sic tema *m* musical; **'theme park** parque *m* temático; **'theme song** tema *m* musical; **'theme tune** tema *m* musical

them•selves [ðem'selvz] *pron reflexive* se; *emphatic* ellos mismos *mpl*, ellas mismas *fpl*; ***they hurt ~*** se hicieron daño; ***when they saw ~ in the mirror*** cuando se vieron en el espejo; ***they saw it ~*** lo vieron ellos mismos; ***by ~*** (*alone*) solos; (*without help*) ellos solos, ellos mismos

then [ðen] *adv* **1** (*at that time*) entonces; ***by ~*** para entonces; ***from ~ on*** desde entonces **2** (*after that*) luego, después **3** *deducing* entonces **4**: ***but ~, you did promise*** pero tú lo prometiste

the•o•lo•gi•an [θɪə'loʊdʒɪən] teólogo *m*

the•o•log•i•cal [θɪə'lɑːdʒɪkl] *adj* teológico; ***~ college*** facultad *f* de teología

the•ol•o•gy [θɪ'ɑːlədʒɪ] teología *f*

the•o•rem ['θɪərəm] MATH teorema *m*

the•o•ret•i•cal [θɪə'retɪkl] *adj* teórico

the•o•ret•i•cal•ly [θɪə'retɪklɪ] *adv* en teoría

the•o•rist ['θɪərɪst] teórico(-a) *m*(*f*)

the•o•rize ['θɪəraɪz] *v/i* teorizar (***about, on*** sobre)

the•o•ry ['θɪrɪ] teoría *f*; ***in ~*** en teoría

ther•a•peu•tic [θerə'pjuːtɪk] *adj* terapéutico

ther•a•pist ['θerəpɪst] terapeuta *m/f*

ther•a•py ['θerəpɪ] terapia *f*; ***be in ~***

estar recibiendo tratamiento terapéutico

there [ðer] *adv* allí, ahí, allá; ***over*** **~** allí, ahí, allá; ***down*** **~** allí *or* ahí *or* allá abajo; **~** ***is / are …*** hay …; **~** ***is / are not …*** no hay …; **~** ***you are*** *giving sth* aquí tienes; *finding sth* aquí está; *completing sth* ya está; **~** ***and back*** ida y vuelta; ***it's 5 miles*** **~** ***and back*** entre ida y vuelta hay cinco millas; **~** ***he is!*** ¡ahí está!; **~, ~!** ¡venga!; **~** ***and then*** en el acto; **~** ***you go!*** F *that's for you* ¡aquí tienes!; *see what I mean* ¡ya te lo decía yo!; **~** ***you go again!*** F ¡otra vez!; ***you'll get*** **~** ***one day*** F *succeed* al final lo conseguirás; **~*'s a good boy!*** ¡bien hecho!; ***we've all been*** **~** F todos hemos pasado por eso

there•a•bouts [ðerə'baʊts] *adv* aproximadamente; ***fifty dollars or*** **~** cincuenta dólares, más o menos

there•af•ter [ðer'æftər] *adv* en lo sucesivo

there•by [ðer'baɪ] *adv* así

there•fore ['ðerfɔːr] *adv* por (lo) tanto

there•up•on [ðerə'pɑːn] *adv* acto seguido

ther•mal ['θɜːrml] **I** *n* corriente *f* térmica **II** *adj* térmico

ther•mal in•su'la•tion aislamiento *m* térmico; **ther•mal 'pa•per** papel *m* térmico; **ther•mal 'print•er** impresora *f* térmica; **ther•mal 'spring** fuente *f* termal; **ther•mal 'un•der•wear** ropa *f* interior térmica

ther•mom•e•ter [θər'mɑːmɪtər] termómetro *m*

ther•mo•nu•cle•ar [θɜːrmoʊ'nuːklɪər] *adj*: **~** ***device*** dispositivo *m* termonuclear

ther•mos flask ['θɜːrməs] termo *m*

ther•mo•stat ['θɜːrməstæt] termostato *m*

these [ðiːz] **I** *adj* estos(-as) **II** *pron* éstos *mpl*, éstas *fpl*

the•sis ['θiːsɪs] (*pl* ***theses*** ['θiːsiːz]) tesis *f inv*

they [ðeɪ] *pron* ellos *mpl*, ellas *fpl*; **~** ***are Mexican*** son mexicanos; **~*'re going, but we're not*** ellos van, pero nosotros no; ***if anyone looks at this,*** **~** ***will see that …*** si alguien mira esto, verá que …; **~** ***say that …*** dicen que …; **~** ***are going to change the law*** van a cambiar la ley

they'd [ðeɪd] F ☞ ***they had***; ***they would***

they'll [ðeɪl] F ☞ ***they will***

they're [ðer] F ☞ ***they are***

they've [ðeɪv] F ☞ ***they have***

thick [θɪk] **I** *adj* **1** *soup* espeso; *fog* denso; *wall, book* grueso; *hair* poblado; *crowd* compacto; ***it's 3 cm*** **~** tiene 3 cm de grosor; ***give s.o. a*** **~** ***ear*** *Br* F dar un sopapo a alguien; **~** ***with smoke*** lleno de humo; ***the furniture was*** **~** ***with dust*** los muebles estaban llenos de polvo; ***they're*** **~** ***on the ground*** F hay muchos; ***they're (as) thick as thieves*** F son uña y carne; ***that's a bit*** **~*!*** *Br* F ¡eso es una pasada! **2** F (*stupid*) corto **II** *adv*: ***lay it on*** **~** F cargar las tintas; ***come*** **~** ***and fast*** llover **III** *n*: ***in the*** **~** ***of …*** en pleno …; ***in the*** **~** ***of the fight*** en primera línea de batalla; ***through*** **~** ***and thin*** contra viento y marea

thick•en ['θɪkən] **I** *v/t sauce* espesar **II** *v/i* espesarse

thick•et ['θɪkɪt] matorral *m*

thick•head•ed [θɪk'hedɪd] *adj* F zoquete

thick•ie ['θɪkɪ], **thick•o** *Br* P torpe *m(f)*, zoquete *m(f)*

thick•ness ['θɪknɪs] **1** grosor *m* **2** F (*stupidity*) estupidez *f*

thick•set ['θɪkset] *adj* fornido

thick•skinned [θɪk'skɪnd] *adj fig* insensible

thief [θiːf] (*pl* ***thieves*** [θiːvz]) ladrón(-ona) *m(f)*

thigh [θaɪ] muslo *m*

thim•ble ['θɪmbl] dedal *m*

thin [θɪn] **I** *adj person* delgado; *hair* ralo, escaso; *soup* claro; *coat, line* fino; ***disappear into*** **~** ***air*** *fig* desaparecer como por arte de magia; ***produce sth out of*** **~** ***air*** *fig* crear algo por arte de magia; ***this is just the*** **~** ***end of the wedge*** *fig pej* esto es sólo el principio; ***be*** **~** ***on the ground*** F ser escaso; ***he's getting*** **~** ***on top*** se está quedando calvo **II** *v/t* (*pret & pp* ***-ned***) *sauce etc* aclarar **III** *v/i* (*pret & pp* ***-ned***) *of mist* despejarse; ***his hair is starting to*** **~** está empezando quedarse sin pelo

thing [θɪŋ] cosa *f*; **~*s*** (*belongings*) cosas *fpl*; ***how are*** **~*s?*** ¿cómo te va?; ***it's a***

T

good ~ you told me menos mal que me lo dijiste; ***what a ~ to do / say!*** ¡qué barbaridad!; ***I couldn't see a ~*** no veía nada; ***an amusing ~*** algo divertido; ***the ~ is that ...*** lo que pasa es que ...; ***first ~ tomorrow*** mañana a primera hora; ***for one ~ ..., and for another*** para empezar..., y para continuar; ***be on to a good ~*** estar en una buena situación; ***know a ~ or two about*** saber bastante sobre; ***just the ~ for ...*** justo lo que hace falta para...

thing•um•a•jig ['θɪŋʌmədʒɪg] F *object* chisme *m*; *person* fulanito *m*

think [θɪŋk] **I** *v/t & v/i* (*pret & pp* ***thought***) pensar; *hold an opinion* pensar, creer; ***I ~ so*** creo que sí; ***I don't ~ so*** creo que no; ***I ~ so too*** pienso lo mismo; ***what do you ~?*** ¿qué piensas *or* crees?; ***what do you ~ of it?*** ¿qué te parece?; ***I can't ~ of anything more*** no se me ocurre nada más; ***I can't ~ of his name*** no me sale su nombre; ***she doesn't ~ that's funny*** no cree *or* piensa que sea divertido; ***~ hard!*** ¡piensa más!; ***I'll ~ about it*** me lo pensaré; ***I'm ~ing about emigrating*** estoy pensando en emigrar; ***he ~s he's clever*** se cree muy listo; ***I can't ~ why ...*** no veo por qué...; ***try to ~ where ...*** intenta recordar dónde...; ***come to ~ of it ...*** ahora que lo pienso ...; ***it makes you ~*** te da que pensar
II *n* F: ***have a ~ about sth*** pensarse algo; ***he's got another ~ coming*** está muy equivocado
◆ **think back** *v/i* recordar (***to sth*** algo)
◆ **think out** *v/t* reflexionar
◆ **think over** *v/t* reflexionar sobre
◆ **think through** *v/t* reflexionar
◆ **think up** *v/t plan* idear

think•er ['θɪŋkər] pensador(a) *m(f)*

think•ing ['θɪŋkɪŋ] **I** *adj*: ***a newspaper for ~ people*** un periódico para la gente que piensa **II** *n*: ***do some ~*** pensar; ***to my way of ~*** en mi opinión

'think tank grupo *m* de expertos

thin•ner ['θɪnər] disolvente *m*

thin-skinned [θɪn'skɪnd] *adj fig* sensible

third [θɜːrd] **I** *adj* tercero; ***~ time lucky*** a la tercera va la vencida **II** tercero(-a) *m(f)*; *fraction* tercio *m*, tercera parte *f*; ***the ~ of May*** el tres de mayo

'third base tercera base *f*; **'third base•man** tercera base *f*, jugador(a) *m(f)* de tercera base; **'third-class** *adj* de tercera; **'third-de•gree** *adj burns* de tercer grado; **third de'gree**: ***give s.o. the ~*** interrogar a alguien con dureza

third•ly ['θɜːrdlɪ] *adv* en tercer lugar

third 'par•ty tercero *m*; **third-par•ty in'sur•ance** seguro *m* a terceros; **third 'per•son** GRAM tercera persona *f*; **'third-rate** *adj* de tercera, de pacotilla F; **Third 'World** Tercer Mundo *m*

thirst [θɜːrst] sed *f*; ***~ for knowledge*** *fig* sed de conocimientos

thirst-quench•ing ['θɜːrstkwenʃɪŋ] *adj* que quita la sed

thirst•y ['θɜːrstɪ] *adj* sediento; ***be ~*** tener sed; ***gardening is ~ work*** la jardinería da mucha sed

thir•teen [θɜːr'tiːn] trece

thir•teenth [θɜːr'tiːnθ] *n & adj* decimotercero

thir•ti•eth ['θɜːrtɪɪθ] *n & adj* trigésimo

thir•ty ['θɜːrtɪ] treinta; ***be in one's thirties*** tener treinta y tantos años; ***in the thirties*** en los (años) treinta

'thirt•y-some•thing *adj* treinta y tantos

this [ðɪs] **I** *adj* este *m*, esta *f*; ***~ one*** éste **II** *pron* esto *m*, esta *f*; ***~ is good*** esto es bueno; ***~ is ...*** *introducing s.o.* éste / ésta es ...; TELEC soy ...; ***like ~*** así; ***~ is what I expected*** es lo que esperaba; ***after ~*** después de esto; ***before ~*** antes de esto **III** *adv*: ***~ big / high*** así de grande / de alto

this•tle ['θɪsl] BOT cardo *m*

thong [θɑːŋ] **1** *on whip* tralla *f*; *on clothing* correa *f* **2** *underwear, bikini bottom* tanga *m* **3** *sandal* chancla *f*

tho•rax ['θɔːræks] ANAT tórax *m inv*

thorn [θɔːrn] espina *f*; ***be a ~ in s.o.'s side*** *fig* no dejar en paz a alguien

thorn•y ['θɔːrnɪ] *adj also fig* espinoso

thor•ough ['θɜːroʊ] *adj search* minucioso; *knowledge* profundo; *person* concienzudo

'thor•ough•bred *horse* purasangre *m*

thor•ough•fare ['θɜːroʊfer] vía *f* pública; ***no ~*** camino *m* privado; (*dead end*) sin salida

thor•ough•ly ['θɜːroʊlɪ] *adv* completamente; *clean up* a fondo; *search* minuciosamente; ***I'm ~ ashamed*** estoy aver-

gonzadísimo; ***I ~ enjoyed it*** lo disfruté muchísimo
those [ðouz] **I** *adj* esos *mpl*, esas *fpl*; *more remote* aquellos *mpl*, aquellas *fpl* **II** *pron* ésos *mpl*, ésas *fpl*; *more remote* aquéllos *mpl*, aquéllas *mpl*
though [ðou] **I** *conj* (*although*) aunque; ***as ~*** como si **II** *adv* sin embargo; ***it's not finished ~*** pero no está acabado
thought[1] [θɒːt] *n single* idea *f*; *collective* pensamiento *m*; ***that's a ~!*** *worth bearing in mind* no hay que olvidarse de eso; ***on second ~*** *or Br* ***~s*** ahora que lo pienso otra vez; ***with no ~ for*** sin pensar en
thought[2] [θɒːt] *pret & pp* ☞ ***think***
thought•ful ['θɒːtfəl] *adj* **1** pensativo; *book* serio **2** (*considerate*) atento
thought•less ['θɒːtlɪs] *adj* desconsiderado
thou•sand ['θauznd] mil *m*; ***~s of*** miles de; ***a ~ and ten*** mil diez
thou•sandth ['θauzndθ] *n & adj* milésimo
thrash [θræʃ] *v/t* golpear, dar una paliza a; SP dar una paliza a
◆ **thrash around** *v/i with arms etc* revolverse
◆ **thrash out** *v/t solution* alcanzar
thrash•ing ['θræʃɪŋ] *also* SP paliza *f*; ***give s.o. a ~*** dar una paliza a alguien
thread [θred] **I** *n* hilo *m*; *of screw* rosca; ***lose the ~*** (***of the conversation***) perder el hilo de la conversación **II** *v/t needle* enhebrar; *beads* ensartar; ***~ one's way through*** abrirse paso por
thread•bare ['θredber] *adj* raído
threat [θret] amenaza *f*; ***under ~ of*** bajo amenaza de; ***death ~s*** amenazas *fpl* de muerte
threat•en ['θretn] *v/t* amenazar; ***~ s.o. with sth*** amenazar a alguien con algo; ***~ to do sth*** amenazar con hacer algo; ***be ~ed with extinction*** estar en peligro de extinción
threat•en•ing ['θretnɪŋ] *adj* amenazador; ***~ letter*** carta *f* con amenazas
three [θriː] tres; ***~ of hearts*** tres de corazones
three-di•men•sion•al [θriːdaɪ'menʃnəl] *adj fig* tridimensional
'three•fold I *adj* triple **II** *adv* tres veces; ***increase ~*** triplicarse
three-piece 'suit terno *m*; **three-piece 'suite** tresillo *m*; **three-'point•er** *in basketball* canasta *f or* lanzamiento *m* de tres puntos; **'three-point line** *in basketball* línea *f* de seis veinticinco; **three-quart•ers** [θriː'kwɔːrtərz] tres cuartos *mpl*; **three-se•conds vi•o'la•tion** *in basketball* tres segundos *m*, zona *f*
thresh [θreʃ] *v/t corn* trillar
thresh•ing ma•chine ['θreʃɪŋ] trilladora *f*
thresh•old ['θreʃhould] *of house*, *new age* umbral *m*; ***on the ~ of*** en el umbral de, en puertas de; ***pain ~*** tolerancia *f* del dolor
threw [θruː] *pret* ☞ ***throw***
thrift [θrɪft] ahorro *m*
thrift•y ['θrɪftɪ] *adj* ahorrativo
thrill [θrɪl] **I** *n* emoción *f*, estremecimiento *m*; ***it was such a ~ for us all to visit you again*** nos hizo mucha ilusión volver a visitarte; ***he gets some sort of ~ out of annoying people*** disfruta *or* goza de alguna manera molestando a la gente **II** *v/t* ***be ~ed*** estar entusiasmado
thrill•er ['θrɪlər] *movie* película de *Span* suspense *or L.Am.* suspenso; *novel* novela de *Span* suspense *or L.Am.* suspenso
thrill•ing ['θrɪlɪŋ] *adj* emocionante
thrive [θraɪv] *v/i* (*pret* ***throve*** *or* ***thrived***, *pp* ***thrived***) *of plant* medrar, crecer bien; *of business*, *economy* prosperar
◆ **thrive on** *v/t adversity* crecerse ante
throat [θrout] garganta *f*; ***force sth down s.o.'s ~*** *fig* hacer tragar algo a alguien
'throat loz•enge pastilla *f* para la garganta
throat•y ['θroutɪ] *adj voice* ronco
throb [θrɑːb] **I** *n of heart* latido *m*; *of music* zumbido *m* **II** *v/i* (*pret & pp* ***-bed***) *of heart* latir; *of music* zumbar; ***my head is still ~bing*** todavía siento que me va a estallar la cabeza
throes [θrouz] *npl*: ***be in the ~ of*** (***doing***) ***sth*** estar luchando con algo; ***the company was in the ~ of reorganization*** la empresa estaba en medio de una compleja reorganización
throm•bo•sis [θrɑːm'bousɪs] trombosis *f*
throne [θroun] trono *m*; ***come to the ~*** acceder al trono
throng [θrɑːŋ] muchedumbre *f*

throt•tle ['θrɑːtl] **I** *n on motorbike* acelerador *m*; *on boat* palanca *f* del gas; *on motorbike* mango *m* del gas **II** *v/t* (*strangle*) estrangular
◆ **throttle back** *v/i* desacelerar
through [θruː] **I** *prep* **1** (*across*) a través de; ***go ~ the city*** atraversar la ciudad **2** (*during*) durante; ***~ the winter / summer*** durante el invierno / verano; ***Monday ~ Friday*** de lunes a viernes **3** (*by means of*) a través de, por medio de; ***arranged ~ him*** acordado por él **II** *adv*: ***wet ~*** completamente mojado; ***watch a film ~*** ver una película de principio a fin; ***read a book ~*** leerse un libro de principio a fin; ***~ and ~*** de los pies a la cabeza
III *adj*: ***be ~*** *of couple* haber terminado; (*have arrived*: *of news etc*) haber llegado; ***you're ~*** TELEC ya puede hablar; ***I'm ~ with ...*** (*finished with*) he terminado con ...
'through bill COM conocimiento *m* de embarque directo
'through flight vuelo *m* directo
through'out **I** *prep* durante, a lo largo de; ***~ the night*** durante toda la noche; ***~ the country*** por todo el país **II** *adv* (*in all parts*) en su totalidad
'through route vía *f* de paso; **'through traf•fic** tráfico *m* de paso; **'through train** *Br* tren *m* directo; **'through•way** autopista *f*
throw [θroʊ] **I** *v/t* (*pret* **threw**, *pp* **thrown**) **1** tirar; *of horse* tirar, desmontar; ***~ s.o. sth*** tirar algo a alguien; ***~ open*** *door etc* echar abajo; ***~ o.s. at s.o.*** *fig*: *in romantic sense* echarse en brazos de alguien; ***~ o.s. into sth*** tirarse a algo; *fig* entregarse a algo, meterse de lleno en algo **2** (*disconcert*) desconcertar **3** *party* dar
II *n* lanzamiento *m*; ***it's your ~*** te toca tirar
◆ **throw about, throw around** *v/t*: ***throw one's money about*** derrochar el dinero
◆ **throw away** *v/t* tirar, *L.Am.* botar
◆ **throw back** *v/t* devolver
◆ **throw down** *v/t* tirar al suelo; ***throw down a challenge to s.o.*** lanzar un desafío a alguien, desafiar *or* retar a alguien
◆ **throw in** *v/t* tirar; ***throw the ball in*** *in soccer* sacar de banda; ***throw sth in*** (***for free***) añadir algo (de regalo)
◆ **throw off** *v/t jacket etc* quitarse rápidamente; *cold etc* deshacerse de
◆ **throw on** *v/t clothes* ponerse rápidamente
◆ **throw out** *v/t old things* tirar, *L.Am.* botar; *from bar, job, home* echar; *from country* expulsar; *plan* rechazar
◆ **throw over** *v/t friend etc* dejar colgado F (***for*** por)
◆ **throw together** *v/t* **1** *make in a rough and ready way* pergeñar **2**: ***a group of people thrown together by fate*** un grupo de gente a los que había unido el destino
◆ **throw up** **I** *v/t* **1** *ball* lanzar hacia arriba; ***throw up one's hands*** echarse las manos a la cabeza **2** (*vomit*) vomitar **II** *v/i* (*vomit*) vomitar
'throw-a•way *adj* **1** *remark* insustancial, pasajero **2** (*disposable*) desechable
throw•er ['θroʊər]: ***be a good ~*** ser un buen lanzador
'throw-in SP saque *m* de banda
thrown [θroʊn] *pp* ☞ **throw**
thru [θruː] ☞ **through**
thrush[1] [θrʌʃ] *bird* zorzal *m*
thrush[2] [θrʌʃ] MED candidiasis *f inv*
thrust [θrʌst] **I** *v/t* (*pret & pp* **thrust**) (*push hard*) empujar; *knife* hundir; ***~ sth into s.o.'s hands*** poner algo en las manos de alguien; ***~ one's way through the crowd*** abrirse paso a empujones entre la multitud **II** *n with knife etc* cuchillada *f*; MIL ofensiva *f*; PHYS, *of rocket* empuje *m*
'thru•way F ☞ **throughway**
thud [θʌd] golpe *m* sordo
thug [θʌg] matón *m*
thumb [θʌm] **I** *n* pulgar *m*; ***be all ~s*** F ser un torpe; ***give sth the ~s up / down*** dar / no dar el visto bueno a algo; ***stick out like a sore ~*** F llamar la atención, cantar **II** *v/t*: ***~ a ride*** hacer autoestop
'thumb in•dex uñero *m*; **'thumb•nail 'sketch** reseña *f*; **'thumb•screw** **1** TECH palomilla *f* **2** *for torture* empulguera *f*; **'thumb•tack** chincheta *f*
thump [θʌmp] **I** *n* **1** *blow* porrazo *m* **2** *noise* golpe *m* sordo **II** *v/t person* dar un porrazo a; ***~ one's fist on the table*** pegar un puñetazo en la mesa **III** *v/i of heart* latir con fuerza; ***~ on the door***

T

aporrear la puerta
◆ **thump out** *v/t tune on the piano* aporrear
thump•ing ['θʌmpɪŋ] **I** *adj headache* horrible **II** *adv*: **~ *great*** F supergrande
thun•der ['θʌndər] **I** *n* truenos *mpl*; ***steal s.o.'s ~*** *fig* quitar el protagonismo a alguien **II** *v/i also fig* tronar **III** *v/t* vociferar
'thun•der•bolt rayo *m*; **'thun•der•clap** trueno *m*; **'thunder•cloud** nubarrón *m* de tormenta
thun•der•ous ['θʌndərəs] *adj applause* ensordecedor
'thun•der•storm tormenta *f* (*con truenos*)
'thun•der•struck *adj* atónito
thun•der•y ['θʌndərɪ] *adj weather* tormentoso
Thurs•day ['θɜːrzdeɪ] jueves *inv*; ***on ~*** el jueves; ***on ~s*** los jueves
thus [ðʌs] *adv* **1** (*in this way*) así **2**: **~ *far*** hasta el momento
thwart [θwɔːrt] *v/t person, plans* frustrar
thyme [taɪm] tomillo *m*
thy•roid gland ['θaɪrɔɪd] (glándula *f*) tiroides *m inv*
ti•ar•a [tɪ'ɑːrə] diadema *f*
Ti•bet [tɪ'bet] Tíbet *m*
Ti•bet•an [tɪ'betən] **I** *adj* tibetano **II** *n* tibetano(-a) *m(f)*
tic [tɪk] MED tic *m*
tick[1] [tɪk] **I** *n* **1** *of clock* tictac *m* **2** (*checkmark*) señal *m* de visto bueno **3** *Br* F: ***in a ~*** en un santiamén F **II** *v/i* **1** *of clock* hacer tictac **2**: ***what makes him ~?*** ¿qué es lo que le va?
◆ **tick away** *v/i* pasar
◆ **tick off** *v/t* **1** *entry in list etc* marcar **2** *Br* F (*tell off*) echar una bronca a
◆ **tick over** *v/i* MOT estar al ralentí
tick[2] [tɪk] *n* ZO garrapata *f*
tick•er ['tɪkər] F (*heart*) corazón *m*
tick•et ['tɪkɪt] **1** *for bus, train, lottery* billete *m*, *L.Am.* boleto *m*; *for airplane* billete *m*, *L.Am.* pasaje *m*; for *theater, concert, museum* entrada *f*, *L.Am.* boleto *m* **2** *for speeding etc* multa *f*; ***he got a speeding ~*** le multaron por exceso de velocidad
'tick•et col•lec•tor revisor(a) *m(f)*
tick•et•ing ['tɪkɪtɪŋ] billetaje *m*
'tick•et in•spec•tor revisor(a) *m(f)*; **'tick•et ma•chine** máquina *f* expendedora de billetes; **'tick•et of•fice** *at station* mostrador *m* de venta de billetes; THEA taquilla *f*, *L.Am.* boletería *f*
'tick•et tout *Br* revendedor(-a) *m(f)*
tick•ing ['tɪkɪŋ] *noise* tictac *m*
tick•ing 'off *Br* F bronca *f* F; ***give s.o. a ~*** echar una bronca a alguien F
tick•le ['tɪkl] **I** *v/t person* hacer cosquillas a **II** *v/i of material* hacer cosquillas; ***stop that, you're tickling!*** ¡para ya, me haces cosquillas!
tickl•ish ['tɪklɪʃ] *adj*: ***be ~*** *person* tener cosquillas
tid•al ['taɪdl] *adj sea* con mareas
'tid•al wave maremoto *m*
tid•dly•winks ['tɪdlɪwɪŋks] *nsg juego consistente en introducir fichas en un contenedor*
tide [taɪd] marea *f*; ***high ~*** marea alta; ***low ~*** marea baja; ***the ~ is in / out*** la marea está alta / baja; ***against the ~*** *also fig* a contra corriente; ***go with the tide*** *fig* dejarse llevar por la corriente
◆ **tide over** *v/t*: ***20 dollars will tide me over*** 20 dólares me bastarán
ti•di•ness ['taɪdɪnɪs] orden *m*
ti•dy ['taɪdɪ] *adj* ordenado; ***that's a ~ sum*** F es una cantidad considerable
◆ **tidy away** *v/t* (*pret & pp* ***-ied***) guardar
◆ **tidy up I** *v/t room, shelves* ordenar; ***tidy o.s. up*** arreglarse **II** *v/i* recoger
tie [taɪ] **I** *n* **1** (*neck~*) corbata *f* **2** SP (*even result*) empate *m*; ***end in a ~*** acabar en empate **3**: ***he doesn't have any ~s*** no está atado a nada
II *v/t* **1** *knot* hacer, atar; *hands* atar; **~ *two ropes together*** atar dos cuerdas; ***my hands are tied*** *fig* tengo las manos atadas; ***be ~d to sth*** *fig* estar relacionado con algo **2**: ***the game was ~d*** iban iguales
III *v/i* SP empatar; ***they ~d for second place*** empataron y compartieron el segundo puesto
◆ **tie down** *v/t also fig* atar
◆ **tie in with** *v/t* encajar con
◆ **tie up** *v/t person, laces* atar; *boat* amarrar; *hair* recoger; ***I'm tied up tomorrow*** (*busy*) mañana estaré muy ocupado; ***I got tied up at the office*** me demoré *or* entretuve en la oficina; ***be tied up*** *of capital etc* estar inmobilizado

T

'tie•break, 'tie•break•er *in tennis* tie-break *m*, muerte *f* súbita
'tie•pin alfiler *m* de corbata
tier [tɪr] **1** *of hierarchy* nivel *m* **2** *in stadium* grada *f*
'tie-up conexión *f* (***between*** entre)
tiff [tɪf] riña *f*
ti•ger ['taɪgər] tigre *m*
tight [taɪt] **I** *adj* **1** *clothes* ajustado, estrecho **2** *security* estricto **3** (*hard to move*) apretado; (*properly shut*) cerrado **4** (*not leaving much time*) justo de tiempo **5** F (*drunk*) como una cuba F **II** *adv* *hold* fuerte; *shut* bien; ***sit ~*** *fig* esperar; ***sleep ~!*** ¡que duermas bien!
tight•en ['taɪtn] *v/t screw* apretar; *control* endurecer; *security* intensificar; ***~ one's grip on sth*** *on rope etc* asir algo con más fuerza; *on power etc* incrementar el control sobre algo; ***~ one's belt*** *fig* apretarse el cinturón
◆ **tighten up** *v/i in discipline, security* ser más estricto
tight•fist•ed [taɪt'fɪstɪd] *adj* agarrado; **tight'fit•ting** *adj* ajustado; **tight'knit** *adj community* unido; **tight-lipped** [taɪt'lɪpt] *adj*: ***be ~ about sth*** no decir ni mu sobre algo
tight•ly ['taɪtlɪ] *adv* ☞ ***tight***
'tight•rope cuerda *f* floja; ***walk a ~*** *fig* estar en la cuerda floja
'tight•rope walk•er funambulista *m/f*
tights [taɪts] *npl Br* medias *fpl*, pantis *mpl*
'tight•wad F rácano(-a) *m(f)*, roñoso(-a) *m(f)*
ti•gress ['taɪgrɪs] tigresa *f*
tile [taɪl] **I** *n on floor* baldosa *f*; *on wall* azulejo *m*; *on roof* teja *f*; ***have a night on the ~s*** F ir de parranda F **II** *v/t floor* embaldosar; *wall* alicatar; *roof* tejar
'til•er *of wall* alicatador(-a) *m(f)*; *of floor / roof*: *albanil que pone el suelo / el tejado*
till[1] [tɪl] ☞ ***until***
till[2] [tɪl] *n* (*for cash*) caja *f* (registradora)
till[3] [tɪl] *v/t soil* labrar
tilt [tɪlt] **I** *v/t* inclinar **II** *v/i* inclinarse **III** *n*: ***at full ~*** F a toda pastilla F
tim•ber ['tɪmbər] madera *f* (de construcción)
'tim•ber yard almacén *m* de madera
time [taɪm] **I** *n* **1** tiempo *m*; ***~ is up*** se acabó (el tiempo); ***for the ~ being*** por ahora, por el momento; ***have a good ~*** pasarlo bien; ***have a good ~!*** ¡que lo paséis bien!; ***all the ~*** todo el rato; ***two / three at a ~*** de dos en dos / de tres en tres; ***at the same ~*** *speak, reply etc* a la vez; (*however*) al mismo tiempo; ***in ~*** con tiempo; ***on ~*** puntual; ***in no ~*** en un santiamén; ***some ~ ago*** hace algún tiempo; ***at the ~*** en ese momento; ***by the ~ you receive this*** para cuando recibas esto; ***for a ~*** durante un tiempo; ***from ~ to ~*** de vez en cuando; ***in two years' ~*** dentro de dos años; ***all in good ~*** todo a su tiempo; ***be ahead of one's ~*** ser un adelantado; ***be behind the ~s*** no andar con los tiempos; ***keep up with the ~s*** estar al día; ***do ~*** F *in jail* estar en la sombra F (***for*** por); ***take your ~*** tómate el tiempo; ***there's no ~ to lose*** no hay tiempo que perder; ***I don't have much ~ for him*** no me cae muy bien
2 (*occasion*) vez *f*; ***the first ~*** la primera vez; ***four ~s*** cuatro veces; ***~ and again*** una y otra vez; ***~ after ~*** una y otra vez; ***every ~ I ...*** cada vez que ...; ***how many ~s?*** ¿cuántas veces?; ***next ~*** (***I ...***) la próxima vez (que ...); ***this ~*** esta vez; ***at ~s*** a veces
3 *of clock*: ***what's the ~?, do you have the ~?*** ¿qué hora es?; ***what ~?*** ¿a qué hora?; ***this ~ tomorrow*** mañana a esta hora
4 MUS: ***in ~*** *march, play* al ritmo (***with*** de), al compás (***with*** de); ***beat ~*** llevar el compás; ***keep ~*** ir al ritmo; ***in 3 / 4 ~*** en tiempo 3 / 4
5 MATH: ***three ~s four equals*** *or* ***is twelve*** tres por cuatro (igual a) doce **II** *v/t* **1** *runner* cronometrar; *worker* controlar el tiempo de; ***he was ~d at 20 seconds*** hizo un tiempo de 20 segundos **2** *event* programar; ***~ sth well*** hacer algo en el momento exacto
'time bomb bomba *f* de relojería; **'time cap•sule** cápsula *f* del tiempo; **'time-card** tarjeta *f*; **'time clock** *in factory* reloj *m* registrador; **'time-con•sum•ing** *adj* que lleva mucho tiempo; **'time dif•fer•ence** diferencia *f* horaria; **time-hon•ored**, *Br* **time-hon•oured** ['taɪmɑːnərd] *adj* ancestral; **'time-keep•er** *in sport* cronometrador(a) *m(f)*; ***be a good ~*** *of watch* ser preciso;

T

'time-lag intervalo *m*; **time-lapse pho'tog•ra•phy** fotografía *f* en intervalos
time•less ['taɪmlɪs] *adj* eterno
'time lim•it plazo *m*
time•ly ['taɪmlɪ] *adj* oportuno
'time ma•chine máquina *f* del tiempo
'time•out SP tiempo *m* muerto; ***take ~*** hacer un descanso
tim•er ['taɪmər] **1** *device* temporizador *m* **2** *person* cronometrador(a) *m(f)*
'time•sav•ing ahorro *m* de tiempo; **'time•scale** *of project* plazo *m* (de tiempo); **'time share** *apartment* apartamento *m* en multipropiedad; **time shar•ing** ['taɪmʃerɪŋ] multipropiedad *f*; **'time sig•nal** señal *f* horaria; **'time sig•na•ture** MUS llave *f* de tiempo; **'time switch** temporizador *m*; **'time-ta•ble** *for train etc* horario *m*; EDU *Br* horario *m*; *for events* programa *m*; **'time warp** salto *m* en el tiempo; **'time zone** huso *m* horario
tim•id ['tɪmɪd] *adj* tímido
tim•ing ['taɪmɪŋ] *of dancer* sincronización *f*; *of actor* utilización *f* de las pausas y del ritmo; ***the ~ of the announcement was perfect*** el anuncio fue realizado en el momento perfecto
tin [tɪn] **1** *metal* estaño *m* **2** *Br* (*can*) lata *f*
tin•foil ['tɪnfɔɪl] papel *m* de aluminio
tinge [tɪndʒ] **I** *n of color, sadness* matiz *m* **II** *v/t*: ***be ~d with*** *fig* estar teñido de
tin•gle ['tɪŋgl] **I** *n* hormigueo **II** *v/i* estremecerse (***with*** de)
tin 'hat MIL F casco *m*
◆ **tin•ker with** ['tɪŋkər] *v/t* enredar con
tin•kle ['tɪŋkl] **I** *n of bell* tintineo *m* **II** *v/i* tintinear
tinned [tɪnd] *adj Br* enlatado, en conserva
tin•ni•tus [tɪ'naɪtəs] zumbido *m*
tin•ny ['tɪnɪ] *adj sound* metálico
'tin o•pen•er *Br* abrelatas *m inv*
tin•sel ['tɪnsl] espumillón *m*
tint [tɪnt] **I** *n of color* matiz *m*; *in hair* tinte *m*; ***have a ~ of red*** tener un matiz rojo **II** *v/t hair* teñir
tint•ed ['tɪntɪd] *glasses* con un tinte; *paper* coloreado
ti•ny ['taɪnɪ] *adj* diminuto, minúsculo
tip[1] [tɪp] *n* **1** *of stick, finger* punta *f*; *of mountain* cumbre *f*; ***it's on the ~ of my tongue*** *fig* lo tengo en la punta de la lengua **2** *of cigarette* filtro *m*
tip[2] [tɪp] **I** *n* **1** *advice* consejo *m*; ***take a ~ from me and ...*** hazme caso *or* sigue mi consejo y... **2** *money* propina *f* **II** *v/t* (*pret & pp* ***-ped***) *waiter etc* dar propina a
◆ **tip in** *v/t in basketball* palmear
◆ **tip off** *v/t* F avisar
◆ **tip over I** *v/t jug* volcar; *liquid* derramar; ***he tipped water all over me*** derramó agua encima mío **II** *v/i* volcarse
'tip-in *in basketball* palmeo *m*
'tip-off 1 F soplo *m* **2** *in basketball* salto *m* inicial
tipped [tɪpt] *adj cigarettes* con filtro
Tip•pex® ['tɪpeks] *Br* Tipp-Ex *m*
tip•ple ['tɪpl] F *alcoholic* bebida *f* alcohólica
tip•py-toe ['tɪpɪtoʊ]: ***on ~*** de puntillas
tip•sy ['tɪpsɪ] *adj* achispado
'tip•top *adj* F perfecto
ti•rade [taɪ'reɪd] diatriba *f* (***against*** contra)
tire[1] [taɪr] *n* neumático *m*, *L.Am.* llanta *f*
tire[2] [taɪr] **I** *v/t* cansar, fatigar **II** *v/i* cansarse, fatigarse; ***he never ~s of telling the story*** nunca se cansa de contar la historia
◆ **tire out** *v/t* agotar, cansar
tired [taɪrd] *adj* cansado, fatigado; ***be ~ of s.o. / sth*** estar cansado de alguien / algo; ***~ out*** cansado
tired•ness ['taɪrdnɪs] cansancio *m*, fatiga *f*
tire•less ['taɪrlɪs] *adj efforts* incansable, infatigable
tire•some ['taɪrsəm] *adj* (*annoying*) pesado
tir•ing ['taɪrɪŋ] *adj* agotador
ti•ro → ***tyro***
tis•sue ['tɪʃu:] **1** ANAT tejido *m* **2** *handkerchief* pañuelo *m* de papel, Kleenex® *m*
'tis•sue pa•per papel *m* de seda
tit[1] [tɪt] *bird* herrerillo *m*
tit[2] [tɪt]: ***give s.o. ~ for tat*** pagar a alguien con la misma moneda
tit[3] [tɪt] V (*breast*) teta *f* V; ***get on s.o.'s ~s*** P cabrear a alguien F
ti•tan•ic [taɪ'tænɪk] *adj* titánico
ti•tan•i•um [taɪ'teɪnɪəm] titanio *m*
titch [tɪtʃ] *Br* F renacuajo(-a) *m(f)*
tit•il•late ['tɪtɪleɪt] *v/t* excitar

T

ti•tle ['taɪtl] **1** *of novel, person etc* título *m* **2** LAW título *m* de propiedad
'ti•tle deed LAW escritura *f* de propiedad; **'ti•tle fight** combate *m* por el título; **'ti•tle•hold•er** SP campeón(-ona) *m(f)*; **'ti•tle page** portada *f*; **'ti•tle role** *personaje que da título a una obra*
tit•ter ['tɪtər] *v/i* reírse tontamente
tit•tle-tat•tle ['tɪtltætl] F chismorreos *mpl*
tiz•zy ['tɪzɪ] F: ***be in a ~*** ponerse histérico
tlc [ti:el'si:] *abbr* (= ***tender loving care***) cariño *m* y cuidados
to [tu:] *unstressed* [tə] **I** *prep* a; ***~ Japan / Chicago*** a Japón / Chicago; ***let's go ~ my place*** vamos a mi casa; ***walk ~ the station*** caminar a la estación; ***~ the north / south of …*** al norte / sur de …; ***give sth ~ s.o.*** dar algo a alguien; ***from Monday ~ Wednesday*** de lunes a miércoles; ***from 10 ~ 15 people*** de 10 a 15 personas
II *with verbs*: ***~ speak, ~ shout*** hablar, chillar; ***learn ~ swim*** aprender a nadar; ***~ be honest with you …*** para ser sincero …; ***nice ~ eat*** sabroso; ***too heavy ~ carry*** demasiado pesado para llevarlo; ***~ be able to do that you will need …*** para poder hacer eso necesitarás …; ***easy ~ understand*** fácil de entender; ***he only does it ~ earn money*** lo hace únicamente por dinero; ***he was the first ~ arrive*** él llegó primero, fue el primero en llegar; ***~ hear her talk*** escuchándola hablar
III *adv*: ***~ and fro*** de un lado para otro
toad [toʊd] ZO sapo *m*
'toad•stool seta *f* venenosa
toad•y ['toʊdɪ] *pej* **I** *n* adulador(a) *m(f)* **II** *v/i* (*pret & pp* ***-ied***): ***~ to s.o.*** adular a alguien
toast [toʊst] **I** *n* **1** pan *m* tostado; ***a piece of ~*** una tostada **2** *drinking* brindis *m inv*; ***propose a ~ to s.o.*** proponer un brindis en honor de alguien **II** *v/t* **1** *bread* tostar **2** *drinking* brindar por
toast•er ['toʊstər] tostador(a) *m(f)*
to•bac•co [tə'bækoʊ] tabaco *m*
to•bac•co•nist [tə'bækənɪst] *Br* estanquero(-a) *m(f)*
to•bog•gan [tə'bɑ:gən] tobogán *m*
tod [tɑ:d]: ***on one's ~*** *Br* F más solo que la una
to•day [tə'deɪ] *adv* hoy; ***a week ~, ~ week*** de hoy en ocho; ***~'s paper*** el periódico de hoy
tod•dle ['tɑ:dl] *v/i of child* dar los primeros pasos
tod•dler ['tɑ:dlər] niño(-a) *m(f)* pequeño(-a)
tod•dy ['tɑ:dɪ] *una bebida alcohólica, agua, azúcar, especias y zumo*
to-do [tə'du:] F revuelo *m*
toe [toʊ] **I** *n* dedo del pie; *of shoe* puntera; ***be on one's ~s*** *fig* estar alerta; ***keep s.o. on his ~s*** *fig* no dejar en paz a alguien; ***tread on s.o.'s ~s*** *fig* meterse en el terreno de alguien **II** *v/t*: ***~ the line*** acatar la disciplina
'toe•nail uña *f* del pie
tof•fee ['tɑ:fɪ] *Br* tofe *m*
'tof•fee ap•ple manzana *f* de caramelo
tof•fee-nosed ['tɑ:fɪnoʊzd] *adj Br* F presumido
to•fu ['tɑ:fu:] tofu *m*
to•geth•er [tə'geðər] *adv* juntos(-as); ***mix two drinks ~*** mezclar dos bebidas; ***don't all talk ~*** no hablen todos a la vez
to•geth•er•ness [tə'geðərnɪs] unión *f*
tog•gle ['tɑ:gl] *fastener* botón *m* de trenca
◆ **toggle between** *v/t* COMPUT pasar de entre
'tog•gle key COMPUT *tecla que activa o desactiva una función*
'tog•gle switch ELEC tecla *f* de conmutación
toil [tɔɪl] **I** *n* esfuerzo *m* **II** *v/i* esforzarse (***at*** en)
toi•let ['tɔɪlɪt] *place* cuarto de baño, servicio *m*; *equipment* retrete *m*; ***go to the ~*** ir al baño
'toi•let bag *Br*, **'toi•let kit** bolsa *f* de aseo
'toi•let pa•per papel *m* higiénico
toil•et•ries ['tɔɪlɪtrɪz] *npl* artículos *mpl* de tocador
'toi•let roll rollo *m* de papel higiénico
to•ken ['toʊkən] **I** *n* **1** (*sign*) muestra *f*; ***as a ~ of*** como muestra de **2** *for gambling* ficha *f* **3** (*gift ~*) vale *m* **II** *adj* simbólico
'to•ken strike huelga *f* de advertencia
told [toʊld] *pret & pp* ☞ ***tell***
tol•er•a•ble ['tɑ:lərəbl] *adj* **1** *pain etc* soportable **2** (*quite good*) aceptable
tol•er•a•bly ['tɑ:lərəblɪ] *adv* aceptablemente
tol•er•ance ['tɑ:lərəns] tolerancia *f*

tol•er•ant ['tɑːlərənt] *adj* tolerante
tol•er•ate ['tɑːləreɪt] *v/t noise, person* tolerar; ***I won't ~ it!*** ¡no lo toleraré!
toll[1] [toʊl] *v/i of bell* tañer
toll[2] [toʊl] *n* (*deaths*) mortandad *f*, número *m* de víctimas
toll[3] [toʊl] *n for bridge, road* peaje *m*; TELEC tarifa *f*; ***take its ~ on*** *fig* haber hecho estragos en
'toll booth cabina *f* de peaje; **'toll bridge** puente *m* de peaje; **'toll-free** *adj* TELEC gratuito; **'toll-free num•ber** teléfono *m* gratuito, *Span* número *m* 900; **'toll road** carretera *f* de peaje
tom [tɑːm] ZO gato *m*
to•ma•to [tə'meɪtoʊ] (*pl* **-oes**) tomate *m*, *Mex* jitomate *m*
to'ma•to juice zumo *m* de tomate; **to-ma•to 'ketch•up** ketchup *m*; **to•ma•to 'sauce** *for pasta etc* salsa *f* de tomate
tomb [tuːm] tumba *f*
'tom•boy niña *f* poco femenina
'tomb•stone lápida *f*
'tom•cat gato *m*
tome [toʊm] tomo *m*
tom•fool•er•y [tɑːm'fuːlərɪ] tonterías *fpl*
to•mog•ra•phy [tə'mɑːgrəfɪ] MED tomografía *f*
to•mor•row [tə'mɔːroʊ] **I** *adv* mañana; ***the day after ~*** pasado mañana; ***~ morning / night*** mañana por la mañana / noche; ***a week ~, ~ week*** de mañana en ocho **II** *n*: ***~'s paper*** el periódico de mañana; ***he's spending money like there's no ~*** está gastando dinero como si se fuera a acabar el mundo
ton [tʌn] tonelada (*907 kg*); ***~s of*** F montones de
tone [toʊn] *of color, conversation* tono *m*; *of musical instrument* timbre *m*; *of neighborhood* nivel *m*; ***~ of voice*** tono de voz
◆ **tone down** *v/t demands, criticism* bajar el tono de
◆ **tone up** *v/t* tonificar
ton•er ['toʊnər] tóner *m*
'ton•er cart•ridge cartucho *m* de tóner
tongs [tɑːŋz] *npl* tenazas *fpl*; *for hair* tenacillas *fpl* de rizar
tongue [tʌŋ] lengua *f*; ***~ in cheek*** en broma; ***bite one's ~*** *also fig* morderse la lengua; ***hold one's ~*** cerrar la boca; ***stick one's ~ out at s.o.*** sacar la lengua a alguien
'tongue twist•er trabalenguas *m inv*
ton•ic ['tɑːnɪk] MED tónico *m*; ***be a real ~*** ser realmente tonificante; ***a gin and ~*** un gin-tonic
'ton•ic (wa•ter) (agua *f*) tónica *f*
to•night [tə'naɪt] **I** *adv* esta noche **II** *n*: ***~'s television programs*** los programas de televisión para esta noche
ton•sil ['tɑːnsl] amígdala *f*
ton•sil•li•tis [tɑːnsə'laɪtɪs] amigdalitis *f*
too [tuː] *adv* **1** (*also*) también; ***me ~*** yo también **2** (*excessively*) demasiado; ***~ big / hot*** demasiado grande / caliente; ***~ much rice*** demasiado arroz; ***eat ~ much*** comer demasiado
took [tʊk] *pret* ☞ ***take***
tool [tuːl] herramienta *f*; ***the ~s of the trade*** *fig* las herramientas de trabajo
'tool•bag bolsa *f* de herramientas; **'tool•bar** COMPUT barra *f* de herramientas; **'tool•box** caja *f* de herramientas; **'tool•kit** juego *m* de herramientas; **'tool•shed** cobertizo *m* para las herramientas
toot [tuːt] F **I** *v/t* tocar **II** *v/i* tocar la bocina **III** *n*: ***a ~ on the horn*** un bocinazo
tooth [tuːθ] (*pl* ***teeth*** [tiːθ]) diente *m*; (*back ~*) muela *f*; ***in the teeth of*** *fig* a pesar de; ***fight ~ and nail*** luchar con uñas y dientes; ***get one's teeth into sth*** hincarle el diente a algo
'tooth•ache dolor *m* de muelas
'tooth•brush cepillo *m* de dientes
tooth•less ['tuːθlɪs] *adj* desdentado
'tooth•paste pasta *f* de dientes, dentífrico *m*
'tooth•pick palillo *m*
toot•sie, toot•sy ['tʊtsɪ] *children's language* dedito *m* del pie
top [tɑːp] **I** *n* **1** *of mountain* cima *f*; *of tree* copa *f*; *of wall, screen, page* parte *f* superior; ***at the ~ of the page*** en la parte superior de la página; ***at the ~ of the mountain*** en la cumbre; ***at the ~ of one's voice*** a grito pelado; ***be ~ of the class / league*** *person, team* ser el primero de la clase / de la liga; ***get to the ~*** *of company, mountain* llegar a la cumbre; ***from ~ to toe*** de la cabeza a los pies; ***from ~ to bottom*** de arriba abajo
2 (*lid*: *of bottle etc*) tapón *m*; *of pen* capucha *f*

3 *clothing* camiseta *f*, top *m*
4 (MOT: *gear*) directa *f*
5: ***on ~*** arriba, en la parte de arriba; ***on ~ of*** encima de, sobre; ***on ~ of each other*** uno encima del otro; ***on ~ of that*** *fig* además de eso; ***are things getting on ~ of you?*** F ¿te estás agobiando demasiado? F; ***come out on ~*** resultar victorioso; ***be over the ~*** (*exaggerated*) ser una exageración
II *adj branches* superior; *floor* de arriba, último; *management*, *official* alto; *player* mejor; *speed*, *note* máximo; ***~ scorer*** pichichi *m*; ***the ~ dog*** F el mandamás; ***~ gear*** directa *f*; ***at ~ speed*** a toda velocidad
III *v/t* (*pret & pp* ***-ped***): ***~ped with …*** *of cake etc* con una capa de … por encima; ***and to ~ it all …*** y para colmo …; ***~ the bill*** encabezar el cartel
◆ **top off** *v/t evening etc* rematar (***with*** con)
◆ **top up** *v/t Br glass*, *tank* llenar
'top cop•y *not photocopy* original *m*; **'top•flight** *adj* F de altos vuelos F; **top 'hat** sombrero *m* de copa; **top 'heav•y** *adj* sobrecargado en la parte superior
top•ic ['tɑːpɪk] tema *m*
top•i•cal ['tɑːpɪkl] *adj* de actualidad
top•less ['tɑːplɪs] *adj* en topless
top-'lev•el *adj* de alto nivel
'top•most *adj branches*, *floor* superior
top-'notch *adj* F de primera F
to•pog•ra•phy [tə'pɑːgrəfɪ] topografía *f*
top•ping ['tɑːpɪŋ] *on pizza* ingrediente *m*; ***with a ~ of whipped cream*** y con nata montada encima
top•ple ['tɑːpl] **I** *v/i* derrumbarse **II** *v/t government* derrocar
◆ **topple over** *v/i* venirse abajo
top-'qual•i•ty *adj* de primera; **top 'se•cret** *adj* altamente confidencial; **'top•soil** capa *f* superficial del suelo; **'top•spin** *in tennis etc*: *efecto resultado de golpear la pelota por arriba*
top•sy-tur•vy [tɑːpsɪ'tɜːrvɪ] *adj* (*in disorder*) desordenado; *world* al revés
'top-up card *Br*: *for cell phone* tarjeta *f* de recarga
torch [tɔːrtʃ] **1** *with flame* antorcha *f* **2** *Br* (*flashlight*) linterna *f*
'torch•light: ***by ~*** con luz de antorchas; ***~ procession*** procesión *f* de antorchas
tore [tɔːr] *pret* ☞ ***tear***
tor•ment I ['tɔːrment] **I** *n* tormento **II** *v/t* [tɔːr'ment] *person*, *animal* atormentar; ***~ed by doubt*** atormentado por la duda
torn [tɔːrn] *pp* ☞ ***tear***
tor•na•do [tɔːr'neɪdoʊ] tornado *m*
tor•pe•do [tɔːr'piːdoʊ] **I** *n* (*pl* ***-oes***) torpedo **II** *v/t also fig* torpedear
tor'pe•do boat torpedero *m*
tor•por ['tɔːrpər] letargo *m*
torque [tɔːrk] PHYS par *m* de torsión
tor•rent ['tɑːrənt] *also fig* torrente *m*; *of lava* colada *f*
tor•ren•tial [tə'renʃl] *adj rain* torrencial
tor•rid ['tɑːrɪd] *adj heat* tórrido; *passion* apasionado
tor•sion ['tɔːrʃn] PHYS torsión *f*
tor•so ['tɔːrsoʊ] torso *m*
tor•toise ['tɔːrtəs] tortuga *f*
'tor•toise•shell carey *m*
tor•tu•ous ['tɔːrtʃʊəs] *adj route*, *procedures* tortuoso
tor•ture ['tɔːrtʃər] **I** *n* tortura; ***it was ~ not knowing*** fue un suplicio estar sin saber nada **II** *v/t* torturar
'tor•ture cham•ber cámara *f* de torturas
To•ry ['tɔːrɪ] *Br* POL **I** *n* tory *m/f*, conservador(a) *m(f)* **II** *adj* tory, conservador
toss [tɑːs] **I** *v/t ball* lanzar, echar; *rider* desmontar; *salad* remover; ***~ a coin*** echar a cara o cruz; ***~ s.o. for sth*** echar algo a cara o cruz con alguien **II** *v/i* **1**: ***~ and turn*** dar vueltas **2**: ***~ for sth*** echarse algo a cara o cruz **III** *n*: ***win the ~*** SP ganar el sorteo inicial; ***I don't give a ~ about it*** *Br* F me importa un pimiento
tot [tɑːt] F **1** *child* crío(-a) *m(f)* **2** *of brandy etc* dedal *m*
◆ **tot up** *v/t* F sumar
to•tal ['toʊtl] **I** *n* total; ***in ~*** en total **II** *adj sum*, *amount* total; *disaster* rotundo, completo; *idiot* de tomo y lomo; *stranger* completo **III** *v/t* (*pret & pp* ***-ed***, *Br* ***-led***) **1**: ***~ing 500 …*** sumando 500… **2** F *car* cargarse F; ***the truck was ~ed*** el camión quedó destrozado
to•tal•i•tar•i•an [toʊtælɪ'terɪən] *adj* totalitario
to•tal•ly ['toʊtəlɪ] *adv* totalmente
tote [toʊt] F *in betting* totalizador *m*
'tote bag bolsa *f* grande
to•tem pole ['toʊtəmpoʊl] tótem *m*

tot•ter ['tɑːtər] *v/i of person* tambalearse
tot•ter•y ['tɑːtərɪ] *adj* tambaleante
touch [tʌʧ] **I** *n* **1** toque *m*; *sense* tacto *m*; ***be soft to the ~*** ser blando al tacto; ***at the ~ of a button*** apretando un botón; ***put the finishing ~es to*** dar los últimos toques a; ***a personal ~*** un toque personal
2: ***get in ~ with s.o.*** ponerse en contacto con alguien; ***lose ~ with s.o.*** perder el contacto con alguien; ***keep in ~ with s.o.*** mantenerse en contacto con alguien; ***we kept in ~*** seguimos en contacto; ***be out of ~*** no estar al corriente; ***the leader was out of ~ with the people*** el líder estaba desconectado de lo que pensaba la gente
3 SP: ***in ~*** fuera
4: ***a ~ of flu*** una gripe ligera
II *v/t* **1** tocar; ***~ wood!*** ¡toca madera! **2** *emotionally* conmover
III *v/i* tocar; *of two lines etc* tocarse
◆ **touch down** *v/i* **1** *of airplane* aterrizar **2** SP marcar un ensayo
◆ **touch off** *v/t crisis etc* desencadenar
◆ **touch on** *v/t* (*mention*) tocar, mencionar
◆ **touch up** *v/t* **1** *photo* retocar **2** *Br*: *sexually* manosear
touch-and-'go *adj*: ***it was ~ whether*** no era seguro si
touch•down ['tʌʧdaʊn] **1** *of airplane* aterrizaje *m* **2** SP touchdown *m*, ensayo *m*
tou•ché ['tuːʃeɪ] *int* ¡touché!
touched [tʌʧt] *adj* **1** (*moved*) conmovido **2** F (*crazy*) tocado del ala
touch•ing ['tʌʧɪŋ] *adj* conmovedor
'touch•line SP línea *f* de banda; **'touch screen** pantalla *f* táctil; **'touch-sen•si•tive** *adj screen* táctil; **'touch-stone** piedra *f* de toque (***of*** de); **touch-tone 'tel•e•phone** teléfono *m* de tonos; **'touch-type** *v/i* escribir a máquina al tacto
touch•y ['tʌʧɪ] *adj person* susceptible
tough [tʌf] *adj* **1** *person*, *meat*, *punishment*, *competition* duro; ***get ~ with s.o.*** ponerse duro con alguien; ***that's ~ on them*** eso es injusto para con ellos; ***well, that's ~, I can't help it*** mala suerte, no puedo evitarlo **2** *question*, *exam* difícil **3** *material* resistente, fuerte
tough•en ['tʌfn] *v/t material*, *person* endurecer
◆ **toughen up** *v/t person* hacer más fuerte
'tough guy F tipo *m* duro F
tou•pee [tuː'peɪ] bisoñé *m*
tour [tʊr] **I** *n of museum etc* recorrido *m*; *of area* viaje *m* (***of*** por); *of band etc* gira *f*; ***give s.o. a ~ of sth*** hacer con alguien un recorrido de algo; ***be on ~*** estar de gira (***in*** por) **II** *v/t area* recorrer **III** *v/i of band etc* estar de gira
◆ **tour around** *v/i* hacer turismo
'tour group grupo *m* de turistas
'tour guide guía *m/f* turístico(-a)
tour•ism ['tʊrɪzm] turismo *m*
tour•ist ['tʊrɪst] turista *m/f*
'tour•ist at•trac•tion atracción turística; **'tour•ist board** oficina *f* de turismo; **'tour•ist class** AVIA, NAUT clase *f* turista; **'tour•ist in•dus•try** industria *f* turística; **tour•i•st in•for'ma•tion of•fice** oficina *f* de turismo; **'tour•ist sea•son** temporada *f* turística; **'tour•ist trade** sector *m* turístico
tour•ist•y ['tʊrɪstɪ] *adj* turístico
tour•na•ment ['tʊrnəmənt] torneo *m*
'tour op•er•a•tor operador(a) *m(f)* turístico(-a)
tou•sled ['taʊzld] *adj hair* revuelto
tout [taʊt] **I** *v/i*: ***~ for business*** intentar hacerse con negocio **II** *n Br* revendedor(a) *m(f)*
tow [toʊ] **I** *v/t car*, *boat* remolcar **II** *n*: ***give s.o. a ~*** remolcar a alguien; ***with his children in ~*** F con sus niños a cuestas
◆ **tow away** *v/t car* llevarse
to•ward [tɔːrd] *prep* hacia; ***we are working ~ a solution*** estamos intentando encontrar una solución; ***they gave me something ~ it*** me dieron una ayuda; ***a contribution ~ sth*** una contribución para algo
'tow•bar barra *f* de remolque
tow•el ['taʊəl] toalla *f*; ***throw in the ~*** *also fig* tirar la toalla
'tow•el rail toallero *m*
tow•er ['taʊər] torre *m*
'tow•er block *Br* bloque *m* (*de pisos, oficinas etc*)
◆ **tower over** *v/t of building* elevarse por encima de; *of person* ser mucho más alto que
tow•er•ing ['taʊərɪŋ] *adj fig* imponente;

be in a ~ rage estar enfadadísimo
town [taʊn] ciudad *f*; *small* pueblo *m*; ***go to ~*** ir al centro; ***really go to ~ on sth*** F dejarse la piel en algo F; ***be out on the ~*** F estar de parranda F
town 'cen•ter, *Br* **town cen•tre** centro *m* de la ciudad / del pueblo; **town 'coun•cil** ayuntamiento *m*; **town 'hall** ayuntamiento *m*; **'town house** casa *f* adosada; **town plan•ning** [taʊn'plænɪŋ] urbanismo *m*
towns•folk ['taʊnzfoʊk] *npl* ciudadanos *mpl*
town•ship ['taʊnʃɪp] municipio *m*
towns•peo•ple ['taʊnzpi:pl] *npl* ciudadanos *mpl*
'tow•rope cuerda *f* para remolcar
'tow truck grúa *f*
tox•ic ['tɑ:ksɪk] *adj* tóxico
tox•ic 'waste residuos *mpl* tóxicos
tox•in ['tɑ:ksɪn] BIO toxina *f*
toy [tɔɪ] juguete *m*
◆ **toy with** *v/t object* juguetear con; *idea* darle vueltas a
'toy store juguetería *f*, tienda *f* de juguetes
trace [treɪs] **I** *n of substance* resto *m*; ***without (a) ~*** sin dejar rastro **II** *v/t* **1** (*find*) localizar; ***he was ~d to …*** se le localizó en …; ***~ a call*** localizar una llamada **2** (*follow*: *footsteps of*) seguir el rastro a **3** (*draw*) trazar
◆ **trace back** *v/t*: ***we can trace our family back to …*** nuestra familia se remonta a …; ***trace the origins / the cause of sth back to sth*** encontrar los orígenes / la causa de algo en algo
'trace el•e•ment CHEM oligoelemento *m*
tra•che•a ['treɪkɪə] ANAT tráquea *f*
trac•ing pa•per ['treɪsɪŋ] papel *m* de calco
track [træk] **1** (*path*) senda *f*, camino *m*; ***be on the wrong ~*** ir por el mal camino; ***be on ~ for …*** ir bien encaminado para …
2 *for horses* hipódromo *m*; *for dogs* canódromo *m*; *for cars* circuito *m*; *for athletics* pista *f*
3 *on CD* canción *f*, corte *m*
4 RAIL vía *f*; ***~ 10*** via 10
5 *of animal etc* rastro *m*; ***keep ~ of sth*** llevar la cuenta de algo; ***lose ~ of*** perder la cuenta de; ***it's time we were making ~s*** es hora de largarse
◆ **track down** *v/t* localizar
track-and-'field e•vents *npl* atletismo *m*
'track•ball COMPUT trackball *m*, ratón *m* de bola
tracked [trækt] *adj*: ***~ vehicle*** vehículo *m* oruga
track•er dog ['trækər] perro *m* rastreador
'track e•vents *npl* atletismo *m* en pista
track•ing sta•tion ['trækɪŋ] estación *f* de seguimiento
track 'rec•ord *fig* historial *m*; ***have a good ~*** tener un buen historial; ***what's her ~ like?*** ¿qué historial tiene?
'track•suit *Br* chándal *m*
tract[1] [trækt] **1** *of land* tramo *m* **2** ANAT: ***digestive ~*** tubo *m* digestivo; ***respiratory ~*** vías *fpl* respiratorias
tract[2] [trækt] *written* panfleto *m*
trac•ta•ble ['træktəbl] *adj* dócil
trac•tion ['trækʃn] **1** MOT tracción *f* **2**: ***his leg is in ~*** MED tiene la pierna en alto
trac•tor ['træktər] tractor *m*
trade [treɪd] **I** *n* **1** (*commerce*) comercio *m* **2** (*profession*, *craft*) oficio *m*; ***be a plumber by ~*** ser un fontanero de profesión **II** *v/i* (*do business*) comerciar; ***~ in sth*** comerciar en algo **III** *v/t* (*exchange*) intercambiar (***for*** por)
◆ **trade in** *v/t when buying* entregar como parte del pago
◆ **trade on** *v/t pej* aprovecharse de
'trade a•gree•ment acuerdo *m* comercial; **'trade as•so•ci•a•tion** asociación *f* profesional; **'trade bar•ri•er** barrera *f* comercial; **'trade def•i•cit** déficit *m* comercial; **'trade di•rec•to•ry** directorio *m* comercial; **'trade dis•count** descuento *m* comercial; **'trade ex•hi•bi•tion** feria *f* de muestras; **'trade fair** feria *f* de muestras; **'trade jour•nal** revista *f* profesional; **'trade•mark** marca *f* registrada; **'trade mis•sion** misión *f* comercial; **'trade name** nombre *m* comercial; **'trade-off**: ***there's always a ~ between speed and quality*** más rapidez siempre significa peor calidad; **'trade price** precio *m* al por mayor
trad•er ['treɪdər] comerciante *m/f*
trade 'se•cret secreto *m* de la casa, secreto *m* comercial

T

trades•man ['treɪdzmən] (*plumber etc*) *electricista, fontanero / plomero etc*
trade 'un•ion *Br* sindicato *m*; **trade 'un•ion•ist** *Br* sindicalista *m/f*; **'trade wind** viento *m* alisio
trad•ing part•ner ['treɪdɪŋ] socio(-a) *m(f)* comercial
tra•di•tion [trə'dɪʃn] tradición *f*
tra•di•tion•al [trə'dɪʃnl] *adj* tradicional
tra•di•tion•al•ly [trə'dɪʃnlɪ] *adv* tradicionalmente
traf•fic ['træfɪk] *on roads, in drugs* tráfico *m*
◆ **traffic in** *v/t* (*pret & pp* ***-ked***) *drugs* traficar con
'traf•fic calm•ing medidas *fpl* viales para reducir la velocidad del tráfico; **'traf•fic cha•os** caos *m inv* circulatorio; **'traf•fic cir•cle** rotonda *f*, *Span* glorieta *f*; **'traf•fic cone** cono *m* de señalización; **'traf•fic cop** F poli *m/f* de tráfico F; **'traf•fic is•land** isleta *f*; **'traf•fic jam** atasco *m*
traf•fick•er ['træfɪkər] *esp in drugs* traficante *m/f*
'traf•fic light semáforo *m*; **'traf•fic po•lice** policía *f* de tráfico; **'traf•fic sign** señal *m* de tráfico; **'traf•fic vi•o•la•tion** infracción *f* de tráfico; **'traf•fic war•den** *Br*: *agente que pone multas por aparcamiento indebido*
trag•e•dy ['trædʒədɪ] tragedia *f*
trag•ic ['trædʒɪk] *adj* tragico
trag•i•cal•ly ['trædʒɪklɪ] *adv* trágicamente
trag•i•com•e•dy [trædʒɪ'kɑːmədɪ] tragicomedia *f*
trag•i'com•ic *adj* tragicómico
trail [treɪl] **I** *n* **1** (*path*) camino *m*, senda *f* **2** *of blood, dust, destruction* rastro *m*; ***be hot on s.o.'s ~*** estar tras la pista de alguien **II** *v/t* **1** (*follow*) seguir la pista de **2** (*tow*) arrastrar **III** *v/i* (*lag behind*) ir a la zaga
trail•er ['treɪlər] **1** *pulled by vehicle* remolque *m* **2** (*mobile home*) caravana *f* **3** *of movie* avance *m*, tráiler *m*
train[1] [treɪn] *n* **1** tren *m*; ***go by ~*** ir en tren; ***on the ~*** en el tren; ***~ set*** tren *m* de juguete **2**: ***~ of thought*** pensamientos *mpl*
train[2] [treɪn] **I** *v/t team, athlete* entrenar; *employee* formar; *dog* adiestrar **II** *v/i of team, athlete* entrenarse; *of teacher etc* formarse
train•ee [treɪ'niː] aprendiz(a) *m(f)*
train•er ['treɪnər] SP entrenador(a) *m(f)*, preparador(a) *m(f)* físico(-a); *of dog* adiestrador(a) *m(f)*
train•ers ['treɪnərz] *npl Br shoes* zapatillas *fpl* de deporte
train•ing [treɪnɪŋ] *of new staff* formación *f*, SP entrenamiento *m*; ***be in ~*** SP estar entrenándose; ***be out of ~*** SP estar desentrenado
'train•ing course cursillo *m* de formación; **'train•ing pe•ri•od** periodo *m* de formación; **'train•ing pro•gram** programa *m* de formación; **'train•ing scheme** plan *m* de formación
'train sta•tion estación *f* de tren
traipse [treɪps] *v/i* F dar vueltas
trait [treɪt] rasgo *m*
trai•tor ['treɪtər] traidor(a) *m(f)*
tra•jec•to•ry [trə'dʒektɔːrɪ] trayectoria *f*
tramp [træmp] **I** *v/i* marchar **II** *n* **1** *pej*: *loose woman* fulana *f* **2** *Br* (*hobo*) vagabundo(-a) *m(f)*
tram•ple ['træmpl] *v/t* pisotear; ***be ~d to death*** morir pisoteado; ***be ~d underfoot*** ser pisoteado
◆ **trample on** *v/t person, object* pisotear
tram•po•line ['træmpəliːn] cama *f* elástica
trance [træns] trance *m*; ***go into a ~*** entrar en trance
tran•quil ['træŋkwɪl] *adj* tranquilo
tran•quil•i•ty [træŋ'kwɪlətɪ] tranquilidad *f*
tran•quil•iz•er ['træŋkwɪlaɪzər] tranquilizante *m*
trans•act [træn'zækt] *v/t deal* negociar
trans•ac•tion [træn'zækʃn] **1** *action* transacción *f* **2** *deal* negociación *f*
trans•at•lan•tic [trænzət'læntɪk] *adj* transatlántico
trans•ceiv•er [træn'siːvər] transceptor *m*
tran•scen•den•tal [trænsen'dentl] *adj* trascendental
trans•con•ti•nen•tal [trænzkɑːntɪ'nentl] *adj* transcontinental
tran•scribe [træn'skraɪb] *v/t* transcribir
tran•script ['trænskrɪpt] transcripción *f*
tran•scrip•tion [træn'skrɪpʃn] transcripción *f*
tran•sept ['trænsept] ARCHI transepto

m, crucero *m*

trans•fer I *v/t* [træns'fɜːr] (*pret & pp* **-red**) transferir **II** *v/i* [træns'fɜːr] (*pret & pp* **-red**) *in traveling* hacer transbordo; *from one language to another* pasar **III** *n* ['trænsfɜːr] transferencia *f*; *in travel* transbordo *m*

trans•fer•a•ble [træns'fɜːrəbl] *adj ticket* transferible

'trans•fer ad•vice FIN comunicación *f* de transferencia; **'trans•fer fee** *for football player* traspaso *m*; **'trans•fer order** FIN orden *f* de transferencia

trans•fig•ure [træns'fɪgər] *v/t* transfigurar

trans•fix [træns'fɪks] *v/t* paralizar (**with** con)

trans•form [træns'fɔːrm] *v/t* transformar

trans•form•a•tion [trænsfər'meɪʃn] transformación *f*

trans•form•er [træns'fɔːrmər] ELEC transformador *m*

trans•fu•sion [træns'fjuːʒn] transfusión *f*

tran•si•ent ['trænzɪənt] **I** *adj* pasajero **II** *n* transeúnte *m/f*

tran•sis•tor [træn'zɪstər] transistor *m*; (*radio*) transistor *m*, radio *f* transistor

trans•it ['trænzɪt]: ***in ~*** en tránsito

'trans•it bill COM certificado *m* de paso

tran•si•tion [træn'sɪʒn] transición *f*

tran•si•tion•al [træn'sɪʒnl] *adj* de transición

tran•si•tive ['trænsətɪv] *adj* LING transitivo

'trans•it lounge *at airport* sala *f* de tránsito

tran•si•to•ry ['trænsɪtɔːrɪ] *adj* ☞ ***transient***

'trans•it pas•sen•ger pasajero(-a) *m(f)* en tránsito

trans•lat•a•ble [træns'leɪtəbl] *adj* traducible

trans•late [træns'leɪt] **I** *v/t* traducir **2**: ***~ words into action*** convertir palabras en hechos **II** *v/i* traducir

trans•la•tion [træns'leɪʃn] traducción *f*

trans'la•tion com•pa•ny agencia *f* de traducciones

trans'la•tion soft•ware software *m* de traducción

trans•la•tor [træns'leɪtər] traductor(a) *m(f)*

trans•mis•sion [trænz'mɪʃn] **1** *of news, program* emisión *f*; *of disease* transmisión *f* **2** MOT transmisión *f*

trans•mit [trænz'mɪt] *v/t* (*pret & pp* **-ted**) *news, program* emitir; *disease* transmitir

trans•mit•ter [trænz'mɪtər] RAD, TV emisora *f*

trans•par•en•cy [træns'pærənsɪ] PHOT diapositiva *f*

trans•par•ent [træns'pærənt] *adj* **1** transparente **2** (*obvious*) obvio

tran•spire [træns'paɪər] *v/i* **1** (*emerge*) saberse **2** (*happen*) ocurrir

trans•plant MED **I** *v/t* [træns'plænt] transplantar **II** ['trænsplænt] transplante *m*

trans•pond•er [træns'pɑːndər] transpondedor *m*

trans•port I *v/t* [træns'pɔːrt] *goods, people* transportar **II** *n* ['trænspɔːrt] *of goods, people* transporte *m*

'trans•port air•craft avión *m* de transporte

trans•port•a•tion [trænspɔːr'teɪʃn] *of goods, people* transporte *m*; ***means of ~*** medio *m* de transporte; ***public ~*** transporte *m* público; ***Department of Transportation*** Ministerio *m* de Transporte

trans•port•er [træns'pɔːrtər] MOT camión *m* de transporte; *aircraft* avión *m* de transporte

trans•pose [træns'pouz] *v/t* **1** invertir **2** MUS transportar

trans•sex•u•al [træns'sekʃʊəl] transexual *m/f*

trans•ship•ment ['trænsʃɪpmənt] COM transbordo *m*

trans•verse ['trænsvɜːrs] *adj* transversal

trans•verse•ly ['trænsvɜːrslɪ] *adv* transversalmente

trans•ves•tite [træns'vestaɪt] travestí *m*, travestido *m*

trap [træp] **I** *n* **1** trampa *f*; ***set a ~ for s.o.*** tender una trampa a alguien **2**: ***keep one's ~ shut*** P mantener cerrado el pico **II** *v/t* (*pret & pp* **-ped**) atrapar; ***be ~ped*** *by enemy, flames, landslide etc* quedar atrapado; ***~ s.o. into doing sth*** engañar a alguien para que haga algo

'trap•door trampilla *f*

tra•peze [trə'piːz] trapecio *m*
tra'peze ar•tist trapecista *m/f*
trap•per ['træpər] trampero(-a) *m(f)*
trap•pings ['træpɪŋz] *npl of power* parafernalia *f*
trash [træʃ] **I** *n* (*garbage*) basura *f*; (*poor product*) bazofia *f*; (*despicable person*) escoria *f* **II** *v/t* (*destroy*) destrozar; *by criticism* poner por los suelos
'trash•can cubo *m* de la basura
'trash i•con COMPUT icono *m* de la papelera
trash•y [træʃɪ] *adj goods, novel* barato
trau•ma ['trɔːmə] PSYCH trauma *f*
trau•mat•ic [trə'mætɪk] *adj* traumático
trau•ma•tize ['traʊmətaɪz] *v/t* traumatizar
trav•el ['trævl] **I** *n* viajes *mpl*; ***do you like ~?*** ¿te gusta viajar?; ***on my ~s*** en mis viajes **II** *v/i* (*pret & pp* **-ed**, *Br* **-led**) **1** viajar; ***be really ~ing*** F ir a toda pastilla F **2** *in basketball* hacer pasos **III** *v/t miles* viajar, recorrer
'trav•el a•gen•cy agencia *f* de viajes; **'trav•el a•gent** agente *m/f* de viajes; **'trav•el al•low•ance** dietas *fpl* de desplazamiento; **'trav•el bag** bolsa *f* de viaje
trav•el•er, *Br* **trav•el•ler** ['trævələr] viajero(-a) *m(f)*
'trav•el•er's check, *Br* **'trav•el•ler's cheque** cheque *m* de viaje
'trav•el ex•pen•ses *npl* gastos *mpl* de viaje
trav•el•ing, *Br* **trav•el•ling** ['trævlɪŋ] **1** viajes *mpl* **2** *in basketball* pasos *mpl*
trav•el•ing 'sales•man, *Br* **trav•el•ling 'sales•man** viajante *m*
'trav•el in•sur•ance seguro *m* de asistencia en viaje
trav•e•log, *Br* **trav•e•logue** ['trævəlɑːg] documental *m* sobre viajes
'trav•el pro•gram, *Br* **'trav•el pro•gramme** *on TV etc* programa *m* de viajes
'trav•el•sick *adj* mareado
'trav•el•sick•ness mareo *m*
trav•erse ['trævərs] *v/t* atravesar
trav•es•ty ['trævəstɪ] parodia *f*; ***a ~ of justice*** una parodia de la justicia
trav•o•la•tor ['trævəleɪtər] pasillo *m* móvil
trawl ['trɔːl] *v/i* **1** NAUT hacer pesca de arrastre **2**: ***~ for information*** rastrear en busca de información; ***~ through documents*** rastrear documentos
trawl•er ['trɒːlər] (barco *m*) arrastrero *m*
tray [treɪ] bandeja *f*
treach•er•ous ['treʧərəs] *adj* traicionero
treach•er•y ['treʧərɪ] traición *f*
trea•cle ['triːkl] *Br* melaza *f*
tread [tred] **I** *n* **1** pasos *mpl* **2** *of staircase* huella *f* (del peldaño) **3** *of tire* dibujo *m* **II** *v/i* (*pret* **trod**, *pp* **trodden**) andar; ***mind where you ~*** cuida dónde pisas; ***~ carefully*** andar con cuidado; *fig* andar con pies de plomo
◆ **tread on** *v/t s.o.'s foot* pisar
trea•son ['triːzn] traición *f*
trea•sure ['treʒər] **I** *n also fig* tesoro *m* **II** *v/t gift etc* apreciar mucho
trea•sur•er ['treʒərər] tesorero(-a) *m(f)*
Trea•sur•y De•part•ment ['treʒərɪ] Ministerio *m* de Hacienda
treat [triːt] **I** *n* placer *m*; ***it was a real ~*** fue un auténtico placer; ***I have a ~ for you*** tengo una sorpresa agradable para ti; ***it's my ~*** (*I'm paying*) yo invito **II** *v/t* **1** tratar; ***he's being ~ed for arthritis*** MED le están tratando la artrosis **2**: ***~ s.o. to sth*** invitar a alguien a algo; ***~ o.s. to sth*** darse el capricho de algo
trea•tise ['triːtɪs] tratado *m* (**on** sobre)
treat•ment ['triːtmənt] tratamiento *m*
treat•y ['triːtɪ] tratado *m*
tre•ble[1] ['trebl] *n* MUS soprano *m*
tre•ble[2] ['trebl] **I** *adv*: ***~ the price*** el triple del precio **II** *v/i* triplicarse
tree [triː] árbol *m*
'tree line límite *m* del bosque; **tree-lined** [triː'laɪnd] *adj* bordeado de árboles; **'tree sur•geon** arboricultor(a) *m(f)*; **'tree trunk** tronco *m* de árbol
trek [trek] **I** *v/i* (*pret & pp* **-ked**): ***we ~ked all the way out to his ranch*** recorrimos un camino largo y penoso hasta su rancho **II** *n* caminata *f*
trel•lis ['trelɪs] *for plants* espaldar *m*
trem•ble ['trembl] *v/i* temblar
tre•men•dous [trɪ'mendəs] *adj* **1** (*very good*) estupendo **2** (*enormous*) enorme
tre•men•dous•ly [trɪ'mendəslɪ] *adv* **1** (*very*) tremendamente **2** (*a lot*) enormemente
trem•or ['tremər] *of earth* temblor *m*
trench [trenʧ] trinchera *f*

'trench coat trinchera *f*
trend [trend] tendencia *f*; (*fashion*) moda *f*
trend•set•ter ['trendsetər] pionero(-a) *m(f)*
trend•y ['trendɪ] *adj* de moda; *views* moderno
tres•pass ['trespæs] *v/i* entrar sin autorización; ***no ~ing*** prohibido el paso
◆ **trespass on** *v/t land* entrar sin autorización en; *privacy* entrometerse en
tres•pass•er ['trespæsər] intruso(-a) *m(f)*; ***~s will be prosecuted*** prohibido el paso
tri•al ['traɪəl] **1** LAW juicio *m*; ***be on ~*** estar siendo juzgado; ***~ by jury*** juicio con jurado; ***stand ~*** ser procesado (***for*** por) **2** *of equipment* prueba *f*; ***have sth on ~*** *equipment* tener algo a prueba; ***by ~ and error*** por ensayo y error
'tri•al bal•ance FIN balance *m* de comprobación; **'tri•al of•fer** oferta *f* de prueba; **tri•al 'pe•ri•od** periodo *m* de prueba; **tri•al 'run** TECH, MOT ensayo *m*; **tri•al sep•a'ra•tion** separación *f* de prueba
tri•an•gle ['traɪæŋgl] triángulo *m*; ***the eternal ~*** el triángulo amoroso
tri•an•gu•lar [traɪ'æŋgjʊlər] *adj* triangular
tri•ath•lon [traɪ'æθlən] SP triatlón *m*
trib•al ['traɪbl] *adj* tribal
tribe [traɪb] tribu *f*
tribes•man ['traɪbzmən] miembro *m* de una tribu
trib•u•la•tion [trɪbjʊ'leɪʃn]: ***trials and ~s*** tribulaciones *fpl*
tri•bu•nal [traɪ'bjuːnl] tribunal *m*
tri•bu•ta•ry ['trɪbjəterɪ] *of river* afluente *m*
trib•ute ['trɪbjuːt]: ***be a ~ to*** ser motivo de orgullo para; ***pay ~ to*** rendir tributo a
trice [traɪs]: ***in a ~*** F en un periquete
tri•ceps ['traɪseps] *npl* tríceps *mpl*
trick [trɪk] **I** *n* **1** (*to deceive, knack*) truco *m*; (*practical joke*) broma *f*; ***play a ~ on s.o.*** gastar una broma a alguien; ***how's ~s?*** F ¿qué tal va todo?; ***dirty ~*** jugarreta *f*; ***be up to one's old ~s*** volver a las andadas; ***that should do the ~*** F con eso debería servir **2**: ***take** or **win a ~*** *in cards* ganar una baza **II** *v/t* engañar; ***~ s.o. into doing sth*** engañar a alguien para que haga algo
trick•er•y ['trɪkərɪ] engaños *mpl*; ***by ~*** con engaños
trick•le ['trɪkl] **I** *n* hilo *m*, reguero *m*; *fig*: *of money* goteo *m* **II** *v/i* gotear, escurrir
trick 'ques•tion pregunta *f* con trampa
trick•ster ['trɪkstər] embaucador(a) *m(f)*
trick•y ['trɪkɪ] *adj* (*difficult*) difícil
tri•cy•cle ['traɪsɪkl] triciclo *m*
tri•fle ['traɪfl] **1** (*triviality*) nadería *f* **2** *Br*: *postre con gelatina de frutas, bizcocho y nata*
◆ **trifle with** *v/t fig* jugar con; ***he is not to be trifled with*** hay que tenerle mucho respeto
tri•fling ['traɪflɪŋ] *adj* insignificante
trig•ger ['trɪgər] *on gun* gatillo *m*; *on camcorder* disparador *m*; ***pull the ~*** apretar el gatillo
◆ **trigger off** *v/t* desencadenar
'trig•ger-hap•py *adj* de gatillo ligero
trig•o•nom•e•try [trɪgə'nɑːmətrɪ] MATH trigonometría *f*
trike [traɪk] F triciclo *m*
tril•by ['trɪlbɪ] sombrero *m* de fieltro
tril•lion ['trɪlɪən] billón *m*; *Br* trillón *m*
tril•o•gy ['trɪlədʒɪ] trilogía *f*
tri•ma•ran ['traɪməræn] NAUT trimarán *m*
trim•ming ['trɪmɪŋ] *on clothes* adorno *m*; ***with all the ~s*** *dish* con la guarnición clásica; *car* con todos los extras
trim [trɪm] **I** *adj* (*neat*) muy cuidado; *figure* delgado **II** *v/t* (*pret & pp* **-med**) *hair, hedge* recortar; *budget, costs* recortar, reducir; (*decorate*: *dress*) adornar **III** *n* **1** (*light cut*) recorte *m*; ***just a ~, please*** *to hairdresser* corte sólo las puntas, por favor **2**: ***in good ~*** en buenas condiciones
◆ **trim off** *v/t* recortar
Trin•i•ty ['trɪnɪtɪ]: ***the Holy ~*** la Santísima Trinidad
trin•ket ['trɪŋkɪt] baratija *f*
tri•o ['triːoʊ] MUS trío *m*
trip [trɪp] **I** *n* (*journey*) viaje; ***he's away on a ~*** está de viaje **II** *v/i* (*pret & pp* **-ped**) (*stumble*) tropezar **III** *v/t* (*pret & pp* **-ped**) **1** (*make fall*) poner la zancadilla a **2** TECH hacer saltar
◆ **trip up I** *v/t* **1** (*make fall*) poner la zancadilla a **2** (*cause to go wrong*) confundir **II** *v/i* **1** (*stumble*) tropezar **2** (*make a*

mistake) equivocarse
tripe [traɪp] *to eat* mondongo *m*, *Span* callos *mpl*
trip•le ['trɪpl] ☞ ***treble***
'trip•le jump triple salto *m*
'trip•le jump•er saltador(-a) *m(f)* de triple salto
trip•lets ['trɪplɪts] *npl* trillizos *mpl*
trip•li•cate ['trɪplɪkət]: ***in ~*** por triplicado
tri•pod ['traɪpɑːd] PHOT trípode *m*
'trip•wire *cable para hacer tropezar a alguien*
trite [traɪt] *adj* manido
tri•umph ['traɪʌmf] triunfo *m*
tri•um•phal [traɪ'ʌmfl] *adj* triunfal
tri•um•phant [traɪ'ʌmfənt] *adj* triunfante; ***be ~*** salir triunfante
triv•i•al ['trɪvɪəl] *adj* trivial
triv•i•al•i•ty [trɪvɪ'ælətɪ] trivialidad *f*
trod [trɑːd] *pret* ☞ ***tread***
trod•den ['trɑːdn] *pp* ☞ ***tread***
trol•ley ['trɑːlɪ] (*streetcar*) tranvía *m*
trom•bone [trɑːm'boʊn] trombón *m*
trom•bon•ist [trɑːm'boʊnɪst] trombonista *m/f*
'troop carr•i•er AVIA, NAUT transporte *m* de tropas
troop•er ['truːpər] MIL soldado *m*; (*policeman*) policía *m/f*; ***swear like a ~*** jurar como un carretero
troops [truːps] *npl* tropas *fpl*
tro•phy ['troʊfɪ] trofeo *m*
trop•ic ['trɑːpɪk] trópico *m*
trop•i•cal ['trɑːpɪkl] *adj* tropical
trop•i•cal 'for•est bosque *m* tropical
trop•i•cal 'rain•for•est selva *f* tropical
trop•ics ['trɑːpɪks] *npl* trópicos *mpl*
trot [trɑːt] **I** *v/i* (*pret & pp* ***-ted***) trotar **II** *n* trote *m*; ***on the ~*** F uno tras otro
◆ **trot out** *v/t* F salir con
trou•ble ['trʌbl] **I** *n* **1** (*difficulties*) problema *m*, problemas *mpl*; ***get into ~*** meterse en líos; ***be in ~*** estar en un lío; ***make ~*** causar problemas; ***there'll be ~*** va a haber problemas; ***run into ~*** tropezar con problemas; ***have ~ with*** tener problemas con; ***have ~ doing sth*** tener problemas haciendo algo
2 (*inconvenience*) molestia *f*; ***go to a lot of ~ to do sth*** complicarse mucho la vida para hacer algo; ***no ~!*** no es molestia; ***put s.o. to ~*** causar problemas a alguien; ***take the ~ to do sth*** molestarse en hacer algo
3 (*disturbance*) conflicto *m*, desorden *m*
II *v/t* **1** (*worry*) preocupar, inquietar **2** (*bother, disturb*) molestar
'trou•ble-free *adj* sin complicaciones; **'trou•ble•mak•er** alborotador(a) *m(f)*; **trou•ble•shoot•er** ['trʌblʃuːtər] (*mediator*) *persona encargada de resolver problemas*; **'trou•ble•shoot•ing** resolución *f* de problemas
trou•ble•some ['trʌblsəm] *adj* problemático
'trou•ble spot POL zona *f* conflictiva
trough [trɑːf] **1** *for animals* abrevadero *m* **2** *atmospheric* frente *m* de bajas presiones
trounce [traʊns] *v/t* SP machacar
troupe [truːp] THEA compañía *f*
trou•sers ['traʊzərz] *npl Br* pantalones *mpl*
'trou•ser suit *Br* traje *m* de chaqueta y pantalón
trous•seau ['truːsoʊ] (*pl* ***-seaux*** ['truːsoʊ], ***-seaus*** ['truːsoʊz]) ajuar *m*
trout [traʊt] (*pl* ***trout***) trucha *f*
trow•el ['traʊəl] paleta *f*
tru•ant ['truːənt]: ***be ~***, ***Br play ~*** hacer novillos, *Mex* irse de pinta, *S.Am.* hacerse la rabona
truce [truːs] tregua *f*
truck[1] [trʌk] camión *m*
truck[2] [trʌk]: ***have no ~ with*** no querer nada que ver con
'truck driv•er camionero(-a) *m(f)*
truck•er ['trʌkər] camionero(-a) *m(f)*
'truck farm huerta *f*
'truck farm•er horticultor(a) *m(f)*
truck•ing ['trʌkɪŋ] transporte *m* por carretera
'truck stop restaurante *m* de carretera
truc•u•lent ['trʌkjʊlənt] *adj* agresivo
trudge [trʌdʒ] **I** *v/i* caminar fatigosamente **II** *n* caminata *f*
true [truː] *adj* **1** verdadero, cierto; ***come ~*** *of hopes, dream* hacerse realidad; ***be ~*** ser verdad **2** *friend, American* auténtico; ***~ love*** amor *m* verdadero; ***stay ~ to one's principles*** ser fiel a los principios de uno; ***~ to life*** fiel a la realidad
'true cop•y copia *f* conforme
truf•fle ['trʌfl] BOT trufa *f*
tru•ism ['truːɪzəm] perogrullada *f*
trul•y ['truːlɪ] *adv* verdaderamente, real-

mente; ***Yours ~*** le saluda muy atentamente

trump [trʌmp] **I** *n* triunfo *m*; ***play one's ~ card*** *fig* jugar la mejor baza de uno **II** *v/t* ganar con un triunfo

◆ **trump up** *v/t pej* falsificar

trum•pet ['trʌmpɪt] trompeta *f*

trum•pet•er ['trʌmpɪtər] trompetista *m/f*

trun•cate [trʌŋ'keɪt] *v/t also fig* truncar

trun•cheon ['trʌntʃən] *Br* porra *f*

trun•dle ['trʌndl] *v/t cart* empujar lentamente

trunk [trʌŋk] **1** *of tree*, *body* tronco *m* **2** *of elephant* trompa *f* **3** (*large case*) baúl *m* **4** *of car* maletero *m*, *C.Am.*, *Mex* cajuela *f*, *Rpl* baúl *m* **5**: ***pair of ~s*** *Br* bañador *m*

'trunk road *Br* carretera *f* troncal

truss [trʌs] MED braguero *m*

◆ **truss up** *v/t* atar

trust [trʌst] **I** *n* **1** confianza *f*; ***place** or **put one's ~ in*** depositar la confianza de uno en; ***take sth on ~*** dar algo por cierto; ***position of ~*** puesto *m* de confianza **2** FIN fondo *m* de inversión; ***hold sth in ~*** tener algo en fideicomiso (***for*** para) **II** *v/t* confiar en; ***~ s.o. to do sth*** confiar en que alguien haga algo; ***~ him!*** *that's typical of him* ¡típico de él!

◆ **trust in** *v/t* tener confianza en

◆ **trust to** *v/t* confiar en

'trust com•pa•ny compañía *f* fiduciaria

trusted ['trʌstɪd] *adj* de confianza

trust•ee [trʌs'tiː] fideicomisario(-a) *m*(*f*)

trust•ful ['trʌstfʊl] *adj* confiado

'trust fund fondo *m* fiduciario

trust•ing ['trʌstɪŋ] *adj* confiado

'trust•wor•thy *adj* de confianza

truth [truːθ] verdad *f*; ***there is some / no ~ in it*** hay algo / no hay nada de verdad en ello; ***to tell (you) the ~*** a decir verdad

truth•ful ['truːθfəl] *adj person* sincero; *account* verdadero

T

try [traɪ] **I** *v/t* (*pret & pp* ***-ied***) **1** probar; ***~ to do sth*** intentar hacer algo, tratar de hacer algo; ***~ not to be stupid!*** ¡no seas tonto! **2** LAW juzgar **II** *v/i* (*pret & pp* ***-ied***): ***he didn't even ~*** ni siquiera lo intentó; ***you must ~ harder*** debes esforzarte más **III** *n* intento *m*; ***can I have a ~?*** *of food* ¿puedo probar?; *at doing sth* ¿puedo intentarlo?

◆ **try for** *v/t* intentar conseguir

◆ **try on** *v/t clothes* probar; ***try it on*** F poner a prueba F

◆ **try out** *v/t new machine*, *new method* probar

◆ **try out for** *v/t team* competir por una posición en

try•ing ['traɪɪŋ] *adj* (*annoying*) molesto, duro

'try•out: ***give sth a ~*** probar algo

T-shirt ['tiːʃɜːrt] camiseta *f*

tub [tʌb] **1** (*bath*) bañera *f*, *L.Am.* tina *f* **2** *for liquid* cuba *f*, *for yoghurt*, *ice cream* envase *m*

tub•by ['tʌbɪ] *adj* rechoncho

tube [tuːb] **1** tubo *m* **2** *Br* (*subway*) metro *m*, *Rpl* subte *m*

tube•less ['tuːblɪs] *adj tire* sin cámara de aire

tu•ber ['tuːbər] BOT tubérculo *m*

tu•ber•cu•lo•sis [tuːbɜːrkjə'loʊsɪs] tuberculosis *f*

tu•bu•lar ['tuːbjələr] *adj* tubular

tuck [tʌk] **I** *n in dress* pinza **II** *v/t* (*put*) meter

◆ **tuck away** *v/t* (*put away*) guardar; F (*eat quickly*) zamparse F; ***be tucked away*** *of house etc* estar escondido

◆ **tuck in I** *v/t children* arropar; *sheets* remeter **II** *v/i* (*start eating*) ponerse a comer

◆ **tuck into** *v/t esp Br* F papear

◆ **tuck up** *v/t* **1** *sleeves etc* remangar **2**: ***tuck s.o. up in bed*** meter a alguien en la cama

Tues•day ['tuːzdeɪ] martes *inv*; ***on ~*** el martes; ***on ~s*** los martes

tuft [tʌft] *of hair* mechón *m*; *of grass* mata *f*

tug [tʌg] **I** *n* **1** (*pull*) tirón *m* **2** NAUT remolcador *m* **II** *v/t* (*pret & pp* ***-ged***) (*pull*) tirar de **III** *v/i* (*pret & pp* ***-ged***) tirar

tug of 'war *juego en el que dos bandos tiran de una soga*

tu•i•tion [tuː'ɪsn] clases *fpl*

tu•lip ['tuːlɪp] tulipán *m*

tum•ble ['tʌmbl] *v/i* caer, caerse

◆ **tumble to** *v/t* F (*realize*) darse cuenta de

'tum•ble•down *adj* destartalado

'tum•ble-dry•er secadora *f*

tum•bler ['tʌmblər] **1** *for drink* vaso *m* **2**

in circus acróbata *m/f*
'tum•ble•weed bledo *m* blanco
tum•my ['tʌmɪ] F tripa F, barriga F
'tum•my ache dolor *m* de tripa *or* barriga
tu•mor ['tu:mər] tumor *m*
tu•mult ['tu:mʌlt] tumulto *m*
tu•mul•tu•ous [tu:'mʌltʃuəs] *adj* tumultuoso
tu•na ['tu:nə] atún *m*
tune [tu:n] **I** *n* melodía *f*; ***be in ~*** *of instrument* estar afinado; ***sing in ~*** cantar sin desafinar; ***be out of ~*** *of singer* desafinar; *of instrument* estar desafinado; ***to the ~ of $6000*** F por valor de 6.000 dólares **II** *v/t instrument* afinar
◆ **tune in** *v/i* RAD, TV sintonizar
◆ **tune in to** *v/t* RAD, TV sintonizar (con)
◆ **tune up I** *v/i of orchestra, players* afinar **II** *v/t engine* poner a punto
tune•ful ['tu:nfəl] *adj* melodioso
tune•less ['tu:nlɪs] *adj* sin melodía
tun•er ['tu:nər] *hi-fi* sintonizador *m*
'tune-up *of engine* puesta *f* a punto
tun•ing fork ['tu:nɪŋfɔ:rk] diapasón *m*
Tu•ni•si•a [tu:'nɪzɪə] Túnez *m*
Tu•ni•si•an [tu:'nɪzɪən] **I** *adj* tunecino **II** *n* tunecino(-a) *m (f)*
tun•nel ['tʌnl] túnel *m*; SP túnel *m* de vestuarios
◆ **tunnel through** *v/t* (*pret & pp* **-ed**, *Br* **-led**) abrir un túnel por
tun•ny ['tʌnɪ] ☞ ***tuna***
tur•bine ['tɜ:rbaɪn] turbina *f*
tur•bo ['tɜ:rbou] turbo *m*
tur•bo•charged ['tɜ:rboutʃɑ:rdʒd *adj*: ***~ engine*** motor *m* turbo
'tur•bo•charg•er MOT turbo *m*; **'tur•bo•jet** turborreactor *m*; **'tur•bo•prop** turbopropulsor *m*
tur•bot ['tɜ:rbət] rodaballo *m*
tur•bu•lence ['tɜ:rbjələns] *in air travel* turbulencia *f*
tur•bu•lent ['tɜ:rbjələnt] *adj* turbulento
turd [tɜ:rd] P **1** cagada P *f* **2** *person* gilipollas P *m/f inv*
tu•reen [tə'ri:n] sopera *f*
turf [tɜ:rf] (*pl* ***turves*** [tɜ:rvz]) césped *m*; *piece* tepe *m*
◆ **turf out** *v/t Br* F echar
tur•gid ['tɜ:rdʒɪd] *adj* **1** MED hinchado **2** *style, language* ampuloso
Turk [tɜ:rk] turco(-a) *m(f)*
Tur•key ['tɜ:rkɪ] Turquía *f*
tur•key ['tɜ:rkɪ] pavo *m*
Turk•ish ['tɜ:rkɪʃ] **I** *adj* turco **II** *language* turco *m*
Turk•ish 'bath baño *m* turco
Turk•ish de'light delicia *f* turca
tur•mer•ic ['tɜ:rmərɪk] GASTR cúrcuma *f*
tur•moil ['tɜ:rmɔɪl] desorden *m*, agitación *f*
turn [tɜ:rn] **I** *n* **1** (*rotation*) vuelta *f* **2** *in road* curva *f*; *junction* giro *m*; ***make a right ~*** girar *or* torcer a la derecha **3** *in vaudeville* número *m*
4: ***take ~s doing sth*** turnarse para hacer algo; ***it's my ~*** me toca a mí; ***it's not your ~ yet*** no te toca todavía; ***miss a ~*** *in game* perder un turno; ***take a ~ at the wheel*** turnarse para conducir *or L.Am.* manejar; ***in ~*** a su vez; ***and he, in his ~, …*** y él, a su vez,…
5: ***do s.o. a good ~*** hacer un favor a alguien
6: ***at the ~ of the century*** a principios de siglo; ***take a ~ for the better / worse*** cambiar a mejor / peor
II *v/t* **1** *wheel* girar; ***~ one's back on s.o.*** dar la espalda a alguien **2** *corner* dar la vuelta a
III *v/i* **1** *of driver, car, wheel* girar; *of person: turn around* volverse; ***~ left / right here*** gira aquí a la izquierda / a la derecha
2 (*become*) volverse, ponerse; ***it has ~ed sour / cold*** se ha cortado / enfriado; ***it ~ed blue*** se volvió *or* puso azul; ***he has ~ed 40*** ha cumplido cuarenta años; ***he ~ed violent*** se puso violento; ***~ professional*** hacerse profesional
3: ***~ to s.o.*** *fig: for help* acudir a alguien; ***not know where to ~*** no saber que rumbo tomar
◆ **turn against** *v/t person* volverse contra; ***turn s.o. against s.o.*** volver a alguien contra alguien
◆ **turn around I** *v/t* **1** *object, car* dar la vuelta a **2** *company* dar un vuelco a **3** (COM: *deal with*) procesar, preparar **II** *v/i of person* volverse, darse la vuelta; *of driver* dar la vuelta
◆ **turn away I** *v/t* (*send away*) rechazar; ***the doorman turned us away*** el portero no nos dejó entrar **II** *v/i* **1** (*walk away*) marcharse **2** (*look away*) desviar

la mirada

◆ **turn back** I *v/t edges, sheets* doblar; ***turn back the clock*** retrasar el reloj; *fig* cambiar el pasado II *v/i of walkers etc* volver; *in course of action* echarse atrás

◆ **turn down** *v/t* **1** *offer, invitation* rechazar **2** *volume, TV, heating* bajar **3** *edge, collar* doblar; ***turn down the bed*** abrir la cama

◆ **turn in** I *v/i* (*go to bed*) irse a dormir II *v/t to police* entregar; ***turn oneself in*** entregarse

◆ **turn off** I *v/t TV, engine* apagar; *faucet* cerrar; *heater* apagar; ***it turns me off*** F *sexually* me quita las ganas F II *v/i of car, driver* doblar

◆ **turn on** I *v/t TV, engine, heating* encender, *L.Am.* prender; *faucet* abrir; F *sexually* excitar F II *v/i of machine* encenderse, *L.Am.* prenderse

◆ **turn out** I *v/t lights* apagar II *v/i*: ***it turned out well*** salió bien; ***as it turned out*** al final; ***he turned out to be ...*** resultó ser ...

◆ **turn over** I *v/i in bed* darse la vuelta; *of vehicle* volcar, dar una vuelta de campana; ***please ~*** dese la vuelta, por favor II *v/t* **1** (*put upside down*) dar la vuelta a **2** *page* pasar **3** FIN facturar **4**: ***turn sth over in one's mind*** dar vueltas a algo

◆ **turn up** I *v/t* **1** *collar* subirse **2** *volume, heating* subir II *v/i* (*arrive*) aparecer

'turn•a•bout, 'turn•a•round vuelco *m*

'turn•coat chaquetero(-a) *m(f)*

turn•ing ['tɜːrnɪŋ] giro *m*

'turn•ing cir•cle MOT giro *m*

'turn•ing point punto *m* de inflexión

tur•nip ['tɜːrnɪp] nabo *m*

'turn•key plant fábrica *f* llave en mano; **'turn•off 1** *from road* salida *f* **2**: ***it / he is a real ~*** es lo menos excitante del mundo; **'turn-on** F *sexual or non-sexual*: ***it / he is a real ~*** me excita enormemente; **'turn•out** *of people* asistencia *f*; **'turn•o•ver 1** FIN facturación *f*; ***staff ~*** rotación *f* de personal **2** *in basketball* pérdida *f*; **'turn•pike** autopista *f* de peaje; **'turn sig•nal** *on car* intermitente *m*; **'turn•stile** torniquete *m* (*de entrada*); **'turn•ta•ble** *of record player* plato *m*

tur•pen•tine ['tɜːrpəntaɪn] CHEM trementina *f*

tur•quoise ['tɜːrkwɔɪz] *adj* turquesa

tur•ret ['tʌrɪt] **1** *of castle* torrecilla *f* **2** *of tank* torreta *f*

tur•tle ['tɜːrtl] tortuga *f* (marina); ***turn ~*** NAUT volcar

tur•tle•neck 'sweat•er suéter *m* de cuello alto

turves [tɜːrvz] *pl* ☞ ***turf***

tusk [tʌsk] colmillo *m*

tus•sle ['tʌsl] pelea *f*

tu•tor ['tuːtər] *at university* tutor *m*; (***private***) ~ profesor(a) *m(f)* particular

tux [tʌks] F ☞ ***tuxedo***

tux•e•do [tʌk'siːdoʊ] esmoquin *m*

TV [tiː'viː] tele *f*, televisión *f*; ***on ~*** en la tele; ***watch ~*** ver la tele

T'V din•ner menú *m* precocinado; **T'V guide** guía *f* televisiva; **T'V mov•ie** telefilm *m*; **T'V pro•gram** programa *m* de televisión

twad•dle ['twɑːdl] F tonterías *fpl*

twang [twæŋ] I *n in voice* entonación *f* nasal II *v/t guitar string* puntear

tweak [twiːk] *v/t* **1** *pull* pellizcar **2** *make fine adjustment to* ajustar, retocar

tweed [twiːd] *material* tweed *m*

tweet [twiːt] *v/i* piar

tweet•er ['twiːtər] tweeter *m*

tweez•ers ['twiːzərz] *npl* pinzas *fpl*

twelfth [twelfθ] *n & adj* duodécimo

twelve [twelv] doce

twen•ti•eth ['twentɪɪθ] *n & adj* vigésimo

twen•ty ['twentɪ] veinte; ***be in one's twenties*** tener veintitantos años; ***in the twenties*** en los (años) veinte

twerp [twɜːrp] F besugo(-a) *m(f)*

twice [twaɪs] *adv* dos veces; ***~ as much*** el doble; ***~ the amount*** el doble; ***you should think ~ before ...*** piénsatelo dos veces antes de ...

twid•dle ['twɪdl] *v/t* dar vueltas a; ***~ one's thumbs*** holgazanear

twig[1] [twɪg] *n* ramita *f*

twig[2] [twɪg] *Br* F I *v/t* (*pret & pp* **-ged**) darse cuenta de II *v/i* (*pret & pp* **-ged**) *understand* caer

twi•light ['twaɪlaɪt] crepúsculo *m*

twin [twɪn] I *n* gemelo *m*; ***~ brother / sister*** hermano gemelo / hermana gemela II *v/t*: ***be ~ned with*** estar hermanado con

'twin beds *npl* camas *fpl* gemelas

twine [twaɪn] I *n* cordel *m* II *v/i* enroscar-

T

se (***around*** alrededor de)
twin-en•gined ['twɪnendʒɪnd] *adj* AVIAT bimotor
twinge [twɪndʒ] *of pain* punzada *f*; ***a ~ of conscience*** un remordimiento de conciencia
twin•kle ['twɪŋkl] **I** *v/i of stars* parpadeo *m*; *of eyes* brillo *m* **II** *n*: ***with a ~ in one's eye*** con un brillo en los ojos
twin•kling ['twɪŋklɪŋ]: ***in the ~ of an eye*** en un abrir y cerrar de ojos
twin•ning ['twɪnɪŋ] emparejamiento *m*
twin 'room habitación *f* con camas gemelas
'twin town ciudad *f* hermana
twirl [twɜːrl] **I** *v/t* hacer girar **II** *of cream etc* voluta *f*
twist [twɪst] **I** *v/t* retorcer; ***~ one's ankle*** torcerse el tobillo; ***his face was ~ed with pain*** tenía el rostro retorcido de dolor; ***be able to ~ s.o. around one's little finger*** *fig* tener totalmente dominado a alguien **II** *v/i of road, river* serpentear **III** *in rope, road* vuelta *f*; *in plot, story* giro *m* inesperado
◆ **twist off** *v/t lid* desenroscar y quitar
twist•er ['twɪstər] F (*tornado*) tornado *m*
twist•y ['twɪstɪ] *adj road* serpenteante
twit [twɪt] *Br* F memo(-a) *m(f)* F
twitch [twɪtʃ] **I** *n nervous* tic *m* **II** *v/i* (*jerk*) moverse (ligeramente)
twit•ter ['twɪtər] *v/i of birds* gorjear
two [tuː] dos; ***the ~ of them*** los dos, ambos; ***in a day or ~*** en un día o dos; ***break / cut sth in ~*** partir / cortar algo por en dos; ***~ of hearts*** dos de corazones; ***in ~s*** en pares; ***put ~ and ~ together*** atar cabos
'two-bit *adj* F de tres al cuarto
two-faced ['tuːfeɪst] *adj* falso
'two•fold I *adj* doble **II** *adv* dos veces
two-hand•ed [tuː'hændɪd] *adj* con las dos manos; **two•pence** ['tʌpəns] *Br* moneda *f* de dos peniques; **'two-piece** (*woman's suit*) traje *m*; **'two-point•er** *in basketball* canasta *f or* lanzamiento *m* de dos puntos, tiro *m* de dos; **two-seat•er** ['tuːsiːtər] AVIA, MOT biplaza *m*; **'two-stroke** *adj engine* de dos tiempos; **'two-time** *v/t* F *girlfriend etc* pegársela a (***with*** con); **two-way 'traf•fic** tráfico *m* en dos direcciones
ty•coon [taɪ'kuːn] magnate *m*
tym•pa•num ['tɪmpənəm] ANAT tímpano *m*
type [taɪp] **I** *n* (*sort*) tipo *m*, clase *f*; ***what ~ of …?*** ¿qué tipo *or* clase de …?; ***she's not my ~*** F no es mi tipo **II** *v/i* (*use a keyboard*) escribir a máquina **III** *v/t with a typewriter* mecanografiar, escribir a máquina
'type•cast *v/t* (*pret & pp* **-cast**) encasillar; **'type•face** tipo *m*; **'type•script** copia *f* mecanografiada; **'type•set** *v/t* componer; **type•set•ter** ['taɪpsetər] tipógrafo(-a) *m(f)*; **'type•writ•er** máquina *f* de escribir; **'type•writ•ten** *adj* escrito a máquina
ty•phoid ['taɪfɔɪd] fiebre *f* tifoidea
ty•phoon [taɪ'fuːn] tifón *m*
ty•phus ['taɪfəs] tifus *m*
typ•i•cal ['tɪpɪkl] *adj* típico; ***that's ~ of you / him!*** ¡típico tuyo / de él!
typ•i•cal•ly ['tɪpɪklɪ] *adv* típicamente; ***~ American*** típicamente americano
typ•i•fy ['tɪpɪfaɪ] *v/t* tipificar
typ•ing ['taɪpɪŋ] mecanografía *f*
'typ•ing er•ror error *m* mecanográfico
typ•ist ['taɪpɪst] mecanógrafo(-a) *m(f)*
ty•po•graph•ic [taɪpə'græfɪk] *adj* tipográfico
ty•pog•ra•phy [taɪ'pɑːgrəfɪ] tipografía *f*
ty•ran•ni•cal [tɪ'rænɪkl] *adj* tiránico
ty•ran•nize ['tɪrənaɪz] *v/t* tiranizar
ty•ran•ny ['tɪrənɪ] tiranía *f*
ty•rant ['taɪrənt] tirano(-a) *m(f)*
tyre *Br* ☞ ***tire***[1]
ty•ro ['taɪroʊ] principiante *m/f*

T

U

u•biq•ui•tous [juː'bɪkwɪtəs] *adj* ubicuo
ud•der ['ʌdər] ZO ubre *f*
UEFA [juː'eɪfə] *abbr* (= ***Union of European Football Associations***) UEFA *f* (= Unión *f* Europea de Fútbol Asociación); ~ ***Cup*** Copa *f* de la UEFA
UFO [juːef'oʊ, 'juːfoʊ] *abbr* (= ***unidentified flying object***) ovni *m* (= objeto *m* volante no identificado)
ugh [ʌx] *int* ¡uf!, ¡uh!
ug•li•ness ['ʌglɪnɪs] fealdad *f*
ug•ly ['ʌglɪ] *adj* feo
UHT [juːeɪʧ'tiː] *abbr* (= ***ultra-heat-treated***): ~ ***milk*** leche *f* uperizada
UK [juː'keɪ] *abbr* (= ***United Kingdom***) RU *m* (= Reino *m* Unido)
U•kraine [juː'kreɪn]: ***the*** ~ Ucrania *f*
ul•cer ['ʌlsər] úlcera *f*; *in mouth* llaga *f*
ul•te•ri•or [ʌl'tɪrɪər] *adj*: ~ ***motive*** móvil *m* oculto
ul•ti•mate ['ʌltɪmət] *adj* (*final*) final; (*basic*) esencial; ***the*** ~ ***car*** (*best, definitive*) lo último en coches
ul•ti•mate•ly ['ʌltɪmətlɪ] *adv* (*in the end*) en última instancia
ul•ti•ma•tum [ʌltɪ'meɪtəm] ultimátum *m*; ***give s.o. an*** ~ dar un ultimátum a alguien
ul•tra•high [ʌltrə'haɪ] *adj*: ~ ***frequency*** ELEC alta frecuencia *f*
ul•tra•light ['ʌltrəlaɪt] *aircraft* ultraligero *m*
ul•tra•son•ic [ʌltrə'sɑːnɪk] *adj* ultrasónico
ul•tra•sound ['ʌltrəsaʊnd] MED ultrasonido *m*; (*scan*) ecografía *f*
ul•tra•vi•o•let [ʌltrə'vaɪələt] *adj* ultravioleta
um•bil•i•cal cord [ʌm'bɪlɪkl] cordón *m* umbilical
um•brage ['ʌmbrɪdʒ]: ***take*** ~ ***at*** disgustarse *or* ofenderse por
um•brel•la [ʌm'brelə] paraguas *m inv*
um'brel•la or•gan•iza•tion *organización que reúne a varios grupos*
um'brel•la stand paragüero *m*
um•pire ['ʌmpaɪr] árbitro *m*; *in tennis* juez *m/f* de silla
ump•teen [ʌmp'tiːn] *adj* F miles de F
ump•teenth [ʌmp'tiːnθ] *adj*: ***for the*** ~ ***time*** F por enésima vez F
UN [juː'en] *abbr* (= ***United Nations***) ONU *f* (= Organización *f* de las Naciones Unidas)
un•a•bashed [ʌnə'bæʃt] *adj* desvergonzado
un•a•bat•ed [ʌnə'beɪtəd] *adv*: ***continue*** ~ continuar con todas sus fuerzas
un•a•ble [ʌn'eɪbl] *adj*: ***be*** ~ ***to do sth*** (*not know how to*) no saber hacer algo; (*not be in a position to*) no poder hacer algo
un•a•bridged [ʌnə'brɪdʒd] *adj* íntegro
un•ac•cept•a•ble [ʌnək'septəbl] *adj* inaceptable; ***it is*** ~ ***that*** es inaceptable que
un•ac•com•pa•nied [ʌnə'kʌmpənɪd] *adj* solo
un•ac•count•a•ble [ʌnə'kaʊntəbl] *adj* inexplicable
un•ac•count•ed [ʌnə'kaʊntɪd] *adj*: ***be*** ~ ***for*** estar en paradero desconocido
un•ac•cus•tomed [ʌnə'kʌstəmd] *adj*: ***be*** ~ ***to sth*** no estar acostumbrado a algo
un•ac•knowl•edged [ʌnək'nɑːlɪdʒd] *adj* negado, no reconocido
un•ac•quaint•ed [ʌnə'kweɪntɪd] *adj*: ***be*** ~ ***with*** desconocer
un•a•dul•ter•at•ed [ʌnə'dʌltəreɪtɪd] *adj fig* (*absolute*) absoluto
un•af•fect•ed [ʌnə'fektɪd] *adj* **1** (*natural*) llano, sencillo **2**: ***be*** ~ ***by*** no ser afectado por
un•a•fraid [ʌnə'freɪd] *adj* impávido; ***be*** ~ ***of sth*** no tener miedo a algo
un•aid•ed [ʌn'eɪdɪd] *adj*: ***do sth*** ~ hacer algo sin ayuda
un•al•tered [ʌn'ɒːltərd] *adj*: ***his will remained*** ~ ***until 1984*** su testamento no sufrió cambio alguno hasta 1984
un•am•big•u•ous [ʌnæm'bɪgjʊəs] *adj* inequívoco
un•am•bi•tious [ʌnæm'bɪʃəs] *adj* conformado
un-A•mer•i•can [ʌnə'merɪkən] *adj* poco americano; *activities* antiamericano
u•na•nim•i•ty [juːnə'nɪmɪtɪ] unanimi-

dad *f*

u•nan•i•mous [juː'nænɪməs] *adj verdict* unánime; ***be ~ on*** ser unánime respecto a

u•nan•i•mous•ly [juː'nænɪməslɪ] *adv vote, decide* unánimemente

un•an•nounced [ʌnə'naʊnst] **I** *adj* inesperado **II** *adv* de manera inesperada

un•an•swer•a•ble [ʌn'ænsərəbl] *adj* **1** *question* sin respuesta **2** *argument* irrefutable

un•an•swered [ʌn'ænsərd] *adj* sin respuesta

un•ap•peal•ing [ʌnə'piːlɪŋ] *adj* poco atractivo

un•ap•pe•tiz•ing [ʌn'æpɪtaɪzɪŋ] *adj* poco apetitoso

un•ap•proach•a•ble [ʌnə'proʊʧəbl] *adj person* inaccesible

un•armed [ʌn'ɑːrmd] *adj person* desarmado; ***~ combat*** combate *m* sin armas

un•asked [ʌn'ɑːskt] *adj question* no formulado

un•as•sist•ed [ʌnə'sɪstɪd] *adv* sin ayuda, independientemente

un•as•sum•ing [ʌnə'suːmɪŋ] *adj* sin pretensiones

un•at•tached [ʌnə'tæʧt] *adj* (*without a partner*) sin compromiso, sin pareja

un•at•tain•a•ble [ʌnə'teɪnəbl] *adj* inalcanzable

un•at•tend•ed [ʌnə'tendɪd] *adj* desatendido; ***leave sth ~*** dejar algo desatendido

un•at•trac•tive [ʌnə'træktɪv] *adj* poco interestante

un•au•thor•ized [ʌn'ɒːθəraɪzd] *adj* no autorizado

un•a•vail•a•ble [ʌnə'veɪləbl] *adj* no disponible

un•a•void•a•ble [ʌnə'vɔɪdəbl] *adj* inevitable

un•a•void•a•bly [ʌnə'vɔɪdəblɪ] *adv*: ***be ~ detained*** entretenerse sin poder evitarlo

un•a•ware [ʌnə'wer] *adj*: ***be ~ of*** no ser consciente de

un•a•wares [ʌnə'werz] *adv* desprevenido; ***catch s.o. ~*** agarrar *or Span* coger a alguien desprevenido

un•bal•anced [ʌn'bælənst] *adj also* PSYCH desequilibrado

un•bear•a•ble [ʌn'berəbl] *adj* insoportable

un•beat•a•ble [ʌn'biːtəbl] *adj team* invencible; *quality* insuperable

un•beat•en [ʌn'biːtn] *adj team* invicto

un•be•com•ing [ʌnbɪ'kʌmɪŋ] *adj* poco favorecedor

un•be•known(st) [ʌnbɪ'noʊn(st)] *adv*: ***~ to her*** sin que ella lo supiera

un•be•liev•a•ble [ʌnbɪ'liːvəbl] *adj also* F increíble; ***he's ~*** F (*very good / bad*) es increíble

un•be•liev•a•bly [ʌnbɪ'liːvəblɪ] *adv* increíblemente

un•bend [ʌn'bend] (*pret & pp* ***-bent***) *v/i fig* distenderse

un•bend•ing [ʌn'bendɪŋ] *adj* intransigente

un•bi•as(s)ed [ʌn'baɪəst] *adj* imparcial

un•blem•ished [ʌn'blemɪʃt] *adj* impecable

un•block [ʌn'blɑːk] *v/t pipe* desatascar

un•born [ʌn'bɔːrn] *adj* no nacido

un•break•a•ble [ʌn'breɪkəbl] *adj plates* irrompible; *world record* inalcanzable

un•bri•dled [ʌn'braɪdld] *adj* irrefrenable

un•bro•ken [ʌn'broʊkən] *adj* intacto; *fig*: *silence* ininterrumpido; *world record* no superado

un•buck•le [ʌn'bʌkl] *v/t* desabrochar

un•bur•den [ʌn'bɜːrdn] *v/t*: ***~ o.s to s.o.*** explayarse con alguien

un•but•ton [ʌn'bʌtn] *v/t* desabotonar

un•called-for [ʌn'kɒːldfɔːr] *adj*: ***be ~*** estar fuera de lugar

un•can•ny [ʌn'kænɪ] *adj resemblance* increíble, asombroso; *skill* inexplicable; (*worrying*: *feeling*) extraño, raro

un•ceas•ing [ʌn'siːsɪŋ] *adj* incesante

un•cer•e•mo•ni•ous•ly [ʌnserɪ'moʊnɪəslɪ] *adv* sin miramientos, rudamente

un•cer•tain [ʌn'sɜːrtn] *adj future, origins* incierto; ***be ~ about sth*** no estar seguro de algo; ***what will happen? – it's ~*** ¿qué ocurrirá? – no se sabe

un•cer•tain•ty [ʌn'sɜːrtntɪ] incertidumbre *f*; ***there is still ~ about his health*** todavía hay incertidumbre en torno a su estado de salud

un•chain [ʌn'ʧeɪn] *v/t* desencadenar, desatar

un•changed [ʌn'ʧeɪndʒd] *adj*: ***even after all these years the village was ~*** incluso después de tantos años el pueblo seguía igual

un•chang•ing [ʌn'ʧeɪndʒɪŋ] *adj* invariable
un•char•ac•ter•is•tic [ʌnkærɪktə'rɪstɪk] *adj* impropio
un•char•i•ta•ble [ʌn'ʧærɪtəbl] *adj* ingrato, desconsiderado
un•checked [ʌn'ʧekt] *adj*: ***let sth go ~*** no controlar algo
un•chris•tian [ʌn'krɪsʧən] *adj* poco cristiano
un•civ•il [ʌn'sɪvl] *adj* grosero
un•civ•i•lized [ʌn'sɪvɪlaɪzd] *adj* incivilizado
un•claimed [ʌn'kleɪmd] *adj* no reclamado
un•cle ['ʌŋkl] tío *m*
un•clear [ʌn'klɪr] *adj* impreciso, confuso; ***I'm still ~ about what I have to do*** no acabo de entender qué es lo que tengo que hacer
Un•cle Sam [ʌŋkl'sæm] tío Sam
un•com•for•ta•ble [ʌn'kʌmftəbl] *adj chair* incómodo; ***feel ~ about sth*** *about decision etc* sentirse incómodo con algo; ***I feel ~ with him*** me siento incómodo con él
un•com•mit•ted [ʌnkə'mɪtɪd] *adj* no comprometido
un•com•mon [ʌn'kɑːmən] *adj* poco corriente, raro; ***it's not ~*** no es raro *or* extraño
un•com•mu•ni•ca•tive [ʌnkə'mjuːnɪkətɪv] *adj* reservado
un•com•plain•ing [ʌnkəm'pleɪnɪŋ] *adj* sumiso
un•com•plain•ing•ly [ʌnkəm'pleɪnɪŋlɪ] *adv* sumisamente
un•com•pli•cat•ed [ʌn'kɑːmplɪkeɪtɪd] *adj* sencillo
un•com•pro•mis•ing [ʌn'kɑːmprəmaɪzɪŋ] *adj* inflexible
un•con•cerned [ʌnkən'sɜːrnd] *adj* indiferente; ***be ~ about s.o. / sth*** no preocuparse por alguien / algo
un•con•di•tion•al [ʌnkən'dɪʃnl] *adj* incondicional
un•con•firmed [ʌnkən'fɜːrmd] *adj* sin confirmar
un•con•scious [ʌn'kɑːnʃəs] *adj* MED, PSYCH inconsciente; ***knock ~*** dejar inconsciente; ***be ~ of sth*** (*not aware*) no ser consciente de algo
un•con•sti•tu•tion•al [ʌnkɑːnstə'tuːʃənl] *adj* inconstitucional
un•con•trol•la•ble [ʌnkən'troʊləbl] *adj anger, children* incontrolable; *desire* incontrolable, irresistible
un•con•trolled [ʌnkən'troʊld] *adj* descontrolado
un•con•ven•tion•al [ʌnkən'venʃnl] *adj* poco convencional
un•con•vinced [ʌnkən'vɪnst] *adj*: ***be ~*** tener dudas (***about*** acerca de)
un•con•vinc•ing [ʌnkən'vɪnsɪŋ] *adj* dudoso, poco convincente
un•cooked [ʌn'kʊkt] *adj* no cocinado
un'cool *adj* F *L.Am.* no chévere F, *Span* no guay F
un•co•op•er•a•tive [ʌnkoʊ'ɑːpərətɪv] *adj*: ***be ~*** no estar dispuesto a colaborar
un•cork [ʌn'kɔːrk] *v/t bottle* descorchar
un•count•a•ble [ʌn'kaʊntəbl] *adj* LING no contable
un•couth [ʌn'kuːθ] *adj* burdo
un•cov•er [ʌn'kʌvər] *v/t* (*remove cover from*) destapar; *plot, ancient remains* descubrir
un•crit•i•cal [ʌn'krɪtɪkl] *adj person* con poca capacidad crítica
unc•tion ['ʌŋkʃn] REL unción *f*; ***extreme ~*** extrema unción
un•cut [ʌn'kʌt] *adj* **1** *grass* sin cortar **2** *movie* íntegro **3** *diamond* en bruto
un•dam•aged [ʌn'dæmɪdʒd] *adj* intacto
un•dat•ed [ʌn'deɪtɪd] *adj* sin fecha
un•daunt•ed [ʌn'dɒːntɪd] *adj* impertérrito; ***carry on ~*** seguir impertérrito
un•de•cid•ed [ʌndɪ'saɪdɪd] *adj question* sin resolver; ***be ~ about s.o. / sth*** estar indeciso sobre alguien / algo
un•de•mand•ing [ʌndɪ'mændɪŋ] *adj job* que requiere poco esfuerzo; *person* poco exigente
un•dem•o•crat•ic [ʌndemə'krætɪk] *adj* antidemocrático
un•de•ni•a•ble [ʌndɪ'naɪəbl] *adj* innegable
un•de•ni•a•bly [ʌndɪ'naɪəblɪ] *adv* innegablemente
un•der ['ʌndər] **I** *prep* (*beneath*) debajo de, bajo; (*less than*) menos de; ***~ the water*** bajo el agua; ***it is ~ review / investigation*** está siendo revisado / investigado **II** *adv* (*anesthetized*) anestesiado
un•der'age *adj*: ***~ drinking*** el consumo de alcohol por menores de edad
'un•der•arm *adv*: ***throw a ball ~*** lanzar

una pelota soltándola por debajo de la altura del hombro

'un•der•brush ☞ ***undergrowth***

un•der•cap•i•tal•ized [ʌndər'kæpɪtlaɪzd] *adj* sin suficiente capital

'un•der•car•riage tren *m* de aterrizaje

un•der'charge *v/t person* cobrar de menos a; ***~ s.o. by $10*** cobrar a alguien 10 dólares de menos

'un•der•class clase *f* marginal

'un•der•class•man *estudiante de primer o segundo año de educación secundaria*

'un•der•clothes *npl* ☞ ***underwear***

'un•der•coat primera mano *f*

'un•der•cov•er *adj agent* secreto

'un•der•cur•rent *fig* sentimiento *m* subyacente

un•der'cut *v/t* (*pret & pp* ***-cut***) COM vender más barato que

un•der•devel•oped [ʌndərdɪ'veləpt] *adj* subdesarrollado

'un•der•dog: ***support the ~*** apoyar al más debil

un•der'done *adj meat* poco hecho

un•der'es•ti•mate *v/t* subestimar

un•der•ex'pose *v/t* PHOT subexponer

un•der•ex•posed [ʌndərɪk'spoʊzd] *adj* PHOT subexpuesto

un•der'fed *adj* malnutrido

'un•der•floor *adj*: ***~ heating*** calefacción *f* subterránea

un•der'foot *adv*: ***the grass was wet ~*** la hierba del suelo estaba mojada; ***be trampled ~*** ser pisoteado

un•der'go *v/t* (*pret* ***-went***, *pp* ***-gone***) *surgery, treatment* ser sometido a; *experiences* sufrir; ***the hotel is ~ing refurbishment*** se están efectuando renovaciones en el hotel

un•der•grad ['ʌndərgræd] F, **un•der'grad•u•ate** estudiante *m/f* universitario(-a) (*todavía no licenciado(a)*)

'un•der•ground I *adj passages etc* subterráneo; POL *resistance, newspaper etc* clandestino **II** *adv work* bajo tierra; ***go ~*** POL pasar a la clandestinidad

'un•der•growth maleza *f*

un•der'hand *adj* (*devious*) poco honrado

un•der'lie *v/t* (*pret* ***-lay***, *pp* ***-lain***) (*form basis of*) sostentar

un•der'line *v/t text* subrayar

un•der•ling ['ʌndərlɪŋ] subordinado(-a) *m(f)*

un•der•ly•ing [ʌndər'laɪɪŋ] *adj causes, problems* subyacente

un•der•manned [ʌndər'mænd] *adj* sin suficiente personal

un•der•men•tioned [ʌndər'menʃnd] *adj Br* susodicho

un•der'mine *v/t s.o.'s position, theory* minar, socavar

un•der•neath [ʌndər'ni:θ] **I** *prep* debajo de, bajo **II** *adv* debajo

un•der•nour•ished [ʌndər'nʌrɪʃd] *adj* desnutrido

un•der'paid *adj* mal pagado

'un•der•pants *npl* calzoncillos *mpl*

'un•der•pass *for pedestrians* paso *m* subterráneo

un•der'pay *v/t* (*pret & pp* ***-paid***) pagar mal

un•der'play *v/t fig* quitar importancia a

un•der•priv•i•leged [ʌndər'prɪvɪlɪdʒd] *adj* desfavorecido

un•der'rate *v/t* subestimar, infravalorar

un•der•rep•re•sent•ed [ʌndəreprɪ'zentɪd] *adj* sin suficiente representación; ***women are ~ in Congress*** las mujeres no están suficientemente representadas en el Congreso

un•der'score *v/t fig* poner de relieve

'un•dersea ☞ ***underwater I***

un•der'sec•re•tar•y 1 POL subsecretario(-a) *m(f)* **2** *Br: civil servant* funcionario(-a) *m(f)*

un•der'sell *v/t* (*pret & pp* ***-sold***) ☞ ***undercut***

'un•der•shirt camiseta *f*

'un•der•shorts ☞ ***underpants***

'un•der•side base *f*

un•der•signed [ʌndər'saɪnd]: ***I, the ~, …*** yo, el abajo firmante,…

un•der•sized [ʌndər'saɪzd] *adj* demasiado pequeño

'un•der•skirt enaguas *fpl*

un•der•staffed [ʌndər'stæft] *adj* sin suficiente personal

un•der•stand [ʌndər'stænd] **I** *v/t* (*pret & pp* ***-stood***) entender, comprender; *language* entender; ***I ~ that you …*** tengo entendido que …; ***they are understood to be in Canada*** se cree que están en Canadá **II** *v/i* (*pret & pp* ***-stood***) entender, comprender

un•der•stand•able [ʌndər'stændəbl] *adj* comprensible

un•der•stand•a•bly [ʌndər'stændəblɪ] *adv* comprensiblemente
un•der•stand•ing [ʌndər'stændɪŋ] **I** *adj person* comprensivo **II** *n* **1** *of problem, situtation* interpretación *f* **2** (*agreement*) acuerdo *m*; ***on the ~ that …*** (*condition*) a condición de que …
un•der'state *v/t production etc figures, costs* recortar; ***~ the extent of the problem*** atenuar la magnitud del problema
un•der•stat•ed [ʌndər'steɪtɪd] *adj* moderado, comedido
'un•der•state•ment: ***that's an ~!*** ¡y te quedas corto!
'un•der•stud•y THEA **I** *n* suplente *m/f* **II** *v/t* ser el suplente de
un•der'take *v/t* (*pret* ***-took***, *pp* ***-taken***) *task* emprender; ***~ to do sth*** (*agree to*) encargarse de hacer algo
un•der•tak•er ['ʌndər'teɪkər] *Br* encargado *m* de una funeraria
'un•der•tak•ing **1** (*enterprise*) proyecto *m*, empresa *f* **2**: ***give an ~ to do sth*** compreterse a hacer algo
un•der-the-'count•er *adj* F ilegal
'un•der•tone **1** tono *m* **2**: ***in an ~*** (en un tono) muy bajo
un•der'val•ue *v/t* infravalorar
un•der'wa•ter **I** *adj* subacúatico **II** *adv* bajo el agua
un•der'way *adj* en curso; ***get ~*** comenzar
'un•der•wear ropa *f* interior
un•der'weight *adj*: ***be ~*** pesar menos de lo normal
'un•der•world **1** *criminal* hampa *f* **2** MYTH Hades *m*
un•der'write *v/t* (*pret* ***-wrote***, *pp* ***-written***) FIN asegurar, garantizar
un•de•served [ʌndɪ'zɜːrvd] *adj* inmerecido
un•de•serv•ed•ly [ʌndɪ'zɜːrvɪdlɪ] *adv* injustamente
un•de•sir•a•ble [ʌndɪ'zaɪrəbl] *adj features, changes* no deseado; *person* indeseable; ***~ element*** *person* persona *f* problemática
un•dies ['ʌndɪz] *npl* F ropa *f* interior
un•dig•ni•fied [ʌn'dɪgnɪfaɪd] *adj* indigno
un•dis•ci•plined [ʌn'dɪsɪplɪnd] *adj* indisciplinado
un•dis•cov•ered [ʌndɪ'skʌvərd] *adj* sin descubrir
un•dis•guised [ʌndɪs'gaɪzd] *adj* evidente, abierto
un•dis•put•ed [ʌndɪ'spjuːtɪd] *adj champion, leader* indiscutible
un•dis•turbed [ʌndɪs'tɜːrbd] *adj* **1** intacto **2**: ***be ~ by*** no inquietarse *or* sobresaltarse por
un•di•vid•ed [ʌndɪ'vaɪdɪd] *adj*: ***give s.o. / sth one's ~ attention*** prestar a alguien / algo total atención
un•do [ʌn'duː] *v/t* (*pret* ***-did***, *pp* ***-done***) *parcel, wrapping* abrir; *buttons, shirt* desabrochar; *shoelaces* desatar; *s.o. else's work* deshacer
un•done [ʌn'dʌn] *adj*: ***leave sth ~*** dejar algo sin hacer; ***come ~*** desatarse
un•doubt•ed [ʌn'daʊtɪd] *adj* indudable
un•doubt•ed•ly [ʌn'daʊtɪdlɪ] *adv* indudablemente
un•dreamt-of [ʌn'dremtəv] *adj riches* inimaginable
un•dress [ʌn'dres] **I** *v/t* desvestir, desnudar; ***get ~ed*** desvestirse, desnudarse **II** *v/i* desvestirse, desnudarse
un•due [ʌn'duː] *adj* (*excessive*) excesivo
un•du•lat•ing ['ʌndjʊleɪtɪŋ] *adj hills, countryside* ondulante
un•du•ly [ʌn'duːlɪ] *adv* **1** *punished, blamed* injustamente **2** (*excessively*) excesivamente
un•dy•ing [ʌn'daɪɪŋ] *adj* eterno
un•earth [ʌn'ɜːrθ] *v/t* descubrir; *ancient remains* desenterrar
un•earth•ly [ʌn'ɜːrθlɪ] *adv*: ***at this ~ hour*** a esta hora intempestiva
un•eas•i•ness [ʌn'iːzɪnɪs] inquietud *f*, intranquilidad *f*
un•eas•y [ʌn'iːzɪ] *adj relationship, peace* tenso; ***feel ~ about*** estar inquieto por
un•eat•a•ble [ʌn'iːtəbl] *adj* incomible
un•e•co•nom•ic [ʌniːkə'nɑːmɪk] *adj* antieconómico, no rentable
un•ed•u•cat•ed [ʌn'edʒəkeɪtɪd] *adj* inculto, sin educación
un•e•mo•tion•al [ʌnɪ'moʊʃənl] *adj* frío, indiferente
un•em•ploy•a•ble [ʌnɪm'plɔɪəbl] *adj* no apto para trabajar
un•em•ployed [ʌnɪm'plɔɪd] **I** *adj* desempleado, *Span* parado **II** *npl*: ***the ~*** los desempleados
un•em•ploy•ment [ʌnɪm'plɔɪmənt] desempleo *m*, *Span* paro *m*

un•end•ing [ʌn'endɪŋ] *adj* interminable
un•en•dur•a•ble [ʌnɪn'dʊrəbl] *adj* insoportable
un•en•vi•a•ble [ʌn'envɪəbl] *adj*: ***have the ~ task of doing sth*** tener (ante sí) la indeseable tarea de hacer algo
un•e•qual [ʌn'iːkwəl] *adj* desigual; ***be ~ to the task*** no estar a la altura de lo que requiere el trabajo
un•e•qual•ed, *Br* **un•e•qual•led** *adj* [ʌn'iːkwəld] inigualable, sin igual
un•e•quiv•o•cal [ʌnɪ'kwɪvəkl] *adj* inequívoco
un•er•ring [ʌn'erɪŋ] *adj judgement*, *instinct* infalible
un•eth•i•cal [ʌn'eθɪkl] *adj* poco ético
un•e•ven [ʌn'iːvn] *adj quality* desigual; *surface*, *ground* irregular
un•e•ven•ly [ʌn'iːvnlɪ] *adv distributed*, *applied* de forma desigual; ***be ~ matched*** *of two contestants* no estar en igualdad de condiciones
un•e•vent•ful [ʌnɪ'ventfəl] *adj day*, *journey* sin incidentes
un•ex•pec•ted [ʌnɪk'spektɪd] *adj* inesperado
un•ex•pec•ted•ly [ʌnɪk'spektɪdlɪ] *adv* inesperadamente, de forma inesperada
un•ex•plained [ʌnɪk'spleɪnd] *adj* inexplicado
un•ex•plored [ʌnɪk'splɔːrd] *adj* por descubrir *or* explorar
un•ex•posed [ʌnɪk'spoʊzd] *adj* PHOT sin revelar
un•fail•ing [ʌn'feɪlɪŋ] *adj* inquebrantable; *support* firme
un•fair [ʌn'fer] *adj* injusto; ***that's ~*** eso no es justo; ***~ competition*** competencia *f* desleal
un•fair•ness [ʌn'fernɪs] injusticia *f*
un•faith•ful [ʌn'feɪθfəl] *adj husband*, *wife* infiel; ***be ~ to s.o.*** ser infiel a alguien
un•fal•ter•ing [ʌn'fɔːltərɪŋ] *adj loyalty*, *love etc* constante
un•fa•mil•i•ar [ʌnfə'mɪljər] *adj* desconocido, extraño; ***be ~ with sth*** desconocer algo
un•fash•ion•a•ble [ʌn'fæʃnəbl] *adj area* impopular; *idea* pasado (de moda), obsoleto
un•fas•ten [ʌn'fæsn] *v/t belt* desabrochar
un•fa•vo•ra•ble, *Br* **un•fa•vou•ra•ble** [ʌn'feɪvərəbl] *adj* desfavorable
un•feel•ing [ʌn'fiːlɪŋ] *adj person* insensible
un•fin•ished [ʌn'fɪnɪʃt] *adj* inacabado; ***leave sth ~*** dejar algo sin acabar
un•fit [ʌn'fɪt] *adj*: ***be ~*** *physically* estar en baja forma; ***be ~ to eat*** no ser apto para el consumo; ***be ~ to drink*** no ser potable; ***he's ~ to be a parent*** no tiene lo que se necesita para ser padre
un•fix [ʌn'fɪks] *v/t part* soltar, desmontar
un•flag•ging [ʌn'flægɪŋ] *adj* invariable, absoluto
un•flap•pa•ble [ʌn'flæpəbl] *adj* impasible
un•flat•ter•ing [ʌn'flætərɪŋ] *adj* poco favorecedor
un•fold [ʌn'foʊld] **I** *v/t sheets*, *letter* desdoblar; *one's arms* descruzar **II** *v/i of story etc* desarrollarse; *of view* abrirse
un•fore•seen [ʌnfɔːr'siːn] *adj* imprevisto
un•for•get•ta•ble [ʌnfər'getəbl] *adj* inolvidable
un•for•giv•a•ble [ʌnfər'gɪvəbl] *adj* imperdonable; ***that was ~ of you*** eso ha sido imperdonable
un•for•tu•nate [ʌn'fɔːrtʃənət] *adj people* desafortunado; *event* desgraciado; *choice of words* desafortunado, desacertado; ***that's ~ for you*** has tenido muy mala suerte
un•for•tu•nate•ly [ʌn'fɔːrtʃənətlɪ] *adv* desgraciadamente
un•found•ed [ʌn'faʊndɪd] *adj* infundado
un•friend•ly [ʌn'frendlɪ] *adj person* antipático; *place* desagradable; *welcome* hostil; *software* de difícil manejo
un•ful•filled [ʌnfʊl'fɪld] *adj election promises* incumplido; *potential* desaprovechado; ***she feels ~*** no se siente realizada
un'funk•y *adj* P *L.Am.* no chévere F, *Span* no guay F
un•furl [ʌn'fɜːrl] *v/t flag* desenrollar; *sails* desplegar
un•fur•nished [ʌn'fɜːrnɪʃt] *adj* sin amueblar
un•gain•ly [ʌn'geɪnlɪ] *adj* torpe
un•gen•tle•man•like [ʌn'dʒentlmənlaɪk], **un•gen•tle•man•ly** [ʌn'dʒentlmənlɪ] *adj* poco caballeroso

un•god•ly [ʌn'gɑːdlɪ] *adj*: ***at this ~ hour*** a esta hora intempestiva
un•gov•ern•a•ble [ʌn'gʌvərnəbl] *adj* ingobernable
un•grate•ful [ʌn'greɪtfəl] *adj* desagradecido
un•guard•ed [ʌn'gɑːrdɪd] *adj* **1** *building, prisoner* sin vigilancia **2** *fig*: ***in an ~ moment*** en un momento de descuido
un•hap•pi•ness [ʌn'hæpɪnɪs] infelicidad *f*
un•hap•py [ʌn'hæpɪ] *adj person, look* infeliz; *day* triste; *customer etc* descontento
un•harmed [ʌn'hɑːrmd] *adj* ileso; ***be ~*** salir ileso
un•health•y [ʌn'helθɪ] *adj person* enfermizo; *conditions, food, economy* poco saludable; ***it's an ~ sign*** es una mala señal
un•heard [ʌn'hɜːrd] *adj*: ***go ~*** ser desoído *or* desestimado
un•heard-of [ʌn'hɜːrdəv] *adj* inaudito
un•help•ful [ʌn'helpfl] *adj person* poco cooperativo; *comment* inservible
un•hes•i•tat•ing [ʌn'hezɪteɪtɪŋ] *adj* decidido
un•hinge [ʌn'hɪndʒ] *v/t*: ***~ s.o.*** *or* ***~ s.o.'s mind*** *fig* perturbar (mentalmente) a alguien
un•ho•ly [ʌn'houlɪ] *adj* F maldito F
un•hurt [ʌn'hɜːrt] *adj*: ***be ~*** salir ileso
un•hy•gi•en•ic [ʌnhaɪ'dʒiːnɪk] *adj* antihigiénico
u•ni ['juːnɪ] *Br* F ☞ ***university***
un•i•den•ti•fied [ʌnaɪ'dentɪfaɪd] *adj* no identificado; *caller* anónimo
un•i•den•ti•fied fly•ing 'ob•ject objeto *m* volante no identificado
u•ni•fi•ca•tion [juːnɪfɪ'keɪʃn] unificación *f*
u•ni•form ['juːnɪfɔːrm] **I** *n* uniforme *m* **II** *adj* uniforme
u•ni•formed ['juːnɪfɔːrmd] *adj* uniformado
u•ni•form•i•ty ['juːnɪfɔːrmətɪ] uniformidad *f*
u•ni•fy ['juːnɪfaɪ] *v/t* (*pret & pp* ***-ied***) unificar
u•ni•lat•e•ral [juːnɪ'lætərəl] *adj* unilateral
un•i•ma•gi•na•ble [ʌnɪ'mædʒɪnəbl] *adj* inimaginable
un•i•ma•gi•na•tive [ʌnɪ'mædʒɪnətɪv] *adj* sin imaginación
un•im•por•tant [ʌnɪm'pɔːrtənt] *adj* poco importante
un•im•pressed [ʌnɪm'prest] *adj* poco impresionado (***by*** por); ***I was ~ by his performance*** su actuación no me dejó boquiabierto; ***be ~ by threats*** no ser intimidado por las amenazas
un•in•hab•i•ta•ble [ʌnɪn'hæbɪtəbl] *adj* inhabitable
un•in•hab•it•ed [ʌnɪn'hæbɪtɪd] *adj building* deshabitado; *region* desierto
un•in•hib•it•ed [ʌnɪn'hɪbɪtɪd] *adj* desinhibido
un•in•jured [ʌn'ɪndʒərd] *adj*: ***be ~*** salir ileso
un•in•spir•ing [ʌnɪn'spaɪrɪŋ] *adj view, performance* sin nada de particular
un•in•sured [ʌnɪn'ʃʊrd] *adj* sin asegurar
un•in•tel•li•gi•ble [ʌnɪn'telɪdʒəbl] *adj* ininteligible
un•in•tend•ed [ʌnɪn'tendɪd] *adj insult* impensado; *outcome* imprevisto
un•in•ten•tion•al [ʌnɪn'tenʃnl] *adj* no intencionado; ***sorry, that was ~*** lo siento, ha sido sin querer
un•in•ten•tion•al•ly [ʌnɪn'tenʃnlɪ] *adv* sin querer
un•in•ter•est•ed [ʌn'ɪntrəstɪd] *adj* indiferente (***in*** a)
un•in•te•rest•ing [ʌn'ɪntrəstɪŋ] *adj* sin interés
un•in•ter•rupt•ed [ʌnɪntə'rʌptɪd] *adj sleep, two hours' work* ininterrumpido
un•in•vit•ed [ʌnɪn'vaɪtɪd] *adj*: ***he asked the ~ guests to leave*** pidió a los invitados que no tenían invitación que se fueran
un•ion ['juːnjən] **1** unión *f* **2** (*labor ~*) sindicato *m*
un•ion•ist ['juːnjənɪst] sindicalista *m/f*
un•ion•ize ['juːnjənaɪz] **I** *v/t* sindicar **II** *v/i* sindicarse
u•nique [juː'niːk] *adj* único
u•ni•sex ['juːnɪseks] *adj* unisex
u•ni•son ['juːnɪsn]: ***in ~*** al unísono
u•nit ['juːnɪt] unidad *f*; ***~ of measurement*** unidad *f* de medida; ***power ~*** fuente *f* de alimentación
u•nit 'cost COM costo *m or Span* coste *m* unitario *or* por unidad
u•nite [juː'naɪt] **I** *v/t* unir **II** *v/i* unirse
u•nit•ed [juː'naɪtɪd] *adj* unido

U•nit•ed 'King•dom Reino *m* Unido; **U•nit•ed 'Na•tions** Naciones *fpl* Unidas; **U•nit•ed 'States (of A'mer•i•ca)** Estados *mpl* Unidos (de América)
u•nit 'price precio *m* unitario
u•nit 'trust sociedad *f* de inversión de capital variable
u•ni•ty ['ju:nətɪ] unidad *f*
u•ni•ver•sal [ju:nɪ'vɜ:rsl] *adj* universal
u•ni•ver•sal 'bar code COM código *m* de barras universal
u•ni•ver•sal•ly [ju:nɪ'vɜ:rsəlɪ] *adv* universalmente
u•ni•verse ['ju:nɪvɜ:rs] universo *m*
u•ni•ver•si•ty [ju:nɪ'vɜ:rsətɪ] **I** *n* universidad *f*; ***he is at ~*** está en la universidad **II** *adj* universitario; ***if you have a ~ education*** si has cursado estudios universitarios
un•just [ʌn'dʒʌst] *adj* injusto
un•jus•ti•fi•a•ble [ʌndʒʌstɪ'faɪəbl] *adj* *cost, price increase etc* inexcusable, imperdonable
un•kempt [ʌn'kempt] *adj appearance* descuidado; *hair* revuelto
un•kind [ʌn'kaɪnd] *adj* desgradable, cruel; ***don't be so ~ to her*** no la trates tan mal
un•known [ʌn'noʊn] **I** *adj* desconocido; ***she's an ~ quantity*** es una incógnita **II** *n* **1**: ***a journey into the ~*** un viaje hacia lo desconocido **2** MATH incógnita f
un•la•dy•like [ʌn'leɪdɪlaɪk] *adj* poco femenino
un•law•ful [ʌn'lɔ:fʊl] *adj* ilegal
un•lead•ed [ʌn'ledɪd] *adj* sin plomo
un•learn [ʌn'lɜ:rn] *v/t* (*pret & pp* ***-ed*** *or* ***-learnt***) *old habits* desaprender
un•leash [ʌn'li:ʃ] *v/t* **1** *dog* desatar **2** *fig anger, violence* descargar (***on*** contra)
un•less [ən'les] *conj* a menos que, a no ser que; ***don't say anything ~ you're sure*** no digas nada a menos que *or* a no ser que estés seguro
un•like [ʌn'laɪk] *prep* (*not similar to*) diferente de; ***it's ~ him to drink so much*** él no suele beber tanto; ***that photograph is so ~ you*** has salido completamente diferente en esa fotografía
un•like•ly [ʌn'laɪklɪ] *adj* (*improbable*) improbable; *explanation* inverosímil; ***he is ~ to win*** es improbable *or* poco probable que gane
un•lim•it•ed [ʌn'lɪmɪtɪd] *adj* ilimitado
un•list•ed [ʌn'lɪstɪd] *adj*: ***be ~*** no aparecer en la guía telefónica
un'list•ed mar•ket FIN mercado *m* sin cotización oficial
un•lit [ʌn'lɪt] *adj street* a oscuras
un•load [ʌn'loʊd] *v/t* descargar
un•lock [ʌn'lɑ:k] *v/t* abrir
un•looked-for [ʌn'lʊktfɔ:r] *adj* inesperado
un•loved [ʌn'lʌvd] *adj* no querido *or* amado
un•luck•i•ly [ʌn'lʌkɪlɪ] *adv* desgraciadamente, por desgracia
un•luck•y [ʌn'lʌkɪ] *adj day, choice* aciago, funesto; *person* sin suerte; ***that was so ~ for you!*** ¡qué mala suerte tuviste!
un•made [ʌn'meɪd] *adj bed* sin hacer
un•man•age•a•ble [ʌn'mænɪdʒəbl] *adj* indomable, rebelde
un•man•ly [ʌn'mænlɪ] *adj* poco masculino
un•manned [ʌn'mænd] *adj spacecraft* no tripulado; *reception desk* sin personal
un•marked [ʌn'mɑ:rkt] *adj* **1** *face* indemne; *police car* de incógnito **2** SP desmarcado
un•mar•ried [ʌn'mærɪd] *adj* soltero
un•mask [ʌn'mɑ:sk] *v/t fig* desenmascarar
un•matched [ʌn'mætʃt] *adj* inigualable, extraordinario; ***be ~*** no tener igual
un•men•tion•a•ble [ʌn'menʃnəbl] *adj* innombrable; ***be ~*** ser tabú
un•mer•ci•ful•ly [ʌn'mɜ:rsɪfʊlɪ] *adv* *tease* despiadadamente, sin compasión
un•mis•tak•a•ble [ʌnmɪ'steɪkəbl] *adj* inconfundible
un•mit•i•gat•ed [ʌn'mɪtɪgeɪtɪd] *adj*: ***be an ~ disaster*** ser un desastre total y absoluto
un•moved [ʌn'mu:vd] *adj*: ***he was ~ by her tears*** sus lágrimas no lo conmovieron
un•mu•si•cal [ʌn'mju:zɪkl] *adj person* sin talento musical; *sounds* estridente
un•named [ʌn'neɪmd] *adj* no identificado
un•nat•u•ral [ʌn'nætʃrəl] *adj* anormal; ***it's not ~ to be annoyed*** es normal estar enfadado
un•ne•ces•sa•ry [ʌn'nesəserɪ] *adj* innecesario
un•nerve [ʌn'nɜ:rv] *v/t* aturdir, descon-

certar
un•nerv•ing [ʌn'nɜːrvɪŋ] *adj* desconcertante
un•no•ticed [ʌn'noʊtɪst] *adj*: ***it went ~*** pasó desapercibido
un•num•bered [ʌn'nʌmbərd] *adj page, check* sin numerar
un•ob•tain•a•ble [ʌnəb'teɪnəbl] *adj goods* no disponible; TELEC desconectado
un•ob•tru•sive [ʌnəb'truːsɪv] *adj* discreto
un•oc•cu•pied [ʌn'ɑːkjʊpaɪd] *adj building, house* desocupado; *post* vacante
un•of•fi•cial [ʌnə'fɪʃl] *adj* no oficial; ***this is still ~ but …*** esto todavía no es oficial, pero …
un•of•fi•cial•ly [ʌnə'fɪʃlɪ] *adv* extraoficialmente
un•o•pened [ʌn'oʊpənd] *adj packet of cereal, jar of coffee etc* sin abrir *or* empezar; *envelope* sin abrir
un•or•tho•dox [ʌn'ɔːrθədɑːks] *adj* poco ortodoxo
un•pack [ʌn'pæk] **I** *v/t* deshacer **II** *v/i* deshacer el equipaje
un•paid [ʌn'peɪd] *adj work* no remunerado; ***~ leave*** baja *f* sin sueldo
un•pal•at•a•ble [ʌn'pælətəbl] *adj food* incomible; *fig*: *truth* amargo, duro
un•par•al•leled [ʌn'pærəleld] *adj* inigualable
un•par•don•a•ble [ʌn'pɑːrdnəbl] *adj* imperdonable
un•per•turbed [ʌnpər'tɜːrbd] *adj* impasible
un•play•a•ble [ʌn'pleɪəbl] *adj* SP *ball, shot etc* imposible (*de devolver, chutar etc*); ***the field is ~*** es imposible jugar en este campo
un•pleas•ant [ʌn'pleznt] *adj* desagradable; ***he was very ~ to her*** fue muy desagradable con ella
un•pleas•ant•ness [ʌn'plezntnɪs] (*arguments*) disputas *fpl*
un•plug [ʌn'plʌg] *v/t* (*pret & pp* **-ged**) *TV, computer* desenchufar
un•pol•lut•ed [ʌnpə'luːtɪd] *adj* no contaminado, limpio
un•pop•u•lar [ʌn'pɑːpjələr] *adj* poco popular; ***this decision was very ~ with the school*** esta decisión no fue bien recibida *or* acogida en el colegio
un•prac•ti•cal [ʌn'præktɪkl] *adj* poco práctico
un•pre•ce•den•ted [ʌn'presɪdentɪd] *adj* sin precedentes; ***it was ~ for a woman to …*** no tenía precedentes que una mujer …
un•pre•dict•a•ble [ʌnprɪ'dɪktəbl] *adj person, weather* imprevisible, impredecible
un•prej•u•diced [ʌn'predʒʊdɪst] *adj* imparcial
un•pre•pared [ʌnprɪ'perd] *adj*: ***be ~ for sth*** no estar preparado para algo
un•pre•ten•tious [ʌnprɪ'tenʃəs] *adj person, style, hotel* modesto, sin pretensiones
un•prin•ci•pled [ʌn'prɪnsɪpld] *adj* sin principios
un•print•a•ble [ʌn'prɪntəbl] *adj* impublicable; *language* vergonzoso, escandaloso
un•pro•duc•tive [ʌnprə'dʌktɪv] *adj meeting, discussion* infructuoso; *soil* improductivo
un•pro•fes•sion•al [ʌnprə'feʃnl] *adj* poco profesional
un•prof•it•a•ble [ʌn'prɑːfɪtəbl] *adj* no rentable
un•prompt•ed [ʌn'prɑːmptɪd] *adj* voluntario, espontáneo
un•pro•nounce•a•ble [ʌnprə'naʊnsəbl] *adj* impronunciable
un•pro•tect•ed [ʌnprə'tektɪd] *adj borders* desprotegido, sin protección; ***~ sex*** sexo *m* sin preservativos
un•pro•vid•ed [ʌnprə'vaɪdɪd] *adj*: ***leave s.o. ~-for*** dejar a alguien sin medios para mantenerse
un•pro•voked [ʌnprə'voʊkt] *adj attack* no provocado
un•pub•lished [ʌn'pʌblɪʃt] *adj* no publicado
un•pun•ished [ʌn'pʌnɪʃt] *adj* impune; ***go ~*** quedar impune
un•put•down•a•ble [ʌnpʊt'daʊnəbl] *adj* F: ***be ~*** *of book* enganchar
un•qual•i•fied [ʌn'kwɑːlɪfaɪd] *adj worker, doctor etc* sin titulación
un•ques•tion•a•bly [ʌn'kwestʃnəblɪ] *adv* (*without doubt*) indiscutiblemente
un•ques•tion•ing [ʌn'kwestʃnɪŋ] *adj attitude, loyalty* incondicional
un•rav•el [ʌn'rævl] *v/t* (*pret & pp* **-ed**, *Br* **-led**) *string, knitting* desenredar;

mystery, *complexities* desentrañar
un•read [ʌn'red] *adj* sin leer
un•read•a•ble [ʌn'ri:dəbl] *adj book* ilegible
un•re•al [ʌn'rɪəl] *adj* irreal; ***this is ~!*** F ¡esto es increíble! F
un•re•al•is•tic [ʌnrɪə'lɪstɪk] *adj* poco realista
un•rea•son•a•ble [ʌn'ri:znəbl] *adj person* poco razonable, irrazonable; *demand*, *expectation* excesivo, irrazonable; ***you're being ~*** no estás siendo razonable
un•rec•og•niz•a•ble [ʌn'rekəgnaɪzəbl] *adj* irreconocible
un•re•cov•ered debt [ʌnrɪ'kʌvərd] *adj*: ***~ debt*** deuda *f* impagada
un•re•fined [ʌnrɪ'faɪnd] *adj sugar* sin refinar
un•re•lat•ed [ʌnrɪ'leɪtɪd] *adj issues* no relacionado; *people* no emparentado
un•re•lent•ing [ʌnrɪ'lentɪŋ] *adj* implacable
un•rel•i•a•ble [ʌnrɪ'laɪəbl] *adj car, machine* poco fiable; *person* informal
un•re•lieved [ʌnrɪ'li:vd] *adj* incesante
un•re•mit•ting [ʌnrɪ'mɪtɪŋ] *adj* ininterrumpido
un•rep•re•sent•a•tive [ʌnreprɪ'zentətɪv] *adj* poco representativo, atípico
un•re•quit•ed [ʌnrɪ'kwaɪtɪd] *adj love* no correspondido
un•re•served [ʌnrɪ'zɜ:rvd] *adj seat, table* no reservado
un•re•serv•ed•ly [ʌnrɪ'zɜ:rvɪdlɪ] *adv* sin reservas
un•rest [ʌn'rest] malestar *m*; (*rioting*) disturbios *mpl*
un•re•strained [ʌnrɪ'streɪnd] *adj emotions* incontrolado
un•re•strict•ed [ʌnrɪ'strɪktɪd] *adj* ilimitado
un•re•ward•ing [ʌnrɪ'wɔ:rdɪŋ] *adj* poco gratificante
un•ripe [ʌn'raɪp] *adj fruit* verde
un•ri•val•ed, *Br* **un•ri•val•led** [ʌn'raɪvld] *adj* inigualable, único
un•road•wor•thy [ʌn'roudwɜ:rðɪ] *adj* que no está en condiciones de circular
un•roll [ʌn'roul] *v/t carpet, scroll* desenrollar
un•ruf•fled [ʌn'rʌfld] *adj person* tranquilo, calmado
un•ru•ly [ʌn'ru:lɪ] *adj* revoltoso; *hair* indomable
un•sad•dle [ʌn'sædl] *v/t horse* desensillar
un•safe [ʌn'seɪf] *adj* peligroso; ***it's ~ to drink / eat*** no se puede beber / comer
un•said [ʌn'sed] *adj*: ***leave sth ~*** dejar algo en el tintero; ***be left ~*** callarse, omitirse; ***some things are better left ~*** algunas cosas es mejor callarlas *or* no decirlas
un•sal(e)•a•ble [ʌn'seɪləbl] *adj* invendible
un•salt•ed [ʌn'sɔ:ltɪd] *adj* sin sal
un•san•i•tar•y [ʌn'sænɪterɪ] *adj conditions, drains* insalubre
un•sat•is•fac•to•ry [ʌnsætɪs'fæktərɪ] *adj* insatisfactorio
un•sat•is•fied [ʌn'sætɪsfaɪd] *adj* insatisfecho (***with*** con)
un•sat•is•fy•ing [ʌn'sætɪsfaɪɪŋ] → ***unsatisfactory***
un•sa•vo•ry [ʌn'seɪvərɪ] *adj person, reputation* indeseable; *district* desagradable
un•scathed [ʌn'skeɪðd] *adj* (*not injured*) ileso; (*not damaged*) intacto
un•sci•en•tif•ic [ʌnsaɪən'tɪfɪk] *adj* poco científico
un•screw [ʌn'skru:] *v/t top* desenroscar; *shelves, hooks* desatornillar
un•script•ed [ʌn'skrɪptɪd] *adj* improvisado
un•scru•pu•lous [ʌn'skru:pjələs] *adj* sin escrúpulos
un•sea•son•a•ble [ʌn'si:znəbl] *adj weather* inusual
un•seat [ʌn'si:t] *v/t* POL destituir a
un•se•cured cred•i•tor [ʌnsɪ'kjʊrd] FIN acreedor(a) *m(f)* no asegurado(-a)
un•se'cured loan préstamo *m* sin garantía
un•seed•ed [ʌn'si:dɪd] *adj* SP que no es cabeza de serie
un•seem•ly [ʌn'si:mlɪ] *adj* impropio
un•seen [ʌn'si:n] *adj* **1** *not visible* invisible; ***do sth ~*** hacer algo sin ser visto **2** *translation* a la vista
un•self•ish [ʌn'selfɪʃ] *adj* generoso
un•sen•ti•men•tal [ʌnsentɪ'mentl] *adj* poco sentimental
un•set•tle [ʌn'setl] *v/t* agitar, excitar
un•set•tled [ʌn'setld] *adj issue* sin decidir; *weather, stock market, lifestyle* inestable; *bills* sin pagar

un•shak(e)•a•ble [ʌn'ʃeɪkəbl] *adj* total, absoluto
un•shav•en [ʌn'ʃeɪvn] *adj* sin afeitar
un•sight•ly [ʌn'saɪtlɪ] *adj* horrible, feo
un•signed [ʌn'saɪnd] *adj* sin firmar
un•skill•ful, *Br* **un•skil•ful** [ʌn'skɪlfʊl] *adj* torpe, desmañado
un•skilled [ʌn'skɪld] *adj* no cualificado
un•so•cia•ble [ʌn'soʊʃəbl] *adj* insociable
un•so•cial [ʌn'soʊʃl] *adj*: ***work ~ hours*** *Br* trabajar fuera del horario habitual
un•sold [ʌn'soʊld] *adj* no vendido
un•so•lic•it•ed [ʌnsə'lɪsɪtɪd] *adj* que no ha sido pedido
un•solved [ʌn'sɑːlvd] *adj* sin resolver
un•so•phis•ti•cat•ed [ʌnsə'fɪstɪkeɪtɪd] *adj person, beliefs* sencillo; *equipment* simple
un•sound [ʌn'saʊnd] *adj fig advice* poco sensato; *argument* poco sólido
un•spar•ing [ʌn'sperɪŋ] *adj*: ***be ~ in one's efforts*** no escatimar esfuerzos (***to do sth*** a la hora de hacer algo)
un•speak•a•ble [ʌn'spiːkəbl] *adj* vergonzoso, incalificable
un•spec•i•fied [ʌn'spesɪfaɪd] *adj* indeterminado, desconocido
un•spoiled [ʌn'spɔɪld], **un•spoilt** [ʌn'spɔɪlt] *adj* intacto
un•spo•ken [ʌn'spoʊkən] *adj* no expresado (oralmente)
un•sport•ing [ʌn'spɔːrtɪŋ], **un•sports•man•like** [ʌn'spɔːrtsmənlaɪk] *adj* poco deportivo; ***~ foul*** falta *f* antideportiva
un•sta•ble [ʌn'steɪbl] *adj* inestable
un•stead•y [ʌn'stedɪ] *adj hand* tembloroso; *ladder* inestable; ***be ~ on one's feet*** tambalearse
un•stint•ing [ʌn'stɪntɪŋ] *adj* generoso; ***be ~ in one's efforts / generosity*** no escatimar esfuerzos / generosidad
un•stop [ʌn'stɑːp] *v/t* (*pret & pp* ***-ped***) *blocked pipe, sink* desatascar
un•stop•pa•ble [ʌn'stɑːpəbl] *adj* imparable
un•stressed [ʌn'strest] *adj* LING inacentuado
un•stuck [ʌn'stʌk] *adj*: ***come ~*** *of sticky label* despegarse; *fig*: *of person* fracasar; *of plan* frustrarse
un•suc•cess•ful [ʌnsək'sesfəl] *adj writer etc* fracasado; *candidate* perdedor; *party, attempt* fallido; ***he tried but was ~*** lo intentó sin éxito
un•suc•cess•ful•ly [ʌnsək'sesfəlɪ] *adv try, apply* sin éxito
un•suit•a•ble [ʌn'suːtəbl] *adj partner, film, clothing* inadecuado; *thing to say* inoportuno
un•suit•a•bly [ʌn'suːtəblɪ] *adv dressed* de manera inadecuada
un•sure [ʌn'ʃɔːr] *adj*: ***be ~ of sth*** no estar muy seguro acerca de algo; ***be ~ of o.s.*** carecer de seguridad en uno mismo
un•sur•passed [ʌnsər'pæst] *adj* incomparable, único
un•sus•pect•ed [ʌnsə'spektɪd] *adj talent, difficulties* insospechado, inesperado; ***he remained ~ for years*** *of spy, terrorist* no levantó sospechas durante años
un•sus•pect•ing [ʌnsəs'pektɪŋ] *adj* confiado
un•sweet•ened [ʌn'swiːtnd] *adj without sweeteners* sin endulcorantes; *without sugar* sin azúcar
un•swerv•ing [ʌn'swɜːrvɪŋ] *adj loyalty, devotion* inquebrantable
un•sym•pa•thet•ic [ʌnsɪmpə'θetɪk] *person* insensible, poco compasivo; *character in book etc* desagradable; ***be ~ to sth*** oponerse a algo
un•tan•gle [ʌn'tæŋgl] *v/t* desenredar
un•tapped [ʌn'tæpt] *adj resources* sin explotar
un•teach•a•ble [ʌn'tiːtʃəbl] *adj child* incapaz de aprender; *subject* imposible de enseñar
un•ten•a•ble [ʌn'tenəbl] *adj* insostenible, indefendible
un•think•a•ble [ʌn'θɪŋkəbl] *adj* impensable
un•think•ing•ly [ʌn'θɪŋkɪŋlɪ] *adv* inconscientemente
un•ti•dy [ʌn'taɪdɪ] *adj room, desk* desordenado; *hair* revuelto
un•tie [ʌn'taɪ] *v/t knot, laces, prisoner* desatar
un•til [ən'tɪl] **I** *prep* hasta; ***from Monday ~ Friday*** desde el lunes hasta el viernes; ***I can wait ~ tomorrow*** puedo esperar hasta mañana; ***not ~ Friday*** no antes del viernes; ***it won't be finished ~ July*** no estará acabado hasta julio **II** *conj* hasta que; ***can you wait ~ I'm ready?*** ¿puedes esperar hasta que esté listo?;

they won't do anything ~ you say so no harán nada hasta que (no) se lo digas

un•time•ly [ʌn'taɪmlɪ] *adj death* prematuro

un•tir•ing [ʌn'taɪrɪŋ] *adj efforts* incansable

un•told [ʌn'toʊld] *adj suffering* indecible; *riches* inconmensurable; *story* nunca contado

un•touched [ʌn'tʌʧt] *adj* **1** *by hand* sin tocar; *building* intacto; ***leave a meal ~*** dejar una comida en el plato **2** *emotionally* indiferente, impasible (***by*** ante)

un•to•ward [ʌntə'wɔːrd] *adj*: ***nothing ~ happened*** no hubo ningún contratiempo

un•trans•lat•a•ble [ʌntræns'leɪtəbl] *adj* intraducible

un•treat•ed [ʌn'triːtɪd] *adj* **1** *illness, injury* sin recibir tratamiento **2** *effluent* sin depurar *or* tratar

un•trou•bled [ʌn'trʌbld] *adj*: ***be ~ by*** no preocuparse por; *by war, natural catastrophe etc* no quedar afectado por

un•true [ʌn'truː] *adj* falso

un•trust•wor•thy [ʌn'trʌstwɜːrðɪ] *adj* de poca confianza

un•used[1] [ʌn'juːzd] *adj goods* sin usar

un•used[2] [ʌn'juːst] *adj*: ***be ~ to sth*** no estar acostumbrado a algo; ***be ~ to doing sth*** no estar acostumbrado a hacer algo

un•u•su•al [ʌn'juːʒl] *adj* poco corriente; ***it is ~ …*** es raro *or* extraño …

un•u•su•al•ly [ʌn'juːʒəlɪ] *adv* inusitadamente; ***the weather's ~ cold*** hace un frío inusual

un•var•nished [ʌn'vɑːrnɪʃt] *adj surface* sin barnizar; *fig*: *truth* sin tapujos

un•var•y•ing [ʌn'verɪɪŋ] *adj* invariable

un•veil [ʌn'veɪl] *v/t memorial, statue etc* desvelar

un•versed [ʌn'vɜːrst] *adj* no versado (***in*** en)

un•voiced [ʌn'vɔɪst] *adj* LING sordo

un•want•ed [ʌn'wɑːntɪd] *adj* no querido *or* deseado

un•war•rant•ed [ʌn'wɑːrəntɪd] *adj* injustificado

un•wa•ver•ing [ʌn'weɪvərɪŋ] *adj stare* fijo; *loyalty* constante; *belief* firme

un•wel•come [ʌn'welkəm] *adj* mal recibido

un•well [ʌn'wel] *adj* indispuesto, mal; ***be ~*** sentirse indispuesto *or* mal

un•whole•some [ʌn'hoʊlsəm] *adj company, influence* poco saludable; *diet* insano, nocivo

un•wield•y [ʌn'wiːldɪ] *adj* difícil de manejar

un•will•ing [ʌn'wɪlɪŋ] *adj* poco dispuesto, reacio; ***be ~ to do sth*** no estar dispuesto a hacer algo, ser reacio a hacer algo

un•will•ing•ly [ʌn'wɪlɪŋlɪ] *adv* de mala gana, a regañadientes

un•wind [ʌn'waɪnd] **I** *v/t* (*pret & pp* ***-wound***) *tape* desenrollar **II** *v/i* (*pret & pp* ***-wound***) **1** *of tape* desenrollarse; *of story* irse desarrollando **2** (*relax*) relajarse

un•wise [ʌn'waɪz] *adj* imprudente

un•wit•ting [ʌn'wɪtɪŋ] *adj* inintencionado

un•wit•ting•ly [ʌn'wɪtɪŋlɪ] *adv* inintencionadamente, sin darse cuenta

un•wont•ed [ʌn'woʊntɪd] *adj* inusitado

un•work•a•ble [ʌn'wɜːrkəbl] *adj* inviable

un•wor•thy [ʌn'wɜːrðɪ] *adj*: ***be ~ of sth*** no ser digno de algo

un•wrap [ʌn'ræp] *v/t* (*pret & pp* ***-ped***) *gift* desenvolver

un•writ•ten [ʌn'rɪtn] *adj law, rule* no escrito

un•yield•ing [ʌn'jiːldɪŋ] *adj resistance* firme, inexorable

un•zip [ʌn'zɪp] *v/t* (*pret & pp* ***-ped***) **1** *dress etc* abrir la cremallera de **2** COMPUT descomprimir

up [ʌp] **I** *adv position* arriba; *movement* hacia arriba; ***~ in the sky / on the roof*** (arriba) en el cielo / en el tejado; ***~ here / there*** aquí / allí arriba; ***be ~*** (*out of bed*) estar levantado; *of sun* haber salido; (*be built*) haber sido construido, estar acabado; *of shelves* estar montado; *of prices, temperature* haber subido; (*have expired*) haberse acabado; ***what's ~?*** F ¿qué pasa?; ***~ to the year 1989*** hasta el año 1989; ***he came ~ to me*** se me acercó; ***what are you ~ to these days?*** ¿qué es de tu vida?; ***what are those kids ~ to?*** ¿qué están tramando esos niños?; ***be ~ to something*** (***bad***) estar tramando algo; ***I don't feel***

U

~ ***to it*** no me siento en condiciones de hacerlo; ***it's ~ to you*** tú decides; ***it is ~ to them to solve it*** (*their duty*) les corresponde a ellos resolverlo; ***be ~ and about*** *after illness* estar recuperado **II** *prep*: ***further ~ the mountain*** más arriba de la montaña; ***he climbed ~ a tree*** se subió a un árbol; ***they ran ~ the street*** corrieron por la calle; ***the water goes ~ this pipe*** el agua sube por esta tubería; ***we traveled ~ to Chicago*** subimos hasta Chicago **III** *n*: ***~s and downs*** altibajos *mpl*

up-and-com•ing [ʌpən'kʌmɪŋ] *adj* prometedor

'up•beat *adj* F positivo, optimista

up•bring•ing ['ʌpbrɪŋɪŋ] educación *f*

up•com•ing ['ʌpkʌmɪŋ] *adj* (*forthcoming*) próximo

up'date[1] *v/t file, records* actualizar; ***~ s.o. on sth*** poner a alguien al corriente de algo

'up•date[2] *n* actualización *f*; ***can you give me an ~ on the situation?*** ¿me puedes poner al corriente de la situación?

up'end *v/t* (*stand on end*) poner derecho; (*turn upside down*: *desk, sofa etc*) poner boca arriba; *drawer, purse etc* poner boca abajo

up'front I *adj* **1** (*honest*) franco **2** *payment* por adelantado **II** *adv* por adelantado; ***be paid ~*** cobrar por adelantado

up'grade[1] *v/t computers etc* actualizar; (*replace with new versions*), *product* modernizar; ***~ s.o. to business class*** cambiar a alguien a clase ejecutiva

'up•grade[2] *n to software package* actualización *f*

up•heav•al [ʌp'hi:vl] *emotional* conmoción *f*; *physical* trastorno *m*; *political, social* sacudida *f*

up•hill I *adv* [ʌp'hɪl] *walk* cuesta arriba **II** *adj* ['ʌphɪl] *struggle* arduo, difícil

up'hold *v/t* (*pret & pp* ***-held***) **1** *traditions, rights* defender, conservar **2** (*vindicate*) confirmar

up•hol•stered [ʌp'hoʊlstərd] *adj* tapizado

up•hol•ster•y [ʌp'hoʊlstərɪ] (*coverings of chairs*) tapicería *f*; (*padding of chairs*) relleno *m*

'up•keep *of buildings, parks etc* mantenimiento *m*

up•lift•ing [ʌp'lɪftɪŋ] *adj experience, sermon* edificante

'up•load *v/t* COMPUT cargar

up'mar•ket *adj restaurant, hotel* de categoría

up•on [ə'pɑ:n] *prep* ☞ ***on***

up•per ['ʌpər] *adj part of sth* superior; *stretches of a river* alto; *deck* superior, de arriba

'up•per•case *adj*: ***~ B*** B mayúscula

up•per-'class *adj accent, family* de clase alta

up•per 'clas•ses *npl* clases *fpl* altas

'up•per•cut *punch* gancho *m* (hacia arriba)

'up•per•most I *adj* superior, de arriba; (*facing upward*) hacia arriba; ***be ~ in a pile*** estar arriba; (*face upward*) estar hacia arriba; ***be ~ in s.o.'s mind*** *fig* ser lo que más preocupa a alguien **II** *adv* arriba; (*facing upward*) hacia arriba

up•pi•ty ['ʌpətɪ] *adj* F creído F

'up•right I *adj citizen* honrado **II** *adv sit* derecho **III** *n* piano *m* vertical

up•right pi'an•o piano *m* vertical

'up•ris•ing levantamiento *m*

'up•roar (*loud noise*) alboroto *m*; (*protest*) tumulto *m*

up'root *v/t also fig* desarraigar

UPS [ju:pi:'es] *abbr* (= ***uninterruptible power supply***) SAI *m* (= sistema *m* de alimentación ininterrumpible)

'up•scale *adj restaurant etc* de categoría

up'set I *v/t* (*pret & pp* ***-set***) **1** *drink, glass* tirar **2** *emotionally* disgustar **II** *adj emotionally* disgustado; ***get ~ about sth*** disgustarse por algo; ***have an ~ stomach*** tener el estómago mal

up'set•ting *adj* triste

'up•shot F (*result, outcome*) resultado *m*

up•side 'down *adv* boca abajo; ***turn sth ~*** *box etc* poner algo al revés *or* boca abajo

up'stairs I *adv* arriba **II** *adj room* de arriba

'up•start advenedizo(-a) *m*(*f*)

up'stream *adv* río arriba

'up•surge brote *m*; *of enthusiasm, interest etc* oleada *f*

'up•swing subida *f*

'up•take 1 FIN respuesta *f* (***of*** a) **2**: ***be quick / slow on the ~*** F ser / no ser muy espabilado F

up'tight *adj* F (*nervous*) tenso; (*inhibited*) estrecho
up-to-'date *adj information* actualizado; *fashions* moderno
up-to-the-'min•ute *adj news* de última hora
'up•town I *adv away from the center*: *walk* hacia las afueras de la ciudad; *live* en las afueras de la ciudad; *toward the center*: *walk* hacia el centro de la ciudad; *live* en el centro de la ciudad **II** *adj* de las afueras de la ciudad; ***in ~ New York*** en las afueras de Nueva York
'up•turn *in economy* mejora *f*
up•turned [ʌp'tɜːrnd] *adj* **1** (*upside down*) boca arriba **2**: ***~ nose*** nariz *f* respingona
up•ward ['ʌpwərd] *adv fly*, *move* hacia arriba; ***~ of 10,000*** más de 10.000
u•ra•ni•um [jʊ'reɪnɪəm] uranio *m*
ur•ban ['ɜːrbən] *adj* urbano
ur•bane [ɜːr'beɪn] *adj* refinado, sofisticado
ur•ban•i•za•tion [ɜːrbənaɪ'zeɪʃn] urbanización *f*
ur•chin ['ɜːrtʃɪn] golfillo(-a) *m*(*f*)
urge [ɜːrdʒ] **I** *n* impulso *m*; ***I felt an ~ to hit her*** me entraron ganas de pegarle; ***I have an ~ to do something new*** siento la necesidad de hacer algo nuevo **II** *v/t*: ***~ s.o. to do sth*** rogar a alguien que haga algo
◆ **urge on** *v/t* (*encourage*) animar
ur•gen•cy ['ɜːrdʒənsɪ] *of situation* urgencia *f*
ur•gent ['ɜːrdʒənt] *adj job*, *letter* urgente; ***be in ~ need of sth*** necesitar algo urgentemente; ***is it ~?*** ¿es urgente?
u•ri•nal ['jʊrənl] **1** *fitting* urinario *m* **2** *place* servicios *mpl*
u•ri•nar•y ['jʊrənərɪ] *adj* urinario
u•ri•nate ['jʊrəneɪt] *v/i* orinar
u•rine ['jʊrɪn] orina *f*
URL [juːɑːr'el] *abbr* (= ***uniform resource locator***) COMPUT URL *f*
urn [ɜːrn] urna *f*
u•rol•o•gist [jʊ'rɑːlədʒɪst] MED urólogo(-a) *m*(*f*)
U•ru•guay ['jʊrəgwaɪ] Uruguay *m*
U•ru•guay•an [jʊrə'gwaɪən] **I** *adj* uruguayo **II** *n* uruguayo(-a) *m*(*f*)
us [ʌs] *pron* nos; *after prep* nosotros (-as); ***they love ~*** nos quieren; ***she gave ~ the keys*** nos dio las llaves; ***he sold it to ~*** nos lo vendió; ***that's for ~*** eso es para nosotros; ***who's that? – it's ~*** ¿quién es? – ¡somos nosotros!; ***all of ~ agree*** todos (nosotros) estamos de acuerdo
US [juː'es] *abbr* (= ***United States***) EE.UU. (= Estados Unidos)
USA [juːes'eɪ] *abbr* (= ***United States of America***) EE.UU. (= Estados Unidos)
us•a•ble ['juːzəbl] *adj* utilizable; ***it's not ~*** no se puede utilizar
us•age ['juːzɪdʒ] uso *m*
USDA [juːesdiː'eɪ] *abbr* (= ***United States Department of Agriculture***) Ministerio *m* de Agricultura
use I *v/t* [juːz] *tool*, *word* utilizar, usar; *skills*, *knowledge*, *car* usar; *a lot of gas* consumir; *pej*: *person* utilizar; ***I could ~ a drink*** F no me vendría mal una copa
II *n* [juːs] uso *m*, utilización *f*; ***be of great ~ to s.o.*** ser de gran utilidad para alguien; ***it's of no ~ to me*** no me sirve; ***is that of any ~?*** ¿eso sirve para algo?; ***it's no ~*** no sirve de nada; ***it's no ~ trying / waiting*** no sirve de nada intentarlo / esperar
◆ **use up** *v/t* agotar
used[1] [juːzd] *adj car etc* de segunda mano
used[2] [juːst] *adj*: ***be ~ to s.o. / sth*** estar acostumbrado a alguien / algo; ***get ~ to s.o. / sth*** acostumbrarse a alguien / algo; ***be ~ to doing sth*** estar acostumbrado a hacer algo; ***get ~ to doing sth*** acostumbrarse a hacer algo
used[3] [juːst] *v/aux*: ***I ~ to like him*** antes me gustaba; ***they ~ to meet every Saturday*** solían verse todos los sábados
use•ful ['juːsfəl] *adj* útil; ***~ life*** vida *f* útil
use•ful•ness ['juːsfʊlnɪs] utilidad *f*
use•less ['juːslɪs] *adj* inútil; *machine*, *computer* inservible; ***be ~*** F *person* ser un inútil F; ***it's ~ trying*** (*there's no point*) no vale la pena intentarlo
use•less•ness ['juːslɪsnɪs] inutilidad *f*
us•er ['juːzər] *of product* usuario(-a) *m*(*f*)
us•er-'friend•ly *adj* de fácil manejo
ush•er ['ʌʃər] (*at wedding*) *persona que se encarga de indicar a los asistentes dónde se deben sentar*

◆ **usher in** *v/t new era* anunciar
ush•er•ette [ʌʃə'ret] *Br* acomodadora *f*
USSR [juːeses'ɑːr] *abbr* (= ***Union of Soviet Socialist Republics***) URSS *f* (= Unión *f* de las Repúblicas Socialistas Soviéticas)
u•su•al ['juːʒl] *adj* habitual, acostumbrado; ***as ~*** como de costumbre; ***the ~, please*** lo de siempre, por favor
u•su•al•ly ['juːʒəlɪ] *adv* normalmente; ***I ~ start at 9*** suelo empezar a las 9
u•surp [juː'zɜːrp] *v/t power, throne* usurpar
u•su•ry ['juːʒʊrɪ] usura *f*
u•ten•sil [juː'tensl] utensilio *m*
u•te•rus ['juːtərəs] útero *m*
u•til•i•tar•i•an [juːtɪlɪ'terɪən] *adj* (*functional*) funcional, práctico
u•til•i•ty [juː'tɪlətɪ] **1** (*usefulness*) utilidad *f* **2**: ***public utilities*** servicios *mpl* públicos
u'til•i•ty pole poste *m* telegráfico
u•til•ize ['juːtɪlaɪz] *v/t* utilizar
ut•most ['ʌtmoʊst] **I** *adj* sumo **II** *n*: ***do one's ~*** hacer todo lo posible
ut•ter ['ʌtər] **I** *adj* completo, total **II** *v/t sound* decir, pronunciar
ut•ter•ly ['ʌtərlɪ] *adv* completamente, totalmente
U-turn ['juːtɜːrn] cambio *m* de sentido; ***do a ~*** *fig*: *in policy etc* dar un giro de 180 grados

V

V ['viː] *abbr* (= ***volts***) V (= voltios *mpl*)
va•can•cy ['veɪkənsɪ] *esp Br* **1** *job* vacante *f*; ***fill a ~*** llenar una vacante **2**: *in hotel* ***vacancies*** habitaciones disponibles; ***'no vacancies'*** 'completo'
va•cant ['veɪkənt] *adj building* vacío; *position* vacante; *look, expression* vago, distraído; ~ *on toilet door* libre; ***situations ~*** *Br* ofertas *fpl* de empleo, colocaciones *fpl*
va•cant•ly ['veɪkəntlɪ] *adv look etc* distraídamente
va•cate [veɪ'keɪt] *v/t room* desalojar
va•ca•tion [veɪ'keɪʃn] **I** *n* vacaciones *fpl*; ***be on ~*** estar de vacaciones; ***go to … on ~*** ir de vacaciones a …; ***take a ~*** tomarse vacaciones **II** *v/i* ir de vacaciones
va•ca•tion•er [veɪ'keɪʃənər] turista *m/f*; *in summer* veraneante *m/f*
vac•cin•ate ['væksɪneɪt] *v/t* vacunar; ***be ~d against…*** estar vacunado contra …
vac•cin•a•tion [væksɪ'neɪʃn] *action* vacunación *f*; (*vaccine*) vacuna *f*
vac•cine ['væksiːn] vacuna *f*
vac•il•late ['væsɪleɪt] *v/i* vacilar, dudar (***between*** entre)
vac•il•la•tion [væsɪ'leɪʃn] vacilación *f*, titubeo *m*
vac•u•ous ['vækjʊəs] *adj* vacuo, vacío
vac•u•um ['vækjʊəm] **I** *n* PHYS, *fig* vacío *m* **II** *v/t floors* pasar el aspirador por, aspirar
'vac•u•um bot•tle termo *m*; **'vac•u•um clean•er** aspirador *m*, aspiradora *f*; **'vac•u•um flask** *Br* termo *m*; **vac•u•um-'packed** *adj* envasado al vacío
vag•a•bond ['vægəbɑːnd] vagabundo(-a) *m(f)*
va•gar•ies ['veɪgəriːz] *npl of weather* antojos *mpl* (***of*** de); *of financial markets* altibajos *mpl* (***of*** de)
va•gi•na [və'dʒaɪnə] vagina *f*
va•gi•nal ['vædʒɪnl] *adj* vaginal
va•gran•cy ['veɪgrənsi] LAW vagancia *f*
va•grant ['veɪgrənt] vagabundo(-a) *m(f)*
vague [veɪg] *adj* vago; ***he was very ~ about it*** no fue muy preciso
vague•ly ['veɪglɪ] *adv answer,* (*slightly*) vagamente; *possible* muy poco
vain [veɪn] **I** *adj* **1** *person* vanidoso **2** *hope* vano **II** *n*: ***in ~*** en vano; ***their efforts were in ~*** sus esfuerzos fueron en vano
va•lence ['veɪləns] CHEM, LING valencia *f*
va•len•cy ['veɪlənsɪ] *Br* ☞ ***valence***
val•en•tine ['væləntaɪn] *card* tarjeta *f* del día de San Valentín; ***Valentine's Day*** día *m* de San Valentín *or* de los enamorados
val•et I *n* ['væleɪ] *person* mozo *m* **II** *v/t* ['vælət] *car* lavar y limpiar
'val•et park•ing servicio *m* de aparca-

coches
'val•et ser•vice *for clothes* servicio *m* de planchado; *for cars* servicio *m* de lavado y limpiado
val•iant ['væljənt] *adj* valiente, valeroso
val•iant•ly ['væljəntlɪ] *adv* valientemente, valerosamente
val•id ['vælɪd] *adj* válido
val•i•date ['vælɪdeɪt] *v/t with official stamp* sellar; *s.o.'s alibi* dar validez a
va•lid•i•ty [və'lɪdətɪ] validez *f*
Val•i•um® ['vælɪəm] Valium *m*
val•ley ['vælɪ] valle *m*
val•or ['vælər] valentía *f*, coraje *m*
val•our *Br* ☞ ***valor***
val•u•a•ble ['væljʊbl] **I** *adj* valioso **II** *n*: ***~s*** objetos *mpl* de valor
val•u•a•tion [væljʊ'eɪʃn] tasación *f*, valoración *f*
val•ue ['vælju:] **I** *n* valor *m*; ***be good ~*** ofrecer buena relación calidad-precio; ***get ~ for money*** recibir una buena relación calidad-precio; ***rise* / *fall in ~*** aumentar / disminuir de valor **II** *v/t s.o.'s friendship, one's freedom* valorar; ***I ~ your advice*** valoro tus consejos; ***have an object ~d*** pedir la valoración *or* tasación de un objeto
val•ue-'ad•ded tax *Br* impuesto *m* sobre el valor añadido
val•ued ['vælju:d] *adj* valorado, apreciado
'val•ue judg(e)•ment juicio *m* de valor
val•ue•less ['væljʊlɪs] *adj* carente de valor
val•u•er ['væljʊər] tasador(a) *m(f)*
valve [vælv] válvula *f*
vamp [væmp] vampiresa *f*, mujer *f* fatal
vam•pire ['væmpaɪr] vampiro *m*
'vam•pire bat vampiro *m* del Uruguay
van [væn] camioneta *f*, furgoneta *f*
van•dal ['vændl] vándalo *m*, gamberro(-a) *m(f)*
van•dal•ism ['vændəlɪzm] vandalismo *m*
van•dal•ize ['vændəlaɪz] *v/t* destrozar (*intencionadamente*)
vane [veɪn] *of propeller* aspa *f*, paleta *f*
van•guard ['vængɑ:rd] vanguardia *f*; ***be in the ~ of*** *fig* estar a la vanguardia de
va•nil•la [və'nɪlə] **I** *n* vainilla *f* **II** *adj* de vainilla
van•ish ['vænɪʃ] *v/i* desaparecer
van•i•ty ['vænətɪ] *of person* vanidad *f*
'van•i•ty case neceser *m*; **'van•i•ty pub•lish•ing** *publicación de una obra financiada por el propio autor*; **'van•i•ty ta•ble** tocador *m*
van•quish ['væŋkwɪʃ] *v/t* conquistar, derrotar
van•tage point ['væntɪdʒ] *on hill etc* posición *f* aventajada
va•por ['veɪpər] vapor *m*
va•por•ize ['veɪpəraɪz] *v/t of atomic bomb, explosion* vaporizar
'va•por trail *of airplane* estela *f*
va•pour *Br* ☞ ***vapor***
var•i•a•ble ['verɪəbl] **I** *adj* variable **II** *n* MATH, COMPUT variable *f*
var•i•ance ['verɪəns]: ***be at ~ with*** estar en desacuerdo con
var•i•ant ['verɪənt] variante *f*
var•i•a•tion [verɪ'eɪʃn] variación *f*
var•i•cose vein [værɪkoʊs'veɪn] variz *f*
var•ied ['verɪd] *adj* variado
var•i•e•gat•ed ['verɪəgeɪtɪd] *adj* variopinto
va•ri•e•ty [və'raɪətɪ] (*variedness, type*) variedad *f*; ***a ~ of things to do*** (*range, mixture*) muchas cosas para hacer; ***~ is the spice of life*** en la variedad está el gusto
va•ri•fo•cal ['verɪfoʊkl] *adj lens* progresivo
var•i•ous ['verɪəs] *adj* **1** (*several*) varios **2** (*different*) diversos
var•nish ['vɑ:rnɪʃ] **I** *n* **1** *for wood* barniz *m* **2** *for fingernails* esmalte *m* **II** *v/t* **1** *wood* barnizar **2** *fingernails* poner esmalte a, pintar
var•y ['verɪ] **I** *v/i* (*pret & pp* ***-ied***) variar; ***it varies*** depende **II** *v/t* (*pret & pp* ***-ied***) variar
vase [veɪz] jarrón *m*
vas•ec•to•my [və'sektəmɪ] vasectomía *f*
Vas•e•line® ['væsəli:n] vaselina *f*
vast [væst] *adj desert, knowledge* vasto; *number, improvement* enorme; ***the ~ majority*** la gran mayoría
vast•ly ['væstlɪ] *adv* enormemente; *different* totalmente; *superior* infinitamente
VAT [vi:eɪ'ti:, væt] *abbr Br* (= ***value-added tax***) IVA *m* (= impuesto *m* sobre el valor añadido)
vat [væt] barril *m*, tanque *m*
Vat•i•can ['vætɪkən]: ***the ~*** el Vaticano

vau•de•ville ['vɒːdvɪl] vodevil *m*
vault[1] [vɒːlt] *n* **1** *in roof* bóveda *f* **2**: **~s** (*cellar*) sótano *m*; *of bank* cámara *f* acorazada
vault[2] [vɒːlt] **I** *n* SP salto *m* **II** *v/t beam etc* saltar
vault•ed ['vɒːltɪd] *adj* convexo, abombado
vault•ing horse ['vɒːltɪŋ] potro *m*
vCJD [viːsiːdʒeɪ'diː] *abbr* (= ***new variant Creutzfeldt-Jakob Disease***) nueva variante *f* de la enfermedad de Creutzfeldt-Jakob
VCR [viːsiː'ɑːr] *abbr* (= ***video cassette recorder***) aparato *m* de *Span* vídeo *or L.Am.* video
VD [viː'diː] *abbr* (= ***venereal disease***) enfermedad *f* venérea
VDU [viːdiː'juː] *abbr* (= ***visual display unit***) monitor *m*
veal [viːl] ternera *f*
vec•tor ['vektər] MATH vector *m*
veer [vɪr] *v/i* girar, torcer; **~ *to the right*** POL dar un giro a la derecha
◆ **veer off** *v/i* girar, torcer
ve•gan ['viːgn] **I** *n* vegetariano(-a) *m(f)* estricto (-a) (*que no come ningún producto de origen animal*) **II** *adj* vegetariano estricto
veg•e•burg•er® ['vedʒɪbɜːrgər] hamburguesa *f* vegetariana
veg•e•ta•ble ['vedʒtəbl] hortaliza *f*; **~s** *pl* verduras *fpl*
veg•e•tar•i•an [vedʒɪ'terɪən] **I** *n* vegetariano(-a) *m(f)* **II** *adj* vegetariano
veg•e•tar•i•an•ism [vedʒɪ'terɪənɪzm] vegetarianismo *m*
veg•e•tate ['vedʒɪteɪt] *v/i* vegetar
veg•e•ta•tion [vedʒɪ'teɪʃn] vegetación *f*
veg•gie•bur•ger ['vedʒɪbɜːrgər] hamburguesa *f* vegetariana
ve•he•mence ['viːəməns] vehemencia *f*
ve•he•ment ['viːəmənt] *adj* vehemente
ve•he•ment•ly ['viːəməntlɪ] *adv* vehementemente
ve•hi•cle ['viːɪkl] *also fig* vehículo *m*
veil [veɪl] **I** *n* velo *m*; ***draw a ~ over sth*** *fig* correr un tupido velo sobre algo **II** *v/t* cubrir con un velo; ***~ed in secrecy*** envuelto en secretismo
vein [veɪn] ANAT vena *f*; ***in this ~*** *fig* en este tono
Vel•cro® ['velkroʊ] velcro *m*
ve•loc•i•ty [vɪ'lɑːsətɪ] velocidad *f*
vel•vet ['velvɪt] terciopelo *m*
vel•vet•y ['velvɪtɪ] *adj* aterciopelado
vend•er ☞ ***vendor***
ven•det•ta [ven'detə] vendetta *f*
vend•ing ma•chine ['vendɪŋ] máquina *f* expendedora
vend•or ['vendər] LAW parte *f* vendedora
ve•neer [və'nɪr] *on wood* chapa *f*; *fig*: *of politeness etc* apariencia *f*, fachada
ven•er•a•ble ['venərəbl] *adj* venerable
ven•er•ate ['venəreɪt] *v/t* venerar
ven•er•a•tion [venə'reɪʃn] veneración *f*
ve•ne•re•al dis•ease [vɪ'nɪrɪəl] enfermedad *f* venérea
ve•ne•tian 'blind persiana *f* veneciana
Ven•e•zue•la [venɪz'weɪlə] Venezuela *f*
Ven•e•zue•lan [venɪz'weɪlən] **I** *adj* venezolano **II** *n* venezolano(-a) *m(f)*
ven•geance ['vendʒəns] venganza *f*; ***with a ~*** con ganas
venge•ful ['vendʒfʊl] *adj* vengativo
ven•i•son ['venɪsn] venado *m*
ven•om ['venəm] *also fig* veneno *m*
ven•om•ous ['venəməs] *adj snake* venenoso; *fig* envenenado
vent [vent] **I** *n for air* respiradero *m*; ***give ~ to*** *feelings* dar rienda suelta a **II** *v/t*: **~ *one's anger on s.o.*** descargarse con alguien
ven•ti•late ['ventɪleɪt] *v/t* ventilar
ven•ti•la•tion [ventɪ'leɪʃn] ventilación *f*
ven•ti'la•tion shaft pozo *m* de ventilación
ven•ti•la•tor ['ventɪleɪtər] ventilador *m*; MED respirador *m*
ven•tri•cle ['ventrɪkl] ventrículo *m*
ven•tril•o•quism [ven'trɪləkwɪzəm] ventriloquia *f*
ven•tril•o•quist [ven'trɪləkwɪst] ventrílocuo(-a) *m(f)*
ven•ture ['ventʃər] **I** *n* (*undertaking*) iniciativa *f*; COM empresa *f* **II** *v/i* aventurarse **III** *v/t*: **~ *to do sth*** aventurarse a hacer algo; **~ *an opinion*** aventurar una opinión (***on*** sobre)
'ven•ture cap•i•tal capital *m* de riesgo
'ven•ture cap•i•tal•ist capitalista *m/f* de riesgo
ven•ue ['venjuː] *for meeting* lugar *m*; *for concert* local *m*, sala *f*
Ve•nus ['viːnəs] ASTR Venus *m*
ve•ran•da [və'rændə] porche *m*
verb [vɜːrb] verbo *m*

ver•bal ['vɜːrbl] *adj* (*spoken*) verbal
ver•bal•ize ['vɜːrbəlaɪz] *v/t* expresar, exteriorizar con palabras
ver•bal•ly ['vɜːrbəlɪ] *adv* de palabra
ver•ba•tim [vɜːr'beɪtɪm] *adv* literalmente
ver•bi•age ['vɜːrbɪɪdʒ] verbosidad *f*, verborragia *f*
ver•bose [vɜːr'bous] *adj* verboso, recargado
ver•dict ['vɜːrdɪkt] LAW veredicto *m*; ***what's your ~?*** ¿qué te parece?, ¿qué opinas?
ver•di•gris ['vɜːrdɪgrɪ] verdete *m*
verge [vɜːrdʒ] *of road* arcén *m*; ***be on the ~ of*** *ruin* estar al borde de; *tears* estar a punto de
◆ **verge on** *v/t* rayar en
ver•i•fi•a•ble [verɪ'faɪəbl] *adj* demostrable, comprobable
ver•i•fi•ca•tion [verɪfɪ'keɪʃn] **1** (*checking*) verificación *f* **2** (*confirmation*) confirmación *f*
ver•i•fy ['verɪfaɪ] *v/t* (*pret & pp* ***-ied***) **1** (*check*) verificar **2** (*confirm*) confirmar
ver•i•ta•ble ['verɪtəbl] *adj* auténtico, verdadero; ***a ~ labyrinth*** un verdadero laberinto
ver•mi•cel•li [vɜːrmɪ'tʃelɪ] *nsg* fideos *mpl*
ver•mil•ion [vər'mɪlɪən] *adj* bermellón
ver•min ['vɜːrmɪn] *npl* bichos *mpl*
ver•min•ous ['vɜːrmɪnəs] *adj* sarnoso, cochambroso
ver•mouth [vɜːr'muːθ] vermut *m*
ver•nac•u•lar [vər'nækjələr] lenguaje *m* de la calle
ver•sa•tile ['vɜːrsətəl] *adj* polifacético, versátil
ver•sa•til•i•ty [vɜːrsə'tɪlətɪ] polivalencia *f*, versatilidad *f*
verse [vɜːrs] verso *m*
versed [vɜːrst] *adj*: ***be well ~ in a subject*** estar muy versado en una materia
ver•sion ['vɜːrʃn] versión *f*
ver•sus ['vɜːrsəs] *prep* SP, LAW contra
ver•te•bra ['vɜːrtɪbrə] vértebra *f*
ver•te•brate ['vɜːrtɪbreɪt] vertebrado (-a) *m*(*f*)
ver•tex ['vɜːrteks] (*pl* ***-tices*** ['vɜːrtɪsiːz], ***-texes***) vértice *m*
ver•ti•cal ['vɜːrtɪkl] *adj* vertical
ver•ti•go ['vɜːrtɪgou] vértigo *m*
verve [vɜːrv] entusiasmo *m*, garbo *m*
ver•y ['verɪ] **I** *adv* muy; ***was it cold? – not ~*** ¿hizo frío? – no mucho; ***the ~ best*** el mejor de todos **II** *adj*: ***at that ~ moment*** en ese mismo momento; ***that's the ~ thing I need*** (*exact*) eso es precisamente lo que necesito; ***the ~ thought*** (*mere*) sólo de pensar en; ***right at the ~ top / bottom*** arriba / al fondo del todo
ver•y large-scale in•te'gra•tion integración *f* a gran escala
ves•i•cle ['vesɪkl] vesícula *f*
ves•sel ['vesl] **1** NAUT buque *m* **2** *dish* vasija *f*, cuenco *m*
vest [vest] **1** chaleco *m* **2** *Br* camiseta *f* interior
vest•ed in•ter•est [vestɪd'ɪntrəst] **1**: ***the ~s*** *pl* los intereses establecidos *or* creados **2**: ***have a ~ in sth*** tener verdadero interés en algo
ves•ti•bule ['vestɪbjuːl] vestíbulo *m*
ves•tige ['vestɪdʒ] vestigio *m*
ves•try ['vestrɪ] REL sacristía *f*
vet[1] [vet] *n* (*veterinary surgeon*) veterinario(-a) *m*(*f*)
vet[2] [vet] *v/t* (*pret & pp* ***-ted***) *applicants etc* examinar, investigar
vet[3] [vet] *n* MIL veterano(-a) *m*(*f*)
vet•e•ran ['vetərən] **I** *n* veterano(-a) *m*(*f*) **II** *adj* veterano
vet•e•ri•nar•i•an [vetərə'nerɪən] veterinario(-a) *m*(*f*)
vet•er•i•nar•y ['vetərɪnerɪ] *adj* veterinario
'vet•er•i•nar•y med•i•cine veterinaria *f*
'vet•er•i•nar•y sur•geon *Br* veterinario(-a) *m*(*f*)
ve•to ['viːtou] **I** *n* (*pl* ***-oes***) veto *m* **II** *v/t* vetar
vex [veks] *v/t* (*concern, worry*) molestar, irritar
vexed [vekst] **1** *adj* (*worried*) molesto, irritado **2**: ***the ~ question of*** la polémica cuestión de
VHF [viːeɪtʃ'ef] *abbr* (= ***Very High Frequency***) VHF *m* (= frecuencia *f* muy alta)
vi•a ['vaɪə] *prep* vía
vi•a•ble ['vaɪəbl] *adj* viable
vi•a•duct ['vaɪədʌkt] viaducto *m*
vi•al ['vaɪəl] frasco *m*
vibes [vaɪbz] *npl* F **1** *vibraphone* vibráfono *m* **2** *fig* vibraciones *fpl*; ***I was getting positive ~ from her*** (ella) me dio

buenas vibraciones
vi•brant ['vaɪbrənt] *adj* **1** *color, voice* penetrante, vivo **2** *personality* dinámico, entusiasta
vi•bra•phone ['vaɪbrəfoun] MUS vibráfono *m*
vi•brate [vaɪ'breɪt] *v/i* vibrar
vi•bra•tion [vaɪ'breɪʃn] vibración *f*
vi•bra•tor [vaɪ'breɪtər] vibrador *m*
vic•ar ['vɪkər] *Br* REL vicario *m*
vic•ar•age ['vɪkərɪdʒ] *Br* REL vicaría *f*
vi•car•i•ous [vaɪ'kerɪəs] *adj* indirecto
vice[1] [vaɪs] vicio *m*; ***the problem of ~*** el problema del vicio
vice[2] *Br* ☞ ***vise***
vice 'pres•i•dent vicepresidente(-a) *m(f)*
'vice squad brigada *f* antivicio
vi•ce ver•sa [vaɪs'vɜːrsə] *adv* viceversa
vi•cin•i•ty [vɪ'sɪnətɪ] zona *f*; ***in the ~ of*** ... *the church etc* en las cercanías de ...; *$500 etc* rondando ...
vi•cious ['vɪʃəs] *adj dog* fiero; *attack, temper, criticism* feroz
vi•cious 'cir•cle círculo *m* vicioso
vi•cious•ly ['vɪʃəslɪ] *adv* con brutalidad
vi•cis•si•tudes [vɪ'sɪsɪtuːdz] *npl fml* vicisitudes *fpl*
vic•tim ['vɪktɪm] víctima *f*
vic•tim•ize ['vɪktɪmaɪz] *v/t* tratar injustamente
vic•tor ['vɪktər] vencedor(a) *m(f)*
Vic•to•ri•an [vɪk'tɔːrɪən] *adj* HIST victoriano
vic•to•ri•ous [vɪk'tɔːrɪəs] *adj* victorioso
vic•to•ry ['vɪktərɪ] victoria *f*; ***win a ~ over ...*** obtener una victoria sobre ...
vid•e•o ['vɪdɪou] **I** *n Span* vídeo *m*, *L.Am.* video *m*; ***have X on ~*** tener a X en *Span* vídeo *or L.Am.* video **II** *v/t* grabar en *Span* vídeo *or L.Am.* video
'vid•e•o ar•cade salón *m* de juegos recreativos; **'vid•e•o cam•e•ra** videocámara *f*; **vid•e•o•cas'sette** videocasete *m*; **vid•e•o•cas'sette re•cord•er** aparato *m* de video *or Span* vídeo; **'vid•e•o clip** videoclip *m*, vídeo *m* musical; **'vid•e•o con•fer•ence** TELEC videoconferencia *f*; **'vid•e•o•disk** videodisco *m*, video disk *m*; **'vid•e•o game** videojuego *m*; **vid•e•o 'nas•ty** *Br*: *película de contenido violente o pornográfico*; **'vid•e•o•phone** videoteléfono *m*; **'vid•e•o re•cord•er** aparato *m* de *Span* vídeo *or L.Am.* video; **'vid•e•o re•cord•ing** grabación *f* en *Span* vídeo *or L.Am.* video; **'vid•e•o screen** *of TV* pantalla *f* del televisor; **'vid•e•o sig•nal** señal *f* de *Span* vídeo *or L.Am.* video; **'vid•e•o•tape I** *n* cinta *f* de video *or Span* vídeo **II** *v/t* grabar en video *or Span* vídeo

vie [vaɪ] *v/i* competir
Vi•et•nam [vɪet'nɑːm] Vietnam *m*
Vi•et•nam•ese [vɪetnə'miːz] **I** *adj* vietnamita **II** *n* **1** *person* vietnamita *m/f* **2** *language* vietnamita *m*
view [vjuː] **I** *n* **1** vista *f*; ***in ~ of*** teniendo en cuenta; ***be on ~*** *of paintings* estar expuesto al público; ***be hidden from ~*** estar oculto *or* escondido; ***in full ~ of the crowd*** a la vista de todos; ***you're blocking my ~*** no me dejas ver **2** *of situation* opinión *f*; ***with a ~ to*** con vistas a **II** *v/t events, situation* ver, considerar; *TV program, house* ver **III** *v/i* (*watch TV*) ver la televisión
view•er ['vjuːər] TV telespectador(a) *m(f)*
'view•find•er PHOT visor *m*
view•ing fig•ures ['vjuːɪŋ] *npl* índice *m* de audiencia
'view•point punto *m* de vista
vig•il ['vɪdʒɪl] vigilia *f*; ***keep ~*** velar (***by*** por)
vig•i•lance ['vɪdʒɪləns] vigilancia *f*
vig•i•lant ['vɪdʒɪlənt] *adj* vigilante, en alerta
vig•i•lan•te [vɪdʒɪ'læntɪ] vigilante *m/f*
vig•or ['vɪgər] (*energy*) vigor *m*
vig•or•ous ['vɪgərəs] *adj shake* vigoroso; *person* enérgico; *denial* rotundo
vig•or•ous•ly ['vɪgərəslɪ] *adv shake* con vigor; *deny, defend* rotundamente
vig•our *Br* ☞ ***vigor***
Vi•king ['vaɪkɪŋ] **I** *n* vikingo(-a) *m(f)* **II** *adj* vikingo
vile [vaɪl] *adj smell* asqueroso; *thing to do* vil
vil•i•fy ['vɪlɪfaɪ] *v/t* difamar, desacreditar
vil•la ['vɪlə] chalet *m*; *in the country* villa *f*
vil•lage ['vɪlɪdʒ] pueblo *m*
vil•lag•er ['vɪlɪdʒər] aldeano(-a) *m(f)*
vil•lain ['vɪlən] malo(-a) *m(f)*
vin•ai•grette [vɪnɪ'gret] GASTR vinagreta *f*

vin•di•cate ['vɪndɪkeɪt] *v/t* (*show to be correct*) dar la razón a; (*show to be innocent*) vindicar; ***I feel ~d*** los hechos me dan ahora la razón
vin•dic•tive [vɪn'dɪktɪv] *adj* vengativo
vin•dic•tive•ly [vɪn'dɪktɪvlɪ] *adv* vengativamente
vine [vaɪn] vid *f*
vin•e•gar ['vɪnɪgər] vinagre *m*
vine•yard ['vɪnjɑːrd] viñedo *m*
vi•no ['viːnoʊ] F vino *m*
vin•tage ['vɪntɪdʒ] **I** *n of wine* cosecha *f* **II** *adj* (*classic*) clásico *m*
vint•ner ['vɪntnər] **1** (*wine merchant*) vinatero(-a) *m(f)* **2** (*wine maker*) vinicultor(a) *m(f)*
vi•nyl ['vaɪnl] vinilo *m*
vi•o•la [vɪ'oʊlə] MUS viola *f*
vi•o•late ['vaɪəleɪt] *v/t* violar
vi•o•la•tion [vaɪə'leɪʃn] violación *f*; (*traffic ~*) infracción *f*
vi•o•lence ['vaɪələns] violencia *f*; ***outbreak of ~*** estallido *m* de violencia
vi•o•lent ['vaɪələnt] *adj* violento; ***have a ~ temper*** tener muy mal genio
vi•o•lent•ly ['vaɪələntlɪ] *adv react* violentamente; *object* rotundamente; ***fall ~ in love with s.o.*** enamorarse perdidamente de alguien; ***he was ~ ill*** vomitó mucho
vi•o•let ['vaɪələt] **1** *color* violeta *m* **2** *plant* violeta *f*
vi•o•lin [vaɪə'lɪn] violín *m*
vi•o•lin•ist [vaɪə'lɪnɪst] violinista *m/f*
VIP [viːaɪ'piː] *abbr* (= ***very important person***) VIP *m*
vi•per ['vaɪpər] *snake* víbora *f*
vi•ral ['vaɪrəl] *adj infection* vírico, viral
Vir•gin ['vɜːrdʒɪn]: ***the ~*** (***Mary***) la Virgen (María)
vir•gin ['vɜːrdʒɪn] virgen *m/f*
vir•gin•i•ty [vɜːr'dʒɪnətɪ] virginidad *f*; ***lose one's ~*** perder la virginidad
Vir•go ['vɜːrgoʊ] ASTR Virgo *m/f inv*; ***be*** (***a***) **~** ser Virgo
vir•ile ['vɪrəl] *adj man* viril; *prose* vigoroso
vi•ril•i•ty [vɪ'rɪlətɪ] virilidad *f*
vi•rol•o•gy [vaɪ'rɑːlədʒɪ] virología *f*
vir•tu•al ['vɜːrtʃʊəl] *adj* virtual
vir•tu•al•ly ['vɜːrtʃʊəlɪ] *adv* (*almost*) virtualmente, casi
vir•tu•al re'al•i•ty realidad *f* virtual
vir•tue ['vɜːrtʃuː] virtud *f*; ***in ~ of*** en virtud de; ***make a ~ of necessity*** hacer de la necesidad virtud
vir•tu•o•so [vɜːrtʃuː'oʊzoʊ] MUS virtuoso(-a) *m(f)*
vir•tu•ous ['vɜːrtʃʊəs] *adj* virtuoso
vir•u•lent ['vɪrʊlənt] *adj* virulento
vi•rus ['vaɪrəs] MED, COMPUT virus *m inv*
'vi•rus de•tec•tion pro•gram programa *m* detector de virus; **'vi•rus e•lim•i•na•tion pro•gram** programa *m* antivirus; **'vi•rus pro•tec•tion** COMPUT antivirus *m*; **'vi•rus scan•ner** COMPUT scanner *m* antivirus
vi•sa ['viːzə] visa *f*, visado *m*
vis-à-vis [viːzɑː'viː] *prep* contra, de cara a
vis•cer•a ['vɪsərə] *npl* ANAT vísceras *fpl*
vis•cer•al ['vɪsərəl] *adj* visceral
vis•cos•i•ty [vɪs'kɑːsətɪ] viscosidad *f*
vis•cous ['vɪskəs] viscoso, glutinoso
vise [vaɪs] torno *m* de banco
vis•i•bil•i•ty [vɪzə'bɪlətɪ] visibilidad *f*
vis•i•ble ['vɪzəbl] *adj object*, *difference* visible; *anger* evidente; ***not be ~ to the naked eye*** no ser visible a simple vista
vis•i•bly ['vɪzəblɪ] *adv different* visiblemente; ***he was ~ moved*** estaba visiblemente conmovido
vi•sion ['vɪʒn] *also* REL visión *f*; ***I had ~s of having to rekey the whole thing*** ya me veía teniendo que teclear todo otra vez
vi•sion•ar•y ['vɪʒnerɪ] **I** *adj* (*far-sighted*) previsor, precavido **II** *n* **1** (*far-sighted person*) previsor(a) *m(f)*, precavido(-a) *m(f)* **2** REL visionario(-a) *m(f)*
vis•it ['vɪzɪt] **I** *n* visita *f*; ***pay a ~ to the doctor / dentist*** visitar al doctor / dentista; ***pay s.o. a ~*** hacer una visita a alguien **II** *v/t* visitar
◆ **visit with** *v/t* **1** (*visit*) visitar **2** (*chat to*) platicar *or Span* conversar con
vis•it•a•tion [vɪzɪ'teɪʃn] **1** REL aparición *f* **2** *hum* (*visit*) visita *f*
vis•it•ing card ['vɪzɪtɪŋ] tarjeta *f* de visita
'vis•it•ing hours *npl at hospital* horas *fpl* de visita
vis•i•tor ['vɪzɪtər] (*guest*) visita *f*, (*tourist*), *to museum etc* visitante *m/f*
'vis•i•tors' book libro *m* de visitas
vi•sor ['vaɪzər] visera *f*

vis•ta ['vɪstə] vista *f* (***of*** de)
vis•u•al ['vɪʒʊəl] *adj* visual
vis•u•al 'aid medio *m* visuale; **'vis•u•al arts** *npl* artes *fpl* plásticas; **vis•u•al dis'play u•nit** monitor *m*
vis•u•al•ize ['vɪʒʊəlaɪz] *v/t* visualizar; (*foresee*) prever
vis•u•al•ly ['vɪʒʊlɪ] *adv* visualmente
vis•u•al•ly im'paired *adj* con discapacidad visual
vi•tal ['vaɪtl] *adj* (*essential*) essencial, fundamental; *piece of evidence, clue* clave; ***it's absolutely ~ that ...*** es imprescindible que ...; ***of ~ importance*** de vital importancia
vi•tal•i•ty [vaɪ'tælətɪ] *of person, city etc* vitalidad *f*
vi•tal•ly ['vaɪtəlɪ] *adv*: ***~ important*** de importancia vital
vi•tal 'or•gans *npl* órganos *mpl* vitales
vi•tal sta'tis•tics *npl of woman* medidas *fpl*
vit•a•min ['vaɪtəmɪn] vitamina *f*
'vit•a•min pill pastilla *f* vitamínica
vit•ri•ol•ic [vɪtrɪ'ɑːlɪk] *adj* virulento
vi•va•cious [vɪ'veɪʃəs] *adj* vivaz
vi•vac•i•ty [vɪ'væsətɪ] vivacidad *f*
viv•id ['vɪvɪd] *adj color* vivo; *memory, imagination* vívido
viv•id•ly ['vɪvɪdlɪ] *adv* **1** (*brightly*) vivamente **2** (*clearly*) vívidamente
viv•i•sec•tion [vɪvɪ'sekʃn] BIO vivisección *f*
vix•en ['vɪksən] ZO zorra *f*
VLSI [viːeles'aɪ] *abbr* (= ***very large-scale integration***) integración *f* a gran escala
V-neck ['viːnek] cuello *m* de pico
vo•cab ['voʊkæb] F ☞ ***vocabulary***
vo•cab•u•la•ry [voʊ'kæbjʊlerɪ] vocabulario *m*
vo•cal ['voʊkl] *adj* **1** *to do with the voice* vocal **2** *expressing opinions* ruidoso; ***a ~ opponent*** un declarado adversario
'vo•cal cords *npl* cuerdas *fpl* vocales
'vo•cal group MUS grupo *m* vocal
vo•cal•ist ['voʊkəlɪst] MUS vocalista *m/f*
vo•ca•tion [və'keɪʃn] (*calling*) vocación *f*; (*profession*) profesión *f*
vo•ca•tion•al [və'keɪʃnl] *adj guidance* profesional
vo•cif•er•ous [və'sɪfərəs] *adj* vociferante, vehemente
vod•ka ['vɑːdkə] vodka *m*
vogue [voʊg] moda *f*; ***be in ~*** estar en boga
voice [vɔɪs] **I** *n* voz *f* **II** *v/t opinions* expresar
voice-ac•ti•vat•ed ['vɔɪsæktɪveɪtɪd] *adj* activado por voz
'voice box ANAT laringe *f*
voiced [vɔɪst] *adj* LING sonoro
voice•less ['vɔɪslɪs] *adj* LING sordo
'voice mail correo *m* de voz; **'voice-o•ver** voz *f* en off; **'voice rec•og•ni•tion** reconocimento *m* de voz; **'voice vote** voto *m* oral
void [vɔɪd] **I** *n* vacío *m* **II** *adj*: ***~ of*** carente de
vol•a•tile ['vɑːlətəl] *adj personality, moods* cambiante; *markets* inestable
vol-au-vent ['vɑːloʊvɑːn] GASTR vol-au-vent *m*, tartaleta *f*
vol•can•ic [vɑːl'kænɪk] *adj* volcánico
vol•ca•no [vɑːl'keɪnoʊ] (*pl* ***-o(e)s***) volcán *m*
vole [voʊl] ZO ratón *m* de campo
vo•li•tion [və'lɪʃn]: ***of one's own ~*** por decisión *or* elección propia
vol•ley ['vɑːlɪ] **I** *n* **1** *of shots* ráfaga *f* **2** *in tennis, soccer* volea *f* **II** *v/t* volear, golpear en el aire
'vol•ley•ball voleibol *m*, balonvolea *m*
volt [voʊlt] voltio *m*
volt•age ['voʊltɪdʒ] voltaje *m*
vol•u•ble ['vɑːljʊbl] *adj* elocuente, expresivo
vol•ume ['vɑːljəm] **1** *of sound* volumen *m* **2** *of container* capacidad *f* **3** *of book* volumen *m*, tomo *m*; ***speak ~s about s.o.*** decir mucho de alguien; ***her silence spoke volumes*** su silencio lo dijo todo
vol•ume con'trol control *m* del volumen
vo•lu•mi•nous [və'luːmɪnəs] *adj* **1** *item of clothing* amplio, voluminoso **2** *writing* profuso, detallado
vol•un•tar•i•ly [vɑːlən'terɪlɪ] *adv* voluntariamente
vol•un•ta•ry ['vɑːlənterɪ] *adj* voluntario; ***on a ~ basis*** como voluntario
vol•un•teer [vɑːlən'tɪr] **I** *n* voluntario(-a) *m*(*f*) **II** *v/i* ofrecerse voluntariamente
vo•lup•tu•ous [və'lʌptʃʊəs] *adj woman, figure* voluptuoso

V

vom•it ['vɑːmət] **I** *n* vómito *m* **II** *v/i* vomitar

◆ **vomit up** *v/t* vomitar

voo•doo ['vuːduː] vudú *m*

vo•ra•cious [və'reɪʃəs] *adj appetite* voraz

vo•ra•cious•ly [və'reɪʃəslɪ] *adv also fig* vorazmente

vor•tex ['vɔːrteks] (*pl* ***vortexes*** ['vɔːrteksɪs], ***vortices*** ['vɔːrtɪsiːz]) METEO vórtice *m*; *fig* torbellino *m*, espiral *f*

vote [voʊt] **I** *n* voto *m*; ***have the ~*** (*be entitled to vote*) tener el derecho al voto **II** *v/i* POL votar; ***~ for / against*** votar a favor / en contra **III** *v/t*: ***they ~d him President*** lo votaron presidente; ***they ~d to stay behind*** votaron (a favor de) quedarse atrás

◆ **vote in** *v/t new member* elegir en votación

◆ **vote on** *v/t issue* someter a votación

◆ **vote out** *v/t of office* rechazar en votación

vot•er ['voʊtər] POL votante *m/f*

vot•ing ['voʊtɪŋ] POL votación *f*

'vot•ing booth cabina *f* electoral

◆ **vouch for** [vaʊtʃ] *v/t truth of sth* dar fe de; *person* responder por

vouch•er ['vaʊtʃər] vale *m*

vow [vaʊ] **I** *n* voto *m* **II** *v/t*: ***~ to do sth*** prometer hacer algo

vow•el [vaʊl] vocal *f*

voy•age ['vɔɪɪdʒ] viaje *m*

voy•eur [vɔɪ'ɜːr] voyeur *m/f*, mirón (-ona) *m(f)*

VP [viː'piː] *abbr* (= ***Vice President***) vicepresidente(-a) *m(f)*

vul•can•ized rub•ber ['vʌlkənaɪzd] goma *f* vulcanizada

vul•gar ['vʌlgər] *adj person*, *language* vulgar, grosero

vul•gar•i•ty [vʌl'gærətɪ] vulgaridad *f*, ordinariez *f*

vul•ner•a•bil•i•ty [vʌlnərə'bɪlətɪ] vulnerabilidad *f*

vul•ne•ra•ble ['vʌlnərəbl] *adj to attack*, *criticism* vulnerable

vul•ture ['vʌltʃər] buitre *m*

W

wack•o ['wækoʊ] F majareta *m/f*, grillado(-a) *m/f*

wack•y ['wækɪ] *adj* F estrambótico

wad [wɑːd] *of paper*, *absorbent cotton etc* bola *f*; ***a ~ of $100 bills*** un fajo de billetes de 100 dólares

wad•ding ['wɑːdɪŋ] relleno *m*

wad•dle ['wɑːdl] *v/i of duck* caminar; *of person* anadear

wade [weɪd] *v/i* caminar en el agua

◆ **wade in** *v/i Br* F *to conversation* entrometerse

◆ **wade through** *v/t book*, *documents* leerse

wad•er[1] [weɪdər] ORN zancuda *f*

wad•er[2] [weɪdər] *boot* bota *f* de agua

wad•ing pool ['weɪdɪŋpuːl] piscina *f* hinchable

wa•fer ['weɪfər] **1** *cookie* barquillo *m* **2** REL hostia *f*

'wa•fer-thin *adj* muy fino

waf•fle[1] ['wɑːfl] *n to eat* gofre *m*

waf•fle[2] ['wɑːfl] *v/i* F andarse con rodeos

waft [wɑːft] **I** *v/i of smell* flotar; ***the sound of a guitar ~ed in from …*** una música agradable de guitarra venía de … **II** *v/t* llevar

wag[1] [wæg] **I** *v/t* (*pret & pp* ***-ged***) *tail*, *finger* menear **II** *v/i* (*pret & pp* ***-ged***) *of tail* menearse

wag[2] [wæg] *n* payaso *m*

wage[1] [weɪdʒ] *v/t*: ***~ war*** hacer la guerra

wage[2] [weɪdʒ] *n* salario *m*, sueldo *m*; ***~s*** salario *m*, sueldo *m*

'wage claim, 'wage de•mand reivindicación *f* salarial; **'wage earn•er** asalariado(-a) *m(f)*; **'wage freeze** congelación *f* salarial; **'wage ne•go•ti•a•tions** *npl* negociación *f* salarial; **'wage pack•et** *fig* salario *m*, sueldo *m*

wa•ger ['weɪdʒər] **I** *n* apuesta *f*; ***have a ~ on sth*** apostar por algo **II** *v/t*: ***I'll ~ that …*** apuesto a que…

wag•gle ['wægl] *v/t hips* menear; *ears*, *loose screw etc* mover

wag•on, *Br* **wag•gon** ['wægən] **1** *horse-drawn* carro *m*; *covered* carromato *m* **2**

Br RAIL vagón *m* **3**: ***be on the ~*** F haber dejado la bebida

waif [weɪf] niño(-a) *m/f* desamparado(-a); ***~s and strays*** niños desamparados

wail [weɪl] **I** *n of person, baby* gemido *m*; *of siren* sonido *m*, aullido *m* **II** *v/i of person, baby* gemir; *of siren* sonar, aullar

wain•scot•ting ['weɪnskɑːtɪŋ] revestimiento *m*

waist [weɪst] cintura *f*

'waist•band cinturilla *f*; **'waist•coat** *Br* chaleco *m*; **waist-'deep** *adj*: ***the water was ~*** el agua cubría hasta la cintura; **waist-'high** *adj*: ***the grass was ~*** la hierba llegaba hasta la cintura; **'waist-line** cintura *f*; ***watch one's ~*** F cuidar la línea

wait [weɪt] **I** *n* espera *f*; ***I had a long ~ for a train*** esperé mucho rato el tren; ***it was worth the ~*** mereció la pena esperar; ***lie in ~ for s.o.*** acechar a alguien **II** *v/i* esperar; ***have you been ~ing long?*** ¿llevan mucho rato esperando? **II** *v/t*: ***don't ~ supper for me*** no me esperéis a cenar; ***~ table*** trabajar de camarero(-a)

◆ **wait for** *v/t* esperar; ***wait for me!*** ¡espérame!

◆ **wait on** *v/t* **1** (*serve*) servir **2** (*wait for*) esperar

◆ **wait up** *v/i* esperar levantado

wait•er ['weɪtər] camarero *m*

wait•ing ['weɪtɪŋ] espera *f*; ***no ~ sign*** señal *f* de prohibido estacionar

'wait•ing list lista *f* de espera

'wait•ing room sala *f* de espera

wait•ress ['weɪtrɪs] camarera *f*

waive [weɪv] *v/t right* renunciar; *requirement* no aplicar

waiv•er ['weɪvər] LAW renuncia *f*

wake[1] [weɪk] **I** *v/i* (*pret* **woke**, *pp* **woken**): **~ (up)** despertarse **II** *v/t* (*pret* **woke**, *pp* **woken**): **~ (up)** despertar

◆ **wake up I** *v/i* **1** *from sleep* despertarse **2** *fig* espabilarse **II** *v/t* **1** *from sleep* despertar **2** *fig* espabilar

wake[2] [weɪk] *n of ship* estela *f*; ***in the ~ of*** *fig* tras; ***missionaries followed in the ~ of the explorers*** a los exploradores siguieron los misioneros

wake•ful ['weɪkful] *adj* (*unable to sleep*) desvelado; ***she spent a ~ night*** pasó la noche en vela

wak•en ['weɪkən] *v/t* despertar

'wake-up call: ***could I have a ~ at 6.30?*** ¿me podrían despertar a las 6.30?

wak•ing ['weɪkɪŋ] *adj*: ***he spends all his ~ hours studying*** pasa todas las horas que está despierto estudiando

Wales [weɪlz] Gales *m*

walk [wɒːk] **I** *n* **1** paseo *m*; *longer* caminata *f*; ***it's a long / short ~ to the office*** hay una caminata / un paseo hasta la oficina; ***go for a ~*** salir a dar un paseo, salir de paseo; ***it's a five-minute ~*** está a cinco minutos a pie **2** (*path*) camino *m* **3**: ***from all ~s of life*** de toda condición **4** *in baseball* base *f* por bolas **II** *v/i* caminar, andar; *as opposed to driving* ir a pie ***she ~ed over to the window*** se acercó a la ventana; ***I ~ed over to her place*** fui a su casa **III** *v/t* **1** *dog* sacar a pasear **2**: ***~ the streets*** (*walk around*) caminar por las calles **3** *in baseball*: ***he was ~ed*** hizo una base por bolas

◆ **walk in** *v/i* entrar

◆ **walk into** *v/t* **1** *room* entrar **2** (*collide with*) chocarse con

◆ **walk off I** *v/i* marcharse, irse **II** *v/t headache* ir a dar un paseo para librarse de

◆ **walk off with** *v/t prize* hacerse con

◆ **walk out** *v/i of spouse* marcharse; *from theater etc* salir; (*go on strike*) declararse en huelga

◆ **walk out on** *v/t*: ***walk out on s.o.*** abandonar a alguien

◆ **walk over** *v/t*: ***walk all over s.o.*** F (*defeat*) derrotar *or* aplastar alguien (*treat badly*) pisotear a alguien F

'walk•a•bout *Br* F: ***go on a ~*** *of politician* dar un paseo entre la multitud; ***go ~*** (*disappear*) desaparecer

'walk•a•way F (*easy win*) paseo *m*

walk•er ['wɒːkər] **1** (*hiker*) excursionista *m/f* **2** *for baby, old person* andador *m* **3**: ***be a slow / fast ~*** caminar *or* andar despacio / rápido

walk•ie-'talk•ie [wɒːkɪ'tɒːkɪ] walkie-talkie *m*

walk-in 'clos•et vestidor *m*, armario *m* empotrado

walk•ing ['wɒːkɪŋ] (*hiking*) excursionismo *m*; ***~ is one of the best forms of exercise*** caminar es uno de los mejores ejercicios; ***it's within ~ distance*** se

puede ir caminando *or* andando
'walk•ing stick bastón *m*
'walk•ing tour visita *f* a pie
'Walk•man® walkman *m*; **'walk-on part** papel *m* de figurante; **'walk•out** (*strike*) huelga *f*, **'walk•o•ver** (*easy win*) paseo *m*; **'walk-up** *apartamento en un edificio sin ascensor*; **'walk•way** pasarela *f*
wall [wɒ:l] *external*, *fig* muro *m*; *of room* pared *f*; *in soccer* barrera *f*; ***go to the ~*** *of company* quebrar; ***drive s.o. up the ~*** F hacer que alguien se suba por las paredes
wal•la•by ['wɑ:ləbɪ] wallaby *m*
'wall•chart gráfico *m* mural
wal•let ['wɑ:lɪt] (*billfold*) cartera *f*
wall•eyed ['wɒ:laɪd] *adj* bizco
'wall•flow•er *fig* F: ***she was tired of being a ~*** estaba harta de no tener con quién bailar
wal•lop ['wɑ:ləp] **I** *n* F *blow* tortazo *m* F, galletazo *m* F **II** *v/t* F dar un golpetazo a F; *opponent* dar una paliza a F
wal•lop•ing ['wɑ:ləpɪŋ] *adj & adv*: ***a ~*** (***great***) ***hole*** F un agujero enorme F
wal•low ['wɑ:loʊ] *v/i*: ***~ in*** *mud* revolcarse en; ***~ in luxury*** nadar en la abundancia; ***~ in self-pity*** recrearse en la autocompasión
'wall paint•ing pintura *f* mural; **'wall•pa•per I** *n* papel *m* pintado **II** *v/t* empapelar; **'Wall Street** Wall Street *m*, la bolsa de Nueva York; **wall-to-wall 'car•pet** *Span* moqueta *f*, *L.Am.* alfombra *f*
wal•nut ['wɒ:lnʌt] nuez *f*; *tree*, *wood* nogal *m*
wal•rus ['wɒ:lrəs] ZO morsa *f*
wal•rus 'mus•tache, *Br* **wal•rus 'mous•tache** bigote *m* largo
waltz [wɒ:lts] **I** *n* vals *m* **II** *v/i* bailar un vals
wan [wɑ:n] *adj face* pálido *m*
wand•er ['wɑ:ndər] *v/i* (*roam*) vagar, deambular; (*stray*) extraviarse; ***my attention began to ~*** empecé a distraerme
◆ **wander around** *v/i* deambular, pasear
wan•der•ings ['wɑ:ndərɪŋz] *npl* andanzas *fpl*; ***she's off on her ~ again*** está otra vez viajando
'wand•er•lust pasión *f* por viajar
wane [weɪn] **I** *v/i of interest*, *enthusiasm* decaer, menguar; *of moon* menguar **II** *n*: ***be on the ~*** estar decayendo
wan•gle ['wæŋgl] *v/t* F agenciarse F
wan•na ['wɑ:nə] F ☞ ***want to***; ***want a***
wan•na•be ['wɑ:nəbɪ] F **I** *adj* ***a ~ actor / writer*** un aprendiz de actor / escritor **II** *n*: ***an Oprah ~*** una persona que aspira a ser como Oprah
want [wɑ:nt] **I** *n*: ***for ~ of*** por falta de **II** *v/t* querer; (*need*) necesitar; ***~ to do sth*** querer hacer algo; ***I ~ to stay here*** quiero quedarme aquí; ***do you ~ to come too? – no, I don't ~ to*** ¿quieres venir tú también? – no, no quiero; ***you can have whatever you ~*** toma lo que quieras; ***it's not what I ~ed*** no es lo que quería; ***she ~s you to go back*** quiere que vuelvas; ***he ~s a haircut*** necesita un corte de pelo
III *v/i*: ***he ~s for nothing*** no le falta nada
'want ad anuncio *m* por palabras (*buscando algo*)
want•ed ['wɑ:ntɪd] *adj by police* buscado por la policía
want•ing ['wɑ:ntɪŋ] *adj*: ***the team is ~ing in experience*** al equipo le falta experiencia
wan•ton ['wɑ:ntən] *adj* gratuito
WAP phone ['wæpfoʊn] teléfono *m* WAP
war [wɔ:r] *also fig* guerra *f*; ***be at ~*** estar en guerra; ***go to ~ with s.o.*** entrar en guerra con alguien
war•ble ['wɔ:rbl] *v/i of bird* trinar
'war chest POL fondos *mpl*; **'war crime** crimen *m* de guerra; **'war crim•i•nal** criminal *m/f* de guerra; **'war cry** *also fig* grito *m* de guerra
ward [wɔ:rd] **1** *in hospital* sala *f* **2** *child* pupilo(-a) *m(f)* **3** *of city* circunscripción *f* electoral
◆ **ward off** *v/t blow* parar; *attacker* rechazar; *cold* evitar
war•den ['wɔ:rdn] *of prison* director(-a) *m(f)*, alcaide(sa) *m(f)*; *Br of hostel* vigilante *m/f*
'ward•robe *for clothes* armario *m*; (*clothes*) guardarropa *m*
ware•house ['werhaʊs] almacén *m*
wares [werz] *npl* mercancías *fpl*
'war•fare guerra *f*, **'war film** película *f* bélica; **'war•head** ojiva *f*
war•i•ly ['werɪlɪ] *adv* cautelosamente

'war•like *adj* belicoso
'war•lord señor *m* de la guerra
warm [wɔːrm] *adj* **1** *hands, room, water* caliente; *weather, welcome* cálido; ***it's ~er than yesterday*** hace más calor que ayer; ***get ~*** calentarse; ***you're getting ~*** *in game* caliente, caliente **2** *coat* de abrigo
◆ **warm over** *v/t* calentar
◆ **warm up** **I** *v/t* calentar **II** *v/i* calentarse; *of athlete etc* calentar
warm•blood•ed [wɔːrm'blʌdɪd] *adj* ZO de sangre caliente
warmed-o•ver [wɔːrmd'oʊvər] *adj* recalentado; *fig* manido
'war me•mo•ri•al monumento *m* a los caídos en la guerra
warm•heart•ed ['wɔːrmhɑːrtɪd] *adj* cariñoso, simpático
warm•ly ['wɔːrmlɪ] *adv welcome, smile* calurosamente; ***~ dressed*** abrigado
war•mon•ger ['wɔːrmʌŋgər] belicista *m/f*
'war mov•ie película *f* bélica
warmth [wɔːrmθ] calor *m*; *of welcome, smile* calor *m*, calidez *m*
'warm-up SP calentamiento *m*
warn [wɔːrn] *v/t* advertir, avisar; ***~ s.o. against doing sth*** advertir a alguien para que no haga algo
◆ **warn off** *v/t* advertir, prevenir
warn•ing ['wɔːrnɪŋ] advertencia *f*, aviso *m*; SP amonestación *f*; ***without ~*** sin previo aviso
War of In•de'pen•dence HIST Guerra *f* de la Independencia (Americana)
war of 'nerves guerra *f* de nervios
warp [wɔːrp] **I** *v/t wood* combar; *character* corromper **II** *v/i of wood* combarse
'war paint *of warrior* pintura *f* de guerra; ***she's putting on her ~*** *hum* se está pintando
'war•path: ***be on the ~*** estar en pie de guerra
warped [wɔːrpt] *adj fig* retorcido
'war•plane avión *m* de guerra
war•rant ['wɔːrənt] **I** *n* orden *f* judicial **II** *v/t* (*deserve, call for*) justificar
war•ran•ty ['wɔːrəntɪ] (*guarantee*) garantía *f*; ***be under ~*** estar en garantía
'war•ran•ty cer•tif•i•cate certificado *m* de garantía
war•ren ['wɔːrən] madriguera *f*; *fig* laberinto *m*
war•ri•or ['wɔːrɪər] guerrero(-a) *m(f)*
'war•ship buque *m* de guerra
wart [wɔːrt] verruga *f*; ***~s and all*** F con todas las imperfecciones
'war•time tiempos *mpl* de guerra
war•y ['werɪ] *adj* cauto, precavido; ***be ~ of*** desconfiar de
was [wʌz] *pret* ☞ ***be***
wash [wɑːʃ] **I** *n* lavado *m*; ***have a ~*** lavarse; ***that shirt needs a ~*** hay que lavar esa camisa; ***my blue shirt is in the ~*** mi camiseta azul está con la ropa sucia **II** *v/t* lavar **III** *v/i* lavarse
◆ **wash down** *v/t* **1** *clean* lavar con abundante agua **2** *medicine, meal* bajar
◆ **wash up** *v/i* **1** (*wash one's hands and face*) lavarse **2** *Br* (*wash dishes*) lavar los platos
wash•a•ble ['wɑːʃəbl] *adj* lavable
'wash•bag *Br* neceser *m*; **'wash•ba•sin, 'wash•bowl** lavabo *m*; **'wash•cloth** toallita *f*; **'wash•day** día *m* de hacer la colada
washed-out [wɑːʃt'aʊt] *adj* agotado
washed-up [wɑːʃt'ʌp] *adj* F *actor, artist* acabado F
wash•er ['wɑːʃər] **1** *for faucet etc* arandela *f* **2** ☞ ***washing machine***
wash•ing ['wɑːʃɪŋ] (*clothes washed*) ropa *f* limpia; (*dirty clothes*) ropa *f* sucia; ***do the ~*** lavar la ropa, hacer la colada
'wash•ing line cuerda *f* para tender
'wash•ing ma•chine lavadora *f*
'wash•out F *disaster* fracaso *m*
'wash•room lavabo *m*, aseo *m*
was•n't ['wɑːznt] ☞ ***was not***
WASP [wɑːsp] *abbr* (= ***White Anglo-Saxon Protestant***) *blanco, anglosajón y protestante*
wasp [wɑːsp] *insect* avispa *f*
wasp•ish ['wɑːspɪʃ] *adj remark, comment* mordaz
waste [weɪst] **I** *n* desperdicio *m*; *from industrial process* desechos *mpl*; ***it's a ~ of time / money*** es una pérdida de tiempo / dinero **II** *adj* residual; ***~ land*** erial *m* **III** *v/t* derrochar; *money* gastar; *time* perder
◆ **waste away** *v/i* consumirse
'waste•bas•ket papelera *f*
wast•ed ['weɪstɪd] *adj* P como una cuba F
'waste dis•pos•al (unit) trituradora *f* de basuras

waste•ful ['weɪstfəl] *adj* despilfarrador, derrochador
'waste•land erial *m*; **waste'pa•per** papel *m* usado; **waste•pa•per 'bas•ket** papelera *f*; **'waste pipe** tubería *f* de desagüe; **'waste prod•uct** desecho *m*
wast•er ['weɪstər] F inútil *m/f*
watch [wɑːtʃ] **I** *n timepiece* reloj *m*; ***keep ~*** hacer la guardia, vigilar **II** *v/t* mirar; *film, TV* ver; (*look after*) vigilar; ***~ me!*** ¡mírame!; ***~ s.o. doing sth*** mirar a alguien hacer algo *or* cómo hace algo; ***~ it*** ten cuidado; ***you want to ~ it with him*** ten cuidado con él **III** *v/i* mirar, observar
◆ **watch for** *v/t* esperar
◆ **watch out** *v/i* (*be careful*) tener cuidado; ***watch out!*** ¡cuidado!
◆ **watch out for** *v/t* (*be wary of*) tener cuidado con
'watch•band correa *f* de reloj
'watch•dog 1 *dog* perro *m* guardián **2** *fig* organismo *m* regulador
watch•ful ['wɑːtʃfəl] *adj* vigilante
'watch•mak•er relojero(-a) *m(f)*; **watch•man** ['wɑːtʃmən] vigilante *m*; **'watch•strap** *Br* correa *f* de reloj; **'watch•tow•er** atalaya *f*; **'watch•word** consigna *f*
wa•ter ['wɒːtər] **I** *n* agua *f*; ***~s*** NAUT aguas *fpl* **II** *v/t plant* regar **III** *v/i*: ***my eyes are ~ing*** me lloran los ojos; ***my mouth is ~ing*** se me hace la boca agua
◆ **water down** *v/t drink* aguar, diluir
'wa•ter bed cama *f* de agua; **'wa•ter bird** ave *f* acuática; **'wa•ter bot•tle** *for drinking water* cantimplora *f*; **'wa•ter cannon** cañón *m* de agua; **'wa•ter•col•or**, *Br* **'wa•ter•col•our** acuarela *f*; **'wa•ter cool•er** dispensador *m* de agua; **'wa•ter•course** curso *m* de agua; **'wa•ter•cress** berro *m*
wa•tered-down [wɒːtərd'daʊn] *adj fig* dulcificado
'wa•ter•fall cascada *f*, catarata *f*; **'wa•ter•front**: ***a hotel on the ~*** un hotel en primera línea de mar; ***walk along the ~*** pasear por la orilla; **'wa•ter hole** abrevadero *m*; **'wa•ter ice** *Br* sorbete *m*
wa•ter•ing can ['wɒːtərɪŋ] regadera *f*; **'wa•ter•ing hole** *hum* bar *m*; **'wa•ter•ing pot** regadera *f*
'wa•ter jump SP foso *m* de agua; **'wa•ter lev•el** nivel *m* del agua; **'wa•ter lil•y** nenúfar *m*; **'wa•ter•line** línea *f* de flotación; **wa•ter•logged** ['wɒːtərlɑːgd] *adj earth, field* anegado; *boat* lleno de agua; **'wa•ter main** tubería *f* principal; **'wa•ter•mark** filigrana *f*; **'wa•ter•mel•on** sandía *f*; **'wa•ter me•ter** contador *m* del agua; **'wa•ter pipe 1** *for water supply* cañería *f* de agua **2** *for smoking* pipa *f* de agua; **'wa•ter pis•tol** pistola *f* de agua; **'wa•ter pol•lu•tion** contaminación *f* del agua; **'wa•ter po•lo** waterpolo *m*; **'wa•ter•proof** *adj* impermeable; **'wa•ter•shed** *fig* momento *m* clave; **'wa•ter short•age** escasez *f* de agua; **'wa•ter•side** orilla *f*; ***at the ~*** en la orilla; **'wa•ter-ski** *v/i* hacer esquí acuático; **'wa•ter-ski•ing** esquí *m* acuático; **'wa•ter sup•ply** suministro *m* de agua; **'wa•ter ta•ble** capa *f* freática; **'wa•ter•tight** *adj compartment* estanco; *fig* irrefutable; **'wa•ter•way** curso *m* de agua navegable; **'wa•ter wheel** noria *f*; **'wa•ter•wings** *npl* flotadores *mpl* (*para los brazos*); **'wa•ter•works** depuradora *f*; ***turn on the ~*** F ponerse a llorar como una magdalena F
wa•ter•y ['wɒːtərɪ] *adj* aguado
watt [wɑːt] vatio *m*
wave[1] [weɪv] *n in sea* ola *f*; ***don't make ~s!*** *fig* ¡no montes un cirio! F
wave[2] [weɪv] **I** *n* **1** *of hand* saludo *m* **2** *at sports etc event* ola *f* (mexicana) **II** *v/i with hand* saludar con la mano; ***~ to s.o.*** saludar con la mano a alguien **III** *v/t flag etc* agitar
'wave band RAD banda *f* de frecuencia
'wave•length RAD longitud *f* de onda; ***be on the same ~*** *fig* estar en la misma onda
wa•ver ['weɪvər] *v/i* vacilar, titubear
wav•y ['weɪvɪ] *adj hair, line* ondulado
wax[1] [wæks] **I** *n for floor, furniture* cera *f*, *in ear* cera *f*, cerumen *m*; *for legs* cera *f* depilatoria **II** *v/t legs* depilar (con cera)
wax[2] [wæks] *v/i* crecer; ***~ lyrical about sth*** hablar poéticamente de algo
'wax bean frijolillo *m*
waxed pa•per [wækst'peɪpər] papel *m* encerado
wax•en ['wæksən] *adj fig* céreo
'wax mu•se•um museo *m* de cera
'wax•work 1 *model* figura *f* de cera **2**: ***~s*** *sg o pl museum* museo *m* de cera

wax•y ['wæksɪ] *adj* céreo
way [weɪ] **I** *n* **1** (*method*) manera *f*, forma *f*; (*manner*) manera *f*, modo *m*; ***I don't like the ~ he behaves*** no me gusta cómo se comporta; ***it's just the ~ you said it*** es la manera en que lo dijiste; ***this ~*** (*like this*) así; ***in a ~*** (*in certain respects*) en cierto sentido; ***have one's (own) ~*** salirse con la suya; ***OK, we'll do it your ~*** de acuerdo, lo haremos a tu manera; ***OK, have it your ~*** de acuerdo, como tú digas *or* quieras **2** (*route*) camino *m*; ***can you tell me the ~ to …?*** ¿me podría decir cómo se va a …?; ***this ~*** (*in this direction*) por aquí; ***lead the ~*** abrir (el) camino; *fig* marcar la pauta; ***lose one's ~*** perderse; ***be in the ~*** (*be an obstruction*) estar en medio; ***it's on the ~ to the station*** está camino de la estación; ***I was on my ~ to the station*** iba camino de la estación; ***on my ~ to school I met …*** de camino al colegio me encontré con…; ***which ~ did you come?*** ¿por dónde viniste?; ***Easter's still a long ~ off*** todavía falta mucho para Semana Santa; ***it's a long ~ to Rochester*** Rochester queda muy lejos; ***I went the wrong ~*** tomé el camino equivocado;
3: ***by the ~*** (*incidentally*) por cierto, a propósito; ***by ~ of*** (*via*) por; (*in the form of*) a modo de; ***be under ~*** haber comenzado, estar en marcha; ***give ~*** *Br* MOT ceder el paso; (*collapse*) ceder; ***give ~ to*** (*be replaced by*) ser reemplazado por; ***no ~!*** ¡ni hablar!, ¡de ninguna manera!; ***there's no ~ he can do it*** es imposible que lo haga
II *adv* F (*much*): ***it's ~ too soon to decide*** es demasiado pronto como para decidir; ***they are ~ behind with their work*** van atrasadísimos en el trabajo
'way•bill COM conocimiento *m* de embarque; **way 'in** entrada *f*; **way'lay** *v/t* (*pret & pp* **-laid**) **1** *attack* asaltar **2** *fig* abordar; **way of 'life** modo *m* de vida; **way 'out** *also fig* salida *f*; **'way-out** *adj* P estrambótico F; **way•side**: ***fall by the ~*** ser abandonado
way•ward ['weɪwərd] *adj* rebelde
WC [dʌblju:'si:] *abbr Br* (= ***water closet***) váter *m*
we [wi:] *pron* nosotros *mpl*, nosotras *fpl*; ***~ are the best*** somos los mejores; ***they're going, but ~'re not*** ellos van, pero nosotros no
weak [wi:k] *adj* **1** débil; ***get or become ~*** debilitarse **2** *tea, coffee* poco cargado
weak•en ['wi:kn] **I** *v/t* debilitar **II** *v/i* debilitarse
weak-kneed [wi:k'ni:d] *adj* F gallina
weak•ling ['wi:klɪŋ] *morally* cobarde *m/f*; *physically* enclenque *m/f*
weak•ly ['wi:klɪ] *adv* débilmente
weak•ness ['wi:knɪs] debilidad *f*; ***have a ~ for sth*** (*liking*) sentir debilidad por algo
weal [wi:l] *mark* señal *f*
wealth [welθ] riqueza *f*; ***a ~ of*** abundancia de
wealth•y ['welθɪ] *adj* rico
wean [wi:n] *v/t* destetar; ***~ s.o. off sth*** desenganchar a alguien de algo
weap•on ['wepən] arma *f*
weap•on•ry ['wepənrɪ] armamento *m*
weap•on•ry ['wepənrɪ] armamento *m*
'weap•ons of mass de•struc•tion *npl* armas *fpl* de destrucción masiva
wear [wer] **I** *n* **1**: ***~ (and tear)*** desgaste *m* **2**: ***clothes for everyday / evening ~*** ropa *f* de diario / de noche **II** *v/t* (*pret* **wore**, *pp* **worn**) **1** (*have on*) llevar **2** (*damage*) desgastar **III** *v/i* (*pret* **wore**, *pp* **worn**) **1** (*~ out*) desgastarse **2** (*last*) durar
◆ **wear away I** *v/i* desgastarse **II** *v/t* desgastar
◆ **wear down** *v/t* agotar
◆ **wear off** *v/i of effect, feeling* pasar
◆ **wear on** *v/i of time* pasar
◆ **wear out I** *v/t* **1** (*tire*) agotar **2** *shoes* desgastar **II** *v/i of shoes, carpet* desgastarse
wea•ri•ly ['wɪrɪlɪ] *adv* cansinamente
wear•ing ['werɪŋ] *adj* (*tiring*) agotador
wea•ri•some ['wɪrɪsəm] *adj* (*tiring*) fatigoso; (*boring*) aburrido; (*annoying*) pesado
wear•y ['wɪrɪ] **I** *adj* cansado; ***get or become ~*** cansarse **II** *v/t* cansar **III** *v/i*: ***~ of (doing) sth*** cansarse de (hacer) algo
wea•sel ['wi:zl] **1** ZO comadreja *f* **2** *fig* raposo(-a) *m(f)*
◆ **weasel out of** *v/t* F *task* escaquearse de
weath•er ['weðər] **I** *n* tiempo *m*; ***what's the ~ like?*** ¿qué tiempo hace?; ***not in this ~!*** ¡no con este tiempo!; ***be feeling***

under the ~ estar pachucho **II** *v/t crisis* capear, superar
'weath•er-beat•en *adj* curtido; **'weath•er chart** mapa *m* del tiempo; **'weath•er-bound** *adj*: ***the planes / ships were ~*** los aviones / barcos no pudieron salir por culpa del mal tiempo; **'weath•er cock** veleta *f* (*en forma de gallo*); **'weath•er eye**: ***keep a ~ open for sth*** estar atento a algo; **'weath•er fore•cast** pronóstico *m* del tiempo; **'weath•er•man** hombre *m* del tiempo; **'weath•er map** mapa *m* del tiempo; **'weath•er•proof I** *adj* impermeable **II** *v/t* impermeabilizar; **'weath•er sat•el•lite** satélite *m* meteorológico; **'weath•er sta•tion** estación *f* meteorológica; **'weath•er vane** veleta *f*
weave [wiːv] **I** *v/t* (*pret* ***wove***, *pp* ***woven***) tejer **II** *v/i* (*pret* ***wove***, *pp* ***woven***) *move* zigzaguear
weav•er ['wiːvər] tejedor(a) *m*(*f*)
web [web] **1** *of spider* tela *f* **2**: ***the Web*** COMPUT la Web
webbed 'feet [webd] *npl* patas *fpl* palmeadas
'web•mas•ter webmaster *m/f*; **'web page** página *f* web; **'web site** sitio *m* web
wed [wed] *v/t* (*pret* & *pp* ***wed*** *or* ***wedded***) casarse con; ***they were ~ in 1921*** se casaron en 1921; ***be ~ded to an idea / a principle*** estar aferrado a una idea / un principio
we'd [wiːd] F ☞ ***we had***; ***we would***
wed•ding ['wedɪŋ] boda *f*
'wed•ding an•ni•ver•sa•ry aniversario *m* de boda; **'wed•ding cake** pastel *m or* tarta *f* de boda; **'wed•ding day** día *m* de la boda; **'wed•ding dress** vestido *m* de boda *or* novia; **'wed•ding ring** anillo *m* de boda
wedge [wedʒ] **I** *n* **1** *to hold sth in place* cuña *f* **2** *of cheese etc* trozo *m* **II** *v/t*: ***~ a door open*** calzar una puerta para que se quede abierta
wed•lock ['wedlɑːk] matrimonio *m*; ***be born out of ~*** nacer fuera del matrimonio
Wed•nes•day ['wenzdeɪ] miércoles *m inv*
wee[1] [wiː] *adj* F pequeñín; ***a ~ bit*** un poquito; ***the ~ (small) hours*** la madrugada
wee[2] [wiː] F **I** *v/i* hacer pipí F **II** *n*: ***do or have a ~*** hacer pipí F
weed [wiːd] **I** *n* mala hierba **II** *v/t* escardar
◆ **weed out** *v/t* (*remove*) eliminar; *candidates* descartar
'weed-kill•er herbicida *m*
weed•y ['wiːdɪ] *adj* F esmirriado, enclenque
week [wiːk] semana *f*; ***a ~ Tuesday*** del martes en ocho
'week•day día *m* de la semana; **week'end** fin *m* de semana; ***on the ~*** el fin de semana; **'week•long** *adj* que dura una semana; **week•ly** ['wiːklɪ] **I** *adj* semanal **II** *n magazine* semanario *m* **III** *adv* semanalmente
'week•night noche *f* de entre semana
wee•ny ['wiːnɪ] *adj* F pequeñín F
weep [wiːp] *v/i* (*pret* & *pp* ***wept***) llorar
'weep•ing wil•low sauce *m* llorón
weep•y ['wiːpɪ] *adj*: ***be ~*** estar lloroso
wee•vil ['wiːvl] gorgojo *m*
'wee-wee F **I** *n* pipí *m* F; ***do a ~*** hacer pipí F **II** *v/i* hacer pipí F
weft [weft] trama *f*
weigh[1] [weɪ] **I** *v/t* pesar **II** *v/i* pesar; ***how much do you ~?*** ¿cuánto pesas?
◆ **weigh down** *v/t* cargar; ***be weighed down with*** *bags* ir cargado con; *worries* estar abrumado por
◆ **weigh in** *v/i* **1** *of jockey, boxer* pesarse **2** *at airport* facturar el equipaje
◆ **weigh on** *v/t* preocupar
◆ **weigh up** *v/t* (*assess*) sopesar
weigh[2] [weɪ] *v/t*: ***~ anchor*** levar anclas
weight [weɪt] **I** *n* peso *m*; ***put on ~*** engordar, ganar peso; ***lose ~*** adelgazar, perder peso **II** *v/t figures etc* ponderar; ***~ed average*** media *f* ponderada
◆ **weight down** *v/t* sujetar (*con pesos*)
'weight cat•e•go•ry, 'weight di•vi•sion SP peso *m*
'weight•less ['weɪtləs] *adj* ingrávido
'weight•less•ness ['weɪtləsnəs] ingravidez *f*
'weight•lift•er levantador(a) *m*(*f*) de pesas; **'weight•lift•ing** halterofilia *f*, levantamiento *m* de pesas; **'weight train•ing** levantamiento *m* de pesas
weight•y ['weɪtɪ] *adj fig* (*important*) serio
weir [wɪr] presa *f* (*rebasadero*)
weird [wɪrd] *adj* extraño, raro

weird•ly ['wɪrdlɪ] *adv* extrañamente
weird•o ['wɪrdoʊ] F bicho *m* raro F
wel•come ['welkəm] **I** *adj* bienvenido; ***you're ~!*** ¡de nada!; ***you're ~ to try some*** prueba algunos, por favor **II** *n* bienvenida *f* **III** *v/t guests etc* dar la bienvenida a; *fig*: *decision etc* acoger positivamente
weld [weld] *v/t* soldar
weld•er ['weldər] soldador(a) *m(f)*
wel•fare ['welfer] **1** bienestar *m* **2** *financial assistance* subsidio *m* estatal; ***be on ~*** estar recibiendo subsidios del Estado
'wel•fare check *cheque con el importe del subsidio estatal*; **wel•fare 'state** estado *m* del bienestar; **'wel•fare work** trabajo *m* social; **'wel•fare work•er** asistente *m/f* social
we'll [wi:l] ☞ ***we will***
well[1] [wel] *n for water, oil* pozo *m*
well[2] **I** *adv* bien; ***as ~*** (*too*) también; ***as ~ as*** (*in addition to*) así como; ***it's just as ~ you told me*** menos mal que me lo dijiste; ***how ~ is she doing in English?*** ¿qué tal le va en inglés?; ***very ~*** muy bien; ***I couldn't very ~ change my mind*** me era imposible cambiar de opinión; ***it's all very ~ for you to laugh but …*** te puedes reír todo lo que quieras pero …; ***~, ~!*** *surprise* ¡caramba!; ***~ …*** *uncertainty, thinking* bueno …; ***you might as ~ spend the night here*** ya puestos quédate a pasar la noche aquí; ***you might as ~ throw it out*** yo de ti lo tiraría
II *adj*: ***be ~*** estar bien; ***how are you? – I'm very ~*** ¿cómo estás? – muy bien; ***feel ~*** sentirse bien; ***get ~ soon!*** ¡ponte bueno!, ¡que te mejores!
well-ad'vised *adj* sensato; **well-ap'point•ed** *adj* bien acondicionado; **well-'bal•anced** *adj person, diet* equilibrado; **well-be'haved** *adj* educado; **well-'be•ing** bienestar *m*; **well-'born** *adj* de buena familia; **well-'built** *adj also euph* fornido; **well-dis'posed** *adj*: ***be ~ toward s.o.*** tener buena disposición hacia alguien; **well-'done** *adj meat* muy hecho; **well-'dressed** *adj* bien vestido; **well-'earned** *adj* merecido; **well-'found•ed** *adj* fundado; **well-'groomed** *adj* arreglado; **well-'heeled** *adj* F adinerado, *Span* con pasta F; **well-in'formed** *adj* bien informado; **well-in'ten•tioned** bienintencionado; **well-'kept** *adj* **1** *garden, building* cuidado **2** *secret* bien guardado; **well-'known** *adj fact* conocido; *person* conocido, famoso; **well-'made** *adj* bien hecho; **well-'man•nered** *adj* educado; **well-'mean•ing** *adj* bienintencionado; **well-'meant** *adj* bienintencionado; **well-nigh** ['welnaɪ] *adv* casi; ***~ impossible*** prácticamente imposible; **well-'off** *adj* acomodado; **well-'paid** *adj* bien pagado; **well-pro'por•tioned** *adj* proporcionado; **well-'read** *adj*: ***be ~*** haber leído mucho; **well-'thought-of** *adj* prestigioso; ***be ~*** tener prestigio; **well-'timed** *adj* oportuno; **well-to-'do** *adj* acomodado; **well-'versed** *adj*: ***be ~ in sth*** estar versado en algo; **'well-wish•er** admirador(a) *m(f)*; **well-'worn** *adj* gastado
Welsh [welʃ] **I** *adj* galés **II** *n* **1** *language* galés **2** *npl*: ***the ~*** los galeses
◆ **welsh on** *v/t* F **1** *debt* no pagar **2** (*betray*) traicionar
Welsh•man ['welʃmən] galés *m*
'Welsh•wom•an galesa *f*
welt [welt] señal *f*
wel•ter•weight ['weltərweɪt] SP peso *m* welter
went [went] *pret* ☞ ***go***
wept [wept] *pret & pp* ☞ ***weep***
were [wer] *pret* ☞ ***be***
we're [wɪr] ☞ ***we are***
weren't [wɜ:rnt] ☞ ***were not***
were•wolf ['werwʊlf] hombre *m* lobo
west [west] **I** *n* oeste *m*; ***the West*** (*Western nations*) el Occidente *m*; (*western part of a country*) el oeste **II** *adj* del oeste; ***West Africa*** África occidental **III** *adv travel* hacia el oeste; ***~ of*** al oeste de
'west•bound *adj* en dirección oeste
West 'Coast *of USA* Costa *f* Oeste
west•er•ly ['westərlɪ] *adj wind* del oeste; *direction* hacia el oeste
west•ern ['westərn] **I** *adj* occidental; ***Western*** occidental **II** *n movie* western *m*, película *f* del oeste
West•ern•er ['westərnər] occidental *m/f*
west•ern•ized ['westərnaɪzd] *adj* occidentalizado
'west•ern•most *adj* más occidental
West 'In•di•an I *adj* antillano **II** *n* antillano(-a) *m(f)*
West In•dies ['ɪndi:z] *npl*: ***the ~*** las

W

Antillas
west•ward ['westwərd] *adv* hacia el oeste
wet [wet] *adj* mojado; (*damp*) húmedo; (*rainy*) lluvioso; ***get** or **become** ~* mojarse; ***~ paint** as sign* recién pintado; ***be ~ through*** estar empapado
'wet•back mojado(-a) *m(f) Mex*
'wet•back la•bor mano *f* de obra espaldamojada
wet 'blan•ket F aguafiestas *m/f inv*
'wet suit *for diving* traje *m* de neopreno
we've [wiːv] ☞ ***we have***
whack [wæk] F **I** *n* **1** (*blow*) porrazo *m* F **2** (*share*) parte *f* **II** *v/t* dar un porrazo a F
whacked [wækt] *adj* F hecho polvo F
whack•ing ['wækɪŋ] F *adj & adv*: ***a ~ (great) hole*** un agujero enorme F
whack•y ['wækɪ] *adj* F estrambótico
whale [weɪl] **1** ballena *f* **2**: ***have a ~ of a time*** F pasarlo bomba
whal•er ['weɪlər] *boat* ballenero *m*
whal•ing ['weɪlɪŋ] caza *f* de ballenas
wharf [wɔːrf] (*pl* **wharves** [wɔːrvz]) embarcadero *m*
what [wɑːt] **I** *pron* qué; ***~ is that?*** ¿qué es eso?; ***~ is it?*** (*what do you want*) ¿qué quieres?; ***~?*** (*what do you want*) ¿qué?; (*what did you say*) ¿qué?, ¿cómo?; *astonishment* ¿qué?; ***~ about some dinner?*** ¿os apetece cenar?; ***~ about heading home?*** ¿y si nos fuéramos a casa?; ***~ for?*** (*why*) ¿para qué?; ***so ~?*** ¿y qué?; ***~ is the book about?*** ¿de qué trata el libro?; ***~ gave you that idea?*** ¿ se puede saber qué te ha dado esa idea?; ***take ~ you need*** toma lo que te haga falta
II *adj* qué; ***~ university are you at?*** ¿en qué universidad estás?; ***~ color is the car?*** ¿de qué color es el coche?; ***~ a house!*** ¡vaya casa!; ***~ a big ...!*** ¡qué ... tan grande!
what•ev•er [wɑːt'evər] **I** *pron*: ***I'll do ~ you want*** haré lo que quieras; ***~ gave you that idea?*** ¿se puede saber qué te ha dado esa idea?; ***~ the season*** en cualquier estación; ***~ people say*** diga lo que diga la gente **II** *adj* cualquier; ***you have no reason ~ to worry*** no tienes por qué preocuparte en absoluto
whats•it ['wɑːtsɪt] F chisme *m*
what•so•ev•er [wɑːtsoʊ'evər] ☞ ***whatever II***
wheat [wiːt] trigo *m*
'wheat germ germen *m* de trigo
whee•dle ['wiːdl] *v/t*: ***~ sth out of s.o.*** camelar algo a alguien
wheel [wiːl] **I** *n* rueda *f*; (*steering ~*) volante *m* **II** *v/t bicycle* empujar **III** *v/i of birds* volar en círculo
◆ **wheel around** *v/i* darse la vuelta
'wheel•bar•row carretilla *f*; **'wheel-base** MOT empate *m*; **'wheel brace** MOT llave *f* de cruz; **'wheel•chair** silla *f* de ruedas; **'wheel clamp** cepo *m*
wheeled [wiːld] *adj*: ***two / four-~*** de dos / cuatro ruedas
wheel•er-deal•er [wiːlər'diːler] F chanchullero(-a) *m(f)* F
wheel•ie ['wiːlɪ] F: ***do a ~*** hacer un caballito F
wheel•ing and deal•ing [wiːlɪŋən-'diːlɪŋ] F chanchullos *mpl* F
wheeze [wiːz] **I** *n sound* resoplido *m* **II** *v/i* resoplar
whelk [welk] buccino *m*
when [wen] **I** *adv* cuándo; ***~ do you open?*** ¿a qué hora abren?; ***say ~*** ya dirás basta *or* cuándo **II** *conj* cuando; ***~ I was a child*** cuando era niño
whence [wens] *adv* de dónde
when•ev•er [wen'evər] *adv* (*each time*) cada vez que; ***call me ~ you like*** llámame cuando quieras; ***I go to Paris ~ I can afford it*** voy a París siempre que me lo puedo permitir
where [wer] **I** *adv* dónde; ***~ from?*** ¿de dónde?; ***~ to?*** ¿a dónde? **II** *conj* donde; ***this is ~ I used to live*** aquí es donde vivía antes
where•a•bouts [werə'baʊts] **I** *adv* dónde **II** *npl*: ***nothing is known of his ~*** está en paradero desconocido
where'as *conj* mientras que
where'by *adv* a través del cual
where•up'on *conj* tras lo cual
wher•ev•er [wer'evər] **I** *conj* dondequiera que; ***sit ~ you like*** siéntate donde prefieras **II** *adv* dónde
where•with•al ['werwɪðɔːl] medios *mpl*
whet [wet] *v/t* (*pret & pp* **-ted**) *appetite* abrir
wheth•er ['weðər] *conj* si; ***I don't know ~ to tell him or not*** no sé si decírselo o no; ***~ you approve or not*** te parezca bien o no
whey [weɪ] suero *m*

which [wɪʧ] **I** *adj* qué; **~ *one is yours?*** ¿cuál es tuyo? **II** *pron* **1** *interrogative* cuál; ***take one, it doesn't matter ~*** toma uno, no importa cuál **2** *relative* que; ***an idea ~ is ...*** una idea que está ...
which•ev•er [wɪʧ'evər] **I** *adj*: **~ *color you choose*** elijas el color que elijas **II** *pron*: **~ *you like*** el que quieras; ***use ~ of the methods you prefer*** utiliza el método que prefieras
whiff [wɪf] (*smell*) olorcillo *m*
while [waɪl] **I** *conj* **1** mientras **2** (*although*) si bien **II** *n* rato *m*; ***a long ~*** un rato largo; ***for a ~*** durante un tiempo; ***I lived in Tokyo for a ~*** viví en Tokio una temporada; ***I'll wait a ~ longer*** esperaré un rato más
◆ **while away** *v/t* pasar
whilst [waɪlst] ☞ ***while* I 1**
whim [wɪm] capricho *m*; ***do sth on a ~*** hacer algo por capricho
whim•per ['wɪmpər] **I** *n* gimoteo *m* **II** *v/i* gimotear
whim•si•cal ['wɪmzɪkl] *adj* curioso
whim•sy ['wɪmzɪ] capricho *m*
whine [waɪn] *v/i* **1** *of dog* gimotear **2** F (*complain*) quejarse
whin•er ['waɪnər] quejica *m/f*
whinge [wɪndʒ] *v/i Br* F quejarse (***about*** de)
whin•ny ['wɪnɪ] **I** *v/i* relinchar **II** *n* relincho *m*
whip [wɪp] **I** *n* látigo *m* **II** *v/t* (*pret & pp* ***-ped***) **1** (*beat*) azotar; *cream* batir, montar **2** F (*defeat*) dar una paliza a F
◆ **whip away** *v/t* retirar rápidamente
◆ **whip up** *v/t* (*arouse*) agitar
'whip•cord cuerda *f* de látigo
'whip•lash MED esguince *m* cervical
'whipped cream [wɪpt] nata *f* montada
whip•pet ['wɪpɪt] lebrel *m*
whip•ping ['wɪpɪŋ] **1** (*beating*) azotes *mpl* **2** F (*defeat*) paliza *f* F
'whip•ping boy cabeza *m/f* de turco
'whip•ping cream nata *f* para montar
'whip•round F colecta *f*; ***have a ~*** hacer una colecta
whir [wɜːr] *v/i* (*pret & pp* ***-red***) zumbar
whirl [wɜːrl] **I** *n*: ***my mind is in a ~*** me da vueltas la cabeza **II** *v/i* dar vueltas
'whirl•pool 1 *in river* remolino *m* **2** *for relaxation* bañera *f* de hidromasaje
'whirl•wind I *n* torbellino *m* **II** *adj*: ***a ~ romance*** un romance arrasador

whirr *Br* ☞ ***whir***
whisk [wɪsk] **I** *n kitchen implement* batidora *f* **II** *v/t eggs* batir
◆ **whisk away** *v/t* retirar rápidamente; ***he was whisked away to the airport*** se lo llevaron rápidamente al aeropuerto
whis•kers ['wɪskərz] *npl of man* patillas *fpl*; *of animal* bigotes *mpl*
whis•key ['wɪskɪ] whisky *m*
whis•per ['wɪspər] **I** *n* **1** susurro *m*; ***say sth in a ~*** susurrar algo, decir algo en voz baja **2** (*rumor*) rumor *m* **II** *v/t & v/i* susurrar
whis•per•ing cam•paign ['wɪspərɪŋ] campaña *f* de difamación
whist [wɪst] whist *m*
whis•tle ['wɪsl] **I** *n sound* silbido *m*; SP pitido *m*; *device* silbato *m*, pito *m* **II** *v/t & v/i* silbar
whis•tle-blow•er ['wɪslblouər] denunciante *m/f*
whis•tle-stop 'tour gira *f* relámpago
white [waɪt] **I** *n* **1** *color* blanco *m* **2** *of egg* clara *f* **3** *person* blanco(-a) *m(f)* **II** *adj* blanco; ***her face went ~*** se puso blanca
'white•bait pescadito *m*; **'white•board** pizarra *f* blanca; **white 'Christ•mas** Navidades *fpl* blancas; **white 'cof•fee** *Br* café *m* con leche; **white-col•lar 'crime** delito *m* de guante blanco; **white-col•lar 'work•er** *persona que trabaja en una oficina*; **white 'el•e•phant** mamotreto *m*; **'white flag** bandera *f* blanca; **'white•goods** *npl* electrodomésticos *mpl*; **white-'hot** *adj* candente; **'White House** Casa *f* Blanca; **white 'knight** COM caballero *m* blanco; **white 'lie** mentira *f* piadosa; **white 'meat** carne *f* blanca
whit•en ['waɪtn] *v/t* blanquear
'white•out *for text* Tipp-Ex® *m*; **white 'sauce** besamel *f*; **white 'spir•it** *Br* aguarrás *m inv*; **white su•prem•a•cist** [waɪtsuː'preməsɪst] defensor(a) *m(f)* de la supremacía blanca; **white 'trash** F chusma *f* blanca; **'white•wash I** *n* cal *f*; *fig* encubrimiento *m* **II** *v/t* encalar; **white-wa•ter ca•noe•ing** [waɪtwɑːtərkə'nuːɪŋ] descenso *m* de aguas bravas en canoa; **white-wa•ter raft•ing** [waɪtwɑːtə'ræftɪŋ] descenso *m* de aguas bravas en bote; **white 'wed•ding** boda *f* de blanco; **white 'wine** vino *m* blanco
whi•ther ['wɪðər] *adv* adónde

whit•ing ['waɪtɪŋ] pescadilla *f*
whit•ish ['waɪtɪʃ] *adj* blanquecino
Whit•sun ['wɪtsn], **Whit Sun•day** [wɪt'sʌndeɪ] Pentecostés *m*
whit•tle ['wɪtl] *v/t wood* tallar
◆ **whittle down** *v/t* reducir
whiz(z) [wɪz]: ***be a ~ at*** F ser un genio de
◆ **whizz past** *v/i of car* pasar zumbando
'whizz•kid F prodigio *m/f*; ***a computer ~*** un prodigio *or* as en computadoras
who [huː] *pron* **1** *interrogative* ¿quién?; ***~ do you want to speak to?*** ¿con quién quieres hablar?; ***I don't know ~ to believe*** no sé a quién creer **2** *relative* que; ***an artist ~ tries to ...*** un artista que intenta ...
who'd [huːd] ☞ ***who had***; ***who would***
who•dun•(n)it [huː'dʌnɪt] *libro o película centrados en la resolución de un caso*
who•ev•er [huː'evər] *pron* quienquiera; ***~ can that be calling at this time of night?*** ¿pero quién llama a estas horas de la noche?
whole [hoʊl] **I** *adj* entero; ***the ~ town / country*** toda la ciudad / todo el país; ***it's a ~ lot easier / better*** es mucho más fácil / mucho mejor **II** *n* totalidad *f*; ***the ~ of the USA*** la totalidad de los Estados Unidos; ***on the ~*** en general
'whole•food alimentos *mpl* integrales; **whole-heart•ed** [hoʊl'hɑːrtɪd] *adj* incondicional; **whole-heart•ed•ly** [hoʊl-'hɑːrtɪdlɪ] *adv* incondicionalmente; **whole•meal 'bread** *Br* pan *m* integral; **'whole note** MUS semibreve *f*; **'whole-sale I** *adj* **1** al por mayor; ***~ price*** precio *m* al por mayor **2** *fig* indiscriminado **II** *adv* al por mayor; **whole•sal•er** ['hoʊlseɪlər] mayorista *m/f*; **whole•some** ['hoʊlsəm] *adj* saludable, sano; **'whole-wheat** *adj* integral
who'll [huːl] ☞ ***who will***
whol•ly ['hoʊlɪ] *adv* completamente
whol•ly owned sub'sid•i•ar•y subsidiaria *f* en propiedad absoluta
whom [huːm] *pron fml* quién; ***~ did you see?*** ¿a quién vio?; ***the person to ~ I was speaking*** la persona con la que estaba hablando
whoop [wuːp] **I** *n* grito *m* **II** *v/i* gritar
whoop•ing cough ['huːpɪŋ] tos *f* ferina
whoops [wʊps] *int* huy
whoosh [wʊʃ] **I** *n* zumbido *m* **II** *v/i* pasar zumbando
whop•per ['wɑːpər] F **1** *something big*: ***I caught a real ~ the other day*** el otro día pesqué una pieza de campeonato; ***the neighbors' cat is a real ~*** el gato de los vecinos es una pasada de grande **2** *lie* trola *f*
whop•ping ['wɑːpɪŋ] *adj* F enorme
whore [hɔːr] prostituta *f*
'whore•house prostíbulo *m*
whorl [wɜːrl] espiral *f*
who's [huːz] ☞ ***who is***; ***who has***
whose [huːz] **I** *pron* **1** *interrogative* de quién; ***~ is this?*** ¿de quién es esto? **2** *relative* cuyo(-a); ***a country ~ economy is booming*** un país cuya economía está experimentando un boom **II** *adj* de quién; ***~ bike is that?*** ¿de quién es esa bici?
whup [wʌp] *v/t* (*pret & pp* ***-ped***) F dar un repaso a F
why [waɪ] *adv* por qué; ***that's ~*** por eso; ***~ not?*** ¿por qué no?
wick [wɪk] pabilo *m*
wick•ed ['wɪkɪd] *adj* **1** malvado, perverso **2** P (*brilliant*) dabuten P, *L.Am.* chévere F
wick•er ['wɪkər] *adj* de mimbre
wick•er 'bas•ket cesta *f* de mimbre; **wick•er 'chair** silla *f* de mimbre; **'wick•er•work** cestería *f*
wick•et ['wɪkɪt] **1** *in station, bank etc* ventanilla *f* **2** *Br* SP palos *mpl*
wide [waɪd] *adj* ancho; *experience, range* amplio; ***be 12 feet ~*** tener 12 pies de ancho
wide-an•gle 'lens PHOT gran angular *m*; **wide a'wake** *adj* completamente despierto; **wide-eyed** [waɪd'aɪd] *adj* **1** con los ojos abiertos de par en par **2** *fig* ingenuo
wide•ly ['waɪdlɪ] *adv used, known* ampliamente; ***~ read*** muy leído
wid•en ['waɪdn] **I** *v/t* ensanchar **II** *v/i* ensancharse
wide-'o•pen *adj* abierto de par en par; **wide-'rang•ing** *adj* amplio; **'wide screen** pantalla *f* panorámica; **'wide-spread** *adj* extendido, muy difundido
wid•ow ['wɪdoʊ] **I** *n* viuda *f* **II** *v/t*: ***be ~ed by sth*** quedarse viudo como resultado de algo
wid•ow•er ['wɪdoʊər] viudo *m*

width [wɪdθ] anchura *f*, ancho *m*
wield [wi:ld] *v/t weapon* empuñar; *power* detentar
wife [waɪf] (*pl* ***wives*** [waɪvz]) mujer *f*, esposa *f*
wig [wɪg] peluca *f*
wig•gle ['wɪgl] *v/t* menear
wig•wam ['wɪgwæm] tipi *m*
wild [waɪld] **I** *adj animal* salvaje; *flower* silvestre; *teenager, party* descontrolado; (*crazy: scheme*) descabellado; *applause* arrebatado; ***be ~ about sth*** (*enthusiastic*) estar loco por algo; ***go ~*** (*express enthusiasm*) volverse loco; (*become angry*) ponerse hecho una furia; ***run ~*** *of children* desahogarse **II** *npl*: ***the ~s*** los parajes remotos
wild 'boar jabalí *m*; **'wild card** comodín *m*; COMPUT wildcard *m*, comodín *m*; **'wild•cat I** *n* gato *m* montés **II** *adj*: ***~ strike*** huelga *f* salvaje
wil•de•beest ['wɪldəbi:st] ñu *m*
wil•der•ness ['wɪldərnɪs] desierto *m*, yermo *m*
'wild•fire: ***spread like ~*** extenderse como un reguero de pólvora; **wild-'goose chase** búsqueda *f* infructuosa; **'wild-life** flora *f* y fauna; ***~ program*** TV documental *f* sobre la naturaleza
wild•ly ['waɪldlɪ] *adv applaud* enfervorizadamente; ***I'm not ~ enthusiastic about the idea*** la idea no me emociona demasiado
'wild pitch *in baseball* lanzamiento *m* malo
wil•ful *Br* ☞ ***willful***
will[1] [wɪl] *n* LAW testamento *m*; ***write*** *or* ***make one's ~*** escribir *or* hacer el testamento
will[2] [wɪl] *n* (*willpower*) voluntad *f*; ***the ~ to win*** la voluntad para ganar; ***where there's a ~ there's a way*** querer es poder
will[3] [wɪl] *v/aux*: ***I ~ let you know tomorrow*** te lo diré mañana; ***~ you be there?*** ¿estarás allí?; ***I won't be back until late*** volveré tarde; ***you ~ call me, won't you?*** me llamarás, ¿verdad?; ***I'll pay for this – no you won't*** esto lo pago yo – no, ni hablar; ***the car won't start*** el coche no arranca; ***~ you tell her that …?*** ¿le quieres decir que …?; ***~ you have some more tea?*** ¿quiere más té?; ***~ you stop that!*** ¡basta ya!
will•ful ['wɪlfəl] *adj person* tozudo, obstinado; *action* deliberado, intencionado
wil•lies ['wɪlɪz] *npl*: ***give s.o. the ~*** F dar canguelo a alguien F
will•ing ['wɪlɪŋ] *adj* dispuesto; ***be ~ to do sth*** estar dispuesto a hacer algo
will•ing•ly ['wɪlɪŋlɪ] *adv* gustosamente
will•ing•ness ['wɪlɪŋnɪs] buena disposición *f*
wil•low ['wɪlou] BOT sauce *m*
wil•low•y ['wɪlouɪ] *adj* esbelto
'will•pow•er fuerza *f* de voluntad
wil•ly-nil•ly [wɪlɪ'nɪlɪ] *adv* (*at random*) a la buena de Dios
wilt [wɪlt] *v/i of plant* marchitarse
wi•ly ['waɪlɪ] *adj* astuto
wimp [wɪmp] F enclenque *m/f* F, blandengue *m/f* F
wimp•ish ['wɪmpɪʃ] *adj* F blandengue F
win [wɪn] **I** *n* victoria *f*, triunfo *m* **II** *v/t & v/i* (*pret & pp* ***won***) ganar
◆ **win back** *v/t* recuperar
wince [wɪns] *v/i* hacer una mueca de dolor
winch [wɪntʃ] **I** *n* torno *m*, cabestrante *m* **II** *v/t* elevar con cabestrante
wind[1] [wɪnd] **I** *n* viento *m*; (*flatulence*) gases *mpl*; ***get ~ of sth*** enterarse de algo **II** *v/t*: ***be ~ed*** quedarse sin respiración; ***he was ~ed by the ball*** se quedó sin aliento *or* respiración cuando le golpeó la pelota
wind[2] [waɪnd] **I** *v/i* (*pret & pp* ***wound***) zigzaguear, serpentear; ***~ around*** enrollarse en **II** *v/t* (*pret & pp* ***wound***) enrollar
◆ **wind down I** *v/i of party etc* ir finalizando **II** *v/t* **1** *car window* bajar, abrir **2** *business* ir reduciendo
◆ **wind up I** *v/t* **1** *clock* dar cuerda a **2** *car window* subir, cerrar **3** *speech, presentation* finalizar; *business, affairs* concluir; *company* cerrar **4** *Br* F: *tease* tomar el pelo a **II** *v/i* (*finish*) concluir; ***wind up in hospital*** acabar en el hospital; ***I wound up agreeing with him*** terminé *or* acabé dándole la razón
'wind-bag F cotorra *f* F; **'wind•break** parapeto *m* (*contra el viento*); **'wind-fall** *fig* dinero *m* inesperado; **'wind farm** parque *m* de energía eólica
wind•ing ['waɪndɪŋ] *adj* zigzagueante, serpenteante

'wind in•stru•ment instrumento *m* de viento
wind•lass ['wɪndləs] TECH torno *m*
wind•less ['wɪndlɪs] *adj* sin viento
'wind•mill molino *m* de viento
win•dow ['wɪndoʊ] *also* COMPUT ventana *f*; *of car* ventana *f*, ventanilla *f*; ***in the ~*** *of store* en el escaparate *or L.Am.* la vidriera
'win•dow box jardinera *f*; **'win•dow clean•er** *person* limpiacristales *m/f inv*; **'win•dow dress•ing 1** escaparatismo *m* **2** *fig* cortina *f* de humo; **'win•dow en•ve•lope** sobre *m* con ventana; **'win•dow•pane** cristal *f* (*de una ventana*); **'win•dow seat** *on plane*, *train* asiento *m* de ventana; **'win•dow shade** persiana *f*; **'win•dow-shop** *v/i* (*pret & pp* ***-ped***): ***go ~ping*** ir de escaparates *or L.Am.* vidrieras; **'win•dow•sill** alféizar *m*
'wind•pipe tráquea *f*; **'wind pow•er** energía *f* eólica; **'wind pump** bomba *f* eólica; **'wind•screen** *Br*, **'wind•shield** parabrisas *m inv*; **'wind•shield wip•er** limpiaparabrisas *m inv*; **'wind•sock** manga *f* catavientos; **'wind•surf•er** *person* windsurfista *m/f*; *board* tabla *f* de windsurf; **'wind•surf•ing** el windsurf; **wind-swept** ['wɪndswept] *adj* golpeado por el viento; **'wind tun•nel** túnel *m* de viento; **'wind tur•bine** turbina *f* eólica
wind•up ['waɪndʌp] *Br* tomadura *f* de pelo
wind•ward ['wɪndwərd] NAUT *adv* hacia barlovento
wind•y ['wɪndɪ] *adj* ventoso; ***a ~ day*** un día de mucho viento; ***it's very ~ today*** hoy hace mucho viento; ***it's getting ~*** está empezando a soplar el viento
wine [waɪn] **I** *n* vino *m* **II** *v/t*: ***~ and dine s.o.*** agasajar a alguien
'wine bar *Br bar especializado en vinos*; **'wine bot•tle** botella *f* de vino; **'wine cel•lar** bodega *f*; **'wine glass** copa *f* de vino; **'wine list** lista *f* de vinos; **'wine mak•er** viticultor(a) *m(f)*; **'wine mer•chant** comerciante *m/f* de vinos
win•er•y ['waɪnərɪ] bodega *f* vinícola
wing [wɪŋ] **1** ala *f* **2** SP *position* ala *f*; *player* extremo *m/f*
wing•er ['wɪŋər] SP extremo *m/f*
'wing mir•ror retrovisor *m* lateral *or* exterior; **'wing nut** TECH palomilla *f*; **'wing•span** envergadura *f*
wink [wɪŋk] **I** *n* guiño *m*; ***I didn't sleep a ~*** F no pegué ojo **II** *v/i of person* guiñar, hacer un guiño; ***~ at s.o.*** guiñar *or* hacer un guiño a alguien
win•kle ['wɪŋkl] bígaro *m*
◆ **winkle out** *v/t*: ***winkle sth out of s.o.*** sonsacar algo a alguien
win•ner ['wɪnər] ganador(a) *m(f)*, vencedor(a) *m(f)*; *of lottery* acertante *m/f*
win•ning ['wɪnɪŋ] *adj* ganador
'win•ning post meta *f*
win•nings ['wɪnɪŋz] *npl* ganancias *fpl*
◆ **win•now out** ['wɪnoʊ] *v/t weaker teams etc* apartar
win•o ['waɪnoʊ] F borrachín(-ina) *m(f)* F
win•ter ['wɪntər] **I** *n* invierno *m* **II** *v/i* pasar el invierno
win•ter•ize ['wɪntəraɪz] *v/t* MOT preparar para el invierno
win•ter sports [wɪntər'spɔːrts] *npl* deportes *mpl* de invierno
'win•ter•time invierno *m*; ***in*** (***the***) ***~*** en invierno
win•try ['wɪntrɪ] *adj* invernal
wipe [waɪp] *v/t* limpiar; *tape* borrar
◆ **wipe out** *v/t* (*kill*, *destroy*) eliminar; *debt* saldar
wip•er ['waɪpər] ☞ ***windshield wiper***
wire [waɪr] **I** *n* alambre *m*; ELEC cable *m*; ***get one's ~s crossed*** *fig* confundirse **II** *v/t* ELEC cablear
'wire cut•ters *npl* cizallas *fpl*
wire•less ['waɪrlɪs] radio *f*
wire 'net•ting tela *f* metálica; **'wire•tap** escucha *f* telefónica; **wire 'wool** estropajo *m* de aluminio
wir•ing ['waɪrɪŋ] ELEC cableado *m*
'wir•ing di•a•gram diagrama *m* de la instalación eléctrica *or* de conexiones
wir•y ['waɪrɪ] *adj person* fibroso
wis•dom ['wɪzdəm] *of person* sabiduría *f*; *of action* prudencia *f*, sensatez *f*
'wis•dom tooth muela *f* del juicio
wise [waɪz] *adj* sabio; *action*, *decision* prudente, sensato
◆ **wise up** *v/i* F abrir los ojos; ***wise up to sth*** F darse cuenta de algo
'wise•crack F chiste *m*, comentario *m* gracioso
'wise guy *pej* F sabelotodo *m*
wise•ly ['waɪzlɪ] *adv act* prudentemen-

te, sensatamente

wish [wɪʃ] **I** *n* deseo *m*; ***best ~es*** un saludo cordial; ***make a ~*** pedir un deseo **II** *v/t* desear; ***~ s.o. well*** desear a alguien lo mejor; ***I ~ed him good luck*** le deseé buena suerte; ***I ~ that you could stay*** ojalá te pudieras quedar **III** *v/i*: ***~ for*** desear

'wish•bone espoleta *f*

wish•ful 'think•ing ['wɪʃfəl] ilusiones *fpl*; ***that's ~ on her part*** que no se haga ilusiones

wish•y-wash•y ['wɪʃɪwɑːʃɪ] *adj person* anodino; *color* pálido

wisp [wɪsp] *of hair* mechón *m*; *of smoke* voluta *f*

wist•ful ['wɪstfəl] *adj* nostálgico

wist•ful•ly ['wɪstfəlɪ] *adv* con nostalgia

wit [wɪt] **1** (*humor*) ingenio *m*; *person* ingenioso(-a) *m*(*f*) **2**: ***be at one's ~s' end*** estar desesperado; ***keep one's ~s about one*** mantener la calma; ***be scared out of one's ~s*** estar aterrorizado

witch [wɪʧ] bruja *f*

'witch•craft brujería *f*; **'witch doc•tor** hechicero *m*; **'witch•hunt** *fig* caza *f* de brujas

with [wɪð] *prep* con; ***shivering ~ fear*** temblando de miedo; ***a girl ~ brown eyes*** una chica de ojos castaños; ***are you ~ me?*** (*do you understand*) ¿me sigues?; ***~ no money*** sin dinero

with•draw [wɪð'drɒː] **I** *v/t* (*pret* ***-drew***, *pp* ***-drawn***) *complaint*, *money*, *troops* retirar **II** *v/i* (*pret* ***-drew***, *pp* ***-drawn***) *of competitor*, *troops* retirarse

with•draw•al [wɪð'drɒːəl] *of complaint*, *application*, *troops* retirada *f*; *of money* reintegro *m*

with'draw•al symp•toms *npl* síndrome *m* de abstinencia

with•drawn [wɪð'drɒːn] *adj person* retraído

with•er ['wɪðər] *v/i* marchitarse

with•er•ing ['wɪðərɪŋ] *adj fig* fulminante

with'hold *v/t* (*pret & pp* ***-held***) *information* ocultar; *payment* retener; ***but his parents withheld their consent*** pero sus padres no le dieron el consentimento

with'in *prep* (*inside*) dentro de; *in expressions of time* en menos de; ***~ five miles of home*** a cinco millas de casa; ***we kept ~ the budget*** no superamos el presupuesto; ***it is well ~ your capabilities*** lo puedes conseguir perfectamente; ***~ reach*** al alcance de la mano

with'out *prep* sin; ***~ looking / asking*** sin mirar / preguntar; ***~ an umbrella*** sin paraguas

with'stand *v/t* (*pret & pp* ***-stood***) resistir, soportar

wit•less ['wɪtlɪs] *adj* estúpido; ***scare s.o. ~*** dar un susto morrocotudo a alguien

wit•ness ['wɪtnɪs] **I** *n* testigo *m/f* **II** *v/t accident*, *crime* ser testigo de; ***I ~ed his signature*** firmé en calidad de testigo

'wit•ness stand estrado *m* del testigo

wit•ti•cism ['wɪtɪsɪzm] comentario *m* gracioso *or* agudo

wit•ty ['wɪtɪ] *adj* ingenioso, agudo

wives [waɪvz] *pl* ☞ ***wife***

wiz•ard ['wɪzərd] **1** mago *m* **2** *fig* genio *m*; ***financial ~*** genio de las finanzas

wiz•ened ['wɪznd] *adj* arrugado

WLTM [dʌbljuːeltiː'em] *abbr* (= ***would like to meet***) me gustaría conocer

WMD [dʌbljuːem'diː] *abbr* (= ***weapons of mass destruction***) armas *fpl* de destrucción masiva

wob•ble ['wɑːbl] *v/i* tambalearse

wob•bly ['wɑːblɪ] *adj* tambaleante

woe [woʊ] desgracia *f*; ***~ betide you if you're late*** ay de ti si llegas tarde; ***his tale of ~*** *hum* sus desgracias

woe•ful ['woʊfʊl] *adj* espantoso

wok [wɑːk] wok *m*, *sartén típica de la cocina china*

woke [woʊk] *pret* ☞ ***wake***

wok•en ['woʊkn] *pp* ☞ ***wake***

wolf [wʊlf] **I** *n* (*pl* ***wolves*** [wʊlvz]) *animal* lobo *m*; *fig* (*womanizer*) don juan *m* **II** *v/t*: ***~*** (***down***) engullir

'wolf whis•tle silbido *m*

'wolf-whis•tle *v/i*: ***~ at s.o.*** silbar a alguien (*como piropo*)

wolves [wʊlvz] ☞ ***wolf***

wom•an ['wʊmən] (*pl* ***women*** ['wɪmɪn]) mujer *f*

wom•an 'doc•tor médica *f*; **wom•an 'driv•er** conductora *f*; **wom•an hat•er** ['wʊmənheɪtər] misógino *m*

wom•an•hood ['wʊmənhʊd] feminidad *f*

wom•an•ize ['wʊmənaɪz] *v/i* ir detrás de mujeres
wom•an•iz•er ['wʊmənaɪzər] mujeriego(-a) *m(f)*
wom•an•kind [wʊmən'kaɪnd] las mujeres
wom•an•ly ['wʊmənlɪ] *adj* femenino
wom•an 'priest mujer *f* sacerdote
womb [wu:m] matriz *f*, útero *m*
wom•en [wɪmɪn] *pl* ☞ ***woman***
wom•en's lib [wɪmɪnz'lɪb] la liberación de la mujer; **wom•en's lib•ber** [wɪmɪnz'lɪbər] partidario(-a) *m(f)* de la liberación de la mujer; **wom•en's room** ['wɪmɪnzru:m] baño *m* de mujeres
won [wʌn] *pret & pp* ☞ ***win***
won•der ['wʌndər] **I** *n* (*amazement*) asombro *m*; ***no ~!*** ¡no me sorprende!; ***it's a ~ that …*** es increíble que … **II** *v/i* preguntarse; ***I've often ~ed about that*** me he preguntado eso a menudo **III** *v/t* preguntarse; ***I ~ if you could help*** ¿le importaría ayudarme?
won•der•ful ['wʌndərfəl] *adj* maravilloso
won•der•ful•ly ['wʌndərfəlɪ] *adv* (*extremely*) maravillosamente
'won•der•land paraíso *m*
won•ky ['wɑ:ŋkɪ] *adj Br* F cojo
wont [woʊnt] *esp lit* **I** *adj*: ***be ~ to do sth*** acostumbrar a hacer algo **II** *n*: ***as was his ~*** como era costumbre suya
won't [woʊnt] ☞ ***will***[3]
woo [wu:] *v/t woman* cortejar; *supporters* atraer
wood [wʊd] **1** madera *f*; *for fire* leña *f* **2** (*forest*) bosque *m*
'wood•cock ORN chocha *f* perdiz
'wood•cut grabado *m* sobre madera
'wood•cut•ter leñador(a) *m(f)*
wood•ed ['wʊdɪd] *adj* arbolado
wood•en ['wʊdn] *adj* **1** (*made of wood*) de madera **2** *performance*, *tone* acartonado
wood•land ['wʊdlənd] bosque *m*; **'wood•louse** cochinilla *f*; **wood•peck•er** ['wʊdpekər] pájaro *m* carpintero; **'wood•pile** montón *m* de leña; **'wood•shed** leñera *f*; **'wood•wind** MUS sección *f* de viento de madera; **'wood•work** carpintería *f*; **'wood•worm** ZO carcoma *f*
wood•y ['wʊdɪ] *adj hillside* boscoso; *plant* leñoso
woof [wʊf] *int* guau
woof•er ['wʊfər] woofer *m*
wool [wʊl] lana *f*
wool•en, *Br* **wool•len** ['wʊlən] **I** *adj* de lana **II** *n* prenda *f* de lana
wool•y, *Br* **wool•ly** ['wʊlɪ] *adj* **1** de lana **2** (*vague*) vago
woo•zy ['wu:zɪ] *adj* F atontado
word [wɜ:rd] **I** *n* palabra *f*; ***I didn't understand a ~ of what she said*** no entendí nada de lo que dijo; ***is there any ~ from …?*** ¿se sabe algo de …?; ***I've had ~ from my daughter*** (*news*) he recibido noticias de mi hija; ***you have my ~*** tienes mi palabra; ***have ~s*** (*argue*) discutir; ***have a ~ with s.o.*** hablar con alguien; ***the ~s*** *of song* la letra **II** *v/t article*, *letter* redactar
word•ing ['wɜ:rdɪŋ]: ***the ~ of a letter*** la redacción de una carta
'word•play juegos *mpl* de palabras; **word 'pro•cess•ing** procesamiento *m* de textos; **word 'pro•ces•sor** *software* procesador *m* de textos
word•y ['wɜ:rdɪ] *adj* verboso
wore [wɔ:r] *pret* ☞ ***wear***
work [wɜ:rk] **I** *n* (*job*) trabajo *m*; (*employment*) trabajo *m*, empleo *m*; ***out of ~*** desempleado, *Span* en el paro; ***be at ~*** estar en el trabajo; ***I go to ~ by bus*** voy al trabajo en autobús **II** *v/i of person* trabajar; *of machine*, (*succeed*) funcionar; ***how does it ~?*** *of device* ¿cómo funciona? **III** *v/t* **1** *employee* hacer trabajar **2** *machine* hacer funcionar, utilizar **3**: ***you'll have to ~ your way back to fitness*** tendrás que trabajar duro para volver a estar en forma
◆ **work off** *v/t bad mood*, *anger* desahogarse de; *flab* perder haciendo ejercicio
◆ **work out** **I** *v/t problem*, *puzzle* resolver; *solution* encontrar, hallar **II** *v/i* **1** *at gym* hacer ejercicios **2** *of relationship etc* funcionar, ir bien
◆ **work out to** *v/t* (*add up to*) sumar
◆ **work up** *v/t appetite* abrir; ***work up enthusiasm*** entusiasmarse; ***work up a sweat*** sudar; ***get worked up*** (*get angry*) alterarse; (*get nervous*) ponerse nervioso
◆ **work up to** *v/t*: ***have you told her yet? – I'm working up to it*** ¿se lo has dicho ya? – estoy en ello

work•a•ble ['wɜːrkəbl] *adj solution* viable
work•a•day ['wɜːrkədeɪ] *adj* de todos los días
work•a•hol•ic [wɜːrkə'hɑːlɪk] F *persona obsesionada con el trabajo*
'work•bench TECH banco *m* de carpintero; **'work•book** EDU libro *m* de ejercicios; **'work camp** campo *m* de trabajo; **'work•day** (*hours of work*) jornada *f* laboral; (*not a holiday*) día *m* de trabajo
work•er ['wɜːrkər] trabajador(a) *m*(*f*); ***she's a good ~*** trabaja bien
work•ers' 'comp subsidio *m* de enfermedad
'work•force trabajadores *mpl*
'work hours *npl* horas *fpl* de trabajo
work•ing ['wɜːrkɪŋ] funcionamiento *m*
'work•ing cap•i•tal capital *m* circulante; **'work•ing class** clase *f* trabajadora; **'work•ing-class** *adj* de clase trabajadora; **'work•ing con•di•tions** *npl* condiciones *fpl* de trabajo; **work•ing 'day** ☞ ***workday***; **'work•ing hours** ☞ ***work hours***; **work•ing 'knowledge** conocimientos *mpl* básicos; **'work•ing lunch** almuerzo *m* de trabajo; **work•ing 'moth•er** madre *f* que trabaja; **'work•ing pop•u•la•tion** población *f* activa
'work•load cantidad *f* de trabajo; **'work•man** obrero *m*; **'work•man•like** *adj* competente; **'work•man•ship** factura *f*, confección *f*; **'work•mate** compañero(-a) *m*(*f*) de trabajo; **work of 'art** obra *f* de arte; **'work•out** sesión *f* de ejercicios; **'work per•mit** permiso *m* de trabajo; **'work•place** lugar *m* de trabajo; **'work•room** taller *m*; **'work sheet** hoja *f* de ejercicios; **'work•shop** *also seminar* taller *m*; **'work•shy** *adj* perezoso; **'work•sta•tion** estación *f* de trabajo; **'work sur•face** encimera *f*; **'work•top** encimera *f*; **work-to-'rule** *Br* huelga *f* de celo
world [wɜːrld] mundo *m*; ***the ~ of computers / of the theater*** el mundo de la informática / del teatro; ***out of this ~*** F sensacional
world-'class *adj* de categoría mundial; **World 'Cup** Mundial *m*, Copa *f* del Mundo; **world-'fa•mous** *adj* mundialmente famoso
world•ly ['wɜːrldlɪ] *adj* mundano
world 'pow•er potencia *f* mundial; **world 're•cord** récord *m* mundial *or* del mundo; **World 'Se•ries** *nsg in baseball* Serie *f* Mundial; **world 'war** guerra *f* mundial; **'world•wide I** *adj* mundial **II** *adv* en todo el mundo; **'world(•wide) rights** *npl* derechos *mpl* de explotación mundiales
worm [wɜːrm] gusano *m*
'worm-eat•en *adj* carcomido
'worm•hole 1 agujero *m* de gusano **2** *in space* picadura *f* de gusano
worn [wɔːrn] *pp* ☞ ***wear***
worn-'out *adj shoes, carpet, part* gastado; *person* agotado
wor•ried ['wʌrɪd] *adj* preocupado
wor•ried•ly ['wʌrɪdlɪ] *adv* con preocupación
wor•ri•some ['wʌrɪsəm] *adj* preocupante
wor•ry ['wʌrɪ] **I** *n* preocupación *f* **II** *v/t* (*pret & pp* **-ied**) preocupar **III** *v/i* (*pret & pp* **-ied**) preocuparse; ***don't ~, I'll get it!*** ¡no te molestes, ya respondo yo!
wor•ry•ing ['wʌrɪɪŋ] *adj* preocupante
worse [wɜːrs] **I** *adj* peor; ***get ~*** empeorar; ***and to make things ~ ...*** y por si fuera poco… **II** *adv* peor
wors•en ['wɜːrsn] *v/i* empeorar
wor•ship ['wɜːrʃɪp] **I** *n* culto *m* **II** *v/t* (*pret & pp* **-ped**) adorar, rendir culto a; *fig* adorar
wor•ship•(p)er ['wɜːrʃɪpər] fiel *m*
worst [wɜːrst] **I** *adj & adv* peor **II** *n*: ***the ~*** lo peor; ***if (the) ~ comes to (the) ~*** en el peor de los casos
worst-case scen'a•ri•o el peor de los casos
worth [wɜːrθ] *adj*: ***$20 ~ of gas*** 20 dólares de gasolina; ***be ~ ...*** *in monetary terms* valer …; ***the book's ~ reading*** valer la pena leer el libro; ***be ~ it*** valer la pena
worth•less ['wɜːrθlɪs] *adj person* inútil; ***be ~*** *of object* no valer nada
worth'while *adj* que vale la pena; ***be ~*** valer la pena
wor•thy ['wɜːrðɪ] *adj* digno; *cause* justo; ***be ~ of*** (*deserve*) merecer
would [wʊd] *v/aux*: ***I ~ help if I could*** te ayudaría si pudiera; ***I said that I ~ go*** dije que iría; ***I told him I ~ not leave unless ....*** le dije que no me iría a no ser que …; ***~ you like to go to***

the movies? ¿te gustaría ir al cine?; ~ ***you mind if I smoked?*** ¿le importa si fumo?; ~ ***you tell her that ...?*** ¿le podrías decir que ...?; ~ ***you close the door?*** ¿podrías cerrar la puerta?; ***I ~ have told you but ...*** te lo habría dicho pero ...; ***I ~ not have been so angry if ...*** no me habría enfadado tanto si ...
'would-be *adj*: ~ ***authors*** los aspirantes a escritores
would•n't ['wʊdnt] ☞ ***would not***
wound[1] [wu:nd] **I** *n* herida *f* **II** *v/t with weapon, remark* herir
wound[2] [waʊnd] *pret & pp* ☞ ***wind***[2]
wound•ed ['wu:ndɪd] *adj* herido
wove [woʊv] *pret* ☞ ***weave***
wo•ven ['woʊvn] *pp* ☞ ***weave***
wow [waʊ] **I** *int* ¡hala! **II** *v/t* F *impress* deslumbrar
wran•gle ['ræŋgl] **I** *v/i* discutir, pelear (***with*** con; ***over*** por) **II** *n* discusión *f*, pelea *f*
wrap [ræp] *v/t* (*pret & pp* **-ped**) *parcel, gift* envolver; ***he ~ped a scarf around his neck*** se puso una bufanda al cuello
◆ **wrap up** *v/i against the cold* abrigarse
wrap•per ['ræpər] *for candy etc* envoltorio *m*
wrap•ping ['ræpɪŋ] envoltorio *m*
'wrap•ping pa•per papel *m* de envolver
'wrap-up *summary* resumen *m*
wrath [ræθ] ira *f*
wreak [ri:k] *v/t*: ~ ***havoc*** hacer estragos; ~ ***revenge*** vengarse
wreath [ri:θ] corona *f* de flores
wreathe [ri:ð] *v/t*: ***~d in mist / smoke*** envuelto en niebla / humo
wreck [rek] **I** *n* restos *mpl*; ***be a nervous ~*** ser un manojo de nervios **II** *v/t ship* hundir; *car* destrozar; *plans, marriage* arruinar
wreck•age ['rekɪdʒ] *of car, plane* restos *mpl*; *of marriage, career* ruina *f*
wreck•er ['rekər] grúa *f*
wreck•ing com•pa•ny ['rekɪŋ] empresa *f* de auxilio en carretera
wren [ren] ORN chochín *m*
wrench [rentʃ] **I** *n tool* llave *f* **II** *v/t* (*pull*) arrebatar; ~ ***one's wrist*** hacerse un esguince en la muñeca
wrest [rest] *v/t*: ~ ***sth from s.o.*** arrebatar algo a alguien
wres•tle ['resl] *v/i* luchar
◆ **wrestle with** *v/t problems* combatir
wres•tler ['reslər] luchador(a) *m(f)* (de lucha libre)
wres•tling ['reslɪŋ] lucha *f* libre
'wres•tling con•test combate *m* de lucha libre
wretch [retʃ]: ***poor ~*** pobre desgraciado(-a) *m(f)*
wretch•ed ['retʃɪd] *adj* **1** (*unhappy*) desdichado **2** *headache, weather* horrible
wrig•gle ['rɪgl] *v/i* (*squirm*) menearse; *along the ground* arrastrarse; *into small space* escurrirse
◆ **wriggle out of** *v/t* librarse de
◆ **wring out** [rɪŋ] *v/t* (*pret & pp* **wrung**) *cloth* escurrir
wring•ing ['rɪŋɪŋ] *adv*: ~ ***wet*** empapado
wrin•kle ['rɪŋkl] **I** *n* arruga *f* **II** *v/t clothes* arrugar **III** *v/i of clothes* arrugarse
wrin•kly ['rɪŋklɪ] F viejarrón(-ona) *m(f)* F
wrist [rɪst] muñeca *f*
'wrist•band muñequera *f*
'wrist•watch reloj *m* de pulsera
writ [rɪt] LAW mandato *m* judicial
write [raɪt] **I** *v/t* (*pret* **wrote**, *pp* **written**) escribir; *check* extender **II** *v/i* (*pret* **wrote**, *pp* **written**) escribir
◆ **write away for** *v/t* solicitar por escrito
◆ **write down** *v/t* escribir, tomar nota de
◆ **write off** *v/t* **1** *debt* cancelar, anular **2** *Br* F *car* destrozar **3** (*regard as unimportant: person*) tener a menos
◆ **write out** *v/t* **1** *name etc* escribir; *check, receipt* hacer **2** (*make a clean copy of*) pasar a limpio **3**: ***he was written out of the series*** suprimieron el papel que tenía en la serie
◆ **write up** *report* redactar
'write-down FIN depreciación *f*
'write-off **1** COM condonación *f* **2** *Br* F siniestro *m* total
writ•er ['raɪtər] escritor(a) *m(f)*; *of book, song* autor(a) *m(f)*; ***he's a neat ~*** su letra es muy clara
'write-up reseña *f*
writhe [raɪð] *v/i* retorcerse
writ•ing ['raɪtɪŋ] **1** *words, text* escritura *f*; ***I like his ~*** me gusta cómo escribe; ***in ~*** por escrito; ***that's a good piece of ~*** está muy bien escrito **2** (*hand~*) letra *f*
'writ•ing desk escritorio *m*
'writ•ing pa•per papel *m* de escribir

writ•ings ['raɪtɪŋz] *npl* obra *f*
writ•ten ['rɪtn] *pp* ☞ **write**
wrong [rɒːŋ] **I** *adj answer, information* equivocado; *decision, choice* erróneo; **be ~** *of person* estar equivocado; *of answer* ser incorrecto; *morally* ser injusto; ***what's ~?*** ¿qué pasa?; ***there is something ~ with the car*** al coche le pasa algo; ***you have the ~ number*** TELEC se ha equivocado
II *adv* mal; **go ~** *of person* equivocarse; *of marriage, plan etc* fallar
III *n* mal *m*; ***right a ~*** deshacer un entuerto; ***he knows right from ~*** sabe distinguir entre el bien y el mal; ***be in the ~*** tener la culpa
'wrong•do•er malhechor(a) *m(f)*;
wrong•do•ing ['rɒːŋduːɪŋ] fechoría *f*;
wrong'foot *v/t* sorprender
wrong•ful ['rɒːŋfəl] *adj* ilegal
wrong•ly ['rɒːŋlɪ] *adv* erróneamente
wrote [rout] *pret* ☞ **write**
wrought i•ron [rɔːt'aɪərn] hierro *m* forjado
wrought-'i•ron *adj* de hierro forjado
wrung [rʌŋ] *pret & pp* ☞ **wring**
wry [raɪ] *adj* socarrón
WWW ['dʌbljuːdʌbljuːdʌbljuː] *abbr* (= ***World-Wide Web***) WWW *f*
WYSIWYG ['wɪzɪwɪg] *abbr* (= ***What You See Is What You Get***) WYSIWYG, *se imprime lo que ves*

X

xen•o•pho•bi•a [zenou'foubɪə] xenofobia *f*
xen•o•pho•bic [zenə'foubɪk] *adj* xenófobo
X•mas ['eksməs, 'krɪsməs] F ☞ ***Christmas***
X-rat•ed ['eksreɪtɪd] *adj no recomendable a menores de 18 años*
X-ray ['eksreɪ] **I** *n* rayo *m* X; *picture* radiografía *f* **II** *v/t* radiografiar, sacar un radiografía de
xy•lo•phone [zaɪlə'foun] xilofón *m*

Y

Y [waɪ] *abbr* F ☞ ***YMCA, YWCA***
yacht [jɑːt] yate *m*
yacht•ing ['jɑːtɪŋ] vela *f*
yachts•man ['jɑːtsmən] navegante *m* (*en embarcación de vela*)
yachts•wom•an ['jɑːtswumən] navegante *f* (*en embarcación de vela*)
yak [jæk] *v/i* (*pret & pp* ***-ked***) F parlotear F
yam•mer ['jæmər] *v/i* F (*yell*) gritar; (*nag*) dar la lata F
Yank [jæŋk] F yanqui *m/f*
yank [jæŋk] *v/t* tirar de
Yan•kee ['jæŋkɪ] F yanqui *m/f*
yap [jæp] *v/i* (*pret & pp* ***-ped***) **1** *of small dog* ladrar (*con ladridos agudos*) **2** F (*talk a lot*) parlotear F, largar F
yard[1] [jɑːrd] **1** *of prison, institution etc* patio *m*; *behind house* jardín *m* **2** *for storage* almacén *m* (*al aire libre*)
yard[2] [jɑːrd] *measurement* yarda *f*
yard•man ['jɑːrdmən] RAIL obrero *m* ferroviario; **'yard•sale** *chamarileo en el jardín de un particular*; **'yard•stick** patrón *m*
yarn [jɑːrn] **1** (*thread*) hilo *m* **2** F (*story*) batallita *f* F
yawn [jɒːn] **I** *n* **1** bostezo *m* **2**: ***be one big ~*** F ser un aburrimiento F **II** *v/i* bostezar
yawn•ing ['jɒːnɪŋ] *adj*: ***a ~ gap*** un abismo
yeah [je] *int* F sí
year [jɪr] año *m*; ***I've known her for ~s*** la conozco desde hace años; ***we were in the same ~*** *Br. at school* éramos del mismo curso; ***be six ~s old*** tener seis años (de edad); ***~ in, ~ out*** todos los años, año tras año; ***~ after ~*** todos los años, año tras año; ***all ~ round*** du-

Y

rante todo el año
'year•book EDU anuario *m* escolar; **'year-end ac•counts** *npl* cuentas *fpl* de fin de ejercicio; **'year•long** *adj* de un año
year•ly ['jɪrlɪ] **I** *adj* anual **II** *adv* anualmente
yearn [jɜːrn] *v/i* anhelar
◆ **yearn for** *v/t* ansiar
yearn•ing ['jɜːrnɪŋ] anhelo *m*
yeast [jiːst] levadura *f*
yell [jel] **I** *n* grito *m* **II** *v/i & v/t* gritar
yel•low ['jelou] **I** *n* amarillo *m* **II** *adj* amarillo; F (*cowardly*) cobarde
yel•low 'card tarjeta *f* amarilla; ***show s.o. the ~*** sacarle la tarjeta amarilla a alguien; **yel•low 'fe•ver** fiebre *f* amarilla; **yel•low 'pag•es** *npl* páginas *fpl* amarillas
yelp [jelp] **I** *n* aullido *m* **II** *v/i* aullar
yep [jep] *int* F si
yes [jes] **I** *int* sí; ***she said ~*** dijo que sí **II** *n* sí *m*; ***is that a ~ or a no?*** ¿eso es que sí o que no?
'yes•man *pej* pelotillero *m*
yes•ter•day ['jestərdeɪ] **I** *adv* ayer; ***the day before ~*** anteayer; ***~ afternoon*** ayer por la tarde; ***I wasn't born ~*** no nací ayer **II** *n* ayer *m*
yet [jet] **I** *adv* todavía, aún; ***as ~*** aún, todavía; ***have you finished ~?*** ¿has acabado ya?; ***he hasn't arrived ~*** todavía *or* aún no ha llegado; ***is he here ~? – not ~*** ¿ha llegado ya? – todavía *or* aún no; ***~ bigger / longer*** aún más grande / largo; ***the fastest one ~*** el más rápido hasta el momento; ***he has ~ to win a major title*** todavía le queda por ganar un título importante **II** *conj* sin embargo; ***~ I'm not sure*** sin embargo no estoy seguro
yew [juː] BOT tejo *m*
Y-fronts ['waɪfrʌnts] *npl Br* calzoncillos *mpl*
Yid•dish ['jɪdɪʃ] LING yídish *m*
yield [jiːld] **I** *n from fields etc* cosecha *f*; *from investment* rendimiento *m* **II** *v/t fruit, good harvest* proporcionar; *interest* rendir, devengar **III** *v/i* (*give way*) ceder; *of driver* ceder el paso
yip•pee [jɪ'piː] *int* yupi
YMCA [waɪemsiː'eɪ] *abbr* (= ***Young Men's Christian Association***) YMCA *f* (= Asociación *f* de Jóvenes Cristianos)
yob [jɑːb] *Br* gamberro *m*
yo•ga ['jougə] yoga *m*
yog•hurt ['jougərt] yogur *m*
yolk [jouk] yema *f*
you [juː] *pron singular* tú, *L.Am.* usted, *Rpl, C.Am.* vos; *formal* usted; *plural*: *Span* vosotros, vosotras, *L.Am.* ustedes; *formal* ustedes; ***~ are clever*** eres / es inteligente; ***do ~ know him?*** ¿lo conoces / conoce?; ***~ go, I'll stay*** tú ve / usted vaya, yo me quedo; ***~ never know*** nunca se sabe; ***~ have to pay*** hay que pagar; ***exercise is good for ~*** es bueno hacer ejercicio
young [jʌŋ] **I** *adj* joven **II** *npl*: ***the ~*** los jóvenes, la juventud
young•ish ['jʌŋɪʃ] *adj* bastante joven
young•ster ['jʌŋstər] joven *m/f*
your [jʊr] *adj singular* tu, *L.Am.* su; *formal* su; *plural*: *Span* vuestro, *L.Am.* su; *formal* su; ***~ house*** tu / su casa; ***~ books*** tus / sus libros
you're [jʊr] F ☞ ***you are***
yours [jʊrz] *pron singular* el tuyo, la tuya, *L.Am.* el suyo, la suya; *formal* el suyo, la suya; *plural* el vuestro, la vuestra, *L.Am.* el suyo, la suya; *formal* el suyo, la suya; ***a friend of ~*** un amigo tuyo / suyo / vuestro; ***~ ...*** *at end of letter* un saludo
your•self [jʊr'self] *pron reflexive* te, *L.Am.* se; *formal* se; *emphatic* tú mismo *m*, tú misma *f*, *L.Am.* usted mismo *m*, usted misma *f*, *Rpl, C.Am.* vos mismo *m*, vos misma *f*; *formal* usted mismo *m*, usted misma *f*; ***did you hurt ~?*** ¿te hiciste / se hizo daño?; ***when you see ~ in the mirror*** cuando te ves / se ve en el espejo; ***by ~*** (*alone*) solo; (*without help*) tú solo, tú mismo, *Rpl, C.Am.* vos solo, vos mismo, *L.Am.* usted solo, usted mismo; *formal* usted solo, usted mismo
your•selves [jʊr'selvz] *pron reflexive* os, *L.Am.* se; *formal* se; *emphatic* vosotros mismos *mpl*, vosotras mismas *fpl*, *L.Am.* ustedes mismos *mpl*, ustedes mismas *fpl*; *formal* ustedes mismos *mpl*, ustedes mismas *fpl*; ***did you hurt ~?*** ¿os hicisteis / se hicieron daño?; ***when you see ~ in the mirror*** cuando os veis / se ven en el espejo; ***by ~*** (*alone*) solos; (*without help*) vosotros

solos, *L.Am.* ustedes solos, ustedes mismos; *formal* ustedes solos, ustedes mismos
youth [ju:θ] **1** juventud *f* **2** (*young man*) joven *m*
'youth club club *m* juvenil
youth•ful ['ju:θfəl] *adj* joven; *fashion, idealism* juvenil
'youth hos•tel albergue *m* juvenil
you've [ju:v] F ☞ ***you have***
yo-yo ['joʊjoʊ] yoyó *m*
yuck [jʌk] *int* F buaj F
yuck•y ['jʌkɪ] *adj* F asqueroso
Yu•go•slav [ju:goʊ'slɑ:v] HIST **I** *adj* yugoslavo **II** *n* yugoslavo(-a) *m(f)*
Yu•go•slav•i•a [ju:gə'slɑ:vɪə] HIST Yugoslavia *f*
Yule•tide ['ju:ltaɪd] Navidad(es) *f(pl)*
yum•my ['jʌmɪ] *adj* F rico F, delicioso; ***he's so ~*** es un encanto
yup [jʌp] F sí
yup•pie ['jʌpɪ] F yupi *m/f* F
YWCA [waɪdʌblju:si:'eɪ] (= ***Young Women's Christian Association***) YWCA *f* (= Asociación *f* de Jóvenes Cristianas)

Z

Zam•bi•a ['zæmbɪə] Zambia *f*
za•ny ['zeɪnɪ] *adj* loco, excéntrico
zap [zæp] F *v/t* (*pret & pp* ***-ped***) **1** (COMPUT: *delete*) borrar **2** (*kill*) liquidar F **3** (*hit*) golpear **4** (*send*) mandar rápidamente **5** *Br*: ***~ channels*** hacer zapping, cambiar de canal **6**: ***~ sth in the microwave*** meter algo en el microondas **II** *v/i*: ***~ along the motorway*** ir a toda velocidad por la autopista
◆ **zap along** *v/i* F (*move fast*) volar F
◆ **zap up** *v/t* animar, alegrar
zapped [zæpt] *adj* F (*exhausted*) hecho polvo F
zap•per ['zæpər] *Br*: *for TV channels* telemando *m*, mando *m* a distancia
zap•py ['zæpɪ] *adj* F *car, pace* rápido; (*lively, energetic*) vivo
zeal [zi:l] celo *m*
zeal•ous ['zeləs] *adj* ferviente, entusiasta
ze•bra ['zebrə] cebra *f*
ze•bra 'cross•ing *Br* paso *m* de cebra
ze•ro ['zɪroʊ] (*pl* ***-o(e)s***) cero *m*; ***10 degrees below ~*** 10 bajo cero
◆ **zero in on** *v/t* (*identify*) centrarse en
ze•ro-e'mis•sion *adj* que no emite gases contaminantes; **ze•ro 'growth** crecimiento *m* cero; **ze•ro-'tol•er•ance** tolerancia *f* cero
zest [zest] entusiasmo *m*
zig•zag ['zɪgzæg] **I** *n* zigzag *m* **II** *v/i* (*pret & pp* ***-ged***) zigzaguear
zilch [zɪltʃ] F nada de nada
zil•lion ['zɪlɪən] F: ***I've a ~ things to do*** tengo tropecientas cosas que hacer F
zinc [zɪŋk] cinc *m*
zip [zɪp] *Br* cremallera *f*
◆ **zip up** *v/t* (*pret & pp* ***-ped***) **1** *dress, jacket* cerrar la cremallera de **2** COMPUT compactar
'zip code código *m* postal
'zip fas•ten•er *Br* cremallera *f*
zip•per ['zɪpər] cremallera *f*
zit [zɪt] F *on face* grano *m*, espinilla *f*
zo•di•ac ['zoʊdɪæk] zodiaco *m*; ***signs of the ~*** signos *mpl* del zodiaco
zom•bie ['zɑ:mbɪ] F (*idiot*) estúpido(-a) *m(f)* F; ***feel like a ~*** (*exhausted*) sentirse como un zombi
zone [zoʊn] **I** *n* zona *f* **II** *v/t area* destinar; ***be ~d for*** destinarse a
'zone de•fense *in basketball* defensa *f* en zona
zon•ing re•stric•tions ['zoʊnɪŋrɪstrɪkʃnz] *npl* reglamentación *f* urbanística
zonked [zɑ:ŋkt] *adj* P (*exhausted*) molido P
zoo [zu:] zoo *m*
zo•o•log•i•cal [zu:ə'lɑ:dʒɪkl] *adj* zoológico
zo•ol•o•gist [zu:'ɑ:lədʒɪst] zoólogo(-a) *m(f)*
zo•ol•o•gy [zu:'ɑ:lədʒɪ] zoología *f*
zoom [zu:m] *v/i* F (*move fast*) ir zumbando F
◆ **zoom in on** *v/t* PHOT hacer un zoom sobre
'zoom lens zoom *m*
zuc•chi•ni [zu:'ki:nɪ] calabacín *m*

Spanish verb conjugations

In the following conjugation patterns verb stems are shown in normal type and verb endings in *italic* type. Irregular forms are indicated by **bold** type.

Notes on the formation of tenses.

The following stems can be used to generate derived forms.

Stem forms	Derived forms
I. From the **Present indicative**, *3rd pers sg* (mand*a*, vend*e*, recib*e*)	**Imperative** *2nd pers sg* (¡mand*a*! ¡vend*e*! ¡recib*e*!)
II. From the **Present subjunctive**, *2nd* and *3rd pers sg* and all plural forms (mand*es*, mand*e*, mand*emos*, mand*éis*, mand*en* - vend*as*, vend*a*, vend*amos*, vend*áis*, vend*an* - recib*as*, recib*a*, recib*amos*, recib*áis*, recib*an*)	**Imperative** *1st pers pl*, *3rd pers sg* and *pl* as well as the negative imperative of the *2nd pers sg* and *pl* (no mand*es*, mand*e* Vd., mand*emos*, no mand*éis*, mand*en* Vds. - no vend*as*, vend*a* Vd., vend*amos*, no vend*áis*, vend*an* Vds. - no recib*as etc*)
III. From the **Preterite**, *3rd pers pl* (mand*aron*, vend*ieron*, recib*ieron*)	**a) Imperfect Subjunctive I** by changing ...ron to ...*ra* (mand*ara*, vend*iera*, recib*iera*) **b) Imperfect Subjunctive II** by changing ...ron to ...*se* (mand*ase*, vend*iese*, recib*iese*) **c) Future Subjunctive** by changing ...ron to ...*re* (mand*are*, vend*iere*, recib*iere*)
IV. From the Infinitive (mand*ar*, vend*er*, recib*ir*)	**a) Imperative** *2nd pers pl* by changing ...r to ...*d* (manda*d*, vende*d*, recibi*d*) **b) Present participle** by changing ...ar to ...*ando*, ...er and ...ir to ...*iendo* (or sometimes ...*yendo*) (mand*ando*, vend*iendo*, recib*iendo*) **c) Future** by adding the *Present* tense endings of ***haber*** (mand*aré*, vend*eré*, recib*iré*) **d) Conditional** by adding the *Imperfect* endings of ***haber*** (mand*aría*, vend*ería*, recib*iría*)
V. From the **Past participle** (mand*ado*, vend*ido*, recib*ido*)	all **compound tenses** by placing a form of ***haber*** or ***ser*** in front of the participle.

First Conjugation

⟨**1a**⟩ **mandar.** No change to the written or spoken form of the stem.

Simple tenses

Indicative

	Present	**Imperfect**	**Preterite**
sg	mand*o*	mand*aba*	mand*é*
	mand*as*	mand*abas*	mand*aste*
	mand*a*	mand*aba*	mand*ó*
pl	mand*amos*	mand*ábamos*	mand*amos*
	mand*áis*	mand*abais*	mand*asteis*
	mand*an*	mand*aban*	mand*aron*

	Future	**Conditional**
sg	mand*aré*	mand*aría*
	mand*arás*	mand*arías*
	mand*ará*	mand*aría*
pl	mand*aremos*	mand*aríamos*
	mand*aréis*	mand*aríais*
	mand*arán*	mand*arían*

Subjunctive

	Present	**Imperfect I**	**Imperfect II**
sg	mand*e*	mand*ara*	mand*ase*
	mand*es*	mand*aras*	mand*ases*
	mand*e*	mand*ara*	mand*ase*
pl	mand*emos*	mand*áramos*	mand*ásemos*
	mand*éis*	mand*arais*	mand*aseis*
	mand*en*	mand*aran*	mand*asen*

	Future	**Imperative**
sg	mand*are*	—
	mand*ares*	mand*a* (no mand*es*)
	mand*are*	mand*e* Vd.
pl	mand*áremos*	mand*emos*
	mand*areis*	mand*ad* (no mand*éis*)
	mand*aren*	mand*en* Vds.

Infinitive: mand*ar*
Present participle: mand*ando*
Past participle: mand*ado*

Compound tenses

1. **Active forms**: the conjugated form of ***haber*** is placed before the *Past participle* (which does not change):

Indicative

Perfect	*he* mand*ado*	**Future perfect**	*habré* mand*ado*
Pluperfect	*había* mand*ado*	**Past conditional**	*habría* mand*ado*
Past anterior	*hube* mand*ado*		
Past infinitive	*haber* mand*ado*	**Past gerundive**	*habiendo* mand*ado*

Subjunctive

Perfect	*haya* mand*ado*	**Future perfect**	*hubiere* mand*ado*
Pluperfect	*hubiera* mand*ado* *hubiese* mand*ado*		

2. **Passive forms**: the conjugated form of ***ser*** (or ***haber***) is placed before the *Past participle* (which does not change):

Indicative

Present	*soy* mand*ado*	**Past anterior**	*hube sido* mand*ado*
Imperfect	*era* mand*ado*	**Future**	*seré* mand*ado*
Preterite	*fui* mand*ado*	**Future perfect**	*habré sido* mand*ado*
Perfect	*he sido* mand*ado*	**Conditional**	*sería* mand*ado*
Pluperfect	*había sido* mand*ado*	**Past conditional**	*habría sido* mand*ado*

Infinitive		**Gerundive**	
Present	*ser* mand*ado etc*	**Present**	*siendo* mand*ado*
Past	*haber sido* mand*ado*	**Past**	*habiendo sido* mand*ado*

Subjunctive

Present	*sea* mand*ado*	**Pluperfect**	*hubiera sido* mand*ado* *hubiese sido* mand*ado*
Imperfect	*fuera* mand*ado* *fuese* mand*ado*		
Future	*fuere* mand*ado*	**Future perfect**	*hubiere sido* mand*ado*
Past	*haya sido* mand*ado*		

Infinitive	**Present Indicative**	**Present Subjunctive**	**Preterite**

⟨1b⟩ cambiar. Model for all …*iar* verbs, unless formed like *variar* ⟨1c⟩.

cambi*o*	cambi*e*	cambi*é*
cambi*as*	cambi*es*	cambi*aste*
cambi*a*	cambi*e*	cambi*ó*
cambi*amos*	cambi*emos*	cambi*amos*
cambi*áis*	cambi*éis*	cambi*asteis*
cambi*an*	cambi*en*	cambi*aron*

Infinitive	Present Indicative	Present Subjunctive	Preterite
⟨**1c**⟩ **variar.** *i* becomes *í* when the stem is stressed.			
	varí*o*	varí*e*	vari*é*
	varí*as*	varí*es*	vari*aste*
	varí*a*	varí*e*	vari*ó*
	vari*amos*	vari*emos*	vari*amos*
	vari*áis*	vari*éis*	vari*asteis*
	varí*an*	varí*en*	vari*aron*
⟨**1d**⟩ **evacuar.** Model for all …*uar* verbs, unless formed like *acentuar* ⟨1e⟩.			
	evac*uo*	evac*ue*	evac*ué*
	evac*uas*	evac*ues*	evac*uaste*
	evac*ua*	evac*ue*	evac*uó*
	evac*uamos*	evac*uemos*	evac*uamos*
	evac*uáis*	evac*uéis*	evac*uasteis*
	evac*uan*	evac*uen*	evac*uaron*
⟨**1e**⟩ **acentuar.** *u* becomes *ú* when the stem is stressed.			
	acent**ú***o*	acent**ú***e*	acentu*é*
	acent**ú***as*	acent**ú***es*	acentu*aste*
	acent**ú***a*	acent**ú***e*	acentu*ó*
	acentu*amos*	acentu*emos*	acentu*amos*
	acentu*áis*	acentu*éis*	acentu*asteis*
	acent**ú***an*	acent**ú***en*	acentu*aron*
⟨**1f**⟩ **cruzar.** Final *z* in the stem becomes *c* before *e*. Model for all …*zar* verbs.			
	cruz*o*	cru**c***e*	cru**c***é*
	cruz*as*	cru**c***es*	cruz*aste*
	cruz*a*	cru**c***e*	cruz*ó*
	cruz*amos*	cru**c***emos*	cruz*amos*
	cruz*áis*	cru**c***éis*	cruz*asteis*
	cruz*an*	cru**c***en*	cruz*aron*
⟨**1g**⟩ **tocar.** Final *c* in the stem becomes *qu* before *e*. Model for all …*car* verbs.			
	toc*o*	to**qu***e*	to**qu***é*
	toc*as*	to**qu***es*	toc*aste*
	toc*a*	to**qu***e*	toc*ó*
	toc*amos*	to**qu***emos*	toc*amos*
	toc*áis*	to**qu***éis*	toc*asteis*
	toc*an*	to**qu***en*	toc*aron*

Infinitive	Present Indicative	Present Subjunctive	Preterite

⟨**1h**⟩ **pagar.** Final *g* in the stem becomes *gu* (*u* is silent) before *e*. Model for all *…gar* verbs.

	Present Indicative	Present Subjunctive	Preterite
	pag*o*	pa**gu***e*	pa**gu***é*
	pag*as*	pa**gu***es*	pag*aste*
	pag*a*	pa**gu***e*	pag*ó*
	pag*amos*	pa**gu***emos*	pag*amos*
	pag*áis*	pa**gu***éis*	pag*asteis*
	pag*an*	pa**gu***en*	pag*aron*

⟨**1i**⟩ **fraguar.** Final *gu* in the stem becomes *gü* before *e* (*u* with dieresis is pronounced). Model for all *…guar* verbs.

	Present Indicative	Present Subjunctive	Preterite
	fragu*o*	fra**gü***e*	fra**gü***é*
	fragu*as*	fra**gü***es*	fragu*aste*
	fragu*a*	fra**gü***e*	fragu*ó*
	fragu*amos*	fra**gü***emos*	fragu*amos*
	fragu*áis*	fra**gü***éis*	fragu*asteis*
	fragu*an*	fra**gü***en*	fragu*aron*

⟨**1k**⟩ **pensar.** Stressed *e* in the stem becomes *ie*.

	Present Indicative	Present Subjunctive	Preterite
	piens*o*	**piens***e*	pens*é*
	piens*as*	**piens***es*	pens*aste*
	piens*a*	**piens***e*	pens*ó*
	pens*amos*	pens*emos*	pens*amos*
	pens*áis*	pens*éis*	pens*asteis*
	piens*an*	**piens***en*	pens*aron*

⟨**1l**⟩ **errar.** Stressed *e* in the stem becomes *ye* (because it comes at the beginning of the word).

	Present Indicative	Present Subjunctive	Preterite
	yerr*o*	**yerr***e*	err*é*
	yerr*as*	**yerr***es*	err*aste*
	yerr*a*	**yerr***e*	err*ó*
	err*amos*	err*emos*	err*amos*
	err*áis*	err*éis*	err*asteis*
	yerr*an*	**yerr***en*	err*aron*

⟨**1m**⟩ **contar.** Stressed *o* of the stem becomes *ue* (*u* is pronounced).

	Present Indicative	Present Subjunctive	Preterite
	cuent*o*	**cuent***e*	cont*é*
	cuent*as*	**cuent***es*	cont*aste*
	cuent*a*	**cuent***e*	cont*ó*
	cont*amos*	cont*emos*	cont*amos*
	cont*áis*	cont*éis*	cont*asteis*
	cuent*an*	**cuent***en*	cont*aron*

Infinitive	Present Indicative	Present Subjunctive	Preterite

⟨1n⟩ agorar. Stressed *o* of the stem becomes *üe* (*u* with dieresis is pronounced).

	Present Indicative	Present Subjunctive	Preterite
	agüero	agüere	agoré
	agüeras	agüeres	agoraste
	agüera	agüere	agoró
	agoramos	agoremos	agoramos
	agoráis	agoréis	agorasteis
	agüeran	agüeren	agoraron

⟨1o⟩ jugar. Stressed *u* in the stem becomes *ue*; final *g* of the stem becomes *gu* before *e* (*see* ⟨1h⟩); *conjugar*, *enjugar* and *enjugarse* are regular.

	Present Indicative	Present Subjunctive	Preterite
	juego	juegue	jugué
	juegas	juegues	jugaste
	juega	juegue	jugó
	jugamos	juguemos	jugamos
	jugáis	juguéis	jugasteis
	juegan	jueguen	jugaron

⟨1p⟩ estar. *Present indicative 1st pers sg* in …*oy*, otherwise regular, but note the stressed *a*; the *Present subjunctive* has a stress on the *e* in the endings (apart from *1st pers pl*); *Preterite etc* as ⟨21⟩. Otherwise regular.

	Present Indicative	Present Subjunctive	Preterite
	estoy	esté	estuve
	estás	estés	estuviste
	está	esté	estuvo
	estamos	estemos	estuvimos
	estáis	estéis	estuvisteis
	están	estén	estuvieron

⟨1q⟩ andar. *Preterite* and derived forms like *estar* as in ⟨21⟩. Otherwise regular.

	Present Indicative	Present Subjunctive	Preterite
	ando	ande	anduve
	andas	andes	anduviste
	anda	ande	anduvo
	andamos	andemos	anduvimos
	andáis	andéis	anduvisteis
	andan	anden	anduvieron

⟨1r⟩ dar. *Present indicative 1st pers sg* in …*oy*, otherwise regular. *Present subjunctive 1st* and *3rd pers sg* takes an accent. *Preterite etc* follow the regular second conjugation. Otherwise regular.

	Present Indicative	Present Subjunctive	Preterite
	doy	dé	di
	das	des	diste
	da	dé	dio
	damos	demos	dimos
	dáis	deis	disteis
	dan	den	dieron

Second Conjugation

⟨**2a**⟩ **vender.** No change to the written or spoken form of the stem.

Simple tenses

Indicative

	Present	**Imperfect**	**Preterite**
sg	vend*o*	vend*ía*	vend*í*
	vend*es*	vend*ías*	vend*iste*
	vend*e*	vend*ía*	vend*ió*
pl	vend*emos*	vend*íamos*	vend*imos*
	vend*éis*	vend*íais*	vend*isteis*
	vend*en*	vend*ían*	vend*ieron*

	Future	**Conditional**
sg	vender*é*	vender*ía*
	vender*ás*	vender*ías*
	vender*á*	vender*ía*
pl	vender*emos*	vender*íamos*
	vender*éis*	vender*íais*
	vender*án*	vender*ían*

Subjunctive

	Present	**Imperfect I**	**Imperfect II**
sg	vend*a*	vend*iera*	vend*iese*
	vend*as*	vend*ieras*	vend*ieses*
	vend*a*	vend*iera*	vend*iese*
pl	vend*amos*	vend*iéramos*	vend*iésemos*
	vend*áis*	vend*ierais*	vend*ieseis*
	vend*an*	vend*ieran*	vend*iesen*

	Future	**Imperative**
sg	vend*iere*	—
	vend*ieres*	vend*e* (no vend*as*)
	vend*iere*	vend*a* Vd.
pl	vend*iéremos*	vend*amos*
	vend*iereis*	vend*ed* (no vend*áis*)
	vend*ieren*	vend*an* Vds.

Infinitive: vend*er*
Present participle: vend*iendo*
Past participle: vend*ido*

Compound tenses

Formed with the *Past participle* together with ***haber*** and ***ser***, see ⟨1a⟩.

⟨2b⟩ vencer. Final *c* of the stem becomes *z* before *a* and *o*. Model for all …*cer* verbs where the …*cer* is preceded by a consonant.

Infinitive	Present Indicative	Present Subjunctive	Preterite
	venzo	venza	vencí
	vences	venzas	venciste
	vence	venza	venció
	vencemos	venzamos	vencimos
	vencéis	venzáis	vencisteis
	vencen	venzan	vencieron

⟨2c⟩ coger. Final *g* of the stem becomes *j* before *a* and *o*. Model for all …*ger* verbs.

Infinitive	Present Indicative	Present Subjunctive	Preterite
	cojo	coja	cogí
	coges	cojas	cogiste
	coge	coja	cogió
	cogemos	cojamos	cogimos
	cogéis	cojáis	cogisteis
	cogen	cojan	cogieron

⟨2d⟩ merecer. Final *c* of the stem becomes *zc* before *a* and *o*.

Infinitive	Present Indicative	Present Subjunctive	Preterite
	merezco	merezca	merecí
	mereces	merezcas	mereciste
	merece	merezca	mereció
	merecemos	merezcamos	merecimos
	merecéis	merezcáis	merecisteis
	merecen	merezcan	merecieron

⟨2e⟩ creer. Unstressed *i* between two vowels becomes *y*. Past participle: *creído*. Present participle: *creyendo*.

Infinitive	Present Indicative	Present Subjunctive	Preterite
	creo	crea	creí
	crees	creas	creíste
	cree	crea	creyó
	creemos	creamos	creímos
	creéis	creáis	creísteis
	creen	crean	creyeron

⟨2f⟩ tañer. Unstressed *i* is omitted after *ñ* and *ll*; compare ⟨3h⟩. Present participle: *tañendo*.

Infinitive	Present Indicative	Present Subjunctive	Preterite
	taño	taña	tañí
	tañes	tañas	tañiste
	tañe	taña	tañó
	tañemos	tañamos	tañimos
	tañéis	tañáis	tañisteis
	tañen	tañan	tañeron

Infinitive	Present Indicative	Present Subjunctive	Preterite

⟨**2g**⟩ **perder.** Stressed *e* in the stem becomes *ie*; model for many other verbs.

	pierd_o_	**pierd**_a_	perd_í_
	pierd_es_	**pierd**_as_	perd_iste_
	pierd_e_	**pierd**_a_	perd_ió_
	perd_emos_	perd_amos_	perd_imos_
	perd_éis_	perd_áis_	perd_isteis_
	pierd_en_	**pierd**_an_	perd_ieron_

⟨**2h**⟩ **mover.** Stressed *o* in the stem becomes *ue*. …*olver* verbs form their *Past participle* with …*uelto*.

	muev_o_	**muev**_a_	mov_í_
	muev_es_	**muev**_as_	mov_iste_
	muev_e_	**muev**_a_	mov_ió_
	mov_emos_	mov_amos_	mov_imos_
	mov_éis_	mov_áis_	mov_isteis_
	muev_en_	**muev**_an_	mov_ieron_

⟨**2i**⟩ **oler.** Stressed *o* in the stem becomes *hue*… (when it comes at the beginning of the word).

	huel_o_	**huel**_a_	ol_í_
	huel_es_	**huel**_as_	ol_iste_
	huel_e_	**huel**_a_	ol_ió_
	ol_emos_	ol_amos_	ol_imos_
	ol_éis_	ol_áis_	ol_isteis_
	huel_en_	**huel**_an_	ol_ieron_

⟨**2k**⟩ **haber.** Many irregular forms. In the *Future* and *Conditional* the *e* after the stem *hab*… is dropped. Future: *habré*. Imperative *2nd pers sg*: *he*.

	he	**hay**_a_	**hube**
	has	**hay**_as_	**hub**_iste_
	ha	**hay**_a_	**hubo**
	h_emos_	**hay**_amos_	**hub**_imos_
	hab_éis_	**hay**_áis_	**hub**_isteis_
	han	**hay**_an_	**hub**_ieron_

⟨**2l**⟩ **tener.** Irregular in most forms. In the *Future* and *Conditional* the *e* coming after the stem is dropped and a *d* is inserted. Future: *tendré*. Imperative *2nd pers sg*: *ten*.

	teng_o_	teng_a_	**tuve**
	tien_es_	teng_as_	**tuv**_iste_
	tien_e_	teng_a_	**tuvo**
	ten_emos_	teng_amos_	**tuv**_imos_
	ten_éis_	teng_áis_	**tuv**_isteis_
	tien_en_	teng_an_	**tuv**_ieron_

	Infinitive	Present Indicative	Present Subjunctive	Preterite

⟨2m⟩ **caber.** Irregular in many forms. In the *Future* and *Conditional* the *e* coming after the stem is dropped. Future: *cabré*.

	quep_o_	**quep**_a_	**cupe**
	cab_es_	**quep**_as_	**cup**_iste_
	cab_e_	**quep**_a_	**cupo**
	cab_emos_	**quep**_amos_	**cup**_imos_
	cab_éis_	**quep**_áis_	**cup**_isteis_
	cab_en_	**quep**_an_	**cup**_ieron_

⟨2n⟩ **saber.** Irregular in many forms. In the *Future* and *Conditional* the *e* coming after the stem is dropped. Future: *sabré*.

	sé	**sep**_a_	**supe**
	sab_es_	**sep**_as_	**sup**_iste_
	sab_e_	**sep**_a_	**supo**
	sab_emos_	**sep**_amos_	**sup**_imos_
	sab_éis_	**sep**_áis_	**sup**_isteis_
	sab_en_	**sep**_an_	**sup**_ieron_

⟨2o⟩ **caer.** In the *Present ...ig...* is inserted after the stem. Unstressed *i* between vowels changes to *y* as with ⟨2e⟩. Past participle: *caído*. Present participle: *cayendo*.

	ca**ig**_o_	ca**ig**_a_	ca_í_
	ca_es_	ca**ig**_as_	ca_íste_
	ca_e_	ca**ig**_a_	ca**y**_ó_
	ca_emos_	ca**ig**_amos_	ca_ímos_
	ca_éis_	ca**ig**_áis_	ca_ísteis_
	ca_en_	ca**ig**_an_	ca**y**_eron_

⟨2p⟩ **traer.** In the *Present ...ig...* is inserted after the stem. The *Preterite* ends in *...je*. In the *Present participle i* changes to *y*. Past participle: *traído*. Present participle: *trayendo*.

	tra**ig**_o_	tra**ig**_a_	tra**je**
	tra_es_	tra**ig**_as_	tra**j**_iste_
	tra_e_	tra**ig**_a_	tra**jo**
	tra_emos_	tra**ig**_amos_	tra**j**_imos_
	tra_éis_	tra**ig**_áis_	tra**j**_isteis_
	tra_en_	tra**ig**_an_	tra**j**_eron_

⟨2q⟩ **valer.** In the *Present ...g...* is inserted after the stem. In the *Future* and *Conditional* the *e* coming after the stem is dropped and a *...d...* inserted. Future: *valdré*.

	val**g**_o_	val**g**_a_	val_í_
	val_es_	val**g**_as_	val_iste_
	val_e_	val**g**_a_	val_ió_
	val_emos_	val**g**_amos_	val_imos_
	val_éis_	val**g**_áis_	val_isteis_
	val_en_	val**g**_an_	val_ieron_

Infinitive	Present Indicative	Present Subjunctive	Preterite

⟨2r⟩ **poner.** ...*g*... is inserted in the *Present*. Irregular in the *Preterite* and *Past participle*. In the *Future* and *Conditional* the *e* coming after the stem is dropped and a ...*d*... inserted. Future: *pondré*. Past participle: *puesto*. Imperative *2nd pers sg*: *pon*.

Present Indicative	Present Subjunctive	Preterite
pongo	ponga	puse
pones	pongas	pusiste
pone	ponga	puso
ponemos	pongamos	pusimos
ponéis	pongáis	pusisteis
ponen	pongan	pusieron

⟨2s⟩ **hacer.** In the *1st* person of the *Present Indicative* and *Subjunctive g* replaces *c*. Irregular in the *Preterite* and *Past participle*. In the *Future* and *Conditional* the *ce* is dropped. In the *Imperative sg* just the stem is used with ...*c* changing to ...*z*. Future: *haré*. Imperative *2nd pers sg*: *haz*. Past participle: *hecho*.

Present Indicative	Present Subjunctive	Preterite
hago	haga	hice
haces	hagas	hiciste
hace	haga	hizo
hacemos	hagamos	hicimos
hacéis	hagáis	hicisteis
hacen	hagan	hicieron

⟨2t⟩ **poder.** Stressed *o* in the stem changes to ...*ue*... in the *Present* and the *Imperative*. Irregular in the *Preterite* and *Present participle*. In the *Future* and *Conditional* the *e* coming after the stem is dropped. Future: *podré*. Present participle: *pudiendo*.

Present Indicative	Present Subjunctive	Preterite
puedo	pueda	pude
puedes	puedas	pudiste
puede	pueda	pudo
podemos	podamos	pudimos
podéis	podáis	pudisteis
pueden	puedan	pudieron

⟨2u⟩ **querer.** Stressed *e* in the stem changes to *ie* in the *Present* and *Imperative*. Irregular in the *Preterite*. In the *Future* and *Conditional* the *e* coming after the stem is dropped. Future: *querré*.

Present Indicative	Present Subjunctive	Preterite
quiero	quiera	quise
quieres	quieras	quisiste
quiere	quiera	quiso
queremos	queramos	quisimos
queréis	queráis	quisisteis
quieren	quieran	quisieron

Infinitive	Present Indicative	Present Subjunctive	Preterite

⟨2v⟩ ver. *Present indicative 1st pers sg*, *Present subjunctive* and *Imperfect* are formed on the stem *ve…*, otherwise formation is regular using the shortened stem *v…* Irregular in the *Past participle*. Past participle: *visto*.

	ve*o*	**ve***a*	**vi**
	ves	**ve***as*	*viste*
	ve	**ve***a*	*vio*
	vemos	**ve***amos*	*vimos*
	veis	**ve***áis*	*visteis*
	ven	**ve***an*	*vieron*

Infinitive	Present Indicative	Present Subjunctive	Imperfect Indicative	Preterite

⟨2w⟩ ser. Totally irregular with several different stems being used. Past participle: *sido*. Imperative *2nd pers sg*: *sé*. *2nd pers pl*: *sed*.

	so**y**	se*a*	**er***a*	**fu***i*
	er*es*	se*as*	**er***as*	**fu***iste*
	es	se*a*	**er***a*	**fue**
	so*mos*	se*amos*	**ér***amos*	**fu***imos*
	so**i***s*	se*áis*	**er***ais*	**fu***isteis*
	so*n*	se*an*	**er***an*	**fu***eron*

⟨2x⟩ placer. Used almost exclusively in the *3rd pers sg*. Irregular forms: *Present subjunctive* *pl***eg***a* and *pl***egue** as well as *plazca*; *Preterite* *pl***ugo** (or *plació*), *pl***ugu***ieron* (or *placieron*); *Imperfect subjunctive* *pl***ugu***iera*, *pl***ugu***iese* (or *placiera*, *placiese*); *Future subjunctive* *pl***ugu***iere* (or *placiere*).

⟨2y⟩ yacer. Used mainly on gravestones and so used primarily in the *3rd pers*. The *Present indicative 1st pers sg* and *Present subjunctive* have three forms. The *Imperative* is regular; just the stem with *c* changing to *z*. *Present indicative*: *ya***zc***o*, *ya***zg***o*, *ya***g***o*, *yaces* etc; *Present subjunctive*: *ya***zc***a*, *ya***zg***a*, *ya***g***a* etc; *Imperative yace* and *ya***z**.

⟨2z⟩ raer. The regular forms of the *Present indicative 1st pers sg* and *Present subjunctive* are less common than the forms with inserted *…ig…* as in ⟨2o⟩: *ra***ig***o*, *ra***ig***a*; but also *ra***y***o*, *ra***y***a* (less common). Otherwise regular.

⟨2za⟩ roer. As well as their regular forms the *Present indicative 1st pers sg* and *Present subjunctive* have the less common forms: *ro***ig***o*, *ro***ig***a*, *ro***y***o*, *ro***y***a*.

Third Conjugation

⟨3a⟩ **recibir.** No change to the written or spoken form of the stem.

Simple tenses

Indicative

	Present	**Imperfect**	**Preterite**
sg	recib*o*	recib*ía*	recib*í*
	recib*es*	recib*ías*	recib*iste*
	recib*e*	recib*ía*	recib*ió*
pl	recib*imos*	recib*íamos*	recib*imos*
	recib*ís*	recib*íais*	recib*isteis*
	recib*en*	recib*ían*	recib*ieron*

	Future	**Conditional**
sg	recib*iré*	recib*iría*
	recib*irás*	recib*irías*
	recib*irá*	recib*iría*
pl	recib*iremos*	recib*iríamos*
	recib*iréis*	recib*iríais*
	recib*irán*	recib*irían*

Subjunctive

	Present	**Imperfect I**	**Imperfect II**
sg	recib*a*	recib*iera*	recib*iese*
	recib*as*	recib*ieras*	recib*ieses*
	recib*a*	recib*iera*	recib*iese*
pl	recib*amos*	recib*iéramos*	recib*iésemos*
	recib*áis*	recib*ierais*	recib*ieseis*
	recib*an*	recib*ieran*	recib*iesen*

	Future	**Imperative**
sg	recib*iere*	—
	recib*ieres*	recib*e* (no recib*as*)
	recib*iere*	recib*a* Vd.
pl	recib*iéremos*	recib*amos*
	recib*iereis*	recib*id* (no recib*áis*)
	recib*ieren*	recib*an* Vds.

Infinitive: recib*ir*
Present participle: recib*iendo*
Past participle: recib*ido*

Compound tenses

Formed with the *Past participle* together with ***haber*** and ***ser***, see ⟨1a⟩.

⟨3b⟩ esparcir. Final *c* of the stem becomes *z* before *a* and *o*.

Infinitive	Present Indicative	Present Subjunctive	Preterite
	esparzo	esparza	esparcí
	esparces	esparzas	esparciste
	esparce	esparza	esparció
	esparcimos	esparzamos	esparcimos
	esparcís	esparzáis	esparcisteis
	esparcen	esparzan	esparcieron

⟨3c⟩ dirigir. Final *g* of the stem becomes *j* before *a* and *o*.

Infinitive	Present Indicative	Present Subjunctive	Preterite
	dirijo	dirija	dirigí
	diriges	dirijas	dirigiste
	dirige	dirija	dirigió
	dirigimos	dirijamos	dirigimos
	dirigís	dirijáis	dirigisteis
	dirigen	dirijan	dirigieron

⟨3d⟩ distinguir. Final *gu* of the stem becomes *g* before *a* and *o*.

Infinitive	Present Indicative	Present Subjunctive	Preterite
	distingo	distinga	distinguí
	distingues	distingas	distinguiste
	distingue	distinga	distinguió
	distinguimos	distingamos	distinguimos
	distinguís	distingáis	distinguisteis
	distinguen	distingan	distinguieron

⟨3e⟩ delinquir. Final *qu* of the stem becomes *c* before *a* and *o*.

Infinitive	Present Indicative	Present Subjunctive	Preterite
	delinco	delinca	delinquí
	delinques	delincas	delinquiste
	delinque	delinca	delinquió
	delinquimos	delincamos	delinquimos
	delinquís	delincáis	delinquisteis
	delinquen	delincan	delinquieron

⟨3f⟩ lucir. Final *c* of the stem becomes *zc* before *a* and *o*.

Infinitive	Present Indicative	Present Subjunctive	Preterite
	luzco	luzca	lucí
	luces	luzcas	luciste
	luce	luzca	lució
	lucimos	luzcamos	lucimos
	lucís	luzcáis	lucisteis
	lucen	luzcan	lucieron

⟨3g⟩ concluir. A *y* is inserted after the stem unless the ending begins with *i*. Past participle: *concluido*. Present participle: *concluyendo*.

Infinitive	Present Indicative	Present Subjunctive	Preterite
	concluyo	concluya	concluí
	concluyes	concluyas	concluiste
	concluye	concluya	concluyó
	concluimos	concluyamos	concluimos
	concluís	concluyáis	concluisteis
	concluyen	concluyan	concluyeron

Infinitive	Present Indicative	Present Subjunctive	Preterite

⟨3h⟩ **gruñir.** Unstressed *i* is dropped after *ñ*, *ll* and *ch*. Likewise *mullir*: *mull***ó**, *mull***e***ron*, *mull***e***ndo*; *henchir*: *hinch***ó**, *hinch***e***ron*, *hinch***e***ndo* Present participle: *gruñendo*.

	gruñ*o*	gruñ*a*	gruñ*í*
	gruñ*es*	gruñ*as*	gruñ*iste*
	gruñ*e*	gruñ*a*	**gruñó**
	gruñ*imos*	gruñ*amos*	gruñ*imos*
	gruñ*ís*	gruñ*áis*	gruñ*isteis*
	gruñ*en*	gruñ*an*	**gruñe***ron*

⟨3i⟩ **sentir.** Stressed *e* of the stem becomes *ie*; unstressed *e* remains unchanged before endings starting with *i*, but before other endings it changes to …*i*…; likewise *adquirir*: stressed *i* of the stem becomes *ie*; unstressed *i* remains unchanged in all forms. Present participle: *sintiendo*.

	sient*o*	**sient***a*	sent*í*
	sient*es*	**sient***as*	sent*iste*
	sient*e*	**sient***a*	**sint***ió*
	sent*imos*	**sint***amos*	sent*imos*
	sent*ís*	**sint***áis*	sent*isteis*
	sient*en*	**sient***an*	**sint***ieron*

⟨3k⟩ **dormir.** Stressed *o* of the stem becomes *ue*; unstressed *o* is unchanged when the ending starts with *i*; otherwise it changes to …*u*… Present participle: *durmiendo*.

	duerm*o*	**duerm***a*	dorm*í*
	duerm*es*	**duerm***as*	dorm*iste*
	duerm*e*	**duerm***a*	**durm***ió*
	dorm*imos*	**durm***amos*	dorm*imos*
	dorm*ís*	**durm***áis*	dorm*isteis*
	duerm*en*	**duerm***an*	**durm***ieron*

⟨3l⟩ **medir.** The *e* of the stem is kept if the ending contains an *i*. Otherwise it changes to …*i*… whether stressed or unstressed. Present participle: *midiendo*.

	mid*o*	**mid***a*	med*í*
	mid*es*	**mid***as*	med*iste*
	mid*e*	**mid***a*	**mid***ió*
	med*imos*	**mid***amos*	med*imos*
	med*ís*	**mid***áis*	med*isteis*
	mid*en*	**mid***an*	**mid***ieron*

Infinitive	Present Indicative	Present Subjunctive	Preterite

⟨3m⟩ **reír.** As *medir* ⟨3l⟩; when *e* changes to *i* any second *i* belonging to the ending is dropped. Past participle: *reído*. Present participle: *riendo*.

	rí*o*	**rí***a*	re*í*
	rí*es*	**rí***as*	re*íste*
	rí*e*	**rí***a*	**ri***ó*
	re*imos*	**ri***amos*	re*ímos*
	re*ís*	**ri***áis*	re*ísteis*
	rí*en*	**rí***an*	**ri***eron*

⟨3n⟩ **erguir.** As *medir* in the *Present indicative*, *Subjunctive* and *Imperative*. Other forms follow *sentir* with initial *ie*… changing to *ye*… Present participle: *irguiendo*. Imperative: *irgue*, *yergue*.

	irg*o*, **yerg***o*	**irg***a*, **yerg***a*	*erguí*
	irgu*es*, **yergu***es*	**irg***as*, **yerg***as*	ergu*iste*
	irgu*e*, **yergu***e*	**irg***a*, **yerg***a*	irgu*ió*
	ergu*imos*	**irg***amos*, **yerg***amos*	ergu*imos*
	ergu*ís*	**irg***áis*, **yerg***áis*	ergu*isteis*
	irgu*en*, **yergu***en*	**irg***an*, **yerg***an*	irgu*ieron*

⟨3o⟩ **conducir.** Final *c* of the stem, as with *lucir* ⟨3f⟩, becomes *zc* before *a* and *o*. *Preterite* is irregular with *…je*.

	condu**zc***o*	condu**zc***a*	condu**je**
	conduc*es*	condu**zc***as*	condu**j***iste*
	conduc*e*	condu**zc***a*	condu**jo**
	conduc*imos*	condu**zc***amos*	condu**j***imos*
	conduc*ís*	condu**zc***áis*	condu**j***isteis*
	conduc*en*	condu**zc***an*	condu**j***eron*

⟨3p⟩ **decir.** In the *Present* and *Imperative e* and *i* are changed, as with *medir*; in the *Present indicative 1st pers sg* and in the *Present subjunctive c* becomes *g*. Irregular *Future* and *Conditional* based on a shortened *Infinitive*. *Preterite* has *je*. Future: *diré*. Past participle: *dicho*. Present participle: *diciendo*. Imperative *2nd pers sg*: *di*.

	dig*o*	**dig***a*	**dije**
	dic*es*	**dig***as*	**dij***iste*
	dic*e*	**dig***a*	**dijo**
	dec*imos*	**dig***amos*	**dij***imos*
	dec*ís*	**dig***áis*	**dij***isteis*
	dic*en*	**dig***an*	**dij***eron*

Infinitive	Present Indicative	Present Subjunctive	Preterite

⟨3q⟩ oír. In the *Present indicative 1st pers sg* and *Present subjunctive* *…ig…* is inserted after the *o…* of the stem. Unstressed *…i…* changes to *…y…* when coming between two vowels. Past participle: *oído*. Present participle: *oyendo*.

	oigo	oiga	oí
	oyes	oigas	oíste
	oye	oiga	oyó
	oimos	oigamos	oímos
	oís	oigáis	oísteis
	oyen	oigan	oyeron

⟨3r⟩ salir. In the *Present indicative 1st pers sg* and the *Present subjunctive* a *…g…* is inserted after the stem. In the *Future* and *Conditional* the *i* is replaced by *d*. Future: *saldré*. Imperative: *2nd pers sg*: *sal*.

	salgo	salga	salí
	sales	salgas	saliste
	sale	salga	salió
	salimos	salgamos	salimos
	salís	salgáis	salisteis
	salen	salgan	salieron

Infinitive	Present Indicative	Present Subjunctive	Imperfect Indicative	Preterite

⟨3s⟩ venir. In the *Present* two changes: either a *…g…* is inserted after the stem or *e*, *ie* and *i* follow the same changes as *sentir*. In the *Future* and *Conditional* the *i* is dropped and replaced by *d*. Future: *vendré*. Present participle: *viniendo*. Imperative *2nd pers sg*: *ven*.

	vengo	venga	venía	vine
	vienes	vengas	venías	viniste
	viene	venga	venía	vino
	venimos	vengamos	veníamos	vinimos
	venís	vengáis	veníais	vinisteis
	vienen	vengan	venían	vinieron

⟨3t⟩ ir. Totally irregular with several different stems being used. Present participle: *yendo*

	voy	vaya	iba	fui
	vas	vayas	ibas	fuiste
	va	vaya	iba	fue
	vamos	vayamos	íbamos	fuimos
	vais	vayáis	ibais	fuisteis
	van	vayan	iban	fueron

Imperative: **ve** (no **vay***as*), **vay***a* Vd, **va***mos*, *id* (no **vay***áis*), **vay***an* Vds.

Notas sobre el verbo inglés

a) Conjugación

1. **El tiempo presente** tiene la misma forma que el infinitivo en todas las personas menos la **3ª** del singular; en ésta, se añade una *-s* al infinitivo, p.ej. *he brings*, o se añade *-es* si el infinitivo termina en sibilante (ch, sh, ss, zz), p.ej. *he passes*. Esta *s* tiene dos pronunciaciones distintas: tras consonante sorda se pronuncia sorda, p.ej. *he paints* [peɪnts]; tras consonante sonora se pronuncia sonora, *he sends* [sendz]; *-es* se pronuncia también sonora, sea la *e* parte de la desinencia o letra final del infinitivo, p.ej. *he washes* ['wɑːʃɪz], *he urges* ['ɜːrdʒɪz]. Los verbos que terminan en *-y* la cambian en *-ies* en la tercera persona, p.ej. *he worries*, *he tries*, pero son regulares los verbos que en el infinitivo tienen una vocal delante de la *-y*, p.ej. *he plays*. El verbo *to be* es irregular en todas las personas: *I am*, *you are*, *he is*, *we are*, *you are*, *they are*. Tres verbos más tienen forma especial para la tercera persona del singular: *do-he does*, *go-he goes*, *have-he has*.

   En los demás tiempos, todas las personas son iguales. **El pretérito** y **el participio del pasado** se forman añadiendo *-ed* al infinitivo, p.ej. *I passed*, *passed*, o añadiendo *-d* a los infinitivos que terminan en *-e*, p.ej. *I faced*, *faced*. (Hay muchos verbos irregulares: v. abajo). Esta *-(e)d* se pronuncia generalmente como [t]: *passed* [pæst], *faced* [feɪst]; pero cuando se añade a un infinitivo que termina en consonante sonora o en sonido consonántico sonoro o en *r*, se pronuncia como [d]: *warmed* [wɔːrmd], *moved* [muːvd], *feared* [fɪrd]. Si el infinitivo termina en *-d* o *-t*, la desinencia *-ed* se pronuncia [ɪd]. Si el infinitivo termina en *-y*, ésta se cambia en *-ie*, antes de añadirse la *-d*: *try-tried* [traɪd], *pity-pitied* ['pɪtiːd]. **Los tiempos compuestos del pasado** se forman con el verbo auxiliar *have* y el participio del pasado, como en español: **perfecto** *I have faced*, **pluscuamperfecto** *I had faced*. Con el verbo auxiliar *will* (*shall*) y el infinitivo se forma **el futuro**, p.ej. *I shall face*; y con el verbo auxiliar *would* (*should*) y el infinitivo se forma **el condicional**, p.ej. *I should face*. En cada tiempo existe además una forma continua que se forma con el verbo *be* (= estar) y el participio del presente (v. abajo): *I am going*, *I was writing*, *I had been staying*, *I shall be waiting*, etc.

2. **El subjuntivo** ha dejado casi de existir en inglés, salvo en algún caso especial (*if I were you*, *so be it*, *it is proposed that a vote be taken*, etc.). En el presente, tiene en todas las personas la misma forma que el infinitivo, *that I go*, *that he go*, etc.

3. **El participio del presente** y **el gerundio** tienen la misma forma en inglés, añadiéndose al infinitivo la desinencia *-ing*: *painting*, *sending*. Pero **1)** Los verbos cuyo infinitivo termina en *-e* muda la pierden al añadir *-ing*, p.ej. *love-loving*, *write-writing* (excepciones que conservan la *-e*: *dye-dyeing*, *singe-singeing*); **2)** El participio del presente de los verbos *die*, *lie*, *vie*, etc. se escribe *dying*, *lying*, *vying*, etc.

4. Existe una clase de verbos ligeramente irregulares, que terminan en consonante simple precedida de vocal simple acentuada; en éstos, antes de añadir la desinencia *-ing* o *-ed*, se dobla la consonante:

lob	lob*bed*	lob*bing*	compel	compel*led*	compel*ling*
wed	wed*ded*	wed*ding*	control	control*led*	control*ling*
beg	beg*ged*	beg*ging*	bar	bar*red*	bar*ring*
step	step*ped*	step*ping*	stir	stir*red*	stir*ring*
quit	quit*ted*	quit*ting*			

Los verbos que terminan en *-l*, *-p*, aunque precedida de vocal átona, tienen doblada la consonante en los dos participios en el inglés escrito en Gran Bretaña, aunque no en el de Estados Unidos:

travel	traveled, *Br* travel*led*,	travel*ing*, *Br* travel*led*

Los verbos que terminan en *-c* la cambian en *-ck* al añadirse las desinencias *-ed*, *-ing*:

traffic	traffi*cked*	traffi*cking*

5. **La voz pasiva** se forma exactamente como en español, con el verbo *be* y el participio del pasado: *I am obliged*, *he was fined*, *they will be moved*, etc.

6. Cuando se dirige uno directamente a otra(s) persona(s) en inglés se emplea únicamente el pronombre *you*. *You* se traduce por el *tú*, *vosotros*, *usted* y *ustedes* del español.

b) Los verbos irregulares ingleses

Se citan las tres partes principales de cada verbo: infinitivo, pretérito, participio del pasado.

alight - alighted, alit - alighted, alit
arise - arose - arisen
awake - awoke - awoken, awaked
be (am, is, are) - was (were) - been
bear - bore - borne
beat - beat - beaten
become - became - become
begin - began - begun
behold - beheld - beheld
bend - bent - bent
beseech - besought, beseeched - besought, beseeched
bet - bet, betted - bet, betted
bid - bid - bid
bind - bound - bound
bite - bit - bitten
bleed - bled - bled
blow - blew - blown
break - broke - broken
breed - bred - bred
bring - brought - brought
broadcast - broadcast - broadcast
build - built - built
burn - burnt, burned - burnt, burned
burst - burst - burst
bust - bust(ed) - bust(ed)
buy - bought - bought
cast - cast - cast
catch - caught - caught
choose - chose - chosen
cleave (*cut*) - clove, cleft - cloven, cleft
cleave (*adhere*) - cleaved - cleaved

cling - clung - clung
come - came - come
cost (*v/i*) - cost - cost
creep - crept - crept
crow - crowed, crew - crowed
cut - cut - cut
deal - dealt - dealt
dig - dug - dug
do - did - done
draw - drew - drawn
dream - dreamt, dreamed - dreamt, dreamed
drink - drank - drunk
drive - drove - driven
dwell - dwelt, dwelled - dwelt, dwelled
eat - ate - eaten
fall - fell - fallen
feed - fed - fed
feel - felt - felt
fight - fought - fought
find - found - found
fit - fitted, fit - fitted, fit
flee - fled - fled
fling - flung - flung
fly - flew - flown
forbear - forbore - forborne
forbid - forbad(e) - forbidden
forecast - forecast(ed) - forecast(ed)
forget - forgot - forgotten
forgive - forgave - forgiven
forsake - forsook - forsaken
freeze - froze - frozen
get - got - got, gotten
give - gave - given
go - went - gone
grind - ground - ground
grow - grew - grown
hang - hung, (*v/t*) hanged - hung, (*v/t*) hanged
have - had - had
hear - heard - heard
heave - heaved, NAUT hove - heaved, NAUT hove
hew - hewed - hewed, hewn
hide - hid - hidden
hit - hit - hit
hold - held - held
hurt - hurt - hurt
keep - kept - kept
kneel - knelt, kneeled - knelt, kneeled
know - knew - known
lay - laid - laid
lead - led - led
lean - leaned, leant - leaned, leant
leap - leaped, leapt - leaped, leapt
learn - learned, learnt - learned, learnt
leave - left - left
lend - lent - lent
let - let - let
lie - lay - lain
light - lighted, lit - lighted, lit
lose - lost - lost
make - made - made
mean - meant - meant
meet - met - met
mow - mowed - mowed, mown
pay - paid - paid
plead - pleaded, pled - pleaded, pled
prove - proved - proved, proven
put - put - put
quit - quit(ted) - quit(ted)
read - read [red] - read [red]
rend - rent - rent
rid - rid - rid
ride - rode - ridden
ring - rang - rung
rise - rose - risen
run - ran - run
saw - sawed - sawn, sawed
say - said - said
see - saw - seen
seek - sought - sought
sell - sold - sold
send - sent - sent
set - set - set
sew - sewed - sewed, sewn
shake - shook - shaken
shear - sheared - sheared, shorn
shed - shed - shed
shine - shone - shone
shit - shat, shitted - shat, shitted
shoe - shod - shod
shoot - shot - shot
show - showed - shown
shrink - shrank - shrunk

shut - shut - shut
sing - sang - sung
sink - sank - sunk
sit - sat - sat
slay - slew - slain
sleep - slept - slept
slide - slid - slid
sling - slung - slung
slink - slunk - slunk
slit - slit - slit
smell - smelt, smelled - smelt, smelled
smite - smote - smitten
sneak - sneaked, snuck - sneaked, snuck
sow - sowed - sown, sowed
speak - spoke - spoken
speed - sped, speeded - sped, speeded
spell - spelt, spelled - spelt, spelled
spend - spent - spent
spill - spilt, spilled - spilt, spilled
spin - spun, span - spun
spit - spat - spat
split - split - split
spoil - spoiled, spoilt - spoiled, spoilt
spread - spread - spread
spring - sprang, sprung - sprung
stand - stood - stood
stave - staved, stove - staved, stove
steal - stole - stolen
stick - stuck - stuck
sting - stung - stung
stink - stunk, stank - stunk
strew - strewed - strewed, strewn
stride - strode - stridden
strike - struck - struck
string - strung - strung
strive - strove - striven
swear - swore - sworn
sweep - swept - swept
swell - swelled - swollen
swim - swam - swum
swing - swung - swung
take - took - taken
teach - taught - taught
tear - tore - torn
tell - told - told
think - thought - thought
thrive - throve, thrived - thrived
throw - threw - thrown
thrust - thrust - thrust
tread - trod - trodden
understand - understood - understood
wake - woke, waked - woken, waked
wear - wore - worn
weave - wove - woven
wed - wed(ded) - wed(ded)
weep - wept - wept
wet - wet(ted) - wet(ted)
win - won - won
wind - wound - wound
wring - wrung - wrung
write - wrote - written

Currículum vitae

JULIE DELGADO

201-331-1289
c/ Garrison 19, Oakland, Nueva Jersey 07436
juliedelgado@yahoo.com

EXPERIENCIA LABORAL

Escritora y correctora freelance: *septiembre de 2001-actualmente*
Clientes destacados:
Scholarly Books Inc., Nueva York, Nueva York.
FotoTravels, Little Falls, Nueva Jersey.
Children of Bellevue, Bellevue Hospital, Nueva York, Nueva York.

Profesora de inglés: *septiembre de 2000-marzo de 2001*
The English Language School, Tczew, Polonia.
Benedict-Schule, Hamm, Alemania.
Enseñanza de inglés para nivel principiante, intermedio y avanzado.
Preparación de clases atractivas y dinámicas, con actividades en el aula.

Correctora de producción: *octubre de 1999-septiembre de 2000*
The Tipps Company, Nueva York, Nueva York.
Corrección de tarjetones de deportes y espectáculos, y del empaquetado.
Aprobación de elementos de texto y diseño de los productos de la empresa.

Editora y redactora publicitaria: *marzo de 1998-junio de 1999*
Americana Book Clubs, Mahwah, Nueva Jersey.
Escritura de ejemplar de catálogo y de notas de ventas para clubs de lectura americanos y canadienses.
Redacción mensual de las hojas informativas de las publicaciones *Girl Connection* y *Ready to Read*.
Corrección y edición de todas las páginas del catálogo.

Asistente creativa: *1997-1998*
New Entertainment Inc., Nueva York, NuevaYork.
Redacción de borradores para campañas publicitarias de espectáculos.
Asistencia creativa y administrativa del presidente y director creativo.

FORMACIÓN

Brooklyn College, Brooklyn, Nueva York.
Master de Escritura Creativa, Poesía.

Fairleigh Dickinson University, Teaneck, Nueva Jersey.
Licenciada en Filología Inglesa, especialización en Escritura.

INFORMÁTICA

Excelente dominio de Microsoft Word, WordPerfect, QuarkXPress, FilemakerPro.
Nociones generales de Excel.

Résumé

JULIE DELGADO

201-331-1289
19 Garrison Street, Oakland, New Jersey 07436
juliedelgado@yahoo.com

EXPERIENCE

Freelance Writer and Proofreader: September 2001-Present
Clients include:
Scholarly Books Inc., New York, New York
FotoTravels, Little Falls, New Jersey
Children of Bellevue, Bellevue Hospital, New York, New York

English Language Instructor: September 2000-March 2001
The English Language School, Tczew, Poland
Benedict-Schule, Hamm, Germany
Taught beginner-, intermediate- and advanced-level English language classes
Created dynamic and engaging lesson plans and classroom activities

Production Proofreader: October 1999-September 2000
The Tipps Company, New York, New York
Proofread sports and entertainment cards and packaging
Approved text and design elements on company products

Editor and Copywriter: March 1998-June 1999
Americana Book Clubs, Mahwah, New Jersey
Wrote catalog copy and sales pieces for American and Canadian Book Clubs
Authored monthly *Girl Connection* and *Ready to Read* newsletters
Proofread and edited all catalog pages

Creative Assistant: 1997-1998
New Entertainment Inc., New York, New York
Drafted copy for entertainment advertising campaigns
Provided creative and administrative assistance for President and Creative Director

EDUCATION

Brooklyn College, Brooklyn, New York
Master of Fine Arts in Creative Writing, Poetry

Fairleigh Dickinson University, Teaneck, New Jersey
Bachelor of Arts in English, Writing Concentration

COMPUTER SKILLS

Proficient in Microsoft Word, WordPerfect, QuarkXPress, FilemakerPro
Familiarity with Excel

Numerals – Numerales

Cardinal Numbers – Números cardinales

0 cero *zero, Br tb nought*
1 uno, una *one*
2 dos *two*
3 tres *three*
4 cuatro *four*
5 cinco *five*
6 seis *six*
7 siete *seven*
8 ocho *eight*
9 nueve *nine*
10 diez *ten*
11 once *eleven*
12 doce *twelve*
13 trece *thirteen*
14 catorce *fourteen*
15 quince *fifteen*
16 dieciséis *sixteen*
17 diecisiete *seventeen*
18 dieciocho *eighteen*
19 diecinueve *nineteen*
20 veinte *twenty*
21 veintiuno *twenty-one*
22 veintidós *twenty-two*
30 treinta *thirty*
31 treinta y uno *thirty-one*
40 cuarenta *forty*
50 cincuenta *fifty*
60 sesenta *sixty*
70 setenta *seventy*
80 ochenta *eighty*
90 noventa *ninety*
100 cien(to) *a hundred, one hundred*
101 ciento uno *a hundred and one*
110 ciento diez *a hundred and ten*
200 doscientos, -as *two hundred*
300 trescientos, -as *three hundred*
400 cuatrocientos, -as *four hundred*
500 quinientos, -as *five hundred*
600 seiscientos, -as *six hundred*
700 setecientos, -as *seven hundred*
800 ochocientos, -as *eight hundred*
900 novecientos, -as *nine hundred*
1000 mil *a thousand, one thousand*
1959 mil novecientos cincuenta y nueve *one thousand nine hundred and fifty-nine*
2000 dos mil *two thousand*
1 000 000 un millón *a million, one million*
2 000 000 dos millones *two million*

Notes:

i) In Spanish numbers a comma is used for decimals:

1,25 **one point two five** uno coma veinticinco

ii) A period is used where, in English, we would use a comma:

1.000.000 = 1,000,000

Numbers like this can also be written using a space instead of a comma:

1 000 000 = 1,000,000

Ordinal Numbers – Números ordinales

1°	primero	**1st**	*first*
2°	segundo	**2nd**	*second*
3°	tercero	**3rd**	*third*
4°	cuarto	**4th**	*fourth*
5°	quinto	**5th**	*fifth*
6°	sexto	**6th**	*sixth*
7°	séptimo	**7th**	*seventh*
8°	octavo	**8th**	*eighth*
9°	noveno, nono	**9th**	*ninth*
10°	décimo	**10th**	*tenth*
11°	undécimo	**11th**	*eleventh*
12°	duodécimo	**12th**	*twelfth*
13°	decimotercero	**13th**	*thirteenth*
14°	decimocuarto	**14th**	*fourteenth*
15°	decimoquinto	**15th**	*fifteenth*
16°	decimosexto	**16th**	*sixteenth*
17°	decimoséptimo	**17th**	*seventeenth*
18°	decimoctavo	**18th**	*eighteenth*
19°	decimonoveno, decimonono	**19th**	*nineteenth*
20°	vigésimo	**20th**	*twentieth*
21°	vigésimo prim(er)o	**21st**	*twenty-first*
22°	vigésimo segundo	**22nd**	*twenty-second*
30°	trigésimo	**30th**	*thirtieth*
31°	trigésimo prim(er)o	**31st**	*thirty-first*
40°	cuadragésimo	**40th**	*fortieth*
50°	quincuagésimo	**50th**	*fiftieth*
60°	sexagésimo	**60th**	*sixtieth*
70°	septuagésimo	**70th**	*seventieth*
80°	octogésimo	**80th**	*eightieth*
90°	nonagésimo	**90th**	*ninetieth*
100°	centésimo	**100th**	*hundredth*
101°	centésimo primero	**101st**	*hundred and first*
110°	centésimo décimo	**110th**	*hundred and tenth*
200°	ducentésimo	**200th**	*two hundredth*
300°	trecentésimo	**300th**	*three hundredth*
400°	cuadringentésimo	**400th**	*four hundredth*
500°	quingentésimo	**500th**	*five hundredth*
600°	sexcentésimo	**600th**	*six hundredth*
700°	septingentésimo	**700th**	*seven hundredth*
800°	octingentésimo	**800th**	*eight hundredth*
900°	noningentésimo	**900th**	*nine hundredth*
1000°	milésimo	**1000th**	*thousandth*
2000°	dos milésimo	**2000th**	*two thousandth*
1 000 000°	millonésimo	**1,000,000th**	*millionth*
2 000 000°	dos millonésimo	**2,000,000th**	*two millionth*

Note:

Spanish ordinal numbers are ordinary adjectives and consequently must agree:

her 13th granddaughter
su decimotercera nieta

Fractions and other Numerals – Números quebrados y otros

$^1/_2$	medio, media	*one half, a half*
$1^1/_2$	uno y medio	*one and a half*
$2^1/_2$	dos y medio	*two and a half*
$^1/_3$	un tercio, la tercera parte	*one third, a third*
$^2/_3$	dos tercios, las dos terceras partes	*two thirds*
$^1/_4$	un cuarto, la cuarta parte	*one quarter, a quarter*
$^3/_4$	tres cuartos, las tres cuartas partes	*three quarters*
$^1/_5$	un quinto	*one fifth, a fifth*
$3^4/_5$	tres y cuatro quintos	*three and four fifths*
$^1/_{11}$	un onzavo	*one eleventh, an eleventh*
$^5/_{12}$	cinco dozavos	*five twelfths*
$^1/_{1000}$	un milésimo	*one thousandth, a thousandth*
	siete veces más grande	*seven times as big, seven times bigger*
	doce veces más	*twelve times more*
	en primer lugar	*first(ly)*
	en segundo lugar	*second(ly)*
7 + 8 = 15	siete y (*or* más) ocho son quince	*seven and* (*or plus*) *eight are* (*or is*) *fifteen*
10 – 3 = 7	diez menos tres resta siete, de tres a diez van siete	*ten minus three is seven, three from ten leaves seven*
2 x 3 = 6	dos por tres son seis	*two times three is six*
20 ÷ 4 = 5	veinte dividido por cuatro es cinco	*twenty divided by four is five*

Dates – Fechas

1996	mil novecientos noventa y seis	*nineteen ninety-six*
2005	dos mil cinco	*two thousand* (*and*) *five*

el diez de noviembre, el 10 de noviembre
(on) the 10th of November, (on) November 10

el uno de marzo, *L.Am.* **el primero de marzo**, **el 1° de marzo**
(on) the 1st of March, (on) March 1

Abbreviations
Abreviaturas

and	&	y
see	☞	véase
registered trademark	®	marca registrada
abbreviation	*abbr*	abreviatura
abbreviation	*abr*	abreviatura
adjective	*adj*	adjetivo
adverb	*adv*	adverbio
agriculture	AGR	agricultura
anatomy	ANAT	anatomía
architecture	ARCHI	arquitectura
Argentina	*Arg*	Argentina
architecture	ARQUI	arquitectura
article	*art*	artículo
astronomy	AST	astronomía
astrology	ASTR	astrología
attributive	*atr*	atributivo
motoring	AUTO	automóvil
civil aviation	AVIA	aviación
biology	BIO	biología
Bolivia	*Bol*	Bolivia
botany	BOT	botánica
British English	*Br*	inglés británico
Central America	*C.Am.*	América Central
Caribbean	*Carib*	Caribe
chemistry	CHEM	química
Chile	*Chi*	Chile
Colombia	*Col*	Colombia
commerce, business	COM	comercio
comparative	*comp*	comparativo
computers, IT term	COMPUT	informática
conjunction	*conj*	conjunción
Southern Cone	*CSur*	Cono Sur
Cuba	*Cu*	Cuba
sports	DEP	deporte
contemptuous	*desp*	despectivo
determiner	*det*	determinante
Ecuador	*Ecuad*	Ecuador
education (schools, universities)	EDU	educación, enseñanza (sistema escolar y universitario)
electronics, electronic engineering	EL	electrónica, electrotecnia
electronics, electronic engineering	ELEC	electrónica, electrotecnia
Spain	*Esp*	España
especially	*esp*	especialmente
euphemistic	*euph*	eufemismo
familiar, colloquial	F	familiar
feminine	*f*	femenino
feminine noun and adjective	*f/adj*	sustantivo femenino y adjetivo
railroad	FERR	ferrocarriles
figurative	*fig*	figurativo
financial	FIN	finanzas
physics	FÍS	física
formal	*fml*	formal
photography	FOT	fotografía
feminine plural	*fpl*	femenino plural
feminine singular	*fsg*	femenino singular
gastronomy	GASTR	gastronomía
geography	GEOG	geografía
geology	GEOL	geología
geometry	GEOM	geometría
grammar	GRAM	gramática
historical	HIST	histórico
humorous	*hum*	humorístico
IT term	INFOR	informática
interjection	*int*	interjección
interrogative	*interr*	interrogativo
invariable	*inv*	invariable
ironic	*iron*	irónico
ironic	*irón*	irónico
law	JUR	jurisprudencia
Latin America	*L.Am.*	América Latina
law	LAW	jurisprudencia
linguistics	LING	lingüística
literary	*lit*	literario
masculine	*m*	masculino
masculine noun and	*m/adj*	sustantivo masculino y